Encyclopedia of

# American Poetry

## THE TWENTIETH CENTURY

DISCARDED
from the Nashville Public Library

# Encyclopedia of American Poetry

## The Twentieth Century

Edited by Eric L. Haralson

FITZROY DEARBORN PUBLISHERS

Chicago • London

FITZROY DEARBORN PUBLISHERS
919 North Michigan Avenue, Suite 760
Chicago, IL 60611
USA

*or*

FITZROY DEARBORN PUBLISHERS
310 Regent Street
London W1R 5AJ
UK

**British Library and Library of Congress Cataloguing in Publication Data are available.**

ISBN 1-57958-240-0

First published in the USA and UK 2001

Indexed by Jackie Orihill, Chicago, Illinois
Typeset by Impressions Book and Journal Services, Inc., Madison, Wisconsin
Printed by Edwards Brothers, Ann Arbor, Michigan
Cover design by Peter Aristedes, Chicago Advertising and Design, Chicago, Illinois

In Memory of Jerome Notkin, with love for Janice

# CONTENTS

# EDITOR'S NOTE

It has to be living, to learn the speech of the place.
It has to face the men of the time and to meet
The women of the time.
—Wallace Stevens, "Of Modern Poetry"

To hear the poets tell it, poetry is what gets lost in translation. Poetry issues from the continual extinction of the author's personality. It makes nothing happen (although it is a way of happening), and in a certain mood, we are inclined to dismiss it as so much contemptible "fiddle." Nothing that can be said about poetry is worth saying.

By these standards, this project takes on a tall order, for it aspires to find many things worth saying about American poetry of the last century, a period of literary history in which American poetry really came into its own (with all due regard for Dickinson, Whitman, and a handful of their peers). This book indeed seeks to "translate"—or in other words, to explicate with care and tact—a broad selection of poems; it also aims to recover the "personality" and life stories of the women and men who created such an abundant wealth of writing; and it further invites the reader to consider all that poetry has "made happen" both in the way of formal evolution and as a mode of intervention in the complex politics of the so-called American century.

In practical terms, these objectives are served by the following organization of contents:

- Entries on individual **poets** feature a critical treatment of the poet's achievements; a capsule biography; a list of her or his published books of poetry; and, as appropriate, a list of the poet's selected criticism and "other writings" (such as memoirs, correspondence, or translations).
- Entries on landmark **poems** offer close readings of the work thus distinguished and situate it within a historical and biographical context. These entries follow the relevant poet entries, so that five works by Robert Frost, from "Desert Places" to "The Road Not Taken," are addressed immediately after the Frost entry, four works by Adrienne Rich, from *An Atlas of the Difficult World* to "A Valediction Forbidding Mourning," are discussed after the Rich entry, and so forth.
- Entries on major **topics** offer in-depth analysis of formal developments in 20th-century American poetry, under such headings as "Free Verse," "Long Poem," and "Prosody and Versification"; of distinct schools or movements, such as "Beat Poetry," "Black Mountain School," "Objectivism," and "Language Poetry"; of poetry engaged in social and cultural politics, such as "Gay and Lesbian Poetry," "Religion and Poetry," and "War and Anti-War Poetry"; of the vibrant verse that has emerged from different ethnic traditions within our national literature, such as "Asian American Poetry," "Harlem Renaissance," "Hispanic Poetry," and "Native American Poetry"; of verse of the Americas with which United States writing has conducted an intimate and intricate dialogue, such as "Canadian Poetry" and "Caribbean Poetry"; and of such crucial aspects of publication and reception as the marketing, teaching, and cultural valuation of poetry, such as "Anthologies, Textbooks, and Canon Formation," "Prizes," "Little Magazines and Small Presses," and "Literary Theory and Poetry."

All entries—poet, poem, or topic—provide a "further reading" list of key secondary sources on the subject of the given entry. Finally, certain poet entries are cross-referenced to topic entries where the poet in question comes in for additional treatment.

To borrow once again from the poets themselves, the goal of this volume is to demonstrate that this extraordinary body of poetry is important not because of any "high-sounding interpretation," but because it has proven useful, in varied ways, to our culture. Throughout, we strive to honor American verse as a source of genuine meanings; as a process of finding, if not always satisfaction, then "what will suffice"; and as a force that can open "chambers of possibility," restore feeling, and revitalize desire. At the end of the day, we are all interested—in the largest sense of the word—in poetry.

My wish, then, for those who consult this book is that reading it will do for you what editing it has done for me: greatly expand and enrich your appreciation of the power, beauty, and profundity of 20th-century American poetry. If this sounds like boasting, it is boasting on behalf of my team of almost 200 contributors, whose expertise and diligent labor will be apparent on every page. Beyond the contributions of these excellent scholars, the project has enjoyed the guidance of an advisory board made up of some of the most distinguished poets and critics (and poet-critics) working in American letters today. Without their insights, this volume would be a diminished thing, and although their names are listed elsewhere, I am pleased to repeat them here in a gesture of recognition for their generous and authoritative counsel: Christopher Beach, Charles Berger, Edward Halsey Foster, Dana Gioia, Elizabeth Gregory, John Hollander, Yusef Komunyakaa, Paul Mariani, Elisa New, Geoffrey O'Brien, Marjorie Perloff, and Linda Wagner-Martin. Without prejudicing the case, I must add that my debt to John Hollander is now ancient, even if he remains young.

My sense of gratitude to Fitzroy Dearborn Publishers almost defies description. George Walsh rescued the precursor volume—the *Encyclopedia of American Poetry: The Nineteenth Century*—from publishing oblivion, and his steadfast support is much appreciated. Paul Schellinger has been a model editorial director, firmly and sensitively steering the project through each phase of development. Other valued colleagues at Fitzroy Dearborn who were indispensable to making this big book "go" are Audrey Berns, Anne-Marie Bogdan, Jessica House, Thad King, Elizabeth Nishiura, and Heather Sabel. Gretchen Knapp and Bruce Owens copyedited every line and lineament of the monster, with keen intelligence and unfailing delicacy. Kudos, as well, to Peter Aristedes for selecting an eye-fetching piece of cover art, just as he did for the 19th-century poetry encyclopedia. But my greatest thanks and highest praise are reserved for my commissioning editor, Chris Hudson, who deserves more credit than anybody for making this reference work a reality. Chris is a volume editor's dream—tirelessly dedicated, infinitely wise and helpful, and wonderfully witty when comic relief is called for (as happened once or twice). To my fellow authors in the field I say: you should be so lucky!

It is a pleasure to close with words of thanks and love to those who have been the real poetry in my life—Susan, Sara, and Lucas, Kay and Howie, Janice and Jerry.

ERIC L. HARALSON
*State University of New York at Stony Brook*

# ADVISERS

Christopher Beach

Charles Berger
*University of Utah*

Edward Halsey Foster
*Stevens Institute of Technology*

Dana Gioia

Elizabeth L. Gregory
*University of Houston*

John Hollander, Jr.
*Yale University*

Yusef Komunyakaa
*Princeton University*

Paul L. Mariani
*Boston College*

Elisa New
*Harvard University*

Geoffrey O'Brien
*The Library of America*

Marjorie G. Perloff
*Stanford University*

Linda C. Wagner-Martin
*University of North Carolina*

# CONTRIBUTORS

Edward A. Abramson
Genevieve Abravanel
Alex Albright
Karen Alkalay-Gut
Elizabeth Arnold
G. Douglas Atkins
Steven Gould Axelrod
Anne Baker
Robert Baker
Jack Barbera
Michael Basinski
Christopher Beach
Michael D. Berndt
Robert Bertholf
Joel Bettridge
Michael Boughn
Melissa Bradshaw
Douglas Branch
Jewel Spears Brooker
Richard Buckstead
Sidney J. Burris
Peter J. Bushyeager
Jennifer A. Bussey
Cynthia Cameros
Katey Kuhns Castellano
Isaac Cates

Mary Ann Caws
Randolph Chilton
Paul Christensen
Henry Claridge
J. Elizabeth Clark
William Clarkson
David Clippinger
Alicia Cohen
Nadia Herman Colburn
Philip Coleman
Richard Collins
Nicole E. Cortz
Kathleen Crown
Catherine Cucinella
Stephen Cushman
Adenike Marie Davidson
William V. Davis
Anthony Dawahare
Joe Francis Doerr
David C. Dougherty
James Dougherty
Camille Dungy
Reshmi Dutt
Craig Dworkin
Sean Elliott
James F. English
Andrew Epstein
Dan Featherston
Paul J. Ferlazzo
Thomas Fink
Norman Finkelstein
Ann Fisher-Wirth
Hilene Flanzbaum
Edward Halsey Foster
Jeff Foster
Thomas Gardner
James Gibbons
Dobby Gibson
Jonathan Gill
Lorrie Goldensohn
Maggie Gordon
Elizabeth Grainger
Gary Grieve Carlson
Piotr Gwiazda
James C Hall
Nick Halpern
Linda Hamalian
George Hart
Burton Hatlen
Edward Haworth Hoeppner
Eric Hayot
Kristin K. Henson
Trenton Hickman
Mark Hillringhouse
Michael Hinds
Tyler Hoffman
Brooke Horvath
W. Scott Howard
Andrew Howe
Tim Hunt
Richard A. Iadonisi
David Garrett Izzo
Millie Jackson
Lisa Jarnot
Ymitri Jayasundera
Lee M. Jenkins
Jeannie Sargent Judge
Daniel Kane
Jim Keller
Jack Kimball
Nancy Kuhl
Kimberly Lamm
Benjamin S. Lawson
Anna Leahy
Michael Leddy
Cecilia Hae-Jin Lee
Jonathan Levin
Deshae E. Lott
Scott MacPhail
David E. Magill
Douglas Mao
David Marriott
Dawn Lundy Martin
Robert K. Martin
David Mason
Susan McCabe
Janet McCann
Mary A. McCay
Philip McGowan
Mark Melnicove
Sandra Merriweather
Ann-Marie Mikkelsen
Bronwyn Mills
Elizabeth Mills
Fiona Mills
Robert Miltner
Will Montgomery
Sharon L. Moore
Candice Maureen Moton
Adrienne Munich
Erika Nanes
Elisa New
Peter Nickowitz
Peter O'Leary
John Olson
Liesl Marie Olson
Ted Olson
Ranen Omer Sherman
William Orem
Robert S. Oventile
Benjamin Paloff
Catherine N. Parke
John Parras
Cyrus R.K. Patell
Catherine Paul
Ian Peddie
Nancy J. Peterson
Rhonda Pettit
Roxane V. Pickens
Donna Potts

Luca Prono
Stephen Rachman
Sharon Raynor
Jeffrey Rhyne
Kelly L. Richardson
Pat Righelato
Jeannette E. Riley
Gary Roberts
Corinne Robins
John F. Roche, Jr.
Augusta Rohrbach
Rachel Rubinstein
Kathy Rugoff
Nicole Sarrocco
Melita C. Schaum
William J. Scheick
Julie M. Schmid
Sarah Schoon
Leonard Schwartz
Harold Schweizer
Mark Scroggins
Katrina Shilts
Ernest J. Smith
Cheryl Spector
Nicholas Spencer
Thaine Stearns
Karen F. Stein
Lisa M. Steinman
Derrick Stone
Anthony Szczesiul
Bruce Taylor
Douglas Taylor
Michelle L. Taylor
Troy Thibodeaux
Catherine Tramontana
Jane Gentry Vance
Sherri Lynn VandenAkker
Peter Van Egmond
Christina Veladota
Michael W. Vella
Bryan Walpert
Krista Walter
Gary P. Walton
Linda S. Watts
Michael Wenthe
Jeff Westover
Rosemary Gates Winslow
Tim Woods
Jake Adam York
David R. Zauhar

# LIST OF ENTRIES

# A

## Agrarians. *See* Fugitives and Agrarians

## Conrad Aiken 1889–1973

As an innovator both in both poetry and prose fiction, Conrad Aiken forecast styles and genres that would later make other poets and writers famous. He waited many years for recognition of his 1920s and 1930s work, which his contemporaries underappreciated. Traumatized as a child when his father shot his mother and then himself—Aiken heard the shots and found their bodies—he said that he "found himself possessed of them forever." Aiken spent the rest of his life writing poetry of psychological exploration, first grounded in Freud and Jung, then moving toward his own hybrid sense of Eastern mysticism in a Western context. Seeking through his deliberately musical poetry the form and order wrenched from him as a child, Aiken plunged into his inner self and attempted to relate that self to the greater world. Critic Malcolm Cowley called him the "priest of consciousness."

After losing his parents, Aiken suffered the second trauma of being separated from his siblings, who were adopted by a family in Philadelphia while he was taken in by a very elderly aunt in New Bedford. Aiken entered Harvard in 1907, befriending T.S. Eliot with whom he shared a mutual interest in poets, poetic theory, language, and their own poems. At Harvard Aiken composed *The Clerk's Journal* (1911), which features similar themes that were employed to greater effect in Eliot's "The Love Song of J. Alfred Prufrock" (also written in 1911).

In 1912 Aiken married and began his career as a writer. Verse was his first love, but Aiken supported himself by writing reviews, criticism, short stories, and novels. His criticism is now considered prescient, and stories such as "Silent Snow, Secret Snow"—prose versions of his metaphysically introspective inquiries—are much-anthologized classics. His first and second marriages were disrupted by his compulsive affairs, the obsessive quality of which was hardly understood in his time. Guilt pervaded his poetry thereafter.

Most critics—including Aiken himself—dismissed his first published volume of verse, *Earth Triumphant* (1914), as derivative, mainly of John Masefield. *Turns and Movies* (1916) departed from the first volume, depicting the nights of the Vaudeville circuit Aiken loved, where he pursued his illicit liaisons. The blunt, edgy images depict dysfunctional, chaotic relationships. At this time Ezra Pound was promoting Imagism, which called for a new poetic vocabulary to counter fin-de-siècle floridity in favor of a more pruned, viscerally direct language. While Aiken would not claim to be a Pound disciple per se, in 1915 he became a good friend of the poet John Gould Fletcher, a member of the Imagist movement. Fletcher published *Goblins and Pagodas* from the same publisher as *Turns and Movies* in 1916, and the two friends thought of the volumes as companion pieces.

From 1914 until 1930 Aiken lived mainly in England and wrote verse from passion while living off his prose. His audacity was often better understood by his close coterie of friends than by critics. From 1915 to 1920 Aiken composed a sequence of long poems, subtitled "symphonies": *The Jig of Forslin* (1916), *The Charnel Rose* (1918), *Senlin: A Biography* (1918), *The House of Dust* (1920), and *The Pilgrimage of Festus* (1923). He considered them a single long work of musical "movements" meant for one book, but they were published separately, lessening their overall impact. Rhythmically intricate, deft and fluid, the poems used a facile sonority as counterpoint to disturbing images that suggested much more between the lines than in them. Critics of his era praised Aiken's technique but chided him for elevating style over substance, focusing more on the *in* than the *in-between.* The substance of these poems did not become apparent until after World War II, when W.H. Auden's *Age of Anxiety* encouraged more psychological readings of poems. In 1949 the "movements" were finally published together as *The Divine Pilgrim* to greater appreciation.

Aiken's 1929 *Selected Poems* earned the Pulitzer Prize; his future work received more attention. *Preludes for Memnon* (1931) and its sequel, *Time in the Rock: Preludes to Definition* (1936, when he returned to America permanently), are considered his greatest achievement. Fugues rather than symphonies, these poems layer stanzas with superimposed themes reiterated and reinforced in variations rather than repetitions. Aiken forsakes the violent, disturbing aspects of consciousness explored in his earlier work for calmer meditations such as those Eliot would later pursue in his *Four Quartets*.

In 1937 a mellowed Aiken married again and found a bliss that informed his subsequent work, although consciousness remained at the center of works such as *And in the Human Heart* (1940), *Brownstone Eclogues* (1942), and *The Kid* (1947). *Ushant* (1952) is a stream-of-consciousness autobiography that would influence some of the Beat writing of the 1950s. Aiken turned to light verse with *A Seizure of Limericks* (1964) and two books of children's verse: *Cats, Bats and Things with Wings* (1965) and *Tom, Sue and the Clock* (1966). *Thee* (1967) is a Taoist meditation on spirit that never mentions God.

While Aiken's popularity resurged in the 1950s, it later subsided. He was a unique poet who served his art rather than promoted it, an innovator of the introspective perambulations that are integral to so much contemporary poetry.

DAVID GARRETT IZZO

**Biography**
Born in Savannah, Georgia, 5 August 1889. Attended Harvard University, Cambridge, Massachusetts (President, *Harvard Advocate*), 1907–10, 1911–12, A.B. 1912; contributing editor, *The Dial*, 1916–19; American correspondent, *Athenaeum*, London, 1919–25, and London *Mercury*, 1921–22; Instructor, Harvard University, 1927–28; London correspondent, *New Yorker*, 1934–36; fellow, 1947, and consultant in poetry, 1950–52, Library of Congress, Washington, D.C. Received Pulitzer Prize, 1930; Shelley Memorial Award, 1930; Guggenheim fellowship, 1934; National Book Award, 1954; Bollingen Prize, 1956; Academy of American Poets fellowship, 1957; American Academy Gold Medal, 1958; Huntington Hartford Foundation Award, 1960; Brandeis University Creative Arts Award, 1967; National Medal for Literature, 1969; member, American Academy, 1957. Died in Savannah, Georgia, 17 August 1973.

**Poetry**
*Earth Triumphant, and Other Tales in Verse*, 1914
*The Jig of Forslin: A Symphony*, 1916
*Turns and Movies, and Other Tales in Verse*, 1916
*Nocturne of Remembered Spring, and Other Poems*, 1917
*The Charnel Rose, Senlin: A Biography, and Other Poems*, 1918
*The House of Dust: A Symphony*, 1920
*Punch: The Immortal Liar*, 1921
*The Pilgrimage of Festus*, 1923
*Priapus and the Pool, and Other Poems*, 1925
*(Poems)*, edited by Louis Untermeyer, 1927
*Selected Poems*, 1929
*John Deth: A Metaphysical Legend, and Other Poems*, 1930
*Preludes for Memnon*, 1931
*The Coming Forth by Day of Osiris Jones*, 1931
*Landscape West of Eden*, 1934
*Time in the Rock: Preludes to Definition*, 1936
*And in the Human Heart*, 1940
*Brownstone Eclogues, and Other Poems*, 1942
*The Soldier*, 1944
*The Kid*, 1947
*The Divine Pilgrim*, 1949
*Skylight One: Fifteen Poems*, 1949
*Collected Poems*, 1953
*A Letter from Li Po, and Other Poems*, 1955
*Sheepfold Hill: Fifteen Poems*, 1958
*Selected Poems*, 1961
*The Morning Song of Lord Zero: Poems Old and New*, 1963
*A Seizure of Limericks*, 1964
*Preludes*, 1966
*Thee*, 1967
*Collected Poems, 1916–1970*, 1970
*The Clerk's Journal, Being the Diary of a Queer Man: An Undergraduate Poem, Together with a Brief Memoir of Dean LeBaron Russell Briggs, T.S. Eliot, and Harvard, in 1911*, 1971
*A Little Who's Zoo of Mild Animals* (for children), 1977
*Selected Poems*, 1980

**Selected Criticism**
*A Reviewer's ABC: Collected Criticism of Conrad Aiken from 1916 to the Present*, edited by Rufus A. Blanshard, 1958; as *Collected Criticism*, 1968

**Other Writings:** play, short stories (*Among the Lost People*, 1934), novels (*Blue Voyage*, 1927), an autobiography (*Ushant*, 1952), children's poetry (*Cats, Bats and Things with Wings*, 1965; *Tom, Sue and the Clock*, 1966), correspondence (*Selected Letters*, edited by Joseph Killorin, 1978).

**Further Reading**
Butscher, Edward, *Conrad Aiken, Poet of White Horse Vale*, Athens: University of Georgia Press, 1988
Cowley, Malcolm, "A Priest of Consciousness," in *The Flower and the Leaf: A Contemporary Record of American Writing since 1941*, New York: Viking, 1985
Hoffman, Frederick John, *Conrad Aiken*, New York: Twayne, 1962
Martin, Jay, *Conrad Aiken: A Life of His Art*, Princeton, New Jersey: Princeton University Press, 1962
Spivey, Ted R., *Time's Stop in Savannah: Conrad Aiken's Inner Journey*, Macon, Georgia: Mercer University Press, 1997

# Will Alexander 1948–

Will Alexander, a Los Angeles poet of African-American descent, has been prolific (if sometimes partially hidden) since the publication of his first book, *Vertical Rainbow Climber* (1987). His published work (which often includes his own drawings) straddles multiple genre classifications and often seems invested in calling into question the very category of poetry. Most important, because of his fondness for archaic usage, for neologism, and for a sentence (and poetic phrase) style that accumulates rather than sorts—what Harryette Mullen has called a "hyper-hypotactic sentence"—Alexander constantly risks dismissal as being merely willfully obscure. "I'm consumed with trying to find my own language," Alexander has stated, but if the reader is willing to come to terms with both the urgency and the character of that quest, the poet has foregrounded the possibility of a productive (multi)valence, and the quest is thus unlikely to be rejected as narcissism. That impressive escape is, perhaps, a result of his willingness to talk of (if nothing else) biological and aesthetic genealogies and their interesting convergence.

Never to be mistaken as an ideologue, Alexander has described his creative output as marked by a peculiar doubleness, rooted in the differing approaches to life he saw embodied by his parents. His father he describes as "steady" and about locality, home, and power in this world; his mother, however, is about magic, intuition, transcendence, and clairvoyance. This dual inheritance and gift provides the poet with a singular means to approach the "primeval," which, in Alexander's poetics (and criticism), is the eternal shared past. This is not strictly an archaeological or a political conception of "past" but rather an attempt to get back to a paradoxically unreachable genesis moment of human consciousness. Like other counter-Enlightenment figures, Alexander is convinced that present change is dependent on fundamental encounter with the mediation of language, a coming to terms with what is permanently lost.

Alexander's most accomplished work of poetry, *Asia and Haiti* (1995), is organized around an unusual dialogue between the world situations of late-20th-century Tibetan Buddhists (conquered by the Chinese communists) and the endlessly contested Caribbean black republic. While by no means "history poems" per se, the two long compositions that make up the dialogue alternately rely on discernible narratives of liberation and enslavement and the jarring dissonance created by the surprising juxtaposition of the title locations. They are noteworthy for their command of geography, history, and cosmology and, coincidentally, a casual disregard for comprehensiveness, objectivity, and interpretation as measured response. While a student of the poems could certainly become knowledgeable about the geographic places, their incomplete or staggered presentation is intended to invite or establish not "mastery" but some alternative consciousness. A similarly conspicuous and adept admixture of palpability and fabrication (if not hallucination) can be found in an important early prose poem, "Mountain Slope Swimming in Detroit" (1987). Affiliating impossible physical action with a rich panorama of city landmarks, milestones, and ephemera, somehow the poem productively rants against urban disrepair and hate while never swaying from its surrealist commitment into didactic explication. History and myth are not so much exacting and alternating terms here as they are an interestingly protean dyad; one becomes the other, partaking of its mental currency and offering reassurance toward its inevitable incompleteness.

A further doubleness in Alexander's creativity might be marked by the ways in which it is appropriate to simultaneously locate him inside and outside typical delineations of African-American poetry. He has pointed out the importance of the African-American surrealist poet Bob Kaufman to his development but has also claimed Arthur Rimbaud as the poet who clarified his own calling to write. (See his important essay "Bob Kaufman: The Footnotes Exploded," in *Conjunctions* 29 [1997].) Since Alexander's poetry has little truck with African-American vernacular, is distant from specific confrontation with the peculiarities of American race relations, and is hard to place relative to the influence of the preeminent African-American Modernists (Gwendolyn Brooks, Robert Hayden, or Langston Hughes), it is unlikely that his work will be readily canonized within any consensus academic accounting of African-American poetics. Still, his reliance on "found language" is reminiscent of some accounts of black aesthetics in which improvisatory virtuosity is seen as definitive of black difference or singularity; moreover, his continued valorization of Kaufman itself points out how accounts of black poetic achievement continue to be circumscribed by narrowed expectations. In general, Alexander, like African-American poets Nathaniel Mackey, Harryette Mullen, and Ed Roberson, has found that it is wholly possible to effectively exist at the crossroads of American experimental poetries and post-1960 African-American avant-gardism. Multiplicity in influence (and perhaps even agenda) prevents neither psychic clarity nor specific kinds of allegiance. However, noting as further influences Aimé Césaire, Federico García Lorca, Octavio Paz, and Antonin Artaud and as further contemporary conversation partners Clayton Eshleman, Fanny Howe, Philip Lamantia, and Leslie Scalapino, Alexander incessantly describes and builds an anti-provincial intellectuality and commitment to the dismissal of conventional artistic categories.

Unfortunately, Alexander's work has yet to receive the kinds of sustained attention necessary to unpacking his valorization of the "arcane." Part of this is likely a result of his intimidating array of sources (see, for instance, the essay "Isolation and Gold," in *Towards the Primeval Lightning Field* [1998]), but part, too, may be a suspicion on the part of critics that a traditional exegesis will not serve to reveal the tangible pleasures of Alexander's poetry, relying as it does on a sustained unhinging of "tradition," "exegesis," and so on. This, however, is too pessimistic an assessment. As Alexander has said, "The work finds an audience," by which he might mean not only that his books will be conventionally distributed but also that some process is already at work by which his poetry's strangeness will produce both wonder and understanding.

JAMES C. HALL

**Biography**

Born 27 July 1948 in Los Angeles, California. Attended University of California-Los Angeles, B.A. 1972; since 1996 has taught at University of California-San Diego, New College, San Francisco, Hofstra University, Hempstead, New York, and State University of New York at Buffalo. Received Whiting grant, 2000–01. Living in Los Angeles.

**Poetry**
*Vertical Rainbow Climber,* 1987
*Arcane Lavender Morals,* 1994
*Asia and Haiti,* 1995
*The Stratospheric Canticles,* 1995
*Above the Human Nerve Domain,* 1998
*Towards the Primeval Lightning Field,* 1998

**Other Writings:** novels (*Pandora's Hatchery,* 1994), novella (*Alien Weaving,* 2001), plays (*Conduction in the Catacombs,* 1997), and essays (*Singing in the Magnetic Hoofbeat,* 2002).

**Further Reading**

Joron, Andrew, "On Alexandrian Philosophy," in *Towards the Primeval Lightning Field,* by Will Alexander, Oakland, California: O Books, 1998
Mullen, Harryette, "'Hauling Up Gold from the Abyss': An Interview with Will Alexander," *Callaloo* 22, no. 2 (1999)

---

# Miguel Algarín 1941–

Miguel Algarín has nurtured "Nuyorican" (New York Puerto Rican) poetry and theater in the Lower East Side of Manhattan for almost three decades. Founder of the Nuyorican Poets Café, Algarín is one of the most important promoters of performance poetry in the contemporary United States. He arrived in New York City in the summer of 1951, when he was nine years old. Although he had experienced some degree of racism from fairer-skinned islanders as a child in his native Puerto Rico, the race tensions of mid-20th-century New York City certainly affected his life greatly. Despite their hardscrabble existence in neighborhoods fraught with poverty, drug use, and violence, Algarín's parents infused his youth with a love of culture. He subsequently earned his undergraduate and master's degrees, and pursued doctoral work in comparative literature in subjects ranging from Shakespeare to Pablo Neruda. Algarín ultimately refused to officially complete his doctorate at Rutgers University, objecting to the "intelligentsia industry" that he felt doctoral programs had become. Instead he published his thesis, a translation of Neruda's *Song of Protest,* with William Morrow in 1976. Ironically, despite Algarín's refusal to formally complete his doctoral degree at Rutgers, the university not only hired Algarín as a professor in its English department but also awarded him tenure.

Algarín's introduction to Neruda's *Song of Protest* explains not only the importance of Neruda's book to Puerto Ricans who want to understand their own history through anti-imperialist eyes, but also many of Algarín's motivations in writing his own poetry. "History," writes Algarín, "is personalized. It is attached to the individual. History, made concrete and contemporary, nourishes the memory of the individual and of the whole nation." First and foremost Miguel Algarín's poetry aims to nourish the Nuyorican community of "Loisaida" (the Nuyorican renaming of Manhattan's Lower East Side). It also invites a larger audience to read against the grain of histories that have sorted people of different nations and colors in awkward sociopolitical configurations, arrangements that often obscure the common experiences shared by all people.

Algarín's poetry often returns to what he calls "the zero-point place": home, or that place where one feels a sense of belonging. His readers should prepare themselves for the multi-lingualism native to his own, distinctively Nuyorican, zero-point place. Rather than a strict bilingualism, in which English and Spanish alternate in discrete strophes on the page, multi-lingualism embraces a hybrid, jostling "Spanglish," a linguistic synthesis of the two languages. Just as the Nuyoricans figured prominently in Algarín's poetry find themselves in a "neither/nor" relationship with the larger United States and Puerto Rico ("neither" accepted as part of the mainstream" U.S. "nor" as "authentic" Puerto Ricans), Algarín's poetry straddles a divide between North American and Caribbean poetic traditions. As Algarín wrote in his 1975 introduction to *Nuyorican Poetry: An Anthology of Puerto Rican Words and Feelings* (the first published anthology of Nuyorican poetry, which he co-edited with poet Miguel Piñero):

> Everything is in English in the U.S.A., yet there is also a lot of Spanish, and Spanish is now gaining. The mixture of both languages grows. The interchange between both yields new verbal possibilities, new images to deal with the stresses of living on tar and cement. There is at the edge of every empire a linguistic explosion that results from the many multilingual tribes that collect around wealth and power.

The multi-lingual tribe of the Nuyoricans featured so prominently in Algarín's poetry, in fact, may be even more important to the poet than the language and politics of Loisaida. When Algarín tackles large sociopolitical portraits, he grounds his views in his own interpersonal relationships. If he worries about the AIDS epidemic, as in his popular poem "HIV," he worries about the way the disease "contaminates" the sexual expressions between people in love. When he talks about the globalization of Nuyorican aesthetics via multimedia technology in "Nuyorican Angel of Wordsmithing," his goal in using "MTV Unplugged" to "reach millions" across the world is to "interact *live,*" to demonstrate "how a verse can heal human pain." In this way Algarín shows his readers how global forces so often come down to local, human passions: love, hate, anger, lust, longing, and sadness. Even when he takes his readers on a fantastic journey into the cybernetic future of *Body Bee Calling from the 21st Century* (1982), where some would speculate that computers and bionics may have reduced human contact, Algarín posits a world redeemed by "embracing [the] certain sweetness" of lovemaking's inefficiencies. As Efraín Barradas notes in the introduction to *Body Bee,* this commitment to the flow of life implicit in such human contact lies in the tradition of Walt Whitman's "Song of Myself." In this vision of America the burgeoning democratic spirit must necessarily be characterized not just by diversity and industry but also by the sexuality of the masses.

Just as Whitman characterizes his bardic poetry as a "song," so Algarín sings his poems—literally. For Algarín the poem lives only partially on the page. Each time he performs one of his poems, it comes alive in a combination of speech and song, sometimes rich and resonant, sometimes keening and pained. By varying the performance of his poems Algarín reaffirms the alternating voice that his aesthetic privileges and also nods to the oral tradition in Caribbean poetry, which shares rhythmic roots with the lively beats of *salsa, merengue, bomba, mambo,* and other lively musical genres of Caribbean origin.

Algarín's role as a poet and editor certainly energizes much of what has come to be known as Nuyorican literature. He incorporates into that tradition not only an awareness of the Lower East Side neighborhoods that Nuyoricans call home but also a sense of how a Nuyorican presence in New York City corresponds to a stake in the future of a multicultural American literary tradition.

Trenton Hickman

**Biography**

Born in Santurce, Puerto Rico, 11 September 1941. Attended University of Wisconsin, Madison, B.A. 1963; Pennsylvania State University, Philadelphia, M.A. 1965; Rutgers University, New Brunswick, New Jersey. Lecturer, Brooklyn College, Brooklyn, New York, 1965–67; Instructor, Middlesex County College, Edison, New Jersey, 1968; Assistant Professor, then Associate Professor, Rutgers University, New Brunswick, New Jersey, from 1971; editor of Nuyorican Press; director of El Puerto Rican Playwrights'/Actors' Workshop, 1974; executive director of Nuyorican Theater Festival; founder of Nuyorican Poets Cafe, 1975; visiting poet, Naropa Institute, Boulder, Colorado, 1978. Received Samuel Rubin Foundation grant, 1975; Peabody Foundation grant; New York State Council of the Arts grant. Living in New York City.

**Poetry**

*Mongo Affair,* 1978
*On Call,* 1980
*Body Bee Calling from the 21st Century,* 1982
*Time's Now/Ya Es Tiempo,* 1986
*Love Is Hard Work; Memorias de Loisaida,* 1997

**Other Writings:** plays (*The Murder of Pito,* 1976), translation of Spanish poetry (*Song of Protest,* by Pablo Neruda, 1976), television programs (*Side Show, the Making of a Play,* 1975); edited collections of poetry (*Nuyorican Poetry: An Anthology of Puerto Rican Words and Feelings* [co-edited with Miguel Piñero], 1975).

**Further Reading**

Acosta-Belén, Edna, "Beyond Island Boundaries: Ethnicity, Gender, and Cultural Revitalization in Nuyorican Literature," *Callaloo* 15, no. 4 (Autumn 1992)
Aparicio, Frances, "On Sub-Versive Signifiers: U.S. Latina/o Writers Tropicalize English," *American Literature* 66, no. 4 (December 1994)
Hernández, Carmen Dolores, *Puerto Rican Voices in English,* London: Praeger, 1997 (contains an interview with Algarín)
Phillips, J.J., et al., editors, *The Before Columbus Foundation Poetry Anthology: Selections from the American Book Awards, 1980–1990,* New York: Norton, 1992

---

# Julia Alvarez 1950–

One of the most important Latina poets to emerge in the final decades of the century, Julia Alvarez writes poetry that straddles the cultural and linguistic borders between an early life in the Dominican Republic and a subsequent upbringing in the United States. Alvarez identifies herself as "Dominican, hyphen, American," anxious to reject the either/or fallacy that she feels both the dominant Anglo-American culture and the Latino minority cultures of the United States wish to foist upon her. Instead she insists on the importance of essential ties to what she calls a past "torn" and "broken" by competing languages, fraught gender roles, and disparate social realities.

Julia Alvarez was born in New York City to Dominican parents who returned to the Dominican Republic shortly after her birth. Alvarez, whose well-educated parents belonged to landed families of means, enjoyed a life of relative ease during her early years in the Caribbean. This idyllic life of privilege abruptly ended when her father, who had involved himself with resistance groups committed to the overthrow of then-dictator Rafael Trujillo, was forced suddenly to flee his homeland with his family to avoid imprisonment, torture, and likely execution at the hands of Trujillo's secret police. Alvarez and her family suddenly plunged into an economically less-privileged life in Queens, New York, where she and her sisters did not speak the language and no longer occupied a prominent standing in the community. In the autobiographical paragraph Alvarez has published on her Middlebury College website, she refers to this sudden entry into New York life as "land[ing]" in "English." In the United States, Alvarez's Spanish would gradually yield to a "Spanglish" increasingly colonized by English.

For Alvarez, arriving in the United States meant arriving in a land of books. By her own account she hardly read literature of her own volition while in the Dominican Republic; in New York, she read every chance she could get. By the time she entered her teenage years, she knew that she wanted to be a writer. Upon winning several student writing competitions, she gained even more resolve to pursue her chosen career. During the late 1970s she worked as a poet in public schools in Kentucky, Delaware, and North Carolina and in 1978 received funding from the National Endowment for the Arts to create a bilingual program. In 1979 she was awarded the John Atherton Scholarship in Poetry by the Bread Loaf Writers' Conference.

The publication of her first book of poems, *Homecoming* (1984), preceded what would be her first serious experimentation with the genres of the short story and the novel, although Alvarez makes it clear in one autobiographical statement that she "never abandoned poetry." Indeed, poetry won her a National Endowment for the Arts grant in 1987. After publishing two successful novels, *How the García Girls Lost Their Accents* (1991) and *In the Time of the Butterflies* (1994), Alvarez published a second book of poems, *The Other Side/El Otro Lado* (1995). In 1996 she reissued an expanded version of her first book of poems, *Homecoming: New and Collected Poems. Something to Declare* (1998) collects two dozen of her personal essays, many of which speak to her "hyphenated" existence as a Dominican-American writer in the United States.

*Homecoming* details the scores of domestic duties that a traditional mother inculcates in her daughter: bed-making, dusting, sewing, mending, cleaning, hanging the wash, and so on. Despite the narrator's resistance to these lessons and to the gender inequities she perceives in them, Alvarez finally likens her writing to these "arts" of "woman's work" taught to her in her youth. *Homecoming* also explores the unrealistic romantic expectations promoted in popular women's magazines and fairy tales. Ultimately the poems conclude that it is better to be one of the "unstoried women who [form] the mere backdrop" to the "beauty" and "betrayals" of pop-culture "heroines" than it is to lead a life aboard the "jailhouse train" of unfulfilled expectations. The most significant group of poems in *Homecoming,* the ambitious sonnet sequence "33," contains a sonnet for each of the poet's 33 years (the reissue of *Homecoming* in 1996 contains 46 sonnets). After first asking what it means to be a single Dominican-American woman approaching middle age, the sonnets finally make a larger gesture toward all aging readers of the poems:

Those of you lost and yearning to be free,
who hear these words, take heart from me.
I once was in as many drafts as you.
But briefly, essentially, here I am.
Who touches this poem touches a woman.

*The Other Side/El Otro Lado* delves deeper into the cultural rift where Alvarez makes her home as a writer, featuring an increased interspersion of Spanish words in the English poems and a more careful questioning of what it means to be "bilingual" and "bicultural." These later poems also explore issues of desire and sexuality as important components in the making of herself as a writer. "Bookmaking," a poem selected by Mark Strand for inclusion in *The Best American Poetry 1991,* links her love of books to her love of the human body, intertwining insights Alvarez gleans from a visit to the book displays at New York City's Pierpont Morgan Library with accounts of her love affair with a bookmaker. "Now the words become flesh," Alvarez writes, blending eroticism and bibliophilia until sexuality and textuality become difficult to distinguish:

the seam of the spine
centered in the jacket of the shoulders,
    the ligaments tooled in the plates
of the clavicles, the legible bones
    of the wrists and the ankles.

The poetry of Julia Alvarez advances a prominent Latina voice in the final two decades of the 20th century, framing broad issues of knowing one's own identity by scrutinizing her own identities as a woman, a Latina, and a poet. While the most important poetic accomplishments of her career may well occur in the 21st century, her contribution has already been substantial and impressive.

TRENTON HICKMAN

**Biography**

Born in New York City, 27 March 1950. Attended Connecticut College, New London, 1967–69; Middlebury College, Vermont, B.A. 1971; Syracuse University, New York, M.F.A. 1975; Bread Loaf School of English, Ripton, Vermont, 1979–80; poet-in-the-schools, Kentucky, Delaware, North Carolina, 1975–78; Instructor, Phillips Andover Academy, Andover, Massachusetts, 1979–81; Visiting Assistant Professor, University of Vermont, Burlington, 1981–83; visiting writer, George Washington University, Washington, D.C., 1984–85; Assistant Professor, University of Illinois, Urbana, 1985–88; since 1988 Associate Professor, Middlebury College, Vermont. Received Academy of American Poetry Prize, 1974; Syracuse University fellowship, 1974–75; La Reina Press Award, 1982; Bread Loaf Writers' Conference fellowship, 1986; General Electric Foundation Award, 1986; National Endowment for the Arts grant, 1987–88; Ingram Merrill Foundation grant, 1990. Living in Middlebury, Vermont.

**Poetry**

*Homecoming,* 1984; revised edition, as *Homecoming: New and Collected Poems,* 1996
*The Other Side/El Otro Lado,* 1995

**Other Writings:** novels (*How the García Girls Lost Their Accents,* 1991; *In the Time of the Butterflies,* 1994), children's literature (*The Secret Footprints,* 2000), essays (*Something to Declare,* 1998); edited anthologies of poetry (*Old Age Ain't for Sissies,* 1979).

**Further Reading**

Barak, Julie, "'Turning and Turning in the Widening Gyre': A Second Coming into Language in Julia Alvarez's *How the García Girls Lost Their Accents,*" *MELUS* 23, no.1 (1998)
Rosario-Sievert, Heather, "Conversation with Julia Alvarez," *Review: Latin American Literature and Arts* 54 (1997)
Umpierre, Luz Maria, "Sexualidad y metapoesía: Cuatro poemas de Julia Álvarez," *The Americas Review: A Review of Hispanic Literature and Art of the USA* 17, no. 1 (1989)
Vela, Richard, "Daughter of Invention: The Poetry of Julia Alvarez," *Postscript* 16 (1999)

## American Indian Poetry. *See* Native American Poetry

---

## A.R. Ammons 1926–2001

Despite being one of the great American poets of the 20th century, A.R. Ammons irascibly refused to adhere to the labels set upon him by critics. His work has never been easy to categorize, and his career was marked by sudden turns that seem intended to confuse the issue of what kind of poet he is. For many, he remains the prototypical American Romantic: *The Dictionary of Literary Biography* in 1996 called him the "foremost living representative of the American Romantic tradition in poetry." His Romanticism was always rather skeptical, however, and his views of nature too dependent on humankind's frail and fumbling interactions with it for him to be seen as purely Romantic.

Nevertheless, Ammons is still often called a nature poet, although others see him as a scientific one; he is an Old Testament prophet or a gross hedonist; self-reflective or all encompassing; obsessed with cataclysmic events or quotidian ones; smitten with beauty or obsessed with trash; a master of short, observational lyrics that define moments, or of long, contemplative poems that seek the grandest themes and subjects as represented in a single, all-encompassing image. Too playful for some, too serious for others; too obscure or too simple. In short, he typifies Whitman's famous self-proclamation: "I contain multitudes."

A prodigious writer, Ammons published nearly 30 books in the last 35 years of the 20th century. His influences were the Bible, Robert Browning, Whitman, Lao-Tse, and William Carlos Williams. Although critics often cite Emerson as an influence, Ammons admitted that he did not read Emerson much until Harold Bloom suggested an Emersonian influence. His dominant influences were more experiential than literary: his farm childhood, his family, and his interest in science.

Stylistically, Ammons remained iconoclastic. In the process he also confounded more than a few critics, for he appeared, at least on the surface, to eschew the critics and what they said. He seemed at times more an anti-poet than one anxious for acceptance, sometimes making fun of both critic and poet at the same time, and often managing to downplay the importance of both. Ammons moved back and forth between the lyric and the long poem as easily as he moved from the narrative to the observational to the meditation. He unabashedly employed the spontaneous poetics for which Jack Kerouac was so roundly chastised by critics of a previous generation. Like Cummings, he rarely used capitalization and often laughed at the many interpretations generated by his idiosyncratic use of the colon, his punctuation mark of choice. He also maintained a consistent and engaging interest in how poems are structured, and in the relationship between shape and structure in the physical world and in the poem itself. To that end, much of Ammons' poetic concern is for the dichotomy between the individual and the many, the self and others, the poem and the world. He finds metaphors to explore that dichotomy all about him. Poems are everywhere in the world, he said, if one can but find them. Form in the world echoes form in the poem, but "The writings about the stone do not replace the stone. Nothing can replace the stone." Of poetry itself, he said, "Nothing that can be said about it in words is worth saying." Many of his poems are self-reflective discussions of his methods of composition, sometimes imitating the flow of thought itself. For Ammons, poetry about writing poetry is also poetry about being alive in the world.

Over the course of his long career, Ammons also switched thematic gears at will. At his best he bridges seemingly impossible gaps. Nature and science go as much hand-in-hand in Ammons' poetic world as do the cataclysmic and quotidian. He demonstrates, sometimes going to great lengths, that one cannot appreciate beauty without understanding trash, that great moments mean nothing without the mundane that surrounds them. In fact, his poems often seek to define the moment when beauty starts to turn, inexorably, into something else. Despite humanity's desire for the concretely knowable, "concretion is a myth," he said. "Look into any so-called 'solid object' and it breaks down into this, that and the other until finally there may be nothing going on there but motion" ("From the Wind to the Earth: An Interview with A.R. Ammons," in Schneider, 1999). For Ammons, poems are motion, process.

Whether because he lived most of his life in New York or because so few, relatively speaking, of his poems reclaim the landscapes of his youth, Ammons avoided for most of his career being labeled a "Southern" writer. In his poems he never strayed very far from the farm he grew up on, however, in the swampy lowlands of North Carolina. In fact, had not the Depression forced his father to sell the family farm, Ammons believed that he himself would have spent his life as a farmer. The impact of the Depression on his childhood never left him, despite how far in years and miles he traveled. He often wrote about the indelible imprint those years made upon him and his poetic sensibilities:

> I love the land and the terrible dependency on the weather and the rain and the wind. It betrays many a farmer, but makes the interests of the farmer's life tie in very immediately with everything that's going wrong meteorologically. . . . That's where I got my closeness and attention to the soil, weeds, plants, insects, and trees. ("An Interview," in Ammons, 1996)

In addition to occasional narratives about Carolina roots, his poems often reflect his fine eye and ear for the small moments afforded by daily existence, his ongoing interest in land and landscapes, weather, cycles, and, particularly, his concern with boundaries. An image from his U.S. Navy experience—he joined near the end of World War II—indelibly marks most of his poetry. From the bow of his ship, the *U.S.S. Gunason,* he had been observing an island on the distant horizon, when he realized that

> the water level was not what it was because of a single command by a higher power but because of an average result of a host of actions—runoffs, wind currents, melting glaciers. ("The *Paris Review* Interview," in Ammons, 1996)

Because of this "interior illumination," he began to "apprehend things in the dynamics of themselves." The "line" where land meets ocean, he realizes, would reveal itself on closer inspection to be rising and falling with the tides: the line is fluid and alive, not fixed.

Although he had been writing since high school, it was not until his stint in the Navy that Ammons found time and inclination to seriously pursue poetry. Despite some early encouragement, it would be another decade, however, before his first poems would start finding their way into print. In the meantime, he returned to North Carolina to study biology, botany, and chemistry at Wake Forest College. He spent a year after graduation as a school principal, started but did not complete graduate work at the University of California at Berkeley, and then settled in southern New Jersey, where he began what he believed would be his career as an executive at a glass manufacturer operated by his father-in-law.

Ammons' first collection, *Ommateum,* was self-published in 1955; it sold 16 copies in five years. Still, he continued to write: "I spent twenty years writing on my own without any recognition" ("The *Paris Review* Interview"). Things began turning for him quickly in July 1963, when he gave a now-famous reading at Cornell University and was subsequently asked why he did not teach. "Why don't you ask me?" he replied. He joined the faculty in 1964.

At Cornell Ammons quickly began to see the results of his years of work in obscurity. *Expressions of Sea Level* (1964) was followed by *Corsons Inlet* and *Tape for the Turn of the Year,* both published in 1965, *Northfield Poems* (1966), and *Selected Poems* (1968). *Tape* was his first dramatic experiment in form, composed on an adding machine tape and concluded when the tape ran out. By 1975 he had published 11 volumes of poetry, including his *Collected Poems, 1951–1971* (1972), which received the National Book Award, and the long poem *Sphere: The Form of a Motion* (1974), which was awarded the Bollingen Prize. By this point Ammons' critical reputation had been established, primarily by Harold Bloom's astute criticism and his insistence that Ammons was "a major visionary . . . the Poet that Emerson prophesied as necessary for America" (1986).

*The Snow Poems* (1977) marked a turn both in Ammons' poetry and in its reception. It was critically panned by virtually everyone except for William Harmon and Helen Vendler. Ammons' own comments on the book make it seem more an anti-poem, something composed to fly in the face of both contemporary poetry and its critics, than an attempt to please his readers:

> I had meant to write a book of a thousand pages . . . because I wanted to say here is a thousand pages of trash that nevertheless indicates that every image and every event on the planet and everywhere else is significant and could be great poetry, sometimes is in passages and lines. But I stopped at three hundred pages. I had worn myself and everybody else out. ("An Interview")

*The Snow Poems* typifies his belief that "poems are not written in order to be studied or discussed but to be encountered."

Soon after, Ammons returned to more lyrical and accessible work, winning the National Book Critics Circle Award for *A Coast of Trees* (1981) and publishing two other slim volumes of lyrics within the next two years. It was not until *Garbage* (1993), however, that his critical reputation seemed fully restored. It earned for him another National Book Award and has been lauded as "a brilliant book," "a dazzling dance of purposes and speculations, made of whatever material it finds at hand." *Garbage,* like most of his long poems, began with a single image, a notion of the garbage heap as the central metaphor for contemporary American society. In this important work Ammons contemplates what it means to be disposable, and how it feels to be living in a world increasingly filled with waste in all its various forms.

Ammons had a massive coronary in 1989, and in 1998 he suffered a hematoma followed by brain seizures and had to have emergency surgery. His poetic output remained prodigious: *Brink Road* (1996) and *Glare* (1997) continue his explorations of the long poem, spontaneous composition, and many of his thematic interests such as garbage and the peripheries of things. In addition to the prizes given to his individual books, Ammons was also awarded the Frost Medal, a MacArthur fellowship, and the Academy of American Poets' prestigious Tanning Prize, at $100,000 the largest literary prize in the United States.

Since he was first noticed in the mid-1960s, critical response to Ammons' poems has generally been favorable if not laudatory, except for the period surrounding *The Snow Poems.* Bloom and Vendler dominated early discussions of his work, but Steven Schneider has led a shift in recent years that recognizes Ammons as a poet with an ecological conscience grounded in the scientific. For Ammons the simplest walk was fraught with heightened meaning. He found adventure in the smallest places, such as a few drops of water in a seashell, or collected on a leaf where a wasp drinks thirstily. He found high drama in a blue jay eating a cicada, aesthetic wonder and abject horror in garbage mounds, poetry in the silence of pauses. He fashioned in the process a truly American and individualized body of work that will stand as a monument to the 20th century.

ALEX ALBRIGHT

**Biography**

Born in Whiteville, North Carolina, 18 February 1926. Attended Wake Forest College, North Carolina, B.S. 1949; University of California, Berkeley, 1950–52; served in the United States Naval Reserve, 1944–46; principal, Hatteras Elementary School, North Carolina, 1949–50; executive vice-president, Friedrich and Dimmock, Inc., Millville, New Jersey, 1952–62; Assistant Professor, 1964–68, Associate Professor, 1969–71, from 1971 Professor of English, and from 1973 Goldwin Smith Professor of Poetry, Cornell University, Ithaca, New York; Visiting Professor, Wake Forest University, 1974–75; poetry editor, *Nation,* 1963. Received Bread Loaf Writers Conference scholarship, 1961; Guggenheim fellowship, 1966; American Academy traveling fellowship, 1967, and award,

1977; Levinson Prize (*Poetry,* Chicago), 1970; honorary Litt.D., Wake Forest University, 1972, University of North Carolina, Chapel Hill, 1973; National Book Award, 1973, 1993; Bollingen Prize, 1974; MacArthur fellowship, 1981; National Book Critics Circle Award, 1982; Fellow, American Academy of Arts and Sciences, 1982; Rebekah Johnson Bobbitt Poetry Prize, 1994; Frost Medal, 1994; Ruth Lilly Poetry Prize, 1995; Tanning Prize, 1998. Died in Ithaca, New York, 25 February 2001.

**Poetry**
*Ommateum, with Doxology,* 1955
*Expressions of Sea Level,* 1964
*Corsons Inlet,* 1965
*Tape for the Turn of the Year,* 1965
*Northfield Poems,* 1966
*Selected Poems,* 1968
*Uplands,* 1970
*Briefings: Poems Small and Easy,* 1971
*Collected Poems, 1951–1971,* 1972
*Sphere: The Form of a Motion,* 1974
*Diversifications,* 1975
*The Snow Poems,* 1977
*The Selected Poems, 1951–1977,* 1977; revised edition, as *The Selected Poems,* 1986
*Highgate Road,* 1977
*For Doyle Fosco,* 1977
*Poem,* 1977
*Six-Piece Suite,* 1979
*Selected Longer Poems,* 1980
*A Coast of Trees,* 1981
*Worldly Hopes,* 1982
*Lake Effect Country,* 1983
*Easter Morning,* 1986
*Sumerian Vistas,* 1987
*The Really Short Poems of A.R. Ammons,* 1990
*Garbage,* 1993
*The North Carolina Poems,* 1994
*Brink Road,* 1996
*Glare,* 1997
*Strip,* 1997

**Other Writings:** essays (*Set in Motion: Essays, Interviews, and Dialogues,* edited by Zofia Burr, 1996), edited collection of poetry (*The Best American Poetry 1994* [with David Lehman], 1994).

**Further Reading**
Ammons, A.R., *Set in Motion: Essays, Interviews, and Dialogues,* edited by Zofia Burr, Ann Arbor: University of Michigan Press, 1996
Bloom, Harold, editor, *A.R. Ammons,* New York: Chelsea House, 1986
Kirschten, Robert, *Approaching Prayer: Ritual and the Shape of Myth in A.R. Ammons and James Dickey,* Baton Rouge: Louisiana State University Press, 1998
Kirschten, Robert, editor, *Critical Essays on A.R. Ammons,* New York: G.K. Hall, and London: Prentice Hall, 1997
Lehman, David, "Archie," *American Poet* (Summer 1998)
*Pembroke Magazine* 18 (1986) (A.R. Ammons issue)
Schneider, Steven P., *A.R. Ammons and the Poetics of Widening Scope,* Rutherford, New Jersey: Fairleigh Dickinson University Press, and London: Associated University Presses, 1994
Schneider, Steven P., editor, *Complexities of Motion: New Essays on A.R. Ammons's Long Poems,* Madison, New Jersey: Fairleigh Dickinson University Press, and London: Associated University Presses, 1999
Scigaj, Leonard M., *Sustainable Poetry: Four American Ecopoets,* Lexington: University Press of Kentucky, 1999

## Easter Morning

In his essay "A Poem Is a Walk," A.R. Ammons claims that "the purpose of a poem is to go past telling, to be recognized by burning." His poem "Easter Morning" moves the reader to that "fresh . . . particular" of insight, to the "unstructured sources of our beings" (*Set in Motion,* 1996). Even as he seeks to return the reader to something beyond language, Ammons identifies nonverbal feelings as the motivation behind his verbal expression in poetry. He claims that his poems come from and are "a way of releasing anxiety," revealing that one such source of anxiety has been the death of Elbert, his 18-month-old younger brother. Although the death occurred when Ammons was four, he says, "I still carry images of that whole thing." In a video recording of "Easter Morning," he explains that the poem, written in Ithaca, New York, just after the death of his wife's father in 1978, also recalls his childhood home of New Hope, North Carolina. The poem was "not worked up, it's just written out." He continues, "I just sat down and wrote the poem . . . basically just the way it is . . . under the pressure of feeling for my own family and for Phyllis' family." Admitting the intense grief that the poem exposes, he adds, "It touched me; I cried for most of the writing of it."

Since its first publication in *Poetry* (April 1979) and its central position in *A Coast of Trees* (1981), which won the National Book Critics Circle Award, "Easter Morning" has been viewed as one of Ammons' best and most characteristic poems as well as one of the great lyrics in English. Readers of 17th-century English poetry will hear its echoes and revisions of George Herbert's concrete poem "Easter Wings." Ammons' poem, unlike Herbert's, is divided into six sections of unequal length and forms one long, unfolding meditation, more of a walk than a bird. It dwells on paradox, on "blessings and / horrors," and, as the poet says, on "what the loss of life and the gaining of life can mean." The title's homophonic play on "morning/mourning" suggests just such verbal as well as emotional indeterminacy; in the morning moves the mourning.

Here stalks an ancient grief, such as one finds in the Anglo-Saxon elegies "The Wanderer" or "The Seafarer," where the *ubi sunt* lament of the lone speaker cries out for meaning in a broken life, the ruined world he inhabits. The same human longings motivate the lyric "I" of "Easter Morning" who speaks in the present about the past he always bears. The poem's complex verb-tense shifts demonstrate that the past's losses continue to haunt the speaker's present. "I have a life that did not become," begins the speaker, showing that the present ("have") contains a past ("did") of loss, the negative ("not") denying what might have "become." The arrested life, "astonished," inhabits the poem as a ghostly unbeing, "a child," an undeveloped psychic double for the "old man" who speaks the words of the poem. Although the man, in existential perplexity, declares

> it is to his grave I most
> frequently return and return
> to ask what is wrong, what was
> wrong . . .

the child is unable to provide insight or to help him "see it all by / the light of a different necessity." That enlightened seeing is the goal of the speaker's quest throughout the poem.

In the third section of the poem, the speaker journeys from the single grave of the child to the "graveyard," but he does not let his audience know where he has arrived until, almost as a macabre aside, he describes "everybody" as

> waiting, particularly, but not for
> me. . . .
> . . . all in the graveyard
> assembled, done for, the world they
> used to wield, have trouble and joy
> in, gone. . . .

Such loss evokes "crying out for / help," the call for someone to "fix this," but there is nothing but "flurry" and "bitter / incompletions." The "knots of / horror, silently raving" and the "empty ends not / completions, not rondures . . ." form double "knots" of "not[s]," such deep negation being all that the "child in me that could not become" finds. From this negative world of the dead, which is the center of the poem, the speaker acknowledges their powerlessness to ease his fear of "change," with its "blessings and / horrors." He grants that the troop of "great ones who / were to return" are not going to "fix this" and "can't come / back with help." Physically alone then, the speaker can only "stand on the stump / of a child" and "yell as far as [he] can" from his own particular "place" in the universe, the one to which he feels inextricably bound:

> . . . I cannot leave this place, for
> me it is the dearest and the worst,
> it is life nearest to life which is
> life lost: it is my place. . . .

Passing from the grave to the graveyard to the "stump / of a child," the speaker discovers his paradoxical knot of truth about "life," that "the life nearest to life" is actually "life lost." That is why his place is at once "the dearest and the worst." The "branches not lofting / boughs into space" and "the barren / air that holds the world that was [his] world" evoke his wordless, physical response, his "tears."

The hope for light and enlightenment that brought him to the grave finds a further paradoxical indeterminacy in the words "burn out," which simultaneously denote both light and dark. A "still" change follows the "flash high-burn / momentary structure of ash" in the last section of the poem, as the speaker moves from "ash" to "Easter morning." The pace of the poem quickens, as the six short declarations joined by colons carry the speaker toward his final vision.

What the man sees replaces the "empty ends," the "bitter incompletions" of the "barren air" with "a sight of bountiful / majesty and integrity." In the flight of the "two great birds," he sees "patterns and routes," a "breaking / from them," and a "return." He sees a "circle," the "rondures" and "completions" he lacked earlier, in the birds' "dance sacred as the sap in / the trees." The use of present participles—"oaring," "looking," "coasting," "resting," "rising," "falling," "having," and "breaking"—to describe the birds underscores their action, their free flight in contrast to the man's earlier entrapment on the "place" where he "must stand and fail." The poem's last lines take the speaker and his audience literally into the light, described as a "flood of burn breaking across us now / from the sun." The references to "breaking," describing both the birds and the man, form a verbal connection between them and suggest that the high "dance" belongs to the man as well.

"Easter Morning" depicts a spiritual journey and verbally walks the reader on that path, joining not only the child and the old man but also the audience within that simple "us." The poem's tone is conversational, and its focus looks to the universally sacred despite the embedded puns on "ash" and "sun," which obviously have Christian connotations. Its resolution is quiet, contemplative. However, Ammons has said that the "really great poet feels as deeply as anyone" yet in his art "touches" and "controls . . . lightly with delicate gestures" and brings the reader to "a quietness" (Stahl, 1986). Such is the graceful power of "Easter Morning."

ELIZABETH MILLS

**Further Reading**


Ammons, A.R., "The Art of Poetry LXXIII," *The Paris Review* 38, no. 139 (Summer 1996)

Ammons, A.R., "A Poem Is a Walk," in *Set in Motion: Essays, Interviews, and Dialogues,* by Ammons, edited by Zofia Burr, Ann Arbor: University of Michigan Press, 1996

Buell, Frederick, "The Solitary Man: The Poetry of A.R. Ammons," *Pembroke Magazine* 18 (1986)

Lehman, David, "Where Motion and Shape Coincide," *Parnassus* 9 (Fall/Winter 1981)

Lepkowsji, Frank J., "'How Are We to Find Holiness?' The Religious Vision of A.R. Ammons," *Twentieth Century Literature* 40 (1994)

Reiman, Donald H., "A.R. Ammons: Ecological Naturalism and the Romantic Tradition," *Twentieth Century Literature* 31, no. 1 (1985)

Schneider, Steven P., *A.R. Ammons and the Poetics of Widening Scope,* Rutherford, New Jersey: Fairleigh Dickinson University Press, and London: Associated University Presses, 1994

Soifer, Mark, "The Precise Magic of A.R. Ammons," *Pembroke Magazine* 18 (1986)

Stahl, Jim, "The Unassimilable Fact Leads Us On," *Pembroke Magazine* 18 (1986)

Stephenson, Shelby, "A.R. Ammons: The Dance of a Visionary," *Pembroke Magazine* 18 (1986)

Vendler, Helen, "Reason, Shape, and Wisdom," *The New Republic* (April 1981)

## Garbage

As *Tape for the Turn of the Year* (1965), "Essay on Poetics" (1972), "Hibernaculum" (1972), *Sphere: The Form of a Motion* (1974), and *The Snow Poems* (1977) amply demonstrate, A.R. Ammons is a master of the long, meandering, meditative poem in the tradition of Wallace Stevens. The 121-page *Garbage* (1993) is arguably Ammons' most aesthetically realized and thematically cogent long poem.

Like *Tape for the Turn of the Year, Garbage* was composed on adding machine tape: "I think of this tape // (this is another tape, a little wider, just about / pentameter) as the showboat churning down the // Mississippi with the banks, the fast currents, / the sandbars, drenchings. . . ." In an interview with Steven P. Schneider (1999), Ammons stated that *Garbage,* written in 1989 "over a period of two or three months . . . was entirely improvisational," neither "premeditated nor . . . ever revised." This buoyant improvisational quality permeates the entire text, which consists of 18 sections, averaging five pages each, of free-verse couplets (sections 1, 3, and 15 end with a single line, and section 6 includes one tercet). The colon, as in a good deal of Ammons' other work, is the dominant way of signifying a pause. One of the few periods in the text comes at the very end.

In *Garbage*'s "'fractal organization,'" Daniel Tobin (1999) finds "relationships of scale in both nature and poetry . . . evident in the grand shifts of perception from microscopic and subatomic to galactic and universal." Helen Vendler (1999) perceives "generic ingredients" in nearly all of the sections: "a) An emotional meditation in the first person . . . ; b) A narrative; c) A scene; d) One or more aphorisms; e) Something ugly or frightening . . . ; f) Something beautiful or reassuring . . . ; g) Remarks about poetry." She notes that Ammons' "interweaving" of these elements "makes any canto seem a farrago of cross-cuts and jump-starts," and that he utilizes a variety of voices—"the rustic, the scientific, the faux-naif, the philosophical, the descriptive, the religious." Sometimes Ammons seems at once to deliver an evocation of spiritual sublimity *and* parody. Early in the poem, gritty, acutely rendered images of processes of men, machines, and incineration atop the garbage mound's "ziggurat" are poised against high-flown abstraction:

> the driver gets out of his truck
> and wanders over to the cliff on the spill and
>
> looks off from the high point into the rosy-fine
> rising of day, the air pure, the wings of the
>
> birds white and clean as angel-food cake: holy, holy,
> holy, the driver cries and flicks his cigarette
>
> in a spiritual swoop that floats and floats before
> it touches ground: here, the driver knows,
>
> where the consummations gather, where the disposal
> flows out of form, where the last translations
>
> cast away their immutable bits and scraps,
> flits of steel, shivers of bottle and tumbler,
>
> here is the gateway to beginning, here the portal
> of renewing change. . . .

Frequently, Ammons alludes to excesses that have contributed so heavily to pollution and "waste management" dilemmas, but he never elaborates an ideological critique or earnestly moralizes. The nightmares of "toxic waste, poison air, beach goo, eroded / roads" are even seen as "possibilities" for positive change and regeneration, ones that "draw nations together" rather than encourage dangerous conflict. Ammons can (seriously?) joke that "the planet is going to // be fine, as soon as the people get off," but he can also consider human ecological resourcefulness. Reporting that "the people at / Marine Shale are said to be 'able to turn // wastes into safe products': but some say these / 'products are themselves hazardous wastes,'" he realizes that

> poetry is itself like an installation at Marine
>
> Shale: it reaches down into the dead pit
> and cool oil of stale recognition and words and
>
> brings up hauls of stringy gook which it arrays
> with light and strings with shiny syllables and
>
> gets the mind into vital relationship with
> communication channels. . . .

In section 1, which does not mention garbage but focuses on the poet's own mortality and need to adapt to circumstances of aging, Ammons meditates on opportunities for "elegance," "simplicity," and "moderation." After a quirky lecture on the virtues of soybeans, he declares, "Social Security can provide / the beans, soys enough," since his "house" is "paid for" and his "young'un / is raised"; materialism for the middle-class individual is no vice but a waste of energy: "nothing one can pay cash for seems // very valuable: that reaches a high enough / benchmark for me—high enough that I wouldn't // know what to do with anything beyond that, no / place to house it, park it, dock it, let it drift // down to. . . ."

Implicitly advocating the moderation of human egotism, *Garbage* holds that nature is the center/origin and that human beings (and their "styrofoam verbiage") are secondary. Further, as Leonard Scigaj (1998) states, "*Garbage* emphasizes homologous shared relationships between humans and various orders of sentient life." In section 2, the speaker announces that the poem "about the pre-socratic idea of the // dispositional axis from stone to wind, wind / to stone (with my elaborations, if any) // is complete before it begins. . . ." As a "scientific poem," *Garbage* asserts "that nature models values, that we / have invented little (copied), reflections of // possibilities already here. . . ." According to Fredrick Buell (1999), Ammons is questioning the emphasis on representation and ideology in recent U.S. cultural theory because "the work of science, like the idea of 'nature,' is not . . . reducible to politically-interested social constructions." Death, decay, and (re)generation dwarf human efforts to create values. However, human beings, Ammons continually emphasizes, "are not . . . / divorced from higher, finer configurations" since

> tissues and holograms of energy circulate in
> us and seek and find representations of themselves
>
> outside us, so that we can participate in
> celebrations high and know reaches of feeling

and sight and thought that penetrate (really
penetrate) far, far beyond these our wet cells. . . .

In its own circulation of "tissues and holograms of energy," *Garbage* is an abundant "celebration" of diverse late-20th-century difficulties and possibilities.

THOMAS FINK

**Further Reading**

Buell, Fredrick, "Ammons's Peripheral Vision: *Tape for the Turn of the Year* and *Garbage*," in *Complexities of Motion: New Essays on A.R. Ammons's Long Poems,* edited by Steven P. Schneider, Madison, New Jersey: Fairleigh Dickinson University Press, and London: Associated University Presses, 1999

Schneider, Steven P., *A.R. Ammons and the Poetics of Widening Scope,* Rutherford, New Jersey: Fairleigh Dickinson University Press, and London: Associated University Presses, 1994

Schneider, Steven P., "From the Wind to the Earth: An Interview with A.R. Ammons," in *Complexities of Motion: New Essays on A.R. Ammons's Long Poems,* edited by Schneider, Madison, New Jersey: Fairleigh Dickinson University Press, and London: Associated University Presses, 1999

Scigaj, Leonard M., "'The World Was the Beginning of the World': Agency and Homology in A.R. Ammons's *Garbage*," in *Reading the Earth: New Directions in the Study of Literature and the Environment,* edited by Michael P. Branch, Moscow: University of Idaho Press, 1998

Tobin, Daniel, "A.R. Ammons and the Poetics of Chaos," in *Complexities of Motion: New Essays on A.R. Ammons's Long Poems,* edited by Steven P. Schneider, Madison, New Jersey: Fairleigh Dickinson University Press, and London: Associated University Presses, 1999

Vendler, Helen, "*The Snow Poems* and *Garbage*," in *Complexities of Motion: New Essays on A.R. Ammons's Long Poems,* edited by Steven P. Schneider, Madison, New Jersey: Fairleigh Dickinson University Press, and London: Associated University Presses, 1999

## Sphere: The Form of a Motion

A.R. Ammons' second book-length poem, *Sphere: The Form of a Motion,* was published in 1974 and won the Bollingen Prize in Poetry that year. Generally praised by critics, it is widely regarded as one of Ammons' most successful book-length long poems. *Sphere* is divided into 155 numbered sections, with each section consisting of four stanzas of three lines each. The poem is, essentially, one long sentence with almost no punctuation. There are commas and colons, but there is no end stop until the poem, after 79 pages, reaches its end. It is a memorable ride. *Sphere* is a deeply original and wonderfully seductive poem.

Ammons himself speaks of *Sphere* as a breakthrough volume. He had long been attracted to the philosophical problem of "the One and the Many," and the central visual image of *Sphere,* that of the earth as recently photographed from outer space, helped Ammons to think of multiplicity and unity as reconcilable. In *Sphere,* he tells us, he "was able to manage the multifariousness of things and the unity of things so much more easily than I ever had before. I saw a continuous movement between the highest aspects of unity and the multiplicity of things, and it seemed to function so beautifully that I felt I could turn to any subject matter and know how to deal with it." It is as if the image of the earth in space might also be an image of a mind in the world.

Ammons does seem to be able "to turn to any subject matter and know how to deal with it," but he did not always have this ability. The static, constricted, prophetic voice he used in his first book, *Ommateum* (1955), constituted the book's power as well as its limitation. His attempts to introduce a variety of voices into his poetry suggested a poetics, and it is one that he discusses explicitly throughout his subsequent poems. (A cheerfully didactic tone is, after all, one of the voices he taught his poems to accommodate.) By the time he wrote *Sphere,* he had developed a deep confidence in and excitement about his poetic voice(s). In section 44 of *Sphere,* he tells us that his central aim is simply to "attract and hold attention":

this measure moves
to attract and hold attention: when one is not holding one,
that is a way of holding: dip in anywhere, go on until the

attractions fail: I angle for the self in you that can be
held, had in a thorough understanding: not to persuade
you,
enlighten you, not necessarily to delight you, but to hold

you:

The poet attracts and holds our attention by allowing us to watch him try to put his whole mind on the page. (Many first-time readers of *Sphere* will take pleasure in their dawning sense of the outrageousness of the project.) The whole mind, for Ammons, will need many different ways of speaking to express its entirety, and another attractive element of the poem is Ammons' use of various dictions. Scientific language, for example, is present throughout the poem. *Sphere* is also notable for its use of slang. Words such as "snag-gaggling" and "do-funnies" and "gol-danging" and "gurble" fill the poem. Appealing in particular, for some readers, is the constant back-and-forth motion between these ways of speaking.

Motion is, after the first book, crucial to Ammons' poetics; a whole mind on the page would be a dismal thing unless that mind were in constant motion. Such motion must never be simply willed, however. Accidents must be allowed. In *Sphere,* the reader is given not simply the poet's thoughts or meditations but also the thoughts that he *happens* to think. Characteristically, Ammons will then praise his poem for its ability to accommodate the interruption and keep moving. Sometimes he offers us jaunty progress reports, but there are also fresh and arresting meditations on form. Again, form must be, as the subtitle of the poem indicates, "the form of a *motion.*" He does not want to write "well-wrought" poems. In section 13, he tells us that "the shapes nearest shapelessness awe us most," and in section 138 he writes, famously, "I don't know about you, / but I'm sick of good poems, all those little rondures / splendidly brought off, painted gourds on a shelf. . . ." Such a poetics has its risks, of course, and Ammons' thrillingly implausible but persuasive lack of anxiety about those risks offers the reader another source of pleasure. Aware of all the ways in which such a poem can go astray ("we have so many ways to go wrong // and so often go wrong"), Ammons insists that the poem must be allowed to take those ways. He is willing to risk, even asks us to enjoy, "the dull / continuum of the omnium-gatherum."

He really does gather everything up. Readers unsympathetic to Ammons often think of his poems as cold, abstract, windy; he might be putting his whole mind on the page, such readers argue, but it is always only a *mind*. In fact, *Sphere,* like his other poems, is full of powerful emotion, powerfully expressed. The poet gives himself a body and a history. He takes up everyday concerns, both trivial and pressing. He writes about his childhood, about bodily pain, about death in the family. Unsympathetic readers may also feel that he is, so to speak, fixated on motion. Ammons, no doubt, would answer that fixation is, for him, what agony was for Whitman: one of his changes of garments; and a poem such as *Sphere* is about the exuberance with which it uses the space the poet has won for it. We live vicariously inside the deeply attractive way of being that the poem celebrates. What would it feel like to be in creative possession of a whole mind and to be able to take pleasure in the constant motions and countermotions within that mind?

*Sphere* is an exhilaratingly happy poem, but it is never complacent. Although he finds his most optimistic speculations vindicated everywhere he looks (within or without), the poet is not "at one" with nature or with himself. The dedicatory poem tells us that the poet had not been able to find in nature an image of his "longing." Part of the work of the poem is to imagine a world in which such longing will find images of itself *everywhere*. His longing is for constant motion, and this is a longing that can be satisfied, if not forever, at least for the duration of a book-length poem—hence the happiness. Motion, because it answers to his deepest appetites, is spoken of affectionately. There are varieties of motion, he tells us: motion can mean moseying or floating or sailing. A student of all the varieties of motion, he insists perhaps most of all on the freedom to move between kinds of motion. At the very end of the poem, offering us the image of the earth sailing through space, he imagines his happiness as belonging to everyone, and one feels that his deepest purpose in the poem has been to make us believe that his happiness is within our reach.

NICK HALPERN

**Further Reading**


Bloom, Harold, "The Breaking of the Vessels," in *A.R. Ammons,* edited by Bloom, New York: Chelsea House, 1986

Davie, Donald, "Cards of Identity," in *Critical Essays on A.R. Ammons,* edited by Robert Kirschten, New York: G.K. Hall, and London: Prentice Hall, 1997

Holder, Alan, *A.R. Ammons,* Boston: Twayne, 1978

Schneider, Steven P., "From the Wind to the Earth: An Interview with A.R. Ammons," in *Complexities of Motion: New Essays on A.R. Ammons's Long Poems,* edited by Schneider, Madison, New Jersey: Fairleigh Dickinson University Press, and London: Associated University Presses, 1999

Spiegelman, Willard, "Myths of Concretion: Myths of Abstraction: The Case of A.R. Ammons," in *The Didactic Muse: Scenes of Instruction in Contemporary American Poetry,* by Spiegelman, Princeton, New Jersey: Princeton University Press, 1989

Vendler, Helen, "A.R. Ammons: Dwelling in the Flow of Shapes," in *The Music of What Happens: Poems, Poets, Critics,* Cambridge, Massachusetts: Harvard University Press, 1988


---

# Bruce Andrews 1948–

A central figure in what would come to be known—with whatever utility—as Language poetry, Bruce Andrews has maintained a consistently uncompromising position at the most radical extreme of the literary avant-garde. In numerous books of poetry and a collection of innovative critical essays, the significance of his writing has developed in direct proportion to its restiveness.

Andrews spent the summer of 1968 in Paris, and significantly, his earliest poetry dates from the moment immediately following the Situationist-inspired revolution of May of that year. Following his stay in France Andrews continued his undergraduate study of political science, writing a dissertation comparing French and American imperialism in Southeast Asia and later becoming a professor of political science at Fordham University. From this perspective outside both English departments and the creative writing programs that were proliferating in the 1970s, Andrews has developed a particularly sophisticated politics of poetic practice.

In terms similar to those of his colleague Jed Rasula ("The Politics of, the Politics in," 1987), Andrews differentiates between the thematic and formal politics of writing, calling for a poetry not *about* politics but actually *as* politics. One would locate that political practice of writing neither in a poem's ability to mobilize its audience nor in its thematic content, but rather in what is signified by its form, enacted by its structures, and implicit in its philosophy of language. One would also consider the poem as a material object: how it was produced, distributed, and exchanged. Moreover, the politics of a poem (in contradistinction to the politics *in* the poem) would hinge on how the language positions its reader *vis-à-vis* both the writer and language itself. Accordingly, Andrews' exceedingly demanding writing has often been seen as a prime example of the kind of poetry that requires a high degree of reader participation, thus transforming the author's authoritarian monologue into a more egalitarian and productive dialogue.

The particular difficulty of Andrews' poetry is also the source of its distinction; even within the tradition of the avant-garde there are few texts as radically anti-semantic. Andrews' poems do not simply mask or distance their referential "meaning" but actually oppose the very grounds of reference itself. The work is not merely difficult to explicate; it actually puts the very notion of explication into question. "There is nothing to decipher," as he writes in the early essay "Text and Context" (1977), "There is nothing to explain." Emphasizing the opaque materiality and artifice of language—the insubordination of words—his poetry challenges and frustrates the conception of language as either transparent or instrumental. The politics of such difficulty are manifest; Andrews' poems aggressively refuse assimilation to any conventionally available mode of reading, obviating the status quo by demanding new ways of thinking about and engaging language. To alter consciousness by disrupting language has long been the dream of a politicized avant-garde, but Andrews' poetics provide an especially sophisticated version of the revolution of the word, positing linguistic structures as analogous to social formations and recognizing the social ground against which even the most abstract play of the signifier occurs.

The most abstract of Andrews' own poetry was written in the early and mid-1970s. His most distinctive work from this period isolates small constellations of grammatically and thematically disjunctive words, discrete syllables, and phonemes. Often creating unprecedented combinations of letters, these poems are clearly analogues to the revolutionary *zaum'* [transrational] language of the Russian Futurists, as well as to contemporary experimental writing by Carl Andre, Clark Coolidge, and Peter Inman. Andrews' early poetry focuses attention on the edges of linguistic particles and the way in which nonreferential aspects of language can organize thematically disparate and grammatically disjunctive vocabularies. More generally, these poems explore the fits and faults of stress and pressure at which different discourses intersect. In "Swaps Ego" (1978), for instance, specialized vocabularies are re-contextualized by the collision between the scientific language of what seems to be some sort of linguistics text with what appears to be names drawn from a sporting paper such as *The Daily Racing Form*. In the resultant mesh of language, themes only latent in the source texts emerge newly animated by the tension between atomized words and the pull of an emergent syntax: "Distinctly Luck Coal Stern," "Limited Capital Cupola Plosive," "Noise Hypotenuse." The language of these poems is motivated along multiple, but unprivileged axes; the reader does not know which suggestions of "meaning" to focus on. The collision of irreconcilable elements—the racing form names and the linguistics text—frustrates both the referential pull of the signs (the original meanings of the words in their usual contexts) and the inevitable, if tenuous, invitations of even the most paratactic syntax to establish conceptual associations (the suggestive new "meanings" the words seem to acquire simply from being arranged together). In these poems language idles, the gears grating.

Near the end of the 1970s, as evinced in works like "Confidence Trick" and "I Guess Work the Time Up" (1980–81), the units of composition in Andrews' poems began to include larger, more syntactically coherent phrases and to incorporate the confrontational and controversial samples of social discourse that would characterize *I Don't Have Any Paper So Shut Up (or, Social Romanticism)* (1992). While the highly ironized and ventriloquizing transcriptions of public speech in these works may initially appear more accessible than the earlier nonlexical work, the writing is still significantly anasemantic. Although the content of these phrases is frequently provocative and offensive—"suck the testicles," "*sink* the boat people"—the emphasis is less on the particular content of the phrases than on the social work undertaken by such language. The disjunctive and irreconcilable contexts of the phrases underscore the sorts of social and psychological constructions that language enables, enacts, and structures.

Coincident with this marked stylistic shift, Andrews' compositional process changed as well. Habitually jotting down individual words, or small constellations of words on small pieces of paper, Andrews amasses a large amount of material that is then organized into larger structures, often at a much later date. With that montage (the physical, material dimension of which should not be overlooked), the emphasis in writing thus shifts from expressive production to editing.

Indeed editing, in a broader sense, has been an important part of Andrews' contribution to contemporary writing. The term "language-centered" writing was coined by Andrews in the early 1970s, and between 1978 and 1981 he co-edited the eponymous journal *L=A=N=G=U=A=G=E* with Charles Bernstein. The journal provided a key critical forum for the community of poets whose work was being published simultaneously in magazines such as *Hills* (edited by Bob Perelman), *Roof* (edited by James Sherry), *Tottel's* (edited by Ron Silliman), and *This* (edited by Robert Grenier and Barrett Watten). Featuring critical, theoretical, and review essays—frequently in the form of collaged texts and various modes of "composition as explanation"—*L=A=N=G=U=A=G=E* sought to emphasize the type of work that has made Andrews' own poetry so distinctive. In "Poetry as Explanation, Poetry as Praxis" (1988) he described it as

> a spectrum of writing that places its attention primarily on language and ways of making meaning, that takes for granted neither vocabulary, grammar, process, shape, syntax, program, or subject matter.

CRAIG DWORKIN

*See also* Language Poetry

**Biography**
Born in Chicago, Illinois, 1 April 1948. Attended Johns Hopkins University, Baltimore, Maryland, B.A. and M.A. 1970; Harvard University, Cambridge, Massachusetts, 1971–75, Ph.D.; administrative assistant in arts and humanities program, Bureau of Research, United States Office of Education, Washington, D.C., 1969; assistant to the director, President's Commission on International Trade and Investment Policy, Washington, D.C., 1970; consultant to planning staff, National Institute of Education, 1971; since 1975 member of the Political Science Department, Fordham University, Bronx, New York; co-editor, *Toothpick*, 1974; editor, with Charles Bernstein, *L=A=N=G=U=A=G=E* journal of poetics, 1978–81; member of the editorial collective, *New Political Science*, 1979–82. Living in New York City.

**Poetry**
*Edge* (includes prose), 1973
*Corona*, 1973
*Vowels*, 1976
*Praxis*, 1978
*Film Noir*, 1978
*Sonnets: (Memento Mori)*, 1980
*Jeopardy*, 1980
*R and B*, 1981
*Wobbling*, 1981

*Love Songs,* 1982
*Excommunicate,* 1982
*Factura,* 1987
*Give 'Em Enough Rope,* 1987
*Both Both* (with Bob Cobbing), 1987
*Getting Ready to Have Been Frightened,* 1988
*Only/Transblucency,* 1990
*Standpoint,* 1990
*Executive Summary,* 1990
*I Don't Have Any Paper So Shut Up (or, Social Romanticism),* 1992
*STET, SIC and SP,* 1992
*Tizzy Boost,* 1993
*Divestiture-E,* 1993
*Divestiture-A,* 1994
*Blue Horizon,* 1994
*Strictly Confidential,* 1994
*Ex Why Zee: Performance Texts* (with Sally Silvers), 1995
*Spectacular Diseases,* 1998
*Four Poems,* 2000

**Selected Criticism**
*Paradise and Method: Poetics and Praxis,* 1996

**Other Writings:** plays, nonfiction.

**Further Reading**


Baudrillard, Jean, *Pour une critique de l'économie politique du signe,* Paris: Gallimard, 1972; as *For a Critique of the Political Economy of the Sign,* translated by Charles Levin, St. Louis, Missouri: Telos Press, 1981

Brecht, Bertolt, *Brecht on Theatre: The Development of an Aesthetic,* translated by John Willett, New York: Hill and Wang, and London: Methuen, 1964; 2nd edition, London: Methuen, 1974; New York: Hill and Wang, 1982

Debord, Guy, *La Societé du spectacle,* Paris: Buchet/Chastel, 1967; as *Society of the Spectacle,* translated by Donald Nicholson-Smith, Detroit, Michigan: Black and Red, 1970; new edition, 1977

Deleuze, Gilles, and Félix Guattari, *Mille plateau,* Paris: Minuit, 1980; as *A Thousand Plateaus: Capitalism and Schizophrenia,* translated by Brian Massumi, Minneapolis: University of Minnesota Press, 1987; London: Athlone, 1988

McCaffery, Steve, *North of Intention: Critical Writings, 1973–1986,* New York: Roof Books, 1986

Perelman, Bob, "Building a More Powerful Vocabulary: Bruce Andrews and the World (Trade Center)," *The Arizona Quarterly* 50, no. 4 (1994)

Silliman, Ron, "Review of *Wobbling,*" *Sagetrieb* 1, no. 1 (1982)

Smith, Rod, editor, *Ariel* 9, Washington, D.C.: Edge Books, 1999

Watten, Barrett, *Total Syntax,* Carbondale: Southern Illinois University Press, 1985

Watten, Barrett, "Social Formalism: Zukofsky, Andrews, and Habitus in Contemporary Poetry," *North Dakota Quarterly* 55, no. 4 (Fall 1987)


---

# Maya Angelou 1928–

Although her early poetry collection *Just Give Me a Cool Drink of Water 'fore I Diiie* (1971) was nominated for a Pulitzer Prize, Maya Angelou's poems receive much less critical attention and acclaim than her autobiographies. Her autobiographies have been praised for their honest, vibrant depictions of African-American women's lives in the United States and abroad and, because of their broad dissemination, have fostered social transformations regarding black awareness and equal rights. Angelou's nonfiction explicitly details her pains: divorced parents; childhood rape; unwed teenage motherhood; sexual prostitution; and diverse discriminations in Arkansas, California, and even Africa because she is black, female, non-Muslim, non-Arab, and six-feet tall. Although her poetry also addresses her displacement from and desire to belong to a community, the majority of print responses to her poetry appear as essays in reference works or as book reviews in major newspapers or periodicals such as *Library Journal, Horn Book Magazine,* and *Booklist,* rather than in exclusively literary publications.

Angelou herself considers her poetry and plays among her works of autobiography. During an interview with Dolly Aimee McPherson (1990), she asserted that "every writer writes autobiographically anyway, whether he's Eugene O'Neill or Arthur Miller or Paul Laurence Dunbar." Social oppression operates in every human life on some level, Angelou contends, and writers—male, female, white, black, playwright, poet—capture such experiences and respond to them. More so than O'Neill, Miller, and Dunbar, Angelou provides hope for an individual's ability to confront oppression and to cultivate grace, beauty, wisdom, and joy in the process. Her poetry, like her prose, shows personas in pain but celebrating life nonetheless. Her poetry merits attention not only for its ability to enhance a reader's understanding of her autobiographical prose but also as autobiographical writing in its own right, rich and varied in voice, plot, and theme.

Angelou's prose can similarly enhance a reader's understanding of her poetry and its influences. *I Know Why the Caged Bird Sings* (1969) takes its title from the last line in "Sympathy," a poem composed by late-19th-century African-American poet Paul Laurence Dunbar; *The Heart of a Woman* (1981) echoes the title of a 1918 volume of poetry by Harlem Renaissance poet and playwright Georgia Douglas Johnson. Her prose reveals her long-held fondness for African-American speech in the family, in the community, in the pulpit, on the lectern, on the page. Prose works describing her role, at the request of Dr. Martin Luther King, Jr., as the northern coordinator for the Southern Christian Leadership

Conference place Angelou's poems in an illuminating context of political activism. Her account of her own five years of silence following a childhood rape, and her ensuing discovery of poetry (first of others, then her own) as the medium back to the speaking world, reveals the foundation of her deeply held belief in the transforming power of poetry.

Attributes of African-American oral performances appear in Angelou's poetry, but the political climate during which she began publishing her poetry did not necessitate rhetorical clichés associated with Uncle Toms and Aunt Jemimas. Angelou identifies violent behaviors toward women and African-Americans wherever she may find them: in homes, communities, and cultures. Accordingly, Angelou's poems do not flinch from harsh criticism of intimates or strangers. In *Just Give Me a Cool Drink of Water 'fore I Diiie,* Angelou asserts that, given the violence she witnesses, "I have no pity." She berates herself for her apathy; but rather than restore in herself any initial sympathy she might have had for the oppressors, she strives to cultivate more courage to articulate her outrage: "My sin lies in not screaming loud"; "Deafened and unwilling [to speak out] / We aided in the killing." By her next volume of poetry, *Oh Pray My Wings Are Gonna Fit Me Well* (1975), Angelou declaimed her position more forcefully:

Here then is my
Christian lack:
If I'm struck then
I'll strike back.

Other transformations occurred between texts as well. In *Just Give,* she mourned her losses and beseeched others to value her, seemingly finding one rejection or loss after another. In *Oh Pray,* however, she invokes her audience to

Give me your hand.

Make room for me
to lead and follow
you
beyond this rage of poetry.

Although Angelou knew and respected Malcom X, her tone takes a turn away from anger and toward forgiveness. The change parallels her forgiveness of herself, her own growing self-confidence and self-respect, which allowed her to condemn wrongs without condemning the violators, as in "Phenomenal Woman" and "Life Doesn't Frighten Me," both from *And Still I Rise* (1978).

Angelou's early poetry, with its cycle of renewed hope and ensuing hurts, contained signs of the renewal of innocence that would strongly characterize her later poems. This later work emphasizes the need for individual self-respect, arguing that therein lies an abundance of power and blessings. One could argue that Angelou's move toward more inclusive, inspirational poetry corresponded with her attainment of greater financial and political power. But this style mimics the blues tradition of using laughter or a lively beat rather than tears to cope with hardships. Early works like "Times-Square-Shoeshine-Composition" and "Harlem Hopscotch" in *Just Give* and "Song for the Old Ones" in *Oh Pray* reflect this technique as much as later poems like "Woman Work" in *And Still I Rise* and "A Good Woman Feeling Bad" in *Shaker, Why Don't You Sing?* (1983). Her later poems encourage connections among individuals by demonstrating that life can be improved by cultivating respect for differences as well as commonalities.

Angelou's autobiographies—whether prose or poetry—call for transformations: transformation of anger into love, transformations outside one's self and in one's social matrix but also—just as importantly—transformations within one's self. She insists that an individual must not be silenced for long, must not become anesthetized by life's traumas, but rather must learn from experience and re-create one's self without denying the past and all of its baggage. Angelou said during an interview on 30 July 1981:

> All of my work, my life, everything I do is about survival, not just bare, awful, plodding survival, but survival with grace and faith. While one may encounter many defeats, one must not be defeated. In fact the encountering may be the very experience which creates the vitality and the power to endure. (McPherson, 1990)

Out of violence, out of silence, Maya Angelou creates beauty and finds power in her poetry, passing her lessons on to her readers.

Deshae E. Lott

**Biography**

Born in St. Louis, Missouri, 4 April 1928. Attended schools in Arkansas and California; worked as actress, singer, composer, television host and interviewer; associate editor, *Arab Observer,* Cairo, 1961–62; assistant administrator, School of Music and Drama, University of Ghana Institute of African Studies, Legon and Accra, 1963–66; freelance writer for *Ghanaian Times* and Ghanaian Broadcasting Corporation, both Accra, 1963–65; feature editor, *African Review,* Accra, 1964–66; Lecturer, University of California, Los Angeles, 1966; writer-in-residence, University of Kansas, Lawrence, 1970; visiting professor, Wake Forest University, Winston-Salem, North Carolina, 1974; Wichita State University, Kansas, 1974; and California State University, Sacramento, 1974; since 1981 Reynolds Professor, Wake Forest University; writer for Oprah Winfrey television series *Brewster Place;* northern coordinator, Southern Christian Leadership Conference, 1959–60; member, American Revolution Bicentennial Council, 1975–76; member, advisory board, Women's Prison Association; since 1975 member, board of trustees, American Film Institute; wrote and delivered presidential inaugural poem, 1993. Received Yale University fellowship, 1970; Rockefeller grant, 1975; *Ladies Home Journal* Award, 1976; honorary Litt.D., Smith College, Northampton, Massachusetts, 1975; Mills College, Oakland, California, 1975; Lawrence University, Appleton, Wisconsin, 1976. Living in Winston-Salem, North Carolina.

**Poetry**

*Just Give Me a Cool Drink of Water 'fore I Diiie,* 1971
*Oh Pray My Wings Are Gonna Fit Me Well,* 1975
*And Still I Rise,* 1978
*Poems,* 1981
*Shaker, Why Don't You Sing?* 1983

*Now Sheba Sings the Song,* 1987
*I Shall Not Be Moved,* 1990
*Wouldn't Take Nothing for My Journey Now,* 1993
*On the Pulse of Morning: The Inaugural Poem,* 1993
*The Poetry of Maya Angelou,* 1993
*The Complete Collected Poems of Maya Angelou,* 1994
*Phenomenal Woman: Four Poems Celebrating Women,* 1994
*A Brave and Startling Truth,* 1995

**Other Writings:** plays, screenplays, television play, television documentaries (*Trying to Make It Home,* 1988), autobiography (*I Know Why the Caged Bird Sings,* 1969), nonfiction, children's literature.

**Further Reading**

Courtney-Clarke, Margaret, editor, *Maya Angelou: The Poetry of Living,* New York: Clarkson Potter, 1999; London: Virago, 2000
Cudjoe, Selwyn R., "Maya Angelou: The Autobiographical Statement Updated," in *Reading Black, Reading Feminist: A Critical Anthology,* edited by Henry Louis Gates, Jr., New York: Meridian, 1990
Essick, Kathy M., "The Poetry of Maya Angelou: A Study of the Blues Matrix as Force and Code," Ph.D. Diss., University of Indiana, Pennsylvania, 1994
Georgoudaki, Ekaterini, *Race, Gender, and Class Perspectives in the Works of Maya Angelou, Gwendolyn Brooks, Rita Dove, Nikki Giovanni, and Audre Lorde,* Thessaloniki, Greece: Aristotle University of Thessaloniki, 1991
McPherson, Dolly Aimee, *Order out of Chaos: The Autobiographical Works of Maya Angelou,* New York: Lang, 1990; London: Virago, 1991
Neubauer, Carol E., "Maya Angelou: Self and a Song of Freedom in the Southern Tradition," in *Southern Women Writers: The New Generation,* edited by Tonette Bond Inge, Tuscaloosa: University of Alabama Press, 1990
Ramsey, Priscilla R., "Transcendence: The Poetry of Maya Angelou," *A Current Bibliography on African Affairs* (new series) 17, no. 2 (1984–85)
Sahar, Annette D., Sebastian M. Brenninkmeyer, and Daniel C. O'Connell, "Maya Angelou's Inaugural Poem," *Journal of Psycholinguistic Research* 26, no. 4 (1997)
Smith, Sidonie A., "The Song of the Caged Bird: Maya Angelou's Quest after Self-Acceptance," *Southern Humanities Review* 7 (1973)

---

# Anthologies, Textbooks, and Canon Formation

If a student of poetry were to visit campuses—whether small community colleges or Ivy League universities, whether in California, Kansas, or Maine—and look at all the syllabi for courses that contain American poetry, the student would notice a substantial overlap among the poems and poets being taught. Wallace Stevens' "The Snow Man" would appear on almost every instructor's list, as would Marianne Moore's "Poetry." Similarly, after examining the anthologies of American literature used by all the professors in these colleges and universities, the student would notice that the poets listed in the tables of contents were, with a few exceptions, the same.

How does this happen? How does a certain poet, or group of poets, get included in an anthology? Why do certain poems get reprinted over and over again, taught and re-taught, while thousands of poems and scores of poets go unnoticed? Most important, who decides which poems students will read and which they will not?

The answer to these questions can be found in the complicated process called "canon formation," the term scholars use to describe the way in which certain works are repeatedly chosen to be taught, memorized, and written about by students and literary critics. These chosen works are then said to be part of the literary canon. In the case of poetry, canon formation is a distinctly academic process. Because poetry has little economic viability and a rather small readership, the decisions about which poems get taught are made inside universities, by professors who teach and also by professors who, by and large, put together college textbooks and anthologies. Anthologization is an especially potent force in the formation of the poetry canon because individual volumes of poetry usually do not stay in print for very long. The survival of a poem often depends on whether or not it has been included in an anthology—more specifically, an anthology that itself has longevity. Thus professors and students are limited first by the choices that anthologists make, and second by how much a particular anthology is used. Those collections that are not bought by professors rapidly disappear from publishers' lists, along with many of the poems contained within.

Professors and anthologists, then, wield a great deal of power in constructing a canon. So who are these anthologists, one asks, and how do readers know they can be trusted? It seems a logical question, but strangely enough, no one asked it for more than half of the 20th century because consensus on the canon among professors and editors was so strong. By the end of the 20th century, however, critics and readers had become more skeptical. Scholars argued that the previous consensus had been possible only because the people who made the decisions were themselves so similar: white men of fairly well-to-do backgrounds, many of whom had been educated in Ivy League institutions and taught by professors like themselves.

By 1960 the process of canonization came under fire as universities began to reflect changes in the economic and political structure of the country. In the late 1940s and 1950s the G.I. Bill enabled many men who would not previously have been able to afford it to go to college or graduate school. In the 1960s the women's liberation movement took hold and black nationalist groups grew; in the 1970s the interest in ethnic derivation, as well as the increase of new immigrants, transformed universities. By the 1980s, as creative writing grew into an academic discipline, many poets and fiction writers had become faculty. Thus many different potential anthologists entered the academic establishment. An anthologist could be a 35-year-old Asian-American man who grew up in Chinatown in New York City, educated at City College; a 60-year-old woman, a native of New England and a graduate of Harvard; or an African-American man who grew up in the South and attended the University of Mississippi, his tuition paid by the government. Is there any reason to assume that their lists of the best poems would be the same or would share any overlap? The answer to these questions is no, and yes, depending upon one's position.

Postmodern critics as well as those groups whose works had been largely excluded from the canon argued that the literary canon was only an expression of cultural power. Their argument, greatly oversimplified, went as follows: when someone chooses what he or she thinks is best, he or she is expressing personal values and interests. If that person wields more cultural authority than another person, then his or her decisions will carry more weight; thus decisions about canonization are just the expression of (and an attempt to retain) political and cultural power. Although this argument seemed fairly obvious to some, to more traditional critics it seemed like heresy. They argued that literary qualities were immutable and transcendent, and that there were standards that everyone—regardless of race, creed, class, or gender—could appreciate. This issue has been debated long and hard behind university walls and in academic journals, and some would say it occupied scholars for the better part of the second half of the 20th century. The rise and prominence of French theory and theorists, principally Deconstruction and Historicism, also contributed to the ferocity of this discussion.

While the protracted debate about what and who to teach has at times seemed overwhelming, there can be no doubt that universities, syllabi, textbooks, and anthologies changed as a result. Women writers are more fully represented in anthologies and syllabi, as are minority and dissident writers. As universities began to offer courses in minority literatures, publishing houses had to adapt their lists of textbooks and anthologies to accommodate these changing syllabi. This trend was notable as early as the 1960s, when several important anthologies of African-American literature emerged. Arnold Adoff's *The Poetry of Black America* (1973) recovered lost poems and poets in an attempt to make a new canon. Florence Howe's *No More Masks!* (1973), which collected poetry written by women, was dedicated to

> our sisters
> in jail
> underground
> at war
> whose lives are their poems.

By the 1990s, W.W. Norton, the preeminent publisher of college textbook anthologies, published a best-selling collection of African-American literature, of Southern American literature, and of Jewish-American literature. Nor is it uncommon to find offerings in Native American, in Asian-American, and in Latino-American literature on publishers' lists. A not-atypical poetry anthology, *Unsettling America* (1994) collects the work of diverse ethnic and political voices and announces in its introduction that the editors "chose poems that directly address the instability of American identity and confront the prevalence of cultural conflict and exchange within the United States."

If all the poems in these anthologies have not become canonized, their presence has broadened the scope of what might be considered canonical in the next generation. Clearly the canon looks different than it did 50, or even 20, years ago, but variations of race, gender, and class have also remained within a certain spectrum. For instance, professors who have wanted to add a woman to their syllabi have overwhelmingly chosen Elizabeth Bishop or H.D.; professors who have wanted to represent more heavily the contribution of African-American writers have by and large chosen Gwendolyn Brooks or Langston Hughes. Moreover, the presence of traditional white male writers may have been trimmed, but it still remains substantial. A reader simply would not find an anthology of American literature that does not include T.S. Eliot's "The Waste Land" or Ezra Pound's "In a Station of the Metro." Thus, although the canon has shifted with political and cultural tides, there are still many points of consensus; what the academy deems canonical has stretched but not lost its shape.

Despite the challenges to canonicity that occurred in the second half of the 20th century, standards of evaluation have never strayed too far from the century's principal artistic movement: perhaps no word has dominated the evaluation of American poetry in the 20th century more than the word "Modernism." Indeed, the values of Modernism and its associate, Postmodernism, have spelled out the formula to which critics respond. When exactly modern poetry begins is open to interpretation; certainly scholars have called some 19th-century poets "modern." It has become popular, for instance, to understand Emily Dickinson's crisis of faith as a precursor to later Modernist ennui. Calling Dickinson a precursor to modern poetry has substantially elevated her place in the 20th-century canon. Similarly, the *Norton Anthology of Modern Poetry* begins with Walt Whitman, also a 19th-century writer, a radical stylist who also paved the way for later Modernist innovation.

There can be no doubt, however, that a gathering storm of Modernist energy, what Ezra Pound called a "vortex," grew between 1910 and 1920. The *annus mirabilus* of Modernism, 1922—which saw the publication of James Joyce's *Ulysses,* William Faulkner's *The Sound and the Fury,* and T.S. Eliot's "The Waste Land"—forever changed the canons of American poetry. The most important anthologies of the 20th century have included "modern" in their title, from Louis Untermeyer's influential *Modern American Poets* (1919) up to Norton's modern and postmodern anthologies, the virtual Goliaths of the field. For many editors a 20th-century poem was not worth studying unless it fell under the heading "modern."

Modernism, a radical way to use language, to reinvent forms, and to challenge cultural norms, saw the world afresh. As an ideological system, it reacted against conventional institutions, and national affiliations were of course among these. Thus in the early decades of the 20th century anthologists tried to shed the 19th-century ideal of Americanism as a literary value. With Modernism came the radical idea that the best American poets resist the national climate, rather than support and express the cultural values of their time. T.S. Eliot, perhaps the most influential poet and critic of the century, could not even decide whether he was European or American, and in fact, both British and American anthologists claim him.

With "The Waste Land," however, Eliot wanted to transcend national identity and write a poem with universal, rather than local, applications. Revolutionary for many reasons, "The Waste Land" was initially remarkable for its difficulty: when it first appeared, it seemed incomprehensible. Eliot defended it in his canon-making essay, "The Metaphysical Poets":

> We can only say that it appears likely that poets in our civilization must be difficult. Our civilization comprehends great variety and complexity. . . . The poet must become more and more comprehensive. More allusive, more indirect, in order to force, to dislocate if necessary, language into meaning.

Considering how central "The Waste Land" has become to the study of 20th-century poetry, it is important to remember the great controversy the poem initiated. Such a moment of controversy often precedes an artifact's entrance into the canon. In the first years of the poem's publication, many critics accused Eliot of willful obscurity, impenetrability, and incomprehensibility. Other critics immediately attempted to decipher the poem's vast array of classical and mythical allusions, its fractured narrative, and its alternating voices. When the dust cleared, not only was "The Waste Land" considered the preeminent poem of the age, but Eliot was, as American poet Delmore Schwartz called him, the undisputed "dictator of the literary world." Moreover, the characteristics of the poem—once considered liabilities by some—were now clearly seen as virtues; difficulty, obscurity, ambiguity, allusiveness, and fragmentation became necessary for the modern poem to accurately represent the complexities of modern life. Innovative poetry came to be more highly valued than the merely commonplace.

The degree to which Eliot's own essays dictated the response to "The Waste Land" has been documented. As one anonymous reviewer observed as early as 1923, "Thank goodness Eliot finally wrote the poem to which he can apply his own critical theories." The critical theories were not only applied to his poetry, however, but to many other poems and poets of that era as well. Additionally, Eliot was not the only poet/critic who gained prominence at that time: Ezra Pound, Conrad Aiken, Allen Tate, John Crowe Ransom, and Randall Jarrell, to name a few, wrote literary essays that justified the kinds of poems they themselves were writing. Several consequences emerged from this pairing of the poet-critic. First, modern poetry seemed to become more and more removed from a general readership, becoming an elite and elevated discourse that only poets, critics, and professors seemed to understand. Second, as literary study became further and further removed from popular discourse, the divide between the popular and the academic or "literary" became a wide, unbridgeable chasm. What ultimately emerged was a cynical, even censorious, view of mass culture derived from Eliot, who firmly upheld the very important divide. In other words, for Modernist critics, a popular artist—almost by definition—could not be much good. The commonplace was quickly deemed unliterary.

"New Criticism," a scholarly school that descended from the Southern Agrarian movement, a group that also prized their distance from mass culture, followed the precepts of Modernism. Several of the New Critics, themselves poet/critics, became interested in discussing the poem primarily as a "literary document" rather than an ethical or historical one. The editors of a highly influential textbook of this period, *Understanding Poetry* (1938, still in print), Robert Penn Warren and Cleanth Brooks, both New Critics, advocated study of the poem as a formal document. That meant probing its surface for all the potentialities of language. These prescripts arose in opposition to what the poem might mean in a political, cultural, or biographical context.

It is impossible to overstate just how significant New Criticism has been in the development of the canon of 20th-century American poetry. Generations of scholars trained to read poems "closely" valued poems that yielded fruitfully to this type of inquiry. Poems that could be dissected, analyzed, explained, and endlessly and variously interpreted were prized more heavily than poems that had easily accessible and cogent messages. Professors became interpreters, specially trained individuals with the knowledge to decode obscure or even indecipherable passages. As Gerald Graff (1987) has pointed out, part of the success of the New Critical approach was the advantage it offered to professors. Graff explains,

> I remember the relief I felt as a beginning assistant professor when I realized that by concentrating on the text itself I could get a good discussion going about almost any literary work without having to know anything about its author, its circumstances of composition, or the history of its reception.

Modernism, an international aesthetic movement, and New Criticism, a formal, sometimes almost scientific mode of inquiry, were not hospitable to political writers. The large number of political poems written during the early decades of the 20th century seemed to disappear as anthologists, following Modernist guidelines, banished political poems from anthologies and textbooks for almost 50 years. When a poet like Langston Hughes, an outspoken Communist and activist, was anthologized, editors included only his mildest, most apolitical poems. Indeed, the recovery and publication of Hughes' strident political voice, as well as that of other Harlem Renaissance poets, has been a job for literary critics in the closing decades of the 20th century. Similarly, the other leftist poets of the 1930s and 1940s also began to reappear in American anthologies. The *Heath Anthology of American Literature* (2nd edition, 1994), for instance, made it a point to resurrect writers like Genevieve Taggard and Kenneth Fearing under the heading, "A Sheaf of Political Poetry in the Modern Period."

Indeed, one can understand the canon of American poetry at the end of the 20th century as a response to, or a correction of, Modernist principles of evaluation. If William Carlos Williams was right that the publication of "The Waste Land" was the great catastrophe to American letters, and that it destroyed the national idiom for almost half a century, then Williams might have found cause for celebration in the changing canon of Postmodernism. Other anthologies, like Joel Conarroe's *Eight American Poets* (1994), have sought to reconstruct a canon of "classic" American poets.

In the reappraisal of Modernism and the subsequent revisions of the canon, Eliot, his poetry, and his criticism, as well as New Criticism have come under attack. Not only did political writers slowly re-enter the canon, but those premodern writers who were more accessible and popular, such as Edwin Arlington Robinson and Edna St. Vincent Millay, have also regained status. Beat poets like Allen Ginsberg and Robert Creeley have also been anthologized in both *Postmodern American Poetry* (Hoover, 1996) and *Contemporary American Poetry* (Poulin, 1996). Although it seems somewhat ironic that writers who launched their careers challenging authority are now part of the literary canon, often the writers who at first seem the most extreme are the writers later embraced as visionary. The entrance of Beat writers into the canon also illustrates the rising importance that postmodern critics have given to popular culture. Rather than bemoaning the presence of film, television, or the Internet, postmodern art and theory have explored their presence in contemporary consciousness. A 1999 anthology of poems about popular culture, *Real Things* (Elledge and Swartwout), would not have been possible or even desirable two decades earlier.

But even as certain evaluative principles of Modernism continue to be challenged, a surprising consistency remains in what professors and critics value. John Ashbery, perhaps the most critically esteemed poet of the 20th century, writes notoriously difficult poems, and the complaints about his work—incomprehensibility, obscurity, ambiguity—are not unlike those first leveled at Eliot. Ashbery's fans, as Eliot's were, are among the most important literary critics in the country, and their opinions go a long way toward the construction of the canon. In the 1990s, work had already begun in probing the seemingly impenetrable surfaces of Ashbery's poems. If literary history repeats itself, it will not be long before a whole critical lexicon springs up to deal with his "difficulty."

Hilene Flanzbaum

**Further Reading**


Eliot, T.S., *The Selected Prose of T.S. Eliot,* edited by Frank Kermode, New York: Harcourt Brace Jovanovich, and London: Faber, 1975

Golding, Alan, "The History of the American Poetry Anthology," in *Canons,* edited by Robert von Hallberg, Chicago: University of Chicago Press, 1984

Graff, Gerald, *Professing Literature,* Chicago: University of Chicago Press, 1987

Nelson, Cary, *Repression and Recovery: Modern American Poetry and the Politics of Cultural Memory, 1910–1945,* Madison: University of Wisconsin Press, 1989

Pearce, Roy Harvey, *The Continuity of American Poetry,* Princeton, New Jersey: Princeton University Press, 1961

Perkins, David, *A History of Modern Poetry,* 2 vols., Cambridge, Massachusetts: Harvard University Press, 1976, 1987

Perloff, Marjorie, *Wittgenstein's Ladder: Poetic Language and the Strangeness of the Ordinary,* Chicago: University of Chicago Press, 1996

Shetley, Vernon, *After the Death of Poetry: Poet and Audience in Contemporary America,* Durham, North Carolina: Duke University Press, 1993

Smith, Barbara Herrnstein, *Contingencies of Value,* Cambridge, Massachusetts: Harvard University Press, 1988

Von Hallberg, Robert, *American Poetry and Culture,* Cambridge, Massachusetts: Harvard University Press, 1985


---

# David Antin 1932–

The poetry of David Antin is an extension of his life as an art critic, a performance artist, and a translator and reflects his deep interest in science, philosophy, and linguistics. His poetry, in this regard, challenges the boundary of what constitutes a poem and, thereby, embodies the postmodern characteristic of pushing at the preconceived notions of the genre of poetry by blending the visual with the performative, poetic, scientific, and philosophical.

Born on 1 February 1932 in New York City, Antin spent the majority of his first 25 years in and around New York and, subsequently, is often associated with other New York poets, such as Jerome Rothenberg and Armand Schwerner. After earning a B.A. in science from the City College of New York (now the City University of New York) in 1955, Antin dedicated himself to both poetry and art criticism, and his early, more imagistic poetry is heavily influenced by the visual artists of New York City and especially by Pop and Postpop painters such as Warhol, Lichtenstein, and Wesselman. Employing methods similar to those of these painters, Antin's early poetry engages popular culture and especially the way that meaning is created, structured, and negotiated in and by language.

In December 1960 Antin married Eleanor Fineman, a highly acclaimed performance artist, and the couple continued to live and work in New York City. During the period between 1962 and 1966, Antin translated various scientific works into English, all of which were high-level studies of mathematics and/or physics, and traces of the ideas from those texts are evident in many of the early poems as well as in Antin's poetic mode of inquiry.

In 1966 Antin earned an M.A. in linguistics from New York University, where his graduate project concentrated on the language structure of Gertrude Stein, who, along with Charles Olson, the Black Mountain poets, and the Objectivists, was an important early influence on his work. Antin's interest in science and linguistics is clearly evident in his writings and especially in his sustained interrogation of how the structuring and codifying of meaning alters the social modes of communication. In the late 1960s, Antin broke with an image-based poetry, which he describes as "more decorative than meaningful and incapable of addressing the kinds of things that were coming insistently to my mind . . . language and politics." The scientific mode of inquiry and his interest in linguistics offered a lens for him to consider the social aspects of language and meaning, and the fusing of the scientific and the linguistic is evident in his book *Definitions* (1967). "Definitions for Mendy," for example, is a sustained meditation on the scientific, linguistic, and emotional aspects of loss. The poem opens with an almost clinical "definition" that serves as the ideational fulcrum for the poem as a whole:

loss is an unintentional decline in or disappearance of
a value arising from a contingency
a value is an efficacy a power a brightness
it is also a duration.

A number of different perspectives and structures for understanding loss are given throughout the poem—all of which bear on the issue of coming to terms with the death of Mendy. The conclusion renders the difficulty of comprehending death by fusing scientific language with a poetic mode of description:

the eye cannot discriminate true intensities of light
only their ratios
similarly the ear
cannot distinguish among sounds that are very high or low
in the dark all cats are black
what color are they in a blinding light

How the mind comprehends and rationalizes things such as death, loss, and duration is questioned, and, like the larger body of Antin's writing, the poem explores the relationship of language and value.

Antin's early poems challenge the traditional conception of the poem as a recapitulation of an experience and propose a more fluid, associationally rich poetry that is more akin to the cognitive processes of the mind. The process-oriented poetry in the books from the late 1960s and early 1970s, such as *Autobiography* (1967), *Definitions* (1967), and *Code of Flag Behavior* (1968)—all of which are collected in *Selected Poems: 1963–1973* (1991)—develops the poetic prototype of what would emerge as Antin's signature poetic mode, the "talk" poem, with its propensity for sustained inquiry and meditation. The first talk poem appeared in 1972 in *Talking*.

Antin describes these poems as

> improvised talk pieces [where] I go to some particular place to create—in public, as improvisations. I go to a particular place with something in mind but no clear way of saying it, and in the place I come to I try to find some way to deal with what I am interested in, in a way that is meaningful to both the audience and myself. ("David Antin," Contemporary Authors Online, 2000)

The poem, therefore, is a heightened version of Charles Olson's conception of "Projective Poetry," whereby the poem is the means and vehicle of discovery of content, as in Olson's tenet that "form is an extension of content." Antin elevates projective poetry to the performative level. Such talks reveal Antin's shrewd and engaging mind grappling with a concept or idea in a startlingly fresh way. A passage from his talk poem "the river" from *What It Means To Be Avant-Garde* (1993) aptly depicts the gist of such poems:

because talking for me is the closest I can come
as a poet to thinking and I wanted for a long
time a kind of poetry of talking not a poetry of thought
but a poetry of thinking since getting so close to the
process of thinking was what I thought the poem was

The energy and force of the thinking is the heart of the talk poem and brings his poetry closer to the realm of performance art since it engages an idea or a concept within the dynamic of a social setting.

The last 20 years of Antin's writing career have been dedicated to the talk poem, yet it should not be overlooked that Antin continues to push at the boundaries of poetry and the conception of an audience in other ways as well. In 1987, he began "SKYPOEM," a long poem to be written gradually in the air, thereby proposing an even more "public" poetry.

Since 1972 Antin has taught full-time the structure of art, the history of criticism, and other courses in the Visual Arts Department of the University of California, San Diego. His wife, Eleanor Antin, also teaches in the program, and they currently live in La Jolla, California.

DAVID CLIPPINGER

**Biography**

Born in Brooklyn, New York, 1 February 1932. Attended City College, New York, B.A. 1955; New York University (Lehman Fellow), 1964–66, M.A. in linguistics 1966; freelance editor and translator, 1956–57; chief editor and scientific director, Research Information Service, New York, 1958–60; freelance editor and consultant, Dover Press, New York, 1959–64; curator, Institute of Contemporary Art, Boston, 1967; Director of the University Art Gallery and Assistant Professor of Visual Arts, 1968–72, Professor of Visual Arts, 1972–92, and Emeritus Professor, University of California, San Diego; founding editor, with Jerome Rothenberg, *Some/Thing*, New York, 1964; contributing editor, *Alcheringa*, New York, 1972–80; member of the editorial board, University of California Press, San Diego, 1972–76, and since 1979, *New Wilderness*. Received Longview Award, 1960; University of California Creative Arts Award, 1972; Guggenheim fellowship, 1976; National Endowment for the Arts fellowship, 1983. Living in La Jolla, California.

**Poetry**

*Definitions*, 1967
*Autobiography*, 1967
*Code of Flag Behavior*, 1968
*Meditations*, 1971
*Talking*, 1972
*After the War (A Long Novel with Few Words)*, 1973
*Talking at the Boundaries*, 1976
*Who's Listening Out There?* 1980
*Tuning*, 1984
*Selected Poems: 1963–1973*, 1991
*What It Means To Be Avant-Garde*, 1993

**Other Writings:** essays, translations of German mathematics and physics texts.

**Further Reading**

Alpert, Barry, "Post-Modern Oral Poetry: Buckminster Fuller, John Cage, and David Antin," *Boundary 2: A Journal of Postmodern Literature* 3 (1975)
Altieri, Charles, "The Postmodernism of David Antin's *Tuning*," *College English* 48, no. 1 (1986)

Lazer, Hank, "Thinking Made in the Mouth: The Cultural Poetics of David Antin and Jerome Rothenberg," in *Picturing Cultural Values in Postmodern America,* edited by William Doty, Tuscaloosa: University of Alabama Press, 1995

Perloff, Marjorie, *The Poetics of Indeterminacy: Rimbaud to Cage,* Princeton, New Jersey: Princeton University Press, 1981; London: Turnaround, 2000

Sayre, Henry, "David Antin and the Oral Poetics Movement, " *Contemporary Literature* 23, no. 4 (1982)

## Antiwar Poetry. *See* War and Antiwar Poetry

## Rae Armantrout 1947–

Rae Armantrout burst onto the American literary scene in the late 1970s with refreshing metaphors and inventive narratives. Her poetry constitutes a growing awareness of complex contingent relationships between the world and language itself. Primarily interested in the way the mind creates associations, Armantrout breaks away from conventional metaphors, linear narratives, and traditional ways of sense-making to compose refreshingly innovative thematic and imagistic connections. Her poetry developed from early subversive counter-narratives into increasingly sophisticated play with syntax, sentences, prose poetry, and voice, all of which explicitly address the arbitrary nature of language and truth. By the 1980s and early 1990s Armantrout had established herself as an avant-garde poet in an age of postmodernism and cultural materialism. Her poetry points to the panoply of inter-related social and linguistic threads that construct identity.

From her earliest work, *Extremities* (1978), to *Made to Seem* (1995), Armantrout develops an astute perception of the provisional possibilities of truth-making and truth-telling. Skeptical and subversive, each volume questions assumptions of a universal standard of truth and authenticity, opposing the construction of familiar narratives of authority or conformity with parodic versions of the same story. "Generation" revises the Hansel and Gretel tale by eliminating the characters and setting of the story, leaving the reader with a more abstract and open-ended representation. The narrative is less a matter of what really transpires in the woods than it is a careful attention to the choices a writer makes when constructing a narrative. Such extreme measures foreground writing (and reading) as a matter of choice.

Armantrout's second volume of poems, *The Invention of Hunger* (1979), is comprised of 19 parts made of prose sentences and sentence fragments. Much of the work details the disjunctive relationships between generations of family members and the fragmented representations of identity in these contexts. *Precedence* (1985) and *Necromance* (1991) build upon the fictive notions of identity. Both works move out of the more personal and familial contexts, however, into broader commentaries on American culture. Armantrout's contention with conventional narratives plays out in her resistance to authority and social structures in increasingly unexpected and cryptic narratives. Several poems from both works, such as "Fiction" and "Bases," foreground the fragile connections between the real and imagined, paying close attention to fabrications and romantic illusions of "true" or "authentic" American identity. Moreover, the poems lay bare the devices of these simulations by pointing out the parameters of their construction. Armantrout continually examines the modes of telling the story rather than completing the actual story itself. Questioning rather than answering, foregrounding authorship, she plays with signifiers, leaving out images or ideas to undermine the assumption that the speaker and/or author will locate meaning for the reader.

*Made to Seem* (1995) continues this counteracting process against conventional "natural-ness." While many poems in *Necromance* ("Fiction," "Pairs," "Context," "Necromance") play with voice and challenge "narrative sense-making," they often seem to have no definitive voice at all. These lines from "Attention" are representative:

Ventriloquy
is the mother tongue.

Can you colonize rejection
by phrasing your request,
"Me want?"

Song: "I'm not a baby.
Wa, Wa, Wa.

I'm not a baby.
Wa, Wa, Wa.

I'm crazy
like you."

The "you"
in the heart of
molecule and ridicule.

In *Made to Seem* the speakers of the poems *seem* more real, more ordinary, and sound more conventional in their language—making them even more deceptive, ultimately. Rather than use as many direct questions as she does in the former volume, in *Made to Seem* Armantrout opts for the conversation, using a lot of "we" and "you" and "us" as a way of inclusion in a larger discussion ("Sit-Calm," "The Creation," "Incidence," "Crossing"). In each of these poems the narrative seems easy to follow, building on the conversation as if writer and reader are acquaintances or friends. Once the reader is comfortable with the poem's context, however, seemingly ordinary relationships are turned in on themselves. The reader is never completely safe, nor does meaning come as naturally as it may seem.

Armantrout's poetry helps to clarify these questions of sense-making but does not completely alienate the reader with feelings of meaninglessness, instead drawing fresher images and metaphors out of the disrupted assumptions of meaning. She argues for a kind of displacement of meaning in which the metaphor becomes more of an "oblique association" than something "natural" or "appropriate" to the context. While she may counter traditional narrative techniques in her poetry, an approach that at first seems to put off or limit the reader's understanding of the poem, she ultimately uses the poetic structure to reinvent new forms within it.

Other avant-garde poets, such as Ron Silliman, Susan Howe, Lyn Hejinian, and Charles Bernstein, use similar inventive techniques. Armantrout's counterparts make up an innovative portion of the Language poets or Language writers. The Language movement emerged during the 1980s, inspired by reader-response and Derridean theories, with their suspicious approaches to the interpretation of texts. These poets seek intuitive associations or renovations in images rather than original innovations in ideas. Their narrative and poetic renovations lead into the Language movement's critique of traditional capitalist, or "bourgeois," culture. If Language poets can renovate the images—the structure of the text—perhaps they may transform the social matrix out of which traditional narrative assumptions and conventions arise. Rather than create new images, Armantrout and the others challenge hegemonic conceptualizations of art by breaking poetic form, utilizing parataxis and the new sentence, and commenting on the power and instability of ideological frameworks.

Language writing and Armantrout's Language poetry in particular rework the limitations of structure and convention, social positions and roles, by foregrounding devices by which these structures shape thoughts and perceptions. Her work renovates identities by reconstructing the relationship between language and the world. By calling into question the constructs of authority and familiarity, Armantrout touches upon the unreliability of the universal American narrative, and, at the same time, opens up the possibilities for new relationships to language, to poetry, and to American culture.

NICOLE E. CORTZ

**Biography**

Born in Vallejo, California, 13 April 1947. Attended California State University, San Diego, 1965–68; University of California, Berkeley, B.A. 1970; California State University, San Francisco, M.A. 1975; teaching assistant, California State University, San Francisco, 1972–74; Lecturer, California State University, San Diego, 1980–82, and since 1980, University of California, San Diego. Received California Arts Council fellowship, 1989; Fund for Poetry Award, 1993. Living in San Diego, California.

**Poetry**

*Extremities,* 1978
*The Invention of Hunger,* 1979
*Precedence,* 1985
*Necromance,* 1991
*Made to Seem,* 1995
*The Pretext,* 2000

**Selected Criticism**

*Not "Literary Practitioners of Deconstruction,"* 1989

**Other Writings:** memoirs (*True,* 1998).

**Further Reading**

Golding, Alan, "The New American Poetry Revisited, Again," *Contemporary Literature* 39, no. 2 (1998)
Hoeppner, Edward Haworth, "Referential Politics: The Body, Technology, and the Poetic Avant-Garde," *Southern Humanities Review* 31, no. 1 (1997)
Kalaidjian, Walter, *Languages of Liberation: The Social Text in Contemporary American Poetry,* New York: Columbia University Press, 1989
Leddy, Michael, "'See Armantrout for an Alternative View': Narrative and Counternarrative in the Poetry of Rae Armantrout," *Contemporary Literature* 35, no. 4 (1994)
Moramarco, Fred S., and William John Sullivan, *Containing Multitudes: Poetry in the United States Since 1950,* New York: Twayne, and London: Prentice Hall, 1998
Perelman, Bob, *The Marginalization of Poetry: Language Writing and Literary History,* Princeton, New Jersey: Princeton University Press, 1996
Perloff, Marjorie, *Poetic License: Essays on Modernist and Postmodernist Lyric,* Evanston, Illinois: Northwestern University Press, 1990
Perloff, Marjorie, "The Coming of Age of Language Poetry," *Contemporary Literature* 38, no. 3 (1997)
Perloff, Marjorie, *Poetry On and Off the Page: Essays for Emergent Occasions,* Evanston, Illinois: Northwestern University Press, 1998
Peterson, Jeffrey, "The Siren Song of the Singular: Armantrout, Oppen, and the Ethics of Representation," *Sagetrieb* 12, no. 3 (1993)

# John Ashbery 1927–

John Ashbery is undoubtedly one of the most important and influential American poets of the second half of the 20th century. Throughout a prolific career that has spanned more than five decades, Ashbery has been a consistently adventurous poetic explorer whose challenging and distinctive oeuvre has altered the definition of what poetry can be. Although he has always been a controversial figure, with the response to his work polarized between those who regard him as a preeminent poet who has done much to reinvent American poetry, and those who find his writing to be overrated, self-indulgent, and willfully difficult, few would deny his significance to American literature. Furthermore, the overriding themes of his writing—the nature of consciousness, language, and temporality; the ubiquity of randomness and indeterminacy; the instability of the self; the encroachment of the information age's proliferating media on the inner life; the impossibility of closure and fixed absolutes—reflect and express the philosophical and cultural temper of the times, making Ashbery an exemplary poet of his age.

Ashbery's poetry tends to provoke strong reactions because of its experimental handling of language and poetic form: his poems resist conventional explanation and paraphrase, refuse to present a coherent speaking self that can be identified with the poet, and lack traditional subject matter and easily grasped significance. As he points out, rather than addressing "a particular subject and treating it formally in a kind of essay," "my poetry . . . has an exploratory quality and I don't have it all mapped out before I sit down to write" (Packard, 1974). Ashbery readily admits that this quality leads his poetry in unpredictable and even bewildering directions but defends such unsettling journeys into the unknown as an integral part of his work's *raison d'être:*

> [M]y intention is to communicate and my feeling is that a poem that communicates something that's already known by the reader is not really communicating anything to him and in fact shows a lack of respect for him[.] (Packard, 1974)

Unlike many poets, Ashbery is less concerned with relating a specific event than with conveying what he calls "the experience of experience":

> [T]he particular occasion is of less interest to me than the way a happening or experience filters through me. . . . I'm trying to set down a generalized transcript of what's really going on in our minds all day long. (Poulin, 1981)

In Ashbery's pluralistic worldview, "things are in a continual state of motion," so any attempt to fit the overwhelming flux and variety of experience into a coherent, tidy explanation is viewed with skepticism (Stitt, 1983). Because he is much more interested in process than any finished product, the actual subject of his poems is often the "poem creating itself," the process of its own coming into being (Poulin, 1981).

Ever elusive, Ashbery's writing always seems to be on the verge of revealing something that trembles just out of reach. This uncanny ability to tantalize with possible meanings that are continually deferred or undermined is one of Ashbery's distinctive strengths. Certain stylistic features run through nearly all of his work, including the use of intentionally vague and shifting pronouns (which he has said helps "to reproduce the polyphony that goes on inside me"); the creation of indeterminate, rapidly changing, often surreal narrative situations; the collaging of various discourses, including clichés and slangy conversational speech; and a wild mix of tones and diction that can swing from the high poetic to the ridiculous in the space of a line (Stitt, 1983; Packard, 1974).

Although he is associated with New York City and the poetry of the "New York School," Ashbery grew up on a rural farm. Extremely precocious and interested in art, poetry, and music from an early age, he had a rather isolated childhood, marked by the haunting death of his nine-year-old brother when Ashbery was 13. He attended Harvard, where he began to write poetry in earnest and met the poets Kenneth Koch and Frank O'Hara, who would become his closest friends and artistic allies. He also steeped himself in the writers who would influence his work, such as W.H. Auden, Wallace Stevens, Gertrude Stein, and Marianne Moore, as well as French poets from Stephane Mallarmé and Arthur Rimbaud to the surrealists. After graduating, Ashbery moved to New York, where he earned an M.A. in English from Columbia University and found himself at the center of a thriving community of experimental poets and painters that included Koch, O'Hara, James Schuyler, Barbara Guest, and the artists Jane Freilicher and Larry Rivers. Together these poets, who would later be given the name "the New York School," rejected the closed, traditional forms of the academic poetry then dominant in favor of a more open-ended, exploratory, and playful poetics of process. Like the other New York poets, Ashbery found inspiration for this project in Abstract Expressionist painting, Surrealism, French and American avant-garde poetry, the aleatory music of John Cage, and popular culture.

In 1955 the manuscript of Ashbery's first book, *Some Trees* (1956), was chosen by Auden for the Yale Younger Poets Prize, an award that effectively launched his career. While these early poems are still relatively traditional, showing the strong influence of Stevens, Auden, and French poetry, they feature Ashbery's characteristic voice, verbal brilliance, and range of concerns. Among them are the much-anthologized and atypical poem "The Instruction Manual," a rather straightforward reverie about escaping from a dull publishing job on an imaginary trip to Guadalajara on the wings of poesy, and the title poem, a gentle yet oblique piece about covert and illicit love. Critics have recently addressed the link between the evasive reticence of these early poems and Ashbery's discomfort, as a homosexual, with self-revelation at a time of McCarthyism and repressive homophobia, an evasiveness that underlies all of his explorations of the protean, unstable nature of identity.

Ashbery also received a Fulbright scholarship in 1955 to study in France for a year, but he enjoyed living there so much that he extended his stay for most of a decade. In France he researched the eccentric French writer Raymond Roussel for a doctoral dissertation he never completed and began writing art criticism steadily, which he would continue to do for many years. In 1962 Ashbery published his controversial second volume, *The Tennis Court Oath,* a book comprised of highly experimental and radically disjunctive poems written at a time when Ashbery was "baffled as to what to do in poetry" (Packard, 1974). In works like the long collage poem "Europe," with its fragmentary phrases and isolated words, Ashbery was self-consciously "taking poetry apart to try to understand how it works" (Osti, 1974). While some of his most ardent supporters, like Harold Bloom, view the book as a regrettable detour on Ashbery's path to greatness, the volume has had a major influence on later experimental poets, such as the Language poets, who take it to be a foundational text of postmodernist poetry and the poet's most groundbreaking book. Although Ashbery himself sees *The Tennis Court Oath* as transitional and feels less close to it than his other works, there is no doubt that the volume stands as a significant moment in his evolving aesthetic.

In *Rivers and Mountains* (1966) Ashbery began "trying to fit [poetry] back together" in arresting new formations after the rigorous "dismembering of language" in his previous book, with poems like the dense, swirling "Clepsydra" revealing his growing interest in "how time feels as it is passing" (Osti, 1974; Kostelanetz, 1981). The long poem "The Skaters" signals a departure from the austere and fractured poems of his second book, and can be seen as Ashbery's breakthrough into full stride. This expansive and exuberant masterpiece, in which the questing poet is seen paradoxically "continuing but ever beginning / My perennial voyage," is by turns conversational, lyrical, parodic, and meditative, as well as highly self-conscious about the process of its own composition (Ashbery, *The Mooring of Starting Out,* 1997).

Ashbery finally returned from France in late 1965 to live in the United States permanently and began working as an executive editor for *Art News* in New York. Following the death of his father (1964) and the shocking accidental death of his dear friend Frank O'Hara (1966), Ashbery's poetry became increasingly elegiac and concerned with temporality and transience, as exemplified in the ruminative, lyrical poems in *The Double Dream of Spring* (1970), one of Ashbery's finest volumes. "In a way the passage of time is becoming more and more *the* subject of my poetry as I get older," he explained in an interview (Packard, 1974).

By the end of the 1960s Ashbery had again grown restless with his poetry and decided to break new ground with a triad of long poems in prose, the critically praised volume *Three Poems* (1972). One of Ashbery's major achievements and a favorite of his, this innovative sequence is a central expression of his philosophical and aesthetic outlook. By creating "an open field of narrative possibilities" in the poems' onrushing, serpentine language, Ashbery hit on a more inclusive, discursive, and meditative style that would become his dominant mode (Ashbery, *Three Poems,* 1972). The ecstatic response to Ashbery's next book, *Self-Portrait in a Convex Mirror* (1975), marked a crucial turning point in his career: although he had been gradually gaining acceptance after years of indifference and even hostility from reviewers dismayed by the difficulty of his work, the 1976 National Book Award, Pulitzer Prize, and National Book Critics Circle Award suddenly vaulted Ashbery into relative stardom. The book's long title poem is regarded by many to be Ashbery's masterpiece, although the poet himself has often commented disparagingly about the poem and its celebrity. A brilliant and moving contemplation of a painting by the 16th-century Italian painter Francesco Parmigianino, the poem considers the problems of rendering the contingent self in art while musing on the complexities of subjectivity, perception, time, and the vexed relationship between art and life.

After reaching this pinnacle Ashbery continued to write at the height of his powers. His equally masterful next book, *Houseboat Days* (1977), features a number of frequently anthologized poems ("Syringa," "Street Musicians," "The Other Tradition," "And *Ut Pictura Poesis* Is Her Name"), only to be followed by yet another bold and perhaps less successful experiment with form, the long poem "Litany" in *As We Know* (1979), which appears in two parallel columns and is "meant to be read as simultaneous but independent monologues" (Ashbery, *As You Know,* 1979). Ashbery has remained remarkably productive through his 60s and 70s, publishing six books in the 1990s alone—nearly twice as many as in any other decade of his career—each filled with provocative poems. Highlights of this later phase include the book-length poem *Flow Chart* (1991), a massive compendium of Ashberyean concerns with an autobiographical slant, and a shorter book-length poem about the fantastic, irrevocable realms of childhood, *Girls on the Run* (1999). In the latter, Ashbery once again takes a work of art as a point of departure—in this case, the strange paintings of an "outsider" artist, the recluse Henry Darger.

More than any other post–World War II poet, Ashbery has managed to bridge the "experimental" and the "mainstream." Perfecting what he has called "a kind of fence-sitting / Raised to the level of an esthetic ideal" in "Soonest Mended," he has remained open to the impulses and techniques of the avant-garde and to the resources of poetic tradition at once. Lauded in both academic and experimental circles, he has remained free from any camp or movement. Ashbery has always stressed the importance, even the necessity, of independence for the artist, and has consistently championed those he sees as staunch individualists, outsiders, and eccentrics, such as Roussel, Stein, and artists like Fairfield Porter, Jasper Johns, and Joseph Cornell. He greatly admires—and emulates—such self-reliant figures who defiantly go their own way, avoiding dogma and programs, creating works that resist assimilation and categorization. In his own poetry Ashbery elegantly balances playfulness and pathos, mystery and revelation, randomness and meaning like no one else. With his startling inventiveness, his aesthetic and conceptual daring, and his dazzling verbal textures, Ashbery has had a tremendous impact on American poetry.

ANDREW EPSTEIN

*See also* New York School; Surrealism

**Biography**

Born in Rochester, New York, 28 July 1927. Attended Harvard University, Cambridge, Massachusetts (member of the editorial board, *Harvard Advocate*), A.B. in English 1949; Columbia University, New York, M.A. in English 1951; New York University, 1957–58; copywriter, Oxford University Press, New York, 1951–54, and McGraw-Hill Book Company, New York, 1954–55; co-editor, *One Fourteen,* New York, 1952–53; art critic, European Edition of New York *Herald Tribune,* Paris, 1960–65, and *Art International,* Lugano, Switzerland, 1961–64; editor, *Locus Solus* magazine, Lans-en-Vercors, France, 1960–62; editor, *Art and Literature,* Paris, 1963–66; Paris correspondent, 1964–65, and executive editor, 1965–72, *Art News,* New York; Professor of English, 1974–80, and Distinguished Professor of English, 1980–90, Brooklyn College; since 1991 Professor of English, and currently Charles P. Stevenson, Jr., Professor of Languages and Literature, Bard College, Annandale-on-Hudson, New York; poetry editor, *Partisan Review,* New Brunswick, New Jersey, 1976–80; art critic, *New York* magazine, 1978–80; art critic, *Newsweek*, New York, 1980–85. Received Fulbright fellowship, 1955, 1956; Poets Foundation grant, 1960, 1964; Ingram Merrill Foundation grant, 1962, 1972; Harriet Monroe Memorial Prize, 1963, 1974; Guggenheim fellowship, 1967, 1973; National Endowment for the Arts grant, 1968, 1969; American Academy Award, 1969; Shelley Memorial Award, 1973; Frank O'Hara Prize, 1974; National Book Critics Circle Award, 1976; Pulitzer Prize, 1976; National Book Award, 1976; Rockefeller grant, for playwriting, 1979–80; English Speaking Union Prize, 1979; Academy of American Poets fellowship, 1982; Bard College Charles Flint Kellogg Award, 1983; Mayor's Award (New York), 1983; Bollingen Prize, 1984, 1985; Lenore Marshall Award (*Nation*), 1985; Wallace Stevens fellowship, 1985; MacArthur Foundation fellowship, 1985; MLA Commonwealth Award in Literature, 1986; Frost Medal, 1995; American Academy of Arts and Letters Gold Medal for Poetry, 1997; Litt.D., Long Island University, Southampton, New York, 1979; member, American Academy, 1980; American Academy of Arts and Sciences, 1983. Living in New York City and Hudson, New York.

**Poetry**
*Some Trees*, 1956
*The Tennis Court Oath*, 1962
*Rivers and Mountains*, 1966
*The Double Dream of Spring*, 1970
*Penguin Modern Poets 19*, with Lee Harwood and Tom Raworth, 1971
*Three Poems*, 1972
*The Vermont Notebook*, 1975
*Self-Portrait in a Convex Mirror*, 1975
*Houseboat Days*, 1977
*As We Know*, 1979
*Shadow Train*, 1981
*A Wave*, 1984
*Selected Poems*, 1985; revised edition, 1987
*April Galleons*, 1987
*Flow Chart*, 1991
*Hotel Lautrémont*, 1992
*Three Books: Poems*, 1993
*And the Stars Were Shining*, 1994
*Can You Hear, Bird?* 1995
*The Mooring of Starting Out: The First Five Books of Poetry*, 1997
*Wakefulness*, 1998
*Girls on the Run: A Poem*, 1999
*Your Name Here: Poems*, 2000

**Selected Criticism**
*Reported Sightings*, 1989
*Other Traditions*, 2000

**Other Writings:** plays, novel (*A Nest of Ninnies*, with James Schuyler, 1969), nonfiction, editions of collected poetry (*The Best American Poetry 1988*), translations of French literature.

**Further Reading**
Blasing, Mutlu Konuk, "John Ashbery: The Epidemic of the Way We Live Now," in *Politics and Form in Postmodern Poetry: O'Hara, Bishop, Ashbery, and Merrill*, Cambridge and New York: Cambridge University Press, 1995
Bloom, Harold, editor, *John Ashbery*, New York: Chelsea House, 1985
Imbriglio, Catherine, "'Our Days Put on Such Reticence': The Rhetoric of the Closet in John Ashbery's *Some Trees*," *Contemporary Literature* 36, no. 2 (1995)
Keller, Lynn, *Re-Making It New: Contemporary American Poetry and the Modernist Tradition*, Cambridge and New York: Cambridge University Press, 1987
Kostelanetz, Richard, "John Ashbery," in *The Old Poetries and the New*, Ann Arbor: University of Michigan Press, 1981
Lehman, David, *The Last Avant-Garde: The Making of the New York School of Poets*, New York: Doubleday, 1998
Lehman, David, editor, *Beyond Amazement: New Essays on John Ashbery*, Ithaca, New York: Cornell University Press, 1980
Osti, Louis, "The Craft of John Ashbery," *Confrontation* 9 (Fall 1974)
Packard, William, editor, *The Craft of Poetry: Interviews from the New York Quarterly*, Garden City, New York: Doubleday, 1974; revised edition, as *The Poet's Craft: Interviews from the New York Quarterly*, New York: Paragon House, 1987
Poulin, A., Jr., "The Experience of Experience: A Conversation with John Ashbery," *Michigan Quarterly* 20, no. 3 (Summer 1981)
Schultz, Susan M., editor, *The Tribe of John: Ashbery and Contemporary Poetry*, Tuscaloosa: University of Alabama Press, 1995
Shapiro, David, *John Ashbery: An Introduction to the Poetry*, New York: Columbia University Press, 1979
Shoptaw, John, *On the Outside Looking Out: John Ashbery's Poetry*, Cambridge, Massachusetts: Harvard University Press, 1994
Stitt, Peter, "The Art of Poetry 33," *Paris Review* 90 (Winter 1983)
Ward, Geoff, *Statutes of Liberty: The New York School of Poets*, New York: St. Martin's Press, and London: Macmillan, 1993

## Clepsydra

John Ashbery's "Clepsydra" was written in 1965 and published a year later in *Rivers and Mountains*, Ashbery's third book. "Clepsydra" marks a crucial change in the direction of Ashbery's poetry in which the competing discourses of lyric poetry and verbal disjunction typical of Ashbery's second book, *The Tennis Court Oath* (1962), are synthesized into playful yet adamantly philosophical lines. This new style would find its densest expression in the massive prose poetry of *Three Poems* (1972) and its lightest manifestation in the more "reader-friendly" books of the 1990s, including *Can You Hear, Bird?* (1995) and *Wakefulness* (1998). "Clepsydra" has secured an oddly conditional laudatory reception. Responses range from Bloom's awed dismissal—he termed "Clepsydra" a "beautiful failure" (Bloom, 1985)—to later readings of the poem as directly influenced by and responding to Emily Dickinson.

A clepsydra is an ancient water clock used by the Greek and Chinese. John Shoptaw (1994) has pointed out that the clepsydra was used to time lawyers' arguments in court. If one imagines that lawyers' arguments are defined precisely by their provision of differing interpretations based on an identical event or series of events, one can begin to understand "Clepsydra" as a poem that is a particularly porous and debatable event unto itself. The poem invites multiple interpretations ("arguments") from multiple readers ("lawyers"), resisting the safety of easy paraphrase or discernible narrative. This conception of a poem as a field where countless interpretations can converge and play is typical of Ashbery's oeuvre; near the end of "Clepsydra" Ashbery goes so far as to say, "It is because everything is relative." The momentary appearance of truth as it manifests itself within an individual interpretation leads to the almost simultaneous slippage of truth as competing interpretations come to the foreground.

Beyond introducing philosophical themes that continue to obsess Ashbery, "Clepsydra" marks a formal shift in basic writing practice. For example, even in his "experimental" phase Ashbery's line breaks were relatively conventional, at times conforming to metrical rules, *vers libre* breath stops, or simply conceptual shifts in content. In his notoriously difficult poem "Europe" (from *The Tennis Court Oath*) Ashbery's lines break where syntactical sense demands it; its first stanza reads like the beginning of a list poem in which both ideas and objects are materialized:

> To employ her
> construction ball
> Morning fed on the
> light blue wood
> of the mouth
> cannot understand
> feels deeply.

For the first time in Ashbery's work, however, "Clepsydra" uses the poetic line to stretch, turn, and twist in a sometimes frustratingly elusive manner:

> Each moment
> Of utterance is the true one; likewise none are true,
> Only is the bounding from air to air, a serpentine
> Gesture which hides the truth behind a congruent
> Message, the way air hides the sky, is, in fact,
> Tearing it limb from limb this very moment: but
> The sky has pleaded already and this is about
> As graceful a kind of non-absence as either
> Has a right to expect. . . .

This train of thought continues for another six lines before coming to a full stop. The excerpt above is certainly a "serpentine / Gesture" to be reckoned with for its various interpretive possibilities and its aesthetics as a run-on and nearly circular, solipsistic sentence that compares in scale and expressive potential with the "Torqued Ellipses" sculptures of Richard Serra.

If one reads "Clepsydra" as a text that suggests future ambition in Ashbery's poetry, one need look no farther than the initial half-sentence in the first line, "Hasn't the sky?" "Hasn't the sky?" works as a generically epic convention: it marks the poem as commencing *in media res* and thus points back to Modernist epics like Ezra Pound's *Cantos* (which begins "And then went down to the ship"), as well as to Kenneth Koch's comic epic *Ko; or, A Season on Earth* (1959). While "Clepsydra" never reaches epic scale in terms of length, it nevertheless shows that Ashbery is conceptually on his way to writing the longer poems of his later career.

"Clepsydra" engages a strangely secular and even heretical consciousness, husbanding its own nonsense into a mimetic reflection of a preconscious *and* post-apocalyptic physical universe. In marked contrast to the Book of Genesis' exegesis on the Word of God and its role in creation, Ashbery writes,

> But there was no statement
> At the beginning. There was only a breathless waste,
> A dumb cry shaping everything in projected
> After-effects orphaned by playing the part intended for
> them,
> Though one must not forget that the nature of this
> Emptiness, these previsions,
> Was that it could only happen here, on this page held
> Too close to be legible, sprouting erasures, except that they
> Ended everything in the transparent sphere of what was
> Intended only a moment ago, spiraling further out, its
> Gesture finally dissolving in the weather.

Ashbery's debt to Blake is apparent here in that rationality—an intellectual intervention into "this / Emptiness"—is deemed an annihilative force. Indeed, Blake's idealized non-binary mythic worlds are alluded to in later lines when Ashbery refers coyly to a "sphere of pure wisdom and / Entertainment" that "we shall never see." Close readings are disappearing acts, "this page held / Too close to be legible." The moment one interrogates the page, it dies in a sense, "spiraling further out, its / Gesture finally dissolving in the weather." One can see why Harold Bloom (1985) writes that "'Clepsydra' gives the uncanny effect of being a poem that neither wants nor needs readers."

For all its seriousness, however, "Clepsydra" remains a poem of pleasure, one that invites the reader to dally, loll, and play on the margins of sense and rationality: "He was out of it of course for having lain happily awake / On the tepid fringes of that field or whatever." Joining Ashbery on the field of "Clepsydra" is certainly a worthwhile if often perplexing game.

DANIEL KANE

**Further Reading**


Bloom, Harold, "The Charity of the Hard Moments," in *John Ashbery,* edited by Bloom, New York: Chelsea House, 1985

Gilson, Annette, "Disseminating 'Circumference': The Diachronic Presence of Dickinson in John Ashbery's 'Clepsydra,'" *Twentieth Century Literature* 44, no. 4 (1998)

Howard, Richard, "John Ashbery," in *John Ashbery,* edited by Harold Bloom, New York: Chelsea House, 1985

Kostelanetz, Richard, "How To Be a Difficult Poet," *New York Times Magazine* (23 May 1976)

Lehman, David, editor, *Beyond Amazement: New Essays on John Ashbery,* Ithaca, New York: Cornell University Press, 1980

Ross, Andrew, *The Failure of Modernism: Symptoms of American Poetry,* New York: Columbia University Press, 1986

Shoptaw, John, *On the Outside Looking Out: John Ashbery's Poetry,* Cambridge, Massachusetts: Harvard University Press, 1994

## Flow Chart

Preeminent literary critics such as Harold Bloom have long seen John Ashbery "joining that American sequence that includes Whitman, Dickinson, Stevens, and Hart Crane." Perhaps more than any of his other work, the long-term evaluation of his magnum opus *Flow Chart* (1991), which fellow poets such as Alfred Corn deem his "most important book," will determine whether he fulfills his christening as the poet of the age.

Weighing in at 216 pages, *Flow Chart* is Ashbery's longest book-length poem and is generally considered to be his most challenging work since *The Tennis Court Oath* (1962). It remains arguably the grandest exercise of his highly original style. More so than his other book-length poems, such as *Three Poems* (1972) and *Girls on the Run* (1999), *Flow Chart*'s aspirations are more distinctly traceable to its forerunners, especially Wordsworth's *The Prelude* (1805) and T.S. Eliot's *The Waste Land* (1922). Typically, Ashbery only briefly hints at such lofty intentions before quickly both confusing and defusing them by a sudden shift in register:

> The words, distant now, and mitred, glint. Yet not one
> Ever escapes the forest of agony and pleasure that keeps
> them
> In a solution that has become permanent through inertia.
> The force
> Of meaning never extrudes. And the insects,
> Of course, don't mind.

The original idea for the book came from Ashbery's friend Trevor Winkfield, who proposed Ashbery write a 100-page poem about his mother not long after she died in 1987. While the poem that became *Flow Chart* is not, ultimately, "about" Ashbery's mother, it was produced within Winkfield's proposed constraints: an even 100-page single-spaced typewritten manuscript was translated into a 216-page bound text. Winkfield's inspiration is somewhat commemorated by the flow chart-like design he created for the cover of the original edition.

Ashbery began composing the poem on 8 December 1987, with plans to finish the 100th page on 28 July 1988, his 61st birthday. Although not part of the published version, date tags on the source manuscript trace the poet's progress for "future scholars to come," as Ashbery himself has said. Ashbery followed this same diary format while creating several of his earlier long poems. It is therefore not difficult to recognize any of these poems' kinship with Marcel Proust's *À la recherche du temps perdu* (1922–32; *Remembrance of Things Past*), a text to which Ashbery has openly admitted turning for inspiration over the years. He has described *Flow Chart* as

> a kind of continuum, a diary, even though it's not in the form of a diary. It's the result of what I had to say on certain days over a period of six months, during the course of thinking about my past, the weather outside. I free-associate and come up with all kinds of extra material that doesn't belong—but does. (Dinitia Smith, "Poem Alone," *New York* [20 May 1991])

Despite what the circumstances of its composition might lead one to believe, *Flow Chart* is not autobiographical, at least not in the traditional sense. As much as the poem suggests a central consciousness, it also constantly switches—or suddenly abandons—the governing pronoun without notice. Proper names are used once and then never again. Yet traditional sentence structure is carefully, even eloquently, maintained. This technique (if it can be called conscious technique) and the effect it produces are uniquely Ashbery's.

On the other hand, the poem is a kind of celebration of the autobiographical act, an almost physical representation of the effects of time on recorded detail. The poem focuses on everything in general and nothing—no single person's autobiography—in particular. Helen Vendler tried to describe the poem as follows:

> [*Flow Chart* is] a two-hundred-and-fifteen-page lyric; a diary; a monitor screen registering a moving EEG; a thousand and one nights; Penelope's web unraveling; views from Argus' hundred eyes; a book of riddles; a ham-radio station; an old trunk full of memories; a rubbish dump; a Bartlett's *Familiar Quotations;* a Last Folio; a vaudeville act. . . . It makes Ashbery's past work (except for those poems in *The Tennis Court Oath* . . .) seem serenely classical, well ordered, pure, shapely, and above all, *short.* (Vendler, 1992)

Ashbery described another of his better-known long poems, "Self-Portrait in a Convex Mirror" (1975), a poem to which *Flow Chart* bears many similarities, as "a kind of history of its own coming into being." *Flow Chart* also contains passages that say as much:

> I suppose it does congeal slowly, like those footprints a
> primate
> made one morning zillions of years ago, and that says
> *something* about spontaneity
> as well as one's right to privacy.

Such fluctuation in register and ingenuousness is typical of an Ashbery poem. *Flow Chart* constantly makes wild moves between pathos and bathos:

> In the meantime, look sharp, and sharply at
> What is around you; there is
> Always the possibility something may come of something,
> and that is our
> Fondest wish though it says here I'm not supposed to say
> so, not now, not
> In this place of wood and sunlight, this stable or retiring
> room or whatever you
> Want to call it.
>
> Excuse me while I fart. There, that's better. I actually feel
> relieved.

The poem is written in free verse, with line structure governed solely by the width of the source manuscript page. The edition of the poem does not recreate the appearance of the source manuscript, instead wrapping longer lines beneath themselves in the style of poet C.K. Williams. There is a notable exception to the poem's free verse in its elaborate near-conclusion: a double sestina that borrows its end-words from Swinburne's sestina "The Complaint of Lisa." While startling to the uninitiated, such fantastic parlor games are typical of Ashbery's work.

Many critics have attempted to ease readers' discomfort with Ashbery's work by encouraging them to read it through the lens of modern art. Ashbery himself has said of his style, "I attempt to use words abstractly, as an artist uses paint." The experience of reading *Flow Chart* is very much akin to the experience of regarding one of the massive abstract canvases of Ashbery's contemporary New York School painter friends. As with standing in front of a wall-sized Jackson Pollock canvas, to make any attempt at assembling the random into the singularly representational is to be quickly frustrated and defeated.

In a sense the reader has to make the Zen-like transformation into "being" Ashbery. The critic Helen Vendler has written that the only way she can read Ashbery is

> by entering some bizarrely tuned pitch inside myself . . . [where I can] find myself on Ashbery's wavelength, where everything at the symbolic level makes sense. The irritating (and seductive) thing about this tuning in is that it can't be willed: I can't make it happen when I am tired or impatient. But when the frequencies meet, the effect on me is Ashbery's alone, and it is the form of trance. (Vendler, 1992)

*Flow Chart,* in both scope and length, proves the ultimate test.

Dobby Gibson

**Further Reading**

Benfey, Christopher, "Flow Chart," *The New Republic* 204, no. 24 (17 June 1991)

Bloom, Harold, editor, *John Ashbery,* New York: Chelsea House, 1985

Lehman, David, editor, *Beyond Amazement: New Essays on John Ashbery,* Ithaca, New York: Cornell University Press, 1980

Schultz, Susan M., editor, *The Tribe of John: Ashbery and Contemporary Poetry,* Tuscaloosa: University of Alabama Press, 1995

Shoptaw, John, *On the Outside Looking Out: John Ashbery's Poetry,* Cambridge, Massachusetts: Harvard University Press, 1994

Vendler, Helen, "A Steely Glitter Chasing Shadows," *The New Yorker* (3 August 1992)

## Self-Portrait in a Convex Mirror

Published in the middle of Ashbery's career, "Self-Portrait in a Convex Mirror" (1975) has sparked more critical interest than any of his other poems. There are good reasons for its popularity: the poem itself is a stunning meditation on the nature of identity and its relationship to experience or perception, death, and the passage of time. It is also the most plainly discursive of Ashbery's major works. Before publication the poem was heavily revised—something of an anomaly for Ashbery—and although "Self-Portrait" is by no means simple, its solemnity makes it a bit more approachable than the wider-ranging syntactical and structural play that is often the hallmark of his work.

In its opening line "Self-Portrait" refers to Francesco Parmigianino, a Mannerist painter who copied his reflection in a convex mirror onto a half-sphere of wood. A response to this painting, the six sections of the poem include: a meditation on the values implicit in the painting's composition; a reflection on the relationship between the self and the phenomenal world; an examination of time and possibility; a reassessment of the painting's impact on the observer; a discussion of the influence of the immediate world on the act of reflection; and a consideration of change and death that regards the difficult nature of love, objects to mimetic art, and underscores the speaker's immersion in time's progress.

Parmigianino's almost "angelic" face occupies the center of the painting, showing "tenderness, amusement and regret." The problem it presents, as the poem's opening lines demonstrate, is that the artist is "sequestered." The convex mirror chooses to reflect "only what he saw," which is "glazed" and "embalmed." In the expression on Parmigianino's face "the soul establishes itself," but because "the distance increases / Significantly" on the surface of the mirror, between the artist and the world, "the soul is a captive" that longs "to be free." Before the first section of the poem concludes, the speaker asserts that "the soul is not a soul": it holds "no secret, is small, and it fits / Its hollow perfectly: its room, our moment of attention." This "moment of attention"—as far as art is concerned—is represented in Parmigianino's work by the hand that holds the brush, a hand that, because of the mirror's distortions, is larger in the painting than is the face above it. While the mirrored face invites and rejects the soul's existence, the hand insists that "there are no words for the surface," no words "to say what really is." Despite what one might long for, appearances *are* reality, what the end of section one calls a "visible core." As a consequence, there is "no way out of the problem of pathos vs. experience."

The middle sections of "Self-Portrait" probe this problem and ultimately attempt to find a solution by joining the self to its ongoing experience. The second section folds the past into the present, so that memory becomes part of the "magma of interiors" that shapes the self, the "dreaming model," and the third section of the poem considers the future, the horizon of possibilities "sweeping out from us." The "room" that the self inhabits contains this "flow like an hourglass"; in passing through time and trying to find significance in events "something like living occurs, a movement / Out of the dream into its codification." Section four tells the reader that the effort to discover a unitary meaning, the "consonance of the high Renaissance," is as impossible as it might be to recognize an angel who "looks like everything / We have forgotten." There must be another way to look at life, the fifth section suggests—life as it happens, immediate and resistant to code, the landscape "alive with filiations, shuttlings," the "backing of the looking glass." This other life is grounds for "a new preciosity," a challenger pounding on the gates of an amazed Castle," banging at the door of the "sequestered self," of the classical artist's dream of "consonance." For some readers the optimism expressed here will carry through to the poem's conclusion. Parmigianino's argument has grown "stale," and "another life"—a compound of memory, self, appearances, and immediacy—can supplant the outmoded desire for transcendence, the secret soul, and the false immortality promised by art. Rejecting the singular for the plural, the poem suggests that

It,
Not we, are the change; that we are in fact it
If we could get back to it.

The last section of "Self-Portrait"—nearly half of the entire poem—demands a careful reading, however, because it responds to the "new preciosity" while it continues to consider the values represented in the convex mirror.

The sixth section of "Self-Portrait" begins by returning to Parmigianino's face, attention "locking into place" like death. Mirrors are often problematic in Ashbery's work: "The Skaters" hopes there is time

. . . to utterly destroy
That too-familiar image
Lurking in the glass
Each morning, at the edge of the mirror

and "Fragment" calls the mirror a "stiff enclave" that contains "so much authority / And intelligence in such a miserable result." "Self-Portrait" holds forth against the ominous suggestions of limitation and mortality that mirrors represent but, like "another life," it cannot hold forth forever. The act of attention, the process involved in the creation of art, cannot be endless. The products of art, Parmigianino's portrait and the poem itself, might feed the desire for permanence, for transcendent meaning and immortality, but they are delimited by time. Love, a cousin to high art and the desires it represents, "once / Tipped the scales but now is shadowed and invisible." It is "around somewhere," but "cannot be sandwiched / Between two adjacent moments," leaving a vague

. . . sense of something that can never be known
Even though it seems likely that each of us
Knows what it is.

A large part of the sixth section carries on almost cheerfully in the face of finality, praising the "never-to-be-defined daytime," the "present we are always escaping from / And falling back into," but "*This* thing, the mute, undivided present," cannot fairly compete with the notion of eternity. One might be happy understanding that "all time / Reduces to no special time," the poem suggests, if one did not also understand that "no special time" must inevitably end. Consciousness of death creates a distance in the midst of life, an "otherness" that is "all there is to look at / In the mirror." These conclusions darken the last pages of "Self-Portrait." The landscape that earlier seemed so promising, the "backing of the looking glass," becomes at last "the gibbous / Mirrored eye of an insect." At the end of the poem, whether looking to the self or toward the world, the speaker—and the reader—are caught in a reflection:

And each part of the whole falls off
And cannot know it knew, except
Here and there, in cold pockets
Of remembrance, whispers out of time.

Edward Haworth Hoeppner

**Further Reading**

Altieri, Charles, *Self and Sensibility in Contemporary American Poetry,* Cambridge and New York: Cambridge University Press, 1984

Bloom, Harold, editor, *John Ashbery,* New York: Chelsea House, 1985

Edelman, Lee, "The Pose of Imposture: Ashbery's 'Self-Portrait in a Convex Mirror,'" *Twentieth Century Literature* 32, no. 1 (1986)

Hoeppner, Edward Haworth, *Echoes and Moving Fields: Structure and Subjectivity in the Poetry of W.S. Merwin and John Ashbery,* Lewisburg, Pennsylvania: Bucknell University Press, and London: Associated University Presses, 1994

Kinzie, Mary, "Irreference: The Poetic Diction of John Ashbery, Part I," *Modern Philology* 84, no. 3 (1987)

Kinzie, Mary, "Irreference: The Poetic Diction of John Ashbery, Part II," *Modern Philology* 84, no. 4 (1987)

Lehman, David, editor, *Beyond Amazement: New Essays on John Ashbery,* Ithaca, New York: Cornell University Press, 1980

Lieberman, Laurence, *Unassigned Frequencies: American Poetry in Review, 1964–77,* Urbana: University of Illinois Press, 1977

Perloff, Marjorie, "Transparent Selves: The Poetry of John Ashbery and Frank O'Hara," *Yearbook of English Studies* 8 (1979)

Vendler, Helen, "Understanding Ashbery," *The New Yorker* (16 March 1981)

## The Tennis Court Oath

"The Tennis Court Oath" is the title poem of John Ashbery's book by the same name published in 1962. The poem consists of 49 lines of free verse divided into six stanzas of varying length. The title of the work suggests two possible sources for its inspiration: one an historical event, and the other a famous work of art. However, only one of these is actually relevant to the poem. Historically, The Tennis Court Oath was a key episode of the French Revolution. It earned its name when a crowd of commoners known as the "Third Estate," having been locked out of a meeting of the Estates General, gathered in solidarity on a nearby tennis court and vowed to remain there united in protest until the Constitution was reformed with certain concessions granted to them. Ashbery's poem neither retells nor refers to this incident. Second, the title is that of a well-known painting by the French Neoclassicist Jacques-Louis David (1748–1825) in which the historical protest is depicted. In David's painting, the oath-takers of the Third Estate are portrayed as patriots and heroes of the Revolution. What Ashbery found to be most intriguing about David's painting is that it was never completed, and this notion of "incompleteness" is central to his poem. Ashbery was fascinated by the unfinished work's combination of an ironic expression of heroism with a lack of completeness. He saw this combination as being congruous to the methods employed and the themes expressed in his poem, in which the first-person speaker remains permanently "incomplete."

The key to understanding how "The Tennis Court Oath" works is the poem's first line. The phrase "What had you been thinking about" is a question that cannot be answered with any real satisfaction because thoughts are internal events unique to the person who generates them. Thoughts cannot be transferred completely intact from the mind of one person to another, thus "thinking" itself remains forever incomplete. And yet Ashbery's opening line suggests a way for the reader to comprehend the many incomplete sentences that arise and disappear at random throughout the piece. After encountering the opening line, the reader will understand that one is expected to give oneself over entirely to the poem's non sequiturs, and allow meaning itself to be constructed from their juxtaposition with one's own thoughts. Thus, the overall meaning of the poem will differ from reader to reader, and from time to time, according to each individual's or time period's unique response to it.

To enhance this effect, the poet has purposely left the lines in the poem unpunctuated, so that the reader must approach each one with some confusion before deciding for himself how to interpret its meaning. Ashbery's intention is to use language in its most minimal configuration, stripped of all the trappings and sign posts designed to lead one through a written work so that meaning can be precisely conveyed. His concern is not with the precise conveyance of meaning, but rather with the true nature of thought. It is "thinking" itself Ashbery wishes to investigate, thus his poem proceeds accordingly as a stream of consciousness through which flow fragments of only partially comprehensible incidents, images, and assertions. A bit like Pound's notion of the "Vortex," the poem may be thought of as a catalyst for the reader's intellectual response to it. However, Ashbery is in no way a Modernist in sensibility, but rather a Postmodernist whose goal lies in the creation of a kind of interactive text that, by virtue of its incompleteness, is resistant to stability, classification, and finitude.

What is discernibly and undeniably concrete in the poem are its many nightmarish images. The first stanza contains the lines "the face studiously bloodied," "I go on loving you like water but," and "there is a terrible breath in the way all of this." There is a sense of disappointment: "You were not elected president, yet won the race," and a general foreboding: "I worry." In subsequent stanzas, the poem gathers disorienting momentum. Like a dream encountered *in medias res*, it vacillates quickly between the grotesque and the sublime. The predominant motifs of danger and expedition are put through many variations. In the second stanza a "water beetle head" that "reflects all" seems to provide the most effective and appropriate representation for the poem's refracted and diffused imagery, while the implications of travel appear to waver between the mundane in the line "I thought going down to mail this" and the exotic with "are incomparable the lovely tent / mystery you don't want surrounded the real / you dance." Stanza three builds on this imperfect exoticism as a nameless "mulatress" approaches but never reaches "[some]one in yon house" of stanza four. Stanza five exhibits a dark psychological inwardness underlying scenes of some violent import: "blood," "The doctor," "sharp edge," and "cry" are interposed by the insinuative "reading it carelessly as if to tell you your fears were justified." In the final stanza, one senses some relief in the line "there was no turning back but the end was in sight," before the poem concludes abruptly and ambiguously.

Ashbery was living in Paris at the time the poem was written. While there, he was introduced to a variety of the new traditions of linguistic experimentation then surfacing in French poetry, as well as to the generally anti-hermeneutic outlook that dominated the 1960s. In many ways, "The Tennis Court Oath" is illustrative of the techniques and philosophies to which Ashbery had been newly exposed. The poem is explosively dadaistic in form; radically "open" and disjunctive. Words are spattered onto the page in a style full of wild leaps, discontinuities, and fragments. A general sense of chaos predominates. Ashbery has described this "cut-up" strategy as a way of "taking poetry apart to try to understand how it works." He was experimenting with poetry's limits, seeing to what degree the elements of a poem could appear unrelated and yet have some mysterious poetic and imaginative connection for the mind to resolve.

Joe Francis Doerr

**Further Reading**


Andrews, Bruce, "Misrepresentation: A Text for 'The Tennis Court Oath' of John Ashbery," in *In the American Tree,* edited by Ron Silliman, Orono, Maine: National Poetry Foundation, 1986

Ashbery, John, "The Invisible Avant-Garde," in *The Avant-Garde,* edited and compiled by Thomas B. Hess and Ashbery, New York: Macmillan, 1968

Bloom, Harold, editor, *John Ashbery,* New York: Chelsea House, 1985

Fredman, Stephen, *Poet's Prose: The Crisis in American Verse,* Cambridge and New York: Cambridge University Press, 1990

Kermani, David K., *John Ashbery: A Comprehensive Bibliography, Including His Art Criticism, and with Selected Notes from Unpublished Materials,* New York: Garland, 1976

Kinzie, Mary, "Irreference: The Poetic Diction of John Ashbery, Part I," *Modern Philology* 84, no. 3 (1987)

Kinzie, Mary, "Irreference: The Poetic Diction of John Ashbery, Part II," *Modern Philology* 84, no. 4 (1987)

Lehman, David, editor, *Beyond Amazement: New Essays on John Ashbery,* Ithaca, New York: Cornell University Press, 1980

Ross, Andrew, "Taking 'The Tennis Court Oath,'" in *The Tribe of John: Ashbery and Contemporary Poetry,* edited by Susan M. Schultz, Tuscaloosa: University of Alabama Press, 1995

Shapiro, David, *John Ashbery: An Introduction to the Poetry,* New York: Columbia University Press, 1979

# Asian American Poetry

In the preface to their groundbreaking collection *Aiiieeeee! An Anthology of Asian American Writers* (1974), Frank Chin, Jeffery Paul Chan, Lawson Fusao Inada, and Shawn Hsu Wong note that "Asian Americans are not one people but several—Chinese Americans, Japanese Americans, and Filipino Americans." The "Asian-American sensibility" that the volume seeks to represent depends on being "American born and raised"; it features writers who, the editors claim, "got their China and Japan from the radio, off the silver screen, from television, out of comic books, from the pushers of white American culture that pictured the yellow man as something that when wounded, sad, or angry, or swearing, or wondering whined, shouted, or screamed 'aiiieeeee!'" Taking aim at the stereotype of Asian-Americans as the model minority, the editors lament that "seven generations of suppression under legislative racism and euphemized white racist love have left today's Asian Americans in a state of self-contempt, self-rejection, and disintegration." As of 1974, they maintain, fewer than "ten works of fiction and poetry have been published by American-born Chinese, Japanese, and Filipino writers," not because "in six generations of Asian Americans there was no impulse to literary or artistic self-expression" but because mainstream American publishers were only interested in publishing works written by Asian-Americans that were "*actively inoffensive* to white sensibilities."

*Aiiieeeee!* was intended to counter the accepted wisdom that a literature that could be called "Asian-American" simply did not exist. "My writer's education owes a big debt to this first *Aiiieeeee!*" writes the Filipino-American novelist and poet Jessica Hagedorn:

> The energy and interest sparked by *Aiiieeeee!* in the Seventies was essential to Asian American writers because it gave us visibility and credibility as creators of our own specific literature. We could not be ignored; suddenly, we were no longer silent. Like other writers of color in America, we were beginning to challenge the long-cherished concepts of a xenophobic literary canon dominated by white heterosexual males. Obviously, there was room for more than one voice and one vision in this ever-expanding arena.

In 1990, the editors of *Aiiieeeee!* produced a sequel titled *The Big Aiiieeeee!* which dropped the requirement of birth on U.S. soil but restricted itself to Chinese-American and Japanese-American literature. In narrowing its focus, *The Big Aiiieeeee!* contributed to the perception that Asian-American literature essentially consists of literature by Chinese- and Japanese-Americans, with sporadic contributions by writers of Southeast Asian and Asian-Indian descent.

By the end of the 20th century, however, critics working in the field of Asian-American literature preferred to include under the rubric of "Asian-American literature" texts written by people of Asian descent who were either born in or migrated to North America. Although the term "Asian-American" had been invented for the purpose of promoting political solidarity among Americans of Asian descent, the idea of a unifying "Asian-American" sensibility that depends on being born in North America has come to seem stifling, particularly after the sharp increase in Asian immigration that followed the 1965 Immigration and Nationality Act, which abolished the quotas that favored immigrants from northern European countries. By century's end, the label "Asian-American" had been broadened to include native and naturalized Americans of not only Chinese, Japanese, and Filipino but also Bangladeshi, Burmese, Cambodian, Indian, Indonesian, Korean, Laotian, Nepalese, Thai, and Vietnamese descent. This new diversity was not represented, however, in the Asian-American literary canon, which continued to be dominated by Chinese- and Japanese-American authors, with increasing contributions from writers of Korean, Filipino, and South Asian descent.

The original *Aiiieeeee!* anthology contained fiction and drama but no poetry, and in general Asian-American poetry has lagged behind the other genres in achieving prominence on the literary landscape. *The Big Aiiieeeee!* however, brought attention to a recently recovered tradition of Chinese-American poetry, written by immigrants arriving in the San Francisco Bay Area during the first two decades of the century. During this period, poetry appeared in two daily newspapers written in Cantonese and published in San Francisco's Chinatown: the *Chung Sai Yat Po,* which was established in 1900 and began issuing a daily literary supplement in 1908, and the *Sai Gat Yat Po,* which was established in 1909. Chinatown had a number of literary societies that sponsored poetry competitions, and in 1911 the prominent bookseller Tai Quong Company published an anthology of 808 vernacular poems titled *Jinshan ge ji* ("Songs of Gold Mountain," after the popular name given to the United States by Chinese sojourners); a second volume, published in 1915, collected an additional 832 folk rhymes. Together, these poems present a rich account of the experience of early Chinese immigrants in the United States; many express the loneliness, despair, and frustration of discovering that American practices do not always live up to American ideals: "So, liberty is your national principle," writes one of these anonymous poets. "Why do you practice autocracy? / You don't uphold justice, you Americans, / You detain me in prison, guard me closely. . . . When can I get out of this prison and free my mind?" An additional set of 135 poems, which had been scribbled in Cantonese on the walls of the Angel Island Immigration Station by those detained there, were preserved when two detainees copied them down and brought them to San Francisco.

The only Chinese-American poet included in *The Big Aiiieeeee!* is Wing Tek Lum, who was born and raised in Honolulu. His first volume of poetry, *Expounding the Doubtful Points* (1987), was awarded the Before Columbus Foundation's American Book Award. It contains poignant lyrics about family life, describing the poet's difficult relationship with his father ("a gruff old fut"), who died of cancer, and—in sharp contrast to the tendentious mother-son relationships that are found in many works by male Asian-American writers—his more tender relationship with his mother, who died of cancer when he was 16. Other poems treat sociopolitical issues, such as the melting pot, pluralism, and Eurocentrism, while still others, such as "To Li Po," meditate on the practice of poetry. Another American Book Award winner, Mei-Mei Berssenbrugge, also cites Li Po as a part of her "poetic tradition"; as befits a writer who was born in Beijing of Chinese and Dutch parents and raised in Massachusetts, she includes among her other influences Sappho, Dante, Yeats, Vallejo, Rilke, Stein, Whitman, Dickinson, Pound, and Ashbery as well as Tu Fu and Wang Wei.

Lum and Berssenbrugge, like most Chinese-American poets, are interested in finding ways to make use of traditional Chinese poetics and the long history of Chinese poetry within the context of modern poetry written in English. Other Chinese-American poets with similar interests include Arthur Sze, who studied Chinese literature at the University of California, Berkeley; Li-Young Lee, who describes his poetry as a process of "serious and passionate apprenticeship, which involves a strange combination of awe and argument, with the Masters"; and Carolyn Lau, who invokes Chinese philosophy in poems such as "A Footnote to a Dispute among Confucius's Disciples." Paradoxically, such interests put these poets squarely within a central tradition of American Modernist poetry: Conrad Aiken, Amy Lowell, Ezra Pound, William Carlos Williams, and many other "American" poets of the early 20th century sought inspiration by turning to China.

Other poets, however, view traditional Chinese culture with more ambivalence. In "My Father's Martial Art," Stephen Liu portrays traditional Chinese culture as an anachronism in modern America. The narrator of Marilyn Chin's "We Are Americans Now, We Live in the Tundra" sings "a blues song" to China and bids "farewell" to her "ancestors / Hirsute Taoists, failed scholars." Moreover, women poets such as Chin, Diana Chang, Genny Lim, Diane Mark, Nellie Wong, and Merle Woo often fault traditional Chinese culture for its misogyny and discover that finding a poetic voice is often linked to rebellion against patriarchal traditions personified in the figure of the father and implicit in the communal life of Chinatown.

The typical American Chinatown began as a segregated ghetto for immigrants who were still designated "aliens ineligible to citizenship" under the provisions of the Nationality Act of 1870, so that in the early years of the 20th century they were largely communities of immigrant bachelors. Planning merely to sojourn in the United States in order to earn money, many early immigrants found it too expensive to bring their wives with them, and in 1870 the ratio of Chinese men to women in the United States was 14 to 1. This gender imbalance was frozen into place by the provisions of the Chinese Exclusion Act of 1882, which prohibited further immigration from China, and by the fact that Chinese men were forbidden by U.S. law to marry white women. Chinatown thus becomes a symbol in Chinese-American writing for traditional Chinese values, including patriarchy, and for U.S. racial oppression; and for many Chinese-American poets, particularly those who are the children of pre–World War II immigrants, it is often Chinatown that is their primary link to Chinese tradition.

Finding themselves caught between cultures, many Chinese-American poets lace their work with history and politics. A powerful example is Alan Lau's "Water that Springs from a Rock," which merges the lyrical and the historiographic as it recounts the massacre of Chinese workers for the Union Pacific Railroad in Rock Springs, Wyoming, in 1885. Genny Lim, Nellie Wong, and Merle Woo write about the ways in which Chinese women have been objectified by white male culture, while poems such as Arthur Sze's "Listening to a Broken Radio" and John Yau's "Rumors" question the value of the American dream. A humorous but apt dramatization of the project of Chinese-American poetry can be found in the meal prepared by the narrator of Wing Tek Lum's "T-Bone Steak":

No, it was not
Chinese, much less
American, that pink piece
sitting in my rice bowl. It was,
simply, how our family
ate, and I
for one am grateful for
the difference.

Twentieth-century Chinese-American poetry makes use of a set of recurrent motifs: traditional Chinese culture, the idea of the United States as the "Gold Mountain," working on the railroads, the bachelor culture of Chinatown, the feminization of Chinese culture, and racial discrimination. In contrast, the history of 20th-century Japanese-American poetry centers on a single historical moment: World War II and its immediate aftermath. Japanese-American poetry written in English during the 20th century was produced almost exclusively by nisei (second-generation) and sansei (third-generation) authors. The issei, first-generation immigrants who came to the United States mainland and to Hawaii between 1885 and 1924, did write poetry that was published in Japanese-language newspapers on the West Coast and in Hawaii, usually in haiku or in other traditional Japanese poetic forms. One issei poet, Bunichi Kagawa, not only published in Japanese-language newspapers but also wrote poems in English, which were collected in the volume *Hidden Flame* (1930). From the 1920s on, nisei writers began publishing in the English-language sections of Japanese-American newspapers, and for the most part their poetry is strongly influenced by Western literary conventions. Chiye Mori was one of the first poets to explore the political dimension of nisei identity: her poem "Japanese American" (1932) likens the nisei to "clay pigeons traveling swiftly and aimlessly / On the electric wire of international hate / Helpless targets in the shooting gallery of political discord."

The bombing of Pearl Harbor in 1941 and the subsequent internment of 110,000 Japanese and Japanese-Americans produced feelings of bewilderment and betrayal among many of the nisei, whose rights as U.S. citizens were completely ignored by the U.S. government. Some, such as the members of the Japanese American Citizens League (JACL), sought to prove their loyalty as Americans by supporting the U.S. government's wartime policies toward American Japanese, while others remained bitterly disillusioned, particularly after the government sought to recruit nisei volunteers into the armed forces in 1942. The English-language magazines that were produced in three of the internment camps—*Trek* (Topaz, Utah), *Tulean Dispatch* (Tule Lake, California), and *The Pen* (Rowher, Arkansas)—reflect the struggle between these perspectives, although critical points of view were blunted by government censorship. The wartime poetry of Toyo Suryemoto uses a facade of natural metaphors to convey the bitterness and despair brought about by internment.

This split perspective about the necessity of internment continues in Japanese-American writing after the war. In prose, it is reflected in the gap between the conciliatory rhetoric of Monica Sone's autobiography *Nisei Daughter* (1953) and John Okada's bitterly ambivalent novel *No-No Boy* (1957), which details the postwar struggles of a former internee who was imprisoned after refusing to swear loyalty to the U.S. government while in camp. Issei poets such as Shumpa Kiuchi and Shusei Matsui wrote poems that hearkened back to heroic traditions in Asian literature, while many nisei authors, writing in the JACL's national paper, *Pacific Citizen,* and in such Japanese-American newspapers as *Rafu*

*Shimpo* (Los Angeles) and *Hokubei Mainichi* (San Francisco), devoted themselves to forgetting the miseries of internment and reintegrating themselves into U.S. culture. Hisaye Yamamoto's celebrated story "Seventeen Syllables" charts the gap that grows between a young and increasingly Americanized nisei woman and her mother; the daughter, Rosie, pretends to appreciate the haiku that her mother has just composed because she is ashamed to reveal just how shaky her command of Japanese really is.

The poet Mitsuye Yamada, born in Japan and therefore an issei but raised among nisei in the United States, cuts across the grain of these generalizations. Her first collection, *Camp Notes* (1976), brings together pieces written during and after her internment at Minidoka and poems written during the 1970s. Written with an ironic detachment and an eye for poignant detail, her poems adopt the anti-racist and anti-patriarchal attitudes that are usually found in sansei writing about the war. Writing in the aftermath of the civil rights movements of the 1960s and the Vietnam War, sansei poets such as Lawson Fusao Inada and Janice Mirikitani sought to make their poetry a vehicle for the reconstruction of Japanese-American identity. In the introduction to his second volume of poetry, *Legends of Camp* (1993), Inada writes, "More and more, artist and audience are becoming one—for the greater cause of community and mutuality . . . I began functioning as a *community* poet—with new people, places, and publications to work with." Sharing Inada's sense of political commitment, Mirikitani adds a strain of self-reflectiveness, meditating occasionally on the limits of what poetry and thought can accomplish. After listening to the experiences of a Vietnam veteran, the speaker of "Jungle Rot and Open Arms" asks,

> so where is my
> *political education?* my
> *rhetorical answers* to everything? my
> *theory into practice?* my
> *intensification of life in art?*

Some sansei writers have sought to ground their poetry in a new regionalism: Juliet Kono's collection *Hilo Rains* (1988) explores the ways in which three generations of her family have been shaped by the land of Hawaii, while Garrett Kaoru Hongo writes about Hawaii and other communities where Asian-Americans live, seeking to draw connections across regional and ethnic boundaries.

Cathy Song is another poet whose work crosses ethnic boundaries. Born in Honolulu to a Chinese mother and a Korean father, Song's poetry is deeply rooted in both the Hawaiian landscape and her dual Asian heritage. Her first collection, *Picture Bride* (1983), draws inspiration from Korean and Chinese traditions, even as it uses memories and images drawn from family life to explore the ways in which these traditions are restrictive, particularly for women. Myung Mi Kim, a Korean who came to the United States at the age of nine, found herself influenced by what is perhaps the best-known Korean-American text in academic circles, Theresa Cha's formally experimental *Dictée* (1982), which explores the aftereffects of the Japanese colonization of Korea while taking aim at U.S. national narratives of assimilation. Kim's first collection, *Under Flag* (1991), portrays the fragmentation of Korean-American subjectivities as a result of the loss of language and homeland and the corrosiveness of U.S. racism. Kim has characterized her use of language as "an English that behaves like Korean, an English shaped by a Korean," a kind of third language "beyond what is systematically Korean and English." The question of whether Korean immigrants should produce literature written in Korean or English is debated among Korean-American intellectuals. The poet Ch'oe Yun-hong has suggested that Koreans' lack of interest in the problems of Korean-Americans has discouraged the production of American poetry written in Korean, and scholars of Korean literature have suggested that Korean-American literature should distinguish itself by turning to English and focusing on immigrant life rather than memories of Korea. Ch'oe suggests that the harshness of life for many Korean-Americans has fueled a "desire for poetry," but at the end of the 20th century, Korean-American poetry remains an underdeveloped segment of Asian-American poetry.

Another as yet underdeveloped but increasingly vibrant area is Filipino-American poetry. Because the majority of Filipino immigrants have seemed to take pride in their Americanization, Filipinos have been regarded as an "invisible minority," with many Americans unaware of the existence of a Philippine-American War in 1899. One of the earliest Filipino-American poets to publish in the United States was José García Villa, who lived the bohemian life in Greenwich Village and counted among his friends W.H. Auden, E.E. Cummings, and Edith Sitwell. In addition to short stories, Villa wrote poetry that was strongly influenced by the intellectual climate of Modernism. His contemporary Carlos Bulosan is perhaps best known for his autobiography *America Is in the Heart* (1946), but he also wrote poems that continued his exploration of what it means to be an outsider in U.S. culture while still believing in the nation's ideals. In the aftermath of the 1960s, Filipino-American poets began to explore the contours of U.S. racial discrimination. Serafin Syquia wrote paeans to solidarity among U.S. ethnic minorities in poems such as "i can relate to tonto" (1972), while Sam Tagatac's "A Chance Meeting between Huts" (1975) focused on an "act / of recognition" between two Asian-Americans who learn to see outside of U.S. stereotypes. In "Rapping with One Million Carabaos in the Dark" (1974), Alfred Robles tells his fellow Filipino-Americans to "put down your white mind / . . . / & burn up all that white shit / that's keeping your people down." The success of Jessica Hagedorn's novel *Dogeaters* (1990) sparked new interest in Filipino-American literature and was followed by the publication in 1996 of two anthologies—*Returning a Borrowed Tongue: An Anthology of Contemporary Filipino Poetry in English* (edited by Nick Carbó) and *Flippin': Filipinos on America* (edited by Luis H. Francia and Eric Gamalinda)—that contain a richly diverse set of Filipino and Filipino-American poets.

Poetry by Americans of South Asian descent was also a growing field at the end of the 20th century despite the fact that South Asians are still being omitted from mainstream collections, such as Shawn Wong's *Asian American Literature: A Brief Introduction and Anthology* (1996). In his first volume of poetry, *The Loss of India* (1964), Zulfikar Ghose, born in prepartition India and Pakistan, explores the dislocation that occurs when a South Asian chooses to write in English and to live in the West. Writing in both English and Kannada, the Indian-born poet and translator A.K. Ramanujan explores the dynamics of the Hindu family, weaving together past and present, India and Chicago, his adopted home. The list of significant South Asian poets working in North America includes two Canadians of Sri Lankan descent, Rienzi Crusz and Michael Ondaatje, the latter best known for his Booker Prize–

winning novel *The English Patient* (1992); Agha Shahid Ali, whose 1979 volume *In Memory of Begum Akhtar* invokes a long tradition of Urdu poetry; and Meena Alexander, who was born in India and raised in the Sudan before settling permanently in New York. To the exploration of postcolonial identity that marks the work of all the South Asian writers mentioned here, Alexander adds a commitment to feminist aesthetics and politics. In an essay titled "Is There an Asian American Aesthetics?" Alexander maintains that art "is always political, even if it is mostly abstract, even if it is a simple visual image of a leaf falling from a tree."

The idea that art and politics are inextricably connected has become a staple of Asian-American poetry, particularly as new voices emerge from the shadows of cultural marginalization. Perhaps the dramatic monologues written by Ai, the daughter of a Japanese father and a mother who is a mixture of black, Choctaw, and Irish, might serve as an emblem for 20th-century Asian-American poetry. "It's time to cross the border / and cut your throat with two knives," says a character in Ai's *Killing Floor* (1979). Whether or not their ethnic background is mixed like Ai's, Asian-American poets recognize that they live in a state of cultural hybridity, caught between cultures. In their poetry, hybridity is portrayed more often than not as a state of violence. For these writers, the beauty of poetry is its ability to transform violence into art and thus despair into hope.

CYRUS R.K. PATELL

**Further Reading**

Cheung, King-Kok, editor, *An Interethnic Companion to Asian American Literature,* Cambridge and New York: Cambridge University Press, 1997

Cheung, King-Kok, editor, *Words Matter: Conversations with Asian American Writers,* Honolulu: University of Hawai'i Press, 2000

Cheung, King-Kok, and Stan Yogi, editors, *Asian American Literature: An Annotated Bibliography,* New York: Modern Language Association of America, 1988

Hom, Marlon K., editor and translator, *Songs of Gold Mountain: Cantonese Rhymes from San Francisco Chinatown,* Berkeley: University of California Press, 1987

Kim, Elaine H., *Asian American Literature: An Introduction to the Writings and Their Social Context,* Philadelphia, Pennsylvania: Temple University Press, 1982

Lai, Him Mark, Genny Lim, and Judy Yung, editors and translators, *Island: Poetry and History of Chinese Immigrants on Angel Island, 1910–1940,* San Francisco: HOC DOI, 1980

Lim, Shirley Geok-lin, and Amy Ling, editors, *Reading the Literatures of Asian America,* Philadelphia, Pennsylvania: Temple University Press, 1992

Lowe, Lisa, *Immigrant Acts: On Asian American Cultural Politics,* Durham, North Carolina: Duke University Press, 1996

Patell, Cyrus R.K., "Emergent Literatures," in *The Cambridge History of American Literature, Prose Writing, 1940–1990,* volume 7, edited by Sacvan Bercovitch, Cambridge and New York: Cambridge University Press, 1999

Takaki, Ronald, *Strangers from a Different Shore: A History of Asian Americans,* Boston: Little Brown, 1989; updated and revised edition, 1998

---

## W.H. Auden 1907–73

Virtually the whole of W.H. Auden's achievement in poetry, drama, opera libretti, and critical prose may be said to be governed by two convictions: first, that the poet must not lie; second, that although individuals never cease to be responsible for the suffering of others, happiness must balance guilt. Although widely regarded as one of the 20th century's dominant poetic figures, Auden has seemed to some frustratingly protean, his formal versatility and willingness to rethink his opinions seeming to deprive his corpus of the coherence usually found in major writers. It has become clear with time, however, that Auden's work is held together by a number of enduring concerns, among which none are more central than poetic truthfulness and human responsibility.

Auden's most pointed statement on poetic honesty appears in his foreword to the *Collected Shorter Poems, 1927–1957* (1966), in which he explains that he omitted certain poems because "they were dishonest, or bad-mannered, or boring." A dishonest poem, he writes, is "one which expresses, no matter how well, feelings or beliefs which its author never felt or entertained." As an example, he cites the closing lines of "Spain" (1937): "History to the defeated / may say alas but cannot help nor pardon." It would have been bad enough, he observes, if he "had ever held this wicked doctrine, but that [he] should have stated it simply because it sounded . . . rhetorically effective is quite inexcusable." In fashioning the 1966 collection, he omitted not only "Spain" but also several other of his most famous poems, including "September 1, 1939." Both remain absent from the *Collected Poems* (1976), whose editor, Edward Mendelson, strove to honor Auden's own intentions in assembling the volume.

The 1966 collection did not mark Auden's first intervention in the shaping of his canon or his first revulsion from insincerity, however. In earlier collections (1945 and 1950), he had already rewritten or excluded poems he no longer felt to be true to the beliefs that had generated them. He also articulated this concern for honesty within such lyrics as "Mundus et Infans" (1942), in which he writes of "what only the / Greatest of saints become— someone who does not lie." In 1939 he had discovered, in concluding an address to the Foreign Correspondents' Dinner Forum in New York, that he "could make a fighting demagogic speech and have the audience roaring." He later described this feeling as degrading as well as exciting ("I felt just covered with dirt afterwards") and vowed never again to speak at a political meeting. That Auden was one of the most scrupulous of writers is not to be doubted, and yet—one of the great ironies of his career—he found his integrity questioned far more frequently than most of his fellows. The facility with which he ranged through voices and positions in his early poetry led some critics to mistake experiment for expediency; in later years, his fidelity to his own intellectual development (especially as realized in the revisions) invited the mistrust of those who believed that a work's first incarnation is its truest.

Chronicles of literary history routinely describe Auden's influence on other poets in terms of an ambivalent retreat from the High Modernism of Eliot, Pound, and the later Yeats, but few have noted how Auden's commitment to poetic honesty illuminates an ambivalence at the heart of High Modernism itself. On one hand, Auden's devotion to precision aligns him with the early Pound's belief that the modern poet's responsibility is to keep the tools of communication clean (even as his horror of demagoguery distances him from the later Pound, eagerly broadcasting his views over Rome radio). On the other hand, Auden's resistance to untruth frequently places him in opposition to the Modernist embrace of myth as a valid structuring principle for poetry and life. Negative models on this front included Rilke and (less explicitly) Eliot, but the greatest source of consternation was Yeats, who in 1935 told Laura Riding that poets should be good liars. In 1960, Auden named theatricality the great flaw of the masculine imagination and called Yeats one of that imagination's great exemplars. In a letter of 1964 he referred to Yeats as "a symbol of my own devil of unauthenticity, of everything which I must try to eliminate from my own poetry, false emotions, inflated rhetoric, empty sonorities." It was Auden's aversion to certain deployments of myth, however, that most specifically marked his distance from the writer who produced *A Vision*. In a 1942 review in *Partisan Review* of Louise Bogan's poetry he aligned myth with a mistaken belief that poetry can develop apart from life, and numbered the Yeats of the lunar phases (along with mythifiers of history and the id) among those Modern poets who ask "of a general idea, not Is It True?, but Is It Exciting? Is It Poetically Useful?"

Auden's dislike of such recourse to myth was clearly shaped by his coming of age as an English person in the aftermath of the Great War and as a poet in the 1930s. With others of his generation he had witnessed the terrible costs of nationalist and militarist fictionalizing, and in Fascism and Nazism he would see such fictions deployed more effectively and disastrously still. Unlike many of his peers, however, he was led by his unease with this kind of storytelling to avoid placing his poetry in the service of particular political lines. It is therefore another great irony of his reception that Auden gained early notice as a propagandist and in some quarters is still remembered principally as the court poet of the 1930s left. Although his rise to public recognition had begun, in a sense, even before he left Oxford in 1928, it jelled around the publication of the anthologies *New Signatures* (1932) and especially *New Country* (1933), edited by the Communist writer Michael Roberts: the contributors to these collections quickly became known as "the Auden group," and Auden was touted as the representative of a new generation advocating a revolutionary politics. This was not an unreasonable inference, given that one of his entries was entitled "A Communist to Others," but in fact Auden only briefly considered joining the Communist party, and the poem in question has nothing to say about Communist principles or practice. Rather, it concentrates on the mendacity of the British ruling class, which Auden regarded as his own but believed destined for a well-deserved dissolution:

A host of columbines and pathics
Who show the poor by mathematics
    In their defence
That wealth and poverty are merely
Mental pictures, so that clearly
Every tramp's a landlord really
    In mind-events.

Some have regarded the text as a sort of dramatic monologue, in which case it becomes still less legible as the enunciation of a party line. In any case, Auden would never again write even so nearly partisan a poem.

Auden's poetry is not apolitical, however. Much of his writing is pervaded not only by an awareness of suffering in the world, but also by a left-leaning belief that the lessening of this suffering may require the remaking of social institutions. Wary of party-line myths as Auden was, he was also alert to the ways in which myths of other kinds could distract from—or, worse, excuse—human misery. After his return to Christianity in 1940, Auden aligned himself, tellingly, with the activist Protestantism of Paul Tillich and Reinhold Niebuhr, and against followers of Karl Barth who believed that the transcendental nature of the kingdom of heaven made social reform irrelevant to Christian concerns. For Auden the central contradiction of living was that one can always be doing more to alleviate the wretchedness of others, although no one can live wholly selflessly all the time. Guilt is thus structurally inescapable and understandable to the compassionate intelligence, yet undiminished by its universality.

Auden's writings from both before and after 1940 testify amply to his recognition that the comforts of some are bought at the price of others' deprivation. In "A Summer Night" (1933), he asks,

    what doubtful act allows
Our freedom in this English house
Our picnics in the sun,

a question that both evokes Yeats' "Ancestral Houses" and anticipates Walter Benjamin's 1940 notation (which may have remained unknown to Auden but profoundly influenced later generations of British intellectuals) that no document of civilization is not also a document of barbarism. In Auden's most famous longer work, "The Sea and the Mirror" (1944), the astute Caliban observes, "We should not be sitting here now, washed, warm, well-fed . . . unless there were others who are not here," others whose poverty makes possible "our" provision. Of all his variations on this theme, however, the one that may have meant the most to Auden himself appears in the sequence "Horae Canonicae" (1949–54), which he always gave a place of importance in later collections. In the "Nones" section, composed in 1950, implication in the murder of Christ appears as the archetype or essence of continuous responsibility for others' injury:

        wherever
The sun shines, brooks run, books are written,
    There will also be this death.

. . . .

we have time
To misrepresent, excuse, deny,
Mythify, use this event
While, under a hotel bed, in prison,
Down wrong turnings, its meaning
Waits for our lives[.]

Whether Auden recognized how he himself mythifies the crucifixion in this instance is an open question, as is the more general one of whether, in poems like "The Shield of Achilles" (1952), his employment of mythology is best described as critically ironic or ambivalently admiring. (This latter possibility finds support in places like 1948's "In Praise of Limestone," wherein Auden's speaker cherishes statues that "obviously doubt" the "antimythological myth" of the poet of disenchantment.)

Whatever his investment in demythologizing, however, Auden clearly did not believe his major function to be that of calling attention to misery: although he insisted that poetry must not turn away from evils, he stated no less emphatically that its primary function has to do with what is good. In his most expansive declaration of a poetics, 1956's "Making, Knowing and Judging," he emphasizes that "every poem is rooted in imaginative awe," and that although poetry can accomplish many things, "there is only one thing that all poetry must do; it must praise all it can for being and for happening." In 1950 Auden wrote feelingly of "our duty to be happy," and his poetry from the late 1950s and after finds him much occupied with domestic order and creature comforts—a turn that led several critics to lament a once ambitious poet's decline into technically splendid triviality and others to regard his whole corpus as frivolous.

Yet it would be a mistake to describe Auden's trajectory as one of increasing interest in praising and diminishing interest in guilt, for these elements appear in close proximity throughout his career. In his famous Yeats elegy of 1939 Auden concludes by exhorting the poet to "Teach the free man how to praise," having asserted in an earlier section that poetry "makes nothing happen" and is instead a "way of happening, a mouth." Just a year before, however, he had written (in one of the extraordinary "Sonnets from China," also known under the title "In Time of War"):

Certainly praise: let the song mount again and again
For life as it blossoms out in a jar or a face,
For the vegetable patience, the animal grace;
Some people have been happy; there have been great men.

But hear the morning's injured weeping, and know why:
Cities and men have fallen; the will of the Unjust
Has never lost its power; still, all princes must
Employ the Fairly-Noble unifying Lie.

For Auden the function of ritual and the ontology of happening go together. Like other forms of praise, poetry is both a recollection of other events and an event in itself; insofar as it is the latter, it should be purely good, but insofar as it is the former, it needs to include ugliness. Or as he put it in a note of 1950 (later incorporated into "The Virgin and the Dynamo," 1962), every poem "is an attempt to present an analogy to that paradisal state in which Freedom and Law, System and Order are united in harmony[.]" Thi effect of this perfection will be evil

to the degree that beauty is taken, not as analogous to, but identical with goodness . . . and the conclusion drawn that, since all is well in the work of art, all is well in history. But all is not well there.

This last quotation illuminates two of the most prominent characteristics of Auden's mature verse: its didacticism and its embrace of traditional forms. Auden's earliest poetry was not primarily didactic: although full of declarative sentences, poems such as the one later called "The Secret Agent" (1928) unfolded narratives whose facts were obscure and whose meanings were opaque. It was just this quality of hard-edged reticence that inspired devotion in Auden's first enthusiasts, however; one of his best received works of the 1930s was *The Orators* (1932), which many reviewers praised but which few pretended to understand. Even harder to decipher than *The Waste Land* in certain respects, Auden's early poems are also noteworthy for their thematic and sonic toughness. Many were occupied with normatively masculine and unpoetic phenomena such as machines and spying, and many were energized by Auden's casual adaptation of the Anglo-Saxon alliterative line. (This last feature constitutes another link to Pound, and to a poetic tradition that Tom Paulin has named "Gothic": a "northern and consonantal" tradition marked by a "fricative, spiky, spoken texture" and encompassing Donne, Jonson, Browning, Hardy, and Frost.)

The virtues of Auden's early style appear most intriguingly, perhaps, in a poem that also incorporates a new direction. In "It was Easter as I walked in the public gardens" (later titled "1929," after its year of composition), Auden uses his jagged contours to render something like pre-linguistic consciousness but locates this very rendering in the mind of an adult speaker meditating on human life in general:

Is first baby, warm in mother,
Before born and is still mother,
Time passes and now is other,
Is knowledge in him now of other,
Cries in cold air, himself no friend.

The last section of "It was Easter" concludes on the characteristically mystifying note of the early poetry but begins with a line heralding Auden's new didactic strain: "It is time for the destruction of error." In the next few years, Auden would perfect the mode of conversational but firm declaration that was to sustain him for the next four decades, the mode of, "The eyes of the crow and the eye of the camera open / Onto Homer's world, not ours" ("Memorial for the City," 1949) and

though one cannot always
Remember exactly why one has been happy,
There is no forgetting that one was. ("Good-bye to the
Mezzogiorno," 1958)

Biographers agree that from an early age Auden liked dispensing wisdom, and that as he grew older he grew increasingly rigid in his daily routine. In the poet's own view his predilection for quietly sweeping statements was bound up with an affinity for traditional poetic structures, as a 1942 letter reveals. In order to purge his poetry of "its whiff of the hearty scoutmaster," he told his correspondent Stephen Spender, he would have to "deprive

[him]self of the support of strict conventional forms," but he never seriously undertook that project. Although he did develop new resources for poetry in English, he almost never ventured into fragmentation, typographical disruption, or even irregular stanzas and is rightly seen as a leading figure in the reaction against High Modernism's opening-up of form. In a series of aphorisms composed near the end of his life, Auden at his most conservative wrote, "Blessed be all metrical rules that forbid automatic responses, / force us to have second thoughts, free from the fetters of Self." What underlay his formal inclination, however, was less a love of impersonality than a taste for a world in which maximum freedom would not imply maximum disorder. In the magnificent conclusion of his 1939 elegy for Freud, he relays both his affection for libido's disruptive capabilities and his esteem for its sublimated, productive aspect: "Sad is Eros, builder of cities, / And weeping anarchic Aphrodite."

The Freud elegy is especially important, formally speaking, because it was the first of many important poems that Auden would write in syllabic verse, which he later described as a way of "achieving a balance between freedom and order." Auden surely discerned a kindred spirit in Marianne Moore, who shared his combination of humility and self-confidence, his love for the world, his intellectuality, and his commitment to a poetry fusing restraint and innovation. In 1939 he told her, "Like Rilke, you really do 'Praise,'" and he eventually adapted the syllabic construction for which she was known to his own purposes. But syllabic verse was far from the only technical possibility he vitalized. One of the first major 20th-century poets to revisit the now standard sestina and villanelle, Auden also made a case for rhyme royal in his "Letter to Lord Byron" (1936) and for both the long philosophical poem and the neoclassical rhymed couplet in "New Year Letter" (1940). In works like "For the Time Being" (1941–42), "The Sea and the Mirror," "The Age of Anxiety" (1944–46), "Horae Canonicae," "Bucolics" (1952–53), and "Thanksgiving for a Habitat" (1958–64), he perfected the art of linking poems in several forms into coherent sequences. In 1959 he assembled 50 short prose meditations on love and poetry into "Dichtung und Wahrheit," a text like nothing else of its time. Auden did not by himself inspire postwar poetry's extended engagement with traditional patterns, but his virtuoso performances did play a crucial exemplary role.

If 1939 has usually been regarded as the watershed in Auden's career, this is so not only because that year produced the Freud and Yeats elegies, but also because it witnessed the poet's emigration to the United States. In the short term this departure helped to diminish Auden's cachet in Britain, not least because it left him open to the charge of deserting his country in its hour of need. In fact, he seems to have had several motivations for the move, none of which included fear for personal safety. His installation in New York and environs did, however, enhance Auden's influence on American writing. In the 1930s his work captivated savvy Americans from a distance, as Elizabeth Bishop would later recall, but in subsequent decades he touched immediately and consequentially poets like Richard Howard, James Merrill (who made him one of the principal ghosts of *The Changing Light at Sandover*), Sylvia Plath, James Schuyler, and Richard Wilbur. Also crucial was Auden's tenure as editor of the Yale Series of Younger Poets, which on his recommendation published first books by (among other eventual luminaries) Adrienne Rich, W.S. Merwin, John Ashbery, James Wright, and John Hollander. In spite of these American genealogies and his acquisition of American citizenship in 1946, however, Auden continues to be treated principally as a British poet, perhaps because postwar British and Irish poetry (less forcefully diversified, in the long run, by avant-gardist imperatives) seems to evoke him more consistently than its American counterpart.

Since Auden's death his admirers have profited from the care and insightfulness of his literary executor. In addition to publishing richly nuanced critical studies, Mendelson has complemented the *Collected Poems* with a *Selected Poems,* reprinting original rather than revised texts, and has been releasing singly the components of a multi-volume edition of Auden's complete works (also using earliest published versions). Filling out the Auden canon are Mendelson's 1977 *The English Auden,* which gathers poems, essays, and dramatic writing through 1939; Katherine Bucknell's 1994 edition of Auden's juvenilia; and three volumes of *Auden Studies* edited by Bucknell and Nicholas Jenkins and combining primary with secondary material. Auden's reputation as one of the great poets of the 20th century has only grown more secure, although his work's resistance to many traditional manifestations of ambition has required some rethinking of the criteria for major poetry. It is instructive that one study (McDiarmid, 1990) tries less to liberate Auden from the accusation of triviality than to draw from his playfulness a serious argument about poetry's limitations, while another (Boly, 1991) argues that Auden's concern is to help readers resist the operations of rhetoric by making them more attentive to what happens when they read.

Studies like these notwithstanding, Auden has not benefited as much as might have been expected from strong interest in the intersections of politics and language. The more potent renewal of enthusiasm at century's end, arguably, has come from an aspect of his life and work that he might have been surprised to find figuring so large: his sexuality. Burgeoning interest in gay writing has brought to the forefront the sometimes conflicted but never closeted figure who began his sexual education early and (in the company of Christopher Isherwood) advanced it in interwar Berlin; the maritally inclined romantic who found a mate and collaborator (but only briefly a lover) in Chester Kallman; and the sometimes campy conversationalist who long after his conversion was given to speaking of "Miss God." Complementing attention to these biographical Audens, moreover, is a renewal of fascination with another textual Auden, the writer of such luminous meditations on desire as "Lay your sleeping head, my love" (1937), "Law Like Love" (1939), and "First Things First" (1957). Nor is this fascination limited to the kinds of audiences who routinely purchase books of poetry. Following a moving adaptation of "Stop all the clocks" (1936) to the demands of gay elegy in the film *Four Weddings and a Funeral,* Faber released a special edition of ten Auden poems called *Tell Me the Truth about Love;* named for a line from a 1938 poem, the volume has since sold more than 250,000 copies. How Auden might have reacted to the phenomenon no one can know, of course. But he would not have been wholly displeased, surely, to find truth as well as love in the title of his best-selling work to date.

DOUGLAS MAO

**Biography**

Born in York, England, 21 February 1907. Attended Oxford University, Oxford, England, 1925–28, B.A. 1928;

schoolmaster, Larchfield Academy, Helensburgh, Scotland, and Downs School, Colwall, England, 1930–35; co-founder, Group Theatre, 1932; stretcher-bearer, Spanish Civil War, 1937; teacher, St. Mark's School, Southborough, Massachusetts, 1939–40; faculty member, American Writers League School, New York, 1939; teacher, New School for Social Research, New York City, 1940–41, 1946–47; faculty member, University of Michigan, Ann Arbor, 1941–42, Swarthmore College, Pennsylvania, 1942–45, Bryn Mawr College, Pennsylvania, 1943–45, Bennington College, Vermont, 1946, Barnard College, New York, 1947; editor, Yale Series of Younger Poets, 1947–62; co-founder, The Reader's Subscription Book Club, 1951; Professor, Smith College, Northampton, Massachusetts, 1953; Chancellor, Academy of American Poets, 1954–73; Professor, Oxford University, Oxford, England, 1956–61; co-founder, Mid-Century Book Society, 1959. Received King's Gold Medal for Poetry, 1937; Guggenheim fellowships, 1942, 1945; American Academy of Arts and Letters Award of Merit Medal, 1945, and Gold Medal, 1968; Pulitzer Prize, 1948; Bollingen Prize, 1954; National Book Award, 1956; Feltrinelli Prize, 1957; Guinness Award, 1959; Poetry Society of America Alexander Droutzkoy Memorial Award, 1959; honorary Litt.D., Swarthmore College, 1964; Austrian State Prize for European Literature, 1966; National Endowment for the Arts grant, 1966; National Medal for Literature of National Book Committee, 1967. Died in Vienna, Austria, 28 September 1973.

**Poetry**

*Poems,* 1930
*The Orators: An English Study,* 1932; revised editions, 1934, 1966
*Poems,* 1934
*Look, Stranger!* 1936; as *On This Island,* 1937
*Spain,* 1937
*Another Time,* 1940; revised editions, 1946, 1996
*Some Poems,* 1940
*The Double Man,* 1941
*For the Time Being,* 1944; revised edition, 1945
*The Collected Poetry of W.H. Auden,* 1945
*The Age of Anxiety: A Baroque Eclogue,* 1947; revised edition, 1948
*Collected Shorter Poems, 1930–1944,* 1950
*Nones,* 1951; revised edition, 1953
*The Shield of Achilles,* 1955
*The Old Man's Road,* 1956
*Selected Poetry of W.H. Auden,* 1959
*Homage to Clio,* 1960
*W.H. Auden, A Selection,* 1961
*Collected Shorter Poems, 1927–1957,* 1966
*About the House,* 1965
*The Platonic Blow,* 1965
*Marginalia,* 1966
*Selected Poems,* 1968
*Collected Longer Poems,* 1968
*City without Walls, and Other Poems,* 1969
*Academic Graffiti,* 1971
*Epistle to a Godson, and Other Poems,* 1972
*Thank You Fog: Last Poems,* 1974
*Collected Poems,* 1976
*The English Auden: Poems, Essays, and Dramatic Writings, 1927–1939,* 1977
*Selected Poems,* 1979
*Collected Poems,* 1991
*The Complete Works of W.H. Auden,* 1993
*Juvenilia: Poems, 1922–1928,* 1994
*Tell Me the Truth about Love,* 1994

**Selected Criticism**

*The Enchafed Flood: The Romantic Iconography of the Sea,* 1950; revised edition, 1985
*The Dyer's Hand, and Other Essays,* 1962
*Forewords and Afterwords,* 1973
*In Solitude, for Company: W.H. Auden after 1940,* 1995
*Lectures on Shakespeare,* 2001

**Other Writings:** essays (*Selected Essays,* 1964), plays (*The Dance of Death,* 1933), correspondence (*Letters from Iceland,* 1937; revised edition, 1969), travel memoirs (*Journey to a War* [with Christopher Isherwood], 1939); translations of German literature (*Italian Journey, 1786–1788,* by Johann Wolfgang von Goethe, 1962), Greek literature (*The Portable Greek Reader,* 1948), French literature (*The Knights of the Round Table,* by Jean Cocteau, 1957), Swedish literature (*Evening Land* [translator with Leif Sjöberg], by Pär Lagerkvist, 1975), Icelandic poetry (*Norse Poems* [translator with Paul Taylor], 1981), and Icelandic libretti (*The Rake's Progress: Opera in Three Acts,* 1951); edited anthologies of poetry (*The Oxford Book of Light Verse,* 1938; *Poets of the English Language* [editor with Norman Holmes Pearson], 1950).

**Further Reading**

Boly, John R., *Reading Auden: The Returns of Caliban,* Ithaca, New York: Cornell University Press, 1991
Bucknell, Katherine, and Nicholas Jenkins, editors, *Auden Studies,* 3 vols., Oxford: Clarendon Press, and New York: Oxford University Press, 1990–95
Davenport-Hines, Richard, *Auden,* New York: Pantheon, and London: Heinemann, 1995
Fuller, John, *W.H. Auden: A Commentary,* Princeton, New Jersey: Princeton University Press, and London: Faber and Faber, 1998
Hecht, Anthony, *The Hidden Law: The Poetry of W.H. Auden,* Cambridge, Massachusetts: Harvard University Press, 1993
Hynes, Samuel, *The Auden Generation: Literature and Politics in England in the 1930s,* Princeton, New Jersey: Princeton University Press, New York: Viking Press, and London: Bodley Head, 1976; new edition, London: Pimlico, 1992
McDiarmid, Lucy, *Auden's Apologies for Poetry,* Princeton, New Jersey: Princeton University Press, 1990
Mendelson, Edward, *Early Auden,* New York: Viking, and London: Faber, 1981
Mendelson, Edward, *Later Auden,* New York: Farrar Straus and Giroux, and London: Faber, 1999
Smith, Stan, *W.H. Auden,* Oxford and New York: Blackwell, 1985
Wasley, Aidan, "Auden and Poetic Inheritance," *Raritan* 19, no. 2 (1999)

## In Memory of W.B. Yeats

W.H. Auden's "In Memory of W.B. Yeats" (first published in *New Republic* [8 March 1939]) is a Modernist elegy on the occasion of the death of William Butler Yeats in the south of France, 28 January 1939. Two days earlier Auden had arrived from England in New York harbor during a snowstorm, making this his first American poem. Auden portrayed Yeats' death as a tragedy for the world of letters, a tragedy that also reflects the general disorder on the eve of World War II. Yeats was both a private and a public figure, a lyric autobiographer and a prophetic poet on a grand historical scale, but his weaknesses for rich women, the occult, and reactionary politics qualified Auden's admiration. Like "A Pact," in which Ezra Pound comes to terms with his differences with Walt Whitman, "In Memory of W.B. Yeats" is Auden's vehicle for coming to terms with Yeats as a great poet whose anti-democratic ideals Auden, a radical socialist, found abhorrent.

Part One begins on an objective note, emphasized by the sincerity of its variable free verse, with a description of the weather in New York at the time of Yeats' death. The elegiac tone undercuts this detachment, however, transforming scientific into symbolic terms. In the "dead of winter" all nature, commerce, and public life have come to a standstill, yet elsewhere life goes on in the rhythms of nature: wolves run through "evergreen forests" and rivers flow past "fashionable quays." But however one measures the impact of the poet's death, Auden notes, "What instruments we have agree / The day of his death was a dark cold day." Auden's change of this line (originally "O all the instruments agree") suggests that Auden is striving for objectivity by avoiding too exact an echo of Yeats' own line ("O sages standing in God's holy fire") from "Sailing to Byzantium," while providing the obligatory echo common to elegy.

Describing Yeats' "last afternoon as himself," however, the third stanza echoes the metaphor of the body in "Sailing to Byzantium" as "no country for old men" by developing an extended metaphor of Yeats as a country to himself, his provinces in revolt, squares empty, and suburbs gone silent. The electrical "current of his feelings" has "failed," but while his life force has been extinguished, Yeats "became his admirers." Like Osiris, the Egyptian god of fertility, Yeats is (in his works) "scattered among a hundred cities" and "given over to [the] unfamiliar affections" of his readers: "The words of a dead man / Are modified in the guts of the living." In the ecology of reading, Yeats is consumed and digested, his life force not destroyed but recycled.

In Part One's final stanza, Auden confronts his ideological differences with Yeats over economics and social justice. Auden compares the brokers of capitalism to "beasts," evoking Yeats' image of the "rough beast" that "Slouches towards Bethlehem" in his apocalyptic poem "The Second Coming." Yeats believed the poor to be a necessary economic evil who must become "fairly accustomed" to their sufferings, but Auden wrings irony from "fairly" to suggest that the poor can never see such a system as fair but can become only *slightly* or *relatively* accustomed to their lot, even if "each in the cell of himself is almost convinced of his freedom." Nevertheless, a select group of readers—"a few thousand"—will look back on the day Yeats died as "a day when one did something slightly unusual."

In the single stanza of Part Two (not included in the poem's first publication), the tone shifts as Auden addresses Yeats familiarly: "You were silly like us: your gift survived it all." Its iambic hexameter, a classical meter, like its thematic movement from the particular to the universal, shows Auden striving to extract a general lesson from Yeats' life and death by putting aside his disagreements to measure the man's faults against the poet's "gift." Auden divorces the transitory and "silly" concerns of Yeats' personal life (his love life in the "parish of rich women") and political views (his engagement in Ireland's struggles, changeless as "her madness and her weather") from what can be seen *sub specie aeternitatis*.

This clears the way for Auden's own *ars poetica*—"poetry makes nothing happen"—which reflects the Modernist idea that poetic discourse is unique, and the poem a self-sufficient, autotelic object, an end in itself and not polemical or didactic. Like a river that springs from a place "where executives / Would never want to tamper," poetry flows from real feelings of "isolation and busy griefs," but survives less as a set of beliefs than as "A way of happening." The premise "poetry makes nothing happen," then, takes on an additional meaning: poetry has no practical effect in the world, but by making what did not exist (nothing) come into existence (happen), the poem endures in a way that the everyday world of the "Raw towns that we believe and die in" cannot.

Part Three concludes on a traditionally elegiac note. In six quatrains of rhymed iambic tetrameter couplets suitable for prayers, Auden lays "an honoured guest" to rest: "Let the Irish vessel lie / Emptied of its poetry." Revising the poem for *Collected Shorter Poems* (1966), Auden omitted three stanzas that repeat Part Two's suggestion that time will pardon Yeats, like Rudyard Kipling and Paul Claudel, for "writing well." Choosing instead to proceed directly to the present threat of another war in Europe, Auden raises the tone of his argument with Yeats' ideology. Instead of blaming Yeats for the "nightmare of the dark" in which "All the dogs of Europe bark," Auden invokes Yeats the poet to combat the "Intellectual disgrace" and to "persuade us to rejoice" with the humanity of his poetry's "unconstraining voice." Here Auden is again paying homage to Yeats' "Sailing to Byzantium," in which Yeats invokes the "the singing-masters" of his soul to "clap its hands and sing, and louder sing / For every tatter in its mortal dress."

Auden concludes by returning to nature metaphors, asking that the buried poet (Osiris-like) make fertile the fields of poetry: "With the farming of a verse / Make a vineyard of the curse." In Yeats' "Adam's Curse," the title refers to God's curse that man work for a living after expulsion from the Garden of Eden. While Yeats' poem is a love poem to Maud Gonne, Auden makes the curse a political and aesthetic duty to "Sing of human unsuccess / In a rapture of distress" and to

> Let the healing fountain start,
> In the prison of his days
> Teach the free man how to praise.

That these last two lines are inscribed on Auden's tomb in Poets' Corner of Westminster Abbey may be ironic, since they are from an elegy critical of its subject. "In Memory of W.B. Yeats" is an excellent example of Auden's poetic resourcefulness of tone, voice, and prosody, some of which one can say he learned from Yeats. But the poem is also a tribute, if an argumentative tribute, to the senior poet of the elder generation, in which Auden respectfully resolves their ideological differences by weaving strands of Yeats' verse into his own *ars poetica*.

RICHARD COLLINS

**Further Reading**

Bold, Alan, editor, *W.H. Auden: The Far Interior,* London: Vision, and Totowa, New Jersey: Barnes and Noble, 1985
Callan, Edward, *Auden: A Carnival of Intellect,* New York: Oxford University Press, 1983
Fuller, John, *W.H. Auden: A Commentary,* Princeton, New Jersey: Princeton University Press, and London: Faber and Faber, 1998
Hartmann, Charles O., "Verse and Voice," in *Conversant Essays: Contemporary Poets on Poetry,* edited by James McCorkle, Detroit, Michigan: Wayne State University Press, 1990
Hecht, Anthony, *The Hidden Law: The Poetry of W.H. Auden,* Cambridge, Massachusetts: Harvard University Press, 1993
McDiarmid, Lucy, *Auden's Apologies for Poetry,* Princeton, New Jersey: Princeton University Press, 1990
Smith, Stan, *W.H. Auden,* Oxford and New York: Blackwell, 1985

## In Praise of Limestone

"In Praise of Limestone," one of W.H. Auden's most accomplished poems, was first published in July 1948 in *Horizon,* subsequently included in *Nones* (1951), and slightly revised for reprinting in succeeding collections. Written in sinuous syllabic lines, the poem is a Horatian ode sustaining comfortable tempo and conversational tone without ever lapsing into the garrulity or digressiveness that would mar some of Auden's later compositions. As the first poem Auden wrote on the island of Ischia in the Bay of Naples, it also marks the beginning of his interest in Italy and affection for the Mediterranean people and country.

The poem opens by celebrating the Italian limestone landscape, with its tangible slopes, statues, fountains, caves, "short distances and definite places," and commending the simple lives led by its inhabitants, unmolested by grandiose inclinations and fantasies of transcendence. Auden suggests that humanity is naturally homesick for this landscape, because it forms an allegory of the human body with its expressly maternal contours and vaguely erotic arrangements. He asserts the common values of life, viewing limestone country as the only truly human landscape because it promotes moderation in judgment, ambition, love, and spirituality. It is a landscape of innocence, signifying not only proximity between human community and its natural habitat, but also freedom from intellectual arrogance and absolutist temptations.

Auden then contrasts people who live in the moment with those who view their lives as ceaseless processes of education and self-perfection. While the landscape emanates an air of peacefulness and innocence, with the locals climbing the slopes "Arm in arm, but never, thank God, in step," it also bears discernible signs of hopelessness and resignation. The southern habitat is self-sufficient, but also surrendered to the reality of death and sin. The poem underscores the distinction between "the inconstant ones," ordinary people attached to life in obscurity and moderation, and "the best and the worst of us," those who leave the Edenic landscape of rock and water and move into "immoderate soils" in pursuit of higher ambitions and ideals. Auden associates these fugitives from the limestone country with mountains, plains, and seas: the solidity and permanence of mountain granite lures future saints, the malleability of clay and gravel plains seduces politicians and social reformers, while the "oceanic whisper" entices the "really reckless," or nihilists.

But at this point in the poem Auden makes a surprising admission. The voices of granite, gravel, clay, and the ocean "were right / And still are." The limestone landscape has its own imperfections. It is, like the human body, constantly changing and susceptible to decay. It is not a site of escape or even a place of return. The modern poet (presumably a reference to Wallace Stevens) calling "The sun the sun, his mind Puzzle," the modern scientist only concerned with "Nature's / Remotest aspects," and even the speaker (or Auden) himself "reproached, for what / And how much you know" refuse the reality of the flesh. They reject a chance for restored authenticity and spontaneity realizable only when they have abandoned their quest for transcendence and recognized the mutable body—exemplified by the limestone landscape—as their true home. But is this ever possible? After all, "this land is not the sweet home that it looks": the poet, the scientist, and the speaker are justified in their search of abstraction and understanding. Although the poem celebrates harmony between nature and human beings and promotes the holiness of physical love, it also admits the inevitability of human demands for something other than what simple mundane reality can offer. In the intentionally anti-climactic final passages, Auden envisions moderate existence in the limestone country reconciled with ideals of "faultless love" and spiritual meditations on "the life to come."

Because of its discreet references to a solitary listener, the poem can be viewed as a personal address to Auden's lover, Chester Kallman, whose glimpses we catch especially in the original, more explicit version of the poem: "the nude young male . . . lounges / Against a rock displaying his dildo." Regarded as such, the poem presents an argument to transcend time in uninhibited eroticism, even if it ultimately results in faithlessness and absence. More conspicuously, "In Praise of Limestone" reflects Auden's childhood fascination with lead mines. With the transformation of English lead-mine country into Edenic limestone landscape of southern Italy, the poem, like other important pieces written in Ischia, explores the contrast between the northern Protestant culture, predicated on guilt and self-improvement, and the culture of the Mediterranean world based on shame and self-acceptance. The northern environment of exclusion and isolation, superficiality and speculation, counters the communal epicureanism and decadence of the south's simple residents, but it is eventually dependent on these values as well. Ten years after writing "In Praise of Limestone," Auden reached the same conclusion in his farewell to the Mediterranean world of marble landscapes and modest temperaments, "Good-bye to the Mezzogiorno."

PIOTR GWIAZDA

**Further Reading**

Bucknell, Katherine, and Nicholas Jenkins, "'In Praise of Limestone': A Symposium," in *"In Solitude, for Company": W.H. Auden after 1940: Unpublished Prose and Recent Criticism,* Oxford: Clarendon Press, and New York: Oxford University Press, 1995
Fuller, John, *W.H. Auden: A Commentary,* Princeton, New Jersey: Princeton University Press, and London: Faber and Faber, 1998

Hecht, Anthony, "On W.H. Auden's 'In Praise of Limestone,'" *New England Review* 2 (1979)

Johnson, Richard, *Man's Place: An Essay on Auden,* Ithaca, New York: Cornell University Press, 1973

Mendelson, Edward, *Later Auden,* New York: Farrar Straus and Giroux, and London: Faber, 1999

## Musée des Beaux Arts

There are many reasons why "Musée des Beaux Arts" (1938) should be one of W.H. Auden's best known and most widely anthologized poems. To those who value lyric compression, it offers 21 lines of extraordinary complexity, yet does so with a feeling of ease and a directness that make it accessible even on a first reading. To those in search of characteristic Auden, it offers the coolly assured didacticism for which that poet was famous. To those seeking representative early 20th-century lyric, it offers a typically modern preoccupation with pain and evil as well as that interweaving of the conversational and the momentous often considered one of the period's major innovations. To readers whose expectations have been formed by mainstream post–World War II poetry it offers crisp images and a cleanly stated moral, linked together by the consciousness of a thoughtful observer. And to connoisseurs of interart relations, it offers a superb addition to an ekphrastic tradition (Wordsworth's "Peele Castle," Keats' "Ode on a Grecian Urn," Rilke's "Archaïscher Torso Apollos" ["Archaic Torso of Apollo"]) in which the lyric speaker is moved to reflection by a work of visual art.

But while "Musée des Beaux Arts" fills all of these roles admirably, the ways in which it does so are usually less straightforward than they may seem, and the extent to which it does so is sometimes less than complete. Consider, for example, the question of its representativeness as an Auden lyric. From its first words ("About suffering they were never wrong, / The Old Masters"), the poem is marked by Auden's characteristically definite declaration, the commitment to telling as well as showing that constituted one of his major breaks with Modernism in the Imagist line. "Musée des Beaux Arts" depends much more heavily on showing than is usual for Auden, however, and insofar as it seems to focus on particular paintings, its manner of showing is atypical as well. Although hardly a poet without pictures, Auden was famously fond of abstract statement, and when he did use images preferred generic elements to detailed particulars (a city, a mountain, or a tree rather than London, a mountain dotted with scrub pines, or the tree at his window). The poems in which Auden does rely on intimate description and highly individual objects—the shield of Achilles, the limestone landscape, even the body of Yeats in his Yeats elegy—have been among his most celebrated, but this recognition may say more about readerly taste than about Auden's peculiar strengths.

Moreover, the form of "Musée des Beaux Arts" is uncharacteristically open. Although all but one of its lines finds a rhyme, the rhyme scheme is highly asymmetrical, and enormous variation in line length—from five to 22 syllables and from two to eight beats—helps to conceal the rhymes so well that some readers never notice them. In addition, 14 of the line endings are enjambed, and the enjambment is frequently severe: "skating / On a pond"; "may / Have heard"; "the green / Water." None of this is usual for Auden, who tended to foreground rhyme when using it, who preferred to adhere to one stanza form through the whole of a poem, and who normally maintained a higher ratio of end-stopped lines to sharply enjambed ones. "Musée des Beaux Arts" thus reads more like free verse than almost anything else Auden wrote, which is to say that when presented as archetypal Auden in anthologies or literary histories, it may obscure the extent of his break with the High Modernism of writers like Pound, Williams, and the 1920s Eliot. The reader encountering Auden only in this lyric and one or two others may see his poetry more as a dilution of Modernist innovations than as a deliberate reversal or meaningful revision, and may have trouble understanding why his work was so important to poets of succeeding generations.

On the thematic side, "Musée des Beaux Arts" is in a sense *more* representative of Auden than will be evident to the reader who understands it principally as the record of a meditation prompted by a particular painting. Auden wrote the poem while in Brussels, where the Musées Royaux des Beaux-Arts house the *Landscape with the Fall of Icarus* as well as two other Brueghels alluded to in the first stanza, *The Numbering at Bethlehem* and *Winter Landscape with Skaters.* (A fourth Brueghel clearly involved in the poem, *The Massacre of the Innocents,* hangs in the Kunsthistorisches Museum in Vienna.) Auden had been thinking about the relation between those who suffer and those who do not since the beginning of his poetic career, however, and found it especially preoccupying through much of 1938 and 1939. The other poems he wrote in December 1938 all concern suffering and responsibility in some way, as do sections from "A Voyage" written the previous January (two mention suffering explicitly in their last lines), the "Sonnets from China" of mid-1938, several important poems from 1939, including "Voltaire at Ferney" and "September 1, 1939," and a compellingly large part of his subsequent writing.

Where not viewed as itself coldly indifferent, "Musée des Beaux Arts" has usually been treated as an admonition, an indictment, or a lament: with an understatement designed to render the banality of evil more rather than less disturbing, it is argued, the poem condemns people's habitual inattention to the miseries of others and by implication exhorts its reader to avoid this failing. Such a reading is clearly supported by the references to how "everything turns away / Quite leisurely from the disaster" and to "the expensive delicate ship" that "Had somewhere to get to and sailed calmly on." In both instances, the non-suffering are rendered more culpable by their comfortableness (they have nothing else as urgent to attend to) and by a language of affluence that evokes the class antagonism that absorbed Auden in the 1930s. Moreover, the title of the poem, along with the expensive delicacy of the ship, seems to bring art itself under the shadow of blame, recalling how going to a museum to see beautiful ("beaux") representations of injuries—or reading a poem about disaster, for that matter—might constitute a leisurely turning-away disguised as a turning-toward. This last point seems further supported by the handling of rhyme: many readers will notice it, if they notice it at all, only when they get to the second-stanza couplets ("away"/ "may" and "green"/"seen"). The poem invites a formal replication of the inattention it decries.

It should be clear, however, that this very effect can extenuate as readily as indict. By inducing "complicity" with the inattentive, the poem could be emphasizing not how the reader participates in evil, but rather how no one can be attentive to everything all the time, and by extension, how inattention to suffering (however wrong or harmful) may not be the kind of social problem subject to complete resolution through sheer moral exertion. A sonnet from earlier in the year (beginning "They are and suffer; that is all they do") renders with striking concentration the impossibility of sharing pain:

Even a scratch we can't recall when cured,
But are boisterous in a moment and believe

In the common world of the injured. . . .

In the Yeats elegy of early 1939, Auden would famously defend poetry in spite of the fact that it not only "makes nothing happen" but also may absorb attention that could go elsewhere. And in the Voltaire poem Auden shows movingly how the sense of responsibility can become an obsession:

So, like a sentinel, he could not sleep. The night was full of
  wrong,
Earthquakes and executions. Soon he would be dead,
And still all over Europe stood the horrible nurses
Itching to boil their children. Only his verses
Perhaps could stop them: He must go on working.
  Overhead
The uncomplaining stars composed their lucid song.

Voltaire's commitment is at once neurotic and admirable, but whether to be commended or blamed, it says nothing about the case of the stars, which can only be believed capable of intervening in human affairs by the kind of superstition that Voltaire himself (and Auden with him) resisted.

In this respect it seems important that in "Musée des Beaux Arts" those who ignore great things transpiring nearby are humble beings, figures who might bring their admiration to the large event but who have neither the power nor the eminence to affect it in other ways. Auden names children skating, dogs, and a horse in the first stanza, and while the ploughman of the second may be culpably indifferent to the "forsaken cry" (assuming he hears it), his activity of ploughing counterbalances the "leisurely" used to describe the general turning away. The sun can no more intervene than can the stars in "Voltaire at Ferney." And although the ship may seem especially irritating in its unruffled progress, the predicating claim that it "must have seen" the disaster can only be true if one imagines it to be sensate or takes the line to refer to the crew (unlikely to be either "expensive" or "delicate"). It may be, then, that the error invited by the poem is not that of failing to attend, but that of laying blame in the wrong manner or in the wrong place, as on an object that cannot see or a horse with no moral part in its owner's actions. Even the pivotal "leisurely" finally mitigates the poem's disapprobation, for although the word is here used (correctly) as an adverb, the reader will be more accustomed to seeing it as an adjective. The adverbial sense suggests that the turning away is a matter of volition, but the adjectival overtone counters with a hint that "everything"—notably not "everyone"—in the painting is leisurely by nature. The adverbial makes turning away a matter of doing, but the adjectival makes it a matter of being.

Is the point of "Musée des Beaux Arts" therefore to legitimate indifference, or even to exonerate human beings from blame for their failures to help each other? To say so would be to ignore the force of those devices, mentioned earlier, that *have* led readers to understand this poem as admonitory. It would seem more accurate to say that although "Musée des Beaux Arts" foregrounds this central guilt, it also frames it in terms of an ethical contradiction: people can always be doing more to alleviate others' suffering, yet were they to listen constantly for cries and wait unremittingly for miracles (instead of eating, opening windows, or walking dully along), they would risk violating their own lives' claims to intrinsic, rather than merely instrumental, meaning. If, as many readers have suggested, the first stanza anticipates Auden's 1940 return to Christian belief, it is appropriate that the Nativity and the Crucifixion should come mediated through Brueghel, in the very liveliness of whose canvases Auden seems to have discerned a claim not on behalf of the secular as opposed to the religious, but on behalf of a vital quotidian that any credible Christianity would have to embrace. In "The Old and the New Masters" (1965) Randall Jarrell revised Auden by insisting, "About suffering, about adoration, the old masters / Disagree," and by seeing a Copernican step away from anthropocentrism in those pictures where the Crucifixion is exiled to "one corner of the canvas." Although William Carlos Williams' "Landscape with the Fall of Icarus" (1962) is a very different poem from Jarrell's, it too finds in its painting a demotion of legendary event, here in favor of pulsing nature:

the whole pageantry

of the year was
awake tingling

. . .

there was

a splash quite unnoticed
this was
Icarus drowning.

In Auden's poem, however, miracles, martyrdoms, and disasters retain their importance. The complication is that ordinary life, too, is allowed to lay its extraordinary claim.

DOUGLAS MAO

**Further Reading**

Bartel, Roland, "Icarus Poems since Auden's 'Musée des Beaux Arts,'" *Classical and Modern Literature* 2 (1982)

Caws, Mary Ann, "A Double Reading by Design: Breughel, Auden, and Williams," *Journal of Aesthetics and Art Criticism* 41, no. 3 (1983)

Fry, Paul H., *A Defense of Poetry: Reflections on the Occasion of Writing,* Stanford, California: Stanford University Press, 1995

Heffernan, James, *Museum of Words: The Poetics of Ekphrasis from Homer to Ashbery,* Chicago: University of Chicago Press, 1993

Riffaterre, Michael, "Textuality: W.H. Auden's 'Musée des Beaux Arts,'" in *Textual Analysis: Some Readers Reading,* edited by Mary Ann Caws, New York: Modern Language Association of America, 1986

## September 1, 1939

"September 1, 1939" is well known for having one of the most colorful histories of revision of any poem in W.H. Auden's canon. Auden had arrived in America from England on 26 January 1939, and many of his countrymen in Great Britain considered his move, coinciding with rumors of war, to be cowardly at least and perhaps even traitorous. From his newly adopted home Auden followed the troublesome events in Europe closely, and on 1 September 1939, the day that Hitler invaded Poland, Auden wrote out a draft of the poem. Within a year he was regularly attending Holy Communion in the Episcopal Church—his return to the Anglicanism of his childhood had been gradual—but his own distinctive Christian humanism lay behind the last and notorious line of the penultimate stanza: "We must love one another or die." Several years later Auden soberly pronounced the line "a damned lie," contending that one must die regardless of love; accordingly, in his *Collected Poetry* (1945) and *Collected Shorter Poems* (1950) the entire stanza in which the line appeared was deleted. In 1955, at the behest of an editor who wanted to reprint the complete poem, Auden changed the line to the more realistic, "We must love one another and die." He finally abandoned the poem altogether, however, and it was not included in Edward Mendelson's *Collected Poems* (1976). The original version of the poem reappeared for the first time in *The English Auden* (1977), which Mendelson edited, and is readily available in *Selected Poems* (1979), also edited by Mendelson.

Although Auden's fervent wish to see the poem removed from his body of work was matched and finally overcome by his readers' will to save the poem, this contest of wills reveals much that is central to the subject matter of the lyric. The poem is unique inasmuch as it was inspired by an isolated military action that would ultimately lead to World War II, and its sense of foreboding and impending doom seems clairvoyant at times. Several of the poem's most passionate defenders—Anthony Hecht and Joseph Brodsky, for example—lived through the conflict and were perhaps better equipped to recognize the sense of imminent cataclysm that pervades the poem and distinguishes each of its nine 11-line stanzas. What Auden's readers have found to be dramatically evocative about the poem Auden himself ultimately considered imprecise and vague. But the first stanza, with its "unmentionable odour of death," figures prominently in any discussion of the poem's connection with the vast tragedy that lay in wait for Europe, America, and Asia:

I sit in one of the dives
On Fifty-Second Street
Uncertain and afraid
As the clever hopes expire
Of a low dishonest decade:
Waves of anger and fear
Circulate over the bright
And darkened lands of the earth,
Obsessing our private lives;
The unmentionable odour of death
Offends the September night.

Of course the portrayal of an *imminent* cataclysm must be necessarily vague, and even in the first stanza, this vagueness gives rise to the kinds of generalizations that would ultimately anger many of Auden's critics. In that stanza alone, however, several of the themes that had already occupied Auden, and would continue to do so until he died, are clearly present: psychology and neurosis; the conflict between the individual and the state; and the individual's moral responsibility in times of national crisis. These are the themes that engage Auden in this poem and in varying guises throughout his career. The poem's solution to these tensions, arriving in the last line of the last stanza, is eloquent, dignified, and vague:

May I . . .
Beleaguered by the same
Negation and despair,
Show an affirming flame.

It is a general solution to a generally articulated problem, yet the poetry of its stately trimeter has been largely convincing to readers.

As Auden aged he began to distrust idealism of all sorts, which probably led him to reject first the stanza that advises humanity to love one another or die and ultimately to reject the entire poem in which the advice appeared. Most readers recognize a degree of extremity in Auden's rejection of the poem, but as he remade his life, returning to the Anglican Church and taking up residence in America, he most likely grew impatient with the poem's penchant for social analysis, a legacy of the Marxist decade of the 1930s to which the poem recognizably belongs. Significantly, each of the 11-line stanzas comprises a single complete sentence, mostly in iambic trimeter. The long sentence allows Auden to argue at some length the point of each stanza, thoroughly increasing the poem's polemical effect, while the shorter three-beat line, the rhythmical unit of the argument, gives the poem an almost aphoristic quality: "All I have is a voice / To undo the folded lie," for example, or "Who can reach the deaf, / Who can speak for the dumb?" A decade or so later, beside the confessional verse of the 1950s, Auden's poetry sounded didactic and impersonal to unsympathetic readers. There are clearly signs of this quality in several of the poem's more well-known phrases: "The strength of Collective Man," or "There is no such thing as the State / And no one exists alone." The poem has continued, however, to occupy a prominent place in Auden's canon because of its remarkable ability to blend the personal ("I *will* be true to the wife") with the apocalyptic ("We must love one another or die"); it ponders the uncertain future of a nation's citizens when their collective fate might well lie beyond their individual control. Accordingly, the poem falls midway between the obscure lyrics of Auden's youth and the occasional verse of his later years and so remains a powerful vehicle both of social criticism and personal revelation.

SIDNEY BURRIS

**Further Reading**

Bahlke, George W., editor, *Critical Essays on W.H. Auden,* New York: Hall, 1991
Brodsky, Joseph, *Less Than One: Selected Essays,* New York: Farrar Straus and Giroux, and London: Viking, 1986
Burris, Sidney, "Auden's Generalizations," *Shenandoah* 43, no. 3 (1993)
Carpenter, Humphrey, *W.H. Auden: A Biography,* Boston: Houghton Mifflin, and London: Allen and Unwin, 1981

Fuller, John, *W.H. Auden: A Commentary,* Princeton, New Jersey: Princeton University Press, and London: Faber and Faber, 1998
Hecht, Anthony, *The Hidden Law: The Poetry of W.H. Auden,* Cambridge, Massachusetts: Harvard University Press, 1993
McDiarmid, Lucy, *Auden's Apologies for Poetry,* Princeton, New Jersey: Princeton University Press, 1990
Mendelson, Edward, *Later Auden,* New York: Farrar Straus and Giroux, and London: Faber, 1999

## Avant-Garde. *See* Experimental Poetry/The Avant-Garde

## Awards. *See* Prizes

# B

## Imamu Amiri Baraka (LeRoi Jones) 1934–

Amiri Baraka is widely acknowledged as one of the most important African-American poets of the 20th century. His defining contributions to the Black Arts movement of the 1960s have ensured his lasting legacy in American letters. That said, Baraka's poetic development—from European literary Modernism to a Black Aesthetic, from black nationalism to revolutionary socialism—has been a unique and contested odyssey. It is certainly not by chance that his works have been the object of violently contrasting commentaries and appropriations by critics, cultural commentators, and fellow writers. Despite the many violent reversals of his poetic career, Baraka has consistently sought to define his poetry in opposition to European or Anglo-American Modernism, to explore instead the structures and forms of a black popular Modernism. There is, then, an underlying continuity of poetic concern in Baraka's varied expressions of black opposition.

Since the 1950s, Baraka has published more than a dozen highly influential works, among them his well-known collections of poetry *Preface to a Twenty-Volume Suicide Note* (1961), *The Dead Lecturer* (1964), *Black Magic: Collected Poetry, 1961–1967* (1969), *It's Nation Time* (1970), *Hard Facts* (1976), *Poetry for the Advanced* (1979), *Reggae or Not!* (1981), *In the Tradition* (1982), *Heathens* (1994), and *Wise, Why's, Y's* (1995). In his first volume of poetry, *Preface to a Twenty-Volume Suicide Note,* comprising poems written from 1958 to 1961, Baraka employs free-verse forms in an oblique and often elliptical style. The influence of William Carlos Williams' experiments with the "irregular foot" and Charles Olson's ideas of projective, or syllabic, verse are clearly present, as is the Beat aesthetic of Allen Ginsberg and Jack Kerouac. In many of these early poems, Baraka's pursuit of an expressive poetry combining lyric realism, jazz rhythms, and abrupt turns of image and syntax is indebted to the formal innovations of Anglo-American Modernism, but he is also at pains to resolve the double bind of a black vernacular and a High Modernist aesthetic. As a result of this at times impossible translation, many of Baraka's early poems suffer from a kind of formally confused idiom as he struggles to achieve the necessary "destruction of the old temple" ("The Plumed Serpent"), while still seemingly unable to progress beyond an alienated and narcissistic self. The moving title poem treats existential themes of alienation and angst and is typical of this stylistic irresolution:

> Lately, I've become accustomed to the way
> The ground opens up and envelops me
> Each time I go out to walk the dog.
> Or the broad edged silly music the wind
> Makes when I run for the bus . . .
>
> Things have come to that.

The use of the first person is also typical of Baraka's early poetic self-image: a self doomed to irony, unable to figure any redemptive community beyond the alienated inner landscape of the black ego. In the poem "Hymn for Lanie Poo," for example—which takes as its motto Rimbaud's "*vous êtes des faux Nègres*"—the structure of alienated irony reaches its apotheosis as Baraka pours scorn on himself, as well as on the exotic primitivism of "*die schwartze Bohemein.*" Baraka's attempts to go beyond this structure of identification and resistance, and thus achieve a more stable poetic idiom, turn to music, especially jazz, as the poet seeks to travel beyond "the cold insensitive roads" on a journey into "what / we wanted to call 'ourselves'" ("Bridge"). Here Baraka visualizes the "changes" of music via the poet's "sliding through" into "unmentionable black." Despite such gestures to cultural continuity and transformation, the dominant tone of Baraka's first volume can be found in the ending of "Notes for a Speech," the poem that concludes the collection on a note of cultural estrangement and despair:

> Africa
> is a foreign place. You are
> as any sad man here
> american.

Not until his second volume, *The Dead Lecturer* (1964), did Baraka's search for a black Modernist idiom or jazz measure lead him to a radical restaging of the culture and poetics of European Modernism, using a language marked more by anger than resignation. Gone is the elegiac lyricism of Baraka's first volume, replaced now by sardonic rage and vengeful irony as he scrutinizes the whole thematics of white bohemianism for its aesthetic contributions to "political art" ("Short Speech to My Friends"), rejecting that thematics as "a heap of broken feeling" ("Duncan Spoke of a Process"). This aesthetics of commitment, albeit willfully crude and antagonistic, signifies a new concern with the social ramifications of poetry. A major turning point in Baraka's poetic development, this new concern emerges out of a period of deep self-questioning triggered by his 1960 visit to Cuba. In *The Autobiography of LeRoi Jones* (1984), he comments, "Cuba split me open," adding that the trip was "a turning point in my life." There Baraka encountered political Third World artists and intellectuals who challenged his aesthetic and political convictions and insisted that his lack of interest in politics was itself political, that the modesty he espoused in separating art and politics was, in reality, that of a "cowardly bourgeois individualist." Moreover, he failed to counter their charge that his desire to cultivate the soul could not for a moment suffice in the "ugliness [he] live[d] in." Baraka's initial response, full of resentful bewilderment, later changed as he conceded the force of these arguments in his move to a new politicized awareness and black aesthetics of protest.

Baraka's quest for awareness begins with the question "What are influences?" ("Betancourt"). Conducting dialogues with W.B. Yeats (the "Crow Jane" sequence), William Carlos Williams ("A Contract for the Destruction and Rebuilding of Paterson"), and Valéry ("Valéry as Dictator"), among others, Baraka's yearning for change passes through the rarefied aestheticism of his earlier poetry in favor of an aesthetics of commitment. In "The Politics of Rich Painters," spoken cadences are dispersed through collage to denounce the commodification of formerly avant-gardist art, including his former Abstract Expressionist friends in Greenwich Village:

> You know the pity
> of democracy, that we must sit here
> and listen to how he made his money.

The open violence of this new, populist Modernism is motivated by a concern with ethnic, as against narrowly personal, freedoms of expression. In the essay "Expressive Language," for example, Baraka insists that "Black speech as a poetic reference" should enter into an alliance with "the cleansed / purpose" of a black aesthetic ("Black Dada Nihilismus"). In "Black Dada Nihilismus," which can be taken as emblematic of this aesthetic, Baraka uses tropes of sexual violence and racial revenge to negotiate the idiomatic and literary concerns of a radical black poetics. The poem enjoins its (presumably black male) readers to "Rape the white girls. Rape / their fathers. Cut the mothers' throats." In the course of this virulent anti-white fantasy, Baraka also aspires to an exorcism of Western culture via a cathartic immersion in black culture. The conflict between black ego and white bohemianism has been resolved, but through regression to a violent fantasy: indeed, Baraka's search for cathartic immersion becomes the signature of his espousal of a Black Aesthetic throughout the 1960s, especially during his black nationalist phase.

During these transitional years Baraka changed his name from LeRoi Jones to Amiri Baraka. He wrote essays, notably *Blues People* (1963), "the first real attempt to place jazz and the blues within the context of American social history"; *Home* (1966), a collection of social and political ideas that Baraka developed between 1960 and 1965; and *Black Music* (1967), a study of outstanding contemporary jazz musicians. He has also produced and published some 20 plays, among them *Dutchman* (1964); a television play, "The Death of Malcolm X" (1969); and the popular and shocking collection *Four Black Revolutionary Plays* (1969). The Obie Award–winning *Dutchman* was widely celebrated; Norman Mailer, for instance, claimed that it was "the best play in America." Baraka's national success as a playwright went hand in hand with a growing black chauvinistic sensibility. An admirer of Malcolm X and a convert to that leader's revolutionary political doctrines of black nationalism, Baraka's poetics of blackness (indebted equally to ethical and political ideals of solidarity) became more pronounced after Malcolm's assassination in 1965. Abandoning and repudiating his Greenwich Village lifestyle, beliefs, wife and two children, as well as friends, Baraka decided to head uptown to Harlem in the name of race solidarity.

In Harlem, Baraka established the Black Arts Repertory/School. His writing from the mid-1960s through the end of the decade is avowedly nationalist, dedicated to overcoming white racism. Baraka's nationalist poetry is widely seen as the founding moment of the Black Arts movement of the 1960s. In addition to editing, with Larry Neal, an anthology of black writing, *Black Fire* (1968), Baraka published *Black Magic: Collected Poetry, 1961–1967* (1969), a collection of poems written seeking to establish race consciousness. The volume opens with "An Explanation of the Work," written in 1968, in which Baraka dismisses most of his early poetry as "a cloud of abstraction and disjointedness, that was just whiteness." The new affirmation of racialism, however, also leads to an abstract, concrete poetry in which meaning is displaced by pure spontaneity ("Vowels 2") and black poems are presented as weapons for the complete destruction of the white world. That destruction, demanded by the Black Arts movement's wish for a radical reordering of the Western cultural aesthetic, leads Baraka to develop a separatist symbolism, mythology, critique, and iconology. Viewing the black poet as first and foremost an educator and agitator, Baraka's poetry becomes a rhetorical reflection of the racial ideology that precedes it; he presents his poems as political messages written to effect social change. As a result, the dominant motifs of these poems are those of a fiercely didactic and imperious anti-white rhetoric. The poem "Black Art" provides an exemplary instance of this trend, calling for

> . . . poems that wrestle cops into alleys
> and take their weapons leaving them dead
> with tongues pulled out and sent to Ireland. Knockoff
> poems for dope selling wops or slick halfwhite
> politicians Airplane poems . . .
> . . . Setting fire and death to
> whities ass. Look at the Liberal
> Spokesman for the jews clutch his throat
> & puke himself into eternity . . .
> . . . Another bad poem cracking
> steel knuckles in a jewlady's mouth

The imperious rhetoric of such poems, the result of a language of hatred, is already compromised by the anti-bourgeois sentiments of the white avant-garde that act as the prototypes for Baraka's anti-white rhetoric. Even though Baraka uses black figures of speech—such as the dozens, scatting, shouts, chants, blues, and the uneven, syncopated rhythms of jazz—his repeated affirmation of the need for "a black poem. And a / black world" does not take this need beyond the level of a prescriptive exclusionism and can only disallow (while unwittingly repeating) the avant-garde rhetoric of European Modernism.

This failure probably explains Baraka's shift from the nationalist poetry of the 1960s to the fully-fledged Marxist-Leninism of *Hard Facts* (1976), a work that returns to the formal obliquities of *Black Magic* without the racist rhetoric. Indeed, in the "Introduction," Baraka asserts that he now disowns the "reactionary nationalism" of his former "narrow nationalist and bourgeois nationalist stand," repudiating it in favor of "Socialist Revolution." Such a conversion from race to history, however, is still indebted to a didactic idea of poetry: comparing the two phases, he states: "They were similar in the sense I see art as a weapon of revolution. It's just now that I define revolution in Marxist terms." In brief, Baraka still sees committed art as the way of overcoming the dichotomy between the accessible and the esoteric, black ideology and the poetic forms of Modernism. In "History on Wheels," for example, which denounces "a class of exploiters, / in black face," Baraka's anti-bourgeois rhetoric has come full circle. His attack on "the feverish nearreal fantasy" of Hollywood in "A New Reality Is Better Than a New Movie!" also repeats his ethical demand that true art should emerge from the rigorous consequence of attacking inner and outer alienation: "Inside beyond our craziness is reality" ("Reggae or Not!"). This is also why, in insisting on the political dimensions of writing, Baraka continues to adhere to an expressive aesthetic. In later works, such as *In the Tradition* (1982) and *Wise, Why's, Y's* (1995), Baraka's use of language-as-process continues to treat words as acts that refuse the quietism of any final communication, or judgment.

DAVID MARRIOTT

*See also* Black Arts Movement

**Biography**

Born Everett LeRoi Jones in Newark, New Jersey, 7 October 1934; changed name to Amiri Baraka in 1968. Attended Rutgers University, New Brunswick, New Jersey, 1951–52; Howard University, Washington, D.C., 1953–54, B.A. 1954; served in the United States Air Force, 1954–57; teacher, New School for Social Research, New York, 1961–64 and summers 1977–79, State University of New York, Buffalo, summer 1964, and Columbia University, New York, 1964 and spring 1980; Visiting Professor, San Francisco State College, 1966–67, Yale University, New Haven, Connecticut, 1977–78, and George Washington University, Washington, D.C., 1978–79; Assistant Professor, 1980–82, Associate Professor, 1983–84, and since 1985 Professor of African Studies, State University of New York, Stony Brook; founder, *Yugen* magazine and Totem Press, 1958–62; editor, with Diane di Prima, *Floating Bear* magazine, 1961–63; founding director, Black Arts Repertory Theatre, Harlem, New York, 1964–66; since 1966 founding director, Spirit House, Newark; involved in Newark politics as member of the United Brothers, 1967, and Committee for Unified Newark, 1969–75; chair, Congress of Afrikan People, 1972–75. Received Whitney fellowship, 1961; Obie Award, 1964; Guggenheim fellowship, 1965; Yoruba Academy fellowship, 1965; National Endowment for the Arts grant, 1966, Award, 1981; Dakar Festival Prize, 1966; honorary Litt.D., Malcolm X College, Chicago, 1972; Rockefeller grant, 1981; Before Columbus Foundation Award, 1984; American Book Award, 1984; member, Black Academy of Arts and Letters. Living in Stony Brook, New York.

**Poetry**

*Preface to a Twenty-Volume Suicide Note,* 1961
*The Disguise,* 1961
*The Dead Lecturer,* 1964
*Black Art,* 1966
*A Poem for Black Hearts,* 1967
*Black Magic: Collected Poetry, 1961–1967,* 1969
*It's Nation Time,* 1970
*In Our Terribleness: Some Elements and Meaning in Black Style* (with Fundi [Billy Abernathy]), 1970
*Spirit Reach,* 1972
*Afrikan Revolution,* 1973
*Hard Facts,* 1976
*Poetry for the Advanced,* 1979
*Selected Poetry,* 1979
*AM/TRAK,* 1979
*Spring Song,* 1979
*Reggae or Not!* 1981
*In the Tradition,* 1982
*Thoughts for You!* 1984
*An Amiri Baraka/Leroi Jones Poetry Sampler,* 1991
*The LeRoi Jones/Amiri Baraka Reader* (includes prose), 1991
*5 Boptrees,* 1992
*Heathens and Revolutionary Art: Poems and Lecture,* 1994
*Wise, Why's, Y's,* 1995
*Funk Lore: New Poems, 1984–1995,* 1996

**Other Writings:** plays (*Dutchman,* 1964; *Money: A Jazz Opera* [with George Gruntz], 1982; *Primitive World* [music by David Murray], 1984), screenplays, novel (*The System of Dante's Hell,* 1965), short stories (*Tales,* 1967), essays and books on African-American culture and politics (*Blues People,* 1963; *Home,* 1966; *Black Music,* 1967), autobiography (*The Autobiography of LeRoi Jones,* 1984); edited collections of literature (*Confirmation; An Anthology of African American Women* [with Amina Baraka], 1983).

**Further Reading**

Benston, Kimberly W., editor, *Imamu Amiri Baraka (LeRoi Jones): A Collection of Critical Essays,* Englewood Cliffs, New Jersey: Prentice Hall, 1978
Gayle, Addison, Jr., editor, *The Black Aesthetic,* Garden City, New York: Doubleday, 1971
Harris, William J., editor, *The LeRoi Jones/Amiri Baraka Reader,* New York: Thunder's Mouth Press, 1991; 2nd edition, 2000
Henderson, Stephen, *Understanding the New Black Poetry: Black Speech and Black Music as Poetic References,* New York: Morrow, 1972
Sollors, Werner, *Amiri Baraka/LeRoi Jones: The Quest for a "Populist Modernism,"* New York: Columbia University Press, 1978

## Black People: This Is Our Destiny

Published in the section "Black Art" of the collection *Black Magic* (1969), "Black People: This Is Our Destiny" exemplifies the shift toward black nationalism and ethnic separatism that characterizes the poetry of Amiri Baraka in the late 1960s and that the poet would reject in the 1970s in favor of a Marxist-Leninist approach. The poem carries to its extreme consequences Baraka's polemics against the rationalism of Western society by reversing the cultural dynamics of civilization traditionally invoked by white Westerners: the "primitives" will civilize the world, this is black people's destiny ("the primitives the first men who evolve again to civilize the world"). Baraka thus becomes both committed poet and black magician: the former sings the political reversal brought about by the magic of the latter.

In "An Explanation of the Work," the prefatory note to *Black Magic,* Baraka distances himself from *The Dead Lecturer* (1964) and *Preface to a Twenty-Volume Suicide Note* (1961), his earlier collections of poetry, claiming that they were the result of a "twisted society" and "European influence" and that they amounted to "a cloud of abstraction and disjointedness, that was just whiteness." On the contrary, *Black Magic* will focus on that "spirituality always trying to get through, to triumph, to walk across these dead bodies europeans call their minds." The preface announces the major contrasts that run throughout the collection and that inform "Black People: This Is Our Destiny": white versus black, sterile rationality (the "Explanation" associates the white mind to a dead body) versus spirituality and black magic. Baraka takes on a more committed and a decidedly separatist poetic persona.

From the very title "Black People: This Is Our Destiny," it is clear that Baraka is addressing black people directly, as a leader of a nation would. The poem (not to be confused with "Black People!," the text that ends the collection and that was cited as legal evidence against Baraka in the 1967 trial following the Newark riots) constructs a gendered ethnic pride and black nationalism by declaring black men "holy," "harmonized with creation," and longing for "the purity of the holy world." As in other poems collected in *Black Magic,* such holiness is coupled with a militaristic stance: black people have "the war" in their hearts. "Black People: This Is Our Destiny" affirms racial self-love and turns on its head the usual stereotype of racial self-hatred, which is employed in juxtaposition in other poems in the collection, such as "The Deadly Eyes." Black identity is strongly affirmed and linked to a movement of ascension (". . . in the holy black man's / eyes that we *rise,* whose race is only *direction up,* where / we go to meet the realization of makers *knowing who we are*"). Black men become part of a new creation and communion that encompasses "all existing forms of life, the gases, the plants, the ghost minerals the spirits the souls." As it is clear from this list, in this process spirituality pervades materiality, and tellingly the punctuation disappears to give a sense of togetherness. It is such a union of opposites that allows us to make sense of the first five lines, which play off against one another the geometric form of the straight line and that of the circle.

The poem invites the reader to read this union of contrastive forms in the materiality of the text itself since it consists of 19 long, straight lines (with the addition of a 20th line consisting simply of the word "world"), while its circularity is emphasized by the absence of a full stop at the end and by rhetorical devices, such as the polyptoton "embraced embracing" and the chiasmus "the storm of peace" / "a peaceful storm." As is often the case in Baraka's poems, there are no rhymes, and to create a sense of rhythm, the text relies on intonation (as suggested by the punctuation) and repetitions. Therefore, the poem takes on the heritage of the African-American oral tradition.

Tellingly, "rhythm," a word that signals Baraka's interest in African-American music, is invoked just before the call to the primitives to civilize the world. This is the last section of the text, and it stands apart from the rest of it thanks to the pause marked by the dots: ". . . vibration holy nuance beating against itself, a rhythm a playing." In this way, Baraka links the political content of the poem (the reversal of roles between civilized and primitives, between rationalism and irrationalism) with the African-American cultural tradition of oral art and music. Ethnic pride becomes both the content and the form of the poem, thus sustaining Baraka's critique of the use of form as mere aesthetic escapism, which the poet finds typical of white culture ("Gatsby's Theory of Aesthetics," "Kenyatta Listening to Mozart," and "Form Is Emptiness"). "Black People: This Is Our Destiny" is certainly characterized by that "convincing sense of integration" that Lloyd Brown (1980) has detected in the best poems of the collection *Black Magic:* "a compelling blend of magic as the essence of spirituality, magic as the chant of ethnic awakening, and magical chant as the sound, or tonal design, of politically committed poetry."

LUCA PRONO

**Further Reading**

Brown, Lloyd W., *Amiri Baraka,* Boston: Twayne, 1980

Davidas, Lionel, *Chemins d'identité: LeRoi Jones/Amiri Baraka et le fait culturel africain-américain,* Kourou, French Guiana: Ibis Rouge, 1997

Hudson, Theodore R., *From LeRoi Jones to Amiri Baraka: The Literary Works,* Durham, North Carolina: Duke University Press, 1973

Lacey, Henry C., *To Raise, Destroy, and Create: The Poetry, Drama, and Fiction of Imamu Amiri Baraka (LeRoi Jones),* Troy, New York: Whitston, 1981

Sollors, Werner, *Amiri Baraka/LeRoi Jones: The Quest for a "Populist Modernism,"* New York: Columbia University Press, 1978

Woodard, Komozi, *A Nation within a Nation: Amiri Baraka (LeRoi Jones) and Black Power Politics,* Chapel Hill: University of North Carolina Press, 1999

## A Poem Some People Will Have to Understand

Amiri Baraka's "A Poem Some People Will Have to Understand" (1969) appeared in "Sabotage," one of three volumes included in *Black Magic* (1969), his first collection of poetry inspired by black nationalism. In these poems the narrator is unlike the young speaker of Baraka's previous works; he begins to speak for himself and to articulate to others his resolutions for political and social change in the external world, promoting black awareness through attacks on white racism and Western culture.

The "Sabotage" poems in *Black Magic* evolved out of Baraka's Greenwich Village period from 1961 to 1963. Although Baraka worked on "Sabotage" during those years, it was not published in the form of a collection until 1969. He wanted to be confident in his message, fully committed to the context of the poems, and certain that he would not mind offending those people with whom he once associated. As Henry Lacey (1981) has noted, these poems are

> marked by an ever-increasing use of Afro-American allusions. In this manner, Baraka tells the former associates that he has different ideals and speaks from a different frame of reference.

With the poems in "Sabotage," "Baraka starting stripping away his ornate style, a style he identified with whiteness" (Harris, 1985), and began using the black chant and scream and black jazz forms. These poems, especially "A Poem Some People Will Have to Understand," were Baraka's way of taking a direct action in the world by attacking American society.

Baraka wrote "A Poem Some People Will Have to Understand" to his black middle-class and white liberal friends, the "Some People" of the title, to express his concern for them and their attitudes about his political interests. The first lines of the poem—

> Dull unwashed windows of eyes
> and buildings of industry. What
> industry do I practice? A slick
> colored boy. 12 miles from his
> home. I practice no industry.
> I am no longer a credit
> to my race

—express his artist-intellectual friends' image of him and their belief that he relinquished his place with the other "credits" to his race like George Washington Carver, Joe Louis, and Ralph Bunche. In their eyes he is just a colored boy 12 miles from home, practicing "no industry." Baraka, on the other hand, seeks a change in the condition of black people but has realized that the liberal protocol has not affected or even improved this condition:

> All the pitifully intelligent citizens
> I've forced myself to love.
> We have awaited the coming of a national
> phenomenon. Mystics and romantics, knowledgeable
> workers
> of the land.
> But none has come.
> (repeat)
> but none has come.
> Will the machinegunners please step forward?

The liberals are ironically labeled as the mystics and romantics who have had little or no effect on the social condition of black people, despite their ideals. Baraka is ready to take the necessary political action, and he disassociates with his friends who are either incapable of or refuse to take this same action. "A Poem Some People Will Have to Understand" publicly renounces his former friends and way of thinking.

Baraka sees no other alternative to political and social inequity but violence, and that is what "some people will have to understand" and accept. Baraka calls for the machinegunners to step forward because of his "feelings of urgency and impatience towards those he perceived of as standing in the way" (Harris, 1991). This poem places both political art and political action in opposition to the concept of art for art's sake.

SHARON D. RAYNOR

**Further Reading**

Benston, Kimberly W., *Baraka: The Renegade and the Mask,* New Haven, Connecticut: Yale University Press, 1976

Brown, Lloyd W., *Amiri Baraka,* Boston: Twayne, 1980

Harris, William J., *The Poetry and Poetics of Amiri Baraka: Jazz Aesthetic,* Columbia: University of Missouri Press, 1985

Harris, William J., editor, *The LeRoi Jones/Amiri Baraka Reader,* New York: Thunder's Mouth Press, 1991; 2nd edition, 2000

Hudson, Theodore R., *From LeRoi Jones to Amiri Baraka: The Literary Works,* Durham, North Carolina: Duke University Press, 1973

Lacey, Henry C., *To Raise, Destroy, and Create: The Poetry, Drama, and Fiction of Imamu Amiri Baraka (LeRoi Jones),* Troy, New York: Whitston, 1981

---

# Beat Poetry

The reputation of the poetry written by Beat generation writers has suffered not from neglect but from the excessive media attention generated on its first appearances in the late 1950s. This attention, coming in the form of articles and photo spreads in popular magazines such as *Time* and *Life,* created an undue emphasis on the lifestyle aspects of something called the "beatnik" rather than on the substance of the poetry. All poetic movements are diminished by those imitators who grasp only the mannerisms of the masters without the hard-earned technique, but the reputations of the Beat writers have suffered even more as a result of the media hyperbole generated by the early furor. To this day, many of the prominent members of the Beat generation are not treated like the serious artists that they are.

The term "beatnik," in fact, is the hostile creation of an unsympathetic San Francisco journalist named Herb Caen. This amalgamation of the word "beat" with the name of the Soviet satellite "Sputnik" managed to associate a talented and diverse group of writers with something threatening, otherworldly, and un-American. The Beats, while certainly not to be confused with the Cold Warriors and the liberal academics who defined the mainstream of American intellectual life after World War II, were more likely to see themselves as living up to the potential for freedom and independence offered by the United States. Furthermore, the actual meaning of the term "Beat" is in fact ambiguous enough to cover a range of implications favored by the various writers associated with the movement. Some say that it originated in the

New York underworld, from which emerged Times Square hustler Herbert Huncke, who in the 1940s introduced the word to novelist William S. Burroughs and Allen Ginsberg as a synonym for "downtrodden." A decade later, Jack Kerouac, who had been born and raised in the Roman Catholic Church, endowed the word with a more overtly religious connotation when he realized, on entering a cathedral, that the word "beat" is embedded in the words "beatitude" and "beatific."

Just as the word covers a wide range of social and spiritual connotations, the poetry associated with the Beat generation is also diverse and varied, so much so that it would be futile to define or even attempt to characterize the Beat poet or poem in any way except provisionally. How else could one account for the street lyrics of poets such as Jack Micheline and Ray Bremser, or the haiku variations of Kerouac and Lew Welch, or the Buddhist meditative lyrics of Gary Snyder, Philip Whalen, and Joanne Kyger, not to mention the book-length epics published by Snyder (*Mountains and Rivers without End,* 1996) and Diane di Prima (*Loba,* 1998)? Part of the appeal of Beat poetry to its many readers rests precisely in this diversity and unpredictability. Thus, speaking generally and without attempting to define the standard Beat writer or Beat poem, one can only offer tentative characteristics shared by many of the participants in the movement.

The Beat generation consists of writers born mostly but not exclusively between the years 1920 and 1940. They published their first books in the late 1950s through the early 1970s, almost always with small, independent publishers. In terms of Western poetry, most of the Beats have roots in the British Romantic poets, such as William Blake (Ginsberg) or Percy Bysshe Shelley (Gregory Corso). However, unlike their vociferous critics, many Beats were far more cosmopolitan. In addition to the carefully studied Eastern influences on Snyder and Whalen (and later Ginsberg), Lawrence Ferlinghetti (Ph.D. from the Sorbonne and owner of City Lights Books) learned from several French writers, many of whom he translated into English and almost all of whom were unknown to American critics of the 1950s. Ed Sanders, furthermore, possessed an M.A. in classics from New York University, enabling him to adapt the idiom of Greek poetry to life in the 1960s. Besides these international sources, the Beats were far more willing than their contemporaries to embrace uniquely American literary sources, such as Walt Whitman, and musical forms, such as jazz and blues.

In addition to being learned (although not in ways generally acknowledged by the tastemakers of their time), most of the Beats valued some degree of spontaneity. Herein comes to play both the jazz influences and the Romantic tendency to value the unmediated experience, tendencies expressed by both the schooled poets, such as Ginsberg, Snyder, Whalen, and Ferlinghetti, and the unschooled poets, such as Micheline, Corso, and Bremser. However, unlike the British Romantic poet William Wordsworth, who in his "Preface to *Lyrical Ballads*" theoretically advocated writing poetry that used the language of ordinary people, the Beats actually encouraged their friends from the margins of society to write prose and poetry.

Even with the characteristics offered so far, certain writers who are indisputably Beat have not been covered. Michael McClure, for instance, was neither Buddhist nor street poet. He was, however, one of the few writers to work in the theater and as a songwriter (he receives credit on the Janis Joplin hit "Mercedes Benz"). His former wife, Joanna McClure, shares many similarities with Jack Kerouac, right down to the type of notebook preferred for drafting poems, but her bohemian lifestyle did not prevent her from developing an expertise in early childhood development and parent education. In short, a comprehensive definition of "Beat" is impossible, but it is safe to say that the concerns of all the poets were marginal to mainstream life of the 1950s. Beat poetry, in other words, emerged in this space marked off by the marginal life of street people and bohemians on the one hand and an intense, ecumenical spirituality on the other.

A final factor to consider is that, despite appearances, Beat poetry did not spring spontaneously from the pages of Madison Avenue lifestyle magazines. Rather, the poetry of Ginsberg, Kerouac, Corso, Snyder, Kyger, di Prima, and Ferlinghetti emerged where and when it did because each of the poets involved had studiously prepared him- or herself. This preparation enabled each of the poets to build creatively on the foundations laid by their predecessors. Because literary San Francisco was so far ahead of the rest of the country and because the nation was gripped by the Cold War, the Beats were initially presented as an anomaly, a minor disruption of day-to-day life. However, a study of their works indicates that it is actually grounded in an extensive range of traditions. Ferlinghetti's academic background has already been mentioned. Ginsberg's own extensive reading is often overshadowed by his pronouncements in favor of spontaneous composition, but by his mid-20s he had already accumulated a tremendous knowledge of poetics and prosody. Gary Snyder developed a recognized expertise in Asian languages as well as ecology—the latter largely on his own since there was little attention paid to environmental issues in the 1940s and 1950s, when he came of age.

The specifics of all the Beat poets' training are as different as the poets themselves. Suffice it to say that each of them was generally more learned than the dominant media images of the period would indicate. However, the fact that the movement emerged in San Francisco owes much to the city itself. A poetry scene had already been established there primarily through the combined (although at times conflicting) efforts of Kenneth Rexroth, Josephine Miles (a scholar and poet at Berkeley), and the poet Ruth Witt-Diamant, who ran a reading series at San Francisco State College as early as the 1940s (decades before the vogue of public readings by poets reached the rest of the country); and, by 1953, Ferlinghetti had already established City Lights Bookstore. Before Ginsberg and Kerouac had even arrived on the scene from New York, San Francisco had already nurtured talented younger poets such as those just mentioned as well as William Everson, Robert Duncan, and Jack Spicer.

If Beat poetry can be said to have a specific origin in time and place, the birth of the Beat generation as a public force occurred with a poetry reading on 13 October 1955 at the Six Gallery in San Francisco. Allen Ginsberg had recently moved to Berkeley to pursue a graduate degree at the University of California. There he became acquainted with the established poets of the Bay Area as well as with younger writers, such as McClure, Snyder, Whalen, and Philip Lamantia. At Rexroth's urging, Ginsberg invited the other four poets to read at a former garage that had recently been converted to an art gallery. Rexroth served as a master of ceremonies that evening, while Jack Kerouac built the audience's enthusiasm by passing around a jug of wine. Each of the five poets read breakthrough work, culminating with the first public reading of Ginsberg's "Howl," which was soon to become famous. While none of the other poets attained quite the stature of Ginsberg in terms of mass media exposure, each of them went on to a long, successful, and varied career in poetry. All of them, except Lamantia, retained a lifelong identification with the Beat generation.

Although the term "Beat" was not at the time in widespread public use, the New York poets associated with the term had been using it for years. In fact, novelist and Beat fellow traveler John Clellon Holmes had already published an article in the *New York Times Magazine* called "This Is the Beat Generation" (16 November 1952). While not specifically addressing literary developments (indeed, almost none of the major writers associated with the movement had even been published by this date), Holmes was the first to take the term public. In the late-1950s backlash against Ginsberg's *Howl, and Other Poems* (1956) and Jack Kerouac's novel *On the Road* (1957), the name took on more sinister connotations, and the term "beatnik" became a national commonplace in several uncomplimentary articles and photo spreads treating a literary movement as a form of social deviance. Thus, a particular image of these poets took hold with the public, an image suggesting a lack of hygiene and a penchant for spewing forth words of detached pomposity to a roomful of snapping fingers and bongo drums. Caricatured on television in the form of the character Maynard G. Krebs on *The Life and Loves of Dobie Gillis,* the image of the beatnik overwhelmed the poetry written by the Beat generation. By 1960, FBI Director J. Edgar Hoover could address the Republican National Convention declaring that the three major threats to national security were communism, homosexuality, and beatniks.

Despite this negative publicity (which of course attracted some positive attention from disaffiliated sectors of the public), the Beat poets continued to work and to engage the world through poetry. While the Beat movement coalesced in San Francisco in the early and middle 1950s, writers subsequently associated with the movement came from all over the United States. By the time *Howl, and Other Poems* was facing an obscenity trial in 1958, independent magazines had emerged in several cities, and previously disparate communities started to come together under one banner. In 1958, administrators at the University of Chicago censored an issue of the *Chicago Review* that featured Beat writings, so the magazine's graduate student editors Paul Carroll and Irving Rosenthal formed *Big Table* magazine. By 1961 in New York, LeRoi Jones (later Amiri Baraka) and Diane di Prima published *Floating Bear,* and a year later Ed Sanders opened Peace Eye Bookstore and began publishing *Fuck You/A Magazine of the Arts.* Attention was also drawn to Los Angeles, which already featured an active scene revolving around Venice Beach, where Lawrence Lipton, Stuart Perkoff, and others had been publishing work and even performing poetry to jazz accompaniment for more than a decade. Lipton had published in 1959 a sociological essay called *The Holy Barbarians,* a book that gave the first full-length, inside account of the emerging bohemian movement as a national phenomenon. The interesting feature of Lipton's book is the historical dimension: while scenes were popping up all over the country where previously poetry was not part of daily life, Lipton traces the origin of these developments to the various bohemias of Paris, New York, and Chicago in the 1920s and 1930s. Lipton's probing account offers an interesting antidote to the superficial and misleading stories then appearing in the major news and style magazines and still goes a long way toward explaining the significance of Beat poetry. Historian John Arthur Maynard (1991) describes Lipton's Venice West scene and, for the most part, the social tendencies of the Beat poets in general when he writes, "They lived on subsistence incomes in the shabbiest part of town, held jobs no longer than they had to, and considered the sacrifice worth it if it freed them from the false values and phony satisfactions of conventional life. . . . Instead of amassing possessions and staring into the television set, they wrote poetry, painted pictures, made collages."

By the 1960s, the Beats were a global phenomenon. Ginsberg and Corso lived in the famous "Beat Hotel" in Paris, where they met poet Harold Norse and several other artists from Europe and the United States. Ginsberg appeared at political protests around the world and was even deported from Cuba and Czechoslovakia for his activities. In San Francisco, Snyder, Kyger, Ferlinghetti, and di Prima were often asked (and still are to this day) to contribute poems to gatherings on behalf of environmental and spiritual causes. At a time when American poetry became more and more associated with the classroom, the writers associated with the Beat generation would often place themselves and their poetry literally at the barricades. For this, they were criticized, and to be fair, the poetry sometimes (although not often) suffered. However, unlike mainstream poets, the Beat writers through the decades bravely faced dismissal from the established poets in order to make poetry a public art once again.

Interest in the Beat generation continues into the 21st century. While some of the leading practitioners have died, a few continue to publish innovative volumes of poetry. For example, the last decade of the 20th century saw the publication of the previously mentioned volumes by Snyder and di Prima as well as major collections by McClure, Corso, and Ted Joans. Courses devoted to the Beat writers are staples at many colleges and universities.

Scholarly attention is expanding as well. Much research is still directed at the major figures, such as Ginsberg, Corso, and Kerouac, but women and minority writers who contributed to the movement are also attracting sustained critical attention. For example, scholar Brenda Knight published an extensive anthology titled *Women of the Beat Generation: The Writers, Artists, and Muses at the Heart of a Revolution* (1996). The next year saw publication of *A Different Beat: Writings by the Women of the Beat Generation* (Richard Peabody, editor, 1997). These books bring together hard-to-find writings by authors known and virtually unknown. These two anthologies are especially encouraging because there is almost no overlap in their contents, a fact that shows the tremendous energy and diversity of the women who have been all too often overlooked and that also suggests that there remain further discoveries for inquiring scholars. Indeed, as Ronna Johnson and Maria Damon (1999) characterize the contributions of the "skipped Beats," they "did not so much criticize mainstream American life as try to assert their places as artists and members of the Beat community. They were invisible as artists to their male peers, and are invisible today in the popular perception of the Beat era." Still, despite that invisibility, women writers have made major contributions to the understanding of Beat culture, primarily through memoirs, which Johnson and Damon acknowledge when they mention "popular interest in *Minor Characters* (by Joyce Johnson), Hettie Jones' *How I Became Hettie Jones,* Carolyn Cassady's *Off the Road,* Bonnie Bremser's *Troia: Mexican Memoirs,* and Diane di Prima's *Memoirs of a Beatnik.*" However, as the authors conclude, recent scholars have shown, rightfully, that "there is a substantial Beat women's literature that goes beyond memoir."

A definitive history of poetry written by the Beat generation cannot yet be written largely because the work, as well as our understanding of it, continues to evolve. There will always be readers looking for poetry with the critical edginess that characterizes Beat writing, and since the work of many writers associated with the movement is ongoing, readers will not soon run out of the kinds of poems and poets that can change their lives. This latter feature, finally, is the defining characteristic of Beat writing: the power to change individual lives in ways that other contemporary poems and poets cannot. For this reason, the poetry of the Beat generation will continue to attract positive attention from its supporters and strong criticism from its detractors for quite some time.

DAVID R. ZAUHAR

*See also* Performance Poetry; San Francisco Renaissance

**Further Reading**

Cherkovski, Neeli, *Whitman's Wild Children: Portraits of Twelve Poets,* South Royalton, Vermont: Steerforth Press, 1999

Davidson, Michael, *The San Francisco Renaissance: Poetics and Community at Mid-Century,* Cambridge and New York: Cambridge University Press, 1989

Delattre, Pierre, *Episodes,* St. Paul, Minnesota: Graywolf Press, 1992

Ferlinghetti, Lawrence, and Nancy J. Peters, *Literary San Francisco,* San Francisco: City Lights Books, Harper and Row, 1980

Johnson, Ronna C., and Maria Damon, "Recapturing the Skipped Beats: Women and Minorities in the Beat Generation," *Chronicle of Higher Education* (1 October 1999)

Maynard, John Arthur, *Venice West: The Beat Generation in Southern California,* New Brunswick, New Jersey: Rutgers University Press, 1991

Miles, Barry, *The Beat Hotel,* New York: Grove Press, 2000

Plimpton, George, editor, *The Beat Writers at Work: Paris Review Interviews,* New York: Modern Library, and London: Harvill, 1999

Skau, Michael, *A Clown in a Grave: Complexities and Tensions in the Works of Gregory Corso,* Carbondale: Southern Illinois University Press, 1999

Sterritt, David, *Mad to Be Saved: The Beats, the Fifties, and Film,* Carbondale: Southern Illinois University Press, 1998

Watson, Steven, *The Birth of the Beat Generation: Visionaries, Rebels, and Hipsters, 1944–1960,* New York: Pantheon, 1995

---

# Ben Belitt 1911–

Better known as a translator than as a poet, Ben Belitt has been celebrated by prestigious and loyal readers without attracting substantial fame or anthologization. His poems, published in only six volumes over the span of nearly 50 years, present an ornate, demanding language that his friend Howard Nemerov (1972) identified as "not only difficult but in other ways unfashionable." By this, Nemerov meant that Belitt's poetry, committed to precise description and a dizzying density of sound, requires not only close attention but also multiple careful readings; hard work, after all, is rarely popular. In poems such as "The Bathers: A Triptych," Belitt asks us to imagine "marinations, / emollients: Job in a sitzbad, / dipping the nib of his quill in the optics of Newton," as he describes David's painting of the dying Marat. Yet, as Nemerov and Robert Boyers (1973) remind us, there is great pleasure in this idiosyncrasy, these overlooked but "exquisite" lyrics.

Belitt's early life was tragic, although it figures only obliquely in his adult writings. His childhood in the care of Manhattan's Hebrew Orphan Asylum and his subsequent retrieval by his mother after six years appear in his autobiographical poem "The Orphaning" and in the prose memoir titled "From the Bookless World." (After his mother remarried, she brought Belitt to Lynchburg, Virginia, the home of her second husband; Belitt later attended the University of Virginia.)

Leaving graduate school in 1936 to become assistant literary editor at *The Nation,* Belitt moved from the romanticized Virginia of his adolescence directly into Manhattan's literary inner circles, mentored by Joseph Wood Krutch and Eda Lou Walton. Walton first introduced Belitt to the works of Hart Crane and Gerard Manley Hopkins: the deeply personal, intensely wrought dictions of both poets resonate still in Belitt's verse. Among his other duties at *The Nation,* Belitt reviewed a biography of Keats, already an important figure in his imaginative life, and three books by Wallace Stevens, whose consanguinity of "the logic and the music of the poem" (the phrase is from Belitt's 6 November 1937 review of *The Man with the Blue Guitar*) remains also a hallmark of Belitt's technique.

After two years in New York, Belitt moved to Bennington, Vermont, where he has lived since 1938 as a professor of literature at Bennington College. Working in the richly interdisciplinary and experimental atmosphere there, Belitt collaborated (or, as he wrote, "collided") with the legendary choreographer Martha Graham and with the scholar Wallace Fowlie, who first turned Belitt's attention to the translation of poems. Belitt produced his *Four Poems by Rimbaud: The Problem of Translation* (1947) because, in Belitt's words, "My knowledge of French was such that, although I could imagine what the tension and the weight of the idiom was in French, I could not get close enough to the excitement of the sound without touching it with English and, as Keats says, 'proving it on my own pulses.'" After these initial efforts on the French Modernists, Belitt was drawn to Federico García Lorca and the modern Spanish-language poetry that made his reputation: Antonio Machado, Eugenio Montale, Rafael Alberti, Jorge Luis Borges, and most significantly Pablo Neruda, who chose Belitt as his translator for several volumes of poetry. Belitt's translation of García Lorca's *Poet in New York* (1955) became the standard translation of that important text, and it has been suggested, although Belitt denies it, that this translation influenced Allen Ginsberg's *Howl* (1956) and the San Francisco Sound of the 1950s.

Belitt's method of translation honors imagination over literal fidelity. In his essays on translation in *Adam's Dream* (1978), he claims that the translator must preserve the "pleasure and not [the] truth" of the original poem. Translators, Belitt insists, cannot afford to believe in the "Incorruptible Form": translation is a "sweaty empiricism in which everything is . . . a choice." This epistemology of translation explicitly takes part in the metaphors of quantum physics—a "poetics of uncertainty" proven and driven by every semantic choice—and in his criticism Belitt invokes Werner Heisenberg as easily as S.T. Coleridge. In the essays of *The Forgèd Feature: Toward a Poetics of Uncertainty* (1995), he connects the quantum-physical "dynamics of uncertainty" to Keats' notion of "Negative Capability," making the translator (or poet) the one perceiver who can preserve (or imitate) the essential unresolvability of the actual world. As Belitt said in a 1999 internet interview, "The power of what a poem does is to make the thing more dubious."

The poets who seem most prominent in Belitt's personal canon are also the poets for whom this "poetics of uncertainty" seems most apt: Hart Crane; Gerard Manley Hopkins, whose work provides the titles for *The Double Witness* (1977) and *The Forgèd Feature;* and John Keats, whose spirit rises to confront Belitt in the powerful title poem of his collected works, *This Scribe, My Hand* (1998). In that great meditation, as the noise of traffic ("demotic with engines and klaxons") swirls around Keats' grave in Rome, Belitt finds himself overcome by the "murderous" violence of writing and the terrible silence of poetic anonymity. Seeing the places that Keats had seen in Rome, he begins to sense poetry as "a hashish of blood" on the palate, later slipping "on the blood and the ink / toward the exigent bed" where Keats died. Drawing on imagery as various as his high school botany lessons, the Russian film *Potemkin,* Sumerian cuneiform, street violence, and Wordsworth, Belitt revolves, like a man possessed, around Keats' proposed epitaph ("Here lies a man whose name was writ on water") and the poem's eventually terrifying refrain—terrifying because it carries with it the silence it implies—"*Nobody listens.*"

For a poet as skilled, as demanding, and as careful as Belitt, no fate could be less appropriate. By eschewing the fashionable for the difficult, by producing only at lengthy intervals, and by devoting his career to translation and teaching, Belitt has done little to court fame, although he has done much to deserve it.

Isaac Cates

**Biography**

Born in New York City, 2 May 1911. Attended the University of Virginia, Charlottesville, B.A. 1932 (Phi Beta Kappa), M.A. 1934, 1934–36; served in the United States Army Infantry, 1942–44; editor-scenarist, Signal Corps Photographic Center Combat Film Section, 1945–46; assistant literary editor, *The Nation,* New York, 1936–37; since 1938 member of the English Department, and currently Professor of literature and languages, Bennington College, Vermont; taught at Mills College, Oakland, California, 1939, and Connecticut College, New London, 1948–49. Received Shelley Memorial Award, 1936; Guggenheim fellowship, 1946; Oscar Blumenthal Award, 1957, and Union League Civic and Arts Foundation Prize, 1960 (*Poetry,* Chicago); Brandeis University Creative Arts Award, 1962; National Institute of Arts and Letters Award, 1965; National Endowment for the Arts grant, 1967; Russell Loines Award, 1981; Rockefeller Foundation grant, 1984; Williams/Derwood Award, 1986. Living in Bennington, Vermont.

**Poetry**

*The Five-Fold Mesh,* 1938
*Wilderness Stair,* 1955
*The Enemy Joy: New and Selected Poems,* 1964
*Nowhere but Light: Poems, 1964–1969,* 1970
*The Double Witness: Poems, 1970–1976,* 1977
*Possessions: New and Selected Poems, 1938–1985,* 1986
*Graffiti, and Other Poems,* 1990
*The Poetry of Ben Belitt: An Anthology of Poems and Readings,* 1990
*This Scribe, My Hand: The Complete Poems of Ben Belitt,* 1998

**Other Writings:** essays (*Adam's Dream,* 1978; *The Forgèd Feature: Toward a Poetics of Uncertainty,* 1995), translations of Spanish poetry (*Poet in New York,* by Federico García Lorca, 1955; *A la pintura,* by Rafael Alberti, 1972; *Skystones,* by Pablo Neruda, 1981).

**Further Reading**

Belitt, Ben, "From the Bookless World: A Memoir," in *Contemporary Authors: Autobiography Series,* edited by Adele Sarkissian, Detroit, Michigan: Gale Research, 1985
Boyers, Robert, "To Confront Nullity: The Poetry of Ben Belitt," *Sewanee Review* 81 (1973)
Hutton, Joan, "Antipodal Man: An Interview with Ben Belitt," *Midway: A Journal of Discovery in the Arts and Sciences* 10, no. 3 (1970)
Kinzie, Mary, "A Servant's Cenotaph," *Salmagundi* 87 (1990)
Landis, Joan Hutton, "A 'Wild Severity': Towards a Reading of Ben Belitt," *Salmagundi* 22–23 (1973)
*Modern Poetry Studies* 7, no. 1 (1976) (special issue on Belitt)
Nemerov, Howard, "The Fascination of What's Difficult," in *Reflexions on Poetry and Poetics,* by Nemerov, New Brunswick, New Jersey: Rutgers University Press, 1972
*Salmagundi* 87 (1990) (special issue on Belitt entitled "The Poetry of Ben Belitt: An Anthology of Poems and Readings")
*Voyages* 1, no. 1 (1967) (special issue on Belitt)

# Stephen Vincent Benét 1898–1943

From 1928 with the publication of his verse epic *John Brown's Body* until his untimely passing in 1943, Stephen Vincent Benét was one of the most popular and beloved writers in the United States. The commercial success of his lyrical and dramatic history of the American Civil War was unprecedented and propelled Benét into the forefront of literary recognition, which he sustained with poetry, fiction, libretti, and radio scripts that tackled social issues such as the Great Depression, the rise of Fascism, and support for the Allied forces at the outset of World War II and then for the United States after Pearl Harbor. In addition, Benét's short story "The Devil and Daniel Webster" appeared in the *Saturday Evening Post* in 1937 and became an American legend. If Benét's good friend Archibald MacLeish could be described as an American Stoic, then Benét was an "American Visceral" who wore his heart on his pen.

Benét was born in Bethlehem, Pennsylvania, to Colonel James Walker and Frances Neill Benét. His parents were progressive, and his father was an expert in the appreciation of poetry. Stephen was the youngest of three children. His brother William and sister Laura also became poets and writers. Benét published his first book of verse, *Five Men and Pompey* (1915), at age 17, and it featured dramatic monologues by Roman figures. A penchant for the dramatic became a Benét standard. Benét attended Yale University and was recognized as a rising star by such future literary luminaries as Thornton Wilder (his Yale classmate and friend), Malcolm Cowley, John Peale Bishop, and F. Scott Fitzgerald. While at Yale, Benét published two more volumes of verse: *Young Adventure* (1918) and *Heavens and Earth* (1920). Both feature youthful exuberance and sonorously lyrical fluidity in a manner more 19th century than 20th. A strong influence on Benét's verse at this time was the poet Vachel Lindsay, whom Benét met twice at Yale. Lindsay was the first poet as performance artist, and his recitals were electrifying theatrical events.

With a master's degree earned from Yale in 1921, Benét ventured to Paris, where he met Rosemary Carr, who was as a journalist there for the *Chicago Tribune*. His courtship featured love poems that are cleverly playful. (In 1925, many of these were collected in *Tiger Joy*.) Stephen and Rosemary married in 1921, and she became his muse and moral compass. They would have three children, and their marriage was the great love story behind the rest of his life and work.

In New York City, Benét worked only as a writer. In 1922, he published the two long poems that marked the beginning of his poetic maturity. *The Ballad of William Sycamore* in *The New Republic* and *King David* in *The Nation* were a blend of style and substance that predicts the landmark epic still to come.

In the 1920s, Benét struggled to earn money as a writer. Although the poems in *Tiger Joy* (1925) received critical praise and comparisons to Thomas Hardy, Benét turned to fiction and drama for an income. In this regard, the poetic turning point for Benét was a Guggenheim fellowship earned in 1926, which meant that he would not have to worry about writing for an income. The Benéts returned to Paris, where the grant would stretch further. Benét spent the next two years writing *John Brown's Body*.

*John Brown's Body* (1928) was perhaps the first truly American verse epic and certainly the first of the 20th century. The 15,000 lines chronicle the five years of the Civil War with extended and well-defined portrayals of Brown, Lincoln, Lee, Davis, Grant, Jackson, and many others as well as fictional creations exemplifying composites of slaves, farmers, soldiers, and their families. While his epic has the classic structure of Homer and Virgil, the story, in all its Homeric detail, is unabashedly American. The book's release was highly anticipated. It made the front page of literary reviews alongside Aldous Huxley's novel *Point Counterpoint* and took the Pulitzer Prize for Poetry. *John Brown's Body* became a national bestseller and has never been out of print since. Benét's success encouraged contemporaries to try more poetic epics, novels in verse, and verse plays over the next 20 years, ranging from MacLeish's *Conquistador* (1932) to W.H. Auden's *The Age of Anxiety* (1947), also Pulitzer winners. Margaret Mitchell credited Benét's poem as the inspiration for *Gone with the Wind*.

Financial success was brief, as Benét lost all his income to the stock market crash. Once again he turned to prose to earn his way and became a master of the short story. He did not publish new verse again until collaborating with Rosemary on *A Book of Americans* (1933), a collection of children's poems about American themes and personas. In 1933, he became editor of the prestigious Yale Younger Poets series (his successor was Auden), and many of his choices became poets of international standing.

In 1936, Benét returned to adult verse with fury in *Burning City*. The Depression had motivated him to side with Franklin Roosevelt and against special interests. The poems, such as " Ode to Walt Whitman," are written in declamatory and very modern free verse. There are also early concerns about Fascism a year before the Spanish Civil War caught everyone's attention. Already respected and popular when *The Devil and Daniel Webster* appeared in 1937, Benét became an influential public figure and a writer for democracy. In 1940, the antifascist poem "Nightmare at Noon" was published in *Life* magazine and became a national sensation. Benét wrote radio plays that were heard by millions of Americans every week. Benét, only 44, died in March 1943 from a heart attack. *Western Star*, a planned verse epic about the settling of America, was not completed; nonetheless, the book-length opening sections were published posthumously and won Benét a second Pulitzer Prize in 1944.

Benét's work has been reprinted in anthologies regularly since 1943, and *John Brown's Body* ensures his continued place alongside the important American poets of the 20th century.

DAVID GARRETT IZZO

**Biography**

Born in Bethlehem, Pennsylvania, 22 July 1898. Attended Yale University, New Haven, Connecticut (Chairman, *Yale Literary Magazine*, 1918), 1915–18, 1919–20, A.B. 1919, M.A. 1920; the Sorbonne, Paris, 1920–21; worked for the State Department, Washington, D.C., 1918; worked for advertising agency, New York, 1919; lecturer and radio propagandist for the liberal cause, 1930s and early 1940s; editor, Yale Younger Poets series. Received Poetry Society of America Prize, 1921; Guggenheim fellowship, 1926; Pulitzer Prize, 1929, 1944; O. Henry Award, 1932, 1937, 1940; Shelley Memorial Award, 1933; American Academy Gold Medal, 1943; Member, 1929, and Vice President, National Institute of Arts and Letters. Died 13 March 1943.

**Poetry**
*Five Men and Pompey,* 1915
*Young Adventure,* 1918
*Heavens and Earth,* 1920
*The Ballad of William Sycamore, 1790–1880,* 1923
*King David,* 1923
*Tiger Joy,* 1925
*John Brown's Body,* 1928
*The Barefoot Saint,* 1929
*Ballads and Poems, 1915–1930,* 1931
*A Book of Americans* (with Rosemary Benét), 1933
*Burning City,* 1936
*The Ballad of the Duke's Mercy,* 1939
*Nightmare at Noon,* 1940
*Listen to the People: Independence Day 1941,* 1941
*Selected Works of Stephen Vincent Benét* (includes prose), 1942
*Western Star,* 1943
*The Last Circle: Stories and Poems,* 1946
*Selected Poetry and Prose,* edited by Basil Davenport, 1960

**Other Writings:** plays, radio plays, screenplays (*All That Money Can Buy* [with Dan Totheroh], 1941), novels, short stories (*O'Halloran's Luck and Other Short Stories,* 1944), nonfiction (*A Summons to the Free,* 1941); edited collections of literature (*Tamburlaine the Great,* by Christopher Marlowe [editor with Monty Woolley], 1919).

**Further Reading**
Fenton, Charles, *Stephen Vincent Benét: The Life and Times of an American Man of Letters, 1898–1943,* New Haven, Connecticut: Yale University Press, 1958
Izzo, David Garrett, "A Centenary Tribute," in *The Dictionary of Literary Biography Yearbook 1997,* Detroit, Michigan: Gale Research, 1998
Ludington, Townsend, "Introduction," in *Stephen Vincent Benét: The Devil and Daniel Webster, and Other Writings,* New York: Penguin, 1999
Stroud, Parry Edward, *Stephen Vincent Benét,* New York: Twayne, 1962

---

# Charles Bernstein 1950–

A seminal figure in the development and practice of Language poetry in the 1970s and 1980s, Charles Bernstein has emerged as a prominent and prolific poet of late-20th-century American poetics. As co-editor with Bruce Andrews of the influential small magazine called *L=A=N=G=U=A=G=E,* Bernstein helped shape the climate of a radical poetics that emerged in the early 1970s, centered in New York City and San Francisco. Along with other journals, such as *Hills, Tottels, Poetics Journal,* and *This,* the *L=A=N=G=U=A=G=E* magazine was a collection of statements on poetics, poems, theoretical ideas, and extracts from pertinent theorists that disseminated a broad range of literary and extraliterary ideas to like-minded practicing writers. Now with more than 20 books of poetry and three collections of essays published with such presses as Sun and Moon, Harvard University Press, and the University of Chicago Press, Bernstein is David Gray Professor of Poetry and Letters at the State University of New York at Buffalo, from where he has continued to make a significant impact on the development of contemporary poetry in the United States.

As with many of the Language poets, the issues of comprehension and representation figure large in Bernstein's work. His poetry edges tentatively toward sense, gesturing to an unease about the production of meaning, to the contract of reference in communication that somehow gets broken in the saying. He is interested in interruption and a poetics of constellation, a practice that he describes in his essay "Semblance" (1981) as "working at angles to the strong tidal pull of an unexpected sequence of a sentence—or by cutting off a sentence or a phrase midway and counting on the mind to complete where the poem goes off in another direction, giving two vectors at once—the anticipated projection underneath and the actual wording above." For example, his poetry substitutes syllables or letters to produce unexpectedly different signifiers in familiar phrasal constructions ("Would you do me the flavor of buying that sty?"), as in Bernstein's poem "Outrigger" in *The Sophist* (1987). The same impulse has also produced an investigation into alternative syntactical structures and their effect on meaning and opening up the links between temporality and language. Upsetting the rules of conventional grammar, Bernstein practices "scissoring / the syntax of language (that is, cutting / *against* expected breaks of the / grammatical phrase or unit of / breath" (*My Way,* 1999).

Elsewhere, Bernstein has shown a marked interest in the preoccupations of the "Objectivist" poetics of Louis Zukofsky, especially the interest in sound. Introducing a collection of "Language" writing in *The Paris Review,* Bernstein pointedly remarks on the characteristic attention given to the *sound* of words:

> Hints, then, of a writing that takes as its medium, or domain of intention, every *articulable* aspect of language. It's as if a new scanning of consciousness were possible by introduction of the *music* of its constituting. And by this means to make *audible* the thinking field: to get access to the lens (the mixed metaphor is again ideology) through which the world's meanings are formed into *audibilities.* ("Language Sampler," collected in Bernstein, *Content's Dream* [1986], italics added)

Bernstein continues, describing the writing as a "multimodal process," which while questioning the ideologies inherent in conventional syntax, simultaneously lays claim to

> a syntax—to put it indefensibly—of pure music, of absolute attention to the ordering of sound's syllables. . . . Not that this is "lyric" poetry, insofar as that term may assume a musical, or metric, *accompaniment* to the words: the music

> rather is built into the sequence of the words' tones, totally saturating the texts' sound. "Indefensibly," that is, because there really is no pure music any more than there is a pure language since any material practice becomes itself a mode. (*Content's Dream*)

Bernstein concludes his introduction by speaking about the music of language as a "resonating of the wordness of language" (*Content's Dream*). These remarks directly confront the trends in which language is increasingly being seen to be *unsound,* the mixed metaphor here informing the whole of Bernstein's irony.

Wittgenstein's philosophical investigations into language frequently and persistently return to the role of sound in language as meaning (or misunderstanding—i.e., not hearing). Deeply indebted to this philosopher, this is a factor that Bernstein is at pains to emphasize in his own work:

> In*hear*ing in a poetics of vision or reflection (as if to counter a visualist frame of reference in these terms) is a poetics of sound. Words returned to a sonorousness that does not require the validity of fixed images, of sight and in sight, nor deny its common roots with visibility. (*Content's Dream*)

There is an unequivocal break here with any secret desire for the primacy of the eye, or the object-oriented, reifying vision evident in earlier Modernist poetics. The multiplicity brought about by a return to the sonority of words is a mosaic not only of images but of the senses as well. Sight based on the eye/I is singular in its isolation of "reality," and by resorting to sight, perceptions are compartmentalized and hierarchized, and the indivisible individual rests on "other" divisions. The experiments with language by recent avant-garde writers reveal that resonances are dissonances, not harmonies. Yet these multiplicities are felt to be an enrichment rather than a disordered chaos in language:

> Polyvalences and polysyllables occurring overall throughout the poem create a music of the text, a music that has to do with the rhyming/comparing/vectoring of possible meanings, creating *chords* of the simultaneous vectors of the several interpretations of each poly-entendre, and with the combination of these chords with other chords, durationally, in the sequence of the writing, and simultaneously, in the overall structure. The overall "sound" of the work is actually more important to listen for than the linear prosodic sequences, since the relation of the "chords" reinforces the sound resonances and echoes creating an intense overall vibration that adds a dynamic of dimensional depth to the sound of any given linear movement. (*Content's Dream*)

Bernstein emphasizes the "music of the text," which occurs in the vectoring potential of words, setting up resonances through a matrix of semantic possibility. Hence the insistent emphasis on *hearing* that pervades his poetics: the basis for understanding as a matter of echoes, repercussions, and sounds that vibrate or resonate only at certain accidental moments. Bernstein perceives music as nodes of meaning in much the same sense as mordents, "tune being the variety of ways meaning congeals, not so much as a plotted act of creation but rather, retrospectively, as the accumulation of occurrences, occurrences being non-systematic formations, accidents in the literal sense" (*Content's Dream*). The string of chords that weaves the dynamic texture of the language exists in the movement, repetition, alteration, and improvisation of sounds.

Bernstein constantly emphasizes that language does not operate in an isolated, self-contained sphere but in an interactive social sphere. The fact that "language speaks" forces or prompts a response: indeed, the very understanding of words engages people in a hearing of sounds that are *culturally* induced. Thus, in his important verse essay "Artifice of Absorption," Bernstein draws a distinction between poetry that is "absorptive" ("rhapsodic, spellbinding, / mesmerizing, hypnotic, total, riveting, / enthralling") and poetry that is "impermeable" ("artifice, boredom, / exaggeration, attention scattering, distraction, digression, interruptive, transgressive") (*A Poetics,* 1992). In other words, Bernstein argues that poetry that is absorptive depends on realism, transparency, and continuity, whereas the anti-absorptive is characterized by the artificial, the opaque, and discontinuous. Rather than being seduced by a text of romantic affirmation, Bernstein uses radical formal experimentation and "opaque and nonabsorbable elements" (*A Poetics*) to force the reader into participating in the process of constituting the text's meaning. Thus, poems such as "eLecTrIc" in *Poetic Justice* (1979) or "Like DeCLAraTionS in a HymIE CEMetArY" in *The Sophist* use capital letters to interrupt and disrupt the textual line, producing an intensity and rhythmic energy in the process. On other occasions, the text is left deliberately open, inviting the reader to add to the text as a participating "author," as in many of the poems in *Controlling Interests* (1980). Elsewhere, Bernstein puts together a patchwork of different discourses, encouraging the reader to make any bridging connections or metaphorical analogies, as, for example, in this extract from "The Klupzy Girl":

> Sense of variety: panic. Like
> my eye takes over from the front
> yard, three pace. Idle gaze—years
> right down the window. Not clairvoyance,
> predictions, deciphering—enacting. Analytically,
> i.e., thoughtlessly. Begin to push and cue
> together. Or I originate out of this
> occurrence, stoop down, bend on. The
> Protest-ant's voice within, calling for
> this to be shepherded, for moment's
> expression's enthroning. Able to be
> alibied (contiguity of vacuity). Or
> do you think you can communicate
> telepathetically? Verena read the epistle
> with much deliberateness. If we are
> not to be phrasemongers, we must
> sit down and take the steps that will
> give these policies life. I fumbled clumsily
> with the others—the evocations, explanations,
> glossings of "reality" seemed like stretching
> it to cover ground rather than make
> or name or push something through. (*Islets/Irritations,*
> 1983)

This is a passage from a poem that uses found material, parodies of other literary genres, and an effacement of the writing self to interrogate the failures and weaknesses of realism as a literary mode. One can read the poem as embedding within itself a self-reflexive commentary on how to read. The "sense of variety" equated with "panic" is the result of a poetry that does not "fit" an accepted sameness, of a multiplicity of othernesses and differences upsetting received aesthetic forms. The poem rejects transparency and interpretive forecasts for the performative dimension, or "enacting." That is, the poem requires analytic reading but redefines this as "thoughtless" reading, or not using preformulated ideas and models. Rather than "shepherding" language as an expression of an epiphanic moment and intuiting the meaning "telepathetically," the poem obstructs this by disjunction, disconnection, and disfiguration, forcing deliberation. If we are to *read* a text rather then merely collude with prepared aesthetic significances and judgments, then we have to accept language as a series of duplicities and multiplicities rather than singularities and univocalities. The section finishes with a critique of the realist conception of language as merely a hypnotic veneer of words on the world that precludes a sincere investigative attempt to "name or push something through."

It is evident from "The Klupzy Girl" that the conventional expressivist self of romantic poetry has been erased and that the poem does not resort to the "I" as the final point of reference. The poem focuses principally on writing as a production of meanings, a process that seeks to engage the reader in the construction of the text rather than allowing words to be registered or heard passively. Bernstein's poetry continually asks one to read *writing* rather than *meanings,* interrogating the construction of the text as much as the words themselves. The "exchange" of meaning is an active process instead of a static paradigm of rules. It is to write with what Bernstein describes as "a recharged use of the multivalent referential vectors that any word has," showing reference to be not "a one-to-one relation to an 'object' but a perceptual dimension . . . [that] roams over the range of associations suggested by the word" (Andrews and Bernstein, editors, *The L=A=N=G=U=A=G=E Book,* 1984).

Bernstein's poetic strategy is often one of defamiliarization, as the opening lines of "The Klupzy Girl" indicate:

> Poetry is like a swoon, with this difference:
> it brings you to your senses. (*Islets/Irritations*)

This strategy of defamiliarization reorients language through the blockage of flow and exchange, thereby throwing a spanner in the works of semantic circulation, urging poetry as a practice of "anti-conformity": "I care most for poetry that disrupts business as usual, including literary business: I care most for poetry as dissent, including formal dissent; poetry that makes sounds possible to be heard that are not otherwise articulated" (*A Poetics*). Bernstein's allegiance is to a poetics that approaches otherness without subsuming it: "Poetry can, even if it doesn't, throw a wedge into this engineered process of social derealization: find a middle ground of care in particulars, in the truth of details and their constellations—provide a site for the construction of social and imaginative facts and configurations avoided or overlooked elsewhere" (*A Poetics*). Inevitably, this propels that poet more "outward, centrifugally, to the unknown and peripheral, than toward a constant centripetal regrouping and reshoring through official verse culture's enormously elastic and sophisticated mechanism of tokenization that targets, splits off, and decontextualizes; essentializing the mode of difference and incorporating the product (never the process) into its own cultural space" (*A Poetics*).

As Bernstein has said of his poetic practice, "I prefer the wrong way—anything better than the well-wrought epiphany of predictable measure—for at least the cracks and flaws and awkwardnesses show signs of real life" (*A Poetics*). That errant way produces a sort of glimpse of another social structure, another sexual ideology, another life world, through the current language of the day. To this degree, Bernstein's poetry poses an alternative to a coercive moral absolutism on the one hand and to an inchoate postmodernist relativism on the other.

TIM WOODS

*See also* Language Poetry

**Biography**

Born in New York City, 4 April 1950. Attended Harvard University, Cambridge, Massachusetts, 1968–72, A.B. in philosophy 1972 (Phi Beta Kappa); Simon Fraser University, Burnaby, British Columbia (King fellow), 1973–74; writer on medical and health topics; Visiting Lecturer, University of Auckland, 1986, and University of California, San Diego, 1987; Visiting Professor, Queens College, City University of New York, 1988; faculty member and series coordinator, Wolfson Center for National Affairs, New School for Social Research, New York, 1988; Lecturer in Creative Writing Program, Princeton University, New Jersey, 1989 and 1990; Visiting Butler Chair Professor, 1989, and since 1990 David Gray Professor of Poetry and Letters, State University of New York, Buffalo; editor, with Bruce Andrews, *L=A=N=G=U=A=G=E,* New York, 1978–81, and of poetry anthologies for *Paris Review,* 1982, and *Boundary 2,* 1987. Received National Endowment for the Arts fellowship, 1980; Guggenheim fellowship, 1985; University of Auckland Foundation fellowship, 1986; New York Foundation for the Arts fellowship, 1990. Living in New York City.

**Poetry**

*Asylums,* 1975
*Parsing,* 1976
*Shade,* 1978
*Poetic Justice,* 1979
*Senses of Responsibility,* 1979
*Legend* (with others), 1980
*Controlling Interests,* 1980
*Disfrutes,* 1981
*The Occurrence of Tune* (photographs by Susan Bee Laufer), 1981
*Stigma,* 1981
*Islets/Irritations,* 1983
*Resistance,* 1983
*Amblyopia,* 1985
*Veil,* 1987
*The Sophist,* 1987
*Four Poems,* 1988
*The Nude Formalism,* 1989
*The Lives of the Toll Takers,* 1990
*Rough Trades,* 1990
*The Absent Father in Dumbo,* 1990
*Dark City,* 1994

*Log Rhythms,* 1998
*My Way: Speeches and Poems,* 1999
*Republics of Reality: Poems, 1975–1995,* 2000

**Other Writings:** essays (*A Poetics,* 1992), translations of French literature.

**Further Reading**

Glazier, Loss Pequeño, "An Autobiographical Interview with Charles Bernstein," *Boundary 2* 23, no. 3 (Fall 1996)
Lazer, Hank, "Charles Bernstein's Dark City: Polis, Policy, and the Policing of Poetry," *American Poetry Review* 24, no. 5 (September–October 1995)
Nathanson, Tenney, "Collage and Pulverization in Contemporary American Poetry: Charles Bernstein's *Controlling Interests,*" *Contemporary Literature* 33, no. 2 (Summer 1992)
Naylor, Paul, "(Mis)Characterizing Charlie: Language and the Self in the Poetry and Poetics of Charles Bernstein," *Sagetrieb* 14, no. 3 (Winter 1995)

---

## Ted Berrigan 1934–83

In 25 years of writing, Ted Berrigan created a poetry that melded intelligence, emotion, and wit in unexpected ways, a poetry of what he calls in Sonnet LIII "baffling combustions." Berrigan's poetry can be at once dazzlingly opaque and utterly clear, full of dense verbal collage and unashamed sentiment, blatantly appropriative yet singularly original. Although typically identified as a poet of the New York School, Berrigan also pronounced himself "a late beatnik," and his work indeed encompasses multiple possibilities in the New American Poetry, veering from painterly abstraction to the "I do this I do that" mode of Frank O'Hara to expansive autobiographical statements of great pathos. His sense of poetic form is also surprising in its variety: while a poem such as "Tambourine Life" suggests the open-field poetics of Black Mountain, with the poem taking shape in the act of composition, its form an extension of its content, Berrigan was also a profoundly radical formalist who took on the unlikely project of reanimating the sonnet and who suggested that it may also be true that content is an extension of form.

It was Berrigan's radical formalism that established him as a poet in *The Sonnets* (1964), first published by his own "C" Press. While Berrigan's avowed intention to become "big" by means of a sonnet sequence might seem naive in retrospect, his approach to sonnet form drew on important currents in modern and postmodern art and writing. As he explained in a 1978 interview, "My technical achievement in *The Sonnets* was to conceive the sonnet as fourteen units of one line each," and he often described the poems in terms of blocks and bricks, the poet building the poem unit by unit. Berrigan's investigation of the possibilities of discontinuous form was influenced by the fractured surfaces of Cubist collage, the line-by-line shifts of Guillaume Apollinaire's poem "Lundi Rue Christine" (a Berrigan favorite), the cut-up texts of William Burroughs, the chance operations of John Cage, and the use of found materials in writing and visual art, particularly in John Ashbery's *The Tennis Court Oath* (1962) and the work of Marcel Duchamp. *The Sonnets* in fact began with found materials, as Berrigan made the first poems of what became the sequence by going through his own failed poems and choosing lines intuitively to make oblique, suggestive collages. The sequence also freely appropriates from Ashbery, O'Hara, Rilke, Rimbaud, and Shakespeare, among others, with lines quoted, translated, or transliterated to add distinctive tones. Much of the art of *The Sonnets,* however, lies in Berrigan's own tonal brilliance, particularly his use of repetition to make bits of language into resonant motifs: "feminine marvelous and tough," "my dream a white tree," "Dear Chris, hello."

What distinguishes *The Sonnets* from much postmodern writing is an insistence on the presence of an individual imagination and a feeling, perceiving self within the text. As Alice Notley (1999) observes, "*The Sonnets* is not, as is sometimes stated, concerned with the rejection of the 'psychological I.'" Berrigan often spoke of "I" as a character within his poems: here an "I" records events and complications among itself, friends, and lovers, sometimes in individual lines that become parts of an overall texture, sometimes in entire poems, as in Sonnet XXXVI, which seems both homage to and parody of Frank O'Hara. *The Sonnets* ends with a remarkable claim of poetic selfhood: Sonnet LXXXVIII, "A Final Sonnet," reprises motifs from the sequence, moves on to borrow (and relineate) Prospero's renunciation of magic in *The Tempest,* and ends in a moment of direct address, "Dear Chris, hello," suggesting that even in the absence of magic and other voices, the poet is able to continue speaking.

In the years following *The Sonnets,* Berrigan published with numerous small poet-run presses, and he became an inspiring figure amid the writing community associated with the Poetry Project at St. Mark's Church on Manhattan's Lower East Side. He made numerous collaborative works, most notably with artists Joe Brainard and George Schneeman and poet Ron Padgett. *Bean Spasms* (1967), a volume whose title suggests its general atmosphere of intellectual high jinks, collects many Berrigan-Padgett collaborations. In the late 1960s and 1970s, Berrigan's own poetry came to dwell increasingly on his daily life circumstances. His poems pay tribute to friends and lovers and heroes ("People Who Died"), record difficulties with ill health and poverty ("Today's News"), and find their scenes in different places on the visiting-professor circuit ("Today in Ann Arbor"). "Tambourine Life" and "Things to Do in Providence" are among Berrigan's finest poems of dailiness, with moments of hilarity and unexpected sadness. Poems such as "Soviet Souvenir" and "Peking" from the sequence "Easter Monday" return to the dense collages of *The Sonnets.* Berrigan's work in the 1970s also includes autobiographical statements, such as "Red Shift," whose fierce, eloquent claims to an abiding presence in the world are all the more moving in light of the poet's ill health: "Alone & crowded, unhappy fate, nevertheless / I slip softly into the air / The world's furious song flows through my costume."

In his final years, Berrigan discovered a new possibility for a radically formalist poetry: the poems of his final writing project, *500 American Postcards,* were handwritten on postcards. Berrigan regarded the postcard as a form, a fixed space determining (along with the variable of handwriting) the size of the poem. The resulting poems range from very brief postcard-like messages ("Angst" and "Salutation") to short poems of opaque lyrical beauty ("Paris, Frances" and "Buenos Aires"). A selection of poems from this project was published after Berrigan's death as *A Certain Slant of Sunlight* (1988). The title poem is one of Berrigan's finest, an ekphrasis of a photograph, and a poignant recollection of his mother and his childhood.

In the years since his death, interest in Berrigan's poetry has grown tremendously. Much of his work has come back into print, together with new volumes of interviews and talks, and Berrigan has been the subject of memoirs, critical essays, a volume of homage, and an annotated checklist of publications. As the poet Anne Waldman has said, "Ted is back" (Fischer, 1998). In his formal and tonal innovations, in his emotional range and humor, Ted Berrigan remains a unique presence in postmodern American poetry.

MICHAEL LEDDY

*See also* New York School

**Biography**

Born in Providence, Rhode Island, 15 November 1934. Attended University of Tulsa, Oklahoma, B.A. 1959, M.A. 1962; served in United States Army, 1954–57; founded "C" Press and "C" magazine, 1963; teacher, St. Mark's Poetry Project, New York City, 1966–67; visiting lecturer, Writers' Workshop, University of Iowa, Iowa City, 1968–69; teacher, University of Michigan, Ann Arbor, 1969, Yale University, New Haven, Connecticut, 1970, State University of New York at Buffalo, 1970, Essex University, England, 1973–74, Stevens Technical Institute, Hoboken, New Jersey, 1980, and Naropa Institute (now University), Boulder, Colorado, 1970s and 1980s; poet-in-residence, Northeastern Illinois University, Chicago, 1969–76, and City College of the City University of New York, 1982; member, board of advisors, St. Mark's Poetry Project. Received Poetry Foundation Award, 1964. Died in New York City, 4 July 1983.

**Poetry**

*A Lily for My Love: 13 Poems,* 1959
*The Sonnets,* 1964; revised editions, 1967, 1982, 2000
*Bean Spasms* (with Ron Padgett), 1967
*Living with Chris,* 1968
*Many Happy Returns,* 1969
*Doubletalk* (with Anselm Hollo), 1969
*In the Early Morning Rain,* 1970
*Memorial Day* (with Anne Waldman), 1971
*The Drunken Boat,* 1974
*A Feeling for Leaving,* 1975
*Red Wagon,* 1976
*Nothing for You,* 1977
*Train Ride,* 1978
*Carrying a Torch,* 1980
*So Going around Cities: New and Selected Poems, 1958–1979,* 1980
*In a Blue River,* 1981
*The Morning Line,* 1982
*A Certain Slant of Sunlight,* 1988
*Selected Poems,* 1994
*Great Stories of the Chair,* 1998

**Other Writings:** novel (*Clear the Range,* 1977), plays (*Seventeen* [with Ron Padgett], 1964), memoir (*Back in Boston Again* [with Tom Clark and Ron Padgett], 1972), talks and interviews (*Talking in Tranquility: Interviews with Ted Berrigan,* 1991; *On the Level Everyday: Selected Talks on Poetry and the Art of Living,* 1997).

**Further Reading**

Bernstein, Charles, "Writing Against the Body," in *Content's Dream: Essays, 1975–1984,* Los Angeles: Sun and Moon Press, 1986
Clark, Tom, *Late Returns: A Memoir of Ted Berrigan,* Bolinas, California: Tombouctou, 1985
Fischer, Aaron, *Ted Berrigan: An Annotated Checklist,* New York: Granary, 1998
Foster, Edward, *Code of the West: A Memoir of Ted Berrigan,* Boulder, Colorado: Rodent Press, 1994
Lewis, Joel, "'Everything Turns into Writing': The Sonnets of Ted Berrigan," *Transfer* 2, no. 1 (1988/89)
Notley, Alice, "A Certain Slant of Sunlight," *American Poetry Review* 28, no. 2 (1999)
Padgett, Ron, *Ted: A Personal Memoir of Ted Berrigan,* Great Barrington, Massachusetts: The Figures, 1993
Rifkin, Libbie, "'Worrying about Making It': Ted Berrigan's Social Poetics," *Contemporary Literature* 38, no. 4 (1997)
Selinger, Eric, "That Awkward Grace," *Parnassus* 21, nos. 1–2 (1996)
Waldman, Anne, editor, *Nice to See You: Homage to Ted Berrigan,* Minneapolis, Minnesota: Coffee House Press, 1988

# Wendell Berry 1934–

An accomplished essayist, fiction writer, and poet since the mid-1950s, Wendell Berry has explored one central theme in virtually all his writing, regardless of the genre: the interconnectedness of nature and culture, particularly as manifested in agriculture. Berry's poetry has attracted a loyal readership since the late 1960s and has garnered critical attention since the early 1970s. The emergence of ecocriticism in the 1990s strengthened Berry's literary standing. Although a friend of several Beat writers, Berry rejected the Beat movement's emphasis on stylistic experimentation, intellectual esotericism, and individualism. Some critics have compared Berry's poetry to that of Gary Snyder, who has similarly championed community and who has likewise explored the interrelationship between humans and the natural world. Berry's worldview, however, has remained for the most part solidly grounded in Western cultural tradition; he has not embraced Eastern philosophies as fully as Snyder.

Wendell Erdman Berry was born in Henry County, Kentucky, to parents who both hailed from longtime Henry County farm families. His father, an attorney and advocate for small-scale farming, left a promising political career in Washington, D.C., in the 1920s to return to his native county. This foreshadowed Wendell Berry's own mid-1960s decision to settle in Henry County rather than in the urban centers of art, academia, and political influence. The Depression-era environment in which Berry was raised, a landscape of self-sufficient family farms bordered by heavily forested river valleys, resembled pioneer days; at an early age he learned to value traditional rural community life. Much of his work is set in the Kentucky countryside between the World Wars, and his nonfiction frequently reflects upon the predicament of agricultural folkways and traditional rural wisdom in the postwar prosperity.

Initially an undisciplined student who preferred outdoor activities over formal education, Berry matured rapidly as a writer, first winning collegiate literary contests, then placing poems and short stories in local and national publications, and finally receiving a Wallace Stegner fellowship at Stanford University (1958–59). Shortly thereafter Berry won a Guggenheim Foundation fellowship (1961–62) and *Poetry* magazine's Vachel Lindsay Prize (1962). His first published book, *November Twenty-Six, Nineteen Hundred Sixty-Three* (1964), consisted of just one poem, an elegy for recently slain President John F. Kennedy. Most of the poems in Berry's breakthrough volume, *The Broken Ground* (1964), evoke the universality of rural life and reveal the stylistic traits found in much of his early poetry: commonplace and occasionally archaic language; generalized, often overtly symbolic nature imagery; and a quietly prophetic, wizened persona. *Openings* (1968) combines protest poems such as "Against the War in Vietnam" with poems that reflect his deepening interest in local history, such as "My Great-Grandfather's Slaves." That volume also includes Berry's widely anthologized lyric poem "The Peace of Wild Things," in which the poet lauds the spiritual blessings possible for receptive humans in the natural world. *Findings* (1969) is comprised of three long poems that explore the psychological role of old houses—and by metaphorical extension, human history—in the lives of their occupants. Berry writes,

> Love has visualized a house,
> and out of its expenditure
> fleshed the design
> at this cross ways
> of consciousness and time. . . .

The focal point of *Farming: A Hand Book* (1970) is a group of related poems narrated by Berry's "Mad Farmer" persona, celebrating the organic and often radical vision of farmers. *The Country of Marriage* (1973) concerns relationships. Some of that volume's poems are overtly sentimental; for instance, "Kentucky River Junction," dedicated to author Ken Kesey, typifies Berry's career-long penchant for paying tribute to his personal friendships publicly via published poems. Two of that volume's other poems, "At a Country Funeral" and the title poem (an ode to the institution of marriage), convey the complexity of human relationships without sentimentality. The descriptive and didactic poems in *Clearing* (1977) are artfully constructed meditations on the meaning of place and the past:

> All the lives this place
> has had, I have. I eat
> my history day by day.

*A Part* (1980) addresses a wide range of themes, including love, relationships, history, farming, and politics. Two poems, acknowledging Berry's growing literary reputation, admonish followers and imitators to "stay home." *The Wheel* (1982) illuminates the Hindu/Buddhist concept of the mandala (the Wheel of Life) by chronicling in various poems significant stages of human life (birth, coming of age, marriage, middle years of hard work and responsibility, old age, and death). *Collected Poems, 1957–1982* (1985) gathers all the poems written through 1982 that Berry claimed he would "care to have reread."

By the 1980s Berry was demonstrating a heightened commitment to poetic form. Whereas much of his early poetry could be characterized as *vers libre*, Berry's poems in *Sabbaths* (1987), *Sabbaths, 1987–1990* (1992), and *A Timbered Choir: The Sabbath Poems, 1979–1997* (1998) employ traditional forms, regularly metered lines, and rhyme. Thematically, the "Sabbaths" volumes constitute Berry's sustained effort to reconcile perceived polarities in Western thought (heaven versus earth, humanity versus the natural world, Christian theology versus modern science).

In *Entries* (1994), his principal volume of new poetry published during the 1990s, Berry reinterprets familiar themes (death, love, relationships, nature, spirituality, and work) while also revealing a new inclination on his part toward Orientalism ("Noguchi Fountain") and Confessionalism ("To My Mother"). *The Selected Poetry of Wendell Berry* (1998) offers an overview of his life's work in poetry through the late 1990s. In 1994 Berry received the prestigious T.S. Eliot Award for Creative Writing.

TED OLSON

**Biography**

Born in Henry County, Kentucky, 5 August 1934. Attended the University of Kentucky, Lexington, A.B. 1956, M.A. 1957; Stanford University, California (Stegner Fellow), 1958–59; taught at Stanford University, 1959–60, and New York University; member of the English Department, University of Kentucky, 1964–77, and 1987–94; starting in 1977 staff member, Rodale Press, Emmaus, Pennsylvania. Received Guggenheim fellowship, 1961; Vachel Lindsay Prize, 1962; Rockefeller fellowship, 1965; Bess Hokin Prize (*Poetry*, Chicago), 1967; National Endowment for the Arts grant, 1969; T.S. Eliot Award for Creative Writing, 1994; Aiken Taylor Award, 1995. Living in Port Royal, Kentucky.

**Poetry**

*November Twenty-Six, Nineteen Hundred Sixty-Three*, 1964
*The Broken Ground*, 1964
*Openings*, 1968
*Findings*, 1969
*Farming: A Hand Book*, 1970
*The Country of Marriage*, 1973
*Clearing*, 1977
*A Part*, 1980
*The Wheel*, 1982
*Collected Poems, 1957–1982*, 1985
*Sabbaths*, 1987
*Sabbaths, 1987–1990*, 1992
*Entries*, 1994
*The Selected Poems of Wendell Berry*, 1998
*A Timbered Choir: The Sabbath Poems, 1979–1997*, 1998

**Selected Criticism**

*Standing by Words*, 1983

**Other Writings:** short stories, novels, essays, biography (*Harlan Hubbard: Life and Work*, 1990).

**Further Reading**

Angyal, Andrew J., *Wendell Berry*, New York: Twayne, 1995
Decker, William, "'Practice Resurrection': The Poesis of Wendell Berry," *North Dakota Quarterly* 55, no. 4 (Fall 1987)
Fields, Kenneth, "The Hunter's Trail: Poems by Wendell Berry," *Iowa Review* 1 (Winter 1970)
Hass, Robert, "Wendell Berry: Finding the Land," *Modern Poetry Studies* 2 (1971)
Merchant, Paul, editor, *Wendell Berry*, Lewiston, Idaho: Confluence Press, 1991
Murphy, Patrick D., "Two Different Paths in the Quest for Place: Gary Snyder and Wendell Berry," *American Poetry* 2, no. 1 (Fall 1984)
Scigaj, Leonard M., "The Long Hunter's Vision: Wendell Berry," in *Sustainable Poetry: Four American Ecopoets*, by Scigaj, Lexington: University Press of Kentucky, 1999
Triggs, Jeffrey Alan, "Moving the Dark to Wholeness: The Elegies of Wendell Berry," *Literary Review* 31, no. 3 (Spring 1988)
Waage, Frederick O., "Wendell Berry's History," *Contemporary Poetry* 3, no. 3 (1978)

---

## John Berryman 1914–72

"I am a half-closed book," John Berryman wrote in "Dream Song 159," reflecting on the complicated relationship between life and art that lies at the center of much of his writing. With large sections of his work dominated by the themes of dispossession and loss, absence and betrayal, and survival and recovery, Berryman's writing is often difficult to separate from a disturbing autobiographical impulse and, indeed, from the myths that have surrounded him since, if not long before, his death by suicide at the age of 57 in 1972. This has meant that Berryman's claim that "I am not writing an autobiography-in-verse, my friends" from the poem "Message" (*Love and Fame*, 1970) has seldom been taken very seriously by his critics. Berryman was a contemporary and acquaintance of other middle-generation or Confessional poets, including Robert Lowell, Randall Jarrell, Delmore Schwartz, and Theodore Roethke, and Berryman scholars have rarely disputed the assumptions that have allowed this group of writers to be represented as America's midcentury *poètes maudits*.

A poet frequently obsessed with nomenclature and naming in his work, Berryman was born John Allyn Smith on 25 October 1914 in McAlester, Oklahoma. In the early 1920s, his family moved from Oklahoma, finally settling in 1925 in Tampa, Florida, where a year later the poet's father would die in mysterious circumstances (Giroux, 1996). Ten weeks later, Berryman's mother married John Angus McAlpin Berryman, and the family moved to Jackson Heights, New York City; it was at this time that he became John Allyn McAlpin Berryman, although his name was not legally changed until 1936. Berryman entered Columbia College in 1932, where he became acquainted with his future publisher, Robert Giroux, and the writers Thomas Merton and E.M. Halliday. Under the patronage and encouragement of Mark Van Doren, Berryman excelled at Columbia and published his first poems and reviews in *The Columbia Review* (then edited by Giroux) in 1935. In 1936, he had his first publication in a national magazine when "Notes on E.A. Robinson" was published in *The Nation*. In the same year, after graduating Phi Beta Kappa with an English major and a philosophy minor, Berryman was awarded a Euretta J. Kellett scholarship to study for two years at Clare College, Cambridge.

In many respects, Berryman's time at Cambridge was a period of passionate apprenticeship when, as he later admitted, he wished not only to resemble but also "to be" W.B. Yeats (*The Freedom of the Poet*, 1976). It was hardly surprising, then, that when Berryman's poems appeared alongside those of Mary Bernard, Randall Jarrell, W.R. Moses, and Marion O'Donnell in *Five Young American Poets* (1940) they were criticized for their obsessive use of Yeatsian imagery and tone, as is evident in such pieces as "Meditation," "The Curse," and "Ceremony and Vision."

Nevertheless, Berryman's time at Cambridge afforded him valuable introductions to the London literary world and to the work of writers such as Dylan Thomas, Louis MacNeice, and W.H. Auden, with whom he would develop an important intertextual dialogue in his own early work. Significant to note also is the fact that while at Cambridge, Berryman became the first American scholar to win the prestigious Oldham Shakespeare Prize, an early acknowledgment of his later contribution to Shakespeare scholarship. Berryman recalled many of the experiences and personalities of his two-year stint at Cambridge in the first three sections of his 1970 collection *Love and Fame.* In the intervening 30 years, however, between his return to the United States in 1938 and the publication of his major work, *The Dream Songs,* in 1969, Berryman moved impressively away from the overbearing Yeatsian tenor of his early efforts, writing works of radical thematic originality and rare technical brilliance, expanding our idea of the modern long poem while simultaneously examining and evaluating the nature and expression of personal and national origins and limits in poetry.

In the year of his return to the United States from England, Berryman published poems in *The Southern Review,* then edited by Cleanth Brooks and Robert Penn Warren. As part-time poetry editor of *The Nation* in 1939 and 1940, he befriended the poet Delmore Schwartz, to whose "sacred memory" he would later dedicate the last four books of *The Dream Songs,* published as *His Toy, His Dream, His Rest* in 1968. Throughout the 1940s, in a decade he once termed "the decade of survival," Berryman taught at Wayne State, Harvard, and Princeton Universities, although he was also unemployed for long periods during this time. Classified 4-F for the draft because of poor eyesight and a diagnosis of petit mal, Berryman's first individual collection, the New Directions pamphlet *Poems,* was published in 1942, the same year he married Eileen Mulligan (later Eileen Simpson), novelist and author of the important memoir *Poets in Their Youth* (1982). Criticism of his early work, however, instilled in Berryman a deep desire to move away from his earlier influences. Signs of his success in achieving a new style were evident in some of the poems of his first major collection, *The Dispossessed,* which was published in 1948. Nevertheless, although *The Dispossessed* contained important and original pieces, such as "Winter Landscape," "The Ball Poem," and "Desire Is a World by Night," Berryman's work was still clearly affected by the metrical and imagistic examples of his early masters, and only a handful of poems (the nine songs of the "The Nervous Songs" sequence being the most significant) achieved true originality of style and tone. Those few poems, as Randall Jarrell wrote at the time of the book's publication, signaled the beginning of an important change of direction in the development of Berryman's early work, a change that Jarrell (for one) looked forward to "with real curiosity and pleasure" (see Jarrell, *Kipling, Auden and Co.,* 1980).

No one could have foreseen what Berryman was in fact already working on for over a year when *The Dispossessed* was published in 1948. *The Dispossessed* had shown Berryman to be a serious and able verbal technician, a master of poetic diction and form in the lyric voice and mode. In 1947 and 1948, however, Berryman began work on two projects that would help establish him as a major original poet of his time. *Berryman's Sonnets,* or *Sonnets to Chris,* is a sequence of 117 sonnets that Berryman began composing in 1947; although it was not published until 1967, this sequence may be read retrospectively as a clear indication of the advent of Berryman's unique voice in the late 1940s. More important, however, is the example of *Homage to Mistress Bradstreet,* which Berryman began writing in 1948 and, when it was first published in *The Partisan Review* in 1953, was hailed by Edmund Wilson as "the most distinguished long poem by an American since *The Waste Land.*" When *Homage to Mistress Bradstreet* was finally published in book form in 1956, Wilson's praise was repeated by many of America's finest and most respected contemporary literary critics, from Conrad Aiken to Robert Fitzgerald. In the context of the trajectory of Berryman's career, *Homage to Mistress Bradstreet* marks his relatively late discovery of an individual style. With *Homage,* however, Berryman made a unique contribution to the development of American poetry in the 20th century. The poem's importance lies not only in Berryman's masterful use of syntax and voice and in his brilliant handling of the long poem form; it also heralded a radical and imaginative reappraisal of the entire American poetic tradition, interrogating the issue of national origins by presenting the figure of the 17th-century Puritan poet Anne Bradstreet as a peculiar (and precarious) founding mother, with whose phantom Berryman charts a difficult but passionate affair in the course of the poem.

In 1955, encouraged by the universally positive reception given to *Homage to Mistress Bradstreet,* Berryman began work on a few stanzas that marked the tentative beginning of the long poem that would occupy much of his thought over the next decade and a half. Arising, in all probability, out of a manuscript of unpublished dream analysis that he had given the title *St. Pancras Braser,* but inspired also by the complex psychoanalytical work that formed the centerpiece of his critical biography of Stephen Crane published in 1950, *The Dream Songs* would complete the task that Berryman had begun with *Homage to Mistress Bradstreet* and permanently alter our understanding of the nature and limits of the American long poem. At once seductively playful and intellectually challenging in its range of social, cultural, political, and philosophical references and allusions, *The Dream Songs* has nevertheless been surprisingly slow in inspiring the kind of serious theoretical engagement that has marked much contemporary literary study. Preferring instead to read *The Dream Songs* in terms of the development of Confessional poetry, much analysis has failed to consider the inadequacy of certain interpretive labels in themselves and the necessarily reductive readings they encourage. Future Berryman criticism will surely seek to move analysis of his work beyond the ostensibly biographical focus of Confessional analysis and explore some of the deeper issues that *The Dream Songs* addresses, issues concerning the relationship between self and society, race and history, the ethics and politics of literary production, and the borders and origins of American postmodernism.

Throughout the 1950s and 1960s, Berryman was admitted to the hospital for alcoholism on numerous occasions. Indeed, from 1959 until the end of his life, he was hospitalized at least once a year. Through the break-up of his first and second marriages (in 1953 he became separated from Eileen Mulligan and in 1956 married Ann Levine, from whom he was divorced in 1959), Berryman nevertheless remained active and creative throughout the last and most difficult decade of his life. His success in that final decade was in part related to the dedication of his third wife, Kate Donahue, whom he married in 1961 and with whom he set up house in Minneapolis in 1964. In 1966, Berryman spent an important year living in Dublin, where he attempted to finish *The Dream*

*Songs* and oversaw the publication of a collection of *Short Poems* (which included the 1958 chapbook *His Thought Made Pockets and the Plane Buckt* and the significant elegy on the death of John F. Kennedy, "Formal Elegy") and, 20 years after their composition, *Berryman's Sonnets.* In 1969, Berryman was awarded the National Book Award and the Bollingen Prize for *His Toy, His Dream, His Rest,* the final collection (the last four books) of *The Dream Songs;* he was also made a Regents' Professor of Humanities at the University of Minnesota in the same year.

*Love and Fame,* first published in 1970, was the last of Berryman's books published during his lifetime. It was also the book that, in a sense, revealed the poet's disillusionment with the attention and fame that the success of *The Dream Songs,* in particular, had brought him. The retrospective structure of the first three sections of *Love and Fame* exposes a figure intent on refiguring his past as part of a movement toward spiritual illumination and transcendence. The surface autobiographical focus of the book, however, yields to a deeper allegorical plane of meaning where Berryman suggests that modern man is in a state of spiritual and ethical crisis. This is most evident in poems such as "Have a Genuine American Horror-&-Mist on the Rocks" and "To a Woman," but it is also present in the sequence "Eleven Addresses to the Lord," which ends the book, where the poet cries out for a god of rescue. Such divine intervention, however, never came for Berryman, and on the morning of 7 January 1972 he leapt to his death from the Washington Avenue Bridge over the Mississippi River in Minneapolis.

Berryman's posthumous works have been many and varied. *Delusions, Etc.,* published in the year of Berryman's death, is a book of poems that, although very uneven, contains many important pieces, such as his elegies for Dylan Thomas and Georg Trakl, and *Opus Dei,* the nine-part "layman's winter mockup" that begins the book. The latter piece, when considered alongside "Eleven Addresses to the Lord" from *Love and Fame,* confirms Berryman's position as one of the most important religious poets of the 20th century. In 1973, *Recovery,* an unfinished novel that deals in painful detail with Berryman's treatment for alcoholism and his involvement with Alcoholics Anonymous, was published with an introduction by Saul Bellow. A collection of prose, *The Freedom of the Poet* (which includes the important interview-essay "One Answer to a Question: Changes" and the short story "The Imaginary Jew"), was published in 1976. *Henry's Fate, and Other Poems (1967–1972),* a collection of some of the Dream Songs that Berryman had culled from the earlier work, was published in 1977. Berryman's impressive contribution to Shakespeare scholarship was published as *Berryman's Shakespeare* in 1999 and was enthusiastically welcomed by Shakespeare scholar Anne Barton in the *New York Review of Books* (23 November 1999) and by Hugh Kenner in the *Times Literary Supplement* (17 September 1999). Considering Berryman's posthumous publication profile, one cannot help but feel that, had he not met the tragic end he did, he would almost certainly have grown into the same late brilliance as his esteemed precursor, W.B. Yeats.

Berryman's career as a poet and scholar, like Yeats' in some respects, vacillated between periods of suffering and success, frequently misperceived personal failure, and sometimes overwhelming public fame. Regarded by Donald Davie (1976) as "not only one of the most gifted and intelligent Americans of his time, but also one of the most honorable and responsible," Berryman may finally be read as a writer less concerned with the details of his private life and more with the changing climate of American cultural life during his relatively brief but highly productive career. Contrary to the stubbornly dominant critical view that Berryman was principally a Confessional poet, a label against which he railed "with rage and contempt" in a *Paris Review* interview toward the end of his life (reprinted in Thomas, 1988), recent studies have suggested that his work may be read as a significant register of American cultural feeling in the decades following World War II, poems that probe the workings of the inner mental and emotional life while simultaneously gauging the contemporary social weather.

PHILIP COLEMAN

*See also* Confessional Poetry

**Biography**

Born John Allyn Smith in McAlester, Oklahoma, 25 October 1914. Attended Columbia College, New York (Rensselaer Prize, 1935), 1932–36, A.B. 1936 (Phi Beta Kappa); Clare College, Cambridge (Kellett fellow, 1936–37, Oldham Shakespeare scholar, 1937), 1937–38, B.A. 1938; Instructor in English, Wayne State University, Detroit, Michigan, 1939–40, and Harvard University, Cambridge, Massachusetts, 1940–43; Instructor in English, 1943, Associate in Creative Writing, 1946–47, Resident Fellow, 1948–49, and Hodder Fellow, 1950–51, Princeton University, Princeton, New Jersey; Lecturer in English, University of Washington, Seattle, 1950; Elliston Professor of Poetry, University of Cincinnati, 1952; creative writing teacher, University of Iowa, Iowa City, 1954; Assistant Professor, 1955–56, Associate Professor, 1957–62, Professor, 1962–72, and Regents' Professor of Humanities, 1969–72, University of Minnesota, Minneapolis; United States Information Service Lecturer, India, 1957; Visiting Professor, University of California, Berkeley, 1960, and Brown University, Providence, Rhode Island, 1962–63; poetry editor, *The Nation,* 1939. Received Rockefeller fellowship, 1944–46, 1956; Shelley Memorial Award, 1949; Levinson Prize (*Poetry,* Chicago), 1950; Guggenheim fellowship, 1952, 1966; Harriet Monroe Award, 1957; Brandeis University Creative Arts Award, 1959; Ingram Merrill Foundation grant, 1964; Loines Award, 1964; Pulitzer Prize, 1965; Academy of American Poets fellowship, 1967; National Endowment for the Arts grant, 1967, and senior fellowship, 1971; Bollingen Prize, 1969; National Book Award, 1969; honorary Litt.D., Drake University, Des Moines, Iowa, 1971; member, American Academy, American Academy of Arts and Sciences, and Academy of American Poets; Chancellor, Academy of American Poets, 1968. Died in Minneapolis, Minnesota, 7 January 1972.

**Poetry**

*Five Young American Poets* (with others), 1940
*Poems,* 1942
*The Dispossessed,* 1948
*Homage to Mistress Bradstreet,* 1956
*Homage to Mistress Bradstreet, and Other Poems,* 1959
*77 Dream Songs,* 1964
*Berryman's Sonnets,* 1967
*Short Poems,* 1967
*His Toy, His Dream, His Rest: 308 Dream Songs,* 1968
*The Dream Songs,* 1969

*Love and Fame,* 1970; revised edition, 1972
*Delusions, Etc.,* 1972
*Selected Poems, 1938–1968,* 1972
*Henry's Fate, and Other Poems (1967–1972),* edited by John Haffenden, 1977
*Collected Poems, 1934–1972,* edited by Charles Thornbury, 1986

**Selected Criticism**
*The Freedom of the Poet,* 1976
*Berryman's Shakespeare,* 1999

**Other Writings:** novel (*Recovery,* 1973), biography (*Stephen Crane,* 1950); edited collections of literature (*The Arts of Reading* [with Ralph Ross and Allen Tate], 1960).

**Further Reading**

Conarroe, Joel, *John Berryman: An Introduction to the Poetry,* New York: Columbia University Press, 1977
Davie Donald, "Problems of Decorum," *New York Times Book Review* (25 April 1976)
Giroux, Robert, "Henry's Understanding," *Yale Review* (April 1996)
Haffenden, John, *John Berryman: A Critical Commentary,* New York: New York University Press, and London: Macmillan, 1980
Haffenden, John, *The Life of John Berryman,* Boston: Routledge and Kegan Paul, 1982
Kelly, Richard J., and Alan K. Lathrop, editors, *Recovering Berryman: Essays on a Poet,* Ann Arbor: University of Michigan Press, 1993
Mariani, Paul, *Dream Song: The Life of John Berryman,* New York: Morrow, 1990; 2nd edition, Amherst: University of Massachusetts Press, 1996
Stitt, Peter, "John Berryman: The Dispossessed Poet," *Ohio Review* 15, no. 2 (1974)
Thomas, Harry, editor, *Berryman's Understanding,* Boston: Northeastern University Press, 1988
Travisano, Thomas, *Midcentury Quartet: Bishop, Lowell, Jarrell, Berryman, and the Making of a Postmodern Aesthetic,* Charlottesville: University Press of Virginia, 1999
Vendler, Helen, *The Given and the Made: Recent American Poets,* London and Boston: Faber and Faber, 1995

## The Dream Songs

*The Dream Songs* (1969) was originally published in two collections: the Pulitzer Prize–winning *77 Dream Songs* (1964) and *His Toy, His Dream, His Rest* (1968). Between the publication of *Homage to Mistress Bradstreet* (1956) and *77 Dream Songs* Berryman had begun experimenting with the three six-line stanza form in which the Songs, with some minor exceptions, are written. This poetic form, together with the poetic persona of Henry in *The Dream Songs,* would dominate Berryman's career, and further Songs were planned for publication in the provisionally titled collections "Addenda" and "Parega." The character of Henry rises again in the poems published posthumously in 1977, *Henry's Fate, and Other Poems (1967–1972),* five years after Berryman's suicide. *77 Dream Songs* maps the first three of the entire collection's seven books, with each book in this first volume containing 26, 25, and 26 Songs respectively. Although a noted stylist and poetic technician in his other collections and his criticism, Berryman's systematic structuring of the remaining sections of *The Dream Songs* became more haphazard: the four books of *His Toy, His Dream, His Rest* contain 14, 54, 133, and 107 poems respectively.

*The Dream Songs* is not a comprehensible and unified text nor does it seek to provide a coherent, easy read as "Dream Song 366" testifies: "These Songs are not meant to be understood, you understand. / They are only meant to terrify & comfort." The work's open-ended nature, the initially difficult syntax and thought processes at work, and the occasional failure (particularly in the later books) to remain within the three six-line stanza form make this a text that demands attention and repeated reading. Moreover, understanding an individual Song in isolation from its placement within a section or indeed within the collection as a whole is difficult: Berryman structured this poetic event around a high degree of textual interdependency and cross-reference. Many of the early critical appraisals dwelt on the biographical similarities between Berryman and his character Henry in the Songs, but more recent scholarship has opened up the discussions of Berryman's text to a range of textual and theoretical analyses. *The Dream Songs* charts a set of alternative landscapes: the internal spaces of an individual psyche; real and tangible locations within the contemporary United States of Berryman's time; and considerations of political and cultural territories outside America, particularly in Europe and Asia, in the 1960s. Although the action that does occur throughout the 385 Dream Songs centers on the life and experiences of Henry, this is not to say that these poems are wholly divorced from an actual and realized social and political world. On the contrary, Berryman navigates a complex of interwoven themes, the dimensions of which incorporate the personal in conjunction with the universal, situating the private in tandem with the public. Central to this poetic project is the crisis of identity, in particular that of American identity in the 1960s following the assassination of John F. Kennedy and the nation's later involvement in the Vietnam War. An art of opposition and tension frames Berryman's work: alternative streams of philosophy and thought (Western as opposed to Eastern, psychoanalysis as against religion); competing individualized characters (Henry and his interlocutors throughout); an ordered presentation of "reality" clashing with the fragmented representations of such a reality. Each of the oppositions established by Berryman contributes to the construction of a unique poetic dynamic.

Originally planned as a creation epic, *The Dream Songs* operates ultimately (noted by Matterson in his study [1988]) as a survival epic. Many of the Songs are elegiac in mood, and Berryman will be remembered, among other things, as *the* elegist of his generation, the so-called "middle generation" of American poets. In his recollections of fellow writers such as Delmore Schwartz, Randall Jarrell, and Sylvia Plath, Berryman registers—through Henry—the fact of human survival amid the despair and disintegration of modern life. Each of the books either opens or closes with progression and continuance in the face of the tragic consequences of such continuation. Henry moves between the demands of calibrated time and the cyclical motion of the seasons as the recorder of the losses of this world, losses among which he is not numbered. Knowledge of the human condition and acceptance of the fallen state of mankind are central coordinates in the journeys of Berryman's version of the American anti-hero. Although there are concordances between Berryman and the poetic persona of Henry, biographical readings are both reductionist in approach and mistaken: as Berryman's prefatory note to the work explains, "The poem, then, whatever its wide cast of characters, is essentially about an imaginary character (not the poet, not me) named Henry." Discord strikes a prominent note in the poetic voices of *The Dream Songs*. The contemplation of loss, the consequences of various suicides and deaths, the disconnection from the past and from a previously solid, stable identity—all speak of *The Dream Songs*' wrestlings with history (personal and national) and its mappings of "the geography of grief" ("Dream Song 172").

*The Dream Songs* stands as Berryman's greatest poetic achievement; as his reputation continues to grow almost 30 years after his death, critics and readers alike turn to this volume to investigate and understand the unique art of John Berryman. Although his previous works had displayed at turns the heavy influence of writers as disparate in time and style as Shakespeare, Keats, and Yeats, *The Dream Songs* marked Berryman's emergence into his own poetic voice, a voice that straddled the transition in American poetry from Modernism to the development of a new poetics of fragmentation and loss situated within the landscape of postmodern uncertainty.

PHILIP MCGOWAN

**Further Reading**

Bawer, Bruce, *The Middle Generation: The Lives and Poetry of Delmore Schwartz, Randall Jarrell, John Berryman, and Robert Lowell,* Hamden, Connecticut: Archon Books, 1986

Berryman, John, *The Freedom of the Poet,* New York: Farrar Straus and Giroux, 1976

Bloom, Harold, editor, *John Berryman,* New York: Chelsea House, 1989

Kelly, Richard J., and Alan K. Lathrop, editors, *Recovering Berryman: Essays on a Poet,* Ann Arbor: University of Michigan Press, 1993

Mariani, Paul, *Dream Song: The Life of John Berryman,* New York: Morrow, 1990; 2nd edition, Amherst: University of Massachusetts Press, 1996

Matterson, Stephen, *Berryman and Lowell: The Art of Losing,* London: Macmillan, and Totowa, New Jersey: Barnes and Noble, 1988

Perloff, Marjorie, "*Poètes Maudits* of the Genteel Tradition: Lowell and Berryman," in *Robert Lowell: Essays on the Poetry,* edited by Steven Gould Axelrod and Helen Deese, Cambridge: Cambridge University Press, 1986

Thomas, Harry, editor, *Berryman's Understanding: Reflections on the Poetry of John Berryman,* Boston: Northeastern University Press, 1988

Vendler, Helen, *The Given and the Made: Recent American Poets,* London and Boston: Faber and Faber, 1995

## Homage to Mistress Bradstreet

When *Homage to Mistress Bradstreet* was first published in the *Partisan Review* in 1953, it was hailed by Edmund Wilson as "the most distinguished long poem by an American since *The Waste Land.*" Considered by many critics to be John Berryman's finest poem, although not strictly speaking a *long* poem (consisting of 55 eight-line and two nine-line stanzas), it was begun in March 1948 and completed almost exactly five years later in 1953. It was Berryman's first major breakthrough as a poet, the poem against which the imitations and affectations of his first book, *The Dispossessed* (1948), paled into critical insignificance. With *The Dispossessed,* reprinted in 1956 in a beautiful Farrar, Straus and Cudahy edition with illustrations by Ben Shahn, Berryman began what is, in an important sense, a profoundly passionate love poem during a period in his personal life when he had just come out of an affair, many details of which became raw material for his sonnet sequence *Sonnets to Chris,* first published as *Berryman's Sonnets* in 1967. *Homage to Mistress Bradstreet* charts the course of the poet's imagined amorous tryst with a real historical figure: Anne Bradstreet (c. 1612–72), the Puritan and first American poetess or "Tenth Muse," writer of what Berryman termed "bald abstract didactic rime." The poem is less concerned with describing the erotic details of their transhistorical relationship—although it does this, too—than it is with suggesting questions pertaining to the nature of personal and national origins, the limits of dialogue and imagination, and the role of the writer in a restrictive society. The poem's Cold War context demands that we read it in these terms.

Through the five-year period of the poem's composition and final publication, Berryman spent terms working in no fewer than five universities, from Princeton to the University of Washington (Seattle), then to Iowa, Harvard, Cincinnati, and finally to Minnesota, where he stayed from 1955 until his death in 1972. During this period, Berryman's first marriage, to the novelist Eileen Simpson, ended. It was an intense and precarious period for Berryman, financially and domestically, when he had to try to balance the practical difficulties of his personal life with, as one commentator has noted, "the burden of trying to be scholar, teacher, poet" (Haffenden, 1980). *Homage to Mistress Bradstreet* bears all the hallmarks of Berryman's tripartite creative career, being at once an astute reconstruction of a historical personality as well as an instructive and useful example of Modernist reinvention and intertextual assimilation, while also standing out as his most achieved, if not his finest, poem. Although there has been some dissent (see, e.g., Carol Johnson's early essay [1964] on Berryman's failings), most critics have agreed that Berryman succeeded in portraying a vivid picture of Puritan life and Anne Bradstreet's experience of it; Robert Lowell once referred to the work as "the most resourceful historical poem in our literature." This achievement, however, was not the poet's principal aim. Rather, *Homage to Mistress Bradstreet* was written, as Berryman said in his interview-essay "One Answer to a Question: Changes" in 1965, as an experiment in narrative: "Narrative!" he boomed, "Let's have narrative, and at least one dominant personality, and no fragmentation! In short, let us have something spectacularly NOT *The Waste Land*" (*The Freedom of the Poet,* 1976).

How does *Homage to Mistress Bradstreet* rebel against the example of Eliot's great poem and at the same time take its place as a masterpiece of American late Modernist poetry? First, Berryman's poem is an attempt to rejuvenate the Eliotic poetic by subjecting it to a rigorous formalism. *Homage to Mistress Bradstreet* is, as one critic has put it, "a masterful technical achievement" (Gelpi, 1969), in which Berryman borrows an eight-line stanza form from Hopkins ("The Wreck of the Deutschland") and Yeats ("In Memory of Major Robert Gregory") and wields it to his own brilliant purpose. While the poem is largely regular in meter and rhyme, following a 5-5-3-4-5-5-3-6 basically iambic metrical schema with an a-b-x-b-c-c-x-a rhyme scheme, it nevertheless produces some wonderful surprises, as in the movement from stanza 20 to stanza 21 (they are numbered), where the poetess, giving birth, is described as follows:

> [20]
> hide me forever I work I thrust I must free
> now I all muscles & bones concentrate
> what is living from dying?
> Simon I must leave you so untidy
> Monster you are killing me Be sure
> I'll have you later Women do endure
> I can *can* no longer
> and it passes the wretched trap whelming and I am he
>
> [21]
> drencht & powerful, I did it with my body!
> One proud tug greens Heaven. Marvellous,
> unforbidding Majesty.
> Swell imperious bells. I fly.
> Mountainous, woman not breaks and will bend:
> sways God nearby: anguish comes to an end.
> Blossomed Sarah, and I
> blossom. Is that thing alive? I hear a famisht howl.

Berryman's strict adherence to formal pattern nowhere impedes his delivery, and in these stanzas and many others, his use of enjambment and impeccable syntactic control produce effects that subsume the external poetic apparatus, allowing content and form to merge in an exciting, if sometimes eccentric, exploration of character and theme.

Second, Berryman rebels against Eliot's call for the impersonality of the poet by boldly inscribing himself into the poem. *Homage to Mistress Bradstreet* has four main sections: an exordium, or introductory section (1–4.8); a second section (5–25.3) that presents the poetess herself telling of the difficulties of colonial life, her barrenness, and then her eventual, late, first childbirth and life as a mother and wife in colonial New England; a third section (25.3–39.3) that is largely a dialogue between Berryman and Bradstreet; and then a fourth section (39.4–53.8) that culminates in the final sickness of the poetess and her passing into history and Berryman's present in the coda (54–57). Berryman's dialogue with the poetess allows him to enter into a dialogue with American history that is marked by an intense desire to understand the American (Cold War) present, where "foxholes hold men, / reactor piles wage slow upon the wet brain rime." In a manner similar to the way in which William Carlos Williams places the threat of nuclear holocaust alongside his more intimate personal concerns in "Asphodel, That Greeny Flower" (1955), Berryman's *Homage to Mistress Bradstreet* embodies a range of questions and tensions, from the poet's problematic private life to his uneasiness with recent developments in contemporary America, such as the production and stockpiling of nuclear weapons.

*Homage to Mistress Bradstreet,* then, is a scrupulously well structured poem that marks Berryman's relatively late but brilliant discovery of his own voice. Building on experiments with syntax and form that were already present in some of his earlier poems ("The Nervous Songs" especially), the work launched Berryman to the forefront of contemporary poetry and paved the way for the more sustained (if not so well executed) effort that was to become *The Dream Songs,* which he began in 1955. Complete with notes (a parody of those provided by Eliot in *The Waste Land* or a helpful reader's aid through the poem's intertextual maze), *Homage to Mistress Bradstreet* is not so much "about the woman," as Berryman writes in his first annotation, as it is about *the poet:* his or her role in society and in history, his or her posthumous reception and fate. The poet's fate, however, is ours, and Berryman's meditation on America's colonial beginnings through the personality of Anne Bradstreet ends with an open-ended reflection on an uncertain Cold War future: "Hover, utter, still, / a sourcing whom my lost candle like the firefly loves." That "sourcing" is directed toward the past *and* the future, like Paul Klee's *Angelus Novus* (as Walter Benjamin, in his "Theses on the Philosophy of History," has noted). It is no accident, indeed, that in a note to this poem—which is also a profound meditation on history—Berryman points the reader to a painting by Klee, just as it is no accident that some recent critics have found the poem relevant for its oblique but effective powers of cultural critique.

PHILIP COLEMAN

**Further Reading**

Conarroe, Joel, *John Berryman: An Introduction to the Poetry,* New York: Columbia University Press, 1977

Gelpi, Albert, "Homage to Berryman's 'Homage,'" *Harvard Advocate* 103 (1969)

Haffenden, John, *John Berryman: A Critical Commentary,* New York: New York University Press, and London: Macmillan, 1980

Holder, Alan, "Anne Bradstreet Resurrected," *Concerning Poetry* 2 (1969)

Johnson, Carol, "John Berryman and Mistress Bradstreet: A Relation of Reason," *Essays in Criticism* 14 (1964)

Kunitz, Stanley, "No Middle Flight: Berryman's 'Homage to Mistress Bradstreet,'" in *Berryman's Understanding,* edited by Harry Thomas, Boston: Northeastern University Press, 1988

Nims, John Frederick, "Screwing Up the Theorbo: Homage in Measure to Mr. Berryman," in *Berryman's Understanding,* edited by Harry Thomas, Boston: Northeastern University Press, 1988

Simpson, Eileen, *Poets in Their Youth: A Memoir,* New York: Random House, and London: Faber, 1982

Travisano, Thomas, *Midcentury Quartet: Bishop, Lowell, Jarrell, Berryman, and the Making of a Postmodern Aesthetic,* Charlottesville: University Press of Virginia, 1999

# Frank Bidart 1939–

Frank Bidart's poems have the density of a tragic drama, a philosophical meditation, or a Faulknerian novel. They show us interior landscapes of failure and horror, crime and guilt, desire and regret, blindness and blankness. Telling of failed love and artistic struggle—and of the inability of our culture, our cosmology, to sustain and to support—Bidart has produced some of the most powerful and profound poems of the postmodern era.

Bidart was born in Bakersfield, in the Central Valley of California, in 1939. He received his B.A. in English from the University of California, Riverside, and his M.A. from Harvard University, where he studied with Robert Lowell. At Harvard, he became a friend of both Lowell and Elizabeth Bishop, two poets who have had an enduring influence on his life and art. Bidart teaches at Wellesley College, where he is a professor of English. His books of poetry include *Golden State* (1973), *The Book of the Body* (1977), *The Sacrifice* (1983), *In the Western Night: Collected Poems, 1965–1990* (1990), and *Desire* (1997). He is also editing Robert Lowell's *Collected Poems* (forthcoming). His books have won many prizes, including the Lila Wallace–Reader's Digest Award, the Shelley Memorial Award, the Morton Dauwen Zabel Award, the Bernard Connors Prize, and the Lannan Foundation Poetry Award. The critic Harold Bloom has stated that Bidart "writes narrative so harrowing in design and detail that all of his acute intelligence, moral force, and devoted skill at language may continue to be neglected, since very few readers can sustain poems so uncompromising in facing reductive and very unpleasant truths." Poet Louise Glück has remarked that "the importance of Bidart's work is difficult to overestimate; certainly he is one of the crucial figures of our time."

Bidart's first volume, *Golden State,* presents us with both selves and anti-selves. One anti-self is the child-rapist and killer who speaks the poem "Herbert White." Discoursing from the nadir of moral and psychic horror, this self-divided character tries to defeat the meaninglessness that threatens him through acts of extreme violence that he alternately brags of and denies. Ultimately, both his brazenness and his denials fail to work their magic, and in a suicidal moment of incipient sanity he recognizes himself: "I hope I fry. / —Hell came when I saw / MYSELF."

A character representing the poet's self speaks another of Bidart's most brilliant poems, the title poem "Golden State." The narrator—a child of divorce, like Herbert—attempts to recall his significant interactions with his remote and self-absorbed father, who has just died. This long memory poem joins a tradition of post–World War II poems about the father that includes Theodore Roethke's "My Papa's Waltz," Robert Lowell's "Commander Lowell," and Sylvia Plath's "Daddy." Like the predecessor poems, "Golden State" tells a story of oedipal conflict and domestic rupture as a way of gaining leverage on even larger issues. It exposes the tarnish on the "Golden State" of California—and on American culture. It reveals the failure of fathers to father and of families to shelter. However, in its dialogism and uncertainties, the poem goes well beyond its precursors. "Golden State" extensively quotes the father's utterances. As it does so, he recedes as an object of the son's control and gradually emerges as a mysterious and fully voiced other. The narrator has tried to make the father into a character in order to release himself from the father's grip. However, in a surprising twist he finds that "no such knowledge is possible;—/ as I touch your photographs, they stare back at me / with the dazzling, impenetrable, glitter of mere life." Bidart's art can make no more sense of life than Herbert White's violence can. The father triumphs over the son's will to power and over the pretensions of poetry. Yet the text does succeed in less obvious ways, discovering freedom in alterity and beauty in the sheer bareness of contemporary life.

Another stunning poem is "Ellen West," initially published in *The Book of the Body.* Partly invented and partly based on a psychiatric case study by Ludwig Binswanger, this poem carries Bidart's dialogic experimentation even further by alternating between Ellen West's voice and that of her sympathetic but uncomprehending doctor. The poem manifests debts to the dramatic monologues of Robert Browning and Randall Jarrell, to the genres of novel and case history, and to such late-20th-century texts of psychological extremity as Lowell's "Waking in the Blue," Bishop's "Visits to St. Elizabeths," Plath's *The Bell Jar,* and Anne Sexton's "You, Dr. Martin." Although the poem is not objective in the manner of Eliot or Pound, it is not personal in the manner of Lowell or Sexton, either. It both extends and overturns Lowell's poetic tradition by moving from autobiography to biography. Then, doubling back on itself, it implies authorial obsessions within the subject of the biography. Ellen West, like Maria Callas, who functions as a kind of Shakespearean foil, is a struggling artist figure, although unlike Callas she is a failed one. The two characters echo each other in terms of conflicts about self-expression, the body, food, gender, sexuality, and love. "The ideal of being thin," asserts the title character, "conceals the ideal / *not* to have a body." As her name suggests, these conflicts are endemic to the "West." The title character's refusal to be appropriated by any discourse or normative ideology ties her to other such refusals by women, lesbians and gays, minorities, and outcasts, but it also positions her as specific, unique, and free, much like the unpossessable father in "Golden State."

In "The War of Vaslav Nijinsky," first published in *The Sacrifice,* Bidart constructs another powerful, polyphonic meditation on guilt, the body, and history. Oscillating between Nijinsky's voice in verse and the voices of his wife and other observers in prose, the poem traces the ballet dancer's final descent into madness. His madness is at once historical (reflecting the guilt of World War I), philosophical (as Nijinsky contemplates Nietzsche), personal (as he deals with a conflicted sexual identity and a divided self resembling both Herbert White's and Ellen West's), and creative (as he prays, "*Let this be the Body / through which the War has passed*").

"The Second Hour of the Night," the longest and most ambitious poem in *Desire,* is a tripartite exploration of desire and desolation. The first part, a pastiche of passages drawn from Hector Berlioz's memoir, narrates the tragic failures and deepening loneliness of Berlioz's wife, the actress Henriette-Constance Berlioz-Smithson. The second part re-creates the myth of Myrrha and Cinyras in a manner comparable to texts by H.D., Plath, and Lowell. In Bidart's harrowing retelling, the myth evokes the compulsion, intensity, and pain of unlawful desire—as well as its ubiquity. The poem's enigmatic final part suggests the interpenetrations of memory, death, and longing.

Bidart has given us a series of greatly original and greatly disturbing poems. They stretch the limits of language and genre. In a style never quite seen before, they plumb the depths of guilt, suffering, passion, forgiveness, and love.

STEVEN GOULD AXELROD

**Biography**

Born in Bakersfield, California, 1939. Attended the University of California at Riverside, B.A. 1962; Harvard University, Cambridge, Massachusetts, M.A. 1967; currently Professor of English, Wellesley College, Massachusetts; has also taught at the University of Massachusetts, Boston, and Brandeis University, Waltham, Massachusetts. Received Guggenheim fellowship, 1979; Morton Dauwen Zabel Award, 1995; O.B. Hardison, Jr., Poetry Prize, 1996; Shelley Memorial Award, 1997; Lannan Foundation Poetry Award, 1998. Living in Cambridge, Massachusetts.

**Poetry**

*Golden State,* 1973
*The Book of the Body,* 1977
*The Sacrifice,* 1983
*In the Western Night: Collected Poems, 1965–1990,* 1990
*Desire,* 1997

**Further Reading**

Ferry, Anne, *The Title to the Poem,* Stanford, California: Stanford University Press, 1996
Glück, Louise, *Proofs and Theories: Essays on Poetry,* Hopewell, New Jersey: Ecco Press, 1994; Manchester: Carcanet, 1999
Gray, Jeffrey, "'Necessary Thought': Frank Bidart and the Postconfessional," *Contemporary Literature* 34, no. 4 (1993)
Pinsky, Robert, *The Situation of Poetry: Contemporary Poetry and Its Traditions,* Princeton, New Jersey: Princeton University Press, 1976
Williamson, Alan, *Eloquence and Mere Life: Essays on the Art of Poetry,* Ann Arbor: University of Michigan Press, 1994

---

# Elizabeth Bishop 1911–79

During her lifetime, Elizabeth Bishop published only five books of poetry: *North and South* (1946), *Poems: North and South—A Cold Spring* (1955), *Questions of Travel* (1965), *The Complete Poems* (1969), and *Geography III* (1976). About once a decade, a book of hers would collect its major literary award from one of the prominently named arts foundations in America—Guggenheim, Pulitzer, or Rockefeller. Throughout her lifetime, Bishop's precise and understated art, with its brilliant but deceptively simple surfaces, drew admirers. Of the first book, Marianne Moore wrote, "Elizabeth Bishop is spectacular in being unspectacular" (Schwartz and Estess, 1983). In his sonnet "Calling," Robert Lowell addressed Bishop in midcareer as the "unerring Muse who makes the casual perfect." James Merrill, after Bishop's death, remarked, "Poetry was a life both shaped by and distinct from the lived one," and spoke affectionately of "her own instinctive, modest, lifelong impersonations of an ordinary woman" (Schwartz and Estess, 1983). Yet from this reticence, with its refusal of elevated style or epic scope, rises the poetry praised by nearly every major poet writing in the English language since midcentury.

Within a perfectly conventional narrative frame, unmarked by surreal distortions of time or space, Bishop fires her scenes and objects with almost preternatural attentions. Her gift for unexpected correspondences signals for us the deep order of otherness always inherent in being, as her poems suggest the crowded, hovering flux of our own reality. Using all of her five senses, Bishop glides readily from maps to fish houses to band concerts, from mechanical toys to invented animals or to historical or fancied monologue. Her ears note the "ferocious obbligatoes" of the mosquitoes in "Florida"; in "A Cold Spring," she tunes in to the bullfrogs' "sounding, / slack strings plucked by heavy thumbs." In "Sandpiper," she stands on a shoreline where "The beach hisses like fat." Or catching up a size, a smell, a posture, and a color and texture of misery in one swift, persuasive go, she opens "The Prodigal" with this description of the sty that confines the dark biblical sibling:

> The brown enormous odor he lived by
> was too close, with its breathing and thick hair.

In poem, story, and parable, Bishop performs odd juxtapositions, sharp little dramas of perceptual amplification or miniaturization. When we look at the incurved dogwood petal of "A Cold Spring," its fresh bloom put in terms of a mysterious brutality, it is "burned, apparently, by a cigarette butt." When we inspect the clapboard churches of "The Moose," their large, solemn, and distant selves "ridged as clamshells" company with the hard rind of a mollusk. Each thing or act startles us with a resemblance that reshuffles our understanding of the ties of the world. Often gay, occasionally sour or somber, the voice of the poem is balanced and in control, even as control is threatened: it bespeaks an integral life, but one trembling in solution and on edge with fantastic possibility.

It is never the eyes alone that engage Bishop. At the climax of "At the Fishhouses," the visual and aural combine forces with the tactile, ending brilliantly and poignantly with the taste and feel of northern seawater:

> If you should dip your hand in,
> your wrist would ache immediately,
> your bones would begin to ache and your hand would burn
> as if the water were a transmutation of fire

that feeds on stones and burns with a dark gray flame.
If you tasted it, it would first taste bitter,
then briny, then surely burn your tongue.

As with all of Bishop's metaphors, this metaphor for knowledge establishes itself so unshakably that it contains an utterly physical presence, drawing on all five senses in commanding sequence.

Brought to prominence by her superb technique, Bishop's poetry initially made interest in her life subordinate to interest in the practice of her art. She was born in Worcester, Massachusetts, and then in her infancy moved abruptly to Nova Scotia after her father's death and her mother's subsequent mental breakdown and permanent institutionalization in Halifax. After the age of five, she never saw her mother again. Bishop remained in Canada. Shortly after, her paternal grandparents returned her, like a misplaced parcel, to the United States. After a childhood and adolescence marked by asthma and other psychic and bodily ailments, as well as frequent domestic removals and changes of caregiver, Bishop finally made it to a good preparatory school and then, with family help, to Vassar College. After college, a small independent income enabled her to travel with a violent aimlessness through France, England, Ireland, Mexico, Morocco, Key West, and elsewhere; ultimately, she migrated for more than a decade and a half to Brazil.

Bishop's truly loved homes can be counted on the fingers of one hand. An uneasy shuttle between Key West and New York ended in the loss of the first house, in Key West. Then came Samambaia, a country residence shared with her Brazilian lover, Lota de Macedo Soares. For some period after her estrangement from Lota and after Lota's suicide, Bishop lived at Casa Mariana, a small, historic edifice that she restored with the help of an American lover and from whom she fled after that relationship fell apart. Fever and a wracking illness pushed Bishop back to the United States for treatment. Returning permanently to Boston in the 1970s, after a series of moves from the West Coast to the East and back again, Bishop made her final home in a renovated wharf building in Boston Harbor.

But by 1969, with the publication of *The Complete Poems,* the trajectory of a life within particular houses and places had unfolded. Bishop lamented to Robert Lowell,

> I worry a great deal about what to do with this accumulation of exotic or picturesque or charming detail, and I don't want to become a poet who can only write about South America.

How can I go on living here, she asked him, "and yet be a New Englander herring-choker bluenoser at the same time" (*One Art: Letters,* 1994). Because she recognized the fruitful dialectic between her southern life and her northern memory, Brazil as focusing lens gave her an approach to autobiography and led her to the masterly late poems of *Geography III* (1976).

There in Brazil, for the first time secure in house and partner, Bishop's earlier poems sketching the rigors of love gave way to affectionate but unsentimental accounts of her Nova Scotian childhood. The brilliant prose memoirs of 1953, such as "In the Village" and "Gwendolyn," nudged earlier veiled and brittle dramatizations of a problematic sexual identity out of the way as the loop back to childhood brought Bishop a fresh narrative of her life. In Adrienne Rich's words, her poems began to embody "a need to place herself in the actual, to come to terms with a personal past, with family and class and race, with her presence as a poet in cities and landscapes where human suffering is not a metaphor" (*Boston Review* 8 [April 1983]).

Homeless and virtually orphaned from childhood, Bishop was deeply at home in the far-flung parts of the world that she domesticated in the confines of her art. The "country mouse" of her 1961 memoir of that title, she nevertheless remained a citizen of far larger worlds. Bishop, the child accustomed to oil lamps at night and to daytime streets filled with horse and buggy traffic, deals in one of her final poems with the meshing lights of an international airport, seen from the altitude of a landing plane. As a traveling child, Bishop named the Pullman-car sink at which she washed herself, in good farm terms, a "hopper"; she who began writing in thick chalk on the heavy slates of a provincial Canadian elementary school typed the last poem, "Five Flights Up," of her last published book, *Geography III,* while looking out at the world from the dawn of an entirely urban apartment building. Nevertheless,

Yesterday brought to today so lightly!
(A yesterday I find almost impossible to lift.)

Or to erase. The Canadian village culture familiar to Bishop's teacher-mother and grandmother gathered in reading societies at which people read Browning out loud; her own education at Vassar included literary talk in speakeasies over illicit wine. Just as her personal history split between America and Canada and later, as she navigated the continental drop between Brazil and the United States, between North and South America, she began to see how her own interior was similarly bifurcated emotionally and psychologically. She was the divided woman who wore jeans in Rio to luncheon, served by a butler in livery, who yet also wrote poems about women's breasts and about lying in bed together during thunderstorms—poems never to see publication during Bishop's lifetime.

The first Elizabeth Bishop to emerge as an American poet of stature projected her complicated life onto the screens of fairly safe, sexually neutral subjects: animals, fantastic objects, travel, and childhood. But fair copies and drafts of Bishop poems, such as "Vaguely Love Poem" and "It Is Marvellous," as well as the magical "Apartment in Leme," have received journal publication, raising provocative issues of both control and definition of an oeuvre. Bishop made no sign of wishing to have such poems published; in fact, she protested vigorously at the publication of unfinished work by Marianne Moore. Each person drawing from the archives containing these papers must decide for her- or himself as to the value, order, and propriety of their circulation; inevitably, the work exposed shifts the perspective on Bishop's art.

After the 1976 publication of *Geography III* and its more openly autobiographical poems, readers began to write about the darker, more plangent tones of Bishop's register of the human comedy, paying a heightened attention to its subtly placed class and cultural politics. Enthusiastically rejecting previous assumptions of the sexual neutrality of Bishop's poems, readers now crowd to decode her readings of the female body and to trace the doubled perspectives of lesbian experience in published poems such as "Insomnia" and "Exchanging Hats," with their wordplay on experiences of inversion.

Skeptics argue the proprieties of Bishop's use of Brazilian materials. Brett Millier (1993) assesses Bishop's project in her

Brazilian poems as a record of culture collision in which the poems "at their best, are aware of their outsider's perspective, and at their most naive, participate fully in the paternalistic culture." Other critics have wrestled to describe the exact combination of gender sensitivities and awareness of imperialist policies and indigenous vulnerability that Bishop sets going in a poem such as "Brazil, January 1, 1502." The poem stitches a free tapestry on which the tiny, nail-hard conquistadors advance against retreating Indian women: with which group does Bishop align herself, if she does? But poems such as "Going to the Bakery" and "Under My Window" arguably recall, while undermining, any of the blunt, ideological binaries, living and acting as they do beyond the simpler assignments of national consciousness.

With precision and subtlety, Bishop brings together these issues of cross-cultural division and alienated identity without a hint of the programmatic or forced. Overwhelmed by history and geography, the six-going-on-seven-year-old protagonist of "In the Waiting Room" sits in a dentist's office during the Great War, staring at the pages of the *National Geographic.* Cannibalism, racial confrontation, and bodily mutilation in tribal ritual thrust themselves at the little girl who reads, "too shy to stop" or turn away in rebellion from her membership in the human family. Sitting there in Worcester, Massachusetts, however, she knows that she is "an *I,* . . . an *Elizabeth,*" and that she is "one of them." Yet the poem does not finish here. Helplessly, inevitably, Bishop evades what the poet William Blake called the idiocy of generalization and, in the dazzling register of her experience, plunges us back into the minute particulars that are this poet's illuminating care.

Within her different orders of species, the benign toy horse and brittle dancer of "Cirque d'Hiver," facing each other, for instance, are like all the mesmerizing citizens of Bishop's diverse kingdoms who deal with the flashing alternation of sameness/difference, with exhilaration or with alarm and sometimes both. Like life itself, Bishop's poems remain in flux: now past the century of their origin, they still summon from fresh sets of readers what she singled out in George Herbert's "Love Unknown": the "new, tender, and quick."

Lorrie Goldensohn

**Biography**

Born in Worcester, Massachusetts, 8 February 1911. Attended Vassar College, Poughkeepsie, New York, 1930–34, A.B. 1934; consultant in poetry, Library of Congress, Washington, D.C., 1949–50; poet-in-residence, University of Washington, Seattle, 1966, 1973; Lecturer in English, Harvard University, Cambridge, Massachusetts, 1970–79. Received Houghton Mifflin Poetry Prize fellowship, 1945; Guggenheim fellowship, 1947; American Academy grant, 1951; Shelley Memorial Award, 1953; Pulitzer Prize, 1956; Amy Lowell traveling fellowship, 1957; Chapelbrook fellowship, 1962; Academy of American Poets fellowship, 1964; Rockefeller fellowship, 1967; Ingram Merrill Foundation grant, 1969; National Book Award, 1970; Harriet Monroe Poetry Award, 1974; Neustadt Prize, 1976; National Book Critics Circle Award, 1977; L.L.D., Smith College, Northampton, Massachusetts, 1968, Rutgers University, New Brunswick, New Jersey, 1972, and Brown University, Providence, Rhode Island, 1972; Chancellor, Academy of American Poets, 1966; member, American Academy, 1976; Order of Rio Branco (Brazil), 1971. Died in Cambridge, Massachusetts, 6 October 1979.

**Poetry**

*North and South,* 1946
*Poems: North and South—A Cold Spring,* 1955
*Questions of Travel,* 1965
*Selected Poems,* 1967
*The Complete Poems,* 1969
*Geography III,* 1976
*Complete Poems, 1927–1979,* 1983

**Other Writings:** travel literature (*Brazil* [with the editors of *Life* magazine], 1962), translation of Portuguese literature (*The Diary of Helena Morley,* by Alice Brant, 1957), correspondence (*One Art: Letters,* edited by Robert Giroux, 1994); edited collections of poetry (*An Anthology of Twentieth-Century Brazilian Poetry* [with Emanuel Brasil], 1972).

**Further Reading**

Barry, Sandra, *Elizabeth Bishop: An Archival Guide to Her Life in Nova Scotia,* Halifax: Elizabeth Bishop Society of Nova Scotia, 1996
Costello, Bonnie, *Elizabeth Bishop: Questions of Mastery,* Cambridge, Massachusetts: Harvard University Press, 1991
Fountain, Gary, and Peter Brazeau, *Remembering Elizabeth Bishop: An Oral Biography,* Amherst: University of Massachusetts Press, 1994
Goldensohn, Lorrie, *Elizabeth Bishop: The Biography of a Poetry,* New York: Columbia University Press, 1992
Harrison, Victoria, *Elizabeth Bishop's Poetics of Intimacy,* Cambridge and New York: Cambridge University Press, 1993
Kalstone, David, *Becoming a Poet: Elizabeth Bishop with Marianne Moore and Robert Lowell,* New York: Farrar Straus and Giroux, and London: Hogarth Press, 1989
Lombardi, Marilyn May, editor, *Elizabeth Bishop: The Geography of Gender,* Charlottesville: University Press of Virginia, 1993
Millier, Brett C., *Elizabeth Bishop: Life and the Memory of It,* Berkeley: University of California Press, 1993
Schwartz, Lloyd, and Sybil P. Estess, editors, *Elizabeth Bishop and Her Art,* Ann Arbor: University of Michigan Press, 1983
Travisano, Thomas J., *Midcentury Quartet: Bishop, Lowell, Jarrell, Berryman, and the Making of a Postmodern Aesthetic,* Charlottesville: University Press of Virginia, 1999

# The Armadillo

Confusion over the meaning of Elizabeth Bishop's "The Armadillo" (which first appeared in the 22 June 1957 issue of *The New Yorker*) is typical of critical reactions to poems from *Questions of Travel* (1965). The existence of too many viewpoints and too much information in *Questions of Travel,* Bishop's third collection, suggests that she had not gained aesthetic control of many of the poems; she also was still coming to terms with the meaning of her experience living in Brazil. In that sense "The Armadillo," which describes the fire balloons the Brazilians sent up during the festival of St. John's Eve, is typically ambiguous in its perspective. In later poems, such as "Crusoe in England," Bishop had fully assimilated her Brazilian experiences. Nevertheless, "The Armadillo" is a critical transitional poem for Bishop and for American poetry. Like "Electrical Storm" and "Song for a Rainy Season," it marks the beginning of a movement away from a strictly aesthetic response to her experience in Brazil to a more personal response. Robert Lowell credited "The Armadillo" with leading him toward the looser, more personal style of "Skunk Hour," the poem that ushered in his breakthrough collection of Confessional poetry, *Life Studies:*

> The dedication [of "Skunk Hour"] is to Elizabeth Bishop, because rereading her suggested a way of breaking through the shell of my old manner. Her rhythms, idiom, images and stanza structure seemed to belong to a later century. "Skunk Hour" is modeled on Miss Bishop's "The Armadillo," a much better poem and one I had heard her read and later carried around with me. Both "Skunk Hour" and "The Armadillo" use short line stanzas, start with drifting description, and end with a single animal.

The poem opens with an appreciative description of the festival and the "frail, illegal fire balloons"; as they drift upward, "the paper chambers flush and fill with light / that comes and goes, like hearts." The man-made balloons begin to resemble nature itself. By the time they are high in the sky, they resemble:

> planets, that is—the tinted ones:
> Venus going down, or Mars,
> or the pale green one.

The beauty of the balloons is deceptive, however. "[R]eceding, dwindling, solemnly / and steadily forsaking" the people below, when caught in a downdraft that threatens to blow them against a cliff or house, the balloons are "suddenly turning dangerous."

As the balloons are appreciated for their beauty, their danger is missed. First the balloons disrupt the lives of the animals:

> The flame ran down. We saw the pair
> of owls who nest there flying up
> and up.

The armadillo runs away "hastily, all alone." The imagery of this destruction—the owls that are "stained bright pink" and the baby rabbit "a handful of intangible ash / with fixed, ignited eyes"—suggests that the balloons, for all their beauty, have upset the natural order. By the final stanza, the balloons have begun to threaten the people below. Criticizing its earlier aestheticization of the balloons, the poem warns,

> *Too pretty, dreamlike mimicry!*
> *O falling fire and piercing cry*
> *and panic, and a weak mailed fist*
> *clenched ignorant against the sky!*

This final stanza, set off from the rest of the poem by italic type, is the source of the critical debate over the meaning of the poem. It appears to comment not only on the narrator's previously aestheticized description but also on the Brazilians, who are judged "ignorant" for first sending up the balloons and later panicking when the flames fall down to earth. To whom does the "weak mailed fist" belong? Was Bishop sympathizing with superstitious Brazilians or not? Other poems in *Questions of Travel* present Bishop's native Nova Scotia and adopted Brazil through many pairs of eyes. In "Arrival at Santos" the "I" is Bishop herself; in "Manuelzinho," the persona is Lota de Macedo Soares, Bishop's life partner. In "The Riverman" the persona is an Amazonian riverman about whom Bishop had read. Many of these personae undercut one another; for example, the riverman who speaks to river spirits is presented sympathetically. What, then, is the meaning of the authorial intrusion at the end of "The Armadillo"? Penelope Laurans sees "The Armadillo" as a sympathetic response to Lowell's objections to the Dresden fire-bombing. Brett Millier (1993) has argued that the fist is that of "the ignorant, victimized lower class."

Some critics have argued that the poems in *Questions of Travel* are mired in a profusion of details. Bishop may have added the final stanza to "The Armadillo" in order to give hierarchical organization to its details. If that was Bishop's intention, however, it failed. It is certain that the final stanza was added in the second draft; at second glance, Bishop reconsidered the aestheticized portrait the poem draws of the St. John's festival, acknowledging the portrait is "Too pretty, dreamlike mimicry!"

In other ways early drafts of "The Armadillo" read very close to the final version. In the first draft Bishop's diction tends toward the formal. For example, Bishop had originally written: "Once they're against the sky we often / confuse them with the stars." She revised these lines to the more informal: "Once up against the sky it's hard / to tell them from the stars." She had also written in her first draft:

> frail, illegal fire-balloons . . .
> climb the mountain height
> and float above it towards a saint
> still honored in these parts.

She dramatized the movement of the balloons in her next draft as "rising toward a saint." Similarly, in the first draft, she does not emphasize the fear of the glistening armadillo: the animal left "without haste." In the second draft the frightened armadillo leaves "hastily."

All in all, the majority of Bishop's revisions give the poem fuller dramatization and a more casual tone. This looser, more natural diction that so influenced Robert Lowell was, therefore, the product of some conscious crafting. She also gave the poem the dedication "For Robert Lowell" when it was collected in *Questions of Travel,* perhaps reciprocating the gesture of Lowell's dedication of "Skunk Hour" to herself.

Cynthia Cameros

**Further Reading**

Goldensohn, Lorrie, *Elizabeth Bishop: The Biography of a Poetry,* New York: Columbia University Press, 1992

Kalstone, David, *Becoming a Poet: Elizabeth Bishop with Marianne Moore and Robert Lowell,* New York: Farrar Straus and Giroux, and London: Hogarth Press, 1989

McPherson, Sandra, "'The Armadillo': A Commentary," *Field* 31 (Fall 1984)

Merrin, Jeredith, *An Enabling Humility: Marianne Moore, Elizabeth Bishop, and the Uses of Tradition,* New Brunswick, New Jersey: Rutgers University Press, 1990

Millier, Brett C., *Elizabeth Bishop: Life and the Memory of It,* Berkeley: University of California Press, 1993

Schwartz, Lloyd, and Sybil P. Estess, editors, *Elizabeth Bishop and Her Art,* Ann Arbor: University of Michigan Press, 1983

## Crusoe in England

Influenced, perhaps, by Robert Lowell's *Life Studies* (1959) and other Confessional poetry, Elizabeth Bishop's poetry became more autobiographical in *Geography III* (1976), which includes "Crusoe in England." Although Bishop had written about her youth in poems such as "First Death in Nova Scotia" and "Manners," she had never before written in the highly personal manner of "In the Waiting Room," "One Art," or "Crusoe in England." Robinson Crusoe was a useful character on which Bishop could hang a personal exploration of her life in Brazil, her home for almost 16 years. Crusoe was marooned on an island near Brazil; Bishop lived in Petropolis, Ouro Preto, and Rio de Janeiro, Brazil, "marooned" far away from the American literary scene. Crusoe was an older man narrating his earlier adventures in Defoe's novel; Bishop was almost 60 upon the first publication of "Crusoe in England" in the 6 November 1971 issue of *The New Yorker.* At the time Bishop was having difficulty moving on after the death of her companion, Lota de Macedo Soares, as she told a friend in a 1970 letter:

> Since she died, Anny—I just don't seem to care whether I live or die. I seem to miss her more every day of my life. I try hard to live in the present, as everyone always says—but the present is so hideous to me. (Bishop, 1994)

In order to move on, writing about her personal life in Brazil was not enough for Bishop. She decided that she needed to say goodbye to life in Brazil altogether. Bishop finally finished "Crusoe in England" when she returned home to New England.

The first stanza introduces Robinson Crusoe, a narrator who is already well-known to readers of Daniel Defoe's 18th-century novel of the same name: a fictional English character who was marooned on an island near Brazil until, after 28 years, he was rescued and returned to England. Bishop's Crusoe, like Defoe's, tells his tale as an older man residing in his homeland. In the poem this older Crusoe has recently read about the discovery and naming of a newly born island and is dismayed to find that it has already been named, mapped, and entered into the English geographies, whereas his own has been "still / un-rediscovered, unrenamable." His attempts to convey his experience on the island have not yet been understood by his readership, so he writes this poem to set the record straight.

One of the myths about his experience that Crusoe tries to deconstruct is the Christian myth that his was an island of heathen cannibals. Rather than a Christian god, Crusoe was the giant of the island:

> Well, I had fifty-two
> miserable, small volcanoes I could climb
> with a few slithery strides—.

He could see all 52 volcanoes from the edge of the highest one, and they all looked to be dwarfs with "their heads blown off." Left without the reassuring existence of a Christian god, Crusoe grew frightened:

> If I had become a giant,
> I couldn't bear to think what size
> the goats and turtles were,
> or the gulls, or the overlapping rollers

Without a higher power to assign meanings to the world around him, Crusoe was left with the responsibility of creating the meanings himself. To accept himself as the "giant" of the island, Crusoe had to accept responsibility for his fate: "'Do I deserve this? I suppose I must.'" By accepting responsibility for his fate, he felt more deeply and was able to pity himself for the first time: "So the more pity I felt, / the more I felt at home."

Further deconstructing the binary of "civilized" and "primitive," Crusoe describes the domes of the turtles as hissing "like teakettles"; the folds of lava—black, red, white, and gray—as "marbled colors"; the waterspouts as "glass chimneys, flexible, attenuated." The natural world of the island flows into the civilized world of England. Contrary to Defoe, Bishop does not present England and the island as two separate, opposing worlds. One of the perils for her Crusoe of these blurred boundaries between the natural world of the island and the civilized world of England, however, is the loss of a sense of his own identity. The goats and gulls mistook Crusoe for one of them. The rain and the turtles hissed together and got on Crusoe's nerves. The mixing of identities was so extreme that when Crusoe innocently dyed a baby goat red, the result was tragic: "his mother wouldn't recognize him." Crusoe's own empowerment through breaking down these binaries, the poem suggests, could have had tragic results, too.

He might have gone mad, for example, as his dream of slitting a baby's throat suggests. Even though they come from different cultures, the arrival of Friday restored Crusoe's identity as a human being: "Just when I thought I couldn't stand it / another minute longer, Friday came." Crusoe explains that European Christians, like Defoe, have misunderstood Friday's positive influence: "(Accounts of that have everything all wrong.)" Defoe's Christian portrayal of Friday as a heathen cannibal failed to show that "Friday was nice." The terms "heathen" and "Christian" overlooked the greater similarity between the two men: both were sexual humans. Crusoe thought of Friday in sexual terms: "I wanted to propagate my kind, / And so did he, I think, poor boy."

When Crusoe was rescued and returned to England, he had the novel pain of his skepticism of the Christian faith: "Now I live here, another island, / that doesn't seem like one, but who decides?" Crusoe himself has already answered that question: those who control the naming of islands decide, forcing him to write to deconstruct the myths of the past. Now he lives among objects like the "uninteresting lumber" that lack the meaning of his homemade objects like the knife:

> The knife there on the shelf—
> it reeked of meaning, like a crucifix.
> It lived. How many years did I
> beg it, implore it, not to break?
> I knew each nick and scratch by heart,

the bluish blade, the broken tip,
the lines of wood-grain on the handle . . .

In the final stanza Crusoe tells the reader that he is to be commemorated by the local museum. They want everything,

The flute, the knife, the shrivelled shoes,
my shedding goatskin trousers
(moths have got in the fur),
the parasol that took me such a time
remembering the way the ribs should go.

Mazzaro (1980) sees the final stanza as the key to the poem. Here Crusoe recognizes that self-definition comes from reverie: countering the museum keeper's judgment and the limits of biological propagation as seen in the death of Friday. Through his imagination, Crusoe is able to overcome the limits of other things.

The genesis of "Crusoe in England" began long before the first publication dates in 1971 and 1976. In August 1964 Bishop first mentioned to Robert Lowell that she had been up late working on a poem about Crusoe. In 1965 she reported that the restoration of an 18th-century slave church in Ouro Preto, Santa Eugenia, had uncovered a mural of Crusoe. The first draft, entitled "Crusoe at Home," was a mere fragment, comprised of only the first three stanzas of the final version, but Bishop had already chosen to write Crusoe's account of his life on the island in the past tense: "Well, I had fifty-two / miserable little volcanoes[.]" Middle drafts were entitled "Last Days of Crusoe." Parts of the middle and end of the poem came to Bishop in short images that she later developed into complete stanzas. The fourth stanza first appears in much abbreviated form:

self-pity—what is wrong so wrong about it anyways
Do I deserv [sic] this? Somehow I must
or did I chose it? I don't remember chosing it
there must have been a moment when I actually
chose this?

The character of Friday appears in the third draft, blending two images Bishop later separated and developed:

If only Friday had been a owoman [sic]
I wanted to propagate my kind
so did he, I think, poor boy
We'd pet the baby goats
baa baa baa I still can't shake
it out of my ears.

Parts of that development were scattered about the draft. Bishop knew the ending for the poem by the third draft, where it appears in the middle with a note scribbled next to it, "end." In another place on the draft, Bishop wrote: "And Friday, my dear Friday, died of measles, / seventeen years ago come march."

In addition to leaving behind her painful memories of her life with Lota de Macedo Soares in Brazil, "Crusoe in England" suggests that Bishop also needed to return to New England to reconnect with her forgotten past there. Did Bishop, like Crusoe, feel that she was losing her identity? In a letter from 1970 she recorded simultaneous breakthroughs in her writing and her grieving:

> My own affairs seem to be going very well in spite of this awfulness. I have been drunk once, for a few hours, since Christmas—that's all. I have stopped smoking. I am now the poetry critic for *The New Yorker*. . . . And I have just—Sunday—accepted the invitation to take over Robert Lowell's courses at Harvard for the fall term, while he's in England. . . . I've also just sold *The New Yorker* the first poem I have been able to finish in over three years ["In the Waiting Room"] and really can't believe this. I have finished two more old ones and am well along with a brand-new one. (Bishop, 1994)

*Geography III* won the 1977 National Book Critics Circle Award.

Cynthia Cameros

**Further Reading**

Bishop, Elizabeth, *One Art: Letters,* edited by Robert Giroux, New York: Farrar Straus and Giroux, 1994

Curry, Renee R., "Augury and Autobiography: Bishop's 'Crusoe in England,'" *Arizona Quarterly* 47, no. 3 (Autumn 1991)

Diehl, Joanne Feit, "At Home with Loss: Elizabeth Bishop and the American Sublime," in *Coming to Light: American Women Poets in the Twentieth Century,* edited by Diane Wood Middlebrook and Marilyn Yalom, Ann Arbor: University of Michigan Press, 1985

Kalstone, David, *Becoming a Poet: Elizabeth Bishop with Marianne Moore and Robert Lowell,* New York: Farrar Straus and Giroux, and London: Hogarth Press, 1989

Mazzaro, Jerome, "The Poetics of Impediment: Elizabeth Bishop," in *Postmodern American Poetry,* Urbana: University of Illinois Press, 1980

Millier, Brett C., *Elizabeth Bishop: Life and the Memory of It,* Berkeley: University of California Press, 1993

## In the Waiting Room

Elizabeth Bishop's poem "In the Waiting Room" introduces the final book of Bishop's poetic career, *Geography III* (1976), and anticipates the book's determination to upset the dichotomies between domestic and foreign, quotidian and exotic. It also engages Bishop's poetry in a larger debate about how an imperialist United States views the rest of the world, especially the so-called "savage" regions, and details a young girl's destabilized self-awareness in relation to this imperialist gaze.

Bishop composed "In the Waiting Room," which originally appeared in *The New Yorker* in 1971, during a time of intense self-assessment following the death of Bishop's long-time companion, Lota de Macedo Soares, and Bishop's departure from Brazil, where she had lived with Lota for 15 years. Bishop, who spent her childhood in Nova Scotia and New England, and who lived as an adult in Key West, Washington, D.C., New York, Brazil, and Massachusetts (among other places), always viewed herself as something of an "expatriate" wherever she resided. This perceived personal displacement would build throughout Bishop's life and poetic career. In a 1970 letter Bishop asserts that "the trouble is, I really don't know where or how I want to live any more." Although it would be a mistake to read "In the Waiting

Room" as a purely autobiographical poem, the poem does hint at Bishop's effort to retrace her migrations back to one childhood moment, to reconstruct how "Elizabeth" decided to live in relation to the larger world, even if it was as a perpetual expatriate.

The poem takes place in a dentist's office in Worcester, Massachusetts, the city of Bishop's birth, during the dark of a winter afternoon. The "Elizabeth" of the poem waits for her "Aunt Consuelo" (Bishop had no aunt by that name) to finish her appointment and encounters among the drab accoutrements of the room ("arctics and overcoats, / lamps and magazines") a copy of *National Geographic*. This issue, dated "February, 1918," advances an encapsulated view of the world as generated by the imperialist "geographic" project of the politically assertive United States, showing

the inside of a volcano,
black, and full of ashes;
then it was spilling over
in rivulets of fire.
Osa and Martin Johnson
dressed in riding breeches,
laced boots, and pith helmets.
A dead man slung on a pole
—"Long Pig," the caption said.
Babies with pointed heads
wound round and round with string;
black, naked women with necks
wound round and round with wire
like the necks of light bulbs.
Their breasts were horrifying.
I read it straight through.
I was too shy to stop.

The magazine, really a composite of many *Geographics* (despite Bishop's repeated insistence that she actually read a single issue containing all these images), juxtaposes unfettered violence with measured restraint, exotic "savagery" with familiar Anglo "civilization." It is not the carefully-laced anthropologist Johnson who seduces the young Elizabeth, but the half-naked women and their "exotic" children, whose images hurl Elizabeth into a vertigo of identity:

I—we—were falling, falling,
our eyes glued to the cover
of the *National Geographic,*
February, 1918.

As the young Elizabeth tries to stabilize her sense of self with what she sees as "concrete" aspects of her life and surroundings—her name and age, the "shadowy gray knees," "trousers," "skirts," "boots," and "different pairs of hands" around her in the room—she understands that even her sense of those reassuring details is not absolute but defined in relation to the very swirl of "foreign" images that has set her awareness adrift.

You are a *I,*
you are an *Elizabeth,*
you are one of *them,*

she finally dares to realize. No longer is "Elizabeth" simply a proper noun corresponding neatly to a compartmentalized, isolated person: Elizabeth is now a category, a subset of the "*them*" that the reader understands to include at least Elizabeth, the "foolish, timid" Aunt Consuelo, and the bare-breasted women from the magazine, if not everything Elizabeth has known. "What similarities," asks the Elizabeth of the poem, "held us all together / or made us all just one?"

"In the Waiting Room" does not posit a cut-and-dried answer. Instead, acknowledging that "nothing / stranger could ever happen" than the personal and cultural vertigo it introduces in its lines, it leaves the reader to ponder the multivalent situation of identity in what appears to be Bishop's own postmodern, postcolonial refiguring of John Donne's dictum, "No man is an island." In such a light, the poems that follow "In the Waiting Room" in *Geography III* extend Bishop's "strange" unsettling of binaries: "Crusoe in England," which appears immediately after "In the Waiting Room," portrays Robinson Crusoe living a disturbed, unsettled life in England in the wake of his "rescue" from an uncharted, "savage" island; "The Moose" brings a "wild" animal into contact with humans in the midst of a nondescript, foggy Canadian forest; and "One Art" illustrates that the "losses" that come by converting the foreign into the domestic and vice versa mean that one never becomes accustomed to "the art of losing things."

Some critics would fault "In the Waiting Room" for not tackling in a more overt way other significant issues in Bishop's own struggle to sort out personal identity, particularly those matters surrounding the public depiction of her own sexuality. Still, Bishop's gesture in the poem is wide, ambitious, and surprisingly political in ways that her earlier poems are not. "In the Waiting Room" poses many subtle questions to an America embroiled in the Vietnam War and other disputes "abroad" while painfully engaged at "home" in its redefinition of what it means to be American. Bishop's questions disquiet readers seeking easy definitions of personal, public, and political identity.

TRENTON HICKMAN

**Further Reading**

Colwell, Anne, *Inscrutable Houses: Metaphors of the Body in the Poems of Elizabeth Bishop,* Tuscaloosa: University of Alabama Press, 1997

Costello, Bonnie, *Elizabeth Bishop: Questions of Mastery,* Cambridge, Massachusetts: Harvard University Press, 1991

Dickie, Margaret, *Stein, Bishop, and Rich: Lyrics of Love, War, and Place,* Chapel Hill: University of North Carolina Press, 1997

Diehl, Joanne Feit, *Elizabeth Bishop and Marianne Moore: The Psychodynamics of Creativity,* Princeton, New Jersey: Princeton University Press, 1993

Doreski, Carole Kiler, *Elizabeth Bishop: The Restraints of Language,* New York: Oxford University Press, 1993

Fountain, Gary, and Peter Brazeau, *Remembering Elizabeth Bishop: An Oral Biography,* Amherst: University of Massachusetts Press, 1994

Goldensohn, Lorrie, *Elizabeth Bishop: The Biography of a Poetry,* New York: Columbia University Press, 1992

Kalstone, David, *Becoming a Poet: Elizabeth Bishop with Marianne Moore and Robert Lowell,* New York: Farrar Straus and Giroux, and London: Hogarth Press, 1989

Lombardi, Marilyn May, *The Body and the Song: Elizabeth Bishop's Poetics,* Carbondale: Southern Illinois University Press, 1995

Lombardi, Marilyn May, editor, *Elizabeth Bishop: The Geography of Gender,* Charlottesville: University Press of Virginia, 1993

MacMahon, Candace W., *Elizabeth Bishop: A Bibliography, 1927–1979,* Charlottesville: University Press of Virginia, 1980

McCabe, Susan, *Elizabeth Bishop: Her Poetics of Loss,* University Park: Pennsylvania State University Press, 1994

Millier, Brett C., *Elizabeth Bishop: Life and the Memory of It,* Berkeley: University of California Press, 1993

Parker, Robert Dale, *The Unbeliever: The Poetry of Elizabeth Bishop,* Urbana: University of Illinois Press, 1988

Schwartz, Lloyd, and Sybil P. Estess, editors, *Elizabeth Bishop and Her Art,* Ann Arbor: University of Michigan Press, 1983

Stevenson, Anne, *Elizabeth Bishop,* New York: Twayne, 1966

Stevenson, Anne, *Five Looks at Elizabeth Bishop,* London: Bellew, 1998

Travisano, Thomas J., *Elizabeth Bishop: Her Artistic Development,* Charlottesville: University Press of Virginia, 1988

## One Art

Elizabeth Bishop's much-anthologized poem "One Art" is a villanelle. The villanelle took on its standardized form in France in the late 17th century as a 19-line poem divided into five stanzas. The standard villanelle has only two rhymes, and certain lines repeat in the following pattern: A1 b A2 // a b A1 // a b A2 // a b A1 // a b A2 // a b A1 A2. The form enjoyed renewed popularity in the later 19th century, when it made its way to England, and has remained popular to this day. In addition to Bishop, 20th-century American poets Dylan Thomas, W.H. Auden, Theodore Roethke, Sylvia Plath, and James Merrill, among others, have all used the form to good effect (*Princeton Encyclopedia of Poetics*).

Bishop's biographer Brett Millier reports that Bishop had envisioned "One Art" as a villanelle from the start and consciously employed the number 2—as the villanelle has two rhymes (two rivers, two cities)—in the poem to highlight the loss of love, the primary subject of the poem: when the poet loses her love in the last stanza, she is no longer part of a couple (Millier, 1993). Lloyd Schwartz notes that "One Art" has a "double" meaning: "both learning not to mind [losing] and learning to lose more. Though the latter may be easier than the former, the 'expert' ironically suggests practice: *Lose something every day . . . Then practice losing farther, losing faster*" (quoted in Schwartz and Estess, 1983).

Of course, the achievement of any exceptional poem—and "One Art" is indeed exceptional—lies in its universal appeal. Bishop's poem succeeds because it chronicles loss in terms familiar to everyone: ultimately, "loss"—of objects, time, relationships, and finally of life itself—is the "art" we will all come to "master," willingly or not. "One Art" also chronicles Bishop's own formidable losses. The poem, in Millier's words, is really an "elegy for [Bishop's] whole life" (Millier, 1993).

David Kalstone (1989) notes that "One Art"—like many of Bishop's poems—takes memory and loss as its subject. In such poems Bishop pays homage to those who bear their inevitable yet devastating losses with quiet dignity. Indeed, in writing "One Art" as a villanelle, Bishop underscores her deep regard for these individuals: she meets the strict demands of the form while recounting her own pain, just as they meet their daily responsibilities while suffering their own pain. Moreover, the poem transforms pain into an enduring work of art.

The losses that Bishop catalogs in "One Art" increase in magnitude. Bishop opens with things commonly lost that do not have inherent value but that cause "fluster": "door keys, the hour badly spent." However, these seemingly innocuous losses signal profound losses. The "door keys" become "three loved houses"; the houses become "two cities, lovely ones"; the cities become "some realms I owned"; the realms become "two rivers"; and ultimately these become a whole "continent." The "hour badly spent"—emphasized by "I lost my mother's watch"—indicates the loss of time. Interestingly, this lost "time" seems less a nod to the speaker's approaching death (Bishop wrote the poem in her mid-60s) than a lament for the past, most notably her childhood years in Nova Scotia, a brief and relatively happy spell in Key West, and her 15 happy years in Brazil. (Bishop identifies the "three loved houses" as those in Key West, Florida; Petropolis, Brazil; and Ouro Preto, Brazil [cited in Schwartz and Estess, 1983].) Of course, the poem also chronicles the loss of relationships—indirectly in the first four stanzas and directly in the last. (Bishop's father died of Bright's disease when she was an infant, her mother was institutionalized with mental illness when Bishop was a young girl, and she had few satisfying or enduring romantic relationships in the course of her lifetime.)

The fact that the speaker documents the disappearance of the physical world—nations, rivers, and even a whole continent—suggests the inevitability and enormity of loss. Yet the speaker regards the loss of love as the most grave of all: "even losing you" culminates her long, sad catalog. Bishop's increasingly strained romantic relationship with Alice Methfessel in the fall of 1975 occasioned "One Art." However, the poem clearly mourns Lota de Macedo Soares, Bishop's lover of some 15 years with whom she lived in Brazil and whom she lost in 1967 to suicide. (Millier titles her chapter on Lota's death "The Art of Losing.") Although Bishop survived some ten years after losing Lota and even managed to find love again with Alice, she could no longer bear living in Brazil without Lota; she moved back to the United States and spent the majority of her last years in Boston, where she taught at Harvard University.

"One Art" puts forward a heroic stance toward loss. The speaker seems to accept loss, if not with ease at least with dignity and grace. (Yet, as Millier notes, the last stanza shifts to the future perfect tense, which suggests that the speaker has not yet fully come to terms with her loss.) Many readers new to Bishop's work mistakenly confuse the restraint evident in poems such as "One Art" with a lack of feeling. Bishop's early mentor, Marianne Moore, succinctly captures her protégée's unique poetic temperament in these lines from a review of *North and South,* Bishop's first collection of poems: "Elizabeth Bishop is spectacular in being unspectacular. Why has no one ever thought of this, one asks oneself, why not be accurate and modest?" (cited in Schwartz and Estess, 1983). Rather than Berryman and Lowell—the latter a dear friend to Bishop—Bishop resembles her reticent contemporary Randall Jarrell, an early and ardent champion of Bishop's work. Jarrell beautifully articulates Bishop's stance toward the world, in "One Art" and elsewhere, in these lines: "Instead of crying, with justice, 'This is a world in which no one can get along,' Miss Bishop's poems show that it is barely but perfectly possible" (cited in Schwartz and Estess, 1983).

SHERRI LYNN VANDENAKKER

**Further Reading**

Bloom, Harold, editor, *Elizabeth Bishop,* New York: Chelsea House, 1985

Costello, Bonnie, *Elizabeth Bishop: Questions of Mastery,* Cambridge, Massachusetts: Harvard University Press, 1991

Doreski, Carole Kiler, *Elizabeth Bishop: The Restraints of Language,* New York: Oxford University Press, 1993

Harrison, Victoria, *Elizabeth Bishop's Poetics of Intimacy,* Cambridge and New York: Cambridge University Press, 1993

Kalstone, David, *Becoming a Poet: Elizabeth Bishop with Marianne Moore and Robert Lowell,* New York: Farrar Straus and Giroux, and London: Hogarth Press, 1989

Lombardi, Marilyn May, *The Body and the Song: Elizabeth Bishop's Poetics,* Carbondale: Southern Illinois University Press, 1995

Millier, Brett C., *Elizabeth Bishop: Life and the Memory of It,* Berkeley: University of California Press, 1993

Schwartz, Lloyd, and Sybil P. Estess, editors, *Elizabeth Bishop and Her Art,* Ann Arbor: University of Michigan Press, 1983

Stevenson, Anne, *Five Looks at Elizabeth Bishop,* London: Bellew, 1998

Travisano, Thomas J., *Midcentury Quartet: Bishop, Lowell, Jarrell, Berryman, and the Making of a Postmodern Aesthetic,* Charlottesville: University Press of Virginia, 1999

---

# Black Arts Movement

The Black Arts movement was described by Larry Neal, one of its major figures, in a 1968 essay as the "aesthetic and spiritual sister of the Black Power concept" ("The Black Arts Movement"). Some call it "the most audacious, prolific, and socially engaged literary movement in America's history" (Salaam, 1997). From its inception in 1965, Black Arts contested the petition and protest literature that had evolved during the Civil Rights movement, promoting "Black Power" instead. The movement affirmed "the integral relationship between black art and black people" and

> proposed the participation of artists of all categories in letters, music, and the theater in the exemplification of the experience and values of African and African American life. (Long, 1997)

Its legacy in American poetry includes the use of Black English Vernacular (BEV), call and response, music, and performance or spoken word to enhance the poem.

The Black Arts movement got its start when Amiri Baraka (then LeRoi Jones), who evolved out of the 1950s Beat generation, moved to Harlem from Greenwich Village. According to Haki R. Madhubuti, Baraka was the acknowledged father of the Black Arts movement, the central theorist and practitioner who created the term "Black Arts," which originated in writing groups like Umbra. The first post–Civil Rights Black literary group to establish a distinct radical voice, Umbra founded On Guard for Freedom, a 1960 Black nationalist literary organization, and the Harlem Writers Guild, a writers' group focusing primarily on fiction. The Black Arts movement established its characteristic aesthetic within these writing groups. Whereas the writers of the Harlem Writers Guild concentrated more on fiction that was more difficult to publish, other writers focused on performance poetry that used the black vernacular, themes, slogans, and chants from the culture. After the breakup of Umbra some writers formed the Uptown Writers movement. Along with New Music musicians they performed poetry all over Harlem and helped Amiri Baraka found the Black Arts Repertory Theatre/School (BART/S). BART/S was designed to create and teach plays that emphasized the meaning of the lives of Black people and brought art, music, poetry, and drama to the streets of Harlem. Baraka soon returned to Greenwich Village, however, and BART/S began to fall apart.

The concept of the Black Arts movement continued despite the demise of BART/S because of its strong connection to the Black Power movement. From the mid- to late 1960s the assassination of Martin Luther King, Jr., and the riots in Watts, Detroit, Newark, and Cleveland created a radical revolution. Baraka's poem "Black Art" was the centerpiece of the Black Arts literary movement. The poem was reminiscent of the confrontational social structure of the era; one section proclaims:

> We want "poems that kill."
> Assassin poems, poems that shoot
> guns. Poems that wrestle cops into alleys
> and take their weapons leaving them dead
> with tongues pulled out and sent to Ireland.

The advocacy for artistic and political freedom resulted in a militant artistic movement. The establishment of three organizations, the Revolutionary Action Movement (RAM), US (as opposed to "them"), and the Chicago-based Nation of Islam helped further characterize the style and direction of the movement. Chicago, home of the *Negro Digest/Black World* and Haki Madhubuti's Third World Press, became a haven for the Black Arts movement, as did the San Francisco Bay Area, home of the *Journal of Black Poetry* (founded in 1966 by Dingane Joe Goncalves) and *Black Scholar*.

The development of Black Theater groups, poetry performances, and journals tied the Black Arts writers to the community. In the 1960s and 1970s several significant theaters were formed: the National Black Theater, founded by Barbara Ann Teer; the New Lafayette Theater, developed by Ed Bullins; and the Negro Ensemble Company (NEC), founded by Robert Hooks in 1967. Other Harlem theaters include Ernie McClintock's Afro-American Studio, Mical Whitaker's East River Players, the New Heritage Repertory Theater, and the Hadley Players. These theaters served as key facilities for films, meetings, lectures, and study groups. The development of Black Arts theaters and cultural centers spread rapidly across the country due to the national distribution of magazines and various publication opportunities. *Freedomways* and Dan Watt's *Liberator* solicited the writings of young Blacks; *Liberator* published many of the early critical essays of the Black Arts movement. *Black Dialogue,* founded in 1964, was the first major Black Arts literary publication. At the time Goncalves edited the poetry section of the journal; after the massive influx of poetry he decided to start the *Journal of Black Poetry,* which also featured revolutionary poets from African, Caribbean, and Asian cultures. Dudley Randall's Broadside Press in Detroit functioned as an important publisher of many poets.

Askia Toure arose as the most influential poet of the Black Arts movement. Throughout the movement he served in various capacities as contributing editor, editor-at-large, and staff writer for different journals and magazines. His long poem *Juju: Magic Songs for the Black Nation* was published by Third World Press in 1970 and was followed by his 1973 collection *Songhai!* He won the American Book Award in 1989 for *From the Pyramid to the Projects: Poems of Genocide and Resistance. Dawnsong,* an epic in lyric poetry, was published in 1999.

Other major artists of the movement were Ed Bullins, Larry Neal, Addison Gayle, Hoyt Fuller, Haki R. Madhubuti (Don L. Lee), and Sonia Sanchez. Ed Bullins wrote 50 plays, receiving the Obie Award for *The Fabulous Miss Marie* (1971) and a National Book Critics Circle Award for *The Taking of Miss Janie* (1975). He also edited the issue of *Drama Review* that featured essays and plays by the major writers of his generation. Ben Caldwell, Jimmy Garrett, John O'Neal, Ron Milner, Woodie King, Jr., Bill Gunn, and Adam David Walker joined with the early writers of this era to produce writings for the journal.

Larry Neal is often considered the Black Arts movement's "spiritual journeyman" (Engelhardt, 1997). His two collections of poetry, *Black Boogaloo: Notes on Black Liberation* (1969) and *Hoodoo Hollerin' Bebop Ghosts* (1974), addressed various themes of the era, such as mythology, history, and language. Neal also produced two plays, *The Glorious Monster in the Bell of the Horn* (1976) and *In an Upstate Motel: A Mortality Play* (1980), worked in association with Amiri Baraka to create the Black Arts Repertory Theater, and wrote films for both television and private companies. The author of several critical essays on various artists and subjects, Neal edited the *Journal of Black Poetry,* the *Cricket,* and *Liberator* magazine, but his own writing did not receive critical acclaim until after his death. His work is featured in the 1989 collection *Visions of a Liberated Future: Black Arts Movement Writings.*

Addison Gayle was another major contributor to the Black Arts movement. He edited *Black Expressions: Essays by and about Black Americans in the Creative Arts* (1969), an anthology of Black critical writings. In 1970 Gayle published *The Black Situation,* a collection of essays about his personal growth and development in the wake of both the Civil Rights and Black Power movements. *The Black Aesthetic* (1971), perhaps Gayle's most well-known work, compiled the works of various African-American authors and theorists. Gayle continued to advocate a strong link between artistic creativity and the political and social endeavors of African-Americans throughout his teaching career and in other publications. These include *Oak and Ivy: A Biography of Paul Laurence Dunbar* (1971), *Claude McKay: The Black Poet at War* (1972), *Way of a New World* (1975), *Richard Wright: Ordeal of a Native Son* (1980), and his autobiography *Wayward Child: A Personal Odyssey* (1971).

Another leading contributor to the Black Arts movement, Hoyt Fuller, went abroad to live in France and Spain after becoming disillusioned with racism in America, later traveling to Africa due to his interest in Sekou Toure of Guinea. These experiences are portrayed in his only book, *Return to Africa* (1971). Fuller did return to America in 1960 and became the editor of the *Negro Digest;* in only a few years the journal's revival became the sourcebook of the Black Arts movement. It was renamed *Black World* to indicate its emphases on both African and African-American Diaspora. Although the journal reflected Fuller's views on political, social, health, and spiritual issues, its publication was stopped when he relocated to Atlanta and started another journal, *First World.* Fuller also created, along with Haki R. Madhubuti, the Organization of Black American Culture (OBAC), which sought to influence cultural activities in the arts.

Haki R. Madhubuti, who changed his name from Don L. Lee because of the influence of the Black Arts movement, founded Third World Press in 1967. In the same year his first collection of poetry appeared from Randall's Broadside Press, *Think Black.* Six other books followed, and Madhubuti joined other members of the Black Arts movement in reading and selling their poetry at Black Arts conferences. Many of his works are as political as his activities, most notably a collection of essays entitled *Enemies: The Clash of Races* (1978). His 1987 collection of poetry *Killing Memory, Seeking Ancestors* explores the late-century re-emergence and transformation of issues—political, spiritual, health—that affected the lives of Blacks in the 1960s. The poems in *The Great Wait* reflect his love of jazz music and critique the Black community for what he sees as its passive stance toward self-improvement. Madhubuti's work also includes a collection of critical essays (*Gifted Genius: Writings from the Frontline of the Black Arts Movement,* 1996) and two collections of love poems.

Sonia Sanchez, another core leader of the movement, was born Wilsonia Driver. She published her first collection, *Homecoming,* in 1969. After moving to Harlem she became very involved with Baraka and Neal and immersed herself in political activism and poetry, rejecting white Western values to become the militant female voice of the 1960s. She helped establish the first Black Studies program and fought for radical reform of a racist agenda and a corrupt economic system. Her work focuses on the music—blues and jazz—and heroes of the African-American community, paying homage to Malcolm X, Bobby Hutton, John Coltrane, and Billie Holiday. A writer of children's books, love poems, plays, and her autobiography *A Blues Book for Blue Black Magical Women* (1974), Sanchez received the American Book Award in 1985 for *Homegirls and Handgrenades* (1984). She has received numerous other awards, including a National Endowment for the Arts fellowship, the Lucretia Mott Award, and the Paul Robeson

Social Justice Award. Sanchez remains committed to the central theme of her works: the return to Blackness.

The Black Arts movement can be more comprehensively understood through the anthologies published in the 1960s and 1970s. *Black Fire* (1968), edited by Baraka and Neal, "stands as a definitive movement anthology" (Salaam, 1997). Contributors in *Black Fire* are of the Black Power/Black Consciousness generation that addressed its works to Africa, Asia, and Latin America. Other anthologies included *For Malcolm X, Poem on the Life and the Death of Malcolm X* (1969), edited by Dudley Randall and Margeret Taylor Goss Burroughs; Gayle's *The Black Aesthetic* (1971); *New Black Voices* (1972), edited by Abraham Chapman; and *Drumvoices, The Mission of Afro-American Poetry: A Critical History* (1976), edited by Eugene Redmond. *The Black Woman* (1970, edited by Toni Cade Bambara) was the first anthology of Black feminist works, and Stephen Henderson's *Understanding the New Black Poetry* (1972) provided a comprehensive examination of the Black Arts poetic aesthetic.

Major internal and external factors contributed to the breakup of the Black Arts movement around 1974. In May of that year the nationalists and Marxists in the African Liberation Support Committee split; Africa began denouncing race-based struggles in the Sixth Pan-African Congress in Tanzania; and Baraka's Congress of Afrikan People became a Marxist organization. The Black Arts movement also suffered from commercialization and capitalism. Corporate mainstream America targeted certain artists of the movement, and the Black community could not compete economically with new offers to publish and produce the works of the artists. Neither the Black Arts nor the Black Power movement was ever able to recover from these devastating blows.

SHARON D. RAYNOR

**Further Reading**

Bambara, Toni Cade, *The Black Woman: An Anthology,* New York: Mentor, 1970

Cook, Williams, "The Black Arts Poets," in *The Columbia History of American Poetry,* edited by Jay Parini and Brett Candlish Millier, New York: Columbia University Press, 1993

Engelhardt, Elizabeth Sanders Delwiche, "Haki R. Madhubuti," in *The Oxford Companion to African American Literature,* edited by William L. Andrews, Frances Smith Foster, and Trudier Harris, New York: Oxford University Press, 1997

Harris, William J., editor, *The LeRoi Jones/Amiri Baraka Reader,* New York: Thunder's Mouth Press, 1991; 2nd edition, 2000

Jones, LeRoi, and Larry Neal, editors, *Black Fire: An Anthology of Afro-American Writing,* New York: Morrow, 1968

Long, Richard, "Hoyt Fuller," in *The Oxford Companion to African American Literature,* edited by William L. Andrews, Frances Smith Foster, and Trudier Harris, New York: Oxford University Press, 1997

Salaam, Kalamu ya, "Black Arts Movement," in *The Oxford Companion to African American Literature,* edited by William L. Andrews, Frances Smith Foster, and Trudier Harris, New York: Oxford University Press, 1997

---

# Paul Blackburn 1926–71

The work of Paul Blackburn, a committed organizer of poetry readings in New York bars and coffeehouses in the 1950s and 1960s, displays aspects of the Beat, New York School, Black Mountain, and Projectivist poetics that were current in his milieu. In many ways, however, his sense of line, point of view, and poetic practice stand markedly apart.

Blackburn's poems show the intense awareness of breath and line that characterize Charles Olson's work, but Blackburn is the more personal and musical writer. His work features the sometimes scatological outrageousness of the Beats along with the New York School's vivid social or "street" energy, but strikes a less glitzy, mordant tone and offers a sort of dark patience that is entirely different from Frank O'Hara and his colleagues' fast, celebratory poetry. Finally, while Blackburn placed himself firmly outside of New Criticism and other influential academic power structures of the period, he nonetheless exhibited a scholarly streak in his translations of Lorca, the early fictions of Julio Cortazar, and, most notably, the Troubadour poets of 11th-, 12th-, and 13th-century Provence.

Rather than courting publishers and critics, Blackburn opted for an intense grassroots involvement as a promulgator of the downtown Manhattan poetry community. As a result, although he was quite prolific, most of his books appeared in ephemeral small-press editions that quickly went out of print. It was only after the posthumous publication of *Proensa* (1978), his anthology of Troubadour translations, and *The Collected Poems of Paul Blackburn* (1985) that the full range of his achievement became apparent. Blackburn's commitment to providing public venues for his contemporaries lives on through the tapes of readings he organized at the Deux Magots and Metro coffeehouses. These audio recordings, now housed at the library of the University of California at San Diego, constitute an invaluable oral history of this key period in American poetry.

Paul Blackburn was born in 1926 and spent his early years in Vermont. His mother, poet Frances Frost, was selected for the Yale Series of Younger Poets in 1929. Within a year of the award, she separated from her husband, moved to New York City to pursue a writing career, and left Blackburn and his younger sister with her parents. When he was 14, Blackburn rejoined his mother in New York City. She encouraged his growing interest in poetry, which ultimately led him to study at New York University with poet, critic, and teacher M.L. Rosenthal.

Like many poets of his generation, Blackburn began corresponding with Modernist pioneer Ezra Pound and visited him at St. Elizabeths Hospital outside of Washington, D.C. As a result of pro-fascist activities in Italy during World War II, Pound had been declared insane and was institutionalized. At St. Elizabeths Pound held court for a steady stream of young American poets. As he was for many others, Pound became an important influence for Blackburn. He encouraged Blackburn's enthusiasm for Troubadour poetry and was instrumental in having Blackburn's work appear in the magazine *New Directions* (1951). Pound also introduced him to Robert Creeley who in turn put him in touch with Charles Olson and other Black Mountain poets, as well as poet Cid Corman, the editor of *Origin,* which published a good sampling of Blackburn's 1950s poems.

Although Blackburn was grouped with the Black Mountain poets in Donald Allen's landmark anthology *The New American Poetry* (1960), his connection with this school was hardly definitive. However, he did share with Olson and others a focus on "composition by field," which utilizes the entire surface of the page, with irregular line indentations and breaks to deconstruct the quatrain in favor of a music-like notation of spoken performance.

In the spring of 1954 Blackburn and his new wife traveled to Mallorca, Spain, and Toulouse, France, after he received a Fulbright fellowship to study the Provençal language and its literature. They remained abroad until 1957, when they returned to New York and the marriage broke up. During this European sojourn his first book, *The Dissolving Fabric* (1955), was published by Creeley's Mallorca-based Divers Press. A slender book of only 14 poems, it presents early manifestations of key Blackburn themes.

"Death and the Summer Woman" explores sensuality and all the attendant fear it had for him:

> . . . the brown easy
> slope of back and shoulders moving into surf,
> how you lower your head when I try to look at you,
> a hot sunny innocence, yet sea-green coolness
>
> and your eyes know us;
> your open palms, the sweated tracings
> show the door stands open.
> But the trap of will
> will trip it snap shut like brass
> the slightest touch,
> haul you hooked inside and kill the season, Death
> smiling cool at you the whispered
>
> "no"

In later years this theme—and its underlying threat—would unfortunately often manifest itself through an objectification of women that can be extremely off-putting by contemporary standards. "The Birds" introduces a motif that continued to develop in poems such as "Purse-Seine," which appears in *The Nets* (1961). "The Birds"—specifically, gulls—are strangely prescient, powerful, coldly objective observers. Poet and critic Clayton Eshleman discusses this recurring image in his reminiscence of Blackburn that appeared in the Blackburn issue of the magazine *SixPack* (7–8 [1974]). He characterizes the bird imagery as "the presence of the creation itself, the confirmation that Blackburn allows himself."

Blackburn's major collection, *The Cities* (1967), incorporates work from the early 1950s through the mid-1960s. At this point the Blackburn urban persona was in full force, particularly in a genre for which he was a primary proponent: the subway poem. "Clickety-Clack" and "The Yawn" are two prime examples that appear in this volume. In the former poem, he writes,

> I took
> a coney island of the mind
> to the coney
> island of the flesh
> the brighton local
> riding
> past church avenue, beverly, cortelyou, past
> avenues h & j
> king's highway, neck road, sheepshead bay,
> brighton, all the way to stillwell
> avenue
> that hotbed of assignation
> clickety-clack . . .

After a second failed marriage and a bitter period characterized by poems that often seemed about self-obliteration, Blackburn became revitalized during a 1967 Guggenheim fellowship trip to Europe. He met his third wife en route and began to develop his final body of work, *The Journals* (1975), which consists of seemingly offhand poems that effortlessly utilize daily reportage, as in this journal poem dated "12. VI 71":

> THE 2 A.M.
> of a summer night in Cortland, this street
> high on the hill is
> virtually (virtuously) soundless, it
> has the virtue of near
> silence . The far
> sound of a truck, mile away on the interstate,
> a bird or two waking up (hence thee, fear), two
> faucets that run (do not drip to the nearest), the
> sound of my fat pen
> writing this down .
>
> The bath room faucets sound like the overrun
> of a fountain in Granada .
> The birds go back to sleep.
> The truck climbs away north toward Homer, Preble,
> Tully, Syracuse . Just the sound of fountain, no breeze.
>
> How say goodnite to you all, dear friends?
> Easy.
> Goodnite! The bed
> awaits my head,
> waits on the
> sound of this pen
> stopping now .

As poet Robert Kelly notes in his introduction, these poems "demonstrate the way his work knew to go, the power of music that he could charm out of everything that came his way[.] . . . [N]o idle dailiness was without its seed of connection."

*The Journals* covers the period from May 1967 to July 1971, only two months before Blackburn's death from esophageal cancer. Kelly aptly describes much of the work in this book as a "*carni vale*, a joyous farewell to the flesh of the world."

PETER J. BUSHYEAGER

See also Black Mountain School

**Biography**
Born in St. Albans, Vermont, 24 November 1926. Attended New York University, University of Wisconsin, B.A. 1950; University of Toulouse, France, 1954–55; Lecturer, University of Toulouse, 1955–56; assistant editor, Funk and Wagnalls, New York City, 1959–60; poet-in-residence, City University of New York, 1966–67; Assistant Professor, State University of New York, Cortland, 1970–71; co-founder of poetry reading programs at Judson Church, St. Mark's Church, Dr. Generosity's coffeehouse, New York City; director of poetry reading and interview program on WBAI radio, 1964–65. Received Fulbright fellowship, 1954–55; Guggenheim fellowship, 1967–68. Died in Cortland, New York, 13 September 1971.

**Poetry**
*The Cities*, 1967
*In. On. Or about the Premises*, 1968
*Early Selected Y Mas*, 1972
*Halfway Down the Coast*, 1975
*The Journals*, 1975
*Against Silences*, 1980
*The Collected Poems of Paul Blackburn*, 1985
*The Parallel Voyages*, 1987
*The Selected Poems of Paul Blackburn*, 1989

**Other Writings:** translations of selected Provençal poets from French (*Proensa*, 1978), and Spanish literature (*Cronopios and Famas*, 1999); edited anthologies of poetry (*Lorca/Blackburn: Poems of Federico García Lorca*, 1979).

**Further Reading**


Economou, George, "Introduction," in *Proensa: An Anthology of Troubadour Poetry*, edited by Economou, Berkeley: University of California Press, 1978

Eshleman, Clayton, "Introduction," in *The Parallel Voyages*, edited by Eshleman, Tucson, Arizona: SUN/Gemini Press, 1987

Jarolim, Edith, "Introduction," in *The Collected Poems of Paul Blackburn*, edited by Jarolim, New York: Persea Books, 1985

Kelly, Robert, "Introduction," in *The Journals*, edited by Kelly, Los Angeles: Black Sparrow Press, 1975

*SixPack* 7–8 (1974) (special issue on Blackburn edited by Pierre Joris and W.R. Prescott)


---

# Black Mountain School

Black Mountain College, near Asheville, North Carolina, was open for 23 years, from 1933 until 1956. This remarkably innovative, iconoclastic liberal arts college was founded during the Depression and endured into the conservative Eisenhower years. Only several hundred faculty and 1,200 students were associated with Black Mountain, but from this lively community important 20th-century aesthetic principles would emerge. Poets, novelists, painters, sculptors, printmakers, musicians, and dancers, among others, were inspired in an educational environment that fostered creativity, individuality, originality, experimentation, and cross-pollination among the arts. Quite a few of its faculty were refugees from war-torn Europe.

Black Mountain poets are very much part of the American experience. They include Charles Olson, Robert Creeley, Robert Duncan, and Hilda Morley, who taught there; Edward Dorn, Joel Oppenheimer, Jonathan Williams, and John Wieners, who studied there; and Paul Blackburn, Paul Carroll, Larry Eigner, and Denise Levertov, who are associated with the group because they published in *Black Mountain Review* or *Origin*, two magazines from the 1950s that featured the work of Black Mountain poets. With the exception of Hilda Morley, they were given what would become major recognition through their appearance in Donald Allen's anthology *The New American Poetry: 1945–1960* (1960). Morley was on the Black Mountain campus for several years, and she wrote highly engaging Projectivist poetry, as Brian Conniff (1993) argues. She has been overlooked, he observes, partly because she did not promote herself and as a woman was not encouraged to publish by Olson and his colleagues.

The preface to Allen's anthology, outlining five groups of avant-garde poets, is alluded to in virtually every discussion of Black Mountain poetry and most histories of 20th-century American poetry. Allen also included excerpts from the poets' statements on their poetics and brief biographies. Martin Duberman (1972) observes that Michael Rumaker and Irving Layton are sometimes also identified as Black Mountain poets. Paul Christensen (1979) considers Amiri Baraka, Ed Sanders, Gilbert Sorrentino, and Cid Corman to be "poets on the fringe" because they published in journals associated with the Black Mountain poets or were in Olson's circle. Corman founded and edited the magazine *Origin*, which had an unparalleled role in the 1950s in publishing early work by Olson, Creeley, Levertov, and other promising writers in the Pound or Williams vein. Levertov first appeared in its second issue in 1951. Her greatest influence was William Carlos Williams, although Olson's poetics were also significant. She would go on to publish many books of poetry, essays, and translations and would emerge as a major voice in American poetry written since World War II. While the principles of Projectivist prosody permeated her work, she was drawn to several themes, including Jewish mysticism and Christian revelation. In addition, she dealt with the brutality of the Vietnam War.

Black Mountain College was founded by John Andrew Rice, a professor of classics who had left Rollins College, a traditional liberal arts college in Florida. Rice was Black Mountain's first rector and Charles Olson its final one, from 1951 to 1956. Both Olson's writing and his personal presence had a major role in the direction of the college and its legacy in the course of 20th-century American poetry. Black Mountain College is important not only for the art and literature produced at the time but also owing to the impact of its aesthetics and poetics. However, although the poets associated with the college rejected traditional poetry, T.S. Eliot's poetics, and New Critical arguments and generally accepted Charles Olson's argument for Projective verse in his seminal essay of that title published in 1950, their work differs considerably in form and content. As a result, the Black Mountain School does not constitute a single well-defined aesthetic. Generally, however, the poets write in free verse, use run-on lines and enjambment, include informal diction, and avoid conventional poetic forms and familiar literary and biblical allusions. They treat subjects including love, sexuality, philosophy, art, history, and geography in poetry that is loosely structured and open-ended rather than rigorously structured and resolved through unifying metaphors. They also have a strong predilection for the spoken word. In addition, as Edward Halsey Foster (1995) maintains, "Black Mountain poetry is located in time; in the occasion of its composition; and above all, in the physiological and psychological identity of the poet." Black Mountain poetry thus stands in marked contrast to the highly regarded academic poetry of its day—work by T.S. Eliot, John Crowe Ransom, and others praised by the New Critics.

The Black Mountain poets universally celebrate the poetry and poetics of Ezra Pound and William Carlos Williams and view themselves as their descendants: Pound's exhortation to "make it new" and Williams' "no ideas but in things" are at the core of their work. The poetry of Walt Whitman, Ralph Waldo Emerson, and other various Romantic poets also figures to a greater or lesser extent in their poetry. The Black Mountain poets were an influence on other poets. Stephen Fredman maintains that "a second wave of projectivist writers appeared and intermingled with the first including Robert Kelly, Jerome Rothenberg, Ronald Johnson, and Theodore Enslin among other writers" (see Fredman's *The Grounding of American Poetry: Charles Olson and the Emersonian Tradition,* 1993). Black Mountain poetry coincided with similar innovations of the Beat and San Francisco poets and has associations with the work of the Language poets.

Olson's "Projective Verse," a manifesto in the Pound tradition, defines poetry as a process and emphasizes the humanity and individuality of its maker. Olson maintains that the vital source of poetry is speech, not the written word. The heart of poetry lies in the syllable and line. "And the line comes (I swear it) from the breath," claims Olson. He continues,

> Let me put it baldly. The two halves are:
> the HEAD, by way of the EAR, to the SYLLABLE
> the HEART, by way of the BREATH, to the LINE

Not unlike Pound's Vorticism in some respects, Olson's Projective verse maintains that the source of a poem is energy and its discharge, but for Olson the energy is human and physical. Poetry is projective, as each perception leads directly to another, and, as Olson quotes from Robert Creeley, "form is never more than an extension of content." In addition to rejecting various dimensions of literary tradition, Olson discards several Western cultural assumptions, including the hierarchical construct that human beings are separate from and above the rest of nature. Olson admired Mayan and other Indian civilizations. As a result of Greek dualist thinking and its impact on European tradition, humanity has become separate from the world, Olson argues in his essay "Human Universe" (1965). Thus, inheritors of Western culture are alienated from their geography and their history. Olson was very much influenced by the British philosopher Alfred North Whitehead, who viewed humanity in a dialectical relation with the universe. Olson's concept of the relationship between humanity and history was presented as a series of lectures at Black Mountain and published in *The Special View of History* (1970). These perceptions and others are treated extensively in theme and in structural innovation in Olson's major work *The Maximus Poems* (1983). "The Kingfishers," published in 1949, was a groundbreaking exploration of his new poetic. His philosophical perspective and predilection for open-ended free verse are shared by other Black Mountain poets.

Beginning in 1950, Olson and Robert Creeley wrote a series of letters sharing their perspectives on poetry. Three years later on Olson's request, Creeley became editor of *Black Mountain Review* for its seven-issue duration from 1954 to 1957. In the early 1950s, Creeley founded Divers Press in Mallorca and went on to publish work by Olson, Paul Blackburn, Larry Eigner, and Robert Duncan. Creeley was on the Black Mountain College campus several times and briefly taught there in the mid-1950s before moving to San Francisco.

Pound and Williams figure significantly in Creeley's perspective. To a lesser extent, so do Louis Zukofsky, George Oppen, and Charles Reznikoff. Creeley was also drawn to the improvisation of contemporary jazz and to the non-referential dimension of Abstract Expressionist painting, including Jackson Pollock's work.

Creeley has published many collections of poetry, including *For Love: Poems, 1950–1960* (1962), *Words* (1967), and *Selected Poems* (1991), as well as books of fiction and essays. He also served as editor of Charles Olson's *Selected Writings* (1966) and *Selected Poems* (1993). Creeley's poems often address the nature of love and his relationships with women in spare lyric poetry of short run-on lines that approximate moments of awareness of experience, examples of which are "A Form of Woman" and "The Window." In addition, some of his poems in *Words* and *Pieces* (1968) call attention to how language functions and creates meaning, as Foster (1995) points out.

In his role as editor of *Black Mountain Review,* Creeley helped promote the experimental poetry of the Beat writers and the poets of the San Francisco Renaissance. Poems by Black Mountain poets and members of these two groups appeared in the final issue of *Black Mountain Review* with Allen Ginsberg serving as a contributing editor. Creeley had a considerable impact on the history of 20th-century American poetry, as his own work and the work of others he published link the early moderns, first, to the Black Mountain poets; second, to the San Francisco Beat poets; and, third, to postmodern Language poets, including Susan Howe and Charles Bernstein, the latter two poets associated with the State University of New York at Buffalo, where Creeley teaches.

Creeley also recognized the strengths of Hilda Morley's poetry, including the poet's acute attention to nature and her compassion for human beings. Creeley wrote the preface to her first collection, *A Blessing Outside Us* (1976), and Denise Levertov wrote the preface to her second book, *What Are Winds and What Are*

*Waters* (1983). Morley went on to publish several more collections, including *To Hold in My Hand: Selected Poems* (1983) and *Turning* (1998). Although she taught literature and writing at Black Mountain College, as a woman with an interest in writers such as T.S. Eliot and Henry James she received no encouragement from Charles Olson. Nevertheless, her poetry, like Olson's Projective verse, achieves a sense of immediacy through the use of enjambment and spare lines that are indented nearly to the right margin. Morley was also engaged by music and the visual arts, references to which appear in numerous poems. Among other things, Morley's poetry contributes to the body of work that responded to the innovative and interdisciplinary spirit of the Black Mountain environment.

Robert Duncan had connections with several groups of poets. As a very young man, he was associated with Anaïs Nin, Kenneth Patchen, and Henry Miller. In the 1940s, he joined Kenneth Rexroth's small group of poets that included Philip and Everson Lamantia, and later that decade he associated with Bay Area poets Robin Blaser and Jack Spicer while taking classes at Berkeley. Denise Levertov's poem "The Shifting," which appeared in *Origin* in 1952, sparked Duncan's interest in Black Mountain poetics. He was also very much taken with Olson's conception of Projectivist verse. He and Olson would correspond until Olson's death, and Duncan remained a strong supporter of Olson's poetics. He taught at Black Mountain in 1956 and then returned to San Francisco, where he became the assistant director of that city's Poetry Center.

Duncan's collections *Letters* (1958) and *The Opening of the Field* (1960) strongly reflect Black Mountain aesthetics. In the former, poems are dedicated to various Black Mountain and San Francisco poets, and the introduction argues for poetry that is discontinuous, suggesting that consciousness and creation are in process. Many of the poems are playful, replete with enjambment and run-on lines. The collection was inspired partly by Duncan's reading of parts of the *Zohar,* a medieval Jewish mystical text treating the relationship between the letters in the Bible and mystical truth. *The Opening of the Field* also treats cosmic themes and contains references to the Atlantis myth, to the Bible, and to poets and poetry. The "field" of the title refers not only to a meadow as a place connected to higher realities but also to the field of poetry, a place of movement and change. Through open poetry, Duncan attempts to let cosmic reality be uncovered.

Edward Dorn, who attended Black Mountain College in 1950 and again in 1954, praises Olson's poetics in *What I See in the Maximus Poems* (1960) and dedicated the collection of poems *Geography* (1965) to his mentor. Of the poets on the Black Mountain campus, Dorn was the most overtly political, and he frequently criticized American imperialism. *Gunslinger,* a groundbreaking long poem that was published in progress in several volumes over a period of years and eventually in *Slinger* (1975), mixes voices and vernaculars in a mock epic of American Western culture. A postmodern parody of the American hero and the myths of American history, it lambastes unbridled greed for wealth and power. Dorn's critique parallels Olson's discontent with Western culture, and his study of Native American culture echoes Olson's interest in the Mayans. A prolific writer, Dorn also translated the work of Cesar Vallejo and other Latin American poets.

Joel Oppenheimer, a student at the college from 1950 to 1953, spent almost two years in Olson's workshops and published in *Black Mountain Review* and with Jonathan Williams' Jargon Press. Oppenheimer was also influenced by Creeley, Williams, E.E. Cummings, and the music of Miles Davis. Employing simple diction, an unadorned straightforward voice, enjambment, lowercase letters, and slashes instead of apostrophes, Oppenheimer's poems explore the psychology of love, friendship, and sexuality. Although he spent most of his life in New York, where he served for many years as a contributing editor to the *Village Voice,* Oppenheimer's experience at Black Mountain was central to his work. He went on to have a significant role in promoting poetry as director of St. Mark's Poetry Project and also as director of the Teachers and Writers Collaborative in New York City in the late 1960s. His articles for the *Village Voice,* like his poetry, reflect his compassionate existentialism, including his respect for human dignity and his anxiety over the abuse of power in government.

Jonathan Williams, a native of western North Carolina, attended Black Mountain College in the early 1950s and founded Jargon Press in 1951. As the editor and designer of Jargon Press, Williams played an important role in promoting Black Mountain poets, publishing poetry by Olson, Creeley, Duncan, and Levertov, as well as verse by other writers including Kenneth Patchen, Lorine Niedecker, and Mina Loy. Williams is an enthusiastic supporter of nontraditional poetry, a critic of American culture, and a strong proponent of democracy and ecology. His poems are witty, satirical, erudite, and playful, and they often incorporate the language of casual conversation, road signs, and graffiti. In its allusions to writers, painters, and musicians such as Olson, Pound, Creeley, Gustav Mahler, and Miles Davis, his poetry reflects the interdisciplinary spirit of the Black Mountain community. Of his work, *An Ear in Bartram's Tree* (1969), *Mahler* (1969), and *Blues & Roots/Rue and Bluets* (1971) have received the most critical attention.

Inspired by an issue of *Black Mountain Review* and by an Olson reading in 1954, John Wieners attended Black Mountain College after earning a degree in English from Boston College. Although highly regarded by Projectivist poets—Duncan in particular praised the close alliance of form and emotion in Wieners' poetry—Wieners is more often associated with the Beat poets. In the late 1950s, he lived in San Francisco and participated in coffeehouse readings with Allen Ginsberg, Jack Spicer, Lawrence Ferlinghetti, Bob Kaufman, and others. Ginsberg wrote the foreword to Wieners' *Selected Poems, 1958–1984* (1986). Many of his poems in collections such as *The Hotel Wentley Poems* (1958) and *Nerves* (1970) treat homosexual relationships as well as experiences with drugs or alcohol in the context of urban landscapes. Some of his later poems in the 1970s are more political, dealing with racism, the Vietnam War, and gay and women's rights.

Paul Blackburn was not a student or faculty member at Black Mountain College, but he did publish in *Origin* and in *Black Mountain Review.* He also published several books with Creeley's Divers Press. In addition to his own work, he also translated the poetry of the Troubadours and Federico García Lorca. Pound's translations and references to the Provençal poets instigated Blackburn's interest in translation. Indeed, Blackburn was heavily influenced by Pound's poetics and corresponded with him. On Pound's suggestion, he wrote to Creeley, and this led to contact with other Black Mountain poets. As Sherman Paul (1978) observes, Blackburn's poem "Shop Talk" praises the vital link between Olson's group and Pound, Williams, and Marianne Moore, and it advocates open-field poetry. His poetry often mixes formal and informal diction and uses unusual word spacing and alignment to suggest a poem's oral performance. In the years before he died of cancer in his mid-40s, he focused on the experience of loneliness, sexual desire, and looming mortality. His most widely discussed volume of poetry, *The Journals* (1975), chronicles the last years of his life.

Larry Eigner, who, like Blackburn, was not affiliated with Black Mountain College, first came into contact with the Black Mountain poets in 1949 when he wrote to Cid Corman after listening to his radio program. Soon after Eigner published in *Origin*, in *Black Mountain Review*, and with Divers Press. His first collection, *From the Sustaining Air* (1953), was edited by Robert Creeley. Eigner, perhaps of all the poets of his generation, comes closest to achieving Williams' dictum "no ideas but in things."

Eigner was unable to travel much because of a severe disability; he suffered complications from cerebral palsy from an injury at birth. While his physical movement may have been somewhat limited, his sensitivity and powers of observation were not. His poetry employs enjambment, stark juxtaposition of objects and observations, minimal punctuation and capitalization, and innovative word and line spacing. Many of his poems convey not only the objects of his perception but also the act of their apperception. Eigner was embraced by the Language poets, and his work appeared in the first issue of *L=A=N=G=U=A=G=E* (1976). The poet Robert Grenier edited Eigner's *Waters/Places/A Time* (1983), *Windows/Wall/Yard/Ways (Lines Squares Paths Worlds Backwards Sight)* (1994), and *readiness enough depends on*, published after Eigner's death in 1998.

Although he was a poet, Paul Carroll is best known for his work as an editor. Often categorized as a Beat poet, Carroll is also associated with the Black Mountain poets since he published Robert Duncan and John Wieners. He worked with Irving Rosenthal as poetry editor of the *Chicago Review* for several years, publishing work by William S. Burroughs, Lawrence Ferlinghetti, Jack Kerouac, and Ginsberg, among other writers. Carroll and Rosenthal started the journal *Big Table* after the *Chicago Review* was severely criticized for obscenity and a new staff put into place. The new magazine received similar criticism but prevailed in a court case, and five issues appeared. In the mid-1960s, Carroll founded Big Table Publishing Company, a subdivision of Follett. Several of its publications, including the anthology *The Younger American Poets* (1968), which Carroll edited, and the collection of essays *The Poem in Its Skin* (1968), which he wrote, had lasting reputations.

This commitment to little magazines and to promoting avant-garde poetry is part of Pound's legacy and a telling characteristic of the Black Mountain poets. Important articles published in the 1990s by Marjorie Perloff, Paul Breslin, and Brian Conniff call into question various other constructs of Black Mountain poetry maintained by scholars and critics for 30 years. Among other topics, these critical writings take up the definition of Black Mountain poetry, the focus on Olson, and the lack of attention given to Hilda Morley.

KATHY RUGOFF

**Further Reading**


Altieri, Charles, *Self and Sensibility in Contemporary American Poetry*, Cambridge and New York: Cambridge University Press, 1984

Breslin, Paul, "Black Mountain Reunion" (review of various books by and about Black Mountain poets), *Poetry* 176, no. 3 (2000)

Christensen, Paul, *Charles Olson: Call Him Ishmael*, Austin: University of Texas Press, 1979

Conniff, Brian, "Reconsidering Black Mountain: The Poetry of Hilda Morley," *American Literature* 65, no. 1 (1993)

Duberman, Martin, *Black Mountain: An Exploration in Community*, New York: Dutton, 1972

Foster, Edward Halsey, *Understanding the Black Mountain Poets*, Columbia: University of South Carolina Press, 1995

Fox, Willard, *Robert Creeley, Edward Dorn, and Robert Duncan: A Reference Guide*, Boston: G.K. Hall, 1989

Harris, Mary Emma, *The Arts at Black Mountain College*, Cambridge, Massachusetts: MIT Press, 1987

Paul, Sherman, *Olson's Push: Origin, Black Mountain, and Recent American Poetry*, Baton Rouge: Louisiana State University Press, 1978

Perloff, Marjorie, "Whose New American Poetry? Anthologizing in the Nineties," *Diacritics* 26, nos. 3–4 (1996)


---

## R.P. Blackmur 1904–65

A major American critic of the 20th century, R.P. Blackmur published three volumes of poems in his lifetime. Famously self-schooled (he never graduated from high school), he had a distinguished career as a professor of English at Princeton University. From his early 1930s pieces in *Hound and Horn* to his posthumously published lectures, *A Primer of Ignorance* (1967), Blackmur's work is by turns acute, obscure, penetrating, and aphoristic. Along with T.S. Eliot, William Empson, John Crowe Ransom, Cleanth Brooks, and Robert Penn Warren, he played an influential role in explicating a relationship to literature commonly associated with the New Criticism. Founder of the Gauss seminars at Princeton, Blackmur was, in the 1950s, perhaps *the* central critic and critical personality, one who, in R.W.B. Lewis' estimation, seemed "pretty well assured of being one of the two or three very likely to endure." As Edward Said summed it up, "He is without question the finest, the most patient and resourceful explicator of difficult literature produced in mid-twentieth-century America." In its moment, his poetry was respected and generally taken quite seriously. It certainly played an important role in his emerging reputation as a wide-ranging man of letters, especially early in his career. In fact, he first went to Princeton in 1940 as an "associate" to Allen Tate in the Program of Creative

Arts. Abstract, lyrical, studded with literary allusion, carefully wrought, and explicitly political, Blackmur's verse evokes the influence of the towering Modernists Pound and Yeats and the 19th-century American figures Ralph Waldo Emerson and Henry James but above all Eliot. Like Eliot (T.S.), Blackmur went by initials (R.P.), adopting similar critical postures, quoting him in his verse, and modeling *Hound and Horn* after Eliot's *Criterion*. However, unlike Eliot's, Blackmur's poems have not "established themselves as exerting much pressure upon contemporary poetry," as Denis Donoghue delicately put it in introducing *Poems of R.P. Blackmur* (1977), and it does not seem likely that they ever will. Nevertheless, like his criticism, his poems are often beautiful in their rigorous play of mind, in their faith in the power of mind, and in the struggle they represent of getting matter into language.

Richard Palmer Blackmur was born on 21 January 1904 in Springfield, Massachusetts. Between 1905 and 1910, the family lived in New York City, where Blackmur's father worked on Wall Street. In 1910, the family moved to Cambridge, Massachusetts. He was expelled from Cambridge High and Latin School in 1918 after a quarrel with the headmaster. Between 1918 and 1925, Blackmur hovered around Harvard Square, working a series of menial jobs. In 1925, he formed a partnership in a bookshop, Dickson and Blackmur. In 1928, Blackmur began his career in earnest as a freelance critic and poet. He became managing editor of *Hound and Horn,* was removed from that position in 1930, but continued as a contributor until the demise of the magazine in 1934. Also in 1930, he married a painter, Helen Dickson, and lived in the Boston area, spending summers in the Dickson farmhouse in Maine, the setting for the striking early poems in *From Jordan's Delight* (1937). He published his first collection of critical essays, *The Double Agent,* in 1935 and began work on a biography on Henry Adams (never completed but published in 1980).

In 1940, Blackmur accepted a one-year appointment at Princeton University. In 1942, he published his second collection of verse, *The Second World.* He was appointed Alfred Hodder Memorial Fellow at Princeton (1943); Fellow of the School of Economics and Politics, Institute for Advanced Study, Princeton (1944–46); and Resident Fellow in Creative Writing (1946–48). In 1947, he published a third collection of verse, *The Good European.* In 1951, he divorced and became a full professor at Princeton. In 1956, he was elected to the National Institute of Arts and Letters. He served as an Honorary Consultant in American Letters to the Library of Congress (1960–64). In 1961, Blackmur was made the Pitt Professor of American History and Institutions and Fellow of Christ's College, Cambridge. In 1964, he was elected to the American Academy of Arts and Sciences. Blackmur died on 2 February 1965, in Princeton.

While Blackmur's poetry and essays are undoubtedly associated with New Criticism and his currency has risen and fallen with its popularity, he was probably the least stereotypical of New Critics. He was certainly committed to the practice of extended close reading, and his faith in form and craftsmanship led him to criticize the expressive fallacy—the belief that intensity of feeling can be transferred to poetry and to the reader solely through inspiration. Like Eliot's poetry, Blackmur's can be bookish and austere. Many of his poems derive from other texts and authors (e.g., Catullus in "Phasellus Ille," *Hamlet* in "Miching Mallecho," or Twain in "Nigger Jim"), and it requires an intimate familiarity with the original to divine the connection. However, Blackmur was not as committed to the autonomy of the literary work as much as to the process by which experience is transformed into literature. Far from being one who tended to isolate literature from history or biography, Blackmur was often explicitly political, and his great, unrealized biographies of Henry Adams and Henry James reflect his abiding, if tortured, commitment to the historical in the search for literary meaning. Blackmur was the New Critical master of the provisional or contingent statement.

Like all New Critics, Blackmur celebrated the power of words. He was fond of quoting Elizabeth Sewell: "Words are the mind's one defense against possession by thought or dreams." His poetry frequently articulates, as Denis Donoghue has pointed out, the process of finding the right words. In the final section of the title poem in *From Jordan's Delight,* the poet attempts to gloss the naming of this windswept, sea-shattered Maine island, Jordan's Delight (off the coast from his wife's summer place):

> Some irony out of the common mind,
> Some wisdom gathered, and returned, like night,
> Saw half-united, half at odds, the blind
> Conjunction in the name, Jordan's Delight.
> What Jordan's that?—Some journeyman of despair
> Lived here and died fishing foul weather fair.
>
> And What delight?—Some bleak and gallant face,
> Lonely in words, but under words at home,
> Might look, might almost see, a first wind-trace,
> What hardness rock and flower overcome.
> It is the sea face that we hidden wear
> So still, rises, rejoices, and is bare.

By ascribing to irony the mythic or social production of meaning through the act of naming such a bleak landscape a "delight," Blackmur gives the poem its allegorical purchase. The concrete, almost regionalist subject matter, in good New Critical fashion, is transformed. Blackmur ascribes to culture (the common mind) the properties of language (irony) and connects the optimism of the name with the physical attitude or formation of the craggy island itself. This strategy invokes a kind of sly, cheerfully existential brand of survival. It also links the formation of words with the formation of things. It is attentive to the process by which things get named and the play of meaning entailed in that process.

The process of wrestling the inchoate into form (or finding this impossible) is Blackmur's constant theme, applied even to Europe in the aftermath of World War II, as in the lyrical commentary in "The Good European: 1945":

> *(Secreto: For All the Living)*
>
> It is not the burned out houses,
> not food nor transport loss, that rouses
> massive resentment and self-rape
> and pleads disorder as amazed escape.
>
> It is the ragging in the mind
> as thought goes doggo, kind on kind,
> and all that had been common will,
> is spoil divided at the kill.
>
> Concert and conflict disengaged
> leaves even natural prayer outraged.

In five couplets, Blackmur articulates the mental and emotional disconnection that the war had engendered. "Thought is the bomb for personnel," he would explain in another section. He attempts to articulate the mechanism by which language and thought are denatured and to reassert a faith in the search for form and language in experience. "The Second World" presents the reader with this article of faith:

> Who that has sailed by star
> on the light night air,
> first hand on the tiller,
> second on the nibbling sheet,
>
> who, looking aloft then aback,
> has not one moment lost
> in the wind's still eye
> his second world
> and the bright star
> before the long shudder fills on
> the windward tack?

Like Robert Frost kneeling at his well-curb looking for a glimpse of a pebble of quartz or truth, Blackmur's lyrics return again and again to the scene in which meaning is recognized, only to be lost or, at best, provisionally fathomed. In a sense, this poem might be an allegory for Blackmur's vision of the condition of the modern poet. As he put it in *Language as Gesture,*

> It is almost the mark of genuine merit in our time—the poet who writes serious works with an intellectual aspect which are nonetheless poetry—that performs his work in the light of an insight, a group of ideas, and a faith, with the discipline that flows from them, which taken together form a view of life most readers cannot share, and which furthermore, most readers feel as repugnant, or sterile, or simply inconsequential.

Not only a poet but a theorist of poetry, Blackmur articulated the predicament of the Modernist author. Like the speaker sailing at night, the poet and the critic merge, torn between the tiller and the sail, the sea's surface and the wind. The tension between the turbulent world and the attempt to follow the process of composition, the sense that this labor is redemptive, although arduous and unpopular, amount to a critical and aesthetic creed. That Blackmur's creed was irreducible to dogma, that his forms were relentlessly traditional, and that his faith in literature as secular incarnation has grown passé may explain his centrality to the 1950s and his marginality at the beginning of the 21st century.

STEPHEN RACHMAN

**Biography**

Born in Springfield, Massachusetts, 21 January 1904. Clerk, Dunster House Bookshop, Cambridge, Massachusetts, 1926; editor, *Hound and Horn,* 1928–30; Resident Fellow, Princeton University, Princeton, New Jersey, 1940–43, 1946–48; Fellow, Institute for Advanced Study, Princeton, New Jersey, 1944–46; Associate Professor, 1948–51, and Professor, 1951–65, Princeton University; Fellow of Christ's College, 1961, and Pitt Professor, 1961–62, Cambridge University, Cambridge, England. Received Guggenheim fellowship, 1936–37, 1937–38; honorary Litt.D., Rutgers University, 1958; M.A., Cambridge University, 1961; Library of Congress Fellow in American Letters, 1961–64. Died in Princeton, New Jersey, 2 February 1965.

**Poetry**

*From Jordan's Delight,* 1937
*The Second World,* 1942
*The Good European, and Other Poems,* 1947
*Poems of R.P. Blackwell,* 1977

**Selected Criticism**

*The Double Agent: Essays in Craft and Elucidation,* 1935
*The Expense of Greatness,* 1940
*Language as Gesture: Essays in Poetry,* 1952
*Form and Value in Modern Poetry,* 1952
*The Lion and the Honeycomb: Essays in Solicitude and Critique,* 1955
*New Criticism in the United States,* 1959
*Eleven Essays in the European Novel,* 1964
*A Primer of Ignorance,* 1967
*Studies in Henry James,* 1983

**Other Writings:** biographies (*Henry Adams,* 1980), collected lectures (*Lectures in Criticism,* 1949); edited anthologies of literature (*American Short Novels,* 1960).

**Further Reading**

Cone, Edward T., Joseph Frank, and Edmund Keeley, editors, *The Legacy of R.P. Blackmur: Essays, Memoirs, Texts,* by Blackmur, New York: Ecco Press, 1987
Donoghue, Denis, editor, *Selected Essays of R.P. Blackmur,* by Blackmur, New York: Ecco Press, 1986
Fraser, Russell, *A Mingled Yarn: The Life of R.P. Blackmur,* New York: Harcourt Brace Jovanovich, 1981
Jones, James T., editor, *Outsider at the Heart of Things: Essays,* by Blackmur, Urbana: University of Illinois Press, 1989

# Robin Blaser 1925–

Robin Blaser's work has long been associated with the most radical and innovative streams in American writing while at the same time laying claim to a place in a tradition that extends from Pound, Whitman, Dante, Lucretius, and Ovid back to Homer. During a period when American poetry has been dominated largely by the lyric (and its dark, noisy twin, the anti-lyric), Blaser's work has opened up new formal possibilities for the epic and philosophical impulses of poetry, impulses that insist on poetry's role as agent in the "composition of the world." In this pursuit, Blaser, together with Jack Spicer, developed the idea of the serial poem and in his masterwork, *The Holy Forest* (1993), gave it one of its fullest realizations.

Robin Francis Blaser was born in Denver, Colorado, on 18 May 1925. Both his father and his maternal grandmother worked for the railroad, and most of Blaser's youth was spent in small communities near or even on the railroad tracks (the family lived in a railroad car for some time) in the high plains of Idaho. Both the landscape and the social world of those American spaces figure centrally in Blaser's imagination and his work. Sophia Nichols, his maternal grandmother, was especially important to the young Blaser, telling him stories of Odysseus and the gods, launching his imagination into the "circuitously Odyssean" orders of *The Holy Forest,* while his great grandmother Ina read him passages from Emerson's essays.

After short stays at Northwestern University and the College of Idaho, Blaser made his way in 1944 to the University of California, Berkeley, where he was initiated into the world of poetry in the company of two other students, Robert Duncan and Jack Spicer. Together, Duncan, Spicer, and Blaser ignited what became known as the Berkeley Renaissance, an enormous outpouring of innovative poetic activity whose repercussions are still being felt in American writing. Inspired by important teachers such as medievalist Ernst Kantorowicz and poet Josephine Miles, the three poets poured themselves into a thorough study of modern writers that influenced their work throughout their lives.

After graduating with an M.A. and an M.L.S. in 1955, Blaser moved to Boston, where he worked as a librarian at the Widener Library at Harvard University. During that time, he became close to a number of East Coast poets, including Charles Olson, John Wieners, Steve Jonas, John Ashbery, and Frank O'Hara. Their work became crucial to the development of Blaser's own unique poetics. He first came to national attention when several of his early poems were included in Donald Allen's groundbreaking anthology *The New American Poetry* (1960). Blaser moved to Vancouver, British Columbia, in 1966 to teach at Simon Fraser University. He became a Canadian citizen in 1972.

In an important essay on the work of Jack Spicer called "The Practice of Outside," Blaser writes, "Poetry is necessary to the composition or knowledge of the 'real.'" Elsewhere, he calls this business "cosmology," thus linking himself to the work of poets such as Homer, Ovid, Lucretius, and Dante, all of whom at various points enter *The Holy Forest.* This impulse toward "the composition of the real" emerges immediately in *Cups,* his first book (although not his first published book), where the elements of that world are made up of images and stories from the poet's childhood resonant with mythic significance and the astonishment of language itself.

Although not published until 1968, *Cups* was composed from 1959 to 1960, making it the initiatory work of *The Holy Forest.* The first lines of the poem—"Inside I brought / willows, the tips / bursting, blue / iris (I forget / the legend of long life / they represent) / and the branch of pepper tree"—introduce many of the concerns that run through the whole of *The Holy Forest:* the question of the composition of the self, the relation of the inner and outer worlds, the nature of the creative act (poetics), and the transformational (and often terrifying) energy of Eros. They also mark the poet's entrance into the eponymous Holy Forest.

*The Moth Poem* (1964) was Blaser's first published book. *Les Chimères: Translations of Nerval* (1965), *Cups* (1968), *Image-Nations 1–12 and The Stadium of the Mirror* (1974), *Image-Nations 13–14* (1975), *Harp Trees* (1977), *Image-Nation 15* (1981), *Syntax* (1983), *The Faerie Queene and The Park* (1987), and *Pell Mell* (1988) followed, although in Blaser's case publication chronology does not reflect order of composition. Many of the poems had earlier incarnations in little magazines, chapbooks, and broadsides. *The Holy Forest,* published by Coach House Press in 1993, includes all these poems as well as some that had seen only magazine publication (*Charms* and *Streams*) and some previously unpublished work (*Streams II* and *Exody*).

That said, it should be made clear that the "books" of *The Holy Forest* are not discrete books per se. Brought together in its entirety (to date), *The Holy Forest* is an immense labyrinth. In the serial poem, order manifests itself not in some preordained form (whether regular or irregular) but in a constant moving forward, a revelatory unfolding. *The Holy Forest* is full of twisting, turning, and looping paths that cross and recross, constantly opening into the unprecedented and the unexpected. Like Dante's dark wood, we (and the poet) are simply in it, waiting to see what comes next. Unlike Dante's wood, however, no guide appears to lead us through, a signal fact of our current circumstance. This does not mean that we have no teachers, only that our teachers are companions rather than guides. Throughout his work, Blaser has remained committed to antithetical modes of thinking (composing) the world. From the tarot and the hermetic occult to the recent philosophical work of Gilles Deleuze, Jean Luc Nancy, Giorgio Agamben, Mark C. Taylor, and Stanley Cavell (among others), Blaser's reading among his companions in thought leaves a residue that contributes significantly to the poem's community of mind.

In addition to *The Holy Forest,* Blaser has edited books of poetry by Jack Spicer, Louis Dudek, and George Bowering. He has written a number of important essays, including "The Fire," "The Practice of Outside," "The Violets: Olson and Whitehead," "Poetry and Positivisms," and "The Recovery of the Public World." Blaser's latest work is the libretto for English composer Harrison Birtwhistle's opera *The Last Supper* (2000). In it, Blaser recalls the apostles to time and the flesh where they are asked by the Ghost to reconsider their exclusion of Judas and its catastrophic repercussions within the "Western Mind."

MICHAEL BOUGHN

*See also* Canadian Poetry (Anglophone)

**Biography**

Born in Denver, Colorado, 18 May 1925; naturalized Canadian citizen, 1972. Attended Northwestern University, Evanston,

Illinois, 1943; College of Idaho, Caldwell, 1943–44; University of California, Berkeley, B.A. 1952, M.A. 1954, M.L.S. 1955; librarian, Harvard University Library, Cambridge, Massachusetts, 1955–59; assistant curator, California Historical Society, 1960–61; librarian, San Francisco State College Library, 1961–65; lecturer, 1966–72, Professor of English, 1972–86, Professor, Centre for the Arts, 1980–84, and since 1986 Professor Emeritus, Simon Fraser University, Burnaby, British Columbia; co-founder, *Measure,* 1957; editor, *Pacific Nation,* 1967–69. Received Poetry Society Award, 1965; Canada Council Award, 1970, grant, 1989–90. Living in Vancouver, British Columbia.

**Poetry**

*The Moth Poem,* 1964
*Les Chimères: Translations of Nerval* (versions of Gérard de Nerval), 1965
*Cups,* 1968
*Image-Nations 1–12 and The Stadium of the Mirror,* 1974
*Image-Nations 13–14,* 1975
*Harp Trees,* 1977
*Image-Nation 15,* 1981
*Syntax,* 1983
*The Faerie Queene and The Park,* 1987
*Pell Mell,* 1988
*The Holy Forest,* 1993
*Robin Blaser, Barbara Guest, Lee Harwood* (with others), 1996

**Other Writings:** essays, libretto (for Harrison Birtwhistle's opera *The Last Supper,* 2000); edited collections of poetry (*The Collected Books of Jack Spicer,* 1975; *Selected Poems: Particular Accidents,* by George Bowering, 1980; *Infinite Worlds: The Poetry of Louis Dudek,* 1988).

**Further Reading**


Boughn, Michael, "Exody and Some Mechanics of Splendor in Emerson and Blaser," *Talisman* 15 (Winter 1995/96)
Conte, Joseph, "Seriality and the Contemporary Long Poem," *Sagetrieb* 11, nos. 1–2 (Spring–Fall 1992)
Creeley, Robert, "Robin Blaser's Holy Forest," *Brick* 47 (Winter 1993)
Marlatt, Daphne, "Eratic/Erotic Narrative: Syntax and Mortality in Robin Blaser's 'Image-Nations,'" *West Coast Line* 29, no. 2 (Fall 1995)
Mossin, Andrew, "In the Shadow of Nerval: Robert Duncan, Robin Blaser, and the Poetics of (Mis)Translation," *Contemporary Literature* 38, no. 4 (Winter 1997)
Nichols, Miriam, "Robin Blaser's 'Syntax': Performing the Real," *Line* 3 (Spring 1983)
Nichols, Miriam, "Robin Blaser's Poetics of Relation: Thinking without Bannisters," *Sagetrieb* 9, nos. 1–2 (Spring–Fall 1990)
Quartermain, Peter, "The Mind as Frying Pan: Robin Blaser's Humour," *Sulfur* 37 (Fall 1995)
Watts, Charles, and Edward Byrne, *The Recovery of the Public World: Essays on Poetics in Honour of Robin Blaser,* Burnaby, British Columbia: Talonbooks, 1998


---

# Robert Bly 1926–

Robert Bly is an extremely private person who has lived his life quite publicly; and, just as he has often changed directions in his life, he has often revised his poems to reflect those changes. Bly seems to have taken to heart Rilke's famous line "Du musst dein Leben ändern" ("You must change your life") and applied it to both his life and his work. Because of Bly's tendency to make such abrupt changes, the old Romantic dichotomy that insists on the essential separation between the public and the private breaks down in him as he brings together and intermixes the private and public and the "inner" and "outer" worlds in his poems, just as they are, he would argue, inseparably mixed together in life. The fusing of these dichotomies in large part accounts for Bly's wide-ranging, ever-changing, frequently controversial work.

Despite his increasingly public visibility in the 1980s and 1990s as a media guru, spokesman for the men's movement, critic, editor, social commentator, political demonstrator, and translator, it is as a poet that Bly has always made his most important impact, and he is now, as he has been for almost 40 years, one of the most innovative and important and one of the most imitated and influential poets of the 20th century.

Bly's first book, *Silence in the Snowy Fields* (1962), was a powerful debut. Almost single-handedly, it created, authenticated, and popularized the "deep image" movement in American poetry. By "trusting" the unconscious leaps of the mind, Bly's deep image poems "leap" from one image to another and often end with a suggestion of the imminent presence of the mysterious or the numinous. Poems such as "Driving Toward the Lac Qui Parle River," a paradigm of such deep image poems, were immediately celebrated and widely imitated.

Throughout the time of the Vietnam War, Bly was an active and outspoken critic of the war. He participated in antiwar demonstrations, gave poetry readings against the war, supported the draft resistance, and marched on the Pentagon. Surprisingly enough, *The Light around the Body* (1967)—a book that applied the deep image trappings of *Silence in the Snowy Fields* to poems that were fierce, angry, outspoken antiwar poems, extremely critical both of the war in Vietnam (and by extension all wars) and of the political defenses mounted for and in support of war—won the National Book Award. Poems, too, Bly argued, could be "political acts" with serious political themes and could influence the way people live their lives and the way life could or should be lived. In this book, he put his argument into practice. "Driving through Minnesota during the Hanoi Bombings" typifies Bly's tactics. In it, "instants" of a bucolic scene in Minnesota suddenly dissolve and then fuse with the distant war, becoming "crystals" in which people are tortured and killed in the rice fields of Vietnam.

"Counting Small-Boned Bodies," one of Bly's best-known and most frequently anthologized poems, is perhaps his most memorable antiwar poem.

*Sleepers Joining Hands* (1973) synthesizes Bly's early career and anticipates much of what was to come. A hybrid book, it contains short lyrics, two long poems, and a substantial prose essay in which Bly describes the sources of many of his poems. This essay, together with the long poem at the center of the book, "The Teeth Mother Naked at Last," describes and documents the influence of "Great Mother" culture, Jungian psychology, and "new-brain" studies that Bly often uses to support, summarize, and synthesize the seemingly antithetical inner and outer elements of his work. In the final long title poem of the book, Bly describes how, ideally, the public and private worlds might—and in his view should—merge as "All the sleepers in the world join hands."

Bly's next two major books, *The Morning Glory* (1975; early partial edition published in 1969) and *This Body Is Made of Camphor and Gopherwood* (1977), represent some of his finest, most distinctive work. Both are books of prose poems, a genre new to American poetry. Again, Bly's example was quickly followed by others, and, almost immediately, the "genre-less genre" of the prose poem became critically popular and widely practiced. Always anxious to support his poetic shiftings with theoretical or autobiographical buttressing, Bly described this turn (both his own and others) to the prose poem as an attempt to alleviate the abstract tendencies he saw surfacing in American society. Perhaps he was equally concerned, as critics had pointed out, that much of his own recent work had become too abstract. He wanted, he said, to "heal the wound of abstraction" while continuing to speak "in a low voice to someone he is sure is listening."

The next turn in Bly's career was really a return or a turning back. *This Tree Will Be Here for a Thousand Years* (1979; extensively revised in 1992) contains more "snowy fields" poems. Even though these poems are reminiscent of Bly's earliest work, they introduce a new tone and a more somber, brooding tenor to his voice. Much darker than the poems of *Silence in the Snowy Fields, This Tree Will Be Here for a Thousand Years* marks a major shift in Bly's career. In addition, as his life and work continued to influence each other, his poems began to elicit startlingly diverse responses from critics, some of whom seemed disturbed by these reciprocal relationships. Some of these responses were, therefore, as much as anything responses to Bly's life, to his various and often controversial political activities, and to his growing popular successes. One example of such diverse responses can be seen in the differing reactions to several well-known lines:

> Sometimes when you put your hand into a hollow tree
> you touch the dark places between the stars.

Called simply "a remark" by one critic (Weinberger, 1979), others attested to Bly's accuracy in describing the "sudden epiphany" (Kramer, 1983) that he defines here and described the lines as a significant example of the kind of "intuitive moments" that are "perhaps the principal reward" (Nelson, 1984) of reading Bly's work.

*The Man in the Black Coat Turns* (1981) was another insistently hybrid book, containing poems in lines as well as prose poems. It represents yet another new beginning for Bly, personally and poetically. A much more personal if not more private book than any he had published to date, these poems focus on fathers and male consciousness, and they parallel Bly's activities with men's groups during this period of his life. As might be expected, such overtly masculine poems again made for a rather bifurcated critical response, primarily positive, but somewhat divided along sexual lines. Bly, however, was quick to counter such criticism in his next book, *Loving a Woman in Two Worlds* (1985), which might be read as a sequel to *The Man in the Black Coat Turns*. Here Bly turned forcefully from a concentration on male consciousness to focus on female consciousness. These poems, often developed in terms of the metaphor of the body (first introduced early in Bly's career), are explicit love poems that deal with bodies in overtly sexual ways.

Bly's *Selected Poems* (1986) followed almost immediately. As usual, it was an unusual book. The old habit of revising earlier poems, sometimes drastically, was clearly in evidence. Although Bly had often argued that poems ought to reflect changes in the poet's life and felt that he was therefore simply bringing things "up to date" with these revisions, some of them made considerable demands on readers familiar with his work from the beginning, and this practice often frustrated (or infuriated) these readers. In addition, Bly's "selection" from his earlier work was distinctly thin, and he shifted or reshuffled previously published poems in terms of thematic (or other) new groupings, even inserting totally "new" poems, some never before published, into the old sequences. It was as if he was attempting to direct or influence the reading of his career—an impression supported by the inclusion of explanatory prefaces for each section of the book.

However, Bly was turning to much more visible things than poetry at this period of his life. Indeed, his next book was not poetry at all. For some time, Bly had been making public appearances with men's groups and had been identified by the media as a kind of guru or cult figure. Thus, *Iron John: A Book about Men* (1990) represents the kind of literary activity for which Bly was best known during the early 1990s. It drastically changed his life. Positively, it resulted in increased recognition and attention, but because for many there appeared to be an inherent conflict between a public personality and a private lyric poet, in an ironic twist this popular success somewhat diminished Bly's poetic reputation.

In *What Have I Ever Lost by Dying? Collected Prose Poems* (1992), Bly reprinted (again often in revised versions) prose poems from earlier books. Like so many of his poems, these focused fixedly on the actual and often ended in vivid metaphors or epiphanic visions that slashed out in new directions or surprised in surprising ways. A good example is "A Hollow Tree." Beginning with a straightforward statement and the simple description of bending "over an old hollow cottonwood stump" and looking inside, the poem suddenly turns to intricate metaphor and ambiguous meaning:

> Its Siamese temple walls are all brown and ancient. The walls have been worked on by the intricate ones. Inside the hollow walls there is privacy and secrecy, dim light.

The stanza ends, literally enough, with another simple statement: "And yet some creature has died there." The poem itself ends,

> On the temple floor feathers, gray feathers, . . . Many feathers. In the silence many feathers.

The hollow stump has been transformed into a temple where some sort of sacrifice seems to have been carried out, and the reader is left to make connections that go beyond the poem. In his essay "The Prose Poem as an Evolving Form" (*Selected Poems,* 1986), clearly thinking of this poem, Bly wrote, "When the human mind honors a stump . . . by giving it human attention in the right way, something in the soul is released; and often through the stump we receive information we wouldn't have received by thinking or by fantasy." Yet, he warns, readers must also be wary: "I say to the reader, beware. Readers who love poems of light . . . may end as a mound of feathers and a skull on the open boardwood floor" ("Warning to the Reader").

*Meditations on the Insatiable Soul* (1994) simultaneously summarizes Bly's long career and anticipates yet another new turn, another beginning. Here, arranged in separate sections, are early lyric meditations, "father" poems (including a powerful series about his own father), prose poems, poems on political and psychological themes, and poems haunted by myth and history. This recapitulation of Bly's career can also be seen in *Morning Poems* (1997). In the first poem, as if speaking simultaneously to himself and to the reader, Bly writes, "It seems you've travelled years to get here." These short lyrics, both morning and mourning poems, revisit Bly's earlier themes, but they also add new emphases and suggest a turn toward final conclusions. In "Reading Silence in the Snowy Fields" Bly summarizes his entire career by going back to his earliest beginnings, revisiting and revising himself yet again. However, here he also seems to criticize his early work for its anonymity. Thus, for all his public presence and for the detailed documentation of so much of his public life in so many private poems, Bly seems to think that he has been too reticent too often. Yet even this suggests another new turn, another beginning.

*Eating the Honey of Words: New and Selected Poems* (1999), Bly's second "selected poems," is his most recent collection. In addition to including poems from each of his major collections, Bly includes here nine "new" poems that, characteristically, he inserts into the sequences where they belong chronologically. Clearly, Bly is still revising both his life and his work.

William V. Davis

*See also* Deep Image Poetry

**Biography**

Born in Madison, Minnesota, 23 December 1926. Attended St. Olaf College, Northfield, Minnesota, 1946–47; Harvard University, Cambridge, Massachusetts, B.A. (magna cum laude) 1950; University of Iowa, Iowa City, M.A. 1956; served in the United States Naval Reserve, 1944–45; since 1958 founding editor, *The Fifties* magazine (later *The Sixties* and *The Seventies*), and The Fifties Press (later The Sixties Press and The Seventies Press), Madison, Minnesota; 1966 co-chair, American Writers against the Vietnam War. Received Fulbright fellowship, 1956; Amy Lowell traveling fellowship, 1964; Guggenheim fellowship, 1965, 1972; American Academy grant, 1965; Rockefeller fellowship, 1967; National Book Award, 1968. Living in Moose Lake, Minnesota, and Minneapolis.

**Poetry**

*Silence in the Snowy Fields,* 1962
*The Lion's Tail and Eyes: Poems Written out of Laziness and Silence* (with James Wright and William Duffy), 1962
*The Light around the Body,* 1967
*Sleepers Joining Hands,* 1973
*The Morning Glory: Prose Poems,* 1975 (early partial edition published in 1969)
*Old Man Rubbing His Eyes,* 1975
*This Body Is Made of Camphor and Gopherwood: Prose Poems,* 1977
*This Tree Will Be Here for a Thousand Years,* 1979; revised edition, 1992
*The Man in the Black Coat Turns,* 1981
*Loving a Woman in Two Worlds,* 1985
*Selected Poems,* 1986
*What Have I Ever Lost by Dying? Collected Prose Poems,* 1992
*Meditations on the Insatiable Soul: Poems,* 1994
*Morning Poems,* 1997
*Eating the Honey of Words: New and Selected Poems,* 1999

**Selected Criticism**

*American Poetry: Wildness and Domesticity,* 1990

**Other Writings:** nonfiction (*Iron John: A Book about Men,* 1990; *Remembering James Wright,* 1991), translations of poetry (*Neruda and Vallejo: Selected Poems,* 1971; *Selected Poems of Rainer Maria Rilke,* 1981), edited collections of poetry and criticism (*The Winged Life: Selected Poems and Prose of Thoreau,* 1986; *The Rag and Bone Shop of the Heart: Poems for Men* [with James Hillman and Michael Meade], 1992).

**Further Reading**


Breslin, James E.B., *From Modern to Contemporary: American Poetry, 1945–65,* Chicago: University of Chicago Press, 1984
Davis, William V., *Understanding Robert Bly,* Columbia: University of South Carolina Press, 1988
Davis, William V., *Robert Bly: The Poet and His Critics,* Columbia, South Carolina: Camden House, 1994
Davis, William V., editor, *Critical Essays on Robert Bly,* New York: G.K. Hall, 1992
Kalaidjian, Walter B., *Languages of Liberation: The Social Text in Contemporary American Poetry,* New York: Columbia University Press, 1989
Kramer, Lawrence, "A Sensible Emptiness: Robert Bly and the Poetics of Immanence," *Contemporary Literature* 24 (1983)
Lacey, Paul A., *The Inner War: Forms and Themes in Recent American Poetry,* Philadelphia, Pennsylvania: Fortress Press, 1972
Nelson, Howard, *Robert Bly: An Introduction to the Poetry,* New York: Columbia University Press, 1984
Sugg, Richard P., *Robert Bly,* Boston: Twayne, 1986
Weinberger, Eliot, "Gloves on a Mouse," *The Nation* (17 November 1979)


## Counting Small-Boned Bodies

"Counting Small-Boned Bodies" is the central poem in *The Light around the Body* (1967), Bly's controversial National Book Award–winning book, a book remembered and celebrated (or castigated) primarily for its outspoken portrayal and caustic criticism of U.S. involvement in the Vietnam War. This poem is one of Bly's best known, and it is perhaps his most powerful condemnation of the Vietnam War and of war in general. It is a classic example of Bly's contention that "a poem can be a political act" (see "On Political Poetry," *The Nation,* 24 April 1967). For Bly, at least during this period of his career, poems not only could be but should be "political acts."

Bly has said that during the Vietnam War the "practice of doing ugly things, then describing them in bland words . . . became national policy" (see *Selected Poems,* 1986), and during the 1960s, Bly published a number of poems in which such "ugly things" were vividly described—and condemned. His long antiwar poem "The Teeth Mother Naked at Last" (*Sleepers Joining Hands,* 1973) is a conspicuous and noteworthy example of these condemnatory poems, but "Counting Small-Boned Bodies," despite its brevity, is as strong a condemnation of war as Bly has written.

The poem exists in two slightly but significantly different versions. Bly revised the original version in *The Light around the Body* for inclusion in his *Selected Poems* by changing the exclamation points at the end of the first and second stanzas to periods and by changing the crucial final word of the central line of the second stanza from "get" to "fit," the same word he had used at the end of the central line of the third stanza. (In *Eating the Honey of Words: New and Selected Poems* [1999], Bly used the original version of the poem.)

Like so many of his poems, "Counting Small-Boned Bodies" makes use of the "deep images" and the imaginative "leaps" for which Bly is well known. Such "leaps" and such "deep images," as Bly describes them, make for poems that "trust" the unconscious without excluding the intellect. Such poems, which have come to be known as "deep image" poems (although Bly prefers to describe them, in terms of his own work, as poems of the "deep mind"), "think in flashes," involve "great spiritual energy," and, even if "irrational," attempt to be psychologically accurate and to express accurately the truths of "inward reality" (see Bly 1961, 1975, 1980). These "deep image" poems are perhaps Bly's most definitive signature on poetry's page.

"Counting Small-Boned Bodies" recounts the ghoulish practice, common during the Vietnam War, of announcing the daily casualties on the nightly television news broadcasts. The speaker of the poem, conscious that he is caught in an awkward situation but clearly intrigued with his assignment, tries to make his task more acceptable to a potentially hostile audience by obsessively counting the bodies over and over again and then, rather ingeniously, suggesting imaginative ways to decrease the size of the corpses—always referred to only as "bodies"—in an attempt to minimize the terror and the potential audience shock.

The poem consists of a single-line first stanza followed by three tercets, each containing two long lines enclosing one shorter one. Each tercet begins identically: "If we could only make the bodies smaller." In each of these tercets, the speaker takes a somewhat different approach to describing, and thereby attempting to deal with, the problem he faces. He suggests,

If we could only make the bodies smaller,
The size of skulls,
We could make a whole plain white with skulls in the
moonlight!

If we could only make the bodies smaller,
Maybe we could get
A whole year's kill in front of us on a desk!

If we could only make the bodies smaller,
We could fit
A body into a finger-ring, for a keepsake forever.

This anonymous speaker's voice, which seems so calm and unperturbed, coming to the reader as if from a television set, is also somewhat terrifying because it seems almost simultaneously to be a kind of echo of the reader's own subconscious "voice," or the voice of the collective unconscious, implicating everyone even as it attempts to smooth over the gruesome details of the war, that classic example throughout all history of man's inhumanity to man. Indeed, in many of his most biting and blatantly political poems, as well as in his most outspoken poems of social commentary and condemnation, Bly has often used the strategy of implying a universal psychic substratum to a situation that he wishes to highlight or condemn.

The speaker of this poem, then, imaginatively reconstructs these terrible truths of the war by suggesting that if the bodies were smaller, "the size of skulls," they might be beautiful and shine "in the moonlight." If they could be made even smaller, a "whole year's kill" (a phrase shockingly reminiscent of a hunter's quota) might be collected together and displayed like souvenirs or mementos on a desk. Made even smaller still, they might be made into finger rings to be kept as "keepsake[s] forever." By this kind of ingenious, almost insane logic, the bodies, made smaller, are brought closer and closer, and thus, rather than being distanced by their decreased size, they are made even more terrifying by their increased proximity. This is exactly the kind of thinking and logic, Bly implies, that allows war to exist, persist, and be justified. The poem almost shouts out the message that war and the rational used to justify it need to be highlighted, castigated, and condemned.

Bly's condemnation of war has never been more blatant or more scathing than it is here, and this short lyric poem, perhaps the most powerful antiwar statement in Bly's entire canon, is perhaps also the classic paradigm of this genre in 20th-century American poetry.

William V. Davis

**Further Reading**

Bly, Robert, "Some Notes on French Poetry," *The Sixties* 5 (1961)

Bly, Robert, *A Poetry Reading against the Vietnam War,* Madison, Minnesota: The Sixties Press, 1966

Bly, Robert, "On Political Poetry," *The Nation* (24 April 1967)

Bly, Robert, *Leaping Poetry: An Idea with Poems and Translations,* Boston: Beacon Press, 1975

Bly, Robert, "On Unfinished Poets: An Interview with Scott Chisholm," in *Talking All Morning,* Ann Arbor: University of Michigan Press, 1980

Bly, Robert, "Recognizing the Image as a Form of Intelligence," *Field* 24 (1981)

Davis, William V., "'Hair in a Baboon's Ear': The Politics of Robert Bly's Early Poetry," *The Carleton Miscellany* 18 (1979–80)

Davis, William V., *Understanding Robert Bly,* Columbia: University of South Carolina Press, 1988
Haskell, Dennis, "The Modern American Poetry of Deep Image," *Southern Review* (Australia) 12 (1979)
Kalaidjian, Walter B., *Languages of Liberation: The Social Text in Contemporary American Poetry,* New York: Columbia University Press, 1989
Nelson, Howard, *Robert Bly: An Introduction to the Poetry,* New York: Columbia University Press, 1984
Sugg, Richard P., *Robert Bly,* Boston: Twayne, 1986

## Driving Toward the Lac Qui Parle River

"Driving Toward the Lac Qui Parle River" is a classic example of the kind of poem Bly is famous—or infamous—for. It is also a classic example of what has come to be called a "deep image" poem, or as Bly, one of the most outstanding proponents of deep image poetry, would prefer to call it, poetry of the "deep mind."

"Deep mind" poetry, as Bly has defined it, derives from a dichotomy initially defined by Jacob Boehme, the 17th-century German mystic. Boehme suggested that men are bifurcated in terms of the ways they think and the ways they live in the world, which he described as the difference between the "inward" and the "outward" man. Bly's critical writings and the epigraph to his first book of poems, *Silence in the Snowy Fields* (1962)—"We are all asleep in the outward man"—explicitly reveal Boehme's influence. In *The Light around the Body* (1967), Bly quotes Boehme on the relationship between the "two worlds" of the social and spiritual realms, worlds that often clash or intersect in Bly's poetry. As a result of his being caught up in such a duality, man must "speak in two languages, and . . . must be understood also by two languages."

Bly makes his most definitive statement on deep image poetry in his essay "Recognizing the Image as a Form of Intelligence" (1981). Bly suggests that "deep images" join the "light and dark worlds" of the inward and outward man in such a way that "when a poet creates a true image," he also gains "knowledge" by "bringing up into consciousness" connections that most people have "forgotten." Deep images "trust" the unconscious and are filled with "great spiritual energy." Even if seemingly irrational, Bly argues, deep images are psychologically accurate in terms of "inward" reality and thus are also "right" even in terms of "outward" reality.

"Driving Toward the Lac Qui Parle River," published in *Silence in the Snowy Fields,* might be regarded as a paradigm of the deep image poem. Indeed, Lawrence Kramer (1983) has described this poem as "decisive" among contemporary deep image poems, which he calls poems of "immanence," written as fragments of "a lost, privileged presence" that create a "pattern of apotheosis" and that, after "groping forward metonymically," often end in a kind of "mystical vision."

"Driving Toward the Lac Qui Parle River" describes a drive at dusk in Minnesota "from Willmar to Milan," two small towns not far from where Bly was born. The first of the three stanzas is largely descriptive; except for the reference to the soybeans "breathing" there is no hint of the deep images to come, nor of the epiphany in the final stanza. At the end of the first stanza the speaker seems to identify himself with the "old men" who are contentedly "sitting before their houses on car seats," saying simply, "I am happy." The second stanza is self-contained by the "small world of the car" plunging through the "deep fields of the night," the only sound to be heard that of "the noise of crickets."

These first two stanzas are so straightforward that most readers are probably not prepared for the third stanza, in which the speaker seems to witness something miraculous in the midst of this bucolic landscape and simple setting. Indeed, he seems to have a glimpse of the deeper inward world before he ends his journey in this outer world:

> Nearly to Milan, suddenly a small bridge,
> And water kneeling in the moonlight.
> The lamplight falls on all fours in the grass.

These images suggest the immediate or imminent presence of the numinous, something that demands homage from even ordinary phenomena, water and light, "kneeling" and then "fall[ing] on all fours." They seem to prostrate themselves before something unseen, something sensed but not known or fully understood by the speaker as he travels through a darkened landscape that he otherwise knows so well. Whatever has happened—and it is clear that what has happened is "inside" the speaker's metaphoric mind, not "outside" in the world he witnesses—it has happened quickly and almost as quickly vanished. The speaker, like the reader, is left with a sense of having witnessed something mysterious, or even miraculous, even if he cannot name it or fully define what it means.

The poem ends somewhat anti-climactically with the destination reached, the moon shining full on the river as if to "cover" it, and "[a] few people . . . talking low in a boat." The river is the actual Lac Qui Parle river in western Minnesota referred to in the title of the poem, but it is also "the river that speaks," as the translation of the river's name suggests. It is as if nature has found words, and these words are "driving toward" something essential both to nature and to man in nature: something that can be seen perhaps only fleetingly, but which can change the ways men look at things and the ways they live their lives.

Finally, like the "talking" river, this "talking" poem can say nothing more. Just as the light on the river is covered by the moonlight, so any more meaning to be drawn from this experience is also covered in mystery.

WILLIAM V. DAVIS

**Further Reading**

Bly, Robert, "Recognizing the Image as a Form of Intelligence," *Field* 24 (1981)
Breslin, James E.B., *From Modern to Contemporary: American Poetry, 1945–65,* Chicago: University of Chicago Press, 1984
Davis, William V., *Understanding Robert Bly,* Columbia: University of South Carolina Press, 1988
Haskell, Dennis, "The Modern American Poetry of Deep Image," *Southern Review* (Australia) 12 (1979)
Kramer, Lawrence, "A Sensible Emptiness: Robert Bly and the Poetics of Immanence," *Contemporary Literature* 24 (1983)

Lacey, Paul A., *The Inner War: Forms and Themes in Recent American Poetry*, Philadelphia, Pennsylvania: Fortress Press, 1972

Nelson, Howard, *Robert Bly: An Introduction to the Poetry*, New York: Columbia University Press, 1984

Rehder, Robert, "Which Way to the Future?" in *Critical Essays on Robert Bly*, edited by William V. Davis, New York: G.K. Hall, 1992

## The Teeth Mother Naked at Last

In one of the introductory sections of his *Selected Poems* (1986), Robert Bly argues that the Vietnam War changed the way we lived. "The Teeth Mother Naked at Last," his long, meditative harangue on war, is Bly's most outspoken response to that war and to the changes it created. Bly called "Teeth Mother" a poem of "judgment." The poem focuses, often in graphic detail, on the specific horrors of the Vietnam War and on America's involvement in it, but Bly is equally interested in describing the effects of war in general on the human psyche. In his preface to *A Poetry Reading against the Vietnam War* (1966), a diverse collection of materials related to the Vietnam War that could be considered a companion volume to "The Teeth Mother Naked at Last" and to Bly's other antiwar poems in *The Light around the Body* (1967), Bly states that the "really serious evil" of war "is the harm it will do" to men "inwardly." In "The Teeth Mother Naked at Last," Bly attempts to illustrate and to describe the kinds of damage that war has had on the "inward" man.

Bly's title refers to the Teeth (or Stone) Mother, one of the mothers of the ancient mystic cult of The Great Mother. This "Teeth Mother" interferes with spiritual growth and works to destroy man's conscience. In Jungian psychology (by which Bly has been significantly influenced), the Teeth Mother is associated with the destruction of the psyche. Bly's long essay "I Came Out of the Mother Naked," his explication of the role of the Teeth Mother at work in the world, draws heavily on Jung, on Johann Bachofen's *Mother Right* (1861), and on Erich Neumann's *The Great Mother: An Analysis of the Archetype* (1963). This essay immediately follows the poem in *Sleepers Joining Hands* (1973).

Several sections of "The Teeth Mother Naked at Last" were originally published individually in *The Nation* (25 March 1968) and in Bly's play *The Satisfaction of Vietnam* (1968). The "complete" poem has been published in four rather different versions: by City Lights Books (1970), as revised for *Sleepers Joining Hands*, in a further revised version in the *Selected Poems*, and as revised yet again in *Eating the Honey of Words: New and Selected Poems* (1999). This most recent revision incorporates small changes in lineation and stanza structure and revamps the structural divisions of the poem. More important, however, is the fact that in this most recent version, Bly has progressively softened some of his most outspoken and inflammatory rhetoric and many of the most blatant antiwar statements from the earlier versions either by eliminating them altogether or by appreciably toning them down. Even so, many of the most scathing antiwar passages—which remain the theme and focus of the poem in all its versions—have remained consistent throughout each of the various versions. One example is this passage, in which some of the most horrible atrocities of the Vietnam War are visited on children, even infants:

> The six-hour infant puts his fists instinctively to his eyes to
> keep out the light.
> But the room explodes;
> The children explode;
> Blood leaps on the vegetable walls.

Bly says, "This is what it's like for a rich country to make war" (*Sleepers* version, cut in *Eating the Honey of Words*).

Clearly, "The Teeth Mother Naked at Last" represents Bly's abiding interest in both social and political themes, and it stands as his most definitive condemnation of those who overstep or violate traditional societal or humanitarian boundaries, even for so-called positive political ends. Bly minces no words and spares no one: "The ministers lie, the professors lie, the television reporters lie, the priests lie." These lies "mean that the country wants to die" (*Selected* version, amended to "mean we have a longing to die" in *Eating the Honey of Words*). "The Teeth Mother Naked at Last," then, in any of its versions, remains one of the most sustained and important antiwar poems of the 20th century.

The poem opens with helicopters (called "death-bees") lifting "beautifully" from the decks of warships to bomb the Vietnamese people in their "vegetable-walled" villages. Such inhumane actions have been rationalized by "lies." At the center of the poem, Bly asks, "Why are they dying?" No direct answer is ever given—apparently because there is no acceptable or believable answer. In the latter half of the poem, the speaker returns to his psychic "animal brain" in an attempt to deal with, or to escape from, the atrocities of the war:

> If one of those children came toward me with both hands
> in the air, fire rising along both elbows,
> I would suddenly go back to my animal brain.

Since such terrors cannot be dealt with rationally or logically, the speaker, at the very end of the poem, attempts to escape them through sleep, and he does not desire to be awakened from this sleep. His dream, which takes him "down" into the depths of the psyche, where poetry has its source, simultaneously catapults him "upward" into an apocalyptic dream or vision in which the "Teeth Mother," "naked at last," rises from the "underneath" waters of the psyche to point to a possibility for psychic renewal, a renewal that may affect the "outward" man as well as the "inward" one and that may eventually lead to social and political changes or even to the end of war:

> Let us drive cars
> Up
> The light beams
> To the stars . . .
>
> Then return to earth crouched inside the drop of sweat
> That falls
> From the chin of the Protestant tied in the fire.
> (*Eating the Honey of Words* version)

These images, as interesting and enigmatic as any in Bly's canon, seem to suggest man's mastery of technology, risen to the highest heights of the heavens, but crumbling back to earth and descending on a believer, a martyr to mankind, who has been condemned for, and is dying for, his beliefs. From such devotion, even unto death, and only through poetry, there may yet come new life.

William V. Davis

**Further Reading**

Davis, William V., "'At the Edges of the Light': A Reading of Robert Bly's *Sleepers Joining Hands*," *Poetry East* 4/5 (1981)

Davis, William V., *Understanding Robert Bly,* Columbia: University of South Carolina Press, 1988

Davis, William V., *Robert Bly: The Poet and His Critics,* Columbia, South Carolina: Camden House, 1994

Kalaidjian, Walter B., *Languages of Liberation: The Social Text in Contemporary American Poetry,* New York: Columbia University Press, 1989

Lacey, Paul A., *The Inner War: Forms and Themes in Recent American Poetry,* Philadelphia, Pennsylvania: Fortress Press, 1972

Libby, Anthony, "Robert Bly Alive in Darkness," *Iowa Review* 3, no. 3 (1972)

Libby, Anthony, *Mythologies of Nothing: Mystical Death in American Poetry, 1940–70,* Urbana: University of Illinois Press, 1984

Mersmann, James F., *Out of the Vietnam Vortex: A Study of Poets and Poetry against the War,* Lawrence: University Press of Kansas, 1974

Nelson, Howard, *Robert Bly: An Introduction to the Poetry,* New York: Columbia University Press, 1984

Sugg, Richard, "Robert Bly and the Poetics of Evolutionary Psychology," *Journal of Evolutionary Psychology* 6, no. 1–2 (1985)

---

# Louise Bogan 1897–1970

At her death in 1970, Louise Bogan had been relegated to the position of a brilliant minor poet who had chosen not to follow in the path of Ezra Pound, T.S. Eliot, and other Modernist poets. Rather, she chose traditional forms of poetry and developed an intellectual style in the tradition of the English metaphysical poets. However, at the end of the century, 100 years after her birth, she is being reassessed as a major formalist voice in American poetry, and there has been an acknowledgment that women artists like Bogan faced difficulties that their male counterparts did not, difficulties that Bogan herself recognized but never tried to respond to because she saw herself as an observer of life, not an observer of women's lives or a poet speaking only as a woman. Now, at the beginning of a new century, her observer's vision seems clear and quite remarkably astute and uncluttered by prejudice or ideology.

Always attracted to form in poetry, Bogan wrote "The Pleasures of Formal Poetry" (1953) to illustrate her commitment to traditional meter and rhyme. For Bogan, poetic form was closely tied to musical form, and her poetry depended on musical measures not simply to convey human feelings but to create a balance between sound and silence.

Form for Bogan also depended on patterns of meaning, and her own personal experiences as well as her connection with Roman Catholic liturgy and with her Celtic heritage influenced both the richness and the depth of her poetic language. However, being Irish had, for Bogan, a negative side. In a *Partisan Review* interview in 1939, the poet admitted that being Irish caused her much difficulty in her formative years because of the prejudice against the Irish in New England. However, she felt that her mother's Irish heritage added to the richness of her poetic gift. Her relationship with her mother was not always tranquil, and much of her poetry centers on the conflict between a maternal force and the poet trying to free herself from that past.

Bogan first began publishing poetry in the Girls' Latin School publication *Jabberwock,* and she continued to publish poetry in the Boston University *Beacon.* These early poems are formal in style and romantic in content. Shortly after her marriage to Curt Alexander, a new element entered her poetry. Two poems, "Betrothed" and "The Young Wife," published in 1917 in *Others,* indicate that she had lost the romantic idealism that permeated the premarital poetry. Her separation from Alexander after only a few years of marriage and the change of tone in her poetry during the brief marriage suggest unhappiness in her life and in the relationship. "Betrothed," which was reprinted several times and even appeared in her last volume, *The Blue Estuaries: Poems, 1923–1968* (1968), posits that love is "beauty and sorrow," and the emphasis is on what one expects from love, only to find something quite different.

Bogan's first volume of poetry, *Body of This Death* (1923), reveals that Bogan was quite aware of and clearly influenced by the early Symbolists whom she read about in Arthur Symons' book *The Symbolist Movement in Literature* (1899). The poems in her first volume constitute a quest for symbols to express the power of sin and death in human life.

Her second book of poems, *Dark Summer* (1929), highlights the paradoxes and conflicts in Bogan's life and in her writing, and the title poem contains all the tensions and conflicts of "the storm in the sky" that "mounts, but is not yet heard." Bogan was beset during the writing of these poems by uncertainties about her poetry, her personal life, and her religious beliefs.

*The Sleeping Fury* (1937) was a watershed volume that confirmed that Bogan's poetic voice had not been silenced by several bouts of mental stress and illness. In the eponymous poem the subconscious preoccupations that sickened Bogan are brought to the fore, and the poet pulls the tensions and competing images together. The Furies, Greek avengers, become the symbols for unresolved conflicts in Bogan's personal relationships. The Fury in the poem is addressed directly as "You with your whips and shrieks, bearer of truth and of solitude." It is in this poem that Bogan tackles her difficult and painful relationship with her mother and with the world her mother represented.

During the 1930s and 1940s, Bogan began to be recognized as a major poetic voice and was awarded Guggenheim fellowships in 1933 and 1937. She became a Fellow in American Letters at the Library of Congress in 1944 and held the Chair of Poetry there in 1945–46. Other awards followed, including the Harriet Monroe Poetry Award (1948) and a fellowship from the American Academy of Poets (1959). She also published *Poems and New Poems* (1941) and *Collected Poems, 1923–1953* (1954). Her final volume of poetry, *The Blue Estuaries,* is a compilation of all her previous volumes and clearly shows Bogan's development and maturation as an important voice in American poetry.

In addition to writing poetry, Bogan was, for several years, a contributor of short stories to *The New Yorker* and other journals. Those stories depict the illusory nature of relationships between men and women. Throughout the 1930s, Bogan continued to write prose but always felt that "prose [was] so terribly unsatisfactory." Prose offers ways of avoiding confrontation with life, but poetry, Bogan maintained, reveals all that has been repressed in life and thus, at its best, presents a truer picture of human experience than prose.

Bogan also published three volumes of criticism, a collection of journal entries and letters that comprise a sort of autobiography, and several translations and anthologies. At the time of her death in 1970, Bogan was working on a book of criticism entitled *A Poet's Alphabet: Reflections on the Literary Art and Vocation.* It was edited and published posthumously in 1970.

Mary A. McCay

**Biography**

Born in Livermore Falls, Maine, 11 August 1897. Attended Boston University, 1915–16; freelance writer, New York, 1919–25; poetry editor, *The New Yorker,* 1931–69; fellow, 1944, and consultant-in-poetry, 1945–46, Library of Congress, Washington, D.C.; Visiting Professor, University of Washington, Seattle, 1948, University of Chicago, 1949, University of Arkansas, Fayetteville, 1952, Salzburg Seminar in American Studies, 1958, and Brandeis University, Waltham, Massachusetts, 1964–65. Received Guggenheim fellowship, 1933, 1937; Harriet Monroe Poetry Award, 1948; American Academy grant, 1951; Bollingen Prize, 1955; Academy of American Poets fellowship, 1959; Brandeis University Creative Arts Award, 1961; National Endowment for the Arts grant, 1967; honorary L.H.D., Western College for Women, Oxford, Ohio, 1956; honorary Litt.D., Colby College, Waterville, Maine, 1960; member, American Academy, 1951, and Academy of American Poets, 1954. Died in New York City, 4 February 1970.

**Poetry**

*Body of This Death,* 1923
*Dark Summer,* 1929
*The Sleeping Fury,* 1937
*Poems and New Poems,* 1941
*Collected Poems, 1923–1953,* 1954
*The Blue Estuaries: Poems, 1923–1968,* 1968
*Uncollected Poetry and Prose,* 1975

**Selected Criticism**

*Achievement in American Poetry, 1900–1950,* 1951
*Emily Dickinson: Three Views* (with Archibald MacLeish and Richard Wilbur), 1960
*A Poet's Alphabet: Reflections on the Literary Art and Vocation,* edited by Robert Phelps and Ruth Limmer, 1970

**Other Writings:** essays, memoirs, translations of German literature (*The Sorrows of Young Werther, and Novella,* by Goethe [with Elizabeth Mayer and W.H. Auden], 1971); edited selections of poetry (*The Golden Journey: Poems for Young People* [with William Jay Smith], 1965).

**Further Reading**

Bowles, Gloria, *Louise Bogan's Aesthetic of Limitation,* Bloomington: Indiana University Press, 1987
Colasurdo, Christine, "The Dramatic Ambivalence of Self in the Poetry of Louise Bogan," *Tulsa Studies in Women's Literature* 13, no. 2 (1994)
Collins, Martha, editor, *Critical Essays on Louise Bogan,* Boston: G.K. Hall, 1984
Dodd, Elizabeth, *The Veiled Mirror and the Woman Poet: H.D., Louise Bogan, Elizabeth Bishop, and Louise Glück,* Columbia: University of Missouri Press, 1992
Frank, Elizabeth, *Louise Bogan: A Portrait,* New York: Knopf, 1985
Peterson, Douglas L., "The Poetry of Louise Bogan," *Southern Review* 19, no. 1 (Winter 1983)
Ridgeway, Jaqueline, *Louise Bogan,* Boston: Twayne, 1984
Upton, Lee, "The Re-Making of a Poet: Louise Bogan," *Centennial Review* 36, no. 3 (1992)
Upton, Lee, "Coming to God: Notes on Dickinson, Bogan, Cixous," *Denver Quarterly* 27, no. 4 (Spring 1993)

## Medusa

First published in *The New Republic* in 1921, "Medusa" is one of Louise Bogan's most anthologized works, one that represents an early model for feminist poetry in the 20th century. Ever confrontational, Bogan chose the lyric style when it was out of fashion; she did not ally herself with the burgeoning feminist movement, speaking out against feminist positions in her criticism. In a 1963 review, she observed that "women's poetry continues to be unlike men's, all feminist statements to the contrary notwithstanding." Her poems reveal an avid exploration of what critics have called an "ambivalence" about her subject position as a woman. Yet "Medusa" complicates that historical perspective. "Medusa" appears in her first collection, *Body of This Death* (1923), as one of many poems about relationships, emotional trauma, and ultimately, although Bogan did not claim this as her subject matter, the position of women in society. "Medusa" was later reprinted in the first section of *The Blue Estuaries: Poems, 1923–1968* (1968), maintaining a central place in Bogan's work as a complicated rendering of female subjectivity.

Written after Bogan's marriage to Lieutenant Curt Alexander ended in 1918 and after her lover John Coffey left her, "Medusa" presents the stark encounter between the speaker and the mythological Medusa, a woman changed by Athena into a monster with snakes for hair. Medusa provides a complex figure for a poetic consideration of the feminine. In the myth, Medusa petrified anyone who caught sight of her, until she was stalked and slain by Perseus. When Perseus cut off her head, her children, Pegasus and Chrysaor, were born from the wound. Medusa embodies the feminine, for before her transformation she was a beautiful woman; in her monstrosity, however, she is incapable of giving birth until her death.

As a sequel to Bogan's poem "A Tale," "Medusa" focuses on a literal and metaphoric barren landscape. The speaker comes to a house "in a cave of trees, / Facing a sheer sky." At the outset of the poem there is motion, a marked contrast to the eerie stillness beginning in stanza three. The speaker moves to the house, a bell prepares to "strike," and the sun "wheel[s] by." The next stanza continues the theme of movement as the speaker describes Medusa peering into a window: "When the bare eyes were before me." While the mythological Medusa petrified those unlucky enough to cross her path, Bogan's Medusa appears to be no victim of Athena's curse. Instead, this Medusa stalks. Predatory and vicious, she is out of her element, in a foreign landscape, seeking her victim's gaze through the window.

Another possible analysis is that Medusa's appearance in the window represents powerlessness and danger for both Medusa and the speaker. The speaker describes Medusa as "Held up at a window," as if the monster were not moving under her own power. Perhaps more ominous than the stalking Medusa is the conquered Medusa, the one controlled by a greater power. This reading suggests the speaker's powerlessness as well: as a creature like Medusa, who is both woman and not, the speaker will share Medusa's fate.

"Medusa" exhibits the rigorous thematic and stylistic control typical of Bogan's poetry, the formal structure of the poem lending to its interpretation; her strict adherence to form has been called masculine. Written in five stanzas, of which all but stanza two are quatrains of alternating long and short lines, the lines of "Medusa" are themselves snake-like. Stanza two, which introduces Medusa, is subtly different, containing five lines with an altered line-length pattern (long, short, long, long, short).

The structural movement of the long and short lines continues throughout the poem, contrasting with the internal stasis of the poem's last three stanzas. The earlier movement in the poem comes to a halt after Medusa and the speaker exchange glances. Nothing moves, as Bogan reveals:

> This is a dead scene forever now.
> Nothing will ever stir.
> The end will never brighten it more than this,
> Nor the rain blur.

Several critics, Theodore Roethke first among them, have suggested it is not simply the speaker's fear that accounts for this stasis. Roethke reads the dead scene as a dream-like sequence in which the speaker perseverates, unable to move away from the Medusa, in perpetual agony, literally terrified. His Jungian analysis suggests that the house, approached in stanza one "in a cave of trees," is a "womb within a womb." The confrontation with the Medusa is ultimately a confrontation, muses Roethke, with the Anima, or man-in-the-woman. In this interpretation, Medusa represents Bogan's continuing exploration of a woman's freedom, suggesting perhaps that, to be truly free, the speaker must become man (Medusa usually froze men; the speaker therefore assumes a masculine role in her confrontation with the goddess).

Roethke further speculated that the Medusa represents Bogan's mother, with whom the poet had a troubled relationship. Critic Lee Upton explores this idea of the mother/daughter relationship at the center of the poem by reading the window of the house as a mirror (in the myth, the only way one can safely view Medusa is in a mirror). In this reading the halting of motion constitutes a suspended moment in which Medusa and the speaker recognize themselves in one another. They are at once separate, independent beings and entwined by a history of physical intimacy as mother and daughter. Upton notes the importance of assonance and word repetitions in the poem and how these create a mirroring effect, the language mimicking the static moment.

Like the speaker, or perhaps as a reflection of the speaker, the scene remains static as well. "The water will always fall, and will not fall, / And the tipped bell make no sound." The speaker is left to look at the barren landscape, punctuated only by the yellow dust that no longer blows away in the wind. The poem moves into a frozen landscape where the speaker is not only locked in a gaze with Medusa but also locked in her own thoughts. Elizabeth Frank observes that Bogan is ultimately silenced in this poem, "locked inside her own speech," as Medusa and the speaker reach an impossible stasis.

The fascination surrounding "Medusa" and its author continues today. Feminists in recent years have rescued Bogan in countless new analyses of her work, and many of these analyses characterize "Medusa" as an important poem depicting the challenges of living as a woman during Bogan's lifetime. Bogan herself would likely have dismissed these readings, as she considered her life private and her poetry nonconfessional. Indeed, Ruth Limmer quotes Bogan in the introduction to the poet's autobiography: "If they [future research students] can know everything to begin with, how in hell can they go on eating up their tidy little fellowships researching? And I believe the less authentic records are, the more 'interesting' they automatically become."

J. ELIZABETH CLARK

**Further Reading**


Bawer, Bruce, "Louise Bogan's Angry Solitude," *New Criterion* 3, no. 9 (1985)

Bowles, Gloria, "Louise Bogan: To Be (Or Not To Be?) Woman Poet," *Women's Studies* 5 (1977)

Colasurdo, Christine, "The Dramatic Ambivalence of Self in the Poetry of Louise Bogan," *Tulsa Studies in Women's Literature* 13, no. 2 (1994)

Collins, Martha, editor, *Critical Essays on Louise Bogan*, Boston: G.K. Hall, 1984 Couchman, Jane, "Louise Bogan: A Bibliography of Primary and Secondary Materials, 1915–1975: Parts I–III," *Bulletin of Bibliography and Magazine Notes* 33 (1976)

Frank, Elizabeth, *Louise Bogan: A Portrait,* New York: Knopf, 1985

Moore, Patrick, "Symbol, Mask, and Meter in the Poetry of Louise Bogan," *Women and Literature* 1 (1980)

Roethke, Theodore, "The Poetry of Louise Bogan," *Michigan Quarterly Review* 6 (1967)

Upton, Lee, "The Re-Making of a Poet: Louise Bogan," *Centennial Review* 36, no. 3 (1992)
Upton, Lee, *Obsession and Release: Rereading the Poetry of Louise Bogan,* Lewisburg, Pennsylvania: Bucknell University Press, and London: Associated University Presses, 1996

## Women

The widespread inclusion of Louise Bogan's "Women" in recent anthologies has created an impression of her career that is at once accurate and misleading. The impression is accurate insofar as it reflects the real centrality of the poem to Bogan's work. As Gloria Bowles (1987) points out, Bogan "set special store by the poem early in her career since she had it reprinted for private distribution in 1929," and she reprinted it in every book she published after its first publication in February 1922 in *Measure* (Knox, 1990). However, the impression is misleading insofar as it suggests the "backwardness" of Bogan's views concerning women. In the 1970s, "Women" frequently appeared in anthologies of women's poetry, but many readers of such collections did not respond to Bogan's poem favorably: "'Women,'" writes Bowles, "has been read as a 'self-hate,' and thus a 'woman-hating,' poem." Bowles' description of the cool response to "Women" by some feminists points to the contradictions embedded within the language and rhetorical situation of the poem itself. As critics have observed, however, this reading of "Women" is neither the only one possible nor the most nuanced. "We need to understand," Bowles argues, "that Bogan at once includes and excludes herself from [the] indictment" of women she makes in the poem. Despite the critical controversy surrounding the text, then, it is clear that Bogan's poem makes the status of women its central concern.

Bowles' remarks reflect the ambiguity and irony that characterize Bogan's poem as a whole. The "meaning" of "Women" varies according to how one views the poem's speaker, tone, and language. If, for example, one imagines the speaker of "Women" to be a man (like the speakers of "The Frightened Man" and "Juan's Song"), the tone of the poem emerges somewhat differently than it does if the speaker is taken to be a woman. As spoken by a man, the successive pronouncements about women more likely express bewildered condescension than sympathetic irony. The male speaker presumably makes his remarks with an arrogant confidence in the value of his abilities by defining them against the putative deficiencies of women. From this point of view, the speaker establishes his sense of superiority by constituting "women" as the inferior "other" that provides the basis for male supremacy.

In fact, an additional complication of this reading might be that, as the poetic creation of a woman, Bogan's male speaker is an imagined puppet in the hands of an ironic female "master" whose attitude differs from that of her speaker. According to this scenario, the speaker's confidence becomes the butt of the poet's unspoken ridicule, for the speaker ticks off a series of qualities and behaviors commonly attributed to women that the poet, or the reader, regards as myopic stereotypes. Whether male or female, Bogan's speaker may be an unreliable narrator, in which case readers will question the claims that she or he makes about women. The poem underscores the difference between the actual diversity among women and the monolithic representation of them in the poem's series of assertions.

While such speculations about speaker and tone may appear to ignore the biographical context of the poem's composition (Bogan did, after all, express doubts about the adequacy of women's poetry), the poet's views on women and their artistic achievement continued to evolve after she published "Women." Bowles points out that "in a reading of the poem at the Library of Congress" decades after the poem's initial publication, Bogan "said that over the years she had learned to appreciate, admire, and value women." Her remark reflects the ambiguity already latent within the poem, which registers a subtle sense of a woman's position in a male-dominated world. One may read the speaker's comments about women's behavior either as a straightforward condemnation of behaviors innate to women or as an ironic critique of social contexts that predispose women to assume such self-defeating postures, but a fuller interpretation of the poem might combine something of both positions.

If one reads "Women" as the text of a speech delivered by a woman instead of a man, the words appear to suggest that the speaker harbors an embittered, ambivalent perspective regarding the situation of women in general and of female artists in particular. At the same time that she berates women for not having a lively "wilderness in them" and for failing to be self-reliant, the speaker may also value the wary prudence that she attributes to them. Her claim that "They use against themselves that benevolence / To which no man is friend" is doubly satirical, for it both damns masculine egotism and laments the self-destructive excesses of feminine generosity. At the same time that the poem condemns the "eager meaninglessness" of women's "love," moreover, it values the exuberant abandon of the inner "wilderness" that women lack, and it appreciates the passionate yearning that prompts "A shout and a cry." In contrast to the broad freedom of nature ("wilderness"; "Snow water going down under culverts / Shallow and clear"), women's lives are cramped ("in the tight hot cell of their hearts"), secondhand and hungry ("dusty bread"), anesthetized or stunted ("They do not see," "They do not hear"), passive ("They wait"), and defensive ("They stiffen"). In the phrase that begins the last two lines, "As like as not," Bogan foregrounds the discrepancy between the possibility that "life" *ought* to offer to women and the sinister threat that it *actually* poses. From this perspective, the poem registers a vexed sense of the double-bind that women face within a patriarchal culture that worships self-reliance and defines autonomy in masculine terms. In her catalogs of the things that women fail to do or that "They cannot think of," Bogan's speaker suggests that women are deprived of the sustenance that would allow "life" to step "over their door-sills." Subsisting on a "provident" but meager diet, women exist like ghosts in tomblike, lifeless houses. The anger that drives Bogan's declarations makes them serve as denunciations that both diagnose and decry the predicament of women.

Jeff Westover

**Further Reading**

Aldrich, Marcia, "Lethal Brevity: Louise Bogan's Lyric Career," in *Aging and Gender in Literature: Studies in Creativity,* edited by Anne M. Wyatt-Brown and Janice Rossen, Charlottesville: University Press of Virginia, 1993

Bowles, Gloria, *Louise Bogan's Aesthetic of Limitation,* Bloomington: Indiana University Press, 1987
Colasurdo, Christine, "The Dramatic Ambivalence of Self in the Poetry of Louise Bogan," *Tulsa Studies in Women's Literature* 13, no. 2 (1994)
Collins, Martha, editor, *Critical Essays on Louise Bogan,* Boston: G.K. Hall, 1984
DeShazer, Mary, "'My Scourge, My Sister': Louise Bogan's Muse," in *Coming to Light: American Women Poets in the Twentieth Century,* edited by Diane Wood Middlebrook and Marilyn Yalom, Ann Arbor: University of Michigan Press, 1985
Dodd, Elizabeth, *The Veiled Mirror and the Woman Poet: H.D., Louise Bogan, Elizabeth Bishop, and Louise Glück,* Columbia: University of Missouri Press, 1992
Knox, Claire E., *Louise Bogan: A Reference Source,* Metuchen, New Jersey: Scarecrow Press, 1990
Moore, Patrick, "Symbol, Mask, and Meter in the Poetry of Louise Bogan," *Women and Literature* 1 (1980)
Ridgeway, Jaqueline, *Louise Bogan,* Boston: Twayne, 1984
Upton, Lee, *Obsession and Release: Rereading the Poetry of Louise Bogan,* Lewisburg, Pennsylvania: Bucknell University Press, and London: Associated University Presses, 1996

---

## Arna Bontemps 1902–73

Although not as well known as other Harlem Renaissance writers (e.g., Langston Hughes, Countee Cullen, and Jean Toomer), Arna Bontemps influenced the development of African-American poetry as a poet, an editor, and a colleague. His vibrant poetry reclaimed the past for African-Americans, his various anthologies documented that history, and his friendly influence encouraged other African-American writers to express their legacy in verse and prose.

Bontemps was born in Alexandria, Louisiana, on 13 October 1902 but moved to Los Angeles with his family at the age of three because of several racial incidents. He spent his formative years under the competing influences of his father, who pushed him to act "less colored," and his uncle, who provided Bontemps with access to black culture and history. Their opposing views on blackness crystallized for Bontemps the conflict for African-Americans between a need for heritage and a desire to break with the horrors of the past, leading him to devote his career to documenting African-American heritage and supporting black identity.

In 1924, Bontemps moved to New York and joined the Harlem literary circle. He began to publish poems in literary magazines, earning praise from his fellow poets and awards from various groups. He won *Opportunity*'s Alexander Pushkin Award for Poetry in 1926 for his poem "Golgotha Is a Mountain" and repeated as winner in 1927 for "The Return." *The Crisis* also awarded Bontemps first prize in 1927 for "Nocturne at Bethesda." These poems, along with "A Black Man Talks of Reaping" and "Reconnaissance," became his most famous poems.

Bontemps' poetry never included the direct protestations of his contemporaries. His poems were subdued meditations on recurring themes: the return to the past as racial memory, the black as alien and exile, the usefulness of Christianity and other Western myths to alleviate black suffering, and the ability of the African-American people to endure such suffering and prevail against hardship. "Golgotha Is a Mountain" links Christ's suffering to blacks across space and time. Yet "Nocturne at Bethesda" exposes the inability of Christianity to provide meaning to black suffering and pain, suggesting instead that the answer lies in racial memory. "The Return" combines personal emotion and racial consciousness in the depiction of two lovers whose greatest joy lies in the remembrance of an Edenic ancestral Africa. "Reconnaissance" also figures a return to primitive Africa: the poet seeks truth in the past, finding it in a return to the jungle. "A Black Man Talks of Reaping" is Bontemps' most overt protest poem. It argues powerfully that it is improper and unnatural for any human not to reap what he sows, ending with an implied threat of rebellion against black exploitation. These poems typify Bontemps' poetic project: engaging with the past as a means of defining black identity. Yet, despite its recognition at the time, Bontemps' poetry does not receive the recognition it deserves today.

Bontemps stopped writing poetry seriously in 1931. While he did publish a book of children's poetry (*Golden Slippers,* 1941), he chose instead to focus on fiction and drama. Yet Bontemps still acted as a proponent of African-American poetry in his role as an editor, producing the volumes *The Poetry of the Negro, 1746–1949* (1949, co-edited with Hughes) and *American Negro Poetry* (1963). He also collected 23 of his Harlem Renaissance poems in the volume *Personals* (1963), a volume that reflects Bontemps' youthful wonder. The collection is infused with the spirit of possibility as seen through the eyes of a young man defining himself and accepting his heritage. In addition, *Personals* constitutes an archive of Bontemps' strongest poems as he judged them through wisdom and experience.

Perhaps as important as his printed works, however, are Bontemps' friendships with other Harlem Renaissance poets. When he arrived in New York, Bontemps began relationships with Hughes, Cullen, and other African-American artists. He collaborated with these poets, discussing ideas and reading poems. Bontemps' friendship with Hughes would last a lifetime. They exchanged letters even after Bontemps left Harlem, continuing to support each other's work. Together, they encouraged the development and recognition of African-American poetry in the United States.

In 1943, Bontemps earned his M.L.S. degree from the University of Chicago and became the head librarian of Fisk University. Once at Fisk, Bontemps was able to create the Langston Hughes Renaissance Collection through his friendship with Hughes and their connections with many figures of the Harlem Renaissance.

Bontemps continued to publish collections of African-American folklore and poetry and to write biographies, novels, plays, and histories until his sudden death on 4 June 1973.

DAVID E. MAGILL

**Biography**

Born in Alexandria, Louisiana, 13 October 1902. Attended Pacific Union College, Angwin, California, B.A. 1923; University of Chicago, M.L.S. 1943; teacher, Harlem Academy, New York City, 1924–31, Oakwood Junior College, Huntsville, Alabama, 1931–34, Shiloh Academy, Chicago, Illinois, 1935–37, and Illinois Writers' Project, 1937–38; Librarian, Fisk University, Nashville, Tennessee, 1943–65; Professor, University of Illinois, Chicago, 1966–69; Visiting Professor and Curator of James Weldon Johnson Collection, 1969; writer-in-residence, Fisk University, 1970–73; member, Metropolitan Nashville Board of Education, National Association for the Advancement of Colored People, PEN, American Library Association, Dramatists Guild, Sigma Pi Phi, and Omega Psi Phi. Received Poetry Prize, *The Crisis* magazine, 1926; Alexander Pushkin Poetry Prize, 1926, 1927; Short Story Prize, *Opportunity,* 1932; Julius Rosenwald fellowships, 1938–39, 1942–43; Guggenheim fellowship, 1949–50; Jane Adams Children's Book Award, 1956; Dow Award, Society of Midland Authors, 1967; honorary L.H.D., Morgan State College, Baltimore, Maryland, 1969. Died in Nashville, Tennessee, 4 June 1973.

**Poetry**

*Personals,* 1963

**Other Writings:** novels (*Drums at Dusk,* 1939), children's literature (*Popo and Fifina: Children of Haiti* [with Langston Hughes], 1932; *Lonesome Boy,* 1955), plays (*Free and Easy,* 1949), biographies (*Free at Last: The Life of Frederick Douglass,* 1971), histories (*One Hundred Years of Negro Freedom,* 1961), correspondence (*Arna Bontemps-Langston Hughes Letters, 1925–1967,* 1980); edited anthologies of poetry (*American Negro Poetry,* 1963), literature, (*The Harlem Renaissance Remembered,* 1972), and folklore (*The Book of Negro Folklore* [with Langston Hughes], 1958).

**Further Reading**

Bontemps, Arna, *Arna Bontemps-Langston Hughes Letters, 1925–1967,* edited by Charles H. Nichols, New York: Dodd Mead, 1980

Davis, Arthur P., *From the Dark Tower: Afro-American Writers, 1900 to 1960,* Washington, D.C.: Howard University Press, 1974

Fleming, Robert E., *James Weldon Johnson and Arna Wendell Bontemps: A Reference Guide,* Boston: G.K. Hall, 1978

Harris, Violet J., "From Little Black Sambo to Pope and Fifina: Arna Bontemps and the Creation of African American Children's Literature," *The Lion and the Unicorn* (June 1990)

Jones, Kirkland C., "Arna Bontemps," in *Dictionary of Literary Biography,* volume 48: *American Poets, 1880–1945: Second Series,* edited by Peter Quartermain, Detroit, Michigan: Gale Research, 1986

Jones, Kirkland C., *Renaissance Man from Louisiana: A Biography of Arna Wendell Bontemps,* Westport, Connecticut: Greenwood Press, 1992

Reagan, Daniel, "Achieving Perspective: Arna Bontemps and the Shaping Force of Harlem Culture," *Essays in Arts and Sciences* 25 (October 1996)

---

# Kamau Brathwaite 1930–

Long considered to be one of the foremost voices in West Indian poetry and criticism, Kamau Brathwaite has devoted his career to finding ways of transforming the English language to enable it to capture the characteristic rhythms of Caribbean life and culture. For Brathwaite, poetry acts as a force for communal affirmation and unification, particularly when it serves the project of rediscovering origins. In his autobiographical essay "Timehri" (1974), Brathwaite links Caribbean poetic practice to the "recognition of an ancestral landscape" that "involves the artist . . . in a journey into the past and hinterland which is at the same time a movement of possession into present and future. Through this movement of possession we become our selves, truly our own creators, discovering word for object, image for word."

The transformation of Brathwaite's own name is an example of this process of self-discovery. He was born Lawson Edward Brathwaite in Bridgetown, Barbados, on 11 May 1930. His first book of poetry, *Rights of Passage* (1967), is attributed to "Edward Brathwaite," but as he recounts in the volume *BarabajanPoems* (1994), he was given the Kikuyu name "Kamau" in 1971 during an impromptu ritual at the home of the Kenyan writer Ngugi wa Thiong'o in Tigoni, Limuru. Recollecting the event years later on the occasion of Brathwaite's receiving the 1994 Neustadt Prize for Literature, Ngugi described "Kamau" as "the name of a generation that long ago had struggled with the elements to tame the land and made us what we now were." For Brathwaite, the importance of that ceremony lay not only in its timing—"it took place for me as an adult rather than as a child carried to the baptismal font"—but also in its public affirmation of a "cultural position/commitment/orientation." In 1987, during a visit to Barbados to deliver the 12th Sir Winston Scott Memorial Lecture at the invitation of the Central Bank of Barbados, Brathwaite changed his name legally, shortening it to "Kamau Brathwaite," thus giving equal weight to the African and British aspects of his cultural inheritance.

Brathwaite was educated at Harrison College in Barbados, where he and several friends founded a newspaper, the *Harrisonian,* for which he wrote a column on jazz and in which he would publish several poems in 1949–50. His first major publication was the poem "Shadow Suite," which appeared in *Bim,* the Barbadian literary journal published by Frank Collymore, whom Brathwaite describes as his "literary godfather." Like much of Brathwaite's early poetry, "Shadow Suite" is indebted to the work of T.S. Eliot, and only two of the poem's eight sections draw on the Caribbean motifs that would animate Brathwaite's mature work. In 1949, Brathwaite received the Barbados Island Scholarship to Cambridge University, where he read history at Pembroke College, graduating with an honors degree in 1953. After spending another year at Cambridge earning a certificate in education, Brathwaite traveled in 1955 to what is now Ghana, working for the Ministry of Education for seven years. Throughout this period, he continued to publish poems, stories, and essays in *Bim,* but in 1953 he found another outlet for his work, the BBC's *Caribbean Voices* program, which would present more than 50 of Brathwaite's poems, some as yet unpublished, from 1953 to 1958. Inspired in part by Eliot's phonograph recordings, Brathwaite developed an interest in recording his own poetry, sometimes to musical accompaniment, and increasingly sought to portray his verse as the written record of an oral art form.

The essays that appeared in *Bim* established Brathwaite as an important West Indian critical voice, but his international reputation as a poet resulted from the publication of his first three books of poetry—*Rights of Passage* (1967), *Masks* (1968), and *Islands* (1969)—which appeared together in 1973 as a single volume titled *The Arrivants: A New World Trilogy.* The first book of the trilogy was completed while Brathwaite was serving as a lecturer in history at the Mona, Jamaica, campus of the University of the West Indies and the next two while he was pursuing a doctorate in history at the University of Sussex in England. Although *The Arrivants* does not display the verbal difficulty and density—or the typographical experimentation—of Brathwaite's later work, it does set out many of the poet's abiding thematic concerns, particularly his interest in uncovering the African roots of the Caribbean psyche. "Where is the nigger's home?" Brathwaite asks in *Rights of Passage.* The first words of that volume—"Drum skin whip / lash"—immediately evoke the horror of the middle passage, in which the slave is transformed into a kind of African drum, beaten incessantly by the slaver's whip. *Rights of Passage* goes on to chart the movement of Caribbean peoples further into exile in the cities of North America and Europe; in the second book, *Masks,* this rootlessness is transformed by the rediscovery of Africa, particularly in the final three sections, which describe a modern Caribbean poet's pilgrimage to his ancestors' homeland. In the aftermath of this journey, the West Indies portrayed in *Islands* is a place marked by the presence of Africa: through poems with titles such as "Ananse," "Legba," "Ancestors," and "Vèvè," Brathwaite creates a communal voice that speaks for the African diaspora, and the trilogy ends with the image of "hearts / no longer bound / to black and bitter / ashes in the ground / now waking / making / making / with their / rhythms some- / thing torn / and new."

After completing his doctorate, Brathwaite returned to his teaching job in Jamaica and continued his exploration of Caribbean culture, publishing *Folk Culture of the Slaves in Jamaica* (1970), *The Development of Creole Society in Jamaica, 1700–1820* (1971), *Contradictory Omens: Cultural Diversity and Integration in the Caribbean* (1974), and *Our Ancestral Heritage: A Bibliography of the English-Speaking Caribbean* (1977). His next volume of poetry, *Other Exiles* (1975), presented poems written between 1950 and 1975 that, in contrast to *The Arrivants,* emphasized the personal rather than the communal; it was followed in 1976 by *Black + Blues,* which explored Brathwaite's Jamaican experience. With the support of a Guggenheim fellowship in 1972–73, Brathwaite began the trilogy *Ancestors,* which would eventually comprise the volumes *Mother Poem* (1977), *Sun Poem* (1982), and *X/Self* (1987). The first two volumes are set in the Caribbean, but *X/Self* stages a poetic appropriation of Europe, offering a fantasia on ancient Roman history that traces "our slavery" to the burning of Rome. In this trilogy, particularly in the final volume, Brathwaite intensifies his use of what he calls "calibanisms," the wordplay that results from the pressures of colonial exploitation, which he had begun to explore in *Black + Blues.* In his later work, such as *BarabajanPoems* and the docu-poem *TrenchTownRock* (1994), Brathwaite makes use of what he calls "Sycorax video style," which adds computer-generated typographical diversity to his other modes of formal and linguistic experimentation, creating a poetry that continually provokes and unsettles its readers.

Perhaps the most personal of Brathwaite's published work is *The Zea Mexican Diary* (1993), a collection of journal entries, letters, and meditations that record the poet's grief during and after the terminal illness of his wife, Doris Monica, in 1986, which coincided with the final revisions to *X/Self.* The volume moves from disbelief to rage and finally to acceptance and the ability to celebrate the life of a woman who was "the perfect wife of/for the poet."

In 1991, Brathwaite joined the Department of Comparative Literature at New York University, a department that includes Ngugi wa Thiong'o. He is currently at work on a volume of literary criticism that continues his project of shaping a distinctive Caribbean poetic sensibility at once indebted to and at odds with its British and American predecessors.

Cyrus R.K. Patell

*See also* Caribbean Poetry

**Biography**

Born in Bridgetown, Barbados, 11 May 1930. Attended Harrison College, Barbados; Pembroke College, Cambridge (Barbados Scholar), 1950–54, B.A. (honors) in history 1953, Cert. Ed. 1954; University of Sussex, Falmer, 1965–68, D.Phil. 1968; education officer, Ministry of Education, Ghana, 1955–62; Tutor, University of the West Indies Extra Mural Department, St. Lucia, 1962–63; Lecturer, 1963–76, Reader, 1976–82, and Professor of social and cultural history, 1982–91, University of the West Indies, Kingston, Jamaica; Visiting Professor, Southern Illinois University, Carbondale, 1970, University of Nairobi, 1971, Boston University, 1975–76, University of Mysore, India, 1982, Holy Cross College, Worcester, Massachusetts, 1983, and Yale University, New Haven, Connecticut, 1988; Visiting Fellow, Harvard University, Cambridge, Massachusetts, 1987; plebiscite officer in the Trans-Volta Togoland, United Nations, 1956–57; founding secretary, Caribbean Artists Movement, 1966; since 1970 editor, *Savacou* magazine, Mona, Jamaica; since 1991 Professor, New York University. Received Arts Council of Great Britain bursary, 1967; Camden Arts Festival Prize, London, 1967; Cholmondeley Award, 1970; Guggenheim fellowship, 1972;

City of Nairobi fellowship, 1972; Bussa Award, 1973; Casa de las Américas Prize, 1976; Fulbright fellowship, 1982–83, 1987–88; Institute of Jamaica Musgrave Medal, 1983; Neustadt Prize for Literature, 1994. Living in New York City.

**Poetry**

*The Arrivants: A New World Trilogy,* 1973
*Rights of Passage,* 1967
*Masks,* 1968
*Islands,* 1969
*Days and Nights,* 1975
*Other Exiles,* 1975
*Black + Blues,* 1976
*Ancestors* (trilogy)
*Mother Poem,* 1977
*Sun Poem,* 1982
*X/Self,* 1987
*Soweto,* 1979
*Word Making Man: A Poem for Nicólas Guillèn,* 1979
*Third World Poems,* 1983
*Jah Music,* 1986
*Sappho Sakyi's Meditations,* 1989
*MiddlePassages,* 1992
*Shar/Hurricane Poem,* 1992
*BarabajanPoems,* 1994
*TrenchTownRock,* 1994

**Other Writings:** plays (*Four Plays for Primary Schools,* 1964; *Odale's Voice,* 1967), nonfiction (*The Development of Creole Society in Jamaica, 1770–1820,* 1971; *History of the Voice: The Development of Nation Language in Anglophone Caribbean Poetry,* 1984; *Roots: Essays in Caribbean Literature,* 1986, revised edition, 1993; *The Zea Mexican Diary,* 1993); edited collections of literature (*Iouanaloa: Recent Writing from St. Lucia,* 1963; *New Poets from Jamaica,* 1979).

**Further Reading**

Bobb, June D., *Beating a Restless Drum: The Poetics of Kamau Brathwaite and Derek Walcott,* Trenton, New Jersey: Africa World Press, 1998
Brathwaite, Doris Monica, *A Descriptive and Chronological Bibliography (1950–1982) of the Work of Edward Kamau Brathwaite,* London: New Beacon, 1988
Brathwaite, Kamau, *Conversations with Nathaniel Mackey,* Staten Island, New York: We Press, 1999
Brown, Stewart, editor, *The Art of Kamau Brathwaite,* Bridgend, Mid Glamorgan, Wales: Seren, 1995
Lewis, Maureen Warner, *Notes to Masks,* Benin City, Nigeria: Ethiope, 1977; revised edition, as *E. Kamau Brathwaite's Masks: Essays and Annotations,* Mona, Jamaica: Institute of Caribbean Studies, 1992
Naylor, Paul, *Poetic Investigations: Singing the Holes in History,* Evanston, Illinois: Northwestern University Press, and London: Taylor and Francis, 1999
Rohlehr, Gordon, "Islands," *Caribbean Studies* 10 (January 1971)
Savory, Elaine, "The Word Becomes *Nam:* Self and Community in the Poetry of Kamau Brathwaite and Its Relation to Caribbean Culture and Postmodern Theory," in *Writing the Nation: Self and Country in the Post-Colonial Imagination,* edited by John C. Hawley, Amsterdam and Atlanta: Rodopi, 1996
Torres-Saillant, Silvio, *Caribbean Poetics: Toward an Aesthetic of West Indian Literature,* Cambridge and New York: Cambridge University Press, 1997
*World Literature Today* 68, no. 4 (1994) (special issue entitled "Kamau Brathwaite: 1994 Neustadt International Prize for Literature")

---

# Joseph Brodsky 1940–96

Few anglophone writers could easily relate to the circumstances under which Joseph Brodsky developed his poetic consciousness. Born in Leningrad, Brodsky survived the Nazi siege of his native city only to struggle against its post–World War II poverty and anti-Semitism. He abandoned formal education in his early teens to help support his family. While drifting through a succession of odd jobs he proved to be an exemplary autodidact, acquiring a near-native command of Polish and English in order to read the original texts of Czeslaw Milosz and the English metaphysical poets, with whom he has some affinity. But Brodsky's lack of a steady profession, as well as his early efforts at composing poems on unsanctioned themes, led him to be charged with "social parasitism" in 1964. It was the publicity surrounding his trial, and not his considerable merits as a poet, that first brought Brodsky to Western attention. The Soviet authorities sentenced him to five years' hard labor in Arkhangelsk, a bleak region in the far north, but public outcry (including protests by such cultural luminaries as Anna Akhmatova) led to his early release in 1965. Brodsky was then forced into exile in 1972, emigrating to the United States. He became a citizen five years later.

This information is, by the poet's own insistence, inessential to an understanding of his work. Packed with allusions to the literature, myths, and history of global (especially Western) antiquity, Brodsky's poems nevertheless read as self-contained artifacts, each a finely wrought specimen of aural resonance, narrative concision, and emotional control. At the same time his peculiar biography helps explain how he fits into the larger picture of contemporary American poetry, beginning with the fact that his poems appeared in the West long before they could be widely enjoyed in his native country. (Until the fall of the Soviet Union, Brodsky's poems could be read in Russia only in small, *samizdat* editions.) His first collection, *Stikhotvoreniya i poemy* (1965; Lyrics and Longer Poems), was published in New York. A selection of translations drawing from this collection, *Elegy to John Donne, and Other Poems*, appeared in London two years later. These early poems reveal him as a young master of the elegy and the dramatic monologue that, in their later development, would elicit frequent comparisons between Brodsky and Robert Lowell, whose work Brodsky greatly admired. This terrifically productive period in the early 1960s also demonstrates his interest in revisiting older narratives drawn from such diverse sources as the Old Testament, Greco-Roman myth, and Russian cultural history. As in "The Great Elegy to John Donne," perhaps his first major poem, Brodsky avoided artful rehashing of a received drama and instead exploited and embellished those aspects of the common narrative that were uncommon, drawing personal, often poignant conclusions from minute or altogether fabricated details:

> I'll follow, in the torment of desire,
> to stitch this parting up with my own flesh.
> But listen! While with weeping I disturb
> your rest, the busy snow whirls through the dark,
> not melting, as it stitches up this hurt—
> its needless flying back and forth, back, forth!
> It is not I who sob. It's you, John Donne:
> you lie alone. Your pans in cupboards sleep,
> while snow builds drifts upon your sleeping house—
> while snow sifts down to earth from highest Heaven.

Brodsky's next three collections—*Ostanovka v pustyne* (1970; A Stop in the Desert), *Konets prekrasnoi epokhi* (1977; End of a Beautiful Epoch), and *Chast' rechi* (1977; A Part of Speech), which appeared in re-edited translations as *Selected Poems* (1973) and *A Part of Speech* (1980)—complicated and deepened the poet's use of allusion, locating the speaker's life in the received narrative. Poems like "Odysseus to Telemachus" cannot help but reflect the poet's frustration with his homeland and the difficulties its political apparatus has forced upon him:

> I don't know where I am or what this place
> can be. It would appear some filthy island,
> with bushes, buildings, and great grunting pigs.

While continuing to address issues of universal human consequence, from the struggle against mortality to questions of social ethics and responsibility, these poems increasingly fold those concerns into the dilemmas of a speaker who has lost his faith in culture or suffers from moral exhaustion. Poems written after Brodsky's expulsion from the Soviet Union bear the imprint of exile and uncertainty—a sense of having been betrayed by that which the poet most loves ("Letters from the Ming Dynasty")—at the same time that they evidence a broader range of settings and themes ("The Thames at Chelsea").

The reappearance of characters and motifs from the Mediterranean tradition through Brodsky's last English collections, *To Urania* (1988) and *So Forth* (1996), has prompted some critics to discuss him as a classicist. This moniker seems appropriate to the extent that, like his friends Seamus Heaney and Derek Walcott, Brodsky finds in Western art and legend a series of cultural codes that transcend both time and geography, a versatile currency for communicating troublesome individual truths. This may partly account for his broad appeal among Western readers, culminating in his being awarded the Nobel Prize in 1987, while also explaining what many Soviet critics found so appalling in his work. Thinking of Brodsky as a classicist, however, fails to encompass his distinctive poetic style, a combination of formal rhymes interrupted by irregular lines and multiple registers of diction. It also ignores his grounding in two 20th-century poetic traditions: he is heir to the Russian Acmeists, including Akhmatova and Osip Mandelstam, but he also shows the influence of Lowell, W.H. Auden, and Robert Frost, among others.

Brodsky's works in English translation fall into multiple categories, since there is a noteworthy difference in quality and style between those poems translated by other poets, those poems Brodsky translated himself, and poems originally written in English. From his first introduction to an anglophone public, his poems have been rendered in exquisite English by diligent scholars and accomplished poets, among them George L. Kline, Anthony Hecht, and Richard Wilbur. These poems stand out for their faithful recasting of Brodsky's originals and their creative and insightful solutions to the problems and complexities his work inevitably presents. Translations executed by the poet himself are of uneven quality, and poems first composed in English typically lack the linguistic flair of his Russian. But if he had mixed success as an English poetic stylist, his prose, most of which he wrote in English, is superb. His critical and autobiographical essays, collected in *Less Than One* (1986, winner of the National Book Critics Circle Award) and *On Grief and Reason* (1995), are supple and natural, full of wit and thoughtful reflections on poetry and exile, the two subjects with which he was most intimately acquainted.

Benjamin Paloff

**Biography**

Born in Leningrad, Soviet Union, 24 May 1940. Attended public schools in Leningrad until 1956; stoker, sailor, photographer, geologist's assistant, coroner's assistant, farm laborer, Soviet Union, 1956–72; poet-in-residence, University of Michigan, Ann Arbor, 1972–80; Adjunct Professor, Columbia University, New York City, 1978–85; Professor, Mount Holyoke College, South Hadley, Massachusetts, 1981–96; co-founder, American Poetry and Literacy Project, 1993. Received honorary Litt.D., Yale University, New Haven, Connecticut, 1978; Mondello Prize, 1979; National Book Critics Circle Award, 1986; MacArthur fellowship, 1981; Guggenheim fellowship, 1987; Nobel Prize, 1987; Poet Laureate of the United States, 1991–92. Died in Brooklyn, New York, 28 January 1996.

**Poetry**

*Stikhotvoreniya i poemy* (Lyrics and Longer Poems), 1965
*Elegy to John Donne, and Other Poems*, 1967
*Ostanovka v pustyne* (A Stop in the Desert), 1970
*Selected Poems*, 1973
*Konets prekrasnoi epokhi* (End of a Beautiful Epoch), 1977
*Chast' rechi* (A Part of Speech), 1977
*A Part of Speech*, 1980
*Novye stansy k Avguste* (New Stanzas for August), 1983
*To Urania*, 1988
*Selected Poems*, 1992
*So Forth*, 1996
*Collected Poems in English*, 2000

**Other Writings:** essays (*Less Than One: Selected Essays,* 1986; *On Grief and Reason,* 1995), children's poetry (*Discovery,* 1999), plays (*Marbles: A Play in Three Acts,* 1989), travel writing (*Watermark,* 1992), translations of English and Polish into Russian and of Russian into Hebrew; edited anthology of poetry (*Modern Russian Poets on Poetry: Blok, Mandelstam, Pasternak, Mayakovsky, Gumilev, Tsvetaeva* [with Carl Proffer], 1976).

**Further Reading**

Bethea, David M., *Joseph Brodsky and the Creation of Exile,* Princeton, New Jersey: Princeton University Press, 1994

Brown, Edward James, *Russian Literature Since the Revolution,* New York: Collier, 1963; revised and enlarged edition, Cambridge, Massachusetts: Harvard University Press, 1982

Godzich, Wlad, "Brodsky and the Grounding of Poetry," *Georgia Review* 49, no. 1 (1995)

Polukhina, Valentina, *Joseph Brodsky: A Poet for Our Time,* Cambridge: Cambridge University Press, 1989

Polukhina, Valentina, *Brodsky Through the Eyes of His Contemporaries,* New York: St. Martin's Press, 1992

Rigsbee, David, *Styles of Ruin: Joseph Brodsky and the Postmodernist Elegy,* Westport, Connecticut: Greenwood Press, 1999

---

# William Bronk 1918–99

Bronk's Dartmouth professors included Sidney Cox, one of the first critics to defend Robert Frost as a major poet. Bronk met Frost through Cox, and Frost's influence on Bronk's early work is easily detected. Samuel French Morse, another of Cox's students, introduced Bronk to Wallace Stevens' poetry. Critics have made much of the Stevens/Bronk connection, and Stevens' influence is obvious in Bronk's early work, but there is little in the sound and structure of the later poems to remind one of the older poet. Bronk shared with Stevens the notion that any "world" is a fiction imagined by the mind, but his source for this was not Stevens but rather New England transcendentalism.

Rooted in Kantian metaphysics, transcendentalism saw each person closeted within a potentially solipsistic privacy: the individual's sense of the world has more to do with the subjective act of perception than with the objective nature of things. Ralph Waldo Emerson's solution to this isolation lay in his belief that "There is one mind common to all individual men. Every man is an inlet to the same and to all of the same" (Emerson, "History," in *Essays: First Series,* 1841). Bronk considered Emerson overly abstract but found Henry David Thoreau's adaptation of Emersonian idealism useful to his own work. Thoreau's greater particularity and his ability to root conceptions of transcendental truth in personal experience appealed to Bronk, and Thoreau became the primary figure in his personal canon.

For Bronk, transcendence is rare but does occur and is the subject of several poems, such as "Metonymy as an Approach to the Real World":

> Once in a city blocked and filled, I saw
> the light lie in the deep chasm of a street,
> palpable and blue, as though it had drifted in
> from say, the sea, a purity of space.

Central to Thoreau's transcendentalism was the Romantic doctrine of correspondence, which posits direct analogies between the world of spirit and the world of matter and that the spirit can be represented in terms of the matter in a poem. Frost, who admitted his debt to Thoreau, was the principal American poet of his generation to adopt this idea. Conceivably Bronk was led to it by way of his enthusiasm for Frost, but he soon found in Thoreau notions even more fruitful for his work than the doctrine of correspondence.

Although Bronk believed that correspondence could from time to time be discovered, like Thoreau he saw the universe as essentially silent. There was no analogy, no correspondence, through which this could be expressed, and, wrote Bronk, "in spite of [Thoreau's] earnest attempt to translate the silence into English, it would remain little better than a sealed book" (*The Brother in Elysium,* 1980). Although unable to evoke the essential silence of being, poetry could at least express what the world is not. To that end Bronk constructed a "negative" poetry in which any given version of "reality" turns out to be true to nothing but itself: "Oh, it is always *a* world," he wrote in "At Tikal," "and not *the* world" (italics added).

In 1938 Bronk entered the Harvard M.A. program but left at the end of the semester because, as he said in an interview a half-century later, "poetry wasn't treated [there] in any sense as an art" (Foster, 1994). He then set himself the task of evaluating three of his 19th-century predecessors: Thoreau, Whitman, and Melville. The book that resulted, *The Brother in Elysium* (1980), concerns the isolated and radically skeptical individual in search of friendship and community. Like Thoreau, Bronk suggests that genuine friendship, and hence community, is rarely achieved.

Insofar as Bronk's work is political (and little could be more suspect to writers like him than politics), it is anarchistic, positioning the individual as radically isolated but aware that any other prospect would be a dreamscape. Paradoxically, that isolation is not sterile but offers its own prospect in "The Mind's Landscape on an Early Winter Day":

> The mind is always lost and gropes its way,—
> lost, even when the senses seize the world
> and feed as though there never could be loss.
> It is this winter mind, the ne'erdowell
> that never finds a plan, that tells us see.
> And we open our eyes and feel our way in the dark.

Bronk had little interest in poetic communities and the personal politics that inform them. He consistently refused to let his work be published by journals and publishing houses that he thought were more interested in his name than in the poetry itself. His early work reached the world largely through the efforts of Cid Corman's journal, *Origin,* and Origin Press, which published Bronk's first book, *Light and Dark,* in 1956. His second, *The World, the Worldless,* did not appear until 1964, when Bronk was 46. Published by June Oppen in association with New Directions, it is considered by some critics to be Bronk's best and sold enough copies to warrant a second printing.

James Weill's Elizabeth Press became Bronk's publisher in 1969, issuing *The Empty Hands* and then in rapid succession ten other books collected together with the first two in *Life Supports: New and Collected Poems* (1981, republished shortly afterward by North Point Press) and *Vectors and Smoothable Curves: Collected Essays* (North Point, 1983). *Life Supports* won the American Book Award in 1982. Bronk, now 64, had finally achieved a measure of the fame many of his contemporaries had known for many years.

Some critics included Bronk with the Objectivists; others saw him as a forerunner of the Language poets. He himself denied both classifications, arguing that his work cut its own path, free of associations and poetic traditions. He resisted allegiance to any single group or tradition, refusing to compromise his work by using it to advance any personal or political cause. The seriousness of his enterprise is suggested by his final poem, an *ars poetica* that conveys his sense of poetry as essentially impersonal and transcendental:

Art isn't made; it's in the world almost
unseen but found existent there. We paint,
we score the sound in music, we write it down.

Edward Halsey Foster

**Biography**
Born in Fort Edward, New York, 17 February 1918. Attended Dartmouth College, Hanover, New Hampshire, A.B. 1938; served in the United States Army, 1941–45; owner and manager of a lumber business, Hudson Falls, New York, until 1978. Received American Book Award, 1982; Lannan Literary Award for Poetry, 1991. Died 22 February 1999.

**Poetry**
*Light and Dark,* 1956
*The World, the Worldless,* 1964
*The Empty Hands,* 1969
*That Tantalus,* 1971
*To Praise the Music,* 1972
*Silence and Metaphor,* 1975
*My Father Photographed with Friends and Other Pictures,* 1976
*The Meantime,* 1976
*Finding Losses,* 1976
*The Force of Desire,* 1979
*Life Supports: New and Collected Poems,* 1981
*Careless Love and Its Apostrophes,* 1985
*Manifest, and Furthermore,* 1987
*Death Is the Place,* 1989
*Living Instead,* 1991
*Some Words,* 1992
*The Mild Day,* 1993
*Our Selves,* 1994
*Selected Poems,* 1995
*The Cage of Age,* 1996
*All of What We Loved,* 1998
*Metaphor of Trees and Last Poems,* 1999

**Other Writings:** essays (*The Brother in Elysium: Ideas of Friendship and Society in the United States,* 1980; *Vectors and Smoothable Curves: Collected Essays,* 1983).

**Further Reading**
Clippinger, David, editor, *The Body of This Life: Reading William Bronk,* Jersey City, New Jersey: Talisman House, 2001
Corman, Cid, *William Bronk: An Essay,* Carrboro, North Carolina: Truck Press, 1976
Foster, Edward Halsey, interviewer, "Conversations with William Bronk," in *Postmodern Poetry: The Talisman Interviews,* by Foster, Hoboken, New Jersey: Talisman House, 1994
Foster, Edward Halsey, *Answerable to None: Berrigan, Bronk, and the American Real,* New York: Spuyten Duyvil, 1999
Kimmelman, Burt, *The "Winter Mind": William Bronk and American Letters,* Madison, New Jersey: Fairleigh Dickinson University Press, and London: Associated University Presses, 1998
*Sagetrieb* 7, no. 3 (1988) (special issue on Bronk edited by Burt Kimmelman and Henry Weinfield)
*Talisman* 2 (1989) (special issue on Bronk edited by Edward Halsey Foster)

## The Force of Desire

William Bronk's *The Force of Desire* was first published in 1979 by St. Elizabeth Press and later reprinted in *Life Supports: New and Collected Poems* (1981). The original book, comprised of 66 untitled three-line poems, also includes seven etchings by Eugene G. Canadé, a painter and lifelong friend of Bronk's. The etchings, which hung in Bronk's house in Hudson Falls, New York, neatly complement the spare but philosophically intense poetry of *The Force of Desire,* and the concise linear patterns and nonrepresentational shapes echo Bronk's own interrogation of the boundaries that delineate the human perception of the world, the "real," and truth.

The concise philosophical character of the poetry is further accentuated by a spare poetic form, namely, the three-line stanza, which is a continuation of the formal structure established in three prior books of poetry: *Finding Losses* (1976) is made up of four-line poems, *Silence and Metaphor* (1975) utilizes two-stanza poems with four lines each, and *To Praise the Music* (1972) is made up of unrhymed sonnets, what Bronk refers to as his "fourteen-liners." Nevertheless, for a poet whose prowess is developing and maintaining a sustained and detailed meditation on the nature of reality, being confined to only three lines would seem to reduce such ideas to mere epigraphs. Yet despite their brevity, the poems of *The Force of Desire* are evocative ruminations that are poignant and insightful.

Written at a time when Bronk faced periodic hospitalization for life-threatening emphysema that was complicated by his severe asthma, *The Force of Desire* is strong in its meditative tone and brutal honesty, especially in regard to Bronk's interrogation of his own death:

> I can be glad in my death that, selfless,
> the beauty of the world goes on; and then more:
> even worldless, that beauty still.

For its philosophical rigor and honest concision, *The Force of Desire* is regarded as one of his more accomplished books for its nuanced exploration of an ideational theme that has been the mainstay of Bronk's career, namely, the inability of language and knowledge to grasp the "real" and "truth" and, subsequently, the irreparable separation of the human from the "real." As Bronk writes,

> These are invented words and they refer
> to inventions of their own and not to a real world
> unresembled, inexpressible.

The chasm between the "real" and the human manifests in *The Force of Desire* in three different ideational themes: the separation of the "real" world or truth from the fictitious ones that we construct, the schism that inhibits the individual from knowing another person as well as she knows herself, and the infinite distance between the human and the divine.

While *The Force of Desire* continues to explore themes central to all of Bronk's poetry, the poems share less with the abstract reflections that dominate the earlier books. Like the poem cited previously that discusses Bronk's death, the poems of *The Force of Desire* gesture more toward the intensely personal tone and content of the later work: *Our Selves* (1994), *The Cage of Age* (1996), and *All of What We Loved* (1998). Moreover, the intimacy achieved in *The Force of Desire* has not only to do with the issue of Bronk's death but also that of his life—and especially the people who define and mark that life:

> The morning door is open to the outer world:
> the pleasure of edges, clear shapes and names.
> Its air is the sharp pain of your separateness.

The "pain" of separation of one individual from one another is a common thread in all of Bronk's work, but the occasion of that "sharp pain of your separateness" is specific in its reference. The audience for the book is clearly more particularized than in prior works, with the poems addressing specific friends and documenting the intimacy of friendship:

> Oh God, you feel the lust of your desire
> helpless in its despair of any speech.
> Mutely, I touch my friends to tell them so.

The poems of *The Force of Desire,* in this light, illuminate in a strikingly candid way how the philosophical issues that dominate Bronk's poetry are also central to his personal life.

In addition to the space between people, a recurring focus of *The Force of Desire* is the state of humankind after the fall from divine grace. For Bronk, the fall from God extends beyond the expulsion from the Garden of Eden and original sin and manifests as the perpetual absence of divinity:

> Lord, I cannot see You; I
> have nothing else to examine but my mind.
> It is extraneous. I look for You there.

The divine is infinitely hidden and separate, which fuels the distinctively agnostic stance and the tone of spiritual longing:

> As I am, Lord, there are little things I know
> whereas You have places of ignorance
> I know nothing of and cannot attain to.

The primary human condition is ignorance coupled with impotence, and the poems continually brush up against the limitations of human thinking, even chiding the reader that

> First, is to learn we have no power of our own.
> Second, an Outside Power is impotent too.
> The strength we acquire is to live with powerlessness.

To recognize powerlessness is to discover a sense of strength in impotence, which is central to the economics of desire in Bronk's poetry. The challenge, subsequently, is that human desire cannot and will not be fulfilled, and, moreover, the poem cannot transcend its own inherent limitations of language, form, and ideas. The strength of *The Force of Desire,* as well as Bronk's poetry as a whole, is the relentless interrogation of the boundaries that limit human experience—the bars that separate the human from truth—as well as the "force" of desire that manifests as the will to live, a relentless striving in the face of inevitable failure.

Bronk's poetry, in this light, is heroic even as it negotiates the seemingly self-negating assertion that all words are inventions and all human forms are false, including poetry. *The Force of Desire* is a testament to the intrinsic relationship of poetry and the impossibility of articulating a world that remains in perpetual flux:

> The poem is momentary though it has not
> the same moment always. Changes occur
> and it changes with them. The moment is felt.

What is felt in Bronk's poetry is the current of desire, surging in and through the poems as they wrestle with an unknown and unknowable world.

DAVID CLIPPINGER

**Further Reading**

Clippinger, David, "Luminosity, Transcendence, and the Certainty of Not Knowing," *Talisman* 14 (1995)

Clippinger, David, "The Act and Place of Poetry: William Bronk's 'Our Selves,'" *Sagetrieb* 16, no. 3 (1997)

Clippinger, David, editor, *The Body of This Life: Reading William Bronk,* Jersey City, New Jersey: Talisman House, 2001

Ernest, John, "William Bronk's Religious Desire," *Sagetrieb* 7, no. 3 (1988)

Ernest, John, "Fossilized Fish and the World of Unknowing: John Ashbery and William Bronk," in *The Tribe of John:*

*Ashbery and Contemporary Poetry,* edited by Susan M. Schultz, Tuscaloosa: University of Alabama Press, 1995
Finkelstein, Norman, "The World as Desire," *Contemporary Literature* 23, no. 4 (1982)
Finkelstein, Norman, "Bronk, Duncan and the Far Border of Poetry," *Sagetrieb* 12, no. 3 (1993)
Kimmelman, Burt, *The "Winter Mind": William Bronk and American Letters,* Madison, New Jersey: Fairleigh Dickinson University Press, and London: Associated University Presses, 1998
Weinfield, Henry, "'The Cloud of Unknowing': William Bronk and the Condition of Poetry," *Sagetrieb* 7, no. 3 (1988)

## The World, the Worldless

William Bronk's poetry bears witness to the illusory nature of everyday reality, of visual and other sensual perceptions, natural specimens, and the natural world. One might suspect that testimony so uncompromising and restricted would shut down its own poetic possibilities; paradoxically, however, the poems in *The World, the Worldless* (1964) open up a new path for verse. This new path addresses Boolean logarithms and the disordering findings of quantum physics through a lyricism that George Oppen has described as "absolutely coherent in thought and in form, [and] staggeringly profound."

Published by New Directions, *The World, the Worldless* came into print largely because of George and Mary Oppen, and George Oppen's discussions with his sister June Degnan, an assistant to James Laughlin at New Directions at that time. Oppen had written Bronk in 1962 after first reading Bronk's poetry in the influential magazine *Origin;* the alliance thus initiated continued for two decades until Oppen's death. The two writers reinforced each other's views of how contemporary social and scientific upheavals would necessarily influence poetic discourse. One result of their friendship is *The World, the Worldless,* Bronk's second published collection, but his first to be distributed nationwide and to receive critical attention. Gilbert Sorrentino, in reaction to Bronk's transformation of the seemingly tangible world into the worldless region of the unknown, wrote in *Poetry* that this was "a place to be respected, and feared: a little suspect."

The verse of *The World, the Worldless* does indeed reveal a primary shift in poetic discourse. Bronk's poems are detailed meditations on the news in physics, mathematics, and related disciplines, news that began to circulate widely beyond scientific communities in the mid–20th century (most of the poems date from the mid-1950s to the year of publication). Poem titles provide clear proof of scientific preoccupation as a major organizing principle for the collection: "The Nature of the Universe"; "Boolean Algebra: $X^2 = X$"; "The Extensions of Space"; "The World in Time and Space"; "The Annihilation of Matter"; and so on. In the poem "How Indeterminacy Determines Us" Bronk engages cosmological data and physics to achieve solemn lyric effects. The poem begins,

> We are so little discernible as such
> in so much nothing, it is our privacy
> sometimes that startles us: the world is ours;
> it is only ours. . . .

The poem's argument sounds new because it forges a brisk and intimate connection between the verifiable enormity of the universe ("so much nothing") and the epistemic consequences ("We are so little discernible" and "our privacy"). In another example of this kind of argument, in "The Thinker Left Looking Out the Window," Bronk describes the thinker as a bewildered reader (a trope for the poet and his audience), since "what he had in mind was planetary" and "proliferated schemes / the same for the tiniest or most immense." In such a disoriented "looking out" the reader's thought of "the natural world" is a trap, "a series of planes" that are somehow parallel and receding, "either a universe / or basic and particled atom." The disequilibrium is cosmos-wide, Bronk suggests, the same as experienced in the down-to-earth natural environment that "is trapped where it looks" and as experienced in the universe beyond that "shifts with us like a shadow."

*The World, the Worldless* also includes Bronk's earliest poems about Incan ruins at Machu Picchu in Peru, a special focus of Bronk's attention mid-career leading to the critically acclaimed essays in *The New World* (1974). As early as 1956 Bronk started visiting Copán, Mayan ruins in Honduras, and by the time *The World, the Worldless* was published he had discovered what he described in correspondence with Charles Olson as one place where the "fiction" of time was invented. As a consequence, he said, "I go [there] to look in the mirror hoping to see us in the prism of the remote." Poems in *The World, the Worldless* document Bronk's linkage between these ancient places and the deepening enigmas of physics and cosmology. In "The Beautiful Wall, Machu Picchu" his depiction of the laid stones partly illuminates this link, his worldless view and, perhaps, his own place in that view: "abstract austerities, unimitative[.]" The stones

> . . . say of the world there is nothing to say.
> Who had to spend such easing care on stone
> found grace inherent more as idea than in
> in the world, loved simple soundness in a just joint.
> And the pieces together once though elsewhere apart.

From these lines one might draw the troubling conclusion that a particularly praiseworthy quality like grace is only "idea" and thus not "in the world." This conclusion is at once a warranted and simplistic summation of Bronk's views expressed in the poem and throughout *The World, the Worldless.* In the perhaps more familiar and surely more intimate context in "My House New-Painted," the poet more directly assesses the perceived world as a product of imagination. Bronk regards his "particular" 100-year-old house with pleasure; he is pleased it is "firmed," he insists,

> by its shiny paint, [pleased it] should show the metaphor
> of a material world, though it is plainly that
> and nothing more—as spirit was nothing more—
> could have such power now, summon it
> as though from an actual world it meant to claim.

The argument here pulses with the same dimension-bending effect of Bronk's contrastive affinity between parallel and receding planes, between the universe and basic atom. The intimacy of a house, the conundrum of spirit, in effect all things that might give pleasure, are metaphors of "a material world" but "nothing more." The force of "nothing more" underscores that matter is only particles in empty space and also suggests that over time everything humankind imagines is nothing. *The World, the Worldless* looks out across space and time to the unknowable and unflinchingly faces its uncertainty, bringing the unknown into new and astonishing proximity.

Jack Kimball

**Further Reading**


Chawla, Louise, *In the First Country of Places: Nature, Poetry, and Childhood Memory,* Albany: State University of New York Press, 1994

Conte, Joseph Mark, "Constant and Variant: Semantic Recurrence in Harry Matthews, William Bronk, and Robert Creeley," in *Unending Design: The Forms of Postmodern Poetry,* by Conte, Ithaca, New York: Cornell University Press, 1991

Ernest, John, "Fossilized Fish and the World of Unknowing: John Ashbery and William Bronk," in *The Tribe of John: Ashbery and Contemporary Poetry,* edited by Susan M. Schultz, Tuscaloosa: University of Alabama Press, 1995

Finkelstein, Norman, *The Utopian Movement in Contemporary American Poetry,* Lewisburg, Pennsylvania: Bucknell University Press, and London: Associated University Presses, 1988; revised edition, 1993

Foster, Edward Halsey, "William Bronk's *The Brother in Elysium:* The Authority of Form," *Sagetrieb* 7, no. 3 (1988)

Kimmelman, Burt, *The "Winter Mind": William Bronk and American Letters,* Madison, New Jersey: Fairleigh Dickinson University Press, and London: Associated University Presses, 1998

*Sagetrieb* 7, no. 3 (1988) (special issue on Bronk edited by Burt Kimmelman and Henry Weinfield)

Sorrentino, Gilbert, "William Bronk," in *Something Said: Essays,* by Sorrentino, San Francisco: North Point Press, 1984

Taggart, John, "Reading William Bronk," in *Songs of Degrees: Essays on Contemporary Poetry and Poetics,* by Taggart, Tuscaloosa: University of Alabama Press, 1994

*Talisman* 2 (1989) (special issue on Bronk edited by Edward Halsey Foster)


---

# Gwendolyn Brooks 1917–2000

African-American poet Gwendolyn Brooks was always firmly invested in the black community. Her poetry is characterized by her intimate portrayals of the everyday lives of African-Americans, particularly women; a breadth of style ranging from Italian *terza rima* to sonnets to jazz and blues; and a profound concern with social issues. Brooks' vignettes about black life are neither simplistic nor one-sided. Overall, her work reveals a deep love of the African-American community and an unshakeable belief in humanity.

Brooks was born in Kansas to parents who vigorously supported her writing, proclaiming her destiny to be a poet when she was just seven years old. Rejected at a young age because of her dark skin, Brooks took solace in her writing, and, consequently, many of her poems examine the negative impact of Eurocentric notions of beauty on the African-American community. Her poems also explore intra-racial prejudice through the recurring image of the rejected dark-skinned woman in poems such as "the ballad of chocolate Mabbie."

In 1945 Brooks published her first volume, *A Street in Bronzeville,* under the editorial direction of Richard Wright. In this collection, she adeptly uses a variety of poetic modes, including the blues as well as ballad and sonnet forms, to examine the struggles of ordinary blacks living in the Bronzeville section of Chicago. She elevates ordinary lives to heroic status suggesting that, although life in Bronzeville may be hard, its inhabitants are not without hope. Brooks also uses her poetry to address social concerns in poems such as "The Mother," which explores abortion and its aftermath, and "Negro Hero," which exposes hypocritical American military rhetoric dictating that black men must fight for American democracy overseas, yet be denied basic human rights within their own country. This volume received praise for both its artistry and its treatment of racial themes.

Her next volume, *Annie Allen* (1949), addresses social issues in greater depth, centering on the growth and experiences of a young black woman. As in her earlier work, Brooks adroitly mixes traditional and unconventional forms and language. "The Anniad," for example, is a mock epic in which Brooks deliberately alludes to Homer's *The Iliad,* detailing Annie's burgeoning maturity and growing disillusionment with young married life. Brooks states, "Think of sweet and chocolate, / Left to folly or to fate, / Whom the higher gods forgot, / Whom the lower gods berate." In 1950, Brooks won the Pulitzer Prize for *Annie Allen,* becoming the first African-American writer to be so honored.

*Maud Martha* (1953), Brooks' only novel, returns to the subject of the dark-skinned woman suffering prejudice. Demystifying marriage and motherhood by exposing their burdensome undercurrents, the novel centers on the experiences of a mother and a wife forced to confront an often harsh reality once her romantic dreams of love and marriage have been shattered. *Bronzeville Boys and Girls* (1956), Brooks' first book of children's poetry, returns to Chicago's Bronzeville section to depict the lives of children there, whose hardships, despair, and loneliness are overcome by love, friendship, and creativity. This volume received praise for its rhythmic simplicity and universality.

In her next volume, *The Bean Eaters* (1960), Brooks focused on the inherent strength and resilience displayed by African-Americans in the daily struggle to survive. "We Real Cool," perhaps her most recognized poem, depicts youth's lack of ambition and admonishes the young to meet life's challenges: "We real cool. We / Left school . . . We / Jazz June. We / Die soon." In "The *Chicago Defender* Sends a Man to Little Rock," written on the occasion of the integration of Little Rock Central High School in 1957, Brooks deftly avoids simplistically portraying southern whites as monstrous beings by ironically revealing their humanity, thus defying readers' expectations. Although the speaker acknowledges the violence polarizing this community, in the end the black reporter can only conclude, "They [the whites] are like people everywhere." Brooks achieves a similar affect in "A Bronzeville Mother Loiters in Mississippi. Meanwhile, a Mississippi Mother Burns Bacon." The white woman over whom Emmett Till was lynched gradually moves from naïve romantic notions about her husband's supposedly chivalrous act to growing horror as she recognizes the undeniable brutality of her "Fine Prince" and, more importantly, her own complicity as a "milk-white maid." In "Jessie Mitchell's Mother" Brooks subtly condemns the intra-racial prejudice of a light-skinned mother toward her darker-hued daughter.

The 1960s, marked as they were by the turbulent struggle for racial equality, were a watershed time for Brooks. She dedicated herself to teaching and enjoyed a growing popularity, culminating in her appointment as the Poet Laureate of Illinois in 1968. In 1967 she attended the Fisk University Writers' Workshop, which precipitated a marked transformation in her conception of herself racially and of her poetry. Afterward, she expressed her commitment to the Black Arts movement by focusing her work on the struggle for equality and the celebration of Blackness. She also began a series of writing workshops for the Blackstone Rangers, a Chicago street gang, and worked with young writers such as Don L. Lee (Haki Madhubuti), Walter Bradford, Carolyn Rodgers, and Etheridge Knight. Around this time Brooks left her publishing company, Harper and Row, in favor of Dudley Randall's Broadside Press and, later, Haki Madhubuti's Third World Press. With this gesture, she hoped to encourage the support and patronage of black-owned publishing houses.

Her long-awaited volume *In the Mecca* (1968) expanded Brooks' use of free verse and focused on the cavernous, violence-plagued Chicago housing project known as the Mecca. The title poem depicts the growing trepidation of Mrs. Sallie Smith, a domestic worker, as she searches for her youngest child, who is lost in the Mecca. Sallie's search leads her to confront various occupants of the Mecca who display different ways of coping with daily brutalities. Although Brooks had always grounded her work in the concerns of the African-American community, *In the Mecca* revealed a greater commitment to the struggle for racial equality and adherence to a new Black consciousness. Accordingly, the subject matter here includes Medgar Evers, Malcolm X, the Blackstone Rangers, and two sermons on the "warpland" (America).

Throughout the 1970s and 1980s Brooks' poetry progressively shifted away from her characteristically woman-identified vision toward a more male-centered vision. Her intimate portraits of black women are replaced by poems such as "Boys, Black," encouraging young boys to maintain their health and develop a Black consciousness, and "The Life of Lincoln West," in which a young black boy, spurned because of his dark skin, prides himself in being "the real thing" because of his African features. Other poems heroize various black men including Steven Biko, John O. Killens, Haki Madhubuti, Paul Robeson, and Keorapetse Kgositsile. Notably, these volumes, including *Riot* (1969), *Family Pictures* (1970), and *Beckonings* (1975), were published by Black presses and received little critical attention. This may be due to the pronounced political content of poems such as "Riot," which openly urges blacks to rebel, if necessary, in order to gain social justice. Despite their more aggressive stance, the poems in these volumes also advocate solidarity within the African-American community and the forging of communal bonds.

During this same time, Brooks continued her interest in encouraging young writers with the publication of several children's volumes: *Aloneness* (1971); *Mayor Harold Washington; and Chicago, The I Will City* (1983); *The Near-Johannesburg Boy, and Other Poems* (1987); and *Winnie* (1988), a book celebrating Winnie Mandela. Brooks' body of work is uniquely marked by her commitment to encourage and support young poets. She personally established and funded numerous poetry contests, regularly gave readings and workshops around the country, and wrote several books, including *Young Poet's Primer* (1981) and *Very Young Poets* (1983), on the art of writing poetry.

Brooks' style is grounded in traditional Euro-American poetic forms, such as the ballad and the sonnet, yet she is distinctly Modernist in her unique appropriation of these forms through jazz and blues rhythms, common folk sayings, and Black English vernacular. Her fundamental belief in the human spirit and commitment to building a humane society place her within the tradition of American democratic writers such as Whitman, Emerson, and Thoreau; she successfully managed to speak for poor and working-class blacks while simultaneously attaining critical praise. Her adept rendering of themes concerning women, such as motherhood, beauty, marriage, and abortion, also garnered her a particular following among feminists. Despite its emphasis on women's concerns and the African-American community, however, Brooks' poetry is notable for its objectivity and humanistic tone. Her work has acquired an immense and loyal readership across racial and gender lines.

Fiona Mills

**Biography**

Born in Topeka, Kansas, 7 June 1917. Attended Wilson Junior College, Chicago, graduated 1936; publicity director, NAACP Youth Council, Chicago, 1930s; teacher, Northeastern Illinois State College, Chicago, Columbia College, Chicago, and Elmhurst College, Illinois; Rennebohm Professor of English, University of Wisconsin, Madison, 1969; Distinguished Professor of the arts, City College, City University of New York, 1971; editor, *Black Position* magazine; consultant-in-poetry, Library of Congress, Washington, D.C., 1985–86. Received Guggenheim fellowship, 1946; American Academy grant, 1946; Pulitzer Prize, 1950; Thormod Monsen Award, 1964; Ferguson Memorial Award, 1964; Anisfield-Wolf Award, 1968; Poet Laureate of Illinois, 1968; Black Academy Award, 1971; Shelley Memorial Award, 1976; Frost Medal, 1988; New York Public Library Award, 1988; National Endowment for the Arts Award, 1989; Jefferson Lecturer, National Endowment for the Humanities, 1994; Academy of American Poets fellowship, 1999; 51 honorary degrees from American universities. Died in Chicago, Illinois, 3 December 2000.

**Poetry**

*A Street in Bronzeville,* 1945
*Annie Allen,* 1949
*Bronzeville Boys and Girls* (for children), 1956
*The Bean Eaters,* 1960
*Selected Poems,* 1963
*We Real Cool,* 1966
*The Wall,* 1967

*In the Mecca*, 1968
*Riot*, 1969
*Family Pictures*, 1970
*Black Steel: Joe Frazier and Muhammad Ali*, 1971
*Aloneness* (for children), 1971
*Aurora*, 1972
*Beckonings*, 1975
*To Disembark*, 1981
*Black Love*, 1982
*Mayor Harold Washington; and Chicago, The I Will City* (for children), 1983
*The Near-Johannesburg Boy, and Other Poems* (for children), 1987
*Blacks*, 1987
*Winnie* (for children), 1988
*Gottschalk and the Grand Tarantelle*, 1988
*Children Coming Home*, 1991

**Other Writings:** novel (*Maud Martha*, 1953), autobiography, children's literature, writing handbooks (*Very Young Poets*, 1983); edited poetry collections (*Jump Bad: A New Chicago Anthology*, 1971).

**Further Reading**

Bloom, Harold, editor, *Gwendolyn Brooks*, Philadelphia, Pennsylvania: Chelsea House, 2000
Evans, Mari, editor, *Black Women Writers (1950–1980): A Critical Evaluation*, Garden City, New York: Anchor Press/ Doubleday, 1984
Madhubuti, Haki R., editor, *Say That the River Turns: The Impact of Gwendolyn Brooks*, Chicago: Third World Press, 1987
Melhem, D.H., *Gwendolyn Brooks: Poetry and the Heroic Voice*, Lexington: University Press of Kentucky, 1987
Mootry, Maria K., and Gary Smith, editors, *A Life Distilled: Gwendolyn Brooks, Her Poetry and Fiction*, Urbana: University of Illinois Press, 1987
Tate, Claudia, editor, *Black Women Writers at Work*, New York: Continuum, 1983
Wright, Stephen Caldwell, editor, *On Gwendolyn Brooks: Reliant Contemplation*, Ann Arbor: University of Michigan Press, 1996

## A Bronzeville Mother Loiters in Mississippi. Meanwhile, a Mississippi Mother Burns Bacon.

"A Bronzeville Mother Loiters" directly precedes "The Last Quatrain of the Ballad of Emmett Till" in Brooks' volume *The Bean Eaters* (1960). Brooks cleverly connects the two by placing "Ballad" conspicuously in the second line, by means of enjambment:

> From the first it had been like a
> Ballad. It had the beat inevitable. It had the blood.
> A wildness cut up, and tied in little bunches,
> Like the four-line stanzas of the ballads she had never quite
> Understood—the ballads they had set her to, in school.

Brooks won the Pulitzer Prize for Poetry in 1950 for *Annie Allen*, a work that highlighted both the sonnet and epic forms. *Bean Eaters* marked her departure from traditional poetic form, and its contents were highly political in nature, coinciding with the Civil Rights movement. "A Bronzeville Mother Loiters" intentionally avoids standard ballad stanzas, and instead of relating a simple folk story, it offers a story of incongruities and complexity.

Much of the dynamic between the poem's two very different mothers is articulated in the title itself. Bronzeville, as a place-marker of identity, is decidedly black, northern, and urban; it specifically denotes a black neighborhood in Chicago. The Bronzeville mother is clearly out of her element down south in Mississippi. Although the Mississippi mother is physically in the proper setting, there is something askew suggested by her burning bacon, for how could a decent, dutiful southern mother—black or white—desecrate the pig, which is stereotypically connected to the South and its people? The word "meanwhile" establishes a link between women who are seemingly removed from each other. Their bond is tenuous, held together by a comma, and yet in the poem's counter-legend, the "maiden mild" and "that snappy-eyed mother" are united by much more: the inexplicable murder of the so-called Dark Villain, as southern mythology would cast Emmett Till.

> [A] blackish child
> Of fourteen, with eyes still too young to be dirty,
> And a mouth too young to have lost every reminder
> Of its infant softness.

The Mississippi mother recalls that she never understood ballads in school, just as she does not understand this one: she does not fit her role as maiden fair, and neither does the Fine Prince or the Dark Villain. Yet she is scripted to be the innocent, delicate flower "pursued / by the Dark Villain. Rescued by the Fine Prince." The background is this: in August 1955, Emmett Till, 14-year-old son of Mamie Bradley, arrived in Money, Mississippi. It is uncertain precisely what code of conduct, endemic to the racially volatile South, Till violated in his encounter with the white store clerk Carolyn Bryant, but whatever the offense (whistling at her, touching her, or simply saying "bye, baby"), he paid for it with his life. Bryant's husband and a friend abducted Till, beat him, and then shot him in the head and threw his body (loaded down with a massive cotton gin fan) into the Tallahatchie River. An all-white jury found them not guilty.

In media coverage of this sensational murder case, Carolyn Bryant was silent. "A Bronzeville Mother Loiters" gives her voice, as the Mississippi mother who becomes increasingly aware that her husband's actions were neither chivalrous nor necessary. She realizes that she does not want the Fine Prince's version of protection or love, for

> . . . under the magnificent shell of adulthood, just under,
> Waited the baby full of tantrums.
> It occurred to her that there may have been something
> Ridiculous in the picture of the Fine Prince
> Rushing (rich with the breadth and height and
> Mature solidness whose lack, in the Dark Villain, was
>   impressing her,
> Confronting her more and more as this first day after the trial
> And acquittal wore on) rushing

With his heavy companion to hack down (unhorsed)
That little foe.

The actuality of a little boy destroyed by two grown men in the name of racial and sexual preservation is incongruous and monstrous enough to force "maiden mild" to see herself outside of societal mythology:

The one thing in the world that she did know and knew
With terrifying clarity was that her composition
Had disintegrated. That, although the pattern prevailed,
The breaks were everywhere.

The Mississippi mother, trapped in a construct of southern femininity (weak and genteel), coexists with the Fine Prince, the proud white Mississippi male, the racist, who is also trapped. He is trapped by a misguided and outmoded southern chivalric code ("Still, it had been fun to show those intruders / A thing or two") and a violent belief in his own righteousness ("What he'd like to do, he explained, was kill them all. . . . / Nothing could stop Mississippi. . . . / And, what was so good, Mississippi knew that. / Nothing and nothing could stop Mississippi"). Brooks ends "A Bronzeville Mother Loiters" by uniting the two mothers. They are unified through intense hatred for the Fine Prince. The Bronzeville mother has eyes like "exclamation points," while the Mississippi mother is filled with "a hatred for him burst into glorious flowers." Lost in all this hate and "the last bleak news of the ballad" is the "little foe" himself.

Sharon L. Moore

**Further Reading**

Bolden, B.J., *Urban Rage in Bronzeville: Social Commentary in the Poetry of Gwendolyn Brooks, 1945–1960,* Chicago: Third World Press, 1999

Goldsby, Jacqueline, "The High and Low Tech of It: The Meaning of Lynching and the Death of Emmett Till," *Yale Journal of Criticism* 9, no. 2 (1996)

Kent, George E., *A Life of Gwendolyn Brooks,* Lexington: University Press of Kentucky, 1990

Melhem, D.H., "Gwendolyn Brooks: An Appreciation," *Humanities* 15, no. 3 (1994)

Mootry, Maria K., and Gary Smith, editors, *A Life Distilled: Gwendolyn Brooks, Her Poetry and Fiction,* Urbana: University of Illinois Press, 1987

Taylor, Henry, "Gwendolyn Brooks: An Essential Sanity," *Kenyon Review* 13, no. 4 (Fall 1991)

Wright, Stephen Caldwell, editor, *On Gwendolyn Brooks: Reliant Contemplation,* Ann Arbor: University of Michigan Press, 1996

## A Street in Bronzeville

Gwendolyn Brooks' first collection of poetry, *A Street in Bronzeville* (1945) celebrates and investigates the lives of urban blacks. The poems explore the lives, loves, deaths, and days of various inhabitants of a neighborhood Brooks names Bronzeville. In a book that intricately explores attitudes toward race, class, and gender, Brooks both uses and subverts formal poetic traditions as she deftly defines the lives of her characters. The poems in *A Street in Bronzeville* articulate the characters' joys and frustrations, addressing the precarious space in which they live: "We are things of dry hours and the involuntary plan, / Grayed in, and gray." These characters have little time for "dreams," which make "a giddy sound," and must instead focus on issues of survival such as "rent" or "feeding a wife" ("kitchenette building"). Even under such circumstances, the inhabitants of Bronzeville create beauty and life where they can:

He looks in his mirror, loves himself—
The neat curve here; the angularity
That is appropriate at just its place
. . . .
Here is all his sculpture and his art
And all his architectural design.

In this and other sections of the "The Sundays of Satin-Legs Smith," one of four of the book's longer poems, Brooks points to the ways that Smith "designs his reign, / That no performance may be plain or vain," simultaneously delineating his majestic nature and commenting on what and whom society considers culturally acceptable:

At Joe's Eats
You get your fish or chicken on meat platters.
With coleslaw, macaroni, candied sweets,
Coffee and apple pie. You go out full.
(The end is—isn't it?—all that really matters.)

Brooks suggests that although Satin-Legs Smith does not live in a gardened world of fine sculpture, architecture, and cuisine, he manages to sustain himself with the tools to which he has access.

Although Brooks celebrates her character's ability to make the best of what he has, she is quick to point out that this is a merely adequate means of survival: "Would you have him think . . . of baroque, / Rococo. You forget and you forget." There are art forms, the narrator suggests, more appropriate to this black urban experience than those borrowed from Europe:

Down these sore avenues
Comes no Saint-Saens, no piquant elusive Grieg . . .
And not the shapely tender drift of Brahms.
But could he love them? Since a man must bring
To music what his mother spanked him for
When he was two: bits of forgotten hate,
Devotion: whether or not his mattress hurts:
The little dream his father humored: the thing
His sister did for money . . . all his skipped desserts.

In "The Sundays of Satin-Legs Smith" and many other poems in *A Street in Bronzeville,* Brooks suggests that there must be an art form specific to the lives and needs of urban blacks.

Brooks' style throughout the book supports this assertion. Although she bases many of these poems on traditional poetic forms, she is not confined by them. The last piece in this book, "Gay Chaps at the Bar," is a sonnet series, but the sonnets vary in the degree to which they adhere to the rules of the form. The series, about the reaction of black soldiers to their involvement in World War II, illustrates the men's frustration with a structure and order that has damaged their bodies and spirits. The part of these men that still strives for reason and a place in their American/Western European culture strives for the order represented by the sonnet:

We still wear our uniforms, follow
The cracked cry of the bugles, comb and brush
Our pride and prejudice, doctor the sallow
Initial ardor, wish to keep it fresh. ("the progress")

When these speakers articulate this desire for place and structure, the poem moves toward iambic pentameter. The soldiers know a certain "soberness" that does not allow them to blindly enjoy such a life, however:

But suddenly, across my climbing fever
Of proud delight—a multiplying cry.
A cry of bitter dead men who will never
Attend a gentle maker of musical joy. ("piano after war")

The soldiers have to stow what they love, including a belief in order and purpose, until after the war. Their hope is that "when the devil days of . . . hurt / Drag out their last dregs," they will find their way home and find their "taste will not have turned insensitive / To honey and bread old purity could love" ("my dreams my works, must wait till after hell").

Brooks renders the sonnet both useful and useless. Its confining form, which she adheres to strictly with the number of lines she uses and loosely with off-rhyme and her intermittent iambic pentameter, conveys the life of structure and order promised to these soldiers. The men's ideas will not be fully contained in this Western tradition, however, just as the black American soldiers were not fully incorporated into the Army in World War II. The soldiers understand a certain failure inherent in the pomp and circumstance accompanying their precarious occupation:

For even if we come out standing up
How shall we smile, congratulate: and how
Settle in chairs? Listen, listen. The step
Of iron feet again. And again wild.

This excerpt from "the progress," the last poem in the series, again shows how Brooks approaches and then retreats from iambic pentameter. The lines indicate the speaker's disillusionment; he fears that he will be unable to do something so simple as "settle" into a chair. The gap at the end of the poem intensifies the space of disorder into which the soldier topples.

Although there are spaces of chaos, there are also spaces of refuge in Bronzeville. Satin-Legs Smith finds refuge each Sunday in the different women he takes to Joe's Eats. The poem "the soft man" indicates the church as the place "to which you creep on Sundays. And you cool / in lovely sadness." In "Sadie and Maud" Brooks suggests that the conventional routes are not necessarily the ones by which to attain happiness—

Maud, who went to college
Is a thin brown mouse.
She is living all alone
In this old house

—whereas Sadie, who "scraped life / With a fine-tooth comb" and had two children out of wedlock, lived a high and happy life. Love, too, is a place of refuge, Brooks suggests. In "when you have forgotten Sunday: the love story," the speaker asserts that when her lover has forgotten all the comforts she and he shared on Sundays, he will have "forgotten me well." The natural ease and comfort of the day off the two spend together epitomizes their "love story" and the solace they find in one another.

Along with love, war, and art, Brooks explores attitudes about race, class, and beauty in this volume of poetry. Her commentary on the attitudes held by and about the inhabitants of Bronzeville ranges from scathing to humorous to heartbreaking. A hunchback girl's view of heaven is a place where she can "walk straightly through most proper halls / Proper myself. Princess of properness" ("hunchback girl: she thinks of heaven"), whereas a proper girl who has "stayed in the front yard all [her] life" wishes she could "peek at the back / Where it's rough and untended" ("song in the front yard"). Brooks calls into question the desire many of the occupants of Bronzeville hold for people with light skin and straight hair. In the poem "patent leather" the "other guys" question why the man with "patent-leather hair" is able to attract "that cool chick down on Calumet." "The ballad of chocolate Mabbie" spins the sad tale of a girl whose love spurns her for "a lemon-hued lynx / With sand-waves loving her brow." In perhaps the most biting commentary on the dangers of the color line, "The Ballad of Pearl May Lee," the speaker "cut[s her] lungs with laughter" over the lynching of a man named Sammy who "paid with [his] hide and [the speaker's] heart" for a "taste of pink and white honey."

Using folk forms such as the blues and the ballad as well as formal poetic styles like the sonnet, Brooks creates life and music for the inhabitants of *A Street in Bronzeville*. Her lyrical styling of everyday subject matters and the clear images and language she uses to define lofty ideas make this first book by Gwendolyn Brooks an outstanding piece of craft and poetry.

Camille Dungy

**Further Reading**


Bolden, B.J., *Urban Rage in Bronzeville: Social Commentary in the Poetry of Gwendolyn Brooks, 1945–1960,* Chicago: Third World Press, 1999

Brooks, Gwendolyn, *Report from Part One,* Detroit, Michigan: Broadside Press, 1972

Brooks, Gwendolyn, *Report from Part Two,* Chicago: Third World Press, 1996

Kent, George E., *A Life of Gwendolyn Brooks,* Lexington: University Press of Kentucky, 1990

McLendon, Jacquelyn, "Gwendolyn Brooks," in *African American Writers: Profiles of Their Lives and Works—From the 1700s to the Present,* edited by Valerie Smith, Lea Baechler, and A. Walton Litz, New York: Scribner, and Toronto: Collier Macmillan Canada, 1991

Melhem, D.H., *Gwendolyn Brooks: Poetry and the Heroic Voice,* Lexington: University Press of Kentucky, 1987

Mootry, Maria K., and Gary Smith, editors, *A Life Distilled: Gwendolyn Brooks, Her Poetry and Fiction,* Urbana: University of Illinois Press, 1987

# Sterling A. Brown 1901–89

Born on 1 May 1901 into middle-class respectability, Sterling Allen Brown was the sixth child and only son of the Reverend Sterling Nelson Brown, a professor of religion at Howard University and minister of Lincoln Temple Congregational Church, and Adelaide Allen. Reverend Brown often spoke of his friendships with noted African-American leaders such as Frederick Douglass and Booker T. Washington. Brown's mother graduated valedictorian of her class at Fisk; although his father's life was inspirational, the poet credits his mother with introducing him to poetry and encouraging his literary career.

Intellectuals such as W.E.B. DuBois influenced Brown as a child. He attended the famous Dunbar High School, noted for its distinguished teachers and for graduating the nation's leading African-Americans. At the age of 17, Brown entered Williams College, began writing poetry, and graduated Phi Beta Kappa in 1922. He then entered Harvard University and earned a masters degree in 1923. The anthology *Modern American Poetry* (1921) influenced him greatly, as he came to identify with poets such as Robert Frost and Edwin Arlington Robinson.

Accepting a teaching position at Virginia Seminary in Lynchburg proved significant to Brown's career and personal life. There he met his future wife of more than 50 years, Daisy Turnbull, and also found his poetic voice and the muse for his poetry—the African-American folk community. In 1929, he joined the faculty at Howard University, where he remained until his retirement in 1969.

In 1927, Brown won first prize in a writing contest sponsored by *Opportunity* magazine for the poem "When de Saints Go Ma'ching Home." Over the next three years, several of his poems were published in *Crisis, Opportunity, Contempo,* and *Ebony and Topaz.* In 1932, Brown published his first volume of poetry, *Southern Road,* in which he challenged black stereotypes, created a blues and spiritual aesthetic, and extended dialect beyond the traditional use of comedy and misery. James Weldon Johnson heralded Brown, along with Langston Hughes, as one of two major folk poets of the New Negro movement. Alain Locke named Brown "The New Negro Folk Poet." Yet Brown often is forgotten in the group of major poets of this era, with Hughes, Countee Cullen, and Claude McKay taking center stage. Although *Southern Road* was met with critical praise, Brown's commitment to blues, jazz, and folk images was not popular among his peers on the Howard University faculty, who considered them unacademic. Brown is credited with influencing and enlightening students, such as Amiri Baraka, in the dorms at Howard with his music collection.

*Southern Road* is divided into four sections—"The Road So Rocky," "On Restless River," "Tin Roof Blues," and "Vestiges"—and includes work songs, spirituals, blues, and ballads as well as memorable portraits based on characters he came to know in Virginia. In the folk tradition, his poems express the grim conditions of life but also the heroism and courage of survival. "Strong Men," considered Brown's signature poem, celebrates the tenacity to succeed or persevere despite oppression that Brown found among African-American men. Poems such as "Virginia Portrait" and "Sister Lou" reflect a feminine dignity in age and in the capacity to await death with grace. "Old Lem" presents an old man exhausted by the fight against mob violence. "Southern Road" addresses the hardships on a chain gang and the tragic injustices of racial oppression. "The Last Ride of Wild Bill" explores the "bad man" and rejoices in his beating the system that attempts to suppress him.

Brown also incorporates music through the blues poems "Ma Rainey," "Memphis Blues," and "St. Louis Blues" and the spirituals "Crossing" and "When de Saints Go Ma'ching Home." In "Ma Rainey," Brown expresses the importance of humor as a coping strategy. *Southern Road* also contains five poems about Slim Greer, a trickster and folk hero who is another figure of determination. Not all the poems in this volume are in dialect form. Brown also includes sonnets addressed to his wife as well as lyrics on romantic love and nostalgically remembered places.

When Brown failed to find a publisher for his second volume of verse, *No Hiding Place,* he turned his creative energy to writing criticism, compiling anthologies, and leaving a legacy through his students. He argued against "a double standard of judgment which is dangerous to the future of Negro writers." In 1975, Brown published a second collection of poetry, *The Last Ride of Wild Bill, and Eleven Narrative Poems; Southern Road* was also reprinted. In 1980, Michael S. Harper edited *The Collected Poems of Sterling A. Brown,* which includes material from the previously rejected collection.

The onset of the Black Arts movement revived interest in Brown. He was seen as a pioneer in the blues and black aesthetics, finally receiving the acclaim that his achievements deserved. He died of leukemia in Takoma Park, Maryland, on 17 January 1989.

Adenike Marie Davidson

**Biography**

Born in Washington, D.C., 1 May 1901. Attended Williams College, Williamstown, Massachusetts, 1918–22, A.B. 1922 (Phi Beta Kappa); Harvard University, Cambridge, Massachusetts, A.M. 1923; teacher at Virginia Seminary and College, Lynchburg, 1923–26, Lincoln University, Jefferson City, Missouri, 1926–28, and Fisk University, Nashville, Tennessee, 1929; Professor of English, Howard University, Washington, D.C., 1929–1969; Visiting Professor, New York University, New School for Social Research, New York, Vassar College, Poughkeepsie, New York, and University of Minnesota, Minneapolis; literary editor, *Opportunity* magazine, 1930s; editor, *Negro Affairs* (Federal Writers' Project), 1936–39; on staff, *American Dilemma.* Received Guggenheim fellowship, 1937; Lenore Marshall Prize, 1981; received honorary degrees from 13 colleges and universities; Poet Laureate of the United States, 1984. Died in Takoma Park, Maryland, 17 January 1989.

**Poetry**

*Southern Road,* 1932
*The Last Ride of Wild Bill, and Eleven Narrative Poems,* 1975
*The Collected Poems of Sterling A. Brown,* edited by Michael S. Harper, 1980

**Selected Criticism**

*Negro Poetry and Drama,* 1937

**Other Writings:** essays (*A Son's Return: Selected Essays of Sterling A. Brown,* 1996), poetry study guide (*Outline for the*

*Study of the Poetry of American Negroes,* 1931), biography (*James Weldon Johnson* [with A.B. Spingarn and Carl Van Vechten], 1941); edited collections of literature (*The Negro Caravan: Writings by American Negroes,* 2 vols. [with Arthur P. Davis and Ulysses Lee], 1941).

**Further Reading**

Benston, Kimberly W., "Sterling Brown's After Song: 'When de Saints Go Ma'ching Home' and the Performance of Afro-American Voice," *Callaloo* 5, no. 1–2 (1982)

Gabbin, Joanne V., *Sterling A. Brown: Building the Black Aesthetic Tradition,* Westport, Connecticut: Greenwood Press, 1985

Henderson, Stephen E., "The Heavy Blues of Sterling Brown: A Study of Craft and Tradition," *Black American Literature Forum* 14, no. 1 (1980)

Manson, Michael Tomasek, "Sterling Brown and the 'Vestiges' of the Blues: The Role of Race in English Verse Structure," *MELUS* 21, no. 1 (Spring 1996)

O'Meally, Robert G., "'Game to the Heart': Sterling Brown and the Badman," *Callaloo* 5, no. 1–2 (1982)

Rowell, Charles H., "Sterling A. Brown and the Afro-American Folk Tradition," in *The Harlem Renaissance Re-Examined,* edited by Victor A. Kramer, New York: AMS Press, 1987

Sanders, Mark A., *Afro-Modernist Aesthetics and the Poetry of Sterling A. Brown,* Athens: University of Georgia Press, 1999

Smith, Gary, "The Literary Ballads of Sterling Brown," *College Language Association Journal* 32, no. 4 (June 1989)

Stuckey, Sterling, "Introduction," in *The Collected Poems of Sterling A. Brown,* edited by Michael S. Harper, Chicago: TriQuarterly Press, 1996

Thomas, Lorenzo, "Authenticity and Elevation: Sterling Brown's Theory of the Blues," *African American Review* 31, no. 3 (Fall 1997)

# Ma Rainey

Sterling A. Brown's poem "Ma Rainey" is distinctive mainly for its use of dialect and its blues theme and style. An answer to the rejection by early 20th-century New Negro intellectuals of the use of meaningless and cartoonish black dialect, Brown's poetry demonstrated his ability to carefully and respectfully portray a range of African-American thought and feeling.

Sterling Brown is often regarded as a Harlem Renaissance poet but is more precisely a member of the New Negro movement. Brown was highly critical of the group of artists who resided in Harlem and managed their craft with the aid of white patronage. He likewise resisted critical attempts to view black America through the lens of New York's black urbanites. Convinced of both the ability of African-American artists to support themselves through the black community and the existence of a wider range of African-American experiences that cut across regional and class lines, Brown consciously avoided the New York City scene, choosing instead to make his home in Washington, D.C. (where he taught at Howard University), exploring black communities in both the urban and rural South and Midwest.

Apart from his disregard for the professional decisions made by Harlem greats like Langston Hughes, Countee Cullen, and Zora Neale Hurston, Brown nonetheless shared their philosophical and literary mindset, guided in part by Alain Locke's seminal 1925 essay "The New Negro." The early 1920s marked an important shift in the way that African-Americans saw themselves, said Locke. It was a movement toward a self-conscious effort to regain control of the re/presentation of black identity and black life. Embracing the new Modernist emphasis on social realism and the common people, Brown and others sought to paint a picture of African America that was more fully developed than any that had been crafted to date. And as critics have observed, Brown was the most successful in giving that picture movement and life, showing black folk culture across the United States as dynamic and richly expressive through the revised use of dialect and blues metaphor.

"Ma Rainey" was originally published in 1930 as part of Benjamin A. Botkin's *Folk-Say, A Regional Miscellany, II.* It was eventually included in Brown's first volume of published poetry, *Southern Road* (1932). The people he encountered while traveling and teaching in rural Virginia and Missouri, as well as at Fisk University in Nashville, Tennessee, inspired the poems that make up *Southern Road.* Like Hurston, Brown interacted with his students and their families as an educator and in part as a sort of cultural anthropologist, seeking out the myriad of people one could call "black folk." His ability to understand the qualities of their speech patterns and the feelings they expressed in their voices led him to compose dialectic poetry that was accurate in its linguistic form and moving in its expression. "Ma Rainey" remains a significant example of this accomplishment. The poem is also successful in another regard; called *the* blues poem by nearly all of its critics and admirers, "Ma Rainey" highlights what the blues can mean to African-American folk communities by using a typical aspect of black life—the blues singer's performance at a popular "juke-joint"—to illustrate the depth of feeling and simple eloquence displayed by black folk. The poem is a careful interplay between the folk and a narrator. In parts II and IV, Brown's narrator is a respectful observer who is of the people (as seen through his dialect) but also apart from them (outlining their collective story).

The poem recounts a painful memory for poor black communities in the South: the Mississippi flood of 1929. In this devastating incident, foreshadowed in the second part of the poem and remembered in the fourth, scores of black Americans lost their homes and their possessions, suffering further when later overlooked in relief efforts that targeted whites. Water imagery pervades the poem. Part II, for example, describes the swell of humanity who survived the tragedy and lived to remember it through their bluesy muse:

> Dey comes to hear Ma Rainey from de little river settlements,
> From blackbottom cornrows and from lumber camps;
> Dey stumble in de hall, jes a-laughin' an' a-cacklin',
> Cheerin' lak roarin' water, lak wind in river swamps.
>
> An' some jokers keeps deir laughs a-goin' in de crowded aisles,
> An' some folks sits dere waitin' wid deir aches an' miseries,
> Till Ma comes out before dem, a-smilin' gold-toofed smiles
> An' Long Boy ripples minors on de black an' yellow keys.

With rivulets and pools of admiring and hopeful fans crowding "de hall," Rainey, the performer, emerges as the ultimate blues heroine. She is the symbol and the definition of blues, a representative of the folk and their bittersweet lives, especially equipped with the gift of strength and healing:

O Ma Rainey,
Sing yo' song;
Now you's back
Whah you belong.
Git way inside us,
Keep us strong. . . .
O Ma Rainey,
Li'l an' low;
Sing us 'bout de hard luck
Roun' our do';
Sing us 'bout de lonesome road
We mus' go. . . .

The story of the actual 1929 rains are recalled in the fourth part of the poem when Rainey croons "Backwater Blues":

*'It rained fo days an' de skies was dark as night,*
*Trouble taken place in de lowlands at night.*

*'Thundered an' lightened an' the storm begin to roll*
*Thousands of people ain't got no place to go.*

*'Den I went an' stood upon some high ol' lonesome hill,*
*An' looked down on the place where I used to live.'*

An' den de folks, dey natchally bowed dey heads an' cried,
Bowed dey heavy heads, shet dey moufs up tight an' cried,
An' Ma lef' de stage, an' followed some de folks outside.

The blues mood that so profoundly affects Rainey's audience becomes a pervasive sentiment that affects the reader. The story of Rainey's performance is literally quoted by an audience member, but the narrator provides the final, powerful commentary that echoes his, the audience's, and even the reader's collective response: "Dere wasn't much more de fellow say: / She jes' gits hold of us dataway."

An understudied New Negro poet and intellectual who gave as good a glimpse of African-American folk life as Zora Neale Hurston, Brown remains an important contributor to the 20th-century African-American literary tradition. He once said of the existing poor attempts at black dialect, "better poets could have smashed the mold" (*Negro Poetry and Drama,* 1937). Few poets were as adept at wielding that hammer as Sterling Brown.

Roxane V. Pickens

**Further Reading**

Benston, Kimberly W., "Sterling Brown's After Song: 'When de Saints Go Ma'ching Home' and the Performance of Afro-American Voice," *Callaloo* 5, no. 1–2 (1982)

Brown, Sterling A., *A Son's Return: Selected Essays of Sterling A. Brown,* Boston: Northeastern University Press, 1996

Henderson, Stephen E., "The Heavy Blues of Sterling Brown: A Study of Craft and Tradition," *Black American Literature Forum* 14, no. 1 (1980)

Rowell, Charles H., "'Let Me Be with Ole Jazzbo': An Interview with Sterling A. Brown," *Callaloo* 14, no. 4 (1991)

Sanders, Mark A., *Afro-Modernist Aesthetics and the Poetry of Sterling A. Brown,* Athens: University of Georgia Press, 1999

Thomas, Lorenzo, "Authenticity and Elevation: Sterling Brown's Theory of the Blues," *African American Review* 31, no. 3 (1997)

# Southern Road

*Southern Road* (1932) is Sterling Brown's first and most well-known volume of poetry. A wide range of notable critics and poets, from Alain Locke to Louis Untermeyer, praised *Southern Road* when it first appeared and placed Brown on an equal footing with such contemporaries as Langston Hughes, Countee Cullen, and Claude McKay. In his introduction to the volume, James Weldon Johnson declared that "Brown's work is not only fine, it is also unique." Since Brown's second book of poetry, *No Hiding Place* (c. 1936), was not published until 1980 (its contents were included in *The Collected Poems of Sterling A. Brown*) and his only other published volume of verse, *The Last Ride of Wild Bill* (1975), also appeared relatively late, *Southern Road* still stands as Brown's chief contribution to American poetry.

*Southern Road* is composed of four parts. The first two parts focus on the centrality of black folk culture in the South, while the latter parts explore the detrimental social and literary consequences of the loss of that culture for northern blacks and black poets who employ traditional English verse forms. The volume aims to preserve and transmit the southern folk tradition to younger generations of black Americans who may not know or understand the lives and culture of their parents and foreparents. The volume's epigraph, taken from a spiritual, presents the problem that Brown hopes to address: "O de ole sheep dey knows de road, / Young lambs gotta find de way." The southern road on which the "lambs" must find their way represents the means to a better place, socially and spiritually. The southern road may beckon like freedom, as in the poem "Long Gone," or it may serve as a means of escape from violence or exploitation, as in "Slim Lands a Job?," or as a way to share in the collective experience of hearing Ma Rainey sing the blues.

Yet the title poem, innovatively written as a blues adaptation of a work song, reminds us that the southern road is built by the black prison labor of the chain gangs, by people whose only crime in the Jim Crow South was being black. The southern road thus also functions as a sign of immobility, of arrest by the white man who "Damn[s] yo' soul" if you are black—a potential dead end. Nonetheless, Brown views the southern "road" (in the sense of a way of life), precisely because it is "rocky," as the very location for the production of a rich culture of resistance. Thus, like other modern black American poetry, *Southern Road* adapts African-American expressive forms, such as the blues, work songs, spirituals, and a southern black dialect, in an attempt to represent the social and linguistic power of the black vernacular tradition. The blues, which emerges from these conditions, for example, expresses not simply despair or hopelessness but, as Brown stated in an interview, "strength; it's stoicism; it's fortitude; it's humor; it's directness" (1998). The vernacular expressive forms provide a forum for the transmission of the hard lessons of survival in the South.

It is also along the southern road that Brown finds exemplary heroic and legendary black figures for the younger generation to emulate. As he suggests in "Strange Legacies," Brown's heroes are black men and women not typically associated with political resistance (as are Frederick Douglass or Nat Turner). Rather, they are boxers (Jack Johnson), railroad steel drivers (John Henry), and an "Old nameless couple" who, despite circumstances, were not defeated and can teach fortitude, "Muttering, beneath an unfriendly sky, / '*Guess we'll give it one mo' try. / Guess we'll give it one mo' try.*'" One of his best and frequently anthologized poems, "Strong Men," which significantly closes Part I ("The Road So Rocky"), presents this idea even more forcefully by depicting a history of resistance. Brown shows that all the unknown efforts of black people to make a better life in the South, including those depicted in the poetic snapshots he provides in the volume, are part of a larger historical narrative leading to inevitable victory. Despite slavery, wage slavery, domestic servitude, dehumanization, and co-opted leaders, "The strong men keep a-comin' on / The strong men git stronger." Brown seems in perfect agreement with Hughes' radical sentiment expressed in "Open Letter to the South" (also published in 1932) that, for him, "no more, the migration to the North. / Instead: migration into force and power— / Tuskegee with a new flag on the tower!" Like Hughes and other Depression-era writers influenced by the Communist Party of America during the "Red Decade," Brown suggests that blacks must fight it out in the South against oppression.

Indeed, flight to the North for Brown equaled the loss of a cultural tradition of revolt. Hence, Part III, "Tin Roof Blues," represents the blacks who have taken the northern road as either longing to return to the South or, as in the case of the younger generation, ignorant of the sustaining southern folk culture of their ancestors. "They have forgotten, they have never known," Brown writes in "Children's Children," "Long days beneath the torrid Dixie sun / In miasma'd rice swamps . . . / With these [folk] songs, sole comfort. / They have forgotten / What had to be endured—." On the contrary, they know only popularized and, for Brown, inauthentic parodies of black culture and have assimilated the values of a predominantly white society. Thus, they have "sleek hair cajoled to Caucasian straightness" or, as in "Sporting Beasley," they delude themselves that they have attained equality by playing the part of a "dicty" (or nouveau riche), with top hat, Prince Albert coat, spats, and cane. For Brown, the farther blacks are removed from their folk culture, the weaker they, including their poets, become. Undoubtedly, Part IV, "Vestiges," underscores this point with its Romantic poems on life, love, beauty, and loss, far and falsely removed, as in "Mill Mountain," from "Intolerable things . . . / Bringing oblivion to trivial cares." In short, *Southern Road* is nothing less than a defense and poetic development of southern black culture as a powerful means to fight racism and class oppression.

Anthony Dawahare

**Further Reading**


Anderson, David, "Sterling Brown's Southern Strategy: Poetry as Cultural Evolution in *Southern Road,*" *Callaloo* 21, no. 4 (1998)

Benston, Kimberly W., "Sterling Brown's After Song: 'When de Saints Go Ma'ching Home' and the Performance of Afro-American Voice," *Callaloo* 5, no. 1–2 (1982)

Gabbin, Joanne V., *Sterling A. Brown: Building the Black Aesthetic Tradition,* Westport, Connecticut: Greenwood Press, 1985

Rowell, Charles H., "'Let Me Be with Ole Jazzbo': An Interview with Sterling A. Brown," *Callaloo* 14, no. 4 (1991)

Sanders, Mark A., "Sterling A. Brown's Master Metaphor: *Southern Road* and the Sign of Black Modernity," *Callaloo* 21, no. 4 (1998)

Smethurst, James Edward, *The New Red Negro: The Literary Left and African American Poetry, 1930–1946,* Oxford and New York: Oxford University Press, 1999


---

## Charles Bukowski 1920–94

Charles Bukowski dominated and defined more than three decades of American outsider poetry by mastering a brutally frank and realistic anti-poetry. He abandoned literary ornament and tender philosophical insight to report factually from the underbelly and dark side of American life and published profusely in the anti-academic and anti-corporate world of the small press and little magazine. Bukowski's reputation as a sarcastic, cantankerous curmudgeon endeared him to legions of loyal fans. As the premier American outlaw poet, Bukowski portrayed himself as a working-class alcoholic gambler and a skid-row bohemian bum. He was not a member of the Beat generation or any other literary movement, nor is he considered a literary innovator. Nevertheless, his books continue to outsell the majority of well-respected poets, and a vibrant and vast literary underground of poets, editors, and publishers honor him for his inspiration and mimic his candid style.

Henry Charles Bukowski, Jr., was born in Andernach, Germany, in 1920; his father was an American soldier and his mother a German citizen. In 1922 the family emigrated to Los Angeles. Bukowski's tyrannical father often savagely beat him. The Depression fueled the elder Bukowski's rage and strengthened his faith in patriotism, middle-class ideals, and the American dream. Disdain for conformity and middle-class hypocrisy became major themes in Bukowski's poetry. Horrible acne left his face scarred, and sensitive Bukowski spent his teenage years alone in blue-collar Los Angeles. His insecurity and cynicism eventually drove him to society's fringe, and L.A.'s skid row became his home.

The 1940s and early 1950s were formative years, during which Bukowski drank heavily and read voraciously. His literary masters were Robinson Jeffers and Ernest Hemingway. Like Jeffers, Bukowski admired toughness and violent, base human emotions. A poem from this period, "Hello" (*Matrix* 9, no. 2 [Summer 1946]), celebrates and champions the life of a Negro junk wagon driver:

riding your high board with whip
I see a chariot, a gaiety, a basilic
  dance
blood in horses, blood in you, blood
  sounding

The imagery of stars, blood, roses, and wombs represents the vibrant natural force Bukowski glamorized in his portrayal of the social outsider's less complicated, more naturalistic life.

Bukowski's life on skid row culminated in his hospitalization at age 35 with a severe bleeding ulcer. Miraculously surviving this near death experience, Bukowski was reinvigorated and began to write poetry. In 1960, nearing his 40th birthday, he published his first small book, *Flower, Fist and Bestial Wail.* The title of the book defines the essence of Bukowski's writing. The flower symbolizes nature or the natural world, a world of instinctual actions and reactions, which for Bukowski included poetry, while the fist represents civilization and the laws of society. The clash between nature and civilization provokes the bestial howl, Bukowski's own despair. He saw himself as a prisoner, frozen between raw nature and the equally awesome beauty of pure soaring imagination. Bukowski, for example, wrote in his poem "The Tragedy to the Leaves":

I awakened to dryness and the ferns were dead,
the potted plants yellow as corn;
my woman was gone
and the empty bottles like bled corpses
surrounded me with their uselessness;
the sun was still good, though
(*It Catches My Heart in Its Hands,* 1963)

The hard-edged beauty and spontaneity of his poetic voice, which he called "bar talk," link Bukowski with other post–World War II poets.

As the 1960s progressed, Bukowski's poetry attracted small press publishers. John Edgar Web published Bukowski's *It Catches My Heart in Its Hands* (1963) and *Crucifix in a Deathhand* (1965), and Doug Blazek's Mimeo Press published Bukowski's first book of prose, *Confessions of a Man Insane Enough to Live with Beasts* (1965). Writing a weekly column, "Notes from a Dirty Old Man," for an alternative newspaper won Bukowski a readership beyond poetry. His anarchistic and obstinate attitude fit youth culture and philosophy, and Bukowski became an obscure heroic figure. Meeting John Martin, the editor of Black Sparrow Press, changed his life: Martin published Bukowski's *At Terror Street and Agony Way* (1968) and *The Days Run Away Like Wild Horses over the Hills* (1969). With Martin's financial support Bukowski left his job at the postal service to write full time.

Devoting all of his energy to his craft, Bukowski quickly produced his first autobiographical novel. *Post Office* (1970) introduced Bukowski's thinly veiled persona, Henry Chinaski, the self-centered, sometimes crude, sometimes melancholy American underground man. Chinaski appeared in the novels *Women* (1978), *Ham on Rye* (1982), *Hollywood* (1989), and in much of Bukowski's other prose.

Black Sparrow published a steady stream of Bukowski's poetry in the 1970s and 1980s. Hundreds of poems appeared in large collections such as *Mockingbird Wish Me Luck* (1972), *Love Is a Dog from Hell: Poems, 1974–1977* (1977), and *Dangling in the Tournefortia* (1981). Bukowski's popularity grew enormously, and readers increasingly demanded new, more outrageous work. Turning away from the reflective, mournful poems of his early career, Bukowski began to chronicle his daily raucous adventures. His poetry became more realistic, personal, immediate, and narrative, as in this passage from "dark shades":

I never wear dark shades
But this red head went to get
A prescription filled on Hollywood Blvd.
And she kept haggling and working at
Me, snapping and snarling.
I left her at the prescription counter
And walked around and got a large tube of
Crest and giant bottle of Joy.
Then I walked up to
The dark shade display rack and bought
The most vicious pair of shades
I could find.
(*Love Is a Dog from Hell,* 1977)

He created an image of himself as a deviant, sarcastic madman poet. Bukowski said in a *New York Quarterly* interview, "I am 93 percent the person I present in my poetry; the other 7 percent is where art improves upon life" (Bukowski, 1985).

In 1985 Bukowski married Linda Lee Beighle, and in 1987 his screenplay *Barfly* became a major motion picture. Bukowski was a prolific writer, particularly toward the end of his life, and translations of his work made him wealthy: he drove a black BMW and owned a home in San Pedro, California. Nonetheless, the last book of poems published during his lifetime (*The Last Night of the Earth Poems,* 1992) is still rich in satire, anti-authoritarian tirades, and cynicism worthy of Diogenes. In poems like "The Creative Act" and "Death Is Smoking My Cigars," he reveals that poetry and the act of writing kept his identity anchored in the word throughout his life.

Bukowski died of leukemia in 1994 and remains American poetry's anti-hero. He has been immortalized in the United States and throughout Europe for his solitary independence and for his festering critiques of academic poetry and American society.

MICHAEL BASINSKI

**Biography**

Born in Andernach, Germany, 16 August 1920; emigrated to the United States in 1922. Attended Los Angeles City College, 1939–41; editor, *Harlequin,* Wheeler, Texas, then Los Angeles, and *Laugh Literary* and *Man the Humping Guns,* both Los Angeles; columnist, *Open City,* Los Angeles, then Los Angeles *Free Press.* Received LouJon Press Award; National Endowment for the Arts grant, 1974. Died 9 March 1994.

**Poetry**

*Flower, Fist and Bestial Wail,* 1960
*It Catches My Heart in Its Hands: New and Selected Poems, 1955–1963,* 1963
*Crucifix in a Deathhand: New Poems, 1963–1965,* 1965

*At Terror Street and Agony Way,* 1968
*The Days Run Away Like Wild Horses over the Hills,* 1969
*Penguin Modern Poets 13* (with Philip Lamantia and Harold Norse), 1969
*Mockingbird Wish Me Luck,* 1972
*Me and Your Sometimes Love Poems,* 1972
*While the Music Played,* 1973
*Burning in Water, Drowning in Flame: Selected Poems, 1955–1973,* 1974
*Love Is a Dog from Hell: Poems, 1974–1977,* 1977
*Play the Piano Drunk Like a Percussion Instrument until the Fingers Begin to Bleed a Bit,* 1979
*Dangling in the Tournefortia,* 1981
*War All the Time: Poems, 1981–1984,* 1984
*You Get So Alone at Times That It Just Makes Sense,* 1986
*The Rooming House Madrigals: Early Selected Poems, 1946–1966,* 1988
*Septuagenarian Stew* (includes stories), 1990
*In the Shadow of the Rose,* 1991
*The Last Night of the Earth Poems,* 1992
*Run with the Hunted: A Charles Bukowski Reader,* edited by John Martin, 1993
*Heat Wave,* 1995
*Betting on the Muse: Poems and Stories,* 1996
*Bone Palace Ballet: New Poems,* 1997
*What Matters Most Is How Well You Walk through the Fire,* 1999
*Open All Night: New Poems,* 2000

**Other Writings:** play, screenplay (*Barfly,* 1987), short stories, novels (*Post Office,* 1970; *Pulp,* 1993); edited poetry collection.

**Further Reading**

Brewer, Gay, *Charles Bukowski,* New York: Twayne, and London: Prentice Hall, 1997
Bukowski, Charles, "Craft Interview with Charles Bukowski," *New York Quarterly* 27 (Summer 1985)
Cherkovski, Neeli, *Hank: The Life of Charles Bukowski,* New York: Random House, 1991
Harrison, Russell, *Against the American Dream: Essays on Charles Bukowski,* Santa Rosa, California: Black Sparrow Press, 1994
Locklin, Gerald, *Charles Bukowski: A Sure Bet,* Sudbury, Massachusetts: Water Row Press, 1996
Sounes, Howard, *Charles Bukowski: Locked in the Arms of a Crazy Life,* New York: Grove Press, and Edinburgh: Rebel, 1998

---

## Witter Bynner 1881–1968

Early in his long career, Witter Bynner appeared poised to become a major figure in American literature. In 1902, after graduating from Harvard University, where he had worked on the *Advocate* at the invitation of Wallace Stevens, Bynner joined the editorial staff of *McClure's.* While there, he worked alongside Willa Cather, met Henry James, and urged the printing of stories by O. Henry; Bynner also oversaw the first American publication of poems from A.E. Housman's *A Shropshire Lad.* Mark Twain supported Bynner's decision to quit *McClure's* in 1906 and devote himself full time to writing and lecturing on literary topics. When Ezra Pound's father sent his son to Bynner to determine whether he should further his poetic study in Europe, Bynner encouraged Pound to go abroad, and in 1910 he arranged for the publication of Pound's first book at the press that had published Bynner's 1907 volume.

Despite Bynner's personal connections with some of the giants of 20th-century poetry, his poetic affinities did not bind him to the work of Stevens, Pound, or other High Modernists. Bynner preferred the simpler language and emotional accessibility of Housman and Millay, and his own verse was never showy, complicated, or densely allusive. His first books, *An Ode to Harvard* (1907) and *The New World* (1915), echo Poe in their versification and Whitman in their sentiments. Bynner's comments about Wordsworth in "An Ode to Harvard" offer a sound approach to his own work: "I, who'd scoffed at first / At the simple-minded worst, / Brought devotion to the best and simple-hearted." At his best, Bynner's early work achieves the thoughtful declaration of heartfelt emotions in direct but moving language, as in "Driftwood" and "The Dead Loon" from *Grenstone Poems* (1917).

In 1916, after composing many of the Grenstone lyrics, Bynner contrived a literary hoax to spoof such poetic trends as Imagism and Vorticism. Together with his friend Arthur Davison Ficke, Bynner fabricated the "Spectric" school of poetry. Adopting the pseudonyms Emanuel Morgan and Anne Knish, Bynner and Ficke published parodic poems that some took quite seriously, although others recognized the burlesque intent behind such lines as "Then you came—like a scream / Of beeves." Formally, Bynner's Spectra poems resemble his prior work, but they distinguish themselves in their tone and range of subjects. As Emanuel Morgan, Bynner allowed himself to write funny, satirical verse that had the capacity to startle with its unexpected juxtapositions. Even after the hoax was exposed in 1918, Bynner retained some of his alter ego's freedom and boldness in verses published under his own name.

Bynner published one more book as Emanuel Morgan, 1920's *Pins for Wings;* it summed up some of poetry's leading lights with devastating acerbity in one to three lines (T.S. Eliot: "the wedding cake / of two tired cultures"). *Guest Book* (1935) continued Bynner's satirical portraits of his contemporaries with a sequence of sonnets, based on his acquaintances, describing types (thus Robinson Jeffers, Edna St. Vincent Millay, and Amy Lowell become "Jeremiah," "Liar," and "Poetess," respectively).

In his more serious verse, Bynner turned away from the intellectualizing, European-inflected work of the Modernists to find an alternative model of poetry in the straightforward but evocative work of the T'ang poets. In 1917, Bynner had traveled with Ficke to Japan and China; their trip bore lasting consequences for Bynner's thought and poetry. In 1918, he began an 11-year effort to translate some 300 T'ang poems, using texts prepared by Berkeley professor Kiang Kang-hu. *The Beloved Stranger* (1919) first catches a note of the Chinese poetry that now captivated Bynner, and such poems as "The Wall," "Lightning," and "Horses" are among his best short lyrics. *A Canticle of Pan* (1920), published before his second trip to China, includes more poems about Asia as well as Bynner's first Chinese translations.

In 1922, Bynner moved to Santa Fe, New Mexico, where he lived for the rest of his life. The next year, he traveled with Frieda and D.H. Lawrence to Mexico, where he eventually bought a second house. Bynner became an advocate for Native American rights, and his poetry began to take account of his new geographic and cultural surroundings, starting with the sensitive depiction of Native American and Hispanic cultures in the poems of *Caravan* (1925).

Bynner reached a creative pinnacle in 1929, when he published three books crucial to his poetic development. After 11 years of work, he finished *The Jade Mountain,* his fine translation of classical Chinese poems into subtle free verse. An expanded version of its introduction appeared separately as *The Persistence of Poetry,* a statement of poetic principles in which Bynner defines poetry as "passionate patience." He also published *Indian Earth,* a volume of his own verses about the indigenous peoples of the southwestern United States and Mexico; many consider it his finest book.

With *Eden Tree* (1931), Bynner attempted a great poem in the style of his now-famous Modernist contemporaries. The book-length poem, unusually personal for Bynner, considers human relations—including a sidelong avowal of Bynner's homosexuality—through the prism of biblical and personal mythologies. Bynner's blending of traditional materials with personal revelations ultimately fails to convince intellectually or emotionally, and his poem was neither an artistic nor a critical success.

A volume of Bynner's *Selected Poems* (1936), edited by his lover Robert Hunt, also failed to secure the attention that Bynner, now 55 years old, had long sought. Thereafter, Bynner scaled back his poetic ambitions, casting himself exclusively as a lyric poet. His next books, *Against the Cold* (1940) and *Take Away the Darkness* (1947), restrict themselves to short lyrics, some of which—notably "The Wintry Mind" and "Spring and a Mother Dead"—are quite finely wrought and moving, while "Defeat" fills ten taut lines with careful observation and controlled indignation over the treatment of African-American soldiers during World War II. In 1955, Bynner released a new volume of selected poems, revealingly titled *Book of Lyrics;* this collection effaced any sense of development throughout his career by loosely arranging poems according to the seasons.

Bynner's last book, *New Poems 1960,* appeared when he was nearly 80. A remarkable turn to experimentation, *New Poems 1960* recalls the wildness of the Spectra poems in its enigmatic (and at times bizarre) verses, which Bynner claimed to have recorded from his dreams. This volume was well received, and it brought Bynner some welcome attention before a severe stroke disabled him in 1965. Since his death in 1968, Bynner has been remembered chiefly for his Chinese translations, the Spectra hoax, and the Witter Bynner Foundation for Poetry, but he also deserves attention for his sympathetic verses about Native American and Mexican cultures and for the austere beauty of his best lyrics.

MICHAEL WENTHE

**Biography**

Born in Brooklyn, New York, 10 August 1881. Attended Harvard University, Cambridge, Massachusetts, A.B. 1902; editor, McClure, Phillips and Co., New York City, 1902–06; editor, Small, Maynard and Co., Boston, Massachusetts, 1907–15; Instructor, University of California, Berkeley, 1918–19. Received Boylston and Bowdoin Prizes (Harvard University), 1902; Phi Beta Kappa Poet, Harvard University, 1911, University of California, 1919, and Amherst College, Massachusetts, 1931; Poetry Society of America Gold Medal, 1954; honorary Litt.D., University of New Mexico, Albuquerque, 1962. Died in Santa Fe, New Mexico, 1 June 1968.

**Poetry**

*An Ode to Harvard, and Other Poems,* 1907
*The New World,* 1915
*Grenstone Poems,* 1917
*The Beloved Stranger,* 1919
*Pins for Wings,* 1920
*A Canticle of Pan, and Other Poems,* 1920
*Caravan,* 1925
*Indian Earth,* 1929
*Eden Tree,* 1931
*Guest Book,* 1935
*Selected Poems,* 1936; revised edition, 1978
*Against the Cold,* 1940
*Take Away the Darkness,* 1947
*Book of Lyrics,* 1955
*New Poems 1960,* 1960
*The Works of Witter Bynner,* 1978
*The Selected Witter Bynner: Poems, Plays, Translations, Prose, and Letters,* 1995

**Other Writings:** plays (*Cake,* 1926), essays (*The Persistence of Poetry,* 1929), travel memoirs (*Journey with Genius,* 1951), correspondence (*Selected Letters,* 1981), translations from Greek (*Iphigenia in Tauris,* 1915), translations from Chinese (*The Jade Mountain,* 1929), translation from French (*A Book of Love,* by Charles Vildrac, 1923); edited collections of sonnets (*The Sonnets of Frederick Goddard,* 1931).

**Further Reading**

Kraft, James, *Who Is Witter Bynner?* Albuquerque: University of New Mexico Press, 1995
Smith, William Jay, *The Spectra Hoax,* Middletown, Connecticut: Wesleyan University Press, 1961; 2nd edition, Ashland, Oregon: Storyline Press, 2000
Stanford, Donald E., "The Best of Bynner," *Hudson Review* 36 (Summer 1983)

# C

## John Cage 1912–92

John Cage's work has been called "strangely beautiful," and it is richly deserving of both terms. He became famous primarily as the 20th century's most radical musician rather than for the poetry, essays, and various *objets d'art* that he created in a long and productive lifetime. His most famous piece remains the notorious *4'33" for Piano* (1952), a composition in three movements that is silent from beginning to end. The first performance was met with the hallmark outrage, but unlike *Rites of Spring,* Cage's elliptical opus remains nearly as far off the aesthetic spectrum as it was half a century ago. The same may be said of his output in general, in which it is possible to find scores for amplified pencils, essays that include exacting instructions as to when the speaker must cough, and poetry that may be read in any direction.

As a result, the image of Cage that has survived is that of a Dada prankster who wanted either to destroy art altogether or simply pull the sheep's wool over the eyes of a gullible and foolish century. Neither comes close to the truth, except perhaps in that the Dadaist comedy of long-term mentor Marcel Duchamp partly influenced Cage's openness to artistic possibilities generally considered absurd. His work is neither Dada nor a late creation of the anti-art schools (Futurism) that opened the century. Rather, Cage's oeuvre remains idiosyncratic in the best sense of the word, his *idée fixe* the "exploration of nonintention," the separation of the artist entirely from the art itself, which is produced by means of indeterminacy and randomness.

Although his influence extends from the earth installation of Walter de Maria to the collages of friend Robert Rauschenberg to electronic music as a whole, the only clear precedent that one can find to Cage's approach is in Zen Buddhism and his beloved Meister Eckhardt. The first Zen lectures that he attended by Daisetz Suzuki in the 1940s were pivotal, and in his influential book *Silence* (1961), he writes often of what Zen can mean for America in the 20th century. True to Roshi form, however, Cage quipped to comparative-religion guru Alan Watts that what he did should not be "blamed" on Zen.

As were prior iconoclasts, Cage was drawn to the poetry of Gertrude Stein, E.E. Cummings, and James Joyce. He composed mixed-genre pieces on all three authors' works, including *Three Songs* (1932; Stein) for voice and piano, *Forever and Sunsmell* (1942; Cummings) for voice and percussion, and *Nowth upon Nacht* (1985; Joyce) for voice and piano. His most ambitious poetic work, however, is the extensive series *Writings through Finnegans Wake.*

*Writings* has been realized as pure text, as music, and as performance. In the first category, it includes the variously structured *Writing through Finnegans Wake* (1976), *Writing for the Second Time through Finnegans Wake* (1977), and so on (up to a fifth time, titled *Muoyce,* in 1980). Under the title *Roaratorio, An Irish Circus on Finnegans Wake* (1979), it was read by Cage to the taped accompaniment of a barrage of sounds, including ambient recordings from various locations around Ireland and more or less coordinated examples of noises being described in the text. As performance, a combination reading/tape/live musical show was delivered on several occasions, with singer Joe Heaney and a cast of Irish folk musicians. Finally, Cage wrote up a score with the title ——, —— *Circus on* ——, in which the blank spaces represent the ability of any written work to be transformed through this method into sound.

Both playful and daunting, *Writings* best exemplifies Cagian method as applied to the poetic process. Using Joyce's High-Modernist opus as a source text, no version of *Writings* technically contains anything penned by Cage himself. Rather, he applied what he has called a "mesostic" process to the book, the neologism designating an acrostic that is centered on the page. The "mesostic string" is the letter series JOYCEJAMES; each letter is sought in turn and, when found, printed along with the word or grouping of words in which it appears. Specific details of the process differ from version to version and are often decided by means of chance operations.

The end result is a thin, trailing line of "found" text, resembling both the ultra-minimalist "zings" of stripe painter Barnett Newman and, at times, Ezra Pound's edge-clipped fragments in the style of Sappho:

pftJschute
Of finnegan
that the humptYhillhead of humself
is at the knoCk out
in theE park

Jiccup
the fAther
My shining
thE
Soft (X, 1)

The decision to utilize Joyce's already neologistic novel contributes much to both the ambiguity and the richness of this kind of meta-writing. When Cage applies a similar mesostic rule to Samuel Beckett's 1937 poem "They Come," for example, the result is more immediately readable but perhaps less rewarding.

In mesostic writing, it is the artist's intention (always a difficult word with Cage) to divorce himself completely from the process of poetry making, so that he and the reader together can discover novelty and surprise. It is, in fact, the same impulse that lies behind *4′33″*, now understood not to be about silence per se but rather about opening up a space in which performer and audience alike can make discoveries (Frank Zappa's 1993 recording captures a creaking piano stool, while Peter Greenaway's filmed version records the activity of the camera itself). Similarly, *Writings* is best approached not as a work of deconstruction or of unreachably academic intellectualism but rather as an invitation to wander through this field of verbal flowers and uncover whatever may be found.

Cage applied his mesostic approach to a number of different sources, ranging from newspaper articles to essays by Buckminster Fuller and Henry David Thoreau. The resultant pieces stand in relation to poetry as the first inclusion of text stood to pre-Cubist painting: a startling "neither this, nor this" (Cage's credo). Not surprisingly, Cage's poetic influence can be seen in the present generation, most notably at the interface between poetry and the visual arts: word-installation artists such as Jenny Holzer, Barbara Kreuger, and (to a lesser extent) Laurie Anderson owe much to Cage's willingness to disregard traditional divisions between art forms; and, after the star of *musique concrète* has fallen, Cage's musical thought is maintained in the silence-rich work of Toru Takemitsu and in the montage-opening of most pop songs.

The same may be said of Cage's poetry as he himself said in praise of the music of Christian Wolff: that all one can do with it is to "suddenly listen." The reader of Cage's work will be confused, even angered; however, making less rather than more of an attempt to make sense of it, one finds oneself "suddenly reading," perhaps even suddenly alive.

WILLIAM OREM

**Biography**

Born in Los Angeles, California, 5 September 1912. Attended Pomona College, California, 1928–30; freelance library researcher, 1934–35; accompanist and teacher, Cornish School, Seattle, Washington, 1936–38; faculty member, School of Design, Chicago, Illinois, 1941–42; musical director, Merce Cunningham Dance Company, New York City, 1944–66; teacher, New School for Social Research, New York City, 1955–60; Research Professor and Associate, Center for Advanced Studies, Wesleyan University, Middletown, Connecticut, 1960–61; composer-in-residence, University of Cincinnati, Ohio, 1967; Research Professor, Center for Advanced Studies, University of Illinois, Urbana-Champaign, 1967–69; member of summer faculty, Mills College, Oakland, California, 1938–39, and Black Mountain College, 1950–52; founded New York Mycological Society. Received Guggenheim fellowship, 1949; National Academy of Arts and Letters Award, 1949; Woodstock Art Film Festival First Prize, 1951; Thorne Music Fund grant, 1967–69; Comandeur de l'ordre des Arts et Lettres, French Ministry of Culture, 1982. Died 12 August 1992.

**Poetry**

*Diary: How to Improve the World (You Will Only Make Matters Worse) Continued, Part 3,* 1967
*M: Writings '67–'72,* 1973
*Writing through Finnegans Wake,* 1976
*Writing for the Second Time through Finnegans Wake,* 1977
*Empty Words: Writings '73–'78,* 1979
*X: Writings '79–'82,* 1983
*Composition in Retrospect,* 1993

**Other Writings:** biography (*Virgil Thomson: His Life and Music* [with Kathleen Hoover], 1959), essays (*Silence: Selected Lectures and Writings,* 1961), correspondences (*The Boulez-Cage Correspondence,* 1993), musical compositions (*Cheap Imitations,* 1972).

**Further Reading**

Kostalanetz, Richard, "Talking about *Writings through Finnegans Wake,*" *TriQuarterly* 54, no. 2 (1982)
Kostalanetz, Richard, "The Aesthetics of John Cage: A Composite Interview," *Kenyon Review* 9, no. 2 (1987)
Perloff, Marjorie, *The Poetics of Indeterminacy: Rimbaud to Cage,* Princeton, New Jersey: Princeton University Press, 1981
Perloff, Marjorie, "'Unimpededness and Interpenetration': The Poetics of John Cage," *TriQuarterly* 54, no. 2 (1982)
Perloff, Marjorie, and Charles Junkerman, editors, *John Cage: Composed in America,* Chicago: University of Chicago Press, 1994
Revill, David, *The Roaring Silence: John Cage, a Life,* New York: Arcade, and London: Bloomsbury, 1992

---

# Canadian Poetry (Anglophone)

Challenging the notion that modernity is primarily about the *new,* Octavio Paz has usefully argued that it is rather "never itself; it is always *the other.* The modern is characterized not only by novelty, but by otherness." If we locate modernity here, in Paz's *other,* then Canada arguably was among the last of the American nations to develop a truly modern poetry of its own. A number of factors contributed to that situation, but one of the most important had to do with the question of the relation to authority (especially colonial authority) that has haunted Canada's national development from its inception.

The same Anglo-Saxon colonizers occupied and founded both the United States and Canada. The eventual distinction between them arose out of an internal argument over whether the traditional (and, it was believed, sacred) relation to authority should prevail over what came down to the desire for less taxes. In what became the United States, those in support of less taxes won the argument through force of arms, and those who continued to adhere to a belief in the sanctified authority of the king and his right to assign whatever taxes he saw fit were run out of town by the rebels after having their property confiscated. Many fled north of the 49th parallel, to Canada.

By the mid–19th century, thinkers such as Ralph Waldo Emerson in the United States had extended the argument over authority to the question of culture. Writers in the United States began to develop poetry consciously at odds with the poetry being written in England. Walt Whitman, especially, and Emily Dickinson broke profoundly with the authority of the old forms transmitted through English Romanticism and Victorian verse and developed native New World poetries that were radically other than the regular metrics and end rhymes of preformed English verse.

In Canada, on the other hand, those English forms were embraced, even as the developing nation itself continued to embrace its ties to the authority of the British Empire and the English crown. The result was often a skilled imitation of a Romanticism that had largely passed on in the mother country almost a half-century earlier. Poets such as Charles Roberts (1860–1944), Archibald Lampham (1861–99), and Bliss Carman (1861–1929) dominated Canadian writing up until the mid-1920s, well after Modernism had taken root in much of the rest of the world. That situation began to seriously change only in the late 1940s, and then in the 1960s and 1970s exploded into an unprecedented creative frenzy that propelled Canadian writing to the forefront of innovative work not only in the Americas but around the world as well.

The first stirrings of new possibilities in Canada occurred in 1925 in Montreal at McGill University when A.J.M. Smith (1902–80) and Frank Scott (1899–1985) founded the *McGill Fortnightly Review.* Students at McGill, they were unhappy with the neo-Romantic, nature-centered verse then dominating Canada. Their effort broke with the antique 19th-century models, but their ideas of the modern were themselves largely derivative of work they had been exposed to in England—the Georgians associated with Harold Munro's bookshop, the early Imagist poems that had been left behind some ten years before, and to some degree Eliot. Smith and Scott's own verse, typically characterized by end rhymes and meter, imitated the most conservative aspects of Eliot's poetics, overlooking or evading the crisis of form that is central to Modernism's undertaking. Both Smith, an academic who later emigrated to the United States and gained U.S. citizenship, and Scott, a social democratic lawyer, also inclined toward satire in their work, a mode generally inhospitable to innovative breaks with tradition.

Two poets, W.W.E. Ross (1894–1966) and Raymond Knister (1899–1932), did begin to make unprecedented moves toward a specifically Canadian Modernism in the 1920s, although the careers of both were cut short. Ross took his lead from early Imagism, mastered it, and began to push beyond toward a verse engaged with the materialities and otherness of language. The result is a poetry of remarkable intensity and subtle musicality increasingly involved in the physical arrangement of words on a page. Aside from some small chapbooks, Ross' poems were not available until *Shapes and Sounds* was published in 1968 two years after Ross' death. Ross worked as a geophysicist at an observatory and had little contact with any literary scenes. Reticent about submitting his work to public scrutiny, he never played an active part in the national literary life and wrote very little during the last 30 years of his life. In retrospect, however, his poetry provided hints of further possibilities to young writers of the 1960s and 1970s.

Like Ross, Knister was not closely associated with any of the existing "schools" of poetry, although he was close to other writers, such as Dorothy Livesay and Leo Kennedy. Much of Knister's work focused on the pastoral and, like Ross', took its lead from Imagism. While it was less engaged with the materiality of language, it eschewed rhymes and regular meter, and it moved toward an intense musicality within a simple and precise diction stripped of pretensions. Whereas Ross became silent for the last 30 years of his life, Knister drowned at the age of 33, with much work unpublished. Thus, two of the most innovative writers of the 1920s lapsed into an early silence.

Knister's friend Dorothy Livesay (1909–96) began her long and diverse writing career at about the same time. Deeply affected by the economic and political injustices of the time, she moved from early Imagist-influenced verse to Marxist-inflected documentary poems in the 1930s and 1940s. Again, though, the influences on her were predominantly English, especially the early Auden and Spender. Her work during this period is marked by the priority of politics over verse and has a distinct propagandistic edge. Livesay, however, is an example of a remarkable phenomenon in Canadian poetry—the older, established poet who, rather than resting on one's accomplishments, goes "back to school" with younger writers and renews one's energies and forms. Livesay's most enduring work was arguably *The Unquiet Bed* (1967), illustrated by poet and artist Roy Kiyooka (1926–94). It was written after she had returned from a stay in Africa and moved to Vancouver, where she systematically investigated the work of the younger poets then involved in turning the entire Canadian writing scene on its head. The lessons she learned in poetics and prosody led her to an entirely new kind of verse in which an awareness of language assumes a place of priority.

After years of relative silence, A.J.M. Smith ensconced his sense of Canadian Modernism in *The Book of Canadian Poetry: A Critical and Historical Anthology* (1943), some 20 years after publishing the *McGill Fortnightly Review.* Praised by conservative critic Northrop Frye, among others, *The Book of Canadian Poetry* became the first textbook of Canadian verse. Its central distinction between a "native" (romantic) and a "cosmopolitan" school, however, did not sit well with the many poets who had sprung up in Canada since Smith left for the United States. Smith's anthology was countered by *Other Canadians* (1947), edited by John Sutherland (1919–56).

Sutherland, a young writer and editor living in Montreal, was deeply involved in current polemics that pitted not "romantics" against "cosmopolitans" but a New World realist tradition against the Old World metaphysical aesthetics of Eliot and his imitators. As the editor of the little magazines *First Statement* and later *Northern Review,* Sutherland was active in promoting writers such as Louis Dudeck (1918–), Raymond Souster (1921–), and Irving Layton (1912–), poets who had openly broken, in terms of both language and content, with the legacy of English colonialism. He also published first books by Layton, Souster, Miriam Waddington (1917–), and Anne Wilkinson (1910–61) in what he called the *New Writers Series.* Sutherland was finally better known for his criticism than for his poetry, but his contribution to the development of Canadian poetry was crucial. Prophetically, he proposed a period in which Canadian writing would turn to U.S. examples as a way of breaking with England, "a half-way house from which Canadian poetry will pass towards an identity of its own" (Introduction, *Other Canadians: An Anthology of the New Poetry in Canada, 1940–1946,* 1947).

Sutherland's introduction to *Other Canadians* stands as a harbinger of the enormous changes in store for Canadian poetry. The poets he published in his magazine, including Dudeck, Souster, Layton, and Waddington, went on to rewrite Canadian verse. Not that their writing is similar, although they do all share a sense of political and literary discontent. At the moment of Sutherland's magazine and anthology, they shared with Sutherland fundamental agreements on what they opposed, and that, more than anything else, led to sense of cohesion and unity.

Dudeck, under the influence of Ezra Pound, moved from early lyric work to the long meditative poem in books such as *Europe, En México,* and *Atlantis,* forging a mode that became widespread in Canadian poetry. Dudeck's poetry is intellectually bold and philosophical in its address. He has always held that poetry is of the mind—that poetry is thought—and without being abstract has pursued that route into an art of ideas. Imitative of Pound in the beginning, his work quickly developed its own sensibility. A sharp critic and editor as well as writer, Dudeck went on to edit *Contact* with Souster and to found his own magazine, *Delta,* which ran from 1957 to 1966.

If Dudeck began under the sign of Pound, then Souster began under the sign of William Carlos Williams. Like Williams, his working life was spent in pursuits other than poetry, in his case as a banker. Unlike Williams, Souster has never ventured far from the short, image-based observational poem. He nevertheless played a crucial role in the development of modern Canadian poetry, not only as a poet but also as a publisher, an editor, and a mentor to young writers.

For most of his writing career, Souster has produced short, lucid poems about the unobserved marvels of the everyday world. Although the individual poems are short, the accumulation over the years has led to a substantial body of work, what critic and poet Bruce Whiteman (1984) has called a world "in constant construction." After Sutherland abandoned his early support for modern poetry and the Anglo-centric university-based writers and critics launched an attack on the new poetries, cutting off publication venues, Souster founded the magazine *Contact* in 1952 as an outlet for innovative new work. It was the only magazine publishing such poetry for its two-year run. The first issue carried an important polemic by Dudeck encouraging young poets to fight for the modern poetic imagination.

In the same year, recognizing the dearth of local publishers, Souster, along with Dudeck and Layton, founded Contact Press, arguably the most important Canadian press during the 1950s. After *Contact* folded in 1954, Souster went on to found and edit *Combustion* beginning in 1957. It had close links with various innovative magazines and poets in the United States and developed connections that Souster had been building for years with writers such as William Carlos Williams, Charles Olson, Robert Creeley, and others. Most important, Souster dedicated his energies to nurturing and publishing young Canadian writers and laying the groundwork for the creative explosion of the 1960s and 1970s.

Layton was the third member of this seminal group. An immigrant from Romania who grew up in Montreal, Layton brought to his poetry an imagination of 19th-century Romantic passion fueled by massive sexual energy and an unbridled ego. In the 1950s and 1960s, Layton presented himself as a pagan rebel-prophet whose life was constituted of the same grand gestures as his poetry. His attacks on conventionality made him a celebrity in the 1960s. Layton accomplished some memorable poems and was involved in the crucial early battles that prepared for the poetry that followed.

A number of interesting, innovative writers rose up in the turbulence of the changes taking place in Canadian writing. Earle Birney (1904–95), although older than the *First Statement* writers, began writing at a later age. His initial work is dependent largely on irony for its force, but, like Dorothy Livesay and Phyllis Webb, some of his later work was influenced by younger poets, especially bpNichol, and reveled in the materiality of language. Al Purdy (1918–2000) and Milton Acorn (1923–86), a carpenter from Prince Edward Island, were friends for much of their lives and shared a commitment to the struggles and lives of common people and a poetry and language that celebrated those realities. Phyllis Webb (1927–) is another of those remarkable Canadian poets who keeps reinventing her writing over and over again. She works in a poetics in which the question is not the point of departure but, rather, the very flesh and bones of the poem. D.G. Jones (1929–), first published in *Contact,* initially wrote a painterly poetry that recently has located itself in surprising densities of language and thought. Leonard Cohen (1934–) went on to set his poetry to music, becoming a hugely successful popular songwriter and singer.

Two events in the early 1960s signaled the onset of a period of remarkable innovation in Canadian poetry. The first was the birth of the magazine *Tish* in Vancouver in 1961. The second was the founding in 1964 of Coach House Press by Stan Bevington and Wayne Clifford in Toronto. In both cases, many of the writers associated with the organizations maintained strong relationships with poets in the United States, especially those connected to Black Mountain College, the San Francisco Renaissance, and the Beat movement, all centers of explosive formal innovation. In most cases, those ties fed a two-way exchange, with the Canadians frequently as influential among the U.S. poets as vice versa.

In 1959, Warren Tallman (1921–94), a professor at the University of British Columbia and one of the few academics to teach the poetry of Dudeck, Souster, and Layton, invited one of his wife's friends from her student days in Berkeley to read in Vancouver. Some 40 people attended Robert Duncan's first Vancouver reading in the Tallmans' living room. It generated a tremendous amount of excitement, and two years later, when Tallman initiated the Festival of Contemporary Arts, the artists he chose to inaugurate it were Robert Duncan and W.D. Snodgrass. Later he would invite Robert Creeley, Edward Dorn, Michael McClure, Jack Spicer, and Lew Welch. The excitement generated by the event led several poets who were students at the University of British Columbia, including George Bowering (1938–), Frank

Davey (1940–), Fred Wah (1939–), David Dawson (1942–), and Jamie Reid (1941–), to begin a small mimeographed magazine called *Tish*. Conceived as a monthly "local" newsletter, *Tish* began to push poetic form farther than it had ever been taken in Canada, almost immediately stirring up a storm of excitement (and rage) that shadowed its eight-year run.

Almost immediately, Vancouver became recognized as an important North American literary center, for the first time shifting the literary balance of Canada away from Montreal and Toronto. Warren Tallman continued to further that process. The success of the Festival of Contemporary Arts encouraged him to organize the 1963 Vancouver Poetry Conference, an event that included Charles Olson, Robert Creeley, Allen Ginsberg, Philip Whalen, Denise Levertov, Robert Duncan, and Canadian Margaret Avison, who had recently been featured in Sid Corman's *Origin*. The conference galvanized not only Vancouver and the rest of Canada but much of the United States as well.

Robin Blaser (1925–) arrived in Vancouver from San Francisco in 1966 to begin teaching at Simon Fraser University, becoming a naturalized Canadian in 1973. Over the next 34 years, as teacher, poet, and mentor, Blaser fired the imaginations of countless young writers in Vancouver, adding immeasurably to the creative ferment of a city that over the years produced innovative writers as significant and diverse as George Bowering, Daphne Marlatt (1942–), Gerry Gilbert (1936–), Barry MacKinnon (1944–), George Stanley (1934–), Sharon Thesen (1946–), Frank Davey, Fred Wah, and Lisa Robertson (1961–) and eventually led to the foundation of the Kootney School of Writing. Other important presses and magazines that sprang up in the wake of *Tish* included *Iron*, blewointmentpress, and Talonbooks.

*Tish* immediately influenced a number of writers in central Canada as well. David McFadden (1940–), Victor Coleman (1944–), and bpNichol (1944–88) were among the many who responded to the energy of the Vancouver scene as it reverberated across Canada. One of the most significant results of that spread was the founding of Coach House Press in 1964 in Toronto to further the publication of the new writing. Initially run by printer Stan Bevington and Wayne Clifford, editorship passed to poet Victor Coleman between 1966 and 1974 and then to an editorial collective from 1974 to 1992. Over the years of its operation, Coach House published books by every significant Canadian writer and several U.S. writers as well. Among those associated with the press are Margaret Atwood (1939–), Gwendolyn MacEwen (1941–87), Michael Ondaatje (1943–), Victor Coleman, bpNichol, Roy Kiyooka, Christopher Dewdney (1951–), and Steve McCaffery (1947–). As with *Tish*, the energy Coach House generated spread and encouraged the growth of other small presses. Both House of Anansi, started by poets Dennis Lee (1939–) and David Godfrey in 1967, and Oberon Press, founded the same year, went on to become important Canadian publishers.

The energy, imagination, and inventiveness of the 1960s and 1970s, although less explosive, made Canadian writing some of the most significant and innovative in the Americas. The increasingly widespread and strong sense of Canada's important role in the postcolonial reimagining of America fueled that process. While much of that thinking flowed out of the history sketched here, the ongoing importance of immigration needs to be emphasized as well. Large-scale immigration, already important in giving Canada writers such as Michael Ondaatje, Daphne Marlatt, and Robin Blaser, continued to contribute new blood, feeding new and surprising energies into the nation's poetry and prose. The coming of age of second- and third-generation immigrant children such as Fred Wah, Roy Kiyooka, and many others has also contributed to the formal inventiveness and complex postcolonial thematic concerns that have advanced the rethinking not only of Canada but of America as a whole.

Michael Boughn

**Further Reading**

Barbour, Douglas, editor, *Beyond Tish*, Edmonton, Alberta: NeWest, 1991

Blodgett, E.D., *Configuration: Essays in the Canadian Literatures*, Downsview, Ontario: ECW Press, 1982

Bowering, George, *A Way with Words*, Ottawa, Ontario: Oberon Press, 1982

Davey, Frank, *Reading Canadian Reading*, Winnipeg, Manitoba: Turnstone Press, 1988

Dudeck, Louis, and Michael Gnarowski, editors, *The Making of Modern Poetry in Canada*, Toronto, Ontario: Reyerson Press, 1967

Tallman, Warren, *In the Midst: Writings 1962–1992*, Vancouver, British Columbia: Talonbooks, 1992

Whiteman, Bruce, *Raymond Souster and His Works*, Toronto, Ontario: ECW Press, 1984

Woodcock, George, *George Woodcock's Introduction to Canadian Poetry*, Toronto, Ontario: ECW Press, 1993

## Canon Formation. *See* Anthologies, Textbooks, and Canon Formation

# Caribbean Poetry

It is impossible to address the subject of Anglophone Caribbean poetry without being aware of its difficult start. Growing as it has from the legacy of colonialism, Caribbean culture, according to Louis James' *Caribbean Literature in English* (1999), possesses "an essentially subversive quality" that pervades its poetry and expressive arts. It had to be subversive to exist in the first place. Disentangling a falsified genealogy has been part of the exercise of West Indian poetry finding its voice.

Some scholars have christened the dulled pentameter of colonials genuflecting toward their European homes the first Caribbean poetry: from the perspective of these colonials, certainly nothing could come from an African or from among the decimated Amerindian population that remained on the islands, no matter what paternal experiment attempted their education. Thus, the story of the educated free black Francis Williams (d. c. 1762–74), who wrote a Latin ode to honor the incoming governor of Jamaica, has mythological resonance. Writing in a recent review of early Caribbean literature, Derek Walcott makes the point that Edward Long, slavery advocate and Williams' contemporary, translated the poem and published it in his *History of Jamaica* (1774) in hopes of showing the author up. Williams' skill showed up Long instead.

However, note that Williams bested the colonizer in his own tongue, not Williams'—and to a great degree that has been the available strategy from post-emancipation time until the later 20th century, largely through the agency of British colonial education. That members of the white European plantocracy and its milieu should be characterized as the forefathers of Caribbean poetry rankles still. Thus, St. Lucian Nobel laureate Walcott references canonical Anglophone literature as well as the music of Caribbean patois, yet he typically fumes at the efforts of Thomas W. Krise's *Caribbeana: An Anthology of English Literature of the West Indies, 1657–1771* to claim early plantocracy's work as West Indian patrimony. The poet dismisses these as nothing but attempts of a "desperate archivist, eager to find anything that will give the Caribbean past dignity, . . . exaggerated importan[ce] if not reverence." Nevertheless, Walcott believes that an African legacy is hopelessly lost, and that idea has been hotly disputed among Caribbean intellectuals, especially in the 20th century.

Intrinsic to this tangled argument is Kamau Brathwaite's reading of the Caliban/Prospero paradigm from Shakespeare's *The Tempest.* Both Brathwaite and Walcott have debated the work of Scots physician and poet James Grainger, especially his lengthy *Sugar Cane* (1764). Grainger's poem was hailed by Samuel Johnson as, at last, a poem competitive with British work and modeled on Virgil's *Georgics,* a popular pastoral form much imitated at the end of the 17th century (James, 1999). Walcott complains that Grainger's methodical "Caribbean Georgics" drag on interminably when the whole of it could be summed up as follows:

> What soil the Cane effects: what
> care demands;
> Beneath what signs to plant; what
> ills await;
> How the hot nectar best to
> christallize [sic];
> And Africa's sable progeny to
> treat.

Brathwaite disagrees. He quotes Grainger's poetic goal to construct something new out of the raw materials of the place: "as the face of this country was wholly different from that of Europe, so whatever hand copied its appearances, however rude, could not fail to enrich poetry with many new and picturesque images" (Brathwaite, 1986). Brathwaite appends to the introductory verse Walcott quoted previously the verse's original closing couplet:

> A Muse that long hath wander'd in the groves
> Of myrtle-indolence, attempts to sing.

Walcott sniffs that anchoring Caribbean poetry in "watery rhapsodies over cane fields and bamboo groves" is a threadbare legacy and "a forced amnesia," given the absence of recorded culture among the unlettered slave population. Brathwaite agrees to the damage loosed on subjugated people. However, he studiously points out that what disqualifies Grainger from candidacy as a completely Caribbean poet is his voice:

> [Voice] can transform the scene, even though its elements are local, into something quite "other." In the *Sugar Cane* this happens when Grainger contemplates "nature." At once the "Caribbean" disappears, and we find ourselves in English autumn, anticipating Keats. (Brathwaite, 1986)

Thus, it is not simply skill at the master's own game, the slow rejection of past brutalities, or even the inclusion of local flora and fauna rather than nonexistent English landscapes. The voice is what the Caribbean poet must struggle for. Indeed, were the Anglophone Caribbean simply to link itself to the British poetic tradition, little might follow. Or, to quote the famous Calypsonian from Grenada, Sparrow,

> I. According to the education you get when you small
> You'll grow up with true ambition and respect from one
> and all
> But in my days in school they teach me like a fool
> The things they teach me I should be a block-headed mule.
>
> Pussy has finished his work long ago
> And now he resting and thing
> Solomon Agundy was born on a Monday
> The Ass in the Lion skin
> Winkin Blinkin and Nod
> Sail off in a wooden shoe
> How the Agouti lose he tail and Alligator trying to get
> monkey liver soup.
>
> II. The poems and the lessons they write and send from
> England
> Impress me they were trying to cultivate comedians
> Comic books made more sense
> You know it was fictitious without pretence
> But like Cutteridge wanted to keep us in ignorance.
> . . . .
>
> III. . . .

Peter Peter was a pumpkin eater
And the Lilliput people tie Guilliver
When I was sick and lay abed
I had two pillows at my head
I see the Goose lay the golden egg
The Spider and the Fly
Morocoy with wings flying in the sky
They beat me like a dog to learn that in school
If me head was bright I woulda be a damn fool.
(*Voiceprint,* 1989)

The reference to Cutteridge is to a text of English verse that every West Indian school child was forced to learn. Cutteridge would hardly acknowledge the richness of oral culture among transported Africans and Amerindians who survived. Rather, this is preserved in Caribbean music and religious practices and buried in the music and vocabulary of Caribbean English. Indeed, since the Caribbean oral tradition (expressed in popular culture) clearly antedates the written, it is as much the forebear of Caribbean poetry as is any written tradition—"Who hath ears to hear, let him hear," as the King James version of the Bible, familiar to Anglophone West Indian ears, would say. Oddly, though, Walcott is reticent about the issue of popular culture that feeds West Indian poetry, claiming that "the vocal tradition, apart from calypso, *conte,* reggae, and hymn, is audible in the best West Indian fiction." This "apart from" is a whole world, and it is a shame that he has not expanded on these exceptions.

Consider the case of Jamaican transplant to the United States Claude McKay. His first books of poetry, *Songs of Jamaica* and *Constab Ballads* (both published in 1912), were written while he was still living in Jamaica. Here is one of the *Songs,* resonating with the voices of home:

Merry voices chatterin',
Nimble feet dem patterin',
Big an' little, faces gay,
Happy day dis market day.

Sateday! de marnin' break,
Soon, soon market-people wake;
An' de light shine from de moon
While dem boy, wid pantaloon
Roll up ober dem knee-pan,
'Tep across de buccra lan'
To de pastur whe' de harse
Feed along wid de jackass,
An' de mule cant' in de track
Wid him tail up in him back,
All de ketchin' to defy
No ca' how dem boy might try.

In de early marnin'-tide,
When de cocks crow on de hill
An' de stars are shinin' still,
Mirrie by de fireside. . . .

The poem is not Caribbean merely by accent but also in the use of "him" as "his," the repetitious "soon soon," the nation language "buccra" and "knee-pan," the use of "dem" (as in Akan, a West African language) to pluralize, and the failure to acknowledge a collective noun such as feet (so that in imitation of standard English, "feet" and "people," for example, become "feets" and "peoples"). The application of "dem" to feet, then, is consistent with an Africanized grammar. All these locate the poem in the Caribbean, although a reader may wince at the Victorian rhythm and rhyme (probably the influence of his mentor, Walter Jekyll, an expatriate Englishman with a reputation for his investigation of Jamaican folklore). McKay's work corroborates some of Brathwaite's comments on voice, yet McKay's voice simultaneously rings of empire. With all its facility, his subsequent poetry, written in exile, seems dated, even mediocre, and voiceless by comparison, as in this sonnet from the 1953 *Selected Poems:*

Throughout the afternoon I watched them there,
Snow-fairies falling, falling from the sky,
Whirling fantasies in the misty air,
Contending fierce for space supremacy.
And they flew down a mightier force at night,
As though in heaven there was a revolt and riot,
And they, frail things had taken panic flight
Down to the calm earth seeking peace and quiet.

Contemporaneous with McKay were W.A. Roberts, Louis Simpson, Philip Sherlock, Jamaica's Thomas MacDermot, and Belize's James Martinez. The latter two, according to Paula Burnett, exemplify the ambivalence that Caribbean poets shared toward the use of the vernacular: MacDermot's gaze still fixed on the British empire, and he was more at ease in the neutral tones of "standard" English; Martinez wrote best in vernacular (Introduction, *The Penguin Book of Caribbean Verse in English,* 1986). Later, in the 1930s, the poems of Una Marsdon, one of the first women poets of note, show a vacillation between standard English and vernacular. Note the ironic contrast between the two selections here:

Lord gie you chile de spirit
Let her shout
Lord gie you chile de power
An let her pray—

They tell us
That our skin is black
But our hearts are white.

We tell them
That their skin is white
But their hearts are black.

Marsdon also satirizes the Caribbean woman's dilemma, long before it was fashionable, in "To Wed or Not To Wed," a parody of Hamlet's famous soliloquy.

A sparse 1920s and 1930s gave way to a 1940s in which a real movement toward a Caribbean literature began to take off under the influence of Frank Collymore. Collymore taught at Combermere School in Bridgetown, Barbados, until 1963; and while he himself wrote "verse both serious and whimsical" and a few short stories (James, 1999), his real strength lay in encouraging others. He was studiously apolitical, and it is hard to believe that the author of the almost naive lines from "Homage to Planters" (in *Collected Poems,* 1959) could have been mentor to the likes of the novelist George Lamming, Kamau Brathwaite, A.J. Seymour, Edward Baugh, Derek Walcott, and many others whom "Colly" and *Bim*, the little magazine he founded in 1942, encouraged:

> . . . I do not know
> Much about sugar kings,
> But I salute with gratitude
> The loving care which wrings
> Such beauty from the soil and o'er
> Our land its patchwork flings

Nearly every West Indian writer of stature has been published in *Bim*. Indeed, although other little magazines—such as A.J. Seymour's *Kyk-over-al* in Guyana and *Focus* under Elizabeth Manley's direction—also flourished at this time, *Bim* outlasted nearly all of them. As Burnett (1986) notes, *Caribbean Voices*, Henry Swanzy's Caribbean service BBC radio program, was also a moving force from 1945 to 1958.

Toward the end of this period, the young Walcott emerged, as did Wilson Harris, who first began as a poet. Continuing their careers were Seymour, George Campbell, Shake Keane, Kamau (originally Edward) Brathwaite, and, in the 1950s, the very political, imprisoned Martin Carter, with his *Poems of Resistance* (1954). In the 1960s, focus on the vernacular became more pronounced. One may cite Claude McKay as a forebear to poet and performer Louise Bennett, who affirmed Jamaican nation language in a way that he never did. For a long time a prophet without honor in her own country because she did not disdain the folk vernacular, she is now recognized by numerous Anglophone Caribbean poets. A radio performer and columnist for Kingston's *Daily Gleaner*, she also made her mark as a serious folklorist and oral historian. After a brief stint in New York circles from 1953 to 1955, Bennett returned home and worked for the Jamaican government and also lectured in drama at the University of the West Indies, Mona. She received numerous accolades for her work, but, as she notes,

> From the beginning, nobody ever recognized me as a writer. "Well, she is 'doing' dialect"; it wasn't even writing you know. Up to now a lot of people don't even think I write. . . . I did start to write before I started to perform. (Mervyn Morris' introduction to Bennett's *Selected Poems*, 1987)

Indeed the debate between acknowledging or denying folk culture as root, between an ambivalent attachment to the British canon and Europe in general, or bemoaning home's hopelessness or sterility—all this has taken up more than its share of time in Caribbean circles. As James (1999) points out, "'Literary' usage . . . left the social prejudice against West Indian English largely intact. In 1966 this began to change when Louise Bennett's *Jamaica Labrish* [gossip] was published." The debate is not over, considering, for example, that the latest minister of education in Barbados has issued a policy banning the use of any song not in standard English in the schools.

With Miss Lou, as Bennett was called, on the airwaves and the 1960s driving creativity as it did, Caribbean poetry blossomed. Certainly Brathwaite extended the possible range of what now becomes difficult to call simply "vernacular." Pointing to the complex origins of Caribbean English and its infusion with African languages, he has encouraged the use of the term "nation language," referring to the ethnic identification in the consciousness of descendants of enslaved Africans and its subversion of the tongue of the slave owner. Even Walcott, "Roddy brother/Teacher Alex son," does not lose that Caribbean inflection ("Sainte Lucia," 1976).

Yet another factor persists, and that is the fact of exile. Early exiles were E.A. Markham, James Berry, A.L. Hendricks, Shake Keane, and Andrew Salkey (who was also a novelist). Before junketing back and forth to teach at New York University, Brathwaite had already read for two degrees in London and taught in Ghana. Walcott migrates, too. The slightly younger group coming up behind them—the succinct Mervyn Morris (Jamaica), the more theatrical and "dangerously styled" Dennis Scott (Jamaica; *Caribbean Quarterly* [March 1984]), the more formalistic Wayne Brown (Trinidad), and the fragmented Anthony McNeill (also of Jamaica)—did their time abroad as well. E.M. Roach did not leave, and, although novelist Ian MacDonald rated him in the company of Walcott, Brathwaite, Bennett, McKay, and the intense Martin Carter, staying took its toll. At the start, Roach seemed to hold natural gloom at bay, as in "I Walk Abroad":

> Join my voice to the frog-throat in the pond,
> To the cricket shrill and bird-cry in the wood;
> I sign my name upon the papyrus
> Of plantain leaves broad in my garden,
> I'm halo'd with the sun. (Introduction, *The Flowering Rock*, 1992)

However, this was followed by lines such as

> silence
> silence
> a man has passed
> into the heart of darkness ("At Quinham Bay," in *The Flowering Rock*)

Roach succumbed to despair, and in 1974 he drowned himself. He moved from affirming the landscape and his region's Africanness to a position perceived as much less radical by many around him and finally to more and more silence. According to Kenneth Ramchand, Roach finally ended by declaring the need of Caribbean men to "fight / those last and hardest battles with ourselves" ("At Quinham Bay").

One question that Roach's sad passing might raise is how Caliban fails, a question that Brathwaite posed several times into the late 1990s. In his view, the failure of federalism; the increasing silence and then dying out of a voice such as Roach's; the assassination of Walter Rodney, author of *How Europe Underdeveloped Africa* (1972), in Guyana; the difficulties of the ordinary folk who have never left—these and other features plague Caliban's Caribbean and its artists:

> Language, as all (ex-)colonials know, is Caliban's big problem/monster. . . . The political or whatever other revolt has to buck up sooner or later (and sooner better than letter) on the forts and greathouses of language. (*Caribbean Quarterly* [March 1984])

Like the weed that pushes through concrete, however, Caribbean poets, in residence and in exile, continue despite Caliban's fortunes. Part of this survival may indeed be the result of greater acceptance of West Indian English as a rightful poetic. North American jazz, although influential, has never supplanted the freshness and wit of calypso or, in Brathwaite's phrase, the "linguistic strategies" of Rastafarian culture and the influence of such groups as the Shaker Baptists; and all these have been sources for poets of the latter part of the 20th century and beyond. Nor is it possible to divide up writers solely on the basis of genre: Fred D'Aguiar, for example, is both poet and a novelist, as is David Dabydeen. One of the more interesting developments is the voice of Caribbean women. As Olive Senior, a Jamaican poet and fiction writer living in Canada, understates, "Caribbean women shoulder the most tremendous burdens." Among women poets of note is Grace Nichols, who wrote the much-quoted lines

> I have crossed an ocean
> I have lost my tongue
> from the root of the old
> one
> a new one has sprung. (*i is a long-memoried woman,* 1983)

So, too, is Lorna Goodison, who writes,

> My mother raises rare blooms
> and waters them with tea
> her birth water sand like rivers
> my mother now is me. . . .
> I am becoming my mother
> brown/yellow woman
> fingers smelling always of onions. (*Caribbean Poetry Now,* 1992)

Goodison's is a quiet voice, whereas others, such as Pam Mordecai, write and perform today with the orality of a Louise Bennett. In 1984, Trinidadian Dionne Brand raged in response to the U.S. invasion of Grenada in her poem sequence *Chronicles of a Hostile Sun,* as did poet and novelist Merle Collins of Grenada. Marlene Nourbese Philip's verse/prose *Looking for Livingston* (1991) presents a woman's confrontation with the British male explorer. It seems that Caribbean women continue to be heard, in performance as well as on the printed page.

In conclusion, Caribbean poetry in the Americas is significant in many ways. It puts issues of coming to voice after being colonized into high relief. Descendants of Africans throughout the Americas link to the Caribbean, and aesthetic connections between Africa and the Caribbean are demonstrable. Finally, the music of West Indian English, having evolved from a blend of folk, popular, and literary aesthetics, is one of the most vital and interesting forms of expression in the world. That Caribbean poetry survives well outside the academy is an inspiration.

BRONWYN MILLS

**Further Reading**

Brathwaite, Edward Kamau, *Roots,* Havana: Casa de las Americas, 1986; Ann Arbor: University of Michigan Press, 1993

Brown, Stewart, editor, *Caribbean Poetry Now,* London: Hodder and Stoughton, 1984; 2nd edition, London and New York: Arnold, 1992

Brown, Stewart, Mervyn Morris, and Gordon Rohlehr, editors, *Voiceprint: An Anthology of Oral and Related Poetry from the Caribbean,* Harlow, Essex: Longman, 1989

Burnett, Paula, editor, *The Penguin Book of Caribbean Verse in English,* London and New York: Penguin, 1986

James, Louis, *Caribbean Literature in English,* New York and London: Longman, 1999

Markham, E.A., editor, *Hinterland: Caribbean Poetry from the West Indies and Britain,* Newcastle upon Tyne: Bloodaxe, 1989

McDonald, Ian, and Stewart Brown, selectors, *The Heinemann Book of Caribbean Poetry,* Oxford and Portsmouth, New Hampshire: Heinemann, 1992

---

## Hayden Carruth 1921–

Hayden Carruth is one of America's most prolific writers. The author of more than 20 volumes of poetry and four books of criticism, Carruth has worked as editor-in-chief of *Poetry* (1949–50) and as poetry editor for *Harper's* (1977–82). *The Voice That Is Great within Us* (1970), also edited by Carruth, is regarded by critics as an influential anthology of the 20th century. Although he has stated that his early poetic influences included Shakespeare and Mother Goose—the latter for its syncopated line (Scheele, 1996)—his own experiences have also inspired his work, particularly his years as a resident of Johnson, Vermont, a locale that prompted his many poems about rural life. He has spent time in psychiatric hospitals, and much of his work deals with the struggle between sanity and madness. What has had the strongest effect on Carruth's poetry, however, is jazz. Carruth himself says, "What is more important, yet at the same time more difficult to discuss . . . the influence on writing of the other arts; in my case, particularly the influence of jazz" (quoted in Swiss, 1985). By employing the cadences of jazz music, Carruth has created poetry of intellectual and rhythmic complexity, and his poems reflect a deep belief in both cultural and environmental responsibility.

Carruth was born in Waterbury, Connecticut, in 1921. He earned his B.A. in journalism from the University of North Carolina (1943), after which he served two years as a member of the Army Air Corps during World War II. After the war, he attended graduate school at the University of Chicago, where he received his M.A. in English (1947) and first became interested in writing poetry. His first book, *The Crow and the Heart* (1959), is still regarded as one of his best. This volume includes "The Asylum," a long poem that James Dickey has described as "the finest sonnet sequence that I have read by a contemporary poet" (quoted in Swiss, 1985). This poem addresses Carruth's experience in a psychiatric hospital and calls into question the different definitions of the word "asylum." In "The Asylum," Carruth establishes an important theme of his career: the tension between the chaos of insanity and the order achieved through rural farm life and the changing of the seasons (Cooley and Hoey, 1996).

The "sonnets" of "The Asylum" are written in a 15-line verse form of Carruth's invention. This form, known as "paragraphs," is rhymed complexly and consistently in an intricate rhyme (ABABAACCDEDEFEF) and metrical scheme (554355445354555); the paragraph employs the irregular formalism of a Renaissance ode or elegy (e.g., Milton's "Lycidas" could well be regarded as a formal antecedent). In "The Asylum," the form is employed quite strictly, using only the variations allowed by traditional English prosody: inverted first feet, cataleptic lines, and so on (Miller, 1998). When Carruth uses this form again in "Paragraphs," a poem that appears in *From Snow and Rock, from Chaos* (1973), he utilizes it in a looser fashion. He allows himself liberty in varying the rhyme scheme and the metrical pattern. The result is a poem that moves intuitively down the page as it addresses directly the jazz musicians who have inspired Carruth's work. "Oh I loved you Pete Brown. And you were a brother / to me Joe Marsala. And you too sweet Billy Kyle. / You Sidney Bechet. And Benny Carter." However, more important perhaps, "Paragraphs" comments on Vermont's landscapes as corporations threaten to destroy the beauty of the state. Carruth writes,

> half the forests lay in slashed ruin,
> the river's blue was more likely not sky
> but the paintworks in Hardwick
> cleaning its vats again. And yet
> somehow
> it was absorbed, humanity sick
> with greed, with loathing, somehow was taken in
> by earth, water, mountain . . .

Although Carruth uses this paragraph form in other works, such as *Contra Mortem* (1967), the most well known example of his sonnet invention is *The Sleeping Beauty* (1982). A tour de force, this book-length poem in 125 sections is regarded by many to be Carruth's finest creation. The poem offers a medley of voices as it revisits the classic fairy tale. The sleeping princess is dreaming, and "as in all dreaming / Is heard the echo of coincidental voices." These "coincidental voices" emerge as characters such as the prince and a man named Amos, a rural farmer who speaks in the dialect of a northern Vermonter. In this poem, Carruth again explores the theme of environmental responsibility—Amos speaks about the "trillionaires" guilty of buying up property and "shoving some farmer off his land."

*The Sleeping Beauty* is a socially conscious poem, but many of its sections have a hallucinatory quality appropriate for the dream state of the princess. At times erotic, this poem turns the innocence of the prince's kiss to a scene of violent rape. The men of the princess' dreams are all historical figures associated with the letter "H," such as Hamlet, Hegel, and Homer. As Matthew Miller (1998) states, "If there is a 'philosophy of Hayden Carruth,' this is the book to which one should turn to find it. In it, Carruth sets in motion a world that is immediately recognizable because it is the historical world Americans and Europeans all share."

Carruth is one of America's most underrated poets. At nearly 80 years of age, he has graced us with his vast poetic vision, one not limited to the "paragraph" form. He is a virtuoso of strict form, which is evident in work such as *Asphalt Georgics* (1985), but other volumes (e.g., his latest collection, *Scrambled Eggs and Whiskey* [1996]) demonstrate a wide range of form and craft. Although he has not received the critical attention that he deserves, Carruth has been an important influence on 20th-century American poetry. In fact, Anthony Robbins (1993) calls Carruth "one of the finest American poets of this century." This jazz-inspired poet who first brought his readers inside the walls of "The Asylum" continues to be an innovative poetic force.

CHRISTINA VELADOTA

**Biography**

Born in Waterbury, Connecticut, 3 August 1921. Attended the University of North Carolina, Chapel Hill, B.A. 1943; University of Chicago, M.A. 1947; served in the United States Army Air Corps during World War II; editor, *Poetry,* Chicago, 1949–50; associate editor, University of Chicago Press, 1950–51, and Intercultural Publications Inc., New York, 1952–53; Visiting Professor, Johnson State College, Vermont, 1972–74, University of Vermont, Burlington, 1975–78, and St. Michael's College, Winooski, Vermont; since 1979 Professor of English, Syracuse University, New York; poetry editor, *Harper's,* New York, 1977–82; since 1971 editorial board member, *Hudson Review,* New York. Received Vachel Lindsay Prize, 1954, Bess Hokin Prize, 1956, Levinson Prize, 1958, Eunice Tietjens Memorial Prize, and Morton Dauwen Zabel Prize, 1968 (*Poetry,* Chicago); Harriet Monroe Award, 1960; Bollingen Prize, 1962; Carl Sandburg Prize, 1963; Emily Clark Balch Prize (*Virginia Quarterly Review*), 1964; Guggenheim fellowship, 1965, 1979; National Endowment for the Arts grant, 1967, 1968, 1974, 1984, fellowship, 1988; Shelley Memorial Award, 1978; Lenore Marshall Prize, 1979; Whiting Foundation Award, 1986; Senior Fellow, National Endowment for the Arts, 1988; Ruth Lilly Poetry Prize, 1990; National Book Critics Circle Award, 1992; Lannan Award, 1995; National Book Award, 1996. Living in Munnsville, New York.

**Poetry**

*The Crow and the Heart, 1946–1959,* 1959
*Journey to a Known Place,* 1961
*The Norfolk Poems, 1 June to 1 September 1961,* 1962
*North Winter,* 1964
*Nothing for Tigers: Poems, 1959–64,* 1965
*Contra Mortem,* 1967
*For You,* 1970
*The Clay Hill Anthology,* 1970
*From Snow and Rock, from Chaos: Poems, 1965–1972,* 1973
*Dark World,* 1974
*The Bloomingdale Papers,* 1974
*Brothers, I Loved You All,* 1978
*The Sleeping Beauty,* 1982
*If You Call This Cry a Song,* 1983
*Asphalt Georgics,* 1985
*The Oldest Killed Lake in North America: Poems, 1979–1981,* 1985

*The Selected Poetry of Hayden Carruth,* 1985
*Tell Me Again How the White Heron Rises and Flies Across the Nacreous River at Twilight Toward the Distant Islands,* 1989
*Collected Shorter Poems, 1946–1991,* 1992
*Collected Longer Poems,* 1993
*Scrambled Eggs and Whiskey, Poems, 1991–1995,* 1996

**Selected Criticism**
*Working Papers: Selected Essays and Reviews,* edited by Judith Weissman, 1982
*Effluences from the Sacred Caves: More Selected Essays and Reviews,* 1983

**Other Writings:** novel, essays (*Reluctantly: Autobiographical Essays,* 1998); edited poetry anthologies (*The Voice That Is Great within Us,* 1970; *The Bird Poem Book: Poems on the Wild Birds of North America,* 1970).

**Further Reading**
Cooley, John R., and Allen Hoey, "Hayden Carruth: Overview," in *Contemporary Poets,* 6th edition, edited by Thomas Riggs, Detroit, Michigan, and London: St. James, 1996
Miller, Matthew, "A Love Supreme: Jazz and the Poetry of Hayden Carruth," *Midwest Quarterly* 39, no. 3 (1998)
Robbins, Anthony, "Hayden Carruth: An Interview by Anthony Robbins," *American Poetry Review* 22, no. 5 (1993)
Scheele, Roy, "Hayden Carruth: The Gift of Self," *Poets and Writers Magazine* 24, no. 3 (1996)
Swiss, Thomas, "'I Have Made This Song': Hayden Carruth's Poetry and Criticism," *Sewanee Review* 93, no. 1 (1985)
Tillinghast, Richard, "Chants and Chain Saws," *New York Times Book Review* (December 1992)
Weiss, David, editor, *In the Act: Essays on the Poetry of Hayden Carruth,* Geneva, New York: H. and W. Smith Colleges Press, 1990

## Chicago Renaissance. *See* Midwestern Poetry Renaissance

## Chinese American Poetry. *See* Asian American Poetry

## John Ciardi 1916–86

Truly a modern man of letters, John Ciardi lived a life almost completely devoted to language, as editor, translator, critic, lecturer, teacher, and, most importantly to him, poet. He earned a fortune (as well as envious disdain from some other poets) from royalties, lecture fees, and editorial salaries, but he never stopped pursuing his scholarly interests. Ciardi followed the disciplined, erudite tradition of Wallace Stevens and belonged to the more formal generation of Richard Wilbur, Karl Shapiro, and Elizabeth Bishop. Although many of his later poems reveal details about his family life, his loves, and his World War II experience as a tail gunner, he could never be described as a "confessional" poet such as Robert Lowell, and he steadfastly resisted the free-form jazzy style of the Beat movement.

Ciardi was born in 1916 in Medford, Massachusetts, to Italian immigrant parents. His father's death in a freak automobile accident three years later figures mythically in several poems. Ciardi's Italian heritage of temperament and language shaped his personality and his literary and scholarly interests, culminating in his translation of Dante's *Divina Commedia* (1977), published over a 25-year period. Randall Jarrell wrote in *The Yale Review* in 1953 that Ciardi's *Inferno* translation "has more narrative power, strength of action, than any other I know." Ciardi's translations, which some have called the benchmark of Dante translation, are still widely read and admired. After graduating from Tufts University in 1938, Ciardi attended the University of Michigan on a Hopwood Award and completed his first book of poems, *Homeward to America* (1940), the first of more than 20 books of poetry, counting two books of limericks written with Isaac Asimov.

In 1940 Ciardi received a fellowship to the Bread Loaf School of English, as it was called then, where he met fellow first-time authors Eudora Welty and Carson McCullers. Ciardi would continue his association with Bread Loaf for more than 30 years, eventually becoming its director. The 1940s were a pivotal period for young American men, and Ciardi enlisted in the Army and wound up in the Air Corps as an aerial gunner on a B-29. He saw his share of combat in the Pacific and made it out with a fistful of medals and a wry sense of having cheated death more than once, which figures in many of his poems. Following the war, Ciardi married Judith Hostetter (the "Judith" of his love and marriage poems), and they had three children.

Ciardi's lifetime career of teaching at various universities and colleges began at Harvard in 1946. He also began a 20-year association with *The Saturday Review of Literature,* the most important popular culture periodical of the 1950s, where he served as poetry editor and wrote a regular column, "Manner of Speaking," primarily on language. He was a frequent guest lecturer at colleges all across America, charming undergraduates with his limitless knowledge of poetry and his spellbinding basso profundo delivery. At *The Saturday Review,* however, Ciardi angered the public with a scathing review of Anne Morrow Lindbergh's *The Unicorn, and Other Poems* (1957). Mrs. Lindbergh was the wife of the famous aviator and a figure of great public sympathy, and many readers found Ciardi's essay extreme. Ciardi himself was unrepentant, however, even when faced with a lack of support from his editor-in-chief, Norman Cousins. In 1958 Ciardi sparked controversy again when he described Robert Frost's "Stopping by Woods on a Snowy Evening" as expressing the death wish of its speaker. Years later Ciardi would still have to defend his argument as legitimate interpretation, if not fact.

Ciardi's other editorial efforts include *Mid-Century American Poets* (1950), a highly acclaimed anthology that includes such poets as John Frederick Nims, Karl Shapiro, Randall Jarrell, Theodore Roethke, Richard Wilbur, and Peter Viereck as well as poems of his own. He also produced an anthology for collegiate poetics courses called *How Does a Poem Mean?* (1959), a textbook to rival the phenomenally successful and lucrative *Sound and Sense* anthology by Laurence Perrine (1956). In the 1960s Ciardi began to isolate himself, however unwittingly, from the emerging poets who would establish themselves in the 1970s. He was writing in the old tradition of Robert Frost, with whom he shared the gift of playfulness in gruesome or even terrifying situations. Several poems Ciardi mockingly entitled "elegy" of one kind or another.

Going his own way at the expense of the regard of his contemporaries, Ciardi could be heard on National Public Radio in a regular short segment called "Words in Your Ear." Despite his declining health, he continued to speak on college campuses. His work, like Frost's, stressed masculine sympathy with language and experience. And like Frost and Wallace Stevens, Ciardi found a loving humanism in poetry, expressed in his "Elegy Just in Case":

> Darling, darling, just in case
> Rivets fail or engines burn,
> I forget the time and place
> But your flesh was sweet to learn.
>
> In the grammar of not yet
> Let me name one verb for chance,
> Scholarly to one regret:
> That I leave your mood and tense.

PETER VAN EGMOND

**Biography**

Born in Medford, Massachusetts, 24 June 1916. Attended Bates College, Lewiston, Maine, 1934–36; Tufts University, Medford, Massachusetts, B.A. 1938; University of Michigan (Hopwood Award), M.A. 1939; served in U.S. Army Air Force, 1942–45; Instructor, Kansas State University, 1940–42, 1946; Briggs-Copeland Instructor, 1946–48, and Assistant Professor, 1948–53, Harvard University, Cambridge, Massachusetts; Lecturer, 1953–54, Associate Professor, 1954–56, and Professor, 1956–61, Rutgers University, New Brunswick, New Jersey; editor, Twayne Publishers, New York City, 1949; Lecturer, 1947–72, and Director, 1955–72, Bread Loaf Writers' Conference, Middlebury, Vermont; Lecturer, Salzburg Seminar in American Studies, 1951; poetry editor, *The Saturday Review,* 1956–72; host, CBS's "Accent," 1961–62, and National Public Radio's "Words in Your Ear," 1980–86; Fellow, American Academy of Arts and Sciences, National Institute of Arts and Letters; Director, 1955–57, and President, 1958–59, National College English Association. Received Oscar Blumenthal Prize, 1943; Harriet Monroe Memorial Award, 1955; Prix de Rome, American Academy of Arts and Letters, 1956–57; Junior Book Award, Boys' Clubs of America, 1962; honorary Litt.D., Tufts University, 1960; honorary L.H.D., Kalamazoo College, 1964, Bates College, 1970, Washington University, 1971, and Ohio Wesleyan University, 1971. Died in Metuchen, New Jersey, 30 March 1986.

**Poetry**

*Homeward to America,* 1940
*Other Skies,* 1947
*Live Another Day,* 1949
*From Time to Time,* 1951
*As If: Poems New and Selected,* 1955
*I Marry You: A Sheaf of Love Poems,* 1958
*Thirty-Nine Poems,* 1959
*In the Stoneworks,* 1961
*In Fact,* 1962
*Person to Person,* 1964
*This Strangest Everything,* 1966
*An Alphabestiary,* 1966
*The Achievements of John Ciardi,* 1969
*Lives of X,* 1971
*The Little That Is All,* 1974
*Limericks, Too Gross* (with Isaac Asimov), 1978
*For Instance,* 1979
*A Grossery of Limericks* (with Isaac Asimov), 1981
*Selected Poems,* 1984
*The Birds of Pompeii,* 1985
*Poems of Love and Marriage,* 1988
*Echoes: Poems Left Behind,* 1989
*The Collected Poems of John Ciardi,* 1997
*Limericks* (with Isaac Asimov), 2000

**Selected Criticism**

*Poetry: A Closer Look* (with James M. Reid and Laurence Perrine), 1963

**Other Writings:** essays (*Manner of Speaking,* 1972; *Ciardi Himself: Fifteen Essays in the Reading, Writing, and Teaching of Poetry,* 1989), memoir (*Saipan: The War Diary of John Ciardi,* 1988), correspondence (*The Selected Letters of John Ciardi,* 1991), children's poetry (*I Met a Man,* 1961) and literature (*The Wish-Tree,* 1962), dictionaries (*A Browser's Dictionary,* 1980), translations of Italian literature (*Dante's Divine Comedy,* 1977); edited anthologies of poetry (*Mid-Century American Poets,* 1950).

**Further Reading**

Cargas, Harry J., "Poetry and the Poet: An Interview with John Ciardi," *America* 13 (January 1973)
Cifelli, Edward M., "Ciardi on Frost: An Interview," in *Frost: Centennial Essays,* compiled by the Committee on the Frost

Centennial of the University of Southern Mississippi, Jackson: University Press of Mississippi, 1974
Cifelli, Edward M., *John Ciardi: A Biography,* Fayetteville: University of Arkansas Press, 1997
Clemente, Vince, editor, *John Ciardi: Measure of the Man,* Fayetteville: University of Arkansas Press, 1987
Jerome, Judson, "Ciardi's Art," *Writer's Digest* 69 (October 1985)

---

## Amy Clampitt 1920–94

The 1983 publication of Amy Clampitt's *The Kingfisher* drew the kind of critical praise rarely granted new poets. According to Edmund White in *The Nation,* this collection, Clampitt's third after the privately printed *Multitudes, Multitudes* (1974) and the cooperative venture that resulted in *The Isthmus* (1982), heralded "one of the most brilliant debuts in recent American literary history" (16 April 1983). *The Kingfisher* was a remarkable volume for a writer already 63 years old and established Clampitt's reputation as an accomplished poet with a body of work that was at once both erudite and literary.

In *The Kingfisher* Clampitt gave notice of her trademark ability to render nature in dense poetic vocabulary:

> Where at low tide the rocks, like the
> back of an old sheepdog or spaniel, are
> rugg'd with wet seaweed, the cove
> embays a pavement of ocean, at times
> wrinkling like tinfoil, at others
> all isinglass flakes. ("The Love")

Clampitt spent her career combing the strata of meaning generated by observation and experience, often by exploring geology, botany, zoology, and architecture. Throughout her work, Clampitt makes repeated points of comparison between the seemingly arbitrary sense of nature and the human desire to make sense of it. In "Beach Glass," an early poem from the opening section of *The Kingfisher,* the poet draws an analogy between beach debris and ideas, with both

> turned over and over as gravely
> and gradually as an intellect
> engaged in the hazardous
> redefinition of structures
> no one has yet looked at.

*What the Light Was Like* (1985), a much darker volume than *The Kingfisher,* continued to evoke nature as a fundamental concern. This volume is dominated by the impressive eight-part sequence "Voyages: A Homage to John Keats." "Voyages," ostensibly a depiction of Keats, is in fact Clampitt's first sustained meditation on the value of literary tradition, another theme to which she would frequently return. Prompted by a desire "not to have to forge some totally new thing," Clampitt sought to fill what she saw as a void created by her Midwestern birth and often speculated on her own role in the literary tradition. In this way she is able to invoke Keats not only as an English Romantic who can help make sense of the emptiness of the Midwestern prairies, but also as a grandee of the literary tradition. Along the way the poem refers to such luminaries as Mandelstam, Crane, Coleridge, predecessors all, and from this point on the dominant theme in Clampitt's work would be the vexing problem of tradition, both literary and otherwise. In "Voyages" and much of her later work, the literary tradition is a sustaining presence. The following lines from "The Elgin Marbles" refer at least as much to Clampitt as they do to Keats:

> Now, primed on *Lear,*
> Milton, Gibbon, Wordsworth, he'd set himself
> to re-imagining an epic grandeur, such as
> (if it arrived at all) came battered
> and diminished, fallen like Lucifer,
> or else dismantled, fragmentary, lowered and
> transported, piece by piece, like the heroic
> torsos, the draperied recumbent hulks Lord Elgin
> took down from the Parthenon.

"It's not the command of knowledge that matters," Clampitt wrote in her essay collection *Predecessors, Et Cetera* (1991), "but the company. It's the predecessors." Both George Eliot and Margaret Fuller are accorded poems in *Archaic Figure* (1987), and at various times the volume also makes mention of Dorothy Wordsworth, George Eliot, Marx, Freud, Tolstoy, Chopin, Lewis Carroll, Simone Weil, and Virginia Woolf.

*Archaic Figure* grew out of Clampitt's travels to Greece—the voyage was also a metaphor of which she made much use—and in style it is as allusive and dense as any of her poetry. Split into four sections, *Archaic Figure* is informed by female experience, with Clampitt again reaching back, this time to classical mythology, to establish what the epigraph from Virginia Woolf's *The Common Reader* identifies as "the ancient consciousness of women." That consciousness is played back and forth across history, with the plight of women as its chief concern, and reaches its impressive apogee in "An Anatomy of Migraine," in which Clampitt summons "a gathering of shades," "an elite / vised by the same splenetic coronet" of migraine—and of tradition. Although *Archaic Figure* is perhaps Clampitt's most introspective collection, in terms of linguistic complexity and observational detail it stands comparison with any of her work.

Clampitt's last two collections, *Westward* (1990) and *A Silence Opens* (1994), continued to address her predecessors. In poems such as "Having Lunch at Brasenose" and "John Donne in California" she began to develop a skepticism of historiography that finds expression in the beautiful "Matoaka." The question of history, its uses and abuses, was by this point a familiar motif, and

Clampitt continued to scrutinize the past with an eye as keen as that which she brought to her observations on nature. Some critics argued that her work was too detailed, too literary or too prosaic, but she was, she declared, wary "about being co-opted."

In June 1994, three months before ovarian cancer claimed her life, Clampitt married her long-time companion Harold Korn. Almost 26 years earlier Howard Moss had accepted "The Sun Underfoot Among the Sundews" for *The New Yorker,* and during the intervening two and a half decades Clampitt produced a rich and fulfilling body of work. Her learned diction, fluid meter, and humane spirit mark her as unique among contemporary American poets.

IAN PEDDIE

**Biography**

Born in New Providence, Iowa, 15 June 1920. Attended Grinnell College, Iowa, B.A. (honors) in English 1941 (Phi Beta Kappa); Columbia University, New York, 1941–42; secretary and promotion director, Oxford University Press, New York, 1943–51; reference librarian, National Audubon Society, New York, 1952–59; freelance editor and researcher, New York, 1960–77; editor, E.P. Dutton, New York, 1977–82; writer-in-residence, College of William and Mary, Williamsburg, Virginia, 1984–85, and Amherst College, Massachusetts, 1986–87; taught at Smith College. Received Guggenheim fellowship, 1982; Academy of American Poets fellowship, 1984; American Academy and Institute of Arts and Letters award, 1984; D.H.L., Grinnell College, 1984; MacArthur fellowship, 1992. Died 10 September 1994.

**Poetry**

*Multitudes, Multitudes,* 1974
*The Isthmus,* 1982
*The Kingfisher,* 1983
*The Summer Solstice,* 1983
*A Homage to John Keats,* 1984
*What the Light Was Like,* 1985
*Archaic Figure,* 1987
*Manhattan: An Elegy, and Other Poems,* 1990
*Westward,* 1990
*A Silence Opens,* 1994
*The Collected Poems of Amy Clampitt,* 1997

**Other Writings:** essays (*Predecessors, Et Cetera: Essays,* 1991); edited poetry collection (*The Essential Donne,* 1988).

**Further Reading**

Fairchild, Laura, "Amy Clampitt: An Interview," *The American Poetry Review* 16, no. 4 (1987)
Hosmer, Robert E., Jr., "Amy Clampitt: The Art of Poetry," *The Paris Review* 126 (1993)
Longenbach, James, *Modern Poetry after Modernism,* New York: Oxford University Press, 1997
McClatchy, J.D., *White Paper on Contemporary American Poetry,* New York: Columbia University Press, 1989
Vendler, Helen, *The Music of What Happens: Poems, Poets, Critics,* Cambridge, Massachusetts: Harvard University Press, 1988
Vendler, Helen, *Soul Says: On Recent Poetry,* Cambridge, Massachusetts: Harvard University Press, 1995
Weisman, Karen A., "Starving before the Actual: Amy Clampitt's 'Voyages: A Homage to John Keats,'" *Criticism* 36, no. 1 (1994)
White, Edmund, "Poetry as Alchemy," *The Nation* 236 (16 April 1983)

---

# Lucille Clifton 1936–

Lucille Clifton, former poet laureate of Maryland, writes strikingly simple, unrhymed, epigrammatic poetry about her life, her family, and the lives of African-Americans. She has written several series on biblical subjects, with poems about Adam and Eve, David, and Mary. In these poems, she re-presents biblical figures as complex human subjects, using colloquial language and expressing the worries and uncertainties that they may have experienced but that are not included in the biblical accounts. She asserts that she is interested primarily in trying to render big ideas in a simple way. Although her language is simple, she brings wide-ranging literary knowledge and personal wisdom to her poems. Her lyrics tend to the celebratory as they explore topics that range from her family, prominent African-Americans, women's bodies, and her own "big hips" and "nappy hair" to a re-imagining of the lives of biblical characters, such as Jonah, Moses, and the Virgin Mary.

Clifton's early poems appeared in the 1960s and 1970s. During this period, a group of writers affiliated with the Black Arts movement sought to further black American culture and to promote political activism for civil rights. While others writing at that time (e.g., Don L. Lee and Nikki Giovanni) put forth such ideas in heightened rhetoric and violent imagery, Clifton's voice was trenchant without the violence, stridency, and profanity employed by some of her contemporaries. Her first book, *Good Times* (1969), describes ghetto life in a series of vignettes of her family and neighborhood. With tongue in cheek, she speaks of "the inner city / or / like we call it / home." Her inner city is a place where some suffer but where others may find happiness in their links to family and friends despite poverty. Her second book, *Good News about the Earth* (1972), includes poems addressed to a series of heroes, such as Malcolm X and Bobby Seale and Eldridge Cleaver, the latter two members of the Black Panther Party. The third section of *Good News,* titled "some jesus," uses gentle humor and simple language to depict biblical figures, such as Adam and Eve, Cain, Moses, Job, Daniel, and Jonah. Clifton often situates these characters in African or Caribbean settings, as when Jonah in the whale remembers mangoes and yams and thinks "if I had a drum / I would send to the brothers / —Be care full of the ocean."

In *An Ordinary Woman* (1974), Clifton addresses Kali, a Hindu goddess of destruction and death. The poet speaks of our human complexity through acknowledging our affinity to this devouring mother. "I am one side of your skin, / she sings, softness is the other, / you know you know me well, she sings, / you know you know me well."

Clifton's memoir *Generations: A Memoir* (1976) crosses the line between prose and poetry as it depicts the history of her family in America, from the arrival of her great-great-grandmother, Caroline Donald Sale, sold into slavery, to her own children. The memoir is a celebration of survival in the face of slavery, racism, and poverty. Clifton begins each section with a quotation from Walt Whitman, thus linking her family's history to his celebration of the diversity of America's people. The story is one of mixed tragedy and triumph, as the family endured slavery and emerged. Clifton's epigraph asserts that Caroline Sale was born free in Dahomey and "died free in America in 1910." Further, she concludes, "We go on . . . the line goes on." In her memoir, Clifton assumes the role of the griot, the African oral storyteller who passes on the record of the tribal history.

In *Two-Headed Woman* (1980), a very Caribbean Virgin Mary speaks in her own voice, a dramatic departure, for Mary's voice has seldom been heard in American culture. Clifton depicts Mary as a working-class young woman who speaks in a Caribbean vernacular, experiences eroticism, and worries about the choices she must make.

*Next* (1987) continues with poems on American and South African history and contains elegiac poems about the death of her husband, Fred. *Quilting: Poems, 1987–1990* (1991) titles its sections with the names of traditional quilt designs. Quilting is perhaps a metaphor for the work of any creative artist, the piecing together of fragmentary materials (ideas, words, sounds, and fabric scraps) into beautiful and potentially useful artifacts. This book continues to develop Clifton's central themes: women's bodies, African-American history, and re-imaginings of biblical characters. She celebrates menstruation in the delightful "poem in praise of menstruation" that begins "if there is a river / more beautiful than this." The last section, called "tree of life," continues Clifton's exploration of the relationship between good and evil in a series of poems on Lucifer as seen through the eyes of Adam, Eve, and the fallen angel himself.

*The Book of Light* (1993) pursues the Lucifer story in its concluding section, an eight-part conversation representing a reconciliation between Lucifer and God titled "brothers." The Leda of Greek mythology (mother of Helen of Troy through a rape by Zeus in the form of a swan) meditates on her life, thinking "always pyrotechnics: / . . . . You want what a man wants, / next time come as a man / or don't come." Other figures here are Atlas, Clark Kent and Superman, Cain, Sarah, and Ruth and Naomi of the Bible. In the middle of the book, Clifton invites us:

> won't you celebrate with me
> what i have shaped into
> a kind of life? i had no model.
> born in babylon
> both nonwhite and woman
> what did I see to be except myself?
> . . . .
> come celebrate
> with me that everyday
> something has tried to kill me
> and has failed.

Clifton is a deeply spiritual person, and her poems reflect that trait. She continues to probe for the meaning of ordinary and extraordinary events and to explore what it means to be an African-American and a woman in America.

KAREN F. STEIN

**Biography**

Born in Depew, New York, 27 June 1936. Attended Howard University, Washington, D.C., 1953–55; Fredonia State Teachers College, New York, 1955; claims clerk, New York State Division of Employment, Buffalo, 1958–60; literature assistant, U.S. Office of Education, Washington, D.C., 1969–71; visiting writer, Columbia University School of the Arts, 1972–76; poet-in-residence, Coppin State College, Baltimore, 1972–76; visiting writer, George Washington University, Washington, D.C., 1982–83; Professor of literature and creative writing, University of California, Santa Cruz, 1985–91; since 1989, Distinguished Visiting Professor, St. Mary's College, Maryland. Received YM-YWHA Poetry Center Discovery Award, 1969; National Endowment for the Arts grant, 1970, 1972; American Library Association Coretta Scott King Award, 1974; Juniper Prize, 1980; Lannan Award, 1996; Poet Laureate for the state of Maryland, 1976–85; since 1999, Chancellor, Academy of American Poets. Living in Columbia, Maryland.

**Poetry**

*Good Times*, 1969
*Everett Anderson* series (for children), 1970–83
*Good News about the Earth*, 1972
*An Ordinary Woman*, 1974
*Two-Headed Woman*, 1980
*Good Woman: Poems and a Memoir, 1969–1980*, 1987
*Next: New Poems*, 1987
*Ten Oxherding Pictures*, 1989
*Quilting: Poems, 1987–1990*, 1991
*The Book of Light*, 1993
*The Terrible Stories*, 1995
*Selected Poems*, 1996
*Dear Creator: A Week of Poems for Young People and Their Teachers* (for children), 1997
*Blessing the Boats: New and Selected Poems, 1998–2000*, 2000

**Other Writings:** family history (*Generations: A Memoir*, 1976), children's literature.

**Further Reading**

Clifton, Lucille, "A Simple Language," in *Black Women Writers (1950–1980): A Critical Evaluation*, edited by Mari Evans, Garden City, New York: Anchor Press/Doubleday, 1983

Hull, Akasha, "In Her Own Images: Lucille Clifton and the Bible," in *Dwelling in Possibility: Women Poets and Critics on Poetry*, edited by Yopie Prins and Maeera Schreiber, Ithaca, New York: Cornell University Press, 1997

Madhubuti, Haki, "Lucille Clifton: Warm Water, Greased Legs, and Dangerous Poetry," in *Black Women Writers (1950–1980): A Critical Evaluation,* edited by Mari Evans, Garden City, New York: Anchor Press/Doubleday, 1983

McCluskey, Audrey T., "Tell the Good News: A View of the Works of Lucille Clifton," in *Black Women Writers (1950--1980): A Critical Evaluation,* edited by Mari Evans, Garden City, New York: Anchor Press/Doubleday, 1983

Rushing, Andrea Benton, "A Simple Language," in *Coming to Light: American Women Poets in the Twentieth Century,* edited by Diane Wood Middlebrook and Marilyn Yalom, Ann Arbor: University of Michigan Press, 1985

---

# Confessional Poetry

"Confessional poetry" as a label was first applied, disapprovingly, to Robert Lowell's *Life Studies* (1959) in a review by M.L. Rosenthal in *The Nation.* With its religious, psychological, and judicial connotations, the term has been contentious. John Drury articulates both sides of the argument over the merits of Confessional poetry: at best it "explores previously forbidden subjects with honesty and directness," and at worst it "wallows in emotional excess . . . in the guise of autobiography" (*The Poetry Dictionary,* 1995).

In the first book-length study of the subject, *The Confessional Poets* (1973), Robert Phillips ascribes some specific characteristics, many of which still seem viable. Confessional poetry, he notes, is therapeutic and/or purgative, displaying moral courage. Its personal narratives often portray unbalanced, afflicted, or alienated protagonists, using irony and understatement for detachment. The self is a poetic symbol around which is woven a personal mythology, written in ordinary speech and using open forms. There are no barriers between the reader and the poet, or barriers of subject matter. Personal failure, mental illness, and alienation are common themes in poems that are generally anti-establishment (Phillips, 1973).

The constituency of the group of poets who have become known as Confessional has also engendered much debate. Some include writers of a previous generation, such as Theodore Roethke, Delmore Schwartz, and Randall Jarrell, or those who were clearly tangential and went on to do different kinds of work, such as Maxine Kumin, Alan Dugan, and James Merrill. Still other poets are still labeled Confessional despite more direct associations with other schools and/or movements, such as Allen Ginsberg, Amiri Baraka, Carolyn Kizer, and Adrienne Rich. It is generally agreed, however, that the core of the movement exists within and among certain works from the late 1950s to the late 1960s.

In addition to Lowell's *Life Studies* these central works include his *Notebooks, 1967–1968* (1969), whose subject matter was revisited in *History* (1973), *For Lizzy and Harriet* (1973), and *The Dolphin* (1973). Also essential to any understanding of this movement are: W.D. Snodgrass' *Heart's Needle* (1959) and his small-press, limited edition *Remains* (1970), published under the pseudonym S.S. Gardons; Anne Sexton's *To Bedlam and Part Way Back* (1960), *All My Pretty Ones* (1962), and *Live or Die* (1966); John Berryman's *77 Dream Songs* (1964) and *Berryman's Sonnets* (1967); and Sylvia Plath's posthumous *Ariel* (1965), perhaps the most broadly popular and famous Confessional work. Certain prose pieces of—to one degree or another—fictionalized autobiography contributed to the scope and definition of Confessional poetry. These include the fragment "1 Revere Street," which appeared in Lowell's *Life Studies,* as well as novels such as Plath's *The Bell Jar* (1963) and Berryman's *Recovery* (1973).

A canon of Confessional poems would have to include Lowell's already classic "Skunk Hour," as well as "Memories of West Street and Lepke," "Waking in the Blue," and "Home After Three Months Away." "Skunk Hour," which did for postmodern poetry what "The Love Song of J. Alfred Prufrock" did for modern, contains the line "My mind's not right." It was a tepid enough admission by current standards but held shocking implications in its day, especially when written by Robert Lowell, the heir of High Modernism as bestowed by T.S. Eliot and already a winner of the Pulitzer Prize for *Lord Weary's Castle* (1946) when he was only 30. Also significant are Anne Sexton's "For John, Who Begs Me Not to Enquire Further," " The Double Image," "You, Doctor Martin," and "Her Kind," and a handful of Berryman's Dream Songs, perhaps numbers 1, 4, 13, 22, 29, and 77. Sylvia Plath's "Ariel," "Daddy," and "Lady Lazarus" have already achieved iconic status.

The entire 12-section sequence that makes up the title poem of *Heart's Needle* would more than suffice as perhaps the purest example of the Confessional genre. It recounts the poet's separation and divorce, his estrangement from his young daughter, his remarriage, and his second daughter's birth in a metrically elegant and subtly rhymed seasonal progression from winter to spring over the span of two and a half years. Interwoven with minor themes such as his own writer's block and the general paralysis of the Cold War era, the narrative tacks toward an epiphany more succinctly expressed in another famous poem included in the same volume, "April Inventory": "I have not learned how often I can win, can love, but choose to die."

Structuring his poem as a series of dramatic vignettes, Snodgrass employs imagery of deep resonance and universal implications. Musing on his impending separation from his daughter while they are planting in a spring garden, the poet writes:

> These mixed seeds are pressed
> With light loam in their steadfast rows.
> Child, we've done our best.
> Someone will have to weed and spread
> The young sprouts. Sprinkle them in the hour
> When shadow falls across their bed.
> You should try to look at them every day
> Because when they come to full flower I will be away.

Even when the poet and his daughter are together, the imagery underscores the fleeting nature of their good times, as section seven demonstrates:

> Here in the scuffled dust
> is our ground of play.
> I lift you on your swing and must
> shove you away,
> see you return again,
> drive you off again, then
>
> stand quiet till you come.
> You, though you climb
> higher, farther from me, longer,
> will fall back to me stronger.
> Bad penny, pendulum,
> you keep my constant time
>
> to bob in blue July
> where fat goldfinches fly
> over the glittering fecund
> reach of our growing lands.
> Once more now, this second,
> I hold you in my hands.

If it was Lowell who was first called a Confessional poet, it was also Lowell who publicly, if somewhat self-servingly, designated Snodgrass' "Heart's Needle" as the early paradigm of the genre.

There were intimate connections between the Confessional poets who lived and visited, studied and taught in and around Boston. All were white, all relatively affluent; Snodgrass, Sexton, and Plath were all students of Lowell at one time or another, although there is ample evidence that he learned as much from them as they did from him. All of *Heart's Needle* and much of *To Bedlam and Part Way Back* predate *Life Studies.* As Jeffrey Meyers (1987) has noted,

> They encouraged and criticized each other in interviews, letters, reviews, essays, eulogies; even rewrote, adapted and imitated each other's lines. They competed for lectures, jobs, grants, advances, loans, patrons and awards, for readers, recognition and praise, for success and security.

They shared other common ground as well: unhappy childhoods, weak or absent fathers, overbearing mothers. They counted among them more than their share of stormy marriages tossed by infidelity, alcoholism, addictions to prescription drugs, violence, serious illness, mental breakdowns, incarcerations, electroshock treatments, and suicide. Their turmoil became the stark subject of their poetry. Tales told boldly as biographical facts, regardless of accuracy, and spoken—literally, at public readings—without the shield or safety net of a dramatic persona became part of each poet's personal mythology.

Some would say that all poetry is autobiographical; even if not directly representative of experiences and details of the poet's life, it is informed in very essential ways by a vision crafted by those experiences and colored by those details. Perhaps the degree of explicit personal details distinguishes the Confessional from the merely autobiographical poet. The roots of the confession in literature extend along the Western tradition from Sappho, Catullus, Augustine, and Rousseau to Wordsworth, Coleridge, and Byron, and further to Rilke, Baudelaire, and Verlaine. At the very beginnings of poetry in the United States—Whitman and Dickinson—one might even find something particularly American, a Protestant form of individual confession with no middleman or second party involved.

Much has been made—by the participants themselves and others—of the mental health of the Confessional poets. All spent their later years in and out of analysis. For Lowell and Sexton, writing was part of the prescribed therapy. The fact that the process of psychoanalysis was similar to the process of poetry, at least their own poetry, was not lost on any of these writers. Lowell, Berryman, Sexton, Roethke, Plath, and Snodgrass wrote what they, their critics, and their readers agree is some of their best work during periods of mania or depression. Roethke seemed most comfortable writing during his many stays in the hospital; during the months of despair preceding her suicide, Plath wrote or rewrote almost all of the poems that made up *Ariel.* Anne Sexton admitted to the *Paris Review* in 1968:

> My doctors tell me that I understand something in a poem that I haven't integrated into my life. In fact I may be concealing it from myself while I was revealing it to my readers. Poetry, after all [all art] milks the unconscious. Which is why, I suppose, we are all told that confession is good for the soul.

This intricate relationship between art and madness extends from Dionysus, the origin of the idea that the artist is possessed of and by a "dangerous gift [which] place[s] the creative mind on a lonely height and threaten[s] to topple him into the abyss of insanity" (Meyers, 1987). Rimbaud called for a "self-destructive, deliberate derangement of all the senses that would enable the tormented, sacrificial, even insane artist" (from a letter dated 15 May 1871). Jean-Paul Sartre also believed that a writer's talent was closely connected to his capacity for self-ruin:

> In relation to Gauguin, Van Gogh and Rimbaud, I have a distinct inferiority complex because they managed to destroy themselves. . . . I am more and more convinced that, in order to achieve authenticity, something has to snap. (*War Diaries,* 1984)

Legend has it that Sexton, Plath, and George Starbuck used to have long "three martini lunches" at which they discussed their suicide attempts. As Sexton recalled, "We three were stimulated by it, as if death made each of us a little more real at the moment" (see *Anne Sexton: A Biography,* by Diane Wood Middlebrook, 1991).

In a similar fashion the idea that great artists must suffer ranges across the history of Western poetry. Lowell himself in a letter to Theodore Roethke three weeks before the latter's death put it directly: "It's this, to write we seem to have to go at it with such single-minded intensity that we are always on the point of drowning" (Meyers, 1987). Berryman took Miranda's lines from *The Tempest* as an epigram for his autobiographical novel *Recovery,* published one year after his suicide in 1972: "Oh I have suffered / With those that I saw suffer."

According to David Perkins in *A History of Modern Poetry: From the 1890's to the High Modernist Mode* (1976), central to any exploration of poetry is an examination of how its conventions reflect "premises about reality." Certainly there were, both culturally and more specifically in terms of literary history, many contemporary "premises about reality" that contributed to the rise of some of the particular conventions of Confessional poetry. Some critics see a "notable drift, at every level, away from the public affairs and towards an introspection, the cult of the personal" during this period in American history (Gray, 1990). Others claim that "much of this writing displays the narcissism, the therapeutic questing, and the doubt about the authenticity of all relations with others that runs through much of the wider culture" (Bradbury and Temperly, 1981).

This was, after all, what Lowell labeled the "tranquilized fifties" and Snodgrass called the "torments of demented summer," dominated, according to John Berryman, by "a squeamish comfy ruin-prone proud national mind." The post–World War II era was an age of widespread abundance and heightened materialism, but also engendered a mass feeling of social dislocation, alienation, and neurosis. A cultural milieu of conformity prevailed. Confessional poetry was just one expression of anti-establishment sentiment toward this climate of repression.

Within the closer confines of literary history in the 1950s, Confessional poetry emerged in direct opposition to the poetic conventions created by the previous generation of Modernists and upheld by the New Critics. If the common wisdom held that poetry should be removed, formal, difficult, and allusive, then this new poetry would be direct, informal, accessible, and unguarded. Urged on by, or at least contemporaneous with, the candor of the Beat movement and its emphasis on the essential worth of individual, immediate, and everyday experience, the Confessional poets were caught up in the trend toward public readings. Whereas the 1950s and the New Critics

> had emphasized the created and crafted object, the iconic texts, the [1960s] insisted on spontaneous and open acts of creation and performance, emphasizing the role of chance, randomness, and pure confession. Dispensing with ideas of permanence, they emphasized the magic moment of impermanence, the event rather than the assessment. (Bradbury and Temperly, 1981)

Critics, however, were not necessarily pleased with this shift toward the personal and spontaneous, neither as it was happening then nor in later years. Representative of their central complaints is the charge that "Individual 'madness' under scrutiny finally becomes neither heroic nor pathetic, but simply clinical" (Molesworth, 1979). This viewpoint holds that

> The poetry of moral enervation, whose master spokesman was J. Alfred Prufrock, has become, successively, a poetry of plangent egoism and a poetry of psychological vacuity. Pried asunder from both an audience and a social value, many contemporary American poets have become caretakers of their own obsessions, tending a ground both desiccated by defensive irony and overgrown with psychologized imagery, but seldom visited by outsiders.

Ironically, the trends that allowed Confessional poetry to flourish in the early and mid-1960s eventually led to its decline when the wide-ranging developments in America's cultural modes rather suddenly overtook it. What had seemed to Snodgrass and Sexton in the late 1950s as the most taboo subjects became the topic of widespread and ordinary discourse. In comparison to the excesses of the Beat poets, the lives of the Confessional poets paled to near respectability. The shock of their revelations was simply subsumed by the sexual revolution, drug experimentation, and the counterculture of a new generation.

Any summary evaluation of Confessional poetry must be undertaken within the broadest possible context, however. The degree to which this body of work—in particular the work of Sexton and Plath—was instrumental in stimulating the rise of poetry written by and about women in the 1970s, for example, has not yet been established. Confessional poetry may in fact be a part of a larger shift in American culture and poetry in the decades after World War II, a shift that encompasses the Beats as well as the explosion of new writing about gender, ethnicity, and sexual orientation. This era stands as one of the most complex and vital periods of American poetry.

BRUCE TAYLOR

**Further Reading**

Bradbury, Malcolm, and Howard Temperly, editors, *Introduction to American Studies,* London and New York: Longman, 1981; 3rd edition, 1998

Davison, Peter, *The Fading Smile: Poets in Boston, 1955–1960, from Robert Frost to Robert Lowell to Sylvia Plath,* New York: Knopf, 1994

Gray, Richard, editor, *American Poetry of the Twentieth Century,* London and New York: Cambridge University Press, 1990

Meyers, Jeffrey, *Manic Power: Robert Lowell and His Circle,* New York and London: Macmillan, 1987

Middlebrook, Diane Wood, "What Was Confessional Poetry?" in *The Columbia History of American Poetry,* edited by Jay Parini, New York: Columbia University Press, 1993

Mills, Ralph J., *Cry of the Human: Essays on Contemporary American Poetry,* Urbana: University of Illinois Press, 1975

Molesworth, Charles, *The Fierce Embrace: A Study of Contemporary American Poetry,* Columbia: University of Missouri Press, 1979

Perkins, David, *A History of Modern Poetry,* volume 1: *From the 1890's to the High Modernist Mode,* Cambridge, Massachusetts: Belknap Press, 1976

Phillips, Robert S., *The Confessional Poets,* Carbondale: Southern Illinois University Press, 1973

# Clark Coolidge 1939–

"I am the Horn without Stop," Clark Coolidge writes in the poem "Names of the Lessons." Unending improvisatory invention is indeed the hallmark of Coolidge's poetry. From his first published book in 1966, he has focused on what he terms "the Tonality of Language," the flow "from meaning to meaning, and that sideslippage between meanings." As poet Ron Silliman (1978) suggests, "What Clark Coolidge is about, literally, is the reinvention of language."

Coolidge's work draws on an unusual array of influences. In Samuel Beckett, Coolidge finds an exemplary dedication to the work of writing; Coolidge has often cited Beckett's dictum "To find a form that accommodates the mess, that is the task of the artist now." The language investigations of Gertrude Stein and Louis Zukofsky helped shape Coolidge's interest in the materiality of language, and John Ashbery's collaging of found texts in *The Tennis Court Oath* (1962) gave Coolidge early on a sense of the formal possibilities of discontinuity and fragmented syntax in poetry. Jack Kerouac is the writer of greatest importance to Coolidge's work: Coolidge has attested that the improvisatory freedom of what Kerouac called "spontaneous bop prosody" made him feel that he too could be a writer. Jazz itself, particularly bop, is a pervasive influence in Coolidge's work (he is himself a drummer): the improvising soloist surging forward in time, riding on a pulse and building momentum, becomes for Coolidge a model for the poet in the act of composition.

Coolidge's work began with what he later described as "an interest in single words to generate a larger structure." In early works, such as *Flag Flutter and U.S. Electric* (1966), *Ing* (1968), and *Space* (1970), Coolidge can be seen "transforming / the common language into an irreducible variation," generating a language material that is uniquely his own ("From Notebooks (1976–1982)," 1983). The early poetry is preoccupied with arrangement (a favorite Coolidge word), offering language constructs that foreground relations of sound and meaning among words and word fragments (e.g., "bunkum," "mica," "mote," "cian," and "tion") with little regard for conventional possibilities of syntax. Coolidge's commentary on the poem "ounce code orange" (from *Space*) in his talk "Arrangement" gives a sense of the generative play of meaning in the early poetry.

After *Space*, Coolidge took up more procedural possibilities. *Suite V* (1973) uses the page as a field for a pair of four-letter words ending in "s," inviting the reader to ponder relations between words in white space. *The Maintains* (1974) is a noun-laden work (the title itself transforms either the article "the" or the verb "maintains" into a noun) drawing on the language of dictionary definitions and moving toward a rudimentary syntax in its final pages. *Polaroid* (1975) explores other parts of speech—adjectives, adverbs, prepositions, and pronouns: "Of what can it such," the poem begins, inquiring as to the materials that make a poem possible. *Quartz Hearts* (1978) marks a shift in interest to the sentence as a unit of composition. The language investigations of these works deeply influenced the development of Language poetry, although Coolidge does not call himself a "Language poet" and professes a lack of interest in the theoretical discourse associated with Language poetry.

Coolidge's next book, *Own Face* (1978), has come to be recognized as a breakthrough work, marking a shift to a newly lyrical and personal poetry, with moments of humor, mystery, and oblique beauty. While the poems resist explication and paraphrase, they are often grounded in recognizable contexts of phenomena and circumstance—listening to music ("Mozart on a Sunday"), glancing out a window ("How I Open"), or looking at old photographs ("Album—A Runthru"). However, Coolidge's run through a photograph album makes for something quite different from first-person confessionalism: "Here the shadow has more flavor than my / trains, elbow on livingroom floor, bangs that / curl, opera broadcast, The Surreptitious Adventures of / Nightstick." *Solution Passage: Poems, 1978–1981* (1986) and *Sound as Thought: Poems, 1982–1984* (1990) offer further explorations of the lyric, with a number of sonnets that reflect the influence of Ted Berrigan and Bernadette Mayer.

In the 1980s, Coolidge began to publish works in prose, offshoots of a writing project called the "prosoid" work, a still-unpublished work in prose once projected to reach 1,000 pages. *American Ones (Noise and Presentiments)* (1981) and "Weathers" (1986) are among the results. Most notable among Coolidge's prose works is *Mine: The One That Enters the Stories* (1982), which remains, with *Own Face,* the best introduction to his work. "I live in composition," Coolidge writes in *Mine,* a work that foregrounds the activity of writing and returns again and again to what Coolidge calls in an interview "the Beckett image of the man in the room with nothing but a pen and paper and usually one window." In the spirit of Beckett's *The Unnamable,* the poet's task in *Mine* is to continue, to go on: "To tell the tale, to wax unrepentant, to overlook the middle for all its ends, to form all cast out on the sea a lining, to wait until the glance all sufficiently watches." Mining consciousness and language, Coolidge (an accomplished caver) undertakes what poet Michael Palmer (1983) has characterized as "a continual process of descent and resurfacing, fraught with immediate and necessary risks."

In the late 1980s and 1990s, Coolidge remained extraordinarily prolific. Four works from these years suggest some of his abiding concerns. *The Crystal Text* (1986) is a book-length meditation that starts from a quartz crystal on the poet's desk, as Coolidge attempts to find a language in the transparent yet resistant object: "I want to hear the one thing speak that / cannot speak." *The Book of During* (1991), known as Coolidge's "sex book," considers its subject in terms at once abstract and starkly erotic, "juicings down on any possible sphere." The poems of *The Rova Improvisations* (1994) form what Coolidge calls "two parallel surges of improvisation," the first written while he listened to recordings of the Rova Saxophone Quartet and the second while he read through the first. Nowhere is Coolidge's commitment to a jazz aesthetic more clearly revealed. In *Keys to the Caverns* (1995), Coolidge returns to the subterranean territory of *Mine:* "These are the only dark corners illuminated by magnesium fire to be opened to the public. Make your bent leaf room and the rest ash of it." Coolidge remains dedicated to a wholly original aesthetic of exploration and improvisation.

MICHAEL LEDDY

**Biography**

Born in Providence, Rhode Island, 26 February 1939. Attended Brown University, Providence, 1956–58; editor, *Joglars* magazine, Providence, 1964–66; since 1977 Adjunct Faculty,

Poetics Department, Naropa Institute, Jack Kerouac School for Disembodied Poetics; Writer-in-Residence, American Academy in Rome, 1984–85. Received National Endowment for the Arts grant, 1966; New York Poets Foundation Award, 1968. Living in Petaluma, California.

**Poetry**
*Flag Flutter and U.S. Electric,* 1966
*Clark Coolidge,* 1967
*Ing,* 1968
*Space,* 1970
*Moroccan Variations,* 1971
*The So,* 1971
*Suite V,* 1973
*The Maintains,* 1974
*Polaroid,* 1975
*Own Face,* 1978
*Quartz Hearts,* 1978
*Smithsonian Depositions, and Subject to a Film,* 1980
*American Ones (Noise and Presentiments),* 1981
*A Geology,* 1981
*Mine: The One That Enters the Stories,* 1982
*Research,* 1982
*The Crystal Text,* 1986
*Solution Passage: Poems, 1978–1981,* 1986
*Melencolia,* 1987
*At Egypt,* 1988
*Mesh,* 1988
*The Symphony,* 1989
*Sound as Thought: Poems, 1982–1984,* 1990
*Supernatural Overtones,* with Ron Padgett, 1990
*Baffling Means: Writings/Drawings,* with Philip Guston, 1991
*The Book of During,* 1991
*Odes of Roba,* 1991
*Lowell Connector: Lines and Shots from Kerouac's Town,* with Michael Gizzi and John Yau, photographs by Bill Barrette and Celia Coolidge, 1993
*On the Pumice of Morons: The Unaugural Poem,* with Larry Fagin, 1993
*Registers: (People in All),* 1994
*The Rova Improvisations,* 1994
*Keys to the Caverns,* 1995
*For Kurt Cobain,* 1995
*The Names,* 1997
*Alien Tatters,* 2000
*Bomb,* with collages by Keith Waldrop, 2000
*On the Nameways: Volume One,* 2000

**Other Writings:** play (*To Obtain the Value of the Cake Measure from Zero,* with Tom Veitch, 1970), prose (*Now It's Jazz: Writings on Kerouac and The Sounds,* 1999).

**Further Reading**

Bernstein, Charles, "Maintaining Space: Clark Coolidge's Early Works," in *Content's Dream: Essays, 1975–1984,* Los Angeles: Sun and Moon Press, 1986
Campbell, Bruce, "The Place between the Name and the Thing," *Temblor* 7 (1988)
Grenier, Robert, "Notes on Coolidge, Objectives, Zukofsky, Romanticism, and &," in *In the American Tree,* edited by Ron Silliman, Orono, Maine: National Poetry Foundation, 1986
Mack, Anne, and Jay Rome, "Truth in the Body of Falsehood," *Parnassus* 15, no. 1 (1989)
Nielsen, Aldon L., "Clark Coolidge and a Jazz Aesthetic," *Pacific Coast Philology* 28, no. 1 (1993)
Palmer, Michael, Review of *Mine: The One That Enters the Stories, Sulfur* 8 (1983)
Rasula, Jed, Review of *Solution Passage: Poems, 1978–1981, Sulfur* 17 (1986)
*Stations* 5 (1978) (special issue edited by Ron Silliman entitled "A Symposium on Clark Coolidge")
Watten, Barrett, "Total Syntax: The Work in the World," in *Total Syntax,* Carbondale: Southern Illinois University Press, 1985
Ziarek, Krzysztof, "Word for Sign: Poetic Language in Coolidge's *The Crystal Text," Sagetrieb* 10, nos. 1–2 (1991)


---

## Gregory Corso 1930–2001

Gregory Corso is perhaps the least-known major poet of the Beat movement, despite being one of its original founders. Although he lacks a famous seminal work such as Ginsberg's *Howl* or Kerouac's *On the Road,* Corso exhibited perhaps the widest range of any of the original Beats, excelling in both traditional and experimental form. He was comfortable using conventional stanza and verse formations but also participated in some of the more eccentric experiments of the Beats, including William S. Burroughs' "cut up," a practice in which an established poem (by Rimbaud, for instance) would be cut up and reconfigured as a new poem, line by line.

Corso's first work, *The Vestal Lady on Brattle, and Other Poems* (1955), was published privately and failed to garner much recognition. Three years later City Lights published *Gasoline.* This volume gained him more recognition, partially because Ginsberg, now infamous for the "obscenity" of *Howl,* wrote the introduction. In the epigraph to *Gasoline* Corso acknowledged the source of his creativity as "from a dark river within." This typified his new approach to poetry, one that indicated his movement away from more classical forms toward the experimental work of Ginsberg and Burroughs. *Gasoline* caught the attention of several literary figures, including William Carlos Williams and Randall

Jarrell, and established Corso as one of the central figures in the burgeoning Beat movement. *Gasoline* continued in the vein of *Vestal Lady,* examining the beauty inherent in death and destruction in poems such as "Don't Shoot the Warthog":

> The child trembled, fell,
> and staggered up again,
> *I screamed his name!*
> And a fury of mothers and fathers
> sank their teeth into his brain.
> . . . .
> *I screamed the name!* and they came
> and gnawed the child's bones.
> *I screamed the name:* *Beauty*
> *Beauty* *Beauty* *Beauty*

Beauty, in the form of a child, is sacrificed in this poem, revealing Corso's fascination with the aesthetics of death and destruction, in which the death of beauty causes a new vision of beauty to emerge.

Due to a disagreement with Lawrence Ferlinghetti at City Lights, Corso signed on with New Directions, which would publish his work for the next 20 years. *The Happy Birthday of Death* (1960) is perhaps Corso's most critically acclaimed work, containing some of his most well-known poems: "Bomb," "Power," and "Marriage." This volume continued to explore death but stylistically was quite superior to Corso's first two collections. Written in the shape of a mushroom cloud, "Bomb" commemorates the August 1945 bombing of Hiroshima. This poem is typical of the Beat paranoia concerning the nuclear age and their conviction that the bomb marked the end of one historical epoch and the beginning of another:

> Budger of history Brake of time you Bomb
> Toy of universe Grandest of all snatched-sky I
> cannot hate you
> . . . .
> They'd rather die by anything but you Death's finger is
> free-lance
> Not up to man whether you boom or not Death has
> long since distributed its
> categorical blue I sing thee Bomb Death's
> extravagance Death's jubilee

Corso's early ambivalence toward death as creator of both horror and beauty reached its zenith in "Bomb." In other passages of the poem Corso likens the bomb to music, to the Olympic games, and to the Second Coming of Christ.

"Power," another poem in this collection, is undoubtedly Corso's most controversial work. Accused by many (including Ferlinghetti) of celebrating fascism, "Power" sought to examine the beauty inherent in cruelty:

> Know my Power
> I resemble fifty miles of Power
> I cut my fingernails with a red Power
> In buses I stand on huge volumes of Spanish Power
> . . . .
> We are ready to fight with howitzers! this is Love
> This has never been my Love
> Thank God my Power

Although this poem does acknowledge the aesthetics of cruelty, it is far from a celebration of fascism: the "power" Corso refers to is not that of brutality, but rather of the fertile imagination and its ability to transform.

*The Happy Birthday of Death* also contained some humorous poems, such as "Marriage." Corso's partial turn toward the comic was indicative of his general shift in focus from death to creation. Corso's next collection of poetry, *Long Live Man* (1962), further explored his new preoccupation with life and the creative power of the poet to make spiritual transformations. This new optimism perhaps mirrored the similar feelings of political vitality that were sweeping the nation.

This optimism did not last, however. *Elegiac Feelings American* (1970) is a much more somber collection, mirroring the vastly changed political climate in the nine years since *Long Live Man.* Kerouac's premature death in 1969 came as a blow to the Beats, and Corso (along with Ginsberg) viewed it as emblematic of the death of 1960s optimism and social progress. "Elegiac Feelings American," the centerpiece of the collection, is dedicated to the memory of Jack Kerouac:

> How inseparable you and the America you saw yet was
> never there to see; you and America, like the tree and the
> ground, are one the same; yet how like a palm tree in the
> state of Oregon . . . dead ere it blossomed, like a snow
> polar loping the Miami—

Most of the poems in this volume address the new America promised in the early 1960s yet never delivered. Some optimism is retained through the power of creative imagination to recognize beauty, however. This bittersweet optimism is also present in Corso's next volume of poetry, *Herald of the Autochthonic Spirit* (1981). *Herald* deals with the inevitable march of age, although Corso suggests that imagination is powerful enough to transcend this truth and recognize the beauty inherent in life. *Mindfield,* published by Thunder's Mouth in 1989, contains mostly previously published poems. Corso has also published several plays, including *This Hung-Up Age* (1955) and *Happy Death* (1965), and a novel, *The American Express* (1961).

Andrew Howe

*See also* Beat Poetry

**Biography**

Born in New York City, 26 March 1930. Manual laborer, 1950–51; reporter, Los Angeles *Examiner,* 1951–52; merchant seaman, 1952–53; attended Harvard University, Cambridge, Massachusetts, 1954–55; Faculty, Department of English, State University of New York, Buffalo, 1965–70. Died in New York City, 17 January 2001.

**Poetry**

*The Vestal Lady on Brattle, and Other Poems,* 1955
*Gasoline,* 1958

*Bomb,* 1958
*A Pulp Magazine for the Dead Generation* (with Henk Marsman), 1959
*The Happy Birthday of Death,* 1960
*Minutes to Go* (with others), 1960
*Selected Poems,* 1962
*Long Live Man,* 1962
*The Mutation of the Spirit: A Shuffle Poem,* 1964
*There Is Yet Time to Run through Life and Expiate All That's Been Sadly Done,* 1965
*The Geometric Poem: A Long Experimental Poem, Composite of Many Lines and Angles Selective,* 1966
*10 Times a Poem,* 1967
*Penguin Modern Poets 5* (with poems by Corso, Lawrence Ferlinghetti, and Allen Ginsberg), 1968
*Elegiac Feelings American,* 1970
*Egyptian Cross,* 1971
*Ankh,* 1971
*(Poems),* 1971
*The Night Last Night Was at Its Nightest,* 1972
*Earth Egg,* 1974
*Herald of the Autochthonic Spirit,* 1981
*Writings from Unmuzzled Ox Magazine,* 1981
*Four Poems,* 1981
*Wings, Wands, Windows,* 1982
*Hitting the Big 5–0,* 1983
*Mindfield: New and Selected Poems,* 1989
*Gregorian Rant,* 1993
*Poems, Interviews, Photographs,* edited by Ron Whitehead and Kent Fielding, 1994

**Other Writings:** plays (*This Hung-Up Age,* 1955; *Happy Death,* 1965), novel (*The American Express,* 1961), parodies; edited poetry collection (*Junge Amerikanische Lyrik* [with Walter Höllerer], 1961).

**Further Reading**

Bartlett, Lee, editor, *The Beats: Essays in Criticism,* Jefferson, North Carolina: McFarland, 1981
Chassman, Neil A., editor, *Poets of the Cities: New York and San Francisco, 1950–1965,* New York: Dutton, 1974
Cook, Bruce, *The Beat Generation,* New York: Scribner, 1971
Gaiser, Carolyn, "Gregory Corso: A Poet, the Beat Way," in *A Casebook on the Beat,* edited by Thomas Parkinson, New York: Cromwell, 1961
Grunes, Dennis, "The Mythifying Memory: Corso's 'Elegiac Feelings American,'" *Contemporary Poetry: A Journal of Criticism* 2, no. 3 (1977)
Harney, Steve, "Ethnos and the Beat Poets," *Journal of American Studies* 25 (December 1991)
Howard, Richard, "Gregory Corso: 'Surely There'll Be Another Table,'" in *Alone with America: Essays on the Art of Poetry in the United States Since 1950,* edited by Howard, enlarged edition, New York: Atheneum, 1980
Skau, Michael, *"A Clown in a Grave": Complexities and Tensions in the Works of Gregory Corso,* Carbondale: Southern Illinois University Press, 1999
Tytell, John, *Naked Angels: The Lives and Literature of the Beat Generation,* New York: McGraw-Hill, 1976
Wilson, Robert A., *A Bibliography of Works by Gregory Corso, 1954–1965,* New York: Phoenix, 1966

---

# Jayne Cortez 1936–

Jayne Cortez has been writing, publishing, recording, and performing her poetry for more than 30 years. She was an influential member of the Black Arts movement of the 1960s and 1970s, and her poetry is revolutionary in content and often surreal in form. Among the many themes Cortez addresses in her poetry are racism, sex and sexism, alienated labor, environmental politics, and the threat of nuclear destruction. Her poems champion people's resistance to oppression and celebrate the redemptive power of poetry and music, particularly jazz.

Cortez co-founded the Watts Repertory Theater Company in Los Angeles, and her first book, *Pisstained Stairs and the Monkey Man's Wares* (1969), is dedicated to the company and written for its members to perform. Its long, free-verse poems contain praise songs to blues and jazz musicians Huddie "Leadbelly" Ledbetter, Ornette Coleman, Dinah Washington, Theodore "Fats" Navarro, Clifford Brown, Billie Holiday, and John Coltrane. The best known of these poems, "How Long Has Trane Been Gone," with its titular reference to James Baldwin's novel *Tell Me How Long the Train's Been Gone* (1968), is among the best of the many elegies written by Black Arts poets to celebrate the life of jazz musician and cultural icon John Coltrane. Another poem in this volume that has captured the attention of critics, if only for the controversy it has aroused, is "Race." Violently homophobic, the poem depicts gay black men as collaborating with white males in the oppression of blacks and chillingly asserts that "we must slaughter these / our [gay] sons to bring a revolution on." Although Cortez has said that she has had "second thoughts" about this early poem, she has never publicly apologized for it.

In her second book, *Festivals and Funerals* (1971), Cortez's use of surreal—or what critic D.H. Melhem refers to as "supersurreal"—images comes into full flower. Cortez elaborates on the text's unifying metaphor, comparing the florid profusion of imagery in her poems to a festival: "I use dreams, the subconscious, and the real objects, and I open up the body and use organs, and I sink them into words, and I ritualize them and fuse them into events. I guess the poetry is like a festival" (Melhem, 1990).

The text's title poem is a lament for fallen heroes Patrice Lumumba and Malcolm X. With the incantatory power of a chant or war cry, it uses incremental repetition and parallel structures to increase its impact on the reader. "I'm a Worker," based on

Cortez's firsthand experience working in a shirt factory in Los Angeles, deals with exploitation, alienated labor, and the emergent class consciousness of a garment industry employee. One of the earliest Black Arts poems to address working-class issues, "I'm a Worker" is significant for its incorporation of Marxist thematics several years before poet Amiri Baraka's *Hard Facts* (1975). "To the Artist Who Just Happens To Be Black" revisits the ground covered by Langston Hughes' famous essay "The Negro Artist and the Racial Mountain" and offers the same negative assessment of black artists who think that their work should be free of racial content.

*Coagulations* (1984) collects poems from three earlier books: *Scarifications* (1973), *Mouth on Paper* (1977), and *Firespitter* (1982). In "I Am New York City," Cortez personifies the city, capturing its capacity for cruelty and indifference through monstrous, sometimes grotesque imagery. "For the Poets" reads like the directions of a sorcerer to her apprentice, calling out the names of the items she needs to cast the spell that is the poem itself. Each line ends with the sounds "ah," "a," "oh," or "uh-hun," reminding one of the emphatic exclamations African-American preachers use to punctuate their sermons. "For the Brave Young Students in Soweto" recalls the resistance and martyrdom of the students who joined in protest against the racist educational policy of the South African government during the Soweto uprising of 1976. "If the Drum Is a Woman" draws on the nationalist image of the ideal black woman (e.g., "African queen," "mother of the black nation") and uses it as the basis for an incisive critique of physical and sexual abuse. "Rape" addresses similar issues, but more acerbically. Comparing the rape of a woman to a declaration of war, the poem applauds the violent retribution rape victims Inez Garcia and Joan Little visited on their attackers. The repeated inquiry "what was [she] supposed to do[?]" points to the justness of their responses as well as their limited options for redress.

*Poetic Magnetic* (1991) contains transcribed poems from two previous recordings: *Maintain Control* (1986) and *Everywhere Drums* (1990). In the foreword, Cortez comments on the unique role that music and technology have come to play in her poetic performances: "By using music and technology I'm trying to extend the poet's role, which means, the poet in this situation becomes the band, the pen, paper, books, research, instruments, words and all the possibilities of the technology." Yet, as many of the poems in this volume indicate, Cortez is no technophile. "Stockpiling," for instance, depicts an apocalyptic vision of environmental devastation and then inquires of the reader, "And even if you think you have a shelter / that can survive this stockpiling / of communal graves / tell me / Where are you going[?]" "Push Back the Catastrophes" similarly condemns the use of technology to create weapons of death and destruction. Instead of this self-destructive use of technology, Cortez suggests that we focus on creating the conditions that will allow us to "breathe clean air / to drink pure water to plant new crops. . . ."

To paraphrase the opening lines of the poem "Find Your Own Voice," from Cortez's most recent book, *Somewhere in Advance of Nowhere* (1996), one might argue that very early in her career Cortez had found her own voice and used it, and that with each new book, recording, live performance, and film she continues to use her own voice and find it. Cortez's consistent concern with timely social issues, her profound moral vision, and her unparalleled ability to move audiences through a unique combination of poetry and music guarantee her an important place in the history of 20th-century American poetry.

DOUGLAS TAYLOR

**Biography**

Born in Ft. Huachuca, Arizona, 10 May 1936. Artistic director, Watts Repertory Theater Company, Watts, California, 1964–70; writer-in-residence, Livingston College of Rutgers University, New Brunswick, New Jersey, 1977–83. Received Creative Artists Program Service Poetry Award, New York State Council of the Arts, 1973, 1981; National Endowment for the Arts fellowship, 1979–80; Before Columbus Foundation American Book Award, 1980; New York Foundation for the Arts Award, 1987. Living in New York City.

**Poetry**

*Pisstained Stairs and the Monkey Man's Wares,* 1969
*Festivals and Funerals,* 1971
*Scarifications,* 1973
*Mouth on Paper,* 1977
*Firespitter,* 1982
*Coagulations: New and Selected Poems,* 1984
*Poetic Magnetic,* 1991
*Somewhere in Advance of Nowhere,* 1996

**Other Writings:** screenplays (*War on War,* 1982).

**Further Reading**

Brown, Kimberly N., "Of Poststructuralist Fallout, Scarification, and Blood Poems: The Revolutionary Ideology Behind the Poetry of Jayne Cortez," in *Other Sisterhoods: Literary Theory and U.S. Women of Color,* edited by Sandra Kumamoto Stanley, Urbana: University of Illinois Press, 1998
Christian, Barbara T., "There It Is: The Poetry of Jayne Cortez," *Callaloo* 9 (1986)
Lee, Don L., "Toward a Definition: Black Poetry of the Sixties," in *The Black Aesthetic,* edited by Addison Gayle, Jr., Garden City, New York: Doubleday, 1971
Melhem, D.H., *Heroism in the New Black Poetry,* Lexington: University Press of Kentucky, 1990
Redmond, Eugene B., *Drumvoices: The Mission of Afro-American Poetry: A Critical History,* Garden City, New York: Anchor Press, 1976

# Hart Crane 1899–1932

Although Hart Crane was a child of the Midwest, it never moved him nor found a significant place in his mature poetry. For Crane was above all a poet of the city, and the city was New York, never captured as well as by Crane. Crane's parents had an unhappy marriage with separations, final divorces, and remarriages, which enabled him to see himself as a divided young man torn between maternal and paternal (he adopted his mother's maiden name for his first name), East and West, rural and urban, ecstasy and contemplation. Crane's homosexuality allowed him to see himself as a tormented Modernist or Symbolist, even as he was increasingly celebrating his passionate encounters in what Whitman had called the "city of orgies."

Crane was only 16 when he published his first poems. They testify to his remarkable ability to absorb the lessons of the many poets he was reading voraciously while living, as he felt, in exile in Ohio. Crane was imitating and mocking Cummings and translating Laforgue. His poem "C 33" was a tribute to Oscar Wilde, representing the forgotten artist suffering for his art as well as the homosexual outsider punished for his desires. These early poems illustrate well the tensions in Crane's work: sentimentality interwoven with Modernist irony. This divided consciousness would be the source of many contradictions, in particular of "The Bridge," both in Crane's structures and in critical responses. In poetic terms Crane was trying to wed Whitman to Eliot, no easy task, especially during the 1920s, when a dry, hard aesthetic dominated, leaving no place for Crane's sailor-lovers.

Although in some ways Crane never resolved these contradictions, and indeed made his poetry out of their tensions, *White Buildings* (1926) stakes out Crane's position as the foremost Modernist of his time. The political and social themes of "The Bridge," on which he had begun working at the same time, were largely absent in his first volume. There were some exceptions, such as "Black Tambourine," which stemmed from Crane's interest in the Harlem Renaissance, and "Chaplinesque," a tribute to the movies. Chaplin is a perfect figure for Crane, allowing the poet to celebrate the comedy of Chaplin along with the need for affection. Crane's "moon in lonely alleys" is borrowed from the Symbolists. Evoking his self-portrait, and punning on his name, Crane asks, "What blame to us if the heart live on?"

Crane's New York is captured in "Possessions," a poem of largely unfulfilled desire, seen as a "fixed stone of lust." The poem seeks to go beyond physical desire to a purer world of the ideal, a heart of fire. Crane's dense language recalls his enthusiasm for the Metaphysical poets, particularly Donne, and his ability to make a drama of sexual cruising out of these figures of desire. Although rarely a mythical poet like Eliot or Yeats, Crane did draw on an American mythology—"The Bridge" has obvious links to Copland's "Appalachian Spring"—and made one major attempt to relocate classical and Renaissance mythology in the city. "For the Marriage of Faustus and Helen" takes the attempt to cross space and time, to bridge the gap between history and the modern, masculine and feminine, as one of its structural themes.

"Faustus and Helen" is noticeably a response to Eliot, one that both borrows and rewrites, and is in some ways a draft of "The Bridge." The speaker, working perhaps as Crane had in advertising, seeks escape from "stenographic smiles and stock quotations." Leaving the day behind, he seeks a world of night. Helen is present, as in Marlowe, as a figure of beauty, not quite extinguished by the world of advertising. Crane's praise of Helen locates him as a searcher after beauty, which can be located anywhere. In response to Eliot's nostalgia for an earlier, better age, Crane transforms Harlem into a source of physical pleasure "poised in traffic." To Crane love remains love, even in forms conventionally thought of as degraded. The second section of the poem is set in Harlem, where pleasure, like so much desire in Crane, includes a "guilty song." The poem concludes with scenes of World War destruction and links the military to the sexual: "the mounted, yielding cities of the air."

More successful than "Faustus," Crane's "Voyages" remains, along with some of Auden's best work, one of the great love poems of the 20th century. The six-part poem that concludes the volume celebrates Crane's love for Emil Opffer. Opffer's many sea journeys made him an elusive object of desire; in the poem Crane seeks consolation for what he recognizes to be the inevitability of loss. The first of the "Voyages," written before the larger structure, offers a number of warnings about a transgressive love; "there is a line / You must not cross nor ever trust beyond it." The center of the poem, the end of part 3, is the moment of sexual consummation, seen spiritually (as "reliquary hands") and physically ("admitted through black swollen gates"). The two lovers are finally destroyed by time and distance, a "tidal wedge." In the end, Crane suggests, it is not physical love that survives but rather the expression of the love in language. The "unbetrayable reply" is found in the "imaged Word," the timeless place of art.

Crane's lasting reputation seems certain to depend primarily on his American epic, "The Bridge," which drew on American materials to propose hope in the place of despair in response to Eliot. In this Crane is the poetic antecedent of composers such as Copland or Thomson. Crane had relatively little interest in Europe, at least by the standard of other Americans in Paris such as Gertrude Stein or Marsden Hartley. Although Crane could draw upon the example of the *Iliad* for the "Cape Hatteras" section, he was more importantly drawing on Rip Van Winkle, Emily Dickinson, and Isadora Duncan. If Eliot's poem ends alongside the Thames, piecing together the fragments, Crane's speaker finds himself crossing the Brooklyn Bridge, toward an ecstatic passion that echoes Plato's *Symposium*.

The poem opens with an ode to Brooklyn Bridge, which Crane took as a modern triumph of human dream and technology. Although the poet has had a glimpse in the seagull's flight of the "Liberty" that is symbolized by the statue in the harbor, he must forsake this visionary realm for a mundane world with "some page of figures to be filed away." The bridge's engineering feat is a sign of the human capacity for transcendence, a modern miracle of vision. The crossing of the bridge, recalling Whitman, also recalls Columbus' journey to the New World. All of these crossings are signs of the triumph of the imagination as well as gestures toward communication and desire.

Columbus speaks in the second section, and realizes that he has succeeded in his mission: "I thought of Genoa; and this truth, now proved / That made me exile in her streets." At the same time Columbus' journey brings a prophetic warning: "Rush down the plenitude, and you shall see / Isaiah counting famine on this lee!" The American dream contains within itself the danger of waste and greed; from the beginning one wonders if the explorers and settlers had come for God or for gold.

The long second part of the poem is devoted to the native past, portrayed through the land itself. The speaker imaginatively crosses the continent, thereby completing the mission of Columbus, but now learning the ways of nature rather than imposing a new order. Although the America of the 1920s was devoted to commerce and speed, one can interrupt the transcontinental journey to explore the "other" America, the hobos and blacks, left behind by a myth of progress. The core of the poem is the meeting of the east-west and north-south axes, and the triumphal vision of the orgasmic meeting of the river and the sea. The destruction of the native peoples, now mere "dead echoes," leads the speaker toward a symbolic act of union with the past. He joins in a ritual erotic dance with Maquokeeta, a dance that can at least in the imagination bring back "the tribal morn." The union of the speaker and the native chief allows the speaker to go beyond the world of order into an ecstatic world that joins time and space.

While the native provides one form of passage to the past, there is another vision that goes down instead of up. Crane mirrors the crossing of the Brooklyn Bridge with a subway tunnel that finds paradise by going through hell, not above it. Here the guiding spirit is Poe and his visions of destruction and madness from the darkest side of American life, the insistent crude sexuality, the absence of love. Crane sees no way to the ideal except through the real; this is the crucial nature of his modified idealism. The ideal can only be reached through suffering. Accomplishing his journey, the speaker finds an "intrinsic Myth," one that comes out of the earth and experience rather than from a heavenly truth. Crane's chthonic vision is his answer to the melancholy and loss of *The Waste Land.*

"The Bridge" took many years to complete, and met with a mixed response, many Modernist readers finding Crane's reliance on Whitman offensive and aesthetically inconsistent. Crane himself seemed unable to go forward from his great work. He was also tormented by the inability of many of his friends to accept his homosexuality. His last project was for another long poem, this one on the encounter of native peoples and European settlers. It was a difficult project, one that would presumably have required more Spanish than Crane could muster. Although he got a Guggenheim grant to Mexico, he spent most of his time drinking heavily and trying to prove his heterosexual competence. While returning by boat to the States, Crane was pushed, or he jumped, overboard and drowned.

ROBERT K. MARTIN

**Biography**

Born in Garrettsville, Ohio, 21 July 1899. Worked in munitions plant, Cleveland, Ohio, 1918; reporter, Cleveland *Plain Dealer,* 1918–19; advertising manager, *Little Review,* and clerk, Rheinthal and Newman, both New York, 1919; worked for his father in Akron, Ohio, and Cleveland, 1920–21; advertising copywriter, Cleveland, 1922–23; worked at office jobs in advertising and sales, New York, 1923–25; received money from financier Otto Kahn, 1925 and 1927. Received Guggenheim fellowship, 1931. Died 27 April 1932.

**Poetry**

*White Buildings,* 1926
*The Bridge,* 1930
*The Complete Poems of Hart Crane,* edited by Waldo Frank, 1933; revised edition, 1958
*Seven Lyrics,* 1966
*The Complete Poems and Selected Letters and Prose of Hart Crane,* edited by Brom Weber, 1966
*Ten Unpublished Poems,* 1972
*Porphyro in Akron,* 1980
*The Poems of Hart Crane,* edited by Marc Simon, 1986
*Complete Poems,* edited by Harold Bloom, 1991

**Other Writings:** memoirs (*Robber Rocks: Letters and Memories of Crane, 1923–1932,* edited by Susan Jenkins Brown, 1969), collections of correspondence (*The Letters of Hart Crane, 1916–1932,* edited by Brom Weber, 1965; *Letters of Crane and His Family,* edited by Thomas S.W. Lewis, 1974).

**Further Reading**

Edelman, Lee, *Transmemberment of Song: Hart Crane's Anatomies of Rhetoric and Desire,* Stanford, California: Stanford University Press, 1987
Lewis, R.W.B., *The Poetry of Hart Crane: A Critical Study,* Princeton, New Jersey: Princeton University Press, 1967
Martin, Robert K., *The Homosexual Tradition in American Poetry,* Austin: University of Texas Press, 1979; expanded edition, Iowa City: University of Iowa Press, 1998
Unterecker, John, *Voyager: A Life of Hart Crane,* New York: Farrar Straus and Giroux, 1969
Weber, Brom, *Hart Crane: A Biographical and Critical Study,* New York: Bodley, 1948; corrected edition, New York: Russell and Russell, 1970
Weber, Brom, editor, *The Letters of Hart Crane, 1916–1932,* New York: Hermitage House, 1952
Yingling, Thomas, *Hart Crane and the Homosexual Text: New Thresholds, New Anatomies,* Chicago: University of Chicago Press, 1990

## At Melville's Tomb

"At Melville's Tomb" is the penultimate poem in Hart Crane's astonishing first book, *White Buildings* (1926), a collection of 22 poems. Composed in October 1925 in four quartets of pentameter, "At Melville's Tomb" is a paradigmatic Crane poem that establishes many themes the poet returns to in later work, such as the "Voyages" sequence, "The Broken Tower," and the poems of *The Bridge* (1930). At the same time it provides an introduction into Crane's poetic style and serves as a lesson in how to read his highly impacted and densely allusive poetry.

Crane originally submitted his poem to Harriet Monroe, editor of *Poetry* magazine, in 1926. Monroe found the poem "elliptical" and "obscure" and wanted to print a prose explanation with it. Crane's response to Monroe in a now-famous letter explains his poem as well as his poetic practice in general:

> [A]s a poet I may very possibly be more interested in the so-called illogical impingements of the connotations of words on the consciousness . . . than I am interested in the preservation of their logically rigid significations. . . .

Crane went on to propose his "logic of metaphor" and explained the way that he extends language in his poetry, and in "At

Melville's Tomb" in particular, by focusing on the "illogical impingements of the connotations of words." The poem's "apparent illogic operates so logically in conjunction with its context in the poem as to establish its claim to another logic, quite independent of the original definition of the word or phrase or image thus employed" (Crane, 1966).

True to Crane's characterization, "At Melville's Tomb" embodies an apparent illogic that nonetheless works logically. The poem opens with the image of Melville watching the sea from the perspective of a ledge. What lies "beneath the wave[s]" is of interest because on the sea floor rests the "dice of drowned men's bones," the remnants of the sailors who lost their lives without being able to reveal their "embassy," a message that remains undelivered. Crane explained the genealogy of the dice imagery in his letter to Monroe:

> Dice bequeath an embassy, in the first place, by being ground . . . in little cubes from the bones of drowned men by the action of the sea, and are finally thrown up on the sand, having "numbers" but no identification. These being the bones of dead men who never completed their voyage, it seems legitimate to refer to them as the only surviving evidence of certain messages undelivered, mute evidence of certain things. . . . Dice as a symbol of chance and circumstance is also implied.

The word "dice" is thus both a metaphor for bones being awash on the sea floor and a metonym for the gambling life of sailors. Such multiple meanings combined into a single image, phrase, or word characterizes Crane's impacted poetic style.

In the second stanza, Crane depicts death as a generous basket of plenty that provides a "scattered chapter" and a "livid hieroglyph," that is, the bones of dead sailors:

> The calyx of death's bounty giving back
> A scattered chapter, livid hieroglyph,
> The portent wound in corridors of shells.

The bones constitute incomplete messages that both dissipate and retain their secrets, representing the sailors' inability to communicate their stories. The image of a "scattered chapter" could also refer to the poem itself, the language of which embodies such nonspecific signification by resisting the temptation to ground itself in any single meaning. Many contemporary critics read the poem as a metaphor for Crane's complicated relationship to his homosexuality: the undelivered message of the sailors can be read as the poet's own inability to express openly his homosexual desire.

The frustrated communications of the dice, embassy, chapter, and hieroglyph contrast with the "Compass, quadrant and sextant" of the final stanza, scientific instruments used to read the otherwise unintelligible horizon. Throughout the poem Crane reinforces this idea of unintelligibility by coupling words that would seem to be oxymoronic: a "chapter" that is "scattered," a "hieroglyph" that is "livid," and "answers" that are "silent." Crane uses these illogical combinations to enhance meaning, however, to foreground their creation of a new logic within the poem's context—to impinge, as he put it, on their connotations for the reader. The poem's excess language thus belies the sailors' wordless messages and perhaps the poet's own unspoken feelings as well. "At Melville's Tomb" ends with a reiteration of the power of the sea, an image of the sea inherited from Walt Whitman's "Sea Drift" poems and from Melville's *Moby-Dick*. A source of life and death, the sea "keeps" the "fabulous shadow" of secret, undelivered messages as well as messages that are knowable.

Crane's early death by suicide at the age of 32—he leapt off a cruise ship into the Caribbean Sea—casts an ironic shade over "At Melville's Tomb," in which the poet aggrandizes the power of the sea. "At Melville's Tomb" illustrates Crane's precocious talents and reminds readers of his potential as a poet who, like the sailor's embassy, remains a "scattered chapter."

PETER NICKOWITZ

**Further Reading**

Berthoff, Warner, *Hart Crane: A Re-Introduction,* Minneapolis: University of Minnesota Press, 1989

Clark, David, editor, *Critical Essays on Hart Crane,* Boston: G.K. Hall, 1982

Crane, Hart, *The Complete Poems and Selected Letters and Prose of Hart Crane,* edited by Brom Weber, New York: Liveright, 1966

Edelman, Lee, *Transmemberment of Song: Hart Crane's Anatomies of Rhetoric and Desire,* Stanford, California: Stanford University Press, 1987

Hammer, Langdon, *Hart Crane and Allen Tate: Janus-Faced Modernism,* Princeton, New Jersey: Princeton University Press, 1993

Hammer, Langdon, and Brom Weber, editors, *O My Land, My Friends! The Selected Letters of Hart Crane,* New York: Four Walls Eight Windows, 1997

Lewis, R.W.B., *The Poetry of Hart Crane: A Critical Study,* Princeton, New Jersey: Princeton University Press, 1967

Mariani, Paul, *The Broken Tower: A Life of Hart Crane,* New York: Norton, 1999

Nickowitz, Peter, "Infinite Mischief: The Rhetorical Distortion of Identity in the Poems of Hart Crane, Elizabeth Bishop, and James Merrill," Ph.D. Diss., New York University, 1999

Yingling, Thomas, *Hart Crane and the Homosexual Text: New Thresholds, New Anatomies,* Chicago: University of Chicago Press, 1990

# The Bridge

Hart Crane's second book, a 1,200-line poem begun in 1923, published in 1929 in Paris and in America in 1930, *The Bridge* is the major production of his career as well as one of the most misunderstood poems of the 20th century. It presents Crane's "myth of America," his answer to T.S. Eliot's *The Waste Land* (1922). The Brooklyn Bridge, the poem's emblem, stands in opposition to the eternal catastrophe of Eliot's London Bridge, a "harp and altar" invoked to "condense eternity" and coalesce America's history into a visible and usable form that could sustain a bright and prosperous future.

Crane condenses American history by fusing similar although temporally disparate acts. In "Ave Maria" Columbus returns from his discovery of "Cathay" and wakes to realize he has sailed from the country of safety, that "between two worlds, another, harsh, // This third, of water, tests the word." He finds his partner in "The Harbor Dawn," in which the 20th-century narrator wakes to the necessity of abandoning a lover's arms for the journey of the day. In "Van Winkle" this figure walks to the subway where he becomes, in "The River," a luxury-train passenger who later embarks on a Mississippi riverboat. Riverboat gives way to canoe in "The Dance," canoe to trail-runner, trail to wagon-road in "Indiana," and wagon-road to sea-lane in "Cutty Sark." In "Cape Hatteras" airplane supersedes boat, and space-ship airplane. Together, these sections detail a constant outward motion articulated in various eras and by several means, an extroversion Waldo Frank, Crane's friend, identified in *Our America* (1919) at the heart of American history and culture.

This extroversion reaches its extreme in "Cape Hatteras" as Crane's history of travel ends in a fiery plane crash that suggests spatial conquest creates as many questions as it answers. Crane addresses Walt Whitman, his figure of visionary power, who has braved spiritual frontiers beyond space:

Years of the Modern! Propulsions toward what capes?
But thou, *Panis Angelicus,* hast thou not seen
And passed that Barrier that none escapes—
But knows it leastwise as death-strife?—O, something
green,
Beyond all sesames of science was thy choice
Wherewith to bind us throbbing with one voice,
New integers of Roman, Viking, Celt—
Thou, Vedic Caesar, to the greensward knelt!

Whitman returns, a Christ, to instruct the testing of inner territories, which Crane sees as final frontiers. The conquest of these inner territories, Crane suggests, could answer the spiritual paucity identified in *The Waste Land.*

"Three Songs," "Quaker Hill," and "The Tunnel" illuminate this paucity and the necessity of fathoming the spirit. In "Three Songs" a fantastic mistress, a burlesque dancer, and an unattainable female paragon distract from the recognition of spiritual crisis. "Quaker Hill" identifies a similar numbness in weekenders oblivious to the Quakers' achievement:

This was the Promised Land, and still it is
To the persuasive suburban land agent
In bootleg roadhouses where the gin fizz
Bubbles in time to Hollywood's new love-nest pageant.
Fresh from the radio in the old Meeting House
(Now the New Avalon Hotel) volcanoes roar
A welcome to highsteppers that no mouse
Who saw the Friends there ever heard before.

Crane completes his orchestration in "The Tunnel," often regarded as the most pessimistic and troublesome section of *The Bridge.* On the subway he muses,

The phonographs of hades in the brain
Are tunnels that re-wind themselves, and love
A burnt match skating in a urinal.

In his despair the ghost of Edgar Allan Poe appears. Crane asks:

And when they dragged your retching flesh,
Your trembling hands that night through Baltimore—
That last night on the ballot rounds, did you,
Shaking, did you deny the ticket, Poe?

Poe shares with Whitman and Columbus—and Emily Dickinson and Isadora Duncan, addressed in "Quaker Hill"—a resolve in trial, a faith that might fill the spiritual void at the end of conquest. Poe appears in the extreme of Crane's doubt and of the subway's descent to suggest that doubt and descent are first steps toward the resolution of this spiritual and cultural crisis. Naming the need indicates a solution, an introversion to balance extreme extroversion.

This discovery precipitates the turn toward the surface, to dawn and "Atlantis" reversing the City-in-the-Sea imagined in "Cape Hatteras." In this final section the Brooklyn Bridge figures a choral weaving of the poem's themes and a vision of unparalleled positivity:

Through the bound cable strands, the arching path
Upward, veering with light, the flight of strings,—
Taut miles of shuttling moonlight syncopate
The whispered rush, telepathy of wires.
Up the index of night, granite and steel—
Transparent meshes—fleckless the gleaming staves—
Sibylline voices flicker, waveringly stream
As though a god were issue of the strings. . . .

Cathay, Atlantis, America interweave. The history of human conquest is condensed into the Bridge, whose resistance to gravity, a motion in stasis, indicates the stasis in motion Crane prescribes for America's cultural ailment, a stable center for the outward-moving.

Many critics recommend reading "Atlantis" first, the first-written section whose coordinations solve many of the poem's mysteries. But this notion proceeds on the view that *The Bridge* is a failure, a view promulgated by Yvor Winters and Allen Tate soon after the poem's publication and taken as fact until recently. A critical reassessment now underway seeks to prove the poem as worthy and effective in the form Crane chose for it. The poem is difficult and often opaque, but as readers master Crane's poetic grammar, characterized by hypotaxis and extreme compression and fusion of image, its fogs clear, a half-century's negative criticism ebbs, and *The Bridge* rises to assume its place with *The Waste Land* and *The Cantos* as one of the 20th century's most daring poetic experiments and most important poetic visions.

JAKE ADAM YORK

**Further Reading**

Bennett, Maria F., *Unfractioned Idiom: Hart Crane and Modernism,* New York: Peter Lang, 1987

Berthoff, Warner, *Hart Crane: A Re-Introduction,* Minneapolis: University of Minnesota Press, 1989

Bloom, Harold, editor, *Hart Crane,* New York: Chelsea House, 1986

Brunner, Edward, *Splendid Failure: Hart Crane and the Making of "The Bridge,"* Urbana: University of Illinois Press, 1985

Frank, Waldo, *Our America,* New York: Boni and Liveright, 1919; reprint, New York: AMS Press, 1972

Giles, Paul, *Hart Crane: The Contexts of "The Bridge,"* Cambridge and New York: Cambridge University Press, 1986

Hammer, Langdon, and Brom Weber, editors, *O My Land, My Friends! The Selected Letters of Hart Crane,* New York: Four Walls Eight Windows, 1997

Irwin, John, "Hart Crane's 'Logic of Metaphor,'" in *Critical Essays on Hart Crane,* edited by David Clark, Boston: G.K. Hall, 1982
Martin, Robert K., *The Homosexual Tradition in American Poetry,* Austin: University of Texas Press, 1979; expanded edition, Iowa City: University of Iowa Press, 1998
Yingling, Thomas, *Hart Crane and the Homosexual Text: New Thresholds, New Anatomies,* Chicago: University of Chicago Press, 1990

## Voyages

"Voyages" first appeared in its entirety as the last poem in Hart Crane's *White Buildings* (1926). It embodies many of the recurrent images of the book (hands, whiteness, the sea) and develops the themes of "To Herman Melville," which immediately precedes it. Both poems treat the sea paradoxically as man's destroyer and as the harbinger of literary immortality. Melville becomes immortal by surrendering himself to the sea; strongly influenced in imagery and syntax by *Moby-Dick,* "Voyages" traces the poet's journey through an intense but transitory love affair, which becomes a union with the sea in the poem's metaphor.

"Voyages" immediately won a high critical reputation. Yvor Winters and Allen Tate wrote enthusiastically about "Voyages" in essays that were extremely critical of Crane's other poems. Robert Lowell praised "Voyages II" in interviews, and his own "The Quaker Graveyard in Nantucket" was influenced by the sequence. Recent critics such as Gregory Woods and Langdon Hammer emphasize the importance of "Voyages" as a homosexual love poem representing a libertarian and subversive Modernism that opposes the heterosexual and authoritarian values of such influential Modernists as Ezra Pound and T.S. Eliot.

In 1924 Crane fell in love with Emil Opffer, a ship's officer. He wrote to Waldo Frank (21 April 1924) that "the sea has thrown itself upon me," describing himself as "transubstantiated." "Voyages," conceived of as a sequence of six parts in November 1924, "transubstantiates" the affair with Opffer into an archetypal love between the poet and a nameless, unfaithful beloved.

Crane wrote to Gorham Munson (late August 1922) that "Voyages I," entitled "Poster" in the January 1923 issue of *Secession,* was "nothing more profound" than a "'stop, look and listen' sign." Its conclusion was "merely bold and unambitious like a skull and cross-bones insignia." His decision in 1924 to use the poem to begin "Voyages" increased its resonance. It establishes the sea as an erotic but dangerous presence; the speaker wants to warn some children playing on the shore of the dangers of both the ocean and their own sexuality:

> there is a line
> You must not cross nor ever trust beyond it
> Spry cordage of your bodies to caresses
> Too lichen-faithful from too wide a breast.
> The bottom of the sea is cruel.

This passage reveals the stylistic debt to Elizabethan love poetry that permeates "Voyages." The suggestion that the children would be caressed and drowned by a broad-breasted masculine sea refers to Christopher Marlowe's *Hero and Leander* in which Neptune caresses and almost drowns the swimming Leander. The last line, described as a "skull and cross-bones," anticipates the "piracy" of sexual infidelity in "Voyages V," but the warning is both unheard and too late. These children who "flay each other" and "Fondle" their phallic "shells and sticks" already display sexual characteristics.

"Voyages II," beginning with a conjunction, immediately qualifies its predecessor. Despite its cruelty, the sea spares the "pieties of lovers' hands." The image of hands praying or caressing recurs in "Voyages," and Crane's source is again Elizabethan poetry. In *Hero and Leander,* "lovers parlèd by the touch of hands," and Romeo and Juliet also explore the religious and erotic potential of hands: "palm to palm is holy palmers' kiss."

"Voyages II" establishes the poem's universe as a written text. The waves are "scrolls of silver snowy sentences," and the sea's "palms" (punning on palm trees) "Pass superscription of bent foam." Crane's essay "General Aims and Theories," written simultaneously with "Voyages," argues that every poem creates a "new *word,* never before spoken." At the conclusion of "Voyages" Crane celebrates the creation of "The imaged Word," which, unlike a lover, cannot be betrayed: "It is the unbetrayable reply / Whose accent no farewell can know."

The promise of this "Word," evocative of the creation myth of Genesis, first appears at the end of "Voyages II." Crane prays to remain inspired until his mortality is "answered" by "The seal's wide spindrift gaze toward paradise." "Seal" has a secondary meaning: a wax seal guarantees a pact, lovers "seal" their promises with kisses. Belle Isle in "Voyages VI" represents a "fervid covenant."

In "Voyages III" the poet travels through "black swollen gates" to ecstasy. These gates simultaneously suggest waves engulfing a ship, vaginal or anal penetration, and William Blake's "doors of perception" in *The Marriage of Heaven and Hell,* which, if cleansed, allow everything to "appear as it is, infinite." The last line anticipates an orgasm that is also a spiritual pilgrimage: "Permit me voyage, love, into your hands . . ." The statement is incomplete, ending with an ellipsis rather than a period. In "Voyages IV" contrived oxymorons ("Madly meeting logically") and excessive alliteration ("Portending," "port," "portion") also convey the poet's loss of certainty. The "bright insinuations" found in his beloved's embrace, despite the phrase's lyricism, suggest deviousness. The betrayal of "Voyages V" is suspected; its discovery becomes poignantly inevitable: "In all the argosy of your bright hair I dreamed / Nothing so flagless as this piracy."

The rhyming quatrains of "Voyages VI," a formal contrast to the blank verse of the previous sections, express the poet's determination to transform the flux of experience into the fixed structures of art. He desires a confirmation of his vocation as a visionary poet:

> let thy waves rear
> More savage than the death of kings,
> Some splintered garland for the seer.

Like Shakespeare's Richard II, recalling "sad stories of the death of kings," the poet seeks a lyrical wisdom through suffering. The garland is "splintered" and imperfect, however; poetry is a consolation for loss but not a cure. The "Belle Isle" of artistic perfection, like its surrounding rainbows, is intangible. The biblical covenant between God and Noah, symbolized by the rainbow, becomes a "fervid covenant" between the poet and the "Word" of the freshly created poem. Crane wins his "garland," but his triumph is founded on betrayal. The inspiring sea remains "cruel" and full of "dungeons" where drowned swimmers lift "their lost morning eyes."

SEAN ELLIOTT

**Further Reading**

Beach, Joseph Warren, "Hart Crane and *Moby Dick*," in *Hart Crane: A Collection of Critical Essays*, edited by Alan Trachtenberg, Englewood Cliffs, New Jersey: Prentice Hall, 1982

Berthoff, Warner, *Hart Crane: A Re-Introduction*, Minneapolis: University of Minnesota Press, 1989

Hammer, Langdon, *Hart Crane and Allen Tate: Janus-Faced Modernism*, Princeton, New Jersey: Princeton University Press, 1993

Hammer, Langdon, "Introduction and Commentary," in *O My Land, My Friends! The Selected Letters of Hart Crane*, edited by Hammer and Brom Weber, New York: Four Walls Eight Windows, 1997

Paul, Sherman, *Hart's Bridge*, Urbana: University of Illinois Press, 1972

Woods, Gregory, *Articulate Flesh: Male Homo-Eroticism and Modern Poetry*, New Haven, Connecticut: Yale University Press, 1987

Yingling, Thomas, *Hart Crane and the Homosexual Text: New Thresholds, New Anatomies*, Chicago: University of Chicago Press, 1990

---

# Adelaide Crapsey 1878–1914

Adelaide Crapsey is known for one major poetic innovation: the creation of the only serious poetic form to have emerged in the United States, the cinquain, a poem consisting of five lines, the first and last of which is one stress, with the second, third, and fourth lines gradually increasing in length. It is also described as being syllabic, but the intricacies of the form are often enhanced by the interrelationship between stress and syllable count. Thus, the following poem is regular as far as both syllables and stress are concerned:

"Niagara Seen on a Night in November"

How frail
Above the bulk
Of crashing water hangs,
Autumnal, evanescent, wan,
The moon.

The evenness of the rhythm supports the appearance of a serene, oriental word picture, disguising the numerous transformations of reality in the scene. The moon is depicted as frail and wan, while Niagara appears powerful and loud. However, the quiet monosyllables of the moon frame and control the rushing falls and reverse the effect of power.

The following example of a lesser-known poem, however, has far too many syllables for a standard cinquain, although the number of stresses is the same:

"Now Barabbas Was a Robber"

No guile?
Nay, but so strangely
He moves among us. . Not this
Man but Barabbas! Release to us
Barabbas!

In the last four lines, only the stress count is regular by cinquain norms. The effect is of a channeled emotional excitement as well as the sense of a growing loss of control. Each of Crapsey's cinquains operates with this kind of metrical complexity, adding an additional dimension to simple thematic or imagistic poems.

This discovery was not an accident. Crapsey had been trained in the metrics of English poetry and researched the intricacies of the relationship between syllable and stress for at least a decade. However, her work was never completed and, like her poems, was published only posthumously.

Although Crapsey seemed to have no personal connection with the Imagists who were in London and Paris during her visit in 1911, it is clear that she either was influenced by some contact with Pound or Lowell or was nurtured from the same sources. Although most of her cinquains were written between 1911 and a few months before her death in 1914, they were initiated during her month's stay in Paris in the summer of 1909, when she was probably reading William N. Porter's *A Thousand Verses from Old Japan*, a translation of the Hyaku-Nin-Isshiu ("Single Verses by a Hundred People," 1909), and translating haikus from French translations.

In many ways, this form was not only a product of intense research but also her unique biography. Louise Townsend Nicholls, a student of Crapsey's, once noted that the form had "likeness to her own abbreviated, but perfected life. The five lines, one-stress, two-stress, three-stress, four-stress, and then caught back suddenly again to one-stress, were her life, her young, joyful life, broadening and straining—and then, with a faint grasp of terror at the unfulfillment of promises which life and love and art had made, but still undaunted, caught back again to one" ("Adelaide Crapsey's Poems," *New Republic* 33 [31 January 1923]).

What was this life, and how did it resemble the cinquain? Born on 9 September 1878 in Brooklyn, New York, Crapsey grew up in Rochester, New York, where her father, an Episcopal minister, brought his growing family at the beginning of a very promising career. At Vassar College, she became friendly with Jean Webster, who shared with her a belief in socialism and women's equality and who used Crapsey's unusual independent personality as the model of many of her heroines, most notably Judy Abbott in *Daddy Long-Legs*. On graduation in 1901, however, Webster went on to develop her writing career, and Crapsey became a teacher and scholar, held back by ill health and numerous family tragedies, including the deaths of her elder siblings, but anticipating both a poetic and a scholarly career. After two years teaching at the same school where she had studied before college (1901–03), Kemper Hall in Kenosha, Wisconsin, she began studies in Rome but was called back to Rochester to aid her family in her father's notorious trial for heresy, of which he was convicted in 1907. Financial considerations that followed made further studies impossible, and she began teaching in Miss Lowe's School in Stamford, Connecticut, until ill health forced her to seek rest and a better climate again in Rome, London, and Paris.

An offer to teach at Smith College in Northampton, Massachusetts, brought her home in 1911, and it began to appear that her teaching renown and her studies of metrics would bring her some recognition as an academic. She had also been working steadily on her poetry, writing cinquains as well as free verse. However, in the summer of 1913, she collapsed and was finally diagnosed with the tuberculosis that had been with her for almost a decade. She was sent to Saranac Lake, New York, where the cold mountain air was said to be health promoting, and for the last year of her life she was isolated in a cottage with only a nurse and occasional visitors. Despite severe restrictions on her writing and the severe limitations of her health, she managed to write several of her most famous cinquains, such as "Snow" and a plaintive long poem, "To the Dead in the Graveyard by My Window." In September, it was agreed that the cure at Saranac Lake had failed, and she was returned to Rochester, where she died on 8 October 1914. On her deathbed, Crapsey learned from Jean Webster that her poem "The Witch" had been accepted by *Century* magazine, and her long-delayed poetic career was to begin. Almost a year after her death, a friend, Claude Bragdon, whose wife was visited by Crapsey's ghost, discovered the existence of a manuscript prepared with the wish that it be published. *Verse* (1915) immediately influenced numerous literary, artistic, and critical figures. From the painter Marsden Hartley to poets as different as Carl Sandburg and Lola Ridge, the figure of Crapsey and her poems was a source of inspiration.

Expanded editions of *Verse* were brought out in 1922 and 1934 through the efforts of Crapsey's friend Esther Lowenthal, who was also instrumental in the publication of her research, *A Study of English Metrics* (1918).

KAREN ALKALAY-GUT

**Biography**

Born in Brooklyn Heights, New York, 9 September 1878. Attended Vassar College, A.B. 1901; School of Classical Studies, the American Academy in Rome, 1904–05; teacher, Kemper Hall, Kenosha, Wisconsin, 1901–03; Miss Lowe's School, Stamford, Connecticut, 1906–08; Instructor in poetics, Smith College, Northampton, Massachusetts, 1911–13. Died in Rochester, New York, 8 October 1914.

**Poetry**

*Verse,* 1915; revised editions, 1922, 1934
*The Complete Poems and Collected Letters of Adelaide Crapsey,* 1977

**Other Writings:** nonfiction (*A Study of English Metrics,* 1918).

**Further Reading**

Alkalay-Gut, Karen, *Alone in the Dawn: The Life of Adelaide Crapsey,* Athens: University of Georgia Press, 1988
Butscher, Edward, *Adelaide Crapsey,* Boston: Twayne, 1979
Osborn, Mary Elizabeth, *Adelaide Crapsey,* Boston: Humphries, 1933
Smith, Susan Sutton, editor, *The Complete Poems and Collected Letters of Adelaide Crapsey,* Albany: State University of New York Press, 1977
Winters, Yvor, *In Defense of Reason,* Chicago: Swallow Press, 1947

---

# Robert Creeley 1926–

While introducing Robert Creeley at his 70th birthday celebration in 1996, poet Susan Howe painted the definitive picture of Creeley by likening his poetic concerns to those of Walt Whitman. Howe invoked a passage from Creeley's introduction to the book that he also edited, *Whitman: Selected Poems* (1973), in which he noted Whitman's desire for "absolute communion with others." Howe observed that, like Whitman, Creeley has exhibited in his poetry a supreme desire for such communion since the publication of his first work in the Harvard magazine *Wake* in 1946. For more than 50 years, he has been an indefatigable advocate of poetic experimentation, challenging established canons of literary taste. Through his own distinctive use of language, he has led by example in the exploration of the linguistic, lyrical, and musical foundations of poetry.

Robert White Creeley was born in Arlington, Massachusetts, but was brought up in the nearby rural community of West Acton, where he moved, at the age of four with his mother and sister, after his father's death. A year later, he lost his left eye to an infection resulting from an earlier injury. He spent his secondary school years as a scholarship student at Holderness School in Plymouth, New Hampshire, where he contributed to school publications. Following his three years at Holderness, Creeley entered Harvard University in the fall of 1943 but left a year later to join the American Field Service in the India-Burma theater of World War II serving as an ambulance driver. He married Ann McKinnon in 1946 and reentered Harvard, but with one term to go before receiving a degree, he dropped out for good. In 1948, he went to New Hampshire to try subsistence farming. During this period, he forged a close friendship with the poet Cid Corman, who hosted a radio program in Boston called *This Is Poetry.*

In the years following the war, Creeley became interested in the ideas expressed in William Carlos Williams' *The Wedge* (1944) and Ezra Pound's *Make It New* (1934), and in 1949 he began corresponding with Pound and Williams. In 1950, he wrote to these and other poets in hopes of obtaining their help in establishing a new literary magazine. The attempt failed but prompted a long correspondence with Charles Olson and aided Corman in launching *Origin,* the magazine that was to become the vehicle for Creeley's early success. Creeley and his wife moved to France in 1951 in search of a less expensive way of life. The following year, they moved to Mallorca, where they lived until their divorce in 1955. There they set up the Divers Press and printed books by Creeley himself (including *The Gold Diggers* [1954], 11 stories), Robert Duncan, Olson, and others. Mallorca would also provide Creeley with both the inspiration and the setting for his only novel, *The Island* (1963). In 1954, at Olson's invitation, Creeley accepted a teaching position at Black Mountain College (spring of 1954 and fall of 1955), where he founded and edited the *Black Mountain Review* and took a bachelor's degree in 1955.

Creeley's first three books of poetry, *Le Fou* (1952), *The Kind of Act of* (1953), and *The Immoral Proposition* (1953), appeared in quick succession while he was living abroad. His next two, *All That Is Lovely in Men* (1955) and *If You* (1956), were published shortly after his return to the United States. He left Black Mountain in 1956 and went to San Francisco, where he met Beat generation writers Allen Ginsberg, Jack Kerouac, Kenneth Rexroth, and Gary Snyder. Later that year, he settled in Albuquerque, New Mexico, and then remarried and taught at a boys' school until 1959. That year, he worked as a tutor on a coffee plantation in Guatemala before returning to New Mexico. By the time he took a master of arts degree from the University of New Mexico in 1960, he had seven books of poetry to his credit. The year 1960 was a turning point for Creeley. In May, *Poetry* magazine published ten of his new poems and awarded him its Levinson Prize. That same month, several of Creeley's poems appeared in Donald Allen's critical anthology *The New American Poetry: 1945–1960.* Not long after, Creeley began a new career in academe, accepting a teaching post at the University of New Mexico in 1961–62.

Although Creeley published several books of poetry during the 1950s, he did not receive widespread recognition until 1962, when his poetry was made readily available to the public for the first time with the appearance of *For Love: Poems, 1950–1960.* Dedicated to his second wife, Bobbie Hoeck, the book established Creeley as a serious poet and addressed many of the themes that occur throughout his work, particularly his focus on language and his preoccupation with human relationships. *For Love,* which includes the frequently anthologized "I Know a Man" and "Ballad of the Despairing Husband," contains 123 poems divided into three sections arranged by chronology: 1950 to 1955, 1956 to 1958, and 1959 to 1960. All but four of the poems included in the collection had been previously published in *The Whip* (1957), *A Form of Woman* (1959), or in periodicals. *For Love* was nominated for a National Book Award in 1962 and continues to be one of Creeley's most successful books commercially. Other critically acclaimed books by Creeley include *Words* (1967), *A Day Book* (1972), *Dreams* (1989), and *Life and Death* (1998).

Creeley's poetry owes a great deal to various 20th-century movements, most notably Projectivism, whose leading theoretician was Charles Olson. In his 1950 essay "Projective Verse," Olson set forth the poetics of what would become the Projectivist movement, or Black Mountain School. The central tenet of Projectivism is the rejection of artificial or "closed" poetic constructions based on meter and stanza in favor of an organically produced free verse emphasizing the kinetics of poetic form. In Olson's theory, the poem is a "high-energy construct" that embodies or enacts "the process" of its own creation. Its most important component is the line, which "pushes" forward moment by moment according to the natural rhythm of the poet's breathing. Olson insisted it is the breath that must generate the shape, meter, and duration of the line of poetry. His theory privileges the act of writing itself over what he derides as the overwrought polish of formal poetry and asserts that what a poet wishes to express will itself determine the structure of the poem that he makes. The well-known statement attributed by Olson to Creeley that "form is never more than an extension of content" is evidence of Projectivism's profound influence on Creeley.

In addition to Olson, Creeley lists as influences William Carlos Williams and Allen Ginsberg, but he is also quick to include the enduring influence of jazz music on his writing as well. Olson's notion of the line pushed into being by the poet's breath finds a close corollary with the musical constructs of jazz, which itself eschews formal arrangement in favor of spontaneity and improvisation. As Ginsberg reassured Creeley that he could "write directly from that which you feel," so the musicians Creeley has most admired have demonstrated to him that emotions can be expressed artistically and lucidly without being constrained by proscribed form.

The typical Creeley poem may be characterized as a brief improvisation on a fleeting meditation that begins and ends in mid-thought. Its lines are invariably short, and its dominant concerns are for the subject of love and the emotions accompanying intimate relationships. Intellectually, it shares an affinity with the compacted psychological meanderings typical of the sonnet, expressing a generalization forming the heart of the poem that is customarily introduced by an epigrammatic statement gradually dissolved by a series of terse enjambments into a moment of resolution. Creeley is a master of the tentative conclusion, and his best poems are capped by such astute speculations. Although frequently oblique and aphoristic, these are always astonishing in conception. For example, "Air: The Love of a Woman" (1962) begins with the meditation "The love of a woman / is the possibility / which surrounds her as hair / her head, as the love of her / follows and describes / her." This reverie is interrupted in the second stanza by an acute awareness of the inevitability of death, the destroyer of life and relationships. In the two stanzas that follow, the deciding factor in the struggle between life and death emerges as the poem itself captures the "aura" of love that remains even after death. The final line speaks of the creative existential courage that Creeley finds in poetry: "Then sing, of her, of whom / it will be said, he / sang of her, it was the / song he made which made her / happy, so she lived."

Creeley has received numerous awards besides the Levinson Prize for his work, including two Guggenheim fellowships, the Shelley Memorial Award, and the Robert Frost Medal, both from the Poetry Society of America. He was elected to the American Academy and Institute of Arts and Letters in 1987 and received a Distinguished Fulbright fellowship to serve as the Bicentennial Chair in American Studies at the University of Helsinki in 1988–

89. Although he has held many visiting posts over the years and has been affiliated with several universities, including the University of British Columbia and San Francisco State College, Creeley has worked at the State University of New York, Buffalo (UB), since 1966, where he served as professor of English from 1967 to 1978. He was subsequently named David Gray Professor of Poetry and Letters at UB and has been reappointed for the five-year term many times since. He married his third wife, Penelope, in 1976.

In 1989, Creeley began a two-year tenure as New York State's official poet laureate, an experience that he claims led him to a moment of "consummate truth," helping him shake a half-century's feelings of inadequacy. In 1997, true to his enduring desire to connect with the human community, he began instructing UB undergraduates again, hoping to infuse his students with a love of language and with new ways of perceiving and connecting with the world. One of these new ways proved to be through the medium of computer technology and electronic communication. Creeley has been an advocate of UB's resourceful Electronic Poetry Center since its inception in 1994. The subject of his recent book *Daybook of a Virtual Poet* (1999) is, in fact, a record of e-mail exchanges between Creeley and high school students who participated in an experimental "on-line" honors poetry course. The effort demonstrates Creeley's fearless approach to innovation and his ongoing interest in the relationship between experimental poetry, language, and community.

In 1999, Creeley was awarded Yale University Library's coveted Bollingen Prize for Poetry, one of the most prestigious awards of its kind in the United States, and later that same year he was elected to the Board of Chancellors of the American Academy of Poetry along with several other pioneering writers who represent minority forms, themes, and approaches to *fin-de-siècle* American life.

Among the poems read by Creeley at his 70th birthday celebration was a new composition titled "Histoire de Florida" (1998). Written over a three-week period while Creeley was involved in a workshop, "Histoire de Florida" is a kind of daybook that sums up many of the concerns that have so long preoccupied the poet. Creeley described the poem as a means of getting at

> something that in its own way has to do with the preoccupation of living dearly and particularly with other people. [It is a] daily preoccupation and activity, and also a curious taking stock of trying to not just define oneself, but to get located—what were one's defining imaginations of whatever it was that one seems to have as a life.

Creeley lives and works in Buffalo, New York.

JOE FRANCIS DOERR

*See also* Black Mountain School

**Biography**

Born in Arlington, Massachusetts, 21 May 1926. Attended Holderness School, Plymouth, New Hampshire; Harvard University, Cambridge, Massachusetts, 1943–44, 1945–46; Black Mountain College, North Carolina, B.A. 1955; University of New Mexico, Albuquerque, M.A. 1960; served in the American Field Service in India and Burma, 1944–45; farmer near Littleton, New Hampshire, 1948–51; Instructor, Black Mountain College, spring 1954 and fall 1955; teacher in a boys' school, Albuquerque, 1956–59, and on a finca in Guatemala, 1959–61; Visiting Lecturer, 1961–62, and Visiting Professor, 1963–66, 1968–69, 1978–80, University of New Mexico; Lecturer, University of British Columbia, Vancouver, 1962–63; Visiting Professor, 1966–67, Professor, 1967–78, David Gray Professor of Poetry and Letters, 1978–89, and since 1989 Samuel P. Capen Professor of Poetry and Humanities, State University of New York, Buffalo; Visiting Professor, San Francisco State College, 1970–71, and State University of New York, Binghamton, 1985, 1986; operated the Divers Press, Palma de Mallorca, 1953–55; editor, *Black Mountain Review*, North Carolina, 1954–57, and associated with *Wake, Golden Goose, Origin, Fragmente, Vou, Contact, CIV/n,* and *Merlin* magazines in early 1950s, and other magazines since; since 1983, advisory editor, *American Book Review* and *Sagetrieb*, and since 1984 *New York Quarterly;* since 1984 contributing editor, *Formations*. Received D.H. Lawrence fellowship, 1960; Levinson Prize, 1960; Guggenheim fellowship, 1964, 1971; Rockefeller grant, 1965; Shelley Memorial Award, 1981; National Endowment for the Arts grant, 1982; DAAD fellowship, 1983, 1987; Leone d'Oro Premio Speziale (Venice), 1984; Frost Medal, 1987; Member, 1987, and Chancellor, 1999, American Academy; Distinguished Fulbright fellowship, 1988–89; New York State poet, 1989–91; Honorary D.Litt., University of New Mexico, 1993; Horst Bienek Lyrikpreis (Munich), 1993. Living in Buffalo, New York.

**Poetry**

*Le Fou*, 1952
*The Kind of Act of*, 1953
*The Immoral Proposition*, 1953
*A Snarling Garland of Xmas Verses*, 1954
*All That Is Lovely in Men*, 1955
*Ferrini and Others*, with others, 1955
*If You*, 1956
*The Whip*, 1957
*A Form of Woman*, 1959
*For Love: Poems, 1950–1960*, 1962
*Distance*, 1964
*Two Poems*, 1964
*Hi There!* 1965
*Words* (single poem), 1965
*About Women*, 1966
*Poems, 1950–1965*, 1966
*For Joel*, 1966
*A Sight*, 1967
*Words* (collection), 1967
*Robert Creeley Reads* (with recording), 1967
*The Finger*, 1968
*5 Numbers*, 1968
*The Charm: Early and Uncollected Poems*, 1968
*The Boy*, 1968
*Numbers*, 1968
*Divisions and Other Early Poems*, 1968
*Pieces*, 1969
*Hero*, 1969
*A Wall*, 1969

*Mazatlan: Sea*, 1969
*Mary's Fancy*, 1970
*In London*, 1970
*The Finger: Poems, 1966–1969*, 1970
*For Betsy and Tom*, 1970
*For Benny and Sabina*, 1970
*As Now It Would Be Snow*, 1970
*America*, 1970
*Christmas: May 10, 1970*, 1970
*St. Martin's*, 1971
*Sea*, 1971
*1.2.3.4.5.6.7.8.9.0.*, 1971
*For the Graduation*, 1971
*Change*, 1972
*One Day after Another*, 1972
*A Day Book* (includes prose), 1972
*For My Mother*, 1973
*Kitchen*, 1973
*His Idea*, 1973
*Sitting Here*, 1974
*Thirty Things*, 1974
*Backwards*, 1975
*Away*, 1976
*Presences*, 1976
*Selected Poems*, 1976
*Myself*, 1977
*Thanks*, 1977
*The Children*, 1978
*Hello: A Journal, February 23–May 3, 1976*, 1978
*Later* (single poem), 1978
*Desultory Days*, 1978
*Later: New Poems*, 1979
*Corn Close*, 1980
*Mother's Voice*, 1981
*The Collected Poems of Robert Creeley, 1945–1975*, 1982
*A Calendar*, 1983
*Mirrors*, 1983
*Memories*, 1984
*Four Poems*, 1984
*Memory Gardens*, 1986
*The Company*, 1988
*7and6*, with illustrations by Robert Therrien and prose by Michel Butor, 1988
*It*, with illustrations by Francesco Clemente, 1989
*Dreams*, 1989
*Windows*, 1990
*Have a Heart*, 1990
*Places*, 1990
*Selected Poems, 1945–1990*, 1991
*Gnomic Verses*, 1991
*The Old Days*, 1991
*Echoes*, 1994
*Loops: Ten Poems*, 1995
*Life and Death*, with paintings by Francesco Clemente, 1998
*Personal: Poems*, 1998
*So There: Poems, 1976–1983*, 1998
*En Famille: A Poem*, 1999
*For Friends*, 2000

**Selected Criticism**
*A Sense of Measure*, 1973
*Was That a Real Poem and Other Essays*, edited by Donald Allen, 1979
*The Collected Essays of Robert Creeley*, 1989

**Other Writings:** play, novel (*The Island*, 1963), short stories (*The Gold Diggers*, 1954); edited poetry collections (*Whitman: Selected Poems*, 1973).

**Further Reading**

Altieri, Charles, *Self and Sensibility in Contemporary American Poetry*, Cambridge and New York: Cambridge University Press, 1984
Butterick, George, editor, *Charles Olson and Robert Creeley: The Complete Correspondence*, Santa Barbara, California: Black Sparrow Press, 1980
Clark, Tom, *Robert Creeley and the Genius of the American Common Place: Together with the Poet's "Autobiography,"* New York: New Directions, 1993
Creeley, Robert, *The Collected Prose of Robert Creeley*, New York and London: Boyars, 1984
Creeley, Robert, "Autobiography," in *Contemporary Authors Autobiography Series* 10 (1989)
Creeley, Robert, "Introduction to 'Histoire de Florida,'" in *Robert Creeley: A 70th Birthday Celebration* (videorecording), Buffalo, New York: Vincent Gregory, 1996
Edelberg, Cynthia Dubin, *Robert Creeley's Poetry: A Critical Introduction*, Albuquerque: University of New Mexico Press, 1978
Fredman, Stephen, *Poet's Prose: The Crisis in American Verse*, Cambridge and New York: Cambridge University Press, 1983; 2nd edition, 1990
Von Hallberg, Robert, *American Poetry and Culture, 1945–1980*, Cambridge, Massachusetts: Harvard University Press, 1985
Wilson, John, editor, *Robert Creeley's Life and Work: A Sense of Increment*, Ann Arbor: University of Michigan Press, 1987

## Anger

"Anger" is part of Robert Creeley's third major collection of poems, *Words*, published in 1967. Creeley, a founding member of the Black Mountain School of poetry, was born into a middle-class family in Arlington, Massachusetts, during the spring of 1926. Raised in a comfortable but emotionally restrictive Protestant New England environment, Creeley often reflects on the conflicts inherent in intimate human communications. "Anger" is one such poem. In it, Creeley examines a particular moment of domestic life and grapples with discordant emotions of love and hatred.

Creeley opens the poem by giving the reader a clear sense of physical location. The poem is arranged with a cinematographer's eye for detail, as if a movie camera were slowly panning across the room. There is a feeling of unsettling quiet, interrupted by reminders of the outside world:

The children
sleep, the dog fed,
the house around them

is open, descriptive,
a truck through the walls,
lights bright there,

glaring . . .

Having intimated that this is a scene in which an argument has just taken place between a husband and wife, Creeley begins to distance himself, and in the second section of the poem he attempts to view the emotion of anger more philosophically. It is once again possible to compare the poem to the work of a visual artist engaged in the study of a physical object. Creeley describes the emotion of anger from many angles, but in the end he concedes, "I rage. / I rage, I rage."

The next section of the poem is crucial and serves as the center of the work, both physically on the page and thematically. Creeley obscures the location of the angry voice by replacing the pronoun "I" with "you." The reader is then thrust into the narrative with the accusation "You did it." Through this sudden shift of voice, the universality of anger in human life is made more clear. The excruciating emotion of the scene is also conveyed through the physical form of the poem: short phrases of thought are clustered in sections of two- and three-line stanzas, creating an uncomfortable sense of the silences surrounding the words. In a letter to fellow poet Charles Olson in 1950, Creeley suggested that within a poem "form is never more than an extension of content." Olson recorded this idea in his seminal essay "Projective Verse" (1950), and it became one of the major precepts of contemporary American poetry. During a time when more traditional poets adhered to strict rules of meter and rhyme in the composition of their poems, Creeley's idea stood out and influenced an entire generation of writers. "Anger" serves as a good example of this theory of composition.

What appears to be a relaxed sense of meter and stanza structure is complemented by an underlying mastery of craft. While Creeley is considered to be a writer of free verse, his work is not free of technical skill, and within his writing there exists a subtle attention to tradition. It is no accident that Creeley opens the book *Words* with a quotation by American Modernist poet William Carlos Williams, a writer who influenced Creeley in several ways. "Anger" resembles many of Williams' poems in its abbreviated lines and in its sparse delivery of images that nonetheless lead to profound revelations of emotion.

Creeley's formal style also derives from his study of American jazz music compositions. In the fourth section of the poem, Creeley writes, "The rage / is what I / want, what / I cannot give / to myself." By breaking the lines in unexpected places, he again achieves a sense of urgency and panic. It is also important to note that this poem was written during the mid-1960s, at a time when many young people in the United States and Europe were reevaluating social mores and calling for more open emotionality and expression. Published at a time when political activists were promoting nonviolent protest and sexual liberation, Creeley's "Anger" stands out as a poem that is daring and yet also reactionary.

While "Anger" focuses intently on emotionality, the author does not prioritize love over hatred. In this sense, the poem serves as important social commentary. Despite the peace movement of the 1960s, there was an anger that pervaded American society, particularly in relation to the politics of the Civil Rights movement, the assassinations of John F. Kennedy and Malcolm X, and the escalating violence of the Vietnam War. In the sixth and final section of "Anger," Creeley again turns his gaze outward toward an unspecified social sphere. The personal anger that emerged at the beginning of the poem is conflated with the aggression and ambivalence that are intrinsic to human life. The "you" becomes ambiguous, simultaneously representing the author, the reader, society, and the emotion of anger itself. Creeley ends the poem with the admonishment

All you say you want
to do to yourself you do
to someone else as yourself

and we sit between you
waiting for whatever will
be at last the real end of you.

Throughout "Anger," Creeley voices a frustration with humankind's frailty and with his own erratic capacity to love others. He also points to a frustration with words themselves as tools of expression. As he writes in the introduction to the collection, "Words will not say anything more than they do, and my various purposes will not understand them more than what they say." With this, the title of the collection, *Words,* takes on a new dimension. As anger and hatred are intrinsic to the human condition for Creeley, so too does language intrinsically fall short of expressing all that the author intends.

LISA JARNOT

**Further Reading**

Altieri, Charles, "Robert Creeley's Poetics of Conjecture: The Pains and Pleasures of Staging a Self at War with Its Own Lyrical Desires," in *Self and Sensibility in Contemporary American Poetry,* by Altieri, Cambridge and New York: Cambridge University Press, 1984

Chung, Ling, "Predicaments in Robert Creeley's *Words,*" *Concerning Poetry* 2, no. 2 (Fall 1969)

Clark, Tom, *Robert Creeley and the Genius of the American Common Place: Together with the Poet's "Autobiography,"* New York: New Directions, 1993

Creeley, Robert, *A Quick Graph: Collected Notes and Essays,* edited by Donald Allen, San Francisco: Four Seasons Foundation, 1970

Creeley, Robert, *Contexts of Poetry: Interviews, 1961–1971,* edited by Donald Allen, Bolinas, California: Four Seasons Foundation, 1973

Fox, Willard, III, *Robert Creeley, Edward Dorn, and Robert Duncan: A Reference Guide,* Boston: G.K. Hall, 1989

Olson, Charles, *Selected Writings,* edited and with an introduction by Robert Creeley, New York: New Directions, 1966

Wilson, John, editor, *Robert Creeley's Life and Work: A Sense of Increment,* Ann Arbor: University of Michigan Press, 1987

## The Door

Robert Creeley's "The Door" is composed in the place between hope and despair, between destination and origin; it is a poem concerned with the present moment and the moment always yet to come. "The Door" appeared in 1959, first in *Poetry* magazine and later in Creeley's book *A Form of Woman*. In 1962 *A Form of Woman* became the second section (poems 1956–58) of his first complete collection of poems, *For Love*. "The Door" stands out in the collection not only for its length and its use of modified quatrains—a style that grounds much of Creeley's formal practice—but also for its lyric effect, its focus on the domestic space, and its concern for poetic tradition as well as Creeley's contemporaries, subjects that would continue to occupy his imagination in the following decades.

A sense of composition as exploration drives the lyric in "The Door": the poem is a locating device that discovers and names its surroundings. Each stanza re-approaches the object of desire (the door, and later the Lady), so that the speaker (and as a result the reader) finds his position continually changing. The door remains fixed only in that it remains the goal:

> But I see the door,
> and knew the wall, and wanted the wood,
> and would get there if I could
> with my feet and hands and mind.

The Lady remains out of reach: there is only the glimpse of her "skirt" in the "sunlight." It is the approach itself that matters, not necessarily entrance or possession of the Lady. The poet's primary need is to follow the vision of the poem begun in the first stanza, "the vision which echoes loneliness," and to trust that vision in its various guises as the source of meaning and value. This pursuit of vision is an act of uncertainty. The poem embodies the conflict between movement and non-movement: "Running to the door, I ran down / as a clock runs down"; "There is nothing to do but get up. / My knees were iron, I rusted in worship, of you." The poet fuses the act of writing with the act of living through poetic dialogue. Each address tries to communicate something and thus make the next step toward the object of desire ("The Door" does not valorize pursuit for its own sake), but the poem questions whether real progress is ever made—whether the address is ever heard or responded to—as the poet "goes on walking" and "will go on talking forever."

Within each stanza and shifting position, the lyric of exploration takes place at the level of the individual line, with the poet practicing a certain economy of words, cutting back on description while foregrounding each stressed beat; every word at once creates a sparse image and an essential sound:

> In my mind I see the door,
> I see the sunlight before me across the floor
> beckon to me, as the Lady's skirt
> moves small beyond it.

In this sense, "The Door" does not seek to transcend the speaker's world but chooses to search out and understand where he is and where he is going:

> Running to the door, I ran down
> as a clock runs down. Walked backwards,
> stumbled, sat down
> hard on the floor near the wall.

To reach the door depends on vision, a vision that takes place in a telescoping domestic sphere, in a "room," by the "wall," in a "garden." In this domestic environment the poem picks up ordinary objects of daily encounters as material from which the poem, and thus life, is made, but these objects always reach out toward a larger context, or perhaps more precisely, use individual domestic life to generate vision. A vision is always a guide that points the pilgrim, the knight, the poet toward the object of the quest. Indeed, the door is such a guide and the Lady is the muse; as Arthur Ford (1978) has noted, she stands as a parallel figure to Robert Graves' White Goddess, an unattainable figure who becomes the source of poetry. Although at one point the poet is able to possess her—

> I walked away from myself,
> I left the room,
> I found the garden,
> I knew the woman
> in it, together we lay down

—it becomes strikingly unclear if the woman in the garden is the Lady after all or if she is just a "woman" in the garden. Moreover, to gain the woman, he must leave himself, and finally she slips away.

This focus on the quotidian and on the activity of living and writing a poem makes Creeley's dedication of "The Door" to Robert Duncan of primary importance. In the context of *For Love,* the investment that Creeley has in the people around him—his family, friends, and fellow poets Olson, Levertov, Williams, and Pound—reveals his insistence on creating a place within poetry for his imagined company. While a certain loneliness pervades "The Door," it is a loneliness emphasized by what is around it: people and places. "The Door" and its container, *For Love,* seem to say: "Do not just look at a thing, or at me in isolation; look at the other poems around me—mine and those of other poets; look at the people within them, and the people without."

In a note for *The Collected Poems of Robert Creeley, 1945–1975* (1982), Robert Duncan writes, "Visionary and oracular, Creeley has been a worker in the deep romantic vein. . . . He loves the daily popular tunes, the ring of contemporary coinage, flashes of wry and sardonic humor, the lover's chagrin—for the sake of the human condition they are immediacies of, but it is a music of heaven and hell he listens for in it all." This note affirms the company of Creeley's poetry; not only does Duncan see Creeley's work as a pursuit of "the human condition" and its daily existence from moment to moment, but he also agrees with the manner of that pursuit, echoing Creeley's own lines in "The Door" back to him:

> I will go to the garden.
> I will be a romantic. I will sell
> myself in hell,
> in heaven also I will be.

Certainly Creeley and Duncan worked to find a world through poetry, both their own and each other's, and in doing so they continued the conversation that "The Door" began.

Joel Bettridge

**Further Reading**

Butterick, George, editor, *Charles Olson and Robert Creeley: The Complete Correspondence,* Santa Barbara, California: Black Sparrow Press, 1980

Clark, Tom, *Robert Creeley and the Genius of the American Common Place: Together with the Poet's "Autobiography,"* New York: New Directions, 1993

Conniff, Brian, *The Lyric and Modern Poetry: Olson, Creeley, Bunting,* New York: Peter Lang, 1988

Ford, Arthur, *Robert Creeley,* Boston: Twayne, 1978

Terrell, Carroll, editor, *Robert Creeley: The Poet's Workshop,* Orono, Maine: National Poetry Foundation, 1984

## For Love: Poems, 1950–1960

Robert Creeley's poems are exceptional in their impassioned concision, unpretentious but highly focused lexicon, and offbeat cadences. These characteristics are apparent in work collected in his first trade edition, *For Love: Poems, 1950–1960.* Issued in 1962, the volume was circulated nationally to wide acclaim, the poetry judged as "spare and tender" by Allen Ginsberg and as a "plea for the heart, for the return of, into the work of language" by Charles Olson. *For Love* was nominated for the American (now "National") Book Award and has been Creeley's bestseller, in print in various editions for decades.

The poems, composed during a tumultuous period in which Creeley divorced his first wife and remarried, speak to intuitions developed while falling in and out of particular exigencies of love, "warmth of a night perhaps, the misdirected intention come right," as Creeley writes in his preface. The majority of pieces consist of couplets and quatrains of sometimes breathtaking brevity addressing what Creeley sees as marital confusion and isolation. The work is gathered in chronological sections of decreasing durations: 1950–55; 1956–58; 1959–60. Some poem titles—"The Wife," "The Bed," "A Marriage," and the ironically rhymed sing-song "Ballad of the Despairing Husband"—forecast the scale of intimacy.

The opening of "Ballad" makes plain what is at stake: "My wife and I lived all alone, / contention was our only bone." Still, "Ballad" contains another bone. The third quatrain, as originally written and as it appeared earlier in Donald Allen's *The New American Poetry* (1960), begins: "Oh come home soon, I write to her. / Go fuck yourself, is her answer." For the first edition of *For Love* publisher Charles Scribner, Jr., insisted the word "fuck" be replaced by the more respectable "screw." Donald Hutter, Creeley's editor, unable to persuade Scribner "of the acceptability of any vernacular in a meritorious book of the sixties," recalls this incident with "a swell of frustration." "Fuck" as first inscribed was restored in later editions.

Intriguing events led to the publishing of *For Love,* Scribner's first one-author book of poetry since 1954. The writer Michael Rumaker, Creeley's colleague from Black Mountain College, had a selection of his stories featured in Scribner's short-story series, and he in turn recommended Creeley to the publisher. As a result, two years prior to the publication of *For Love,* Scribner anthologized prose by Creeley in *Short Story 3.* Scribner then asked to see a new book-length manuscript. Counter to Creeley's initial intent, a decade's worth of verse (most of which had been the basis for Creeley's M.A. thesis at the University of New Mexico and previously published by small presses) was reconstituted as the hugely successful *For Love.* In correspondence Creeley explained:

> I was trying to connect with James Laughlin's New Directions—he had said he would be interested in a new collection of poems. . . . [T]o satisfy Scribner's legal provision (that they get first look at what new manuscript I might have) and to clear the decks for going to ND, I made a book of all I'd written and gave it to them to look at, presuming that they would turn it down. They didn't.

Tonal and narrative twists animate *For Love* in evidence of how Creeley follows William Carlos Williams' directive to "think with the poem." In "The Whip" a narrator talks of two women, one "my love . . . a feather, a flat // sleeping thing," the other

> above us on
> the roof [a] woman I
>
> also loved

The reader might assume the second woman is prescience or memory of an intuition, and, if so, the first—"a feather"—more a composite of mind than substance. Surprisingly, the woman on the roof whom

> . . . I
>
> also loved, had
> addressed myself to in
>
> a fit she
> returned.

"Feather" and "on the roof" may serve as signs of the ethereal, but emotional qualities in the misgivings Creeley conveys prosodically bring them down to earth. Shortness of breath, stressful hesitations at line endings ("I"; "had"; "in") are purposeful. Creeley relates in correspondence that the woman on the roof "is a real person, really up there (at 52 Spring Street, NYC)" and thus she has really "returned," as the poem argues. She registers (making a racket upstairs?) as a material part of the narrator's "night turning in bed." The first woman is a real person, too, who wakes:

> Ugh,
> she said beside me, she put
>
> her hand on
> my back

A year before *For Love* appeared, Creeley noted elsewhere: "The local is not a place but a place in a given man . . . brought by love to give witness to in his own mind." Poem after poem Creeley brings the reader close to him, into his local place. Yet he speaks responsibly for America's 1960s generation and for many others as well when he observes in "The Kind of Act of" that there is "no more giving in / when there is no more sin." *For Love* earned immediate and sustained popularity because Creeley's place is familiar to a culture that engages inclusive experience and graceful romance. The poem "Song" starts:

What I took in my hands
grew in weight, You must
understand it
was not obscene.

In insisting that we "understand," Creeley will never seem more doctrinaire, nor sound more like his New England ancestors, nor strike a more devout pose for the cause of living "in a prayer" so unpuritanical. Indeed, he disclosed in an interview soon after the release of *For Love* that he does not choose subject matter, never "setting out to write a poem literally about something," but finds "articulation of emotions in the actual writing" (*Contexts of Poetry: Interviews, 1961–1971,* edited by Donald Allen, 1973). Creeley's strategy is unembarrassed and fearless: love and other forces of nature are brought to breath, not by giving in to them, but by giving them witness "in his own mind," that is, natural emotions are rendered into poems to think with, to live.

Jack Kimball

**Further Reading**


Altieri, Charles, "Robert Creeley's Poetics of Conjecture," in *Self and Sensibility in Contemporary American Poetry,* by Altieri, Cambridge and New York: Cambridge University Press, 1984

Clark, Tom, *Robert Creeley and the Genius of the American Common Place: Together with the Poet's "Autobiography,"* New York: New Directions, 1993

Conte, Joseph, "One Thing Finding Its Place with Another: Robert Creeley's *Pieces,*" in *Unending Design: The Forms of Postmodern Poetry,* by Conte, Ithaca, New York: Cornell University Press, 1991

Foster, Edward Halsey, "Robert Creeley, Poetics of Solitude," in *Understanding the Black Mountain Poets,* by Foster, Columbia: University of South Carolina Press, 1995

Fredman, Stephen, "'A Life Tracking Itself': Robert Creeley's *Presences: A Text for Marisol,*" in *Poet's Prose: The Crisis in American Verse,* by Fredman, Cambridge and New York: Cambridge University Press, 1983; 2nd edition, 1990

Paul, Sherman, *The Lost America of Love: Rereading Robert Creeley, Edward Dorn, and Robert Duncan,* Baton Rouge: Louisiana State University Press, 1981

Terrell, Carroll, editor, *Robert Creeley: The Poet's Workshop,* Orono, Maine: National Poetry Foundation, 1984

Von Hallberg, Robert, "Robert Creeley and John Ashbery: Systems," in *American Poetry and Culture, 1945–1980,* by Von Hallberg, Cambridge, Massachusetts: Harvard University Press, 1985

Wilson, John, editor, *Robert Creeley's Life and Work: A Sense of Increment,* Ann Arbor: University of Michigan Press, 1987


---

# Countee Cullen 1903–46

Countee Cullen was a major poet of the Harlem Renaissance, an African-American literary movement that flourished during the 1920s. His poetic reputation rests on the four books of poetry he published between 1925 and 1929. Cullen's most notable work is a volume of verse titled *Color* (1925), which is in many ways representative of writings from the Harlem Renaissance. Thematically, many of his poems explore how African-Americans struggle with what W.E.B. DuBois termed "double-consciousness," a dualistic, embattled identity composed of a sense of black cultural difference and Americanness. The two widely anthologized poems from *Color,* "Incident" and "Heritage," for example, represent the dilemma of maintaining and/or attaining a securely affirmative African-American identity in a racist society. The short poem "Incident" depicts the moment when the poem's persona realizes at age eight that he is viewed by whites as different and inferior. While "Once riding in old Baltimore, / Heart-filled, head-filled with glee," he is insulted by another child with a racial epithet. The impact of the incident is so profound that it is all he remembers of his eight-month trip to Baltimore.

"Heritage," considered by most critics to be Cullen's best poem, examines more deeply African-American "double-consciousness." The poem's persona is an African-American who explores his African heritage to understand its meaning for himself, "one three centuries removed / From the scenes his fathers loved." In rhyming couplets, the poem explores the cognitive distance the persona feels in relation to Africa, a "book one thumbs / Listlessly, till slumber comes." Indeed, the poem asks whether Africa is anything more than picture-book fantasies of an Edenic jungle depicted by modern black writers and artists. He answers affirmatively, but, for him, Africa resides not so much in the mind as in the body. That is, exploiting popular pseudo-scientific theories of "racial identity," he affirms an African self that courses through his veins: Africa is more of a "blood memory" than a cognitive memory. However, because he has intellectually assimilated to America, he fears "the dark blood dammed within / Like great pulsing tides of wine." He fears, in other words, that he will become intoxicated by his African self and lose his "civilized," humble Christian self. Hence, he tells himself that "All day long and all night through / One thing only must I do: / Quench my pride and cool my blood, / Lest I perish in the flood." Unresolved, the poem ends by expressing the troubling dualism of his identity and his desire to continue to "damn" his African self, suggesting that he has internalized the contempt for blacks in a racist America.

"Heritage" is also exemplary of another feature of Cullen's major poetry: primitivism. Like many Harlem Renaissance writers, as well as modern writers in general, Cullen maintains that

African-Americans possess a primitive self that originates from the "jungles" of Africa. Culture or civilization is a facade of sorts over the primitive, African self. The primitive self can function as a threat to the "civilized" identity, as in "Heritage," but it usually functions as a point of pride. Cullen celebrates this primitive self in essentially Romantic terms. The primitive is more spontaneous and vital than the civilized self and closer to nature. Hence, in *Color,* the poems "Atlantic City Waiter," "Pagan Prayer," and "Fruit of the Flower" all portray a repressed but ultimately irrepressible primitive self that manifests itself in subtle ways. "Atlantic City Waiter," for example, depicts a black waiter whose movements betray "Ten thousand years on jungle clues." Black Americans are represented through the dyadic model of a "civilized" appearance or "mask" versus a "primitive" essence: "Sheer through the acquiescent mask / Of bland gentility, / The jungle flames like a copper cask / Set where the sun strikes free." While fraught with difficulties, Cullen's recuperation of the "primitive" self was part and parcel of one of the central ways that writers from the Harlem Renaissance reevaluated some of the stereotypes of black Americans in hopes of fostering race pride.

Much of Cullen's poetry is also characterized by religious themes and figures. Especially noteworthy is one of his longer narrative poems titled "The Black Christ," the title poem of a book of poetry he published in 1929. In this poem, Cullen develops a familiar theme of African-American literature, namely, that black Americans are Christ-like figures unjustly crucified by whites. Cullen's poem centers on a young southern black man named Jim who kills a white man for insulting him and his white girlfriend as they enjoy together the arrival of spring. Jim is lynched by a white mob yet is miraculously resurrected. His resurrection quells the doubts that he and his brother had about God's existence and salvation for black people. Characteristically, Cullen narrates the poem in a Romantic voice. The real crime for Jim is that the intrusion of racism into the beautiful spring day was tantamount to letting "the winter in once more" and thus killing spring, the Romantic symbol of growth, renewal, and, as in Percy Bysshe Shelley's poetry, revolutionary change. Yet the poem suggests that even the long winter of racism must come to an end, as Jim's resurrection symbolizes the rebirth of hope for black Americans. Even death contributes to freedom since each lynching "resurrects" another Jim who will be guided by "a thousand black men, long since gone" who also sought freedom. Again, for Cullen, one's black heritage and ancestors live on in the present and, in this poem, can provide spiritual and political guidance.

Stylistically, Cullen's poetry is conventional, relying on the lyric, the Petrarchan and Shakespearean sonnet forms, the Spenserian stanza, and the ballad. His greatest influences were John Keats and Edna St. Vincent Millay, the latter on whom he wrote his undergraduate thesis at New York University. Enamored of Keats, he writes of his continuing importance to him: "'John Keats is dead,' they say, but I / Who hear your full insistent cry / In bud and blossom, leaf and tree, / Know John Keats still writes poetry" ("To John Keats, Poet. At Spring Time," 1925). Cullen thus takes a position against a number of his black literary contemporaries, most notably Langston Hughes, who argued that black poets should use uniquely African-American expressive forms, such as the spirituals, black dialect, and the blues and jazz forms, to adequately represent black Americans. Fully aware of his minority position in the Harlem Renaissance, Cullen clearly suggests his preference for English poetic conventions in a foreword he wrote to his anthology of poetry by black Americans titled *Caroling Dusk* (1927): "As heretical as it may sound, there is the probability that Negro poets, dependent as they are on the English language, may have more to gain from the rich background of English and American poetry than from any nebulous atavistic yearnings toward an African inheritance." In a review he wrote of Hughes' first major book of poetry, *The Weary Blues* (1926), Cullen goes so far as to suggest that "jazz poetry" is an oxymoron.

Ultimately, Cullen's defense of traditional poetic forms was linked to his defense of himself as a poet, a difficult profession for black Americans since critical opinion had historically concluded that blacks could not be poets, let alone first-rate poets. He anticipates the surprise that the literary establishment may express on encountering *Color* by beginning the book with the lyric "Yet Do I Marvel," wherein he marvels that God would "make a poet black, and bid him sing!" He therefore viewed the emerging careers of vernacular poets such as Hughes as dangerous. "If I am going to be a poet at all," Cullen proclaimed, "I am going to be a POET and not a NEGRO POET. This is what has hindered the development of artists among us."

Cullen's use of traditional forms is not without innovation, however. Indeed, to write almost exclusively of black subjects in conventional form is to produce a new class of poetry that subtly asserts the equal "fitness" and importance of black life for high art. For example, like many English poets before him, Cullen wrote a number of carpe diem poems. Since the carpe diem poem pleads for the consummation of love before death, it always represents a heightened interest for the object of desire. Of course, traditionally, for English poetry, the love object has been a white English woman. The racial politics of the object of such an English poem becomes clearer when we read one of Cullen's poems beside it, such as "To a Brown Boy" (1925). Here the object of desire is a "brown girl" whose value is equal to any other woman, even a "queen": "That brown girl's swagger gives a twitch / To beauty like a queen; / Lad, never dam your body's itch / When loveliness is seen."

Cullen's use of the ballad form also refunctions the form for some of the egalitarian aims of the Harlem Renaissance. In 1927, Cullen published *The Ballad of the Brown Girl: An Old Ballad Retold.* Written in popular ballad form, it tells of the disastrous consequences of an aristocrat's decision to marry a "brown girl" for her riches instead of a southern "lily maid" for love. The spurned white woman arrives uninvited to the wedding ceremony and insults the Lord and the brown girl by stating that "only the rose and rose should mate, / Oh, never the hare and the hound." When the Lord refuses to heed to the brown girl's request for revenge, she stabs the white woman. The Lord then in effect lynches the brown girl by hanging her with a noose made of her long hair, and, overcome with madness, he then kills himself. The brown girl is represented as a regal woman who kills out of pride for her "brown" self rather than committing suicide from shame as told in legend "of a dusky queen" who "Had loved in vain, and died of it, / By her own slim twilight hand." In other words, Cullen uses the ballad form here to condemn the devaluation of this black woman by a racist ideology that equates interracial marriage to different species pairing off, as if the black woman was not of the human species. The mythical setting and aristocratic personages of the traditional English ballad form also allow Cullen to treat a contemporaneous and controversial topic as if it happened long ago. He thereby stems immediate rejection of the poem's topic by readers unsympathetic to direct political statements concerning the unjustness and harmfulness of racist ideas and practices.

Historically, Cullen has occupied a minor place in American literary history. Like other black writers, he was virtually ignored by the American literary establishment until the 1960s, when there emerged a renewed interest in Harlem Renaissance writers. However, even among scholars of the Harlem Renaissance, Cullen's work has not figured prominently. One of the contributing causes of Cullen's continuing neglect has been the importance given by black literary studies to black vernacular oral and literary traditions. His rejection of African-American expressive forms has earned him little favor among contemporary critics. Moreover, since Cullen wrote during the heyday of Modernism, he has not figured into contemporary reassessments of Modernism. Presently, except for *Color,* his books of poetry are out of print; selections of his poetry are anthologized.

ANTHONY DAWAHARE

*See also* Harlem Renaissance

**Biography**

Born Countee Leroy Porter in Louisville, Kentucky, 30 May 1903; adopted by Frederick Asbury Cullen, 1918. Attended New York University, B.A. 1925 (Phi Beta Kappa); Harvard University, Cambridge, Massachusetts, A.M. 1926; assistant editor and columnist, *Opportunity* magazine, 1927; taught French, Frederick Douglass Junior High School, New York, 1934–46. Received John Reed Memorial Prize (*Poetry,* Chicago), 1925; Spingarn Award (*Crisis* magazine), 1925; Harmon Foundation Literary Award, 1927; Guggenheim fellowship, 1928. Died in New York City, 9 January 1946.

**Poetry**

*Color,* 1925
*Copper Sun,* 1927
*The Ballad of the Brown Girl: An Old Ballad Retold,* 1927
*The Black Christ, and Other Poems,* 1929
*The Medea, and Some Poems,* 1935
*The Lost Zoo (A Rhyme for the Young, but Not Too Young),* 1940
*On These I Stand: An Anthology of the Best Poems of Cullen,* 1947
*My Soul's High Song: The Collected Writings of Countee Cullen, Voice of the Harlem Renaissance,* edited by Gerald Early, 1991

**Other Writings:** plays (*The Third Fourth of July* [with Owen Dodson], 1946), novel (*One Way to Heaven,* 1932), children's literature; edited collections of poetry (*Caroling Dusk: An Anthology of Verse by Negro Poets,* 1927).

**Further Reading**

Baker, Houston A., Jr., *A Many-Colored Coat of Dreams: The Poetry of Countee Cullen,* Detroit, Michigan: Broadside Press, 1974
Early, Gerald, "Introduction," in *My Soul's High Song: The Collected Writings of Countee Cullen, Voice of the Harlem Renaissance,* edited by Gerald Early, New York and London: Anchor, 1991
Lomax, Michael L., "Countee Cullen: A Key to the Puzzle," in *The Harlem Renaissance Re-Examined,* edited by Victor A. Kramer, New York: AMS, 1987; London: AMS Press, 1988; revised and expanded edition, edited by Kramer and Robert A. Russ, Troy, New York: Whitson, 1997
Shucard, Alan R., *Countee Cullen,* Boston: Twayne, 1984
Tuttleton, James W., "Countee Cullen at 'The Heights,'" in *The Harlem Renaissance: Revaluations,* edited by Amrijit Singh, William S. Shiver, and Stanley Brodwin, New York and London: Garland, 1989

## Heritage

Published in Countee Cullen's first book of lyric verse, *Color* (1925), "Heritage" explores the conflict at the core of much of his poetry: How does an African-American reconcile the legacy of African heritage with the circumstances of life in America? "Heritage," through expert use of form, language, image, and example, defines the speaker's struggle for identity.

The title and the opening lines of the poem immediately present the question to which the rest of the poem responds: "What is Africa to me[?]" As "one three centuries removed / From the scenes his fathers loved," the speaker cannot immediately answer. The quest to understand history and thus self continues throughout the poem, with Cullen using repetition to underscore the speaker's continuous return to questions of identity. The second stanza introduces the reader to whom and where the speaker is currently and to whom and where he imagines himself capable of being:

So I lie, who all day long
Want no sound except the song
Sung by wild barbaric birds
Goading massive jungle herds,
. . . .
So I lie, who always hear,
Though I cram against my ear
Both my thumbs, and keep them there,
Great drums throbbing though the air.

Three times in this stanza, and several times more throughout the poem, the refrain "So I lie" leads into his imagined struggles; the speaker passively explores his knowledge of Africa as if it were "a book one thumbs / Listlessly, till slumber comes." He does not consciously remember Africa, although echoes of communal memory still come upon him when he is least resistant. Although he struggles against the urges brought on by this persistent blood-memory, he still strongly desires the abundant and free life he believes would be available in Africa. The speaker's fond reference to the animals, people, and music of this native home reveals his belief in Africa as a space of savage and unhindered freedom that calls to the speaker, "Strip!" and, "Come and dance."

Despite the speaker's blood-allegiance to Africa, the poem is restrained by formal Western conventions. The conflict that ensues suggests that the poem's speaker is not so much passive as prisoner to the circumstances of his life. He can "find no peace / Night or day." This inability to sleep or rest manifests itself most incessantly

When the rain begins to fall;
Like a soul gone mad with pain
I must match its weird refrain;
Ever must I twist and squirm,
Writhing like a baited worm,
While its primal measures drip
Through my body[.] . . .
In an old remembered way
Rain works on me night and day.

Although the poem is written in trochaic trimeter, each line has an extra masculine foot to emphasize the drum-like meter of the poem and, thus, subverts Western metrical convention. Possessed body and soul by the drumming rhythm of rain and blood, the speaker can stop his ears or try to sleep but is forever overcome by throbbing memories and a desire to search for some scarcely buried self.

The speaker's impulse to reconcile his African heritage to his American existence nearly overwhelms his reserve throughout the course of the poem:

So I lie, whose fount of pride,
Dear distress, and joy allied,
Is my somber flesh and skin,
With the dark blood dammed within
Like great pulsing tides of wine
That, I fear, must burst the fine
Channels of the chafing net
Where they surge and foam and fret.

His happiness and distress both stem from his black skin. The persistent enjambment of these lines mimics the speaker's fears that his skin and mind will not be able to contain the more abandoned heritage he takes as part of the legacy of his dark skin. The poem is written in rhymed couplets but for two exceptions, when the rhyme mimics the longed-for abandon and trips ahead of itself, running into tercets. Throughout the poem Cullen uses enjambment, as he does above, to distract the reader from the restrained, rhymed couplets, and to create a sense of boundless movement.

This alternating use of form to convey both Western and African heritage reveals itself in another understanding of the repeated phrase, "So I lie." If "lie" is read with its alternate definition, the line suggests the speaker attempts to deceive himself and others, to repress his African heritage. The speaker will not be able to rest, however—literally or figuratively—until he is able to fully understand and accept both where he is and from whence he has come.

This poem explores the conflict inherent in the dual-consciousness of the African-American; this term, "African-American," was coined by Cullen's one-time father-in-law, W.E.B. DuBois. Likewise, "Heritage" both contains classical Western aesthetic form—embodied in rhymed couplets and regular meter—and rebels against its constraints using constant enjambment, the drum rhythm of trochaic meter (in defiance of the typical iambic meter of the English language), and the extra beat at the end of each line. It is a poem both American and African.

The middle of the poem gives great prominence to the importance of being able to worship in the manner of one's choice:

Quaint, outlandish heathen gods
Black men fashion out of rods,
Clay, and brittle bits of stone
In a likeness like their own,
My conversion came high-priced;
I belong to Jesus Christ,
Preacher of humility;
Heathen gods are naught to me.

Is this high price of conversion based on the sacrifices Jesus Christ made, because of which Christians must know humility and eschew their "heathen" traits, or is the loss of the gods "his fathers loved" the great price of conversion? Here Cullen expresses the double blessing and double curse of having lost and gained two sorts of gods, two cultures, two identities.

In this section the reader truly senses the conflict and frustration that require the speaker to "play a double part":

Ever at Thy glowing altar
Must my heart grow sick and falter,
Wishing He I served were black[.]

Although the speaker claims to be worshiping the same Jesus as his Christian fellows, like the "Black men" of his heritage he "fashion[s] dark gods too." These dark gods share his pain, as well as his "Dark despairing features" and "dark rebellious hair." Only through such a creation and recreation of self, spirit, and God can the speaker find some source for true comfort, the opportunity to "Quench [his] pride and cool [his] blood / Lest [he] perish in the flood."

The poem ends with this acknowledgment:

Not yet has my heart or head
In the least way realized
They and I are civilized.

The speaker lives in fear of the condemning flood, the engulfing fire, and the judgment that might be brought upon him if he fully allows himself to explore his African heritage. To survive he must constrain his impulses toward heathen abandon and give in to the god of humility he accepted upon his conversion to the Western faith and life. He must forever battle against both his mind and his heart, since these will not, and seemingly cannot, fully accept the "high-priced" consequences of being "civilized."

CAMILLE DUNGY

**Further Reading**

Baker, Houston A., Jr., "Many-Colored Coat of Dreams: The Poetry of Countee Cullen," in *Afro-American Poetics: Revisions of Harlem and the Black Aesthetic,* edited by Baker, Madison: University of Wisconsin Press, 1988

Canaday, Nicholas, "Major Themes in the Poetry of Countee Cullen," in *The Harlem Renaissance Remembered,* edited by Arna Bontemps, New York: Dodd Mead, 1972

Early, Gerald, editor, *My Soul's High Song: The Collected Writings of Countee Cullen, Voice of the Harlem Renaissance,* New York and London: Anchor, 1991

Lomax, Michael L., "Countee Cullen: A Key to the Puzzle," in

*The Harlem Renaissance Re-Examined,* edited by Victor A. Kramer, New York: AMS Press, 1987; London: AMS Press, 1988; revised and expanded edition, edited by Kramer and Robert A. Russ, Troy, New York: Whitson, 1997

Onyeberechi, Sydney, *Critical Essays: Achebe, Baldwin, Cullen, Ngugi, and Tutuola,* Hyattsville, Maryland: Rising Star, 1999

Perry, Margaret, *A Bio-Bibliography of Countee P. Cullen, 1903–1946,* Westport, Connecticut: Greenwood, 1971

---

# E.E. Cummings 1894–1962

E.E. Cummings was the beneficiary of contemporary revolutions in poetry and painting: Ezra Pound's Imagism (1912), whose highly concentrated language drew on the visual imagination, and Gertrude Stein's experiments in prose in *Tender Buttons* (1914), based on the Cubist paintings of Picasso and Braque. Both innovative rebellions from orthodoxy met with derision from critics while forging new perspectives and modes of expression. Cummings immersed himself in the Modernist ferment and invented a style of verse that looked dismembered on the page but is well-crafted poetry when read aloud.

Cummings' first book is *Tulips and Chimneys* (1923), which contains some of his wittiest poems. His Imagist leanings can be read in the title, which perceives an underlying form in a flower and a chimney pot, which are made to serve as images of spring and winter, youth and age. The poems under "Tulips" celebrate first love and range over many forms, some of them exploded stanzas with even their words fragmented and left sprawling down the page; the poems under "Chimneys" explore winter emotions in a variety of sonnets in standard 14-line forms.

The opening poem, "Epithalamion," is a witty, slightly twisted marriage poem that skillfully employs iambic pentameter and an eight-line stanza with an intricate rhyme scheme (abcadcbd) while torturing syntax and taking liberties with decorum. This marriage poem welcomes the lustful energies of Cummings' favorite season, spring. The poem is calculated to shock the reader with its blunt interpretations of Greek mythological love while offering an impressive imitation of Spenser's baroque style. This and other formal poems in the opening section of the book confirm Norman Friedman's observation that Cummings was well trained in classical poetry at Harvard University and an able craftsman in the formal mode despite his reputation as a trailblazer of new poetry.

In the next section, "Chansons Innocentes" (Innocent Songs), one meets the familiar, unorthodox Cummings. In his untitled "balloonMan" poem, spring is hailed as the beginning of puberty, where children at play are confronted suddenly by the "goat-footed // balloonMan" whose fragile balloons stand for perishable illusions and easily burst innocence. Cummings' ear for children's nonsense lyrics is keen here and elsewhere; his rhythms are fluid and light, and his language has the nervousness and jumpy logic of Dixieland jazz, just then coming into vogue.

"Buffalo Bill's / defunct" is among Cummings' most famous poems, an elegy for the arch symbol of indestructible youth, drawn from the myth of the cowboy and the perpetual youthfulness of America's Wild West. This cliché is wielded lightly to deliver a brief meditation on how "Mister Death" can claim even the youngest and boldest, "your blue-eyed boy." While the language is slangy and urbane, the shape of the poem dramatizes the quick draw and pistol-blazing of Buffalo Bill's Wild West Show act. This alone is an important innovation in poetry, where words are scattered to the right and spliced together to reenact the visual sensation of a rapidly fired gun.

The "Chimneys" section begins with "Sonnets-Realities" and a wry tribute to "the Cambridge ladies," who once hosted tea parties for Harvard's eligible bachelor undergraduates and who appear in this poem as grim guardians of virtue, both proffering and withholding their charming daughters. (These same "daughters" are featured in Eliot's "The Love Song of J. Alfred Prufrock" and likened to indifferent mermaids at the poem's close.) The sight of old dowagers conducting a ritual of high society gives Cummings a glimpse into middle-aged respectability and a sterile world of faded customs and thus a gate into the world of winter. Other poems feature the ravages of urban life, as with the girl "kitty," who at 16 is already a prostitute. Others remark on the despair at being jilted or spurned or lament the season: "I think i too have known / autumn too long." Death is an impending condition on all who once loved or who carry the torch forlornly.

Cummings, like Wallace Stevens, divided New England into summer as the season of imagination and liberty and winter as the season of reality and death. While their criticisms of lingering Puritanism are wry and only half serious, both writers squirmed at regional pragmatism and longed for an imaginary haven of perpetual summertime and amorous freedom. For Cummings, that realm belonged exclusively to children and young adults, who were not yet wage earners and bitter realists. Cummings would retreat to that state of mind often in his poetry, but his poems after 1940 slowly give up his pastoral Eden of satyrs and Jazz Age flappers to talk about the responsibilities of adult love.

*&* (1925), the title of Cummings' next book, alludes to the fact that these poems and the following collection, *XLI Poems* (1925), were parts of the original manuscript of "Tulips and Chimneys" but were excluded from the published version for reasons of length. Both books follow the general plan of the first and develop many of the same themes; they contain impressionist poems, portraits, and miscellaneous short poems. The title of *Is 5* (1926) is explained in a sardonic foreword as violating the basic arithmetic of two plus two equals four. The poems have the same disregard for predictable formulas and contain many of Cummings' most popular poems, including "Poem, or Beauty Hurts Mr. Vinal," "Jimmy's got a goil," "she being Brand," "next to of course god america i," and "my sweet old etcetera."

Cummings' tone mixes satire and amorous whimsy; the target of much of his wit is the same American "booboisie" that H.L. Mencken and Sinclair Lewis spared no pains to skewer in their own satires—Americans prospering from unregulated stock markets and a postwar boom and making a gospel of their materialism. While other poets were still writing in a decorously formal language, Cummings, like William Carlos Williams, was exploring the American speech idiom, in particular a New York accent, as in "Jimmy's got a goil." Street life in the 1920s is vividly sketched in these poems, with their sprawling lines but tightly framed lyric patterns. The voice of many of these poems is a slightly cranky, common citizen who observes the passing scene with a blend of impatience, wonder, and erotic interest.

*W (ViVa)* (1931) fleshes out this tireless satirist of the greedy and the mean spirited and indulges an ear for the broadest accents, as in "oil tel duh woil doi sez" and "buncha hardboil guys from duh A.C. fulla / hooch." Much fun is poked at politicians of this troubled era, as in his mock tribute to Warren Harding, "the only man woman or child who wrote / a simple declarative sentence with seven grammatical / errors." A favorite Cummings poem crops up here in "I sing of Olaf glad and big," a mock-heroic idyll of a brave "conscientious object-or," and so on for 70 poems of relentless wordplay and shape changing.

*No Thanks* (1935) directs its title to all the presses (duly listed in the "Initial Dedication") that rejected the manuscript after Cummings published his memoir of a trip to Russia, *Eimi* (1933), in which he scorns Stalinist totalitarianism. A glimpse of his attitude may be seen in his mocking lyric "kumrads die because they're told." He was spurned by editors angry at his seeming betrayal of the Left. However, this book begins Cummings' most vigorous period of experiment in poetic form and contains some of his best work.

The classic "tmetic" style is here: breaking up words into their characters and syllables, segmenting words with internal parentheses around roots and endings, or inserting pronouns and adjectives into the phrase to suggest movement, punning sense, or merely to interrupt the obvious course of a thought. Cummings' eye is keenly sensitive to the pictorial dimension of mere letters on the page and anticipates a century of typographical restlessness with his loops and swirls and descents of language to mimic action.

Using his considerable skills as a draftsman, Cummings set the poem in motion on the page, giving words a new liveliness and visual humor, as in his celebrated poem "r-p-o-p-h-e-s-s-a-g-e-r," a favorite of anthologists. Here the leap of the grasshopper is brilliantly reproduced in the tumble, shredding, and final reconstruction of the word. Another of his classic pieces of visual dramatization, "o pr," drops the letter "o" from everything that follows as a baseball is thrown out by the president to start the season. Only in the first line does one see the "o" appear. Another, "b / eLl / s?," or "Bells," splinters and fragments the word "bells" down the page as Cummings attempts to show us the swinging of church bells in different steeples. Sometimes this visual cleverness can become self-indulgent and merely puzzle pictures. His humor, always brimming with irreverence and erotic undertones, is nowhere better demonstrated than in "may I feel said he," where two lovers exchange one-liners in a brief but hilarious seduction.

However, Cummings' best poems are not far from the world of cartoons and comic book illustrations; they share a similarly grotesque humor and mock-epic hyperbole. Eventually, his experiments in graphic language would find their way into advertising and even painting, where tortured writing played a prominent role in the canvases of Pop art.

*Collected Poems* (1938), itself only a selection of recent work, came next in Cummings' prolific career and was, like his first published book, the prose memoir *The Enormous Room* (1922), the basis of his enormous popularity by 1940. *Complete Poems, 1910–1962* (1981) takes a small sample from the 1938 book and calls it "New Poems." A brief introduction distinguishes individuals from what he calls "mostpeople": snobs and those who pursue material success without enjoying their lives. "You and I" are dreamers, natural poets for whom the work is written.

These playful notions of two societies, an adult world of careerists and a fringe of idealists and fantasists, go to the heart of Cummings' beliefs. He saw himself as a minstrel of the young and a satirist of the rest of society. While his techniques grew and diversified into plays, memoirs, "nonlectures," and a wellspring of new poetry, his emotions remained those of an unrepentant sentimentalist and romantic. Cummings' poems might be described as Valentines wrapped in a Modernist wit.

"(of Ever-Ever Land i speak" shows how idealists "like us" live in the real world perhaps more than do pragmatists, with their visions of glory to come. "Down with hell and heaven / and all the religious fuss / infinity pleased our parents / one inch looks good to us." Or take this bit of verbal play: "Q:dwo / we know of anything which can / be as dull as one englishman / A: to." Or "my specialty is living / said a man (who could not earn his bread / because he would not sell his head." The gentle sort of Marxism exhibited in these poems is always on the side of playful grouses against a world of commerce, as in the poem "economic secu / rity is a curious excu // se . . . for pu // tting the arse / before the torse." "Above all things be glad and young," Cummings declares at the end of these poems.

Cummings was a talented performer of his own work and in great demand as a reader on the college circuit after World War II. His readings were recorded and sold well, and it was this popularity that inspired a vast new outpouring of poems, including *1 x 1* (1944) and *Xaipe* (1950); the very successful *95 Poems* (1958), the last volume published during his lifetime; and the posthumous edition of his final work, *73 Poems* (1963). The writing is fluid and effortless and carries on the lighthearted but often barbed social commentary of his earlier years. However, a more sober and didactic tone characterizes his love poetry hereafter, in part the result of a successful and long-lasting marriage to his third wife, Marion Morehouse.

This more preacherly turn of Cummings' wit may be seen in "when serpents bargain for the right to squirm," a series of paradoxical propositions leading to the compromise to believe "in that incredible / unanimal mankind." As before, he plunders the Mother Goose rhymes for models for his own eccentric songs, which he peppered with slang and cranky humor; and his old nemesis, the Soviet Union, comes in for some verbal whacking, as in "o to be in finland / now that russia's here)." The shape of his poems settled down to conventional lyric form, short irregular stanzas with less of the visual play of his best work.

Much of Cummings' late work is light, airy, and forgettable, but for occasional whimsy or punning. His best work is concentrated in the flamboyant lyricism and radical forms of the 1930s, but the public remained faithful to him throughout his long and fertile career. By the late 1950s, he was regarded as a public treasure and enjoyed the respect of an adoring readership. Like Robert Frost, his contemporary, Cummings expressed the dry sardonic humor and individuality of New England character, with its pungent speech and thinly disguised moral idealism. If Frost likened free verse to playing tennis without a net, Cummings made netless tennis a romp of improvised humorous movements that concealed a similar dedication to craft and traditional forms. He never abandoned the sonnet or the irregular ode, which he is partly responsible for modernizing for use in the 20th century.

PAUL CHRISTENSEN

*See also* Light Verse

**Biography**

Born in Cambridge, Massachusetts, 14 October 1894. Attended Harvard University, Cambridge, 1911–16 (co-founder, Harvard Poetry Society, 1915), A.B. (magna cum laude) in Greek 1915, A.M. 1916; served in the Norton-Harjes Ambulance Service, 1917; interned in France, 1917–18; served in the United States Army, 1918–19; worked at P.F. Collier and Company, mail-order books, New York, 1917; writer, *Vanity Fair,* New York, 1925–27; artist with paintings in several group and individual shows, Paris, New York City, and Rochester, New York, 1932–57; Charles Eliot Norton Professor of Poetry, Harvard University, 1952–53. Received *Dial* Award, 1925; Guggenheim fellowship, 1933, 1951; Levinson Prize (*Poetry,* Chicago), 1939; Shelley Memorial Award, 1945; Academy of American Poets fellowship, 1950; Harriet Monroe Poetry Award, 1950; Eunice Tietjens Memorial Prize (*Poetry,* Chicago), 1952; National Book Award, 1955; Bollingen Prize, 1958; Ford Foundation grant, 1959; Oscar Blumenthal Prize (*Poetry,* Chicago), 1962. Died in Madison, New Hampshire, 3 September 1962.

**Poetry**

*Tulips and Chimneys,* 1923; complete edition, 1937; revised edition, edited by George James Firmage, 1976
*&,* 1925
*XLI Poems,* 1925
*Is 5,* 1926
*W (ViVa: Seventy New Poems),* 1931; revised edition, edited by George James Firmage, 1979
*No Thanks,* 1935; revised edition, edited by George James Firmage, 1978
*Collected Poems,* 1938
*50 Poems,* 1940
*1 x 1,* 1944
*Xaipe,* 1950; revised edition, edited by George James Firmage, 1979
*Poems, 1923–1954,* 1954
*95 Poems,* 1958
*100 Selected Poems,* 1959
*Selected Poems, 1923–1958,* 1960
*73 Poems,* 1963
*Poems, 1905–1962,* edited by George James Firmage, 1973
*Complete Poems, 1910–1962,* 2 vols., edited by George James Firmage, 1981
*Etcetera: The Unpublished Poems,* edited by George James Firmage and Richard S. Kennedy, 1983
*Hist Whist and Other Poems for Children,* edited by George James Firmage, 1983
*Selected Poems,* 1994
*Little Tree* (for children), 1999
*22 and 50 Poems,* edited by George James Firmage, 2000

**Other Writings:** plays (*Santa Claus: A Morality,* 1946), memoirs (*The Enormous Room,* 1922), travel literature, children's literature, correspondence (*Selected Letters,* edited by F.W. Dupee and George Stade, 1969), translation of French literature (*The Red Front,* by Louis Aragon, 1933).

**Further Reading**

Cohen, Milton A., *Poet and Painter: The Aesthetics of E.E. Cummings' Early Work,* Detroit, Michigan: Wayne State University Press, 1987
Friedman, Norman, *E.E. Cummings: The Art of His Poetry,* Baltimore, Maryland: Johns Hopkins University Press, and London: Oxford University Press, 1960
Friedman, Norman, *E.E. Cummings: The Growth of a Writer,* Carbondale: Southern Illinois University Press, 1964
Friedman, Norman, *(Re)valuing Cummings: Further Essays on the Poet, 1962–1993,* Gainesville: University Press of Florida, 1996
Kennedy, Richard S., *E.E. Cummings Revisited,* New York: Twayne, and Oxford: Macmillan, 1994
Kidder, Rushworth M., *E.E. Cummings: An Introduction to the Poetry,* New York: Columbia University Press, 1979
Webster, Michael, *Reading Visual Poetry after Futurism: Marinetti, Apollinaire, Schwitters, Cummings,* New York: Peter Lang, 1995

## anyone lived in a pretty how town

Most readers of E.E. Cummings' work would agree that Cummings' use of language is at the very least problematic. His attempt to democratize language by abandoning strict adherence to the accepted rules of punctuation and capitalization is just one of his many idiosyncrasies. His poems are certainly iconoclastic both thematically and grammatically: they seem to self-consciously "deconstruct" on the page. Accordingly, the structuralist theories of Roland Barthes and Jacques Derrida may provide a useful framework to interpret one of his most anthologized poems, "anyone lived in a pretty how town" from his collection *50 Poems* (1940).

Structuralists like to point out that any text is the functioning of a system. Consider, for example, the following combination of words: "Mary runs to the store." The reader can interpret this sentence using standard rules of English. Since a sentence must have a subject and a predicate, "Mary" is in the subject slot and reads as a noun. "Runs" in the verb slot functions as part of the predicate. These two words are compatible within the rules of the system of the sentence. The reader can substitute other words in those slots, however: "*Gliph* goes to the store," or "Mary *slurges* to the store." "Gliph" is still understandable as a noun simply because it is in the noun slot, and "slurges" as a verb because it is in the verb slot. These kinds of substitutions within a system are called paradigmatic. They are important because of the difference the reader can discern between items that may be substituted in the same slot.

A radical text like Cummings' poem forces the reader to make paradigmatic substitutions in his lines in order to approach some kind of traditional interpretation, since it would be very difficult to say just what Cummings' "intentions" were. For example, the poem begins:

anyone lived in a pretty how town
(with up so floating many bells down)
spring summer autumn winter
he sang his didn't he danced his did.

From the first line of "anyone lived in a pretty how town" the poet forces the reader to construct a meaning from his already radically interpolated syntax. Thus for the first word, "anyone" (which is sitting in the subject slot of the sentence), the reader might substitute: everyman/everywoman, an individual, a human, an average Joe, an American, and so on. This single word suggests a cluster of meanings that all have validity. Moreover, since "anyone" is an indefinite pronoun, the poet seems to be *intentionally* inviting the reader to substitute any number of particular subjects to the sentence. For "how" (which seems to be sitting in an adjective position), the reader might substitute: cow, Midwestern, small, nondescript, average or middle class. In fact, Cummings can be seen as having *already* substituted his words for the ones expected in a simple declarative sentence—"An average person lived in a small Midwestern town"—specifically to prevent any single univocal reading.

Linguists like to point out that because the act of reading always forces a reader to discriminate between possible substitutions in any given slot, the reader cannot help but consider highly subjective possibilities, derived from a personal cache. Thus "how" could be read as "cow," "grandpa's farm," "last summer," or "boring," depending on the reader. This whole chain of paradigmatic substitutions is established and held in the mind at once in what Derrida might call "traces" of signification (meanings). Some substitutions are more apropos, but the other "traces" cannot, nor should they be, discounted. A text such as Cummings' poem, consciously written to have a plurality of interpretive meanings, is what Roland Barthes calls a "writerly" text. A reader cannot easily consume it, as he or she would a more traditional or "readerly" text.

Another way to approach "anyone lived in a pretty how town" is to examine what A.J. Griemas has called its "isotopies" or patterns. In this poem, these isotopies illustrate rhythms of diurnal and climactic change, seasonal change, and human generation. With these patterns, the poet also sets up an opposition between "anyone" and the social and cosmological forces that are arrayed against "anyone" in a kind of parable of the individual human life. Time passes in such isotopies as "spring summer autumn winter" and "sun moon stars rain," while lines such as "someones married their everyones" allude to traditional social structures. Cummings suggests traditional belief systems by the metonymic association of bells with churches and schools in the line "(with up so floating many bells down)" and the struggle of "anyone" in "he sang his didn't he danced his did." Passages like

Women and men . . .
cared for anyone not at all
they sowed their isn't they reaped their same

address the dehumanizing effect of social conformity, a negation of possibility ("their isn't") resulting in "same," unaltered repetition. In the poem's conclusion, the human life cycle ends in anonymity: "one day *anyone* died I guess / (and *noone* stooped to kiss his face)" (emphasis added). Here the opposition of "anyone" and "noone" comes to its climax as the presence and consciousness of the former are negated by the latter. Life's repetitive cycle continues, however: as the seasons rotate "summer autumn winter spring," the bells "(both dong and ding)" as the men and women "[reap] their sowing"—that is, their sameness.

GARY P. WALTON

**Further Reading**


Friedman, Norman, *(Re)valuing Cummings: Further Essays on the Poet, 1962–1993,* Gainesville: University Press of Florida, 1996

Gee, James Paul, "Anyone's Any: A View of Language and Poetry through an Analysis of 'anyone lived in a pretty how town,'" *Language and Style: An International Journal* 16, no. 2 (Spring 1983)

Kennedy, Richard S., *E.E. Cummings Revisited,* New York: Twayne, and Oxford: Macmillan, 1994

Rotella, Guy, editor, *Critical Essays on E.E. Cummings,* Boston: G.K. Hall, 1984

Steinmann, Theo, "The Semantic Rhythm in 'anyone lived in a pretty how town,'" *Concerning Poetry* 11, no. 2 (1998)


# i sing of Olaf glad and big

One of E.E. Cummings' most famous anti-war poems, "i sing of Olaf glad and big" is frequently anthologized in both selections of the poet's work and anthologies of 20th-century war poetry. In its anti-military rhetoric and championship of an outsider abused by unjust force, the poem represents the worldview guiding not only Cummings' World War I poems but also *The Enormous Room* (1922), his experimental prose memoir of his wartime imprisonment in France on suspicion of disloyalty. In its juxtaposition of formal and colloquial diction, its strategic use of typography and punctuation, and its combination of rhythmic levity and scathing satire, it characterizes Cummings' unique contribution to 20th-century satiric and political poetry.

First published in *W (ViVa)* (1931), "i sing of Olaf glad and big" has its origins in Cummings' unwilling, unhappy service in the U.S. Army in the final year of World War I. Having returned to the United States in January 1918 after his stint in the Norton-Harjes Ambulance Service and subsequent internment in the French prison La Ferté-Macé, he was drafted and served at Camp Devens, Massachusetts, from July 1918 to January 1919. One of his fellow privates there, a man whom Cummings would later call Olaf, made his opposition to violence and unwillingness to handle weapons clear to his commanding officers. "Olaf" quickly disappeared from Camp Devens and was rumored to be at the military prison at Fort Leavenworth, Kansas (Kennedy, 1980). Out of his memory of this Swedish-American pacifist, his understanding of the reportedly brutal treatment of men at military prisons, and his own antagonism toward the conformist values of the military system he encountered at Camp Devens, Cummings created the dual elegy and satire of "i sing of Olaf glad and big."

From its opening lines the poem announces its engagement with and departure from the Western tradition of writing about the heroic and violent encounters of war. Cummings replaces Virgil's famed opening to *The Aeneid*—"I sing of arms and a man"—with a description of the good-natured pacifist who is the subject of his song:

i sing of Olaf glad and big
whose warmest heart recoiled at war:
a conscientious object-or[.]

Cummings' mid-word insertion of a hyphen, typical of his use of punctuation to expand linguistic meaning, suggests that Olaf's status as an objector to war secures simultaneously his status as an "object." The next stanza narrates explicitly Olaf's status as an object of violence, a literally naked "helplessness," within the military order. The violent scene described takes place not on the battlefield but in the mundane setting of an Army barracks and its lavatory:

his wellbelovéd colonel(trig
westpointer most succinctly bred)
took erring Olaf soon in hand;
but—though an host of overjoyed
noncoms(first knocking on the head
him)do through icy waters roll
that helplessness which others stroke
with brushes recently employed
anent this muddy toiletbowl,
while kindred intellects evoke
allegiance per blunt instruments—
Olaf(being to all intents
a corpse and wanting any rag
upon what God unto him gave)
responds,without getting annoyed
"I will not kiss your fucking flag"

straightway the silver bird looked grave
(departing hurriedly to shave)

The poem's tetrameter doggerel, with its irregular rhyme scheme and deliberate awkwardness of rhythm and phrasing, underscores the incongruities that drive the poem's cruel ironies. Classical heroic speech may be an inappropriate medium in which to tell this war story, but so is the superficially jocular language that Cummings employs. Just as the speaker's seemingly carefree tone contrasts with the shocking seriousness of Olaf's torture, the ideal of patriotic service for one's country conflicts with both the "allegiance" to abuse demonstrated by the noncommissioned officers and the permissive neglect shown in the "silver bird" colonel's hurried departure to tend to his appearance.

Through these contradictions and through his description of Olaf's unwavering conviction, Cummings depicts this conscientious objector as a martyr for his pacifist beliefs. Even as he is attacked by "all kinds of officers / (a yearning nation's blueeyed pride)," whose torture culminates in sexual abuse "by means of skilfully applied / bayonets roasted hot with heat," Olaf refuses to renounce his beliefs and chooses instead to "ceaselessly repeat / 'There is some shit I will not eat.'" In the poem's concluding stanzas Olaf's martyrdom becomes clear, as does the speaker's conviction that in his defiant assertions, Olaf is braver and more "American" than anyone, including the nation's president:

our president,being of which
assertions duly notified
threw the yellowsonofabitch
into a dungeon,where he died

Christ(of His mercy infinite)
I pray to see;and Olaf,too

preponderatingly because
unless statistics lie he was
more brave than me:more blond than you.

Olaf's status as a martyr overcomes his treatment as an "object"; Cummings' summarizing prayer and his strategic use of capitalization throughout the poem reinforce Olaf's self-sacrificing significance. Whereas the poem's speaker is represented by Cummings' trademark lowercase "i," Olaf's quoted first-person statements employ the uppercase "I." Indeed, the only capitalized words in the entire poem are "Olaf," Olaf's spoken "I," "God," "Christ," and the pronoun "His" in reference to Christ. Given Cummings' expressive use of capitalization (and miscapitalization) throughout his oeuvre, his selective capitalization in this poem can be viewed as purposefully lifting Olaf to a mythic level above the hypocritical failings of freedom's defenders. Although some critics have seen "i sing of Olaf glad and big" as providing a mostly surface treatment of its topic, the poem compels careful consideration of its methods even as it boldly conveys its satiric bite.

The 1930s proved a decade in which Cummings' individualism isolated him from the prevailing Communist commitments of his fellow avant-garde artists. Yet Cummings remained an advocate of the dispossessed against what he saw as the tyranny of collectivist movements in the 20th century. At the same time, as "i sing of Olaf glad and big" demonstrates, he was willing to satirize the failings of democracy and its institutions. As the volume title *ViVa* implies, Cummings hails "long live!" not to official authority or powerful individuals but to individuals who, despite their denigrated, powerless positions in society, uphold human courage and dignity.

CATHERINE TRAMONTANA

**Further Reading**

Cohen, Milton A., "The Political Cummings: Iconoclast or Solipsist?" *Spring: The Journal of the E.E. Cummings Society* 6 (1997)

Forché, Carolyn, editor, *Against Forgetting: Twentieth-Century Poetry of Witness*, New York: Norton, 1993

Friedman, Norman, *(Re)Valuing Cummings: Further Essays on the Poet, 1962–1993*, Gainesville: University Press of Florida, 1996

Heusser, Martin, *I Am My Writing: The Poetry of E.E. Cummings*, Tübingen, Germany: Stauffenburg, 1997

Kennedy, Richard S., *Dreams in the Mirror: A Biography of E.E. Cummings*, New York: Liveright, 1980; 2nd edition, New York and London: Liveright, 1994

Kennedy, Richard S., *E.E. Cummings Revisited*, New York: Twayne, and Oxford: Macmillan, 1994

Rotella, Guy, editor, *Critical Essays on E.E. Cummings*, Boston: G.K. Hall, 1984

Versluys, Kristiaan, "'The Season 'Tis, My Lovely Lambs': E.E. Cummings' Quarrel with the Language of Politics," *Dutch Quarterly Review of Anglo-American Letters* 17, no. 3 (1987)

## my father moved through dooms of love

At once an elegy for the poet's father and a parable of any human being who "live[s] his soul," "my father moved through dooms of love" synthesizes E.E. Cummings' linguistic invention, romantic individualism, and move toward social responsibility. First published in *50 Poems* (1940) 14 years after the sudden death of Edward Cummings in a 1926 car accident, this much-anthologized poem marks Cummings' emotional reconciliation with his father. As a young man establishing himself as an avant-garde artist in the late 1910s and early 1920s, Cummings rebelled against his father, a Unitarian minister, Harvard sociologist, and all-around forceful personality. Just as Cummings challenged poetic and typographic conventions, he defied the social and religious conventions that his father represented. By 1940, however, having established his independence and suffered the early death of his father, Cummings paid tribute to Edward Cummings' religious and civic virtues by interpreting them through the frame of his own individualistic values.

Like "anyone lived in a pretty how town," another poem from *50 Poems* that has become an anthology favorite, "my father moved through dooms of love" combines rhymed quatrains with syntactic deviations to narrate its mythic story. One of Cummings' longest poems, the 17-stanza poem is sometimes faulted for being too long. Yet its slant rhymes, well-timed repetitions, and use of pronouns, verbs, and adverbs as nouns prevent monotony of rhythm or language. The poem's opening stanzas introduce a distinctive linguistic equation that becomes a metaphor for the model of humanity praised throughout the poem:

> my father moved through dooms of love
> through sames of am through haves of give,
> singing each morning out of each night
> my father moved through depths of height
>
> this motionless forgetful where
> turned at his glance to shining here;
> that if(so timid air is firm)
> under his eyes would stir and squirm
>
> newly as from unburied which
> floats the first who,his april touch
> drove sleeping selves to swarm their fates
> woke dreamers to their ghostly roots
>
> and should some why completely weep
> my father's fingers brought her sleep:
> vainly no smallest voice might cry
> for he could feel the mountain grow.

The meaning of the linguistic formula "through x of y," puzzling at first, becomes clearer on repetition. The phrase juxtaposes opposing aspects of life while establishing a relationship between them; hence, the ideals of love, being ("am"), and giving are truly known only in comparison with their alternatives of despairing "dooms," conformist "sames," and self-serving "haves." That the father described "moved through" these negations of ideals suggests both that he successfully negotiated the pitfalls of humanity and that he experienced the "dooms" but was able to triumph through "love" of other people. In his influence on struggling individuals—the hesitant person designated an "if" and the sad, questioning girl described as a "why"—the father is an inspirer, a leader, and a consoler.

As the poem moves through the seasonal cycle from spring to winter and again to spring, the father emerges as divine in his very humanness, a view consonant with Edward Cummings' Unitarianism. He is a creator ("Lifting the valleys of the sea / my father moved through griefs of joy"), a compass of otherworldly joy ("joy was his song and joy so pure / a heart of star by him could steer"), and a vessel of quite worldly needs ("his flesh was flesh his blood was blood: / no hungry man but wished him food"). By further identifying the father with the natural world ("his anger was as right as rain") and the nourishment that sustains life ("his sorrow was as true as bread"), Cummings transforms an elegy for his father into a more universal statement on life, death, and rebirth.

The poem's concluding stanzas reiterate the father's role in the processes of physical and spiritual renewal by construing him as an agent of love over hate, good over evil:

> My father moved through theys of we,
> singing each new leaf out of each tree
> (and every child was sure that spring
> danced when she heard my father sing)
>
> then let men kill which cannot share,
> let blood and flesh be mud and mire,
> scheming imagine,passion willed,
> freedom a drug that's bought and sold
>
> giving to steal and cruel kind,
> a heart to fear,to doubt a mind,
> to differ a disease of same,
> conform the pinnacle of am
>
> though dull were all we taste as bright,
> bitter all utterly things sweet,
> maggoty minus and dumb death
> all we inherit,all bequeath
>
> and nothing quite so least as truth
> —i say though hate were why men breathe—
> because my father lived his soul
> love is the whole and more than all

Through his careful manipulation of parallel syntax beginning with the lines "let blood and flesh be mud and mire / scheming imagine,passion willed," Cummings achieves an expansive description of the world's failings in an economy of words. At the same time, the difficult, confused syntax used to describe the imperfect world appropriately gives way to the straightforward phrasing of the final couplet. Thus, by poem's end, love recognized as a salvific wholeness clarifies the confusions and contradictions inherent in "dooms of love."

In retrospect, Cummings saw the writing of "my father moved through dooms of love" as a crucial moment in his poetic development, opening the way for a greater sense of responsibility and a new moral dimension to enter his work (Kennedy, 1980). His father's life as a man of courage and compassion, a man whose moral character was so apparent that "no liar looked him in the head," compelled Cummings to merge his credo of individualism with an awareness of what truly living one's soul and holding to the ideal of "we" can offer to a society threatened by conformity and division. As a breakthrough poem in Cummings' oeuvre and an example of how meaningful and effective his linguistic innovation could be, "my father moved through dooms of love" stands out as a memorable 20th-century elegy and an affirmation of the power of the individual soul.

Catherine Tramontana

**Further Reading**

Dougherty, James P., "Language as a Reality in E.E. Cummings," in *Critical Essays on E.E. Cummings,* edited by Guy Rotella, Boston: G.K. Hall, 1984

Fairley, Irene R., *E.E. Cummings and Ungrammar: A Study of Syntactic Deviance in His Poems,* Searington, New York: Watermill, 1974

Friedman, Norman, *(Re)valuing Cummings: Further Essays on the Poet, 1962–1993,* Gainesville: University Press of Florida, 1996

Heusser, Martin, *I Am My Writing: The Poetry of E.E. Cummings,* Tübingen, Germany: Stauffenburg, 1997

Kennedy, Richard S., *Dreams in the Mirror: A Biography of E.E. Cummings,* New York: Liveright, 1980; 2nd edition, New York and London: Liveright, 1994

Kennedy, Richard S., *E.E. Cummings Revisited,* New York: Twayne, and Oxford: Macmillan, 1994

Överland, Orm, "E.E. Cummings' 'my father moved through dooms of love': A Measure of Achievement," *English Studies: A Journal of English Language and Literature* 54, no. 2 (1973)

---

# J.V. Cunningham 1911–85

The story of classicism in 20th-century American poetry has yet to be written, but any such story will include J.V. Cunningham. From the early 1930s to the early 1980s, Cunningham composed original verse that drew directly from ancient Latin and Greek poetry as well as from its English Renaissance imitations. He also made some memorable translations (e.g., of Statius' invocation to Sleep). He was a brilliant epigrammatist and is generally regarded as the genre's foremost American practitioner; the Roman poet Martial and the English poets Ben Jonson, Robert Herrick, and Walter Savage Landor are often invoked as his exemplary predecessors. Like them, Cunningham combined witty wordplay, sharp observation, and a plain style to produce short poems that are by turns sophisticated or uncouth. As he once responded in an epigram to a disapproving critic, "I like the trivial, vulgar, and exalted." Cunningham also liked the aural felicities of rhyme and iambic meter and eschewed the revolution in poetic phrasing brought about by Modernism and free verse, preferring to write in "the predestined space" of regular formal patterns where "chance and craft" may "redeem" an inherently graceless vernacular.

Despite his seemingly anachronistic use of older forms, Cunningham throughout his career wrote about contemporary topics in convincing and often startlingly vigorous ways. For example, his treatment of adult love can be tender or coarse but is always up to date. Here is "Love's Progress" in its entirety: "Pal was her friend, her lover, and, dismissed, / Became at last her lay psychiatrist." The winking puns in the second line on "lay" and the concluding syllable "-trist" reveal the obvious but unstated sexual frustration in Pal's "progressive" relationship to his ex-lover. This sly satirical couplet is part of a long tradition of epigrams on indiscreet subjects; that the tradition is now rarely practiced accounts in part for Cunningham's preference for it.

His first volume of poetry, *The Helmsman* (1942), is his most diverse in meter, stanza form, and diction, and it is correspondingly, in the poet's own judgment, his most "obscure" book. It contains several extended conceits in the English Metaphysical manner that do not achieve the clarity of Cunningham's mature style; the most successful of these poems are "The Dogdays" and "This Tower of Sun." In his early essay "The Quest of the Opal" (1950), Cunningham described the book as a "history" of his endeavor to achieve his "native style," which he deemed to be an "exactitude of statement" arrived at through the dual pursuits of "sensibility" (a poetry of "feeling") and "simplicity" (a poetry of unstrained thoughtfulness). Whether writing lyrics, odes, or epigrams, he was striving for a classical directness—formal, crisp, laconic—that could precisely present reasoning and passion. This goal is realized in assured poems such as "Lector Aere Perennoir," "The Symposium," and "For My Contemporaries," all of which deal with the larger significance of their own pure style.

An important part of Cunningham's poetics of direct statement is his frequent use of the grammar and vocabulary of philosophical propositions; logical distinctions and syllogistic structures are common in his poems. With this spare and rigorous language, he contemplated the self's commitments to others in a contingent universe. If racy satires on sex lie at one end of his poetic spectrum, at the other are his abstract examinations of the ethical decision to love another person, as in "Choice":

> Allegiance is assigned
> Forever when the mind

Chooses and stamps the will.
Thus, I must love you still
Through good and ill.

The strict argument of this stanza should be considered in light of the poet's conclusion that, as proposed by the title of a related poem, "All Choice Is Error." Cunningham's work as a whole attempts to understand what, for the philosophical lover, follows from this belief. Some insight into his theory of interpersonal commitment can be gotten from a medley of paragraphs excised from "The Quest of the Opal" and later published together as "The Journal of John Carden" (1961).

Cunningham's second collection, *The Judge Is Fury* (1947), also contains many abstract love poems, of which the most accomplished are "The Phoenix," "Passion," "The Metaphysical Amorist," and "Haecceity." Even more noteworthy is the volume's closing "journal" of 43 epigrams, which by its segregation indicates that Cunningham had begun to realize his own particular contribution to American poetry. The epigrams maintain the concision of his exacting lyric stanzas but not their severe angularity; it is as if poems of only one verse unit—a single paragraph, even a single sentence-couplet—offered the poet a more fitting space to work in. The language of the epigrams is formal and intellectual but also fluid and apt, as in this clever sententious poem about desire titled "Motto for a Sundial": "I who by day am function of the light / Am constant and invariant at night."

Most of the poems that Cunningham wrote after 1945 until the end of his career were miscellaneous epigrams that, from time to time, he gathered into new volumes, such as *Doctor Drink* (1950) and *Some Salt* (1967). An important exception is *To What Strangers, What Welcome* (1964), a fractured "sequence" of 15 poems "in whose succession there is an implicit structure." In his essay "Several Kinds of Short Poem" (1966), Cunningham recounted the narrative of this sequence with characteristic brevity: "A traveler drives west; he falls in love; he comes home." The implied story allows the poet to carry out, in different styles and tones, a "spiritual" exploration of an "illicit" encounter.

Over time, Cunningham extended his stylistic range by using more everyday idioms. However, although his writing could be hard, poignant, comical, or downright naughty, he always aimed for the effect of unlabored artfulness created by precise syllabic arrangements. Remarkable later poems include "Consolatio Nova" (a short blank-verse meditation on the death of his publisher, Alan Swallow) and "Montana Fifty Years Ago" (an unusually naturalistic depiction of childhood memories). An epigram written in 1980 after his retirement as an English professor at Brandeis University is a near perfect example of the classical terseness that he left as his poetic legacy:

After so many decades of . . . of what?
I have a permanent sabbatical.
I pass my time on actuarial time,
Listen to music, and going to bed,
Leave something in the bottom of the glass,
A little wastefulness to end the day.

GARY ROBERTS

**Biography**

Born James Vincent Cunningham in Cumberland, Maryland, 23 August 1911. Attended Stanford University, Stanford, California, A.B. 1934, Ph.D. 1945; Instructor, Stanford University, 1937–45; Assistant Professor, University of Hawaii, Honolulu, 1945–46; Assistant Professor, University of Chicago, 1946–52, and University of Virginia, Charlottesville, 1952–53; Professor, Brandeis University, Waltham, Massachusetts, 1953–80, and Professor Emeritus, 1980–85; Visiting Professor, Harvard University, Cambridge, Massachusetts, 1952, University of Washington, Seattle, 1956, Indiana University, Bloomington, 1961, University of California, Santa Barbara, 1963, and Washington University, St. Louis, Missouri, 1976. Received Guggenheim fellowship, 1959, 1966; National Institute of Arts and Letters grant, 1965; National Endowment for the Arts grant, 1966. Died in Waltham, Massachusetts, 30 March 1985.

**Poetry**

*The Helmsman,* 1942
*The Judge Is Fury,* 1947
*Doctor Drink,* 1950
*The Exclusion of a Rhyme,* 1960
*To What Strangers, What Welcome,* 1964
*Some Salt,* 1967
*The Collected Poems and Epigrams of J.V. Cunningham,* 1971
*The Poems of J.V. Cunningham,* 1997

**Selected Criticism**

*The Quest of the Opal: A Commentary on "The Helmsman,"* 1950
*Woe or Wonder: The Emotional Effect of Shakespearean Tragedy,* 1951
*Tradition and Poetic Structure: Essays in Literary History and Criticism,* 1960
*The Renaissance in England,* 1966
*Dickinson, Lyric and Legend,* 1980

**Other Writings:** essays (*The Collected Essays of J.V. Cunningham,* 1976); edited anthologies of literature (*In Shakespeare's Day,* 1970).

**Further Reading**

Cunningham, J.V., *The Collected Essays of J.V. Cunningham,* Chicago: Swallow Press, 1976
Donoghue, Denis, *Connoisseurs of Chaos: Ideas of Order in Modern American Poetry,* New York: Macmillan, 1965; London: Faber, 1966; 2nd edition, New York: Columbia University Press, 1984
Shapiro, Alan, *In Praise of the Impure: Poetry and the Ethical Imagination: Essays, 1980–1991,* Evanston, Illinois: TriQuarterly Books, 1993
Steele, Timothy, editor, *The Poems of J.V. Cunningham,* Athens: Ohio University Press, 1997
Winters, Yvor, *Forms of Discovery: Critical and Historical Essays on the Forms of the Short Poem in English,* Chicago: Swallow Press, 1967

# D

## Dada

We are all presidents of Dada, declared the Papa-Dada of them all, Tristan Tzara: "I say: there is no beginning, and we are not trembling, we are not sentimental" (Tzara, 1970). Dada was the most revolutionary aesthetic movement probably ever to hit Zurich, for its original happenings took place in the Cabaret Voltaire in that city. Democratic, iconoclastic, scandalous, speedy, violent ("Streaming in all colors and bleeding among the leaves of all the trees"), noisy, and paradoxical ("Darkness is productive if it is a light so white and pure that our neighbors are blinded by it"), Dada shouted its anti-logic against Cartesian thought and bourgeois thinking of every kind. Tzara, Hugo Ball, Emmy Hennings, Hans Arp, Sophie Tauber-Arp, Richard Huelsenbeck, Johannes Baader, together with Louis Aragon, Philippe Soupault, and André Breton in their pre-Surrealist period, all were Dadas. Dada was, from beginning to end, funny. It neither took itself seriously, nor seriously expected that the audience would take it that way. No recipes, just spontaneously comic: "Freedom, freedom: not being a vegetarian I'm not giving any recipes" ("Note on Poetry," in Tzara, 1970).

Dada led to the more organized manifestations of Surrealism, founded by André Breton and Louis Aragon, with Philippe Soupault, who wrote together with Breton in 1921 the "automatic" text (meant to unleash the unconscious) called "Magnetic Fields," as much a founding document as the first Manifesto of Surrealism in 1924. Dada, so celebratedly nihilistic, was a hobbyhorse (one of the meanings of its name) and a negation of everything, and at the same time a joyous proclamation of non-seriousness. It was anti-war in a wartime atmosphere. It defined itself as intensity. Whereas Surrealism was to define itself as a replay of Romanticism ("but how prehensile!"), Dada was clearly and radically opposed to anything smacking of the Romantic:

> Humidity of ages past. Those who feed on tears are happy and heavy; they slip them on to deceive the snakes behind the necklaces of their souls. The poet can devote himself to calisthenics. But to obtain abundance and explosion, he knows how to set hope afire TODAY. Tranquil, ardent, furious, intimate, pathetic, slow, impetuous, his desire boils for enthusiasm, that fecund form of intensity. ("Note on Poetry"; originally published in *DADA* 4–5 [1919])

When, after the 1916–17 manifestations in Zurich and Hanover, Dada came to Paris with Tristan Tzara, it did not last past 1923, when it officially committed suicide, and Tzara became, for a while, more or less a Surrealist. It was in his Surrealist period, from 1925 to 1931, that he wrote his great epic poem, *Approximate Man,* the French-language equivalent of T.S. Eliot's *The Waste Land.* Published in 1931, it is at once a lament of homelessness and imperfection ("what am I / a disconsolate starting point where I return smoking the word in the corner of my mouth") and a triumph of resolution:

> for the fire of anger varies the flickering of the subtle remains according to the mumbling modulations of hell that your heart strains to hear among the giddy salvos of stars and stony in my garments of schist I have pledged my waiting to the oxidized desert of torment to the unshakable advent of its flame (Tzara, 1970)

But that is reckoning without the various continuations of Dada in the Merz movement of Kurt Schwitters and Raoul Hausmann, in the later Fluxus movement in the United States, and in particular without the double genius of Marcel Duchamp and Francis Picabia, both of whom came early to the United States and continued Dada in their own ways that they had started far before. True Dada was always international in feeling, demonstrated in particular by the cases of Tzara, a Roumanian, moving from Switzerland to Paris, Picabia, a Spaniard shuttling between Paris and New York, and the Frenchman Duchamp, who lived in New York. Together, Duchamp and Picabia exhibited in the New York Armory show of 1913, and came then into contact with the American avant-garde gathered around Alfred Stieglitz and his 291 Gallery, and around the *Little Review,* of which Picabia became an editor. Then he began his Dada journal *391* in Barcelona in 1917, continued it in New York with numbers 5–7 in the same year, printed number 8 in Zurich in 1919, and numbers 9–19 in Paris from 1919 to 1924. In 1921 he renounced Dada and the element of moralizing that frequently entered with the trial against Maurice Barrès, defender of patriotism and staid close-to-home values, and thus guilty of a crime against freedom of the mind. If Barrès was found guilty in this period by the Dada spirit, this accusation was the ancestor of the 1924 Surrealist pamphlet "A

Corpse," directed at Anatole France (guilty of being a "comic" character, a "master" writer, a necessity of the bourgeois imagination). Both Dada and Surrealism thrived on accusations.

Duchamp, recognized as a genius by André Breton, who was to remain in awe of him, created an art style in the form of found objects: the Urinal he signed "R. Mutt"; the shovel called "In Advance of a Broken Art"; the iron bed originally advertising Sapolin Paint, which he labeled "Apolinère Enameled"; and the "Large Glass," with its Bachelors and its Bride. When it broke on being transported, he promptly welcomed the crack and made it part of the spontaneous object. Having abandoned "retinal" art, which pleased only the eye and not the mind, Duchamp devoted himself to chess and to the idea of transportable art. His Valise, or the suitcase in which were small models of all his pieces, traveled with him and replicated itself all over the world. The accompanying text is no less a masterpiece than the "Large Glass." Everything about Duchamp was touched with genius, and he in turn radiated his tongue-in-cheek brilliance into the American art scene. At the end of his life, he was working on his post-masterpiece masterpiece called "Etant Donnés . . .", composed of a door with eyeholes, through which the viewer spies on a nude outstretched in the grass, her crotch exposed, holding aloft a lamp, behind which flows a stream. "Given the waterfall, etc.," it reads, in a title composed of the elements in the construction.

One of Duchamp's more memorable creations was that of his female alter ego Rrose Sélavy, whose sayings and whose character represented him but also herself. She lent her voice to the Surrealist poet Robert Desnos, who asked Duchamp's permission to have her visit him. "I do not own her," said Duchamp, "and she is free to travel." And so Rrose Sélavy inhabited France as well as the United States. She saw "la vie en rose," of course, and was the very concretization of Eros (Eros is life.)

Dada in America had an immense influence on the Beat poets, and on such conceptual painters as Andy Warhol. In the 1960s, Tzara's play *The Gas Heart* (first performed in 1921) was performed once more in an art gallery, where the players (Nose, Ear, etc.) recited their parts while in front of them Warhol and other artists acted the same parts, mute. The audience was at once mystified and charmed. Dada characters walked the streets, like the Baroness Elsa von Freytag-Loringhoven, outlandish and mad, and the author of texts as bizarre as her outfits. Irresistible and irritating, Dada swept society and the world of art. It has had, in fact, as lasting an impact as Surrealism.

Robert Motherwell's edition of *The Dada Painters and Poets* (1951), published by George Wittenborn, whose art gallery and bookstore was the focus of much of the movement, made an impression unlike any other. The Beat poet Allen Ginsberg thanked Motherwell profusely for having given his inspiration to the Beat movement. Contemporary poetry has likewise benefited from the Dada impulse, whose intensity was lasting, like its smile.

MARY ANN CAWS

*See also* Surrealism

**Further Reading**

Caws, Mary Ann, *The Poetry of Dada and Surrealism: Aragon, Breton, Tzara, Eluard, and Desnos,* Princeton, New Jersey: Princeton University Press, 1970

Foster, Stephen, and Rudolf Kuenzli, editors, *Dada Spectrum: The Dialectics of Revolt,* Iowa City: University of Iowa, 1978

Hale, Terry, Paul Lenti, and Ian White, editors, *Four Dada Suicides: Selected Texts of Arthur Cravan, Jacques Rigaut, Julien Torma, and Jacques Vaché,* London: Atlas, 1995

Huelsenbeck, Richard, editor, *Dada Almanach,* Berlin: Reiss, 1920; as *Dada Almanac,* London: Atlas Press, 1993; 2nd edition, 1998

Lippard, Lucy, editor, *Dadas on Art,* Englewood Cliffs, New Jersey: Prentice Hall, 1971

Motherwell, Robert, editor, *The Dada Painters and Poets: An Anthology,* New York: Wittenborn Schultz, 1951; 2nd edition, Boston: G.K. Hall, 1981

Sawelson-Gorse, Naomi, editor, *Women in Dada,* Cambridge, Massachusetts: MIT Press, 1998

Tzara, Tristan, *Approximate Man, and Other Writings,* Detroit, Michigan: Wayne State University Press, 1970

Young, Alan, *Dada and After: Extremist Modernism and English Literature,* Manchester: Manchester University Press, and Atlantic Highlands, New Jersey: Humanities Press, 1981

## Deconstructionism. *See* Literary Theory and Poetry

# Deep Image Poetry

The Deep Image movement is a study in the fluidity and ambiguity of poetry movements in general. Their outlines are clear only to historians; for those in the actual moment of their happening, a movement is diaphanous, a function of friendships, shared geography, or momentary common interests, but always with a residue of hard reality and some important cultural content. It is also likely that a movement confirms the power of an aesthetic to enter into the politics and social activism of a time and thus can act as a shield or banner for the writer's cause.

The emergence of Deep Image came at a time when journalists and critics alike had begun noticing a rash of movements in poetry named for their geographical locations. The "Black Mountain School" took its name from the small liberal arts college located in Black Mountain, North Carolina; the New York School was associated with the Museum of Modern Art and the "city of the gods," the Abstract Expressionist painters, as Frank O'Hara, a poet and curator of the museum, called them. The San Francisco Renaissance was another such movement, headed by Kenneth Rexroth and including such notable Beat writers as Allen Ginsberg, Gary Snyder, Philip Whalen, Lawrence Ferlinghetti, Gregory Corso, and Jack Kerouac. It would seem by 1960 that all groups except the Deep Image poets had been accounted for by region, if not by aesthetic stance, in Donald Allen's inaugural anthology, *The New American Poetry, 1945–1960* (1960).

The phrase "deep image" was first recorded in an untitled prose poem by Jerome Rothenberg printed on the inside cover of the journal *Poems from the Floating World,* published by his own Hawk's Well Press in 1960. A final passage reads:

> The deep image rises from the shoreless gulf: here the poet reaches down among the lost branches, till a moment of seeing: the poem. Only then does the floating world sink again into darkness, leaving a white shadow, and the joy of our having been here together.

The sea implied here is defined in the preceding stanza as a "connection that floats / between men." Hence a poem is a descent into the collective waters of human imagination to wrest a figure from among the "lost branches," and when brought to the surface represents a momentary joyful reunion of what was once the tribal or universal amity of human beings.

Deep image, in Rothenberg's terms, is the language of undivided life, in which the collective status of being includes not only human beings but also nature itself. His poetry has never diverted from this principle. One may trace a specific evolution of the idea of collective language from its inception here to his anthologies of "world imagination" and outward into the 1970s movement he created under the name of "ethnopoetics," with many of the original Deep Image writers still with him. The sentiments of the Deep Image movement clearly respond to the Holocaust with an overt plea for connectedness after a half-century of racial strife and pogroms throughout the world.

The importance of Deep Image lies in the fact that hardly anything theoretical or aesthetic had been done with Pound's original conception of Imagism of 1912, when the role of image became central to modernist lyric. In any true image, Pound wrote, the writer captures in a few words the movement of formal energy as it passes from one medium to another, as in his figure of the "rose in the iron dust," in which a magnet has drawn together iron filings into the gravitational shape of rose petals. Whenever form leaps from one physical instance to another, one glimpses nature's creativity, and with it the vision of a paradisal earth of living things in concert with one another through the spiritual powers of moving, transcendent "forms."

Emersonian transcendentalism plays an important role in Pound's idea of the Image, but Pound intended the movement to correct certain vices of runaway moral discursiveness that had crept into poetry in the 19th century. The image eliminated the need for commentary and evoked a sense of conscious nature that the poet reached through imagination alone, the unique power of mind to draw on *a priori* knowledge to recognize order in nature. In other words, the imagination was a repository of innate knowledge about forms that it recognized in nature as they moved through matter. This is the soul of poetry, according to Pound, and lyric poetry was therefore essentially visual, eidetic, a perception of forms and shapes.

For several decades thereafter poets toyed with Imagism and perfected its rhetorical and linguistic potentials, advancing to the idea of the ideogram, or the idea made exclusively of pictorial elements. The ideogram was Pound's approximation of the hieroglyphic and the pictographic characters of Chinese writing, forms of expression rooted in visual experience and only partly abstracted into phonic symbols. Another generation opened the Imagist poem to serial writing, a pathway of extended lyric still rooted in visual data and called Objectivism. But even with Charles Olson's latest embroidery on the notion of the Image in his "Projective Verse" essay of 1950, the original idea of Image was still adamantly visual, eidetic, and impersonal.

Deep Image added a subjective dimension for the first time—not only subjective but also intensely personal and therapeutic. Rothenberg was thinking of the archetypes when he coined his phrase "deep image"; it meant the same thing, a relic idea lying in the sediments of evolutionary intelligence, a part of the old sea floor of the mind where nothing was defined or separated from the continuum of life. To put the archetype into circulation in 1960 as a tool of personal lyric and as a means of self-healing in poetry was to toss a wrench into the post–World War II emphasis on competitive individuality. At the end of the gray 1950s, a paramilitary civilian culture run by veterans of World War II emphasized loyalty to corporate employers (the "organization man") and uniformity in public life (the "gray flannel suit"). All this was upended with the eruption of a new sense of pre-individual intelligence lying at the bottom of the Jungian depths. To dredge up such an active ingredient of pre-conscious life was to let loose a new energy of the primitive into poetry, and thus interface with not only Beat poetry, but also with the emerging youth rebellions across the spectrum of middle-class life.

In that sense the Deep Image movement anticipated a variety of calls to group activism and collective unity: the Civil Rights movement, the peace marches later in the decade, the "happenings" in the art world, and the myriad forms of Woodstock that ended the "hippie era." Deep Image prefigures the turn by some poets to performance poetry, the revival of oral culture that would extend to experiments in open theater and to the popular "rock operas" of the era, at which audiences were invited to join actors in the finales of Brechtian populist celebrations.

In essence Deep Image responded not only to the horrors of World War II but also to the alienation of the postwar era, combining an urge toward collectivism with a personal desire for therapy and liberation. The theories of Jungian depth psychology offered a vigorous sense of self-integration through the "talking cure" as well as through the process of bringing the deep unconscious to the surface through art.

Robert Kelly's "Notes on the Poetry of the Deep Image," published in his journal *Trobar* in 1961, sought to anchor the movement within the Pound/Olson tradition and to retain the visual emphasis of lyric poetry. He added a significant nuance to the poetic, however, by suggesting that images transform "the perceived world." What this transforming mechanism might be, Kelly does not say; his primary interest is to confirm that new poetry will spring from the release of repressed content in the unconscious, and that strings of unsevered association will come with it, setting up high-energy flows of imagistic language. A bit of politics creeps into the "Notes" as Kelly tries to supplant Olson's emphasis on line and syllable, technical features of the projective poem, with the psychologically charged deep image.

The introduction of Jungian theory radically altered Pound's original concept of the epiphany of nature. If Imagism looked for unity in nature, Deep Image sought for unity in human consciousness, a transcendent unity allied to Jung's theory of the collective unconscious. In both definitions of lyric's core, the idea of higher order is not lost, merely transposed. For Pound, order (and its rhyme scheme) lay in the shifting materiality of the surrounding world; for Kelly and Rothenberg, order lay in the depths of the mind, where individuality vanished into primitive holism.

The release of buried archetypes was a mode of self-integration, a healing technique. Diane Wakoski and Clayton Eshleman joined the movement and introduced thematic sequences of highly personal lyrics that turned on problem-solving, a kind of literary depth analysis performed poem by poem until the dilemma, loneliness or maladjustment to others, was "solved." The deep image was a medicinal charm, a healing talisman from the buried past that cleansed the strident materialism and bickering individuality that characterized modern life. Wakoski's monologues involved a series of mythical suitors who entered her imaginary life as surrogates for her missing father; the King of Spain, George Washington, motorcycle riders, and one-night stands represent for her the transformation of barren modernity into a pastoral landscape of lovers and sensual pleasures.

For Eshleman the escape from Indiana, his mythologized purgatory of middle-class provincialism, is achieved through the ardors of Reichian sex therapy, exorcisms of the taboos instilled in him as a child, and through vigorous Boschian fantasies of other worlds. Ultimately he would embrace the art of paleolithic caves as the source of archetypal imagination. Armand Schwerner would contrive a primal language out of his own typographic symbols to communicate with the origins of intelligence.

Much European and South American poetry of the 1950s featured a disruptive, paralogical lyricism that seemed to suggest the release of painful psychic content borne from long experience with war and revolution. This leaping logic, as Robert Bly called it, allowed the reader to perceive the gaps in language where unconsciousness revealed itself. By permitting such unassimilated content into the language of self, the whole person emerged. This letting-go struck Deep Image poets, who were also translators of poetry, as a healthy response to political upheaval. They advocated deep image to open up and invigorate what they felt was a dry, often mechanical American lyric style that repressed unconscious angst.

Rothenberg's search for the collective binding power of images led him to anthologize a variety of experimental work from around the world, and from so-called primitive or primal literatures—chants, spells, mantras, healing songs, and the like. Kelly emphasized surreal language and myth in lyric poetry; Eshleman and Wakoski wrote unmediated autobiographical poetry about their adolescence and troubled early adulthood. David Antin and Armand Schwerner explored spontaneous structures of language, "talk poetry," and the strategies of decentralized texts in which an authorial voice splinters into what Schwerner called *pluriloges*, or texts with many intervening voices.

Robert Bly was not part of the original circle of Deep Imagists but was a friend of Robert Kelly and Rothenberg at the time they were formulating the poetic. Bly was struck by the power of surrealistic imagery coming from other cultures, in the work of Cesar Vallejo of Peru, Georg Trakl of Germany, and the Chilean poet Pablo Neruda. Translation of these poets by Bly, James Wright, and later by W.S. Merwin, Mark Strand, and Marvin Bell were published in Bly's journal *The Fifties*, later *The Sixties* and *The Seventies*, and in Bly's press of that name. The public interest in this new poetry soon spread to mainstream journals like *The New Yorker*, where other South Americans like Jorge Borges began appearing in translation. Bly sensed an opening in American tastes for a new kind of poetry that was less literal and autobiographical and more open to myth, magic, folklore, and daydreams. It was the dawning of Magic Realism in all its forms.

Bly made the case that poetry abroad was richer for the fact that Catholic cultures did not inhibit the expression of unconscious thought but rather encouraged and celebrated its disruptive, energizing influences. In a highly polemical essay, "A Wrong Turning in American Poetry," he contrasts the Spanish poet Antonio Machado's poetry, "strange without being neurotic," with the poetry of Pound, Eliot, and Marianne Moore, suggesting that anyone who "follows them will freeze to death." American poetry "is without spiritual life," Bly wrote, and "the beginning of spiritual life is a horror of emptiness." A worship of objects is not enough, he argues, for feeding the soul's hunger for unconscious knowledge. This nurture comes in abundance from Spain and Germany, cultures only beginning to push out through the rubble of war and fascism, with the poets leading the way toward redemption.

American poetry venerates its own materialism through the modernist embrace of an objective world, but without the subjective richness of the deep image. "In this country is a poetry without even a trace of revolutionary feeling—in either language or politics," Bly wrote, going on to lament that "in the last twenty years there have been almost no poems touching on political subjects." Part of the problem is the adamant injunction against such topics under the regime of the New Critical poets, John Crowe Ransom and Allen Tate, then-editors of *The Kenyon Review* and *The Southern Review*. Worse, Bly reports, "The poetry we have now is a poetry without the image. . . . If there is no image how is the unconscious going to make its way into the poem?"

A "puritan fear of the unconscious" led to a rigidly practical life, and in this and other essays published in *The Fifties*, Bly quotes passages from other American poets with derisive comments about their gray language and repressed emotions. In his preface to *American Poetry: Wildness and Domesticity* (1990), however, he admits, "one-sidedness becomes elaborate in 'A Wrong Turning in American Poetry.'" Even so, movements require foils and antagonists, and Bly eagerly provided them as part of a definition of his sense of deep image.

As James E.S. Breslin notes in *From Modern to Contemporary: American Poetry, 1945–1965* (1984), Bly did not provide an actual theory of the deep image. He proselytized for more access to the unconscious and attracted other poets to his journal and press through his advocacy of Deep Image lyricism, but one can infer a signal difference between his brand of Deep Image and that of Rothenberg and Kelly. Bly stresses the integrative function of Deep Image for the individual; it does not lead to the collective human spirit or to the primal nature of human beings, as Rothenberg argued. As Bly told an interviewer, "I don't believe that a bridge has to be made between the individual and society—if [the poet] goes inward far enough, he'll find society" (Power, 1976).

Bly's sense of the term does imply a turn to autobiography with the motive of healing the disintegrating self of modern life, a premise that would take him from early Deep Image writing to a prominent role first in the anti–Vietnam War movement and later in the men's movement of the 1990s. The therapeutic powers of poetry lay at the heart of his interest in the deep image, in so far as venting repressed emotion (and language) helped consolidate the self polarized by American life. In 1976 he remarked, "The issue is to try to heal oneself first" (Power, 1976). Bly's emphasis was always on the individual psyche and its needs, not on the group spirit or the revival of collective cultural expression.

Early signs of Deep Image in Bly's work occur in his first published book, *Silence in the Snowy Fields* (1962), which slips odd details—animations of barns and other objects—into ordinary phrasing and in general presents the familiar world through dream logic or a child's visions. In "Snowfall in the Afternoon," set in the Minnesota winter, a barn is seen advancing like a ship in a storm, a ship on which "All the sailors on deck have been blind for many years." The eruption of unlikely or provocative images set a new standard for the conventional lyric.

But the success of this book did not deter Bly from complaining that the autobiographical mode was too narrow a frame for the times. In his second book, *The Light around the Body* (1967), Bly expanded his reference to contemporary politics, corporate commerce, and the first protests against the Vietnam War. These are bolder poems by far, with strikingly disruptive phrasings in which subjects clash or collide into abrupt political declarations. The style made Bly famous and a guru of political youth.

By 1976, however, Bly remarked, "I don't use the term deep image . . . I don't like it. In my opinion all images are deep" (Power, 1976). James Wright, whose early work reflects a similar use of the deep image to disrupt the predictable flow of lyric, was closely associated with Bly in the 1960s. Louis Simpson, another member of the loose-knit second group of Deep Imagists, perfected his own style of image dissonance, as in his famous closing line about Whitman, "The open road leads to the used car lot." The method of these writers might be described as dislocating the particular, inflating reference when context demanded constraint. Under the pressure of such lyrics ordinary details become fluid and dream-like, no longer subject to the rules of empirical logic. The melting of reality in this poetry anticipated the art forms and culture of the psychedelic era of the later 1960s, when the distortions of LSD and marijuana performed a similar transformation on the ordinary. For the reading public, Magic Realism in fiction under Donald Barthelme soon eclipsed the poetry of deep image.

PAUL CHRISTENSEN

**Further Reading**

Bellamy, Joe D., editor, *American Poetry Observed: Poets on Their Work,* Urbana: University of Illinois Press, 1984

Bly, Robert, *American Poetry: Wildness and Domesticity,* New York: Harper and Row, 1990

Breslin, James E.B., *From Modern to Contemporary: American Poetry, 1945–1965,* Chicago: University of Chicago Press, 1984

Christensen, Paul, *Minding the Underworld: Clayton Eshleman and Late Postmodernism,* Santa Rosa, California: Black Sparrow Press, 1991

Myers, Jack, and David Wojahn, editors, *A Profile of Twentieth-Century American Poetry,* Carbondale: Southern Illinois University Press, 1991

Power, Kevin, "Robert Bly," *Texas Quarterly* 19, no. 3 (1976); reprinted in *American Poetry Observed: Poets on Their Work,* edited by Joe D. Bellamy, Urbana: University of Illinois Press, 1984

---

# James Dickey 1923–97

James Dickey came onto the literary scene in 1960 with his first book of poems, *Into the Stone, and Other Poems,* in which he presents himself as a war veteran, a survivor of violence and death. Other poets had written about World War II with equal force, and it is likely Dickey's brand of documentary lyricism would have aged quickly and not propelled him to the stature of a major poet. With his second book, however, *Drowning with Others* (1962), Dickey liberated southern poetry from constraints imposed on it by the previous generation of agrarian poets—principles that demanded orthodox meter and the use of conventions of traditional English poetry.

Dickey introduced themes into poetry from fiction writers such as William Faulkner, Flannery O'Connor, and Eudora Welty—the decline of southern civilization, the industrializing of rural life, and the mysteries and terrors of sexual love. Dickey rhapsodized over the lingering wilderness of the South, where he set many scenes of initiation into the mysteries of nature. His vision is of a world of ordinary men braving the adversities of wild rivers; night camps where bears lurk and sometimes clawed open a tent; hunting adventures, as in his first novel, *Deliverance* (1970), and even a fishing adventure ("The Shark's Parlor" in *Buckdancer's Choice,* 1965) in which a wild shark is hauled into a living room where it thrashes until the house is devastated; and other acts that transform ordinary southern men into heroes.

It was this second vision that gave Dickey a national voice in which he seemed to redeem the South that had fallen into disgrace since the Civil War. The burden of a lost war vanishes under the spell of his sensuous, detailed storytelling, in which regional stereotypes blossom into complex characters wracked by guilt, as in the celebrated poem "The Lifeguard" (*Drowning with Others*), where a teenager fails to save a drowning child at a summer camp and now hides in the boathouse. The dread and accompanying desire to fantasize saving a life in the speaker transcends the immediate situation to become a mythic event embodying the horrors of war in general.

"The Lifeguard" is written in anapestic meter, the meter perfected by Edwin Arlington Robinson, the poet of the imaginary Maine town of Tilbury, where so many citizens faced calamity, despair, and suicide under the elaborate guise of seeming "normal." Robinson told his stories in compressed, ironic poetry driven by a stark suspense until the last line. Dickey made a careful study of Robinson's technique as a student at Vanderbilt University, and his ghost may be felt all through Dickey's early work. The theme of penetrating below the surface dominates the period of his work that Dickey called "the early motion," from 1960 to 1967. Drowning is one metaphor of that penetration, falling is another; many poems reach out to read the minds of animals or to contact the dead. Mainly, his poetry is the attempt to go under the surface of the South itself, to enter the imagination of the region below its defenses and protective surface.

Working with spare, muscular diction and strict rhythms was one way to reveal and even psychoanalyze regional life, but this cautious strategy slowly gave way to looser, more flexible rhythms in his third book, *Helmets* (1964), where even the targets are more subtle and interesting. In "Winter Trout," a hatchling "nourished a dream of living / Under the ice" as the speaker rhapsodizes over the freedom that fish must know. The speaker is a hunter with bow and arrow who later stands poised to kill such a winter trout but misses and then plunges his hand into the ice to retrieve his arrow point. The cold is the alien otherworld buried below a boundary, and his hand nearly freezes "As a sign of the penalties / For breaking into closed worlds."

It was this intimacy with personal detail that led Dickey to write about sexual initiation, as in the poem "Cherrylog Road." The poem is a deliberate collision of pastoral themes against the harsh industrial wasteland of Beat poetry—a love bower cast among the hulks of old cars in a rural junkyard where the swain, a motorcycle rider, awaits his beloved in a decaying and suggestively named Pierce-Arrow. The whole poem relishes its sexual puns and the swaggering masculinity of the lover, "restored" after lovemaking, atop his "bicycle fleshed / With power."

Even "Cherrylog Road" conveys a certain willingness to die in order to pass over or through the boundary of "ice." It ends with the rider "Wringing the handlebar for speed, / Wild to be wreckage forever." Dickey's brooding on death as the final boundary separating him from forbidden experience appears across his work and has led some readers to compare him to Hemingway; the comparison is not without merit since both writers were preoccupied with ordeals of courage and lyrical meditations on the meaning of death. Ice is Dickey's metaphor for the gateway into other worlds, and he once observed that he found belief in reincarnation, if only to fuel his desire to become a bird after being human.

In the third section of *Helmets* are various meditations on death, including "Breath," an eloquent lyric on water as the otherworld of spirits and on the danger one faces being suspended above it in a boat, where the speaker "felt my fear apportioned to the sharks, / Which fell to sands // Two hundred feet down within cold." "The Ice Skin" tracks the metaphor of ice as the last boundary of life through a number of objects: tree limbs breaking in an ice storm, stalled aircraft covered in ice, and staring through "a window of ice." Even the drunks in "Bums, On Waking" are seen flirting with real death as they awaken at the end of the poem "With water moving over their legs." In "Goodbye to Serpents," a farmer slashes the wound in his foot from a snake's bite to watch blood flow serpentlike into the river in a kind of ritual suicide that kills not him but all the nature around him. In another poem, "In the Child's Night," sleeping in winter is akin to dying or, to use another metaphor from earlier in the book, to becoming the "quiet body like a fish. . . . To pass into the star-sea, into sleep."

The fourth part of *Helmets* continues the theme of death and dying with "Drinking from a Helmet," in which a soldier on the front lines takes a drink as other soldiers fight and are killed around him. Water and death converge in the poem to form a single image of passing through the boundary, with the soldier's own haggard face reflected in the water he is drinking as if he were devouring himself into his own body: "A cool, trembling man / Exactly my size, swallowed whole." The poem is a reprise of all the major images of the book, from trees cracking in ice storms to death by water or by violence, to the survivor standing alone in his cramped foxhole, faced with a reflected and shimmering otherworld in his helmet.

Already a certain oratorical richness had crept into Dickey's line, replacing the more rigidly exacting anapestic meters of his earliest work. Dickey was raising the lyric threshold toward a more florid style heard in southern pulpits and in the political oratory of the region—lush, musical, loosely structured, homiletic, but intensified by driving rhythms difficult to maintain as his line grew longer and more complex. The solution was to break up the phrasing into smaller units while maintaining the long line for its look of involution.

In "The Firebombing," the opening poem of his most celebrated book, *Buckdancer's Choice* (1965), for which he received the National Book Award, the long-line poem first appears with breaks to mark off the fits and starts of language in the mind. The pauses, Dickey once observed, mark the gaps in the firing of the imagination, over which language must sometimes leap like the electric spark in a spark plug. The momentary silences show hesitation or a forked path in consciousness, after which the poem plunges ahead. This new measure is specially suited to the voice of a former bomber pilot, now a parent and suburbanite, recalling his raids over cities such as the one he now lives in. However, even so, he does not feel any guilt for dropping napalm onto huddled families below; he never saw the result of his raids. They were Japanese families, and, as Dickey noted about the poem in *Self-*

*Interviews* (1970), the life below was as foreign as anything he could imagine.

"The Firebombing" is especially influential among Vietnamese poets attempting to explain in peacetime the delayed traumas of their own combat experience. Dickey plunges into the subject with an expansive, rolling speech that moves along on waves of emotional recollection. Here and there, words are spaced apart for emphasis or to mark the confused feelings of the speaker. The new style of elliptical line was firmly established by this book and culminates in the long, dithyrambic lyrics at the close of the book in "Coming Back to America," which tells the story of Americans returning to their homeland to find themselves momentarily disoriented.

It was this style of open, expansive lyric that would attract a new generation of lyric poets to write of the New South, led by Dave Smith and featuring a poetry that swelled with the sonorities of the Sunday sermon and the rolling meters of Dickey's middle style. "Falling," Dickey's most noted poem, appears at the end of *Buckdancer's Choice,* in which a stewardess plunges to her death over a Midwest cornfield. Her thoughts are recorded from beginning to end as she takes the familiar leap from one side of life to the other, in the cold, clear sky over Kansas, stripping off her clothing so as to die "beyond explanation" to those who find her below.

The speech here is ecstatic, entranced, a molten rush of lyric energies reminiscent of the Beat prose of Jack Kerouac. The poem is a relentless chant of pulsing phrases flowing down the page from margin to margin, with only the suspense of certain death at the end of it. It would lead Dickey to consider other extreme situations of pain or excitement that would further explode the lyric frame of his work in *The Eye-Beaters* (1970) and *The Strength of Fields* (1977, revised 1979). To shape the unwieldy line he had been developing, Dickey resorted to a "plumb line" effect by centering the lines in imitation of Alexander Calder's mobiles. The lines appear to float more lightly in this configuration and to sustain the syntactic complexity of his language. His poetry had turned to aging and its infirmities and to madness, blindness, and accidents to capture the disorderly states of mind caused by such emergencies. His lyric forms had become baroque and the language often overwrought in his zeal to find the highest pitch of troubled emotion.

*Puella* (1982), Dickey's monologues as a young girl reaching puberty, marks an outer limit to this more figurative style, as does *The Zodiac* (1976) before it; both books assume a different identity entirely, a young girl and a mad Dutch poet who drinks himself to death. Both take lyric poetry to the breaking point, where language seems about to implode on itself from its mounting complexities.

Critics were dubious about the worth of this new direction in his writing; it was considered a falling off of his more disciplined early narrative style, with its terse lines and clear rhythmic signatures. Dickey had declared himself an experimenter and did not wish to repeat his successes or even remain what he ruefully described as a "*New Yorker* poet," where many of his best poems had debuted. Instead, he longed to be seen as a daring and innovative stylist, even in middle life; his poems imitated the sprawling fieldlike compositions of the Black Mountain School, but he was never accorded the rank of an avant-garde writer.

Instead, his reputation rests on the achievement of his early work, where he liberated southern regional lyric from its classical restraints and gave other writers the freedom to explore their own southern experience.

PAUL CHRISTENSEN

**Biography**

Born in Atlanta, Georgia, 2 February 1923. Attended Clemson College, South Carolina, 1942; Vanderbilt University, Nashville, Tennessee, B.A. (magna cum laude) 1949 (Phi Beta Kappa), M.A. 1950; served as a pilot in the U.S. Army Air Force during World War II and as a training officer in the Air Force during the Korean War; taught at Rice University, Houston, 1950, 1952–54, and University of Florida, Gainesville, 1955–56; copywriter, McCann-Erickson, New York, 1956–59, and Burke Dowling Adams, Atlanta, Georgia, 1960–61; copy chief and creative director, Liller Neal Beattie and Lindsay, Atlanta, 1959–60; poet-in-residence, Reed College, Portland, Oregon, 1963–64, San Fernando Valley State College, Northridge, California, 1964–66, University of Wisconsin, Madison, 1966, and Milwaukee, summer 1967, and Washington University, St. Louis, spring 1968; consultant in poetry, Library of Congress, Washington, D.C., 1966–68; Franklin Distinguished Professor, Georgia Institute of Technology, Atlanta, fall 1968; Professor of English and writer-in-residence, University of South Carolina, Columbia, 1969–97; associate editor, *Esquire* magazine, early 1970s, and *Sewanee Review;* advisory editor, *Shenandoah* literary review; member of board of directors, *Charleston* magazine; member of board of governors, South Carolina Academy of Authors. Received Vachel Lindsay Prize, 1959; Longview Foundation Award, 1960; Guggenheim fellowship, 1962; Melville Cane Award, 1965; National Book Award, 1966; American Academy grant, 1966; Médicis Prize, for novel, 1971; received honorary degrees from 13 American universities; member, American Academy. Died in Columbia, South Carolina, 19 January 1997.

**Poetry**

*Into the Stone, and Other Poems,* 1960
*Drowning with Others,* 1962; selection, as *The Owl King,* 1977
*Helmets,* 1964
*Two Poems of the Air,* 1964
*Buckdancer's Choice,* 1965
*Poems, 1957–1967,* 1967
*The Achievement of James Dickey: A Comprehensive Selection of His Poems, with a Critical Introduction,* edited by Laurence Lieberman, 1968
*The Eye-Beaters, Blood, Victory, Madness, Buckhead and Mercy,* 1970
*The Zodiac,* 1976
*The Strength of Fields,* 1977; revised edition, 1979
*Veteran Birth: The Gadfly Poems, 1947–1949,* 1978
*Head-Deep in Strange Sounds: Free-Flight Improvisations from the UnEnglish,* 1979
*Falling, May Day Sermon, and Other Poems,* 1981
*The Early Motion,* 1981
*Puella,* 1982
*Värmland,* 1982
*The Central Motion: Poems, 1968–1979,* 1983

*False Youth: Four Seasons,* 1983
*For a Time and Place,* 1983
*Intervisions* (photographs by Sharon Anglin Kuhne), 1983
*Bronwen, the Traw, and the Shape-Shifter: A Poem in Four Parts* (for children), 1986
*The Eagle's Mile,* 1990
*The Whole Motion: Collected Poems, 1945–1992,* 1992
*James Dickey: The Selected Poems,* 1998

**Selected Criticism**
*Spinning the Crystal Ball: Some Guesses at the Future of American Poetry,* 1967
*Babel to Byzantium: Poets and Poetry Now,* 1968
*The Water-Bug's Mittens: Ezra Pound, What We Can Use* (lecture), 1979
*The Poet Turns on Himself,* 1982

**Other Writings:** play, screenplay (*Deliverance,* 1972), novels (*Deliverance,* 1970; *To the White Sea,* 1993), editions of collected poetry.

**Further Reading**
Baughman, Ronald, editor, *The Voiced Connections of James Dickey: Interviews and Conversations,* Columbia: University of South Carolina Press, 1984
Bloom, Harold, editor, *James Dickey,* New York: Chelsea House, 1987
Kirschten, Robert, editor, *Critical Essays on James Dickey,* New York: G.K. Hall, 1994
Kirschten, Robert, editor, *Struggling for Wings: The Art of James Dickey,* Columbia: University of South Carolina Press, 1997
Van Ness, Gordon, *Outbelieving Existence: The Measured Motion of James Dickey,* Columbia, South Carolina: Camden House, 1992
Weigl, Bruce, and T.R. Hummer, editors, *The Imagination as Glory: The Poetry of James Dickey,* Urbana: University of Illinois Press, 1984

# Drowning with Others

*Drowning with Others* (1962), James Dickey's second book of poems, published when he was 39 years old, was conceived under two very different poetic influences: the spare, narrative poetry of Edwin Arlington Robinson, which showed Dickey how to use anapestic meter to tell mesmerizing and suspenseful stories, and the lush, sometimes opaque rhetorical style of the Welsh poet Dylan Thomas, whose star was very high in this era. Each style represents a different aspect of Dickey's creativity, and the two potential voices are at war with each other throughout the volume, as if fighting for ultimate dominance in his future work. But neither voice quite conquers the other; for the rest of his life Dickey would move between a lean, muscular narrative style to tell regional stories and another that blew out all the stops to lyricize feverishly and often bombastically over puberty (*Puella,* 1982), blindness (*The Eye-Beaters,* 1970), madness (*The Zodiac,* 1976), and aging (*The Strength of Fields,* 1977).

*Drowning with Others* is the battleground of other conflicts as well. The stylistic instability running throughout the book, ranging from taut, laconic verses to sprawling and overwrought language, suggests that Dickey was still trying to find an appropriate voice as American culture swung from the Eisenhower years into the new "Camelot" presidency of John F. Kennedy. A sudden flowering of imagination accompanied this sweeping change of governmental philosophy, taking the nation from war into what promised to be a greening of America, to borrow Charles Reich's description of the era in his 1970 book of that title.

Dickey seems torn between a vision of rebirth and renewal and a despair over the disappearance of the old regional South he knew as a child. An essentially urban poet from metropolitan Atlanta, his task in this and later books is to create a mythical South of wilderness and visionary experience, and to construct a persona with easy access to the spiritual underworld of dead Civil War soldiers, the souls of animals, and the lingering ethos of a culture long dependent upon a fertile but mysterious natural world.

The book opens with one of his most famous poems, "The Life Guard," with its southern Gothic touches and its spell-binding atmosphere of a pool at night and an anguished life guard confessing his remorse at failing to save a drowning child. That child might well have been himself, whom he now recovers as an image of "water water water," as if to say he has only the fabricated image of whatever that lost child might be. The poem, crafted in nearly perfect anapestics, shows a very steady skill at storytelling. The underlying sense is that the poet will dredge memory for the rest of the book, and attempt to recreate or re-flesh things that merely haunt him now. This task will be carried out with mixed results, but Dickey reminds the reader of his intention in the closing poem, "In the Mountain Tent," whose last line is, "'I shall rise from the dead,' I am saying."

The poems that follow in section one of the four-part book explore the relation between human beings and animals, and especially the ritual relations of the hunt. Dickey's work here, in the best section of the book, joins contemporary poets like James Wright and Robert Bly in importing into poetry a new "magical realism" of spells, miracles, visions, and magical tableaux—where the animal becomes totemized and "spiritual." In "The Summons," blowing on a grass blade awakens the hidden part of nature, which then comes out into the open to be shot by both a figurative and a literal bow and arrow. "Night / things are waking fast," he reports in "For the Nightly Ascent of the Hunter Orion over a Forest Clearing," in which he confers upon himself certain shamanistic powers. Whether in reaction to Cold War science or the new romanticism of nuclear-age culture, Dickey's hunger to "reach nature" ripples outward across the entire spectrum of American poetry in the early 1960s, culminating in the larger visions of Carlos Castañeda's *The Teachings of Don Juan* (1968).

Dickey's mythologizing is cautious, and he is careful to state his thoughts in elegant, highly disciplined lyrics, many of them conventional in form. As he remarked in essays and interviews, he was an heir to the Agrarian poets, and had studied at Vanderbilt University, home to major Agrarian poets and the New Critics. Taking their view of southern culture as a place of cherished traditions and sacred battles, Dickey seems torn between a reverence for southern nostalgia and a desire to remap the region culturally as a source of American strength. He envisions the southern woods as a fountain of youth and masculinity, the site of ordeals in courage, where boys are transformed by hunting and violence into men.

It is in this logical framework that Dickey moves to the theme of war in the next section, a less resolute poetry that sketches a lurid vision of an execution in "Between Two Prisoners," and experiments in a richer, more opaque lyric style in "Drowning with Others," where the language becomes a series of butted-together, slightly feverish metaphors in the manner of Dylan Thomas' late poetry. The weakest poem of the lot is "The Owl King," where Dickey is at a loss for what to do with his exotic material on wood gods and borrowed romantic symbolism.

Section three returns to southern experience, and no where better than in "Hunting Civil War Relics at Nimblewill Creek," where Dickey fuses together two important themes of the book, the dead of war and his own deceased and ghostly brother, whom he accompanies in a highly figurative, even humorous search for relics, while "the dead regroup." This is Dickey in his proper voice, as the punning, myth-making, keenly observant and lyrically flush bard. The style and approach anticipate such classic short lyrics of his canon as "Cherry Log Road" and other masterpieces in the new southern idiom. Section four might well be summarized from a line in "Snow on a Southern State," where Dickey admits, "I labor / To change wholly into my spirit." While the sense of that line may not be altogether plausible or even clear, it suggests the intended motif of the section as a series of transformations of self from one sort of person—his practical, logic-bound self (the one who wrote advertising for Coca-Cola and other corporate clients)—to a new self, still blinking at the identity of poet, not quite sure what limits to impose on this persona. "To Landrum Guy" offers a rather pretentious commiseration with a man turned 60 just now writing poems, from the bard of Georgia, a persona that does not quite gel in this poem, even if it reveals a difficult ego being born here.

The quieter lyrics of "Facing Africa," in which the poet looks to Africa for magic and vision, are better, more appropriate to this poet turning himself into a regional "magus," as he calls himself in the opening poem of the section. "In the Mountain Tent" prepares the way for many poems on hiking, hunting, and the escape back to nature for rejuvenation that will follow in his productive and highly successful career.

If it had not been for Dickey's reexamination of southern life, its psychological bonds to nature and the past, and for his desire to push the envelope of lyric form to its maximum amplitude, the next generation of southern poets would not have had much ground on which to build their own poetry. Dave Smith, David Bottoms, and a host of other writers owe their liberation and new directions to Dickey, who is trying out his themes and strategies in this book, which succeeds as much as it fails, and gave even himself a destination to move toward—a mystical, brooding, sometimes troubling, even heroic sense of the South.

PAUL CHRISTENSEN

**Further Reading**

Bowers, Neil, *James Dickey: The Poet as Pitchman,* Columbia: University of Missouri Press, 1985

Kirschten, Robert, editor, *Struggling for Wings: The Art of James Dickey,* Columbia: University of South Carolina Press, 1997

Suarez, Ernest, *James Dickey and the Politics of Canon: Assessing the Savage Ideal,* Columbia: University of Missouri Press, 1993

Van Ness, Gordon, *Outbelieving Existence: The Measured Motion of James Dickey,* Columbia, South Carolina: Camden House, 1992

Weigl, Bruce, and T.R. Hummer, editors, *The Imagination as Glory: The Poetry of James Dickey,* Urbana: University of Illinois Press, 1984

## Falling

James Dickey's "Falling" is a crucial text in his canon, representing simultaneously what is most vital and contentious in his work. One hundred and seventy-five lines long, it is Dickey's most convincing experiment with page-wide lines in a poem of significant duration. The poem describes the accidental fall of a female flight attendant from a commercial airliner to her death below on Kansas farmland. The epigraph for the poem (taken from the *New York Times* but scanned by Dickey) is a remarkable piece of found poetry in its own right:

> A 29-year-old stewardess fell . . . to her death tonight
> when she was swept through an emergency door that
> suddenly sprang open. . . . The body . . . was found
> . . . three hours after the accident.

The authorial text of "Falling" exploits the gaps in the journalistic account, saving the woman from journalistic pathos by writing her into varieties of mythic reincarnation as she plummets. Primarily, the poem is about making mythic capital out of the found; this is its fascination, while it has also given rise to allegations of opportunism and voyeurism on Dickey's part.

Sympathetic readings of "Falling" have countered such criticism by emphasizing the radical energies of Dickey's writing and the exuberant consequences of the woman's conversion from a fetishistic object of desire into an archetypal subject, an empowering and activist presence on earth. It has been represented by some critics as Dickey's attempt at a radical feminism, a response to the allegations of macho belligerence that were aimed at Dickey's perceived ambivalence about the Vietnam War. "Falling" was the last poem in the collection *Poems, 1957–1967* (1967), and it can be read as an intertextual riposte to "The Firebombing," the earlier poem of Dickey's that had provoked most criticism. In this sense, "Falling" can be read as atonement for those poems that had appeared to endorse violence within the terms of a masculine ethics; furthermore, it suggests that Dickey felt compelled to write against the rigidly gendered persona that he had created for himself.

"Falling" is a poem of reversal, Dickey's first proper attempt at writing from a feminine perspective, preparing him for the future volume *Puella* (1982). The falling woman removes her clothing and enacts in turn a carnivalesque sexual awakening of the Kansas people who behold her fall, as they experience desire and then transgress beyond their societal roles—farm girls "feeling the goddess in them struggle and rise brooding," "Boys finding for the first time their loins filled with heart's blood / Widowed farmers . . . / Arisen at sunrise." The fall of the woman is described as being restorative and generative for the entire nation, reverberating out from Kansas to "all levels of American breath."

Earth is made heaven in this poem, the paradigmatic fall from grace is reversed; similarly, the woman reverses the masculine archetype of the faller as a tragic overreacher, Icarus or Satan. Her fall is an escape from the containment of technology and commodification, symbolized by the plane and her uniform:

The states when they black out and lie there rolling when
they turn
To something transcontinental move by drawing moonlight
out of the great
One-sided stone hung off the starboard wingtip some
sleeper next to
An engine is groaning for coffee and there is faintly coming
in
Somewhere the vast beast-whistle of space. In the galley
with its racks
Of trays she rummages for a blanket and moves in her slim
tailored
Uniform to pin it over the cry at the top of the door. As
though she blew

The door down with a silent blast from her lungs frozen
she is black
Out finding herself with the plane nowhere and her body
taking her by the throat
The undying cry of the void falling living beginning to be
something
That no one has ever been and lived through screaming
without enough air
Still neat lipsticked girdled by regulation her hat
Still on her arms and legs in no world

The woman now begins to experiment with her predicament and her body, "hung high up in the overwhelming middle of things"; as she takes on new identities and acquires the supernatural power of transformation, she also shape-changes in language, moving between complex syntax to bare participles:

There is time to live
In superhuman health seeing mortal unreachable lights far
down seeing
An ultimate highway with one late priceless car probing it
arriving
In a square town and off her starboard arm the glitter of
water catches
The moon by its one shaken side scaled, roaming silver My
God it is good
And evil lying in one after another of all the positions for
love
Making dancing sleeping

Dickey's Nietzschean vocabulary implies that she is a spiritual revolutionary, refusing morbidity and embracing her newfound deity; her last words at the poem's climax represent an ecstatic release from mortality into divinity:

Feels herself go go toward go outward breathes at last fully
Not and tries less once tries tries AH, GOD—

She is Dickey's "Energized Woman," the performer of an antirepressive rite that represents the alleviation of the agony of her own death and the arid predicament of the nation. "Falling" is an ambitious, problematic poem; it is a uniquely energizing and vivid reading experience, proving that Dickey could write in opposition to the negative perception of him as a monotonously macho poet.

Michael Hinds

**Further Reading**

Baughman, Ronald, *Understanding James Dickey,* Columbia: University of South Carolina Press, 1985
Bowers, Neal, *James Dickey: The Poet as Pitchman,* Columbia: University of Missouri Press, 1985
Dickey, James, *Self-Interviews,* New York: Doubleday, 1970
Hodge, Marion, "James Dickey's Natural Heaven," in *Critical Essays on James Dickey,* edited by Robert Kirschten, New York: G.K. Hall, 1994
Kirschten, Robert, "Form and Genre in James Dickey's 'Falling': The Great Goddess Gives Birth to the Earth," in *Critical Essays on James Dickey,* edited by Kirschten, New York: G.K. Hall, 1994
Lieberman, Laurence, "James Dickey: The Deepening of Being," in *James Dickey,* edited by Harold Bloom, New York: Chelsea House, 1987

---

# Diane di Prima 1934–

Throughout her career Diane di Prima has sought to return to the community what she sees as the life-sustaining force of the imagination. Like that of so many of her Beat contemporaries, di Prima's work reflects the philosophic and aesthetic influence of Walt Whitman and William Carlos Williams. In "Rant," she writes:

The imagination is not only holy, it is precise
it is not only fierce, it is practical
men die everyday for the lack of it,
it is vast and elegant[.]

Di Prima's free verse is based upon a view of poetry as a form of political activism: "THE ONLY WAR THAT MATTERS IS THE WAR AGAINST THE IMAGINATION / ALL OTHER WARS ARE SUBSUMED IN IT," she writes, and poetry offers the means by which individuals may combat that war.

In 1961 di Prima founded *The Floating Bear: a newsletter* with the poet LeRoi Jones (who later became Amiri Baraka). In the introduction to the collected issues of the *Bear,* she says one of their concerns was "speed: getting this new, exciting work into the hands of other writers as quickly as possible," which meant their ideas "would be in the hands of a few hundred writers within two or three weeks. It was like writing a letter to a bunch of friends." This service to their community shaped di Prima's poetics by bringing her into contact with what would become some of the most well-known voices of that generation, including Frank O'Hara, Allen Ginsberg, William Burroughs, Robert Duncan, Denise Levertov, and John Ashbery.

In spite of its raison d'être, *Memoirs of a Beatnik* (1969) proves a thoughtful, vivid account of the New York Beat "scene" in which she began her career. This written-for-hire erotica remains one of di Prima's most readily available works, unfortunately, perhaps because in it she chronicles the male-dominated Beat movement, a role often left to the "chicks." Jack Kerouac called di Prima the "other best girl poet," next to Barbara Moraff (Friedman, 1996). In fact di Prima often stands as the representative woman poet of the age.

In contrast to the inherent sexism of Beat culture, di Prima grounds her poetics in female fertility and creativity. In response to Gary Snyder's comment that

> The female is fertile, and discipline
> (contra naturam) only
> confuses her,

di Prima writes in "The Practice of Magical Evolution":

> i am a woman and my poems
> are woman's: easy to say
> this. the female is ductile[.]

Di Prima's recurrent themes of female creativity, fertility, and motherhood fuse with Beat slang and immediacy to create a feminine aesthetics. The poet herself identifies as kindred spirits such female literary predecessors and contemporaries as Lenore Kandel, Audre Lorde, H.D., Laura Riding, Adrienne Rich, and Djuna Barnes, as well as singers Bessie Smith, Joan Baez, and Janis Joplin.

It is appropriate that di Prima should claim an affinity with singers as well as poets, because her work so often draws on oral tradition. The ritual repetitions and rhythms of such forms reflect the influence of Tibetan Buddhism and the Western magical tradition as early as *This Kind of Bird Flies Backward* (1958). Dedicated to what she sees as the healing, magical, and revolutionary potential of poetry, her work includes incantations, chants, spells, and songs.

*Revolutionary Letters* (1979) captures the spirit of rebellion, anarchy, and community activism that permeates di Prima's body of work, and because it reflects so well the spirit and concerns of the period it is one of her most acclaimed volumes. The poet attributes her sense of commitment to social justice to her maternal grandfather. In "April Fool Birthday Poem for Grandpa," she recalls "how you would love us all, would thunder your anarchist wisdom" and responds:

> . . . well I want you to know
> we do it for you, and your ilk, for Carlo Tresca,
> for Sacco and Vanzetti, without knowing
> it, or thinking about it[.]

Set against an urban landscape, di Prima's poetry gives voice to outsiders and others silenced by economic, racial, and gender prejudice.

Published originally in 1973 and in expanded editions in 1976, 1978, and 1998, *Loba* is a feminine epic that simultaneously mourns and celebrates women's experience in the latter half of the 20th century. This continually evolving mythology is perhaps di Prima's most important work to date, bringing together the poet's recurrent concerns of the imagination, revolution, and healing in the creation of the archetypal wolf goddess, Loba. Di Prima juxtaposes images of contemporary women with those of women throughout world mythology, all of which, she says, are manifestations of the Loba. In the opening section, called "Ave," the Loba says:

> I am you
> and I must become you
> I have been you
> and I must become you
> I am always you
> I must become you.

Di Prima's political activism expresses itself in her dedication to publication, performance, and education as well as to her writing. She has continually worked to make poetry a vital force in society, co-founding the New York Poets Theatre in 1961 and establishing the Poets Press in 1965 and Eidelon Editions in 1972. During the 1970s she participated in the Poetry-in-the-Schools program, teaching in reform schools, on reservations, and in prisons. She has also assisted in the development of several programs for poetry and the arts, including the Buddhist Naropa Institute, The Poets Institute in Point Reyes, California, and the San Francisco Institute of Magical and Healing Arts.

Maggie Gordon

*See also* Beat Poetry

**Biography**

Born in New York City, 6 August 1934. Attended Swarthmore College, Pennsylvania, 1951–53; contributing editor, *Kulchur* magazine, 1960–61; co-editor, with LeRoi Jones, 1961–63, and editor, 1963–69, *Floating Bear* magazine; associated with *Yugen, Signal, Guerilla,* San Francisco *Sunday Paper,* and *Rallying Point;* publisher, Poets Press, 1965–69, and Eidolon Editions, San Francisco, 1972–76; founder, with Alan Marlowe, New York Poets Theatre, 1961–65; associated with Wingbow Press, Berkeley, California; teacher in the Poetry-in-the-Schools program, 1971–75; visiting faculty member, Naropa Institute, Boulder, Colorado; artist-in-residence, Napa State Hospital, 1976–77; since 1980 Core Faculty member, New College of California, San Francisco. Received National Endowment for the Arts grant, 1966, 1973; Coordinating Council of Little Magazines grant, 1967, 1970. Living in San Francisco.

**Poetry**

*This Kind of Bird Flies Backward,* 1958
*The Monster,* 1961
*The New Handbook of Heaven,* 1963
*Unless You Clock In,* 1963

*Combination Theatre Poem and Birthday Poem for Ten People,* 1965
*Poems for Freddie,* 1966; as *Freddie Poems,* 1974
*Haiku,* 1967
*Earthsong: Poems, 1957–59,* edited by Alan S. Marlowe, 1968
*Hotel Albert,* 1968
*Revolutionary Letters,* 1968; as *Revolutionary Letters, Etc.,* 1971; as *Revolutionary Letters, Etc., 1966–1978,* 1979
*L.A. Odyssey,* 1969
*The Book of Hours,* 1970
*Kerhonkson Journal 1966,* 1971
*Prayer to the Mothers,* 1971
*So Fine,* 1971
*XV Dedications,* 1971
*The Calculus of Variation,* 1972
*Loba, Part 1,* 1973
*North Country Medicine,* 1974
*Brass Furnace Going Out: Song, after an Abortion,* 1975
*Selected Poems, 1956–1975,* 1975; revised edition, 1977
*Loba as Eve,* 1975
*Loba, Part 2,* 1976
*Loba, Parts 1–8,* 1978; revised edition as *Loba,* 1998
*Revolutionary Letters,* 1979
*The Selected Poems of Diane di Prima,* 1989
*Pieces of a Song: Selected Poems,* 1990
*Seminary Poems,* 1991
*No More* (with others), 1991
*22 Death Poems,* 1996
*Dinners and Nightmares* (includes prose), 1998

**Other Writings:** plays, novels (*Memoirs of a Beatnik,* 1969), short stories, translations of French and Latin literature (*The Man Condemned to Death,* by Jean Genet [translator with others], 1963); edited collections of poems (*War Poems,* 1968).

**Further Reading**

Friedman, Amy L., "'I Say My New Name': Women Writers of the Beat Generation," in *The Beat Generation Writers,* edited by A. Robert Lee, East Haven, Connecticut, and London: Pluto, 1996
Kirschenbaum, Blossom S., "Diane di Prima: Extending *La Famiglia,*" *MELUS* 14, nos. 3–4 (Fall–Winter 1987)
Knight, Brenda, *Women of the Beat Generation: The Writers, Artists, and Muses at the Heart of a Revolution,* Berkeley, California: Conari Press, 1996
McNeil, Helen, "The Archeology of Gender in the Beat Movement," in *The Beat Generation Writers,* edited by A. Robert Lee, East Haven, Connecticut, and London: Pluto, 1996
Ostriker, Alicia S., *Stealing the Language: The Emergence of Women's Poetry in America,* Boston: Beacon Press, 1986
Waldman, Anne, "An Interview with Diane di Prima," in *The Beat Road,* edited by Arthur Knight and Kit Knight, California, Pennsylvania: Knight, 1984
Waldman, Anne, and Marilyn Webb, editors, *Talking Poetics from the Naropa Institute,* 2 vols., Boulder, Colorado: Shambhala, 1978

## Hilda Doolittle. *See* H.D. (Hilda Doolittle)

## Edward Dorn 1929–99

Edward Dorn was an immensely and diversely skilled poet whose wit, intelligence, and uncompromising predilection toward heresy made him one of the great satirists of 20th- century American writing. He naturally inclined from his first work toward the political possibility of the poem. That, combined with an attraction to the 18th century ("a total century of insult . . . a brilliant century. It invented the modern.") and an unyielding inclination toward independent thought, led Dorn to locate his work utterly outside any legitimizing structures of power, literary or otherwise: "I think the function of the poet in present day America . . . would be to stay as removed as possible from all permanent associations with power." It led to a practice of writing that, as the English poet Tom Raworth noted in his obituary of Dorn, left Dorn "almost *persona non grata* in the . . . literary and academic climate of his homeland."

Born Edward Merton Dorn in Villa Grove, Illinois, on 2 April 1929, the poet grew up in poverty during the Great Depression. He was educated in a one-room schoolhouse and later went to the University of Illinois for two years, before heading west, where he worked in an aircraft plant in Seattle. In 1950, Dorn enrolled in Black Mountain College in North Carolina. After he dropped out and then returned to Black Mountain, his interest shifted from art to writing. In the interim, Charles Olson had taken over as rector of the college. Olson encouraged his student to take up the American West as his poetic material, publishing a pamphlet called "Bibliography on America for Ed Dorn." Dorn, in turn, produced a significant meditation on place and poetry called "What I See in the Maximus Poems" (1960), which became his first published work.

After graduating from Black Mountain in 1955, Dorn and his wife eventually returned to the Pacific Northwest, where they eked out a marginal existence. Their experiences became the subject matter for Dorn's novel, first published as *The Rites of Passage* (1965) and later retitled *By the Sound.* In 1960, Donald Allen included some of Dorn's early work in his groundbreaking anthology *The New American Poetry,* introducing Dorn to a wide audience of young, enthusiastic poets and poetry readers. A few years later, LeRoi Jones (later Amiri Baraka) included several of Dorn's short stories in another influential anthology called *The Moderns,* further increasing his exposure.

From 1961 to 1965, Dorn taught at Idaho State University at Pocatello. Those years saw the publication of his early lyrical work, poems marked by a spare but striking musicality and a deep sympathy for the lives and concerns of the ordinary working people he grew up with, poems such as "Like a Messenger on Sunday," "The Argument Is," and "A Country Song." *The Newly Fallen* was published by LeRoi Jones' Totem Press in 1961 and was followed three years later by *Hands Up!* which contained "Vaquero" and "On the Debt My Mother Owed to Sears Roebuck" as well as "The Land Below," Dorn's first attempt at a long narrative poem. These poems are frequently dark and taut with anger, and already Dorn was pushing away from lyricism toward the sustained political attentions of his later work.

In 1965, with the support of Donald Davie, Dorn became a Fulbright lecturer at the University of Essex in England. With a brief break, he stayed there for five years. He was already in correspondence with several English poets, including J.H. Prynne, Lee Harwood, Tom Raworth, and Tom Pickard. Fulcrum Press published his next two books, *Geography* (1965) and *The North Atlantic Turbine* (1967), which initiate Dorn's increasing turn toward the book as a unit of composition.

Discursive, intellectual, argumentative, moral, and political, the poems of *Geography* and *The North Atlantic Turbine* mark Dorn's coming of age as a poet of consequence. In these books, the materials of his life were projected outward into the figures of a cosmology rather than turned inward toward lyric self-absorption, a distinction between what he later called "inside real" and "outsidereal." Near the end of *The North Atlantic Turbine,* "An Idle Visitation" marks the first appearance of a figure that came to dominate his life for the next decade: "The cautious Gunslinger / of impeccable personal smoothness / and slender leather encased hands."

*Slinger,* as it was originally called, was written in sequential installments between 1966 and 1975. Conceived as a mock epic in the tradition of *The Dunciad* or *The Rape of the Lock, Slinger* exploded onto a poetry scene then still deeply under the spell of Charles Olson's vast and daring reimagination of the epic *The Maximus Poems* . In many ways undercutting the seriousness of the master he still "wore on his sleeve," Dorn wrote a deeply ironic poem founded on puns, jokes, and verbal slapstick. In place of Maximus and the various figures of history and myth that populate *The Maximus Poems,* Dorn peopled his mock epic with characters out of cartoons and comic books: a talking Stoned Horse variously named Heidegger and Lévi-Strauss, a saloon keeper named Lil, Dr. Flamboyant, the Gunslinger, and a character named "I" who dies and is resurrected as secretary to Parmenides.

During the course of their "epic" journey toward Las Vegas to find Howard Hughes (a journey that is never completed), the political/economic/philosophical systems that uphold the industrial/technological devastation of the West and, by extension, the "world" are relentlessly discussed, analyzed, deconstructed, and most importantly made fun of. Humor in the poem is not simply a tactic; it is the poem's crucial, philosophical gesture. As "I" says late in the poem, "Entrapment is this society's / Sole activity, I whispered / and only laughter / can blow it to rags."

While much of the rest of Dorn's work for the next 25 years was overshadowed by the enormous accomplishment of *Gunslinger,* he continued to develop a poetry of deep satirical intelligence and cutting wit while also writing some enduring love poetry: *Twenty-Four Love Songs* was published by Harvey Brown's Frontier Press in 1969, followed by *Songs: Set Two, a Short Count* in 1970. *Recollections of Gran Apacheria,* a brilliant homage to the Apaches, came out in 1974. *Hello, La Jolla* (1978) and *Yellow Lola* (1981) demonstrate Dorn's continuing interest in 18th-century form in a series of biting epigrammatic pronouncements on contemporary culture and politics. *Abhorrences* (1990) followed the spirit of these books with its short, savage observations of American culture in the age of Reagan. *Way West: Stories, Essays and Verse Accounts, 1963–1993* followed in 1993, and in 1997 came *High West Rendezvous: A Sampler,* reflecting his continuing attention and dedication to the "outsidereal" spaces of the American West.

From 1977 until his death in 1999, Dorn was on the faculty of the University of Colorado in Boulder. In addition to his poetry, he and his wife edited *Rolling Stock,* a wide-ranging tabloid-size journal that included poetry, fiction, political analysis, reviews, and a column on golf. He also produced several translations of Latin American writers in collaboration with Gordon Brotherston. At the time of his death, he was working on *Languedoc Variorum: A Defense of Heresy and Heretics,* a long poem on the heretical spirit that he celebrated so enthusiastically in his life.

MICHAEL BOUGHN

*See also* Black Mountain School

**Biography**

Born in Villa Grove, Illinois, 2 April 1929. Attended the University of Illinois, Urbana, 1949–50; Black Mountain College, North Carolina, 1950–51, 1954–55; reference librarian, New Mexico State Library, Santa Fe, 1959; taught at Idaho State University, Pocatello, 1961–65; Visiting Professor of American Literature (Fulbright Lecturer, 1965–66, 1966–67), University of Essex, Wivenhoe, England, 1965–68, 1974–75; visiting poet, University of Kansas, Lawrence, 1968–69; taught at Northeastern Illinois University, Chicago, 1970–71, and Kent State University, Ohio, 1973–74; Regents Lecturer, University of California, Riverside, 1973–74; writer-in-residence, University of California at San Diego, La Jolla, 1976, and from 1977, University of Colorado, Boulder; editor, *Wild Dog* magazine, 1964–65; editor, *Rolling Stock* newspaper; from 1983 editor, *Rolling Rock* magazine. Received National Endowment for the Arts grant, 1966, 1968; D.H. Lawrence fellowship, 1969. Died in Denver, Colorado, 10 December 1999.

**Poetry**
*Paterson Society,* 1960
*The Newly Fallen,* 1961
*From Gloucester Out,* 1964
*Hands Up!* 1964
*Idaho Out,* 1965
*Geography,* 1965; revised edition, 1968
*The North Atlantic Turbine,* 1967
*Song,* 1968
*Gunslinger, Book I,* 1968
*The Midwest Is That Space between the Buffalo Statler and the Lawrence Eldridge,* 1968
*Gunslinger, Book II,* 1969
*Gunslinger 1 and 2,* 1969
*Twenty-Four Love Songs,* 1969
*The Cosmology of Finding Your Spot,* 1969
*Ed Dorn Sportcasts Colonialism,* 1969
*Songs: Set Two, a Short Count,* 1970
*Spectrum Breakdown: A Microbook,* 1971
*A Poem Called Alexander Hamilton,* 1971
*The Cycle,* 1971
*The Kultchural Exchange,* 1971
*Old New Yorkers Really Get My Head,* 1972
*The Hamadryas Baboon at the Lincoln Park Zoo,* 1972
*Gunslinger, Book III: THE WINTERBOOK, Prologue to the Great Book IIII Kornerstone,* 1972
*Recollections of Gran Apacheria,* 1974
*The Collected Poems, 1956–1974,* 1975
*Manchester Square* (with Jennifer Dunbar), 1975
*Gunslinger/Slinger,* 1975
*Hello, La Jolla,* 1978
*Selected Poems,* edited by Donald Allen, 1978
*Yellow Lola: Formerly Titled Japanese Neon (Hello, La Jolla, Book II),* 1981
*Captain Jack's Chaps; or, Houston, MLA,* 1983
*Abhorrences,* 1990
*The Denver Landing, 11 Aug 1993,* 1993
*Way West: Stories, Essays, and Verse Accounts, 1963–1993,* 1993
*High West Rendezvous: A Sampler,* 1997

**Other Writings:** short stories, novel (*The Rites of Passage,* 1965; reprinted as *By the Sound,* 1971), essays, translations of Latin American poetry (*Image of the New World: The American Continent Portrayed in Native Texts,* edited by Gordon Brotherston, 1979).

**Further Reading**
Davidson, Michael, "Archeologist of Morning: Charles Olson, Edward Dorn, and Historical Method," *ELH* 47 (1980)
Dewey, Anne, "The Relation between Open Form and Collective Voice: The Social Origin of Processual Form in John Ashbery's *Three Poems* and Ed Dorn's *Gunslinger,*" *Sagetrieb* 11, nos. 1–2 (Spring–Fall 1992)
Elmborg, James K., *"A Pageant of Its Time": Edward Dorn's "Slinger" and the Sixties,* New York: Lang, 1998
Fox, Willard, *Robert Creeley, Edward Dorn, and Robert Duncan: A Reference Guide,* Boston: Hall, 1989
Hatlen, Burton, "Toward a Common Ground: Versions of Place in the Poetry of Charles Olson, Edward Dorn, and Theodore Enslin," *Sagetrieb* 15, no. 3 (Winter 1996)
McPheron, William, *Edward Dorn,* Boise, Idaho: Boise State University, 1988
Paul, Sherman, *The Lost America of Love: Rereading Robert Creeley, Edward Dorn, and Robert Duncan,* Baton Rouge: Louisiana State University Press, 1981
Von Hallberg, Robert, *American Poetry and Culture, 1945–1980,* Cambridge, Massachusetts: Harvard University Press, 1985
Wesling, Donald, editor, *Internal Resistances: The Poetry of Edward Dorn,* Berkeley: University of California Press, 1985

## Gunslinger

Edward Dorn's *Gunslinger* was composed and published between 1966 and 1975, the most turbulent decade in the last half of the 20th century. It was a decade that saw the rise of the counterculture and mass resistance to the U.S. war against Vietnam, the transformation of the post–World War II United States into a mass consumer society, and the triumph of mass popular culture over all other forms of cultural expression. During those ten years, the United States nearly tore itself apart in a struggle over the interpretation of the fundamental values of the nation. Dorn, whose poetry had always had a political focus and who was a longtime admirer of the satiric spirit and literary forms of the 18th century, embodied that profound ruckus in *Gunslinger* in the form of a mock epic, perhaps the only poem of its kind in 20th-century American writing.

Dorn was a student of Charles Olson at Black Mountain College in the 1950s and was influenced by his teacher in a number of ways. Perhaps most important, like Olson, Dorn rejected the omnipresent personal lyric as a viable poetic form (in *Gunslinger,* a character named "I" dies and is later reborn as secretary to Parmenides). In addition, Olson bequeathed to Dorn "the West" as his poetic material, a charge that Dorn took seriously. Both issues come together to shape *Gunslinger.*

Olson, working critically in the wake of Ezra Pound and William Carlos Williams, had turned to the primary epic as the form necessary to the demands of the historical moment. The result was *The Maximus Poems,* a vast and daring push past the literary toward a recuperation of primordial energies that Olson felt was a necessary political move in the United States in the 1950s and 1960s. Dorn was sympathetic to Olson's position, although not uncritical in his own right of Olson's straight-ahead take on the epic. Unlike Olson, who proposed to leap over all literature between Homer and Melville, Dorn was attracted early on to the satirical spirit of the 18th century as well as its poetic forms, among them the mock epic. The mock epic allowed Dorn the scope and length he required to unleash his complex poetic energies while satisfying his deep attraction to satire.

*Gunslinger,* or *Slinger* as it is also referred to, consists of five books: *Gunslinger, Book I* (1968); *Gunslinger, Book II* (1969); *The Cycle* (1971); *Gunslinger, Book III: THE WINTERBOOK, Prologue to the Great Book IIII Kornerstone* (1972; called simply "Book III" in the collected poem); and *Book IIII,* first published as part of the completed poem (titled *Gunslinger* on the spine and

*Slinger* on the cover) in 1975. The four numbered sections track the "epic" journey of a group of characters through the western United States toward an apocalyptic encounter with industrialist Howard Hughes. "The Cycle" introduces Hughes to the poem (under his middle name, Robarts) and describes in surrealistic detail his departure from Boston for Las Vegas in November 1966 and the events of that trip.

The poem openly invokes a number of American myths. At the center of it is the figure of the Gunslinger himself, a man "of impeccable personal smoothness / and slender leather encased hands / folded casually / to make his knock." Described later as a "son of the sun," the Gunslinger, who is later called Slinger and, still later, Zlinger, is a manifestation of the hero/outlaw mythos of the American West imbued with metaphysical power. He is utterly present in the world, and his presence holds the world in place. One of Slinger's traveling companions says of him,

the sun, the moon
and some of the stars are
kept in their tracks
by this Person's equilibrium
or at least I sense some effect
on the perigee and apogee of all
our movements in this, I can't quite say,
man's presence.

Hughes, on the other hand, embodies an opposing American myth of personal power accumulated through acquisition of wealth, a kind of monstrous Horatio Alger. The confrontation between these two opposing forces—one grounded in the vast spaces and peoples of the American West and the other in the technological, world-devouring drive of European culture—provides the poem with its central conflict. Crucially, the apocalyptic confrontation between them never occurs. In fact, Slinger sleeps through the "climactic" moment, as if such business was finally of no interest to him. The world that *Gunslinger* satirizes is a world beyond apocalypse.

In addition to Slinger and Robarts, the poem is peopled with a hilarious assortment of unlikely traveling companions, including a talking horse who is variously called Heidegger or Lévi-Strauss, Lil (another archetypal figure from American television westerns), the Poet, "I," Kool Everything, Dr. Flamboyant, and a Talking Barrel. Combining the language and imagery of cartoons, drug culture, rock songs, techno-speak, pulp fiction, television westerns, and popular slang, *Gunslinger* invokes the world of mass popular culture at the moment it was recognized as the dominant and unequaled cultural experience in the United States.

In so doing, however, *Gunslinger* proposes itself in terms that make it the apotheosis of resistance to the processes of commodification that are central to that culture. At one point in the poem, the resurrected, metamorphosed "I" says, "Entrapment is this society's / Sole activity, I whispered / and only laughter / can blow it to rags." In the current cultural climate, the commodification of poetry is tied to careerism in the university English department (Universe City, as Dorn has it in the poem). The laughter central to *Gunslinger*—elicited by the poem's vicious and hilarious critique of the academy, its flippant disregard for any "rules" of poetry, its enthusiastic embrace of the outlaw drug culture, and its enormous range of reference to events contemporaneous with the composition of the poem—make the poem almost unteachable in the current academic climate. It thus resists its transformation into some kind of exchange value within an academic economy, a status that some other "oppositional" poetries actually seek.

In *Gunslinger,* Dorn uses the possibilities inherent in the form of the mock epic to push it beyond its traditional limits. Like *The Dunciad* or *Mac Flecknoe, Gunslinger*'s humor is centered in large part on its moral outrage over social and cultural stupidities. However, as in *The Rape of the Lock,* the epic form itself (as much as its subject matter) is also a focus of the poem's humor. For Pope, it was a way of dealing with Milton. For Dorn, it was a way of addressing Olson, whom, he asserted, he still "wore . . . on his sleeve." *Gunslinger* gently and with great good humor mocks its own "epic" processes. It pokes fun at the idea of the primary epic as a viable form in a culture given over to the banal and the pompous, even as it makes that culture the butt of satirical hilarity.

MICHAEL BOUGHN

**Further Reading**


Davidson, Michael, "To Eliminate the Draw: Narrative and Language in *Slinger,*" in *Internal Resistances: The Poetry of Edward Dorn,* edited by Donald Wesling, Berkeley: University of California Press, 1985

Dewey, Anne, "The Relation between Open Form and Collective Voice: The Social Origin of Processual Form in John Ashbery's *Three Poems* and Ed Dorn's *Gunslinger,*" *Sagetrieb* 11, nos. 1–2 (Spring–Fall 1992)

Elmborg, James K., *"A Pageant of Its Time": Edward Dorn's "Slinger" and the Sixties,* New York: Lang, 1998

Foster, Thomas, "'Kick(ing) the Perpendiculars Outa Right Anglos': Edward Dorn's Multiculturalism," *Contemporary Literature* 38, no. 1 (Spring 1997)

Jenkins, Grant, "*Gunslinger*'s Ethics of Excess: Subjectivity, Community, and the Politics of the Could Be," *Sagetrieb* 15, no. 3 (Winter 1996)

Lockwood, William J., "Art Rising to Clarity: Edward Dorn's Compleat *Slinger,*" in *Internal Resistances: The Poetry of Edward Dorn,* edited by Donald Wesling, Berkeley: University of California Press, 1985

# Rita Dove 1952–

Rita Dove has brought African-American expression into the mainstream of American poetry. Her own family history of early 20th-century migration from the rural South to industrial Akron became an exemplary journey affirming black entitlement to the American dream in her Pulitzer Prize–winning poem, *Thomas and Beulah* (1986). Dove has continued to position civil rights as essential to the cultural freedoms of all Americans.

Dove's work has been markedly international as well, beginning with *The Yellow House on the Corner* (1980). Published when Dove was 28, after periods of living in Germany, it juxtaposes explorations of European history and cultural mythology with American investigations, both historical and contemporary. "The Bird Frau" expresses the disorientated anxieties and anticipations of a half-starved German mother in wartime and illustrates Dove's historical imagination, her readiness to inhabit another consciousness. "Robert Schumann, Or: Musical Genius Begins with Affliction," a comic celebration of the itch of creativity, is an early example of her continuing interest in music, both as subject and as formal inspiration. Poems of American history include "The Transport of Slaves from Maryland to Mississippi," which dramatizes an 1839 incident in which a slave woman prevented a wagonload of slaves from escaping by helping the wounded Negro driver give the alarm to the white owners. Dove is absorbed by the specific situation in which the personal might override the political; in her poetry, slavery is a human predicament as well as a cultural evil. The geographical and metaphorical range matches the bold historical range of this volume: travel not only stimulates the transforming powers of the poet's imagination, but also serves as a metaphor for them. The title, *The Yellow House on the Corner,* signifies local origin and global village. Dove's formal economy and lyric flight are evident in the justly famous "Geometry," in which the analogy between proving a theorem and writing a poem is taken to "where they've intersected," at which point the metaphorical imagination releases the elements "to some point true and unproven."

*Museum* (1983) is a more exigent examination of cultural origins and ideological attitudes, less buoyant than *The Yellow House on the Corner,* always conscious of the processes of the historicizing imagination, the way in which the cultural gaze reworks artifacts and legends. "Agosta the Winged Man and Rasha the Black Dove" addresses the uncomfortable burden conferred on those who seek historical truth and find it unexpectedly painful and personally relevant. Based on the 1929 Christian Schad painting of that title, the poem underplays the shock of finding that a black woman with Dove's own name was routinely exhibited as a freak in 1920s Berlin. The precise and complex visual layout formally and austerely traces questions of representation. These historicist preoccupations recur in the series of poems on Italian and Greek legends and in "The Sailor in Africa," a poem of notable comic poise on colonialist enterprise in pursuit of the slave trade, based on a Viennese card game circa 1910. The volume concludes with "Parsley," a registration of the consciousness of Trujillo, the dictator of the Dominican Republic. Overall Dove expresses her preoccupation with historical representation, both the larger political frame and the more personal family history, with considerable narrative ingenuity in *Museum.* Dove's next volume, *Thomas and Beulah,* combined narrative and lyric in a formally innovative long poem sequence loosely based on her grandparents' lives and responded to what she has called "the underside of history" (*The Poet's World,* 1995).

*Grace Notes* (1989), a title suggestive of musical embellishment, also indicates Dove's feminist intent to note the conditions and possibilities for black American women 50 years on from the opening poem, "Summit Beach, 1921," whose date and location signify racial segregation. Autobiographical, sometimes confessional, poems of motherhood explore the "black mother, cream child" relationship. Some of the most notable poems, such as "Ozone," critique the damaged culture in which parents raise children. Others express this awareness of a fallen condition symbolically, with a sensibility akin to Rilke's (whom Dove particularly admires). "Horse and Tree" depicts childhood as the "sap" that "ascends" in the natural cycle, just as the fairground carousel on which children ride rises and falls. "Mississippi" also uses symbolism, to fuse carnal discovery and the geographical exploration of "the New World, before maps," the "falling down / river" prefigured.

The cultural workings of myth and an awareness of the vulnerabilities of modern motherhood unite in *Mother Love* (1995), a sonnet sequence based on the Demeter/Persephone myth. Dove noted in her introduction that she composed *Mother Love* "in homage and as counterpart to Rilke's *Sonnets to Orpheus.*" The sequence sustains a continuous parallel between the contemporary and the antique, sometimes through antiphony: "Grief: the Council" alternates the response of American neighbors to Persephone's abduction—gossip and social platitudes—with Demeter's own grief-stricken abdication of her role as universal earth mother. Lyrical and witty (Hades, Persephone's seducer, is a middle-aged painter in Paris), ironically feminist, the sonnets display a modern sensibility, addressing the randomness of violence in the opening poem, "Heroes," and gender roles in the title poem. This contemporary stance is not at odds with a mythic universalizing mode: "Lamentations" recalls the reader from the elegiac mode with a reminder that nature's sensual music is culturally mediated and that to hear Pan's pipes "and not answer / is to deny this world."

*On the Bus with Rosa Parks* (1999) highlights the role ordinary black women played in the struggle for civil rights. Dove pays homage in poems to lesser-known figures Claudette Colvin and Mary Louise Smith as well as to Rosa Parks and her historic refusal in 1955 to move to the back of a bus in Montgomery, Alabama. "Lady Freedom Among Us," written during Dove's period as Poet Laureate (1993–95), commemorates the return of the Statue of Freedom to the Capitol Dome. The touch of black phrasing and the pun on U.S. in the title indicate Dove's confidence in ethnic diversity as the norm "among us." Published in a limited fine art edition and also on the Internet, "Lady Freedom Among Us" speaks directly to the American people, imperatively, individually:

> don't lower your eyes
> or stare straight ahead to where
> you think you ought to be going

Genuinely populist, this volume reflects Dove's readiness to reach out and broaden the audience for poetry.

The timing and historical nature of *On the Bus with Rosa Parks* almost necessitate millennial reflections. "Revenant," the title poem of a section devoted to ghostly revisitings, somberly stages the rituals of the body politic, "the black hood of the condemned," and its failures, "Gauze bandages over the wounds of State." Dove's historical imagination reaches back here symbolically to condense the human spirit suffering through centuries. In sometimes colloquial, seemingly artless language, Dove uses the bus as a democratic symbol of the struggle for individual freedom as well as for an inclusive culture. She never forgets that its passengers are afforded only a partial, fleeting glimpse—"the view chopped square / and dimming quick"—of their own journey.

Travel, marriage to a German writer, and grants to live periodically in Europe have conferred upon Dove what Henry James has called "the complex fate" of the international American writer. Dove herself addresses the particular comedy of the *black* American writer abroad in "The Venus of Willendorf," an ironic narrative of her reception as an "exotic" in provincial Austria. Rita Dove is Associate Editor and occasional contributor to *Callaloo,* the African-American journal, yet she was not part of the Black Arts movement of the 1960s, rejecting the narrowness of its aims. In a 1991 interview published in *Callaloo,* she said that her interest in politics and history always lay in the individuals "whose histories make them react to the world in different ways." Her play *The Darker Face of the Earth* (1996) and her poems highlight individual predicament and achievement. In linguistic terms, her spare use of black vernacular and folk idiom links her with predecessors such as Langston Hughes in only the loosest way. Her work lies closer to the eclecticism of Melvin B. Tolson, to whose collection of poems she wrote an introduction praising his narrative gifts and his ear for rhythm and inflection.

Dove's innovative poetics have been most evident in her experiments with the long poem sequence, in the successful fusion of lyric and narrative in *Thomas and Beulah, Mother Love,* and poems such as "Cameos." In this she has been part of a remarkable flowering of women poets, including Judy Grahn, Brenda Maria Osbey, and Susan Howe, celebrated by Lynn Keller in *Forms of Expansion: Recent Long Poems by Women* (1997) for extending the boundaries of the genre of the long poem. As a woman poet, however, Dove has retained her individuality, avoiding postmodern opacity and gender bias, focusing often on family relationships in ordinary lives; like Elizabeth Bishop, Dove always grounds her work in the specific. Dove has the added quality of being able to create extended works entering into and dramatizing the consciousness of those very different from herself.

The autobiographical strand in Dove's poetry might seem to position her in the line of confessional poetry, heir to Lowell, Plath, and Sexton. In one sense, her poems about family, marriage, and parenting are in Middle America territory, written from within the experience of consumer capitalism: she holds no illusions about standing aside from it. Her imagination is both culturally critical, at times satiric, *and* mythic, universalizing. More fully sharing in typical American values and aspirations than Lowell, Dove is nevertheless, in historical and aesthetic range, and in her acute mapping of the ideological pressures and political topographies that shape the individual and the family, one of his successors. These qualities can be found in an early poem, "Corduroy Road," about the lumberjacks who created the westward trail of logs laid parallel (resembling corduroy wale) across the continent:

> What prevails a man to hazard his person in the Wisconsin
> Forests
> is closer to contrition than anything: the wild honey
> blazing from outstretched palms, a skunk bagged and eaten
> in tears.

American mythology and history, the cultural cost of "blazing" the human trail westward, the official language of documents, and the rigors of frontier life converge with characteristic economy in this "masculine" poem. The shift to Edenic immediacy and the individual staggering toward the reader are powerfully realized. Rita Dove is not a confessional poet, nor a polemicist in the mode of Adrienne Rich; rather, her imagination finds the point where, as in her poem "Geometry," the personal and the political, the private moment and the larger cultural shift, have intersected.

PAT RIGHELATO

**Biography**

Born in Akron, Ohio, 28 August 1952. Attended Miami University, Oxford, Ohio, B.A. (summa cum laude) 1973; University of Tübingen, West Germany, 1974–75; University of Iowa, Iowa City, M.F.A. 1977; research assistant, 1975, and teaching assistant, 1976–77, University of Iowa; Assistant Professor of creative writing, 1981–84, Associate Professor, 1984–87, Professor of English, 1987–89, Arizona State University, Tempe; since 1989 Commonwealth Professor of English, University of Virginia, Charlottesville; writer-in-residence, Tuskegee Institute, Alabama, 1982; Rockefeller Foundation residency, Bellagio, Italy, 1988; since 1984 member of the editorial board, *National Forum;* since 1986 poetry editor, *Callaloo;* advisory editor, since 1987, *Gettysburg Review,* and since 1988, *Tri-Quarterly;* since 1987 commissioner, Schomburg Center for the Preservation of Black Culture, New York Public Library. Received Fulbright fellowship, 1974–75; National Endowment for the Arts grant, 1978, fellowship, 1982; Ohio Arts Council grant, 1979; Guggenheim fellowship, 1983; Lavan Younger Poets Award, 1986; Pulitzer Prize, 1987; H.D.L., Miami University, 1988; Mellon fellowship, 1988–89; University of Virginia Center for Advanced Studies fellowship, 1989–92; Harvard University Phi Beta Kappa poet, 1993; NAACP Great American Artist Award, 1993; Carl Sandburg Award, International Platform Association, 1994; United States Poet Laureate/Consultant in Poetry, Library of Congress, 1993–95; Heinz Award in the Arts, 1996; Levinson Prize, *Poetry* magazine, 1998; Special Consultant in Poetry, Library of Congress, 1999–2000. Living in Charlottesville, Virginia.

**Poetry**

*Ten Poems,* 1977
*The Only Dark Spot in the Sky,* 1980
*The Yellow House on the Corner,* 1980
*Mandolin,* 1982
*Museum,* 1983
*Thomas and Beulah,* 1986
*The Other Side of the House,* 1988

*Grace Notes,* 1989
*Selected Poems,* 1993
*Lady Freedom Among Us,* 1994
*Mother Love: Poems,* 1995
*On the Bus with Rosa Parks: Poems,* 1999

**Other Writings:** short-story collection (*Fifth Sunday,* 1985), novel (*Through the Ivory Gate: A Novel,* 1992), essays (*The Poet's World,* 1995), play (*The Darker Face of the Earth,* 1996).

**Further Reading**

Booth, Alison, "Abduction and Other Severe Pleasures: Rita Dove's *Mother Love,*" *Callaloo* 19, no. 1 (1996)
Cavalieri, Grace, "Rita Dove: An Interview," *American Poetry Review* 24, no. 2 (1995)
Costello, Bonnie, "Scars and Wings: Rita Dove's *Grace Notes,*" *Callaloo* 14, no. 2 (1991)
Cushman, Stephen, "And the Dove Returned," *Callaloo* 19, no. 1 (1996)
Keller, Lynn, *Forms of Expansion: Recent Long Poems by Women,* Chicago: University of Chicago Press, 1997
Lofgren, Lotta, "Partial Horror: Fragmentation and Healing in Rita Dove's *Mother Love,*" *Callaloo* 19, no. 1 (1996)
Rampersand, Arnold, "The Poems of Rita Dove," *Callaloo* 9, no. 1 (1986)
Vendler, Helen, "The Black Dove: Rita Dove, Poet Laureate," in *Soul Says: On Recent Poetry,* by Vendler, Cambridge, Massachusetts: Harvard University Press, 1995
Vendler, Helen, "Rita Dove: Identity Markers," in *The Given and the Made: Strategies of Poetic Redefinition,* Cambridge, Massachusetts: Harvard University Press, 1995; as *The Given and the Made: Recent American Poets,* London: Faber and Faber, 1995

## "Ö"

It is not surprising that a phrase from "Ö," first published in *The Ohio Review* (20, no. 2 [1979]), supplies the title for Rita Dove's first full collection of poems. *The Yellow House on the Corner* (1980) is markedly the product of travel, international and wide-ranging in its concerns, and Ö, the Swedish word for "island," as the poem tells us, is also a universal expression of wonder. The poem is not only about making poetry but about adjusting from the known to the unknown, and it may very well represent Dove's own career, which has been, as she stated in her introduction to *Selected Poems* (1993), one of finding in the ordinary and the familiar "some disclosure, some *connection,* waiting to be seen."

In "Ö" metaphor itself becomes a mode of travel, and translation from one culture or language to another elicits the same elation as the transformations of metaphor:

> One word of Swedish has changed the whole
> neighborhood.
> When I look up, the yellow house on the corner
> is a galleon stranded in flowers.

The foreign language has the enchanting capacity to make everything new, uprooting the neighborhood for a historical and transcontinental voyage via an archaic galleon.

The incongruity of the "galleon stranded in flowers" renders both the known and the unknown strange. The word *stranded* suggests being left behind or shipwrecked on a beach, but here it is transformed in an amusing predicament: stranded in a suburban garden. As with the windows in the poem "Geometry," the intersections of metaphor are an expansive liberation. Paradoxically, the speaker does not need to go anywhere to change her sense of place, to envisage the neighborhood as an island to discover. "Island" itself is transformed from being insular in the sense of being cut off from change, like the "Families [who] refuse to budge," into the fabulous, ready to be discovered by the eager explorer. Such an imagination is not soothed by the contemporary suburban sound of a "leaf-mulcher"; it "could be the horn-blast from a ship," a romantic call to metaphorical transformation.

This is also a poem about the art of poetry. The title's single letter turns out to be a word capable of generating an entire poem. The first stanza begins with an instruction, "Shape," drawing the reader into the activity, a process that is then ascribed a single, unambiguous meaning: "Shape the lips to an *o,* say *a.* / That's *island.*" The reader understands the word by its basic translation only until the second stanza, when that "One word" changes everything by inspiring the speaker's flight of fancy. The speaker's imagination shifts from isolating literal meaning (translation) to discovering the word as a vehicle to a remote destination, the multiple meanings of metaphor. The process is initially involuntary, a visual gift: "When I look up, the yellow house . . . / is a galleon." Soon, however, the imagination, symbolized here by the "wind" and "backyard breezes," domesticated versions of Romantic imagery for poetic energy, becomes active. The speaker assumes fellowship with the reader by this stage, using only the slightest details to sustain the poem: "We don't need much more to keep things going." Imagination is not a faculty reserved exclusively for poets, Dove suggests, for "if, one evening, the house . . . took off . . . neither I nor my neighbor / would be amazed."

For all its liberations, the poem holds on to the sense of precision in translation. The poet is and is not like the translator. The paradox is explored as the poem turns the corner into the final stanza, the enjambment highlighting the luck, the randomness of discovery, like a buried treasure:

> Sometimes
>
> a word is found so right it trembles
> at the slightest explanation.

The poet, like the translator, recognizes the "right" word, but for the poet the word is "found," not selected for a static or fixed meaning. The ambiguity in "trembles" is finely expressed: in one sense, human fear is attributed to the inanimate object in the notion that the poetic word "trembles" at the thought of being explained, as if it were alive and did not want to be pinned down. In another sense "trembles" suggests the delicate, active potency of the word, its transformational latency. In the conclusion to the poem, the wonder of the process is deliberately flattened to the matter-of-fact language that reports the completed poem: "You start out with one thing, end / up with another." In artistic terms this transformation is satisfactory, but in terms of personal adjustment to change, unsettling.

*The Yellow House on the Corner,* published when she was 28, was the breakthrough collection that made Rita Dove's name. When her *Selected Poems* was published in 1993, Dove wrote a new poem as preface entitled "In the Old Neighborhood," an affectionate return to the familiar and known. Similarly, "Ö" celebrates origins as well as where it will "end / up." But to compare it with the later poem is to be aware of how "Ö" articulates the *beginning* of an artistic journey into the poetic function of language. It is characteristic that Dove does not choose an elaborate, formal, "literary" register to express the transformations and extensions that language grants the known world of reality. The youthful delight is in the voyage into the unknown, scattering the "cardinals," the winds blowing from fixed points, as if the compass has been "Done with" (Emily Dickinson, poem 249). Even the present, the window of the house, "extends its glass forehead to sea," as if straining into the salt wave like a ship's figurehead, pressing forward into the future.

Pat Righelato

**Further Reading**

McDowell, Robert, "The Assembling Vision of Rita Dove," in *Conversant Essays: Contemporary Poets on Poetry,* edited by James McCorkle, Detroit, Michigan: Wayne State University Press, 1990

Schneider, Steven, "Coming Home: An Interview with Rita Dove," *Iowa Review* 19, no. 3 (1989)

Taleb-Khyar, Mohammed B, "An Interview with Maryse Condé and Rita Dove," *Callaloo* 14, no. 2 (1991)

"'The Underside of the Story': A Conversation with Rita Dove," in *The Post-Confessionals: Conversations with American Poets of the Eighties,* edited by Earl J. Ingersoll, Judith Kitchen, and Stan Sanvel Rubin, Rutherford, New Jersey: Fairleigh Dickinson University Press, and London: Associated University Presses, 1989

Van Dyne, Susan, "Siting the Poet: Rita Dove's Refiguring of Traditions," in *Women Poets of the Americas: Toward a Pan-American Gathering,* edited by Jacqueline Vaught Brogan, Notre Dame, Indiana: University of Notre Dame Press, 1999

Vendler, Helen, "An Interview with Rita Dove," in *Reading Black, Reading Feminist,* edited by Henry Louis Gates, Jr., London: Penguin, and New York: Meridian, 1990

## Thomas and Beulah

In *Thomas and Beulah* (1986), awarded the Pulitzer Prize for Poetry in 1987, Rita Dove re-creates the lives of her grandparents to document and celebrate the history of an ordinary African-American family. The book is a series of highly compressed, allusive poems depicting the events in their lives and in American society during the period from 1900 to 1969. The poems are linked by their narrative thread and by common images and motifs. Music recurs throughout, as do images of a canary, a mandolin, the color yellow, and water.

Intrigued by her grandmother's stories that she had heard as a child, Dove began to write poems to help her better understand her grandparents. Because both her grandparents were dead when she began the project, she asked her mother for details about their lives, working from the known to imagine the rest of their stories. Eventually, she wrote 23 poems about her grandfather, whom she calls Thomas, and 21 about her grandmother, whom she calls Beulah.

In a videotaped interview with Bill Moyers, she comments that memory is more important than truth, explaining that the events of life are remembered not so much in their chronological linearity but as moments that stand out as if they were pearls on a string. Following her analogy of strung pearls, Dove writes the life of her grandparents as a series of private memories narrated sequentially, first by Thomas and second by Beulah. *Thomas and Beulah* is the story of a marriage of ordinary people, spoken through the viewpoints of husband and wife. Dove writes carefully crafted, tightly knit poems, condensed and precise, drawing on the spoken word but rich in implication. A single detail stands for a complex emotion. For example, we learn a great deal about Beulah's father from two details: the dog crawls under the stove and the gate slams when he comes home. Each poem has its own form; some are in two-line stanzas, others in irregular stanzas. Alliteration and slant rhyme are frequent devices.

We see their marriage evolve as a series of experiences remembered differently by each of the partners. For example, Thomas plays the mandolin to court Beulah, and he magnanimously gives her his yellow silk scarf ("Courtship"), but we learn later that Beulah would "much prefer a pianola" and thinks his scarf too bright. A gnat flies into Thomas' eye, causing it to tear, and Beulah interprets the tear as a sign that he is sensitive.

The book narrates an important era in African-American history: the northward migration of thousands of African-Americans in the early decades of the 20th century. Beulah's family moved from Georgia to Akron, Ohio, in 1906; Thomas arrived in Akron from Tennessee in 1921. The migration changed the demographics of both North and South and provided workers for northern industry, contributing to the urbanization of northern cities. The concentration of African-Americans in places such as Harlem in New York or the south side of Chicago led to the development of jazz and to the flowering of culture in the Harlem Renaissance. The lives of Dove's grandparents mirror the circumstances of their times, such as the Depression, racism, and World War II. Because she is black, Beulah irons dresses in the back of the dress shop and is not allowed to sell dresses to the white customers. Thomas works as a riveter in an airplane factory during World War II and wishes that he could be a combatant instead of working in a defense plant (or, if not that, at least work on the plane engines rather than the wings).

Thomas begins as a devil-may-care dandy, a singer dressed in a houndstooth vest traveling on a riverboat with his friend Lem, who plays the mandolin. Lem drowns when Thomas dares him to swim to a nearby island. Thomas is haunted by Lem's memory. He leaves the riverboat, courts Beulah, and becomes a husband, a metalworker, and the father of four daughters. He works in factories, stops playing his mandolin, and joins the church gospel choir.

Both protagonists find escape from the strains of daily life in fantasy: Thomas in his music, in womanizing, and in haunting memories of his friend Lem; Beulah in the hope of a trip to France and, when that becomes impossible, in reading about France.

Another escape is in solitude, when Beulah experiences reverie and becomes "nothing." Although Dove does not romanticize the lives or marriage of Thomas and Beulah, nevertheless their commitment to each other emerges. After her husband has died, Beulah thinks "we were good, / though we never believed it."

Karen Stein

**Further Reading**

Cavalieri, Grace, "Rita Dove: An Interview," *The American Poetry Review* 24, no. 2 (1995)

Cook, Emily Walker, "'But She Won't Set Foot / in His Turtle-Dove Nash': Gender Roles and Gender Symbolism in Rita Dove's *Thomas and Beulah*," *College Language Association Journal* 38, no. 3 (1995)

Keller, Lynn, "Sequences Testifying for 'Nobodies': Rita Dove's *Thomas and Beulah* and Brenda Marie Osbey's *Desperate Circumstance, Dangerous Woman*," in *Forms of Expansion: Recent Long Poems by Women*, edited by Keller, Chicago: University of Chicago Press, 1997

Schneider, Steven, "Coming Home: An Interview with Rita Dove," *The Iowa Review* 19, no. 3 (1989)

Vendler, Helen, "Rita Dove: Identity Markers," *Callaloo* 17, no. 2 (1994)

---

## Robert Duncan 1919–88

Robert Duncan was a central poet in the San Francisco Renaissance of poetry in the 1950s and 1960s. Kenneth Rexroth provided the foundation for the emergence of a group of poets—Madeline Gleason, Helen Adam, Jack Spicer, Robin Blaser, Robert Duncan, and later Michael McClure and Joanne Kyger—who were based in San Francisco but not enveloped in the Beat movement. Duncan was a native Californian (as distinct from Beat writers Allen Ginsberg and Jack Kerouac, who came to San Francisco from the East Coast), a learned man who read extensively in medieval history, occult movements, and spiritual literature of all kinds. Duncan brought this information and an articulate intelligence to poetry. Even before he met Charles Olson in 1947, he was formulating a poetics based on open field composition, which he derived from Gestalt psychology and Modernist art. From 1951 until his death he lived with the painter Jess Collins, and together they developed a poetics of collage in painting and poetry that made new directions in American writing possible.

After his mother died in childbirth, Robert Duncan was adopted by a theosophist couple who chose the baby after casting astrological charts. He grew up as Robert Edward Symmes (his first poems were published under that name), reverting to his original surname in 1942. He was raised in Bakersfield, California, where his adopted father, an architect, had an office. His grandmother had been an elder in a Hermetic order similar to Yeats' Order of the Golden Dawn. The tales told and read to Duncan as a child by his parents and the appropriately named Aunt Fay were as lasting and important as any of his later influences. A high school English teacher introduced him to the work of D.H. Lawrence and H.D., especially her poem entitled "Heat." In the long prose study called "The H.D. Book," he derives his life as a poet in part from his teacher's instruction and her dedication to literature. By the time he was 18 he had accepted his homosexuality and the calling to devote his life to writing poetry.

He attended the University of California at Berkeley from 1936 to 1938, publishing his first poems in school magazines and learning about the poetry of Ezra Pound, T.S. Eliot, and Gertrude Stein before leaving for New York. There he became part of the circle of Anaïs Nin that included Kenneth Patchen, George Barker (an early influence along with Edith Sitwell), Jean Cocteau, and the French Surrealists. In New York he followed exhibitions in art galleries and museums, and witnessed the emergence of Abstract Expressionism. His article "The Homosexual in Society" appeared in the magazine *Politics* in 1944 and has become a benchmark document for gay activism and individual freedom. He returned to Berkeley in the spring of 1946, met Jack Spicer and Robin Blaser, and reconnected with Kenneth Rexroth in San Francisco. Again he attended Berkeley (1948–50), studying medieval and Renaissance civilization. In 1952 he joined the group of poets publishing in *Origin* magazine after responding to a poem by Denise Levertov published there. His association with the *Black Mountain Review* then followed. His poetry and prose appear prominently in Donald Allen's landmark anthology, *The New American Poetry* (1960).

The highly rhetorical poems in his first book, *Heavenly City, Earthly City* (1947), were followed by two defining poems: "The Venice Poem," which appeared in *Poems, 1948–1949* (1949), proposed a symphonic form as a way to structure a long poem, and *Medieval Scenes* (1950) proposed "serial form," in which each of the ten poems can be considered independently as well as within the series as a whole. The latter's open-ended structure provided the basis for two later serial poems, "The Structure of Rime," which begins in *The Opening of the Field* (1960), and "The Passages Poems," which begins in *Bending the Bow* (1968). Both series continue through the final volume, *Ground Work II: In the Dark* (1987). Duncan derived the principles of "serial form" in company with Jack Spicer and Robin Blaser. This concept of form is a major and defining contribution to American poetry after 1945.

In the 1950s Duncan carried on intense correspondences with Denise Levertov and Charles Olson, and *Origin*, a magazine edited by Cid Corman, became the center of his poetic focus. Between 1950 and 1953 he wrote the poems for *A Book of Resemblances* (1966), a book to which Jess Collins contributed drawings. "An Essay at War" is the most heavily revised of any of Duncan's poems; it shows him shedding the rhetorical structures of his early poems and entering the period when sounds and tones would lead him toward meaning:

The design of a poem
    constantly
under reconstruction,
    changing, pusht forward;
alternations of sound, sensations;
    the mind dance
wherein thot shows its pattern :
    a proposition
    in movement.

*Letters,* written between 1953 and 1956, appeared in 1958. The first poem, "For a Muse Meant," was originally sent to Denise Levertov; other poem-letters are to Helen Adam, Philip Lamantia, Charles Olson, Robert Creeley, and James Broughton.

By 1960, when Duncan published his first major book, *The Opening of the Field,* he had arrived at a concept of composition that extended the principles of serial form to include the composition of a whole book of poems as an integrated work, not simply a collection of isolated lyrics. The opening poem, "Often I Am Permitted to Return to a Meadow," introduces the concept of open field composition and the search for the female muse of poetry. Poetry takes place within a body of information that includes the poet's experience, Duncan suggests, but is not dominated by it. He uses the image of children dancing in a ring to represent the act of poetry itself.

It is only a dream of the grass blowing
east against the source of the sun
in an hour before the sun's going down

whose secret we see in a children's game
of ring a round of roses told.

Other poems like "The Dance," "The Maiden," and "Poetry, a Natural Thing" advance and amplify these ideas. The serial poem "The Structure of Rime" begins in this volume and is as embedded in its internal reference system as "A Poem Beginning with a Line by Pindar," which is longer and more expansive. The latter poem enforces "the tone leading of vowels" in Duncan's poetics, substantiating his view that a poem has a musical structure that leads the formation of words and generates the content of the poem. The story of Cupid and Psyche presents the longing for love as coinciding with the desire for poetry and fixes Duncan firmly in the greater Romantic tradition of American poetry.

*Roots and Branches* (1964), Duncan's next book, contains well-known poems like "A Sequence of Poems for H.D.'s 73rd Birthday," "Apprehensions," and "The Continent." It further explores the myths and occult literature that Duncan knew so well. "The Structure of Rime" continues in this volume, folded into parts of longer poems and as individual poems. The autobiographical sections of "A Sequence of Poems for H.D.'s 73rd Birthday" and the frequent appearance of Dante and Blake suggest that Duncan is laying out the foundations of a spiritual vision based in Dante and a poetic vision based in Blake. "There is no life that does not arise / melodic from scales of the marvelous," he writes in "Close," from "Apprehensions," asserting again his place in a tradition.

In *The Truth and Life of Myth* (1968), a long essay on his personal attachment to occult stories and ancient myths, he proposes a mythopoeic creation of an imaginary world. Blake, Shelley, and Wallace Stevens had made such proposals before him. In *Bending the Bow* (1968), he began another serial poem, "The Passages Poems." There are 30 of these poems interspersed within the volume. "Tribal Memories," the first, appeals to Mnemosyne, the Mother, grand universal memory, as the source of all myths and stories. Quotations from Blake, Jakob Boehme, Charles Baudelaire, John Adams, Dante, Charles Olson, Thomas Carlyle, and Victor Hugo and etymologies from *The Oxford English Dictionary* appear juxtaposed with the "soft luminous threads" of his own imagining. The result is a majestic imagined universe, a "*grand collage*" in which all parts of the human experience can appear with equal authority. Duncan champions the ability of the poet as a spiritual agent to create a universe that, although fictional, exists as an idealized version of reality:

I am beside myself with this
    thought of the One in the World-Egg,
enclosed,    in a shell of murmurings,

    rimed round,
    sound-chamberd child.

"The Soldiers, Passages 26" and "Eye of God, Passages 29" explore the national anxiety over the Vietnam War, the climatic statement being reached in "Up Rising, Passages 25," a poem containing one protracted sentence, a rant against the crippling pressures of war and politically corrupt leaders who put private claims before the public good:

this specter that in the beginning Adams and Jefferson
  feard and knew
would corrupt the very body of the nation
    and all our sense of our common humanity,
this black bile of old evils arisen anew,
takes over the vanity of Johnson;
and the very glint of Satan's eyes from the pit of the
  hell of
America's unacknowledged, unrepented crimes that I
  saw in Goldwater's eyes
now shines from the eyes of the President
  in the swollen head of the nation.

"My Mother Would Be a Falconress," a poem about his relationship with his mother told in a parable of a falcon, appears along with his translations of Gérard de Nerval's poems entitled "The Chimeras," a sequence of poems that precipitated a break in friendship with Robin Blaser in 1963. Duncan has assembled a poetics of expression that allows all kinds of poems to enter the field of action of his grand mythopoeic collage.

When *Caesar's Gate: Poems, 1949–1950* (1955) was reprinted in an enlarged edition in 1972, Duncan added a statement that he would not publish a new book of poems until 1983. He did publish pamphlets, like *Tribunals* (1970), a collection of poems including "Before the Judgment, Passages 35," a triumphant visionary poem that asserted the strength and value of human life against the horrible waste of war. Duncan's friendship and poetic affinity with Denise Levertov were broken by their different responses to the Vietnam War. In an earlier essay, "Man's Fulfillment in Order and Strife" (1969), Duncan set out a system of Blakean oppositions that depicted the struggle between war and peace as part of a necessary contention between two halves of the same whole, part of an even larger cosmic struggle between dualities. This period of the 1970s was as troubled for Duncan as it was for American culture in general.

By the time he gathered his poems for his final two volumes, *Ground Work: Before the War* (1984) and *Ground Work II: In the Dark* (1987), Duncan held a more pessimistic view of humanity. Great poems like "Achilles' Song" establish the general tone of these volumes, the attempt to piece the world together again:

I do not know more than the Sea tells me,
told me long ago,     or I overheard Her
  telling distant roar upon the sands,
waves of meaning in the cradle of whose
  sounding and resounding power I
slept.

The "Dante Études" relocates the geography of his imagination from the hearth and household to the spiritual universe of Dante's vision. The powerful "Circulations of the Song" is perhaps his finest love poem. In his early love poems the elegiac tone and solitude dominate; in this late love poem he finds powerful fulfillment and joy.

In the wide Universe
  emptying Itself into me, thru me,
in the myriad of lights falling,
let us speak of the little area of light
  this lamp casts.
Let us speak of what love there is.
Let us speak of how these perishing
  things
uphold me     so that

  I fall

    into *Place*.

"In Blood's Domaine" and other of the "Passages Poems," however, Duncan brings in the Angel Syphilis to illustrate war's suffocation of the spirit and the congestion of the public well-being by corrupt government. To the end Duncan held his position that poetry could mythologize the actual world in order to know it, and in doing so extended the Romantic imagination into a body of passionate and informed poems.

ROBERT BERTHOLF

*See also* Black Mountain School; Long Poem; San Francisco Renaissance

**Biography**

Born Edward Howard Duncan in Oakland, California, 7 January 1919; adopted in 1920 and given the name Robert Edward Symmes; took original surname in 1942. Attended the University of California, Berkeley, 1936–38, 1948–50; editor, *Experimental Review,* 1938–40, *Phoenix,* and *Berkeley Miscellany,* 1948–49; teacher at Black Mountain College, North Carolina, 1956; assistant director of Poetry Center (Ford grant), 1956–57, and lecturer in the Poetry Workshop, 1965, San Francisco State College; Lecturer, University of British Columbia, Vancouver, 1963. Received Guggenheim fellowship, 1963; National Endowment for the Arts grant, 1966 (two grants); Shelley Memorial Award, 1984; Cody Award, 1985; Before Columbus Foundation Award, 1985; National Poetry Award, 1985. Died in San Francisco, California, 3 February 1988.

**Poetry**

*Heavenly City, Earthly City,* 1947
*Poems, 1948–1949,* 1949
*Medieval Scenes,* 1950; revised edition, 1978
*The Song of the Border-Guard,* 1952
*Caesar's Gate: Poems, 1949–1950,* 1955; enlarged edition, 1972
*Letters,* 1958
*Selected Poems,* 1959; revised edition, 1977
*The Opening of the Field,* 1960
*Roots and Branches,* 1964
*Writing, Writing: A Composition Book of Madison, 1953,* 1964
*Wine,* 1964
*Uprising,* 1965
*A Book of Resemblances: Poems, 1950–1953,* 1966
*Fragments of a Disordered Devotion,* 1966
*Of the War: Passages 22–27,* 1966
*The Years as Catches: First Poems, 1939–1946,* 1966
*Boob,* 1966
*Epilogos,* 1967
*The Cat and the Blackbird,* 1967
*Christmas Present, Christmas Presence!* 1967
*Bending the Bow,* 1968
*My Mother Would Be a Falconess,* 1968
*Names of People,* 1968
*The First Decade: Selected Poems, 1940–1950,* 1968
*Derivations: Selected Poems, 1950–1956,* 1968
*Play Time, Pseudo Stein,* 1969
*Achilles' Song,* 1969
*Poetic Disturbances,* 1970
*Bring It Up from the Dark,* 1970
*Tribunals: Passages 31–35,* 1970
*In Memoriam Wallace Stevens,* 1972
*Poems from the Margins of Thom Gunn's Moly,* 1972
*A Seventeenth-Century Suite,* 1973
*An Ode and Arcadia* (with Jack Spicer), 1974
*Dante,* 1974
*The Venice Poem,* 1975
*Veil, Turbine, Cord, and Bird,* 1979
*The Five Songs,* 1981
*Ground Work: Before the War,* 1984
*A Paris Visit: Five Poems,* 1985
*The Regulators,* 1986
*Ground Work II: In the Dark,* 1987
*An Essay at War,* 1988
*Notebook Poems: 1953,* edited by Robert Bertholf, 1991
*Upon Hearing Leonard Wolf's Poem on a Madhouse, January 13, 1947,* 1991
*Selected Poems,* edited by Robert Bertholf, 1993
*Copy Book Entries,* 1996

**Selected Criticism**

*The Sweetness and Greatness of Dante's Divine Comedy, 1265–1965,* 1965

**Other Writings:** plays, essays (*The Truth and Life of Myth,* 1968; *Fictive Certainties: Essays,* 1985).

**Further Reading**

Auping, Michael, *Jess: A Grand Collage, 1951–1993,* Buffalo, New York: Albright-Knox Art Gallery, 1993

Bertholf, Robert, *Robert Duncan: A Descriptive Bibliography,* Santa Rosa, California: Black Sparrow Press, 1986

Bertholf, Robert, and Ian Reid, editors, *Robert Duncan: Scales of the Marvelous,* New York: New Directions, 1979

*Boundary* 2 8, no. 2 (1980) (special issue on Duncan)

Faas, Ekbert, *Young Robert Duncan: Portrait of the Poet as Homosexual in Society,* Santa Barbara, California: Black Sparrow Press, 1983

*Ironwood* 22 (1983) (special issue on Duncan)

Johnson, Mark Andrew, *Robert Duncan,* Boston: Twayne, 1988

*Sagetrieb* 4, nos. 2/3 (1985) (special issue on Duncan)

## Doves

Robert Duncan's poem "Doves" was written as an elegy to the Modernist poet H.D. (Hilda Doolittle). Doolittle, who died in September 1961, had been an influence on Duncan's poetry from the time he first read her work at 17. Duncan was known as a poet of the Black Mountain School of poetry, but his work was strongly influenced by Modernism, and particularly by a movement within Modernism called Imagism that originated in a manifesto written by Ezra Pound, H.D., and Richard Aldington in 1912. The main precepts of Imagism were that poems should deal directly with the objects present in the physical world, that the poet should use only those words necessary to create a clear image for the reader, and that the poet should compose the poem based on the music inherent in words rather than on a set pattern of meter. Throughout Duncan's career as a writer he paid homage to the Modernists and specifically to H.D.

"Doves" appeared in Duncan's second major book of poems, *Roots and Branches* (1964), which also includes another long poem written for H.D. called "A Sequence of Poems for H.D.'s 73rd Birthday." While at the beginning of "Doves" Duncan mentions a stroke that H.D. suffered during June of 1961, he actually began the composition of this poem some months later during September of 1961. At the time of the poem's initial draft he was unaware of H.D.'s death that very week. When informed of the event a few days later, he completed the fourth and final section of the poem.

H.D.'s death had a significant emotional impact on Duncan: she was the surrogate mother of his poetry, the "Mother of mouthings" in the poem, and his actual mother had died just nine months earlier. Like H.D., Duncan had been raised in a family where non-traditional religious studies were central to daily home life; both Duncan and H.D. incorporated childhood stories of Christian religion, Egyptian legend, and Greek mythology into their poems. In "Doves" Duncan uses the Christian symbol representing the Holy Spirit and the spirit inside the physical body, the dove, to illustrate his own belief that H.D.'s soul was freed from her body in death.

Duncan also makes reference to "the Lady." This figure is present in H.D.'s work in various manifestations: sometimes as the figure of Mary from Christian tradition, sometimes as Isis of the Egyptians, and sometimes as the goddess Aphrodite of the Greeks. In "Doves" Duncan uses the Lady not only as a religious symbol but also as a way of paying respect to H.D., whom he thought of as a royal figure in poetry. The Lady is an almost archetypal presence in the mythological landscape of the poem, in which day is personified and the Lady or "Queen of the Tree's Talking" walks alone:

> where the Day slept
> after noon, in the light's blur and shade
> the Queen of the Tree's Talking
> hears only the leaf sound,
> whirrr of wings in the boughs

"Doves" also illustrates the usual musical quality of Duncan's writing in accordance with the tenets of Imagism. "Mother of mouthings" uses alliteration and assonance to create what Ezra Pound called a "melopoeia" or musical pattern that gestures toward the importance of speech and sound in H.D.'s own poetry. Both Duncan and H.D. are rendered mute in the poem—H.D. by a stroke and Duncan by grief. In sections one and three of the poem, words are replaced with the cooing of doves, and in the final section of the work, Duncan remarks upon his own muteness:

> I wanted to say something,
> that my heart had such a burden,
> or needed a burden in order to say something.

As he often does, Duncan suggests the magic potential of words themselves, a belief he and H.D. shared. In an ironic turn, however, the legacy of her poetry, the magical words she has left for him and all her readers, is a pitiful substitute for her actual being: "Now from your courses the flame has fled / making but words of what I loved."

LISA JARNOT

**Further Reading**

Altieri, Charles, "The Book of the World: Robert Duncan's Poetics of Presence," *Sun and Moon: A Quarterly of Literature and Art* 1 (Winter 1976)

Bertholf, Robert, editor, *A Great Admiration: H.D./Robert Duncan Correspondence, 1950–1961,* Venice, California: Lapis Press, 1992

Bertholf, Robert, and Ian Reid, editors, *Robert Duncan: Scales of the Marvelous,* New York: New Directions, 1979

Davidson, Michael, *The San Francisco Renaissance: Poetics and Community at Mid-Century,* Cambridge and New York: Cambridge University Press, 1989

Duncan, Robert, "Beginnings: Chapter 1 of the H.D. Book, Part 1," *Coyote's Journal* 5–6 (1966)

Duncan, Robert, "The H.D. Book: Rites of Participation," *Caterpillar* 1 (October 1967)

Faas, Ekbert, *Young Robert Duncan: Portrait of the Poet as Homosexual in Society,* Santa Barbara, California: Black Sparrow Press, 1983

# A Poem Beginning with a Line by Pindar

"A Poem Beginning with a Line by Pindar" is one of Robert Duncan's most complex and interesting works. Written in 1957, it was conceived of as a central part of his first major collection, *The Opening of the Field* (1960). Throughout his career Duncan drew from the influence of fellow writers of the Black Mountain School; in "A Poem Beginning with a Line by Pindar" he illustrates their precepts while drawing from a wider range of Western poetry and art.

The poem makes use of a fragment from the First Pythian Ode of the Greek lyric poet Pindar and was in fact inspired by the ambiguity of its phrase, "the light foot hears you and the brightness begins." Duncan, who was raised in an unconventional family where gnostic religion was studied and practiced, often incorporated ancient myths into his writing. In this poem he invokes the image of Cupid and Psyche from Greek and Roman mythology as he remembers it represented in a painting by Goya. In the myth, Cupid, the son of Venus, falls in love with a woman named Psyche. He courts her, but conceals his identity from her. Out of curiosity Psyche shines a light on her mysterious husband and accidentally burns him with her oil lamp. Cupid flees and Psyche must complete a number of tasks in order to be reunited with him. Duncan uses this myth as a metaphor for humankind's curiosity and the perils associated with it. The image of fire, as in the fire of Psyche's lamp, can be viewed as a representation of the modern age's experiments with atomic energy.

Early in the poem Duncan establishes the landscape of American history and poetry as a place of mythologies equal to that of the Greeks. Like the Romantic poet Shelley, Duncan juxtaposes the role of the poet with the role of the political legislator. He asks the reader to understand the landscape of a poem as a small version of the landscape of a country and sets out to name a number of American legislators of poetry and politics:

It is toward the old poets
    we go, to their faltering,
their unaltering wrongness that has style,
    their variable truth,
    the old faces,
words shed like tears from
a plenitude of powers time stores.

In the lines that directly follow this passage Duncan alludes to the American poet William Carlos Williams, one of the "old poets," who suffered a series of strokes during the early 1950s. With the line "What if lilacs last in this dooryard bloomd?" he refers to Whitman's elegy for Abraham Lincoln. Duncan laments the fact that Whitman's cry for democracy in the United States has not been fully answered. At the end of section II he speaks of American presidents Harding, Wilson, Taft, and Roosevelt, asking "Where among these did the spirit reside / that restores the land to productive order?" Duncan also includes two other quotations from Whitman—"The theme is creative and has vista" and "He is the president of regulation"—again pointing out the relationship between poet and legislator.

Duncan's idea of a poem as a "field" or "vista" was inspired by the writings of the Black Mountain poet Charles Olson. Olson's 1950 essay "Projective Verse" described the page of the poem as a "projective" field upon which energy is discharged in clusters of words, measured by the poet's breath. Duncan compares the activity of writing a poem to the activity of inhabiting the natural world:

    I see always the under side turning,
fumes that injure the tender landscape.
    From which up break
lilac blossoms of courage in daily act
    striving to meet a natural measure.

It is not uncommon for Duncan's poetry to leap from myth to myth, building a new narrative out of a collage of sources; in the first two sections of "A Poem Beginning with a Line by Pindar" he moves from the myths of the Greeks and Romans to myths of American history. It is no accident, then, that the third section was written as an homage to Charles Olson, whose own poetry was concerned with the myths of American peoples.

Duncan briefly returns to the story of Cupid and Psyche, outlining the tasks that Psyche is forced to complete at the hands of Venus. He then introduces another writer, the Modernist poet Ezra Pound. Pound enters the poem as Williams had earlier: as a source of inspiration who is nonetheless an "old man at Pisa / mixd in whose mind." Here Duncan touches upon Pound's incarceration in an Italian prison camp after the end of World War II. Like Psyche, Pound was faced with a trial, having been accused of treason against the United States. In this section the physical form of the poem begins to shift in response to Olson's call for "projective verse":

                    West
from east    men push.

Duncan also makes it clear that where there is myth, there is the figure of the hero. He describes American heroes who sprawl across the landscape as words sprawl across the poem:

            Solitary first riders advance into legend.

    This land, where I stand, was all legend
in my grandfather's time: cattle raiders,
    animal tribes, priests, gold.
It was the West. . . .

The poem that began with an ancient source now includes a more contemporary landscape. Duncan points out that the myth of Cupid and Psyche still has meaning and that

Psyche travels
life after life, my life, station
    after station,
to be tried

    without break.

In the fourth and final section of the poem Duncan returns to autobiographical ground while also reminding the reader of "the foot" of Pindar's First Pythian Ode that opened the poem. Here the word *foot* refers to both the meter of the original Greek ode and the dance of words in a contemporary lyric poem. Duncan then incorporates a myth from his own life, his memory of a childhood dream:

On the hill before the wind came
the grass moved toward the one sea,
blade after blade dancing in the waves.

He uses this image in other poems in *The Opening of the Field* as well, particularly in the first poem, "Often I Am Permitted to Return to a Meadow." For Duncan the dream is a reminder that he too inhabits "the field" of poetry.

"A Poem Beginning with a Line by Pindar" is one of Robert Duncan's most significant works. In it he establishes his belief in "the truth" of mythological sources, using line and form in the tradition of the Black Mountain poets. As a means of summary he tells the reader: "We have come so far that all the old stories / whisper once more."

LISA JARNOT

**Further Reading**

Bertholf, Robert, and Ian Reid, editors, *Robert Duncan: Scales of the Marvelous,* New York: New Directions, 1979

Davidson, Michael, *The San Francisco Renaissance: Poetics and Community at Mid-Century,* Cambridge and New York: Cambridge University Press, 1989

Duncan, Robert, *Fictive Certainties: Essays,* New York: New Directions, 1985

Faas, Ekbert, *Young Robert Duncan: Portrait of the Poet as Homosexual in Society,* Santa Barbara, California: Black Sparrow Press, 1983

MacIntyre, Wendy, "Psyche, Christ, and the Poem," *Ironwood* 11, no. 2 (Fall 1983)

Olson, Charles, "Projective Verse," in *Selected Writings of Charles Olson,* edited by Robert Creeley, New York: New Directions, 1966

Thurley, Geoffrey, "Robert Duncan: The Myth of Open Form," in *The American Moment: American Poetry in Mid-Century,* by Thurley, London: Arnold, 1977; New York: St. Martin's Press, 1978

# E

## Richard Eberhart 1904–

Richard Eberhart's output over his 60-year career establishes him as a significant 20th-century poet. In addition to his admirable body of lyrical verse, Eberhart proved to be an excellent ambassador for the art, occupying a number of teaching jobs as well as positions like Consultant to the Library of Congress. Often deeply mystical, Eberhart's writing is at times a worthy contribution to nature poetry as well. Although no single volume from his lengthy career stands out as a generation-defining collection, each book consistently featured several outstanding poems, a few great ones, and, as even his most ardent supporters admit, a few bad ones.

After graduating from college Eberhart entered business literally at the lowest level, selling ties in the basement of the Marshall Field department store in Chicago. In addition he made forays into advertising and marketing and began publishing poetry in nationally circulating magazines, landing eight poems in the November 1927 issue of *Poetry* magazine. While just one of these poems survived to reappear in Eberhart's definitive *Collected Poems* (1988), each of the original eight clearly marks the transition from his juvenilia to his mature work. The single poem collected years later, "Cover Me Over," is an early manifestation of Eberhart's major theme: the centrality of death as a natural part of life.

Eberhart's subsequent development as a poet was delayed, although probably enhanced, by a series of voyages he took in 1927. Working his way around the world westward on steamships, Eberhart wound up at Cambridge University, where he earned a second B.A. in 1929. While in England Eberhart encountered representatives of a wider literary world. One night, for instance, Eberhart attended a debate between George Bernard Shaw and G.K. Chesterton. He would frequently discuss poetry with poets and critics like I.A. Richards, F.R. Leavis, and, on one memorable side-trip to Ireland, William Butler Yeats.

It is fortunate that Eberhart made so much of his opportunities in England as his return to the United States coincided with the onset of the Great Depression. Eberhart's first job stateside, which he called "a vision of Hell," was in a slaughterhouse. While obviously unpleasant and certainly not "literary" in any conventional sense, the requirements of the job certainly contributed to his understanding of death as a part of life's process.

In spite of the Depression and his inability to find rewarding work, Eberhart published *A Bravery of Earth* (1930). Unusual for a first book, the volume is not a collection of previously published poems, but rather a book-length autobiographical poem that reviewers and critics frequently compared to Wordsworth's *The Prelude*. While less formal in terms of meter and structure than Wordsworth's volume, Eberhart's book similarly weaves philosophical insight and personal experience to produce some stunning passages. At that early stage of his career, however, Eberhart found it hard to sustain the poem for its full 127 pages. Difficult to find and long out of print, fragments of *A Bravery of Earth* were reprinted in various editions of Eberhart's selected and collected poems.

The potential that some reviewers recognized in *A Bravery of Earth* was partially fulfilled by some of the 31 lyrics collected in *Reading the Spirit* (1936). Two poems stand out in this volume and, it has been argued, set the tone for the remainder of Eberhart's career. An autobiographical self-assessment and *ars poetica*, the poem "1934" brings together images of strife found both in modern urban life and as well as in nature. This combination permits Eberhart to depict the struggles faced by a young poet in a world recently transformed. Perhaps Eberhart's most anthologized piece, "The Groundhog" depicts the cycle of a dead animal's decaying corpse. The image allows Eberhart to focus on his major themes: death, nature, regeneration, and creativity, and on the connection between spirit and matter:

> It has been three years, now.
> There is no sign of the groundhog.
> I stood there in the whirling summer,
> My hand capped a withered heart,
> And thought of China and of Greece,
> Of Alexander in his tent;
> Of Montaigne in his tower,
> Of Saint Theresa in her wild lament.

While Eberhart was establishing his reputation with these poems, he began teaching at St. Mark's Prep School, where Robert Lowell was his student in the 1930s. Shortly before the outbreak of World War II, Eberhart married and began teaching at Cambridge School in Massachusetts. When war broke out Eberhart joined the Navy, serving from 1942 to 1946 as an aerial gunnery instructor. Perhaps because he was accustomed to creating under adverse circumstances, Eberhart published two volumes during the war years, *Song and Idea* (1940) and *Poems, New and Selected*

(1944). The latter volume featured one of the best poems written about World War II, "The Fury of Aerial Bombardment." In the second stanza he writes

> You would feel that after so many centuries
> God would give man to repent; yet he can kill
> As Cain could, but with multitudinous will,
> No farther advanced than in his ancient furies.

When the war ended Eberhart took work at the Butcher Polish Company (owned by his father-in-law) before returning to teaching in 1953. The 1950s also saw the publication of two more important books: *Undercliff* (1953) and *Great Praises* (1957). As the decade drew to a close Eberhart received one of the highest accolades available to a poet when he was named Consultant in Poetry for the Library of Congress, serving a term from 1959–61. In 1960 Eberhart was elected to the National Institute of Arts and Letters, and in 1962 he received the prestigious Bollingen Prize. From 1963–66 he was Consultant in American Letters at the Library of Congress, and in 1966 he received the Pulitzer Prize for his most widely read volume, *Selected Poems, 1930–1965* (1965). The 1960s ended with Eberhart's 1969 election as a Fellow in the Academy of American Poets and receipt of the Academy's prize for lifetime achievement.

Eberhart remained prolific, publishing, in addition to his *Selected Poems, The Quarry* (1964), *Thirty-One Sonnets* (1967), and *Shifts of Being* (1968). In the remaining decades of the 20th century, however, Eberhart's production slowed somewhat, culminating with his magisterial *Collected Poems* (1988). While not yet as widely read as his 1965 *Selected Poems,* this work is a testament to Eberhart's skill and his durability as a poet, and also a fitting tribute.

Eberhart's faults are those of a minor poet: his lesser poems fall back on a limited range of mannerisms, some of them personal, some generational. He is distinct among his generation for his commitment to profound reflection, rigorous formalism, and accessibility. Given these standards, it is no surprise that his poems fell short occasionally, nor that readers have been willing to overlook these flaws for the excellence found in his better work.

DAVID R. ZAUHAR

**Biography**

Born in Austin, Minnesota, 5 April 1904. Attended the University of Minnesota, Minneapolis, 1922–23; Dartmouth College, Hanover, New Hampshire, B.A. 1926; St. John's College, Cambridge, B.A. 1929, M.A. 1933; Harvard University, Cambridge, Massachusetts, 1932–33; served in the United States Naval Reserve, 1942–46, Lieutenant Commander; basement floorwalker, Marshall Field and Company, Chicago, 1926–27; slaughterhouse worker, New York, 1929; tutor to the two Procter daughters (of Procter and Gamble), 1929–30, the son of King Prajadhipok of Siam, 1930–31, and the son of Prime Minister Kridakava; English teacher, St. Mark's School, Southboro, Massachusetts, 1933–41, and Cambridge School, Kendal Green, Massachusetts, 1941–42; assistant manager to vice-president, Butcher Polish Company, Boston, 1946–52; now honorary vice-president and member of the board of directors; Visiting Professor, University of Washington, Seattle, 1952–53, 1967, 1972; Professor of English, University of Connecticut, Storrs, 1953–54; Visiting Professor, Wheaton College, Norton, Massachusetts, 1954–55; Resident Fellow in creative writing and Gauss Lecturer, Princeton University, New Jersey, 1955–56; Professor of English and poet-in-residence, 1956–68, Class of 1925 Professor, 1968–70, Professor Emeritus, 1970–80, and since 1986 poet-in-residence, Dartmouth College; Elliston Lecturer, University of Cincinnati, 1961; Visiting Professor, Columbia University, New York, 1975, University of California, Davis, 1975, and University of Florida, Gainesville, winters, 1974–82; Wallace Stevens Fellow, Timothy Dwight College, Yale University, New Haven, Connecticut, 1976; Honorary Fellow, St. John's College, Cambridge, 1986; founder, 1950, and first president, Poets' Theatre, Cambridge, Massachusetts; member, 1955, and since 1964 director, Yaddo Corporation; consultant in poetry, 1959–61, and honorary consultant in American letters, 1963–69, Library of Congress, Washington, D.C. Received Guarantor's Prize, 1946, and Harriet Monroe Memorial Prize, 1950 (*Poetry,* Chicago); New England Poetry Club Golden Rose, 1950; Shelley Memorial Award, 1952; Harriet Monroe Memorial Award, 1955; American Academy grant, 1955; Bollingen Prize, 1962; Pulitzer Prize, 1966; Academy of American Poets fellowship, 1969; National Book Award, 1977; President's Medallion, University of Florida, 1977; Poet Laureate of New Hampshire, 1979; World Academy of Arts and Letters Diploma Award, 1981; Sarah Josepha Hale Award, 1982; Frost Medal, 1986; Litt.D., Dartmouth College, 1954; Skidmore College, Saratoga, New York, 1966; College of Wooster, Ohio, 1969; Colgate University, Hamilton, New York, 1974; Franklin Pierce College, Rindge, New Hampshire, 1978; St. Lawrence University, Canton, New York, 1985; Plymouth State College, New Hampshire, 1987; since 1972 honorary president, Poetry Society of America; member, American Academy, 1960, and American Academy of Arts and Sciences, 1967. Living in Hanover, New Hampshire.

**Poetry**

*A Bravery of Earth,* 1930
*Reading the Spirit,* 1936
*Song and Idea,* 1940
*A World-View,* 1941
*Poems, New and Selected,* 1944
*Rumination,* 1947
*Burr Oaks,* 1947
*Brotherhood of Men,* 1949
*An Herb Basket,* 1950
*Selected Poems,* 1951
*Undercliff: Poems, 1946–1953,* 1953
*Great Praises,* 1957
*The Oak,* 1957
*Collected Poems, 1930–60, Including 51 New Poems,* 1960
*The Quarry: New Poems,* 1964
*The Vastness and Indifference of the World,* 1965
*Fishing for Snakes,* 1965
*Selected Poems, 1930–1965,* 1965
*Thirty-One Sonnets,* 1967
*Shifts of Being,* 1968
*The Achievement of Richard Eberhart: A Comprehensive Selection of His Poems,* edited by Bernard F. Engle, 1968
*Three Poems,* 1968

*Fields of Grace,* 1972
*Two Poems,* 1975
*Collected Poems, 1930–1976,* 1976
*Poems to Poets,* 1976
*Hour, Gnats,* 1977
*Survivors,* 1979
*Ways of Light: Poems, 1972–1980,* 1980
*New Hampshire: Nine Poems,* 1980
*Four Poems,* 1980
*Florida Poems,* 1981
*The Long Reach: New and Uncollected Poems, 1948–1984,* 1984
*Snowy Owl,* 1984
*Throwing Yourself Away,* 1984
*Spite Fence,* 1984
*Collected Poems, 1930–1986,* 1988
*Maine Poems,* 1989
*New and Selected Poems, 1930–1990,* edited by Jay Parini, 1990

**Selected Criticism**
*Poetry as a Creative Principle* (lecture), 1952
*Of Poetry and Poets,* 1979

**Other Writings:** plays, editions of collected poetry.

**Further Reading**

Brooks, Cleanth, "A Tribute to Richard Eberhart," *South Atlantic Quarterly* 50, no. 4 (November 1985)
Engel, Bernard F., *Richard Eberhart,* New York: Twayne, 1971
Lea, Sydney, Jay Parini, and M. Robin Barone, editors, *Richard Eberhart: A Celebration,* Hanover, New Hampshire: Kenyon Hill, 1980
Mills, Ralph J., *Contemporary American Poetry,* New York: Random House, 1965
Mills, Ralph J., *Richard Eberhart,* Minneapolis: University of Minnesota Press, 1966
*Negative Capability* 6, nos. 2–3 (Spring–Summer 1986) (special issue devoted to Eberhart)

---

# T.S. Eliot 1888–1965

When T.S. Eliot died in London in 1965, he was regarded as the most important poet to have written in English in the 20th century. His obituary in the *Times Literary Supplement* (London) was entitled "The Most Influential English Poet of His Time"; and in *Life* magazine, a memorial essay ended with "Our age beyond any doubt has been, and will continue to be, the Age of Eliot." His reputation, although often challenged, has survived decades of reassessment. In June 1998, *Time* magazine published a special issue on artists and entertainers of the past 100 years. Picasso was named the artist of the century, Stravinsky the composer, Joyce the novelist, and Eliot the poet. This list is a reminder that Eliot is part of a watershed in the history of Western art, and *The Waste Land* (1922), his early showpiece, is the century's signature poem. Poets in Europe and America have been profoundly influenced by his work; moreover, as Richard Ellmann once noted, for most of the 20th century, poets writing in Swahili, Japanese, Chinese, or Hindi were more likely to have been influenced by Eliot than by any poet who had written in their own language.

Eliot's poetry can best be understood in the context of his early years. He was born in Missouri in 1888 into a distinguished family recently transplanted from New England. His family lineage included founding members of the Massachusetts Bay Colony, a president of Harvard University, and three presidents of the United States. The poet grew up in downtown St. Louis, not far from the Mississippi River. Although tireless in their service to St. Louis, the Eliots never felt entirely at home in the West. They summered in Massachusetts and sent their sons to Harvard University. After graduation, Eliot studied for a year at the Sorbonne in Paris, returned to Harvard for graduate study in philosophy, and finished his education at Oxford University in England. In 1915, he married an English woman, Vivienne Haigh-Wood, a disillusioning union for both parties. Settling permanently in London, Eliot worked from 1925 until his death as an editor/director at the publishing firm of Faber and Faber in Bloomsbury. In 1927, he became a British citizen and a member of the Church of England. In 1948, he was awarded the Nobel Prize for Literature and the Order of Merit. His first marriage ended with the death of his wife in 1947, and in 1958 he married Valerie Fletcher (nearly 40 years his junior), a redemptive union that consecrated his last years.

The first of many crucial connections between Eliot's life and art is his acute consciousness of history—his own and that of his generation and his civilization—and of the ways in which the past constantly impinges on the present and the present on the future. His well-known critical concept of tradition asserts continuity between past and present, and his most celebrated poem, *The Waste Land,* concerns a crisis both in his own history and in the history of Western civilization. A second connection is a profound sense of homelessness. In 1919, he wrote his brother that, in London, "one remains always a foreigner" and "is always coming up against differences of feeling that make one feel humiliated and lonely." This feeling of estrangement haunts his poetry from "Prufrock" through "The Hollow Men." A third connection between life and art is evident in Eliot's thoroughly urban imagination, the formative experience being his childhood in St. Louis. In "The Influence of Landscape upon the Poet" (1960), he said that, in childhood and early youth, "for nine months of the year my scenery was almost exclusively urban, and a good deal of it seedily, drably urban at that." In reference to his poems, he remarked that "My urban imagery was that of St. Louis, upon which that of Paris and London had been superimposed." His unforgettable city images—the half-deserted streets, the prostitutes, the stray cats—were etched on his mind in the streets of St.

Louis. The river imagery that pervades his poetry from beginning to end can also be traced to St. Louis. In a 1930 letter quoted in an appendix to *American Literature and the American Language* (1953), Eliot claimed that "Missouri and the Mississippi have made a deeper impression on me than any other part of the world." Great dark rivers flow through his major poems, carrying "empty bottles, sandwich papers, cardboard boxes." And in *The Dry Salvages* (1941), one of his last poems, the Mississippi River at flood-time is an implacable brown god, bearing its booty beneath the Eads Bridge in St. Louis. A final intersection between life and art can be seen in the uneasiness about sexual love revealed in the early poems and drafts. This ambivalence was underscored by his failed marriage, a disaster that not only became part of the theme and style of *The Waste Land,* but pointed toward a turn to divine love in mid-life and a new style in *Ash-Wednesday* (1930), a style that prefigured that of *Four Quartets* (1943), arguably his finest poem.

Eliot's poetry can be divided into three periods, each with its distinctive style and its major works. The first coincided with his studies in Boston and Paris and culminated in "The Love Song of J. Alfred Prufrock" in 1911; the second coincided with World War I and the personal distress in his marriage and culminated in *The Waste Land* in 1922; and the third coincided with his alarm at the rise of Fascism and Nazism and his consolation in embracing the Christian faith, culminating in *Four Quartets* in 1942. The last 25 years of his creative life were devoted primarily to writing plays, of which the most popular is *The Cocktail Party* (1950).

In 1909–11, while still a student, Eliot wrote four poems—"Portrait of a Lady," "Preludes," "Rhapsody on a Windy Night," and "The Love Song of J. Alfred Prufrock"—that are landmarks in American poetry. In these strikingly modern poems, first published separately in 1915, he began his life-long exploration of "overwhelming questions" about the self, society, and the world. On one level, these poems are about language and art. Each announces itself as a major genre in 19th-century art, and then proceeds to call that genre into question through irony. In the case of "The Love Song," the genre is dismantled before the poem even begins, for one cannot imagine a "J. Alfred Prufrock" either singing or loving. On another level, these poems explore the tension between existential and social issues, between the mutually defining structures of the self and society. They deal with isolation and the inadequacies of language and of love for breaking out of the self. Stylistically, they are Expressionistic; like the paintings of Edvard Munch, they objectify feelings ranging from tedium to terror, from angst to eager longing. Prufrock conducts the reader through labyrinthine streets of a modern city that turns out to be a modern mind, and in its hopelessness and horror, a modern hell. The poem begins as a dramatic monologue in the manner of Robert Browning, but soon reveals itself to be an interior monologue framed at one end with a shocking conceit comparing the evening to a patient etherized upon a surgery table, and at the other end, with a metaphor associating surfacing into the world of "human voices" with drowning.

Eliot's early poems were collected in 1917 in *Prufrock and Other Observations.* His next major poem, "Gerontion," appeared in *Poems* (1919, 1920). Like "The Love Song of J. Alfred Prufrock," "Gerontion" descends from the dramatic monologue, but is bolder, more comprehensive. The earlier poem is a portrait of an individual mind, but "Gerontion" is a portrait of the Mind of Europe, a container for fragments of history from the Battle of Thermopylae in 480 B.C.E. to the Treaty of Versailles in 1918. Gerontion, as his name indicates, is very old; born in ancient Greece, he survives as a desiccated creature "waiting for rain" on the doorstep of modern Europe. Like Prufrock, he is an intellectual. His dry thoughts are "tenants of the house" of his brain which is a tenant in a decrepit body domiciled in a "decayed house" in a stony yard in war-ravaged Europe at the end of history, itself a house of horrors with "many cunning passages, contrived corridors." Thematically, "Gerontion" anticipates *The Waste Land,* and Eliot at one stage considered using it as a prelude to the larger work.

*The Waste Land,* composed over several years and published in 1922, is at once an expression of personal despair and a reflection of postwar culture. Eliot's genius enabled him to deal simultaneously with such issues as his illness and failed marriage and larger issues such as the upheavals in politics, philosophy, and science that surrounded World War I. The title and much of the symbolism were taken from Sir James Frazer's *Golden Bough* and Jessie Weston's Arthurian studies. Frazer argued that all myths descended from a single ancestor or monomyth. In his reconstruction, the monomyth describes a land in which a king and his people are so interrelated that impotence in the ruler leads to sterility in the people and devastation in the land. This myth had special relevance to early 20th-century culture: God had been declared dead, the earth had been violated by war, political leaders had proven impotent, an entire generation of young men had been slaughtered in France and Belgium, and survivors resembled ghosts on the streets of the city. The ancestor myth itself is not present in *The Waste Land,* but is generated in the reader's mind by juxtaposition of fragments of its many variants and, as in Joyce's *Ulysses,* by a complex web of references. The poem features many voices from many times and places, and together they reveal shifting perspectives on situations in which failures of leadership, community, and love have produced a wasteland. The use of slivers of myth to generate structure and the use of shifting perspectives are hallmarks of *The Waste Land*'s radical form. Another aspect of form is the juxtaposition without transition of fragments—some no more than a single word. Bits of myth, literature, religion, and philosophy from many times and cultures are combined with snatches of music and conversation so contemporary they could have come from yesterday's newspaper. Meaningless in themselves, the fragments in this literary collage become powerfully suggestive in their juxtaposition and in the way they echo and explain one another as they generate larger wholes. "These fragments I have shored against my ruins," then, is more than a statement by a character within the poem; it is also a hint for the reader.

The analysis of modernity evident in "Gerontion" and *The Waste Land* continues in Eliot's next poem, his darkest, "The Hollow Men" (1925). In five sections, the poem dramatizes spiritual vacuity in a "cactus land" where "dead men" raise their hands to images of stone. It begins with a ritualistic chant by figures whose heads are stuffed with straw and ends with a version of apocalypse, "This is the way the world ends / Not with a bang but a whimper." This surrealistic poem is stylistically simpler than *The Waste Land,* with fewer allusions. Influenced by nursery rhymes and Christian liturgy, it anticipates the language and style of *Ash-Wednesday* (1930), the first major poem after the poet's 1927 conversion to Anglo-Catholicism. Ash-Wednesday is the first day of Lent in the Christian calendar, a day in which penitents acknowledge their mortality and begin the self-examination that leads to Easter. The Ash-Wednesday motif of repentance or turning provides both theme and structure, as the narrator alternates between struggle and peace, movement and stillness. Eliot also makes structural and thematic use of the Incarnation, a unique intersection of human and divine, time and eternity, and movement and stillness that figures in all his subsequent work, including *Four Quartets*. In his early work, Eliot had struggled to make art possible in the chaos of contemporary history; he now tries to make life, of which art is only a part, possible.

Eliot's major poetic achievement during the 1930s was *Burnt Norton,* conceived as an independent work, but becoming during the war the first of four parallel poems that together constitute *Four Quartets*. This magnificent sequence—*Burnt Norton* (first published in *Collected Poems, 1909–1935,* 1936), *East Coker* (1940), *The Dry Salvages* (1941), and *Little Gidding* (1942)—is a meditation on time and timelessness, history and consciousness, life and language. As indicated by the title, it has structural affinities with music, including the use of statement/counter statement and theme/variation, but as Eliot warns in his essays, the analogy should not be pushed too far. More significant is his focus on the isolated moment, the fragment of time that takes its meaning from and gives its meaning to a pattern, a pattern at once in time, continuously changing until the supreme moment of death completes it, and also out of time. Since the individual exists only in a sequence of moments, he can never know the whole pattern, but in certain moments he can glimpse the pattern in miniature. These timeless moments in time—"the moment in the rose-garden, / The moment in the arbour where the rain beat"—constitute pledges that time can be conquered. Eliot associates this moment of sudden illumination with the Word-made-flesh, the Incarnation; and also with the word-made-art, poetry. The part-pattern configuration is both the main subject and the main principle of form in *Four Quartets*.

Each of the *Quartets* is related to one of the four elements, and each to a specific place having significance for the poet. Burnt Norton is an English country house that Eliot visited in the summer of 1934 with Emily Hale, a woman he had loved in his youth and perhaps loved still. East Coker is the village in Somersetshire from which in the 17th century Eliot's family had emigrated to America and to which his own ashes would be returned. The Dry Salvages are treacherous rocks near the Massachusetts coast where Eliot had passed his childhood summers. Little Gidding is a 17th-century religious community near Cambridge, which Eliot visited in 1936. Each of these places is associated with Eliot's part-pattern, stillness-movement theme. He insists on the importance of specific places just as he does of specific moments. The timeless moment, in fact, can only occur in a specific place, such as a rose garden or a draughty church. The places are only fragments of the pattern; they constitute, nevertheless, the means to transcendence. "Only through time time is conquered" (*Burnt Norton*); only through place place is conquered. *Little Gidding,* which Eliot considered his finest poem, was composed during World War II and combines references to the bombing of London with references to the English Civil War, a reminder that his masterpiece, like Milton's, is a theodicy, a vindication of the ways of God to man, issuing in the splendid finale—"All manner of thing shall be well / When the tongues of flame are in-folded / Into the crowned knot of fire / And the fire and the rose are one."

*Four Quartets* was Eliot's last major poem, but not his last poetic achievement. Long interested in verse drama, he had already written two important plays, *Murder in the Cathedral* (1935) and *The Family Reunion* (1939). After the war, he resumed work in the theater, writing *The Cocktail Party* (1950), *The Confidential Clerk* (1954), and *The Elder Statesman* (1958). Any account of Eliot's influence in 20th-century letters must note that he was also a major literary critic, shaping the taste of two generations with his early essays, collected in *The Sacred Wood* (1920) and *Selected Essays* (1932). Moreover, he founded and edited *The Criterion,* one of his generation's most prestigious journals, and for decades, as an editor at Faber and Faber, he worked to nurture younger poets. Eliot's greatest triumph, however, remains his poetry, two lines of which are inscribed on his memorial in Westminster Abbey—"The communication of the dead is tongued with fire beyond the language of the living" (*Little Gidding*).

Jewel Spears Brooker

*See also* Long Poem; Religion and Poetry; Symbolism

**Biography**

Born Thomas Stearns Eliot in St. Louis, Missouri, 26 September 1888; became British citizen, 1927. Attended Harvard University, Cambridge, Massachusetts (board member, *Harvard Advocate,* 1909–10; Sheldon Traveling Fellowship, 1914), 1906–10, 1911–14, A.B. 1909, A.M. in English 1910; the Sorbonne, Paris, 1910–11; Merton College, Oxford, 1914–15; teacher, High Wycombe Grammar School, Buckinghamshire, 1915–16, and Highgate Junior School, London, 1916; tutor, University of London Extension Board, Southall, 1916–19; clerk in the Colonial and Foreign Department, then in charge of the Foreign Office Information Bureau, Lloyd's Bank, London, 1917–25; editor, then director, Faber and Gwyer, 1925–28, and Faber and Faber, publishers, London, 1929–65; assistant editor, *The Egoist,* London, 1917–19; regular contributor, *Times Literary Supplement,* London, from 1919; founding editor, *The Criterion,* London, 1922–39; member of the editorial board, *New English Weekly,* London, 1934–44, and *Christian News Letter,* Oxford, 1939–46; Clark Lecturer, Trinity College, Cambridge, 1926; Charles Eliot Norton Professor of Poetry, 1932–33, and Theodore Spencer Memorial Lecturer, Harvard University, 1950; Page-Barbour Lecturer, University of Virginia, Charlottesville, 1933; Visiting Fellow, Institute for Advanced Studies, Princeton University, New Jersey, 1948. Received Nobel Prize for Literature, 1948; New York Drama Critics Circle Award, 1950; Hanseatic-Goethe Prize (Hamburg), 1954; Dante Gold Medal (Florence), 1959; Order of Merit (Bonn), 1959; Emerson-Thoreau Medal, 1960; U.S. Medal of Freedom, 1964; received honorary degrees from 19 colleges and universities; Honorary Fellow, Magdalene College, Cambridge, 1948, and Merton College, Oxford, 1949; O.M. (Order of Merit), 1948; Officer, Legion of Honor, and Commander, Order of Arts and Letters (France), 1950; honorary member, American Academy; Foreign Member, Accademia dei Lincei (Rome) and Akademie der Schönen Künste. Died in London, 4 January 1965.

**Poetry**

*Prufrock and Other Observations,* 1917
*Poems,* 1919
*Ara Vos Prec,* 1920; republished as *Poems,* 1920

*The Waste Land,* 1922; republished as *"The Waste Land": A Facsimile and Transcript of the Original Drafts Including the Annotations of Ezra Pound,* edited by Valerie Eliot, 1971
*Poems, 1909–1925,* 1925
*Journey of the Magi,* 1927
*A Song for Simeon,* 1928
*Animula,* 1929
*Ash-Wednesday,* 1930
*Marina,* 1930
*Triumphal March,* 1931
*Murder in the Cathedral* (play), 1935
*Words for Music,* 1935
*Collected Poems, 1909–1935,* 1936
*The Family Reunion* (play), 1939
*Old Possum's Book of Practical Cats,* 1939
*The Waste Land, and Other Poems,* 1940
*East Coker,* 1940
*Later Poems, 1925–35,* 1941
*The Dry Salvages,* 1941
*Little Gidding,* 1942
*Four Quartets* (including *Burnt Norton, East Coker, The Dry Salvages, Little Gidding*), 1943
*Selected Poems,* 1948
*The Undergraduate Poems,* 1949
*The Cocktail Party* (play), 1950
*Poems Written in Early Youth,* edited by John Hayward, 1950
*The Confidential Clerk* (play), 1954
*The Cultivation of Christmas Trees,* 1954
*The Elder Statesman* (play), 1958
*Collected Poems, 1909–1962,* 1963
*The Complete Poems and Plays of T. S. Eliot,* 1969
*The Complete Poems and Plays, 1909–1950,* 1980
*The Waste Land, Prufrock, and Other Poems,* 1998
*Inventions of the March Hare: Poems, 1909–1917,* edited by Christopher Ricks, 1998

**Selected Criticism**
*The Sacred Wood,* 1920
*Selected Essays,* 1932; revised edition, 1950
*The Use of Poetry and the Use of Criticism,* 1933
*The Music of Poetry,* 1942
*Poetry and Drama,* 1951
*American Literature and the American Language,* 1953
*On Poetry and Poets,* 1957

**Other Writings:** essays (*The Idea of a Christian Society,* 1939; *Notes Towards the Definition of Culture,* 1948), nonfiction (*Reunion by Destruction: Reflections on a Scheme for Church Unity in South India Addressed to the Laity,* 1943), correspondence (*The Letters of T.S. Eliot,* 1988), translation of French literature (*Anabasis: A Poem,* by Saint-John Perse, 1930; revised editions, 1938, 1949, 1959); edited collections of literature (*Literary Essays of Ezra Pound,* 1954).

**Further Reading**

Ackroyd, Peter, *T.S. Eliot,* London: Hamish Hamilton, 1984; as *T.S. Eliot: A Life,* New York: Simon and Schuster, 1984
Brooker, Jewel Spears, *Mastery and Escape: T.S. Eliot and the Dialectic of Modernism,* Amherst: University of Massachusetts Press, 1994
Brooker, Jewel Spears, and Joseph Bentley, *Reading "The Waste Land": Modernism and the Limits of Interpretation,* Amherst: University of Massachusetts Press, 1990
Gordon, Lyndall, *T.S. Eliot: An Imperfect Life,* New York: Random House, 1998
Gray, Piers, *T.S. Eliot's Intellectual and Poetic Development, 1909–1922,* Atlantic Highlands, New Jersey: Humanities Press, 1982
Moody, A. David, editor, *The Cambridge Companion to T.S. Eliot,* Cambridge and New York: Cambridge University Press, 1994
Schuchard, Ronald, *Eliot's Dark Angel: Intersections of Life and Art,* New York: Oxford University Press, 1999
Sigg, Eric, *The American T.S. Eliot,* Cambridge: Cambridge University Press, 1989
Smith, Grover Cleveland, *T.S. Eliot's Poetry and Plays: A Study in Sources and Meanings,* Chicago: University of Chicago Press, 1950; 2nd edition, 1974
Southam, B.C., *A Student's Guide to the Selected Poems of T.S. Eliot,* London: Faber and Faber, 1968; 6th edition, as *A Guide to the Selected Poems of T.S. Eliot,* London: Faber and Faber, 1994; San Diego, California: Harcourt Brace, 1996


## Ash-Wednesday

*Ash-Wednesday* was the first long poem that T.S. Eliot wrote after his pivotal Modernist work, *The Waste Land* (1922). Taking its title from the Christian holiday that marks the beginning of a season of renunciation before Easter, the poem also marks Eliot's turn to Anglicanism and political conservatism. *Ash-Wednesday* originally consisted of six separate pieces written between 1927 and 1930, some of which were published separately and not in the order in which they finally appeared. While some critics applauded this poem for demonstrating maturity and a "growth beyond desire," others received it with hostility, complaining that Eliot's poetry had declined under the influence of Anglicanism. Compared to *The Waste Land*'s frantic search through the mythic past for redemption, *Ash-Wednesday* points toward a future with the infinite and remains firmly grounded in Christian, specifically Anglo-Catholic, symbolism and iconography.

Published in 1930 after Eliot became a British subject and converted to high-church Anglicanism, the subject matter of the poem dramatizes Eliot's own spiritual search for a divine order. His conversion not only signaled a break with the nihilistic strain of his past work but also brought about his break with Modernism's infatuation with alienation and disorder. At the same time, *Ash-Wednesday* remains stylistically Modernist in its use of imagism, free verse, and dense allusions. Eliot himself confirmed these observations in a letter: "Between the usual subjects of poetry and 'devotional' verse there is a very important field still very unexplored by modern poets—the experience of a man in search of God, and trying to explain to himself his intenser human feelings in terms of the divine goal. I have tried to do something of that in 'Ash Wednesday.'" Although written in the form of a dramatic monologue that seems to refer to the poet's life, the poem tells us very little about the speaker; its content reaches beyond a personal narrative into philosophy and theology, especially through Eliot's use of images that illustrate the ancient struggle between spirit and flesh.

*Ash-Wednesday* is difficult to explicate because of its use of numerous "objective correlatives" that force the reader to infer "intenser human feelings" rather than directly understand them. What remains clear, despite the dense allusions and images, is the mood of the poem, which conveys the speaker's resignation and turn to God. In the first lines, two hopes appear to be relinquished: the hope for worldly achievements and the hope for spiritual transcendence.

Because I do not hope to turn again
Because I do not hope
Because I do not hope to turn
Desiring this man's gift and that man's scope
I no longer strive to strive towards such things
(Why should the aged eagle stretch its wings?)
Why should I mourn
The vanished power of the usual reign?

In an allusion to Shakespeare's 29th sonnet, the speaker gives up his envy of the talent and intellect of others and the accompanying desire for worldly success. At the same time, the image of an eagle that is unable to stretch its wings and leave behind worldly concerns indicates the difficulty and incompleteness of the speaker's spiritual aspirations. Despite his profound recognition of his worldly and spiritual limitations, part I ends decisively with two lines from the "Angelus," an Anglican prayer to Mary—"Pray for us now and at the hour of our death"—bespeaking his resolve that, regardless of the outcome, the speaker will continue in his faith.

In part II, the Lady enters, accompanied by three leopards that "fed to satiety / On my legs my heart my liver and that which had been / contained / In the hollow round of my skull." All that is left of the speaker after this feast are dry bones, which revisits a major theme from *The Waste Land,* where Eliot made use of the same image from the Old Testament book of Ezekiel. Again the question is asked, "Shall these bones live?" Unlike in Ezekiel, in *The Waste Land* the bones do not come to life; there they serve as a symbol of religious failure. In *Ash-Wednesday,* the bones sing out, "We are glad to be scattered, / we did little good to each other." Here conversion is represented by dry bones singing in joy that the carnal is subdued, rejoicing in the cyclic nature of repentance and renewal instead of demanding transcendence. Alluding to the mystic theology of St. John of the Cross, these bones now exemplify the spiritual paradox that the bliss accompanying conversion leads to spiritual aridity.

The cyclic theme of conversion and despair continues in part III with allusions to the spiral staircase of Dante's *Inferno:* "At the second turning of the second stair / I left them twisting, turning below." Finding "strength beyond hope and despair," the speaker climbs up the stairs and again encounters the Lady, who resembles Dante's Beatrice. The Lady, who "made strong the fountains and made fresh the springs," returns, wearing the blue color of the Virgin Mary. Through this biblical allusion, she becomes a feminine complement to Christ. In Eliot's earlier poems, women chatter meaninglessly or trap and emasculate male speakers, but here in *Ash-Wednesday* the woman is represented as a sacred, if silent, guide into conversion. Although Christ-like, the Lady also has fleshly attributes: "Brown hair is sweet, brown hair over the mouth blown." In contrast to *The Waste Land,* where the hyacinth girl exclusively connotes fertility and sexuality, Eliot's depiction of women in *Ash-Wednesday* has attained greater complexity. The conflation of the divine Virgin with the fleshly Lady symbolizes the convert's struggle with the dueling entities of flesh and spirit. Soon, however, this "silent sister" withdraws into contemplation; her inaccessibility has lead many critics to understand her as representative of Eliot's ambivalent feelings toward women.

The poem concludes with a philosophical and theological treatise that acknowledges spiritual conversion not as a momentary decision but as an ongoing "time of tension between dying and birth":

Suffer us not to mock ourselves with falsehood
Teach us to care and not to care
Teach us to sit still
Even among these rocks,
Our peace in His will
And even among these rocks
Sister, mother
And spirit of the river, spirit of the sea,
Suffer me not to be separated

And let my cry come unto thee.

The prayer to "care and not to care" amounts to one of the many difficult paradoxes in the poem, signaling the incomprehensibility of God and the incompleteness of all acts of the flesh. Although many critics believe that this poem espouses a straightforward Anglo-Catholic faith, the intercessor with God addressed in the previous quotation, the spirit of the river and sea, corresponds to Eliot's earlier interest in ancient fertility rites. Anglo-Catholic imagery and theology dominate the lines of *Ash-Wednesday,* yet Eliot is neither making an attempt to convert others nor bearing witness to an uncomplicated conversion. In that sense, while *Ash-Wednesday* testifies to a Christian faith, it also must be read as a modern poem because of its acknowledgment of the deep uncertainties, complexities, and paradoxes of that faith.

KATEY KUHNS CASTELLANO

**Further Reading**

Bush, Ronald, "'Explaining to Himself': *Ash Wednesday,*" in *T.S. Eliot: A Study in Character and Style,* by Bush, Oxford and New York: Oxford University Press, 1983

Daumer, Elisabeth, "Charlotte Stearns Eliot and *Ash-Wednesday*'s Lady of Silences," *ELH* 65, no. 2 (1998)

Kwan-Terry, John, "*Ash Wednesday:* A Poetry of Verification," in *The Cambridge Companion to T.S. Eliot,* edited by A. David Moody, Cambridge and New York: Cambridge University Press, 1994

Leavell, Linda, "Eliot's Ritual Method: *Ash-Wednesday,*" *The Southern Review* 21, no. 4 (1985)

Loucks, James F., "Eliot's *Ash Wednesday,* I," *ANQ* 8, no. 2 (1995)

Montgomery, Marion, "T.S. Eliot Circa 1930: The Recovery of Permanent Things," *Modern Age* 37, no. 3 (1995)

## Four Quartets

Regarded as the culminating achievement of T.S. Eliot's later career, the *Four Quartets* has become one of the cornerstones of literary Modernism. Much praised and widely read at the time of its publication, the poems mark the articulation of Eliot's religious convictions and the summation of his beliefs in cultural tradition in a stylistically complex and densely allusive fashion. Yet the publication of the *Four Quartets* has a curious history. Originally, "Burnt Norton" was published in 1936 in Eliot's *Collected Poems, 1909–1935,* having been written from material originally drafted for the play *Murder in the Cathedral* and conceived of as a separate poem in its own right. However, with the publication of "East Coker" in 1940 in *New English Weekly,* Eliot began to think of these two poems as parts of a larger poem. With the approbation of his friend John Hayward, "The Dry Salvages" was published in *New English Weekly* in 1941, followed by "Little Gidding" in 1942. The complete *Four Quartets* was published in the United States in 1943 and in Britain the following year.

The poems derive some of their power from a juxtaposition of the personal-confessional with the public events of history and World War II. Although centered on places of symbolic importance to Eliot, the poems are not topographical and resist merely describing these places. "Burnt Norton" focuses on a Cotswold Garden; "East Coker" focuses on a Somerset village from where Eliot's own ancestor, Andrew Eliot, traveled to the New World in 1669 in search of religious freedom; "The Dry Salvages" mixes the landscapes of the Mississippi River in Missouri and New England; and "Little Gidding" focuses on the home of Nicholas Ferrar, a significant 17th-century Anglican businessman. The poems are meditations prompted by the places, combining philosophical, theological, and symbolic imagery in an analysis of the intersection of time and eternity. The famous opening of "Burnt Norton"—"Time present and time past / Are both perhaps present in time future, / And time future contained in time past" (*BN* I, 1–3)—indicates this preoccupation with temporality that forms the basis for the philosophical exploration of the poem. The poems explore how humans, shaped by and steeped in time, experience the divine and eternal, and all the poems are concerned with the tension between temporality, history, immortality, and eternity. In their attempts to represent this mystical experience, the poems investigate the metaphysical point of union between humans and God and aim to communicate the fundamentals of Christian faith and experience in a modern idiom. Utilizing ideas from the medieval Christian tradition of the *via negativa* (the "negative way") derived from the work of mystics such as St. John of the Cross and Julian of Norwich, the poems balance the known with the unknown and are constructed within a rhetoric of mystical paradoxes, such as "where you are is where you are not" (*EC* III, 46) or "neither movement from nor towards, / Neither ascent nor decline" (*BN* II, 65–66). Permeated by this profoundly nostalgic and Anglican vision of history, the *Four Quartets* culminates in the deeply religious vision of 17th-century Little Gidding framed by the war-torn London of the Blitz. Ultimately, the poems appear to be deeply conservative in their politics, implicitly expressing support for the "big three" of British institutional establishment: monarchy, nation, and church.

Much has been made of the implicitly musical structure of the poems, many critics seeking to delineate the repeated patterns that loosely unite the poems' movements. As with a musical work, the poems appear to state various themes that they then develop, repeat, explore, and recapitulate. The first "movement" in each poem appears to contain a musical "statement" that is followed by a second movement that opens in rhyme and continues in a more colloquial or discursive manner. The third movement is often considered to be the core of each poem, followed by a short lyrical "interlude" in the fourth movement, while the fifth and final movement reverses the structure of the second movement and generally relates the philosophical issues of the poem to the artistic problems of using language. These final movements have produced some of the more famous sections of the poem, with their anxiety-stricken passages over the slipperiness and intractability of language for the modern-day artist: "Words strain, / Crack and sometimes break, under the burden, / Under the tension, slip, slide, perish, / Decay with imprecision, will not stay in place, / Will not stay still" (*BN* V, 149–53). This anxiety about the instability of language is tied to the more general insecurity about cultural order and social equilibrium in the *Four Quartets,* as "Little Gidding" shows a poet policing language to prevent words from growing insubordinate and creating a semantic world in which "every word is at home / *Taking its place* to support the others" (*LG* V, 217–18, italics added).

Heavily allusive and intertextual, the poems borrow from and gesture to works by, among others, Heraclitus, Shakespeare, Dante, Milton, Whitman, Shelley, Mallarmé, Yeats, and Gide, and also to the Bible. The four poems have been associated with the four seasons and the four elements, and early critical efforts focused on emphasizing the continuities with the imagery and preoccupations of Eliot's earlier poetry and tracing the internal interrelations of the poems. However, since the late 1960s, critical attention has begun to respond to the separate poems and their varying degrees of success rather than poetic unity. Succeeding critical attention from Marxist or poststructuralist perspectives has focused on the poem's metaphysics of the word, its structural metaphors, and its intertextual references.

Tim Woods

**Further Reading**

Blamires, Harry, *Word Unheard: A Guide through Eliot's "Four Quartets,"* London: Methuen, and New York: Barnes and Noble, 1969

Cooper, John Xiros, *T.S. Eliot and the Ideology of "Four Quartets,"* Cambridge and New York: Cambridge University Press, 1995

Ellmann, Maud, *The Poetics of Impersonality: T.S. Eliot and Ezra Pound,* Brighton, Sussex: Harvester Press, and Cambridge, Massachusetts: Harvard University Press, 1987

Gardner, Helen, *The Composition of the "Four Quartets,"* London and Boston: Faber, 1978

Murray, Paul, *T.S. Eliot and Mysticism: The Secret History of "Four Quartets,"* New York: St. Martin's Press, and London: Macmillan, 1991

## Gerontion

"Gerontion" is a pivotal poem in T.S. Eliot's oeuvre. It marks the turn away from the fragments that Eliot wrote (most of which he never published) in preparation for his long poem *The Waste Land* (1922) toward a unified poem and vision. Eliot originally wanted to include "Gerontion" as an introduction to *The Waste Land,* but Ezra Pound, who edited Eliot's manuscript down to approximately half its original length, dissuaded him from the idea. Nevertheless, it can be helpful to see the character in "Gerontion," whose title, roughly, means "little old man," as a kind of Tiresias—the central hermaphroditic prophetic figure of *The Waste Land.* Moreover, the vision of spiritual and cultural emptiness of "Gerontion" is illuminated by and itself illuminates *The Waste Land.*

"Gerontion" takes the form of an interior monologue and should be read as such. Although it would be wrong to interpret the poem as autobiographical, it can be helpful to view the poem in the context of Eliot's own experiences during and in the aftermath of World War I. Eliot wrote "Gerontion" in May–June 1919; the past years had been arduous ones for him. Eliot had spent the war years in London, a city he found increasingly oppressive, putting in long hours during the week working in a bank. His marriage to his wife, Vivienne, had almost from the first (1915) been full of tension, and the war years only accentuated both husband's and wife's nervous anxieties and sense of frustrated entrapment. When the Americans entered the war, Eliot tried to enlist, but as a result of a lifelong hernia, he was deemed unfit for service, and so he found himself, as one of the few men of fighting age not participating in the war, outside the main activity of his generation.

"Gerontion" opens with the speaker, "an old man in a dry month . . . waiting for rain." The image of rain here, as in *The Waste Land,* is of physical, spiritual, and cultural rejuvenation that never arrives. The man is aware of his own removal from the world; the speaker has not taken part in the decisive battles of his day ("nor fought in the warm rain"), and later in the poem he laments his physical insensibility. "I have lost my sight, smell, hearing, taste and touch: / How should I use them for your closer contact?" "Gerontion" speaks in the voice of a man who finds both his personal life and the life of his times futile. The poem deplores man's failure to learn from history:

> Think now
> History has many cunning passages, contrived corridors
> And issues, deceives with whispering ambitions [. . .]
> Gives too late
> What's not believed in [. . .]

Gerontion's impotence and distance from a vision of salvation can be compared to that of Eliot's early character Prufrock, but Gerontion takes on larger, more historical, and also more specifically religious connotations than does Prufrock. Gerontion's house, for example, can be read simultaneously as his home, his decrepit body, and also the house of a decrepit civilization itself:

> My house is a decayed house,
> And the jew squats on the window sill, the owner,
> Spawned in some estaminet of Antwerp

The blatant anti-Semitism of these lines—the stereotypical image of the Jew is used here to symbolize a depraved, money-driven society—has been the subject, along with Eliot's anti-Semitic remarks elsewhere, of recent criticism. Within the poem, the image of the Jew is used in the context of its theme of failed Christian revelation.

Eliot formally converted to Anglicanism in 1927, but even in his earliest works he expresses a desire for spiritual renewal and an interest in the idea of sainthood. From 1914 on, Eliot's interest in and attraction to Christianity became increasingly pronounced, and the essential emptiness that runs throughout "Gerontion" can be read as a failure to find religious meaning and faith. "I have lost my passion," the old man Gerontion declares, meaning both passion in the vulgar sense and the Christian passion of Christ's suffering. In the poem's second stanza, Eliot alludes to a 17th-century Nativity sermon by Lancelot Andrewes in which the "sign taken for wonders" is the infant Christ who remains essentially mute, difficult to understand. So Eliot writes, "'We would see a sign!' / The word within a word, unable to speak a word, / Swaddled with darkness." As in "Prufrock" and later in *The Waste Land,* the failed revelation in "Gerontion" is a failure not only of religious understanding but also of language itself; language remains incomprehensible, cut off from the essential insight toward which it should lead.

There is more literary allusion in "Gerontion" than in Eliot's earlier poems. Eliot quotes and misquotes as if to emphasize language's complexity and slipperiness, a technique that was to be one of the signature features of *The Waste Land.* "Gerontion" alludes to a wide range of sources, from, among others, *Measure for Measure* in its epigraph, to biographical details from Edward Fitzgerald's life, to *The Education of Henry Adams.* Similarly, the poem navigates among different moods and cultural modes—from the serious to the sarcastic, from the highbrow to the satiric. Throughout "Gerontion," Eliot offers moments of failed revelation that segue into parodic scenes of contemporary life. In its often bitter (and, because of the anti-Semitism, unpleasant) cultural lampooning, "Gerontion" bears resemblance to the other poems published in Eliot's second volume of poetry, *Poems* (1920), in which "Gerontion" appeared (after having first appeared in the volume *Poems* published by Virginia and Leonard Woolf's Hogarth Press in an edition of 250 copies in May 1919). However, in its ruminative tone and in its poetic form, "Gerontion" stands out, distinct from the quatrain poems that make up most of Eliot's 1920 volume *Poems.*

NADIA HERMAN COLBURN

**Further Reading**


Gish, Nancy K., *Time in the Poetry of T.S. Eliot: A Study in Structure and Theme,* Totowa, New Jersey: Barnes and Noble, and London: Macmillan, 1981

Gordon, Lyndall, *Eliot's Early Years,* Oxford and New York: Oxford University Press, 1977

Grant, Michael, editor, *T.S. Eliot: The Critical Heritage,* 2 vols., London and Boston: Routledge and Kegan Paul, 1982

Julius, Anthony, *T.S. Eliot, Anti-Semitism, and Literary Form,* Cambridge and New York: Cambridge University Press, 1995

Rajan, Balachandra, *The Overwhelming Question: A Study of the Poetry of T.S. Eliot,* Toronto and Buffalo, New York: University of Toronto Press, 1976

Smith, Grover Cleveland, *T.S. Eliot's Poetry and Plays: A Study in Sources and Meanings,* Chicago: University of Chicago Press, 1950; 2nd edition, 1974

## The Love Song of J. Alfred Prufrock

T.S. Eliot's first volume of poetry, *Prufrock and Other Observations,* was published in 1917; the 500 copies did not sell out until 1922. The mostly dismissive reviews found the title poem "clever" but "banal" or "incoherent" and "neither witty nor amusing." Eventually, Ezra Pound's early praise of "Prufrock" as "the best poem I have yet had or seen from an American" turned out to be prophetic. Today "Prufrock" is one of the most widely anthologized poems, and critical commentaries continue to examine the complicated linguistic, philosophical, and psychological dimensions of the poem.

Mostly written while Eliot stayed in Paris during the year 1911, "Prufrock" is a loosely connected collage of fragments. Its original title was "Prufrock among the Women," which alludes to Eliot's early preoccupations with stifling bourgeois superficiality, social alienation, and sexual ambiguity. The published title, "The Love Song of J. Alfred Prufrock," has been discussed in terms of its ironic juxtaposition of such romantic notions as love and song with a name—derived from a St. Louis furniture wholesaler—whose verbosity appears to be purposely anti-romantic. Thus, the title exemplifies the major tensions in the poem between self and self-consciousness, between (sexual) desire and fear, or between lyrical authenticity and the social prattle of women who (although they are mentioned only twice) seem endlessly to "come and go / Talking of Michelangelo."

The invitation, "Let us go then, you and I," announces the first of many intentions to be thwarted. Fraught with intimations of mental and narrative instability, the famous third line, "Like a patient etherized upon a table," brutally disrupts any notions of a predictable plot. The romantic, opening apostrophe eventually reveals that we are overhearing the voice of a solitary speaker whose intended visit to a tea party may never have taken place. Rather than in terms of an external plot, one might thus understand "Prufrock" as a Cubist collage whose emotional content or intent the protagonist can explain neither to himself nor to others. "It is impossible to say just what I mean!" he exclaims late in the poem. The poem's Cubist style suggests Henri Bergson's influence, whose lectures in philosophy Eliot attended while in Paris. In light of Bergson's concept of time as duration, Prufrock's imaginary journey can be read as a spatial metaphor for a heterogeneous sense of temporality where past, present, and future do not appear as linear but overlap and collide in discordant scenes, voices, and images.

If the poem's avant-garde style amounts to a self-referential aesthetic that has lost its connection to the external world, it also mirrors, or constructs, Prufrock's self-enclosed mind. Escape from his tormenting solipsism is offered only at the beginning and end of the poem and only at the cost of utter loss of consciousness, by ether or drowning. In the claustrophobic middle of what Hugh Kenner (1959) has called a "fin de siècle inferno," we find Prufrock caught in the same stereotypes he purports to critique. No one has ever returned from here, says Guido da Montefeltro in the epigraph from Dante's *Inferno,* suggesting that Prufrock's predicament will be as inescapable as that of a soul in hell. The poem demonstrates this inescapability in Prufrock's solitude, famously rendered in one of Eliot's many subaqueous images:

> I should have been a pair of ragged claws
> Scuttling across the floors of silent seas.

Prufrock's obsessive rehearsals of heroic roles "to force the moment to its crisis" and the tantalizing revelations proffered in his "overwhelming" questions are all foiled by the poem's inexorable movement from present to impossibility, from dream to nightmare, from youth to old age, or from the present tense to that indicator of supreme futility: the past subjunctive.

Within these fated parameters, Prufrock prepares his faces, questions, furtive glances, and tentative approaches, only to be stalled by instantaneous self-consciousness, self-doubt, or self-mockery. Perhaps that is why he seeks his own voice in so many other voices: those of Ecclesiastes, the Gospels, Dante, Shakespeare, Donne, Marvell, Dostoyevsky, Baudelaire, James, Swinburne, Nerval, Jules Laforgue—the latter being the "wholly self-conscious," as Eliot wrote in the Clark lectures, whose lamentations and ennui pervade the poem. All that these exhausted voices can prove is that they cannot diagnose Prufrock's modern condition; he is "the hollow voice of a twentieth century corpse," as Jonathan Raban (1971) has put it. Morbid, melancholic, and more than a little mad, he is a Hamlet figure, even if such associations are vehemently denied: "No! I am not prince Hamlet, nor was meant to be." However, Prufrock protests too much: his feelings are as excessive as Eliot claimed Hamlet's were. Like Hamlet, Prufrock lives in an age past the possibilities of heroic, tragic action:

> Shall I part my hair behind? Do I dare to eat a peach?
> I shall wear white flannel trousers, and walk upon the
> beach.

If heroic action once engendered a sense of a corollary significance and inexpendability of the self, the poem can be read as an elegy on the death of classical traditions and values. This and Prufrock's obsessive references to body parts—"arms that lie along a table"—refer not only to the poem's fragmented, Cubist style but also to a concept of human life bereft of substance and reduced to mere function. It is against such reduction that Prufrock whispers his never enacted resistance. We will hear him again as Sweeney, as Tiresias, or as the "young man carbuncular" in *The Waste Land* and later in the voices of *The Hollow Men.*

Both cosmic and comic, the closing lines of "Prufrock" admit once more Prufrock's desire to transcend his stifling social and mental predicament. However, the allusion to John Donne's line from "Song," "Teach me to hear mermaids singing," underscores the failure of this protagonist's desire for an authentic encounter—sexual or metaphysical. What remains and what may account for the lasting appeal of "The Love Song of J. Alfred Prufrock" is the particular pathos of his failure, a pathos that has ever since been associated with the modern.

HAROLD SCHWEIZER

**Further Reading**

Ackroyd, Peter, *T.S. Eliot,* London: Hamish Hamilton, 1984; as *T.S. Eliot: A Life,* New York: Simon and Schuster, 1984

Bergonzi, Bernard, *T.S. Eliot,* New York: Macmillan, 1972; 2nd edition, 1978
Bush, Ronald, *T.S. Eliot: A Study in Character and Style,* Oxford and New York: Oxford University Press, 1983
Habib, M.A.R., *The Early T.S. Eliot and Western Philosophy,* Cambridge and New York: Cambridge University Press, 1999
Kenner, Hugh, *The Invisible Poet: T.S. Eliot,* New York: McDowell Obolensky, 1959; London: Allen, 1960
Moody, A. David, *Thomas Stearns Eliot: Poet,* Cambridge and New York: Cambridge University Press, 1979; 2nd edition, 1994
Moody, A. David, editor, *The Cambridge Companion to T.S. Eliot,* Cambridge and New York: Cambridge University Press, 1994
Raban, Jonathan, *The Society of the Poem,* London: Harrap, 1971
Schuchard, Ronald, *Eliot's Dark Angel: Intersections of Life and Art,* New York: Oxford University Press, 1999
Wagner-Martin, Linda, editor, *T.S. Eliot: A Collection of Criticism,* New York: McGraw-Hill, 1974

## The Waste Land

The most representative, if not the greatest, poem of the 20th century is, outside Ezra Pound's *Cantos,* perhaps also the most difficult. In a celebratory essay on "The Metaphysical Poets" (1921), T.S. Eliot issued a programmatic statement clarifying that "poets in our civilization, as it exists at present, must be *difficult.*" Eliot certainly follows his own prescription in *The Waste Land* (1922), immediately successful and massively influential.

The first-time reader is jarred, unnerved, and (likely) both attracted and repulsed by its "self-sufficient juxtaposition without copulae of themes and passages in a dense mosaic" (Kenner, 1959). In its comprehensiveness, allusiveness, indirection, and dislocations, the poem clutches at social and personal malaise, spiritual bankruptcy, and cultural deracination. Not much grows "Out of this stony rubbish" depicted, and it is often monstrous, perverted, and corrupt. Yet, from the beginning, ironic evocation of Chaucer's *Canterbury Tales* to the end ("Datta. Dayadhvam. Damyata. / Shantih shantih shantih" ["Give. Sympathize. Control. / The Peace which passeth understanding," from the Hindu fable *The Upanishad*]), the reader cannot but feel in the presence of something numinous and elusive, whose own roots reach deep into tradition—poetic, philosophical, and religious.

The poem poses the question of how to read it. An answer lies in Eliot's own suggestion for coming at another difficult poem, *The Divine Comedy.* In *Dante* (1929), he advises to "begin with detail, and [then] approach the general scheme." What Eliot says of *The Divine Comedy* applies to *The Waste Land:* enjoyment of it "is a continuous process. If you get nothing out of it at first, you probably never will; but if from your first deciphering of it there comes now and then some direct shock of poetic intensity, nothing but laziness can deaden the desire for fuller and fuller knowledge." Start with the poetry, with details of the poetic texture, rather than "the general scheme." Do not, then, be either caught up in or put off by the "learned" notes Eliot added, probably to stretch the poem to a requisite length for printing. The poem is traditional in meaning, if disjunctive and fragmentary in form. We know that Pound—to whom *The Waste Land* is warmly dedicated: "il miglior fabbro" ("the better craftsman")—hacked along at it and in the revisionary process made the poem what it is: not at all a dramatic monologue, there being only what has been called a zone of consciousness. No wonder one feels adrift, as if bereft of footholds, the condition the poem exposes and explores.

Although we might enter the poem at any "direct shock of poetic intensity," I do so at perhaps the most obvious: its fragmentariness in the context of verses about fragments: "You cannot say, or guess, for you know only / A heap of broken images" (section I, 21–22) and "These fragments I have shored against my ruins" (V, 431). Such allusions (e.g., to the Book of Ezekiel) are not necessary to a preliminary grasp of the poem. What to make of these fragments, paralleling the quester's condition *in* the poem? The reader is clearly implicated: "You! hypocrite lecteur!—mon semblable-mon frère!" Eliot makes poetry out of the fragments, allusions, shards of civilization, the "stony rubbish" of lives spent in desperation or indifference—not the subject matter makes poetry, he insisted, but the use to which it is put, how it is wrenched and dislocated into tension and intensity, working to make poetry of the unpoetical. The reader's job is to make sense, connect, see, and understand just as the poet did, just what the protagonist struggles toward. In the Holy Grail myth, to which Eliot's notes lead us via the work of Sir James Frazer and Jessie L. Weston, the Knight-Errant has, on arrival at the Chapel Perilous in section V, but to ask the meaning of what he has seen, and the diseased land will be restored to health. For the reader, too, the job is hard: the individual far from being invited to reach a private meaning, for the intrusion of personality is as disastrous in reader as in poet.

Much is clear, as early as the opening inversion of *The Canterbury Tales,* of religious pilgrimage, renewal; we moderns prefer winter and forgetfulness, journeys to Canterbury having deteriorated into meaningless ski trips (and spring breaks). Human life is no waste land, but postwar "civilization" is. We are responsible for having made this mess, and we can find a way out of it. Eliot gives us the bits and pieces with which to work. Required, says *Little Gidding,* is "prayer, observance, discipline, thought and action."

One such piece, relatively easy to deal with in and of itself, is the story in "The Fire Sermon" (section III) of the "typist home at teatime" and her indifferent tryst with "the young man carbuncular," "A small house agent's clerk," "One of the low on whom assurance sits / As a silk hat on a Bradford millionaire." The scene is important—and accessible in its familiar theme and depiction—connecting with other representations of lust, apathy, and meaninglessness (e.g., in "A Game of Chess," from Cleopatra-like splendor to the bar scene revealing Lil's abortion). The central section both geographically and thematically, "The Fire Sermon" also introduces us to Tiresias (what he "*sees,* in fact, is the substance of the poem," avers Eliot in a note), instances other sexual encounters, and suggestively renders a positive scene "Beside a public bar in Lower Thames Street": "Where fishmen lounge at noon: where the walls / Of Magnus Martyr hold / Inexplicable splendor of white and gold." Hints thus appear in fragments, although the lines "On Margate Sands . . ." sound the familiar lament of a sated lover: "'I can connect / Nothing with nothing.'" Such connections include the section's last lines, which evoke St.

Augustine's confession of lust and the Buddha's teaching that all things are on fire, with passion, hatred, and egotistical clutching.

These lines resonate with section IV, "Death by Water." What as spring rain stirs "Dull roots" here brings death, although the suggestion appears of sacrifice preceding rebirth, which carries over into "What the Thunder Said": "Here is no water but only rock." Suggestive images accumulate—from the journey of Christ's disciples to Emmaus (there is a "third who walks always beside you"), past the destruction of "Jerusalem Athens Alexandria / Vienna London / Unreal," to "a damp gust / Bringing rain," perhaps, and the intensity of "Datta, Dayadhvam, Damyata." Arguably the poem's most suggestive and intense moment occurs with Dayadhvam, or "Sympathize," which in another Trinity points to Christ and the Incarnation:

*Dayadhvam:* I have heard the key
Turn in the door once and turn once only
We think of the key, each in his prison
Thinking of the key, each confirms a prison
Only at nightfall, ethereal rumors
Revive for a moment a broken Coriolanus

Eliot's notions of the individual and tradition, presented in "Tradition and the Individual Talent" (1920), are never far from play: "What happens [or should, with the poet] is a continual surrender of himself as he is at the moment to something which is more valuable. The progress of an artist is a continual self-sacrifice, a continual extinction of personality." Because we cannot or do not surrender (our lust, our indifference), we cannot sympathize. The culprit being our own egotism, the key lies in breaking out of our imprisonment within the self.

That key Eliot only hints at in *The Waste Land.* Perhaps he, too, then understood at best darkly. As important as it is, *The Waste Land* does not tell the whole story; it should be read, and read along with *Ash-Wednesday* and *Four Quartets.*

G. DOUGLAS ATKINS

**Further Reading**


Bolgan, Anne C., *What the Thunder Really Said: A Retrospective Essay on the Making of "The Waste Land,"* Montreal: McGill-Queen's University Press, 1973

Brooker, Jewel Spears, *Mastery and Escape: T.S. Eliot and the Dialectic of Modernism,* Amherst: University of Massachusetts Press, 1994

Charity, A.C., *"The Waste Land" in Different Voices,* edited by A.D. Moody, London: Arnold, 1974; New York: St. Martin's Press, 1975

Cuddy, Lois A., and David H. Hirsch, editors, *Critical Essays on T. S. Eliot's "The Waste Land,"* Boston: G.K. Hall, 1991

Eliot, T.S., *"The Waste Land": A Facsimile and Transcript of the Original Drafts Including the Annotations of Ezra Pound,* edited by Valerie Eliot, London: Faber and Faber, and New York: Harcourt Brace Jovanovich, 1971

Gardner, Helen, *The Art of T.S. Eliot,* London: Cresset, 1949; New York: Dutton, 1950

Kenner, Hugh, *The Invisible Poet: T.S. Eliot,* New York: McDowell Obolensky, 1959; London: Allen, 1960

Kirk, Russell, *Eliot and His Age: T.S. Eliot's Moral Imagination in the Twentieth Century,* New York: Random House, 1971; revised edition, LaSalle, Illinois: Sugden, 1984

Southam, B.C., *A Student's Guide to the Selected Poems of T.S. Eliot,* London: Faber and Faber, 1968; 6th edition, as *A Guide to the Selected Poems of T.S. Eliot,* London: Faber and Faber, 1994; San Diego, California: Harcourt Brace, 1996


---

# Clayton Eshleman 1935–

Over the course of Clayton Eshleman's voluminous career two central themes have emerged. Eshleman's own childhood in Depression-era Indianapolis, recounted in his first full-length book of poems, *Indiana* (1969), is a study in repressive child rearing and the wounding of the consciousness of an artist that would haunt his succeeding books. A second theme, beginning in *Hades in Manganese* (1981), addresses the coming to consciousness of the species, as witnessed in the art of the caves of southern France, notably Lascaux, the "Sistine Chapel" of primordial art. The birth of mind involved separating human identity from what Eshleman calls the "animal continuum," when imagination began producing images from its still undivided knowledge of animal and human lore roughly 50,000 years ago. The birth of the ego was not without anguish, pain, loneliness, and ultimately exile—the same exile Eshleman experienced as a child in Indianapolis.

Both readings of self and world derive from the Cold War era and its brooding over global death from nuclear warfare and the growing sense that European civilization had prospered on the backs of the colonialized Third World. Guilt, remorse, the Holocaust, and the arms race all had their impact on mid-20th-century American culture and on Eshleman's turn toward dark interpretations of the venality and craven self-interest of the modern human spirit.

Fueling the introspection in Eshleman's poetry was the Deep Image movement begun in the late 1950s by Jerome Rothenberg. The "deep image" is presumably dredged up from a stratum under consciousness, containing what the psychotherapist Carl Jung called an archetype. The archetypes are the original grains of primordial continuity in the pre-human imagination; when brought to the surface they seem altogether foreign and untranslatable. These ideas attracted Eshleman and also Diane Wakoski, Armand Schwerner, Robert Kelly, and David Antin among other poets. Even though the "movement" lasted only a few months, the writers involved went on using the deep image as the basis of their work.

The practice of Deep Image poetry led to a new kind of lyricism in which the self is healed through an imagistic mode of self-analysis. Unlike Confessionalism, a Freudian-based method of poetic self-analysis, Deep Image poetry tries to escape the self through appeals to community and immersion into the collective human psyche. Eshleman's overt aim in this context is to join a world once subjugated by white cultures, with which he associates the subjugated and repressed body.

*Indiana* achieves a formidable statement of Deep Image goals through its scrutiny of childhood traumas and vexations. "The Book of Yorunomado" establishes the rhapsodic pattern of Eshleman's poetry: a breezy, sinuous unfolding of biographical lore flowing through epigram, narrative vignette, and lyric interlude, closing on a resolution to open the psyche to new experience:

> When the female principle takes over,
> it is, as has been said, the darkening
> of the light.
>
> Goodbye all I've ever known . . .

The image of the caterpillar emerges here as the sign of rebirth. Denial of the natural body lies at the core of the book; restrictive parenting moves inexorably toward separating the human being from its "beast origins," a process of winnowing out wild nature from a pliant, conforming human will.

The boundaries marking off acceptable reality left an unknown dark of woods, figuratively Dante's *selva obscura,* but also the actual Butler woods (a small park near Eshleman's childhood home in Indianapolis) featured in *Indiana.* His father Ira was an efficiency engineer at a local slaughterhouse, and his return home each day for lunch wearing a blood-spattered lab coat signified a second universe of knowledge from which the boy was denied. The father as figure of authority is turned over in the poems "The Creek" and "Bear Field" in an attempt to uncover the motives of repression.

Eshleman's poetry career coincides with his career as a translator of poetry, mainly of Spanish and French writers who embody the liberated consciousness he strives for in his own self-portraits. His best work is devoted to Cesar Vallejo, the native voice of Peru who expressed the Indian imagination after centuries of Spanish colonial rule. Eshleman's *Complete Posthumous Poems of Cesar Vallejo* received the National Book Award in 1979. As editor of several quarterlies, including *Caterpillar* (1967–1973) and *Sulfur* (1981–2000), Eshleman assembled poems and graphic art of the postmodern era, showing different sides of the issue of alienation and the use of "depth" aesthetics to achieve an enriched awareness.

In *Fracture* (1983), Eshleman's chief work, he pursues a bolder course in interpreting cave art, urging not only a reading of the paintings as allegories of the birth of the ego, but as a vast anticipation of epic literature and the Bible. The "invention of hell" begins with depictions of trident-like figures emerging out of darkness who later become the devils of medieval Christianity. Hell is the unconscious, the unknown self, and, according to Eshleman, its ties to primordial nature are vilified by a culture of fear. The artist is the one who reenters hell as an Orphic figure to reconnect imagination with its ultimate source in wild nature.

In the major poem of this collection, "Visions of the Fathers of Lascaux," Eshleman takes rhapsodic lyric to its limits. Fluid form and dizzying switches of point of view are driven by a richly encoded allegorical speech depicting the creation of Adam within the terms of Eshleman's interpretation of cave art:

> my language shat in its stall
> terrified stagy by waterhole as the Fathers fixed
> the potential to dream and scrawl the clouds of animality
>   as they shredded
> to open a blue immensity as if the sky
> were entrance of an earthcave we were always
> on the verge of leaving and so we remain
> thresheld in gravity even though
> the autonomous animal gods are departing

Eshleman comes close to realizing in "Visions" one of the 20th-century writer's central aims, to merge the literal terms of autobiography with the universality of mythic narrative. While no single Eshleman poem ultimately transforms personal detail into myth, the collective poem written over 12 full-length books of poetry organizes a labyrinthine map of self touching on many mythological heroes and episodes of world myth.

In *From Scratch* (1998), a title playing on the means by which early pictographs recorded the first images, Eshleman expresses his main theme—the birth and rebirth of the soul—in a unique blend of cartoon fantasy, epic exaggeration, allegory, and grotesque humor. "Notes on Exile and Paradise" is both characteristic and exemplary:

> I pass up under the Spider Queen's veil,
> lift up her festering egg-sac smile
> that the radiance behind her moth-stained tusks
> might clarify my passage.

Eshleman's style is unique in modern poetry, and his argument about human origins—based on a mixture of history, archaeology, and his own idiosyncratic decodings of ancient art—is akin to other monuments of 20th-century epic longing, including Pound's *Cantos*, Simon Rodia's "Watts Towers," and the *tableaux* of Max Ernst.

Paul Christensen

*See also* Deep Image Poetry

**Biography**

Born in Indianapolis, Indiana, 1 June 1935. Attended Indiana University, Bloomington, 1953–61, B.A. in philosophy 1958, M.A. 1961; Instructor, University of Maryland Eastern Overseas Division, Taiwan, Korea, and Japan, 1961–62; Instructor in English, Matsushita Electric Corporation, Osaka, Japan, 1962–64; Instructor, New York University American Language Institute, 1966–68; member of School of Critical Studies, California Institute of the Arts, Valencia, 1970–72; taught at University of California, Los Angeles, 1975–77; taught in an inner-city high school in Los Angeles (California Arts Council grant), 1977–78; Visiting Lecturer in creative writing, University of California, San Diego, Riverside, Los Angeles, and Santa Barbara, 1979–86; Dreyfuss poet-in-residence, and Lecturer, California Institute of Technology, Pasadena, 1979–84; since 1986 Professor of English, Eastern Michigan University, Ypsilanti; editor, *Folio,* 1959–60; publisher, Caterpillar Books, 1966–68, and editor, *Caterpillar* magazine, 1967–73; reviewer, *Los Angeles Times Book Review,* 1979–86;

founder and editor, *Sulfur* magazine, 1981–2000. Received National Translation Center Award, 1967, 1968; Union League Civic and Arts Foundation Prize (*Poetry,* Chicago), 1968; National Endowment for the Arts grant, 1969, fellowship, 1979, 1981; Coordinating Council of Literary Magazines grant, 1969, 1970, 1971, 1975; PEN Award, for translation, 1977; Guggenheim fellowship, 1978; National Book Award, for translation, 1979; National Endowment for the Humanities grant, 1980, fellowship, 1981; Soros Foundation travel grant, 1986; Michigan Arts Council grant, 1988. Living in Ypsilanti, Michigan.

**Poetry**
*Indiana,* 1969
*Altars,* 1971
*Coils,* 1973
*The Gull Wall: Poems and Essays,* 1975
*What She Means,* 1978
*Nights We Put the Rock Together,* 1980
*Hades in Manganese,* 1981
*Fracture,* 1983
*The Name Encanyoned River: Selected Poems, 1960–1985,* 1986
*Hotel Cro-Magnon,* 1989
*Under World Arrest,* 1994
*From Scratch,* 1998

**Selected Criticism**
*Novices: A Study of Poetic Apprenticeship,* 1989

**Other Writings:** essays (*Antiphonal Swing: Selected Prose, 1962–1987,* 1989), translations of Spanish, Hungarian, and French literature (*The Complete Posthumous Poems of Cesar Vallejo,* 1979; *Lyric and Dramatic Poetry, 1946–1982,* by Aimé Césaire [translator with Annette Smith], 1990); editions of collected literature (*A Caterpillar Anthology: A Selection of Poetry and Prose from Caterpillar Magazine,* 1971).

**Further Reading**
Arnold, A, James, "Inscribing the Fall," *The Virginia Quarterly Review* (Winter 1983)
Christensen, Paul, *Minding the Underworld: Clayton Eshleman and Late Postmodernsim,* Santa Rosa, California: Black Sparrow Press, 1991
Christensen, Paul, et al., "Six Writers on Eshleman," *Temblor* 6 (1987)
Tuma, Keith, "An Interview with Clayton Eshleman," *Contemporary Literature* 1 (Summer 1960)
Wakoski, Diane, "The Visionary Poetry of Clayton Eshleman," *American Poetry* 3 (1984)
Weinberger, Eliot, *Works on Paper: 1980–1986,* New York: New Directions, 1986

---

## William Everson 1912–94

Known also as Brother Antoninus, William Everson was a poet whose life not only informed his writing but also generated the dynamic that makes his poetry interesting. His books have crisis-laden, religious, and mythic titles, whether *The Crooked Lines of God, The Masks of Drought,* or *Prodigious Thrust.* Likewise, his books are endorsed by striking pronouncements and provocative descriptions, such as "All the verse of the celebrated San Francisco poet written before his crisis of religious faith," which adorns the cover of *The Residual Years: Poems, 1934–1948,* or the assessment by critic Albert Gelpi that Everson is "the most important religious poet of the second half of the twentieth century." Everson's literary friendships were numerous and vital, including among them Kenneth Rexroth, Gary Snyder, and Robert Duncan. He was instrumental to the San Francisco Renaissance that dominated midcentury poetry and poetic innovation. As a young William Everson, he was known as an autochthonous California poet, heir to the mantel of Robinson Jeffers; as Brother Antoninus, he was known for a while as the "Beat Friar," as prone to writing verses of divine affliction as he was to writing protest poems for People's Park in Berkeley; and then as William Everson once again, this time old and wizened, he was known as the writer of a vivid Lawrentian-Jungian fusion, producing epic sequences of archetypal and sexual force.

Everson's religious conversion defines his career: his best verse relates to this experience directly or indirectly. In 1948, on Christmas Eve, Everson converted to Catholicism rather dramatically during a vigil Mass at St. Mary's in San Francisco. Shortly afterward, he separated from his second wife, poet and artist Mary Fabilli, and entered the Dominican priory of St. Albert's in Oakland as a lay brother. He changed his name to Brother Antoninus and would remain a Dominican for the next 19 years. Before his conversion, as a young poet, Everson wrote lean, pantheistic and agnostic poetry, clearly under the sign of Jeffers, whom he never met. Most of these early poems are short, meditative reflections of the California natural world, toward which the poet expressed a variety of animistic devotion. "These Are the Ravens," which was the title poem to his first collection (1935), is exemplary:

> These are the ravens of my soul,
> Sloping above the lonely fields
> And cawing, cawing.
> I have released them now,
> And sent them wavering down the sky,
> Learning the slow witchery of the wind,
> And crying on the farthest fences of the world.

In this poem, and in many others like it, Everson sees himself reflected in, and somehow alienated from, the natural world. This is a disposition clearly derived from his hero Jeffers. However, unlike Jeffers, Everson did not take to writing long-verse narratives from biblical or mythical originals. Instead, Everson took his life as his subject, demonstrated in the powerful verse sequence "Chronicle of Division," which tells the story of his estrangement and divorce from his first wife.

The poetry of Brother Antoninus typically litanized the need for rectification from adverse habits and thoughts. The poems from this period bristle with the religious intensity of a convert, echoing St. Augustine as much as Thomas Merton, Everson's contemporary who made conversion and monasticism momentarily trendy. Lines from "The Screed of the Flesh" are a good example of Everson's own contribution to the midcentury Catholic revival, in his case a kind of venomous loathing of the impoverished spiritual self:

> The mouth of my soul was utterly stopped with the wadded
> rag of my self,
> As the truthful man who would speak of truth is gagged
> and kept from speaking;
> As the mouth of a man of terrible truths is stuffed with a
> wad of rags,
> So I gagged my soul with the stuff of self, I gagged it and
> led it away.

This poem appeared in *The Crooked Lines of God* (1959), a book that was nominated for a Pulitzer Prize, a sign of Brother Antoninus' visibility. This same book contains "A Canticle to the Waterbirds," if not Everson's best poem, certainly his most popular. A catalog of West Coast bird life, beginning with the utterly memorable line "Clack your beaks you cormorants and kittiwakes," this poem is at once his most Jeffers-like poem and yet his most Catholic, an idiosyncratic joining of Audubon and Aquinas. The "migratory terns and pipers who leave but the temporal clawtrack written on sandbars" are also "utterly seized in God's supremacy," feathered proof of it.

Love drew Everson out of his religious habits, quite literally, when he shed them during a poetry reading in 1969, announcing that he was leaving the Dominican Order to marry. Some of the intensity of Everson's erotic life was forecasted in *The Rose of Solitude* (1967), an agonistic book in which the poet recalls in an elaborate verse sequence his experience of falling in love with a young woman who had come to seek his counsel at the priory and the conflict that these feelings caused him because of his monastic vows. The erotic potency of his poetry rather luridly—albeit couched in Jungian terms—comes to life in *River-Root: A Syzygy* (1976), a long poem recounting a fight between a couple and the coitus that ensues on their reconciling. However, the best, most intensely felt poetry Everson wrote is collected in *The Masks of Drought* (1980), published when the poet was 68. In this powerful book, Everson chronicles the California drought of 1976–77 in terms of his own sexual impotence, evoking these events in the guise of the myth of the Fisher King. These poems are bleak and austere, bringing together Everson's early pantheism with Christian rectitude. In "Kingfisher Flat" (the name of Everson's home), we find both the "lordly phallus" who would "Quench its ardour in the uterine fens" and the "wisdom and delight" of the poet "crucified in bed." The poem ends,

> Deeper than the strict
> Interdiction of denial or the serpentine coiling of time,
> Woman and earth lie sunk in sleep, unsatisfied.
> Each holds that bruise to her heart like a stone
> And aches for rain.

During the last years of his life, Everson worked on a verse autobiography titled *Dust Shall Be the Serpent's Food,* which was half completed when he died in 1994.

Mention should be made of one other factor that contributed to Everson's poetry: his work as a printman. While Everson was imprisoned during World War II in Waldport, Oregon, for his conscientious objection, he founded a press, Untide Press (making an anagram of "United"), using an old handpress kept at the military base prison. Thus began his career as a printer, which he pursued throughout his life, even up to his death, when he was running the Lime Kiln Press out of Santa Cruz, California. Everson set the type for a number of his own books of poetry, including *The Crooked Lines of God* and *The Poet Is Dead* (1964), the dirge he wrote for Jeffers, and these books are remarkably beautiful compositions. He also famously reset into verse the prose preface to Whitman's 1855 *Leaves of Grass,* revealing the bardic poem within Whitman's thoughts on America. Perhaps his most famous production was the *Psalter,* which was to commemorate the first new Latin translation of the Psalms, commissioned by Pope Pius XII, since the Vulgate translation, which was at the time already 1,500 years old. This was an incredibly ambitious project undertaken shortly after Everson entered the Dominican priory, one that would ultimately take up nearly three years of Everson's time, to be abandoned on being one-quarter completed. It was eventually put together and bound in a partial edition that dissatisfied the perfectionist Everson. However, even today it is regarded as one of the two or three finest examples of hand pressing in the United States.

The final assessment of Everson as a poet is yet to be made. His output was prodigious and has not yet been completely reckoned. In each of his three phases, he can strike the reader as monofocal and reductive: in his early phase, he too quickly equates the harshness of the natural world with the harshness of human emotion; as Brother Antoninus, he seems capable only of striking the notes of sinfulness and piety; and in his later phase, there is the simplified Jungian dynamic always at work, particularly regarding sex as mythical union. Throughout, he suffers some of the habits of his master Jeffers, most especially an abrupt and clunky use of metaphor. However, despite and perhaps even because of these, Everson's poetry is always genuine, impassioned, vivid, and even liturgical. His command of language is utterly convincing. His awe at the natural world was undiminished throughout his writing life, just as his awe at the divine life the natural world signified became increasingly intense, even after he left formal religious life. When the final assessment is made, Everson may be regarded as the truly great California poet, deserving the literary company of Jeffers, Rexroth, and Snyder and perhaps better than each.

Peter O'Leary

*See also* San Francisco Renaissance

**Biography**

Born in Sacramento, California, 10 September 1912. Attended Fresno State College, California, 1931, 1934–35; cannery worker and laborer for the Civilian Conservation Corps, 1933–34; farmer, mid-1930s; conscientious objector during World War II; with the Civilian Public Service, 1943–46; co-founder,

Untide Press, 1943, and director, Fine Arts Group, 1944–46, both Waldport, Oregon; staff member, University of California Press, Berkeley, 1947–49; member of the Catholic Worker Movement, 1950–51; Dominican lay brother (Brother Antoninus), 1951–69; poet-in-residence, Kresge College, University of California, Santa Cruz, 1971–81; master printer, Lime Kiln Press, Santa Cruz, California, 1971–81. Received Guggenheim fellowship, 1949; Shelley Memorial Award, 1978; National Endowment for the Arts grant, 1982; Lifetime Achievement Award, National Poetry Association; Body of Work Award, PEN Center USA West. Died 2 June 1994.

**Poetry**

*These Are the Ravens,* 1935
*San Joaquin,* 1939
*The Masculine Dead: Poems, 1938–1940,* 1942
*X War Elegies,* 1943
*Waldport Poems,* 1944
*War Elegies,* 1944
*The Residual Years: Poems, 1940–1941,* 1944; revised edition, 1948; enlarged edition, as *The Residual Years: 1934–1948,* 1968; revised and enlarged edition, 1997
*Poems MCMXLII,* 1945
*A Privacy of Speech: Ten Poems in Sequence,* 1949
*Triptych for the Living,* 1951
*At the Edge* (as Brother Antoninus), 1958
*A Fragment for the Birth of God* (as Brother Antoninus), 1958
*An Age Insurgent* (as Brother Antoninus), 1959
*The Crooked Lines of God: Poems, 1949–1954* (as Brother Antoninus), 1959
*There Will Be Harvest,* 1960
*The Year's Declension,* 1961
*The Hazards of Holiness: Poems, 1957–1960* (as Brother Antoninus), 1962
*The Poet Is Dead: A Memorial for Robinson Jeffers* (as Brother Antoninus), 1964
*The Rose of Solitude* (as Brother Antoninus), 1964
*The Vision of Felicity* (as Brother Antoninus), 1966
*The Blowing of the Seed,* 1966
*Single Source: The Early Poems of William Everson, 1934–1940,* 1966
*In the Fictive Wish,* 1967
*The Rose of Solitude* (collection, as Brother Antoninus), 1967
*The Achievement of Brother Antoninus: A Comprehensive Selection of His Poems with a Critical Introduction* (as Brother Antoninus), introduction by William Stafford, 1967
*A Canticle to the Waterbirds* (as Brother Antoninus), 1968
*The Springing of the Blade,* 1968
*The City Does Not Die* (as Brother Antoninus), 1969
*The Last Crusade* (as Brother Antoninus), 1969
*Who Is She That Looketh Forth as the Morning?* (as Brother Antoninus), 1972
*Gale at Dawn,* 1972
*Tendril in the Mesh,* 1973
*Black Hills,* 1973
*Man-Fate: The Swan Song of Brother Antoninus,* 1974
*River-Root: A Syzygy for the Bicentennial of These States,* 1976
*Missa Defunctorum,* 1976
*The Mate-Flight of Eagles,* 1977
*Blackbird Sundown,* 1978
*Rattlesnake August,* 1978
*The Veritable Years: Poems, 1949–1966,* 1978
*Cutting the Firebreak,* 1978
*Blame It on the Jet Stream!* 1978
*The Masks of Drought,* 1980
*Eastward the Armies: Selected Poems, 1935–1942, That Present the Poet's Pacifist Position Through the Second World War,* edited by Les Ferriss, 1980
*Renegade Christmas,* 1984
*In Medias Res,* 1984
*Mexican Standoff,* 1989
*The Engendering Flood,* 1990
*The Blood of the Poet: Selected Poems,* edited by Everson and Albert Gelpi, 1993

**Selected Criticism**

*Robinson Jeffers: Fragments of an Older Fury,* 1968
*Archetype West: The Pacific Coast as a Literary Region,* 1976
*Earth Poetry: Essays and Interviews,* 1980
*The Excesses of God: Robinson Jeffers as a Religious Figure,* 1988
*Naked Heart: Talking on Poetry, Mysticism, and the Erotic,* 1992

**Other Writings:** essays, edited poetry collection (*The Double Axe and Other Poems,* by Robinson Jeffers, 1977), biography (*Prodigious Thrust,* 1996).

**Further Reading**

Bartlett, Lee, "Creating the Autochthon: Kenneth Rexroth, William Everson, and 'The Residual Years,'" *Sagetrieb* 2, no. 3 (Winter 1983)
Bartlett, Lee, *William Everson: The Life of Brother Antoninus,* New York: New Directions, 1988
Davidson, Michael, *The San Francisco Renaissance: Poetics and Community at Mid-Century,* Cambridge and New York: Cambridge University Press, 1989
Labrie, Ross, "Sexuality and Mysticism in the Poetry of William Everson," *Christianity and Literature* 44, no. 1 (Autumn 1994)
Parkinson, Thomas, "William Everson: Pacifist Poet and Printer Emerges from Waldport, 1945–1949," *American Poetry* 4, no. 2 (Winter 1987)
Zimmerman, Lee, "An Eye for an I: Emerson and Some 'True' Poems of Robinson Jeffers, William Everson, Robert Penn Warren, and Adrienne Rich," *Contemporary Literature* 33, no. 4 (Winter 1992)

# Expatriate Poetry

Following World War I, and again after World War II, many American writers and artists sought refuge in Europe. To the self-exiled artist, Europe represented a place of freedom far from the strictures of middle-class values. American expatriates alienated themselves from the culture of their homeland, where the moral code included a "good life" but left out the freedom for experimentation with style, subject, and form that would make many of them well known. An international community of writers and artists who inspired, critiqued, and promoted each other's work gathered in European cities during the periods between the wars and after the wars. The cosmopolitan cities of Paris and London influenced many American poets to push the boundaries and meet the challenge of Ezra Pound's command to "make it new."

World War I was the "Great War" or the "war of wars" for its generation. New technological warfare changed the face of war and held the power to destroy human spirits as well as lives, completing the dehumanization of mankind that began in the 19th century with the Industrial Revolution. Poetic styles and subjects reflected the abhorrent scenes on the battlefields; a dissonant tone showed disillusionment with America and life in general. Disenfranchised poets presented themselves as spokespersons for their generation. By 1925 the generation of poets who matured during World War I broke completely with the "old school" of the 19th century as well as with the Chicago School of poetry. Expatriate poets no longer reflected on the fireside and home as John Greenleaf Whittier or William Cullen Bryant had in the late 19th century; instead they created the anti-heroes of modern life, such as T.S. Eliot's J. Alfred Prufrock or Ezra Pound's Hugh Selwyn Mauberley. Hugh Selwyn Mauberley felt "out of key with his time," while Prufrock went out into a world that is "like a patient etherized upon a table." These characters illustrated the emptiness felt by many. Poets who had spent time in the war as soldiers or volunteers were acutely aware of this emptiness and sought to make sense of the death and chaos that surrounded them in the war. Archibald MacLeish, E.E. Cummings, and Harry Crosby all spent the war as volunteer ambulance drivers. MacLeish also served as a captain of field artillery on the front. These experiences colored their vision of the world and influenced the poetry they wrote afterward.

Several movements emerged from the work of these expatriate poets, known as the "Lost Generation," including Imagism, Vorticism, Objectivism, and Symbolism. Artistic schools such as Cubism also influenced poetic works. Poets often challenged themselves by experimenting with more than one theory or form, crossing over to new movements as old ones became out of date and their poetic visions grew and changed. Experimentation forms the cornerstone of many of these movements. Expatriate poets felt more freedom to abandon the traditional rhyme schemes and patterns and play with language. In Europe they also gained a wider vision of the world through influential encounters with other writers. The expatriates did not completely give up traditional aspects of poetry or references; however, many relied on their classical educations for knowledge of schools and forms of poetry from prior centuries. Without the background in these poetic traditions, they could not have broken or reworked them.

The Imagist movement began with Ezra Pound in 1912. The circle of poets who gathered in London "emphasized the virtues of clarity, compression, and precision" (see *The New Princeton Encyclopedia of Poetry and Poetics,* edited by Preminger and Brogan, 1993). Imagism was their reaction against 19th-century Romanticism and the traditions of 19th-century poetry. It was dedicated to "rejuvenating poetic language and form through the objective presentation of visual images." Concentrating on the object and the relation between word and meaning, the Imagists rejected the flowery prose of their predecessors. Pound's two-line poem "In a Station of the Metro" may be one of the finest examples of Imagist poetry: "The apparition of these faces in the crowd: / Petals on a wet, black bough." Pound explained that he had seen a "beautiful face, and then another and another" in the metro (see *Norton Anthology of Modern Poetry,* edited by Ellmann and O'Clair, 1988). He searched for a way to capture the faces but could not find one; a year later, he captured the image in two lines that paint a picture of what he saw and experienced in that moment.

Ezra Pound was not alone in the Imagist movement, although he was the leader for a time. Other poets in the circle included H.D. (Hilda Doolittle), Amy Lowell, and William Carlos Williams. British poets Richard Aldington and F.S. Flint and Irish author James Joyce were also part of the group. Pound sought publicity and venues for publication for the poets, and was keenly interested in the technique of Imagism. *Des Imagistes* (1914), an anthology of Imagist poetry, marked the end of Pound's involvement in the group, however, when Pound disagreed with Amy Lowell about the direction of the Imagist movement. Lowell was publishing competing anthologies that Pound dismissed as "Amygism" because he thought she was diluting the movement's original principles. Lowell took over the leadership of the movement for two more years while Pound abandoned Imagism for Vorticism.

Vorticism, a movement founded by Wyndham Lewis in 1914, was also based on the visual. It stood for all that is "abstract and nonrepresentational in art" (Preminger and Brogan, 1993). The essential element in Vorticism was energy, according to Pound; the poem must go beyond mere images and create energy. "Oread," by H.D, demonstrates what Pound described.

Whirl up, sea—
whirl your pointed pines,
splash your great pines
on our rocks,
hurl your green over us,
cover us with your pools of fir.

The movement of the sea that H.D. captures, along with the visual comparison to the pines, seizes the essence of Vorticism. It is ironic that H.D. wrote one of the finer examples of Vorticist poetry since she criticized Pound's involvement in the movement.

T.S. Eliot, sometimes referred to as a neo-Symbolist, was one of the poets who became associated with Symbolism, a 19th-century school and theory. Eliot claimed that he had not found a model for poetry until he read Arthur Symon's *The Symbolist Movement in Literature.* Eliot "invited [readers] to tackle the enigma of the poem" (Preminger and Brogan, 1993), modifying Symbolism to connect with the modern reader through narration and description. "The Hollow Men," "Ash-Wednesday," and "The Waste

Land" all reflect Eliot's use of symbolism and allegory. "The Hollow Men" are more than mortal men; they represent the culture that has turned shallow and empty, while "The Waste Land" contemplates both the world out of sync and Eliot's personal life in fragments that depict the atrocities of modern life. Eliot also contributed to the poetic theory through his essay "Tradition and the Individual Talent," in which he set forth his theory on the "objective correlative": a work must include a "particular emotion," he argued, and must reveal that emotion, rather than just describe it. Eliot's theory influenced his generation and succeeding ones as well.

Objectivism began with Louis Zukofsky's stint as guest editor of the February 1931 issue of *Poetry*. Poets who practiced Objectivism in the 1930s began with an object, which then inspired verbal associations. Ezra Pound was one of the few expatriates who associated himself with the movement for a brief time.

Artistic movements also influenced the expatriates. E.E. Cummings spent time in Paris and Europe, first as a volunteer in World War I and later as a writer. The paintings of Picasso, the sights of Paris, and the bohemian life he experienced all inspired his poetic style. From Picasso and Cubism, Cummings drew inspiration for his sparse lines and vivid images. The visual character of his poetry has been described by Marianne Moore as "a kind of verbal topiary-work." Cummings' poem "in Just/spring" uses sparse language to paint vivid images. The reader feels the excitement of the children through words run together: "and eddieandbill come / running from marbles" and "bettyandisbel come dancing / from hop-scotch and jump-rope and . . ."

The various movements that shaped the expatriate poets' work also shaped the Modernist movement. Not only did they inspire the poets residing in Europe, they influenced those who remained in the United States. Poets did not necessarily remain tied to one movement. They learned the elements, incorporated them into their poems, and then moved on to develop even more complex works. As the world continued to change between the wars, and as groups of poets moved from London and the United States to Paris, poetic style continued to evolve.

Poets who left the United States during the early decades of the 20th century often felt their lives were out of step with cultural expectations. Women poets, who tend to be grouped together by sexual orientation or schools of thought, may have felt more disconnected than their male counterparts. Female expatriates found space in Europe to examine and write about the oppressive nature of patriarchy, developing new modes of expression. Gertrude Stein, remarkably productive as a writer in many genres, constructed prose poetry that countered male forms. Younger women had different experiences than women born in the 19th century. H.D., for example, began as part of Pound's circle but later moved on to Paris. Stein sought social liberation, while Kay Boyle became more international and political, putting her at odds with Stein and her group.

H.D. (Hilda Doolittle) was the "most perfect" of the Imagist poets for her "innovative musical rhythms, crystalline lines, and stark images" (Scott, 1990). Although praised early as an Imagist, H.D. went on to develop her style and experiment with prose poetry. She challenged culturally assigned gender identities, which sometimes made her work controversial. H.D. was not widely published during her lifetime but still pursued the creative outlets that London and later Paris afforded her.

Another significant aspect of life in Europe for the expatriates was the active publishing scene. Little magazines and presses showcased the expatriate poets as well as poets who remained at home. Founded on both sides of the Atlantic, these publications quickly took on an international flavor. *Poetry*, originally founded by the Chicago School, showcased Pound, Eliot, Marianne Moore, and H.D., among others. *The Egoist* and the Egoist Press became a venue for the Imagists and later for avant-garde writers. As many as 20 publishers produced works of English-language authors in the 1920s and 1930s in France.

Harry and Caresse Crosby were a pivotal couple in the careers of many expatriate authors. Minor poets themselves, the Crosbys established Black Sun Press, first known as Editions Narcisse. The press began as a self-publishing venture for Harry and Caresse's poetry but later published authors such as Archibald MacLeish, Kay Boyle, Hart Crane, and Pound in beautifully designed limited editions that presented poetry as works of art. Caresse carried on the publishing ventures on her own after Harry's suicide.

The generation of writers who fled to European shores before and after World War I provided a foundation for later generations. Their experimentation and freedom showed younger writers that it was possible to find a place where their avant-garde work would be accepted. After World War II a group of expatriates again left American shores for Europe, this time settling primarily in Paris. Writers were still disillusioned with American society, but for different reasons. African-American writers such as James Baldwin left to escape racism and homophobia. Baldwin noted,

> [T]he American writer in Europe is released, first of all, from the necessity of apologizing for himself. . . . It is not necessary for him, there, to pretend to be something he is not, for the artist does not encounter in Europe the same suspicion he encounters here [in the United States]. (Sawyer-Lauçanno, 1992)

Like the previous generation, many young poets came to study. Lawrence Ferlinghetti, John Ashbery, and Harry Matthews all began their time in Paris as students. Allen Ginsberg, Gregory Corso, Peter Orlofsky, and William Burroughs, collectively known as the Beats, came to Paris in the mid-1950s. Already established in San Francisco, the group traveled to escape the limitations and censorship of the United States. Unlike the "Lost Generation," the expatriates of the 1940s and 1950s defied labels, immersing themselves in French culture and life, often living in the seedier areas of Paris.

Once again English-language publishing became important in France. The presses of the 1920s and 1930s had closed, leaving few outlets for expatriates to publish works abroad. A new generation of small reviews and magazines struggled at first, but many eventually succeeded. *The Paris Review, Merlin, Zero,* and *Points,* among others, presented new authors unknown by readers. Most included an international sampling of poets, rather than restricting themselves to American exiles. Like the magazines in the decades prior to World War II, these publications sought to publish those writers considered avant-garde.

*The Paris Review,* which is still in publication, is perhaps the most famous publication of the era. Conceived by Peter Matthiessen and Harold (Doc) Humes, the magazine published both known and unknown writers. From its inception *The Paris Review* sought to be more literary than its American counterparts;

*The Paris Review* published quality literature of all genres, rather than just criticism and politically motivated articles. To increase its audience the magazine featured a well-known author in each issue. George Plimpton joined the staff as editor, and most of the authors who lived in Paris during the 1950s had something to do with the publication in one way or another. When the founders and many of the expatriates returned to the United States in the late 1950s, *The Paris Review* began to focus on writers in America. Still, as William Styron wrote, it retained the original intent to publish "the good writers and good poets, the non-drumbeaters and the non-axe-grinders. So long as they're good" (Sawyer-Lauçanno, 1992).

Expatriate writers and artists of the first half of the 20th century invigorated literature with new perspectives. Their work evolved in ways that would have been impossible had they remained on American shores. Although most of them returned to the United States eventually, the flavor of the international community continued to influence their work.

Millie Jackson

**Further Reading**

Sawyer-Lauçanno, Christopher, *The Continual Pilgrimage: American Writers in Paris, 1944–1960,* New York: Grove Press, and London: Bloomsbury, 1992

Scott, Bonnie Kime, editor, *The Gender of Modernism: A Critical Anthology,* Bloomington: Indiana University Press, 1990

# Experimental Poetry/The Avant-Garde

The word *experimental* goes back to the days of Francis Bacon, the 16th-century natural scientist who challenged the ancient practice of working from general laws to determine the identity of things; he reversed the process and worked from evidence to induce the laws of nature. *Experiment,* like *essay,* means "to try." In a way poetry had grown old in the 19th century by relying on certain deductive forms of thought and expression that the 20th century challenged.

The result was a turn to experiment in verse, with early French efforts at breaking up old formulas by turning to *vers libre,* or free verse: a method of writing in which rhythm is not imposed but is found latent within the accents of unfettered language. In closed or formal verse order is imposed upon language, whereas in "open" or free verse, order is discovered within the unmediated flow of speech. Where order is to be found—in the artist's will or in the materials an artist works with—is a metaphysical question that lies at the heart of 20th-century art.

Experimental poetry attempts to reveal order within the writer's working materials, allowing language to reveal its own meanings and patterns rather than imposing the writer's meaning onto the words. Late in the 20th century this culminated in popular "found" poetry, in which scraps of paper blowing in the street, notices on bulletin boards, and other printed ephemera were quoted in whole or in part as poems.

The history of experimental poetry may be said to have begun with Stéphane Mallarmé's last poem, *Un coup de des n'abolira le hasard* (1887), "a throw of the dice will not eliminate chance." Mallarmé applied every kind of typographical diversity to the printed poem, including a large format page with the type sprawled across it (thanks to the new technology of lithography) to map out the course of a ship in a great storm. The tossing boat whipped by high winds and great swells is a figure for the poet at sea with his composition, attempting to direct a process subject to influence by every surrounding variable, from noise to bodily functions. The poem enshrines the contingency of composition and the ineffable latent power of words to form their own patterns.

Mallarmé demonstrated that the edges of the poem could be made porous and receptive to the white space around it. The poem was no longer exclusive and bounded by artificial conventions; rather, it was open to silences, leaps of thought, and the interference of rhyming syllables that might divert the logic to a new subject. The poem was as free as water to seek its own level and shape, but whatever that shape might be, it had come from within the materials, and not from the will of the writer.

Once the drift of experimental writing became clearer to critics at the start of the century, it was roundly rejected as an exercise in writing gibberish, or worse, a pretext for certain poetasters to indulge in obscurity and verbal chaos for their own sake. The reception of Gertrude Stein's prose poems in *Tender Buttons* (1911) was especially hostile and cause for many newspaper parodies.

The formal lyric that had evolved since Petrarch and Dante's era bore direct relation to Christian prayer. While the poem had gone through many permutations since the 12th century, it had never really departed from its essential expression as elevated words directed to a divine ear. Even love poetry was prayerful and venerated the beloved as a divinity. But the poem emerging in the Darwinian revolution was curiously post-Christian in attitude and called the divine directly from nature. Some wary critics of the period accused the new poetry of being a revival of pagan religion, of "nature worship," and indeed, there is some truth to the notion. Pound made frequent, overt reference to pagan religion in his poetry and strident criticisms of Christianity in his prose.

The tradition of experimental poetry is complicated by the fact that it has not one but two broad lines of descent throughout the 20th century. Ezra Pound formulated a new poetic he called "Imagism," in which the poet records a perception in the fewest words possible; "direct treatment of the thing," he called it. The "thing" may be either a natural event or an idea, a thought, an emotion from within. Whatever the subject was, imagination held the power to perceive its form within the particles of experience and to record its manifestation in spare, unembellished language. Pound first noticed the feasibility of this method in a poem by his colleague and friend, H.D., who, as the story goes, handed him a new lyric work ("Oread") for him to edit down. This he did until he found a single relation at the core of the poem: the waves of the sea transposing their form onto a forest of firs bowed by wind.

"Oread" captured a moment in which "form" leapt from one material to another, from water to trees, but the "wave" endured and left its pattern behind in the particulars. Pound applied the method to his own poem, "In a Station of the Metro," in which a crowd of commuters waiting for a train is depicted as resembling the petals of fruit blossoms on a branch. Pound would later call the arrangement of petals by their biological name, "phyllotaxis," meaning that the radiality of odd-numbered petals is constant among a broad range of flowering shrubs and trees. The commuters represent strangers in the industrial landscape coming together in a purely random event. The radiality of the flower leaps from the garden to travel into the underground to this crowd of faces, unifying the accidental.

Imagism provided a solution to the problem of form in the free-verse poem by anchoring language to a perception of unity occurring in the landscape. Chaos would not occur if the poem were rooted in an observation of order. An important motif of Pound's *Cantos* is "the rose in the iron dust," which he had gleaned from Allen Upward's report of an experiment in which a magnet placed under iron filings produced a gravitational field resembling the petals of a rose. The transformation of radiality from the rose to iron filings satisfied all of Pound's longings for a new sacred vision, of form passing freely out of nature into the industrial world of iron and mechanical life.

William Carlos Williams, a fellow Imagist, wrote another classic in the Imagist mode. In "The Red Wheelbarrow," the "so much depends" of the opening line refers to the power of nature to attract particulars into a unifying whole, in this case the harmony created by a red wheelbarrow "beside the white chickens." The juxtaposition of these two colors occurs in most of the flags of nations and in other patriotic symbols, in the colors of emergency vehicles, and so on. That known formula of color symbolism, however, was found "by accident" in a fisherman's backyard one snowy morning when Williams was buying fish. Imagism's central tenet is that the "form" is found in nature, not imposed by means of "concepts," arguments, or other extraneous means of ordering detail. Later Charles Olson and Robert Creeley would expand the notion of Imagism in their formulation that "form is the extension of content."

Mina Loy and Lorine Niedecker were also Imagists, but of their own means and styles. Loy's wide vocabulary in science and mathematics in *Lunar Baedeker & Time-Tables* (1958) brought to poetry a new diction and range of metaphors from fields often viewed as alien to art. Niedecker's focus on detail and the miniature world of wetlands flora in *My Life by Water* (1970) contributed an exacting naturalistic authenticity. The intensely visual focus of Imagist poetry welcomed writers whose powers of observation were trained in other fields, including photography and painting. Even E.E. Cummings participated on the edges of Imagism through his knowledge of abstract painting. His poems intensify the visual aspects of written language on the page, including exploded punctuation and the fragmentation of words into their visual components as letters and punning symbols.

A second experimental tradition was launched by T.S. Eliot, Pound's friend of the London years (1910–20), about whom he wrote appreciatively to Harriet Monroe, then-editor of the Chicago quarterly *Poetry*, that Eliot "had modernized himself." By this he meant that Eliot had read himself out of the 19th-century poetic conventions that other American poets continued to use. At Harvard Eliot had read widely in French Symbolism and had imitated the styles of Charles Baudelaire and Jules Laforgue, an ironic lyricism describing the *demi-monde* of Paris. Eliot projected a similar sort of absinthe state of mind onto Cambridge and Boston.

Eliot had also stripped lyric of traditional artifice; the poem moved in brief strophes from idea to idea, flowing with the drift of emotion to whatever caught the speaker's attention. "The Love Song of J. Alfred Prufrock"—which first appeared in *Poetry* in 1915 over the hesitations of Monroe, who did not understand the poem—revolutionized American poetry. It showed how unity could be achieved without the old conventions by dwelling on the speaker's psychology and perspective. The projection of subjective states onto the world colored and distorted reality in exact proportion to the mental distress of the viewer. This coded language allowed Eliot to use objects and events as metaphors of a central unifying feeling, thus integrating a seeming chaos of detail into a coherent argument. Eliot had come upon form within the subjective mind, whereas Pound found form outside the imagination, in the events of nature.

Wallace Stevens enriched Eliot's Symbolist method by offering a more colorful and whimsical lyricism, projecting a playful subjectivity unclouded by Eliot's sexual themes. *Harmonium* (1923) masterfully evokes the mind enjoying its fictions and what-ifs about the American landscape, but always with an underlying truth about self or the moral imagination. Hart Crane's lyrics were more in line with Eliot's in their exploration of sexual desire in *White Buildings* (1926) and in his long mythological poem, *The Bridge* (1930). Robert Lowell's poetry continued the Eliot tradition through yet another version of the sorrows of human love in *Life Studies* (1959), a book that launched a new mode of lyric at midcentury known as Confessionalism.

Because Symbolism was dependent upon strong, recognizable states of feeling in which the world is deformed, Symbolist poets tend to dwell on the dark side of human nature, on illness, divorce, guilt, and religious anguish. To this degree the Symbolist mind is still very much attached to poetry's basis in prayer, since much of the motivation of Symbolist lyric is to seek deliverance from or to understand the sources of anguish or suffering. The Symbolist mode attempts to know the human soul through its symbols and diffractions of an objective world.

Lowell's New England–Confessional style was countered by a more oblique Symbolist lyric in the work of John Ashbery and the New York School of poets. Associated with the Abstract Expressionist painters and the Museum of Modern Art, Ashbery demoted the representational values of poetry and stressed instead the inner voice as it rambled and discoursed on a fraying, disintegrating world of impressions and sensations. Contradiction, paradox, riddles, and echoed reformulations uprooted argumentative continuity and logical development, frustrating many readers. The parodic quality of the eloquence, always lustrous and animated, as in his award-winning *Self-Portrait in a Convex Mirror* (1975), brought Symbolist writing into the debates on reality, subjectivity, and truth during the Watergate years.

Ashbery may have laid the groundwork for the Language poets, who took Ashbery's circumlocutions to a new frontier of arbitrary structures in which sense was almost lost altogether. The Language poem followed sound patterns or visual punning or merely accumulated the debris of exhausted speech into a kind of verbal sculpture depicting the persona's paranoia or helpless entrapment in modern technological life. Charles Bernstein formulated the poetics of Language poetry and edited a journal devoted to the movement. Many practitioners have kept the style vigorously alive on the West Coast, including: Lyn Hejinian, poet and editor of Tuumba Press; Douglas Messerli, poet and editor of Sun and Moon Press; Leslie Scalapino; Barrett Watten; Michael Palmer; and Bruce Andrews.

Contemporary Symbolist writing in and out of the Language movement seems to have reached an impasse of sorts, having discovered that the inmost subjective voices are not necessarily logical or grammatical but are instead composed of disjunctive waves of speech based willy-nilly on nonsense rhymes, sensations, and colliding fragments of thought. Beyond lies a non-linguistic void where further disintegration seems unrecordable. A retrenchment to more representational uses of speech seems imminent.

Pound's more difficult and exacting mode of poetry attracted fewer poets and did not reach wide public attention or find its way into the textbooks and anthologies of American literature until the 1960s. As a result there is no conventionalized form of Imagist poetry or any standardized methods of writing it. Each generation has had to confront the problems of compression and brevity, to try to expand the frame of the lyric, and to justify discursiveness. The direction of Imagist poetry since 1910 has been toward wider ranges of comment around the centralizing perception of a formal relation occurring in nature.

The Objectivist movement of the 1930s did reorient the Imagist poem by making it perform in serial forms. George Oppen's *Discrete Series* (1934) goes beyond the bounds of the single poem as found in Williams' *Spring and All* (1930) by creating small perceptual vignettes that develop parts of a larger central idea, in this case the changing significance of water on another transparent medium, glass. The serial form of the Imagist lyric takes on a cinematic quality as it moves the single unifying perception through different contexts and situations, each time discovering a nuance or latent content in the relation. Other Objectivist poets—Charles Reznikoff, Carl Rakosi, and Louis Zukofsky—developed long poems variously deploying the Imagist technique. Rakosi used legal documents as objects in which a certain legal, religious, or racial relation is constant, as in the color pattern of a mosaic. Zukofsky's *"A"* (1978) features a multitude of mathematical, musical, and literary passages to create a large mosaic displaying underlying unities of theme and structure.

But the further evolution of Imagism was obscured by the hardships of the Depression and the outbreak of World War II. It was not until midcentury that Beat poetry, under the leadership of Allen Ginsberg, gave Imagism a new excitement in *Howl, and Other Poems* (1956) and set in motion the youth culture of the Cold War years. Charles Olson also took up Pound's poetics with "projective verse," in which the rigors of Imagist procedure are relaxed somewhat to record the fluidities of consciousness in the act of perception. Such verse projects the movement of language itself as it inspects, coordinates, links, and relates the data of an experience into a final encompassing perception. In the inaugural poem of what became known as Black Mountain poetry, "The Kingfishers" (1949), Olson pokes fun at Eliot's masterpiece, *The Wasteland* (1922), by inverting his religious symbol of Christ as fisher king back to a mere bird. He then articulates the stages by which his speaker reaches the revelation that he is no longer a product of the Old World but the heir of New World indigenous cultures in Mexico and Central America. This declaration of identity also initiates the postmodern turn toward native cultures and against the imperialism of European and Western industrial powers.

The celebration of the American landscape and its native history in projective poetry coincided with the "Green Revolution" and the ecology movements. Poets as diverse as Robert Duncan, Robert Creeley, Paul Blackburn, and Ed Dorn ignored the Anglo-American tradition and crafted their perceptual lyrics out of local history and specific environmental contexts, often with a political edge advocating conservation, ecological responsibility, and moral indignation against the wastefulness of industrial capitalism. Gary Snyder's poetry illustrates the dual nature of late-20th-century Imagist practice in following a path between Pound's rigorous lyric procedures and the desire to polemicize the politics of environmental degradation. In *Turtle Island* (1974), for which he received the Pulitzer Prize, Snyder speaks out directly in "Plain Talk" to address his readers on the need for greater restraint in the use of natural resources.

A younger generation of Imagists has emerged since 1970 with a poetry celebrating cultural and biological diversity. It is clear that the theological questions posed by Pound's original formulation of Imagism continue to haunt the imagination of poets today. The search for a divine principle in nature has proved elusive, or has tended to create didactic and idiosyncratic visions of the sacred.

The history of experimental poetry, while split and in some ways dialectical, reflects the larger struggle of 20th-century American culture to discover the role of self in the post-industrial world and the meaning of experience outside Christian teachings.

PAUL CHRISTENSEN

**Further Reading**

Allen, Donald Merriam, *The New American Poetry: 1945–1960,* New York: Grove Press, 1960

Allen, Donald Merriam, and Warren Tallman, editors, *The Poetics of the New American Poetry,* New York: Grove Press, 1973

Altieri, Charles, *Enlarging the Temple: New Directions in American Poetry during the 1960s,* Lewisburg, Pennsylvania: Bucknell University Press, 1979

Dijkstra, Bram, *The Hieroglyphics of a New Speech: Cubism, Stieglitz and the Early Poetry of William Carlos Williams,* Princeton, New Jersey: Princeton University Press, 1969

Kenner, Hugh, *The Pound Era,* Berkeley: University of California Press, 1971

Lazer, Hank, *Opposing Poetries,* Evanston, Illinois: Northwestern University Press, 1996

Longenbach, James, *Modern Poetry after Modernism,* New York: Oxford University Press, 1997

Perloff, Marjorie, *Poetic License: Essays on Modernist and Postmodernist Lyric,* Evanston, Illinois: Northwestern University Press, 1990

# F

## Lawrence Ferlinghetti 1919–

Lawrence Ferlinghetti is one of the most important poets of the San Francisco Renaissance, which included Kenneth Rexroth, Gary Snyder, and Kenneth Patchen. Although he has always distanced himself from the label "Beat poet," he is invariably linked to Beat writers such as Allen Ginsberg, Jack Kerouac, and William Burroughs. Poet, dramatist, artist, and publisher, Ferlinghetti's contributions to 20th-century poetry and to the arts in general are multitudinous.

Ferlinghetti was born in Yonkers, New York, on 24 March 1919, a few months after his father died. In a tragic twist, his mother was committed to an asylum for the insane only a few months after his birth, and so the young boy was sent to France to be raised by a female relative. It was not until his return to the United States, at the age of five, that Ferlinghetti learned to speak English, and it was during the 1920s at boarding school where he began writing poetry. Ferlinghetti attended Columbia University at the same time that Allen Ginsberg and Jack Kerouac did, although he apparently never made their acquaintance. Returning to France, he earned a doctoral degree in poetry at the Sorbonne in Paris with a dissertation titled "The City as Symbol in Modern Poetry: In Search of a Metropolitan Tradition." Appropriately enough, in 1951 Ferlinghetti moved to San Francisco, where he would help found the center of that city's poetic tradition.

In Ferlinghetti's poetry, the reader can see the author's persistent struggle to know himself and the world around him. The poems that arise from this effort are infused with a genuine sense of struggle as the author examines the possibility of integrating himself with the reality that he experiences. Rising above the poet's sense of loss, including a sense of personal abandonment, and converting it into a philosophical strength, the poems deal openly and frankly with the everyday world. Ferlinghetti's poet-in-the-world is the figure of the compassionate comic Charlie Chaplin, who represents the "Little Man" in each of us:

> a little charleychaplin man
>             who may or may not catch
>
> her fair eternal form
>        spreadeagled in the empty air
> of existence ("15")

This Chaplinesque persona is able to ask effective and dangerous questions without threatening or isolating his audience. He questions anything that seeks to codify human expression and freedom, whether it be government, politics, large institutions, or the conventional poetic form.

In 1952, Ferlinghetti and Peter Martin, who was publishing a small magazine on popular culture and cinema called *City Lights* (after the Chaplin film of the same name), started a bookstore of the same name. The bookstore immediately became (and still remains) a place where writers, especially local poets, and a literate public would meet, talk, and discuss poetry. In 1955, Ferlinghetti bought out Martin and started a publishing venture, City Lights Books, of which his volume *Pictures of the Gone World* (1955) was the first volume published in the now famous Pocket Poets series. Other Pocket Poets included Kenneth Rexroth, Robert Duncan, Denise Levertov, Gregory Corso, and Jack Kerouac. The most well known of these Pocket Poet books is Allen Ginsberg's *Howl, and Other Poems* (1956). The publication of *Howl* drew the wrath of authorities, and an obscenity trial followed in which *Howl* was finally declared to be a work of literature and not pornography.

In his first book, *Pictures of the Gone World,* Ferlinghetti found a coherent voice for the expression of his diverse influences and experiences: his Chaplinesque comic-sad voice projected into a realm of public significance, as in "26":

> Reading Yeats I do not think
>                     of Ireland
> but of midsummer New York
>                 and of myself back then
>    reading that copy I found
>                 on the Thirdavenue El
>
>        the El
>            with its flying fans
>    and its signs reading
>                SPITTING IS FORBIDDEN

This poem, as representative of Ferlinghetti's philosophy, balances the world of hardened lives against the world of "High Art," as suggested by Yeats. This balance clearly and finally falls to the side of humanity.

*A Coney Island of the Mind* (1958), his next book, is divided into three sections: "A Coney Island of the Mind," "Oral

Messages," and "Poems from *Pictures of the Gone World.*" The longer, first section begins with Ferlinghetti's powerful statement of the human condition as he sees it:

In Goya's greatest scenes we seem to see
the people of the world
exactly at the moment when
they first attained the title of
'suffering humanity'
They writhe upon the page
in a veritable rage
of adversity

The poems in this collection move beyond simply detailing the ironies and adversities of life by attempting to transform the poet-artist into the role of experiencing consciousness. The result of this transformation is that the poet-as-experiencing-consciousness becomes the mirror for our contemporary reality: "The poet's eye obscenely seeing / sees the surface of the round world." This new type of poetics necessitated a new subject matter, one that focuses on the everyday actions and reactions of the poet to the external world, so that the poems become a record of his existence and of his engagement with the world.

This populist view of poetry—that poetry speaks of the world to people in the world—was one that Ferlinghetti clearly shared with other San Francisco poets. His concern for the world and his political beliefs have been called radical; he championed Castro's revolution and visited Cuba in 1960; in the 1980s, as a sympathetic investigator of the Sandanista revolution, he visited Nicaragua. Ferlinghetti remains a grand example of the Chaplinesque "Little Man" who tries to make his own neighborhood a better neighborhood: a neighborhood of inclusion rather than of exclusion.

The section titled "Oral Messages" contains prose-like pieces that were conceived and developed "specifically for jazz accompaniment and as such should be considered as spontaneous spoken 'oral messages' rather than as poems for the printed page." They are fluid, inchoate pieces, venues for the poet-as-critic to speak without formal constraints, to speak using his own voice, the voice of the jazz generation, as in the opening lines of "I Am Waiting":

I am waiting for my case to come up
and I am waiting
for a rebirth of wonder
and I am waiting for someone
to really discover America

His book *A Far Rockaway of the Heart* (1997), a sequel to *A Coney Island of the Mind,* begins with the same note of public awareness and concern that made his earlier volume one of the most popular books of poetry ever published in the United States:

Everything changes and nothing changes
Centuries end
and all goes on
as if nothing
ever ends
As clouds still stop in mid-flight
like dirigibles caught in cross-winds
And the fever of savage city life
still grips the streets

In 1998, Ferlinghetti was appointed as San Francisco's first poet laureate.

DERRICK STONE

*See also* Beat Poetry; San Francisco Renaissance

**Biography**

Born in Yonkers, New York, 24 March 1919. Attended the University of North Carolina, Chapel Hill, B.A. in journalism 1941; Columbia University, New York, M.A. 1948; Sorbonne, Paris, Doctorat de l'Université 1950; served in the United States Naval Reserve, 1941–45; employed by *Time* magazine, New York, 1945–46; French teacher, San Francisco, 1951–53; co-founder, 1952, with Peter D. Martin, and since 1955 owner, City Lights Bookstore, and editor-in-chief, City Lights Books, San Francisco; delegate, Pan American Cultural Conference, Concepción, Chile, 1960; exhibited paintings at the Ethel Guttmann Gallery, San Francisco, 1985. Received Etna-Taormina Prize (Italy), 1968. Living in San Francisco, California.

**Poetry**

*Pictures of the Gone World,* 1955; revised and enlarged edition, 1995
*A Coney Island of the Mind,* 1958
*Tentative Description of a Dinner Given to Promote the Impeachment of President Eisenhower,* 1958
*One Thousand Fearful Words for Fidel Castro,* 1961
*Berlin,* 1961
*Starting from San Francisco,* 1961; revised edition, 1967
*Where Is Vietnam?* 1965
*Penguin Modern Poets 5* (with poems by Corso, Ginsberg, and Ferlinghetti), 1968
*The Secret Meaning of Things,* 1968
*Tyrannus Nix?* 1969; revised edition, 1973
*Back Roads to Far Places,* 1971
*Open Eye, Open Heart,* 1973
*Who Are We Now?* 1976
*Northwest Ecolog,* 1978
*Landscapes of Living and Dying,* 1979
*The Populist Manifesto* (with an interview with Jean-Jacques Lebel), 1981
*Endless Life: Selected Poems,* 1981
*Over All the Obscene Boundaries: European Poems and Transitions,* 1984
*Wild Dreams of a New Beginning,* 1988
*When I Look at Pictures,* 1990
*These Are My Rivers: New and Selected Poems, 1955–1993,* 1993
*A Far Rockaway of the Heart,* 1997

**Other Writings:** plays (*Unfair Arguments with Existence,* 1963), fiction (*Her,* 1960), nonfiction (*Literary San Francisco: A Pictorial History from Its Beginnings to the Present Day* [with Nancy J. Peters], 1980), correspondence (*Dear Ferlinghetti/ Dear Jack: The Spicer-Ferlinghetti Correspondence,* 1962), translations of Russian poetry (*Dogalypse,* by Andrei Voznesensky, 1972); edited collections of poetry and journals.

**Further Reading**

Charters, Samuel Barclay, *Some Poems/Poets: Studies in American Underground Poetry since 1945,* Berkeley, California: Oyez, 1971

Cherkovski, Neeli, *Ferlinghetti: A Biography,* New York: Doubleday, 1979

Hopkins, Crale D., "The Poetry of Lawrence Ferlinghetti: A Reconsideration," *Italian Americana* 1, no. 1 (Autumn 1974)

Kherdian, David, *Six Poets of the San Francisco Renaissance: Portraits and Checklists,* Fresno, California: Giligia Press, 1967

Meltzer, David, editor, *The San Francisco Poets,* New York: Ballantine Books, 1971

Silesky, Barry, *Ferlinghetti: The Artist in His Time,* New York: Warner, 1990

Skau, Michael, *"Constantly Risking Absurdity": The Writings of Lawrence Ferlinghetti,* Troy, New York: Whitson, 1989

Smith, Larry, *Lawrence Ferlinghetti, Poet-at-Large,* Carbondale: Southern Illinois University Press, 1983

Vestere, Richard, "Ferlinghetti: Rebirth of a Beat Poet," *Identity Magazine* (March 1977)

---

# Carolyn Forché 1950–

Carolyn Forché is a poet, a journalist, a translator, and an international activist whose poems link history and verse together to provide a compelling commentary of witness to pressing issues of social justice. In *Against Forgetting: Twentieth-Century Poetry of Witness* (1993), Forché writes that poets who witnessed and recorded the major armed conflicts of the 20th century performed an important literary and social function by moving acts of atrocity into print circulation. Forché introduces a new term to describe the location of her poetic project, "the social," which is situated between political and personal poetry. "The social," Forché writes, "is a place of resistance and struggle, where books are published, poems read, and protest disseminated. It is the sphere in which claims against the political order are made in the name of justice." Forché's use of this term responds to her discomfort with the narrow American understanding of the word "political."

One of seven children born in working-class Detroit to tool and die maker Michael Sidlosky and his wife, Louise, Forché developed an early interest in the world outside her immediate environment. Her childhood and adolescence were marked by a fascination with foreign cultures, fostered by her relationship with her Slovakian grandmother, Anna, who appears in all three of Forché's books of poetry. Forché avidly considered the relationship among cultures, language, history, and contemporary events, as evidenced by her various areas of academic interest in her study for her B.A. at Michigan State University (1972) in creative writing, English literature, French, Russian, Spanish, Serbo-Croatian, and Tewa. After college, she earned an M.F.A. from Bowling Green State University (1975).

At Michigan State University, Forché took part in protesting the Vietnam War. At age 19, she was briefly married to a fellow protester who was greatly affected by the war. She then fell in love with a poet named John Michael Brennan. His suicide, the effects of the Vietnam War on Forché's friends and companions, and her exploration of her personal history and that of the Pueblo Indians led to her first book of poetry, *Gathering the Tribes* (1976), which won the 1975 Yale Series of Younger Poets Award. At the heart of *Gathering the Tribes* is a longing for community and for the reclamation of lost voices—here her grandmother Anna's and the Pueblo Indians'—that has come to define Forché's poetic style.

In 1977, Forché took a trip to Spain to translate exiled Salvadoran Claribel Alegría's poetry into English. She sought the translation work during a period of writer's block following the publication of *Gathering the Tribes.* Her association with Alegría proved to be a turning point in her poetry career, as she explains in "A Lesson in Commitment." After spending the summer in Spain, Forché returned to San Diego to teach and soon after was awarded a Guggenheim fellowship. One night, Alegría's nephew, Leonel Gomez Vides, appeared at her door with an invitation to travel to El Salvador. Gomez Vides suggested that the role of a North American poet observing the increasingly horrific political situation in El Salvador would be pivotal in exposing the injustices in his country.

From this 72-hour visit, Forché was persuaded to begin a series of journeys to El Salvador over the next two years (1978–80), where she worked with Monsignor Oscar Romero and many others in the resistance movement. With the publication of *The Country Between Us* (1981), which chronicled her experiences in El Salvador, Forché was thrust into the heart of the debate about the role of poetry in North America. A winner of the Lamont Poetry Selection of the American Academy of Poets, this second book was simultaneously praised and panned (particularly by critic Eliot Weinberger) for its political content.

With poems such as "The Colonel" and "Ourselves or Nothing," Forché demonstrated a keen ability to walk the line between fact and fiction, journalism and poetry, calling on and representing voices other than her own in an effort to expose the dire situation in El Salvador. "The Colonel" is a prose poem that recounts the story of a dinner at a military leader's home. Forché tantalizes the reader in the beginning of the poem, stating "What you have heard is true. I was in his house." His tyranny, told in his anger toward North America and realized in a bag of human ears, brought the grisly events of El Salvador to the United States, much as Gomez Vides had hoped. Forché uses the human ears as animate objects to carry a message: "Some of the ears on the floor caught this scrap of his voice. Some of the ears on the floor were pressed to the ground." Foreshadowing her next major poetic work, *The Country Between Us* linked the oppression in El Salvador with prior historical events such as the Holocaust in poems such as "Ourselves or Nothing." Forché ends the poem that recalls, among other places and events, "Belsen, Dachau, Saigon, Phnom Penh / and the one meaning Bridge of Ravens" by emphasizing connections between people. She writes: "we hover in a calm protected world like / netted fish, exactly like netted fish. / It is either the beginning or the end / of the world, and the choice is ourselves / or nothing." Lyrically and imagistically, Forché exposes the commonalities of human history, of countries, and, most important, of people linked by strife, desperation, and hope. Following the publication of *The Country Between Us,* in 1984 she married photographer Henry Mattison, with whom she had a son, Sean, in 1986.

Some critics have placed Forché within a strictly American poetry tradition that includes William Carlos Williams and Theodore Roethke because of her use of voices, particularly those of disenfranchised or "lost" voices within history. Forché's style and content, however, are rarely limited by national borders or strictly American influences. Her work draws on poets as diverse as Alegría, Terrence Des Pres, T.S. Eliot, and Czeslaw Milosz as well as on philosopher Walter Benjamin. Acknowledging both her American literary roots and her fervent interest in cross-cultural poetry, she identifies an affinity with Muriel Rukeyser and Wislawa Szymborska.

These international influences are most strongly realized in Forché's latest two works, *Against Forgetting* and *The Angel of History* (1994). *Against Forgetting* is an anthology of poems gathered from the major conflicts of the 20th century, from the Armenian Genocide to World War II to the ongoing struggle for democracy in China. *The Angel of History,* which draws its title from Walter Benjamin's *Illuminations,* was published some 12 years after *The Country Between Us* as the culmination of more than a decade's worth of collected notebooks and writings in many voices. As a sort of *Waste Land* for the end of the 20th century, the collection works to reconcile memory and history, victory and loss. The poems in this ambitious and difficult work grieve for the people affected by some of the major tragedies of the century, from the atomic bomb and the Holocaust to the death squads of Latin America.

J. ELIZABETH CLARK

**Biography**

Born in Detroit, Michigan, 28 April 1950. Attended Michigan State University, East Lansing, B.A. in international relations and creative writing 1972; Bowling Green State University, Ohio, M.F.A. 1975; Visiting Lecturer, Michigan State University, 1974; Visiting Lecturer, 1975, and Assistant Professor, 1976–78, San Diego State University; Visiting Lecturer, University of Virginia, Charlottesville, 1979, 1982–83; Assistant Professor, 1980, and Associate Professor, 1981, University of Arkansas, Fayetteville; Visiting Lecturer, New York University, 1983, 1985, and Vassar College, Poughkeepsie, New York, 1984; Adjunct Associate Professor, Columbia University, New York, 1984–85; writer-in-residence, State University of New York, Albany, 1985; Visiting Associate Professor, University of Minnesota, Minneapolis, Summer 1985; Visiting Writer, New York State Writers Institute, Skidmore College, Saratoga Springs, New York, 1985; Professor, George Mason University, Fairfax, Virginia, 1988–; on faculty, New York State Summer Writers Institute, Skidmore College, 2000–; journalist for Amnesty International in El Salvador, 1978–80, and Beirut correspondent, "All Things Considered" radio program, 1983; poetry editor, *New Virginia Review,* 1981. Received Yale Series of Younger Poets Award, 1975; *Chicago Review* Award, 1975; Devine Memorial Prize, 1975; Bread Loaf Writers' Conference Tennessee Williams fellowship, 1976; National Endowment for the Arts fellowship, 1977, 1984; Guggenheim fellowship, 1978; Emily Clark Balch Prize (*Virginia Quarterly Review*), 1979; Lamont Poetry Selection Award, 1981; Poetry Society of America Alice Fay di Castagnola Award, 1981; *Los Angeles Times* Book Prize for poetry, 1994; honorary Litt.D., Russell Sage College, Troy, New York, 1985. Living in Fairfax, Virginia.

**Poetry**

*Gathering the Tribes,* 1976
*The Country Between Us,* 1981
*The Angel of History,* 1994

**Other Writings:** essays, nonfiction (*History and Motivations of U.S. Involvement in the Control of the Peasant Movement in El Salvador: The Role of the AIFLD in the Agrarian Reform Process, 1970–1980* [with Reverend Philip Wheaton], 1980), translations of Spanish and French poetry (*Flowers from the Volcano,* 1983; *The Selected Poems of Robert Desnos* [with William Kulik], 1991; *The Complete Rimbaud,* 1995), annotated bibliography (*Women in the Labor Movement, 1835–1925: An Annotated Bibliography* [with Martha Jane Soltow], 1972); edited poetry anthology *(Against Forgetting: Twentieth-Century Poetry of Witness,* 1993).

**Further Reading**

Balakian, Peter, "Carolyn Forché and the Poetry of Witness: Another View," *Agni* 40 (1994)
Forster, Imogen, "Constructing Central America," *Red Letters: A Journal of Cultural Politics* 16 (1984)
Greer, Michael, "Politicizing the Modern: Carolyn Forché in El Salvador and America," *The Centennial Review* 30, no. 2 (1986)
Helle, Anita, "Elegy as History: Three Women Poets 'By the Century's Deathbed,'" *South Atlantic Review* 61, no. 2 (1996)
Mann, John, "Carolyn Forché: Poetry and Survival," *American Poetry* 3, no. 3 (1986)
Mitchell, Nora, and Emily Skoler, "History, Death, Politics, Despair," *New England Review* 17, no. 2 (1995)
Montenegro, David, "Carolyn Forché: An Interview," *American Poetry Review* 17, no. 6 (1988)
Rea, Paul, "The Poet as Witness: Carolyn Forché's Powerful Pleas from El Salvador," *Confluencia* 2, no. 2 (1987)
Smith, Leonora, "Carolyn Forché: Poet of Witness," in *Still the Frame Holds: Essays on Women Poets and Writers,* edited by Sheila Roberts and Yvonne Pacheco Tevis, San Bernardino, California: Borgo Press, 1993
Taft-Kaufman, Jill, "Jill Taft-Kaufman Talks with Carolyn Forché," *Text and Performance Quarterly* 10, no. 1 (1990)

# Robert Francis 1901–87

Highly respected yet never widely known, Robert Francis wrote poetry, an autobiography, a novel, a memoir of Robert Frost, and two collections of short essays on poetry. In "Bouquets" (*Like Ghosts of Eagles,* 1974), he wrote a poetic and personal philosophical credo, asserting the values of minimalism. The poem claims that one flower is sufficient; more would dilute the effect:

> One flower at a time, please
> however small the face.
>
> Two flowers are one flower
> too many, a distraction
> . . . .
> One flower at a time. I want
> to hear what it is saying.

The poem explains the poet's "passion for economy with words" and justifies a life lived simply and intensely, the life that Francis elected for himself.

After graduating from Harvard University in 1923, Francis became a teacher but found the job uncongenial and decided to live thriftily so that he could spend more time writing. He grew much of his own food and lived on minimal earnings obtained chiefly from teaching the violin privately. He had a two-room house, which he named Fort Juniper, built near Amherst, Massachusetts. It had electricity and running water, but Francis chose not to own a telephone, a television, or an automobile for most of his life. His chief pleasures were walking, playing the violin, cultivating his garden, reading, writing, and conversing with friends. Because of his dedication to simplicity and to a high moral standard (he was a vegetarian and a conscientious objector in World War II), he has often been compared to the American Transcendental poet and essayist Henry David Thoreau, who spent a year living simply and economically at Walden Pond and wrote his famous book *Walden* about that experience. Francis lived a simple life yet insisted that, although he read and admired Thoreau, he lived as he did entirely for reasons of thrift and economy and not out of a desire to emulate Thoreau. During World War II, he was assigned to work on a farm in lieu of military service. This was one of his few departures from his beloved Fort Juniper. Another was when he received a grant to live and write in Rome for a year.

He suffered a dry spell from 1944 through 1960, when he had difficulty getting his poems published; *The Face against the Glass* (1952) was printed at his own expense. As his poetry became better known, he was invited to teach poetry workshops in the summers and occasionally gave poetry readings or talks during the rest of the year. Fees for these lectures helped supplement his income.

Francis wrote chiefly short lyrical poems in the realist tradition about rural New England, often finding lessons for human life in the world he observed. He had a gentle yet sly Yankee humor that found expression in his poems and essays. A central theme of his poetry is an examination of nature in both its sunny and its dark aspects. Because of his New England humor and subject matter, he has frequently been compared to Robert Frost, another Northeastern poet who explored similar themes. Indeed, Francis admired Frost's work and considered him a mentor, and the two became friends. According to Andrew Stambuk (1999), Francis learned from Frost but "took Frost's advice [to take a stance of detached engagement] more to heart than Frost ever did."

Another important theme in Francis' work is art and artistry. He praised the art that he found in work done well, such as in athletic events or in chores, in cutting wood or in peeling apples. In "Excellence," he describes the skill of the pole-vaulter who wins because he jumps an inch higher than the second-place competitor. These poems allude to writing poetry as well, as in "Catch" and "Pitcher," which describe both the baseball player pitching a ball and the poet pitching a poem to an audience:

> His art is eccentricity, his aim
> How not to hit the mark he seems to aim at.
>
> . . . He
> Throws to be a moment misunderstood.
>
> Yet not too much. Not errant, arrant, wild,
> But every seeming aberration willed.
>
> Not to, yet still, still to communicate
> Making the batter understand too late.

While many of his poems rhyme, Francis experimented with other writing techniques. One device he used was word counting, in which each line contains the same number of words. The poem "Artist" employs this device:

> He cuts each log in lengths exact
> As truly as truth cuts a fact.
>
> When he has sawed an honest pile
> Of wood, he stops and chops awhile. . . .

The exact log lengths match the exact line lengths of the poem, as the poem celebrates the arts of woodcutting and poetry.

Francis loved language and wordplay, and some of his poems celebrate words. One poem was inspired by arranging compound words to produce a picture of the New England rural landscape:

> backroad leafmold stonewall chipmunk
> underbrush grapevine woodchuck shadblow
>
> woodsmoke cowbarn honeysuckle woodpile
> sawhorse bucksaw outhouse wellsweep
>
> backdoor flagstone bulkhead buttermilk
> candlestick ragrug firedog brownbread. . . . ("Silent Poem")

Alliteration and assonance knit this poem together in a patchwork pattern of sounds, and the traditional New England images generate a visual pattern.

In his autobiography, Francis describes his life and his efforts to publish his work. He wrote two books of short essays that convey his attitudes toward poetry and other poets: *The Satirical Rogue on Poetry* (1968) and *Pot Shots at Poetry* (1980). An interview with Philip Tetreault and Kathy Sewalk-Karcher appears in *Pot Shots.* Here Francis talks about his poetic experiments and his preference for writing about "plain country folk." He explains that he seeks to "confront the actual, recognizable world that we share with one another."

It is time for a reappraisal and revaluation of Robert Francis. Several recent articles about him have appeared. Perhaps this indicates a renewed interest in his work.

KAREN F. STEIN

**Biography**
Born in Upland, Pennsylvania, 12 August 1901. Attended Harvard University, A.B. 1923, Ed.M. 1926; instructor at summer writing workshops and conferences and lecturer at universities throughout the United States. Received Shelley Memorial Award, 1939; Golden Rose of New England Poetry Club, 1942–43; Phi Beta Kappa poet, Tufts University, 1955; Prix de Rome fellowship, American Academy of Arts and Letters, 1957–58; Phi Beta Kappa poet, Harvard University, 1960; Amy Lowell Traveling Scholar, 1967–68; Brandeis University Creative Arts Award in Poetry, 1974; honorary L.H.D., University of Massachusetts, 1970. Died in Northampton, Massachusetts, 13 July 1987.

**Poetry**
*A New Zealand Harp,* 1926
*Stand with Me Here,* 1936
*Valhalla, and Other Poems,* 1938
*The Sound I Listened for,* 1944
*The Face against the Glass,* 1952
*The Orb Weaver,* 1960
*Come Out into the Sun: Poems New and Selected,* 1965
*Like Ghosts of Eagles: Poems, 1966–1974,* 1974
*Robert Francis: Collected Poems, 1936–76,* 1976
*Late Fire, Late Snow: New and Uncollected Poems,* 1992

**Selected Criticism**
*The Satirical Rogue on Poetry,* 1968
*Pot Shots at Poetry,* 1980

**Other Writings:** novel (*We Fly Away,* 1948), autobiography (*The Trouble with Francis,* 1971), interviews (*Frost, A Time to Talk: Conversations and Indiscretions Recorded by Robert Francis,* 1972), memoirs (*Travelling in Amherst: A Poet's Journal, 1931–54,* 1986)

**Further Reading**
McNair, Wesley, "Triumph of Robert Francis," *Harvard Review* 11 (1996)
Stambuk, Andrew, "Learning to Hover: Robert Frost, Robert Francis, and the Poetry of Detached Engagement," *Twentieth Century Literature* 45, no. 4 (1999)
Tetreault, Philip, and Kathy Sewalk-Karcher, "Francis on the Spot: An Interview," in *Pot Shots at Poetry,* by Robert Francis, Ann Arbor: University of Michigan Press, 1980

---

# Kathleen Fraser 1937–

In Kathleen Fraser's poetry and prose, one finds a daring and breathtakingly original writer who pushes the boundaries of what language and form can achieve. Her linguistic and formal experiments, along with her attentiveness to feminist poetics, come together to form the kind of poem that presents itself as an inquiry, a journey—a poem that does not attempt answers but instead raises multiple questions. Fraser is most successful in her exploration at midcareer—in the liberating poems of *Boundayr* (1988), in which she embraces the notion of error as a means of composition, and in "Giotto: Arena," a long multi-voiced poem collected in *When New Time Folds Up* (1993).

Amounting to 13 books of poetry, numerous essays (many of which are collected in *Translating the Unspeakable: Poetry and the Innovative Necessity* [1999]), and translations, Fraser's work represents a significant postmodern moment in which process, language, form, and the experience of gender converge. Feminist journals in the 1970s would seem a likely place for Fraser's work, but American feminism favored a transparent poetic language (one whose meaning was easily understood) and shunned theoretical frameworks. At the same time, Frank O'Hara's New York School, which had once been a sort of home for Fraser, was male dominated and therefore began to feel stifling. In response to the omission of experimental writing from feminist little magazines and the lack of female representation in contemporaneous anthologies of experimental writing, Fraser eventually founded *HOW(ever)* (1983–91), a radical journal of innovative women's writing.

Fraser moved to New York City in 1959 with aspirations of becoming a journalist, shortly after earning a B.A. in English literature from Occidental College in Los Angeles. In New York, she embraced her first love—poetry—and began attending workshops and readings and eventually publishing a "certain kind of good poem," three of which were published in *The New Yorker.* While there, Fraser studied with Stanley Kunitz, whom she found stifling, and Kenneth Koch, whom she found liberating. Koch brought her back to the playfulness of language that she recalled so fondly from her childhood when her father would recite the nonsensical verse of Lewis Carroll. That deep fascination with the malleability of language is evident in most of her collections after 1979. *Each Next* (1980), *Something (Even Human Voices in the Foreground, a Lake)* (1984), and *Boundayr* (1988) all to varying degrees exemplify Fraser's devotion to destabilizing language and interrogating the spaces between traditional notions of meaning and the creation of meaning.

In one of her most important essays, "The Tradition of Marginality" (1989), Fraser describes a powerful memory of one of her first role models, Madame Curie. What appeals to Fraser about Curie is her sense of what is possible outside of conventional knowledge—her quest "for that element which has not been imagined or named" and her finding it, finally, in "an unheard-of departure from the laws of nature" (Fraser, 2000). Like Curie, Fraser had to unlearn her education in order to see a wider field of possibility. The process of unlearning the patriarchal tradition of poetry and its attendant means of expression took the form of unearthing the genealogy of Modernist women poets such as H.D., Gertrude Stein, Mina Loy, Marianne Moore, and Virginia Woolf. This lineage would prove to be increasingly important to Fraser as she became more angered by the omission of women experimentalists from conversations on poetry.

*Magritte Series* (1977), published as a chapbook by Lyn Hejinian, makes a departure from the poetry of Fraser's first collections, *Change of Address, and Other Poems* (1966) and *In Defiance of the Rains* (1969), in which her verse is more aligned with the project of other 1960s feminists; she disrupts poetic convention by articulating the substance and pertinence of women's experiences. However, in *Magritte Series,* Fraser is more conscientiously engaging in an exploration of possibilities of line breaks, the field of the page, language fragmentation, and subversion of normative syntax. "L'Invention Collective" begins,

> of the marigolds, of blue vinyl suitcase, of crud all over the
> stove
> she'd left shiniest
> two to bring light to,
> yes, a shelf in reach where the little both of them could
> begin
> could make his clean start as fresh as Watermelon slice (oh
> where was her life?)

Gertrude Stein's influence is apparent here. The half-rhyme of "slice" and "life" as well as the playfulness of that word pairing bring to mind the lilting and generously mischievous voice in Stein's *Lifting Belly.*

Generally, however, *New Shoes* (1978), which includes "Magritte Series," is considered to be Fraser's transitional text. In it, she moves away from the New York School's investment in the representation of the ordinary and the accidental to a concern with exploring the interconnectedness of gendered experience and language. For Fraser, the different manners of expression emblematic of experimental writing are necessary innovations for her personally and for women's writing as a whole. Her "writing process as a lyric poet [had begun] to seem very limiting" (Hogue, 1999). Also, she was developing a growing interest in the means of speaking through gender. She was asking questions such as "How might the 'theme of interruption [that] has often been alluded to in describing the character of the daily lives of women' [*Translating the Unspeakable*] be represented in the form and voice (or voices) of the poem?"

"The ambivalence," writes Fraser, "for women artists around the issues of children and mates will never be resolved" (Fraser, 2000). The voice of the poem, then, needs to represent, in some way, the nature of that existence. Fraser developed a "newly evolved" poetic form in order to attempt to articulate what that kind of expression might look like. She called it "The Gestate," a form of "unnumbered discrete phrases, unfolding and proliferating as rapidly or as slowly as one's perceptions do . . . while welcoming those unexpected and mysterious and necessary leaps in perception" (Fraser, 2000).

Avant-garde art, by its very nature, exists away from its mainstream counterpart. However, as is well known, many of the most profound artists are to be found in those far reaches. Fraser is there now, writing poetry that is beautiful, challenging, and defiant.

DAWN LUNDY MARTIN

**Biography**

Born in Tulsa, Oklahoma, 22 March 1937. Attended Occidental College, Los Angeles, B.A. in English 1959; Columbia University and New School for Social Research, both New York, 1960–61; San Francisco State University, 1976–77, Doctoral Equivalency in creative writing; Visiting Professor, Writers' Workshop, University of Iowa, Iowa City, 1969–71; writer-in-residence, Reed College, Portland, Oregon, 1971–72; Director of the Poetry Center, 1972–75, Associate Professor of Creative Writing, 1975–78, and since 1978 Professor, San Francisco State University; founding editor, *HOW(ever).* Received YM-YWHA Discovery Award, 1964; National Endowment for the Arts grant, 1969, and fellowship, 1978. Living in San Francisco, California.

**Poetry**

*Change of Address, and Other Poems,* 1966
*Stilts, Somersaults, and Headstands: Game Poems Based on a Painting by Peter Breughel* (for children), 1968
*In Defiance of the Rains,* 1969
*Little Notes to You from Lucas Street,* 1972
*What I Want,* 1974
*Magritte Series,* 1977
*New Shoes,* 1978
*Each Next,* 1980
*Something (Even Human Voices in the Foreground, a Lake),* 1984
*Notes Preceding Trust,* 1987
*Boundayr,* 1988
*When New Time Folds Up,* 1993
*Il Cuore: The Heart: Selected Poems, 1970–1995,* 1995

**Other Writings:** essays (*Translating the Unspeakable: Poetry and the Innovative Necessity,* 1999), children's literature; edited collections of essays (*Feminist Poetics: A Consideration of the Female Construction of Language,* 1984).

**Further Reading**

Fraser, Kathleen, *Translating the Unspeakable: Poetry and the Innovative Necessity,* Tuscaloosa: University of Alabama Press, 2000
Hogue, Cynthia, "An Interview with Kathleen Fraser," *Contemporary Literature* 39, no. 1 (1999)
Juhasz, Suzanne, "The Journal as Source and Model for Feminist Art: The Example of Kathleen Fraser," *Frontiers* 8, no. 1 (1984)
Kinnahan, Linda A., *Poetics of the Feminine: Authority and*

*Literary Tradition in William Carlos Williams, Mina Loy, Denise Levertov, and Kathleen Fraser,* Cambridge and New York: Cambridge University Press, 1994

Taylor, Linda, A., "'A Seizure of Voice': Language Innovation and a Feminist Poetics in the Works of Kathleen Fraser," *Contemporary Literature* 33, no. 2 (1992)

---

# Free Verse

Free verse is poetry that is structured in ways other than traditional forms of meter, line, rhyme, and stanza. A poet writing free verse may devise any sort of structuring system but may not eliminate structure nor separate structure from meaning; most readers still expect coherence and congruence of form and meaning in a well-constructed poem.

In the absence of a governing metrical system the vast majority of 20th-century free verse in English draws structure from the phonological and syntactic systems of the language. Free verse often incorporates traditional forms but is freed to varying extents, depending on the poem or style, from the technical constraints of formal tradition. Many free-verse poems are consciously written against the background of the formal tradition, and this background is often brought powerfully into the foreground. In free verse, then, meaning often depends in part on its rejection of the formal verse tradition. Because of its relationship to the formal tradition, a definition of free verse must include historical as well as structural considerations.

Free verse was a rare experiment in the 17th and 18th centuries. In the 19th century British Romantics accelerated experimentation, devising new structures from traditional metrical, line, rhyme, and stanza forms. By the 20th century free verse dominated American poetry, almost subsuming it during the midcentury decades. American free verse has evolved largely from the verse Walt Whitman first published in *Leaves of Grass* in 1855; Whitman's long lines, structured by rhythmic phrasing in which fragments reminiscent of metrical forms appear, echo biblical and Homeric cadences. In a move to identify and write a distinctly American poetry, Whitman proclaimed traditional forms "dead" and the American poem free of its British and European past.

Since this beginning, American free verse has been associated with American themes: independence, freedom, democratic individualism, self-expression, inclusion, and growth and expansiveness of self and nation. Declaring the American poem to be true and living poetry, Whitman called for a looser, natural structure in the preface to *Leaves of Grass:*

> The poetic quality is not marshalled in rhyme or uniformity . . . but in the life of these. . . . The rhyme and uniformity of perfect poems show the free growth of metrical laws and bud from them as unerringly and loosely as lilacs or roses on a bush, and take shapes as compact as the shapes of chestnuts and oranges[.]

American poets after Whitman have followed his expansive attempt to create a collage of all life and experience. The line as rhythmic contour and stanza length and shape have been the two main avenues for expressive reshaping, allowing a poet to diverge from conventional forms. Rhyme did not disappear, for the most part, but turned inward from line-end.

Whitman's rhythmic phrases established the basic unit types that would be used thereafter, most often shortened and given tighter contexts. His rhythmic units occur in several types, each with a different accentual contour cut from the cloth of a literate spoken language as regularized shapes of the phonological phrase, a sound unit over which an accentual contour moves to highlight the prominent word in which meaning is focused. Whitman's verse tends to fall into units with two or three prominence peaks (accents) in a rising contour, with a fair number of one-peak and four-peak units. Because of isochrony, the long and short phrasal units create various speeds, allowing for great expressive variety, a rhythm that William Carlos Williams likened to the sea's advance and retreat on a shore. In the poems of 1860 and after, the greater regularity of unit types often gives the verse a highly musical quality.

Within Whitman's phrasal units arise fragments of traditional meters such as ballad meter or iambic trimeter or pentameter, often at the opening or close of a stanza. But no single type of metrical form ever becomes dominant for more than a few feet, so that rhythmic phrasing carries the dominant structure forward, absorbing the metrical fragments into the unit types. Traditional stanzas of couplets, tercets, quatrains, and so on are almost absent, replaced by long lines of phrasal units. Full rhyme is absent or suggested in assonance. Sonnets, for example, need not have 14 lines or traditional rhyme scheme. This short lyric illustrates the main features of Whitman's free verse practice, the prelude to American free verse:

> When I heard the learn'd astronomer,
> When the proofs, the figures, were ranged in columns
> before me,
> When I was shown the charts and diagrams, to add, divide,
> and measure them,
> When I sitting heard the astronomer where he lectured with
> much applause in
> the lecture-room,
> How soon unaccountable I became tired and sick,
> Till rising and gliding out I wander'd off by myself,
> In the mystical moist night air, and from time to time,
> Look'd up in perfect silence at the stars.

The oratorical tone is delivered in heightened cadences, in virtue of their existences in lines of poetry and in the accumulation of accentual units (phonological phrases) possessing most often two or three peaks. A pensive, measured tone is enforced by frequent commas, which slow the rhythm of thought, and longer lines without commas, which must therefore be read more rapidly, with fewer accents and many unaccented syllables, as many as five in a row. The sheer accumulation of unaccented syllables precludes scanning in metrical feet. Iambic and anapestic feet can be heard, but rarely more than three of a kind in a row. The exception is the last line, which achieves a strict iambic pentameter that is striking in this context of long cadenced lines. The pentameter closes the stanza in a traditional form, as if to reinforce with traditional finality the meaning of wandering outside the stuffy lecture room, where reason and tradition prevail and do not satisfy the speaker, into the "mystical . . . night." Traditional rhyme is also absent, but frequent assonance occurs mid-line and at line-end. The first line offers occurrences of "er" in two of the three strong beats and again in a light beat syllable at the end of the line. This sound is repeated frequently throughout the poem and occurs at the end of the poem mid-line ("perfect") and with a slight variation in the last word ("stars"). While avoiding end-rhyme, assonance at line-end, particularly "m," is common. The verse itself is comprised of eight lines of narrative meditation typical of a Petrarchan sonnet octave. Was Whitman thinking of the poem as a sonnet? He considered any short lyric a sonnet, rejecting form as definitive of any poem. But here he seems to write an octave and reject the sestet, which typically explores and complicates the rhetorical argument raised in the octave, perhaps because, as the poet says, there can be no argument but silence beyond seeing the stars in the vastness of the night sky. Because there can be no argument, the sestet is silence—not there.

Whitman's style of verse became quickly and widely popular, imitated by a large number of poets. Few wrote with much mastery, seeming not to sense Whitman's structure and choosing to use little structure of their own. Notable exceptions are Stephen Crane, Carl Sandburg, Vachel Lindsay, and Edgar Lee Masters. By the turn of the century free verse was hugely popular, with Masters the most widely read poet in America. Masters himself satirized the "little" poet who too late realizes he spent his life writing little French stanzas and "such little iambics / While Homer and Whitman roared in the pines" ("Petit the Poet," in *Spoon River Anthology,* 1916).

The prevalence and popularity of free verse of the type Masters wrote—loose conversational lines with little more than a conversational structure—spurred the generation of poets led by Ezra Pound to reject the long Whitmanian phrasal line. The experiments in free-verse form conducted by several of these poets established the major styles of free verse that were written and explored further in the ensuing decades. Pound's principles for writing verse, published in the *Imagist* in 1912, called for short poems in which image and sound structure fused intellect and emotion. To produce this effect Pound advocated "Direct treatment of the 'thing,'" banned any words extraneous to the treatment, and advocated composing "in the sequence of the musical phrase, not in the sequence of the metronome." Discursive material would be thereby eliminated as well as any words needed merely to fill out a metrical pattern or explain something as opposed to presenting directly. Free-verse cadence or a mix of metrical forms would replace a galloping regularity.

The next year, 1913, Marianne Moore, young and just starting out, traveled to New York City and viewed the first exhibit of Cubist art in the country. Taken with it, she began to call her poems "compositions" and began building a new line that was defined both visually and prosodically. Her early drafts of "The Fish," for instance, enclose the line as in a fence, a rhyme at each end:

> Wade through black jade.
> Of the crow blue mussel shells, one
> Keeps adjusting the ash heaps."

The first published version of the poem (*The Egoist,* 1918) maintains the rhyme pattern in quatrains. By 1919, for publication in *Others,* she had opened the tight quatrains into spacious sestets by lifting a line-initial rhyme up above its previous location into a line of its own. In this she had settled on her famous line, determined by strict syllabic count and visual disposition on the page, just as she was about to give up the manner for a freer verse at Pound's urging regarding a draft of "A Grave" she had sent him. Originally arranged in three septets of lines ranging from 10 to 19 syllables each, Moore rewrote "A Grave" more loosely, with end-stopped long lines similar to Whitman's. It is the most unmeasured of her poems, fitting the subject: the inability for the human being to take the sea's measure. The poems following it determine their degrees of visual measure variously line by line and poem by poem, with a return after 1930 to a syllabic patterning less strict than in her early work. Her readings, as marked on the copies she used for the purpose, indicate she deliberately ignored line boundaries in sound structure. Her frequent internal rhymes and controlled rhythmic phrasing influenced many late-century poets (James Dickey, Larry Lieberman, Mary Oliver) as well as her contemporaries, such as William Carlos Williams, whom she knew.

Following the publication of Moore's syllabic poems Williams began to enjamb lines that previously had consisted of a single (phonological) phrase. Until that point Williams had sounded like Whitman with shorter lines (Gates, 1987). *Spring and All,* written in 1922 and published in 1923 in response to *The Waste Land* (for which he had an intense distaste), exhibits Williams' first sustained effort at a new structural style. By breaking lines in the middle of syntactic units but retaining the integrity of the line, a double meaning, often a double image, resulted from the two syntactic/semantic units. Williams thought of himself as forming a new prosodic unit, which he called at first the "rhythmic unit." His prosody creates a double rhythm and a double meaning, both of which register in the mind of the reader despite the fact that they cannot be read aloud simultaneously (although Williams apparently tried). Here is a well-known lyric from *Spring and All:*

> so much depends
> upon
>
> a red wheel
> barrow
>
> glazed with rain
> water
>
> beside the white
> chickens

Williams establishes and maintains a pattern of a two-stressed line followed by a one-stressed line throughout. The lines could also scan as two iambic pentameters if not for the back-to-back unstressed syllables in "water / beside." The poem counts on the traditional integrity of line for its effects, so that when the eye hits "wheel," "rain," and "white," one image and its meaning arise in the mind only to be revised to another image and meaning. When read silently, both the first and the revised intonation pattern can exist in the mind, but when read aloud, the voice cannot read the intonations for both meanings. A reader must either choose between the two or give an intonation that does not commit to either, which is what Williams did when he read his poems aloud. Williams' other poems do not bear such a strict rhythmic pattern, but they do depend on the effects of the double meaning caused by radical syntactic breaks.

Spanning these changes was the poetry of T.S. Eliot, whose early composition "The Love Song of J. Alfred Prufrock" had helped to spur Pound's Imagist directives. Both he and Pound continued to experiment with and call for combining rhythmic traditions, of English and other national poetries. Poetic rhythm, they suggested, should be formed of fragments taken from tradition:

> The poem comes before the form, in the sense that a form grows out of an attempt to say something; just as a system of prosody is only a formulation of the identities in the rhythms of a succession of poets influenced by each other. (T.S. Eliot, "The Music of Poetry," 1942)

*The Waste Land* contains passages of alliterative stressed verse, ballad, blank verse, and conversational and biblical rhythmic phrasing, all running through a free-verse fabric. Stanza forms are fragments as well: ballad quatrains, heroic couplets, and a fragmented sonnet at the end of Part III.

American free verse in the remainder of the 20th century further explored the territory blazed by these poets. Langston Hughes adapted Whitman to a shorter line and incorporated blues structures. The Black Mountain poets explored rhythmic and visual relations initiated by Williams, and the Beat poets returned to Whitman's long line, often making it even longer and intoning it in one breath.

Most of this poetry relies on visual shape, the convention of line integrity, and rhythmic phrasing for the quantitative sound structure, with the phrases themselves, but not the whole context, scannable as traditional metrical feet. Eliot and Pound proclaimed this the modern manner of writing: the incorporation of metrical traditions and rhythms, the "ghost of meter" appearing as bricks, and brick laid on brick in evolving structures and styles.

ROSEMARY GATES WINSLOW

*See also* Prosody and Versification

**Further Reading**


Berg, S., and R. Mezey, *Naked Poetry: Recent American Poetry in Open Forms,* Indianapolis, Indiana: Bobbs Merrill, 1969

Bollobás, Eniko, *Tradition and Innovation in American Free Verse: Whitman to Duncan,* Budapest: Akadémiai Kiadó, 1986

Cooper, G. Burns, *Mysterious Music: Rhythm and Free Verse,* Stanford, California: Stanford University Press, 1998

Cushman, Stephen, *William Carlos Williams and the Meanings of Measure,* New Haven, Connecticut: Yale University Press, 1985

Gates, Rosemary L., "Forging an American Poetry from Free Verse: Williams after Whitman," *Poetics Today* 8, nos. 3–4 (1987)

Hartman, Charles O., *Free Verse: An Essay on Prosody,* Princeton, New Jersey: Princeton University Press, 1980

Longenbach, James, *Modern Poetry after Modernism,* New York: Oxford University Press, 1997

New, Elisa, *The Line's Eye: Poetic Experience, American Sight,* Cambridge, Massachusetts: Harvard University Press, 1998

Perloff, Marjorie, *The Poetics of Indeterminacy: Rimbaud to Cage,* Princeton, New Jersey: Princeton University Press, 1981


---

# Robert Frost 1874–1963

There has long been a discrepancy between the popular image and the actual reality of Robert Frost, the man and poet. In the popular consciousness, he is seen as a cracker-barrel versifier, a grandfatherly farmer-poet full of practical Yankee wit and wisdom. The public likes his poems with settings in the picturesque New England countryside and honors him as one of America's historic luminaries for having graced a U.S. postage stamp. He is probably best remembered for having read a poem at the inauguration of President John F. Kennedy.

However, those who have studied Frost closely have known a darker reality in the man. To them, he is ironic, skeptical, and competitive. He is a man who has suffered and caused the suffering of others close to him. If his inner demons appear to be under control, it is only because his iron will and mocking intelligence take pride in not showing weakness. The easy moral lessons that his poems appear to provide on a first reading turn out to be complex and ambiguous on closer inspection.

The vision of something "terrifying" associated with Frost was first articulated by Lionel Trilling in a speech that he gave at a dinner on 26 March 1959 celebrating Frost's 85th birthday. Portions of the speech were reprinted by J. Donald Adams in the *New York Times Book Review* on 12 April of that year. Adams offered a reply to some of the things that Trilling had said about Frost, prompting a series of letters to the editor published in the 26 April issue of the *Book Review* agreeing with Adams and condemning Trilling's speech. The letters were written by prominent individuals, many from the field of literature. The stir caused by this exchange, no doubt brief and minor by contemporary standards, reverberates to this day in Frost scholarship. Although Trilling's speech appears now quite harmless, the entire episode shows to what extent the image of America's beloved Frost was revered and protected by loyal readers.

The English were the first to recognize Frost as a major poet. Frustrated with his life in the United States, at 38 years of age Frost sold the farm in Derry, New Hampshire, that he had inherited from his grandfather and moved with his family to England. There, for the first time in his life, he had the pleasure and stimulation of literary discussions with other poets. He met several Georgian poets (Lascelles Abercrombie, Wilfred Gibson, F.S. Flint, and Edward Thomas) and Imagists (T.E. Hulme and Ezra Pound). David Nutt and Company in London brought out his first two books, *A Boy's Will* (1913) and *North of Boston* (1914). By the time Frost returned to the United States in 1915, he had found an American publisher, Henry Holt and Company, and the beginnings of a world-class career. Before his death 48 years later in 1963, Frost would publish nine more books of poetry, hold many appointments as poet-in-residence and visiting professor at leading American colleges and universities (notably Harvard, Dartmouth, and Michigan), and earn numerous honorary doctorates, awards, and other honors, including the Congressional Medal and four Pulitzer Prizes.

Frost was a master of the lyric and the meditation narrative forms of poetry. He saw himself as part of the great tradition of English literature and was a traditionalist in his use of meter, rhythm, rhyme scheme, stanzaic patterns, and occasionally blank verse. However, in temperament and philosophical point of view, Frost was a Modernist. Like many of his contemporaries whose formative experiences were shaped by a post-Darwinian world marked by industrial urbanization, conflicting ethnic and political values culminating in world war, and a growing doubt about customary religious practice, Frost was pessimistic about mankind's ideals. His poems articulate the struggle of a man on his own in an indifferent universe trying to come to terms with loss, doubt, and fear.

Skeptical about traditionalist supports available to other men, Frost relies on the individual and existentialist values of reason, courage, sympathy, and commitment to make meaning out of things. "Design" is probably his most powerful expression of the individual confronting cosmic indifference. It is a Petrarchan sonnet that rhetorically asks the question, "Is the world designed and protected by a creator?" The poet pictures a world in miniature where all the living elements appear unnatural and out of place. Death and nihilism seem to rule, and the poet dares the reader to find a divine plan in any of it.

Another sonnet localizes this cosmic sense of loneliness and despair into the individual heart and soul of man. "Acquainted with the Night" is a dark portrait of the homeless and isolated self, drifting in an urban wasteland searching for love. Using Dante's terza rima to write an irregular sonnet of four three-line stanzas and a couplet, Frost creates a modern vision of hell on earth. A man filled with guilt and longing wanders on a rainy night unable to look the night watchman in the eye as he searches for a guide, a word, a feeling that will offer peace. In the end, all he finds is "One luminary clock against the sky" ironically proclaiming "the time was neither wrong nor right." Instead of unity and wholeness, the poet offers relativity and instability. The poem ends with the same existential affirmation that opened the poem: "I have been one acquainted with the night." This is the human condition, the poet seems to say, and our search for release is futile. Frost's craftsmanship is uniquely evident in this poem, as the "fractured" sonnet form of the poem is a perfect match for the disturbing Modernist content.

One of Frost's most popular and often-quoted poems is "Stopping by Woods on a Snowy Evening." Although popularly thought of as a homey statement of endurance and commitment by a busy but devoted man, the poem is actually more skeptical and the lesson less assuring. Frost the word magician lulls the reader with a picture postcard setting for the poem and a simple singsong musical sound. Beneath the sugary exterior of four four-line stanzas of regular iambic tetrameter with a linking rhyme scheme is the voice of a poet confronting the emptiness of existence and contemplating self-destruction as an easy escape. The isolation of the first stanza emphasizes his detachment physically and psychologically from the community. He refers with some apprehension to an absentee land speculator who owns the vacant country land and would be suspicious if he knew the poet were eyeing his property. In the second and third stanzas, the small horse, hardworking and practical, urges the poet to the security of his farm on this darkest night by giving "his harness bells a shake." The setting, although picturesque, is hostile to man and beast and void of comfort. The poet ignores the warning and listens to the only other sound there is "Of easy wind and downy flake." His next remark in the fourth stanza, that "The woods are lovely, dark, and deep," seems to counter the mere physical concerns of the horse with the poet's higher aesthetic response to his environment. However, the reader wonders why the poet juxtaposes this immediately with the line "But I have promises to keep." Promises, obligations, and commitments to life are what rescue him, we realize, not from his contemplation of natural beauty but from his wish to escape into it, to lose his identity in it. The famous repetition of "And miles to go before I sleep," which closes the poem, emphasizes that he must wait not for the ordinary sleep found in a secure homestead but for the deep endless sleep of death found in nature. The existentialist poet accepts his fate and his life's work and moves on.

In Frost's poetry, one finds that there is hope for the meaningful life and expectation of human solidarity in primarily one thing: work. This is expressed, for example, in a group of well-made meditation narratives: "After Apple Picking," "Mowing," "The Tuft of Flowers," and "The Wood Pile." In each poem, Frost describes an experience relating to work in an agricultural or rural setting and expands on it to make the point, among others, that it is only in the job well done that one finds something to hold on to. The rural tasks that Frost writes about of haying, harvesting, and wood chopping are symbolic of all human labor. Whatever the work is, Frost seems to say, it is never easy. Furthermore, it is physically and psychically exhausting and full of frustration and tedium. However, Frost affirms that work is all we have that connects us with the world and with one another. Frost's respect for work goes beyond the traditional Yankee notion of profit making or the New England Puritan's idea of punishment resulting from the fall of man. For Frost, work is the existential acceptance of the life that must be lived. An individual finds position in the world through work, shares in the common heritage of all humans to work, and develops meaning and understanding through the necessity of doing something well.

Mostly from letters and recorded conversations, we know that the English writers of greatest influence on Frost were Chaucer,

Shakespeare, Wordsworth, Browning, and Arnold. Among the Americans, the most important to him were Dickinson, Thoreau, and Emerson. He referred to Dickinson as the greatest of all woman poets, and his much-used copy of her poems is filled with scribbles and pencil marks next to favorite poems. Besides the ideas of *Walden,* he valued what he called the "unversified poetry of *Walden.*" However, it was Emerson who was Frost's greatest mentor. Not only was Frost inspired by Emerson's notions of individuality, self-identity, and freedom, but he admired Emerson's colloquial style. He writes that the style of Emerson's poem "Monadnoc" taught more to him about the art of writing than anything else.

Frost's poetic theories are scattered in letters, speeches, book prefaces, and several essays. Although his ideas about poetry do not have the far-reaching cultural implications of a T.S. Eliot, they show that Frost was a serious, self-conscious theorist about his craft. Like Eliot, Frost was temperamentally conservative with a deep respect for the tradition of English poetry and for the objectivity of the artist. Sounding like Eliot in his essay "Tradition and the Individual Talent," Frost wrote, "A poem is best read in the light of all other poems ever written. We read A the better to read B. . . . We read B the better to read C, C the better to read D, D the better to go back and get something more out of A. Progress is not the aim, but circulation" ("The Prerequisites," *Selected Prose,* 1966).

Once criticized as a young poet because his poems were considered too close to plain talk, Frost was struck by the truth that it was, in fact, plain talk that he was trying to capture in his poems. This idea is best expressed in his principle of versification known as "the sound of sense." Frost sought to capture the unique patterns of common speech and the tone of voice of an actual character speaking in the poem. This reproduction of actual talk formed the basis of the poem's meaning that the poet reworked in meter. As he describes it, "An ear and an appetite for these sounds of sense is the first qualification of a writer, be it of prose or verse. But if one is to be a poet, he must learn to get cadences by skillfully breaking the sounds of sense with all their irregularity of accent across the regular beat of the meter" (To John T. Bartlett, 4 July 1913, *Selected Letters,* 1964).

Frost beautifully described the purpose of poetry in an essay he wrote to serve as a preface for the first edition of his collected poems. In "The Figure a Poem Makes" (1939), he wrote that a poem produces "a clarification of life—not necessarily a great clarification, . . . but a momentary stay against confusion." For Frost, the poem gives back to the reader what the confusion and pain of living has caused him to forget. "No tears in the writer, no tears in the reader. . . . For me the initial delight is in the surprise of remembering something I didn't know I knew."

Frost's centrality in American literature is assured. Research and scholarship relating to his life and work continue to develop, and analysis of his poetry continues to serve the interests of changing scholarly trends. Frost understood deeply the forces of his age and raised an independent voice to evaluate them. Anthologies of American literature and the world's great poetry always include sizable selections of Frost. It seems clear that his insights into the hearts and minds of humanity, sometimes dark but always truthful, will continue to be valued as long as readers of poetry flourish.

Paul J. Ferlazzo

*See also* Prosody and Versification

**Biography**

Born in San Francisco, California, 26 March 1874. Attended Dartmouth College, Hanover, New Hampshire, 1892; Harvard University, Cambridge, Massachusetts, 1897–99; mill worker and teacher, Lawrence, Massachusetts, 1892–97; farmer, Derry, New Hampshire, 1900–12; English teacher, Pinkerton Academy, Derry, 1905–11; conducted course in psychology, State Normal School, Plymouth, New Hampshire, 1911–12; poet-in-residence, Amherst College, Massachusetts, 1916–20; Visiting Lecturer, Wesleyan University, Middletown, Connecticut, 1920, University of Michigan, Ann Arbor, 1921–23, 1925–26, Dartmouth College, Yale University, New Haven, Connecticut, and Harvard University; co-founder, Bread Loaf School, Middlebury College, Vermont, 1920; poetry consultant, Library of Congress, Washington, D.C., 1958; presented and read presidential inaugural poem, "The Gift Outright," 1961. Received Levinson Prize (*Poetry,* Chicago), 1922; Pulitzer Prize, 1924, 1931, 1937, 1943; New England Poetry Club Golden Rose, 1928; Loines Award, 1931; American Academy Gold Medal, 1939; Academy of American Poets fellowship, 1953; Sarah Josepha Hale Award, 1956; Emerson-Thoreau Medal, 1959; U.S. Senate Citation of Honor, 1960; Poetry Society of America Gold Medal, 1962; MacDowell Medal, 1962; Congressional Gold Medal, 1962; Bollingen Prize, 1963; received honorary degrees from 44 colleges and universities; member, National Institute of Arts and Letters, 1916; member, American Academy. Died in Boston, Massachusetts, 29 January 1963.

**Poetry**

*A Boy's Will,* 1913
*North of Boston,* 1914
*Mountain Interval,* 1916
*Selected Poems,* 1923
*New Hampshire: A Poem with Notes and Grace Notes,* 1923
*West-Running Brook,* 1928
*Collected Poems,* 1930; revised edition, 1939
*A Further Range,* 1936
*Selected Poems,* 1936
*A Witness Tree,* 1942
*Come In and Other Poems,* edited by Louis Untermeyer, 1943; revised edition, as *The Road Not Taken,* 1951
*A Masque of Reason,* 1945
*Poems,* 1946
*Steeple Bush,* 1947
*A Masque of Mercy,* 1947
*Complete Poems of Robert Frost,* 1949
*Aforesaid,* 1954
*Selected Poems,* 1955
*In the Clearing,* 1962
*You Come Too: Favorite Poems for Young Readers,* 1967
*The Poetry of Robert Frost,* edited by Edward Connery Lathem, 1969
*The Pocket Book of Robert Frost Poems,* 1971
*Robert Frost: Poetry and Prose,* edited by Edward Connery Lathem and Lawrence Thompson, 1972

*Robert Frost's Poetry Written Before 1913: A Critical Edition,* edited by Andrew Angyal, 1976
*A Swinger of Birches: Poems of Robert Frost for Young People,* 1982
*Birches* (for children), 1988
*Frost in Spring: An Anthology in Memoriam,* edited by John H. Morgan, 1989
*Sweet and Bitter Bark: Selected Poems by Robert Frost,* 1992
*Collected Poems, Prose and Plays,* 1995
*Early Poems,* edited by Robert Faggen, 1998
*Mountain Interval; and, New Hampshire: Poems,* 1999

**Selected Criticism**
*Frost on Writing,* edited by Elaine Barry, 1973

**Other Writings:** plays (*The Cow's in the Corn,* 1929), essays (*Selected Prose,* edited by Hyde Cox and Edward Connery Lathem, 1966), children's literature, correspondence (*Family Letters of Robert and Elinor Frost,* edited by Arnold Grade, 1972).

**Further Reading**

Bloom, Harold, editor, *Robert Frost,* New York: Chelsea House, 1986
Brower, Reuben, *The Poetry of Robert Frost: Constellations of Intention,* New York: Oxford University Press, 1963
Gerber, Philip L., editor, *Critical Essays on Robert Frost,* Boston: G.K. Hall, 1982
Kearns, Katherine, *Robert Frost and a Poetics of Appetite,* Cambridge and New York: Cambridge University Press, 1994
Lentricchia, Frank, *Robert Frost: Modern Poetics and the Landscapes of Self,* Durham, North Carolina: Duke University Press, 1975
Lynen, John, *The Pastoral Art of Robert Frost,* New Haven, Connecticut: Yale University Press, 1960
Marcus, Mordecai, *The Poems of Robert Frost: An Explication,* Boston: G.K. Hall, 1991
Parini, Jay, *Robert Frost: A Life,* London: Heinemann, 1998; New York: Holt, 1999
Poirier, Richard, *Robert Frost: The Work of Knowing,* Oxford and New York: Oxford University Press, 1977
Potter, James L., *Robert Frost Handbook,* University Park: Pennsylvania State University Press, 1980

## Desert Places

Robert Frost lacks neither critical nor popular acclaim. Yet if in 1959 Lionel Trilling could startle Frost's admirers by adjudging him "a terrifying poet," that is because Frost, then as now, has seemed to many readers a crusty New Englander dispensing folksy wisdom. Yet however disturbing Trilling's assessment, perhaps more dismaying was Yvor Winters' contention that Frost is "a spiritual drifter" who flirts with profound moral questions that he fails to answer seriously or carefully. "Desert Places" reveals the extent to which Trilling and Winters are correct in their assessments.

"Desert Places," which appeared in 1934 in *The American Mercury* magazine before being collected in *A Further Range* (1936), was written during a dark period for both Frost, plagued by a series of illnesses, and the United States, caught in the grip of the Great Depression (see Parini, 1999). In keeping with this personal and national depression, "Desert Places" presents the poet brought up short during a solitary journey by a sight that gives him pause:

> Snow falling and night falling fast, oh, fast
> In a field I looked into going past,
> And the ground almost covered smooth in snow,
> But a few weeds and stubble showing last.

What captures the poet's attention is the disappearance of the familiar world beneath the descending dark and snow (both symbols of death and loss). Possibly more troubling is the erasure of the specifically man-made world represented by the field (the "stubble" indicating its cultivation), which, as Albert J. von Frank (1974) explains, figures "nature given purpose and identity by man."

In stanza two, the field becomes an obliterated "it" subsumed by the dark chaos of the encircling trees. All signs of life are likewise extinguished: "All animals are smothered in their lairs." In this scene of increasing gloom and lifeless nothingness, even the poet's sense of self becomes attenuated: "I am too absent-spirited to count; / The loneliness includes me unawares." Yet stanza three insists that "lonely as it is, that loneliness / Will be more lonely ere it will be less," both the darkening, snow-deepening landscape and the poet's spirit reduced to a condition of impersonality, inarticulateness, and emptiness: "A blanker whiteness of benighted snow / With no expression, nothing to express."

Stanza four opens with a reference that has caused disagreement among Frost's critics: "They cannot scare me with their empty spaces / Between stars—on stars where no human race is." To whom does the pronoun that begins this passage refer? Cleanth Brooks and Robert Penn Warren (*Understanding Poetry,* 1938) suggest that the reference is to astronomers; von Frank, on the other hand, argues that the pronoun refers to "nature itself" most generally and to the woods of stanza two more specifically (von Frank, 1974). The woods seem the likeliest candidate, having served earlier as a synecdoche of what threatens to overwhelm whatever meaning and order humans have managed to scratch on the earth's surface (those plowed fields). However, reference to astronomers does make sense insofar as it is they whose findings have encouraged a view of the universe inhospitable to humankind. However, if the reference is vague, Frost's point is clear: he cannot be frightened by nature's lack of human meaning, its essential otherness, because he has within himself his own "desert" (forsaken, deserted, and inhospitable) places, his own alienated loneliness: "I have it in me so much nearer home / To scare myself with my own desert places" (on Frost's preoccupation with solitude, see Strong [1988] and Wallace [1984]).

The poem that emerges from this summary would seem to validate Trilling's view of Frost as a terrifying poet who here conjures a wintry, indifferent, lifeless world in which the poet stands spiritless, empty, and alone. "[B]enighted" in line 11 furnishes additional gloom insofar as it carries the meaning not only of something overtaken by darkness but also of intellectual or moral ignorance. Indeed, James Ellis (1965), arguing that Frost took his title from a passage in Nathaniel Hawthorne's *The Scarlet Letter,* sees in the poem the depiction of a "moral wilderness" the response to which is "anguish." Edward Stone (1974), extending Ellis' reading, finds "Desert Places" a rebellious exercise in "illicit" atheism.

Yet it is possible to read the poem otherwise. If it is true, as Frost insists, that what he sees is not especially frightening to him because he recognizes within himself the spiritual or emotional or intellectual equivalent of these external "desert places," the poem that he has written belies by its passionate existence its contention that the poet is an "absent-spirited," expressionless blank with "nothing to express." Further, Frost is commonsensical enough to observe that the scene "Will be more lonely *ere* it will be less" (line ten, emphasis added); that is, this state of mind will pass with the return of day, of spring, or after a thaw. Just so, his bleak mood, although deepening, will doubtless also pass. Indeed, Paul A. Orlov (1986) finds "Desert Places" transcending nihilism and "subverting the grim subject matter [Frost's] poem is 'about'" by the poet's insistence on meaningful artistic design (the poem is, for example, rhymed and metered) and on the significance of interpreted experience (what Frost offers and found important enough to do). Similarly, von Frank (1974) deems the poem modern in its implicit demonstration that nothing has meaning for good or ill until the human mind supplies it and that the mind's unlimited freedom in rendering things meaningful is a powerful tribute to the poet's "shaping imagination."

If "Desert Places" remains a terrifying poem, this is less because it reveals a set of existential circumstances inimical to human well-being and more because it shows us our implication in whatever our lives and world come to signify. If Frost is spiritually adrift in this poem, he is so only if we conclude that reliance on one's own meaning-making abilities constitutes the espousal of an illicit self-apotheosis.

BROOKE HORVATH

**Further Reading**

Ellis, James, "Frost's 'Desert Places' and Hawthorne," *The English Record* 15 (1965)

Orlov, Paul A., "The World's Disorder and the Word's Design in Two Poems by Robert Frost," *Journal of the Midwest Modern Language Association* 19, no. 2 (1986)

Parini, Jay, *Robert Frost: A Life,* London: Heinemann, 1998; New York: Holt, 1999

Poirier, Richard, *Robert Frost: The Work of Knowing,* Oxford and New York: Oxford University Press, 1977

Stone, Edward, "Other 'Desert Places': Frost and Hawthorne," in *Frost: Centennial Essays II,* edited by Jac L. Tharpe, Jackson: University Press of Mississippi, 1976

Strong, Paul, "Robert Frost's 'Nighthawks'/Edward Hopper's 'Desert Places,'" *Colby Library Quarterly* 24, no. 1 (1988)

Trilling, Lionel, "A Speech on Robert Frost: A Cultural Episode," in *Robert Frost: A Collection of Critical Essays,* edited by James M. Cox, Englewood Cliffs, New Jersey: Prentice Hall, 1962

von Frank, Albert J., "'Nothing That Is': A Study of Frost's 'Desert Places,'" in *Frost: Centennial Essays II,* edited by Jac L. Tharpe, Jackson: University Press of Mississippi, 1976

Wallace, Patricia, "Separateness and Solitude in Frost," *Kenyon Review* 6, no. 1 (1984)

Winters, Yvor, *The Function of Criticism: Problems and Exercises,* Denver, Colorado: Swallow, 1957

# Design

It would be difficult to say anything new about Robert Frost's poem "Design," so often and so extensively has it been commented on. Indeed, one Frost biographer observed, in an attempt at originality, that the whiteness of the spider and flower in "Design" is a play on the maiden name of Frost's wife—an observation that another Frost biographer (Parini) described as absurd and irrelevant. "Design" has been commented on so much because it powerfully engages one of humanity's oldest and most troubling questions: whence comes evil?

As early as January 1912, Frost sent to a friend a version of "Design" titled "In White." That draft, like "Design" itself, is a sonnet that describes in its octave a white spider atop a white flower, holding up a dead white moth, and that asks in its sestet philosophical questions about the octave's tableau. By the time the poem was first published in *American Poetry 1922: A Miscellany,* it had achieved its final state, with tighter and more resonant language, a self-assured tone, and a more pointed and disturbing concluding couplet. Frost did not include "Design" in either of his next two volumes of poetry, but finally, 14 years after its first publication, he did put it in the volume *A Further Range* (1936). More than a decade later, Randall Jarrell could rightly claim that "Design" was among both the best—and the least—known of Frost's poems. Jarrell's admiring commentary on "Design" in his essay "To the Laodiceans" initiated the poem's ascent to the high status it occupies today.

The design in question in Frost's poem is twofold: not only an aesthetic arrangement in white, what Jarrell called "a little albino catastrophe," but also, and more important, a teleological composition suggesting purpose in nature, "the Argument from Design with a vengeance" (Jarrell, 1953). Here is the poem in its entirety:

I found a dimpled spider, fat and white,  
On a white heal-all, holding up a moth  
Like a white piece of rigid satin cloth—  
Assorted characters of death and blight  
Mixed ready to begin the morning right,  
Like the ingredients of a witches' broth—  
A snow-drop spider, a flower like a froth,  
And dead wings carried like a paper kite.

What had that flower to do with being white,  
The wayside blue and innocent heal-all?  
What brought the kindred spider to that height,  
Then steered the white moth thither in the night?  
What, but design of darkness to appall?—  
If design govern in a thing so small.

Simply put, the Argument from Design is that the presence of design implies a designer: if one finds order in the universe, from the microcosm (the structure of a snowflake) to the macrocosm (the movement of heavenly bodies), the existence of a designer or creator of the universe is implied. In *Pragmatism* (1907), a book that Richard Poirier suggests is the probable source of Frost's poem, William James notes that those employing the Argument from Design traditionally considered the Divine Designer to be benevolent but that Darwin pointed to many things in nature that, if designed, would suggest a malevolent designer. "*Here*, all depends upon the point of view," James continues. "To the grub under the bark the exquisite fitness of the woodpecker's organism to extract him would certainly argue a diabolical designer" (cited in Poirier, 1977).

A perception of the diabolical is not wanting in Frost's "Design," nor has it gone unnoticed by Jarrell and critics writing after him. The albino spider, blighted flower (a heal-all is normally blue, as the speaker notes in the sestet), and dead moth are "Like the ingredients of a witches' broth"; they are "Mixed ready to begin the morning right" if, one presumes, one is dancing around a bubbling cauldron with evil intention. Moreover, the pun on "right" with "rite" and the spider's "holding up" its victim convey the feeling of an unholy ritual, a black Mass. Frost heightens our unease when he links imagery of positive connotation to inappropriate objects: we are more likely to associate "dimpled" and "fat" with a cute baby than with a spider, and the sense of innocent play invoked by a paper kite seems betrayed when the image is linked to dead wings. Similarly, the name "heal-all" is ironic, as the flower was not able to heal itself and, by its blighted whiteness, even served to camouflage the predator while luring the prey.

The first question of the poem's sestet implies that it is not just the heal-all but innocence itself that has somehow been blighted, and the verbs "brought" and "steered" in subsequent questions imply a death-dealing agency operating behind the scene. When the suggestion is made in the concluding couplet of an operative "design of darkness to appall," what has been implied all along is named. "Appall," to fill with horror or dismay, is an apt word here, for it derives from "to grow or make pale." It is as if the whiteness of the octave's dramatis personae, a whiteness associated in this poem with death rather than purity (the "rigid satin cloth" invoking a coffin lining rather than a wedding gown), has the power not only to shock but also to infect the viewer. Then the poem springs its final surprise in a last-minute almost throwaway "if" clause that raises the possibility that, after all, there may be no malevolent designer behind the octave's Grand Guignol. However, this escape hatch only leads to the unnerving alternative that evil in nature is the result of chance and that there is no ultimate purpose to make sense of things.

"Design" is central to a critical controversy over whether Frost is a poet of terrifying vision. Some have noted that, as there is no moral evil in nature, the perception of it in "Design" comes from the imagination of the poem's speaker. For David Perkins, Frost is a poet in the tradition of Romantic irony who in "Design" neither asserts nor denies the reality of evil but merely uses it as a topic to play with. The poem itself, of course, is a small thing in which design governs (with a vengeance, Frost constructing a sonnet with only three rhymes). Was Frost's purpose to appall, or was he being mischievous? Probably both.

Jack Barbera

**Further Reading**


Cook, Reginald, *Robert Frost: A Living Voice,* Amherst: University of Massachusetts Press, 1974

Isaacs, Elizabeth, *An Introduction to Robert Frost,* Denver, Colorado: Swallow, 1962

Jarrell, Randall, *Poetry and the Age,* New York: Knopf, and London: Faber and Faber, 1953

Kemp, John C., *Robert Frost and New England: The Poet as Regionalist,* Princeton, New Jersey: Princeton University Press, 1979

Lentricchia, Frank, *Robert Frost: Modern Poetics and the Landscapes of Self,* Durham, North Carolina: Duke University Press, 1975

Marcus, Mordecai, *The Poems of Robert Frost: An Explication,* Boston: G.K. Hall, 1991

Monteiro, George, *Robert Frost and the New England Renaissance,* Lexington: University Press of Kentucky, 1988

Parini, Jay, *Robert Frost: A Life,* London: Heinemann, 1998; New York: Holt, 1999

Perkins, David, "Robert Frost and Romantic Irony," *South Carolina Review* 22, no. 1 (Fall 1989)

Poirier, Richard, *Robert Frost: The Work of Knowing,* Oxford and New York: Oxford University Press, 1977


## Home Burial

Robert Frost told biographer Lawrance Thompson that in his many public and private performances, he never read "Home Burial" because it was "too sad" for him to say out loud. Inevitably, this sadness recalls Frost's biography. Although the poet claimed that "Home Burial" originated in the darkening marital situation between his wife's sister and her husband after the death of their first child in 1895, Frost's own life also could have inspired the poem, he and his wife Elinor having lost two of their children, a three-year-old son, Elliott, in 1900 and an infant daughter, Elinor, in 1907. At the same time, however, in acknowledging the overwhelming sadness of "Home Burial," Frost may also have been pointing beyond its biographical genesis and confirming the unique and powerful pathos of the poem itself.

Claiming to have written "Home Burial" at The Bungalow in Beaconsfield, England, in 1912 or 1913, Frost first published the poem in *North of Boston* (1914) and subsequently included it in every edition of his selected or collected poems. Although Frost never made major changes in the poem, Richard Poirier argues persuasively that three minor emendations of punctuation made by Edward Connery Lathem for his 1969 edition of *The Poetry of Robert Frost* (two of the emendations wholly on his own authority) sacrifice much of the poignancy in Frost's representation of the estrangement between wife and husband. Poirier himself follows the text of the poem in the 1949 *Complete Poems of Robert Frost.*

In his essay "Education by Poetry" (first published in 1931), Frost offers several formulations that bear directly on the drama and pathos of "Home Burial": "Poetry provides the one permissible way of saying one thing and meaning another. People say, 'Why don't you say what you mean?' We never do that, do we, being all of us too much poets. We like to talk in parables and in hints and in indirections—whether from diffidence or some other instinct." In "Home Burial," a dramatic dialogue between Amy and her unnamed husband, Frost probes many aspects of marriage, grief, and isolation, but he grounds his probing in memorable instances of "saying one thing and meaning another."

With the careful precision of stage directions, this blank-verse poem opens by showing a man standing at the bottom of a staircase looking up at his wife, Amy, who is looking back over her shoulder as she starts down the stairs, changes her mind, and steps back to look a second time at whatever she sees. When the husband climbs the stairs to discover for himself that she has been looking out a window at the little family graveyard, where he has recently buried their dead male child, Amy slips past him, descends the stairs, goes to the door as he sits down, and eventually opens it to flee the house as someone comes down the road outside. Aside from these simple actions, the rest of "Home Burial" consists of what the woman and man say to each other, and in their exchange lies the real drama of the poem.

An early example of saying one thing and meaning another surfaces in the husband's first extended speech, after he has asked his wife what she has been looking at; climbed the stairs to see for himself, "Mounting until she cowered under him" (a line rich both in assonance and in sexual suggestiveness, as some readers have noted); and been challenged by Amy to tell her what he has found. In response, he describes "The little graveyard where my people are! / So small the window frames the whole of it. / Not so much larger than a bedroom, is it?" The comparison of graveyard to bedroom cannot help but suggest the death of something between husband and wife in the latter, and with this indirect hint spoken by the husband, Frost's title suggests both the literal burial of a child at home and at least two figurative burials: the burial of a home once animated by marital love and the live burial of the estranged couple in a home that now consists of nothing but a forced and alienated domesticity.

A further and more complex instance of saying one thing and meaning another appears in the second of Amy's two long speeches in the latter half of the poem. Having interrupted her husband's first extended speech with a memorable instance of epizeuxis, "Don't, don't, don't, don't," Amy answers his question, "Can't a man speak of his own child he's lost?" with the crushing rejoinder "I don't know rightly whether any man can." With this bitter exchange, Frost sharply focuses "Home Burial" on the problem of how one speaks about loss. The woman believes the man lacks any ability to speak about their shared loss in an appropriate way, a way that refuses to turn "back to life," as she puts it near the end of her second long speech, from a grief so huge. However, in her condemnation of his inarticulateness, she misses the indirect hinting of his words, which she quotes back to him: "I can repeat the very words you were saying: / 'Three foggy mornings and one rainy day / Will rot the best birch fence a man can build.'" Recoiling from "talk like that at such a time!," Amy then asks, "What had how long it takes a birch to rot / To do with what was in the darkened parlor," resorting to this final circumlocution, intensified by assonance, to avoid referring directly to the child's dead body.

Rhetorical as her question sounds, "Home Burial" suggests that talking about a rotting fence has everything to do with talking about the loss of a child. Although the poem represents many of the husband's deficiencies and limitations, as when it shows him attempting to soothe his wife with the patronizing line "There, you have said it all and you feel better," it also balances the representation by showing that Amy fails to hear the man's remarks about a birch fence as making a little poem about loss and his sense of powerlessness in the face of it. In "Home Burial," then, Frost not only focuses on how different people necessarily speak about loss in different ways but also offers us a meditation on his own hinting, indirect parables of loss and how to read them.

STEPHEN CUSHMAN

**Further Reading**


Brodsky, Joseph, "On Grief and Reason," in *Homage to Robert Frost,* by Brodsky, Seamus Heaney, and Derek Walcott, New York: Farrar Straus and Giroux, 1996; London: Faber, 1997

Hoffman, Tyler, *Robert Frost and the Politics of Poetry,* Hanover, New Hampshire: University Press of New England, 2001

Jarrell, Randall, "Robert Frost's 'Home Burial,'" in *The Third Book of Criticism,* by Jarrell, New York: Farrar Straus and Giroux, 1965; London: Faber, 1975

Kearns, Katherine, *Robert Frost and a Poetics of Appetite,* Cambridge and New York: Cambridge University Press, 1994

Kilcup, Karen L., *Robert Frost and Feminine Literary Tradition,* Ann Arbor: University of Michigan Press, 1998

Lentricchia, Frank, *Robert Frost: Modern Poetics and the Landscapes of Self,* Durham, North Carolina: Duke University Press, 1975

Oster, Judith, *Toward Robert Frost: The Reader and the Poet,* Athens: University of Georgia Press, 1991

Poirier, Richard, *Robert Frost: The Work of Knowing,* Oxford and New York: Oxford University Press, 1977


## Mending Wall

Robert Frost's reputation and style solidified in the 1914 volume *North of Boston,* which featured several of the greatest narrative poems of the 20th century. These blank-verse dramas depicted the culture of rural New England, not with picture-postcard vistas but rather with interior landscapes. The psychology of the Frost New Englander extended beyond geography, representing an America that could have been left behind in the Modernist attempts to sophisticate and globalize American verse. Frost's interests were local, inward; like Wordsworth and Coleridge in the previous century in England, he set out to discover the inherent poetry of the everyday, in speech and image. "The Death of the Hired Man" and "Home Burial" clearly depict conversations between two characters narrated by a more removed, somewhat omniscient voice. "Mending Wall," the opening poem of the volume, may be as much a dramatic narrative as these poems, only with a more directly involved speaker. Necessitating its more meditative tone is the lack of verbal exchange between these two characters, the speaker and his neighbor. Instead, the poet gives us a psychological portrait of their mostly unspoken dialogue as it takes place in its both realistic and symbolic landscape.

Beginning more as a meditation, the speaker's "I" does not appear until line six; his companion, the neighbor, is first mentioned in line 12. The two landowners have agreed to meet periodically to maintain the fence that defines the line between their properties. This utilitarian action takes on higher levels of significance in the poem, first as a kind of social function: "Oh, just another outdoor game, / One on a side." The speaker continues the game playing verbally, questioning his neighbor's insistence on the barrier. Without livestock, he argues, there seems to be nothing to keep in or keep out.

The refrain of the neighbor's saying, "Good fences make good neighbors," handed down generation to generation, adds to the scene the quality of ritual. They cast "spells" to balance the stones; in one syntactically odd passage, the speaker playfully suggests "elves" as the source of the wall's deterioration. These instances of superstition and folklore culminate with an image of the neighbor as a primitive, "a stone grasped firmly by the top / In each hand, like an old-stone savage armed." The neighbor remains in "darkness," one greater than the shade of the trees. However, this darkness of old ways and stubborn dedication to them interest the speaker; he makes his challenges as if he knows the outcome and makes no serious attempt to change his neighbor's outlook. It is as if he is goading the neighbor to articulate these views aloud for another listening party—the reader.

The relationship between these two as they walk side by side develops as one of older and younger, old-timer and outsider. The story becomes a parable of the transmission of wisdom within the tribe, the preservation of tradition greater than the seemingly everyday farm tasks they pursue. The tension derives from the younger man's desire to understand the reason for their actions—for the speaker, the natural force is unity, "Something there is that doesn't love a wall, / That wants it down." Balancing his repetition of this assertion is the old farmer's repetition of his father's aphorism about good fences. Where their differences meet and press against one another defines the line between their two selves, just as the line of the wall defines the land, which is a metonym for each in line 24: "He is all pine and I am apple orchard."

Frost's diction conspires to keep the reader slightly at bay, the lines of the poem creating yet another fence of complex syntax that must be unraveled. Lines such as "But they would have the rabbit out of hiding" effect the tone of an ancient dialect in translation. Neolithic echoes in vocabulary include "frozen-ground-swell" and "old-stone," as Frost places the scene outside historical time, adding authority to its conclusions about the deeper truths of human interaction.

Occasional lapses in metrics in this blank-verse poem, beginning with the first line's opening trochee, stand out, as do the gaps created by the fallen stones in the wall. This fluctuation in rhythm also lends a colloquial cadence to the poem. In addition to its metrical structure, the poem is mortared with alliterative patterns that add the kind of cohesion that rhyme would in a rhyming form. Passages such as "sends the frozen-ground-swell" show a chiastic, or mirroring, alliterative pattern between the "s" and "r" sounds, while phrases such as "neighbor know beyond" display an interlocking pattern between the "n" and "b" sounds. These patterns of likeness and difference replicate in the syntax: a chiastic pattern of vocabulary and consonance can be seen in the line "To each the boulders that have fallen to each," while "seen them made or heard them made," "walling in or walling out," and even "good fences make good neighbors" all use repetition to highlight the tension between sameness and difference.

An everyday chore gives us a glimpse into human nature and beyond, into a chthonic realm, in this poem, which balances a tone both serious and comic. This mixture of gravity and humor characterizes many Frost poems as he creates in his work a record of what it is to be a New Englander, an American, an individualist. He teases us with wordplay—"to whom I was like to give offense"—and with questions about our beliefs, our habits, and our respect for the beliefs and habits of others. Above all, he demonstrates the reaction of the poet to his world, his calling to observe order and meaning in action, translating his experience into art.

Nicole Sarrocco

**Further Reading**


Beacham, Walton, "Technique and the Sense of Play in the Poetry of Robert Frost," in *Frost: Centennial Essays II*, edited by Jac L. Tharpe, Jackson: University Press of Mississippi, 1976

Brodsky, Joseph, "On Grief and Reason," in *Homage to Robert Frost*, by Brodsky, Seamus Heaney, and Derek Walcott, New York: Farrar Straus and Giroux, 1996; London: Faber, 1997

Cook, Reginald, *Robert Frost: A Living Voice*, Amherst: University of Massachusetts Press, 1974

Kemp, John C., *Robert Frost and New England: The Poet as Regionalist*, Princeton, New Jersey: Princeton University Press, 1979

Liebman, Sheldon W., "Robert Frost, Romantic," *Twentieth Century Literature* 42, no. 4 (1998)

McNair, Wesley, "Robert Frost and Dramatic Speech," *Sewanee Review* 106, no. 1 (1998)

Monteiro, George, *Robert Frost and the New England Renaissance*, Lexington: University Press of Kentucky, 1988

Poirier, Richard, *Robert Frost: The Work of Knowing*, Oxford and New York: Oxford University Press, 1977

Thompson, Lawrance Roger, *Fire and Ice: The Art and Thought of Robert Frost*, New York: Holt, 1942


# The Road Not Taken

In 1912 Robert Frost gave up his secure teaching post at the State Normal School in Plymouth, New Hampshire, and traveled with his wife and children to England. "The Road Not Taken" has often been interpreted as expressing his risky decision to leave America for an uncertain future in a country where he could write poetry in peaceful poverty. Some have also suggested that the poem refers to Frost's wondering in 1915 whether to join the British army. Frost himself always claimed, however, that the poem was inspired by the man who would become his closest friend, the Welsh poet Edward Thomas. He probably began writing "The Road Not Taken" (penning just the final stanza) in Thomas' home, The Gallows at Ryton Dymock, Gloucestershire, "on a big fluffy sofa." Upon his return to New Hampshire in 1915 Frost read through Thomas' letters, which he felt often expressed Thomas' attitude of discontent over alternatives not experienced. In addition he saw Thomas as having chosen an isolated life very much off the main road. Frost said that he told Thomas: "No matter which road you take, you'll always sigh, and wish you'd taken another." Frost sent the earliest known manuscript version to Thomas in late April or very early May 1915. At first he called the poem "Two Roads," but he seems to have mentioned the final title in the next letter to Thomas. The final title was first used in public when Frost read the completed poem at Tufts College (5 May 1915). It was first published in *Mountain Interval* (1916).

"The Road Not Taken" is one of Frost's most popular and anthologized poems, showing the energizing effect that his stay in England had upon his poetic life. The poem works so well in part because of his brilliant use of ambiguity to describe the difficult but necessary process of making choices in life, a theme that would be central to his work. It features a regular metrical pattern (predominantly iambic tetrameter), rhyme scheme (*abaab*), and the conversational tone favored by Frost.

The speaker arrives in the midst of a forest and stops where two paths cross, trying to decide which one to take. It being autumn ("a yellow wood"), the forest floor is partially obscured by many newly fallen leaves, and one path bends into the undergrowth, making it impossible to see its destination. The speaker can only peer down it. He turns to the other path, "as just as fair," and invents a reason for choosing it: "it was grassy and wanted wear." When he is honest with himself and tries to be objective, however, the speaker must admit that they "really are about the same."

The poem is ultimately about the speaker, not the paths, since despite his desire to see them as different, he must admit that they "equally lay / In leaves no step had trodden black." Choosing the path that he tries to convince himself "wanted wear" indicates that the speaker is an individualist ("one traveler") rather than one of the crowd. Here, as in other poems, nature is not Frost's primary concern, but human beings. Thus, perhaps desirous of retaining his individuality, of being true to himself, the speaker is forced to use little more than whim to choose which path to take. The important aspect of this choice is that he *wants* to choose the less-traveled road; that he cannot tell which one it is does not lessen the importance of his desire. Simultaneously, however, he would love to experience whatever possibilities the other path has to offer as well. So desirous is he of doing this that he feels he must return one day to take the other one—"Oh I kept the first for another day!"—hence the implied anguish of the title. Ultimately he gives in to reality, admitting that he doubts "if I should ever come back."

In the final stanza Frost presents a set of ambiguities that lie within the speaker and, by implication, are part of the human condition. The speaker states that even as he chooses, he knows any choice is likely to be unsatisfactory as it eliminates other choices. One day, "ages and ages hence," he will look back on this moment with a "sigh." The speaker—and the reader—do not yet know whether it will be a sigh of despair or a sigh of relief and joy; perhaps it will be a sigh of resignation that every choice is made without knowing all of its consequences in the future. This reflects the human dilemma: required to make important, even crucial, decisions without adequate information or insight, without knowing who one will become "ages hence," nor how situations will develop, one still must choose.

The final two lines complete the ambiguity in the poem, as in the life situation it describes. The speaker informs the reader that he did, after all, take the road "less travelled by." As he could not tell which one this was, he must be referring to his *intention*. This focus may be seen in the repetition of the word "I" at both the end and beginning of lines, both repetition and position stressing its centrality to the poem; it is this intention that has "made all the difference." Again, as previously with the word "sigh," the reader must question the meaning of the word "difference": is it a difference for the better or for the worse? Or is it an undistinguished difference? Whatever the end result, something in human nature forces a decision one way or another; that human quality is what makes "all the difference."

EDWARD A. ABRAMSON

**Further Reading**


Bagby, George, *Frost and the Book of Nature,* Knoxville: University of Tennessee Press, 1993

Cady, Edwin H., and Louis J. Budd, editors, *On Frost,* Durham, North Carolina: Duke University Press, 1991

Meyers, Jeffrey, *Robert Frost: A Biography,* Boston: Houghton Mifflin, 1996

Monteiro, George, *Robert Frost and the New England Renaissance,* Lexington: University Press of Kentucky, 1988

Oster, Judith, *Toward Robert Frost: The Reader and the Poet,* Athens: University of Georgia Press, 1991

Poirier, Richard, *Robert Frost: The Work of Knowing,* Oxford and New York: Oxford University Press, 1977

Potter, James L., *Robert Frost Handbook,* University Park: Pennsylvania State University Press, 1980


---

# Fugitives and Agrarians

With the publication in 1930 of *I'll Take My Stand: The South and the Agrarian Tradition* by "Twelve Southerners," a group of writers whose work had appeared in *The Fugitive* magazine gave intellectual expression to a body of conservative ideas about art and its relationship to regionalism that was to have a considerable influence both on southern literature (especially on what came to be called "the Southern Renascence") and on American literature more generally, most notably in the field of literary criticism. Not all the essayists included in *I'll Take My Stand* (the title comes from the Confederate song "Dixie") were "Fugitives," but three poets were the shaping spirits behind the collection—Donald Davidson, John Crowe Ransom, and Allen Tate—and they included an essay by Robert Penn Warren, a younger poet whose contribution to what has been called the "Renaissance" in the South's literary culture of the 1930s and 1940s is considerable (other notable literary contributors to *I'll Take My Stand* were the Imagist poet John Gould Fletcher and the novelist Andrew Lytle). To isolate poets as critical contributors to what is, in effect, a symposium on the state of society in the South as it appeared to the reflective intelligence at the end of the 1920s, in which agricultural, economic, industrial, and cultural ideas (they may as well be called proposals, for the collection is more a manifesto than the symposium it has been described as) are analyzed, would suggest that this is a volume of essays of a diagnostic literary kind. The introduction to the volume, significantly subtitled "A Statement of Principles," expressed a common purpose: "All the articles bear in the same sense upon the book's title-subject: all tend to support a Southern way of life against what might be called the American or prevailing way; and all as much agree that the best terms in which to represent the distinction are contained in the phrase, Agrarian *versus* Industrial." The diagnosis, in other words, takes on something of the character of a call to arms, but none of the contributors was, in any serious sense, seeking to reignite battles over ways of living that had ended at Appomattox Court House in April 1865. Rather, they were seeking a partial restitution of values that had helped sustain the South in its antebellum years, conveniently the same values that were very much at odds with the pervasive forces of modernity that were shaping post–World War I America. The contributors to *I'll Take My Stand* shared what might be called a Jeffersonian outlook on life: for them, the traditional society is essentially an agricultural community in which socio-economic conditions are indivisibly woven together with moral behavior to create a harmonious whole. Sustaining this society are the institutions of Christian religion (largely Protestant, of course, although Allen Tate was to convert to Roman Catholicism in his later years) and those myths and symbols by which any society understands itself and by which it explains its relationship to both the physical and the metaphysical world. In opposition to this stands the world of business, industry, progress, rationality, and above all science. (Donald Davidson, one of the guiding spirits behind both the Fugitive movement and its Agrarian offspring, spoke of saving "the South from civilization.") The contributors to the volume, therefore, attempted (and not entirely unsuccessfully) to analyze the disparate aspects of society in ways that lead to a common conclusion. Thus, essays on the economy, education, the position of the black American in both the Old and the New South, religion, and the arts (particularly the literary arts) are held together by the commitment to finding something positive and worth preserving in antebellum southern culture. For John Crowe Ransom, the "South is unique on this continent for having founded and defended a culture which was according to the European principles of culture," while for Frank Lawrence Owsley, the "life of the South was leisurely and unhurried for the planter, the yeoman or the landless tenant. It was a way of life, not a routine of planting and reaping merely for gain"—a society, in other words, whose values were rooted in its very soil. Some attention has been given to the impact of the Scopes trial of 1925 (a court trial in Dayton, Tennessee, in which John Scopes, a high school teacher of biology, was found guilty of violating a state law that forbade the teaching of Darwinian evolutionary theory) and to the influence of distributist economic thought (notably in the social writings of English Catholics such as Hilaire Belloc and G.K. Chesterton) on southern Agrarianism, but there is much that is indigenously and inescapably "southern" in the character of the Fugitive and Agrarian vision.

Many of those who contributed to *I'll Take My Stand* were connected with the arts—poets, novelists, critics, and occasionally all three—and thus the volume, for all its socio-economic considerations, has much to say about the role of the arts and, indeed, the artist in a traditional society. Donald Davidson's essay "A Mirror for Artists" gives voice to the concern as to whether the arts are cherished in an industrial civilization. For Davidson (and many of his contemporaries, both southern and northern), the values of Puritan New England had fostered the growth of a business-oriented culture and were inimical to the creative arts. Moreover, the machine could not be "mastered" for aesthetic purposes, and thus Davidson rejected one important strain of the Modernist agenda—the view that "machine civilization" yielded both a subject and an aesthetic method. Art could grow only in an organic society, and the very heterogeneity of industrial civilization worked against the creative imagination. Davidson, along with the three other major Agrarian writers (Ransom, Tate, and Warren), wrote much about the issues of regionalism and sectionalism (the latter frequently *contrasted* with the former), arguing that the vitality of creative expression was a matter of the writer's rediscovering his relation to his immediate world and its sustaining traditions. This might be a matter of rediscovering his relationship to the past of his region, its history, although the Agrarians never successfully demonstrated how this was to be for a South whose defeat in war and subsequent reconstruction had effectively expunged much of what gave it a different social and historical identity from the rest of the United States. Ransom, in his essay "The Aesthetic of Regionalism" (first published in the January 1934 issue of *American Review*), emphasizes the degree to which a regional economy sustained artistic endeavor (and by the arts he means more than just the creative arts, including architecture, dress, language, manners, pastimes, and speech, among other of what we might now call anthropological features of culture):

> The arts make their appearance in some ascending order, perhaps indicated like this: labour, craft, and business insist upon being transacted under patterns which permit the enjoyment of natural background; houses, tools, manufactured things do not seem good enough if they are only effective but must also be ornamental, which in a subtle sense means natural; and the fine arts arise, superficially pure or non-useful, yet faithful to the regional culture and to the moral patterns to which the community is committed.

For Ransom, the poet's role was prophetic and pedagogical. The idea that poetry is a special kind of knowledge, that it is a way of thinking (Ransom's word for this is "ontological"), and that the individual poem in paraphrase can only ever be a pale imitation of the original is the Agrarian's reply to the claims of science and, at the same time, seeks to give to poetry a status *equal* to that of science. These ideas, reshaped for the purposes of teaching poetry and turning literary criticism away from its belletristic character, were to dominate the New Criticism and the professional study of English for much of the middle period of the 20th century. With the loosening of the ties that held Fugitives and Agrarians together (Ransom moved north to Kenyon College in Ohio in 1937 and Tate to the University of Minnesota), it fell to *The Southern Review,* a literary quarterly founded at Louisiana State University in Baton Rouge, the third periodical in the South to carry such a title, to articulate and represent the southern position, and under the editorships of Cleanth Brooks, C.W. Pipkin, and Robert Penn Warren, it became one of America's most distinguished journals.

*I'll Take My Stand* was the intellectual expression of the Fugitive movement of poets (and other fellow travelers) that had centred on the little bimonthly magazine *The Fugitive,* edited and published from Vanderbilt University in Nashville, Tennessee, between the years 1922 and 1925. Fugitive verse in the hands of its more important creators, such as Davidson, Ransom, Tate, and Warren, was in many respects the expression of a sentiment articulated by Ransom in his preface to the first edition of *The Fugitive* of April 1922: "*The Fugitive* flees from nothing faster than the high-caste Brahmins of the Old South." The intellectual "caste" of the Old South was thus associated, implicitly, with a sentimental, melodramatic, romantic, and backward-looking literary culture, although it is obviously a matter of some irony that charges of this kind were also leveled at the Fugitives themselves, who were seen by W.J. Cash, in his influential *The Mind of the South* (1941), as "the spiritual heirs of Thomas Nelson Page" (Page's novels and short stories offer a romantic vision of the South in the years before and during the Civil War and frequently dramatize the alleged brutality of northern military rule of the South in the years immediately afterward). In a recollection published in 1942, Tate defined the Fugitives as "an intensive and historical group as opposed to the eclectic and cosmopolitan groups that flourished in the East. There was a sort of unity of feeling, of which we were not then very much aware, which came out of—to give a big name—a common historical myth," and this definition, when placed alongside Cash's more cynical assessment, points to the essential paradox (one might see it more simply as a contradiction) that lies at the heart of Fugitive-Agrarian literary efforts. The Fugitives were Modernists opposed to the forces of modernity. Their art embodied many of those features, both technical and thematic, that we characteristically associate with the "discoveries" of Modernism: the emphasis on irony and ambiguity, the appeal to classical and thus anti-romantic ideals of poetic expression, the cultivation of an impersonal voice, and the belief in the transcendent, spiritual, and "ordering" power of art. However, with this went a rejection of much of what we associate with modernity: science, rationality, the secular society, the city, the growth of the nation-state, and above all industrialization and its by-product, consumerism. The Old South, by which the Fugitives meant the South before the Civil War, thus became a repository of those values and traditions that were antithetical to the forces of modernity.

The consequences of the South's defeat and the social and moral repercussions of that defeat are addressed with varying degrees of explicitness in Fugitive verse. Davidson's account in "The Tall Men" eschews ambiguity and indirectness:

The Union is saved. Lee has surrendered forever.
Today, Lorena, it is forbidden to be
A Southerner. One is an American now;
Propounds the pig's conception of the state—
The constitution of, by, for the pig—
Meanwhile pushing his trotters well in
The trough.

In "Antique Harvesters," one of Ransom's more well-known poems and one of the few in which he writes specifically about his region, the address is more subtle, and the South is imaged as an integrated, harmonious culture whose rituals and ceremonies are charged with what Ransom sees as the proper relation between man and land:

Here come the hunters, keepers of a rite;
The horn, the hounds, the lank mares coursing by
Straddled with archetypes of chivalry;
And the fox, lovely ritualist, in flight
Offering his unearthly ghost to quarry;
And the fields, themselves to harry[.]

Similarly, Allen Tate, in his "Ode to the Confederate Dead," both mourns and celebrates those who died in the major battles of the Civil War, presenting the South as a heroic society sure enough of itself and its beliefs to permit the transcendence of self and death that heroic action demands:

Turn your eyes to the immoderate past,
Turn to the inscrutable infantry rising
Demons out of the earth—they will not last.
Stonewall, Stonewall, and the sunken fields of hemp,
Shiloh, Antietam, Malvern Hill, Bull Run.
Lost in that orient of the thick-and-fast
You will curse the setting sun.

This quality of elegiac regionalism in Tate's poetry does not necessarily presuppose a southern context. Like many of his contemporaries whose education exposed them to the great poetical achievements of classical antiquity (in this Tate, of course, has affinities with T.S. Eliot), Tate's "classicism" is used both as a way of eschewing romantic subjectivity and as thematic device in which the grandeur of the ancient past (much of it, of course, of a pastoral or bucolic kind) can be juxtaposed with the debasements of the present. In three poems, particularly, the figure of Aeneas straddles past and present. In "The Mediterranean," the search for order amid the chaos of modernity is imaged in the wanderings of the defeated Trojans, while in "Aeneas at Washington" a more explicit parallel is articulated between the defeat of Troy and the defeat of the South:

That was a time when civilization
Run by the few fell to the many, and
Crashed to the shout of men, the clang of arms[.]

In "Aeneas in New York," the epical hero inhabits a world torn between the extremes of J.P. Morgan and Karl Marx's *Das Kapital.* In Tate's only novel, *The Fathers* (1938), the destructive effects of the Civil War on the old order of the South are imaged in the decline of the Buchan family, whose home at Pleasant Hill stands, symbolically, for the refinements of Virginia's antebellum civilization. (With the novel, Tate was, to some extent, exploiting the popularity of southern Civil War fiction in the 1930s: the great commercial success of Stark Young's *So Red the Rose* [1934]—Young wrote the concluding essay for *I'll Take My Stand*—was exceeded two years later by Margaret Mitchell's *Gone with the Wind* [1936], which sold a million copies in its first year of publication. Even a "serious" writer such as William Faulkner contributed to this literature of a lost cause, notably with *The Unvanquished* [1938].)

Robert Penn Warren, whose writings as a literary critic and novelist have tended to eclipse his poetry, was the youngest of the four major poets associated with southern Agrarianism. Where for Davidson and Ransom the Agrarian stance was, in part, a seriously political response to the encroachments of modernity and nationalism, for Warren it took the form of a philosophical and moral attitude to experience. Warren's lyric poetry is often tragic in character, depicting man's plight, the fragility of his place in the universe, and the burden of the past. The rich resources of the land, however, provide some compensatory pleasures, and in his early volumes, such as *Thirty-Six Poems* (1936) and *Eleven Poems on the Same Theme* (1942), Warren's imagery frequently evokes the beauties and plenitude of nature in a way that suggests a kinship with Romanticism and Transcendentalism, although he is too much a skeptical poet of the age of Modernism to accept the pantheistic certitudes of Wordsworth and Emerson. Like Eliot's and Tate's, the tone of his early verse is ironic and paradoxical and shows the influence of the Metaphysical poets whom Eliot had championed in his critical writings. Later volumes of his poetry mark the growth of his interest in narrative forms, notably in *Brother to Dragons* (1953; revised edition, 1979), a historical verse drama that recounts the murder of a slave who is hacked to death for breaking a pitcher cherished by the mother of his master (the master was a nephew of Thomas Jefferson). The historical subject here is intimately connected to Warren's Agrarianism and his strong sense of the weight of the southern past. In his essay for *I'll Take My Stand*, "The Briar Patch," Warren meditated on the uncertain position of the black American in the new, increasingly industrialized South and what he took to be the likelihood of continuing "friction and difference" between white and black. *Brother to Dragons* reasserts Warren's vision of slavery, and its effects, as a historical burden that neither black nor white can easily shed.

Henry Claridge

*See also* New Criticism

**Further Reading**

Bradbury, John M., *The Fugitives,* Chapel Hill: University of North Carolina Press, 1958
Conkin, Paul Keith, *The Southern Agrarians,* Knoxville: University of Tennessee Press, 1988
Cowan, Louise, *The Fugitive Group,* Baton Rouge: Louisiana State University Press, 1959
Dorman, Robert L., *Revolt of the Provinces: The Regionalist Movement in America, 1920–1945,* Chapel Hill: University of North Carolina Press, 1993
*Fugitives: An Anthology of Verse,* New York: Harcourt Brace, 1928
*I'll Take My Stand: The South and the Agrarian Tradition,* New York: Harper, 1930
Karanikas, Alexander, *Tillers of a Myth: Southern Agrarians as Social and Literary Critics,* Madison: University of Wisconsin Press, 1969
Purdy, Rob Roy, editor, *Fugitives' Reunion: Conversations at Vanderbilt, May 3–5, 1956,* Nashville, Tennessee: Vanderbilt University Press, 1959
Rubin, Louis D., Jr., *Writers of the Modern South: A Faraway Country,* Seattle: University of Washington Press, 1963
Stewart, John Lincoln, *The Burden of Time: The Fugitives and the Agrarians,* Princeton, New Jersey: Princeton University Press, 1965
Young, Thomas Daniel, *Waking Their Neighbours Up: The Nashville Agrarians,* Athens: University of Georgia Press, 1982
Young, Thomas Daniel, "The Fugitives: Ransom, Davidson, Tate," in *The History of Southern Literature,* edited by Louis D. Rubin, Jr., et al., Baton Rouge: Louisiana State University Press, 1985

# G

## Gay and Lesbian Poetry

Not only the European, but also the American tradition of lesbian and gay poetry may be said to begin with the woman who has lent it two names: Sappho ("sapphic") of Lesbos ("lesbian"). We have little biographical information about Sappho, but she has remained a central figure of admiration, struggle, and textual tribute, as Page du Bois (1996) has shown. Sappho is essential in the creation of a lesbian and gay tradition that is explicitly feminist and political. The virtually total destruction of Sappho's work is the most terrifying example of the elimination of a tradition of writing by women, especially when it is eroticized; at the same time, the state of Sappho's texts (entirely in fragments) seemed to the Modernists, such as H.D. (Hilda Doolittle), to provide a model for a minimalist writing that was precise and compact. More recently, Sappho has provided a model for a counter-tradition that established a lyric voice as a form of resistance to those other Greek forms, the epic and the philosophical dialogue.

Sappho is indeed mentioned in Plato's *Phaedrus,* termed "the fair Sappho," in a figure that favors the poet over the poetry. There is also a strong affinity between Plato's description of the lover's reaction to the beloved and Sappho's Fragment 31, as du Bois shows. But Plato, famously, attempts to transcend the physical, going from desire to sublimation, while Sappho locates the physical reaction to desire—speechlessness, trembling, cold sweat. Sappho's resistance to the philosophical tradition of idealism (like that of Whitman to Emerson and the American Transcendentalists) is needed to preserve the "lower" body, the so-called feminine, against the claims of the "higher," masculine soul. Sappho's troubled link to Greek philosophy is accompanied by her anti-epic structures. The most striking aspect of Sappho's work is her use of the first person, her insistence on the personal (in one fragment, she would rather see her beloved Anactoria than an infantry "full-armed").

Among American women Modernists, H.D. stands out, partly because of the way she made a reclaiming and rewriting of ancient Greece into a condition of her own emergence as a woman and lesbian; in this project Sappho was of course crucial, as DuPlessis (1986) argues. Like Byron, H.D. made special use of Greece as "a sign of female cultural authority" and a place for an alternative sexuality. Sappho's "lost" texts stand for a "lack of female presence" and "cultural silence about lesbianism." H.D.'s "reconstructions" of several fragments use Sappho's texts as a starting place for recapturing the radical claim to subjectivity in what remains. Such strategies recall the florid voice of Swinburne more than the strict control of Modernism, which was necessary for women writers of the early 20th century, who needed to break with a sentimental, decorative poetry and create a new hard edge. In a different approach, Paula Bennett (1993) calls attention to female erotic imagery such as flowers and pearls, derived from Dickinson, that defines an explicitly female body of work, as in H.D.'s "At Baia."

If Sappho was struggling to find a voice different from that of the male tradition, male poets were themselves using a counter-epic form of the pastoral. The pastoral, one of the most important Renaissance forms, came to the authors of the 16th century in a line of descent from Theocritus to Vergil. In this tradition, the country setting and lower-class characters allow for a frankness of desire and sexuality. Theocritus' Idyll 5, a singing contest, is also marked by delightfully salacious sexual competition, as in these often censored lines, "When I bugger you, you'll feel it. / Your she-goats / will bleat, and your rams will screw them."

Poets of the English Renaissance sustained this tradition, and it has continued to have cultural power, especially in its sub-genre, the pastoral lament in which a friend is mourned after death not only by the speaker but by nature itself. This is the tradition of Tennyson's "In Memoriam," his lament for the dead Arthur Hallam, as well as of Shelley's "Adonais" and, on the American scene, of many recent poems responding to the multiple losses of AIDS, particularly the work of Thom Gunn.

Less directly related to this classical past reborn in the Renaissance, but similarly locating love in a world of nature and in the thematics of the outcast, the American poet Walt Whitman introduced a new democratic poetics as part of his utopian vision of brotherhood, as Fone (1992) has shown. The "Calamus" poems, first added to *Leaves of Grass* in 1860, constitute a sequence on male love at once anguished and triumphant that is a vital precursor to 20th-century gay poetry. Adopting the rural swain persona of the pastoral, as in "In Paths Untrodden," Whitman celebrates the male lovers as "two natural and nonchalant persons."

Whitman's impact on later poets was enormous, for he had effected a revolution in prosody by the refusal of metrical verse. One of his most important followers was Hart Crane, whose long poem *The Bridge* (1930) was a response to the tragic and despairing vision of T.S. Eliot's *The Waste Land* (1922). Critics such as Martin (1979, 1998) have traced the homosexual text in Crane's work. Crane was able to imagine a national recovery from the dangers of industrialism and greed through the example of Whitman. As Whitman had learned to face the possible failure of his vision in the slaughter of the Civil War, Crane would follow Whitman's path toward the prospect of a national rebirth, reclaiming Whitman's Open Road as an emblem for a change in consciousness. The Brooklyn Bridge becomes for Crane the means of ecstatic union and passionate love. Crane was the first modern poet in America to respond so strongly to Whitman's example, although later poets would almost all learn from it.

Lesbian poetry in the 20th century is largely political poetry. The connections between the feminist movement and lesbian experience give a hard edge to poems that, although they celebrate, must also challenge. Judy Grahn's work illustrates this link, especially in a poem such as "A History of Lesbianism," which juxtaposes the "women-loving-women" and the "trials and hatreds" of "male domination." Grahn also celebrates the erotic encounters of women, in a poem such as the concrete "fortunately the skins." Grahn's working-class origins and her own work experience permit her to celebrate the "common woman," the survivor. Grahn recognizes the links among racism, homophobia, class privilege, and misogyny. Her political poems of the 1970s are gradually eclipsed by a new set of concerns, based on mythology and ecology, in which the female body and the earth are similarly called upon as sources of a new consciousness.

Grahn's collection of essays *The Highest Apple: Sappho and the Lesbian Poetic Tradition* (1985) is a crucial document in the reclaiming of a lesbian poetic past. Underlying the search for the lesbian tradition is a belief in a women-centered universe and the worship of the goddess. What was essential about Sappho for Grahn was the sense of writing out of a female-bonded community. The tradition that Grahn sketches is broad enough to include H.D., Gertrude Stein, Dickinson, as well as more contemporary figures. Amy Lowell, protected by her wealth and social standing, was a sharp antagonist to the works of Ezra Pound and challenged his misogyny. Her poems create special, protected space that offers intimacy and privacy. Although Pound liked to include Lowell as an Imagist poet, his deep sexual hostility was expressed in his snide reference to "Amygism." Lowell adopted a male persona in a number of her poems and used imagery of flowers to suggest a female ambiance. Although her personal life was dominated by the love of women, Lowell remained discreet.

For a writer such as Audre Lorde, the return to mythology is more concrete than in Grahn's essays. Lorde writes out of her experience as a Black woman, joining those two identities. Her long stay in Berlin permitted her to reflect upon the vast hatred and evil of oppression, and their embodiment in German history. The term "lesbian" is to be taken in the largest sense, to include women of various sexualities who share lives and experience, and who forge a shared identity. Lorde calls for a sense of community, and her sense of herself includes a search for strong matriarchal figures, African women who can provide strength and resistance.

The best-known and most highly regarded (at least to a larger audience) of modern lesbian poets is Adrienne Rich, who came to fame early, as a Yale Younger Poet. Even her early poems of the 1950s, although written in traditional forms, point to her later development as a feminist and lesbian theorist. "Aunt Jennifer's Tigers" is a testament to silent resistance. Although "the massive weight of Uncle's wedding band / Sits heavily upon Aunt Jennifer's hand," and Aunt Jennifer has been "mastered," her tigers express the survival and even victory, in time, of tigers "proud and unafraid."

In Rich's more recent poems, the concern has shifted from the personal to the national. "An Atlas of the Difficult World" is a major work in the American literary tradition, taking its place alongside the national epics of Whitman and Crane (or, more recently, Alfred Corn). References to those sources are subtly woven into the text. The speaker continues to love the land and its inhabitants even as she will not "hear how he beat her after the earthquake, / tore up her writing, threw the kerosene / lantern into her face." Her Whitmanic catalogs can only be deceptive and ironic: "This is the desert where missiles are planted like corns / This is the breadbasket of foreclosed farms." Her celebration of the Oakland Bridge in section five is an extended riff on Crane's *The Bridge*. Liberty is, as in Crane's wordplay, "chained," and her marginal glosses, echoing Crane's, bespeak instead loss and confusion: "Where are we moored? / What are the bindings?" And yet Rich has a certainty about her audience that Whitman could not share. For Rich "I know you are reading this poem, and will make possible running / up the stairs / to a new kind of love." Whitman's workingman lovers lead to but also give way to the "sensate" hands of a woman.

It is not surprising that the Greek Alexandrian poet C.P. Cavafy has served as a crucial model for a number of contemporary gay male writers, since Cavafy's tone, mixing the ironic and the elegiac, is suitable for conveying the feelings of loss and desire that are so often a part of urban gay life. In particular, Cavafy wrote a number of poems entitled "Days of . . . ," with a year indicated, that record apparently random sexual encounters with young men whose beauty offers a glimpse of the ideal that must inevitably elude us. Mark Doty, the most distinguished young gay male poet, has made brilliant use of the model of Cavafy in a volume whose title indicates Doty's connection to Cavafy, *My Alexandria* (1993). "Days of 1981" records an early sexual experience to the music of the Supremes that is "strangely exhilarating." Nothing comes of this meeting, aside from momentary sexual pleasure, but, as in Cavafy's "Days of . . ." poems, the young man brings "perfected longing and release." Alongside Doty's tributes to Cavafy are his complex reworkings of Hart Crane, who has come to replace Whitman as the central figure of American gay poetry. "Almost Blue," from the same volume, uses multiple fragments from *The Bridge* to call forth an urban reality that Doty calls a "long amalgam of ardor and indifference."

By the 1940s and 1950s most gay poets were no longer satisfied with a style of suggestion and allusion. The poets of the post-war period wanted to write directly of their sexual experiences. These erotic poems, such as Paul Goodman's "Making Love" series, are witty and ironic and yet realistic. In one, "For G. Aet. 16" Goodman recalls a comic cruising of a bartender, "'You're beautiful,' I said, 'I love you' / I met him half an hour ago / but he was and I did." The longing and loss seem to recall Cavafy's poems of desire. Goodman's openness about his sexual encounters will be echoed in more radical forms by the Beats, and especially by Allen Ginsberg and his continuation of the Whitman tradition, notably in *Howl, and Other Poems* (1956). Ginsberg brings together the long poetic line of Whitman and the biblical verse structures of anaphora in an oral poetry of lament. In "A Supermarket in California" Ginsberg undercuts the Whitman tradition of celebration for the sake of the lonely bard: "I saw you, Walt Whitman, childless, lonely old grubber . . . eyeing the grocery boys."

In the latter half of the 20th century American poetry was imagined as divided between a West Coast poetry influenced by the Beats and a more erudite and formal poetry associated with the East Coast and the university world. One of the disagreements on this issue arose when James Merrill was awarded the Bollingen Prize in 1973 and the *New York Times* editorialized against this choice. The division was never that simple. Robert Duncan was of course associated with the West Coast, but he was as learned as any university poet, although favoring mythic sources rather than cultural ones. Duncan also saw himself in a largely female tradition, working throughout his career on "The H.D. Book" and affiliating himself with Grahn. In the East the dominant gay voice of the 1950s was Frank O'Hara, whose lively, mischievous verse in celebration of momentary pleasures captured an emerging gay world. O'Hara insouciantly "tall[ies] up the merits of each / of the latrines" of Manhattan in his poem "Homosexuality," and in "At the Old Place" the poet and his friends plan for an evening of dancing in a gay bar.

It is hard to imagine any contemporary gay poet who has not had to try to come to terms with AIDS and the losses it has brought. Rafael Campo, a Harvard physician of Hispanic origin, brings several perspectives to bear. Campo is able to write with great sympathy of people with AIDS, even as he recognizes a more general world of illness and violence. Campo is particularly strong in his portrayal of drag. He celebrates the absurd and brave gesture of "her Final Show," the drag queen who wears pearls and Opium for her death. The camp style evokes the earlier poet James Merrill. Merrill was another poet of New York City, although he was equally at home in Greece, or at his house in Stonington, Connecticut. His camp style and urbane wit make him a crucial figure in American poetry. His "Matinees" keeps an ironic distance from its recognition of the centrality of art and artifice to life. Merrill has many admirers who have followed in his poetic tradition, notably J.D. McClatchy and Daryl Hine. Their mastery of verse forms and their adroit use of sound owe much to Merrill's wonderful rhyming, a literary surface that barely conceals a ground of psychic pain.

Gender may be performed in these poems, but race is a more complex matter. Reginald Shepherd's work deals repeatedly with the black man as abjected object of desire. Shepherd's poems, often set in a gay bar, call up the cultural association of whiteness and beauty. "Skin Trade" deals with the difficult subject of whiteness in the context of a culture that prizes white over black. The black gay man, such as Shepherd or Marlon Riggs, may find his desire for a white body at odds with a political need to be true to his race. Shepherd writes of such matters in forms that are deeply marked by the past—his frequent echoes of Eliot come to mind—and yet that seek a radical re-imaging of the force of racism in a white culture.

ROBERT K. MARTIN

**Further Reading**

Bennett, Paula, "Critical Clitoridectomy: Female Sexual Imagery and Feminist Psychoanalytic Theory," *Signs* 18 (1993)

Du Bois, Page, *Sappho Is Burning,* Chicago and London: University of Chicago Press, 1996

DuPlessis, Rachel Blau, *H.D.: The Career of That Struggle,* Bloomington: Indiana University Press, 1986

Fone, Byrne R.S., *Masculine Landscapes: Walt Whitman and the Homoerotic Text,* Carbondale: Southern Illinois University Press, 1992

Forster, E.M., *Pharos and Pharillon,* Berkeley, California: Creative Arts, 1980 (originally published in 1923)

Martin, Robert K., *The Homosexual Tradition in Modern Poetry,* Austin: University of Texas Press, 1979; revised edition, Iowa City: University of Iowa Press, 1998

Woods, Gregory, *Articulate Flesh: Male Homo-Eroticism and Modern Poetry,* New Haven, Connecticut: Yale University Press, 1987

Woods, Gregory, *A History of Gay Literature: The Male Tradition,* New Haven, Connecticut: Yale University Press, 1998

---

## Allen Ginsberg 1926–97

The most important poet to emerge from the Beat movement, Allen Ginsberg is, along with Robert Lowell, arguably the most influential poet of the second half of the 20th century. Ginsberg's raw power, spiritual depth, and technical innovation were driving forces in the shift that saw American poetry in the 1950s move away from a New Critical emphasis on formal, metrical, witty, ironic, and allusive verse toward verse that was at once more personal and more political. Thus it is important to juxtapose the prominent poet with his public figure as prophet, guru, activist, critic, and model of alternative lifestyle. Ginsberg emerged as a nationally recognized spokesperson for innovation, dissent, and disaffected youth, combining the spheres of poetry and politics so the two were inextricably intertwined.

Ginsberg's earliest poems were largely traditional, reflecting two key influences: the poet's father, a high school English teacher and poet of some renown, and Mark Van Doren and Lionel Trilling, both of whom taught Ginsberg while he attended Columbia University off and on beginning in 1943. Even when he wrote in the style of the New Critics, however, Ginsberg's works demonstrated his sense of dissatisfaction with the culture surrounding him, permeated as they were by a figure termed by Ginsberg the "shroudy stranger," a lonely, desperate outcast based in part on Ginsberg's homosexuality. The "shroudy stranger" is a frequent element in *The Gates of Wrath* (1972), poems written from 1948 to 1952.

This move beyond traditional verse was accelerated by Ginsberg's expulsion from Columbia in 1945 for scrawling obscenities in the dust of his dorm window and for being caught in bed with his friend and fellow writer Jack Kerouac. Drawn to an "underworld" of drugs, crime, and gay bars, Ginsberg soon rejected traditional verse forms and methods of composition, falling under the influence of William S. Burroughs and Kerouac. A January 1947 meeting with Neal Cassady (the model for Dean Moriarty in Kerouac's *On the Road*) was significant both because Ginsberg fell in love with Cassady, beginning a one-sided relationship that lasted for years, and because Ginsberg, like Kerouac, fell under the spell of Cassady's spontaneity and verbal sleights-of-hand. From this point on, Ginsberg's poems would be written "spontaneously," free of the restraints of the "well-wrought urn."

In 1949 Ginsberg was sentenced to spend time in Columbia Presbyterian Psychiatric Institute because of his friendship with Herbert Huncke, a friendship Huncke abused by using Ginsberg's apartment as a receptacle for property that Huncke and some of his accomplices had stolen. During his eight months at the Institute Ginsberg met Carl Solomon, and long conversations and exchanges of poems with Solomon (to whom "Howl" is dedicated) taught Ginsberg to "Act boldly, [and] think with Caution—even timorously" because "They censor words" (*Journals: Early Fifties, Early Sixties,* 1977).

The period following Ginsberg's release from the Institute was crucial for him. Returning to his hometown of Paterson, New Jersey, Ginsberg struck up a friendship with William Carlos Williams, whose work he had long admired. This friendship led Ginsberg to produce poetic rhythms that reflected actual speech rhythms, as Williams' did. The connection with Williams also locates Ginsberg as a Romantic poet and points to his literary inheritance from Walt Whitman and Herman Melville, from whom he learned the long poetic lines that typify his major works. In addition to such stylistic influences, Ginsberg was deeply attracted to spirituality as a way of breaking down personal identity, finding a sense of belonging, and enhancing poetic production. A key figure in this spiritual quest was William Blake, who Ginsberg believed spoke to him in a 1948 vision, and who stamped Ginsberg's writing with the seemingly polar yet inseparable themes of ecstasy and horror, innocence and experience. Ginsberg's own spiritual questing took a different direction, into Asian philosophy (specifically, Zen Buddhist thought and meditation) as a path to awareness of the wholeness of all things.

All of these elements coalesced in Ginsberg's most influential volume, one of the most significant poetic works of the 20th century: *Howl, and Other Poems* (1956), written after Ginsberg moved to San Francisco. *Howl* reinvigorated and revalidated the Beat movement at a time when "Beat" had become popularized and stereotyped as the beret-sporting, finger-snapping "beatniks." The title poem was influenced not only by the writers and writings mentioned earlier, but also by peyote ("certainly one of the world's great drugs" [*Journals: Early Fifties, Early Sixties*]); haiku, with its intense compression and omission of logical connectives (what Ezra Pound termed "superposition" decades earlier); and Paul Cezanne's overlapping geometric figures, which Ginsberg saw as a way to add depth. Attacked or ignored by most critics at first, "Howl" was immediately adopted as the Beat manifesto and celebrated by the counterculture. In the poem Ginsberg contrasts a hipster's dream world of drugs, madness, and homosexuality with "Moloch's" straight world of money, machinery, and war to criticize the deadening effects of mainstream 1950s convention. Other important poems from *Howl* include "Sunflower Sutra" and "In the Baggage Room at Greyhound." The latter is at once despairing and hopeful as the poet, in his capacity as a baggage handler, provides a Whitmanesque list of material possessions that surround him in the baggage room loft, a "grayish-green whale's stomach interior"; by the end of the poem, however, the poet recognizes that both this job and the life it represents are fit only "for the poor shepherds," and not for himself: "I am a communist," he proclaims. The former is an affirmation of the holiness and blessedness of existence, in which contemplation of a sunflower (pointed out by Jack Kerouac) leads the poet to conclude the following:

> —We're not our skin of grime, . . .
> . . . we're all
> beautiful golden sunflowers inside, we're bles-
> sed by our own seed & golden hairy naked ac-
> complishment-bodies growing into mad black
> formal sunflowers in the sunset

The volume raised a serious challenge to traditionalist poetry of the 1950s, and its focus on previously forbidden and "unliterary" topics led to a highly publicized obscenity trial for its publisher Lawrence Ferlinghetti, a trial that simultaneously opened the door for more open and honest poetry and propelled both Ginsberg and the Beat movement into national prominence.

*Kaddish, and Other Poems* (1961), a more mature volume than its celebrated predecessor, reflects Ginsberg's growing interest in hallucinogens as a way of exploring the inner space of the mind. Manifested in experiments with such drugs as LSD, mescaline, psilocybin, morphine, and dexadrine, poems like "Mescaline, "Lysergic Acid," and "Laughing Gas" attempt to record different altered states in fragmentary fashion. This volume is most noteworthy for its title poem, however, an elegy for the poet's mother Naomi Levy, whose long mental illness, institutionalization for paranoid delusions, and death in 1956 had a profound effect on Ginsberg. "Kaddish" is a poem of psychological anguish in which he examines both his deep love for his mother and the pain her affliction causes him. While the poem—especially the deeply moving recollection of Ginsberg's last visit with his mother in Pilgrim State Hospital—is confessional and serves as the "kaddish" (the Jewish burial rites), "Kaddish" moves beyond the personal. It positions his mother as an emblem of all those persecuted for their religion, politics, ideologies, and social status—unlike "Howl," which generalized grief for the many with Whitmanesque catalogs. Other poems from *Kaddish* that fuse elegy and social commentary include "To Aunt Rose," "At Apollinaire's Grave," and especially "Death to Van Gogh's Ear," which begins, "Money has reckoned the soul of America," and continues to criticize a society that rejects the spiritual, creative, and artistic (Van Gogh) in favor of the material, the "million automobiles" that Detroit churns out. Like the poem about Van Gogh (which identifies America as "lacklove"), "To Aunt Rose" mourns the "tears of sexual frustration" shed not only by Ginsberg's aunt but by all those who suppress the urges of the body.

Ginsberg spent the period from March 1961 to July 1963 in travels to France, Morocco, Greece, Israel, India, Vietnam, and Japan, taking the opportunity to learn from different spiritual and philosophical sages. From philosopher Martin Buber in Israel and different Indian holy men with whom he studied Hindu thought and meditation practices, Ginsberg came to focus on interpersonal relationships and contentment within the body rather than attempting to reach transcendence by moving beyond physical limitations. This shift from consciousness-raising through hallucinogens to consciousness-raising through meditation and yoga, recorded in the poem "The Change," is evidenced in two of the volumes that Ginsberg produced during the decade of the 1960s: *Reality Sandwiches* (1963) and *Planet News: 1961–1967* (1968). In the former he collects poems written from 1953 to 1960, depicting the Beat lifestyle and sensibility and tracing his own coming of age, often in what critics have noted as loose, rambling, and sentimental verse. The poems in *Planet News* express Ginsberg's sympathy for developing nations and criticism of Western nations for their repressive economic and military policies. No longer is he concerned with "the greatest minds of a [Beat] generation," but rather with the suffering and exploitation of masses of humans. These poems rely on the rhythm, breath, and elemental sounds of Hindu mantras, and are thus transformed into poetic prayers. Specifically, these prayers are often directed at the youth of America, with whom Ginsberg was in constant contact owing to his performances on university campuses during the mid- to late 1960s. Operating in the Whitmanesque role of poet-prophet, Ginsberg felt it was his mission to enlighten young people to the evils of America's involvement in Vietnam and its puritanical repression of open sexuality. "Wichita Vortex Sutra" is a clear example of the commingled poet and preacher, as it criticizes the "vortex" of illusion and corruption into which middle America has fallen.

During the 1960s Ginsberg complemented his public readings and performances with participation in various protests, peace marches, and sit-ins. As time passed the poet became almost secondary to the public figure, and the poetry secondary to the spiritual activism. Nonetheless, he continued to produce volumes reflecting both his hopes and his fears for America. *The Fall of America* (1972) is pessimistic and grim, connecting the landscape devastated by industry, spiritual pollution caused by war in Asia, and personal suffering (his own aging and injuries suffered in a 1968 auto accident) and mortality (the death of Neal Cassady in 1968 and Jack Kerouac in 1969). In *Mind Breaths: Poems, 1972–1977* (1978), Ginsberg demonstrates the influence of the Buddhist abbot Chogyam Trungpa, who instructed the poet in *shamatha*, a form of meditation in which the practitioner concentrates on his or her own breathing. Poems such as "What Would You Do If You Lost It?" and "Thoughts Sitting Breathing" suggest a oneness of body and mind and a meditative approach to the materiality of life.

During the last decade of his life Ginsberg continued to read on university campuses and to serve as spokesperson for the avant-garde while returning to New Jersey to live on a small farm. He died one of the great figures of American poetry, a relentless crusader against materialism and imperialism and a technically innovative poet who voiced the despair and anxiety of several generations of Americans.

RICHARD A. IADONISI

*See also* Beat Poetry

**Biography**

Born in Newark, New Jersey, 3 June 1926. Attended Columbia University, New York, 1943–45, 1946–48, A.B. 1948; served in the Military Sea Transport Service; book reviewer, *Newsweek*, New York, 1950; market researcher, New York, 1951–53, and San Francisco, 1954; freelance writer; participant in many poetry readings and demonstrations; from 1971 director, Committee on Poetry Foundation, New York; co-founder, 1974, and director, 1974–83 (from 1984 emeritus), Kerouac School of Poetics, Naropa Institute, Boulder, Colorado; Distinguished Professor, Brooklyn College, New York, 1986. Received Guggenheim fellowship, 1965; National Endowment for the Arts grant, 1966, 1987; American Academy grant, 1969; National Book Award, 1974; National Arts Club Gold Medal, 1979; *Los Angeles Times* Award, 1982; member, American Academy, 1973. Died in New York City, 5 April 1997.

**Poetry**

*Howl, and Other Poems*, 1956; revised edition, 1971; annotated edition, 1986
*Empty Mirror: Early Poems*, 1961
*Kaddish, and Other Poems, 1958–60*, 1961
*Reality Sandwiches, 1953–60*, 1963
*Penguin Modern Poets 5* (poems by Ginsberg, Lawrence Ferlinghetti, and Gregory Corso), 1963
*T.V. Baby Poems*, 1967
*Planet News, 1961–1967*, 1968
*Airplane Dreams: Compositions from Journals*, 1968
*Ankor Wat*, 1968
*Iron Horse*, 1972
*The Gates of Wrath: Rhymed Poems, 1948–1952*, 1972
*Bixby Canyon Ocean Path Word Breeze*, 1972
*The Fall of America: Poems of These States, 1965–1971*, 1972
*Sad Dust Glories*, 1975
*First Blues: Rags, Ballads, and Harmonium Songs, 1971–1974*, 1975
*Mind Breaths: Poems, 1972–1977*, 1978
*Poems All over the Place: Mostly Seventies*, 1978
*Mostly Sitting Haiku*, 1978; revised edition, 1979
*Plutonian Ode: Poems, 1977–1980*, 1982
*Collected Poems, 1947–1980*, 1984
*White Shroud: Poems, 1980–1985*, 1986
*Cosmopolitan Greetings: Poems, 1986–1992*, 1994
*Making It Up: Poetry Composed at St. Marks Church on May 9, 1979*, 1994
*Selected Poems, 1947–1995*, 1996
*Illuminated Poems* (illustrated by Eric Drooker), 1996
*Death and Fame: Poems, 1993–1997*, 1999

**Selected Criticism**

*Allen Verbatim: Lectures on Poetry, Politics, Consciousness*, edited by Gordon Ball, 1974
*Composed on the Tongue: Literary Conversations, 1967–1977*, edited by Donald Allen, 1980

**Other Writings:** plays, nonfiction (*Chicago Trial Testimony*, 1975), journals, letters.

**Further Reading**

Fiedler, Leslie, *Waiting for the End*, New York: Stein and Day, 1964; London: Cape, 1965
Hyde, Lewis, editor, *On the Poetry of Allen Ginsberg*, Ann Arbor: University of Michigan Press, 1984

Kramer, Jane, *Allen Ginsberg in America*, New York: Random House, 1969; as *Paterfamilias: Allen Ginsberg in America*, London: Gollancz, 1970

Martin, Robert K., *The Homosexual Tradition in American Poetry*, Austin: University of Texas Press, 1979; expanded edition, Iowa City: University of Iowa Press, 1998

Morgan, Bill, *The Response to Allen Ginsberg, 1926–1994: A Bibliography of Secondary Sources*, Westport, Connecticut: Greenwood Press, 1996

Mottram, Eric, *Allen Ginsberg in the Sixties*, Brighton, East Sussex, and Seattle, Washington: Unicorn Bookshop, 1972

Portugés, Paul, *The Visionary Poetics of Allen Ginsberg*, Santa Barbara, California: Ross-Erikson, 1978

Sanders, Edward, *The Poetry and Life of Allen Ginsberg: A Narrative Poem*, Woodstock, New York: Overlook Press, 2000

Schumacher, Michael, *Dharma Lion: A Critical Biography of Allen Ginsberg*, New York: St. Martin's Press, 1992

Tytell, John, *Naked Angels: Kerouac, Ginsberg, Burroughs*, New York: Grove Press, 1991

## America

Allen Ginsberg's "America" was written in January 1956. At the time Ginsberg lived in Berkeley, California, where he completed several of the poems that would be included in his early and influential book *Howl, and Other Poems* (1956). *Howl* is of particular historical importance both for its publishing history and for its central place in the literature of the mid-century movement known as the San Francisco Renaissance. Printed in Europe, the volume was seized by United States customs agents in 1957, and Lawrence Ferlinghetti of City Lights Books was charged with obscenity for his role in its publication. Later that year a judge in San Francisco dismissed the case, deciding that, although some people might find the book offensive, as a whole the work contained redeeming social content.

Ginsberg opens his ode to America by speaking to the country directly, as if he were having a private conversation with another person. With the opening line—"America I've given you all and now I'm nothing"—Ginsberg emphasizes the alienation that many young intellectuals felt during the 1950s. With the end of World War II came a narrowing of cultural values and a conservatism in politics that many people in the United States found alarming. In "America" Ginsberg presents the reader with a catalog of the important issues of the time period. He speaks of the anxieties related to the atomic age and the Cold War, the phenomenon of anti-Communist sentiment in the United States, and the move to impose stricter moral codes in American society. The form of "America" is derived partly from the poetry of Walt Whitman in its series of long, unrhymed lines organized as a list. Whitman was a major influence on Ginsberg's writing and politics. Ginsberg shared with Whitman the view that American democracy would eventually triumph, despite the country's internal strife and external conflicts. Raised in a household where socialist politics were highly valued, Ginsberg early on sought to combine historical facts and autobiographical anecdotes in his writing. This passage from "America" is characteristic:

> America when I was seven momma took me to Communist Cell meetings they sold us garbanzos a handful per ticket a ticket cost a nickel and the speeches were free everybody was angelic and sentimental about the workers it was all so sincere you have no idea what a good thing the party was in 1853

As the poem progresses, Ginsberg creates a portrait of himself as a young writer, a political activist, and a homosexual.

"America" helped to cement Ginsberg's role as a spokesperson for the Beat Generation of the 1950s and for the counterculture and anti-war movements of the 1960s. Alongside friends such as Jack Kerouac, Neal Cassady, Gregory Corso, and William Burroughs, Ginsberg contributed to a body of literature that critiqued the culture of the period. During the 1950s public acknowledgment of one's own deviance was dangerous, as society often seemed closed and hostile toward people who violated the rules of acceptable conduct. In "America" Ginsberg systematically challenges many of the social mores that he finds too restrictive, particularly in statements such as "I smoke marijuana every chance I get." Radical political views such as those expressed in "America" were grounds for investigation by government agencies such as the House Un-American Activities Committee (HUAC), formed in the 1950s to monitor the threat of communism in the United States. Ginsberg not only implicates himself in these activities but also uses his poem to give voice to a number of figures persecuted at the hands of the United States government:

> America free Tom Mooney
> America save the Spanish Loyalists
> America Sacco and Vanzetti must not die
> America I am the Scottsboro Boys.

Here Ginsberg collects a disparate group of people: labor leader Tom Mooney, who was erroneously imprisoned in 1919; the Spanish Loyalists who fought against Fascism during the Spanish Civil War; Italian anarchists Sacco and Vanzetti, who were executed on false murder charges in 1927; and nine young black men known as the Scottsboro Boys who were arrested and jailed under questionable circumstances in Alabama in 1931. In bringing together these names Ginsberg illustrates the universality of suffering at the hands of government. He identifies with the plight of such individuals throughout the poem.

While the tone of "America" is sometimes humorous, the humor is used to expose the tragic nature of American policies leading up to the Cold War. Toward the end of the poem Ginsberg points out the absurdity of American fears about other peoples, mocking the cultural paranoia that was so much a part of the 1950s American mindset:

> America you don't really want to go to war.
> America it's them bad Russians.
> Them Russians them Russians and them Chinamen.
>         And them Russians.
> The Russia wants to eat us alive. The Russia's power mad.
>    She wants to take our cars
>         from out our garages.
> Her wants to grab Chicago. Her needs a Red Reader's
>    Digest.

Her wants our auto plants in Siberia. Him big bureaucracy
running our fillingstations.
That no good. Ugh. Him make Indians learn read. Him
need big black niggers. Hah.
Her make us all work sixteen hours a day. Help.

Because of his candid statements about politics throughout his career, Allen Ginsberg was viewed by the Federal Bureau of Investigation and other governmental agencies as a threat to national security. In "America" as in many other poems, however, he expresses a loyalty to his country and a deep concern for its future. Attempting to reconcile himself with the society in which he lives, Ginsberg asks that he and all other individuals be accepted as part of the country's "natural resources," or as he says in the poem's closing lines, "America I'm putting my queer shoulder to the wheel."

LISA JARNOT

**Further Reading**


Charters, Samuel Barclay, *Some Poems/Poets: Studies in American Underground Poetry since 1945,* Berkeley, California: Oyez, 1971

Davidson, Michael, *The San Francisco Renaissance: Poetics and Community at Mid-Century,* Cambridge and New York: Cambridge University Press, 1989

Ginsberg, Allen, *Journals: Early Fifties, Early Sixties,* edited by Gordon Ball, New York: Grove Press, 1977

Hahn, Stephen, "The Prophetic Voice of Allen Ginsberg," *Prospectus: Annual of American Cultural Studies* 2 (1976)

Hyde, Lewis, editor, *On the Poetry of Allen Ginsberg,* Ann Arbor: University of Michigan Press, 1984

Miles, Barry, *Ginsberg: A Biography,* New York: Simon and Schuster, 1989; London: Viking Press, 1990

Peters, Nancy J., "The Beat Generation and San Francisco's Culture of Dissent," in *Reclaiming San Francisco History: Politics, Culture,* edited by James Brook, Chris Carlsson, and Nancy J. Peters, San Francisco: City Lights, 1998

Rumaker, Michael, "Allen Ginsberg's 'Howl,'" *Black Mountain Review* (Autumn 1957)


# Howl

Along with Jack Kerouac's *On the Road* (1957) and William Burroughs' *Naked Lunch* (1959), "Howl" (including "Footnote to Howl") marks the high point of Beat Generation literary achievement and is arguably the best-known American poem published since T.S. Eliot's "The Waste Land" (1922). Written in August 1955—Ginsberg would recall large chunks of the poem "typed out madly in one afternoon" (Merrill, 1988)—"Howl" caused a sensation when Ginsberg performed it at San Francisco's Six Gallery in the fall of 1955, as much for its shattering of poetic conventions as for its expression of "revolutionary individuality" and its restoration to American poetry of a "prophetic consciousness" (Ginsberg, 1986). Published a year later as part of *Howl, and Other Poems* (1956), "Howl" became a *cause célèbre* when poet-publisher Lawrence Ferlinghetti and his bookstore manager were arrested for selling an "obscene" book. The precedent-setting trial that ensued insured Ginsberg's fame even as the court found the poem protected by the First Amendment because, in the words of Judge Clayton Horn, it was not "without redeeming social importance."

But however influential the poem might be for its confessional immediacy and prosodic innovations, "Howl" stands as the signature poem of the 1950s and a manifesto of the Beats (and, later, of the 1960s counterculture) because it gives voice to what Gregory Stephenson (1990) has described as "the personal and social consequences of trying to achieve . . . transcendence" amid a materialistic culture. "Howl" is, as its famous opening line declares, a vision of "the best minds" of Ginsberg's generation "destroyed by madness, starving hysterical naked" and the poet's search for an alternative wherein everything and everyone are parts of a visionary company of holiness.

Employing the language of the street, jazz phrasings, long lines reminiscent of Walt Whitman, surreal metaphors, and a rhetorical stance evocative of the Lamentations of Jeremiah, the opening section of "Howl," running eight pages in the original edition, is a single sentence comprised largely of relative clauses. Part I catalogs the atrocities committed against those "angelheaded hipsters" whose refusal or inability to conform takes them down what William Blake termed the "road of excess" in their often self-destructive quest for salvific love and transcendent wisdom. They are holy misfits "who cowered in unshaven rooms in underwear, burning their money in wastebaskets and listening to the Terror through the wall," who "ate fire in paint hotels or drank turpentine in Paradise Alley" while "listening to the crack of doom on the hydrogen jukebox" and, wherever they went, "[left] no broken hearts."

Part II of "Howl" targets the source of such defeat, despair, and discontent: Moloch, the biblical god of abominations to whom children were sacrificed, here depicted as a state of mind and, according to Stephenson (1990), "the ruling principle of our age." Moloch is responsible for all of America's woes: its materialism, indifference, ignorance, brutality, sexual repression: "Moloch whose love is endless oil and stone! Moloch whose soul is electricity and banks! . . . Moloch whose fate is a cloud of sexless hydrogen! Moloch whose name is the Mind!"

If Moloch (the establishment, the powers that be, the conformist mainstream) "frightens [the individual] out of natural ecstasy"—what Ginsberg described in a letter to poet Richard Eberhart as "the mechanical feelingless inhuman world we live in and accept" (Ginsberg, 1986)—it is possible, Ginsberg affirms, to "Wake up in Moloch!" Part III of "Howl" and the "Footnote to Howl" dramatize the effects of such an awakening. Part III is a litany of solidarity with Carl Solomon, to whom the poem is dedicated (Ginsberg had met Solomon when both were patients at Columbia Presbyterian Psychiatric Institute) and whom Ginsberg uses to symbolize all oppressed members of his generation driven crazy by the world in which they are forced to live. "Carl Solomon! I am with you in Rockland [Mental Hospital] / where you're madder than I am," the poet begins, repeating "I am with you in Rockland" as refrain as he howls his empathetic comradeship within the "armed madhouse" wherein both men find themselves.

Ginsberg's commitment to Solomon helps effect that awakening hypothesized in Part II, and the speaker can now see the world rhapsodically. "Footnote to Howl" can therefore close the poem by chanting the sacredness of everything: "The world is holy! The soul is holy! The skin is holy! The nose is holy! The tongue and cock and hand and asshole holy!" As throughout, Ginsberg's strategy, in the words of Peter Georgelos (1995), is to deploy his long poetic lines as "a kind of battering ram against all forms of enclosure" in order to "break out into a wider experience of life."

An exercise in radical imagination, the poem charts a course from despair and defeat to what Ginsberg (1986) has described as

> self-realization, self-acceptance and the consequent and inevitable relaxation of protective anxiety and selfhood and the ability to see and love others in themselves as angels.

This vision of a counterculture founded on love and the divinity inherent in everyone and everything moved many readers throughout the 1950s and 1960s. "Howl" continues to speak to all those who hope to find, at the end of a dark night spent walking "on the snowbank docks" with "their shoes full of blood," "the supernatural extra brilliant intelligent kindness of the soul" and to praise it.

BROOKE HORVATH

**Further Reading**


Casale, Frank D., "Madness, Speech, and Prophecy in Allen Ginsberg's 'Howl,'" *Spectacle* 1, no. 2 (1998)

Foster, Edward Halsey, *Understanding the Beats,* Columbia: University of South Carolina Press, 1992

Georgelos, Peter, "Allen Ginsberg and the American Jeremiad," *Kerouac Connection* 27 (Winter 1995)

Ginsberg, Allen, *Howl: Original Draft Facsimile, Transcript, and Variant Versions, Fully Annotated by Author, with Contemporaneous Correspondence, Account of First Public Reading, Legal Skirmishes, Precursor Texts, and Bibliography,* edited by Barry Miles, New York: Harper and Row, 1986

Merrill, Thomas F., *Allen Ginsberg,* New York: Twayne, 1969; revised edition, Boston: Twayne, 1988

Miles, Barry, *Ginsberg: A Biography,* New York: Simon and Schuster, 1989; London: Viking Press, 1990

Ostriker, Alicia, "'Howl' Revisited: The Poet as Jew," *American Poetry Review* 26 (July–August 1997)

Sanders, Ed, *The Poetry and Life of Allen Ginsberg: A Narrative Poem,* Woodstock, New York: Overlook Press, 2000

Stephenson, Gregory, *The Daybreak Boys: Essays on the Literature of the Beat Generation,* Carbondale: Southern Illinois University Press, 1990

Watson, Steven, *The Birth of the Beat Generation: Visionaries, Rebels, and Hipsters, 1944–1960,* New York: Pantheon, 1995


## Kaddish

September 1960: for 30 hours straight Allen Ginsberg typed in a fury at his desk in his apartment on Second Avenue in Manhattan's Lower East Side. Fueled by benzedrine and dexedrine, he wrote the final revisions to his long poem "Kaddish," an elegy to his mother Naomi, who died in a mental institution on 9 June 1956 after suffering for decades from incurable paranoid delusions. Ginsberg took the name of his five-part poem (which he had begun while crying alone one night in November 1957 in a Paris café) from the 2,500-year-old Jewish prayer for the dead. After a partial appearance in *The New American Poetry: 1945–1960* (1960), "Kaddish" was published in its entirety in *Kaddish, and Other Poems* (1961), book number 14 in Lawrence Ferlinghetti's City Lights Pocket Poets series. The poem's text appears virtually unchanged in Ginsberg's *Collected Poems* (1984) and *Selected Poems* (1996).

So uncertain was he of his achievement that in the letter to Ferlinghetti he included with the manuscript, Ginsberg worried that he might be sending along "a huge white elephant." In a 1966 essay, "How *Kaddish* Happened," by then convinced of the poem's immortality, Ginsberg reflected upon his earlier doubts:

> Defeat like that is good for poetry—you can go so far out you don't know what you're doing, you lose touch with what's been done before by anyone, you wind up creating a new poetry-universe. "Make it new" saith Pound, "Invention," said W.C. Williams. That's the "Tradition"—a complete fuckup so you're on your own. (Allen and Tallman, 1973)

Ginsberg believed his poem required complete candor to succeed. The outburst in Paris (he believed he wrote best when crying) became Part IV of the poem. The rest of his first draft exploded out of him in a 40-hour non-stop session boosted by morphine, methamphetamine, and dexedrine in November 1958, soon after moving back to New York:

> . . . downtown Manhattan, clear winter noon, and I've been up all night, talking, talking, reading the Kaddish aloud,
> listening to Ray Charles blues shout blind on the phonograph
> the rhythm the rhythm—and your memory in my head three years after—

When he stopped, he had filled up 58 pages of onion-skin typing paper with ballpoint pen scratchings, having broken through to feelings and memories about his mother that he had repressed or been afraid to write down before.

Ginsberg had sent his father, Louis, an early draft in May 1959. "Some lines are heartwrenching," Louis averred, "what with not only you but me being at that time in the middle of anguish." Of a line about Naomi's "beard about the vagina," Louis wrote, "It's bad taste and offends my sensibilities." Replying in defense, Ginsberg was earnest, self-righteous:

> The line about the "beard around the vagina" is probably a sort of very common experience and image that children have who see their parents naked and it is an archtypical [sic] experience and nothing to be ashamed of. It looks from the outside, objectively, probably much less shocking than it appears to you, I think—it's a universal experience which almost everyone has had though not many poets have referred to it but it can do no harm to be brought to consciousness.

"The decision is yours," wrote back Louis, clearly sensing that he had about as much chance of winning this argument as the ones he had had over the years with strong-willed Naomi. He signed off, pointedly, "In words begin responsibilities" (Schumacher, 1992)—an allusion to a work by Delmore Schwartz.

No expression of what can happen when madness takes down a family had ever been so rawly rendered in English poetry, making "Kaddish" the most extreme of Confessional poems—which is not to say that it was the most sublime. Its meaning hit the reader between the eyes with pointed rhetorical dashes and expansive lines, just as in "Howl," but it was choppier, more telegraphic, not so messianic or excessively self-conscious. At the center of the poem sounded a voice of prophecy akin to the Hebrew patriarchs of old; this prophet was a woman, however, the poet's mother, a discard of society. In a review when the book first came out, Harvey Shapiro called Naomi Ginsberg "the most bizarre muse in English lit" (Hyde, 1984). Totally dispossessed of everything except for the passion of her visions, she expressed truths that were out of mind and yet at times immensely appealing in their tenderness, humor, Jewish folksiness, and candor. The wisdom of madness is an old theme, but that is not what made Naomi so disturbingly new. Passages like the following startled readers, to say the least:

> One time I thought she was trying to make me come lay her—flirting to herself at sink—lay back on huge bed that filled most of the room, dress up round her hips, big slash of hair, scars of operations, pancreas, belly wounds, abortions, appendix, stitching of incisions pulling down in the fat like hideous thick zippers—ragged long lips between her legs—What, even, smell of asshole?

Ginsberg seemed to spare nothing about what was for him a brutal experience: the loss of his mother, first to madness, then to institutionalization, and finally to death.

"For years, Allen could not understand why his mother had deserted him," said Louis (Miles, 1989), and the poem reflects his devastation:

> "The Horror" I weeping—to see her again—"The Horror"—as if she were dead thru funeral rot in—"The Horror!"
>
> I came back she yelled more—they led her away—"You're not Allen—" I watched her face—but she passed by me, not looking—

If she was mad, he was mad, too. The speaker was only beginning to understand how hard he would have to work to heal himself, to redeem not just himself, but her as well; and not just her, but ultimately, the world in which such horror is possible.

Mark Melnicove

**Further Reading**

Allen, Donald, and Warren Tallman, editors, *Poetics of the New American Poetry,* New York: Grove Press, 1973

Caveney, Graham, *Screaming with Joy: The Life of Allen Ginsberg,* New York: Broadway, 1999

Hyde, Lewis, editor, *On the Poetry of Allen Ginsberg,* Ann Arbor: University of Michigan Press, 1984

Miles, Barry, *Ginsberg: A Biography,* New York: Simon and Schuster, 1989; London: Viking Press, 1990

Ostriker, Alicia, "'Howl' Revisited: The Poet as Jew," *American Poetry Review* 26 (July–August 1997)

Schumacher, Michael, *Dharma Lion: A Critical Biography of Allen Ginsberg,* New York: St. Martin's Press, 1992

---

## Dana Gioia 1950–

Although Dana Gioia had been working as a poet, editor, critic, and translator since his undergraduate years at Stanford University, he did not publish his first full-length collection of poems, *Daily Horoscope* (1986), until he was 35 years old. Most of the poems included in that volume were composed over the previous decade and tirelessly revised while Gioia worked as a business executive. A few of them, such as "Men after Work," "Waiting in the Airport," "The Man in the Open Doorway," and "A Short History of Tobacco," took as their starting points the white-collar working world (or the language of that world) that had rarely appeared in American verse. Gioia seemed an anomaly: a businessman-poet who had been listed in *Esquire* in 1984 as one of the "men and women under forty who are changing America." Since then Gioia has indeed made an impact on American letters, especially poetry, but that impact has been due more to his criticism and his editions of textbooks and anthologies. His poems, although widely reviewed, have been less fully understood.

*Daily Horoscope* is not only the product of a businessman-poet; it is also the debut of a powerfully elegiac voice. Gioia's poetry is rooted in the spartan clarities of the Stanford School and poets such as Yvor Winters, J.V. Cunningham, and Timothy Steele. Because he often writes in rhyme and meter, he was from the start associated with other poets whom hostile critics called New Formalists. Eventually the name simply stuck and was taken up by the poets themselves. The label, however, ignores Gioia's frequent use of free verse and his avoidance of "form for form's sake." "The Burning Ladder," the lyric that opens *Daily Horoscope,* contrasts human aspirations with their limits in a world in which "Gravity" is "Always greater than desire." The poem announces Gioia's visionary stance: he is more muted and self-effacing than the Beats or the Confessional poets, but no less insightful about modern life. Poems like "In Cheever Country" and "Eastern Standard Time" dare to suggest that suburban life contains subjects worthy of art. Other poems, such as "In Chandler Country," "An Elegy for Vladimir de Pachman," and "Four Speeches from Pygmalion," derive from Gioia's wide reading. "Cuckoos" is a lyric of great beauty and simplicity, while "Lives of the Great Composers" adapts the complexities of the verbal fugue invented by Weldon Kees.

*Daily Horoscope* is a book of variety and accomplishment. Poems such as "My Secret Life," "The Journey, the Arrival and the

Dream," and "The Room Upstairs" are among the best short monologues or narratives of the 1980s and 1990s. Two strong narrative poems anchor Gioia's second collection, *The Gods of Winter* (1991), as well. In "Counting the Children" a Chinese-American accountant is forced to confront his own fears of human vulnerability. "The Homecoming," a chilling monologue in the voice of a serial killer, is also in lucid blank verse:

> I walked back to the kitchen quietly
> and saw her busy working at the sink.
> She must have heard me come into the room,
> but if she did, she wouldn't turn around.
> And I came up behind her all at once.
> Then it was over—over just like that.

*The Gods of Winter* also contains some of Gioia's most personal poems, including the poems in the opening sequence—beginning with "Prayer" and concluding with "Planting a Sequoia"—that deal with the death of an infant son. "The Next Poem," a sort of *ars poetica* composed long before but deliberately excluded from *Daily Horoscope,* is found alongside "The Silence of the Poets" and "My Confessional Sestina," poems that make light of literary pretensions, and "Money," a brief tour de force based on the challenging dictum of Wallace Stevens: "Money is a kind of poetry." Perhaps due to personal grief, this second volume is less reserved than Gioia's first, but one can readily locate the unifying elegiac voice of both books.

A final point to make about Gioia's poems is that they are written by a seasoned Californian. Poems like "Rough Country"—which begins "Give me a landscape full of obstacles"—"California Hills in August," and "Becoming a Redwood" speak not only of Gioia's critical and spiritual positions but also of his strong identification with his region.

As a critic Gioia displays an acute knowledge not only of world literature but also of music and economics. He has a rare ability to think of the place of poetry in almost sociological terms. This is also the most controversial aspect of his work. In *Can Poetry Matter?* (1992), the title essay argues that poets themselves have contributed to their marginalization in the broader culture, and that the proliferation of creative writing programs has not generally improved the state of the art. In response, defenders of such programs charged that Gioia's position outside the academy made him a dangerous conservative, but the book was also greeted with passionate support in many quarters, not just among New Formalists. Gioia had struck a nerve. Interestingly, some of the ideas in the book that once seemed controversial—such as the idea that poets cannot afford to ignore the educated common reader—are now taken almost for granted in discussions of poetry. The book is also notable for "Notes on the New Formalism," "Business and Poetry," and its pieces on Weldon Kees, Robinson Jeffers, and Ted Kooser.

If Gioia is a kind of populist, he is also a learned critic and translator who has published versions of Montale and Seneca and has co-edited two volumes of translations from the Italian. Add to this his textbooks and other anthologies, his uncollected criticism and music reviews, his libretto for *Nosferatu,* and new poems appearing in numerous small magazines, and it becomes increasingly apparent that Gioia's growing prominence is the product of great industry. The controversy surrounding some of his ideas may not entirely disappear, but one thing is certain: Gioia is becoming one of the most challenging and important figures in contemporary letters.

David Mason

*See also* New Formalism

**Biography**

Born in Los Angeles, California, 24 December 1950. Attended Stanford University, Palo Alto, California, B.A. 1973, M.B.A. 1977; Harvard University, Cambridge, Massachusetts, M.A. 1975; development manager, General Foods Corporation, White Plains, New York, 1977–87, marketing manager, 1988–90, vice president, 1990–92; since 1992 freelance writer; member, board of directors, Wesleyan University Writers Conference, 1985–. Received Frederick Bock Prize (*Poetry*), 1986; Poetry Book Society (London) main selection, 1991; Poets' Prize, 1992; *Publisher's Weekly* Best Books Award, 1992; American Literary Translator's Award, 1992. Living in Santa Rosa, California.

**Poetry**

*Daily Horoscope,* 1986
*The Gods of Winter,* 1991
*Interrogations at Noon,* 2001

**Selected Criticism**

*Can Poetry Matter?: Essays on Poetry and American Culture,* 1992

**Other Writings:** libretto (*Nosferatu,* 2000), translations of Italian literature (*Mottetti: Poems of Love,* by Eugenio Montale, 1990); edited anthologies (*New Italian Poets* [with Michael Palma], 1990; *Literature: An Introduction to Fiction, Poetry, and Drama* [with X.J. Kennedy], 1998).

**Further Reading**

Feirstein, Frederick, editor, *Expansive Poetry: Essays on the New Narrative and the New Formalism,* Santa Cruz, California: Story Line Press, 1989; revised edition, as *New Expansive Poetry: Theory, Criticism, History,* edited by R.S. Gwynn, Ashland, Oregon: Story Line Press, 1999
Foley, Jack, *O Powerful Western Star,* Oakland, California: Pantograph, 2000
Jarman, Mark, and David Mason, editors, *Rebel Angels: 25 Poets of the New Formalism,* Brownsville, Oregon, Story Line Press, 1996
Lindner, April, *Dana Gioia,* edited by John P. O'Grady, Boise, Idaho: Boise State University Press, 2000
Mason, David, *The Poetry of Life and the Life of Poetry: Essays and Reviews,* Ashland, Oregon: Story Line Press, 2000
Shetley, Vernon, *After the Death of Poetry: Poet and Audience in Contemporary America,* Durham, North Carolina: Duke University Press, 1993
Stevenson, Anne, *Between the Iceberg and the Ship: Selected Essays,* Ann Arbor: University of Michigan Press, 1998
Walzer, Kevin, *The Ghost of Tradition: Expansive Poetry and Postmodernism,* Ashland, Oregon: Story Line Press, 1999

# Nikki Giovanni 1943–

Born Yolande Cornelia Giovanni, Jr., Nikki Giovanni published her first book of poetry, *Black Feeling, Black Talk,* in 1968. She has since published over 20 volumes and anthologies of poetry and prose focused largely on issues of social and political justice. Over the course of her career Giovanni passed through phases of militancy, radicalism, and pacifism. Although much of Giovanni's early poetry was the product of an intense awareness of a race war that had spiraled to such extreme lows that peace seemed impossible (*A Poetic Equation,* 1983), many of her later poems center on the importance of relationships with family, friends, and the broader community. Ultimately she argues that for the Black community, true revolution is about claiming the power of self-discovery and self-actualization.

Giovanni began her career during the Black Arts movement. Her early work reflected the revolutionary social and political agendas of the black liberation movements as well as her own record of social activism: *Black Feeling, Black Talk* (1968) and *Black Judgement* (1969) question the advances and failures of the Civil Rights movement and react to drastic changes in social values and desires:

> Tomorrow is too late to properly arm yourself
> See can you do an improper job now
> See can you do something, anything, but move now ("Poem [No Name No. 3]")

The construction of language in *Black Feeling, Black Talk* and *Black Judgement* mirrors the social context and ideologies of the period, demanding that freedom and justice be granted to Black Americans. Giovanni uses colloquial language to make her poetry accessible to the populace, carefully applying rhythmic language and vivid imagery to illustrate her messages. Giovanni and the New Black Poets, of whom she was an important member, felt it was the responsibility of the artist to "draw a new picture" of the ideal future for the Black person in America (*Black Judgement*). She believed that making art and literature available to America's Black population would awaken social consciousness in such a way as to instigate revolution: "Ammunition for gun and mind must be smuggled in / Support your local bookstore" ("Of Liberation"). Guns and minds were, Giovanni claimed, equally powerful weapons.

At the time, however, many dreams of the early 1960s had faded away, and most of Giovanni's heroes were killed, imprisoned, or forced into exile. "Adulthood," from *Black Judgement,* is punctuated with a litany of dead revolutionaries:

> . . . hammarskjold was killed
> and lumumba was killed
> and diem was killed
> and kennedy was killed
> and malcolm was killed

For Giovanni, these deaths brought into focus questions regarding the validity, possibility, and means of revolution. Poems such as "Poem for Black Boys," "The True Impact of Present Dialogue, Black vs. Negro," "Of Liberation," and "Adulthood" were intended to enlighten unaware Blacks and support the efforts of those already fighting for social change.

Giovanni pursued political change through concrete measures as well as through her poetry. In 1965 she reestablished Fisk University's chapter of the Student Nonviolent Coordinating Committee (SNCC), staking her claim as an important figure in the Black power struggle. By organizing Cincinnati's first Black Arts Festival in 1967, she added Cincinnati to the increasing number of cities with Black theater troupes. Later that year she attended the Detroit Conference of Unity and Art, beginning a long-term friendship with H. Rap Brown, the charismatic leader of SNCC, just one of the bonds she formed with many of the Black liberation spokespeople. The 1970 foundation of her communications company, NikTom, Ltd., made her a contributor to the Black fight for control over production and distribution. Giovanni followed the advice of the day's rhetoric and assumed the responsibility for the publication and distribution of her work. Borrowing money from friends, Giovanni printed copies of *Black Feeling, Black Talk* herself, with unprecedented success. By 1970 Broadside Press and William Morrow, two major publishers of the writings of the Black Arts movement, were both eager to distribute and publish her work.

Giovanni did not adhere dogmatically to the concrete agenda of the Black Arts movement, however, and has continued to eschew the boundaries of other aesthetic movements. These lines from "A Poem Off Center" are characteristic of her independent spirit:

> if you write a political poem
> you're anti-semitic
> if you write a domestic poem
> you're foolish
> if you write a happy poem
> you're unserious
> if you write a love poem
> you're maudlin
> of course the only real poem
> to write
> is the go to hell writing establishment poem

Although she is vocal about gender issues in books such as *My House* (1972), *The Women and the Men* (1975), and *Cotton Candy on a Rainy Day* (1978), Giovanni does not wish to be labeled a feminist poet. Her prose and poetry insist upon personal and poetic freedom as fiercely as they call for racial and gender awareness and equality. According to Giovanni, an artist must see the world from a variety of perspectives; although one of these perspectives, especially at the beginning of her poetic career, needed to be political, the personal and domestic are equally important. Family and friends are featured prominently in her work. Poems such as "Nikki-Rosa" and "Ego-Tripping" attempt to show that a Black person who is comfortable with his or her own identity, personal strengths, and the strengths of community and family can achieve a revolution.

In particular Giovanni has praised intergenerational community throughout her career. She is deeply attached to the symbiotic relationship between the young and the old. Her books *Grandmothers: Poems, Reminiscences, and Short Stories about the Keepers of Our Traditions* (1996) and *Grandfathers* (1999, with the same subtitle) address the legacy of wisdom passed from the old to the young. Giovanni also believes that the younger generation's youth and vitality are crucial to older people. She has also published many books for children and young adults.

Giovanni has always been interested in making her poetry accessible to all readers. *Those Who Ride the Night Winds* (1983), like the poetry grounded in the Black Arts movement, takes drastic formal risks: all but a few of the book's poems use ellipses rather than line breaks. This poetic technique, rather than spinning from any particular aesthetic philosophy, is meant to make the poetry easier to read. She regularly experiments with poetic forms and techniques, as well as with the language and music of her work, seeking accessible and meaningful poetic styles. Not only does Giovanni continually seek to revise and rethink past stances, she also strives in her revisions to create a more fulfilling present and a future with the possibility of contentment. In *Those Who Ride the Night Winds, Love Poems* (1997), and *Blues: For All Changes,* the mature poet finds the state that is natural for her.

The final poem of *Those Who Ride the Night Wind,* "A Song for New-Ark," like many of Giovanni's poems, incorporates Black musical nuances. Song is used throughout her books to clarify the poet's mission:

> . . . When I write I want to write . . . in rhythm . . . regularizing the moontides . . . to the heart/beats . . . of the twinkling stars . . . sending an S.O.S. . . . to day trippers . . . urging them to turn back . . . toward the Darkness . . . to ride the night winds . . . to tomorrow

Newark, New Jersey, is often considered the home of the Black Arts movement; Giovanni posits her re-visionary poem on the site of her own beginnings. She writes a song calling her readers back into the "Darkness," inviting them to thoroughly explore themselves and their Blackness. She sings a song of pride in community and pride in self.

CAMILLE DUNGY

**Biography**

Born in Knoxville, Tennessee, 7 June 1943. Attended Fisk University, Nashville, Tennessee, 1960–61, 1964–67, B.A. (magna cum laude) in history 1967; University of Pennsylvania School of Social Work, Philadelphia, 1967; Columbia University, New York, 1968; Assistant Professor of Black Studies, Queens College, Flushing, New York, 1968; Associate Professor of English, Livingston College, Rutgers University, New Brunswick, New Jersey, 1968–72; Visiting Professor of English, Ohio State University, Columbus, 1984; Professor of creative writing, Mt. St. Joseph on the Ohio, 1985–87; Commonwealth Visiting Professor of English, 1987–89, and since 1989 Professor of English and Gloria D. Smith Professor of Black Studies, Virginia Tech, Blacksburg, Virginia; founder, NikTom Publishers, New York, 1970–74; editorial consultant, *Encore* magazine, Albuquerque, New Mexico. Received Ford grant, 1968; National Endowment for the Arts grant, 1969; D.H.L., Wilberforce University, Ohio, 1972; D.Litt., University of Maryland, Princess Anne, 1974, Ripon University, Wisconsin, 1974, Smith College, Northampton, Massachusetts, 1975, and Mt. St. Joseph on the Ohio, 1983; Langston Hughes Award, 1996; NAACP Image Award for Literature, 1998. Living in Blacksburg, Virginia.

**Poetry**

*Black Feeling, Black Talk,* 1968
*Black Judgement,* 1969
*Re: Creation,* 1970
*Black Feeling, Black Talk/Black Judgement,* 1970
*Poem of Angela Yvonne Davis,* 1970
*Spin a Soft Black Song* (for children), 1971; revised edition, 1985
*My House,* 1972
*Ego Tripping and Other Poems for Young Readers* (for children), 1973
*The Women and the Men,* 1975
*Cotton Candy on a Rainy Day,* 1978
*Vacation Time* (for children), 1980
*Those Who Ride the Night Winds,* 1983
*Selected Poems of Nikki Giovanni,* 1996
*Love Poems,* 1997
*Blues: For All Changes: New Poems,* 1999

**Other Writings:** essays (*Sacred Cows . . . and Other Edibles,* 1988); edited poetry collection (*Night Comes Softly: An Anthology of Black Female Voices,* 1970).

**Further Reading**

Chapman, Abraham, editor, *New Black Voices: An Anthology of Contemporary Afro-American Literature,* New York: New American Library, 1972
Elder, Arlene, "A *MELUS* Interview: Nikki Giovanni," *MELUS* (Winter 1982)
Fowler, Virginia, *Nikki Giovanni,* New York: Twayne, and Toronto: Macmillan Canada, 1992
Giovanni, Nikki, *A Poetic Equation: Conversations between Nikki Giovanni and Margaret Walker,* Washington, D.C.: Howard University Press, 1974; revised edition, 1983
"Nikki Giovanni: On Race, Age, and Sex," *Black Collegian* (December–January 1970–71)
Palmer, Roderick, "The Poetry of Three Revolutionists: Don L. Lee, Sonia Sanchez, and Nikki Giovanni," *CLA Journal* (September 1971)
Tate, Claudia, "Nikki Giovanni," in *Black Women Writers at Work,* edited by Tate, New York: Continuum, 1983

# Louise Glück 1943–

In her first collection, Louise Glück writes, "such of my own lives / I have cast off" ("Gemini," in *Firstborn*), and it is just such a sense of continual reinvention of identity and poetics that gives shape to her career. Because writing each volume has involved, according to the poet, this kind of self-conscious "casting off"—of syntax, of vocabulary, of themes, and of forms—each book is, in some ways if not entirely, distinct from the one preceding it.

Glück's literary analyses in *Proofs and Theories: Essays on Poetry* (1994) provide insight into her own poetry and poetics, which she is often more reticent to discuss. Throughout her work, Glück writes of poetry as a vocation. Her characteristic tone of mystical authority expresses a concept of the poet as a medium who gives flesh to abstract spiritual truth. In "Phenomenal Survivals of Death in Nantucket," she writes,

> Awake I see Nantucket but with this bell
> Of voice I can toll you token of regions below visible:
> . . . .
> . . . I have been past
> what you hear in a shell.

Returning from beyond the realm of human experience, she is compelled to convey revelation to the community. From the mythical Persephone of "Pomegranate" (*The House on Marshland,* 1975) and Orpheus of *Vita Nova* (1999) to the lyric speaker who tells of her own maternity in *Firstborn* (1968) and anorexia in *Descending Figure* (1980), Glück's personae have all been to what she envisions as "The Edge" (the title of the middle section of *Firstborn*). Her mystic speakers are, like the poet herself, vehicles by which truth is made manifest.

Glück's poetry bears obvious resemblance to some recent predecessors and contemporaries: the New England landscape and the obsessive scrutiny of suffocating familial relationships echo Robert Lowell and Sylvia Plath; her myth-narrative lyric is reminiscent of the appropriation of myth in both Plath and Anne Sexton, akin to Adrienne Rich and Jorie Graham. Yet Glück is conscious of writing after Postmodernism. She reclaims elements of Modernism—myth, personae, and form—in reaction to the exclusion she sees in contemporary attempts to sustain the Confessional mode. She perceives the virtuoso "confession" of Modernist Wallace Stevens, Plath, or more recently Sharon Olds as denying the reader entry into the poem as either "respondent [or] analogue." Glück's mythic tone and personae descend from T.S. Eliot, and both are heir to Emily Dickinson's whispered confidences that invite readers' participation by selection and collusion.

Despite its immaturity, *Firstborn* demonstrates a mythic sensibility and use of archetypal symbolism and fictional personae foreshadowing the hallmarks of Glück's later poetry. It is perhaps for this reason that despite its sometimes derivative and affected stylistics, Glück's inaugural volume met with critical reception that predicted her becoming a major literary force. *The House on Marshland* is often identified as being her "breakthrough" volume, so it is significant that it includes her first use of narrative personae drawn specifically from classical and Judeo-Christian myth. Some of its personae poems, including "The Murderess," "Gretel in Darkness," and "*Brennende Liebe,*" as well as "For My Mother" (which has its origins in the fairy tale *Sleeping Beauty*), are among her most widely acclaimed and memorable pieces.

Glück's poetry and her poetics are grounded in the biological, psychological, and spiritual experience of being a woman—a daughter, a sister, a lover, and a mother—in late-20th-century America. In *Descending Figure,* she offers her experience of adolescent anorexia—particularly in the poem "Dedication to Hunger"—as metaphor for poetry. Like the anorexic who discovers that to survive she must admit her body's frailty and insatiable desire, the poet must be committed to communication despite the insufficiencies of language. Glück's ongoing formal experimentation—from "Bridal Piece" in *Firstborn* to the elegy that is *Vita Nova*—reflects an attempt to compensate for the failures of language and to reconcile the spiritual desire that she shares with Eliot with her commitment to the sensual world more descendant of William Carlos Williams. *The Wild Iris* (1992) makes explicit this attempt to synthesize spiritual longing and a sense of immanence, and in this too we hear echoes of Dickinson. The human voice speaking the recurring "Matins" and "Vespers" poems of *The Wild Iris* is one among many, as Glück literally gives voice also to aspects of nonhuman nature and to an abstract sacred.

*The Triumph of Achilles* (1985), although perhaps least characteristic, contains some of Glück's most anthologized poems—including "Mock Orange," "Mythic Fragment," and "The Mountain"—perhaps because of its relative accessibility; it reflects an effort to be clear that becomes at times didactic. *Ararat* (1990) is her most overtly personal volume, and in it she explores the metaphoric origins of literary confession in religious communal ritual. Set in the year following her father's death, *Ararat* marks a pivotal moment in her work. Here and in the volumes preceding it, the relationships in the poet's family of origin are central concerns. Later collections—*The Wild Iris, Meadowlands* (1996), and *Vita Nova*—consider instead the individual's, particularly the poet's, relationship to the larger community.

Both *Meadowlands* and *Vita Nova* are metapoetic, and both focus on the poet's own second divorce. Yet in the former, an epic, poetry serves as metaphor for the deteriorating marriage, while in the latter, an elegy, the divorce is metaphor for art. Although the tone changes—the colloquialism of some of the poems reveals an ironic sense of humor not heard previously—the notion of the inextricability of mortality and desire remains. In *Vita Nova,* she writes,

> to be noticed by the Fates
> is some distinction after all.
>
> Or should one say, to have honored hunger,
> since the Fates go by that name also. ("The Queen of
> Carthage")

Here again, desire is inseparable from the "dedication to hunger" that is the poet's vocation. In her eighth volume, the poet casts off another life and is yet again set to begin anew.

Maggie Gordon

**Biography**

Born in New York City, 22 April 1943. Attended Sarah Lawrence College, Bronxville, New York, 1962; Columbia

University, New York, 1963–65; taught at Goddard College, Plainfield, Vermont, 1971–72, 1973–74, 1976–80, University of Virginia, Charlottesville, 1973, University of North Carolina, Greensboro, 1973, University of Iowa, Iowa City, University of Cincinnati, Ohio, 1978, Warren Wilson College, Swannanoa, North Carolina, 1978–80, Columbia University, 1979, University of California at Berkeley, 1982, at Davis, 1983, and at Irvine, 1984; Scott Professor of poetry, 1983, and since 1984 member of the faculty, Williams College, Williamstown, Massachusetts; Regents Professor, University of California, Los Angeles, 1985–87. Received Academy of American Poets Prize, 1966; Rockefeller fellowship, 1967; National Endowment for the Arts grant, 1969, 1979, fellowship 1988–89; Eunice Tietjens Memorial Prize (*Poetry*, Chicago), 1971; Guggenheim fellowship, 1975, 1987–88; American Academy Award, 1981; NBCC Award, 1985; Melville Cane Award, 1986; Sara Teasdale Memorial Prize, 1986; Rebekah Johnson Bobbitt National Prize for Poetry, 1992; William Carlos Williams Award, 1993; Pulitzer Prize, 1993; Lannan Literary Award, 1999; Chancellor, Academy of American Poets, 1999. Living in Cambridge, Massachusetts.

**Poetry**

*Firstborn,* 1968
*The House on Marshland,* 1975
*Descending Figure,* 1980
*The Triumph of Achilles,* 1985
*Ararat,* 1990
*The Wild Iris,* 1992
*The First Four Books of Poems,* 1995
*Meadowlands,* 1996
*Vita Nova,* 1999

**Selected Criticism**

*Proofs and Theories: Essays on Poetry,* 1994

**Further Reading**

Bonds, Diane, "Entering Language in Louise Glück's *The House on Marshland:* A Feminist Reading," *Contemporary Literature* 31, no. 1 (Spring 1990)

Dodd, Elizabeth Carolina, *The Veiled Mirror and the Woman Poet: H.D., Louise Bogan, Elizabeth Bishop, and Louise Glück,* Columbia: University of Missouri Press, 1992

Keller, Lynn, "'Free / of Blossom and Subterfuge': Louise Glück and the Language of Renunciation," in *World, Self, Poem: Essays on Contemporary Poetry from the "Jubilation of Poets,"* edited by Leonard M. Trawick, Kent, Ohio: Kent State University Press, 1990

Matson, Suzanne, "Without Relation: Family and Freedom in the Poetry of Louise Glück," *Mid-America Review* 14, no. 2 (1994)

McMahon, Lynne, "The Sexual Swamp: Female Erotics and the Masculine Art," *Southern Review* 28, no. 2 (Spring 1992)

Townsend, Ann, "The Problem of Sincerity: The Lyric Plain Style of George Herbert and Louise Glück," *Shenandoah* 46, no. 4 (Winter 1996)

Upton, Lee, *The Muse of Abandonment: Origin, Identity, Mastery in Five American Poets,* Lewisburg, Pennsylvania: Bucknell University Press, and London: Associated University Presses, 1998

Vendler, Helen, "Louise Glück," in *Part of Nature, Part of Us: Modern American Poets,* by Vendler, Cambridge, Massachusetts: Harvard University Press, 1980

---

# Jorie Graham 1951–

Jorie Graham is perhaps the most ambitious descendant of Wallace Stevens at work in contemporary writing. Throughout her career she has returned to Stevens' crucial notion, expressed in "Of Modern Poetry," that in order to be living, poetry must actively trace the movements of a "mind in the act of finding / What will suffice." The development of the intellectual reach and stylistic complexity of her poetry can be linked to her success in enacting or making visible more and more of the mind's drama on the page, in the act of writing. Consistently, what draws her mind into action is a confrontation with some aspect of the world that resists easy assimilation and forces a new response.

In her introduction to *The Best American Poetry 1990,* Graham describes her confrontation with resistance in these terms:

> It compelled me to let go. The frontal, grasping motion frustrated, my intuition was forced awake. I felt myself having to "listen" with other parts of my sensibility, felt my mind being forced back down into the soil of my senses.

The two predecessors behind Graham's confrontations with the limits of that frontal, grasping motion are Emily Dickinson and Elizabeth Bishop, whose work she also attempts to extend. Bishop's sense of exhilaration at the "constant re-adjustment" ("The Gentleman of Shalott") forced on attempts to describe the world and Dickinson's charged, desperate claim that

> I know that He exists.
> Somewhere—in Silence—
> He has hid his rare life
> From our gross eyes

are everywhere entwined in Graham's work.

Graham's first two books concentrate on emblems of the mind's forced-awake encounters with resistance. *Hybrids of Plants and of Ghosts* (1980) captures the mind's placement in the world in a glance that simultaneously takes in the goal-directed movement of migrating geese and the endlessly-revised, thickening webs of spiders ("The Geese"). *Erosion* (1983) often looks to paintings to capture that tension. A Madonna by Piero della Francesca both invites the "nimble-fingered" viewer to enter mystery and quietly turns away ("San Sepolcro"), while a pair of paintings proclaim the beauty and attraction of story and structure as well as the terrible cost of such pleasures ("Two Paintings by Gustav Klimt"). In "At Luca Signorelli's Resurrection of the Body" an imagining of the resurrection of bodies at the end of time testifies both to the desire to arrive at some resting point and the impossibility of the same.

With *The End of Beauty* (1987) Stevens' "mind in the act of finding" comes more clearly into the foreground. "Vertigo" offers a typical Graham situation in scenic form. The poet is on the edge of a cliff; looking out, she sees a bird held in an updraft—held, she notes, as if by the mind's "intelligence" so that each of its parts is broken free and made knowable. When the bird flares away, a series of dizzying questions follows, and the poet is reminded of the less certain claims of the body as she leans out:

> Oh it has vibrancy, she thought, this emptiness, this intake
> just prior to
> the start of a story, the mind trying to fasten
> and fasten, the mind feeling it like a sickness this wanting
> to snag, catch hold, begin [. . .]

*The End of Beauty* brought Graham to the attention of many readers. Helen Vendler commented on "the rapture of the contemplating mind" in Graham that, while "not a new topic in poetry . . . tends to be forgotten in our pragmatic America" (*Soul Says*, 1995). What most caught the attention of readers was the way she charted that sense of desperate vertigo—poems riddled with blanks or questions, their paces slowed and speeded up as the mind cast around for something solid—as well as the ambitious backdrop she read her mental gestures against: Adam and Eve, Orpheus and Eurydice, Apollo and Daphne, all of these pairs becoming figures for the mind's live confrontation with what cannot be grasped.

*Region of Unlikeness* (1991) and *Materialism* (1993) consolidate the achievements of *The End of Beauty*. Instead of playing out the tension between mind and world as it is displayed in paintings or emblems or stories, Graham turns to her own memories: hearing that Kennedy had been shot, watching a grandmother descend into confusion, grappling with a student's suicide attempt. Prodding at these resistant memories by slowing them or reading them against wildly different contexts in order to hold them fast or arrive at a likeness, she is reduced time and again to a sense of poised alertness "(Where the hurry is stopped) (and held) (but not extinguished) (no)" ("Soul Says"). *Materialism* moves even more firmly into the present-tense act of writing. Taking as its guide Bishop's probing, skidding eye, the book attempts to enter the world through the discipline of description. A Monarch butterfly becomes a "bright new world the eyes would seize upon" ("Subjectivity"), while a winter storm becomes

> a splinter colony, new world, possession
> gripping down to form,
> wilderness brought deep into my clearing ("The Dream of
> the Unified Field")

As these two quotations suggest, what tends to shatter these descriptions and open the poet to new ways of knowing is the Bishop-like realization that her descriptive efforts share something with such larger and obviously tainted human drives as colonialism or the drive to possess.

Graham was awarded the Pulitzer Prize for *The Dream of the Unified Field* (1995), a selection of poems from her first five books. Two difficult books followed. *The Errancy* (1997) focuses not on description or memory but on the wandering, errant act of thinking itself. The volume's cover reproduces a painting by René Magritte of Pascal's coat. The coat, into which Pascal had sewn "irrefutable proof of the existence of God," floats torn and riddled against a night sky:

> floats in illustration
> of what was once believed, and thus was visible—
> . . . .
> floats before us asking to be worn[.] ("Le Manteau de
> Pascal")

Indeed, the poems in this volume, against a chorus of angelic commentary on the limits of human thought, attempt to wear that old coat again, thought becoming "a stammering, an unattachedness" ("Emergency"), a drive "dwindling yet increasingly aswarm" ("Studies in Secrecy"), a "bad fit that the mind be made to awaken" ("How the Body Fits on the Cross"). *Swarm* (2000), the most Dickinson-like of Graham's volumes, displays her encounter with resistance through the voice of a lover calling to, pleading with, attempting to rouse a beloved. Just as the previous books explored the vibrancy and newly-wakened uncertainty of the moment when the world withheld itself, so these poems—fragmented, haltingly-voiced—call the beloved and the reader to an experience with what remains ever outside the lover's embrace:

> I knock on the front
> whispering open up, forgive us,
> can you grow any more silent? ("The Veil")

"Probity" praises that resistance:

> we numb the intelligence
> we push against your law without regret
> we enter my body harder because of the wall

Graham's work, probing silence and pushing against limits, is a powerful, still-developing exploration of what is awakened in language when the intelligence is numbed and the body comes alive.

THOMAS GARDNER

**Biography**

Born in New York City, 9 May 1951. Attended the Sorbonne, Paris; New York University, B.A. 1973; University of Iowa, Iowa City, M.F.A. 1978; Assistant Professor of English, Murray State University, Kentucky, 1978–79, and California State University, Humboldt, 1979–81; workshop instructor, Columbia University, New York, 1981–83; staff member, University of Iowa Writers' Workshop, 1983–99; Boylston Professor of Rhetoric and Oratory, Harvard University, Cambridge, Massachusetts, 1999–. Received Academy of American Poets Prize, 1977; Ingram Merrill Foundation grant, 1981; Bunting fellowship, 1982; Guggenheim fellowship, 1983;

National Endowment for the Arts grant, 1984; Whiting Award, 1985; Lavan Award, 1991; Morton Zabel Award, 1992; Pulitzer Prize in letters, 1996; O.B. Hardison, Jr., Poetry Prize, 1997; Chancellor, Academy of American Poets, 1997. Living in Cambridge, Massachusetts.

**Poetry**
*Hybrids of Plants and of Ghosts,* 1980
*Erosion,* 1983
*The End of Beauty,* 1987
*Region of Unlikeness,* 1991
*Materialism,* 1993
*The Dream of the Unified Field: Selected Poems, 1974–1994,* 1995
*The Errancy,* 1997
*Swarm,* 2000

**Other Writings:** edited poetry anthologies (*The Best American Poetry 1990,* 1990; *Earth Took of Earth: 100 Great Poems of the English Language,* 1996).

**Further Reading**
Altieri, Charles, "Jorie Graham and Ann Lauterbach: Towards a Contemporary Poetry of Eloquence," *Cream City Review* 12 (Summer 1988)
Bedient, Calvin, "Like a Chafing of the Visible," *Salmagundi* 120 (Fall 1998)
Costello, Bonnie, "Jorie Graham: Art and Erosion," *Contemporary Literature* 33, no. 2 (Summer 1992)
Gardner, Thomas, *Regions of Unlikeness: Explaining Contemporary Poetry,* Lincoln: University of Nebraska Press, 1999
Longenbach, James, *Modern Poetry after Modernism,* New York: Oxford University Press, 1997
Selinger, Eric Murphy, "In Each Other's Arms, or No, Not Really," *Parnassus* (Spring 1999)
Spiegelman, Willard, "Jorie Graham's 'New Way of Looking,'" *Salmagundi* 120 (Fall 1998)
Vendler, Helen, *The Breaking of Style: Hopkins, Heaney, Graham,* Cambridge, Massachusetts: Harvard University Press, 1995
Vendler, Helen, *The Given and the Made: Strategies of Poetic Redefinition,* Cambridge, Massachusetts: Harvard University Press, 1995
Vendler, Helen, *Soul Says: On Recent Poetry,* Cambridge, Massachusetts: Harvard University Press, 1995

---

## Angelina Weld Grimké 1880–1956

Although Angelina Weld Grimké never published a volume of poetry, she often found publishers for her poems in local newspapers and in prominent journals, such as *Opportunity* and *The Crisis.* During the 1920s, she was recognized as one of the leading female poets of the Harlem Renaissance, or the New Negro movement, and her poetry was included in the three main anthologies of the period: Alain Locke's *The New Negro* (1925), Charles S. Johnson's *Ebony and Topaz* (1927), and Countee Cullen's *Caroling Dusk* (1927).

Grimké began writing at a young age, and, as early as 1893 at the age of 13, she received public praise for her first published poem. Also known for several polemical plays against lynching, one of which, *Rachel,* was staged in 1916 and later published in 1920, and for several short stories, the majority of which also deal with the lynching theme, Grimké is recognized primarily for her contribution to American poetry. Paradoxically, her poetry has historically been denied a place in Modernist, feminist, lesbian, African-American, and Romantic poetic traditions because of its resistance to the boundaries of a single tradition.

Some of Grimké's early poems, for example, express desire for other women. Indeed, she had had a female lover, Mamie Burrill, by the age of 16 but then seems to have denied herself love relationships thereafter. Unpublished in her lifetime, "Caprichosa" (1901) and "Rosabel" (date unknown unless noted) are two poems in which a woman is the subject of a female speaker's desire. Published or nearly published poems, such as "El Beso" (1909), "A Mona Lisa" (1927), and "My Shrine," encode female-female desire either by avoiding the use of third-person pronouns ("El Beso") or by assuming the voice of a male speaker ("My Shrine"). Critic Gloria Hull (1987) notes that Grimké sometimes wrote love lyrics, a tradition in which the speaker was male, using female speakers but replaced "she" with "he" in her identifications of the speakers during the "typescript stage" in order to mask the poems' explicit lesbian relationships. Grimké's assumption of a male voice was a common strategy for female poets of the early 20th century. Her appropriation of the masculine, Romantic love lyric both enables her to express her love for women and implicates her in the ideology that prohibits love between women.

That Grimké both borrows and departs from earlier poetic traditions is patent in her later, more successful poems. In "The Black Finger" (1923), one of her most anthologized poems (along with "Tenebris," "A Winter Twilight," and "El Beso"), Grimké demonstrates a distinctively modern (if not postmodern) sensibility by combining two poetic traditions: the Imagist and the Romantic. While some critics have noted this combination as Grimké's failure to write in one tradition or the other, part of the poem's innovation is its successful blending of the two traditions. Moreover, "The Black Finger" shows Grimké's celebration of black strength and beauty. The ironic questioning in the poem's final line—"Why, beautiful finger, are you black? / And why are you pointing upwards?"—does not weaken the imagistic subtlety of the tree's black beauty; rather, it parodies white poetical traditions and their ideological refusals of black beauty.

Grimké's remarks about her writing reveal a "double-consciousness" about the influences of disparate literary traditions in her work. In a 1925 letter to a young student who had written to her, Grimké describes her writing in Romantic terms (Hull, 1987). In an undated address to a reading group, she describes the importance of race consciousness to her writing ("Remarks on Literature"). When paired, the two remarks adumbrate a richly textured tension of identifications with different poetic, racial, and cultural traditions.

While Grimké did write poems that state aggressive black resistance to white racism and others that celebrate the "New Negro," poems with explicit racial themes seem to be only a small minority of her total output. In "Beware Lest He Awakes" (1902) and "Trees," Grimké takes up the lynching theme that dominates her drama and her fiction. In "Tenebris" (1924), through the figure of a tree "Against the white man's house," she remembers the violence of white racism and warns of the stability, resilience, and power of black peoples and cultures.

In Grimké's "nature lyrics," where images of marginalized times, spaces, peoples, and concepts dominate her poetic landscape, one can find a consistent voice of resistance against a belief in the fixity of difference and its potential to subordinate other people(s). Through these images, her speakers variously express anguish ("Dusked Lilies"), contentment ("My Star"), and ambivalence ("A Winter Twilight," 1923) about their "naturally" imposed solitude. Grimké sometimes wrote her nature lyrics in pairs—"At the Spring Dawn" (1923) and "At the Autumn Dusk," "Dawn" (1923) and "Dusk" (1924), and even "Lullaby (1)" and "Lullaby (2)"—a strategy that further questions the naturalization of fixed polar opposites, for that fixity underlies both white racism and pro-black claims for a "truer" black voice (*The New Negro,* 1925). Grimké seems to suggest through her poetry that claims for a singular black voice marginalize the other black voices of the Harlem Renaissance and thus replicate the exclusionism of white traditions. Indeed, Grimké seems to have given up the fight against her own marginalization and stopped writing in 1928, when she began nursing her father until his death in 1930. Only then, after the peak of the Harlem Renaissance, did she move to New York, where she remained in relative solitude until her own death in 1956.

Because historical and contemporary critics have expected Grimké to renounce imitation of 19th-century poetic traditions and to embrace specific forms of black expression popularized by the male poets of the New Negro movement, they have failed to recognize her blending of styles and forms as a consistent poetic project that expresses her ambivalent resistance to personal and cultural forces that define the world in simple, oppositional categories. What such assessments share is their expectation that Grimké imitate others; as a result, her poetic work largely continues to suffer the very marginalization against which the poems themselves express their struggles.

Grimké's scrapbooks, letters, manuscripts, and unpublished writings can be found in the Angelina W. Grimké Collection, Manuscript Division, Moorland-Spingarn Research Center, Howard University, where there also exists a special collection, the Archibald H. Grimké Collection, of her father's writings.

JEFFREY RHYNE

**Biography**

Born in Boston, Massachusetts, 27 February 1880. Attended Boston Normal School of Gymnastics, graduated 1902; Harvard University, Cambridge, Massachusetts, summers 1904–10; English teacher, Armstrong Manual Training School, 1902–07, and M Street High School, 1907–26, both Washington, D.C. Died in New York City, 10 June 1956.

**Poetry**

*The Selected Works of Angelina Weld Grimké,* 1991

**Other Writings:** play (*Rachel,* 1920); contributed to poetry anthologies (*The New Negro,* 1925), periodicals (*Opportunity,* 1923).

**Further Reading**

Herron, Carolivia, "Introduction," in *Selected Works of Angelina Weld Grimké,* by Grimké, edited by Herron, New York: Oxford University Press, 1991

Honey, Maureen, "Survival and Song: Women Poets of the Harlem Renaissance," *Women's Studies* 16 (1989)

Hull, Gloria T., *Color, Sex, and Poetry: Three Women Writers of the Harlem Renaissance,* Bloomington: Indiana University Press, 1987

Perry, Margaret, *Silence to the Drums: A Survey of the Literature of the Harlem Renaissance,* Westport, Connecticut: Greenwood Press, 1976

Shockley, Ann Allen, "Afro-American Women Writers: The New Negro Movement, 1924–1933," in *Rereading Modernism: New Directions in Feminist Criticism,* edited by Lisa Rado, New York: Garland, 1994

---

# Allen Grossman 1932–

As Allen Grossman writes in an epigraph to the volume *Of the Great House* (1982), poems have always been a way for human beings to "help one another to the world." That the making of verse out of words and sounds is hard human labor and that the service the poet performs is arduous and also obscure—these facts allow the lyric to stand for all those labors that humans achieve despite and by means of recalcitrant materials. Adamic, Emersonian, a gatherer of fossils, and a hewer of stones, Grossman's poet has nothing but his lines to bear the voice and his voice nothing but its memory of other lines to hold, and thence to bestow, the tidings of those past voices we still require. In Grossman's poetry, the world to which we help one another is our world, yes, but also that made before us by other voices and that eventually to be found by other hearers. As such, the poem must honor by allusion, bringing others into the music of the poem; by immediacy, inhabiting its own most implicated time and place;

and by vigilant address, ever remembering the expectant and sometimes puzzled interlocutor who must be taught from the beginning.

What is a beginning, and where is listening's starting place? In the mother's voice? In the father's silence? In the schoolroom with its disorderly desks? In birdsong or plainsong? In the abc? These, no more or less obscure than the classical age or the canonical singers, remain outside, alien, hard, unalive, or inaccessible. They remain encased in their archaic structures, in their weird cities or towns, or in their superannuated histories until we take them in. They wait on us, wait for us, to discern that threshold, a line where difference may be felt as relation. A lover and a teacher, tender and strict, the lyric persona that Grossman inhabits is urged by passion but ever attentive to passion's office. Radical, breaching boundaries, he yet keeps faith with the fact of limits and with the narrow fate of all particulars. Token of these (and tool, too) is the poetic line.

Grossman cherishes form, and he maintains and renews the forms of the past, letting his lines sound the meters, flow into the shaped stanzas, and return again and again to those places of origin where, apostrophic, his precursors broke silence with speech. Homer, Caedmon, Milton, Wordsworth; Whitman, Crane, Stevens, Yeats—the poets from whom Grossman learns the most are explainers of all human culture. Sinai, Troy, America's Great Plains, and Poland—the sound of this last now mutilated, tattooed by catastrophe: it is Poland of Death—such are the sites of creation, emergence, violence, and terror to which Grossman's poetry returns. At these old and resonant places, his verse finds what Whitman calls "the origin of all poems": there, again and again, his own voice, the voice of the present, finds both fecundity and weariness, youth and the exhaustion, whose only outlet is, paradoxically, song. The poet is Greek and Hebrew, Christian and Jew. Heroic, the poet wrests form, presents his wrought shield, in a light never any less new or beautiful than light ever was; but sorrowful, too, and going sometimes unarmed with elegy, Grossman's speaker suffers history's onslaughts and suffers, too, the contraction of imagination, the despair of form, that narrows sufferers and flattens singing. It is, as he allows, "a bitter logic" that governs his poetic principle, that principle a definition of Being itself. For this reason, the dialectic of Hellenism and Hebraism and the scholar-poet's toil to contain them find, Grossman argues, no vessel more adequate than the poem. Polemics coarsen the feelings, and politics strand our profundity in the topical. The ecumenical abstracts the person into estimable purpose while orthodoxy forgets the questioner, the addressee who must begin at beginnings. Only the poem, and the poet who shapes it in our hearing, comprehends what these other modes do not.

Grossman's definition of the poet's (and his own) career begins in the "The Sands of Paran," first published in *A Harlot's Hire* (1961). There, the speaker, finding his voice in the struggle to know the unknown Moses, ponders the difficulty of being misunderstood. He would recover "not the dream, / But the confrontation, not the nice complement / Of olive and cedar, but the complex face / That talked with Moses there, and spoke on stone." In these lines, the poet rejects lighter lyrical consolations while committing himself to speech's more toilsome business. The stone on which the Hebrew God speaks, its carven message incised, wounding its own matter, will always transmit more than the Divine intended or the faithful would receive. It is, the poems demonstrate, the nature of media to snag, garble, transfigure, and refract Being into representation, to profane it in the course of sounding its profundity. However, the material clash and the mental clangor of our clumsy instruments—the thud of the "hammer," the fall of the "the bright nails scattered on the ground, the scraping of the "key" in the "hard lock"—these tools, metaphors for many makings, are talismans of the human effort that emits some music and some love, too. The playing of the song, the use of the instrument, is a lesson, then, in a kind of love that is ineluctably human. Earth, as Frost had it, is the right place for it.

Therefore, on his ancient tools, Grossman the poet plays, softly or louder, songs that honor and sustain the uncanny persistence of human effort. He wonders, in a poem addressed to his father's generation,

How did the
Dead soldiers, as they arose in the dark,
Put on their shoes? That is what they did, when
I was a child; they arose
And put on their shoes, somehow; and walked into
Their graves.

The speaker of "The Book of Father Dust" never answers this question; rather, he takes the arc, the tension, the resignation, and the high ambition of this question into his own "still / Morning of outcome." This "Morning," an interval bracketed by his own birth and death, accrues urgency as the death of the past generation resets the clock of present outcome. The poet's aim, to use his own time as if it were already memory, already retrospective, gives voice to that dust which, in its morning, strapped on heroic, doomed sandals. As the soldiers, already dead, put on their shoes, the poet makes covenant with the past, strapping on the phylacteries of his father's, of every father's, obscurity and pathos. In these lines, the project of all Grossman's poems—a project of human holding and keeping—reiterates its pledge:

I marry Louis

My author—the dust.
I take the dry yellow rubberband from
Around his wallet,

and wind it on my
Book (in which
Will yet be bound by love in one volume
The scattered leaves of the whole world)

ELISA NEW

**Biography**

Born in Minneapolis, Minnesota, 7 January 1932. Attended Harvard University, Cambridge, Massachusetts, B.A. 1955, M.A. 1957; Brandeis University, Waltham, Massachusetts, Ph.D. 1960; Assistant Professor, Professor, Brandeis University, 1983–91; Professor, Johns Hopkins University, Baltimore, Maryland, 1991–. Received Garrison Award, 1955; Academy of American Poets Award, 1955; Outstanding Teachers Award (Brandeis), 1965; Council for Advancement and Support of Education "Professor of the Year," 1987. Living in Baltimore, Maryland.

**Poetry**

*A Harlot's Hire,* 1961
*The Recluse, and Other Poems,* 1965

*The Woman on the Bridge over the Chicago River,* 1979
*Of the Great House,* 1982
*The Bright Nails Scattered on the Ground: Love Poems,* 1986
*The Ether Dome, and Other Poems: New and Selected (1979–1991),* 1991
*The Philosopher's Window, and Other Poems,* 1995
*How to Do Things with Tears,* 2001

**Selected Criticism**
*Poetic Knowledge in the Early Yeats: A Study of the Wind among the Reeds,* 1969
*Against Our Vanishing: Winter Conversations with Allen Grossman on the Theory and Practice of Poetry,* edited by Mark Halliday, 1981; revised edition, as *The Sighted Singer: Two Works on Poetry for Readers and Writers,* 1992
*The Long Schoolroom: Lessons in the Bitter Logic of the Poetic Principle,* 1997

**Further Reading**
Bromwich, David, "The Poetry of Allen Grossman," *New Republic* (18 December 1976)
Bromwich, David, "Prophetic Dreaming," *Parnassus* 8, no. 1 (1980)
Durante, Janice Floyd, "A Conversation with Allen Grossman," *Boulevard* 6, no. 2–3 (Fall 1991)
Halliday, Mark, "A Conversation with Allen Grossman Concerning 'Of the Great House,'" *Ploughshares* 7, no. 2 (1981)

---

# Barbara Guest 1920–

Barbara Guest is a poet central to, yet curiously independent of, two of the most important "schools" of postwar avant-garde American poetry. Her early career developed within the context of the New York art and poetry scene of the 1950s and 1960s, while her more recent work has been affiliated with the Language poetry movement of the 1980s and 1990s. Yet Guest's work also stands apart from both these groups. While early poems such as "Parachutes, My Love, May Carry Us Higher" were widely anthologized and acclaimed for their surreal lyric delicacy, other early work already indicated her willingness to experiment more radically than her contemporaries with stanza, line length, and syntax and to work toward a more precise condensation of sound and imagery. In her later writing, this vein becomes dominant, marking Guest as one of the most prescient of the postmodern poets.

Early in her career, Guest moved from California to New York, where she became associated with poets such as John Ashbery, James Schuyler, Kenneth Koch, and Frank O'Hara as well as painters such as Grace Hartigan and Robert Goodnough. Her early poetic influences included Anglo-American Modernists such as T.S. Eliot and H.D. (the subject of a biography by Guest) as well as French avant-garde writers such as Breton and Mallarmé. As an editor for the influential journal *Art News* during the early 1950s, Guest also was keenly attuned to the rise of Abstract Expressionism and undoubtedly inspired by its gestural spontaneity and rejection of a utilitarian "realism." Throughout her career, her poetry has revealed a painterly sensibility: a tendency to use the language of color and art as metaphors for a poetic project marked by surrealistic yet finely tuned juxtapositions of images and sounds. In "A Reason," she contrasts the "clutch" of "this mustard feeling" with the understated exuberance of "Well wild wild whatever / in wild more silent blue," and in "Roses" she reflects on a specific painting:

> The roses of Juan Gris from which
> we learn the selflessness of roses
> existing perpetually without air,
> the lid being down, so to speak,
> a 1912 fragrance sifting
> to the left corner where we read
> "The Marvelous" and escape.

The search for the "marvelous" is often at the core of Guest's poetics, embodied in her consistent references to classical and medieval worlds, times and places necessarily both real and imagined. Early poems, such as those in *Archaics* (1962), rewrite events from Greek myths as whimsical snapshots of a world neither ancient nor modern, while the indecisive and amorous "Knight of the Swan" wanders through a typographically fragmented and metaphorically ambiguous narrative.

Guest delights in blurring distinctions, lingering on the relationships between words and silences or spaces, colors, and blackness as she works toward what she terms the ordinary world "encased in an extraordinary kind of thought." The result is lines that are liquid but taut, colloquial yet chiseled, reflecting a keen ear that resists the harmonic fade-out or anticipated poetic closure in favor of a teasing "artful dare" to her readers. In an important early volume, *The Blue Stairs* (1968), "A Handbook of Surfing" alternates short choppy lines, such as "knee songs and thigh grippers / foam slashers bone knockers / surf kindlers in the riddle splash," with prose passages and extended lines evocative of the epic, referencing Homer, Wordsworth, and Shakespeare. In later volumes, such as *Moscow Mansions* (1973) and *The Countess from Minneapolis* (1976), her subjects range from the witty "The Poetess (after Miró)" to displaced Europeans in the American Midwest, while in the evocative *The Türler Losses* (1979) she composes a book-length meditation on language, loss, and temporality.

Guest moves easily among a range of poetic forms, eschewing traditional metrics and conventional implementations of poetic devices such as rhyme, assonance, and consonance. She tends toward irregular stanzas, longer and shorter lines, refracted lines and phrases, and eventually single words as her poetic units of choice. Emphasizing the visual effect of her poems, she often dispenses with conventional punctuation and spacing, as in the haunting "The Farewell Stairway" as well as "Chalk," a recent poem constructed by a process of literal erasure. Her dense fieldings of words forge delicate layers of sound and meaning, constructing what might be called elaborate "collages" of language (collage being Guest's own medium of choice in the visual arts). Yet, as a woman in the mainly male realm of poetry, Guest often has not received the critical attention that she deserves. Despite her inclusion in John Bernard Myers' anthology *The Poets of the New York School* (1969) and Donald Allen's *The New American Poetry* (1960), critical appraisals of the group have ignored Guest's presence in the interest of examining the work of and friendships among the four central male poets. Guest's poetry—often difficult and rarely "confessional" in the mainstream sense—was long overlooked by the feminist academic establishment as well. Recent articles, however, particularly by younger avant-garde women poets who look to her as a model, have begun to correct this oversight.

Since the late 1980s, Guest's reception has dramatically altered as critics and writers associated with the Language school of poetry have called attention to her increasingly spare, elegant lines and interest in the "thingness" of language itself. Guest has been adopted as both a forerunner and a current practitioner of Language poetry. Her most recent books, *Fair Realism* (1989), *Defensive Rapture* (1993), and *Selected Poems* (1995), have received wide acclaim and cemented her place within an avant-garde canon. Guest remains singular in her approach, however, and is more reluctant than some of her younger colleagues to reject a certain lyrical tone even while she moves toward a poetics of purer sound and image. Instead, even her most recent poetry is reflective of a certain productive "tension," leading her to comment of her own work, "I am always leaving out, and still I am too full of saying."

ANN-MARIE MIKKELSEN

**Biography**

Born in Wilmington, North Carolina, 6 September 1920. Attended the University of California, Berkeley, A.B. 1943; editorial associate, *Art News*, New York, 1951–54. Received Yaddo fellowship, 1958; Longview Foundation Award, 1960; National Endowment for the Arts grant, 1980; American Awards in Literature, 1996; Frost Medal, 1999. Living in Berkeley, California.

**Poetry**

*The Location of Things*, 1960
*Poems: The Location of Things, Archaics, The Open Skies*, 1962
*The Blue Stairs: Poems*, 1968
*Moscow Mansions: Poems*, 1973
*The Countess from Minneapolis*, 1976
*The Türler Losses*, 1979
*Biography*, 1980
*Quilts*, 1980
*The Nude* (lithographs by Warren Brandt), 1986
*Musicality* (illustrations by June Felter), 1988
*Fair Realism*, 1989
*Defensive Rapture*, 1993
*Selected Poems*, 1995
*Stripped Tales* (with Anne Dunn), 1995
*Quill, Solitary Apparition*, 1996
*If So, Tell Me*, 1999
*Symbiosis*, 2000

**Other Writings:** plays, novel (*Seeking Air*, 1978), short stories (*The Confetti Trees*, 1998), biography (*Herself Defined: The Poet H.D. and Her World*, 1984).

**Further Reading**

Bernstein, Charles, "Linebreak: Interview with Barbara Guest," recorded 16 October 1995 (*http://wings.buffalo.edu/epc/linebreak/programs/guest/*)
Diggory, Terence, *Grace Hartigan and the Poets: Paintings and Prints, March 25–April 18, 1993*, Saratoga Springs, New York: Skidmore College, 1993
Duncan, Erika, "Encounters: Hearing a Poet, but Understanding Little," *New York Times* (25 September 1994)
Fraser, Kathleen, "One Hundred and Three Chapters of Little Times: Collapsed and Transfigured Moments in the Fiction of Barbara Guest," in *Breaking the Sequence: Women's Experimental Fiction*, edited by Ellen G. Friedman and Miriam Fuchs, Princeton, New Jersey: Princeton University Press, 1989
Hillman, Brenda, "The Artful Dare: Barbara Guest's *Selected Poems*," *Talisman* 16 (1996)
Hillringhouse, Mark, "Barbara Guest: An Interview," *American Poetry Review* 21 (1992)
Lehman, David, *The Last Avant-Garde: The Making of the New York School of Poets*, New York: Doubleday, 1998
Lundquist, Sara, "Reverence and Resistance: Barbara Guest, Ekphrasis, and the Female Gaze," *Contemporary Literature* 38 (1997)
Myers, John Bernard, *The Poets of the New York School*, Philadelphia: Graduate School of Fine Arts, University of Pennsylvania, 1969

# Louise Imogen Guiney 1861–1920

Louise Imogen Guiney was a lifelong professional writer. Beginning in her early 20s, when her first poems and essays appeared in magazines and newspapers in her hometown of Boston, then still the literary capital of the United States, until her death at age 59 in England, Guiney wrote substantively in a variety of genres: poetry, fiction, and nonfiction prose (biography, essays, scholarly-critical editions, translations, and letters). She published seven books of poetry, two collections of essays and two of short fiction, three biographies, and editions of work by Matthew Arnold, Hurrell Froude, Lionel Johnson, James Clarence Mangan, Katherine Philips, Thomas Stanley, and Henry Vaughan, to name a few, as well as translations of Louise Morvan and St. Francis of Assisi. None of this considerable body of work is still in print, although 11 of her poems are reprinted in two late-20th-century anthologies (see Kilcup, 1996; Gray, 1997).

Guiney was born in Roxbury, Massachusetts, the only child of Irish Catholic parents, and educated at the Catholic Elmhurst Academy in Providence, Rhode Island, from which she graduated in 1879. Her father, Patrick Robert Guiney, who is generally thought to have been the single most influential figure in her life, was a lawyer by training and brigadier general in the Union army during the Civil War. When he died in 1877, after prolonged invalidism resulting from war wounds, his daughter undertook to support herself and her mother by writing. Unable to survive by writing alone, she served as postmistress of Auburndale in 1894, resigning under duress from apparent anti-Catholic and anti-female prejudice, then worked in the Boston Public Library Catalogue Room. She lived with her mother and aunt until she moved to Oxford, England, permanently in 1901. She returned twice to the United States to visit her mother, nursing her and subsequently her aunt through their final illnesses. She also cared for three orphaned female relatives who joined her household in the 1910s. Any assessment of Guiney's literary production and career must recognize these substantial and continuous responsibilities, a pattern not uncommon for the eldest unmarried daughter in a family and in Guiney's case undertaken by one whose own health was often poor.

Guiney's early work—a first collection of poems, *Songs at the Start* (1884), dedicated to John Boyle O'Reilly (editor of the *Boston Pilot*), and first collection of essays, *Goose-Quill Papers* (1885), dedicated to Oliver Wendell Holmes, Sr.—were well received. A sign of her admission into the elite Boston literary circle that included Francis Parkman, Brooks Adams, George Parsons Lathrop, and James and Annie Fields was the commission to write a memorial ode on General Ulysses S. Grant. Her poetry appeared in prestigious literary magazines, including *Harper's* and the *Atlantic Monthly.* Well into the 1910s, her poetry continued to be well received by such notable writer-editors as Willa Cather. Zoë Akins, who reprinted Guiney's "Irish Peasant Song" in her anthology of contemporary American poetry, *In the Shadow of Parnassus* (1915), praised her poetry for being "consistently high in quality, and rare in spirit" (*In the Shadow of Parnassus,* 1994).

When a revised and enlarged edition of Guiney's *Happy Ending* (1927) was published seven years after her death, the "Publisher's Note" could still legitimately claim that Guiney's "place in our literature is secure." A decade later, when the *Recusant Poets* (1938–39) appeared, it was still possible to claim that her "reputation among poets is secure." This edition of poetry by Catholic poets of the Cavalier period (Thomas More, Henry Parker, Thomas Langdon, Henry Howard, Nicholas Grimald, Thomas Lodge, and Ben Jonson, among them), so Grace Guiney, her editor and cousin, notes in the preface, will enhance an "already impressive" reputation as historian and critic.

Guiney's qualities of "high courage, both physical and moral; a gay heart and a vivid imagination; an enlightened intellect; a 'passion for perfection'; a love of poetry and history" ("Preface," *Recusant Poets*), apparent in both her life and her work and often associated with her father, were also qualities characterizing the New Woman of the late 19th century. This figure of "boldness and radiant vigor" was born of what John Higham (1965) and more recently T.J. Jackson Lears (1981) describe as "a profound spiritual reaction . . . a hunger to break out of the frustrations, the routine, and the sheer dullness of urban-industrial culture" (Higham, 1965). Remarks in a letter to her father, dated 3 December 1876, express this quintessence of the vigorous New Woman: "Welcome to old Winter! I am glad enough to see the ice and snow once more—there is something so energetic, so invigorating in the cold weather, far preferable to the lazy, dreamy summer months" (*Letters of Louise Imogen Guiney,* 1926). One of her subsequent essays that argues for more impetuously vigorous reading of literature demonstrates the robustly revisionist intellectual counterpart to her agenda of physical vigor: "To enter a library honorably, is not to go clam-digging after useful information, nor even emotions. . . . To read well is to make an impalpable snatch at whatever item takes your eye, and run. . . . The Muse is dying nowadays of over-interpretation" ("A Bitter Complaint of the Ungentle Reader," *Patrins,* 1897).

Guiney's passion for 17th-century English poetry and interest in Celticism combined with a searching, if skeptical, interest in the newly emerging Modernist poetics—its lyric sparseness, powerfully yet impersonally articulated emotion, and belief in the autonomy of the work of art—to create her signature poetic style. Later Modernists Amy Lowell and Louise Bogan acknowledged their debt to Guiney, so several critics have noted. Jessie B. Rittenhouse identified the demanding energy of Guiney's poetry: "it has no flaccid thought. There is fibre in all she writes; fibre and nerve" (*The Younger American Poets,* 1906). Alice Brown, Guiney's friend and sometime collaborator, described the poet and her work as "austerely beautiful in the modern world" to account for why she had become a "victim of majorities" (*Louise Imogen Guiney,* 1921). Guiney's description of Henri de La Rochejacquelein, a Vendean hero whose achievements she admired as representing the "spectacle of a strong soul," is the kind of insight that typically can emerge only from hard-won self-analysis: "He represents, in the economy of things, the waste which is thrift, the daring which is prudence, the folly which is ineffable" (*"Monsieur Henri," A Foot-Note to French History,* 1892). Guiney might have been speaking of herself.

Guiney's wittily serious definition of happiness not only mirrors the temperamental qualities reflected in her lifelong engagement with 17th-century poetry but also expresses with uncanny precision the fortunes of her reputation as a writer: "Perfect happiness, which we pretend is so difficult to get at, lies at either end of our sentient pole: in being intimately recognized, or else in evading recognition altogether" ("On the Delights of an Incognito," *Patrins,* 1897). Between intimate recognition on the one hand and complete evasion on the other stands the poet unperturbed, a figure who in her persona, mission, and craft combines elements both ethereal and martial that embody a creed lyrically expressed in "The Poet's Chart" ("Ten Colloquies," *Happy Ending*):

Where shall I find my light?

Turn from another's track:
Whether for gain or lack,
Love but thy natal right. . . .

Whence shall I take my law?

Neither from sires nor sons,
Nor the delivered ones,
Holy, invoked with awe.
Rather, dredge the divine
Out of thine own poor dust,
Feebly to speak and shine. . . .

CATHERINE N. PARKE

**Biography**

Born in Roxbury, Boston, Massachusetts, 7 January 1861. Worked as journalist; postmistress, Auburndale, Massachusetts; worked in cataloging department, Boston Public Library, 1899–1901; editor, with Alice Brown, *Pilgrim Scrip.* Died in Chipping Campden, Gloucestershire, England, 2 November 1920.

**Poetry**

*Songs at the Start,* 1884
*The White Sail, and Other Poems,* 1887
*A Roadside Harp,* 1893
*Nine Sonnets Written at Oxford,* 1895
*"England and Yesterday": A Book of Short Poems,* 1898
*The Martyrs' Idyl, and Shorter Poems,* 1899
*Happy Ending: Collected Lyrics,* 1909; revised edition, 1927

**Other Writings:** essays (*Goose-Quill Papers,* 1885), short stories (*Lovers', Saint Ruth's, and Three Other Tales,* 1895), children's literature, nonfiction (*Three Heroines in New England Romance: Their True Stories* [with Harriet Prescott Spofford and Alice Brown], 1894), correspondence (*Letters of Louise Imogen Guiney,* 2 vols., edited by Grace Guiney, 1926), translations of French literature (*The Secret of Fougereuse: A Romance of the Fifteenth Century,* by Louise Morvan, 1898); edited collections of literature (*Recusant Poets* [with Geoffrey Bliss], 1938–39).

**Further Reading**

Fairbanks, Henry G., *Louise Imogen Guiney,* New York: Twayne, 1973
Gilbert, Sandra M., and Susan Gubar, *No Man's Land: The Place of the Woman Writer in the Twentieth Century,* 3 vols., New Haven, Connecticut: Yale University Press, 1988–94 (see especially volumes 1 and 2)
Gray, Janet, editor, *She Wields a Pen: American Women Poets of the 19th Century,* London: Dent, and Iowa City: University of Iowa Press, 1997
Higham, John, "The Reorientation of American Culture in the 1890's," in *The Origins of Modern Consciousness,* edited by John Weiss, Detroit, Michigan: Wayne State University Press, 1965
Kilcup, Karen L., editor, *Nineteenth-Century American Women Writers: An Anthology,* Oxford: Blackwell, 1996; Cambridge, Massachusetts: Blackwell, 1997
Lears, T.J. Jackson, *No Place of Grace: Antimodernism and the Transformation of American Culture, 1880–1920,* New York: Pantheon, 1981
Leggott, Michele J., "Louise Imogen Guiney," in *Dictionary of Literary Biography,* volume 54: *American Poets, 1880–1945,* 2 vols., edited by Peter Quartermain, Detroit, Michigan: Gale Research, 1987 (see especially volume 1)
Parke, Catherine N., editor, *In the Shadow of Parnassus: Zoë Akins's Essays on American Poetry,* Selinsgrove, Pennsylvania: Susquehanna University Press, and London: Associated University Presses, 1994
Walker, Cheryl, *The Nightingale's Burden: Women Poets and American Culture Before 1900,* Bloomington: Indiana University Press, 1982
Walker, Cheryl, *Masks, Outrageous and Austere: Culture, Psyche, and Persona in Modern Women Poets,* Bloomington: Indiana University Press, 1991

---

# Thom Gunn 1929–

Born and raised in England, Thom Gunn moved permanently to northern California in 1954 and calls himself "an Anglo-American poet" based on his openness to both British and American poetic traditions (*Shelf Life,* 1993). Originally critics grouped Gunn with the British "Movement" poets of the 1950s—Philip Larkin, Donald Davie, Elizabeth Jennings, and others—in light of his return to "traditional resources in structure and method," but Gunn refuses that classification, expressing a disinterest in all literary movements of the last 40 years (see Gunn's *The Occasions of Poetry: Essays in Criticism and Autobiography,* edited by Clive Wilmer, 1982, 1985). In particular he has sought to distance himself from the New Formalism, a poetic school committed to the exclusive use of traditional measures, insisting instead on the continuity between free verse and meter.

Gunn's first book of poetry, *Fighting Terms,* which he wrote while a student at Cambridge, was published in 1954, the same year he emigrated to America. In *Fighting Terms* Gunn demonstrates his adept handling of fixed forms; the rhetoric of the poems is shaped largely by his readings in the Elizabethans, particularly Shakespeare and Donne. Sartre also influences this early work, and in the opening poem entitled "The Wound," set in the aftermath of the Trojan War, the poet asserts his existential independence: "I was myself; subject to no man's breath." Gunn's second book, *The Sense of Movement* (1957), extends his "quest of the heroic in the modern world" ("An Interview with Thom Gunn," *Paris Review* [Summer 1995]). Citing Yvor Winters (his teacher at Stanford University in the mid-1950s), Yeats, and Sartre as influences on that book, Gunn explores the idea of the "will." In "On the Move" he meditates on a gang of American motorcyclists whose actions offer a partial solution to the aimlessness of modern life:

> On motorcycles, up the road, they come:
> Small, black, as flies hanging in heat, the Boys,
> Until the distance throws them forth, their hum
> Bulges to thunder held by calf and thigh.

*My Sad Captains* (1961) includes poems written in both meter and syllabics, the latter a form not often used by poets in English. It represents a departure from Gunn's earlier work insofar as he tries to find a way "of incorporating the more casual aspects of life, the non-heroic things in life, that are of course a part of daily experience and infinitely valuable" ("Interview"). The first poem in the book, "In Santa Maria del Popolo," illustrates Gunn's greater emphasis on humanistic concerns; the old women kneel in the church, "too tired" for the heroic gesture, "the large gesture of solitary man, / Resisting, by embracing, nothingness."

Although Gunn does not regard his book *Touch* (1967) very highly ("some of that book seems to me distinctly inferior in that I really wasn't quite sure how to connect the poetry of everyday life and the heroic poetry"), in "Misanthropos," a series of linked poems about a man who thinks he is the sole survivor of a nuclear holocaust, he is able to make that connection, as he considers the communal nature of the poet as individual. In 1966 Gunn also collaborated on *Positives* with his brother Ander, writing poem-captions in a free-verse form inspired by William Carlos Williams to accompany his brother's photographs.

The poems in *Moly* (1971), a book named for the magical herb given by Hermes to Odysseus to protect him from Circe's incantation, are mostly about metamorphosis; many of them were written when Gunn was taking LSD. Some of the poems in *Moly* are in traditional meters, and Gunn has said that he opted for such meters in an attempt to assert some control over the basically uncontrolled drug experience. "The Geysers," a sequence of poems named for an area of hot springs in northern California where hippies bathed naked, and "Moly" celebrate the 1960s West Coast dreams of sexual and hallucinogenic freedom in heroic couplets.

*Jack Straw's Castle* (1976) includes a range of autobiographical poems in which Gunn reflects on his childhood and adolescence. In "Autobiography" he declares his interest in "the sniff of the real," an interest that shapes the entire book. It is also the first of Gunn's books to clearly address his homosexuality, and at the close of the title poem the reader finds the male speaker in bed with another man, "loose-twined across the bed / Like wrestling statues." *The Passages of Joy* (1982) continues to explore his gay identity as well as the value of friendship. Its highlights include the erotic imagery of his free-verse pinball lyric "Bally *Power Play*" ("His haunches are up against the wood now / the hard edge which he presses") and the elegy "Talbot Road," written upon the death of Gunn's close friend Tony White.

In *The Man with Night Sweats* (1992) Gunn writes about homosexual experience in the age of AIDS. Divided into four sections, the book chronicles the spread of AIDS as it shadows sexual relationships and shows sexual risk to be a potentially fatal enterprise. Poems like the second section's single elegy ("A Sketch of the Great Dejection") register the sorrow that comes with loss. Most of the poems in Gunn's pamphlet *Undesirables* (1988) are incorporated into the third section of the book, which presents a gallery of social outcasts, including hustlers, the homeless, and gay men, and reminds readers of the full compass of AIDS. The final section features a sequence of elegies in a range of traditional poetic forms for friends who have died from AIDS. The book ends in a poem of consolation ("A Blank"), in which a gay man's decision to adopt a son reconstitutes love in the face of grief and despair; the speaker admires the father's "self-permission" and lauds his bold decision "To educate, guide, feed, keep warm, / And love a child to be adopted, though / The child was still a blank then on a form."

Gunn has published two collections of critical and autobiographical prose that shed light on his poetry and poetics, *The Occasions of Poetry: Essays in Criticism and Autobiography* (1982) and *Shelf Life: Essays, Memoirs, and an Interview* (1993). Gunn's *Collected Poems,* which contains most of his published poetry through *The Man with Night Sweats,* came out in 1994.

TYLER HOFFMAN

**Biography**

Born in Gravesend, Kent, 29 August 1929. Attended University College School, London; Trinity College, Cambridge, B.A. 1953, M.A. 1958; Stanford University, California, 1954–55, 1956–58; served in the British Army, 1948–50; member of the English Department, 1958–66, and since 1975 Visiting Lecturer, now Senior Lecturer, University of California, Berkeley; poetry reviewer, *Yale Review,* New Haven, Connecticut, 1958–64. Received Levinson Prize (*Poetry,* Chicago), 1955; Maugham Award, 1959; Arts Council of Great Britain Award, 1959; American Academy grant, 1964; Rockefeller Award, 1966; Guggenheim fellowship, 1971; W.H. Smith Award, 1980; Sara Teasdale Prize, 1988; *Los Angeles Times* Kirsch Award, 1988; Lenore Marshall Poetry Prize, 1993; MacArthur fellowship, 1993; American Academy of Arts and Letters Award of Merit Medal, 1998. Living in San Francisco, California.

**Poetry**

*Fighting Terms,* 1954; revised edition, 1958
*The Sense of Movement,* 1957
*My Sad Captains, and Other Poems,* 1961
*Selected Poems* (with Ted Hughes), 1962
*Positives* (photographs by Ander Gunn), 1966
*Touch,* 1967
*Poems, 1950–1966: A Selection,* 1969
*Moly,* 1971
*Corgi Modern Poets in Focus 5* (poems by Gunn, Ezra Pound, Bernard Spencer, Sylvia Plath, Fleur Adcock, and John Ormond), edited by Dannie Abse, 1971
*Moly, and My Sad Captains,* 1971
*Jack Straw's Castle,* 1976

*Selected Poems, 1950–1975,* 1979
*The Passages of Joy,* 1982
*The Man with Night Sweats,* 1992
*Collected Poems,* 1994
*Boss Cupid,* 2000

**Selected Criticism**
*The Occasions of Poetry: Essays in Criticism and Autobiography,* edited by Clive Wilmer, 1982; expanded edition, 1985

**Other Writings:** essays (*Shelf Life: Essays, Memoirs, and an Interview,* 1993); edited collections of poetry (*Selected Poems of Fulke Greville,* 1968; *Ben Jonson,* 1974).

**Further Reading**

Bold, Alan Norman, *Thom Gunn and Ted Hughes,* Edinburgh: Oliver and Boyd, 1976
Dyson, A.E., editor, *Three Contemporary Poets: Thom Gunn, Ted Hughes, and R.S. Thomas: A Casebook,* London: Macmillan, 1990
Hoffman, Tyler, "Representing AIDS: Thom Gunn and the Modalities of Verse," *South Atlantic Review* 65, no. 2 (Spring 2000)
"An Interview with Thom Gunn," *Paris Review* (Summer 1995)
Woodcock, Bruce, "'But Oh Not Loose': Form and Sexuality in Thom Gunn's Poetry," *Critical Quarterly* 35 (1993)

# H

## Marilyn Hacker 1942–

Variously seen as a rampant feminist, a retrograde formalist, and the creator of a new and sometimes jarringly explicit lesbian poetics, Marilyn Hacker has provided one of the most visible and important links between feminism and formalism in late-20th-century American poetry. Hacker's trademark talent rests on her ability to bring the quotidian—motherhood, sex, Bloomingdale's—into received forms such as the Petrarchan sonnet, the pantoum, and the sestina. Writing personal, confessional poetry almost exclusively in rhyme and meter, Hacker has consistently set her work apart from the open forms that gained an ideological foothold in the 1960s and 1970s.

The author of eight volumes of poetry and translator of the French poet Claire Malroux's selected poems (*Edge,* 1996), Hacker uses her impressive metrics to bring eroticism, doubt, longing, and mourning into the fold of what her poetry frequently calls "dailiness." Hacker's early efforts met with widespread acclaim when her first collection, *Presentation Piece* (1974), won both the Lamont Prize and the National Book Award. The collection introduces Hacker's dazzling facility with the sestina, including the important "Forage Sestina," in which she meditates on form through the conceit of a crumbling building: "Falling words / erode veined gullies in the nearer wall. / This is to see if only structure / communicates." Notably, this volume, which received as much mainstream praise as Hacker would attract for some time, does not contain any obvious lesbian content.

Unlike Adrienne Rich, whose desire to write politically engaged, overtly lesbian poetry led her to renounce traditional structures, Hacker found or modified forms to accommodate her increasingly feminist, increasingly lesbian themes. While she identifies Rich as an important influence, Hacker takes pains to differentiate herself from a view of form as necessarily patriarchal and oppressive. In an interview, she insists, "Traditional forms, or for that matter, invented forms, aren't in any way inimical to women's poetry, feminist poetry. . . . Traditional narrative and lyric forms have been used by women for centuries—even if our professors of Western literature never mentioned Marie de France or Christine de Pisan" (Hammond, 1980).

It is no surprise that Hacker's defense of form as feminist and engaged makes recourse to literary history. As she puts it in a colloquy with Richard Howard, "There's a wonderful line of John Hollander's on borrowing that I actually did borrow. . . . The line is 'writing is a difficult form of reading'" (Hacker and Howard, 2000). Hacker's poetry shows her to be widely read both in her contemporaries, such as Howard, Hollander, Hayden Carruth, Eavan Boland, and Marie Ponsot, as well as in Shakespeare, Petrarch, and other canonical masters of her chosen forms, and in those women writers, from Sappho to Edna St. Vincent Millay, who have importantly defined and reshaped the forms she uses. Despite the query in her third volume, *Taking Notice* (1980), "Can a woman / learn writing from a man," Hacker frequently cites the importance of male writers to her development. Auden's early, friendly interest in her work—"He told me my sestina was not a sestina" (Hacker and Howard, 2000)—proved helpful, sending her back to study prosody as well as helping her to decide when to opt for modified or invented forms. Hacker also exchanged ideas with writers by editing several literary journals. From 1977 to 1982, she served on the editorial collective of the *Little Magazine;* from 1982 to 1986, she edited the feminist literary journal *13th Moon;* and from 1990 to 1994, she served as editor of the *Kenyon Review.* Hacker's influence can be strongly felt in the vitality of these journals, and she has been given credit for the "discovery" of younger American writers such as Rafael Campo.

Throughout her development, Hacker has balanced a feminist realism with her formal virtuosity. The title sonnet sequence of her second volume, *Separations* (1976), mourns the end of her relationship with the father of her daughter, Iva. By *Taking Notice,* the title sonnet sequence is openly lesbian: "The two women sit one row / ahead, kissing. I look at them, look away. / They are more edifying than the play." Her fourth volume, *Assumptions* (1985), contains the important, witty "Grafitti from the Gare Saint-Manqué," with lines such as "We hope chairpersons never ask: why are / unblushing deviants abroad on grants? / My project budget listed: Entertain / another Jewish Lesbian in France." Tracking her anxiety about subsisting on grants, constantly traveling between Paris and the United States, and supporting her young daughter, Hacker's poems maintain an élan, as well as sexual openness, in the face of various hardships.

Yet it was not until Hacker's fifth volume, *Love, Death, and the Changing of the Seasons* (1986), that her edgy explicitness emerged full blown, to a mixed reception of praise and uneasiness. For her lesbian audience, this collection provided what one writer calls "a lesbian classic" (Gardinier, 1993). With opening epigraphs from Shakespeare's sonnets and Ezra Pound, the volume gestures toward its traditional heritage while presenting a sonnet cycle of lesbian love. Written to a younger woman, with an implicit nod to Shakespeare's young man, the cycle brings the characteristic yearnings of the sonnet to bear on Hacker's topic: "Didn't Sappho say her guts clenched up like this? / Before a face suddenly numinous, / her eyes watered, knees melted. Did she lactate / again, milk brought down by a girl's kiss?"

Her sixth volume, *Going Back to the River* (1990), came out in the same year that Norton published her *Selected Poems, 1965–1990.* This selection highlights a number of Hacker's important poems, including her early "Villanelle," "Feeling and Form," and "The Ballad of Ladies Lost and Found." Hacker's next collection, *Winter Numbers* (1994), ends with a long meditation on her struggles with breast cancer. Her latest collection, *Squares and Courtyards* (2000), includes the widely praised poems "The Boy" and "Again, the River." Increasingly, Hacker's poetry has turned to issues of fate, mortality, and her Jewish heritage. Even with this shift in attention, Hacker maintains the supple formalism that is uniquely hers, using decisively modern content to make traditional forms relevant for contemporary readers.

Genevieve Abravanel

*See also* New Formalism

**Biography**

Born in New York City, 27 November 1942. Attended Washington Square College, New York University, B.A. 1964; Art Students League, New York; worked as teacher, postal worker, and editor of books, magazines, and trade journals; antiquarian bookseller, London, 1971–76; editor, *City Magazine,* 1967–70, *Quark,* 1969–70, *Little Magazine,* 1977–82, *13th Moon,* 1982–86, and *Kenyon Review,* 1990–94; Lecturer, George Washington University, Washington, D.C., 1976; George Elliston poet-in-residence, University of Cincinnati, Ohio, 1988; distinguished writer-in-residence, American University, Washington, D.C., 1989; Visiting Professor, State University of New York at Binghamton, 1990. Received YM-YWHA Discovery Award, 1973; Lamont Poetry Selection Award, 1973; National Endowment for the Arts grant, 1974, 1985; National Book Award, 1975; Jenny McKean Moore fellowship (George Washington University), 1976; Guggenheim fellowship, 1980; New York State Council on the Arts grant, 1980; Ingram Merrill Foundation fellowship, 1984; Coordinating Council of Little Magazines Editor's fellowship, 1984; Lambda Literary Award, 1990, 1994; Lenore Marshall Poetry Prize, 1995; Bernard F. Conners Prize (*Paris Review*), 1995; Poets' Prize (Nicholas Roerich Museum), 1996; John Masefield Memorial Award (Poetry Society of America). Living in New York City and Paris.

**Poetry**

*Presentation Piece,* 1974
*Separations,* 1976
*Taking Notice,* 1980
*Assumptions,* 1985
*Love, Death, and the Changing of the Seasons,* 1986
*Going Back to the River,* 1990
*The Hang-Glider's Daughter: New and Selected Poems,* 1990
*Selected Poems, 1965–1990,* 1994
*Winter Numbers,* 1994
*Squares and Courtyards,* 2000

**Other Writings:** translations of French literature (*A Long-Gone Sun,* by Claire Malroux, 2000); edited collections of literature (*Woman Poet: The East,* 1982).

**Further Reading**


Campo, Rafael, "About Marilyn Hacker," *Ploughshares* (Spring 1996)

Finch, Annie, "Marilyn Hacker: An Interview on Form by Annie Finch," *American Poetry Review* 25, no. 3 (1996)

Gardinier, Suzanne, "Marilyn Hacker," in *Lesbian Writers of the United States: A Bio-Bibliographical Critical Sourcebook,* edited by Sandra Pollack and Denise D. Knight, Westport, Connecticut, and London: Greenwood Press, 1993

Hacker, Marilyn, and Richard Howard, "The Education of the Poet: A Colloquy with Richard Howard and Marilyn Hacker," *Antioch Review* (Summer 2000)

Hammond, Karla, "An Interview with Marilyn Hacker," *Frontiers: A Journal of Woman's Studies* 5, no. 3 (Fall 1980)

Honicker, Nancy, "Marilyn Hacker's *Love, Death, and the Changing of the Seasons:* Writing/Living within Formal Constraints," in *Freedom and Form: Essays in Contemporary American Poetry,* edited by Esther Giger and Agnieszka Salska, Lodz, Poland: Wydawnictwo Uniwersytetu Lodzkiego, 1998

Johnson, Judith, "Poetics: A Conversation with Marilyn Hacker," *13th Moon: A Feminist Literary Magazine* 9, nos. 1–2 (1991)

Keller, Lynn, "Measured Feet 'in Gender-Bender Shoes': The Politics of Form in Marilyn Hacker's *Love, Death, and the Changing of the Seasons,*" in *Feminist Measures: Soundings in Poetry and Theory,* edited by Lynn Keller and Cristanne Miller, Ann Arbor: University of Michigan Press, 1994


---

# Rachel Hadas 1948–

"Particular and universal, / elegy, artifact, intrusion: / nothing to do but join the dots I saw," writes Rachel Hadas in section XI of "Art," as if describing the course and content of her protean body of work. From themes of love, loss, motherhood, mythology, dreams, and AIDS in her own work to translations of Tibullus, Baudelaire, and Konstantine Karyotakis, Hadas redefines herself every time she writes. Thus far, her career encompasses eight books of original verse and several well-received translations and book-length essays on the writing process. Her career has been widely lauded with awards ranging from a Guggenheim fellowship to an Ingram Merrill Foundation grant to an award in literature from the American Academy of Arts and Letters. Hadas' important poetic voice records the world around her with a formal dexterity, connecting the quotidian to the past through the ghosts who inhabit her dreams. Her poems are adept at stopping in the moment, full of lush description.

The daughter of Elizabeth Chamberlayne Hadas and famous Columbia University classics professor Moses Hadas, Rachel Hadas had an early introduction to high literary society. Not surprisingly, she sees Greek and Latin poetry as important influences. Much of Hadas' work is centered on the idea of transitions, as she moves from one urgent poetic moment to the next. One of these important movements in Hadas' life prefigured her first book, *Starting from Troy* (1975). Following her graduation from Radcliffe in 1969, she traveled to Greece, where she married Stavros Kondylis and became fluent in Greek. At one point, she was arrested and imprisoned on charges of setting fire to an olive oil factory—the "victim" of what Gloria Glickstein Brame calls "xenophobia gone mad in their peasant village." Poems such as "Landlady" demonstrate Hadas' talent for descriptive moments that leap from the page full of life and vigor.

Hadas' life and career turned again as she returned to the United States, divorcing Kondylis and pursuing graduate studies. She earned an M.A. from the Writing Seminars at Johns Hopkins in 1977 and a Ph.D. from Princeton in 1982. *Slow Transparency* (1983) demonstrates her expertise in writing poems that slow life to carefully rendered moments. This important period of transition established several key relationships that influence Hadas' later writing. She married again, to composer George Edwards. Their son, Jonathan, and her friendships with James Merrill, Alan Ansen, David Kalstone, and Charles Barber provide much of the basis for Hadas' considerations of love and loss in her later work, beginning with *A Son from Sleep* (1987).

Hadas is perhaps most well known for *Unending Dialogue: Voices from an AIDS Poetry Workshop* (1991). After the death of David Kalstone, among others, Hadas felt compelled to join the AIDS community by teaching a poetry workshop at the Gay Men's Health Crisis (GMHC) Center in New York City. The poems composed in this workshop, together with Hadas' own poetry and two essays, comprise *Unending Dialogue*. In this book, Hadas establishes two new themes, moving from transitions and motherhood to a preoccupation with the presence of those who have died but continue to influence her thoughts and dreams. Hadas also develops a fascination with the difficult place of silence in the world. Inspired by ACT UP's slogan "Silence = Death," Hadas began to explore how words and poems can counter death.

*Unending Dialogue* is unique in its reconciliation of the varied participants in the creative writing workshop. It presents the poetry of gay men dying from AIDS-related complications alongside the poetry of their teacher, who is allied with the AIDS community yet distinctly separate from it. As in *Living in Time* (1990), Hadas places her own poetry in the midst of a larger essay meditating on the poetry and situation of AIDS and on her relationships with the men in the workshop in *Unending Dialogue*. The move between prose and poetry allows Hadas to develop her ideas of craft and the relationship between language and life.

Hadas has a love for formal poetry, which is evident in her connection to poets such as Merrill and more ancient predecessors such as Sappho and in her use of forms such as the sestina, terza rima, and pantoum. However, *Unending Dialogue* presents a different side to Hadas, as her subject matter moves from her everyday world to a global health crisis. "Less Than Kind" demonstrates Hadas' entrance into a world dominated by newspaper headlines about drug abuse and syphilis. Hadas deftly expresses her own subject position as an HIV-negative woman, a caretaker within the HIV/AIDS community, and the way in which this relationship to AIDS leaves her with a profound sense of uselessness. Stopping the moment, for Hadas, takes on a new urgency. In "Taking Sides," she writes, "Our task today: to write against the clock," revealing both the despair and the possibilities involved in the act of writing poetry.

*Mirrors of Astonishment* (1992) returns to verse imbued with the "poetic mundane," as in "Learning to Talk" and "The Bath." The difference, however, is that, with the loss of her mother, her friend Charles Barber, and many of the men in the workshop, Hadas now brings the ghosts of the dead into the world of the living. *The Empty Bed* (1995), in many ways a sequel to *Unending Dialogue,* demonstrates the continuation of this movement in Hadas' work with poems such as "The Friend," recalling isolated moments in order to explain the sum total of a companionship. Hadas' newest theme is dreams, perhaps a necessary extension of the effort to reconcile enjoyment of life with instances of profound loss. Hadas urged her students in the GMHC workshop to write against the clock. Her readers revel in every poem, each an opportunity to see Hadas' stopped moments.

J. ELIZABETH CLARK

**Biography**

Born in New York City, 8 November 1948. Attended Radcliffe Institute, Harvard University, Cambridge, Massachusetts, B.A. 1969; Johns Hopkins University, Baltimore, Maryland, M.A. 1977; Princeton University, New Jersey, Ph.D. 1982; Instructor, 1980–81, Assistant Professor, 1982–87, Associate Professor, 1987–92, and since 1992 Professor, Rutgers University, Newark, New Jersey; teacher, Columbia University, New York City, 1992, 1993, and Princeton University, Hellenic Studies Program, 1995, Creative Writing Program, 1996. Received Vermont Council of the Arts grant, 1975–76; MacDowell Colony fellowship, 1976; Bread Loaf Writers' Conference scholar, 1976; Ingram Merrill Foundation Award, 1977, 1994; Guggenheim fellowship, 1988–89; American Academy of Arts and Letters Literature Award, 1990; Elizabeth Matchett Stover Poetry Award, 1991; Sharp Family Foundation Award, 1995. Living in New York City.

**Poetry**

*Starting from Troy,* 1975
*Slow Transparency,* 1983
*A Son from Sleep,* 1987
*Pass It On,* 1989
*Living in Time,* 1990
*Mirrors of Astonishment,* 1992
*The Empty Bed,* 1995
*Halfway down the Hall: New and Selected Poems,* 1998

**Selected Criticism**
*Form, Cycle, Infinity: Landscape Imagery in the Poetry of Robert Frost and George Seferis*, 1985
*Merrill, Cavafy, Poems, and Dreams*, 2000

**Other Writings:** essays (*The Double Legacy*, 1995), translations of Greek and French literature (*Other Worlds Than This: Translations*, 1994); edited anthologies of poetry (*Unending Dialogue: Voices from an AIDS Poetry Workshop* [with Charles Barber], 1991).

**Further Reading**
Glickstein Brame, Gloria, "Rachel Hadas: A Poet's Life," *ELF: Eclectic Literary Forum* (*www.pce.net/elf/archives/v7n1006a.htm*)
Helle, Anita, "Elegy as History: Three Women Poets 'By the Century's Deathbed,'" *South Atlantic Review* 61, no. 2 (1996)
Upton, Lee, "Women's Creation Stories," *Denver Quarterly* 23, no. 2 (1988)
Watkins, Ann Vreeland, "Rachel Hadas, Poet and Essayist: A Bibliography, 1965–1993," *Bulletin of Bibliography* 51, no. 2 (1994)

---

# Theresa Hak Kyung Cha 1951–82

Before her untimely death at the age of 31, Theresa Hak Kyung Cha was a promising innovator of experimental film, slide projections, sculpture, audio recordings, performance art, and poetry. Her work challenges assumptions about history, narrative, language, and in particular conceptions of immigrants; through powerful and often dislocating ideological and grammatical interrogations of cultural, geographic, and social positions, she recuperates an alternative sense of self and identity in a postcolonial, feminist, racially marked world. Her experiments with the sense of displacement and fragmentation mark an important stage in postmodernist, multicultural, and feminist writing. By addressing, resisting, and reconstructing an alternative idea of the "nation," she articulates a multiple, even self-contradictory, sense of identity, most notably with Asian-American female subjects. In addition this articulation explores the processes of memory, communication, and transcendence of the self through the redemption of suffering, an influence inspired by her childhood traditions of Catholicism and Confucianism.

Hak Kyung Cha was born in Korea; during the chaos of the Korean War her family moved about the country before settling first in Hawaii and then in northern California. These experiences lend to her profound observations on not only the colonialism in war-torn Korea, but also on the problematic American representations of Asians. Her works attempt to construct Asian-American identity by blurring the boundaries between definitive categories of race, gender, culture, history, and language as well as between genres such as autobiography and biography. Often mixing techniques of the lyric and the prose poem, her works use English, French, and Asian languages to alert her readers to their own subjectivity and the need to reevaluate their conceptions of language and identity.

As a student at the University of California at Berkeley during the 1970s, Hak Kyung Cha studied the noted theorists Roland Barthes, Jacques Derrida, and Jacques Lacan. The psychologist A.R. Luria and his theories on memory were also influential in her work. At Berkeley Hak Kyung Cha received bachelor's degrees in comparative literature and art, a master's degree in art, and a master of fine art's degree. These studies led to postgraduate work in film-making and theory at the Centre d'Études Americaine du Cinéma in Paris, where she came into much contact with artists and writers such as Christian Metz, Thierry Kuntzel, Monique Wittig, and Raymond Bellour. After her return to California Hak Kyung Cha gained recognition for her performances and films, which play with the process of breaking apart and reconstructing formal visual and linguistic strategies.

In 1980 Hak Kyung Cha moved to New York City and produced two works: *Apparatus* (1980), an anthology of writings on the film apparatus, and her most important work, *Dictée* (1982), a collage of narratives and images that traces names, histories, and fictive characters embodied in the voices of nine female Muses. Each of the nine self-contained sections forms a composite of narrative—autobiographical, biographical (Yu Guan Soon, Joan of Arc), historical (documents, photographs), classical (evocation of the Nine Muses, Sappho), visual (diagrams, maps, pictures, handwritten notes)—in which she continually demands that readers reevaluate and rearticulate identity from an immigrant, feminist, religious, multi-historical perspective. This culling and piecing together of fragmented narratives highlights the constructed nature of memory and language, illuminating the political, linguistic, familial, and psychological dimensions of identity formation. The disruptions in the text—tri-lingualism (Korean, French, English), mother tongue, dictation, and translation—foreground the reader as a collaborator responsible for the shaping of identity. Hak Kyung Cha challenges the hegemony of nation and family, exploiting the tensions beneath layers of historical sediment:

> Scratch. Marking. Uncontainable. She knows during. While she says to herself she does not account for the sake of history. Simulated pasts resurrected in memoriam. She hears herself uttering again re-uttering to re-vive. The forgotten. From stone. Layers. Of stone upon stone her self stone between the layers, dormant. No more. She says to herself she would return time to itself. To time itself. To time before time. To the very first death. From all deaths. To the one death. One and only remaining. From which takes place annunciation. A second coming.

Each self-contained section of *Dictée* becomes the site of linguistic and historical interrogation of the physical body as the immigrant subject. The metaphor of the body weaves throughout the text with diagrams and descriptions of blood, body parts (particularly the tongue), and rituals of cutting and splicing the body. These recurring and often violent images explicitly connect to Hak Kyung Cha's deeply postmodern imperative, tracing the literal effects of colonization as well as its figurative effects on dictation and speech.

Influenced by postmodern notions of deconstruction and reader-response theory, feminist identity politics, psychoanalysis, and avant-garde poetics, in *Dictée* Hak Kyung Cha confronts the slipperiness of language and of identity construction, particularly that of the immigrant female subject's memory and experience. For Hak Kyung Cha the writer and reader are jointly responsible for the construction of meaning. Moreover, this relationship is contingent on specific historical moments and positioned by personalities of race, gender, and culture. *Dictée* represents a collaboration between the writer and the reader in which no privileged voice asserts a limiting narrative authority; language is not connected to any body, *Dictée* suggests, but rather is the fragmentarily represented voice of many separate individuals.

In *Dictée* each individual female voice embodies multiple subjectivities, garnering various narratives and resisting universal truth-making. In several sections Hak Kyung Cha writes of the mother tongue, utterance and speech, the act of dictation and translation, and its atrophied disuse. Through the acts of speaking and writing the subject can perform identity, physically remember, and document her journey into recollection, thus reclaiming her memory of home. Wordplay, syntactical fragments, and multiple points of view disrupt the linear narrative, calling attention to the process of writing and the nature of speech. Many sections, for example, elaborate on the immigrant or colonial subject's broken speech, in which she stutters, stops, and transposes syntax:

> Contractions. Noise. Semblance of noise.
> Broken speech. One to one. At a time.
> Cracked tongue. Broken tongue.
> Swallows. Inhales. Stutter. Starts. Stops before starts.
> About to. Then stops. Exhale
> swallowed to a sudden arrest.

Particularized to the very notion of pauses and exhalations, this awareness links itself to the act of constructing an articulation all the while conscious of the physical act in itself. Not only is speech mental, it is physical. It takes energy. By flouting grammatical and linguistic conventions, Hak Kyung Cha emphasizes the formal features of language construction and the normative ways in which readers accept such paradigms.

Just seven days after the publication of *Dictée,* Theresa Hak Kyung Cha was brutally murdered by a stranger in New York City. At the time she was prominently poised to become an influential voice in experimental poetry and art. Her inclusion of mixed media, exercise in dislocation and fragmentation of formal structures, and articulation of the exile's experience chronicle her attempts to create a simultaneously singular and complex voice for the American subject, thus opening new possibilities for understanding the postmodern condition.

NICOLE E. CORTZ

**Biography**

Born in Pusan, Korea, 4 March 1951. Attended University of San Francisco, California; University of California, Berkeley, B.A. in comparative literature 1973, B.A. in art 1975, M.A. in art 1977, M.F.A. 1978; Centre d'Études Americaine du Cinéma, Paris, 1976; editor and writer, Tanam Press, 1980; instructor in video art, Elizabeth Seton College, New York, 1981; artist-in-residence, Nova Scotia College of Art and Design, 1982. Died in New York City, 5 November 1982.

**Poetry**

*Dictée,* 1982

**Other Writings:** cinema studies (*Apparatus, Cinematographic Apparatus: Selected Writings,* 1980), screenplays (*Exilée,* 1980).

**Further Reading**

Alarcón, Norma, and Elaine Kim, editors, *Writing Self, Writing Nation: A Collection of Essays on "Dictée" by Theresa Hak Kyung Cha,* Berkeley, California: Third Woman Press, 1994

Chang, Julia, "'Transform This Nothingness': Theresa Hak Kyung Cha's *Dictée,*" *Hitting Critical Mass* 1, no. 1 (1993)

Keller, Lynn, and Cristanne Miller, editors, *Feminist Measures: Soundings in Poetry and Theory,* Ann Arbor: University of Michigan Press, 1994

Lew, Walter K., *Excerpts from, Dikte = Dikte: for Dictée,* Seoul: Yeul Eum, 1992

Martin, Stephen-Paul, *Open Form and the Feminine Imagination: The Politics of Reading Twentieth Century Innovative Writings,* Washington, D.C.: Maisonneuve Press, 1988

Min, Eun Kyung, "Reading the Figure of Dictation in Theresa Hak Kyung Cha's *Dictée,*" in *Other Sisterhoods: Literary Theory and U.S. Women of Color,* edited by Sandra Kumamoto Stanley, Urbana: University of Illinois Press, 1998

Shih, Shu-mei, "Nationalism and Korean American Women's Writing: Theresa Hak Kyung Cha's *Dictée,*" in *Speaking the Other Self: American Women Writers,* edited by Jeanne Campbell Reesman, Athens: University of Georgia Press, 1997

Spahr, Juliana M., "Postmodernism, Readers, and Theresa Hak Kyung Cha's *Dictée,*" *College Literature* 23, no. 3 (1996)

Stephens, Michael Gregory, *The Dramaturgy of Style: Voice in Short Fiction,* Carbondale: Southern Illinois University Press, 1986

Wolf, Susan, "Theresa Cha: Recalling Telling ReTelling," *Afterimage* (Summer 1986)

# Donald Hall 1928–

Poet, essayist and autobiographer, critic, editor, dramatist, and professor of English, Donald Hall was educated at Harvard, Oxford, and Stanford Universities. After teaching for 18 years at the University of Michigan (1957–75), Hall left academia to live and write at Eagle Pond Farm in rural New Hampshire, where his grandparents once lived. Since the mid-1970s, much, although not all, of Hall's work has taken a distinctly pastoral turn, especially in volumes such as *Seasons at Eagle Pond* (1987) and *Winter Poems from Eagle Pond* (1999), his most recent book. However, Hall is less a poet of nature than of people and human relationships mediated by the natural world, and, since a child, has been concerned with intersections of city and country, culture and nature. *Exiles and Marriages* (1955), his first major collection, includes, for example, "Elegy for Wesley Wells," a poem about the loss of his maternal grandfather, who died while Hall was studying in England. The elegy's consolation hinges on the promise that the poet will eventually return to New Hampshire to follow his own calling: "Soon I will come to cross the hilly sea, / And take my work again, / And walk again, among the familiar hills." Memory and nature engender redemptive work for Hall. The cycle of life and death yields, in many of his poems, a celebration of pleasure infused with a sense of loss that has understandably moved some critics to call his writing "elegiac" and "metaphysical."

Hall is known for combining simple, direct language with surrealistic imagery in poetry that emphasizes patterns of sound appealing to emotion and imagination. He affirms that successful works convey a process of discovery for author and reader alike: "Many poems begin for me without any sense of where they will go; then the voyage of revision is pure discovery" (Woodruff, 1993). In theory, for Hall, a poem's psychological dimension accommodates *any* reader's open mind; however, as some critics have noted, such an ideal is difficult to achieve in practice. Since his first chapbook, *(Poems)* (1952), Hall has published some 17 volumes of poetry and numerous prose works and edited collections, including: a play based on the work of Robert Frost, *An Evening's Frost* (1965); *As the Eye Moves: A Sculpture by Henry Moore* (1970), a tribute to the eminent sculptor's work; various books on the craft of writing, such as *The Weather for Poetry* (1982) and *Poetry and Ambition* (1988); several works for children, including *Ox Cart Man* (1979); and two volumes on sport, *Dock Ellis in the Country of Baseball* (1976) and *Fathers Playing Catch with Sons: Essays on Sport (Mostly Baseball)* (1985), which reflect Hall's stated desire to have been a great athlete had he not become a poet. In 1995 Hall's wife, the poet Jane Kenyon, died of leukemia. Two of his recent collections are dedicated to her memory: *The Old Life* (1996) and *Without* (1998).

Hall began writing poetry at the age of 12 and first published his work at 16, the year he met Robert Frost at the Bread Loaf Writers Conference. As an undergraduate working for the *Harvard Advocate,* he conversed with Dylan Thomas and T.S. Eliot. Years later, while poetry editor for the *Paris Review,* he interviewed Ezra Pound. Hall recollects these meetings and conversations in *Remembering Poets: Reminiscences and Opinions* (1978), where he observes: "Three [of these men] were models of persistence in art, of endurance and courage; the fourth was a virtual suicide, a counterexample. Endurance is as admirable as energy." Other poets who have strongly influenced Hall's writing include, among many others, Bly, Creeley, Hill, Kinnell, Moore, Rich, Simpson, Snodgrass, Wright, and Yeats.

Hall's poetry moves through three cycles of growth and change that may be succinctly described as formalist, vatic, and synthetic. His earliest work follows formal and generic principles of meter and rhyme and frequently involves exilic themes. Hall's poems began to change direction in the late 1950s, as he recounts in a 2000 interview with Ian Hamilton: "By 1956 I began to feel uncomfortable in the iambic. . . . From syllabics I took the leap to various types of free verse. I felt this necessity to break out of the cage I had made for myself, even before [Ginsberg's] *Howl.*" *A Roof of Tiger Lilies* (1964) perhaps best illustrates Hall's first transition into a style of writing concerned less with poetic form than with the emotional and psychological forces a poem may reveal. This new mode, as Hall often remarks, attempts to bring together two ancient poetic traditions: that of *vates* (i.e., the poet as divinely inspired visionary) and that of *poiein* (i.e., the poet as master craftsman, or maker). Most of Hall's readers agree that *Kicking the Leaves* (1978) and *The Happy Man* (1986) together signal the next important transition in his career—a time when, according to Liam Rector (1989), "Hall began to find not only the *image* but the *book* of his poetry." His synthesis of writing styles culminates in *The One Day* (1988), a long poem in three sections published in the year of Hall's 60th birthday that collects 17 years of writing. The book opens with Picasso's assertion that "every human being is a colony" and accordingly delivers, in an elliptical poetic form, a meditation on the meaning of life from the perspective of two narrators (one male, one female) who convey the experiences of multiple personae.

Hall readily expresses his suspicion of literary criticism, workshop writing, and literary careerism in general but remains committed nonetheless to the value of poetry according to an ethic of ambition, which he articulates in *Poetry and Ambition* (1988): "Maybe ambition is appropriately unattainable when we acknowledge: *No poem is so great as we demand that poetry be.*" He thrives on revision, sometimes moving a single piece through at least 100 drafts, as he did with "Ox Cart Man" before submitting the text for publication. For Hall, inspiration yields the least amount of the poetic process; writing, the greatest of work, pleasure and discovery.

W. SCOTT HOWARD

**Biography**

Born in New Haven, Connecticut, 20 September 1928. Attended Harvard University, Cambridge, Massachusetts (Garrison and Sergeant Prizes, 1951), B.A. 1951; Oxford University (Henry fellow; Newdigate Prize, 1952), B.Litt. 1953; Stanford University, California (creative writing fellow), 1953–54; junior fellow, Society of Fellows, Harvard University, 1954–57; Assistant Professor, 1961–66, and Professor of English, 1966–75, University of Michigan, Ann Arbor; poetry editor, *Paris Review,* Paris and New York, 1953–62; member of the editorial board for poetry, Wesleyan University Press, Middletown, Connecticut, 1958–64; consultant, Harper and Row publishers, 1964–81; Deacon, South Danbury Church, New Hampshire. Received Lamont Poetry Selection Award, 1955; Edna St. Vincent Millay Memorial Prize, 1956; Longview Foundation

Award, 1960; Guggenheim fellowship, 1963, 1972; Sarah Josepha Hale Award, 1983; Lenore Marshall Award, 1987; NBCC Award, 1989; *Los Angeles Times* Award, 1989; Ruth Lilly Prize, 1994; honorary Litt.D., Presbyterian College, Clinton, South Carolina, Colby College, Waterville, Maine, and Daniel Webster College, Nashua, New Hampshire; honorary L.H.D., Plymouth State College, New Hampshire; Poet Laureate of New Hampshire, 1984. Living in Danbury, New Hampshire.

**Poetry**

*Exiles and Marriages,* 1955
*The Dark Houses,* 1958
*A Roof of Tiger Lilies,* 1964
*The Alligator Bride: Poems New and Selected,* 1969
*The Yellow Room: Love Poems,* 1971
*The Town of Hill,* 1975
*Kicking the Leaves,* 1978
*The Toy Bone,* 1979
*The Happy Man,* 1986
*Seasons at Eagle Pond,* 1987
*The One Day: A Poem in Three Parts,* 1988
*Old and New Poems,* 1990
*The One Day, and Poems, 1947–1990,* 1991
*The Museum of Clear Ideas,* 1993
*The Old Life,* 1996
*Without,* 1998
*Winter Poems from Eagle Pond,* 1999

**Selected Criticism**

*Marianne Moore: The Cage and the Animal,* 1970
*Remembering Poets: Reminiscences and Opinions—Dylan Thomas, Robert Frost, T.S. Eliot, Ezra Pound,* 1978
*Goatfoot Milktongue Twinbird: Interviews, Essays, and Notes on Poetry, 1970–76,* 1978
*The Weather for Poetry: Essays, Reviews, and Notes on Poetry, 1977–81,* 1982
*Poetry and Ambition: Essays, 1982–88,* 1988

**Other Writings:** plays (*An Evening's Frost,* 1965), short stories (*The Ideal Bakery,* 1987), children's literature, essays; edited collections of literature (*The Faber Book of Modern Verse,* 1965; *American Poetry: An Introductory Anthology,* 1969).

**Further Reading**


Collins, Floyd, "Loss and Redemption," *Gettysburg Review* 11, no. 4 (1998)
Flint, R.W., "Kicking Over the Traces," *Parnassus* 7, no. 1 (1978)
Hall, Donald, and Ian Hamilton, *Donald Hall in Conversation with Ian Hamilton,* London: Between the Lines, 2000
Hansen, Tom, "On Writing Poetry: Four Contemporary Poets," *College English* 44, no. 3 (1982)
Haskell, Dennis, "The Modern American Poetry of Deep Image," *Southern Review* 12 (1979)
Orr, Gregory, "A Reading of Donald Hall's *Kicking the Leaves,*" *Iowa Review* 18, no. 1 (1988)
Rector, Liam, editor, *The Day I Was Older: On the Poetry of Donald Hall,* Santa Cruz, California: Story Line Press, 1989
Steinman, Lisa, "Dialogues between History and Dream," *Michigan Quarterly Review* 26, no. 2 (1987)
Walsh, Chris, "'Building the House of Dying': Donald Hall's Claim for Poetry," *Agni* 47 (1998)
Woodruff, Jay, "Donald Hall: 'Ox Cart Man,'" in *A Piece of Work: Five Writers Discuss Their Revisions,* edited by Woodruff, Iowa City: University of Iowa Press, 1993


---

## Joy Harjo 1951–

Seeking ways to transform hatred into love, weaving together the mundane and the visionary, Joy Harjo has become a celebrated figure in contemporary women's and Native American poetry. Born to Muscogee (also known as Creek) and Cherokee-French-Irish parents and raised in an urban setting, Joy at 19 years old changed her last name from Foster to Harjo to claim her Muscogee heritage and to link her identity to her paternal grandmother, Naomi Harjo, an acclaimed painter. Harjo intended to become an artist herself but changed her major to English after hearing Simon Ortiz read his poetry and meeting Leslie Marmon Silko, who gave Harjo her first typewriter. The influence of both writers is seen in Harjo's poetry. Like Silko's short stories and novels, Harjo's poems emphasize survival and regeneration by showing how the old ways—stories, dances, spiritual beliefs—continue to provide meaning in the contemporary world. From Ortiz, Harjo learned that poetry could be written in a natural speaking voice, that poetry need not follow a Modernist aesthetic of fragmentation, difficult allusiveness, and irony.

Harjo published her first chapbook of poetry, *The Last Song* (1975), while still an undergraduate. Its nine poems were later reprinted in Harjo's first full-length volume of poetry, *What Moon Drove Me to This?* (1979). Even in these early poems many of Harjo's major themes and images are present. "I Am a Dangerous Woman" and her Noni Daylight poems show compassion for and insight into the lives of anguished women. Other poems ("The Last Song" and "3 A.M.") reveal a fierce attachment to the land. Harjo delicately renders the contemporary world of pain for American Indians while simultaneously celebrating the life-force in lovemaking, children, and language. The speaker in "3 A.M." appeals to a TWA agent at an airport to find some way of getting her back to "old oraibi, third mesa . . . the center of the world," and in these early poems (as in her later work) blackbirds, crows, coyotes, and horses are present as spiritual guides.

The poems in *What Moon Drove Me to This?* are conventional in form, but as her career developed Harjo became more innovative in her approach to form. In *She Had Some Horses* (1983;

revised edition, 1997) she plays with typography in poems such as "One Cedar Tree" and "Late Summer Leaving" to form a line that breathes and modulates. Prose-poem paragraphs in "For Alva Benson, and for Those Who Have Learned to Speak" and "The Woman Hanging from the Thirteenth Floor Window" tell poignant stories. Repetition in "Remember," "She Had Some Horses," and "I Give You Back" transforms these poems into chants or prayers, so that reading them aloud becomes a kind of cure. In this way Harjo firmly rejects W.H. Auden's famous lament that "poetry makes nothing happen." Rejecting Modernist paralysis, she instead crafts a visionary poetry that creates openings in which "dynamic possibility" can occur (Harjo, 1996).

*Secrets from the Center of the World* (1989) continues Harjo's development as an innovator. A collaboration with astronomer-photographer Stephen Strom, *Secrets from the Center of the World* pairs Harjo's lyrical prose poems with Strom's impressive landscape photographs of Navajo territory and the Four Corners area. Harjo perfects the innovations of her earlier volumes, creating a varied repertoire of line rhythms and lengths, verse paragraphs, chant-like stanzas, and other word-musical effects. Her next volume, *In Mad Love and War* (1990), established her reputation as a major poetic voice. In the mid-1980s Harjo began to play the saxophone—an instrument she chose because it "sounds close to the human voice" (Harjo, 1996)—and the poems of *In Mad Love and War* pay tribute to a variety of musical genres and to a host of musicians, including Billie Holiday, Charlie Parker, John Coltrane, Aretha Franklin, and Nat King Cole.

In some of the most notable poems Harjo uses musical effects to create moving poems of witness. "For Anna Mae Pictou Aquash" commemorates the AIM activist who was found murdered on the Pine Ridge Reservation in February 1976; "Strange Fruit," a riff on the Billie Holiday song of that same title, mourns Jacqueline Peters, a woman lynched when she tried to organize a local chapter of the NAACP; "Resurrection" is based on Harjo's 1983 visit to Nicaragua, where she heard staggering stories of torture and death, but also of survival and courage. An important part of family history sanctions these beautiful, political poems. Harjo's great-great-grandfather, Monahwee, led the Red Stick War against Andrew Jackson in the early 19th century to oppose the removal of the Creek Nation from Alabama to Oklahoma. Although the Creek Nation lost and was removed in 1832, Harjo relates Monahwee's rebellion against the policy of removal to her writing poetry as a way to protest injustice and transform the world (Harjo, 1996): "What I mean," Harjo insists in the prose poem "Transformations," "is that hatred can be turned into something else, if you have the right words, the right meanings, buried in that tender place in your heart where the most precious animals live."

In the early 1990s Harjo's search for strong connections between poetry and music led her to co-found the musical group Poetic Justice, which performs some of her poems set to a music that Harjo has described as "TRIBAL-JAZZ-REGGAE." The title of their 1997 CD, *Letter from the End of the Twentieth Century,* comes from one of the most important poems in Harjo's acclaimed volume *The Woman Who Fell from the Sky* (1994). In "Letter from the End of the Twentieth Century," the spirit of a dead man unexpectedly reaches out in love to forgive his murderer. Reconciliation and the power of love to transform oneself and one's community in spite of tremendous pain and devastation are the connective tissues of this volume. Harjo has described her poetry as an attempt "to make th[e] spiritual realm more manifest, obvious" (Harjo, 1996). The most remarkable poems in this volume bring inspiring visions down to earth, as in the title poem "The Woman Who Fell from the Sky," in which Lila, simultaneously a young woman searching for direction in life and the legendary Sky Woman, falls from the sky into the arms of a young man, Johnny, a runaway who is also called Saint Coincidence, as he stands in front of a Safeway grocery store.

In *The Woman Who Fell from the Sky* Harjo places an italicized meditation or narrative tale at the end of almost every poem; the effect is to amplify meaning by looking again at the situation from a new perspective. She continues using this combination of poem followed by prose tale in *A Map to the Next World* (2000), which also shows the influence of Harjo's move to Hawaii in its evocation of the land and ocean.

Like the feminist writers and poets—Audre Lorde, June Jordan, Alice Walker, and Adrienne Rich—who have influenced her career, Joy Harjo is a word-warrior. Although she remains cautious about whether the word "feminist" is an appropriate label for herself or her work, she does insist that her poetry is "woman-identified" and that "empowerment" is central to her poetry (Harjo, 1996). Taking up the situation of distressed peoples in contemporary America—the suffering and heartbroken, those who long for connection—and crafting a visionary poetry that encompasses both the sacred and the profane, Harjo is one of the most important Native American poets of the 20th century.

Nancy J. Peterson

*See also* Native American Poetry

**Biography**

Born in Tulsa, Oklahoma, 9 May 1951. Attended the University of New Mexico, Albuquerque, B.A. 1976; University of Iowa, Iowa City, M.F.A. 1978; Anthropology Film Center, Santa Fe, New Mexico, 1982; Instructor, Institute of American Indian Arts, Santa Fe, 1978–79, 1983–84; Lecturer, Arizona State University, Tempe, 1980–81; Assistant Professor, University of Colorado, Boulder, 1985–88; Associate Professor, University of Arizona, Tucson, 1988–90; Professor, University of New Mexico, Albuquerque, 1991–97; Visiting Professor, University of Montana, 1985; writer and consultant, Native American Public Broadcasting Consortium, National Indian Youth Council, National Endowment for the Arts, 1980–83; writer-in-residence, Navajo Community College, 1978; University of Alaska Prison Project, 1981; Institute of Alaska Native Arts, 1984. Received National Endowment for the Arts fellowship, 1978; Arizona Commission on the Arts Creative Writing fellow, 1989; American Indian Distinguished Achievement Award, 1990; Josephine Miles Award, PEN Oakland, 1991; William Carlos Williams Award, Poetry Society of America, 1991; American Book Award, 1991; Wittner Bynner Poetry fellowship, 1994; Lifetime Achievement Award, Native Writers' Circle of America, 1995; Oklahoma Book Arts Award, 1995; Delmore Schwartz Memorial Award, 1995; Mountains and Plains Booksellers Award, 1995. Living in Honolulu, Hawaii.

**Poetry**

*The Last Song,* 1975
*What Moon Drove Me to This?* 1979
*She Had Some Horses,* 1983; revised edition, 1997

*Secrets from the Center of the World,* 1989
*In Mad Love and War,* 1990
*The Woman Who Fell from the Sky,* 1994
*A Map to the Next World: Poems,* 2000

**Other Writings:** children's literature (*The Good Luck Cat,* 2000), screenplay (*Origin of Apache Crown Dance,* 1985), television plays, short stories (in *Talking Leaves: Contemporary Native American Short Stories,* 1991); edited collections of literature (*Reinventing the Enemy's Language: North American Native Women's Writing* [with Gloria Bird], 1997).

**Further Reading**

Allen, Paula Gunn, *The Sacred Hoop: Recovering the Feminine in American Indian Traditions,* Boston: Beacon Press, 1986; revised edition, 1992
Donovan, Kathleen M., *Coming to Voice: Feminist Readings of Native American Literature,* Tucson: University of Arizona Press, 1998
Harjo, Joy, *The Spiral of Memory: Interviews,* edited by Laura Coltelli, Ann Arbor: University of Michigan Press, 1996
Harjo, Joy, and Poetic Justice, *Letter from the End of the Twentieth Century* (CD), Silverwave Records, SD 914, 1997
Jahner, Elaine A., "Knowing All the Way Down to Fire," in *Feminist Measures: Soundings in Poetry and Theory,* edited by Lynn Keller and Cristanne Miller, Ann Arbor: University of Michigan Press, 1994
Lincoln, Kenneth, *Sing with the Heart of a Bear: Fusions of Native and American Poetry, 1890–1999,* Berkeley: University of California Press, 2000
Pettit, Rhonda, *Joy Harjo,* Boise, Idaho: Boise State University Press, 1998
Scarry, John, "Representing Real Worlds: The Evolving Poetry of Joy Harjo," *World Literature Today* 66, no. 2 (1992)
Wilson, Norma C., "Joy Harjo," in *Native American Writers of the United States,* edited by Kenneth M. Roemer, Detroit, Michigan: Gale, 1997

---

# Harlem Renaissance

At the height of the Harlem Renaissance, Lester A. Walton, a black journalist, wrote that art was in a position to establish a kind of unity between white and black America. However, art was no closer to uniting disparate races and ethnicities than it was to uniting the black community as a whole. Carl Van Vechten, a white novelist, photographer, and patron of black art, landed squarely in the minefield of color consciousness on the 1926 publication of *Nigger Heaven.* The novel, set in the exotic world of Harlem night life, raised questions about his possible racism and/or his decidedly poor taste. Some members of the black literary community, W.E.B. DuBois chief among them, felt betrayed by Van Vechten's title and his decision to deal exclusively with the "wilder" aspects of black Harlem. DuBois wrote in *The Crisis* (the journal of the National Association for the Advancement of Colored People [NAACP]) that *Nigger Heaven* was a "a blow in the face" of black Americans; he saw Van Vechten's novel as an "affront to the hospitality of black folk and the intelligence of white" ("The Intelligence of White," 1926). These concerns echo the very real fear during the Harlem Renaissance that one segment of the black community (however illegitimate or legitimate) would become representative of the disparateness of black experience. This rift did not spontaneously arise with the Harlem Renaissance, however. Its roots can be located in the history of black people in America.

Blacks have had an intensely hoary relationship with America. Captured from their native African shores, shipped as steerage across the Middle Passage, and enslaved as chattel in a "new" world, African-Americans had no autonomy, no voice, no power, and ultimately no home in America. The first blacks were brought to America as indentured servants in 1619, and in 1641 Massachusetts became the first colony to legalize slavery. Slavery silenced a people and effectively rendered the race "invisible" on the American landscape. The African people who had been uprooted and transplanted to a foreign soil were considered less than human. Their languages, cultures, and families were eradicated, and from the moment of the first slave auction, African-Americans ceased to be flesh-and-blood beings and became instead the stereotyped figment of their masters' imaginations. They were chattel: exploited in fields, violated in cabins, and whipped in yards, all in God's name. Black people were alternately "darkies," "niggers," "mammies," or "wenches" but rarely human beings. Blackness became a commodity of the white master, and black people became the object of white domination.

Color has become a windowless room from which millions of blacks are unable to escape, the four walls papered with the common negative associations of blackness and black people found in art, literature, and general popular culture. There have always been those who resisted, who attempted to carve out a place in a racist wasteland; there have always been those who spoke for the innumerable silent. Each wave of artists, writers, and critics that attempts to find the door does so by providing an "authentic" definition of blackness. Clearly, then, language, literacy, and artistic creation are powerful tools in the struggle to maintain dominance and in the struggle to subvert that dominance.

The earliest extant poetic expression by an African-American dates back to Jupiter Hammon, born a slave on Long Island in 1711, although Lucy Terry is credited with having written the first poem by an African-American in 1755 (the poem no longer exists). Hammon's poem "An Evening Thought, Salvation by Christ, with Penetential Cries" was published in 1760, although this work was not "rediscovered" until nearly two centuries later. Literary critics have glossed Hammon's work as significant for its position as the first published work by an African-American;

however, the role of "unofficial" progenitor of African-American poetic expression is conferred upon Phillis Wheatley. Wheatley's poetry volume *Poems on Various Subjects: Religious and Moral* was published in 1773. Thus, regardless of which figure marks its beginning, African-American literary expression has poetry at its roots, although the strength of those roots has been questioned. For example, critics have endlessly debated Hammon's and Wheatley's artistic skills. Some find Wheatley merely imitative, others find her voice and vision distorted by a wholesale acceptance of racist rhetoric, while still others find her poetry subtly subversive of that very racism. Regardless, Hammon and Wheatley provided the foundation for later African-American artisans.

The slave narrative tradition that followed in the 19th century was an attempt on the part of escaped slaves, with the help of northern abolitionists, to rewrite black people into existence. Slave narratives were enormously popular throughout the 19th century, and although they were not wholly successful in reconfiguring blackness from the object of white manipulation to the power position of speaking subject, as Henry Louis Gates, Jr., states in *The Signifying Monkey* (1988), the narratives did create the literary foundation for the Harlem Renaissance: "What was at stake for the earliest black authors was nothing less than the implicit testimony to their humanity, a common humanity which they sought to demonstrate through the very writing of a text of an ex-slave's life." Books such as Harriet Jacobs' *Incidents in the Life of a Slave Girl* (1861) and Frederick Douglass' *Narrative of the Life of Frederick Douglass* (1845) called attention to the sexual, physical, and mental indignities that four million of their brothers and sisters were enduring in slavery. Despite these and other literary efforts, the white gaze continually constructed and misconstrued 19th-century black life. This white gaze did not have access to the reality of black experience, for, as Paul Laurence Dunbar (the first black poet to gain nationwide recognition) wrote in "We Wear the Mask" (1897), "we [African-Americans] wear the mask that grins and lies, / It hides our cheeks and shades our eyes." The writers of the Harlem Renaissance attempted to shift this focus and lift that veil.

Alain Locke wrote in his foreword to *The New Negro* (1925), perhaps the manifesto of the Renaissance, that "Negro life is not only establishing new contacts and founding new centers, it is finding a new soul. We have, as the heralding sign, an unusual outburst of creative expression." Redefining the race problem and more specifically race representation had the potential to unify the artistic community. However, there was no consensus about how this creative energy should be spent. Some artists attempted to reconceptualize Africa, to shift the association of Africa and African people with words such as "dark," "primitive," and "savage" to progressive words such as "creative," "beautiful," and "resilient." Some artists attempted to privilege the Folk, to give voice to black folk (black southern folk) and to posit the Folk as the very essence of blackness. Still other artists attempted to deify the Talented Tenth, to show, as DuBois wrote in "Of the Training of Black Men," a "loftier respect for the sovereign human soul that seeks to know itself and the world about it; that seeks a freedom for expansion and self-development; that will love and hate and labor in its own way, untrammeled alike by old and new" (*The Souls of Black Folk,* 1903). Ultimately, the fissure running through the heart of the Harlem Renaissance separated not only the Folk from the bourgeois Talented Tenth but also one "authentic" representation of blackness from another.

The Harlem Renaissance was not a coherent movement, driven by a singular cause or held together by a singular vision. The Renaissance, like the nation, was diverse and diffuse. In fact, it is even difficult to pinpoint the period's beginning or end. It is clear, however, that black people in America were increasingly on the move around the turn of the century. Between 1910 and 1920, about half a million southern blacks moved north. They sought refuge from racist violence, opportunity for industrial employment, and freedom to be full citizens of their country. World War I, perhaps the single most violent confrontation in human history, ironically afforded African-Americans a period of peace in an otherwise tumultuous time. America needed blacks as relatively cheap labor in the North, and the nation needed black men as fodder in the war overseas. There existed within the black community a belief that if they fought valiantly, if they worked patriotically, then certainly black people would find acceptance and respect on their "native" American soil. Despite America's triumph, on their return home black soldiers, along with their families and the larger community as a whole, were faced with renewed racial tension and increased racist violence. While the nation settled into peacetime, African-Americans were just beginning their real battle, this one domestic. A convenient marker, then, for the start of the Renaissance is 1919.

Running parallel to the Harlem Renaissance was, of course, the Roaring Twenties (with its decadent opulence) and the Modernist period in American literature (with its rejection of tradition and form). Much of the nation was experiencing an era of wealth and renewed social freedom. Women, for instance, increasingly stepped outside their prescribed "feminine" role; African-Americans attempted to do the same. As Alain Locke highlights in *The New Negro,* "Neither labor demand, the boll weevil nor the Ku Klux Klan is a basic factor. . . . The wash and rush of this human time on the beach line of the northern city centers is to be explained in terms of . . . a chance for the improvement of condition." Dissatisfied with their lot, African-American leaders such as Locke, DuBois, Arthur Huff Fauset, Arthur A. Schomburg, Charles S. Johnson, James Weldon Johnson, and William Stanley Braithwaite looked to the arts as a means to carve out a new and more accurate description of who African-Americans were and what their lives were like. Indeed, the success of these new creative efforts would presumably result in social acceptance not only for the artists themselves but also for the larger group. As Locke states, hope for a shift in the African-American's place in society "rests in the revaluation by white and black alike of the Negro in terms of his artistic endowments and cultural contributions."

The year 1919 marks not only the end of World War I but also the publication of Claude McKay's "If We Must Die"—an intriguing juxtaposition, for the former indicates a cease-fire, while the other is a kind of call to arms: "We must meet the common foe! / Though far outnumbered let us show us brave, / . . . Like men we'll face the murderous, cowardly pack / Pressed to the wall, dying, but fighting back!" McKay, a native of Jamaica, is one of the Renaissance's most well-known poets (the other two being Countee Cullen and Langston Hughes). McKay's poetry is largely steeped in primitivism, an embrace and even elevation of primitive (i.e., untainted) man as the last uncorrupted bastion of preindustrialized society. McKay closely associated this primitive state with his remembered island home. "The Tropics in New York" provides a particularly clear illustration of McKay's version of primitivism:

Bananas ripe and green, and ginger root,
Cocoa in pods and alligator pears,
And tangerines and mangoes and grape fruit,
Fit for the highest prize at parish fairs. . . .
My eyes grew dim, and I could no more gaze;
A wave of longing through my body swept,
And, hungry for the old familiar ways,
I turned aside and bowed my head and wept.

McKay juxtaposes New York with a natural beatific tropical setting, clearly positioning the latter as idyllic and desirable. "The Tropics in New York" leaves an impression that this island life of bananas and "mystical blue skies" is McKay's and thus African-Americans' home, away from industrial/modern accoutrements. His vision, then, embraces the kind of seemingly stereotyped image of blackness that so many African-Americans of the day (e.g., fellow poets Arna Bontemps, Jessie Redmon Fauset, Angelina Weld Grimké, and Georgia Douglas Johnson) tried to deny or, at least, to transcend.

Langston Hughes, 12 years McKay's junior but ideologically aligned, similarly located blackness in the Folk, a folk residually connected to mother Africa and residing in urban northern ghettoes, primarily Harlem. Hughes' use of black dialect, his embrace of "ordinary" black people, and his creative employment of form made him perhaps *the* literary darling of the Harlem Renaissance. The publication of Hughes' first volume of poetry, *The Weary Blues* (1926), coincided with the publication of his "revolutionary" essay "The Negro Artist and the Racial Mountain." Hughes' voice, as articulated in these works, was one of independence not only from racist white America but also from so-called bourgeois black America. Hughes, speaking for other young black artists, boldly declared,

> We Negro artists who create now intend to express our individual dark skinned selves without fear or shame. If white people are pleased, we are glad. If they are not, it doesn't matter. We know we are beautiful and ugly too. If colored people are pleased, we are glad. If they are not, their displeasure doesn't matter either. We build our temples for tomorrow, strong as we know how, and we stand on top of the mountain, free within ourselves. ("The Negro Artist and the Racial Mountain," *The Nation* 122 [1926])

The freedom that Hughes refers to is presumably the freedom to write out of and about the multiplicity of African-American experience. Interestingly, however, Hughes' voice in *The Weary Blues* is limited to one "authentic" blackness while his critical essay damns another: an "elitist" black middle class. Perhaps "High to Low" best expresses the central artistic/poetic schism running through the Harlem Renaissance:

God knows
We have our troubles, too—
One trouble is you:
you talk too loud,
cuss too loud,
look too black,
don't get anywhere,
and sometimes it seems
you don't even care. . . .
you let me down—
me, trying to uphold the race
and you—
well, you can see,
we have our problems,
too, with you.

No longer defined outwardly, African-Americans and their voices, in the form of artists and intellectuals, were no closer to an internally unified definition of blackness.

Langston Hughes with writers Wallace Thurman and Zora Neale Hurston and artists Aaron Douglas, John P. Davis, Bruce Nugent, and Gwendolyn Bennett (also a poet) were the founding editors of *Fire!!* This was a young and supposedly radical group of Harlem Renaissance writers who had grown increasingly tired of "genteel" and "dishonest" middle-class depictions of black life. *Fire!!* attempted to present the experiences of common black people, experiences that the Talented Tenth presumably avoided. One of the works featured in this ill-fated journal was Countee Cullen's poem "From the Dark Tower." Cullen, essentially a lyric poet and thusly a traditionalist in form, dealt primarily with issues of religion, love, and death while infusing these universal concerns with considerations of race ("Two Who Crossed a Line"), racism ("Incident" and "Uncle Jim"), and protest ("Scottsboro"). "Incident" basically follows the pattern of a ballad stanza (rhyming in lines two and four, four metrical feet in lines one and three, and three metrical feet in lines two and four). Utilizing a traditional format (unlike Hughes, for instance), Cullen highlights the "tradition" of racism in American society:

Once riding in old Baltimore,
Heart-filled, head-filled with glee,
I saw a Baltimorean
Keep looking straight at me.

Now I was eight and very small,
And he was no whit bigger,
And so I smiled, but he poked out
His tongue, and called me, "Nigger."

I saw the whole of Baltimore
From May until December;
Of all things that happened there
That's all that I remember.

Interestingly, those poets whose artistic creations fall thematically outside the Folk-infused visions of McKay, Hughes, and Cullen are women. This fact alone certainly raises gender as an issue in the Harlem Renaissance. Does the Folk continue to endure because it has some inherent connection to authentic black experience, or does it endure because its most vocal proponents were men? Whatever the answer, Georgia Douglas Johnson, like fellow poets Jessie Fauset, Anne Spencer, and Helene Johnson (Angelina Weld Grimké to a lesser extent), is historically relegated to second-tier status. Born on 10 September 1886 in Atlanta, Georgia, Johnson was a good student who exhibited a natural talent for music. Writing, specifically poetry writing, would eventually override her interest in music. In the same year that McKay penned his rebellious "If We Must Die," Johnson published "Shall I Say, 'My Son, You Are Branded?,'" an expression of the great difficulty facing black people in America. Signified, marginalized, and vilified by the color of their skin, African-Americans, Johnson posits, must confront and surpass the limitations others place on that blackness. Although the poem is not as overtly subversive as McKay's "If We Must Die," Johnson nonetheless couches a defiant tone in the mother's voice. The poem is at once a black feminist statement of resistance ("shall I with love prophetic bid you dauntlessly arise, / spurn the handicap that binds you, taking / what the world denies?") and an expression of traditional maternal instinct ("shall I mark the young light fading through / your soul-enchanneled eye"), and thus thematically complex. Yet one would be hard-pressed to find this poem or any other of Johnson's works in a recent anthology.

Jessie Redmon Fauset was a central Harlem Renaissance figure; nevertheless, she has subsequently and rather effectively been excised from its history. Her four novels, numerous short stories, poetry, reviews, editorials, and nonfiction essays are relatively invisible on the landscape of critical inquiry into this period. She was an independent, well-educated, and eloquent voice, and she created narratives of import and vision. Fauset often gave her poems French titles ("La Vie C'est la Vie" and "Douce Douvenance"), and she translated poems from their French originals ("The Pool" by Amedee Brun and "Oblivion" by Massillon Coicou). This fact alone has led some critics to label Fauset and her work elitist and endemic of black bourgeois pretension. Unfortunately, Fauset was also a northern middle-class woman whose very identity was inconsistent with established expectations of her race and gender. As with fellow Renaissance writers Nella Larsen and Dorothy West, critics irrepressibly attach Fauset's work to black middle-class decorum and to stylistic gentility. Renaissance artists were expected to racially mark their creations; the question was, How should these works be marked? not Should they be marked at all? Therefore, a poem such as Fauset's "Noblesse Oblige" was atypical:

Lolotte, who attires my hair,
Lost her lover, Lolotte weeps,
Trails her hand before her eyes;
Hangs her head and mopes and sighs,
Mutters of the pangs of hell. . . .
Love's dart lurks in my heart too,—
None may know the smart
Throbbing underneath my smile.

Feminist scholars such as Judith R. Berzon, Hazel Carby, Ann duCille, Deborah E. McDowell, Carolyn Sylvander, and Claudia Tate have of late rescued Larsen, West, and, to a lesser extent, Fauset from obscurity. Like the son in Johnson's poem and Johnson herself, Fauset and her fictional and poetic creations remain "foully tethered, bound forever" by critical misinterpretation and bias.

Black journals (*Opportunity*, the official arm of the Urban League, and *The Crisis*) and literary anthologies (James Weldon Johnson's *The Book of American Negro Poetry*, 1922, 1931; Cullen's *Caroling Dusk*, 1927; and Langston Hughes and Arna Bontemps' *The Poetry of the Negro, 1746–1949*, 1949) were invaluable to Renaissance writers, in particular those artists for whom these publications were their only outlet (Frank Horne, Anne Spencer, Helene Johnson, and Effie Lee Newsome chief among them). This dynamic clearly suggests the relationship between the ability to publish and the ability to succeed and endure. Those Harlem Renaissance poets who published individual volumes of poetry remain on the literary landscape, and those who did not are, for the most part, footnotes to the period.

SHARON L. MOORE

**Further Reading**

Baker, Houston A., Jr., *Afro-American Poetics: Revisions of Harlem and the Black Aesthetic*, Madison: University of Wisconsin Press, 1988
Bloom, Harold, editor, *Black American Poets and Dramatists of the Harlem Renaissance*, New York: Chelsea House, 1995
Bontemps, Arna, editor, *The Harlem Renaissance Remembered*, New York: Dodd Mead, 1972
Cooper, Wayne F., *Claude McKay: Rebel Sojourner in the Harlem Renaissance: A Biography*, Baton Rouge: Louisiana State University Press, 1987
Favor, Martin J., *Authentic Blackness: The Folk in the New Negro Renaissance*, Durham, North Carolina: Duke University Press, 1999
Honey, Maureen, editor, *Shadowed Dreams: Women's Poetry of the Harlem Renaissance*, New Brunswick, New Jersey: Rutgers University Press, 1989
Hull, Gloria T., *Color, Sex, and Poetry: Three Women Writers of the Harlem Renaissance*, Bloomington: Indiana University Press, 1987
Johnson, Eloise E., *Rediscovering the Harlem Renaissance: The Politics of Exclusion*, New York: Garland, 1997
Wall, Cheryl A., *Women of the Harlem Renaissance*, Bloomington: Indiana University Press, 1995
Wintz, Cary D., editor, *The Politics and Aesthetics of "New Negro" Literature*, New York and London: Garland, 1996

---

# Michael S. Harper 1938–

As a poet, editor and inspirational mentor, Michael S. Harper has distinguished himself as a major figure in American poetry and in African-American letters. Since the appearance of his first volume, *Dear John, Dear Coltrane* (1970), Harper has furthered the legacy of Langston Hughes and other poets who have brought the rhythm, mood, and vitality of jazz and blues into poetry. At the same time Harper is a poet of conscience who persistently examines and reevaluates American history, including some of its darker moments, in an effort to help heal what he has called America's "amnesia."

Even with its attendant violence and injustice, history as process is an important theme for Harper, as it also was for one of Harper's acknowledged literary forbears, the poet Robert Hayden. In the short poem "American History" from *Dear John, Dear Coltrane,* Harper imaginatively links the 1963 bombing of a church in Alabama to "middle passage blacks" hiding underwater from redcoats in Charleston Harbor. While the poem may suggest the disturbing notion of history repeating itself in a cycle of racial oppression, it can also be read as an affirmation of the continuing struggle for justice and equality. In a 1972 interview Harper characterized the aim of "Dear John, Dear Coltrane" as "redemptive" in that, like Coltrane's music, it attempts to internalize pain and suffering and to transform those feelings in "a kind of cultural process."

Harper's blending of personal history with cultural and national history reveals the influence of African-American musical forms throughout his career. His second volume, *History Is Your Own Heartbeat* (1971), contains a poetic sequence titled "Ruth's Blues" that presents the health problems of his mother-in-law as a metaphor for some of America's lingering national ills. In the poem Ruth has been separated from family members for an extended period of time in part because of economic and racial social inequities. Her blues are in many ways America's blues, and in discussing the sequence in a 1984 interview, Harper spoke of the blues as an "art form" that makes use of "real things a person incorporates into his or her own life to fortify and sustain the living." The blues are a way to say "'yes' to life no matter what it is," a way of sustaining not just oneself but also one's immediate family and even humanity in general. In "Blue Ruth: America," he writes:

I am telling you this:  
the tubes in your nose,  
in the esophagus,  
. . . .  
is America:  
I am telling you this:  
*history is your own heartbeat.*

Song and survival are certainly at the heart of Harper's work in the genre of the elegy. Both *Dear John, Dear Coltrane* and *Nightmare Begins Responsibility* (1975), Harper's fifth major book of poems, contain several elegies for two sons lost in infancy. "We Assume," "Reuben, Reuben," "Deathwatch," "Nightmares Again," and "Nightmare Begins Responsibility" are among Harper's major achievements in the genre. But even in poems of personal loss, such as "Deathwatch," Harper undertakes the bold task of broadening his theme of loss to encompass America's history of racial strife:

. . . you witness  
your parents sign the autopsy  
and disposal papers  
shrunken to duplicate  
in black ink  
on white paper  
like the country  
you were born in, unreal, asleep,  
silent, almost alive.

Harper uses elegy to illuminate broader social issues in other poems as well, for musicians such as Charlie Parker and Bessie Smith, and more overtly in poems for important social figures such as Malcolm X and Martin Luther King, Jr.

After the limited edition *Photographs: Negatives: History as Apple Tree* (1972; contains poems he incorporated into a larger volume that year, *Song: I Want a Witness*), Harper expanded the breadth of his poetic vision in his fourth full volume, *Debridement* (1973). The first part of the book, "History as Cap'n Brown," explores the history of black resistance to slavery in America, with the historical figure of John Brown serving as central metaphor. The book's title sequence is one of the few works by an African-American poet dealing with the social aftermath of the Vietnam conflict. "Debridement" is loosely based on the actual experiences of a highly decorated African-American Vietnam veteran who returns to his hometown of Detroit only to find that American society has no place for him. After health and financial struggles, he is gunned down by a store owner who owes him money and then buried with full military honors in Arlington National Cemetery. In "The Family of Debridement," the poem's final sequence, Harper captures the sense of juxtaposition:

*Store manager: "I first hit him with two bullets*  
*so I pulled the trigger until my gun was empty."*  
. . . .  
*Subject buried on grass slope, 200 yards*  
*east of Kennedy Memorial,*  
*overlooking Potomac and Pentagon,*  
*to the south,*  
*Arlington National Cemetery.*

*Army honor guard in dress blues,*  
*Carried out assignment with precision*

A highly improvisational sequence, "Debridement" raises important questions about the role of people of color in the American military system and their reintegration into society after service.

After *Nightmare Begins Responsibility* Harper won the Melville Cane Award and received a National Book Award nomination for *Images of Kin: New and Selected Poems* (1977), which included selections from all his previous volumes. During this period Harper also began some of the vital editorial work that has contributed greatly to African-American letters. *Chant of Saints: A Gathering of Afro-American Literature, Art, and Scholarship* (1979), co-edited with Robert B. Stepto, remains one of the most significant and unique interdisciplinary collections of material in its field. As editor of *The Collected Poems of Sterling A. Brown* (1980), Harper brought back into print the work of an important poet in the oral folk tradition, and with *Every Shut Eye Ain't Asleep: An Anthology of Poetry by African Americans Since 1945* (1994), co-edited with Anthony Walton, he provided a selection of verse by both well- and lesser-known poets, offering readers an opportunity to trace influence and lineage in the second half of the 20th century. He continued this work with *The Vintage Book of African American Poetry* (2000), again co-edited with Anthony Walton.

His own poetry has continued to expand in breadth and range with *Healing Song for the Inner Ear* (1985) and *Honorable Amendments: Poems* (1995). Both of these volumes continue to offer many tribute-poems to figures from the world of jazz, African-American culture and letters, as well as significant historical figures. *Honorable Amendments* explores America's vision of democracy within a global context, what Harper has described previously as "the tension between stated moral idealism and brutal historical realities." His 2000 collection, *Songlines in Michaeltree: New and Collected Poems,* continues to contribute to the collective dialogue about American culture and history.

ERNEST J. SMITH

**Biography**

Born in Brooklyn, New York, 18 March 1938. Attended City College of Los Angeles, A.A. 1959; California State University, Los Angeles, B.A. 1961, M.A. in English 1963; University of Iowa, Iowa City, M.F.A. 1963; University of Illinois, Urbana, 1970–71; statistics teacher, Pasadena City College, California, 1962; Instructor in English, Contra Costa College, San Pablo, California, 1964–68; poet-in-residence, Reed College and Lewis and Clark College, Portland, Oregon, 1968–69; Associate Professor, California State University, Hayward, 1970; Associate Professor, 1971–73, since 1973 Professor of English, and since 1983 Kapstein Professor, Brown University, Providence, Rhode Island; Visiting Professor, Harvard University, Cambridge, Massachusetts, 1974, 1977, and Yale University, New Haven, Connecticut, 1976; Benedict Distinguished Professor of English, Carleton College, Northfield, Minnesota, 1979; Elliston poet, University of Cincinnati, Ohio, 1979; National Humanities Distinguished Professor, Colgate University, Hamilton, New York, 1985; American specialist, International Congress of Africanists State Department tour of Africa, 1977; council member, Massachusetts Council on Arts and Humanities, 1977–80; board member, Yaddo Artists Colony; original founding member, African Continuum, St. Louis, Missouri. Received American Academy Award, 1972; Black Academy of Arts and Letters Award, 1972; Guggenheim fellowship, 1976; National Endowment for the Arts grant, 1977; Melville Cane Award, 1977. Living in Providence, Rhode Island.

**Poetry**

*Dear John, Dear Coltrane,* 1970
*History Is Your Own Heartbeat,* 1971
*Photographs: Negatives: History as Apple Tree,* 1972
*Song: I Want a Witness,* 1972
*Debridement,* 1973
*Nightmare Begins Responsibility,* 1975
*Images of Kin: New and Selected Poems,* 1977
*Rhode Island: Eight Poems,* 1981
*Healing Song for the Inner Ear,* 1985
*Songlines: Mosaics,* 1991
*Honorable Amendments: Poems,* 1995
*Songlines in Michaeltree: New and Collected Poems,* 2000

**Other Writings:** edited collections of literature (*Chant of Saints: A Gathering of Afro-American Literature, Art, and Scholarship* [with Robert B. Stepto], 1979; *The Collected Poems of Sterling A. Brown,* 1980; *Every Shut Eye Ain't Asleep: An Anthology of Poetry by African Americans Since 1945* [with Anthony Walton], 1994; *The Vintage Book of African American Poetry* [with Anthony Walton], 2000).

**Further Reading**

Bibby, Michael, *Hearts and Minds: Bodies, Poetry, and Resistance in the Vietnam Era,* New Brunswick, New Jersey: Rutgers University Press, 1996
Callahan, John F., "'Close Roads': The Friendship Songs of Michael S. Harper," *Callaloo* 13, no. 4 (1990)
Dodd, Elizabeth, "Another Version: Michael S. Harper, William Clark, and the Problem of Historical Blindness," *Western American Literature* 33, no. 1 (1998)
Lieberman, Laurence, *Beyond the Muse of Memory: Essays on Contemporary American Poets,* Columbia: University of Missouri Press, 1995
Lloyd, David, "Interview with Michael S. Harper," *TriQuarterly* 65 (1986)
Nicholas, Xavier, editor, "Robert Hayden and Michael S. Harper: A Literary Friendship," *Callaloo* 17, no. 4 (1994)
Ramazani, Jahan, *Poetry of Mourning: The Modern Elegy from Hardy to Heaney,* Chicago: University of Chicago Press, 1994
Randall, James, "An Interview with Michael S. Harper," *Ploughshares* 7, no. 1 (1981)
Stepto, Robert B., "Michael S. Harper, Poet as Kinsman: The Family Sequences," *Massachusetts Review* 17 (1976)
Young, Al, Larry Kart, and Michael S. Harper, "Jazz and Letters: A Colloquy," *TriQuarterly* 68 (1987)

## Dear John, Dear Coltrane

*Dear John, Dear Coltrane* (1970), Michael S. Harper's powerful first book, establishes many of the themes and techniques for which he is now known. Nominated for the National Book Award, *Dear John, Dear Coltrane* represented a real achievement for Harper, who wrote the book over ten years, struggling with poetic conventions such as voice, line, idiom, imagery, and diction. His success in creating a synthesis of original form and content marks him as a leading contemporary poet; Harper is as well known for his style as he is for his subject matter. *Dear John, Dear Coltrane* demonstrates Harper's use of jazz improvisation as formal poetic device, a technique that many poets have come to emulate. He borrows from jazz greats such as John Coltrane, Billie Holiday, and Elvin Jones as well as old spiritual songs; this style informs the content, as at the heart of all of Harper's poems is a difficult negotiation of living in the United States as a participant in the African-American struggle for freedom. Harper utilizes American history as a poetic site through which present-day racial tensions are intimately connected to the history of slavery in the United States. *Dear John, Dear Coltrane* uses the deaths of many African-Americans, from jazz musicians to Harper's infant son Reuben to Malcolm X to the four girls blown up in an Alabama church at the height of the civil rights struggle, to suggest a poetic unity within the African-American community. Using historical figures and events, personal relationships, and travel, *Dear John, Dear Coltrane* is a redemptive book, seeking reconciliation between history and all those it has affected.

Harper opens the collection with "Brother John," which clearly establishes race as a major theme of the book. Harper challenges racist language; in particular, his assertion "I'm a black man," repeated throughout the poem, stands against the use of "boy" by many whites in addressing African-American men. Harper emphasizes the theme of race by beginning and ending the poem with the stanza

Black man:
I'm a black man;
I'm black; I am—
A black man; black—
I'm a black man;
I'm a black man
I'm a man; black—
I am—

Harper's celebration of black identity is achieved through stanzas about jazz players Charlie "Yard Bird" Parker, Miles Davis, and John Coltrane. The reader's introduction to Coltrane, in particular, initiates a redemptive theme: that even in the course of personal and historical tragedies, art (in this case jazz) holds the possibility for celebration, joy, and hope. Many other poems in the collection, such as "Where Is My Woman Now," written for Billie Holiday, continue this complicated celebration, marking both the achievements and the death of an important individual.

As he links history to individuals, Harper makes no distinction between prominent historical figures and individuals who were important to him. Charlie Parker's life and music are as important to understanding history as is the death of a child. "We Assume: On the Death of Our Son, Reuben Masai Harper" and "Reuben, Reuben" present the death of one of Harper's two infant sons who died soon after birth, a tragedy that came to figure greatly in future poems and collections, such as *Nightmare Begins Responsibility* (1975). The 28 painful hours of Reuben's tiny life, Harper asserts, are as important as John Coltrane's life is.

*Dear John, Dear Coltrane* works as a creation of an alternate American history that presents prominent historical figures alongside others previously unknown to history. "American History" reveals this most poignantly as Harper compares the deaths of the four little girls—Denise McNair, Carole Robertson, Cynthia Wesley, and Addie Mae Collins—who died in the 15 September 1963 explosion at the Sixteenth Street Baptist Church in Birmingham, Alabama, to the deaths of more than 500 black slaves in Charleston Harbor who were "in a net, under water / in Charleston harbor / so *redcoats* wouldn't find them." The poem suggests that in American history black history has been left untold. Harper's poetic project, then, is to retrieve individual figures, to tell their stories and find connections between them.

"Dear John, Dear Coltrane," like other poems in the collection, retells history by focusing on a particular historical figure. A eulogy for Coltrane (whom Harper knew), the poem hinges on the chant-like repetition of the words "a love supreme," as Harper unfolds the story of Coltrane's life from his birth and childhood in Hamlet, North Carolina, to his music, his drug use, and his relationship with God. In Coltrane, Harper finds a hero, a teacher, and someone who used history—the black musical experience—to create something new and inspiring, something Harper takes on as his own project in *Dear John, Dear Coltrane.*

J. ELIZABETH CLARK

**Further Reading**


Callahan, John F., "'Close Roads': The Friendship Songs of Michael S. Harper," *Callaloo* 13, no. 4 (1990)

Lenz, Günter H., "Black Poetry and Black Music: History and Tradition: Michael Harper and John Coltrane," in *History and Tradition in Afro-American Culture,* edited by Günter H. Lenz, Frankfurt and New York: Campus, 1984

"Michael S. Harper: American Poet," *Callaloo* 13, no. 4 (1990)

Moyers, Bill D., "Michael Harper," in *Language of Life,* by Moyers, edited by James Haba, New York: Doubleday, 1995

Randall, James, "An Interview with Michael S. Harper," *Ploughshares* 7, no. 1 (1981)

Rowell, Charles H., "'Down Don't Worry Me': An Interview with Michael S. Harper," *Callaloo* 13, no. 4 (1990)

Young, Al, Larry Kart, and Michael S. Harper, "Jazz and Letters: A Colloquy," *TriQuarterly* 68 (1987)


## Nightmare Begins Responsibility

*Nightmare Begins Responsibility* (1975), Michael S. Harper's fifth major book of poetry, is among his most well known. Widely acclaimed for its complex stories of individual courage, this collection presents Harper's interpretation of W.H. Auden's phrase "we are a collectivity of individuals." Continuing the idea that history provides a locus for poetry, a theme Harper developed in his first four books, *Nightmare Begins Responsibility* reveals the larger history of African-American life in the United States through individual stories of grief, struggle, and joy. *Nightmare Begins Responsibility* was so popular that Harper reprinted it as a section of his later collection *Images of Kin* (1977).

As part of his project to expand the meaning of being "American" to include black experience, Harper unites the many figures in his poems as "kin," a group of people as disparate as Frederick Douglass, Bessie Smith, Harper's mentor and teacher Sterling A. Brown (to whom a section of the book is dedicated), and Harper's immediate family, all of whom have similar life experiences and share ancestral heritage. In the poem "Kin," Harper suggests that sometimes "kin" are chosen rather than inherited through blood relations.

*Nightmare Begins Responsibility* portrays both subtle and blatant acts of discrimination against African-Americans, and Harper vividly describes the way individuals absorb this adversity into everyday life. In "Grandfather," Harper tells the story of the burning of his grandfather's Catskill home by white neighbors in 1915. The angry mob surrounds the house, guided by the belief that "the death of a lone black / family is *the Birth of a Nation.*" The grandfather carries on, but he is overcome by the weight of the white world. While he survives an incident as catastrophic as the burning of his house, he nevertheless imagines a bleak future for his grandson.

As if in response to the grandfather's resignation, Harper makes the following plea in "No. 24": "Do not forget Birmingham." Harper writes the history of resistance, lest it be forgotten. "Do not unhook your tongue- / broken grammar with commercials; / do not sell your restricted / billboard home secure," he writes: maintain your cultural identity, keep hold of your ancestors. Harper extends this point in "Gains," lamenting the inability of an uncle and nephew to relate to each other after the nephew leaves home and tries to assimilate to white culture.

"Nightmare Begins Responsibility" invokes William Butler Yeats' phrase "in dreams begin responsibility" and Etheridge Knight's notion of the importance of acknowledging those who have influenced families and their development, even if they are no longer living. In this poem Harper watches one of his sons die from hyaline membrane disease in an intensive care unit. The poem employs a jazz-like rhythm, a hallmark of Harper's innovative style. The poem begins with the helpless father filled with the distrust of white power, represented here by the white uniforms of the white doctors and nurses. The father is kept isolated from the baby; his "gloved stickshifting gasolined hands" contrast with the white hands caring for the child, suggesting class distinctions. Harper repeats the words "distrusting" and "white" in the poem, creating a scene that invokes the historical oppression recorded in other poems. Harper is well aware that some hospital procedures and care are extended to those of certain races and classes but not to others. Accordingly, his distrust is born of the historical prejudices revealed in earlier poems.

This poem, however, offers a redemptive moment as Harper acknowledges the work of the "*white-doctor-who-breathed-for-him-all-night.*" Distrust gives way to "panebreaking heartmadness" as Harper realizes that no matter what, the child will die. "Nightmare Begins Responsibility" is a difficult poem, one in which Harper confronts his own prejudices. In an interview with Bill Moyers, Harper noted that at the heart of the poem is the father's understanding that, once the worst nightmare is realized—the impending death of the baby—he must move on, away from placing prejudicial blame, to a responsibility for the children who are living. In this moment, Harper extends his hand to heal the world, seeking to overcome the supremacy of white culture for a more united, more diverse America.

J. ELIZABETH CLARK

**Further Reading**

Brown, Joseph A., "Their Long Scars Touch Ours: A Reflection on the Poetry of Michael Harper," *Callaloo* 9, no. 1 (1986)

Callahan, John F., "The Testifying Voice in Michael Harper's *Images of Kin*," *Black American Literature Forum* 13 (1979)

Dodd, Elizabeth, "Another Version: Michael S. Harper, William Clark, and the Problem of Historical Blindness," *Western American Literature* 33, no. 1 (1998)

Keen, Suzanne, "Inescapable Responsibility," *Callaloo* 13, no. 4 (1990)

Lloyd, David, "Interview with Michael S. Harper," *TriQuarterly* 65 (1986)

"Michael S. Harper: American Poet," *Callaloo* 13, no. 4 (1990)

Moyers, Bill D., "Michael Harper," in *Language of Life*, by Moyers, edited by James Haba, New York: Doubleday, 1995

Stepto, Robert B., "Let's Call Your Mama and Other Lies about Michael S. Harper," *Callaloo* 13, no. 4 (1990)

---

# Robert Hass 1941–

Robert Hass' work marks the coming together of two different poetic currents. The first is the work of the Modernists: Pound, Eliot, Stevens, and, most powerfully, Frost. The Modernists, for Hass, "in insisting on brokenness rather than wholeness, that the relation between words and things is not a given," made it clear "that poetry stands in the middle of a wasteland still, a wreckage of all previous metaphysics that made us feel at home in the world" ("An Interview with Robert Hass," in Gardner, 1999). Frost passes on a Modernism that both acknowledges and finds generative the fragility of the forms within which humanity thinks and lives, insisting that poetry reveals "metaphor in its strength and in its weakness" and teaches "how far you may expect to ride it and when it may break down with you" (Frost, "Education by Poetry," 1931). Poetry, for Hass and Frost, demonstrates how to hold oneself within a landscape where, as Frost puts it:

> The background is hugeness and confusion shading away from where we stand into black and utter chaos; and against the background any small man-made figure of order and concentration. What pleasanter than that this should be so? ("Letter to 'The Amherst Student,'" 1935)

The second current that Hass draws from is that of Eastern literature, particularly the work of such masters of the image as the Japanese poets Issa, Buson, and Basho. Hass' translations of these writers appeared as *The Essential Haiku* in 1994. In an important essay in his collection *Twentieth Century Pleasures: Prose on Poetry* (1984), Hass comments that the image, as used by these writers—"no one of them feels like whole truth and they do not last"—offers an opportunity for "quiet attention." Such poems, understanding their limits as "man-made figures," Hass writes, "marry the world, but they do not claim to possess it, and in this they have the power and the limitations of intimate knowledge."

Hass' first book, *Field Guide* (1973), won the Yale Series of Younger Poets Prize. It works out the relationship between the fragility of form and an attentiveness to the world in two primary areas: poems about the Bay Area California landscape where Hass was born and poems about houses or other shared domestic spaces. The California poems are written out of an often thwarted desire to connect to the landscape in a simple and transparent way. Desiring to "own what is familiar" ("Maps"), the poet describes the coast's dry hills and beaches, recites its names, and remembers its history. However, he continually finds that simple bond—that figure of order and concentration—broken and complicated by the dark background Frost speaks of, in this case the troubled history of the area, still alive in the very names and nouns the poet lovingly handles. So, for example, the poet tries to locate himself in "Palo Alto: The Marshes" by naming components of his world:

Walking, I recite the hard
explosive names of birds:
egret, killdeer, bittern, tern.
Dull in the wind and early morning light,
the striped shadows of the cattails
twitch like nerves.

The explosive, twitching uneasiness here, the reader discovers, is produced by the poet's absorption in an earlier conflict between settlers of this region, a conflict in a sense still tugging at him as he tries, imaginatively, to wrest the landscape back from its despoilers:

my eye performs
the lobotomy of description.
Again, almost with yearning,
I see the malice of . . . ancient eyes.

At the same time, however, many of these uneasy coast poems, although unable through simple description to reestablish a stable home, do discover within their conflicted forms quiet, haiku-like moments of attention, as in "Maps":

Late summer—
red berries darken the hawthorns
curls of yellow in the laurels

your body and the undulant
sharp edges of the hills

Something similar goes on in *Field Guide*'s domestic poems. "House" thinks about the fragility of the "premises" the poet inhabits. It begins with the speaker luxuriating in the stability of a Saturday morning. He stands at a window, breakfast underway, music filtering in from another room: "coffee & bacon & Handel / & upstairs asleep my wife." Suddenly,

old dusks break over me,
      the thick shagged heads
of fig trees near the fence
      & not wanting to go in
. . . .
& all that terror
      in the house

He realizes, that is, that the premises he inhabits, his home and marriage, are never entirely free from childhood terrors, rendering the form within which he now dwells deeply contingent and vulnerable. Such forms are like the body: finite, exhausted, breaking down, but also stirring, awake, alive.

In *Praise* (1979) the fragile premises that the poet examines are first linguistic, then often move to metaphorically equivalent domestic or social situations. In "Heroic Simile," for example, Hass compares the fall of a swordsman in Kurosawa's *Seven Samurai* to the fall of a pine, then deliberately extends the simile to its breaking point. The swordsman falls like a pine that was so big that a woodsman and his uncle traveled from a village and spent days cutting it up, and so on. Eventually the comparison stalls. Just as the act of describing the California coast or dwelling with an imagination of domestic stability gave way, so this form breaks down:

They have stopped working
because they are tired and because
I have imagined no pack animal
. . . .
and there's nothing I can do.
The path from here to that village
is not translated.

Within that incomplete translation, however, a great deal gets accomplished. Within the simile's limits an entire world is sketched in. It is like the rich intimacy of a couple leaving the Kurosawa movie, uninterested in blazing a path from one world to another, but nonetheless charged and alive to each other:

A man and a woman walk from the movies
to the house in the silence of separate fidelities.
There are limits to imagination.

The most widely read poem in *Praise,* "Meditation at Lagunitas," is the volume's most direct examination of the generative limits of language. The poem begins with the speaker meditating on a conversation late the night before in which a friend had been expounding what he took to be "all the new thinking" about language: that is, the idea that

because there is in this world no one thing
to which the bramble of *blackberry* corresponds,
a word is elegy to what it signifies.

While the idea is not in fact a new one, as the speaker remarks, the tone of his friend's voice during that conversation, his attitude toward contingency, was clearly disturbing:

We talked about it late last night and in the voice
of my friend, there was a thin wire of grief, a tone
almost querulous. After a while I understood that,
talking this way, everything dissolves: *justice,*
*pine, hair, woman, you* and *I.*

In fact, he admits, he found his friend's whining grief to be a seductive way of talking, a response he himself had engaged in last night as he remembered embracing a woman he had loved and feeling her almost dissolve in his arms. Longing and desire had prompted a wish for something far beyond what her immediate presence could provide. But now, thinking again about that way of talking, the poet realizes that there are other responses to human limits that do not leave the world for dead. This poem speaks of these responses as "tenderness"; other poems use the terms "attentive" or "intimate." Such responses—both linguistic and social—come fully alive as the poet realizes how temporary or tentative they are and how powerful is the world he brushes up against: "Such tenderness, those afternoons and evenings, / saying *blackberry, blackberry, blackberry.*"

The most ambitious poem in the book, "Songs to Survive the Summer," prompted by the poet's desire to comfort a child learning about death, catalogs a series of linguistic gestures that both acknowledge fragility and yet embrace the world: jokes, songs, poems, recipes, tales, letters, names. Such gestures are both "croon[ed]" and "broken." Each is, the poet admits, the "frailest stay against / our fears." Such ordinary gestures are the haiku of daily life, however, like a worthless wooden nickel carried in a pocket,

> lustered
> by the steady thoughtlessness
> of human use.

In *Human Wishes* (1989) Hass quite boldly extends the forms and the areas of his investigations. In addition to the meditative lyrics and quick-hitting catalogs of his previous volumes, *Human Wishes* examines Hass' familiar issues under the pressure of prose or sprawling, nonconsecutively analytical lines. The scope of these poems opens out as well, the poet wrestling with such tentative, "habitable" ("Spring Drawing") forms as marriage, the family, or memory, forms within which one might attend to the world's "swellings and diminishings" ("Tall Windows").

"Museum," for example, a striking prose poem, describes a couple in a museum restaurant on a Sunday morning. Sleepy, almost without thinking, "hardly exchang[ing] a look," they work out what Hass calls an "equitable arrangement": drinking coffee, reading the paper, passing their baby back and forth. They are surrounded by an exhibit that, although they seem unaware of its implications, brings out the powerful fragility of the form they have constructed. In a moment, all could be different:

> All around them are faces Käthe Kollwitz carved in wood of people with no talent or capacity for suffering who are suffering the numbest kinds of pain: hunger, helpless terror. But this young couple is reading the Sunday paper in the sun, the baby is sleeping, the green has begun to emerge from the rind of the cantaloupe, and everything seems possible.

Similar moments occur in a long poem entitled "Santa Barbara Road" in which the poet, in an attempt to "marry" himself back to the place where he had raised his family, sorts through a number of memories. All of the memories, as is true also of the family itself, are charged but fragile. They offer rich forms made all the more striking by the briefness of their insights. The poet remembers bathing his daughter and, almost inadvertently, introducing her to the precariousness of identity:

> "Who are you?"
> the rubber duck in my hand asked Kristin
> once, while she was bathing, three years old.
> "Kristin," she said, laughing, her delicious
> name, delicious self. "That's just your name,"
> the duck said. "Who are you?" "Kristin,"
> she said. "Kristin's a name. Who are you?"
> the duck asked. She said, shrugging,
> "Mommy, Daddy, Leif."

One notion of identity taken away, she reestablishes herself in another form—the web of father, mother, brother—which, the other poems in the volume suggest, is itself equally susceptible to fracture and dissolution. As with watching the couple in the museum, the poet is struck here by the new form's clarity, beauty, and impermanence: its human finitude.

Such forms, other poems in the volume suggest, are powerful because, like a memory that fails to settle into its place within an otherwise straightforwardly organized life, they refuse to be taken for granted. They remain live and open-eyed:

> When the memory of that time came to her, it was touched by strangeness because it formed no pattern with the other events in her life. It lay in her memory like one piece of broken tile, salmon-colored or the deep green of wet leaves, beautiful in itself but unusable in the design she was making. ("Novella")

Marriage, the volume suggests, has a similar open-eyed fragility to it. A couple in "The Apple Trees at Olema" comes upon "two old neglected apple trees" as they walk along the California coast. The limbs look rotten, but the trees are "wild with blossom and a green fire / of small new leaves." The couple is driven by different rhythms, demonstrating once again the vulnerability of form. She is shaken by the blossoms' raw flaring desire. He is exultant, sensing an expression of an unspoken version of himself. Turning to her for confirmation, he finds none, and loses the image while she slowly takes in the image and receives the blossoms. As the poet writes, "This is as sad or happy / as the tide," a given part of the inevitable slippage and fracturing of all human arrangements. When the couple reunites and shares a response to a bird flashing through the meadow, the poet compares that formal, delicate gesture to the grave vulnerability of a small boy walking in a hotel. Like all forms in Hass, the shape he makes and momentarily puts his weight on is both fragile and fleeting:

> He holds the number
> of his room close to the center of his mind
> gravely and delicately, as if it were the key,
> and then he wanders among strangers all he wants.

*Sun Under Wood* (1996) extends Hass' concerns in significant ways. Formally the poems are quite free, often mixing prose with lyric meditations or haiku-like bursts with elaborately extended stories within stories. More important, the book continually calls attention to itself as a piece of writing. Poems are sometimes followed with poetic "notes" or second thoughts; the poet often halts in mid-stride to puzzle over what he does when he writes. Quite often he brings the reader into the writing scene itself, sitting at a desk, or taking a break, pretending in language. The point seems to be that language itself is one of the temporary, finite forms of human life; language and time—"we live our lives in language and in time, / craving" ("English: An Ode")—become simply the broadest possible extensions of the fragile houses, coasts, and relationships of the previous books.

Hass' interest in the movement from finitude to open-eyed attentiveness is also extended in this book. Finitude now includes the never satisfied, "half-mated longing [carried] up out of childhood" ("Dragonflies Mating"), the moment in a relationship "when everything broken is broken / and everything dead is dead" ("Faint Music"), or the various forms of "emptiness" the world is "honeycombed with," "the whole botched world" ("Regalia for a Black Hat Dancer"). One repeated image for the pain of finitude is divorce: "my throat so swollen with some unsortable mix / of sorrow and desire I couldn't swallow" ("Regalia"). Another is the poet's mother's drinking:

> When I couldn't wake her, I decided to sit with her until she woke up. I must have been ten years old: I suppose I wanted for us to look like a son and mother who had been picnicking, like a mother who had fallen asleep in the warm light and

scent of orange blossoms and a boy who was sitting beside
her daydreaming, not thinking about anything in particular.

You are not her singing, though she is what's
broken in a song.
She is its silences. ("My Mother's Nipples")

Song is this volume's term for the watchfulness that an acknowledgment of fragility creates. The blank or tormented space where the mother should be, rendering tenuous every form of connection attempted thereafter, is also what allows one to sing, addressing the world openly because its notes are never settled. As "Faint Music" puts it, tracing the collapse of a relationship:

I had the idea that the world's so full of pain
it must sometimes make a kind of singing.
And that the sequence helps, as much as order helps—
First an ego, and then pain, and then the singing.

What many of the poems in this volume do, then, is attempt to enter pain or emptiness or shame and work out such a "sequence," poetry rising into song as the various "unsortable mix[es]" of emotions are handled and sized up. The strongest of these is "Regalia for a Black Hat Dancer," a poem that in sorting out the sorrows of divorce eventually comes to see that in pain one can only

lie down in . . . swift opposing currents

. . . two emptinesses, I suppose, the one
joy comes from, the one regret, disfigured intention, the
longing
to be safe or whole flows into when it's disappearing.

This has been Hass' central problem and insight throughout his career: he longs to make some sort of form in order to be safe or whole, but that form, under pressure, eventually gives way, leaving him torn by regret or disfigurement, and joy. That joy, this last volume insists, is never found without the shadowy pressure of regret: "I last but a minute. I walk on nothing. / Coming and going I do this dance in the air." One must acknowledge both currents to take in life, "to see its size" ("Regalia").

THOMAS GARDNER

**Biography**

Born in San Francisco, California, 1 March 1941. Attended St. Mary's College, Moraga, California, B.A. 1963; Stanford University, California (Woodrow Wilson fellow; Danforth fellow), 1964–67, M.A. 1965, Ph.D. 1976; taught at the State University of New York, Buffalo, 1967–71, St. Mary's College, 1971–74, 1975–89, and University of Virginia, Charlottesville, 1974; since 1989 Professor of English, University of California, Berkeley; poet-in-residence, The Frost Place, Franconia, New Hampshire, 1978. Received Yale Series of Younger Poets Award, 1972; U.S.-U.K. Bicentennial Exchange fellowship, 1976; William Carlos Williams Award, 1979; Guggenheim fellowship, 1980; American Academy Award, 1984; MacArthur Foundation fellowship, 1984–89; NBCC Award, for criticism, 1985; PEN/BABRA Award, for translation, 1986; National Book Critics Circle Award, 1996; Poet Laureate of the United States, 1995–1997. Living in Berkeley, California.

**Poetry**

*Field Guide,* 1973
*Praise,* 1979
*Five American Poets,* with others, 1979
*Human Wishes,* 1989
*Sun Under Wood,* 1996

**Selected Criticism**

*Twentieth Century Pleasures: Prose on Poetry,* 1984
*An Unnamed Flowing: The Cultures of American Poetry,* 2001

**Other Writings:** translations of Polish literature (*Facing the River,* by Czeslaw Milosz, 1995); edited collections of poetry (*Rock and Hawk: A Selection of Shorter Poems,* by Robinson Jeffers, 1987; *Poet's Choice: Poems for Everyday Life,* 1998).

**Further Reading**

Altieri, Charles, *Self and Sensibility in Contemporary American Poetry,* Cambridge and New York: Cambridge University Press, 1984
Bedient, Calvin, "Man Is Altogether Desire?" *Salmagundi* 90–91 (Spring–Summer 1991)
Berger, Charles, "Poetry Chronicle: Dan Pagis and Robert Hass," *Raritan* 10, no. 1 (Summer 1990)
Doody, Terrence, "From Image to Sentence: The Spiritual Development of Robert Hass," *American Poetry Review* 26, no. 2 (March/April 1997)
Gardner, Thomas, *Regions of Unlikeness: Explaining Contemporary Poetry,* Lincoln: University of Nebraska Press, 1999
Miklitsch, Robert, "Praise: The Poetry of Robert Hass," *Hollins Critic* 17, no. 1 (1980)
Shapiro, Alan, "'And There Will Always Be Melons': Some Thoughts on Robert Hass," *Chicago Review* 33, no. 3 (Winter 1983)

# Robert Hayden 1913–80

Robert Hayden occupies an important transitional role in the history of African-American poetry. His work and career offer a link between the Harlem Renaissance poets who preceded him and the Black Nationalist writers and their respondents who began to gain prominence at the end of his life. While he is most often read as an important poet in the tradition of African-American writing, Hayden's work also demonstrates the inextricably entwined nature of any history of either American or African-American poetry in the 20th century.

Hayden was born and grew up in the poor black neighborhood of Detroit called Paradise Valley. Named Asa Bundy Sheffey at birth, Hayden was left with a neighboring family by his mother when she decided to pursue a stage career in the east. The Haydens renamed Robert and did their best to raise him as one of their own, but the sense of a misplaced or ambiguous identity would become a major theme of his poetry, as in "'Mystery Boy' Looks for Kin in Nashville" (1970), in which a voice promises: "We'll go and find them, we'll go / and ask them for your name again."

Hayden read widely in the popular poets of his day, including Sandburg and Millay, and sought out the work of other African-American writers such as Cullen and Dunbar. Music was his early passion, and although he had to give up performance because of deteriorating eyesight, the phrasing and rhythms of popular, folk, religious, and classical song styles would all inflect his poetry. He studied poetry under Auden and later took a teaching position at Fisk University in Nashville, which he often blamed for his relatively light poetic output.

Hayden is best known for his historical poems and his mastery of a wide range of lyric forms. His first collection, *Heart-Shape in the Dust* (1940), contains mostly apprentice pieces that he chose not to reprint in subsequent collections. Hayden's emerging style is nonetheless evident in the mix of voices of the long choral poem "These Are My People" and in descriptive passages like this one from "Sunflowers: Beaubein Street":

> The Negroes here, dark votaries of the sun,
> Have planted sunflowers round door and wall,
> Hot-smelling, vivid as an August noon.
> Thickets of yellow fire, they hold in thrall
> The cruel, sweet remembrance of Down Home.

The title of Hayden's next book of poems was intended to be *The Black Spear*. Although Hayden eventually withdrew this manuscript from consideration for publication, much of its contents appears (often in revised forms) in subsequent volumes, and its themes and techniques remained dominant strains in Hayden's writing. This collection, which won the University of Michigan's Hopwood Award for 1942, was intended to answer Stephen Vincent Benét's call for a "black-skinned epic." "Middle Passage," the poem for which Hayden is best known, is, in terms of ambition, the most epic of the poems. In it Hayden adapts an Eliot-like sampling of historical and mythical sources to suggest that the African's journey to slavery in America is the heroic birth of a new people: "voyage through death / to life upon these shores." "Frederick Douglass" and "O Daedalus, Fly Away Home," also from *The Black Spear,* demonstrate the range of Hayden's formal accomplishments. The former is a sonnet in monument to the hero of its title, and the latter employs traditional ballad form and a colloquial voice to retell the traditional slave folk story of flying back to Africa.

"Homage to the Empress of the Blues," from the chapbook *The Lion and the Archer* (1948), continues Hayden's play with poetic voice and his fusion of the rhetoric of high-art poetry with black folk culture in a tribute to the blues singer Bessie Smith. The densely layered "A Ballad of Remembrance" fuses aspects of the mythic and the mundane, the sacred and the profane, and formal and informal speech simultaneously in a portrait of a Mardi Gras–like street scene:

> Quadroon mermaids, Afro angels, black saints
> balanced upon the switchblades of that air
> and sang.

Widely disparate and variously disguised, these are the voices in which Hayden will sing in much of his subsequent career.

When Hayden won the Third World Festival of Negro Arts' Grand Prix in 1966 for the volume *A Ballad of Remembrance* (1962), he had yet to find a mainstream publisher for his works. Soon after the festival, however, he was able to publish his *Selected Poems* (1966) with October House, making his poetry available to a wider readership. *Selected Poems* includes his famous lyric of belated recognition of his father's love, "Those Winter Sundays," in which the poet asks: "What did I know, what did I know / of love's austere and lonely offices?" "Runagate Runagate" juxtaposes the voices of escaped slave and slave-catcher in visceral encapsulation of the misery of slavery, while "Mourning Poem for the Queen of Sunday," about a murdered former choir singer, employs the rhythms of the hymn to question the value of a visionary Christianity for life on this earth.

At the peak of the Black Nationalist period in the late 1960s, Hayden was dismissed as an irrelevant formalist and attacked for his insistence that he was a "poet who happened to be a Negro" rather than the inverse. Hayden maintained that poetry and what he called propaganda must be kept separate even as he continued to give voice to the forgotten and ignored subjects of American and African-American history. In "The Dream" (*Words in the Mourning Time,* 1970), for instance, Hayden presents another variation on the dialogue poem, in this case counterpoising the dream that motivates a black soldier in the Civil War with the inadequacy of emancipation for an old slave woman who has long dreamed of her deliverance in apocryphal terms:

> That evening Sinda thought she heard the drums
> and hobbled from her cabin to the yard.
> The quarters now were lonely-still in willow dusk
> after the morning's ragged jubilo,
> when laughing crying singing the folks went off
> with Marse Lincum's soldier boys.
> But Sinda hiding would not follow them: those
> Buckras with their ornery
> funning, cussed commands, oh they were not
> the hosts the dream had promised her.
>
> and hope when these few lines reches your hand they will fine
> you well. I am tired some but it is war you know and ole jeff
> davis muss be ketch an hung to a sour apple tree like it says

in the song I seen some akshun but that is what I listed for not to see the sights ha ha More of our peeples coming every day the Kernul calls them contrybans and has them work aroun the Camp and learning to be soljurs. How is the wether home. Its warm this evening but theres been lots of rain

In the mid-1970s Hayden served a two-year stint as Consultant in Poetry to the Library of Congress and continued to write on the nature of identity, to juxtapose multiple voices, and to set the present in a complex historical context. In the longer "American Journal," the multiple competing identities and voices of Americans are viewed from the perspective of an alien spacecraft. Closer to home, in "Elegies for Paradise Valley" he reveals what might now be called the multicultural nature of America, writing about a black man's view of Gypsies:

They take on as bad as Colored Folks,
Uncle Crip allowed. Die like us too
. . . .
aliens among the alien: thieves,
carriers of sickness: like us like us.

Like the teachings of the Baha'i faith that sustained Hayden through his adult years, his poems require close study and the moral fortitude to recognize the specific individuality of others.

SCOTT MACPHAIL

**Biography**

Born Asa Bundy Sheffey in Detroit, Michigan, 4 August 1913. Attended Detroit City College (now Wayne State University), 1932–36, B.A. 1942; University of Michigan, Ann Arbor (Hopwood Award, 1938, 1942), 1938–44, M.A. in English 1944; writer and researcher, Federal Writers Project (Works Progress Administration), Detroit, 1936–40; Teaching Assistant in English, University of Michigan, 1944–46; Assistant Professor, 1946–53, Associate Professor, 1954–66, and Professor of English, 1967–69, Fisk University, Nashville, Tennessee; Visiting Professor, 1968, and Professor of English, 1969–80, University of Michigan; poet-in-residence, Indiana State University, Terre Haute, summer 1967; Bingham Professor, University of Louisville, Kentucky, spring 1969; poet-in-residence, University of Washington, Seattle, summer 1969, Denison University, Granville, Ohio, 1971, and Connecticut College, New London, 1974; staff member, Bread Loaf Writers Conference, Middlebury College, Vermont, 1972; from 1967 poetry editor, *World Order* (Baha'i magazine); from 1970 consultant, Scott Foresman, publishers, Glenview, Illinois; Consultant in Poetry, Library of Congress, Washington, D.C., 1976–78. Received Rosenwald fellowship, 1947; Ford Foundation grant, 1954; Third World Festival of Negro Arts (Dakar, Senegal) Poetry Prize, 1966; American Academy Loines Award, 1970; Academy of American Poets fellowship, 1975; honorary Litt.D., Grand Valley State College, Allendale, Michigan, 1975; honorary L.H.D., Brown University, Providence, Rhode Island, 1976, Benedict College, Columbia, South Carolina, 1977, and Wayne State University, 1977; member, American Academy, 1979. Died in Ann Arbor, Michigan, 25 February 1980.

**Poetry**

*Heart-Shape in the Dust,* 1940
*The Lion and the Archer* (with Myron O'Higgins), 1948
*Figure of Time,* 1955
*A Ballad of Remembrance,* 1962
*Selected Poems,* 1966
*Words in the Mourning Time,* 1970
*The Night-Blooming Cereus,* 1972
*Angle of Ascent: New and Selected Poems,* 1975
*American Journal,* 1978; revised edition, 1982
*Robert Hayden: Collected Poems,* edited by Frederick Glaysher, 1985

**Other Writings**: essays (*Collected Prose,* edited by Frederick Glaysher, 1984), children's literature; edited collections of literature (*The United States in Literature* [with James E. Miller, Jr., and Robert O'Neal], 1973).

**Further Reading**

Conniff, Brian, "Answering 'The Waste Land': Robert Hayden and the Rise of the African American Poetic Sequence," *African American Review* 33, no. 3 (1999)
Fetrow, Fred M., *Robert Hayden,* Boston: Twayne, 1984
Fetrow, Fred M., "Portraits and Personae: Characterization in the Poetry of Robert Hayden," in *Black American Poets Between Worlds, 1940–1960,* edited by R. Baxter Miller, Knoxville: University of Tennessee Press, 1986
Friedlander, Benjamin, "Robert Hayden's Epic of Community," *MELUS* 23, no. 3 (1998)
Hatcher, John, *From the Auroral Darkness: The Life and Poetry of Robert Hayden,* Oxford: Ronald, 1984
Williams, Pontheolla T., *Robert Hayden: A Critical Analysis of His Poetry,* Urbana: University of Illinois Press, 1987

## Elegies for Paradise Valley

The eight ballad-like poems that constitute Robert Hayden's "Elegies for Paradise Valley," which first appeared in his last collection, *American Journal* (1978), offer a bracing reflection on the poet's early years in the Detroit ghetto, ironically called "Paradise Valley," where he was born and raised. Arguably one of his finest works, "Elegies for Paradise Valley" exemplifies two of Hayden's acclaimed Modernist techniques: tonal variation and narrative fusion. The text's eight sections range in mood from hatred to love, bewilderment to rapture, and shift seamlessly in perspective from the narrator's voice to those of several other, baroque characters. Hayden's poem also critiques the materialism and violence of American culture as well as the commercialization of mourning, thereby signaling this work's participation in a tradition of modern poetic elegies that resist conventional themes of spiritual consolation.

In "Some Remembrances" (1984), Hayden notes that the poem's title refers to the entire ghetto, neither only to Beacon Street (where he lived until the age of 10 or 11) nor only to St. Antoine, the notoriously sordid, vibrant boulevard where the young poet was exposed to a kaleidoscope of raw activity: "Shootings, stabbings, blaring jazz, and a liveliness, a gaiety at once desperate and releasing, at once wicked—Satan's playground—and good-hearted." Although completed late in his career, "Elegies for Paradise Valley" cuts to the core of Hayden's romantic realism that was strongly informed by his childhood years in Detroit, as he writes of himself in "Some Remembrances": "these streets recalled for him voices, faces he had loved and whose loss even now, after how many years—close to forty maybe—he mourned." Within this context, Hayden's elegies concern four personal experiences: a junkie's death in the alley outside his bedroom window; a funeral, in the front room of the Hayden's home, for the murdered Uncle Crip; a séance to contact Uncle Crip that Hayden's foster mother, Sue Ellen, arranged with a counterfeit gypsy, Madam Artelia; and the poet's own exuberant, imaginative encounters with Uncle Crip's spirit.

In each of these scenes, Hayden excels as a symbolist confronting historical fact, deftly modulating both the tone of his writing and the transitions in narrative perspective, a change in one often inter-animating a shift in the other. The first elegy, for example, begins with a cool, detached recording of the junkie's death that transforms into a cogent evaluation of racism:

> My shared bedroom's window
> opened on alley stench.
> A junkie died in maggots there.
> I saw his body shoved into a van.
> I saw the hatred for our kind
> glistening like tears
> in the policemen's eyes.

The poem's action of witnessing, which Hayden articulates in a disturbingly calm, rational manner, hinges here on the repetition of "I saw" in lines four and five that amplifies the narrator's uncanny equanimity into quiet rage. This shift in mood complements a change in perspective from the speaker's objectified point of view to an imagined look through the policemen's eyes. In turn, that projection, rife with irony, reinforces the distance between perceiver and perceived, as the poet reveals—through the incisive simile, "like tears"—a veil of false sympathy that imperfectly covers racism.

In the third elegy, Hayden similarly alters the poem's tone from detached reporting to an ironic reflection, yielding trenchant transitions in perspective. After this section's first two stanzas have somewhat dispassionately described the setting of Uncle Crip's funeral, we overhear first the mourners' private conversations, then the narrator's interior experience:

> Beautiful, our neighbors
> murmured; he would be proud.
> Is it mahogany?
> Mahogany—I'd heard
> The victrola voice of
>
> dead Bert Williams
> talk-sing that word as macabre
> music played, chilling
> me. Uncle Crip
> had laughed and laughed.

The neighbors' utterance of the word "mahogany"—as if consolation could be secured by a mere coffin—transports Hayden to the memory of listening to the Bert Williams recording that had so amused Uncle Crip, engendering then a laugh that now reverberates hauntingly in this text as a sarcastic commentary on his own funeral's obsequiousness.

The following elegy (section four) recounts the bogus séance that Hayden vicariously experienced with his mother and Aunt Roxie. Hayden writes all but one line in the first three stanzas with a mood of disengagement and from a single character's perspective. Then, in the middle of the fourth stanza, at the entrance to the darkened room beyond which Hayden may not proceed, the poem shifts in tone and point of view, thereby undercutting the event's authenticity:

> You greet us, smiling, lay your hand
> in blessing on my head, then lead
>
> the others into a candlelit room
> I may not enter. She went into a trance,
> Auntie said afterward, and spirits
> talked, changing her voice to suit
> their own. And Crip came.
>
> Happy yes I am happy here,
> he told us; dying's not death. Do not grieve.
> Remembering, Auntie began to cry
> and poured herself a glass of gin.
> Didn't sound a bit like Crip, Ma snapped.

The work's remaining four elegies continue to offer many transitions in mood but fewer changes in narrative perspective as Hayden speaks with increasing strength about his own imaginative meetings with Uncle Crip's spirit. Sections six and eight in particular bring the two together as they dance "to Jellyroll / Morton's brimstone / piano on the phonograph, / laughing . . . face[s] foremost into hell." Through this concluding image of Hayden and Uncle Crip dancing together in hell, "Elegies for Paradise Valley" resists traditional themes of elegiac consolation that would have been so familiar to the young poet, having been raised a devout Baptist. In the early 1940s, Hayden and his wife became believers of the Baha'i faith, which holds (among 12 central principles) the convictions that spiritual truths must be freely investigated by individuals and that all religions grow from a common ground. Written late in his life, these eight elegies look backward, from the vantage of liberated spirituality, to the poet's childhood when Hayden perhaps first confronted his own ambivalence about moralistic dichotomies between the worlds of the living and the departed.

W. SCOTT HOWARD

**Further Reading**

Cooke, Michael G., *Afro-American Literature in the Twentieth Century,* New Haven, Connecticut: Yale University Press, 1984

Davis, Arthur P., "Robert Hayden," in *From the Dark Tower: Afro-American Writers, 1900 to 1960,* Washington, D.C.: Howard University Press, 1974

Davis, Charles T., "Robert Hayden's Use of History," in *Modern Black Poets,* edited by Donald B. Gibson, Englewood Cliffs, New Jersey: Prentice Hall, 1973

Fetrow, Fred M., *Robert Hayden,* Boston: Twayne, 1984

Fetrow, Fred M., "Portraits and Personae: Characterization in the Poetry of Robert Hayden," in *Black American Poets Between Worlds, 1940–1960,* edited by R. Baxter Miller, Knoxville: University of Tennessee Press, 1986

Glaysher, Frederick, "Re-Centering: The Turning of the Tide and Robert Hayden," *World Order* 17, no. 4 (1983)

Harper, Michael S., "Remembering Robert Hayden," *Michigan Quarterly Review* 21, no. 1 (1982)

Hatcher, John, *From the Auroral Darkness: The Life and Poetry of Robert Hayden,* Oxford: Ronald, 1984

Williams, Pontheolla T., *Robert Hayden: A Critical Analysis of His Poetry,* Urbana: University of Illinois Press, 1987

Williams, Wilburn, Jr., "Covenant of Timelessness and Time: Symbolism and History in Robert Hayden's 'Angle of Ascent,'" *Massachusetts Review* 18, no. 4 (1977)

## Middle Passage

Robert Hayden's three-part poem "Middle Passage" focuses on three aspects of the American understanding of slavery and its effects: clarity of vision, the weave of history, and transformation from slave to a self-determining individual. The term "middle passage" refers to the crossing of the Atlantic by slave ships in the 18th and 19th centuries, in which one in six Africans died and countless others suffered illness, insanity, and rape. Hayden initially defines the term ironically as a "voyage through death / to life upon these shores," a refrain that he will revise at the poem's close. The form of the poem, a montage of voices and events, not only demonstrates Hayden's accomplishment with the long poem, but the role poetry can play in representing this history clearly. No single point of view can tell the complete story, he suggests: seemingly disparate elements must be woven together, even if loosely, to come near some kind of truth.

Hayden's tapestry of voices includes that of the poet, which provides the poem's frame and moral conscience. The speaker's use of historical detail and irony are echoed in the poem's other voices: a crewman of a slave ship recording his anxiety, a survivor of a slave ship fire referred to as a "deponent," a slave trader recounting his experiences in Africa, and a survivor of the *Amistad,* a Spanish slave ship overtaken by its human cargo. Each voice also has its own form of telling. The poet offers a short catalog of slave and slave ship names, as well as a thread of subtle moral commentary that moves toward transcendence. Other forms include journal entries, official reports and testimony, a conversational account, and Protestant prayers and hymns. Hayden leaves out the voices of African slaves for historical accuracy; locked in other languages and denied legitimacy, none among them could tell the story or imagine the horrors to come.

Section one of the poem contains complex voices and issues that run parallel to the complex nature of the slave trade and its links to religion. Hayden refuses to explain this complexity; instead he lets each account, with its revealing ironies, speak for itself. The names of the slave ships—"*Jesus, Estrella* [star], *Esperanza* [hope], *Mercy*"—stand in stark contrast to the treatment of the Africans and suggest the hypocrisy of using Christianity to justify the slave trade. Later in the first section a prayer offered by a white ship captain or crew member asks for "safe passage to our vessels bringing / heathen souls unto Thy chastening." Lines from Protestant hymns, interspersed throughout the section, become ironic prayers for guidance, coming as they do from slave traders morally blind to their acts. Hayden links this moral blindness to physical blindness. "Ophthalmia" attacks both slaves and slave ship personnel, prompting a crew member to ask in his journal, "Which one of us / has killed an albatross?" This allusion to Coleridge's "Rime of the Ancient Mariner" suggests the bizarre, nightmarish reality of the slave trade and will be invoked again in section three of the poem.

The allusion to Shakespeare's *The Tempest* in sections one and three also serves Hayden's probing of religious hypocrisy. The first act of Shakespeare's play invokes a transformation into "something rich and strange." Hayden's version takes a different direction:

> Deep in the festering hold thy father lies,
> of his bones New England pews are made,
> those are altar lights that were his eyes.

As Charles T. Davis (1973) points out, the passage mocks the less-than-spiritual transformation the Africans undergo. When Hayden returns to this allusion in section three, the father still festers in the ship's hold and "the corpse of mercy"—echoing the name of one of the slave ships—"rots with him." The slavers thus damn themselves as well as their passengers.

Section two is the shortest section of the poem, consisting of six quatrains largely in blank verse and spoken by a single voice. The voice, a retired slave trader, recalls the purchase of Africans from African tribal chiefs for "tin crowns that shone with paste" and "red calico and German-silver trinkets." This exploitation echoes that of land purchases from Native Americans made by early colonists. Here, the lush African landscape has become a lucrative slave factory from which "there was wealth aplenty to be harvested." This section is linked to the first via its discussion of sexual relations between white slave traders and African women. In section one the women are raped; in section two the sex appears consensual, but there is the suggestion of forced prostitution since the women are part of the tribal king's effort to conduct business with the slave traders.

The tone of section two, however, plays a vital role in weaving together the three parts of "Middle Passage." The speaker shows no remorse and admits he would "be trading still / but for the fevers melting down my bones." Although his language is conversational and relaxed, there is a coldness in his attitude that also appears in the "Deponent" stanzas in section one and in the testimony regarding the mutiny of the *Amistad* in section three. The formality of the language of "official" documentation reflects the moral distance white slave traders placed between themselves and their work.

In addition to the testimony of the white *Amistad* survivor in section three, the poet's voice returns to draw together the poem's concerns with vision, history, and transformation. The voice of the poet addresses those enslaved in and to the past, outlining the projection of white guilt onto black victims in terms of the flawed vision experienced previously in the poem: "But, oh, the living look at you / with human eyes whose suffering accuses you." The need to weave the strands of the slave past into a coherent and honest history becomes more acute through Hayden's diction. He refers to the slave ships at the poem's beginning with "their bright ironical names" as "Shuttles in the rocking loom of history."

Cinquez, the African slave who led the revolt against the *Amistad* and was later returned to Africa, symbolizes the transformation from slave to man, the "life that transfigures many lives." The refrain "voyage through death / to life upon these shores" closes the poem. With the figure of a free Cinquez behind it, the refrain can now suggest hope for a better life.

"Middle Passage" is the product of extensive research and years of revision. Hayden was inspired to write the poem after reading Stephen Vincent Benét's *John Brown's Body* (1928), a book-length blank-verse poem that called for a black voice to tell the story of slavery. Hayden's earliest version was written entirely in blank verse, but he moved toward a more Modernist version using fragmentation and collage under the influence of T.S. Eliot. Versions of the poem appeared in 1941 (*Phylon* magazine), 1945 (*Cross Section* magazine), 1962 (*A Ballad of Remembrance*), and 1966 (*Selected Poems*).

It might be useful to think of "Middle Passage" as an anti-epic, even though the poem tells a story of epic proportions. No decisive battle, let alone war, is won, as Americans are still dealing with the long-term effects of slave culture. No central figure appears in the poem to represent a unified community with common values. Hayden knew there were many key figures in this history, as evidenced by his poems about Frederick Douglass, Nat Turner, and Harriet Tubman. Perhaps the central figure of "Middle Passage" is the reader who, by reading the poem, journeys through a complex and painful past in order to get beyond it.

Rhonda Pettit

**Further Reading**

Davis, Charles T., "Robert Hayden's Use of History," in *Modern Black Poets,* edited by Donald B. Gibson, Englewood Cliffs, New Jersey: Prentice Hall, 1973

Glaysher, Frederick, "Re-Centering: The Turning of the Tide and Robert Hayden," *World Order* 17, no. 4 (1983)

Hatcher, John, *From the Auroral Darkness: The Life and Poetry of Robert Hayden,* Oxford: Ronald, 1984

Mullen, Harryette, and Stephen Yenser, "Theme and Variations on Robert Hayden's Poetry," *Antioch Review* 55 (Spring 1997)

Nicholas, Xavier, "Robert Hayden and Michael S. Harper: A Literary Friendship," *Callaloo* 17, no. 4 (Fall 1994)

Williams, Pontheolla T., *Robert Hayden: A Critical Analysis of His Poetry,* Urbana: University of Illinois Press, 1987

---

# H.D. (Hilda Doolittle) 1886–1961

In one of the rarest matchmakings in poetry, the life of H.D. and her writings meld in a perfect Greek spirit. "If I could walk to Delphi, I should be healed," she said to her partner Bryher (Winifred Ellerman), in a time of her greatest illness (*Paint It Today,* 1992). If her upbringing by her Moravian family in Pennsylvania marked—with a certain seductive mysteriousness—all her words and much of her living, so did her early involvement with Ezra Pound, which her *End to Torment: A Memoir of Ezra Pound* (1979) recalls in two phases. In the later reflection she thought of

> what supremely matters. Sheath upon sheath of self seems peeled away. I begin to understand this "strange man" as the *London Times* of April 9 called him. . . . I was not equipped to understand the young poet.

H.D.'s triple autobiography—*Paint It Today* (written 1921, published 1992), *Asphodel* (1921–22, 1992), and *HERmione* (1926–27, 1981)—leads the reader through her sense of failure from her year at Bryn Mawr College and her hopeless affair with Frances Gregg, who then married a university lecturer, Louis Wilkinson; through her own marriage to Richard Aldington—whose affair with Dorothy Yorke led to their separation in 1918, and their divorce in 1938; through her affair with the Scot Cecil Gray in 1919, from which her daughter Perdita was born; and then through her fascinating analysis with Freud, to her lifelong attachment to Bryher. These volumes are among the best examples of High Modernist style, at once lyric and profound, adventuresome and readable, deeply serious and yet witty. The best known, *HERmione,* mingles observation of the material with the emotional in a tight fit, its perceptions immediate and its impact intense:

> Now playing with an éclair under a pink lampshade, the thing became more difficult. Now facing George across a white small cloth with cream sort of inserted edges and squares and triangles on the cloth and an inset little dolphin, ramping in its little square of insertion, it was the more difficult.

*Asphodel* traces the journey of Hermione Gart (H.D.), Fayne Rabb (Frances Gregg), and her mother to France and London. George Lowndes (Ezra Pound) is in love with Hermione, who in turn loves Fayne:

> I, Hermione, tell you I love you Fayne Rabb. Men and women will come and say I love you. I love you Hermione, you Fayne. Men will say I love you Hermione but will anyone ever say I love you Fayne as I say it?

This was as open a declaration of lesbian love as possible during H.D.'s lifetime; her own partner Bryher married twice for appearance. H.D.'s writing, on the other hand, was openly about loving. *Paint It Today* ends, "Let him love today who never has loved, for tomorrow, who knows where flits the creature of his loving."

H.D. is best known for her restrained classical verses and as Ezra Pound's "H.D. Imagiste." In her poetry she is an Imagist in the sense that the drastic energies of Vorticism led to a single surprising image, radiating out into the entire text. Her seminal *Tril-*

*ogy* (1973) goes far past that early label to a broader vision and epic form. About this text, written in London during the World War II bombing raids she termed an "orgy of destructions," H.D. claimed:

> This is not the "crystalline" poetry that my early critics would insist on. It is no pillar of salt nor yet of hewn rock-crystal. It is the pillar of fire by night, the pillar of cloud by day. (Friedman, 1981)

During the raids H.D. worked with Bryher in the Tea Kettle, their restaurant, which was itself bombed and so "more open than usual." This terrible time was, however, good for poetry.

H.D. noted parallels between ancient Egypt and modern London and called on the teachings of "this old Janus, this beloved light-house keeper, old Captain January"—that is, Freud, with whom she underwent analysis starting in 1933. She later wrote *Tribute to Freud* (1956) in the same form as her memoir of Pound. Her fascination with Egypt led to her superb and celebrated long poem *Helen in Egypt* (1961).

H.D. is far more than an autobiographical novelist and learned poet, however. Some of her less well-known writings, such as the small volume *Notes on Thought and Vision* (written 1919, published 1982), have a freshness that strikes new readers still more strongly than work already accepted into the canon of High Modernism. H.D. herself claimed to have had a vision in 1920, in her hotel room on Corfu:

> We lovers of modern poetry are reminded of the great Cubist poet the Jew Max Jacob's vision of Christ on his wall—through which he was converted to Catholicism. (Which did not stop the Nazis from tearing him away from his meditation to send him off to his death.)

Of this vision, Freud said it was her hidden desire to "found a new religion," in which she was both scribe and priestess. H.D. believed that Freud's work on the unconscious would save humanity; in her *Notes on Vision* she divided the spirit into body, mind, and over-mind.

Much of *Notes on Thought and Vision* calls on H.D.'s early Moravian upbringing. In the Moravian church the soul is conceived as feminine, *anima;* in H.D.'s vision the "s" on the chalice (for *Spiritus Sanctus*) represents both Sophia, the female Gnostic Holy Spirit, and Sappho, classic symbol of lesbian love. The new Eve—like Sappho and real-life lesbian heroines such as Nathalie Barney and her lover Renée Vivien in Paris, about whom H.D. loved to read—unravels the Christian conception of Eve as terrible temptress who brings about the Fall. In this revision of the Genesis story, humanity is not given over to sin and death in the Fall; instead Eve brings the Book of Life.

These surprising *Notes* invoke Sappho directly as

> A song, a spirit, a white star that moves across the heaven to mark the end of a world epoch or to presage some coming glory.
> Yet she is embodied—terribly a human being, a woman, a personality as the most impersonal become when they confront their fellow beings . . .
> Aristocratic—indifferent—full of caprice—full of imperfection—intolerant.

"You were," H.D. says, addressing Sappho as Plato had addressed a young beloved, "the morning star among the living."

Among H.D.'s other writings, *The Gift* (1982) stands out. It is the story of H.D.'s brilliant father, Professor Charles Doolittle, whose absentmindedness actually "froze him to the telescope," so that his beard and whiskers had to be thawed out, according to Perdita Schaffner, his granddaughter. The whole family was marked with the title's "gift," whose uncertain nature makes up the lyric gist of the book. *The Gift* is about making "things," about the kind of Christianity Moravianism is, about secrets and rituals: the Ritual of the Wounds, the Wunden Eiland, the Power, the "s" on the chalice. *The Gift* ends with an initiation by bombardment and its excruciating noise—another ritual, another baptism by fire: "The sound accumulates, gathers sound. . . . 'It's the all-clear,' says Bryher. 'Yes,' I say."

MARY ANN CAWS

*See also* Expatriate Poetry; Imagism

**Biography**

Born in Bethlehem, Pennsylvania, 10 September 1886. Attended Bryn Mawr College, Pennsylvania, 1905–06; closely associated with the Imagist movement after 1912; editor, *Egoist* magazine, 1916–17; joint founder, *Close Up* film journal, Territet, Switzerland, 1927–33. Received Levinson Prize (*Poetry,* Chicago), 1938; Harriet Monroe Memorial Prize, 1958; Brandeis University Creative Arts Award, 1959; American Academy Award of Merit Medal, 1960. Died in Zurich, Switzerland, 27 September 1961.

**Poetry**

*Sea Garden,* 1916
*Choruses from the Iphigenia in Aulis by Euripides,* 1916
*The Tribute, and Circe: Two Poems,* 1917
*Choruses from the Iphigenia in Aulis and the Hippolytus by Euripides,* 1919
*Hymen,* 1921
*Heliodora, and Other Poems,* 1924
*Collected Poems,* 1925
*(Poems),* edited by Hughes Mearns, 1926
*Red Roses for Bronze,* 1931
*The Usual Star,* 1934
*Nights* (as by John Helforth), 1935
*What Do I Love?* 1943
*The Walls Do Not Fall,* 1944
*Tribute to the Angels,* 1945
*By Avon River,* 1949; revised edition, 1986
*Selected Poems,* 1957
*Helen in Egypt,* 1961
*Two Poems,* 1971
*Hermetic Definition,* 1972
*Trilogy* (includes *The Walls Do Not Fall, Tribute to the Angels, The Flowering of the Rod*), 1973
*The Poet and the Dancer,* 1975
*Priest, and a Dead Priestess Speaks,* 1983
*Collected Poems, 1912–1944,* edited by Louis Martz, 1983
*Selected Poems,* edited by Louis Martz, 1988
*Vale Ave,* 1991

**Other Writings:** plays (*Ion,* from the play by Euripides, 1937; revised version, 1985), novels, children's literature, nonfiction

(*Tribute to Freud,* 1956; *Notes on Thought and Vision: The Wise Sappho,* 1982), autobiography (*HERmione,* 1981; *Paint It Today,* 1992; *Asphodel,* 1992), memoir (*The Gift,* 1982), poem cycle (*Temple of the Sun,* 1972).

**Further Reading**

Buck, Claire, *H.D. and Freud: Bisexuality and a Feminine Discourse,* New York: St. Martin's Press, and Hemel, Hempstead: Harvester Wheatsheaf, 1991

Chisholm, Diane, *H.D.'s Freudian Poetics: Psychoanalysis in Translation,* Ithaca, New York: Cornell University Press, 1992

Friedman, Susan Stanford, *Psyche Reborn: The Emergence of H.D.,* Bloomington: Indiana University Press, 1981

Friedman, Susan Stanford, *Penelope's Web: Gender, Modernity: H.D.'s Fiction,* Cambridge and New York: Cambridge University Press, 1990

Guest, Barbara, *Herself Defined: The Poet H.D. and Her World,* Garden City, New York: Doubleday, 1984

## Helen in Egypt

H.D.'s epic *Helen in Egypt* (1961) is a feminist reconsideration of the Modernist long poem, which is often perceived as dominated by male poets, such as T.S. Eliot, Ezra Pound, William Carlos Williams, and others. Published by Grove Press shortly before H.D.'s death in 1961, *Helen in Egypt* blends feminism, mysticism, the Modernist conception of the palimpsest, and the issue of female subjectivity into a poem of great lyric, emotional, and philosophical force.

*Helen in Egypt* takes as its starting point a 50-line fragment from the Greek lyric poet Stesichorus of Sicily (c. 640–555 B.C.). H.D., like other Modernists interested in using poetry as a means to recover and re-present fragments (palimpsests) of past writers, builds on the central theme of Stesichorus and his Pallinode, namely, that Helen was never in Troy. She had been transposed or translated from Greece into Egypt. Helen of Troy was a phantom, substituted for the real Helen by jealous deities. The Greeks and the Trojans alike fought for an illusion.

Against this backdrop, *Helen in Egypt* explores how Helen came to be in Egypt and recasts her story in an attempt to fill in obvious textual blanks. The poem questions the issue of the relation of the "real" to "illusion" as embodied by the figure of Helen. Therefore, more than simply retelling Helen's story, H.D. raises the question of Helen's subjectivity and her "voice." In this regard, the poem explores the nature of Helen's subjectivity in relation to the patriarchal versions of her story, but H.D. places Helen at the center of the narrative, thereby refuting her passive image as the cause and/or trophy-prize of the Greek-Trojan War. Subsequently, *Helen in Egypt* advances a feminist critique and might be considered the literary and philosophical prototype for contemporary feminist scholarship and poetry.

Structurally, *Helen in Egypt* is divided into three sections—"Pallinode," "Leuke`," and "Eidolon"—each of which is comprised of seven books of eight three-line stanzas. ("Eidolon," however, has only six books as well as an additional six-stanza section titled "Eidolon.") Each book also includes a prose introduction that paraphrases, repeats, and accentuates key aspects of the poetry. H.D. added the prose introductions after completing the verse epic. While the suturing of prose to the poetic narrative was not part of the original design, such blending further contributes to the multifaceted and multivocal narrative texture of the work.

The overarching trajectory of the narrative is Helen's transformation from an image, or "ghost," into a person and then a guide and sage for others: she moves from being powerless to realizing the potentiality of her own being and from passivity to action. At the beginning of the poem, Helen is unable to "read" herself and the hieroglyphs that tell her story. She states,

I can not "read" the hare, the chick, the bee,
I would study and decipher
the indecipherable Amen-script.

In the first section, Helen confronts her absence as an inability to comprehend her voice and identity, and the poem follows her as she "studies and deciphers" the images of her subjectivity that unfold as a stream of her memories and personal history as well as her relationship with three main male characters who recur throughout the 304-page poem and represent various love interests of Helen: Achilles, Theseus, and Paris.

Some readers of H.D. have argued that these three men are loose masks for people in H.D.'s own personal history: Achilles represents Lord Dowding and/or her husband, Richard Aldington; Paris mirrors the figures of Ezra Pound and/or D.H. Lawrence; and Theseus, who serves as Helen's valuable guide, is a foil for Sigmund Freud, who was H.D.'s psychoanalyst. (H.D.'s relationship with Freud is discussed at length in her *Tribute to Freud* [1956].) Some have read Helen's quest for and triumph of subjectivity as representative of H.D.'s own interrogation of her poetic/writerly life as well as her sense of self. Much of H.D.'s work is fictionalized autobiography, and *Helen in Egypt* certainly bears the imprint of aspects of her life and perhaps her relationship with these men.

Nevertheless, the governing philosophical and spiritual principle of *Helen in Egypt* is love, and the poem focuses on the love stories of Helen's life. Helen's romantic involvement with Achilles, Paris, and Theseus is retold in the poem, and those various relationships represent different facets of the conflicting narratives of her self. As a guide to Helen, Theseus divulges his law of love to her, "that only love, the Immortal, / brings back love to old-love, / kindles a spark from the past," which is the catalyst for Helen's transformation and leads to a deeper understanding of her self. She recognizes that love has the potential to reconcile the various dimensions of her fractured and seemingly disjunct subjectivity, which are presented in the lines "Helen – Helen – Helen – Helen – / there was always another and another and another / the rose has many petals." Once Helen realizes the force of love, she concludes that she no longer needs to "untangle the riddle." Rather, she understands that love is a gift, and instead of clinging to a hierarchy of selves (or the narratives of the self), she embraces the image of the self as the accumulation of love's infinite potential.

Yet, despite the claim that she need not untangle the riddle, H.D. reintroduces the question that sparked Helen's quest: "How [to] reconcile [the] Trojan and Greek" both as the tension between Achilles and Paris and as conflicting textual narratives. While "Helen seems to wish to return to an easier 'formula,'" the poem argues that "It is not so simple," which is accentuated by the structure of the text as well. That is, the conclusion offered by

*Helen in Egypt* is deeply open ended, whereby the final lines read, "the seasons revolve around / a pause in the infinite rhythm / of the heart and of heaven." The image of the perpetual seasons is striking, but, more important, it marks a refusal to claim that the conclusion is final. The rejection of poetic closure serves an important purpose deeply interwoven with the subject matter. By allowing the poem to remain open, Helen's subject position, as rendered in the poem, is merely a "pause" and not a full stop. H.D.'s story of Helen, therefore, is not definitive, and Helen's subjectivity is not fixed: the openness of the poetic structure, therefore, reinforces the lesson that Helen discovers of her own will to power as the infinite flowing of love that refutes closure and silencing.

In this light, *Helen in Egypt* is significant because it not only presses the Modernist epic in a new direction but also anticipates feminist modes of critique that emerged nearly 20 years after its publication. *Helen in Egypt* bridges modern and postmodern poetry, practice, and theory, and H.D.'s text, in this regard, established a path that other contemporary women poets, such as Susan Howe, Rachel Blau DuPlessis, Rosmarie Waldrop, Barbara Guest, and others, have continued to follow.

David Clippinger

**Further Reading**

Davis, Dale, "*Heliodora*'s Greece," in *H.D.: Woman and Poet,* edited by Michael King, Orono, Maine: National Poetry Foundation, 1986

DuPlessis, Rachel Blau, "Romantic Thralldom in H.D.," in *Signets: Reading H.D.,* edited by Susan Stanford Friedman and Rachel Blau DuPlessis, Madison: University of Wisconsin Press, 1990

Friedman, Susan Stanford, *Psyche Reborn: The Emergence of H.D.,* Bloomington: Indiana University Press, 1981

Guest, Barbara, *Herself Defined: The Poet H.D. and Her World,* Garden City, New York: Doubleday, 1984

Ostriker, Alicia, "No Rule of Procedure: The Open Poetics of H.D.," in *Signets: Reading H.D.,* edited by Susan Stanford Friedman and Rachel Blau DuPlessis, Madison: University of Wisconsin Press, 1990

# Trilogy

Although it clearly can be read as a continuous sequence, H.D.'s *Trilogy* actually consists of three long poems originally published as separate works. The first of these is "The Walls Do Not Fall," written in 1942 and originally published in England in 1944. This was followed by "Tribute to the Angels," which was written in 1944 and appeared in 1945, and "The Flowering of the Rod," which was written in 1946 and first appeared in print only in 1973 as part of *Trilogy,* published in the United States by New Directions. The proximity of the three poems' dates of composition and the clear overlaps of concern therein, however, mark out the work as one continuous whole.

H.D. wrote the poems in London, where she lived and where she experienced the Luftwaffe bombardment of the city during the German offensive. From 7 September to 15 September 1940, thousands of people were killed, and large stretches of the city were destroyed. Many more raids were to follow. *Trilogy* was written under the influence of these raids. It is often referred to as the great civilian war poem of World War II, given the circumstances of its period of composition; certainly, it is this experience of war that is its spur and the experience of destruction that is its premise. This is most powerfully felt in the 43 sections of "The Walls Do Not Fall." The title of the poem is extraordinarily optimistic; despite the bombardment and the barbarism, despite the metal of British train tracks being torn up to make bullets and guns, the human imagination provides grounds for both metamorphosis and preservation so that indeed "the walls do not fall." The first section of the poem establishes an analogy between war-torn London and ancient Egypt, an analogy important for *Trilogy* as a whole:

> There as here, ruin opens
> the tomb, the temple; enter,
> there as here, there are no doors;
>
> the shrine lies open to the sky
> the rain falls, here, there
> sand drifts; eternity endures

The poem pursues this enduring eternity, finding it not so much in immortal life as by everlasting presence. The metaphor of an oyster transforming itself into a pearl ("master mason planning / the stone marvel") is a telling one, as is the spinning of the silkworm, whose beautiful artifact outlasts the artist who spins it. Much of the vocabulary of the poem is derived from Egypt: "asp," "erect serpent," "Thoth," "Ra," "Osiris," and "Pharaoh" form the mythopoetic foundation of the poem, which begins with a dedication "to Karnak 1923," where H.D. had earlier had her mystical vision. However, the poem draws from other religious and mythic traditions as well: "Jehovah," the "Christos-Image," and "the Holy Ghost" all mingle here, the names of multiple divinities contributing to the poem's monition of the eternal. The poem asserts that "idols and their secret is stored / in man's very speech" and ends "possibly we will reach haven, / heaven." The implication of "The Walls" could not be more clear: art-making is human liberation, and language itself, like silk, shell, and other inanimate forms of beauty, is our only salvation.

However, Louis Martz, in his introduction to the *Collected Poems, 1912–1944* (1983), asserts that "The Walls Do Not Fall" is preliminary: "the secret is not yet found. It is discovered in the second part, 'Tribute to the Angels,' a sequence wholly unified and sustained, moving forward confidently under the guidance of Hermes Trismegistus, inventor of language, father of alchemy, founder of Egyptian culture; and with the support of the book of Revelation, in which she boldly and wittily finds her role as prophet justified." Whether or not we regard "The Walls Do Not Fall" as preliminary, surely Martz is right that in "Tribute to the Angels" we pass over into a more explicitly religious poetry. It is here that H.D. makes her sturdiest stand in a kind of secret knowledge in which the vocabulary of religion wielded for poetic end is overtaken by religion's substance. The poet assumes a full-blown prophetic stance. Yet because of its multiple prongs (Egyptian, Jewish, Christian, and hermetic), it is doubtful that H.D's religious vision could ever be reduced to a doctrine. The tone here is often highly declarative and yet insists in its conclusion on the priority of image: "not *vas spirituale,* / not *rosa mystica* even, / but a cluster of garden-pinks / or a face like a Christmas rose."

The last section of *Trilogy,* "The Flowering of the Rod," is more diffuse in nature, ranging through the various poetic and religious possibilities offered in the first two sections. It is also perhaps the most personal of H.D.'s *Trilogy* compositions:

I go where I love and where I am loved,
into the snow;

I go to the things I love
with no thought of duty or pity;

I go where I belong, inexorably
as the rain that has lain long

in the furrow; I have given
or would have given

life to the grain;
but if it will not grow or ripen

with the rain of beauty,
the rain will return to the cloud;

the harvester sharpens his steel on the stone;
but this is not our field,

we have not sown this;
pitiless, pitiless, let us leave

The place-of-a-skull
to those who have fashioned it.

Perhaps it is in "The Flowering of the Rod" that poetry as its own ecstasy and poetry as religious imagination find a perfect equivalence. Beginning as it does in times of war, *Trilogy* is a poem that succeeds in harvesting a language of rapture from the most destructive of fields.

LEONARD SCHWARTZ

**Further Reading**

Duncan, Robert, "The H.D. Book, Part 2," *Montemora* 8 (1981)

Robinson, Janice S., *H.D., The Life and Work of an American Poet,* Boston: Houghton Mifflin, 1982

Scalapino, Leslie, "Re-Living," *Poetics* 4 (May 1984)

---

# Anthony Hecht 1923–

In a generation dominated by the influence of the "confessional poets" and their experimental poetic autobiographies, Anthony Hecht revived neoclassical poetic forms such as the sonnet, the villanelle, and the sestina, aligning himself thus with such formalist poets as Howard Nemerov, John Hollander, Randall Jarrell, and Richard Howard. Hecht's poems remind one of a well-tended garden in which patient cultivation has produced a poetic "sanctuary from hostilities of disorder or danger" (*On the Laws of the Poetic Art,* 1995). Although their form always strives toward a "celebration of an order" (Howard, 1980), Hecht's poems often implicitly or explicitly accommodate horrific subject matter so that the decorum of his style might serve to foreground the discordant nature of violence and cruelty. The meticulous patience required to contain specific historical, social, and psychological traumas in such rigorous form has produced a poetic oeuvre whose moral and aesthetic achievement has been summed up as an eloquent rage against loss, pain, and violence (Gross, in Lea, 1989).

Hecht was inducted into active duty in the U.S. Army during World War II. While serving in Czechoslovakia and Germany, his unit discovered mass graves of charred bodies; he also helped to liberate the Flossenburg concentration camp (German, 1989). After the war, Hecht attended Kenyon College on the G.I. Bill and studied with John Crowe Ransom, whose formal influence remains evident throughout Hecht's writing. The subject matter of his poems does not divulge his own experience; even in a recent interview, he questions how much one can morally write about the war if one emerges from it "comparatively smoothly." However, "in this poetic era of arrogant solipsism and limp narcissism," as Hecht explains, "when great, shaggy herds of poets write only about themselves, or about the casual workings of their rather tedious minds—it is essential to our sanity, salutary to our humility, with a minimal obeisance to the truth to acknowledge . . . the vast alterity, the 'otherness' of the world, that huge corrective to our self-sufficiency" (*Obbligati,* 1986).

According to some critics, Hecht's first volume of poetry, *A Summoning of Stones* (1954), lacked emotional and thematic depth. While that volume was perhaps too hastily described as "exhibitionistic" in regard to its emphasis of complicated forms, others saw it as a lyrical "ecstatic vision" (Howard, 1980). His second volume, *The Hard Hours* (1967), redresses the perceived weaknesses of the first volume, demonstrating a "marked ascendance of theme over form, a message within a frame that does not call undue attention to itself" (German, 1989). The widely anthologized poem "More light! More light!" for example, recounts a grizzly medieval incident of a man being burned at the stake; then the poem moves forward in time to a scene in which a Pole is required by a Nazi soldier to bury two Jewish prisoners alive. After his valiant refusal, the Polish prisoner is partially buried alive himself until there is "No light, no light in the blue Polish eye." He then consents to bury the Jews, only to be shot and left to die after his task is done. This horrific story is neatly tucked into rhyming quatrains, presumably so that, in Alicia Ostriker's words, "poetic control may signify a self-control without which one would simply explode with grief and fear" (Lea, 1989).

In the same volume, "Behold the Lilies of the Field" appears to critique the romanticized self-indulgence of confessional therapy poems: the first stanza opens with an unmistakable reference to the confessional style, a patient complaining to his therapist about his mother's lack of warmth and her "mechanical enthusiastic show." In the second section, however, this satiric reference turns toward a traumatic memory of "what I saw them do to the emperor." Here, a Roman emperor is repeatedly tortured as the patient recalls, "And I was tied to a post and made to watch." Such recounting of violence and cruelty, whether psychological or historical, frequently disrupts the formal preoccupations of the poet—reminding him (and us) of the larger universal context that the poet must address. While Hecht acknowledges in "Rites and Ceremonies" that "The contemplation of horror is not edifying, / Neither does it strengthen the soul," his moral outrage serves as a gauge to measure the relevance and responsibility of art—an art opposed throughout his work to "Art for the sake / Of money, glamour, ego, self-deceit" ("Green: An Epistle").

Even poems ostensibly about his children do not escape being tainted with the trauma of the Holocaust. In the poem "It Out Herod's Herod. Pray you, Avoid it," the ironic juxtaposition of the iambic trimeter implies the fast and easy resolution of his children's television formula, "The Good outcast the Bad." The father revokes all such illusions when he reminds himself that evil runs rampant in the world. His love makes him want to protect his children, even though his faith in his ability to do so falters in the reality of evil: "And that their sleep be sound / I say this childermas / Who could not, at one time / Have saved them from the gas." In an ambiguous god-like voice, the father confirms this prayer when he admits in the poem "Adam" that "there will be / Many hard hours . . . They are our common lot" while at the same time asking the child to "believe in a father's love." Ambivalence about the beauty and pain of existence is further explored in "The Vow." The poem tells the story of a miscarriage with the fetus returning in dreams, claiming, "Truly it is the best of all fates / Not to be born." Despite Hecht's unflinching perusal of human evil, in this poem life, although painful, is reaffirmed in the Old Testament prophet Daniel's voice: "The flames are lit / That shall refine us; they shall not destroy / a living hair."

Hecht's third volume of poetry, *Millions of Strange Shadows* (1977), continues this quest for redemptive vision. Alicia Ostriker defines its difference from *The Hard Hours* as "an attempt to transcend despair without resorting to self-delusion" (Lea, 1989). "Green: An Epistle" traces some catastrophic evolutionary beginnings, "an everlasting war," to a mythological "Third Day" and closes with an invocation of a supreme aesthetic "single image, / Utterly silent, utterly at rest"—an image, too, of the death wish, or of a reprieve from the struggle for survival, implicit in the aesthetic. Despite intermittent moments of aesthetic redemption, Hecht continues to explore the phenomenon of human evil. "The Feast of Stephen" has seemingly innocent beginnings; the boys' "sparring dance, adrenal life" in the locker room is described as an "unfocused ballet of self-love." However, this masculine beauty quickly exposes its other side: the man "Who loves Beethoven and collects Degas" turns into an SS commandant, and the half-naked young men in their stunning "self-conscious grace" are stoning Stephen to death.

Although his lyric poems have accommodated disruptive scenes of violence and trauma, in *The Venetian Vespers* (1979), Hecht broadens his poetic register to include dramatic monologues after Robert Browning so as to allow for character development and a more dramatic clash between the violent and the aesthetic. The title poem, one of his "anatomies of melancholy" as J.D. McClatchy puts it, has been read as similar to Eliot's *The Waste Land* or "Gerontion." The beautiful city of Venice here becomes the site of a narrative suspended between dream and decline, a site for the narrator's introspection into "intuitions of a living desolation / That last a lifetime." In perusing the melancholic events of his life, the narrator concludes, "Something profoundly soiled, pointlessly hurt / And beyond cure in us yearns for this costless / Ablution, this impossible reprieve." Predictably, this reprieve can only be found in fleeting moments of aesthetic appreciation: "To give one's attention to such a sight / Is a sort of blessedness." Only in lyric time can the narrator flee "Into the refuge of the present tense" or "the blessed stasis of a painting" where the soul will be "drenched in fine particulars." The poem repeats here Hecht's aesthetic moment in which escapism, fulfillment, and death wish are held in precarious balance. For in the next section this beautiful moment quickly vanishes: "Seeing is misbelieving," as if to cast doubt on the authenticity of the previous aesthetic reprieve.

A similar questioning of the aesthetic occurs in the first scene of "The Deodand," in which Parisian women are dressing up like members of a harem while "consulting the authority / Of a painting, perhaps by Ingres or Delacroix." The scene is lavish and enticing, and the reader is drawn into the scene until the narrator asks, "What is all this but crude imperial pride . . . The exploitation of the primitive"—and we are alerted to a subliminal allegory of colonial exploitation that this role play acts out. For as the second section of the poem abruptly turns to another "dress up" scene, the women's enactment is unmasked as unwitting collaboration with the violent reality of the imperial project. A more grisly satire than the women's role play, a young legionnaire, a French colonist captured by the Algerian natives, is outfitted in women's clothing and blonde wig, and as part of the display, the natives cut off all his fingers so that he must beg to be fed by others while being taken from town to town on a leash.

The widely anthologized "Book of Yolek" in *The Transparent Man* (1990) employs a sestina whose melodious form is bitterly juxtaposed to the terrible story of the five-year-old Yolek, who has bad lungs and who is sent on a death march to the concentration camps in the sweltering heat of August. The poem seeks to restrain this horror spatially through the consistent use of six-line stanzas and psychologically through the repetition of the final words of each line, and, as in many of Hecht's poems, the restraint of form here amplifies the aesthetic as capable of sustaining inexorable suffering. The repetition and conclusion utilized in this work affirm that although the Holocaust is over historically, the memory of the Holocaust should and will continue to haunt us as the poem eerily concludes, "He will walk in as you're sitting down to a meal." In a similar exploration, "The Transparent Man" confronts the reader with the suffering of a dying cancer patient whom no one wants to acknowledge. Tired of reading books because he no longer cares about "How things work out, or whether they even do," the patient finds comfort in contemplating the leafless "Delicate structures of sycamores, / The fine articulation of beeches" outside his window, an aesthetic observation again intimately tied to a death wish, suspending momentarily this patient's suffering.

Exploring similar themes, "Presumptions of Death" is the title of the first section of Hecht's most recent volume, *Flight among the Tombs* (1996). Accompanied by the woodcuts of Leonard Baskin, its 22 poems, all composed in regular forms, imaginatively personify death as painter, poet, inquisitor, or Oxford don, among others. Regularity of form, meter, and rhythm here or elsewhere remains ambiguous as to its ability to contain the stories the poem tells. In three sestets with a rhyme scheme after Herbert, "Death the Painter" announces "I have sought out and arrested everyone / Under my watchful eye all human creatures / Convert to a *still life*." Both death and the aesthetic share a universality and an ultimate stasis, making explicit the intimate conjunction of death and the aesthetic in Hecht's poetry. The Italian octave "Death as a Member of the Haarlem Guild of St. Luke" carries a "honed scalpel delicate enough" to create great works of art. However, this art, like the painter's, is mere "trompe l'oeil" as the aesthetic is once again riddled with ambiguities. For this carving hand is "called in doubt"; most "settle for a simple box of pine" rather than deal with the complexities of the aesthetic.

Selected for *The Best of the Best American Poetry* by Harold Bloom, the philosophic villanelle "Prospects," from the second section of *Flight among the Tombs,* optimistically puts forth a moment hopeful about aesthetic redemption: "We have set out from here for the sublime." This confidence in the redemptive qualities of art, according to John Hollander (1997), gives the reader a "rather remarkable glimpse at what art can mean," requiring that we "must get past the scene of an old crime" by way of an aesthetic capable of mediating human suffering. Despite doubts or lack of direction, the speaker confidently concludes, "I have no doubt we will arrive on time." Hecht's poetry, a cultivated garden of human pain, points us to the transcendent qualities of art and the paradoxical nature of beauty and death.

KATEY KUHNS CASTELLANO

**Biography**

Born in New York City, 16 January 1923. Attended Bard College, Annandale-on-Hudson, New York, B.A. 1944; Columbia University, New York, M.A. 1950; served in the U.S. Army during World War II; taught at Kenyon College, Gambier, Ohio, 1947; University of Iowa, Iowa City, 1948; New York University, 1949; Smith College, Northampton, Massachusetts, 1956–59; Bard College, 1962–67; member of the Department of English, Rochester University, New York, from 1967; poetry consultant, Library of Congress, Washington, D.C., 1982–84; since 1985 University Professor, Georgetown University, Washington, D.C.; Fulbright Professor in Brazil, 1971; Hurst Professor, Washington University, St. Louis, Missouri, 1971; Visiting Professor, Harvard University, Cambridge, Massachusetts, 1973, and Yale University, New Haven, Connecticut, 1977; faculty member, Salzburg Seminar in American Studies, 1977; trustee, American Academy in Rome, Italy, from 1983. Received American Academy in Rome fellowship, 1951; Guggenheim fellowship, 1954, 1959; *Hudson Review* fellowship, 1958; Ford fellowship, for drama, 1960, for verse, 1968; Brandeis University Creative Arts Award, 1964; Rockefeller fellowship, 1967; Loines Award, 1968; Pulitzer Prize, 1968; Academy of American Poets fellowship, 1969; Litt.D., Bard College, 1970, Georgetown University, 1981, Towson State University, Maryland, 1983, and Rochester University, 1987; Bollingen Prize, 1983; Eugenio Montale Award, 1983; Monroe Award, 1987; Ruth Lilly Prize, 1988; Tanning Prize, 1997; Frost Medal, 2000; Chancellor (now Emeritus), Academy of American Poets; member, American Academy, and American Academy of Arts and Sciences. Living in Washington, D.C.

**Poetry**

*A Summoning of Stones,* 1954
*The Hard Hours,* 1967
*Millions of Strange Shadows,* 1977
*The Venetian Vespers,* 1979
*Collected Earlier Poems,* 1990
*The Transparent Man,* 1990
*Flight among the Tombs,* 1996

**Selected Criticism**

*The Pathetic Fallacy* (lecture), 1985
*Obbligati: Essays in Criticism,* 1986
*The Hidden Law: The Poetry of W.H. Auden,* 1993
*On the Laws of the Poetic Art,* 1995

**Other Writings:** translations of Latin poetry (*Seven Against Thebes,* by Aeschylus [with Helen Bacon], 1973; *Poem upon the Lisbon Disaster,* by Voltaire, 1977); edited collections of poetry (*Second Sight: Poems,* by Jonathan Aaron, 1982; *Eve Names the Animals,* by Susan Donnelly, 1985).

**Further Reading**

German, Norman, *Anthony Hecht,* New York: Lang, 1989
Hollander, John, "On Anthony Hecht," *Raritan* 17 (Summer 1997)
Howard, Richard, *Alone with America: Essays on the Art of Poetry in the United States since 1950,* New York: Atheneum, 1969; enlarged edition, 1980
Jacobs, Kathryn, "Hecht's 'The Ghost in the Martini,'" *The Explicator* 58, no. 1 (Fall 1999)
Lea, Sydney, editor, *The Burdens of Formality: Essays on the Poetry of Anthony Hecht,* Athens: University of Georgia Press, 1989
Lindsay, Geoffrey, "'Laws That Stand for Other Laws': Anthony Hecht's Dramatic Strategy," *Essays in Literature* 21, no. 2 (1994)

# Lyn Hejinian 1941–

Lyn Hejinian is among the most prominent of the avant-garde Language poets, a group as well known for generating innovative poetics and political philosophy as for creating highly experimental and challenging poetry. At once intellectually rigorous and personally engaging, Hejinian's texts are touchstones of postmodern American poetry. A large part of her influence is due to the success of *My Life* (1980, 1987), an ongoing prose-like poetic project whose crossover appeal as an "autobiography" has won her consistent attention from the academic establishment.

After a childhood spent in both Massachusetts and California, Hejinian graduated from Harvard University during the early 1960s but soon returned to San Francisco. By the 1970s, she had become part of a growing group of younger writers in the Bay Area who felt disaffected by mainstream poetry. Rejecting the dominant "Confessional" or "Romantic" lyric form, Hejinian, along with Barrett Watten, Ron Silliman, Carla Harryman, and Rae Armantrout, among others, formulated a poetics with such varied influences as Russian formalism; Continental philosophy; Modernists such as Gertrude Stein, James Joyce, and Ezra Pound; and the New York and Black Mountain Schools of poetry. Emphasizing the importance of revolutionary poetic forms, they focused on "language as such" in order to reflect their concern with the highly ideological premises of all textual representation. Their self-described "utopian" project eventually involved a number of poets in collaborative publishing efforts of manifestos and poetry, including Hejinian's own Tuumba Press as well as the journals *L=A=N=G=U=A=G=E* (edited by Charles Bernstein and Bruce Andrews) and *Poetics Journal* (edited by Hejinian and Watten).

Hejinian's earliest major work, *Writing Is an Aid to Memory* (1978), both a poem and an *ars poetica* of sorts, begins with a preface in which the poet calls attention to her "desire" to explore the world as well as the "restlessness" characteristic of language that embodies such a "desire." The poem is comprised of 42 sections, each consisting of anywhere between 3 and 150 lines, and is typographically "open," with irregularly spaced and syntactically fragmented lines and words often broken down into syllables or phonemes. No single "I" or "subject" appears to narrate the poem, the authorial presence being disrupted and dispersed by the text's formal irregularities. Instead, the poem playfully mocks lyric conventions, such as the "classic clink of feet," calling attention instead to words that are ambiguously "rub tinged" in phrases that range from the reflective ("the push of music for a long meaning") to the enigmatic ("genre find two of gence object screen object ble").

These experiments with form and subjectivity are revisited in *My Life,* a procedural poem shaped by the arbitrary number of Hejinian's own age: originally consisting of 37 sections of 37 sentences each, it was revised eight years later to 45 sections of 45 sentences and continues to be expanded. This text, read as both prose and poetry, incorporates elements of autobiography, reportage, lyric, and epic, confounding generic conventions on multiple levels. The text's title suggests the story of an individual, presumably the author, yet the reader encounters no definitive speaker or "I," much less any kind of straight narrative. The traditional genre of autobiography, marked by its authoritative, often male, speaker, is replaced by a text that seeks to undermine all that the form and subject represent. The reader is left to him- or herself to decipher the observations of everyday life ("A pause, a rose, something on paper"), clichés, memories, statements of poetics, and philosophical observations that make up the poem. *My Life* perhaps can be read most clearly as a manifestation of Hejinian's observation that "subjectivity is not an entity but a dynamic," while "form is an activity" for the poet and reader alike. Foregrounding a highly conscious mode of reading and writing outlined by important essays such as "The Rejection of Closure," "Strangeness," and "The Person and Description," the poem invites the reader into the process of poetic composition and linguistic exploration.

While *My Life* has received the bulk of the critical attention, Hejinian has written a number of other significant works, including "The Guard" (1984; in *The Cold of Poetry,* 1994) and *The Cell* (1992). Composed in reference to Hejinian's understanding of how, "if language induces a yearning for comprehension, for perfect and complete expression, it also guards against it," "The Guard" at first glance looks like a fairly traditional poem, comprised of eight sections of left-justified stanzas consisting of six to ten lines. The musings on language, memory, music, and sexuality as well as the surreally dense juxtapositions of syntax, however, are unmistakably Hejinian's: "Anyone who could believe can reveal / it can conceal." *The Cell* is a different kind of text again: a long serial poem, it is in part a diary with dated entries marking points between 6 October 1986 and 21 January 1989. The overall format contrasts with the individual sections, which seem to be "cells" of "description." Again, the deceptively conventional, quasi-lyric fragments belie their possible embodiment of "the smallest unit of imagination / in time, a retrospection / A unit of space so / small it seems to be / going backwards." Manifesting the "restlessness" of a language that continually attempts new kinds of "description," *The Cell* brings Hejinian's poetic project to a new level of intensity.

In recent years, Hejinian has become interested in the Russian avant-garde, an interest facilitated by visits to Leningrad during the late 1980s and early 1990s. *Oxota* (1991), a text playfully subtitled "A Short Russian Novel," chronicles several of her visits with Russian friends, poets, and visual artists in a series of 270 "free sonnets." These trips also resulted in a collaborative account of experiences in Russia (*Leningrad,* 1991) as well as in numerous translations by Hejinian of the work of Russian poet Arkadii Dragomoshchenko. Still based in San Francisco, Hejinian is one of the most active and consistently innovative of her contemporaries, continually embarking on collaborative projects with other poets and artists while producing new and thoughtful reflections on postmodern poetics, theory, and culture.

ANN-MARIE MIKKELSEN

*See also* Language Poetry

**Biography**

Born in San Francisco, California, 17 May 1941. Attended Harvard University, Cambridge, Massachusetts, B.A. 1963; founder, 1976, and editor, 1976–84, Tuumba Press, Berkeley, California, and since 1981 editor, *Poetics Journal;* faculty member, graduate Poetics Program at New College of California; co-director, with Travis Ortiz, of Atelos (cross-genre literary project); works as assistant to private investigator in capital crime defense and death row appeals. Received California Arts Council writing fellowship; Poetry Fund grant; National Endowment for the Arts fellowship, for translation; Poetics Function (Leningrad) Award for Independent Literature, 1989. Living in Berkeley, California.

**Poetry**
*A Thought Is the Bride of What Thinking,* 1976
*A Mask of Motion,* 1977
*Writing Is an Aid to Memory,* 1978
*Gesualdo,* 1978
*My Life* (prose poem), 1980; revised edition, 1987
*Redo,* 1984
*The Guard,* 1984
*Individuals* (with Kit Robinson), 1988
*The Cell,* 1992
*The Cold of Poetry,* 1994
*Wicker: A Collaborative Poem* (with Jack Collom), 1996
*Guide, Grammar, Watch, and the Thirty Nights,* 1996
*The Little Book of a Thousand Eyes,* 1996
*Hearing* (with Leslie Scalapino), 1998
*The Traveler and the Hill, and The Hill,* 1998
*Sight* (with Leslie Scalapino), 1999
*Happily,* 2000
*Chartings* (with Ray DiPalma), 2000

**Selected Criticism**
*The Language of Inquiry,* 2000

**Other Writings:** novels (*The Hunt,* 1991; revised edition, as *Oxota: A Short Russian Novel,* 1991), nonfiction (*Leningrad: American Writers in the Soviet Union* [with Michael Davidson, Ron Silliman, and Barrett Watten], 1991), translations of Russian literature (*Description,* by Arkadii Dragomoshchenko, 1990).

**Further Reading**
Armantrout, Rae, "Feminist Poetics and the Meaning of Clarity," *Sagetrieb* 11 (1992)
Beach, Christopher, "Poetic Positionings: Stephen Dobyns and Lyn Hejinian in Cultural Context," *Contemporary Literature* 38 (1997)
Clark, Hilary, "The Mnemonics of Autobiography: Lyn Hejinian's *My Life,*" *Biography* 14 (1991)
Jarraway, David, "*My Life* through the Eighties: The Exemplary L=A=N=G=U=A=G=E of Lyn Hejinian," *Contemporary Literature* 33 (1992)
Perloff, Marjorie, "The Word as Such: L=A=N=G=U=A=G=E Poetry in the Eighties," in *The Dance of the Intellect: Studies in the Poetry of the Pound Tradition,* by Perloff, Cambridge and New York: Cambridge University Press, 1985
Perloff, Marjorie, "The Return of the Numerical Repressed: From Free Verse to Procedural Play," in *Radical Artifice: Writing Poetry in the Age of Media,* by Perloff, Chicago: University of Chicago Press, 1991
Perloff, Marjorie, "How Russian Is It: Lyn Hejinian's *Oxota,*" in *Poetry On and Off the Page: Essays for Emergent Occasions,* by Perloff, Evanston, Illinois: Northwestern University Press, 1998
Quartermain, Peter, "Syllable as Music: Lyn Hejinian's *Writing Is an Aid to Memory,*" *Sagetrieb* 11 (1992)
Ratcliffe, Stephen, "Private Eye/Public Work," *American Poetry* 4 (Spring 1987)
Spahr, Juliana, "Resignifying Autobiography: Lyn Hejinian's *My Life,*" *American Literature* 68 (1996)

---

## Victor Hernández Cruz 1949–

Growing out of a childhood rooted in Aguas Buenas, Puerto Rico, and transplanted to the cold, rough tenements of Manhattan's Lower East Side, Victor Hernández Cruz's poetry blends tropical language, cadence, and rhythm with a street-smart, gritty English and a bittersweet sense of irony. It is, in Hernández Cruz's own words, an "interesting kind of a contradiction" that textures these lines, appearing sometimes in English, other times in Spanish, and occasionally in Spanglish born of both. Similarly, Hernández Cruz fills his work with an equally varied array of images that attest to his keen sense of what it means to straddle cultural borders. In his most recent book, *Panoramas* (1997), Hernández Cruz writes, "Seeing two languages collide, melt, struggle, fight, sabotage each other is one of the greatest shows on earth—the sensations that feed and stimulate writing come right along with linguistic warfare."

For Hernández Cruz, this baptism by "linguistic warfare" came early in life. While most poets must wait until adulthood to see their first book of poems in print, this was not the case with Hernández Cruz, whose book *Papo Got His Gun* (1966) was published by Calle Once when he was only 16 years old. His first book to garner critical attention, however, was *Snaps* (1969). Published in a year of racial tension and political upheaval, it has been viewed by some as oddly disengaged from the "collective sense" that dominates the poetry written by Cruz's Latino contemporaries during the period, opting instead for a style that looks inward at Hernández Cruz's own sensibilities as often as it examines the tumult in the exterior world. The poems in *Snaps* evidence Hernández Cruz's early interest in concrete poetry and the arrangement of the poem on the page.

Certainly, Hernández Cruz's subsequent books of poetry—*Mainland* (1973), *Tropicalization* (1976), *By Lingual Wholes* (1982), and *Red Beans* (1991)—more overtly engage his bifurcated heritage and the assets and liabilities of his community's hybrid heritage. *Mainland* depicts New York and other North American cities from the perspective of the outsider traveling through their urban landscapes, both awed by and ashamed of the scenes found there. Many of the poems draw directly on Hernández Cruz's own history, as these first lines from "The Man Who Came to the Last Floor" reveal:

> There was a Puerto Rican man who
> came to New York
> He came with a whole shopping bag
> full of seeds strange to the big
> city

This image of the countercolonization of New York City by "strange" Caribbean people and their "seeds" forecasts patterns of images found in later Hernández Cruz poems. In *Tropicalization,* for example, we read of New York Puerto Ricans thinking of "Uncle Listo" who sits "cooling himself with a fan / in that imaginary place / called Puerto Rico." In *By Lingual Wholes,* a group of "scientists / from Columbia University" find their curiosity piqued by "an old / tenement apartment / occupied by a family named González" whose "plaster of Paris" statue weeps tears that contain the word "JEHOVAH" when examined under a microscope. Hernández Cruz's Latino characters unsettle the landscapes they inhabit even as these landscapes discomfit them.

Sometimes Hernández Cruz illustrates the United States' tense relationships with its Caribbean neighbors from the American point of view, as frustrated gringos try to navigate terrains that work by different rules than theirs. In "Problems with Colonialism," a poem included in the "Islandis: The Age of Seashells" section of Hernández Cruz's *Rhythm, Content, and Flavor: New and Selected Poems* (1988), a North American dirty with tropics-induced diarrhea finds his toilet paper stolen as he sits in the blacked-out darkness of his San Juan hotel room. Frustrated and spiteful, the tourist decides to use what he thinks is a hotel blanket to clean himself, only to find when the lights come back on that he has soiled his own white shirt that he had left on the bed. While the scatology of the scene might drive some readers to reject the poem for what they perceive as simple, crass irony, the piece's larger implied statement seems difficult to dismiss—for good or ill, through colonial rule the United States has bound its future to Puerto Rico's at some fundamental level. Any underhandedness toward its colonies will surely undermine the United States itself, and Hernández Cruz's poetry offers a powerful reminder of this link.

That Hernández Cruz weaves politics into his poetry does not diminish the musicality of the verse. Far from being ponderous pronouncements of postcolonial angst, his poems float on the rhythms of guitars, maracas, and tambores and capture the syncopation of the jazz heard in the best New York clubs. In this sense, the hybridity of the musical strains that underlies Hernández Cruz's work echoes the blend of English and Spanish in his verse. As he writes in his introduction to *Panoramas,* "The music of the guitar and the music of the drum came together in the ears and hearts of a bilingual generation bred in the States. Everything was jumping with Symphony Sid in the city; he had a late-night radio program playing the New York-based Cuban and Puerto Rican music. . . . My generation developed a boogaloo with Latin rhythms and English lyrics."

In addition to receiving the more staid Guggenheim and New York Poetry Foundation awards, Victor Hernández Cruz also boasts such trophies as the "Heavyweight Poetry Champion of the World" from poetry slams in Taos, New Mexico. He lives in Puerto Rico.

Trenton Hickman

**Biography**

Born in Aguas Buenas, Puerto Rico, 6 February 1949; emigrated to the United States in 1954; editor, *Umbra* magazine, 1967–69; co-founder, East Harlem Gut Theater, New York, 1968; Guest Lecturer, University of California, Berkeley, 1970; member of Ethnic Studies Department, San Francisco State College, 1971–72; worked for the San Francisco Art Commission; founder, with Ishmael Reed, Before Columbus Foundation. Received Creative Arts Public Service Award, 1974, 1978; National Endowment for the Arts fellowship, 1981; Guggenheim fellowship, 1991. Living in Aguas Buenas, Puerto Rico.

**Poetry**

*Papo Got His Gun,* 1966
*Snaps,* 1969
*Mainland,* 1973
*Tropicalization,* 1976
*By Lingual Wholes* (includes prose), 1982
*Rhythm, Content, and Flavor: New and Selected Poems,* 1988
*Red Beans: Poems,* 1991
*Selections from Poets at Work: Contemporary Poets—Lives, Poems, Process* (with Jayne Cortez and Simon Ortiz), edited by Betty Cohen, 1995
*Panoramas* (includes prose; bilingual English and Spanish edition), 1997

**Other Writings:** short stories (*Rumba on Ice,* 1996); edited collections of literature (*Paper Dance: 55 Latino Poets* [with Leroy Quintana and Virgil Súarez], 1995).

**Further Reading**

Acosta-Belén, Edna, "The Literature of the Puerto Rican National Minority in the United States," *Bilingual Review* 5, nos. 1–2 (1978)

Aparicio, Frances, "Salsa, Maracas, and Baile: Latin Popular Music in the Poetry of Victor Hernández Cruz," *Multi-Ethnic Literatures of the United States* 16, no. 1 (1989)

Aparicio, Frances, "On Sub-Versive Signifiers: U.S. Latina/o Writers Tropicalize English," *American Literature* 66, no. 4 (1994)

# Edward Hirsch 1950–

A combination of critical acclaim and popular appeal has propelled Edward Hirsch's career from its beginning. Starting with his first book, *For the Sleepwalkers* (1981), which won the Lavan Younger Poets Award, Hirsch has been honored with a breathless series of prestigious distinctions, including the Delmore Schwartz Award (1985), a Guggenheim fellowship (1985), the National Book Critics Circle Award (1987), the American Academy of Arts and Letters' Rome Prize (1988), the Modern Language Association's William Riley Parker Prize (1992), and a MacArthur fellowship (1998). These accolades have been bestowed on Hirsch the poet, but he has another successful role: that of an advocate for the genre itself. His article "How to Read These Poems" originally appeared in *DoubleTake* magazine (Fall 1996) and was designed to help expand the audience for poetry. Printed in pamphlet form, it was then distributed throughout the United States in bookstores. That work eventually expanded to a book, a reader's guide for all levels of poetry enthusiasts. The reader is the final focus of all Hirsch's prose and poetry and has been called by Hirsch the "hero" of his books.

Hirsch's first volume, *For the Sleepwalkers,* introduces a style of poetry that could be called part confessional in its intimacy and yet neo-romantic in its meditative tone. He embraces form, but only inasmuch as it serves the content or, more important, the emotion expressed. A sestina, for instance, "At Kresge's Diner in Stonefalls, Arkansas," makes use of a repetitive form to depict the repetitive lives of a diner waitress and truck driver. The poems have a shapeliness without mechanism; his use of three-line stanzas in particular lends a deliberate, quiet evenness.

The title poem of *For the Sleepwalkers* exemplifies Hirsch's type of personal meditation. A soul in need of connection is couched in a setting recalling Coleridge's "Frost at Midnight"—moonlight, mirrors, windblown branches, owl music. The speaker wants not only to participate in the sublime experience of the sleepwalkers with their "desperate faith" but also to include the reader as well by saying "something wonderful" to allow us entry into "the skin of another life."

*Wild Gratitude* (1986) explores the artist's experience of high emotion through a multitude of stimuli, ranging from the "strange, gawky" house with "large, awkward hands" in "Edward Hopper and the House by the Railroad" to the elegance of a hook shot in "Fast Break." The city of Chicago, Hirsch's birthplace, figures prominently in *The Night Parade* (1989). Images in this book become closer and more intimate and rely on familiarity itself for their unexpected quality. Often childhood memories surface as magic—the mystery of a grandmother's Murphy bed—or in haunting specificity and detail, as in "My Father's Back." Words function as images themselves; the familiar language of "A Short Lexicon of Torture in the Eighties" transforms into something strange and chilling when imbued with sinister meaning.

The arrival of *Earthly Measures* in 1994 drew a fresh raft of praise from critics who hailed it as the full maturity of Hirsch's poetic voice. It is populated with international figures from the realms of art and history, ranging from Simone Weil to Art Pepper, yet still includes poems of family and personal sentiment, as in "Summer Surprised Us" and "Blunt Morning." "Sortes Virgilianae" blends the sense of exoticism and antiquity found in many of the poems with the intense personal quest begun by the poet in "For the Sleepwalkers"; in what could be a companion poem, a fortune-teller reaches out to that wanderer in the night, urging him to become "more than a shadow / Among shadows." Positioned to close one of the book's sections, this poem embodies the idea of spiritual quest that runs through the entire volume.

*On Love* (1998) pursues a favorite topic of this and many other poets: love and its many forms. Poetic form is, in a way, the second subject of the book, especially in the section titled "On Love." All these poems are dramatic monologues—a style that Hirsch had adopted in earlier poems—spoken by an international panel of voices from the literary history of the past century. All are composed in tight forms based on repeated end words rather than rhyme—variations on the sestina form also seen in Hirsch's earlier work. The incantatory effect achieved by the repetition lends to these treatises on love the sense of prayers being offered up either to the reader or on behalf of the reader. Each speaker speaks with the authority of his or her artistic sensibilities but also backed by the force of a life completed—of lessons learned and reflected on. In the concluding eight-line stanza of the final poem, spoken by the French writer Colette, each line ends with the word "love." The final sentences condense in length until the last short pair: "Savor the world. Consume the feast with love." The quiet echo of love itself ends the volume, a transmutation of the 24 voices through the single voice of the poet.

Lack of a sympathetic readership has been the perennial complaint of poets. Hirsch has addressed this need by taking an active role in the rehabilitation of poetry's image, both in his prose and in his public readings and lectures. His 1999 book *How to Read a Poem* speaks with the voice not only of the poet but of the lover of poetry as well, not as a critic but as an admirer. Its scope and knowledge offer much to enthusiasts without excluding readers who are just beginning their study. Unlike much literary criticism, the book's main focus is to heighten the enjoyment of poetry rather than to expose flaws or hidden agendas in individual works.

Another work illustrates Hirsch's understanding of the effect of one art form on another. *Transforming Vision: Writers on Art* (1994), edited by Hirsch and published by The Art Institute of Chicago, brings together works of art from the institute and works of literature inspired by the various pieces. The book includes a diverse group of artists and writers, from the Impressionists to Joseph Cornell, from Willa Cather to Philip Levine. In his introduction, Hirsch refers to the works as examples of "intimacies attained," perhaps as much a statement of the goals of his own poems.

Through a variety of articles and his position as adviser to the acclaimed magazine *DoubleTake,* Hirsch has been able to promote the work of newer or lesser-known poets to a more general readership, introducing English-speaking audiences to many contemporary poets outside our own culture, particularly Eastern European and Latin American authors. For many years, the call among American poets was for the development of a uniquely American voice. Along with poets such as James Wright and W.S. Merwin, Hirsch demonstrates how the new goal for art is to become less nationalistic and more inclusive, to dissolve borders and transcend nationality.

Hirsch's expansive interests and influences create a climate for the extremely personal and individual nature of his own work. His poems choose for subjects the fierce moments of the soul, with each action a reflection of the deep emotion that fires it. He is a generous poet—to his poems, to other poets, and most especially to his readers, whom he addresses through the ghost of Paul Valéry in *On Love:* "I wish you all a form of radiance."

Nicole Sarrocco

**Biography**

Born in Chicago, Illinois, 20 January 1950. Attended Grinnell College, B.A. 1972; University of Pennsylvania, Ph.D. 1979; Assistant Professor, 1979–82, and Associate Professor, 1982–85, Wayne State University, Detroit, Michigan; Associate Professor, 1985–88, and since 1988 Professor, University of Houston, Texas. Received Watson fellowship, 1972–73; Academy of American Poets Award, 1975–77; Amy Lowell traveling fellowship, 1978–79; Ingram Merrill Award, 1978–79; American Council of Learned Societies fellowship, 1982; Lavan Younger Poets Award, 1983; Delmore Schwartz Award, 1985; Guggenheim fellowship, 1985–86; National Book Critics Circle Award, 1987; Rome Prize, American Academy of Arts and Letters, 1988; William Riley Parker Prize, Modern Language Association, 1992; MacArthur fellowship, 1998; Member of PEN, Phi Beta Kappa. Living in Houston, Texas.

**Poetry**

*For the Sleepwalkers,* 1981
*Wild Gratitude,* 1986
*The Night Parade,* 1989
*Earthly Measures,* 1994
*On Love,* 1998

**Selected Criticism**

*How to Read a Poem and Fall in Love with Poetry,* 1999
*Responsive Reading,* 1999

**Other Writings:** edited anthologies of criticism (*Transforming Vision: Writers on Art,* 1994).

**Further Reading**

Curtis, Gregory, "Poets and Pedestrians," *Texas Monthly* 24, no. 1 (1996)
Eimers, Nancy, "Edward Hirsch," in *The Dictionary of Literary Biography,* volume 120: *American Poets Since World War II,* Matthew J. Bruccoli, editorial director, Detroit, Michigan: Gale, 1978–
Seaman, Donna, "Edward Hirsch: The *Booklist* Interview," *Booklist* 95, no. 14 (15 May 1999)

---

# Hispanic American Poetry

Although Hispanic-American poetry may be said to have blossomed during the 1960s, it is by no means a purely 20th-century phenomenon. The Chicano and U.S. Puerto Rican writers who came to notice during that decade saw themselves as part of a tradition of literature by Hispanic authors (written most often in Spanish but occasionally also in English) that existed on what is now U.S. soil as far back as the 16th century. The expedition of Juan de Oñate (1598–1608) produced the first New World example of the European tradition of epic poetry, *Historia de la Nueva México* (1610), written by Gaspar Pérez de Villagrá (1555–1620). The poem's 30 cantos, full of allusions to classical epic and Christian doctrine, culminate with the brutal suppression of the Acoma pueblo. In the aftermath of the conquest of Nueva España (which later became Mexico), Spanish speakers created a vibrant oral culture that was a New World descendant of the medieval Spanish peninsular tradition of ballads and dramas. In the mid–19th century, this Spanish culture, which had displaced the indigenous Native American culture, was itself displaced as a result of the Mexican-American War, which ended in 1848 with the Treaty of Guadalupe Hidalgo. The history of Chicano expression begins with the resulting Americanization of a vast area that had once been part of Mexico, and U.S. Puerto Rican poetry continues to contend with the cultural aftershocks of Spain's loss of Puerto Rico to the United States in 1898.

The two dominant strains of 20th-century Hispanic-American poetry thus have much in common: Chicano poetry and U.S. Puerto Rican poetry share a Latin American heritage, a deep connection to Spanish language and culture, the experience of being a minority within U.S. culture, and an abiding interest in racial and ethnic mixing (*mestizaje*). Both poetic traditions make frequent use of "code switching" between English, Spanish, and other vernacular forms, a kind of linguistic *mestizaje* that serves not only to represent accurately the sociocultural situations of their communities but also to empower bilingual readers. Spanish represents the most visible and viable challenge to the hegemony of the English language in the United States, and the debates over bilingual education have been driven largely by the issue of classroom instruction in Spanish. The use of Spanish by U.S. Hispanic poets, either exclusively or in combination with English, serves as a challenge to the idea that "American literature" should be written in English.

There are, however, significant differences between these two dominant traditions of Hispanic-American poetry. Chicanos have a far more conflicted attitude toward their Spanish heritage, in part because Mexican culture underwent two periods of anti-Hispanism, once after independence in 1821 and then again during the revolution of 1910. Many of the important early Chicano writers sought to emphasize their Indian heritage as the key to Chicano identity. In contrast, many Puerto Rican writers rebelled against the process of Americanization that began in 1898 when Spain ceded Puerto Rico to the United States and continued with the granting of U.S. citizenship to Puerto Ricans in 1917. A Hispanist strain of Puerto Rican poetry arose that sought to achieve a "pure" poetry of lyricism, metaphor, and strong identification with Spanish culture. In addition, Chicano poetry arises from a continental sense of geography, born in northern Mexico, while U.S. Puerto Rican poetry is very much part of a Caribbean tradition of island writing. The history of European imperialism transforms this geographic distinction into a racial distinction: Chicano culture views itself primarily as a mixture of Native American and Spanish heritages, while Puerto Rican culture emphasizes its mixture of Spanish and black.

The roots of 20th-century Chicano literature lie in the tradition of resistance to what many Mexican-Americans still consider to be the "occupation" of America by the U.S. government. As a result of the Treaty of Guadalupe Hidalgo, Mexico ceded all its territories north of the Rio Grande to the United States, territories that spanned the present-day states of Arizona, California, Nevada, New Mexico, Utah, and half of Colorado. Although approximately 2,000 of the area's Spanish-speaking residents chose to relocate to Mexico, more than 80,000 remained on their lands and automatically became American citizens, and they were allowed to maintain their language and cultural traditions. Although Article IX of the treaty guaranteed Mexicans remaining in the Southwest "the enjoyment of all the rights of citizens of the United States according to the principles of the Constitution," those Mexicans who stayed to become American citizens found that they were treated as second-class citizens: they constituted an ethnic minority within American national culture, and they were soon victimized by unscrupulous white Americans. "A pre–Civil War type of carpetbagger moved into the territory to make his fortune," writes the Chicano fiction writer and scholar Américo Paredes, "preying upon the newly created Americans of Mexican descent. The Mexican's cattle were killed or stolen. The Mexican was forced to sell his land; and if he did not, his widow usually did after her husband was 'executed' for alleged cattle rustling. Thus did the great Texas ranches and the American cattle industry begin" (Paredes, 1979).

The flowering of Chicano literature is often considered to be the result of the Chicano movement, which arose during the early 1960s in tandem with other movements aimed at gaining civil rights for disenfranchised minority groups. The etymology of the term "Chicano" is still hotly disputed among Chicano scholars. The most likely derivation is from "Mexicano," with the "x" pronounced the way it was at the time of the Spanish Conquest, as "sh." However, the term "Chicano," which came to prominence during the student movements of the 1960s, has not been universally accepted by those whom it is intended to describe. Various other terms have gained currency in different regions, however: for example, "Hispano" and "Spanish American" have been the preferred terms in southern Colorado and northern New Mexico, while "Mexicano" has been widely accepted in southern Texas and in many of the border regions. The first major literary work produced by the movement was *I Am Joaquín,* an epic poem written in 1967 by Rodolfo "Corky" Gonzales, who founded the Crusade for Justice in Colorado. In his introduction to the poem, Gonzales describes *Joaquín* as "a call to action" for Chicanos "as a total people, emerging from a glorious history, traveling through social pain and conflicts, confessing our weaknesses while we shout about our strength."

The construction of a heroic tradition is the project of much early Chicano writing, and the publication in 1958 of Américo Paredes' groundbreaking study *"With His Pistol in His Hand": A Border Ballad and Its Hero* is often cited by the Chicano writers of the 1960s as an inspiration because it made them aware of an existing literary tradition of proto-Chicano writing and because it served as proof that Chicano writers could indeed be published in the United States. The *corrido* is a narrative ballad, generally anonymously composed, that is sung or spoken to musical accompaniment. Related to ballad forms that had been brought by the Spanish to Mexico, the *corrido* flourished in the border region south of Texas, where relations between Mexican- and Anglo-Americans were particularly troubled. In contrast to earlier ballad forms, which generally dealt with incidents from daily life, the *corrido* emphasizes drama and conflict, particularly the resistance of an individual to forces of oppression along the border. Its protagonist is often the Mexican cowboy, the *vaquero.* True to its name, which is derived from the verb *correr,* "to run," the *corrido* generally offers a swiftly paced story, most often told in stanzas of four eight-syllable lines.

With the decline of the communal village that accompanied the building of 15,000 miles of railroad track between 1880 and 1910, many peasants were forced to become migrant workers—*braceros*—who increasingly traveled across the border to work in the United States, where they often competed with freed slaves for work and suffered from racial discrimination. Although the Mexican Revolution of 1910 produced what Paredes calls "the Greater Mexican heroic *corrido,*" it also produced a massive influx of new *braceros* who migrated to the United States to fill the need for cheap foreign labor in the aftermath of the Chinese Exclusion Acts. It is thought that as many as 100,000 Mexican immigrants entered the United States during the years surrounding the Mexican Revolution; with the outbreak of World War I in 1914, a second wave of immigration began that would bring more than one million Mexican immigrants to the United States by the end of the 1920s. Throughout this period, as its subject shifted from the *vaquero* to the *bracero,* the *corrido* remained the primary cultural form through which the suffering of Mexicans in United States found expression.

Early Chicano poets concerned themselves with the creation of a cultural identity that was distinct from the Anglo-American dominant culture. Foremost among these poets is Alurista, whose poetry reaches back to pre-Columbian indigenous myths in order to forge a new mythology centered on the Chicano homeland, Aztlán. In the Nahuatl language of ancient Mexico, "Aztlán" means "the lands to the north," and it is used by Chicanos today to refer to what is now the southwestern United States. Aztlán is thought to be the homeland of the ancestors of the Aztecs, the place where they made an alliance with their god of war, Huitzilopochtli, who promised to lead them out of Aztlán. The resulting migration southward led to the establishment of the new Aztec nation of Tenochtitlán, which would eventually be conquered by Hernán Cortés in 1521. The modern invocation of Aztlán was codified at the Chicano Youth Conference held in Denver, Colorado, in March 1969, which produced a document, titled "El Plan Espiritual de Aztlán," that "declare[d] the Independence of our Mestizo Nation."

For Alurista, the playwright Luis Valdez, and other Chicano poets such as Gloria Anzaldúa, Inés Hernández, Miguel Mendéz, and Lin Romero, emphasizing Aztlán as the source of Chicano culture was a way of emphasizing the Native American roots of Chicano identity and thus of de-emphasizing its roots in the Spanish conquistadors, the first invaders and occupiers of America, forerunners in that sense of the U.S. government. Anzaldúa and Cherríe Moraga are two poets who rewrite the mythology of Aztlán in response to what they see as the oppressive misogyny that runs throughout much Chicano culture. Other poets, such as Sandra Cisneros and Lorna Dee Cervantes, make use of pre-Columbian mythologies more warily, careful to indicate the constructed nature of the myths of Aztlán. As early as 1972, the poet and essayist E.A. Mares argued, unfashionably, "We are not Aztecs, and we are far from Aztlán," cautioning in his essay "El Lobo y El Coyote: Between Two Cultures" against the danger of marginalizing individuals and cultural productions that do not fit within the conception implicit in the idea of Aztlán.

Chicano poetry in the 1960s and 1970s is a poetry of elegy and protest. The writings of José Montoya, J.L. Navarro, Abelardo (Delgado), and Tino Villanueva portray the frustrations of the Chicano experience: whether in the *barrio* or in the fields where migrant workers toil, a Chicano's life is marked by feelings of loss, dislocation, self-division, and hopelessness. For example, Abelardo's "Stupid America" (1969) laments the destructive effects of Anglo ignorance and prejudice: "stupid america, see that chicano / with a big knife / in his steady hand / he doesn't want to knife you / he wants to sit on a bench / and carve christfigures / but you won't let him." The *pinto* poetry of Raúl Salinas and Ricardo Sánchez focuses on the convict's experience, which serves as an allegory for the oppressiveness of U.S. culture. Chicano protest poetry concerns itself above all with the needs of *la raza:* it is hortatory, didactic, and communal in orientation. Moreover, many of these poets—most notably Alurista, Montoya, and Sánchez—make extensive use of code switching as a way of signifying resistance to the process of Americanization.

The mid-1970s, however, saw the emergence of a new strain of Chicano poetry that shifted its emphasis away from the public to the private, seeking to create idiosyncratic, personal voices in a lyric mode. Writing primarily in English, Gary Soto uses a stripped-down style to treat a wide range of subjects; his first book, *The Elements of San Joaquin* (1977), is divided into three parts, treating the laborer's life in the fields, the violence of modern urban society, and the difficulties of interpersonal relationships. Several of the poems in *The Tale of Sunlight* (1978) draw on Latin-American magical realism, while his poems of the 1980s focus more closely on themes drawn from family life. The title of Bernice Zamora's first volume, *Restless Serpents* (1976), may serve as an emblem of her poetic technique: in contrast to serpents "carved" into the "balustrades" of "the castle of the weary wealthy" in the volume's opening poem, "Stone Serpents," the "restless serpents" of the title poem are vital, creative, and rebellious, "coiling, / recoiling, pricking the master's veins." Zamora's interest in vitality leads her to explore the nature of love and sexuality, and she portrays the serpent as a figure of bisexuality and fecundity. Other poets who exemplify this new phase of Chicano poetics are Lorna Dee Cervantes and Alberto Ríos as well as Alma Villanueva.

If the development of Chicano poetry can be sketched very broadly as a movement from the communal to the personal, from an emphasis on social protest to an emphasis on aesthetics, the development of island-based Puerto Rican poetry can be sketched as nearly its opposite. After 1917, Puerto Rican poets resisted the attempts of the United States to Americanize the island by reaffirming their Hispanic heritage, looking instead to the *arielista* and *criollista* movements present throughout Latin America. The *arielistas* were followers of José Enrique Rodó, a Uruguayan who called for Latin Americans to emulate Ariel rather than Caliban, to embrace the humanistic values inherited from Spain rather than the materialism of the United States. The *criollistas* of the 1930s and 1940s were intellectual and often academic poets who turned to a "pure" poetry rooted in the island's natural landscape and folklore. After Puerto Rico became a commonwealth in 1952, a new generation of poets rebelled against both of these movements, producing a separatist poetry that is almost anti-poetic, emphasizing naturalistic representation and social awareness. At the close of the 20th century, these two traditions continue to contend with one another in island-based Puerto Rican poetry.

The Puerto Rican diaspora has traditionally been centered in New York. From 1917 through World War II, first-generation Puerto Rican immigrants, such as Bernardo Vega and Jesus Colón, wrote accounts of their struggles to adjust to life in the United States, while Rafael Hernández and other songwriters produced popular music using island forms such as the *bolera* and the *plena* that explored what it meant to be a Riqueño. The period of intensifying immigration that followed the war and lasted through the mid-1960s was a troubled time that saw many in the Puerto Rican community sink into poverty, relegated to temporary, low-paying jobs or welfare. The pain of this time is powerfully expressed in the poetry of Julia de Burgos, whose poetry combines the aesthetics of the island Hispanist movements with an acknowledgment of the impact of her American context. Written in Spanish, de Burgos' poetry maps the personal onto the social: her personal experience as a woman dominated by the patriarchal traditions of Catholic Puerto Rico, ignored by critics and other poets, and driven to alcoholism becomes an allegory of Puerto Rico's situation as an occupied territory.

Out of the cultural ferment of the late 1960s in New York arose a vibrant group of Puerto Rican poets who call themselves "Nuyoricans," adopting what had been a disparaging term used by island Puerto Ricans. Conceiving of poetry as a public and popular form, these poets gathered at Nuyorican Poets' Café, located in Manhattan at 505 East Sixth Street, where they were visited by such legends of the Beat generation as William Burroughs, Gregory Corso, and Allen Ginsberg. Their abiding subjects are the agony of the inner city and the need to decolonize the Puerto Rican mind, whether in New York or in Puerto Rico. Early Nuyorican poetry was written primarily in English and heavily indebted to its Beat and African-American predecessors as well as to the eminent Modernist poet William Carlos Williams, who shunned his Puerto Rican heritage. Increasingly, the most prominent Nuyorican poets—Miguel Algarín, Angel Figueroa, Martin Espada, Sandra Maria Esteves, Tato Laviera, Pedro Pietri, and Miguel Piñero—have begun to develop more complex voices: their poetry becomes less reliant on earlier models; less interested in conceiving of a liberated Puerto Rico as mythified, utopian space; and more willing to experiment with multilingual code switching. Victor Hernández Cruz is sometimes grouped with the Nuyoricans, although his work was not included in the anthology edited by Algarín and Piñero in 1975. Indeed, his poetry does not share their aesthetic commitments, relying heavily on verbal abstraction rather than emotion and exhortation.

Gradually, poets with roots in Cuba, the Dominican Republic, and other countries in Central and Latin America are beginning to add their distinctive voices to the annals of Hispanic-American literature. Given the increasing critical attention devoted to women poets such as Anzaldúa, Moraga, Zamora, Cervantes, Alma Villanueva, and the Dominican Julia Alvarez, it seems likely that the 21st century will see the blossoming of a distinctive Hispanic-American feminist poetry.

Cyrus R.K. Patell

**Further Reading**

Arteaga, Alfred, *Chicano Poetics: Heterotexts and Hybridities,* Cambridge and New York: Cambridge University Press, 1997

Bruce-Novoa, *Chicano Poetry: A Response to Chaos,* Austin: University of Texas Press, 1982

Bruce-Novoa, *RetroSpace: Collected Essays on Chicano Literature, Theory, and History,* Houston, Texas: Arte Público Press, 1990

Candelaria, Cordelia, *Chicano Poetry: A Critical Introduction,* Westport, Connecticut: Greenwood Press, 1986

Flores, Juan, *Divided Borders: Essays on Puerto Rican Identity,* Houston, Texas: Arte Público Press, 1993

Límon, José Eduardo, *Mexican Ballads, Chicano Poems: History and Influence in Mexican-American Social Poetry,* Berkeley: University of California Press, 1992

Mohr, Eugene V., *The Nuyorican Experience: Literature of the Puerto Rican Minority,* Westport, Connecticut, and London: Greenwood Press, 1982

Paredes, Américo, "The Folk Base of Chicano Literature," in *Modern Chicano Writers: A Collection of Critical Essays,* edited by Joseph Sommers and Tomás Ybarro-Frausto, Englewood Cliffs, New Jersey: Prentice Hall, 1979

Patell, Cyrus R.K., "Emergent Literatures," in *The Cambridge History of American Literature, Prose Writing, 1940–1990,* volume 7, edited by Sacvan Bercovitch, Cambridge and New York: Cambridge University Press, 1999

Pérez-Torres, Rafael, *Movements in Chicano Poetry: Against Myths, Against Margins,* Cambridge and New York: Cambridge University Press, 1995

Sánchez, Marta Ester, *Contemporary Chicana Poetry: A Critical Approach to an Emerging Literature,* Berkeley: University of California Press, 1985

---

# Daniel Hoffman 1923–

Even in his first published book of poems, *An Armada of Thirty Whales,* chosen by W.H. Auden for the Yale Younger Poets series in 1954, Daniel Hoffman had a vigorous style of writing—wiry, intense, driven by a disciplined metrical ear, and having a clear sense of what he wanted to say. The early poems were steeped in a contemporary sense of irony and Audenesque detachment, the rhetorical conventions of Cold War skepticism—very smart stuff, with an urbane finish drawn from close study of Wallace Stevens' whimsical humor. In his title poem to this debut volume, Hoffman could outdo Stevens at his own game when he writes of the whales "exulting gigantically [as] / each trumpets a sousaphone wheeze." That intensity and finish might have spelled trouble in the ensuing years, where the one-page poem became the cliché of the writing schools and the mainstay of books thereafter. Anything longer might spill over into uncharted regions of psyche and occasion the unregulated speech of the bohemians, a fringe culture of experimental poetry with which Hoffman would have nothing to do. Hoffman's ideology, not a pronounced part of his poetry but a rich layer of tacit assumption all the same, is Anglo-American and grows out of an age of earlier certainties about right and wrong, left and right. Like Denise Levertov, he too disliked the poetry of no punctuation and of barbarous spontaneity.

However, as time went on and Hoffman's career as poet grew, the well-wrought-urn school of poetry began to lose some of its appeal. In the wake of Vietnam and Watergate and into the profligate years of the Reagan era, small poems were mocking testimonies to a bygone era of neat categories and uncontested absolutes. The world of politics was melting all that down, and Hoffman's poetry grew more thorny, difficult, and suggestive.

"History alters all it touches," he wrote in "Aphrodite" in *Broken Laws* (1970), launching his new work into questions about what and when we know things, how to see—and the answer is now to measure a "landscape of sensible / Disaster." With the poem "The Center of Attention," from the book of that title, Hoffman captures the fever of the Watergate era with a suicide's foiled attempt at leaping off a high building. The crowd below loses interest the moment he is rescued, as if another Nixon gets to go free.

*Brotherly Love* (1981) is, to quote Ezra Pound on his *Cantos,* "a poem about history," in this case a sequence of constantly shifting lyric short forms to record the relations between William Penn and the Delaware Indians resident in colonial Pennsylvania. The task of the opening third of this book is to understand the "mind" on both sides of the racial divide, to offer readings of the Lenni Lenape creation myth (the *Wampum Olum*), and to slip into Penn's mind to discover the sources of his fairness in the making of a celebrated treaty of peace. The book's title bears specifically on this one instance of a successful relation between colonial Americans and native people.

The underlying text of this long exploration of racially distinct imaginations is a commentary on the Vietnam War. It is a plea for decency based on a remarkable historical precedent that does not seem to have influenced the future of race relations in "this flawed / Commonweal." The poem is tacit on the subject of Vietnam or of race in general but subtly evokes them at every turn of its historical argument. Indeed, part 2 of the book, "The Opening of Joy," is a running account of the villains of British imperialism and its singular antihero, William Penn, who chose justice over the usual tendency toward tyranny and exploitation. Hence the moral purpose of the book: to study the unique figure of an unsung Quaker hero in colonial America.

However, in "The Structure of Reality," the concluding third section, relations break down, and the deed, recounted in its original legal language, becomes a reminder of promises not kept and of terms violated by Penn's heirs. The sale of land by the Delaware permanently "debarred" them from reentering their homeland, a fact that provokes foiled and bloody rebellions, a prologue to centuries of racial strife. The will of the possessors stiffened against the dispossessed and marks a peculiar pattern of events to come. The closing poem of the book celebrates the abiding spirit of Penn atop the dome of City Hall in Philadelphia, as an inspiration if not the principle of life in our time.

With *Middens of the Tribe* (1995), Hoffman made his boldest attempt yet at the long poem, an interlocking series of monologues involving several households connected by the slender thread of a doctor making house calls and attending to accidents in the opening poem. The work has antecedents, notably Edgar Lee Master's *Spoon River Anthology* (1916), which offers the principle of ghosts standing up from their tombstones in a cemetery to tell their secrets. Hoffman has his own device for allowing us access to the voices of "neither the / living, nor the dying," who will "confide in you—you'll keep their secrets?"

Brief as it is, a mere 77 pages of close writing, the work is highly compressed and moves in leaps from voice to voice, detailing the thoughts of a young blond-haired woman in love with a magician who saws her in half each evening while she laments his infidelities and whose pregnancy ends in disaster—a monster delivered stillborn by the doctor. The main story is of a wealthy, miserly investor, a Dickensian character who surrounds himself with paintings of nudes and dreams of seducing his hired help. His sons and daughter are estranged, and his wife dies in bitterness. However, the old man lasts to the end of the tale, giving up his secrets to the son who goes through his papers, free at last. Another son plies his trade as an archaeologist, commenting here and there on his research into the Cromlech people, a unified clan against the sordid, fractious, and alienated families of the main narrative.

These "middens," or trash heaps, that the poems search through reveal the secretive, furtive passions of a host of characters making up midcentury America. The failure at the heart of American culture is the inability to communicate and break down barriers; everyone lives in isolation, in ignorance of the sufferings and longings of others. It is a book about loneliness and the frailty of human life, which the poems vigorously anatomize. The real hero of the piece is the narrator's own boisterous, powerful language breaking down the doors to let in a cleansing sunlight into everyone's moldy privacy.

PAUL CHRISTENSEN

**Biography**

Born in New York City, 3 April 1923. Attended Columbia University, New York, A.B. 1947 (Phi Beta Kappa), M.A. 1949, Ph.D. 1956; served in the United States Army Air Force, 1943–46, Legion of Merit; Instructor in English, Columbia University, 1952–56; Visiting Professor, University of Dijon, France, 1956–57; Assistant Professor, 1957–60, Associate Professor, 1960–65, and Professor of English, 1965–66, Swarthmore College, Pennsylvania; since 1966 Professor of English, since 1978 poet-in-residence, and since 1983 Felix E. Schelling Professor of English, University of Pennsylvania, Philadelphia; Fellow of the School of Letters, Indiana University, Bloomington, 1959; Elliston Lecturer, University of Cincinnati, Ohio, 1964; Lecturer, International School of Yeats Studies, Sligo, Ireland, 1965; consultant in poetry, 1973–74, and honorary consultant in American letters, 1974–77, Library of Congress, Washington, D.C. Received YMHA Introductions award, 1951; Yale Series of Younger Poets award, 1954; Ansley prize, 1957; American Council of Learned Societies fellowship, 1962; Columbia University Medal for Excellence, 1964; American Academy grant, 1967; Ingram Merrill Foundation grant, 1971; National Endowment for the Arts fellowship, 1975; Hungarian PEN Medal, 1980; Guggenheim fellowship, 1983; Hazlett Memorial award, 1984; since 1972 Chancellor, Academy of American Poets. Living in Swarthmore, Pennsylvania.

**Poetry**

*An Armada of Thirty Whales*, 1954
*A Little Geste, and Other Poems*, 1960
*The City of Satisfactions*, 1963
*Striking the Stones*, 1968
*Broken Laws*, 1970
*Corgi Modern Poets in Focus 4* (with others, edited by Jeremy Robson), 1971
*The Center of Attention*, 1974
*Able Was I Ere I Saw Elba: Selected Poems, 1954–1974*, 1977
*Brotherly Love*, 1981
*Hang-Gliding from Helicon: New and Selected Poems, 1948–1988*, 1988
*Middens of the Tribe*, 1995

**Selected Criticism**

*The Poetry of Stephen Crane*, 1957
*Form and Fable in American Fiction*, 1961
*Barbarous Knowledge: Myth in the Poetry of Yeats, Graves, and Muir*, 1967
*Poe Poe Poe Poe Poe Poe Poe*, 1972
*"Moonlight Dries No Mittens": Carl Sandburg Reconsidered*, 1979
*Faulkner's Country Matters: Folklore and Fable in Yoknapatawpha*, 1989

**Other Writings:** edited collections of literature and criticism (*The Red Badge of Courage and Other Stories*, by Stephen Crane, 1957; *American Poetry and Poetics: Poems and Critical Documents from the Puritans to Robert Frost*, 1962; *Harvard Guide to Contemporary American Writing*, 1979).

**Further Reading**

Allen, John Alexander, "Another Country: The Poetry of Daniel Hoffman," *Hollins Critic* (15 October 1978)

Hoffman, Daniel, *Words to Create a World: Interviews, Essays, and Reviews of Contemporary Poetry*, Ann Arbor: University of Michigan Press, 1993

Howard, Richard, *Alone with America: Essays on the Art of Poetry in the United States since 1950*, New York: Atheneum, 1969; enlarged edition, 1980

Spears, Monroe K., "A Major Poet," *The Southern Review* 11 (Summer 1975)

Sylvester, William, "Daniel Hoffman's Poetry of Affection," *Voyages* 3 (Winter 1970)

---

# John Hollander 1929–

Born in New York City in 1929, John Hollander is the author of 27 volumes of poetry and several books on poetic form, technique, and allusion, as well as the editor of several anthologies. In the manner of the neoclassical poets of the 17th century, Hollander's poetry displays immense knowledge of prosody in a dense weave of philosophical, literary, and theological allusions. His many honors include a Bollingen Prize in Poetry, the Melville Cane Award, a MacArthur Foundation fellowship, and the Ambassador Book Award.

Hollander's first book, *A Crackling of Thorns* (1958), reveals the influence of masters of Modern style such as Yeats, Stevens, and Pound. Auden, who selected the collection for the Yale Series of Younger Poets in 1958, emphasized its technical invention and literary allusion in his introduction. Later in Hollander's career some critics would fault him for employing "complication for complication's sake" (Vendler, 1975), or for indulging his "terrifying knowledgeability" (Davie, 1975), but Hollander argued that "every prosodic pattern or verse scheme of rhetorical style is, apart from its content, *expressive*"—a lesson he attributed to Auden himself (McClatchy, 1982). Featuring verse forms such as sestinas, sonnets, and villanelles, as well as allusions ranging from Greek myth to Old Testament Apocrypha to Wallace Stevens, *A Crackling of Thorns* is in the tradition of the New Criticism and the literary culture of New York in the 1940s and 50s. These lines from "The Observatory" are representative:

> How vainly open eyes amaze
> Themselves with the synoptic gaze!
> And cloud the mediant air between.
> The image and the object seen,
> Whose public face may never ask
> The one behind it to unmask.

As if in answer to his critics, in his widely used introduction to English verse, *Rhyme's Reason* (1981), Hollander contended that "the sense must seem an echo to the sound." He has also expressed his wish to write poems that "know more about themselves" than he does:

> [S]omething you do for the sake of rhyme alone is probably *not* going to be very good. But something you do for the sake of rhythm may very often be remarkable. You may discover something you didn't know in an effort to get the cadence right; you may bring to the surface a word you'd hidden from yourself. (McClatchy, 1982)

Since 1969 Hollander has relied on syllabics to violate Modernism's sense of "the musical phrase" and to shift the reader's attention away from the "lyric's lull" and toward "the meter-making argument, the particular myth a poem is making up out of itself" (McClatchy, 1982). Despite his intense interest in prosody, Hollander's critical work argues that even at a late time of myth-making, the contemporary poem, like the Renaissance one, must ultimately do its teaching by mythographic means.

His own myths are not necessarily biblical or classical, however. *Movie-Going, and Other Poems* (1962) relies on more contemporary allusions to the poet's memories of the movie houses and films of his youth. As in his first volume, the poems advocate the imagination as a means of staving off dark and painful aspects of reality:

> And still, now as always, once
> The show is over and we creep into the dull
> Blaze of mid-afternoon sunshine, the hollow dole
> Of the real descends on everything and we can know
> That we have been in some place wholly elsewhere, a night
> At noonday, not without dreams, whose portals shine. . . .

Later works incorporated such personal myth-making with the biblical mythology of Hollander's Jewish heritage. *Visions from the Ramble* (1965), which some consider Hollander's finest collection, renders individual, national, and religious consciousness divided between the European past and what Hollander terms "the American moment" in a geography of imagination that "takes absence and loss, exile and diaspora, as basic preconditions" (Lehman, 1984). The collection moves from the secular world of "The Ninth of July" to the Hebrew world of "The Ninth of Ab" and includes 14 interrelated poems based on Hollander's youth as well as a "proem" focusing on Central Park.

*Tales Told of the Fathers* (1975) opens with a long, complex poem entitled "The Head of the Bed" and has been read as a despairing statement on the condition of American poetry. Harold Bloom concludes that the "two countries" of the poem represent "life and the dream," and that Lilith, the mythical figure that informs the poem, serves as the destructive muse of poetry. Bloom's essay on the poem, which appears with the separate publication of the poem in the Godine Chapbook Series, contends that "Hollander's remarkable achievement is to have so dreamed his own nightmares as to have joined, if not quite the universal, at least the national predicament of poetry" (1974).

*Reflections on Espionage: The Question of Cupcake* (1976) departed from the serious tone, although not subject, of Hollander's previous work. This long farce began as a little verse written in the form of a communication between a spy with the code name "Cupcake" and a control named "Lyrebird." Hollander described it as "a kind of allegorical diary about the life of artists and, always even more importantly, about the life of the imagination which every humane person has to try to live as well" (McClatchy, 1982).

*Spectral Emanations: New and Selected Poems* (1978) features a similar synthesis between playful methodology and philosophical exploration. *Spectral Emanations* fuses the story of the sacred *menorah* taken from the destroyed Second Temple with an allegorical solar spectrum. The seven parts of the title poem each correspond to one of the colors of the spectrum, used as metaphors for states of consciousness; the poem's protagonist, Roy G. Biv, endeavors to combine the lessons of each color into the "white light of truth." Critics David Lehman and Harold Bloom have both noted that the mediated vision achieved through Hollander's incorporation of prose into his poetry is reminiscent of *midrashim,* rabbinical commentaries. For example, "Green" concludes with a series of prose paragraphs, one of which illustrates verdancy as a spiritual state: "I feel strangely young, as if I had acquired new qualities: the power to charm, a speaking and cheerful gaze, an aura of fragility that was somehow nonetheless being projected, and thus remaining uncoarsened by any defenses of its own. I am to embark not on a night journey, but upon a pastoral cycle of magic and simplifications."

An important milestone in Hollander's career, *Blue Wine, and Other Poems* (1979) continues the theme of the search for truth in the title poem:

When some unexpected visitor
Drops in and sees these bottles of blue wine, and does not
ask
At the time what they mean,
he may take some drops home with him
In the clear cup of his own eye, to see what he will see.

It also continues Hollander's exploration of themes such as the nature of reality and the role of imagination. The quality of light and color, from which emerges the integral imagery of "Blue Wine," is revisited in poems like "August Carving," in which a sculptor carves two joined figures, commemorating "a knowledge as of a distant light composed here by the green of fields."

In his review of *Tesserae* (1993) and *Selected Poetry* (1993) for *New Republic,* Vernon Shetley remarked on Hollander's strict avoidance of anything that might seem merely an expression of personality, as if the poet had taken to heart, much more fully than its author, Eliot's dictum that poetry should embody "emotion which has its life in the poem and not in the history of the poet." Even in poems such as "Movie-Going" and "The Ramble," which clearly have autobiographical roots, Hollander eschews the confessional in favor of fidelity to the poem as a self-contained entity that does not demand the reader's acquaintance with personal details of the poet's life.

While Hollander's long-standing interest in poetic theory is reflected in works such as *Modern Poetry: Modern Essays in Criticism* (1968) and *The Work of Poetry* (1997), he has also expressed his distress over the "academicization of literary theory." In "The Practice of Theory and the Theory of Practice" he notes:

> The growing substitution of bureaucratized "theory" as the subject of study in literature departments is fueled by the lack of literary experience of the students and, by now, of two younger generations of teachers. And this poverty—this dearth of literary possession—has been accompanied by a lack of logical, rhetorical and general conceptual sophistication. (*Remapping the Boundaries: A New Perspective in Comparative Studies,* 1997)

This lack of literary experience may account for the critical neglect of Hollander's own work in his lifetime. The intricate weave of allusions, sophisticated prosodic technique, and unfashionable emotional remove do not lend themselves to a quick or impressionistic reading. In contrast to the mixed critical response with which Hollander's poetry has been greeted, however, his anthologies and works on poetic form have few detractors. His edition of *American Poetry: The Nineteenth Century* (1994), two volumes of verse including sonnets, ballads, folk songs, and epic poetry, received unanimous praise. Alexander Theroux of *The Chicago Tribune* even argued that Hollander's anthology should be "required reading for every person who purports to care about our nation's cultural history" (20 March 1994).

DONNA POTTS

**Biography**

Born in New York City, 28 October 1929. Attended Columbia University, New York, A.B. 1950 (Phi Beta Kappa), M.A. 1952; Indiana University, Bloomington, Ph.D. 1959; Junior fellow, Society of Fellows, Harvard University, Cambridge, Massachusetts, 1954–57; Lecturer, Connecticut College, New London, 1957–59; Instructor, 1959–61, Assistant Professor, 1961–64, and Associate Professor of English, 1964–66, Yale University, New Haven, Connecticut; Professor of English, Hunter College, City University of New York, 1966–77; since 1977, Professor of English, and currently Sterling Professor of English, Yale University; Gauss Lecturer, Princeton University, New Jersey, 1962, 1965; Visiting Professor, Indiana University, 1964; Lecturer, Salzburg Seminar in American Studies, 1965; Overseas Fellow, Churchill College, Cambridge, 1967–68; since 1977 Fellow, Ezra Stiles College, Yale University; member of the poetry board, Wesleyan University Press, 1959–62; editorial assistant for poetry, *Partisan Review,* New Brunswick, New Jersey, 1959–65; contributing editor, *Harper's* magazine, New York, 1969–71. Received Yale Series of Younger Poets Award, 1958; American Academy grant, 1963; National Endowment for the Arts fellowship, 1973; Levinson Prize (*Poetry,* Chicago), 1974; Guggenheim fellowship, 1979; Modern Language Association Shaughnessy Medal, 1982; Bollingen Prize, 1983; Litt.D., Marietta College, Ohio, 1982, Indiana University, 1990; Chancellor, Academy of American Poets; member, American Academy, and American Academy of Arts and Sciences. Living in New Haven, Connecticut.

**Poetry**
*A Crackling of Thorns*, 1958
*Movie-Going, and Other Poems*, 1962
*A Beach Vision*, 1962
*A Book of Various Owls* (for children), 1963
*Visions from the Ramble*, 1965
*The Quest of the Gole* (for children), 1966
*Philomel*, 1968
*Types of Shape*, 1969; revised edition, 1991
*The Night Mirror*, 1971
*Town and Country Matters: Erotica and Satirica*, 1972
*Selected Poems*, 1972
*The Head of the Bed*, 1974
*Tales Told of the Fathers*, 1975
*Reflections on Espionage: The Question of Cupcake*, 1976
*Spectral Emanations: New and Selected Poems*, 1978
*In Place*, 1978
*Blue Wine, and Other Poems*, 1979
*Looking Ahead*, 1982
*Powers of Thirteen*, 1983
*A Hollander Garland*, 1985
*In Time and Place*, 1986
*Some Fugitives Take Cover*, 1988
*Harp Lake*, 1988
*Tesserae*, 1993
*Selected Poetry*, 1993
*The Gazer's Spirit: Poems Speaking to Silent Works of Art*, 1995
*Figurehead, and Other Poems*, 1999

**Selected Criticism**
*Modern Poetry: Modern Essays in Criticism*, 1968
*Rhyme's Reason: A Guide to English Verse*, 1981
*Melodious Guile: Fictive Pattern in Poetic Language*, 1988
*The Work of Poetry*, 1997

**Other Writings:** play; edited collections of literature and criticism (*The Oxford Anthology of English Literature* [with others], 2 vols., 1973; *Poetics of Influence*, by Harold Bloom, 1988; *The Essential Rossetti*, 1990; *American Poetry: The Nineteenth Century*, 1994).

**Further Reading**

Auden, W.H., "Introduction," in *A Crackling of Thorns*, by John Hollander, New Haven, Connecticut: Yale University Press, 1958
Bloom, Harold, "The Sorrows of American-Jewish Poetry," *Commentary* 53 (March 1972)
Bloom, Harold, "The White Light of Trope: An Essay on John Hollander's 'Spectral Emanations,'" *Kenyon Review* 1, no. 1 (1979)
Davie, Donald, "Gift of the Gab," *The New York Review of Books* (2 October 1975)
Hammer, Langdon, "Working through Poems: An Interview with John Hollander," *Southwest Review* 80 (Autumn 1995)
Howard, Richard, "John Hollander," in *Alone with America: Essays on the Art of Poetry in the United States since 1950*, by Howard, New York: Atheneum, 1969; enlarged edition, 1980
Lehman, David, "The Sound and Sense of the Sleight-of-Hand Man," *Parnassus: Poetry in Review* 12 (Fall/Winter 1984)
McClatchy, J.D., "Speaking of Hollander," *The American Poetry Review* 11, no. 5 (September–October 1982)
Vendler, Helen, "A Quarter of Poetry," *The New York Times Book Review* (6 April 1975)
Wark, Wesley, "Interview with John Hollander," *Queen's Quarterly* 100, no. 2 (Summer 1993)


## Kinneret

First published in a limited edition (1986), John Hollander's "Kinneret" next appeared in *Harp Lake* (1988) and then in *Selected Poetry* (1993). "Kinneret" gathers allusions to Plato's forms, ancient Rome's occupation of Galilee, the apostle Paul's distinction between the spirit and the letter, and Shakespeare's *Hamlet* into the singular *ekphrasis* that the poem's words and letters achieve. Hollander's concern with *ekphrastic* poetry finds critical expression in *The Gazer's Spirit* (1995). An *ekphrastic* poem imitates a plastic aesthetic object, usually a painting, by capturing the object's spatial form and visual qualities in the temporal, nonvisual medium of language. A peak achievement is to paint an image with words that fuses movement over time with stillness in space (Krieger, 1967).

A poem that emblematizes itself is also *ekphrastic:* "The poem as emblem, under the *ekphrastic* principle, seeks to create itself as its own object" (Krieger, 1991 [emphasis added]). Such a poem refers to the world by referring to itself. "'*Poems get to be about the world by being about how to talk about it*,'" Hollander argues: "Poetry is a use of language in which language is opaque rather than transparent, and in which what is being said about the world immediately becomes part of the world as it comes to be uttered" (Hollander, 1998 [emphasis in the original]). "Kinneret" attempts an *ekphrasis* of itself as an artwork struggling to refer to its own being in the world.

The poem is named after Kinneret, the harp-shaped lake that the Christian gospels refer to as the Sea of Galilee. The lake's name may derive from the Hebrew word *kinnôr* (harp). Building on this confluence of phenomenal contour, linguistic derivation, and musical association, Hollander weaves the poem's verbal medium into a visual form: "Kinneret," the harp that musically paints an image of the "lake-shaped instrument" that the poem would be.

An aspiring verbal icon, the poem marks its closure's limits even as it celebrates *ekphrastic* moments. The poem's words and images fuse together and break apart. The relationship between language and vision is a fluid interplay between the limpid reflection of one in the other and the sharp disjoining of the two: "I harp on the two flowing themes of still / Water and jagged disconnectedness." The poem desires the "jagged disconnectedness" to flow smoothly together with the "still / Water." However, the poem's ambition to unify opposites (e.g., the "flowing" and the "still") yields to its playful creation and evasion of form and meaning.

This play inheres in the poem's quatrains. Each quatrain's unity resides in a disjunction. Hollander notes that he borrowed the "disjunct form" of the quatrains "from the Malay *pantun*." In *pantun*s, the first and third and the second and fourth lines rhyme. The first two lines form a sentence, as do the last two, but the sentences seem unrelated. They are "superficially connected" by the rhyme scheme and by "some common construction, scheme, pun, assonance," or other surface feature. "Below the surface," the sentences are connected "by some puzzlingly deeper parable." Hollander gives us a "self-descriptive example":

"Catamaran"

Pantuns in the original Malay
Are quatrains of two thoughts, but of one mind.
Athwart these two pontoons I sail away,
Yet touching neither; land lies far behind.

Reading "Kinneret" is like sailing a series of catamarans out onto the "lake-shaped instrument" that the poem is. The reader pilots each quatrain, clinging to neither of its two thoughts but supported by each, so as to fathom the "deeper parable" connecting them. One of the poem's deeper parables concerns theological and philosophical anxieties about letters and poetry.

Hollander relates the marriage of language and sense to a theological question: are letters agents of death or life? Paul insists that "the letter kills, but the Spirit gives life" and that the Mosaic law is a "ministry of death, chiseled in letters on stone tablets" (2 Corinthians 3:6–7, New Revised Standard Version). Hollander animates the letters that Paul voids of life:

The wind was working on the laughing waves,
Washing a shore that was not wholly land.
I give life to dead letters: from their graves
Come leaping even X and ampersand.

Like God's generative spirit moving over the waters, Hollander's "wind" works the "waves" into "laughing" existence. As God's breath animates the clay that becomes Adam, so the poet breathes "life" into "dead letters." "[L]eaping" to life from its Pauline grave, "X" dismantles the opposition between spirit and letter.

Besides Paul's abjection of graven letters, Hollander also disputes Plato's devaluation of poetry in favor of the rational cognition of universal forms. For the poet, sunlight becomes, if not an enemy, at least an antagonist: "In bright, chaste sunlight only forms are seen." Such Platonic sunlight reveals a universal form behind particulars, an abstract idea that underlies variety. This light is "chaste," that is, free of the idiomatic qualities of any given language. The phonic and graphic particulars of a language are poetry's prime resource. For example, English allows poets to alliterate the letter "g" to evoke an idiomatic hue: "Only in English does the grass grow green." Neither a Platonic form nor such a form's sensory embodiment controls this alliteration's meaning. Hollander challenges the notion that words, say, green, *grün,* and *verde,* are semantically unified by an idea, be it a Platonic form or a Lockean sensation. Instead, "Kinneret" asserts, "Off-color language gives the world its hue."

To reflect the sun's light is no achievement: "The merest puddle by the lowest hill / Answers the flashing sunlight none the less." However, when the sun departs, the theme of "still / Water" reaches its apotheosis: "The sun is blind now; only the stars awake / To see the whole world mirrored in the sea." And the moon, not the sun, has brought an exalted moment to the poem's speaker: "This miracle the moonlight once gave me: / The sky lay still; the broad water walked on." The "sky" was "still," but the "water" mirroring it "walked on." This shimmering unity of stillness and movement defines the "surfaces" the "mind's eye . . . turned" to when it "wearied" of its "distrust" of appearances. These are the singular *ekphrastic* "surfaces" that Hollander's poem gives us to contemplate as we wrestle with the complex "parable[s]" that lurk beneath.

ROBERT S. OVENTILE

**Further Reading**

Hollander, John, *The Gazer's Spirit: Poems Speaking to Silent Works of Art,* Chicago: University of Chicago Press, 1995

Hollander, John, *The Poetry of Everyday Life,* Ann Arbor: University of Michigan Press, 1998

Krieger, Murray, "The Ekphrastic Principle and the Still Movement of Poetry; or *Laokoön* Revisited," in *The Play and Place of Criticism,* by Krieger, Baltimore, Maryland: Johns Hopkins University Press, 1967

Krieger, Murray, *Ekphrasis: The Illusion of the Natural Sign,* Baltimore, Maryland: Johns Hopkins University Press, 1991

Yenser, Stephen, "Bright Sources," *Yale Review* 77, no. 1 (1987)

---

# Bob Holman 1948–

From his early work with live performance to his later work with emergent technologies, Bob Holman has been a central figure in contemporary American poetry and played an integral role in the renaissance of performance poetry. A self-described poetry activist, he introduced the "poetry slam" to New York audiences and has been a multimedia pioneer of the movement to bring poetry into mainstream culture through video, television, and the Internet. Holman has published six collections and made numerous audio and video recordings of poetry. His works include *Bicentennial Suicide* (1976), a novel for performance that he co-authored with Bob Rosenthal, *Tear to Open* (1979), *8 Chinese Poems* (1980), *Sweat and Sex and Politics* (1984), *Cupid's Cashbox* (1985), and *Panic*DJ!* (1988). In 1994 he co-edited *Aloud: Voices from the Nuyorican Poets Café* with Miguel Algarín. Holman's collected works, *The Collect Call of the Wild,* appeared in 1995.

Since performing his own poetry in New York's East Village in the late 1960s, Holman has devoted his career to reclaiming poetry as a performed art. A long-time New Yorker, Holman was active in the 1970s and 1980s with the Poets' Theater Workshop, where he directed productions of Tristan Tzara's *The Gas Heart* and Antonin Artaud's *Jet of Blood,* as well as with St. Mark's

Poetry Project, where he ran the Monday night reading series for three years and later served as project coordinator with Bernadette Mayer. In 1985 Holman began hosting a live performance series called The Double Talk Show with Pedro Pietri, his co-host for the Poets in the Bars series as well. Holman's own *Panic*DJ!*, a rap-poetry performance series, ran from 1980 to 1990 and culminated in a film collaboration with Carl Teitelbaum. Holman is most well known, however, as emcee of the Friday Night Poetry Slam at the Nuyorican Poets Café, a position he held from 1989 to 1996.

In all his poems and performances Holman references a diverse range of influences, from Dada and Surrealism to popular musical and vernacular forms. In "Rock 'n' Roll Mythology" Holman synthesizes rock music, televangelism, and vaudeville, constructing a hybrid poetic language. "57 Gazillion Lung-Tongue Varieties," included in *The Collect Call of the Wild*, shows the influence of the hip-hop aesthetic with its "samples" from Marx, Whitman, Ezra Pound, slam poet Emily XYZ, and William Carlos Williams. This poem, like Holman's other work, attempts to reclaim poetry as a culturally and politically relevant art form for audiences beyond the academy by linking poetry and national identity:

Hey US!
Get up!
Stand up!
Pay up
The Bill of Writes!

Hey, Poets!
Time to fill up
Swirling Void Hole
At empty center
Of National Consciousness Doughnut!

Our Whole's got a hole in it!
From which Soul of the Nation is leaking—

Hey, US!
It's time to Re-soul!

Poets of the World, re-write!
Rewrite History as
57 Gazillion

Lung-Tongue

Varieties

One of the first poets to experiment with poetry and video, from 1987 to 1994 Holman produced *Poetry Spots* for New York public television, for which he won several awards. Modeled after music videos, *Poetry Spots* used short segments of fresh new voices to bring poetry back into the cultural mainstream. Holman also co-produced "Words in Your Face," a half-hour program of poetry videos, for Twin Cities Public Television's *Alive TV* series (1991). "Words in Your Face" was so popular that it was rebroadcast as part of the series' tenth-anniversary special in 1994.

*The United States of Poetry* (1995) continues Holman's history of collaborative multimedia poetics. Produced by Washington Square Films, the video-production company Holman founded with Josh Blum, this encyclopedic poetry-video series first aired on PBS affiliates around the nation in February 1995. The series follows up on "Words in Your Face" and like its precursor reclaims poetry as a lively, culturally relevant art form. It synthesizes performances by contemporary poets with a music-video aesthetic and captures the vitality of live performance events such as the open-mike night or the poetry slam. *The United States of Poetry* articulates a new hybrid poetic form, one that references a diverse range of expressive cultures, from street poetry and rap to radical Modernism, the Beats, and the historical avant-garde.

*The United States of Poetry* replaces the local poetry venue with the shared cultural space of television. The product of a 13,500-mile journey across the nation, this two-and-a-half-hour series reflects Holman's Whitmanesque poetic vision. Holman and his co-producer bring together 68 poets from diverse geographical regions, age groups, and ethnicities to reconstruct the body politic. One of the driving forces behind this poetry video project was Holman's desire to document an American poetic tradition. The other was to use the medium of television to introduce a wide range of poets and poetic styles to a large, geographically and economically diverse audience.

From 1996 to 1999 Holman served as executive producer of the now-defunct Mouth Almighty Records/Mercury, the first spoken-word subsidiary of a major recording label. His own poetry CD, *In with the Out Crowd*, was released in 1998.

Holman and Marjory Snyder co-author weekly columns on contemporary poetry for the About.com website. Holman is currently working on *The World of Poetry*, an interactive poetry website, with Josh Blum.

Julie M. Schmid

*See also* Performance Poetry

**Biography**

Born in LaFollette, Tennessee, 10 March 1948; director of readings, St. Mark's Poetry Project, 1977–84; producer, *Poetry Spots* (PBS), 1987–94; director of poetry slams, Nuyorican Poets Café, New York City, 1989–96; co-producer, "Words in Your Face" (PBS), 1991; co-producer, *Rap Meets Poetry* series (MTV), 1993–; producer, *Mouth Almighty* and *The United States of Poetry* (PBS), 1995; Visiting Professor, Bard College, Annandale-on-Hudson, New York, 1998–. Received New York Foundation for the Arts fellowship, 1993, 2001; National Endowment for the Arts grant, 1994, 1997; New York State Council on the Arts grant, 1994, 1997; Lannan Foundation grant, 1994; Emmy Award, 1997, 1998; Bessie for Performance Excellence, 1993. Living in New York City.

**Poetry**

*Tear to Open: This This This This This This*, 1979
*8 Chinese Poems*, 1980
*Sweat and Sex and Politics*, 1984
*Cupid's Cashbox*, 1985
*Panic*DJ!* 1988
*The Collect Call of the Wild*, 1995

**Other Writings:** biographies (*Good Old George: The Life of George Lansbury*, 1990), novels (*Bicentennial Suicide: A Novel to Be Performed* [with Bob Rosenthal], 1976); edited anthologies of poetry (*Aloud: Voices from the Nuyorican Poets Café* [with Miguel Algarín], 1994).

**Further Reading**

Beach, Christopher, *Poetic Culture,* Evanston, Illinois: Northwestern University Press, 1999
Damon, Maria, "Was That 'Different,' 'Dissident,' or 'Dissonant'? Poetry (n) the Public Spear: Slams, Open Readings, and Dissident Traditions," in *Close Listening: Poetry and the Performed Word,* edited by Charles Bernstein, Oxford and New York: Oxford University Press, 1998
Foster, Edward Halsey, "Bob Holman, Performance Poetry, and the Nuyorican Poets Café," *Multicultural Review* 2, no. 2 (1993)
Gates, Henry Louis, Jr., "Sudden Def," *The New Yorker* 71 (19 June 1995)

---

# Fanny Howe 1940–

Working from the American Transcendental tradition that she perceives through the political and cultural turmoil of the 1950s and 1960s, Fanny Howe is unique in contemporary poetry for her exploration of religious faith, politics, and suffering. Howe renders the way these themes unpredictably strengthen and complicate one another with a seriousness that rejects what she describes as "the prettiness of the reports coming in from a poetry that is the equivalent of an I.Q. test" (Howe, 1996). With a detached yet tender voice that carries her precise and grim perceptions, Howe's contemplative style recalls the melancholic voice and harsh vision of T.S. Eliot's "Preludes."

Howe is prolific in both poetry and fiction, and her work in both these genres allows her to draw from their structures of meaning and play them off each other, helping to sustain thematic coherence within her often-fractured poetic narratives of religious experience. *The Quietest* (1992) is an example of Howe's use of an extended form that vacillates between poetry and narrative in order to enact the vicissitudes of religious experience. The prose pieces control through narration and visualization: "of the two souls which occupy the person in a sort of figure eight, the upper one looked back to the lower one." The poetry serves to break up coherent images and express desires for the ecstatic. A theme in many of Howe's poems, the idea that composing poetry allows for and is analogous to religious dedication, lies within the logic of the following lines:

Mad God, mad thought.
Take me for a walk.
Stalk me. Made God.
Wake me talking.
Believe in what I made.

Howe's work has not always represented religious desire so directly, but an early novel, the eerie *Forty Whacks* (1969), represents the desire to submit to authority, and writing about daily life—its constant movement between the quotidian and the profound—best expresses the details of that submission. The main character in *Forty Whacks* is a young woman writing in a journal that she sends to her analyst. Her journal chronicles her new life creating and destroying an oedipal triangle that imitates the family she fled. As with many of Howe's characters and voices, the narrator is victim and perpetrator simultaneously, her fallibility obvious but not easily condemned. Her story ends violently, but the violence is veiled. Howe delves into the violence of the familial and domestic but does not represent it graphically or gratuitously; yet she does not avoid allowing her language to suggest the brute effects of violence, as the title *Forty Whacks* attests.

Howe's first book of poetry, *Eggs* (1970), contains tightly crafted and acerbic poems that deal primarily with unrequited love. Religion is just one small part of this volume's tough constellation, but *Eggs* does reveal an important tendency in Howe's work: representing spiritual submission with vivid imagery. In the poem "Afterword," Howe tinges a particularly visual image with a sarcasm aimed at the ego's use of religion: "I made an angel of myself / and hung from an icicle / choking." In *The Amerindian Coastline Poem* (1975), Howe's previous forms—precise and tight—open to encounter the space of the page, the voices of others, and the densely metaphoric images of the ocean's shore. This book enacts a struggle between Howe's ability to render thought as it moves through spiritual questions with sharp visual imagery and a need to avoid grounding poetic experience in a physical actuality that is recognizable as this world: "Here then is / my article of faith in the void / I want to / be good without thinking I am good / to clear the sky of rocks or be one." In *For Erato: The Meaning of Life* (1984), a book composed of philosophical and religious aphorisms that distill a voice of vulnerability, Howe suggests an agency beyond the individual by personifying natural elements and representing their movement as a desire for expression. The colors of the sky "dripped to the East, the name for one span of nowhere, as if they too wanted to speak in the dark."

As Howe's poetry developed, expressions from a discernible persona became rare—a choice that she links to both craft and content. In her "Artobiography" (1985), Howe states that she "want[s] to abolish the personal, or hurl it to the furthest point; and polish the impersonal, until its dazzle unfocuses complete clarity, as with everything good." In *Introduction to the World* (1986), an experiment with a disciplined format and time span, Howe highlights language as her subject, allowing her to destabilize a simple link between herself and the world. In the afterthoughts of this volume, Howe acknowledges the presence of others within the language that worked through her: "I was at no time the only one writing these poems, for the taking of the language from outside heralded a further loss of myself." In "Close Up," the poem that opens *The End* (1992), Howe continues to destabilize the integral presence of the writer by contemplating the phantasm of herself and her reflection, both composed with an inspired idea of writing: "The woman's face on the other side of this pane— / Paper or fate? / Written in light, in either case." This loss of the self, this negation of an essentialized identity that occurs when the poet highlights language's exteriority, has political dimensions for Howe, allowing her to imaginatively become the victims of the brutal political landscape she perceives. She is interested less in public politics than in individuals who helplessly absorb, distort, and inflict on themselves the brute power of the outside world. In the poems that comprise *(Sic)* (1988), Howe writes in the voice of an impoverished woman in prison, articulating her reflections on the tragic inevitability of her life, its imprisoning and mutually reinforcing perceptions and actualities: "I couldn't look through the window of the television, I would break my fingers on the stones."

In many of Howe's poems, but particularly in her collection *Robeson Street* (1985), she renders a grim urban milieu that harkens back to Robert Lowell's cynical representations of Boston in *Life Studies* (1959) and *For the Union Dead* (1964). However, while *Robeson Street* is a portrait of capitalism insinuating its injustices wherever she looks, it is also interspersed with unsentimental images of children and the questions of meaning and the demands for hope that they inspire. Howe's latest book-length works, *O'Clock* (1995) and *Forged* (1999), continually stitch demands for hope and desires for meaning to the landscape; these poems manage to be incessantly shaped and polished but still convey a passionate attentiveness to the ragged texture of the everyday. Of Gerard Manley Hopkins' words, Howe writes, "They aim for a heightened place—paradise" (Howe, 1984). The spiritual suffering in these books by Howe refuses to settle in metaphysical abstraction or the material world, so Howe renders moments of redemption in her words' restlessly hopeful aims.

KIMBERLY LAMM

**Biography**

Born in Buffalo, New York, 15 October 1940. The daughter of playwright and actress Mary Manning and law professor Mark DeWolfe Howe, and sister of the poet Susan Howe. Attended Stanford University, Palo Alto, California, 1958–62; lecturer, Tufts University, Medford, Massachusetts, 1968–72; Poetry-in-the-Schools program, Massachusetts, 1973; lecturer, Emerson College, Boston, Massachusetts, 1973–74; lecturer, Columbia University, New York City, 1974–77; visiting writer, Massachusetts Institute of Technology, Cambridge, 1978–87; Professor of Writing and American Literature, University of California, San Diego, 1987–; associate director, University of California Study Center, London, England, 1993–95. Received McDowell Colony fellowship, 1965, 1990; National Endowment for the Arts grant, 1970, 1991; Bunting Institute fellowship, 1974; St. Botolph Award, 1976; Writers Choice Award, 1984; *Village Voice* Fiction Award, 1988. Living in San Diego, California.

**Poetry**

*Eggs,* 1970
*The Amerindian Coastline Poem,* 1975
*For Erato: The Meaning of Life,* 1984
*Robeson Street,* 1985
*Introduction to the World,* 1986
*The Lives of a Spirit,* 1987
*(Sic),* 1988
*The End: Poems,* 1992
*The Quietest,* 1992
*O'Clock,* 1995
*One Crossed Out,* 1997
*Forged,* 1999
*Selected Poems,* 2000

**Other Writings:** novels (*Forty Whacks,* 1969; *In the Middle of Nowhere,* 1984), short stories, juvenile novels (*The Blue Hills,* 1981).

**Further Reading**

Howe, Fanny, "The Ecstatic," *Ironwood* 12, no. 2 (1984)
Howe, Fanny, "Artobiography," in *Writing/Talks,* edited by Bob Perelman, Carbondale: Southern Illinois University Press, 1985
Howe, Fanny, "Weil Over Void," in *Primary Trouble: An Anthology of Contemporary Poetry,* edited by Leonard Schwartz, Joseph Donahue, and Edward Foster, Jersey City, New Jersey: Talisman House, 1996
Payne, Johnny, "Letters from Nowhere: Fanny Howe's *Forty Whacks* and Feminine Identity," in *Anxious Power: Reading, Writing, and Ambivalence in Narrative by Women,* edited by Carol J. Singley and Susan Elizabeth Sweeney, Albany: State University of New York Press, 1983
Vickery, Ann, "Finding Grace: Modernity and the Ineffable in the Poetry of Rae Armantrout and Fanny Howe," *Revista Canaria de Estudios Ingeles* 37 (November 1998)

---

## Susan Howe 1937–

Poet, critic and theorist, artist, and professor of English, Susan Howe was educated as a painter at the Boston Museum School of Fine Arts, receiving her diploma in 1961. Howe turned to writing in the 1970s, crafting, in her earliest works, a unique style and voice, as Marjorie Perloff (1990) observes: "she seems to have had no apprentice period during which she wrote derivatively 'in the style' of X or Y." Howe has published 14 books of poetry—including *The Liberties* (1980), for which she received an American Book Award—and four critical works, most notably *My Emily Dickinson* (1985) and *Pierce-Arrow* (1999), which have established her reputation as a scrupulous textual scholar and poetic theorist. Howe's audience reaches beyond the United States, as illustrated by the recent translation into French of *Melville's Marginalia* (1997). Although her texts often articulate principles central to language poetry (such as the indeterminate conditions of: linguistic reference, subjectivity, and the construction of gender), Howe's writing also affirms visionary experiences even in the absence of belief that pervades 20th-century American literary culture. These latter characteristics reveal her work's haunting singularity.

In the prologue to *The Europe of Trusts* (1990), Howe notes the extent to which world events from the late 1930s and early 1940s marked her childhood and later shaped her historical imagination:

> I became part of the ruin. . . . For me there was no silence before armies. . . . This is my historical consciousness. I have no choice in it. In my poetry, time and again, questions of assigning *the cause* of history dictate the sound of what is thought. . . . I wish I could tenderly lift from the dark side of history, voices that are anonymous, slighted—inarticulate.

Peter Quartermain (1992) sees Howe as a poet "burdened by history: The burden, of retrieving from erasure and marginality those (women) who have been written out." Howe's rigorously innovative poetry and poetics are consistently grounded in a cluster of topical interests—biography, historiography, linguistics, philosophy, and metaphysics—attesting to her wide reading and ongoing concern with the cultural work of experimental writing. "Her poetry," Paul Naylor (1999) reflects, "ranges across vast tracts of English, Irish, and American history in the service of a resolute investigation of the 'dark side' of colonialism and imperialism."

The difficulty of Howe's poetry has moved some critics to call her work "unreadable" and "sibylline." However, Linda Reinfeld (1992) affirms that "Susan Howe is no sophist. She writes not only in the name of the devil but in her own name as well: she believes in the power of her art and the power of her self." Howe's texts frequently employ any number of experimental techniques, such as fragmentary syntax, unacknowledged quotations and blocks of discourse (either of which may appear in altered states), photographic mirroring, structures of apposition, and erasure. Howe also juxtaposes those destabilizing strategies with more traditional poetic elements: eye rhyme, repetition, free verse, prose poetry, and stanza-like verse columns. These characteristics together create a poetics that demands the reader's active interpretation. Although Howe's poetry often verges on alienating her audience, such a risk turns on a greater wager—that of creating open literary systems that invite readers to discover the vivid otherness of both poetic language and the subjects with which Howe's texts engage.

Howe's writing may be described succinctly as a dialogue between drama, history, and painting—a perspective that emphasizes the combined influences of: her mother, Mary Manning Howe (who wrote plays and had been an actress on the Dublin stage); her father, Mark DeWolfe Howe (who was a professor of law at Harvard University with a keen interest in American colonial history); and Howe's own study of both acting (in Dublin after finishing high school) and painting (at the Boston Museum School of Fine Arts). Howe frequently begins a composition by working with fragments of discourse (i.e., biographical or historical anecdotes, literary puzzles, or cultural mythologies) and then shaping those discontinuous narrative elements into a canvass, or field, of questioning and answering, always critically attentive to the role of language as a mediator of human experience.

In *Hinge Picture* (1974), for example, Howe imagines a primordial writer who endures great anxieties over the origin of language because of the weight of history that such a beginning involves. *Secret History of the Dividing Line* (1978) similarly engages with notions of the emergence of language and human consciousness, the "dividing line" serving as a trope for that which separates language, nature, and culture. *The Liberties* (1980) investigates the linguistic construction of feminine identity through the story of Hester Johnson, or "Stella," and Rebecca Dingley, both of whom Swift encouraged to move to Ireland to become his lifelong companions. *Defenestration of Prague* (1983), arguably Howe's most complex text, works within and against a single historical event from 1617—when Calvinist rebels threw Catholic officials from windows in Prague, thereby instigating the Thirty Years' War—which Howe juxtaposes against religious and political conflicts in Ireland. *Articulation of Sound Forms in Time* (1987) examines the strange tale of Hope Atherton, first minister of Hatfield, Connecticut, who was lost during the aftermath of the Turner's Falls massacre in 1676 only to return to his congregation and perish as a social outcast because of his unbelievable survival experience with native tribes.

Poets and philosophers who have strongly informed Howe's writing include, among many others, Beckett, Derrida, Dickinson, H.D., Melville, Milton, Moore, Olson, Shakespeare, and Williams. Although shaped by metaphysical, symbolist, existential, avant-garde, and poststructuralist traditions, Howe's texts evade ready classification because her work engages vigilantly, from one poem to another, with the particularities of the different subjects within and against which she writes. In a *Talisman* interview (1990), Howe compares her poetry and poetics to the algebraic theory of "singularity," or, as she summarizes, "the point chaos enters cosmos, the instant articulation . . . [when] there is a leap into something else." In fine, such leaps distinguish the aporetic and finite matter of language—the enabling conditions of Howe's exuberance.

W. Scott Howard

**Biography**

Born in Boston, Massachusetts, 10 June 1937. Attended Museum School of Fine Arts, Boston, B.F.A. in painting 1961; Butler Fellow in English, 1988, and since 1989 Professor of English, State University of New York, Buffalo; Visiting Scholar and Professor of English, Temple University, Philadelphia, Pennsylvania, spring 1990; Distinguished Fellow, Stanford Institute of the Humanities, winter 1998. Received Before Columbus Foundation Award, 1980; American Book Award, 1981; New York State Council of the Arts residency, 1986; Pushcart Prize, 1987; New York City Fund for Poetry grant, 1988; Guggenheim fellowship, 1996; Chancellor, Academy of American Poets, 2000. Living in Buffalo, New York.

**Poetry**

*Hinge Picture,* 1974
*The Western Borders,* 1976
*Secret History of the Dividing Line,* 1978
*Cabbage Gardens,* 1979
*The Liberties,* 1980
*Pythagorean Silence,* 1982

*Defenestration of Prague,* 1983
*Articulation of Sound Forms in Time,* 1987
*A Bibliography of the King's Book; or, Eikon Basilike,* 1989
*The Europe of Trusts: Selected Poems,* 1990
*Singularities,* 1990
*The Nonconformist's Memorial,* 1993
*Frame Structures: Early Poems, 1974–1979,* 1996
*Melville's Marginalia,* 1997

**Selected Criticism**

*My Emily Dickinson,* 1985
*The Birth-Mark: Unsettling the Wilderness in American Literary History,* 1993
*Pierce-Arrow,* 1999

**Further Reading**

*The Difficulties* 3, no. 2 (1989) (special issue on Howe edited by Tom Beckett)

DuPlessis, Rachel Blau, "'WHOWE': On Susan Howe," in *The Pink Guitar: Writing as Feminist Practice,* by DuPlessis, New York and London: Routledge, 1990

Howard, W. Scott, "'Writing Ghost Writing': A Discursive Poetics of History; or, Howe's 'Hau' in Susan Howe's 'A Bibliography of the King's Book; or, Eikon Basilike,'" *Talisman* 14 (1995)

Naylor, Paul, "Susan Howe: Where Are We Now in Poetry?" in *Poetic Investigations: Singing the Holes in History,* by Naylor, Evanston, Illinois: Northwestern University Press, 1999

O'Brien, Geoffrey, "Voyage of Reconnaissance: Susan Howe," in *Bardic Deadlines: Reviewing Poetry, 1984–95,* by O'Brien, Ann Arbor: University of Michigan Press, 1998

Perloff, Marjorie, "'Collision or Collusion with History': Susan Howe's 'Articulation of Sound Forms in Time,'" in *Poetic License: Essays on Modernist and Postmodernist Lyric,* by Perloff, Evanston, Illinois: Northwestern University Press, 1990

Quartermain, Peter, "And the Without: An Interpretive Essay on Susan Howe," in *Disjunctive Poetics: From Gertrude Stein and Louis Zukofsky to Susan Howe,* by Quartermain, Cambridge and New York: Cambridge University Press, 1992

Reinfeld, Linda, "Susan Howe: Prisms," in *Language Poetry: Writing as Rescue,* by Reinfeld, Baton Rouge: Louisiana State University Press, 1992

"Susan Howe," in *Electronic Poetry Center,* State University of New York, Buffalo, website (*www.wings.buffalo.edu/epc/*)

*Talisman* 4 (1990) (special issue on Howe edited by Edward Foster)

## Pythagorean Silence

*Pythagorean Silence* was first published in 1982 as a special supplement of *Montemora,* and its blending of scholarly critique and innovative poetic form clearly marked Susan Howe as a dominant poet in contemporary literature. The poem was reprinted in 1990 as part of *The Europe of Trusts* with an added preface titled "THERE ARE NOT LEAVES ENOUGH TO CROWN TO COVER TO CROWN," wherein Howe states that her poetry is driven by a desire "to break out into perfect primeval consent. I wish I could tenderly lift from the dark side of history, voices that are anonymous, slighted—inarticulate." Marjorie Perloff characterizes Howe's poetics as the merging of poetry and ethics—a "poethics" of history, textuality, and culture. Yet her poetry is not merely historical or scholarly in scope: in addition to the voices of history, her poetry is haunted by voices from Howe's life and her family. Poetry for Howe is both an extended analysis of a particular cultural moment and an explication of how her subjectivity intersects with that event; her poetry filters the historical through the personal and vice versa.

The historical focus of *Pythagorean Silence* is World War II and especially the effect of war on Howe, her mother, and the culture at large. The centerpiece for *Pythagorean Silence* is the bombing of Pearl Harbor, which had personal repercussions for Howe since it prompted her father, the prominent legal historian and scholar Mark DeWolfe Howe, to enlist in the United States Army. Subsequently, in the poem, the images of war are juxtaposed with Howe's memories as she examines the effect of war on cultural and personal consciousness. As Howe writes,

> From 1939 until 1946 in news photographs, day after day I saw signs of culture exploding into murder. Shots of children being herded into trucks by hideous helmeted conquerors—shots of children who were orphaned and lost—shots of the emaciated bodies of Jews dumped into mass graves on top of more emaciated bodies—nameless numberless men women and children, uprooted in a world almost demented.

The central motif is loss, and the poem searches for "survivors" and lost voices lurking in a tapestry of textual, cultural, and historical points of reference. "Voices I am following," Howe explains, "lead me to the margins" (*The Birth-Mark,* 1993). The mode is elegiac and follows any discovered evidence of the marginalized and lost: "My mind's eye elegaic Meditation / embracing something / some history of Materialism." The search is textual, and the poem pursues passages as they open:

> a sentence or character
> suddenly
>
> steps out to seek for truth fails
> falls
>
> into a stream of ink Sequence
> trails off

Any sentence or character is worthy of deep and sustained rumination since it marks some human voice.

The various facets of loss are presented as silence, absence, deprivation, violence, war, mystery, poverty, and truth throughout the three sections of *Pythagorean Silence*—"Pearl Harbor," "Pythagorean Silence," and an untitled third section. Moreover, each section includes literary, historical, and philosophical figures that amplify specific characteristics of loss. "Pearl Harbor," the first section of the book, employs the biblical figures of Herod who "had all of the little children murdered!" and "Rachel weeping for her children" to signify the dimensions of grief and murder in war. The dominant tone of "Pearl Harbor" is grief—the "cry [that] / silences / whole / vocabularies / of *names* / for / *things.*" That cry gestures to Rachel as well as to Howe and her mother and signifies the collective loss of their children/father/husband. The poetic technique of the poem creates a palimpsest of the literary, historical, and personal that details grief and how that grief obliterates language and signifies loss and silence.

The second section of the book, "Pythagorean Silence," is presented in 17 parts that revolve around the figure of the mathematical philosopher and mystic Pythagoras. Since Pythagoras did not preserve his ideas in writing, his "voice" (or its "silence") raises the question of authenticity and certainty. The gap of certainty, the silent abyss of cultural and personal memory, is central to the section, and the poem asks, "How far / back through Memory does memory / extend a gap / in knowledge before all people / tell / historical past the historical / truth." The poem thereby questions the possibility of ascertaining the truth and includes mathematical philosophers—Pythagoras, Anaximander, Plato, and Sir Issac Newton, all of whom pursue truth and divine order in numbers, measures, and forms—as examples of the human urge to extract the "truth" from silence. Juxtaposed against this philosophical questioning is the figure of Penelope, who (like Rachel in the first section) mirrors Howe's mother waiting for her husband to return from war:

> We hear her walking in her room
> moving through measured
>
> velocity
> Passing away according to restless
>
> necessity
>
> Irascible unknowably disorderly
> irrational
>
> Poverty my mother and Possession
>
> my father
> Time to set our face homeward
>
> shadow-emperor

Pythagoras' ordered universe is contrasted with her mother's "measured" steps, which represent uncertainty, poverty, and the irrational, all of which are extensions of her mother's love. The obliteration of language by grief in "Pearl Harbor" becomes the mark of love in the second section, and silence and loss achieve a deeper human tone in the poem. While the focus sifts through a range of cultural referents, the gravitational pull is toward an explication of the personal and the "shadow" of its truth. The scholarly machinations of *Pythagorean Silence* ultimately interrogate the issues of memory, personal history, subjectivity, and love. Howe writes that her poetry searches "for some trace of love's infolding through all the paper in all the libraries I come to" (*The Birth-Mark*).

The final, untitled section presents ideas and events from the prior two in an impressionistic pastiche of words that are loaded with connotations. The effect reinforces the central themes of memory, loss, and silence as words drift from the anchor of their referents. The elliptical form mirrors the slippage of meaning and truth as each word offers a trace of meanings that elide certainty. For example, the line "timid satyr vesper winnow" does not follow the sequence of the sentence and suggests, rather, a loose affiliation that is connotative, open, and, for Howe, the embodiment of the poetic. The form and the content of the section and the poem as a whole emphasize writing as process, thereby depicting the act of poetry as engaging a field of meanings—what the poet Charles Olson called "composition by field." In *Pythagorean Silence* and its scholarly, linguistic, and musical form, that poetic field is framed by the bombing of Pearl Harbor and the concomitant issues of memory, language, childhood, philosophy, loss, love, history, and war. *Pythagorean Silence* is an important book because it reveals a way of thinking through philosophy and history without abandoning the human and the poetic. By refusing to bracket off meaning and impose closure, the poem remains ethical in that the voices are free from censure and vibrantly alive.

David Clippinger

**Further Reading**


Butterick, George F., "The Mysterious Vision of Susan Howe," *North Dakota Quarterly* 55, no. 4 (1987)

Ma, Ming-qian, "Articulating the Inarticulate: Singularities and the Counter-Method in Susan Howe," *Contemporary Literature* 36, no. 3 (1987)

Ma, Ming-qian, "Poetry as History Revised: Susan Howe's 'Scattering as Behavior Toward Risk,'" *American Literary History* 6, no. 4 (1994)

Middleton, Peter, "On Ice: Julia Kristeva, Susan Howe and Avant-Garde Poetics," in *Contemporary Poetry Meets Modern Theory,* edited by Antony Easthope and John O. Thompson, Toronto: University of Toronto Press, and New York and London: Harvester Wheatsheaf, 1991

Nicholls, Peter, "Unsettling the Wilderness: Susan Howe and American History," *Contemporary Literature* 37, no. 4 (1996)

Perloff, Marjorie, "'Collision or Collusion with History': The Narrative Lyric of Susan Howe," *Contemporary Literature* 30, no. 4 (1989)

Quartermain, Peter, *Disjunctive Poetics: From Gertrude Stein and Louis Zukofsky to Susan Howe,* Cambridge and New York: Cambridge University Press, 1992

# Langston Hughes 1902–67

Langston Hughes is best known as the "poet laureate" of the Harlem Renaissance, an African-American literary movement that flourished in the 1920s. Hughes had a prolific career as a poet, publishing seven books of poetry, four pamphlets of poetry, and numerous miscellaneous poems. His reputation has been based largely on the poetry he published in the 1920s, although the poems he published after the Harlem Renaissance have increasingly received critical acclaim and demonstrate his range as a poet.

From the start of his career, Hughes prided himself on being a black poet whose inspiration came from the black "folk," that is, the working class and poor with whom he identified. His clearest definitive statement of principles is an essay he published in *The Nation* in 1926, titled "The Negro Artist and the Racial Mountain." In this essay, he argues that the cultural forms one employs as an artist or consumes as a spectator signify one's racial and class identification. He thus criticizes black poets such as Countee Cullen who scorned black folk culture in favor of "high" cultural forms to appease their desire to belong to the white bourgeoisie. Hughes proudly proclaims that his poetry is "racial in theme and treatment, derived from the life I know."

In his poetry Hughes adapted African expressive forms, such as spirituals, work songs, and the blues, because he believed they authentically express the ways that black people have experienced and resisted slavery, racial discrimination, and oppression. Moreover, he saw jazz as inherently oppositional to an oppressive, urbanized American society. He writes that jazz is the "eternal tom-tom beating in the Negro soul—the tom-tom of revolt against weariness in a white world, a world of subway trains and work, work, work" ("The Negro Artist and the Racial Mountain"). The black folk and their vernacular culture have a similar status for Hughes as did peasant life and culture for the Romantic Wordsworth: the folk are the repositories of vitality, truth, rebellion, and beauty in an otherwise dreary modern world characterized by repetitive, meaningless labor concentrated in urban centers.

Hughes powerfully illustrates these views in what critics have considered one of his major volumes of poetry, *The Weary Blues* (1926). *The Weary Blues* contains a number of poems written in blues and jazz forms, all of which depict black folk in a variety of humble occupations and pastimes. Included are poems about blues and jazz clubs, portraits of black prostitutes and virgins, love poems, urban laments, and lyric poems about being black and about black history. The title poem, one of Hughes' most popular, is a prime example of a poem "racial in theme and treatment." The poem tells of a blues pianist in a Harlem bar who, "Droning a drowsy syncopated tune," sings the "weary blues." The poem adapts the 12-bar blues form, particularly in its transcription of the blues singer's three phrases, the first two that repeat themselves and the third that completes the first two phrases. In this and other such poems, Hughes clearly challenged the prevalent "high" poetical forms of English verse, such as the sonnet, that Cullen so assiduously defended. Hughes declared that "popular" culture (in the sense of a "people's culture") is fit material for poetry. He thus participates in a progressive tradition of American vernacular poetry extending from Walt Whitman to Carl Sandburg, both major influences on Hughes.

Much of Hughes' poetry celebrates his African and African-American heritage. Early on in his career, he began writing poems that provided counterhistories to those of the dominant American culture that viewed Africa and Africans as uncivilized. In poems such as "The Negro Speaks of Rivers" (1921) and "Negro" (1922), Hughes writes of the monumental contributions of Africans and African-Americans to world culture. In "Negro," for example, he depicts a history of black enslavement yet shows how slavery and wage slavery have been the hidden secret of civilization. "I have been a worker," he affirms, "Under my hands the pyramids arose. / I made mortar for the Woolworth Building." Also noteworthy in these poems is that Hughes' personae express the voice of a collective black consciousness. In "The Negro Speaks of Rivers," he writes that he has "known rivers" of great significance in black history, such as the Euphrates, Nile, and Mississippi, and his "soul has grown deep like the rivers." In other words, Hughes' poetic self is transhistorical and transpersonal, a kind of Emersonian "Oversoul" that is one with African and African-American peoples.

However, Hughes' celebration of his African identity is not free from a strain of primitivism that runs through his early work as well as through much modern American poetry. The black folk retain an essential "primitive" identity whose origins lie in African agrarian cultures. Hence, employing the savage/civilized binary opposition endemic to the discourse of primitivism, Hughes equates civilization with a circus that cages black people who once lived freely in the "jungles" of Africa ("Lament for Dark People," 1924). In "Poem" (1925), Hughes, like Cullen, identifies a biological basis for his African identity since "the tom-toms of the jungles beat in [his] blood." This notion of an essential primitive African self also resonates with modern nationalist discourses that greatly influenced Hughes and other black writers: in opposition to the experience of urban alienation, Hughes posits the rebellious presence of a primitive self communally linked to others by "blood" and "soil." Indeed, in the last section of *The Weary Blues,* titled "Our Land," he expresses desire for an African homeland instead of "this land where life is cold." Hughes thus attempts to invert the values of a racist discourse that claimed that the "primitive" was inferior to the "civilized" while at the same time showing how the "primitive" creates "civilization."

In the past two decades, a number of major studies of Hughes' poetry from the 1930s have been published, significantly revising the established perception of Hughes as simply the poet laureate of the Harlem Renaissance. During the Great Depression, Hughes, like a number of writers and intellectuals, moved to the political Left and allied himself with the Communist Party of the United States. Outraged by the mass unemployment, the rise of Fascism, and continuing racism in the United States, Hughes expanded his long-standing sympathy for the black working class to include white workers and the international proletariat in general. During the 1930s, he wrote scores of poems that express his revolutionary hopes for an egalitarian society free from exploitation and discrimination of all kinds. In fact, his previous "race pride" is replaced by a "workers' pride." In an address he gave before the Second International Writers' Congress in 1937, he even argued for the end of racial categorization, which he viewed as a means for ruling classes to divide and conquer the working class, and claimed that he represented "the end of race." The spirit of Hughes' radical poetry is nicely embodied in a stanza from "One More 'S' in the U.S.A." (1934), a poem in which he calls for a

Soviet America: "But we can't join hands together / So long as whites are lynching black, / So black and white in one union fight / And get on the right track. / By Texas, or Georgia, or Alabama led / Come together, fellow workers / Black and white can all be red." Hughes' radical poetry displays a wider range of style, as he virtually abandons the blues lyric (which he viewed as no longer appropriate for his optimism and agitational goals) and writes in the colloquial voice of a second-generation urban worker.

Hughes' diversion from the principles he set forth in "The Negro Artist and the Racial Mountain" did not last long, however. During World War II, he continued to write poems against Fascism in Europe and in the United States (i.e., the segregated South), but his attention increasingly turned once again to black Americans and black expressive forms. As early as 1942, he published a volume of verse titled *Shakespeare in Harlem,* which, as he explains in a prefatory note, is "a book of light verse. Afro-Americana in the blues mode. Poems syncopated and variegated in the colors of Harlem, Beale Street, West Dallas, and Chicago's South Side." Yet, as *Shakespeare in Harlem* attests, Hughes' radicalization during the Depression years left its mark, since his postwar poems demonstrate a greater insight into the class issues that affect black Americans. His black protagonists and personae express more clearly their "blues" and their hopes in relation to the problems of unemployment and class exploitation. In "Out of Work," for example, Hughes' persona laments his class problems in blues form: "I walked the streets till / De shoes wore off my feet. / I done walked de streets till / De shoes wore off my feet. / Been lookin' for a job / So's that I could eat."

Another important facet of Hughes' aesthetic is its link to Modernism. Hughes' poetry had always been experimental, and he clearly modeled some of his poems on Modernist montage. Like other Modernists, he used montage to represent the modern experience of social fragmentation while simultaneously recomposing the image fragments in a meaningful way. One of his earliest montage poems, "Advertisement for the Waldorf-Astoria" (1931), published during the Great Depression, satirizes an ad published in *Vanity Fair* announcing the opening of the luxury New York hotel. Hughes juxtaposes fragments of the ad, such as "All the luxuries of private home" and "A lease, if you prefer, or an arrangement terminable at will," with images of homeless families who, at most, can "choose the Waldorf as a background for [their] rags." He also satirizes the ad by extending it to blacks in Harlem: "*Hallelujah! Undercover driveways! / Ma soul's a witness for de Waldorf-Astoria!*"

Not until the 1950s, however, did Hughes compose an entire volume of verse in montage form. *Montage of a Dream Deferred* (1951) uses the bebop form of jazz, popular at the time and itself Modernist, to represent the problems and aspirations of the black community in Harlem. In his prefatory note to the volume, he writes that it, "like be-bop, is marked by conflicting changes, sudden nuances, sharp and impudent interjections, broken rhythms, and passages sometimes in the manner of the jam session, sometimes the popular song, punctuated by the riffs, runs, breaks, and distortions of the music of a community in transition." The volume contains verbal snapshots of life in Harlem, from the streets to the bars and the homes. It shows how Harlemites (and by implication all black Americans) are part of black community because of their shared experiences and their "dream deferred" of a decent life in America free from racism and class inequality. It is within the montage form of bebop that Hughes hopes to unite black Americans to struggle together for the realization of their dream. Hence, in a number of places throughout the poem, the poem's title and refrain are put in the form of a question whose answer spells unity: "Good morning, daddy! / Ain't you heard / The boogie-woogie rumble / Of a dream deferred?"

Hughes' last phase of writing converged with the Civil Rights movement and anti-colonial movements worldwide. He poetically engages the major events and issues of the day, such as increasing heroin use among urban black youth, political strategy for black liberation, the Vietnam War, mass demonstrations, police violence, and southern church bombings. Hughes' poetry from the 1960s also displays a greater sense of frustration and anger over America's treatment of people of color. In "The Backlash Blues" (1967), Hughes shows the interrelation of a number of these issues when he writes from the perspective of a black parent: "Mister Backlash, Mister Backlash, / Just who do you think I am? / Tell me, Mr. Backlash, / What do you think I am? / You raise my taxes, freeze my wages, / Send my son to Vietnam." The image of the "backlash" links the slaver's whip with contemporary enslavement, suggesting a lack of progress. The poem ends with a threat to white America: "What do you think I got to lose? / I'm gonna leave you, Mister Backlash, / Singing your mean old backlash blues. / *You're the one, / Yes, you're the one / Will have the blues.*" While Hughes stood for integration, here he voices the growing black nationalist sentiment that, should white America resist integration, blacks must form their own self-determined, self-sufficient communities.

As a multi-talented and complex poet whose work speaks to many different interests both within and outside academia, from Modernism to Civil Rights, Hughes is a major voice in 20th-century American poetry. To date, no other black American poet has garnered as much critical acclaim as Hughes, whose lifelong concern for social justice will continue to attract ever more readers of his poetry.

ANTHONY DAWAHARE

*See also* Harlem Renaissance

**Biography**

Born in Joplin, Missouri, 1 February 1902. Attended Columbia University, New York, 1921–22; Lincoln University, Pennsylvania (Witter Bynner Award, 1926), 1926–29, B.A. 1929; member of the Music and Writers war boards during World War II; English teacher in Mexico, 1920–21; seaman, 1923–24; busboy, Wardman Park Hotel, Washington, D.C., 1925; Madrid correspondent, Baltimore *Afro-American,* 1937; columnist ("Simple"), Chicago *Defender,* 1943–67, and New York *Post,* 1962–67; founded Harlem Suitcase Theatre, New York, 1938, New Negro Theatre, Los Angeles, 1939, and Skyloft Players, Chicago, 1941; Visiting Professor of creative writing, Atlanta University, 1947; poet-in-residence, University of Chicago Laboratory School, 1949. Received Harmon Gold Medal, 1931; Rosenwald fellowship, 1931, 1940; Guggenheim fellowship, 1935; American Academy grant, 1946; Anisfield-Wolf Award, 1953; Spingarn Medal, 1960; honorary Litt.D., Lincoln University, 1943, Howard University, Washington, D.C., 1963, and Western Reserve University, Cleveland, 1964; member, American Academy, 1961, and American Academy of Arts and Sciences. Died in New York City, 22 May 1967.

**Poetry**
*The Weary Blues,* 1926
*Fine Clothes to the Jew,* 1927
*Dear Lovely Death,* 1931
*The Negro Mother, and Other Dramatic Recitations,* 1931
*The Dream-Keeper, and Other Poems,* 1932
*Scottsboro Limited: Four Poems and a Play in Verse,* 1932
*A New Song,* 1938
*Shakespeare in Harlem,* 1942
*Jim Crow's Last Stand,* 1943
*Lament for Dark Peoples, and Other Poems,* edited by H. Driessen, 1944
*Fields of Wonder,* 1947
*One-Way Ticket,* 1949
*Montage of a Dream Deferred,* 1951
*Selected Poems,* 1959
*Ask Your Mama: 12 Moods for Jazz,* 1961
*The Panther and the Lash: Poems of Our Times,* 1967
*Don't You Turn Back* (for children), edited by Lee Bennett Hopkins, 1969
*Collected Poems of Langston Hughes,* 1994
*The Sweet and Sour Animal Book* (for children), 1994
*The Block: Poems* (for children), 1995
*Carol of the Brown King: Nativity Poems* (for children), 1998
*Langston Hughes: Poems,* edited by David Roessel, 1999

**Other Writings:** plays (*Five Plays,* includes *Mulatto, Soul Gone Home, Little Ham, Simply Heavenly, Tambourines to Glory,* edited by Webster Smalley, 1963), screenplay (*Way Down South* [with Clarence Muse], 1939), radio plays, fiction (*Simple's Uncle Sam,* 1965), children's literature, nonfiction (*Good Morning, Revolution: Uncollected Social Protest Writings,* edited by Faith Berry, 1973), autobiography (*The Big Sea: An Autobiography,* 1940), translations of Spanish literature (*Selected Poems of Gabriela Mistral,* 1957); edited collections of literature (*The Best Short Stories by Negro Writers: An Anthology from 1899 to the Present,* 1967).

**Further Reading**
Appiah, K.A., and Henry Louis Gates, Jr., editors, *Langston Hughes: Critical Perspectives, Past and Present,* New York: Amistad, 1993
Berry, Faith, *Langston Hughes, Before and Beyond Harlem,* Westport, Connecticut: Hill, 1983
Bloom, Harold, editor, *Langston Hughes,* New York: Chelsea House, 1988
Dawahare, Anthony, "Langston Hughes's Radical Poetry and the 'End of Race,'" *MELUS* 23, no. 3 (Fall 1998)
Mullen, Edward J., editor, *Critical Essays on Langston Hughes,* Boston: G.K. Hall, 1986
Rampersad, Arnold, *The Life of Langston Hughes,* 2 vols., Oxford and New York: Oxford University Press, 1988

## Montage of a Dream Deferred

When *Montage of a Dream Deferred* was published in 1951, Langston Hughes' reputation as the "Poet Laureate of the Negro Race" was firmly enshrined in the American imagination. However, despite his overwhelming success with other literary endeavors, including *The Weary Blues* (1926) and the long-running drama *Mulatto* (1935), the verse collection *Montage of a Dream Deferred* was rejected by his longtime publisher, Knopf. It was later published by Henry Holt, but to unenthusiastic reviews. *Montage of a Dream Deferred* is Hughes' experimental meditation on the changes that took place in Harlem during the Great Depression and World War II. Although the volume consists of 91 distinct poems, Hughes wanted the pieces to be read as a single unit. To capture the frustration and fragmentation in the lives of Harlem's residents, Hughes turned to the broken rhythms and improvisation of bebop. In so doing, Hughes merged the individualist impulse of Modernism with African-American literary tradition, thus creating an Afromodernist aesthetic.

In a prefatory note to the volume, Hughes explains the influences behind *Montage of a Dream Deferred:* "In terms of current Afro-American popular music and the sources from which it has progressed—jazz, ragtime, swing, blues, boogie-woogie, and be-bop—this poem on contemporary Harlem, like be-bop, is marked by conflicting changes, sudden nuances, sharp and impudent interjections, broken rhythms, and passages sometimes in the manner of the jam session, sometimes the popular song, punctuated by the riffs, runs, breaks, and distortions of the music of a community in transition." Bebop had emerged during the 1940s as a response to and rejection of the commercialization of jazz and thus promoted itself as a more rebellious musical expression. Hughes capitalized on the spirit of resistance engendered by bebop, writing *Montage of a Dream Deferred* as a rejection of American racism and inequality. The volume consists of dramatic monologues and dialogues of Harlem residents that, taken as a whole, capture the vibrancy and spirit of black life. Like bebop, *Montage* employs sudden changes in tone and mood (see, for example, the shift from sensual love in "Juke Box Love Song" to bald anger in "Ultimatum") as the multiple speakers respond to each other. Nevertheless, the voices also harmonize into one communal tenor.

Although the volume experiments with a mainstream Modernist poetic form, it is nonetheless marked by Hughes' sharp critique of the world around him. Hughes had long been well acquainted with the Harlem community, but the Harlem that he encountered in 1951 no longer resembled the Harlem of the 1920s, with its lively culture and its hopefulness about the future. "Dream Boogie," the first poem in the volume, brings to bear the potency of unrealized dreams: "Good morning, daddy! / Ain't you heard / The boogie-woogie rumble / Of a dream deferred?" Although thoroughly ensconced in the language of bebop, the message of unrealized hope is quite clear. The refrain "Ain't you heard?" resonates throughout the volume, and Hughes is careful to point out that even the wealthier Harlem residents are not free from hardship. "Lady's Boogie," in particular, addresses the ever-present specter of social inequality:

> See that lady
> Dressed so fine?
> She ain't got boogie-woogie
> on her mind—
>
> But if she was to listen
> I bet she'd hear,
> Way up in the treble
> The tingle of a tear.
>
> *Be-Bach!*

"Harlem," perhaps the most well-known poem from the collection, weaves together anger, poverty, and death and suggests that a dream deferred will "fester" or "crust and sugar over—or does it explode?"

*Montage of a Dream Deferred* captured the spirit of the times and stands as a testimony to Hughes' considerable talent and his love for Harlem. Although Arthur P. Davis argued in a 1951 review in the *Journal of Negro History* that a few of the poems are "protest pieces of a type definitely outmoded," the collection's insights into urban life still strike a chord with 21st-century readers.

MICHELLE L. TAYLOR

**Further Reading**

Hokanson, Robert O'Brien, "Jazzing It Up: The Be-Bop Aesthetic of Langston Hughes," *Mosaic* 31 (1998)

Peters, Erskine, "Rhythmic Manipulation and Instrument Simulation in *Montage of a Dream Deferred,*" *Literary Griot* 5 (1993)

Rampersad, Arnold, "Langston Hughes and Approaches to Modernism in the Harlem Renaissance," in *The Harlem Renaissance: Revaluations,* edited by Amritjit Singh, William S. Shriver, and Stanley Brodwin, New York and London: Garland, 1989

## The Negro Speaks of Rivers

Published in *The Crisis* in 1921, "The Negro Speaks of Rivers" was written when Langston Hughes was only 19 years old and is still one of Hughes' most recognizable poems. It expresses the inner thoughts of a young African-American on a journey to meet the unknown, using the motif of rivers to reflect upon the history of African-Americans and Hughes' own history. Its publication launched his career.

A train ride to visit his father in Mexico inspired the poem. In his autobiography *The Big Sea* (1940), Hughes describes how his thoughts about his father during the train ride evolved into "The Negro Speaks of Rivers":

> Now it was just sunset and we crossed the Mississippi, slowly, over a long bridge. I looked out of the window of the Pullman at the great muddy river flowing down toward the heart of the South, and I began to think what that river, the old Mississippi, had meant to the Negroes in the past—how to be sold down the river was the worst fate that could over take a slave in bondage. Then I remembered reading how Abraham Lincoln had made a trip down the Mississippi on a raft, and how he had seen slavery at its worst, and had decided within himself that it should be removed from American life. Then I began to think of other rivers in our past—the Congo, and the Niger, and the Nile in Africa—and the thought came to me: "I've known rivers," and I put it down on the back of an envelope I had in my pocket, and within the space of ten or fifteen minutes, as the train gathered speed in the dusk, I had written this poem.

In this seminal poem Hughes attempts to find his place in the world: within his immediate family, within the African-American community, within America, within the human family. For the speaker the image of the river functions as a trigger to the past. The particular rivers in the poem—the Euphrates, the Congo, the Nile, and the Mississippi—have a strong sense of history attached to them, which the poet evokes with visceral imagery: "I've known rivers ancient as the world and older than the flow of human blood in human veins." The image of blood also evokes questions of family and race, which were foremost on the mind of the young poet on the journey to meet his estranged father. In America the amount of black blood determined whether a person was classified as black or white; the light-complected Hughes often dealt with this question of color. His concerns may have intensified while going to visit his father, an African-American who relocated to Mexico because of his dislike of other African-Americans.

"The Negro Speaks of Rivers" also stands out as one of Hughes' finest because it attempts to validate the African and African-American presence in the world. Its emphasis on a sense of belonging is central to understanding the poem's meaning; the speaker appears to be attempting to find a connection to the world. The long rivers mentioned in the poem are major landmarks of the countries in which they are located, with the ability to sustain and nourish life; each functions as a major link in the life chain, providing a valuable resource for those who "build a hut" and "bathe" along its shores. The river's ability to assist with shelter and physical comforts while continuing to ebb and flow parallels the struggles of the African-American race.

The poem also contains the refrain, "My soul has grown deep like the rivers," a reference to W.E.B. DuBois, to whom the poem is dedicated. DuBois had explored the concept of the soul in *The Souls of Black Folk* (1903); Hughes draws on the idea that the soul can transcend time and space to allow the poem's speaker to relate to the heritage evoked by the rivers.

SANDRA MERRIWEATHER

**Further Reading**

Appiah, K.A., and Henry Louis Gates, Jr., editors, *Langston Hughes: Critical Perspectives, Past and Present,* New York: Amistad, 1993

Bloom, Harold, editor, *Langston Hughes,* New York: Chelsea House, 1988

Miller, R. Baxter, *The Art and Imagination of Langston Hughes,* Lexington: University Press of Kentucky, 1989

Rampersad, Arnold, "The Origins of Poetry in Langston Hughes," *Southern Review* 21, no. 3 (Summer 1985)

Sundquist, Eric J., "Who Was Langston Hughes?" *Commentary* 102, no. 6 (1996)

## The Weary Blues

*The Weary Blues* was Langston Hughes' first collection of poetry and established his reputation as one of the most notable poets of the period now known as the Harlem Renaissance. The volume includes a number of previously published poems, chief among them "The Negro Speaks of Rivers," which originally appeared in a 1921 issue of *The Crisis,* and the title poem, which won first prize in a 1925 *Opportunity* magazine literary contest. *The Weary Blues* is notable for its meditations on African-American music, race, and spirituality, all of which capture the complexities of African-American life during the 1920s.

The collection is separated into seven sections, and, as the title suggests, the blues aesthetic operates on a variety of levels throughout. Historically, blues music has functioned as a folk history of the African-American experience, telling of survival and transcendence in a hostile world. Hughes was very interested in the blues as both a musical and a literary form and was one of the first writers to incorporate it into his work. Hughes uses the blues as a structural device, insofar as the stanzas in "The Weary Blues" conform to the 8- and 12-bar patterns of many blues songs. More important, however, he uses the blues form to capture the struggle of African-Americans in the early 20th century. Such is the case in section one, also titled "The Weary Blues," which includes such blues-inflected poems as "The Weary Blues" and "Blues Fantasy."

"The Weary Blues" describes a blues musician during a performance:

> With his ebony hands on each ivory key
> He made that poor piano moan with melody.
> O Blues!
> Swaying to and fro on his rickety stool
> He played that sad raggedy tune like a musical fool.
> Sweet Blues!
> Coming from a black man's soul.

Although the musician is weary, the power of the performance nevertheless affords him a sense of redemption, as evidenced by the refrains "O Blues!" and "Sweet Blues!" His performance gives expression to the experience of African-Americans in a white world, as indicated by his "ebony hands on each ivory key." However, despite the melancholy, the poem ultimately suggests that the blues is just as much an expression of joy as it is of sorrow.

Hughes was very much concerned with the relationship between poetry and race. While section two, "Dream Variations," explores the possibility of escaping racial tension through a return to nature, section three, "The Negro Speaks of Rivers," deals explicitly with racial protest. The poem "The Negro Speaks of Rivers" conjures memories of the African past and the horrors of slavery but ultimately suggests that African-Americans will transcend racial injustice by asserting their pride in a shared racial heritage. "The Cross" explores the racial dilemma resulting from miscegenation and specifically questions the issue of racial purity:

> My old man died in a fine big house.
> My ma died in a shack.
> I wonder where I'm gonna die,
> Being neither white nor black?

The middle sections of the collection, "Black Pierrot," "Water-Front Streets," and "Shadow in the Sun," deal more with psychology and aesthetic principles than with race. For example, the poems in "Black Pierrot" examine the poet's desire for freedom and individuality. The poems in "Water-Front Streets" explore feelings of loneliness and sorrow, as do the poems in "Shadow in the Sun."

The final section of the collection, "Our Land," constitutes the political center of the work. The poems in this section examine race and the meaning of America for people of African descent. In "Mother to Son," which contains the often-quoted lines "Well, son, I'll tell you: / Life for me ain't been no crystal chair," a mother tells her son that he can persevere despite life's inevitable difficulties. Also in this section is "I, Too," which condemns America for its racism while also promoting a more equitable society. Appropriately, "I, Too" is the final poem in the collection.

MICHELLE L. TAYLOR

**Further Reading**


Chinitz, David, "Literature and Authenticity: The Blues Poems of Langston Hughes," *Callaloo* 19 (1996)

Grendel, Hartmut, "The Role of Music in the Self-Reflexive Poetry of the Harlem Renaissance," in *Poetics in the Poem: Critical Essays on Self-Reflexive Poetry,* edited by Dorothy Z. Baker, New York: Lang, 1997

Miller, R. Baxter, *The Art and Imagination of Langston Hughes,* Lexington: University Press of Kentucky, 1989

Tracy, Steven C., *Langston Hughes and the Blues,* Urbana: University of Illinois Press, 1988

Trotman, C. James, editor, *Langston Hughes: The Man, His Art, and His Continuing Influence,* New York and London: Garland, 1995


---

# Richard Hugo 1923–82

The considerable critical attention paid to Richard Hugo since his death achieves a consensus that disparate perspectives rarely do. This is due in part to the fact that Hugo was acutely aware of his own legacy as a man of letters, leaving both a collection of essays on poetry and teaching (*The Triggering Town,* 1979) and the mostly autobiographical papers and interviews collected posthumously as *The Real West Marginal Way* (1986). In almost polemical tones, both collections speak to Hugo's faith in the study of creative writing and the value of the local. Regarding the former, Hugo believed that the writing produced in an instructive venue was of secondary importance to the collaborative consideration of the essential, lasting human questions that are the writer's domain and, for Hugo, directly related to place. Much as he depicted in his now-famous essay on craft, "The Triggering Town," Hugo's own poems begin with a fixed and local point, often a setting of some emotional significance to the speaker, and push outward toward a broader human significance, frequently closing with a stunning, even jarring new image or metaphor.

Readers will immediately notice that a disproportionate number of Hugo's titles include place names. But whereas a lesser poet might be disparaged for overemphasizing the local, critics have generally acknowledged the importance of Hugo's approach to regionalism and the versatility with which he has applied it, drawing a poem's occasion from the Pacific Northwest, where he was born and spent most of his life, as well as from Montana, Italy, and, in his last full-length collection (*The Right Madness on Skye,* 1980), the landscape of a remote Scottish island.

Before taking up serious studies in poetry Hugo served as a World War II bombardier in Italy. His experiences there and his return travels two decades later formed the basis of several poems, including "G.I. Graves in Tuscany" and other works in *Good Luck in Cracked Italian* (1969). The war also had a profound effect on the poet's interest in the interplay of good and evil, the relationship between the solitary man and nature, and the role of nostalgia in present-day life, concerns that would develop and recast themselves in poems and essays for the remainder of Hugo's career.

Hugo returned to Seattle after his military service and received bachelor's and master's degrees from the University of Washington, where, like his close friends James Wright and David Wagoner, he was a student of Theodore Roethke. As Hugo would later write, Roethke's influence was immeasurable, not only teaching Hugo a love for the modern canon, including Auden, Yeats, and Hopkins, but also leading him away from the strict formalism prevalent in creative writing courses at the time. Even in his earliest extant poems the speaker makes passionate connections between himself, his physical surroundings, and weighty metaphysical or historical dilemmas without descending into the maudlin or portentous or resorting to overtly formal gestures. Hugo was also engaged from the beginning with the textures of language, and his poems exploit the tension between casual phrasings and lines in a heightened lyrical register. He was nearly 40 when, after 12 years of working at the Boeing Company, he published his first book, *A Run of Jacks* (1961), which demonstrates a surprising clarity of vision and a mature style. The success of that collection led to a teaching job at the University of Montana, where he lived from 1964 until his death of leukemia.

Hugo's second collection, *Death of the Kapowsin Tavern* (1965), is formally very similar to his first, although it harbors an even stronger faith in local nostalgia. As Hugo writes in the title poem, "Nothing dies as slowly as a scene." The unhurried death of landscapes forms the crux of these early poems, but the physical decay of buildings is counterbalanced by memory's attentive, not altogether faithful reconstruction of necessary details, since the speaker recognizes that his nostalgia is more about himself than the particular place.

Following a Rockefeller fellowship in Italy and the publication of *Good Luck in Cracked Italian,* Hugo shifted his regional interests closer to home, locating his poems in the landscape of Montana. His next two collections, *The Lady in Kicking Horse Reservoir* (1973) and *What Thou Lovest Well, Remains American* (1975), are probably his most accomplished works, achieving a more tenuous balance between the cold, objective minutiae of a place and the raw emotional investment of the individual. Poems like "Degrees of Gray in Phillipsburg," "Farmer, Dying," and "The Lady in Kicking Horse Reservoir" find new intensity as personal revelations break free from the constraints of local description, as in the second stanza of the latter poem:

> Lie there lily still. The spillway's closed.
> Two feet down most lakes are common gray.
> This lake is dark from the black blue Mission range
> climbing sky like music dying Indians once wailed.
> On ocean beaches, mystery fish
> are offered to the moon. Your jaws go blue.
> Your hands start waving every wind.
> Wave to the ocean where we crushed a mile of foam.

This is not to say that Hugo's insistence on the local typically constrains his poems' progress or execution; on the contrary, a principal pleasure of reading Hugo is watching the personal or human implications emerge from the setting with all the struggle and necessity of a slow hatching. The speaker's attitude toward the place is usually ambivalent, opposing sentimental attachment with disappointment, anger, or disgust; this tension creates the poem's sometimes urgent lyricism.

Hugo was a master of the second-person narrative, and in *31 Letters and 13 Dreams* (1977) he explores the possibilities of that technique. The "dream" poems are written in the second person, guiding the reader through scenes drawn from memory and imagination. The "letter" poems, on the other hand, are first-person monologues addressed to Hugo's poet-friends and, by extension, to the reader as well, as in these lines from "Letter to Logan from Milltown":

> I'm in Milltown. You remember that bar, that beautiful bar
> run by Harold Herndon where I pissed five years away
> but pleasantly. And now I can't go in for fear
> I'll fall sobbing to the floor. God, the ghosts in there.

This is the most programmatic and rich in personal detail of all Hugo's collections, but because those details do not have to work as hard to break free of the setting, these poems are somewhat less compelling than those that followed in *White Center* (1980), *The Right Madness on Skye,* and the new poems published after his death.

In his last work Hugo asserts himself again as a poet of place, although this time there is a pervading sense of loss and mortality both in the man and the locale, revealing a strong connection not only to James Wright but also to William Stafford. Hugo's project, however, was wholly his own, and he stands out among his contemporaries for his ability to turn landscape into an act of imagination and human inquiry.

Benjamin Paloff

**Biography**

Born in Seattle, Washington, 21 December 1923. Attended the University of Washington, Seattle, B.A. 1948, M.A. 1952; served in the United States Army Air Corps during World War II, bombardier; worked for Boeing Company, Seattle, 1951–63; member of the English Department, then Professor of English, University of Montana, Missoula, from 1964; editor, Yale Younger Poets series, from 1977. Received Northwest Writers Award, 1966; Rockefeller fellowship, 1967; Guggenheim fellowship, 1977; Academy of American Poets fellowship, 1981. Died in Seattle, Washington, 22 October 1982.

**Poetry**
*A Run of Jacks*, 1961
*Five Poets of the Pacific* (with others), edited by Robin Skelton, 1964
*Death of the Kapowsin Tavern*, 1965
*Good Luck in Cracked Italian*, 1969
*The Lady in Kicking Horse Reservoir*, 1973
*What Thou Lovest Well, Remains American*, 1975
*31 Letters and 13 Dreams*, 1977
*Selected Poems*, 1979
*White Center*, 1980
*The Right Madness on Skye*, 1980
*Making Certain It Goes On: The Collected Poems of Richard Hugo*, 1983

**Selected Criticism**
*The Triggering Town: Lectures and Essays on Poetry and Writing*, 1979

**Other Writings:** novels (*Death and the Good Life*, 1981), memoirs (*The Real West Marginal Way: A Poet's Autobiography*, edited by Ripley S. Hugo, Lois Welch, and James Welch, 1986).

**Further Reading**

Allen, Michael S., *We Are Called Human: The Poetry of Richard Hugo*, Fayetteville: University of Arkansas Press, 1982
Holden, Jonathan, "West Marginal Way: Richard Hugo's Poetry as Self-Psychoanalysis," *Mid-American Review* 16, no. 1 (1995)
Levinger, Larry, "Poet Richard Hugo: The Open Field Beyond," *Ploughshares* 18 (1992)
Myers, Jack, editor, *A Trout in the Milk: A Composite Portrait of Richard Hugo*, Lewiston, Idaho: Confluence Press, 1982
Pinsker, Sanford, *Three Pacific Northwest Poets: William Stafford, Richard Hugo, and David Wagoner*, Boston: Twayne, 1987

---

## Humorous Verse. *See* Light Verse

---

# I

## David Ignatow 1914–97

Working largely independently of his own generation's critical establishment and schools of poetry, David Ignatow produced a significant body of work that found recognition by a later generation. Concise, sometimes biting, his poems explore the sense of absurdity to which the search for a unified and consistent meaning in life can lead.

Born and raised in Brooklyn, New York, David Ignatow was involved in the family bindery business, despite his early avocation as a poet. As a result—and as reflected in his early work—he seemed trapped by his limited high school education, his business, and his family obligations. Not until the 1960s and 1970s, when he received numerous awards including the Bollingen Prize, two Guggenheim fellowships, and the National Institute of Arts and Letters Award, was he able to begin his second career as a college professor.

Ignatow's influences include Walt Whitman, who, like Ignatow, exhibited a strong empathy with Americans outside the mainstream of society, those who suffer from "disease, / . . . heartbreak and insanity" ("Communion"). Ignatow acquired the "consoling, Whitmanesque idea that since men are part of the natural cycle of cyclic renewal, they never perish entirely," notes Christopher Brown in the *Dictionary of Literary Biography* (1980). William Carlos Williams also influenced Ignatow, largely for his use of common idiom and a plain-talk, prose-like vernacular. Moreover, Williams was Ignatow's model for poetically rendering the urban landscape with direct honesty.

Although not necessarily a confessional poet in the strictest sense, Ignatow's inclusion of details relating to the intricacies and tribulations of his personal and economic life make him "the most autobiographical of writers" (Brown, 1980). Ignatow's poetry, which blends honest emotion, intellectual engagement, and technical skill, eschews Romanticism in lieu of direct confrontation with personal and social realities; his poems use direct statements with few poetic devices. Terse and effective, this flat style confronts the difficult issues of 20th-century America head-on. His prose poems feature lyrical first-person narrative, faux-allegorical Surrealism, and the epiphanic sense of encounter with the world. The combination of direct address with the fabulous quality of the narratives produces satiric, self-reflexive fantasies; these poems strive more for bitter laughter than for social reformation.

There are three stages in David Ignatow's work. His early work, which includes *The Gentle Weight Lifter* (1955) and *Say Pardon* (1961), is characterized by short lyric poems that concentrate on the evils of business, money-grubbing, and exploitation of the many for the profit of the one. Ignatow also considers depression, as well as sexuality and its relationship to romantic love. Solitary speakers—sometimes as personae, sometimes as symbols—tread predominantly urban and American landscapes.

Work from Ignatow's middle stage includes *Figures of the Human* (1964), his first work to receive critical praise, *Rescue the Dead* (1968), which Christopher Brown calls Ignatow's "finest" book (1980), and *Tread the Dark* (1978). Under the growing influence of the Surrealists Ignatow began using the prose poem in addition to the short lyric in the 1960s. This middle work "presents a more surreal vision of social violence and insanity" (Brown, 1980). Ignatow told Scott Chisholm in a *Tennessee Poetry Journal* interview:

> I'm dealing personally with violence because I think of myself as a metaphor for the whole society. The way I see American society, the individual is at the center of his culture. That's forced on him. . . . If violence is the great and important thing in [the poet's] work, it's only because it's been proven to the one overriding experience we have had in this country and which we will probably continue to have—a sense of violence about ourselves. (1970)

In "Triptych," a poem about a mugging, for example, Ignatow ironically indicates social acceptance of violence by acknowledging, "I should believe that a man being mugged in his own / apartment is part of the order of things," so much so, in fact, that he invokes the sinister figure directly: "Kill me when you must, mugger." Because Ignatow sees violence as both personal and societal, he writes scathing social critiques against the Vietnam War, as in "My President Weeps," in which he takes on the personal guilt of the President's national policy:

> My
> President, my poems that are stained with blood . . .
> . . . poems that have
> holes in them the size of shrapnel wounds, poems that
> peel off from paper like napalmed skin, poems that
> crumple together like the gassed.

A growing acceptance of aging and death also begins to emerge during this middle stage, as in "The Pleasure":

When I watch myself
grow old and grey,
I am authentic, I say.

Late work includes *Whisper to the Earth* (1981), *Leaving the Door Open* (1984), and the posthumous *Living Is What I Wanted: Last Poems* (1999). In these works nature becomes the healer, the balance to urban and societal ills. Ignatow expressed increasing acceptance of coming death, of "the last of living," as he calls it in "63. It is wonderful to die . . ." (*Leaving the Door Open*). He writes of dying

without recriminations towards myself and
others, free of guilt at my shortcomings, happy to have
lived,

so that he may die "in pleasure with myself. I did not fail my / life." For Ignatow, one arrives ultimately at the idea of hope. After all, the artist brings hope to the process of writing and makes discoveries each time he practices his art. In the quasi-religious–sounding poem "58. I am lifted from my sadness," Ignatow sees "everything as a gift / with which to make a life." This act, this affirmation, becomes

the religion I've been searching for
and now it is gone into this writing—
simply a hope and hope alone
to me is a reality.

Even in his final book of poems, written the year before he died, he looked squarely at his life and at the gift that his writing life was. He wrote in "All Living Is Lying,"

[how p]atient we wait
so that
once dead
we'll know perhaps just who we were,
with others thinking back on us.

By turning autobiography into art, David Ignatow earned a reputation as "a poet of great range and power" who dealt "as honestly as any could with modern existence" (Brown, 1980).

ROBERT MILTNER

**Biography**
Born in Brooklyn, New York, 7 February 1914. Attended Brooklyn public schools; employed as salesman, public relations writer, editor, shipyard handyman, newspaperman, and treasurer and president of a bindery firm; associate editor, *American Scene* magazine, 1935–37; literary arts editor, *New York Analytic* magazine, 1937; co-editor, *Beloit Poetry Journal,* Wisconsin, 1949–59; poetry editor, *The Nation,* New York, 1962–63; consulting editor, *Chelsea* magazine, New York, 1969–71; editor-at-large, *American Poetry Review,* Philadelphia, 1973–76. Instructor, New School for Social Research, New York, 1964; Visiting Lecturer, University of Kentucky, Lexington, 1965–66; Lecturer, University of Kansas, Lawrence, 1966–67, and Vassar College, Poughkeepsie, New York, 1967–68; Adjunct Professor, Southampton College, Long Island University, 1967–68, and from 1969, Columbia University, New York; Visiting Professor, New York University, 1985; poet-in-residence, 1968–84, and Professor Emeritus, York College, City University of New York, and Walt Whitman Birthplace Association, Huntington Station, New York, 1987. Received American Academy Award, 1964; Shelley Memorial Award, 1966; Rockefeller fellowship, 1968; Guggenheim fellowship, 1968, 1973; National Endowment for the Arts grant, 1970; Creative Artists Public Service grant, 1976; Bollingen Prize, 1977; Wallace Stevens fellowship, 1977; honorary Litt.D., Long Island University, 1987; President, Poetry Society of America, 1981. Died 17 November 1997.

**Poetry**
*Poems,* 1948
*The Gentle Weight Lifter,* 1955
*Say Pardon,* 1961
*Figures of the Human,* 1964
*Rescue the Dead,* 1968
*Earth Hard: Selected Poems,* 1968
*Poems, 1934–69,* 1970
*Facing the Tree,* 1973
*Facing the Tree: New Poems,* 1975
*Selected Poems,* edited by Robert Bly, 1975
*The Animal in the Bush: Poems on Poetry,* 1977
*Tread the Dark: New Poems,* 1978
*Sunlight: A Sequence for My Daughter,* 1979
*Conversations,* 1980
*Ten Poems,* 1981
*Whisper to the Earth: New Poems,* 1981
*Leaving the Door Open,* 1984
*New and Collected Poems, 1970–1985,* 1986
*Despite the Plainness of the Day: Love Poems,* 1991
*Shadowing the Ground,* 1991
*If We Knew,* illustrations by Glenn Mott, 1992
*Against the Evidence: Selected Poems, 1934–1994,* 1993
*I Have a Name,* 1996
*At My Ease: Uncollected Poems of the Fifties and Sixties,* 1998
*Living Is What I Wanted: Last Poems,* 1999

**Other Writings:** memoirs, short stories (*The End Game and Other Stories,* 1996), notebooks, correspondence, translations of Ukrainian poetry; edited collections of poetry (*Walt Whitman: A Centennial Celebration,* 1963; *The Wild Card: Selected Poems, Early and Late by Karl Jay Shapiro* [with Stanley Kunitz], 1998).

**Further Reading**
Brown, Christopher, "Ignatow, David," in *Dictionary of Literary Biography,* volume 5: *American Poets Since World War II,* part 1, edited by Donald J. Greiner, Detroit, Michigan: Gale Research, 1980
Chisholm, Scott, "An Interview with David Ignatow," *Tennessee Poetry Journal* 3 (Winter 1970)
Ignatow, David, *The Notebooks of David Ignatow,* edited by Ralph J. Mills, Jr., Chicago: Swallow Press, 1973

Ignatow, David, *Open between Us: David Ignatow,* edited by Ralph J. Mills, Jr., Ann Arbor: University of Michigan Press, 1980

Ignatow, David, *Talking Together: Letters of David Ignatow, 1946 to 1990,* edited by Gary Pacernick, Tuscaloosa: University of Alabama Press, 1992

Lavenstein, Richard, "A Man with a Small Song," *Parnassus* 4 (Fall/Winter 1975)

Mazzarro, Jerome, "The Poetry of David Ignatow," *Boundary 2* 4 (Fall 1975)

Melange, Gerard, "The Art of Poetry XIII: David Ignatow," *Paris Review* 76 (Fall 1979)

Terris, Virginia R., editor, *Meaningful Differences: The Poetry and Prose of David Ignatow,* Tuscaloosa: University of Alabama Press, 1994

Wagner, Linda W., *American Modern: Essays in Fiction and Poetry,* Port Washington, New York: Kennicat Press, 1980

Ziegler, Alan, "An Interview with David Ignatow," *Some* 3 (Winter 1973)

# Imagism

In its brief official life Imagism produced many theories about what Imagism actually was, four anthologies of poetry, and the beginnings of several of the century's important poetic careers. Names associated with Imagism include Ezra Pound, H.D., T.S. Eliot, D.H. Lawrence, John Gould Fletcher, Amy Lowell, and Richard Aldington. Looking at their work, however, it would be difficult to say what these poets have in common; indeed the Imagists themselves had a difficult time describing the principles that lay behind their work. Perhaps because of this, Imagism has something like a dual history. The first, a history of names and places, manifestos written and repudiated, personal conflicts won and lost, gives a sense of the historical conditions and events under which the Imagists gathered themselves, published, and dispersed. The second history is of necessity more vague. Leaving behind the dates and names, it tries to determine Imagism's legacy from a historical perspective: how various poets gave voice to a general set of poetic principles in a vital moment in 20th-century literature's attempt to understand the world.

The story of Imagism begins in 1908 London, at evenings hosted by the English writer T.E. Hulme. More a theorist than a poet himself, Hulme and his guests used these weekly "poet's club" gatherings to articulate their dissatisfaction with contemporary English poetry and discuss techniques that might change it. Hulme's theories on art were much influenced by his reading of the French philosopher Henri Bergson, who argued that thinking cut people off from the true nature of things. The goal of art, from this point of view, was to use analogy, image, and rhythm to open the mind to truly "knowing" reality. Bergson believed the artist could reach beyond the merely rational and wrote that the "poet is he with whom feelings develop into images, and the images themselves into words which translate them while obeying the laws of rhythm" (*Time and Free Will,* 1910).

Hulme used Bergson to articulate a more general theory of the history of poetry. Whereas the Victorian poetry of the late 19th century used words in a sentimental way, with little regard to their referents in reality, Hulme believed in a new poetic era of "dry, hard, classical verse" that would pierce through the veil of the intellect and get at reality itself. Writing in *The New Age* in 1909, Hulme told readers that the new poetry would choose "fresh epithets and fresh metaphors, not so much because they are new and we are tired of the old, but because the old cease to convey a physical thing and become abstract counters" (Coffman, 1951).

The phrase *Les imagistes* first appeared in 1912 in a prefatory note to Pound's *Ripostes.* There he referred both to a "School of Images" and "the forgotten school of 1909." A short while later Harriet Monroe, editor of the Chicago-based review *Poetry,* wrote a note about the mysterious and unnamed *Imagistes* at Pound's behest. But the first work to appear under its name was H.D.'s: two poems signed "H.D. Imagiste" (at Pound's suggestion) appeared in *Poetry*'s January 1913 issue. In the same issue Pound wrote a short note about the group, saying that "one of their watchwords is Precision, and they are in opposition to the numerous and unassembled writers who busy themselves with dull and interminable effusions." Three months later *Poetry* published Pound's article "A Few Don'ts by an Imagiste" and an essay on Imagism signed by F.S. Flint (written in collaboration with Pound). Among the Imagist principles Flint identified were direct treatment of the "thing," whether subjective or objective; the use of absolutely no word that did not contribute to the presentation; and composition in sequence of the musical phrase, not in sequence of a metronome. Pound's list of don'ts opened with an attempt at defining the Image by declaring it

> that which presents an intellectual and emotional complex in an instant of time. . . . It is better to produce one Image in a lifetime than to produce voluminous works. . . . [Poets should not] use such an expression as "dim lands of *peace.*" It dulls the image. It mixes an abstraction with the concrete. It comes from the writer's not realizing that the natural object is always the adequate symbol.

This much theory for a movement with only two poems to its name struck some, including Aldington, as ridiculous. As he wrote in *Life for Life's Sake* (1941), "I didn't like his insistence that the poems should be signed: 'H.D. Imagist,' because it sounded a little ridiculous." Only through Pound, however, could Aldington and H.D. get their poems published in *Poetry.*

Although Imagism may initially have been a marketing ploy, it did seem to have some descriptive value. Here is H.D.'s "Hermes of the Ways," which appeared in the January 1913 issue:

The hard sand breaks,
and the grains of it
are clear as wine.

Far off over the leagues of it,
the wind,
playing in the wide shore,
piles little ridges,
and the great waves
break over it.

But more than the many-foamed ways
of the sea,
I know him
of the triple path-ways
Hermes
who awaits.

The poem offers clear echoes of Hulme's "dry, hard, classical verse" in the diction as well as the subject matter. If there is an image here, it seems to come especially in the first stanza, which in likening the clarity of the sand to wine performs what would prove to be a typically Imagist gesture: the unromantic vision of the "thing" itself through comparison or metaphor. By subordinating rhyme and meter to her vision and the necessities of the poem, H.D. signaled her move away from poetry written to metronomes.

The early history of Imagism is thus intimately tied to Pound. Although he did at first come up with the label *Imagisme* as a way of creating a stir and getting published—a prelude to his next "circus act," as Humphrey Carpenter puts it—the principles he defined seemed at least to be describing poems like "Hermes" as it existed on the page. The principles and don'ts published in *Poetry,* while never strictly followed by any of the poets who published under the Imagist label, not only described but also inspired some of their work. As an idea Imagism catalyzed both in the public eye and in the private writing-rooms some of the things a certain group of writers felt to be true about poetry; in the end, its historical value may be not that it explained their work but that it offered, if briefly, an impetus to create more of it.

Around the same time Pound first read H.D.'s "Hermes of the Ways," perhaps inspired by H.D., perhaps in order to try his hand at her *Imagisme,* he wrote the two-line poem "In a Station of the Metro," which Monroe published in *Poetry*'s April 1913 issue: "The apparition of these faces in the crowd: / Petals on a wet, black bough." The stark play of black on white in this poem may reflect Pound's familiarity with East Asian painting, and the haiku-like form gives a further suggestion of the East. The petals and the bough work against the title's mechanical "Metro," staging the clash between a "natural" culture and an "industrial" one, East and West. "Station" occasions its meaning by juxtaposing well-known opposites, allowing each half of the binary (industrial West/natural East) to create new knowledge about its counterpart. At the same time the momentary appearance of the East in the West here points to the possibility of an Eastern understanding of Western experience, a vision of the smoke-and-steel West mediated by an Eastern emphasis on the colors and shapes of nature. Pound's faces, like H.D.'s grains of sand, exist primarily as they are *seen.* But they are more than simply the faces in the Metro; the comparison to the petals opens up a whole new dimension of meaning and possibility. The poet's eye does not simply expose what the poet happened to see but also pretends to be giving voice to a higher truth: a truth, in Bergsonian terms, beyond the rationalizations of the modern intellect.

Following the publication of "Station" Imagism received some attention in American circles, with Wallace Rice writing in *The Dial* that "*Poetry* is being turned into a thing for laughter." Negative attention was better than none at all, however, and with an eye to reaction in London and the United States, Pound began to look for a publisher for an Imagist anthology. In spring 1914 *Des Imagistes: An Anthology* was published in London and the United States. Inside were nine poems by Aldington, seven by H.D., six by Pound, five by Flint, and one each by Ford Maddox Hueffer, William Carlos Williams, Skipwith Cannell, Amy Lowell, Allen Upward, John Cournos, and James Joyce. The anthology received some notice in the United States, most of it negative, and precious little in London, where quite a few copies were returned to the bookshop.

After 1914 Pound seemed to lose interest in Imagism as a movement and started work on a new aesthetic philosophy with Wyndham Lewis: Vorticism. Imagism, orphaned, would not have lasted had it not been for the efforts of the Boston poet Amy Lowell, who stepped in when Pound lost interest and helped push through the publication of three more Imagist anthologies. After a protracted wrangle with Lowell about the use of the word *Imagiste*—Pound at one point threatened a lawsuit, and wrote to her publisher seeking to stop publication—he eventually was mollified by the change from "*Imagiste*" to "Imagist," and by the titles of the anthologies, which called themselves *Some Imagist Poets,* leaving open the possibility that other Imagists were out there working separately. The other Imagists were glad to be rid of Pound's dictatorship and considered briefly dropping the name "Imagism" entirely. John Gould Fletcher wrote:

> Couldn't we call ourselves the Independents or the Vitalists or the young America group or something like that and dissasociate [*sic*] ourselves from any –isms except free verse and definite treatment of the subject? (Coffman, 1951).

Lowell, who saw value in Imagism's marketability, disagreed. Since she was bankrolling the publication, the others went along and in 1915 *Some Imagist Poets: An Anthology* appeared in Boston from Houghton Mifflin. It had six contributors: H.D., Aldington, Flint, Lowell, Fletcher, and D.H. Lawrence. A preface articulated the principles these poets held in common, a commitment to "use the language of common speech, but to employ always the *exact* word, not the nearly-exact, nor the merely decorative word," and an intention to "produce poetry that is hard and clear, never blurred or indefinite." New volumes of the anthology appeared in 1916 and 1917, after which the Imagists as a group agreed that the project had outlived its usefulness.

A survey of Imagist poetry reveals a propensity not only toward the image and "hard" language, but also to the kind of comparison made in Pound's "In a Station of the Metro." Here is Amy Lowell's poem "The Fisherman's Wife":

When I am alone,
The wind in the pine trees

Is like the shuffling of waves
Upon the wooden sides of a boat.

And here is Aldington's "New Love":

She has new leaves
After her dead flowers,
Like the little almond-tree
Which the frost hurt.

In "The Fisherman's Wife" the narrator's loneliness at home, more or less ordinarily described in the first two lines, is revealed in the third and fourth lines to be an echo of her husband's loneliness on the sea. It is as though the world of sound (the wind in the trees, the shuffling of the waves) vibrates to the tune of her emotion, connecting her, despite their distance, to her husband on the water. Aldington's "New Love" depends on a similar turn around the word "like." The reader knows in the first two lines that the poem is comparing a woman to a tree but cannot know why. The third and fourth lines explain the comparison: the woman has been hurt and is recovering in some way. They also add a hard visual detail to the image; she is not like any tree, but like an almond tree damaged by frost. Both poems present a relatively ordinary situation (loneliness, being hurt) in terms of the natural world. Such comparisons may seem to contradict the principle of "direct treatment of the thing," but for the Imagists any direct perception of real life had to overcome the tendency to see things as ordinary. For Aldington as for Lowell, comparison produced a sense of getting at last to the genuine *truth* of a situation as it excited beyond simple description.

Perhaps because such comparisons attempted as much as possible to create, as Pound had written, "an intellectual and emotional complex in an instant of time," there are few long Imagist poems. Of all the Imagist poets H.D. held truest to Imagism's founding principles, so it is perhaps appropriate that one of the most successful, and most astonishing, Imagist poems is her "Adonis":

I
Each of us like you
has died once,
each of us like you
has passed through drift of wood-leaves,
cracked and bent
and tortured and unbent
in the winter frost—
then burnt into gold points,
lighted afresh,
crisp amber, scales of gold-leaf,
gold turned and re-welded
in the sun-heat.
Each of us like you
has died once,
each of us has crossed on old wood-path
and found the winter leaves
so golden in the sun-fire
that even the wood-flowers
were dark.

II
Not the gold on the temple-front
where you stand,
is as gold as this,
not the gold that fastens your sandal,
nor the gold reft
through your chiselled locks
is as gold as this last year's leaf,
not all the gold hammered and wrought
and beaten on your lover's face,
brow and bare breast
is as golden as this.
Each of us like you
has died once,
each of us like you
stands apart, like you
fit to be worshipped.

Even though this poem is relatively long, it retains, by virtue of its repetitions, something of the structure of short Imagist poems. The phrase "each of us like you," which appears four times in the poem, establishes the poem's first major comparison (between "us" and "you"). Between these repetitions H.D. gives a lengthy Imagistic description of the precise shade of gold "turned and rewelded / in the sun heat." The result is a poem that revolves around one larger Image (of the gold) separated into several small descriptions, and ends with a surprising comparison of "us" to Adonis. As with so many Imagist poems, the precise appreciation of the nature of the gold allows for an insight into a more general truth: that the Greeks' age, to which H.D. looked back so often for inspiration, might, as though through the purity of the gold itself, bring itself still breathing into the modern era. The poem is then something like Pound's "Station," committed to a poetry whose vision transcends history, a poetry in which the diffuse and distant past can, if one looks at the world in just the right way, come alive.

Imagism had as many admirers as detractors in its short life, and certainly the movement's commitment to a seemingly too-theoretical set of principles made it easy to mock (even the Imagists got in on this, as when Aldington parodied Pound's "Station" as "The apparition of these poems in a crowd: / White faces in a black dead faint"). But the magnesium flare of its brief history articulated and extended a more generally modern interest in visual epistemology, in the way one knows things by *seeing* them. That interest, as well as the interest in free verse, has remained a vital part of 20th-century American poetry. One finds it elsewhere in the modern period, in the poetry of William Carlos Williams for instance. It extends later into the century in the form of concrete poetry, which takes Imagism's commitment to the visual presentation of reality to a typographic extreme. Although it remains half-forgotten, at the end of the century interest in Imagism resurged, primarily attributable to its attention to Chinese and Japanese poetry. Regardless of the critical judgment of the movement in general, however, many of the Imagists remain important today. Their work can be profitably read with an eye both for its expression of a certain modern spirit, and also for what it still has to teach: that at its best, a poetry committed to visual description can, however briefly, move beyond everyday perceptions of life to glimpse the infinite.

ERIC HAYOT

**Further Reading**


Coffman, Stanley K., *Imagism: A Chapter for the History of Modern Poetry,* Norman: University of Oklahoma Press, 1951

Gage, John T., *In the Arresting Eye: The Rhetoric of Imagism,* Baton Rouge: Louisiana State University Press, 1981

Gross, Harvey, *Sound and Form in Modern Poetry: A Study of Prosody from Thomas Hardy to Robert Lowell,* Ann Arbor: University of Michigan Press, 1964; 2nd edition by Gross and Robert McDowell, 1996

Harmer, J.B., *Victory in Limbo: Imagism, 1908–1917,* New York: St. Martin's Press, and London: Secker and Warburg, 1975

Hsieh, Ming, *Ezra Pound and the Appropriation of Chinese Poetry: Cathay, Translation, and Imagism,* New York: Garland, 1998

Huang, Guiyou, *Whitmanism, Imagism, and Modernism in China and America,* Selingsgrove, Pennsylvania: Susquehanna University Press, 1997

Hughes, Glenn, *Imagism and the Imagists: A Study in Modern Poetry,* Stanford, California: Stanford University Press, and London: Oxford University Press, 1931

Pratt, William, and Robert Richardson, editors, *Homage to Imagism,* New York: AMS Press, 1992

# J

## Japanese American Poetry. *See* Asian American Poetry

---

## Randall Jarrell 1914–65

Randall Jarrell's dedication to poetry could be unnerving. As part of a lengthy tribute to his old friend and fellow poet, Robert Lowell (1967) wrote,

> I have never known anyone who so connected what his friends wrote with their lives, or their lives with what they wrote. This could be trying: whenever we turned out something Randall felt was unworthy or a falling off, there was a coolness in all one's relations with him. You felt that even your choice in neckties wounded him.

Also,

> His mind, unearthly in its quickness, was a little boyish, disembodied, and brittle. His body was a little ghostly in its immunity to soil, entanglements, and rebellion.

Yet Lowell adds, "Jarrell was the most readable and generous of critics of contemporary poetry."

This assessment brings into play many elements of Jarrell's achievement. From Lowell, we can deduce the profound seriousness of Jarrell's commitment to literature, which led to the richness and variety of his poems and literary criticism, and the depth of his work in translation. However, "boyish" and "brittle" does not explain the buoyant tickle of wit, the wicked good humor, spreading through Jarrell's novel satirizing academia (*Pictures from an Institution,* 1954) and all his essays.

The best of his critical prose was celebratory. Many essays triggered a revaluation of their subjects: through the intensity of Jarrell's admiration, new facets of Rudyard Kipling, Walt Whitman, and Robert Frost were turned to the light. Whitman, Leslie Fiedler reminds us, had been "declared officially dead" (Lowell, 1967) before Jarrell's influential essay came along in 1952 to resurrect him. While his own wide interests drove him through books about history, psychology, philosophy, music, and painting, Jarrell complained about the tameness of professional critics. "Readers," he declared, "real readers are almost as wild a species as writers"; everywhere, it is the freshness and the feisty immediacy of Jarrell's voice that we come to heed.

The quips that some of his essays bred were infamous, and his friends were not immune to their sting. Of Lowell's characters in *The Mills of the Kavanaughs,* Jarrell said, "I doubt that many readers will think them real; . . . the heroine is some sort of symbiotic state of the poet. (You feel, 'Yes, Robert Lowell would act like this if he were a girl'; but whoever saw a girl like Robert Lowell?)" Of Marianne Moore, whom he admired, he said, "Some of her poems have the manners or manner of ladies who learned a little before birth not to mention money, who neither point nor touch, and who scrupulously abstain from the mixed, live vulgarity of life." After his poetry had been reviewed by Jarrell, Karl Shapiro could say, "I felt as if I'd been run over but not hurt." Jarrell's judgment was fierce but also trusted.

The poet who produced new versions of the Brothers Grimm was deeply schooled in folk myth and wrote his own haunting fables for children. His preoccupation with German culture, which he mocks in the poem "Deutsch durch Freud" (1950), nonetheless generated his translation of Johann Wolfgang von Goethe's *Faust* as well as the strange, remote, and glowing unearthliness of his recastings of Rainer Maria Rilke's shorter lyrics.

Reading Jarrell, from the dense, ornate qualification of the early poems influenced by Allen Tate to the limpid simplicity of style in *The Lost World* (1965), we are led to a peculiar mix of formal elegance and homey directness, grounded in William Blake's minute particulars and yet afloat in all the tributaries of the ineffable and mysterious. Jarrell's are poems of great ambition and reach, even when reach faltered and the poems collapse from the weight of their rhetoric or flatten into scrap observation. He is a prolific poet, but one not governed by a tight and visibly consistent aesthetic: those who read Jarrell narrowly will always come on passages, if not whole poems, to deplore. However, for the reader open to his style of risk, the pleasures of a frisky wit and the shine of his precise and varied diction—its surprising music—as well as the depth of Jarrell's moral and emotional intelligence will always satisfy.

Jarrell's best-known poems describe war and childhood. Others are striking because of their gender-switching personae: no lyric poet of the 20th century has written so well and so imaginatively from inside the skin of the opposite sex. These subjects developed over time. Initially, the war poems grew from the Marxist shadings of Jarrell's early years and then took on a more persuasive local texture through his noncombatant Army service on American airbases in World War II.

Perhaps because of his noncombatant status, Jarrell's poems about war range widely. He did not hesitate to write in the voice of downed pilots, prisoners of war, concentration camp inmates, battlefield corpses, or refugee Jews, but, however varied his personae may have been, the voice was sorrowing, afflicted, and in clear opposition to conventional odes of glory. Much like James Dickey, another American poet drawn to the romance of flight, Jarrell grew up wrapped in boyhood fantasies about the greatness of pilot aces in World War I. The World War II poem that remains the most famous, however, is "The Death of the Ball Turret Gunner," in which a fetally positioned gunner wakes to death before ever having had a chance at life: "When I died they washed me out of the turret with a hose."

Jarrell's nearly 50 war poems do not stand off in a crowd by themselves; they relate to subjects and images thronging the rest of his poetry. The hapless boy victims of "Second Air Force" (1944)—or even, lower down on the scale of heroic costume, "The Sick Nought" (1943)—are recognizable kin to the disposable citizen, the office worker camouflaged in her bureaucratic nullity, of a much later poem, "The Woman at the Washington Zoo" (1960). The dehumanizing anonymity of the modern state, as well as the modern army, has robbed from each of these figures the power to act, reducing them to pawns of corporate- and state-sponsored violence and repression. "In bombers named for girls, we burned / the cities we had learned about in school—" cry the dead pilots of "Losses" (1944), in unison with the burned civilians who can only call back, in response to the death of heroes, "We are satisfied if you are; but why did I die?"

Jarrell's fliers inhabit a high, cold, and lonely grandeur in which the carriers on seas far below them define a warscape of intense and elemental sweep. However, the mood is insistently anti-heroic; Jarrell never obscures the burning cities or the mass graves at the heart of global war. Jarrell's soldiers die in bombing raids and, foretelling the increasing incidence of friendly fire in 20th-century industrial warfare, in airbase accidents. Yet in the somber tenderness of these pieces, he does not omit from mention that soldiers are not only the killed but also the killers, as his soldiers are seen to participate in the bloodshed welling from even the just war.

Poem after poem features a dreaming, mythic child or the child-like mass recruit, caught up in a dangerous and depersonalizing bureaucracy that, like jail, presents its inmates with a fixed sentence. Whether the prison invoked is the Nazi *Lager* or a camp in Colorado for German soldiers or the prison of the army itself, war and the modern state infantilize and nullify choice. Jarrell's originality lies in this central insight: he pairs the diminished soldier with the anxious and diminished dweller of the postmodern world. Both in wartime and postwar, each class of protagonist confronts both death and life, suffering the contrast of their infinite imaginative longing with the reality of the wounded will. Mutilated by war, the pilot of "Siegfried" stumbles "to the toilet on one clever leg / Of leather, wire, and willow"; released and rehabilitated, he asks, "—*What will you do now?*" and answers, "*I don't know*—" much as the woman speaker of "Next Day" (1963) looks down into the coffin of her friend's "undressed, operated-on, dressed body," saying,

> I stand beside my grave
> Confused with my life, that is commonplace and solitary.

Each of these speakers faces an oncoming death and inexplicable fading within their ordinary, bewildering dailiness.

Quite ahead of his time, although not without an intermittent sexist condescension, Jarrell understood how gender functions to limit personal capacity. He rewrote the predicament of the woman boxed into a life of purely material domesticity several times, once in the long, slow poem "At the End of the Rainbow" (1954), then again in quick poems such as "In Montecito" (1963). Most memorably in "The Woman at the Washington Zoo" and "Next Day" the female speakers plead for change and recognition.

Recent readers, such as James Longenbach (1997), have noticed how Jarrell's assumption of female identity allowed him emotive tenderness and a terrifying personal vulnerability. In the gender conventions of his time, female personae could express feelings denied by men. When Jarrell makes his male saint face the pangs of aging and death in "Jerome," he has him face it accompanied by a faithful lion and in the stiffened placidity of a mellow wisdom and faith. However, without the harness of irony, readers trained to a Modernist cool tended to find Jarrell's preoccupation with fears of death, with aging and impotence embedded in a scene of prosaic or suburban domesticity, a less-than-dignified subject.

Jarrell's child protagonists proliferated in his final book, *The Lost World* (1965). In long narrative sequences, he made luxuriant use of period detail from the golden time in 1926–27, when he was allowed a blissful domesticity with his grandparents in an apparently modest home in a workaday Hollywood, California. He has a pet rabbit and a crystal set; at a friend of the family's farm, he meets the Metro Goldwyn Mayer lion, Tawny. The eerie, luminous poems that he made of this transient world, which he was put into and then pulled back from by his divorcing mother, trace the jarring transitions and betrayals against which children have no defense.

Lowell came to describe Jarrell's "governing and transcendent vision of childhood" as rooted in a tradition spanning Wordsworth and Rilke. William Pritchard (1990) agrees with the contours of this vision but whisks Jarrell out of the school of Rilke and Wordsworth into that of Robert Frost because of Jarrell's reliance on a Frost-like dramatic technique. In contrast, Thomas Travisano (1999) finds these poems of the vulnerable speaker the expression of a developing postmodern aesthetic, one challenging the deficiencies of impersonality in the Modernist tradition of poets such as T.S. Eliot and Ezra Pound.

Yet none of these approaches entirely encompasses the magical hold of poems like "Seele im Raum" (1951), whose fusions of the fantastic, the dreamt, and the familial convey a piercing distress of the heart utterly recognizable to child, parent, man, and woman. Like Elizabeth Bishop's poem playing on a misprint of "Man-moth" (for "mammoth"), Jarrell's punning, fortuitous confusion of *eland,* the beast, with the German *elend,* or "miserable," opens a gap in language through which new insights and new worlds slip into our hands.

"A Quilt Pattern" and "The Black Swan" (both 1951) make full use of syntactical, spatial, and genre disruptions. These poems and other strong poems like them are fractionally naturalistic in setting but also inhabit fairy tale, dream, and memory. In these mixed modes, Jarrell recovers new versions of childhood traumas of death, sexuality, parental loss, and identity confusion. The poems do bring us back strongly, despite Pritchard's disclaimers, to the childhood terrors of Blake's *Songs of Experience* and to Wordsworth's skaters and mountain predators. Some time having passed since the boy Wordsworth stalked the Cumberland fells or Blake roamed the streets of London observing chimney sweeps, it is inevitable that Jarrell represent modernity, even forms of postmodernity. Jarrell and others have profited from new rhythms and modes of dramatizing speech in lyric poems and have made innovative use of modern candors and consciousness of gender problems. However, the Romantic anxiety about vulnerability to death and transience still troubles the modern and contemporary poet examining her or his place in the linkage between the human, the material, and the world of others. In this distinguished and enduring community of poets stretching from Wordsworth and Rilke to Robert Frost and Elizabeth Bishop, Jarrell takes his rightful place.

LORRIE GOLDENSOHN

*See also* War and Antiwar Poetry

**Biography**

Born in Nashville, Tennessee, 6 May 1914. Attended Vanderbilt University, Nashville (editor, *Masquerader*), B.S. in psychology 1936 (Phi Beta Kappa), M.A. 1939; served as celestial navigation tower operator in the United States Army Air Corps, 1942–46; Instructor in English, Kenyon College, Gambier, Ohio, 1937–39, University of Texas, Austin, 1939–42, and Sarah Lawrence College, Bronxville, New York, 1946–47; Associate Professor, 1947–58, and Professor of English, 1958–65, Woman's College of the University of North Carolina (later University of North Carolina at Greensboro); Lecturer, Salzburg Seminar in American Civilization, 1948; Visiting Fellow in creative writing, Princeton University, New Jersey, 1951–52; Fellow, Indiana School of Letters, Bloomington, summer 1952; Visiting Professor of English, University of Illinois, Urbana, 1953; Elliston Lecturer, University of Cincinnati, Ohio, 1958; acting literary editor, *The Nation,* 1946–47; poetry critic, *Partisan Review,* New Brunswick, New Jersey, 1949–53, and *Yale Review,* 1955–57; editorial board member, *American Scholar,* 1957–65; consultant in poetry, Library of Congress, Washington, D.C., 1956–58. Received Guggenheim fellowship, 1946; American Academy grant, 1951; National Book Award, 1961; University of North Carolina Gardner Award, 1962; American Association of University Women Award, 1964; Ingram Merrill Award, 1965; honorary L.H.D., Bard College, Annandale-on-Hudson, New York, 1962; member, American Academy, 1961; Chancellor, Academy of American Poets, 1965. Died in Chapel Hill, North Carolina, 14 October 1965.

**Poetry**

*Five Young American Poets* (with others), 1940
*Blood for a Stranger,* 1942
*Little Friend, Little Friend,* 1945
*Losses,* 1948
*The Seven-League Crutches,* 1951
*Selected Poems,* 1955
*Uncollected Poems,* 1958
*The Woman at the Washington Zoo: Poems and Translations,* 1960
*Selected Poems, Including the Woman at the Washington Zoo,* 1964
*The Lost World: New Poems,* 1965
*The Complete Poems,* 1969
*The Achievement of Jarrell: A Comprehensive Selection of His Poems,* edited by Frederick J. Hoffman, 1970
*Jerome: The Biography of a Poem,* 1971

**Selected Criticism**

*Poetry and the Age,* 1953
*The Third Book of Criticism,* 1969
*No Other Book: Selected Essays,* 1999

**Other Writings:** play (*The Three Sisters,* adaptation of a play by Chekhov, produced 1964), fiction (*Pictures from an Institution: A Comedy,* 1954), children's literature (*The Bat Poet,* 1964), essays (*A Sad Heart at the Supermarket: Essays and Fables,* 1962), translations of German literature (*The Ghetto and the Jews of Rome,* by Ferdinand Gregorovius, translator with Moses Hadas, 1948; *Goethe's Faust, Part I,* 1976); edited collections of literature (*Six Russian Short Novels,* 1963).

**Further Reading**

Ferguson, Suzanne, *The Poetry of Randall Jarrell,* Baton Rouge: Louisiana State University Press, 1972
Ferguson, Suzanne, editor, *Critical Essays on Randall Jarrell,* Boston: G.K. Hall, 1983
Flynn, Richard, *Randall Jarrell and the Lost World of Childhood,* Athens: University of Georgia Press, 1990
Jarrell, Mary von Schrader, *Remembering Randall: A Memoir of Poet, Critic, and Teacher Randall Jarrell,* New York: HarperCollins, 1999
Longenbach, James, *Modern Poetry after Modernism,* Oxford and New York: Oxford University Press, 1997
Lowell, Robert, Peter Taylor, and Robert Penn Warren, *Randall Jarrell, 1914–1965,* New York: Farrar Straus and Giroux, 1967
Pritchard, William H., *Randall Jarrell: A Literary Life,* New York: Farrar Straus and Giroux, 1990
Quinn, Mary Bernetta, *Randall Jarrell,* Boston: Twayne, 1981
Travisano, Thomas, *Midcentury Quartet: Bishop, Lowell, Jarrell, Berryman, and the Making of a Postmodern Aesthetic,* Charlottesville: University Press of Virginia, 1999

## Thinking of the Lost World

"Thinking of the Lost World" appears as the last poem in *The Lost World* (1965), Randall Jarrell's final volume of poetry, published shortly before his death in 1965. The poem is the companion piece to the longer "The Lost World," also written in 1963; a reading of the longer poem enhances an understanding of the shorter, since the two share numerous images. In *Remembering Randall* (1999), her memoir of her husband, Mary von Schrader Jarrell says:

> For Randall 1963 was the time to write his long, autobiographical poem, *The Lost World*. . . . At just this time Randall's mother sent him an old Christmas card box from the twenties containing the letters he had written her from California when he was twelve.

These letters were the inspiration for "The Lost World" and "Thinking of the Lost World," and although these poems are deeply personal and highly autobiographical, recalling a period of time Jarrell spent with his grandparents in Hollywood, California in 1926, they go well beyond sentimental autobiography. A knowledge of Jarrell's autobiography expands understanding of the poems, but Jarrell universalizes the experience so that readers do not need much background information about the poet's life to *feel* and *experience* his poetry, because the poems engage readers in their own acts of creative imagination. The poems attest to a dramatic change in Jarrell's point of view on life in general, but especially on childhood and the power of the poetic, creative, and "childlike" imagination.

Many readers view "Thinking of the Lost World" as pessimistic because after its Romantic Proustian opening, in which the flavor of a spoonful of chocolate tapioca evokes in the speaker memories of his childhood, the bulk of the poem employs a seemingly sober, nostalgic, adult tone. References to polluted Los Angeles, a child's destroyed tree house (symbol of a fantasy world), and other elements from the "lost world" of childhood take on greater pessimistic significance when read in the context of "The Lost World," as do the repeated and critically debated references to emptiness and nothing at the end of the poem.

In accord with this apparently pessimistic tone the speaker says he and his wife had revisited California a few years earlier and found the experience unsatisfactory: "Back in Los Angeles, we missed / Los Angeles." Viewing the city through metaphorically clouded adult eyes, they saw only the pollution and destruction, the remnants of a seemingly unrecoverable childhood happiness. As the poem continues, however, the tone becomes more optimistic. A close reading, especially of the poem's ending, reveals the speaker's recaptured sense of childlike wonder at both his past and present lives, which he comes to realize are ultimately inseparable. In a figurative, psychological, and even mythological sense, he is always "Moving between the first world and the second," between adulthood and childhood. The speaker comes to realize that his childhood world was never really lost, and that he is recreating in his poetry the fantasy worlds (represented by the tree house and other objects described in "The Lost World") he imagined as a child, thereby illustrating a powerful link between the childhood and the poetic imagination.

The key to understanding the poem lies in the seemingly oxymoronic juxtaposition of the words "happiness" and "nothing" in the final lines, when the speaker says, "I hold in my own hands, in happiness, / Nothing: the nothing for which there's no reward." In the worldly, ego-encapsulated view, "nothing" implies emptiness and loss, the absence of "things" (the type of "nothing" Jarrell speaks of when referring to pain, for example, at the end of "90 North"). However, when viewed in terms of the negative theology, "nothing" takes on very different connotations. Jarrell does not present "nothing" in strictly orthodox theological terms as the all-creating God, as theologians do, but rather in the secularized Romantic sense of the deific, creative Imagination. Jarrell does in this poem apparently adhere in secularized terms to Henry Suso's idea that

> men call this Nothing "God," and it is itself a most essential Something. And here man knows himself to be one with this Nothing, and this Nothing knows itself without the action of the intellect[.] (*Little Book of Truth,* translated by James M. Clark, n.d.)

When the adult becomes empty of material things of this world, according to this branch of thought, he is most childlike and, paradoxically, most complete, most able aesthetically to re-create and enjoy the "no-thing-ness" of the imagination. The fallen adult's emptiness and inner despair are the result of his loss of childhood perception, a theme familiar in Wordsworth, one of Jarrell's favorite poets. In Jarrell's poem, however, that adult emptiness is redeemed in the metaphorical transformation of the adult into the child. The fallen man reclaims the clear-sighted vision of the imagination that knows "without the action of the intellect" when he says "I seem to see / A shape in tennis shoes and khaki riding-pants / Standing there empty-handed; I reach out to it / Empty-handed, my hand comes back empty, / And yet my emptiness is traded for its emptiness. . . ."

The end of "Thinking of the Lost World" comprises Jarrell's poetic testimony that he has finally achieved in the most autobiographical of his poems the transformation he has sought in various personae throughout his career. The "Lost World" and the "nothing" the speaker happily holds in his hands are the imagined work, the poem, the book, and thereby the lost world of childhood and fantasy, a world that the speaker realizes was never really lost because it was and is imagined: "for me nothing is gone," the poet says. He has come to realize that to achieve transformation and the "happiness" that it brings, he must empty himself of the adult world and become again like the child he was in Hollywood in 1926 (and in some sense still is), the child who possessed nothing except a vivid and even divine (or at least divinely inspired) imagination, "the nothing for which there's no reward" but itself.

KATRINA SHILTS

**Further Reading**


Bryant, J.A., Jr., *Understanding Randall Jarrell,* Columbia: University of South Carolina Press, 1986

Ferguson, Suzanne, *The Poetry of Randall Jarrell,* Baton Rouge: Louisiana State University Press, 1972

Flynn, Richard, *Randall Jarrell and the Lost World of Childhood,* Athens: University of Georgia Press, 1990

Jarrell, Mary von Schrader, *Remembering Randall: A Memoir of Poet, Critic, and Teacher Randall Jarrell,* New York: HarperCollins, 1999

Pritchard, William H., *Randall Jarrell: A Literary Life,* New York: Farrar Straus and Giroux, 1990

# Robinson Jeffers 1887–1962

Robinson Jeffers is most often acknowledged as the California poet of Tor House (an edifice of rock he built himself) who immortalizes the stark beauty of the Carmel coastline. Although his works are not well known to most students of American poetry, Jeffers is an important contributor to the Modernist period in American letters and a powerful poet in his own right. Recently, a number of scholars and literary critics have seen fit to revisit the many remarkable poems Jeffers published between 1924 and 1937, his most productive years. *Tamar* (1924), *Roan Stallion* (1925), *Cawdor* (1928), and *Solstice* (1935) are the volumes that have attracted the most attention. In these as well as his other collections, readers will find a poetic voice deeply engaged with philosophical and aesthetic conflicts that occupied Walt Whitman, T.S. Eliot, Ezra Pound, William Butler Yeats, Stephane Mallarmé, and other great Modernists. Most scholars agree that his later works—*The Double Axe* (1948), *Hungerfield* (1954), and *The Beginning and the End* (1963)—generally lack the conviction or intensity of his earlier poems.

Jeffers' lack of representation in poetry anthologies and the relatively limited notice he has received in the popular culture raises the question of this poet's precise place in American literary history. If Jeffers is not always included on syllabi or in overviews of American poetics, it may have to do with his reception by the critics of his day. Jeffers certainly had followers and supporters, including William Everson, Czeslaw Milosz, Langston Hughes, and other literary contemporaries, but those who exerted the most lasting influence, namely the New Critics, uniformly rejected his work. From a New Critical perspective, Jeffers' poetry, written for the most part in free verse, was deemed simply unpoetic; it supposedly lacked the complex irony, linguistic precision, and elaborate symbolism that came to define great poetry for reigning critics and canon shapers such as Cleanth Brooks and John Crowe Ransom. Yvor Winters dismissed Jeffers' verses as "unpretentious trash." Such an unwarranted "expert" condemnation no doubt influenced the trajectory of this poet's career.

Many other readers have also failed to comprehend Jeffers' artistic perspective, although perhaps this is understandable. Readers often find it necessary to locate the individual poet within a literary movement of school of thought. Jeffers seems to have at best ambiguous relationships to both Modernism and Romanticism, the latter being the movement against which many moderns defined their new perspectives and avant-garde practices; he fits comfortably into neither movement and thus seems "out of place" in the literary canon.

Certainly, Jeffers does seem nostalgically to embrace a Wordsworthian perspective. The better portion of his works insists on the need to forgo human religion and revel instead in "Organic wholeness, the wholeness of life and things, the divine / beauty of the universe" ("The Answer," 1937). Like the Romantics, Jeffers values nature above all and seeks answers in the apprehension of a cosmic reality. Not surprisingly, he lived his life in retreat and often portrayed "man" as both tragic and foolish for daring to place himself above animals or the natural world. Like Henry David Thoreau, he removed to the "woods," although for Jeffers a mere pond a few miles from the village would never suffice. His natural sanctuary was not a private bower but the jutting rocks and windy crags of the rugged central California coast. Philosophically as well as geographically, Jeffers locates himself at continent's end, where sea meets land and where life originated. As he conveys in "Meditation on Saviors" (1928), "I pledged myself a while ago not to seek refuge, neither in death nor / in a walled garden, / In lies nor gated loyalties, nor in the gates of contempt, that / easily lock the world out of doors."

However, contrary to the Romantics, Jeffers rejects imagination as an important creative or reflective faculty. In "Prelude"(1937), Jeffers challenges William Wordsworth's ars poetica. In this poem, he condemns the imagination as "the traitor of the mind" that makes fables and clings to old mythologies, thus prohibiting the unmediated experience of reality he so desires. To assert, as he does in "Boats in a Fog," that "all the arts lose / Virtue / Against the essential reality / Of creatures going about their business among the equally / Earnest elements of nature" is likewise to reject the Romantics' faith in the imagination as a divine source of wisdom. In addition, Jeffers refuses to believe that poetry can achieve an unmediated expression of truth and nature. Instead, he maintains, the goal of a poet should be to abandon linguistically any desire to construct a symbolic world that would separate him or her from nature. Jeffers feels that the essentially inhuman being of nature requires a new mode of representation, one that would avoid the alienating, artificial "poetic" language of tradition. There "only remains to invent the language to tell" of his *discovery* of nature, he promises. Yet he is forced by his own critique of mediation to accept the inefficacy of language to represent nature. Acknowledging his own desire to be humanly understood, he concedes, "Scraps and metaphors will serve" ("Prelude").

Jeffers' reference to using "scraps" invokes Eliot's famous final lines of *The Waste Land* (1922), where he proposes that he has shored fragments against his ruins. Although Jeffers and Eliot are opposed when it comes to the value of nature in itself and to the writing of poetry, they, along with many other Modernists, grapple with the desire to create a linguistic art form capable of infusing new life into what appears to them a horribly decadent civilization. It is thus more accurate to view Jeffers as a critic of modernity than a Romantic or a strict anti-Modernist. He is, as critic Tim Hunt argues, an anti-modern Modernist, and, like Eliot, his disparagement of humanity is actually a very modern response to advances in the fields of anthropology, biology, geology, and astronomy that seemed to diminish the importance of human beings in the order of things. Jeffers' poetry registers what Friedrich Nietzsche had prophesized in the late 19th century—that "the death of God" or any metaphysical belief that places human beings at the center of the universe will inevitably result in a monumental identity crisis for humankind; and, like naturalists Stephen Crane and Theodore Dreiser, Jeffers apprehends a universe utterly indifferent to the selfish, egotistical pleas of humanity. God and religion are simply fantasies devised to ward off the existential truth: life is a natural process devoid of predestination or inherent significance. Thus, for Jeffers, human desire always betrays the truth of the universe. Civilization—urbanization, mass political movements for progressive social change, industrialization, and science—is, in the end, no more than an elaborate phantasm and a "transient sickness" ("New Mexican Mountain," 1932). As he writes in "The Answer," we must not love "man" but "the divine beauty of the universe." Jeffers calls this philosophy "inhumanism."

However, Jeffers is no misanthrope, as some New Critics thought. Rather, he rejects our self-centeredness, our need to find affirmation for being in the material world, and our tendency to transmit such a need into false beliefs in the supernatural. For Jeffers, our inability to come to terms with our place in the natural realm and with our mortality, along with our profound capacity for arrogance and violence, are the primary causes of environmental devastation, political turmoil, and war. His critique of the vanity of politics becomes very clear in the poems he wrote in the late 1930s. While World War II was in the making, he deflated even the noblest desires to make a just world as doomed to failure because of the essential disposition of humans to desire power over others: "not to be duped," he cautions, "By dreams of universal justice or happiness. / These dreams will not be fulfilled" ("The Answer"). Ironically, for Jeffers, human survival depends on a kind of philosophical negation of humanity—our rejection of anthropocentric perspectives and religions that place us at the center of existence or in primary relation to God.

While such a view certainly smacks of cynicism—a cynicism all the more pronounced when compared to the writings of American poets such as Langston Hughes, Edwin Rolfe, and Kenneth Fearing, who sided with the Left in their condemnation of Fascism—Jeffers' inhumanist position nonetheless aims to subvert the nihilistic tendency of modern life by alerting us to our connection with nature. For him, the human is an aspect of nature; therefore, it is false to conceive of humanity as somehow opposed to or inevitably alienated from the reality of an organically unified realm. His point of attack is that of an ecologist. He mourns the effects of Western expansion and corporate development but particularly the destruction of what we now refer to as the "environment."

Interestingly, like his Modernist counterparts, Jeffers critique of modernity and search for a new poetic form leads him to incorporate Greek myths and biblical allusions as an essential component, particularly in some of his longer poems. This technique has misled or confused some readers since Jeffers attacks mythology and religion as illusory. It is therefore helpful to view his use of familiar myths as a means of enacting an existential drama—the tragedy of human existence—rather than as an affirmation of the supernatural. Whereas modern poets often use nature as a vehicle for reflection on the tragedy of human mortality from the Christian perspective (since, in this view, humankind has "fallen" away from nature), Jeffers offers an alternative perspective. For example, in the stark tableau of a falcon on a stone precipice, we should not find the familiar emblem of salvation or redemption but a countersymbol: "Not the cross, not the hive, / But this; bright power, dark peace; / fierce consciousness joined with final / Disinterestedness" ("Rock and Hawk," 1935). In short, his inhumanist philosophy circumvents our tendency to project our fears and needs onto the natural world, but he often invokes religious or mystical figures to make the point that the search for salvation is doomed to failure. Sadly, Christian history is "one vast / poem drunk with the wine of his blood," Jeffers suggests in "Theory of Truth" (1938). Humanity will not find truth until it has "turned its love from / itself and man, from parts to the whole." However, Jeffers is doubtful that humans will ever be able to transcend their fables and superstitions. Culture has severed us from nature and thus from truth.

Twenty-first-century students who approach Jeffers poetry with renewed or fresh interest may feel less daunted by his seemingly pessimistic outlook than did his contemporaries. Jeffers' urgent appeal to end the destruction of the environment carries more force now than ever before. His cynicism about political engagement may likewise strike a chord in the contemporary reader. As an anti-modern Modernist, then, Jeffers may very well play an important role in the making of a postmodern perspective. Whether or not this proves to be the case, Jeffers' uncompromising poetry continues to provoke, challenge, and move his readers with compelling ideas and images whose significance resists the traditional boundaries of literary history.

KRISTA WALTER

**Biography**

Born in Pittsburgh, Pennsylvania, 10 January 1887. Attended the University of Western Pennsylvania (now University of Pittsburgh), 1902–03; Occidental College, Los Angeles (editor, *Aurora*), 1903–05, B.A. 1905; University of Southern California, Los Angeles, 1905–06, 1907–10; University of Zurich, 1906–07; University of Southern California Medical School, 1908–10; studied forestry at the University of Washington, Seattle, 1910–11. Received Academy of American Poets fellowship, 1958; Shelley Memorial Award, 1961; honorary L.H.D., Occidental College, 1937, University of Southern California, 1939; member, American Academy; Chancellor, Academy of American Poets, 1945–56. Died in Carmel, California, 20 January 1962.

**Poetry**

*Flagons and Apples*, 1912
*Californians*, 1916
*Tamar, and Other Poems*, 1924
*Roan Stallion, Tamar, and Other Poems*, 1925
*The Women at Point Sur*, 1927
*Poems*, 1928
*An Artist*, 1928
*Cawdor, and Other Poems*, 1928
*Dear Judas, and Other Poems*, 1929
*Stars*, 1930
*Apology for Bad Dreams*, 1930
*Descent to the Dead: Poems Written in Ireland and Great Britain*, 1931
*Thurso's Landing, and Other Poems*, 1932
*Give Your Heart to the Hawks, and Other Poems*, 1933
*Return*, 1934
*Solstice, and Other Poems*, 1935
*The Beaks of Eagles*, 1936
*Such Counsels You Gave to Me, and Other Poems*, 1937
*The Selected Poetry*, 1938
*Two Consolations*, 1940
*Be Angry at the Sun*, 1941
*The Double Axe, and Other Poems*, 1948
*Hungerfield, and Other Poems*, 1954
*The Loving Shepherdess*, 1956
*The Beginning and the End, and Other Poems*, 1963
*Selected Poems*, 1965
*The Alpine Christ, and Other Poems*, edited by William Everson, 1973
*Brides of the South Wind: Poems, 1917–1922*, edited by William Everson, 1974
*Granite and Cypress*, edited by William Everson, 1975
*The Women at Point Sur, and Other Poems*, 1977

*The Double Axe, and Other Poems,* edited by William Everson, 1977
*Dear Judas, and Other Poems,* 1977
*What Odd Expedients, and Other Poems,* edited by Robert Ian Scott, 1981
*Rock and Hawk: A Selection of Shorter Poems by Robinson Jeffers,* edited by Robert Hass, 1987
*Selected Poems: The Centenary Edition,* edited by Colin Falk, 1987
*Point Lobos: A Portfolio of Fifteen Poems by Robinson Jeffers and Fifteen Photographs by Wolf von dem Bussche,* 1987
*Songs and Heroes,* 1988
*The Collected Poetry of Robinson Jeffers,* 3 vols., edited by Tim Hunt, 1988–91
*Tea at Tor House,* 1993
*Meditation on Saviors,* 1994
*The Collected Early Verse of Robinson Jeffers, 1903–April 1914,* 1997
*The Collected Poetry of Robinson Jeffers,* 2000
*The Selected Poetry of Robinson Jeffers,* 2001

**Other Writings:** plays (*Tragedy Has Obligations,* 1973), correspondence (*The Selected Letters of Robinson Jeffers, 1897–1962,* edited by Ann N. Ridgeway, 1968).

**Further Reading**

Brophy, Robert, *Robinson Jeffers: Myth, Ritual, and Symbol in His Narrative Poems,* Cleveland, Ohio: Press of Case Western Reserve University, 1973
Everson, William, *Robinson Jeffers: Fragments of an Older Fury,* Berkeley, California: Oyez, 1968
Karman, James, editor, *Critical Essays on Robinson Jeffers,* Boston: G.K. Hall, 1990
Zaller, Robert, *The Cliffs of Solitude: A Reading of Robinson Jeffers,* Cambridge and New York: Cambridge University Press, 1983
Zaller, Robert, editor, *Centennial Essays for Robinson Jeffers,* Newark: University of Delaware Press, and London: Associated University Presses, 1991

# Hurt Hawks

Part II of Robinson Jeffers' frequently anthologized lyric "Hurt Hawks" opens, "I'd sooner, except the penalties, kill a man than a hawk"—a claim that still has the power to startle more than 70 years after the poem first appeared in the 8 February 1928 issue of *The Nation* and then in Jeffers' *Cawdor, and Other Poems* (1928). To some, the line has seemed evidence that Jeffers was deeply misanthropic; critics inclined to this reading have tended to condemn his work as a nihilistic rejection of modern civilization. To others, the line has seemed more an attempt to shock the reader into recognizing—and valuing—the beauty of nonhuman nature; those inclined to this reading have argued that Jeffers' work celebrates a nature in which humanity is one element among many. In one important way, these conflicting reactions converge. In both, the poem and its infamous line are seen as essentially didactic gestures. The poem is a kind of teaching, and its harsh physical details of the hawk's condition ("The broken pillar of the wing jags from the clotted shoulder, / The wing trails like a banner in defeat") serve to intensify the message. The disagreement is not so much over the poem's character as over what to make of its message.

While the didactic claims in "Hurt Hawks" are important to the poem, several factors suggest that other elements are also important—elements that may complicate the nature and implications of the speaker's claim that he would rather "kill a man than a hawk." First, the poem derives from Jeffers' own experience. In a 6 January 1927 letter, he notes that his sons then had a "broken-winged hawk" as a pet, and in a 3 March 1927 letter, he mentions shooting the hawk on 1 March (*Selected Letters,* 1968). The timing of shooting the hawk points to a second factor: that he probably wrote the poem in two stages. In Part I, the speaker evokes the suffering of the injured hawk and responds to its refusal to be "humble[d]" by its "incapacity" and "pain." Challenged by its "intrepid readiness" and "terrible eyes," the speaker claims that the hawk, "Intemperate and savage," still "remembers" the "wild God" that "you communal people . . . have forgotten." The use of present tense in the lines suggests that Jeffers wrote them while the hawk was alive. If so, Part I was probably at first the complete poem; the correspondence shows that Jeffers sent his publisher a poem titled "The Hurt Hawk" in mid-February 1927 before he shot the hawk. This piece apparently became Part I of "Hurt Hawks" when he wrote and added Part II sometime after shooting the hawk.

As this compositional process suggests, the finished poem is two different responses to the encounter with the injured hawk. In Part I, the speaker is challenged by the way the hawk endures his pain and incapacity and is moved to acknowledge and invoke a God in nature who is only "sometimes merciful." The speaker's recognition that God's nature is "Beautiful and wild" rather than merciful and loving implicitly indicts the "communal people" for their failure to recognize God's nature; it also confronts the speaker with the need to accept the reality of the hawk's pain as the price of knowing the "Beautiful and wild"—the price of knowing God. In Part II, the speaker also confronts a challenge. Faced with the hawk's "unable misery," "the bones too shattered for mending," he offers the mercy that the "wild God" had withheld ("We had fed him six weeks, I gave him freedom / . . . I gave him the lead gift"). In killing the hawk, the speaker places his need to be merciful above God's desire to be "Beautiful and wild"; he acts (at least in part) from the perspective of the "communal people" who have forgotten the "wild God." He also destroys the figure that, through its sacrificial pain, has mediated his recognition of the "wild God." Implicitly at least, these dilemmas are intensely emotional for the speaker. To kill the hawk, despite its suffering, even perhaps because of its suffering, is to deny God and to destroy a being that participates more fully in God than the "communal people." If so, the notorious claim that opens Part II—"I'd sooner, except the penalties, kill a man than a hawk"—is a dramatic gesture that is more than a rejection of humanity; it registers both the speaker's dismay at having had to kill the hawk and his conflicting relationships to nature, pain, the "wild God," and the "communal people."

The way these two encounters with the figure of the hawk, the poem's two parts, play against each other and drive both the speaker's various didactic claims and his emotional responses suggest that "Hurt Hawks" is a dramatic poem more than a didactic one. The arguments in it are less its conclusion and more a part of how the speaker wrestles with his reactions to the hawk's pain and his act of killing it, as suggested by the way the poem ends not with a concluding claim but a final, complex moment of vision. The poem offers one final hint that it should be read dramatically, with close attention to the speaker's emotional stake in his material and his claims. Some of Jeffers' early admirers suggested an affinity between him and the hawks that he celebrated in this and other poems (an identification that Jeffers seemed to share). The title suggests that there are two "hawks" in the poem, even though the injured hawk of Part I is apparently the same hawk that is shot in Part II. Implicitly, the second hawk of the title is the speaker, who is hurt both by the pain of the actual hawk and by the decision to kill it.

TIM HUNT

**Further Reading**

Brophy, Robert, editor, *Robinson Jeffers: Dimensions of a Poet,* New York: Fordham University Press, 1995

Carpenter, Frederic Ives, *Robinson Jeffers,* New York: Twayne, 1962

Karman, James, *Robinson Jeffers: Poet of California,* San Francisco: Chronicle Books, 1987; revised edition, Brownsville, Oregon: Story Line Press, 1995

Karman, James, editor, *Critical Essays on Robinson Jeffers,* Boston: G.K. Hall, 1990

Ridgeway, Ann N., editor, *The Selected Letters of Robinson Jeffers, 1897–1962,* Baltimore, Maryland: Johns Hopkins University Press, 1968

Thesing, William B., editor, *Robinson Jeffers and a Galaxy of Writers: Essays in Honor of William H. Nolte,* Columbia: University of South Carolina Press, 1995

Zaller, Robert, editor, *Centennial Essays for Robinson Jeffers,* Newark: University of Delaware Press, and London: Associated University Presses, 1991

## Shine, Perishing Republic

Critics (but not readers) avoided Robinson Jeffers' poetry in the mid–20th century, especially formalists such as the New Critics, because of its content as well as its form. Jeffers is primarily a nature poet, and his worldview is based in his vision of a post-Darwinian universe in which humanity plays a minor role at best. In addition Jeffers wrote in free verse, usually using long lines and employing direct statement, techniques devalued by New Critics. "Shine, Perishing Republic," a short lyric written in the early 1920s and originally published in *Tamar, and Other Poems* (1924), provides an excellent example of Jeffers' typical themes and poetics.

"Shine, Perishing Republic" consists of five couplets, with lines containing between 20 and 27 syllables; the unstressed syllables are uncounted, and each line has nine or ten stressed syllables. Jeffers' long line makes what would be a brief text, in another poetic idiom, a more substantial poem. A contemporary Modernist poem in couplets, say Williams' "Red Wheelbarrow," with no more than three words per line, produces a decidedly different effect. The tension and structure that an Imagist-Objectivist poet achieves by means of line breaks, fragmented syntax, and omitted punctuation, Jeffers achieves by means of parallelism, rhetorical figures, and direct statement. The poem itself has a tripartite structure: the first two couplets establish parallel metaphors that express Jeffers' concept of history, the third states his main point, and the last two make personal modifications of his general statement.

The poem expounds one of Jeffers' lifelong themes: the permanence of nature versus the transience of culture. In this case Jeffers views the America of the emerging Jazz Age from his isolated position on the West Coast and proclaims it decadent and corrupt. The controlling metaphor of the first couplet is molten metal being cast into a mold: "While this America settles in the mould of its vulgarity, heavily thickening to empire, / And protest, only a bubble in the molten mass, pops and sighs out, and the mass hardens[.]" The unformed "metal" of the people, their character as the "demos," is being shaped, or indeed misshapen, by the vulgarity of the form it is being cast into. Jeffers shows his individualist, and somewhat aristocratic, disdain for "this" America in his diction: "vulgarity" derives from the Latin *vulgus,* the common people, and "mass," used here twice, also has a negative connotation. Moreover, this metaphor establishes a concrete image of nation-building as a cultural process. The speaker foresees that his own protest against this state of decline is itself a part of the process, however, and thus meaningless as countermand. By making this whole couplet a subordinate clause, the poet uses sentence structure to indicate that his poem has a larger statement to make.

The main clause introduces the metaphor that Jeffers wishes to emphasize: "I sadly smiling remember that the flower fades to make the fruit, the fruit rots to make earth. / Out of the mother; and through the spring exultances, ripeness and decadence; and home to the mother." In this couplet Jeffers makes his first significant rhetorical move. Rather than simply opposing nature to culture, the speaker naturalizes the cultural process of decadence, reconnecting it to its literal meaning of decay. Now, instead of the human-made artifact, the cast metal, society is seen as participating in natural cycles of growth and decay. Jeffers derives this perspective from German historian Oswald Spengler, whose *The Decline of the West* theorized that history moves in cyclical periods of ascent and decline.

Taking this long view, the speaker can turn his protest to praise, and this ironic turn is the center of the poem: "You making haste haste on decay: not blameworthy; life is good, be it stubbornly long or suddenly / A mortal splendor: meteors are not needed less than mountains: shine, perishing republic." In urging the republic on in its decline into empire, the speaker can praise the beauty of the process while maintaining his distance from it, another typical Jeffers stance. This distance allows him to see both the decline and its beauty. Yet another metaphor expresses the theme of transience versus impermanence, one that naturalizes both terms: the endurance of mountains and the splendid but brief flash of a meteor.

The final two couplets modify the position reached in the central couplet and personalize the poem by apostrophizing the poet's twin sons:

> But for my children, I would have them keep their distance
> from the thickening center; corruption
> Never has been compulsory, when the cities lie at the
> monster's feet there are left the mountains.

And boys, be in nothing so moderate as in love of man, a
clever servant, insufferable master.
There is the trap that catches noblest spirits, that caught—
they say—God, when he walked on earth.

Although the speaker has claimed that "meteors are not needed less than mountains," in the fourth couplet he betrays his true commitment: he would rather his sons remain in the free and enduring mountains. His last bit of advice expresses the seed of his Inhumanist philosophy codified in the 1940s; he requires moderation in the love of fellow beings. Alluding to God's incarnation in Christ, the speaker refers to excessive love for man as a trap. As Jeffers has said in other poems, he believes people should love the coast opposite humanity in order to achieve freedom from the painful and deluded anthropocentric worldview.

The aloof stance required to imagine this view has drawn charges of cruelty and fascism against Jeffers. It is one thing to criticize a frivolous society during an economic boom, and another to express such sentiments during a depression or war, as in fact Jeffers did in companion poems to "Shine, Perishing Republic." In the 1930s he wrote "Shine, Republic," which expresses similar sentiments but in a more public manner, and which he read at the Library of Congress as part of an address on freedom. Prior to the outbreak of World War II he wrote "Shine, Empire," the most topical of these poems, referring to Roosevelt and Hitler. If the coming war seen in naturalized terms is too much for many readers to take, the failure of the later poems underscores the success of the earlier one. "Shine, Perishing Republic" stands as an example of Jeffers' free-verse poetics at their most muscular and vital. Against the experimentalism of his Modernist contemporaries, Jeffers demonstrates the power of rhetoric and direct statement to express complex emotion and political protest.

George Hart

**Further Reading**

Beers, Terry, "*. . . A Thousand Graceful Subtleties": Rhetoric in the Poetry of Robinson Jeffers,* New York: Peter Lang, 1995

Brophy, Robert, editor, *Robinson Jeffers: Dimensions of a Poet,* New York: Fordham University Press, 1995

Everson, William, *The Excesses of God: Robinson Jeffers as a Religious Figure,* Stanford, California: Stanford University Press, 1988

Hunt, Tim, "A Voice in Nature: Jeffers' *Tamar, and Other Poems,*" *American Literature* 61, no. 2 (1989)

Nickerson, Edward A., "Freedom, Democracy, and Poetry: What Robinson Jeffers Really Said at the Library of Congress," *The Library Chronicle of the University of Texas at Austin* (new series) 40 (1987)

Thesing, William B., editor, *Robinson Jeffers and a Galaxy of Writers: Essays in Honor of William H. Nolte,* Columbia: University of South Carolina Press, 1995

---

# Georgia Douglas Johnson 1886–1966

Georgia Douglas Johnson—poet, playwright, composer, and teacher—was born in Atlanta, Georgia. Most sources date her birth year as 1886, but her obituary gives 1880 as her starting point. Although her parents are listed as George and Laura Camp, little is known about her childhood or her parents. Her appearance (very fair skinned with angular features), the absence of any discussion about her family history, and a preoccupation with miscegenation in her poetry and dramas allude to a mixed-race heritage. Johnson was formally educated in music and at first dreamed of becoming a composer. She soon settled for schoolteacher and assistant principal in the Atlanta school system, before marrying Henry Lincoln Johnson, an African-American politician and lawyer, several years her senior. They relocated to Washington, D.C., in 1910, and Johnson gave birth to two sons.

The new environment proved profitable for Johnson. Their house became a literary hub during the Harlem Renaissance, and despite her husband's disapproval, Johnson became a leading figure. She was considered "the foremost woman poet of the race" and was better known and more widely published than any of the other African-American female poets of this time. Johnson produced three volumes of poetry in ten years; no other African-American woman published a single volume of poetry during the Harlem Renaissance. In 1916, her first poems appeared in *The Crisis,* the magazine of the National Association for the Advancement of Colored People (NAACP). Her first volume, *The Heart of a Woman* (1918), made her reputation. Johnson became the first African-American woman since Frances Ellen Watkins Harper to be widely recognized as a poet, drawing comparisons to Sara Teasdale and Edna St. Vincent Millay. Her second volume, *Bronze: A Book of Verse* (1922), was a change in theme and an attempt to connect more deeply with the issues of the Harlem Renaissance. *An Autumn Love Cycle* (1928) is considered by some to be her best volume. After taking a lengthy hiatus to successfully pursue playwriting, Johnson published her fourth volume, *Share My World* (1962), which includes poems written to and for friends, some from earlier collections, and a series of inspirational essays.

Johnson's first volume of poetry was a collection of love poems expressing feminine sensibility and a longing for love. In her attempt to appeal to all women, white and black alike, she received harsh criticism for an apparent lack of concern for racial issues. Although this critique may have some basis, her poems do reveal an awareness of sexism and the oppressive nature of traditional female roles. The title poem likens a woman's heart to a caged bird. In "Smothered Fires," she presents a woman suppressing her "burning flame." In "When I Am Dead," the speaker delays a "blooming legacy" until her death and funeral. Other poems in this collection—"Foredoom," "Omega," "Despair," "Illusions," and "My Little Dreams"—refer to dead hopes and dreams as well as the solitude Johnson finds to be a frequent part of womanhood. Some poems, such as "Dead Leaves," focus on nature and the seasons. This collection, as well as most of her poetry, shows the influence of classical and Victorian verse. Some of her poems have been described as "perfect lyrics." Ironically, although her husband did not approve of his wife's longing for a literary career, *The Heart of a Woman* is dedicated to him, leading critics to a biographical reading of the themes found in this volume.

Johnson composed the poems in her second volume, *Bronze,* as an attempt to show her solidarity with the struggle against racism and racial oppression. With 65 poems and nine sections, the volume deals entirely with blackness, addressing race riots, lynchings, and random violence; the dominant image is that of the "mantle"—similar to W.E.B. DuBois' image of a veil—a cloak of darkness enveloping the community. Whereas her first volume included only two poems about motherhood and/or children, one section is devoted entirely to the struggles of black motherhood. It generally follows a movement from despair and entreaty to confidence and determination. The last section of the volume, "Appreciations," includes praise poems and sonnets to specific individuals such as W.E.B. DuBois and Abraham Lincoln. She experiments with sonnets, quatrains, and free verse. "Aliens" is a unique treatment of the tragic mulatto character, "Black Woman" presents a potential mother who refuses to bring a black child into this world of "cruelty and sin," and "Homing Braves" is a salute to proud black soldiers returning from World War I. Although her second volume received mixed reviews, it further enhanced her reputation as a poet.

Johnson became a widow in 1925, and while Lincoln's death allowed her free time to write, she found herself without financial support. While she continued the literary evenings at her home (which helped to make her well known) and created a New Negro Renaissance in Washington, D.C., she also was forced to seek employment in jobs ranging from substitute teacher to labor inspector. Her third volume of poetry, *An Autumn Love Cycle,* marks a return to her original themes and tells the story of an older woman's romantic affair. This is considered by most to be her best collection. While she uses nature images as metaphor for a lover, the speaker is concerned with passing time and the aging process. The collection reflects a pondering over love lost—but gratitude at having loved at all.

Johnson's last collection, *Share My World,* is a small volume that was published privately. During the many years separating her third and fourth volumes, Johnson's poems continued to appear in various newspapers, magazines, and anthologies. Not much criticism has been published about Johnson as a poet. Despite the quantity and quality of her work, she is often considered a "minor" poet of the Harlem Renaissance, living in the shadow of the more well-known male poets Langston Hughes and Countee Cullen.

ADENIKE MARIE DAVIDSON

*See also* Harlem Renaissance

**Biography**

Born in Atlanta, Georgia, 10 September 1886. Attended Atlanta University, Georgia, Howard University, Washington, D.C., Oberlin College, Ohio; taught school in Atlanta; commissioner of conciliation in Department of Labor, Washington, D.C., 1925–34. First Prize in drama contest, *Opportunity* magazine, 1927; honorary Litt.D., Atlanta University, 1965. Died in Washington, D.C., 14 May 1966.

**Poetry**

*The Heart of a Woman, and Other Poems,* 1918
*Bronze: A Book of Verse,* 1922
*An Autumn Love Cycle,* 1928
*Share My World: A Book of Poems,* 1962
*The Selected Works of Georgia Douglas Johnson,* 1997

**Other Writings:** plays (*Plumes,* 1927).

**Further Reading**


Dover, Cedric, "The Importance of Georgia Douglas Johnson," *Crisis* 59 (December 1952)
Fletcher, Winona, "Georgia Douglas Johnson," in *Dictionary of Literary Biography,* edited by Thadious M. Davis and Trudier Harris, Detroit, Michigan: Gale, 1984
Hull, Gloria T., *Color, Sex, and Poetry: Three Women Writers of the Harlem Renaissance,* Bloomington: Indiana University Press, 1987
Roses, Lorraine Elena, and Ruth Elizabeth Randolph, *Harlem's Glory: Black Women Writing, 1900–1950,* Cambridge, Massachusetts: Harvard University Press, 1996
Tate, Claudia, "Introduction," in *The Selected Works of Georgia Douglas Johnson,* by Georgia Douglas Johnson, New York: Hall, and London: Prentice Hall International, 1997


---

## James Weldon Johnson 1871–1938

Heralded in his time as the "Dean of Negro Letters," James Weldon Johnson literally made it his business that blacks succeed in the arts as part of a larger program of "racial uplift." One of the most notable successes was his own; his name is linked with countless "firsts," including first African-American to hold a visiting professorship at New York University and, subsequently, designer of the first African-American studies course to be taught at a white mainstream university. Had he lived to continue the program he was developing at NYU, as one critic noted, African-American studies would have been born in the late 1930s instead of in the 1960s with the Black Arts movement. Johnson achieved on many levels, composing in collaboration with his brother what is known as the Negro National Anthem, "Lift Every Voice and Sing," as well as popular songs for Broadway. He drew together anthologies of black poetry, spirituals, and sermons and, in the novel he wrote, predicted the cultural value of ragtime before anyone else had reckoned it. His success is little short of astonishing, especially when one considers the racial terrain of the country during his lifetime.

Johnson's case offers a glimpse into what must be seen as the special qualities that enabled his success. For, as Carl Van Vechten noted in a letter he wrote to Johnson after reading *Along this Way* (1933), Johnson's autobiography,

> I suppose you know that, aside from what unpleasantness racial prejudice has played, you have had a most enchanted and charmed life, full of luck, pleasure, rewards, and what not. People who benefit from luck—I am one of them and SO I KNOW—however are indebted to their own prowess more than is generally suspected. In other words, while you were working and playing in tin-pan alley you were unconsciously fitting yourself mentally, socially, etc. for a diplomatic career; your service in South America, in turn, made you invaluable to the NAACP. And all of this fed the future college professor and made him fat with the kind of ideas which inspire college students.

Most are inclined to agree with Van Vechten's appreciation of Johnson's "prowess" here, but a closer look at his poetic efforts might reveal more about the relationship between race and literary production with which James Weldon Johnson so masterfully contended.

Born and raised in Florida, Johnson took education as his first vocation. He became principal of the middle school he graduated from and helped to develop it into a high school during his tenure. Later he took up the study of law and became—despite the prejudices of his examiners—the first African-American to pass the Florida bar. His first major poetic achievement came with the 1917 publication in the *New York Times* of "Fifty Years," a poem commemorating the 50th anniversary of the Emancipation Proclamation. Striking themes that alternate between celebration, gratitude, and the need to continue struggling, the poem is both a keepsake and a brandishing iron. With a celebratory "O brothers mine, today we stand" the poem begins, "Where half a century sweeps our ken. / Since God, through Lincoln's ready hand, / Struck off our bonds and made us men." But the tone soon changes to one of admonition:

> For never let the thought arise
> That we are here on sufferance bare;
> Outcasts, assylumed 'neath these skies,
> And aliens without part of share.
>
> This land is ours by right of birth,
> This land is ours by right of toil;
> We helped to turn its virgin earth,
> Our sweat is in its fruitful soil.

Calling the United States a "haughty land," the poem recognizes the need to overcome the pervading racism of its white citizenry and thus typifies Johnson's program.

Famous for speaking out against dialect as the major poetic mode for African-American writers, Johnson argued that dialect had only "two stops, one for pathos and one for humor." Although many disagree with his assessment of dialect, particularly considering the richness of Zora Neale Hurston's work, Johnson's assessment rests largely on literary history as he knew it and especially on the thwarted career of his friend and fellow poet Paul Laurence Dunbar. By the end of his career, Dunbar, dubbed the "Poet Laureate of the Negro Race" by William Dean Howells, resented being confined to dialect poetry by both his publishers and his readership. Johnson discusses this example explicitly in his introduction to *The Book of American Negro Poetry* (1922), and it was never far from his mind when pronouncing his views on dialect elsewhere. One feature of this discussion that many neglect to mention is the important proviso "at present," making Johnson's condemnation of dialect conditional. His interest was to commemorate and break new ground for blacks; he considered dialect an impediment to those goals at that time. Subsequent work in dialect, notably that used by Langston Hughes, met with Johnson's approval.

Part of Johnson's genius lay in knowing how to find a middle ground that permits success with dignity. For instance, together with his brother Rosamond and the white composer Robert Cole, Johnson transformed what were then called "coon songs" into popular ballads of the Broadway stage. In the hit song "Run Brudder Possum" he replaced the word "coon" with a character's name, among other significant changes. In rewriting the song, Johnson's aim was to disassociate black people from the lowly circumstances of the cotton field, highlighting instead the beauty and pathos of the artistry over the circumstances of production. One might also see his rejection of dialect in the poetry, sermons, and spirituals he published as consistent with this effort.

In addition to the two volumes of his own poetry, Johnson also published one of the first anthologies of African-American poetry as well as a series of sermons in a beautifully crafted book he called *God's Trombones* (1927). In an effort to make the book's form as spectacular as its content, Johnson made stipulations about the book's physical composition an explicit part of the contract with the publisher. Illustrated by the celebrated Harlem Renaissance artist Aaron Douglas, *God's Trombones* represents still another effort on Johnson's part for racial uplift. Eschewing dialect in his recovery of folk sermons that had their origins in slave culture, Johnson called the sermons God's "trombones" rather than "trumpets" as they had traditionally been called because of the special properties of the instrument. Played with a "slide" instead of through the trumpet's percussive "stops," the trombone, in Johnson's view, possesses "above all others [instruments] the power to express the wide and varied range of emotions encompassed by the human voice—and with greater amplitude" (see preface to *God's Trombones,* 1927). Taken in a broader context, Johnson's evaluation of the trombone is a controlling metaphor for black literary and cultural production. In his view the trombone renders a broader swath of sentiment, muted and nuanced by the mechanics of the instrument itself. Thus, as also demonstrated by his evaluation of dialect, Johnson placed value on merging with white culture so as to be understood by it.

Johnson achieved a place in American culture as a "race man" through a multitude of venues. Additional publications include *The Autobiography of an Ex-Colored Man* (1912, 1927), *Fifty Years, and Other Poems* (1917), *Black Manhattan* (1930), *Saint Peter Relates an Incident of the Resurrection Day* (1930), and *Negro Americans, What Now?* (1934). Johnson's edited volumes of poetry and song include *The Book of American Negro Poetry* (1922), *The Second Book of American Negro Poetry* (1931), and with his brother, Rosamond, *The Book of American Negro Spirituals* (1925) and *The Second Book of American Negro Spirituals* (1926). In addition to Johnson's own significant literary production he also served on selection committees for the Guggenheim Foundation, reviewed books for publication by the major presses of the day, and functioned as a cultural commentator from the pages of the *New York Age*. His institutional accomplishments include his role as a founding member of the American Society for Composers, Authors and Publishers (ASCAP) and his many years of service as Secretary of the NAACP.

AUGUSTA ROHRBACH

**Biography**

Born in Jacksonville, Florida, 17 June 1871. Attended Atlanta University, A.B. 1894, A.M. 1904; Columbia University, New York; principal, Stanton Central Grammar School for Negroes, Jacksonville; helped found Jacksonville *Daily American;* admitted to Florida bar; practiced law in Jacksonville, 1897–1901; co-writer with his brother, J. Rosamond Johnson, of popular songs and light opera, 1901–06; United States Consul, Puerto Cabello, Venezuela, 1906–09, and Corinto, Nicaragua, 1909–12; Executive Secretary, National Association for the Advancement of Colored People, 1916–30; Spence Professor of creative literature, Fisk University, Nashville, Tennessee, 1930–38; Visiting Professor of creative literature, New York University, 1934; columnist, *New York Age;* director, American Fund for Public Service; trustee, Atlanta University. Received Spingarn medal, 1925; Du Bois Prize for Negro Literature, 1933; honorary Litt.D., Talladega College, Alabama, 1917, Howard University, Washington, D.C., 1923; member, Academy of Political Science. Died in Wiscasset, Maine, 26 June 1938.

**Poetry**

*Fifty Years, and Other Poems,* 1917
*Self-Determining Haiti,* 1920
*God's Trombones: Seven Negro Sermons in Verse,* 1927
*Saint Peter Relates an Incident of the Resurrection Day,* 1930
*Saint Peter Relates an Incident: Selected Poems,* 1935
*Lift Every Voice and Sing: Selected Poems,* 1993
*The Creation: A Poem,* 1993
*The Selected Writings of James Weldon Johnson* (includes prose), 1995
*Complete Poems,* 2000

**Other Writings:** plays (*Shakespeare in Harlem* [with Langston Hughes], 1959), novel (*The Autobiography of an Ex-Colored Man,* 1912), nonfiction (*Negro Americans, What Now?* 1934), songs (*Lift Ev'ry Voice and Sing* [*Negro National Anthem*], 1900), autobiography (*Along This Way: The Autobiography of James Weldon Johnson,* 1933); edited collections of literature (*The Book of American Negro Poetry,* 1922; revised edition, 1931).

**Further Reading**

Andrews, William, "The Representation of Slavery and the Rise of Afro-American Literary Realism, 1865–1920," in *African American Autobiography: A Collection of Critical Essays,* edited by Andrews, Englewood Cliffs, New Jersey: Prentice Hall, 1993
Fleming, Robert E., *James Weldon Johnson,* Boston: Twayne, 1987
Johnson, James Weldon, *The Selected Writings of James Weldon Johnson,* 2 vols., edited by Sondra Kathryn Wilson, Oxford and New York: Oxford University Press, 1995
Levy, Eugene, *James Weldon Johnson: Black Leader, Black Voice,* Chicago: University of Chicago Press, 1973
Price, Kenneth M., and Lawrence J. Oliver, editors, *Critical Essays on James Weldon Johnson,* New York: G.K. Hall, and London: Prentice Hall International, 1997

## God's Trombones

The trombone is the only wind instrument that possesses a full range of tones equivalent to the range of the human voice. When devising a title for his 1927 collection of verse sermons, *God's Trombones,* James Weldon Johnson decided that the trombone best symbolized the vast range, tone, and timbre of a traditional African-American preacher's voice. He also recognized the trombone's close associations with 1920s jazz bands, and his title indicates the convergence of the secular and the sacred in African-American culture.

Johnson, who began his artistic career as a musician in collaboration with his brother, Rosamond Johnson, and their partner, Bob Cole, draws on a musical metaphor and a musical approach to notation to convey a distinctive oratorical style. In his preface to *God's Trombones,* Johnson explains that he uses line arrangements to convey the dramatic tempos of the preacher's voice and dashes to suggest "a certain sort of pause that is marked by a quick intaking and an audible expulsion of breath."

Johnson's portrayal of his subject matter and of a living, spoken language stands as an important achievement for literary Modernism. In 1920, *The Freeman,* a Chicago magazine focused on political and social criticism, initially published the first verse sermon in the collection "The Creation." "The Creation" appeared again in Alain Locke's epoch-building anthology *The New Negro* (1925). The poem's early publication date and its later inclusion in Locke's anthology indicate Johnson's significant role as an innovator in the Harlem Renaissance movement to transform African-American vernacular poetics. *God's Trombones* also includes illustrations by the Harlem Renaissance's most famous painter, Aaron Douglas, and bold calligraphy by C.B. Falls.

The visual impact of Douglas' and Falls' artistry coupled with the written language of the verse sermons in *God's Trombones* suggest the energy and power of skillful improvisation. In "The Prodigal Son," for example, Douglas' drawing of two women and a man surrounded by images of dice, cards, money, alcohol, and trombones follows Falls' formal and austere calligraphy, and in his first lines the preacher proclaims, "Young man— / Young man— / Your arm's too short to box with God." Readers must actively make connections as the visual symbolism and the language of the text combine biblical imagery with contemporary life.

In its rendition of a vernacular style, the language of these poems demands to be heard as well as read. Like a musician who improvises on a composed melody, the reader must actively participate in the process of conjuring and creating the sounds of the text. Through this active participation, the reader symbolically becomes a member of the preacher's congregation. Johnson thus bridges the gap between observer and participant in these poems, an approach that also conjoins spoken and written language. His subtle techniques dismantle the constrained, stilted language of conventional poetic dialect usage. The first stanza of "The Creation" illustrates the way that Johnson captures nuances of spoken language:

And God stepped out on space,
And he looked around and said:
I'm lonely—
I'll make me a world.

In these lines, the personification of divine authority and the vernacular usage of "me" indicate a distinctive tone and style of speech.

Throughout *God's Trombones,* the silent page calls the reader's attention to the sounds of its language. "The Crucifixion" emphasizes sound through repetition and emphatically punctuated lines:

On Calvary, on Calvary,
They crucified my Jesus.
They nailed him to the cruel tree,
And the hammer!
The hammer!
The hammer!
Rang through Jerusalem's streets.
The hammer!
The hammer!
The hammer!
Rang through Jerusalem's streets.

In this stanza, Johnson portrays the authoritative, bellowing capacity of the preacher's wide vocal range.

Johnson's preacher-speaker compels his audience through his mixture of ancient and contemporary images and his fusion of vernacular idioms with the English of the King James Bible. Johnson portrays the African-American folk preacher as a figure of oratorical force and poetic sublimity who wields significant social and political power by unifying the diverse members of his congregation. The preacher inspires his audience through the Moses and Pharaoh story in "Let My People Go." When Moses triumphs and the Israelites go free, the preacher prophesies victory in present battles against oppression:

Listen!—Listen!
All you sons of Pharaoh.
Who do you think can hold God's people
When the Lord God himself has said,
Let my people go?

Through the verse sermons, the preacher rouses his audience to action. In the preliminary prayer poem, "Listen Lord—A Prayer," the prayer leader appeals to God to give the preacher strength and guidance so that he can move his congregation:

Lord God, this morning—
Put his eye to the telescope of eternity,
And let him look upon the paper walls of time.
Lord, turpentine his imagination,
Put perpetual motion in his arms,
Fill him full of the dynamite of thy power,
Anoint him all over with the oil of thy salvation,
And set his tongue on fire.

This stanza illustrates the style of earthy spirituality that Johnson captures in his collection of verse sermons. In these images, tools of this world, sanctioned by divine authority, give the spiritual leader the power to move his congregation. A "telescope" can metaphorically provide access to understanding eternity's dominion over illusory "paper walls of time." Mineral spirits of "turpentine" can burn the preacher's imagination and drive him to reach his fullest potential. "Perpetual motion" in the physical universe can animate him in the struggle for spiritual transcendence. Finally, images of "dynamite," "oil," and "fire" summon the explosive power of the preacher's voice so that he can inspire his congregation, assuage their pain and tribulations in this life, and give them fortitude to persevere.

Each of Johnson's verse sermons, including this preliminary prayer poem, reveals a facet of the traditional African-American folk preacher's style and voice. The collection as a whole delineates the complexity and magnitude of the preacher's presence as an orator. His charismatic performance and compelling voice arise from the silent pages of *God's Trombones* and demand to be witnessed and heard.

Kristin K. Henson

**Further Reading**


Baker, Houston A., Jr., *Modernism and the Harlem Renaissance,* Chicago: University of Chicago Press, 1987

Edwards, Brent, "The Seemingly Eclipsed Window of Form: James Weldon Johnson's Prefaces," in *The Jazz Cadence of American Culture,* edited by Robert G. O'Meally, New York: Columbia University Press, 1998

Fleming, Robert E., *James Weldon Johnson,* Boston: Twayne, 1987

Fleming, Robert E., "James Weldon Johnson's 'God's Trombones' as a Source for Faulkner's Rev'un Shegog," *College Language Association Journal* 36, no. 1 (1992)

Hutchinson, George, *The Harlem Renaissance in Black and White,* Cambridge, Massachusetts: Harvard University Press, 1995

Johnson, James Weldon, *Along This Way: The Autobiography of James Weldon Johnson,* New York: Viking Press, 1933; reprint, with an introduction by Sondra Kathryn Wilson, New York: Da Capo Press, 2000

Kirschke, Amy Helene, *Aaron Douglas: Art, Race, and the Harlem Renaissance,* Jackson: University Press of Mississippi, 1995

Price, Kenneth M., and Lawrence J. Oliver, editors, *Critical Essays on James Weldon Johnson,* New York: G.K. Hall, and London: Prentice Hall International, 1997

Sundquist, Eric J., *The Hammers of Creation: Folk Culture in Modern African-American Fiction,* Athens: University of Georgia Press, 1992

# Ronald Johnson 1935–98

Ronald Johnson's poetry is visionary, architectonic, and playfully polysemous. His poetic models are William Blake, Christopher Smart, and Walt Whitman. He learned poetry from Charles Olson, Louis Zukofsky, and Robert Duncan, and he learned how to make things with words from such autodidactic builders as the Facteur Cheval, Raymond Isidore, and Simon Rodia. He was as devoted to Thoreau's *Journals* as to L. Frank Baum's *Wizard of Oz.* He was born in western Kansas, in the midst of the American prairie; lived in New York; walked through England; and traced the Appalachian Trail with Jonathan Williams, finally settling in San Francisco. He wrote several books of poetry, and his masterpiece, *ARK* (1980, 1984, 1996), is one of the most idiosyncratic, intelligent, and enjoyable poems ever written by an American. While he was alive, Guy Davenport called him "America's greatest living poet." Robert Duncan believed that Johnson's *ARK* stirred "long-stored feelings of the radiant structural beauty and mystery of the universe."

Perhaps the cornerstone of Johnson's poetics is concrete poetry—the international poetry movement of the 1960s and 1970s that treated words as physical objects—which he examined in as visionary a light as he did the natural world, science, or the poetry of Milton. In a line such as "earthearthearth," which appeared originally in *Songs of the Earth* (1970), his suite of concrete responses to Mahler's musical piece of the same name, and was included in BEAM 24 of *ARK,* Johnson enjoins his readers to "hear the art" and to see the "hearth" that is the earth. Johnson understood that vision is as much an optical phenomenon as it is a spiritual one. Likewise, Johnson's poetry involves a great deal of quotation and found imagery. These are not placed in the poems haphazardly but are carefully arranged in meticulous collages, so that quoted matter illuminates the work at hand. Johnson's poems are built from the sonic and visual qualities of the words themselves. As he put it himself, "It's as lucid as Euclid."

His early work was first collected in *A Line of Poetry, a Row of Trees* (1964), published by Jonathan Williams' Jargon Society, and then recollected in *Valley of the Many-Colored Grasses* (1969), which added a section of new poetry titled "The Different Musics," the poems of which greatly anticipate the formal and material innovations that distinguish *ARK.* The poems in this book are very much in the mode of the emerging projective verse of the time, which means that the figure of Olson looms large over them. His themes were the prairie, the natural world, and those who wrote of that world: Bartram, Audubon, Thoreau, Emerson, and Whitman. The poetry bristles with the Orphic pleasure of naming things, as in these lines from "Quivira":

> Canceas, Cansez, Kansies, Konza: the Indian word
> meaning smoky,
> from an atmospheric condition
> in the fall of the year, called
> Indian Summer:
> smoke in the air,
> in Quivira.

Johnson was likewise able to see Olson as a mythic six-foot bear, pulling bark off a tree.

In *The Book of the Green Man* (1967), Johnson recounts his year walking through England in the form of a seasonal poem; the book was published the same year as Bunting's "Briggflatts," the other great British seasonal poem of that time. This poem is as much a journal of his two years walking through England as it is a resurrection of the tellic druid god of the title, in the form of the Jolly Green Giant. Johnson spent several years directly engaged in the making of concrete poetry, closely affiliated with Ian Hamilton Finlay, whose Wild Hawthorn Press published some of Johnson's poetry. Perhaps his involvement with concrete poetry came to greatest fruition in *Eyes and Objects* (1976), made up of poems that stand for an imaginary art exhibition, in which the poet sought to make poems that literally stood as sculpture. One of the poems, titled "World-Framed Page" and subtitled "molecules on void," is simply a blank sheet of paper.

In 1977, Johnson published *RADI OS,* a book of enduring interest. Inspired by a piece of music by Lukas Foss in which the composer took a piece by Handel and "poked holes in it," Johnson created a poem out of "Paradise Lost" in which he aerated Milton, as if under the direction of Blake. The result is very much unlike Milton yet completely Miltonic. Seemingly in kind with the aleatory techniques of the chance poetics of Jackson Mac Low and John Cage, Johnson's poem is in fact utterly different; indeed, it is yet another act of vision. In *RADI OS,* Johnson uses the Miltonic imagination and vocabulary to see the world anew, such that there is no longer a Fall but the Rising of man into the cosmos. *RADI OS* is one of the truly unique books in American letters.

However, Johnson's masterpiece is his epic poem *ARK.* Begun in 1970 and completed in 1991, *ARK* is a poetic, visual cathedral to language as well as a figurative vessel to carry it into the next millennium, conceived in the antique form of Noah's famous ark but transformed over the course of the poem into a rocket launched into the stars. Composed in 99 parts, made up of three sections of 33 poems apiece, *ARK* is a structurally inhering poem that praises the cosmos, which it evokes not through a Dantean journey through a dark woods but by venturing over the rainbow from Kansas into mythic Oz. Johnson claims to have invented a new poetic form for *ARK.* Whether true or not, he certainly generated some of the most visually exciting page displays in recent American poetry. Most of the poems are constructed along a central axis, so that the poetry evokes limitless symmetries, reflecting the bilateral brain and body as well as the cosmological Tree of Life, which is the image of the universe the poem portrays. BEAM 19, typical of the early sections of the poem, runs,

> lilac, winedark
> sun-gold in chopped scarlet
> starred
> equilateral equangular quinquangles
> (like those balls stitched twelve patchwork of color)
> skiey Okeanos
> clouds like loud chords
> —whose contours their contours pun—
> out of a drop of water-that-does-not-wet-the-hand
> become a blue mirrored ball on emerald lawn
> (with dandelions for
> miles)

The heroic legend of Odysseus vies with Pythagorean observations spied in a mundane, sunny yard, where the sun-gold in the dandelions reflects the light from the creation of the universe, spraying out in a rainbow of colors, the *arc-en-ciel* that the title of the poem puns on. The poem is divided into 33 Beams, which make up the Foundations, and then 33 Spires, which give the poem its vertical dimension. It concludes with 33 Arches, which make up the Ramparts of the poem. This construction takes place—like creation itself—in a day: the Foundations progress from dawn to high noon, the Spires from noon to sundown, and the Ramparts move through midnight, to conclude with a dazzling final evocation of Oz, Souzaphones at a bandstand, Aristotle and Job, a vision of the Primordial Man who is also the Tree of Life, and finally a rocket ship being launched into the morning stars. Although *ARK* belongs in the company of Olson's *Maximus Poems,* Zukofsky's "*A*," Williams' *Paterson,* Pound's *Cantos,* and Duncan's "Passages," there is nothing else quite like *ARK* in American letters. Few other poems yield such consistent readerly pleasure.

Johnson spent the last years of his life writing poems of a narrower scope. His "Blocks to Be Arranged in a Pyramid," which was written in memoriam AIDS, is admittedly a darker poetic project. The poem is made up of spare, haunting quatrains that avoid any conventional sense, instead evoking intense associations, as in "So darksparkling souls / as flame licketh up / consuming flesh / speak in cataract." While Johnson's poetry has earned its place in the lineages of Black Mountain and Objectivist poetries, it has not yet found the audience it deserves. No other poetry of its kind so successfully combines intelligence, ambition, craft, music, ebullience, and play. As Thom Gunn remarked, when the final reckoning of American 20th-century poetry has been made, Johnson may be regarded as one of its greatest practitioners.

PETER O'LEARY

**Biography**

Born in Ashland, Kansas, 25 November 1935. Attended Columbia University, New York, B.A. 1960; served in the United States Army, 1954–56; poet-in-residence, University of Kentucky, Lexington, 1970–71, and University of Washington, Seattle, 1972; led the Wallace Stegner Advanced Workshop at Stanford University, 1991; poet-in-residence, University of California, Berkeley, 1994. Received Inez Boulton Award (*Poetry,* Chicago), 1964; National Endowment for the Arts grant, 1969, 1974; National Poetry Series, 1984. Died in Topeka, Kansas, 4 March 1998.

**Poetry**

*A Line of Poetry, a Row of Trees,* 1964
*Assorted Jungles: Rousseau,* 1966
*Gorse/Goose/Rose, and Other Poems,* 1966
*Sun Flowers,* 1966
*Io and the Ox-Eye Daisy,* 1966
*The Book of the Green Man,* 1967
*The Round Earth on Flat Paper,* 1968
*Reading 1 and 2,* 2 vols., 1968
*Valley of the Many-Colored Grasses,* 1969
*Balloons for Moonless Nights,* 1969
*The Spirit Walks, the Rocks Will Talk,* 1969
*Songs of the Earth,* 1970
*Maze/Mane/Wane,* 1973
*Eyes and Objects,* 1976
*RADI OS I–IV,* 1977
*ARK: The Foundations 1–33,* 1980
*ARK 50: Spires 34–50,* 1984
*ARK,* 1996
*To Do as Adam Did: Selected Poems,* 2000

**Other Writings:** cookbooks, translations of French nonfiction (*Sports and Divertissements,* by Erik Satie, 1965).

**Further Reading**

Davenport, Guy, "Ronald Johnson," in *The Geography of the Imagination,* San Francisco: North Point Press, 1981
Folsom, Ed, "Whispering Whitman to the Ears of Others: Ronald Johnson's Recipe for *Leaves of Grass,*" in *The Continuing Presence of Walt Whitman,* edited by Robert K. Martin, Iowa City: University of Iowa Press, 1992
O'Leary, Peter, "*ARK* as a Spiritual Phenomenon: An Approach to Reading Ronald Johnson's Poem," *Sagetrieb* 14, no. 3 (Winter 1995)
O'Leary, Peter, "An Interview with Ronald Johnson," *Chicago Review* 42, no. 1 (1996)
Selinger, Eric, "'I Composed the Holes': Reading Ronald Johnson's *RADI OS,*" *Contemporary Literature* 33, no. 1 (1992)
Selinger, Eric, "Important Pleasures and Others: Michael Palmer, Ronald Johnson," *Postmodern Culture: An Electronic Journal of Interdisciplinary Criticism* 4, no. 3 (1994)
Stratton, Dirk, *Ronald Johnson,* Boise, Idaho: Boise State University, 1996

---

## LeRoi Jones. *See* Imamu Amiri Baraka (LeRoi Jones)

---

# June Jordan 1936–

An activist, teacher, and prolific writer in many genres, June Jordan challenges her readers to think about who they are and how they use the language of everyday life. Her writings include children's books, novels, essay collections, plays, and a libretto for an opera, as well as ten books of poetry. Her poems are occasional poems in the best sense: they emerge from and address particular audiences, historical moments, and linguistic formations as these audiences, moments, and languages come to the forefront of struggles for human freedom and dignity. Jordan's work should be read in light of her affiliations with the black nationalist and feminist movements of the 1960s and 1970s, but these affiliations provide no simple key to her work. Her poetry is consistently critical of set identities and meanings, and is noteworthy for its resistance to oppression and limits (as they are manifested in "proper" language, political institutions, and everyday activities, for instance) more than for the articulation of any particular ideology or aesthetics.

Jordan grew up in Brooklyn the daughter of Jamaican immigrant parents. She comments that her early family life and schooling taught her how to fight. While the slight Jordan may not have won many fights against the bullies of her family and neighborhood, she learned that if she fought hard she could at least earn some peace: "nobody fought me twice. They said I was 'crazy'" (*Civil Wars,* 1981). Jordan's poetry is of a similar battling nature: she uses words to fend off the violence of those who attack her or the peoples she speaks of and for in her verse.

Jordan's poetry ranges widely in form and theme, but one consistent aspect of her writing is its rhetorical self-consciousness—that is, her poems are oriented toward provoking a response in the reader, and they foreground the occasion of their writing and reading. She calls attention to the fact that her writings serve a function at a particular historical or personal moment for their audience, and she crafts a poetic that bridges the gaps between reader and poet, that forces a recognition of shared interests, identity, or passion between reader and poet, reader and other readers.

Her first collection, *Some Changes* (1971), gathers poems that were written during the 1960s, and many of its selections are inflected by the Black Arts aesthetic of the period. They stress the poet's role in giving shape to and serving the needs of a nationalist black audience. "Okay Negroes" is a poetic calling out of the "Negroes" in Jordan's audience. The poem ends with two questions sandwiched around a command:

> you think who's gonna give you something?
>
> Come a little closer.
> Where you from?

The poet forces a self-identifying response from her audience at the same time that she moves them closer to herself (and each other). The function of this poem is to simultaneously prompt self-critique and engender a communal identity in its audience.

Jordan is a pioneer in the use of Black English, especially in her attempts to offer a systemized accounting of it. For Jordan a struggle over the form of writing is part of a larger battle by African-Americans, those whom white America has classified as "nonstandard," to assert self-identity. "The problem is that we are saying *language,* but really dealing with power," she explains in her important essay collection *Civil Wars.* The link between power and language, and the use of poetry to wrest or resist language's power, are central themes in many of her works. "Getting Down to Get Over" (1972) articulates resistance to the particular burdens of oppression that African-American women have borne. It begins with a list of the many generic, and often dismissive and insulting, names that have been applied to African-American women. The poem then turns from exorcising these hurts to taking control, assertively self-naming, a transformation enabled by the survival of African-American women in the past:

> momma
> teach me hot to hold a new life
> momma
> help me
> turn the face of history
> *to your face.*

The rhetorical function of Jordan's poems is often announced at their start: many of her poem titles name the poem's form, audience, and/or moment, as in "1977: Poem for Mrs. Fannie Lou Hamer" and "A Song for Soweto." The fitting of the language to the function of the poem is a central component of Jordan's craft; often the success of her best poems depends on the subtle and yet seemingly effortless selection of voice, tone, and form to negotiate the orientation of speaker and audience toward one another. Jordan's famous poem about rape, "Case in Point," provides a horrific example of exactly the kind of language use that her poetry fights against. The poem ends with the image of the rapist who

> rammed
> what he described as his quote big dick
> unquote into my mouth
> and shouted out: "D'ya want to swallow
> my big dick; well, do ya?
>
> He was being rhetorical.

Jordan's speaking from her own experiences counters this silence; she speaks from and to the silences in the languages of domination.

While Jordan is best known in the United States for her advocacy for African-Americans in her poetry and for her feminist writings, in both of which she carefully shapes autobiographical and topical materials, her poetry of resistance is international in scope. "Moving Towards Home," from *Living Room* (1985), suggests the multiple and situational nature of the resistance poet's sense of identity. Jordan writes of her reluctance to speak about the horrors that followed the Israeli invasion of Lebanon, but she is compelled to speak by their violence and the suffering of their victims. By the end of the poem she asserts unity with the people she speaks about:

> I was born a Black woman
> and now
> I am become a Palestinian
> against the relentless laughter of evil.

The sufferings of the victims, their silence enforced by violence and by the euphemisms in official accounts of the massacre, force the poet—a black woman who has suffered her own oppressions but who in this case has better access to the means of representation—to become Palestinian.

Jordan's poetry consistently aspires to a poetic language that builds community, from her early black nationalist writings to her later collections of love poems and more public verse. Like her contemporaries Audre Lorde and Adrienne Rich, Jordan is continually remaking the form and function of contemporary poetry as she fits her poems to the needs of the particular audience she addresses.

Scott MacPhail

**Biography**

Born in New York City, 9 July 1936. Attended Barnard College, New York, 1953–55, 1956–57; University of Chicago, 1955–56; assistant to the producer of the film *The Cool World,* 1964; research associate, Mobilization for Youth Inc., New York, 1965–66; director, Voice of the Children, 1967–70; member of the English Department, City College, New York, 1967–70, 1972–75, and 1977–78, Connecticut College, New London, 1968, Sarah Lawrence College, Bronxville, New York, 1971–75, and Yale University, New Haven, Connecticut, 1974–75; Associate Professor, 1978–82, Professor of English, 1982–89, and director of the Poetry Center and the Creative Writing Program, 1986–89, State University of New York, Stony Brook; Chancellor's Lecturer, 1986, and since 1989 Professor of Afro-American studies and women's studies, University of California, Berkeley; poet-in-residence, Teachers and Writers Collaborative, New York, 1966–68, Macalester College, St. Paul, Minnesota, 1980, Loft Mentor Series, Minneapolis, 1983, and Walt Whitman Birthplace, Huntington, New York, 1988; Reid Lecturer, Barnard College, 1976; playwright-in-residence, New Dramatists, New York, 1987–88; Visiting Professor, Department of Afro-American Studies, University of Wisconsin, Madison, 1988; member of the executive board, Teachers and Writers Collaborative, since 1978, PEN American Center, 1980–84, Poets and Writers Inc. since 1979, American Writers Congress since 1981, Center for Constitutional Rights since 1984, and Authors Guild since 1986; political columnist, *The Progressive* magazine, since 1989, and *City Limits,* London, since 1990. Received Rockefeller grant, 1969; American Academy in Rome Environmental Design Prize, 1970; New York Council of the Humanities Award, 1977; Creative Artists Public Service grant, 1978; Yaddo fellowship, 1979, 1980; National Endowment for the Arts fellowship, 1982; National Association of Black Journalists Award, 1984; New York Foundation for the Arts fellowship, 1985; Massachusetts Council on the Arts Award, 1985; MacDowell Colony fellowship, 1987; Nora Astorga Leadership Award, 1989. Living in Berkeley, California.

**Poetry**

*Some Changes,* 1971
*Poem: On Moral Leadership as a Political Dilemma (Watergate, 1973),* 1973
*New Days: Poems of Exile and Return,* 1974
*Things That I Do in the Dark: Selected Poetry,* 1977; revised edition, 1982
*Passion: New Poems, 1977–1980,* 1980
*Living Room: New Poems, 1980–1984,* 1985
*Lyrical Campaigns: Selected Poems,* 1989
*Naming Our Destiny: New and Selected Poems,* 1989
*Haruiko/Love Poems,* 1994
*Kissing God Goodbye: Poems, 1991–1997,* 1997

**Other Writings:** plays, children's literature, essays (*Civil Wars,* 1981; *Moving Towards Home: Political Essays,* 1989; *Technical Difficulties,* 1994; *Affirmative Acts,* 1998), a guidebook (*June Jordan's Poetry for the People: A Blueprint for the Revolution,* edited by Lauren Muller, 1995), editions of collected poetry (*Soulscript: Afro-American Poetry,* 1970), novels, a memoir (*Soldier: A Poet's Childhood,* 2000).

**Further Reading**


Brogan, Jacqueline Vaught, "From Warrior to Womanist: The Development of June Jordan's Poetry," in *Speaking the Other Self: American Women Writers,* edited by Jeanne Campbell Reesman, Athens: University of Georgia Press, 1997

Erickson, Peter, "After Identity: A Conversation with June Jordan and Peter Erickson," *Transition* 63 (1994)

Freccero, Carla, "June Jordan," in *African American Writers,* edited by Valerie Smith et al., New York: Scribners, 1991

Jordan, June, *Civil Wars,* Boston: Beacon Press: 1981

Jordan, June, "Introduction," in *June Jordan's Poetry for the People: A Revolutionary Blueprint,* edited by Lauren Muller and the Poetry for the People Collective, New York: Routledge, 1995

MacPhail, Scott, "June Jordan and the New Black Intellectuals," *African American Review* 33, no. 1 (1999)


---

# Donald Justice 1925–

Recipient of the Bollingen (1991 with Laura Riding), Pulitzer (1980), and Lamont (1959) prizes for poetry and other prestigious fellowships (e.g., Guggenheim and National Endowment for the Arts fellowships) and for many years an abiding presence at the Iowa Writers' Workshop—as a much-loved and admired teacher of poetry—Donald Justice is paradoxically both a central and elusive figure in American poetry during the last half of the 20th century. He has instructed more poets than perhaps any teacher of his time and many of his students have become poets of established reputation and have developed creative writing programs throughout the United States, poets as different as Jorie Graham, Mark Strand, and Charles Wright. Yet his relatively modest output has left him something of a poet's poet with a small but influential circle of admirers and a number of less enthusiastic reviewers. Dana Gioia, in a volume dedicated to rectifying the problem of Justice's relative critical obscurity, has likened—perhaps hopefully—Justice to Elizabeth Bishop in the mid-1970s before the dramatic rise in her critical reputation. A poet of meticulous seriousness, formal virtuosity, rueful humor, tonal equipoise, and profound learning, Justice's abiding themes are memory and loss, framed both formally and thematically by an engagement with language, poetic tradition, and his own life and body of work.

In an admiring reminiscence of his classmate at Iowa in the 1950s, W.D. Snodgrass mentions that Justice's "intellectual and aesthetic principles seemed fully formed and relatively unshakable" (Goia and Logan, 1997); indeed, Justice's poetry has always exhibited quiet confidence. The book jacket of *The Summer Anniversaries* (1960) notes that he had been "writing poetry seriously for more than a decade, but he has found none of his earliest work worth preserving." This sureness about the aesthetic grounding of his work has remained a constant feature even as he has revised early poems, collected and selected his work. The opening stanza of "The Thin Man," from *Night Light* (1967),

> I indulge myself
> In rich refusals.
> Nothing suffices.

can be taken as wry comment on the poet's aesthetic continence and the mixture of praise and criticism that his work has received. *The Summer Anniversaries* is notable for its formal versatility, its deft rhymes and well-turned sestinas, villanelles, and sonnets. Yet some disparaged its craft and found it derivative—"On the Death of Friends in Childhood" too much like Yeats, "Counting the Mad" with its "This little piggy" pastiche too reminiscent of Bishop's "Visit to St. Elizabeth's." Perhaps because so many of Justice's poems seem to be inspired by other writings—by Gioia's count at least one-quarter of Justice's poems makes use of openly borrowed material—critics have focused on the point of recognition rather than the point of departure. As he writes in *Platonic Scripts* (1984), "Certainly you don't want to imitate. I don't want to imitate poets who write in other languages any more than I want to imitate poets who write in my language; but perhaps I can learn something intangible from them." In the variations that his lyrics deploy, even in early poems such as "Love's Strategems" ("But these maneuverings to avoid / The touching of hands") or in the detached descriptions of "On a Painting by Patient B of the Independence State Hospital for the Insane," Justice displays a notable gift for tonal control that frequently signals a new attitude or treatment. The poems show family resemblance to Robinson and Williams, but the resemblance always stops at a certain point and the intangible something presents itself.

The forms and methods of the early poems would become the explicit themes of Justice's work from the 1960s onward. *Night Light* provides oblique commentary (in Justice's own subdued idiom) on that decade of social and poetic upheaval with poems such as "After a Phrase Abandoned by Wallace Stevens" and "Early Poems" ("How fashionably sad those early poems are. . . . The rhymes, the meters, how they paralyze."). Justice had turned toward syllabics and free verse, and *Night Light* was a showcase for these poems, including poems about the anonymity of interior lives glimpsed from without: "The Suicides," "Hands," "The Tourist from Syracuse," and "Bus Stop"; "To the Hawks" is dedicated to McNamara, Rusk, and Bundy, which reads like a poetic evocation of the notorious Daisy ad of the 1964 presidential campaign (by the time of *Selected Poems* this dedication would acquire an "etc."). The turn toward free verse afforded Justice new ways of creating the patterns and variations that have always interested him: slant rhymes could be retained and new tensions could be exploited between poetic form and the rhythms of speech. This is on display in the first two stanzas of "Men at Forty":

> Men at forty
> Learn to close softly
> The doors to rooms they will not be
> Coming back to.
>
> At rest on a stair landing
> They feel it
> Moving beneath them now like the deck of a ship,
> Though the swell is gentle.

For Justice's work the 1970s were a decade of consolidation, although his major publications were greeted with the same kind of critical division that had marked the earlier ones. In *Departures* (1973) and *Selected Poems* (1979) (which included a selection of previously uncollected poems), the trajectory of Justice's poetic project was fully on display. These volumes charted a course in which the formal or structural self-consciousness that marks his work becomes increasingly latent while the textual origins become more manifest. Poems like "Three Odes," "Fragment: To a Mirror," and "Variations on a Text by Vallejo" all give evidence of this tendency. *Departures* included notes explaining its origins and how some of the poems were created using chance methods inspired by conversations with John Cage (whom Justice encountered while lecturing at the University of Cincinnati). *Selected Poems* brought his work together in a way that emphasized this pattern. It also included striking works such as "First Death," in which the poet recalls the childhood experience of his grandmother's death over the course of three days in June 1933. The poem achieves an elegant tension between the stricture of its rhymed tetrameter couplets and its relatively simple diction to create an elegy to early mourning. Justice found a way to buck the trend of free-verse prosody by way of a traditional structure.

In the last two decades, Justice has branched out while continuing to consolidate his oeuvre and to write with increasing documentary vigor about his past, publishing librettos, criticism, interviews, stories, memoirs, fragments, and notes. *Platonic Scripts* (1984), *The Sunset Maker* (1987), *A Donald Justice Reader* (1991), and *Oblivion* (1998) all present these different genres. *New and Selected Poems* (1995) and *Orpheus Hesitated Beside the Black River: Poems, 1952–1997* (1998) give shape to a career that is as elusive as it is consistently intelligent. In his own work, Justice is a major poet of the minor statement. In his teaching, he has fostered in his students a "conscience about language" but not a commitment to a particular style. His work may indeed function as "platonic scripts," a term Justice derives from his sense of his own creative process. He writes "as if convinced that, prior to my attempt, there existed a true text, a sort of Platonic script, which I had been elected to transcribe or record" (Justice, 1984). This statement reflects Justice's poetic condition: he is searching for the classical perfection of a "true text" but is undercut by a recognition that the poet has to behave "as if convinced." "As if convinced" is not the same as belief and this doubt seems emblematic of Justice's elusive work. He is a fine poet but a quiet one.

Stephen Rachman

**Biography**
Born in Miami, Florida, 12 August 1925. Attended the University of Miami, B.A. 1945; University of North Carolina, Chapel Hill, M.A. 1947; Stanford University, California, 1948–49; University of Iowa, Iowa City, Ph.D. 1954. Visiting Assistant Professor, University of Missouri, Columbia, 1955–56; Assistant Professor, Hamline University, St. Paul, Minnesota, 1956–57; Lecturer, 1957–60, Assistant Professor, 1960–63, and Associate Professor, 1963–66, University of Iowa; Associate Professor, 1966–67, and Professor, 1967–70, Syracuse University, New York; Visiting Professor, University of California, Irvine, 1970–71; Professor of English, University of Iowa, 1971–82; Professor of English, University of Florida, Gainesville, 1982–92; poet-in-residence, Reed College, Portland, Oregon, 1962; Bain-Swiggett Lecturer, Princeton University, New Jersey, 1976; Visiting Professor, University of Virginia, Charlottesville, 1980. Received Rockefeller grant, 1954; Lamont Poetry Selection Award, 1959; Inez Boulton Prize, 1960; Ford fellowship, in theater, 1964; Harriet Monroe Memorial Prize (*Poetry*, Chicago), 1965, 1984; National Endowment for the Arts grant, 1967, 1973, 1980; American Academy Award, 1974; Guggenheim fellowship, 1976; Pulitzer Prize, 1980; Bollingen Prize, 1991; Chancellor, Academy of American Poets, 1997. Living in Iowa City, Iowa.

**Poetry**
*The Summer Anniversaries*, 1960
*A Local Storm*, 1963
*Night Light*, 1967
*Four Poets* (with others), 1967
*Sixteen Poems*, 1970
*From a Notebook*, 1972
*Departures*, 1973
*Selected Poems*, 1979
*Tremayne*, 1984
*The Sunset Maker: Poems/Stories/A Memoir*, 1987
*A Donald Justice Reader: Selected Poetry and Prose*, 1991
*New and Selected Poems*, 1995
*Orpheus Hesitated Beside the Black River: Poems, 1952–1997*, 1998

**Selected Criticism**
*Oblivion: On Writers and Writing*, 1998

**Other Writings:** play (*The Death of Lincoln*, 1988), translations of French poetry (*The Man Closing Up: A Poem*, by Eugene Guillevic, 1973); edited poetry collections (*The Collected Poems of Weldon Kees*, 1960).

**Further Reading**

Gioia, Dana, and William Logan, editors, *Certain Solitudes: On the Poetry of Donald Justice*, Fayetteville, University of Arkansas Press, 1997
Jarman, Mark, "Ironic Elegies: The Poetry of Donald Justice," *Pequod* 16/17 (1984)
Justice, Donald, "Notes of an Outsider," in *Platonic Scripts*, by Justice, Ann Arbor: University of Michigan Press, 1984
Wright, Charles, "Homage to the Thin Man," *The Southern Review* 30, no. 4 (1994)


## Men at Forty

Donald Justice's "Men at Forty" epitomizes what fellow poets and critics have praised throughout his career: a careful attention to phrasing; a sense of emotional restraint amid deep feeling; a direct, accessible language; and a mastery of the elegiac tone. Writing on Justice's poetry in general, Charles Wright (1994) commented on the "nostalgia, sadness, melancholia, and sense of a world lost and a time lost (especially of childhood and adolescence)" that recurs in many of the poems. Unlike so many poems published by his contemporaries in the 1960s, "Men at Forty" is not a clearly autobiographical or explicitly "confessional" poem, a fact indicated by the use of the plural "men" in the title. As in many of his poems, Justice seems to move beyond private sensibility to comment on a condition or feeling common to many.

First published in Justice's second full volume of poetry, *Night Light* (1967), and later in *Poetry* magazine (February 1969), "Men at Forty" has become one of the handful of poems most often selected to represent Justice's work in anthologies of American poetry. It begins by evoking its ostensible subject, namely, men coming into middle age:

> Men at forty
> Learn to close softly
> The doors to rooms they will not be
> Coming back to.

There is a keen sense in this first stanza of an increasing awareness of mortality as one ages, the knowledge that a great deal of what is experienced in life cannot be counted on to occur again. What is striking is the lack of anger or panic in the face of this reality. Rather than "raging against the dying of the light," the men of the poem gracefully accept their aging, even as, in the subsequent stanzas of the poem, they move deeper and more nostalgically into the recesses of memory.

In the second of the poem's five four-line stanzas, the men of the poem's title and first line are presented resting "on a stair landing," feeling it move "beneath them now like the deck of a ship." The stairs may suggest a transition, an ascent or descent into middle age; the sense of being "at rest" does not indicate fatigue so much as a state of reflection, which is what the poem presents in the next two enjambed stanzas:

> And deep in mirrors
> They rediscover
> The face of the boy as he practices tying
> His father's tie there in secret

And the face of that father,
Still warm with the mystery of lather.
They are more fathers than sons themselves now.

Flashing back to the realm of childhood is a common occurrence in Justice's poems, and several critics have noticed how that realm is idyllic, a world the adult may remember and long for, even as he is aware of its remoteness. However, in that act of memory, escape from the bonds of adult awareness may be at least partially achieved. Justice has said in an interview that "one of the motives for writing is surely to recover and hold what would otherwise be lost totally—memory or experience" (Justice, 1984).

The moment of "rediscovery" of the childhood self is nearly epiphanic, a sense that indeed pervades the entire poem. Justice's evocation of the bond between father and son is the poem's most emotionally charged moment, but what is most characteristic of his practice here is how delicately that connection is suggested by the emblems of the necktie and shaving lather. These are symbols of both adulthood and male privacy in that shaving and the tying of the tie are typically conducted in solitude as part of a grooming and dressing ritual. However, when a young boy is allowed to share these activities with his father, an unspoken rite of passage is enacted. The line in which the men of the poem remind themselves that they "are [now] more fathers than sons" announces the poem's gentle move from memory back to the present. The loss of childhood's innocence is a theme many have noticed in Justice's work, and that theme is rendered here in his typically restrained but heartfelt manner.

As the poem moves into its final lines, the men feel something "filling them," something unnamed but "like the twilight sound / Of the crickets, immense." Of course, twilight is a moment of transition, and as the oncoming darkness is faced, again Justice fosters a feeling of fullness, immensity, rather than a sense of fear. Awareness of time's passage, and one's own limited existence within that passage, is indeed an "immense" awareness, but a man may be the better for it, the poem seems to suggest. At the same time, the poem's final line reinforces the sense of adult responsibility and compromise. The sound of the crickets in the night air fills not only the men but also the woods "Behind their mortgaged houses." While the souls of these men are perhaps not completely "mortgaged" in adult middle age, something has been irrevocably lost or at least sacrificed. The realm of youthful promise and freedom is now available only within memory. As Howard Nemerov noted in reviewing Justice's first volume of poetry, *The Summer Anniversaries* (1960), Justice's chief subject is "the journey from innocence to experience" (quoted in Gioia and Logan, 1997).

ERNEST J. SMITH

**Further Reading**

Gioia, Dana, and William Logan, editors, *Certain Solitudes: On the Poetry of Donald Justice,* Fayetteville: University of Arkansas Press, 1997

Jarman, Mark, "Ironic Elegies: The Poetry of Donald Justice," *Pequod* 16/17 (1984)

Justice, Donald, "An Interview with Wayne Dodd and Stanley Plumly," in *Platonic Scripts,* by Justice, Ann Arbor: University of Michigan Press, 1984

Ryan, Michael, "Flaubert in Florida," *New England Review and Breadloaf Quarterly* 7, no. 2 (1984)

Wright, Charles, "Homage to the Thin Man," *The Southern Review* 30, no. 4 (1994)

# K

## Bob Kaufman 1925–86

The details of Bob Kaufman's life are shrouded by legends wrapped in mysteries. Aside from facts concerning his birth, specific jobs that he held, and his undeniable role as a fixture in San Francisco's poetry scene from the mid-1950s to his death, much remains unknown, and much of what is known is of dubious origin. However, despite what one critic calls the "multiple and conflicting account of Kaufman's genealogy, his life story, and other putatively relevant aspects of his life work" (Damon, 2000), Kaufman's poetry, although not extensive, is sufficient to give readers a sense of a fascinating and complicated human being, not to mention a gifted, if troubled, artist.

The fact that Kaufman is so hard to pin down makes his poetry intriguing to so many readers. His earliest poems emerged from the milieu surrounding the San Francisco jazz scene and thus place him in the Beat generation's sphere of influence. Those first poems, collected for the most part in *Solitudes Crowded with Loneliness* (1965), are accomplished works, but many betray a certain uneasiness with his status as a poet and thus make labored references to other writers and artists. Kaufman invokes outsider artists such as Poe, Hart Crane, Albert Camus, Billie Holliday, and Ray Charles almost as if to solidify his own claim to the title. However, his poems are sufficient to the task, and the first book establishes him as an excellent poet and an integral part of the Beat movement. The most important poem in this volume is "Bagel Shop Jazz." Besides being nominated for Britain's Guinness Prize in poetry in 1960 (Kaufman's work, like many American artists from marginalized social groups, received more attention abroad than in prominent American circles), this poem has recently come to be seen as an important document of the Beat generation. The conclusion of the poem summarizes several themes crucial to Kaufman's work:

> Coffee-faced Ivy Leaguers, in Cambridge Jackets
> Whose personal Harvard was a Fillmore District step,
> Weighted down with conga drums,
> The ancestral cross, the Othello-laden curse,
> Talking of Bird and Diz and Miles,
> The secret terrible hurts
> Wrapped in cool hipster smiles,
> Telling themselves, under the talk,
> This shot must be the end,
> Hoping the beat is really the truth
>
> The guilty police arrive.
>
> Brief, beautiful shadows, burned on the walls of the night.

Here Kaufman captures the status of the outsider artist, the "hipster," in American culture. The subjects portrayed at the end of this poem are the African-American creators who, because of their race, are further marginalized. These "Ivy Leaguers," in short, have all the credentials they need to create dynamic art, but they are not members of the power elite: hence the problems with the police that seemed to be a staple of Kaufman's life.

In San Francisco, Kaufman co-founded and edited *Beatitude,* a small magazine essential to forging an identity for the community that came to be known as the Beat poets. There he published perhaps the closest thing to a Beat generation manifesto (with the possible exception of Allen Ginsberg's "Howl"). "The Abomunist Manifesto"—here Kaufman combines the word "Abominable" with "Communist," the word most likely to alarm "square" America—has more to do with the Surrealism of 1920s Paris than with the writings of Karl Marx: for example, "ABOMUNISTS SPIT ANTI-POETRY FOR POETIC REASONS AND FRINK." Later, in the "Abomunist Election Manifesto," Kaufman's parody takes on a more serious air, although retaining its comic pace and rhythm:

> Abomunists demand the abolition of Oakland.
> Abomunists demand low-cost housing for homosexuals . . .
> Abomunists demand statehood for North Beach.
> The only office Abomunists run for is the unemployment office.

The manifesto, in short, makes a case for certain tenets of the bohemian lifestyle while nodding humorously toward the mass-media stereotype of the "beatnik" as a lazy bum. Kaufman, like many of his fellow Beats, had no trouble taking their art seriously while also seeing it as an appropriate vehicle for humor, if not satire.

Kaufman's work took a turn in the mid-1960s, when, for nearly a decade, he wrote nothing at all. These years are usually referred to as Kaufman's silent period. Raymond Foye, the editor of Kaufman's selected poems, *The Ancient Rain: Poems, 1956–1978* (1981), says that Kaufman's lack of writing can be explained by "a ten-year Buddhist vow of silence, prompted by the assassination of President Kennedy. For the next decade he neither spoke nor wrote." Foye then claims that Kaufman ended his silence at the end of the Vietnam War by reciting for a surprised gathering of writers parts of T.S. Eliot's verse play *Murder in the Cathedral.* Other commentators offer a differing interpretation. Maria Damon (1993) suggests, for example, that Kaufman frequently would speak during this period, but only to ask friends for amphetamines. The writer Pierre Delattre (a former minister whose soup kitchen hosted a reading series that featured many prominent San Francisco poets) goes further and claims that Kaufman's silence was caused by an abuse of amphetamines (Delattre, 1992). The exact cause of Kaufman's silence will likely never be known. At the very least, it seems most likely that it emerged from a variety of political, religious, and pharmacological sources.

*The Ancient Rain* was the last collection published during Kaufman's lifetime. Many of the poems in this volume were not in written form but were transcribed from Kaufman's readings at various venues in San Francisco. Some critics would see this as carelessness on Kaufman's part, but readers familiar with the aesthetics of the Beat generation and jazz would know that an improvisational spirit was valued in this community and that it often led to memorable art.

Kaufman's work has attracted a worldwide readership but very little scholarly attention. In fact, nearly every article devoted to Kaufman features a passage in which the critic expresses surprise at the paucity of attention that Kaufman's poetry has generated among scholars. It is hoped that will change as the Beat generation gains its deserved stature in critical circles and researchers begin to explore the outer reaches of this movement. At that point, it will be clear that Kaufman's position at the cultural margins paradoxically places him at the center of the most important artistic activity of his times.

DAVID R. ZAUHAR

*See also* San Francisco Renaissance

**Biography**

Born in New Orleans, Louisiana, 18 April 1925. Attended New School for Social Research, New York City; merchant marine, 1938–58; co-founder (with Allen Ginsberg), *Beatitude* (magazine), 1959. Received National Endowment for the Arts grant, 1981. Died in San Francisco, California, 12 January 1986.

**Poetry**

*Solitudes Crowded with Loneliness,* 1965
*Golden Sardine,* 1967
*The Ancient Rain: Poems, 1956–1978,* 1981
*Closing Time till Dawn* (with Janice Blue), 1986
*Cranial Guitar: Selected Poems,* 1996

**Further Reading**


Christian, Barbara, "Whatever Happened to Bob Kaufman?" in *The Beats: Essays in Criticism,* edited by Bartlett Lee, Jefferson, North Carolina: McFarland, 1981

Damon, Maria, *The Dark End of the Street: Margins in American Vanguard Poetry,* Minneapolis: University of Minnesota Press, 1993

Damon, Maria, "Victors of the Catastrophe: Beat Occlusions," in *Beat Culture and the New America, 1950–1965,* edited by Lisa Phillips, New York: Whitney Museum of Art in association with Flammarion, Paris, 1995

Damon, Maria, "Triangulated Desires and Tactical Silences in the Beat Hipscape: Bob Kaufman and Others," *College Literature* 27, no. 1 (Winter 2000)

Damon, Maria, and Ronna C. Johnson, "Recapturing the Skipped Beats," *The Chronicle of Higher Education* (1 October 1999)

Delattre, Pierre, *Episodes,* St. Paul, Minnesota: Graywolf Press, 1992

Foye, Raymond, "Editor's Note," in *The Ancient Rain: Poems, 1956–1978,* by Bob Kaufman, New York: New Directions, 1981

Nielsen, Aldon Lynn, *Black Chant: Languages of African-American Postmodernism,* Cambridge and New York: Cambridge University Press, 1997


---

# Weldon Kees 1914–55

Although Weldon Kees was championed by poets such as Dana Gioia and Kenneth Rexroth and participated in major artistic movements such as Abstract Expressionism and Beat poetry, he has become an obscure figure in 20th-century American literary history. His Nebraskan origins or the mysterious disappearance that truncated his career might appear to account for Kees' marginalization, but the more likely explanation lies in the poetry itself. Combined with the apocalyptic nihilism noted by Rexroth, Kees' diffident and inward poetic manner produced verse that might seem to lack ambition and distinctiveness. Kees' poetry lacks the lyrical irony and textual innovation of other late Modernists, such as Randall Jarrell or Charles Olson. Instead, his writing appears too commonplace to qualify as heroic Modernism, too disgruntled to attain the playfulness of Postmodern reflexivity.

*The Last Man* (1943), *The Fall of the Magicians* (1947), and *Poems 1947–1954* (1954) contain the majority of Kees' most significant poetry. While certain developments are apparent across these volumes, the technique and concerns introduced in *The Last Man* remain largely consistent throughout his career. The allusions to Baudelaire, Joyce, and Eliot that abound in *The Last Man* demonstrate how heavily the weight of Modernism bears on Kees. In "Midnight" Kees recognizes that such Modernists have become cultural institutions and appeals to the authority of Joyce to validate the fragmentary nature of his own writing. Kees' citation of Eliot in "What the Spider Heard" constitutes not simply a restatement of a Modernist position, however, since he presents the Prufrockian distaste for banality itself with irony. "To a Contemporary" sounds a more urgent note by warning poets that confusion and disintegration will attend those who claim to share Proust's or Baudelaire's experience of memory and culture. The contradictory aspects of Kees' treatment of Modernism are addressed more fully in later poems such as "Dynamite for Operas" and "The End of the Library." Kees regrets the passing of Modernism's cultural grandeur while acknowledging that the commodified Modernism of the mid-century holds scant value as a poetic resource.

Issues such as personal and public memory, the referentiality of language, and the significance of popular and mass culture are also raised in *The Last Man. The Fall of the Magicians* develops many of the themes of *The Last Man* while introducing the important topic of extreme psychological anxiety associated with despair and even madness. Kees' engagement with Modernism critiques the prophecy of the future and nostalgia for the past that result from alienation from the present. Poems like "Lines for an Album" and "Henry James at Newport" lambasted the redemptive role of "authentic" personal memory in *The Last Man;* in *The Fall of the Magicians* "Eight Variations" and "Five Villanelles" extend the critique by attacking banal and unfulfilled prophecies. "That Winter," however, concedes the appeal of nostalgia as a means of countering the psychological collapse and nihilism of "Moving Target," in which rejecting Modernist cultural complaint leads to silence and an implosion of cultural meaning. The Robinson poems are Kees' most celebrated treatments of insanity and social dislocation, but poems such as "The Contours of Fixation" and "Crime Club" most clearly articulate his vision of psychological terror because these emphasize that the crisis of subjectivity is a function of the dissolution of referential meaning.

Kees' interest in representing the referential limits of the sign-in-itself marks his most decisive break with Modernism and the most Postmodern strain in his work. An emotionally provocative meta-fiction, "For My Daughter" is an important and distinguished study of referential limitation. Other earlier poems such as "A Cornucopia for Daily Use" and "Abstracts of Dissertations" compile eclectic cultural references as sequences of monadic motifs rather than avant-garde wholes. In *Poems 1947–1954* Kees uses word collages to question the referent of history. The notion that the purported truths of history are nothing but the shadow play of motivated signs is evident in "The Lives," "A Pastiche for Eve," and "Dead March." Kees' most significant treatment of this theme, in "Interregnum," articulates the arbitrary nature of historical designation as a function of the cultural interregnum of mid-century.

*Poems 1947–1954* also features Kees' most substantial treatment of popular culture, "Travels in North America." This poem marks a development from "Two Cities" in *The Last Man* in that it depicts a complex amalgamation of different cultural forms. Kees' celebration of popular Americana opposes the mass cultural production of a Ford assembly plant and presages the double coding of Postmodernism by offering unexpected conjunctions with art and literature. Kees' passion for art is nowhere more evident than in "A Salvo for Hans Hofmann," and the motel reproductions of Utrillo in "Travels in North America" demonstrate Kees' attempt to imagine a fusion of art and popular culture. For all Kees' nihilism, this cultural imagination is probably the most important achievement of his poetry.

The strongest poetic influences on Kees ranged from Thomas Love Beddoes to Eliot, while prose influences included Proust, Mann, Flaubert, and Kafka. His dearest novels were American, however, and William Carlos Williams' *White Mule* (1937) and F. Scott Fitzgerald's *Tender Is the Night* (1934) had a particularly strong hold on his imagination. Kees disliked Steinbeck, and unlike many of his contemporaries he did not respond to public events by increasing the political dimension of his writing. Kees was associated with most of the major literary and artistic figures of his time, and, as Raymond Nelson (1989) argues, Kees' anxious and everyday sensibility was typical of the generation of tragic American poets that included John Berryman, Delmore Schwartz, Theodore Roethke, Thomas Merton, and others. Kees' poetry has never really been considered as distinctive as that of some of his contemporaries, however, and this perhaps explains why, as Janet Richards (1979) suggests, his influence upon others was minimal.

NICHOLAS SPENCER

**Biography**

Born in Beatrice, Nebraska, 24 February 1914. Attended University of Missouri, Columbia; University of Nebraska, Lincoln, B.A. 1935; staff member, Federal Writers' Project, Lincoln, Nebraska, 1936–37; librarian, Denver, Colorado, 1937–43; writer, *Time Magazine,* from 1943; scriptwriter, Paramount newsreel studio, New York City, from 1943; screenplay writer, San Francisco, California, from 1950. Died in San Francisco, California, 18 July 1955.

**Poetry**

*The Last Man,* 1943
*The Fall of the Magicians,* 1947
*Poems 1947–1954*, 1954
*The Collected Poems of Weldon Kees,* 1960; revised edition, 1975

**Selected Criticism**

*Reviews and Essays, 1936–55,* 1988

**Other Writings:** novels (*Fall Quarter,* 1990), short stories (*The Ceremony, and Other Stories,* 1983), plays (*The Waiting Room,* 1986), correspondence (*Weldon Kees and the Midcentury Generation: Letters, 1935–1955,* 1986), psychology book (*Nonverbal Communication* [with Jurgen Ruesch], 1953).

**Further Reading**


Ballowe, James, "Weldon Kees: Loathed All Roses," *North Dakota Quarterly* 62, no. 3 (1995)

Elledge, Jim, editor, *Weldon Kees: A Critical Introduction,* Metuchen, New Jersey: Scarecrow Press, 1985

Knoll, Robert E., editor, *Weldon Kees and the Midcentury Generation,* Lincoln: University of Nebraska Press, 1987

Nelson, Raymond, "The Fitful Life of Weldon Kees," *American Literary History* 1, no. 4 (Winter 1989)

Richards, Janet, *Common Soldiers: A Self-Portrait and Other Portraits,* San Francisco: Archer Press, 1979; 2nd edition, 1984

## Robinson Poems

In a 1943 review of *The Way Some People Live* by John Cheever, Weldon Kees commented on the limitations of the fiction published in *The New Yorker.* "Its writers must frequently entertain themselves," Kees wrote, "by concentrating on the merely decorative qualities of a scene, a restriction brought on by an understandable hesitancy to explore their material deeply." Although he expressed qualified admiration for Cheever's "acid accounts of pathos in the suburbs," Kees wished that these stories—*New Yorker* fiction to a fault—would more often "work for something more than episodic notation and minor perceptive effects."

These remarks shed light on Kees' four "Robinson" poems written during the 1940s—"Robinson," "Aspects of Robinson," "Robinson at Home," and "Relating to Robinson"—three of which were first printed in *The New Yorker.* (The first of these poems was collected in *The Fall of the Magicians* [1947] and the others in Kees' *Poems 1947–1954* [1954].) Robinson, the central figure in each of these poems, might have stepped out of a Cheever story: dressed "in Glen plaid jacket, Scotch-grain shoes, / Black four-in-hand and oxford button-down," he plays cards at the Algonquin, summers in Maine, and smokes panatela cigars. He is successful and sophisticated but not without his troubles. He drinks a lot. He lulls himself to sleep with luminol. Once married, he now finds himself in bed with a woman identified by her husband's last name. Robinson's portrait emerges as the accumulation of suggestive, if oblique, sketchings. The "merely decorative qualities of a scene" used to such trivial effect in *New Yorker* fiction are foregrounded to emphasize the crushing banality of Robinson's world.

The four poems, taken together, tell the story of how Robinson becomes unhinged. Robinson's madness, however, is never explained or even established unequivocally since the final poem in the sequence, "Relating to Robinson," is told by someone who "had no certainty, / There in the dark, that it was Robinson / Or someone else." This uncertainty is fundamental to all four poems, in which Robinson is an anonymous, shadowy figure even as he occupies center stage.

A sense of unreality pervades these poems from the beginning. The first poem, simply titled "Robinson," describes a room in Robinson's apartment. The poem's governing conceit is that everything in the room ceases to exist when Robinson is not there. After Robinson has gone out, probably to work, his dog "stops barking. . . . His act is over." The room's mirror reflects nothing. Its furniture and decorative objects, including "the tinted photograph of Robinson's first wife," would "fill the room if Robinson came in." Even the pages of Robinson's books are blank.

The description is coolly detached yet not without feeling for Robinson's loneliness. The penultimate stanza tells us that "All day the phone rings. It could be Robinson / Calling. It never rings when he is here." The references to the first wife and to the dog's "act" focus our attention on Robinson's isolation. Like the later poems about Robinson, "Robinson" neither pities nor sentimentalizes his suffering but places it, however ambiguously, in a larger context. The poem's final lines, "Outside, the birds circle continuously / Where trees are actual and take no holiday," are as mysterious as the transformation taking place within Robinson's apartment. The trees, wholly disenchanted, are described in terms that suggest the workplace and its accompanying view of things, although the relation of Robinson to the realm that is "actual and take[s] no holiday" is one of the poem's unresolved questions.

The answer, judging from "Aspects of Robinson," the next poem in the sequence, is that he is both its representative and its victim. The single room has given way to a barrage of displacing images, set within the empty bustle of New York City. Like Ishmael at the opening of *Moby-Dick,* Robinson gazes out to where "the boats / Mourn like the lost." We are also in Hell: "Gray men in overcoats are ghosts blown past the door," suggesting Dante's tortured shades. These "gray men" recall the first stanza of "Robinson": "The world is a gray world, / Not without violence." The deliberately indirect phrasing underscores the subterranean current of violence that will reach its peak in "Relating to Robinson." Here it is still part of the atmosphere, as with the suicide cryptically mentioned in the second stanza. Robinson balances his anguish with an outward appearance of normality. His heart, although "sad," is nonetheless "usual."

In "Robinson at Home," this equilibrium begins to crack. For the first time, Robinson's personality has a history: "This sleep is from exhaustion, but his old desire / To die like this has known a lessening." This fact is set against dreams that cause him to mumble in sleep, "There is something in this madhouse that I symbolize— / This city—nightmare—black." Robinson's confused murmuring seems to be the birth pangs of a consciousness that is indistinguishable from madness. "Relating to Robinson" bears this out. Robinson, or someone who resembles him, is seen by an acquaintance while staring at a plaster Venus in an antique store window. Their eyes meet, then the man who looks like Robinson confronts the other by telling him how "*a day as huge as yesterday in pairs / Unrolled its horror on my face / Until it blocked—.*" The man flees; the poem closes with an image of boats moving silently on the Hudson, recalling those that had "mourn[ed] like the lost" in "Aspects of Robinson."

The significance of Robinson's end is suggested by his haunted fascination with the shop-window Venus, an image of once-vital Eros now degraded. Given the bitterness of Kees' other poems and his almost certain suicide, the poem can be regarded as an indictment of modern life and its stifling impositions. Robinson escapes his trivial world only in madness and the horrified recognition of diminished human possibility.

JAMES GIBBONS

**Further Reading**

Elledge, Jim, editor, *Weldon Kees: A Critical Introduction,* Metuchen, New Jersey: Scarecrow Press, 1985

Gioia, Dana, *Can Poetry Matter? Essays on Poetry and American Culture,* St. Paul, Minnesota: Graywolf Press, 1992

Nelson, Raymond, "The Fitful Life of Weldon Kees," *American Literary History* 1, no. 4 (Winter 1989)

Niemi, Robert, "'Little Gidding' Revisited and Repudiated: Weldon Kees' 'Relating to Robinson,'" *American Poetry* 8 (Fall 1990)

Ross, William T., *Weldon Kees,* Boston: Twayne, 1985

## Robert Kelly 1935–

Since 1961 Robert Kelly has published some 50 collections of poetry and poetic prose. This prolific output is in itself a notable index of Kelly's poetic project: a "making it new" of words, figures, and visions from seemingly all the world's religious and poetic traditions (in which Catholic, Jewish, and Buddhist notes are perhaps most often struck). Yet Kelly's commitment has also always been to a contemporary avant-garde. Kelly addresses this apparent contradiction between archaic religious traditions and poetic avant-gardism in his important 1988 statement "Spirit/ Vanguard Art":

> Power of poetry: to employ propositional language not to make assertions, but to make, for a moment, lush gardens where one is free from assertions, exalted in the fragrance of presentness. . . . Such deconditioned delights, subtle, struggling free from associations yet enduring with pleasure all the temporary ecstasies of them as they slip off, may indeed give the reader of contemporary poetry a taste of such unconditions, dis-situation. And you may wind up trying to live free of the obligation of attending to your own habitual intentions.

This sense of an absolute present nonetheless mediated by complicated spiritual forces as ancient as the garden itself consistently runs through Kelly's oeuvre.

From his first appearance on the NYC literary scene in the late 1950s and his first book, *Armed Descent* (1961), Kelly was associated with the "Deep Image" School, a construct of his and Jerome Rothenberg's invention. In a 1963 interview Kelly defined "Deep Image" this way:

> I want to say that the Image itself, in its development, constitutes the fundamental, basic rhythm of the poem, which all other rhythms—sound rhythms, stress rhythms and so forth—must subserve. (Ossman, 1963)

One of Kelly's early influences here would be Charles Olson (who wrote back to Kelly across an early, privately circulated manuscript "not imageS but IMAGE," leading Kelly to reformulate his position). Behind Olson stands Ezra Pound, in whom the dream of a poetic totality is most powerfully pursued in an American idiom, and within whose tradition Kelly must be seen. Like Pound, Kelly chose to emphasize *phanopoeia,* that is to say, eye over ear or mind, although the latter two find their constituent roles. Unlike his predecessor, however, who conceived of *phanopoeia* as the power "to cast visual images on the screen of the mind," Kelly felt that if the "rhythm" of image were activated, then vision buried deep in the mythopoetic unconscious might be unleashed. Kelly was also close to Paul Blackburn, whose personal poetics and commitment to the daily can also be felt in Kelly's work, alongside the more visionary strain. In the early 1960s Kelly edited the journal *Trobar,* and along with Rothenberg was instrumental in the construction of ethnopoetics, a search for the contemporary relevance of poetry and myth wherever they are found.

The title of Kelly's 1973 volume *The Mill of Particulars* is telling: he sees the poet as a generator of words and images in their most unique and particular facets of being. So Kelly's beautiful "In the Light," collected in *Red Actions: Selected Poems* (1995), specifies endlessly:

> in the light between desire and performance, in the
> mistaken light between
> the rule and the sentence, the bleak
> light over Kaminstein's Hardware,
> lost marriages, all our olive natures
> ancient, goat-gnawed,
> in the dawning light between
> desire and the expression of desire . . .

This side of Kelly's poetry dwells lovingly on the singular in its daily revelation. Coupled with the consistently high-order celebration of heterosexual love and the poet's quest among the sacred vessels of the feminine, the tenor of Kelly's poetry can only be described as maximalist, even desperately joyous. As Kelly writes in *Kill the Messenger Who Brings Bad News* (1979),

> And I ask for help too, Aphrodite,
> fight at my side so I am not in that sad
> terrible way lonely as I hurry towards
> your holy creatures.

Perhaps Kelly's most important single poem is *The Loom* (1975), a 415-page text composed over two years and published as a whole book. Divided into 36 "chapters," the poem weaves together the daily and the mythic until

> Texture
> is not decoration, it is
> a more intimate structure
> yearning for your close
> attention, tension between
> you & and what you see
> more fertile than any valley.

Speech-based but epic in scope, perfectly embodying Kelly's dual commitment to the visionary and the personal, *The Loom* is generally thought of as one of the most important long poems produced in the last 30 years. Excerpts from it are often anthologized; university courses have been devoted to it. Although *The Loom* employs an elliptical line of never more than six words, Kelly is nothing if not an explorer of multiple forms: long lines, generously spaced minimal offerings, prose poems, poetic prose, and generative syntax are all utilized in his work. Robert Creeley's dictum that "form is never more than an extension of content" has rarely been more fully realized.

In 1965 Kelly co-edited with Paris Leary *A Controversy of Poets,* which attempted to establish a truce in the famed anthology wars of that period. *A Controversy* featured poets from the Black Mountain, New York, and San Francisco Renaissance schools (all associated with the avant-garde), but also confessional poets like Robert Lowell as well as workshop poets like Galway Kinnell. Robert Kelly remains a force on the current poetry scene; in his 1999 book *Runes* he writes:

Poetry

is the body's answer
to language

an appropriation
of its lucidity
to its own ever-

lasting sensual
design.

For Kelly, the poem remains the ground on which body and language erotically and spiritually join.

LEONARD SCHWARTZ

*See also* Deep Image Poetry

**Biography**

Born in Brooklyn, New York, 24 September 1935. Attended the City College of New York, A.B. 1955; Columbia University, New York, 1955–58; translator, Continental Translation Service, New York, 1956–58; Lecturer in English, Wagner College, New York, 1960–61; Instructor in German, 1961–62, Instructor in English, 1962–64, Assistant Professor, 1964–69, Associate Professor, 1969–74, Professor of English, 1974–86, since 1981 director of Writing Program, and since 1986 Asher B. Edelman Professor of literature, Avery Graduate School of the Arts, Bard College, Annandale-on-Hudson, New York; Assistant Professor of English, State University of New York, Buffalo, summer 1964; Visiting Lecturer, Tufts University, Medford, Massachusetts, 1966–67; poet-in-residence, California Institute of Technology, Pasadena, 1971–72, University of Kansas, Lawrence, 1975, and Dickinson College, Carlisle, Pennsylvania, 1976; editor, *Chelsea Review,* New York, 1957–60; founding editor, with George Economou, *Trobar* magazine, 1960–64, and Trobar Books, New York, 1962–65; contributing editor, *Caterpillar,* New York, 1969–72; editor, *Los 1,* 1977; since 1964 editor, *Matter* magazine and Matter publishing company, New York, later Annandale-on-Hudson; contributing editor, *Alcheringa: Ethnopoetics,* New York, since 1977, and *Sulfur,* Pasadena, 1981–82. Received New York City Writers Conference fellowship, 1967; *Los Angeles Times* Book Prize, 1980; American Academy Award, 1986; honorary Litt.D., State University of New York, Oneonta, 1994. Living in Annandale-on-Hudson, New York.

**Poetry**

*Armed Descent,* 1961
*Her Body Against Time* (bilingual edition), 1963
*Round Dances,* 1964
*Tabula,* 1964
*Enstasy,* 1964
*Matter/Fact/Sheet/1,* 1964
*Matter/Fact/Sheet/2,* 1964
*Lunes,* with *Sightings* by Jerome Rothenberg, 1964
*Lectiones,* 1965
*Words in Service,* 1966
*Weeks,* 1966
*Songs XXIV,* 1967
*Twenty Poems,* 1967
*Devotions,* 1967
*Axon Dendron Tree,* 1967
*Crooked Bridge Love Society,* 1967
*A Joining: A Sequence for H.D.,* 1967
*Alpha,* 1968
*Finding the Measure,* 1968
*From the Common Shore, Book 5,* 1968
*Songs I–XXX,* 1969
*Sonnets,* 1969
*We Are the Arbiters of Beast Desire,* 1969
*A California Journal,* 1969
*The Common Shore, Books I–V: A Long Poem about America in Time,* 1969
*Kali Yuga,* 1970
*Flesh:Dream:Book,* 1971
*Ralegh,* 1972
*The Pastorals,* 1972
*Reading Her Notes,* 1972
*The Tears of Edmund Burke,* 1973
*Whaler Frigate Clippership,* 1973
*The Mill of Particulars,* 1973
*The Belt,* 1974
*The Loom,* 1975
*Sixteen Odes,* 1976
*The Lady of,* 1977
*The Convections,* 1978
*The Book of Persephone,* 1978; revised edition, 1983
*The Cruise of the Pnyx,* 1979
*Kill the Messenger Who Brings Bad News,* 1979
*Sentence,* 1980
*The Alchemist to Mercury,* 1981
*Spiritual Exercises,* 1981
*Mulberry Women,* 1982
*Under Words,* 1983
*Thor's Thrush,* 1984
*Not This Island Music,* 1987
*The Flowers of Unceasing Coincidence,* 1988
*Oahu,* 1988
*Ariadne,* 1990
*A Strange Market,* 1992
*Mont Blanc,* 1994
*Red Actions: Selected Poems, 1960–1993,* 1995
*A Play with Shepherds,* 1997
*The Time of Voice: Poems, 1994–1996,* 1998
*The Garden of Discourse: Drawings and Poems,* 1999
*Runes,* 1999

**Other Writings:** plays, novels (*The Scorpions,* 1967; *Cities,* 1971), short stories, essays, children's literature; edited a poetry anthology (*A Controversy of Poets: An Anthology of Contemporary American Poetry,* edited with Paris Leary, 1965); founded three literary magazines (*Chelsea Review,* 1957; *Trobar,* 1960; *Matter,* 1964).

**Further Reading**

Kelly, Robert, "Spirit/Vanguard Art," in *Primary Trouble: An Anthology of Contemporary American Poetry,* edited by

Leonard Schwartz, Joseph Donahue, and Edward Foster, Jersey City, New Jersey: Talisman House, 1996
Mackey, Nathaniel, "That Words Can Be on the Page," in *Discrepant Engagement: Dissonance, Cross-Culturality, and Experimental Writing,* by Mackey, Cambridge and New York: Cambridge University Press, 1993
Ossman, David, "Interview with Robert Kelly," in *The Sullen Art: Interviews by David Ossman with Modern American Poets,* by Ossman, New York: Corinth Books, 1963
Rasula, Jed, "Introduction," in *The Alchemist to Mercury,* by Robert Kelly, edited by Rasula, Richmond, California: North Atlantic Books, 1981
Schevill, James, *The Early Poetry of Robert Kelly,* Australia: Millenium Press, 2001

---

# X.J. Kennedy 1929–

Poet X.J. Kennedy wrote in a 1993 journal entry, "Damned if we haven't gone and raised a generation deaf to the music of poetry. The poor fish can't see anything in a poem but its literal meaning. That's the impression I got from an attack on Mother Goose (*Boston Globe,* Nov. 15, 1993), in which the writer viewed with high dudgeon the notion of telling kids about the Old Woman Who Lived in a Shoe and beats her children" (Kuusisto, Tall, and Weiss, 1995). While Kennedy laments the lack of poetic understanding, his 40-year-long career in poetry has worked to counteract this very malaise, introducing and defining the American poetry tradition through his work as a poet, editor, and literary critic since the early 1960s. His defense of Mother Goose further reveals his own penchant for and identification with traditional forms and light verse.

Born Joseph Charles Kennedy in Dover, New Jersey, to Joseph Francis and Agnes (Rauter) Kennedy, a young X.J. (his pseudonym) began writing early, publishing his own science fiction magazine, *Terrifying Test-Tube,* at age 12. Kennedy's childhood and young adulthood followed traditional patterns: he graduated from Seton Hall College in 1950 with a bachelor of science degree and then attended graduate school, receiving an M.A. from Columbia University in 1951.

Following a four-year stint in the U.S. Navy (1951–55), during which time he was responsible for writing and publishing a daily news sheet for the crew, Kennedy studied at the University of Paris. At the University of Michigan (1956–62), he completed all the work for his doctorate except for his dissertation. These five years saw the beginning of Kennedy's serious writing career. He was awarded the Avery Hopwood Award for poetry and essay (1959), a Bread Loaf fellowship (1960), and *Poetry* magazine's Bess Hokin Prize (1961). In 1961, he began work as the poetry editor for the critically prominent *Paris Review,* a post he held until 1964.

Kennedy's critical success came early with the publication of his first book, *Nude Descending a Staircase: Poems, Song, a Ballad* (1961), which received the Lamont Poetry Prize from the American Academy of Poets. In this first collection, Kennedy established his technical brilliance with formal verse, especially elegies and lyric poems, and his penchant for narrative poems. Following the publication of *Growing into Love* (1969) and *Bulsh* (1970), Kennedy again received critical acclaim, sharing the prominent Shelley Memorial Award with Mary Oliver (1970).

Significantly, however, this critical acclaim would fade. While poems such as the elegy "On a Child Who Lived One Moment" indicated potential for a serious poetic career, poems such as the humorous "King Tut" in *Nude* paved the way for the light verse that later dominated Kennedy's style. This love of satire and light verse is most apparent in his work for adults in *Emily Dickinson in Southern California* (1974). In the title poem, with a style and content he continues in nine subsequent parodies, he writes, "I called one day—on Eden's strand / But did not find her—Home— / Surfboarders triumphed in—in Waves— / Archangels of the foam." While Kennedy continued to be prolific in his composition, few of his other collections of poetry for adults received critical acclaim until 1985. Kennedy's love of form and light verse distanced him from an American poetry community celebrating free verse and the confessional poem. In response to this, he and his wife, Dorothy Mintzlaffe, established the short-lived journal *Counter/Measures* (1972–74) as a venue for traditional poets.

Kennedy places himself in the Wolgamot School of poetry, which centers on the literary historian John Barton Wolgamot and includes fellow poets Donald Hall, W.D. Snodgrass, and Keith Waldrop. One of his most tangible contributions to contemporary poetry has come not in his own work but in the form of ten anthologies and textbooks, including the classic *An Introduction to Poetry* (1966), now in its ninth printing.

Kennedy's poems have appeared in such prominent poetic venues as *Anteus, The Atlantic, Field, Harper's, Hudson Review, New Criterion, New Statesman, The Nation, The New Yorker, Paris Review, Poetry,* and *Sewanee Review* as well as in countless anthologies. As his work also translates well for audiences outside the poetry world, Kennedy's poems have been heard and seen in two popular forums: NBC's *Today Show* and the Poetry in Motion project on the London Underground. He has also been featured on public radio and television on Garrison Keillor's *Prairie Home Companion* and *Writer's Almanac* and in *Literary Visions,* program 15, produced by Maryland Public Television. Additionally, his poems are cited in *Bartlett's Familiar Quotations.*

Since 1975, Kennedy has authored, co-authored, and edited 15 collections of verse for children. As a natural extension of his love for formal verse, his poetry for children combines rhyme with nonsense. Well received in the children's literature community, Kennedy has received three significant awards for his children's poetry: the National Council of Teachers of English Teachers' Choice Book (1983) and the School Library Journal book of the year (1983), both for *Knock at a Star: A Child's Introduction to Poetry,* and the American Library Association Notable Book citation for *The Forgetful Wishing-Well: Poems for Young People* (1985).

In 1985, with *Cross Ties: Selected Poems,* a collection celebrating his then 30-year career as a poet, Kennedy again received critical acclaim with a *Los Angeles Times* Book Award. Cited for his dexterity with poetic form and his humorous content, Kennedy's work seemed again to be in vogue. As *Cross Ties* featured poems from many of Kennedy's previously overlooked collections, satires such as "In a Prominent Bar in Secaucas One Day" reveal Kennedy's work in the context of the changing attitudes toward American poetry rather than any significant change in the work itself. "Brats" is reminiscent of the Dickinson poems, calling on a similar language, style, and form: "Stealing eggs, Fritz ran afoul / Of an angry great horned owl. / Now she has him—what a catch!—/ Seeing if his head will hatch." For his contributions to light verse in adult and juvenile poetry, Kennedy was honored by the American Academy of Arts and Letters with the Michael Braude Award for Light Verse in 1989.

In *An Introduction to Poetry,* Kennedy remarks that poetry "makes some memorable imaginative statement that we treasure in itself." While he uses this statement to open an anthology about the work of other poets, it reflects back on his own significant oeuvre. Kennedy has demonstrated that he writes poems and creates a literary history we remember.

J. ELIZABETH CLARK

**Biography**

Born in Dover, New Jersey, 21 August 1929. Attended Seton Hall College, South Orange, New Jersey, B.S. 1950; Columbia University, New York, M.A. 1951; Sorbonne, Paris, Cert. Litt. 1956; served in the United States Navy, 1951–55; Teaching Fellow, 1956–60, and Instructor, 1960–62, University of Michigan, Ann Arbor; teacher, University of North Carolina, Greensboro, 1962–63; Assistant Professor, 1963–67, Associate Professor, 1967–73, and Professor of English, 1973–79, Tufts University, Medford, Massachusetts; Visiting Lecturer, Wellesley College, Massachusetts, 1964, and University of California, Irvine, 1966–67; Bruern Fellow in American Literature, University of Leeds, 1974–75; poetry editor, *Paris Review,* 1961–64; editor, with Dorothy Mintzlaffe Kennedy, *Counter/Measures* magazine, 1972–74. Received Hopwood Award, 1959; Bread Loaf Writers' Conference fellowship, 1960; Lamont Poetry Prize, 1961; Bess Hokin Prize (*Poetry,* Chicago), 1961; National Endowment for the Arts grant, 1967; Shelley Memorial Award, 1970; Guggenheim fellowship, 1973; New England Poetry Club Golden Rose Award, 1974; *Los Angeles Times* award, 1985; American Academy Braude Award for Light Verse, 1989; honorary Litt.D., Lawrence University, Appleton, Wisconsin, 1989. Living in Bedford, Massachusetts.

**Poetry**

*Nude Descending a Staircase: Poems, Song, a Ballad,* 1961
*Growing into Love,* 1969
*Bulsh,* 1970
*Breaking and Entering,* 1972
*Emily Dickinson in Southern California,* 1974
*Celebrations after the Death of John Brennan,* 1974
*Three Tenors, One Vehicle: A Book of Songs* (with James E. Camp and Keith Waldrop), 1975
*One Winter Night in August, and Other Nonsense Jingles* (for children), 1975
*The Phantom Ice Cream Man: More Nonsense Jingles* (for children), 1979
*Did Adam Name the Vinegarroon?* (for children), 1982
*French Leave: Translations,* 1983
*Missing Link,* 1983
*Hangover Mass,* 1984
*Cross Ties: Selected Poems,* 1985
*The Forgetful Wishing-Well: Poems for Young People,* 1985
*Brats* (for children), 1986
*Ghastlies, Goops, and Pincushions: Nonsense Verse* (for children), 1989
*Fresh Brats* (for children), 1990
*Winter Thunder,* 1990
*The Kite That Braved Old Orchard Beach* (for children), 1991
*Talking Like the Rain: A Read-to-Me Book of Poems* (for children), 1992
*Dark Horses: New Poems,* 1992
*The Beasts of Bethlehem* (for children), 1992
*Drat These Brats!* (for children), 1993
*Uncle Switch: Loony Limericks* (for children), 1997

**Other Writings:** literature and writing textbooks (*An Introduction to Poetry,* 1966; *Literature: An Introduction to Fiction, Poetry, and Drama,* 1976; *The Bedford Guide for College Writers* [with Dorothy Mintzlaffe Kennedy], 1987); edited collections of literature (*Messages: A Thematic Anthology of Poetry,* 1973).

**Further Reading**

Goldstein, Thomas, "X.J. Kennedy," in *Dictionary of Literary Biography,* volume 5: *American Poets since World War II,* edited by Donald Greiner, Detroit, Michigan: Gale, 1980
Kuusisto, Stephen, Deborah Tall, and David Weiss, "X.J. Kennedy," in *The Poet's Notebook: Excerpts from the Notebooks of Contemporary American Poets,* edited by Kuusisto, Tall, and Weiss, New York and London: Norton, 1995
Martz, Louis L., "Recent Poetry: The End of an Era," *Yale Review* 59 (Winter 1970)
Waldrop, Bernard, "Squibs," *Burning Deck* 2 (Spring 1963)

# Jack Kerouac 1922–69

Malcolm Cowley, in his "Introduction" to *Leaves of Grass,* points out that the young Walt Whitman's conduct as a poet "resembled that of the Beat Generation. He stayed out of the rat race, he avoided the squares . . . ; he was 'real gone,' he was 'far out'; and he was writing poems in . . . the 'open,' free-swinging style that is prized in Beat Generation literature. Some of them should be read to loud music as a means of glossing over their faults and holding the listener's attention—not to the music of a jazz combo, like beatnik poetry, but perhaps to that of a regimental band."

Indeed, Jack Kerouac himself addresses his poetic father in "Berkeley Song in F Major":

Walt Whitman is striding
Down the mountain of Berkeley
Where with one step
He abominates & destroys
The whole atomic laboratory
Wherein it becomes a jewel
In his heel, O Eloheim!

The poem issues recriminations about modern excesses of "progress" as Whitman strides over the land:

Walt Bluebeard Handsome
Whitman, farewell
—For he also strides
to East & gobbles
Up Burma & Tits
The Mock Top Peaks
Of T h i b e t a—
Returning, like sun
The shield
Around the other side
Where first we thought
We saw him visioning
Down the shuddering mount
Of Berkeley's Atomic
Test Laboratory
Full of mice and men

Then the poem trails off—after presenting a profile view of Allen Ginsberg—with a mystical Whitmanesque insight into Transcendental "essence" among minute creatures—ants and bees.

Now, what is "beat"? The original meaning was "exhausted": "When I met Williams Burroughs, he looked beat." Or it could mean "used up": "San Francisco / San Francisco / You're a muttering bum / In a brown beat suit" ("27th Chorus," *Book of Blues*). In *On the Road* (1957), the term "beatific" is used to describe a hallucinogenic vision. Later, the term was associated with "beatnik," a derisive term for seedy types in dirty jeans and T-shirts who spoke the "hip" language of jazz musicians. Beats were nonpolitical and indifferent to social problems, although Kerouac often deplores the poverty of oppressed peoples in both his prose and his verse.

However, it was in poetry that the Beats sought to liberate the form from academic purists, to democratize it and carry it back to the streets. Just as experiments in jazz music, led by Stan Kenton among others, challenged the orthodoxy of established musical forms, so the new Beat poetry spoke the language of the city streets: that of black urban life and of the hangers-on—prostitutes, thrill-seeking girls, and others participating in all-night sessions of the hippest excess. Kerouac called many of his poems "blues," as in *Mexico City Blues* (1959). In an introductory note to *Book of Blues* (1995), he writes,

> In my system, the form of blues choruses is limited by the small page of the breastpocket notebook in which they are written, like the form of a set number of bars in a jazz blues chorus, and so sometimes the word-meaning can carry one from chorus into another, or not, just like the phrase-meaning can carry harmonically from one chorus to the other, or not, in jazz, so that, in these blues as in jazz, the form is determined by time, and by the musicians's spontaneous phrasing & harmonizing with the beat of the time as it waves & waves on by in measured choruses. It's all gotta be non stop ad libbing within each chorus, or the gig is shot.

Thus, Kerouac suggests an act of performance, like that of a jazz player; in his performance, the hearer or the poem reader participates reciprocally in the act of creating the poem. As another, "establishment" poet put it, the poem has to "speak words that in the ear, / In the delicatest ear of the mind, repeat, / Exactly, that which it wants to hear" (Wallace Stevens, "Of Modern Poetry"). Of course, familiarity with the newest expressions in progressive jazz—those of the newest young composers associated with Stan Kenton—was essential to the fullest participation in the poems, as was, perhaps, the added influence of peyote, gin, or other drugs in a convivial atmosphere.

Obviously, this is verse of the "happening," an entirely different genre from the cerebral poetry of the classroom or private study. Kerouac never sought to bridge the gap between these two poetries, as his friend and poetic mentor Allen Ginsberg would eventually succeed in doing. Ginsberg recognized in his spiritual mentor, Walt Whitman, "*the* Poet of Democracy," that the "literary" level of performance could be cultivated and maintained only by an academic readership. As Whitman was the "father of American poetry," so the Beats continued to use the apparently undisciplined and sometimes disjointed verbiage they associated with his spirit.

The poetry of this movement has also been labeled "Dionysian" by Gregory Corso and others; it is a wild poetry of spontaneous excitement and orgasmic expression, characterized by dithyramic verse. The Beats' emphasis on combining poetry with jazz is therefore not surprising. It is a poetic almost entirely lacking in the discipline found in the more Apollonian verse of such poets as Williams, who, while revealing the same Dionysian tendencies, especially in *Paterson,* manages to control the poetic ego's eroticism and its childlike predilection to "talk dirty."

Like Ezra Pound before him, Kerouac's chief legacy may be his influence on others of his group, including Ginsberg, as well as later "rebels." In the context of the sedate 1950s, the spontaneously composed *On the Road* was lauded as a revolutionary literary work; as a result, Kerouac's subsequent writings were taken seriously and viewed as an expansion of the new gospel of nonconformity and self-expression, as delivered by the cultural hero of the decade. (For example, Kerouac's romantic vision of the American West was seen as radically new, as if the West had hitherto been indistinguishable from the American East.) Whether or not one regards Kerouac as a cultural hero, it is easy to identify the unique poetic vision that infused his poetry. Robert Creeley recognized it early: "Jack had an extraordinary ear, that impeccable ear that could hear patterns and make patterns in the sounds and rhythms of the language as spoken. Extraordinary ear, in the way he could manage such a live and insistently natural structure. Jack was a genius at the register of the speaking voice, a human voice talking. Its effect on my poetry? He gave an absolute measure of what the range of that kind of writing was" (see "Introduction," *Pomes of All Sizes,* 1992).

Kerouac's voice is also a personal voice, like Whitman's. His is a significant contribution to modern American poetics, different from the first-person "I" in Robert Frost's poetry and more like the "he" in Stevens'. Williams also comes to mind, but it is in Ginsberg's work that the Beat movement finds its fullest expression. Kerouac was the experimenter and innovator, as in *On the Road,* but with the increasing reliance on alcohol and other drugs his power and originality were diverted into hallucinatory incantations, ironic in light of the Beats' insistence on spiritual and personal freedom. Edward Halsey Foster, writing in his *Understanding the Beats* (1992), concludes, "At the very least, the Beats constitute an essential link in the specifically American tradition, traceable to Emerson and Thoreau, which insists that the individual is superior to any consensus, and that poetry and fiction, in so far as they testify to this, constitute a sacred task."

Peter Van Egmond

*See also* Beat Poetry

**Biography**

Born Jean Louis Lebris de Kerouac in Lowell, Massachusetts, 12 March 1922. Attended Horace Mann School, New York, 1939–40; Columbia University, New York, 1940–41, 1942; served in the United States Merchant Marines, 1942, 1943, and the United States Navy, 1943; sports reporter, Lowell *Sun,* 1942; from 1944 worked odd jobs; brakeman, Southern Pacific Railroad, San Francisco, 1952–53; fire lookout for United States Agricultural Service, Washington State, 1956; from 1957, full-time writer. Died in St. Petersburg, Florida, 21 October 1969.

**Poetry**

*Mexico City Blues,* 1959
*Heaven, and Other Poems,* edited by Donald Allen, 1977
*Pomes of All Sizes,* 1992
*Old Angel Midnight,* edited by Donald Allen, 1993
*Book of Blues,* 1995
*The Portable Jack Kerouac* (includes prose), 1995
*A Book of Cats and Haikus,* 1997

**Other Writings:** novels (*On the Road,* 1957; revised edition, edited by Scott Donaldson, 1978), screenplay (*Pull My Daisy,* 1959), correspondence (*Dear Carolyn,* edited by Arthur Knight and Kit Knight, 1983).

**Further Reading**

Bartlett, Lee, editor, *The Beats: Essays in Criticism,* Jefferson, North Carolina: McFarland, 1981
Challis, Chris, *Quest for Kerouac,* London and Boston: Faber and Faber, 1984
Charters, Ann, *Kerouac: A Biography,* San Francisco: Straight Arrow Books, 1973; London: Deutsch, 1974
Clark, Tom, *Jack Kerouac,* San Diego, California, and London: Harcourt Brace Jovanovich, 1984
Foster, Edward Halsey, *Understanding the Beats,* Columbia: University of South Carolina Press, 1992
Miles, Barry, *Jack Kerouac: King of the Beats,* New York: Holt, and London: Virgin, 1998; new edition; London: Virgin, 1999
Nicosia, Gerald, *Memory Babe: A Critical Biography of Jack Kerouac,* New York: Grove Press, 1983; London: Viking 1985; new edition, London: Penguin, 1992
Turner, Steve, *Jack Kerouac: Angelheaded Hipster,* New York: Viking, and London: Bloomsbury Press, 1996

## Mexico City Blues

The publication of *Mexico City Blues* in 1959 coincided with a media backlash against the Beats and thus marked a turning point in Jack Kerouac's career as a writer. Already famous for *On the Road* (1957) and his friendship with Allen Ginsberg, Kerouac was crushed by widespread negative reaction to his poetry and did not publish another volume of poems during the remaining 10 years of his life. Reconsideration of *Mexico City Blues* shows that the volume is a significant, if not a prophetic, contribution to American poetry, however. Employing techniques derived from Kerouac's passionate appreciation of jazz, this tightly formulated serial poem also combines two other significant improvisational art forms: Japanese haiku and American blues. In short, rather than the formless jottings of a novelist trying to pass himself off as a poet, *Mexico City Blues* shows Kerouac to be a thoughtful, cosmopolitan artist, one serious about his craft, yet able to take himself lightly when appropriate. The 242 "choruses" (as Kerouac called them) comprising *Mexico City Blues* will repay scholarly inquiry and prosodic investigation for generations to come.

Kerouac composed *Mexico City Blues* in August of 1955 while living in a Mexico City tenement with his friend William Garver. Because the novel that would make him famous had by this time been rejected by dozens of publishers and was still two years away from publication, Kerouac worked on his choruses in near obscurity, possibly without a thought to their eventual publication. This may have allowed him to experiment more than some of his contemporaries. The length of each chorus and the shape of the lines were determined not by conventional prosody, but rather by the size of the reporter's notebook Kerouac always carried and in which he wrote his poems. Like a musician taking a solo, Kerouac worked with a format that shaped the poems but also left room for improvisation. He wrote in the preface that he hoped

> to be considered a jazz poet blowing a long blues in an afternoon jam session. I take 242 choruses; my ideas vary and

sometimes roll from chorus to chorus or from halfway through a chorus to halfway through the next.

In addition to this dedication to the aesthetic of spontaneous composition, Kerouac also intended an extra-literary purpose for his work. As expressed at the end of "1st Chorus," he is on a "mersion of missy." This seemingly throw-away line perfectly embodies the two themes of the poem: the interaction and hoped-for unity of the ethical and the aesthetic, the serious and the comic. The slurring wordplay on the phrase "mission of mercy" signals both the importance of the poem and the playfulness of the poet.

The "211th Chorus" summarizes many of the themes Kerouac pursues in this book while also demonstrating the Buddhist underpinning of his worldview:

All the endless conception of living beings
Gnashing everywhere in Consciousness
Throughout the ten directions of space
Occupying all the direct quarters in & out,
From supermicroscopic no-bug
To huge Galaxy Lightyear Bowell
Illuminating the sky of one Mind—
*Poor!* I wish I was free
of that slaving meat wheel
and safe in heaven dead.

In this chorus Kerouac employs a veritable Homeric catalog of creatures to illustrate Buddhism's "First Noble Truth," that all life is suffering. The "212th Chorus" picks up this theme by asserting,

All of this meat is in dreadful pain
. . . And it quivers, meat, & owner cries
And wishes "Why was I born with a body?"

The human body here is dwarfed not just by the number of species, most of which cannot be seen by the naked human eye, but by the cosmos as a whole. Kerouac seems in these choruses to regret incarnation; the fragmented human mind is tormented by its inability to comprehend the universe, by what Kerouac calls its "arbitrary conceptions" in the "108th Chorus."

*Mexico City Blues* functions like a jazz symphony, synthesizing decidedly American musical forms and Kerouac's interest in Buddhism. Fittingly, the poem ends with a meditation of "Buddhist saints" ("236th Chorus"), one of whom, it turns out, is jazz legend Charlie Parker. "Charley Parker looked like Buddha," says the 239th chorus, and by the "241st Chorus," Parker's music helps Kerouac transcend the agony depicted earlier in the poem:

Charley Parker, pray for me—
Pray for me and everybody
In the Nirvanas of your brain
Where you hide, indulgent and huge,
No longer Charley Parker
But the secret unsayable name
That carries with it merit
Not to be measured from here
To up, down, east, or west—
—Charley Parker, lay the bane,
off me, and every body

San Francisco poet Michael McClure recognizes *Mexico City Blues* as Kerouac's masterpiece. He is among the few readers who considered it from the start to be "a religious poem startling in its majesty and comedy and gentleness of vision" (1982). Allen Ginsberg called it "my favorite work" and "a great classic" (1980). Appreciated at first by only a handful of poets who used Kerouac's writing as a way of making breakthroughs in their own work, *Mexico City Blues* remains available to a broad audience; increased interest in jazz and Buddhism in literary circles can only improve the reception of this neglected poem.

DAVID R. ZAUHAR

**Further Reading**

Belgrad, Daniel, *The Culture of Spontaneity: Improvisation and the Arts in Postwar America,* Chicago: University of Chicago Press, 1998
Berrigan, Ted, "The Art of Fiction XLI: Jack Kerouac," *The Paris Review* 43 (1968)
Charters, Ann, *Kerouac: A Biography,* San Francisco: Straight Arrow Books, 1973; London: Deutsch, 1974
Clark, Tom, *Jack Kerouac,* San Diego, California, and London: Harcourt Brace Jovanovich, 1984
Fields, Rick, *How the Swans Came to the Lake: A Narrative History of Buddhism in America,* Boulder, Colorado: Shambhala, 1981; 3rd edition, Boston and London: Shambhala, 1992
Garon, Paul, *Blues and the Poetic Spirit,* London: Eddison Press, and New York: Da Capo, 1975; revised edition, San Francisco: City Lights, 1996
Ginsberg, Allen, *Composed on the Tongue: Literary Conversations, 1967–1977,* edited by Donald Allen, San Francisco: Grey Fox Press, 1980
Jones, James T., *A Map of "Mexico City Blues": Jack Kerouac as Poet,* Carbondale: Southern Illinois University Press, 1992
McClure, Michael, *Scratching the Beat Surface,* San Francisco: North Point, 1982
McNally, Dennis, *Desolate Angel: Jack Kerouac, the Beat Generation, and America,* New York: Random, 1979
Nicosia, Gerald, *Memory Babe: A Critical Biography of Jack Kerouac,* New York: Grove Press, 1983; London: Viking, 1985; new edition, London: Penguin, 1992
Sorrell, Richard, "The Catholicism of Jack Kerouac," *Studies in Religion* 11 (1982)
Tallman, Warren, "Keroauc's Sound," in *A Casebook on the Beat,* edited by Thomas Parkinson, New York: Crowell, 1961

# Joyce Kilmer 1886–1918

Known variously as a war poet, a sentimental poet, a Catholic poet, and a New Jersey poet, Joyce Kilmer is as fondly recalled in some circles as he is vilified or ignored in others. Despite his active although brief career as a poet, reviewer, editor, and anthologist, Kilmer's contributions to American literary history are most often reduced to the enormous national and international renown of his poem "Trees." This now notorious poem, whether viewed as a symbol of the divide between academic and popular poetic tastes or as enduring proof that poetry can and does have a place in people's everyday lives, has provoked much debate about value and popularity in 20th-century American poetry. Moreover, Kilmer's work as a whole, along with the devotion to the arts shared by the Kilmer family, demonstrates an unabashed moral idealism much in keeping with the Puritan tradition in American poetry even if it is quite at odds with the disillusionment characteristic of much World War I–era poetry.

Although "Trees" was first published in the prestigious *Poetry: A Magazine of Verse* in August 1913, Kilmer's work represented the magazine's more formally conservative impulses, not its eventual association with Modernist poets such as T.S. Eliot, Marianne Moore, and E.E. Cummings. Nevertheless, thanks in large part to the musical version of the poem by Kilmer's mother, Annie Kilburn Kilmer, the poem's concluding statement that "Poems are made by fools like me, / But only God can make a tree" remains among the most frequently quoted lines of 20th-century American poetry. "Trees" was collected in Kilmer's second volume of poems, *Trees, and Other Poems* (1914), a volume that represented to both Kilmer and his critics a maturation of his verse from his first volume of 1911. However, several of his most accomplished poems came a few years later in his third and final volume, *Main Street, and Other Poems* (1917).

This volume contained World War I poems such as "The White Ships and the Red" (inspired by Kilmer's outrage over the sinking of the *Lusitania*), "Rouge Bouquet," and "Prayer of a Soldier in France." Each of these poems combines a recognition of the pain and loss of war with a conviction that a war fought well and nobly for a cause can bring redemption. Kilmer maintained these themes even in his final poem, "The Peacemaker," written in France shortly before his death in July 1918. This Petrarchan sonnet uses paradox to argue that by submitting himself to suffering in war, the soldier creates, in the model of the crucified Christ, life out of death. The paradoxes surveyed in the sonnet's octave—characterized by the lines "That pain may cease, he yields his flesh to pain. / To banish war, he must a warrior be"—are resolved in the sestet by a heavily alliterative pronouncement about freedom:

> What matters Death, if Freedom be not dead?
>   No flags are fair, if Freedom's flag be furled.
> Who fights for Freedom, goes with joyful tread
>   To meet the fires of Hell against him hurled,
> And has for captain Him whose thorn-wreathed head
>   Smiles from the Cross upon a conquered world.

In war poems such as "The Peacemaker" as well as in Kilmer's more numerous poems about the joys and trials of everyday life, critics have seen the influence of Edwin Arlington Robinson's Puritan ethic of endurance and moral courage as well as the metrical patterns and Catholic themes of Kilmer's fellow Catholic convert Coventry Patmore.

Less well known, yet in some ways more interesting, than Kilmer's poetic contribution to American literary history is his contribution as an editor, anthologist, and essayist. Kilmer was an early and influential advocate of Gerard Manley Hopkins in the United States; a journalistic critic of G.K. Chesterton, Francis Thompson, Hilaire Belloc, and William Vaughn Moody; an interviewer of prominent literary figures of his day, such as William Dean Howells, Amy Lowell, and Edwin Arlington Robinson (in *Literature in the Making, by Some of Its Makers,* 1917); and an energetic anthologist of Catholic poetry in English (in *Dreams and Images: An Anthology of Catholic Poets,* 1917). In addition to examining Kilmer's work in each of these roles, readers can reassess his writing and gain a fuller view of his values by looking at essays such as "The Inefficient Library." The varied themes and tonal inconsistencies of his poetic oeuvre come into sharper focus when read through the lens of Kilmer's attitude toward his beloved books: "My library is inefficient and impractical, entertaining and unexacting. Its members have come to me by chance and by momentary inclination." His poems often delight in the "momentary inclination" and indulge in the passing aversion, but Kilmer valued such passionate stances over the dullness of forced efficiency or modern practicality.

Kilmer's current status in 20th-century American poetry is indicated more by his absence in criticism than his presence. Recent revisions of modern American poetry have overlooked Kilmer for several reasons. Kilmer's image as an idealistic gentleman-poet with refined sensibilities does not fare well in an era of revisionism favoring more politically liberal poets. Cary Nelson does not mention Kilmer in his influential *Repression and Recovery: Modern American Poetry and the Politics of Cultural Memory, 1910–1945* (1989) or include Kilmer in the Oxford *Anthology of Modern American Poetry* (2000). Neither traditionally canonical among literary critics nor newly recoverable as a long-overlooked writer, Kilmer has faded out of view. Further, Kilmer's death in 1918 cast him as a poet of naive, prewar sensibility—an American Rupert Brooke—and not as someone with much to offer an understanding of postwar poetry. Rather than provide an entry into the larger landscape of American poetry, the popularity of "Trees" and Kilmer's image as a poet of valor and sincerity create a screen of quaintness beyond which critics, in either praise or censure, increasingly cease to look. Nevertheless, as the author of one of the best-known poems in 20th-century American poetry and as a poet identified by his wartime service, Catholic faith, and regional ties to New Jersey, Kilmer's poetic and journalistic contributions retain a distinctive place within American literary history.

Catherine Tramontana

**Biography**

Born in New Brunswick, New Jersey, 6 December 1886. Attended Rutgers College 1904–06, Columbia University, A.B. 1908; high school Latin teacher, Morristown, New Jersey, 1908–09; definition writer, *Standard Dictionary,* 1909–12; literary editor, *Churchman,* 1912; writer, *The New York Times,* from 1913; served in U.S. military, 1917–18. Posthumously awarded the Croix de Guerre. Died in the Aisne region of France, c. 30 July 1918.

**Poetry**
*Summer of Love,* 1911
*Trees, and Other Poems,* 1914
*Main Street, and Other Poems,* 1917
*Complete Poems,* 1998

**Selected Criticism**
*The Circus, and Other Essays,* 1916; revised edition, *The Circus, and Other Essays and Fugitive Pieces,* 1921

**Other Writings:** interviews (*Literature in the Making, by Some of Its Makers,* 1917); edited poetry anthologies (*Dreams and Images: An Anthology of Catholic Poets,* 1917).

**Further Reading**
Cargas, Harry J., *I Lay Down My Life: A Biography of Joyce Kilmer,* Boston: St. Paul Editions, 1964
Covell, John E., *Joyce Kilmer: A Literary Biography,* Brunswick, Georgia: Write-Fit Communications, 2000
Harmon, William, "[Alfred] Joyce Kilmer," in *Encyclopedia of American Literature,* edited by Steven R. Serafin, New York: Continuum, 1999
Hart, James A., "Joyce Kilmer," in *Dictionary of Literary Biography,* volume 45: *American Poets, 1880=–1945, First Series,* edited by Peter Quartermain, Detroit, Michigan: Gale Research, 1986
Kenney, Blair G., "Woodsman, Spare Those 'Trees'!" *College English* 25, no. 6 (1964)
Kilmer, Kenton, *Memories of My Father, Joyce Kilmer,* New Brunswick, New Jersey: Joyce Kilmer Centennial Commission, 1993

---

## Galway Kinnell 1927–

Galway Kinnell was born on 1 February 1927 in Providence, Rhode Island, to parents who both had immigrated to the United States—his mother from Ireland and his father from Scotland. The fourth of four children, he grew up in Pawtucket, Rhode Island, attending public schools until a scholarship enabled him to enroll in the Wilbraham Academy in Massachusetts for his senior year of high school. In 1944, he entered Princeton University, where he met W.S. Merwin and his future mentor, the man to whom he first showed his poetry, Charles Bell. From 1944 to 1946, Kinnell participated in the U.S. Navy officer training program at Princeton. He graduated summa cum laude in 1948; the next year, he received an M.A. from the University of Rochester. Since then, Kinnell has lived all over the world—in France and Iran on Fulbright fellowships, in Spain and Australia, and in Chicago, Hawaii, and New York—although since purchasing an abandoned farmhouse in northern Vermont in 1961, he has made that state his primary home. Kinnell has taught at many universities in the United States and abroad. In 1981, he accepted a position at New York University, where he became the Samuel F.B. Morse Professor of Arts and Sciences in 1985 and is now the Erich Maria Remarque Professor of Creative Writing.

One of our major American poets, widely praised and often anthologized, Kinnell has published many books of poems and translations as well as a novel set in Iran, *Black Light* (1966); a collection of revised interviews, *Walking Down the Stairs* (1978); and several essays. His books of poems include *What a Kingdom It Was* (1960), *Flower Herding on Mount Monadnock* (1964), *Body Rags* (1968), *The Avenue Bearing the Initial of Christ into the New World: Poems, 1946–1964* (1974), *Selected Poems* (1982), *The Past* (1985), *When One Has Lived a Long Time Alone* (1990), and *Imperfect Thirst* (1994) as well as his masterpiece, *The Book of Nightmares* (1971), and *A New Selected Poems* (2000). He is also a prize-winning translator of, among others, François Villon, Yves Bonnefoy, and Rainer Maria Rilke. His honors include the Shelley Prize from the Poetry Society of America, the Medal of Merit from the National Institute of Arts and Letters, the Pulitzer Prize for *Selected Poems* (for which he was also co-winner of an American Book Award), and a MacArthur Foundation grant. He has served as president of PEN and as State Poet of Vermont. Politically, too, Kinnell has long been active. During the 1960s, he worked on a voter registration campaign for the Congress of Racial Equality in Louisiana, which led to a week in jail and a major poem, "The Last River" (*Body Rags*). He participated in numerous readings protesting the Vietnam War and published powerful antiwar poems, such as "Vapor Trail Reflected in the Frog Pond" (*Body Rags*) and "The Dead Shall Be Raised Incorruptible" (*The Book of Nightmares*). In 1982, he organized an anti-nuclear reading, Poets Against the End of the World, in New York—a concern unforgettably witnessed to in a poem about Hiroshima and Nagasaki, "The Fundamental Project of Technology," which commemorates and grieves for "the children . . . / in scorched uniforms, holding tiny crushed lunch tins" who, simply by virtue of being born, are sent forth throughout time into the nightmare of history, into which

> they will go
> again and again, until the day flashes and no one lives
> to look back and say, a flash, a white flash sparkled. (*The Past*)

Formally, Kinnell's poetry has changed quite a bit over the years. His earliest poems, heavily modeled on Yeats, are in traditional rhyme and meter:

> Overhead the stars stood in their right course.
> Later a mourning dove stirred the night
> With soft cries. I was deaf, and the light
> Out of the east fell on extinguished sight.

My new eyes searched the passion of the stars. ("Passion,"
*The Avenue . . .*)

These early poems from the rare *First Poems, 1946–1954* (1970) are reprinted in *The Avenue Bearing the Initial of Christ into the New World;* sometimes quite lovely, but a bit attenuated and derivative, they give way by the time of *What a Kingdom It Was* to more energetic and variable free-verse cadences and a more colloquial voice:

Children set fires in ashbarrels,
Cats prowl the fires, scraps of fishes burn.

A child lay in the flames.
It was not the plan. Abraham
Stood in terror at the duplicity. ("The Avenue . . .")

By the time of *Body Rags* and *The Book of Nightmares,* Kinnell's sense of poetic organization and line has developed tremendous musicality and freedom. Many of his great longer poems from this period—"The Porcupine," "The Bear," and all ten poems that make up *The Book of Nightmares*—are composed of short bits of narrative or lyrics joined together in sections; line lengths vary from a single syllable to, for example, 21 in the last line of "The Bear." The formal choices are brilliant. Building a long poem out of short lyrics, charged utterances, allows Kinnell to maintain extraordinary intensity, and the varying line lengths, the stunning line breaks, and all the white space around words enable the poems to swell and contract, to breathe, to dance with silence—as in these lines from *The Book of Nightmares:*

You scream, waking from a nightmare.

When I sleepwalk
into your room, and pick you up,
and hold you up in the moonlight, you cling to me
hard
as if clinging could save us. I think
you think
I will never die, I think I exude
to you the permanence of smoke or stars . . . ("Little
Sleep's-Head Sprouting Hair in the Moonlight")

Emily Dickinson asks in a poem, "Dare you see a Soul *at the White Heat?*" *The Book of Nightmares,* a visionary, mythic book that traces the wanderings of the soul through tenderness, violence, anguish, and loss to the barely imaginable place where on the dead body "one flea" is "laughing" ("Lastness"), was written at the "white heat." After its appearance in 1971, it was hard to imagine what Kinnell could write to follow it. In fact, he has continued to develop and be prolific. The births of his daughter and son begin and end *The Book of Nightmares;* since then, as befits his entry into parenthood, he has fully explored the permutations of ordinary experience and has developed a supple, authoritative voice and a fairly consistent free-verse line for meditations, elegies, and lyrics concerning family, nature, the deaths of fellow poets and friends, and the death and birth of love. His most recent poem, an astonishing anatomy of the decay of a vole, bears testimony not only to Kinnell's humor and wisdom but also to his continuing powers of observation and linguistic vitality:

. . . His gape drawn back,
he bares his teeth: uppers
stubby and old-folks yellow, lowers
an inch long, curled inward, like uppers
of beavers if forced to subsist on soft food.
At the last day, when souls go back
to their graves and resume the form
and flesh once theirs, this one
could jump and jig, as if simply risen from a good night's
dead sloom. ("The Quick and the Dead")

In "Oatmeal," a funny yet profound poem about solitude, creativity, the viscous comforts of hot cereal, and Kinnell's love for the poet John Keats, Kinnell imagines the great Romantic composing his ode "To Autumn" while dragging his spoon through glistening furrows of oatmeal and in a stunning leap concludes, "maybe there is no sublime; only the shining of the amnion's tatters" (*When One Has Lived a Long Time Alone*). This line expresses a realization central to all Kinnell's work: the world of the mortal body—of birth, sex, flesh, time, and the fear and fact of and longing for death—is the only locus of glory. Our abjection and terror cannot be winnowed out from our sublimity and beauty. "I am the poet of the body, / And I am the poet of the soul," Walt Whitman announces in "Song of Myself." Like Whitman, whose poetry (along with Yeats', Rilke's, Emily Dickinson's, and William Carlos Williams') has exerted a primary influence on Kinnell's, Kinnell has always been a poet of the body; as he remarks simply in an interview, "The body makes love possible" (*Walking Down the Stairs*). The implications of this are enormous. The poet of the body is a poet of mortality—of love, yes, the rapture of the sexual embrace, the moments and things of this world, but also always of death. Kinnell shares Rilke's desire in the *Duino Elegies* to go forward into life, accepting the whole of death; he takes as the epigraph for *The Book of Nightmares* Rilke's lines

But this, though: death,
the whole of death,—even before life's begun,
to hold it all so gently, and be good . . .

and transforms them into his own more trenchant utterance:

Listen, Kinnell,
dumped alive
and dying into the old sway bed,
a layer of crushed feathers all that there is
between you
and the long shaft of darkness shaped as you,
let go. ("The Hen Flower")

From beginning to end, Kinnell writes powerfully, even obsessively, about the terrors and indignities of death. But "death has two aspects," he remarks in an interview—"the extinction, which we fear, and the flowing away into the universe, which we desire" (*Walking Down the Stairs*). Like Wallace Stevens, he understands death, too, as the mother of beauty and writes of a "kind of glory in our lives which derives precisely from our inability to enter . . . paradise or to experience eternity" ("The Poetics of the Physical World"). This glory fuels Kinnell's love poems, of which "Rapture" is a beautiful example:

The clock shows eight. Hmmm.
With huge, silent effort of great,
mounded muscles the earth has been turning.
She takes a piece of silken cloth
from the drawer and stands up. Under the falls
of her hair her face has become quiet and downcast,
as if she will be, all day among strangers,
looking down inside herself at our rapture. (*Imperfect Thirst*)

Even more deeply, like Rilke and D.H. Lawrence, Kinnell understands death as the ground of our being, the uncreate from which the amnion develops, a source of holiness, of mystery. As early as *Flower Herding on Mount Monadnock,* he writes,

I know that I love the day,
The sun on the mountain, the Pacific
Shiny and accomplishing itself in breakers,
But I know I live half alive in the world,
I know half my life belongs to the wild darkness. ("Middle of the Way," *The Avenue . . .*)

Kinnell's search for a "death of the self" that would not be "a drying up or withering" but "would give me more loves, not fewer. And greater desire, not less" ("Poetry, Personality, and Death") has lasted throughout his life. Now in his 70s, he continues to be one of our most important poets, not only for the proficiency, range, and authority of his work but also for his courage to write the poem of existence out of the whole self, to insist on tenderness in this violent, "footbattered blaze of the earth" ("Vapor Trail Reflected in the Frog Pond," *Body Rags*), to affirm the desperate beauty of what vanishes. "*The wages / of dying is love,*" Kinnell writes in *The Book of Nightmares* ("Little Sleep's-Head . . ."). From beginning to end, he finds his inspiration there. As he concludes in "Freedom, New Hampshire," a moving, early elegy for his brother Derry, who died at age 32,

. . . an incarnation is in particular flesh
And the dust that is swirled into a shape
And crumbles and is swirled again had but one shape
That was this man. When he is dead the grass
Heals what he suffered, but he remains dead,
And the few who loved him know this until they die. (*What a Kingdom It Was*)

ANN FISHER-WIRTH

**Biography**

Born in Providence, Rhode Island, 1 February 1927. Attended Princeton University, New Jersey, A.B. 1948; University of Rochester, New York, M.A. 1949; served in the United States Navy, 1945–46; Instructor in English, Alfred University, New York, 1949–51; supervisor of liberal arts program, University of Chicago, 1951–55; American Lecturer, University of Grenoble, 1956–57; summer session lecturer, University of Nice, 1957; Fulbright Lecturer, University of Iran, Tehran, 1959–60; poet-in-residence/visiting writer, Juniata College, Huntingdon, Pennsylvania, 1964, Reed College, Portland, Oregon, 1966–67, Colorado State University, Fort Collins, 1968, University of Washington, Seattle, 1968, University of California, Irvine, 1968–69, Deya Institute, Mallorca, 1969–70, University of Iowa, Iowa City, 1970, Sarah Lawrence College, Bronxville, New York, 1972–78, Princeton University, New Jersey, 1976, Holy Cross College, 1977, and Macquarie University, Sydney, Australia, 1979; Visiting Professor, Pittsburgh Poetry Forum, 1971, Queens College, New York, 1971, Columbia University, New York, 1972, 1974, 1976, Brandeis University, Waltham, Massachusetts, 1974, Skidmore College, Saratoga Springs, New York, 1975, University of Delaware, Newark, 1978, and University of Hawaii, Manoa, Honolulu, 1979–80; DeRoy Honors Professor, University of Michigan, Ann Arbor, 1987; since 1979 director, Squaw Valley Community of Writers; formerly Samuel F.B. Morse Professor of Arts and Sciences, currently Erich Maria Remarque Professor of Creative Writing, New York University. Received Ford grant, 1955; Fulbright scholarship, 1955; Longview Foundation Award, 1962; American Academy grant, 1962, and Medal of Merit, 1976; Guggenheim fellowship, 1963, 1974; Bess Hokin Prize, 1965, and Eunice Tietjens Memorial Prize, 1966 (*Poetry,* Chicago); Rockefeller grant, 1967; Cecil Hemley Prize, 1968; Brandeis University Creative Arts Award, 1968; National Endowment for the Arts grant, 1969; Ingram Merrill Foundation Award, 1969; Amy Lowell traveling fellowship, 1969; Shelley Memorial Award, 1972; Academy of American Poets Landon Translation Award, 1978; American Book Award, 1983; Pulitzer Prize, 1983; MacArthur fellowship, 1984; member, American Academy, 1981. Living in Sheffield, Vermont, and New York City.

**Poetry**

*What a Kingdom It Was,* 1960
*Flower Herding on Mount Monadnock,* 1964
*Body Rags,* 1968
*First Poems, 1946–1954,* 1970
*The Book of Nightmares,* 1971
*The Avenue Bearing the Initial of Christ into the New World: Poems, 1946–1964,* 1974
*Mortal Acts, Mortal Words,* 1980
*Selected Poems,* 1982
*The Past,* 1985
*When One Has Lived a Long Time Alone,* 1990
*Three Books: Body Rags; Mortal Acts, Mortal Words; The Past,* 1993
*Imperfect Thirst,* 1994
*A New Selected Poems,* 2000

**Other Writings:** novel (*Black Light,* 1966), essays, children's literature, translations of French poetry (*The Poems of François Villon,* 1977; *The Essential Rilke* [with Hannah Liebmann], 1999); edited collection of poetry (*The Essential Whitman,* 1987).

**Further Reading**

Calhoun, Richard J., *Galway Kinnell,* New York: Twayne, 1992
Kinnell, Galway, *Walking Down the Stairs: Selections from Interviews,* Ann Arbor: University of Michigan Press, 1978
Nelson, Cary, *Our Last First Poets: Vision and History in Contemporary American Poetry,* Urbana: University of Illinois Press, 1981

Nelson, Howard, editor, *On the Poetry of Galway Kinnell: The Wages of Dying*, Ann Arbor: University of Michigan Press, 1987

Zimmerman, Lee, *Intricate and Simple Things: The Poetry of Galway Kinnell*, Urbana: University of Illinois Press, 1987

# The Fundamental Project of Technology

Galway Kinnell's "The Fundamental Project of Technology" prophetically evokes nuclear war's threat to humanity. A veteran of struggles for civil rights and against the Vietnam War, Kinnell was active during the 1980s in the nuclear freeze movement. He organized Poets Against the End of the World, an anti-nuclear poetry reading that took place in New York on 26 May 1982 (Gery, 1996). Kinnell first presented the poem in 1982 at Harvard University (Seigel, 1987). It subsequently appeared in *Writing in a Nuclear Age* (1984), in *The American Poetry Review* (July/August 1984), and in Kinnell's *The Past* (1985).

"The Fundamental Project of Technology" is one of Kinnell's strongest poems on a politically charged topic. Kinnell meditates on the flash that "Fat Man," the atomic bomb that the United States detonated over Nagasaki, Japan, registered in the eyes of a witness, Tatsuichiro Akizuki, whose statement "A flash! A white flash sparkled!" serves as the poem's epigraph. The poem's setting is a Japanese museum commemorating the attack. The first stanza focuses on the relics displayed "Under glass"; the second on a visitor, an "old man, possibly a soldier back then" on the day of the blast; and the third on "a group / of schoolchildren" touring the museum. The middle stanza imagines the sounds that people within an atomic explosion's death zone may hear. In the final three stanzas, provoked by the museum's effort to memorialize an event of virtually no temporal duration but of endless consequence and by his poetic attempt to memorialize the sounds that the victims may have heard, Kinnell ponders the relations between technology, memory, and the foreknowledge of death.

The museum's power as a memorial relies on the striking effects that the atomic flash produced in objects as it fixed people in death. Archiving a technologically induced Pompeii, the museum houses "glass dishes which changed / in color; pieces of transformed beer bottles; / a household iron; bundles of wire become solid / lumps of iron" and so on. The flash made objects into images of a past that the museum recalls in the present to warn of a future nuclear catastrophe (Solotaroff, 1987). Kinnell's imagination, through memory's fusion of past and present, recalls images that yield flashes of insight into humanity's fate. The interplay between Kinnell's poetic project and technology's project "to establish deathlessness" by annihilating mortals raises a question: in recollecting the Nagasaki victims' dying moments, how does the poem avoid merely reinforcing the "foreknowledge" of death that drives the "fundamental project of technology"?

Akizuki survived to write about the flash because he stood on the outer edge of what he defined as the "Concentric Circles of Death" ringing the blast. Kinnell, by way of a speculative "If," edges within those circles to imagine what the annihilated may have memorized as the circles of death expanding from Fat Man's ground zero engulfed them:

> If all a city's faces were to shrink back all at once
> from their skulls, would a new sound come into existence,
> audible above moans eaves extract from wind that
> smoothes
> the grass on graves, or raspings heart's-blood greases still,
> or wails infants trill born already skillful at the grandpa's
> rattle,
> or infra-screams bitter-knowledge's speechlessness
> memorized, at that white flash, inside closed-forever
> mouths?

Like the light of the photographer's flash that fixes an image on film of the children visiting the museum ("schoolchildren line up, hold it, grin at a flash-pop"), Fat Man's "flash" disclosed images, many of which survive. Akizuki saw and memorialized the flash. The museum collects images that the flash imprinted in objects. However, the sounds "bitter-knowledge's speechlessness / memorized" do not survive. The dead of Hiroshima, Nagasaki, or a nuclear holocaust to come will never describe their final memories of sound to us.

Only the imagination allows us access to these memories. One glass case contains "a ring of skull- / bone fused to the inside of a helmet" by the explosion's heat. The mind that inhabited that skull, during "bitter-knowledge's speechlessness," may have "memorized" the "infra-screams" that sounded through it as the "flash sparkled." From within death's concentric circles, Kinnell's imagination retrieves sounds, including an enigmatic "new sound," that displace the voice with which the "foreknowledge [of death] terrorizes the contents of skulls."

"Bitter-knowledge" tells mortals that death is coming. This "foreknowledge" grounds "the fundamental project of technology": "To de-animalize human mentality, to purge it of obsolete / evolutionary characteristics, in particular of death." However, mortals' foreknowledge of death is an inescapably aberrant speculation. Based on such "foreknowledge," technology's project displays a fantastic pseudologic, and this "*pseudologica fantastica*'s mechanisms require: / to establish deathlessness it is necessary to eliminate / those who die." To dismantle these "mechanisms," Kinnell gives us a cognition other than the foreknowledge of death. This cognition dissolves the idolatry of technology.

Several nuclear protest poems imagine atomic weapons to enshrine a deity. For example, Allen Ginsberg's "Plutonian Ode" personifies plutonium as a god of death (Gery, 1996). The image of plutonium as death's god is a symptom of, not a cure for, "the fundamental project of technology." Positing such an idol, "bitter-knowledge's" voice prevails over the imagination. Kinnell takes us to a place where, listening to "bitter-knowledge's speechlessness," we learn to disassociate atomic weaponry from any god that either gives us or takes away our mortality:

> Unlike the trees of home, which continually evaporate
> along the skyline, the trees here have been enticed down
> toward world-eternity. No one knows which gods they
> enshrine.
> Does it matter? Awareness of ignorance is as devout
> as knowledge of knowledge. Or more so. . . .

If Kinnell merely gave us foreknowledge of humanity's death, whether by nuclear war or by natural extinction, he would perpetuate rather than short-circuit the project. By predicting the day when "no one lives / to look back and say, a flash, a white flash sparkled," his poem intimates that aberrant foreknowledge. However, the poem also and "more" "devout[ly]" gives us an "awareness" of the "ignorance" inhabiting the foreknowledge of death that seduces us into knowing technology as the avatar of a god that could "establish deathlessness."

Robert S. Oventile

**Further Reading**


Gery, John, *Nuclear Annihilation and Contemporary American Poetry,* Gainesville: University Press of Florida, 1996

Kinnell, Galway, et al., "Poets Against the End of the World," *Poetry East* 9/10 (Winter 1982/Spring 1983)

Schley, Jim, editor, *Writing in a Nuclear Age,* Hanover, New Hampshire: New England Review and Bread Loaf Quarterly, 1984

Seigel, Catherine F., "Corso, Kinnell, and the Bomb," *University of Dayton Review* 18, no. 3 (1987)

Solotaroff, Ted, "Knowing and Not Knowing," in *On the Poetry of Galway Kinnell: The Wages of Dying,* edited by Howard Nelson, Ann Arbor: University of Michigan Press, 1987

Wilson, Rob, "Towards the Nuclear Sublime," in *American Sublime: The Genealogy of a Poetic Genre,* by Wilson, Madison: University of Wisconsin Press, 1991


## Little Sleep's-Head Sprouting Hair in the Moonlight

"A baby's cry is poetry's tuning-fork," Galway Kinnell said once at a poetry reading. Of no poem is the remark more true than of "Little Sleep's-Head Sprouting Hair in the Moonlight," which is tuned to the cries of his little daughter Maud. "Little Sleep's-Head" is the seventh section of Kinnell's masterpiece, *The Book of Nightmares* (1971), a book-length poem made up of 10 poems (each in seven sections), which begins and ends with the births of Kinnell's two children, Maud and Fergus. Like Hart Crane's *The Bridge* and William Carlos Williams' *Paterson, The Book of Nightmares* is a great long poem that accomplishes many things. It carries forward Whitman's project to write what David Powell has called the "proper history" of America into a postmodern era characterized by apocalyptic horror and breakdown, imperialist aggression, travesties of democracy, atrocities of the Korean and especially Vietnam War; it is a poem seared by the dead that will not "*stop burning*" ("The Dead Shall Be Raised Incorruptible"). With Kinnell's characteristic frankness the poem also probes the corruption and fear in the poet's own heart: his depression, his desires both licit and transgressive, his unappeasable restlessness, and his sense that life and writing are nothing more than mined coal waste, "unbreathable goaf / of everything I ever craved and lost" ("The Path Among the Stones"). It traces a dark night of the soul, through despair, not into belief—for as "the Crone" says in "The Shoes of Wandering,"

*poor fool,*
*poor forked branch*
*of applewood, you will feel all your bones*
*break*
*over the holy waters you will never drink*

—but rather into courage and what Kinnell has called "tenderness toward existence."

The epigraph for *The Book of Nightmares* is taken from Rilke's *Duino Elegies* and announces the poet's nearly impossible project:

> But this, though: death,
> the whole of death,—even before life's begun,
> to hold it all so gently, and be good . . .

"From one point of view," Kinnell has said, *The Book of Nightmares* is "nothing but an effort to face death and live with death" (*Walking Down the Stairs,* 1978). Yet what might promise to be distressingly morbid, at least to the American reading public, is in fact very beautiful. As Kinnell has also said, he

> came to feel very free in writing [*The Book of Nightmares*]. I felt I could set down the very worst . . . in total faith that something was sustaining the whole poem that would not allow it to be a record of self-disgust, or hatred of nature, or fear of death, or loneliness, or defeat, but rather ultimately a restorative and healing and, if I can use the word, a happy poem.

That "something" sustaining the poem is love. *The Book of Nightmares* is irradiated by the love of a new father for his children, "those little lumps of clinging flesh" for whom he feels a "terrible, inexplicable closeness." The poem manages that nearly impossible thing, holds "it all" and is "good": holds it as gently as a father holds his frightened daughter.

Children are their parents' hostages to fortune; knowledge of children's fragility teaches parents their own. "Little Sleep's-Head" follows the war poem "The Dead Shall Be Raised Incorruptible," so when in the poem's first line little Maud screams, "waking from a nightmare," the line looks back to the nightmare that is history, and forward to her own mysterious identity, glimpsed in this private hour between father and child. Sleepwalking into her room, her father picks her up; she clings to him "hard, / as if clinging could save us." He acknowledges the illusion of safety a loving parent offers:

> . . . I think
> you think
> I will never die, I think I exude
> to you the permanence of smoke or stars,
> even as
> my broken arms heal themselves around you.

Robert Peters remarks that Kinnell projects his own "spleen" here: "How does he know that little Maud feels lost?" (in Nelson, 1987). But Maud is no "inanimate" creature, despite Peters' phrasing, and she dimly senses already what Gerard Manley Hopkins calls "the blight man was born for" ("Spring and Fall"). Her father therefore utters a broken prayer to pluck her from time, to make her perfect: to "suck the rot from your fingernail," "scrape the rust off your ivory bones," "help death escape through the little ribs of your body," and—the crux—"let nothing of you go, ever." Yet of course this cannot be. Life is bound to death;

consciousness itself dwells "forever / in the pre-trembling of a house that falls."

Section three of "Little Sleep's-Head" returns to section one; little Maud clings to her father because somehow she senses that he, like her, "only sooner . . . will go down / the path of vanished alphabets." In section four the poet imagines his daughter in 2009, as adult as he is now, walking out in the fields of death, longing but unable to merge with the universe. Section five imagines Maud with a lover, learning

to reach deeper
into the sorrows
to come

—to "hold it all so gently," as Rilke says—and to kiss

the mouth
which tells you, *here,*
*here is the world.*

Then, stunningly, in section six, Kinnell extends the chain of love and loss backward through time, imagining himself as a child in his father's eyes as Maud is a child in his, and describes each identity as a "tiny kite" of which "the angel / of all mortal things lets go the string."

Section seven circles round to the beginning: "Back you go, into your crib." The lines are full of an indestructible tenderness. For the moment the dreams are sweet, and "the hours begin to sing." Ultimately, the poem concludes, "*the wages / of dying is love.*"

Ann Fisher-Wirth

**Further Reading**

Calhoun, Richard J., *Galway Kinnell,* New York: Twayne, 1992

Kinnell, Galway, *Walking Down the Stairs: Selections from Interviews,* Ann Arbor: University of Michigan Press, 1978

Nelson, Howard, editor, *On the Poetry of Galway Kinnell: The Wages of Dying,* Ann Arbor: University of Michigan Press, 1987

Powell, David Glenn, "Prophetic Voices, Proper Histories: Walt Whitman's Preface to the 1855 Edition of *Leaves of Grass* and Galway Kinnell's *The Book of Nightmares,*" Ph.D. Diss., University of Mississippi, 2000

Zimmerman, Lee, *Intricate and Simple Things: The Poetry of Galway Kinnell,* Urbana: University of Illinois Press, 1987

---

# Carolyn Kizer 1925–

It would be easy to label Carolyn Kizer simply as a feminist poet; however, there is much more to her work than her feminist point of view. Kizer is known for her mastery of both traditional and free-verse forms. As a poet, editor, translator, teacher, and critic, Kizer embodies her political and personal points of view in her work and in her comments about her work. Frequently, her collections include a mixture of new poems and old poems that are out of print. After graduating from Sarah Lawrence College and attending Columbia University on a Chinese Cultural Fellowship, she studied poetry with Theodore Roethke at the University of Washington. Her achievements include founding *Poetry Northwest* and serving as its editor from 1959 to 1965, serving as U.S. State Department specialist in Pakistan from 1964 to 1965, and directing literary programs for the National Endowment for the Arts from 1966 to 1970. Kizer has been a poet-in-residence at the University of North Carolina and at Ohio University and has taught poetry at Washington University, St. Louis; University of Missouri, Columbia; Barnard College; and the Iowa Writers' Workshop.

In *The Ungrateful Garden* (1961), the first of her eight volumes of poetry, Kizer develops themes regarding nature that will reappear in her later work. In this collection lice and carrion birds appear as grotesque images of nature. Later in her career, while still maintaining a stoic acceptance of nature, her images become less harsh. Nature is neither evil nor benevolent, but a tension remains between nature and humanity. Despite her choice of subject matter, Kizer dispels the notion that she is a "nature poet" in a 1986 interview with Earl Ingersoll and Stan Sanvel Rubin. She claims that she is unsentimental about nature: "My subject is people, or character, let's say. That's what I am really interested in."

According to Mary Ellis Gibson (in Rigsbee, 1990), "Kizer shares with many contemporary poets the project of rewriting cultural history by retelling its myths." The poem "The Ungrateful Garden," for example, relates the story of Midas. "Semele Recycled," included in *Mermaids in the Basement* (1984), modernizes the myth of Dionysus' mother. "After you left me forever / I was broken into pieces." Whereas Semele's body disintegrates upon seeing Zeus in the original myth, the modern Semele is reinvented. With her lover, she "kneel[s] side-by-side in the sand; / [and they] worship each other in whispers." Kizer pursues the psychological meanings of myths in her later career.

Two of Kizer's poems and one collection frequently receive critical attention: "The Great Blue Heron," "Pro Femina," and the Pulitzer Prize–winning collection *Yin* (1984). "The Great Blue Heron," included in *Mermaids in the Basement,* has been called one of her most emotionally-intense pieces. In the poem, dedicated to her mother, Kizer invokes the image of the heron as "tattered" and ghostlike. While standing with her child on a deserted beach, the mother sees the bird for what it is: a harbinger of her death. The heron exists in nature but neither cares for nor despises the humans around it. When the heron flies away on "vast, unmoving wings," it is a "spectral" for the inevitability of death. The poem offers a dark view of the life cycle and what is natural in the realm of the physical world. The bird is not majestic and beautiful, as might be expected; instead, it is ashen, gray, and connected to the burned house. In Kizer's retelling of the phoenix myth there is no rebirth.

"Pro Femina," originally a three-section poem, is a reaction to the sixth satire of Juvenal. Although some critics see the poem as addressing personal anguish, Kizer claims she wrote "Pro Femina" "on a tremendous high. I don't think there is any pain in the poem at all. Its energies come from that tremendous exhilaration" (Lerner and Austin, 1987). Women of letters are her target in this satiric poem, and the relation of art to true womanhood is her focus. The poem's first line, "From Sappho to myself, consider the fate of women. How unwomanly to discuss it!" immediately sets up gender tensions. The first three parts address women's lives and women's roles as poets and writers. Part 1 considers the fate of women from Sappho to the present day; part 2 takes up the role of the independent woman; and part 3 addresses the woman of letters. In all three sections, Kizer challenges the woman artist to retain her independence. Part 4, added later, is titled "Fanny" and is the biography of Fanny Stevenson, Robert Louis Stevenson's wife. Through her diary entries, the reader learns about Fanny's attempts to create through her garden and also the problems she has in keeping her diary sacred. This section has been praised for its sensuous images and the way in which Kizer conveys Fanny's isolation and the sacrifices she makes for her husband's dream and health.

*Yin* includes both "The Great Blue Heron" and the "Fanny" section of "Pro Femina." Like Kizer's earlier work, this volume received praise for its objectivity and for its variety of voices and tones. *Yin,* which is the Chinese term for the feminine principle, also contains Kizer's prose poem "Muse" about her childhood and her mother. This prose piece depicts her relationship with an overzealous mother who was older when she gave birth to her only child. Although Kizer did not become serious about poetry until her mother's death, her mother is given credit for shaping her as a poet.

Two recent poems demonstrate Kizer's wit and political perceptiveness. "On a Line from Valéry (The Gulf War)," collected in *Harping On* (1996), focuses on the bleak prospect of war: "Our crops of wheat have turned to fields of tares, / This dreadful century staggers to its close / And the sky dies for us, its poisoned heirs." In "Parent's Pantoum," a poem for Maxine Kumin, she turns the tables on parents, satirically depicting how two parents relate to their daughters. She describes the mother's desire to "capture their attention. Don't they know that we're supposed to be the stars?" In these poems, Kizer remains imaginative and technically precise.

Kizer will be regarded as an important voice in 20th-century American poetry. She is a poet who is in touch with the world and with human nature.

MILLIE JACKSON

**Biography**

Born in Spokane, Washington, 10 December 1925. Attended Sarah Lawrence College, Bronxville, New York, B.A. 1945; Columbia University, New York, 1945–46; University of Washington, Seattle, 1946–47, 1953–54; founding editor, *Poetry Northwest,* Seattle, 1959–65; U.S. State Department specialist in Pakistan, 1964–65; director of literary programs, National Endowment for the Arts, 1966–70; lecturer or poet-in-residence, University of North Carolina, Chapel Hill, 1970–74, Washington University, St. Louis, 1971, Barnard College, New York, 1972, Ohio University, Athens, 1974, University of Iowa, Iowa City, 1975, Centre College, Danville, Kentucky, 1979, Eastern Washington University, Cheney, 1980, University of Cincinnati, Ohio, 1981, University of Louisville, Kentucky, 1982, State University of New York, Albany, 1982, Columbia School of Arts, New York, 1982, and Bucknell University, Lewisburg, Pennsylvania, 1983; acting director of the graduate writing program, Columbia University, New York, 1972; Professor, University of Maryland, College Park, 1976–77; Professor of poetry, Stanford University, California, 1986; Senior Fellow in the humanities, Princeton University, New Jersey, 1986; Professor, University of Arizona, Tucson, 1989–90. Received Masefield Prize, 1983; American Academy Award, 1985; Pulitzer Prize, 1985; Theodore Roethke Prize, 1988; Frost Medal, 1988; Litt.D., Whitman College, Walla Walla, Washington, 1986, and Mills College, Oakland, California, 1989; Chancellor, Academy of American Poets, 1995–98. Living in Sonoma, California.

**Poetry**

*The Ungrateful Garden,* 1961
*Five Poets of the Pacific Northwest,* with others, edited by Robin Skelton, 1964
*Knock upon Silence,* 1965
*Midnight Was My Cry: New and Selected Poems,* 1971
*Mermaids in the Basement: Poems for Women,* 1984
*Yin: New Poems,* 1984
*The Nearness of You: Poems for Men,* 1986
*Harping On: Poems, 1985–1995,* 1996
*Cool, Calm and Collected: Poems, 1960–2000,* 2000

**Selected Criticism**

*Picking and Choosing: Essays on Prose,* 1995

**Other Writings:** translations of Chinese and other literature (*Carrying Over: Poems from the Chinese, Urdu, Macedonian, Yiddish, and French African,* 1988); editions of collected poetry (*100 Great Poems by Women,* 1990).

**Further Reading**

Bayes, Ronald H., "Franklin Street Days: Carolyn Kizer in North Carolina, 1970–1974," *Pembroke Magazine* 23 (1991)
Ingersoll, Earl, and Stan Sanvel Rubin, "'The Very Separateness of Things': A Conversation with Carolyn Kizer," *Webster Review* 11, no. 2 (1986)
Lerner, Elizabeth, and David Craig Austin, "An Interview with Carolyn Kizer, with William Matthews," *Columbia: A Magazine of Poetry and Prose* 12 (1987)
Leuenberger, Derek T., "Kizer's 'The Great Blue Heron,'" *Explicator* 57, no. 2 (1999)
Rigsbee, David, editor, *An Answering Music: On the Poetry of Carolyn Kizer,* Boston: Ford-Brown, 1990
Taylor, Henry, "Passwords at the Boundary: Carolyn Kizer's Poetry," *Hollins Critic* 34, no. 3 (1997)

# August Kleinzahler 1949–

August Kleinzahler's poetry, with its linguistic resourcefulness and arresting cheerfulness, is immediately appealing to a wide range of readers. His approach to his material feels at once generous to his subjects and flattering to the reader. There is an atmosphere of effortlessness and abundance, as if there will always be more occasions and more poems. Kleinzahler's early books—*The Sausage-Master of Minsk* (1977), *A Calendar of Airs* (1978), *Storm over Hackensack* (1985), *On Johnny's Time* (1988), and *Dainties and Viands* (1989)—are out of print. *Earthquake Weather* (1989) was nominated for the National Book Critics Circle Award. A volume of new and selected poems, *Like Cities, Like Storms,* was published by Picador in Australia in 1992. His most recent books are *Red Sauce, Whiskey and Snow* (1995) and *Green Sees Things in Waves* (1998). In *Live from the Hong Kong Nile Club: Poems, 1975–1990* (2000), Kleinzahler brings together poems from the earlier collections *Storm over Hackensack* and *Earthquake Weather.*

In *Live from the Hong Kong Nile Club,* Kleinzahler divides his poems into "East" and "West," with poems in the first category taking place mostly in New York City and northern New Jersey and poems in the second category taking place mostly in San Francisco. Although the places named are various, landscapes recur. Kleinzahler's poetry is usually urban rather than suburban or rural, and trucks and buses are more common than cars. People are more likely to be in bars or cafeterias than houses. Greyhound bus stations and Dairy Queens are evoked affectionately. Where other poets might find hopelessness, Kleinzahler finds possibility. In "Poetics," he celebrates "the air outside Shop-Rite Liquor / on summer evenings."

Such a poetics is familiar, and Kleinzahler wears, as one reviewer put it, his influences on his sleeve. He has a great number of them, although his style is unmistakably his own. Williams presides over poems such as "Coconut Oil," in which Kleinzahler writes of an "old woman with swollen legs" who

> pulls a hanky from her bag
> wiping away the film
> of grit and sweat
> that's settled on her face.
> With this breeze the next block won't be
> half so difficult.
> She is on her way to the market
> in order to buy
> a nice piece of fish and some soap.

Kleinzahler differs from Williams in his sly insinuation that the ethical, for poets, is one of a number of effects and that vicarious introspection is not more important than self-absorbed play. Some readers will catch echoes of Bunting, Gunn, or Muldoon in Kleinzahler's poems. One critic notes in *Earthquake Weather* the double influence of Ammons and Stevens. Kleinzahler's people have names such as Crazy Jack and Lu and Jimmy the Lush, and he can remind readers of mainstream pop songwriters, such as Tom Waits and Bruce Springsteen. When Kleinzahler alludes to music, as in "Flynn's End," he will characteristically juxtapose "Boccherini and Mississippi Fred." His range of influences is unusually wide and has allowed him to attract the kinds of readers who do not normally like the same poet.

The people in Kleinzahler's poems often have more energy than they know what to do with. Kleinzahler never pretends to know what to do with that energy, either, although he is determined to do justice to it, sometimes by giving the poem wholly over to his characters ("Real Hair" and "Kid Clarinet"). The other side of exuberance, for him, is not despair but a kind of forlornness. "What is more touching / than a used-book store on Saturday night," he asks in the poem "San Francisco/New York," and shows us "the dowdy clientele haunting the aisles: / the girl with bad skin, the man with a tic." The antidote to this sadness is absorption, and Kleinzahler is drawn to figures, such as Joseph Cornell, who are absorbed in their own imaginative worlds. He also notices "the hobbyist in his room" building with matchsticks ("Toys"). He is alert to every variety of self-involvement and guardedly affectionate about certain kinds of pretension. In the poem about the bookstore, he points out the "chronic ass at the counter giving his art speech." In another poem he writes, "leave it for the great soul, the earnest and stentorian sap / to airdrop pronouncements on warming tar roofs." A great soul, for Kleinzahler, is usually eccentric and given to bursts of guileless enthusiasm, which is the tone the poet trusts most. "What a beautiful night for a philosophical debate!" he exclaims in "Follain's Paris."

A great soul is nervous, too. In his latest collection, Kleinzahler quotes Miles Davis: "If you're not nervous, you're not paying attention." What the people in "November in West New York" or "Hot Night on East 4th" are nervously (or excitedly) paying attention to is the possibility of violence. Many kinds of violence are acceptable, though. Violent *weather* might do the trick. Sunlight, in one poem, explodes suddenly "in the window of Coey Loy Meals . . . / showering light over barbecued ducks—" ("Sunset in Chinatown"). A figure in "Heebie-Jeebies" tries to escape the violence, and we watch him as, "his mind in a froth," he "reckons angles, exits and a safe spot to hide." The people in "Like Cities, Like Storms" blow *back:* "these alto and tenor men / blow back cool legato or a rope of cries / against a world pouring down / so hard and fast." It is clear that violence, if it comes, will not break the spell but is simply a continuation of it. In "Warm Night in February," he writes, "I cannot tell you / how it comes or when / but we are left there broken / our voices everywhere scattered." Such events are not calamitous. Kleinzahler can work with scattered voices. Readers may feel that nothing very bad can happen in the poems and that, if something bad does happen, the poet's linguistic resources will be equal to it.

Kleinzahler rarely makes a false move, but there are moves that he does not make at all. His freedom is, in part, a freedom from older notions of poetic ambition. He never does give his "art speech," and he is never the "earnest and stentorian sap" himself. Big ideas do not exert much felt pressure on the poems, nor does the poet seem to believe that abstract thinking would relieve such pressure. Spiritual impulses are treated tenderly and generously but are not allowed to forget their connections with everyday appetites. Souls, after death, we are told, circulate (as jokes do) around the neighborhoods. Politics, for the poet, means the news, and for the people in his poems this means decontextualized, enigmatic phrases glimpsed momentarily in headlines of newspapers before the newspapers blow away in the wind. Critics hoping to find large ideas in his work focus on the poem "Green Sees Things in Waves" and call perceptual instability the real subject of Kleinzahler's work. Perceptual instability and shifts of consciousness do absorb Kleinzahler, but Green is, after all, a character in a poem, and Kleinzahler may be most interested in the dramatic possibilities in Green's particular way of seeing. (He alienated some critics by revealing in the poem that Green "ate quite a pile of acid one time.")

For many readers, Kleinzahler is essentially a comic poet. The humor helps connect the elements of his vision but never does so in predictable ways. In "Indian Summer Night: The Haight," he writes,

> The 43 bus at Carl&Cole
> steps on the comic's line
> but applause and laughter
> waft up the lane.
> A *ranger* on the grass
> bestirs himself,
> spooked
>
> then barks back a laugh of his own,
> an unwholesome laugh,
> stiffening the neighbor cats.
>
> The summer my sister worked at Palisades Park
> I'd stay awake all midnight
> listening.
> When the breeze in the maples were right
> you could hear her
>
> my sister,
> over the loudspeaker a quarter mile away
> telling barkers patrons and freaks
> everybody
> the last voice before the lights went out
>
> —*Thank you. Good night.*

The tone is comic, and it is also generous, grateful. The comic's line is stepped on, but he gets the applause and laughter anyway. The poet is interested in the afterlife of speech, an afterlife that is suggested as well by the relation between summer and Indian summer. The laughter circulates, making temporary, inconsequential connections. The poem moves east, to a summer in the poet's childhood and a memory not of his own summer job but of his sister's. She is on the loudspeaker at Palisades Park calling out to "barkers patrons and freaks / everybody." (The poet uses that last word the way Louis Armstrong does in his autobiography, when he talks about hearing Earl Hines playing a song that thrilled everybody every night. "I was one of the everybodys," Armstrong tells us.) Kleinzahler's impulses are doubly generous in this poem: not only does he want everybody included, but he wants to ascribe that desire to his sister. Lines are stepped on, lights go out, and nothing lasts, but the phrase "*Thank you. Good night.*" (deftly mixing his colloquial and courtly tones) gently suggests that one of the things a poem can do best is try to express as uncomplicated a gratitude as possible. Kleinzahler's work rarely makes any false moves and makes many stirring and surprising ones.

NICK HALPERN

**Biography**

Born in Jersey City, New Jersey, 10 December 1949. Attended University of Wisconsin, 1967–70, University of Victoria, British Columbia, 1973; Visiting Holloway lecturer, University of California, Berkeley, 1987; has taught at Brown University, Providence, Rhode Island, University of California, Berkeley, and Iowa Writers' Workshop, Iowa City. Received Canada Council grant, 1977, 1979; Ontario Arts Council grant, 1978; New Jersey State Council of the Arts grant, 1980, 1985; General Electric Foundation Award, 1983; Bay Area Book Reviewers Association Award, 1985; Guggenheim fellowship, 1989; Lila Wallace-*Reader's Digest* Award, 1991–94; National Endowment for the Arts fellowship; Academy of American Poets Award. Living in San Francisco, California.

**Poetry**

*The Sausage-Master of Minsk,* 1977
*A Calendar of Airs,* 1978
*Storm over Hackensack,* 1985
*On Johnny's Time,* 1988
*Dainties and Viands,* 1989
*Earthquake Weather,* 1989
*Like Cities, Like Storms,* 1992
*Red Sauce, Whiskey and Snow,* 1995
*Green Sees Things in Waves,* 1998
*Live from the Hong Kong Nile Club: Poems, 1975–1990,* 2000

**Other Writings:** edited anthology of poetry (*News and Weather: Seven Canadian Poets,* 1982).

**Further Reading**

Burt, Stephen, "Poetry in Review," *Yale Review* 86, no. 4 (October 1998)

Gunn, Thom, "Responsibilities: Contemporary Poetry and August Kleinzahler," in *Shelf Life: Essays, Memoirs, and an Interview,* by Gunn, Ann Arbor: University of Michigan Press, 1993; London: Faber, 1994

Kleinzahler, August, "Elevated Shtick: S.J. Perelman," in *Hiding in Plain Sight: Essays in Criticism and Autobiography,* edited by Wendy Lesser, San Francisco: Mercury House, 1993

Kleinzahler, August, "Four Poets," *Parnassus* 19, no. 2 (1994)

Vendler, Helen, "A Dissonant Triad: Henri Cole, Rita Dove, and August Kleinzahler," in *Soul Says: On Recent Poetry,* by Vendler, Cambridge, Massachusetts: Harvard University Press, 1995

# Kenneth Koch 1925–

In "The Art of Poetry," the poem in which Kenneth Koch perhaps comes closest to articulating his poetic credo, the poet advises a presumably younger poet:

> A reader should put your work down puzzled,
> Distressed, and illuminated, ready to believe
> It is curious to be alive.

For nearly 50 years Koch's own work has made readers—at least those willing or able to give into his peculiar charms—experience that curiosity of being alive. A sophisticated and a deeply learned man, Koch has nevertheless managed to keep his work infused with an almost childlike curiosity and joy. Although his work has matured and his voice slightly mellowed through a lifetime of experience, the good humor and sense of excitement about being alive and in the world, which characterized the early poems, has not diminished.

Koch is often grouped with John Ashbery, Frank O'Hara, and James Schuyler as a member of the New York School of poetry, if "member" is not too formal a word to use in conjunction with a group whose signature was a determined casualness. These poets, bound by ties of friendship rather than by strict adherence to a poetic creed or formula, had their heyday in New York during the 1950s and early 1960s. If there were no rules for how to be a New York School poet, there was nevertheless a loosely shared aesthetic. Besides finding constant inspiration in the work and proximity of one another, these poets were strongly influenced by the heroic "first generation" of avant-garde, Abstract Expressionist painters like Willem de Kooning, Jackson Pollock, and Robert Motherwell, artists whose canvasses challenged the way people thought about art by eliminating or radically deemphasizing figure and subject. Even more influential was the work of a younger "second generation" of New York painters like Larry Rivers, Fairfield Porter, and Jane Freilicher, who retained much of the first generation's style but brought figure and subject matter back to their work. The poets and painters valued movement, innovation, experimentation. Art could be *about* almost anything, and the traditional places that poets and artists of the past had looked for beauty did not seem particularly more promising than anywhere else: a city sidewalk or, in a flight of surrealistic fancy for Koch, a brassiere factory possibly located in southern France could easily suffice. In his early "On the Great Atlantic Rainway," published in *Thank You* (1962), Koch writes, "And that is the modern idea of fittingness, / To, always in motion, lose nothing." He continues later in the same poem, "Yet always beneath the rainway unsyntactical / Beauty might leap up!" This sense of the self-consciously modern, of motion, of beauty leaping up and accosting one unawares are all characteristic of the New York School aesthetic and have remained central to Koch's sense of poetic possibility.

None of the major New York School poets is afraid of humor, and all have used it regularly in their work. Koch, however, is the most persistently funny of the group, the most dedicated to employing a range of humor, the one regularly described as "zany." He is the New York School clown, but like any clown, he understands the serious edge of humor. His kind of over-the-top, slightly silly humor is strongly influenced by French Surrealist poetry with a dash of American native optimism, the kind of sunny humor that can allow Koch to open a love poem entitled "To You" with lines like

> I love you as a sheriff searches for a walnut
> That will solve a murder case unsolved for years
> . . . .
> I am crazier than shirttails
> In the wind, when you're near, a wind that blows from
> The big blue sea, so shiny so deep and so unlike us.

These lines are a good example of Koch's use of what he explained in an interview with Jordan Davis (1996) as

> One contemporary comic effect [that] comes from a sort of unconscious or irrational "letting go," saying whatever comes into your head in the interests of surprise. Or letting chance do it. . . .

The Koch poem probably most frequently anthologized is also one of the funniest, in a different vein. "Variations on a Theme by William Carlos Williams," a broad parody of Koch's admired poetic predecessor's "This Is Just to Say," makes the reader better appreciate the edge of hilarity that had always been lurking beneath the surface of Williams' famous poem. In Williams' poem the speaker steals and eats the plums that his wife had been

> probably
> saving
> for breakfast,

those plums like the speaker himself, "so sweet / and so cold"; Koch burlesques Williams' speaker, comically exaggerating his coldness and, in a bizarre way, his sweetness:

> We laughed at the hollyhocks together
> and then I sprayed them with lye.
> Forgive me. I simply do not know what I am doing.

The comic, Koch has said, "is part of what is most serious for art to get to—ecstasy, unity, freedom, completeness, Dionysiac things" (Davis, 1996). For all his humor Koch takes poetry extremely seriously; in his own poetry and through his work teaching the writing of poetry at the university level, in public elementary schools, and in nursing homes, he has consistently demonstrated his belief in poetry's restorative power. The kind of real life change that poetry can bring about is for him perhaps a laughing matter, but a serious laughing matter. He explores this sense of the seriously comic in a later poem, "The Boiling Water," published in *The Burning Mystery of Anna in 1951* (1979):

> A serious moment for the water is when it boils
> And though one usually regards it merely as a convenience
> To have the boiling water available for bath or table
> Occasionally there is someone around who understands
> The importance of this moment for the water—maybe a
> saint,

Maybe a poet, maybe a crazy man, or just someone
temporarily disturbed
With his mind "floating," in a sense, away from his deepest
Personal concerns to more "unreal" things.

Koch has spent a career, a lifetime, conscientiously and persistently being that someone "who understands / The importance of this moment for the water," the moment of effervescence, but also of profound transformation.

DOUGLAS BRANCH

*See also* New York School

**Biography**

Born in Cincinnati, Ohio, 27 February 1925. Attended Harvard University, Cambridge, Massachusetts, A.B. 1948; Columbia University, New York, M.A. 1953, Ph.D. 1959; served in the United States Army, 1943–46; Lecturer in English, Rutgers University, New Brunswick, New Jersey, 1953–54, 1955–56, 1957–58, and Brooklyn College, 1957–59; Director of the Poetry Workshop, New School for Social Research, New York, 1958–66; Lecturer, 1959–61, Assistant Professor, 1962–66, Associate Professor, 1966–71, and since 1971 Professor of English, Columbia University; associated with *Locus Solus* magazine, Lans-en-Vercors, France, 1960–62. Received Fulbright fellowship, 1950, 1978; Guggenheim fellowship, 1961; National Endowment for the Arts grant, 1966; Ingram Merrill Foundation fellowship, 1969; Harbison Award, for teaching, 1970; Frank O'Hara Prize (*Poetry*, Chicago), 1973; American Academy Award, 1976; Shelley Memorial Award, 1994; Bollingen Prize, 1995; Rebekah Johnson Bobbitt Poetry Prize, 1996; member, American Academy of Arts and Letters, 1996. Living in New York City.

**Poetry**

*Poems*, 1953
*Ko; or, A Season on Earth*, 1960
*Permanently*, 1960
*Thank You, and Other Poems*, 1962
*Poems from 1952 and 1953*, 1968
*When the Sun Tries To Go On*, 1969
*Sleeping with Women*, 1969
*The Pleasures of Peace, and Other Poems*, 1969
*Penguin Modern Poets 24* (poems by Koch, Kenward Elmslie, and James Schuyler), 1973
*The Art of Love*, 1975
*The Duplications*, 1977
*The Burning Mystery of Anna in 1951*, 1979
*From the Air*, 1979
*Days and Nights*, 1982
*Selected Poems, 1950–1982*, 1985
*On the Edge*, 1986
*Seasons on Earth*, 1987
*Selected Poems*, 1991
*Making It Up: Poems Composed at St. Marks Church on May 9, 1979* (with Allen Ginsberg), 1994
*One Train*, 1994
*On the Great Atlantic Railway: Selected Poems, 1950–1988*, 1994
*Love* (with others), 1995
*The Art of Poetry: Poems, Parodies, Interviews, Essays, and Other Work*, 1996
*Currency* (with others), 1997
*Straits*, 1998
*New Addresses*, 2000

**Other Writings:** plays (*The Gold Standard*, 1996), novel (*The Red Robins*, 1975), short stories, writing handbooks (*Rose, Where Did You Get That Red?* 1973); edited collections of poetry (*Talking to the Sun: An Illustrated Anthology of Poems for Young People* [with Kate Farrell], 1985).

**Further Reading**

Davis, Jordan, "Kenneth Koch: An Interview by Jordan Davis," *American Poetry Review* 25, no. 6 (1996)
Halliday, Mark, "Koch and Sense," *Michigan Quarterly Review* 36, no. 1 (1997)
Hoover, Paul, "Seriousness," *The American Book Review* 8, no. 6 (1986)
Lehman, David, *The Last Avant-Garde: The Making of the New York School of Poets*, New York and London: Doubleday, 1998
O'Hara, Frank, "Another Word on Kenneth Koch," *Poetry* 85, no. 6 (1955)

---

# Yusef Komunyakaa 1947–

Shortly after winning a Pulitzer Prize for his collection *Neon Vernacular: New and Selected Poems* (1993), Yusef Komunyakaa told a *New York Times* interviewer,

> I grew up with guns around me. . . . The rituals of violence. People hunting. Killing hogs, rabbits. Pragmatic violence. . . . In our culture we celebrate violence. All of our heroes have blood on their hands.

Written in free verse, much of Komunyakaa's poetry is devoted to the exploration of American violence, both at home and abroad, and his style makes use of the violent juxtaposition of seemingly heterogeneous ideas that Samuel Johnson identified with metaphysical "wit."

Komunyakaa was born James Willie Brown, Jr., in Bogalusa, Louisiana, a mill town north of Lake Ponchartrain near the Mississippi border. He changed his name for religious reasons, choosing "Komunyakaa" because (according to family legend) it was the original name of a grandfather who emigrated to the United States from the West Indies. He grew up under the eye of a father who was a carpenter and who would have preferred his son to take up a carpenter's tools rather than a poet's pen, a difficult relationship he addresses in "Songs for My Father" from *Neon Vernacular:*

> You banged a crooked nail
> Into a pine slab,
> Wanting me to believe
> I shouldn't have been born
> With hands & feet
> If I didn't do
> Your kind of work.
> You hated my books.

Fraught family relationships are one of Komunyakaa's abiding subjects, as is the experience of growing up in a small segregated Louisiana town in the years before the advent of the Civil Rights movement. Bogalusa serves as the setting for *Magic City* (1992), which begins with a poem called "Venus's-flytraps" that evokes a five-year-old child's fascination with nature and death and secrets—"My mama says I'm a mistake. / That I made her a bad girl."—and ends with "Butterfly-Toed Shoes," a coming-of-age poem about ill-advised, youthful passion that ends badly:

> I didn't see the flash when her husband burst in.
> . . . .
> I'm still backing away
> From the scene, a scintilla
> Of love & murder.

One of the most powerful poems in the volume, "Knights of the White Camellia & Deacons of Defense," elliptically recounts a clash between black "Sons / & daughters of sharecroppers" and members of the Ku Klux Klan.

Equally formative for Komunyakaa was the violence of Vietnam. He grapples with his wartime experiences first in the chapbook *Toys in a Field* (1987) and later in *Dien Cai Dau* (1988), which draws its title from a Vietnamese phrase meaning "crazy" that became U.S. Army slang. In his attempts to evoke the insane contradictions of the war, Komunyakaa draws from personal experience as a military journalist and editor but also ranges farther afield. "Jungle Surrender," inspired by a painting by Don Cooper, presents a voice that tries to hold at bay the memory of "how I helped ambush two Viet Cong / while plugged into the Grateful Dead." Jarring juxtapositions—American and Vietnamese, home and abroad, mundane and horrifying—animate "Eyeball Television," which depicts a soldier who

> sits crouched in a hole
> covered with slats of bamboo,
> recalling hundreds of faces
> from *I Love Lucy, Dragnet,*
> *I Spy, & The Ed Sullivan Show.*

Lurking in the background of these poems about Vietnam is the knowledge that, for the black G.I., going home is at best a mixed blessing: "The One-legged Stool," a prose monologue, likens the Vietcong to "rednecks" in "'Bama . . . and Mississippi," while "Report from the Skull's Diorama" offers the image of "red-bordered / leaflets" that "quiver / back to the ground" beneath "chopper blades," leaflets that

> tell us
> *VC didn't kill*
> *Dr. Martin Luther King.*

The final poem, "Facing It," offers a moving account of a visit to the Vietnam Veterans Memorial in Washington, D.C.: "My black face fades, / hiding inside the black granite."

It was not until 1983, however, that Komunyakaa began to write about the war and its aftermath. By then, he had produced two self-published chapbooks, *Dedications and Other Darkhorses* (1977) and *Lost in the Bonewheel Factory* (1979), as well as his first full-length volume of poetry, *Copacetic* (1984). "It took me 14 years to write poems about Vietnam," Komunyakaa has said. "I had never thought about writing about it, and in a way I had been systematically writing around it" (see Bruce Weber, "A Poet's Values," *New York Times* [2 May 1994]). According to Komunyakaa, it was while renovating a house that year in New Orleans—doing, one might note, the kind of work that his father had always wanted him to pursue—that he wrote his first Vietnam poem, climbing down a stepladder to write down the lines that occurred to him as he was working. "It was," he says, "as if I had uncapped some hidden place in me. Poem after poem came spilling out."

While in New Orleans Komunyakaa also began to explore the ways that jazz music expresses both the pain of racial inequality and the centrality of African-American experience to American culture. Full of homages to jazz artists and using as its title a word coined by the African-American tap dancer Bill "Bojangles" Robinson, Komunyakaa's first volume, *Copacetic,* portrays jazz as a balm that might promote cultural healing. Komunyakaa's continuing interest in the intersections of poetry and jazz has led him to co-edit two collections of "jazz poetry."

In addition to the Pulitzer Prize, Komunyakaa has earned two Creative Writing fellowships from the National Endowment for the Arts (1981, 1987). His 1998 volume *Thieves of Paradise,* which draws upon the full range of Komunyakaa's poetic interests, was a finalist for the National Book Critics Circle Award and received the Morton Dauwen Zabel Award of the American Academy of Arts and Letters, as well as several other prestigious prizes.

Komunyakaa's poetry has been anthologized in volumes devoted to African-American poetry and American Southern poetry, but his work should be seen as part of a longer tradition of vernacular poetry that harkens back to Whitman, with whom Komunyakaa shares a profound interest in the musicality of verse. Whether writing about Australia, Vietnam, or Louisiana, Komunyakaa brings to his subject a vibrant diction that captures the characteristic rhythms both of American speech and of that most American of musical forms, jazz.

CYRUS R.K. PATELL

*See also* War and Antiwar Poetry

**Biography**

Born in Bogalusa, Louisiana, 29 April 1947. Served in U.S. Army, 1965–67; attended University of Colorado, Boulder, B.A. 1975; Colorado State University, Fort Collins, M.A. 1979;

University of California, Irvine, M.F.A. 1980; Associate Instructor, Colorado State University, 1976–78; Instructor, University of California, Irvine, 1980, and University of New Orleans, 1982–84; poet-in-the-schools, New Orleans, 1984–85; Visiting Assistant Professor, 1985–86, Associate Professor, 1986–93, and Professor, 1993–96, Indiana University, Bloomington; currently Professor of the Council of the Humanities and Creative Writing, Princeton University, New Jersey; Visiting Professor, University of California, Berkeley, fall 1991, Visiting Lecturer, spring 1992; editor, *UCCA* and *Riverrun*, University of Colorado, 1973–75; co-editor, *Gumbo: A Magazine for the Arts*, 1976–79. Received First Place Poetry Award, Rocky Mountain Writers' Forum, 1974, 1977; Fine Arts Work Center writing fellowship, Provincetown, Massachusetts, 1980–81; National Endowment for the Arts fellowship, 1981, 1987; Louisiana Arts fellowship, 1985; San Francisco Poetry Award, 1986; American Library Association Best Books for Young Adults Selection, 1988; The Dark Room Poetry Prize, 1989; Thomas Forcade Award, University of Massachusetts, Boston, 1990; *Kenyon Review* Award, 1991; Pulitzer Prize, 1994; Kingsley Tufts Poetry Award, Claremont Graduate School, 1994; Morton Dauwen Zabel Award, 1998. Living in New York City.

**Poetry**
*Dedications and Other Darkhorses*, 1977
*Lost in the Bonewheel Factory*, 1979
*Copacetic*, 1984
*I Apologize for the Eyes in My Head*, 1986
*Toys in a Field*, 1987
*Dien Cai Dau*, 1988
*Magic City*, 1992
*Neon Vernacular: New and Selected Poems*, 1993
*Thieves of Paradise*, 1998
*Talking Dirty to the Gods: Poems*, 2000
*Pleasure Dome: New and Collected Poems*, 2001

**Other Writings:** essays (*Blue Notes: Essays, Interviews, and Commentaries*, 2000); edited anthologies of poetry (*The Jazz Poetry Anthology* [with Sascha Feinstein], 2 vols., 1991, 1996).

**Further Reading**

Asali, Muna, "An Interview with Yusef Komunyakaa," *New England Review* 16, no. 1 (Winter 1994)

Aubert, Alvin, "Yusef Komunyakaa: The Unified Vision—Canonization and Humanity," *African American Review* 27, no. 1 (Spring 1993)

Gotera, Vicente F., "'Depending on the Light': Yusef Komunyakaa's *Dien Cai Dau*," in *America Rediscovered: Critical Essays on Literature and Film of the Vietnam War*, edited by Owen W. Gilman, Jr., and Lorrie Smith, New York and London: Garland, 1990 Gotera, Vicente F., "'Lines of Tempered Steel': An Interview with Yusef Komunyakaa," *Callaloo* 13, no. 2 (Spring 1990)

Johnson, Thomas C., "Interview with Yusef Komunyakaa," *Worcester Review* 19, nos. 1–2 (1998)

Jones, Kirkland C., "Folk Idiom in the Literary Expression of Two African American Authors: Rita Dove and Yusef Komunyakaa," in *Language and Literature in the African American Imagination*, edited by Carol Aisha Blackshire-Belay, Westport, Connecticut, and London: Greenwood Press, 1992

Kelley, Robert, "Jazz and Poetry: A Conversation," *Georgia Review* 46, no. 4 (Winter 1992)

Ringnalda, Don, "Rejecting 'Sweet Geometry': Komunyakaa's Duende," *Journal of American Culture* 16, no. 3 (Fall 1993)

Stein, Kevin, "Vietnam and the 'Voice Within': Public and Private History in Yusef Komunyakaa's *Dien Cai Dau*," *Massachusetts Review* 36, no. 4 (Winter 1995–96)

Suarez, Ernest, "Yusef Komunyakaa," *Five Points* 4, no. 1 (Fall 1999)

## Facing It

Yusef Komunyakaa's "Facing It" appeared first in *Dien Cai Dau* (1988) and was reprinted in his Pulitzer Prize–winning volume *Neon Vernacular: New and Selected Poems* (1993). In "Facing It" the poet explores his complex emotions while visiting the Vietnam Veterans Memorial, remembering the violence he witnessed as a veteran himself and the turmoil he encountered on returning home. "Facing It" acknowledges the significance of the memorial and the reality of living as a Vietnam veteran.

The title of the poem carries several connotations. Although the phrase is not mentioned within the poem, the reader witnesses the narrator "facing" not only his own emotions upon visiting the memorial, but also the images he carries within him of his fallen fellow soldiers and the guilt of having survived the war. From the poem's opening the speaker is overwhelmed by the memorial, which seems to pull him inside:

> My black face fades,
> hiding inside the black granite.
> I said I wouldn't,
> Dammit: no tears.
> I'm stone. I'm flesh.
> My clouded reflection eyes me
> like a bird of prey, the profile of night
> slanted against morning. I turn
> this way—the stone lets me go.
> I turn that way—I'm inside
> the Vietnam Veterans Memorial
> again, depending on the light
> to make a difference.

He witnesses his very own reflection staring back at him and he seems to resist, "turn[ing] this way. . . . turn[ing] that way" before he is engulfed completely in the memorial and his own emotions. The black granite of the memorial is analogous to a mirror, "depending on the light / to make a difference."

This imagery of lightness and darkness, morning and night, black and white is vivid throughout the poem. He writes:

> I go down the 58,022 names,
> half-expecting to find
> my own in letters like smoke.
> I touch the name Andrew Johnson:
> I see the booby trap's white flash.

Komunyakaa intertwines powerful imagery with memories, perhaps of witnessing the violent death of a comrade; seeing the name and touching the granite triggers the "white flash" of the booby trap that is memory itself. He expresses the expectancy of seeing his name upon the wall as one of the dead, in "letters like smoke" that would soon dissipate, as does the illusion of his name on the wall. Komunyakaa gives the names power; they seem to become a part of whomever looks at the memorial:

> Names shimmering on a woman's blouse
> but when she walks away
> the names stay on the wall.
> Brushstrokes flash, a red bird's
> wings cutting across my stare.
> The sky. A plane in the sky.

Once the woman walks away, however, "the names stay on the wall," signifying the permanence of death. Red, the color of blood, again evokes the violence of the war, as does the "plane in the sky" more subtly. Color lines between white and black soldiers are absorbed by this landscape of loss:

> A white vet's image floats
> closer to me, then his pale eyes
> look through mine. I'm a window.
> He's lost his right arm
> inside the stone.

Komunyakaa ends the poem on an abstract note with the image of a woman who seems to be "erasing names" from the wall but turns out to be "brushing a boy's hair." This loving caress is redemptive in the face of the brutal reality of war: no one could bring back the dead or erase their names from the memorial.

SHARON RAYNOR

**Further Reading**

O'Nan, Stewart, *The Vietnam War: The Definitive Collection of American Fiction and Nonfiction of the War,* New York: Anchor Books, 1998

*A Vietnam Remembrance: And Directory of the National Vietnam Veterans Memorial,* Kinston, North Carolina: U.S. Veterans News and Report, 1992

---

# Maxine Kumin 1925–

Maxine Kumin's distinctive poetry invites and defies comparison. Influences whom she herself has named include Frost, Dickinson, and Sexton, as well as Hopkins, Roethke, Cummings, Whitman, Auden, Millay, and Shapiro. Like Frost above all, Kumin takes as her subject nature in general and the rural farm world of New England in particular. Also like Frost, Kumin frequently examines the relationships between humans and the natural world, as, for example, in "Woodchucks" (in her Pulitzer Prize–winning *Up Country,* 1972) and "Splitting Wood at Six Above" (*The Retrieval System,* 1978), both Frost-like in their subjects. She directly acknowledges her preoccupation with Frost in the title *In Deep: Country Essays* (1987), with its echo of Frost's poem "Neither Out Far Nor In Deep," but she also importantly revises his poem's critique by replacing his negatives ("Neither . . . Nor") with her affirmation: "In Deep." As Alicia Ostriker has argued, Kumin reverses Frost's opposition between humanity and nature. She focuses on "Making the Connection" between humanity and the natural world rather than marking their boundaries.

As a nature poet, Kumin turns lovingly, again and again, to her horses (notably in her Amanda poems) and her dogs. She rejoices with the beans, peas, parsnips, and tomatoes in her garden; she celebrates the pleasures of her blackberry harvest in the often-anthologized "Making the Jam without You" (*The Nightmare Factory,* 1970). She splits wood, feeds her animals, and nurtures her farm and family, and in *Nurture* (1989) she makes wickedly funny poetry addressing the plight of endangered species: "Repent," "Homage to Binsey Poplars," and "Thoughts on Saving the Manatee."

Kumin's vision evokes the connectedness often found in Native American traditions. Her animals seem totemic; they share ownership of what we mistakenly think of as "our" planet and even "our" nation, as, for example, in the title poem of *Nurture,* where the speaker offers her farm as a refuge for homeless animals, echoing "The New Colossus" of Emma Lazarus:

> Bring me your fallen fledgling, your bummer lamb,
> lead the abused, the starvelings, into my barn.
> Advise the hunted deer to leap into my corn.

Nature and family, Kumin's central subjects, are represented aptly by the titles of her volumes *Nurture* and *Connecting the Dots* (1996). They are reflected as well in *Women, Animals, and Vegetables: Essays and Stories* (1994), which discusses jam, jicama, her mother, "Mutts," mushrooms, and horses (among other subjects) and which is dedicated to her "sister poets and horse ambassadors." Kumin clearly works hard to harvest her art from and with the natural world that is so rich to her vision. However, the humor, the sense of fun, and above all the sheer artistry of her poetry's music distinguish Kumin's craft. Although as firm in her feminist politics as Adrienne Rich, to whom she is frequently compared, she differs in her comic self-awareness and her rejection of feminist separatism. Occasionally tweaked as poetry's earth mother (as she observes in "Nurture"), Kumin delights in the variety of her roles as gardener, horse lover, daughter (and granddaughter), mother (and grandmother), wife, cook, and poet.

From this carefully cultivated life rises her theme: the naturalness of our mortality, which she neither sentimentalizes nor avoids. Children grow up and leave, parents die, and Anne Sexton, "better sister," poet, is starkly "Dead by her own hand" ("October, Yellowstone Park," in *Connecting the Dots*). The mower neatly slices a toad in two, weasels and rats suck nest eggs, and Dickinson's fly "buzzes me all the way home" in "After the Poetry Reading" (*Connecting the Dots*). Death is unavoidable, but there is always more life coming to continue the dead, as in "The Retrieval System," where Kumin finds uncanny resemblances that "link my lost people / with the patient domestic beasts of my life."

Kumin's poetry is at once "Sad" and "celebratory" ("October, Yellowstone Park"). Memory and the future are connected by the voice of the poet, lamenting and rejoicing, like Shakespeare, urging us "to love that well which thou must leave ere long." Such, surely, is one meaning of the title *Our Ground Time Here Will Be Brief* (1982); such, too, the point of "Territory" (from *The Retrieval System*):

We are not of it, but in it. We are
in it willynilly with our machinery
and measurements, and all for the good.

"All for the good." Kumin's vision typically includes both mare and nightmare, but it is nonetheless typically affirmative. Perhaps the poem "You Are in Bear Country" best represents the qualities of her inimitable voice—its clarity, anguish, playfulness, and final faith. Published in *The Long Approach* (1985), the poem ostensibly offers advice to the tourist visiting bear country but also offers us Kumin's advice on how to live. Suggesting various "ploys" available to those who must "deal with an aggressive bear," the poem concludes with this exchange:

*Is death*
*by bear to be preferred*
*to death by bomb?* Under
these extenuating circumstances
your mind may make absurd
leaps. *The answer's yes.*
Come on in. Cherish
your wilderness.

"*The answer's yes*": to nature's difference, to the inevitability of death, to the mind's resourcefulness, and to the certainty of our home in the wilderness.

The alliteration and rhyme in these poems tell us that we are in Kumin country, a place of infinite privilege but finite life, where bears may eat us, where we slaughter lambs and shoot woodchucks, and where rhyme and rhythm are nurtured into art. Slant rhymes and half rhymes dominate here, and meters and line lengths vary, but, as in the closing couplet of "Encounter in August" (*Nurture*), order finally prevails. Because "This is not Eden," the bear in this poem enters the speaker's garden and hungrily destroys her careful crop of string beans. However,

At last he goes the way the skunk
does, supreme egoist, ambling
into the woodlot on all fours
leaving my trellis flat and beanless
and yet I find the trade-off fair:
beans and more beans for this hour of bear.

Kumin is not a nature poet after all but a nurture poet, for her subjects are growth, change, decay, and birth, along with what each of us makes of such subjects: more growth, change, decay, and birth. What Kumin makes is poetry.

CHERYL SPECTOR

**Biography**

Born in Philadelphia, Pennsylvania, 6 June 1925. Attended Radcliffe College, Cambridge, Massachusetts, A.B. 1946, M.A. 1948; Instructor, 1958–61, and Lecturer in English, 1965–68, Tufts University, Medford, Massachusetts; Lecturer, Newton College of the Sacred Heart, Massachusetts, 1971; Visiting Lecturer/Professor/Writer, University of Massachusetts, Amherst, 1972, Columbia University, New York, spring 1975, Brandeis University, Waltham, Massachusetts, fall 1975, Princeton University, New Jersey, spring 1977, 1979, 1982, Washington University, St. Louis, 1977, Randolph-Macon Women's College, Lynchburg, Virginia, 1978, Bucknell University, Lewisburg, Pennsylvania, 1983, Massachusetts Institute of Technology, Cambridge, 1984, and Atlantic Center for the Arts, New Smyrna Beach, Florida, winter 1984; staff member, Bread Loaf Writers' Conference, 1969–71, 1973, 1975, 1977; poetry consultant, Library of Congress, Washington, D.C., 1981–82; since 1979 Woodrow Wilson Visiting Fellow, Scholar, 1961–63, and since 1972 officer, Society of Fellows, Radcliffe Institute, Cambridge, Massachusetts. Received Lowell Mason Palmer Award, 1960; National Endowment for the Arts grant, 1966; National Council on the Arts fellowship, 1967; William Marion Reedy Award, 1968; Eunice Tietjens Memorial Prize (*Poetry*, Chicago), 1972; Pulitzer Prize, 1973; Radcliffe College Award, 1978; American Academy Award, 1980; Academy of American Poets fellowship, 1985; Levinson Award, 1987; Chancellor, Academy of American Poets, 1995–98; honorary degrees, Centre College, Danville, Kentucky, 1976; Davis and Elkins College, Elkins, West Virginia, 1977; Regis College, Weston, Massachusetts, 1979; New England College, Henniker, New Hampshire, 1982; Claremont Graduate School, California, 1983; University of New Hampshire, Durham, 1984. Living in Warner, New Hampshire.

**Poetry**

*Halfway*, 1961
*The Privilege*, 1965
*The Nightmare Factory*, 1970
*Up Country: Poems of New England, New and Selected*, 1972
*House, Bridge, Fountain, Gate*, 1975
*The Retrieval System*, 1978
*Our Ground Time Here Will Be Brief*, 1982
*Closing the Ring*, 1984
*The Long Approach*, 1985
*Nurture*, 1989
*Looking for Luck*, 1992
*Connecting the Dots*, 1996
*Selected Poems, 1960–1990*, 1997

**Selected Criticism**
*To Make a Prairie: Essays on Poets, Poetry, and Country Living,* 1979

**Other Writings:** novels (*The Designated Heir,* 1974), short stories, essays (*In Deep: Country Essays,* 1987; *Women, Animals, and Vegetables,* 1994), children's literature.

**Further Reading**

Grosholz, Emily, editor, *Telling the Barn Swallow: Poets on the Poetry of Maxine Kumin,* Hanover, New Hampshire: University Press of New England, 1997 (see especially the essay entitled "Making the Connection: The Nature Poetry of Maxine Kumin," by Alicia Ostriker)
Howard, Ben, "Review of *Selected Poems, 1960–1990,*" *Poetry* 172, no. 3 (1998)
Kumin, Maxine, *To Make a Prairie: Essays on Poets, Poetry, and Country Living,* Ann Arbor: University of Michigan Press, 1979
Kumin, Maxine, *Always Beginning: Essays on a Life in Poetry,* Port Townsend, Washington: Copper Canyon Press, 2000
Shomer, Enid, "An Interview with Maxine Kumin," *Massachusetts Review* 37, no. 4 (1996)

---

## Stanley Kunitz 1905–

A craftsman of the tight, precise, and evocative lyric, Stanley Kunitz exemplifies many of the tenets of 20th-century American poetry. Although he came of age with the generation that grew up under the shadow of T.S. Eliot, he is more often associated with Theodore Roethke and others who sought to fuse the best intellectualism of Modernism with the emotional content more commonly associated with Romanticism. He learned and synthesized the idioms of Modernism, the concentrated and allusive style of Yeats, the careful crafting of the intellectual conceits of the Metaphysical poets, and the metrical narrative skills of Robert Frost. He is held in high esteem both by his students for his teaching of poetry and by the poetic community who considers him a "poet's poet." Despite his winning the Pulitzer Prize for poetry in 1958, it was not until the 1980s, when he received both a National Endowment for the Arts fellowship and the Bollingen Prize, that he received full critical acclaim. Critics tend to favor Kunitz's later work, praising it for its lyrical intensity and its meticulous mastery of sound and sense. Poet, biographer, translator, teacher, arts advocate, Stanley Kunitz has influenced both poets and poetry in the century through which he has lived and written.

Kunitz's early work is best characterized by *Intellectual Things* (1930) and *Passport to the War* (1944), books that established his reputation as a craftsman of intellectual considerations in the traditional mode. The author himself describes these volumes as "very intricate, dense, and formal." In his second phase, following his Pulitzer Prize–winning *Selected Poems, 1928–1958* (1958), carrying through *The Testing-Tree* (1971), and continuing even into *Passing Through: The Later Poems, New and Selected* (1995), Kunitz moved into a more emotional and introspective lyricism, engaging the physical world more and writing in free verse, even tending toward the confessional. The publication of *Passing Through: The Later Poems, New and Selected* was a literary event: named a finalist for the National Book Award, it revealed a poet still writing, in his 90s, poems that explore the transfigured moment with deftness, clarity, and insight. Typical of the lyric poetry of his later career, these poems elucidate the essence of being, encounter the physical nature of life, and speak in a voice that synthesizes the eye and the ear. Throughout his career Kunitz has displayed a fine ear for the music of the line and an ability to capture the natural rhythm of speech, illustrating Coleridge's belief that a sense of musical delight identifies the poet.

Kunitz's concerns and themes have remained relatively consistent: familial relationships, disenfranchisement, life and death, generativity and decline, the transparency of language and vision, and especially the quest for the lost father. Kunitz knew such loss first hand. His own father committed suicide just prior to Kunitz's birth. Unable to reconcile her husband's perceived betrayal, Kunitz's mother forbade her son to mention his father's name in the house. This personal history—the silence, the denial, the absence, the loss, and the longing—surfaces in poems such as "The Portrait," "Three Floors," and "Father and Son." In "The Portrait," for example, Kunitz describes how his mother slapped him for drawing a picture of the father he never knew, recalling how "In my sixty-fourth year / I can feel my cheek / burning still." Kunitz's poems explore the archetypal quest for the father, an endemic theme among postmodern poets that has surfaced as the core issue within the men's movement as well. In "Father and Son" the speaker is desperate for the love of the lost father, for his own completion, in the metaphorical house on the hill that offers much but not enough: "I lived on a hill that had too many rooms: / Light we could make, but not enough warmth." The lost father poems are thus both an incantation and a mythical quest, a confession and a calling out, undercut by the irony of the urgent search for an unattainable goal.

Although the reader discovers a sense of loss or nonbeing in many of Kunitz's poems, beyond that pale lies its antithesis, a sense of being and life, change over stasis. Poems like "The Layers" acknowledge that, despite the impossible quest for the lost father, the speaker is nonetheless not who he once was, and, further, that he is "not done with [his] changes": "Yet I turn, I turn, / exalting somewhat / with my will intact to go / wherever I need to go[.]" For Kunitz the term "layering" describes the poetic process of mounting image on image, time on time, thought on thought, event on event, in the way great civilizations are built in successive layers. As such the poem demonstrates how the life of the mind is in fact a buried life, and the poet a kind of archeologist who must dig down through the layers of details in order to discover what lies at the core of the poem.

Despite his Harvard credentials, Kunitz found himself denied a teaching appointment in 1927 due to anti-Semitism. As a result he worked as a journalist, translator, and editor of biographical dictionaries for the W.H. Wilson company in New York until, with Theodore Roethke's help, he began teaching at Bennington. He later taught at Brandeis, Rutgers, Columbia, and Yale, where he served as editor for the Yale Younger Poets series. He has influenced a generation of important contemporary poets including Tess Gallagher, Daniel Halpern, Louise Glück, Olga Broumas, Carolyn Forché, and Robert Hass. He is also a long-time advocate of the arts. He served as consultant in poetry (poet laureate) to the Library of Congress and was instrumental in founding both the Fine Arts Work Center in Provincetown, Massachusetts, and the Poets House in New York. With his appointment as Poet Laureate of the United States in 2000, Stanley Kunitz can be comprehensively seen as a distinct and important voice in 20th-century American poetry, one that provides a living link between late Modernism and the *fin-de-siecle*.

ROBERT MILTNER

**Biography**

Born in Worcester, Massachusetts, 29 July 1905. Attended Harvard University, Cambridge, Massachusetts (Garrison Medal, 1926), A.B. (summa cum laude) 1926 (Phi Beta Kappa), A.M. 1927; served in the United States Army, 1943–45; editor, *Wilson Library Bulletin,* New York, 1928–43; faculty member, Bennington College, Vermont, 1946–49; Professor of English, Potsdam State Teachers College (now State University of New York), 1949–50, and summers 1949–53; Lecturer, New School for Social Research, New York, 1950–57; Visiting Professor, University of Washington, Seattle, 1955–56, Queens College, Flushing, New York, 1956–57, Brandeis University, Waltham, Massachusetts, 1958–59, Yale University, New Haven, Connecticut, 1970–72, Rutgers University, New Brunswick, New Jersey, 1974, Princeton University, New Jersey, 1978, and Vassar College, Poughkeepsie, New York, 1981; director, YM-YWHA Poetry Workshop, New York, 1958–62; Danforth Visiting Lecturer, United States, 1961–63; Lecturer, 1963–67, and Adjunct Professor of Writing, 1967–85, Columbia University, New York; since 1968 associated with the Fine Arts Work Center, Provincetown, Massachusetts; editor, Yale Series of Younger Poets, Yale University Press, New Haven, Connecticut, 1969–77; consultant in poetry, Library of Congress, Washington, D.C., 1974–76; formerly Cultural Exchange Lecturer, U.S.S.R., Poland, Senegal, Ghana, Israel, and Egypt; Senior Fellow in Humanities, Princeton University, 1978; since 1969 Fellow, Yale University; since 1985 president, Poets House, New York. Received Oscar Blumenthal Prize, 1941, and Levinson Prize, 1956 (*Poetry,* Chicago); Guggenheim fellowship, 1945; Amy Lowell traveling fellowship, 1953; Harriet Monroe Award, 1958; Pulitzer Prize, 1959; Ford grant, 1959; American Academy grant, 1959; Brandeis University Creative Arts Award, 1964; Academy of American Poets fellowship, 1968; Lenore Marshall Award, 1980; National Endowment for the Arts Senior fellowship, 1984; Bollingen Prize, 1987; Walt Whitman Award, 1987; National Medal of the Arts, 1993; National Book Award, 1995; Shelley Memorial Award, 1995; Frost Medal, 1999; United States Poet Laureate, 2000; Chancellor, 1970–96, since 1985 Secretary, and since 1996 Emeritus, Academy of American Poets; honorary Litt.D., Clark University, Worcester, Massachusetts, 1961, and Anna Maria College, Paxton, Massachusetts, 1977; honorary L.H.D., Worcester State College, Massachusetts, 1980, and State University of New York, Brockport, 1987. Living in New York City and Provincetown, Massachusetts.

**Poetry**

*Intellectual Things,* 1930
*Passport to the War: A Selection of Poems,* 1944
*Selected Poems, 1928–1958,* 1958
*The Testing-Tree,* 1971
*The Terrible Threshold: Selected Poems, 1940–1970,* 1974
*The Coat without a Seam: Sixty Poems, 1930–1972,* 1974
*The Lincoln Relics,* 1978
*The Poems of Stanley Kunitz, 1928–1978,* 1979
*The Wellfleet Whale, and Companion Poems,* 1983
*Next-to-Last Things* (includes essays), 1985
*Passing Through: The Later Poems, New and Selected,* 1995
*The Collected Poems,* 2000

**Other Writings:** essays, translations of Russian literature (*Stolen Apples,* by Yevgeny Yevtushenko [translator with others], 1971; *Story under Full Sail,* by Andrei Veznesensky [translator with others], 1974); edited biographical dictionaries (*European Authors, 1000–1900: A Biographical Dictionary of European Literature,* co-edited with Vineta Colby, 1967), collections of poetry (*Poems,* by John Keats, 1964; *The Essential Blake,* 1987).

**Further Reading**

*American Poetry Review* 14 (September–October 1985) (special issue entitled "A Special Supplement: Stanley Kunitz")
*Anteus* 37 (Spring 1980) (special issue on Kunitz)
Barber, David, "A Visionary Poet at Ninety," *The Atlantic Monthly* 277, no. 6 (1996)
Guston, Philip, *A Celebration for Stanley Kunitz: On His Eightieth Birthday,* New York: Sheep Meadow Press, 1986
Henault, Marie, *Stanley Kunitz,* Boston: Twayne, 1980
Kunitz, Stanley, *Interviews and Encounters with Stanley Kunitz,* edited by Stanley Moss, New York: Sheep Meadow Press, 1985
Moyers, Bill, "Stanley Kunitz," in *The Language of Life: A Festival of Poets,* by Moyer, edited by James Haba and David Grubin, New York: Doubleday, 1995
Orr, Gregory, *Stanley Kunitz: An Introduction to the Poetry,* New York: Columbia University Press, 1985
Packard, William, "An Interview with Stanley Kunitz," *New York Quarterly* 4 (Fall 1970)
Stitt, Peter, "An Interview with Stanley Kunitz," *The Gettysburg Review* 5, no. 2 (Spring 1992)

# L

## Language Poetry

"Language" poets have developed from the poetic lineage that extends from the Objectivists, Gertrude Stein, the European avant-garde of Dadaism, Surrealism, and Russian Constructivism, and aspects of the Beats and the Black Mountain poets to American poets such as Clark Coolidge, Larry Eigner, Theodore Enslin, and Ted Berrigan. The Language writers' strategic engagement with contemporary theories of language, subjectivity, and aesthetics, which challenge the orthodoxies of canonical and normative poetries, is motivated by deep ethical concerns. In the past two decades, this loose affiliation of Language writers in the United States has increasingly been concerned with the "politics of the referent" in the various relations between language and ideology. Writing, publishing, and reviewing their own poetry and theoretical essays in self-established small journals and "manifesto" magazines such as *L=A=N=G=U=A=G=E, This, Tottels, Poetics Journal, Hills,* and *The Difficulties,* their wide-ranging debates about the production of writing and the function and politics of linguistic structures have sought to put the "poesis" back into poetry. Often plagued by the term "Language poets," the writers who are loosely described by this collective designation live in various areas of the United States and Canada and practice their poetics in different ways. The politics of group identity is both useful and obfuscating, and, rather than thinking of these writers as a formal "school" or "movement" that adheres to a doctrine, the designation is better construed as a dispersed community of writers who share certain overlapping affinities about problems with aesthetic representation and poetic communication. Emerging in New York and San Francisco in the early 1970s, they have developed an intellectual and renegade brand of urban verse that stands in direct opposition to New Critical orthodoxy and New Formalism. Moving beyond the New York School, the Beats, and the Black Mountain poets, they have maintained a prolific output of theory and poetry over the past 30 years.

The eruption of Language writing in the late 1980s—with significant anthologies by Ron Silliman in *In the American Tree* (1986) and Douglas Messerli in *"Language" Poetries* (1987) and important books on poetics, including Bob Perelman's *Writing/Talks* (1985), Bruce Andrews' and Charles Bernstein's compilation *The L=A=N=G=U=A=G=E Book* (1984), Barrett Watten's *Total Syntax* (1985), Steve McCaffery's *North of Intention* (1986), Ron Silliman's *The New Sentence* (1987), and more recently the essays in Charles Bernstein's *The Politics of Poetic Form* (1990) and *A Poetics* (1992)—belies the fact that many of these writers have been active since the early 1970s. In fact, if it is not too early to sketch its history, Language writing appears to have had at least two phases to its development so far. Earlier works—for example, Silliman's *Crow* (1971) and *Mohawk* (1973); Andrews' *Vowels* (1976), *Praxis* (1978), and *Jeopardy* (1980); and David Melnick's *Pcoet* (1975)—often show experiments with single letters, words, or signifiers. For instance, *Crow* explores the phonemic associations and combinations *between* and *in* words by splitting syllables across lines:

ma
chines
shines.

*Mohawk* explores similar patternings of words, repeating in various grids and designs a "core" set of words. Each page works like a template for the variation of the succeeding page.

Yet there are limits to this linguistic exploration through the single-unit focus, ignoring as it does the operations of ideology at work in larger organizational units of form, grammar, and narrative production. Language poets recognized such limitations around the early 1980s, when they began to examine and experiment with larger forms, moving into a second phase. One gets the focus on sentence structures in Barrett Watten's *Complete Thought* (1982) and the dense prose passages and long stanzaic developments in his *1–10* (1980) and *Progress* (1985); the exponentially cumulative structure based on the Fibonacci number series of Silliman's *Tjanting* (1986), the numerological structure of "The Chinese Notebook" in his *The Age of Huts* (1986), and the reporting of the experiences of a day's travel on the Bay Area Rapid Transport system in *BART* (1982); Lyn Hejinian's "life" structure of 37 paragraphs of 37 sentences each, reflecting her age when writing the first edition of *My Life* (1980), and more recently the continued phenomenological investigations into everyday life in *Oxata* (1991) and *The Cell* (1992); and the longer sectionalized poems of Charles Bernstein's collection *The Sophist* (1987). An increasing interest in how forms shape, reinforce, or interfere with language systems and their structures of significance also begins to become apparent. These take a whole variety of shapes, for instance, in experiments with typography, as in Bruce Andrews' *Love Songs* (1982), and in the interaction of different modes of signification, such as the juxtaposition of visual images with text or the juxtaposition of different texts superimposed on one another, as in the collaborative poem *LEGEND* (1980), written by Andrews, Bernstein, Silliman, Ray DiPalma, and Steve McCaffery.

Language poetry has been part of a cutting-edge radicalism in American poetics for the past three decades and during that course of time has produced a variety of significant manifestos and statements that seek to validate and explicate their position and practice. One of these key statements was published in *Social Text,* titled "Aesthetic Tendency and the Politics of Poetry: A Manifesto," jointly written by Ron Silliman, Carla Harryman, Lyn Hejinian, Steve Benson, Bob Perelman, and Barrett Watten (*Social Text* 19–20 [1988]). In this statement, the writers outlined what they took to be the main issues and characteristics of their poetry. They attack the narrowness and provincialism of mainstream literary norms, especially the "expressivist" lyric as the canonical literary form. They perceive this lyrical form to be predicated on a conservative and inhibiting concept of subjectivity that produces a false consciousness of individualism in the European-American poetic tradition. Instead, they propose a reconfigured sense of the self that is more open to the implications of experience, "an openness of self in the present [that] finds language not as simply transparent and instrumental but as a necessity of the world at large—an obstacle as well as advantage." Furthermore, their writing aims at the transformation of speech through writing since "in order to lay bare language's inherent capacity to construct belief, it is necessary at times to disrupt its convention as communicative transparency." Consciously combining the development of theory and poetry as complementary practices, their writing moves away from the "self-sufficient world" to more explicitly social and political issues as articulated in such key essays as "Disappearance of the Word, Appearance of the World" by Ron Silliman (1976, collected in *The New Sentence,* 1987) and Steve McCaffery's symposium on "Politics and the Referent" in the magazine *Open Letter* (1977). This preoccupation with a "contaminated" rather than a "pure" language, with the social medium of language in itself, has caused people to characterize their writing as a demonstration of the "materiality of the sign" and as substituting chains of self-referential language for the representations of the self.

Commenting on the way that this preoccupation with chains of signifiers opens poetry to more than simply the persona, these poets argue that "there is a possibility, an openness to the implications of experience, associated with the *I* here that is more generative of insight than the transcendent elevation of carefully scripted incidents" ("Aesthetic Tendency"). Their poetry focuses principally on writing as a production of meanings, a process that seeks to engage the reader in the construction of the text rather than allowing words to be registered or heard passively. Language poetry continually asks one to read *writing* rather than *meanings,* interrogating the construction of the text as much as the words themselves. The "exchange" of meaning is an active process rather than a static paradigm of rules. Language poetry seeks to exaggerate the state of the reification of signs by foregrounding the material signifier and offering apparently meaningless words in order to draw attention to the production of meaning itself. This strategy, so akin to the defamiliarization techniques advocated by the Russian formalists and Viktor Shklovsky in particular, is clearly evident in Steve McCaffery's suggestion that "a language centred writing dispossesses us of language, in order that we may repossess it again" (in Bernstein and Andrews, 1984).

A direct confrontation of the problems of reification of and in language structures many of the poetic texts, such as Bob Perelman's *a.k.a.* (1979):

> A non-violent perception of identity: only possible in an ideal landscape? The "world." Do I have to kill every living thing, myself included, in order to live my life in order?

The issue that Perelman raises is how to maintain the *objectness* of an object (one might say the unappropriated value of the object). Using a language that is inextricably involved in the social model of exchange relations threatens the object with an alienating appropriation by the identifying and rationalizing process of commodification. Does writing only succeed in the dematerialization and idealization of the perceptible world (writing as a process of putting the world in inverted commas)? Is an extinction of the material relations between "self" and world the necessary corollary to living an ordered existence? Indeed, "what's the most effective line of resistance here?" (*a.k.a.*). It is quickly evident that no attempt can be made to explain the work from a narrative or character position since incoherence would follow, for Perelman is explicitly concerned with the ethics of conceptual form here and in particular the way identification imposes a synchronic, idealist closure on communication, designating the other within a totalizing linguistic system. The act of "naming" identifies, controls, delimits, and enforces a sameness on the other. Perelman's text self-reflexively resists any expressionist paradigm of language and subjectivity, explicitly countering the notion that the "self" can be referred to as the final term, the touchstone, of meaning. Utilizing parallel structures in the juxtaposition of fragments, the sentences prove decidedly contextual. Furthermore, the oscillation between subject positions or sentence positions and also the continual reconsideration of the metaphoric or literal level of the sentence refuses a congealment of language and leaves the synthesis of meaning always in a fluid state of revision. As Ron Silliman has demonstrated in an influential essay titled "The New Sentence," semantic production is seen to occur at the level of the sentence, or indeed at a smaller unit, and does not engage in the attendant reification of the word, object, or system of language as a result. The writing levers open apparently stable and habitual phrases by switching attention to the literalness of the words and "contravening" the rules of grammatical arrangement. An example from elsewhere in the text reads,

> There's an increasing pressure to identify with history, 14 lbs. per square inch. People carry weights and enforce continuity. (*a.k.a.*)

The metaphoricity of "pressure" is ignored, and the word is taken to indicate literal force. The result is to cleverly point out the relationship between the enforcement of certain ideologies (here the notion of historical continuity) and the manner of linguistic paradigms and rhetorical strategies. The questioning of the nature of language to inform one about reality results in a political conclusion about the manipulation of discourse to inform one about specific, ideological "truths." Shifting from emphasizing semantics to syntax, *a.k.a.* makes the word, as Bruce Andrews argues, the basis of "*extensions.* Instead of derivative (sublimate) of previously established connections . . . [to change] the dominance of ideological restrictive notions of what poetry & language can be.

To politicize—not a closure but an *opening*" (Andrews and Bernstein, 1984). It is to write with what Bernstein describes as "a recharged use of the multivalent referential vectors that any word has," showing reference to be not "a one-to-one relation to an 'object' but a perceptual dimension . . . [that] roams over the range of associations suggested by the word" (Andrews and Bernstein, 1984).

This conception of language disrupts the conventional conception of the poet. No longer construed as an expressive, authoritative source in control of words and their reception, the poet is now "invaded" by other dimensions, words, and letters. He or she is a "pcoet." David Melnick's *Pcoet* uses the "multivalent referential vectors" of words as another challenge to the reification of language. The exchange relation of communication is disrupted by a large degree of linguistic "blockage," occurring not only at the level of the sentence but also at the level of the signifier itself:

thoesiu
thoiea
akcorn woi cirtus locqvump
icgja
cvmwoflux
epaosieusl
cirtus locquvmp
a nex macheisoa.

Closely paralleling aspects of Russian formalist "zaum," or transrational poetry, Melnick seems to defy reification of the word or the object by a straight rejection of referentiality altogether. As Melnick states, "The poems are made of what looks like words and phrases but are not. I think these poems look like they *should* mean something more than other wordless poems do. At the same time, you know that you can't begin to understand what they mean" (Melnick, 1978). He appears more interested in how sounds can be utilized to show how a grammar and meaning can occur despite the absence of standard, received aural signifiers. Although Language writers have been accused of nonreferentiality in their writing, a writing stripped of reference, there has been a concerted attempt to acknowledge that writing is engaged in reference but that reference is a various process. As Peter Inman has put it, writing must be "a language of the word instead of the worded, predigested, pre-fabricated, accepted fact" (in Andrews and Bernstein, 1984). *Pcoet* operates through a constant recorrection of the eye by the voice and vice versa. Clearly, strange sounds and signs conceal familiar sounds and signs: there is a "deus ex machina" somewhere in "a nex macheisoa" and a "circumflex" hovering in "cvmwoflux." The absence of a recognizable referent to the sound signifier forces attention onto the way in which one arrives at the quality of words as textures, materials that are as pliable and malleable as much as any other human product, as a dialectic between eye *and* ear. The inclusion of the manuscript-like crossings out, which appear odd on a typewritten final script, indicates the extent to which this text is "incomplete," still in a process of production, revision, and reconsideration—not yet "sealed" as a finished, completed entity.

A different strategy of anti-reification is adopted in Lyn Hejinian's work. She argues that the "open text" "resists the cultural tendencies that seek to identify and fix material, turn it into a product; that is, it resists reduction and commodification" (1985). Hejinian's poetry has persistently maintained that an openness to otherness is an ethical stance. Like *My Life, The Cell* explores the distinction between the experiencing self and the concept of the self: how experiences constantly alter the concept of the self and its relationship to language and its position vis-à-vis what we call referential reality:

Reality moves around making objects
appear as if they belong
where they are.

Hejinian explicitly acknowledges a debt to Objectivist poetics in its insistence on particularities and its ethical "stance" that resists conceptual abstraction in favor of a poetics of respect for alterity:

Zukofsky says, "Emphasize detail 130
times over or there will
be no poetic . . .

Addressing the issue of closure and openness, Hejinian regards closure as a fiction of completeness and as a stultification of experience. Facing up to otherness is explicitly an openness to particularities in which it is an *ethics of form* that is critical:

> I perceive the world as vast and overwhelming: each moment stands under an enormous vertical and horizontal pressure of information, potent with ambiguity, meaning-full, unfixed, and certainly incomplete. What saves this situation from becoming a vast undifferentiated mass of data and situation is one's ability to make distinctions. Each written text may act as a distinction, may be a distinction. The experience of feeling overwhelmed by undifferentiated material is like claustrophobia. One feels panicky, closed in. The open text is one which both acknowledges the vastness of the world and is formally differentiating. It is form that opens it, in that case. (Hejinian, 1985)

It is this sense of closure as "insufferable," as suffocating, that maintains Hejinian's desire to use language as a means of opening to that otherness, to "discover structure, distinction, the integrity and separateness of things" (Hejinian, 1985). A poem such as *The Cell* is thus a phenomenological exploration of the texture of everyday experiences and how language contains and engenders experiences. The process of seeing becomes a principal preoccupation of the poem ("Seeing as if seeing were / solid in itself, and repeatedly / recent"). Avoiding any subjective lyric confessionalism, *The Cell* demonstrates how narrative is embedded in a mixture of elements, the quotidian discontinuities and disruptions, that is a part of that fabric of everyday life in the present:

A situation—which is a
tableau of trivia—no detail
too small and so lacking
narrative.

As in *Writing Is an Aid to Memory* (1978) and *My Life* (1980; revised edition, 1987), the reader is offered a text wherein generative rather than directive patterns and echoes gradually emerge, as a consciousness explores the relationships between memory, present subjectivity, and narrative constructions. Gaps are essential to the form, although these do not preclude linkages and analogies. Thus, while lines may isolate levels of thought for the reader, he or she is also encouraged to see how thoughts multiply and consolidate connections, especially where the unit of thought strays across the line or across the line to the larger paragraph.

Tim Woods

*See also* Literary Theory and Poetry

**Further Reading**


Andrews, Bruce, and Charles Bernstein, editors, *The L=A=N=G=U=A=G=E Book,* Carbondale: Southern Illinois University Press, 1984

Hartley, George, *Textual Politics and the Language Poets,* Bloomington: Indiana University Press, 1989

Hejinian, Lyn, "The Rejection of Closure," in *Writing/Talks,* edited by Bob Perelman, Carbondale: Southern Illinois University Press, 1985

Perloff, Marjorie, *Radical Artifice: Writing Poetry in the Age of Media,* Chicago: University of Chicago Press, 1991

Perloff, Marjorie, *Poetry On and Off the Page: Essays for Emergent Occasions,* Evanston, Illinois: Northwestern University Press, 1998

Reinfeld, Linda, *Language Poetry: Writing as Rescue,* Baton Rouge: Louisiana State University Press, 1992

Watten, Barrett, *Total Syntax,* Carbondale: Southern Illinois University Press, 1984


---

# Gerrit Lansing 1928–

The idea of transformation is at the heart of Gerrit Lansing's poetry. As Lansing states in a poem for Stephen Jonas, "how poetry transforms we disputed oft, / not denying that it does, it sure does." For Lansing, the imaginations of both the poet and the reader are actively involved in creating the source of each poem. Lansing draws from occult traditions such as gnosis, alchemy, "Magick," yoga, and Tantrism as well as from Jungian depth psychology, Reich's principle of orgasm as connection to cosmic creative energy, and the works of Whitman and Emerson.

Lansing was born in Albany, New York, in 1928 and grew up mostly in Gates Mills, Ohio. After ten years in New York City, he moved to Gloucester, Massachusetts, in 1959–60; there he met the poet Charles Olson, who would become a major influence on his poetry. Lansing edited two issues of a poetry magazine called *SET* in 1961 and 1963. His highly influential "The Burden of SET" essays, contained in the two issues of *SET,* call for "a poetic exploration of the swarming possibilities . . . in American life" using the dual axes of history and magic. The latest incarnation of Lansing's ongoing, lifelong serial poem is *Heavenly Tree, Soluble Forest* (1995), which contains poems written between the late 1950s and mid-1990s. The form of this work will structure the remainder of this article.

The first section of the book, "inscriptions," opens with "A Poem of Love in Eleven Lines." Eleven is the number of sections in the book, the number of the letter "k," which renowned magician Aleister Crowley added to spell the word "Magick," a magical number signifying change, and the number just beyond the ten emanations of God in Kabbalah. The poem enacts for the reader a "transformation" from "frozen rocks" to a "warm Flemish landscape." "The Heavenly Tree Grows Downward" envisions resurrection as a "habit" of movement toward the source of the Kabbalah's Tree of Life. In "Reminders," the book's second section, "Stephen Phillips and the Warmth of Summer Nights" imagines the birth of the poet into "the labyrinthine feeling way." "The Great Form Is Without Shape" is a poem of alchemical transmutation in which "the new gods are swarming" in the "seed of the old gods," even as we "are unhanding / what was handed." "The Milk of the stars from Her Paps" is a meditation on the complex and constantly changing nature of female deity, here envisioned variously as Nuit, Kali, and Fortuna.

In the third section, "Explorers," the reader encounters speakers exploring and working at the edges of our familiar world, "Coursing black savannahs, cruising broken cities," as the title poem states. The speaker in "Judgement of the City" walks in "tarnished lights," and yet his eyes "transpose" "this world's bloody meat / to everlasting bloody meat." The title figure in "The Dark Grammarian," although "disdaining human love," works the images of "universal love": "Mournful angels spire down his black syntax / To health." The fifth section, "a place," enacts the poetic creation of a communal space, "making the place by pacing the place," as stated in "The Curve." Similarly, in "Blue Decrepit Town," the movement of driving a car maps a polis, but one whose formative impetus may only be "grabbed by the throat of mind / much later, if at all."

This looking back for sources also informs the sixth section of the work, "some gone." In "The Bereft," the "newly gone" still "move among the living and cry long animadversion in our sobs and indrawn breath." This section is dominated by two poems to Stephen Jonas. In "Amazing Grace and a Salad Bowl," remembering Jonas provokes thoughts of "Boys moving through the blood," "loved ejaculations," and "upturned wild faces." The poem ends with a glimpse of what unites the two men even beyond death, "bright words hanging on the boughs of dawn // Amazing grace." The seventh section, "on earth, particular," and the untitled eighth section of the book move among the ordinary and extraordinary things of this world with an eye to their alchemical poetic transmutation. "Do you want to shine // softly // in the beam of forms? // But handle the stone," we are advised in "Working in the Lower Red Field." "The Castle of Flowering Birds" envisions a gathering of birds "dumb with feeling" and asks the reader to "Acclaim the throbbing animal" as nature becomes an enactment of our own surging possibilities of feeling.

The untitled ninth section of the work is dominated by the long poem "In Erasmus Darwin's Generous Light." The poem condemns the neglect of the "gnostic garden" and the "worship of document." The unmediated experience of nature is exalted over the textual hairsplitting of deconstructive analysis: "Fuck you, Derrida, Erasmus Darwin said, / origin is beautiful as black / and centers whirl around us as we round them in." In the tenth section, "Portals," "Stanzas of Hyparxis" considers man as microcosm, a being able "to receive nine modes of sophic fire." The mysteries of outer space are the mysteries of inner, psychic space: "How far out you go / it is within." In "Behind the Vale and in the Pleasaunce of the Pythagorean Comma," our idea of heaven is envisioned as "the final Mathematic," a consequence of our rationality. Yet "Logick equals Magick," and, ultimately, "Beauty proves itself by being so." "In Northern Earth" is a powerful meditation on death: "Endurance is calamity if earth speak true." However, despite the fact that "the first darkness blinds the human eyes," the poem hints that it is possible to "climb" to the "thousand-petalled sun."

The final section of *Heavenly Tree, Soluble Forest* is the 18-part masterwork "The Soluble Forest," originally published in 1983 as the Analytical Psychology installment of the Olson-initiated *Curriculum of the Soul*. The poem contains much of what is central in Lansing. The sixth part of the poem combines gnostic light with sexuality, and poetic creation becomes a spontaneous orgasm and source of its own illumination: "The Poem comes / in its own cocklight." Finally, the poem and Lansing's serial work end beneath the lunar sign of change and dissolution: "under the moon / the swimming forest dissolves."

ROBERT BAKER

**Biography**

Born in Albany, New York, 25 February 1928. Attended Harvard University, Cambridge, Massachusetts, A.B. (cum laude) 1949; Columbia University, A.M. 1955; worked for George W. Stewart (publisher) and later Columbia University Press, New York; part-owner, Circle West Books, Annapolis, Maryland, and owner, Abraxas Books, Gloucester, Massachusetts, both antiquarian bookstores. Currently lives in Gloucester, Massachusetts.

**Poetry**

*The Heavenly Tree Grows Downward,* 1966
*Analytic Psychology, or, The Soluble Forest Is Swimming Across,* 1983
*Heavenly Tree, Soluble Forest,* 1995

**Further Reading**

Featherston, Dan, "Couple of Thoughts on Lansing's 'Heavenly Tree,'" *Talisman* 15 (1996)
Foster, Edward, "Emerson's Journal and Melville's Grave," *Talisman* 15 (1996)
Podgurski, Robert, "Anagnorisis and the Magickal Ground of *Heavenly Tree/Soluble Forest*," *Talisman* 15 (1996)
Schelb, Edward, "'Sea-Stoned Altitudes and the Constellated Swing': On the Poetry of Gerrit Lansing," *Talisman* 15 (1996)
Stein, Charles, "For Gerrit Lansing and His 'Soluble Forest,'" *Talisman* 15 (1996)
Stroffoloino, Chris, "The Simplicity of Two: Gerrit Lansing's 'Filthy Lucre,'" *Talisman* 15 (1996)

## Latino Poetry. *See* Hispanic American Poetry

## Ann Lauterbach 1942–

An inheritor of Wallace Stevens' speculative eloquence, the work of Ann Lauterbach is unique in contemporary American poetry for its self-consciously philosophical and lyrical investigations into that which it simultaneously creates: a poetic seam of perception linking mind and world. The seam of Lauterbach's poetry is fragile, beautifully precarious, and yet her work also possesses the stern faith that a nuanced and crafted attentiveness to the infinitely various and tentative meetings of mind and world will hinge them together, if only momentarily, and if only to discover the desire for momentary cohesion. Lauterbach's imagination is both intellectually and emotionally inspired, and while she plays with the arbitrariness and contingency of truth and reality, her work is also tenderly respectful of the desire for their assuring configurations and forms.

As the title of her first collection *Many Times, but Then* (1979) suggests, Lauterbach investigates the figures of surprise and anomaly that emerge from the ground of expectation and pattern: moments of experience without a name to shape their intelligibility, the illogical questions the emotions always pose. In "The White Sequence," Lauterbach interrupts the pattern of a litany with a question, "A rule of thumb. / A rule of eye. A rule of heart. What / rules the heart?" Self-reflexive questioning is at the heart of Lauterbach's work, and the poem "Configurations of One" is an almost dizzying displacement of a unified self. The poem drops into increasingly imaginative configurations of time, image, and self-perception, but then shapes itself back into the present by hinging the speaker's imaginative image of herself with the actuality of her desire for another. After asserting that she was in Italy "back / when Giotto was pressing angels / into flat chapel walls," the speaker ends the poem with a frankness modulated by vulnerability: "When you came / into that room last night I was that again."

*Before Recollection* (1987) pursues anomaly within pattern as well, although in this well-regarded collection the patterns of cultural perception are dense, tragic, and intricate. With a brave and clear intelligence, these poems clear a way through a world that makes a refreshing meeting of self and image difficult, layered as it is with ceremony and cliché. At the end of "Moths to Flame," a poem that makes parallels between the capacities to imagine and the possibility for realizing lasting desires in experience, Lauterbach writes, "Every now and then, a stray day / Finds its way to the surface of our unguarded desires / And we couple with it, wrecking all precedent, gaining ground." Emotional depth is guarded by cliché, too, and the often anthologized "Psyche's Dream" adds another dimension of interiority to a literary and mythological image of fantasy's erotic depths in order to reimagine emotional and physical intimacy. The poem opens with the conditional phrase "If dreams could dream" and then realizes this possibility as the binaries of imitation (an object and its image) are relinquished for an encircling sequence of desiring, insatiable, continually refracting versions of the dream that arrives "Nowhere and would not resemble, but would languish / on the other side of place." This unresembling placelessness makes the singularity of intimate gestures actual and felt, and Lauterbach's career-long investment in collaborations with visual artists suggests that various forms of intimacy are not only her work's pursuit but its sustaining ground.

John Ashbery is Lauterbach's most immediate predecessor, her most obvious peer, and there are many productive comparisons between them (the capacity to simultaneously create and follow meandering abstraction; radical juxtapositions effortlessly rendered; an increasingly inclusive and idiosyncratic field of reference). Yet critics also point to a deliberate absence of sustained irony in Lauterbach's work, as well as a unique seriousness of purpose. Lauterbach's seriousness allows her voice to inhabit fissures in reality with an attentiveness that insists on their plausibility. The critic Susan Schultz (1991) writes, "Lauterbach refus[es] to emancipate herself from the liminal spaces she investigates, including the erotic sites that Ashbery tends to elide." In the 1991 collection entitled *Clamor,* Lauterbach discovers liminal spaces that are rare and erotically charged, as slight as a word and placed in hopeful opposition to the noisy space of discourse. In "Revenant," inspired by the reverberation of the world within a word, "I heard it. I heard it as *branch,*" two figures fight for the intimacy of listening despite playing habitual parts in an imaginative landscape of diminished desire, "A shiver of false fire / Warmed us stupidly, and the needles lay about / On the floor and on the pillows." Lauterbach is well known as a poet of the visual, but *Clamor* is a sustained argument for an attentiveness to the intimacy expressed in spoken words before they solidify into the obdurate codes of the visual. In "Untoward," Lauterbach writes, "The instance, allowed to speak, is not yet / Embodied, the big vacancies filled with bigness / As from beyond, or behind, an image."

*And for Example* represents a more recognizably mythological imaginary, although in this 1994 volume Lauterbach shapes fragments of silence to represent all that the recognizable and factual can suggest. The mythological is juxtaposed in various ways with the quotidian; each spoken phrase becomes an example of the dense histories we cannot always perceive, although we live them out, as close and as distant as our minds' images of ourselves. In "The Scene Shifts," Lauterbach writes, "Once she thought she was a banner / above a statue / in one of those parks you read about." The poem then quickly shifts to a voice that embodies that perception: "*I used to live across from that park.*"

Lauterbach is a poet who possesses gifts of the intellect to match her gifts of lyricism, and her many poetically-inspired philosophical tracts are evidence of the ways an eclectic knowledge of many intellectual traditions enriches her work. If there is one intellectual tradition her work best resembles it might be American pragmatism, a tradition that also embraces shifting scenes: the transition between the dense detail of the lived and all the imagination makes possible, the movement between speculative abstraction and an idea's material embodiment. Her most recent collection, *On a Stair* (1997), focuses on language as such—prepositions, pronouns, the pieces of sound that arbitrarily form words—as a delicate hinge between creation and destruction, between the truth of desire and the lies of its realization. *On a Stair* is a collection that takes Lauterbach's attentiveness to elegant craft and the nuances of thought and feeling to a pristine and microscopic intensity, and, consistent with her previous works, the poet's "self" is always guarded possibility. So, the intensely personal, even confessional poem "N/EST," a poem that appears at the end of this volume and bears witness to her reproductive history, comes as a real surprise: an anomalous bloom of the personal against Lauterbach's sustained attention to the craft of the intellect. In "N/EST" the poet's self is hinged tragically and precariously to the actuality of her physical body, the myths of a woman's body, the intricate grooves and tragic scars of her own history, and the commitments and sacrifices of Lauterbach's art: to imaginatively trace intimacy as it becomes lost.

KIMBERLY LAMM

**Biography**

Born in New York City, 28 September 1942. Attended University of Wisconsin, Madison, B.A. 1964; Columbia University, New York City, 1966–67; editor, Thames and Hudson Publishers; teacher, St. Martin's School of Art; director of Literature Program, Institute of Contemporary Art, London, England, 1967–74; curator, Max Protetch Gallery, Art Latitude Gallery, Fabric Workshop; assistant director, Washburn Gallery; consultant, Rosa Esman Gallery, New York City, 1974–85; teacher, Brooklyn College, 1985–89; since 1989, Professor, City University of New York; since 1991, co-director and teacher, summer MFA program, Bard College, Annandale-on-Hudson, New York; has also taught at Columbia University, New York City, Princeton University, Princeton, New Jersey, and University of Iowa, Iowa City. Received Creative Arts Public Service grant, 1978; Guggenheim grant, 1986; New York State Council for the Arts grant, 1988; Ingram Merrill Foundation grant, 1988; Jerome J. Shestack Prize (*American Poetry Review*), 1990; John D. and Catherine T. MacArthur Foundation fellowship, 1993. Living in New York City.

**Poetry**
*Many Times, but Then,* 1979
*Before Recollection,* 1987
*Clamor,* 1991
*And for Example,* 1994
*On a Stair,* 1997

**Other Writings:** artist's books (*Greeks* [with Jan Groover and Bruce Boice], 1985).

**Further Reading**

Altieri, Charles, "Ann Lauterbach's 'Still' and Why Stevens Still Matters," in *Postmodernisms Now: Essays on Contemporaneity in the Arts,* by Altieri, University Park: Pennsylvania State University Press, 1998
Fink, Thomas A., "The Poetry of David Shapiro and Ann Lauterbach," *American Poetry Review* 17 (January/February 1988)
Schultz, Susan M., "Houses of Poetry after Ashbery: The Poetry of Ann Lauterbach and Donald Revell," *Virginia Quarterly Review* 67, no. 2 (Spring 1991)

---

# Li-Young Lee 1957–

Widely respected by critics and admired by audiences, award-winning poet Li-Young Lee's poems evoke emotional complexity through their lyric intensity. Lee's poetry, much of which explores the themes of family, cultural alienation, identity, and memory, has been widely anthologized, and Lee's prose memoir *The Winged Seed: A Remembrance* (1995) has been praised for its intricate interweaving of family history and myth as well as for the beauty and depth of Lee's prose.

Such important American poets as Walt Whitman, Emily Dickinson, Theodore Roethke, and other American romantic writers have influenced Lee's work. In his introduction to *Rose* (1986), Lee's first collection of poems, Gerald Stern noted that in Lee's work one can see the influence of writers such as Keats and Rilke and, "among contemporaries, James Wright, Galway Kinnell, and Philip Levine." Writing from the particular, Asian-American experience toward the universal experiences of love, grief, and longing, Lee works both within and beyond the traditions of American lyric and romantic poetry. Throughout his books, Lee employs an inherited lyric tradition as a way of engaging and negotiating the cultural inheritance of his Chinese family.

Lee's compelling personal and family histories figure prominently in both his poetry and his prose. Born in Jakarta, Indonesia, Lee is the son of Chinese immigrants. His father, Richard K.Y. Lee, was personal physician to Mao Zedong in China before moving with his wife and family to Jakarta. In Indonesia, Richard Lee worked as a university professor until representatives of the then anti-Chinese dictator arrested him in 1958. The Lee family escaped Indonesia in 1959 and spent several years traveling throughout Asia before finally emigrating to the United States in 1964. After settling in Pennsylvania, Lee's father became a Presbyterian minister.

Lee's complex relationship to his father is a recurring theme in his writing. Of *Rose,* Lee's first book of poetry, Roger Mitchell (1989) noted that, although the book is not wholly about Lee's relationship to his father, his father "enters almost all of these poems like a half-bidden ghost." Indeed, throughout *Rose,* the father figure present in the poems takes on an increasingly mythic, otherworldly quality. In "Dreaming of Hair," Lee writes,

> Out of the grave
> my father's hair
> bursts. A strand
> pierces my left sole, shoots
> up bone, past ribs,
> to the broken heart it stitches,
> then down,
> swirling in the stomach, in the groin, and down,
> through the right foot

Here, it is the father's presence tying the son to the human world, even as he reaches for him from another. In his introduction to *Rose,* Stern refers to the father in Lee's poems as "godlike" and states that "the poet's job becomes . . . to withstand him and comprehend him, and variously love and fear him." Much of Lee's writing exhibits this quality of being caught between wholly different realms of experience. In "The Gift," Lee tells of a father removing a metal splinter from his son's hand:

> Had you entered that afternoon
> you would have thought you saw a man
> planting something in a boy's palm,
> a silver tear, a tiny flame.

As is the case in "The Gift," Lee's work consistently fuses simple daily activities, such as removing a splinter, carrying a bag of peaches, or washing one's father's feet, with a mythic, even surreal quality.

Lee's work also examines the conflicted space between two cultures: the Chinese culture of his parents and his heritage and the American culture in which he lives. Lee's poem "Persimmons" addresses this conflict by recounting the speaker's memory of a sixth-grade teacher who brings a persimmon, a "Chinese apple," for the class to sample. The speaker knows, although the teacher does not, that the fruit is not ripe and will not be sweet. In the same poem, Lee recalls teaching his American wife words in Chinese: "Crickets: *chiu chiu.* Dew: I've forgotten / Naked: I've forgotten / *Ni, wo:* you and me." Here and elsewhere in Lee's work, the complicated experience of living between two cultures, the experience of exile, is examined and laid bare. In "Rain Diary," Lee writes that he once asked his father, "Where are we going?":

My question could have been, In what country
will your pillow finally come to rest
and the rain call you home?
His answer would have been the same,
my father of this America and a divided tongue

Lee's second book, *The City in Which I Love You* (1990), further explores the themes of exile, memory, and fractured, bicultural experience. In the first poem in the collection, "Furious Versions," Lee recounts his family's flight into exile in the United States, "republic to republic, / oligarchy to anarchy to democracy, we arrived." Lee is compelled to tell and retell his family's story because "the characters survive through the telling, / the teller survives / by his telling . . . But, no one / can tell without cease / our human / story, and so we / lose, lose." Loss is a consistent theme in *The City in Which I Love You;* the poet contends here with the loss through death of a father and brother, the loss of memory, and even the loss of self. In "This Room and Everything in It," Lee writes, "My body is estrangement."

The long title poem of Lee's second collection is a sort of re-imagining of the biblical poem *The Song of Songs,* from which Lee's poem takes an epigraph. Poet-critic Judith Kitchen (1991) wrote that the poem is informed by "a dense language, thick with urgent rhythms and relentless desire—as though language itself were the other, the body of the beloved." This is, however, not merely a love poem but an exploration into the redemptive qualities of love. Lee's is a complicated desire for the beloved and for the city itself, the "city I call home, in which I am a guest." Later in the poem, he writes,

late in this century and on a Wednesday morning
bearing the mark of one who's experienced
neither heaven nor hell,

my birthplace vanished, my citizenship earned
in league with stones of the earth, I
enter without retreat or help from history,
the days of no day, my earth
of no earth, I re-enter

the city in which I love you

The scope and depth of "The City in Which I Love You" characterizes the ambitious reach of the poems in Lee's second collection. The urgency of language and rhythm that Kitchen identifies in the title poem can also be found in many other poems in the collection, such as "My Father, in Heaven, Is Reading," "This Hour and What Is Dead," and "The Cleaving."

Lee's most recent work continues to explore themes of family and identity, as these lines from "Hurry toward Beginning," a poem recently published in the *Kenyon Review,* attest:

I can't tell what my father said
about the sea we crossed together
from the sea itself, or the rose's noon
from my mother's crying
on the stairs, lost
between a country and a country.

Although he is among the most widely acclaimed poets of his generation as well as one of the most popular, Lee is still a young writer near the beginning of his career. He will no doubt be a significant force in contemporary American poetry for years to come.

NANCY KUHL

*See also* Asian American Poetry

**Biography**

Born in Jakarta, Indonesia, 19 August 1957. Attended University of Pittsburgh, B.A. 1979; University of Arizona, 1979–80; State University of New York, Brockport, 1980–81; has taught at Northwestern University, Evanston, Illinois, and University of Iowa, Iowa City. Received National Endowment for the Arts fellowship, 1986, 1995; I.B. Lavan Award, 1986; Delmore Schwartz Award, 1987; Whiting Writer's Award, 1988; Guggenheim fellowship, 1989; Lamont Award, 1990; American Book Award (Before Columbus Foundation), 1995; Lannan Literary Award, 1995. Living in Chicago, Illinois.

**Poetry**

*Rose,* 1986
*The City in Which I Love You,* 1990

**Other Writings:** memoir (*The Winged Seed: A Remembrance,* 1995).

**Further Reading**

Hesford, Walter A., "'The City in Which I Love You': Li-Young Lee's Excellent Song," *Christianity and Literature* 46, no. 1 (Autumn 1996)
Kaganoff, Penny, "Review of *The City in Which I Love You,*" *Publishers Weekly* 237, no. 30 (1990)
Kitchen, Judith, "Auditory Imaginations: The Sense of Sound," *Georgia Review* 45, no. 1 (Spring 1991)
Marshall, Tod, "To Witness the Invisible: Interview with Li-Young Lee," *Kenyon Review* 22, no. 1 (Winter 2000)
Mitchell, Roger, "Review of *Rose,*" *Prairie Schooner* 63, no. 3 (Fall 1989)
Norris, Kathleen, "Review of *The City in Which I Love You,*" *The Christian Century* 115, no. 28 (1998)
Xiaojing, Zhou, "Inheritance and Invention in Li-Young Lee's Poetry," *MELUS* 21, no. 1 (Spring 1996)

## Lesbian Poetry. *See* Gay and Lesbian Poetry

# Denise Levertov 1923–97

Denise Levertov's place in American poetry is secured by a lifetime exploring spiritual themes, a pilgrimage of poetry. In her first two decades of writing, she centered on the form and detail of inner experience, exploring in the ordinary large and small things of the world what she termed the "authentic," the "Marvelous Truth" ("Matins," *The Jacob's Ladder,* 1961). From the mid-1960s on, her aesthetics of numinous presence was put under great pressure, for a poetry of the expressive self in moments of awareness could not bridge the public, political realities of societal and national upheaval. Yet she insistently explored a variety of forms in which to combine private reflection with a public moral language. Few poets have explored so intensely and written with so much insight and wisdom on the individual's encounter with the most profound matters of political and spiritual life.

Levertov was born in England in 1923 into a deeply religious family. Her mother was descended from a Welsh mystic, and her father was an Anglican clergyman, a convert who had grown up Jewish under the tutelage of his father, who was a Hasidic rabbi and scholar of the Kabbala. Her father translated part of the *Zohar* and maintained throughout his life an interest in merging the two religions. The poet was tutored at home under her mother's guidance and grew up under the daily influence of Hasidism's keen and steady attention to joy and mystery impelled by seeing glory in the ordinary things of the world. Muriel Rukeyser once said that Levertov's poems were "hymns lying over the basis of that deep scholarship" (quoted in *By Herself: Women Reclaim Poetry,* edited by Molly McQuade, 2000).

Beginning as one of the British neo-Romantics, by the age of 21 Levertov had completed her first volume of poems, published as *The Double Image* in 1946. The poems lavished love and attention on the island landscapes and proved to be the last work in that formal and melancholic mode. The same year, she married Mitchell Goodman, an American, and in 1947 she moved with him to the United States. She spent a decade steeping herself in American life and literature, making herself over into what many regarded as one of the finest of the new contemporary American poets.

The thorough and deep transition was made possible by the deeply absorbed spiritual learning, both from books and in daily experience, and by the correspondence she found to it in the American poetic tradition. Hasidism's focus on finding glory in the everyday things of the world enabled a profound view of American poets' celebrations of the everyday world in everyday language and their modes of writing in moments of wonder, letting experience in the moment find the form. The most immediate sources of this American vision and practice were William Carlos Williams and the Black Mountain poets. However, Levertov's wide reading shows up in echoes and quotations throughout her poems of so many others—Wallace Stevens, Emily Dickinson, H.D., and Marianne Moore, to name a few. T.S. Eliot can be counted among her very early influences—she read his work from an early age and, in an impetuous moment when she was 12, sent him some of her poems, to which he responded with a long letter of advice.

For models of form, Levertov looked most to Williams, whose Imagist-turned-Objectivist views—"no ideas but in things"—gave rise to an aesthetics later called "open form" by Charles Olson and others of the Black Mountain group. In this view, a poem is to be alive each moment in constantly beginning instances of experience. The poem is a drama of the poet's thought, making the poem's form an embrace of the poet's speech and the things of the world. Although later in his life Williams would assert that the poem was dispassionate, early on in developing his distinctive prosody he claimed that form was determined in the instant of time in which an emotion was felt in viewing objects in the world. Poetic form captured the shape of the mind and feeling in the moment of seeing. For example, in the 1921 poem "Young Sycamore," Williams begins with an urgent report on his experience seeing a tree: I must tell you / this young tree / whose round and firm trunk / between the wet / pavement and the gutter[.]" From there the poet's vision follows the tree upward in detail, ending "it / thins / till nothing is left of it / but two / eccentric knotted / twigs / bending forward / hornlike at the top[.]"

Many critics at first saw Levertov's work as mere imitation of Williams and judged her as a quite minor poet. Others recognized a daring and wise voice that went far beyond Williams. The extent to which Levertov used and surpassed Williams can be seen in a comparison of "Young Sycamore" with Levertov's statements of her poetics and in her first volume of poems in this vein. In Williams' poem, humility can be inferred from the image of the young small tree bending forward into nothingness—the blank space at the end of the poem. Levertov makes explicit the poet's encounter with spiritual forces. Poetry and the spiritual were inseparable, as this early statement of her poetics makes clear:

> I believe poets are instruments on which the power of poetry plays. But they are also *makers,* craftsmen: it is given the seer to see, but it is then his responsibility to communicate what he sees, that they who cannot see may see, since we are "members one of another."

Taking after Whitman's prophet/priest/poet, Levertov's idea of the poet is distinctly shaped by her merging of the Jewish and Christian religions—Old Testament seer has also to be a New Testament parable teller seeking to bring all into one spiritual body. Continuing this credo, she speaks of the poem as organic in the language of the New Criticism but with the Williams' belief that verse form must be found in the shape of experience:

> I believe every space and comma is a living part of the poem and has its function, and the way lines are broken is a functioning part essential to the poem's life. (reprinted in *The Poet in the World,* 1973)

Form and the "essential force" of the poem must be fused.

Early poems, such as "To a Snake," from her second book, *Here and Now* (1956), are exemplary achievements of this poetics. The lines address the snake in terms of dramatic intimacy, as between lovers:

> Green Snake, when I hung you round my neck
> and stroked your cold, pulsing throat
>         as you hissed to me, glinting
> arrowy gold scales, and I felt
>         the weight of you on my shoulders,
> and the whispering silver of your dryness
>         sounded close as my ears—.

The poem, à la Williams, narrates a high emotional moment with expressed urgency. Line breaks heighten the drama by marking out the pulses of thought and feeling, indicating the energy of moment. At the same time, the instant fuses darkness and light, the snake's "glinting," "gold" beauty seduces as Eve was seduced into sin, flesh and spirit are united but without flaw, without fear, with only joy in the snake's gift of darkness, "along wake of pleasure" that leaves the speaker "returned / smiling and haunted, to a dark morning." Levertov has gone beyond Williams to use metaphor to draw the spiritual implications in clear relief.

*Here and Now* caught the attention of Kenneth Rexroth, who recognized the many virtues that placed Levertov, in his view, as unquestionably the best of the Black Mountain poets, who were to his mind the best of the new generation (review reprinted in *Denise Levertov: Selected Criticism,* edited by Albert Gelpi, 1993). Rexroth saw in Levertov all the virtues of those poets plus a good deal more: she had knowledge and culture without the faults of academic poets; she was learned, but she also possessed humanity and wisdom.

James Wright concurred. Reviewing her fourth book, *With Eyes at the Back of Our Heads* (1959), he took to task those who saw only an imitation of Williams. Wright knew daring exploration of dark energy when he saw it, something that had been largely avoided in the American vision. Thoroughly expert on Rainer Maria Rilke, he recognized that poet's work behind the poems—the attractive force of the dark, the Orpheus figure who travels down into darkness and returns, haunted with loss but singing. Like Rexroth, Wright judged Levertov the finest of the new poets and compared her favorably to Rilke.

While the early poetry relied on distance from the political world, as most did in the isolationism after World War II, the sweeping political upheaval of the 1960s made the poetics of presence difficult, for it offered no public resolution to suffering or a vision for future direction. Heavily involved in the various activist protests—Vietnam, civil rights, and feminist—and troubled by grief for her older sister's death, she began in *The Sorrow Dance* (1966) to track the negative side of darkness and relate personal suffering, loss, and life purposes to social, moral, and political realities. The best known of these poems, the "Olga Poems," are elegies for her sister; they express the tortured pull of unresolved feelings, misguided courage, and anger coupled with love, admiration, and daring. They conclude with recognition of the inability to understand the other, even someone as close as a sister—a humbling experience that was to expand and redeem human experience in the poems she would write from then on.

*Relearning the Alphabet* (1970) expanded on the problem of relating and acting as a person and as a poet in a disordered, conflicted society by attempting to work out a new moral language that could bridge the private and the public experience. "Disasters / of history" and "anguish / of mortality" combine to try to crush the heart, but it cracks only, and still the poet seeks, as before, the hidden: "What / is under the cracked glaze." *To Stay Alive* (1971) contains the best of political poetry. Reprinting "Olga Poems" at the front of the volume, Levertov proceeds to detail 19th- and 20th-century disasters amid echoes of past poetry, to wonder about the individual lives of victims, and to align them with personal grief by using the same terms of reflection and arrive at the same truth. In "What Were They Like," she holds internal dialogue about Vietnam's peasants, but there is no way left to know them because they are gone. The strongest of the dark political poems inverts the incarnation of innocence: "Advent 1966" envisions napalmed babies instead of peace, war instead of love, and monstrosity born instead of humanity and divinity.

Levertov's poetry of the last three decades of her life increasingly deepens the attention to the hard realities of life in terms of a pilgrimage. If joy is harder to come by, it is because it must be relinquished with other necessary losses for the journey into wisdom. The titles of her books are good indications of their more explicitly religious themes as Levertov explores a way to join the public experience of God with the private one, as she continues to try to gather private conviction and a public political voice into one form. The later volumes seek, *Candles in Babylon* (1982) especially, to achieve a synthesis in a poetry of redemption as loving journey. She sees that it is we who must love, who must have mercy, in the midst of our own profound terror. The achieved courage, the humble gratitude for life in the midst of great darkness, is as powerful as ever in the poems of her final months, collected in *This Great Unknowing* (1999); in this collection she is ready to go into the unknown, all the while longing for her beloved earth: "I move among the ankles / of forest Elders, / tread their moist rugs of moss . . . what perplexities and wisdoms they exchange, / unknown to me," and with her eye on the details of the tree in the moment of viewing, moving from tree base to middle to the top, she begins "to wonder / about what rises / so far above me into the light." She has returned to the place traveled in *With Eyes at the Back of Our Heads,* the desired journey into the unknown while looking back at the earthly beauty being left behind.

ROSEMARY GATES WINSLOW

*See also* Black Mountain School; Religion and Poetry

**Biography**

Born in Ilford, Essex, England, 24 October 1923; emigrated to the United States, 1948; naturalized, 1955. Served as a nurse in World War II; worked in an antique shop and bookshop, London, 1946; nurse at British Hospital, Paris, spring 1947; taught at the YM-YWHA Poetry Center, New York, 1964, City College of New York, 1965, and Vassar College, Poughkeepsie, New York, 1966–67; Visiting Professor, Drew University, Madison, New Jersey, 1965, University of California, Berkeley, 1969, Massachusetts Institute of Technology, Cambridge, 1969–70, Kirkland College, Clinton, New York, 1970–71, University of Cincinnati, Ohio, spring 1973, and Tufts University, Medford, Massachusetts, 1973–79; Fannie Hurst Professor (poet-in-residence), Brandeis University, Waltham, Massachusetts, 1981–83; from 1981 Professor of English, Stanford University, California; poetry editor, *The Nation,* New York, 1961, 1963–65, and *Mother Jones,* San Francisco, 1975–78; Honorary Scholar, Radcliffe Institute for Independent Study, Cambridge, Massachusetts, 1964–67. Received Bess Hokin Prize, 1960; Longview Award, 1961; Guggenheim fellowship, 1962; Harriet Monroe Memorial Prize, 1964; Inez Boulton Prize, 1964; Morton Dauwen Zabel Prize, 1965 (*Poetry,* Chicago); American Academy grant, 1966, 1968; Lenore Marshall Prize, 1976; Bobst Award, 1983; Shelley Memorial Award, 1984; Academy of American Poets fellowship, 1995; honorary Litt.D., Colby College, Waterville, Maine, 1970, University of Cincinnati, 1973, Bates College, Lewiston, Maine, 1984, St. Lawrence University, Canton, New York, 1984;

Allegheny College, Meadville, Pennsylvania, 1987; member, American Academy, 1980; corresponding member, Mallarmé Academy, 1983. Died in Seattle, Washington, 23 December 1997.

**Poetry**
*The Double Image,* 1946
*Here and Now,* 1956
*Overland to the Islands,* 1958
*With Eyes at the Back of Our Heads,* 1959
*The Jacob's Ladder,* 1961
*O Taste and See: New Poems,* 1964
*The Sorrow Dance,* 1966
*Penguin Modern Poets 9* (poems by Levertov, Kenneth Rexroth, and William Carlos Williams), 1967
*Relearning the Alphabet,* 1970
*To Stay Alive,* 1971
*Footprints,* 1972
*The Freeing of the Dust,* 1975
*Life in the Forest,* 1978
*Collected Earlier Poems, 1940–1960,* 1979
*Candles in Babylon,* 1982
*Poems, 1960–1967,* 1983
*Oblique Prayers: New Poems, with 14 Translations from Jean Joubert,* 1984
*Selected Poems,* 1986
*Poems, 1968–1972,* 1987
*Breathing the Water,* 1987
*A Door in the Hive,* 1989
*Evening Train,* 1992
*Sands of the Well,* 1996
*The Stream and the Sapphire: Selected Poems on Religious Themes,* 1997
*The Life around Us: Selected Poems on Nature,* 1997
*This Great Unknowing: Last Poems,* 1999

**Other Writings:** short stories (*In the Night,* 1968), essays (*The Poet in the World,* 1973; *Light Up the Cave,* 1981; *New and Selected Essays,* 1992; *Tesserae: Memories and Suppositions,* 1995), translations of French and Bengali poetry (*Black Iris: Selected Poems,* by Jean Joubert, 1988); edited collections of poetry (*Out of the War Shadow: An Anthology of Current Poetry,* 1967).

**Further Reading**

Levertov, Denise, *Denise Levertov: In Her Own Province,* edited by Linda Welshimer Wagner, New York: New Directions, 1979
Levertov, Denise, *Conversations with Denise Levertov,* edited by Jewel Spears Brooker, Jackson: University Press of Mississippi, 1998
Marten, Harry, *Understanding Denise Levertov,* Columbia: University of South Carolina Press, 1988
O'Connell, Nicholas, "A Poet's Valediction: Interview with Denise Levertov," *Poets & Writers* 26, no. 3 (May/June 1998)
*Renascence* 50, nos. 1–2 (Fall/Winter 1997–98) (special issues entitled "Spirit in the Poetry of Denise Levertov")
Rodgers, Audrey T., *Denise Levertov: The Poetry of Engagement,* Rutherford, New Jersey: Fairleigh Dickinson University Press, and London: Associated University Presses, 1993
Sakelliou-Schultz, Liana, *Denise Levertov: An Annotated Primary and Secondary Bibliography,* New York and London: Garland, 1988
*Twentieth Century Literature* 38, no. 3 (Fall 1992) (special issue on Levertov edited by Ronald R. Jansen)
Wagner-Martin, Linda, editor, *Critical Essays on Denise Levertov,* Boston: G.K. Hall, 1991


## Olga Poems

Denise Levertov's "Olga Poems" is a series of short lyrics that progress as a single poem. Written in May through August 1964, the year of her sister Olga's death at age 50, the work is important for its elegiac beauty and for its transitional role in Levertov's movement from a poetics of nature and the self, pleasure and joy, toward a poetics that attempted to synthesize aesthetics and politics. First published in *The Sorrow Dance* (1966), the poem was subsequently included in *To Stay Alive* (1971) because, as Levertov's preface tells us, the subject matter of the new book—the attempt to be a writer with a historical and political consciousness made public—had begun with that poem.

Immediately preceding "Olga Poems" in *The Sorrow Dance,* "A Lamentation" voices Levertov's newfound awareness that darkness in human existence, not just in nature, must be acknowledged and incorporated into her life and poetics. Turning toward grief after denial of grief, she acknowledges that to continue to turn away is to turn away from love. As she turns toward her sister in "Olga Poems" to seek reconciliation, she turns toward the rage at human suffering that her sister had expressed from Levertov's early memories of her. As she seeks union, she must open her view of what art is to include her sister's view.

Nine years older than Denise, Olga was an outspoken political activist, angry at poverty and injustice. As a child she spoke openly in the streets alongside her father in protest of the takeover of European nations by National Socialist regimes. In her adult years, she continued her activism and was often estranged from friends and family. Levertov recalls her in "Olga Poems" as always angry, "mutter[ing] into my childhood / pacing the trampled grass where human puppets" were "stung into alien semblances by the lash of her will." Levertov claims that her sister's protest against human cruelty was too loud, extreme, and even cruel itself in its way:

You wanted
to shout the world to its senses,
did you?—to browbeat

the poor into joy's
republic—
What rage
and human shame swept you
when you were nine and saw
the Ley Street houses,

grasping their meaning as *slum.*

Then Levertov sets her own poetics next to Olga's political activism, as a vision of order detached from human living:

> Where I, reaching that age,
> teased you, admiring
> architectural probity . . .

She concludes the contrast with an acknowledgment of the flame of compassion at the center of Olga's existence: "Black one, black one, / there was a white / candle in your heart."

To approach her sister in grief requires letting in love, and that opening further opens her to the anger that had separated them. The contrast and necessity of finding connection is presented at the poem's onset, where several contrasting images and themes are inextricably intertwined—fire as warmth and warning, natural beauty and social ugliness, pleasure and hurt, flesh in youth and decay, and distance and intimacy:

> By the gas-fire, kneeling
> to undress,
> scorching luxuriously, raking
> her nails over olive sides, the red
> waistband ring—
>
> (And the little sister
> beady-eyed in the bed—
> or drowsy was I? My head
> a camera—)
>
> Sixteen. Her breasts
> round, round, and
> dark-nippled—
>
> who now these two months long
> is bones and tatters of flesh in earth.

Levertov develops the oppositions throughout the work, moving from childhood pleasures and distresses to adult misunderstanding, separation, and longing to the hospital bed, where Olga "lay afloat on a sea / of love and pain," as Levertov herself feels in the poem. Levertov comes to claim her sister's self as part of her own, "As through a wood, shadow and light . . . your life winds in me." They have traveled together through childhood and adulthood, Olga a "tearless Niobe," too sorrowful to express grief or seek out another for comfort and love.

The poem's end envisions Olga in a synecdoche of the eye, hard, dark, and unknowable, like the self—dark as stone but nevertheless alive in spirit, shining with light. In this gesture, Levertov claims her sister's being and struggling in darkness as inseparable from her own pilgrimage through the world. The individual is uplifted and affirmed as of great value by the light and for her expression of light. In 1965, the year following Olga's death, Levertov joined the public opposition to the Vietnam War, and in the poems about the war, Olga reappears as a flame, a figure of light, of suffering protest against suffering, like those who endure self-immolation, destroying their own lives willingly to call attention to human cruelty. While some critics have charged that the "Olga Poems" are obsessed with death, the work may be seen as a successful and beautiful retrieval of love out of suffering. Levertov envisions love as lying inside and outside of us, as light emerging from the self as the self also reflects the light of compassion in the face of the ugliest truths. Indeed, as *The Sorrow Dance* wonders throughout, the darkness may be only anger or dread, pent energy of light waiting to be freed.

ROSEMARY GATES WINSLOW

**Further Reading**


Altieri, Charles, *Enlarging the Temple: New Directions in American Poetry during the 1960s,* Lewisburg, Pennsylvania: Bucknell University Press, and London: Associated University Presses, 1979

Levertov, Denise, *Denise Levertov: In Her Own Province,* edited by Linda Welshimer Wagner, New York: New Directions, 1979

Little, Anne Colclough, and Susie Paul, editors, *Denise Levertov: New Perspectives,* West Cornwall, Connecticut: Locust Hill Press, 2000

Marten, Harry, *Understanding Denise Levertov,* Columbia: University of South Carolina Press, 1988

Middleton, Peter, *Revelation and Revolution in the Poetry of Denise Levertov,* London: Binnacle Press, 1981

*Renascence* 50, nos. 1–2 (Fall/Winter 1997–98) (special issues entitled "Spirit in the Poetry of Denise Levertov")

Rodgers, Audrey T., *Denise Levertov: The Poetry of Engagement,* Rutherford, New Jersey: Fairleigh Dickinson University Press, and London: Associated University Presses, 1993


## A Woman Alone

"A Woman Alone" appeared in Denise Levertov's collection *Life in the Forest* (1978), considered by some critics to be a landmark collection for its deemphasizing of the political motifs that had characterized her earlier work about the Vietnam War. It initiated, writes Albert Gelpi, a "fresh but organic development" in her poetry. Her later collections after *Life in the Forest* displayed, he writes, "the transcendent third term that bridges the rupture between individual epiphany and public calamity" (see *Denise Levertov: Selected Criticism,* 1993). The collection was well received; Harry Marten wrote that the poems were "exquisitely crafted lyrics" that "in their reverence for language and life" continuously bring the reader into "the full province of poetry" (*New England Review and Bread Loaf Quarterly* 2 [Autumn 1979]). Bonnie Costello read the collection as creating new myths but pointed to a certain irreconcilability in the poetry, writing that Levertov's "private and public selves have never really agreed. And while she judiciously measures out her attentions to these quarrelsome, demanding siblings, we still feel that her most natural affection is for the elder, private self, relations with the other always seeming a bit strained, a but superficial" (*Parnassus* 8, no. 1 [1979–80]).

Inspired by Cesare Pavese's poems of the 1930s, narrative poems about persons "other than himself," Levertov writes in her introductory note to *Life in the Forest* that she was impelled by two forces:

> first, a recurring need—dealt with earlier by resort to a diary-like form, a poem long enough to include prose passages and discrete lyrics—to vary a habitual lyric mode, not to

abandon it, by any means, but from time to time to explore more expansive means, and, second, the decision to try to avoid overuse of the autobiographical, the dominant first person of so much of the American poetry—good and bad—of recent years.

"A Woman Alone" appears in the first section of the volume, titled "Homage to Pavese," the last few poems of which deal with Levertov's mother's death in Mexico. The first half of the poem makes skillful use of enjambment, contributing to the breathless motion that sometimes interrupts the stanzas that informally constitute the backbone of the poem; in the second half, the now end-stopped lines begin to crawl across the page, fortifying the narrative's new sense of equanimity and resolution. The rhetorical trajectory of the poem is driven by the temporal cues "when . . . when . . . then . . . now" to describe the experience of, and reflection on, solitude.

"A Woman Alone" represents a woman freed from the ties of domestic partnership (Levertov herself had divorced Mitchell Goodman in 1974). The moment commemorated by the poem is that moment "past the time of mourning," when lovers blur together in memory, evenings with friends last for hours, and the empty side of the bed has been reclaimed by books. The woman in the poem has fears not about loneliness but about the aging of her body because she "feels so much younger and more beautiful than she looks." She imagines herself, finally, with a "sober euphoria," as an "old woman, a wanderer, seamed and brown," and ends the poem with a benediction: "now she can say without shame or deceit, / O blessed Solitude."

If Levertov's poetry is marked, as critics such as Sandra Gilbert have argued, by doubleness, a split self, an irreconcilability between domestic self and artist self or public self and private self, then this poem marks a new fusion, a new reconciliation of the female poet's split selves. Here, the domestic realm is redefined, made over into a woman's private, artistic domain: "When half her bed is covered with books / and no one is kept awake by the reading light / and she disconnects the phone, to sleep till noon . . . / Then / selfpity dries up, a joy / untainted by guilt lifts her." The poem moves easily from this reinscribed domestic space to a limitless global landscape in which she figures imaginatively as a prophetic wanderer: "little luxuries of the middle of life all gone, / watching cities and rivers, people and mountains, / without being watched; not grim or sad, / an old winedrinking woman, who knows / the old roads, grass-grown, and laughs to herself . . . / She knows it can't be: / that's Mrs. Doasyouwouldbedoneby from / *The Water Babies*." Charles Kingsley's didactic book for children is here reread as modeling female self-sufficiency, which the poet cannot attain but means to approximate: "no one can walk the world any more, / a world of fumes and decibels. / But she thinks maybe / she could get to be tough and wise, some way, / anyway."

Critic Linda Kinnahan (1994) notes Levertov's need to occupy seemingly contradictory roles or positions, which Kinnahan traces to Levertov's early preoccupation with issues of gender and her simultaneous indebtedness to certain male mentors (e.g., Charles Olson, Robert Duncan, and Robert Creeley). Levertov's multiple and complicated subject positions—wife, mother, immigrant, and Jew, to name a few—may provide one helpful frame for reading the poem, in that the poem seems less to enact these multiple identities than to escape them altogether, arguing self-sufficiency as well as a kind of self-effacing "watching . . . without being watched." Deborah Pope (1991) reads "A Woman Alone" as a "validation poem that points to new myths." Throughout the poem, the province of the domestic and familial and that of the poet/seer blur and overlap; the split selves that Pope defines in Levertov's poetry as the passive, immobile domestic gender role (that Levertov characteristically reinforces with images of sleeping) and the independent, mobile artist are here redefined and intertwined and made over into an integral whole.

Rachel Rubinstein

**Further Reading**

Gilbert, Sandra, "Revolutionary Love: Denise Levertov and the Poetics of Politics," *Parnassus* 12–13 (1985)

Kinnahan, Linda A., *Poetics of the Feminine: Authority and Literary Tradition in William Carlos Williams, Mina Loy, Denise Levertov, and Kathleen Fraser,* Cambridge and New York: Cambridge University Press, 1994

Marten, Harry, "Review of *Life in the Forest,*" reprinted in *Denise Levertov: Selected Criticism,* edited by Albert Gelpi, Ann Arbor: University of Michigan Press, 1993

Pope, Deborah, "Homespun and Crazy Feathers: The Split Self in the Poems of Denise Levertov," in *Critical Essays on Denise Levertov,* edited by Linda Wagner-Martin, Boston: G.K. Hall, 1991

*Twentieth Century Literature* 38, no. 3 (Fall 1992) (special issue on Levertov edited by Ronald R. Jansen)

---

# Philip Levine 1928–

A self-professed son of Walt Whitman and William Carlos Williams, Philip Levine has written of struggle, failure, and the lost, recording the stories and voices of America's underdogs in plain American language through more than 18 volumes, including *What Work Is* (1991), winner of the National Book Award, and the Pulitzer Prize recipient *The Simple Truth* (1994). Like Robert Frost, Levine did not publish a book until his mid-30s, but whether or not, as he has said, he developed slowly, his has been a long and rich poetic career. His consistently excellent extension of the populist line of American poetry that also includes Edgar Lee Masters and Carl Sandburg has made Levine a major figure in American poetry.

In his earliest work, Levine moves from imaging struggle—as in the skinless animal of "The Horse"—to voicing it—as in

"Animals Are Passing from Our Lives," a widely-anthologized poem in which a pig accepts its own butchery, and the long poem "Silent in America." Here Levine signals his debt to Whitman in his language and his method, in the epigraph from "Song of Myself"—"Vivas for those who have failed"—and in his witness to the power of human connection. A single human touch leads the speaker to pray, "Let me have / the courage to live / as fictions live, proud, careless, / unwilling to die." For Levine, as for Whitman, poetry is a tool for remaking the life and the world, for voicing the silent in their trials.

To record difficulty is to voice not only individual but collective struggle as well, as Levine does in "They Feed They Lion," the title poem of his fifth book (1972). The poem, which Edward Hirsch has called Levine's "hymn to communal rage" and which Levine himself has described as "a celebration of anger," replays linguistically the social violence marked by the 1967 Detroit riot, rendering "lying"—the hypocritical social order against which the riot turned—in black vernacular as "lion" and so charting the production of ferocity from disenfranchisement, showing how "From 'Bow Down' Come 'Rise Up.'" The incantatory rhythms again indicate Whitman's influence as well as the importance that Ginsberg's Whitmanian work had for Levine. *They Feed They Lion* is widely regarded as the book that brought Levine to national attention, important not only for the title poem but also for its extended attention to the city, particularly Detroit, a mainstay of his work.

Compared to earlier volumes, the scope of *1933* (1974) is narrower; its focus on personal loss is particularly palpable in the sequential "Letters for the Dead" and the title poem, an elegy for his father. In his next collection, *The Names of the Lost* (1976), Levine again widens his attention, and the commemorative energies that result make the volume one of his most important. Here, Levine memorably visits the immigrant so central to his work in the narrative mode, as in "On the Birth of Good & Evil During the Long Winter of '28." In this poem, the reader is called to witness "The Hungarian punch-press operator," one of Levine's silent characters. "If he saw / the winter birds scuffing in the cinders, / if he felt this was the dawn of a new day, / he didn't let on." He perseveres into understanding and forgiveness; he releases the resentment for his mother-in-law that he has concentrated in the cap she made him, the thing that, according to Williams' dictum, contains the idea.

*The Names of the Lost* is continually concerned with workers who feel "the cold anger / of machines that have to eat" and those whom "No One Remembers." Levine stops at a graveyard to "walk among none / of my own, to say / something useless / for them." Levine becomes memory, his most constant role, filled again in "New Season" and "Autumn Again," recursive meditations that firm the ground of Levine's mature style. Meanwhile, his interests grow into an engagement with dissident anarchists, remembered in "For the Poets of Chile," "Gift for a Believer," and "On the Murder of Lieutenant José Del Castillo by the Falangist Bravo Martinez, July 12, 1936." The volume itself is dedicated to Buenaventura Durruti, the Spanish anarchist who declared, "We [the workers] carry a new world, here in our hearts. That world is growing this very moment." Levine echoes the sentiment, noting "the world he said is growing here in my heart this moment." This is the faith from which Levine writes "To My God in His Sickness," from which he fashions a religion of "shout[ing] out the holy names / of the lost."

In the following volumes, this religion grows into a sense of a world beautiful in its birth of both loss and gain. In "The Miracle," from *Ashes* (1979), a vision of a dead man travels from his brother to his wife to his son, who, filled with the vision, "looks out on the world he always sees / and thinks, it's a miracle." Here—as in many poems, including "I Could Believe," "Francisco, I'll Bring You Carnations," "Let Me Begin Again," "Belief," "One for the Rose," and "Sweet Will"—the countenancing of loss makes possible and fulfilling an embrace of the actual, an idea that Levine shares with Whitman, Williams, and Hart Crane.

The work of this period, from *The Names of the Lost* through *One for the Rose* (1981), solidified Levine's growing reputation, so much so that Levine was able to bring out, in 1981, *Don't Ask*, a collection of interviews from the 1970s. Levine's anecdotes about the creation of particular works, his explanations of his political principles, and his statements of poetics illuminate both subsequent as well as preceding volumes and make such significant contributions to the study of his work that *Don't Ask* has remained in print for 20 years.

In the latest collections, the commemorative mode reaches a new maturity. Whether Levine writes of immigrants, including his parents; jazz figures such as Sonny Rollins or Coleman Hawkins; Spanish and South American poets, particularly Vallejo; or laborers, including himself, his commitment to remember sanctifies his subjects. In "The Mercy," Levine remembers the ship that brought his mother to America and finds in its story and hers an index of the promise of American life:

> She learns that mercy is something you can eat
> again and again while the juice spills over
> your chin, you can wipe it away with the back
> of your hands and you can never get enough.

In "Smoke," Levine remembers a similar moment of arrival, of waiting for a bus in the smoky air of industrial Detroit, in which he says that he "understood the moon / for the very first time." The journey and the struggle, whether of the immigrant or of the immigrant's child, are acts of discovery and recovery, the motions of achievement.

While Levine has preserved such moments by giving voice or simply by remembering, he has also taken care not to erase the reality of his subjects with commemoration. In "Salt and Oil," "Three young men . . . / on their way home or to a bar" continue to "fade" as in a photograph, but Levine repeatedly insists, "This is not / a photograph, it is a moment / in the daily life of the world." He concludes,

> There is no
> photograph, no mystery,
> only Salt and Oil
> in the daily round of the world,
> three young men in dirty work clothes
> on their way under a halo
> of torn clouds and famished city birds.

Levine removes the men from a history and from the photograph so that they can live in the moment of the halo, in the dignity of their living.

Many of Levine's poems subvert convention and expectation to bestow the poem on the reader or relinquish it to the subject. In

"What Work Is," Levine addresses his readers, only to reject them again—"Forget you. This is about waiting"—and in the end to remove us from any illusion that we can master the poem's subject: "You've never / done something so simple, so obvious, / . . . because you don't know what work is." Such denials attempt to protect the inspiring reality from poetic distortion. In other cases, Levine means to give his readers a space for themselves. The announcement of "A Poem with No Ending" destroys any need to get to the end and so invites readers to linger in Levine's meditative openings. In others, Levine's refusal to complete traditional circuits shows us the subject more clearly. When, in "Making It New," highway workers realize that they will not be able to renew the curb, we find the speaker in a place without transcendence or its promise, where he appreciates his co-worker and the dignity of the moment and where we can see him simply, clearly, himself; thus, Levine rewrites Pound's directive, embracing failure to renew the energies of poetry. In still other instances, Levine's transgressions of the fictive contract argue his honesty and empower readers by opening poetic machinery to them, as in "Magpiety," where a second-person address that acts directly on the reader's imagination is revoked in a gesture that promotes even greater parity between poet and reader by confirming what is suspected:

Out of a sense of modesty
  or to avoid the truth
I've been writing in the second
  person, but in truth
it was I, not you . . .

We see similar operations in "On the Meeting of Garcia Lorca and Hart Crane" and "The Search for Lorca's Shadow," poems dedicated to avoiding any amplification of the named subjects. These poems instead celebrate the human power that makes poems. As such, they participate in the demythologizing begun in "On the Edge," an early poem whose speaker identifies himself as "Edgar Poe" "born / In 1928 in Michigan," and continued memorably in "A Walk with Tom Jefferson," whose title character is not the president but an African-American man hanging on to his life in a dead section of Detroit. In all these poems, Levine empowers his readers by granting them access to the poem, being honest about his work, and opening our cultural mythologies to revision and reliving.

Like Adrienne Rich, Levine is often identified as a major voice in Jewish-American writing, one who, like Rich, has fashioned a poetry of witness and social conscience, an attempt to be not "part of the problem" but part of the solution instead, extending voice to the voiceless and so extending Whitman's project. With Rich and Galway Kinnell, he has written a poetry of vista, following Whitman, Williams, and Crane. Like Frost, his favorite mode has been the dramatic monologue. Although he has not done so in a single poem, as Keats or Whitman did, Levine has expanded the reach of elegy and shaped an American mode that amplifies without embellishment, an application of the ontological poetry of Williams, George Oppen, and H.D. Perhaps Levine remains important because he weaves together so many of the major strands of American poetry, perhaps because he consciously cultivates his relationship with his readers, or perhaps because he writes poems that gain praise again and again.

Perhaps Levine remains important because he has given us something, because he has been consistent in honoring the beliefs and commitments he set down in his preface to *Don't Ask,* where he described his faith as well as anyone has: "I don't believe in victory in my lifetime. I'm not sure I believe in victory at all, but I do believe in the struggle and preserving the names and natures of those who fought, for their sakes, for my sake, and for those who come after."

JAKE ADAM YORK

**Biography**

Born in Detroit, Michigan, 10 January 1928. Attended Wayne State University, Detroit, B.A. 1950, M.A. 1955; University of Iowa, Iowa City, M.F.A. 1957; Stanford University, California (fellowship in poetry, 1957); Instructor, University of Iowa, 1955–57; since 1958 faculty member, and since 1969 Professor of English, California State University, Fresno; Elliston Professor of Poetry, University of Cincinnati, 1976; poet-in-residence, National University of Australia, Canberra, summer 1978; Visiting Professor, Princeton University, New Jersey, 1978, Columbia University, New York, 1978, 1981, 1984, University of California, Berkeley, 1980, and Brown University, Providence, Rhode Island, 1984; taught fall semesters at Tufts University, Medford, Massachusetts, 1981–88; Adjunct Professor, New York University, 1984; University Professor, Brown University, 1985. Received San Francisco Foundation Joseph Henry Jackson Award, 1961; Chapelbrook Award, 1968; National Endowment for the Arts grant, 1969, 1970 (refused), 1976, 1982; Frank O'Hara Prize, 1972, and Harriet Monroe Memorial Prize, 1976 (*Poetry,* Chicago); American Academy grant, 1973; Guggenheim fellowship, 1973, 1980 (twice); Lenore Marshall Poetry Prize (*The Nation*), 1977; National Book Critics Circle Award, 1980; American Book Award, 1980; New England Poetry Society Golden Rose, 1987; Ruth Lilly Award, 1987; B.A.B.R. Award, 1989; National Book Award, 1991; Pulitzer Prize, 1995; Chancellor, Academy of American Poets, 2000. Living in Fresno, California, and New York City.

**Poetry**

*On the Edge,* 1963
*Not This Pig,* 1968
*Red Dust,* 1971
*They Feed They Lion,* 1972
*1933,* 1974
*New Season,* 1975
*On the Edge and Over: Poems Old, Lost, and New,* 1976
*The Names of the Lost,* 1976
*7 Years from Somewhere,* 1979
*Ashes: Poems New and Old,* 1979
*One for the Rose,* 1981
*Selected Poems,* 1984
*Sweet Will,* 1985
*A Walk with Tom Jefferson,* 1988
*New Selected Poems,* 1991
*What Work Is,* 1991
*The Simple Truth,* 1994
*Unselected Poems,* 1997
*The Mercy,* 1998
*They Feed They Lion; and, The Names of the Lost,* 1999

**Other Writings:** essays (*The Bread of Time: Toward an Autobiography,* 1994), interviews (*Don't Ask,* 1981), translations of Spanish poetry (*Off the Map: Selected Poems of Gloria Fuentes* [with Ada Long], 1984); edited collections of poetry (*The Essential Keats,* 1987).

**Further Reading**

Atlantic Unbound Website Poetry Pages: Interview with Philip Levine by Wen Stephenson (*www.theatlantic.com/unbound/poetry/levine.htm*)

Barron, Jonathan N., "New Jerusalems: Contemporary Jewish American Poets and the Puritan Tradition," in *The Calvinist Roots of the Modern Era,* edited by Aliki Barnstone, Michael Tomasek Manson, and Carol J. Singley, Hanover, New Hampshire: University Press of New England, 1997

Buckley, Christopher, editor, *On the Poetry of Philip Levine: Stranger to Nothing,* Ann Arbor: University of Michigan Press, 1991

Chess, Richard, "In the Tradition of American Jewish Poetry: Philip Levine's Turning," *Studies in American Jewish Literature* 9, no. 2 (Fall 1990)

Levine, Philip, *Don't Ask,* Ann Arbor: University of Michigan Press, 1981

Pacernick, Gary, "Staying Power: A Lifetime in Poetry," *Kenyon Review* 21, no. 2 (Spring 1999)

Suarez, Ernest, "Philip Levine," *Five Points* 3, no. 2 (Winter 1999)

## On the Murder of Lieutenant José Del Castillo by the Falangist Bravo Martinez, July 12, 1936

Philip Levine's elegy "On the Murder of Lieutenant José Del Castillo by the Falangist Bravo Martinez, July 12, 1936" first appeared in *The Names of the Lost* (1976), a collection of biographical, historical, and political poems dedicated to Buenaventura Durruti (1896–1936), anarchist of the Spanish Revolution allegedly slain by a soldier of his own brigade. Two other elegies in this volume, "Gift for a Believer" and "For the Fallen," commemorate both Durruti and his comrade Francisco Ascaso. In his preface to *Don't Ask* (1981), Levine describes himself as "an intensely political person, but a man without a party, who—if things keep going as they are—may soon be a man without a country." Indeed, in these three texts, his concerns extend far beyond party lines and the rhetoric of political allegory to celebrate and lament the exuberant folly of human agency.

In these pieces, Levine merges his political philosophy with childhood experiences shaped by historical events, as he also reflects in *Don't Ask:* "I was a boy during the Spanish Civil War. It was the most meaningful war I can remember. Many people from my neighborhood, in Detroit, went off to fight for a free Spain, and most of them who went didn't come home." Levine's elegy for José Del Castillo is the most historically situated of these three poems and works within and against the conditions of fact, rumor and poetic imagination. The text moves from a descriptive account of Castillo's death (lines 1–23) through a transitional, sympathetic representation of imagined eyewitness reactions to the shooting (lines 23–29) and concludes with a bracing, philosophical judgment tempered equally by redemptive prayer and apocalyptic vision (lines 29–37). This three-part structure follows one of the oldest and most resilient generic conventions for the poetic elegy: a rhetorical progression from lament to praise to consolation. Levine's poem thereby participates in a long-standing tradition of poetic works—including, in the American 20th-century canon, Auden's "In Memory of W.B. Yeats" and Sexton's "All My Pretty Ones"—that accommodate the *ubi sunt* motif to a bittersweet solace underscored by qualification of and resistance to spiritual consolation.

Lieutenant Castillo, an officer of the Republican Guardia de Asalto, was targeted by Falangists—a fascist group opposed to Republicans—because he had allegedly been an instructor of the socialist militias. Bravo Martinez claimed responsibility for the execution, which took place at 9:00 P.M. in a park in Madrid. Levine's elegy opens with a direct account of that tragic scene, which the poet imaginatively sets in Barcelona on a busy boulevard, the Ramblas:

When the Lieutenant of the Guardia de Asalto
heard the automatic go off, he turned
and took the second shot just above
the sternum, the third tore away
the right shoulder of his uniform,
the fourth perforated his cheek. As he
slid out of his comrade's hold
toward the gray cement of the Ramblas
he lost count and knew only
that he would not die and that the blue sky
smudged with clouds was not heaven
for heaven was nowhere and in his eyes
slowly filling with their own light.
The pigeons that spotted the cold floor
of Barcelona rose as he sank below
the waves of silence crashing
on the far shores of his legs, growing
faint and watery. His hands opened
a last time to receive the benedictions
of automobile exhaust and rain
and the rain of soot. His mouth,
that would never again say "I am afraid,"
closed on nothing.

The day after Castillo's murder, his companions executed Calvo Sotelo, a monarchist-fascist and one of the organizers of the fascist revolt. Many historians posit the reciprocal killings of Castillo and Sotelo as major turning points in the revolution during the final days before the outbreak of the Civil War on 17 July in Morocco and on 18 July in Spain.

The parks in Madrid, by day, were vibrant places during these turbulent times. By night, however, they were deserted spaces permeated by fear and silence. Levine's elegy offers testimony for what otherwise would have been an event without witnesses (other than the Falangists and Castillo's comrades). Following the poem's first section, Levine introduces a cluster of characters imagined to be present at the time of the shooting:

The old grandfather
hawking daisies at his stand pressed

a handkerchief against his lips
and turned his eyes away before they held
the eyes of a gunman. The shepherd dogs
on sale howled in their cages
and turned in circles.

Here the grandfather and shepherd dogs constitute this work's procession of mourners, thus fulfilling another key generic component of the poetic elegy. These figures not only express their grief for the loss, but more importantly also signify the sympathy of the natural world for Lieutenant Castillo: the grandfather's daisies invoke the traditional gift of cut flowers for the departed soul; the dogs' captive howling and turning articulates the rupture in the animal kingdom that replies to this rending of the human fabric.

In the work's final passage, Levine offers a prayer for Castillo, substituting the voice of the poem's speaker for that of a fallen kindred spirit, one who, like Castillo, has made the ultimate sacrifice in defense of democratic ideals that, as the following lines suggest, originate in the natural world:

There is more
to be said, but by someone who has suffered
and died for his sister the earth
and his brothers the beasts and the trees.
The Lieutenant can hear it, the prayer
that comes on the voices of water, today
or yesterday, from Chicago or Valladolid,
and hangs like smoke above this street
he won't walk as a man ever again.

Water imagery serves as a powerful vehicle of regeneration and resistance in all three of Levine's elegies from *The Names of the Lost* for these heroes of the Spanish Revolution and Civil War. His meditation on Lieutenant Castillo's murder thus concludes with a strongly qualified consolation, as the poem's redemptive "voices of water" transform into mute smoke above the poet's imagined avenue.

W. Scott Howard

**Further Reading**


Barron, Jonathan N., "New Jerusalems: Contemporary Jewish American Poets and the Puritan Tradition," in *The Calvinist Roots of the Modern Era,* edited by Aliki Barnstone, Michael Tomasek Manson, and Carol J. Singley, Hanover, New Hampshire: University Press of New England, 1997

Broughton, Irv, "Philip Levine," in *The Writer's Mind: Interviews with American Authors,* volume 2, edited by Broughton, Fayetteville: University of Arkansas Press, 1990

Buckley, Christopher, editor, *On the Poetry of Philip Levine: Stranger to Nothing,* Ann Arbor: University of Michigan Press, 1991

Chess, Richard, "In the Tradition of American Jewish Poetry: Philip Levine's Turning," *Studies in American Jewish Literature* 9, no. 2 (Fall 1990)

Hirsch, Edward, "The Visionary Poetics of Philip Levine and Charles Wright," in *The Columbia History of American Poetry,* edited by Jay Parini, New York: Columbia University Press, 1994

Jackson, Richard, "The Long Embrace: Philip Levine's Longer Poems," *Kenyon Review* 11, no. 4 (1989)

Jacobsen, Sally A., "Philip Levine on Teaching Poetry: An Interview," in *Poets' Perspectives: Reading, Writing, and Teaching Poetry,* edited by Charles R. Duke, Portsmouth, New Hampshire: Boynton/Cook, 1992

Marchant, Fred, "Cipriano Mera and the Lion: A Reading of Philip Levine," *Imagine* 1, no. 2 (1984)

Molesworth, Charles, "The Burned Essential Oil: The Poetry of Philip Levine," *The Hollins Critic* 12, no. 5 (1975)

Stein, Kevin, "Why 'Nothing Is Past': Philip Levine's 'Conversation' with History," *Boulevard* 9, nos. 1–2 (1994)


---

# Light Verse

Although most readers of poetry would claim the ability to distinguish light verse from more serious poetry, the characteristics most often attributed to this genre may easily be applied to poetry in general. Its primary function is to divert the reader, to entertain, and to please. It appears effortless; the strain of its making is invisible to the audience. It can be used to illuminate, to reveal hypocrisy, or to comment on political or social ills. In the 20th century, Modernist experimentalism and the fascination with novelty might have made it even harder to categorize the gravity of a poet's intentions. Yet light verse has flourished in the 20th century, stretching to encompass a range of topics and styles as wide as the imaginations of the best poets of the time. Blurring distinctions even further is the fact that many great examples of 20th-century light verse came from the major figures of the period rather than from artists who could be identified as comic. Robert Frost, Wallace Stevens, Marianne Moore, Ezra Pound, and even T.S. Eliot have all had moments of playfulness. The term, although viewed by many as dismissive or derogatory, merely indicates the sense of play, an admission of sentiment or humor, even when the poem itself may address weighty topics.

The subject of linear time concerned 20th-century poets especially, and this issue comes up most interestingly in light verse, where attitudes divide sharply down the middle. On one side, the poets of nostalgia demonstrate a reverence for "the good old days" when life was sweet. Appearing primarily in newspapers and periodicals, these poets practiced dialect writing, invoked familiar stereotypes, and relied on the middle-class desire for stability in their audiences. Anecdotes, reminiscences, occasional verse, regional encomiums, and political and social satires rendered often in regular tetrameter quatrains continued the tradition of sentimental and humorous verse from the 19th century and from earlier folk tradition. Signs of this territory include subjects such as the sanctity of the home and hearth, the battle of the sexes, the naive wisdom of children, and the elevation of rural over urban lifestyles. Light in style but not in purpose, these poets provided comfort to those who felt trapped in a world where change was speeding ahead as never before, not only in the world of art but in technology, politics, and social behavior as well. After reading of the nation's woes in the evening paper, families looked forward to the comfort of a pleasing verse, often clipping their favorites for personal anthologies.

Edgar Guest is one of the best remembered of this type of poet. His poems, such as "Home," celebrated the rustic; poems about familial love and care, such as "Lemon Pie," used everyday images to minimize the threat of the outside world, the "little troubles" that could be forgotten in the glow of small, personal joys. His verse provides a direct link to the sentimental tradition of the previous century, as does the work of Ella Wheeler Wilcox, herself a turn-of-the-century artist in whose footsteps continued an array of female poets of friendship, love, and home. One such poet, Elizabeth Whittemore, published "My Friends Are Little Lamps to Me" in *Harper's*. Other magazines publishing such verse included *The Saturday Evening Post* and even *The New Yorker*, whose earlier editorial taste often included clever and picturesque light verse by writers such as E.B. White, with the seasonal reflection "The Lady Is Cold: Intimations at Fifty-Eighth Street." Even in the title, White's use of tradition juxtaposed with contemporary idiom can be seen. This technique characterizes 20th-century light verse, both comic and sentimental. Arthur Guiterman's "On the Vanity of Earthly Greatness," also originally printed in *The New Yorker*, shows him, like E.B. White, to be a practitioner of old-style *vers de societé*, beginning with a title sounding as though it were carved in marble and ending with the colloquial "and I don't feel so well myself."

Embracing the change of the early century was another breed of writers who targeted with humor the very standards upheld by backward-gazing poets. Their nostalgia, when there was any at all, was ironic. The "good old days" for them were not so good after all; the future symbolized the potential for something better. As a result, these poets broke away from traditional forms, utilizing the freedom that Modernism offered. When they used a traditional form, it was often for satiric purposes. Satire was often their weapon of choice as they subverted the old in the process of creating something new. They celebrated difference, novelty, freshness, the authentic over the quaint, and revelation over tradition. However, like the traditionalists, their verses served a higher purpose, only instead of comforting their audience they sought to incite in readers a desire for change.

This is not to say that these poets read easily as altruistic in purpose—in fact, some of the best-loved writers of the period earned admiration through acerbic wit. For instance, Dorothy Parker and her associates do not appear to look toward a better future until one considers her cynicism as a reaction against the old status quo. The laugh in a Dorothy Parker poem is a rueful one, that of the intellectual standing apart from mundane society and commenting on its banality. Her isolation, her desire for renewal of images, as well as her awareness of the past can be seen in poems such as "One Perfect Rose," where she suggests that the symbol for devotion would be more useful if it were a limousine rather than a flower. Parker, as all intellectual humorists occasionally do, implies the slight possibility of improvement. This narrow hope distinguishes the curmudgeon, who is interesting and funny, from the misanthrope, who is neither.

Like Dorothy Parker, Ogden Nash derived his humor from subtle recasting of older styles and forms. Although known primarily as a poet of light verse, he would at times address much weightier issues in poems whose topics tended to be innocent and childlike, such as his animal series, or lighthearted and superficial, such as his social satires and character studies. Nash's command of style enabled him to use the standards of the past to his own comic ends. For instance, a poem such as "Adventures of Isabel" might seem to be an innocent poem aimed at a young audience with its subject matter, use of regular meter, anaphora, and rhyme. However, Nash's ability to break those rules—with lines running notably past their metrical end, made-up or mispronounced words, and elaborate feminine rhyme (ravenous/cavernous) and mosaic rhyme (rancor/drank her)—winks at the reader, the subject, and even the genre of poetry. Nash's wit sought its target—affectation of any kind—in poets as varied as Edgar Guest and Gertrude Stein.

Alongside the heavy-hitters of light verse, Parker and Nash, others flourished in the new style of sharp tongues and keen ears. Margaret Fishback shows a persona much like Parker's, the jaded sophisticate. In "In Extremis," she worries about a love affair in which the most terrible truth is not that her lover bores her but "that I bore myself as well / And that is nothing short of Hell." Samuel Hoffenstein addresses his beloved in a parody of the encomium; in "Your Little Hands," he lists her "little" endearing attributes—little hands, little eyes, little soul—only to end on her "little mind." Morris Bishop, in a kind of dialect poem, lampoons baby talk in "A Tonversation with Baby." All attack the very realms celebrated in sentimental verse: home, love, friendship, and stability.

Both Richard Armour and Phyllis McGinley continue the acerbic tradition of the urbane wits in some ways, yet both also have connections to the sentimental writers as well. In his 1947 book on how to write and sell light verse, Armour offers suggestions on creating effective poems "in the spirit of play." He recommends the use and abuse of rhyme, the effectiveness of everyday subject matter, and the necessity of hiding one's efforts. Illustrating the technique well is his own poem "Phoney Business," a hymn of annoyance to the relentlessly ringing telephone, which contains the rhyme of "habit" and "grab it." McGinley's poems on marriage and children find fault, as in "The Female of the Species Is Hardier Than the Male," the story of an ill-fated shopping trip. However, her humor is not as bitter as, for instance, that of Parker or Hoffenstein, and the poems tend to end harmoniously. Although this kind of clever, metrical, rhymed verse can date poorly, many of the poems retain their humor at least as period pieces, and the best stand up well over time. These techniques are still popular with humorists such as Judith Viorst, who writes of the woes of the modern woman in the tradition of McGinley, and Roy Blount, Jr., who blends regionalism, satire, and topical humor in regular verse, reminiscent of Nash and Armour.

As Modernism became the standard rather than the avant-garde, its flourishes became targets of satire as well. What Ogden Nash's persona of a good-natured, windy, secretly clever dandy was to 19th-century style, Don Marquis' archy the cockroach was to Modernism. With the first in the series in 1927, Marquis presented archy, a poet reincarnated in the body of a cockroach who typed out verses by flinging himself on the typewriter keys. The resulting poems thus lack capitalization or punctuation but are replete with the serious concerns of a meditative insect. His friend Mehitabel, Cleopatra reincarnated as an alley cat, is a flapper; through their exchanges, Marquis comments not only on certain aspects of modern poetry but also on current relations between men and women as well as their changing social roles. As had many previous practitioners of light verse, Marquis finds the animal realm to be an ideal setting for human dramas. His unique and modern application—cockroach as poet—provides the constantly humorous backdrop.

With Marquis, it is easy to see how a poet of light verse may at once embrace the benefits and satirize the foibles of a chosen style. When the boundaries of light verse break into the realm of the century's major poets, distinctions become harder to make. Some examples are easy to characterize: parodies such as Ezra Pound's "Ancient Music" or Kenneth Koch's "Mending Sump" certainly make humor a primary consideration. Poems about Pop culture often register as light verse, such as Marianne Moore's baseball poem "Hometown Piece for Messrs. Alston and Reese," which is also to be sung to the tune of "Hush Little Baby." Almost any verses to be "sung to the tune of" something or another fall into the light verse category. However, one of the primary functions of Modernism has been to admit to the level of "high art" every available subject matter. Thus, poets of fancy such as E.E. Cummings, regionalists such as Carl Sandburg, Beat poets, and New York School poets, with their references to fantasy, nostalgia, and Pop culture, could justify calling some of their works light verse.

Looking at a poem like Cummings' "anyone lived in a pretty how town," the reader might see in its rollicking meter and childlike voice the elements of light verse. For all its seeming effortlessness, the poem is a tour de force of the poet's auditory capabilities, yet so is Ogden Nash's "The Private Dining Room." When examining light verse of the 20th century, it is important to be inclusive rather than exclusive, realizing that the tool of comic observation belonged to all poets of the era and not only those who wrote primarily as humorists. Another Cummings work, "in just spring," illustrates a conscious affect of naïveté and wonder at the world that might formerly have been tolerated only in children's literature. This technique allowed the poet a voice free of associations, one with which he or she might speak in as modern and new a style as the subject he or she addressed—the contemporary world—while still celebrating the traditional rites of spring. The 20th century constantly reinvented itself, and poets were left to develop ways to keep their voices ahead of the times.

Later, poets such as Theodore Roethke and John Berryman, although they had academic backgrounds as poets, exhibited features of light verse quite regularly in their works. For both poets, humor is often an accent to grief, and the subject of their satire becomes their own damaged psyches. Roethke utilizes his senses of language and of rhythm in poems such as "Dolor," with its "inexorable sadness of pencils," and "I Knew a Woman," with its bouncing meter and lilting rhyme, to create a shambling but good-natured jokester persona who smiles through pain. Berryman's *Dream Songs* are light verse poems that went wrong, like a vaudeville character caught in the bad dream of an unhappy poet. The humor is there, but as a twisted grimace, mocking the darkness that is slowly overtaking Henry, the protagonist.

The poems of Kenneth Koch, Frank O'Hara, John Ashbery, and others of the New York School invite scrutiny as examples of light verse. The fancy of earlier poets such as Wallace Stevens may be seen in their work, along with as many Pop-culture references as a Cole Porter lyric. Poems such as O'Hara's "Poem (Lana Turner Has Collapsed!)" fits squarely into the category of humor, and yet there is a seriousness beyond the laugh. Kenneth Koch's parodies intend to be funny; his poem on the state of contemporary poetry, "Fresh Air," is one of the funniest poems of the century and begs to be performed aloud, two previous criteria in definitions of light verse. Perhaps *The Princeton Encyclopedia of Poetry and Poetics* is correct in theory: that the current definition of light verse has been expanded to the point of being relatively useless for purposes of designation. This state of inclusiveness, however, leaves the poets of the 20th century and those moving forward the freedom to be humorous, fanciful, sentimental, or otherwise without losing the chance to be important at the same time. An accountability, in fact, has been created—poets may no longer take themselves too seriously merely because they take on heavier subject matter, or they will be easily subjected to parody.

Contemporary light verse exemplifies many of the same reliable forms and techniques, yet often with an unusual twist. Regional verse, particularly southern, turns the old darkness of the Gothic into tabloid humor in poems such as Susan Ludvigson's "Man Arrested in Hacking Death Claims He Mistook Mother-in-Law for Raccoon." Jim Hall's "Maybe Dat's Your Pwoblem Too" marries a kind of dialect poem with a Pop-culture icon, Spiderman. The element of fancy in Stevens, Cummings, the New York School, and others can still be seen in the works of James Tate, both in comic narratives, such as "The Motorcyclists," and in romps, such as "The Wheelchair Butterfly," and in the poems of Matthew Rohrer in his book *A Hummock in the Malookas* (1995). Somewhere between old-fashioned reminiscences, Roethke's search for magic in the mundane, and Frank O'Hara's streams of conversation, there is Billy Collins, whose poems relay both wit and compassion.

The time-honored light verse forms of the limerick and double dactyl have enjoyed a resurgence in popularity, their strict measures a lure to many New Formalists. George Starbuck and William Cole are among the proficient with the difficult double dactyl; Starbuck has produced many other language-oriented humorous poems, while Cole has edited several volumes of light verse. John Ciardi, William Harmon, and Edward Gorey have all contributed to the long history of the limerick, although the bawdiest limericks all still seem to be authored by "anonymous." Ciardi has many Nash-like comic narratives, while Harmon edited the *Oxford Book of American Light Verse* and co-authored the 1984 parody *Uneeda Review,* a send-up of literary magazines. Gorey's books have a cult following and make him one of the best-known contemporary light verse masters, although he is often more known for the sinisterly funny illustrations accompanying his macabre rhymes.

Parody continues to be a vital part of comic verse; a great many of the poems in the *Oxford* anthologies of light verse are parodies. An entire volume, *The Brand-X Anthology of Poetry,* consists only of parody in a Norton-style reader. One recent parody, "Thirteen Ways of Being Looked at by a Possum," Everette Maddox's delightful homage to Wallace Stevens, demonstrates how the best parodies can pay tribute to the original, create a fresh, new work, and get a laugh all at the same time.

Concrete poems, particularly those post-1960s works with more affinity to graphic than to literary arts, have been called light verse, along with found poems, for which a stronger case can be made. Both forms are connected to the Dada and Surrealist movements, which did a great deal to make serious what had previously been deemed comic. Found poems are almost always funny, if only for the moment of recognition within a new context. In George Hitchcock's "Three Found Poems," for example, each part is assembled from a different how-to handbook, to great comic effect. Popular songs, greeting card verse, and even advertising jingles make up the measures of our everyday consciousness and are perhaps the truly light verse of our day. Fifty years ago it might have been shocking to include Cole Porter lyrics in an anthology of poetry, but now, "heaven knows, anything goes." Perhaps one day a new anthology of American light verse will include Bob Dylan's "Motorpsycho Nightmare," Johnny Cash's "Boy Named Sue," or even "My bologna has a first name / It's O-S-C-A-R . . ."

Nicole Sarrocco

**Further Reading**

Armour, Richard, *Writing Light Verse,* Boston: The Writer, 1947; revised edition, 1958; reprint, as *Writing Light Verse and Prose Humor,* 1971

Asimov, Isaac, and John Ciardi, *Limericks,* New York: Random House, 2000

Auden, W.H., editor, *Oxford Book of Light Verse,* Oxford: Clarendon Press, 1938

Cole, William, editor, *The Fireside Book of Humorous Poetry,* New York: Simon and Schuster, 1959; London: Hamish Hamilton, 1965

Cole, William, editor, *Pith and Vinegar: An Anthology of Short Humorous Poetry,* New York: Simon and Schuster, 1969

Grigson, Geoffrey, editor, *Unrespectable Verse,* London: Lane, 1971; as *The Penguin Book of Unrespectable Verse,* Harmondsworth, Middlesex: Penguin, 1971

Grigson, Geoffrey, editor, *Faber Book of Nonsense Verse,* London and Boston: Faber and Faber, 1980

Harmon, William, editor, *The Oxford Book of American Light Verse,* Oxford and New York: Oxford University Press, 1979

Harmon, William (under the pseudonym "J. Parkhurst Schimmelpfennig"), editor, *Uneeda Review: Like a Hole in the Head,* New York: Lyons Books, 1984

Zaranka, William, editor, *The Brand-X Anthology of Poetry,* Cambridge: Applewood Books, 1981

---

# Vachel Lindsay 1879–1931

Although Vachel Lindsay is not well known today, during the first quarter of the 20th century he was an immensely popular poet, part of the Midwestern "New Poetry" scene that included Carl Sandburg and Edgar Lee Masters. Lindsay's celebrity came largely as a result of his success on the platform; as he calculated in 1925, he had recited his poetry to more than one million Americans. Critics, however, did not always respond positively to what they saw as a trivial and raucous verse that pandered to the masses, sometimes slipping into arcane mysticism. Many missed the important cultural work Lindsay was attempting: to inculcate civic virtues and to re-enfranchise a segment of American society that felt poetry no longer spoke to them. Moreover, although Lindsay is deemed to be at variance with High Modernist canons, not least for his populism, his radical experimentalism is perfectly consistent with that of T.S. Eliot and Ezra Pound, even if history has not treated him as kindly.

Lindsay's early public poetry was written and sold (or given away) on tramps across the country in exchange for the basic necessities of life. In March 1906 he traveled by rail and foot from Florida to Kentucky, and in the spring of 1908 he walked from New York to Ohio. His privately printed *The Tramp's Excuse, and Other Poems* (1909), which features his pen and ink drawings, is based on those experiences and sings the joys of the open road:

> The road will be my bride
> The road will set me free:
> *Strangers with magic bread*
> *Will make a man of me.*

In a 1912 expedition from his hometown of Springfield, Illinois, to Los Angeles, California, he took with him his leaflet *Rhymes To Be Traded for Bread* (1912), which, like *The Tramp's Excuse,* helped secure his passage.

Lindsay's first professionally published book of verse was *General William Booth Enters into Heaven, and Other Poems* (1913). In his introduction he decried print culture, which—despite the inscriptional aesthetic that stamps his earlier books—he believed had severed artist from audience. "General William Booth Enters into Heaven," written in response to the death of the commander-in-chief of the Salvation Army, appeals to the ear, carrying the following headnote: "To be sung to the [Salvation Army] tune of 'The Blood of the Lamb' with indicated instrument." The poem created a craze in America and England, and Lindsay recited it frequently, growing so tired of it that in November 1913 he fumed, "I have recited the General till my jaws ache—4444 times. The silly things think it is the only good poem I ever wrote, simply because it *forces* attention" (*Letters of Vachel Lindsay,* 1979). This volume also contains "The Wedding of the Rose and the Lotus," commemorating the building of the Panama Canal, which Lindsay performed for Woodrow Wilson's cabinet in 1915, thus securing his reputation as a political poet. Explaining in his drawing accompanying the poem that the rose typifies "the genius of the West" and the lotus "the genius of the East," he celebrates that cultural interchange and the peace it promises:

> Flags of the Pacific
> And the Atlantic meet,
> Captain calls to captain,
> Fleet makes cheer with fleet.

Above the drownèd ages
A wind of wooing blows:—
The red rose woos the lotus,
The lotus woos the rose . . .

Lindsay's greatest success came the following year with the publication of *The Congo, and Other Poems* (1914). The first section, "Poems Intended To Be Read Aloud," includes ten chant poems that Lindsay dubbed "the Higher Vaudeville" for their refinement of a rollicking vaudeville aesthetic. The poems in this section come with marginal reading directions that indicate to readers how they should be vocalized. Like "General William Booth," "The Congo" became a staple in Lindsay's performances. No less a literary figure than William Butler Yeats responded enthusiastically when he heard him recite, observing that with Lindsay the "primitive singing of poetry" still survived (Massa, 1970). Although this return to the primitive is in keeping with Modernist poetics more generally, Lindsay's "plea for poetry as a song art, an art appealing to the ear rather than the eye" conflicts with Imagist credo. In 1914 Lindsay indicted the hierophants of Imagism as an "aesthetic aristocracy," "singing on an island to one another while the people perish" (Massa, 1970); conversely, Lindsay worked to democratize art, to reinsert poetry into the public sphere. *The Congo, and Other Poems* also contains several lyric tributes to silent movie stars, and Lindsay's fascination with the new art of cinema led him to write one of the first books on that subject, *The Art of the Moving Picture* (1915).

*The Chinese Nightingale, and Other Poems* (1917) extended Lindsay's reputation as a political poet, as it highlighted his ambivalence about U.S. involvement in World War I. At once sympathetic to Jane Addams' pacifist preachings as well as to President Wilson's decision to commit the country to a just war (despite his own 1916 anti-war platform), Lindsay finally registered for the draft in 1918. In addition to political poems inspired by the war effort and its opponents, the book includes a section of "Poem Games," poems to be chanted by one person while another interprets them in dance.

The publication of *The Golden Whales of California, and Other Rhymes in the American Language* (1920) came at the height of Lindsay's career. It includes "Bryan, Bryan, Bryan, Bryan," his paean to William Jennings Bryan's oratory and political populism, qualities that led Lindsay to declare him a great American "troubadour" (*Letters of Vachel Lindsay*). Lindsay's jazz poem "Daniel" also appears in the book and headlines *The Daniel Jazz, and Other Poems* (1920), which was issued in London to coincide with Lindsay's English recital tour. Although all the poems in *The Daniel Jazz* had been published previously, Lindsay objected to the title (given by the British publisher) since it accentuated his status as a jazz poet, a label that he increasingly disliked as he worried about becoming a fully commercialized poet-entertainer—a performing "freak" (*Letters of Vachel Lindsay*). In his 1924 poem "A Curse for the Saxophone," he makes his distaste for jazz plain, associating the title instrument with Cain, Judas, and John Wilkes Booth, and asserting, "None but an assassin would enjoy this horn. / Let us think of the Irish flute in the morn, / And the songs of Colum and the songs of Yeats, / And forget our jazzes and our razzes and our hates."

Lindsay's standing declined dramatically following his return from England in 1920. At the end of that year his prose work *The Golden Book of Springfield* was published, but no one seemed interested in his recipe for civic improvement. His *Collected Poems* came out in 1923, but by then Lindsay was no longer the celebrity he once had been. His life would end in suicide, his poetic reputation in tatters.

TYLER HOFFMAN

*See also* Midwestern Poetry Renaissance

**Biography**

Born in Springfield, Illinois, 10 November 1879. Attended Hiram College, Ohio, 1897–1900; studied for the ministry; studied art at Chicago Art Institute, 1901, and New York Art School, 1905; pen and ink designer, 1900–10; lecturer on art history, 1905–10; traveled through the United States reciting his poetry for a living, 1906–12; after 1912 was in demand as poetry lecturer and reader; teacher, Gulf Park College, Mississippi, 1923–24. Received Lifetime Achievement Award (*Poetry,* Chicago), 1929; honorary Litt.D., Hiram College, Ohio, 1930; member, American Academy. Died in Springfield, Illinois, 5 December 1931.

**Poetry**

*The Tramp's Excuse, and Other Poems,* 1909
*Rhymes To Be Traded for Bread,* 1912
*General William Booth Enters into Heaven, and Other Poems,* 1913
*The Congo, and Other Poems,* 1914
*The Chinese Nightingale, and Other Poems,* 1917
*The Golden Whales of California, and Other Rhymes in the American Language,* 1920
*The Daniel Jazz, and Other Poems,* 1920
*Going-to-the-Sun,* 1923
*Collected Poems,* 1923; revised edition, 1925
*Going-to-the-Stars,* 1926
*The Candle in the Cabin: A Weaving Together of Script and Singing,* 1926
*Johnny Appleseed, and Other Poems* (for children), 1928
*Every Soul Is a Circus,* 1929
*Selected Poems,* edited by Hazelton Spencer, 1931
*Selected Poems,* edited by Mark Harris, 1963
*The Poetry,* edited by Dennis Camp, 2 vols., 1984–85

**Other Writings:** essays (*The Litany of Washington Street,* 1929), film theory (*The Art of the Moving Picture,* 1915; revised edition, 1922), correspondence (*Letters of Vachel Lindsay,* edited by Marc Chénetier, 1979).

**Further Reading**

Chénetier, Marc, "'Free-Lance in the Soul-World': Toward a Reappraisal of Vachel Lindsay's Works," *Prospects: An Annual of American Cultural Studies* 2 (1976)
Gray, Paul H., "Performance and the Bardic Ambition of Vachel Lindsay," *Text and Performance Quarterly* 9 (1989)
Hummer, T.R., "Laughed Off: Canon, Kharakter, and the Dismissal of Vachel Lindsay," *Kenyon Review* 17, no. 2 (Spring 1995)
Lindsay, Vachel, *Letters of Vachel Lindsay,* edited by Marc Chénetier, New York: Franklin, 1979
Massa, Ann, *Vachel Lindsay: Fieldworker for the American Dream,* Bloomington: Indiana University Press, 1970

Rittenhouse, Jesse, "Vachel Lindsay," *South Atlantic Quarterly* 32 (July 1933)
Ruggles, Eleanor, *The West-Going Heart: A Life of Vachel Lindsay,* New York: Norton, 1959
Ward, John Chapman, "Vachel Lindsay Is 'Lying Low,'" *College Literature* 12 (1985)

## The Congo

Vachel Lindsay's "The Congo," first published in *The Congo, and Other Poems* (1914) under the section heading "Poems Intended To Be Read Aloud," was one of the most popular poems to be produced in America in the 20th century. It is also one of the first modern performance poems in a tradition that would grow to include much Beat, Black Arts movement, and late-20th-century spoken-word poetry. The reading directions that run down the right-hand margin of the printed version establish the poem as score. Frequently anthologized in the first half of the century and recited by Lindsay around the country, "The Congo" has been all but erased from cultural memory, in part because of its divergence from a High-Modernist poetics of difficulty. Subtitled "A Study of the Negro Race," it imagines in racist types and tones the cultures of Africa and black America despite the fact that Lindsay felt his poem to be a positive treatment of black culture and religion. The poem draws on the popular entertainment form of blackface minstrelsy, a staple of the vaudeville stage in Lindsay's day, and serves as an example of what Lindsay termed "the Higher Vaudeville"—that is, a ritualized public poetry that he believed refines the vulgar elements of popular culture into a legitimate art with the power to rebuild a sense of community in a rapidly expanding nation.

The first section of "The Congo," titled "Their Basic Savagery," depicts the riotous antics of "Negroes," what Lindsay considered their essential primitiveness. It begins with the following racialized image of masculinity in an African-American setting: "Fat black bucks in a wine-barrel room, / Barrel-house kings, with feet unstable, / Sagged and reeled and pounded on the table." This view leads to the speaker's "vision" of a performance in the heart of the Congo, and a marginal reading cue informs us that the first two lines are to be "solemnly chanted":

> THEN I SAW THE CONGO, CREEPING THROUGH THE BLACK,
> CUTTING THROUGH THE FOREST WITH A GOLDEN TRACK.
> Then along the riverbank
> A thousand miles
> Tattooed cannibals danced in files;
> Then I heard the boom of the blood-lust song
> And a thigh-bone beating on a tin-pan gong.

The syncopated chant of the African "witch-doctors" includes such nonsense sounds as "Boomlay, boomlay, boomlay, BOOM" and ends in the following refrain, a version of which closes each section of the poem:

> Be careful what you do,
> Or Mumbo-Jumbo, God of the Congo,
> And all of the other
> Gods of the Congo,
> Mumbo-Jumbo will hoo-doo you,
> Mumbo-Jumbo will hoo-doo you,
> Mumbo-Jumbo will hoo-doo you.

As Lindsay explains, "The ill fate and sinister power of Africa" (what he calls variously "hoodoo" and "voodoo") are compensated for by other essentialized black traits as set forth in the second and third sections of "The Congo."

The second section—"Their Irrepressible High Spirits"—moves from a scene of African-American crapshooters who "whoop" and "call" and dance the juba to a scene of a cakewalk, the dance regularly featured in the minstrel show, on the banks of the Congo:

> Just then from the doorway, as fat as shotes,
> Came the cake-walk princes in their long red coats,
> Canes with a brilliant lacquer shine,
> And tall silk hats that were red as wine.
> And they pranced with their butterfly partners there,
> Coal-black maidens with pearls in their hair,
> Knee-skirts trimmed with the jassamine sweet,
> And bells on their ankles and little black feet.

As these images indicate, Lindsay's poetry, like minstrelsy itself, commodified "blackness" and, in doing so, served up a racist counterfeit—one that audiences would pay to see in the belief that what they were seeing was an authentic display of Negroism. "The Congo," along with certain other Modernist poems, effectively constructs "whiteness" through such blackface displays.

Finally, in the third section of the poem, titled "The Hope of Their Religion," Lindsay represents "an idealized Camp-meeting transferred to the banks of the Congo, along with a prophecy of the redemption of the race through religious instinct, and the death of Mumbo-Jumbo" (Lindsay, 1979). Here the image of a black revivalist preacher gives way to a Congo "transfigured" from a land of voodoo worship to an outpost of Christendom, with "the twelve Apostles" hymning the death of heathen ritual and a company of angels hailing a "Redeemed" "negro nation."

Several prominent African-American artists and political activists lambasted "The Congo" for its unremitting racist rhetoric. To Joel E. Spingarn, chairman of the directors of the National Association for the Advancement of Colored People (NAACP), Lindsay expressed his dismay at the black backlash against his work: "My 'Congo' . . . [has] been denounced by the Colored people, for reasons that I cannot fathom. . . . The third section of the Congo is certainly as hopeful as any human being dare to be in regard to any race" (Lindsay, 1979). In his letter of reply to Lindsay, Spingarn laid out his objection: "You look forward to a colored Utopia separate and different from the hope of the white man; they [African-Americans] have only one overwhelming desire; and that is to share in a common civilization in which all distinctions of race are blurred (or forgotten) by common aspirations and common labors" (quoted in Massa, 1970). Lindsay already had heard the same criticism from W.E.B. DuBois, who was not very pleased by Lindsay's racial mimicry or his separatist vision of black culture (Lindsay, 1979).

Although Lindsay attested in 1915 that "The Congo" "never wears out," he would soon grow weary of the popular demand for it (Lindsay, 1979). In 1923, he lamented that "People howl for me to recite . . . the Congo till I am ready to vomit. And they threaten me if I refuse, till I am ready to swear myself crazy" (Lindsay, 1979). Audiences would not let him escape his signature piece, and Lindsay's success and his failure in the marketplace—both during his lifetime and after—are shaped by that fact.

Tyler Hoffman

**Further Reading**

DuPlessis, Rachel Blau, "'HOO, HOO, HOO': Some Episodes in the Construction of Modern Whiteness," *American Literature* 67 (1995)

Gray, Paul H., "Performance and the Bardic Ambition of Vachel Lindsay," *Text and Performance Quarterly* 9 (1989)

Gubar, Susan, *Racechanges: White Skin, Black Face in American Culture,* New York and Oxford: Oxford University Press, 1997

Hummer, T.R., "Laughed Off: Canon, Kharakter, and the Dismissal of Vachel Lindsay," *Kenyon Review* 17, no. 2 (Spring 1995)

Lindsay, Vachel, *Letters of Vachel Lindsay,* edited by Marc Chénetier, New York: Franklin, 1979

Massa, Ann, *Vachel Lindsay: Fieldworker for the American Dream,* Bloomington: Indiana University Press, 1970

Ruggles, Eleanor, *The West-Going Heart: A Life of Vachel Lindsay,* New York: Norton, 1959

---

## Literary Journals. *See* Little Magazines and Small Presses

---

## Literary Theory and Poetry

Unlike the history of music, which needs no apology, the history of poetry is also the history of its defenses, and thus the history of criticism and literary theory. But literary theory and poetry have been antagonists ever since Plato exiled the poets from his utopian republic. Poets lie, he declared, by merely imitating imitations of the truth. Poets corrupt the minds of the young with dangerously inflated emotions while philosophy deals in pure knowledge and pure concepts. But could Plato's pure concepts be conceived without poetic metaphors? Do philosophic concepts repress their own metaphoric origins, as Nietzsche claimed? These questions could also be turned around: Could poetry be recognized or read without assumptions about its genre or purpose or meaning? Is not a reading of literature always informed by certain philosophic concepts?

These mutual implications and repudiations resurface with renewed vigor in the second half of the 20th century. What caused this most recent encounter of poetry with philosophy, or with theory, can be traced back, according to one narrative, to French Symbolist poets of the 19th century. Baudelaire, Rimbaud, Verlaine, and particularly Mallarmé anticipated many 20th-century theoretical insights and determined the Modernists' preference for the intense lyrical fragment over the continuous narrative. The Modernist poem (along with the Romantic lyric and the Metaphysical poems of the 17th century) became in turn the privileged object of study by the New Criticism. A pragmatically pedagogic, rather than explicitly theoretical, approach to the reading of poetry, the New Criticism tacitly perpetuated the ideology of the poem as symbol, that is, the poem as organic, non-referential plenitude of meaning. Although the New Criticism sought tirelessly, and highly successfully, to analyze a poem's verbal polyphonies, ambiguities, tensions, wit, and irony, the New Critics rarely questioned the underlying assumptions that these principles would end up confirming the aesthetic value of the work of art as such: its completeness and perfection in an uncertain and imperfect world. The moralistic or ideological bent inherent in this approach to literature is indebted to the English critic F.R. Leavis and further back in the 19th century to the poet and critic Matthew Arnold. For both critics poetry filled a moral, even spiritual, vacuum left by the discredited authority of religion. Such quasi-spiritual or moral implications linger on in New Critical readings of poetry as verbal icons.

While the beginnings of literary theory are visible already in Plato's banishment of the poets from the state, various commentators propose possible dates for the reemergence of literary theory in the 20th century: the 1958 conference at Indiana University on linguistics and literary studies with Roman Jakobson as keynote speaker, or the Structuralist Controversy in 1966 at Johns Hopkins University where Jacques Derrida delivered his now famous essay "Structure, Sign, and Play in the Discourse of the Human Sciences." These and other seminal intellectual events, chiefly in the 1960s—all of them critically responding to the implicit moral and political conservatism of a Modernist poetics—arguably brought the hegemony of the New Criticism to an end. For the theorist *after* the New Criticism, the poem exists to testify to a number of linguistic, psychological, social, and political predicaments, becoming a self-conscious and intimate witness of its own language as problematically related to truth and reality; it becomes an open process rather than a well-wrought urn.

In spite of such developments the prevalent mainstream or neo-Romantic poetic style still relies on language as a transparent medium for experience, confession, or protest. This tradition has therefore been under attack from a theoretically informed avant-garde opposed to "everyday natural speech itself, with its rule-governed syntax, semantics and pragmatics" (Easthope and Thompson, 1991). The editor of the New Directions anthology of *"Language" Poetries* thus predicts:

> In truth, poetry "as we knew it"'—the poem that functions as a sort of narrative snapshot of experience, by the poet who sees himself or herself . . . as a worker who, separated from ideas (the abstract), creates a primary product (like a coal miner digging coal) which when brought to the surface represents "real" experience—perhaps these notions of poem and poet will not survive. (Messerli, 1987)

Self-consciously addressing the linguistic condition of identity and experience, postmodern poetry overlaps with literary theory not only because such a poetry exemplifies the *linguistic* interests of literary theory but also because language is here deemed primary to any form of psychological or social identity and political resistance. To that effect Marjorie Perloff, a chief apologist for this particular conjunction between literary theory and poetry, claims

> that postmodern "poetry" and "theory" . . . are part of the same larger discourse, that there is no hard and fast division between them, that, on the contrary, some of the most interesting poetry today theorizes its particular positions even as theory comes to us in increasingly "poetic" forms. (1983)

The phrase "the most interesting poetry" demarcates a division between the two poetic traditions mentioned above—the neo-Romantic and the postmodern—judging the first as theoretically naive and implicitly charging that its claims to authentic voice or "lived experience" would be unable to sustain critical analysis. Indeed, so imperious and wide-spread has been the institutionalizing of theory in the last decades of the 20th century that the "great divide between something called theory and something called poetry," according to Perloff (1993), "is only invoked by those nostalgic for a (mythical) past when poetry spoke to us from the heart." Poetry, authenticity, or emotion is here judged as philosophically untenable. Perloff's assertion of a theoretical position at the expense of poetry of emotion may recall Socrates' similar philosophic stance in relation to poetry. It is in such a context that in the second half of the 20th century "the tone of Anglo-American criticism changed" and began to sound "more inquisitive, even inquisitorial" (Edmundson, 1995). Under the powerful influence of such theorists as Roland Barthes, Jacques Derrida, Jacques Lacan, Paul de Man, and the "Yale deconstructivists," theory seemed again to assume the authority of Socratic philosophy under which literature was subjected to conceptual evaluation.

This may be a matter of perception, however. While reducing all things to text, deconstruction insists that the very concepts seeking to subordinate poetry to philosophy are themselves metaphors borrowed from poetry. A deconstructive understanding of method and terminology suggests in turn an analogy with the poet's own efforts to deconstruct cultural assumptions and categories. John Hollander links the very nature of poetry to such mutual implications: the poet's work, he writes, "if it is genuine poetry—will somehow deconstruct such notions as 'form,' 'content,' 'persona,' 'lyric voice,' etc." (Parker, 1985). The affect of literary theory on poetry or of poetry on theory might thus be seen as complementary or reciprocal rather than antagonistic.

This reciprocal relationship is advocated by the so-called Yale deconstructionists (chiefly de Man, Miller, Hartman), who posit that great works of art are great precisely to the extent that they "anticipate explicitly any deconstruction the critic can achieve" (Bradford, 1993). Rather than deconstructing a literary text, the deconstructive critic merely shows how a literary text has "always already" deconstructed itself, how it questions or undermines its own structure and meaning, and how its subversive linguistic self-consciousness may in turn define a literary text as literary. While such a text is not reducible to philosophic concept but retains a polyphonic or indeterminable signification, it is also opposed to romantic idealizations of literary language. Deconstructive readings, particularly of Romantic poetry, aim to demystify the concept of the aesthetic, insofar as that was associated with religious or metaphysical implications. What deconstruction attempts to prove is that (such) literature does not exist: that self, authenticity, originality, genius, inspiration, God and nature, and not least poetry, are all reducible to text, albeit a text that may be conscious of its own textuality.

The aesthetic thus no longer achieves the kind of spiritual wholeness and moral perfection advocated by the New Critics. Poetry, which had since Arnold fulfilled the function of a secular religion, fusing "great" literature with moral value and spiritual truth, is now revealed as being nothing more than a cultural fabrication or the ideology of a politically suspect morality. In this radical critique of authority and linguistic convention, poststructuralist theory echoes and articulates the philosophic and aesthetic revolution by which the radical Modernists—Pound, Stein, Williams—and their American successors, the Objectivists, the Beat poets, the Black Mountain poets, or the New York School, separated themselves from the legacy of Eliot and his conservative tradition. Charles Olson's influential manifesto "Projective Verse" (1950), for example, anticipates the poststructuralist concept of differential rather than referential meaning when he declares,

> The objects which occur at every given moment of composition . . . are, can be, must be treated exactly as they do occur therein and not by any ideas or preconceptions from outside the poem[.] (Allen, 1960)

The particular theoretical affiliations, whether implicit or explicit, of these poetic schools have in the last quarter of the 20th century reemerged in Language poetry, a poetry "characterized by extreme disruption of the linguistic surface often leading to accusations that it was unreadably non-referential writing" (Easthope and Thompson, 1991). Similar accusations have been leveled against poststructuralist theory; both Language poetry and poststructuralist theory aim to critique the notion of the transparency of language; both aim to critique and deconstruct the ideas and preconceptions (to use Olson's terms) used to structure and give meaning to the world.

When Jerome Rothenberg and Joris Pierre define postmodern poetry as a "turning away . . . from totalizing / authoritarian ideologies and individuals" (*Poems for the Millennium,* 1995) this amounts thus to a turning toward the interests of literary theory in the difficult, the heterogeneous, the open-ended, the politically subversive. This interest, however, does not seem mutual; literary theory has largely ignored serious analysis of postmodern poetry, although there seems to be an effort to redress this neglect. While literary theory, despite its often prevalently canonical tastes, has been said to have accomplished the revolution initiated in the Symbolists and Modernists—a revolution that had been stalled by the inherently conservative emphasis of New Critical pedagogy—Rothenberg's and Pierre's anthology intends to go beyond the revolutionary impulse of theory. In the introduction to the first volume of their encyclopedic two-volume edition of *Poems for the Millennium,* they claim not only poetry's anticipation of theoretical insight but also poetry's progressive vision beyond it:

> This rich array of explorations represents a much larger field of experiment and change than has been brought forward, say, in recent controversies about "the death of the author" or "non-referential writing" and similar textual/intertextual modes of conceiving writing and the world.

The poetic experimentation and change that is to be represented in the two volumes is overtly aimed beyond the "textual/intertextual" limitations of poststructuralism. Late 20th-century poetry is to be, in the words of Ed Sanders (quoted in *Poems for the Millennium*),

> "a form of historical writing . . . using every bardic skill and meter and method of the last 5 or 6 generations, in order to describe every aspect (no more secret governments!) of the historical present."

If the *textual* interest of poststructuralist theory has demystified the ideology of the aesthetic, the most recent *historical* focus of postmodern poetry demystifies the poststructuralist reduction of the world to text. From this historical or politicized vantage point, poststructuralism can be seen as nothing more than a *new* New Criticism, having merely replaced the well-wrought urn with an infinite labyrinth of text. But poststructuralism's emphasis on text has nevertheless opened formerly elitist concepts chiefly associated with Arnold and Eliot—Art, the Aesthetic, Literature, the Canon—to the scrutiny of historical and political analysis. Feminists, new historicists, and cultural theorists now study poetry not as an aesthetic object or a self-referential text but as a social or political document. They draw attention to the text's implicit participation in or resistance to particular historical situations. They address the poet's situation within a historically informed critique, inflected by concerns for gender, class, and race. As far as poetic practice is concerned, they now demand, particularly of poetry, a stripping of linguistic excess and flourish, a plainer speaking, a social and political responsibility that would have been anathema to New Critical principles. Thus June Jordan, for example, becomes a

> "people's poet," who wishes to speak not only *of* her own experience but also *for* her community and *to* readers who have the potential to act constructively in both a cultural and a political capacity. (Whitehead, 1996)

This enumeration of the levels of Jordan's poetics—which is significantly described as a dialogic speaking rather than a monologic writing—exemplifies an opening of the formerly closed text to subjective and communal significance, as well as an opening of the aesthetic to ethical concerns and to political action. The poetics of disinterest and distance, advocated by textually or aesthetically centered poets and theorists—Eliot, the New Critics, the poststructuralists—is here replaced by a poetics that becomes the mediator of communal transactions.

But the influence of poststructuralism may be said to extend even into these progressive historical developments. If some feminists have reclaimed terms such as "experience" or "voice" and if their claim were to amount to an appropriation of poetry by social and political necessities, a poststructuralist critique would insist that just as identities are socially and historically constructed, so is "experience," "voice," or "history." What political poetries and historical theories have thus inherited from poststructuralism is a deconstructive stance toward formerly unquestioned terms and hierarchical dichotomies such as man/woman, black/white, West/East, prose/poetry, high art/popular art, and so on. All experiences, whether poetic or political, participate wittingly or unwittingly in such allegedly oppressive binary structures of language and are thus to be theoretically interrogated.

But genuine poetry (to echo Hollander's remarks above) is perhaps genuine to the extent of deconstructing precisely the seemingly ultimate authority theory claims, whether on linguistic or historical grounds. The question of how theory is related to poetry thus arises not only in the postmodern avant-garde (the Language poets) whose concerns largely overlap with those of poststructuralism; it arises particularly in the poetry that speaks with "untheorized," perhaps "untheorizable," resonances. Terms such as "resonances" or "voice" may indicate a radical departure from the conceptual and visual orientations of theory, the etymological meaning of the word "theory" going back to the Greek *theoria,* to look upon, to contemplate. Poetic language, in other words, aims to go beyond the paradigms of theory and proposes a perception generically different from the cerebral detachment implied in theoretical *speculation.* It attempts, perhaps, a hearing rather than a seeing, an untheorizable intuition, or intimation; a venturing, in other words, beyond the rational processes of philosophical concept or historical argument. Thus Denise Levertov claims in her poem "Writer and Reader" that the hearing of poetry may convey

> . . . music
> beyond what I thought I could hear,
> a stirring, a leaping
> of new anguish, of new hope, a poem
> trembling with its own vital power.

In its rhythms, sounds, allusions, and resonances, as well as in its intricate formal properties, poetry affirms, like music or like the inflections of voice, a world beyond the differential linguistic medium as well as beyond the social constructions of reality. This argument recalls Julia Kristeva's distinction between a subconscious *semiotic* process within the controlled *symbolic* structure of language. As one of her commentators explains,

> Such texts could "explode" phonetically, lexically and syntactically the object of linguistics and, by implication, disrupt the

> cozy arrangements about linguistic reification which philosophers of language practise. (Easthope and Thompson, 1991)

If theory declares either the linguistic medium or the historical reality as absolute and all-encompassing, poetry might be defined as generically avant-garde, that is, outside or ahead of the political or philosophical system. But the quarrel here is not so much between poetry and theory as between two different forms of perception: a conceptual versus an experiential perception, objectification versus process. For theory to denigrate poetry or vice-versa is to forget that both poetry and theory endeavor "experiment and change," to recall Rothenberg's and Pierre's formula, a revolution of language, an expansion of as yet inconceivable perceptions. If poetry is to be a viable alternative or complement either to philosophy or to history, if it is to retain a critical and subversive distance from conceptual or material concerns, then it must assert this difference precisely in ways as yet untheorized by conceptual discourse. If such a call implies a reinstatement of the detached and authoritative position poetry held for the New Critics, it is perhaps to show that the relationship of theory and poetry undergoes repeated cycles of debate about its interconnectedness.

HAROLD SCHWEIZER

*See also* Language Poetry

**Further Reading**

Allen, Donald, editor, *The New American Poetry, 1945–1960,* New York: Grove Press, and London: Evergreen Books, 1960
Bradford, Richard, editor, *The State of Theory,* London and New York: Routledge, 1993
Easthope, Antony, and John O. Thompson, editors, *Contemporary Poetry Meets Modern Theory,* Toronto: University of Toronto Press, and New York and London: Harvester Wheatsheaf, 1991
Edmundson, Mark, *Literature against Philosophy, Plato to Derrida: A Defence of Poetry,* Cambridge and New York: Cambridge University Press, 1995
Hosek, Chaviva, and Patricia Parker, editors, *Lyric Poetry: Beyond New Criticism,* Ithaca, New York: Cornell University Press, 1985
Messerli, Douglas, editor, *"Language" Poetries: An Anthology,* New York: New Directions, 1987
Perloff, Marjorie, *Poetic License: Essays on Modernist and Postmodernist Lyric,* Evanston, Illinois: Northwestern University Press, 1983
Perloff, Marjorie, "Poetry in the Theory Wake," *Common Knowledge* 2, no. 3 (1993)
Perloff, Marjorie, *Wittgenstein's Ladder: Poetic Language and the Strangeness of the Ordinary,* Chicago: University of Chicago Press, 1996
Riddel, Joseph N., *The Turning Word: American Literary Modernism and Continental Theory,* edited by Mark Bauerlin, Philadelphia: University of Pennsylvania Press, 1996
Rothenberg, Jerome, and Joris Pierre, editors, *Poems for the Millennium: The University of California Book of Modern and Postmodern Poetry,* 2 vols., Berkeley: University of California Press, 1995–98
Whitehead, Karen, *The Feminist Poetry Movement,* Jackson: University Press of Mississippi, 1996

---

# Little Magazines and Small Presses

Literary publishing in the 20th century was deeply marked by the expanding role of little magazines and small presses. Canonical 19th-century American literature, with notable exceptions, such as Walt Whitman's *Leaves of Grass* and the initial printing of Frederick Goddard Tuckerman's *Sonnets,* was issued by major publishing houses. By the late 20th century, however, readers and critics realized that innovative and avant-garde work was more likely to be published by small editorially driven companies, such as Burning Deck, Talisman, Sun and Moon, Coffee House, Black Sparrow, and City Lights.

Mainstream poets such as Robert Pinsky and Adrienne Rich were published by large corporate entities, but one looked in vain in their lists for such names as Rosmarie Waldrop, Nathaniel Mackey, Susan Howe, Michael Palmer, and Lyn Hejinian. A few innovative poets—Alice Notley, Anne Waldman, and Kenneth Koch, for example—were published by the large houses, but these exceptions were rare. Nor had an earlier generation fared better: no book by Charles Olson was published by a large commercial house, nor was any by William Bronk, Lorine Niedecker, Jack Spicer, or Robert Duncan. Sylvia Plath, Robert Lowell, and other mainstream poets were published by the larger companies, but even writers at the very core of the American poetic tradition, such as Ezra Pound, William Carlos Williams, and H.D., might have gone largely unpublished had it not been for James Laughlin and the family fortune that allowed him to create and sustain New Directions.

Mass-circulation journals also emphasized mainstream over innovative work. In 1995, New York's Lower East Side poet known as "Sparrow" briefly earned literary notoriety when he picketed *The New Yorker* with a sign claiming, "My Poetry is as bad as yours." The magazine then did publish him but afterward returned largely to the mainstream poetry it had traditionally featured.

The history of little magazines in America begins with 19th-century periodicals such as *The Talisman* (1828–30), featuring American authors and edited by William Cullen Bryant, among others, and *The Dial* (1840–44), edited by Margaret Fuller. Immediate forerunners to 20th-century literary magazines included three journals established in the 1890s in direct imitation of *The Yellow Book* (1894–97), a British periodical edited by the American novelist Henry Harland that, more than any other journal of the day, characterized the tone and aura of the *fin de siècle. The*

*Yellow Book* was founded to make money, but its American imitations, *The Chap-Book* (1894–98), *The Lark* (1895–97), and *M'lle New York* (1895–96, 1898–99), were the work of brash young writers and editors concerned more with literature than with profits.

*The Chap-Book* was the best known. Established as the house organ for Stone and Kimball, a publishing enterprise founded by Harvard undergraduates, it was edited at first by Bliss Carman, whose work was then considered somewhat *outré*. *The Chap-Book* featured poetry and prose by young Americans together with works by Mallarmé, Verlaine, and other avant-garde European poets who would have considerable influence on young American writers, such as T.S. Eliot and Wallace Stevens.

*The Chap-Book*'s direct successors included *Poetry* (1912–present), founded and edited in its early years by Harriet Monroe, and *The Little Review* (1914–29), edited by Margaret C. Anderson and Jane Heap. In these journals and dozens of others, poets such as Eliot, Stevens, Pound, and Williams found an audience at the same time that they were being ignored by mass-circulation magazines. *Poetry* was the more famous; Monroe chose Pound as her foreign correspondent and, following his advice, made her journal a chief outlet for, among others, Robert Frost, H.D., Eliot, Williams, and D.H. Lawrence. *The Little Review* also benefited from Pound's advice; he served as foreign editor from 1917 to 1921, recommending works by Yeats and Eliot, among others, and convinced Anderson to publish James Joyce's *Ulysses*, which she did over a period of three years. Moral watchdogs were scandalized, and four issues with Joyce's text were confiscated and burned by postal authorities.

Other prominent little magazines at this time included *Others* (1915–19), edited by Alfred Kreybord with Williams, Lola Ridge, and others; *Contact* (1920–23, 1932), edited by Williams and Robert MacAlmon; and *The Dial* (1920–29), edited by Scofield Thayer and, after 1925, by Marianne Moore. *The Dial* is remembered not only for Moore's incisive reviews but also for the first American appearance of Eliot's "The Waste Land."

These journals were rarely political, at least overtly. *The Fugitive* (1922–25), which published John Crowe Ransom, Allen Tate, Laura Riding, and others, insisted in its first issue, for example, that it would be "neither radical nor reactionary." In fact, these journals were implicitly political, often aligning themselves with anarchist, socialist, and other left-wing movements.

None of these magazines had as much political presence and impact as *The Masses* (1911–17), edited by Max Eastman, Floyd Dell, and John Reed, and its successor, *The Liberator* (1918–24). *The Masses* defended then-radical issues such as feminism and pacifism, horrifying conservative Americans. In 1918, the Department of Justice took the journal to court, charging "conspiracy against the government." The result was a hung jury, a second trial, and another hung jury. The editors then reconstituted their journal as *The Liberator*, embarking on an even more determined political and increasingly Marxist program. At the same time, they published poets and writers such as Carl Sandburg, Randolph Bourne, Claude McKay, and others whose work firmly opposed the status quo.

Most of the important little magazines established early in the century folded before the Depression, and the 1930s and early 1940s were dominated by a new set of literary journals that took politics very seriously. The most widely read was the *New Masses* (1926–present), which published leftist poets Robinson Jeffers, Carl Rakosi, Kenneth Fearing, and Lola Ridge. *Transition* (1927–38), founded by American-born Eugene Jolas and published in Paris, continued to draw on works by earlier Modernist writers, such as Pound. More characteristic of the decade was *Partisan Review* (1934–present), which promulgated socialist realism in its early years before breaking with the Stalinists in 1937. The journal published both Modernists (segments of Eliot's *Four Quartets* first appeared here) and committed leftists and by the end of the decade was the foremost literary periodical in America.

Politically opposite *Partisan Review* and *New Masses* were essentially anarchistic journals, which rejected Soviet and socialist politics and advocated anarchism and individualism. Most famous was James Cooney's *The Phoenix* (1938–40), for which Henry Miller served as the European editor. Impeccably designed and printed, it was the model for Robert Duncan and Sanders Russell's *Experimental Review* (1940–41), and through Duncan its uncompromising individualism filtered into the journals and poetry of the San Francisco Renaissance. During World War II, the New York–based *View* (1940–47), edited by Charles Henry Ford and Parker Tyler, was the chief venue for Surrealists.

Following World War II, little magazines proliferated. Mass-market magazines increasingly published less poetry, and for most writers little magazines became virtually their only outlet aside from poetry readings. Every new literary movement or group of writers, it seemed, called for a new journal, and with the advent of the "mimeograph revolution" in the 1960s, it was no longer possible to keep track of them. A few, such as Ted Berrigan's "*C*" (1963–66), achieved considerable fame among poets but faded after a few issues; others, such as *The World* (1967–present), remain staples of the poetry world.

*The New American Poetry* (1960), Donald Allen's anthology documenting the transformation of American poetry under the aegis of various Black Mountain, Beat, and Objectivist influences, brought together work from poets who, almost without exception, had established themselves through little magazines, such as Cid Corman's *Origin* (1951–84) and Robert Creeley's *The Black Mountain Review* (1954–57). Allen's book left no question that avant-garde poets had little to do with mainstream periodicals and presses and did not need them.

The spring 1958 issue of another key journal, *The Chicago Review*, included work by William S. Burroughs, Allen Ginsberg, and Robert Duncan. Similar contributions appeared in the fall and winter issues, but the latter in particular offended administrators at the University of Chicago, which underwrote the magazine's expenses, and the issue was suppressed. The editors then published the contents as *Big Table*, which drew attention from postal authorities armed with obscenity laws. The trial that resulted was widely publicized. The court decided in the magazine's favor, sales mushroomed, and *Big Table* ceased being a "little magazine."

Like *Big Table*, periodicals such as the New American Library's *New World Writing* (1952–64) and Barney Rosset and Donald Allen's *Evergreen Review* (1957–73) sought and found a substantial readership while pursuing the little magazine's primary objective: the publication of new and challenging writing that the commercial houses were likely to neglect. Among the more prominent journals publishing "the New American poets" were *Kulchur* (1960–66), edited by Lita Hornick and others, and LeRoi Jones' *Yugen* (1958–62) and *The Floating Bear* (1961–71), which he edited with Diane di Prima.

The new journals, of which the mimeograph magazines of the 1960s and 1970s are prime examples, represented a return to the informality of *The Lark* and *M'lle New York*. Most little magazines had cultivated an aura of high seriousness, but the new breed presented itself in a more playful light, owing more to Marcel Duchamp than to T.S. Eliot. As casual as they might seem, however, magazines such as Ted Berrigan's *"C"* (1963–66), Edward Sanders' *Fuck You, a magazine of the arts* (1962–65), Bill Berkson's *Big Sky* (1971–78), and Lewis Warsh and Bernadette Mayer's *United Artists* (1977–83) were as revolutionary as any little magazine earlier in the century. Usually mimeographed and sometimes distributed free among friends, these journals collectively tore away at the notions of art as a privileged, elitist discourse that High Modernists and New Critics had painstakingly constructed.

Less contentious or revolutionary positions were assumed by established journals such as *The Kenyon Review* (1939–present) and *The Hudson Review* (1948–present) and by newer arrivals such as *The Paris Review* (1953–present) and *Ploughshares* (1971–present), guest edited by such luminaries as Seamus Heaney, Derek Walcott, and Rita Dove. Most of these journals featured mainstream poets but included Allen's "New American Poets" as well. *The Paris Review* was famous for promoting New York School writers such as Ted Berrigan and Anne Waldman during the tenure of poetry editor Tom Clark (1964–74). The *Paris Review* was the most admired American literary magazine during much of the second half of the 20th century, although strictly speaking it was so widely distributed that, like *New World Writing* and *Evergreen Review*, it does not warrant being labeled a "little magazine."

In 1971, Robert Grenier and Barrett Watten founded *This* (1971–82), the first journal in the movement that would dominate much innovative American poetry during the second half of the century: Language writing. Grenier's statement in the first issue—"I hate speech"—set the magazine in opposition to the speech-based poetry practiced by followers of Charles Olson and the New York School. *L=A=N=G=U=A=G=E* (1978–81), edited by Bruce Andrews and Charles Bernstein, became the movement's chief outlet for essays and reviews, but the most famous journal to publish the Language writers (and arguably the most prominent journal for innovative work in the closing decades of the century) was *Sulfur* (1981–2000). Founded by Clayton Eshleman, who was not himself a Language writer, the journal embraced a number of traditions, and its eclectic mix placed Language writers beside New York School poets and published both cutting-edge reviews and archival documents involving Objectivists and Black Mountain poets.

Other admired journals that maintained similar eclectic programs were *Talisman: A Journal of Contemporary Poetry and Poetics* (1988–present), edited by Edward Foster; *o·blek* (1987–93), edited by Peter Gizzi and Connell McGrath; and *Temblor* (1985–89), edited by Lee Hickman, whom critic Marjorie Perloff has called "one of the great unsung heroes of the so-called innovative poetry scene." Hickman's taste was exceptionally fine, and if one were to study the history of the poetic avant-garde in post-structuralist America, one would do well to start with the poets and works he chose to publish.

The circulation for these journals rarely exceeded 2,000 copies, and readership consisted primarily of writers and critics. The same readership can be said to have defined the avant-garde—unlike, for example, *Grand Street, The Paris Review,* and the various university-based journals, such as *The Georgia Review* and *The Massachusetts Review,* which attracted a more general readership.

The history of small literary publishers in the United States is less clear than the history of little magazines. Printers and local publishers were ubiquitous in 19th-century America, but large publishers, such as Ticknor and Fields or Harper and Row, were responsible for most poetry and fiction. These were also highly commercial houses despite their focus on excellent writing.

Small publishers in the 20th century, however, have characteristically been interested in literary work and book design but at best secondarily concerned with marketing and profits. In this, their more prominent 19th-century forerunners would be firms such as Stone and Kimball (1893–97), the publishing house founded by Harvard undergraduates who also issued *The Chap-Book,* and Copeland and Day (1883–1900), whose 97 books issued a range of literary figures from Sarah Orne Jewett to Oscar Wilde. Both Stone and Kimball and Copeland and Day were models of typographic care and high literary taste, but both soon discovered that publishing good books did not ensure high profits. By combining an interest in book design (in which they were much aided by designers such as F.W. Goudy, Bruce Rogers, and D.B. Updike) with an interest in good writing, these *fin-de-siècle* firms set the model for the 20th century that has been followed by most of the famous small publishers.

Book publishing has always been an expensive enterprise and therefore has attracted primarily those with resources. The Black Sun Press, for example, was founded in 1927 by a wealthy American couple, Harry and Caresse Crosby, primarily to publish his poetry. The result included some of the more typographically elegant books of the era, including works by James Joyce and D.H. Lawrence. The press ended with Harry Crosby's suicide in December 1929, shortly after the stock market crash.

Not all self-publishers had fortunes such as Crosby's. Vachel Lindsay (1879–1931) traveled around the country supporting himself with readings and sales from his self-published books, including the aptly titled *Rhymes To Be Traded for Bread* (1912).

Among the greatest of all American small publishers was Harry Duncan (1918–97), who founded the Cummington Press (later renamed Abbatoir) in 1939 and on a hand-operated press issued such Modernist icons as Robert Lowell's *Land of Unlikeness* (1944) and Wallace Stevens' *Notes toward a Supreme Fiction* (1942). Duncan, who at one point supported himself and his project by driving a school bus, had difficulty locating and buying good paper for his projects during the war, but he managed without exception to create books as important in the history of American printing as they are as literature.

In 1945, an Iowa businessman gave his state university funds to establish a "Typography Laboratory." In 1956, Duncan was hired as the director of the laboratory, where he remained until 1972, moving then to the University of Nebraska to run its fine-arts press, retiring in 1985. As *Newsweek* reported in 1982, Duncan was "the father of the post–World War II private-press movement." His students, to cite one well-known example, included Allan Kornblum, a New York School poet who began studying with Duncan in 1970. Two years later, Kornblum had his own press and began publishing a magazine and then books under his imprint, The Toothpaste Press. By 1984, 70 books and chapbooks had been published, at which time Kornblum dissolved Toothpaste and moved to Minneapolis, where he established Coffee House Press, which remains one of the premier small publishers in the country, responsible for publishing New York School writers such as Anne Waldman, Paul Violi, and Joseph Ceravolo as well as a very strong list of multicultural titles.

Jonathan Williams (1929–) is another key figure in the small-press movement. He enrolled at Black Mountain College in 1951 and soon after founded Jargon Press to publish innovative writings. Called "the truffle-hound of American poetry," he has published some of the finest poets associated with the Objectivists and the Black Mountain School, including Charles Olson, Robert Creeley, Lorine Niedecker, and Joel Oppenheimer. After Black Mountain College folded, Williams traveled around the country, visiting bookstores with Jargon publications and books from other small publishers, including City Lights, which was becoming famous as the publisher of *Howl* (1956) by Allen Ginsberg and *A Coney Island of the Mind* (1958) by the founder of the press, Lawrence Ferlinghetti.

The fact that Ferlinghetti and Williams were themselves respected poets reminds one that in operations like theirs, the roles of publisher, editor, and author are somewhat more complexly intertwined than in conventional houses.

*Burning Deck* was established as a journal in the early 1960s by Keith Waldrop and others; it folded after four issues, but Waldrop's wife, Rosmarie, took over the Burning Deck name and with it founded one of the most respected houses among innovative poets. John Taggart, Ron Silliman, Barbara Guest, Marjorie Welish, and Lyn Hejinian are a few of its authors.

New Directions may be the most famous literary small publisher of the century. Founded by James Laughlin (1914–97) in 1936 at the urging of Ezra Pound (Pound "had been seeing my poems for months and had ruled them hopeless," Laughlin remembered. "He urged me to finish Harvard and then do 'something' useful."), New Directions initially specialized in anthologies, but the firm's ambitions rapidly expanded, and it became the principal American publisher for Pound, H.D., and William Carlos Williams. It also published poetry in translation by Rilke, Apollinaire, Lorca, and other key Modernists and later became a prominent publisher of such postmodern writers as William Bronk, Bernadette Mayer, Rosmarie Waldrop, and Michael Palmer.

Jargon and New Directions represent, respectively, two different types of small publishers. Jargon has been driven largely by one person; one cannot imagine it without Williams. Certainly Laughlin was critical to the course and personality of his company (volumes often carried the declaration on the copyright page, "New Directions Books are published for James Laughlin by New Directions Publishing Corporation"), but he also had a battery of committed advisers and editors, including, among the most influential, Delmore Schwartz. New Directions is also distributed by one of the larger commercial houses, W.W. Norton; Jargon, on the other hand, was distributed by Inland Book Company, which specialized in small (often very small) publishers until its demise in 1995. Although Jargon publications are available in good bookstores, they are also available, most efficiently perhaps, through the press itself. As a result, a chain bookstore may be more likely to carry a New Directions title than one from Jargon.

The chains devastated much small publishing in the 1990s. Until then, it was customary for independent bookstores of any quality to order and stock small-press books. This, after all, had long been a primary source of virtually all important innovative poets. Major commercial houses might publish Robert Frost and Robert Lowell but not Niedecker, Rexroth, Ted Berrigan, or Susan Howe. Independent bookstores would often stock small-press books until, years later, they finally found their readers. Sometimes the books were delivered to the bookstores by the publisher (Williams is a case in point) and left on consignment. Distribution systems, such as Inland and Small Press Distribution, supplanted that initiative, but the erosion and collapse of the independents brought down both many of these distributors and the small publishers they served. Seeking higher turnover and profit, the chains would reject titles that independents would have accepted reflexively.

Since it was now difficult or impossible for many small-press books to reach an audience, some poets turned to the Internet. On-line magazines became a viable alternative to print publications, but although Internet booksellers seemed at first a good alternative to the chains for book distribution, one could not browse through available titles as readily as it had been possible to do in the independent bookstores.

By the end of the 20th century, the publication of poetry seemed to be capitulating to the imperatives of a market economy. In order to survive, the publisher had to adjust his or her efforts to a marketing system that had little use for serious writing. As if in conspiracy with these demands, the Academy of American Poets began promoting "National Poetry Month," which, wrote Charles Bernstein, "is about making poetry safe for readers by promoting examples of the art form at its most bland and its most morally 'positive.'" That, in turn, meant selling poetry the way one sold movies and had little to do with the way small publishers had traditionally sold books.

Edward Halsey Foster

**Further Reading**

Anderson, Elliott, and Mary Kinzie, editors, *The Little Magazine in America,* Yonkers, New York: Pushcart Press, 1978

Clay, Stephen, *A Secret Location on the Lower East Side,* New York: New York Public Library and Granary Books, 1998

Dennison, Sally, *Alternative Literary Publishing: Five Modern Histories,* Iowa City: University of Iowa Press, 1984

Gunderloy, Mike, *The World of Zines,* New York: Penguin, 1992

*The International Directory of Little Magazines and Small Presses,* Paradise, California: Dustbooks, 1973

Marek, Jayne, *Women Editing Modernism: Little Magazines and Literary History,* Lexington: University Press of Kentucky, 1995

Whittemore, Reed, *Little Magazines,* Minneapolis: University of Minnesota Press, 1963

# Long Poem

In the 20th century, as Lynn Keller and others have noted, the long poem has become a much-practiced and increasingly broadly defined form of writing. Included under the term's umbrella are such extended forms as narrative poems, collage poems, epics, serial poems, prose poems, and lyric and meditative sequences. A common set of ancestors—chiefly Dante, Browning, Whitman, and the early 20th-century Modernists—and a common set of problems hold this form together. Unlike the lyric, which tends to open up a single encounter or exclamation or moment of insight—"look[ing] over and over at the one place where the eye or mind alights," as Helen Vendler puts it—the long poem consistently displays the poet sorting or reading or embracing a diverse set of materials. Each long poem, then, must address the issues of what materials are to be handled and how they are to be handled—especially rich issues in the 20th century. Because of the contrast between the wealth of material it draws from and the tentativeness of the forms it must employ, each poem, almost without exception, finds itself reflecting on the reach and limits of such attempts at ordering. One could say that despite the different approaches to form demonstrated by the many writers who have attempted long poems, a shared investigation of limits draws these poems together.

T.S. Eliot's *The Waste Land* (1922) and Ezra Pound's *Cantos* (1925–72) stand as powerful early examples of this form because of their radical responses to these issues. Facing a world and a self composed of bewilderingly intertwined voices—voices numb or obsessed, petty or strikingly beautiful, what the poem calls shattered, "stony rubbish"—Eliot's speaker attempts to enter so deeply into what is broken and fearful in those voices that some new or fresh turn might "bloom" out of their exhaustion. He draws from high and low culture—Wagner, Dante, Ovid, Shakespeare; street talk, bar talk, half-articulated confessions—attempting, much in the manner of Walt Whitman, to allow "many long dumb voices" ("Song of Myself") to enter and pass through him. The forms Eliot devised to internalize, shatter, and revitalize those voices have now become standard 20th-century devices: ironic juxtapositions, linked fragments, broken-off memories and quotations, rhythmic and imagistic thinking. The poet's work is done to the accompaniment of a steely, self-aware voice, acknowledging the potential self-delusion that is part of such an ambitious task: perhaps it is only the desire for an ending that produces the "drip drop drop drop drop" of water where there is none, or that hears the "rumour" of revival where there is only the play of translation. At the same time, however, the poem suggests that perhaps that broken self-awareness is itself what stirs to life in the poem's "heap of broken images."

*The Cantos* is a more massive work, left unfinished after 50 years of effort and over 750 pages. Wracked by serious errors and false turns—

> How mean thy hates
> Fostered in falsity,
> . . .
> Rathe to destroy, niggard in charity,

the poet despairingly writes about himself in the *Pisan Cantos*—the poem nonetheless has had an enormous, if complicated influence on other long poems of the century. Its first two cantos establish the materials from which Pound will draw and his means of handling them; the more than 100 cantos that follow trace the poet's slow realization of the limits of those ambitions. "Canto I" is primarily composed of a translation of a portion of *The Odyssey* in which Odysseus sails from Circe's island to the underworld to inquire of Tiresias concerning his journey home. As Hugh Kenner has shown, the ritual Odysseus performs in order to give renewed life and speech to the dead—sacrificing beasts and offering the ghosts their blood—is the same ritual the poet/translator performs in bringing to full speech a silent text. The blood in "Canto I" is the English language itself, powerfully worked by the poet to recall its oldest roots. *The Cantos*, then, seek to "gather from the air a live tradition," recalling to full voice lost but still vital forces that might guide the 20th century from Circe's island to Ithaca. "Canto II," composed in part of a passage from Ovid's *Metamorphoses* in which sailors out for slave money kidnap the god Dionysus, not recognizing the drunken youth, proposes that to locate that live, if silent, tradition one must have eyes able to respond to and "worship" such energies. And since those energies swirl together in various forms—high and low, demonic and transcendent—the poet will need to be able both to separate one strand from another and to recombine them in a form that will speak guidance and warning to the reader. This, of course, is the source of the poem's greater beauty—its fluid juxtapositions and grand dissolving collages—and its great difficulty and obscurity.

Pound's reflections on the limits of his ability to achieve such grand ambitions make up some of the most striking sections of the poem. They begin with the quiet acknowledgment in "Canto I" that, if the writer is in some sense an Odysseus, he will eventually "Lose all companions," a prediction borne out in "Canto LXXXI" when, imprisoned after World War II for treason, the poet notes that all that remains after a shipwrecked life are a few shards of poetry, what he had "lov[ed] well." The reflections end, famously, with the acknowledgment in "Canto CXVI" that "I am not a demigod, / I cannot make it cohere." Quite powerfully, however, these acknowledgments of limits consistently point beyond the poet to a broader, unmasterable world. The writer sees himself as "a blown husk that is finished / but the light sings eternal" ("Canto CXV"); he acknowledges that "Knowledge [is merely] the shade of a shade, / . . . [which] the sea's claw gathers [in]" ("Canto XLVII").

H.D.'s *Trilogy* (1944–46), an increasingly influential Modernist work composed in London during the World War II bombings, is propelled by a similar sense that the shattering of forms—buildings, stained glass, narratives, words—might in fact open a new way to wonder. The first poem in the sequence, "The Walls Do Not Fall," compares London's torn-open, roofless buildings to the exposed tombs of ancient Karnak, in Egypt:

> there, as here, ruin opens
> the tomb, the temple; enter,
> there as here, there are no doors:
>
> the shrine lies open to the sky,
> the rain falls, here, there
> sand drifts; eternity endures[.]

Each of the trilogy's poems asks what treasures have been exposed and how their broken shards might now be handled. "The Walls Do Not Fall" uses the image of fire releasing energy to describe the poet's sense of wonders becoming visible. If "the tide is turning," "old thought[s], old convention[s]" are being uncovered and might be heaped up at that boundary line:

> let us go down to the sea,
>
> gather dry sea-weed,
> heap drift-wood,
>
> let us light a new fire
> . . .
> chant new paeans to the new Sun
>
> of regeneration[.]

"Tribute to the Angels" uses the metaphor of alchemy to envision what might be made of London:

> collect the fragments of the splintered glass
>
> and of your fire and breath,
> melt down and integrate,
>
> re-invoke, re-create
> opal, onyx, obsidian,
>
> now scattered in the shards
> men tread upon.

The shattered materials the poet handles include words, the angels around the throne in the book of Revelation, various versions of the veiled goddess of beauty, all of which "are melted, fuse and join / and change and alter," producing various opal-like jewels. The most powerful of these treasures is identified in a dream as the work of poetry itself: "the blank pages / of the unwritten volume of the new." In "The Flowering of the Rod" H.D. begins to write on those blank pages, charting a story that arises for her out of fragments of the gospels. In a sense, as she melts down and combines the various Marys of the stories, and as she searches for new energy behind the conventional images of the magi or Mary anointing the feet of Jesus, H.D. becomes herself the alchemist or transforming fire the trilogy seeks.

In fact, the poet's self-reflective attention to her writing is once again what drives this long poem forward. What shatters in the first poem and crucially redirects her attention is her own confidence in her method:

> arrogance, over-confidence, pitiful reticence,
>
> boasting, intrusion of strained
> inappropriate allusion,

she writes, slashing at her own work. An outside voice, droningly re-contextualizing her fragmentary dreams, provides the pressure that drives her, in reaction, in the second poem, to melt and unite materials in her own way:

> Oh yes—you understand, I say,
> this is all most satisfactory,
>
> *but* she wasn't hieratic, she wasn't frozen[.]

And it is finally the poet herself whose investigative sifting through traditions is figured as Kaspar, the third poem's crucial, visionary figure. All these poems, attempting to move into the "unrecorded" with "no map," pay close attention to their own complications and tensions, convinced that the way forward will be revealed there.

One final Modernist long poem, Wallace Stevens' "The Auroras of Autumn," is primarily meditative in nature. The poem is generated by the response of the speaker to the overwhelming display of the northern lights, what he calls "form gulping after formlessness." The lights make visible the world's constant motion, energy gathering into momentary distinguishable patterns and then opening back out into formlessness:

> The man who is walking turns blankly on the sand.
> He observes how the north is always enlarging the change,
>
> With its frigid brilliances, its blue-red sweeps
> And gusts of great enkindlings, its polar green. . . .

As H.D. did with her shards of history or Pound did with his thirsty ghosts, Stevens' figure would embrace the flowing, enkindled world itself. As with these other poems, the attempt to name or contain such energy inevitably breaks down:

> He opens the door of his house
>
> On flames. The scholar of one candle sees
> An Arctic effulgence flaring on the frame
> Of everything he is. And he feels afraid.

What is distinctive about Stevens' poem is that most of its energy is put into reflecting on the scholar's fear and on what becomes visible about language and form as their limits are forcefully revealed. The reflective parables Stevens employs here have had a significant influence on contemporary writing. "Farewell to an idea," three early cantos of the poem begin, casting aside such ideas about writing as its ability to mark or remember or make transparent in any permanent sort of way. What is left? Two of Stevens' parables offer notable responses. If "the purpose of the poem" can be thought of as the presence of the mother in a house—

> It is the mother they possess,
> Who gives transparence to their present peace.
> She makes that gentler that can gentle be

—what happens when, under the pressure of an unmasterable, flaring world, "she too is dissolved, she is destroyed"? Stevens writes: think of

> . . . the mother as she falls asleep
> And as they say good-night, good-night. Upstairs
> The windows will be lighted, not the rooms.

That is, the purpose of the poem having been set aside—the mother asleep—the darkened house is then able to record, on its windows, the play of the arctic fires it cannot master. It simply holds itself in the presence of powers beyond it. Think of those powers as making up a drama, as a second parable has it:

It is a theatre floating through the clouds,
Itself a cloud, although of misted rock
And mountains running like water, wave on wave.

The role of the writer or scholar of a single candle, then, is to participate in that drama by recording, on his own nerve endings, the attempt to name and contain and then the sudden expansion of scope as the world gulps toward formlessness and declares itself nameless again:

This is nothing until in a single man contained,
Nothing until this named thing nameless is
And is destroyed.

Such testimony, Stevens writes, makes visible "this drama that we live."

Turning to a representative selection of contemporary long poems, one can see how these concerns, particularly the foregrounding of the reflective turn, are continued and extended. Robert Duncan's "Passages"—an open-ended poem, its first 30 sections appearing in *Bending the Bow* (1968) with additional sections in *Ground Work: Before the War* (1984) and *Ground Work II: In the Dark* (1987)—powerfully develops the work of Pound and H.D. Conceived of as an attempt to read the self against what Duncan calls "the grand ensemble" of humanity's created forms, the poem is deeply indebted to Pound's demonstrations of how, through translation, one can recognize contentions or features not directly visible or accessible in oneself in the voices of others. Duncan writes: "We find our company in Euripedes, Plato, Moses of Leon, Faure or Freud, searching out keys to our inner being in the rites of the Aranda and in the painting processes of Cezanne." As in H.D.'s work, Duncan's grand ensemble is still in process; it is a network in which each individual part is potentially linked to, is co-inherent with, all other parts, which means that individual forms are constantly being shattered and recombined in richer and fuller ways. "Passages 2" uses the image of weaving to sketch this poetics:

my mind a shuttle among
        set strings of the music
lets a weft of dream grow in the day time,
            an increment of associations,
    luminous soft threads,
the thrown glamour, crossing and recrossing,
        the twisted sinews underlying the work.

The "twisted sinews" or warp of this evolving tapestry are the "set strings" of humanity's made things that the poet's mind moves in and out of, while the "luminous soft threads" of his attention, crossing those underlying cords and gathering together his own particular "increment of associations," create an aspect of the tapestry's weft.

Duncan's work with those "set strings" is driven by various concerns generated in the act of writing. He reflects on those issues by reading himself against the work of painters, poets, visionaries, and so on. The sections of the poem appearing in *Bending the Bow* were written during the Vietnam War. If what the poet yearned to do as he read himself against the universe of human imaginings was to improvise

passages of changing dark and light
a music dream and passion would have playd
to illustrate concords of order in order,
a contrapuntal communion of all things,

the discovery that a portion of those imaginings was the war itself threw that dream off. The poet continually asks how to read himself against what seems "a medley of mistaken themes / grown dreadful and surmounting dread." Working through paintings (di Cosimo's *A Forest Fire,* Bosch's *Christ Bearing the Cross*), poems and stories (Verlaine's "Saint Graal," Kipling's "The Knife and the Naked Chalk"), and the rhetoric of the Berkeley Free Speech Movement and of President Johnson, the poet eventually comes to see that his native tendency to retreat from conflict and seal himself off in the tongue's music is inadequate. Outrage and horror are also responses to the ensemble's set strings, generating their own patterns of association and thus envisioning an even larger ensemble in which the horror takes its place as simply an opposing figure within a larger design. Driven out into the world by the tension generated on the page, Duncan discovers:

            There is no

    good a man has in his own things except

        it be in the community of every thing;

        no nature he has

but in his nature hidden in the heart of the living[.]

John Berryman's *Dream Songs* is driven by a similar wrestling with limits. Its 385 songs—18-line poems marked by sudden shifts from first to third person and from high lyric eloquence to drunk talk and baby talk—attempt to sing the wonders of the world (its "possibilities") but find themselves hobbled and shattered by the grim realization that "Fate clobber all." As the first song puts it:

Once in a sycamore I was glad
all at the top, and I sang.
Hard on the land wears the strong sea
and empty grows every bed.

What the poems do, then, is unfold this tension, attempting to sing but also charting the nature of song's limitations in a world eroded by the strong seas of time and loss, illness and madness.

The first three books of songs, published in one volume as *77 Dream Songs* (1964), sketch one complete version of the reflective arc repeatedly traced by the poems. The poems in the first book respond to loss by retreating from the world, hurt and voiceless. The writer studies that tendency by talking about himself in the third person, using variations of the pet name Henry to visualize and gain some purchase on his panicked, offended flight:

Huffy Henry hid the day,
unappeasable Henry sulked.
I see his point,—a trying to put things over.
It was the thought that they thought
they could *do* it made Henry wicked & away.
But he should have come out and talked.

In these hair-trigger poems the speaker is notably wounded. It takes only the warning whisper of "Euphoria" by an inner voice to shatter the singer's Whitman-like, expansive, "valved-voice" and reduce him to a child:

—Hand me back my crawl,
condign Heaven. Tighten into a ball
elongate & valved Henry. Tuck him peace.
Render him sightless,
or ruin at high rate his crampon focus,
wipe out his need. Reduce him to the rest of us.

The songs in the second book attempt to work back through memory to the original wounding that has so restricted the singer's voice:

There sat down, once, a thing on Henry's heart
so heavy, if he had a hundred years
& more, & weeping, sleepless, in all them time
Henry could not make good.

These poems eventually focus on the suicide of the poet's father, claiming that although there is no way of erasing that loss it might be faced and understood. Berryman's term for this is *remercy:*

Now full craze down
across our continent
all storms since you gave in, on my pup-tent.
I have of blast & counter to remercy you
for hurling me downtown.

The wounding faced head-on, the third book attempts to speak rather than hide, but to speak from within acknowledged limitations:

I am obliged to perform in complete darkness
operations of great delicacy
on my self.

The songs and speech are shaky, always about to collapse or retreat again, as here, as an inner voice addresses Henry as Mr. Bones and urges him to sing while Henry ambiguously steps forward to meet his vanished world:

I offers you this handkerchief, now set
your left foot by my right foot,
shoulder to shoulder, all that jazz,
arm in arm, by the beautiful sea,
hum a little, Mr. Bones.
—I saw nobody coming, so I went instead.

One can see a final sort of reflection on writing and limits going on in Lyn Hejinian's *My Life* (revised edition, 1987). Composed of 45 prose poems, each in 45 sentences and each focused on one of the poet's 45 years, the book attempts to engage what Hejinian has described as a life's "mass of data":

> I perceive the world as vast and overwhelming; each moment stands under an enormous vertical and horizontal pressure of information, potent with ambiguity, meaningful, unfixed, and certainly incomplete. What saves this from becoming a vast undifferentiated mass of data and situation is one's ability to make distinctions.

Those distinctions are of course inadequate; as every poet working on a long poem eventually acknowledges, no strand of words ever embraces the grand ensemble of the moment or the potential of a life or a culture. But, Hejinian continues, language's very limitations make it such an effective tool for opening up and making visible that mass of information. She calls this an open use of language, one that in foregrounding the inability of words to capture all of the moment leaves the moment charged and infinitely able to be articulated:

> The experience of feeling overwhelmed by undifferentiated material is like claustrophobia. One feels panicky, closed in. . . . The very incapacity of language to match the world allows it to do service as a medium of differentiation.

Looking briefly at the poems, one can get a feel for how this differentiation works. Each poem's set of 45 sentences is deliberately nonconsecutive, thus acknowledging the vastness of what cannot be straightforwardly organized. The poet watches herself as she writes, drawing out various implications about the act of writing being engaged in as she monitors its progress. For example, an early poem focusing on age three, in about the year 1944 when the poet's father apparently "sailed to the war," opens:

> We see only the leaves and branches of the trees close in around the house. Those submissive games were sensual. I was no more than three or four years old, but when crossed I would hold my breath, not from rage but from stubbornness, until I lost consciousness. The shadows one day deeper. Every family has its own collection of stories, but not every family has someone to tell them.

The reader can see the details of a child's life here: leaves and shadows, games, holding her breath. Some of the sentences are in present tense, from the point of view of the child—"We see only the leaves," "The shadows one day deeper"—and some describe that childhood from an adult's perspective, as a past-tense event: "I was no more than three or four," "I would hold my breath," "Those submissive games were sensual." Further, in the absence of a story line, the reader begins to draw connections. Are the closing-in leaves like the descending shadows? Are they both like those games perhaps forced on the child? Is holding the breath a way of asserting oneself against such pressures? And is that like telling one's story within the family? None of these questions are fully answered as the piece goes on, but one can hear repeated references to the deepening shadows of an absent father, to "a life no more free than the life of a lost puppy." Certainly one can hear repeated references to writing and storytelling as acts of distinguishing and steadying the self.

Even more interesting, however, are sentences that seem to comment on the process of articulation begun in these first, apparently random sentences. It is as if the poet is learning about how language functions by holding it up against the lost or overwhelming details of her past: "Because of their recurrence, what had originally seemed merely details of atmosphere became, in time, thematic," she writes, later commenting,

> What follows a strict chronology has no memory. For me, they must exist, the contents of that absent reality, the objects and occasions which now I reconsidered.

Indeed, breaking free of strict chronology in order to create distinction and memory is a move the book repeats over and over, as is creating a form that, in allowing elements to recur, builds and destroys new patterns far beyond their original reference. The point, then, for *My Life* as for all the poems examined here, is that the long poem seems particularly suited for watching language in action: for watching form gather and dissolve and reconfigure itself. This reflective monitoring drives such poems as these forward, their deepest tensions discovered within form itself as it attempts to grasp what often seems beyond the reaches of language.

Thomas Gardner

**Further Reading**


Bernstein, Michael André, *The Tale of the Tribe: Ezra Pound and the Modern Verse Epic,* Princeton, New Jersey: Princeton University Press, 1980

Conte, Joseph, *Unending Design: The Forms of Postmodern Poetry,* Ithaca, New York: Cornell University Press, 1991

Dickie, Margaret, *On the Modernist Long Poem,* Iowa City: University of Iowa Press, 1986

Gardner, Thomas, *Discovering Ourselves in Whitman: The Contemporary American Long Poem,* Urbana: University of Illinois Press, 1989

Keller, Lynn, "The Twentieth-Century Long Poem," in *The Columbia History of American Poetry,* edited by Jay Parini and Brett C. Miller, New York: Columbia University Press, 1993

Keller, Lynn, *Forms of Expansion: Recent Long Poems by Women,* Chicago: University of Chicago Press, 1997

Miller, James E., Jr., *The American Quest for a Supreme Fiction: Whitman's Legacy in the Personal Epic,* Chicago: University of Chicago Press, 1979

Pearce, Roy Harvey, "The Long View: An American Epic," in *The Continuity of American Poetry,* by Pearce, Princeton, New Jersey: Princeton University Press, 1961

Rosenthal, M.L., and Sally M. Gall, *The Modern Poetic Sequence: The Genius of Modern Poetry,* New York: Oxford University Press, 1983


## Audre Lorde 1934–92

A self-defined "Black lesbian mother warrior poet," African-American poet Audre Lorde is perhaps best known for her impassioned stance in works such as her militant volume *New York Head Shop and Museum* (1974). Her work also interrogated the intersection of gender and race, however, most notably in her critique of African-American male complicity in promoting sexual discrimination. Due to her characteristic outspokenness, she repeatedly encountered resistance from many literary circles. Nonetheless, Lorde's poetry, with its honest examination of sometimes controversial subjects delivered in a tight economical style characterized by vivid imagery and highly symbolic language, established her as a major force in the new Black poetry movement. Together with her essays, her poems place her alongside Black feminist scholars Barbara Smith, Barbara Christian, and Gloria T. Hull.

Lorde, who was born in 1934 in New York City, began writing poetry as a child. After receiving a National Endowment for the Arts grant in 1968, she became poet-in-residence at Tougaloo College in Mississippi and published her first volume of poetry, *The First Cities* (1968). This volume diverged from the characteristic militancy of African-American poetry at the time, receiving praise for its seamless blend of nature imagery, impressive phrasing, and quiet reflection. Lorde's poignant depiction of the loss of a father from his young daughter's perspective in "Father Son and Holy Ghost" established her recurring concern with parent-child relationships and the quest for love. Poems such as "Coal" reflect an African-American sensibility: "I am Black because I come from the earth's inside / now take my word for jewel in the open light."

Lorde's second volume, *Cables to Rage* (1970), with poems including "Rites of Passage," dedicated to Martin Luther King, Jr., laid the groundwork for her later emergence as a social activist. The poems in this volume are also autobiographical, culminating in the often-anthologized "Martha" in which Lorde first openly expressed her homosexuality. Issues of identity and relationships inform *From a Land Where Other People Live* (1973), nominated for a National Book Award. Her interest in the strained relationship between mother and daughter resurfaces in "Black Mother Woman," in which she portrays mothers as stifling their daughters, who must break free in order to create self-affirming identities: "I learned from you / to define myself /through your denials—".

In *New York Head Shop and Museum,* hailed as her most political and militant work, Lorde explores Blackness and her role within the African-American community. Poems such as "Now" deploy the aggressively proud rhetorical style of Black Arts movement poetry to express a womanist ethos: "Woman power / is / Black power / is / Human power." She unites "Woman power" with "Black power" under "Human power," thereby eschewing a separatist ideology. Poems such as "The American Cancer Society" and "The Brown Menace" use sarcasm and symbolism to elucidate the African-American experience of daily injustice in white America.

*Coal* (1976), a compilation of poems from her first two books, introduced Lorde to a much broader readership. Significant poems include "Now That I Am Forever with Child," with its loving account of the indestructible bond she feels with her newborn. *Between Our Selves* (1976), a short volume, included the incendiary "Power" in which Lorde angrily rails against the social injustice inherent in the acquittal of a white police officer accused of shooting a ten-year-old African-American boy. She states that "The difference between poetry and rhetoric / is being ready to kill / yourself / instead of your children." Such poems illustrate Lorde's vision of herself both as an artist and a social activist.

Lorde demonstrates her belief in the inherent relationship between African-American literature and African traditions in *The Black Unicorn* (1978), grounding poems such as "Coniagui Women," "Dahomey," and "From the House of Yemanjá" in the beliefs of the Yoruba people. "125th Street and Abomey" seamlessly melds the African-American experience with that of Africa as the speaker walks the Harlem streets, recalling the power of the African goddess Seboulisa. Lorde locates female and, implicitly, Black strength in the bosom of the African continent.

In *Chosen Poems—Old and New* (1982) Lorde continues her denunciation of various social injustices. In "Need: A Choral of Black Women's Voices" Lorde vehemently castigates Black men for their involvement in sexually oppressing Black women. "The Evening News," written in Lorde's characteristic somber tone and laden with haunting images, is notable for its poignant depiction of the brutalities suffered by children under the South African system of apartheid. *Our Dead behind Us* (1986), displaying an African sensibility and militant undertone, demonstrates her expansive scope as she focuses on the experiences of women around the world, including in Grenada, Germany, and South Africa. In "Call" Lorde again employs African mythology to symbolically link the histories of Black women warriors around the world, from Winnie Mandela to Rosa Parks.

Lorde also received accolades for her prose works, including *The Cancer Journals* (1980), *Zami: A New Spelling of My Name* (1982), and *Sister Outsider: Essays and Speeches by Audre Lorde* (1984). *The Cancer Journals,* her first major prose publication, chronicles her battle with cancer. She later won critical acclaim for her autobiographical novel *Zami,* which was touted by her publishers as a "biomythography, combining elements of history, biography and myth." In *Sister Outsider,* a compilation of essays and addresses delivered over a period of six years, Lorde reflected on her development as both a poet and a feminist. *The Marvelous Arithmetics of Distance* (1993), her last volume of poetry, was published after her 1992 death from liver cancer. In poems such as "Today Is Not the Day," Lorde contemplates her encroaching mortality. Characteristically, the poems do not indulge in self-pity but rather celebrate life and love.

Throughout her career, Lorde received mixed reviews and suffered from insufficient exposure to a wider readership. Her work, however, at once personal and political, individual and communal, ensures Lorde a lasting place in the American poetry canon, and confirms her prediction: "my words will be there."

FIONA MILLS

**Biography**

Born in New York City, 18 February 1934. Attended Hunter College, New York, B.A. 1959; Columbia University, New York, M.L.S. 1961; librarian, Mount Vernon Public Library, New York, 1961–63; Instructor, Town School, New York, 1966–68; poet-in-residence, Tougaloo College, Mississippi, 1968; Visiting Professor, Atlanta University, Georgia, 1968; Instructor, City College of New York, 1968–70, and Lehman College, New York, 1969–70; Lecturer, 1970–71, Associate Professor, 1972–78, and Professor of English, 1978–81, John Jay College of Criminal Justice, New York; from 1981 Professor of English, and from 1987 Thomas Hunter Professor, Hunter College; poetry editor, *Chrysalis* and *Amazon Quarterly;* advisory editor, *Black Box;* contributing editor, *Black Scholar;* editor, *Pound* magazine, 1968. Received National Endowment for the Arts grant, 1968, 1981; Creative Artists Public Service grant, 1972, 1976; Broadside Poets Award, 1975; Gay Caucus Book of the Year Award, 1981; Borough of Manhattan President's Award for Literary Excellence, 1987; Before Columbus Foundation Award, 1989; Walt Whitman Citation of Merit, 1991; Poet Laureate of New York, 1991; honorary Litt.D., Oberlin College, Ohio, 1989. Died in St. Croix, 17 November 1992.

**Poetry**

*The First Cities,* 1968
*Cables to Rage,* 1970
*From a Land Where Other People Live,* 1973
*New York Head Shop and Museum,* 1974
*Coal,* 1976
*Between Our Selves,* 1976
*The Black Unicorn,* 1978
*Chosen Poems—Old and New,* 1982
*Our Dead behind Us,* 1986
*Undersong: Chosen Poems Old and New,* 1992
*The Marvelous Arithmetics of Distance—Poems, 1987–1992,* 1993
*Poetry Is Not a Luxury,* 1993
*The Collected Poems of Audre Lorde,* 1997

**Other Writings:** novel (*Zami: A New Spelling of My Name,* 1982), essays (*Sister Outsider: Essays and Speeches by Audre Lorde,* 1984; *A Burst of Light,* 1988), autobiography (*The Cancer Journals,* 1980).

**Further Reading**

Andrews, William L., Frances Foster Smith, and Trudier Harris, editors, *The Oxford Companion to African American Literature,* New York: Oxford University Press, 1997
Bigsby, C.W.E., editor, *The Black American Writer,* 2 vols., New York: Penguin, 1969
Brooks, Jerome, "In the Name of the Father: The Poetry of Audre Lorde," in *Black Women Writers (1950–1980): A Critical Evaluation,* edited by Mari Evans, Garden City, New York: Anchor Books/Doubleday, and London: Pluto, 1983
Christian, Barbara, editor, *Black Feminist Criticism: Perspectives on Black Women Writers,* Elmsford, New York: Pergamon Press, 1985; 2nd edition, New York: Teacher's College Press, 1997

Gayle, Addison, editor, *Black Expression: Essays by and about Black Americans in the Creative Arts,* New York: Weybright and Talley, 1969
Martin, Joan, "The Unicorn Is Black: Audre Lorde in Retrospect," in *Black Women Writers (1950–1980): A Critical Evaluation,* edited by Mari Evans, Garden City, New York: Anchor Books/Doubleday, and London: Pluto, 1983
Tate, Claudia, editor, *Black Women Writers at Work,* New York: Continuum, and Harpenden, Hertfordshire: Oldcastle, 1983

## Coal

Audre Lorde's *Coal,* published in 1976, is a compilation of work from her first two volumes of poetry: *The First Cities* (1968), much of which was written as early as Lorde's high school years, and *Cables to Rage* (1970). Between these earliest collections and their compilation in *Coal,* Lorde published two other collections, which marked a turn toward a more political tone and subject matter: *From a Land Where Other People Live* (1973), which was nominated for the National Book Award, and *New York Head Shop and Museum* (1974). By the time *Coal* was published, Lorde also had already been awarded one of her two National Endowment for the Arts grants, had received two Creative Artists Public Service grants, had been named Woman of the Year at Staten Island Community College, and had been included in numerous poetry anthologies, including *New Black Poetry* (1969). However, *Coal,* which was published by W.W. Norton and was reissued by that press in 1996, was Lorde's first collection with a major publisher and, therefore, with a wider reading audience than the mainly African-American readership of her earlier collections. Lorde's readership also may have increased because her writing was viewed as less strident and aggressive than much of African-American writing at that time. While *The Black Unicorn* (1978) is often considered her strongest poetic work, *Coal* is a solid introduction to Lorde's strongest themes, including the power of language, relationships between women, and the importance of valuing differences.

As Lorde herself says in "Poetry Is Not a Luxury," first published in 1977 and reprinted in *Sister Outsider: Essays and Speeches by Audre Lorde* (1984), "Poetry is the way we help give name to the nameless so it can be thought." She asks women especially to put their experiences and thoughts into words in order to use the power of language. In an interview with Adrienne Rich (*Sister Outsider*), Lorde says that, in high school, she would try "not to think in poems." However, she continued to read and memorize poetry and recited poems in response to questions about how she felt. Moreover, she began composing and memorizing her own poems, some of which appear in *Coal,* because she had feelings for which she had not found existing poems.

Poetry, in particular, allows Lorde's ideas and images to take shape, in part with sound, as in "To a Girl Who Knew What Side Her Bread Was Buttered On," the final poem in *Coal:*

He, through the eyes of the first marauder
saw her, his catch of bright thunder, heaping
tea and bread for her guardian dead
crunching the nut-dry words they said
and, thinking the bones were sleeping,
he broke through the muffled afternoon
calling an end to their ritual's tune
with lightning-like disorder[.]

In this passage, not only does the end rhyme ("marauder" and "disorder," "heaping" and "sleeping," "dead" and "said," and so on) provide an irregular echo, but the internal rhyme ("bread" and "dead") and the repeated consonant and vowel sounds ("heaping" and "tea," "bright" and "bread" and "broke," "lightning-like," the "-ing" words, and so on) simulate the effect of quickening and slowing, and also give the poem a coherence.

Often, relationships between women serve as Lorde's subject matter, particularly mother-daughter relationships. "Story Books on a Kitchen Table" begins, "Out of her womb of pain my mother spat me / into her ill-fitting harness of despair." The poem goes on to show the speaker alone, at least temporarily motherless, and haunted by story books full of "white witches [who] ruled / over the empty kitchen table." In the end, there is no "enchantment / for the vanished mother / of a black girl." Fairy tales are not about reality—poems are.

In numerous poems, Lorde examines human relationships and their connections with nature. In "What My Child Learns of the Sea," the speaker, a mother, ponders what her daughter will learn of the sea and the seasons. The inevitable and amazing process of a child's growing up leads the daughter to become a stranger to her mother, leaving the speaker "already condemned." Lorde's poems, then, commingle the beautiful and the painful to render the complex relationships people have with one another and with their natural, urban, domestic, and political worlds.

The title poem, "Coal," among other poems in the collection, addresses both blackness and the value of diversity as well as Lorde's assertion that women must overcome silence. She begins, "I / is the total black, being spoken"; she goes on to discuss the variety of words—some like snakes, others like sparrows, some business-like, and still others that "bedevil me"—pointing out a particularly poignant ambiguity in the intention and reception of language; and she concludes, "I am Black because I come from the earth's inside / now take my word for jewel in the open light." While Lorde is sometimes criticized for essentializing the black woman as sensual and natural, here the black woman is the very stuff of earth—a part of each of us. Through the language of poetry and as an utterance herself, she also defines herself as "jewel"—as natural, universal, beautiful, and in full view for the audience.

In "Paperweight," Lorde brings her ideas about language and about the mother-daughter relationship together by describing her writing process:

All the poems I have ever written
are historical reviews of some now-absorbed country
a small judgement
hawking and coughing them up
I have ejected them not unlike children.
Now my throat is clear
and perhaps I shall speak again.

All the poems I have ever written
make a small book shaped like another me[.]

So, *Coal* is a version Lorde has made of herself, a voicing of who she once was so that she could move beyond it and to the next articulation. The poem also advocates various uses for the poems themselves: as "magic lanterns," "napkins," "kindling songs," and so on.

Poetic language, then, Lorde asserts, is powerful and necessary both in writing and in reading. In *Coal,* Lorde's view of power—as a black, lesbian, woman, and mother—and of language as necessary and beautiful utterance is her most important legacy, because it establishes American poetry as the place for various representations of the self and for various sounds, images, and voices coming together to render coherent meanings.

ANNA LEAHY

**Further Reading**

Christian, Barbara, editor, *Black Feminist Criticism: Perspectives on Black Women Writers,* Elmsford, New York: Pergamon, 1985; 2nd edition, New York: Teacher's College Press, 1997

Hammond, Karla M., "Audre Lorde: Interview," *Denver Quarterly* 16, no. 1 (Spring 1981)

Keating, AnaLouise, *Women Reading Women Writing: Self-Invention in Paula Gunn Allen, Gloria Anzaldúa, and Audre Lorde,* Philadelphia, Pennsylvania: Temple University Press, 1996

Kimmich, Allison, "Writing the Body: From Abject to Subject," *Auto/Biography Studies: A/B* 13, no. 2 (1998)

Lorde, Audre, *Sister Outsider: Essays and Speeches by Audre Lorde,* Trumansburg, New York: Crossing Press, 1984

Reid, Catherine, and Holly Iglesias, editors, *Every Woman I've Ever Loved: Lesbian Writers on Their Mothers,* San Francisco: Cleis Press, 1997

Rowell, Charles H., "Above the Wind: An Interview with Audre Lorde," *Callaloo* 14, no. 1 (Winter 1991)

Tate, Claudia, editor, *Black Women Writers at Work,* New York: Continuum, and Harpenden, Herfordshire: Oldcastle, 1983

"A Tribute to Audre Lorde," *Standards: An International Journal of Multicultural Studies* 5, no. 1 (Fall 1995)

## Walking Our Boundaries

"Walking Our Boundaries" is a selection from Audre Lorde's volume titled *The Black Unicorn* (1978), a work many critics believe to be her most ambitious and fully articulated. Indeed, Lorde was quite adamant about the unity of this work and the intimate relationship among the poems, so much so that she did not select any work from *The Black Unicorn* for the later volume *Chosen Poems—Old and New* (1982). Lorde opted not to isolate any one poem from the collection "because the wholeness of that sequence/conversation [could not] yet be breached." The works in *The Black Unicorn,* then, have an indelible connection, exemplified by the relationship between the more well-known and more widely anthologized piece "A Litany for Survival" and the lesser-known "Walking Our Boundaries."

Perhaps the single unifying theme of *The Black Unicorn* can be located in the cover illustration of the book: an image of Tji-Wara (or Chi-Wara), an ancient African (specifically Bambara) headdress. For Lorde, the black cultural version of the unicorn, that fabled creature, derives from the spirit of Tji-Wara. Tji-Wara has three main associations: a headdress used in dances to ensure fertility of the seed and of the crop, a name for a goddess of earth and fertility (vegetative and otherwise), and a name for witches to whom some conciliatory offering must be made in order to avoid evil. This image and its various connotations tie a people to their land, to their creations, indeed to their very survival. Thus, Tji-Wara is a kind of connective tissue, and, at least in the context of this volume, it suggests the bond between poems and underscores Lorde's attempt to connect past to present and that present to some unknowable yet hoped for future.

One criticism levied against Lorde is that her work is too polemical, too political, and too personal. Of course, Lorde is famous for having repeatedly stated that the personal is political; for Lorde, the personal is also poetic. She refused to reserve poetry for "the sterile word play that, too often, the white fathers distorted the word *poetry* to mean" (Lorde, 1984). Poetry, like life, is often messy. "Walking Our Boundaries" is not the most noted piece from *The Black Unicorn.* It is, however, a poem that expresses this messiness, that gives voice to issues easily left unspoken, and that possesses a level of subtlety for which Lorde is not often given credit.

In the poem, an unstated parallel is drawn between Lorde's ongoing struggle with cancer and the cyclical (and thus ongoing) struggle of one who attempts to garner an existence from the land. This duality is subtle yet vitally important to a full appreciation of the work. In an interview with Charles H. Rowell conducted on 29 August 1990, Lorde says,

> [A] poem grows out of the poet's experience, in a particular place and a particular time, and the genius of the poem is to use the textures of that place and time without becoming bound by them. Then the poem becomes an emotional bridge to others who have not shared that experience. The poem evokes its own world. (Rowell, 1991)

The specificity of Lorde's life experience is her battle with cancer, a fight she would ultimately lose in 1992. However, as the poem indicates, Lorde is bound neither to images of hospital beds and waiting rooms nor to images of bitter winters and early thaws. While focusing on the latter may be comfortable, it would not be wholly truthful. It would be "safe" to ignore her lesbianism, yet doing so would also be untrue. Given the ominous presence of cancer in Lorde's life, safety held little significance, for as she once wrote, "I was going to die, if not sooner then later, whether or not I had ever spoken myself. My silences had not protected me" (Lorde, 1984).

In "Walking Our Boundaries," Lorde bridges the space between herself and an anonymous audience she cannot know by utilizing a standard poetic metaphor (seasonal transformation). Lines 1 and 2 of "Walking Our Boundaries" provide a fine example: "This first bright day has broken / the back of winter." These lines clearly point to the first thaw that marks a break from winter and anticipates a period of springtime renewal to come. Read within the context of Lorde's ongoing battle with breast cancer, however, the same lines have a different import. "This first bright day" may well indicate Lorde's return to health or at least a period of remission from the disease, with remission providing a break from the winter of serious illness.

It is important to note that this "bright day" is not met alone, just as the struggle, whatever its specific nature, is not faced alone, although Lorde waits until the poem nears its conclusion to reveal that this union exists between women:

The sun is watery warm
our voices
seem too loud for this small yard
too tentative for women
so in love

The two women, presumably Lorde and someone else, a lover, walk the boundaries of their house "stunned that sun can shine so brightly / after all our [their] pain." What is this pain? There is pain involved in watching the ravages of winter on the land, on the "vine," on the "fruit" of a now long-past harvest, but there is also pain in the struggle to survive disease, in whatever form (be it literally cancer or the societal cancers of racism, sexism, homophobia, and the like). Lorde is undoubtedly changed by chemotherapy and by a partial mastectomy; so are those who love her. Yet they (this union of women) endure, indeed survive, not unlike the way in which

part of last year's garden still stands
bracken
one tough missed okra pod clings to the vine
a parody of fruit cold-hard and swollen
underfoot.

What remains after "war," after winter, after cancer, is indeed tough. However, this residue is not just "cold-hard and swollen." This residue is "becoming loam," the substance out of which something strong may be built. This residue, in essence the poem itself, is part of "the compost heap" and is the substance out of which something new will grow:

I do not know when
we shall laugh again
but next week
we will spade up another plot
for this spring's seeding.

SHARON L. MOORE

**Further Reading**


Birkle, Carmen, *Women's Stories of the Looking Glass: Autobiographical Reflections and Self-Representations in the Poetry of Sylvia Plath, Adrienne Rich, and Audre Lorde*, Munich: Fink, 1996

Carr, Brenda, "'A Woman Speaks . . . I Am Woman and Not White': Politics of Voice, Tactical Essentialism, and Cultural Intervention in Audre Lorde's Activist Poetics and Practice," *College Literature* 20, no. 2 (June 1993)

Keating, AnaLouise, *Women Reading Women Writing: Self-Invention in Paula Gunn Allen, Gloria Anzaldúa, and Audre Lorde*, Philadelphia, Pennsylvania: Temple University Press, 1996

Lorde, Audre, *Sister Outsider: Essays and Speeches by Audre Lorde*, Trumansburg, New York: Crossing Press, 1984

Martin, Joan, "The Unicorn Is Black: Audre Lorde in Retrospect," in *Black Women Writers (1950–1980): A Critical Evaluation*, edited by Mari Evans, Garden City, New York: Anchor Books/Doubleday, and London: Pluto, 1983

Perreault, Jeanne Martha, *Writing Selves: Contemporary Feminist Autobiography*, Minneapolis: University of Minnesota Press, 1995

Rowell, Charles H., "Above the Wind: An Interview with Audre Lorde," *Callaloo* 14, no. 1 (Winter 1991)

Steele, Cassie Premo, *We Heal from Memory: Sexton, Lorde, Anzaldúa, and the Poetry of Witness*, New York: St. Martin's Press, 2000

Wilson, Anna, "Rites/Rights of Canonization: Audre Lorde as Icon," in *Women Poets of the Americas: Toward a Pan-American Gathering*, edited by Jacqueline Vaught Brogan and Cordelia Chavez Candelaria, Notre Dame, Indiana: University of Notre Dame Press, 1999


---

## Amy Lowell 1874–1925

When Amy Lowell died suddenly in May of 1925 she was arguably the most powerful woman in American poetry. During a brief and intense career, beginning with the publication of her first volume of poetry in 1912 and lasting until her death 13 years later at the age of 51, she produced six volumes of poetry, two volumes of criticism, a two-volume biography of John Keats, and countless articles and reviews. Three more volumes of poetry were published posthumously, the first of which, *What's O'Clock*, won the 1926 Pulitzer Prize. Since her death, however, she has become little more than a footnote to discussions of more canonical modern poets like Ezra Pound and Robert Frost, and her own work, out of print since 1957, is rarely anthologized and seldom discussed in literary criticism.

The youngest of Augustus and Katherine Lowell's five children, Amy Lowell inherited a name synonymous with power and wealth. The Lowells dominated industry and the arts in Massachusetts from the arrival of the first family member, a British merchant named Percival Lowle, in 1639. Poets James Russell Lowell and Robert Lowell were both distant relations. Although Lowell's lifetime coincides with first-wave feminism, the gains made by women's rights advocates came slowly, if at all, to women in the Lowell family. Lowell's frustration with the limitations placed upon her gender is a frequent theme in her childhood journals and makes sporadic appearances in her poetry as well, most notably in "The Sisters," a meditation on female poets, and "Patterns," in which a woman's tight, corseted clothing represents her repressed sexuality:

Not a softness anywhere about me,
Only whalebone and brocade.
And I sink on a seat in the shade

Of a lime tree. For my passion
Wars against the stiff brocade.

Shortly after the publication of her first book, *A Dome of Many-Coloured Glass* (1912), Lowell read the poems of "H.D. Imagiste" in the January 1913 issue of Harriet Monroe's *Poetry*. The Imagists, a small, loosely-joined group of poets who aligned themselves against "the moralizing, tendentious whinings of the Victorians and the arid and tiresome laudations of the Georgians," strove for a new form of poetic expression, one which stressed the creation of concise, vivid images, not the evocation of sentiment (Heymann, 1980). Lowell recognized in their writings some of the techniques she herself was trying to perfect. Later that year she traveled to England to meet the poets writing under this banner: Ezra Pound, H.D., and Richard Aldington. Enthusiastic about their work and eager to join their movement, she shared her poetry with them. Pound included one of her poems in his 1914 anthology *Des Imagistes* but by the next year had disowned the movement, which he claimed had deteriorated into overly sentimental Amygism.

Lowell, undeterred by Pound's disapproval, determined to bring the struggling poets she had met in England to the American public's attention. For three consecutive years, 1915, 1916, and 1917, she edited *Some Imagist Poets,* featuring poems by H.D., Aldington, D.H. Lawrence, F.S. Flint, John Gould Fletcher, and herself. At the same time she began a publicity campaign to teach the general public the principles of Imagism and Modern poetry. For the rest of her life she spent a great portion of each year touring the country giving lectures and readings, prompting T.S. Eliot to label her a "demon saleswoman" (Heymann, 1980). These were controversial events, more often than not ending with conservative critics accusing her of attempting to destroy poetry; on one occasion they even "charged the podium, demanding that Amy step down."

While Lowell's first book was neither a critical nor commercial success, her next book, *Sword Blades and Poppy Seed* (1914), garnered both critical acclaim and public enthusiasm. This volume also showed Lowell to be an exceptionally versatile poet: made up of Imagist lyrics, ballads, and dramatic monologues in which she experiments with free verse, it included several poems written in what she called polyphonic prose, a form of poetry that looks like prose but employs poetic tools such as rhyme, cadence, alliteration, and assonance.

With her next book, *Men, Women, and Ghosts* (1916), Lowell began to separate her long, narrative and descriptive poems from her shorter lyrical poems. Whereas this volume consists entirely of narrative monologues, and her next, *Can Grande's Castle* (1918), consists of four novella-length studies of war, *Pictures of the Floating World* (1919) is made up solely of lyrics. In *Legends* (1921) Lowell retold and reinterpreted folk tales from several different cultures, while in *Fir-Flower Tablets* (1921) she collaborated with Florence Ascough in translating Chinese poetry. *A Critical Fable* (1922), originally published anonymously, parodied the styles and careers of her fellow poets. After her death in 1925 the remainder of her poems was published in three volumes: the first two, *What's O'Clock* (1925) and *East Wind* (1926), had been prepared by Lowell before her death; Lowell's companion and literary executor Ada Dwyer Russell assembled and edited *Ballads for Sale* (1927) from the poems left uncollected.

In addition to poetry Lowell produced several volumes of literary criticism. With *Six French Poets* (1915) she introduced her favorite contemporary French poets to American audiences. In *Tendencies in Modern American Poetry* (1917), a study of six contemporary poets (Edwin Arlington Robinson, Robert Frost, Edgar Lee Masters, Carl Sandburg, H.D., and John Gould Fletcher) Lowell created a critical genealogy of modern poetry, ending, of course, with Imagism. Finally, she wrote a massive two-volume biography of John Keats (1925), published just months before her death. Ferris Greenslet collected several of her most popular articles and lectures and published them posthumously in *Poetry and Poets* (1930).

Critical evaluations of Lowell have radically shifted. During her lifetime she was praised for her work in polyphonic prose; *Can Grande's Castle* in particular was regarded as a masterpiece. Feminist critics such as Lillian Faderman and Judy Grahn initiated rereadings of her work, focusing their attention primarily on her lyrical poetry, especially the love lyrics written for Ada Dwyer Russell, such as "Madonna of the Evening Flowers," "The Weather-Cock Points South," and "Venus Transiens."

MELISSA BRADSHAW

*See also* Imagism

**Biography**

Born in Brookline, Massachusetts, 9 February 1874. Educated privately; associated with the Imagists in London, 1913, and afterward promoted their work in America as editor, publisher, and patron; Lecturer, Brooklyn Institute of Arts and Sciences, 1917–18. Received Pulitzer Prize, 1926; honorary Litt.D., Baylor University, Waco, Texas, 1920. Died in Brookline, 12 May 1925.

**Poetry**

*A Dome of Many-Coloured Glass,* 1912
*Sword Blades and Poppy Seed,* 1914
*Men, Women, and Ghosts,* 1916
*Can Grande's Castle,* 1918
*Pictures of the Floating World,* 1919
*Legends,* 1921
*Fir-Flower Tablets: Poems Translated from the Chinese* by Florence Ayscough, English versions by Lowell, 1921
*A Critical Fable,* 1922
*What's O'Clock,* edited by Ada Dwyer Russell, 1925
*East Wind,* edited by Ada Dwyer Russell, 1926
*The Madonna of Carthagena,* 1927
*Ballads for Sale,* edited by Ada Dwyer Russell, 1927
*Selected Poems of Amy Lowell,* edited by John Livingston Lowes, 1928
*The Complete Poetical Works,* 1955
*A Shard of Silence: Selected Poems,* edited by Glenn Richard Ruihley, 1957

**Selected Criticism**

*Six French Poets,* 1915
*Tendencies in Modern American Poetry,* 1917

**Other Writings:** play, short stories (*Dream Drops; or, Stories from Fairy Land* [with Elizabeth Lowell and Katherine Bigelow Lowell], 1887), essays (*Poetry and Poets: Essays* [edited by Ferris Greenslet], 1930), biography (*John Keats,* 2 vols., 1925); edited collections of poetry (*Some Imagist Poets,* 3 vols., 1915–17).

**Further Reading**

Benvenuto, Richard, *Amy Lowell,* Boston: Twayne, 1985

Faderman, Lillian, "Warding Off the Watch and Ward Society: Amy Lowell's Treatment of the Lesbian Theme," *Gay Books Bulletin* 1 (Summer 1979)

Galvin, Mary E., *Queer Poetics: Five Modernist Writers,* Westport, Connecticut, and London: Praeger, 1999

Grahn, Judy, *The Highest Apple: Sappho and the Lesbian Poetic Tradition,* San Francisco: Spinsters Ink, 1985

Heymann, C. David, *American Aristocracy: The Lives and Times of James Russell, Amy, and Robert Lowell,* New York: Dodd Mead, 1980

Lauter, Paul, "Amy Lowell and Cultural Borders," in *Speaking the Other Self: American Women Writers,* edited by Jeanne Campbell Reesman, Athens: University of Georgia Press, 1997

Thacker, Andrew, "Amy Lowell and H.D.: The Other Imagists," *Women: A Cultural Review* 4, no. 1 (1993)

Walker, Cheryl, *Masks, Outrageous and Austere: Culture, Psyche, and Persona in Modern Women Poets,* Bloomington: Indiana University Press, 1991

## Patterns

"Patterns" first appeared in *The Little Review* in August 1915 and later served as the opening poem of *Men, Women, and Ghosts* (1916). Although it includes profanity and an explicit female sexual fantasy, the poem was instantly popular and became Lowell's most anthologized work. Possibly set in the 18th century—the unspecified reference to one of the many English campaigns in Flanders leaves the date uncertain—the work suggests an antiwar sentiment that some readers have applied to World War I, which also included considerable combat in both French and West Flanders.

"Patterns" exemplifies the range of the free-verse form celebrated by Lowell, using soliloquy to reveal the private thoughts and feelings of a solitary woman at a poignant moment in her life. That morning, a messenger from the battlefield gave the speaker the terrible news that her fiancé, Lord Hartwell, was killed in Flanders while fighting beside an unnamed duke. We overhear her soliloquy as she walks, with "powdered hair and jewelled fan," in her ornate artificial garden. She is grief-stricken and angry, but as a woman of social standing must not publicly display her feelings. Just as the pleasure garden is defined by "patterned garden-paths," so too she stands "upright . . . / Held rigid to the pattern / By the stiffness of" her brocaded gown. The weight of social conventions and expectations oppresses her as she struggles to suppress her unseemly emotions behind a proper demeanor.

Such suppression is hardly easy at this traumatic juncture in her life. As a result, a virtual dialogue ensues in her mind between a socially determined propriety (what her mind knows she should do) and a personally desired impropriety (what her heart knows she would like to do). She acknowledges this internal conflict when she indicates that her "passion / Wars against the stiff brocade." Throughout "Patterns" this divided sensibility is conveyed both in the aimless circular movement of the protagonist and in a verse cadence that balances precariously between regularity and irregularity.

As a lime-tree-scented wind gently drops a blossom on her bosom, her feelings surge. She fantasizes dropping her gown, the outward symbol of rigid social decorum, and then bathing naked in the garden fountain. Beneath the dripping fountain, she imagines, her body and its desires, customarily concealed beneath the clothing-like layers of convention, would be as open to nature as are the yellow daffodils and the blue star hyacinths (squills) beneath the breeze.

Her fantasy goes further than nude bathing. She imagines that her fiancé finds her there, strokes her, and then playfully chases her (as an enticing Eve-figure) through the garden until she lets him catch her at the shaded center of a hedge maze. With unpatterned sun-drops and water-drops as background, their love is consummated "in the open afternoon."

But the blossom that occasions this reverie is in fact a fallen bloom no longer open to reproductive (regenerative) possibility. It lands where the woman has secreted the missive announcing the death of her lover. The script of this letter "squirmed like snakes" as her eyes well up with tears, and indeed it is as if the serpent from the Garden of Eden has appeared in her personal garden. Mortality was the outcome of the serpent's villainous work in Eden, and the would-be Eve in "Patterns" likewise now identifies with the demise of the fallen flower's prospects. Whereas spring daffodils and star hyacinths will give way to summer roses, then to autumn asters, and finally to snow, there will be no such seasonal progress for her. Their blooms will renew in a seemingly eternal cycle, whereas her aimless circular tread on the patterned paths of the garden—and of her life—is a travesty of such natural design.

The protagonist may be as "Gorgeously arrayed" as the flowers in her garden, but "the softness of [her] body will be guarded from embrace" forever because "the man who should loose [her] is dead." As the name of her deceased lover suggests, the lady's wounded heart will never be well. Lord Hartwell has died "in a pattern called a war," and so too her emotions, including her potential for passionate sexual fulfillment, are no longer "open" to the future; such a possibility has fallen like a prematurely dropped bloom. Her feelings, as bitter as a lime but without the memory of the sweet blossom, will remain suppressed beneath the stiff pattern of her outward social circumstance.

In this poem the notion of patterns represents the work of human consciousness, which attempts to impose order and meaning on the naturally random expression of human desires. Consciousness searches for and creates patterns in what is otherwise the welter of timeless being, and these patterns at once express and enforce the individual's sense of distance from pure being. So humanity creates ordered gardens to control nature, dons clothing and social mores to deny human sexuality—"What is Summer in a fine brocaded gown," the Lady bitterly asks—and engages in military campaigns to fashion unnatural political configurations.

Ironically, consciousness of both psychological and physical loss (mortality) engenders a sense of the beauty of existence, a beauty that always eludes human desire. The protagonist's emotions and her sensual fantasy are so intense precisely *because* her lover has died. For Lowell, such awareness is bittersweet at best. When at the close of her soliloquy the lady asks, "Christ! What are patterns for?" she expresses more than her grief and anger;

she also summarizes Lowell's abiding puzzlement over humanity's apparently unredemptive estrangement from nature. This sense of exile from nature, the result of a pattern-making consciousness, paradoxically creates human desire for a natural beauty or beautiful possibility always beyond its reach.

WILLIAM J. SCHEICK

**Further Reading**

Benvenuto, Richard, *Amy Lowell,* Boston: Twayne, 1985 (see especially pages 72–76)

Damon, S. Foster, *Amy Lowell: A Chronicle,* Boston: Houghton Mifflin, 1935

Gould, Jean, *Amy: The World of Amy Lowell and the Imagist Movement,* New York: Dodd, Mead, 1975

Scheick, William J., "Art of Estrangement: Four Imagiste Poems by Amy Lowell," *The Journal of Imagism* 3 (1998)

## The Sisters

First published in *The North American Review* (1922) and then in the posthumous, Pulitzer Prize–winning *What's O'Clock* (1925), Amy Lowell's "The Sisters" addresses the relationship of gender, tradition, and individual talent. Contemporary readers might recognize in its title a feminist reference to the notion of sisterhood as a community of women who empower each other. "The Sisters" would largely disappoint those utopian or sentimental expectations. Each woman poet, hemmed in by gendered, repressive conventions, the poem concludes, must invent herself. The woman poet, speaking as Lowell herself, longs to recognize in her work past generations of a female tradition, however "little." Lowell emphasizes the diminutive to represent this tiny band of misfits:

Taking us by and large, we're a queer lot
We women who write poetry. And when you think
How few of us there've been, it's queerer still.

Lowell's declarative opening would seem to brook no disagreement. Her meditative voice invites intimacy, but her statement is both true to women writers' isolation from each other and exaggerated. The female tradition was neither as queer nor as little as she asserts. It is true that many older "sisters" would have been unavailable to Lowell's generation, but Lowell herself was certainly aware of some impressive Victorian women poets and some fine poets of her own generation. Her poem, then, is a work of mythopoesis, an act of poetic self-creation. Her internal monologue depicts her own poetic inhibitions as an attribute of the woman poet through time. The poem eventually intimates that what is missing from women's poetic tradition does not depend on how many women poets there have been. Lowell is looking for a model and therefore authorization for an unconstrained women's poetry.

Ironically, Lowell's self-positioning as a singular poet recalls the stance of the solitary Romantic male poets, to whom Lowell had strong affinities. Her two-volume biography of John Keats was in the making when she was writing "The Sisters." In its form, the poem resembles also the internal monologues of the great Victorian male poets whom she read carefully, namely, Alfred Tennyson and, more important, Robert Browning. The Romantic pose is a strong contrast to Lowell's public persona and her own gregarious organizational skills. In her lectures, her essays, and her famous readings, Lowell forged various communities of poets, first an international group of Imagists, then a selection of contemporary American poets. However, the poem itself invites entry into the poet's emotional reality. In Lowell's private space at the top of her mansion, the poet writes of limitation as part of her heritage. In the midst of plenty—of rooms and rooms of her own and access to an international set of writers—Lowell finds herself inhibited by her genes and her chromosomes. In "The Sisters," the poet addresses only three women poets/sisters: the Greek Sappho, the Victorian Elizabeth Barrett Browning, and the New England 19th-century Emily Dickinson. Why these chosen few?

One can only speculate on the answers, but Lowell's characterization of the three reveals her limitations and longings. Lowell, the energetic proselytizer of clear images and strong verse, wishes for a permissible language to figure the female body and acceptable terms to express female desire. "Sapho" comes first in the Bostonian's wished-for sorority. As a poet known in fragments and through scholarly, phantasmic reconstruction, Sappho's very name evokes desire and nostalgia. Lowell inherited her first sister through a great quickening of interest in the turn of the century, which constructed her as a lesbian, a poet of unmediated ability to write her own passionate desire for women:

There's Sapho, now I wonder what was Sapho.
I know a single slender thing about her:
That loving, she was like a burning birch-tree
All tall and glittering fire, and that she wrote
Like the same fire caught up to Heaven and held there,
A frozen blaze before it broke and fell.

Because she was not bound by family labels—"not Miss or Mrs."—Sappho might join with her younger sister to toss their linguistic "reticences . . . Into the wind." The speaker dreams of a common woman's language, unmasked and unfettered, but she knows that every age has filled in the Sapphic fragments "for convenience" and that her Sappho is only a specter. Invoking this ephemeral genius enables Lowell at once to imagine other constructions of family and other, freer "loveliness of words," a poetic language to articulate women's desire.

Lowell next reaches out to "Mrs. Browning," knowing a great deal about her life and appreciating that she could not have called her by her intimate family nickname, "Ba," as actual sisters did. So Mrs. Browning it has to be, both language and body "squeezed in stiff conventions." Lowell addresses the Elizabeth Barrett Browning of popular mythology, the invalid of Wimpole Street, rescued by the poet Robert Browning and whisked off to marriage and motherhood in warm Italy. This queer poet, tied to her sofa, reads Greek and writes her great sonnet sequence, "Sonnets from the Portuguese," only when "fertilized" by her genius husband.

Lowell's aesthetic judgment of Barrett Browning as "not herself so curious a technician" contrasts with Robert Browning, who barges into the poem despite Lowell's efforts to banish him: "I do not like the turn this dream is taking." The charming intimacy of Lowell's admission acknowledges the considerable influence of Mrs. Browning's husband on Lowell's conversational monologue. The ending, where Amy has entertained her three older sisters as if at one of her famous dinner parties, putting them into "the motor" and calling after them "Good night! Good night!," echoes Browning's Andrea del Sarto, who bids farewell to his unfaithful wife ("Go, my love"), who refuses to act as his muse and whom he blames for his failure to become a great artist.

As she turns to Emily Dickinson, her third older sister, Lowell blames her failed relationships with all of them primarily on that "bat-eyed, narrow-minded" Queen Victoria and secondarily on Martin Luther's repressive Christianity. Her villains prey on the "Anglo-Saxon" race, inhibiting its women with sexual prudery and leading them to neurasthenia. "Emily" paid with her body, according to "The Sisters," "only giving / Herself to hard cold paper." Lowell has fun with this virginal, enigmatic Emily, whom she meets in her garden by leaping over a fence rather than primly presenting her card at the Dickinson front door. With Emily, Lowell suggests, she could share secrets—of sexuality and of language—without having to decode them. However, this would be at great price. At its root, the Anglo-Saxon heritage, which Lowell in fact worried about losing in American poetry, constrains its women. Lowell's racial affinity allows her to criticize yet to value her genetic heritage. It blinds her in this poem to many possible sisters. Did she not know the fierce Victorian lyricist Christina Rossetti, whose collected poems had been available, printed in Boston as early as 1909? Lowell's Sappho may substitute for her close contemporaries who idealized the poet of Lesbos: Sara Teasdale, Edna St. Vincent Millay, and H.D. She has not sought out Black sister poets; not her fellow Bostonian, the well-known slave Phillis Wheatley, whose publications most likely rested in the Boston Athenaeum, an institution supported by Lowell herself; not Anne Spencer, her close contemporary, whose poems resemble Lowell's; and not the powerful Georgia Douglas Johnson. Lowell recognizes yet depends on her limitation of race, class, and gender as she seeks models for replication in her own kind:

> Good-bye, my sisters, all of you are great,
> And all of you are marvellously strange,
> And none of you has any work for me.
> I cannot write like you.

"Sad and self-distrustful," Lowell graciously turns from her sisters but finds them understandable, "near" in their very limitations—like family. "The Sisters" shows us Lowell voicing personal regret, speaking, as Virginia Woolf was to do soon after, for the cultural and familial terrors that have kept writing women apart. The language of the poem shows Lowell at a strong moment, creating such memorable images of female self-abandonment and bodily alienation as this image of Emily Dickinson:

> She hung her womanhood upon a bough
> And played ball with the stars—too long—too long—
> The garment of herself hung on a tree
> Until at last she lost even the desire
> To take it down.

At the poem's end, Lowell fancies that her work might provide a place of sisterly recognition:

> I only hope that possibly some day
> Some other woman with an itch for writing
> May turn to me as I have turned to you
> And chat with me a brief few minutes.

Yet, even with her hope, she does not conceive of being able to give more than she herself has taken from her three sisters, nor does she imagine a group of women poets arriving at her door. The "other woman with an itch for writing" visits alone.

ADRIENNE MUNICH

**Further Reading**

Erkkila, Betsy, *The Wicked Sisters: Women Poets, Literary History, and Discord*, Oxford and New York: Oxford University Press, 1992

Walker, Cheryl, *Masks, Outrageous and Austere: Culture, Psyche, and Persona in Modern Women Poets*, Bloomington: Indiana University Press, 1991

---

# Robert Lowell 1917–77

A stylistic innovator and a voice of conscience, Robert Lowell strongly influenced American poetry and culture. His poetry ranged from the complex verbal structures and the quest for redemption that mark his early poetry through the personal memory and secularized despair of his landmark volume, *Life Studies* (1959), to the later emphasis on political and historical issues and finally a concern with aging and death. A pacifist with violent tendencies, Lowell involved himself in a number of political controversies, most notably two with U.S. Presidents. In the 1940s he criticized President Franklin D. Roosevelt for the conduct of World War II, and in the 1960s he rebuked President Lyndon B. Johnson for initiating the Vietnam War. Lowell changed American poetry by expanding its capacity to address both one's personal life and the public sphere. Through his powerful texts and his political interventions, he helped place poetry at the center of American and international culture.

Lowell was born in Boston, the only child of Robert Traill Spence Lowell IV and Charlotte Winslow Lowell. Among his ancestors were Puritan patriarchs Edward Winslow and Josiah Winslow, poets James Russell Lowell and Amy Lowell, astronomer Percival Lowell, and Harvard president Abbott Lawrence Lowell. Despite these illustrious antecedents, Lowell grew up in a family torn between high social aspirations and problematic financial realities, destabilized by his parents' endless and profound conflicts. Moreover, the antecedents themselves were blemished: Josiah Winslow committed brutal acts against Native Americans, James Russell Lowell was a poet "pedestalled for oblivion" (Meyers, 1988), Percival Lowell discovered nonexistent canals on Mars, and Abbott Lawrence Lowell helped send the possibly innocent Sacco and Vanzetti to their deaths. Lowell grew up notably ambivalent about both family and history, the two topics that would eventually drive his poetic career.

Lowell spent two years at Harvard (1935–37), where he earned mediocre grades and received no recognition for his early attempts at writing poetry. After a violent quarrel with his father, he left home, camped out for a summer on the lawn of the poet and critic Allen Tate, and transferred to Kenyon College (1937–40). At Kenyon, he began to come into his own. He studied with poet John Crowe Ransom, befriended fellow student and incipient poet Randall Jarrell, and published poems in the student magazine. He also excelled academically, graduating summa cum laude in Classics. After graduating, he married the brilliant fiction writer Jean Stafford, converted to Roman Catholicism, and did a year of graduate study with Cleanth Brooks and Robert Penn Warren at Louisiana State University (1940–41). Lowell then returned for a year's stay at the home of Allen Tate and his wife, novelist Caroline Gordon. There he wrote the highly rhetorical religious and political poems that appeared in his first book, the privately printed *Land of Unlikeness* (1944).

At about this time Lowell was inducted into the army. Although he had previously attempted to enlist, he now refused the draft, publicly releasing a letter to President Roosevelt criticizing both the bombing of German civilians and the U.S. demand for Germany's unconditional surrender. Sentenced to a year in prison, he served five and a half months, emerging (as he later said) "educated—not as they wished *re*-educated" (*Collected Prose,* 1987).

Two years after his release from prison Lowell published his first major volume, *Lord Weary's Castle* (1946), which won the Pulitzer Prize and established him as the leading poet of his generation. In this book his early rhetorical excess had been tamed and his linguistic complexity heightened. Randall Jarrell wrote that the book concerns a "conflict of opposites" between everything that blinds or binds and everything that grows or changes (Axelrod, 1999). This struggle informs the poems on a number of levels. On the religious plane, it manifests itself in "The Quaker Graveyard in Nantucket" and "Where the Rainbow Ends" as a clash between forces of war and mammon and the possibility of Christian salvation. On the historical plane, it emerges in "At the Indian Killer's Grave" and "Concord" as a contrast between the barbarous genocide of the Native Americans and the pacifism of a Thoreau or a Jesus. On the personal plane, it appears in "Rebellion" and "In the Cage" as an interior battle between violence and remorse. Lowell's vivid, allusive, and inspired language in this volume produces numerous moments of wrenching intensity and rarer occasions of something approaching transcendence.

In *Lord Weary's Castle* Lowell perfected a late Modernist style of poetry that had been current for almost 40 years, combining daring verbal experiment with traditional moral and social belief systems. By the early 1950s that style was no longer working for Lowell or for American poetry. During this period Lowell encountered a series of life-changing alterations. He lost his religious faith, he divorced Jean Stafford and married the critic and novelist Elizabeth Hardwick, his parents passed away, and he began to undergo a series of bipolar episodes that resulted in institutionalization. Moreover, he now questioned the late Modernist style that had brought him fame. In *The Mills of the Kavanaughs* (1951) he tried adapting his dense verbal style to narrative poems with only middling success. Then he reduced himself to virtual silence, touring Europe, teaching in U.S. universities, starting a family (his daughter Harriet Lowell was born in early 1957), and finding himself from time to time in mental hospitals.

By summer of 1957 Lowell was settled in Boston and desperate to be writing poetry again. He had tried composing a prose autobiography but found the project slow going. He had been impressed by hearing Allen Ginsberg read the personal and prophetic poems that had gone into *Howl* (1956), and he had received a different sort of tutelage in personal writing by reading the painful divorce poems of his student W.D. Snodgrass, later published in *Heart's Needle* (1959). Perhaps even more important, he was studying the poetry of friend Elizabeth Bishop and of his new mentor William Carlos Williams. He carried Bishop's "The Armadillo" around in his wallet, and he paid visits to Williams to drink whiskey and discuss poetics. All four of these poets, in different ways, propelled Lowell to invent a new style that was personal, playful, and exploratory. His poems in this style would center on personal and familial memory rather than on cultural prophecy. They would resemble family portraits or a photograph album, and they would have the richness, observation, and humor of good fiction. In late summer of 1957 Lowell drafted the amazing "Skunk Hour." Within a year—and in the midst of another mental collapse and recovery—he completed the rest of the poems that make up his "Life Studies" sequence.

When *Life Studies* was published in 1959 it created a sensation. It brought the self-disclosure and the plot and characters of autobiography into verse for perhaps the first time. Moreover, the poems possessed verbal qualities that were aesthetically exciting: dynamic juxtapositions of distance with revelation, social observation with personal feeling, and lucid narrativity with a complex and beautiful verbal fabric. The "Life Studies" sequence begins by representing Lowell as a young boy silently observing familial conflicts and deaths. It concludes by portraying him as an adult encountering his own marital difficulties, accumulating deaths, and finally the breakdown of his mind and spirit. The angry prophet of *Lord Weary's Castle* became, in *Life Studies,* a frail human being in a dense social universe, confronting an endless series of question marks. Lowell was reborn as a poet, and American poetry was pushed along toward its appointment with postmodernism.

Almost immediately following the publication of *Life Studies,* Lowell and Hardwick moved from Boston to New York, where they became notable members of the literary scene. In the 1960s Lowell published three major volumes of poetry and had two plays produced. Most of this work shows him trying to return from the personal to the public sphere. Keeping his newfound individual voice, he sought to re-address the larger national and international issues that had played such an important role in *Lord Weary's Castle.* The title poem of *For the Union Dead* (1964), for example, meditates on American history scarred by war, racism, and greed. Both an elegy for a courageous Civil War regiment of African-American soldiers and an anatomy of present-day Boston, the poem transforms Lowell's earlier prophetic mode. It depicts Augustus St. Gaudens' bas relief of the heroic Union Army soldiers as being "out of bounds" now in a Boston where "savage servility / slides by on grease." In a similar vein, "Waking Early Sunday Morning," published in *Near the Ocean* (1967), eloquently laments global conditions that produce "small war on the heels of small / war—until the end of time." "Central Park," appearing in the same volume, satirizes New York's class hierarchy.

Lowell's plays also attempt to do political work. *The Old Glory* (first performed in 1964) exposes imperialism and white supremacy by retelling classic tales by Nathaniel Hawthorne and Herman Melville. *Prometheus Bound* (first performed in 1967) questions patriarchy and war through a restaging of Aeschylus' ancient drama.

While Lowell was consciously inserting his writing into the political life of his nation, he was actively involving himself in politics as well. In 1965 he protested the Vietnam War by publicly declining President Johnson's invitation to attend a Festival of the Arts. It was reported that the President's bellow of rage could be heard echoing through the White House. Lowell subsequently joined Allen Ginsberg, Denise Levertov, Norman Mailer, and thousands of other protesters in the 1967 March on the Pentagon, and he acted as a senior adviser to antiwar Senator Eugene McCarthy in the 1968 presidential primaries. Lowell reflected on such activities in a flurry of political essays and in poems included in his last collection of the decade, *Notebook, 1967–1968* (1969). This book, a diary-like collection of unrhymed sonnets patterned around the seasonal cycle, includes poems on various political events as well as historical, literary, and personal topics.

In the 1970s Lowell retreated from the public sphere back to his personal experience. He moved to England in 1970, had a son (Robert Sheridan Lowell) with the writer Caroline Blackwood, divorced Hardwick, and married Blackwood. As these life-changing events occurred, he continued to produce unrhymed sonnets, finally publishing the whole lot in two new volumes, *History* and *For Lizzie and Harriet* (both 1973). He also published a brand new sonnet sequence called *The Dolphin* (1973), which focused on his artistic quest and his love for Blackwood. Opaque, disturbing in its violation of privacies, and often quite beautiful, this latter volume won Lowell a second Pulitzer Prize.

His heart and his marriage to Blackwood both failing, Lowell ultimately moved back to the United States and to Elizabeth Hardwick. He produced one final book of poems, *Day by Day* (1977), a moving account of the complicated conditions of his existence. The volume concludes with a poem called "Epilogue," an *ars poetica* exploring the role personal memory played in this poet's creative life. Several days after the book's publication, Lowell died of heart failure in a New York taxicab, en route home from a visit with Caroline Blackwood and their son.

From his early prophetic words to his last personal and meditative ones, Lowell made himself a central innovator and a dependably fascinating figure in American poetry. He brought Modernist poetry to one sort of blazing conclusion, and then he loosed the forces of change that ultimately produced both postmodernist and multicultural poetry. From almost the beginning of his career to the very end, he wrote texts that have become landmarks on the American scene, including "The Quaker Graveyard in Nantucket," "Skunk Hour," "For the Union Dead," "Waking Early Sunday Morning," and "Epilogue." Such poems matter today as much as they ever did.

STEVEN GOULD AXELROD

*See also* Confessional Poetry; War and Antiwar Poetry

**Biography**

Born in Boston, Massachusetts, 1 March 1917. Attended Harvard University, Cambridge, Massachusetts, 1935–37; Kenyon College, Gambier, Ohio, 1937–40, A.B. (summa cum laude) 1940 (Phi Beta Kappa); Louisiana State University, Baton Rouge, 1940–41; conscientious objector during World War II; served prison sentence, 1943–44; editorial assistant, Sheed and Ward, publishers, New York, 1941–42; teacher, University of Iowa, Iowa City, 1950, 1953, Kenyon School of Letters, Gambier, Ohio, 1950, 1953, Salzburg Seminar on American Studies, 1952, University of Cincinnati, 1954, Boston University, 1955–57, 1959–60, Harvard University, 1958, 1963–70, 1975, 1977, and New School for Social Research, New York, 1961–62; Visiting Fellow, All Souls College, Oxford, 1970; Professor of Literature, University of Essex, Wivenhoe, Colchester, 1970–72; consultant in poetry, Library of Congress, Washington, D.C., 1947–48. Received Pulitzer Prize, 1947, 1974; American Academy grant, 1947; Guggenheim fellowship, 1947, 1974; Harriet Monroe Poetry Award, 1952; Guinness Prize, 1959; National Book Award, 1960; Ford grant, for poetry, 1960, for drama, 1964; Bollingen Prize, for poetry translation, 1962; New England Poetry Club Golden Rose, 1964; Obie Award, for drama, 1965; Sarah Josepha Hale Award, 1966; Copernicus Award, 1974; National Medal for Literature, 1977; Chancellor, American Academy, 1962. Died in New York City, 12 September 1977.

**Poetry**

*Land of Unlikeness,* 1944
*Lord Weary's Castle,* 1946
*The Mills of the Kavanaughs,* 1951
*Life Studies,* 1959; augmented edition, 1959
*Imitations,* 1961
*For the Union Dead,* 1964
*Near the Ocean,* 1967
*Notebook, 1967–1968,* 1969; augmented edition, as *Notebook,* 1970
*The Dolphin,* 1973
*For Lizzie and Harriet,* 1973
*History,* 1973
*Selected Poems,* 1976; revised edition, 1977
*Day by Day,* 1977

**Selected Criticism**

*Collected Prose,* edited by Robert Giroux, 1987

**Other Writings:** plays (*Phaedra and Figaro* [with Jacques Barzun], 1961; *The Old Glory,* 1964; *Prometheus Bound,* 1967), translations of Italian and Greek literature (*Poesie,* by Eugenio Montale, 1960; *The Oresteia of Aeschylus,* 1978); edited collection of memoirs (*Randall Jarrell, 1914–1965* [with Peter Taylor and Robert Penn Warren], 1967).

**Further Reading**

Axelrod, Steven Gould, *Robert Lowell: Life and Art,* Princeton, New Jersey: Princeton University Press, 1978
Axelrod, Steven Gould, editor, *The Critical Response to Robert Lowell,* Westport, Connecticut, and London: Greenwood Press, 1999
Axelrod, Steven Gould, and Helen Deese, editors, *Robert Lowell: Essays on the Poetry,* New York: Cambridge University Press, 1996

Damon, Maria, *The Dark End of the Street: Margins in American Vanguard Poetry,* Minneapolis: University of Minnesota Press, 1993
Doreski, William, *Robert Lowell's Shifting Colors: The Poetics of the Public and the Personal,* Athens: Ohio University Press, 1999
Fein, Richard, *Robert Lowell,* New York: Twayne, 1970; 2nd edition, Boston: Twayne, 1979
Hamilton, Ian, *Robert Lowell: A Biography,* New York: Random House, 1982; London: Faber, 1983
Hart, Henry, *Robert Lowell and the Sublime,* Syracuse, New York: Syracuse University Press, 1995
Mariani, Paul, *Lost Puritan: A Life of Robert Lowell,* New York and London: Norton, 1994
Mazzaro, Jerome, *The Poetic Themes of Robert Lowell,* Ann Arbor: University of Michigan Press, 1965
Meyers, Jeffrey, editor, *Robert Lowell: Interviews and Memoirs,* Ann Arbor: University of Michigan Press, 1988
Perloff, Marjorie, *The Poetic Art of Robert Lowell,* Ithaca, New York: Cornell University Press, 1973
Staples, Hugh B., *Robert Lowell: The First Twenty Years,* London: Faber and Faber, and New York: Farrar Straus and Cudahy, 1962
Stuart, Sarah Payne, *My First Cousin Once Removed: Money, Madness, and the Family of Robert Lowell,* New York: HarperCollins, 1998
Tillinghast, Richard, *Robert Lowell's Life and Work: Damaged Grandeur,* Ann Arbor: University of Michigan Press, 1995
Travisano, Thomas J., *Midcentury Quartet: Bishop, Lowell, Jarrell, and Berryman, and the Making of a Postmodern Aesthetic,* Charlottesville: University Press of Virginia, 1999
Wallingford, Katharine, *Robert Lowell's Language of the Self,* Chapel Hill: University of North Carolina Press, 1988
Williamson, Alan, *Pity the Monsters: The Political Vision of Robert Lowell,* New Haven, Connecticut: Yale University Press, 1974
Witek, Terri, *Robert Lowell and "Life Studies": Revising the Self,* Columbia: University of Missouri Press, 1993
Yenser, Stephen, *Circle to Circle: The Poetry of Robert Lowell,* Berkeley: University of California Press, 1975

## After the Surprising Conversions

Robert Lowell's "After the Surprising Conversions," although a relatively early poem, combines several important technical and thematic elements that characterize Lowell's poetry throughout his career. Written in rhyming couplets of iambic pentameter, the poem is largely a collage of phrases, some taken verbatim, from Jonathan Edwards' *A Faithful Narrative of the Surprising Work of God in the Conversion of Many Hundred Souls,* a prose work better known as *Narrative of the Surprising Conversions* (1737). "After the Surprising Conversions" thus represents an early instance of a technique that would become increasingly important in Lowell's poetry—the reworking of prose (his own prose as well as that of others) into poetic structures. In addition, Lowell's treatment of Edwards, the 18th-century New England minister and theologian, projects onto one figure the whole of Lowell's ambivalence toward his celebrated New England ancestry, toward the history of his native region, and toward the religions that historically characterize that region. Lowell's choice of a public, historical subject as an occasion to explore what may be seen as personal, familial conflicts may also be considered an early instance of his characteristic melding of public and private spheres, the poetic mode that critics would term "Confessional poetry."

Edwards' *Narrative* is itself an odd mixture of the ostensibly private and self-consciously public. Begun as a letter to a fellow pastor but expanded for publication, the *Narrative* is Edwards' account of the religious revival among his Northampton, Massachusetts, congregation that spread into the neighboring towns of Massachusetts, growing into the movement now known as the Great Awakening. As its title indicates, "After the Surprising Conversions" is set in the wake of this revival, and it focuses on an incident that Edwards presents as evidence that the spirit of God seemed to be withdrawing from the community. Edwards' uncle, Joseph Hawley, had become despondent concerning the state of his soul and committed suicide. According to Edwards, "multitudes" in Northampton and the surrounding region were tempted to follow Hawley's example.

Neither in the *Narrative* nor in Lowell's poem does Edwards consider the possibility that Hawley's suicide and the subsequent rash of suicidal impulses may represent reactions to the excesses of the conversion mania his own preaching had fostered. Many readers therefore consider this poem a clear indictment of Edwards and the enthusiastic strain of Calvinism he represents. As a dramatic monologue spoken in Edwards' voice, however, the very form of the poem indicates a more complex relationship between Lowell's perspective and Edwards' pronouncements.

The figure of Edwards looms over Lowell's career from its earliest moments. Lowell turned from work on a biography of Edwards to write the poems of his first book, *Land of Unlikeness* (1944). Furthermore, two of the poems in his second book, *Lord Weary's Castle* (1946), deal directly with the character of Edwards: "After the Surprising Conversions" itself and its companion piece, "Mr. Edwards and the Spider." Lowell would continue to be fascinated by Edwards for his entire poetic career, writing two additional poems concerned with this figure, the last a sonnet from 1973. Such sustained interest in Edwards' work and life would seem to make a position of simple rejection unlikely. Moreover, the ambivalence toward enthusiastic religion evident in the poem is also related in complex ways to the ambivalence Lowell was feeling toward his own religious convictions.

Lowell's interest in Edwards' conversion narratives is directly related to his own conversion to Roman Catholicism five years before this poem was published. Lowell's poetic identity during this period was indistinguishable from his role as Catholic convert, and *Land of Unlikeness* resounds with the fervor of the newly converted. By 1946, however, Lowell's religious conviction had begun to wane, and "After the Surprising Conversions" may well reflect Lowell's struggle to maintain the fervor and euphoria of his own conversion experience.

The complex relationship between Lowell's position and that of Edwards is palpable from the first line of "After the Surprising Conversions." The poem's opening is marked with the formality of Edwards' phrasing, but this formality is balanced by the immediacy of an italicized date and the use of direct address, both elements added by Lowell:

*September twenty-second,* Sir today
I answer. In the latter part of May,
Hard on our Lord's Ascension, it began
To be more sensible. . . .

Lowell has completely removed the antecedent of the pronoun "it" in these lines, creating a rather mysterious sentence from Edwards' syntactically straightforward original: "it began to be very sensible that the Spirit of God was gradually withdrawing from us." This effect, coupled with the peculiarity of the term "sensible" in its now archaic sense of "able to be perceived," marks a distance between Lowell's audience and the world of his speaker. Edwards is speaking from the edge of a world from which God has yet to withdraw; Lowell's world, as perceived in the apocalyptic mood pervading his early work, is a "land of unlikeness," unlike itself because it has destroyed God's image within it.

In marking the distance between Edwards' world and his own, then, Lowell is also drawing a comparison between Edwards' public position and Lowell's role as poet. Although the poem is concerned primarily with a failed conversion, it is also concerned with the relationship between a prophet and his community. Lowell underscores this concern by attributing to Hawley the delusion that "he dreamed / That he was called to trumpet Judgment Day / To Concord," a delusion drawn from a different case history in Edwards' *Narrative.* Both Hawley's suicide and his delusion seem posed to call into question both Edwards' position as minister and Lowell's position, taken in many of his early poems, as poet/prophet.

The poem's irony becomes even more difficult to gauge when the reader considers Lowell's use of natural imagery not present in the original. This imagery is used, for example, to emphasize Hawley's connection to nature: "He / Would sit and watch the wind knocking a tree / And praise this countryside our Lord has made." It appears again in the poem's ending, which returns to the date and direct address of the opening:

September twenty-second, Sir, the bough
Cracks with the unpicked apples, and at dawn
The small-mouth bass breaks water, gorged with spawn.

These images have given rise to completely contradictory readings: at once violent and consoling, decadent, yet full of promise, they are irreducible to a single position. They do, however, indicate a kinship between Lowell's poetics and Edwards' theology—the proclivity for reading the world as divine allegory. Thus, in the act of criticizing Edwards' worldview, Lowell's poem also extends into modern poetry the dominant trait of Edwards' Puritan legacy. Such contradictory impulses are fitting in a poem that heralds many of the contradictions and complications of Lowell's poetic career.

TROY THIBODEAUX

**Further Reading**

Akey, John, G. Giovanni, and John McCluhan, Jr., "Notes on 'After the Surprising Conversions,'" *Explicator* 9, no. 8 (1951)

Allen, Carolyn, "Lowell's 'After the Surprising Conversions': Another Look at the Source," *Notes on Modern American Literature* 3 (1979)

Doreski, William, *Robert Lowell's Shifting Colors: The Poetics of the Public and the Personal,* Athens: Ohio University Press, 1999

Hart, Henry, *Robert Lowell and the Sublime,* Syracuse, New York: Syracuse University Press, 1995

Lensing, George S., "Robert Lowell and Jonathan Edwards: Poetry in the Hands of an Angry God," *South Carolina Review* 6, no. 2 (April 1974)

Mazzaro, Jerome, *The Poetic Themes of Robert Lowell,* Ann Arbor: University of Michigan Press, 1965

Milburn, Michael, "Robert Lowell's Poems and Other People's Prose," *New England Review* 17, no. 4 (1997)

Perloff, Marjorie, *The Poetic Art of Robert Lowell,* Ithaca, New York: Cornell University Press, 1973

Wiebe, Dallas E., "Mr. Lowell and Mr. Edwards," *Wisconsin Studies in Contemporary Literature* 3, no. 2 (1962)

## For the Union Dead

While *Life Studies* (1959) is widely regarded as Robert Lowell's true arrival, "For the Union Dead" is perhaps the most well-known and widely anthologized of his poems. Commissioned and written for the 1960 Boston Festival and delivered on the Boston Common in May of that year, "For the Union Dead" approaches with the candor and ease of *Life Studies* a public ode reminiscent of the prophetic work in *Lord Weary's Castle* (1946).

The poem moves by observation and associative recollection, beginning before "the South Boston Aquarium," which "stands in a Sahara of snow":

Its broken windows are boarded.
The bronze weathervane cod has lost half its scales.
The airy tanks are dry.

Lowell recalls times when his "nose crawled like a snail on the glass," when his "hand tingled / to burst the bubbles / drifting from the cowed compliant fish," and via these images remembers having "pressed against the new barbed and galvanized // fence on the Boston Common," to watch, instead of "the fish and reptile" of the Aquarium, "yellow dinosaur steamshovels . . . gouge their underworld garage." Thus, the Common replaces the Aquarium.

In this replacement, "the bronze weathervane cod" is foiled by "St. Gaudens' shaking Civil War relief," the bronze that depicts Colonel Robert Gould Shaw and the soldiers of the Massachusetts 54th Negro Regiment, seen "shaking over the excavations." Lowell reminds us,

Two months after marching through Boston,
half the regiment was dead;
at the dedication,
William James could almost hear the bronze Negroes
breathe.

However, his real interest is with the representation, not the represented, as is clear when he writes of "Their monument" and "Its Colonel." The monument "sticks like a fishbone / in the city's throat." Its representations are indigestible. Its Shaw "is as lean / as a compass-needle" or a "fishbone"—unnaturally so—and so unnatural that it can be described only with reference to animals: "He has an angry wrenlike vigilance, / a greyhound's gentle tautness." This figure is well beyond the human, "out of bounds now." Even his will has been removed: "when he leads his black soldiers to death, / he cannot bend his back."

Lowell's critical vision encompasses other cultural memory sites, "a thousand small town New England greens," where

The stone statues of the abstract Union Soldier
grow slimmer and younger each year—
wasp-waisted, they doze over muskets
and muse through their sideburns . . .

These figures also retreat from the human, toward the insect. In answer to such distortions, Lowell eschews these monuments:

Shaw's father wanted no monument
except the ditch,
where his son's body was thrown
and lost with his "niggers."

"The ditch"—by which he means both the South Carolina ditch in which Shaw was buried and the excavation on the Common—"is nearer," nearer to true. An absence would be better than a false presence.

Lowell objects to distortions as interested or prone to support interest, as is clear when he describes an advertisement:

on Boylston Street, a commercial photograph
shows Hiroshima boiling

over a Mosler Safe, the "Rock of Ages"
that survived the blast.

The Shaw Memorial is similarly commercial, propagandistic. As it depicts a Union regiment, the first comprised of enlisted African-Americans, the relief advertises Boston's Abolitionist identity, its contribution to the destruction of American slave economy and to the advancement of African descendants in America, which together form a portrait of righteousness and strength. But for Lowell the self-congratulation, however true its bases, must be dismantled since it enables Boston's aloofness in ongoing struggles for civil rights.

Capitalizing on his conflation of Aquarium and Common, Lowell introduces those struggles into the public space of the Common. "When I crouch to my television set," an act extensive of the previous acts of observation, "the drained faces of Negro school-children rise like balloons" in the place of the fish or the "bell-cheeked Negro infantry." These faces float alongside the others in the Common space, and Lowell "tingle[s] / to burst the bubbles," to free them and Colonel Shaw, who "rid[es] on his bubble" and "waits / for the blessèd break." Having identified the enslavement in misrepresentation, Lowell situates the problem in his Common-Aquarium to encourage reckoning. "The old South Boston Aquarium" is a sign of things to be wished for, a release from the city's slavery to a distorted self-image, a slavery demonstrated as "giant finned cars nose forward like fish" and provide Lowell the terms of his final indictment: "a savage servility / slides by on grease."

"For the Union Dead" was first published as "Colonel Shaw and the Massachusetts 54th," the last poem in paperback editions of *Life Studies* published from 1960 until the release of *For the Union Dead* in 1964, and this is a good indication of its tonal kinship with the poems of the earlier volume. However, "For the Union Dead" is as public and intertextually active as the poems of *Lord Weary's Castle.* It recovers ground broken by Lowell's wife, Elizabeth Hardwick, in her 1959 essay "Boston: A Lost Ideal," as it reprises his own "The Quaker Graveyard in Nantucket" and "At the Indian Killer's Grave" and responds to the poem that the title suggests: Allen Tate's "Ode to the Confederate Dead."

In addition, the poem looks forward as well as back. Its spirit of indictment shapes Lowell's adaptation of Melville's "Benito Cereno," a part of *The Old Glory* (1964). Also, its public inflections prepare the way both for the poems of *Near the Ocean* (1967) and for Lowell's emergence as a public intellectual who opposed U.S. involvement in Vietnam just as he had criticized the U.S. war policy in World War II.

While *Life Studies* has far overshadowed the collection *For the Union Dead,* the poem remains perhaps Lowell's most important single poem. Its Common is the crossroads of his career, the site at which he tunes his instruments and communicates with worlds fore and aft the moment in which he has the farthest reach.

Jake Adam York

**Further Reading**

Axelrod, Steven Gould, *Robert Lowell: Life and Art,* Princeton, New Jersey: Princeton University Press, 1978

Axelrod, Steven Gould, editor, *The Critical Response to Robert Lowell,* Westport, Connecticut, and London: Greenwood Press, 1999

Doreski, William, *Robert Lowell's Shifting Colors: The Poetics of the Public and the Personal,* Athens: Ohio University Press, 1999

Hamilton, Ian, *Robert Lowell: A Biography,* New York: Random House, 1982; London: Faber, 1983

Hardwick, Elizabeth, "Boston: A Lost Ideal," in *A View of My Own: Essays in Literature and Society,* by Hardwick, New York: Farrar Straus and Cudahy, and London: Heinemann, 1962

Hart, Henry, *Robert Lowell and the Sublime,* Syracuse, New York: Syracuse University Press, 1995

"In Bounds," in *Robert Lowell: Interviews and Memoirs,* edited by Jeffery Myers, Ann Arbor: University of Michigan Press, 1988

Lowell, Robert, "To President Johnson, 1965," in *Collected Prose,* by Lowell, edited by Robert Giroux, New York: Farrar Straus and Giroux, and London: Faber, 1987

Mariani, Paul, *Lost Puritan: A Life of Robert Lowell,* New York and London: Norton, 1994

Poirier, Richard, "For the Union Dead," in *Critics on Robert Lowell,* edited by Jonathan Price, Coral Gables, Florida: University of Miami Press, 1972; London: Allen and Unwin, 1974

Tillinghast, Richard, *Robert Lowell's Life and Work: Damaged Grandeur,* Ann Arbor: University of Michigan Press, 1995
Williamson, Alan, *Pity the Monsters: The Political Vision of Robert Lowell,* New Haven, Connecticut: Yale University Press, 1974

## Life Studies

Published in 1959, *Life Studies* was Robert Lowell's fourth and most influential collection of poetry. By all accounts, the text signified a dramatic change in both the poet's career and the landscape of American poetry. Hailed as groundbreaking and technically innovative, it authorized a shift in American poetics, confirming a raw, intimate style that was quickly dubbed "confessional" by M.L. Rosenthal in his landmark review "Robert Lowell and the Poetry of Confession." In the almost 40 years following the publication of "The Waste Land" (1922), American poets had written dense, allusive, and difficult works. Critics Allen Tate and John Crowe Ransom, two of Lowell's mentors, were followers and innovators of the New Critics, a school that prized difficulty, ambiguity, and highly wrought syntax. In his earlier books, *Land of Unlikeness* (1944), *Lord Weary's Castle* (1946), and *Mills of the Kavanaughs* (1951), Lowell heeded well the teachings of the generation of poets and critics that came before him, writing in a formal and elevated diction. When *Lord Weary's Castle* won the Pulitzer Prize in 1947, it established Lowell as a critical darling. Yet, even as Randall Jarrell dubbed him "the poet's poet," Lowell wondered whether he could appeal to a larger American readership.

In the 1950s, as the landscape of American poetry slowly began to shift, Lowell's poetics also evolved. Throughout the mid-1950s, San Franciscans had been treated to performances of poetry that inspired everything from hand clapping to rhythmic dancing. In 1957, when Lowell launched a 14-day reading tour of the West Coast, he recited the ornate formal poems of *Lord Weary's Castle* to audiences that stirred restlessly, struggling to decipher his complex syntax and densely packed metaphors. Hoping to engage his audiences, Lowell improvised as he read, explained obscure allusions, translated Latin into English, and altered meter. Always believing himself part statesman and convinced that he had a message for the American people, Lowell began to think about relaxing his style and writing a more accessible type of poetry. Critic Steven Gould Axelrod reads Lowell's transformation as a result of his relationship with William Carlos Williams, whose simplified syntax and flattened language appear to have affected Lowell. Other critics have cited Lowell's relationship with W.D. Snodgrass, the author of *Heart's Needle* (1959) and a student of Lowell's who took his own divorce as a subject for his poetry. Probably his influences were many. Whatever the case, *Life Studies* can be read as Lowell's most successful attempt to make poetry more accessible to a general readership. Sylvia Plath saw *Life Studies* "as an intense breakthrough into very serious, very personal emotional experience." Although the San Francisco writers, or "Beat" poets, were engaged in a similar enterprise, Lowell's transitions were at that time more resonant: Lowell spoke for the poetry establishment, and when he changed, so did the status quo.

*Life Studies* is divided into four sections, the order of which may be partially read as a narrative of Lowell's career evolution. The first section, composed of only four poems, was written at an earlier stage in his career; these poems demonstrate the formal stylistics of his earlier work, although they do show his leaning toward political content, especially in "Inauguration Day 1953," in which he criticizes the new Republican administration. The second section, "91 Revere Street," written in prose, is a seemingly straightforward autobiographical account of his family and his history. Lowell probably wrote in prose for a number of reasons; first, it helped to psychologically prepare him to take up his family as a topic for his poems; second, prose writers had a much wider readership than did poets. "Prose," Lowell maintained, "is in many ways better off than poetry. It's quite hard to think of a young poet today who has the vitality of Bellow or Salinger." In this section, Lowell continued yet made increasingly explicit his condemnation of his Puritan and American roots; as an antidote, he identifies with a distant relation: the Jewish Mordecai Myers.

The third section also contains only four poems, yet they are some of the most interesting and overlooked pieces in the collection. In these poems, directed to the literary figures Ford Madox Ford, Hart Crane, George Santayana, and Delmore Schwartz, Lowell pays these writers something more and something less than a tribute. Each poem examines these writers' professional lives: each considered great, at least by critics; each known for his difficult and anti-democratic notions about art; each dying rather ignominiously without audience and at the nadir of his power; and each at some point thought of by Lowell as a friend, mentor, or role model. Cautionary tales, these poems deliver the moral that an artist who makes no accommodations to his audience ultimately exiles himself.

It is the last section of *Life Studies,* also called "Life Studies," that has attracted the greatest scholarly attention. Not only does it contain two of Lowell's most widely anthologized poems, "Memories of West Street and Lepke" and "Skunk Hour," but the intimacy of the poetry seemed modestly revolutionary. In its painful individual assertions, Lowell's rhetorical style is neither heightened nor revelatory. Although some critics tried to describe Lowell's suffering as representative of the common man's, the reader witnesses something close to an exposé of Lowell's individual circumstances and background. For the wider context of American poetry, however, the changes he initiates are equally compelling. The poems take place in the domestic sphere—in bedrooms and kitchens; their language is compelling and accessible. Lowell takes an even more historically significant step when he projects himself as several of the least powerful members of the American community: he appears as a mental patient ("Waking in the Blue"), a prison inmate ("Memories of West Street and Lepke"), and an abused woman ("To Speak of the Woe That Is Marriage"). In "Home After Three Months Away," Lowell proclaims, "I keep no rank or station, / Cured I am frizzed stale and small." Such a statement directs us to what is perhaps the most important milestone of *Life Studies.* Delivering a message about the marginalized role of the American poet, *Life Studies* is Lowell's attempt to bring the American poet more fully into the public sphere.

HILENE FLANZBAUM

**Further Reading**

Axelrod, Steven Gould, *Robert Lowell: Life and Art,* Princeton, New Jersey: Princeton University Press, 1978

Axelrod, Steven Gould, editor, *The Critical Response to Robert Lowell,* Westport, Connecticut, and London: Greenwood Press, 1999

Parkinson, Thomas, editor, *Robert Lowell: A Collection of Critical Essays,* Englewood Cliffs, New Jersey: Prentice Hall, 1968

Perloff, Marjorie, *The Poetic Art of Robert Lowell,* Ithaca, New York: Cornell University Press, 1973

Rosenthal, M.L., *The New Poets: American and British Poetry since World War II,* London and New York: Oxford University Press, 1967

## The Quaker Graveyard in Nantucket

Written during Robert Lowell's Roman Catholic period and published originally in *The Partisan Review* in 1945, "The Quaker Graveyard in Nantucket" is the central poem of Lowell's first major collection, *Lord Weary's Castle* (1946). It is ostensibly an elegy for Lowell's cousin, "Warren Winslow, Dead at Sea," that opens with the discovery of the body:

> the drowned sailor clutched the drag-net. Light
> Flashed from his matted head and marble feet,
> He grappled at the net
> With the coiled hurdling muscles of his thighs:
> The corpse was bloodless, a blotch of reds and whites,
> Its open, staring eyes
> Were lustreless dead-lights
> Or cabin-windows on a stranded hulk
> Heavy with sand.

Lowell harmonizes with Milton's *Lycidas,* the most famous sea-death elegy and the formal model for the poem. The injunction "ask for no Orphean lute / To pluck life back" echoes Milton's "Weep no more," although Lowell's imperative is decidedly more pessimistic, a refusal of consolation in the face of a final death. The focus is, rather, on a recognition of loss to which, as in *Lycidas,* nature responds sympathetically:

> Whenever winds are moving and their breath
> Heaves at the roped-in bulwarks of this pier,
> The terns and sea-gulls tremble at your death
> In these home waters.

While *Lycidas* is the poem's conventional benefactor, *Moby-Dick* is its mythological one. When the body is returned to the sea, it sinks to "Where the heel-headed dogfish barks its nose / On Ahab's void and forehead." Lowell then asks Winslow, "can you hear / The Pequod's sea wings, beating landward?" Winslow is, like Ahab's men, victim of a thirst for vengeance—a thirst Lowell attributed to the U.S. war effort in his public refusal of the draft three years before. The Navy cruises for "unconditional surrender" (Lowell, "To President Roosevelt"), as Ahab did for Moby-Dick. Realizing Melville's suggestions of the whale's divinity, Lowell's whale is an incarnation of God, "IS, the whited monster." Thus, in its quest, the United States contests God, as did Ahab. The United States trumps the moral order of the world with its own prerogatives, violating its own democratic valuation of national self-determination, as, in *Moby-Dick,* the Quakers counteracted in the whale hunt their refusal to bear arms or harm life, a point toward which Lowell launches the poem with his epigraph from *Genesis* ("Let man have dominion over the fishes of the sea").

Drawing together biblical, Miltonic, and Melvillian scripture, Lowell declares his lineage, one in which the authority of each member is compounded by that of the others to a power Lowell wields in indictment. He drafts recognized agents and modes of judgment into his service so that he may prophesy: "This is the end of the whaleroad and the whale"; "This is the end of running on the waves." Lowell's ascendency is clearest in section V, wherein the killing of the whale triggers Armageddon: "the whale's viscera go and the roll / Of its corruption overruns this world" and "In the great ash-pit of Jehoshaphat / The bones cry for the blood of the white whale." The section ends with the ultimate appeal to authority, a prayer—"Hide, / Our steel, Jonas Messias, in Thy side"—that completes Lowell's identification of the whale with Christ as well as his critique of U.S. war policy while allying him with God, making him and his poem instruments of judgment.

Section VI turns from the poem's primary mythologies to detail an English shrine, in the process of which the revelation of judgment is completed. Lowell recalls a pilgrimage made by the deceased: "Sailor, you were glad / And whistled Sion by that stream." The remembered pilgrimage figures the soul's journey to heaven but, more important, introduces into the poem the figure of "Our Lady of Walsingham":

> As before,
> This face, for centuries a memory,
> *Non est species, neque decor,*
> Expressionless, expresses God.

Whether or not they indicate or express themselves, Lowell suggests, the agents of judgment are ever present. Here is Lowell's ultimate warning. The lack of punitive judgment indicates not indifference but rather, Lowell explains in the final section, God's grace and willingness to let us begin again:

> You could cut the brackish winds with a knife
> Here in Nantucket, and cast up the time
> When the Lord God formed man from the sea's slime
> And breathed into his face the breath of life,
> And blue-lung'd combers lumbered to the kill.
> The Lord survives the rainbow of His will.

As it evinces Lowell's own quest toward an unassailable poetic authority, "The Quaker Graveyard in Nantucket" organizes *Lord Weary's Castle.* It draws together poems such as "The Exile's Return" and "The Holy Innocents," which image the war's ill effects, into a writ of national sins and does so with an eloquence and power recognized by the 1947 Pulitzer Prize. It introduces into the volume the rainbow of possibility that reappears in "The Drunken Fisherman" and "Where the Rainbow Ends," and it establishes *Moby-Dick* as a central mythos that resurfaces repeatedly, as in "Rebellion." In building its critique around Lowell's cousin, "The Quaker Graveyard" prefigures, in the same volume, "At the Indian Killer's Grave"—a national indictment focused through another family member—and the groundbreakingly personal work of *Life Studies* (1959), whose poems build more nakedly on his family and personal experiences. Finally, as a poem of public pronouncement situated in a cultural memory site, "The Quaker Graveyard" foreruns Lowell's great ode, "For the Union Dead."

"The Quaker Graveyard in Nantucket" is the most complete document of Lowell's early prophetic vocalizations in all their profundity and athleticism, of his quest for power, and the best primer for later work in which he develops the persona of secular prophet. If there is one poem that demonstrates the early Lowell more clearly and exhaustively than any other, "The Quaker Graveyard" is it.

JAKE ADAM YORK

**Further Reading**

Axelrod, Steven Gould, *Robert Lowell: Life and Art,* Princeton, New Jersey: Princeton University Press, 1978

Axelrod, Steven Gould, editor, *The Critical Response to Robert Lowell,* Westport, Connecticut, and London: Greenwood Press, 1999

Doreski, William, *Robert Lowell's Shifting Colors: The Poetics of the Public and the Personal,* Athens: Ohio University Press, 1999

Hart, Henry, *Robert Lowell and the Sublime,* Syracuse, New York: Syracuse University Press, 1995

Lowell, Robert, "To President Roosevelt, 1943," in *Collected Prose,* by Lowell, edited by Robert Giroux, New York: Farrar Straus and Giroux, and London: Faber, 1987

Mariani, Paul, *Lost Puritan: A Life of Robert Lowell,* New York and London: Norton, 1994

Staples, Hugh B., *Robert Lowell: The First Twenty Years,* London: Faber and Faber, and New York: Farrar Straus and Cudahy, 1962

Williamson, Alan, *Pity the Monsters: The Political Vision of Robert Lowell,* New Haven, Connecticut: Yale University Press, 1974

---

# Mina Loy 1882–1966

One of the only women to embrace Futurism, Mina Loy strongly influenced avant-garde poetry in America as well as in Europe. Loy, who over the course of her life exhibited paintings, ran a lampshade design shop, and worked as a gallery representative in Paris, published only two books during her lifetime: *Lunar Baedecker* (1923) and *Lunar Baedeker and Time-Tables* (1958). Her distinctive poetic style, however, influenced a number of 20th-century poets, including Ezra Pound, William Carlos Williams, and Denise Levertov.

Loy was born in London in 1882, the first child of Sigmund Lowy, a Hungarian Jewish immigrant, and Julia Bryan, the daughter of an English cabinetmaker. Loy's parents' marriage was an unhappy one. Although her father was one of the more successful tailors in London, her mother was unhappy with their station in life. Moreover, her father's Jewishness troubled Mrs. Lowy, a devout evangelical Christian. Loy revisits her childhood years in her autobiographical long poem "Anglo Mongrels and the Rose" (1923–25). In this poem, she portrays a family ruled over by the English Rose, a cold Victorian matriarch who is embarrassed by her husband's ethnicity and the family's social status.

Loy's upbringing was that of a typical middle-class girl in Victorian England. Both Loy and her younger sister, Dora, were raised by a series of nurses and governesses, and their early education consisted of grammar, arithmetic, English history, and religious training. While Mrs. Lowy believed that her daughters' education should prepare them for marriage, Loy's father was much more supportive of his older daughter's artistic aspirations. Because Loy exhibited talent as an artist, Mr. Lowy enrolled her in art school in 1897. While in art school, Loy was exposed to the work of pre-Raphaelites such as Dante Rossetti and Edward Burne-Jones, whose work influenced her early paintings and poems. From 1900 to 1903, Loy studied in Munich and Paris.

In 1903, Loy married her first husband, artist Stephen Hawies, in Paris. Although they had three children together, the marriage was, by all accounts, not a happy one. In 1906, Loy was elected to the Salon d'Automne in Paris, where she exhibited six paintings. During 1906, Loy and Hawies moved to Florence. Although Hawies left for an extended stay in Australia in 1913, Loy remained in Florence until 1916. These years were essential to Loy's development as a poet. While living in Florence, she met members of the American expatriate community, including Mabel Dodge Luhan, Carl Van Vechten, and Gertrude Stein. It was also during this period that she met and became romantically involved with Italian Futurists F.T. Marinetti and then Giovanni Papini, founder of the Florence Futurists and founder of *Lacerba.*

While Loy's involvement with the Futurist movement lasted only two years (1913–15), these were undoubtedly the most prolific years of her literary career. She addresses her enthusiasm about Futurism in a 1914 letter to Mabel Dodge Luhan when she writes that she is "in the throes of a conversion to Futurism." During this period, she wrote her "Feminist Manifesto" (1914) as well as a number of Futurist-inspired poems and plays. In 1914, she exhibited paintings at the Free Exhibition of International Futurists in Rome. Her first two published works, "Aphorisms on Futurism" and "Songs to Joannes" (an early version of "Love Songs to Joannes"), reflect the typographical innovation and breakdown in syntax and meter outlined in Marinetti's aesthetic manifesto "Destruction of Syntax—Imagination without Strings—Words-in-Freedom" (1913). Many of her works from this period draw on personal experience (e.g., most critics read "Giovanni Bapini" and "Love Songs to Joannes" as *poems à clef* about her affair with Papini). As Roger Conover and Carolyn Burke have pointed out, Loy's poems, plays, and manifestos from this era represent one of the only feminist responses to Futurism. Although

Loy ultimately became disenchanted with Futurism's misogyny, the typographical and aesthetic innovations associated with the movement continued to influence her poetry.

In 1916, Loy left Florence for New York in order to market her clothing and millinery designs. By the time she arrived in New York, she had published poems, plays, and manifestos in journals such as *Camera Work, Rogue, The Dial,* and *Others,* and her position as an avant-garde poet had already been well established. Loy stayed in New York for about a year and while there became a regular in the New York avant-garde scene, which included Marcel Duchamp, Djuna Barnes, William Carlos Williams, and Alfred Kreymborg. In December 1916, she played opposite William Carlos Williams in Kreymborg's one-act play *Lima Beans* at the Provincetown Playhouse in New York City, and in February 1917 she co-edited the Dada journals *The Blind Man* and *Rongwrong* with Marcel Duchamp. In April 1917, Loy took part in a group poetry reading at the Independent Artists Exhibition, where she also exhibited a painting. On 13 February 1917, she was featured in a *New York Evening Sun* article as epitomizing the New Woman. During this period, Loy met and began an affair with proto-Dadaist/pugilist Arthur Cravan.

Loy's divorce from Hawies was finalized in October 1917, and in 1918 she married Cravan in Mexico City. In November 1918, Loy, who was then pregnant, left Mexico City for Buenos Aires, where Cravan was to meet her. Shortly after Loy left, Cravan disappeared. While Cravan was presumed dead, in 1920 Loy returned to the United States to search for him. In April 1919, Loy gave birth to a daughter, and in the summer of 1919 she returned to Florence. By 1923, Loy had resigned herself to Cravan's death. Although their relationship was short-lived, Cravan continued to play a major role in Loy's life and her poetry. He shows up as "Colossus" in Loy's autobiographical long poem "Anglo Mongrels and the Rose" and as the main character in *Colossus,* Loy's unpublished memoir of Cravan. Cravan was also the inspiration behind "The Widows Jazz," which was published in *Pagany: A Native Quarterly* in 1931.

In 1923, Loy moved to Paris, where she opened a lampshade design business. She remained in Paris until 1936. During this period, she wrote and published "Anglo Mongrels and the Rose" and *Lunar Baedecker* (1923). Although she continued to write poetry until the mid-1960s, after 1925 she withdrew from the literary and aesthetic circles that she had frequented in earlier years and published less and less. From 1931 to 1936, she worked as New York gallery owner Julien Levy's representative in Paris and introduced Levy to the works of the Surrealist artists. She also wrote *Insel,* her *roman à clef* about her friend German Surrealist Richard Oelze, during this period, although it was not published until 1991.

Loy returned to New York in 1936, where she lived until 1953. During this period, she continued to write poetry and began constructing mixed-media assemblages. Both her poetry and her assemblages from these years focus on the poor and the socially dispossessed. In "Hot Cross Bum" (1950), for instance, Loy described how the homeless become invisible to the other citizens of New York City. In 1953, Loy moved to Aspen, Colorado, where her two daughters lived. In 1958, Jonathan Williams' press, The Jargon Society, published Loy's *Lunar Baedeker and Time-Tables.* Loy's exhibit "Constructions" opened at New York's Bodley Gallery in April 1959, and in 1962 seven of her poems were published in the edited collection *Between Worlds.*

Loy died in Aspen in September 1966. Two collections of her poetry, *The Last Lunar Baedeker* (1982) and *The Lost Lunar Baedeker* (1996), have been published posthumously. Although Loy faded into relative obscurity after the mid-1930s, in the past 15 years her contribution to the literary avant-garde and to first-wave feminism has been reassessed. Perhaps Loy's most important contribution to 20th-century experimental poetry was her ability to blend stylistic innovation and her quirky brand of feminism. Because of their unique melding of the political and the aesthetic, poems such as "Love Songs to Joannes" and "Anglo Mongrels and the Rose" and prose pieces such as "Aphorisms on Futurism" and "Feminist Manifesto" remain fresh and significant.

Julie Schmid

**Biography**

Born in London, England, 27 December 1882. Studied art, Munich, London, Paris, 1889–1906; nurse, surgical hospital, Florence, Italy, 1914–15; designer, lampshade business, Paris, France, 1923–30. Died in Aspen, Colorado, 25 September 1966.

**Poetry**

*Lunar Baedecker,* 1923
*Lunar Baedeker and Time-Tables,* 1958
*The Last Lunar Baedeker,* 1982
*The Lost Lunar Baedeker: Poems of Mina Loy,* 1996

**Other Writings:** novel (*Insel,* 1991).

**Further Reading**


Arnold, Elizabeth, "Mina Loy and the Futurists," *Sagetrieb* 8, nos. 1–2 (Spring/Fall 1989)

Burke, Carolyn, "Becoming Mina Loy," *Women's Studies* 7 (1980)

Burke, Carolyn, "Getting Spliced: Modernism and Sexual Difference," *American Quarterly* 39 (1987)

Burke, Carolyn, *Becoming Modern: The Life of Mina Loy,* New York: Farrar Straus and Giroux, 1996

Conover, Roger, "Introduction," in *The Last Lunar Baedeker,* by Mina Loy, edited by Conover, Highlands, North Carolina: Jargon Society, 1982; Manchester: Carcanet, 1985

Conover, Roger, "Introduction," in *The Lost Lunar Baedeker,* by Mina Loy, edited by Conover, New York: Farrar Straus Giroux, 1996; Manchester: Carcanet, 1997

DuPlessis, Rachel Blau, "'Corpses of Poesy': Some Modern Poets and Some Gender Ideologies of Lyric," in *Feminist Measures: Soundings in Poetry and Theory,* edited by Lynn Keller and Cristanne Miller, Ann Arbor: University of Michigan Press, 1994

DuPlessis, Rachel Blau, "'Seismic Orgasm': Sexual Intercourse and Narrative Meaning in Mina Loy," in *Mina Loy: Woman and Poet,* edited by Maeera Shreiber and Keith Tuma, Orono, Maine: National Poetry Foundation, 1998

Kouidis, Virginia M., *Mina Loy: American Modernist Poet,* Baton Rouge: Louisiana State University Press, 1980

Schmid, Julie, "Mina Loy's Futurist Theater," *Performing Arts Journal* 18, no. 1 (January 1996)

Shreiber, Maeera, and Keith Tuma, editors, *Mina Loy: Woman and Poet,* Orono, Maine: National Poetry Foundation, 1998

## Love Songs to Joannes

Mina Loy's "Love Songs to Joannes" (1915–17) is remarkable in several regards. This poetry sequence, like Loy's other poetry from the period, constitutes one of the only feminist responses to the Futurist aesthetic. Along with her "Aphorisms on Futurism," which was published in Alfred Stieglitz's *Camera Work* in January 1914, "Love Songs to Joannes" cemented Loy's reputation as an avant-garde poet. Moreover, because of its frank treatment of sex and female sexuality, this poetic sequence also gained Loy her reputation as a New Woman.

The first four poems in the sequence were first published in the inaugural issue of *Others* (July 1915) under the title "Love Songs" and then republished in the 1916 *Others Anthology*. The completed 34-poem sequence was published as "Songs to Joannes" in the April 1917 issue of the magazine. "Love Songs to Joannes" was composed while Loy was living in Florence, and although the poems were published over a two-year period, most of them had been completed by August 1915. "Love Songs" reflects the influence of the Italian Futurist movement on Loy's poetry. Loy first met F.T. Marinetti, the founder of Italian Futurism, and Florence Futurist Giovanni Papini in 1913, soon after her separation from her first husband, Stephen Hawies, and during this period she became romantically involved with both men.

Loy's involvement with the Futurist movement lasted only two years (1913–15). However, these were undoubtedly the most prolific years of her artistic career. While many of her works from this period reference her affairs with Marinetti and Papini, it would be inaccurate to characterize Loy's interest in Futurism as solely romantic. Futurist formal innovations directly influenced Loy's experimental poetics, most notably her innovative use of typography and collage. During this period she wrote a number of Futurism-inspired poems, including "The Effectual Marriage or the Insipid Narrative of Gina and Miovanni" (a poem that also references her failed relationship with Papini), "Three Moments in Paris," and "Sketch of a Man on a Platform." She exhibited a number of paintings at the 1914 Free Exhibition of International Futurists in Rome, and between 1914 and 1916 she also wrote a number of Futurist plays.

It was also during this period that she wrote her "Feminist Manifesto," a document that integrates Futurist typographical innovations with Loy's quirky brand of feminism. Although this manifesto was not published until 1982, it was written in 1914. In it, Loy critiques the institution of marriage as an economic transaction in which the bride exchanges her virginity for financial security. Loy then calls for "psychological upheaval" as well as social change. Addressing other women, she states, "Leave off looking to men to find out what you are not. Seek within yourself to find out what you are. As conditions at the present are constituted you have the choice between Parasitism, Prostitution, and Negation." Loy then goes on to demand the destruction of "the rubbish heap of tradition," including the surgical destruction of virginity in pubescent women as a means to counteract the ongoing subjugation of women.

Like her other writing from this period, "Love Songs to Joannes" reflects Loy's interest in Italian Futurism as well as her nascent feminism. Throughout the 34 poems included in "Love Songs," Loy draws on Futurist poetic techniques and critiques the conventional love lyric. In Poem I, for instance, Loy juxtaposes the language of traditional romance narratives and corporeal language and describes the sex act:

Spawn   of   Fantasies  
Silting the appraisable  
Pig Cupid   his rosy snout  
Rooting erotic garbage  
"Once upon a time"  
Pulls a weed   white star-topped  
Among wild oats   sown in mucous-membrane

Loy opens her poetry sequence with references to the myth of Cupid and Psyche—a theme that she revisits throughout "Love Songs"—and to the fairy-tale romance. As her quotation of the clichéd "Once upon a time" suggests, she refers to these conventional love narratives only to deconstruct them. In opposition to the winged man-child of mythology, Loy's Cupid is defined by his phallic "rosy snout," and references to bodily fluids and male genitalia replace the lofty language of the lyric.

Throughout "Love Songs," Loy emphasizes the physical in order to demystify the sex act. Poem II opens with a description of the beloved's sex organs, the "skin-sack / . . . Something the shape of a man," and throughout the sequence she includes references to bloody fetuses, spermatozoa, "white scum," "seismic orgasms," and the "cymophanous sweat" of lovemaking. Moreover, throughout the sequence, Loy eschews conventional punctuation and syntax in favor of Futurist poetic techniques. As with "Parturition" (1914), in which Loy uses collage and uneven spacing to re-create the rhythms of childbirth, "Love Songs" uses these formal techniques to re-create the rhythms of sex and/or the female orgasm.

"Love Songs" is, as the title suggests, a love poem, and many of the remaining poems in the sequence document the dissolution of the romance. Many are written in the subjunctive mood, and as the sequence progresses, the tone becomes one of regret. As others have argued, much of the regret seems to center on an abortion. The theme of the aborted pregnancy is first introduced in Poem III, and throughout Loy includes references to "bird-like abortions," "vacuums," and "Foetal buffoons." Poem XVII describes what seems to be an abortion procedure:

Red   a warm colour on the battle-field  
Heavy on my knees as a counterpane  
Count counter  
I counted   the fringe of the towel  
Till two tassels clinging together  
Let the square room fall away  
From a round vacuum  
Dilating with my breath

With its almost clinical treatment of love and sex and its references to such taboo subjects as the female orgasm and abortion, the sequence enacts the "absolute demolition" of the "rubbish heap of tradition" that she calls for in her "Feminist Manifesto." As such, "Love Songs to Joannes" exemplifies the melding of experimental poetics and radical politics that typifies Loy's poems, plays, and manifestos. Like much of her work, "Love Songs" remained relatively unread and unstudied during the second half of the 20th century. However, as a result of renewed scholarly interest in Loy's poetry in the past 15 years, the sequence has finally begun to receive the critical attention it deserves.

Julie Schmid

**Further Reading**

Arnold, Elizabeth, "Mina Loy and the Futurists," *Sagetrieb* 8, nos. 1–2 (Spring/Fall 1989)

Burke, Carolyn, "Getting Spliced: Modernism and Sexual Difference," *American Quarterly* 39 (1987)

Burke, Carolyn, "Mina Loy's 'Love Songs' and the Limits of Imagism," *San José Studies* 13, no. 3 (Fall 1987)

Burke, Carolyn, *Becoming Modern: The Life of Mina Loy,* New York: Farrar Straus and Giroux, 1996

DuPlessis, Rachel Blau, "'Corpses of Poesy': Some Modern Poets and Some Gender Ideologies of Lyric," in *Feminist Measures: Soundings in Poetry and Theory,* edited by Lynn Keller and Cristanne Miller, Ann Arbor: University of Michigan Press, 1994

DuPlessis, Rachel Blau, "'Seismic Orgasm': Sexual Intercourse and Narrative Meaning in Mina Loy," in *Mina Loy: Woman and Poet,* edited by Maeera Shreiber and Keith Tuma, Orono, Maine: National Poetry Foundation, 1998

Kouidis, Virginia M., *Mina Loy: American Modernist Poet,* Baton Rouge: Louisiana State University Press, 1980

Schmid, Julie, "Mina Loy's Futurist Theater," *Performing Arts Journal* 18, no. 1 (January 1996)

Shreiber, Maeera, "'Love Is a Lyric / of Bodies': The Negative Aesthetics of Mina Loy's Love Songs to Joannes," in *Mina Loy: Woman and Poet,* edited by Shreiber and Keith Tuma, Orono, Maine: National Poetry Foundation, 1998

# M

## Nathaniel Mackey 1947–

The poetry of Nathaniel Mackey emerges at a complex crossroads of post-1960s literary production. On the one hand, a student of Robert Duncan and the cultivator of a self-consciously aggressive cosmopolitanism, Mackey has built a serial poetics that erodes and erects myths of origin. On the other, firmly rooted within a specific (if multi-disciplinary) tradition of experimental African-American and African diaspora creativity—important members of which would include Will Alexander, Amiri Baraka, Kamau Braithwaite, Anthony Braxton, Don Cherry, John Coltrane, Henry Dumas, Bradford Graves, Wilson Harris, Ed Love, Harryette Mullen, and Ed Roberson—his creative and critical work extend a conversation about the meaning of black creativity in a variety of world systems.

Mackey's use of music and musical tradition is the most effective means at his disposal to bridge this ostensible divide. His poetry utilizes music's status as medium to ancestral presence and absence while simultaneously celebrating the cultural and intellectual accomplishments of specific musicians. As such, it is appropriate that Mackey's first published collection was *Four for Trane* (1978). The poems are dedicated to John Coltrane in the sense that they celebrate his accomplishment, but they are also an attempt to further certain habits of mind that Mackey sees as indicative of Coltrane's presence in the world. (These pieces were eventually included in his first major publication, *Eroding Witness* [1985], selected by Michael Harper for the prestigious National Poetry series.) Similarly, in the crucial serial poem *Song of the Andoumboulou* (I–VII, 1983; VIII–XV, 1993; and XVI–XXXV, 1998), Mackey makes continual and increasingly powerful use of the ambivalent and agonistic relationship between music and speech. Through sustained consideration of the ability of speech and music to obscure and conjure "meaning," Mackey foregrounds a meditation on and a confrontation with human imperfection. His is very much a poetics of humility, and thus incommensurability is Mackey's great theme—the false longing for an Edenic order or the naïve acceptance of easy cultural taxonomies, often illustrated in his work by recourse to the inarticulate, the dissonant, and the jagged, as well as to slippage and incompleteness.

While this poetic method can (quite intentionally) feel abstruse, quite usefully it has translated into a long body of reflection on literary and cultural categorization, including its institutional formations. If the poetry actively sets out to destabilize the comfortable ways in which we designate affiliation and category, Mackey's literary and cultural criticism (*Discrepant Engagement,* 1993) is a more straightforwardly forceful rendering of cause and effect. Through choice of subject matter and articulation of his own diverse aesthetic affinities, Mackey has called into question the commonplace assumption that "black" writers are always to be evaluated, packaged, and read only among other "black" writers. This is not a disavowal of either cultural particularity or communal historical experience. A fundamental part of coming to terms with the incommensurable is to struggle with the play and costs of power in the world. In some ways, the most straightforward component of Mackey's challenge to hegemony has been a thrust against Eurocentrism, although his instinct is always "centrifugal." In other words, although his poetry is fully situated in the diverse provocations of European Modernism and Postmodernism, it extends that contestation with immersion (on different occasions) in Arabic poetics, Native American myth, the iconology of rhythm and blues, the sounds of post-1960s jazz, Rastafarian cosmology, and ethnomusicology. What Mackey challenges most effectively is the assumption of transparency or the demand for utility in black or minority writing. Following Edouard Glissant, Mackey insists that the minority writer has a right to obscurity and, furthermore, that "angularity" or "indirection" may hold more utopian possibility than previously acknowledged. Later components of *Song of the Andoumboulou* rely on the rehearsing and replaying of a mythic journey; in number 34, a moment of respite, a moment to reflect: "Distant / kin long dead brought to life by the / wine we sipped, revenant dead said / to've / died or been dying of thirst . . . / Clink of glass, clink of chains / transmuted. Andoumboulouous trauma, / andoumboulouous launch. Boat of years, / black-orphic lament, boat of / yearning." The possibility of the expedition—maybe a pilgrimage—is rooted in the double sound of clinking chains (and boundedness) and clinking glasses (and sustenance). The puzzling and hopeful simultaneity in Mackey's poetry is reflected in the fact that the dead are brought back to life and yet trapped in a seemingly permanent yearning.

Mackey's formidable and catholic erudition, his rhapsodic poetic style with eloquent incantatory power, and his increasing specificity about our spiritual dilemmas and possibilities have earned him a burgeoning audience that is anxious, perhaps, for a model of cross-cultural engagement distant from the truisms of

1980s- and 1990s-style "multiculturalism." Interestingly, that emerging audience seems to be a challenging and distinctive mix of academic critics, students of black diaspora creativity, and creators and consumers of experimental poetries and other performing arts. Mackey's reception as a poet and nurturance of a diverse audience may also be rooted in his thoughtful work as editor of the highly respected literary and cultural magazine *Hambone.* Harryette Mullen suggests, for instance, that Mackey's accomplishment is "knowing that every tradition is shaped as much from outside as from inside, that gathering and dispersal, systole and diastole are complementary and interactive rather than opposed processes"; furthermore, that accomplishment helps to "overcome the reductive effect of binary systems." Of course, it will not be enough to simply acknowledge a more satisfying complexity. In "Capricorn Rising" (1985), the poem's speaker reflects, "I wake up mumbling, 'I'm / not at the music's / mercy,' think damned / if I'm not, but / keep the thought / to myself." In its dismissal of facile and insincere symmetries, Mackey's poetry seems to demand that we expose ourselves to possession and renewal—a demand not unlike the effect of insistent music in a Pentecostal church.

JAMES C. HALL

**Biography**
Born in Miami, Florida, 25 October 1947. Attended Princeton University, New Jersey, A.B. 1969; Stanford University, Palo Alto, California, Ph.D. 1975; Professor, University of Wisconsin, Madison, 1974–76; University of Southern California, Los Angeles, 1976–79; since 1979 Professor, University of California, Santa Cruz; co-editor, 1974, and since 1982 editor, *Hambone*. Received Woodrow Wilson fellowship, 1969; National Poetry Series Selection, 1985; Whiting Writer's Award, 1993. Living in Santa Cruz, California.

**Poetry**
*Four for Trane,* 1978
*Septet for the End of Time,* 1983
*Eroding Witness,* 1985
*Bedouin Hornbook,* 1986; revised edition, 1997
*Djbot Baghostus's Run,* 1993
*School of Udhra,* 1993
*Whatsaid Serif,* 1998
*Atet, A.D.,* 2001

**Selected Criticism**
*Discrepant Engagement: Dissonance, Cross-Culturality, and Experimental Writing,* 1993

**Other Writings:** essays (*Cante Moro,* 1994); edited anthology of literature (*Moments Notice: Jazz in Poetry and Prose* [with Art Lange], 1993).

**Further Reading**
Donahue, Joseph, "Sprung Polity: On Nathaniel Mackey's Recent Work," *Talisman* 9 (Fall 1992)
DuPlessis, Rachel Blau, "Rootwork," *Sulfur* 35 (Fall 1994)
Funkhouser, Chris, "Charting the Outside," *Poetry Flash* 224 (November 1991)
Lazer, Hank, "'Vatic Scat': Jazz and the Poetry of Robert Creeley and Nathaniel Mackey," *River City* 17, no. 2 (Summer 1997)
Moten, Fred, "Nathaniel Mackey Overheard," *Proliferations* 2 (November 1994)
Mullen, Harryette, "Phantom Pain: Nathaniel Mackey's *Bedouin Hornbook,*" *Talisman* 9 (Fall 1992)
Naylor, Paul, *Poetic Investigations: Singing the Holes in History,* Evanston, Illinois: Northwestern University Press, 1999
Nielsen, Aldon, "Gassire's Lute," *Talisman* 9 (Fall 1992)
O'Leary, Peter, "An Interview with Nathaniel Mackey," *Chicago Review* 43, no. 1 (Winter 1997)
Scroggins, Mark, "Nathaniel Mackey," in *American Poets Since World War II, Fifth Series,* edited by Joseph Conte, Detroit, Michigan, and London: Gale Research, 1996

---

## Archibald MacLeish 1892–1982

Archibald MacLeish wrote poetry and verse plays that would define him as an American Stoic, confronting the issues of his time directly, without gloss or false romanticism. He was a very public artist: a lawyer who turned to poetry; an editor of *Fortune* magazine who quit when it did not support the working class during the Depression; a Roosevelt New Dealer who served F.D.R. as an Assistant Secretary of State and then as Librarian of Congress; and a teacher at Harvard who challenged McCarthyism. These experiences conditioned a poetry that revealed MacLeish's private reaction to the public chaos he embraced.

MacLeish was born into an upper-middle-class family who instilled in him that they were fortunate, but others less so, and that service to his fellow citizens was an admirable endeavor. MacLeish graduated from Yale (1915) then Harvard law, married Ada Hitchcock in 1916, passed the bar in 1919 and practiced in Boston until 1923. He then gave up law and went to France to teach himself poetics while Ada studied classical voice. Aside from two early volumes that he later disavowed, his serious work began abroad. *The Happy Marriage* (1924) and *The Pot of Earth* (1925) reveal his talent but are still derivative of Swinburne, Pound, and Eliot, not so much in style as theme. *Streets in the Moon* (1926) is more independent and features MacLeish's most well-known poem, "Ars Poetica," which states that "A poem should not mean / But be." This new directness, circular rather than linear, posits man as either the center of life's hurricane or else caught in the spin and trying to get back to the center. His first verse play, *No-*

*bodaddy,* also appeared in 1926 and took a stark view of the Adam and Eve and Cain and Abel parables. In the preface MacLeish described what would become a principal theme of his future work: "the condition of self-consciousness in an indifferent universe." For man to cope with this indifference would require a pragmatic stoicism that recognized folly yet did not suffer fools gladly.

*The Hamlet of A. MacLeish* (1928) addressed the cyclical sufferings of the sensitive man, whose past (Hamlet) is not much different than his present (MacLeish). MacLeish challenged poetry to move beyond the past: "Not until contemporary poetry writes the Hamlet of Laforgue and Eliot out of its veins, will poetry occupy, and reduce to the order of recognition, the public-private world in which we live" (*A Time to Speak,* 1940). The critic Edmund Wilson saw the inclusion of MacLeish's name in the title as self-serving and countered with a vicious parody, "The Omelet of A. MacLeish." Wilson's rebuttal would trail MacLeish's success, as would Wilson's continued attacks. MacLeish's reputation never recovered from criticism by Wilson and others who did not believe that a man could be both a successful public figure and a skilled poet.

During the 1930s MacLeish and his poetry became very public as he wove together personal beliefs in verse responses to world events. *Conquistador* (1932) earned the first of three Pulitzer Prizes for MacLeish. This book-length poem considers the Spanish conquest of Mexico as a parable for current events in an oblique, telegraphic staccato new to MacLeish. *Frescoes for Mr. Rockefeller's City* (1933) used plain speech to denounce Nelson Rockefeller for censoring out Lenin's image from artist Diego Rivera's murals in Radio City Hall, murals commissioned to celebrate America. In 1936 the volume *Public Speech* used the same plain language and stark punctuation to awaken the public to the rise of fascism and the continuing Great Depression. MacLeish also wrote three well-received verse plays in the 1930s, *Panic* (1935), about the run on banks, *The Fall of the City* (1937), and *Air Raid* (1938), about European events, the latter two expressly for national radio. *Land of the Free—U.S.A.* (1938) and *America Was Promises* (1939) are guarded paeans that warn Americans to be vigilant in order to protect democracy. During World War II MacLeish served in F.D.R.'s cabinet and published no more verse until *Act Five* in 1948.

*Act Five* signified a return to more personal verse, intricately structured and graduating from the "I" of a private self-consciousness to the "we" of a still-evolving collective consciousness; *Songs for Eve* would continue its themes in 1954. The 1950s also brought MacLeish his second and third Pulitzers, for his *Collected Poems* (1952) and *J.B.: A Play in Verse* (1958). *J.B.* used Job's confrontation with God to question the role of humankind in the universe and was a hit on Broadway, earning a Tony for best play. A later verse play, *Herakles* (1967), addressed similar themes, suggesting that obsession with science robbed society of its humanity.

By the late 1960s an aging MacLeish had become mellower, inserting a gentle humor into the poems of *The Wild Old Wicked Man* (1968) while still grappling with the nature of humanity. MacLeish himself was now without old friends Hemingway, Sandburg, Cummings, and Muir, to whom he wrote sensitive elegies that also touch on his own mortality. Richard Wilbur found these and the many new poems included in MacLeish's *New and Collected Poems* (1976) to be among his most moving and humane verse: still stoic, but less at war with human frailty and more bemused by it.

David Garrett Izzo

**Biography**

Born in Glencoe, Illinois, 7 May 1892. Attended Yale University, New Haven, Connecticut (editor, *Yale Literary Magazine*), 1911–15, A.B. 1915 (Phi Beta Kappa); Harvard Law School, Cambridge, Massachusetts, 1915–17, 1919, L.L.B. 1919; served in the United States Army, 1917–19, Captain; Lecturer in government, Harvard University, 1919–21; attorney, Choate Hall and Stewart, Boston, Massachusetts, 1920–23; editor, *Fortune* magazine, 1938; Librarian of Congress, Washington, D.C., 1939–44; director, United States Office of Facts and Figures, 1941–42, assistant director, Office of War Information, 1942–43, and Assistant Secretary of State, 1944–45, all Washington, D.C.; Chairman of the United States Delegation to the UNESCO drafting conference, London, 1945, and member of the Executive Board, UNESCO, 1946; Rede Lecturer, Cambridge University, 1942; Boylston Professor of Rhetoric and Oratory, Harvard University, 1949–62; Simpson Lecturer, Amherst College, Massachusetts, 1963–67. Received Shelley Memorial Award, 1932; Pulitzer Prize, for poetry, 1933, 1953, for drama, 1959; New England Poetry Club Golden Rose, 1934; Bollingen Prize, 1952; National Book Award, 1953; Sarah Josepha Hale Award, 1958; Tony Award, 1959; National Association of Independent Schools Award, 1959; Academy of American Poets fellowship, 1966; Oscar, for documentary, 1966; Presidential Medal of Freedom, 1977; National Medal for Literature, 1978; American Academy Gold Medal for Poetry, 1979; honorary degrees from 22 colleges and universities; Commander, Legion of Honor (France); Commander, El Sol del Peru; President, American Academy, 1953–56. Died in Boston, Massachusetts, 20 April 1982.

**Poetry**

*Songs for a Summer's Day (A Sonnet-Cycle),* 1915
*Tower of Ivory,* 1917
*The Happy Marriage, and Other Poems,* 1924
*The Pot of Earth,* 1925
*Streets in the Moon,* 1926
*The Hamlet of A. MacLeish,* 1928
*Einstein,* 1929
*New Found Land: Fourteen Poems,* 1930
*Before March,* 1932
*Conquistador,* 1932
*Frescoes for Mr. Rockefeller's City,* 1933
*Poems, 1924–1933,* 1933; abridged edition as *Poems,* 1935
*Public Speech,* 1936
*Land of the Free—U.S.A.,* 1938
*Dedication: Motet for Six Voices* (music by Douglas Stuart), 1938
*America Was Promises,* 1939
*Freedom's Land* (music by Roy Harris), 1942
*Act Five, and Other Poems,* 1948
*Collected Poems, 1917–1952,* 1952
*Songs for Eve,* 1954
*New York,* 1958
*Collected Poems,* 1963
*The Wild Old Wicked Man, and Other Poems,* 1968

*The Human Season: Selected Poems, 1926–1972,* 1972
*New and Collected Poems, 1917–1976,* 1976
*On the Beaches of the Moon,* 1978
*Collected Poems, 1917–1982,* 1985

**Selected Criticism**
*Emily Dickinson: Three Views* (with Louise Bogan and Richard Wilbur), 1960
*Poetry and Experience,* 1961

**Other Writings:** plays (*Nobodaddy,* 1926; *The Great American Fourth of July,* 1975), screenplays (*The Eleanor Roosevelt Story,* 1965), radio plays, television play, essays (*Riders on the Earth: Essays and Recollections,* 1978); edited collections of papers (*Law and Politics: Occasional Papers of Felix Frankfurter, 1913–1938* [with E.F. Prichard, Jr.], 1962).

**Further Reading**
Barber, David, "In Search of an 'Image of Mankind': The Public Poetry of Archibald MacLeish," *American Poetry* 8 (Fall 1990)
Donaldson, Scott, and R.H. Winnick, *Archibald MacLeish, an American Life,* Boston and London: Houghton Mifflin, 1992
Drabeck, Bernard A., Helen E. Ellis, and Seymour Rudin, editors, *Proceedings of the Archibald MacLeish Symposium,* Lanham, Maryland: University Press of America, 1988
Smith, Grover Cleveland, *Archibald MacLeish,* Minneapolis: University of Minnesota Press, and London: Oxford University Press, 1971

---

# Jackson Mac Low 1922–

"Mac Low stands with John Cage as one of the two major artists bringing systematic chance operations into our poetic & musical practice since the Second World War," observes Jerome Rothenberg in the preface to Mac Low's *Representative Works, 1938–1985* (1986). Mac Low offers a fresh new approach to linguistic experience—language as a medium boundless as the ocean. He invites the reader, performer, or listener to participate in a linguistic event not as a piece of inspired address or moral instruction but as a process that is oriented toward indeterminacy rather than toward deliberation and discrimination. Other aspects of his work are discriminating and expository rather than subject to chance, such as some of the transparently essay-like prose poems and stories included in the collection *Pieces o' Six* (1992). Mac Low's achievement as a writer and performance artist is as elusive and indeterminate as consciousness itself. He does not lend himself to easy definition, testifying instead to this very state of indeterminacy as an ongoing interrogation of his own practices and beliefs: "I feel sympathy for my self of the middle 1950s since in the 1980s other changes have been happening in and to me. I find myself questioning all my beliefs and ways of working—questioning though not rejecting."

"I've been a serious pacifist most of my life, & since about '45, I've also identified myself as an anarchist," Mac Low pointed out at a talk at the Naropa Institute in 1975. "What I mean by this," he elaborated, "is that things [could] get done better in society without a coercive force pushing everybody around. In every governmentally organized society, there's always either an army or a police force or both somewhere, if only in the background. But I really think that people can freely act together in sane ways, relatively spontaneously, as long as they are aware, & I think that this is the political side of Dharma."

The word "Dharma" raises an extremely important aspect of Mac Low's work: the seminal influence of Zen Buddhism and, in particular, the Zen Doctrine of No-Mind, which holds that "from the first not a thing is." Mac Low's immersion in Buddhist principles has resulted in a poetry of open-ended possibility rather than a virtuosic exposition of the poet's feelings. "In 1954 I began working in a different way than I had previously, under the influence of Taoism & Buddhism, especially Zen Buddhism, together with ideas implicit, some explicit, in the *I Ching* (*Book of Changes*)," remarks Mac Low. "Largely through contact with John Cage's work & friendship, I became interested in using chance operations & similar means, using words as he & other composers (Earle Brown, David Tudor, Christian Wolff, & Morton Feldman) were using sounds in the early 50's."

"Machault," written in January 1955, was composed by translating the pitches of Guillaume Machault's motet QUANT THESEUS into a gamut of words from T.H. Bilby's *Young Folk's Natural History with Numerous Illustrative Anecdotes* (1987). The result is a brisk repetition of words—substantives and verbs, such as "lasso," "wits," "ran," "circle," "confessed," "proverb," and "obedience"—mingled with lesser parts of speech, such as "it," "by," "as," "so," "that," "his," and "the." Mac Low acknowledges Gertrude Stein as an early influence, and here he effects a technique very similar to Stein's vigorous repetitions, or what Stein referred to as "insistence": "Expressing any thing there can be no repetition because the essence of that expression is insistence, and if you insist you must each time use emphasis and if you use emphasis it is not possible while anybody is alive that they should use exactly the same emphasis." The end result is a language that approximates the condition of music in the immediacy of its presence. Acoustic properties are emphasized over semantic conformity. Normative syntax is broken down; the words are joined by the sheer energy of their naked, unbridled sound:

it wits
wits it it by the by it it
wits the
by by the by lasso)

lasso) it by
by by the lasso) tired lasso) tired obedience

the the
it by

Mac Low is very specific about both his motivations for using chance operations and the techniques themselves. Much of his work is accompanied by extremely detailed information on how it was constructed and the way in which it is to be performed. In general, he explains, "one uses 'objectively hazardous' means, such as random digits, dice, cards, roulette wheels (random-digit tables are really computerized roulette wheels), the methods by which one consults the *Book of Changes,* or methods which look for certain letters at specific places in words . . . to extract from materials selected in some way or other, or taken from a whole environment of possible materials, various elements to include in an art work."

Mac Low further identifies three basic types of chance. There is

> the kind of chance that's directly related to human impulse, such as that used by Jackson Pollock, the painter. Then there is pure chance, like finding a dime on the street, & that's a beautiful kind which very often adds to everything. Systematic chance is a little more pedantic, but it's a way of working with chance. It's a little different also from what William Burroughs started to do around 1960, when he began to cut up texts & put them together. His so-called "cut-up" method is another form of unsystematic chance, but it's a little more removed from the choice of the author than impulsive chance. The cut-up is in-between objective hazard or systematic chance & impulsive chance.

Compositions Mac Low attributes to "human impulse," such as the first group of poems in *Bloomsday* (1984), show many of the features apparent in work produced by systematic chance operations: words cut loose from their referents (although, in much the same manner as Stein, Mac Low does not so much erase the ability of a word to refer as increase its power to refer to more than one thing), phonology privileged over logic, and metaphor and interiority avoided so that the language is actualized close to the surface in much the same way that Pollock's "drip" paintings force the viewer to engage physically with the work. A chief difference apparent in *Bloomsday*'s "impulse" writing lies in the richness of the vocabulary. Unlike the fairly ordinary vocabularies of his more strictly aleatoric pieces, Mac Low here favors dense phrases and exotic words such as "gastronomic inspissation" and "spasmodic corpus hilarity desks," avoiding the use of connectives while crowding nouns, participles, adjectives, and verbs together in a bulky aggregate. One senses a mirthful, blithely anonymous intelligence at play in a wide-open sea of succulent words in gloriously unending combinations. However, how might an uninformed reader enter into one of these texts? How might someone pulling a Mac Low book off the shelf for the first time read the first stanza of "Cohost Provided?":

Freighted scent penumbrae surprise
reported finitude-plumbers' searches
although no flames preen catch-alls
and phrases peel island-flimsy fractions.

Most readers will first delight in the richness of texture and wealth of linguistic events. "Finitude-plumbers" sounds like something out of an improbable science fiction scenario; what could they be searching? Perhaps some mazy domain of metaphysical plumbing. Birdlike flames preen "catch-alls" (receptacles for odds and ends, not unlike the stanzas themselves), whose absence (and, of course, once they have been mentioned, they are not absent at all) does not preclude the "penumbrae surprise" from reporting (or having reported) the "finitude-plumbers' searches." How might a fraction be "island-flimsy?" What is flimsy about an island? How might anything be peeled by something as abstract as a phrase? One could easily unravel this one stanza ad infinitum and never arrive at definitive answers. However, perhaps it is the very indeterminacy of this language that offers some form of enlightenment, if not sheer linguistic excitement.

The Buddhist scholar Yen-kuan Ch'i-an observed that "deliberate thinking and discursive understanding amount to nothing; they belong to the household of ghosts; they are like a lamp in the broad daylight; nothing shines out of them." The use of chance has had a profound impact on the way we perceive the role of the author in the making of a work and the relationship between consciousness, self, and the production of language. It is a giant step away from the romanticism of the exalted individual. This diffusion of the ego into an indeterminate field of linguistic play has profound political implications, particularly for a capitalistic system based on the sanctity of property ownership. It also offers a revolutionary view of language as material, notes Barrett Watten (1997), "the notion that a poem literally can be made of a predetermined, objectified 'language.'" "'Nonintentional' composition, then, does not simply free language from reference and create an illusion of an ahistorical subject," Watten elaborates; "rather, Mac Low's methods . . . show a way out of the expressivist confines of organic form."

Mac Low's output, both in print and in performance, has been prodigious. *Thanks* (1960), Mac Low's most indeterminate work, was first published in La Monte Young's *Anthology* (1963), a primary influence on the Fluxus movement. *Verdurous Sanguinaria* (a play first performed in Yoko Ono's loft in 1961 in what is now the Tribeca district of New York City) established Mac Low's reputation as a major performance poet and helped set the stage for many of the happenings and concept art of the 1960s. *August Light Poems* (1967), *22 Light Poems* (1968), *The Presidents of the United States of America* (1968), *Odes for Iris* (July 1970–November 1971), *Stanzas for Iris Lezak* (1972), *4 Trains* (1974), *The Pronouns* (1979), *Asymmetries* (1980), and *"Is That Wool Hat My Hat?"* (1982) evidence a continually evolving range of chance-operational strategies. *From Pearl Harbor Day to FDR's Birthday* (1982) is significant in that it marks the first poetical work written without the use of aleatoric systems. *French Sonnets* (1984)—a work brimming with superabundant lines, such as "Awless flag stupor armadilla's irascibility many-petaled vent"—is the product of a number of miscellaneous methods, including what Mac Low terms "dipping," "randomly opening my copy of *The Sonnets* volume of the 1914 *Temple Shakespeare* and pointing blindly at the right- or left-hand page." *Bloomsday* (1984), *The Virginia Woolf Poems* (1985), *Words nd Ends from EZ* (1989), *Twenties* (1991), and *Pieces o' Six: Thirty-Three Poems in Prose* (1992) continue the exploratory variety of Mac Low's oeuvre, sections of which are featured chronologically in *Representative Works* (1986).

*Pieces o' Six* marks another milestone in Mac Low's unceasing evolution. As Mac Low remarks in the introduction, the individual prose poems are "very 'different' both from much of my other work and from each other. . . . As the writing of the series proceeded (or as it did sometimes, lagged or even stopped for a while), I found myself writing several kinds of pieces: many paratactic, though often quasi-narrative; some seemingly out-and-out stories; others much like essays, but deceptively so; a few of them collages drawing from various sources by chance-selection and other chance-operational systems or (at least in one notable case) by impulse chance and 'dipping.'"

*42 Merzgedichte in Memoriam Kurt Schwitters* (1994) marks the influence of the German Dada collagist Kurt Schwitters (whose *Merz 83: Drawing,* a collage of cut paper wrappers, announcements, and tickets, adorns the cover of Mac Low's *Representative Works*). *Barnesbook: Four Poems Derived from Sentences by Djuna Barnes* (1996) makes it clear that Mac Low is not about to abandon the systematic use of chance operation in favor of his more intuitive pieces. Mac Low insists that in *Barnesbook* he uses Djuna Barne's words "strictly as material," employing a process by which he strips the words of Barne's sentence-to-sentence and intra-sentence identity. Likewise, *Stein Poems* (1998) is derived from Gertrude Stein's "A Long Gay Book" and determined via Charles O. Hartman's program DIASTEX5, "his latest automation of one of my diastic procedures developed in 1963, using the 3rd paragraph of the source as seed."

John Olson

**Biography**

Born in Chicago, Illinois, 12 September 1922. Attended the University of Chicago, 1939–43, A.A. 1941; Brooklyn College, New York, 1955–58, A.B. (cum laude) in Greek 1958; freelance music teacher, English teacher, translator, and editor, 1950–66; taught at Mannes School of Music, 1966; reference book editor, Funk and Wagnalls, 1957–58, 1961–62, and Unicorn Books, 1958–59, and copy editor, Alfred A. Knopf, 1965–66, all New York; editorial staff member and poetry editor, 1950–54, *Why?* (later *Resistance*), a pacifist-anarchist magazine; instructor, American Language Institute, New York University, 1966–73; poetry editor, *WIN* magazine, 1966–75. Received Creative Artists Public Service grant, 1973, 1976; PEN grant, 1974; National Endowment for the Arts fellowship, 1979; Tanning Prize, 1999. Living in New York City.

**Poetry**

*August Light Poems,* 1967
*22 Light Poems,* 1968
*23rd Light Poem: For Larry Eigner,* 1969
*Stanzas for Iris Lezak,* 1972
*4 Trains, 4–5 December 1964,* 1974
*36th Light Poem: In Memoriam Buster Keaton,* 1975
*21 Matched Asymmetries,* 1978
*54th Light Poem: For Ian Tyson,* 1978
*A Dozen Douzains for Eve Rosenthal,* 1978
*Phone,* 1978
*The Pronouns: A Collection of 40 Dances—for the Dancers—6 February–22 March 1964,* 1979
*Asymmetries 1–260: The First Section of a Series of 501 Performance Poems,* 1980
*Antic Quatrains,* 1980
*From Pearl Harbor Day to FDR's Birthday,* 1982
*"Is That Wool Hat My Hat?"* 1982
*Bloomsday,* 1984
*French Sonnets, Composed between January 1955 and April 1983,* 1984
*The Virginia Woolf Poems,* 1985
*Representative Works, 1938–1985,* 1986
*Words nd Ends from EZ,* 1989
*Twenties, 8–25: Order 9, Travesty from Twenties, 8–25,* 1990
*Twenties: 100 Poems, 24 February 1989–3 June 1990,* 1991
*Pieces o' Six: Thirty-Three Poems in Prose, 1983–1987,* 1992
*"Ezra Pound" and 99 Anagrams,* 1993
*42 Merzgedichte in Memoriam Kurt Schwitters,* 1994
*From Pearl Harbor Day to FDR's Birthday: 7 December 1981–30 January 1982,* 1995
*Barnesbook: Four Poems Derived from Sentences by Djuna Barnes,* 1996
*125 Postcard Poems,* 1996
*Anthology* (with others), 1997
*Stein Poems,* 1998
*20 Forties: 20 Poems from the Series "154 Forties" Written and Revised 1990–1999,* 1999

**Other Writings:** plays (*Two Plays: The Marrying Maiden and Verdurous Sanguinaria,* 1999), radio scripts, musical compositions.

**Further Reading**

Leddy, Michael, "*Pieces o' Six: Thirty-Three Poems in Prose, 1983–1987*" (book review), *World Literature Today* 67 (Autumn 1993)
Lochhead, Judy, "A Chance Operation: The John Cage Tribute" (recording review), *American Music* 13, no. 3 (Fall 1995)
Perreault, John, "The Language Performances of Jackson Mac Low," *Parnassus* (Spring 1989)
Watten, Barrett, "New Meaning and Poetic Vocabulary: From Coleridge to Jackson Mac Low," *Poetics Today* 18, no. 2 (Summer 1997)

---

## Magazines. *See* Little Magazines and Small Presses

---

# Edgar Lee Masters 1868–1950

Around the turn of the 20th century, poems idealizing rural and small-town life were a staple of American newspapers and magazines. The carefully rhymed and metered (if at times mildly colloquial) work of such poets as James Whitcomb Riley offered a reassuring image of what life and community were supposed to be—and perhaps in part had been—before industrialization, the consolidation of capital, waves of immigration, and new modes of communication and transportation began shaping an urban landscape that featured pale children in sweatshops.

When Edgar Lee Masters wrote the poems in *Spoon River Anthology* (1915, 1916)—one of the most popular books in the history of American poetry and his one major achievement as a poet—he was poised between these two worlds. Masters was born in 1868 and raised in western Illinois, where his experiences on his grandparents' farm and in the town where his father practiced law offered both positive memories of rural and small-town life and an understanding of the ways in which it could be constricting, isolating, and destructive. Masters was also a Chicago lawyer, an urban professional who appreciated the cultural life the city supported even as his populist leanings and his experience in the firm of the crusading Clarence Darrow confronted him with the cost of this urban America for ordinary people and its implications for a democratic society.

From this dichotomy of past and present, rural and urban, Masters shaped his poems of the people and region of Spoon River, celebrating agrarianism but also probing the costs of life in such communities. In its critique of small-town life, *Spoon River* anticipates what was later termed "the revolt from the village" typified by Sinclair Lewis' *Main Street* (1920). Yet *Spoon River* is not simply a rejection of the increasingly marginal societies of small-town America. It is also a lament for and a defense of the values and possibilities such communities had embodied. As such, it not only anticipates Lewis but also looks back to a more positive past, as had such local-color writers of the 19th century as Sarah Orne Jewett. In *Spoon River*, the medley of unrhymed, speech-like, confessional epitaphs that Masters fashioned for the people of his imagined community of Spoon River not only indicts and praises but also measures, as if Masters hoped to discover how the strengths of this way of life might be used to revitalize the present.

Masters' earlier poetry was relatively conventional and undistinguished. The *Spoon River* poems, however, are direct and concrete. The decision to have the characters of the poems speak their own epitaphs and offer an account of their lives was probably one factor in Masters' setting aside of meter and rhyme. The example of Carl Sandburg, then causing a stir in Chicago literary circles, was perhaps another. Masters' practice of writing most of the poems in moments grabbed from his routine as a lawyer also probably contributed to their texture and form. He apparently began the series in the spring of 1914 and began sending the poems to William Marion Reedy, a St. Louis editor who had encouraged his work. Over the course of 1914–15, Reedy serialized much of *Spoon River* in *Reedy's Mirror*, printing them under the pseudonym Webster Ford (presumably because the sexual candor of some of the epitaphs might embarrass Masters professionally). In part through Reedy's advocacy, the work attracted a strong following, and this led to the publication of the first version of the *Spoon River* collection in 1915 and the final version in 1916.

Much of the original impact of *Spoon River* derived from the issues it explored: was the promise of Jeffersonian democracy real or an illusion? how had it eroded? could it be revitalized in an urban present? The collection also drew its force from its mapping of how the psychologies and actions of individuals interact within a community, and from its glimpses into the inner reality behind the characters' various public masks. The artistry of the interweaving of different registers of public declamation and private confession as the characters both advance and withhold their revelations and as they understand and misunderstand the nature of their experiences was less noticed at the time. It has still received less attention than the book's argument. In "Julia Miller," for example, Julia recounts the circumstances that led to her suicide by morphine, yet her epitaph ends not with her own words but with a biblical passage that is "the flickering light" as she dies. In the quotation, Jesus offers "paradise," but it is unclear whether this allusion underscores Julia's faith or her doubt, whether it stands as an ironic comment on her life and act or as an affirmation of her dignity and humanity. Because Julia speaks her own poem, the status of her words and the depth and nature of her understanding are unresolved. Throughout the book, these different registers of voice and the characters' mix of insight and blindness ask the reader to recognize that the characters and their actions must be analyzed for their implications—that they are unique and individual and can never be fully revealed, understood, or judged.

Like Whitman, often cited as an influence, Masters was determined to include a wider range of people and experiences than found in the popular poetry of his period. However, unlike Whitman, his focus was on a specific region and its people, and on the resonance of their specific actions and thoughts. Where Whitman tended to invoke individuals in order to subsume them into a transcendental "we," the kosmos for which he was the oracular voice, Masters decidedly roots his people in particular circumstances, however much they might point to the transcendental and at times participate in it. If they are occasionally aware of the community they make from their disparities, they are always set apart in the distinctiveness, the isolation, of the self.

In the years following *Spoon River* Masters published widely. His later work included fiction, biography, drama, autobiography, and commentary in addition to poetry. The later work represents an impressive range of forms and his continued concern with probing American experience, especially in the Midwest. The later work, however, is uneven and perhaps of most interest for the additional context it provides for reading *Spoon River*, his one major achievement.

TIM HUNT

*See also* Midwestern Poetry Renaissance

**Biography**

Born in Garnett, Kansas, 23 August 1868. Attended Knox College, Galesburg, Illinois, 1889; studied law in his father's law office; admitted to Illinois bar, 1891; worked as lawyer, Chicago, 1891–1921; from 1921 full-time writer, New York. Received Levinson Prize (*Poetry*, Chicago), 1916; Twain Medal, 1927; Shelley Memorial Award, 1944; Academy of American Poets fellowship, 1946; member, American Academy of Arts and

Letters, 1942. Died in Melrose Park, Pennsylvania, 5 March 1950.

**Poetry**

*A Book of Verses,* 1898
*The Blood of the Prophets,* 1905
*Songs and Sonnets,* 2 vols., 1910–12
*Spoon River Anthology,* 1915; revised edition, 1916
*The Great Valley,* 1916
*Songs and Satires,* 1916
*Toward the Gulf,* 1918
*Starved Rock,* 1919
*Domesday Book,* 1920
*The Open Sea,* 1921
*The New Spoon River,* 1924
*Selected Poems,* 1925
*The Fate of the Jury: An Epilogue to Domesday Book,* 1929
*Lichee Nuts,* 1930
*The Serpent in the Wilderness,* 1933
*Invisible Landscapes,* 1935
*The Golden Fleece of California,* 1936
*Poems of People,* 1936
*The New World,* 1937
*More People,* 1939
*Illinois Poems,* 1941
*Along the Illinois,* 1942
*Selected Poems,* edited by Denys Thompson, 1972
*The Harmony of Deeper Music: Posthumous Poems,* edited by Frank K. Robinson, 1976
*The Enduring River: Edgar Lee Masters' Uncollected Spoon River Poems,* 1991

**Other Writings:** plays (*Richmond: A Dramatic Poem,* 1934), fiction (*The Tide of Time,* 1937), essays, biographies (*Mark Twain: A Portrait,* 1938); edited collections of literature (*The Living Thoughts of Emerson,* 1940).

**Further Reading**

Burgess, Charles E., "Edgar Lee Masters: The Lawyer as Writer," in *The Vision of This Land: Studies of Vachel Lindsay, Edgar Lee Masters, and Carl Sandburg,* edited by John E. Hallwas and Dennis J. Reader, Macomb: Western Illinois University Press, 1976
Flanagan, John T., *Edgar Lee Masters: The Spoon River Poet and His Critics,* Metuchen, New Jersey: Scarecrow Press, 1974
Hallwas, John E., "Introduction," in *Spoon River Anthology,* by Edgar Lee Masters, edited by Hallwas, Urbana: University of Illinois Press, 1992
Masters, Edgar Lee, *Across Spoon River: An Autobiography,* New York: Farrar and Rinehart, 1936
Primeau, Ronald, *Beyond Spoon River: The Legacy of Edgar Lee Masters,* Austin: University of Texas Press, 1981

---

## William Matthews 1942–97

Author of a dozen books of poetry, William Matthews won the National Book Critics Circle Award for *Time and Money* in 1996 the Ruth Lilly Poetry Prize in 1997. Many of his best poems are printed in *Selected Poems and Translations, 1969–1991* (1992). Born in Cincinnati in 1942, he was Professor of English and director of the writing program at the College of the City University of New York until his death in 1997.

Moving away from the deep imagistic quality of his early books, Matthews began to hit his poetic stride with *Blues If You Want* (1989), a collection of autobiographical poems that rummage through the open file drawers of his life to produce some of the most elegant and heart-wrenching poems of his generation. Not since Frank O'Hara had a poet captured the rapid tempo and offbeat gestures of everyday life in Manhattan and the late-night, smoky haunts of downtown jazz clubs.

There is a strong yet quiet passion in all Matthews' poetry and a bemused if not faintly cynical distance of the wistful onlooker that keeps his poetry from lapsing into sentimentality. He builds his poems the way a photographer shoots from a wide angle and then gradually zooms in for a close-up. In "Smoke Gets in Your Eyes," from *Blues If You Want,* he writes,

> I love the smoky libidinal murmur
> of a jazz crowd, and smoke coiling
> and lithely uncoiling like a choir
> of vaporous cats. . . .

Or take a few lines from "Straight Life," the last poem in the volume:

> . . . I loved how at the onset
> of desire her eyes would go a little milky
> the way water does just before the surface
> of it shimmers when it starts to boil.

The poems in *Blues If You Want* rise out of the depths of the speaker's unconscious "like an odor snarled in the deepest folds of childhood" (from "Mood Indigo"). They convey an awakening to life while exploring the memory of the joys and hardships of growing up. Matthews writes with a sensuous verbal touch from his private lexicon of favorite words, going down for the deep roots of the language. His meditation on the word "promiscuous" leads him to a poem by that title, in *After All* (1998), on the inequality between men and women.

Despite his big-city sophistication, Matthews is at heart a midwestern poet, and this sense of place gives him a unique vantage from which to judge the changing face of America. In "39,000 Feet," a poem comprised of conversations overheard on a plane as it approaches a Midwest airport, the speaker comments upon the country, its landscape, and its people and the destructive progress of suburban sprawl: ". . . the land / we sped so far above was like the land we grew / up on, before the malls and apartment / complexes were named for what had been destroyed."

In "Nabokov's Blues," the opening poem from *Blues If You Want,* a poem in 20 tercets, Matthews addresses the act of writing by narrating the speaker's visit to Nabokov's apartment in Switzerland. As the speaker stands in rapt wonder at the novelist's personal butterfly collection, he writes ". . . I must have been mute, // or whatever I said won from silence nothing / it mourned to lose. / I was back in that small / room, vast by love of each flickering detail, // . . . and thought—wouldn't you know it—about love and art: / you can be ruined ("rurnt," as we said in south- / western Ohio) by a book or improved by / a butterfly. . . ."

There are poems of sudden realization of failed ambition, of certain mythical places in the speaker's distant past, of teenage summer romance, and of drive-in movies. In the poem "Fox Ridge State Park, Illinois, October," the speaker's interior monologue utters,

> . . . I'd have paid
> beyond my wildest dreams of poverty
> and ruin to stand and let my dreams
> subside, as they did slowly
> on their own, as sick of me as I'd come
> to be of them. . . .

Matthews can juggle a hip street vernacular with the musings of a philosopher. In "Morningside Heights, July," from *After All,* he gives the reader the drama of eavesdropping on a couple on a park bench in the middle of a break-up:

> she tells him he must be psychic,
> for how else could he sense, even before she knew,
> that she'd need to call it off? A bicyclist
> fumes by with a coach's whistle clamped
> hard between his teeth, shrilling like a teakettle
> on the boil. I never meant, she says.
> But I thought, he replies. Two cabs almost
> collide; someone yells fuck in Farsi.

In *Time and Money,* the poet's cancer is a force behind each poem, and there is an element of death in every line. In "Time," the speaker laments the many ways time is used or wasted: "Perhaps I should plan how to spend my / . . . time, but wouldn't that, like a home movie, / prove but a way to waste the same time twice?" In "Money," he writes,

> Money's not an abstraction; it's math
> with consequences, and if it's a kind
> of poetry, it's another inexact way,
> like time, to measure some sorrow we can't
> name. . . .

In "Mingus at the Half Note," the jazz legend Charles Mingus kicks out someone who is interrupting the set by talking to his girlfriend, but in Matthews' able hands the incident becomes a haunting poem about art and the importance of being reverent in the presence of something great. In "Mingus in Shadow," from *After All,* Matthews considers how nature has reduced the famous bass player to silence: ". . . but it was great / nature that skewed his cells and siphoned / his force and melted his fat like tallow."

In "Men at My Father's Funeral," from *Time and Money,* Matthews writes, "The ones his age who shook my hand / on their way out sent fear along / my arm like heroin. . . ." Matthews is self-effacing, and although he is stoic in the face of death, he does not depress the reader. It is his awareness of death that gives life to his late poems.

In "Homer's Seeing-Eye Dog," from *Blues If You Want,* the wry poet in the guise of a dog muses about his master's act of writing: "How he got from the dark of sleep / to the dark of waking up I'll never know." As the canine speaker says about his beloved master,

> and of his life all I can say is that
> when he'd poured out his work
> the best of it was gone and then he died.
> He was a great man and I loved him.

These few lines serve as an appropriate benediction to Matthews' great body of work. He was a poet who poured his heart into every poem.

MARK HILLRINGHOUSE

**Biography**

Born in Cincinnati, Ohio, 11 November 1942. Attended Yale University, New Haven, Connecticut, B.A. 1965; University of North Carolina, Chapel Hill, M.A. 1966; Instructor in English, Wells College, Aurora, New York, 1968–69; Assistant Professor, Cornell University, Ithaca, New York, 1969–74, and University of Colorado, Boulder, 1974–78; Associate Professor and director of creative writing, University of Washington, Seattle, 1978–83; from 1983 Visiting Professor, University of Houston and Brooklyn College, and Professor of English, City College of City University of New York; Visiting Lecturer, University of Iowa, and poetry editor, *Iowa Review,* 1976–77; co-founding editor, Lillabulero Press, and *Lillabulero,* 1966–74; editorial board member, Wesleyan University Press, 1969–74; member, 1976–79, and chair, 1978–79, Literature Panel, National Endowment for the Arts; from 1976 advisory editor, L'Epervier Press; from 1977 contributing editor, *Gumbo.* Received National Endowment for the Arts fellowship, 1974, 1983; Guggenheim fellowship, 1980; National Book Critics Circle Award, 1996; Ruth Lilly Poetry Prize, 1997; Ingram Merrill Foundation fellowship. Died in New York City, 12 November 1997.

**Poetry**

*Ruining the New Road,* 1970
*Sleek for the Long Flight: New Poems,* 1972
*Sticks and Stones,* 1975
*Rising and Falling,* 1979
*Flood,* 1982
*A Happy Childhood,* 1984
*Foreseeable Futures,* 1987
*Blues If You Want,* 1989
*Selected Poems and Translations, 1969–1991,* 1992
*Time and Money,* 1996

*Night Life: Poems,* 1997
*After All: Last Poems,* 1998

**Selected Criticism**
*Curiosities,* 1989

**Other Writings:** translations of Latin and French literature (*A World Rich in Anniversaries: Prose Poems,* by Jean Follain [with Mary Feeney], 1979).

**Further Reading**
Chappell, Fred, "Attempts upon Delight: Six Poetry Books," *Kenyon Review* 12, no. 3 (Summer 1990)
Christopherson, Bill, "Late Night Music," *Poetry* 174, no. 2 (May 1999)
Foy, John, "Jiving toward the Heart of Speech," *Parnassus* 21, nos.1–2 (1996)
Harms, James, "Book Reviews: Poetry Collections," *Antioch Review* 54, no. 4 (Fall 1996)
Matthews, William, "The Complaint," *Antaeus* 73–74 (Spring 1994)
"Notes on Current Books: Poetry," *Virginia Quarterly Review* 69, no. 1 (Winter 1993) (reviews, selected poems, and translations by Matthews)
Yezzi, David, "The Sorrow of Thought, the Play of Poetry," *Sewanee Review* 57, no. 2 (Spring 1999)

---

# Bernadette Mayer 1945–

Bernadette Mayer's poetry plays a crucial role in 20th-century avant-garde traditions. Her collage techniques, stream-of-consciousness writing, and chance-operation poems have established her as a respected innovator. Because her work also candidly focuses on relationships—between men and women, parents and children, citizens of communities and their governments—it is also accessible to a wide audience.

During the mid-1960s the Lower East Side of Manhattan became the site of a renaissance of the arts. Poets, painters, choreographers, and musicians congregated to expand the avant-garde aesthetics established by previous movements in Modernism, Surrealism, and Abstract Expressionism. In 1967, after graduating from the New School for Social Research, Mayer and artist Vito Acconci began editing a magazine called *0 to 9*. The magazine allowed her a venue through which she could be in contact with artists and writers she admired, including Robert Smithson and Jasper Johns. She also had the opportunity to witness performances by many artists who lived and worked in New York, including the composer John Cage, performance artist Yoko Ono, and poets Hannah Weiner and Jackson Mac Low. This early foray into the New York art scene reinforced Mayer's burgeoning interest in experimenting with the boundaries between poetry and other genres. She soon was in the midst of a literary community that included protégés of New York School writers John Ashbery and Frank O'Hara. These younger writers, including Ted Berrigan, Joe Brainard, Clark Coolidge, Alice Notley, Ron Padgett, and Anne Waldman, soon became classified as second-generation New York School poets.

While Mayer worked closely with these writers, her work transcends the parameters of any particular group. Like the Surrealist poetry of the early 20th century in Europe, her work involves a study of states of consciousness. The Modernist writings of Gertrude Stein and James Joyce have had a large influence on her work, as have writings in the realms of philosophy, psychology, and political theory. Mayer often integrates other media into her projects; during the early 1970s she collaborated with New York filmmaker Ed Bowes, whose influence can be seen in her book *Moving* (1971), and began teaching writing workshops at the Poetry Project at St. Mark's Church. The Poetry Project was formed in 1967 as a cultural center providing vital arts programming to Lower Manhattan. From 1972 to 1974 Mayer continued her work as an editor, producing a poetry magazine called *Unnatural Acts* with the poet Ed Friedman.

Throughout this period Mayer expanded the parameters of experimentation in her writing. Three subsequent books, *Memory* (1976), *Studying Hunger* (1976), and *Midwinter Day* (1982), were important early pieces in her career as a conceptual artist. In these works she began to set conditions for the scope of her writing, sometimes deciding upon specific time constraints for the projects, for example, as if they were scientific experiments. *Memory* is a record—in words, photographs, and audio material—of events occurring in July 1971. *Studying Hunger* records various states of consciousness while documenting the course of her work as an analysand. *Midwinter Day* presents the events of one particular 24-hour period in her life, moving back and forth between prose and lyric forms, using audiotapes, photographs, and written notes to develop the content of the work.

Because Mayer's work often explores intimate human relationships and immediate physical environments, her interactions with her children often enter into her poetry. Rather than viewing family life as a hindrance to her writing, Mayer incorporated it into the course of her studies: while pregnant with her third child she spent nine months writing letters to friends and family as a means of documenting her thoughts during the course of the pregnancy. The project was published in 1994 as the book *The Desires of Mothers To Please Others in Letters*. Between larger conceptual projects Mayer wrote lyric poems such as those published in her books *Poetry* (1976) and *The Golden Book of Words* (1978). Many of her shorter poems possess a playfulness that is matched with a distinctly contemplative view of the world. For example, in "The Way to Keep Going in Antarctica" (*Poetry*), Mayer opens with the lines: "Be strong Bernadette / Nobody will ever know / I came here for a reason / Perhaps there is a life here / Of not being afraid of your own heart beating / Do not be afraid of your own heart beating / Look at very small things with your eyes / & stay warm."

Like other poets of the New York School, Mayer often writes witty "conversational" poems focusing on the particulars of community formations and the minute examination of everyday urban events, a form most associated with Frank O'Hara. Mayer employs the conversational method in her work while simultaneously experimenting more radically with language's possibilities. In the poem "A Woman I Mix Men Up . . ." (*Mutual Aid,* 1985), Mayer integrates hints of traditional metrical pattern with unexpected disruptive turns of language. She closes the poem with the stanza: "Scatter the dictionaries, they dont / Tell the truth yet, I mix up words with truth / And abstractions with presence, who cares / Without a form who I am, I know I will timely die / But you two, God and this his image the junky bomb / Live forever to destroy the eternal the immortal / In what they used to call Man, now not." In this respect her influence extends to both younger New York School writers and to the more theoretically oriented Language poets who emerged in the 1970s.

In 1980 Mayer returned to New York City and began working at the Poetry Project at St. Mark's Church, coordinating public events and teaching writing workshops that integrated her ongoing studies of poetry, pedagogy, psychology, philosophy, and utopian politics. Mayer also began several new book projects, focusing once again on stretching the boundaries of acceptable verse forms. For the collaborative *Utopia* (1984) Mayer wrote poems and manifestos that touched upon social issues of the era and invited others to join her in a critique of American politics and culture. As she pointed out in the introduction to the book, "I had been wanting to keep a journal of one week of living in New York and every detail of everything that happened at work, home, and in the community, to see if everything about living in the city would be illuminating, funny or useful because it would be about money, work, politics and sex." With these issues in mind, Mayer assigned topics such as "money," "schools," and "housing" to various friends who then contributed their own written statements for the book.

One of Mayer's major contributions to American experimental writing is a growing "experiments list." This list, a collaborative effort on the part of Mayer and her students, catalogs a variety of exercises that make writing a daily practice integrated into all aspects of life. For Mayer these writing exercises serve as a way of democratizing the writing process, making the composition of poetry more practicable for larger groups of people; for this reason her work is often used in classrooms as a pedagogical tool. Mayer's teaching work also contributed to new directions in her own writing. In 1989 she published a book of poems called *Sonnets* that improvised on traditional sonnet forms, and in 1990 she published *The Formal Field of Kissing,* a volume drawing upon her high school study of classical languages and including translations of Greek and Latin poets. *A Bernadette Mayer Reader* (1992), which gathers selections of Mayer's major works, made her writing available to a wider audience.

In the fall of 1994 Mayer suffered a cerebral hemorrhage and was hospitalized for several months. During her recovery she continued to write poetry and to explore the relationship between writing, the physical body, and the mind. Meanwhile three collections of her earlier writings were published: *Proper Name and Other Stories* in 1996, and *Another Smashed Pinecone* and *Two Haloed Mourners* in 1998. Of the many second-generation New York School writers, Bernadette Mayer has emerged as one of the most influential and prolific.

LISA JARNOT

*See also* New York School

**Biography**

Born in Brooklyn, New York, 12 May 1945. Attended New School for Social Research, New York City, B.A. 1967; Barnard College, New York City, 1963; Columbia University, New York City, 1963; College of New Rochelle, New York, 1963; co-editor, *0 to 9,* 1967–69, *Unnatural Acts,* 1972–74, and *United Artists,* 1977–83; teacher, St. Mark's Poetry Project, New School for Social Research, New York City, 1971–74, 1985–94. Received Poets Foundation grant, 1967; National Institute of Arts and Letters grant, 1971; Creative Artists Public Service Program grant, 1976. Living in New York City.

**Poetry**

*Ceremony Latin,* 1964; revised edition, 1975
*Story,* 1968
*Moving,* 1971
*Memory,* 1976
*Studying Hunger,* 1976
*Poetry,* 1976
*Eruditio ex Memoria,* 1977
*The Golden Book of Words,* 1978
*Midwinter Day,* 1982
*Utopia,* 1984
*Mutual Aid,* 1985
*Sonnets,* 1989
*The Formal Field of Kissing,* 1990
*A Bernadette Mayer Reader,* 1992
*The Desires of Mothers To Please Others in Letters,* 1994
*Another Smashed Pinecone,* 1998
*Two Haloed Mourners: Poems,* 1998

**Other Writings:** autobiography, short stories (*Proper Name and Other Stories,* 1996); edited educational text (*The Art of Science Writing* [with Dale Worsley], 1995).

**Further Reading**

Baker, Peter, editor, *Onward: Contemporary Poetry and Poetics,* New York: Lang, 1996

Jarnot, Lisa, "An Interview with Bernadette Mayer," *Poetry Project Newsletter* no. 168 (Spring 1998)

Miller, Jean, "Notes on Bernadette Mayer's Utopia," *HOW(ever)* 4, no. 1 (April 1987) (*www.scc01.rutgers.edu/however/print_archive/0487post.html*)

Spahr, Juliana, "Love Scattered, Not Concentrated Love: Bernadette Mayer's Sonnets," *Jacket* no. 7 (April 1999) (*www.jacket.zip.com.au/jacket07/spahr-mayer.html*)

# Thomas McGrath 1916–90

Thomas McGrath spent his entire career wrestling with the vexing problem of poetry and politics, and his sustained left-wing beliefs have largely led critics to ignore his work. Although the work of this North Dakota–born poet is clearly modernist, lyrical, topical, and at times intensely moving, his reputation suffered from the pervasive critical belief that after 1939 any writer committed to left-wing issues was either a Stalinist or an anachronism. This perception was exacerbated during the difficult early years of the Cold War, and its legacy remained with McGrath until his death in 1990.

McGrath began publishing during a difficult time for left-wing writers. *First Manifesto* (1940), published when he was an M.A. student under Louis Simpson at Louisiana State University, appeared at a time when the American literary left was losing much of the cultural ground it had gained during the 1930s. With its Marx-inspired title, *First Manifesto* lacked the sophistication of his later poetry, and instead relied too much on the influence of Auden and on the kind of lines found in "Letter to Wendell," in which "life is a stone image until it is / Aroused in the synergy of the communal kiss."

After appearing in Alan Swallow's *Three Young Poets* (1942), McGrath worked as a teacher at Colby College in Maine and as a shipyard welder in Kearney, New Jersey. He also spent three years in the army (1942–45). His next volume, *To Walk a Crooked Mile* (1947), bore traces of some of the weaknesses of *First Manifesto,* notably the continued influence of Auden: "Where are you going? Said Manny the Mayor" ("Not for Love") is lifted almost directly from Auden's "Where are you going, said reader to rider." Yet although McGrath had been clearly influenced by British poets of the 1930s, his experiences during the period between his first two volumes influenced him still more. In this respect *Crooked Mile* marked the development of McGrath's own distinct political and poetic voice. In that volume, McGrath began to question the efficacy and the human cost of capitalism in the United States, a move that increased the FBI's already keen interest in him. In "The Drowned Man: Death Between Two Rivers," the figure of the leaning man, that symbol of indecision, formed the framework through which the poet introduced what was a lifelong theme:

At dawn in Wall Street the gentle fishers
Dapple with nets the sunshot sound,
And all but the strongest swimmers are taken.

After a year as a Rhodes Scholar at New College, Oxford (1947–48), McGrath's ideological commitment to the left and lifelong belief in class struggle led him to influences such as the English Marxist Christopher Caudwell as well as fellow poets Brecht and Neruda. *Longshot O'Leary's Garland of Practical Poesie* (1949) paid homage to such ideological legacies; in this volume McGrath fully developed his notion of tactical versus strategic poetry. Inspired by Engels' belief that political poetry disappeared with the passing of political prejudices of any given time, McGrath conceived of a tactical poetry of immediacy, which he called "overtly and directly political." Strategic poetry, McGrath felt, need not have the political immediacy of tactical poetry, and in that respect would possess a potential longevity that tactical poetry largely would not. Poems such as "He's a Real Gone Guy: A Short Requiem for Percival Angleman," "The Isles of Greece," and "First Book of Genesis According to Marshall" are all tactical poems relevant to a particular time and place.

By the early 1950s McGrath had moved to Los Angeles, where he served on the editorial board of *The California Quarterly.* While teaching at Los Angeles State College McGrath was hauled in front of the House Un-American Activities Committee, which he informed that he belonged to the "unaffiliated far left." This resulted in political persecution and the loss of his teaching position, leading McGrath to found the Sequoia School, a workshop for young, ambitious poets. McGrath's students there privately published his 1954 volume *Witness to the Times,* much of which was a collection of previously published work. Although he was still writing during this time, the political climate was such that McGrath was finding it increasingly difficult to make ends meet. Nevertheless, despite working in a toy factory and doing freelance work for the film industry, he still found time to complete *The Gates of Ivory, The Gates of Horn* (1957), a dystopian novel that drew upon McGrath's own experiences of persecution.

At about this time McGrath began his epic four-part poem, *Letter to an Imaginary Friend.* This long, partly autobiographical poem incorporates a history of the American left into a broad Whitmanesque framework. Beginning with a recollection of his childhood on a farm in North Dakota, the poem touches on religion, Native Americans, political persecution, community, collective political action, and a host of other charged issues. Organized through the juxtaposition of adult and child voices as well as through film-like flashbacks, the poem is often intensely personal, and McGrath's painful realization that social revolution in America is as far away as it ever was is a recurring feature. Laments for "what / Was: the possible; that is: the future that never arrived" seem to acknowledge that "the commune must fail in the filth of the American night." With its vast panorama, *Letter to an Imaginary Friend* is successful not only in its Whitman-like song of America, but also in its use of personal memory as a means of illuminating the cultural validity of the American left.

*Letter to an Imaginary Friend* is widely regarded as McGrath's best work, although he continued to write well into the 1980s. *The Movie at the End of the World: Collected Poems* (1973) spawned a television documentary of the same name, and work such as *Trinc: Praises II* (1979), *Waiting for the Angel* (1979), *Passages toward the Dark* (1982), *Longshot O'Leary Counsels Direct Action* (1983), *Echoes inside the Labyrinth* (1983), and the novel *This Coffin Has No Handles* (1984) all enhanced the poet's reputation, despite a lingering hostility toward the American left.

Ian Peddie

**Biography**

Born near Sheldon, North Dakota, 20 November 1916. Attended the University of North Dakota, Grand Forks, B.A. in English 1939 (Phi Beta Kappa); Louisiana State University, Baton Rouge, M.A. in English 1940; New College, Oxford (Rhodes Scholar), 1947–48; served in the United States Army Air Force, 1942–45; English Instructor, Colby College, Waterville, Maine, 1940–41; Assistant Professor, Los Angeles State College, 1950–54, and C.W. Post College, Long Island, New York, 1960–61; Associate Professor, North Dakota State

University, Fargo, 1962–67; from 1969 Associate Professor of English, Moorhead State College, Minnesota; editor, *The California Quarterly,* 1951–54; film writer, 1956–60; founding editor, with Eugenia McGrath, *Crazy Horse,* 1960. Received Swallow Book Award, 1955; Amy Lowell traveling scholarship, 1965; Guggenheim fellowship, 1967; National Endowment for the Arts grant, 1974; Bush Foundation fellowship, 1976, 1981; Before Columbus Foundation Award, 1984; Lenore Marshall Poetry Prize, 1989; honorary Litt.D., University of North Dakota, 1981. Died 20 September 1990.

**Poetry**

*First Manifesto,* 1940
*Three Young Poets* (poems by McGrath, William Peterson, and James Franklin Lewis), edited by Alan Swallow, 1942
*The Dialectics of Love,* 1944
*To Walk a Crooked Mile,* 1947
*Longshot O'Leary's Garland of Practical Poesie,* 1949
*Witness to the Times,* 1954
*Figures from a Double World,* 1955
*Letter to an Imaginary Friend,* 1962
*New and Selected Poems,* 1962
*Letter to an Imaginary Friend, Parts I and II,* 1970
*The Movie at the End of the World: Collected Poems,* 1973
*Voyages to the Inland Sea III* (with others), edited by John Judson, 1973
*Voices from beyond the Wall,* 1974
*A Sound of One Hand,* 1975
*Letters to Tomasito,* 1977
*Open Songs: Sixty Short Poems,* 1977
*Trinc: Praises II,* 1979
*Waiting for the Angel,* 1979
*Passages toward the Dark,* 1982
*Echoes inside the Labyrinth,* 1983
*Longshot O'Leary Counsels Direct Action,* 1983
*Letter to an Imaginary Friend, Parts III and IV,* 1985
*Selected Poems, 1938–1988,* edited by Sam Hamill, 1988
*Death Song,* 1991
*The Bread of This World: Praises III,* 1992

**Other Writings:** novels (*This Coffin Has No Handles,* 1984), children's literature.

**Further Reading**

Des Pres, Terrence, *Praises and Dispraises: Poetry and Politics, the 20th Century,* New York: Viking Press, 1988
Dochniak, Jim, editor, "Surviving as a Writer: The Politics of Poetry/The Poetry of Politics," *Sez* 2 and 3 (1981)
Engel, Bernard F., "Thomas McGrath's Dakota," *Midwestern Miscellany* 4 (n.d.)
Gibbons, Reginald, and Terrence Des Pres, "Thomas McGrath: Life and the Poem," *TriQuarterly* 70 (1987)
McGrath, Thomas, "Language, Power, and Dream," in *Claims for Poetry,* edited by Donald Hall, Ann Arbor: University of Michigan Press, 1991
Rogers, James H., "Vision and Feeling: An Interview with Thomas McGrath," *North Dakota Quarterly* 53, no. 1 (1985)
Stern, Frederick C., editor, *The Revolutionary Poet in the United States: The Poetry of Thomas McGrath,* Columbia: University of Missouri Press, 1988
Whitehead, Fred, editor, "Dream Champ—A Festschrift for Thomas McGrath," *North Dakota Quarterly* 50, no. 4 (1982)

---

# Claude McKay 1889–1948

Although he is counted among the cadre of African-American poets who gained prominence during the Harlem Renaissance, Claude McKay did not become an American citizen until he was 50. However, primarily because he penned what would immediately become the quintessential expression of black militancy with his poem "If We Must Die," he holds an important place in American and African-American literary history. While one would not want to deny his importance in the United States, it is enlightening to consider McKay in an international context. Born in Jamaica in 1889, he spent years in his native land and then took lengthy sojourns in the United States, England, France, and Russia, developing significant parts of his career as a writer and intellectual at each of these locations. Let us begin with his childhood home and early education in Jamaica.

McKay was the youngest of eight surviving children. Both of his parents were educated Christians, and they worked the land as farmers, achieving a degree of prosperity that was notable in part because they were dark-skinned in a postcolonial culture that favored light complexions. Growing up among people who were sensitive to both class and racial prejudice, he developed a degree of consciousness to social and political complexities that would form a major font of inspiration for the poet Claude McKay.

When he was seven years old, McKay left his rural hilltop village in Sunny Ville with his oldest brother, Uriah Theodore (U'Theo). U'Theo had just completed teacher training and taken a post in a town near Montego Bay. There, McKay came into contact with the sophisticated life of the city and saw, through the respect and privilege accorded to his schoolteacher-brother, the fruits of intellectual labor. Of its pleasures, McKay was quick to avail himself. As a precocious child, McKay was given free reign to broaden and strengthen his knowledge through reading the great (British) writers: Dickens, Waverly, and Shakespeare. In his brother's library, McKay also came into contact with the philosophical debates of the day through the work of Thomas Huxley and Matthew Arnold. Thus, his taste for literature and radical thinking grew up simultaneously.

McKay began writing verse at the age of ten, drawing his subjects from local folk and church music. However, from the start, he fitted his creative vision to the rhyme and meter of the English poets who were taught in school. Even his early dialect poetry retains the forms of the English masters, foreshadowing the tension between his radical vision and traditional form that is a consistent feature of his work.

Growing up in Jamaica, McKay knew the ravages of racism firsthand. At the same time, however, because he grew up in a black community among independent farmers and wage earners, he also knew the love and support that comes from the all-black cultural context that had emerged after the long struggle against such endemic forces. His literary career—which began in Jamaica with two published volumes of poetry, *Songs of Jamaica* (1912) and *Constab Ballads* (1912)—flourished in the United States, where he also published three novels, two autobiographies, and countless journalistic articles.

McKay began his career as a poet producing dialect verse. His *Songs from Jamaica* and the poems that preceded it show an early recognition of the difficulties inherent in racial and class conflict. In one early poem, McKay tackles the subject by calling for a return to the country and the folk culture that his childhood Jamaica symbolized: "Come to de hills; dey may be drear, / But we can shun de evil here." While these lines offer a respite from the city, they also acknowledge the limitations ("drear") of country life. So, although these lines point toward McKay's abiding trust in the land and its country ways over the rising industrial capitalism he saw all around him, McKay's view of the country life remains ambivalent. The country does at least permit the subjects of the poem a place to "spend our short days"; however, the speaker adds, "an' still, / Though prisoners, feel somehow free / To live our lives o' misery." Far from the bucolic bliss that many associate with McKay's vision of Jamaica, these lines memorialize the incompleteness of this Edenic setting. Casting the personae as "helpless playthings of a Will," the lines make it clear that the lack of political power renders even the lovely hills of Jamaica a prison to those without the political power ("Will") to control their lives.

The importance of resistance—and the contribution that individual sacrifice can make—is a major source for McKay's larger focus on collectivity as political action. From the time of his earliest publications in Jamaica, he featured his political and social conscience in his poetry, initiating a new strain of protest that had not been fully articulated in black poetry. For instance, many of the poems he published in Jamaica's *Daily Gleaner* and *Jamaica Times* took historical instances of racial and economic oppression as their focus. The sonnet form that he worked in almost exclusively might seem an odd choice for a black Jamaican poet. Many of his poems adopted both the form and the diction of Jamaica's British colonizers, and he used what Wahneema Lubiano has termed "the master's tools" to deliver scathing critiques of colonial oppression. His poetry addresses political themes through a personal focus, using the lyric persona to give voice to unheard views on political and racial oppression. The form also lent the suffering a dignity that traditional poetic form carried with it.

McKay's success with the sonnet as a vehicle for protest poetry was recognized early in his career. In 1912, he won "Honorable Mention" by *T.P.'s Weekly* of London for "Gordon to the Oppressed Natives," calling "O, you sons of Afric's soil" to revolution. In this poem, McKay returns readers to the 1865 Morant Bay Rebellion in Jamaica. The poem takes its title from the mulatto politician George William Gordon, who encouraged blacks to rise up against their colonial oppressors. McKay places Gordon within the context of the English abolition movement through mention of major figures such as Wilberforce and Clarkson. Accessing this history, he also tapped in to the complex association colonial subjects have with their oppressors. Arguing that "Never would an English mind / Bow beneat' such tyranny," the speaker urges, "Rise O people of my kind! / Struggle, struggle to be free."

McKay admired Booker T. Washington and left Jamaica to pursue a program of study at the Tuskegee Institute in 1912. Yet, soon after his arrival there, he chaffed at the regimentation of student life and the lack of intellectual challenge. He transferred to Kansas State College for a two-year program that he did not complete. Instead, McKay ended up in New York. He sent for Eulalie Imelda Lewers, a woman whom he had been dating in Jamaica, and married her on her arrival in the United States in 1914. This relationship, the only formal one that he would ever undertake, ended quickly. Although he never openly acknowledged his homosexuality, references to it pepper his poetry and prose. According to one biographer, his wife never really understood McKay's preferences. Nonetheless, they divorced six months later; she returned to Jamaica and gave birth to McKay's only offspring, a daughter named Hope.

The publication of the poems "Invocation" and "Harlem Dancer" in the radical magazine *Seven Arts* marks McKay's entrance into the U.S. literary scene. His work, featured along with work by established writers such as Amy Lowell and Bertrand Russell, appealed to the editors, who sought to rejuvenate the American scene by publishing material that took a decidedly fresh approach. In McKay's case, his desire, as expressed in "Invocation," to draw on his African past and become, through this connection, "The worthy singer of my world and race" suited him well for inclusion in the pages of *Seven Arts*. Unfortunately, the magazine was too radical for the wealthy patron who had supported it. A year after its inception, funds were withdrawn, and the magazine folded. Taking odd jobs here and there to support himself and to further his writing career, McKay ended up as a Pullman porter during the race riots of 1919. It was at this time that he penned what has remained his best-known poem.

An admirer of the radical magazine *The Masses* and its subsequent incarnation the *Liberator*, McKay sought publication in its pages. He achieved this goal with "If We Must Die" in 1919. On publication, "If We Must Die" garnered enormous attention. Reprinted in many black newspapers, the poem gave voice to the justified rage that blacks across the country were feeling during the Red Scare of 1919. "If We Must Die" became the clarion call of black liberation on its publication and has remained an anthem of black militancy. True to the poem's directive that "Like men we'll face the murderous, cowardly pack / Pressed to the wall, dying, but fighting back," the poem was found crumpled in the hands of a rebelling prisoner killed during the Attica prison riots in 1971. This poem also had a lasting effect on the poet himself. From the publication of "If We Must Die" forward, McKay committed himself fully to being a professional writer.

As time went on, McKay became more involved in the international Socialist movement, and between 1919 and 1921, while he was living in England, his identity as a writer and a radical thinker flourished through an alliance with Sylvia Pankhurst and her *Workers' Dreadnought*. Using his pen in support of the movement, McKay produced what one biographer has called poetry for the proletariat, and although he used a pseudonym for much of this work, his reluctance to use his own name had more to do with the political climate and risk of arrest than with a lack of pride in the work. He published his third collection of poems, *Spring in New Hampshire, and Other Poems* (1920), during this time. The soon-to-be guru of New Criticism I.A. Richards wrote an introduction to the book in which he hailed McKay's efforts as "the first instance of success in poetry" of a "pure blooded Negro." Ironically, McKay did not include many important poems that dealt explicitly with race in this collection, most notably "If We Must Die." He appended those poems to the collection and republished it in an expanded American edition with Harcourt, Brace and Company in 1922.

On his return to the United States, McKay further solidified his relationship with Max Eastman, editor of the *Liberator.* Eastman would serve as an important touchstone and mentor for the rest of McKay's life. For the next year (1921–22), he served as the associate editor under Eastman at the *Liberator.* McKay's aesthetic sensibility continued to develop, and his work at the *Liberator* helped him extend his contacts among what Zora Neale Hurston termed the "niggeratti" of the day. Relationships with important figures in the National Association for the Advancement of Colored People (NAACP), such as Walter White and, more significantly, James Weldon Johnson, would ultimately benefit McKay. In fact, Johnson functioned as an important power broker during the Harlem Renaissance and was instrumental in McKay's receipt of a $500 grant from the Rosenwald Fund to complete work on his first novel, *Home to Harlem* (1928).

With the publication of *Home to Harlem* also came some of the most vituperative criticism that McKay's work would ever receive. The novel depicted a greater swath of black culture than had previous works by black writers, such as Jessie Fauset and Charles Chesnutt. McKay's novel broke with the "talented tenth" agenda to depict blacks as genteel and middle class, reveling in the cultural expressions of the black lower classes. Calling the novel an example of "filth," "dirt," "drunkenness," and "sexual promiscuity," W.E.B. DuBois pilloried McKay for his open violation of the assimilationist code that DuBois and many others promoted. He was accused of pandering to white tastes by following in the footsteps of Carl Van Vechten, whose *Nigger Heaven* (1926) also focused on lower-class blacks. That novel and McKay's were phenomenal successes. As much as McKay's pecuniary problems plagued him all his life, writing off *Home to Harlem* and his later novels as less-than-genuine artistic efforts seems a gross misinterpretation. McKay's commitment to mass culture—although possibly masked by his use of the class-inflected sonnet form—is consistent throughout his writing career, and his relationship with radical politics further suggests the novel as a true celebration of a black culture flourishing outside the limitations of capitalism. Clashes of class and race energize all of McKay's work; the novels are not greater assaults on social regimentation; rather, they simply represent a more open rejection. Subtitling his 1929 novel *Banjo* "a story without a plot" epitomizes the radicalness of his efforts; the subtitle flies in the face of the form itself in ways that his poetry never did.

In his poetry, McKay maintained a strict allegiance to the sonnet despite the increasing use of the syncopated rhythms of jazz, as in the work of his contemporary Langston Hughes and the melodic verse of his countryman Countee Cullen. McKay's efforts to innovate and open up opportunity for black writers took shape more in social action than in literary form. At several points in his career, he put together writers' groups, most notably in a letter that he circulated to establish a Negro Writers' Guild. His interest in groups such as this one served both artistic and political aims. As he had earlier expressed in his 1917 poem "Invocation," McKay believed that writers of color need to nourish one another. At the same time, he saw the parochial world of publishing often barred to those who dared to be different.

After a lifetime of political and social ostracism, McKay took what he termed "a right turn to Catholicism" in 1944. Raised as an agnostic by his brother U'Theo, McKay's conversion was as much a surprise to his contemporaries as it is to his readers today. Worn out and broken by health problems, McKay was perhaps offered a safe haven and a sense of belonging from the Catholic Church. Despite his continued efforts to unite people in his poetry, he never found a community of his own. After much reflection and deliberation, he believed that conversion would provide such community. He died in a church hospital of the pleurisy that had dogged him much of his adult life; this was a week before the reunion he had planned with his daughter, Hope.

Augusta Rohrbach

*See also* Caribbean Poetry; Harlem Renaissance

**Biography**

Born Festus Claudius McKay in Sunny Ville, Clarendon Parish, Jamaica, 15 September 1889. Attended Tuskegee Institute, Alabama, 1912; Kansas State College, Manhattan, 1913–14; apprentice cabinetmaker and wheelwright, 1907–08; joined Jamaican Constabulary, 1909; police officer in Spanish Town, Jamaica, 1911–12; worked at various jobs and opened restaurant in New York, 1914; on staff of *Workers' Dreadnought* communist newspaper, London, 1919–20; associate editor, 1921–22, and co-editor, 1922, *Liberator,* New York; laborer in welfare camp, New York, 1934–35; writer for Works Progress Administration until 1939; worked in a shipbuilding yard, 1943; joined Catholic Church, 1944, and worked for the National Catholic Youth Organization, Chicago, 1944–48. Received Harmon Prize, 1929. Died in Chicago, 22 May 1948.

**Poetry**

*Songs of Jamaica,* 1912
*Constab Ballads,* 1912
*Spring in New Hampshire, and Other Poems,* 1920; expanded edition, 1922
*Harlem Shadows,* 1922
*Selected Poems of Claude McKay,* 1953
*The Dialect Poetry,* 1972
*The Passion of McKay: Selected Poetry and Prose, 1912–1948,* edited by Wayne Cooper, 1973

**Other Writings:** novels (*Home to Harlem,* 1928; *Banana Bottom,* 1933), short stories (*Gingertown,* 1932), autobiography, nonfiction (*Harlem: Negro Metropolis,* 1940).

**Further Reading**

Cooper, Wayne F., *Claude McKay: Rebel Sojourner in the Harlem Renaissance: A Biography,* Baton Rouge: Louisiana State University Press, 1987
Gayle, Addison, *Claude McKay: The Black Poet at War,* Detroit, Michigan: Broadside Press, 1972

Giles, James R., *Claude McKay,* Boston: Twayne, 1976
Hathaway, Heather, *Caribbean Waves: Relocating Claude McKay and Paule Marshall,* Bloomington: Indiana University Press, 1999

## America

Claude McKay's "America" was first published in book form in *Harlem Shadows* (1922), which has been described as the inaugural poetic text of the Harlem Renaissance. That year, which also saw the publication of *The Waste Land* and *Ulysses,* is often taken as the *annus mirabilis* of literary Modernism, yet the relationship between the literature of the Harlem Renaissance and that of Anglo-American Modernism remains unclear. McKay's poem, which has affiliations with the literature of Renaissance England as well as with the Harlem Renaissance, appears to have little congress with the innovations of the Modernist era. "America" is a version not of the "Shakespeherian Rag" of *The Waste Land,* but of the Shakespearean or English sonnet. McKay's America is personified as female, but McKay also replicates the Renaissance sonnet's use of amorous conventions to address political concerns, to discuss, albeit obliquely, the urgent and topical issue of American race relations. This tension between antique form and insistently contemporary subject matter suggests that "America" is a paleo-modernist text, a work that is Modernist in content but not in form. At the same time "America" can be read in terms of the American tradition of apostrophes to the nation, a poetic subgenre to which Allen Ginsberg's "America" also belongs, a poem that, like McKay's, is both love song and jeremiad.

"America" is a mannered poem, with decoratively alliterative opening lines and internal rhyme and para-rhyme. Written in the present tense, McKay's response to America is characterized by its immediacy and physicality: the vocabulary of "throat," "tooth," and "blood" emphasizes that McKay's is first and foremost a visceral response. The sexualized America-as-woman trope—the poet-lover is "erect against her"—is familiar, but the gender roles of the poem are also subjected to the slippage bisexual McKay experienced in life: the poet-lover is feminized by the "bigness" of an America later masculinized as "king." America both nurtures and destroys, feeds and feeds upon the speaker: "she feeds me bread" but "bread of bitterness"; she "sinks into my throat her tiger's tooth."

McKay, who was Jamaican, renders his American residency as monarchy, fashioning himself as the "rebel" who "fronts a king in state." The poet not only "fronts" America, he also affronts or confronts her. "Front" also evokes a facade or cover, perhaps the mask worn by the black writer as trickster, who, according to Houston Baker (1987), engages in the mastery of (the sonnet) form in order to achieve a subversive mastery. It may equally well be the case, however, that McKay's metaphor of sovereignty bespeaks someone who was raised as, and long after the time of writing legally remained, a subject of the British Crown. His use of the historically charged word "rebel" once again suggests McKay's foreignness to the American scene. Wayne Cooper's definition of McKay in his seminal critical biography as "rebel sojourner in the Harlem Renaissance" (1987) underscores not only McKay's rebellion against the artistic mores of the "New Negro" but also his status as sojourner in all his post-Jamaican residencies.

The allure of America is *a priori* for McKay: with the word "although," the poem begins on a subordinate clause that both describes and syntactically enacts the ambivalence of his response. The principal clause, "I love," articulates McKay's positive embrace of America, even though the contrary states of the poem's opening lines return in the compacted form of the oxymoron in line four, the "cultured hell" that is American life. America is seen as both savage ("tiger") and civilized ("cultured"), as both man-made (the locus of skyscrapers, "granite wonders," and "walls") and organic (the natural, primal element of "flood"). The turn of the sestet counters the argument of the octave in the conventional English sonnet, but McKay tweaks this procedure, simply placing a comma between his octave and sestet and reserving the argumentative "turn" until the tenth line. Thus the greater part of McKay's poem charts his qualified celebration of America, his projection of American decline occupying only the last four lines of the poem. Where Ginsberg puts his "queer shoulder to the wheel" of his "America," McKay turns against her, with his final prophecy of the future decline and fall of America, of her monuments, and by extension of modernity and the West.

America's demise is an imaginative projection, a mystical prophecy, not a call to arms. This projection into time to come also reverts to the past in that the last lines of the poem harbor an allusion to Shelley's sonnet "Ozymandias," as McKay "gaze[s] into the days ahead" and sees America's "might and granite wonders" "sinking in the sand." The poem's conclusion is also a prophecy of McKay's own imminent expatriation from his adopted country of America, and, perhaps, of his own impending turn from the form of the sonnet, itself superannuated by "the touch of Time," to other modes of writing.

Lee M. Jenkins

**Further Reading**

Baker, Houston A., Jr., *Modernism and the Harlem Renaissance,* Chicago: University of Chicago Press, 1987
Breiner, Laurence A., *An Introduction to West Indian Poetry,* Cambridge and New York: Cambridge University Press, 1998
Cooper, Wayne F., *Claude McKay: Rebel Sojourner in the Harlem Renaissance: A Biography,* Baton Rouge: Louisiana State University Press, 1987
Hutchinson, George, *The Harlem Renaissance in Black and White,* Cambridge, Massachusetts: Harvard University Press, 1995
North, Michael, *The Dialect of Modernism: Race, Language, and Twentieth-Century Literature,* New York: Oxford University Press, 1994
North, Michael, *Reading 1922: A Return to the Scene of the Modern,* New York: Oxford University Press, 1999

## The Lynching

Claude McKay's poem "The Lynching," published in 1919, the same year as his most famous poem, "If We Must Die," is in the traditional sonnet form. McKay's use of the sonnet at the height of American Modernism may be interpreted as a strategy for reaching an audience resistant to African-American authors and racial themes. At the same time, McKay employs a poetic form of the dominant society to explore and challenge that society's views on the expendable nature of black life.

Written in response to the "Red Summer" of 1919, which witnessed 26 bloody race riots across the country and a record number of African-Americans lynched (especially returning soldiers still in uniform), "The Lynching" begins by focusing on the victim. Line one, "His Spirit in smoke ascended to high heaven," connects him to Christ. The capitalization of "Spirit," which lends the victim a messianic quality, and his ascent into "high heaven" contradict the unspoken justification of the lynching as punishment for some heinous crime.

Lines two and three, "His father, by the cruelest way of pain, / Had bidden him to his bosom once again," complicate the status of human and divine in the poem. First, "father" is not capitalized and thus suggests an earthly father grieving over the death of his child, although the first line has already led the reader to think of the son as divine. The first quatrain ends, "The awful sin remained still unforgiven," returning the reader to the "divine" reading. Yet the lack of capitalization for "father" can be read as the questioning of God, or of the presence of a God, who allows such atrocities. The victim's death, unlike Christ's, does not produce the forgiveness of sin. Readers are left to define the "awful sin"—what it is and to whom it belongs.

The second quatrain continues to emphasize the victim as a Christ figure. Line five, "All night a bright and solitary star," recalls the star of Bethlehem that announced the birth of Christ. However, the parenthetical note that comprises lines six and seven, "(Perchance the one that ever guided him, / yet gave him up at last to Fate's wild whim)," suggests that this star led the victim to his death—presented here as a random rather than a purposeful Fate. The star may also represent the North Star, which led African-American slaves to the North and, so they thought, to freedom. Here, however, the star that is expected to guide one toward freedom hangs over the body of the victim. Line eight, "Hung pitifully o'er the swinging char," offers the reader a clear image of the lynching, hinted at in the first quatrain through "smoke" and "cruelest way of pain."

In the third quatrain, McKay shifts his focus away from the victim and toward the mob. Line nine, "Day dawned, and soon the mixed crowds came to view," suggests a different group than had attended the lynching the night before. The reference to a mixed crowd indicates the presence of women and children. Line ten, "The ghastly body swaying in the sun," extends the horror of the lynching by presenting it in the light of day. McKay saves his strongest indictment for those members of the community traditionally thought of as nurturing and innocent—women and children. Lines 11 and 12, "The women thronged to look, but never a one / Showed sorrow in her eyes of steely blue," dispel the notion of women as gentle and sympathetic, as the blue eyes reveal that the perpetrators of the lynching are European-Americans. The women merely desire to see the body. McKay contrasts this inhuman response with the humanity (and perhaps divine nature) of the victim.

McKay's couplet "And little lads, lynchers that were to be, / Danced round the dreadful thing in fiendish glee" (lines 13 and 14) condemns the future generation. Here children, often thought to be innocent and free of hate, are presented as demonic. If the women are not moved by the horrific spectacle, the children take delight in dancing around the charred body. In calling the victim a "thing" and emphasizing the children's "fiendish glee," McKay indicts the dominant society as more than inhuman for finding pleasure in the torture and murder—the fundamental dehumanization—of an African-American. Moreover, McKay ends the sonnet with a pessimistic view of future race relations. He labels the children "lynchers that were to be," revealing how racism and racial violence are taught and how the next generation has already become indoctrinated in viewing the African-American as subhuman.

Adenike Marie Davidson

**Further Reading**

Condit, John Hillyer, "An Urge Towards Wholeness: Claude McKay and His Sonnets," *College Language Association Journal* 22 (1979)

Gayle, Addison, *Claude McKay: The Black Poet at War,* Detroit, Michigan: Broadside Press, 1972

Keller, James R., "'A Chafing Savage, Down the Decent Street': The Politics of Compromise in Claude McKay's Protest Sonnets," *African American Review* 28, no. 3 (Fall 1994)

Smith, Gary, "The Black Protest Sonnet," *American Poetry* 2, no. 1 (Fall 1984)

Tillery, Tyrone, *Claude McKay: A Black Poet's Struggle for Identity,* Amherst: University of Massachusetts Press, 1992

# The White City

Originally published in the socialist *Liberator* in October 1921 and then collected in the volume *Harlem Shadows* (1922), Claude McKay's "The White City" powerfully thematizes from its very title the exclusion of African-Americans from the urban North and its promises of freedom and integration. The imagery of entrapment and hatred conveyed by the sonnet are typical of McKay's urban landscapes, as shown by other poems, such as "Rest in Peace," "The Desolate City," "The City's Love," and "The White House."

"The White City" is built around several paradoxical and oxymoronic choices on the level of both content and form. The main assumption of the sonnet, conveyed by the first two quatrains, is that it is the poet's "life-long hate," caused by the white city's contempt for his color, that keeps him alive. Excluded by the city, the poet is trapped in a vicious circle where his hatred is continuously renewed by the constant postponement of African-American equality:

> My being would be a skeleton, a shell,
> If this dark Passion that fills my every mood,
> And makes my heaven in the white world's hell,
> Did not forever feed me vital blood.

These lines contain the main paradox of the poem, defining hatred as a vital force, a concept that is emphasized by oxymoron (dark/white, heaven/hell) as well as by the strong enjambment between lines six and eight. In this sonnet, there is no mention of the "one brief golden moment rare like wine" in which the city is "oblivious" to the poet's skin that McKay had described in "The City's Love." The sonnet defies the reader's expectations: the "secret chambers" of the poet's heart contain not love but hatred. No affection is expressed in the poem: there are no images of warmth, conventionally associated in other of McKay's poems with love (take, as an example, the final rhyming couplet of "The City's Love": "The great, proud city, seized with a strange love, / Bowed down for one *flame* hour my pride to prove"). The white city is like "The Desolate City": "cold as death." The poet and the white city remain separate, and urban space can be seen only at a distance and through a veil of mist. The image of the white city, then, is the embodiment of that particular feature of McKay's poetry identified by John Dewey (1953) as the blending of the physical and the human into an indivisible yet distinctive unity. The whiteness of the city is given both by the physical phenomenon of the mist, recalling the fog in Eliot's "Prufrock," and by the marginalization and exclusion of African-Americans (the same happens in the poem "To One Coming North" through the image of the snow, employed so powerfully by Richard Wright in his novel *Native Son*).

This separation of the poet and the city is conveyed by the third quatrain and the final rhyming couplet. In these six lines, McKay poses as the typical Modernist urban observer: the poet who contemplates the city and its masses at a distance. Yet it seems that this position is forced on the poet rather than chosen by him: the city is almost fortified against the poet's gaze ("the fortressed port"). The city is also described as "mighty," which makes the poet appear completely passive and powerless and which alliterates with "mist" in the same line, emphasizing the identification city-mist and therefore "whiteness." The atmosphere of passivity is also established through two of the three verbs referred to the poet ("I see"; "I contemplate") and by the tenth line, in which the city has an active role while humans have a passive one ("The strident trains that speed the goaded mass"). The only solution that the poet finds for his exclusion from the urban landscape is to resort once more to a feeling of hatred. The poet's psychological tension is underscored by the complex syntax of the last lines, and the sonnet ends with its return to the paradoxical reasoning typical of the first two quatrains ("The tides, the wharves, the dens I contemplate, / Are sweet like wanton loves because I hate"). Thus, the structure foregrounds the separation of the poet from the city and his entrapment in a circle of hatred.

The choice of the sonnet to convey such a sustained feeling of hate may seem an odd one at first. Yet it is completely consistent with the rhetoric of reversal espoused by the poem. The sonnet, which is regarded as the quintessential poetic form for the expression of love, is here reversed and employed to express hatred. "The White City" plays throughout its text with the reader's expectations generated by the sonnet form. As William Maxwell (1999) has perceptively remarked, the "life-long hate" is not revealed until line three, and the fourth line "goes on to cast this hate as something the speaker will bear as thousands of other sonnet voices have borne unrequited desire: 'nobly,' while playing an assigned 'part' in a theatricalized text." "The White City" also plays with the structure of the sonnet itself. At first glance, it appears to follow the English or Shakespearean form with its three quatrains and a final rhyming couplet. Yet on close scrutiny, the rhyming couplet is linked syntactically to the last quatrain, thus forming a sestet, the concluding part of the Italian sonnet.

With its inversion of the northern cityscapes from mythic Promised Land to territory of exploitation, "The White City," a typical embodiment of McKay's urban poems, reveals, as Felipe Smith (1998) has noticed, "how entrapment in this myth of AMERICA is the form that social exclusion often takes." McKay is thus the forerunner of the other African-American intellectuals, such as the "poet Langston Hughes and novelists Richard Wright, Ann Petry, Ralph Ellison, and James Baldwin, who would explore the contradictions of the urban ghetto's proximity but incomplete access to the wealth and power of America."

Luca Prono

**Further Reading**


Cooper, Wayne F., *Claude McKay: Rebel Sojourner in the Harlem Renaissance: A Biography,* Baton Rouge: Louisiana State University Press, 1987

Dewey, John, "Introduction," in *Selected Poems of Claude McKay,* by McKay, New York: Bookman, and London: Harcourt Brace Jovanovich, 1953

Maxwell, William J., *New Negro, Old Left: African-American Writing and Communism between the Wars,* New York: Columbia University Press, 1999

Smith, Felipe, *American Body Politics: Race, Gender, and Black Literary Renaissance,* Athens: University of Georgia Press, 1998

Tillery, Tyrone, *Claude McKay: A Black Poet's Struggle for Identity,* Amherst: University of Massachusetts Press, 1992


---

# James Merrill 1926–95

James Merrill occupies a unique position in American poetry, a position he described in a typically witty phrase as "arch-conservative. More arch than conservative" (*Recitative: Prose by James Merrill,* 1986). Primarily a lyric and narrative poet, Merrill combined, like Blake and Yeats, the strengths of "autobiography-in-verse" (Kalstone, 1977) and the prophetic impulse, but he also sustained the satirical verse tradition of Pope, Byron, and W.H. Auden. His ideal reader, Merrill said, should keep "one eye on the ever-emerging (self-revising) whole, and another on the details" (*Recitative*). Once he broke out of his early aestheticism, Merrill formed a poetic persona in which his reading, his love of opera, his lived experience, and his experiments with the Ouija board allowed him to explore the various connections between material and spiritual phenomena. Never abandoning his early penchant for word play, Merrill's later poetry shows a more relaxed mastery of poetic forms and a deepening connection to lived experience. As Merrill said of C.P. Cavafy, "Formality in the later work appears, so to speak, informally" (*Recitative*).

Merrill's poetry cannot be understood without attention to his biography, especially his parents' divorce, his travels in Europe, and his homosexuality, all of which Merrill himself discusses in his coming of age memoir, *A Different Person* (1993). Privileged by birth, aristocratic and apolitical by temperament, Merrill found himself an outsider in mid-century America, so much so that he said he felt "American in Europe and exotic at home," and for many years lived part of each year in Greece. The son of Charles Merrill, one of the founders of the financial firm Merrill Lynch and of Safeway stores, he was able to live as he wished and to pursue poetry with complete freedom from having to make a living. The divorce of his parents in 1939 is a subject that he returns to repeatedly, notably in "The Broken Home" and "Lost in Translation." After a brief stint in the Army, Merrill graduated in 1947 from Amherst College, where he wrote his senior thesis on Marcel Proust, who along with Auden was the greatest influence on his poetry. Merrill wrote two novels, *The Seraglio* (1957), a portrait of his father, and *The (Diblos) Notebook* (1965), set in Greece, as well as plays, including the Surrealist one-act *The Bait* (1953). His relationships with several men in addition to his companion David Jackson figure prominently in his work. His affair with Kimon Friar, his teacher at Amherst and translator of modern Greek poetry, had a leavening effect, while the death of Hans Lodeizen in 1950 had a sobering influence.

The essays, reviews, interviews, and talks collected in *Recitative* reveal Merrill's literary debts, notably his discovery of the "irresistibly gaudy and irresistibly abstract" vocabulary of Wallace Stevens, and his respect for Elizabeth Bishop, whose "sanity and levelheadedness and quirkiness of mind" tempered the influence of such "male giants" as Stevens, Ezra Pound, and Auden. Merrill compares the work of his Modernist predecessors to "one of these plate-glass banks where you can look in and see the vaults, see all of the workings and all the precautions they've taken against being robbed." For Merrill, as for his contemporaries the Confessional poets and the New York School, poetry was a far more personal performance, "an act of self-purification" in which the clarity arrived at is "unforeseeable."

From the beginning, with *First Poems* (1951), Merrill was interested in discovering meaning in linguistic structures, relying upon puns, metaphor, and symbolism to create a world within the space of the poem. Asked about the importance of domestic spaces in his poetry, Merrill pointed out that "stanza" is Italian for "room." In *The Country of a Thousand Years of Peace* (1959) Merrill branched out into the world, in part due to his travels and the death of Hans Lodeizen. Merrill came into his own, however, with *Water Street* (1962), the result of his having moved with David Jackson in 1954 from New York to the secluded coastal village of Stonington, Connecticut. The volume begins with his impatience with the changing landscape of New York in "An Urban Convalescence" and ends in "A Tenancy" with his settling down in the house on Water Street, where he can

> Invite the visitors to sit.
> If I am host at last
> It is of little more than my own past.
> May others be at home in it.

This invitation stakes out Merrill's poetic territory, a modest and semi-domestic space in which he might reach his own conclusions about his experience.

Merrill's middle period begins with *Nights and Days* (1966), in which a new candor informs his approach to such personal material as his parents' breakup ("The Broken Home") and his homosexuality ("Days of 1964"). The title of the latter poem pays homage to Cavafy, the Alexandrian poet of homoerotic desire, who like Merrill chronicled the "laughter, love and pain" in hopes that love would "climb when it needed to the heights / Even of degradation." "Charles on Fire" introduces Merrill's persona Charles, an observant figure of bemused detachment. Such detachment can also be seen in "The Thousand and Second Night," in which Merrill conducts a metapoetic parody of a classroom discussion of the earlier parts of the poem, complete with students' interruptions and stage directions. The halting self-explication of the professor reflects Merrill's distrust of ideas and words, and his compensating trust in form. "Words might frustrate me," said Merrill, "forms never did; neither did meter" (*Recitative*). Ideas, on the other hand, seemed fickle and unreliable:

> early on I began to understand the relativity, even the reversibility, of truths. . . . the ability to see both ways at once isn't merely an idiosyncrasy but corresponds to how the world needs to be seen: cheerful *and* awful, opaque *and* transparent. The plus and minus signs of a vast, evolving formula. (*Recitative*)

In *The Fire Screen* (1969) and *Braving the Elements* (1972), Merrill appears to be engaging the world at large, as though in preparation for the metaphysical point of view he adopts after *Divine Comedies* (1976). A transitional book largely about Merrill's life in Greece, *The Fire Screen* examines the illuminating and destructive element of fire as memory and art. "Matinees," a sequence of eight sonnets, plays variations on Merrill's love of music, especially opera, which he began to attend about the time of his parents' divorce. *Braving the Elements* expands Merrill's concerns further, even into political commentary in "18 West 11th Street," although the accidental bombing of this address by activists in 1970 does connect to his own history since he grew up at this address. Using the Ouija board as a motivating conceit, Merrill embarks on a radical new experiment in *Divine Comedies* with "The Book of Ephraim," a narrative poem that will become the first book of the trilogy *The Changing Light at Sandover* (1982).

While *The Changing Light at Sandover* marks Merrill's maturity, it can also be seen as a step in his development. Like Aeschylus' addition of the second character in Greek drama, the Ouija board experiment gave Merrill access to voices other than his own, allowing him to explore the conversational mode even more than in his plays and novels. Although this long poem's ambitious theme is cosmological, for most readers the real interest will be the human and spiritual conversations about the sources of Merrill's poetic inspiration and the instability of language and memory. More personal than prophetic, more literary than philosophical, the poem's colloquy with the dead is a sort of interview, seminar, or theatrical performance in which two sides of Merrill's psyche, the traditional and the postmodern, debate the relative values between the will of form and the accidents of innovation, culture versus autobiography.

Merrill's final three volumes of poetry—*Late Settings* (1985), *The Inner Room* (1988), and *A Scattering of Salts* (1995)—continue to explore the familiar terrain of the meanings of childhood, travels, possessions, and houses, but with an unsettling sense of leave-taking. Still master of metaphor, Merrill describes a "Page from the Koran" sold at auction as

black
Scorpions of Kufic script—their ranks
All trigger tail and gold vowel-sac.

This is not Merrill's alphabet, but he respects its mystery, like that of all language, like an undiscovered country. The same attention is given to the scene in "Palm Beach with Portuguese Man-of-War," in which "the anemone's flame chiffon gown" is compared to "those downtown in the boutiques."

In *The Inner Room* Merrill looks back on his life and work, and forward to his legacy: "*My monumental chronicles drag on. / Life glitters once, an epigram, and—gone*" ("Walks in Rome"). In Part IV's "Prose of Departure" the postcard-like vignettes of travel in Japan crystallize into rhyming haiku stanzas of his own design (rhyming *aba*), then conclude in prose by stepping "ashore, in our clumsiness hoping not to spill these brief impressions." While this volume is unified by the knowledge that time is running out, there may still be time for "insight too prompt and vital for words" ("Losing the Marbles"), or to hold a brief for beauty by emphasizing the "sweet, unemphatic" everyday scene, although "someone / else's eye be grazing those Greek horizons" that once belonged to him ("David's Watercolor"). The emphasis of urgency can be heard in the Hopkins-like sprung rhythm of "Arabian Night": "Then ('there' of course, also) insight's / dazzle snaps at gloom, like a wick when first lit" to illuminate and "solve a life-long riddle: a face no longer / sought in dreams but worn as my own."

The valedictory tone is most evident, however, in *A Scattering of Salts,* published immediately after Merrill's death. Its opening and closing poems provide a frame in which to see the world from two points of view. "A Downward Look" from an airplane yields an elaborate conceit that the clouds below are bathtub suds (formed by "a scattering of [bath] salts"), but not without the sinister sense of an ending when "a wrinkled, baby hand / Happens upon the plug." "An Upward Look" from the grave suggests that the riddles of life will remain unsolved, "halves of a clue" continuing to be assembled "by the departing occupier."

Merrill's unwillingness to arrogate to himself a persona of greatness is perhaps best seen in his "Self-Portrait in Tyvek (TM) Windbreaker" from *A Scattering of Salts.* Merrill depicts himself in caricature, wearing a synthetic warm-up jacket of technologically advanced fabric, "Unrippable stuff first used for Priority Mail." Like other Americans, who "Shrug off accountability by dressing / Younger than their kids," Merrill takes an interest in the signs of the times, addressing the issues and pop cultural icons of the day, from the GNP and political correctness to Oprah and the Gap. Although his interest is satirical, he knows that even in such homely things poetry can be found, almost accidentally:

The eloquence to come
Will be precisely what we cannot say
Until it parts the lips.

At Merrill's death in 1995, his place in American poetry was already assured. Not only had he won most of the major prizes for poetry, including two National Book Awards, the Bollingen Prize, the Pulitzer Prize, the National Book Critics Circle Award, and the first Bobbitt National Prize, Merrill also influenced a generation of poets in search of an authentic way of speaking richly of common experience. Unlike the declamations of the Modernists, the self-analyses of the Confessional poets, or the bohemian postures of the Beats and the New York School, Merrill's experiments in formal verse showed that autobiographical subjects could be addressed in a poetry of linguistic play that could be made to reveal the meaning inherent in the accidental structures of language, whether these are the discourses of high art or popular culture. As a postmodern formalist, Merrill deftly orchestrated colloquial and formal diction to provide readers with a poetic comedy of manners for the late 20th century. Merrill's sense of play never left him. J.D. McClatchy describes how, the day before his death in 1995, Merrill was still playing with words in deadly earnest and with sharp irony as he described his hospital room: "A room with every last convenience" (Rotella, 1996).

RICHARD COLLINS

**Biography**
Born in New York City, 3 March 1926. Attended Amherst College, Massachusetts, B.A. 1947; served in the United States Army, 1944–45. Received Oscar Blumenthal Prize, 1947, Levinson Prize, 1949, Harriet Monroe Prize, 1951, Eunice Tietjens Memorial Prize, 1958, and Morton Dauwen Zabel Prize, 1966 (*Poetry,* Chicago); National Book Award, 1967, 1979; Bollingen Prize, 1973; Pulitzer Prize, 1977; *Los Angeles Times* Award, 1983; National Book Critics Circle Award, 1983; Bobst Award, 1984; National Arts Club Medal of Honor, 1988; Rebekah Johnson Bobbitt Prize, 1989; honorary Litt.D., Amherst College, 1968; member, American Academy, 1971; chancellor, Academy of American Poets, 1979. Died in Arizona, 6 February 1995.

**Poetry**
*First Poems,* 1951
*The Country of a Thousand Years of Peace, and Other Poems,* 1959; revised edition, 1970
*Selected Poems,* 1961
*Water Street,* 1962
*Nights and Days,* 1966
*The Fire Screen,* 1969
*Braving the Elements,* 1972
*The Yellow Pages: 59 Poems,* 1974
*Divine Comedies,* 1976
*Mirabell: Books of Number,* 1978
*Scripts for the Pageant,* 1980
*The Changing Light at Sandover,* 1982
*From the First Nine: Poems, 1947–1976,* 1982
*Late Settings,* 1985
*The Inner Room,* 1988
*Selected Poems, 1946–1985,* 1992
*A Scattering of Salts,* 1995
*Selected Poems,* 1996
*Last Poems,* 1998

**Other Writings:** plays (*The Bait,* 1953), novels (*The [Diblos] Notebook,* 1965), essays (*Recitative: Prose by James Merrill,* 1986), autobiography (*A Different Person: A Memoir,* 1993); edited collection of poetry (*The Singing Underneath,* by Jeffrey Harrison, 1988).

**Further Reading**

Adams, Don, *James Merrill's Poetic Quest,* Westport, Connecticut: Greenwood Press, 1997

Bloom, Harold, editor, *James Merrill,* New York: Chelsea House, 1985

Kalstone, David, *Five Temperaments: Elizabeth Bishop, Robert Lowell, James Merrill, Adrienne Rich, John Ashbery,* New York: Oxford University Press, 1977

Labrie, Ross, *James Merrill,* Boston: Twayne, 1982

Lehman, David, and Charles Berger, editors, *James Merrill: Essays in Criticism,* Ithaca, New York: Cornell University Press, 1983

Moffett, Judith, *James Merrill: An Introduction to the Poetry,* New York: Columbia University Press, 1984

Rotella, Guy, editor, *Critical Essays on James Merrill,* New York: G.K. Hall, 1996

Vendler, Helen, *Part of Nature, Part of Us: Modern American Poets,* Cambridge, Massachusetts: Harvard University Press, 1980

Von Hallberg, Robert, *American Poetry and Culture, 1945–1980,* Cambridge, Massachusetts: Harvard University Press, 1985

Yenser, Stephen, *The Consuming Myth: The Work of James Merrill,* Cambridge, Massachusetts: Harvard University Press, 1987

# The Changing Light at Sandover

*The Changing Light at Sandover* (1982) is the final title James Merrill gave to the epic that chronicles his experiences at a Ouija board with his collaborator David Jackson. The poem consists of three parts: "The Book of Ephraim," initially included in *Divine Comedies* (1976); *Mirabell: Books of Number* (1978); and *Scripts for the Pageant* (1980). *The Changing Light at Sandover* also includes "Coda: The Higher Keys," which first appeared in the complete edition. Composed from transcripts of Merrill and Jackson's communications with deceased friends and otherworldly spirits via the homemade board, the trilogy revises universally accepted facts and fables concerning Earth's distant past and imminent future. It also interweaves the story of its unorthodox composition with pertinent episodes from the poet's life. The trilogy received the National Book Critics Circle Award in 1983.

First indications of Merrill's interest in artistic possibilities of the Ouija board can be found in his novel *The Seraglio* (1957) and poems such as "Voices from the Other World" and "The Will." Merrill's early lyrical and narrative poetry combines cultivated aestheticism and tacit autobiography, a discreet sense of craft and a guarded confessional impulse that make intricacies of personal life, both past and present, seem its only valuable subject matter. This is certainly the thematic scope of the trilogy's first installment, "The Book of Ephraim," which the poet fashioned irregularly for almost 20 years. Based on informal conversations with a frivolous Greek youth from the first century A.D., the poem concerns itself with the mediums' dead friends and family, like Dutch poet Hans Lodeizen, avant-garde filmmaker Maya Deren, and Merrill's father. Ephraim also instructs Merrill and Jackson about reincarnation, the bureaucracy of the afterlife's nine stages, and its elaborate system of patrons and representatives. The poem frequently alludes to the method of its own composition, expressing Merrill's skepticism about the undertaking, featuring characters of his lost novel, and recording his travels around the world during the two previous decades.

The poem takes a surprisingly different turn in *Mirabell* and *Scripts.* Although each of these two installments is much lengthier than "Ephraim," both took Merrill only two years to transcribe and prepare for print. Despite its occult character, in these sections the poem purports to be a poem of science. Strangely beautiful passages about dense scientific topics become more and more frequent: "ALL ELEMENTS OF LIFE ARE IN THE ROCKS & SEDIMENT / OF EARTH'S CRUST WE OURSELVES ARE AT HOME IN ITS MOLTEN HEART. / CONSIDER THE CRUST HERE MOLECULAR CONSTRUCTIONS MOVE / AT UNMARKD SPEEDS & TIME IS MEASURED IN MILLENIA." With the assistance of Greek friend Maria Mitsotáki and English poet W.H. Auden, the mediums can only witness as their private preoccupations give way to public concerns; Earth's survival in the aftermath of scientific and technological progress now emerges as the poem's major theme. JM and DJ (as they are frequently designated) communicate with bat-like fallen angels that also style themselves as subatomic particles. One of them, their current guide Mirabell, informs the mediums about the bat-angels' task to fashion a race of perfect human beings by cloning selected souls with admixtures of mineral or vegetal densities in otherworldly research laboratories. They "THIN & PRUNE & CLONE" human population. As the result of their "V" work, a new happy race improved by song and poetry will eventually return paradise to the planet.

The hero who gradually emerges from *Mirabell* and *Scripts* is the so-called Scribe, embodied by JM himself while he is transcribing the messages from the board. The poet has been appointed by God Biology to "RENOVATE THE HOUSE OF MAN" with "MIND WORDS REASON LIGHT." In *Scripts* Mirabell is replaced by Michael and Gabriel, the Angel of Light and the Angel of Fire and Death. Alongside their brothers Emmanuel and Raphael, the two archangels dictate to Merrill and Jackson 25 lessons about rewards and risks of contemporary science, a chain of scribes communicating divine messages to human beings, the five immortal souls known simply as the Five, God Biology, his twin Nature, and other secrets of the universe.

In addition to its occult atmosphere and pseudoscientific argument, the trilogy testifies to Merrill's ambition to be admitted into a company of literary masters; it is a controlled fantasy of becoming a great poet. It is a dazzling performance in verse artistry, as rhymed and unrhymed pentameter, fourteeners, terza rima, villanelles, sonnet sequences, and a canzone attest Merrill's right to be called the most technically accomplished poet in American poetry. On a less explicit level, in composing his trilogy Merrill situates himself with regard to the visionary tradition of Dante, Milton, and Blake, as well as the tradition of poetic wit; reading *Sandover* is an exhilarating although sometimes unnerving walking tour through what the spirit of Auden identifies as the "rosebrick manor" of poetic tradition haunted by miscellaneous literary voices from the past. Among a great number of dead souls that inhabit what is variously called the "imaginative space" or "metaphorical sphere" of the poem, well over 50 are poets or novelists, to which one might add scores of film directors, musicians, painters, philosophers, politicians, and scientists, altogether with the Nine Muses. Sandover itself is the schoolroom in which JM and DJ learn the lessons about creation and apocalypse; it is also, thanks to "the sly economy of dream," wherever the poet and his partner happen to be with their language tool, the Ouija board, at hand. The board itself stands for the whole of literature that has been written, the very poem Merrill is writing, and language in its elementary state.

In his engagement with the personal and literary past, Merrill does not make any attempt to readjust to it or reinvent himself in respect of the dead. He does the opposite: he allows the past to reinvent or readjust itself according to his own memories of the past, imaginatively enriched by experiences of the present. Subscribing to the Proustian view of memory as time recaptured, Merrill lets the past become a part of the continuing life and vice versa. This explains why Merrill's synthesis of epic and autobiography at the Ouija board does not effectively end but keeps returning in his later work, in sequels "From the Cutting-Room Floor" published in *Late Settings* (1985), a *Paris Review*–style interview with dead literati published in that same notable journal, and lastly in his farewell to the world of unascertainable truths and unverifiable spirits, the poem "Nine Days," which appeared in his final poetry collection, *A Scattering of Salts* (1995).

PIOTR GWIAZDA

**Further Reading**

Adams, Don, *James Merrill's Poetic Quest,* Westport, Connecticut: Greenwood Press, 1997

Bloom, Harold, editor, *James Merrill,* New York: Chelsea House, 1985

Kalaidjian, Walter, "A Poetics of Errancy: James Merrill's *The Changing Light at Sandover,*" in *Languages of Liberation: The Social Text in Contemporary American Poetry,* by Kalaidjian, New York: Columbia University Press, 1989

Lehman, David, and Charles Berger, editors, *James Merrill: Essays in Criticism,* Ithaca, New York: Cornell University Press, 1983

Materer, Timothy, *James Merrill's Apocalypse,* Ithaca, New York: Cornell University Press, 2000

Merrill, James, "The Plato Club," *Paris Review* 34, no. 22 (Spring 1992)

Polito, Robert, *A Reader's Guide to James Merrill's "The Changing Light at Sandover,"* Ann Arbor: University of Michigan Press, 1994

Rotella, Guy, editor, *Critical Essays on James Merrill,* New York: G.K. Hall, 1996

Spiegelman, Willard, "The Sacred Books of James Merrill," in *The Didactic Muse: Scenes of Instruction in Contemporary American Poetry,* by Spiegelman, Princeton, New Jersey: Princeton University Press, 1989

Yenser, Stephen, *The Consuming Myth: The Work of James Merrill,* Cambridge, Massachusetts: Harvard University Press, 1987

## Lost in Translation

In "Lost in Translation," James Merrill weaves together memories of his governess, the texts of Paul Valéry's poem "Palme" and Rainer Maria Rilke's translation of it, and a giant jigsaw puzzle he pieced together in childhood. From these materials, Merrill fashions an elegant meditation on translation, loss, and solace. The poem was written in 1972, first published in *The New Yorker* and then collected in *Divine Comedies* (1976), where it rubs shoulders with a number of other ambitious poems, including "The Book of Ephraim," the first part of *The Changing Light at Sandover.* Like *Sandover,* "Lost in Translation" balances elegy with wit.

Merrill's poem begins in "the library," where a "card table . . . stands ready" for a "puzzle which keeps never coming." In this scene, Merrill both commits himself and undercuts his commitments, offering phrases that assert and deny the ideas they express. As in *Sandover,* where the "Yes & No" of the Ouija board forms such an important part of the poem's structure that it functions as the title of an entire section, Merrill shows himself to be of two minds in "Lost in Translation," describing the boy's waiting for the puzzle as a moment "Full of unfulfillment." Similarly, the arrival of the puzzle is not simply delayed or not delivered; it "keeps never coming." Like such paradoxical phrases, the poem's closing lines draw on the trope of translation in a way that seeks to overcome loss though the transfiguring power of metaphor but that does so in an equivocal way. This cagey saying and unsaying occurs throughout "Lost in Translation" and all of Merrill's major poetry.

Before the puzzle arrives, the speaker of the poem interpolates a memory that joins past to present by way of Merrill's epigraph from Rilke's translation of Valéry. Merrill makes the meaning of this fragment important to his poem when he characterizes "Palme" as "That sunlit paradigm whereby the tree / Taps a sweet wellspring of authority" and savors a phrase from the poem, "*Patience dans l'azur*" ("Patience in the blue"). Merrill mines the images and language of Valéry's poem throughout his own, archly echoing the Frenchman in the first words of his next verse paragraph ("Out of the blue . . .").

While literary allusion provides an occasion for Merrill's verbal play, the role of Valéry's poem in "Lost in Translation" is not simply rhetorical. This becomes clear in a telling digression in which the speaker describes the recent performance of "A medium" in another library. "All except him," the speaker explains,

                    have seen
Panel slid back, recess explored,
An object at once unique and common
Displayed, planted in a plain tole
Casket.

The medium goes on to describe the provenance and identity of the object to his audience. Despite the bravado of his description, he correctly identifies the item as "Plywood, Piece of a puzzle" and adumbrates its value for the speaker without divulging its full meaning. "But hidden here is a freak fragment," he declares,

Of a pattern complex in appearance only.
What it seems to show is superficial
Next to that long-term lamination
Of hazard and craft, the karma that has
Made it matter in the first place.

In Merrill's formulation, hazard is as important as craft in the laminations of experience, and the poem emphasizes the vagaries of chance with its initial image of the card table. However, craft remains part of the formulation of what makes things "matter," for Merrill's use of Valéry's palm tree as one of his poem's organizing images reflects his effort to show the unsuspected connections between different moments in time. The revelations of the medium may provoke "A sudden dread" on the part of the speaker, but the strength of that reaction confirms the significance of the link between the various periods of his life. Those days ("*Tage*") of Rilke's epigraph that had seemed so empty ("*leer*") and worthless ("*wertlos*") turn out to have far-reaching roots and "drink from everywhere."

Nonetheless, the poem's work of commemoration offers only partial comfort. While the painfully awaited puzzle magically "assembles" itself "on the shrinking Green" of the card table, its "Consolidations" last only an instant beyond the narrative of its composition. Once the puzzle is done, the poem's speaker narrates its disassembly with a smart but rueful dispatch: "All too soon the swift / Dismantling." The speaker describes this process with the same playfulness with which he described its making, but—in a fine touch—he adds the suspense of a slight caesura:

Lifted by two corners,
The puzzle hung together—and did not.
Irresistibly a populace
Unstitched of its attachments, rattled down.
Power went to pieces as the witch
Slithered easily from Virtue's gown.
The blue held out for time, but crumbled, too.

That crumbling blue, the "Heaven" that the boy and his governess had pieced together, makes for a quotidian apocalypse in the domestic world of the poem. It registers loss, but with such a light and clever hand that the loss becomes transfigured. The remembered bits of puzzle at least momentarily heed the bilingual counsel of the governess ("Patience, chéri. Geduld, mein Schatz"), a counsel that merges with the words of Valéry and Rilke.

This counsel culminates in the poem's closing lines, in which Merrill's puns grow more pronounced. Along with the literary translations performed by Rilke and Merrill himself, there is the dream of another kind of translation. In the metaphor of Valéry's palm tree, loss is borne (perhaps even borne away) through the slow patience of the tree's transfigurations. The world's gritty nourishment becomes its sustaining, golden sap, for the roots of those apparently wasted days work away in the desert ("racines avides / Qui travaillent les deserts"). Likewise, in the physics of Merrill's universe,

nothing's lost. Or else: all is translation
And every bit of us is lost in it
(Or found—I wander through the ruin of S
Now and then, wondering at the peacefulness)
And in that loss a self-effacing tree,
Color of context, imperceptibly
Rustling with its angel, turns the waste
To shade and fiber, milk and memory.

Just as Wallace Stevens argued that "the final belief is to believe in a fiction, which you know to be a fiction," so Merrill gracefully inveigles his reader into finding an angel in a mythical tree, into accepting loss by conceiving it as a change of form, an almost mystical translation, or "bearing away," in an almost redemptive moment of self-loss, of not-quite-rapt transport. "For Merrill," Lynn Keller (1987) writes, "all art acts as the coconut palm does, translating loss, absence, waste into something substantial and nourishing." Merrill's poem reveals the ways in which the revisiting of one's life provides the occasion for transforming otherwise painful experience into something bearable and meaningful.

JEFF WESTOVER

**Further Reading**

Blasing, Mutlu Konuk, *Politics and Form in Postmodern Poetry,* Cambridge and New York: Cambridge University Press, 1995
Bloom, Harold, editor, *James Merrill,* New York: Chelsea House, 1985
Keller, Lynn, *Re-Making It New: Contemporary American Poetry and the Modernist Tradition,* Cambridge and New York: Cambridge University Press, 1987
Mehlman, Jeffrey, "Merrill's Valéry: An Erotics of Translation," in *Rethinking Translation: Discourse, Subjectivity, Ideology,* edited by Lawrence Venuti, London and Boston: Routledge and Kegan Paul, 1992
Merrill, James, *Recitative: Prose by James Merrill,* edited by J.D. McClatchy, San Francisco: North Point Press, 1986
Nadel, Alan, "Replacing the Waste Land: James Merrill's Quest for Transcendent Authority," *College Literature* 20, no. 2 (1993)
Rotella, Guy, "James Merrill's Poetry of Convalescence," *Contemporary Literature* 38 (1997)
Rotella, Guy, editor, *Critical Essays on James Merrill,* New York: G.K. Hall, 1996
Yenser, Stephen, *The Consuming Myth: The Work of James Merrill,* Cambridge, Massachusetts: Harvard University Press, 1987

---

# W.S. Merwin 1927–

Poet, short-story writer, essayist, translator, autobiographer, dramatist, and editor, William Stanley Merwin received his B.A. in English in 1947 from Princeton University (where he studied with John Berryman and R.P. Blackmur) and subsequently completed one year of graduate study. While at Princeton, Merwin began a correspondence with Ezra Pound that continued for several years. From 1949 to 1950 in Portugal he worked as a tutor to the children of the Princess de Braganza and in Mallorca, Spain, to the children of Robert Graves. In the early 1950s, Merwin worked in Europe as a translator of French, Latin, Portuguese, and Spanish; produced literary broadcasts for the BBC in London; and bought a farmhouse in southwestern France, where he lived through much of the 1960s, spending a portion of those later years in New York. These international experiences were not only foundational for many of Merwin's early translations, such as *The Poem of the Cid* (1959) and *The Song of Roland* (1963), but also for later collections of prose and poetry, such as, respectively, *The Lost Upland* (1992) and *The Vixen* (1996), both of which eulogize the ancient farming country above the Dordogne River. Merwin returned to the United States in 1956 and, since 1975, has resided in Hawaii, where he cultivates a small forest of endangered trees and plants.

Allegories of translation and travel shape Merwin's explorations of the major themes that reach across his career: exile, identity, imagination, love, memory, morality, mutability, and the phenomenal relationships among nature, poetic language, and the soul. One of our most prolific poets, he is also one of the most difficult to place within a specific literary tradition because his poetry transforms from book to book. In fact, as many critics note, Merwin's writing changes within and between each collection, signaling, at distinct turning points, future directions for his work's form, style, and themes. His texts thereby engender the pattern of an open synecdoche, linking individual poems not only to their immediate contexts within single volumes but also to previous and forthcoming collections. Author of more than 20 books of poetry and translator of more than 20 works—including *Transparence of the World: Poems by Jean Follain* (1969) and *Vertical Poetry: Poems by Roberto Juarroz* (1988)—Merwin has also published two dramatic works, *Darkling Child* (1956) and *Favor Island* (1957), as well as two collections of short fiction, *The Miner's Pale Children* (1970) and *Houses and Travellers* (1977).

The reception of Merwin's writing is not without controversy, as his work has generated strong criticism and high praise. Several critics have lamented Merwin's iconoclasm and his poetry's rhetorical predictability, including Vendler (1980), who compiled a "Merwin Dictionary" of words the poet seemed to overuse. Nelson and Folsom (1987) observe that "no other contemporary poet has been as universally recognized as a major talent and simultaneously so criticized, prodded, reprimanded and challenged at every stage of his career." Since 1949, Merwin has lived on the margins of American culture, offering only minimal statements on his own poetics, the most familiar of which may be "Notes for a Preface" (1966), which underscores the ethical singularity of the poet's vision:

> The encouragement of poetry itself is a labor and a privilege like that of living. It requires, I imagine, among other startlingly simple things, a love of poetry, and possibly a recurring despair of finding it again, an indelible awareness of its parentage with that biblical waif, ill at ease in time, the spirit. No one has any claims on it, no one deserves it, no one knows where it goes.

In addition to Berryman, Blackmur, Graves, Pound, and the poets whose works he has translated, writers who have influenced Merwin's poetry and prose include (among many others) Auden, Bishop, Crane, Frost, Moore, Nemerov, Roethke, Stafford, Thoreau, and Wright. His work has also been compared with that of Ashbery, Baudelaire, Beckett, Kinnell, and Snyder as well as with the Expressionist paintings of Matisse. Merwin's style has often been described as oneiric and vatic, while his texts have been linked with various literary movements and techniques, such as deconstruction, deep imagery, ecopoetry, existentialism, and surrealism.

As a poet, Merwin is perhaps best known for characteristics and topics that distinguish his first six volumes, from *A Mask for Janus* (1952) through *The Lice* (1967): cerebral, often difficult poetry drawing symbolic imagery from medieval and mythic traditions; the universal cycle of birth, death, and regeneration; the search for identity in modern society; tensions between soul and body, art and experience; humanity's reckless relationship with the natural world; and a despair for civilization infrequently tempered by hope in individual human actions. Yet there are noteworthy formal and thematic variations within this first grouping of texts. *Green with Beasts* (1956) announces a movement away from the traditional metrical and stanzaic forms in *A Mask for Janus* and *The Dancing Bears* (1954) toward more experimental patterns of language, or what Merwin calls "the time of the poem . . . a way of hearing how poetry happens in words" ("On Open Form," 1969). This stylistic shift—emphasizing a heightened sense of the poem's textuality, process, and the concomitant erasure of the poet's identity from the page—intensifies through *The Drunk in the Furnace* (1960) and *The Moving Target* (1963), near the end of which Merwin abandons punctuation, a characteristic that persists in his most recent works. In an interview with Nelson and Folsom published in Merwin's *Regions of Memory: Uncollected Prose, 1949–82* (1987), the poet reflects on that farewell:

> I saw that if I could use the movement of the verse itself and the movement of the line—the actual weight of the language as it moved—to do the punctuation, I would both strengthen the texture of the experience of the poem and also make clear its distinction from other kinds of writing. . . . Punctuation as I looked at it after that seemed to staple the poem to the page, but if I took those staples out the poem lifted itself right up off the page. A poem then had a sense of integrity and liberation that it did not have before.

Merwin's themes also change in his books from the 1960s, turning away from classical motifs and toward more personal subjects, possibly revealing influences from his meetings, while in Boston for two years, with Hall, Hughes, Lowell, Plath, and Rich.

Poets and critics alike have hailed *The Lice* as one of the most significant volumes of poetry since World War II. Published in 1967, the book offers several poems—for example, "The Animals," "The Asians Dying," and "For a Coming Extinction"—that excoriate the hubris and ignorance of civilized humanity at war with both itself (in Vietnam) and the natural world. The volume's dominant motifs of alienation, negation, and spiritual deprivation reply to the tenor of the 1960s but also articulate a turning point at the core of Merwin's epistemology from a poetics of loss toward one of potential regeneration—a theme that he also expresses in "Notes for a Preface": "absolute despair has no art, and I imagine the writing of a poem, in whatever mode, still betrays the existence of hope, which is why poetry is more and more chary of the conscious mind, in our age." "Is That What You Are," from *The Lice,* speaks powerfully of this resilient although fallen, unorthodox divinity through the image of mankind as a creature paradoxically winged with both hope and grief:

> New ghost is that what you are
> Standing on the stairs of water
>
> No longer surprised
>
> Hope and grief are still our wings
> Why we cannot fly
>
> What failure still keeps you
> Among us the unfinished
>
> The wheels go on praying . . .

Since the 1970s, as many readers have remarked, each new book of poetry by Merwin performs a transformation in his poetics, prompting some critics to regret his writing's lack of a consistent style. *The Carrier of Ladders* (1970) and *Writings to an Unfinished Accompaniment* (1973) signal a transition toward a synthesis of Merwin's earliest, formal work and his more personal, experimental texts. While continuing the critique of modern society most prominent in *The Lice,* the poems in these two collections move toward affirmations (however tentative) of human community. *The Carrier of Ladders* in particular articulates another theme that becomes prevalent in Merwin's later work: the transient, tragic beauty of existence. Merwin's interest in classical Chinese poetry strongly informs three subsequent volumes—*The Compass Flower* (1977), *Feathers from the Hill* (1978), and *Finding the Islands* (1982)—in which he writes introspective, personal poems (occasionally in haiku tercets) about the sanctity of life, love, and nature. His following work in prose, *Unframed Originals* (1982), and a collection of poems, *Opening the Hand* (1983), each meditate on autobiographical subjects, especially Merwin's relationship with his father. Some of the poems in *Opening the Hand* also concern interconnections between natural phenomena and poetic language. *The Rain in the Trees* (1988) unites both of these themes, as the poet listens to the voices of the dead, human and also natural, mourning the disappearance of aboriginal cultures and landscapes in Hawaii.

*Travels* (1993) begins an important transition from Merwin's earlier concerns with seeking human community toward new examinations of the making and unmaking of human culture, identity, and history. A prefatory poem, "Cover Note," intimates those more general, symbolic dimensions, while several long, narrative pieces explore the particularized, interior experiences of historical figures, such as naturalist Georg Eberhard Rumpf, poet Arthur Rimbaud, Native American Little Finger Nail, and Amazon explorer Manuel Cordova. Merwin's latest volumes, *The Folding Cliffs: A Narrative* (1998) and *The River Sound* (1999), have each received both strong praise, as arguably his finest poetry yet written, and criticism, as stylistically difficult. While individual texts from *Travels* underscore Merwin's interest in poetry and history, *The Folding Cliffs* amplifies that interdisciplinary perspective into the scope of an epic. Set in late 19th-century Hawaii, this ambitious narrative in verse tells the moralistic story of one aboriginal family's attempt to resist the government's seizure of leprosy victims. *The River Sound* returns to the more familiar topics of autobiography, landscape, memory, and especially the power of poetic language: for example, "Lament for the Makers" celebrates many of the poets who have shaped Merwin's vision, "Testimony" delivers a last will and testament, and "The Stranger" offers a parable about the balance (or lack thereof) between civilization and nature.

Some of Merwin's early, public works in prose, such as "Ecology, or the Art of Survival" (1958), "Act of Conscience" (1962), and "A New Right Arm" (1963), garnered for him a reputation as an anti-imperialist, environmentalist, and pacifist. While he has since then continued to write in response to social causes—most notably environmental concerns—Merwin also defends his own aesthetic and personal distance from politics. For example, in "To Name the Wrong" (1962), he cautions that

> There is, for instance, the danger that [the poet's] gift itself, necessarily one of the genuinely private and integral things he lives for, may be deformed into a mere loudspeaker, losing the singularity which made it irreplaceable, the candor which made it unreachable and unpredictable.

Merwin also argues for the autonomy of poetry in "Milton: A Revisitation" (1967) and most recently in the foreword to his translation of Dante's *Purgatorio* (2000), where he extols literary works that survive the particulars of place and time: "If a poem is not forgotten as soon as the circumstances of its origin, it begins at once to evolve an existence of its own, in minds and lives, and then even in words, that its singular maker could never have imagined." Passages such as these suggest the metaphysical ground of Merwin's secular vision. His writing mediates the antithetical spheres of culture and nature through the music of spirit that uncompromised poetic language makes humanly possible. Merwin's enduring fascination with earthly themes of translation and travel, things marvelous and mutable, reveals the poet's ongoing quest for the liminal imprint of the luminous world.

W. Scott Howard

**Biography**

Born in New York City, 30 September 1927. Attended Princeton University, New Jersey, A.B. 1947; tutor in France and Portugal, 1949, and to Robert Graves' children in Mallorca, Spain, 1950; freelance translator, London, 1951–54; playwright-in-residence, Poet's Theatre, Cambridge, Massachusetts, 1956–57; poetry editor, *The Nation,* 1962; associate, Théâtre de la Cité, Lyons, France, 1964–65. Received Yale Series of Younger Poets Award, 1952; *Kenyon Review* fellowship, 1954; American Academy grant, 1957; Arts Council of Great Britain bursary, 1957; Rabinowitz research fellowship, 1961; Bess Hokin Prize, 1962, and Harriet Monroe Memorial Prize, 1967 (*Poetry,* Chicago); Ford grant, 1964; Chapelbrook Award, 1966; PEN Translation Prize, 1969; Rockefeller grant, 1969; Pulitzer Prize, 1971; Academy of American Poets fellowship, 1973; Shelley Memorial Award, 1974; National Endowment for the Arts grant, 1978; Bollingen Prize, 1979; Aiken Taylor Award, 1990; Maurice English Award, 1990; Lenore Marshall Poetry Prize (*The Nation*), 1994; Tanning Award, 1994; Ruth Lilly Poetry Prize, 1998; member, American Academy. Living near Haiku, Hawaii.

**Poetry**
*A Mask for Janus,* 1952
*The Dancing Bears,* 1954
*Green with Beasts,* 1956
*The Drunk in the Furnace,* 1960
*The Moving Target,* 1963
*The Lice,* 1967
*The Carrier of Ladders,* 1970
*Writings to an Unfinished Accompaniment,* 1973
*The First Four Books of Poems* (contains *A Mask for Janus, The Dancing Bears, Green with Beasts,* and *The Drunk in the Furnace*), 1975
*The Compass Flower,* 1977
*Feathers from the Hill,* 1978
*Finding the Islands,* 1982
*Opening the Hand,* 1983
*The Rain in the Trees,* 1988
*Selected Poems,* 1988
*The Second Four Books of Poems* (contains *The Moving Target, The Lice, The Carrier of Ladders,* and *Writings to an Unfinished Accompaniment*), 1993
*Travels,* 1993
*The Vixen,* 1996
*Flower and Hand: Poems, 1977–1983,* 1997
*The Folding Cliffs: A Narrative,* 1998
*The River Sound,* 1999

**Other Writings:** plays (*Darkling Child,* 1956; *Favor Island,* 1957), short fiction (*The Miner's Pale Children,* 1970; *Houses and Travellers,* 1977), essays, translations of Spanish, French, Italian, Greek, Sanskrit, and other literature (*The Poem of the Cid,* 1959); edited collections of poetry (*The Essential Wyatt,* 1989).

**Further Reading**

Brunner, Edward J., *Poetry as Labor and Privilege: The Writings of W.S. Merwin,* Urbana: University of Illinois Press, 1991

Byers, Thomas B., "W.S. Merwin: A Description of Darkness," in *What I Cannot Say: Self, Word, and World in Whitman, Stevens, and Merwin,* Urbana: University of Illinois Press, 1989

Davis, Cheri, *W.S. Merwin,* Boston: Twayne, 1981

Frazier, Jane, *From Origin to Ecology: Nature and the Poetry of W.S. Merwin,* Madison, New Jersey: Fairleigh Dickinson University Press, 1999

Hix, H.L., *Understanding W.S. Merwin,* Columbia: University of South Carolina Press, 1997

Hoeppner, Edward Haworth, *Echoes and Moving Fields: Structure and Subjectivity in the Poetry of W.S. Merwin and John Ashbery,* Lewisburg, Pennsylvania: Bucknell University Press, and London: Associated University Presses, 1994

Irwin, Mark, editor, *Many Mountains Moving: A Tribute to W.S. Merwin,* Boulder: University of Colorado Press, 2001

Nelson, Cary, and Ed Folsom, editors, *W.S. Merwin: Essays on the Poetry,* Urbana: University of Illinois Press, 1987

Scigaj, Leonard M., "Closing the *Ecarts* through the Moment of Green: W.S. Merwin," in *Sustainable Poetry: Four American Ecopoets,* by Scigaj, Lexington: University Press of Kentucky, 1999

Vendler, Helen, "W.S. Merwin," in *Part of Nature, Part of Us: Modern American Poets,* by Vendler, Cambridge, Massachusetts: Harvard University Press, 1980


# The Chinese Mountain Fox

"The Chinese Mountain Fox," a short lyric poem included in W.S. Merwin's 1999 collection *The River Sound,* is a fine example of both the poet's later style and his typical subject matter, that of humankind's increasing alienation from the natural world. The myth that Merwin creates of the mysterious mountain fox—"legend" is the word the poem actually uses—is born, like Merwin's later style itself, of an intersection of the natural world with an elemental, almost primal language. It is a style now widely imitated.

The transformation that Merwin and his work went through during the 1960s is well documented. Understanding this transformation is not essential to reading "The Chinese Mountain Fox," although it does allow for a more complete understanding of the relationship between the poem and the poet. Put briefly, his early work, typically formal and generally reflective of the medieval poetry that he was translating at that time, gave way in the 1960s to a much freer style as the poet confronted what he has since called the "new and urgent questions" of the age. "It seemed clearer to me than ever," Merwin wrote of his experience during that time, "that the menace of military destruction and the accelerating devastation of what was left of the natural world were effects of the same impulse."

As a result of these concerns, during the creation of the poems that resulted in his collections *The Moving Target* (1963) and *The Lice* (1967), Merwin began to abandon the sentence in search of a more essentialist style, one that used only the most crucial tools of the English language. Among other developments, Merwin's poems began to abandon punctuation, which he began "to feel . . . stapled the poems to the page. Whereas I wanted the poems to evoke the spoken language." Merwin's poetry also shifted in content as he began to explore, among other things, the widening separation between humankind and nature. An increasing personal commitment to pacifism and environmentalism led the poet to move to Hawaii, where he has lived for many years restoring the devastated landscape of a former sugar plantation to its natural state.

As Peter Davison has described Merwin's later style, "The vivid movement and activity of his poetry, which seem to flow up from an underground river that lies beneath mere speech, as though written in some pre-verbal language of which all later languages have proved to be a mere translation." It is this later style and subject matter for which the poet is best known and appreciated, and "The Chinese Mountain Fox" serves as a wonderful introduction to the way in which both manifest themselves in many of his shorter lyric poems.

True to Merwin's later style, all the poems in *The River Sound* collection, including "The Chinese Mountain Fox," contain no punctuation. Instead of punctuation, the pacing of "The Chinese Mountain Fox" is governed by the stanza and the caesura, the combination of which lends the rhythm and brief pauses necessary for the reader to digest a poem composed of a complete utterance. The four-line stanzas of six syllables and loose a-b-a-b end rhymes are meticulously constructed of spare prepositional phrases and liberally used conjunction links. It is a subtle form that creates an effect on the reader not unlike incantation. It is this effect, common to Merwin's work, that has prompted many to identify him with the oracular poets.

In the context of "The Chinese Mountain Fox," the incantation is an appropriate rhythm and tone for the poet to have invoked, as the poem serves as a kind of brief, historical ode to a most mysterious animal—so mysterious as to be left unnamed save for the title of the poem. As the last line of the poem says, this is a history of the animal "before it had a name." As Michael Thurston (1999) wrote of "Testament," another poem in *The River Sound* collection, "Merwin recognizes that . . . proper nouns are meaningless now, their significance, like their referents, 'blown away to dust.'" The poem serves as the final "putting down on paper" of an oral history of the fox—although it might have been almost any animal—seemingly the result of folktales passed down through generations telling of strange confrontations with the natural world. "The Chinese Mountain Fox" reminds us, Thurston says, "that we have at our disposal, however threatened, failed, and faulty, our capacity for remembering."

The poem retrospectively finds the fox among an unspecified "they" and time period from the perspective of "our day." In this setting, the magic of the creature, "part lightning and part rust," appearing "out of nowhere / as they were wont to say," is rediscovered for a modern audience:

but it was never where
they had thought it would be
and showed the best of their
beliefs successively

to be without substance
shadows they used to cast
old tales and illusions
out of some wishful past

The fox moves through the poem almost like a rumor: "the fiction was passed down / with undiminished trust / while the sightings began / to be unusual / second-hand dubious." What is truly unique about the poem is that unlike a typical poem that chooses to celebrate an animal, it is much less concerned with describing the fox than it is with describing—or even reproducing—the effect that the fox has had on those who have been fortunate enough to have seen it:

perhaps at the same place
where they themselves had just
been standing that live face
looking as though it must

have been following them
would have appeared with no
warning they could fathom
or ever come to know

If to name something is, indeed, to possess it, then the body of the poem's refusal to name the fox as such is perhaps its most poignant celebration of the creature's mystery and power. The poem celebrates the creature without forcing assimilation. The destruction of the fox as a result of the destruction of his habitat, Merwin seems to reminds us, is not the same as capture:

never had it been caught
poised or hunted down
by packs of dogs or shot
hung up mounted or worn

In the 1950s, Merwin had planned on publishing a bestiary titled *The Ark of Silence*, whose focus was to be on what animals could teach humans without a common language, through their very silence. "The Chinese Mountain Fox" almost seems as if it could be a relic from this abandoned project. It is in this sense that "The Chinese Mountain Fox" is tied to even the poet's earliest work: its style echoes classical forms; its subject, the fox, alludes to ancient myth.

DOBBY GIBSON

**Further Reading**

Brunner, Edward J., *Poetry as Labor and Privilege: The Writings of W.S. Merwin*, Urbana: University of Illinois Press, 1991

Byers, Thomas B., *What I Cannot Say: Self, Word, and World in Whitman, Stevens, and Merwin*, Urbana: University of Illinois Press, 1989

Hix, H.L., *Understanding W.S. Merwin*, Columbia: University of South Carolina Press, 1997

Hoeppner, Edward Haworth, *Echoes and Moving Fields: Structure and Subjectivity in the Poetry of W.S. Merwin and John Ashbery*, Lewisburg, Pennsylvania: Bucknell University Press, and London: Associated University Presses, 1994

Thurston, Michael, "Poetry in Review," *Yale Review* 87, no. 3 (July 1999)

# The Drunk in the Furnace

W.S. Merwin's often-anthologized poem "The Drunk in the Furnace" announces a change of style and subject in his work and provides in itself an ironic, ambiguous perspective on contemporary poetry in America. Published only eight years after Merwin's first book, *A Mask for Janus* (1952), which was chosen for the Yale Younger Poets series by W.H. Auden, "The Drunk in the Furnace" nevertheless represents a change in Merwin's approach to poetry and even his definition of it.

Merwin's early poems are formal and some would claim ornamental. As a young poet he wrote poems about myth and animal poems that gave his animals medieval bestiary-style meanings; his tightly formal poems were similar to those of Robert Graves. These poems often portrayed the sea and its creatures emblematically. "Leviathan" is a good example, with its elaborate reworking of biblical territory and heavy symbolic freight. The poem, based in part on the Old English *Exeter Book*, begins in imitation of its source: "This is the black sea-brute bulling through wave-wrack, / Ancient as ocean's shifting hills." "The Drunk in the Furnace," in contrast, seems to mock Merwin's previous allegiances while mapping out new territory for his poetry.

"The Drunk in the Furnace," the title poem of Merwin's 1960 collection, marks an important transition between his early and middle styles. The poems following would be more personal, less elaborate, and more direct. "Drunk" is a complex, layered poem that suggests a new kind of Orpheus figure and indeed a new image of the poet and audience. The derelict's pounding away on the iron sides of the furnace for an audience of waifs and strays is appalling and appealing, and the poem has its own clangy music to it, very unlike the formal control of Merwin's early work.

The poem is patterned but teasingly irregular. It consists of four seven-line stanzas that have shortened first and last lines and that use off-rhyme, assonance, and consonance to produce dramatic effects. The poem describes an abandoned furnace in a trash-filled gully that the townspeople notice has become inhabited: smoke rising "like a pale resurrection" indicates that someone has made his home there—"established / His bad castle." Blind drunk, the derelict makes a great racket:

> Where he gets his spirits
> It's a mystery. But the stuff keeps him musical:
> Hammer-and-anvilling with poker and bottle
> To his jugged bellowings, till the last groaning clang
> As he collapses onto the rioting
> Springs of a litter of car-seats ranged on the grates,
> To sleep like an iron pig.

The scene in the poem repels and attracts at once, leading to contradictory interpretations. The adult country dwellers pay no attention to the clamor but listen to the preacher's hellfire-and-brimstone sermons while the youngsters crowd to the brash dissonant music of the drunk. The children "flock like piped rats to its siren / Crescendo, and agape on the crumbling ridge / Stand in a row and learn." Although they may be listening to a pied (pie-eyed?) piper, the only alternative music is song of hate and fear. The drunk's music is aggressive, original, grotesque, and interesting. It is music by an outlaw for a degenerate time, and yet there is a tremendous excitement to it—its very outrageousness is appealing not only to the "witless offspring" who stand in a row to listen but also to the reader, drawn to the sound of "Hammer-and-anvilling" and "jugged bellowings."

Merwin has adapted elements of his own experience into this poem; his grandfather was an alcoholic, and his father was a Presbyterian minister for whom the poet wrote hymns as a child. A minister-father notwithstanding, it was a tough upbringing. Moreover, Merwin had been away in London during the early part of the 1950s, making his living as a translator in London while publishing in the United States. The second half of the decade was a time of shuttling back and forth between countries and traveling abroad. He thus had created a distance between himself and his upbringing. On his return, making poetry in America must have seemed to him an awesome, if not impossible, task.

There are double meanings throughout the poem: the drunk "sleep[s] like an iron pig," bringing pig iron to mind, and "Where he gets his spirits" is a double mystery: no one knows where he gets the liquor and where he gets the élan or zest to continue this performance day after day for the enthralled audience, of whom he is probably not even aware. Indeed, the poem is filled with ironies—that the furnace is a dwelling, that it parallels the hell of which the preacher likes to preach, and that music is made from iron. Perhaps the greatest irony is the use of the ideas and images of Christianity as a backdrop for the drunk in his "bad castle." The drunk makes a wonderful contrast with the preacher, who preaches in the "tar-paper church / On a text about stoke-holes which are sated never"; the drunk becomes by the parallel a prophet himself as well as a poet—an Elijah of the junk heap, with an obscure but compelling message.

Merwin is a constantly changing and evolving poet; "The Drunk in the Furnace" phase is a step on the road toward the primitivist, elemental imagery for which he is most commonly known. It shows his passage from a young poet influenced by Wallace Stevens and Robert Graves to a midcareer poet whose views of his earlier work and the possibilities of his profession are somewhat dim but who is working toward full achievement of his own distinctive voice. The poem itself is a fine conjunction of grim message and high spirits, with its own lively and dissonant music.

Janet McCann

**Further Reading**


Bowers, Neal, "Jeffers and Merwin: The World Beyond Words," in *Robinson Jeffers and a Galaxy of Writers: Essays in Honor of William H. Nolte,* edited by William B. Thesing, Columbia: University of South Carolina Press, 1995

Byers, Thomas B., *What I Cannot Say: Self, Word, and World in Whitman, Stevens, and Merwin,* Urbana: University of Illinois Press, 1989

Collins, Floyd, "Forms Open and Closed: The Poetry of W.S. Merwin," *Gettysburg Review* 7, no. 1 (Winter 1994)

Cook, Albert, "Metrical Inventions: Zukofsky and Merwin," *College Literature* 24, no. 3 (October 1997)

Frazier, Jane, "W.S. Merwin and the Mysteries of Silence," *South Dakota Review* 32, no. 1 (Spring 1994)

Hix, H.L., *Understanding W.S. Merwin,* Columbia: University of South Carolina Press, 1997

Nelson, Cary, and Ed Folsom, editors, *W.S. Merwin: Essays on the Poetry,* Urbana: University of Illinois Press, 1987

Sanderlin, Reed, "Merwin's 'The Drunk in the Furnace,'" *Contemporary Poetry: A Journal of Criticism* 2, no. 1 (1975)

Trengen, Linda, and Gary Storhoff, "Order and Energy in Merwin's 'The Drunk in the Furnace,'" *Concerning Poetry* 13, no. 1 (1980)

# Robert Mezey 1935–

For over 40 years, Robert Mezey has quietly developed his craft as a poet, despite a determined dearth of critical attention. Mezey's early works, in the late 1950s and early 1960s, revealed a fresh voice attempting to examine a wide range of different human experiences while operating within the confines of more traditional verse. In *The Wandering Jew* (1960), the title poem examines such issues as spirituality and sexuality:

I was adrift
And much in need of something I had seen.

At morning and at evening in my head,
A girl in clear silk over nothing on
Smiled with her eyes and all the while her hands
Played with the closing and opening of her gown.
. . . .
Sucking for milk and honey at her breasts,
I strained against her till I ground on bone,
And still I heard a whispering of the past
When I awoke beside her in the dawn.
. . . .
Taste your own bondage in the lives of others—
Isn't it bitter, indigestible food?
If all the wretched of the earth were brothers,
How could I find their father in my god?

This poem, although couched in a traditional, rhymed verse that Mezey would later abandon, captures the essence of Mezey's poetry: ambivalent, complicated, and metaphorical. In one character (the "girl" of the poem), desire, faith, and dejection are brought together in a single, powerful articulation. Mezey's early poetry evidenced a determined analysis of religion, particularly Judaism.

Mezey's next notable collection of verse, *White Blossoms* (1965), displayed the author's increased maturity, as traditional, rhymed stanzas were dropped in favor of more open styles, and a wider range of subjects were explored with a more powerful voice. Many of the poems in this collection focus on nature, and landscapes are often described as primitive and brutal, as in the poem "There":

It is deep summer. Far out
at sea, the young squalls darken
and roll, plunging northward,
threatening everything. I see
the Atlantic moving in slow
contemplative fury
against the rocks, the beaten
headlands, and the towns sunk deep
in a blind northern light.

The relentless power and brutality of nature is often drawn against individual human desire, a desire rooted in both emptiness and hope. In "White Blossoms," the poet drives along a silent roadway at night, contemplating the foliage captured in his headlights:

It is at such moments I
am called, in a voice so pure
I have to close my eyes and enter
the breathing darkness just beyond
my headlights. I have come back,
I think, to something I had
almost forgotten, a mouth
that waits patiently, sighs, speaks
and falls silent. No one else
is alive. The blossoms are
white, and I am almost there.

Mezey's imagery is powerful and his technique solid, suggesting a primitive vitality in sensory experience that can be discerned but never quite captured whole.

Perhaps Mezey's finest undertaking is *The Door Standing Open* (1970), a compilation of poetry from several of his earlier books. This volume represents more than just a collection of older poems with the inclusion of several new works; instead, it acts like a blueprint of Mezey's formal progression as an artist. His thematic progression is also readily noticeable. Some of the older poems are not merely reprinted but are in fact rewritten. It is interesting to note how Mezey's ideas regarding his own poetry have changed over time. The new poems collected in this volume are tighter in form, and a greater control over emotional sensation is practiced. In "At the Point," brutality, religion, and hopelessness once again find articulation in a single stanza:

In the valley the taut fences
stretch pitilessly to the horizon
and all those who want to be someplace else
must follow them.
The hawks and owls crucified on the wire
have long since returned to their own country,
and the mouse trembles in ecstasy,
lost in the shadow of their wings.

The Christ imagery in the poem references the crueler, predator species. Again, an ambivalence toward religion is drawn against the hopelessness of human desire.

Over the next 15 years, Mezey would continue to grow more experimental in both form and content. In *Evening Wind* (1987), a compilation of poems from four of his chapbooks following *The Door Standing Open,* Mezey examined the limits of language and expression: "Wants a pond a thyme, a wight rabid set out to sikh for / wisdom. Sot high and low, yeast and vest" ("Prose and Cons"). Reminiscent of Joyce in his unrelenting use of puns and portmanteau words, "Prose and Cons" signaled a break away from Mezey's earlier works. In another section of the compilation, "Couplets," 30 pages of unrhymed "couplets" are strung together not by a consistent narrative but instead through general themes (love, family, and despair): "An infant screams in the darkness of the crib; / A man might as well step off the edge of the precipice / . . . It was all good clean fun that had no future / And now it doesn't even have a past." The final section of *Evening Wind,* named for the title of the compilation, reveals just how wide a formal range Mezey has become comfortable with, as the poems here are confidently written in the more traditional style with which Mezey began his career.

In addition to his poetry, Mezey is also an editor of some note. He co-edited two editions of *Naked Poetry,* a respected compilation of work by post–World War II poets. Mezey also edited *Poems from the Hebrew* (1973), a collection of Hebrew poems translated into English and ranging from Old Testament psalms to contemporary poetry. His latest publication is the introduction to the new collection of Hardy poems, where he argues that Hardy's poetry should be just as canonical as his prose.

ANDREW HOWE

**Biography**
Born in Philadelphia, Pennsylvania, 28 February 1935. Attended Kenyon College, Gambier, Ohio, 1951–53; University of Iowa, Iowa City, 1956–60, B.A. 1959; Stanford University, California (Poetry fellow, 1961), 1960–61; served in the United States Army, 1953–55, discharged as subversive; worked as a probation officer, psychology technician, social worker, and copywriter; Instructor, Case Western Reserve University, Cleveland, Ohio, 1963–64, and Franklin and Marshall College, Lancaster, Pennsylvania, 1965–66; Assistant Professor, Fresno State University, California, 1967–68; Associate Professor, University of Utah, Salt Lake City, 1973–76; since 1976 Professor of English and poet-in-residence, Pomona College, Claremont, California. Received Lamont Poetry Selection Award, 1960; Ingram Merrill Foundation fellowship, 1973, 1988; Guggenheim fellowship, 1977; American Academy Award, 1983; National Endowment for the Arts fellowship, 1987; Bassine Citation, 1987. Living in Claremont, California.

**Poetry**
*The Wandering Jew,* 1960
*The Lovemaker,* 1961
*White Blossoms,* 1965
*The Book of Dying,* 1970
*The Door Standing Open: New and Selected Poems, 1954–1969,* 1970
*Evening Wind,* 1987
*Natural Selection,* 1995
*Collected Poems, 1952–1999,* 2000

**Other Writings:** translations of Hebrew (*Poems from the Hebrew,* 1973) and Spanish literature; edited collections of poetry (*Selected Poems,* by Thomas Hardy, 1998).

**Further Reading**
"*The Book of Dying*" (book review), *Virginia Quarterly Review* 47, no. 2 (Spring 1971)
"*The Door Standing Open* and *The Book of Dying*" (book reviews), *Poetry* 118, no. 5 (August 1971)
"*Evening Wind*" (book review), *Virginia Quarterly Review* 64, no. 3 (Summer 1988)
Flinker, Noam, "The Dying of the Light: American Jewish Self-Portrayal in Henry Roth and Robert Mezey," in *The Jewish Self-Portrait in European and American Literature,* edited by Hans Jürgen Schrader, Elliott M. Simon, and Charlotte Wardi, Tübingen, Germany: Niemeyer, 1996
"*White Blossoms*" (book review), *Poetry* 109, no. 3 (December 1966)

---

# Midwestern Poetry Renaissance

Literary history conventionally dates the Midwestern Poetry Renaissance from 1912 to 1919 and locates this movement's most vivacious, accomplished, and memorable activity in Chicago and St. Louis. The principal writers and cultural agents usually associated with the Renaissance (sometimes spelled *renascence* by its participants in order to emphasize invigorating renewal and rebirth, not mere newness and novelty) include Zoë Akins, Sherwood Anderson, Willa Cather, Arthur Davison Ficke, Alice Corbin Henderson, Orrick Johns, Vachel Lindsay, Edgar Lee Masters, Harriet Monroe, John G. Neihardt, William Marion Reedy, Carl Sandburg, Sara Teasdale, and Eunice Tietjens. Some of these poets have remained familiar names or grown in luster and significance; some have not. Still others have subsequently become better known for literary accomplishments other than their early poetry: Akins, for instance, for her Hollywood screenwriting career and success as a playwright, including a Pulitzer Prize for drama; Anderson and Cather almost solely for their fiction; and Monroe for her founding editorship of the seminal Chicago-based *Poetry: A Magazine of Verse.* Monroe's first number of *Poetry* in 1912 has served symbolically as the threshold date of this movement, while the end of World War I in November 1918 has served to mark its end, encompassing this "smaller" movement within a larger cultural pattern that divides pre- and post-War thinking, feeling, and imagining into the time before Modernism and the beginning of the Modernist era.

Ford Madox Ford perceived an international movement, however, characterized by what he called "Middle Westishness," "the symptom of an enormous disillusionment . . . and an enormous awakening" that both embraced and transcended region (*Transatlantic Stories,* 1926). Ford's insight serves as touchstone for a revisionist argument to enlarge the understanding of the Midwestern Poetry Renaissance by expanding somewhat the conventional time frame and even more so the geography and agenda associated with this movement.

To begin this revision involves returning briefly to the years 1912–19, conventionally associated with the Midwestern Poetry Renaissance. They are not without historical logic, although they speak chiefly from East Coast and Modernist perspectives, to identify cultural and aesthetic occurrences that happened "in" the Midwest region of the United States. Arguably this span encompasses a particularly concentrated, motivated, articulate, visible, and vigorously productive period in the cultural agenda and practice of poetry. During these years St. Louis and Chicago were perceived by the East Coast cultural establishment to be making either impressive or upstart claims, depending on the viewer. These cities, often rivals, jointly shaped a mission to strengthen American poetry by reconnecting it with previously strong but still under-appreciated traditions and parent figures—in particular Walt Whitman and Emily Dickinson—pursuing varieties of experimentation, defining new forms of social and political commitment to energize poetry by fusing it with contemporary life, and allying this new poetry less diffidently with poetry internationally.

H.L. Mencken called St. Louis the liveliest town in pre–World War I America (*The End of American Innocence,* 1959); William Marion Reedy was central to the St. Louis arts scene for almost 30 years and served as literary mentor to many young writers in this city and the greater Midwest. In 1893 Reedy began developing the old *St. Louis Mirror* into a prestigious nationally and internationally circulated weekly newspaper of politics and arts. In his editor's column of 4 March 1909, Reedy defined what he saw as the task of the new American poets to fulfill their national responsibility to the arts:

> Not only have we not produced a great love-lyric. We have not been able to produce a good national anthem and "The Battle Hymn of the Republic" is a rather sanctimonious performance. To sum up the whole subject, we have produced a great many books in this country, but when we judge things by the great standards, mighty little literature, in more than one hundred and thirty years of nationality and love-making.

In short, Reedy believed that literature, especially poetry, and writers themselves must contribute to the nation.

Characteristically, Reedy responded enthusiastically to the new writing in *The Potter's Wheel.* This handmade monthly of creative writing and visual arts was founded in 1904 by a women artists' collective, including poets Sara Teasdale, Vine Colby, and Celia Harris, as well as photographers Williamina and Grace Parrish. They fashioned their project after the British pre-Raphaelite movement of the second half of the 19th century; the magazine's social, political, and aesthetic program was a call for new freedoms for women (escape from constraints of proper young womanhood) and for art (liberation from outworn conventions). Reedy also gave insightful critical encouragement to Edgar Lee Masters, whose *Spoon River Anthology* debuted in the *Mirror* (1914). Ezra Pound wrote from abroad to praise Reedy's courage in publishing this Chicago poet's innovative free-verse epitaphs (discussed later). Monroe always felt she had been scooped by Reedy, and Masters called him, with admiring irony, the "Literary Boss of the Middle West."

Reedy was committed to supporting and developing a new American poetry to fuse political life with poetry, as Max Putzel (1963) has observed, in a manner he respected in Dickinson, Whitman, and William Butler Yeats. He encouraged and published or reprinted many new young poets from the greater Midwest and beyond: Amy Lowell, Edna St. Vincent Millay, Yone Noguchi, and Pound, among them. His consistent mentoring and showcasing of new talent earned his magazine the epithet, "the *Mirror* school of poetry."

In 1915 Reedy assigned one of his young journalists, Zoë Akins, to write a series of essays on contemporary American poetry. Her essays, entitled *In the Shadow of Parnassus: A Critical Anthology of Contemporary Poetry,* are part of a larger pattern of women's formative role in the Midwestern Poetry Renaissance. Akins, herself a poet and member of the St. Louis arts scene (briefly an actress, then drama reviewer before she turned to poetry and playwriting), wrote this weekly column from 19 February to 13 August 1915. In 23 essays she reviewed the work of over 60 contemporary poets, including but also ranging well beyond the Midwest: Cather, Johns, Lindsay, Masters, Monroe, David O'Neil, and Teasdale, among those from the heartland; William Rose Benét, Anna Hempstead Branch, Robert Frost, Amy Lowell, Edna St. Vincent Millay, Pound, Edwin Arlington Robinson, and Witter Bynner, among those from other parts of the United States or abroad. These writers, many of whom began their careers in the 1910s, were members of what Akins was later to refer to as the "'poetical movement' which was everywhere in this country just before the great war" (*The Hills Grow Smaller,* 1937).

Akins' first article in the *Parnassus* series identified the onset of "a national awakening to the finest and final utterance of a people,—poetry," an awakening dependent on a large and committed audience. She encouraged readers and especially publishers to be alert to the possibility that the next

> Great Poet may be some lad on a Western farm whose untyped manuscripts the verse-writing editors scarcely trouble to examine [because they] are very busy with one another and with their verse-writing friends in Gotham. (*In the Shadow of Parnassus,* 1994)

Akins believed an exciting, pervasive experimental energy characterized the current "generation" of poets, who shared a common aesthetic ethos rather than age; Monroe was in her early 50s when she founded *Poetry,* Reedy in his late 40s when he began systematically supporting the new poetry and poets, and Masters in his mid-40s when *Spoon River* had its spectacular success. Although Akins clearly recognized and articulated the movement, it has typically been obscured by, seen as precursor of, or absorbed into the Modernist story of 20th-century poetry. Literary history has not uncommonly given a Whig interpretation to the origins and unfolding of 20th-century poetry, placing its paradoxical origins in Victorian propriety and conservatism, seeing it foreshadowed in fin-de-siècle decadence and turn-of-the-century innovation, and finding its complete expression in the Modernist revolution.

The Midwestern Poetry Renaissance, not improperly called a *rebellion,* so Henry F. May observes, is woven of a "curious and inescapable duality," a duality perhaps mistakenly seen through the lens of Modernism's signature tropes of paradox and irony and hence absorbed into the later program. The ideas, sources, and even the geographical location of the Midwest poets' varied activity, May continues, manifest themselves in oppositional pairs:

> Its most common article of faith was the importance of spontaneous, individual free expression in brand-new terms. . . . Yet very early, within the rebel ranks, a few proclaimed an exactly opposite creed. Against democratic spontaneity, this minority raised the standard of art, of discipline, even of tradition. (*The End of American Innocence,* 1959)

Reedy, for instance, inveighed against too much intellectuality in American poetry, on the one hand, yet criticized with equal emphasis, in a letter to Teasdale, poetry that did not give evidence of the "constant unremitting application of the file." For her part Monroe noted that although the new poetry was committed to overturning every convention of Victorian poetry or of any preceding poetry not a classic (poetic diction, theory, abstraction, remoteness, verbosity, and eloquence), this revisionist commitment implied no thoughtless disrespect for tradition.

These poets broke with what they perceived to be outworn traditions, aiming to revitalize poetry by vying with the novel and drama to approach what Monroe called the "actual life of our time" (*The New Poetry,* 1917). It would not be unfair to say that these writers' project was fundamentally a civic endeavor to bring democratic, scientific, humane, and liberating values to poetry. They experimented with various untraditional meters, rhythms, and rhymes, often disagreeing with one another yet also conceiving of themselves collectively and even cooperatively. Free verse became the banner-cry for reinvigorating traditional prosody, although not a union card; a fairly healthy respect for prosodic diversity perdured. Poets took inspiration from Celtic, European, and Oriental influences and models. They cultivated intense, often telegraphically lyric passion through vigorously compressed imagery and impressionism. They explored vernacular speech and varieties of unpoetic or unconventional subject matter, while also cultivating traditional verse forms such as the sonnet (Frost, Akins, and Millay), epitaph (Masters), and meter such as blank verse (most notably Frost). Experimenting with technique was important to these new poets, but as Monroe observed, the distinguishing quality of their undertaking was not experimentation for its own sake but rather the attempt to approximate a concrete and immediate realization of life.

In the first issue of *Poetry* Monroe developed a statement of the "motive for the magazine" in her epigraph borrowed from Whitman: "To have great poets there must be great audiences too." Poetry alone, of all the fine arts "in the huge democracy of our age," she continued, "has been left to shift for herself in a world unaware of its immediate and desperate need of her." To underscore the necessity of a "reciprocal relation between artist and public," Monroe paid poets for their work, insisted upon the political importance of this economic commitment to art, allied herself with no single movement or group, and chose widely and eclectically from work by poets nationally and internationally. *Poetry*'s first number included poems by Pound (then living abroad), Rabindranath Tagore, and Yeats (who also lectured in Chicago in 1914, at *Poetry*'s invitation), alongside American poets Henderson, Fannie Stearns Davis, Ficke, H.D., and Lindsay. In the November 1914 number of *Poetry* Monroe published Wallace Stevens' "Phases," generally agreed to be the most significant first appearance of this poet's mature work. If New York editors needed reminding from Akins to keep their eyes open for a manuscript from a "lad on a Western farm" who might be the next great poet, Monroe apparently did not need such reminding about an as yet lesser-known East Coast poet.

Meanwhile another influential magazine of new writing, *The Little Review* (1914–29), was founded in Chicago by Margaret C. Anderson. Anderson published poetry, prose fiction, and nonfiction, although the magazine became more familiarly associated with fiction, including serialization of James Joyce's *Ulysses* and a special issue on Henry James. T.S. Eliot, William Carlos Williams, Lowell, Masters, and Carl Sandburg numbered among the poets published in this magazine before it moved first to the West Coast (San Francisco), then to the East Coast (New York). Anderson's publication of both poetry and fiction was emblematic of an intersection and cross-fertilization of these two genres during this period. This phenomenon seems to have been rather more common in the Midwest than elsewhere. Here nearly all the new writers, as May has noted about Chicago's Anderson and Floyd Dell, subsequently better known for their fiction, thought of themselves as poets. Poetry seems to have been, for this generation of writers, the master form to reckon with and steer one's course by.

As prologue to discussing four poems by Masters, Millay, Sandburg, and Teasdale, selected to represent something of the variety and energy of this movement, a brief anecdote suggesting one aspect of its historico-cultural complexity, both in its own time and as perceived by subsequent literary historians and critics, may be of use. The actors in this factual parable are Eliot, Monroe, and Pound. Eliot was born in St. Louis and, although a second-generation native of the city, is rarely associated with the Midwest, except for having left it to attend Harvard. Graduating from college in 1910, he moved to Europe in 1914, became a British citizen in 1927, and did not return to the United States until 1932. Later asked about his early St. Louis years (Had he read Reedy's *Mirror?* Did he know or know of Teasdale during their overlapping years in St. Louis?), he said he did not recall either (*The Man in the Mirror,* 1963). Pound, by contrast, living in England when he received Monroe's August 1912 letter announcing her new magazine, responded with immediate enthusiasm. He praised the proposed magazine as the only one in America "which is not an insult to the serious and to the dignity of this art" (*A Poet's Life,* 1938). In their next exchange Pound agreed to serve as *Poetry*'s foreign editor. At his urging Monroe published Eliot's "The Love Song of J. Alfred Prufrock" in the June 1915 number of *Poetry* and the following year his "Figlia Che Piange." Much of subsequent Modernism turned toward Pound and Eliot and hence transatlantically. Meanwhile the Poetry Society of America, founded in New York City by Jessie B. Rittenhouse in 1910, became by virtue of its distinguished reading series and awards increasingly central to the kind of national and international organization of poets and poetry that magnetizes the cultural imagination. In addition the major literary publishers remained headquartered in New York. The basic direction of the next phase of new poetry was, in short, eastward.

Work by four poets, Masters, Teasdale, Millay, and Sandburg, embodies several aspects of the energetic diversity of the Midwestern Poetry Renaissance. Millay, although an East Coast poet by birth, is included to demonstrate that this movement was neither merely regional nor limited in its vision and aim to the central United States.

Masters' *Spoon River Anthology* (1915, 1916), stark free-verse epitaphs revealing the secret lives of townspeople buried in a small Midwestern cemetery, published first in Reedy's *Mirror* (1914), became the poet's signature collection. A Chicago lawyer by profession, Masters had previously published several volumes of prose and verse, beginning in the late 19th century, none notably successful. Moved, so the story goes, by Chicago's lively iconoclastic art scene, strong yet encouraging criticism from Reedy, Mackail's translation of epitaphs in the *Greek Anthology,* and a visit from his mother that reminded him of childhood days, Masters undertook this series of short free-verse portraits. Admired by some as energizing heir to Whitman, criticized by others as a dangerous pessimist, Masters achieved the greatest success of his literary life in this series of interconnected poems, spoken to the living from beyond the grave. In "Mollie McGee," for instance, the title character trenchantly describes her wretched life as an abused wife, posthumously calling out for attention to her plight and hence perhaps also that of other women similarly abused. Free-verse prosody imitates colloquial rhythms, while varying line lengths produce dramatic emphasis as when, for instance, McGee recounts her own death in the single unadorned line, "I sank into the grave." Direct address to the reader in many of the epitaphs, often using questions to initiate these brief compelling narratives ("Have you seen walking through the village / A man with downcast eyes and haggard face?"; "Did you ever hear of Editor Whedon . . . ?"; "Do the boys and girls still go to Siever's / For cider, after school, in late September?"), accumulates into a powerful taxonomy of passion, pettiness, boredom, pathology, and secular and spiritual insight.

Teasdale, although a highly successful poet in her own time, does not appear regularly in major late-20th-century anthologies, such as *The Norton Anthology of Modern Poetry* (1988), *The Gender of Modernism* (1990), the Oxford *Anthology of Modern American Poetry* (2000), or even (unlike her contemporaries Cather, H.D., Lowell, and Millay) in anthologies devoted to women writers, such as *The Norton Anthology of Literature by Women* (1996) and *The Prentice Hall Anthology of Women's Literature* (2000). The qualities and resources of Teasdale's success in the 1910s and 1920s—her meditative, lyric, often elegiac focus on women and love and "concern with minor beauties," for which even contemporaries sometimes faulted her (*In the Shadow of Parnassus,* 1994)—have not proved to be of either developing or continuing interest as have the ecstasies, eros, and politics of Millay, for instance, who is more comprehensible to feminist revision of the early-20th-century poetry canon. Teasdale was popular for her spiritually exalted, highly passionate yet often whispered first-person meditations on themes regarding sublime intersections among passion, knowledge, poetry, life, and the after-life in such poems as "The Answer," "On the Dunes," and "'What Do I Care?'" (*The New Poetry,* 1926). She regularly used rhyme and a variety of meters at a time when being new tended to be associated with free verse. Her reputation also became associated with the sonnet, a form that, although not used commonly in this period, was also being revitalized by Millay and Frost. Teasdale's *The Answering Voice* (1917; revised edition, 1928)—a collection of love poems by 19th- and 20th-century women poets including Akins, Emily Brontë, Elizabeth Barrett Browning, Cather, Dickinson, Lowell, Millay, Christina Rossetti, and Edith Wharton—offers a fascinating historical survey of female/feminine expressions of passion. In her forward to the second enlarged edition, Teasdale notes perceptively that if "the passion called love has not changed appreciably during recorded time," ideas about it have, particularly in the 20th century, by virtue of better education for women, their growing economic independence, and the "universal tendency to rationalize all emotion."

Millay, a sensationally popular East Coast poet who achieved something like cult status in her lifetime, was only 20 years old when "Renascence" was chosen for the 1912 *Lyric Year* anthology as one of the year's best 100 poems. Selected from among 10,000 entries by 2,000 poets (a remarkable figure indicating the poetic fervor and fever of the era), "Renascence" is an ecstatic first-person expression of the speaker's encounter with mortality and infinity, two aspects of Millay's subsequent poetic and political commitment to women's issues. She combines Dickinson's characteristic surreal landscape of soul—"All I could see from where I stood / Was three long mountains and a wood"—with Whitman's expressive physicality, although spiritualized, as in the couplet, "God, I can push the grass apart / And lay my finger on Thy heart!" Millay's "Renascence" was voted first prize by the volume editor, Ferdinand Earle, but not by the other two judges: George Woodberry, a versatile man of letters and an academic specialist in comparative literature, and African-American poet-critic-editor William Stanley Braithwaite. First prize was awarded to St. Louis native Orrick Johns for his socially progressive but aesthetically conservative poem "Second Avenue."

Johns wrote this oratorical plea for internationalized democracy, reinvigorated by humanely egalitarian political, moral, and artistic values in tetrameter quatrains, using alternating rhyming lines, and invoking the kind of poetic diction (exclamations such as "Lo"), allusions (such as references to the Muses), and tone (as, for example, series of rhetorical questions) that were going out of style. In addition to Johns, *The Lyric Year* published poems by other Midwestern poets (Akins, Ficke, Lindsay, Teasdale, Edith M. Thomas, Edith Wyatt), a higher percentage of women in this group even than in the notable 40 percent of the volume as a whole. Reedy, who clearly need not be defended against the charge of being a provincial editor, had previously printed or sponsored in the *Mirror* 20 of the 100 poets published in this New York City–published anthology. He admired Millay's "Renascence" for its "wonderful poignancy" (*Mirror,* 1912) and subsequently reprinted it. In her series of essays on contemporary poetry Akins also praised this poem's visionary expression.

Sandburg's "Chicago," with its still-arresting opening line, "Hog-butcher for the world," remains the poem perhaps most familiarly associated with the Midwestern Poetry Renaissance. Published in Monroe's *Poetry* (1914) and subsequently appearing as the title poem of Sandburg's *Chicago Poems* (1916), "Chicago" embodies the new poetry's commitment to the following principles: technical experimentation and reinvigoration (consciously crafted colloquial, idiomatic diction and free-verse prosody); precise, vivid, unflinching observation of commonplace particularity in actual American life; expression of the "spirit of the time"; complex optimism; and emphasis on pragmatic relevance to daily life. Sandburg's varied career-long work as poet-cum-social liberal, biographer and author of other socio-political nonfiction prose, and collector-anthologist of American poetry, song, folklore, and folk history reads as if conceived in response to Reedy's 1909 call for contemporary writers to begin in earnest the project of writing the long-awaited honest, passionate, unsanctimonious national literature.

Ultimately, the Midwestern Poetry Renaissance begins earlier, ranges more widely geographically (both nationally and internationally), and embodies a more complex, distinctive, and influential agenda and practice than are typically associated with it. The beliefs, knowledge, and work of this movement's participants—a number of whom did leave the Midwest and many of whose careers have been used to narrate the story of Modernism—repay efforts to refocus them freshly, accurately, and with greater appreciation of their influence in their own time and after.

Catherine N. Parke

**Further Reading**

Cahill, Daniel, *Harriet Monroe,* New York: Twayne, 1973

Gilbert, Sandra, and Susan Gubar, *No Man's Land: The Place of the Woman Writer in the Twentieth Century,* volume 1: *The War of the Words,* volume 2: *Sexchanges* (3 vols. total), New Haven, Connecticut: Yale University Press, 1988, 1989

May, Henry F., *The End of American Innocence: The First Years of Our Own Time, 1912–1917,* New York: Knopf, 1959

Monroe, Harriet, *A Poet's Life: Seventy Years in a Changing World,* New York: Macmillan, 1938

Parke, Catherine N., editor, *In the Shadow of Parnassus: Zoë Akins's Essays on American Poetry,* Selinsgrove, Pennsylvania: Susquehanna University Press, 1994

Putzel, Max, *The Man in the Mirror: William Marion Reedy and His Magazine,* Cambridge, Massachusetts: Harvard University Press, 1963

---

# Edna St. Vincent Millay 1892–1950

Once recognized as the voice of her generation, Edna St. Vincent Millay presents an intriguing study of paradox. Acknowledgment of her place in American letters came early to this poet. Millay wrote "Renascence" when only 19, and it received immediate acclaim when it appeared in *The Lyric Year* (1912). In 1923, she won the Pulitzer Prize for poetry for "The Ballad of the Harp-Weaver," thus becoming the first woman to win a Pulitzer, and a 1931 survey published in the *New York Times* identified Millay as "the chief glory of contemporary American literature" (in Thesing, 1993). However, by the time of her death in 1950, Millay's position as a critical poetic voice had evaporated. Indeed, this failure of her literary reputation underwrites most of the scholarship on Millay. William Thesing underscores this shift in Millay's standing among critics by turning to what he terms "a haunting prophecy," delivered in 1957 by Karl Shapiro: "I look in vain for the time when men will be so civilized as to appreciate this poet who wrote so voluminously and so passionately and so expertly, almost to no avail" (Thesing, 1993). Shapiro rightly points to Millay's large opus, to the emotion that propels both her sentimental and her political works, to her mastery of the sonnet, and to her lack of a sustained literary reputation.

Besides poetry, Millay's oeuvre includes plays, translations, and short stories. Millay published in avant-garde publications, and writing under the pseudonym Nancy Boyd she made a living publishing her fiction in popular culture magazines. She published 11 volumes of poetry before her death with two additional volumes appearing posthumously. However, *Renascence* (1917), *A Few Figs from Thistles* (1920), *Second April* (1921), *The Harp-Weaver, and Other Poems* (1923), *The Buck in the Snow* (1928), and *Wine from These Grapes* (1934) are her most important volumes and contain her most significant poems: "Renascence," "Spring," "The Ballad of the Harp-Weaver," "Justice Denied in Massachusetts," "Wine from These Grapes," and "An Ungrafted Tree."

Critics immediately embraced Millay's first published volume of poems, *Renascence* (1917). The emotion, freshness, and sincerity of the poems enraptured these early critics, as did the youth of the poet. Words and phrases such as "brilliant child," "simple, little-girl language," "emotion of youth," "the young, girlish poet herself," and "wide-eyed naïf" appear in both early and late reviews of *Renascence,* and these descriptions refer to the subject of the poems, to the tone of the works, and to Millay's poetic personae. "Renascence," the title poem of this volume, garners the most attention for its scope and vision. The poem's persona refuses the boundedness of limited sight, narrowed vision, and incomplete understanding; instead, the speaker brashly proclaims, "God, I can push the grass apart / And lay my finger on Thy heart!" "Renascence" does indeed emerge as an ambitious poem by a very young poet; however, its importance does not lie only in its monumental vision or its youthful fervor. The poem presents a glimpse of a negotiation with a world reluctant to yield to unrestrained ambition and unconstrained creativity. While seemingly conforming to the American tradition of Transcendentalism, "Renascence" possesses a hint of metaphysical mysticism. While early critics of the poem praised it for its freshness and exuberance, scholars today find it a "deeply strange and disturbing work" (Walker, 1991). As today's scholars revisit Millay's work, they struggle to identify her place within an American poetic tradition.

Although Millay lived and wrote during the height of Modernism, critics generally do not recognize her as a participant in that movement. Her retention of conventional forms and her strong lyrical and sentimental voice seemingly separate Millay's poetry from that of T.S. Eliot or Ezra Pound as well as from the work of Marianne Moore and Gertrude Stein. This separation, however, need not place Millay outside Modernism; rather, the form and voice of Millay's poetry represent a rejection of a Modernism dictated by Eliot or Pound, as they present an alternative or redefined Modernism. Millay's poetry offers a negotiation of the varied currents that run through literary Modernism: a nostalgic sense of absence and loss, an acknowledgment of disconnection and alienation, a disintegration of traditional values and paradigms, and a call for a disinterested and impersonal poetic voice. Current scholars of Modernism insist on extending the boundaries of traditional Modernism and on recognizing the existence of multiple Modernisms. This insistence provides a way in which to reconsider Millay's poetry in relation to Modernism.

As a celebrated member of the avant-garde, Millay, as well as her work, became well known for political radicalism, feminism, and the free-thinking spirit of bohemianism, all of which flourished during her years in Greenwich Village (1917–21). Millay came to the Village with already established feminist, political, and radical sentiments; however, the distinctive bohemian atmosphere of this milieu, with its commitment to open and honest expression of one's self, transformed these sentiments into convictions. Here Millay came into contact with a variety of artists and writers, some of the age's most brilliant personalities: Max Eastman, John Reed, Theodore Dreiser, Malcolm Cowley, Kenneth Burke, Paul Robeson, E.E. Cummings, Hart Crane, Wallace Stevens, and Edmund Wilson.

Millay circulated as a central figure among this gathering of writers and artists, and, as Cheryl Walker (1991) points out, Millay "became the symbol of Greenwich Village bohemianism" with the publication of *A Few Figs from Thistles.* This volume unabashedly celebrates sexual freedom and advocates a woman's entitlement to sexual pleasure. *A Few Figs* (1920), containing the oft-quoted "First Fig," apparently exemplified the "sexual defiance of the post-war generation" (Klemans, in Thesing, 1993). The hedonistic and cynical tone that marks "First Fig" characterizes much of Millay's early poetry. Wit, coupled with her skillful use of irony in the poems in *A Few Figs,* effectively established Millay as "the It-girl of the hour" (Walker, 1991). However, besides the openly unconventional sexual attitude that "First Fig" expresses, an acknowledgment of the impermanence and ephemeral aspect of human connection also emerges, and this recognition sounds strikingly Modernist.

Allen Tate identifies Millay as a "distinguished example" of the "second order" of poets. Writing after the height of Modernism, in a 1931 review of Millay's *Fatal Interview* (a 52-sonnet sequence recounting a love affair), Tate praises Millay's technical mastery of the Shakespearean form and identifies her ability to make personal the language of 19th-century poetry as both her "distinction" and her "limitation," echoing the sentiments of many of Millay's reviewers (in Thesing, 1993). Indeed, her poetry utilizes pre-20th-century forms, tropes, and at times emotions. However, Millay did write of her age, and her poetry does express the anxieties of early 20th-century America.

In *Second April,* published in 1921, the poet presents an honest, haunting, and sometimes bleak look at love. "Sonnet XV" ("Only until this cigarette is ended"), while reinforcing the transience of love, lacks the ironic playfulness of "First Fig." Instead, the persona of "Sonnet XV" deliberately permits memory of a past love to emerge only at the end of a day and only for a brief moment: "Only until this cigarette is ended, / A little moment at the end of all." This memory does not come unbidden to the speaker, nor does it present uncensored content; rather, it appears, lingers, and ends at the will of the persona. The persona will forget the lover's face, "the colour and the features, every one," yet he or she will retain the "words" and the "smiles" of the beloved. Thus, the rigid 14 lines of the sonnet contain and restrain the recollections of lost love as Millay utilizes the sonnet form to order the chaos of potentially overwhelming and destructive emotions.

In many ways, Millay, like Eliot, recognized the "disintegrating forces of her time," and, again like Eliot, Millay's poetry did not always present an optimistic view (Klemans, in Thesing, 1993). "Spring," the opening poem in *Second April,* clearly acknowledges this disintegration as well as the disillusionment and the crisis of meaning that marked High Modernism. After questioning the purpose of April's return, the speaker states, "Beauty is not enough." The speaking I of "Spring" admits to knowledge ("I know what I know"), and the poem reveals the knowledge as twofold: acknowledgment of the regenerative aspect of spring and certainty that "Life in / itself is nothing." This poem establishes *Second April* as a distinctively different collection of poems than Millay's first two collections, and it further makes clear her move away from the "girl poet" of "Renascence."

Discussions of Millay's place in American letters inevitably include mention of her person. Reviewers and scholars consistently remark on Millay's coppery red hair and engaging green eyes, her exhibitionism, and her vitality. On occasion, critics explicitly write as if Millay's poetry functions as an extension of her body: "her poems were as well-turned as her own slim ankle" (Engle, in Thesing, 1993), and in 1950 John Ciardi acknowledged the difficulty of separating Millay the person from "the presence contrived by the poems" (in Thesing, 1993). This focus on the body, the person of Millay, and this inability to distinguish the poet from the persona point to yet another factor in Millay's failure to sustain her literary reputation: sentimentality. Sentiment suggests embodiment, and her embodied, sentimental, emotional poetry places Millay in a precarious literary position. Her works borrow from and echo 19th-century poetry as they manifest as modern while simultaneously rejecting Modernism's experimentation.

In the 1920s, two events occurred that directly affected Millay's work: her 1923 marriage to Eugen Jan Boissevain afforded Millay financial security and the time to work, and the 1927 execution of Nicola Sacco and Bartolomeo Vanzetti for murder initiated her turn to political poetry. The two men were executed on 23 August 1927, one day after Millay's poem "Justice Denied in Massachusetts" appeared in the *New York Times.* Millay published four subsequent poems dealing with the Sacco-Vanzetti execution: "Hangman's Oak," "The Anguish," "To Those without Pity," and "Wine from These Grapes" (*The Buck in the Snow,* 1928). Millay does not explicitly name Sacco or Vanzetti in any of these poems, but she does sound a bitter indictment against a country where "Evil doth overwhelm" ("Justice Denied"). Through its allegorical structure, "Justice Denied" depicts a democracy threatened by diminishing political freedoms, and it warns that this denial of justice leaves future generations "a blighted earth to till / With a broken hoe."

These poems, written and published in the late 1920s, mark a shift in Millay's literary and public popularity. The somber intensity of her political voice underpins even her more sentimental verse, and her poetry seems to lose the witty brashness so engaging in her earlier works. The 1920s proved the most celebrated in Millay's career, and her success during this decade lingered into the 1930s; however, Millay's conscious choice to write propaganda poetry during World War II further undermined her standing as a serious poet. Millay herself acknowledged the consequences of this choice writing to a friend: "I have one thing to give in the service of my country,—my reputation as a poet" (in Thesing, 1993). Millay astutely predicted the loss of her poetic reputation, yet her political and social commitment overrode her desire for a place in America's literary canon. Millay seemed to understand that her popularity, both within literary circles and with the reading public, rested in the "gay impudence of her girlhood" and perhaps in the "sensitive curiosity of her more mature work" (Deutsch, in Thesing, 1993). However, neither her earlier political poetry nor this later propaganda offers a satisfactory explanation for the cracks in Millay's literary reputation. Her retention of older poetic forms, the sentimentality of her verse, and the conflation of poet and poetic persona all contributed to the devaluation of Millay's work.

Millay does, however, hold a significant place within American poetics, and feminist attention to this poet enhances the paradoxical aspect of that place. Beginning in the late 1970s and continuing to the present, feminist scholars have sought a recuperation of Millay within a feminist canon, finding in her poems female personae actively participating in poetic speech. In addition,

Millay's work renders women's experiences appropriate subject matter for poetry, and her poems often make clear women's struggles within a patriarchal society. This feminist recuperation of Millay, however, does not prove unproblematic. Millay's poetry also signals a capitulation to the mandates of patriarchy, and her poetry seems at times to exemplify traditional patriarchal expectations of the woman as poet. Nevertheless, the anxiety caused by the conflation of Millay as woman, poet, and persona emerges as her legacy to American poetry. The legend of Millay does not force a revaluation of her place in a literary canon; rather, it demands a reexamination of the place of poetry in America.

CATHERINE CUCINELLA

*See also* Midwestern Poetry Renaissance

**Biography**

Born in Rockland, Maine, 22 February 1892. Attended Barnard College, New York, 1913; Vassar College, Poughkeepsie, New York, 1914–17, graduated 1917; actress and freelance writer, New York, 1917–21; associated with the Provincetown Players, 1917–19; contributor, 1920, and European correspondent, 1921–23, *Vanity Fair.* Received Pulitzer Prize, 1923; Levinson Prize, 1931; Gold Medal of the Poetry Society of America, 1943; honorary Litt.D., Tufts University, Medford, Massachusetts, 1925, University of Wisconsin, Madison, 1933, and Colby College, Waterville, Maine, 1937; honorary L.H.D., New York University, 1937; member, American Academy of Arts and Letters, 1940. Died in Austerlitz, New York, 19 October 1950.

**Poetry**

*Renascence, and Other Poems,* 1917
*A Few Figs from Thistles,* 1920
*Second April,* 1921
*The Ballad of the Harp-Weaver,* 1922
*The Harp-Weaver, and Other Poems,* 1923; republished as *Poems,* 1923
*(Poems),* edited by Hughes Mearns, 1927
*The Buck in the Snow, and Other Poems,* 1928
*Poems Selected for Young People,* 1929
*Wine from These Grapes,* 1934
*Conversation at Midnight,* 1937
*Huntsman, What Quarry?* 1939
*Make Bright the Arrows: 1940 Notebook,* 1940
*Collected Sonnets,* 1941
*Collected Lyrics,* 1943
*Mine the Harvest: A Collection of New Poems,* edited by Norma Millay, 1954
*Collected Poems,* edited by Norma Millay, 1956
*Sonnets and a Few Poems,* 1982
*Take Up the Song: Poems,* 1986
*Grace from Simple Stone,* 1992
*Edna St. Vincent Millay, Selected Poems: The Centenary Edition,* 1992
*Early Poems,* 1999
*Edna St. Vincent Millay,* 1999
*Selected Poems,* 1999
*First Fig, and Other Poems,* 2000

**Other Writings:** plays (*The Princess Marries the Page,* 1932), short stories, nonfiction (*Fear,* 1927), translation of French literature (*Flowers of Evil,* by Baudelaire [with George Dillon], 1936), correspondence (*Letters of Edna St. Vincent Millay,* edited by Allan Ross MacDougall, 1952).

**Further Reading**


Aimone, Joseph, "Millay's Big Book; or, The Feminist Formalist as Modern," in *Unmanning Modernism: Gendered Re-Readings,* edited by Elizabeth Jane Harrison and Shirley Peterson, Knoxville: University of Tennessee Press, 1997

Clark, Suzanne, "'Jouissance' and the Sentimental Daughter: Edna St. Vincent Millay," *North Dakota Quarterly* 20, no. 10 (1986)

Fairley, Irene R., "Edna St. Vincent Millay's Gendered Language and Form: 'Sonnets Form an Ungrafted Tree,'" *Style* 29, no. 1 (1995)

Freedman, Diane P., editor, *Millay at 100: A Critical Reappraisal,* Carbondale: Southern Illinois University Press, 1995

Newcomb, John Timberman, "The Woman as Political Poet: Edna St. Vincent Millay and the Mid-Century Canon," *Criticism* 37, no. 2 (1995)

Nierman, Judith, and John J. Patton, editors, *An Annotated Bibliography of Works about Edna St. Vincent Millay, 1974–1993, with Supplement (1912–1973),* College Park: University of Maryland Woman's Studies, 1996

Thesing, William B., editor, *Critical Essays on Edna St. Vincent Millay,* New York and Oxford: G.K. Hall, 1993

Walker, Cheryl, *Masks Outrageous and Austere: Culture, Psyche, and Persona in Modern Women Poets,* Bloomington: Indiana University Press, 1991

Walker, Cheryl, "Antimodern, Modern, and Postmodern Millay: Contexts of Revaluation," in *Gendered Modernisms: American Women Poets and Their Readers,* edited by Margaret Dickie and Thomas Travisano, Philadelphia: University of Pennsylvania Press, 1996


# Justice Denied in Massachusetts

"Justice Denied in Massachusetts," by Edna St. Vincent Millay, is a political poem written in response to the proposed execution of Nicola Sacco and Bartolomeo Vanzetti in Boston, Massachusetts, on 23 August 1927. Although the poem never refers to the men or the event, it is appropriate to consider the trial and the sentencing as the antecedent scenarios for the poem in order to comprehend the speaker's tone and attitude. Sacco and Vanzetti, arrested in May 1920, were charged with the murder of two men during a payroll robbery in Braintree, Massachusetts, on 15 April 1920. The trial attracted national and international attention. Many people—artists, intellectuals, newspaper editors, public figures, and ordinary people—believed that the two men were guilty of nothing more than holding radical views in an extremely conservative political climate; even those who thought that Sacco and Vanzetti might be guilty agreed that the men did not receive a fair trial. Millay maintained that justice had not been served by the court system and would not be served by the execution of the two men.

On 22 August, the day before the executions, Millay met personally with Governor Alvan Fuller, asking him to grant clemency to the two men. In a letter sent to the governor shortly after this visit, she called on Fuller to become a hero in this dark hour by sparing the lives of Sacco and Vanzetti: "There is need in Massachusetts of a great man tonight," she wrote. "It is not too late for you to be that man" (MacDougall, 1952).

A native New Englander, Millay was familiar with the Commonwealth of Massachusetts and its history. She knew how fiercely proud its citizens were of their legacy: the commitment to liberty and independence that kindled the spirits of earlier radicals, such as Samuel Adams, Paul Revere, and Benjamin Franklin, who was born in Boston in 1709, and the courage and fervor of its outspoken Abolitionist poets and orators. She knew, too, the sinister aspects of Massachusetts history: the Salem witch trials of 1692 that left a dark cloud over the port city for years. She appealed to Governor Fuller's sense of his place in the annals of Massachusetts history. However, when all approaches failed, she read this poem to the anxious crowd gathered on the aptly named Salem Street.

Published in *The Buck in the Snow* (1928), "Justice Denied in Massachusetts" is an address to those who stand with the speaker, those who realize that the demoralizing effects of injustice are long lasting. Millay builds this poem on an agricultural metaphor that incorporates both classical and religious traditions. The sun will not shine on a nation whose injustices must be punished. Just as the murder of Laius brought blight and famine to Thebes in *Oedipus Rex,* the legal murders of Sacco and Vanzetti will produce formidable consequences for Massachusetts and a blight on the nation as a whole. With the eloquence of a Sophoclean chorus, Millay speaks calmly but bitterly of the fate at hand, noting that the curse will affect this generation and the next; even their "children's children" will suffer.

The poem's 36 lines are divided into four stanzas: the first, third, and fourth stanzas contain seven lines each; the second stanza has 15. The lines vary in length and meter. Some of the lines, especially the shorter ones, have end rhyme. Occasionally, a word in the middle of a long line will rhyme with the end word in a short line; for example, "seed" at the end of line four rhymes with "weed" in the middle of line six. Some of the rhymes, like some of the images, recur in their mournful beauty, emphasizing with somber references the fate that the people cannot quit.

In the first stanza, the speaker questions us:

> Let us then abandon our gardens and go home
> And sit in the sitting-room.
> Shall the larkspur blossom or the corn grow under this cloud?

The question is merely rhetorical, however, because the gardens will not grow. The sunless day and the overarching cloud ensure that the cold earth will spoil any fruitful seed that attempts to live even as they force the quack grass and weeds to overtake the land and bend the blades of the hoe. The image of the bent blade, powerless against the stalks, controverts the words of the prophet Isaiah, who promised a time of peace when swords would be turned into ploughshares; here, injustice has turned ploughshares into broken hoes. The alliteration in this stanza emphasizes that "those who hunger and thirst after justice" will not be "satisfied" (unlike the promise that Jesus made in the Sermon on the Mount), at least not here and not now. Now, those who seek justice will leave the *garden* and *go,* will *sit* in the *sitting*-room; they *cannot conquer* injustice.

Stanza two whittles the first and second lines of stanza one into one crabbed line, indicating the decreasing quality of life. The stanza focuses on the lost promises of August in Massachusetts, the "Bay State." Generally in August the warm bay breezes wash across the fields of ripened corn while the farmers gather hay for feed against the long winter to come. At the same time, the farm families harvest the fruits that will keep them in preserves for another year. This stanza, with its rhyming short lines and its alliteration (*warm winds* and *warmed . . . withered* the *weed*), calls forth the pleasant scenes of other years before turning to the present when "We shall *die* in *darkness,* and *be buried* in the rain."

In the third stanza, the speaker recalls the illustrious past that "we" have inherited and squandered. We have forfeited liberty, peace, and prosperity because we have allowed our leaders to let evil—intolerance, secrecy, and injustice—devour our nation:

> Furrows sweet to the grain, and the weed subdued—
> See now the slug and mildew plunder.
> Evil does overwhelm
> The larkspur and the corn;
> We have seen them go under.

The fourth stanza abbreviates the opening lines even further, causing the poem to turn in on itself:

> Let us sit here, sit still,
> Here in the sitting-room until we die;
> At the step of Death on the walk, rise and go;

The sitting-room is not a parlor but an antechamber for death, the consequence of permitting Evil into the garden; so, like Adam and Eve, we leave our descendants far less and far worse than what we inherited:

> Leaving to our children's children this beautiful doorway,
> And this elm,
> And a blighted earth to till
> With a broken hoe.

Although many readers hold that this poem announces the complete and permanent ruin of the nation, there seems to be, in the image of the "beautiful doorway," one lovely place left. It seems more than an invitation for death to come in; it suggests perhaps that, after the passing of the generations responsible for the present social ills, the nation may yet recover.

JEANNIE SARGENT JUDGE

**Further Reading**

Atkins, Elizabeth, *Edna St. Vincent Millay and Her Times,* Chicago: University of Chicago Press, 1936

Brittin, Norman A., *Edna St. Vincent Millay,* New York: Twayne, 1967; revised edition, Boston: Twayne, 1982

Gurko, Miriam, *Restless Spirit: The Life of Edna St. Vincent Millay,* New York: Crowell, 1962

MacDougall, Allan Ross, editor, *Letters of Edna St. Vincent Millay,* New York: Harper, 1952

Sheean, Vincent, *The Indigo Bunting: A Memoir of Edna St. Millay,* New York: Harper, 1951

## Renascence

The circumstances surrounding the publication of Edna St. Vincent Millay's narrative poem "Renascence" describe a fantastic narrative of adolescent artistic triumph. When Millay finished the poem in 1912, she was a 20-year-old woman living in Camden, Maine, with no immediate means for achieving her fervent desire to be a well-published poet. "Renascence" was not her first publishing venture; she had published rather extensively in the popular children's magazine *St. Nicholas* throughout her youth. Having outgrown the magazine's age limit for contributors and won its most coveted literary prize, Millay published nothing for two years and made no plans to leave Maine or attend college.

Millay had begun writing "Renascence" at the age of 18 and submitted it to the immensely competitive anthology *The Lyric Year* at the suggestion of her mother. Millay sent it and another piece to the anthology's editors and awaited the decision that would make possible her life as a poet. Her bravado would be rewarded, for soon an acceptance arrived addressed to "E. Vincent Millay, Esq."

"Renascence" was one of the 100 poems selected for the anthology, and although it was not awarded the cash prize that Millay was promised by one enthusiastic editor, it brought her a far more valuable reward: attention from benefactors who eventually supported her matriculation at Vassar College. In 1917, she published her first book of poems, with "Renascence" as the title work. The poem was at the thematic heart of the book and remains one of Millay's best-received works. Harriet Monroe, who founded *Poetry* magazine in 1912, described it in 1918 as "the only thrill I received from . . . [the] anthology, *The Lyric Year*. . . . Reading it once more, after six years' discipline in modern poetry, I am thrilled again."

There is much to be thrilled by in "Renascence," from its lyric vision to its unfailing iambic tetrameter and satisfyingly rhymed couplets. At a time when many other poets of comparable talent turned to the inventiveness of the new, Millay was here occupied with traditional formal and visionary concerns. In the poem's first stanza, Millay describes a landscape that confines her, scenic as it may be. The physical constraints of the natural world surround the speaker; her vision is limited wherever she looks by the landmarks of the familiar:

All I could see from where I stood
Was three long mountains and a wood;
I turned and looked another way,
And saw three islands in a bay.

The well-known panorama, delineated by geographic markers that form the boundaries of the speaker's vision, serves as her point of inspiration through seeming deprivation. "These were the things that bounded me," Millay writes. Her gaze on the horizon, she surveys her landscape with a knowing look. When they are presented again at the end of the stanza, the mountains and the wood have already lost some of their charm. Millay evokes the tedium of the world she describes through the repetition, cleverly altering the phrasing so as to remark on it while maintaining her exacting tetrameter:

Straight around till I was come
Back to where I'd started from;
And all I saw from where I stood
Was three long mountains and a wood.

As the speaker takes the measure of the world around her, its confines become increasingly claustrophobic. Her frustrated scream, in contrast to the polished lines that describe it, still acts as a commentary on its constraints, for "Infinity / Came down and settled over me; / Forced back my scream into my chest." The scream is rejected, forced back into the body of the presumptuous speaker, and silence is enforced so that something might be learned.

The vision that Millay describes is a revelation rich in negative detail. Sin and loss have become the poem's subject, and the speaker internalizes the wretchedness of her vision. In one of the inversions for which she would become known, Millay writes,

—Ah, fearful pawn:
For my omniscience paid I a toll
In infinite remorse of soul.

The visionary ability to see and feel collective suffering continues, the antithesis of the "bounded" limitations of her physical vision. Only when the speaker has seen and felt too much, has experienced "pity like the pity of God," does Infinity again intervene, inspiring the subject with a longing for the ultimate release from suffering, death.

The quietest moment of "Renascence," with its sentimental crashings and dramatic turns, comes when the speaker imagines herself buried, "so gladly dead." For then, described so that the reader too can perceive its gentle rhythm, "The pitying rain began to fall; / I lay and heard each pattering hoof. . . . / And seemed to love the sound far more / Than ever I had done before." It is the quiet, regular sound of the rain that compels the speaker; it is the natural meter that allows her to experience the unbounded joy and delight of the poem's conclusion.

As the liberating rain washes away the grief and earth that entombed her, the speaker's vision returns to the world around her and she sees "A last long line of silver rain, / A sky grown clear and blue again." In joy, she is inspired by the sensual world around her. Every sense is greeted with glory, and she promises that the scream that inaugurated her experience of woe, and thus permitted her rebirth into delight, will now be tempered as a hushed response to the divine, to "Thy radiant identity." Yet her exuberance will not be reigned in, and she exults, "God, I can push the grass apart / And lay my finger on Thy heart!" The image of the speaker insinuating her fingers into an earthly crevice and there finding the very pulse of God is ecstatically corporeal, startling in its immediacy. Beneath the spot where she stood at the poem's beginning, seeing in everything around her limitation, divine promise quickens the earth and renews the poet.

The poem ends where it began, but all is changed utterly. The landscape is no longer a confinement but a marker of possibility in which "The world stands out on either side / No wider than the heart is wide." The seemingly limitless promise of the poet's vision is tempered by a keen awareness of the killing power of self-limitation, for "he whose soul is flat—the sky / Will cave in on him by and by." In these last lines, all is possible for one with limitless imagination and impossible for one whose soul is pinched and flat; it is the measure of an individual's soul that metes out her fate. The dual consciousness of Millay's final stanza, in which jouissance coexists with doom, expansiveness with implosion, describes an awareness that informs her later work and that was to preoccupy her for years to come.

Elizabeth Grainger

**Further Reading**


Brittin, Norman A., *Edna St. Vincent Millay,* New York: Twayne, 1967; revised edition, Boston: Twayne, 1982

Clark, Suzanne, "'Jouissance' and the Sentimental Daughter: Edna St. Vincent Millay," *North Dakota Quarterly* 20, no. 10 (1986)

Freedman, Diane P., editor, *Millay at 100: A Critical Reappraisal,* Carbondale: Southern Illinois University Press, 1995

Gurko, Miriam, *Restless Spirit: The Life of Edna St. Vincent Millay,* New York: Crowell, 1962

Thesing, William B., editor, *Critical Essays on Edna St. Vincent Millay,* New York and Oxford: G.K. Hall, 1993


---

# Czeslaw Milosz 1911–

For many Americans, Czeslaw Milosz is linked to two 20th-century struggles against totalitarianism. A member of the Polish resistance against the Nazis and an exile from the former Soviet bloc, Milosz has sometimes been idealized in America, particularly after he received the Nobel Prize in 1980, for his political commitments in a way that oversimplifies his achievements as a poet. Milosz speaks of his "discomfort when my image is too noble" and prefers the reaction of those readers who are sensitive to the "meditative" side of his oeuvre, "which I find more comfortable and suitable" (Czarnecka and Fiut, 1987). Nevertheless, the presence—one might say the burden—of politics is everywhere in Milosz's work. Many of his poems are explicitly political or "civic-minded," as Milosz describes them in a nearly disparaging fashion (Czarnecka and Fiut, 1987). He insists that his poetry is a reluctant if necessary engagement with history and politics. His true calling, he claims, was the natural sciences, and his poems often celebrate the singularity of things and places with awe, however tempered with irony, for nature's mysteriousness. He realizes, however, that an escape from history is neither possible in good faith nor desirable despite its seductive pull: "Yes, I would like to be a poet of the five senses, / That's why I don't allow myself to become one," he wrote in "In Milan" (1955). Like Ezra Pound, a poet with whom he otherwise shares little affinity, Milosz has sought to bring the lyric poem into history.

Milosz published his first poems while a student (1929–34) at Stefan Batory University in Wilno (Vilnius). While a student, he co-founded the "Żagary" group of poets and, during a visit to Paris in 1931, met his cousin, the French poet Oskar Milosz, whose visionary poems would have a lifelong influence on the younger Milosz. At the time, however, his poetry was exceedingly "civic-minded." The poems in his first collection, *Poemat o czasie zastygłym* (1933; A Poem on Frozen Time), like much of the poetry of the "Żagary" group, were in large part inspired by Marxism. Although Milosz came to dislike *Poemat o czasie zastygłym* and disowned his first anthology, *Antologia poezji społecznej* (1933; Anthology of Social Poetry), edited with Zbigniew Folejewski, these publications earned him a prize from the Union of Polish Writers and a grant from the National Cultural Fund that allowed him to live in France for a year. While there, he wrote several poems, including "Hymn" and "The Gates of the Arsenal," that show the influences of Surrealism and an apocalyptic strain of Polish Romanticism already evident in his earlier poetry. The poems written in Paris were collected in *Trzy zimy* (1936; Three Winters).

Milosz spent most of World War II in Warsaw. A member of the socialist resistance, he edited an anthology of anti-Nazi poetry, translated Jacques Maritain's anti-Vichy writings, and took part in clandestine poetry readings. While employed as a janitor at the Warsaw University library, he began studying English and soon translated Shakespeare's *As You Like It* and Eliot's *The Waste Land* into Polish. Milosz's own wartime poetry was published secretly. Although many of these poems are about the war, others, such as those in the sequence "The World," are lyrical works. Milosz describes "The World," written in ironic imitation of the poems found in school primers, as "an identification with a naïve view of the world" in its creation of "an artificial world as a defense against the horror" of World War II (Czarnecka and Fiut, 1987); it complements poems directly concerned with the brutalities of the Nazi occupation, such as "Campo dei Fiori" and "The Voices of Poor People." Its "naïve" evocation of the sensuous world of childhood, however precipitated by the pressures of war, is also a version of the lyricism that Milosz has defended throughout his career as necessary to the preservation of humane values. In the introduction to his anthology *A Book of Luminous Things* (1996), Milosz writes, "Since poetry deals with the singular, not the general, it cannot—if it is good poetry—look at things of this earth other than as colorful, variegated, and exciting, and so, it cannot reduce life, with all its pain, horror, suffering, and ecstasy, to a unified totality of boredom or complaint. By necessity poetry is therefore on the side of being and against nothingness."

In 1945, his manuscripts having survived the war, Milosz published *Ocalenie* (Rescue), his only book to appear in postwar Poland until 1980. Later that year, he accepted a diplomatic post from the newly established government and traveled to the United States. Working in New York and then in Washington, D.C., Milosz wrote numerous poems addressing the moral realities of postwar Europe, often through satiric portraiture; "Child of Europe" (1946) coolly mocks the justifications of those who "After the Day of the Lie gather in select circles, / Shaking with laughter when our real deeds are mentioned." Most of these poems were not published until years later, with the exception of "Traktat moralny" ("Treatise on Morals"), which improbably escaped censorship and appeared in 1948.

Milosz's relationship with the Polish authorities became increasingly strained, and in 1951 he requested political asylum in France, where he would reside for the next decade. There he began his involvement with Instytut Literacki, a publishing house run by Polish émigrés. Over the next four decades, Instytut Literacki published Milosz's work in its journal *Kultura,* commissioned translations, and issued the first Polish editions of nearly all of Milosz's writings. In 1953, Milosz published *Światło dzienne* (Daylight), which gathered unpublished poems from the late 1940s and those written in France. He also wrote *Zniewolony umysł* (1953; *The Captive Mind*), a study of totalitarianism, and two semi-autobiographical novels, *Zdobycie władzy* (1953; *The Seizure of Power*) and *Dolina Issa* (1955; *The Issa Valley*). *The Captive Mind,* translated quickly into French, German, and English, was soon recognized by many as a devastating study of Communism in Eastern Europe. For many years, Milosz was known in the United States as a political essayist, as his poetry would not be extensively translated into English until the 1970s. While in France, he also wrote *Rodzinna Europa* (1959; *Native Realm*), a collection of autobiographical essays; translated many of Simone Weil's writings into Polish; and wrote *Traktat poetycki* (1957; A Treatise on Poetry), which is in part a verse history of 20th-century Polish poetry in the manner of Karl Shapiro's *Essay on Rime* (1945). In the poems collected in his next book, *Król Popiel i inne wiersze* (1962; King Popiel and Other Poems), Milosz considered metaphysical questions, such as original sin, resurrection, and the relation of the particular to the universal, and placed less emphasis on political concerns.

In 1960, Milosz left France to accept a position as lecturer in the Department of Slavic Languages and Literature at the University of California, Berkeley; he was named professor the following year. During his first few years in Berkeley, in addition to writing his own poems and essays, he translated poems of Whitman and Jeffers into Polish and translated Polish poems into English for his anthology *Post-War Polish Poetry* (1965). He also wrote poems inspired by the California landscape and published *Widzenia nad Zatoka San Francisco* (1969; *Visions from San Francisco Bay*), a collection of essays about his exile in the United States. Nevertheless, despite strong ties to several American poets (notably Robert Hass, one of his translators), Milosz has been influenced by American poetry in a relatively muted way. Many of his poems written in the United States consider his Lithuanian past or address historical concerns rooted in European experience. Although he acknowledges that the histories of the United States and Europe are intertwined, he often equates America with "nature" or an ahistorical mode of being that is set against the traumas of 20th-century Europe.

Milosz's collections from the 1960s and 1970s include *Gucio zaczarowany* (1965; Bobo's Metamorphosis), *Miasto bez imienia* (1969; City without a Name), and *Gdzie wschodzi słońce i kędy zapada* (1974; From the Rising of the Sun). In these books, Milosz became increasingly skeptical of poetry's ability to represent experience, a skepticism that only intensified the poet's quest to do so. This theme is taken up explicitly in poems such as "The Language Changed" and "Ars Poetica?," one of Milosz's most anthologized poems. In "Ars Poetica?" Milosz imagines an unattainable form that would be free from the limits of poetry and prose; his frustration with conventional forms sheds light on works (such as the majestic "From the Rising of the Sun") that combine poetry and prose and on his increasing use of an expansive, biblical line for much of his later work. (In the 1970s, Milosz began translating books of the Bible.) In addition, the poetry from the 1960s and the 1970s often looked to Milosz's past, a trend that continued in his later work.

Milosz's impact on American poetry first registered after the publication of *Selected Poems* (1973), his first collection to be translated into English. Subsequent English collections include *Bells in Winter* (1978), *The Separate Notebooks* (1984), *Unattainable Earth* (1986), *Provinces* (1991), *Facing the River* (1995), and *Road-Side Dog* (1998). Milosz has supervised the English translations of his poetry and has at times collaborated with his translators; he has also translated poems into English unaided. Working with several gifted translators, including Robert Hass and Robert Pinsky, Milosz has been well served by the English versions of his poetry; their quality is one of the reasons why he has been so widely read in America.

In 1980, Milosz was awarded the Nobel Prize for Literature. The award prompted the Polish government to allow his work to be published again in Poland, and, in June 1981, Milosz visited Poland after 30 years of exile. Later that year, he was awarded the Charles Eliot Norton Chair at Harvard University and delivered six lectures on poetry, later published as *The Witness of Poetry* (1983). Since then, Milosz's position as a major figure in world literature has been secure. The inescapable notoriety brought on by the Nobel Prize did not significantly affect the quality of his later work. He continued to explore the philosophical, metaphysical, and political themes of his earlier poetry, and he also wrote moving poems about aging and death. Many of the poems in *Facing the River* are about a trip to Lithuania and fuse observations on his homeland, virtually unrecognizable after decades of exile, with meditations on his old age.

Milosz has taken up important questions, literary and otherwise, raised by the troubled 20th century and has sought the answers by thinking as a poet. In the prose poems of his most recent book, *Road-Side Dog,* he contemplates poetry's future—"perhaps even poetry survives among a generalized savagery"—and reflects on the century that has just passed:

> I went on a journey to acquaint myself with my province, in a two-horse wagon with a lot of fodder and a tin bucket rattling in the back. . . . And always we were barked at by a dog, assiduous in its duty. That was the beginning of the century; this is its end. I have been thinking not only of the people who lived there once but also of the generations of dogs accompanying them in their everyday bustle, and one night—I don't know where it came from—in a predawn sleep, that funny and tender phrase composed itself: a road-side dog.

This passage represents what is best in Milosz's work: his witness of a vanished past, his sympathy for humble things, and his sense of awe before the origin of a phrase. These qualities, as well as Milosz's probing responses to the deformations of history and politics, have made his voice necessary and enduring.

James Gibbons

**Biography**

Born in Szetejnie, Lithuania, 30 June 1911. Attended University of Vilnius, Lithuania, master of law, 1934; programmer, Polish

National Radio, 1935–39; cultural attaché, Polish Embassy, Washington, D.C., 1946–50, Paris, France, 1950–51; freelance writer, Paris, 1951–60; Visiting Lecturer, 1960–61, Professor of Slavic languages and literatures, 1961–78, and since 1978 Professor Emeritus, University of California, Berkeley. Received National Culture Fund scholarship, 1934; Prix Littéraire Européen, 1953; Marian Kister Literary Award, 1967; Jurzykowski Foundation Award, 1968; Institute for Creative Arts fellowship, 1968; Polish PEN Award for translation, 1974; Wandycz Award, 1974; Guggenheim fellowship, 1976; honorary Litt.D., University of Michigan, 1977; Neustadt International Literary Prize for Literature, 1978; University Citation, University of California, 1978; Zygmunt Hertz Award, 1979; Nobel Prize for Literature, 1980; honorary doctorate, Catholic University, Lublin, Poland, 1981, and Brandeis University, 1983; Bay Area Book Reviewers Association Poetry Prize, 1986; Robert Kirsh Award for poetry, 1990; National Medal of Arts, 1990. Living in Berkeley, California.

**Poetry**

*Poemat o czasie zastygłym* (A Poem on Frozen Time), 1933
*Trzy zimy* (Three Winters), 1936
*Ocalenie* (Rescue), 1945
*Światło dzienne* (Daylight), 1953
*Traktat poetycki* (A Treatise on Poetry), 1957
*Król Popiel i inne wiersze* (King Popiel, and Other Poems), 1962
*Gucio zaczarowany* (Bobo's Metamorphosis), 1965
*Miasto bez imienia* (City without a Name), 1969
*Gdzie wschodzi słońce i kędy zapada* (From the Rising of the Sun), 1974
*Selected Poems,* 1973; revised edition, 1980
*Bells in Winter,* 1978
*The Separate Notebooks,* 1984
*Unattainable Earth,* 1986
*The Collected Poems, 1931–1987,* 1988
*Provinces: Poems, 1987–1991,* 1991
*Facing the River: New Poems,* 1995
*Poezje Wybrane/Selected Poems* (bilingual edition), 1996
*Road-Side Dog,* 1998

**Selected Criticism**

*The History of Polish Literature,* 1969; 2nd edition, 1983
*Emperor of the Earth: Modes of Eccentric Vision,* 1977
*The Witness of Poetry,* 1983

**Other Writings:** novels (*Dolina Issa* [*The Issa Valley*], 1955), essays (*Zniewolony umysł* [*The Captive Mind*], 1953; *Rodzinna Europa* [*Native Realm*], 1959; *Widzenia nad Zatoka San Francisco* [*Visions from San Francisco Bay*], 1969), correspondence (*Striving towards Being: The Letters of Thomas Merton and Czeslaw Milosz,* 1997), translation of Polish poetry (*Selected Poems,* by Zbigniew Herbert, 1968; revised edition, 1986); edited anthologies of poetry (*Antologia poezji społecznej* [Anthology of Social Poetry], 1933; *Post-War Polish Poetry,* 1965; *A Book of Luminous Things: An International Anthology of Poetry,* 1996).

**Further Reading**

Birkerts, Sven, "Czeslaw Milosz," in *The Electric Life: Essays on Modern Poetry,* by Birkerts, New York: Morrow, 1989
Czarnecka, Ewa, and Aleksander Fiut, *Podrozny Swiata: Rozmowy z Czeslawem Miloszem,* New York: Bicentennial, 1983; as *Conversations with Czeslaw Milosz,* translated by Richard Lourie, San Diego, California, and London: Harcourt Brace Jovanovich, 1987
Davie, Donald, *Czeslaw Milosz and the Insufficiency of Lyric,* Knoxville: University of Tennessee Press, and Cambridge: Cambridge University Press, 1986
Fiut, Aleksander, *Moment Wieczny: Poezja Czeslawa Milosza,* Paris: Libella, 1987; as *The Eternal Moment: The Poetry of Czeslaw Milosz,* translated by Theodosia S. Robertson, Berkeley: University of California Press, 1990
Hass, Robert, *Twentieth Century Pleasures: Prose on Poetry,* Hopewell, New Jersey: Ecco Press, 1984
Malinowska, Barbara, *Dynamics of Being, Space, and Time in the Poetry of Czeslaw Milosz and John Ashbery,* New York: Lang, 2000
Mozejko, Edward, editor, *Between Anxiety and Hope: The Poetry and Writing of Czeslaw Milosz,* Edmonton: University of Alberta Press, 1988
Nathan, Leonard, and Arthur Quinn, *The Poet's Work: An Introduction to Czeslaw Milosz,* Cambridge, Massachusetts: Harvard University Press, 1992
Vendler, Helen, "Czeslaw Milosz," in *The Music of What Happens: Poems, Poets, Critics,* by Vendler, Cambridge, Massachusetts: Harvard University Press, 1988
Volynska-Bogert, Rimma, and Wojciech Zaleswski, *Czeslaw Milosz: An International Bibliography, 1930–1980,* Ann Arbor: University of Michigan Press, 1983

## Ars Poetica?

"Ars Poetica?" is too brief to be described as Milosz's summary statement on the art of poetry. Nevertheless, its 36 lines, rendered in unrhymed quatrains in the version Milosz translated with Lillian Vallee, included in *The Collected Poems, 1931–1987* (1988), convey an accurate sense of the place and purpose of poetry that Milosz elucidated more carefully in his 1981–82 Charles Eliot Norton lectures (published as *The Witness of Poetry* in 1983) and in his various critical and autobiographical writings. On the one hand a meditation on the limits of lyric and its place in the modern world, "Ars Poetica?" also challenges conventional assumptions about poetic creation itself, offering astute insights into the notions of inspiration and imagination. "In the very essence of poetry there is something indecent," Milosz writes in the fifth line of the poem, going on to suggest in the first two lines of the third stanza, "That's why poetry is rightly said to be dictated by a daimonion, / though it's an exaggeration to maintain that he must be an angel." Milosz reiterated that claim in the first of his Norton lectures, where he said that "all my life I have been in the power of a daimonion, and how the poems dictated by him came into being I do not quite understand" (Milosz, 1983). Nevertheless, Milosz's experience of man's inhumanity to man (e.g., during the early 1940s, when he lived in Nazi-occupied Poland) is frequently registered in his work; when he writes in "Ars Poetica?" that for him poems were often written "under unbearable duress," one must appreciate that he witnessed and lived through some of the 20th century's most terrible and terrifying circumstances.

From a literary historical perspective, the importance of Milosz's consideration of the conditions of poetic creation in "Ars Poetica?" is important not least because, written in the late 1960s, it intervenes in the history of Anglo-American poetry and the overwhelming tendency toward confessionalism that dominated critical assessments of much of the poetry of the period in the work of Anne Sexton (1928–74), John Berryman (1914–72), and others. In the sixth stanza, Milosz writes,

There was a time when only wise books were read,
helping us to bear our pain and misery.
This after all, is not quite the same
as leafing through a thousand works fresh from psychiatric
clinics.

In these lines, Milosz is clearly referring to the recent proliferation of poetry dealing with emotional trauma and psychiatric health. However, he is concerned less with denying or castigating the so-called confessional voice than with advancing a project that seeks to reveal the universal ground of human feeling. He acknowledges that "the world is different from what it seems to be / and we are other than how we see ourselves in our ravings."

That observation is crucial because it describes something of the dynamic between self and world in Milosz's work, and it reveals an ecstatic tendency in his best poetry where "invisible guests come in and out at will." This means that Milosz's poems frequently deny the kind of recalcitrant categorizations that bedeviled much American poetry that was being published in the 1960s. The question mark in the title signifies Milosz's sense of control while also suggesting an ironic strategy—evaded by the author in interviews and in the poem's fifth stanza—that hinders any trite critical summation of his work. In an interview with Ewa Czarnecka, Milosz denied that the poem is ironic and added, "I have no desire to write statements" (Czarnecka and Fiut, 1987). Nevertheless, his subtle dissembling of certain poetic categories—inspiration, composition, and confession—in the poem suggests that he is more profoundly familiar with the nature of irony than he may be prepared to admit.

No discussion of Milosz's work can avoid the question of translation, and in "Ars Poetica?" he broaches the question on which his reputation in the United States and the English-speaking world so stubbornly rests. In the fourth stanza, he asks,

What reasonable man would like to be a city of demons,
who behave as if they were at home, speak in many
tongues,
and who, not satisfied with stealing his lips or hand,
work at changing his destiny for their convenience?

Perhaps Milosz is hinting in these lines at the way that Russian and Eastern European poetry has been fetishized in the English-speaking world and the way that some critics have come close to suggesting that the sufferings of Mandelstam or Ratushinskaya are sufficient to describe their power and achievement. The last stanza of "Ars Poetica?" makes this point, if obliquely, when Milosz writes,

What I'm saying here is not, I agree, poetry,
as poems should be written rarely and reluctantly,
under unbearable duress and only with hope
that good spirits, not evil ones, choose us for their
instrument.

"Ars Poetica?" begins with a statement about poetics: "I have always aspired to a more spacious form / that would be free from the claims of poetry or prose," suggesting that the poet has an active role in the mediation of the "sublime agonies" "dictated by [the] daimonion." Rather than reducing his work to some form of recondite ahistoricism, however, Milosz's description of poetry in these terms emphasizes the preeminent importance of the questioning voice, the philosophical stance, in his work. "Poetry witnesses us," he argues in "Starting from My Europe" (Milosz, 1983). Milosz's poetic project, therefore, provokes questions about the nature of poetry and its place in the world, forcing us in the process to reconsider those prejudices and opinions that we frequently intractably hold, neither confirming nor denying what we already know but persistently challenging us to rethink, in the general sense, the meaning of "Ars Poetica."

PHILIP COLEMAN

**Further Reading**

Czarnecka, Ewa, and Aleksander Fiut, *Podrozny Swiata: Rozmowy z Czeslawem Miloszem,* New York: Bicentennial, 1983; as *Conversations with Czeslaw Milosz,* translated by Richard Lourie, San Diego, California, and London: Harcourt Brace Jovanovich, 1987

Milosz, Czeslaw, *The Witness of Poetry,* Cambridge, Massachusetts: Harvard University Press, 1983

# Campo dei Fiori

Composed in war-torn Poland in the spring of 1943, "Campo dei Fiori" was first published in the underground anthology *From the Abyss* in 1944. The anthology, which was created by poets living in Nazi-occupied Warsaw and dedicated to the city's Jewish inhabitants, did not reach the shores of the United States until 1945. The poem also appeared in Milosz's *Ocalenie* (1945; Rescue), was later republished in *The Collected Poems, 1931–1987* (1988), and is now posted on the website of the Museum of Tolerance Multimedia Learning Center in the exhibition "Dignity and Defiance: The Confrontation of Life and Death in the Warsaw Ghetto." The poem's calm mood belies its darker thematic messages, creating a subtle irony typical of much of Czeslaw Milosz's work. The discrepancy between the speaker's lucid tone and the horrific suffering the poem treats as its subject results in an unsettling juxtaposition with which the audience, as well as the poem's persona, must come to terms. This opposition is reinforced throughout the poem by the juxtaposition of concrete images against abstract meditations and reflections as well as by the way the poem contrasts the individual or personal life against a larger historical background.

Interested in helping Western audiences understand the character of his native Eastern Europe, Milosz often seeks ways of bridging the gap between East and West, as he does in "Campo dei Fiori" by beginning the poem in contemporary Italy before moving the setting to wartime Poland. The Campo dei Fiori is a famous square frequented by tourists in Rome; Milosz perhaps draws on the square's popularity as an invitation to his Western audience and renders the stanza doubly enticing by filling it with bright, almost cliché images that appeal to the senses: "baskets of olives and lemons," "rose-pink fish; / armfuls of dark grapes / heaped on peach-down." Thus the reader is shocked after learning in the second stanza that a man was burned by a mob "on this same square." Indeed, the rest of the poem casts a kind of shadow back on the first stanza; a rereading of the poem's opening reveals the darker connotations of "splattered," "wreckage," "dark," "heaped," and "peach-down." Even in these ostensibly innocuous opening lines, the poem prepares the reader for the splattered blood, the wreckage of war, heaped corpses, and lives ended in youth that are broached later in the work.

In the year 1600, the Italian philosopher Giordano Bruno was burned at the stake in Campo dei Fiori for refusing to renounce astronomical theories that clashed with Church ideology. Milosz alludes to this event both to emphasize the suffering of a man condemned for his ideas and to comment on the ultimate indifference of the people who witnessed Bruno's execution. As Milosz envisions it, "Before the flames had died / the taverns were full again." The allusion to Bruno also underscores Milosz's broader concern with the ideological struggle between rationalism and religious faith as exemplified in the philosophy of St. Thomas Aquinas.

In the third stanza, the poem jumps to analogous events in 1940s wartime Poland, where Milosz himself witnessed the brutalities of the Nazi occupation. As Polish residents attend a carnival in Warsaw, a nearby Jewish ghetto (sealed off from the main city by walls) is burned, and its inhabitants are killed: "The bright melody [of a carnival tune] drowned / the salvos from the ghetto wall." The points seem obvious: the general populace is ignorant of or indifferent to the suffering of others, and tragedy and beauty exist side by side in our world. Indeed, the carnival goers in the fourth stanza are actually entertained by the ashes floating in the sky: the sky-carousel riders "caught petals in midair"—petals here being a metonymic trope for ashes issuing from the burning ghetto—and the "same hot wind" that issued from the burning ghetto also "blew open the skirts of the girls" enjoying themselves at the carnival.

Lest the reader should be too quick to conclude with simple didactic lessons from such figures, juxtapositions, and analogies, Milosz in the fifth stanza forestalls the most obvious glosses precisely by making them explicit:

Someone will read as moral
that the people of Rome or Warsaw
haggle, laugh, make love
as they pass by martyrs' pyres.
Someone else will read
of the passing of things human,
of the oblivion
born before the flames have died.

By explicitly stating the major themes of the poem, Milosz preempts the audience's finalization of the work; while not denying the truth or accuracy of such conclusions, Milosz suggests that there are other messages he wishes to convey. The fifth stanza is an act of self-reflection on the poet's part that perhaps reflects his desire to extend the poem beyond the obvious interpretations.

Thus, in the final three stanzas of "Campo dei Fiori," Milosz meditates on "the loneliness of the dying"—a state of alienation or utter distance brought about not so much by the fact of death as by the fact that it is impossible for the dying to express their feelings about it. The condemned Bruno, for instance, "could not find / in any human tongue / words for mankind" as he faced death, nor, Milosz says, can any person facing imminent death communicate to others what he or she is experiencing, for "our tongue becomes for them / the forgotten language of an ancient planet." Ultimately, the final stanza acknowledges, hope rests only with the poet figure who, moved by the plight of human suffering and dying, is compelled to write about it and so, Milosz believes, "kindle" "rage" in his or her audience.

JOHN PARRAS

**Further Reading**

Fiut, Aleksander, *Moment Wieczny: Poezja Czeslawa Milosza,* Paris: Libella, 1987; as *The Eternal Moment: The Poetry of Czeslaw Milosz,* translated by Theodosia S. Robertson, Berkeley: University of California Press, 1990

Milosz, Czeslaw, "Campo dei Fiori," Simon Wiesenthal Center Multimedia Learning Center Online: Museum of Tolerance Multimedia Learning Center Online: "Dignity and Defiance: The Confrontation of Life and Death in the Warsaw Ghetto" (*http://motlc.wiesenthal.org/exhibits/dignitydefiance/18.html*)

Milosz, Czeslaw, Zniewolony umysl, Paris: Instytut Literacki, 1953; as *The Captive Mind,* translated by Jane Zielonko, London: Secker and Warburg, and New York: Knopf, 1953

Milosz, Czeslaw, *The History of Polish Literature,* New York: Macmillan, 1969; 2nd edition, Berkeley: University of California Press, 1983

Milosz, Czeslaw, *The Witness of Poetry,* Cambridge, Massachusetts: Harvard University Press, 1983

Mozejko, Edward, editor, *Between Anxiety and Hope: The Poetry and Writing of Czeslaw Milosz,* Edmonton: University of Alberta Press, 1988

Nathan, Leonard, "Czeslaw Milosz: The Laureate of Exiles," *Georgia Review* 49, no. 1 (Spring 1995)

Nathan, Leonard, and Arthur Quinn, *The Poet's Work: An Introduction to Czeslaw Milosz,* Cambridge, Massachusetts: Harvard University Press, 1992

# Modernism

The adjective "modern," says the *Oxford English Dictionary,* means "of or pertaining to the present and recent times," and it derives from the Latin *modo,* "just now." "Modern" was apparently first used by an English writer in 1585, and it has generated two nouns that are crucial to discussions of cultural history: "modernity" and "Modernism." All of us experience our lives as a succession of temporal moments: we have no choice but to live in "the present," and for each of us "now" is constantly changing. However, when we speak of "the modern age" or of "modernity" (earliest recorded appearance in 1627), our experience of temporality becomes self-conscious, a condition that can be grasped and discussed in the abstract rather than merely a sequence of moments. "Modernity" further implies a determinate historical period in which, presumably, entire societies have become acutely conscious of temporality and change, of an inescapable contrast between "then" and "now."

In modernity, change, the calling into question of all traditional certainties, becomes the enduring condition of our experience. The experience of modernity is usually accompanied by a sense, sometimes inculcated by a systematic barrage of propaganda, that "now" represents an advance over "then," that history is a record of "progress." Nevertheless, modernity often induces a state of acute anxiety. In modernity, Marx and Engels suggested in the *Communist Manifesto,* "all that is solid melts into air," as the traditional sanctities binding together parent and child, master and servant, give way to capitalist relations of production. (For a rich development of this theme, see Marshall Berman's classic book [1982].) The result is a constant erosion of those networks of relationship, localized in both space and time, that have traditionally created for human beings a sense of personal identity and mutual trust. For these relationships, modernity substitutes, in all spheres of life, impersonal processes administered by "experts."

Is the historical period of modernity over? Have we, in the closing decades of the 20th century, passed beyond modernity and entered a new historical epoch, postmodernity? Increasingly it seems that what we sometimes call "postmodernity" is merely an advanced stage of modernity, marked by the growing hegemony of an electronically disseminated mass culture and a pervasive cynicism about the possibility of social or political change. At the dawn of the 21st century, Western societies appear to have entered such a stage of late modernity—as, meanwhile, less developed regions, such as Central America and Indonesia, are still experiencing the earlier stages of modernity.

When did modernity begin? Recently, the term "early modern" has become the preferred label for what we once called the Renaissance. Presumably, the early modern period was succeeded by a full-blown modernity, with the 18th century as the transition stage. This chronology suggests that modernity is related in some way to the series of revolutions—political, industrial, social, and cultural—that began in the 18th century and rolled through Western societies in the 19th century and on into the 20th. Furthermore, as the "modern" societies of Europe and North America achieved domination over parts of other continents during the 19th century, societies that felt left behind set themselves a conscious goal of "modernization"—thus generating yet a third form of the modern. In different ways, Bismarck's Germany, Atatürk's Turkey, Lenin's Russia, and Nehru's India all pursued the goal of modernization. Now modernity becomes not a condition that simply happens to us but a systematic *project,* requiring a willed marshaling of resources toward a predetermined goal, usually defined in economic and social terms.

"Modernity" and "Modernism" are clearly interrelated, a connection underscored by the title of a scholarly journal founded in the 1990s, *Modernism/Modernity.* Although the two terms overlap, we do need to distinguish between them. According to the *Oxford English Dictionary,* "Modernism" was first used in the current sense in the 1860s. "Modernism" has in turn generated "Modernist," which may be used either as a noun ("the major Modernists") or as an adjective ("a Modernist poet"). The "-ism" suffix tells us that we are here concerned not with a generalized historical condition (as in "modernity") or with a conscious social project (as in "modernization") but rather with an ideological position, a belief system: in its grammatical form, "Modernism" is analogous to words such as "communism," "socialism," "fascism," or "populism," all of which name belief systems. Yet all the examples listed name specifically *political* ideologies, and no political movement has stormed the battlements under the banner of "Modernism." Instead, "Modernism" has come to denote primarily a set of beliefs and attitudes shared by certain writers and other artists.

The shared root suggests that Modernism represents a certain kind of response to modernity, and so we might initially define "Modernism" as *a belief that modern life is an appropriate subject of art and an effort to develop forms of artistic expression appropriate to modernity.* In the closing pages of *A Season in Hell,* a founding moment of Modernism, Rimbaud declares, "il faut être absolument moderne"—"we must be absolutely modern." A few decades later, the speaker of William Carlos Williams' "The Wanderer" cries out, "How shall I be a mirror to this modernity?" Yet at the same time, Modernism is by no means coextensive with modernity. By any definition, the new condition of existence that we call modernity was well established in northern Europe and North America by the beginning of the 19th century, during the artistic epoch generally labeled the "Romantic Period," and writers whom no critic would want to label "Modernists"—for example, Blake, Wordsworth, and Dickens—were already working out a considered response to modernity. Rather, Modernism emerges as a conscious movement only relatively late in the 19th century, as writers and artists begin to employ the label "modern" to describe the condition in which they find themselves living.

Furthermore, if the birth of Modernism postdates by many decades the advent of modernity, the term "Modernism" now seems to describe an epoch that has ended. Frederick R. Karl, for example, dates the epoch of Modernism as 1885 to 1925; and, while William R. Everdell sees Modernism as having a somewhat longer life span, he too sees the Modernist moment as now fading into history. The sense that Modernism no longer represents a live artistic option has been reinforced by the emergence of the term "Postmodernism," which possesses a degree of cogency that "postmodernity" lacks. The term "Postmodernism" simply suggests that the Modernist generation has been succeeded by a new generation of artists who are unwilling to go on simply repeating the gestures of the Modernists—and, indeed, the story of art since World War II has been in large measure an attempt to come to terms with the legacy of Modernism.

Some scholars tend to use "Modernism" as a general label for the historical period, implying that artistic/cultural production between 1885 and anywhere from 1925 to 1940 can be subsumed under the general rubric of "Modernism." This tendency is apparent, for example, in a justly famous critical anthology edited in 1976 by Malcolm Bradbury and James McFarlane titled *Modernism: A Guide to European Literature, 1890–1930.* A similar tendency to treat "Modernism" as a period term is apparent in Frank Lentricchia's *Modernist Quartet* (1994), which discusses the work of four American poets: Robert Frost, Wallace Stevens, Ezra Pound, and T.S. Eliot. Lentricchia simply assumes that we will all accept "Modernist" as an appropriate label for these poets. In practice, he sees all four of his poets as responding to a common cultural situation characterized by a growing split between the arts and the accelerating engine of mass production. However, for Lentricchia, it appears that anyone caught up in that situation was a "Modernist," no matter how he or she chose to respond to that split.

Other scholars—such as William Everdell and Peter Nicholls—attempt to give content to the label "Modernism" by using it to describe some specific currents running through the artistic world of the last decades of the 19th century and the first decades of the 20th. The work of literary critics such as Hugh Kenner and Marjorie Perloff, even when they are not specifically addressing the word "Modernism," has also served to give content to this concept. This article will follow the precedent of these critics in treating "Modernism" as a label, not for everything that happened in the arts during the early 20th century, but rather for certain deliberate efforts to remake the formal vocabulary of the arts, in ways that would be appropriate to the experience of modernity.

It makes a good deal of sense to group together as "Modernists" the composers Schoenberg, Bartók, and Ives, the painters Seurat, Picasso, and Dove, the poets Apollinaire, Lorca, and Eliot, the dramatists Pirandello, Brecht, and O'Neill, or the novelists Joyce, Proust, and Faulkner (at least the Faulkner of the 1930s). However, is it really useful to apply this label to such contemporaries as the American painters Thomas Hart Benton and Norman Rockwell, the novelists Maxim Gorky and Theodore Dreiser, the composers Sir Edward Elgar and Howard Hanson—or the poets Robert Frost and Edwin Arlington Robinson? To suggest that Robinson and Frost might not have been Modernists is by no means to denigrate the value of their work. However, it does seem useful to distinguish between the poets and other artists who sought to create new forms suited to what they saw as new forms of human experience—that is, the experience of modernity—and those who regarded inherited artistic forms as perfectly adequate to present a human experience that is implicitly defined as eternal and unchanging.

As Christopher Butler points out in *Early Modernism: Literature, Music, and Painting in Europe, 1900–1916* (1994), the early decades of the 20th century saw the emergence of a generation of "heroic figures . . . Matisse, Picasso, Stravinsky, Schoenberg, Marinetti, Pound, Eliot, Apollinaire—[who] developed radically new conventions for their respective arts." A range of formal vocabularies that had endured since the Renaissance all came into question during this period: in painting, the illusion of three-dimensional space, constructed through the application of the "laws" of perspective; in music, the diatonic scale with its attendant harmonies; in fiction, the linear narrative and the controlling authorial point of view; and in poetry, the metrical line and the unitary lyric voice.

The first symptoms of the breakup of these formal vocabularies can be detected in the mid- to late 19th century. The Impressionist movement in painting had already subordinated the illusion of the object in space to "an aesthetic of painting—to light, to the harmony of tones, to the vibrant pattern of brushstrokes, and to novel freedom of composition" (Schapiro, 1997). In the 1890s, Mahler was exploring new tonal possibilities, while Henry James and Joseph Conrad opened up new narrative perspectives in fiction. As early as the poetry of Whitman and Rimbaud, one finds new rhythmic measures and a calling into question of traditional notions of lyric subjectivity. These new artistic possibilities came to a head in the years before World War I, with Cubism and Fauvism in painting, atonality in music, and the radical experiments in narrative perspective of Proust and Joyce. In poetry, the important shifts were the efforts by Pound and others to "break the back of the iamb" and the use of collage and other nonlinear methods of juxtaposition to open up what Marjorie Perloff calls a "poetics of indeterminacy," a poetry that would explore new kinds of relationships between the signifier and the signified.

In addition to calling into question traditional artistic forms, Modernism also redefined the relationships among the arts and among national cultures. From the beginning, Modernist innovators in the various arts were often in dialogue with one another, as suggested by, for example, the rich tradition of commentary on French painting by poets from Baudelaire to Apollinaire. So too, Ezra Pound, inevitably at the center of any discussion of American Modernist poetry, wrote a substantial quantity of music and art criticism, while American Modernists as different as Gertrude Stein and Williams assembled significant collections of modern paintings. It is also striking that the rich critical literature on Frost includes no books on his relationship to the visual arts, as contrasted to at least five books on the role of the visual arts in Williams' poetry (by Dijkstra, Schmidt, Diggory, MacGowan, and Sayre).

As for the international scope of Modernism, it is significant that many American Modernists were expatriates, as Pound, Eliot, H.D., and Stein all chose to live in Europe. Others, including Williams, sought opportunities to pay briefer visits to the continent; and Williams, Stevens, and Marianne Moore lived near New York City, the primary contact point for Americans with what was happening in Europe. The writings of the American Modernists also have identifiable affiliations with transnational literary movements. Thus, Eliot's work can usefully be read in relationship to French symbolism, while Williams' work has affinities with both French and Spanish surrealism. In contrast, Frost's decision to reject London and return to New England seems to be the key moment in his poetic career, and it would seem gratuitous at best to try to read the work of Robinson and Frost in relationship to such transnational movements as surrealism.

At this point, then, we may offer a more refined definition of "Modernism" as *an international movement that cut across all the arts and sought to create new formal vocabularies adequate to the experience of modernity.* As already noted, the definition proposed here challenges the widespread tendency to use "Modernism" as a period label. Furthermore, this definition also implicitly disputes a narrower conception of Modernism (as developed by, for example, Ricardo Quinones) that essentially equates it with a tradition of closed, "impersonal" literary works. This critical tradition emphasizes the ways in which Modernism represents a break with Romanticism, and it tends to see Stephen

Dedalus' theory of the autonomous work of art, as outlined in Joyce's *A Portrait of the Artist as a Young Man* (1916), as central to Modernism.

A tendency to view so-called "High" Modernism as an essentially conservative movement is also apparent in Matei Calinescu's attempt to draw a sharp line between Modernism and the avant-garde. When Calinescu finds in any artwork a spirit of radical critique, he labels that work avant-garde, for he assumes that by definition the ethos of Modernism is essentially conservative. So too, Ihab Hassan's famous dichotomy of Modernism and Postmodernism sees Modernism as a reactionary movement characterized by "Romanticism/Symbolism, Form (conjunctive, closed), Purpose, Design, Hierarchy, Mastery/Logos, Art Object/Finished Work, Distance, Creation/Totalization/Synthesis" in contrast to a Postmodernism defined by "Pataphysics/Dadaism, Antiform (disjunctive, open), Play, Chance, Anarchy, Exhaustion/Silence, Process/Performance/Happening, Participation, Decreation/Deconstruction/Antithesis" (Hassan, 1986). Unfortunately for Hassan's neat dichotomy, the poetry of Pound, Williams, the Eliot of *The Waste Land,* Moore, and other putatively Modernist writers displays, at least intermittently, most of the qualities that he would associate with Postmodernism. While rejecting a broad conception of Modernism as encompassing everything that happened in the early decades of the 20th century, then, the definition proposed here also rejects theories such as Hassan's that would reduce Modernism as uniform and highly conservative.

The attempts of critics such as Quinones, Calinescu, and Hassan to draw narrow boundaries around Modernism result in large measure from a failure to recognize the complexity of this movement. On this score, Peter Nicholls' brilliant 1995 book *Modernisms* offers a useful alternative model. He suggests that we can distinguish two primary currents within literary Modernism, one deriving from Baudelaire and the other from Rimbaud. The Baudelairian mode is essentially ironic. The Baudelairian poet confronts a social reality that has become irresolvably alien, insofar as its "surface momentum conceals its inner sameness, its unceasing production of the safe limits of the bourgeois world" (Nicholls, 1995). The threat posed by this world is the loss of what Walter Benjamin called "aura," the uniqueness of the work of art, as all commodities become copies of something else and as people too become commodities. Baudelaire responds to this alien social world by assuming the posture of the "dandy," whose every gesture displays the ineffable superiority of his own taste and his contempt for the mass culture created by bourgeois society. However, the dandy knows that he will ultimately lose since he stands alone against the mob, and so his posture "suggests that irony is a necessary defence against modernity even as it seems to assume that to be distinctively modern the poet must be ironic" (Nicholls, 1995).

However, there is, Nicholls suggests, a second current within Modernism, ecstatic rather than ironic, represented by Rimbaud. Baudelaire's self-lacerating ironies are encased within traditional poetic forms, but Rimbaud abandons these forms along with the traditional lyric "I," so that the "half-fascinated, half-anguished self-scrutiny of the Baudelairian dandy" gives way to "an expansive opening of the ego which projects a writing freed from the necessity of self-defence" (Nicholls, 1995). In the subsequent history of Modernism, the ironic, Baudelairian heritage is emphasized by critics such as Quinones, while Calinescu would label Rimbaud as an exemplar of the avant-garde or even the postmodern. However, Nicholls' model emphasizes the ways in which these two tendencies intertwine, allowing us to see how, for example, Eliot's high-Mandarin postures only half conceal certain subversive, anarchic (and intermittently homoerotic) forces working beneath the surface.

According to the definition proposed here, then, what American poets can usefully be read as Modernists? A provisional list must include Ezra Pound (clearly, as Hugh Kenner argues in *The Pound Era* [1971], central to any discussion of American Modernism) and his friends and associates William Carlos Williams, Marianne Moore, H.D., T.S. Eliot, and E.E. Cummings. In addition, other American poets who have been or could be read as Modernists include Gertrude Stein, Wallace Stevens, Mina Loy, Hart Crane, Melvin Tolson, and Laura Riding (despite her attack on so-called Modernism in the 1927 pamphlet that she co-authored with Robert Graves). Langston Hughes, Charles Reznikoff, and Louis Zukofsky stand on the outer edge of this Modernist generation, ambiguously Modernist and "Postmodernist." It may also be useful to define a school of "Chicago Modernists," including Carl Sandburg, Edgar Lee Masters, and Vachel Lindsay; for although these poets contributed no useful formal inventions to American poetry and have therefore been of steadily diminishing interest to later generations, they did consciously set out to make their poetry a mirror of modernity, and they were Modernists at least in their chosen subject matter.

The definition of Modernism proposed here encompasses the work of all these poets and helps bring into focus what is distinctive about their work. At the same time, it is important to note that the list does not include several notable American poets who were more or less contemporary with those listed, including Edwin Arlington Robinson, Robert Frost, Robinson Jeffers, John Crowe Ransom, Edna St. Vincent Millay, Louise Bogan, Allen Tate, and Yvor Winters, the last of whom began as a Modernist poet but later consciously rejected the Modernist mode. Frost, for example, remained committed to an iambic-based metric, his work does not call into question the position of the lyric subject, and his quest for a stable center of values suggests a rejection of modernity itself. In all these ways, his work falls outside the definition of Modernism proposed here.

Modernism in the broad sense was a utopian movement, seeking to create a new culture that would allow humans to come to terms with modernity. This utopian impulse is perhaps most fully evident in the Bauhaus movement in Germany and in Modernist architecture in general. A classic statement of utopian Modernism as extending across all the arts is *Foundations of Modern Art* (1928) by Amédée Ozenfant. The new culture envisioned by the Bauhaus members and by Ozenfant has clearly not come to pass. Instead, both the rise of Fascism in the first half of the 20th century (in a symbolic moment, Hitler closed the Bauhaus in one of his first acts after coming to power) and then, in the last half of the century, the resurgence of various kinds of fundamentalisms, all promising a recovery of the certainties of premodernity, attest to the failure of the Modernist project.

Only in the visual arts did Modernism even partially fulfill its promise. The vast audiences that turn out for shows of the work of Van Gogh and Matisse suggest that Modernist painting did indeed persuade large numbers of people to see the world in new ways, and most histories of 20th-century art are in fact histories of Modernism in art. Modernist poetry, in contrast, has never won for itself a mass audience, and whatever poetry survives as part of mass culture (greeting card verse, country and western music, rap, and "slam" poetry) generally eschews Modernist forms in favor of rhyme and meter. The Modernist poets created an arcane, difficult art, and they challenged their readers to rise to a new level of understanding. A Modernist poet such as Pound insists that his readers should know everything that he knows, and *The Cantos* carries the implication that any reader who does not recognize all the references is unforgivably ignorant. However, only a small band of devoted cultists has had the energy or the desire to rise to this challenge posed by Pound's poem. Born out of an impulse to shock the bourgeoisie, Modernist poetry continues to startle, challenge, and offend, and the reading public has repaid the poets with a general indifference: indeed, it has recently become fashionable to blame the Modernists for destroying the audience for poetry.

Nevertheless, we can distinguish among later American poets a distinct lineage that has followed the precedent established by the Modernists, including the Objectivists, the members of the Black Mountain School, the poets of the San Francisco Renaissance, the poets of the New York School, and the Language poets. These later groups of poets have sometimes criticized the Modernists for clinging to the Romantic cult of the "genius"—the sense that the poet stands apart from ordinary mortals as an "unacknowledged legislator of mankind." The heirs of the Modernists have also often criticized the prevalence of racist and sexist stereotypes among their predecessors. For example, anti-Semitism scars the writings not only of Pound but also of Eliot, Williams, and Cummings. In the notorious case of Pound, racism, sexism, and the cult of the genius combined into an explicit Fascism, and Eliot's political and social views are only a little less distasteful.

However, while critiquing the retrograde social attitudes of some of the Modernists, poets such as Louis Zukofsky, Charles Olson, Robert Duncan, Frank O'Hara, Susan Howe, and hundreds of other poets have also preserved a commitment to the open poetic forms pioneered by the Modernists. These younger writers have recognized in the formal innovations of the Modernist masters a way of opening the poem itself to the tides of history and to the steadily widening possibilities of experience that modernity has brought to us. Thus, the efforts of the Modernists to "make it new" have served as an example of a rigorous commitment to the craft of poetry. In addition, the Modernists have left an invaluable repository of specific poetic strategies on which poets continue to draw as we enter the 21st century.

BURTON HATLEN

**Further Reading**


Berman, Marshall, *All That Is Solid Melts into Air: The Experience of Modernity,* New York: Simon and Schuster, 1982; 2nd edition, London: Verso, 1983

Bradbury, Malcolm, and James McFarlane, editors, *Modernism: A Guide to European Literature, 1890–1930,* New York and London: Penguin, 1991

Butler, Christopher, *Early Modernism: Literature, Music, and Painting in Europe, 1900–1916,* Oxford: Clarendon Press, 1994

Calinescu, Matei, *Faces of Modernity: Avant-Garde, Decadence, Kitsch,* Bloomington: Indiana University Press, 1977; revised edition as *Five Faces of Modernity: Modernism, Avant-Garde, Decadence, Kitsch, Postmodernism,* Durham, North Carolina: Duke University Press, 1987

Everdell, William R., *The First Moderns: Profiles in the Origins of Twentieth-Century Thought,* Chicago: University of Chicago Press, 1997

Hassan, Ihab, "The Culture of Postmodernism," in *Modernism: Challenges and Perspectives,* edited by Monique Chefdor, Ricardo Quinones, and Albert Wachtel, Urbana: University of Illinois Press, 1986

Karl, Frederick R., *Modern and Modernism: The Sovereignty of the Artist, 1885–1925,* New York: Atheneum, 1985

Kenner, Hugh, *The Pound Era,* Berkeley: University of California Press, 1971; London: Faber, 1972

Lentricchia, Frank, *Modernist Quartet,* Cambridge and New York: Cambridge University Press, 1994

Nicholls, Peter, *Modernisms: A Literary Guide,* Berkeley: University of California Press, and London: Macmillan, 1995

Ozenfant, Amédée, *Art,* Paris: Budry, 1928; as *Foundations of Modern Art,* translated by John Rodker, New York: Brewer Warren and Putnam, and London: Rodker, 1931

Perloff, Marjorie, *The Poetics of Indeterminacy: Rimbaud to Cage,* Princeton, New Jersey: Princeton University Press, 1981

Perloff, Marjorie, *The Futurist Moment: Avant-Garde, Avant Guerre, and the Language of Rupture,* Chicago: University of Chicago Press, 1986

Quinones, Ricardo J., *Mapping Literary Modernism: Time and Development,* Princeton, New Jersey: Princeton University Press, 1985

Schapiro, Meyer, *Impressionism: Reflections and Perceptions,* New York: Braziller, 1997


---

# Marianne Moore 1887–1972

Marianne Moore is distinctively difficult yet paradoxically inclusive and inviting. Her most famous "ars poetica" begins, "I, too, dislike it," anticipating (even identifying with) a peeved reader of modern poetry ("Poetry"). As the poem explains, "we / do not admire what / we cannot understand." Moore's poems cannot be mistaken for anyone else's. William Carlos Williams praised her poems as "not easy to quote convincingly" ("Spring & All" [1923], in *Imaginations,* 1970). Moore, also a favorite of Eliot, H.D., and Pound, stands out as a bold innovator in Modernism. Asserting the primacy of individual voice, she aspires to an "intonation of gusto" that aims toward "a magnetism, an ardor, a refusal to be false" ("The Accented Syllable," *The Complete Prose,* 1986).

Like other aspects of Moore's work, her publication history is complicated. Her *Collected Poems,* first published in 1951, does not reflect her many variants and her ongoing revision of poems throughout her career. (One dramatic instance of this appears in *The Complete Poems of Marianne Moore* [1967]: "Poetry," a three-line version of the original 30-line poem from 1919, is happily included in the "Notes.") She began publishing poems in 1915 in *The Egoist, Poetry,* and *Others,* the most forerunning magazines of her time. By 1921, her first volume, *Poems,* was published in England by the Egoist Press. *Observations,* her next book, emerged in two slightly different editions in 1924 and then in 1925. Moore's 1935 *Selected Poems* is generally recognized as her most significant collection, comprised of work from her earlier volumes and poems written between 1929 and 1935. Her poems between 1915 and 1920 and again between 1932 and 1936 are in syllabics, a prosody uncommon in English; otherwise, her poems are free verse.

From 1925 to 1929, Moore served as editor of the eminent journal *The Dial.* During this period, she became an arbiter of critical tastes in her almost 200 pieces, including reviews of the work of her contemporaries Stevens, Eliot, Cummings, H.D., and Williams. These essays, along with critical prose on multiple subjects written throughout her career, are collected in *The Complete Prose* (1986). For Moore, the function of criticism was to illuminate texts and to protect them from an insensitive public allegorized in her 1915 "To a Steam Roller": "You crush all the particulars down / into close conformity." While Moore published no poetry during her years at *The Dial,* her essays enacted methods similar to those of her poems and provide the terms by which to appreciate them. Characterized by diverse allusions, her "impressionistic" style reflected, chameleon-like, the writing of those she reviewed. Making it her policy to review only those works she could praise, the basis for her criticism was one of sympathy.

Most critics concur that Moore wrote her best poetry before 1940. However, she published several other volumes, including *The Pangolin, and Other Verse* (1936), *What Are Years?* (1941), and *Nevertheless* (1944). In addition, in 1954 she published a translation of *The Fables of La Fontaine,* a major undertaking that took eight years to finish. By the 1950s, after her *Collected Poems* won the Bollingen Prize, the National Book Award, and the Pulitzer Prize, Moore was established as a key Modernist, and her work became regularly anthologized and the subject of critical studies.

Like Dickinson before her and Plath after her, Moore is often mythologized for her eccentricities. Among her signatures in the 1950s were her donning a black tricorn hat (in George Washington style) and her avid following of the Brooklyn Dodgers. Her work remains, nevertheless, private (this partly accounts for the many images of armor and weaponry in her work) and accords with the Modernist rejection of a romantic emphasis on feeling and self. Moore's cool dissection of external phenomena usurps the sentimental models of the woman poetess of the 19th century. While Moore is subtly subversive and feminist, as in her long 1923 poem "Marriage" ("experience attests / that men have power / and sometimes one is made to feel it"), she seems to willfully obscure her gender.

Since Moore was absorptive of multiple influences and a voracious reader, it is difficult to fix her lineage. She named Montaigne, Molière, and Chaucer as the figures most formative of her sensibility. When asked by Pound for her influences, she listed the visual artist Gordon Craig, Thomas Hardy, Henry James, and the minor prophets of the Bible. An inveterate collector, Moore constantly transplants language from its familiar settings. Moore has been aptly called a "kleptomaniac of the mind" to describe her innovative wide-ranging use of material from multiple sources (Costello, 1981). Unlike Eliot, who "steals" from the high-cultural archive of literary tradition, Moore freely borrows from scientific journals, fashion magazines, travel guides, museum pamphlets, personal letters, overheard conversations, and literary texts. ("Four Quartz Crystal Clocks" uses language almost verbatim from an advertisement enclosed in a telephone bill.) The poet filled and indexed multiple "commonplace books" with quotations she did not want to lose. Moore uses quotations not to fortify some monumental vision but to constellate otherwise disparate elements. In collagist fashion, she will at times use only a portion of a quotation. For instance, she uses a fragment of a Tolstoy sentence to assert an opposite meaning to what his full sentence declares; her alteration claims, "'nor is it valid / to discriminate against business documents and // school-books'" ("Poetry," 1919). Like Whitman and Williams, Moore widens the scope of what is considered suitable poetic material.

"Silence" (1924), a 14-line poem in which 11 and a half lines are enclosed in quotation marks, begins with the phrase "My father used to say" (also not her own). Her ironically verbose quotation ends in the sentence "'The deepest feeling always shows itself in silence; / not in silence, but restraint.'" The quotation reveals as it conceals and is characteristic of Moore's layering, self-modifying style. The "deepest feeling" remains opaque. Despite Moore's gift for precision, her poems rarely emerge from direct experience. Even "An Octopus" (1924), inspired by her visit to Mount Rainier in Washington State, relies heavily on an information pamphlet provided by the Forest Service. Quotations become one way of restraining personal revelation while also remaining true to its fragmentation.

Many of Moore's poems comment on the artistic process of making experience aesthetic or the inverse, of constructing "'imaginary gardens with real toads in them'" ("Poetry," 1919). Precisely designed and controlled, Moore's forms are never perfect but point to their own idiosyncratic structure. An arborealist performing delicate acts of flight and synthesis, she moves between the erudite and the colloquial, the learned observation and the immediate perception, the distant to the more personal, from abstract assertion to minute particular, as with this characteristic passage from "Critics and Connoisseurs" (1916):

> There is a great amount of poetry in unconscious
> fastidiousness. Certain Ming
> products, imperial floor-coverings of coach-
> wheel yellow, are well enough in their way but I have seen
> something
>
> that I like better—a
> mere childish attempt to make an imperfectly bal-
> lasted animal stand up,
> similar determination to make a pup
> eat his meat from a plate.

I remember a swan under the willows in Oxford,
    with flamingo-colored, maple-
        leaflike feet. It reconnoitered like a battle-
    ship.

Shifting between the myopic and the farsighted, the ground of her many-faceted poems is never entirely stable. Her associative logic and enjambments suspend us between stanzas.

Moore's bold experimentalism is evident early on in her arrangement of words. She reinvents syllabics, varying the number of syllables in each line in a stanza, and then, with mathematical precision, repeats the pattern in consecutive stanzas. This self-acknowledged "counter" movement liberates words from their syntax and sets them on the page as visual linguistic paste. As in the previous passage, she innovates in line breaks, dividing "bal- / lasted. "Those Various Scalpels" (1919) defamiliarizes her anatomized subject whose hair, for example, becomes "the tails of two / fighting-cocks head to head in stone— / like sculptured scimitars." The weapons are Moore's as she sharply divides her edgy lines. "The Fish" (1921), her first animal poem, crystallizes her ongoing concern with the relationship between artifice and nature. Through syllabics and an elaborate rhyme scheme, even single words (articles or parts of words) are granted their own lines. The poem, with its interior rhymes and consonantal crispness, itself becomes a "defiant edifice," with "all the physical features of ac- / cident—lack," expressive of its creator's temperament, a survivor's gusto.

Moore's nature is never completely natural but is self-consciously filtered through her idiosyncratic sensibility. "The Steeple-Jack" (1932) traverses the natural and the aesthetic to produce a fluid, sinuous syntax: "a sea the purple of the peacock's neck is / paled to greenish azure as Durer changed / the pine green of the Tyrol to peacock blue and guinea / gray." The function of art is not to impose order; instead, "it is a privilege to see so much confusion." In a virtuoso catalog, another of Moore's notable tactics, she out-Whitmans Whitman in ecstatic inclusivity. The first of several stanzas will here have to suffice:

                                the trumpet-vine,
fox-glove, giant snap-dragon, a salpiglossis that has
spots and stripes; morning-glories, gourds,
or moon-vines trained on fishing twine

Her lexicon is heterogeneous, spanning the human, animal, and vegetable worlds ("crab-claw ragged sailors with greenbracts—toad-plant"). Moore delights in nature but moreover in the fecundity of language.

In her second syllabic phase between 1932 and 1936, Moore expands her menagerie of animal poems (which attain generic status in her work). These creatures, often "supreme in their abnormality" ("The Monkeys") and given emblematic, moral significance, can express the poet's sense of personal isolation, struggle, or idiosyncratic difference. For instance, her "unconfiding frigate-bird hides / in the height and in the majestic / display of his art" and in flying is "able to foil the tired / moment of danger" ("The Frigate Pelican"). This bird is "seldom successless" because it "realizes Rasselas's friend's project / of wings uniting levity and strength." "The Plumet Basilisk" admires the creature's "regal and excellent awkwardness." "The Pangolin," perhaps Moore's most famous poem about "Another armored animal," highlights it as neglected artisan: "the night miniature artist engineer is, / yes, Leonardo da Vinci's replica—/ impressive animal and toiler of whom we seldom hear." Animals survive, and through them we discover fortitude as well as peculiarity: "Among animals, one has a sense of humour. / Humour saves a few steps, it saves years" ("The Pangolin").

While Moore's immediate themes are not monumental, her poems reflect an intense examination of mortality and its bearing on aesthetics. "A Grave," a poem inspired by the sinking of the *Lusitania,* dispels the romance of the sea and her own activity ("[it] is a collector, quick to return a rapacious look"), explicit about our denial, "as if it were not that ocean in which / dropped things are bound to sink." "No Swan So Fine" (1932) further associates possession with an art object's deathliness:

                        No swan,
with swart blind look askance
and gondeliering legs, so fine
    as the chintz china one with fawn-
brown eyes and toothed gold
collar on to show whose bird it was.

Moore's return to syllabics in the 1930s registers a heightened anxiety, as subdued as it is palpable, about containment. "The Steeple-Jack" offers this ominous scene: "on a sidewalk / a sign says C.J. Poole, Steeple-Jack, / in black and white; and one in red / and white says / Danger." The "danger" remains unspecified but related to the difficulty of living in a world with only nominal faith: "he is gilding the solid- / pointed star, which on a steeple / stands for hope."

Moore is a major figure. She manages to navigate between the extremely polarized positions of Williams, in his iconoclastic disavowal of tradition in favor of the American landscape, and of Eliot, in his reverence for the European past and its literary monuments. The most significant immediate influence Moore exerted was on Elizabeth Bishop, whose early career was shaped by her friendship with the older poet. Bishop inherits a close scrutiny of objects along with an interrogation of their stability. Moore's unique lineation and use of quotation and space has made her an important influence on postmodern poets, including Alice Notley, Kathleen Fraser, and Jorie Graham. Moore remains a spur to invention.

SUSAN MCCABE

**Biography**

Born in Kirkwood, Missouri, 15 November 1887. Attended Bryn Mawr College, Pennsylvania, 1905–09, A.B. 1909; Carlisle Commercial College, Pennsylvania, 1909–10, diploma 1910; head of Commercial Studies Department, United States Industrial Indian School, Carlisle, 1911–15; private tutor and secretary, New York, 1918–21; part-time librarian, Hudson Park Branch, New York Public Library, 1921–25; acting editor, 1925, and editor, 1926–29, *The Dial;* teacher, Cummington School, Massachusetts, 1942; Visiting Lecturer, Bryn Mawr College, 1953; Ewing Lecturer, University of California, 1956. Received *Dial* Award, 1924; Levinson Prize (*Poetry,* Chicago), 1933; Hartsook Memorial Prize, 1935; Shelley Memorial Award, 1941; Harriet Monroe Poetry Award, 1944; Guggenheim fellowship, 1945; American Academy grant, 1946, and Gold Medal, 1953; Pulitzer Prize, 1952; National Book

Award, 1952; Bollingen Prize, 1952; Poetry Society of America Gold Medal, 1960, 1967; Brandeis University Creative Arts Award, 1962; Academy of American Poets fellowship, 1965; MacDowell Medal, 1967; National Medal for Literature, 1968; received honorary degrees from 12 colleges and universities; member, American Academy, 1955. Died in New York City, 5 February 1972.

**Poetry**
*Poems,* 1921
*Observations,* 1924; revised edition, 1925
*Selected Poems,* 1935
*The Pangolin, and Other Verse,* 1936
*What Are Years?* 1941
*Nevertheless,* 1944
*Collected Poems,* 1951
*Like a Bulwark,* 1956
*O To Be a Dragon,* 1959
*The Arctic Ox,* 1964
*Tell Me, Tell Me: Granite, Steele, and Other Topics,* 1966
*The Complete Poems of Marianne Moore,* 1967
*Selected Poems,* 1969
*Unfinished Poems,* 1972
*The Complete Poems of Marianne Moore,* edited by Clive E. Driver, 1981

**Selected Criticism**
*Poetry and Criticism,* 1965

**Other Writings:** play, lectures, essays (*The Complete Prose of Marianne Moore,* edited by Patricia C. Willis, 1986), correspondence (*The Selected Letters of Marianne Moore,* 1998), translations of French literature (*The Fables of La Fontaine,* 1954).

**Further Reading**

Costello, Bonnie, *Marianne Moore: Imaginary Possessions,* Cambridge, Massachusetts: Harvard University Press, 1981
Erickson, Darlene Williams, *Illusion Is More Precise than Precision: The Poetry of Marianne Moore,* Tuscaloosa: University of Alabama Press, 1992
Goodridge, Celeste, *Hints and Disguises: Marianne Moore and Her Contemporaries,* Iowa City: University of Iowa Press, 1989
Heuving, Jeanne, *Omissions Are Not Accidents: Gender in the Art of Marianne Moore,* Detroit, Michigan: Wayne State University Press, 1992
Leavell, Linda, *Marianne Moore and the Visual Arts: Prismatic Color,* Baton Rouge: Louisiana State University Press, 1995
Martin, Taffy, *Marianne Moore, Subversive Modernist,* Austin: University of Texas Press, 1986
Miller, Cristanne, *Marianne Moore: Questions of Authority,* Cambridge, Massachusetts: Harvard University Press, 1995
Schulman, Grace, *Marianne Moore: The Poetry of Engagement,* Urbana: University of Illinois Press, 1986
Slatin, John M., *The Savage's Romance: The Poetry of Marianne Moore,* University Park: Pennsylvania State University Press, 1986
Stapleton, Laurence, *Marianne Moore: The Poet's Advance,* Princeton, New Jersey: Princeton University Press, 1978; 2nd printing with corrections, 1978
Willis, Patricia C., *Marianne Moore: Vision into Verse,* Philadelphia, Pennsylvania: Rosenbach Museum and Library, 1987

# The Fish

Marianne Moore's "The Fish" has long garnered the attention of literary critics. T.S. Eliot, in his introduction to Moore's *Selected Poems* (1935), quoted lines from "The Fish" to illustrate Moore's masterful use of "light rhyme," that is, rhyme that works subtly against the syntactic sense of a poem. More recent critics have explored the poem's non-hierarchical structure (Holley) and conspicuous craft (Miller), established it as an example of Cubist technique in poetry (Joyce and Leavell), and even considered its status as a war poem (Slatin and Tramontana). Although "The Fish" is one of Moore's best-known and most-anthologized poems, it continues to intrigue critics and readers. Elusive in its dense juxtaposition of images and complicated in its patterned syllabic stanzas, "The Fish" is both a landmark poem within Moore's oeuvre and an exemplary work of Modernist American poetry.

"The Fish" is an early model of Moore's distinctive combination of syllabic verse—in which line length is determined by the number of syllables, not the number of accentual stresses or metrical feet—and the visual patterning of unique stanzas. The memorable opening of the poem sets the pattern of rhyme, indentation, and line length maintained throughout the poem:

> THE FISH
> wade
> through black jade.
>     Of the crow-blue mussel-shells, one keeps
>     adjusting the ash-heaps;
>         opening and shutting itself like
>
> an
> injured fan.

By making the title double as the first two words of the poem and carrying the enjambment of lines across stanzaic breaks, Moore foregrounds the way in which her stanzaic pattern works independently of her words' syntactic meaning. Linda Leavell (1995) compares Moore's abstracting of form in this way to Cubism's separation of form and content in painting but emphasizes that such abstracted form does not preclude the coordination of syntax and line breaks for emphasis. When, in the penultimate stanza of "The Fish," Moore achieves a monosyllabic first line by dividing "ac- / cident" onto two lines, the conspicuously broken word underscores the "external / marks of abuse" that "stand out on" the cliff described.

Indeed, in the context of the aquatic scene depicted in "The Fish," the tension between Moore's abstract stanzaic pattern and the syntactic flow of her words actually helps reveal some of the poem's concerns. The repetitive actions described in the poem—the mussel-shell "opening and shutting itself," the shafts of sun moving "in and out" of crevices, the assorted marine life forms sliding "each on the other"—are mimicked by the expansion and contraction of lineation as the stanzaic pattern repeats itself. Similarly, the line breaks and heavy enjambment slow the reader's progress through the many images presented, reinforcing the sense of suspended time conveyed by the repeated actions. In these and other ways, the poem's syllabic pattern becomes less arbitrary in relation to the poem's presentation of the eerily beautiful scene.

At the same time, however, there remains in the poem an element of arbitrariness and uncertainty, especially in its concluding statements about destruction and survival:

All
external
    marks of abuse are present on this
    defiant edifice—
        all the physical features of

ac-
cident—lack
    Of cornice, dynamite grooves, burns, and
    hatchet strokes, these things stand
        out on it; the chasm-side is

dead.
Repeated
    evidence has proved that it can live
    on what can not revive
        its youth. The sea grows old in it.

Despite the report-like conclusiveness of these lines, a clear meaning or lesson remains elusive. The damage to the "defiant edifice" described as "dynamite grooves, burns, and / hatchet strokes" sounds very much like the result of deliberate human destruction, not accident. The reader's attempts to grasp the paradox that "it can live / on what can not revive its youth" are thwarted by ambiguity about whether "it" refers only to the cliff as the "defiant edifice" or to the sea as well. The subtle rhymes and syllabic lines carry us promptly to the poem's end, yet the juxtaposed images and statements do not seem to progress to a conclusion so much as present themselves for repeated consideration.

"The Fish," like many of Moore's poems, appeared in versions quite different from the version printed in her *Complete Poems* (1967) and examined here. First published in the August 1918 issue of *The Egoist* in somewhat straightforward four-line stanzas, "The Fish" was composed of eight six-line syllabic stanzas when published in Alfred Kreymborg's *Others for 1919: An Anthology of the New Verse* and in her first two volumes, *Poems* (1921) and *Observations* (1924). By its 1935 appearance in *Selected Poems*, the six-line stanzas had been reduced to five-line stanzas, and "The Fish" had become the version that readers find in the *Complete Poems*. As is the case with other Moore poems, such as "Poetry" and "The Frigate Pelican," tracing the multiple versions of "The Fish" and understanding the contexts and consequences of those versions can yield significant new perspectives. John Slatin (1986), for example, recovers "The Fish" as a war poem of extreme indirection by linking an earlier version of it to a poem with which it is paired in *Observations*. Slatin shows how the opening image of "The Fish" has its metaphoric origin in "Reinforcements," a poem in which men going to war are matter-of-factly and unheroically likened to a school of fish. Other critics have considered how Moore's revisions reflect the shifts in her aesthetic preferences from the late 1910s through the 1930s.

Whether valued as an enigmatic statement about destruction and survival, an inter-artistic translation of Cubist vision into the medium of poetry, or a poem originating in contemplation of war and mortality, "The Fish" addresses issues central to 20th-century poetry. In its innovative rhyme and meter, its treatment of form and content, and its resistance to straightforward interpretation, "The Fish" illuminates the intersecting currents of Modernism and of Moore's distinctive craft.

Catherine Tramontana

**Further Reading**


Costello, Bonnie, *Marianne Moore: Imaginary Possessions,* Cambridge, Massachusetts: Harvard University Press, 1981

Holley, Margaret, *The Poetry of Marianne Moore: A Study in Voice and Value,* Cambridge and New York: Cambridge University Press, 1987

Joyce, Elisabeth W., *Cultural Critique and Abstraction: Marianne Moore and the Avant-Garde,* Lewisburg, Pennsylvania: Bucknell University Press, and London: Associated University Presses, 1998

Leavell, Linda, *Marianne Moore and the Visual Arts: Prismatic Color,* Baton Rouge: Louisiana State University Press, 1995

Miller, Cristanne, *Marianne Moore: Questions of Authority,* Cambridge, Massachusetts: Harvard University Press, 1995

Ranta, Jerrald, "Marianne Moore's Sea and the Sentence," *Essays in Literature* 15, no. 2 (Fall 1988)

Slatin, John M., *The Savage's Romance: The Poetry of Marianne Moore,* University Park: Pennsylvania State University Press, 1986

Tramontana, Catherine, "The Courage of Their Peculiarities: Eccentricity and the Modernist Poetics of Marianne Moore, Edith Sitwell, and E.E. Cummings," Ph.D. Diss., Rutgers, the State University of New Jersey, 2000


# Marriage

Published in 1923, just a year after the appearance of *Ulysses* and *The Waste Land,* Marianne Moore's "Marriage" is a landmark of High Modernism and one of her most ambitious and important works. "Marriage" is a long, complicated collage of statements and quotations regarding the institution of marriage and its problems as well as a critical exploration of gender roles and the relations between men and women. This remarkable masterpiece stands apart from the rest of Moore's work for several reasons: it is her longest and one of her most difficult, experimental works; it is perhaps her most openly feminist poem in its critique of marriage and patriarchy; and with its contradictory attitudes, it is also among her most ambivalent and complex. Critics have argued that the persona that accrued around Moore—the reserved, prim, asexual spinster writer of elegant and moralistic poems—has often obscured the radical energy of her poetry, perhaps best exemplified by this aesthetically and politically subversive poem. In an important essay Moore's friend William Carlos Williams astutely highlighted the poem's kaleidoscopic quality, praising its "rapidity of movement" and calling the poem an "anthology of transit" (Tomlinson, 1969). "There is nothing missing," Williams avowed, "but the connectives." With its jagged discontinuities, sustained indeterminacy, and its iconoclasm, "Marriage" is a classic and influential Modernist poem.

It may seem strange that Moore, who never married, lived most of her life with her mother, and was famously reticent about her personal life, would write a highly regarded poem about marriage and gender dynamics, but in actuality Moore was extremely interested in and troubled by the subject. Keenly aware of the overwhelming societal pressure to marry, especially for young women like herself, Moore remained skeptical of sacrificing her fiercely held independence to any permanent union. She feared that marriage artificially binds two complex, changing, and often incompatible beings into a false and impossible unity. Furthermore, because of the power dynamics in a patriarchal society, Moore felt that such a bond can severely constrain a woman's potential, particularly if the woman is a free thinking, creative artist.

Critics have noted that several crucial events in Moore's life caused the subject of matrimony to be personally vexing to her and helped spark the composition of "Marriage." First, her brother married against their mother's wishes, which unsettled the extremely close-knit family; second, it was rumored that Scofield Thayer, the editor of the literary journal *The Dial,* courted and proposed to Moore only to be rejected; and finally, there was the sudden, shocking marriage of her close friend, the writer and wealthy heiress Bryher (Winifred Ellerman). Much to the surprise of the New York avant-garde, Bryher, who was the lover of Moore's dear friend, the poet H.D. (Hilda Doolittle), married the struggling bohemian writer Robert McAlmon in 1921. Suspicious of McAlmon's intentions and the marriage's seriousness, fearful of its impact on her friend's creativity and freedom, Moore was utterly baffled by the entire situation, which she called "an earthquake," wondering why her friend would submit to an arrangement so threatening to her writing and her liberty (Stapleton, 1978).

The strong emotions and philosophical and cultural questions provoked by these events stimulated Moore's poem. Early in 1922 she began the long process of composing this poem in her notebook by jotting under the heading "Marriage": "I don't know what Adam and Eve think of it by this time / I don't think much of it" (Keller and Miller, 1987). Although the finished poem, which appeared as a chapbook in 1923, refers to marriage as something "requiring all one's criminal ingenuity / to avoid!" it is far from resolved in its attitudes about the matter. In fact, with its shifting viewpoints and contradictions, the poem is a study of uncertainty and ambivalence, as it carries on a protracted internal argument. Rather than giving any definitive answer about marriage, Moore explores this strange phenomenon from a dizzying variety of perspectives, fully aware that no single or simple explanation can accommodate something so complex: "Psychology which explains everything," she writes near the beginning, "explains nothing, / and we are still in doubt." Indeed, the pervasive enigma of romantic relationships and marriage is a major theme of the poem, and the final movement begins with the acknowledgment that "'Everything to do with love is mystery.'"

From the beginning "this institution, / perhaps one should say enterprise," is both celebrated—"this fire-gilt steel / alive with goldenness; how bright it shows"—and critiqued:

> Unhelpful Hymen!
> a kind of overgrown cupid
> reduced to insignificance
> by the mechanical advertising
> parading as involuntary comment.

Moore presents marriage as an intractable paradox: "this amalgamation which can never be more / than an interesting impossibility" is alternately a situation in which two people who wish to be alone decide to "'be alone together,'" a "'strange paradise,'" "'a very trivial object indeed,'" and a "rare . . . striking grasp of opposites."

Moore quickly introduces two opposed archetypal beings, Eve and Adam, who dominate the poem and serve as vehicles for her ironic commentary on the battle of the sexes. Both are portrayed with a mixture of positive and negative terms: they are beautiful yet flawed, "alive with words" yet thoroughly narcissistic. At the center of the poem is a heated dialogue between this generic "He" and "She," a vicious conversation that highlights the strife between the genders, in which Moore clearly critiques male domination and misogyny:

> She says, "Men are monopolists
> of 'stars, garters, buttons
> and other shining baubles'—
> unfit to be the guardians
> of another person's happiness.'
> He says, . . . you will find that
> 'a wife is a coffin,'
> that severe object
> with the pleasing geometry
> stipulating space not people,
> refusing to be buried
> and uniquely disappointing.

Despite the irresolution and multiplicity of the poem, at its heart lies Moore's understated yet chilling observation that

> experience attests
> that men have power
> and sometimes one is made to feel it.

This capacious, challenging poem erupted out of Moore's turbulent attitudes about the conflict between "liberty" and "union" and the seemingly irreconcilable nature of independence and marriage. Innovative in its use of collage and ellipsis, groundbreaking in its feminist cultural critique and its inclusion of so many perspectives and types of discourse, "Marriage" surely stands among the masterpieces of 20th-century American poetry.

ANDREW EPSTEIN

**Further Reading**

Bergman, David, "Marianne Moore and the Problem of 'Marriage,'" *American Literature* 60, no. 2 (1988)

Heuving, Jeanne, *Omissions Are Not Accidents: Gender in the Art of Marianne Moore,* Detroit, Michigan: Wayne State University Press, 1992

Holley, Margaret, *The Poetry of Marianne Moore: A Study in Voice and Value,* Cambridge and New York: Cambridge University Press, 1987
Joyce, Elizabeth W., "The Collage of 'Marriage': Marianne Moore's Formal and Cultural Critique," *Mosaic* 26, no. 4 (1993)
Keller, Lynn, and Cristanne Miller, "'The Tooth of Disputation': Marianne Moore's 'Marriage,'" *Sagetrieb* 6, no. 3 (1987)
Martin, Taffy, *Marianne Moore, Subversive Modernist,* Austin: University of Texas Press, 1986
Miller, Cristanne, *Marianne Moore: Questions of Authority,* Cambridge, Massachusetts: Harvard University Press, 1995
Molesworth, Charles, *Marianne Moore: A Literary Life,* New York: Atheneum, 1990
Parisi, Joseph, editor, *Marianne Moore: The Art of a Modernist,* Ann Arbor: University of Michigan Research Press, 1990
Stapleton, Laurence, *Marianne Moore: The Poet's Advance,* Princeton, New Jersey: Princeton University Press, 1978; 2nd printing with corrections, 1978
Tomlinson, Charles, editor, *Marianne Moore: A Collection of Critical Essays,* Englewood Cliffs, New Jersey: Prentice Hall, 1969

# The Pangolin

Also called a scaly anteater, a pangolin is a long-tailed, scale-covered mammal found in Africa and Asia that uses its long snout and sticky tongue to eat ants and termites. Marianne Moore's poem "The Pangolin," like so many of her animal poems, offers wonder-filled descriptions of the pangolin's body and behavior, a contemplation of human nature, and a compelling commentary on relationships between humans and the natural world. Unlike many of her poems that first saw publication in little magazines, "The Pangolin" first appeared in *The Pangolin, and Other Verse* (1936), of which only 120 copies were printed. The poem reached a wider audience in *What Are Years?* (1941) and *Collected Poems* (1951), and remains in print in *The Complete Poems of Marianne Moore* (1967).

By opening "Another armored animal" Moore gestures to other animal poems such as "He 'Digesteth Harde Yron'" and "The Jerboa" that emphasize animals' self-protection. Moore's descriptions of the pangolin combine scientific precision with a layperson's wonder:

scale
lapping scale with spruce-cone regularity until they
form the uninterrupted central
tail-row!

The result is a sense of the animal's looks and of its strangeness. She calls the pangolin an

uninjurable
artichoke which simpletons thought a living fable
whom the stones had nourished, whereas ants had done
so,

thereby musing on the animal's unusual digestive processes and on humanity's inability to comprehend something so unlike itself. Continuing the precise observations, she introduces valuation:

he draws
away from danger *unpugnaciously,*
with no sound but a *harmless* hiss; keeping

the *fragile grace* of the Thomas-
of-Leighton Buzzard Westminster Abbey wrought-iron
vine, or
rolls himself into a ball that has
power to defy all effort to unroll it [emphasis added]

The pangolin prefers to avoid conflict rather than to triumph; the speaker's details signify her approval.

Beyond these differences, pangolins are, like humans, tool-users. By granting the pangolin tools—for instance, his "tail, graceful tool, as prop or hand or broom or ax"—Moore humanizes him. Conversely, she pangolinizes humans: their use of machines does not surpass the animal world, but rather aspires to its level:

A sail boat

was the first machine. Pangolins, made
for moving quietly also, are models of exactness,
on four legs; on hind feet plantigrade,
with certain postures of a man. Beneath sun and moon,
man slaving
to make his life more sweet, leaves half the flowers worth
having,
needing to choose wisely how to use his strength;
a paper-maker like the wasp; a tractor of
foodstuffs,
like the ant; spidering a length
of web from bluffs
above the stream; in fighting, mechanicked
like the pangolin; capsizing in

disheartenment.

Pangolins are the basis for comparison for sailboat and sailor alike.

The "graceful" modifying the pangolin's tail is hardly a throw-away; rather, it triggers a rumination on grace. Moore already mentioned the fragile grace of the wrought-iron vine, and she further calls the pangolin

a thing
made graceful by adversities, con-

versities.

Such repetition by a poet known for her adventurous word-choice emphasizes that this "grace" is revealed not just in individual movements, but also in the pangolin's entire being. "To explain grace requires / a curious hand"—a hand engaged with the world around it. In struggling to define grace, people have muddled it:

If that which is at all were not forever,
why would those who graced the spires
with animals and gathered there to rest, on cold luxurious
low stone seats—a monk and monk and monk—between
the thus
ingenious roof-supports, have slaved to confuse
grace with a kindly manner, time in which to pay a
debt,
the cure for sins, a graceful use
of what are yet
approved stone mullions branching out across
the perpendiculars?

Humans can only try to *define* the multifaceted nature of grace. The pangolin, made graceful by adversities, possessing a graceful tail, and showing the grace of wrought-iron decoration, *demonstrates* grace in its varieties. A person driven by curiosity rather than definitions will find a more precise explanation of grace, the poem suggests, outside the limits of human expectations.

A focus for intertwined contemplations of grace, self-preservation, and the similarities between animals and humans, Moore's pangolin prompts analysis of human behavior. Although similar to the pangolin in tool-use, humans differ because "Among animals, *one* has a sense of humor. / Humor saves a few steps, it saves years." In emphasizing humor as singularly human, Moore acknowledges the unique position of humans in the animal kingdom without granting them hierarchical superiority.

Although Moore's pangolin merits emulation, the human is hardly condemned. By asking the reader to compare the two creatures rather than offering a verdict herself, Moore encourages the curious hand she advocates. The human being is worth watching as much as the pangolin: "there he sits in his own habitat, / serge-clad, strong shod." Like the pangolin, he wears armor; his desire to control his environment while simultaneously dreading it makes him "the prey of fear." While humans envision themselves the fiercest of the fierce in some imaginary habitat diorama, they do not see this most ever-present predator. Fear leaves humankind "curtailed, extinguished, thwarted by the dusk, work partly done," but thereby open to the hope and salvation of each new day. The speaker closes with a paean

to the alternating blaze,
"Again the sun!
anew each day; and new and new and new,
that comes into and steadies my soul."

Like the adversities that give the pangolin grace, Moore suggests, fear brings humanity strength and salvation.

CATHERINE PAUL

**Further Reading**

Costello, Bonnie, *Marianne Moore: Imaginary Possessions,* Cambridge, Massachusetts: Harvard University Press, 1981

Holley, Margaret, *The Poetry of Marianne Moore: A Study in Voice and Value,* Cambridge and New York: Cambridge University Press, 1987

Martin, Taffy, "Portrait of a Writing Master: Beyond the Myth of Marianne Moore," *Twentieth Century Literature* 30, nos. 2–3 (1984)

Merrin, Jeredith, "'To Explain Grace Requires a Curious Hand': Marianne Moore and the Literary Tradition," *Poesis* 6, no. 1 (1984)

Molesworth, Charles, "Moore's Masterpiece: The Pangolin's Alternating Blaze," in *Marianne Moore: Woman and Poet,* edited by Patricia C. Willis, Orono, Maine: National Poetry Foundation, 1990

Quinn, Bernetta, "The Artist as Armored Animal: Marianne Moore, Randall Jarrell," in *Marianne Moore: Woman and Poet,* edited by Patricia C. Willis, Orono, Maine: National Poetry Foundation, 1990

Roessel, David, "Pangolins and People: A Study of Marianne Moore and Her Notes," *English Language Notes* 27, no. 3 (1990)

Schulman, Grace, *Marianne Moore: The Poetics of Engagement,* Urbana: University of Illinois Press, 1986

Schulze, Robin G., "Marianne Moore's 'Imperious Ox, Imperial Dish' and the Poetry of the Natural World," *Twentieth Century Literature* 44, no. 1 (1998)

Stapleton, Laurence, *Marianne Moore: The Poet's Advance,* Princeton, New Jersey: Princeton University Press, 1978; 2nd printing with corrections, 1978

# Poetry

Known as much for the dramatic differences among its textual variants as for its memorable phrases, Marianne Moore's "Poetry" endures as a remarkable and highly teachable 20th-century American poem. The complicated history of its publication challenges the assumptions of scholars about what constitutes a poet's definitive oeuvre while the frankness of its opening statement about poetry—"I, too, dislike it"—provokes students to examine their expectations about the value of writing and reading poetry. As a poem about poetry, the work invites examination as a self-reflexive statement of Moore's Modernist aesthetic. As the premier example of Moore's career-long method of revising her poems, "Poetry" calls special attention to the personal, social, and historical contingencies that shape poetic creation and interpretation.

First published in the avant-garde magazine *Others* in July 1919 as a five-stanza poem in syllabic verse, "Poetry" appeared in print in multiple versions over the next 50 years. Bonnie Honigsblum (1990) identifies four basic versions of "Poetry," each of which contributes to the complicated story of Moore's method of revision: the five-stanza, 30-line version first published in 1919; a 13-line version written in free verse without stanzas and printed only once in 1925; a three-stanza, 15-line version first appearing in 1932; and a scant three-line version that appears in *The Complete Poems of Marianne Moore* (1967) accompanied by a revision of the original five-stanza version as its footnote. Although the first printings of these four versions appeared chronologically, the variants were at times printed concurrently in different publications, showing Moore's openness to simultaneous alternate versions of her poems. While scholars committed to preserving a more complete Moore oeuvre than that presented in the *Complete Poems* have successfully identified the many variants of "Poetry," scholars and general readers alike have found that accounting for the reasons behind Moore's continual and often radical revisions proves a more difficult task.

Nevertheless, scholars suggest both discrete reasons for particular revisions and larger theoretical rationales for Moore's revisions of "Poetry" and other poems. As Honigsblum (1990) explains, for instance, the 13-line free-verse version of "Poetry" printed for the first and last time in *Observations* (1925) represents Moore's period of experiment with free verse in the early 1920s, after which she returned to her preferred technique of writing in uniquely patterned stanzas of syllabic verse. As a result the next version of "Poetry" returned to a syllabic form, albeit a form somewhat different than that of the original 1919 poem. On a more theoretical level, Honigsblum argues that multiple and changing factors influenced Moore's revisions over time, including the views of her editors, critics, fellow Modernists, and family. Similarly, Robin Gail Schulze (1996), in an article on Moore's poem "The Frigate Pelican," emphasizes that Moore's revisions foreground the process-oriented, historically contingent nature of her Modernist poetic practice. By cutting "Poetry" down to three lines for her *Complete Poems* and simultaneously printing a longer version of the poem in the volume's notes, Moore calls attention to the shifting nature not only of her texts but also of the reader's meaning-making encounters with those texts.

The many textual variants of "Poetry" and the instability of those variants over time call into question the very task of explicating Moore's poem. Which version is the "best" or "final" version? Does understanding Moore's "Poetry" require that a reader examine all of the different versions of it? By examining the two variants most readily available, those in the *Complete Poems,* the reader finds that the poem's thematic concern with defining poetry and the "genuine" anticipates the interpretive difficulties that the poem's multiple variants set into motion. The three-line version of "Poetry," in its brevity and matter-of-fact tone, is deceivingly simple:

> I, too, dislike it.
> Reading it, however, with a perfect contempt for it, one
> discovers in
> it, after all, a place for the genuine.

What does Moore mean by "perfect contempt," and why does it lead to an affirmative discovery about poetry? How can poetry progress, in the space of three lines, from being unlikable to being "a place for the genuine"? The longer version of "Poetry" printed in the notes to *Complete Poems* elaborates on the contradictions of this aphoristic statement by indicating what the speaker values both in and out of poetry:

> Hands that can grasp, eyes
> that can dilate, hair that can rise
> if it must, these things are important not because a
>
> high-sounding interpretation can be put upon them but
> because they are
> useful. When they become so derivative as to become
> unintelligible,
> the same thing may be said for all of us, that we
> do not admire what
> we cannot understand. . . .

Nor does Moore's speaker admire excluding "'business documents and // school-books'" from her definition of poetry. She requires instead that poets be "'literalists of / the imagination'—above / insolence and triviality" and be able to present "'imaginary gardens with real toads in them.'" This latter requirement, a quoted phrase that stands as Moore's most famous statement of Modernist paradox and as her most quoted line, is just one of the many compelling ideas that gets lost in the radically shortened three-line version.

And yet the spirit of the excised lines—their focus on the contradictions inherent in poetry—remains even in the shortest version of "Poetry." Read in light of the poem's long publication history, the three-line version's epigrammatic and elusive brevity bears witness to Moore's concern with the genuine by preventing the poem from becoming a stale anthology piece. Further, even without studying every variant of the poem in depth, readers can recognize that Moore's aesthetic makes room for the ambivalence and complexity of ongoing understanding. The presence of multiple versions, the curious avowal of both dislike and appreciation, and the famous formulation of "'imaginary gardens with real toads in them'" all defy a settled, definitive assessment of Moore's "Poetry" and poetry in general.

CATHERINE TRAMONTANA

**Further Reading**


Costello, Bonnie, *Marianne Moore: Imaginary Possessions,* Cambridge, Massachusetts: Harvard University Press, 1981

DuPlessis, Rachel Blau, "No Moore of the Same: The Feminist Poetics of Marianne Moore," *William Carlos Williams Review* 14, no. 1 (1988)

Gregory, Elizabeth, *Quotation and Modern American Poetry: "'Imaginary Gardens with Real Toads,'"* Houston, Texas: Rice University Press, 1996

Honigsblum, Bonnie, "Marianne Moore's Revisions of 'Poetry,'" in *Marianne Moore: Woman and Poet,* edited by Patricia C. Willis, Orono, Maine: National Poetry Foundation, 1990

Miller, Cristanne, *Marianne Moore: Questions of Authority,* Cambridge, Massachusetts: Harvard University Press, 1995

Peterson, Jeffrey D., "Notes on the Poem(s) 'Poetry': The Ingenuity of Moore's Poetic 'Place,'" in *Marianne Moore: Woman and Poet,* edited by Patricia C. Willis, Orono, Maine: National Poetry Foundation, 1990

Schulman, Grace, "Conversation with Marianne Moore," *Quarterly Review of Literature* 16 (1969)

Schulze, Robin Gail, "'The Frigate Pelican''s Progress: Marianne Moore's Multiple Versions and Modernist Practice," in *Gendered Modernisms: American Women Poets and Their Readers,* edited by Margaret Dickie and Thomas Travisano, Philadelphia: University of Pennsylvania Press, 1996


## The Steeple-Jack

"Prosody is a tool; poetry is a 'maze, a trap, a web,'" Marianne Moore writes in the introduction to the *Marianne Moore Reader* (1958). A poet at once stoic and didactic, Moore piles up details and offers ceaseless revisions that sometimes becomes a trap for the reader. Why all these lists of flora and fauna? From the start,

Moore sought and found revelation in studying the intimate surfaces of things, as in the surface of a seashell. Her unique, dry-voiced, sharp observations were sounded in her earliest poems of the late 1910s. Investigating the mystery of her first major work, "The Steeple-Jack," an apparently seamless achievement, will help clarify her poetic process.

"The Steeple-Jack" begins like a travelogue describing a town that Moore later identified as "both Brooklyn and various New England towns I had visited." In its opening line the poet announces, "Dürer would have seen a reason for living in a town like this." The poem goes on to evoke the grays, browns, and greens of the German artist's watercolors, only to undercut his melancholy with the phrase "with eight stranded whales to look at." The whales, according to Moore, had been found in Brooklyn Bay, and thus Moore, the precisionist writer, makes her entrance on the poem's first page. She then continues to set the scene: "one by one in twos and threes the sea gulls flying back and forth" above a "sea the purple of a peacock's neck . . . paled to greenish azure."

According to the poet and critic Donald Hall (1970), we enter Moore's fictitious New England town to discover that "Danger, unspecific but pervasive, is Moore's main theme." However, if that is true, it is a danger located in precise details, and in "The Steeple-Jack" Moore congratulates the reader for being able to experience the shifting weather, the "whirling fife and drum of the storm which activates poem and landscape and above all conditions for living adjacent to sea and fog." Danger is a factor in "The Steeple-Jack" even as Moore protests, "It could not be dangerous living in a town like this of simple people." The reader does not, in fact, meet any of the town's "simple people." Only C.J. Poole, a college student named Ambrose, and the Hero are cited, the last two of whom reappear in their own separate poems.

"The Steeple-Jack" was first published in 1932 as part of a three-part sequence under the title "Part of a Novel, Part of a Poem, Part of a Play." In 1935, it underwent a curious change when it appeared in Moore's *Selected Poems* cut in two. The first part of the poem acquired the title "The Steeple-Jack" and is the lead poem in her 1935 book. Another section of "Part of a Novel, Part of a Poem, Part of a Play" appears as the second poem in this volume under the title "The Hero," which describes "a man able to live without fictions" and "who shrinks at what it is flies out on muffled wings." Finally, the third part of the original poem, under the title "The Student," was published in Moore's 1941 collection *What Are Years?* All three personae—the Steeple-Jack, the Hero, and Ambrose (the Student)—are introduced in the Steeple-Jack's town, where "each in his way is at home." Moore makes no claim for the hero as a climber but as one "who covets nothing he has let go," even while, unlike the Steeple-Jack, he does not bring hope to the reader. In C.J. Poole the Steeple-Jack, we have already discovered Moore's true hero, one who places "danger-signs by the church while he is gilding the solid pointed star."

The clarity of the artist's vision unfolds through concrete details of this town, of this specific place we think we know. Wallace Stevens, in a tribute to Moore in 1948, wrote, "The encyclopedia provides the reality of an isolated fact. Ms. Moore's reality is significant. An aesthetic integration is a reality." For the poet, Stevens insists, "reality is not the thing, it is the aspect of the thing. In short, the poet's own individual reality."

In *Marianne Moore: The Poetry of Engagement* (1986), critic Grace Schulman finds that, in "The Steeple-Jack," "the town is meditative and it lends itself to the poet's creation of a form that will dramatize thought." Some of the physical details in the poem seem slightly fantastic, such as the ocean with "waves as formal as the scales on a fish," in Moore's structured universe. It is specificity that Moore champions in this and the majority of her later poems. Detail seen unflinchingly, observed up close in Moore's poetry, is at once heroic and enlightening. Detail properly marshaled becomes art.

The world of Moore's imagination comes complete with lush vegetation, and "cats not cobras to keep down the rats" inhabit a life in poetry on the page. "The Steeple-Jack" has put out a sign warning of danger, has climbed up to gild the star on the steeple, and by this action has united the town with its church, which the author murmurs would be a fit haven "for waifs, children, animals and presidents who have repaid sin-driven senators by not thinking about them." The poem in turn has since become a haven for its generations of readers.

CORINNE ROBINS

**Further Reading**

Hall, Donald, *Marianne Moore: The Cage and the Animal,* New York: Pegasus, 1970

Moore, Marianne, *A Marianne Moore Reader,* New York: Viking Press, 1958

Nitchie, George W., *Marianne Moore: An Introduction to the Poetry,* New York: Columbia University Press, 1969

Schulman, Grace, *Marianne Moore: The Poetry of Engagement,* Urbana: University of Illinois Press, 1986

Tomlinson, Charles, editor, *Marianne Moore: A Collection of Critical Essays,* Englewood Cliffs, New Jersey: Prentice Hall, 1969

---

## Howard Moss 1922–87

Howard Moss served as the poetry editor for *The New Yorker* from 1950 to 1987. During this span, he helped advance the careers of many young poets, including Sylvia Plath, James Dickey, Anne Sexton, and Mark Strand. Moss' editing accomplishments have often obscured the fact that he was also a talented writer, producing a large body of poetry and criticism.

Moss' first collection of verse, *The Wound and the Weather* (1946), received mixed reviews. On the whole, critics felt that

Moss' strict adherence to traditional forms of meter and rhyme limited his abilities. The truth of this criticism is clearly seen in "Waterwall Blues," one of the volume's better poems:

> I gnarled me where the spinster tree
> Unwound its green hosanna
> And built its sorrow, leaf by knee,
> A lachrymal cabana.
>
> The selfsame night I cracked my cowl,
> Unwound myself with Anna;
> Speech by speech and howl by howl
> O don't you cry Susanna.

*The Toy Fair* (1954) followed in a similar vein. However, it was clear that Moss was maturing as a writer, as the thematic quality of his work had grown more complicated. Howard Nemerov, in a review for the *Atlantic Monthly,* acknowledged *The Toy Fair* as "one of the most accomplished collections of lyric poetry to appear since the war."

Moss' next two collections of verse, *A Swimmer in the Air* (1957) and *A Winter Come, a Summer Gone* (1960), were very similar to *Toy Fair,* using wit to explore a wide range of themes, yet still limited by traditional form. In 1965, however, Moss published *Finding Them Lost, and Other Poems,* a collection that represented a step in a new direction. Moss' work had grown more overtly metaphorical, examining images of life and death. Furthermore, his style had begun to relax, moving more toward free verse. These changes are evident in the first stanza of "The Pruned Tree," which acts as a metaphor for innocence and experience:

> As a torn paper might seal up its side,
> Or a streak of water stitch itself to silk
> And disappear, my wound has been my healing,
> And I am made more beautiful by losses.
> See the flat water in the distance nodding
> Approval, the light that fell in love with statues,
> Seeing me alive, turn its motion toward me.
> Shorn, I rejoice in what was taken from me.

Moss' next collection, *Second Nature* (1968), dealt in large part with the theater. In addition to his poetry, Moss was also noted as a playwright. He wrote four plays, including *The Folding Green* (first produced 1954) and *The Palace at 4 A.M.* (1972). After a highly acclaimed collection of his old poems in *Selected Poems* (1971), Moss published two collections of original verse after an eight-year hiatus: *A Swim off the Rocks: Light Verse* (1976) and *Tigers and Other Lilies* (1977). The former included a wide range of witty verse, ranging from "light" to heavily satirical. Although many critics ignored it, some realized the range of Moss' ability. The collection attracted the attention of Harold Bloom, who called it "a superb book of light verse." *Tigers and Other Lilies* consists of poems written for children. Once again, Moss demonstrated his versatility, although critics primarily ignored the work.

Moss' next work, *Notes from the Castle* (1979), deservedly received much more attention. In many ways, this collection of verse encapsulates the zenith of his ability. Moss' use of metaphor is never more cleverly woven, and throughout the collection he ties nature to humanity in interesting and fresh ways. Stylistically, *Notes from the Castle* is Moss' best, as he blends his mastery of traditional forms with his burgeoning interest in free verse. This progression in both style and content is noticeable in "Gravel":

> The most gentle of the small stones
> Has fallen in love
> With the ordinary flower beds of summer
> Lying helpless till winter effects
> The divorce of sunlit wood and violet,
> The slow parting of shadow and hydrangea.
>
> Among these dead, these small leftover
> Fragments of something once colossal—
> The glacier moving southward with its ice—
>
> There is one lying in the path of stillness,
> One awakening to a grand piano
> Somewhere in the house

As Stephen Gardner notes, "In the later volumes, [Moss'] poems exhibit more flexibility, stretching the confines of the line and adding the dramatic value of the conversational." The maturity of Moss' writing carried through to his next collection, *Rules of Sleep* (1984). Similar to *Notes from the Castle,* this collection cultivates a more pronounced awareness of the rapid passage of time, focusing on more pessimistic themes, such as death and abandonment. Moss published another collection of poetry, *New Selected Poems,* in 1985.

In addition to poetry and drama, Moss is also credited for his contributions to literary criticism. Over the years, he published many essays on poets, including W.H. Auden, Dylan Thomas, John Keats, and Elizabeth Bishop. He also published essays on playwrights (William Shakespeare and Anton Chekhov) and novelists (Henry James, Leo Tolstoy, and Marcel Proust). In addition to focusing solely on authors, Moss also interrogated basic trends within literature, such as the following discussion of genres:

> I would say that the distinction between fiction writers and poets is becoming obsolete, that it might be more useful to think of authors as mirror-writers or window-writers. . . . In America the two schools stem from two major figures, both poets, who may be viewed as their source: Emily Dickinson, the mirror, and Walt Whitman, the window.

Moss' essays were collected in three volumes: *Writing against Time* (1969), *Whatever Is Moving* (1981), and *Minor Monuments* (1986). In addition to these collections, Moss also published extended studies of authors in *The Magic Lantern of Marcel Proust* (1962) and *Chekhov* (1972).

ANDREW HOWE

**Biography**

Born in New York City, 22 January 1922. Attended University of Michigan, Ann Arbor, 1939–40; University of Wisconsin, Madison, B.A. 1944; Harvard University, Cambridge, Massachusetts, 1942; Columbia University, New York City, 1977; book reviewer, *Time* magazine, 1944; instructor, Vassar College, Poughkeepsie, New York, 1944–46; fiction editor, *Junior Bazaar,* 1947; editorial staff, 1948, and poetry editor,

1950–87, *The New Yorker;* judge, National Book Award, 1957, 1964; Hurst Professor, Washington University, St. Louis, Missouri, 1972; Adjunct Professor, Barnard College, New York City, 1975, Columbia University, 1977, University of California, Irvine, 1979, and University of Houston, Texas, 1980; member of PEN, Authors Guild, American Academy, and Institute of Arts and Letters. Received Janet Sewall David Award, 1944; American Academy and Institute of Arts and Letters Award, 1968; Ingram Merrill Foundation grant, 1972; National Book Award, 1972; National Endowment for the Arts Award, 1984; Academy of American Poets fellowship, 1986; Lenore Marshall Poetry Prize (*The Nation*), 1986. Died in New York City, 16 September 1987.

**Poetry**
*The Wound and the Weather,* 1946
*The Toy Fair,* 1954
*A Swimmer in the Air,* 1957
*A Winter Come, a Summer Gone: Poems, 1946–1960,* 1960
*Finding Them Lost, and Other Poems,* 1965
*Second Nature,* 1968
*Selected Poems,* 1971
*Instant Lives,* 1974; revised edition, 1985
*Buried City,* 1975
*A Swim off the Rocks: Light Verse,* 1976
*Notes from the Castle,* 1979
*Rules of Sleep,* 1984
*New Selected Poems,* 1985

**Selected Criticism**
*The Magic Lantern of Marcel Proust,* 1962
*Writing against Time,* 1969
*Whatever Is Moving,* 1981
*Minor Monuments: Selected Essays,* 1986

**Other Writings:** children's literature (*Tigers and Other Lilies,* 1977), plays (*Two Plays: The Palace at 4* A.M. *[and] The Folding Green,* 1980), French translations (*The Cemetery by the Sea,* 1985); edited collections and volumes of poetry (*Keats,* 1959; *The Poet's Story,* 1973).

**Further Reading**


Garber, Frederick, "Geographies and Languages and Selves and What They Do," *American Poetry Review* 14, no. 5 (September–October 1985)
Howard, Richard, *Alone with America: Essays on the Art of Poetry in the United States Since 1950,* New York: Atheneum, 1969
Jacobsen, Josephine, "The Spirit and the City," *The Nation* 223 (October 1976)
Lieberman, Laurence, *Unassigned Frequencies: American Poetry in Review, 1964–1977,* Urbana: University of Illinois Press, 1977
Malkoff, Karl, *Crowell's Handbook of Contemporary American Poetry,* New York: Crowell, 1973
McClatchy, J.D., "Grace and Rude Will," *Poetry* 82 (August 1978)
Packard, William, *The Craft of Poetry: Interviews from "The New York Quarterly,"* New York: Doubleday, 1974
Schramm, Richard, "A Gathering of Poets," *Western Humanities Review* 26 (Fall 1972) Smith, Dave, "Castles, Elephants, Buddhas: Some Recent American Poetry," *American Poetry Review* 10, no. 3 (May–June 1981)
White, Edmund, "Midas' Touch," *Poetry* 78 (March 1974)


---

# Harryette Mullen 1953–

Born in Alabama and raised in still-segregated Texas, Harryette Mullen is the author of four books of poetry and much critical prose. Placement of Mullen's work is a complex task. On the one hand, she has rarely shown up in mainstream African-American poetry anthologies, despite having clear roots in black aesthetic concerns and producing a richly allusive poetry that challenges readers' command of African diasporic culture. On the other, despite clearly sharing concerns with feminist experimentalists, Language poets, poststructuralist theorists, and postmodernist performance artists and poets, neither has she been clearly taken up by a predominantly Euro-American avant-garde. This critical hesitancy is slowly changing. A recent wave of critics has not been put off by her diverse sources and has discovered the means by which to make those sources speak to each other and discover shared concerns. More important, however, are the ways in which Mullen has made this segregation the focus of her poetics and critical work. Mullen is a crucial voice in American poetry for the aesthetic contribution of the creative work, its culture-critical texts and subtexts, and for her further interventions in the public sphere to insist upon the "mongrel" character of all cultural phenomena. She has powerfully insisted that there is no permanent contradiction between her having Melvin Tolson, Gwendolyn Brooks, the Umbra poets (especially Lorenzo Thomas and Tom Dent), *and* Gertrude Stein as poetic models. Indeed, she has "taken as her text" the overlap (or maybe "underlap") between the explicit and implicit agendas suggested by such an informal genealogy.

The trajectory of her career adds some narrative weight to that which might otherwise seem strictly a confusion. Coming of age as a writer at the University of Texas in the mid-1970s, she was initiated into the affirmative and reconstructive concerns of black aesthetic criticism. *Tree Tall Woman* (1981) is strong work in that mode and brought her a predominantly African-American audience. Black aesthetic criticism (and poetry) was never as monolithic as its detractors sometimes suggest, but it is certainly true that after this first book Mullen's work became much more centrifugal in its thrust. Through graduate study at the University of California at Santa Cruz, where she had an opportunity to read further in poststructuralist theory, anthropology, contemporary poetics, and gained further command of the diversity of African and African-derived cultural forms, Mullen began to shape a poetry much more self-conscious of language-derived and language-specific meaning. The work begins to interrogate culture and language and provocatively combine lyric and culture-critical sensibilities. *Trimmings* (1991) and *S*PeRM**K*T* (1992) are at once an engagement with the work and legacy of Gertrude Stein (especially her *Tender Buttons*) and the furthering of a unique black feminist agenda. Mullen neither assumes that Stein's avant-gardism is invested in the most common of racist cultural assumptions nor does she assume that Stein (or her text) is above such a figuring of blackness. What seems crucial to Mullen is that Stein's work provides an important starting point for an interrogation of "tradition," and further that the work provides a toolbox of sorts to understand the relationship between language and the social construction of race and gender.

Mullen's recent work is related to but not strictly derivative of Stein. While Mullen makes important use of Stein's strategies of defamiliarizing common words and phrases, her own work is heavily invested in the aesthetic and culture-critical productiveness of puns. Mullen suggests that puns can be used as "levers" to make meaning. The pun provides pleasure—erotic and intellectual—but can also be generatively disorienting. The best puns draw a reader's attention to how language conspires to make our experience of the world seem natural and unmediated. *Muse and Drudge* (1995), a book-length poem, embeds multiple puns (among, of course, many other tropes) within a long series of carefully constructed quatrains. The poem's presentation of bits and pieces of remembered ephemera, sometimes self-consciously altered by the poet, sometimes quoted directly, from African-American folklore, the blues, classical and contemporary literature, advertising and other mass media, sometimes utilizing engaging rhyme, sometimes not, creates an incantatory catalogue toward the revision of seemingly all of American culture. The poem often simulates the feeling of remembering only part of a joke. While one cannot reconstruct for oneself the specific cultural signs that generate the pleasure, there is often an inexplicable re-experience of that enjoyment. The incompleteness, however, pushes the reader to encounter his or her own cultural knowledge in such a way as to ask questions about its origins and purpose. In a conversation with critic Calvin Bedient (1996), Mullen suggests that the phrase "stark strangled banjo" (from *Muse and Drudge*) is exemplary of this strategy; it is at once funny, incomplete, and a vigorous push to the reader to encounter the nation's unexamined formative myths. Another way to describe Mullen's poetic strategy is to say that *Muse and Drudge* surrenders to the necessity, beauty, and humor of coincidence; not surrender in the sense of displacing of agency, but rather in the sense of a full embrace of a full and open production of meaning. Despite the potential loss of some part of an audience because of difficulty or opaqueness, the poem warms to the prospect of shared inquiry.

This energetic critique of conventional (i.e., canonical) African-American literary production has been supplemented by a critical writing and scholarship that seeks to undermine the very institutional forces that would seek to permanently marginalize her work. She has written a striking critique ("African Signs and Spirit Writing," 1996) of the privileging of orality in recent African-American literary criticism (especially the work of Henry Louis Gates, Jr.) that insists upon the unsustainability of a hermeneutic that would posit a single "black" way of speaking or writing. The work reconstructs a tradition of African-derived visionary writing that is both reflexive and committed to the work of material and spiritual transformation. Mullen has also attempted to draw attention to the work of other poets and artists whose orientation could be described as "writerly" or broadly experimental. Indeed, there is a striking optimism in both the later critical and poetic work, as the contours of an important and vigorous writing community (if not "tradition") begin to emerge. The prospects for a fuller evaluation of Mullen's work are increased as the work of African-American poets like Will Alexander, C.S. Giscombe, Erica Hunt, Stephen Jonas, Nathaniel Mackey, Ed Roberson, and Jay Wright begins to seem less an aberration and more like one conversation among many. As Mullen's work—both creative and critical—also insists upon acknowledgment of familial and intellectual engagement with Charles Bernstein, Adrienne Rich, Leslie Scalapino, Ron Silliman, Gertrude Stein, and many other non-African-American poets and artists, we are likely to become less and less satisfied with the conventional ways of describing the work of American poetry, and that may be Mullen's greatest accomplishment.

JAMES C. HALL

**Biography**

Born in Florence, Alabama, 1 July 1953. Attended University of Texas, Austin, 1971–75, B.A. in English 1975; University of California, Santa Cruz, 1985–90, Ph.D. in Literature, 1990; poet-in-residence, Texas Commission on the Arts, Artists in the Schools Program, 1978–80; Instructor, 1989–90, and Assistant Professor, 1990–95, Cornell University, Ithaca, New York; Associate Professor, University of California, Los Angeles, 1995–. Received Texas Institute of Letters grant, 1981; Helene Wurlitzer Foundation of New Mexico grant, 1982; Gertrude Stein Award, 1994–95; Rockefeller fellowship (University of Rochester), 1994–95. Living in Los Angeles, California.

**Poetry**

*Tree Tall Woman,* 1981
*Trimmings,* 1991
*S*PeRM**K*T,* 1992
*Muse and Drudge,* 1995
*Blues Baby: Early Poems,* 2001

**Further Reading**

Bedient, Calvin, "The Solo Mysterioso Blues: An Interview with Harryette Mullen," *Callaloo* 19, no.3 (1996)
Frost, Elizabeth, "Signifyin(g) on Stein: The Revisionist Poetics of Harryette Mullen and Leslie Scalapino," *Postmodern Culture* 5, no.3 (1995)
Frost, Elizabeth, "'Ruses of the lunatic muse': Harryette Mullen and Lyric Hybridity," *Women's Studies* (1998)
Hogue, Cynthia, "Interview with Harryette Mullen," *Postmodern Culture* 9, no. 2 (1999)
Mullen, Harryette, "African Signs and Spirit Writing," *Callaloo* 19, no.3 (1996)
Mullen, Harryette, "Incessant Elusives: Oppositional Poetics of

Erica Hunt and Will Alexander," in *Holding Their Own: Perspectives on the Multi-Ethnic Literatures of the United States,* edited by Dorothea Fischer-Hornung and Heike Raphael-Hernandez, Tübingen: Stauffenburg, 2000

Mullen, Harryette, "Poetry and Identity," *West Coast Line* 19 (Spring 1996)

Spahr, Juliana, *Everybody's Autonomy: Collective Reading and Collective Identity,* Tuscaloosa: University of Alabama Press, 2001

Thomas, Lorenzo, *Extraordinary Measures: Afrocentric Modernism and 20th Century American Poetry,* Tuscaloosa: University of Alabama Press, 2000

# N

## Vladimir Nabokov 1899–1977

The writer of 17 novels, as well as numerous translations, critical works, biographies, and entomological papers, Vladimir Nabokov has generally been regarded by critics as a prose stylist, and his poetry has rightly been read as a secondary facet of his prodigious oeuvre. Nabokov began his youthful writing career as a poet, however, publishing his first poem in 1916 in the distinguished Russian journal *Vestnik Evropy* and self-publishing at age 17 a volume titled *Stikhi* (poems or verses), which contained 68 poems that he wrote between 1915 and 1916. He continued to write poetry throughout his life, primarily in his native Russian (over 500 Russian poems are extant) but also in his adopted language, English (over 20 poems). In addition, Nabokov translated the work of several Russian poets into English, most notably Pushkin's *Eugene Onegin* (4 vols., 1964). Finally, poetry plays a prominent role in several of his novels, both thematically and with the presence of original poems in the narratives.

Nabokov was born in Russia into a wealthy aristocratic family that was forced into exile during the 1919 Bolshevik Revolution. He studied at Trinity College, Cambridge, for the next three years and then, after his father's assassination in 1922, moved to Berlin, living there until 1937 amid the large Russian émigré population. He married Véra Slonim in April 1925, the same year in which he completed his first Russian novel, *Mary.* They had a son, Dmitri, in 1934, who would later translate his father's Russian novels into English. In 1937, needing work to support his family, Nabokov left Berlin and its increasingly repressive Nazi regime, settling in France. On the eve of the German invasion in 1940, the family fled to the United States. In America, Nabokov initially divided his time among roles as a lecturer, lepidopterist, critic, translator, and creative writer, accepting teaching posts at Wellesley, Stanford, Harvard, and Cornell. He published several books in English between 1941 and 1955, including the novels *The Real Life of Sebastian Knight* and *Bend Sinister,* an early version of his autobiography *Speak, Memory,* and critical studies on three Russian poets and on Nikolai Gogol. The most famous of Nabokov's novels were written beginning in 1955, including *Lolita* (1955), *Pnin* (1957), *Pale Fire* (1962), and *Ada* (1969). Largely because of the fame engendered by *Lolita* and with the wealth that came with it, the Nabokov family returned to Europe in 1959, settling in Montreux. Nabokov died in 1977.

Most critics of Nabokov's poetry have concurred with him that the large volume of poems written before 1925 represents less mature work than the more polished poetry of his later stages. While there are far fewer poems after 1925, they tend to reflect more of the imaginative creativity that was developing simultaneously in his novel writing. Many of his poems introduce a narrative rather than depending on purely lyrical expression; Nabokov said about his work from the 1920s and 1930s that he specifically undertook to address the problem of plot and story in the short poem. Late in his life, he expressed a view linking the genres even more closely, stating in an interview that poetry and artistic prose were more alike than different (Nabokov, *Strong Opinions,* 1973). In general, Nabokov's poems are formally conservative, relying on conventional meters, traditional stanza forms, and strict rhyme schemes. Yet within these formal restrictions, he attempted to compose poetry that hinted at wonders beyond the ordinary, suggesting mysterious and even mystical elements.

In many ways, Nabokov's approach to writing poetry mirrored one of his other passions: the construction of chess problems. He articulates this relationship explicitly in his introduction to *Poems and Problems* (1970), a collection of his Russian poems (presented on facing pages both in Russian and translated into English) together with the English poems he had published in a 1959 volume and 18 original chess poems. "Problems are the poetry of chess," he asserts, suggesting in turn that poetry is bound by arbitrary borders and rules within which the poet is free to create imaginatively.

The transition from writing in his native Russian to composing in American English presented several challenges for Nabokov. The foremost of these problems in respect to his Russian poetry was its translation into English. His insistence on "rigid fidelity" to the original in translating his or another writer's work was a position challenged by other critics and translators, especially after he published his translation, with commentary, of *Eugene Onegin.* Yet with his employment of English came another concern: his memories of Russia engendered verbal associations in his mother tongue, so writing poems in his adopted language required new subjects and memories, which he felt were less deeply rooted. Nabokov's English poems, most of which were published in *The New Yorker* between 1942 and 1957, on initial reading appear lighter in tone and theme than the early Russian poetry. However, they also exemplify what Nabokov called the "robust style" of his later work, offering multiple levels of significance in addition to the seemingly carefree literal meaning of the poem (*Poems and Problems*). Many of his best poems, both Russian and English, self-reflexively concern the making of poetry and the role of the poet. In this vein, the speaker in "The Room" meditates on the previous inhabitant of the chamber that he now occupies and summarily asserts, "A poet's death is, after all, / a question of technique, a neat enjambment, a melodic fall."

Poetry also has a significant presence in several of Nabokov's novels. Humbert Humbert fashions himself as a kind of poetry dilettante, writing poems to and about Lolita. *Pale Fire* offers perhaps the most elaborate poetic ruse: a 999-line poem by John Shade, which gives the novel its name, framed by a foreword and commentary by Charles Kinbote, the poet's devoted disciple. All this creation is, of course, Nabokov's. His last Russian-language novel, *The Gift* (serialized 1937–38, 1952), contains more than 20 poems, some only fragments, all composed by the novel's hero, Fyodor Godunov-Cherdyntsev, who, like his author, shifts from writing poetry to writing prose. Attesting to his conviction that, as poetry, it could stand on its own, Nabokov included more than a dozen pages of poems from *The Gift* in *Stikhi*, his final volume of poetry, a collection of his Russian poetry published posthumously in 1979.

THAINE STEARNS

**Biography**

Born in St. Petersburg (now Leningrad), Russia, 23 April 1899; left U.S.S.R. in 1919; became United States citizen, 1945. Attended Trinity College, Cambridge, 1919–22, B.A. (honors) 1922; Instructor in Russian literature and creative writing, Stanford University, California, summer 1941; Lecturer in comparative literature, Wellesley College, Massachusetts, 1941–48; part-time research fellow, Museum of Comparative Zoology, Harvard University, Cambridge, Massachusetts, 1942–48; Professor of comparative literature, Cornell University, Ithaca, New York, 1948–59; Visiting Lecturer, Harvard University, spring 1952. Received Guggenheim fellowship, 1943, 1953; American Academy grant, 1951, and Award of Merit Medal, 1969; Brandeis University Creative Arts Award, 1953; National Medal for Literature, 1973. Died in Montreux, Switzerland, 2 July 1977.

**Poetry**

*Stikhi* (Poems), 1916
*Dva Puti: Al'manakh* (Two Paths: An Almanac), 1918
*Gornji Put'* (The Empyrean Path), 1923
*Grozd'* (The Cluster), 1923
*Stikhotvoreniya, 1929–1951* (Poems), 1952
*Poems,* 1959
*Poems and Problems,* 1970
*Stikhi* (Poems), 1979

**Selected Criticism**

*Lectures on Literature,* edited by Fredson Bowers, 1980

**Other Writings:** novels (*Lolita,* 1955; *Pale Fire,* 1962; *Ada,* 1969), short stories (*Details of a Sunset and Other Stories,* 1976), plays (*The Man from the USSR and Other Plays,* translated by Dmitri Nabokov, 1984), memoirs, essays, lectures, translations of Russian literature (*The Song of Igor's Campaign: An Epic of the Twelfth Century,* 1960; *Eugene Onegin,* by Alekandr Pushkin, 1964).

**Further Reading**

Boyd, Brian, *Vladimir Nabokov: The Russian Years,* Princeton, New Jersey: Princeton University Press, 1990; London: Chatto and Windus, 1992
Boyd, Brian, *Vladimir Nabokov: The American Years,* Princeton, New Jersey: Princeton University Press, 1991; London: Chatto and Windus, 1992
*Russian Literature Triquarterly* 24 (1991) (special issue on Nabokov edited by D. Barton Johnson)
Scherr, Barry P., "Poetry," in *The Garland Companion to Vladimir Nabokov,* edited by Vladimir E. Alexandrov, New York: Garland, 1995
Smith, G.S., "Notes on Prosody," in *The Garland Companion to Vladimir Nabokov,* edited by Vladimir E. Alexandrov, New York: Garland, 1995
Soloukhin, Vladimir, "Poet Vladimir Nabokov," *Moskva* 6 (1989)
Wood, Michael, *The Magician's Doubts: Nabokov and the Risks of Fiction,* London: Chatto and Windus, 1994; Princeton, New Jersey: Princeton University Press, 1995

---

# Narrative Poetry

Narrative poetry, broadly defined, is driven by plot and character and privileges story over subjectivity while maintaining the rhythms and compression associated with poetry rather than prose. One of three traditionally identified categories of poetry, narrative poetry differs from dramatic poetry, which eliminates the narrator to allow characters to interact directly, and differs from lyric poetry, which presents the subjective experience of a speaker whose meditations may or may not involve other characters. The parameters of narrative poetry and the characteristics that distinguish it both from narrative prose and lyric poetry have been widely debated, particularly in connection with its late 20th-century American revival as New Narrative, or "expansive," poetry.

Although narrative has been associated with the fable and the ballad, its most consistent association is with the epic. This association grew problematic in the 20th century with the publication of such American Modernist epics as Ezra Pound's *The Cantos* and long poems such as T.S. Eliot's *The Waste Land,* both characterized by fragmentation and juxtaposition, techniques that render it difficult to characterize the modern American epic as narrative in the strict sense of coherent plot and character. Late 20th-century proponents of narrative argue that the emphasis on fragmentation and juxtaposition in Modernist poetics led to a continued lack of interest among poets in narrative verse. American practitioners in the early part of the century, such as Edwin Arlington Robinson and Robinson Jeffers, were consequently relegated to minor canonical status. Instead, American Modernist and Postmodernist poetics have focused variously on the image or word or poem itself as "thing," such as in the work of William Carlos Williams and the Objectivists; on autobiography in the Confessional poem; on the poem as field of composition in Projective verse; and, in the case of Deep Image and American Surrealism, on the workings of the subconscious—movements that Robert McDowell argues have emphasized "the poet's interior landscape rather than the poet's place in the larger community" (in Jarman, 1989).

A number of reasons have been suggested for the lack of interest in narrative poetry among American poets and critics through the late 20th century. One theory is that early Modernists began to see modern life as chaotic and without purpose, a lifestyle characterized by speed and technological change; hence, their poetry reflected the spirit of the times, with less interest in logical structure, the clear cause and effect of narrative, or characters who maintain a coherent profile. Jonathan Holden (1991) argues that the dominance of New Criticism in the middle of the century, with its emphasis on close reading, would seem to favor the shorter lyric. Frederick Feirstein (1983) suggests that the popularity of television contributed to a preference for the lyric sequence, with its short experiences and quick peaks, as a substitute for the narrative long poem. Some critics suggest that much storytelling simply is handled better in prose and, therefore, has been placed in the domain of the short story and novel, although Holden argues that prose writers took up storytelling only because Modernist poetics inherited from Pound and Eliot a contempt for literature "that smacked of the communal or even of the 'common.'"

The communal is precisely what the so-called New Narrative or Neo-Narrative movement claimed to seek through its revival of narrative poetry in the 1980s. These poets and critics allied themselves with the New Formalist movement to promote "expansive poetry," a term attributed to Wade Newman in an essay on the movement in 1989 and taken up by two anthologies of New Narrative and New Formalist criticism: *Expansive Poetry* (1989), edited by Frederick Feirstein, and *New Expansive Poetry* (1999), edited by R.S. Gwynn. The goal of expansive poetry, according to its proponents, was to expand the range of technique available to the poet beyond the lyric, to augment the range of subject matter beyond autobiography or the poetic process itself to issues that concern a broader community, and to reach a broader audience from whom contemporary poetry had grown distant. McDowell, for example, says that narrative offered "a means to escape from the unremarkable first person" (1998).

Major figures in the narrative aspect of the expansive movement (those who figure prominently in the anthologies) include Dick Allen, Dana Gioia, Feirstein, Jarman, and McDowell; the latter two also edited *The Reaper,* a quarterly journal in the 1980s founded to champion and define narrative poetry. However, if those associated with expansive poetry were among the most vocal proponents of narrative, they were not alone. The 1980s and 1990s saw the publication of a number of narrative poems, some by poets directly associated with the expansive movement, some not: book-length epics, such as Frederick Turner's *The New World* (1985) and *Genesis* (1988); Rita Dove's *Thomas and Beulah* (1986), a book-length sequence of narrative poems; long poems such as Anthony Hecht's *The Venetian Vespers* (1979); and books of individual shorter narrative poems by poets as diverse as Philip Levine, Larry Levis, Stephen Dobyns, Robert Hass, and Robert Pinsky—the latter two, along with Dove, former poets laureate of the United States.

If proponents and critics of narrative poetry agree that narrative staged a revival in the 1980s and 1990s, they have not come to terms on a definition of narrative poetry or a prescription for how to write it. Despite the inherent tension between Modernist aesthetics and narrative, some critics have argued for narrative structure as embedded or implied even in Modernist works characterized by fragmentation and juxtaposition. Alan Robinson (1987) notes, for example, that T.S. Eliot's *The Waste Land* receives such a structure from its reliance on the Grail legend. Margaret Dickie (1986) makes an interesting argument for an "inside narrative" of such Modernist long poems as *The Cantos* and William Carlos Williams' *Paterson*—a "narrative of composition, the continuous stages through which these discontinuous poems passed from idea to expression." Arguing that Williams wrote "story poems," Vern Rutsala (1985) cites, among other poems, section XVIII of *Spring and All* (1923), a pivotal Modernist work noted for its sudden shifts, disrupted syntax, and experiments in form. However, attempts to cast these Modernist works as narrative poems are grounded more in the desire to recharacterize the poems themselves than to delimit narrative poetry and, further, risk stretching the definition of narrative poetry until it becomes meaningless. Any attempt to characterize narrative poetry, then, would seem to have to distinguish between poems with narrative elements and narrative poems per se that rely on an identifiable plot and developed characters to derive the poem's "meaning."

If, for many critics, the identification of a narrative poem comes down to the dominant role of "story," that term becomes problematic on closer inspection. Poets active in the expansive movement cite Jeffers, Robinson, and Frost as predecessors of the New Narrative; Jarman (1989) characterizes the narratives of all three as "linear and not spatial, coherent and not fragmented," in opposition to "Eliot's and Pound's deliberately skewed and fragmented approaches to the narrative mode." However, these three poets approach narrative in manners diverse enough to problematize a clear definition of narrative poetry. Jarman, for example, says that Frost's poems are of interest for what his characters say rather than for his plots, underscoring a continued twofold source of debate about narrative: to what extent must it be driven by a fully formed plot, and how is that plot to unfold?

McDowell and Jarman in *The Reaper Essays* (1996) insist accordingly that the narrative poem must have the following: a beginning, middle, and end; observation; compression of time; consistent characterization; characterization through "presentation," not "proclamation"; understatement to develop drama and tension; humor; identifiable location; memorable characters; and a compelling subject. However, their prescriptions are too narrow for some. Holden (1991) suggests that narrative is based not in a clear plot but in voice, the "digressions" and "asides" and "hesitations" characteristic of storytelling. He offers C.K. Williams' "The Gas Station" as an example:

The gas station? Texaco, Esso—I don't know. They were
just words anyway then, just what their signs said.
I wouldn't have understood the first thing about monopoly
or imperialist or oppression.

For Holden, as exemplified in this poem, narrative lies in the sense that the speaker is "thinking out loud"; the story "is nothing special. It couldn't be said to have 'plot' in E.M. Forster's sense of that term." David Wojahn (1989) rejects what he considers *The Reaper*'s implicit call for "strict linear disclosure," for narrative poems that tell "only one story"; instead, he suggests a place in narrative poetry for "fractured narratives or poems that incorporate several narrative strands." The range of what some poets and critics consider narrative is clear in Louse Glück's praise for narrative poems by both Dobyns and Pinsky: Dobyns, she says, effectively uses his material to create a story whose effect is similar to what we would expect from prose. However, she says that readers do not respond to Pinsky's narrative poetry as they do to fiction "because outcome isn't an issue"; Pinsky's poems, Glück says, are "essentially meditative, the poems elaborating themselves in coils and spirals" (1997).

Pinsky's poem "Shirt" (1990) is an example of the type of poem that moves from one narrative to another: it begins with a description of the back, seams, and stitches of his shirt before moving to an imagined scene at the sweatshop where it was made, then to a scene, almost journalistic in tone, about the 1911 fire at the Triangle Factory. The poem describes a man who helps girl after girl onto a windowsill and lets them drop:

He stepped to the sill himself, his jacket flared
And fluttered up from his shirt as he came down,
Air filling up the legs of his gray trousers—

Pinsky's poem does not linger on the scene but jumps to descriptions of other types of shirts and workers, linking the poet George Herbert to a "black / Lady in South Carolina" named Irma who works as a shirt inspector, before returning to his own shirt. The several minor narratives in this poem contribute to a larger narrative of the shirt's production and its history.

Thomas M. Disch (1999) suggests the primary questions to ask of a "good" narrative poem are "is it a good story?" and "does it have a satisfying resolution?" However, this comment begs a distinction between the narrative poem and narrative prose, a distinction critical to any attempt to treat narrative poetry as a distinct category. Wojahn (1989) prefers "poems that can perform according to the rules we would normally require of a short story—plot, character, conflict," but he criticizes many narrative poems for following the rules of fiction too closely, which he says results in excessive exposition. Along similar lines, Disch suggests that the difference between verse and prose narrative lies in the "blanks" left by the poet for the reader's imagination; the poetic narrative's goal, then, is to "suggest as much as possible with maximum compression." Some critics suggest that the difference between narrative poetry and narrative prose lies in the use of form. McDowell notes that some New Narrative poets reject free verse for received form, citing Feirstein's use of rhymed couplets in *Manhattan Carnival* (1981) and the use of meter and rhyme in Turner's *The New World*. Although some critics have gone so far as to say that verse narratives are most likely to occur in conventional forms, Louis Simpson (1998) argues that a sustained narrative is just as effective in free verse and, further, can present "the speech of a modern world, which meter and rhyme cannot." David Mason (1999) suggests that the verse line is an advantage to poetry, helping to make verse narratives memorable and contributing to the drama of the story. Robert Morgan (1982), reviewing Fred Chappell's four-volume *Midquest* (1981), also points to the line as a differentiating factor, characterizing Chappell's work as "lyric narrative, implying that the local texture of the lines is as interesting and concise as lyric poetry, while the overall movement of each piece is essentially narrative."

If it proves difficult at times to distinguish narrative poetry from narrative prose, Morgan's comment suggests it can be difficult to distinguish narrative poetry from lyric poetry as well. Glück differentiates between the two categories, arguing that lyric offers "the emblematic or paradigmatic" by stopping time, while narrative "seeks to locate the endless unfolding of time not as a still point but an underlying pattern or implication," finding "in shift and movement what lyric uses stopped time to manifest" (1997). Still, the terms begin to blur in practice when Wojahn criticizes many narrative poems for insufficient "abstract discourse and lyricism" and praises William Matthews' poem "Whiplash" for its willingness "to work meditation into an essentially narrative framework" (1989).

The role of personal meditation poses the greatest problem since it is a technique characteristic of lyric, of the poem that presents the perspective of the "I," rather than focusing on other characters as some critics insist narrative poetry must do. When does a poem move so far from story to meditation that it is no longer narrative? If poets return to narrative in part to "spring open the jail of the self"—another of *The Reaper*'s demands—to what extent can the narrative poem operate from the speaker's point of view? Or, to put it another way, to what extent can the speaker, particularly when the reader is invited to view the speaker as an aspect of the author, be a primary or even the essential character in the story without the poem's slipping into lyric?

One approach to these questions is to offer a place for the lyric or meditative in narrative poetry as long as these aspects work on behalf of the story rather than on behalf of the speaker's emotions. Tony Whedon attempts to bridge narrative goals and lyric style in his description of "memory narrative" (a term he borrows from Wojahn); Whedon (1988) describes these as "psychological poems" that devise "solutions . . . for dealing with [the] past." Rather than focus on the image, as in Modernist poetry, to show the truth of the "thing," memory narratives for Whedon "transform" images through "a meditation on their relation to time." These poems frequently move in an associative rather than linear fashion to tell their stories.

Michael Collier's "The Welder" (1995) offers an example of a narrative that is based in the memory of the speaker and presents its story in nonlinear fashion. The poem begins with the speaker's crossing a bridge at sunset, noticing the "match-flare sun in the rear-view mirror." The image sparks a memory:

And in the orange burst and flare, I saw the dark
splayed figure of my high-school friend dropping down
out of the white sky, a black heavy cross falling toward
the rising and flattening earth where his father,

standing in the landing field among the bright cloth X's
of targets, followed the descent through binoculars.

The image of the father, imagined by the speaker to be "standing in the field, his hand / held up against the shocking white of the sky," reminds the speaker of another memory, this one further in the past: the same father placing his welder's helmet over his head, placing his hands in gloves. When the father began to weld, "we could not look / directly at the flame's blue snap" but instead "found it muted in the corner of the visor." In memory, the flame's reflection becomes

a star burning and glowing in its moment of creation
before it disappeared on the horizon—a slow
hiss of escaping gas, light fast and precise
that dwarfed us as it passed.

Although Whedon does not offer this poem as an example, "The Welder" is characteristic of those poems that use memory to present a narrative in a nonlinear fashion, in this case moving further and further into the past to make sense of the present, to "offer solutions" to what has happened in the past. In this case, the speaker attempts to make sense of the death of his friend and does so through a transformation of images from one narrative to another: the descent of the "son" paralleling the descent of the "sun," which in turn gives resonance to and is given resonance by the welding flame, sunlike with its "gas" and its disappearance on the horizon. An exchange of images in many ways drives this poem but does so only within the crucial context of the unfolding of the stories themselves.

One might argue that this poem sets itself clearly in the lyric mode: the poem presents a meditation from the point of view of the speaker; it articulates the speaker's emotional state (a speaker the reader is invited to identify with the author) and therefore seems to rely on the subjective experience that expansive poets reject in the name of narrative. Still, the difference between "personal" narrative poems like this one and non-narrative lyric poems may be that the former are, to quote Wojahn (1989), "narrated with a coolness that seeks perspective rather than with an immediacy which seeks simple disclosure," so that "autobiography becomes a means to an end rather than an end itself."

Any attempt to define narrative poetry must ultimately be satisfied with such broad concerns as an emphasis on plot over autobiography, the privileging of events and actions over the image as "thing," and a notion of the poem as vehicle for a story or stories to produce "meaning" rather than as a form that draws primary attention to itself as a process. Such concerns unite narrative poets in theory who in practice differ significantly as to the proper form of narrative verse, the extent to which a story must be linear, the amount and type of detail or exposition required or permitted, and the extent to which characters other than the narrator must be developed. Narrative poetry, finally, is concerned with what its proponents consider the primary impulse to tell a story to an audience, a story that addresses the myriad and particular experiences of human life.

BRYAN WALPERT

*See also* New Formalism

**Further Reading**


Dickie, Margaret, *On the Modernist Long Poem,* Iowa City: University of Iowa Press, 1986

Disch, Thomas M., "North American Addresses: Three Verse Narratives," in *New Expansive Poetry: Theory, Criticism, History,* revised edition, edited by R.S. Gwynn, Ashland, Oregon: Story Line Press, 1999

Feirstein, Frederick, "The Other Long Poem," *Kenyon Review* 5, no. 2 (1983)

Glück, Louise, "Story Tellers," *American Poetry Review* 26, no. 4 (1997)

Holden, Jonathan, "Contemporary Verse Storytelling," *Southern Review* 27 (Spring 1991)

Jarman, Mark, "Robinson, Frost, and Jeffers, and the New Narrative Poetry," in *Expansive Poetry: Essays on the New Narrative and the New Formalism,* edited by Frederick Feirstein, Santa Cruz, California: Story Line Press, 1989

Jarman, Mark, and Robert McDowell, *The Reaper Essays,* Brownsville, Oregon: Story Line Press, 1996

Mason, David, "Other Lives: On Shorter Narrative Poems," in *New Expansive Poetry: Theory, Criticism, History,* revised edition, edited by R.S. Gwynn, Ashland, Oregon: Story Line Press, 1999

McDowell, Robert, "The New Narrative Poetry," in *Expansive Poetry: Essays on the New Narrative and the New Formalism,* edited by Frederick Feirstein, Santa Cruz, California: Story Line Press, 1989

McDowell, Robert, "Why I Write Poems That Tell Stories," *Sewanee Review* 106, no. 1 (1998)

Morgan, Robert, "Midquest," *American Poetry Review* 11, no.4 (1982)

Robinson, Alan, "James Fenton's 'Narratives': Some Reflections on Postmodernism," *Critical Quarterly* 29, no. 1 (1987)

Rutsala, Vern, "'The Truth About Us': William Carlos Williams," *New England Review and Bread Loaf Quarterly* 8, no. 1 (1985)

Simpson, Louis, "Reflections on Narrative Poetry," in *Claims for Poetry,* edited by Donald Hall, Ann Arbor: University of Michigan Press, 1998

Walzer, Kevin, *The Ghost of Tradition: Expansive Poetry and Postmodernism,* Ashland, Oregon: Story Line Press, 1998

Whedon, Tony, "Three Mannerists," *American Poetry Review* 17, no. 3 (1988)

Wojahn, David, "Without a Deep Delight: Neo-Narrative Poetry and Its Problems," *Denver Quarterly* 23, nos. 3–4 (1989)

## Ogden Nash 1902–71

A master of light, whimsical, and sometimes nonsensical verse, Nash started his writing career at Doubleday Page Publishers, where he wrote his first children's book with Joseph Algers, *The Cricket of Carador*, in 1925. After six years of writing advertising copy as an editor and publicist at Doubleday, Nash claimed, he began his career in humorous poetry by scribbling one afternoon. His scribbles were to become a poem called "Spring Comes to Murray Hill," which he threw away. Upon some thought, however, he retrieved it from the wastebasket and sent it to *The New Yorker*. His first piece of satiric verse was published in 1930.

After "Murray Hill" Nash's work began to appear in other periodicals. He was prolific enough that he published a collection of his poetry, *Hard Lines*, in 1931. *Hard Lines* sold out seven printings in its first year and catapulted Nash into his role as the master of light verse. In 1932 Nash left Doubleday to join the editorial staff of *The New Yorker*. His steady and lengthy affiliation with the magazine helped establish its distinctive tone and sense of humor. According to poet Archibald MacLeish, Nash "altered the sensibility of his time." Even after the widespread reception of his first book, however, Nash still insisted that the whole thing was an accident. He had already become quite popular with the general public through his work in *The New Yorker* and "Information Please," a radio quiz show. Eventually he began to write full-time, publishing over two dozen books of poetry and prose in his lifetime.

In an environment in which people cared little about poetry, Nash managed to be one of the most popular and most quoted poets of his time, coining such phrases as "candy is dandy but liquor is quicker." His turn of the phrase, his puns, and his nonsensical rhymes appealed to people of all ages. While speaking in the Library of Congress auditorium, Nash suggested that the average man, surviving the perils of the nuclear age, needed not only missiles, submarines, and a fallout shelter, but also a few lighthearted laughs to save him.

Although the *Atlantic Monthly* heralded Nash as "God's gift to the United States" for his insightful commentary on 20th-century America, his work had international appeal. He was known as the Everyman of his time, the poet of the ordinary and universal. His poems were humorous not only because they made people laugh, but also because they contained some truth of human experience. His signature style used exaggeration, an element of surprise, and absurdity juxtaposed with the universal experience with which the average reader can identify. He was well regarded by critics and the public alike for his inventive titles, his unlikely rhymes, and his ridiculous play on words. Throughout his career a variety of publications from the *Boston Herald* to the *Saturday Review of Literature* sang critical praise for his work.

Although a great fan of Edward Lear and the limerick, Nash possessed a style that was very irregular indeed. Sometimes his poems contained only a handful of words; at other times they went on for several lines before ending in a clever or sometimes nonsensical rhyme. On many occasions he invented a word to fit the rhyme: "Each spring they beautify our suburb, the ladies of the garden cluburb" ("Correction: Eve Delved and Adam Span"). His other rhymes include such sets as nostrilly/tonsilly/irresponsilly ("Fahrenheit Gesundheit") and tortoises/porpoises/corpoises ("Don't Cry, Darling, It's Blood All Right").

Not only are his lines and rhymes irregular, but the length of his poems varied greatly. Some verses would go on for pages at a time, while others began and ended abruptly in two lines. It is quite possible that Nash has written one of the shortest poems in the English language, "Reflection on a Wicked World": "Purity is obscurity." The themes of his poems varied wildly as well. From getting eyeglasses as an old man to traveling in Europe, no subject was too banal or far-fetched for Nash. His middle-class life and family provided no end of inspiration. He wrote of proud parenting, the folly of being a husband, suburban crowds, diets, vacations, fatherhood, and anything else he could think of.

Through his numerous volumes Nash became well established as a writer of light verse. Even after Hollywood expressed interest in his work, poetry remained his primary source of income. Although none of his screenplays were produced, his work was optioned several times, providing enough money for him and his wife to travel to Europe. Eventually he returned to the East Coast to continue writing verse. He also lectured extensively throughout the United States and England. Through his lecture tours he developed a deep respect and keen understanding of his fellow man, which his work reflected. His television appearances in the 1950s (such as "Masquerade Party") also helped increase his popularity.

Nash also renewed his interest in children's literature in the 1950s. He believed that his writing was not just for kids, but rather lay in a gray area between child and adult worlds. In his numerous volumes for children, such as *Custard the Dragon* (1959), Nash continues his setting for universal truth. Nash's approach to children is neither condescending nor mocking, however; in fact, his whimsical yet serious attitude toward the young has gained him respect among children of all ages.

When he was not writing poetry, Nash appeared on various radio game and comedy shows in the 1940s and wrote scores for TV shows in the 1950s, including lyrics for the show "Peter and the Wolf." In 1943 Nash collaborated with Kurt Weill and S.J. Perelman on *One Touch of Venus*, a musical comedy. He continued to write, publish, and lecture until very close to the end of his life.

CECILIA HAE-JIN LEE

*See also* Light Verse

**Biography**
Born in Rye, New York, 19 August 1902. Attended Harvard University, Cambridge, Massachusetts, 1920–21; teacher, St. George's School, 1922–23; bond salesman on Wall Street, New York, 1924; worked in advertising department of Doubleday Page Publishers, New York, 1925–31; on editorial staff, *The New Yorker*, 1932, and regular contributor thereafter; screenwriter in Hollywood, 1936–42; panelist, "Masquerade Party" radio program, 1950s. Received Sarah Josepha Hale Award, 1964; member, American Academy; member, National Institute of Arts and Letters. Died in Baltimore, Maryland, 19 May 1971.

**Poetry**
*Hard Lines*, 1931
*Free Wheeling*, 1931
*Happy Days*, 1933

*Four Prominent So and So's* (music by Robert Armbruster), 1934; republished as *Four Prominent Bastards Are We,* 1934
*The Primrose Path,* 1935
*The Bad Parent's Garden of Verse,* 1936
*I'm a Stranger Here Myself,* 1938
*The Face Is Familiar: Selected Verse,* 1940; revised edition, 1954
*Good Intentions,* 1942; revised edition, 1956
*Many Long Years Ago,* 1945
*Selected Verse,* 1946
*Versus,* 1949
*Family Reunion,* 1950
*The Private Dining Room, and Other New Verses,* 1952
*You Can't Get There from Here,* 1957
*The Christmas That Almost Wasn't,* 1957
*Verses from 1929 on,* 1959; republished as *Collected Verse from 1929 on,* 1961
*Everyone But Thee and Me,* 1962
*Marriage Lines: Notes of a Student Husband,* 1964
*Santa Go Home: A Case History for Parents,* 1967
*There's Always Another Windmill,* 1968
*Bed Riddance: A Posy for the Indisposed,* 1970
*The Old Dog Barks Backwards,* 1972
*I Wouldn't Have Missed It: Selected Poems of Ogden Nash,* edited by Linell Smith and Isabel Eberstadt, 1975
*A Penny Saved Is Impossible,* 1981
*Selected Poems,* 1983
*Selected Poetry of Ogden Nash: 650 Rhymes, Verses, Lyrics, and Poems,* 1995

**Other Writings:** plays, screenplays (*The Shining Hour* [with Jane Murfin], 1938), children's literature (*Custard the Dragon,* 1959), essays; edited collections of literature (*The Moon Is Shining Bright as Day: An Anthology of Good-Humored Verse,* 1953).

**Further Reading**

Allen, Everett S., *Famous American Humorous Poets,* New York: Dodd Mead, 1968
Crandell, George W., *The Ogden Nash Collection at the University of Texas: A Catalogue of the Correspondence,* Austin: University of Texas Press, 1981
Crandell, George W., *Ogden Nash: A Descriptive Bibliography,* Metuchen, New Jersey: Scarecrow Press, 1990
Smith, Linnell Nash, compiler, *Loving Letters from Ogden Nash: A Family Album,* Boston: Little Brown, 1990
Stuart, David, *The Life and Rhymes of Ogden Nash,* Lanham, Maryland: Madison Books, 2000

---

# Native American Poetry

Kenneth Lincoln, in his *Native American Renaissance* (1983), observes that, a generation before most contemporary Indian writers were born, Ezra Pound and other Modernists prepared a non-Indian audience for the new nativism, defined by

> its organic forms and subjects: the eidetic image, the musical cadence, the intrinsic song of spoken language, the visionary passion that charges words with meaning, the nonformalist rediscovery of art *in* things.

Lincoln characterizes the Native American Renaissance as "a written renewal of oral traditions translated into Western literary forms" and traces its origins to the 1960s, when writers such as N. Scott Momaday were recognized by the mainstream literary establishment for their literary achievements. Substantial collections of Native American poetry, such as *Carriers of the Dream Wheel* and *Voices of the Rainbow: Contemporary Poetry by American Indians,* both published in 1975, may be seen as the products of this period of integration and renewal. Contemporary Native American poets, while well schooled in the Western literary tradition, continue to draw on a range of tribal values and traditions: the oral tradition, the cyclical notion of time, a land ethic that emphasizes the relation between nature and human nature, the importance of tribal and ancestral connections to the individual, and various poetic and narrative traditions.

Native American writers emphasize the need to preserve tribal values and traditions in order to maintain a sense of personal identity. Many, in fact, view their work as an important means of preserving their culture. Joseph Bruchac (1987b) contends that

> Survival is one of the major themes in contemporary Native American writing—survival of the old ways, survival of Indian nations, personal survival, and, in the long run, the survival of the whole biosphere.

He further notes:

> The shared themes of survival, of the aliveness of all creation, of the necessity for balance, and of the making power of words are some of the concepts which are part of what might be called a "Pan-Indian" consciousness.

Perhaps for this reason, N. Scott Momaday's Pulitzer Prize–winning *House Made of Dawn* (1968), with its message that a person caught between two cultures can survive, resonated for many Native American writers. Momaday's earliest books of poetry, *Angle of Geese* (1974) and *The Gourd Dancer* (1976), rely on conventional Western poetic form, but also, in several cycles of poems, including "Plainview" and "The Gourd Dancer," on Native beliefs, in particular the concept of a speaking land and the sense of the presence of the past.

Like Momaday, Simon Ortiz, of the Acoma Pueblo tribe in New Mexico, relies on the theme of survival in poems such as "Survival This Way." He also renders the landscape as a living force: "Not only the plants but even the mountains and canyons are growing, living presences that respond to the blessing of the rain" ("Survival"). His recurrent themes are

> the community of the land, the life of the earth's body, the tragedy of losing touch with that life, the search to recover and the struggle to retain its substantial exhilaration. (Wiget, 1985)

Because of the importance of the oral tradition in Ortiz's culture, he regards words not as objects but as "acts with power to organize experience."

Prior to the incursion of Western culture, most Native American tribes depended on the oral transmission of tribal lore; thus, language and poetry were more highly regarded than in Western cultures dependent on writing as a means of communication. Duane Niatum (1984) points out that, because Native American communities were held together by an oral tradition, poetry has traditionally played an essential role in all aspects of Native American life. Likewise, N. Scott Momaday (Kiowa) observes that, because of the nature of the oral tradition, language is understood to be a vital and powerful thing in itself. Song is even believed to have healing power. Whereas the Romantic tradition, creative writing programs, and the Confessional school in American poetry encourage readers to conflate the voices of the poet and the speaker, the oral tradition in Native American poetry relies on interplay between individual and collective expression (McAdams, 1995).

Niatum also observes that American Indian poetry illuminates the present moment by some aspect of the past; time is cyclical rather than linear. This understanding of time leads to the emphasis on ancestral connections: "One of the oldest tribal values is the sense and need for supporting the continuity among generations." Niatum explains that

> what is meant by ancestral connections is a belief the Native American has in never looking upon the land or rivers or lakes surrounding his village without seeing the homes and paths of his grandfathers and grandmothers. So that, "by singing, the soul of the singer is put in harmony with the essential essence of things."

This sense of wholeness is extended to the Native American's relation to the natural world, both animate and inanimate; the modern, Western way of defining self and the world in terms of fragmentation and disunity is foreign to the Native American sensibility. Native American poets celebrate a sense of wholeness, a view of the body as a landscape of the mind.

The work of Leslie Marmon Silko (Laguna Pueblo) illustrates this focus on the relationship to the land and the importance of oral tradition. Silko relies on tribal mythology as a means of interpreting contemporary events and has published a volume of poetry, *Laguna Woman* (1974), several poems in anthologies, as well as a mixture of prose and poetry in *Storyteller* (1981). In Silko's poetry natural elements such as water, butterflies, and sunlight are used to celebrate human sexuality as well as to emphasize the human connection to the natural world. Hunting serves as a metaphor for human relationships, death as a metaphor for sexual union.

Other prominent Native American writers include Maurice Kenny (Mohawk), who writes in a parallel way about the landscape of the Northwest, emphasizing connections between land and history and drawing on the rhythms of Walt Whitman as well as those of Native Ghost Dance songs. Peter Blue Cloud (Mohawk), author of two books of poetry, draws on images from the natural world of the forest, the Mohawk origin myth of the world built on a turtle's back, and the Iroquoian story of how corn came to the people in the person of a young girl. Blue Cloud, like poets Karoniaktatie (Alex Jacobs), Norman Russell, and Barney Bush (*My Horse and a Jukebox,* 1980), deliberately omits punctuation and uses lowercase "i." These poets regard "capitalization and punctuation as unnatural barriers between themselves and the living creation around them" (Bruchac, 1987b).

Lance Henson, a Southern Cheyenne poet, explores his people's close yet unsentimental relationship with the natural world and their traditional ceremonies. His collections include *Naming the Dark* (1976), *Mistah* (1977), and *Buffalo Marrow on Black* (1981). Henson relies on powerful images in part to "probe the layers of the unconscious" in a manner similar to that of Western thinkers such as Freud and Jung, but also to render the Native conception of the self.

Hopi/Miwok poet Wendy Roses relies more on non-Indian concepts that show the influence of Western civilization. In her first two volumes, however, *Hopi Roadrunner Dancing* (1973) and *Long Division: A Tribal History* (1976), Rose nonetheless draws on a Native vision, rendering the earth as alive. *Academic Squaw* (1977) explores the conflict inherent in being an anthropologist and an Indian, the "dilemma of being a student in a discipline which has treated one's own ancestors as little more than bones to be dug up and labeled" (Bruchac, 1987b). *Builder Kachina: A Home-Going Cycle* (1979) centers on the figure of the kachina, the supernatural beings responsible in Hopi legend for managing all the forces of the world. In this and other collections Rose reveals the dialogic nature of Native American poetry in poems that mark the boundaries of her life, yet also, in the European-derived way, express her individuality (Fast, 1995). *Lost Copper* (1981) includes Rose's previous work as well as many new poems. Andrew Wiget (1985) claims that "of all the native poets now writing, none, with the possible exception of Momaday, has more consistently reasserted the creation of personal identity through art [than Rose]."

James Welch (Blackfeet/Gros Ventre) has written a collection of poetry, *Riding the Earthboy 40* (1971), whose thematic concerns reflect those of his novels. His influences include the South American Surrealists as well as the Native American land ethic: "the weight of history, especially the burden of ancient animosities between whites and Indians, rests heavily on the land" (Wiget, 1985).

Duane McGinnis Niatum (Klallam/Irish) is the author of a half-dozen collections of poetry, including three major collections. Like Momaday, he draws on the Western tradition of art and literature while also paying homage to tribal traditions. His work revolves around three recurrent themes: sexual and romantic encounters, the nature of his mixed heritage, and reclamation of his Klallam heritage. In his poems

> the sea, the gulls, berries, cedars, shamans, wolves, salmons, bears, smoke, and all the other cultural symbols of Northwest Coast tribal life, even native language words, are invoked

> almost as talismans, touchstones of a deep and private affective memory. (Wiget, 1985)

Joy Harjo (Creek) and Ray A. Young Bear (Mesquakie) both have attempted to develop systems of personal symbols in order to create alternate contexts of meaning. Both have turned not only from Western conventions but also from tribal ones to achieve a synthesis of multiple voices. Harjo, the author of *What Moon Drove Me to This?* (1979), a commentary on contemporary Indian life, contends that one of Native America's most important contributions to mainstream literature is a land-based language that recognizes a sense of place. The poems in this, her first collection, use sun and moon imagery to explore cycles of fulfillment and abandonment and alternate realities and identities. In collections such as *She Had Some Horses* (1983), *Secrets from the Center of the World* (1989), and *In Mad Love and War* (1990), Harjo focuses on her identity as a woman, and the way in which many Indian cultures have devolved into male-centered, male-dominated cultures.

Young Bear, in his collection *The Invisible Musician* (1990), employs a collective voice and establishes a kind of play between his role as individual artist/poet and traditional singer. His use of surrealism in *Winter of the Salamander* (1980) allows him, like Henson, to draw on Western theories of the unconscious as well as Native theories about the nature and origin of the self. Young Bear, as well as Linda Hogan (Chickasaw) and other contemporary Native American poets, subverts the

> homogenizing of voice and person of dominant mode poetics by constructing voice in the interstices between individual and collective, between the "literary" and the "oral." (McAdams, 1995)

Harjo, Hogan, Rose, and Paula Gunn Allen (Laguna/Sioux/Lebanese) are all engaged in reexamining their roles as women based on traditional Native values. Hogan's first book, *Calling Myself Home* (1978), in suggesting the transformations of persons not only into animals but also into natural elements and objects, recreates the vital connection between nature and human nature that even her state's name, Oklahoma (which in Choctaw simultaneously means "red earth" and "red people"), demonstrates. In an interview Hogan claimed that "if you believe that the earth, and all living things, and all the stones are sacred, your responsibility really is to protect those things" (Coltelli, 1990). *Daughters, I Love You* (1981) again emphasizes transformation and explores the way in which women have been represented in culture. Hogan "reinvents 'voice' as a site of 'play' rather than as a fixed category." Her "The History of Red" remaps identity "by constructing a persona that need not be singular and unified in order to be coherent." By delaying the use of the pronouns "me" or "I" until the ninth stanza—nearly the end of the poem—so that "we" as collective pronoun precedes a clear reference to the speaker, Hogan insists that the poem's "we" be read as collective *and* historical. By the time the singular speaker of the poem is introduced, it is clear that Hogan has "reconstructed it retrospectively to include the speaker's 'mothers,' who appeared in the third stanza" (McAdams, 1995).

Paula Gunn Allen acknowledges that her own mixed heritage has enabled her to deal with a variety of cultural styles, and she views American Indian literature as multi-ethnic because it does not represent a unified common culture, language, or tribal heritage. She acknowledges that influences on her culture include everything from Western literature and music to Catholicism to the rhythm of Arabic songs, chants, and dances. Her poetry moves from the fragmented syntax and abruptly broken images of her first book of poetry, *Coyote's Day Trip* (1978), to *A Cannon Between the Knees* (1981), which is more reflective, mature, and unified in tone and theme. Several poems celebrate Native women and their focus on connections, relationships, and creativity. *Shadow Country* (1982), features black-and-white and color art. Gunn's other collections of poetry include *Wyrds* (1987) and *Skin and Bones* (1988).

Robin Riley Fast (1995) contends that, because many contemporary Indian writers are of mixed race and acknowledge the influence of both Western and tribal traditions, their poetry is generally dialogic, with "antecedents in traditional song, chant, and story, forms that are generally anonymous, tribal, or communal rather than authored by one person." To convey the effect of multiple influences and mixed origins, Native American poets employ several devices that foreground dialogism. These devices include the intermixing of English and Native languages, the placing of traditional figures in contemporary contexts, puns, the use of colloquial expressions in contexts that undermine their intent, the use of multiple speakers or of a single voice using both direct and indirect discourse, the use of multiple levels or registers of discourse, and allusions to historical events or cultural references in contexts that foreground contrasting interpretations (Fast, 1995). Native American writing, like other American ethnic writing, may be viewed as "border writing" in several ways: the reservation is a borderland, and the Native American in mainstream society exists in a borderland in cultural, spiritual, and emotional terms.

Although contemporary Native American poets wish to promote a sense of community, many fear that

> a preoccupation with background and cultural issues undervalues their work and misleads the reader by directing attention away from the creative strategies of art to the unalterable realities of inheritance. (Wiget, 1984)

Many Native poets lament the arrival of the "white shaman," white poets like Gary Snyder, Jerome Rothenberg, and James Koller, who argue that "their art licenses them to appropriate to their own purposes language, images, and prosodic structures originating in Native American tribal literatures." This appropriation is viewed by Native American poets as a form of cultural imperialism, the effect of which is "the promotion of a dulled esthetic based on a neo-primitivist's conception of 'Indianness' as a body of trivialized conventional images" (Wiget, 1984). Paula Gunn Allen laments the fact that Gary Snyder received a Pulitzer Prize for *Turtle Island* (1974), in which he appropriates Native culture, whereas Simon Ortiz was not awarded a Pulitzer Prize for his authentic representation of Native life and culture in *Going for the Rain* (1976). This aesthetic has also made it difficult for Native American poets to place poems on "non-Indian" themes and has led to the "fatal presumption that all Indians are poets, or at least marketable as poets, a confusion of art and ethnicity that promotes novelty instead of achievement" (Wiget, 1984).

DONNA L. POTTS

**Further Reading**

Bromley, Anne, "Renegade Wants the Word: Contemporary Native American Poetry," *The Literary Review* 23, no. 3 (Spring 1980)

Bruchac, Joseph, "Many Tongues: Native American Poetry Today," *North Dakota Quarterly* (Fall 1987)

Bruchac, Joseph, "Survival Comes This Way: Contemporary Native American Poetry," in *A Gift of Tongues: Critical Challenges in Contemporary American Poetry,* edited by Marie Harris and Kathleen Aguero, Athens: University of Georgia Press, 1987

Coltelli, Laura, *Winged Words: American Indian Writers Speak,* Lincoln: University of Nebraska Press, 1990

Fast, Robin Riley, "Borderland Voices in Contemporary Native American Poetry," *Contemporary Literature* 36, no. 3 (Fall 1995)

Lincoln, Kenneth, *Native American Renaissance,* Berkeley: University of California Press, 1983

McAdams, Janet, "We, I, 'Voice,' and Voices: Reading Contemporary Native American Poetry," *Studies in American Indian Literatures* 7, no. 3 (Fall 1995)

Milton, John, *The American Indian Speaks,* Vermillion: University of South Dakota Press, 1969

Milton, John, *American Indian II,* Vermillion: University of South Dakota Press, 1971

Niatum, Duane, "History in the Colors of Song: A Few Words on Contemporary Native American Poetry," in *Coyote Was Here: Essays on Contemporary Native American Literary and Political Mobilization,* edited by Bo Schöler, Aarhus, Denmark: SEKLOS, 1984

Roemer, Kenneth, "Bear and Elk: The Nature(s) of Contemporary Indian Poetry," *Journal of Ethnic Studies* 5 (1977)

Rupert, J., "The Uses of Oral Tradition in Six Contemporary Native American Poets," *American Indian Culture and Research Journal* 4 (1980)

Scarberry-Garcia, Susan, "Simon Ortiz," in *Dictionary of Literary Biography,* volume 175: *Native American Writers of the United States,* edited by Kenneth Roemer, Arlington: University of Texas Press, 1997

Wiget, Andrew, "Sending a Voice: The Emergence of Contemporary Native American Poetry," *College English* 46, no. 6 (October 1984)

Wiget, Andrew, "Contemporary Poetry," in *Native American Literature,* by Wiget, Boston: Twayne, 1985

---

# Howard Nemerov 1920–91

One of the most notable of those poets who came of age during World War II, Howard Nemerov grew up in New York City. Son to cultivated Jewish parents, he was an excellent student at the Feldstone School and then at Harvard University. He graduated from college to the war, flying first for Canadian and then for American forces. Discharged in 1945, he took a job at Hamilton College and so began a distinguished career as fiction writer, essayist, and poet while teaching at several prestigious colleges and universities. He spent nearly 20 years at Bennington College in Vermont, which had many writers and artists on the faculty, and more than 20 years at Washington University in St. Louis, where he numbered Stanley Elkin and Mona Van Duyn among his friends.

Those few facts suggest many of Nemerov's most common subjects. Combat experience informs several poems in his first collection of 1947, and the book's central theme is death. Combat memories return remarkably in the 1987 volume *War Stories,* and his sense of "the good war" underlies a number of political poems, including the powerful "On Getting out of Viet Nam." Death remained an important theme through to his last and posthumous volume, which closes on the "inveterate infantile hope / That the road ends but as the runway does." The wonderful title of the poem (and the book) is "Trying Conclusions."

The move to the country in Vermont brought nature into the poetry and opened for Nemerov the line of poetry that plays natural renewal against terminations. Nemerov's nature, seldom simple, can tempt the mind to the hyperingenious. In "The Blue Swallows," the speaker looks down on the birds from a bridge and sees "the swallow's tails as nibs / Dipped in invisible ink, writing," one might imagine, "Some cabalistic history." There the "spelling mind" distracts from the truth: "Finding again the world, That is the point." Yet nature has truths to tell. In "The Goose Fish," two lovers embracing on a moonlit shore imagine themselves "emparadised" until they see at their feet the "hugely grinning head" of a dead fish. No simple memento mori, the fish becomes "emblem" of their love, first "comedian," then "Rigid optimist," and finally a patriarch who explains no better than most the ironic joke that amuses him and that amuses and troubles the reader.

Nemerov's academic career provided the stuff of many poems. Light verse mocks committee meetings, full professors, careerism, grants, readings, and literati, and dozens of poems connect with what he read and taught—poems, writers, and the nature of language and of poetry itself. An "unobserving Jew," his assaults on puffed piety are fierce, and he finds more truth in classical mythology than in the promises of religion. However, allusions to the Old Testament are rich, as are, more surprisingly, those to St. Augustine, Dante, the New Testament, and the life of Christ. He was heavily influenced by the High Modernists, especially Eliot, Auden, Yeats, and Stevens, and described himself as "imitative" at the start, a poet who valued "irony, difficulty, erudition, and the Metaphysical style." He moved away from the metaphysical armory in time and came to value more highly "simplicity and the appearance of ease in the measure" and "the detachment of a single thought from its ambiguous surroundings" ("Attentiveness and Obedience"). By his third book of poems, *The Salt Garden*

(1955), he had found his own secure voice—witty, ironic, contemplative, and in a measure sad. He continued to gain power through the publication of *The Collected Poems* (1977), which won the National Book Award and the Pulitzer Prize, and four solid books followed *The Collected Poems*. Nemerov was poet laureate of the United States from 1988 to 1990.

It is true that Nemerov's mature verse is seldom obscure, but his range of thought and his wit can be challenging. That wit turned at times to scathing imprecations and epigrams aimed at weak poets (one of whom falls "flat on his ars / Poetica") and at the trend toward free and often longer poems represented in the influential 1969 anthology *Naked Poetry*. Finding much in that movement boring and flabby, he remained a formalist against the mode. The wit also turned often—too often some would say—to jokes and to sometimes execrable puns. These diversions deserve attention, however, for Nemerov thought and wrote persuasively about the connection between poems and jokes in "Bottom's Dream," "Poetry and Meaning," and other essays. Nemerov saw that both joke and poem demand economy of expression. In both, the expected order of things is suddenly reversed when the unexpected (often an absurdity) impinges on the established sense of the way things are. That intrusion then leads to a new and deeper understanding—something hidden is revealed. Allusion, metaphor, situational irony, and even the pun can serve this process well. In addition, Nemerov felt that meter and rhyme contributed importantly to an effect of "decisiveness and finish, of absolute completion to which nothing need be added nor could be added" when expectation leads to "a fulfillment which is simultaneously exact and surprising."

"On an Occasion of National Mourning" treats the aftermath of the space shuttle *Challenger* explosion in 1986. Nemerov traces the public's indulgence in "silvery platitudes" and devotion to an investigation determined to banish such errors from the earth; and so "the nation rises again," Nemerov writes, "Remembering the shuttle, forgetting the loom." In that closing line, the word "shuttle" suddenly loses its connection to the space program and plunges through centuries to an ancient craft and an ancient metaphor carrying a tragic view of life. Watching various shuttles fly back and forth, the nation forgot the fabric of existence.

That is an instance of "getting something right" in language "to keep out windy time / And the worm." In "Lion and Honeycomb," the speaker makes clear that this rightness has to do not with great monuments but with things "Perfected and casual as to a child's eye / Soap bubbles are, and skipping stones."

For Nemerov, language matters above all. He quotes Erich Heller approvingly: "Be careful how you interpret the world, it *is* like that." His most profound poems explore the ways in which nature responds to language and the ways in which language becomes part of the material world. Nemerov tends to play this theme in the epistemological manner of Stevens rather than the bardic manner of Emerson, but he claims that in language "the living and the dead speak simultaneously" ("Attentiveness and Obedience"). In "The Makers," he imagines those primal poets of the origins of language who "worded the world" and then vanished from it,

> Leaving no memory but the marvelous
> Magical elements, the breathing shapes
> And stops of breath we build our Babels of.

The movement from wording the world to Babel and the vision of our words and selves as breathing shapes articulated by stops of breath—these magical elements suggest the scope of Nemerov's poetic project.

WILLIAM CLARKSON

**Biography**

Born in New York City, 1 March 1920. Attended Harvard University, Cambridge, Massachusetts (Bowdoin Prize, 1940), A.B. 1941; served in the Royal Canadian Air Force, 1942–44, and the United States Army Air Corps, 1944–45; Instructor in English, Hamilton College, Clinton, New York, 1946–48; literature faculty member, Bennington College, Vermont, 1948–66; Professor of English, Brandeis University, Waltham, Massachusetts, 1966–69; Hurst Professor of English, 1969–76, and Edward Mallinckrodt Distinguished University Professor, 1976–1991, Washington University, St. Louis, Missouri; Visiting Lecturer, University of Minnesota, Minneapolis, 1958–59; writer-in-residence, Hollins College, Virginia, 1962–64; consultant in poetry, Library of Congress, Washington, D.C., 1963–64; Associate Editor, *Furioso*, 1946–51. Received American Academy grant, 1961; New England Poetry Club Golden Rose, 1962; Brandeis University Creative Arts Award, 1962; National Endowment for the Arts grant, 1966; Theodore Roethke Award, 1968; Guggenheim fellowship, 1968; St. Botolph's Club Prize, 1968; Academy of American Poets fellowship, 1970; Pulitzer Prize, 1978; National Book Award, 1978; Bollingen Prize, 1981; received honorary degrees from seven colleges and universities; fellow, American Academy of Arts and Sciences, 1966; member, American Academy, 1976; Chancellor, Academy of American Poets, 1977; Poet Laureate of the United States, 1988–90. Died in University City, Missouri, 5 July 1991.

**Poetry**

*The Image and the Law*, 1947
*Guide to the Ruins*, 1950
*The Salt Garden*, 1955
*Small Moment*, 1957
*Mirrors and Windows*, 1958
*New and Selected Poems*, 1960
*The Next Room of the Dream: Poems and Two Plays*, 1962
*Five American Poets* (with others), edited by Ted Hughes and Thom Gunn, 1963
*Departure of the Ships*, 1966
*The Blue Swallows*, 1967
*A Sequence of Seven*, 1967
*The Winter Lightning: Selected Poems*, 1968
*The Painter Dreaming in the Scholar's House*, 1968
*Gnomes and Occasions*, 1972
*The Western Approaches: Poems, 1973–1975*, 1975
*The Collected Poems*, 1977
*By Al Lebowitz's Pool*, 1979
*Sentences*, 1980
*Inside the Onion*, 1984
*War Stories: Poems about Long Ago and Now*, 1987
*Trying Conclusions: New and Selected Poems, 1961–1991*, 1991
*A Howard Nemerov Reader* (includes prose), 1991

**Selected Criticism**
*Reflections on Poetry and Poetics,* 1972

**Other Writings:** play, novels (*The Homecoming Game,* 1957), short stories (*Stories, Fables, and Other Diversions,* 1971), essays (*New and Selected Essays,* 1965); edited collections of literature (*Poets on Poetry,* 1966).

**Further Reading**

Bartholomay, Julia, *The Shield of Perseus: The Vision and Imagination of Howard Nemerov,* Gainesville: University of Florida Press, 1972
Bowers, Neal, "An Interview with Howard Nemerov," *Massachusetts Review* 22, no. 1 (1981)
Edgecombe, Rodney Stenning, *A Reader's Guide to the Poetry of Howard Nemerov,* Salzburg, Austria: University of Salzburg, 1999
Kiehl, James, "The Poems of Howard Nemerov: Where Loveliness Adorns Intelligible Things," *Salmagundi* 22–23 (1973)
Labrie, Ross, *Howard Nemerov,* Boston: Twayne, 1980
Meinke, Peter, *Howard Nemerov,* Minneapolis: University of Minnesota Press, and London: Oxford University Press, 1968
Mills, William, *The Stillness in Moving Things: The World of Howard Nemerov,* Memphis, Tennesee: Memphis State University Press, 1975
Nemerov, Alexander, "Modeling My Father," *American Scholar* 62, no. 4 (1993)
Prunty, Wyatt, *"Fallen from the Symboled World": Precedents for the New Formalism,* Oxford and New York: Oxford University Press, 1990
Smith, Raymond, "Nemerov and Nature: 'The Stillness in Moving Things,'" *The Southern Review* 10 (1974)


---

# New Criticism

The New Criticism, as it came to be called from a book by that title written by the poet John Crowe Ransom in 1941, was the first critical movement to enjoy widespread influence in the 20th century. It may also be the first American literary movement to have been launched exclusively by university poets and critics to prepare undergraduate students to read and analyze a limited canon of literary works mainly from the 17th and 20th centuries. The leading figures of the movement, all southerners by birth, were Ransom and Donald Davidson, originally professors at Vanderbilt University in Nashville, Tennessee; Andrew Lytle, a professor and novelist who contributed to an early manifesto of the movement, *I'll Take My Stand: The South and the Agrarian Tradition* (1930), and later edited the *Sewanee Review* (1942–43); and their students Robert Penn Warren, Allen Tate, and Cleanth Brooks, the last the most formidable and prolific practitioner of New Critical methods. Others associated with the movement include the poets Randall Jarrell, himself an able critic and author of *Poetry and the Age* (1953), and two transplanted northerners, Robert Heilman, a critic and professor who moved from Harvard to Louisiana State University in Baton Rouge, and the poet Robert Lowell, who studied poetry under Ransom and Tate at Vanderbilt and Kenyon College, after leaving Harvard in his freshman year.

The New Criticism began at Vanderbilt University, where Ransom published the literary quarterly *The Fugitive* (1922–25), and continued at Louisiana State University, where Brooks and Warren co-edited the *Southern Review* (1933–42) and collaborated on two of the most widely used textbooks on literature, *Understanding Poetry* (1938) and *Understanding Fiction* (1943); a third textbook, *Understanding Drama* (1945), was co-edited by Brooks and Robert Heilman. These and important essay collections demonstrating the analytic methods of New Criticism by Brooks constitute one of the most thoroughgoing attempts to systematize how literature is read and understood. The New Criticism's rigorous attention to the rhetorical processes of literary expression began an era of critical debate about literature and its meanings that flourished at Yale University when Brooks joined its faculty in 1947. After 1960, the New Criticism faced assaults from other critical theorists who have long since replaced its method with historical, social, and cultural modes of literary analysis.

In one sense, the New Criticism arose out of the need to teach reading comprehension to rural youths flocking to the universities on their way to the technical jobs and professions offered by a newly emerging industrialized South of the 1930s. In another, it was the attempt by a generation of southern poets and critics to distinguish their regional culture from the New York literary establishment and, following T.S. Eliot's lead, to link it with that of 17th-century England, the last era before industrialism ended its pastoral economy and secularized literature. From still another point of view, it was the effort by southern conservative intellectuals to dissociate literature from ideology and history, to avoid having to explain or apologize for the tarnished past of a region guilty of secession, civil war, and slavery. By arguing that southern culture still espoused the Christian humanism of earlier English culture, the New Critics defined their region as a bulwark against the spread of social Darwinism and the "pagan culture" of industrial democracy.

The origins of New Criticism may be traced back to the critical pronouncements and attitudes of T.S. Eliot, who lamented the loss of an "undissociated sensibility," or ability to think in terms of both flesh and spirit, last expressed in 17th-century literature (in "The Metaphysical Poets"), and who argued for a lyric poetry in which Christian tradition informed and unified modern subjectivity (in "Tradition and the Individual Talent"). Eliot advocated a return to Christian piety and fellowship with his collection of essays *For Lancelot Andrewes* (1928); his hopes for a religious renaissance were declared in *The Idea of a Christian Society* (1939). He rejected the Modernist turn to other religions in *After Strange*

*Gods* (1934) and demonstrated his idea of a Christian imagination in *The Four Quartets* (1943).

Eliot's role as a leading spokesman for Christian values and for the importance of 17th-century English verse to modern literature influenced Ransom's early poetry and attempts to idealize the South as a culture descended from English values and customs. His poetry depicted a manorial world of quaint gardens and cultivated lives cast into an imaginary South where neither politics nor the modern world intervened. This vision became overtly political when he helped launch the quarterly *The Fugitive,* a title rich in the suggestion that its writers were escaping from an alien world to the north.

When the Scopes trial opened in Dayton, Tennessee, in 1925 over the issue of teaching Darwinism in the public schools, H.L. Mencken and others wrote sardonically of the backward South, prompting Ransom, Davidson, and others to publish a defense of traditional southern values in *I'll Take My Stand.* The writers called their movement Agrarianism, and literary historians have since referred to the group by both names: Fugitives and Agrarians. A second collection of polemical defenses of southern culture appeared in *Who Owns America? A New Declaration of Independence* (1936), featuring many of the same writers.

As Brooks noted after reading *I'll Take My Stand,* the question of defining the South was essentially a "religious one." Ransom published a more strident polemic against secular science in *God without Thunder* (1930), followed by his more general indictment of secularism in modern life, *The World's Body* (1938), in which he affirmed the moral obligations of literature to counter bloodless science. In *The New Criticism* (1941), Ransom offered a narrow view of the poem as argument by means of a system or "structure" of metaphors; like Eliot, Ransom believed in an "impersonal" lyric in which the poet elaborates a view of life through a rhetoric of tropes and irony. Ransom's analytic method works by ferreting out an elusive argument concealed by the relative nature of words. The poem, according to Ransom, is the very opposite of scientific discourse in its use of symbols, emotional formulas, and ambiguous images.

In 1936 Brooks and Warren and a graduate student at Louisiana State, John Purser, published *An Approach to Literature: A Collection of Prose and Verse with Analyses and Discussions;* it covered the major genres (and expository prose) and contained critical introductions that guided students through an exacting method of analysis of each genre, part for part. The method, like Ransom's, required little or no information about author or context for comprehending literary discourse. Meaning was inseparable from its expression in the work and could be understood only by means of parsing and relating the elements composing it.

The method was calculated to avoid impressionism or historical interpretation and seemed to dismiss the importance of aesthetic pleasure in reading, which inspired some critics to rename the book "The Reproach to Literature." Poetry, like drama, expressed emotion through the accumulating motives within the text, not by mere declarations of feeling, as in much romantic lyric. It was a lesson taken from Eliot's essay "Hamlet," where he complained that Hamlet's emotions are without sufficient cause in the play, leading him to formulate the "objective correlative," in which a series of objects or events is thought to provoke a particular emotion in the reader. Brooks and Warren denounced emotional statement as mere sentimentality and dismissed those periods in which sentiment abounded, as in Romantic and Victorian poetry. Literature worked by suggesting its attitudes through irony and paradox, criteria that Brooks came to believe were more crucial than metaphor in grasping the argument of a work. The ideal poem withheld its meaning from being paraphrased, and only by a sort of violence could a poem be reduced to statements of fact and opinion.

The job of New Criticism was to elucidate the strategies by which thought materialized into poetic language and to measure the writer's ability to preserve the ambiguity and complexity of the thought without violating the structural demands of a genre—hence the importance of the sonnet in demonstrating New Critical method, where strict conventions of rhyme and stanzaic pattern provoked the sort of paradoxical discourse perfected in the 17th century. Only New Critical analysis seemed to open the secretive interiors of this lyric mode.

In *Understanding Poetry: An Anthology for College Students* (1938), Brooks and Warren brought together the principles of New Critical method and defined an increasingly selective, some would say fragmentary, literary canon. Obviously, their method depended on a certain kind of poem where linguistic and structural intricacy demanded their method of decoding; the essayistic and discursive styles of 18th-century long poems and Romantic lyrics required some other approach for assessing their merits.

The title *Understanding Poetry* posed its own unintended irony since their formalist approach is only one of many, and their readings were limited to traditional poems. However, the very limitations imposed on the book may have clarified what was before a confusing eclecticism in literary criticism. The rigor and methodology of the book made reading less a matter of sensitivities to psychological stimuli than an acquired skill in methodical analysis. Long after its appearance, *Understanding Poetry* was the standard textbook of freshman and sophomore literature surveys and shaped not only how poetry was to be read but in many ways how it was to be written. Formal verse sprang into vogue in the late 1940s and endured well into the 1960s as if to supply a demand for the very sort of writing New Criticism was intended to explain.

A year after *Understanding Poetry* appeared, Brooks emerged as the foremost proponent of New Critical methods with his study *Modern Poetry and the Tradition* (1939). It was dedicated to his friend and former classmate at Vanderbilt, Allen Tate, whose notion of poetry as a tension between content and "form" gave Brooks his leading principle in the book; another debt is owed to I.A. Richards, whose research in reader comprehension (or lack of it) in *Practical Criticism: A Study in Literary Judgment* (1929), alerted Brooks to the need for a systematic critical method.

Like Eliot, Brooks argues that English poetry took a wrong turn in the late 17th century, when it chose to follow the philosopher Hobbes' premise that poetry was at best a copyist of nature and not a perceiver of designs and intentions. The split between science and art gave the next two centuries a false incentive to simplify the range of poetic discourse and to indulge in emotional excess for lack of serious content. The 20th century, according to Brooks, began to pick up where the 17th left off, partly because of the expansion of psychological imagery made possible by French Symbolist poetry. Poetry was expanding once more into experience previously claimed by science, notably in the areas of psychology and religion. Since Eliot had raised the standard of lyric complexity with his long sequential poems, Brooks argued that the "metaphysical poem" was now returning, demanding a critical method capable of grasping its complexity.

Brooks' definition of a poem is that it reconciles opposites and dissimilarities through a highly charged metaphorical language displaying the poet's wit and irony. With his model poem established in the first four chapters, he moves on to an appreciation of his fellow Fugitive poets, notably Ransom and Warren; in other chapters he makes broad distinctions between new formalist lyric and other kinds of poetry where he finds the gaps in sensibility of the last century growing wider, as in Imagism, with its emphasis on physical reality, and "local color" poetry, which merely celebrated regional life.

Brooks' scheme of things allows him to dismiss the work of Ezra Pound, Hart Crane, Wallace Stevens, William Carlos Williams, W.H. Auden, and even Robert Frost, who have since become major figures of the literary canon; their work did not fit the criteria of his ideal poem. On the other hand, Eliot himself was to praise Brooks' interpretation of *The Waste Land* as a model of perceptive analysis. Others have also said that Brooks' interpretation of this central poem is still the finest ever written, and his analysis of the work of the Irish poet W.B. Yeats shows the power of his method to solve the greatest riddles.

Brooks concludes by noting not only that Hobbes shattered the sensibility on which poetry once thrived by separating imagination from reason but also that, in denying the self its full range of thought in art, tragedy itself disappeared from the English theater. Not only was the poem a reconciliation of opposites under the tension of a poet's urge to pierce through paradox and mystery, but it was a drama of the fully integrated self, whose ambiguities and depths were aroused by the free range of its thoughts among religion, philosophy, emotion, and sexuality. All this shriveled into an art of pathos and sentimentality when the late 17th century placed its faith in reason alone and assigned imagination little more than decorative verbal skills.

However, Brooks' rejection of neoclassical and Romantic verse did not go unchallenged; Richard Harter Fogle, the eminent Romantic scholar, complained that Brooks had rejected "emotion" for irony and condemned the use of plain speech, which might encourage a poet "to make a fetish of unintelligibility." Fogle also complained that the Romantics were far less culpable of dissociating sensibility than was Brooks himself in discrediting everything but irony and wit in poetry. Auden objected to Brooks' dismissal of expressions of belief, which he regarded as little more than propaganda. Ransom lavished praise on the work, as did other members of the New Criticism. On the whole, *Modern Poetry and the Tradition*, despite its tendency toward critical absolutism, was received well and became a standard reference in critical debate.

However, absolutism reared itself once more in *The Well Wrought Urn: Studies in the Structure of Poetry* (1947), which collected Brooks' new essays into his most important contribution to New Criticism. In these essays he parts company not only with Ransom on the value of logic in poetry but also with Yvor Winters' emphasis on rational content as new forms of dualism elevating intellect over feeling. Brooks was sensitive to the criticism leveled at his previous book, where he dismissed two centuries of English poetry as divisive and fragmented; now he takes special pains to include a variety of works from the neoclassical age (Pope and Gray) and a range of poems from among the Romantic poets, but only those that measure up to New Critical analysis. To cover the ground of a larger canon, Brooks redefines lyric poetry as the language of paradox and gives himself the task of showing how paradox may well reside in some of the most cherished classics of English poetry. Even Pope's *The Rape of the Lock* is shown to be more than a satire of English aristocracy, and his analysis of Gray's "Elegy" sifts this plain-spoken poem for residual ambiguities.

Brooks invokes another of his principles in his chapter "The Heresy of Paraphrase," where he is even more unforgiving to those who would attempt to deduce a prose summary of a poem. However, as several critics pointed out in reviews, Brooks himself was offering prose equivalents for each passage of a poem under discussion. Arthur Mizener wryly observed that Brooks was simply validating his own critical paraphrases and damning everyone else's.

Other critics voiced objections to the absolutist bent of *The Well Wrought Urn*. Herbert J. Muller wondered why Brooks' only test for poetry was complexity when the "Twenty-Third Psalm," the prologue to *The Canterbury Tales*, and numerous other poems achieved grandeur through simplicity. Muller also objected to the absolute value of irony when in fact poets were given to forthright statements of belief in accord with their times and audiences. Only in hindsight does a poem acquire the appearance of irony if some of its propositions seem no longer tenable. The failure of Brooks' overall New Critical scheme is a lack of historical relativism to account for changing perceptions and tastes of readers over time.

Each of these complaints anticipated the arrival of other methods of reading and interpretation, with some specializing in discourse analysis and others exploring questions of language and meaning and the issue of authorial intention. The New Criticism raised important issues regarding the nature of literary texts, some of which it could not resolve on its own. After the upheavals of the Vietnam War era, the role of society and history in the meaning of texts became more important than the hermetic formalism of the New Criticism. The New Criticism also raised questions about the American canon, opening the way for feminist and minority ethnic revisions of what should count in the literary tradition.

Perhaps the New Criticism was a way of defining the South at a time of fundamental transition to an industrial economy. Eliot was deemed an essential southerner who had made possible the bridge from a modern and troubled South of the 1930s to an idealized England in the age of Donne. This more usable past not only gave the South a noble tradition on which to nourish a reviving literary culture but also tacitly argued for the nobility of white Christian culture and its southern institutions. The New Critics were quick to denounce writers who attacked the South, including Thomas Wolfe and Erskine Caldwell. Even Faulkner was received with initial caution, until Brooks applied his analytical tools to explain the work of the region's greatest artist. Eudora Welty was welcomed as another ally to the southern literary cause, but not Flannery O'Connor, whose vision of the South was darker and more conflicted.

The New Criticism venerated the work of literature as if it were a sacred text in which the human spirit expressed itself in ineffable but refracted ways, safe from the contaminating influences of Marxism, social Darwinism, and other putative evils of the industrial age. Even its rejection of 18th- and 19th-century discursiveness may have to do in part with the fact that the "northern mind," born of revolution and democratic fervor, was conceived in this era and was alien to the aristocratic traditions that New Critics regarded as the South's heritage.

A lasting benefit of New Criticism is that it proved that literature was not obscure or veiled in inaccessible speech but demanded the highest rigor of analysis to be understood. Poetry rose in stature under New Critical scrutiny; it was treated with the greatest respect and solemnity by highly trained specialists in lyric discourse. Even now, the poem is a subject of serious cultural debate, and on certain readings of the greatest masterpieces of American poetry rest crucial assumptions about the American psyche and its cultural life.

Paul Christensen

*See also* Fugitives and Agrarians

**Further Reading**

Bagwell, J. Timothy, *American Formalism and the Problem of Interpretation,* Houston, Texas: Rice University Press, 1986

Heilman, Robert Bechtold, *The Southern Connection,* Baton Rouge: Louisiana State University Press, 1991

Jancovich, Mark, *Cultural Politics of the New Criticism,* Cambridge and New York: Cambridge University Press, 1993

Patnaik, J.N., *The Aesthetics of the New Criticism,* New Delhi: Intellectual Publishing House, 1982; Atlantic Highlands, New Jersey: Humanities Press, 1983

Winchell, Mark Royden, *Cleanth Brooks and the Rise of Modern Criticism,* Charlottesville: University Press of Virginia, 1996

---

# New Formalism

As a casually organized revival of metered and rhymed poetry among younger American poets in the 1980s, the New Formalism, or Neo-Formalism, was spearheaded primarily by poets who had come of age during the 1960s and 1970s, when the free-verse revolution, instigated by Ezra Pound, T.S. Eliot, and William Carlos Williams, had moved beyond its Modernist origins as an emancipating form to become the accepted orthodoxy in American university creative writing workshops. The New Formalists, many of whom had studied under older formalists such as Yvor Winters and Donald Davie at Stanford, Robert Fitzgerald and Elizabeth Bishop at Harvard, J.V. Cunningham at Brandeis, and Allen Tate at Sewanee, perceived that free-verse conventions had staled and contributed to what they saw as contemporary poetry's tendencies toward solipsism and prosaism, qualities they believed made for unmemorable verse. To remedy this, the New Formalists advocated a return to traditional meters and forms as well as to narrative in order to reintroduce to American poetry the three essential elements they suggested had been suppressed by the free-verse orthodoxy: clarity, music, and objectivity. These qualities, they maintained, would again make intellectual poetry accessible to a general audience.

Coming as it did in the wake of two world wars and the experimentalist age of Modernism, the Vietnam War era produced a poetry born of cultural upheaval that held that formal poetry was antithetical to truth. As a result, younger poets no longer found it profitable to master traditional metrics. Holding up the free verse of Walt Whitman as the paradigm of American poetic virtue, they believed that each poet achieved a personal voice only by creating his or her own idiosyncratic "organic" forms. By the end of the 1960s, the ideology of "open" forms was fueled by the escalation of political activism on American university campuses. Writing poetry for many young people became a way of "finding oneself," of discovering a personal identity and asserting it against a discredited version of an "elitist" past. Thus, the use of "open" forms took on an added political significance, and a wedge was driven between the writers of free verse and what was then called "academic poetry."

Because academia was commonly viewed at the time as being an "ivory tower," a repository of traditional values utterly unmoved by the Zeitgeist of the 1960s, the hostile critics of academic poetry attempted to equate a predilection for writing in meter and rhyme with the advocacy of "Fascism" and the "military-industrial complex." As the poet and critic Lewis Turco (1990) observes,

> Rather than be perceived by their students as members of the American Nazi Party or the Ku Klux Klan, poets on college faculties everywhere during the activist 1960s abdicated their responsibility to provide their pupils with substance and became a caste of "nurturers" rather than teachers.

Thus, the literary establishment of the day, already of the opinion since the rise of the Beat and Confessional poets in the late 1950s that meter and rhyme were outmoded techniques, conceded that formal poetry had become inconsequential.

Despite this prevailing sentiment, there remained many older American poets who never abandoned traditional forms. Some, such as those mentioned previously, were teachers who kept older aesthetic values alive, standing their ground against the onslaught of attacks on their own work by critics who believed measure and rhyme to be "un-American." Many of their students followed their lead and subsequently launched the counter-revolution against what they viewed as the deadening orthodoxy of the free-verse establishment. They professed to be disillusioned with the self-absorption, formlessness, and intellectual vacuity of confessional lyrics, which under the aegis of Whitman, Williams, Allen Ginsberg, and Sylvia Plath had, they alleged, reduced poetry to little more than an individual's tortured response to personal trauma. They sought to remedy such abuses by reclaiming the prosodic heritage of English verse. Despite an educational system that frequently appeared to be hostile to their intentions, the New Formalists schooled themselves in the work of their predecessors, read history, and studied foreign languages and literature hoping to revive those elements of English poetry found even in Pound's visionary free verse but frequently discarded by his successors in favor of the most facile understanding of his notorious axiom "Make it new!" The New Formalists believed that by 1980, Pound's Modernist free verse had degenerated into the prosaic drivel of the poetry workshop or the political ranting of the poetry slam. They supported this claim by pointing out that Pound himself, when asked late in life by the *New York Times* what he felt about the current poetry scene, is said to have exploded in reply, "Disorder! Disorder! I can't be blamed for all this disorder!"

The years 1983, 1985, and 1986 are important dates for New Formalism. The year 1983 witnessed its earliest recognition with the publication of an essay by Lewis Turco titled "The Year in Poetry." Effectively heralding the birth of New Formalism, Turco writes, "One keeps hearing these days rumors and siftings of a return to formalism in American poetry" (1984). The second date saw such rumors develop into a full-fledged movement with the publication of Philip Dacey and David Jauss' *Strong Measures: Contemporary American Poetry in Traditional Forms,* the first major anthology of formal poetry to be published since the so-called War of the Anthologies of the late 1950s and early 1960s waged between the academic poets and the Beat generation. In 1986, the burgeoning movement gained notoriety as it began to draw fire from various sources. In the spring issue of *Sewanee Review,* in an article titled "Six Poets," the critic Thomas Swiss wrote,

> New poems by young writers like Molly Peacock, Baron Wormser, Mary Jo Salter, and Richard Kenney exhibit meter and rhyme. Some of these poets have been called New Formalists, but how does one tell the "new" formalists from the "old" if all these writers are mining the same traditions, exhibiting the same manners?

The implication was clear: the New Formalism was suspicious because it chose to "mine" the traditions many critics and readers believed to be mined out. Hoping to expose the bias in Swiss' remarks, Turco responded by suggesting that the answer to his colleague's question is elementary, that is, that one may distinguish the "new" formalists from the "old" by learning the names of the poets who wrote formally 25 years ago and differentiating them from the names of those poets who were "struggling in the 1980s to throw off the prevailing anti-intellectual egocentricism of the preceding two decades and more" (1990). Thus began the ideological war of words between the supporters of New Formalism and its detractors.

The year 1986 also saw the most remarkable attack on New Formalism. It was launched by the poet and critic Diane Wakoski, who, in an essay titled "The New Conservatism in American Poetry" in the May–June 1986 issue of the *American Book Review,* appeared to have revived the radical 1960s opinion of formal poetry when she referred to John Hollander as "Satan" and to Robert Pinsky as "a nice man, even a good writer but NOT one of the searchers for a new American voice." Wakoski maintained that Hollander and Pinsky were but the vanguard of the conservative literary legions readying themselves for an all-out assault on the free-verse revolution, denouncing the poetry that is the fulfillment of the Whitman heritage, and making defensive jokes about the ill-educated, slovenly writers of poetry who have been teaching college poetry classes for the past decade, allowing their students to write drivel and go out into the world, illiterate of poetry.

It has been proposed that, like so much of the criticism heaped on the New Formalism, Wakoski's impassioned denunciation of the movement was at best ironic as she failed to realize that in 1986 the New Formalism was as revolutionary as Whitman's free verse had been in 1855, the year he published *Leaves of Grass.* Proponents of the movement suggest that both styles are born of the characteristically American predilection of searching for innovative literary expression. They claim that Wakoski's attack is misguided, as she appears to have been unable to perceive that her own generation of anti-intellectuals in 1986 had become the "conservatives" and that the consideration of form and traditional prosody was new, even revolutionary, to the younger poets. Nevertheless, Wakoski's charges echo those leveled on academic poetry in the 1960s, that is, that formalism in poetry denotes the poet's tendency toward political "neoconservatism."

Such charges are, of course, unfounded and inaccurate. Whether one is a traditionalist or an innovator in poetry has nothing to do with one's politics. If, for example, T.S. Eliot was, as many critics have claimed, an arch-traditionalist in religion and a closet Fascist in politics, he was nevertheless one of the most innovative and experimental poets of the early 20th century, as was Pound, Eliot's close friend and mentor. Pound, the poet most responsible for the revival of the "Whitman heritage" so staunchly defended by Wakoski, was the first American poet of the 20th century to champion experimentation in poetry. He was also anything but a political liberal. Being an unabashedly vociferous supporter of Mussolini's Fascist government, Pound very narrowly escaped execution as a traitor to the United States following World War II for the anti-Roosevelt, pro-Fascist broadcasts he made on Italian radio. At the opposite end of the spectrum, one must remember that John F. Kennedy maintained that his favorite poet was Robert Frost, himself an "old formalist" and sometime critic of Roosevelt's New Deal politics. Nevertheless, it was Frost who was invited to give his blessing to Kennedy's "New Frontier" by reading his poem "The Gift Outright" at Kennedy's inauguration in 1961. More recently it was Bill Clinton who, perhaps unwittingly, challenged traditional notions about formal poetry's link to neoconservatism when he invited fellow Arkansan Miller Williams to read his poem "Of History and Hope" at Clinton's 1997 inauguration. Williams is a poet with exceedingly close ties to the New Formalism. He is the author of several books of formal poetry, including *Imperfect Love* (1986) and *Living on the Surface: New and Selected Poems* (1989). In 1986, Williams published *Patterns of Poetry: An Encyclopedia of Forms.*

Mark Jarman and David Mason, editors of the most recent New Formalist anthology, *Rebel Angels: 25 Poets of the New Formalism* (1996), are of the opinion that the New Formalism is simply the latest manifestation of the rebellious streak "bred in the bone of the American character," a character most evident they claim in modern American poetry. In the introduction to the anthology, the editors suggest that just as the flourishing of free verse during the Cold War may itself be seen as a manifestation of American rebelliousness as it suited the chaotic atmosphere of the period, so the move toward a more formal poetry in the present may be seen as the logical reaction to the cultural disorder that preceded it. All things considered, one must not discount the fact that aspects of formalism have managed to survive the onslaught of the free-verse revolution for decades in the most rebellious corners of popular culture—a matter of fact that should quell the theory that meter and rhyme are "un-American." Meter, rhyme, and the ever present quatrain continue to serve as the basis for most lyrical structures in popular music. Indeed, one would find it difficult to consider the lyrics of genres as diverse as country music and heavy metal, or those styles perceived as being more revolutionary such as punk rock, hip-hop, and gangster rap, without also considering their reliance on traditional form, meter, and rhyme. In fact, because of a growing interest in this phenomenon among a new generation weaned to poetry from popular music, there appears to be a nationwide increase in university courses exploring the possibility that popular music may have contributed to a general interest in New Formalist concerns among younger poets as well as the ways in which it has exerted a revitalizing influence on a variety of contemporary poetries, not the least of which is African-American poetry.

The New Formalist movement has been growing and changing rapidly in recent years as poets from diverse backgrounds and perspectives discover in formal poetics a potential tool for vast range and power. The editors of *Rebel Angels* demonstrate that they are acutely aware of this and have collected formal poetry that speaks of innovation. The anthology brings together for the first time a sampling of work by many of the major New Formalists, including Tom Disch, Dana Gioia, Emily Grosholz, R.S. Gwynn, Marilyn Hacker, Rachel Hadas, Sydney Lea, Brad Leithauser, Charles Martin, Molly Peacock, Mary Jo Salter, Timothy Steele, and Frederick Turner—poets "all born since 1940," as the editors are quick to point out in deference to New Formalism's claim of being a movement begun and maintained by "younger poets." Whether or not the anthology lives up to its ambitious aspirations is debatable. For all its promise of being the harbinger of a revolution in American poetry, it is burdened by a fair amount of verse that is at best mundane and mechanical. Even so, the book contains some of the best poetry the New Formalists have to offer.

A fine example of poetry typical of the New Formalism may be seen in Dana Gioia's several contributions to *Rebel Angels*. Gioia, perhaps the best known of the New Formalists for his collections *Daily Horoscope* (1982, revised 1986) and *The Gods of Winter* (1991), is represented by some of his best work, including the often praised narrative poem "Counting the Children" and his sestina "My Confessional Sestina," which opens with "Let me confess. I'm sick of these sestinas / written by youngsters in poetry workshops / for the delectation of their fellow students." The poem could be the New Formalist anthem, being playfully although forcefully critical of both confessional poetry and the workshop mentality. Elsewhere, Gioia's aesthetic concerns are showcased. His "plain" style, often criticized for being too bare, combines with the repetitions of the double triolet in "The Country Wife," producing a mesmerizing effect, as in "The night reflected on the lake, / The fire of stars changed into water. / She cannot see the winds that break / The night reflected on the lake / But knows they motion for her sake."

Marilyn Hacker is proof positive that formal verse cannot be easily dismissed as the voice of neoconservatism, and her inclusion in *Rebel Angels* is a credit to its editors. In the 1980s, when lists of New Formalists first began to appear, Hacker was often left out. Her omission from these lists appears to have been due to the efforts of the various critics who were desperate to find a link between the movement and neoconservatism, and to admit that an outspoken feminist such as Hacker could also be a New Formalist would have contradicted their argument. She is distinguished from most of the other New Formalists by having beaten them into print by several years with the publication of her first book, *Presentation Piece* (1974). She is best represented in *Rebel Angels* by the haunting "Cancer Winter," which chronicles her battle with breast cancer. She is seldom more powerful than in the lines "Cancer, gratuitous as a massacre, / answers to nothing, tempts me to retrieve / the white-eyed panic in the mortal night, / my father's silent death at forty-eight, / each numbered, shaved, emaciated Jew / I might have been. They wore the blunt tattoo, / a scar; if they survived, oceans away. / Should I tattoo my scar? What would I say?"

Other innovative uses of form are found in Brad Leithauser's monosyllabic sonnet "Post-Coitum Tristesse: A Sonnet"—"Why / do / you / sigh / roar / fall / all / for / some / hum / drum / come / —mm? / Hm"—and in what Jarman and Mason call the "irregular meter" of Molly Peacock's verse. In her experimental sonnets, Peacock combines traditional form with a seemingly irrepressible instinct for innovation to create poetry that speaks not only in but of the shape of form and its purpose. Lines such as "It doesn't speak and it isn't schooled, / like a small foetal animal with wettened fur. / It is the blind instinct for life unruled" from "Desire" and "Not to carry / all this in the body's frame is not to see / how the heart and arms were formed on its behalf. / I can't put the burden down. It's what formed / the house I became as the glass ball stormed" from "Those Paperweights with Snow Inside" are windows into Peacock's poetic consciousness, if not into that of the New Formalism as a whole. They seem to cry out that form is determined by experience, that it is as naturally occurring and intrinsic to language as it is to nature itself.

While the New Formalism has certainly managed to reopen the debate about the legitimacy of formal poetry's place in American literature, the verdict is still out on its status as a "revolutionary" movement. Perhaps the true test of any movement's claim to revolutionariness is whether it is accompanied by a genuine change in sensibility. There can be no doubt, for example, that poetic sensibilities were vastly altered by Romanticism at the beginning of the 19th century and again at the start of the 20th with the rise of Modernism. However, can it truly be said that a mere change in technique only, that is, the return to form and meter, constitutes a radical change in poetic sensibility? Critics of the movement maintain, and with good reason, that the answer is no. Others, however, remain convinced that the practice of experimenting with formal poetry is still largely unexplored and that it has just begun to yield results that will satisfy the innate human desire not only for innovation but for pleasing form as well while redressing the imbalance caused by a century of free verse to establish a new era of poetic harmony and order.

Joe Francis Doerr

*See also* Narrative Poetry

**Further Reading**

Dacey, Philip, and David Jauss, editors, *Strong Measures: Contemporary American Poetry in Traditional Forms*, New York and London: Harper and Row, 1985

Feirstein, Frederick, editor, *Expansive Poetry: Essays on the New Narrative and the New Formalism*, Santa Cruz, California: Story Line Press, 1989; revised edition, as *New*

*Expansive Poetry: Theory, Criticism, History,* edited by R.S. Gwynn, Ashland, Oregon: Story Line Press, 1999
Finch, Annie, editor, *After New Formalism: Poets on Form, Narrative, and Tradition,* Ashland, Oregon: Story Line Press, 1999
Jarman, Mark, and David Mason, editors, *Rebel Angels: 25 Poets of the New Formalism,* Brownsville, Oregon: Story Line Press, 1996
McPhillips, Robert, "Reading the New Formalists," *Sewanee Review* 47, no. 1 (Winter 1989)
Prunty, Wyatt, *'Fallen from the Symboled World': Precedents for the New Formalism,* Oxford and New York: Oxford University Press, 1990
Sadoff, Ira, "Neo-Formalism: A Dangerous Nostalgia," *American Poetry Review* 19, no. 1 (January–February 1990)
Swiss, Thomas, "Six Poets," *Sewanee Review* 44, no. 2 (Spring 1986)
Turco, Lewis, "The Year in Poetry," in *The Dictionary of Literary Biography Yearbook: 1983,* edited by Mary Bruccoli and Jean W. Ross, Detroit, Michigan: Gale Research, 1984
Turco, Lewis, "New-Formalism in Contemporary American Poetry," *Poet* 2, no. 3 (1990)
Wakoski, Diane, "The New Conservatism in American Poetry," *American Book Review* 7, no. 4 (May–June 1986)

# New York School

The vitality and optimism of post–World War II America and Manhattan, its cultural capital, are vividly reflected in the poetry movement called the New York School. In the 1950s, as the Abstract Expressionists shifted the center of the international art world to New York City, a small band of poets drew on the energy that was in the air and coalesced as a group that for a time defined the new avant-garde in poetry. Curiously, their commonality was not displayed through a rigorously defined aesthetic, but rather through a shared attitude and subject.

The New York School poets drew inspiration from many places: the energy of the city's streets; Hollywood films; half-heard conversations and gossip at cocktail parties; American words and products like jujubes and Coca Cola that had never before been deemed "poetic"; homosexual camp; ironic humor; and the French Surrealists. They blended these influences to create an alternate poetics and point of view that flew in the face of the established canon of the period. It is a testament to the vigor of the spark they ignited that succeeding groups of poets enthusiastically designated themselves second- and even third-generation members of the New York School. The desire of these younger poets to identify themselves as members of the New York School underscores the group's status as a primary strain of non-academic poetry between the 1950s and early 1970s. Half a century after its founding, the School still has its adherents and countless other poets clearly bear its mark of influence.

Often when the New York School is mentioned in print, the label is preceded by the modifier "so-called." This reflects three facts: the New York "School" is actually a casual gathering of poets with varying styles who are united solely in their often experimental approach to writing and their shared topic, Manhattan's incredible diversity; the poets involved never proclaimed themselves a movement (an art dealer gave them the "New York School" label); and all of the original "members" eschewed the heavy-handed posturing and inevitable literary manifestos that are standard offshoots of any self-proclaimed literary movement. At best, they issued mock manifestos.

While there are a fair number of poets associated with the first-generation New York School, critics generally single out a core group of four individuals: Frank O'Hara, John Ashbery, James Schuyler, and Kenneth Koch. These poets defined the parameters and established the distinctive voice that others would expand.

It is impossible to separate these poets from the time in which they initially established themselves. The 1950s were a vital, curious time in America. On one hand, society in the Eisenhower years was rather inward-looking, with a strong emphasis on conformity. Waves of returning war veterans, anxious to make up for lost time, were quickly establishing families and moving into scores of identical tract houses in newly established suburbs. As a result the American population and the country's mainstream culture shifted away from cities at exactly the time when America's largest city was alive with new ideas and excitement, much of it powered by other veterans with a different agenda—O'Hara, Koch, and Schuyler among them—who returned from overseas tours of duty with newly acquired sophistication and an expanded sense of possibilities.

In the heady, confident aftermath of the war, painters Willem de Kooning, Jackson Pollock, and others made Manhattan the center of the international art scene. O'Hara and his colleagues frequented the gallery openings and ancillary parties and events, wrote reviews of the new artists' shows, added to the burgeoning esprit de corps throughout New York's arts community, and established a beachhead for themselves as published poets.

In general, O'Hara is often seen as the celebrator of Manhattan's urban environment, Koch as the embodiment of the city's urbane humor, Ashbery as the voice of New York's unconscious life, and Schuyler as the codifier of the city's wealth of pleasures and interpersonal relationships.

Frank O'Hara was the first member of the group to achieve widespread recognition. Although his poetry is the most welcoming and seductive of the four, it is fair to say that he achieved literary celebrity before the others for two reasons: his especially close association with the New York art world, and his early death, which transformed him into a mythic figure invoked by both contemporaries and succeeding generations in the ensuing decades.

Perhaps more than his poet colleagues, O'Hara was a fellow conspirator with many of the artists of the period, among them Larry Rivers, Alex Katz, and Willem de Kooning. He posed for their paintings, served as co-creator on a number of collaborative projects, spurred them on with his intense enthusiasm, and acted as their champion through his work as an art critic and ultimately as a curator at the Museum of Modern Art.

It has often been said that O'Hara had a special genius for friendship; dozens of people in New York considered him their "best friend." In the relatively small, intense, cocktail party–driven art world of the 1950s, his interpersonal skills carried a special power. They stitched together a developing community, drew connections between coexisting aesthetics, and helped build artists' reputations. It is not surprising that O'Hara's accidental death at age 40 had a large ripple effect.

His contemporaries often attest to the fact that O'Hara seemed more interested in the act and process of writing than in jockeying for publication. He left behind sheaves of unpublished work; his dedicated friends made sure that it ultimately saw the light of day. O'Hara's work focuses intensely on the small details of daily life: dates, times, days of the week; newspaper headlines; anecdotes about dear friends; soft drink brand names; information about movie stars and the film industry. One of O'Hara's better known poems, "The Day Lady Died," begins with a seemingly rote recitation of the time, location, year, and his schedule for the day:

It is 12:20 in New York a Friday
three days after Bastille day, yes
it is 1959 and I go get a shoeshine
because I will get off the 4:19 in Easthampton
at 7:15 and then go straight to dinner
and I don't know what the people will feed me. . . .

Only in the last stanza and a half is the poem's topic—the death of jazz great Billie Holiday—revealed:

then I go back where I came from to 6th Avenue
and the tobacconist in the Ziegfield Theatre and
casually ask for a carton of Gauloises and a carton
of Picayunes, and a *New York Post* with her face on it

and I am sweating a lot by now and thinking of
leaning on the john door in the *Five Spot*
while she whispered a song along the keyboard
to Mal Waldron and everyone and I stopped breathing.

The accumulation of carefully chosen details places Holiday within a context, however, and makes the poem emotionally compelling. O'Hara's *Collected Poems* (1971) won the National Book Award for poetry in 1972.

For many readers, Kenneth Koch is an appealing, breezy presence. Blessed with a comic genius, he has cheerfully skewered Robert Frost's stylized diction in his poem "Mending Sump" and wittily pled for common sense and room to breathe in his poem/commentary on the Academy called "Fresh Air." This passage from the latter poem is exemplary of Koch's inimitable style:

Until tomorrow, then, scum floating on the surface of
  poetry!
    goodbye for a moment, refuse that happens to land in
      poetry's
    boundaries! adieu, stale eggs teaching imbeciles poetry
      to bol-
    ster up your egos! adios, boring anomalies of these
      same stale
    eggs! . . .

Hello sea! good morning, sea! hello, clarity and excitement,
  you
    great expanse of green—

O green, beneath which all of them shall drown!

His poetry often simultaneously exhibits playfulness and an exquisite aesthetic sense. His most notable poetry collections include *Ko; or, A Season on Earth* (1960), an epic poem written in *ottava rima, The Pleasures of Peace* (1969), and *One Train* (1994).

Koch is also well known for his work as a teacher of poetry and poetry appreciation. *Wishes, Lies and Dreams* (1970) and *Rose, Where Did You Get That Red?* (1973) established innovative techniques for teaching poetry to schoolchildren; *I Never Told Anybody* (1977) offered methods for encouraging poetry writing among nursing-home residents.

Koch tirelessly championed the work of his friends and brought new converts into the New York School fold through his poetry classes at Columbia University and the New School for Social Research. In the 1960s the poets he taught included Bill Berkson, Joseph Ceravolo, Lewis Warsh, Charles North, Ron Padgett, and David Shapiro.

It is easy to consider John Ashbery the mandarin of the New York School. His work started off disjunctive, slippery, and notable for its icy purity. Along the way he increased his ability to abruptly shift diction and offer seemingly rational discourse that more often than not mysteriously dead-ended. In many ways the most rigorously experimental and impersonal, Ashbery ultimately garnered the greatest amount of mainstream approbation; his book *Self-Portrait in a Convex Mirror* (1975) won the Pulitzer Prize, the National Book Award, and the National Book Critics Circle Award in 1976. Unlike O'Hara, there is little autobiographical material in Ashbery's work; he seems more interested in issues of consciousness: misunderstandings, miscommunication, and the passage of time and its erosion of narrative, as in this passage from "Polite Distortions":

The sensible thing is to review, always to review.
In this way new steps are seen to have been already
Invented, while others, old, premature ones may be
Returning to interact with them in a cone of distance
Drawing ever tighter around wrists, throats. Profligate isn't
Anymore, I'll betcha, I'll just betcha, but who can
Know in the violet flood of embarrassment or pure
Terror, put off, put on again. . . .

James Schuyler, the most reticent and least prolific of the four poets, was the last to achieve acclaim. After three decades of writing and four full-length collections of poetry, he won the Pulitzer

Prize in 1981 for the book *The Morning of the Poem* (1980), which featured the long poem of the same name. This work brings into razor-sharp focus many of the strains in Schuyler's work: pointed autobiographical details and an emphasis on dailiness that placed him in O'Hara's constellation; a special relationship with the physical world that manifested itself through vivid descriptions—sometimes of pastoral environments (a practice that distinguished him from his colleagues); and a seemingly ambling sense of line that upon continued reading reveals itself as rigorous and demanding. Here are characteristic lines from "The Morning of the Poem":

> . . . Those woods, that
> island and the bay, I won't forget them soon,
> Nor that same moon I saw last night hang in glory over
> this small
> hill I used to see ride, embosomed, in the fullness
> Of the sky it lit etching the tall, still spruce and casting its
> light on the rippled water that led off and off
> To ocean and to where you cannot see: to go out through
> the
> dining porch among the daisies and the crags
> And moon-bathe. Have you ever swum at night in water so
> cold it's
> like plunging into a case of knives. . . .

On occasion critics draw connections between Schuyler and Elizabeth Bishop, a distinctly non–New York School poet. It is interesting to read the two in tandem and draw one's own conclusions.

By 1970 the original New York School poets had firmly established themselves, although they had yet to receive the awards that would give them the approbation of the literary establishment. Their status was underscored by the appearance that year of *An Anthology of New York Poets,* edited by Ron Padgett and David Shapiro, two members of the burgeoning second generation. This anthology had a lasting influence. While it did not define a canon or mark the beginning of large mainstream publishers' ongoing support, it provided an imprimatur for the first-generation New York School, presented some developing second-generation strains, and ultimately defined the New York style's range of possibilities.

O'Hara's and Schuyler's focus on daily activities and autobiography, Koch's charm and humor, and Ashbery's rapidly shifting tone were joined by a host of new voices. Tom Veitch and Kenward Elmslie emphasized absurdity and camp; Bernadette Mayer and Clark Coolidge brought a new strength to explorations of the word as object or a kernel of meaning. John Giorno employed the techniques of "found" text and repetition. Collage techniques and a revived interest in old forms were the cornerstones of Ted Berrigan's revolutionary *The Sonnets* (1964).

Bernadette Mayer is of particular interest. The only woman represented in the 1970 anthology, her work brought the influence of Gertrude Stein into the New York School mix. Although Mayer's stylistic range is wide, one of her notable modes uses moment-by-moment observations, abstraction, and prose-like structure to emphasize the sensuality of language. *Memory* (1975), one of Mayer's first books, is a journal documenting July 1971; an audiorecording of the text accompanied an exhibition of photographs she had taken during the month the book was written.

Ted Berrigan, a leader of the second generation, initially adopted major elements of Frank O'Hara's style: the signature date/time/location openings, the "I do this, I do that" diction. His *Sonnets* broke new ground, however, and remain an important touchstone in alternative American poetics. Berrigan juggled "found" lines with his own, cut and pasted them, and created a brilliant new structure and surface from the bits and pieces. Recurring lines such as "Dear Chris, hello. It is 3:17 a.m." help foster a fractured autobiographical atmosphere. Some passage achieve, rather appropriately, a high, neo-Shakespearean tone:

> DEAR CHRIS
>
> It is 3:17 a.m. in New York city, yes, it is
> 1962, it is the year of parrot fever. In
> Brandenberg, and by the granite gates, the
> old come-all-ye's streel into the streets. Yes, it is now,
> the season of delight. I am writing you to say that
> I have gone mad. Now I am sowing the seeds which shall,
> when ripe, master the day, and
> portion out the night. . . . ("Sonnet LXXVII")

Ron Padgett, co-editor of *An Anthology of New York Poets* and a close friend of Berrigan's, blended humor and an interest in 20th-century French poetry with the Pop Art sensibility that was rampant in 1960s Manhattan. His *Great Balls of Fire* (1969) is an especially witty and elegant example of his oeuvre.

Many of the new poets in Padgett and Shapiro's anthology used the Poetry Project as their center of operations. Founded in 1966 at historic St. Mark's Church on Manhattan's Lower East Side, the Project and its habitués fostered a literary environment that was distinct from the atmosphere created by the Harvard-educated O'Hara, Koch, and Ashbery. The Poetry Project was a counterculture venue, a focal point for Pop artist Andy Warhol's coterie and other radical art communities. Bumptiously democratic, for many it embodied the literary side of the 1960s. It also nurtured a number of interesting second-generation New York School poets who had not appeared in the anthology. Despite fundamental differences in lifestyle, these new writers admired the work of O'Hara, Schuyler, Ashbery, Koch, et al. and used it as a springboard for their own poems, which flourished in the ensuing decades.

Poet/novelist Lewis Warsh's poetry featured a curious mix of deadpan romanticism and nostalgia. His *Information from the Surface of Venus* (1982) spins out infinite variations on the theme of dislocation; later poetry collections such as *Avenue of Escape* (1995) use successions of long, prose-like fragments to offer complex, multifaceted portraits of emotional states and interpersonal relationships. The first generation of the New York School wrote about film; second-generation Warsh goes one step further by making the literary equivalent of the cinematic jump-cut one of his stylistic trademarks:

> There's a little anger lurking in the corner of my heart
>
> From here, it looks like a scar where the road turns on the
> way to oblivion
>
> I have a relationship with someone other than myself
>
> My father looks up at us & says: you're not my family

Until yesterday, the word "orderly" wasn't part of my
vocabulary. . . .

Artist Joe Brainard established himself as a New York–style poet primarily through his book *I Remember* (1975), which took O'Hara's and Schuyler's interest in the details of daily life and stripped it down to essentials. The book contains a lengthy succession of sentences or brief paragraphs that all begin with "I remember."

Anne Waldman, who served as director of the Poetry Project for many years, distinguished herself as both a tireless proselytizer for the New York School and as a poet. She developed a unique performance-based style that brought new energy and a new audience to the New York School in works such as *Fast Speaking Woman* (1975). Her work combined the street savvy and colloquial energy of O'Hara with an edginess rooted in popular music and chant, as showcased in this passage from "Musical Garden":

Can't give you up, can't stop
clamoring

Can't give you up, sweetheart, my tender
chocolate big-lipped love

Can't give you up, all dear ones, your bright
ears & delicate smiles

Can't give you up, Louis-Ferdinand Celine,
you're obsessed & vitriolic & absolutely
right . . .

During the 1960s and much of the 1970s the Project was home to both first- and second-generation New York School poets. It was also the center of a publishing revolution powered by the eminently affordable mimeo machine, which enabled poets on shoestring budgets to publish magazines and books whose immediacy and lasting impact often belied their humble origins. Notable mimeo publications from this period include the magazines *The World* (the Poetry Project's house organ), *Adventures in Poetry, Telephone, United Artists, Angel Hair,* and *C;* books that originally appeared in mimeograph editions include Ted Berrigan's *Sonnets.*

The Project also nurtured a new style of poetry workshop. Poets who had studied with Koch expanded on his teaching style and offered workshops that emphasized process and appreciation rather than proscribed techniques and standards. Bernadette Mayer became known for her lengthy list of workshop writing experiments, instructions for which ranged from "systematically derange the language: write a work consisting only of prepositional phrases, or, add a gerund to every line of an already existing work" to "write household poems—about cooking, shopping, eating and sleeping."

By the early 1980s yet another crop of interesting poets had emerged from the creative foment at the Poetry Project. Among them was Maureen Owen, who fused humor, a nearly breathless, ecstatic point of view, and Japanese spareness in poems that appeared in a steady stream of playful but intense books that include *Hearts in Space* (1980), *Zombie Notes* (1985), and *Imaginary Income* (1992).

Eileen Myles offered a fast, fearless persona that alternated between toughness and tenderness. Her expansive personality was often the primary driving force for her work in books such as *A Fresh Young Voice from the Plains* (1980). In this respect she can be considered a successor to O'Hara.

Alice Notley's work, which seamlessly veers between disrupted narrative, the serio-comic, and straightforward autobiography, has steadily evolved since her initial publications in the 1970s. Notley, who was married to Ted Berrigan until his death in 1983, has gradually achieved a much wider recognition for her work. Early books include *When I Was Alive* (1980), which features some rhymed poems, and *How Spring Comes* (1981). More recent books, such as the long poem *The Descent of Alette* (1996), which offers a sort of modern myth staged in a nightmarish urban subway setting, and *Mysteries of Small Houses* (1998), which sharply documents specific moments in the poet's life, show the breadth of Notley's poetry and the extent of the New York School's evolution over five decades.

PETER J. BUSHYEAGER

**Further Reading**

Berkson, Bill, and Joe LeSueur, editors, *Homage to Frank O'Hara,* Bolinas, California: Big Sky, 1978

Gooch, Brad, *City Poet: The Life and Times of Frank O'Hara,* New York: Knopf, 1993

Lehman, David, *The Last Avant-Garde: The Making of the New York School of Poets,* New York: Doubleday, 1998

Myers, John Bernard, *Tracking the Marvelous: A Life in the New York Art World,* New York: Random House, 1983

Padgett, Ron, *Ted: A Personal Memoir of Ted Berrigan,* Great Barrington, Massachusetts: The Figures, 1993

Perloff, Marjorie, *Frank O'Hara: Poet among Painters,* Chicago: University of Chicago Press, 1998

Rivers, Larry, and Arnold Weinstein, *What Did I Do? The Unauthorized Autobiography,* New York: HarperCollins, 1992

Waldman, Anne, editor, *Nice To See You: Homage to Ted Berrigan,* Minneapolis, Minnesota: Coffee House Press, 1991

Ward, Geoffrey, *Statutes of Liberty: The New York School of Poets,* New York: St. Martin's Press, and London: Macmillan, 1993

# Lorine Niedecker 1903–70

Of the earth, the mud of flooded land and the marshes of her native Black Hawk Island, Wisconsin, Lorine Niedecker's poems are as powerfully elemental as they show us humans to be—as mineral, copper flowing in our veins, and iron. Butterflies—fragile as spirit—are shown to be actually akin to rock:

Nothing supra-rock
    about it
        simply
Butterflies
    are quicker
        than rock. ("Lake Superior")

Niedecker's vision effects a kind of democratization of the hierarchy of things. In this sense, she is a descendent of Whitman, although in almost every other way—her succinctness, for example, reflecting a lifelong commitment to condensing, her work being her "condensery," as she called it—she is light-years away from Whitman's project of inclusion. Even her cataloging is brutally selective. "I arose from marsh mud," she tells us, from

algae, equisetum, willows,
sweet green, noisy
birds and frogs (untitled fragment)

an earthy, earth-bound beginning reinforced by her decision to remain in her native rural Wisconsin, a world that, in Niedecker's hands, does grant access to more ethereal earth-bound beings, such as those butterflies, beings whose ties to the mineral realm extend everyone's, everything's, connection to the farthest reaches of the universe. She strives for as accurate a description of each object as Gerard Manley Hopkins did, coupling this effort with an unerring ear for sympathetic sounds, far too numerous to do justice to here:

Not all harsh sounds displease—
Yellowhead blackbirds cough
through reeds and fronds
as through pronged bronze.

***

Get a load
    of April's
        fabulous

frog rattle—
    lowland freight cars
        in the night (untitled fragment)

One thinks of William Carlos Williams' "reddish / purplish, forked, upstanding, twiggy / stuff of bushes and small trees" in his famous poem from *Spring and All* (1923)—but Niedecker may actually be exceeding Williams in some places, she has such a fine ear.

These poems celebrate the physicality of sound, that essential component of the art of poetry that seems too often to be lost these days—poetry as sculpted sound. No wonder Niedecker was floored by *Poetry* magazine's February 1931 issue on the Objectivists, whose practitioners were attempting to reclaim Ezra Pound's Imagist aesthetic after Amy Lowell's dilution—"The point of Imagisme is that it does not use images as ornaments" (Pound, "Vorticism," *Fortnightly Review* 96 [1 September 1914], as quoted in Heller, 1985). Louis Zukofsky is more specific in his introduction ("An Objective") to the special issue of *Poetry:* that good writing "*is* the detail, not the mirage of seeing, *of thinking with things as they exist*" (emphasis added). One is reminded of Pound's claim for the natural object as adequate symbol and of his belief that a poet's form is a measure of his or her sincerity. Niedecker seems to have come to these ideas, this aesthetic, on her own, immediately identifying with the Objectivist poems she read in the 1931 issue of *Poetry*—by Zukofsky, George Oppen, Charles Reznikoff, Carl Rakosi, Basil Bunting, and others. She wrote Zukofsky in response to the issue, and they became lifelong friends. Basil Bunting later traveled all the way from England to visit Niedecker in Wisconsin. A few lines from Bunting's "Ode 15" from his *First Book of Odes* (1965) demonstrates a powerful link to Niedecker:

When taut string's note
Passes ears' reach or red rays or violet
Fade, strong over unseen
Forces the word
Ranks and enumerates . . .

Mimes clouds condensed
And hewn hills and bristling forests . . .

However, like Bunting's, Niedecker's attention to human relationships carries as much punch and subtlety of aural effects as do her poems about nature, and her somewhat homespun insights into human behavior—mostly about herself in relation to others—are impressive. In the following untitled fragments she depicts a despair not so desperate as practical, practically caught and held. The speaker has thought these feelings through:

The men leave the car
to bring us green-white lilies
    by woods
These men are our woods
yet I grieve

I'm swamp
as against a large pine-spread—
his clear No marriage
    no marriage
friend

***

My life is hung up
    in the flood
        a wave-blurred
            portrait

Don't fall in love
with this face—
it no longer exists
in water
we cannot fish

***

Stone
and that hard
contact—
the human

On the mossed
massed quartz
on which spruce
grew dense

I met him
We were thick
We said good-bye
on The Passing Years
River

Niedecker expands her net's reach further yet to include political commentary and history—told "slant," indirection being a staple of her method, coming as it does in counterpoint to the personal life as imagined from letters—as in "Thomas Jefferson." However, she is strongest when focusing her attention on the minute particulars of direct experience that, like her view of organic life as qualitatively connected to the so-called inanimate world of rocks, transport her readers well beyond Black Hawk Island, Wisconsin.

ELIZABETH ARNOLD

*See also* Objectivism

**Biography**

Born in Fort Atkinson, Wisconsin, 12 May 1903. Attended Beloit College, Wisconsin, 1922–24; writer, research editor, W.P.A., Madison, Wisconsin, 1938–42; script writer, WHA (radio station), Madison, 1942; stenographer, proofreader, Hoard's, Fort Atkinson, 1944–50; cleaning woman, local hospital, Fort Atkinson, 1957–63. Received Notable Wisconsin Writers Award, 1978. Died in Fort Atkinson, 31 December 1970.

**Poetry**

*New Goose,* 1946
*My Friend Tree,* 1961
*North Central,* 1968
*T and G: The Collected Poems (1936–1966),* 1968
*My Life by Water: Collected Poems, 1936–1968,* 1970
*Blue Chicory,* 1976
*The Granite Pail: The Selected Poems of Lorine Niedecker,* 1985; revised edition, 1996
*From This Condensery: The Complete Writing of Lorine Niedecker,* 1985
*Harpsichord and Salt Fish,* 1991

**Other Writings:** correspondence (*"Between Your House and Mine": The Letters of Lorine Niedecker to Cid Corman, 1960 to 1970,* 1986).

**Further Reading**

Dent, Peter, editor, *The Full Note: Lorine Niedecker,* Budleigh Salterton, Devon: Interim Press, 1983
Gunn, Thom, "Weedy Speech and Tangled Bank: Lorine Niedecker," in *Shelf Life: Essays, Memoirs, and an Interview,* by Gunn, Ann Arbor: University of Michigan Press, 1993; London: Faber, 1994
Heller, Michael, *Conviction's Net of Branches: Essays on the Objectivist Poets and Poetry,* Carbondale: Southern Illinois University Press, 1985
Penberthy, Jenny, *Niedecker and the Correspondence with Zukofsky, 1931–1970,* Cambridge and New York: Cambridge University Press, 1993
Penberthy, Jenny, editor, *Lorine Niedecker: Woman and Poet,* Orono, Maine: National Poetry Foundation, 1996

## Lake Superior

In 1963, when she was 60 years old, Lorine Niedecker married Al Millen, her second husband. After having lived many years alone in her isolated, one-room cabin in rural Wisconsin, she moved to Milwaukee and beyond. She and Millen began taking automobile vacations in the Great Lakes and central Great Plains regions. In 1966, they circumnavigated Lake Superior, driving through Michigan's Upper Peninsula, across the north shore of the lake into Canada, and down through Minnesota. Niedecker kept notes on the trip and did extensive research into the history and geology of the region (the notes are reproduced in Penberthy's *Lorine Niedecker: Woman and Poet* [1996]) before publishing "TRAVELERS: Lake Superior region" in the fall/winter issue of *Arts in Society* (1967). Not satisfied that she had achieved success with a long poem, she continued working on the series. A revised version, simply titled "Lake Superior," appeared in her volume *North Central* (1968), published in London by Fulcrum Press. "Lake Superior" occupies a central place in her work because it initiates the last major phase of her poetics, in which she transmutes her second-generation Modernism, developed under the tutelage of her friend Louis Zukofsky, into a postmodern idiom that expresses the expanding realm of experience of her later years.

Lisa Pater Faranda (1987) explains the major change in focus indicated by the different titles: "The first title emphasizes the transitory contact between travelers and place, which effectually separates them. . . . The second title signals an entrance to an unfamiliar spot, but at the same time naming a specific location offers the possibility of transforming it through intimate, proprioceptive contact into familiar ground, open also to a reader." The revision is important: the final version does not follow a linear, literal journey but rather evokes the circular processes of the mineral cycle, subsuming human history into the larger geologic time scale. Also, the first version numbered the individual poems that constitute the sequence; in rearranging the poems and deleting the numbers, Niedecker achieved a structure that expressed the fluidity of the processes that she was writing about. Rather than a strict sequence, the poem follows, in Joseph Conte's phrase, a "finite serial form." Nonetheless, Niedecker's car trip still structures the series inherently; the last poem looks back at the completed journey:

I'm sorry to have missed
    Sand Lake
My dear one tells me
    we did not
We watched a gopher there

What's more, the poem has a thematic trajectory embodied in the geologic cycle that reveals Niedecker's relationship to the history and geology recounted in the poem. The series begins with "rock" and ends with "stone," and the subtle distinction in usage between these terms reveals the mineral cycle to be a correlative for the individual's journey from source to self.

Such complex structuring indicates Niedecker's affinity with Objectivist poetics, which eschews drawing explicit analogies between the self and nature. Yet Niedecker uses Objectivist principles to establish the connection between human and nonhuman. Through such devices as parataxis, metonymy, and wordplay, she combines personal experience, documentary research, and historical figures into a record of the interpenetration of human consciousness and geologic process in the Lake Superior region. The first poem announces the principle of recirculation:

In every part of every living thing
is stuff that once was rock

In blood the minerals
of the rock

This proclamation initiates the mineral cycle as well as the car trip—the next poem references the point where the travelers cross into Canada (Sault Sainte Marie), and the industry of the Great Lakes seen there is the first example of recirculation: "Iron the common element of earth / in rocks and freighters." The next four sections introduce the early European explorers of the territory—Radisson, Marquette, and Joliet—and Niedecker indicates their simultaneous exploitation of and integration into the land in compressed, telegraphic imagery. For example, Radisson's own description of the lakes is quoted, "'a laborinth of pleasure,'" and Niedecker uses metonymical rather than descriptive images to represent him: "Long hair, long gun." Marquette himself returns to the cyclical round of geologic process:

And at the blue ice superior spot
priest-robed Marquette grazed
azoic rock, hornblende granite
basalt the common dark
in all the Earth

And his bones of such is coral
raised up out of his grave
were sunned and birch bark-floated
to the straits

One aspect of the serial form of the poem is the disruption of the historical sequence as well as the linear journey. In between the early explorers and Henry Rowe Schoolcraft in the 19th century, Niedecker inserts a poem that describes various semi-precious stones that she finds attractive and collects from the roadside gift shops. It introduces a personal element to the history and geology and allows Niedecker a range of wordplay as she puns on the etymology and mineralogy of the names and colors of the stones. In the first stanza, a collage of color—from the deep blue of lapis lazuli to the dark reds and oranges of carnelian—is assembled, and in the second stanza is the first appearance of the poem's speaker:

Greek named
Exodus-antique
kicked up in America's
Northwest
you have been in my mind
between my toes
agate

Here, Niedecker almost directly translates her notes into the poem: "The agate was first found on the shores of a river in Sicily and named by the Greeks. In the Bible (Exodus), this semiprecious stone was seen on the priest's breastplate. . . . Maybe as rocks and I pass each other I could say how-do-you-do to an agate" (quoted in Penberthy, 1996).

Unlike the historical figures, Niedecker's relation to rock is a personalized one; whereas they have passed back into the cycle of recirculation and become part of the "common dark" once again, the speaker meets and identifies with individual stones. This distinction does not privilege her over the explorers—both states of existence are reconnections with one's sources, as the penultimate poem reveals:

The smooth black stone
I picked up in true source park
    the leaf beside it
once was stone

Why should we hurry
    home

The emphasis on rock, the more general term denoting the mass of mineral matter, that began the series shifts to stone, denoting a fragment of rock and implying the polishing and shaping of culture, at the end. The nominative "I" appears only at the end, which connects the lyric subject with the individual stone and the person with the correlative of her geologic sources. Realizing this, she finds her home at the far end of her journey, at the origin of the Mississippi River, and the slant rhyme of "stone" and "home" completes the recirculation announced at the beginning of the series.

GEORGE HART

**Further Reading**

Conte, Joseph Mark, *Unending Design: The Forms of Postmodern Poetry,* Ithaca, New York: Cornell University Press, 1991

Crase, Douglas, "Lorine Niedecker and the Evolutional Sublime," in *Lorine Niedecker: Woman and Poet,* edited by Jenny Penberthy, Orono, Maine: National Poetry Foundation, 1996

Davie, Donald, "Lorine Niedecker: Lyric Minimum and Epic Scope," in *The Full Note: Lorine Niedecker,* edited by Peter Dent, Budleigh Salterton, Devon: Interim Press, 1983
Davie, Donald, "Niedecker and Historicity," in *Lorine Niedecker: Woman and Poet,* edited by Jenny Penberthy, Orono, Maine: National Poetry Foundation, 1996
Faranda, Lisa Pater, "Composing a Place: Two Versions of Lorine Niedecker's 'Lake Superior,'" *North Dakota Quarterly* 55, no. 4 (1987)
Freeman, John, "Blood from a Stone: A Reading of 'Lake Superior,'" in *The Full Note: Lorine Niedecker,* edited by Peter Dent, Budleigh Salterton, Devon: Interim Press, 1983
Hayes, Paul G., "'At the Close—Someone': Lorine's Marriage to Al Millen," in *Lorine Niedecker: Woman and Poet,* edited by Jenny Penberthy, Orono, Maine: National Poetry Foundation, 1996

## My Life by Water

In the 1960s Lorine Niedecker wrestled with theoretical abstractions to describe a new poetics, one that would allow her to express a deeper subjectivity and consciousness but would also remain true to the principles of the minimalist aesthetic she derived from Objectivism. In a letter to her friend and neighbor, Gail Roub, she tried out the term "reflections," but was unsatisfied with that: "or as I think it over now, reflective maybe." The idea was to get the concrete particulars down, in good Objectivist fashion, but then also to get something else in that "overlays all that to make a state of consciousness." At this time Niedecker was working on poems with a strong autobiographical content, looking back at her life and family history, and so "reflection" might evoke the backward glance as that thing that "overlays" the rest of the poem. She continues to Roub:

> I used to feel that I was goofing off unless I held only to the hard, clear image, the thing you could put your hand on but now I dare do this reflection. For instance, *Origin* will have a narrow, longish poem, sensuous, begins "My life / in water" and ends "of the soft and serious / Water." (Faranda, 1986)

This poem, eventually used by Niedecker as the title poem for the British edition of her collected poems (*My Life by Water: Collected Poems, 1936–1968,* 1970), provides an index to many of her themes and techniques.

It is one indication of the poet's feeling that she was betraying her aesthetic of condensing that she considers this poem "longish": it contains a total of only 46 words, arranged in nine stanzas composed of tercets. Niedecker uses this stanza form, based on William Carlos Williams' triadic variable foot, in other poems as well, such as "Paul" (one of a group of poems written in the 1950s for Louis Zukofsky's son) and "Poet's Work," in which she explains her process:

> I learned
> to sit at desk
> and condense
>
> No layoff
> from this
> condensery.

Most important, she used the same tercets in a long poem, "Wintergreen Ridge," written about the same time as "My Life by Water." Kenneth Cox (1996), a critic and admirer of Niedecker's work, believes that this lyric was part of an aborted attempt

> to transfer its technique to another poem about her early life. It was hardly to be expected that a technique developed for the bleak magnificence of "Wintergreen Ridge" would lend itself to a project of nostalgic recollection. "My Life By Water" is probably a piece saved from the wreck before another start was made on the poem that became "Paean to Place."

Indeed, Niedecker returned to a haiku-based, five-line stanza for that poem, but the connection is evident in the similar openings used in both poems. In "Paean to Place" the lines read: "My life // in the leaves and on water." So, despite her fear of "goofing off" from the "condensery," this poem is a condensed autobiography.

Niedecker's tercets condense both the music and subject matter of the poem. The five-liners of "Paean" usually have two rhyming lines, but in the tercets rhyme is eschewed; the poet sings through alliteration, consonance, and assonance. The syntax is also radically condensed, the prepositions often performing double duty through paratactical splicing or line breaks. For example, the fourth and fifth stanzas could be taken as a single causal sentence or broken after "doors" into two separate thoughts on spring:

> Muskrats
> gnawing
> doors
>
> to wild green
> arts and letters . . .

The number of stanzas that begin with prepositions reveals how Niedecker's compression actually gets more music into—and out of—fewer words, while also producing multiple or indeterminate meanings.

Her indeterminate use of prepositions also affects the autobiographical content. Rachel Blau DuPlessis (1992) considers the second line's first word, "by," ambiguous: "My life / by water" "might mean *next to,*" but it

> might at the same time open the much-debated questions of authorship and point of view. Could this really be the "life" of someone, her biography, whose author is water?

Indeterminacies such as these create the complex interplay between particular and universal that Niedecker was perhaps searching for in her "reflective" poetics. The particulars were certainly experienced by one observer who spent her life in this aquatic place. The details are precise and vivid—the sound of frog or board, the gnawing muskrats, the boats pointed toward shore—but they also contribute to "a state of consciousness," one that all readers may share. The compounds of the penultimate stanza evoke the reflective consciousness:

thru birdstart
    wingdrip
        weed-drift[.]

The reader may not be able to say what "birdstart" or "wingdrip" or "weed-drift" refer to exactly but knows, or perhaps feels, what they mean. Certainly these words evoke the seasons, the marshland environment, the common things of place, but, even more, they tell of the "soft" and the "serious" life lived by "Water": both of the delicacy, gentleness, and nurturing offered by water as resource, and the frugality, loneliness, and isolation of the marginal existence.

GEORGE HART

**Further Reading**


Augustine, Jane, "The Evolution of Matter: Lorine Niedecker's Aesthetic," *Sagetrieb* 1, no. 2 (1982)

Cox, Kenneth, "The Longer Poems," in *Lorine Niedecker: Woman and Poet,* edited by Jenny Penberthy, Orono, Maine: National Poetry Foundation, 1996

DuPlessis, Rachel Blau, "Lorine Niedecker, the Anonymous: Gender, Class, Genre, and Resistances," *Kenyon Review* 14, no. 2 (1992)

Faranda, Lisa Pater, editor, *"Between Your House and Mine": The Letters of Lorine Niedecker to Cid Corman, 1960 to 1970,* Durham, North Carolina: Duke University Press, 1986

Heller, Michael, *Conviction's Net of Branches: Essays on the Objectivist Poets and Poetry,* Carbondale: Southern Illinois University Press, 1985

Oderman, Kevin, "Lorine Niedecker: Houses into Hoopla," *Sagetrieb* 7, no. 2 (1988)

Perloff, Marjorie, *Poetic License: Essays on Modernist and Postmodernist Lyric,* Evanston, Illinois: Northwestern University Press, 1990


# Alice Notley 1945–

An immensely prolific poet associated with Manhattan's lower east side and the Beat-influenced contingent of the New York School's second generation, Alice Notley initially pursued fiction writing at Barnard and then at the Iowa Writers' Workshop. Fascinated by poetry's attention to the materiality of language and the compact space of the page, Notley turned to poetry during her second year at Iowa, "so it really turned out that I was more interested in words than I was in stories or a kind of narrative flow" (Foster, 1994). Notley's early poems eschew narrative structure in favor of an almost Steinian playfulness, a quotidian randomness, and a Williams-inspired American vernacular. Later in her career, Notley returned to narrative structure and combined it with a lyric attention to words. *Close to Me and Closer—: (The Language of Heaven)* (1993), *Désamère* (1993), and *The Descent of Alette* (1996) are all "poetic sequences with story-shapes and characters" and expand Notley's consistent experimentation with the role of the poet as a medium for the dead and a spiritual messenger of the living (see Notley's preface to *Close to Me and Closer—: [The Language of Heaven]*). In "Homer's Art" (1990), an essay that articulates the ideas informing the making of *The Descent of Alette,* Notley writes, "What a service to poetry it might be to steal story away from the novel and give it back to rhythm and sound, give it back to the line."

*The Descent of Alette* is a contemporary epic in the tradition of Homer and Dante, yet is written with the intent to recover the ethos and sensibility of pre-Homeric times, when women were, according to Notley, active contributors to culture. The heroine Alette has been chosen as an agent of redemption to plunge the layers of consciousness and misery in a mythical underground world dominated by "the tyrant." *The Descent of Alette* also develops Notley's long-standing interest in voice and enacts the value she places on rendering spiritual and religious concerns in ordinary language. In order to "remind the reader that each phrase is a thing said by a voice," Notley places phrases in quotation marks that mark poetic feet ("Author's Note").

While Notley claims that she is not Alette, this heroine represents a prominent aspect of Notley's persona: an anointed poet of the redemptive and the everyday. This persona, paradoxically humble and elevated, arises in earlier pieces such as "Poem," a poem ending with a question that asserts the necessity of Notley's poetic presence by imagining its absence: "And who will know the desolation of St. Mark's Place / With Alice Notley's name forgotten and / this night never having been?"

In *Mysteries of Small Houses* (1998), Notley continues to develop her attention to the landscape and dwellings in which the events of her life have taken place. One of the many love lyrics that appear in this volume, "April Is Not an Inventory but a Blizzard," attests to the influence of Ted Berrigan on her life and work. With entertaining charm, Notley describes their quirky romantic courtship, a beginning that inspires her "to forget about Plath and James Wright" and "write / I think it's eighty-three poems." In an interview Notley underscores Berrigan's influence when she explains that after meeting him

> everything was different, because after that I knew what poets to read . . . and it all opened up for me, and I knew who I was going to be as a poet and who my models and peers and so on were going to be. And what language I wanted to live in. (Foster, 1994)

While Notley chose to live and work in a poetic language that expresses "the things in-between those talked about in books," a language teeming with the words and sentiments of her everyday life as a woman poet, she also works seamlessly within traditional genres. After Berrigan's death in 1983, Notley wrote her most ambitious elegy, the Whitmanesque "At Night the States," which appears in the collection of the same name. Characteristic of most of Notley's work, "At Night the States" is emotionally lucid, yet its details often slip from logical grasp. Each stanza begins with the title line, and beginning from that refrain, Notley displays the multiple voices and shifting lyrical dictions of loss. "At Night the States" charts Berrigan's voice slipping from presence to absence and into memory as well as the alternately tentative and strong emergence of Notley's solitary voice:

> oh call my name, and if I call
>     it out myself to
> you, call mine out instead as our
>     poets do
> will you still walk on by?

More than any other poetic tropes or themes, Notley's priority has been to consistently render the idiosyncratic texture of individuals' personalities as they are expressed through the human voice. Notley's attention to voice and personality links her to the New York School, especially Frank O'Hara. However, her work does not express the New York School's often evasive urbanity and instead expresses a folksier, grittier attention to the quotidian than can be traced to the Beats. An early poem, "Jack Would Speak through the Imperfect Medium of Alice," reveals her debt to the Beat aesthetic, her impulse to collaborate with both the dead and the living, and her feminine intervention in the primarily male domain of Beat poetry.

Notley's theories about "the feminine" in poetry, her fearless inclusion of the sentimental, and her forthright acknowledgment of her husband's influence attest to her rebellious distinction from feminist strictures and definitions. When discussing her views of gender and the male-dominated literary canon, Notley states, "I put back on it all this femininity it never had—or bring it to light somehow. Suddenly the poetic tradition for me was always there, and it isn't a male, macho, sexist tradition" (Foster, 1994). Notley's work has consistently argued for her voice to speak within, glean from, and communicate with the literary history that precedes her. An early poem, "But He Says I Misunderstood," asserts that there are significant connections among her own life as a wife and a mother, formal innovations, and the way women writers are regarded. According to Notley's assured last line, these connections and the arguments they inspire are in "The Mainstream American Tradition."

KIMBERLY LAMM

*See also* New York School

**Biography**

Born in Bisbee, Arizona, 8 November 1945. Attended Barnard College, New York, B.A. 1967; University of Iowa, Iowa City, M.F.A. 1969. Received National Endowment for the Arts grant, 1980; Poetry Center Award, 1982; G.E. Foundation Award, 1983; Fund for Poetry grant, 1987, 1989. Living in Paris, France.

**Poetry**

*165 Meeting House Lane,* 1971
*Phoebe Light,* 1973
*Incidentals in the Day World,* 1973
*For Frank O'Hara's Birthday,* 1976
*Alice Ordered Me To Be Made: Poems, 1975,* 1976
*A Diamond Necklace,* 1977
*Songs for the Unborn Second Baby,* 1979
*When I Was Alive,* 1980
*Waltzing Matilda,* 1981
*How Spring Comes,* 1981
*Sorrento,* 1984
*Margaret and Dusty,* 1985
*Parts of a Wedding,* 1986
*At Night the States,* 1988
*From a Work in Progress,* 1988
*Homer's Art,* 1990
*The Scarlet Cabinet: A Compendium of Books* (with Douglas Oliver), 1992
*Selected Poems of Alice Notley,* 1993
*To Say You,* 1994
*Close to Me and Closer—: (The Language of Heaven); and, Désamère: Two Books,* 1995
*The Descent of Alette,* 1996
*Mysteries of Small Houses,* 1998

**Other Writings:** play, memoir (*Tell Me Again,* 1981), nonfiction.

**Further Reading**

Foster, Edward, interviewer, "Alice Notley Interview," in *Postmodern Poetry: The Talisman Interviews,* by Foster, Hoboken, New Jersey: Talisman House, 1994
Notley, Alice, "Doctor Williams' Heiresses," *Tuumba* 28 (1980)
Notley, Alice, "Iovis Omnia Plena," *Chicago Review* 44, no. 1 (1998)
Notley, Alice, "A Certain Slant of Sunlight," *American Poetry Review* 28, no. 2 (March/April 1999)

# O

## Objectivism

In discussions of 20th-century American poetry, "Objectivism" refers to the aesthetic principles shared by a group of poets who came together in the early 1930s. Louis Zukofsky was the leader and principal theorist of the group, and he coined the label "Objectivist" to describe their work. The other poets generally grouped as Objectivists include Charles Reznikoff, George Oppen, Carl Rakosi, Lorine Niedecker, and the British poet Basil Bunting. These poets took Ezra Pound and William Carlos Williams as their primary models among the poets of the immediately preceding generation; and Williams, who was for a time in close contact with Zukofsky and other members of the group, sometimes accepted the label "Objectivist" as describing his own work.

The use of the label "Objectivism" to describe the theories and practices of this group of poets must be distinguished from certain other uses of the word. The term "Objectivism" plays an intermittent role in philosophical discourse, where it is sometimes associated with the anti-subjectivist and anti-historicist views of the British philosopher Karl Popper. Richard J. Bernstein defines "Objectivism," in this philosophic sense of the term, as "the basic conviction that there is or must be some permanent, ahistorical matrix to which we can ultimately appeal in determining the nature of rationality, truth, reality, goodness or rightness" (Bernstein, 1983). This philosophic use of the term was also taken up by the radical libertarian novelist and political theorist Ayn Rand, whose views have been popularized by a vocal right-wing cult. The general philosophic meaning of "Objectivism" has some relevance, although only indirectly, to the poetic theories and practices of the Objectivist poets. However, the "Objectivism" of Ayn Rand has no relationship of any sort to the work of these poets, and there is no evidence either that she read their work or that they read her work.

Objectivism crystallized as a literary movement in 1930, when Harriet Monroe, at the suggestion of Ezra Pound, invited Louis Zukofsky to guest edit a special issue of *Poetry* devoted to younger American poets, eventually published as the February 1931 issue. Zukofsky had grown up in a Yiddish-speaking, working-class family in New York and had received both a B.A. and an M.A. from Columbia University, writing a thesis on Henry Adams. In 1930, he was living a bohemian life in New York City, publishing occasionally in literary magazines such as *Poetry* and *Hound and Horn* and moving within the left-wing political circles and the avant-garde literary circles of the city. Zukofsky had earlier become friends with Charles Reznikoff, a law school graduate who, after various abortive career moves, had settled into what became a long career as an editor for a legal publishing firm in New York. Reznikoff had been publishing poems, plays, and autobiographical narratives since 1918, usually at his own expense and often printed on his own basement press.

In 1928, George and Mary Oppen also arrived in New York. Both of the Oppens had grown up on the West Coast, and they had met while students at Oregon State College. Oppen's father was a successful San Francisco businessman; alone among these poets, Oppen had a modest independent income that he often used to support the publications of his friends. After dropping out of college and drifting about the West for a few years, George and Mary set out for New York to join the literary life, making the last leg of the journey on a small boat that they sailed from Detroit through Lake Erie and the Erie Canal and then down the Hudson River. A little after arriving in New York, Oppen read a portion of Zukofsky's "Poem Beginning 'The'" in Pound's magazine *Exile,* and he was delighted to meet this exciting poet (Mary Oppen, 1978). In 1930, while preparing the special issue, Zukofsky also began a correspondence with the Midwestern poet Carl Rakosi, whose work had been appearing in many literary magazines. Finally, during the months in which he prepared the special issue, Zukofsky also saw much of Basil Bunting. Zukofsky and Bunting had met in 1928 as fellow students in Pound's "Ezuversity" in Rapallo, Italy; and in 1930, Bunting, newly married to an American, spent several months in New York. These five poets—Zukofsky, Reznikoff, Oppen, Rakosi, and Bunting—formed the initial core of the Objectivist group.

Harriet Monroe told Zukofsky that he should give an identifying label to the poets in his special issue of *Poetry,* and he came up with the term "Objectivists." Zukofsky generally placed the word in quotation marks, and he avoided the label "Objectivism," for to him the "Objectivists" were not so much a movement as a group of poets who shared some affinities. The label "Objectivist" deliberately echoed the title of Pound's own 1914 anthology *Des Imagistes:* by implication, the "Objectivists" were following in the footsteps of the "Imagists" (or "*Imagistes*") but going them one better in moving beyond the image to re/discover the object itself. However, despite his uneasiness about presenting Objectivism as a "movement," Zukofsky supplemented the poems in the special issue with a theoretic statement, "Program: 'Objectivists' 1931," and with a lengthy critical essay on the themes of "Sincerity" and "Objectification." These texts have all the look of a manifesto—and a manifesto inevitably seems to imply a movement.

In his "Program," Zukofsky sketched a poetic theory to justify the practice of the poets he had drawn together. Specifically, he suggested that an Objectivist poetics is driven by a "desire for what is objectively perfect, inextricably the direction of historic and contemporary particulars." Zukofsky fleshed out this statement by suggesting that "sincerity" and "objectification" are the defining characteristics of an Objectivist poetics. The writing that he called for would be characterized by "sincerity" while offering "the detail, not mirage, of seeing, of thinking with things as they exist, and of directing them along a line of melody." Zukofsky further defines "objectification" as a "rested totality" within which the "apprehension" of the reader is "satisfied completely as to the appearance of the art form as an object." In the critical statements included in the special issue, Zukofsky also identified some older poets whose work is "absolutely essential" to understanding the writing of the younger poets he had selected, including Ezra Pound, William Carlos Williams, Marianne Moore, T.S. Eliot, E.E. Cummings, and Wallace Stevens. However, he points primarily to Charles Reznikoff as an example of a poet whose work displays both sincerity and objectification. (Severely edited versions of these essays are included in *Prepositions,* but for the full text the reader must consult the February 1931 issue of *Poetry.*)

In editing the special issue, Zukofsky selected work not only by his five friends and Williams himself (the issue includes "The Botticellian Trees") but also by a heterogeneous group of other younger writers, including such unlikely candidates as Kenneth Rexroth and John Wheelwright. These last and some of the other poets included in the special issue refused Zukofsky's tutelage or went off in their own directions, and Bunting too resisted being labeled as part of a movement. However, Reznikoff happily assumed the role of exemplary "Objectivist" to which Zukofsky nominated him, and both Oppen and Rakosi also accepted the label. In addition, Lorine Niedecker, after reading the February 1931 issue of *Poetry,* initiated a correspondence with Zukofsky, and there ensued a brief love affair (culminating, probably, in a pregnancy and an abortion), a much longer friendship, and an extended correspondence in which the two poets commented at length on each other's work. Niedecker had been experimenting with surrealist techniques, and her work shows the continuing influence of non-Objectivist currents. However, her reading of the special issue induced in her something like a conversion experience. "I went to school to Objectivism," she later said (quoted in Penberthy, 1993), and her subsequent career is enmeshed with those of the other Objectivists.

By February 1931, Zukofsky and his friends had also begun to plan a publishing company to bring out work that met their aesthetic standards. In 1932, under the imprint of To, Publishers, Zukofsky published *An "Objectivists" Anthology*. Most of the poets in this anthology had been included in the special issue, including Zukofsky himself, Oppen, Reznikoff, Rakosi, Bunting, McAlmon, Rexroth, and Williams, but the anthology discards ten poets included in the special issue and adds Pound, Eliot, and Mary Butts. The anthology does not reprint any poems from the special issue, and the poets in the anthology receive, in most cases, substantially more space than they received in the special issue. Zukofsky also once again contributes a substantial programmatic introduction. Editorial offices for To, Publishers were located in Zukofsky's home, but the books were printed in France, where the Oppens were then living, and then shipped to New York for distribution.

In 1932, To, Publishers also issued Williams' *A Novelette and Other Prose* and a volume including Pound's *How to Read* and the first part of his *The Spirit of Romance.* The press planned to print additional selections of Pound's prose, but the international publishing scheme proved impractical, and To, Publishers suspended operations. However, in 1933, with the Oppens back in New York, the publishing operation returned to life as the Objectivist Press, a collaborative venture of Zukofsky, Oppen, Reznikoff, and Williams that described itself as "an organization of writers who are publishing their own work and that of other writers whose work they think ought to be read." The Objectivist Press published, over the next few years, Williams' *Collected Poems,* several major works by Reznikoff, and Oppen's first book, *Discrete Series.*

In the mid-1930s, however, the members of the Objectivist group began to move in separate directions. George Oppen stopped writing poetry after he and Mary joined the Communist Party and began to devote most of their time to political work. Bunting was in Europe, wrote little between "The Well of Lycopolis" (1935) and "The Spoils" (1951), and then wrote only a few short poems until 1965. Rakosi lived in New York in the late 1930s, and Zukofsky helped him prepare for publication his slim *Selected Poems,* published by New Directions in 1941; but then Rakosi too stopped writing poetry, changed his name to Callman Rawley, and embarked on a successful career as a social worker. Niedecker continued to send her poems to Zukofsky, but otherwise she had essentially no audience. Zukofsky himself married, and his new life centered increasingly on his family. He continued to write, and he published two collections of poems with a small press in Illinois, but his work had so little visibility that Robert Creeley, when he began reading Zukofsky's work in the late 1940s, assumed that the poet was dead.

By the late 1940s, when William Carlos Williams wrote his *Autobiography,* Objectivism had come to seem merely an episode in the career of Williams himself. Williams devotes a little more than a page to the subject in the *Autobiography,* stating that he and Zukofsky were "good friends" but failing to mention that Zukofsky served as the editor of his 1943 volume *The Wedge,* playing Pound to his Eliot by cutting Williams' typescript by more than a fourth and suggesting revisions in individual poems. Williams also describes evenings spent discussing the "Objectivist poem" with Oppen, Zukofsky, and "Charles Regnikoff" (*sic*). "The Objectivist theory," says Williams,

> was this: We had had "Imagism" (*Amygism,* as Pound had called it), which ran quickly out. That, though it had been useful in ridding the field of verbiage, had no formal necessity implicit in it. It had already dribbled off into so called "free verse" which, as we saw it, was a misnomer. There is no such thing as free verse! Verse is measure of some sort. "Free verse" was without measure. . . . Thus the poem had run down. . . . But, we argued, the poem, like every other form of art, is an object, an object that in itself formally presents its case and its meaning by the very form it assumes. Therefore, being an object, it should be so treated and controlled—but not as in the past. For past objects have about them past

> necessities—like the sonnet—which have conditioned them and from which, as a form itself, they cannot be freed. The poem being an object (like a symphony or cubist painting) it must be the purpose of the poet to make of his words a new form: to invent, that is, an object consonant with his day. This was what we wished to imply by Objectivism, an antidote, in a sense, to the bare image haphazardly presented in free verse. (Williams, 1951)

Williams goes on to note, correctly, that these theories owed a significant debt to Gertrude Stein. As a summation of Objectivist theory, Williams' comments are useful, although it should be added that these ideas were largely worked out not in the 1933 conversations in New York but in Zukofsky's 1931 essays for the special issue of *Poetry.*

Issue might also be taken with Williams' final comment on Objectivism in his *Autobiography:* "Nothing much happened in the end." For in the end, quite a bit happened, as the Objectivist poets began to emerge from obscurity during the 1950s and 1960s. *A Test of Poetry,* which Zukofsky had self-published in 1948, was brought out by an English commercial publisher in 1952; in 1956, Jonathan Williams published a substantial collection of Zukofsky's short poems, and in 1959, Cid Corman issued the first half of his long poem *"A,"* with an afterword by Williams. In 1958, George Oppen, after several years of political exile in Mexico, returned to New York, eager to resume his poetic career. By 1962, Oppen had enough new poems to publish a book with New Directions, *The Materials,* followed in quick succession by two more books. Oppen's 1968 book *Of Being Numerous* received the Pulitzer Prize, the only work by an Objectivist poet to receive a "mainstream" poetry prize. Suddenly, the Objectivists were visible—for the first time, actually.

Meanwhile, Oppen had also arranged for the 1962 New Directions publication of a selection of Reznikoff's poetry, under the title *By the Waters of Manhattan.* After one more New Directions book, Reznikoff found a permanent publisher in Black Sparrow, which maintains all of Reznikoff's poetry in print. Rakosi's return to poetry came more slowly. However, in 1965, Andrew Crozier, a young British poet and critic, began to collect Rakosi's work of the 1920s and 1930s. He had difficulty tracking down the poet, who had changed his name, but Crozier finally traced him through Reznikoff, and a letter from the young admirer prompted Rakosi to resume writing poetry. By 1967, he had enough new and older work for a volume, again published by New Directions, titled *Amulet.* Independent of these developments, in 1965 Bunting returned magnificently to poetry with his long (20 pages) poem *Briggflatts,* which was instantly acclaimed by many influential critics as one of the major British poems of the postwar period. In the 1960s, Lorine Niedecker's work also began to find its way into print, in part once again through the good offices of Cid Corman and Jonathan Williams.

Then in 1968, L.S. Dembo, the editor of the journal *Contemporary Literature,* brought Zukofsky, Reznikoff, Oppen, and Rakosi (but not, sadly, Niedecker, although she was living only a few miles away) to the University of Wisconsin, where he interviewed them as part of a seminar on modern poetry. Dembo published the interviews in a 1969 special issue of *Contemporary Literature,* thereby initiating serious critical attention to the work of the Objectivist poets. In the years since, the National Poetry Foundation has published substantial volumes of biographical, critical, and bibliographic work on each of the Objectivist poets, and in 1999 Peter Quartermain and Rachel Blau DuPlessis edited, under the title *The Objectivist Nexus,* a comprehensive volume of critical studies of these poets.

The significance of the Objectivists lies, first, in their determination to carry forward an avant-garde, experimental tradition in American poetry during a time of general aesthetic reaction and, second, in their determination to bring into a poetry a left-wing, Jewish, urban consciousness that had no precedent in American writing. Standard histories of American poetry generally see the experimental work of the Modernist generation (Pound, Williams, Moore, H.D., and Cummings) as succeeded by a return to traditional forms in the work of what Yvor Winters called a "reactionary generation," represented by, for example, Winters himself, John Crowe Ransom, Allen Tate, and Robert Penn Warren. These poets, in turn, sponsored the generation of Robert Lowell, John Berryman, Theodore Roethke, and Randall Jarrell and thus established themselves as the "mainstream" of American poetry. The poets of the "reactionary generation" also founded the New Criticism, which, as codified in Cleanth Brooks and Robert Penn Warren's *Understanding Poetry,* exercised hegemonic control over the teaching of poetry throughout the 1940s and 1950s.

However, as the hegemony of the New Critics has faded, it has become clear that there were many other currents within American poetry during the period from 1930 to 1960—the year in which Donald Allen's anthology *The New American Poetry* graphically demonstrated the inadequacy of the New Critical model of the history of American poetry. Alongside the work of the Southern Agrarians and other aesthetically and politically conservative poets, the 1930s also saw an energetic generation of left-wing poets, including Kenneth Fearing (a friend of Rakosi), Horace Gregory, and Muriel Rukeyser as well as many other poets. Popular in its own time, the work of these poets was effectively effaced in the reaction against Popular Front culture during the McCarthy years. The Objectivists also represented a model of politically engaged poetry: both Oppen and Rakosi eventually joined the Communist Party, Zukofsky wrote poems in praise of Lenin, and Zukofsky, Niedecker, and Oppen were all active in the Progressive Party campaign of 1948. However, the Objectivists were essentially unique among the poets of their generation in combining a radical politics with a commitment to an experimental, innovative poetics in the tradition of their Modernist mentors.

The unique space that the Objectivists sought to establish for themselves led to attacks (or, worse, indifference) from all sides. During the 1930s, the apostles of "socialist realism" within the Communist Party attacked the Objectivist poets as hopelessly obscurantist, while the New Critics simply ignored their work. By the 1950s, the very existence of this movement had been effectively effaced. Fortunately, however, all the Objectivists lived long enough to resume their poetic careers in the 1960s, when the eruption of a countercultural poetics, both politically and aesthetically radical, at last created an audience for their work. Today, it is clear that the Objectivists represent the principal link between the Modernists of the 1920s and the new poetic movements that began to gain momentum in the 1950s, including the Black Mountain School of "Projectivist" poets, the poets of the San Francisco Renaissance, the New York School, and the poets sometimes categorized as members of the "Beat generation."

Burton Hatlen

**Further Reading**

Bernstein, Richard J., *Beyond Objectivism and Relativism: Science, Hermeneutics, and Praxis,* Philadelphia: University of Pennsylvania Press, and Oxford: Blackwell, 1983

DuPlessis, Rachel Blau, and Peter Quartermain, editors, *The Objectivist Nexus: Essays in Cultural Poetics,* Tuscaloosa: University of Alabama Press, 1999

Hatlen, Burton, editor, *George Oppen: Man and Poet,* Orono, Maine: National Poetry Foundation, 1981

Hindus, Milton, editor, *Charles Reznikoff: Man and Poet,* Orono, Maine: National Poetry Foundation, 1984

Oppen, Mary, *Meaning a Life: An Autobiography,* Santa Barbara, California: Black Sparrow Press, 1978

Penberthy, Jenny, *Niedecker and the Correspondence with Zukofsky, 1931–1970,* Cambridge and New York: Cambridge University Press, 1993

Penberthy, Jenny, editor, *Lorine Niedecker: Woman and Poet,* Orono, Maine: National Poetry Foundation, 1994

Terrell, Carroll F., editor, *Louis Zukofsky: Man and Poet,* Orono, Maine: National Poetry Foundation, 1979

Williams, William Carlos, *Autobiography,* New York: Random House, 1951

Zukofsky, Louis, *Prepositions: The Collected Critical Essays of Louis Zukofsky,* London: Rapp and Carroll, and New York: Horizon Press, 1967; expanded edition, Berkeley: University of California Press, 1981

---

## Frank O'Hara 1926–66

Few poets are as important to American poetry in the 20th century as Frank O'Hara. Drawing on influences ranging from modern French poetry to Abstract Expressionist painting, O'Hara created a distinctive poetry of modern urban experience—alert, fast-paced, democratically open to a myriad of phenomena, and flexible enough to allow for quick shifts in tone and focus. His poetry may well represent, as Kenneth Koch has suggested, "the last stage in the adaptation of twentieth-century avant-garde sensibility to poetry about contemporary American experience" (Elledge, 1990). No poet better conveys the excitement of being alive in a great American city.

During his lifetime, O'Hara's work was generally available only in limited samples, primarily *Lunch Poems* (1964) and the poems anthologized in Donald Allen's landmark volume *The New American Poetry* (1960). Living and working apart from the academic poetry world, O'Hara showed no interest in garnering institutional approval of his work, and critics typically regarded him—or dismissed him—as a coterie poet, a member of the "New York School." However, for many young poets in the 1960s—Ted Berrigan and Ron Padgett, among others—O'Hara's example was a decisive one, a model not only of how one might write but also of how one might live, with generosity, wit, and boundless energy. In the years following the publication of *The Collected Poems of Frank O'Hara* (1971), O'Hara has come to be more widely recognized as a poet of extraordinary, prolific innovation, one whose work opened up new ways to imagine the materials and formal possibilities of poetry.

In the late 1940s and early 1950s, O'Hara's poetry developed at a distance from the dominant models then available in American poetry: the well-wrought impersonality of Eliotic modernism, exemplified by the early work of Robert Lowell, and the Poundian mythopoesis of Charles Olson. O'Hara rejected the high seriousness of both models, opting instead for a poetry of seemingly offhand gestures, a poetry that refused to invest its details with symbolic or mythic significance. As he was to sum up his poetics in the mock manifesto "Personism," "You just go on your nerve." The celebrated poem "Why I Am Not a Painter" reveals O'Hara's distance from Eliot and Lowell, Pound and Olson. After recounting several visits to painter Michael Goldberg as he labors to rework a painting, O'Hara offers in contrast an account of his own prose-poem sequence *Oranges: 12 Pastorals:* "One day I am thinking of / a color: orange. I write a line / about orange. Pretty soon it is a / whole page of words." The work of the poet seems like child's play: the comic, irreverent implication is that O'Hara is a poet because it is easier, at least for him, than being a painter; and the casual conversation ("'Sit down and have a drink,'" Mike says) and the happenstance narrative ("I drink; we drink") suggest O'Hara's decided lack of interest in reaching after higher meanings. What readers sometimes miss, however, is that a poem such as "Why I Am Not a Painter," so far removed from poetic traditions of high seriousness, is not merely frivolous or slight. In the course of this seemingly casual narrative, O'Hara makes a complex point about the relations between visual and verbal art, which share materials (Goldberg's painting has a word, "SARDINES," written on its surface; O'Hara's sequence is inspired by a color) but make different demands (the painter reworks the fixed space of the canvas; the poet moves on and on, in a way that seems to spoof Olson's essay "Projective Verse"). The poem's combination of mock solemnity (echoing Bertrand Russell's *Why I Am Not a Christian*), affable wit, and keen insight makes for a complexity of tone, at once comic and serious, not readily assimilated by poetic traditions seeking what O'Hara derisively called in an interview "the important utterance."

O'Hara's own sense of the possibilities of poetry was shaped by an unusual array of influences. His tonal range was influenced by W.H. Auden's colloquialism (O'Hara considered Auden an American poet) and by Vladimir Mayakovksy, from whom he borrowed what James Schuyler called the "intimate yell." Walt Whitman's expansiveness ("my great predecessor," O'Hara calls him in one poem), Hart Crane's linguistic density, and William Carlos Williams' affirmations of ordinary reality are important American influences. O'Hara's own attention to ordinary reality is often tinged with the generous humor of camp: he is likely to celebrate not the austere, Constructivist beauty of a red wheelbarrow but the gaudy delights of "kangaroos, sequins, chocolate sodas!" ("Today"). O'Hara was also strongly influenced by

French poetry: the stylized imagery of the symbolists and surrealists is pervasive in his early work, and Guillaume Apollinaire, another poet among painters, is a major precursor. O'Hara's "lunch poems" have much in common with Apollinaire's "Zone," each poet moving through a great city, shifting his attention between present realities and what is felt or remembered.

Like Apollinaire, O'Hara was deeply attuned to visual art, and critics have often characterized his poetry as an approximation in language of the Abstract Expressionist painting he championed in his museum work and critical writing. Interart analogies are always problematic, and O'Hara's poems, teeming with specific detail—the Camel billboard over Times Square, cheeseburgers and malteds, and names of friends, restaurants, and bookstores—might seem to have little in common with the nonrepresentational surfaces of a Franz Kline or Jackson Pollock. However, as John Ashbery has suggested, Abstract Expressionism gave O'Hara "a conception of art as process," a conception of the poem as "the chronicle of the creative act that produces it" (Elledge, 1990); and in Abstract Expressionism's attention to surface, O'Hara found an alternative to the poetics of symbol and myth, in which meaning lies behind a poem's surface. For O'Hara, surface and meaning are synonymous; as he says with reference to his poem *Second Avenue,* "the one is the other." A poetry of surfaces though need not be simple or transparent: O'Hara's finest poems offer surfaces as richly varied, dense, and surprising as those of a Pollock painting or a city street.

Since the publication of the *Collected Poems,* whose chronological arrangement made it possible to see the course of O'Hara's development, his work has come to be recognized as falling into two broad periods. The first, in the late 1940s and early 1950s, is dominated by what Kenneth Koch has called "experience-inspired outbursts of imaginative creation" (Elledge, 1990). Here symbolist, surrealist, and Abstract Expressionist influences are primary: in such poems as *Oranges: 12 Pastorals,* "Easter," and "Hatred," O'Hara creates dense, opaque language surfaces whose contents resist explication and paraphrase: "The razzle dazzle maggots are summary / tattooing my simplicity on the pitiable" ("Easter"). O'Hara's most difficult work in this mode is the 1953 long poem *Second Avenue* (published in 1960), characterized by Marjorie Perloff (1998) as "O'Hara's most ambitious attempt to do with *words* . . . what the Abstract Expressionists were doing with paint." The poem is not primarily "about" Manhattan's Second Avenue; rather, it is a performance in language, filled with exclamatory energy, rapid shifts in tone, and vivid, discontinuous word clusters whose true context is the poet's imagination: "What spanking opossums of sneaks are caressing the routes!" "Butter. Lotions. Cries. A glass of ice. Aldebaran and Mizar, / a guitar of toothpaste tubes and fingernails, trembling spear." Even O'Hara's most sympathetic readers have had doubts about *Second Avenue:* Perloff, for instance, has wondered "whether verbal structure can be so insistently nonmimetic," particularly in a long poem.

In the mid-1950s, O'Hara's poetry begins to reveal a much greater interest in representing ordinary reality. As O'Hara moves from outbursts of creation to what Koch has called "imaginative illuminations of ordinary experience" (Elledge, 1990), his poetry becomes more relaxed and colloquial, its content more recognizably autobiographical. Here the influence of William Carlos Williams is primary: O'Hara's poems of dailiness, his "lunch poems" and "I do this I do that" poems, take up the familiar Williams premise of the poet on the go, moving through urban space and finding the materials of his poetry in the local conditions. While the city is present in *Second Avenue* only in fleeting glimpses—"umbrella satrap square-carts with hot dogs"—the city is always present in O'Hara's lunch poems, as a living, breathing reality in which the poet participates.

Lunch poems such as "A Step Away from Them," "The Day Lady Died," and "Personal Poem" cannot be mistaken for mere reportage: the poems' stylized surfaces, with their present tense verbs, minimal punctuation, and deliberately casual line breaks, suggest a poet in the act of composition, recording not what happened but what happens. What happens in a lunch poem is not simply a matter of events: it is the poet's attentive responses to reality that give the poem its movement and shape. "Attention is Life," O'Hara once wrote in an essay, and he is always attentive. "A Step Away from Them," for instance, shows a remarkable range of perceptions and cultural references: walking down the street, O'Hara notices or thinks of Coca-Cola, cheeseburgers, papaya juice, cats playing in sawdust, bullfight posters, the 1913 Armory Show, Edwin Denby, Federico Fellini, Giulietta Masina, and Pierre Reverdy, to name only some of the poem's many elements.

What makes O'Hara's lunch poems inimitable is that their seemingly casual movements turn out to have decisive dramatic form. In "A Step Away from Them," O'Hara's evocation of the lively sexual energy of the city in summer is broken by his sudden recollection of friends who have died, after which the poem moves quickly to a quiet, poignant conclusion: "My heart is in my / pocket, it is Poems by Pierre Reverdy." In "The Day Lady Died," the news of Billie Holiday's death interrupts a lunch hour devoted to errands and compels the poet's silence. The camaraderie of lunch with a friend in "Personal Poem" is complicated by the poem's final lines, which imply that the poet's mind has all along been partly elsewhere, preoccupied with difficulties in love. While the surface mannerisms of O'Hara's lunch poems are readily available to other poets (e.g., "It's 11:00 on a Thursday"), the poems' shapes are as individual and inimitable as O'Hara's imaginative and emotional experience.

The range of O'Hara's later poetry extends well beyond his lunch poems. "Meditations in an Emergency" and "In Memory of My Feelings," for instance, are remarkable statements of postmodern selfhood. The "I" of "Meditations" is protean, comically self-aware of its capacity for vertiginous change, even with regard to sexual identity: "Heterosexuality! you are inexorably approaching." "In Memory of My Feelings" also presents a self that resists definition or unity, assuming and shedding multiple identities and celebrating the "Grace / to be born and live as variously as possible." O'Hara's *Odes* (1960)—long, formally varied, and often elevated in diction and tone—bear interesting relations, as Perloff (1998) notes, to his earlier work. O'Hara's friendships with artists led to a number of verbal-visual collaborations in the late 1950s and early 1960s, many of which are reproduced in *In Memory of My Feelings: Frank O'Hara and American Art* (1999), among them the lithographs *Stones* with Larry Rivers, a series of ink and gouache works on paper with Norman Bluhm, and collages and comic strips with Joe Brainard. Between 1959 and 1961, O'Hara wrote a series of love poems during his relationship with the dancer Vincent Warren; a selection was published as *Love Poems (Tentative Title)* in 1965. Love poems such as "An Airplane Whistle (After Heine)" and "Having a Coke with You" are among the clearest examples of O'Hara's sense (expressed in the essay

"Personism") of the poem as a vehicle of intimate communication with another person. O'Hara's last long poem, *Biotherm (For Bill Berkson)* (1990), an elaborate communiqué to a fellow poet, is "a work of complex courtship," as Brad Gooch (1993) describes it, an improvisatory performance to humor and charm its addressee.

As the details of O'Hara's world—rotary phones, unfiltered cigarettes, old movies on late-night television, communism, and Birdland—further recede from view, his poems continue to stand as a passionate response to mid-20th-century American life. What O'Hara says of the objects he celebrates in "Today"—"harmonicas, jujubes, aspirins"—may also be said of his poems: "They / do have meaning. They're strong as rocks."

Michael Leddy

*See also* New York School

**Biography**

Born in Baltimore, Maryland, 27 June 1926. Attended New England Conservatory of Music, Boston, Massachusetts, 1946–50, A.B. 1950; University of Michigan, Ann Arbor (Hopwood Award, 1951), M.A. 1951; served in the United States Navy, 1944–46; on staff, 1951–54, fellowship curator, 1955–64, associate curator, 1965, and curator of the International Program, 1966, Museum of Modern Art, New York; editorial associate, *Art News* magazine, 1954–56; art editor, *Kulchur* magazine, 1962–64. Received Ford fellowship, for drama, 1956; National Book Award, 1972. Died on Fire Island, New York, 25 July 1966.

**Poetry**

*A City Winter, and Other Poems,* 1952
*Oranges,* 1953
*Meditations in an Emergency,* 1956
*Harrigan and Rivers with O'Hara: An Exhibition of Pictures, with Poems,* 1959
*Second Avenue,* 1960
*Odes,* 1960
*Lunch Poems,* 1964
*Love Poems (Tentative Title),* 1965
*In Memory of My Feelings: A Selection of Poems,* edited by Bill Berkson, 1967
*Two Pieces,* 1969
*Odes,* 1969
*The Collected Poems of Frank O'Hara,* edited by Donald Allen, 1971
*Belgrade, November 19, 1963,* 1973
*Hymns of St. Bridget* (with Bill Berkson), 1974
*The Selected Poems of Frank O'Hara,* edited by Donald Allen, 1974
*Early Writing,* edited by Donald Allen, 1977
*Poems Retrieved,* edited by Donald Allen, 1977
*Biotherm (for Bill Berkson),* 1990

**Other Writings:** plays (*Selected Plays,* 1978; *Kenneth Koch: A Tragedy* [with Larry Rivers], produced 1982; *Amorous Nightmares of Delay: Selected Plays,* 1996), essays (*Standing Still and Walking in New York,* 1975), art criticism (*Jackson Pollock,* 1959; *New Spanish Painting and Sculpture,* 1960; *David Smith,* 1966; *Nakian,* 1966; *Art Chronicles, 1954–1966,* 1975; *What's with Modern Art?* 1999); edited collections of literature (*Robert Motherwell: A Catalogue with Selections from the Artist's Writings,* 1965).

**Further Reading**

Berkson, Bill, and Joe LeSueur, editors, *Homage to Frank O'Hara,* Bolinas, California: Big Sky, 1978
Elledge, Jim, editor, *Frank O'Hara: To Be True to a City,* Ann Arbor: University of Michigan Press, 1990
Feldman, Alan, *Frank O'Hara,* Boston: Twayne, 1979
Ferguson, Russell, *In Memory of My Feelings: Frank O'Hara and American Art,* Los Angeles: Museum of Contemporary Art, and University of California Press, 1999
Gooch, Brad, *City Poet: The Life and Times of Frank O'Hara,* New York: Knopf, 1993
Lehman, David, *The Last Avant-Garde: The Making of the New York School of Poets,* New York: Doubleday, 1998
LeSueur, Joe, "Footnote to a Poem by Frank O'Hara," *Arshile* 11 (1999)
Perloff, Marjorie, *Frank O'Hara: Poet among Painters,* Chicago: University of Chicago Press, 1998
Smith, Alexander, *Frank O'Hara: A Comprehensive Bibliography,* New York: Garland, 1980
Ward, Geoff, *Statutes of Liberty: The New York School of Poets,* London: Macmillan, and New York: St. Martin's Press, 1993

## The Day Lady Died

Frank O'Hara's "The Day Lady Died," collected in *Lunch Poems* (1964), is an arresting elegy to the jazz singer Billie Holiday. Known by admirers as "Lady Day," Billie Holiday's intimate voice and style made listeners feel as if she were singing directly to them. Written just after learning of Holiday's death, O'Hara's poem mimics his subject's intimate, jazz-driven musical formulations in this loose and flowing homage.

Although "The Day Lady Died" is an elegy, only the last five lines directly address Holiday's life and death. The rest of the poem is a detailed account of the speaker's mundane urban life:

> It is 12:20 in New York a Friday
> three days after Bastille day, yes
> it is 1959

The title of the poem tells the informed reader that 17 July 1959 is not just an ordinary day, yet the poem's first lines do not highlight this fact. Instead the date and time are tossed off as if they are unimportant: it is not Bastille Day, the day to celebrate the French Revolution and the emergence of a new power structure, not high noon, or any other particularly symbolic hour. It is the 17th of July, just past midday, and nothing spectacular seems to be happening.

The next few stanzas are a thorough account of the speaker's errands: "I will get off the 4:19 in Easthampton / at 7:15 and then go straight to dinner." O'Hara's poems in this style are sometime called "I do this, I do that" poems because they are filled with so many precise details, but part of the power of this poem rests in this specificity of detail. The reader comes to know everything about this man's movements and thoughts:

> and in the GOLDEN GRIFFIN I get a little Verlaine
> for Patsy with drawings by Bonnard although I do

think of Hesiod, trans. Richmond Lattimore or
Brendan Behan's new play or *Le Balcon* or *Les Nègres*
of Genet, but I don't, I stick with Verlaine
after practically going to sleep with quandariness

He spends the majority of the poem's longest stanza deciding what to buy for the woman at whose house he will be eating dinner. Earlier in the poem he claims not to "know the people who will feed" him, although it becomes clear that he does know their names, Patsy and Mike, and their tastes; in fact, Patsy Southgate and Mike Goldberg were friends of O'Hara's. His comments about not knowing them indicate the sense of alienation he feels toward the world. This alienation is underscored by his comments about the woman at the bank whose first name he has only "once heard" and who typically does not trust him enough not to check his balance when he withdraws money. The speaker seems to be alone in the world, despite his city life and his invitation to dinner.

The choices of gifts he considers, Roman or French poetry and art, along with the ease with which he later buys Russian vodka, French cigarettes, and "an ugly NEW WORLD WRITING to see what the poets / in Ghana are doing these days" further develop the speaker's character. He is aware of quality art. He is cutting edge. He is interested in beauty. He is a man who knows great things and where to find them, but his life often leads him to boredom, frustration, and isolation.

The poem's form enhances its casual atmosphere, in which things are simple and slow. The care and time the speaker takes deciding what to bring Patsy causes him nearly to fall asleep. He can "just stroll" into a liquor store and buy what he needs. Although the poem is full of detail, there is no figurative language until its last few lines. The very sparing punctuation—just five commas—allows the poem to flow from one fact to another, one moment to the next.

The most important comma in the poem separates the body of the poem from its end:

then I go back where I came from to 6th Avenue
and the tobacconist in the Ziegfeld Theatre and
casually ask for a carton of Gauloises and a carton
of Picayunes, and a NEW YORK POST with her face on it

After following the speaker through his errands on what has hitherto seemed an unremarkable day, the reader arrives at the moment in which Billie Holiday's life and death are introduced. Having moved without pause through his eating and banking and shopping, the speaker is forced to stop and contemplate the importance of the picture he sees in the paper.

In the poem's final stanza, the tone shifts. The abundance of details are no longer just cataloged facts. For the first time in the poem the speaker's physical condition is highlighted as he is "sweating a lot and thinking of / leaning on the john door in the 5 SPOT." No longer bored by the events of his life, he becomes physically affected by the news he reads and remembers hearing Billie Holiday sing with the jazz pianist Mal Waldron at the 5 Spot, a popular venue for jazz performers frequented by artists and writers of the period. Whereas the bulk of the poem takes place on "the muggy street beginning to sun," this crucial section happens inside the speaker's mind.

The power of the poem's jazz-like styling, lack of punctuation, and nuanced language crests in the last two lines: "while she whispered a song along the keyboard / to Mal Waldron and everyone and I stopped breathing."

Billie Holiday was known for her whispered vocal style, but close to the end of her life much of her vocal strength was gone, forcing her to sing even more softly and intimately. She used this to her advantage, personalizing her songs and her singing habits so that a small room became smaller, commanding her audience's whole attention. O'Hara's poem mimics this style. The lack of punctuation requires careful reading and allows the final line to contain multiple meanings. Was Holiday singing to Mal Waldron and everyone, the effect of which caught the speaker's breath? Or was she singing only to Mal Waldron, so movingly that everyone in the room, including the speaker, stopped breathing? It could also be understood that the memory of Billie Holiday's singing in the 5 Spot causes this shortness of breath. As in a smooth jazz composition that layers multiple sounds and moods, these meanings operate simultaneously, reflecting the immense effect Holiday's life and death has on the speaker. No longer is he bored, disaffected, or isolated; he becomes part of the crowd again, enraptured by the memory of Billie Holiday's song.

Camille Dungy

**Further Reading**

Bowers, Neal, "The City Limits," in *Frank O'Hara: To Be True to a City,* edited by Jim Elledge, Ann Arbor: University of Michigan Press, 1990

Gooch, Brad, *City Poet: The Life and Times of Frank O'Hara,* New York: Knopf, 1993

Perloff, Marjorie, *Frank O'Hara: Poet among Painters,* Chicago: University of Chicago Press, 1998

---

# Sharon Olds 1942–

Sharon Olds was raised in Berkeley, California, as—in her words—a "hellfire Calvinist," just one of the painful legacies she has rejected. She received her B.A. from Stanford in 1964 and her Ph.D. from Columbia in 1972. While at Columbia her poetic models were George Oppen and Gary Snyder; after graduating, as Olds tells it, she vowed to give up all that she had learned and write her own poems, "even if they were bad." A seven-year apprenticeship, which included study with Muriel Rukeyser, led to the publication of Olds' first book, *Satan Says,* in 1980. Winner of the inaugural San Francisco Poetry Center Award, *Satan Says* was followed by *The Dead and the Living* (1984), which won both the Lamont Prize and the National Book Critics Circle Award, *The Gold Cell* (1987), *The Father* (1992), *The Wellspring* (1996), and *Blood, Tin, Straw* (1999).

Virginia Woolf wrote that women must kill the Angel in the House—the role of dutiful daughter or wife, eager to serve and chaste of speech—if they want to become artists. This is the opening move of the title poem of *Satan Says,* in which a jewelry box, a typical gift to girls in the 1950s, becomes a metaphor for cloistered innocence:

I am locked in a little cedar box
with a picture of shepherds pasted onto
the central panel between carvings.
. . . .
I am trying to write my
way out of the closed box
redolent with cedar. Satan
comes to me in the locked box
and says, *I'll get you out. Say*
*My father is a shit.*
. . . .
*Say your mother is a pimp.*
. . . .
*Say shit, say death, say fuck the father.*

The poem continues breaking taboos, saying "the magic words," but finally sticks at anguished ambivalence. Struggling to get free, the daughter discovers, "Oh no, I loved / them too." As Satan urges "*Come out,*" she braces her body tight against escape from the box with its "heart-shaped lock," both site of love and, Satan says, "*your coffin.*"

In many ways this rebellion creates Olds' characteristic terrain. Claiming the freedom to say anything, she plumbs the depths of a childhood scarred by abuse, in which a dangerous but adored alcoholic father eventually divorced a tormented mother whose love for her children metaphorically took the forms of "smothering, knives, / drowning, burning" ("The Forms," in *The Dead and the Living*). One of Olds' best-known poems, "I Go Back to May 1937," imagines confronting her parents as they stand on the brink of their passion and misery, imagines imploring them to

Stop,
don't do it—she's the wrong woman,
he's the wrong man, you are going to do things
you cannot imagine you would ever do,
you are going to do bad things to children[.]

In the end the speaker says nothing to them, concluding, "I want to live." With sardonic honesty she says, "Do what you are going to do, and I will tell about it." Such candor extends as well to Olds' writing about the body, about childbirth, motherhood, and womanhood. "The Language of the Brag" from *Satan Says* describes the desire to do "what you wanted to do, Walt Whitman, / Allen Ginsberg," to discover "some epic use for my excellent body." Olds is one of America's most liberating poets, and partly for this reason has been widely read by both men and women. Few have written more lovingly and insightfully about children. Fewer still have written better about sex, both premarital and in the long intimacy of a passionate marriage. In "True Love," the final poem in *The Wellspring,* she describes making love: "in / complete friendship, we know so fully / what the other has been doing." She continues in a beautiful, looping sentence:

Bound to each other
like mountaineers coming down from a mountain
we wander down the hall to the bathroom, I can
hardly walk, I wobble through the granular
shadowless air, I know where you are
with my eyes closed, we are bound to each other
with huge invisible threads, our sexes
muted, exhausted, crushed, the whole
body a sex—surely this
is the most blessed time of my life. . . .

Olds insists that her "intensely confessional material" is only "*apparently* autobiographical" (Pearlman, 1993), an important caveat to her readers. Grounded in life, her poems have also been shaped into something like myth. This quality of her work becomes evident once one realizes that all her books cover the same ground and tell essentially the same story. A tendency toward obsessive repetitiveness, which seems to grow from the impossible desire once and for all to fix things—to get all of physical, particularly sexual, experience into language; to mitigate suffering or flux by pinning it down in a final form—may be Olds' greatest weakness. But her strengths as a poet are enormous. Michael Ondaatje describes her poems as "pure fire in the hands—risky, on the verge of failing, and in the end leaping up" and speaks of her "roughness and humor and brag and tenderness and completion" (quoted on website). The praise is amply deserved.

ANN FISHER-WIRTH

**Biography**

Born in San Francisco, California, 19 November 1942. Attended Stanford University, California, B.A. (honors) 1964; Columbia University, New York, Ph.D. 1972; lecturer-in-residence on poetry, Theodor Herzl Institute, New York, 1976–80; visiting teacher of poetry, Manhattan Theatre Club, New York, 1982, Nathan Mayhew Seminars, Martha's Vineyard, Massachusetts, 1982, YMCA, New York, 1982, Poetry Society of America, 1983, Sarah Lawrence College, Bronxville, New York, 1984, Squaw Valley Writers' Conference, Olympic Valley, California, 1984–90, Goldwater Hospital, Roosevelt Island, New York, since 1985, Columbia University, New York, 1985–86, and State University of New York, Purchase, 1986–87; Fanny Hurst Chair in literature, Brandeis University, Waltham, Massachusetts, 1986–87; since 1983 Adjunct Professor, and Director, 1988–91, Graduate Program in Creative Writing, New York University. Received Creative Arts Public Service Award, 1978; Madeline Sadin Award, 1978; San Francisco Poetry Center Award, 1980; Guggenheim fellowship, 1981–82; National Endowment for the Arts fellowship, 1982–83; Lamont Prize, 1984; National Book Critics Circle Award, 1985; Poet Laureate of New York, 1998. Living in New York City.

**Poetry**

*Satan Says,* 1980
*The Dead and the Living,* 1984
*The Gold Cell,* 1987
*The Matter of This World: New and Selected Poems,* 1987

*The Sign of Saturn: Poems, 1980–1987,* 1991
*The Father,* 1992
*Liz Lochhead; Roger McGough; Sharon Olds* (poems by Olds, Lochhead, and McGough), 1995
*The Wellspring,* 1996
*Blood, Tin, Straw,* 1999

**Further Reading**

Brown-Davidson, Terri, "The Belabored Scene, the Subtlest Detail: How Craft Affects Heat in the Poetry of Sharon Olds and Sandra McPherson," *The Hollins Critic* 29, no. 1 (1992)
McFarland, Ron, "With Sharon Olds in Idaho," *Weber Studies* 17 (1999) (special poetry supplement)
Moyers, Bill, "Sharon Olds," in *The Language of Life: A Festival of Poets,* edited by James Haba, New York: Doubleday, 1995
Pearlman, Mickey, "Sharon Olds," in *Listen to Their Voices: Twenty Interviews with Women Who Write,* New York and London: Norton, 1993

---

## Mary Oliver 1935–

Mary Oliver, a poet of acute attention and fierce loyalties, is devoted to nature as ecstatically as Emerson and as clear-sightedly as Frost. Like Emerson, she sees in the natural world the manifest patterns of being and perceiving that are necessary to human knowing; and, like Frost, she does not blink at nature's death dealing and takes full account of its neutrality toward human consciousness. While never quailing at the hard facts of mortality, she can pierce through them to win a glimpse of eternity: in "Last Days," in *Twelve Moons* (1979), for example, she writes, "I too love oblivion why not it is full / of second chances."

Her best poems derive from her bodily experience of the woods, the beach, and the meadow, and, through visceral images that re-create this experience, they achieve their deepest, most characteristic effects. A strong countercurrent of literal declaration of meaning also runs in her poems, especially early and later in her career, a habit that only proves the strength of her best poems but that pushes weaker ones toward sentimentality. This vestige of her apprenticeship in traditional lyricism generally and to Edna St. Vincent Millay (on whose estate she worked in her late teens) particularly often serves the tensions between polarities such as life and death, joy and pain, attention and inattention, and loving and preying that energize her work.

Oliver has published nine collections of poems and four books of prose about poetry, the last of which, *Winter Hours* (1999), contains a few prose poems and poems. Her earliest book, *No Voyage, and Other Poems* (1963), while incipient with the later themes, is quite different from her mature work. The poems are more rhetorical, often rhymed; they are more conventional rhythmically; and they address themselves more directly to the human situation, using nature imagery principally as applied metaphor. In shape, tone, and subject, many of the poems are derivative of either Frost or Millay. The endings tend to be epigrammatic, tying up loose ends in a neat moral package.

The 1972 collection *The River Styx* and two chapbooks, *The Night Traveler* (1978) and *Sleeping in the Forest* (1979), are also apprentice works in which many poems stop short of themselves. They tend to center on people, especially the people of childhood: mother, grandmothers, and aunts. She grapples with a youthful, faintly romantic sense of mortality, but "Three Poems for James Wright" introduces real grief. "Farm Country" and "Winter in the Country" are strong early poems about the underside of the food chain, which, even here, she relentlessly refuses to romanticize:

> The terror of the country
> Is prey and hawk together,
> Still flying, both exhausted,
> In the blue sack of weather.

"The Family," also a strong poem, gives notice of her emerging impulse to become part of the natural world.

This idea dominates *Twelve Moons* (1979) and *American Primitive* (1983), in which Oliver comes into her full gift. Poems such as "Sleeping in the Forest," "The Black Snake," "Spring," "Aunt Leaf," and "The Truro Bear" are her first truly ecstatic, fully realized poems. Ever alert, these poems never allow a full drop into timelessness and out of pain: "Entering the Kingdom" pulls back, acknowledging the impossibility of such entrance, for the crows know that she is "No eater of leaves." Yet she can

> . . . stare at the light in the trees—
> To learn something by being nothing
> A little while but the rich
> Lens of attention.

The tension of this balance is itself the subject of one of the best pieces here, "Bone Poem," with its clear presentation of the "litter under the tree / where the owl eats—shrapnel / of rat bones." The accuracy, both physical and metaphysical, of the word "shrapnel" typifies the exactness of her observation and diction. It sets up the unlikeliness of the rhetorical exclamation, "O holy / Protein, o hallowed lime, / o precious clay!," which makes us see

> The cracked bones
>
> Of the owl's most recent feast
> . . . starting
>
> The long fall back to the center—
> The seepage, the flowing
>
> The equity: sooner or later
> In the shimmering leaves

The rat will learn to fly, the owl
Will be devoured.

This difficult "equity" typifies Oliver's poetry.

*American Primitive* (1983), her strongest collection, is deeply American in its vision of human life as part of the natural world, a fact perhaps more easily felt on this new continent. Bringing to deeper consummation such themes in *Twelve Moons* as merging with nature, its fierce neutrality, and the implacability of mortality, many poems here rank among Oliver's best. More than half ring with their own perfection. In this collection, her metaphors tautly rein the energies created by the tensions of her polarities, as in "Lightning," in which each bolt reveals "the landscape / bulging forth like a quick / lesson in creation." She makes palpable that the body wishes to hide but also wants

to flow toward it—strives
to balance while
fear shouts,
excitement shouts, back
and forth—

The concluding metaphor provides no answer but leaves the fiery mystery: "each / bolt a burning river / tearing like escape through the dark / field of the other." Yin and Yang, these opposites become each other. Many of these fine poems ("First Snow," "Flying," "In the Pinewoods, Crows and Owl," "Rain in Ohio," "Something," "Skunk Cabbage," "The Lost Children," "The Fish," "Humpbacks," "A Meeting," and others) reveal the mystery so profoundly that it feels like an answer.

Even a love poem such as "University Hospital, Boston" governs itself with strict metaphor (in the hospital "intricate machines / chart with cool devotion / the murmur of the blood") and rests in the obstinate neutralities of life and death. So does the powerfully sexual "Blossom," one of the high points of the book. All these strains of craft, emotion, and thought come together finally in "In Blackwater Woods," in which clarity of saying, intense attention to the natural scene rendered in sharp metaphors ("cattails / are bursting and floating away over / the blue shoulders / of the ponds"), and the deep humanness of the voice convince us that in the tension it articulates lies some kind of salvation:

To live in this world

you must be able
to do three things:
to love what is mortal;
to hold it

against your bones knowing
your own life depends on it;
and, when the time comes to let it go,
to let it go.

In her subsequent six volumes of poems, she moves out of the stance of the ecstatic nature poet and toward that of the mystic for whom the world's significance lies less in its own reality than in its function as a stepping-stone to ecstasy. While there are still strong poems ("The Journey," "Wild Geese," and "Landscape" in *Dream Work* [1986] and "The Buddha's Last Instruction" and "The Swan" in *House of Light* [1990]) in the later volumes, the "equity " of the polarities gives way to transcendence. Since the poems declare the same happiness over and over, they begin to echo themselves and to say themselves literally rather than creating their realness through images. This movement toward declaration and away from concreteness reaches its climax in *Winter Hours,* in the foreword of which she writes, "I myself am the author of this document; it has no other formal persona, as my books of poems certainly do."

As this movement develops, Oliver relies less and less on short lines dense with imagery and more on longer lines. Finally, the meditative prose poem, which states its meaning quite literally, becomes her mode, that of achieved wisdom rather than that of discovery of the spiritual through the palpably physical. While her work in the late 1980s and the 1990s continues to reveal an inclusive, generous spirit, her finest poetry is that of her middle career, of *Twelve Moons* and *American Primitive.*

Of the eight books Oliver published in the 1990s, four are prose, mainly about the craft of writing and the art of attention to the natural world and to literary models. *A Poetry Handbook* (1994) is an insightful introduction to poetry practice; in it, Oliver manages to convey a sense of the connection of craft to poetry's alchemy. *Rules for the Dance* (1998), while less successful in its instructions (about how to compose metrical verse), is valuable for its anthology of metrical poems, which comprises a catalog of the poets who have shaped Oliver's sensibility (Donne, Blake, the English Romantics, Emerson, Dickinson, Frost, and Elizabeth Bishop).

Oliver's work, awarded both the 1984 Pulitzer Prize (*American Primitive*) and the 1992 National Book Award (*New and Selected Poems*), sets the human in what she sees as its proper context: the natural world. Her voice is principally that of a psalmist. In *Winter Hours,* she says, "I am a performing artist; I perform admiration. / 'Come with me,' I want my poems to say. 'And do the same.'" She writes, "I could not be a poet without the natural world. Someone else could. But not me. For me the door to the woods is the door to the temple." While she sees evil as part of the world, she also, in the best tradition of American Transcendentalism, believes in the soul: "to believe in it exactly as much and as hardily as one believes in a mountain . . . or a fingernail! . . . And the perceived, tactile world is, upon the instant, only half the world!" In her strongest poems, the halves of the whole are equally important, and attention to them is equally urgent, for, as her poetry makes clear, "We are each other's destiny."

JANE GENTRY VANCE

**Biography**

Born in Maple Heights, Ohio, 10 September 1935. Attended Ohio State University, Columbus, 1955–56; Vassar College, Poughkeepsie, New York, 1956–57; Chair of the Writing Department, 1972–73, and member of the writing committee, 1984, Fine Arts Work Center, Provincetown, Massachusetts; Mather Visiting Professor, Case Western Reserve University, Cleveland, 1980, 1982; poet-in-residence, Bucknell University, Lewisburg, Pennsylvania, 1986, and University of Cincinnati, Ohio, 1986; has taught at Sweet Briar College, Sweet Briar, Virginia, and Duke University, Durham, North Carolina; since 1996 Catharine Osgood Foster Chair for Distinguished Teaching, Bennington College, Bennington, Vermont. Received

Poetry Society of America Prize, 1962; Shelley Memorial Award, 1970; National Endowment for the Arts fellowship, 1972; Alice Fay di Castagnola Award, 1973; Guggenheim fellowship, 1980; American Academy Award, 1983; Pulitzer Prize, 1984; National Book Award, 1992; Lannan Award, 1998. Living in Vermont.

**Poetry**

*No Voyage, and Other Poems,* 1963; revised edition, 1965
*The River Styx, Ohio, and Other Poems,* 1972
*Twelve Moons,* 1979
*American Primitive,* 1983
*Dream Work,* 1986
*House of Light,* 1990
*New and Selected Poems,* 1992
*White Pine: Poems and Prose Poems,* 1994
*West Wind: Poems and Prose Poems,* 1997
*The Leaf and the Cloud: A Poem,* 2000

**Other Writings:** poetry handbooks (*A Poetry Handbook,* 1994; *Rules for the Dance: A Handbook for Writing and Reading Metrical Verse,* 1998), essays (*Blue Pastures,* 1995; *Winter Hours,* 1999).

**Further Reading**

Bonds, Diane S., "The Language of Nature in the Poetry of Mary Oliver," *Women's Studies* 21, no.1 (1992)
Burton-Christie, Douglas, "Nature, Spirit, and Imagination in the Poetry of Mary Oliver," *Cross Currents* 46 (Spring 1996)
Fast, Robin Riley, "Moore, Bishop, and Oliver: Thinking Back, Re-Seeing the Sea," *Twentieth Century Literature* 39 (Fall 1993)
Fast, Robin Riley, "The Native American Presence in Mary Oliver's Poetry," *Kentucky Review* 12, no. 1–2 (Fall 1993)
Graham, Vicki, "'Into the Body of Another': Mary Oliver and the Poetics of Becoming Other," *Papers on Language and Literature* 30 (Fall 1994)
McNew, Janet, "Mary Oliver and the Tradition of Romantic Nature Poetry," *Contemporary Literature* 30 (Spring 1989)
Mellard, Joan, "Mary Oliver, Poetic Iconographer," *Language and Literature* 16 (1991)
Russell, Sue, "Mary Oliver: The Poet and the Persona," *Harvard Gay and Lesbian Review* 4, no. 4 (1997)
Swanson, Eleanor, "The Language of Dreams: An Interview with Mary Oliver," *Bloomsbury Review* 10, no. 3 (May/June 1990)

---

# Charles Olson 1910–70

When Charles Olson came of age intellectually in the mid-1930s, the United States was immersed in a prodigious effort to redefine itself as a separate and unique civilization. Harvard inaugurated an American Studies graduate program in 1936, the first of its kind in the United States, and Olson was among its entering class. In the course of that experience—a three-year devotion to American history from the perspectives of geography, botany, physics, and comparative anthropology—Olson developed a love of scientific inquiry into humanistic subjects and brought that love into his own revolutionary essays on poetry, poetics, and American history.

The result was a new way of interpreting American experience and a new poetry. In 1947 Olson published his study of Melville's *Moby-Dick,* a brief but suggestive analysis of the mythical content in the novel entitled *Call Me Ishmael,* in which he links this novel with the history of epic literature. In the course of this study of labor history, the whaling industry, and the figure of Ahab, Olson declares a new "Ishmael," a figure he defines as "post-individual man." According to Olson, Ahab is the last Western hero of the era of migration begun in the ancient exodus out of Mesopotamia. Migration spawned the notion of the hero, since people on the march do not carry with them their heritage or traditions, or the authority of their ancestors, but follow the will of a leader—the self-driven ego, in Olson's perspective.

Ahab, the last of the heroes of migratory history, launched his quest for power against nature in the form of the white whale. His death ends the era of human dispersion since America's western shore is the path back to origins, the East. The lone survivor of the ship is Ishmael, a selfless observer of life who opens an age of rootedness to place and community. Olson hails this figure as the redeemer of the new millennium. Olson's first poems sketch in the attributes and ideals of an Ishmael-ean persona, notably in "The Kingfishers," which renounces an identity tied to Greece and Rome and embraces a New World identity through Mayan and Aztec culture:

> I am no Greek, hath not th'advantage.
> And of course, no Roman:
> he can take no risk that matters,
> the risk of beauty least of all.
>
> But I have my kin, if for no other reason than
> (as he said, next of kin) I commit myself, and,
> given my freedom, I'd be a cad
> if I didn't.

In 1950 Olson published a seminal statement on the new poetics in his essay "Projective Verse," which in one sense is the map of Ishmael's consciousness and thinking about the world. To write in this mode is to ground language in the rhythms of the body. The breath or "breath unit" in composing one's thought provides the limit of each line; the sound of words supersedes their sense. In the second part of the essay Olson explains his philosophy of "objectism," in which the writer decenters attention away from self to become an object among other objects of the landscape, in order to overhear "the secrets objects share."

These early seminal pieces on poetics are pioneering explorations of the biases of ethnocentricity in literature and the role of the privileged observer in Western art. Olson anticipated by several decades the critique of imperialism after Europe withdrew from its colonies in Asia, Africa, and the Pacific island cultures at mid-century. He was an advocate of equality in comparative cultural study and was first on the scene in asking probing questions about the ideological content of grammar and syntax, the alienated "other" in imperialistic discourse, and the pervasive sense of white superiority in America's treatment of other races.

Postmodernism, as formulated by Olson in the early 1950s, laid down the essential elements of the literary avant-garde in the second half of the 20th century. He saw himself and his generation of experimental poets as continuing the work of the Modernists of the 1920s, in particular the poetics of Imagism as developed by Ezra Pound and William Carlos Williams. In essence, Imagism and its successor movements, Objectivism and Projectivism, agreed on the leading principle that nature is alive, dynamic, and self-creating, a reservoir of primal consciousness different from and parent to human consciousness. The poet is more secretary to this natural imagination than an inventor of new worlds. The poet's imagination is the faculty for observing and interpreting how the environment creates and orders its myriad events into a coherent whole. The trajectory of evolution of Pound's original ideas about the Image—the simplest unit of form in nature—to Olson's ideas shows increasing subtlety and flexibility in techniques to capture the moment of natural creativity.

But Olson also argued his differences with the Modernist generation by questioning what appeared to be a persistent ethnocentrism in Pound's idea of history. Olson would push back the wall of cultural time from the Age of Pericles, Pound's historic boundary of Western tradition, and include human history from the last ice age, the Pleistocene era. The dawn of human consciousness bore the evidence of an unmediated and highly creative vision of the world encrypted into origin myths and early rock art. The contemporary mind, Olson suggested, must reorient itself to a primordial aesthetic to correct certain distortions of attitude created by the long descent toward Western cultural imperialism.

Olson saw himself as a reformer at a time when an American empire based on nuclear superiority and military victory seemed imminent. He believed the self had become absolute in the arts and in social philosophy, and the result was a diminished sense of reality and of the diverse world of nature and other cultures. The past itself was disappearing as America rewrote history to support its claim to preeminence among the Western nations.

Olson tested his ideas and newly minted doctrines on literary freedom at Black Mountain College, a small liberal-arts school near Asheville, North Carolina. The school was known already as a center of experimental art and science and for the brilliance of its faculty, which included at one time or another such luminaries of the art world as Josef Albers, the abstractionist Franz Kline, the architect and inventor Buckminster Fuller, the social philosopher Paul Goodman, and novelist and critic Edward Dahlberg. The students drawn to this impoverished but intellectually heady academy included the poets Robert Creeley, Robert Duncan, Ed Dorn, Jonathan Williams, Joel Oppenheimer, and others. Olson became the school's rector and administered over a dwindling enrollment and sinking funds. He ultimately sold off the school's property before closing the doors on one of America's most distinguished schools in 1957.

From the work done under Olson's tutelage, the movement known as Black Mountain poetry emerged, a name derived from its campus publication, the *Black Mountain Review*, which articulated a leading edge of avant-garde writing in its quarterly issues. The Black Mountain movement released a passion to discover the underlying reality of American politics and social movements, and to reveal the hidden hand of forces in commerce and politics shaping the course of American life. The implicit thesis of much Black Mountain poetry of the 1950s was that the sprawling energies of the world's oldest democracy were being driven by market values and not by the natural human instincts of a diverse people.

Out of these historical concerns grew Olson's idea for a long poem that would discover the fundamentals of American identity and thresh the documentary record on the origins of the nation. The poem began to take shape as early as 1953, when the first ten poems of *The Maximus Poems* were published by his former student and poet Jonathan Williams. A second installment of 12 more poems was issued in 1956, and the complete first volume appeared in 1960. Maximus, the narrator of the poem, is based on the life of a second-century Neoplatonic philosopher on the Phoenician coast at Tyre, whose letters were discourses on faith and personal belief. The poems of Olson's work were also called letters, a convention he abandoned in the third and final volume of the work.

Maximus bears close resemblance to other narrators of 20th-century long poems, including the Homeric, sometimes Dantean voice of Pound's *Cantos* (1948), and the figure of Tiresias at the center of T.S. Eliot's *The Waste Land* (1922). These are not only commentators on present-day society but minds enlarged with a vast historic memory stretching back to the beginnings of Western culture. They perceive the present through mythical imaginations and turn literal events into recurrent historical patterns or paradigms. The past is prologue to modern epic poets, who saw their century leaping into the unknown future of technology and social change; their response to the unpredictable nature of modern urban life was to search the past for clues to the fate of post-industrial life.

Maximus replaces Ishmael as Olson's persona in the poetry he wrote in the middle and late 1950s. The new voice reaches toward prophecy and understands history as the key to a developing new metaphysics based on Einstein's theory of relativity and the new theoretical hypotheses of contemporary astronomy and physics. Olson uses the poem as a sketch pad to work out his own hypothesis that the West was engaged in a paradigm shift away from materialism and toward a renewed sense of polytheism and mystery. This new culture rejects Freudian psychology as a post-Enlightenment philosophy of self and embraces Jung for articulating the fundamental notions of the collective unconscious and the mythological content of dreams. The new metaphysic would turn on basic Jungian notions of a sacred universe accessible only through the symbols and archetypes of the imagination.

> Wholly absorbed
> into my own conduits to
> an inner nature or subterranean lake
> the depths or bounds of which I more and more
> explore and know more
> of, in that sense that other than that all else
> closes out and I tend further to fall into
> the Beloved Lake

The first volume of the three-volume *Maximus Poems* analyzes the founding of America, from its inception as an English fishery established to exploit the rich fish supply in the Gulf Stream, to the first colonial charters and settlement diaries, up to the present time. The attempt to find a "shape" to New England history, and thus America's founding, does not yield itself through purely historical means. The story thus far seems to be one of lost dreams and squandered utopian visions of a New World of total freedom and self-realization, as crass commercialism and political deceit take over. The poem exhausts the material record of early New England and moves on, in the second volume, *The Maximus Poems, IV, V, VI* (1968), to locate the American story in a broader analysis of various origin myths in India, Persia, and the Mesopotamian cultures.

The second volume is the crowning achievement of the *Maximus Poems*. Olson weaves myths with commentary on post–World War II America in an array of poetic forms spanning the conventional short lyric to sprawling examples of the projective method taken to its extreme of expressive typography. Cascades of language fill the pages, showing the steps by which his speculative arguments on the nature of mythical history lead to a pessimistic assessment of American experience. Olson wanted to move beyond *Moby-Dick*'s putative myth of the death of the heroic self to some larger vision of America, in order to unfold the myth of nations: their fall from power by virtue of their corrupted visions of the sacred universe around them.

Tucked into the second volume of the *Maximus Poems* is Pound's own version of history as the flowering and decay of human consciousness, as embodied in a philosopher king and his knowing disciples. In this history, the path of enlightenment is not predictable, but its appearance is always marked by a sudden flowering of coherent laws and a prolonged, blissful era of peace and harmony among neighboring states. War is the first sign of social decay from within, and greed and political dishonesty are the final manifestations of an age of discord and lost vision. Olson uses these principles to interpret the rise and fall of modern states, with special emphasis on America as it edged toward conflict with Vietnam and an attendant social discord at home.

Olson reaped the benefit of his leadership in the Black Mountain movement by accepting an offer to teach at the State University of New York at Buffalo, where he trained other poets and the bibliographer of his own work, George Butterick. By then the movement had lost momentum as the Vietnam War took center stage as the cultural dilemma of the period. Rock music and youth leaders soon eclipsed the popularity of poetry as the media of political and social discourse. Olson left Buffalo to devote his time to writing the third volume of the *Maximus Poems* (1975), but was offered a new post at the University of Connecticut at Storrs, where the Olson Archive would one day be organized to preserve his papers.

His stay in Connecticut was cut short by cancer of the liver, which required hospitalization. Olson, an enormous man at six feet seven inches, was shrunken by the disease. After complaining of an earache to his doctor in New York, he was informed that he suffered from inflammation of the Maximus nerve, a detail that astonished and delighted him days before he died. Olson left behind a large body of writing that has influenced the course of American poetry and opened new vistas in historical interpretation of the American Renaissance, his area of greatest interest, as well of the history of race in America.

Paul Christensen

*See also* Black Mountain School

**Biography**

Born in Worcester, Massachusetts, 27 December 1910. Attended Wesleyan University, Middletown, Connecticut, 1928–32, B.A. 1932 (Phi Beta Kappa), M.A. 1933; Harvard University, Cambridge, Massachusetts, 1936–38; Assistant Chief of Foreign Language Division, Office of War Information, Washington, D.C., during World War II; teacher, Clark University, Worcester, and Harvard University, 1936–39; worked for Democratic Party, 1939–44; adviser, Democratic National Committee, late 1940s; Instructor and Rector, Black Mountain College, North Carolina, 1948, 1951–56; teacher, State University of New York, Buffalo, 1963–65, University of Connecticut, Storrs, 1969. Received Guggenheim grant, 1939, 1948; Wenner-Gren Foundation grant, 1952; Longview Foundation Award, 1961; Oscar Blumenthal Prize (*Poetry*, Chicago), 1965; American Academy grant, 1966, 1968. Died in New York City, 10 January 1970.

**Poetry**

*Corrado Cagli March 31 Through April 19, 1947*, 1947
*Y and X*, 1948
*Letter for Melville, 1951*, 1951
*This*, 1952
*In Cold Hell, in Thicket*, 1953
*The Maximus Poems, 1–10*, 1953
*Ferrini and Others* (with others), 1955
*Anecdotes of the Late War*, 1955
*The Maximus Poems, 11–22*, 1956
*O'Ryan 2 4 6 8 10*, 1958; expanded edition, as *O'Ryan 1 2 3 4 5 6 7 8 9 10*, 1965
*The Maximus Poems*, 1960
*The Distances*, 1960
*Maximus, from Dogtown I*, 1961
*Signature to Petition on Ten Pound Island Asked of Me by Mr. Vincent Ferrini*, 1964
*West*, 1966
*Olson Reading at Berkeley*, edited by Zoe Brown, 1966
*Before Your Very Eyes!* (with others), 1967
*The Maximus Poems, IV, V, VI*, 1968
*Reading about My World*, 1968
*Added to Making a Republic*, 1968
*Clear Shifting Water*, 1968
*That There Was a Woman in Gloucester, Massachusetts*, 1968
*Wholly Absorbed into My Own Conduits*, 1968
*Causal Mythology*, 1969
*Archaeologist of Morning: The Collected Poems outside the Maximus Series*, 1970
*Maximus, to Himself*, 1970
*New Man and Woman*, 1970
*May 20, 1959*, 1970
*The Maximus Poems, Volume Three*, edited by Charles Boer and George F. Butterick, 1975
*The Horses of the Sea*, 1976
*Some Early Poems*, 1978
*Spearmint and Rosemary*, 1979
*The Maximus Poems*, edited by George F. Butterick, 1983
*The Chain of Memory Is Resurrection*, 1984

*The Collected Poems of Charles Olson: Excluding the Maximus Poems,* edited by George F. Butterick, 1987
*A Nation of Nothing but Poetry: Supplementary Poems,* edited by George F. Butterick, 1989
*Maximus to Gloucester: The Letters and Poems of Charles Olson to the Editor of the Gloucester Daily Times, 1962–1969,* edited by Peter Anastas, 1992
*". . . The Calyx of the Flower Can Cup All Things within Itself. . . .": A Charles Olson Reader* (includes prose), 1992
*Selected Poems,* edited by Robert Creeley, 1993

**Selected Criticism**
*Call Me Ishmael: A Study of Melville,* 1947

**Other Writings:** plays (*The Fiery Hunt, and Other Plays,* 1977), fiction (*Stocking Cap: A Story,* 1966), essays (*Human Universe, and Other Essays* [edited by Donald Allen], 1965), lectures (*Olson in Connecticut: Last Lectures as Heard by John Cech, Oliver Ford, Peter Rittner,* 1975), correspondence (*Complete Correspondence, 1950–1964,* 1987).

**Further Reading**
Boer, Charles, *Charles Olson in Connecticut,* Chicago: Swallow Press, 1975
Butterick, George F., *A Guide to the Maximus Poems of Charles Olson,* Berkeley: University of California Press, 1978
Christensen, Paul, *Charles Olson: Call Him Ishmael,* Austin: University of Texas Press, 1979
Clark, Tom, *Charles Olson: The Allegory of a Poet's Life,* New York: Norton, 1991
Foster, Edward Halsey, *Understanding the Black Mountain Poets,* Columbia: University of South Carolina Press, 1995
Fredman, Stephen, *The Grounding of American Poetry: Charles Olson and the Emersonian Tradition,* Cambridge and New York: Cambridge University Press, 1993
Halden-Sullivan, Judith, *The Topology of Being: The Poetics of Charles Olson,* New York: Lang, 1991
Paul, Sherman, *Olson's Push: Origin, Black Mountain, and Recent American Poetry,* Baton Rouge: Louisiana State University Press, 1978
Stein, Charles, *The Secret of the Black Chrysanthemum,* Barrytown, New York: Station Hill Press, 1987
Von Hallberg, Robert, *Charles Olson: The Scholar's Art,* Cambridge, Massachusetts: Harvard University Press, 1978

## As the Dead Prey Upon Us

Originally titled "To Alleviate the Dream," then "The Mother Poem" (*Ark II/Moby 1,* 1956–57), Charles Olson's "As the Dead Prey Upon Us" was published under its final name in *The Distances* (1960). Along with Allen Ginsberg's "Kaddish" and Robert Duncan's "My Mother Would Be a Falconress," "As the Dead Prey Upon Us" ranks as one of the great "mother poems" of the 20th century for its exploration of the archetypal figure of mother as Great Creator and Great Destroyer. Despite its thematic importance in relation to Olson's epic, *The Maximus Poems,* as well as its inclusion in *Selected Writings* (1966), there has been very little critical commentary on the poem.

One way of understanding Olson's poetry is to view it as a response to the question he poses in his essay "Human Universe" (1966): "Can one restate man in any way to repossess him of his dynamic?" According to Olson the Western tradition of perceiving discourse as separate from the human organism and its environment has, among other things, led to generalization and abstraction. One way of restoring the human dynamic in poetry, Olson suggests, is to perceive language as "both the instrument of discovery and the instrument of definition."

"As the Dead Prey Upon Us" is in part a rite of passage, a figurative rebirth from the dead mother. It is an address to the dead, who count among poetry's first audience when the ritual use of language was bridgework between the living and the dead, the future and the past. In the Western model, Homer's *Odyssey,* Odysseus receives instruction from the dead, who exist in the underworld and are summoned forth by blood sacrifice. Olson does not merely graft Homer onto his own dreamscape, however. In "As the Dead Prey Upon Us" the dead "are the dead in ourselves" and are projected forward from *inside* the dreamscape and the dream-poem itself: the living are their own underworld and prey upon themselves. Olson's poem does not progress from lament for the dead to some sort of symbolic recovery or "homecoming," either. As he states in "In Cold Hell, in Thicket" (1953), "hell now / is not exterior, is not to be got out of." Rather, "men are now their own wood / and thus their own hell and paradise."

Olson's poem is not so much an attempt to shape the dream ("instrument of definition") as it is an attempt to be shaped *by* the dream ("instrument of discovery"), clinging to its protean narrative in which people and objects are constantly shifting shape and identity. The speaker begins in the dream pushing his car, then finds that "suddenly the huge underbody was above me." The rear tires are "masses of rubber and thread variously clinging together," which morph into "the dead souls in the living room, gathered / about my mother." Modernist poetry often portrays the contemporary as a sort of "hell" or "wasteland" incommensurate with an exulted past or paradise. Olson's hell resists such nostalgia and adheres to the "tawdriness" of an underworld where the dead "pass / beneath the beam of the movie projector" and a record is "playing on the victrola." There is no automotive shop in, say, T.S. Eliot's vision of hell, but in Olson's

> the whole room was suddenly posters and presentations
> of brake linings and other automotive accessories,
>   cardboard
> displays, the dead roaming from one to another

The "dead in ourselves" are entangled in "the nets of being" and "doomed / to mere equipments."

Although other characters shape-shift in the dream-poem, the mother's identity and shape remain constant. She is portrayed as passive, "in a rocker / under the lamp." Her dead weight is not the fecund weight of the Egyptian sky goddess Nut over the earth deity Geb. To suggest such a weight would position the mother in a sexual or generative role in relation to the speaker. At the same time a sexual relationship is implied in the very return to the mother in dream and later when the speaker echoes Odysseus' address to Anticleia: "(o mother, if you had once touched me / o mother, if I had once touched you!)."

The narrative presented in the first several stanzas is not resolved. Instead it is set against another complex of dream characters, including "the Indian woman" who helps the speaker enable "the blue deer / to walk." The "Indian woman" is Viola Barrett, a friend of Olson's mother. The blue deer is mysterious. In *The Maximus Poems* the speaker "was a blue deer" when "Viola Barrett was my mother." Given this context, the Indian woman and speaker double as mother and speaker/son: with the help of his "mother," the speaker enables himself (the blue deer) to walk, talk, and acquire "human possibilities." Another possibility is that this is the shamanic blue deer of the Huichol, a northwest Mexican tribe. Olson studied various indigenous cultures and was no doubt familiar with the blue deer of the Huichol peyote-deer-maize complex. Indeed, there are striking parallels between Olson's poem and the Huichol peyote ritual (see Peter Furst, *The Flesh of the Gods: The Ritual Use of Hallucinogens,* 1972).

The blue deer is "entangled" somewhere between animal and human forms, just as the speaker is entangled in "the five hindrances." These are Buddhism's *Nivarana:* desire, ill will, sloth, compunction, and doubt that "spread out across each plane of being" and "hinder the mind, obstruct insight, and prevent . . . concentration" (Ingrid Fischer-Schreiber, *The Encyclopedia of Eastern Philosophy and Religion,* 1989, page 251). The poem's knot imagery extends beyond *Nivarana,* however. Like the mother archetype, knots are universal symbols of the magical means for creating (conserving) and/or destroying (restricting) vital energies. As Mircea Eliade states, knots "may be either *positive* or *negative,* according to whether one takes the opposites in the sense of 'benefic' or 'malefic'" (*Images and Symbols,* 1961). But the knots in Olson's poem are not "opposites" but rather "contraries" in a Blakean sense: "hindrances" and "vents," "flame" and "wall," an umbilicus linking the speaker both to the dead mother and the living cosmos. Tied to the dead mother, the dream and the dream-poem register profound psychological ambivalence: in the net of being the mother gives birth not only to life but also to death.

There is of course a temporal dimension to "the nets of being," and the "desperateness" is

> that the instant
> which is also paradise (paradise
> is happiness) dissolves

But what is the "wind" that "clears the sodden weights" of images? Key to the poem is "the vent," which can be thought of as the poem itself: a sort of ventriloquy ("belly-speak") of the dream and the dead. Death is "never to die, the ghastliness / of going, and forever coming back, returning to the instants which were not lived," and the speaker's tone is at once remorseful and pleading as he addresses his mother and soul:

> O mother, this I could not have done,
> I could not have lived what you didn't,
> I am myself netted in my own being
>
> I want to die. I want to make that instant, too,
> perfect
>
> O my soul, slip
> the cog

Section two returns to the knot as "vent" for the "death in life." The speaker rejects the Christian notion of eternity: its circumventing of time is "the false cause." Instead of death-in-life configured in relation to idealized time (eternity), each knot is a spatial complex, a "topological corner [that] presents itself, and no sword / cuts it, each knot is itself its fire." This is the Gordian knot, the "riddle of the East," which resonates with the "mother-cord" (umbilicus) and the East as symbolic of origins. As the legend goes, whoever untied the knot (answered the riddle) would rule the East. Alexander the Great could not untie the knot, so he cut it. The knot of being, however, cannot be cut from itself anymore than time can be cut from eternity, or the speaker cut loose from his own origin in mother.

The speaker says that the "nets which entangle us are flames," which recalls Pound's description of an image vortex as "radiant node or cluster." As Hugh Kenner notes, the node or knot is dynamic by virtue of its complex design, its pattern of "self-interference" (*The Pound Era,* 1973). These nets of being are material: one must

> go into everything,
> let not one knot pass
> through your fingers

Olson rejects the slipped cogs of Buddhism's *Nivarana/Nirvana* and Christianity's hell/heaven: the flame is neither conflagration nor purging of the terrestrial nets. Instead the old discourses of hell and heaven are

> earth to be rent, to shoot you
> through the screen of flame which each knot
> hides

Disillusioned by dreams of religious and political utopias, as well as the nightmare of history, "As the Dead Prey Upon Us" calls on readers to awaken to the "human universe" and its "actual earth of value."

DAN FEATHERSTON

**Further Reading**

Bertholf, Robert, "Righting the Balance: *The Distances,*" *Boundary 2* 2, nos. 1–2 (1974)
Butterick, George, *A Guide to the Maximus Poems of Charles Olson,* Berkeley: University of California Press, 1978
Maud, Ralph, *Charles Olson's Reading: A Biography,* Carbondale: Southern Illinois University Press, 1996

# The Kingfishers

"The Kingfishers" is generally regarded as one of the most important poems of the 20th century for its influence on nearly every experimental tradition in postwar American poetry. Originally titled "Proteus" and "The First Proteid," the poem appeared as "The Kingfishers" in *The Montevallo Review* (1, no. 1 [Summer 1950]), then in Olson's collections *In Cold Hell, in Thicket* (1953) and *The Distances* (1960). The appearance of "The Kingfishers" in Donald Allen's *The New American Poetry: 1945–1960* (1960) represented a bridge between Modernism and Postmodernism, combining the rigorous specificity of Pound and Williams with a "stance toward reality" generous enough to engage many of the complexities of postwar America.

"The Kingfishers" is Olson's first significant long poem, priming the pump for his epic *The Maximus Poems*. It is the practice in advance of the theory mapped out in his essay "Projective Verse" (1950) and a response to writer Frances Boldereff's request to "tell me about America—tell me how it is for you" (Maud and Thesen, 1999). Correspondence and drafts of the poem indicate that Olson thought of "The Kingfishers" as an "Anti-Wasteland," a response to T.S. Eliot's negative vision of contemporary civilization as effete ruins set against the grand architecture of an idealized past. According to George Butterick (1989), the great Modernist poems

> were insufficient approaching mid-century; the displacement had been too large with the disclosures of the Nazi death camps and the mushrooming of the Atomic Age within a few months of each other. The extent of evil in the world caused the imagination to stagger.

Thus, "The Kingfishers" is an exploration not only of philosophical paradoxes (i.e., the many and the one, change and permanence) but also of how the benevolence and violence of the human will influence our perceptions of history, culture, and ultimately our human ethos.

Although "The Kingfishers" uses a collage method reminiscent of such Modernist classics as Eliot's "The Waste Land," it does not seek a subordination of the parts into a unified whole. Instead, "The Kingfishers" exemplifies Olson's belief that "the objects which occur at every given moment of composition . . . must be treated exactly as they do occur therein and not by any ideas or preconceptions from outside the poem" (1966). Another primary distinction between many Modernist poems and "The Kingfishers" is Olson's notion of objectism:

> [G]etting rid of the lyrical interference of the individual as ego, of the "subject" and his soul, that peculiar presumption by which western man has interposed himself between what he is as a creature of nature . . . and those other creations of nature which we may . . . call objects.

"The Kingfishers" is divided into three sections. The entire poem hangs from the virgule in the first line, which acts as a kind of unwobbling pivot between contraries of stillness ("What does not change") and action ("is the will to change"). The character Fernand appears early in the poem, never to reappear, "sliding along the wall of the night, losing himself / in some crack of the ruins." He is a sort of one-man chorus, talking cryptically "of Albers & Angkor Vat," "the pool," and "the kingfishers' feathers." Although Fernand "could not go beyond his thoughts," the poem picks up the materials and questions that he leaves unanswered, namely, why "The pool is slime" and "the kingfishers' feathers . . . why / did the export stop?" The kingfishers' feathers take on a variety of complex roles in the poem, representative of aesthetic, economic, cultural, and spiritual value. The "export" may allude to the ancient Cambodian trade of kingfisher feathers (i.e., "Angkor Vat"); also, feathers, especially those of the quetzal, played an important monetary role in Aztec and Mayan civilization. Fernand's "last words"—"The pool is slime"—may refer to the stale waters, as it were, of cultural and historical "wastelands" abandoned or destroyed by the violence of the human will. It is not so important to determine the specific reference for "the pool" as it is to hear in Fernand's statement a foreshadowing of a central issue in "The Kingfishers": the devaluation of histories and cultures by violence and neglect.

Part 2 of section 1 contrasts images of change in relation to the past and the future, the rising and the setting sun. The "E on the stone" (Plutarch: "Know Thyself") faces backward and west toward ancient Greek civilization, while Mao faces forward and east, stating, "la lumière de l'aurore est devant nous!" ("The light of the dawn is before us!"). The legend of the kingfisher also faces west: the bird "got the color of his breast / from the heat of the setting sun!" The E on the stone, Mao's rhetoric, and the kingfisher legend threaten to steer the poem toward symbolism and generalization. Then the actual kingfisher appears. The bird's "features are, the feebleness of the feet . . . / the bill, serrated, sometimes a pronounced beak." However, the dictionary description of the kingfisher is no more useful than the legends, which "will not indicate a favoring wind / or avert the thunderbolt." What is important about the kingfisher is not its description or legends but how it follows natural laws of change, laying its eggs on fish bones "thrown up in pellets by the birds." The "rejectementa" that the kingfisher uses to build its nest reminds us of Fernand's comment that "The pool is slime": as "the young are born" in a "nest of excrement and decayed fish," the human will to change arises out of the "fetid mass" of history.

The third part of section 1 borrows heavily from William H. Prescott's *History of the Conquest of Mexico,* juxtaposing Cortés' violent destruction of Aztec culture with the E at Delphi that "was differently heard // as, in another time, were treasures used." Montezuma attempted unsuccessfully to "avert the thunderbolt" of colonialism by offering Cortés gifts of gold and featherwork. Here we return to Fernand's question ("who cares for their feathers now"), noting how the intrinsic value of gold and feathers was lost on Cortés:

> And all now is war
> where so lately there was peace,
> and the sweet brotherhood, the use
> of tilled fields.

However, the "sweet brotherhood" of precolonial Aztec culture is dubious, and the question of benevolence between indigenous and colonial cultures gets picked up again in section 2. The final part of section 1 returns to a general meditation on change, making reference to the theory of feedback as it relates not only to physics and mathematics but also to ontology and the self vis-à-vis glosses of Heraclitus ("Into the same river no man steps twice") and Plutarch ("To be in different states without a change / is not a possibility").

A recurring theme of "The Kingfishers" is the blurring of distinctions between Eastern and Western civilizations, which in turn makes us question simple dichotomies of the East as the past/birth and the West as the future/death. The Aztec corpse is buried "in a sitting posture," imitating a "living" form, while a child is baptized by a woman who cries out to the fertility goddess Ciao-coatl "with her face to the west." An unlikely bridge between East and West turns up in the Mongolian louse—unique to paleo-Siberians but found in Native American graves, alluding to America as the "light in the east" beyond the Paleolithic ice bridge connecting Asia to the New World. If there is a dichotomy in "The Kingfishers," it has more to do with attitudes toward change, such as the benevolence of Cabeza de Vaca and the violence of Cortés: "the two who first came, each a conquistador, one healed, the other / tore the eastern idols down."

The "old appetite" in section 2 returns our attention to the East and Marco Polo's account of cannibalism in China, which resonates with human sacrifice in the West and the Aztec "temple walls . . . black from human gore." In Olson's study of Melville (*Call Me Ishmael,* 1947), "First Fact" behind civilization is not the Christian Fall from God but cannibalism and man's fall from himself. At the same time, "The Kingfishers" turns back on Dante's Christian image of the divine rose, asking us to "regard the light, contemplate / the flower / whence it arose." The rose puns off Mao's conclusion in section 1 that we must "lever / et agir!" ("rise up and act!"). The density of this section implies that all "light" of benevolence and civilization "arose" out of the human body ("the flower") and the "filth" of violence, cannibalism, and sacrifice: no will to change is immune from "pudor."

In the final section, the speaker separates himself from both Greek and Roman predecessors, who "can take no risk that matters / the risk of beauty least of all." Where "The Waste Land" ends in madness, destruction, and prayerful silence, "The Kingfishers" ends with a commitment to find out "what was slain in the sun." The "honey" can be thought of as whatever "healing" might occur by returning to what is sacrificed or excluded from "the human universe." It is a vision similar to Robert Duncan's "whole symposium," in which "the very form of man has no longer the isolation of a superior paradigm but is involved in its morphology in the cooperative design of all living things, in the life of everything, everywhere" ("Rites of Participation," in *Symposium of the Whole: A Range of Discourse Toward an Ethnopoetics,* edited by Jerome Rothenberg and Diane Rothenberg, 1983).

It is Rimbaud who comes forward as a model for how poetry might renew its commitment to "la terre et les pierres" ("the earth and the stones"). As Olson notes in a draft leading up to "The Kingfishers," the E on the stone is not only "know thyself," "but the extension of the principle, that the end of the knowing is the time, is the E hidden within the statement on the stone" (Butterick, 1989). That is, knowledge of the self must include knowledge of all that has been excluded from history, including violence, destruction, and pudoracracy.

"The Kingfishers" is a response to some of the ethical consequences surrounding two of the greatest changes in 20th-century civilization: the globalization of war and the globalization of economics. What will not change in future readings of "The Kingfishers" is an identification with the benevolence and violence of the human will, as one cannot help but notice affinities between Cortés' 16th-century extermination of the Aztecs and Hitler's 20th-century extermination of the Jews or the failures of any number of revolutionaries to "regard the light, contemplate / the flower." In the 21st century, "The Kingfishers" will no doubt be regarded as a prophetic meditation on the human will to change as we redefine the rights and responsibilities of individual and cultural values within the context of a truly globalized world.

Dan Featherston

**Further Reading**


Altieri, Charles, "Olson's Poetics and the Tradition," *Boundary 2* 2, nos. 1–2 (1974)

Butterick, George, "Charles Olson's 'The Kingfishers' and the Poetics of Change," *American Poetry* 6, no. 2 (1989)

Butterick, George, editor, *Charles Olson and Robert Creeley: The Complete Correspondence,* volume 1, Santa Barbara, California: Black Sparrow Press, 1980

Christensen, Paul, *Charles Olson: Call Him Ishmael,* Austin: University of Texas Press, 1979

Davenport, Guy, "Scholia and Conjectures for Olson's 'The Kingfishers,'" *Boundary 2* 2, nos. 1–2 (1974)

Maud, Ralph, *What Does Not Change: The Significance of Charles Olson's "The Kingfishers,"* Madison, New Jersey: Fairleigh Dickinson University Press, and London: Associated University Presses, 1998

Maud, Ralph, and Sharon Thesen, editors, *Charles Olson and Frances Boldereff: A Modern Correspondence,* Hanover, New Hampshire: University Press of New England, 1999

Olson, Charles, "Projective Verse," in *Selected Writings of Charles Olson,* edited by Robert Creeley, New York: New Directions, 1966

Paul, Sherman, *Olson's Push: Origin, Black Mountain, and Recent American Poetry,* Baton Rouge: Louisiana State University Press, 1978


## The Maximus Poems

Charles Olson's *The Maximus Poems* mark a pivotal point in 20th-century American poetry. They are works of epic imagination that sprawl across both sides of the divide separating Modernism and Postmodernism (the latter term was inaugurated by Olson). In *Maximus,* Olson seeks to stand on the shoulders of his two acknowledged forebears in the writing of the 20th-century American long poem, Ezra Pound and William Carlos Williams. His aim is to produce a work that surpasses both *The Cantos* (1948) and *Paterson* (1946–58), fusing the former's capacity for large historical and cultural syntheses with the latter's emphasis on the absolute specificity of the local, the literal fact of place.

*The Maximus Poems* were begun in 1950 when Olson was teaching at Black Mountain College and finished two decades later, not long before the poet died. The first full volume was published in 1960, the second in 1968, and the third, edited posthumously from a disordered set of manuscripts, in 1975.

Olson's work strays across many fields of knowledge, including ancient philosophy and history, early New England history, geography, geology, non-Euclidean geometry, and the myth and folklore of numerous cultures. Moreover, the stylistic scope of the poems is enormous. They include much matter that formerly were only in rare instances considered proper to poetry—the verbatim inclusion of documentary sources or shipping records, for example.

At the heart of the dense meditations on poetics that produced *The Maximus Poems* is a collapsing of the notions of time and space. History, for Olson, is "the practice of space in time": the poet assumes a role akin to that of the cartographer. Like Pound before him, he rejects linear historical narrative, preferring instead the synchronous reconstellation of diverse past narratives in the mind of the writer situated in the present. Crucially, the writer is also situated in a particular place. The abstraction "history" cannot be thought without the specific incidence of the local, scene of the unceasing self-creation of human collectivities.

Olson sites his epic in the Cape Ann fishing town of Gloucester, Massachusetts, a town that has the potential to match his definition of "polis," or community. Olson moved there permanently in 1957 following the closure of Black Mountain College. The poems are thick with references to the settling of Gloucester in the 1620s, to local fishing exploits, to town characters and friends of Olson, to its geography and economy, and even to the local paper. Gloucester functions at one level as part of a wider critique of American society, but Olson's cultural pessimism is combined with an investment in the role of poetry in effecting a regrounding of human social being.

Olson's poetic is rooted in the particulars of everyday life. His approach is heuristic, applying Herodotus' notion of "istorin," which he interprets as "to find out for oneself":

> I would be an historian as Herodotus was, looking
> for oneself for the evidence of
> what is said . . .
> (*Maximus* I, 100–01)

The practice of history, for Olson, is the involvement of the mind of the poet ("my memory is / the history of time"; *Maximus* II, 86) in an attempt to comprehend space. This attempt to comprehend space begins with Gloucester, becomes a mapping of the westward sweep of power across the globe, and extends into the cross-cultural sway of mythic archetypes. *The Maximus Poems* seek to "do" history and so render its operations intelligible at the level of both the local and the cosmic.

The interpenetration of Olson's themes of time and space occurs most obviously in the composite figure of Maximus, which is subject to numerous reformulations in the poems. He represents, among other personae, the Greek philosophers Maximus of Tyre (itself the main port of the Phoenicians and an ancient precursor of Gloucester) and Apollonius of Tyana, Hercules, Odysseus, Alfred the Great, the 17th-century explorer John Smith and ship's carpenter William Stevens (both involved in the settlement of Gloucester), and sometimes Olson himself. The multiple identities of Maximus allow the figure to become an analogue for human potential, close to Jung's "homo Maximus."

Developing the ideas outlined in such influential essays as his "Projective Verse," Olson established with *The Maximus Poems* a form of poetic utterance that offered great freedoms to succeeding generations of poets. Olson sought to counter the prevailing trend for "confessional" poetry with a poetry that eschewed the "lyrical interference of the individual as ego." In *Maximus*, the damaging separation between subject and object that he argued was symptomatic of abstract thought would be replaced by a kinetic poetry of immediacy and intensities that would necessarily "break open" conventional syntax. The basic building block of this anti-metaphorical, anti-lyrical poetry would be the syllable, organized in lines with a shape determined by the poet's breath. In this way, the materiality of bodily speech opens a window onto the world of objects. Words in *Maximus* are organized in "fields" of force following a logic that is immanent to the poem and that preserves the "proper confusions" of the play of energies operating in the poem. *The Maximus Poems* are, then, poems of "process." Olson's notion of process and his return to the syllable as unit of the line were strongly influenced by the thought of the English philosopher Alfred North Whitehead.

In "On first Looking out through Juan de la Cosa's Eyes" (*Maximus* I, 77–80), Olson discusses the "mappemunde" of Columbus' cartographer. The poetic gaze, Olson suggests, spurning the inward gaze of the "individual as ego," is properly oriented toward the external world. The emphasis in the discovery of America is on the encounter with the new, "first looking":

> . . . The New Land was,
> from the start, even by name was
> Bacalhaos
>                 there,
> swimming, Norte, out of the mists
>
>                                 (out of Pytheus' sludge
>
> out of mermaids & Monsters
> (*Maximus* I, 78)

Olson's poetry seeks to map the data that this outer world offers and, at the same time, to register its shaping force. This mapping is aware of itself as a doubled process, performing its attempts to somehow represent itself to the elusive concreteness of reality in a dynamic play that offers creative priority to neither self nor world.

Olson's concern with cartography finds a parallel in the distribution of words across the page. His typographical experimentation sometimes leads him to break free of the horizontal arrangement of lines altogether. Space is a key element in the arrangement of poetic text, which becomes like a musical score indicating how a poem might be "voiced" by the reader (the musical analogy leans heavily toward dissonance). The typewriter, he argued, enables a new precision in recording the immediacy of the poet's breath. At times, *The Maximus Poems* develop a highly compacted set of relationships between words; at others, the poems read almost as casual speech. Developing from their accumulating variety of registers is a metrical rendering of the irreducibly variegated nature of the human engagement with the world.

Disputes around the settlement of Gloucester in the 17th century are central to the first part of *Maximus*. In subsequent volumes, this is largely displaced by Olson's mythopoeic concerns and cosmological speculation. The declamatory public voice of some of the earlier poems gives way to a more provisional mode of utterance. In keeping with their processual precepts, *The Maximus Poems* do not, in the marshaled disarray of the final volume, have the sense of an argument completed. Although *The Maximus Poems* represent one of Olson's most consistent attempts to apply his holistic ambition and, in so doing, to sketch a mythically based reconception of humanity, their main legacy consists in his concern with process and the concomitant insistence on formal freedom.

Will Montgomery

**Further Reading**

Altieri, Charles, *Enlarging the Temple: New Directions in American Poetry during the 1960s,* Lewisburg, Pennsylvania: Bucknell University Press, and London: Associated University Presses, 1979

Bernstein, Michael André, *The Tale of the Tribe: Ezra Pound and the Modern Verse Epic,* Princeton, New Jersey: Princeton University Press, 1980
Butterick, George F., *A Guide to the Maximus Poems of Charles Olson,* Berkeley: University of California Press, 1978
Byrd, Don, *Charles Olson's Maximus,* Urbana: University of Illinois Press, 1979
Davidson, Michael, "Archeologist of Morning: Charles Olson, Ed Dorn, and Historical Method," *ELH* 47 (1980)
Mellors, Anthony, "Maximal Extent: Charles Olson and C.G. Jung," *Fragmente* (U.K. journal) 8 (1998)
Olson, Charles, *Call Me Ishmael,* New York: Grove Press, 1947; London: Cape, 1967
Olson, Charles, *The Human Universe, and Other Essays,* edited by Donald Allen, San Francisco: Auerhahn Society, 1965
Prynne, J.H., "Review of *Maximus IV, V, VI,*" *The Park* (U.K. journal) 4/5 (1969)
Ross, Andrew, *The Failure of Modernism: Symptoms of American Poetry,* New York: Cambridge University Press, 1986
Von Hallberg, Robert, *Charles Olson: The Scholar's Art,* Cambridge, Massachusetts: Harvard University Press, 1978

---

## Open Form. *See* Free Verse

---

## George Oppen 1908–84

Some poets burst on the scene fully formed and stake their legacy with a first book. Such is the case with George Oppen, whose *Discrete Series* (1934) came into print with an approving preface by Ezra Pound. The manuscript of 32 pages was first sent to Pound by the poet Louis Zukofsky, with a note introducing a bold new innovator to the founder of Imagism. This brief but intense string of interconnected lyric meditations on the sea, boats, and reality took the poem to its experimental limits and solved a riddle of how Imagism could be opened and extended to longer lyric forms. Oppen discovered that by serializing a theme or motif, the austere mode of Imagist writing, with its emphasis on physical experience, could be made discursive without retreating into romanticism or subjectivity.

Oppen was an Objectivist with Zukofsky and others, who specialized in closely detailed observations. It so happens that the word "objective" is the technical term for the lens of a camera, and there are significant links between this form of poetry and the art of photography. Instead of one epiphany as a poem's focus, as in Imagist doctrine, an object or event in an Objectivist poem could be viewed from various perspectives until its intellectual potentials were exhausted. The serialized lyric became Oppen's trademark.

*Discrete Series* takes its title from the mathematical phenomenon of a continuous flow of numbers in which an implicit factor links the numbers in a progression. In poetry, Oppen's factor is a certain object or motif taken from the landscape that reappears in each poem of the sequence, showing not only recurrence but the progressive accumulation of a series as well. The book opens with an oblique comment on boredom as a kind of knowledge, an ironic beginning for a poem about curiosity and close scrutiny. Oppen's point is that in boredom one is not driven by self-interest but merely looks, and in that frame of mind the world becomes liberated from the observer's ego and reveals itself. Maude Blessingbourne, who reappears in later books, is taken from a short story by Henry James, "The Story in It." She lives in a fantasy world of French romances and is the measure of someone who does not "look" much at anything. When she "approached the window as if to see / what really was going on," she is too bored to notice much of anything but the rain. The window separates her from the storm, leaving the world ignored, unknown.

The scene depicts someone in the act of looking out, which prefigures all that happens in the rest of the series of poems; more important, the "factors" in the progression are introduced—the glass boundary between self and world defining both the limits of subjectivity and the threshold of the objective world, and the freely changing medium of water altering the appearance of reality. From here on, these constants will control the discourse on landscape. Water and glass are related—both are transparent, and both take liquid forms.

The first numbered section of "Discrete Series" describes in oblique fragments the interior of an elevator in an office building, calling attention only to the control knob, the "T," for raising or lowering the car; because it is a closed box and obscures the life in the rest of the tower, it is immediately compared to other "boxes" in which things are concealed from view—a Frigidaire and the counters of a soda fountain. The examples move along a strict comparative progression from one sort of box to another, each with knobs to be controlled by the human hand.

In the next passage, the containers shift to a glass of water and to a car. The attention focuses on the idea of a car as another sort of box with windows, with the air outside either frozen or rainy; the gear shift is the knob within this new context. A final passage depicts a woman stepping from a shower, another glass box with faucets as the knobs. The figure of the woman recalls the opening image of Maude Blessingbourne stepping up to a window where the rain pelts down. The lines offer us progressions at many levels, a flow of words carrying before it the accumulating similarities of water, glass, controlling knobs, and women who are bored and somewhat vain. William Carlos Williams called the lyric method of Objectivism an "objectification of significant particulars," and Oppen's poems exactly fulfill that definition by foregrounding things "lost" in ordinary reality, but they also unify experience by recurring in scene after scene.

The development of the series involves permutations on these fixed items—the rain will shift to the sea, and the box will become a boat. The window will turn into a porthole through which the sea may be observed forming a wave; more cars will appear. Women will be present in the scenes that follow, each manifesting something of the character of Maude Blessingbourne tolerating boredom.

Even in this most radical exercise in modern poetry, the "Shape of art" is "More formal / Than a field would be." In choosing one's particulars and emphasizing their recurrence, the randomness of nature becomes limited, but the field (New York City) is clearly present as the sequence casually samples its vast landscape for the presence of these underlying and repeating figures of glass, woman, and so on. A lyric process in which events duplicate and permutate one another seems more akin to musical works than to poetry, as Zukofsky was aware in constructing his own Objectivist sequence, *"A"* (1928–74), where music is the dominant context of his words.

Oppen was in Europe at the time *Discrete Series* was published; Pound and Basil Bunting had introduced him to the literary avant-garde there and were launching his further career when his stay was cut short by the precipitous rise of Fascism. He and his wife, Mary, hurried back to the United States to devote themselves to the struggle against the possibility of Fascism at home. They joined the Communist Party and entered into a world of class conflicts where poetry was "not the most important thing in the world," he later told an interviewer. Oppen would not publish any poetry for the next 28 years.

When *The Materials* appeared in 1962, it broke a long silence from Oppen and from a generation of poets who had gone underground during World War II and the McCarthy years. Oppen had joined the war "to fight Fascism" and returned home to work as a carpenter in Los Angeles; he and Mary then moved to Mexico in 1950 to live in political exile during the era of the "red scares." In 1958, with the end of the McCarthy years, Oppen began writing again.

Oppen's new book was more topical and discursive, less adventurous in experiment or rigor of eye, but Oppen wished to review the experience he had lived for so long in silence. The themes and even some of the crucial motifs of his first book are carried over into *The Materials.* In his opening poem, "Eclogue," Oppen invokes the image of the window where "Flesh and rock and hunger" reveal a world waiting "To be born!" In "Image of the Engine," he writes that "Thru the glass /—If there is someone / In the garden! / Outside, and so beautiful!" The poems are cautious about the postwar age, where Oppen finds community endangered by a rapacious marketplace and greater emphasis on consumption—"the noise of increase," he says in "Return." He summarizes the great surge of immigration to the New World as ending "its metaphysic / In small lawns of home."

*This in Which* (1965), issued three years later, opens with the poem "Technologies," stating Oppen's theme that "The inelegant heart / Which cannot grasp / The World" makes art. The human feud with nature is lamented in "Philai Te Kou Philai," the title taken from the words of Electra after killing her mother, "loved and hated," which Oppen interprets as words directed at nature itself. The natural world is more alien in this poem than in any other; even the animals in the park seem withdrawn, unknowable.

In "Parousia," from "Five Poems about Poetry," Oppen is transparent about the dangers of the new age: "Impossible to doubt the world: it can be seen," but "It cannot be understood, and I believe that is lethal." Even though man may "find his catastrophe," the world "may stand forever." Therein lies both his dread and his hope as a poet writing in the 1960s. Such prescience earned Oppen the respect of younger poets and an enduring reputation as a voice of caution as consumerism reached a breakneck pace, consuming rain forests and fossil fuels, with hardly a river left unpoisoned by industrial pollution. All this Oppen warned against, which may strike the reader now as understated prophecy.

In 1968, Oppen published his most celebrated book, *Of Being Numerous,* for which he received the Pulitzer Prize. The title inscribes his long preoccupation with democracy and his place in it. The opening title sequence sweeps us up in his ongoing meditation on the "things / We live among," which to see "Is to know ourselves." The address is collective and plural, the "we" of America, and the world is now the cities and scraps of nature that make up reality. The "shipwreck / Of the singular" is his reading of the long history of individualism, whereas power and common cause point the way toward community. His earliest themes are present here as well, as in "the rain falls / that had not been falling / and it is the same world," Maude Blessingbourne's casual thought long before.

The "numerous" are both the lumpen proletariat now exploited by the corporations and the raw energies of the nation, "the pure products of America," as Oppen quotes from William Carlos Williams. However, "they carry nativeness / To a conclusion / In suicide" since the nation is still not the home or proper condition of ordinary citizens. These citizens are abused or left in the limbo of "otherness" until each achieves the status of being an individual. There is no link between the one and the many, which is the tragedy of American politics.

Oppen may now clarify what he meant in the opening passage of "Discrete Series," remarking of Blessingbourne (but not by name), "approached the window as if to see . . . // The boredom which disclosed / Everything—." "I should have written," he says, to clarify what Blessingbourne might have seen had she taken advantage of her selfless idleness at the window. "Air so thick with myth the words lucky / And good luck // Float in it." Everything "at the mind's end / Relevant." This sequence and "Some San Francisco Poems" from his next book, *Seascape: Needle's Eye* (1972), are the great achievements of Oppen's poetry: stately, sinuous lyric meditations that can rise to a spare eloquence or become folksy and plain, without loss of rigor or essential purpose—the need for the "known and the unknown [to] / Touch," as he wrote in "Of Being Numerous." America is that unfinished project of great ideals, noble but now corrupt with its own material success.

Oppen's language becomes utterly lucid in the poems of *Seascape,* where he declares, "Time and depth before us, paradise of the real, we / know what it is." The major thrust of his poetry remains "things / and the self." "Prosody // Sings // In the Stones," which is to say, with Williams, "no ideas but in things." These limpid lyrics are purged of self-conscious artistry; passages here come close to the bare eloquence of Pound's final cantos—wispy phrases, some of them unfinished, but jewels of verbal music.

Oppen's last collection, *Myth of the Blaze*, included in *Collected Poems* (1975), consists of nuggets of irreducible lyric wisdom, reformulations of a lifelong exploration of the self's connection to the world. Objects have become the ciphers of a hidden world, and the poem is the expression of nature itself through its own forms and events, which the poet merely transcribes in words—"the poem // discovered // in the crystal / center of the rock image," in which the image is the "transparent // present."

PAUL CHRISTENSEN

*See also* Objectivism

**Biography**

Born in New Rochelle, New York, 24 April 1908. Attended Oregon State University, 1926; co-founder and publisher (with Mary Oppen), To, Publishers, Paris, France, 1930–33; member, Objectivist Press Co-Op, New York City, 1934–36; organizer, Workers Alliance, Brooklyn, New York, 1935–40; factory worker, Detroit, Michigan, 1940–42; served in U.S. Army, 1942–45; carpenter, Los Angeles, 1945–49; operator, furniture factory, Mexico City, 1950–58. Received Pulitzer Prize, 1969; American Academy and Institute of Arts and Letters Award, 1980. Died in Sunnyvale, California, 7 July 1984.

**Poetry**

*Discrete Series*, 1934
*The Materials*, 1962
*This in Which*, 1965
*Of Being Numerous*, 1968
*Collected Poems*, 1972
*Seascape: Needle's Eye*, 1972
*The Collected Poems of George Oppen, 1929–1975*, 1975
*Primitive*, 1978
*The Poems of George Oppen, 1908–1984*, 1990

**Other Writings:** correspondence (*Selected Letters of George Oppen*, edited by Rachel Blau DuPlessis, 1990).

**Further Reading**


Finkelstein, Norman, "Political Commitment and Poetic Subjectification: George Oppen's Test of Truth," *Contemporary Literature* 22, no. 1 (Winter 1981)

Hatlen, Burton, editor, *George Oppen: Man and Poet*, Orono, Maine: National Poetry Foundation, 1981

Kimmelman, Burt, *The "Winter Mind": William Bronk and American Letters*, Madison, New Jersey: Fairleigh Dickinson University Press, and London: Associated University Presses, 1998

Losh, Elizabeth Matthews, "Silent Readings: Lessons in Objectivist Poetics for Contemporary American Poetry," Ph.D. Diss., University of California, Irvine, 1998

McAleavey, David, "Unrolling Universe: A Reading of Oppen's 'This in Which,'" *Paideuma* 10, no. 1 (Spring 1981)

Oppen, George, *Selected Letters of George Oppen*, edited by Rachel Blau DuPlessis, Durham, North Carolina: Duke University Press, 1990

Oppen, Mary, *Meaning a Life: An Autobiography*, Santa Barbara, California: Black Sparrow Press, 1978


## Discrete Series

George Oppen's first book, *Discrete Series* (1934), marked the transition in Modern American poetic movements from the Imagist to the Objectivist style. Like Imagism, Objectivism directly treats the "thing" experienced in an instant. Unlike Imagist poetry, however, Oppen's poetry does not confess with musical phrases the emotional and intellectual truths he finds in awe-striking moments. Instead, its images and syntax show his encounters with a changing environment that call all seeming certainties into question.

In 1929 Louis Zukofsky and George Oppen established To, Publishers, which would later become the Objectivist Press, in Paris. They printed their own poetry as well as that of Williams, Pound, Reznikoff, Rakosi, Bunting, and Niedecker. *Discrete Series*, despite its preface by Ezra Pound, garnered little critical attention beyond that of the Modernist poets themselves until Oppen earned a Pulitzer Prize for *Of Being Numerous* (1968). His contemporary William Carlos Williams, to whose work Oppen's poetry has been compared, did not miss the importance of his work, however. Within three months of reading Oppen's *Discrete Series* Williams responded with the essay "The New Poetical Economy," in which he notes Oppen's significant contribution to American poetry and in turn American culture:

> An imaginable new social order would require a skeleton of severe discipline for its realization and maintenance. Thus by a sharp restriction to essentials, the seriousness of a new order is brought to realization. Poetry might turn this condition to its own ends. Only by being an object sharply defined and without redundancy will its form project whatever meaning is required of it. It could be well, at the same time, first and last a poem facing as it must the dialectic necessities of its day. Oppen has carried this social necessity, so far as poetry may be concerned, to an extreme. (*Poetry* 44 [July 1934])

Oppen's radical deconstruction of syntax may have contributed to the relative lack of critical acclaim his work received. Also contributing to this dearth of attention was Oppen's subsequent 25 years in overt political engagement (joining the Communist Party, serving in World War II, fleeing McCarthyism in Mexico) rather than poetic production, to which he returned in 1958.

In a number of ways Oppen's later work echoed the style that he established in *Discrete Series*. "Of Being Numerous" in *Of Being Numerous*, "A Language of New York" and "A Narrative" in *This in Which* (1965), and "Some San Francisco Poems" in *Seascape: Needle's Eye* (1972) are also serial poems. These differ from other long American poems as well as from traditional epics and extended poems in that they are not mythopoeic, heroic, or didactic: the poems raise questions rather than assert answers. Moreover, all of the poems rely upon noun clauses as the basis of poetic statement and present those nouns or objects as part of an ongoing process. The dialectic among the objects proves both continuous and ruptured; white space, syntactical deviations, and varied signifiers emphasize the images as singularities, while the succession of multiple noun clauses and the reiterations and reconfigurations of common elements through them suggest a collective. In a way, *Discrete Series* served as Oppen's *ars poetica*. In a 1969 post-Pulitzer interview with L.S. Dembo, Oppen explained his use of the mathematical term for his title: in a discrete series each element remains independent and isolated from its neighbors. The effect, although unpredictable, proves cumulative; in a poem the fragments create a whole from which the reader constructs meaning.

*Discrete Series* presents an isolated chain of events from Oppen's observations of New York City. Oppen juxtaposes objects of a culturally-constructed glass menagerie with objects from the natural field that seemingly defy being hidden or destroyed by human creations. An example of the interplay of nature and society near the middle of *Discrete Series* involves a

Closed car—closed in glass—
At the curb,
Unapplied and empty:
A thing among others
Over which clouds pass and the
    Alteration of lighting,
An overstatement
Hardly an exterior.

Oppen equates "A thing" with "An overstatement." The car, the glass, the light, the water (the condensation in clouds) captured by Oppen's representation of this single moment enter the collage of things speaking in the landscape. As a whole, Oppen's serial poem suggests that the scattered and imposed-upon elements ultimately draw together, for their unique moments of expression contain common aspects from the material world. Oppen examines the pieces that together provide an impression of a complicated overall environment. Women, weather, roads, stones, architecture, and machines are among the repeated images.

Glass and water are two of the most diversely and powerfully represented objects in *Discrete Series*. The initial poem of the series describes a bored woman watching "rain falling . . . past the window-glass":

The knowledge not of sorrow, you were
    saying, but of boredom
Is—aside from reading speaking
    smoking—
Of what, Maude Blessingbourne it was,
    wished to know when, having risen,
"approached the window as if to see
    what really was going on";
And saw rain falling, in the distance
    more slowly,
The road clear from her past the window-
    glass—
Of the world, weather-swept, with which
    One shares the century.

The idea that experiential knowledge is framed by the perceiver establishes itself when three voices (the poet, the "you," and Maude Blessingbourne) appear; however, all three refer to the commonality of mediation, of things, of nature in relation to human perception.

Similarly, the next poem, which we "view" through a store window, shows the then-new "big Business" wherein a young man making patrons' sodas splashes water from a sink. Oppen next combines in a poem "water in a glass," a car that "runs on a higher road" during a flood, and a showering woman whose "arm-pits are causeways for water." Later in the series another car appears showing a person "closed in glass," an image similar to the forthcoming depictions of a glass box around "The middle-aged man sliding / Levers in the steam-shovel cab" and a "PARTY ON SHIPBOARD" where nothing can be seen through "the round of the port-hole" but a "Wave," a singular expression of a larger field: the sea. Even the woman he depicts erotically with "hip high" and the sex scene of "love at the pelvis" reflect the wave passing across "a flat bed" in a bedroom. The earth almost narrates the poems, constantly changing material references. The approach disengages the reader in an attempt to show that matter lives and alters itself; but, in doing so, it recombines and reconfigures the same elements. Oppen deliberately leaves his poem seemingly unfinished with the lines "Successive / Happenings / (the telephone)." No matter how distinct the moments in our lives, manufactured roads, vehicles, buildings, and gadgets work to connect us to one another just as grass and prairie, river and ocean do. Throughout the poem, then, the landscape demonstrates a continuum or process involving transmissibility and recurrence, singularity and plurality.

In *Collected Poems* (1975), *Discrete Series* lacks much of the white space found in the page designs of the version Oppen and his wife Mary manually printed in Paris. More than one poem appears on a page, and poems span pages. This arrangement does not present the page-to-page dialectic of Oppen's disjunctive poetics, the distinct and particular parts in conversation, as well as does the original version. Nevertheless, spatially and syntactically, this edition of *Discrete Series* still captures the poet's achievement: among separate words, things, and individuals, Oppen finds a limited, transforming, but inescapable connection of each part to the whole.

DESHAE E. LOTT

**Further Reading**

Dembo, L.S., "The 'Objectivist' Poet: Four Interviews," *Contemporary Literature* 10 (1969)

DuPlessis, Rachel Blau, and Peter Quartermain, editors, *The Objectivist Nexus: Essays in Cultural Poetics,* Tuscaloosa: University of Alabama Press, 1999

Griffin, Jonathan, et al., editors, *Not Comforts, But Vision: Essays on the Poetry of George Oppen,* Budleigh Salterton, Devon: Interim Press, 1985

Hatlen, Burton, editor, *George Oppen: Man and Poet,* Orono, Maine: National Poetry Foundation, 1981

Heller, Michael, "The Mind of George Oppen: Conviction's Net of Branches," in *Conviction's Net of Branches: Essays on the Objectivist Poets and Poetry,* by Heller, Carbondale: Southern Illinois University Press, 1985

*Ironwood* 26 (1985) (special issue on Oppen, edited by Michael Cudihy)

Nicholls, Peter, "Of Being Ethical: Reflections on George Oppen," *Journal of American Studies* 31, no. 2 (1997)
Oderman, Kevin, "Earth and Awe: The One Poetry of George Oppen," *Sagetrieb* 3, no. 1 (1984)
Shoptaw, John, "Lyric Incorporated: The Serial Object of George Oppen and Langston Hughes," *Sagetrieb* 12, no. 3 (1993)
Williams, William Carlos, "The New Poetical Economy," *Poetry* 44 (July 1934)

## Of Being Numerous

"Of Being Numerous" is the title poem of George Oppen's fourth volume of poetry, which was published in 1968 and was awarded the Pulitzer Prize the following year. A shorter version of the poem was published in Oppen's third volume, *This in Which* (1965), under the title "A Language of New York"; thus, we can conclude that Oppen was at work on the poem throughout much of the 1960s, that decade during which the poems of his great "middle period" were composed. It is Oppen's longest and most ambitious poem and, arguably, his masterpiece.

Oppen intended "Of Being Numerous" and the rest of the volume in which it appears to be "a decisive expression of a period" (Oppen, 1990), thinking explicitly of the way *The Waste Land* stands in relation to its time. A sequence, or "serial poem," consisting of 40 relatively brief sections, it is written in Oppen's characteristically condensed and elliptical free verse, with a few sections in prose. Many passages are drawn directly from the poet's wide reading, correspondence, and daily conversation and set in the text in a collage-like fashion. The poem synthesizes all the major themes of Oppen's earlier work and brings to fulfillment the formal experimentation begun in *Discrete Series* (1934), his first book-length sequence. This work, which was written when Oppen was a member of the short-lived group of poets known as the Objectivists, defines the limits beyond which his later poetry would go. Whereas *Discrete Series*, as the title indicates, assumes a disjointed, empirically determined worldview that rigorously eschews any attempt at philosophical integration through the poet's subjective agency, "Of Being Numerous" is an explicitly political poem that attempts to reconcile our experience of discrete, objective phenomena with a pressing sense of the poet's civic as well as aesthetic responsibility. It takes over 30 years for Oppen to move from the extreme Objectivist position of his first book to that of "Of Being Numerous," and much of that time was spent in poetic silence, as Oppen devoted himself to Communist Party activism, served in World War II, and lived in political exile in Mexico. "Of Being Numerous," therefore, is the culmination of a lifetime of thinking about the relationship of the art of poetry both to the object world and to some of the most important public events and social circumstances of the 20th century. The poem, however, is not merely retrospective: written during the Vietnam War, it is informed by the urgency of those times and haunted by the feeling that the struggles of one generation are never resolved but inevitably must be passed on to its successor. Thus, as an open, sequential meditation on time and history, the structure of Oppen's poem makes perfect sense: refusing either formal or thematic closure, it presents us with an accretive linguistic experience that simultaneously unfolds its meaning.

Time and history are to be carefully distinguished in "Of Being Numerous," for on one level the poem can be understood as a confrontation between the engaged historicism of Oppen's Marxism and his equally strong fascination with Heideggerian phenomenology. The history of political struggle, and the role of the artist or intellectual in that struggle, is juxtaposed against the ongoing flow of time, in which "There are things / We live among 'and to see them / Is to know ourselves.'" These are the first lines of the poem, calling attention to the most basic phenomenological conditions of being, "the existence of things, / An unmanageable pantheon." Yet this "pantheon" is always to be experienced in a specific locale, under determinate social conditions. In "Of Being Numerous," that locale is New York City, "A city of the corporations // Glassed / In dreams," which is simultaneously "A world of stoops," the home of millions of common, working individuals. "We are pressed, pressed on each other," declares the poet,

> Obsessed, bewildered
> By the shipwreck
> Of the singular
> We have chosen the meaning
> Of being numerous.

In this early, defining moment in the poem, "the bright light of shipwreck" signifies not merely the loss of individuality in the face of corporate-sponsored mass culture but also the lost possibility of enlightenment, the cherished humanistic dream of the poet or philosopher. "And he fails!" cries Oppen, "He fails, that meditative man!" This failure is due, in part, to the ineluctable predicament of that figure in relation to common humanity:

> 'Whether, as the intensity of seeing increases, one's distance from Them, the people, does not increase'
> I know, of course I know, I can enter no other place

As Henry Weinfield observes, the poet "can neither be isolated from the masses, nor can he merge with them fully: If the former, he risks forfeiting his humanity; if the latter, his originality; in both cases, his poetic identity."

Always dialectical in his thinking and in the process of poetic composition, Oppen moves continually between these poles. Remembering his infantry service in World War II, he observes poignantly how

> I cannot even now
> Altogether disengage
> From those men
>
> With whom I stood in emplacements, in mess tents,
> In hospitals and sheds and hid in the gullies
> Of blasted roads in a ruined country . . .

"How talk / Distantly of 'The People,'" he asks, leveling his criticism equally at leftist intellectuals and, later in the poem, at those writers who deny the importance of common life:

> Stupid to say merely
> That poets should not lead their lives
> Among poets,

They have lost the metaphysical sense
Of the future, they feel themselves
The end of a chain

Of lives, single lives
And we know that lives
Are single

And cannot defend
The metaphysic
On which rest

The boundaries
Of our distances.

In respect to the conditions of poetry in our time, Oppen's heroic insistence on "the metaphysical sense / Of the future" refutes both the naive notion of a "people's poetry" and the equally self-limiting view of the poet in an enclave, a mere professor of "creative writing."

Yet Oppen is also perceptive enough to recognize, as he observes in one of the poem's great understatements, that "It is difficult now to speak of poetry" since "It is not precisely a question of profundity but a different order of experience." Despite the complex and "impenetrable" nature of reality, the poet "must somehow see the one thing." However ambivalently, the later sections of the poem point to the values to which the poet must adhere:

Because the known and the unknown
Touch

One witnesses—.
It is ennobling
If one thinks so.

If to know is noble

It is ennobling.

Since beginning their work, Oppen and his fellow Objectivists emphasize the poet's role as a witness to the immediacies of contemporary life. However, by the time "Of Being Numerous" is written, the poet has also become one who stands in the presence of the unknown, the metaphysical, seeking to know what lies beyond. Like Keats, Oppen advocates negative capability since in the face of the phenomenal world one can never know with certainty; and, again like Keats, Oppen insists "Only that it should be beautiful": for beauty, as it is found in human desire, "is our jubilation / Exalted and as old as that truthfulness / Which illumines speech."

NORMAN FINKELSTEIN

**Further Reading**

Davidson, Michael, *Ghostlier Demarcations: Modern Poetry and the Material Word,* Berkeley: University of California Press, 1997
DuPlessis, Rachel Blau, and Peter Quartermain, editors, *The Objectivist Nexus: Essays in Cultural Poetics,* Tuscaloosa: University of Alabama Press, 1999
Finkelstein, Norman, "Political Commitment and Poetic Subjectification: George Oppen's Test of Truth," *Contemporary Literature* 22, no. 1 (Winter 1981)
Finkelstein, Norman, *The Utopian Moment in Contemporary American Poetry,* Lewisburg, Pennsylvania: Bucknell University Press, and London: Associated University Presses, 1988; revised edition, 1993
Hatlen, Burton, "Opening up the Text: George Oppen's 'Of Being Numerous,'" *Ironwood* 13, no. 2 (Fall 1985)
Hatlen, Burton, editor, *George Oppen: Man and Poet,* Orono, Maine: National Poetry Foundation, 1981
Oppen, George, *Selected Letters of George Oppen,* edited by Rachel Blau DuPlessis, Durham, North Carolina: Duke University Press, 1990

---

# Simon Ortiz 1941–

Simon Ortiz is a poet, essayist, short-story writer, and editor whose writing reflects his concern for the land and for Native American people. A speaking landscape interdependent with people, the animating power of language, and the sacred origin and nature of storytelling are all aspects of Ortiz's poetry that are likewise mainstays of Native American literature. Ortiz's father was famous as a storyteller among his people, and Ortiz speaks with the power associated with orally transmitted tales. Ortiz's poems frequently have a strong narrative thread and employ colloquial diction to capture the sense of place (Wiget, 1985). His tribute to the American Indian oral tradition is simultaneously a tribute to the vernacular tradition exemplified by Whitman and the Beat poets. Ortiz writes:

> Language is more than just a group of words and more than just the technical relationship between sounds and words. Language is more than a functional mechanism. It is a spiritual energy that is available to all. It includes all of us and is not exclusively in the power of human beings—we are part of that power as human beings. (Wiget, 1985)

Ortiz's poetry likewise offers a critique of industrial America's exploitation of land as well as a critique of the disconnectedness between people and land in contemporary American society. Whereas the Indians' conquerors have traditionally regarded land as a commodity to be stolen, sold, or bartered, Indians themselves have regarded land as integral to their identity. In his effort to chronicle the devastating effects of modernity to Indian lands, Ortiz relies on the black humor that has become a staple of Native American literature.

Ortiz's first important collection of poetry, *Going for the Rain* (1976), is divided into four sections: "Preparation," "Leaving," "Returning," and "The Rain Falls." The book's poem prologue bids the *Shiwana* (rainmakers) to return from the other world with blessings for the land and its people. "Preparation" concerns the narrator's preparation for a journey, or in a broader sense, the human preparation for the sacred journey of life. The first poem, "The Creation, According to Coyote," is based on a Keresan Pueblo creation myth in which the people journey upward through successive worlds until they emerge from a hole in the ground onto the earth's surface. In the second section, "Leaving," Ortiz explains that his "main theme" is "to recognize / the relationship I share with everything." He mourns the loss of Indian land as well as the U.S. government's forcible relocation of Indians to cities in the 1950s. "Returning" offers hope that the land will be regenerated and will outlast those who have sought to destroy it. The final section, "The Rain Falls," reiterates a vision of integration with the natural world, incorporating the dominant themes of the collection: "for the morning star / finds that dawn / on its journey / through our single being, / the all that has depth / and completeness, / the single eye / through which we see / and are seen."

In the preface to Ortiz's third collection, *A Good Journey* (1977), he emphasizes the Native American oral tradition as integral to his own work in response to past interview questions such as, "Why do you write?" and "Who do you write for?":

> Because Indians always tell a story. The only way to continue is to tell a story and that's what Coyote says. The only way to continue is to tell a story and there is no other way. Your children will not survive unless you tell something about them—how they were born, how they came to this certain place, how they continued.

As in *Going for the Rain,* Ortiz employs the motif of life as a sacred journey—for the individual as well as the tribe—relying on the figure of Coyote, one of the prime movers of the created universe, to portray the balance between sacred and profane that must be maintained in public and private life. The fourth section of *The Good Journey* includes a critique of industrialized America for its failure to acknowledge the sacredness of life: "For Our Brothers: Blue Jay, Gold Finch, Flicker, Squirrel" is an elegy for the roadkill casualties of industrialized society. In its anticipation of eventual harmony between natural and human worlds, Part 5 of *A Good Journey* invites hope.

In *Fight Back: For the Sake of the People, for the Sake of the Land* (1980), which commemorates "the Pueblo revolt of 1680 and our warrior Grandmothers and Grandfathers," Ortiz contends that "Indian reservations in the U.S. were conceived as convenient surplus labor pools." These poems focus on the Indian working class rather than the singers, dancers, artists, and healers featured in earlier works. The incursion of modernity in this collection takes the form of the atomic bomb testing at White Sands missile range in southeastern New Mexico, which ironically relied on uranium taken from Laguna-Pueblo land. Ortiz suggests that, faced with the threat of total annihilation, the people must rely on the transforming power of words in order to find affirmations for physical and spiritual existence.

*From Sand Creek* (1981), even more overtly political than *Fight Back,* juxtaposes historical narratives on the plight of the American Indian with Ortiz's own personal narratives. Here the railroad symbolizes modernity, and the train symbolizes America on a journey for self-definition. Ortiz's corresponding personal narrative includes reminiscences about his father, who worked for the Santa Fe Railroad.

Ortiz's long 1994 collection, *After and Before the Lightning* (1994), which contains more than 200 poems, is divided into four sections: "The Landscape: Prairie, Time and Galaxy," "Common Trials: Every Day," "Buffalo Dawn Coming," and "Near and Evident Signs of Spring." The collection's two black pages represent storms, which are associated not only with rejuvenating rain and blessings but also with inspiration for storytelling. The final section offers hope, anticipating an eventual reconciliation between self and landscape: "Not alone but one / ball things bin one / snow pine light one / me motion magic one."

Ortiz is also the author of several books of fiction, including three collections of short stories—*Howbah Indians* (1978), *Fightin': New and Collected Stories* (1983), and *Men on the Moon* (1999). His stories rely on the same themes as his poetry, addressing conflicts between white and Indian worldviews, especially in regard to land.

DONNA L. POTTS

*See also* Native American Poetry

**Biography**

Born near Albuquerque, New Mexico, 27 May 1941. Attended Fort Lewis College, Durango, Colorado, 1962–63; University of New Mexico, Albuquerque, 1966–68; University of Iowa, Iowa City (International Writing Fellow), 1968–69; served in the United States Army; public relations consultant, Rough Rock Demonstration School, Arizona, 1969–70, and National Indian Youth Council, Albuquerque, 1970–73; taught at San Diego State University, California, 1974, Institute of American Arts, Sante Fe, New Mexico, 1974, Navajo Community College, Tsaile, Arizona, summers 1975–77, College of Marin, Kentfield, California, 1976–79, and University of New Mexico, 1979–81; editor, *Quetzal,* 1970–73; since 1982 consulting editor, Pueblo of Acoma Press. Received National Endowment for the Arts grant, 1969, 1982; Pushcart Prize for poetry, 1981. Living in Pueblo of Acoma near Albuquerque.

**Poetry**

*Naked in the Wind,* 1970
*Going for the Rain,* 1976
*A Good Journey,* 1977
*Song, Poetry, Language,* 1978
*Fight Back: For the Sake of the People, for the Sake of the Land,* 1980
*From Sand Creek: Rising in This Heart Which Is Our America,* 1981
*A Poem Is a Journey,* 1981
*Woven Stone,* 1991
*After and Before the Lightning,* 1994

**Other Writings:** short stories (*Howbah Indians,* 1978; *Fightin': New and Collected Stories,* 1983; *Men on the Moon,* 1999), children's literature; edited collections of poetry (*These Hearts, These Poems,* 1984).

**Further Reading**

Gingerich, Willard, "The Old Voices of Acoma: Simon Ortiz's Mythic Indigenism," *Southwest Review* 64 (Winter 1979)

Lincoln, Kenneth, "The Now Day Indi'ns/Common Walls: The Poetry of Simon Ortiz," in *Native American Renaissance,* by Lincoln, Berkeley: University of California Press, 1983

Oandasan, William, "Simon Ortiz: The Poet and His Landscape," *Studies in American Indian Literatures* 11 (1987)

Smith, Patricia Clark, "*Canis latrans latrans* in the Poetry of Simon Ortiz," *Minority Voices* 3 (Fall 1979)

*Studies in American Indian Literatures* 8 (Summer/Fall 1984) (special issue on Ortiz)

Wiget, Andrew, *Native American Literature,* Boston: Twayne, 1985

Wiget, Andrew, *Simon Ortiz,* Boise, Idaho: Boise State University Press, 1986

---

# Judith Ortiz Cofer 1952–

To understand Judith Ortiz Cofer's poetry, the reader must trace the source of her insights and outlooks to the landscape that lies between the two cultures of her birth and upbringing. Although Ortiz Cofer was born in Puerto Rico in 1952, her family relocated to the United States by 1955, afterward spending the school year in Paterson, New Jersey, and returning to Puerto Rico in summer.

Her poems address the interstices of two languages and two cultures: English and Spanish, American and Puerto Rican. Ortiz Cofer describes poetry as a means for empowerment, a spiritual discipline that helps both readers and writers become whole. For the poet herself, the use of Spanish words within her poems summons her island heritage. Written largely in English punctuated with Spanish, her poems address the internal and external experience of being caught between two cultures, searching for selfhood and dignity. In this respect, she wants readers to recognize themselves in what she writes.

Ortiz Cofer's work has not been readily recognized within the framework of either American or Puerto Rican literature. Her poems from and about her experience as an immigrant have been overlooked in surveys of American letters. As they are in English (and often about her childhood in the United States), they have not won the favor of critics and writers in her homeland, either. Furthermore, because her work does not fit within the context of Puerto Rican writers based in New York City's Spanish Harlem or Lower East Side, Ortiz Cofer has not been perceived as part of the emerging movement of "Nuyorican" poets writing in "Spanglish," a blend of English and Spanish.

The writer's eclectic history as a reader has affected this "both but neither" status. She describes her own literary education as the traditionally elitist Western background of the undergraduate English major. Her own voice formed over time as her experiences and influences converged, synthesizing the enduring narratives of her childhood, a mixture of folk and fairy tales with the overheard *cuentos* (stories) of her female kin, with canonical classroom reading as she came of age. Ortiz Cofer acknowledges debts to such figures as Modernists James Joyce and Virginia Woolf. After the family moved from New Jersey to Georgia in 1968, Ortiz Cofer also came to know and admire the work of Southern women writers, such as Flannery O'Connor and Eudora Welty. Not until adulthood would she encounter the work of Isabel Allende, Gabriel García Márquez, and other Latin American authors. Readers often locate Ortiz Cofer's work, at least in part, in the context of a new generation of college-educated Latina women writers including Julia Alvarez, Sandra Cisneros, Christina García, Nicholasa Mohr, and Esmeralda Santiago.

In "A Poem," from *Reaching for the Mainland* (1995), the speaker expresses her wish to write a poem capable of rousing readers from their sleep, urging them to locate what they had not as yet realized they had lost. This notion of the poet as an unavoidable irritant who must intervene in the lives of readers pervades Ortiz Cofer's work. Her poems vouch for the otherwise unseen consequence of ordinary moments: the life-story behind a gesture, the yearning that animates a dance, the comforting routines of caregivers tending the dying to their rest. Her work testifies to lives shaped and broken by words as forcefully as by deeds, by perceptions as readily as by historical periods, by longings as much as by leaders. As a result the poems linger thoughtfully on details: the beat of a child's skipped rope, the prayer of ritual, and the hum of a grandmother's unfolding stories of generations.

By the late 1980s Ortiz Cofer began to explore other literary forms. She has worked in fiction, including her Pulitzer Prize–nominated novel, *The Line of the Sun* (1989), which has been compared to Christina García's *Dreaming in Cuban* (1992), Julia Alvarez's *How the García Girls Lost Their Accents* (1991), Sandra Cisneros' *House on Mango Street* (1983), Nicholasa Mohr's *Nilda* (1973), and Esmeralda Santiago's *When I Was Puerto Rican* (1993). She has also written a three-act play, *Latin Women Pray,* first produced in 1984. Her poetry often appears in mixed-genre, multi-vocal texts, such as her semi-fictional essay-memoir *Silent Dancing: A Partial Remembrance of a Puerto Rican Childhood* (1990). In this way Ortiz Cofer has distinguished herself as a writer of creative nonfiction. As a member of the University of Georgia's Creative Writing faculty, Judith Ortiz Cofer pursues a successful career as a writer, critic, educator, lecturer, and workshop leader.

LINDA S. WATTS

**Biography**

Born in Hormigueros, Puerto Rico, 24 February 1952. Attended Augusta College, Georgia, B.A. 1974; Florida Atlantic University, Boca Raton, M.A. 1977; Oxford University, England, 1977; bilingual teacher, public schools in Palm Beach County, Florida, 1974–75; Adjunct Instructor, Palm Beach Junior College, Florida, 1978–80; Adjunct Instructor in English, Broward Community College, Fort Lauderdale, 1978–80; Lecturer, University of Miami, Coral Gables, Florida, 1980–84; Instructor, University of Georgia, Athens, 1984–87, Georgia Center for Continuing Education, Athens, 1987–88, and Macon College, Georgia, 1988–89; special programs coordinator, Mercer University College, Forsyth, Georgia, 1990; since 1992 Associate Professor of English and Creative Writing, University of Georgia, Athens; Visiting Professor, University of Michigan, Ann Arbor, Arizona University, Tucson, and University of Minnesota, Duluth; Scholar of English Speaking Union at Oxford University, 1977; staff member, International Conference on the Fantastic in Literature, 1979–82; fellow, Fine Arts Council of Florida, 1980; scholar, Bread Loaf Writers' Conference, 1981; John Atherton Scholar in Poetry, 1982; member of literature panel of Fine Arts Council of Florida, 1982; member of administrative staff of Bread Loaf Writers' Conference, 1983, 1984. Received Witter Bynner Foundation grant, 1988; National Endowment for the Arts fellowship, 1989; Pushcart Prize, 1990; O. Henry Prize, 1994; Anisfield Wolf Award, 1994. Living in Louisville, Georgia.

**Poetry**

*Peregrina*, 1986
*Terms of Survival*, 1987; revised edition, 1995
*The Latin Deli: Prose and Poetry*, 1993
*Reaching for the Mainland, and Selected New Poems*, 1995
*The Year of Our Revolution: New and Selected Stories and Poems*, 1998

**Other Writings:** contributor to anthologies (*Triple Crown: Chicano, Puerto Rican and Cuban American Poetry*, 1987), play (*Latin Women Pray*, produced 1984), memoirs (*Silent Dancing: A Partial Remembrance of a Puerto Rican Childhood*, 1990), novels (*The Line of the Sun*, 1989), children's literature (*An Island Like You: Stories of the Barrio*, 1995), essays (*Woman in Front of the Sun: On Becoming a Writer*, 2000); edited anthology of criticism (*Sleeping with One Eye Open: Women Writers and the Art of Survival* [with Marilyn Kallet], 1999).

**Further Reading**

Fabre, Genevieve, "Liminality, In-Betweeness and Indeterminacy: Notes toward an Anthropological Reading of Judith Cofer's *The Line of the Sun*," *Annales du centre de recherches sur l'Amerique anglophone* 18 (1993)

Gregory, Lucille, "The Puerto Rican 'Rainbow': Distortions vs. Complexities," *Children's Literature Association Quarterly* 18, no. 1 (Spring 1993)

Grobman, Laurie, "The Cultural Past and Artistic Creation in Sandra Cisneros' *The House on Mango Street* and Judith Ortiz Cofer's *Silent Dancing*," *Confluencia: Revista Hispanica de cultura y literatura* 11, no. 1 (Fall 1995)

Novoa, Juan Bruce, "Judith Ortiz Cofer's Rituals of Movement," *The Americas Review: A Review of Hispanic Literature and Art of the USA* 19, no. 3–4 (Winter 1991)

Novoa, Juan Bruce, "Ritual in Judith Ortiz Cofer's *The Line of the Sun*," *Confluencia: Revista Hispanica de cultura y literatura* 8, no. 1 (Fall 1992)

Ocasio, Rafael, "From Nuyorican Barrio Literature to Issues on Puerto Rican Literature Outside New York City: Nicholasa Mohr and Judith Ortiz Cofer," in *Literature and Ethnic Discrimination*, edited by Michael J. Meyer, Atlanta, Georgia: Rodopi, 1997

Piedra, Jose, "His and Her Panics," *American Journal of Comparative and Cultural Studies* 16, no. 41 (1991)

# P

## Ron Padgett 1942–

A visual humorist, Ron Padgett establishes a new order of interpretive wit for American poetry. His oeuvre is formally disposed to quirky crosscuts in discourse, often addressed to and imitative of cartoon animation. Seasoned with straight-faced exposition on Pluto the dog, Daisy the cow, Fred Flintstone, and so on—as Padgett explains in an interview—his poetry is "down home" American, notwithstanding that he has been based primarily in Manhattan since 1960, and as coeditor of the seminal *An Anthology of New York Poets,* his work has been initially and frequently categorized as second-generation New York School. In early work, Padgett himself points to the influences of first-generation New York School writers John Ashbery, Kenneth Koch, Frank O'Hara, and James Schuyler. What separates Padgett is persistent and entertaining visual surprise—accumulated vision, as the poet Alice Notley expresses it—that yields "a manner of thinking based on the world as a fusion of all its pictorial possibilities."

Padgett's claim to a down-home aesthetic is genuine. Padgett was born and raised in Tulsa, Oklahoma, by parents who were not literary but who indulged his appetite for reading, keeping him in good supply of comic books. His interest in writing developed in part as a result of associations with two childhood friends who were to become important artists in their own right: Joe Brainard and Dick Gallup. At age 15, Padgett, along with his friends, launched *The White Dove Review,* a magazine featuring work by older writers with national reputations. While still in high school, Padgett had the further good fortune of befriending Ted Berrigan, who was enrolled at the University of Tulsa. After Padgett left Oklahoma to attend Columbia University, he, Berrigan, and Brainard met again in Manhattan, collaborating for more than two decades on numerous books of poetry and drawings, giving birth to the so-called Tulsa School sub-branch of the New York School.

Padgett's poems from the 1960s show the influence of Koch (his teacher at Columbia) and other New York School poets. As Michael Leddy (2000) notes, Padgett evinces with lines such as "O astronauts!" Koch's "exclamatory excitement," a quality of O'Hara's verse as well. Of all his precursors, in these first poems Padgett seems under the spell of O'Hara. The opening of Padgett's "Strawberries in Mexico"—

At 14th Street and First Avenue
Is a bank and in the bank the sexiest teller of all time

—can be viewed as a rewrite in Padgett's plain vernacular of opening lines from O'Hara's "Rhapsody": "515 Madison Avenue / door to heaven? portal / stopped realities and eternal licentiousness." Much else appears between the beginning and middle of "Strawberries in Mexico," but midway in the poem the bank at 14th and First has been transformed into a "bright all-yellow building," as Padgett depicts it:

And Frank O'Hara is the building
I'm thinking about him like mad today
(As anyone familiar with his poetry will tell)
And about the way Madison Avenue really
Does go to heaven

In addition to smaller collections, Padgett's later work includes five full volumes of poetry between 1976 and 1995 as well as acclaimed book-length translations from the French of Guillaume Apollinaire, Valery Larbaud, and Blaise Cendrars. The later verse confirms Padgett as a craftsman of deeply ironic poems about language and poetry, that is, metacomposition packed with visual and ruminative events from the perspective of a comedian-observer directing and imparting the composition. The 13-line "Poem" from *Toujours l'amour* (1976) spoofingly labels its persona "a mess" and admits, "I don't know / I may not be much." While hilariously self-deprecating, by line five the text discharges its own exaggerated consciousness: "All surface no inner strength / Poetry not any good / This poem not any good." Midpoint in "The 26 Letters" from *Tulsa Kid* (1979) Padgett illustrates the lot of a language devotee, the "me" in the poem sitting at a typewriter:

3:55 in the morning
with a head cold and a beard
and some tortoise-shell spectacles
attached to my head,
not a bad guy really,
a touch of Sad Sack tonight,
a bit of red and green tomorrow

with a long streak of blue into the future
with orange and black zigzags along the sides

Devices that Padgett repeatedly deploys invoke "the comic strip world," as Clayton Eshleman (1997) observes. Yet "The 26 Letters" overlays highly defined cartooning ("orange and black zigzags" and "a touch of Sad Sack") to draw parallels between the conventions of pictorial illustration and those of language; to expose the finite graphic material of language, as the poem's title implies; and to contend with the substantial limits challenging one who "draws" with words.

More prose forms enter the mix in Padgett's recent collections. Notley (1998) distinguishes between Padgett's use of verse more to "dispel the quotidian" and his turning to prose to acknowledge "direct feeling." For example, "My Room," from *The Big Something* (1990), talks of desire for a place "of my own making" and discontent with the results. "I grew disgruntled," Padgett writes. It "looked dark and mournful, as if someone had died in it." The poem captures impressions of family members, dead and alive, and of a desk lamp given Padgett under humorous circumstances by Ted Berrigan, now deceased. The poem concludes,

> I can hear a brook from my window now. . . . All this confluence in a room I didn't feel comfortable in until a few minutes ago, a room that, broken like a mustang, becomes a friend to man, we who are so desperately in need of friends among the plants and animals of this earth, and yes, the humans too, and the rooms we build around ourselves.

Shifts in subject matter and tone typify Padgett's poetry overall. Sensual impressions merge memories and feelings to mark change ("I didn't feel comfortable . . . until a few minutes ago") that is circumscribed by universal constraints ("rooms we build around ourselves"). Padgett continually contests such limits with good humor and visual certainty, rendering his poems as elegant distillations of dense imagination at play.

Jack Kimball

*See also* New York School

**Biography**

Born in Tulsa, Oklahoma, 17 June 1942. Attended Columbia University, New York (Boar's Head poetry Prize and George E. Woodbeny Award, 1964), A.B. 1964; Fulbright Fellow, Paris, 1965–66; taught poetry workshops at St. Mark's-in-the-Bowery, New York, and poetry writing in New York public schools, 1969–76; writer in the community, South Carolina Arts Commission, 1976–78; associate editor, *Paris Review,* 1968–70; founding editor, Full Court Press, 1973; since 1981 director of publications, Teachers and Writers Collaborative, New York. Received Gotham Book Mart Prize, 1964; Poets Foundation grant, 1965, 1968; Columbia University Translation Center Award, 1976; National Endowment for the Arts fellowship, 1983; Guggenheim fellowship, 1986. Living in New York City.

**Poetry**

*Some Thing* (with Ted Berrigan and Joe Brainard), 1964
*In Advance of the Broken Arm,* 1964
*Sky,* 1966
*Bean Spasms: Poems and Prose* (with Ted Berrigan), 1967
*Tone Arm,* 1967
*100,000 Fleeing Hilda* (with Joe Brainard), 1967
*Bun* (with Tom Clark), 1968
*Great Balls of Fire,* 1969
*Sweet Pea,* 1971
*Sufferin' Succotash* (with Joe Brainard; with *Kiss My Ass,* by Michael Brownstein), 1971
*Poetry Collection,* 1971
*Back in Boston Again* (with Ted Berrigan and Tom Clark), 1972
*Oo La La* (with Jim Dine), 1973
*Crazy Compositions,* 1974
*Toujours l'amour,* 1976
*Arrive by Pullman,* 1978
*Tulsa Kid,* 1979
*Triangles in the Afternoon,* 1980
*How to Be a Woodpecker,* 1983
*How to Be Modern Art* (with Trevor Winkfield), 1984
*Light as Air,* 1989
*The Big Something,* 1990
*Supernatural Overtones* (with Clark Coolidge), 1990
*New and Selected Poems,* 1995

**Selected Criticism**

*The Straight Line: Writings on Poetry and Poets,* 2001

**Other Writings:** plays, short stories (*212 Stories for Andy Warhol,* 1965), novel (*Antlers in the Treetops* [with Tom Veitch], 1973), translations of French literature, travel writing (*Albanian Diary,* 1999); edited collections of poetry (*World Poets,* 3 vols. [editor in chief], 2000).

**Further Reading**

Eshleman, Clayton, "Padgett the Collaborator," *Chicago Review* 43, no. 2 (1997)
Foster, Edward Halsey, "Ron Padgett," in *Postmodern Poetry: The Talisman Interviews,* by Foster, Hoboken, New Jersey: Talisman House, 1994
Guiney, Mortimer, "Reverdy in New York," *World Literature Today* 59, no. 4 (1985)
Leddy, Michael, "Ron Padgett," in *World Poets,* New York: Scribners Reference Books, 2001
Lehman, David, *The Last Avant-Garde: The Making of the New York School of Poets,* New York and London: Doubleday, 1998
Notley, Alice, "Ron Padgett's Visual Imagination," *Arshile* 9 (1998)
Ratcliffe, Stephen, "Supernatural Diet," *Talisman* 10, no. 7 (1991)
Rohrer, Matthew, "Ron Padgett's *New and Selected Poems,*" *Iowa Review* 27, no. 2 (1997)
Shapiro, David, "The New York School, Continued," *New York Times Book Review* (19 September 1976)

# Michael Palmer 1943–

Michael Palmer's poetry is an ongoing philosophical investigation of the relationship of language, culture, history, and the human. Often dreamlike and surreal, his poems explore the tensions implicit in rendering and deciphering the "real" and foreground the linguistic and ideational processes involved in making a world. His poetry focuses on the boundaries of the known and, following a relentless mode of philosophical inquiry, searches for the flaws and absences in the human-made representations of culture and history.

Born in New York City in 1943, Palmer earned a B.A. in French in 1965 as well as an M.A. in comparative literature in 1968 from Harvard University. Deeply interested in Continental literature, Palmer traveled to Europe following his graduation from Harvard and established important connections with contemporary French poets such as Emmanuel Hocquard, whose poetry, including *Theory of Tables* (1994), he would later translate. In addition to the works of Hocquard and other contemporary French poets, Palmer is an avid reader of world literature and has translated the writings of Vicente Nuidobor, contemporary Brazilian poets, Arthur Rimbaud, and others. Palmer returned to the United States in 1969 and moved to San Francisco. He still lives in San Francisco and has been on the faculty of poetics at the New College of California as well as on the faculty at San Francisco State University.

Palmer is often affiliated with the Language poets, which is understandable since his work shares with Language poetry the interrogation of language as the residual trace of sociohistorical pressures. As Palmer remarks about contemporary poets, "I hope we are questioning ways of understanding, seeing, and various crucial orders of assumption about meaning and representation in a culture where most things seem to have become re-presentation." Yet despite his "postmodern" tendencies, Palmer identifies himself as more of a Modernist writer influenced by Robert Creeley, George Oppen, Louis Zukofsky, and other Objectivists; French contemporary poetry; the works of Egyptian/French writer Edmond Jabès; and contemporary theorists such as Maurice Blanchot, Walter Benjamin, and Luce Irigary. The influence of Continental poetry and philosophy has made his work accessible to French audiences, and, subsequently, he frequently has been translated into French and is included in French anthologies of important contemporary American poets, such as *21 + 1: Poetes americains d'aujourd'hui* (1986), edited by Emmanuel Hocquard and Claude-Royet-Journoud.

While Palmer's first chapbook of poetry, *Plan of the City of O,* was printed in 1971 and he continued to publish steadily in the 1970s, *Notes for Echo Lake* (1981) and *First Figure* (1984) were breakthrough works because of their stylistic use of the poetic sequence, a series of poems on the same subject or issue, as well as for the way they conceptualize and interrogate the world. A number of themes emerge in these two books that dominate the body of Palmer's poetry—namely, the relationship of writing, reading, and speaking; the truth of visual and linguistic representations of culture and history; the limitations of knowledge; and the relationship of voice, naming, and being. Both of these works also speak to the influence of the birth of his daughter, Sarah, on his poetry. "French for April Fool's," from *First Figure,* exemplifies these different elements at work in his poetry as well as how his mode of poetic inquiry impacts its style:

> I will name it anything I will name you this
> and it rains bright stones as you say this
>
> Each of us will call it Egypt
> because of the wind
>
> Sarah tripped and fell and spelled nest
> and the wind is to blame for this
>
> The wind has gathered a sequence of things as pure facts

The phrasing of the statements confirms, advances, and complicates the issues under investigation—being, seeing, talking, naming, and knowing—and demonstrates how the poem is a process of inquiry and discovery into the world and the "real."

Palmer's style fully emerges in *Sun* (1988), a masterfully sustained book of poetry that continues to interrogate the possibilities of language and knowing. "Fifth Prose," for example, typifies the strength of the book as a whole, wherein the poem opens with a question of the efficacy of the representation of language:

> Because I'm writing about the snow not the sentences
> Because there is a card—a visitor's card—and on that card
> there are words of ours arranged in a row
>
> and on those words we have written house, we have
>     written
> leave this house, we
> have written be this house . . .

The ability of language to invoke and speak reality is juxtaposed against its inherent artifice. Subsequently, the fictive elements of language, textuality, and poetry constitute an important ideational focal point throughout *Sun* as well as in the larger body of Palmer's poetry.

In the title poem of *Sun,* for example, the fictive is considered from a slightly different angle; that is, language, the material world that it refers to, and also its speaker/writer are subject to violence, decay, death, and erasure. The poem, near its close, includes the words "Lapwing. Tesseract. X perhaps for X," each of which gestures to something that has been lost, is extinct, or has been destroyed. Each is a word without a corresponding referent, or, in linguistic terminology, a signifier without a signified. In this regard, Palmer troubles the certainty and assumed permanency of language, reality, and memory.

Gaps, absences, and margins between words and the world are recurring themes in *Sun* that are continued in *At Passages* (1995), where the poems pursue the "hum of the possible-to-say." As Palmer writes in the opening of "Wheel,"

> You can say the broken word but cannot speak
> for it, can name a precise and particular shade
> of blue, if you can remember the name
> (Woman of the South, New Lilac, Second Sky?)

The book interrogates the "passages" of language as a maze of broken words, implied meanings, and potentialities as well as the processes of creating, discovering, and generating meaning. *The*

*Promises of Glass* (2000) and the prose work *The Danish Notebooks* (1999) further advance the ongoing investigation of language and the possibility of meaning.

Among his generation of writers, Michael Palmer is one of the most consistently intelligent and engaging American poets exploring what constitutes knowledge and how that knowledge is discovered, represented, and communicated.

David Clippinger

**Biography**

Born in New York City, 11 May 1943. Attended Harvard University, Cambridge, Massachusetts, 1961–68, B.A. in French 1965, M.A. in comparative literature 1968; editor, *Joglars* magazine, 1964–66; contributing editor, *Sulfur* magazine. Received National Endowment for the Arts fellowship, 1975; Guggenheim fellowship, 1989; Chancellor, Academy of American Poets, 1999. Living in San Francisco, California.

**Poetry**

*Plan of the City of O,* 1971
*Blake's Newton,* 1972
*C's Songs,* 1973
*Six Poems,* 1973
*The Circular Gates,* 1974
*Without Music,* 1977
*Alogon,* 1980
*Notes for Echo Lake,* 1981
*First Figure,* 1984
*Sun,* 1988
*For a Reading: A Selection of Poems,* 1988
*An Alphabet Underground/Underjordisk Alfabet* (Danish translations by Poul Borum, illustrations by Jens Birkemose), 1993
*At Passages,* 1995
*Coyote Suitcase: Number One* (with others), 1996
*The Lion Bridge: Selected Poems, 1972–1995,* 1998
*The Promises of Glass,* 2000

**Other Writings:** plays, translations of Portuguese literature (*Sky-Eclipse: Selected Poems,* 2000); edited collection of essays (*Code of Signals: Recent Writings in Poetics,* 1983).

**Further Reading**

Clippinger, David, "Making the Dust Rise: Michael Palmer's Interrogation into Being," *Salt Hill Journal* 2 (1996)
Finkelstein, Norman, "The Case of Michael Palmer," *Contemporary Literature* 29, no. 4 (1988)
Jenkins, Grant, "An Interview with Michael Palmer," *Sagetrieb* 12, no. 3 (1993)
Ratcliffe, Stephen, "Reading *Sun,*" *Occident* 103, no. 1 (1990)
Reinfeld, Linda, *Language Poetry: Writing as Rescue,* Baton Rouge: Louisiana State University Press, 1992
Tuma, Keith, "An Interview with Michael Palmer," *Contemporary Literature* 30, no. 1 (1989)

# Sun

"Sun," the title poem of Michael Palmer's sixth volume of poetry (1988), is actually two pieces with the same title. The first piece, composed mainly in unrhymed couplets, appeared in the literary magazine *Sulfur* in 1987 and in the original edition is 20 pages long. The second poem is in the form of brief prose paragraphs and is four pages long. Like so much of Palmer's work, "Sun" deals with the problematic nature of verbal representation under the cultural conditions of postmodernity, and with the impact that the crisis of signification has upon the individual's subjective experience. Yet unlike the elliptical shorter pieces and serial texts that constitute most of Palmer's earlier volumes, "Sun," dramatically situated at the end of its book, is a sustained and insistent poem that gradually rises with mournful, bitter urgency into an outcry against

> The World As It Is
> tango converted to a fugue
>
> black milk, golden hair
> cliffs, bridges, grey lake
>
> and a grave in air

These lines allude to Paul Celan's "Todesfuge," one of the most famous poems written in the wake of the Holocaust. They indicate Palmer's sense that the disasters of modern history cannot be understood apart from daily life, from "The World As It Is," which in turn cannot be understood apart from the linguistic determinants of seemingly mundane experience.

The centralizing vision of "Sun" is of a wholly administered world of capitalist consumption, where "We, the center, offer narratives" in which competing ideologies fluidly transform themselves into their opposites. This vision is both reified and contested by the poem's relentlessly intelligent, self-referential language games and (despite the obvious pain of its discourse) its cool, distanced tone. The jarring discontinuities, disturbing imagery, and densely clustered allusions that impede one's progress through the text are part of "the zero code / system of assemblage and separation" that reveals the poet's dark irony and ineluctable skepticism. As the poet inquires of both himself and his reader,

> Can you decode the birth of the sign
>
> from the miniskirt, the unconscious, TV, the
> mirage
>
> of the referent, the equation
> of A with A

The philosophers, semioticians, and cultural theorists who haunt the pages of "Sun" (and who can be counted as part of the poem's implied readership) may well be able to negotiate these complex hermeneutical transactions—but to what end? For Palmer,

> All these stories are the same
> There is only one story—
> but not really—

The tautological and self-contradictory assertions of the poem induce not a visionary but a "versionary state," a state in which "This I is the I who speaks," implying the radical fragmentation of the self into a series of disjointed utterances.

"Place yourself here as if on a surface," orders one such utterance early in the poem. In "Sun," the surface on which one places oneself is an uncanny site that is both all too familiar and weirdly defamiliarizing, trivialized, and dreadfully serious:

Through the glass box words
pass unrecognised, thinking us

now dead to you, reader,
now an ammonite curve

incomplete, now tablet
of faint scratches, now redness

in margins, now past
and pastness. Now a filament of light

penetrates the image-base
where first glyphs are stored,

Lucy and Ethel, the Kingfish,
Beaver and Pinky Lee

are spoken, die and undie
for you

like a war viewed from poolside
by philosophers and sheiks

senators and dialectician-priests

Here, instead of the scratched clay tablets of antiquity, TV shows from the 1950s provide "the image-base / where first glyphs are stored." The ephemerality of the postmodern simulacrum is represented by the words passing unrecognized through the television's "glass box" and the inane images that "die and undie / for you." The power brokers of contemporary society viewing the war from poolside are frighteningly prophetic of the television coverage of the Gulf War, against which Palmer will protest in *Seven Poems Within a Matrix for War* in his subsequent volume *At Passages* (1995). Yet a strongly self-critical tendency also can be observed at this point in the poem: not only sheiks and senators relax around the TV, but philosophers and "dialectician-priests" as well, an elite class of intellectuals that includes avant-garde artists and poets such as Palmer himself. "Throughout the city," declares Palmer, "there's the sound of broken glass // We have forgotten it / slipped between the pages"—although what rises from the text into which "we" disappear is a "Song to End a World."

This self-critical quality becomes even more explicit in the second of the poems called "Sun," in which a recurrent imperative phrase from the first poem, "Call it . . ." modulates into the terse command "Write this." The move from calling to writing indicates a higher degree of technicality, a further distance from the referent. In the case of "Sun," the result is horrific:

Write this. We have burned all their villages

Write this. We have burned all the villages and the people
in them

Write this. We have adopted their customs and their
manner of dress

Imperialist violence results in new styles for the metropole, as native cultures are expropriated and transformed into commodities. Yet the process of commodification also turns back upon those who would criticize it:

Let go of me for I have died and am in a novel and was a lyric poet, certainly, who attracted crowds to mountaintops. For a nickel I will appear from this box. For a dollar I will have text with you and answer three questions.

The death of the poet (now entombed in an increasingly old-fashioned narrative form) seems to have made little difference to the individual in question. Clown or whore, the corpse of the poet seems perfectly willing to accept his status as a mere entertainer, as the lyric tradition reaches a final state of debasement: "Pages torn from their spines and added to the pyre, so that they will resemble thought." Real thought can be conveyed in poetry—in language—only in spite of itself, for language is a frighteningly neutral instrument of expression. "G for Gramsci or Goebbels," reads one of the last lines of "Sun," one single letter standing for the martyred Italian Communist whose insights into the workings of cultural hegemony bear directly on the poem as well as for the heinous Nazi Minister of Propaganda who fostered the worst forms of totalitarian art. Poised between the two, "The villages are known as These Letters—humid, sunless. The writing occurs on their walls." If Palmer's poem is among these sites of writing, will it, too, be burned? In this dubious sunlight the surrounding shadows are revealed.

NORMAN FINKELSTEIN

**Further Reading**

Campbell, Bruce, "'A Body Disappears into Itself': Michael Palmer's *Sun,*" *Occident* 103, no. 1 (1990)
Finkelstein, Norman, "The Case of Michael Palmer," *Contemporary Literature* 29, no. 4 (1988)
Palmer, Michael, "A Conversation," *American Poetry* 3, no. 1 (1986)
Reinfeld, Linda, "Sun: Light on Michael Palmer," *Occident* 103, no. 1 (1990)

# Dorothy Parker 1893–1967

Dorothy Parker is remembered as the irreverent wit of the Algonquin Round Table. She wrote short stories, plays, and poetry, all of which are imprinted with her unique and cynical worldview. Although she wrote poetry in a variety of forms, including the lyric, ballad, and sonnet, it is her light verse that garnered the most attention among her contemporaries and that continues to draw praise and admiration from modern-day readers. When *Enough Rope* was published in 1926, it soon became a best-seller, and her second collection, *Sunset Gun* (1928), was equally popular. Her third collection came in 1931 and was an extremely pessimistic volume titled *Death and Taxes.* By the time she published her fourth volume of poetry, *Not So Deep as a Well,* in 1936, she had almost stopped writing poetry altogether.

Parker wrote short verses, usually in iambic quatrains or couplets, that offer amusing observations, puns, and clever twists at the end. Her poetry is known for its sensitivity, irony, hyperbole, control, and impeccable timing. She preferred to think of herself as a social satirist rather than as a humorist, and scholars unanimously agree that her best work was her light, witty verse. Critics describe her more serious poetic efforts as predictable and ordinary. Parker admitted that she, like many poets in her day, was particularly fond of Edna St. Vincent Millay's verse. Parker hoped to write like Millay but felt woefully inadequate. In a 1927 review of *Enough Rope,* Edmund Wilson remarked that Parker's poetic personality is quite different than Millay's but no less important. He wrote that Parker writes with emotional complexity and a unique philosophy of love despite the unevenness of the collection as a whole.

The same themes appear throughout Parker's poetry. She frequently wrote about death, loneliness, urban living, and the heartaches that often accompany love. Taken as a whole, her poetry suggests that women must endure inadequate or painful love affairs. Parker either wrote love poetry as a forsaken woman whose man has betrayed or deserted her or wrote as a wisecracking, hardboiled sophisticate who expected the hardships (and boredom) of love. In "One Perfect Rose," she bemoans her luck that she always receives a perfect rose from her lover rather than a perfect limousine. Because of her cynical and traumatic portrayals of love relationships, it is no surprise that she also wrote about dramatic, morbid topics, such as suicide. Perhaps her best-known poem is "The Resume," which is representative of her work in both content and structure: "Razors pain you; / Rivers are damp; / Acids stain you; / And drugs cause a cramp. / Guns aren't lawful; / Nooses give; / Gas smells awful; / You might as well live." Although she wrote about melancholy topics, Parker's particular gift was in making them amusing without completely hiding the pain behind the snicker.

The Algonquin Round Table was a small group of writers in New York City who began meeting in the 1920s at the Algonquin Hotel to exchange witty repartee over lunch or drinks. The group soon caught the attention of journalists, who then covered the gatherings. The Round Table members included Robert E. Sherwood, George S. Kaufman, Robert Benchley, Alexander Woollcott, Franklin Pierce Adams, Harold Ross, and Parker. Parker's reputation for quick sarcasm and clever puns took on a life of its own as a result of the media attention, and there were instances of the other members' one-liners being credited to Parker. After a while, Parker felt burdened by her public personality as a wit. The Round Table disbanded in the 1930s, and looking back on that time, Parker regarded it as pretentious and superficial.

The outcomes of Parker's widespread attention and admiration may not have been all positive. The scholars most familiar with Parker's career note that the early responses to Parker's wit were amusement and mild disbelief. Although these responses were appropriate, Parker's early talent may have been a bit exaggerated, thus making it easy for her to make a living at writing without trying too hard. Some scholars believe that her talent ran much deeper than the light verse for which she is so well known, and had she been pushed to her literary limits, she may have produced more thoughtful, serious works. Late in her career, Parker suspected that the same limitations had befallen her career. She feared that her reputation as a quipster had prevented readers from taking her seriously as a writer.

To many, Parker's poetry represents the spirit of the 1920s and 1930s, when people were frantic and overly honest in social interactions as etiquette and decorum declined. Indeed, Parker herself was a product of a period in American history when women were becoming less concerned with being proper and more interested in expressing themselves. In many ways, Parker is considered a feminist because she disregarded societal expectations in favor of being herself—outspoken, worldly, sexual, and opinionated. The "voice" of her poetry is very much her own—world-weary and bemused.

Perhaps the greatest praise a poet can receive comes from other writers. The comic poet Ogden Nash once said, "The trick about her writing is the trick about Ring Lardner's writing or Ernest Hemingway's writing. It isn't a trick." The novelist Somerset Maugham commented, "Her humor bubbles up and overflows and if there is no one there to enjoy it, it makes no matter. She can no more help being amusing than a peach tree can help bearing peaches. . . . Perhaps what gives her writing its peculiar tang is her gift for seeing something to laugh at in the bitterest tragedies of the human animal."

JENNIFER A. BUSSEY

*See also* Light Verse

**Biography**

Born in West End, New Jersey, 22 August 1893. Played piano at a dancing school, New York, 1912–15; on editorial staff, *Vogue,* 1916–17; staff writer and drama critic, *Vanity Fair,* 1917–20; theater columnist, *Ainslee's,* 1920–33; book reviewer ("Constant Reader"), *New Yorker,* 1925–27; columnist, *McCall's,* late 1920s; book reviewer, *Esquire,* 1957–62; co-founder with Robert Benchley, Robert E. Sherwood, and others, Algonquin Hotel Round Table, 1920. Received O. Henry Award, 1929; Marjorie Peabody Waite Award, 1958. Died in New York City, 7 June 1967.

**Poetry**

*Enough Rope,* 1926
*Sunset Gun,* 1928
*Death and Taxes,* 1931

*Collected Poems: Not So Deep as a Well,* 1936; republished as, *Collected Poetry,* 1944
*The Collected Dorothy Parker* (includes prose), 1939; as, *The Portable Dorothy Parker,* 1976
*Dorothy Parker* (includes prose), 1944
*The Indispensable Dorothy Parker,* 1951
*The Best of Dorothy Parker,* 1952
*Dorothy Parker's Favorites,* 1992
*The Poetry and Short Stories of Dorothy Parker,* 1994
*Not Much Fun: The Lost Poems of Dorothy Parker,* 1996; as *The Uncollected Dorothy Parker,* 1996
*Complete Poems,* 1999

**Selected Criticism**
*Constant Reader,* 1970; as *A Month of Saturdays,* 1971

**Other Writings:** short stories (*Collected Stories,* 1942), plays (*The Ladies of the Corridor* [with Arnaud d'Usseau], produced 1953), screenplays (*A Star Is Born* [with others], 1937; *The Little Foxes* [with others], 1941); edited collections of literature (*The Portable F. Scott Fitzgerald,* 1945).

**Further Reading**

Cowley, Malcolm, editor, *Writers at Work: The "Paris Review" Interviews,* New York: Viking Press, and London: Secker and Warburg, 1958
Gaines, James R., *Wit's End: Days and Nights of the Algonquin Round Table,* New York and London: Harcourt Brace Jovanovich, 1977
Keats, John, *You Might as Well Live: The Life and Times of Dorothy Parker,* New York: Simon and Schuster, and London: Secker and Warburg, 1970
Kinney, Arthur F., *Dorothy Parker,* Boston: Twayne, 1978; as *Dorothy Parker, Revised,* New York: Twayne, and London: Prentice Hall International, 1988
Kronenberger, Louis, "The Rueful, Frostbitten Laughter of Dorothy Parker," *New York Times* (13 December 1936)
Loos, Anita, *A Girl Like I,* New York: Viking, 1966; London: Hamish Hamilton, 1967
Maugham, Somerset W., "Introduction," in *Dorothy Parker,* by Dorothy Parker, New York: Viking, 1944
Wilson, Edmund, "Dorothy Parker's Poems," *The New Republic* 49, no. 633 (1927)

# Kenneth Patchen 1911–72

World-weary already at age 25, Kenneth Patchen proclaimed sardonically in the first lines of the first poem, "'Let Us Have Madness Openly,'" in his first book, *Before the Brave* (1936),

Let us have madness openly, O men
Of my generation. Let us follow
The footsteps of this slaughtered age. . . .

In just 15 lines, the poem announced themes that Patchen stuck with to his death—the insane brutality of modern, industrial existence; his identification with both oppressed and irrepressible humanity; and love, in its deepest idealistic valor, as the light to guide us through the darkness, the light to reform evil, although the odds against it are long.

Kenneth Rexroth called Patchen "the laureate of the doomed youth of the Third World War." He was an important influence on the Beats. The beginning of Allen Ginsberg's 1955 "Howl"—"I saw the best minds of my generation destroyed by madness, starving hysterical naked"—uncannily echoed Patchen. However, whereas the end of "Howl" jauntily advertised the "supernatural extra brilliant intelligent kindness of the soul," an awareness hardly absent from Patchen's poetry, "Let Us Have Madness Openly" down-stopped on a pessimistic note, the possibility of redemption stripped bare, depleted:

We wanted more; we looked to find
An open door, an utter deed of love,
Transforming day's evil darkness;
 but
We found extended hell and fog
Upon the earth, and within the head
A rotting bog of lean huge graves.

Patchen's upbringing in the grim-faced steel-mill towns of eastern Ohio's Mahoning Valley bore heavily on his psyche. Rarely, however, did he make art out of autobiographical facts. The "I" in his poems is usually an amalgam of traits, representative of archetypes or fantasies. An exception to this, "The Orange Bears," from *Red Wine and Yellow Hair* (1949), in its condensation of loss and grief, is one of his best poems:

The orange bears with soft friendly eyes
Who played with me when I was ten,
Christ, before I left home they'd had
Their paws smashed in the rolls, their backs
Seared by hot slag, their soft trusting
Bellies kicked in, their tongues ripped
Out, and I went down through the woods
To the smelly crick with Whitman

In the Haldeman-Julius edition,
And I just sat there worrying my thumbnail
Into the cover—What did he know about
Orange bears with their coats all stunk up with soft coal
And the National Guard coming over
From Wheeling to stand in front of the millgates
With drawn bayonets jeering at the strikers?

I remember you could put daisies
On the windowsill at night and in
The morning they'd be so covered with soot
You couldn't tell what they were anymore.

A hell of a fat chance my orange bears had!

Key elements of Patchen's versification are evident here—driving narrative, felicitous use of slang, keen elocution, gallows humor, insertion of the rhetorical question, and a heavily enjambed open verse that obscured the divide between poetry and prose. Except when writing in street talk, he did not eschew the traditional rhythms of English prosody. Rebel poet that he was, there was nonetheless something refreshingly old-fashioned and reassuring about his voice, not only on the page but in person as well. His dolorous baritone can be heard on the priceless recordings with jazz musicians he made in the late 1950s; there is no better execution of the melding of poetry with jazz from the era that pioneered it.

Patchen wrote, "The meaning is in the wonder." He was the 20th century's most unabashed poet of the utterance "O":

O give us time to guard the winnings
From the winners.
("Thus Far So Nobly Advanced")

O love, it is so little we know of pleasure
Pleasure that lasts as the snow
("The Sea is Awash with Roses")

Oh lonesome's a bad place
To get crowded into
("Lonesome Boy Blues")

Of Patchen's many talents, his mastery of the apothegmatic set him apart from his contemporaries:

Let us continue to waste our lives
Declaring beauty to the world.
("O My Dearest")

Drugging and rouging the Angel, making him kiss any and
every serpent's ass for pay—and there you have the art
of our day.
("'Gentle and Giving' and Other Sayings")

Before the girl picking field daisies
Becomes the girl picking field daisies

There is a moment of some complexity
("The Moment")

Patchen's achievement with the epigram climaxed with his celebrated poem-paintings of the 1960s. Ironically, the joyful sense of awe in much of this work belies the conditions under which he made it. Medical error during a routine operation exacerbated a bad back and confined him to the bedroom of his house in Palo Alto, California. More often than not, intense pain made it impossible for him to work. In the precious time when he felt up to it, he wrote almost nothing but aphorisms, painting them in his distinctive calligraphy, in and among fairy-tale-like animals with human personalities, "a hierarchy of outcasts who endure despite the lack of physical and mental equipment to triumph," as James Schevill (1977) characterized them. In his brilliant exploration of the interface between visual art and poetry, he resembled his hero, William Blake.

Patchen dedicated each of his books to his wife, Miriam. He told her, "I wouldn't have written if we hadn't been together" (Smith, 1991). Their devotion to each other was astounding. The woman as muse—he found her and did not let go, leaving us his most popular legacy, the love poems:

Do I not deal with angels
When her lips I touch?

So gentle, so warm and sweet—falsity
Has no sight of her
O the world is a place of veils and roses
When she is there

I am come to her wonder
Like a boy finding a star in a haymow
And there is nothing cruel or mad or evil
Anywhere
("For Miriam")

With Patchen, there was no separation of the text from the person who authored it. It is necessary to confront his uncompromising beliefs head-on if one is to be moved by his words.

MARK MELNICOVE

**Biography**
Born in Niles, Ohio, 13 December 1911. Attended Experimental College, University of Wisconsin, Madison, 1929–30; Commonwealth College, Mena, Arkansas, 1930; farm worker, gardener, and janitor, across United States and Canada, 1930–33; freelance writer, from 1934; member of staff, New Directions, publishers, Norfolk, Connecticut, 1939–40; artist, individual show of books, graphics, and paintings, Corcoran Gallery, Washington, D.C., 1969. Received Guggenheim fellowship, 1936; Shelley Memorial Award, 1954; National Endowment for the Arts grant, 1967. Died in Palo Alto, California, 8 January 1972.

**Poetry**
*Before the Brave,* 1936
*First Will and Testament,* 1939
*The Teeth of the Lion,* 1942
*The Dark Kingdom,* 1942
*Cloth of the Tempest,* 1943
*An Astonished Eye Looks Out of the Air, Being Some Poems Old and New Against War and in Behalf of Life,* 1945
*Outlaw of the Lowest Planet,* edited by David Gascoyne, 1946
*Selected Poems,* 1946; revised editions, 1958, 1964
*Pictures of Life and Death,* 1947
*They Keep Riding Down All the Time,* 1947
*Panels for the Walls of Heaven,* 1947

*A Letter to God* (with *Patchen: Man of Anger and Light,* by Henry Miller), 1947
*CCCLXXIV Poems,* 1948
*To Say If You Love Someone, and Other Selected Love Poems,* 1948
*Red Wine and Yellow Hair,* 1949
*Poems of Humor and Protest,* 1949
*Fables, and Other Little Tales,* 1953
*The Famous Boating Party, and Other Poems in Prose,* 1954
*Orchards, Thrones, and Caravans,* 1955
*Glory Never Guesses,* 1956
*A Surprise for the Bagpipe Player,* 1956
*When We Were Here Together,* 1957
*Hurrah for Anything: Poems and Drawings,* 1957
*Two Poems for Christmas,* 1958
*Poem-scapes,* 1958
*Pomes Penyeach,* 1959
*Because It Is: Poems and Drawings,* 1960
*A Poem for Christmas,* 1960
*Love Poems,* 1960
*Patchen Drawing-Poem,* 1962
*Picture-Poems,* 1962
*Doubleheader,* 1966
*Hallelujah Anyway,* 1966
*Where Are the Other Rowboats?* 1966
*But Even So,* 1968
*Love and War Poems,* edited by Dennis Gould, 1968
*Selected Poems,* 1968
*The Collected Poems,* 1968
*Aflame and Afun of Walking Faces: Fables and Drawings,* 1970
*There's Love All Day,* edited by Dee Danner Barwick, 1970
*Wonderings,* 1971
*In Quest of Candlelighters,* 1972
*Still Another Pelican in the Breadbox,* edited by Richard G. Morgan, 1980
*Awash with Roses: The Collected Love Poems of Kenneth Patchen,* 1991
*Warmth in the Human Winter: Selected Love and Picturepoems,* 1991
*At the New Year: A Poem,* 1998

**Other Writings:** plays (*Lost Plays,* edited by Richard G. Morgan, 1977), radio play, fiction (*The Journal of Albion Moonlight,* 1941; *Memoirs of a Shy Pornographer,* 1945; *Sleepers Awake,* 1946; *See You in the Morning,* 1948), picture poetry (*What Shall We Do Without Us? The Voice and Vision of Kenneth Patchen,* 1984).

**Further Reading**

Laughlin, James, "Remembering Kenneth Patchen," in *What Shall We Do Without Us? The Voice and Vision of Kenneth Patchen,* by Kenneth Patchen, San Francisco: Sierra Club Books, 1984
Morgan, Richard G., *Kenneth Patchen: An Annotated, Descriptive Bibliography with Cross-Referenced Index,* Mamaroneck, New York: Appel, 1978
Morgan, Richard G., editor, *Kenneth Patchen: A Collection of Essays,* New York: AMS Press, 1977
Mullane, William, editor, *Kenneth Patchen: An Exhibition,* Warren, Ohio: Trumbull Art Gallery and Pig Iron Press, 1989
Rexroth, Kenneth, "Kenneth Patchen: Naturalist of the Public Nightmare," in *Bird in the Bush: Obvious Essays,* by Rexroth, New York: New Directions, 1959
Schevill, James, "The Search for Wonder and Joy," in *Tribute to Kenneth Patchen,* edited by Alan Clodd, London: Enitharmon, 1977
Smith, Larry, "Kenneth and Miriam: When the Wreath Touches the Heart," in *Awash with Roses: The Collected Love Poems of Kenneth Patchen,* by Kenneth Patchen, edited by Larry Smith and Laura Smith, Huron, Ohio: Bottom Dog Press, 1991
Smith, Larry, *Kenneth Patchen: Rebel Poet in America,* Huron, Ohio: Bottom Dog Press, 2000
Veres, Peter, editor, *The Argument of Innocence: A Selection from the Arts of Kenneth Patchen,* Oakland, California: Scrimshaw Press, 1976
Williams, Jonathan, "How Fables Tapped Along the Sunken Corridors," in *Aflame and Afun of Walking Faces: Fables and Drawings,* by Kenneth Patchen, New York: New Directions, 1970

---

# Bob Perelman 1947–

Since the early 1970s, Bob Perelman has attempted to forge a unique, formally experimental poetics. In advancing his theories regarding the avant-garde, Perelman has relied on both poetry and criticism, and it is this mixture of the two, along with his use of satire, that has led some to see him as a latter-day American Alexander Pope. Central to Perelman's mission has been a questioning of the vitality of mainstream American poetry. Perelman is one of the "Language poets" (a group that includes Ron Silliman, Lyn Hejinian, and Rae Armantrout), authors whose interest in the manipulation and foregrounding of language can be traced back through the New York poets (most notably John Ashbery) to Gertrude Stein. In the 1970s, Perelman and other Language poets published magazines and organized conferences, attempting to explore the dimensions of linguistic experimentation. Perelman's own magazine, *Hills,* was published between 1973 and 1980. He was also responsible for organizing numerous formal and informal poetry discussions.

Poems in both *Braille* (1975) and *7 Works* (1978), Perelman's earliest collections, exhibit his early treatment of oedipal concerns, with fathers configured as powerful and dominant and mothers imbued with sensual energy. Oedipal desires are examined in "An Autobiography," a poem that refers not to Perelman's life but to an unfinished Stendhal work:

> My mother was a charming woman and I was in love with her. One night, when by chance I had been put to sleep on the floor of her room on a mattress, this woman, agile as a deer, bounded over my mattress to reach her bed more quickly.
>
> I wanted to cover my mother with kisses, and for her to have no clothes on.
>
> . . . .
>
> I abhorred my father. He brought with him memories of how it feels to be intensely, fiercely hungry. He came and interrupted our kisses.

Perelman's treatment of psychological themes may not, at first glance, seem very experimental, but his early poems were infused with mimicry and collage, leading to an almost kaleidoscopic effect, paving the way for later, more radical forms of experimentation.

After the publication of *a.k.a.* (1979), a work that crumbled the boundaries between prose and poetry, Perelman returned to his poetic roots with *Primer* (1981), a work that evidenced a movement toward foregrounding linguistic concerns. In "Room," Perelman examines the power of language to name:

> The words mention themselves.
> They are literally true.
> Every minute another circle
> Meets them halfway.
>
> The locker locks
> From the inside. I
> is an extensive pun
> Born of this confinement.

The poem continues by extending the power of language to the named: "These objects have the right to remain silent." Perelman thus muddies the distinctions between subject and object. However, this does not presuppose that meaning is just a matter of making new connections. As Robert Glück (1983) mentions in regard to *Primer,* "Although the poems are made up of images, they are not charged with symbolism and they don't generate the force fields of the surreal. These images reject those stakes, that inevitability. They are diffused; meaning becomes a block to move around like the furniture of rhetoric."

Perelman's next three projects—*To the Reader* (1984), *The First World* (1986), and *Face Value* (1988)—represented movement to another linguistic style. In *To the Reader,* Perelman began to move away from distinctive stanzas and to embrace verse-paragraphs, a style he would employ with greater confidence in each succeeding work. *The First World* contains some of Perelman's most noteworthy poems, including "Person" and "Oedipus Rex." As the latter poem uncovers, *The First World* contained an inherent critique of the avant-garde tradition to which Perelman belonged. He had often turned his critical eye on the mainstream, but "Oedipus Rex" represented an interrogation of the Language poet: "I never meant to soliloquize, but since the government's gotten so big and secret, any jerk with an open mouth turns out to be in the center of an infinitely expanding universe of gloom and doom." This critique was further developed in another poem, "The Art Machine":

> The art machine hits the beach running hard.
> But the beach, let's take a breath and think
> about the fact of the beach. Metal treads
> vs. linguistic mucus, oceanic repetition vs.
> one-time bodies, let's really get a two-step going here
> structuralism dressing the baby in pink or blue.

Perelman's next volume, *Face Value,* continued to use linguistic fragmentation to question reality. Slowly, however, Perelman was beginning to move beyond simply trying to "defamiliarize" by forcing disjunction and rupture in meaning. It would become clear in his following works—including *Captive Audience* (1988), *Virtual Reality* (1993), and *Fake Dreams* (1996)—that Perelman was now engaged in a project of "deconcealment," an attempt to foreground not only the linguistic dimensions of a text but also the social underpinnings that art forms outside avant-garde poetics often ignore. This distinction is further developed in Perelman's seminal critical work *The Marginalization of Poetry: Language Writing and Literary History* (1996). However, it is perhaps Perelman's most recent work of poetry, *The Future of Memory* (1998), that brings together all the themes that have led to his current position regarding language. In "Fake Dreams: The Library," two people walk into the men's room of a library, looking to have sex:

> You pointed
> to the magic marker graffiti on
> the beige tiles: 'This place needs
> a woman's touch' answered by 'FINGER
> MY ASSHOLE, CUNT!' This second message
> had been modified by an arrow
> indicating 'CUNT' was to be moved
> from behind to before 'ASSHOLE': 'FINGER
> MY CUNT, ASSHOLE!' We were eager
> to prove syntax was not mere
> vanity and that bodies could use
> it to resist the tyranny of
> elemental words. And wouldn't it be
> nice to get knowledge and pleasure
> on the same page.

This poem in some ways marks the culmination of many of Perelman's developing themes: the manipulation of words to decenter meaning, the power of language to undermine authority, and language as the site of raw but often humorous sexuality.

Andrew Howe

*See also* Language Poetry

**Biography**

Born in Youngstown, Ohio, 2 December 1947. Attended the University of Michigan, Ann Arbor, B.A. in classics 1969, M.A. in Greek and Latin 1970; University of Iowa, Iowa City, M.F.A. in creative writing 1970; University of California, Berkeley, Ph.D. 1990; since 1990 Assistant Professor, University of

Pennsylvania, Philadelphia; editor, *Hills* magazine, 1973–80. Living in Philadelphia, Pennsylvania.

**Poetry**

*Braille*, 1975
*7 Works*, 1978
*a.k.a.*, 1979; enlarged edition, 1984
*Primer*, 1981
*To the Reader*, 1984
*The First World*, 1986
*Face Value*, 1988
*Captive Audience*, 1988
*Two Poems*, 1992
*Virtual Reality*, 1993
*Chaim Soutine*, 1994
*Fake Dreams*, 1996
*The Masque of Rhyme*, 1997
*The Future of Memory*, 1998
*Ten to One: Selected Poems*, 1999

**Selected Criticism**

*The Trouble with Genius: Reading Pound, Joyce, Stein, and Zukofsky*, 1994
*The Marginalization of Poetry: Language Writing and Literary History*, 1996

**Other Writing:** play; edited collection of essays and lectures (*Writing/Talks*, 1985).

**Further Reading**

Armantrout, Rae, "Bob Perelman," in *The L=A=N=G=U=A=G=E Book*, edited by Bruce Andrews and Charles Bernstein, Carbondale: Southern Illinois University Press, 1984
Burnham, Clint, and Deeana Ferguson, "Interview with Bob Perelman," *Boo* 6 (1996)
Glück, Robert, "Bob Perelman," in *Langton Street Residence Program 1982*, edited by Renny Pritikin and Barrett Watten, San Francisco: 80 Langton Street, 1983
Hartley, George, "Jameson's Perelman: Reification and the Material Signifier," in *Textual Politics and the Language Poets*, by Hartley, Bloomington: Indiana University Press, 1989
Jameson, Frederic, "Postmodernism, or the Cultural Logic of Late Capitalism," *New Left Review* 146 (1984)
Monroe, Jonathan, "Poetry, Community, Movement: A Conversation," *Diacritics* 26 (Fall/Winter 1996)
Myles, Eileen, "Perpetual Motion: What Makes Bob Perelman Run?" *Voice Literary Supplement* (November 1993)
Pearson, Ted, "Bob Perelman, '7 Works,'" in *The L=A=N=G=U=A=G=E Book*, edited by Bruce Andrews and Charles Bernstein, Carbondale: Southern Illinois University Press, 1984
Silliman, Ron, "The New Sentences," *Hills* 6/7 (1980)
Silliman, Ron, et al., "Readings and Responses to 'The Marginalization of Poetry,' with a Counter-Response by Bob Perelman," *The Impercipient Lecture Series* 4 (1997)

---

# Performance Poetry

Interpreted broadly, the category of performance poetry might include any poem that is read, sung, recited, acted, or otherwise performed before an audience. In recent decades, however, the term "performance poetry" has emerged to indicate a more specific body of work: poems designed expressly for live performance, often in collaborative or multimedia contexts that incorporate music, dance, or the visual arts. In the United States, performance poetry usually refers to jazz, rap, and hip-hop poetry and to the popular open-mike readings and slam competitions of the Spoken Word movement of the 1990s, although it also includes the more abstract sound-based experiments of the avant-garde. In all these instances, the poem as performance moves decisively off the printed page and into public settings, reclaiming a social space for poetry and expanding its audience.

Performance poetry as a pop-culture phenomenon is a rapidly evolving movement that defies easy definition. To make some general observations: the performance poem is a public, "live event" that emphasizes the oral aspect of poetic composition and reception. Process matters more than product, and the written text is not an aesthetic object or experience but a "score" for the voice in performance. No two performances are the same, and the poems often involve improvisation—out-loud poetic composition as the work unfolds in a public space. Crucial to the performance poem are its extra-literary dimensions—its public setting; the poet-performer's sociocultural background and his or her physical being, voice, and presence on stage; and the audience's experience of sharing a space with a voice that has opened itself up to the risk of contingency. A defining feature of the performance poem is its reliance on interaction with the audience. Instead of developing a purely subjective poetic state, the performance poem is intersubjective, succeeding or foundering on the basis of the quality of feedback and participation it can solicit. The successful performance poet is alert to the audience's expectations and limits, and responds to them during the performance. A performance poem is judged not by its formal characteristics but by its effects on the audience members. The emphasis, then, is on the performance poem's social function—on what a poem can *do* rather than what it *means*.

American performance poetry of the 20th century has developed in two main strands: a genuinely popular, grassroots movement deeply influenced by jazz, rap, and hip-hop and emerging in urban community centers (e.g., the Green Mill Tavern in Chicago and the Nuyorican Poets Café on Manhattan's lower east side) and an avant-garde, sound-based poetry emerging from Modernist and European experimentation with form (e.g., Dada, Surrealism, and Futurism). In recent years, the populist strand of performance poetry has taken the form of the "Spoken Word"—the exuberant poetry readings, slams, and open mikes emerging in such diverse locations as bookstores, cafés, churches, festivals, and community centers. Performance poetry has also thrived on radio, telephones, televisions, feature films, and the Internet and in well-attended annual events (e.g., the traveling National Poetry Slam; the Taos Poetry Circus in New Mexico; the Cowboy Poetry Gathering in Elko, Nevada; and the biennial Dodge Poetry Festival in Waterloo, New Jersey). The ability of the Spoken Word movement to develop these new audiences testifies to the vitality of American poetry's democratic appeal and to its public, social, popular, and political life.

Spoken Word poetry may well be the "people's poetry movement" of the late 20th century since its popular success is often linked to its association with contemporary identity politics. The current wave of Spoken Word poets are largely minority artists, and their poetic "voices" speak of specific cultural identities, whether connected with race, ethnicity, gender, or sexuality. Quite often, the poetic speaker is nearly indistinguishable from the performing poet's body on stage, as the poet stands up before the audience to embody a local (and often bilingual) identity and to defend it against immense pressures to assimilate. Although Spoken Word artists are fundamentally entertainers, they also seek to build and foster communities of the disenfranchised. Much of the poetry is heavily stressed, metrically regular, and marked by extensive use of rhyme, alliteration, and assonance. Relying on quotidian language to speak of everyday life and often speaking in local idioms, dialects, or vernaculars (e.g., Lois-Ann Yamanaka's Hawaiian island pidgin poetry), the language of the class or cultural group to which the performance poet belongs becomes a political issue. Making theater out of social conflict and emphasizing the poem's status as speech act, the Spoken Word challenges our notions of what counts as "literary."

Emerging alongside this popular interest in an oral poetry is a quite different strand of avant-garde poetic performance that emphasizes the poem's sound instead of its voice and its text-based aurality instead of the poet's body on stage. Whereas Spoken Word testifies to a popular demand for a return to "voice" and "presence" as fundamental principles of lyric poetry, language-oriented performance poetry deflects the audience's attention away from personal identification with the poet-performer's personality and toward the complexly sounded material text. Although sound-based poetry might be described as "investigative" rather than community building, it shares with Spoken Word poetry a desire to disrupt the transparency of public language and rescue it from its commodification in mass advertising. These lines of influence, however, cross and recross: Nathaniel Mackey's recording *Strick* mixes the popular realms of jazz and world music with Modernist disjunctions, while Spoken Word artist Tracie Morris takes her hip-hop artistry into the realm of experimental sound poetry.

Compared with the printed poem's assurance of posterity and permanence, the performance poem is sustained only in the collective memory of the audience. Although attempts have been made to preserve the transitory aspects of performance on tapes, CDs, and videos (e.g., Bob Holman's multimedia series *The United States of Poetry*), such efforts usually fail to capture the full range of factors impinging on a given performance. For this reason, literary histories often pass over poetry performances as ephemera, regarding them as perishable events—important only for the moment—rather than as lasting contributions to the culture. Working with cultural studies methods, literary historians and ethnographers are only now beginning to develop a critical vocabulary attentive to poetry performances as cultural practices and to the extraliterary effects of performances on the communities in which they are performed.

The resurgence of interest in performance poetry at the end of the 20th century can be linked to several trends in late-20th-century cultural production, including the democratizing of higher education in the 1960s, the renewed importance of urban centers as a source of popular culture, the widespread influence of electronic media, the increasing availability of visual and acoustic technologies, and the prominent role of identity politics in the public sphere. This much-celebrated resurgence appears remarkable, however, only if viewed against the New Critical tradition of page-bound lyricism, which valued poetry's status as the private discourse of a solitary lyric subject. It is important to remember that the New Critical emphasis on the poem as a highly crafted artifact requiring specialized training to appreciate was itself a relatively new development and was in fact preceded by a long history of "verse speaking" and public poetry reading in the United States.

Early antecedents of contemporary American performance poetry include the "poet-performer movement" of 1870–1930 (Vachel Lindsay and others); the late-19th-century elocutionist movement, imported from Britain, which involved the memorization and public recitation of popular poetry; and Paul Laurence Dunbar's recitals of his dialect-based poems. Influenced by Dunbar, Langston Hughes composed poems that re-created the rhythms of African-American music—particularly blues and jazz—which he later recorded to the jazz accompaniment of Fats Waller and Charles Mingus. In Europe, the Futurists, Dadaists, and other Modernists developed a new field of performance art, an important precursor of avant-garde sound poetry. Although performative poets such as E.E. Cummings and Edna St. Vincent Millay helped keep the oral aspect of American poetry alive, and Dylan Thomas popularized the poetry reading with the thrilling intensity of his 1950s reading tour, poetry performance continued to diminish in importance until after World War II, when an emphasis on poetry's oral roots re-emerged in counterculture poetry.

The staccato breath units of Charles Olson's essay "Projective Verse" (the manifesto of the "New American Poetry") inaugurated the 1950s as the decade of poetry that would be heightened in its sensitivity to the patterns of speech. Just as Olson suggested open form as a kind of excited talk, Allen Ginsberg summed up the fundamentally oral nature of Beat poetics by declaring that "the only poetic tradition is the Voice out of the burning bush." San Francisco poet Bob Kaufman took this ecstatic, automatic Beat poetics to its limit, improvising his own poems on city streets and in cafés. In the early 1960s, Beat-inspired poet Ed Sanders formed the New York City folk-rock band the Fugs; he resurrected the group in 1984 to protest a growing conservatism in American culture. In the early 1970s, Beat poetics and the burgeoning women's liberation movement propelled Anne Sexton to perform with musical backup as the group "Anne Sexton and Her Kind," a precursor to such Spoken Word "divas" as Maggie Estep, who has been called the "MTV Poet Laureate."

The development of performance poetry has been inextricably linked to popular music, particularly the model of African-American music. The jazz aesthetic was a driving force in the emergence of the Beat poets' "spontaneous bop prosody" and Olson's breath-based line. In the late 1950s and early 1960s, Kenneth Rexroth recorded poems live at the Cellar, San Francisco's foremost jazz club; Frank O'Hara wrote poems based on his experiences at New York's Five Spot club; Kenneth Patchen collaborated with Allyn Ferguson's jazz sextet; and Jack Spicer performed with a trio led by Ron Crotty on bass. In 1960, Charles Mingus recorded *A Modern Symposium of Poetry and Music,* a multimedia performance conceived in collaboration with Langston Hughes. Amiri Baraka is our best-known contemporary "jazz poet." His book *Wise, Why's, Y's* (1995) is especially performative, opening with a long, untranscribed improvisation, and with each poem dedicated to a jazz musician. Notable precedents for Spoken Word poetry include the Last Poets' 1970 debut album, with its popular lyric "Niggas Are Scared of Revolution," which reached the Top 10 album charts, and Gil Scott-Heron's popular poem "The Revolution Will Not Be Televised" (1970). While poets such as Jayne Cortez and Quincy Troupe continue the jazz poetry tradition, younger artists, such as Michael Franti (lead vocalist for Disposable Heroes of Hiphoprisy and other bands), Everton Sylvester, and Tracie Morris, have created new poetic forms born, respectively, of rap, reggae patois, and hip-hop.

Combining political urgency with aesthetic pleasure, performance poets have extended the innovations of the Beat, Black Arts, and feminist poetry movements into our time, choosing to serve as community activists, historians, teachers, and agitators. It was the Black Arts movement of the late 1960s that took poetry most deliberately off the page, with such poets as Amiri Baraka, Larry Neal, and Sonia Sanchez literally "taking it to the streets." Poetry also played a central role in the feminist movement, where Adrienne Rich's readings of *Twenty-One Love Poems* and Judy Grahn's readings of *Death of a Common Woman* galvanized feminist and lesbian communities into political action.

The development of a "postliterate" performance poetry was further nurtured by the ethnopoetics movement of the 1970s, which sought to recover oral, "preliterate" poetries from around the world. Like the Beats, the early practitioners of ethnopoetics (including Jerome Rothenberg, Dennis Tedlock, Gary Snyder, and Ed Roberson) viewed the poet as a visionary and shaman, and like the Modernist avant-garde, they valued primitive poetry—tribal songs and ceremonial chants—preferring social and ritualistic language over language that carefully crafted a unique sensibility. Two early participants in the ethnopoetics movement were also innovators in avant-garde poetry: Armand Schwerner's *The Tablets* parodied ethnopoetics strategies using Modernist collage techniques, whereas David Antin used collage techniques to develop poems that could appear indistinguishable from rapid, improvisational "talking." Poets in the Fluxus art movement of the 1960s developed procedural or random compositional methods, including such chance-generated texts as Jackson Mac Low's "Simultaneities." In contrast to populist performances, which rely on the singular voice of the poet-performer, these anti-expressivist, anti-theatrical experiments seek to establish an "authorless" language.

A striking example of the rapidly proliferating venues for contemporary performance poetry is the Nuyorican Poets Café in Loisaida ("Spanglish" for "lower east side"), which has offered "real live poetry" since 1974. A catalyst for the Spoken Word movement, the Café in its initial incarnation (1974–82) served as a base for writers of Puerto Rican heritage living in New York. Reopened in 1989 by Miguel Algarín and Bob Holman, the Café attracted a deliberately multi-ethnic, working-class poetic community as well as the attention of the national media. Its major achievement was the reclaiming of an oral, activist, and communal tradition for poetry, as Algarín suggests in his introduction to *ALOUD: Voices from the Nuyorican Poets Café* (1994): "I knew I had to put the poem into action, and I knew that the whole of the community would have to help me lift the poem off the page."

The Café's popularity beyond the local community is due in large part to its Wednesday and Friday night slams, started by Bob Holman, who was inspired by the poetry slams that Marc Smith had organized at Chicago's Green Mill Tavern as early as 1987. The slam scene, which quickly spread to Boston and San Francisco and beyond, now has a national Grand Slam, an anthology (*Poetry Nation*), and an award-winning documentary (*SlamNation*). The slam courts vulgarity, rage, naked emotionalism, and irony ("The best poet / always loses," explains Holman), even as it is rooted in ancient traditions of linked rhyming and poetry competition, from tenth-century Japanese court poetry to African-American "dozens." Judged by audience members who use an Olympics-style, numbers-based rating system, the mock-competitive venue is a training ground for performance poets: slammers learn how to handle hecklers, how to use a mike, and how to read an audience's reaction to a poem. No genre plays better than another in the Nuyorican slam: poems range from social protest (Martín Espada's history-saturated lyrics) to stand-up comedy (Hal Sirowitz's deadpan delivery of Jewish American humor) to approximations of jazz scat (Julie Patton's idiosyncratic melodies). Among the better-known performers to emerge from the Nuyorican are two young African-American poets: Reg E. Gaines, who wrote the libretto for the commercially successful Broadway musical *Bring in da Noise, Bring in da Funk,* and Paul Beatty, whose first book, *Big Bank Take Little Bank,* was published by the Nuyorican Poets Café Press and sold out its initial printing of 1,000 copies in five months.

Poetry slams have brought to prominence several performance poets who continue to define the medium beyond the circus-like slam environment. Like much Spoken Word poetry, Regie Cabico's raucously funny meditations on life as a young gay Filipino comment on the shifting and hyphenated identities of the post-modern condition. His poem "Check One" begins with a formal and bureaucratic attempt to bribe the respondent into declaring a single identity or affiliation: "*The government asks me to 'check one' if I want money. / I just laugh in their face and say, / 'How can you ask me to be one race?'*" Refusing to fit into "one square box" or to "sing one song," the speaker at first declares, "I stand proudly before you a fierce Filipino." He then complicates and hybridizes that identity, claiming affinities with black, working-poor, gay, and aboriginal communities. Crucial to Cabico's poetics is the wry theatricality of his relationship with the audience. His statement "I stand proudly before you" is part naked emotionalism but also part campy theatricality that subverts any notion of a deep, abiding, or essential self. Cabico's perpetual transformations—his one-man "RegieSpective" traces the life of a young gay Filipino man from his strict Catholic upbringing to his incarnation of M. Butterfly—belie any simplistic notion of the connection between Spoken Word and a naive identity politics.

A Grand Slam winner and the "reigning queen of hip-hop poetry," Tracie Morris writes poems that often "represent" and affirm a particular group. Her popular performance poem "Project Princess," for example, is a feminist ode to the young black women who live in the Brooklyn housing projects where Morris herself grew up. The poem is delivered in a form inspired by the sophisticated play of assonance and consonance in hip-hop: "She's the one. Give her some. Under fire. / Smoking gun. Of which songs are sung, / raps are spun, bells are rung." The hyperperformative aspect of "Project Princess"—the poem's relentless rhymes, unrepentant clichés, and vivid vernacular—is suggested by the outrageousness of the "project princess'" wardrobe—her "multidimensional shrimp earrings," "clinking rings," and "dragon fingers." The power of these performances, both that of the poem and that of the princess, lies in their uncontrollable excess and in the pure pleasure of theatricality as it refuses to constrain itself to fit the demands of mainstream culture. Morris' more recent "sonic improvisations" blur the boundary between verbal and nonverbal expression as she breaks, riffs, scats, rushes, bops, and glides her way through a brief "found" text—for example, Sam Cooke's song lyric "That's the sound of the man working on the chain gang." In a prolonged and visceral "working" of the line, Morris then allows the fragmented syllables to rearticulate themselves, improvisationally, as ecstatic, multivocal, and healing utterances.

The vocal improvisations of bilingual poet-performer Edwin Torres likewise bridge the realms of Spoken Word and sound poetry. Introduced to poetry through the Nuyorican Poets Café and St. Mark's Poetry Project but finding affinities with Futurism, surrealism, and concrete poetry, Torres composes a "NuyoFuturist" poetry with the phoneme as its basic unit. He often begins a performance with a sequence of nonsensical sounds that gradually form into recognizable words: "*chilleeee-moholeeee-eddieeee-yahhhhh-GO! GO! GO! / Gusting, weeping, sorrow, sweeping, boyeeee-gooooo-YAH! YAH! YAH!*" To indicate pitch, volume, and stress, Torres turns to the radically eccentric typography of visual, or concrete, poetry. In doing so, Torres plays with the conventions of identity-based poetry, sometimes in order to thwart them. "Poetry has a foreign ear," Torres explained in a lecture, "a foreign tongue to conversation, to speaking." Although the lexically dense and allusive quality of the poems on his debut CD, *Holy Kid* (1998), might seem to make his poetry less accessible and relevant to a mass audience, Torres has found popular success, appearing on MTV's "Spoken Word Unplugged" and in *Newsweek* and *Rolling Stone.*

Patricia Smith is a dynamic African-American poet, four-time winner of the National Grand Slam, and co-founder of the Boston Slam. A former columnist for the *Boston Globe,* Smith merges poetry and a controversial journalism to develop a poetics of reportage. She often turns to the dramatic monologue in order to bear witness to the marginalized lives of those persons who are seldom included within the "subjective" lyric poem or the "objective" news article. In a recent volume of poetry, *Close to Death* (1995), Smith mixes poems based on her personal knowledge of violence against black men with poems based on interviews she conducted with black men in Boston neighborhoods. Smith's role as performer mediates between her roles as journalist and poet: refusing the autobiographical confessionalism of the pure lyric, she also refuses the distancing stance of the objective reporter, allowing herself to be a medium for the voices of others. In one poem from this book, "Undertaker," Smith shifts from voice to voice, speaking as the mother of a young murdered black man, as the murdered boy, and as the undertaker preparing his body for burial: "But I have explored the jagged gaps / in the boy's body, smoothed the angry edges / of bulletholes. I have touched him in places / no mother knows, and I have birthed / his new face." In this poem, the undertaker's art approximates that of Smith as performance poet, whose intimacies and improvisations with her subjects' voices reinforce her sense of political urgency.

KATHLEEN CROWN

**Further Reading**


Adler, Bill, and Bob Holman, producers, *Grand Slam! Best of the National Poetry Slam* (compact disc), New York: Mouth Almighty Records, 1996

Algarín, Miguel, and Bob Holman, editors, *ALOUD: Voices from the Nuyorican Poets Café,* New York: Holt Books, 1994

Beach, Christopher, *Poetic Culture: Contemporary American Poetry between Community and Institution,* Evanston, Illinois: Northwestern University Press, 1999

Belmont, Bill, producer, and Ann Charters, compiler and annotator, *Howls, Raps, and Roars: Recordings from the San Francisco Poetry Renaissance* (4 compact discs), Berkeley, California: Fantasy Records, 1993 (recorded 1955–70)

Bernstein, Charles, editor, *Close Listening: Poetry and the Performed Word,* Oxford and New York: Oxford University Press, 1998

Blum, Joshua, Bob Holman, and Mark Pellington, compilers, *The United States of Poetry,* New York: Abrams, 1996

Bonair-Agard, Roger, et al., *Burning Down the House: Selected Poems from the Nuyorican Poets Café's National Poetry Slam Champions,* New York: Soft Skull Press, and London: Turnaround, 2000

Brown, Fahamisha Patricia, *Performing the Word: African-American Poetry as Vernacular Culture,* New Brunswick, New Jersey: Rutgers University Press, 1999

Cabico, Regie, and Todd Swift, editors, *Poetry Nation: A North American Anthology of Fusion Poetry,* Montreal, Quebec: Vehicule Press, 1998

Damon, Maria, "When the NuYoricans Came to Town: (Ex)Changing Poetics," *Xcp: Cross-Cultural Poetics* 1 (1997)

Devlin, Paul, director, *SlamNation* (video recording), New York: Cinema Guild, 1998 Feinstein, Sascha, and Yusef Komunyakaa, *The Jazz Poetry Anthology,* 2 vols., Bloomington: Indiana University Press, 1991–96

Glazner, Gary Mex, editor, *Poetry Slam: The Competitive Art of Performance Poetry,* San Francisco: Manic D Press, 2000

Kaufman, Alan, editor, *The Outlaw Bible of American Poetry,* New York: Thunder's Mouth Press, 1999; London: Turnaround, 2000

Morris, Adalaide, editor, *Sound States: Innovative Poetics and Acoustical Technologies,* Chapel Hill: University of North Carolina Press, 1997

# Marge Piercy 1936–

Through her prolific work as both a fiction writer and a poet, Marge Piercy has emerged as a leading creative voice of the late 20th century. She generally explores both the public and the private realm of human experience, illustrating how those spheres often intersect and influence each other. As she states in a 1972 essay with Dick Lourie, "The political is not alien but inherent." Her political concerns include feminism, as she frequently explores the position of women in society, while her personal poetry often concentrates on relationships with family members or lovers. Other recurrent themes include the place of the spiritual and the environment in an increasingly technological world as well as the act of writing itself.

Born on 31 March 1936, Piercy grew up in a household where the personal and political often merged. Her father was involved with unions, while her mother's father had been killed for his participation with labor movements. Her parents, particularly her mother, also helped develop in Piercy skills and ideas that would play a part in her writing. For example, in her essay "Inviting the Muse" (1992), Piercy credits her mother with teaching her "to observe." Elsewhere, she shares how her appreciation of nature comes largely from her mother ("Afterthoughts," 1982).

Piercy started writing when she was still a teenager. In an interview with Sue Walker and Eugenie Hamner (1991), Piercy says that her early influences included the British Romantics, Emily Dickinson, and Walt Whitman. In later interviews such as "Afterthoughts," she has mentioned Allen Ginsberg, Muriel Rukeyser, and T.S. Eliot as being just a few of the other numerous influences she has had. She obtained a degree from the University of Michigan in 1957 and then continued her education at Northwestern University, where she received her M.A. a year later.

In speaking of her first volume, *Breaking Camp* (1968), Piercy states: "Some of the poems are to me very clearly apprentice work; overly literary, overly experimental, overly artsy" (interview with Friedmann and Robson, 1982). Still, in this volume Piercy explores themes that will remain of interest in later poetic works: nature, writing, self, identity, and love. *Hard Loving* (1969) continues many of these themes and also illustrates a strong degree of physicality in poems such as "The Friend."

Her next volume, *4-Telling* (1971), contains Piercy's poems along with three other poets. This was soon followed by her 1973 *To Be of Use,* "a book of feminist consciousness" ("Afterthoughts"). Such social concern is articulated in such well-known poems as "A work of artifice" and "Unlearning to not speak." Piercy followed with *Living in the Open* (1976) and *The Twelve-Spoked Wheel Flashing* (1978), her "solar book" ("Afterthoughts"). Her "lunar book" came next in 1980 with *The Moon Is Always Female* ("Afterthoughts"). Here, Piercy explores relationships with others, including feminists. For example, in "Memo" she addresses several women poets, asserting, "This life is a war we are not yet / winning for our daughters' children. / Don't do your enemies' work for them. / Finish your own." She also details a "lunar cycle" and explores women's spirituality.

Piercy had written so much by the early 1980s that she was able to pull from her earlier collections as well as write new poems for *Circles on the Water: Selected Poems* (1982). *Stone, Paper, Knife* (1983) and *My Mother's Body* (1985) followed. *Available Light* (1988) marked her last collection of the decade, and it shows the continuity of Piercy's writing as she continued to explore themes of trapped women, the influence of the spiritual, and the place of the environment in original and insightful poems such as "Joy Road and Livernois," "I saw her dancing," and "Perfect weather."

In 1992, Piercy published *Mars and Her Children,* a collection that is organized around the colors of the rainbow and the image of the arc. One of her most striking poems, "Apple sauce for Eve," reenvisions this vilified figure, designating her as "the mother of invention." This representation of Eve illustrates Piercy's interest in highlighting women as strong beings, authorized by a spiritual background to know themselves and the world around them. *Eight Chambers of the Heart* (1995) followed and includes newly as well as previously published material. Her 1997 collection *What Are Big Girls Made of?* includes poems dedicated to Audre Lorde and works that focus on women's societal position. Her latest work, *Early Grrrl* (1999), includes pieces from her early volumes, giving readers a fresh chance to see her beginnings.

An overview of Piercy's poetry quickly reveals several important qualities. First, rather than rely on traditional poetic forms, Piercy consistently employs free verse, concrete images, and a personal tone. She explains further this use of the personal in her essay "Mirror Images" (1981): "I speak mostly in my own persona or in a voice that is a public form of it—the spokesperson role. Some poems come out of my own experiences and some poems come from the energy of others' experiences coming through me, but they are all fused in the layers of my mind to my voice." A second, striking feature is how consistently she has published her work, especially considering that she often writes poetry and prose simultaneously. Third, she does not isolate herself behind her poetic persona; rather, she actively connects with her audience by sharing her thoughts on her own writing as well as the work of other writers. This quality is illustrated most clearly by her numerous interviews and her well-designed website. Finally, she sees poetry as more than an artistic exercise; it has the potential to generate real change. As she explains in "Mirror Images," poetry can serve as a healing force, not only for individuals but also for communities "because it can fuse for the moment all the kinds of knowing in its saying." As Ronald Nelson (1991) has discussed, her work seems to have this idea of healing as an underlying theme. Her personal poems are more concerned with self-understanding than self-indulgence, and her political poems, too, while often containing strong critiques of society, appear as a means of encouraging dialogue. Through poetry, then, we may be able to push through self and societal limitations to effect cultural change. Piercy not only sees this challenge to heal for herself but also reminds individual readers of their position, as her last poem from *What Are Big Girls Made of?,* "The art of blessing the day," illustrates: "Bless whatever you can / with eyes and hands and tongue. If you / can't bless it, get ready to make it new."

KELLY L. RICHARDSON

**Biography**

Born in Detroit, Michigan, 31 March 1936. Attended the University of Michigan, Ann Arbor (Hopwood Award, 1956, 1957), A.B. 1957; Northwestern University, Evanston, Illinois, M.A. 1958; Instructor, Indiana University, Gary, 1960–62; poet-in-residence, University of Kansas, Lawrence, 1971; Visiting Lecturer, Thomas Jefferson College, Grand Valley State

Colleges, Allendale, Michigan, 1975; visiting faculty member, Women's Writers Conference, Cazenovia College, New York, 1976, 1978, 1980; staff member, Fine Arts Work Center, Provincetown, Massachusetts, 1976–77; writer-in-residence, College of the Holy Cross, Worcester, Massachusetts, 1976; Butler Chair of Letters, State University of New York, Buffalo, 1977; Elliston Poet-in-Residence, University of Cincinnati, 1986; member of the board of directors, 1982–85, and of the advisory board since 1985, Coordinating Council of Literary Magazines. Received Borestone Mountain Award, 1968, 1974; National Endowment for the Arts grant, 1978; Rhode Island School of Design Faculty Association Medal, 1985; Carolyn Kizer Prize, 1986, 1990; Sheaffer-PEN New England Award, 1989; Golden Rose poetry Prize, 1990; May Sarton Award, 1991. Living in Wellfleet, Massachusetts.

**Poetry**

*Breaking Camp,* 1968
*Hard Loving,* 1969
*4-Telling* (with others), 1971
*To Be of Use,* 1973
*Living in the Open,* 1976
*The Twelve-Spoked Wheel Flashing,* 1978
*The Moon Is Always Female,* 1980
*Circles on the Water: Selected Poems,* 1982
*Stone, Paper, Knife,* 1983
*My Mother's Body,* 1985
*Available Light,* 1988
*The Earth Shines Secretly: A Book of Days* (with Nell Blaine), 1990
*Mars and Her Children,* 1992
*Eight Chambers of the Heart,* 1995
*What Are Big Girls Made of?* 1997
*Written in Bone: The Early Poems of Marge Piercy,* 1998
*The Art of Blessing the Day: Poems with a Jewish Theme,* 1999
*Early Grrrl: The Early Poems of Marge Piercy,* 1999

**Selected Criticism**

*Parti-Colored Blocks for a Quilt,* 1982

**Other Writings:** play, novels (*Three Women,* 1999), nonfiction; edited collections of poetry (*Early Ripening: American Women's Poetry,* 1987).

**Further Reading**

"Afterthoughts: A Conversation between Ira Wood and Marge Piercy," in *Parti-Colored Blocks for a Quilt,* by Marge Piercy, Ann Arbor: University of Michigan Press, 1982
Contoski, Victor, "Marge Piercy: A Vision of the Peaceable Kingdom," *Modern Poetry Studies* 8 (1977)
Doherty, Patricia, *Marge Piercy: An Annotated Bibliography,* Westport, Connecticut, and London: Greenwood Press, 1997
Nelson, Ronald, "The Renewal of the Self by Returning to the Elements," in *Ways of Knowing: Essays on Marge Piercy,* edited by Sue Walker and Eugenie Hamner, Mobile, Alabama: Negative Capability Press, 1991
Piercy, Marge, "Mirror Images," in *Women's Culture: The Women's Renaissance of the Seventies,* edited by Gayle Kimball, Metuchen, New Jersey, and London: Scarecrow Press, 1981
Piercy, Marge, "Interview with Peggy Friedmann and Ruthann Robson," in *Parti-Colored Blocks for a Quilt,* by Piercy, Ann Arbor: University of Michigan Press, 1982
Piercy, Marge, "Inviting the Muse," in *Poets' Perspectives: Reading, Writing, and Teaching Poetry,* edited by Charles R. Duke and Sally A. Jacobsen, Portsmouth, New Hampshire: Boynton/Cook, 1992
Piercy, Marge, and Dick Lourie, "Tom Eliot Meets the Hulk at Little Big Horn: The Political Economy of Poetry," *TriQuarterly* 23–24 (1972)
Rosenbaum, Jean, "You Are Your Own Magician: A Vision of Integrity in the Poetry of Marge Piercy," *Modern Poetry Studies* 8 (1977)
Walker, Sue, and Eugenie Hamner, "Interview with Marge Piercy," in *Ways of Knowing: Essays on Marge Piercy,* edited by Walker and Hamner, Mobile, Alabama: Negative Capability Press, 1991
Wynne, Edith, "Imagery of Association in the Poetry of Marge Piercy," *Publications of the Missouri Philological Association* 10 (1985)

---

## Robert Pinsky 1940–

Robert Pinsky is one of the most powerful forces in contemporary American poetry. His poetry, his critical writing, and his role as poet laureate of the United States from 1997 to 2000 have allowed him to become a major voice in American poetry and to highlight the ways in which poetry interacts with American culture and people.

After recognizing his shortcomings as a saxophone player in his 20s, Pinsky devoted himself to writing poetry. Mentored by Yvor Winters at Stanford University, where Pinsky earned a Ph.D., he first published poems in the *Southern Review* in October 1965 and in the *Southern Review* and *Poetry* between 1969 and 1971. Only a few of these poems made their way into his first poetry collection, *Sadness and Happiness* (1975). These early poems establish Pinsky's attention to craft. "Old Woman," for instance, is a 16-line, beautifully rendered lyric with lush sounds, and "The Destruction of Long Branch" is a poem in couplets that uses lush, natural images but tempers them with "garden apartments," "the martini glass," "creosoted lumps of sewage," and other urban images. In his early work, Pinsky already takes poetic language to task and incorporates colloquial America.

Historically, particularly in the masculine Romantic tradition, the long poem has been seen as a great achievement. However, contemporary American poetry emphasizes the lyric, and the economics of publishing encourages publication of shorter poems. In 1979 Pinsky published the book-length poem *An Explanation of America*. As its title announces, by this time Pinsky viewed himself not only as a craftsman but also as a cultural commentator. Here, in an address to his daughter, he lays out a history of the United States, links contemporary and ancient cultures, and revels in the variety of American society. As the poem's section titles—"Its Many Fragments," "Its Great Emptiness," and "Its Everlasting Possibility"—suggest, Pinsky's America, like his poetry, is defined by both its coherence and its fragmentedness, its order and its disarray, its beauty and its anguish.

Pinsky's next two volumes of poetry begin to focus, while not forgoing attention to craft, more clearly on the self than on the mythological or intellectual. *History of My Heart* (1984), according to James Longenbach (1994), marks

> a turning point in Pinsky's career. . . . While the poems of *History of My Heart* and *The Want Bone* continue this meditation [on the self and society], they do so dramatically, enacting the dialectic as well as explaining it. These poems retain the discursive clarity of the long poem, but their narratives seem (even within their smaller compass) more comprehensive and complex, more a dramatization of a mind thinking than the product of thought (to borrow a distinction Elizabeth Bishop favored).

J.D. McClatchy, too, wrote glowingly of this work in *The New Republic*. Clearly, Pinsky was making his mark.

By 1985 Pinsky had been awarded the William Carlos Williams Prize from the Poetry Society of America, a National Endowment for the Arts fellowship, and a Guggenheim fellowship and had served as the poetry editor for *The New Republic*. In 1988 Pinsky began teaching at Boston University, where he remains on the faculty. Shortly thereafter, he published his fourth collection of poems.

*The Want Bone* (1990) is a particularly strong collection, further solidifying Pinsky's place in American literature, and "Shirt" is one of its emblematic poems. Written in tercets, the poem begins with the shirt itself: "The back, the yoke, the yardage, Lapped seams, / The nearly invisible stitches along the collar." Then the poem moves to Asians making the shirt in a sweatshop; in fact, the poem intermingles the faraway making of the shirt and the speaker's current wearing of it so that both seem immediate. Then the poem recounts the terrible Triangle Factory fire of 1911, an American historical moment in which

> . . . a young man helped a girl to a step
> Up to the windowsill, then held her out
>
> Away from the masonry wall and let her drop.
> And then another. As if he were helping them up
> To enter a streetcar, and not eternity.

After dropping woman after woman, "He stepped to the sill himself, his jacket flared / And fluttered up from his shirt as he came down," an image that recalls a Hart Crane line. The poem remains calm and artistic while at the same time becoming deeply emotional. However, the poem moves beyond the tragedy into a listing of fabric patterns; a recounting of the history of Scottish workers; a mention of Irma, a black woman in South Carolina who inspected the speaker's shirt; and, finally, a discussion of the concept of *shirt* itself. All this interweaving of the personal and the historical occurs in fewer than 50 lines and with a variety of language—or jargon—representative of the poem's scope. In "Shirt," the object becomes intimate, and the speaker and the reader become implicated in the construction and context—historical and linguistic—of the object. *The Want Bone* lies in the tradition of Elizabeth Bishop, with her attention to detail, perspective, and contextualizing of the personal. This work also recalls William Carlos Williams' assertion that there are no ideas but in things. With this collection, Pinsky uses his long-established aesthetic control to achieve compactness, but he also encompasses a greater range of both the personal and the cultural than ever before.

*The Figured Wheel: New and Collected Poems, 1966–1996* was published in 1996 and was nominated for a Pulitzer Prize that year, shortly before Pinsky was named poet laureate. The collection takes its name from the opening poem in *History of My Heart*. As "The Figured Wheel" suggests and as Longenbach (1994) points out, "Virtually all of Pinsky's poems are autobiographical, but they recognize that an autobiography, like the self it narrates, is constituted by a wide array of cultural and historical forces." *The Figured Wheel* is a testament to the ways in which poetry functions as an examination and voicing of both a self and a culture.

In addition to compiling his four earlier poetry collections, the book begins with a gathering of new poems and concludes with a small sampling of translations. In the new work, Pinsky's attention to craft is ever present, and his attention to history and culture abounds. In a poem with a particularly playful title that asks four deaf and visually impaired students, "If You Could Write One Great Poem, What Would You Want It To Be About?" Pinsky might be describing his own work:

> Sign: that it is a language, full of grace,
> That it is visible, invisible, dark and clear,
> That it is loud and noiseless and is contained
> Inside a body and explodes in air
> Out of a body to conquer from the mind.

Poetry, for Pinsky and his readers, is a mental, physical, and emotional act of constraint and unboundedness.

Pinsky is also an accomplished translator. His *The Inferno of Dante* (1994), which was awarded the Harold Morton Landon Prize in Translation and the *Los Angeles Times* Book Prize in 1995, adapts the terza rima with slant rhyme and uses enjambment to offer an exceptionally readable version of the long poem. Few poets have Pinsky's accomplished ear for both traditional form and colloquial English, and few poets have his vast appreciation for history; both talents are highlighted in *The Inferno*. While some critics have questioned the publication of *The Inferno* without its larger context and other critics prefer earlier, more conservative translations of the piece, Pinsky brings Dante's writing to a new audience and reawakens interest in a work important to Western literature.

Pinsky has also published three critical books: *Landor's Poetry* (1968), *The Situation of Poetry: Contemporary Poetry and Its Traditions* (1976), and *Poetry and the World* (1988). The latter two texts garnered critical praise and explore, in accessible rather than academic language, many of the interests and ideas pursued in his poems. *The Situation of Poetry* contextualizes poetry within the world of poetry and links contemporary poetry to a long and rich tradition, whereas *Poetry and the World* places poetry in a larger cultural and sometimes personal context. These critiques of poetry itself and of contemporary poetry's place in literary tradition and in culture situate Pinsky's own work and outline the poet's responsibility to his or her art.

After becoming poet laureate in 1997, Pinsky won the Ambassador Prize, was appointed to the Academy of Arts and Letters, and won the Harold Washington Literary Award. He has also become a computer enthusiast—even writing an essay for the *New York Times Book Review* that links poetry and computer technology—and serves as the editor of *Slate,* an on-line journal. Most recently, he has published *The Sounds of Poetry: A Brief Guide* (1998); *Jersey Rain* (2000), a poetry collection; and *Americans' Favorite Poems* (1999), a collection for which he served as editor. These three books mark an extension of Pinsky talents and interests.

Although criticized by a few as a dumbing down of prosody or an elitist suggestion for common readers, *The Sounds of Poetry* invites readers to appreciate the very aspect of poetry that many readers find daunting, that of sound and patterning. Pinsky points out, "Every speaker, intuitively and accurately, courses gracefully through immensely subtle manipulations of sound." In fact, the point of the guide is merely to help readers become more aware of their expertise, of the importance of sound and patterns in the meaning and feeling of poetry. While he does address meter, he discusses it in terms of the reader's physical involvement with the poem rather than as categorization imposed on the poem. Looking back at Pinsky's own poems, it is easy to see how his view of sound has informed his work. In the opening lines of "Shirt," for instance, the cadence depends on a repetition of sounds—the "k" of "back" and "yoke," the "y" of "yoke" and "yardage," the "a" of "back" and "yardage" and "Lapped," the "i" sounds in the second line—and on the lengthening and shortening of sounds—the quickness of "back" and "yoke," the lingering of "yardage" and "collar." A similar effect is achieved at the end of the poem:

> The buttonholes, the sizing, the facing, the characters
> Printed in black on neckband and tail. The shape
> The label, the labor, the color, the shade. The shirt.

The sound patterning and the syntactical patterning—the listing—recall the process of making a shirt and reinforce the methodical movement of the poem as a whole. For Pinsky, whether poetry is read from a book or on a computer screen, it is ultimately a physical act of the lungs, larynx, and mouth.

In his most recent collection, *Jersey Rain,* Pinsky returns to the Jersey shore of his youth and to concerns of family. He also explores concepts of order, using tercets, alphabetizing subject matter as in "An Alphabet of My Dead" or word order as in "ABC," and employing various sound patterns. His new poems, many of which appeared previously in prestigious journals such as *The New Yorker,* push strict formal elements to their limits while also delving into the self more intimately; these simultaneous challenges, in fact, temper each other so that the poems become trapped neither in game-like formalism nor in sentimentality. As always, Pinsky employs meticulous craft that complements the emotional, cultural—even pop cultural, as in "Victrola" and "To Television"—and physical matter of the poetry.

Perhaps one of Pinsky's most ambitious contributions to American literary history, however, is "The Favorite Poem Project," a project he developed as poet laureate. In celebration of the new millennium, Pinsky collected thousands of letters from ordinary Americans about the poems they deemed important. The culmination of the project is *Americans' Favorite Poems,* which Pinsky edits and briefly introduces, and also a recording of some of these average—as well as a few famous—Americans reading their favorite poems. In this project Pinsky has created yet another way—a lasting and collaborative way—to explain America through poetry.

Pinsky, then, is one of America's most accomplished poets. He has made a career of exploring simultaneously the unified and the fragmentary—the complementary connectedness and disjointedness—of our literature and our world. As he writes in "Jersey Rain," "Now near the end of the middle stretch of road / What have I learned? Some earthly wiles. An art." His poetry, criticism, and public role as poetry advocate have encouraged an inclusiveness and a fuller understanding of the breadth and depth of culture, history, poetry, and the self.

ANNA LEAHY

**Biography**

Born in Long Branch, New Jersey, 20 October 1940. Attended Rutgers University, New Brunswick, New Jersey, B.A. 1962; Stanford University, California (Woodrow Wilson, Stegner, and Fulbright fellow) M.A., Ph.D. 1966; Assistant Professor of humanities, University of Chicago, 1967–68; Professor of English, Wellesley College, Massachusetts, 1968–80; Professor of English, University of California, Berkeley, from 1980; Visiting Lecturer, Harvard University, Cambridge, Massachusetts, 1979–80; Hurst Professor, Washington University, St. Louis, Missouri, 1981; since 1988, faculty member, Department of English, Boston University; from 1978, poetry editor, *The New Republic.* Received Massachusetts Council on the Arts grant, 1974; Oscar Blumenthal Prize (*Poetry,* Chicago), 1978; American Academy Award, 1980; Saxifrage Prize, 1980; Guggenheim fellowship, 1980; William Carlos Williams Award, 1984; *Los Angeles Times* Book Prize, 1995; Shelley Memorial Award, 1996; Lenore Marshall Poetry Prize, 1997; Poet Laureate of the United States, 1997–2000. Living in Newton Corner, Massachusetts.

**Poetry**

*Sadness and Happiness,* 1975
*An Explanation of America,* 1979
*History of My Heart,* 1984
*The Want Bone,* 1990
*The Figured Wheel: New and Collected Poems, 1966–1996,* 1996
*Jersey Rain,* 2000

**Selected Criticism**

*The Situation of Poetry: Contemporary Poetry and Its Traditions,* 1976
*Poetry and the World,* 1988
*The Sounds of Poetry: A Brief Guide,* 1998

**Other Writings:** novel (*Mindwheel* [computerized novel, with programmers Steve Hales and William Mataga], 1985), translations of Italian and Russian literature (*The Separate Notebooks,* by Czeslaw Milosz, translator with Robert Hass, 1984; *The Inferno of Dante: A New Verse Translation,* 1994).

**Further Reading**

Birkerts, Sven, editor, *Tolstoy's Dictaphone: Technology and the Muse,* St. Paul, Minnesota: Graywolf Press, 1996

Erwin, Timothy, "The Extraordinary Language of Robert Pinsky," *Halcyon: A Journal of the Humanities* 16 (1994)

Glück, Louise, "Story Tellers," *American Poetry Review* 26, no. 4 (July–August 1997)

Halliday, Mark, "An Interview with Robert Pinsky," *Ploughshares* 6, no. 2 (1980)

Longenbach, James, "Robert Pinsky and the Language of Our Time," *Salmagundi* 103 (Summer 1994)

Richman, Robert, "At the Intersection of Art and Life," *The New Criterion* 7, no. 10 (June 1989)

Sacks, Peter, "'Also This, Also That': Robert Pinsky's Poetics of Inclusion," *Agni* 36 (1992)

## The Figured Wheel

The title poem of Robert Pinsky's collected work and the first poem in his landmark *The History of My Heart* (1984), "The Figured Wheel" marks a transition from Pinsky's early "discursive" style to the higher, more ambitious mode of *The Want Bone* (1990) and his subsequent work. Where Pinsky's first books tend toward the essay or explanation, "The Figured Wheel" begins an attempt to address and to encompass more: the wheel described in the poem rolls over all human things and all earthly geography; it swallows or gathers in its path all products of human culture.

The poem simply sets out to describe this all-crushing wheel, the imaginary and impossible Destroyer and Prime Mover of the world, humanity, and all its art. The wheel, Pinsky tells us, "rumbles / Through the Antarctic station of American sailors and technicians," rolls over suburban "shopping malls and prisons," and shakes also "the mineral-rich tundra of the Soviet northernmost settlements." As it mills the living and the dead, artists and scientists "festoon" and "illuminate" the wheel with all manner of icons, images, stories, and music—all forms of cultural expression, from "Hopi gargoyles" in the American Southwest to the "dryads" of the Ibo in Nigeria; from toys and zodiacs to "colored ribbons" and "electronic instruments." The wheel is in this sense *figured* (i.e., having figures on it), but it is also *figured* by the poet, as his great catalog of places and artifacts unrolls. The artists that decorate the wheel in life continue to do so from the grave, and some survive in death "by reducing themselves magically / To tiny organisms, . . . / Bits of dry skin, microscopic flakes": this is the mortification of the artist's body and will before the great wheel, in which Pinsky also participates, finally, as the wheel

rolls unrelentingly over

A cow plodding through car-traffic on a street in Iasi,
And over the haunts of Robert Pinsky's mother and father
And wife and children and his sweet self
Which he hereby unwillingly and inexpertly gives up,
  because it is

There, figured and pre-figured in the nothing-transfiguring
  wheel.

In this final line, invoking perhaps Yeats' equally apocalyptic vision of historical change ("Turning and turning in the widening gyre . . ."), Pinsky implicates himself and his work in the wheel's process. He throws himself, too, into his great mill, opening the end of his catalog to include the cataloger—and the catalog itself.

Although its decorations are myriad, little is said about the wheel itself or about its significance. The wheel may be both more menacing and more universal because it lacks structural detail, purpose, or will. Only a single sentence says explicitly what the wheel *is,* and there it is figured as "Jesus oblivious to hurt," as a pig in Gogol that accidentally eats a young chicken without realizing it, and as "the empty armor of My Cid, clattering / Into the arrows of the credulous unbelievers": a juggernaut, without intention or feeling. The wheel, as a symbol, suggests a number of mystical systems—Eastern mandalas, prayer wheels, zodiacs, the medieval European Wheel of Fortune, and even perhaps Wordsworth's "motion and spirit" that "rolls through all things"—but the poem confirms none of these interpretations to the exclusion of others. The figured wheel has suggested many things to Pinsky's critics: Wyatt Prunty (1990) says that it is time, James Longenbach (1997) connects it with history, Langdon Hammer (1996) calls it culture, and Katha Pollitt (1996) suggests that the wheel might be language itself; Andrew Zawacki (1997) may be deliberately perverse when he says that the wheel is "a figure for Pinsky's *oeuvre.*" Most likely, all these definitions are partly correct. The wheel stands for the process, which we might call history or time, by which individual works of culture become parts of a single, monumental body (culture's "monument of its own magnificence," to paraphrase another Yeats figure that Pinsky favors). The wheel is culture as a process, adorned with the works of culture; the wheel is history, chewing both the dead and the living into its own substance and sustenance. This is, apparently, Pinsky's vision of tradition and the individual talent, and if the wheel represents poetry more specifically, it is worth noting that (as poet laureate) Pinsky worked to bring poetry into those "shopping malls and prisons" where the wheel rolls, and that he also traveled to Iasi (of the "cow plodding through car-traffic"), if not to the Antarctic, as a representative of American poetry.

Pinsky himself, in a *Paris Review* interview (1997), emphasizes a different and more geometric significance of the wheel. Asked about the connection between "The Figured Wheel" and his computer game *Mindwheel,* Pinsky answered, "There is something about the circle: each thing reflected by an opposite, and also on a continuum with that opposite—everything contained by a cycle, with each small arc implying the whole." The circle contains multitudes and implies for each thing an opposite. Structurally, "The Figured Wheel" replicates what Pinsky describes here: as a catalog or series of catalogs, the poem tries to comprehend culture's entirety. Pinsky accomplishes this by juxtaposing distant or dissimilar pairs, suggesting thereby the containment of an intervening series. The Ibo counter the Hopi, "the unemployed" oppose "the pampered," and an Antarctic naval station stands near the remote northern reaches of Siberia. Pinsky is a poet greatly given to the pleasures of the list, what Richard Wilbur (1976) calls "the compulsion to designate," and his lists often strive for what Robert Belknap (2000) calls "the pleasurable infinitude of language." This pleasure in the comprehensive, an organizing principle of "The Figured Wheel," is palpable also in the textile lists of Pinsky's "Shirt" (*The Want Bone*) or in his more recent "An Alphabet of My Dead," (*Jersey Rain,* 2000). The ideal inclusiveness of lists, especially as they emerge in Pinsky's prose, hints also at Pinsky's strong hope for inclusion and democracy in contemporary art, a sort of universal suffrage of poetry, whereby we may all contribute to and be comprehended in the grand and unrelenting figured wheel.

ISAAC CATES

**Further Reading**

Belknap, Robert, "The Literary List: A Survey of Its Uses and Deployments," *Literary Imagination* 2, no.1 (2000)

Breslin, Paul, "Review of *The Figured Wheel,*" *Poetry* 170 (1997)

Downing, Ben, and Daniel Kunitz, "The Art of Poetry LXXVI" (interview with Pinsky), *The Paris Review* 39 (1997)

Hammer, Langdon, "Review of *The Figured Wheel,*" *Yale Review* 84 (1996)

Longenbach, James, *Modern Poetry after Modernism,* Oxford and New York: Oxford University Press, 1997

Pollitt, Katha, "World of Wonders" (review of *The Figured Wheel*), *New York Times Book Review* (18 August 1996)

Prunty, Wyatt, *"Fallen from the Symboled World": Precedents for the New Formalism,* Oxford and New York: Oxford University Press, 1990

Wilbur, Richard, "Poetry and Happiness," in *Responses: Prose Pieces, 1953–1976,* by Wilbur, New York and London: Harcourt Brace Jovanovich, 1976; expanded edition, Ashland, Oregon: Story Line Press, 2000

Zawacki, Andrew, "Hope for a Shared Home" (review of *The Figured Wheel*), *Times Literary Supplement* (24 January 1997)

---

# Sylvia Plath 1932–63

Sylvia Plath is at the center of the sometimes controversial movement that has been called Confessional poetry. Her highly emotional poems about her relationship with her father and her use of Holocaust imagery have provoked both high praise and violent criticism. Her recasting of classical mythology to describe her distorted experience of the family myth attracts some readers and alienates others. Her suicide seems almost a literary act, as death and suicide so dominated her poetry. Indeed, Plath's life and work are so entwined that it is difficult to separate them.

Her father's death underlies much of Plath's poetry, from her first work until the last. Of Germanic descent, he was apparently demanding and rigorous, a lover of order (although no Nazi, despite Plath's identification of her father with the Nazis in her poetry). A scholar who disdained taking part in social life, he wrote about bees and kept them; later Sylvia was to follow this precedent. What his daily relationship with his daughter was like is unknown, but his early death—he diagnosed himself incorrectly and refused medical care—caused her to mythologize him into a figure both diabolical and divine who demanded that her life task be to work through their relationship. His German heritage allowed her to portray him as a Nazi, and she invented or assumed Jewish heritage for her mother to illuminate the destructive power of these two strains in herself.

A truly outstanding student, Plath had a story accepted by *Seventeen* before she graduated from high school. She also received a scholarship to Smith College; while she was studying there, her creative abilities won her a trip to New York to spend the summer as a guest editor for *Mademoiselle* magazine, an experience described in detail in her autobiographical novel *The Bell Jar* (1963). Although it had promised to open up her future for her, the trip proved a disaster. Her experiences in the city undermined her confidence, and when she found out on her return home that she had not been accepted into a creative writing course at Harvard, she slipped into a deep depression and attempted suicide.

After hospitalization and recovery, Plath returned to Smith and graduated. She then attended Cambridge University on a Fulbright fellowship, and while in England she met and married the poet Ted Hughes. In 1957 she came back to Massachusetts with Hughes and taught at Smith College for a year but found teaching emotionally debilitating. While in Boston she attended Robert Lowell's poetry classes and learned much from the poet whose 1959 *Life Studies* is often considered the cornerstone of the Confessional school. In 1959 the young couple returned to England and in 1960 Plath celebrated the publication of her first book, *The Colossus.* The title poem describes her obsession with her father as an attempt to clean and reassemble a huge ruined statue, a giant wreck that dwarfs the frantic cleaner:

> Scaling little ladders with gluepots and pails of lysol
> I crawl like an ant in mourning
> Over the weedy acres of your brow
> To mend the immense skull plates and clear
> The bald, white tumuli of your eyes.

In 1962 Plath and Hughes separated, and Plath moved to London with her children. In London she was plagued by financial worries, uncomfortable living conditions, and ill health. A novel that Plath hoped would earn her enough money to alleviate the worst of her financial problems, *The Bell Jar,* recounted her earlier suicide attempt and her recovery. The novel was published in England in January of 1963, under the pseudonym of Victoria Lucas, but Plath committed suicide on 11 February 1963. Her death sparked intense interest in the poetry and made her the center of a literary cult.

Since Plath had never directed otherwise, Hughes inherited her estate and became her literary executor. His edition of *Ariel* appeared in England in 1965 and in America the following year. Hughes published other books of her work later: *Crossing the Water* and *Winter Trees* appeared in England in 1971, and her letters, stories, and journals followed. That her ex-husband was her literary heir has caused problems with the oeuvre; he claims to have destroyed uncomfortable material from the journals, and he rearranged *Ariel* to minimize the effect of poems directed against him.

*The Collected Poems of Sylvia Plath,* edited by Ted Hughes, appeared in 1981 and remains the standard choice for Plath readers. It includes many previously unpublished poems Plath wrote before 1956 as well as the body of her mature work arranged chronologically. It allows the reader to see how Plath's work changed as she grew and to trace the different sources she used in the development of her personal myth. The book also underscores the brevity of her writing life: *The Collected Poems* (exclusive of the appendix of juvenile poems) spans the years 1956–63. Since she lived into only the second month of her last year, her adult writing life lasted just seven years. Even Plath's first poems are carefully crafted and highly original in their use of forms; her "juvenilia" include graceful and image-rich poems in the popular forms such as sonnet and villanelle. In her first major work she struck off on her own to use off-rhyme and syllabics in such a way as to render form nearly invisible but potent. An example is the often-taught "Point Shirley," which describes her return to the house where her grandmother had lived and died. It begins,

From Water-Tower Hill to the brick prison
The shingle booms, bickering under
The sea's collapse.

Slant-rhyme, assonance, consonance, and alliteration are combined with a rocking movement in the lines to catch the motion of the sea and the feel of the permanent and conscienceless landscape that makes her grandmother's life meaningless by undoing her work. There is a sense of hopelessness in much of this work, the notion that this febrile attempt to bring art from death is doomed, because nothing survives. "Point Shirley" concludes:

I would get from these dry-papped stones
The milk your love instilled in them.
The black ducks dive.
And though your graciousness might stream,
And I contrive,
Grandmother, stones are nothing of home
To that spumiest dove.
Against both bar and tower the black sea runs.

Her thinly disguised autobiographical novel *The Bell Jar,* undertaken for practical reasons and in a mood of health, provides some insight into her psychological state. Describing her breakdown after the New York trip and her treatment for mental illness that followed, the book shows her extremely fragile sense of self and her inability to accept any of the few possibilities she saw open to her. She describes her self-image as a hole or a vacancy and discusses the many frantic escapes from herself she considered and/or tried—religion, speed, disguise, flight—before her major suicide attempt. The novel captures the repressive society of the 1950s with its rigidly defined sex roles that allowed little flexibility for someone like Plath, to whom the approved female roles seemed nothing short of death. When *The Bell Jar* was published in England shortly before her suicide, her friends and relatives who were "fictionalized" in it were horrified.

The poetry of Plath's middle period is strangely detached, blunted in affect; there appears to be an attempt to turn personal pain into intellectual abstraction, resulting in poetry that has neither the formal pleasure of her early work nor the emotional intensity of her final poems. "Magi," for instance, begins

The abstracts hover like dull angels:
Nothing so vulgar as a nose or eye
Bossing the ethereal blanks of their face-ovals.

Rather than being stunned by the lines, the reader is left to decipher them. One might generalize to say that in her early work, Plath used form to contain her obsession with death; in her transitional work, she attempted to intellectualize it away; and in her late work, she expressed it directly through obsessive metaphors that had become indistinguishable from reality.

Plath's late work written the year after she separated from Ted Hughes, when she was living by herself with her two children, consists of poems of intense suffering in which the pain of her life is translated to the page, for the most part unmediated by form. Only one or two, including "Daddy," makes use of standard poetic devices. Her suicide in February 1963 ended a brilliant spate of poems. Her last work, dated a week before her suicide, foretells her death. "Edge" begins

The woman is perfected.
Her dead

Body wears the smile of accomplishment.

The dead body is the finished work of the speaker, her product and destiny. It is observed by the moon, a detached goddess without compassion:

The moon has nothing to be sad about,
Staring from her hood of bone.
Her blacks crackle and drag.

Plath's work was not popularly known until after her suicide. Her poems were the most commonly used to illustrate what J.M. Rosenthal called "confessional poetry." Robert Phillips' description of this kind of poetry could be based on her work; it demonstrates nearly all of the 16 characteristics of confessional verse he lists in his book *The Confessional Poets* (1973). These include generalizations that such poetry is subjective, therapeutic, open in form, personal, expressive of self, ironically detached, narrative, and anti-establishment, among other stipulations. Phillips suggests that while the poet strives for personalization rather than universality, successful Confessional poetry creates a persona with which the reader can empathize. Certainly Plath fits his definition and must in part have occasioned it.

Since the term "Confessional poetry" is perceived now as negative, suggesting self-absorption and self-indulgence, many critics prefer other terms, such as personal poetry, poetry of the family, or domestic poetry. But those terms fail to suggest the intensity of personal suffering that defines the poems of John Berryman, Randall Jarrell, Anne Sexton, Robert Lowell, and Sylvia Plath as clearly belonging under one rubric. Moreover, the dismissive attitude taken toward Confessional poetry overlooks the ability of this intense poetry to lure generation after generation of readers into its power.

Feminist criticism has also claimed Plath as a forerunner, someone who was acutely aware of the limitations placed on women just before the storm broke. She wrote at the time when the major feminist statements were beginning to be made, but she did not identify with the dawning movement. She began to write at the time when the great modernists were still alive, mostly looming male presences whose influence must have reinforced her belief that the literary world was all but closed to women. It is uncertain if future Plath study will be able to separate illness from poetry, as Caroline King Barnard Hall (1978) suggests is one fruitful direction of new inquiry, to "focus not on Plath's pathology but on the way she transformed her health and justified anger into art." Some still accept as fair judgment the words written by Richard Wilbur about meeting Plath when she was 20 in "Cottage Street, 1953":

> Sylvia . . . condemned to live,
> Shall study for a decade, as she must,
> To state at last her brilliant negative
> In poems free and helpless and unjust.

JANET MCCANN

*See also* Confessional Poetry

**Biography**
Born in Boston, Massachusetts, 27 October 1932. Attended Smith College, Northampton, Massachusetts (Glasscock Prize, 1955), B.A. (summa cum laude) in English 1955 (Phi Beta Kappa); Newnham College, Cambridge (Fulbright Scholar), 1955–57, M.A. 1957; married poet Ted Hughes, 1956, separated 1962; guest editor, *Mademoiselle* magazine, summer 1953; Instructor in English, Smith College, 1957–58. Received Yaddo fellowship, 1959; Cheltenham Festival Award, 1961; Saxon fellowship, 1961. Died in London, England, 11 February 1963.

**Poetry**
*The Colossus,* 1960
*Ariel,* edited by Ted and Olwyn Hughes, 1965
*Crossing the Water,* edited by Ted Hughes, 1971
*Winter Trees,* edited by Ted Hughes, 1971
*The Collected Poems of Sylvia Plath,* edited by Ted Hughes, 1981
*Selected Poems,* edited by Ted Hughes, 1985
*Above the Oxbow: Selected Writings* (includes prose), 1985

**Other Writings:** play, radio play, novel (*The Bell Jar,* as by Victoria Lucas, 1963), children's literature, journals, collections of correspondence (*Letters Home: Correspondence, 1950–1963,* edited by Aurelia Schober Plath, 1975); edited collection of poetry (*American Poetry Now: A Selection of the Best Poems by Modern American Writers,* 1961).

**Further Reading**

Alexander, Paul, *Rough Magic: A Biography of Sylvia Plath,* New York: Viking Penguin, 1991
Alexander, Paul, editor, *Ariel Ascending: Writings about Sylvia Plath,* New York and London: Harper and Row, 1985
Annas, Pamela J., *A Disturbance in Mirrors: The Poetry of Sylvia Plath,* New York and London: Greenwood Press, 1988
Axelrod, Steven Gould, *Sylvia Plath: The Wound and the Cure of Words,* Baltimore, Maryland: Johns Hopkins University Press, 1990
Draskau, Jennifer, *The Liberation of Sylvia Plath's Ariel: Psychosemantics and a Glass Sarcophagus,* Copenhagen: Department of English, University of Copenhagen, 1991
Hall, Caroline King Barnard, *Sylvia Plath,* Boston: Twayne, 1978; revised edition, as *Sylvia Plath, Revised,* New York: Twayne, and London: Prentice Hall, 1998
Lant, Kathleen Margaret, "The Big Strip Tease: Female Bodies and Male Power in the Poetry of Sylvia Plath," *Contemporary Literature* 34, no. 4 (Winter 1993)
Rose, Jacqueline, *The Haunting of Sylvia Plath,* Cambridge, Massachusetts: Harvard University Press, and London: Virago, 1993
Stevenson, Anne, *Bitter Fame: A Life of Sylvia Plath,* Boston: Houghton Mifflin, and London: Viking, 1989
Sugars, Cynthia, "Sylvia Plath as Fantasy Space; or, The Return of the Living Dead," *Literature and Psychology* 45, no. 3 (1999)
Van Dyne, Susan R., *Revising Life: Sylvia Plath's Ariel Poems,* Chapel Hill: University of North Carolina Press, 1993
Wagner-Martin, Linda, *Sylvia Plath: A Biography,* New York: Simon and Schuster, and London: Chatto and Windus, 1987
Wagner-Martin, Linda, *Sylvia Plath: A Literary Life,* New York: St. Martin's Press, and London: Macmillan, 1999


## Ariel

"Ariel" is a startlingly powerful poem written in October 1962, less than six months before Sylvia Plath's suicide in February 1963. The poem was written on 27 October, among other poems that had more positive and optimistic leanings than did her very last poems. (This group includes the widely anthologized "Lady Lazarus," a much more directly obvious death-rebirth poem.) After trying several other possibilities, Plath made "Ariel" the title poem for her book, which she prepared herself but which her ex-husband and heir, Ted Hughes, revised and rearranged after her death before publishing it in 1965. Powerful, mysterious, and layered, this poem has not received as wide reading as the more easily accessible poem "Daddy," written earlier the same month, but it has earned much critical attention.

Besides being the airy spirit of Shakespeare's *The Tempest,* Ariel was the horse that Plath rode at Devon. The spirit Ariel was in thrall to Prospero until Prospero, at the end of the story, sets Ariel free; he is an "airy spirit" but bound against his will to serve another. Caroline King Barnard Hall (1978) finds this forced servitude germane to the understanding of Plath's poem and comments also on the use of the word "Ariel" in the Bible as a title given to the city of Jerusalem in the book of Isaiah. In Isaiah 29, the prophet tells of the wrath of God that is visited on the city but indicates that the city will be redeemed in the Apocalypse. Thus, the speaker, both as airy spirit and as cursed city, is now in thrall but looks forward to a deliverance that will come only through the violent revision of the order of things.

Plath took great pleasure in riding her horse Ariel at Devon. However, Ted Hughes also told of a frightening experience that Plath had riding in which the horse ran away with her and galloped about two miles home to the stables with Plath hanging around his neck. This experience of having the horse take over the ride and make of his rider only an appendage may have been at least a part of the germ of the poem.

"Ariel" describes a morning ride in which the horse and rider become one as the horse speeds through the landscape toward a mystical point of arrival. The narrative itself plunges forward, and the scenery blurs for the reader as well as the rider as we are propelled toward this point, which appears to be both death and rebirth.

The poem begins with the slow beginning of the ride, the predawn stillness: "Stasis in darkness." Then the rider is hurtled forward and merges with horse to become "God's lioness"—"How one we grow, / Pivot of heels and knees!" The new being formed of horse and rider almost dissolves, although the surroundings would hold her back, the "hooks" of the berries, "black sweet blood mouthfuls." There is a point at which the rider seems both in control and at the mercy of a greater force. "Something else / Hauls me through air," the speaker says, but "white / Godiva, I unpeel—/ Dead hands, dead stringencies." Thus impelled out of the self by speed, she can revise the self, purify it, and remove the dead parts. In other Plath works, speed is a way of achieving a kind of transcendence, even though the speed may be destructive—Plath's fictive double Esther Greenwood is supremely happy in *The Bell Jar,* for instance, as she rockets down the hill on skis toward a crash in which she will break her leg; she also mentions past episodes of speed that brought her fulfillment.

As she escapes, she dissolves: "I / Foam to wheat, a glitter of seas / The child's cry / Melts in the wall." The images may suggest the sexual act, and this implication becomes a part of the trip—that is, the motion forward is sex, death, and rebirth, both a sloughing off of the self and a realization of self. The rider is female, the horse seems to be a male symbol, but together they are "God's lioness."

The conclusion fuses birth and death in the point of arrival. Complete dissolution is the herald of rebirth. Red is the blood color, color of both life and death in Plath. Sometimes the fragile spirit is oppressed by red (as the invalid is overwhelmed by the color in "Tulips"), but sometimes, when stronger, the spirit is exhilarated by the color (as the queen bee, identified with the "self to recover," triumphs in her rebirth as a "red scar in the sky" at the end of "Stings"). This triumphant red seems to be the color at the end of "Ariel":

And I
Am the arrow,
The dew that flies
Suicidal, at one with the drive
Into the red
Eye, the cauldron of morning.

Arrow and dew may be a merging of male and female symbols, but in any case "the red eye" and "the cauldron of morning" are conflated as a death-birth experience with the connotations of both "morning" and "cauldron" (which echoes "caul" but includes the suggestion of witchcraft and magic). The poem takes the reader on the full ride from the waiting, to the frenzied headlong hurtling with the world pulling at the rider with its hooks of desire, to the dissolving of rider into mount and finally of both into sheer motion, body lost in flight. The conclusion suggests both the actual morning—she has ridden from dark to day—and its symbolic equivalent. It is an apocalyptic poem with its clear, consistent metaphor well worked through, and the extended metaphor makes it unusual in Plath's late work.

One of Plath's more difficult and more important poems, "Ariel" shows Plath's vision of what she attempted in her poetry and her life: the transcendence of the old, confining order and the creation of a new self and a new world. It may be compared with other poems of departure, such as Wallace Stevens' "Not Ideas about the Thing, but the Thing Itself," which similarly points to a form of rebirth and was, like "Ariel," a poem intended to sum up a life and serve as its explanation.

JANET MCCANN

**Further Reading**

Alexander, Paul, editor, *Ariel Ascending: Writings about Sylvia Plath,* New York and London: Harper and Row, 1985

Annas, Pamela J., *A Disturbance in Mirrors: The Poetry of Sylvia Plath,* New York and London: Greenwood Press, 1988

Axelrod, Steven Gould, *Sylvia Plath: The Wound and the Cure of Words,* Baltimore, Maryland: Johns Hopkins University Press, 1990

Hall, Caroline King Barnard, *Sylvia Plath,* Boston: Twayne, 1978; revised edition, as *Sylvia Plath, Revised,* New York: Twayne, and London: Prentice Hall, 1998

Rose, Jacqueline, *The Haunting of Sylvia Plath,* Cambridge, Massachusetts: Harvard University Press, and London: Virago, 1993

Van Dyne, Susan R., *Revising Life: Sylvia Plath's Ariel Poems,* Chapel Hill: University of North Carolina Press, 1993

# Daddy

The last six months of Sylvia Plath's life produced much of the work for which she is now known. Plath wrote "Daddy" in October 1962, about five months before her suicide in February 1963. It was one of the poems that she planned to include in her collection *Ariel,* and she read it for BBC radio before it was finally included in *Ariel,* her posthumous collection edited by Ted Hughes and published in England in 1965 (the book was published in the United States in 1966). The poem is unusual among her late poems because it does use rhyme and some other elements of formal poetry, although it uses them nontraditionally.

This poem mythologizes her struggle to separate from her dead father, who continued to dominate her life. She did not claim that the poem was personal but said that it was about myth: preparing a reading for BBC, she said, "Here is a poem spoken by a girl with an Electra complex. Her case is complicated by the fact that her father was also a Nazi and her mother very possibly part Jewish. In the daughter the two strains marry and paralyze each other. She has to act out the awful little allegory once over before she is free of it." These comments, quoted by Ted Hughes in his edition of her work, *The Collected Poems of Sylvia Plath* (1981), are often used to demonstrate that the poem was not "personal." However, Plath would of course want to indicate that the poem was not merely about her life. The Electra myth is her chosen story; her father's powerful hold on her is clear in all her father poems from "The Colossus" on, and his figure is certainly subsumed in the devil-daddy of this late poem. This is an extreme poem, at the edge of sanity, certainly beyond reason. Its intensity must be the reason for its popularity, as it is one of Plath's most anthologized works, if not her most frequently printed single poem, and it may be her most thoroughly analyzed.

The poem's repetitious "oo" rhymes and its banging rhythms give it an effect of being something between a chant and a scream of pain. The tale it tells is of the exorcism of the demon-father, and in fact the poem appears itself to be the exorcism, a performative discourse. The daughter/speaker's relationship with her father is described through a series of metaphors implying suffocation, rejection, and violation. The father himself is compared with malevolent mythic and historic figures: Nazis, vampires, and devils. The story recounts the speaker's attempt to loosen herself from the pull of her dead father by marrying someone like him and then, by dissolving the marriage, to find freedom. It has been noted that the poem was written on the day Plath learned that Hughes had agreed to a divorce. The poem refers to Plath's suicide attempt at age 20 as a previous attempt to join her father:

I was ten when they buried you.
At twenty I tried to die
And get back, back, back to you.
I thought even the bones would do.

But they pulled me out of the sack
And they stuck me together with glue.
And then I knew what to do.
I made a model of you,

A man in black with a Meinkampf look
And a love of the rack and the screw.
And I said I do, I do.
So daddy, I'm finally through.
The black telephone's off at the root,
The voices just can't worm through.

The poem goes on to declare that the ersatz Daddy has been eliminated and therefore that her father can no longer call her on the black telephone from his grave. The last line is a manic cry: "Daddy, daddy, you bastard, I'm through!" "Daddy" has great appeal in the classroom, especially to students new to contemporary poetry. It speaks to those who have family problems that they would like to turn into art, and it helps enlarge the students' notion of what is suitable for poetry.

"Daddy" is often seen as a prime example of so-called confessional poetry. For years, "Sylvia Plath" was the name popularly associated with this movement, although Robert Lowell's *Life Studies* (1959) is generally considered to be the work that defined it and led M.L. Rosenthal to apply the term to the poetry of Lowell, W.D. Snodgrass, and Ann Sexton. (In the 1990s, other confessional poets, such as Ann Sexton and John Berryman, received equal treatment.) "Daddy" illustrates the typical characteristics of confessional poetry: subjectivity, emphasis on the personal, the notion of poetry as therapy, blurring of speaker and poet, and obsessive motifs. According to Robert Phillips in his study *The Confessional Poets* (1973), confessional poetry "uses the self as a poetic symbol around which is woven a personal mythology." This is certainly true of "Daddy" and of Plath's work in general.

Later critics have paid more attention to the nonpersonal interpretations of "Daddy," looking at it as a feminist poem representing the attempt of the female to articulate herself in a male-dominated language and social context. Certainly the demon- father can be seen as a masculine power principle gone wild, and Plath's efforts to communicate are expressed in the poem:

I never could talk to you.
The tongue stuck in my jaw.

It stuck in a barb wire snare.
Ich, ich, ich, ich.
I could hardly speak.

The pain in the attempt to move the tongue around in barbed wire, to form the word "I" in the oppressor's language, is cleverly communicated even by the sound of the word itself.

"Daddy" is an adaptable poem, not limited to its first designated category of "confessional." The subtle and complex relationship between its two poles—Daddy and daughter, Nazi and Jew, violator and victim, oppressor and oppressed—will continue to draw comments and critiques not only from literary critics but from other disciplines as well, such as linguistics and psychology, as its powerful language continues to move readers to want to make it theirs.

JANET MCCANN

**Further Reading**

Annas, Pamela J., *A Disturbance in Mirrors: The Poetry of Sylvia Plath,* New York and London: Greenwood Press, 1988

Axelrod, Steven Gould, *Sylvia Plath: The Wound and the Cure of Words,* Baltimore, Maryland: Johns Hopkins University Press, 1990

Gilbert, Sandra M., "Teaching Plath's 'Daddy' to Speak to Undergraduates," *ADE Bulletin* 76 (Winter 1983)

Hall, Caroline King Barnard, *Sylvia Plath,* Boston: Twayne, 1978; revised edition, as *Sylvia Plath, Revised,* New York: Twayne, and London: Prentice Hall, 1998

Strangeways, Al, *Sylvia Plath: The Shaping of Shadows,* Madison, New Jersey: Fairleigh Dickinson University Press, and London: Associated University Presses, 1998

Van Dyne, Susan R., *Revising Life: Sylvia Plath's Ariel Poems,* Chapel Hill: University of North Carolina Press, 1993

## Lady Lazarus

Sideshow freaks, people returned from the dead, and victims of Nazi concentration camps populate "Lady Lazarus," Sylvia Plath's dramatic, intense, and darkly comic poem about extreme emotional states and attempted suicide. First published posthumously in *Ariel* (1965), its title identifies the speaker with the figure of Lazarus, whom Christ raised from death to life. In the poem this return becomes a comically banal public display as a "peanut-crunching crowd" of onlookers comes to watch her being unwrapped and to gawk at her skeletal figure. Poems such as "Lady Lazarus" voiced many of the tensions about traditional gender role expectations that American women became acutely aware of in the 1960s and that continue to trouble many women.

Sylvia Plath wrote the poem in seven days in October 1962, a time of great emotional intensity and poetic productivity for her. She was writing as many as three poems a day, many of them similarly emotionally charged and dramatic. "Lady Lazarus" is a powerful and chilling indicator of her distraught emotional state, bristling with rage and a kind of desperate bravado. The poem refers to two previous suicide attempts, the first "an accident" when the speaker was ten, the second a serious attempt. Several months after writing "Lady Lazarus" Plath did indeed commit suicide.

Plath's early poems are studied, detached descriptions of landscape and narratives of small daily events. Her later poems are more immediate, looser, more emotionally intense as she began to explore the conflicts she faced trying to reconcile her talent and ambition with the rigid social expectations for women in the post–World War II period. In many of these poems Plath dramatizes her emotions as overwhelmingly larger than life. "Ariel," for example, describes a horseback ride in terms of a suicidal flight into the sun. Another poem, "Colossus," mixes humor and drama to represent her conflicted memory of her father, who died when she was eight. Plath depicts him as an enormous shattered Greek or Roman statue that she is trying to reassemble, in contrast to which she is insignificant and ant-like. "Daddy" combines lilting nursery-rhyme rhythms ("you do not do, you do not do / Any more, black shoe") with the stark horror of Nazi imagery to characterize the speaker's suffering at her father's desertion.

"Lady Lazarus" continues in this vein, combining horror with black humor as it recounts the speaker's attempts at suicide and her return to life, described as a "theatrical / Comeback." The central symbolism graphically compares her to a victim of the Holocaust whose body has been converted into grotesque objects for use and display:

> A sort of walking miracle, my skin
> Bright as a Nazi lampshade,
> My right foot
>
> A paperweight . . .

Her interior suffering is exteriorized as physical annihilation, her private pain publicly dramatized. Lady Lazarus explains that "Dying / Is an art" at which she excels. She anticipates that she will soon die; however, in the last stanza she asserts triumphantly that she will arise again from death and "eat men like air," as if she will return to exact revenge on the men who have betrayed her.

The poem's darkly comic style arises from Lady Lazarus' self-mockery and from a poetic structure that is closer to light verse than to the more formal structures (such as the sonnet, the ode, or the iambic pentameter stanzas of blank verse) traditionally used for serious poetry. It is comprised of 28 three-line stanzas, with short lines and simple words. There is some true rhyme, especially at the start and the end, and a great deal of off-rhyme, linking such groups of words as "cell," "real," "call," and "theatrical," or "woman," "bone," "ten," and "accident." Its diction is slangy and its bizarre heroine a revenant, a woman who miraculously returns from death to become a grotesquely popular sideshow display. As she is unwrapped the crowd watches eagerly, as if watching a "strip tease." She calls herself "a sort of walking miracle," and refers to her suicide attempts with wry self-mockery: "I guess you could say I've a call."

Described as Confessional poetry, poems such as "Lady Lazarus" and similarly self-revealing work by Plath mix politics with personal revelation and the baring of the author's emotions.

KAREN F. STEIN

**Further Reading**


Annas, Pamela J., *A Disturbance in Mirrors: The Poetry of Sylvia Plath*, New York and London: Greenwood Press, 1988

Axelrod, Steven Gould, *Sylvia Plath: The Wound and the Cure of Words*, Baltimore, Maryland: Johns Hopkins University Press, 1990

Bloom, Harold, editor, *Sylvia Plath*, New York: Chelsea House, 1988

Hall, Caroline King Barnard, *Sylvia Plath*, Boston: Twayne, 1978; revised edition, as *Sylvia Plath, Revised*, New York: Twayne, and London: Prentice Hall, 1998

Strangeways, Al, *Sylvia Plath: The Shaping of Shadows*, Madison, New Jersey: Fairleigh Dickinson University Press, and London: Associated University Presses, 1998

Van Dyne, Susan R., *Revising Life: Sylvia Plath's Ariel Poems*, Chapel Hill: University of North Carolina Press, 1993

Wagner, Linda W., editor, *Critical Essays on Sylvia Plath*, Boston: G.K. Hall, 1984

Wagner, Linda W., editor, *Sylvia Plath: The Critical Heritage*, London and New York: Routledge, 1988


---

## Poetry Slams. *See* Performance Poetry

---

## Popular Verse. *See* Light Verse

---

## Poststructuralism. *See* Literary Theory and Poetry

---

## Ezra Pound 1885–1972

Ezra Pound had the most controversial career of any 20th-century American poet, and his overall place in American literature is more fiercely disputed than that of any other Modernist. It has been persuasively argued by Pound's supporters that he had the greatest impact of any single poet on the development of Modernist poetry. Even T.S. Eliot, in dedicating his poem *The Waste Land* to Pound, called him "the better craftsman" ("il miglior fabbro"). Yet at the same time, Pound was a literary vagabond who never felt entirely at home in any culture. Where Eliot settled in England in 1914 and never left, Pound's restless energy led him to London in 1908, to Paris in 1920, and then to Rapallo, Italy, in 1925, where he would remain until the end of World War II. An exile who embraced Italian Fascism during the war and was later indicted for treason, Pound was unique among American writers in the extent of his involvement not only with the art and literature of his time but also with the events of world history in the first half of the 20th century. It is no surprise, then, that when Pound was awarded the Bollingen Prize for poetry in 1949—the first time his poetry had been celebrated in such a public forum—the event unleashed a severe criticism of his role as a poet in history as well as a heated debate concerning the relationship of art to politics.

Pound's comfortable early life in suburban Philadelphia and his education at Hamilton College and the University of Pennsylvania would have seemed to prepare him for the traditional career of a man of letters more than that of a poetic revolutionary. It was Pound's dismissal from his first teaching post at Wabash College in Indiana (for sheltering a young woman overnight in his rooms) that convinced him of his unsuitability for academic life. Pound used the rest of his year's salary to travel to Gibraltar and Venice, where he published his first volume of poetry, *A Lume Spento* (1908). Pound would later refer to these early poems as "stale creampuffs," but it was through these highly derivative poems, with their echoes of William Butler Yeats and others, that Pound perfected his craft and developed his fine ear for the rhythmic and tonal effects of poetry.

Over the next few years, Pound's association with the literary magazine *The New Age* brought him into contact with important writers, artists, and critics as well as economists and politicians. At the same time, he published several more volumes of verse, including *A Quinzaine for This Yule* (1908), *Personae* (1909), *Exultations* (1909), *Canzoni* (1911), and *Ripostes* (1912). His early poetry reflects the influence of an extraordinarily wide range of authors: the Provençal poet Arnaut Daniel, classical poets such as Sappho and Catullus, Italians such as Dante and Cavalcanti, and the English poetic tradition from *Beowulf* and the "Seafarer" poet to Robert Browning and Charles Algernon Swinburne. By 1911, Pound had firmly established himself in London literary circles and had become an important figure in the artistic avant-garde. Along with other expatriate poets, Hilda Doolittle (H.D.) and Richard Aldington, Pound put in place a program for what he called "Imagism," a movement that would have several major tenets. The first of these was that the poem should always involve a "direct treatment of the thing" as opposed to the romanticized or symbolic treatment favored by 19th-century poets. The second was that the poem should use no word that was not absolutely necessary to the composition: Pound wanted to follow French prose writers such as Gustave Flaubert and Guy de Maupassant in finding *le mot juste* (the right word) rather than adopt the overly wordy style of Victorian poets such as Tennyson and Swinburne. "Poetry should be as well written as prose," Pound wrote to poet and editor Harriet Monroe, "departing in no way from speech save by a heightened intensity (i.e. simplicity)."

The third and final rule was that poetry should be composed "in the sequence of the musical phrase" rather than that of the metronome: thus, Pound rejected what he considered the stifling constraint of monotonous pentameter rhythms. With these rules in place, Pound tried to "modernize" poetry in his own work and to encourage the work of other poets—Eliot, William Carlos Williams, and H.D., for example—whom he believed capable of modern writing. Pound edited an anthology of Imagist verse, *Des Imagistes* (1914), which contained the work of H.D., Aldington, Yeats, and others.

On the eve of World War I, however, Pound saw the limitations of the Imagist movement, which he felt had been coopted and sentimentalized by the poet Amy Lowell (who published several Imagist anthologies of her own). Along with the sculptor Henri Gaudier-Brzeska and the painter and novelist Wyndham Lewis, Pound helped found a new movement called Vorticism. The Vorticists encouraged a more dynamic approach to poetry, seeking the hardness and precision of sculpture rather than the static beauty of the image. The movement was to be short-lived—its journal, *BLAST,* folded after two issues, and Gaudier-Brzeska was killed in the war—but it added to Pound's growing reputation as a literary provocateur. Pound also established relationships with various journals—including *The Little Review, Poetry,* and *The Egoist*—and with other writers, including Eliot and Robert Frost. His discovery of Eliot was particularly significant since, Pound believed, Eliot was the only poet to have "modernized himself on his own."

Another event that had a transforming influence on Pound's poetry and poetic ideas was his discovery of the manuscripts of Ernest Fenollosa, an American scholar who had lived in Japan and worked on the translation of Chinese and Japanese poetry. Pound's 1915 volume *Cathay*—a series of loose translations based on Fenollosa's notes—contained some of Pound's best work to date and represented a brilliant use of the poetic "adaptation" to create a new style of lyric poem. The most successful poems in *Cathay,* such as "The River-Merchant's Wife: A Letter" and "Song of the Bowmen of Shu," achieve a freshness and elegance through the directness and simplicity of their language. Pound also took from Fenollosa the notion of the "ideogram," the term Fenollosa used to describe the "simple, original pictures" formed by Chinese characters. Pound responded immediately to the ideogram, or what he later called the "ideogrammatic method," as a way of bringing various images together within language itself. The ideogram inspired another version of Pound's Imagist ideal of the "direct treatment of the thing," and it also provided a structural basis for Pound's composition of longer poetic works.

In 1917, Pound began working on a long poem that would eventually become *The Cantos* and that would take as its primary compositional structure the "ideogrammatic" combination or juxtaposition of different images, ideas, narratives, characters, and historical events. Pound had already experimented in his 1916 volume *Lustra* with longer historical poems, such as "Near Perigord" and "Provincia Deserta," but in his *Cantos* he was more ambitious, hoping to create a modern epic or "poem including history." Pound combined this historical framework with the use of the poetic persona, a technique derived in large part from Browning's long poem "Sordello." After completing the original version of the first three "Cantos" (often referred to as the "Ur-Cantos"), Pound turned his attention to two other projects. *Homage to Sextus Propertius* (first published in *Quia Pauper Amavi* [1919], then as separate volume 1934) is a free translation from the Latin that cast the poet Propertius as a persona for Pound's own dissatisfaction with contemporary society. *Hugh Selwyn Mauberley* (1920), a sequence of shorter lyrics tracing the life and career of a poet based on Pound himself, is a terse and ironic commentary on the situation of the poet and English society after World War I. Pound's most ambitious poem to that point, it is an elegy both for those who died in the war ("There died a myriad, / And of the best, among them") and for his own misguided attempts, in his prewar writings, "to resuscitate the dead art of poetry."

*The Cantos* was to become Pound's lifetime poetic work after he left England in 1921 and moved to Paris. He would continue to write new Cantos and publish them as separate volumes over the next half century: *A Draft of XVI Cantos* (1925) was followed by *A Draft of XXX Cantos* (1930), *Eleven New Cantos: XXXI–XLI* (1934), *The Fifth Decad of Cantos* (1937), *Cantos LII–LXXI* (1940), *The Pisan Cantos* (1948), *Section: Rock-Drill: 85–95* (1955), *Thrones: 96–109* (1959), and *Drafts and Fragments of Cantos CX–CXVII* (1968). A work of over 800 pages, *The Cantos* is both lyric and discursive, a multilingual and allusive modern epic that uses ideogrammatic linkages to combine literary and mythic elements (including a Homeric descent to the underworld and Ovidian metamorphoses) with impressions of such disparate historical figures as the Chinese philosopher Confucius, the American presidents Thomas Jefferson and John Quincy Adams, the Italian Renaissance prince Sigismundo Malatesta, the fascist leader Benito Mussolini, and the economist Major C.H. Douglas. Although Pound finally admitted that he could not "make it cohere," he sought a philosophical structure for *The Cantos* that he defined as being "between KUNG and ELEUSIS," in other words, between an ethic of order and rationality established by Confucian doctrine and a Dionysian celebration of birth, death, and regeneration as represented by the Eleusinian mysteries of ancient Greece. Formally, Pound conceived of *The Cantos* both as a fugue, in which recurring themes are variously rephrased ("the repeat in history"), and as an epic on the model of Dante's *Divine Comedy,* with an Inferno, Purgatorio, and Paradiso. Finally, *The Cantos* can be seen as taking the form of an experimental poetic autobiography in which Pound often speaks in his own voice rather than those of his personae and in which the poet becomes the protagonist of his own poem.

The importance of *The Cantos* as a seminal 20th-century long poem that seeks to redefine the epic in the modern world was recognized by Eliot (Pound's first important critic as well as his friend) and later by such poets as Allen Tate, William Carlos Williams, Louis Zukofsky, Robert Lowell, Robert Duncan, and Charles Olson. Pound's aim, as James Laughlin and Delmore Schwartz wrote in a 1940 essay on *The Cantos,* was nothing less than that of "painting, in vast detail, the mind-body-soul of Twentieth Century man"; in constructing his personal epic, Pound focused not only on the present day but on "the phases of history that have conditioned the nature of his being" (Laughlin and Schwartz, 1972).

*The Cantos* was also preoccupied with the economic issues that were to become an increasing obsession for Pound. In particular, the poem focused on the development of banking and on the damage caused by usury—the lending of money at excessive rates of interest—throughout history. Pound saw a direct relationship between economic conditions and the life of art at a given moment in history; a society's artistic production, its mores, its culture, and even its religion were linked to its economics. During the 1930s, Pound became more interested in economics and politics than in literature: he published several nonliterary books, including *ABC of Economics* (1933) and *Jefferson and/or Mussolini* (1935); he took an active interest in the government and economic programs of Fascist Italy; and he traveled to the United States in 1939, hoping to talk personally with President Roosevelt. Unfortunately, his tendency to associate usury with Jewish moneylenders led him to express views that were increasingly anti-Semitic.

Despite his determinedly expatriate status and his difficult relationship with his homeland, Pound remained an American poet whose poetic tradition looks both back to Walt Whitman (his "pig-headed father") and forward to the work of such poets as Zukofsky, Olson, Duncan, Allen Ginsberg, and Gary Snyder. Pound's experiments with rhythm would help to liberate poetry from the confines of iambic pentameter. At the same time, his more rigorous use of the poetic line and his sculptural sense of poetic form provided an important alternative to the looser free verse of poets such as Whitman and Carl Sandburg. Pound's Imagist ideals—particularly those involving the direct treatment of the visual object and the use of everyday language rather than self-consciously poetic diction—have also had a profound impact on 20th-century poetry; and his avant-garde spirit—captured in his famous Modernist credo "make it new"—has been a source of inspiration to many poets who see themselves as fighting the forces of poetic homogeneity and cultural complacency.

However, it is in *The Cantos,* Pound's magnum opus, that we find his most important legacy for 20th-century poetry. *The Cantos* opened up American poetry to the inclusion of historical sources and documents and to a wider range of languages, cultures, and poetic styles, helping to move modern poetry away from the more narrowly defined set of texts comprising the Anglo-American canon. Further, *The Cantos* established an important model (along with the work of William Carlos Williams and others) for a poetry of "open form" that would be adopted by many of the younger poets of the 1950s and 1960s.

CHRISTOPHER BEACH

*See also* Expatriate Poetry; Imagism; Long Poem; Symbolism

**Biography**

Born in Hailey, Idaho, 30 October 1885. Attended Hamilton College, Clinton, New York, 1903–05, Ph.B. 1905; University of Pennsylvania, Philadelphia, 1901–03, 1907–08, M.A. in Romance languages 1906; on Romance languages faculty, Wabash College, Crawfordsville, Indiana, 1907; reviewer, *New Age,* from 1911; English editor, *Poetry,* Chicago, 1912–19; literary editor, *New Freewoman* (later *The Egoist*), 1913–14; co-founder with Wyndham Lewis, *Blast,* 1914; English editor, *Little Review,* 1917–19; drama and ballet critic, *Athenaeum,* 1920; Paris correspondent, *The Dial,* 1920–23; founding editor, *The Exile,* 1927–28; contributor, *Il Mare,* 1932–40, and *New English Weekly,* 1932–35; promoted "social credit" economic theories, from late 1920s; broadcast over Rome Radio, from 1940 (arrested and jailed for broadcasts by United States Army, 1945); committed to St. Elizabeths Hospital, Washington, D.C., 1946–58. Received Bollingen Prize, 1949; Harriet Monroe Award, 1962; Academy of American Poets fellowship, 1963; National Endowment for the Arts grant, 1966; honorary doctorate, Hamilton College, 1939. Died in Venice, Italy, 1 November 1972.

**Poetry**

*A Lume Spento,* 1908
*A Quinzaine for This Yule,* 1908
*Personae,* 1909
*Exultations,* 1909
*Provença: Poems Selected from Personae, Exultations, and Canzoniere,* 1910
*Canzoni,* 1911
*Ripostes,* 1912
*Cathay,* 1915
*Lustra,* 1916
*Lustra, with Earlier Poems,* 1917
*The Fourth Canto,* 1919
*Quia Pauper Amavi,* 1919
*Hugh Selwyn Mauberley,* 1920
*Umbra: The Early Poems,* 1920
*Poems, 1918–21, Including Three Portraits and Four Cantos,* 1921
*A Draft of XVI Cantos,* 1925
*Personae: The Collected Poems,* 1926; revised edition, 1949; republished as *Personae: Collected Shorter Poems,* 1952; republished as *Collected Shorter Poems,* 1968
*A Draft of the Cantos 17–27,* 1928
*Selected Poems,* edited by T.S. Eliot, 1928
*A Draft of XXX Cantos,* 1930
*Eleven New Cantos: XXXI–XLI,* 1934; republished as *A Draft of Cantos XXXI–XLI,* 1935
*Homage to Sextus Propertius,* 1934
*Alfred Venison's Poems, Social Credit Themes,* 1935
*The Fifth Decad of Cantos,* 1937
*Cantos LII–LXXI,* 1940
*A Selection of Poems,* 1940
*The Pisan Cantos,* 1948
*The Cantos,* 1948; revised edition, 1965; revised edition, as *Cantos No. 1–117, 120,* 1970
*Selected Poems,* 1949
*Seventy Cantos,* 1950; revised edition, as *The Cantos,* 1954, 1964, 1976
*Section: Rock-Drill: 85–95 de los cantares,* 1955
*Thrones: 96–109 de los cantares,* 1959
*Versi prosaici,* 1959
*A Lume Spento, and Other Early Poems,* 1965
*Canto CX,* 1965
*Selected Cantos,* 1967; revised edition, 1970
*Cantos, 110–116,* 1967
*Drafts and Fragments of Cantos CX–CXVII,* 1968
*Selected Poems, 1908–1959,* 1975
*Collected Early Poems,* edited by Michael John King, 1976
*Ezra Pound's Poetry and Prose: Contributions to Periodicals,* 1991
*The Cantos of Ezra Pound,* 1993
*A Selection of Poems,* 1994
*Early Poems,* 1996
*Shakespear's Pound: Illuminated Cantos,* 1999
*Ezra Pound,* 2000

**Selected Criticism**

*The Spirit of Romance,* 1910
*ABC of Reading,* 1934
*Literary Essays,* edited by T.S. Eliot, 1954

**Other Writings:** essays (*Polite Essays,* 1937), radio addresses, political writings (*If This Be Treason,* 1948), correspondence (*Pound and Dorothy Shakespear: Their Letters, 1909–1914,* edited by Omar Pound and A. Walton Litz, 1985), translations of Italian and Chinese literature (*The Sonnets and Ballate of Guido Cavalcanti,* 1912; as *Pound's Cavalcanti Poems,* 1966; *The Classic Anthology Defined by Confucius,* 1954); edited collections of literature (*Des Imagistes,* 1914; *Profile: An Anthology,* 1932).

**Further Reading**

Alexander, Michael, *The Poetic Achievement of Ezra Pound,* Berkeley: University of California Press, and London: Faber and Faber, 1979

Bell, Ian F.A., *Critic as Scientist: The Modernist Poetics of Ezra Pound,* London and New York: Methuen, 1981

Carpenter, Humphrey, *A Serious Character: The Life of Ezra Pound,* London and Boston: Faber and Faber, 1988

Casillo, Robert, *The Genealogy of Demons: Anti-Semitism, Fascism, and the Myths of Ezra Pound,* Evanston, Illinois: Northwestern University Press, 1988

Davie, Donald, *Ezra Pound: Poet as Sculptor,* New York: Oxford University Press, 1964; London: Routledge and Kegan Paul, 1965

Flory, Wendy Stallard, *Ezra Pound and "The Cantos": A Record of Struggle,* New Haven, Connecticut: Yale University Press, 1980

Kenner, Hugh, *The Pound Era,* Berkeley: University of California Press, 1971; London: Faber, 1972; 2nd edition, London: Faber and Faber, 1975

Laughlin, James, and Delmore Schwartz, "Notes on Ezra Pound's 'Cantos': Structure and Music," in *Ezra Pound: The Critical Heritage,* edited by Eric Homberger, London and Boston: Routledge and Kegan Paul, 1972

Lindberg, Kathryne, *Reading Pound Reading: Modernism after Nietzsche,* Oxford and New York: Oxford University Press, 1987

Surette, Leon, *A Light from Eleusis: A Study of Ezra Pound's "Cantos,"* Oxford: Clarendon Press, and New York: Oxford University Press, 1979

## Cathay

Ezra Pound's *Cathay* was 15 translations gathered together in a flimsy volume the color of a brown paper bag. It was also, in 1915, a radical example of the new English poetry, a substantial break from traditional Anglo-American poetics, and a direct challenge to earlier translations of Chinese poetry. As George Steiner (1975) would later remark of the *Cathay* poems, they "altered the feel of the language and set the pattern of cadence for modern verse."

For Pound, *Cathay* marked the beginning of a lifelong interest in Chinese poetry and thought. His first encounter with Chinese material had come in 1913, when he came across Allen Upward's "Scented Leaves—From a Chinese Jar" in *Poetry.* Through Upward, Pound met Mary Fenollosa, widow of the American sinologist Ernest Fenollosa, who was looking for someone to turn her husband's notes on Chinese poetry into a book. On 2 October, Pound wrote to his future wife, Dorothy Shakespear, "I seem to be getting orient from all quarters. . . . I'm stocked up with K'ung fu Tsze [Confucius], and Men Tsze [Mencius], etc. I suppose they'll keep me calm for a week or so." Some short time later, Mary Fenollosa handed Pound the manuscripts of her dead husband's work: preliminary translations of a great many Chinese poems and some Japanese Noh plays to edit and publish as he saw fit. She also gave him £40 to cover expenses. Pound was delighted; he wrote to Shakespear, "There is *no* long poem in chinese. . . . THE period was 4th cent. B.C.—Chu Yüan, Imagiste."

*Cathay*'s poetic innovations included a reliance on free verse and end-stopped lines ("The jewelled steps are already quite white with dew / It is so late that the dew soaks my gauze stockings / And I let down the crystal curtain / And watch the moon through the clear autumn") as well as a commitment to the presentation of experience condensed into an incandescent image ("March has come to the bridge head / Peach boughs and apricot boughs hang over a thousand gates / At morning there are flowers to cut the heart / And evening drives them on the eastward-flowing waters"). Early readers were unsure whether the voice of this new poetry was Pound's or whether it came from the original Chinese poems. Aware of the estranging effect of Pound's meter and syntax, one reviewer for the *Times Literary Supplement* asked, "But is the Chinese language, we wonder, as unusual as Mr. Pound's? If not, he does misrepresent the effect upon a Chinese reader. . . . But for those who, like ourselves, know no Chinese, it does not matter much. The result, however produced, is well worth having, and it seems to us very Chinese."

For literary critics, the genuine Chineseness of *Cathay* remains a vital question. How could Pound, who knew no Chinese in 1915, have produced translations that, some critics feel, reproduce almost perfectly the spirit and tone of the Chinese originals? Consider, for instance, the first four lines of Pound's "The Beautiful Toilet." Fenollosa had left Pound these words, written out beneath the Chinese characters:

| | | | | |
|---|---|---|---|---|
| blue | blue | river | bank | grass |
| luxuriantly spread the willow | luxuriantly spread the willow | garden | in | willow |
| fill/full | fill/full | storied house | on | girl |
| white/brilliant luminous | white/brilliant luminous | just face | window | door |

Pound turned them into

Blue, blue is the grass about the river
And the willows have overfilled the close garden.
And within, the mistress, in the midmost of her youth,
White, white of face, hesitates, passing the door.

Arthur Waley, writing in implied rebuke of Pound several years later, produced this:

Green, green,
The grass by the river bank,
Thick, thick,
The willow trees in the garden.
Sad, sad,
The lady in the tower.

Waley's far more literal translation of the Chinese intends to correct the degree to which Pound's version plays with the content of the Chinese poem, which offers no reason to say, for instance, that the mistress is in the "midmost of her youth." While Pound has not kept the double characters that begin each line—in the second and third lines, there is a repetition of short "i" and double "l" sounds instead—Waley has followed the literal prescriptions of the original text.

Which is the better translation? The answer depends on what one believes a translation should do, and part of *Cathay*'s value is that it made that question a critical one for Anglo-American Modernist poets and for poets who either translated Chinese poetry or found inspiration in it (most famously Gary Snyder). As T.S. Eliot would famously remark of Pound's achievement, "Chinese poetry, as we know it today, is something invented by Ezra Pound." Perhaps more than most, *Cathay* is a book with a dual legacy: while some read it to see how vital new poetic techniques—the image, Pound's free verse, and the end-stopped line—helped Pound reshape English poetry, others take it as a compelling and vibrant example of Modernism's romance with the East.

Such a dual inheritance is perhaps nowhere clearer than in the opening stanzas of "The River-Merchant's Wife: A Letter," in which Pound seems fully identified with his Chinese subject matter and the poet Li Bai:

> While my hair was still cut straight across my forehead
> I played about the front gate, pulling flowers.
> You came by on bamboo stilts, playing horse,
>
> You walked about my seat, playing with blue plums.
> And we went on living in the village of Chokan:
> Two small people, without dislike or suspicion.
>
> At fourteen I married My Lord you.
> I never laughed, being bashful.
> Lowering my head, I looked at the wall.
> Called to, a thousand times, I never looked back.
>
> At fifteen I stopped scowling,
> I desired my dust to be mingled with yours
> Forever and forever, and forever.
> Why should I climb the look out?

Questions of origin aside, then, *Cathay* remains a book of breathtakingly beautiful poetry. Written during a time when Pound's other publications (including the magazine *BLAST*) gave voice to the righteous fire of Pound's harsh politics, *Cathay*, like so much of Pound's Chinese material, presents a breath of quiet calm, an example of the poet at his most empathetic and surefooted.

ERIC HAYOT

**Further Reading**


Baker, Edward H., "Historical Mediation in Two Translations of Ezra Pound," *Paideuma* 17, no.1 (Spring 1988)

Bush, Ronald, "Pound and Li Po," in *Ezra Pound among the Poets*, edited by George Bornstein, Chicago: University of Chicago Press, 1985

Carpenter, Humphrey, *A Serious Character: The Life of Ezra Pound*, London and Boston: Faber and Faber, 1988

Chapple, Anne, "Ezra Pound's *Cathay:* Compilation from the Fenollosa Notebooks," *Paideuma* 17, nos. 2–3 (Fall–Winter 1988)

Chen, Xiaomei, "Rediscovering Ezra Pound: A Postcolonial 'Misreading' of a Western Legacy," *Paideuma* 22, nos. 2–3 (Fall–Winter 1994)

Eliot, T.S., "Introduction," in *Ezra Pound Selected Poems*, edited by T.S. Eliot, London: Faber and Gwyer, 1928

Fenollosa, Ernest Francisco, *The Chinese Written Character as a Medium for Poetry*, New York: Kasper and Horton, and London: Nott, 1936

Hsieh, Ming, *Ezra Pound and the Appropriation of Chinese Poetry: "Cathay," Translation, and Imagism*, New York and London: Garland, 1998

Jang, Gyung-Ryul, "*Cathay* Reconsidered: Pound as Inventor of Chinese Poetry," *Paideuma* 14, nos. 2–3 (Fall–Winter 1985)

Kenner, Hugh, *The Pound Era*, Berkeley: University of California Press, 1971; London: Faber, 1972; 2nd edition, London: Faber and Faber, 1975

Kern, Robert, *Orientalism, Modernism, and the American Poem*, Cambridge and New York: Cambridge University Press, 1996

Qian, Zhaoming, *Orientalism and Modernism: The Legacy of China in Pound and Williams*, Durham, North Carolina: Duke University Press, 1995

Steiner, George, *After Babel*, London and New York: Oxford University Press, 1975; 3rd edition, Oxford and New York: Oxford University Press, 1998

Waley, Arthur, translator, *One Hundred and Seventy Chinese Poems*, London: Constable, 1918


## Homage to Sextus Propertius

Ezra Pound's "Homage to Sextus Propertius" is a 12-part rendition of the work of the Roman poet Sextus Propertius, a contemporary of Horace, Virgil, and Ovid in the first century B.C. The poem can best be described as a rearrangement and reinterpretation of selections from Propertius' love poems to his mistress Cynthia. Pound's first reference to the translation occurs in a 1916 letter to Iris Barry. Advising her to add Catullus and Propertius to her reading list, he went on to say, "And if you CAN'T find any decent translations . . . I suppose I shall have to rig up something" (*The Selected Letters of Ezra Pound, 1907–1941*, 1971).

Yet the question begged by Pound's letter—exactly how to evaluate his translations of Propertius—has aroused strong commentary since its first appearance, when Harriet Monroe published four of its 12 sections in the March 1919 issue of *Poetry*. Pound later noted that he had derived the title of the poem from Debussy, who titled a composition "Hommage à Rameau" to reflect its debt to the work of another composer. His readership did not always detect such nuances, however. In April 1919, immediately after the poem's first publication, the University of Chicago classicist William Gardner Hale published a critique in *Poetry* complaining of Pound's numerous inaccuracies in translation, a charge that has been repeated with varying degrees of intensity many times since.

It can be argued that such pedantry was precisely what Pound intended to satirize in "Homage." In the excessive formality of its diction, as well as in the stilted nature of its word order and syntax, the poem punctures the pretensions of those classical scholars who portray themselves as possessing "mastery" of their borrowed idiom. That is, by deliberately translating Propertius into awkward English, Pound undercuts the claims of classical scholars to cultural authority. One striking example of such satire occurs in Propertius' account of his muse and mistress Cynthia as "with ivory fingers driv[ing] a tune through the / lyre." The ironic contrast between the conventional figure "ivory fingers" and the deliberately clumsy image that follows violates the decorum conventionally associated with English translations from classical literature and, in so doing, calls that decorum, as well as the linguistic politics underlying it, into question.

Why might Pound wish to satirize innocent classics scholars? The answer lies in his own political sympathies. Classical scholars of the late 19th and early 20th centuries generally considered Propertius a brilliantly precocious poet whose work suffered from its emphasis on passion and sensibility. Pound, however, found in Propertius' celebration of love poetry—and in his avoidance of the more traditional epic form—an implicit anti-imperial sentiment similar to Pound's own. That World War I was in progress as Pound wrote also influenced the poem: of the 12 sections of Propertius' work that Pound chose to translate, five are based on poems that protest the Roman celebration of martial values. Years after "Homage" was published, Pound noted that it "presents certain emotions as vital to me in 1917, faced with the infinite and ineffable imbecility of the British Empire, as they were to Propertius some centuries earlier, when faced with the infinite and ineffable imbecility of the Roman Empire" (*Selected Letters*).

Pound's version of Propertius consequently emphasizes the latter poet's ironic tone. As a result, he reinvents Propertius—and himself—as a critic of the destructive power implied by imperial pomposity. In particular, Pound uses highly colloquial diction to downplay or poke fun at the attention to mythology found in the original, as when he attributes to Phoebus the exclamation "'You idiot!'" and refers to the Muses as "keep[ing] their collective nose in my books." At other times, Pound brings out latent ironies by employing secondary rather than primary meanings of the Latin terms, most famously translating "orgia," which literally denotes Bacchic ceremonies, as "orgies." A similarly satiric purpose characterizes Pound's hyperbolic literalism in translating Propertius' description of his poetic practice as "this soft book comes into my mouth."

Perhaps Pound's clearest statement of satirical intent comes in his treatment of the section in which Propertius claims Virgil as his poetic predecessor. In the original, Propertius praises Virgil for his role in propounding the mythology of empire and hints at his own poetic aspirations:

> It pleases Virgil to sing the Actian shores of guardian
>   Apollo,
>       and the brave ships of Caesar,
> Virgil who now brings to life the arms of Trojan Aeneas
>       and the walls founded on Lavinian shores.
> Yield Roman writers, yield Greeks!
>       Something greater than the Iliad is born . . .

Pound's rendition of this passage possesses a notably different tone:

> Upon the Actian marshes Virgil is Phoebus' chief of police,
>       He can tabulate Caesar's great ships.
> He thrills to Ilian arms,
>       He shakes the Trojan weapons of Aeneas,
> And casts stores on Lavinian beaches.
> Make way, ye Roman authors,
>       clear the street, O ye Greeks,
> For a much larger Iliad is in the course of construction

Pound here reduces Virgil to the status of chief clerk in the storehouse of imperial paraphernalia. At the same time, his mockery contains more serious implications, as the mask of Propertius enables Pound to declare his own poetic aspirations to "a much larger Iliad." The first component of that "larger Iliad," the Cantos, would be published in 1922, only a few years after the appearance of "Homage to Sextus Propertius." In many ways, it would not have been possible for Pound to produce his epic without first having written "Propertius": Hugh Kenner (1985) has noted that the Cantos are organized by many of the same devices, such as shifts in tone, that hold together the earlier poem. Viewed in this light, "Homage to Sextus Propertius" both foreshadows and prepares for Pound's transition from the lyric mode to the epic one. More significant, in its ironic combination of what Eliot referred to as "the pastness of the past" with an insistence on that past's relevance, "Homage" embodies a particular strain of Modernist literary enterprise.

ERIKA NANES

**Further Reading**


Alexander, Michael, *The Poetic Achievement of Ezra Pound,* Berkeley: University of California Press, and London: Faber and Faber, 1979

Arkins, Brian, "Pound's Propertius: What Kind of Homage?" *Paideuma* 17, no. 1 (Spring 1988)

Bush, Ronald, "Gathering the Limbs of Orpheus: The Subject of Pound's 'Homage to Sextus Propertius,'" in *Ezra Pound and William Carlos Williams: The University of Pennsylvania Conference Papers,* edited by Daniel Hoffman, Philadelphia: University of Pennsylvania Press, 1983

Froula, Christine, *A Guide to Ezra Pound's Selected Poems,* New York: New Directions, 1983

Hooley, Daniel M., *The Classics in Paraphrase: Ezra Pound and Modern Translators of Latin Poetry,* London and Toronto: Associated University Presses, 1988

Kenner, Hugh, *The Poetry of Ezra Pound,* Lincoln: University of Nebraska Press, 1985

Peacock, Alan J., "Pound's Propertian Distortions: A Possible Rationale," *Paideuma* 17, nos. 2–3 (Fall–Winter 1988)

Thomas, Ron, "The Latin Masks of Ezra Pound," *Studies in Modern Literature* 4 (1983)


## Hugh Selwyn Mauberley

Ezra Pound's *Hugh Selwyn Mauberley* was first published in London in June 1920, and, following F.R. Leavis' attention to the "unrecognized" poem in *New Bearings in English Poetry* (1932), it became the most important of Pound's works apart from the *Cantos.* The poem received constant attention and much praise in the years that followed, but it also suffered sharp attacks by Donald Davie, A.L. French, Marjorie Perloff, and others, and it often frustrated readers attempting to identify the poem's personae. In 1990, Vincent Miller suggested that it had become "perhaps [Pound's] least respected poem" (it was omitted completely from the 1999 *Oxford Anthology of Modern American Poetry*), but his essay holds it rightly to be "one of Pound's major poems" and "essential" to the "development . . . of modernist literature."

The poem is a sequence of 18 discrete poems in two parts. The 13 poems from "Ode" to "Envoi" constitute the first part. The five poems following the subtitle "Mauberley (1920)" constitute the second. The subtitle preceding "Ode," which belongs to the poem as a whole, was originally "Life and Contacts." For a 1957 printing, however, Pound changed the phrase to "Contacts and Life" in order to reflect "the actual order of the subject matter" (cited in Ruthven, 1969).

If we take Hugh Selwyn Mauberley to be the name of a fictitious minor poet who shared much of the London scene and an aesthetic outlook with Ezra Pound, then the "actual order" would move from the contacts each might have made to the life of Mauberley, from the first part of the poem, in other words, to the second.

The "Ode" sets a problem: it presents the case of a minor poet whose work came to little. Wrong in origin ("half savage country"), time ("out of date"), and intention ("wringing lilies from the acorn"), this small-time Odysseus-poet spent too much time with Circe and so "passed from men's memory" at age 31.

Nevertheless, who is this poet, and whose voice dismisses him? Does Pound dismiss Mauberley or Mauberley Pound? Or does Pound dismiss "Pound," some outgrown version of himself? And whose voice do we hear in the poems that follow?

In Hugh Kenner's influential view, reinforced by John Espey's pioneering book *Ezra Pound's Mauberley* (1955), the voice is Pound's except for the final poem, "Medallion," which should be taken as a poem by Mauberley. In the second book-length study of the poem, *Circe's Craft* (1983), Jo Brantley Berryman argues that Mauberley speaks the first 12 poems, whereas the poems from "Envoi" to the end, including "Medallion," are from Pound's point of view. In a recent article that includes a helpful review of this issue, Thomas Grieve claims that the entire sequence is spoken by the fictitious Mauberley. Readers facing the problem would do well to remember the obvious: all the poems in the sequence were written by Pound, but each presents a quite distinctive voice, and nowhere do we confront the reflective personality of the man Ezra Pound himself in lines of personal utterance. In other words, each voice in the poem is to some degree "Pound," and that is true even when we say that a part of the poem is spoken or "written" by another.

Still, one has to identify the poem's voices to talk about the poem, and Espey's view, convincing to many, has worked effectively again and again. If the "Ode" is by Pound, it must be an ironic self-portrait that borrows phrases in circulation and applies them to a younger Pound of, say, 1913–16 (when Pound reached "l'an trentuniesme"). In seeing himself as others saw him, Pound's irony is complicated—he might regret his efforts to wring "lilies from the acorn" and yet be proud of his half-savage origins, and recognize that to be married to Flaubert or "unaffected by 'the march of events'" could mean different things to different people.

From the "Ode," poems II and III describe the literary environment from Pound's point of view in crisp quatrains that lament the commercialization, mechanization, and democratization of the social, political, and aesthetic realms. In overly simple yet effective contrasts, the time-consuming crafted excellence of the past is set against a world of mass production where nothing lasts but "tawdry cheapness." The idea of honoring a hero in the last quatrain of poem III leads to thoughts of the great war in sections IV and V. Here the daring and bravery and beauty of youth plays against the horrors of trench warfare where bodies rotted between the lines ("laughter out of dead bellies") and against the treachery of entrenched political power ("usury age-old and age-thick / and liars in public places").

In "Yeux Glauques" and "'Siena mi fé; disfecemi Maremma,'" Pound gathers particular images to suggest his and Mauberley's immediate aesthetic predecessors first in pre-Raphaelite moments of the 1860s and 1870s and then in the 1890s. One admires at first the dedication to a dangerous idea of beauty and the courage to flout bourgeois values. However, a "foetid" odor builds through these poems, suggesting the decadent and unproductive side of the era by mention of adulterers and pimps and whores, of stillborn books and pickled fetuses.

The next five poems ("Brennbaum" through XII) introduce contacts in a more usual social sense, first three artists, contemporaries of Pound and Mauberley, and then two versions of the audience for art. Mr. Nixon takes a commercial view and advises wily self-promotion; buttering reviewers leads to a creamy yacht. The opposing game of pure art leads to a "'Nineties'" sort of death or the "unpaid, uncelebrated" isolation of the stylist. Brennbaum's immature artificiality sets him close to the effeteness of the 1890s, and his exterior hides, except in the harshest light, his connection to what is evidently his Jewish heritage. In this he is like the respectable woman of Ealing (in poem XI), whose instinctual heritage, whose very thoughts of instinctual satisfaction, have been repressed by a Victorian grandmother. The upper-class Lady Valentine is as commercial a consumer as Mr. Nixon is a producer. A new poet acquaintance might be useful in her climb to ever-higher social strata, and a bohemian acquaintance might be a "friend and comforter" if class warfare should end in proletarian revolution. The last rhyme of socks and flowers ("half-hose has" / "roses") closes the scene on a Brechtian discord.

The discord modulates, however, into the beautiful melody of "Envoi," an imitation of Edmund Waller's song "Go, lovely rose!" (1645). Pound leaves his own strict quatrains here for looser, longer stanzas with delicately varied true and slant rhymes, and, near the close, he makes a sudden departure from the conventional iambic to a haunting falling rhythm as "our two dusts" become "Siftings on siftings in oblivion." Although the speaker proclaims the inadequacy of his book, this poem justly compares to a rose "in magic amber laid, . . . / Braving time." If the sequence is the "farewell to London" that Pound called it in *Personae* (1926), "Envoi" is an evocative valediction.

The second section, "Mauberley (1920)," opens with a spare and allusive introduction to Mauberley's art, which, if fine, is limited, done with a burin and not a brush—"Colourless," "an art / In profile." In "The Age Demanded," Pound's diction inflates pompously to parody Mauberley's self-regard and perhaps his critical if not his poetic style. Pound, who had warned, "Go in fear of abstractions," and was soon to write in Eliot's margin, "Dam per'apsez," says this of Mauberley:

> Invitation, mere invitation to perceptivity
> Gradually led him to the isolation
> Which these presents place
> Under a more tolerant, perhaps, examination. (lines 323–26)

As Odysseus did for Elpenor, Pound plants an oar for the anti-heroic Mauberley, a beached drifter for whom the term "hedonist" is too strong. "Medallion" remains as a sample of Mauberley's poetry. Like "Envoi," the poem treats the song and beauty of a woman in terms of past traditions—Renaissance Italian painting and porcelain, Greek sculpture, and Cretan fresco. However, "Medallion" snaps suddenly from the past into the harsh glare of the present, a glare from the then-new and more efficient gas-filled ("half-watt") electric light bulbs, under which light the eyes turn topaz.

The division of *Mauberley* into so many discrete elements should not obscure the many threads that tie the poems together. The poet-Odysseus parallel fits neatly with sexual motifs. Reproductive incapacity and failure both overt ("eunuch," "still-born") and covert (the autopsy showed Lionel Johnson to be genitally immature, and Dowson engaged prostitutes because their rooms were cheap) connect to a fundamental incapacity to see, and both kinds of failure come together in Mauberley. Confronted by the bedroom eyes ("irides") of the goddess of love, Mauberley "passed, inconscient"; the "mandate / Of Eros" exists for him only in retrospect—he could see the orchid but not its root. That poem's closing quatrain (lines 295–98) adds an epilogue of futility, a metamorphosis into stone of dogs "biting empty air."

Odysseus knew goddesses more fully, avoided metamorphoses, and journeyed with purpose to Ithaca to pass the test of the bed and reestablish dynastic succession. If Pound as poet is not such a hero, he has aspirations; Mauberley is the anti-type. In "Medallion," Mauberley knows the goddess only from an engraving in an art history book; his journey is an aimless drifting. He is still observing the elegance of Circe's hair as his eyes, more than his subject's, turn to stone.

WILLIAM CLARKSON

**Further Reading**

Berryman, Jo Brantley, *Circe's Craft: Ezra Pound's "Hugh Selwyn Mauberley,"* Ann Arbor, Michigan: UMI Research Press, and Epping, Essex: Bowker, 1983

Davie, Donald, *Ezra Pound: Poet as Sculptor,* New York: Oxford University Press, 1964; London: Routledge and Kegan Paul, 1965

Dekker, George, "Ezra Pound's *Hugh Selwyn Mauberley,*" in *The Pelican Guide to English Literature: The Modern Age,* edited by Boris Ford, New York: Penguin, 1978

Espey, John, *Ezra Pound's Mauberley,* Berkeley: University of California Press, 1955

French, A.L., "'Olympian Apathein': Pound's *Hugh Selwyn Mauberley* and Modern Poetry," *Essays in Criticism* 15 (1965); reprinted in *Ezra Pound: A Critical Anthology,* edited by J.P. Sullivan, London and Baltimore, Maryland: Penguin, 1970

Grieve, Thomas F., "Pound's Other Homage: *Hugh Selwyn Mauberley,*" *Paideuma* 27, no. 1 (Spring 1998)

Hoffman, Frederick J., *The Twenties: American Writing in the Postwar Decade,* New York: Viking Press, 1955; revised edition, New York: Collier, 1962

Miller, Vincent, "Mauberley and His Critics," *ELH* 57 (1990)

Perloff, Marjorie, *The Poetics of Indeterminacy: Rimbaud to Cage,* Princeton, New Jersey: Princeton University Press, 1981

Ruthven, K.K., *A Guide to Ezra Pound's "Personae" (1926),* Berkeley: University of California Press, 1969

Witemeyer, Hugh, *The Poetry of Ezra Pound 1908–1920,* Berkeley: University of California Press, 1969

## The Pisan Cantos

The circumstances under which *The Pisan Cantos* (1948) were written account for much of their status among the most conspicuous achievements of the American century. Imprisoned on charges of treason and exposed to the elements in an American army detention camp near Pisa, Italy; isolated from his family, friends, and library; and in constant fear of summary execution in the chaotic atmosphere of a country still riven by Fascism, Pound triumphantly accomplished a longhand transcendence of despair and loss. If Pound's early writings champion the rhetoric of the fragment as a way of passively representing the breakdown of European culture in the aftermath of World War I, *The Pisan Cantos* show Pound actively assembling the shards of memory, history, and experience in order to bring unity to the chaos of a mind that disintegrated along with Europe in the 1930s.

Recent scholarship has challenged the legend, promoted by the text itself, that *The Pisan Cantos* were the singular result of a burst of inspiration produced in an isolated moment—Pound called it "The Pisan Paradise"—of intense physical and psychological pressure, as in "Canto LXXVI":

As a lone ant from a broken ant-hill
from the wreckage of Europe, ego scriptor
The rain has fallen, the wind coming down
out of the mountain

In fact, it was only after being transferred to a tent from the outdoor cage in which he had suffered a terrifying mental collapse in May and June 1945 that Pound began writing out the first version of *The Pisan Cantos* in pencil on pads of paper and even on toilet tissue. He prepared a typewritten manuscript in the evenings later that summer and into the fall, when the camp dispensary was unoccupied.

Following the hermetic cantos of the late 1930s, these writings offered themselves as a singular moment of moral and aesthetic clarity. Pound himself admitted in a note to the military censors monitoring his mail that he had rejected the "intended obscurity" so characteristic of his poems from the 1930s in favor of more direct artistry. At the same time, Pound admitted to practicing the "extreme condensation" that alienated so many of his readers in the 1920s and 1930s, as in this passage from "Canto LXXX":

Tune: kitten on the keys
radio steam Calliope
following the Battle Hymn of the Republic
where the honey-wagon cease from stinking
and the nose be at peace
"mi-hine eyes hev"
well yes they *have*
seen a good deal of it

As with Pound's earlier poetry, this passage gestures toward a variety of materials, including fragments of popular and patriotic songs heard on the radio. Among the other poetic techniques that root *The Pisan Cantos* in the larger poem are the seamless integration of foreign languages and the free, unattributed quotation of his usual textual sources, some from memory, others from materials at hand. In addition to the volume of Mencius and the Chinese dictionary that Pound brought with him when he was first arrested, he had access to newspapers, magazines, and a Bible provided by his captors as well as a poetry anthology he found in the camp latrine. The lessons and poetry of Dante, Villon, and Ecclesiastes, also written in prison or exile, helped Pound achieve a moral authority and vernacular simplicity, especially when recording his ground-level observations of the other prisoners, the weather, plant and insect life, and his own suffering, as in this famous passage from "Canto LXXXIII":

When the mind swings by a grass-blade
        an ant's forefoot shall save you
the clover leaf smells and tastes as its flower

Pound sent the core of the poems that would become *The Pisan Cantos* to his wife, Dorothy, in five "wads" totaling about 300 pages on five occasions in the fall of 1945. Dorothy passed them to Olga Rudge, whose daughter, Mary, typed clean versions, which were sent to Pound's publishers, T.S. Eliot and James Laughlin. Eliot and Laughlin worked with Pound to produce final versions of individual poems for publication in literary magazines in 1946 and 1947. The entire sequence of 11 newly ordered poems was published in the United States in July 1948 by Pound's American publisher, New Directions. Publication in the United Kingdom by Pound's British publisher, Faber and Faber, followed a year later.

In its final form, *The Pisan Cantos* is a Dantesquan confessional narrative that starts with the writer lost in the dark night of total war and ends at sunrise, the poet having survived the crisis. Such formal unity is missing from the original handwritten manuscripts, evidence that Pound's talents as an editor of his own work had also survived. For example, the famous lines linking the martyrdom of the medieval founder of Manichaeanism, the brutal execution of Mussolini, and an image of a rural victim of Italy's political failure were composed at the end of the writing process and placed strategically at the beginning of what would become the first page of the sequence.

On publication, *The Pisan Cantos* was nominated for the 1949 Bollingen Prize of the Library of Congress, igniting a public controversy about the relationship of art and politics. Figures including T.S. Eliot, Allen Tate, and John Berryman defended the nomination by insisting on judging *The Pisan Cantos* on the literary merits. Pound's nomination attracted the disdain of writers such as Karl Shapiro and Robert Frost, who objected to Pound's apparent lack of contrition for morally indefensible positions that culminated in the wartime radio broadcasts he made under the auspices of Italy's Fascist government. In fact, from the moral ambiguity of the opening triptych through the coded mourning of executed Fascist leaders such as Pierre Laval and Vidkun Quisling in "Canto LXXXIV," *The Pisan Cantos* displays an ideological continuity with Pound's wartime views, especially his anti-Semitism, as in "Canto LXXIV":

        The yidd is a stimulant, and the goyim are cattle
In gt/ proportion and go to saleable slaughter
With the maximum of docility.

Yet even such intemperate opinions are accompanied by regret and remorse, as in the following excerpt from "Canto LXXXI," perhaps the best-loved poem of the sequence:

        Pull down thy vanity
Thou art a beaten dog beneath the hail,
A swollen magpie in the fitful sun,
Half black half white
No knowst'ou wing from tail
Pull down thy vanity
                How mean thy hates
Fostered in falsity, niggard in charity,
Pull down thy vanity,
                I say pull down.

Whether the call for awareness and responsibility is directed inward or outward is unclear. Such ambiguity has only reinforced the status of *The Pisan Cantos* as a masterpiece of modern poetry, especially as it reflects the promise and failure of the century at the center of which it stands. The sequence's manic alternation between the clarity and confusion, between the humility and paranoia occasioned by the suffering he endured, makes the sequence a precursor of confessional poets of the 1960s, while Pound's sense of being harassed by the terror of history and culture and healed by the power of nature prefigures the environmental poets of the 1970s.

JONATHAN GILL

**Further Reading**

Bush, Ronald, "'Quiet, Not Scornful'? The Composition of 'The Pisan Cantos,'" in *A Poem Containing History: Textual Studies in the Cantos,* edited by Lawrence Rainey, Ann Arbor: University of Michigan Press, 1997

D'Epiro, Peter, "Whose Vanity Must Be Pulled Down," *Paideuma* 13, no. 2 (Fall 1984)

Kenner, Hugh, *The Pound Era,* Berkeley: University of California Press, 1971; London: Faber, 1972

O'Connor, William Van, and Edward Stone, editors, *A Casebook on Ezra Pound,* New York: Crowell, 1959

Olson, Charles, *Charles Olson and Ezra Pound: An Encounter at St. Elizabeths,* edited by Catherine Seelye, New York: Grossman, 1975

Read, Forrest, "The Pattern of 'The Pisan Cantos,'" *Sewanee Review* 65, no. 3 (Summer 1957)

Surette, Leon, *Pound in Purgatory: From Economic Radicalism to Anti-Semitism,* Urbana: University of Illinois Press, 1999

# Prizes

The earliest documented poetry prizes date from the later sixth century B.C., when festivals of music, poetry, and drama began to be widespread in the cities of east-central Greece (the ancient district of Attica). These festal gatherings were routinely organized in the form of contests or competitions, with poets, playwrights, dramatic troupes, or musical performers competing against one another for prizes awarded by juries. The emphasis was on performance; competing poets were judged not only on the strength of a particular composition, but on the quality of its recitation at the festival.

By the time America began to produce its own literary culture in the late 18th century, much of the festal energy had gone out of literary prizes. Under the auspices of the great universities of early modern Europe and England as well as the national or royal academies and (somewhat later) the professional societies, literary honors had become largely bureaucratic in character. Their main purpose was that of controlling the shape of national languages and literatures through the regulated distribution of cultural credentials and cultural prestige. In America, national literary institutions were relatively late in coming. Although attempts were made as early as 1770 to establish an American institution akin to the French Academy, it was not until 1898 that these efforts met with success in the founding of the National Institute of Arts and Letters, the organization whose smaller and more elite subsidiary, the American Academy of Arts and Letters, founded six years later, would become the country's dominant literary society. This meant that, until the 20th century, the universities assumed the main burden of official literary consecration. Phi Beta Kappa, founded in 1776 at the College of William and Mary (but soon centered on its New England chapters at Yale, Harvard, and Dartmouth), played something of a role in this respect as the nation's first national academic organization. However, Phi Beta Kappa was originally more of a fraternal secret society than an honors society in the modern sense, and it was not until the early 19th century that it began to take its honorific functions quite seriously. Even then, it did not award poetry prizes as such, although an alumnus poet was often honored with an invitation to deliver the "Phi Beta Kappa poem" at the annual Anniversary Day ceremony. Other honors in poetry based at the universities from the later 18th century onward included the title of "Class Laureate" (which Ralph Waldo Emerson held at Harvard in 1821), best-poem prizes (although these were never as numerous or as prestigious as essay contests), and prizes in elocution, such as the Boylston Prize at Harvard, founded in 1817, and the David C. DeForest Prize at Yale, founded in 1823, both of which were open to students reciting their poetry, although the winners were nearly always prose orators.

The emphasis, even within the university, on the public reading of prize poems (which were usually odes) and on the performative skill of the poet signals some vestiges of the classical model. Such traces of prizes' Attican past were even more pronounced in the non-academic, unofficial forms of poetry competition, which could be open to all willing participants and staged as entertainment. One early instance was a 1793 contest for the best lyrical "prologue" to the opening ceremonies of the Federal Street Theatre in Boston, won by Thomas Treat Paine. Three decades later, to promote its 1824 "Shakspeare Jubliee," the same theater held a competition for best ode in honor of Shakespeare. Among the unsuccessful entrants was 17-year-old Henry Wadsworth Longfellow, whose losing ode was nonetheless collected in a book, *Boston Prize Poems,* published later that year. The most famous instance of an open poetry competition was that sponsored by P.T. Barnum as part of his hugely successful advance publicity campaign for the concerts of the Swedish singer Jenny Lind, whom he engaged for a series of American performances in 1850–51. Barnum appointed a jury to choose the best ode from among several hundred submissions and then had that ode set to music for Lind to sing at her New York debut. Surprisingly, perhaps, the winner of this $200 contest, the well-respected poet Bayard Taylor, had delivered the Phi Beta Kappa poem earlier that year at Harvard, suggesting less distance than we might imagine between the poetry prizes of academe and those of commercial entertainment. Unfortunately, apart from this one spectacular example, almost nothing of the early history of America's extracurricular poetry prizes has been excavated by scholars. We know too little about their extent or variety adequately to assess their cultural role and impact. It does appear, however, that by the start of the 20th century the tradition of public poetry competitions, perhaps never very robust, had withered, while the nation was only just beginning to establish the extensive network of society medals, lifetime achievement awards, book-of-the-year prizes, and other honors characteristic of the contemporary poetry scene.

As this virtual industry of poetry prizes has sprung up, it has served in the aggregate to impose a kind of official or consensus taste, as determined and sanctioned by recognized experts (primarily academic critics, book reviewers, and prize-winning poets), on the field of American poetic writing. The festal roots of prizes have not, however, receded entirely beneath the accumulating layers of credentialed officialdom. Prizes have continued to serve as a means of attracting and exciting an audience for poetry, becoming integral to the expanding national machinery of literary hype and celebrity, along with such phenomena as publisher-sponsored reading and lecture tours, bookseller-sponsored poetry reading groups and clubs, nightclub poetry slams, and multi-day poetry festivals such as can now be found from Los Angeles to Provincetown. In this respect, poetry prizes reflect a familiar tension between high and low culture, their commercial (or populist) function as tools of publicity and promotion conflicting in some respects with their perceived loftier (or more elitist) cultural purposes. This tension, which in fact characterizes prizes and awards in all fields of culture, is especially pronounced in respect to poetry, very little of which has more than a nominal commercial value. The very distance of American poets from the major machinery of literary commerce has led to their special dependency on prizes as the chief instrument of material as well as symbolic reward. At every step of the poetic career, from the publishing of a first poem in a little magazine to placing a first book with a university press to finding a steady job and income at a writers' workshop, the poet is either competing for prizes, living off the winnings of prizes, or using prizes received in the past as the primary measure and fungible currency of poetic value. This dependency of those engaged in the "highest" of literary practices on a device reminiscent of P.T. Barnum, the Oscars, and Miss World has naturally ensured a good deal of scandal and complaint from the very beginning, with critics denigrating the major poetry awards as "middlebrow" instruments whereby purely aesthetic values are systematically diluted by commercial ones. Such attacks have, however, tended unwittingly to assist prizes in attracting public attention, thereby augmenting their promotional utility and encouraging rather than containing their proliferation.

In surveying the rise of poetry prizes since the turn of the century, we should note not only the importance of the major institutes, academies, and publishers' groups that begin to emerge at this time but also the powerful influence exerted by the Nobel Prizes in general and the Literature Prize in particular. Much like the great patrons of the Renaissance, the "dynamite king" Alfred Nobel turned his personal fortune into a kind of symbolic capital, ensuring the permanent association of his name with great artistic and intellectual achievements. The effectiveness of this self-memorializing strategy was not lost on other holders of major or even of relatively minor fortunes, and within a year of the first Nobel Prize ceremony in Stockholm (1901), imitative memorial prizes were beginning to appear in various European nations. Such was the case in America as well, where the newspaper baron Joseph Pulitzer, explicitly invoking Nobel, declared in 1902 his intention to establish a set of prizes of national importance in the fields of journalism and letters. Although the first Pulitzers were not presented until 1917 and did not include a poetry award until 1922, they can properly be regarded as part of this turn-of-the-century cultural trend.

The omission of a poetry prize from the original four annual Pulitzer Prizes in Letters was owing to Pulitzer's own indifference to contemporary poetry, no mention of which appears anywhere in the testamentary language of his will. The decision to extend the prizes beyond Pulitzer's original Plan of Award appears to have been urged on the controlling Advisory Board in 1921 by its formidable chair, Nicholas Murray Butler, who held that office by virtue of being president of Columbia University, the institution to which Pulitzer had delegated administrative responsibility for the awards. Butler was aware that the Poetry Society, founded in 1917, had instituted at its inception an annual prize for the outstanding book of poems published in the preceding year, and he arranged for the Society's prize, after a hiatus of two years, to be integrated with the Pulitzer Prizes starting in 1922. To chair the poetry jury and oversee the selection of judges, Butler called on Wilbur Lucius Cross, dean of the Yale Graduate School and editor of the *Yale Review.* The first winner of the newly configured prize was Edwin Arlington Robinson, who, although already 53 years old and seemingly nearing the end of a rather unspectacular career, would go on to win the prize twice more in the next six years, a record that was not surpassed until Robert Frost won his fourth Pulitzer in 1943. The Pulitzer's power seemingly by itself to raise Robinson from the condition of a long-struggling and virtually penniless poet to that of a major cultural celebrity—despite the firm resistance of the American Academy and other traditionalist forces—gave notice that this prize could have more impact on the world of American letters than any poetry award before it.

The Pulitzer is a book-of-the-year award, which distinguishes it from the other main varieties of poetry prize: the lifetime achievement award, the manuscript-competition or "first-book" prize, and the prize for an individual poem. Its rules of eligibility have at times been bent; Edna St. Vincent Millay, for example, close runner-up to Robinson in 1922, was awarded the prize the following year despite not having published a new book in the interim. However, the Pulitzer was officially conceived as a prize for the most outstanding book of verse published in the previous year. Being the earliest such prize in America, it enjoys a distinct symbolic advantage over its many imitators, such as the National Book Award (founded in 1950), the National Book Critics Circle Award (founded in 1974), the Lenore Marshall Prize (founded in 1975 and currently administered by the Academy of American Poets and *The Nation* magazine), and the Kingsley Tufts Memorial Prize (founded in 1992 and administered by the Claremont Graduate Schools). Although many of these newer prizes offer much larger cash awards than the Pulitzer (the Tufts paid $50,000 to its winner in 1999, the Pulitzer just $7,500) and some have managed more consistently to anticipate in their choices the contours of the nation's emerging poetic canon, only one can match the Pulitzer for sheer visibility or for its symbolic force as an instrument of consecration.

That one serious rival to the Pulitzer is the Bollingen Prize, which made a singularly scandalous debut in 1949. The prize had been established the year before by the Library of Congress through a gift of Paul Mellon's Bollingen Foundation. The arrangements had been worked out by one of the great builders of Modernism's institutional base, Allen Tate, who as the national consultant in poetry in 1944 had established within the Library of Congress an endowed body of Fellows in American Letters. Many of the appointments to this body had been made by Tate himself, who in 1949 continued to serve on it with considerable influence, and this was the group that was assigned to jury the new poetry prize. Not surprisingly, therefore, the first Bollingen was awarded, by nearly unanimous vote, to Ezra Pound, a poet of immense importance to the circle of leading Modernists whom Tate had installed as Fellows: a group that included T.S. Eliot, W.H. Auden, Louise Bogan, and Robert Penn Warren, among others. However, Pound was also an unapologetic fascist sympathizer, an anti-Semite, and a wartime propagandist for Mussolini. He had begun work on *The Pisan Cantos,* for which he won the award, while incarcerated by the Allies in a postwar POW camp and, indicted for treason but judged incompetent for trial, had completed the book under continuing confinement at St. Elizabeths mental hospital. Tate and other Fellows presumably hoped that a resounding public affirmation of Pound's poetic achievements, supported by the Library of Congress and hence by the U.S. government, might assist in effecting his release, and this did in fact prove to be the case. In the meantime, however, the fellows, the Library of Congress, Tate, Eliot, and Pound himself had to endure ferocious attacks in the popular and literary press and harangues from outraged congressmen. Indeed, the outcry was so fierce that Congress withdrew from the Library of Congress its license to make awards of this kind—reinstating that power only in 1989, with the founding of the biennial Rebekah Johnson Bobbitt National Prize for Poetry.

As the history of prizes has amply demonstrated, however, nothing succeeds like scandal. Relocated under the auspices of Yale University but able to retain its now famous (or infamous) name, the Bollingen Prize had become the closest thing to a household word among poetry awards and readily managed to transform its scandalous visibility into generally recognized prestige. Today the scandal of Pound's Bollingen remains the single best-known event in the history of American poetry prizes, and it is the Bollingen rather than the Pulitzer that one finds referred to in the *New York Times* as "America's most prestigious poetry award."

Although they are meant to be book-of-the-year awards (or, in the case of the Bollingen and the Bobbitt, every-other-year awards), such prizes tend to favor the most canonical figures, allowing the whole body of a poet's work to outweigh any perceived deficiencies in the most recently published work and leaving the task of recognizing new talent to the many prizes that are specifically set up to judge unpublished first manuscripts. Still, the unpredictable schedule of a poet's publications makes it impossible for book-of-the-year awards to fall consistently on figures of great eminence, and the unavoidable anonymity of many of their winners limits their power to generate much interest among nonreaders of contemporary poetry.

The various lifetime achievement awards, with their huge cash payouts and relatively well-known winners, are closer to the model of the Nobel and can thus appear to nonspecialists to be prizes of greater moment, even if they rarely do more than honor the very poets who are already the most honored. Among these we might of course count the Nobel itself, which, although neither an American prize nor a prize specifically for poetry, remains far and away the most prestigious prize an American poet can hope to win. Only Eliot has done so, and by the time this occurred, in 1948, he had been a naturalized British citizen for some 20 years. Several of America's richest lifetime achievement awards follow the Nobel formula in being named for the wealthy benefactor who created them but administered, wholly or in part, through an established literary society or academy. Examples include two $100,000 awards: the Ruth Lilly Prize of the Modern Poetry Society (first won by Adrienne Rich in 1986) and the Tanning Prize of the Academy of American Poets (first won by W.S. Merwin in 1994). A third $100,000 award, the Lannan Lifetime Achievement Award (again first won by Adrienne Rich, in 1999), is self-administered by the Lannan Foundation and involves no collaboration with an outside literary society. The same is true of the so-called genius awards presented by the John D. and Catherine T. MacArthur Foundation since 1980, the winners of which receive five-year unrestricted grants of $200,000 to $400,000. On average, two MacArthurs are awarded to poets each year, and a glance at the list of recipients (which includes John Ashbery, Joseph Brodsky, Amy Clampitt, John Hollander, Derek Walcott, and Robert Penn Warren) suggests, as with the Guggenheims and other "fellowships" ostensibly intended to support works-in-progress, that where poets are concerned, lifetime achievement is a more potent criterion of selection than any combination of promise and need.

While these self-memorializing prizes are the most valuable in cash terms, there are other lifetime achievement awards of longer standing and arguably greater prestige despite their smaller endowments. Both the National Institute of Arts and Letters and the American Academy of Arts and Letters began a decade after their respective foundings to award Gold Medals on a revolving basis in the different fields of art, including a Medal in Poetry from the Institute and a Medal in Literature from the Academy. Eventually, after decades of sometimes ferocious power struggles between the two overlapping organizations, they achieved a compromise in 1992 whereby the smaller, much better endowed group was reabsorbed into the larger one but its name retained for the now unified entity: the American Academy of Arts and Letters. This current incarnation of the Academy presents a Gold Medal in Poetry every sixth year; the first winner, in 1997, was John Ashbery. Much of the money used to build the Academy and to establish its prizes in the first half of the century was supplied by the railroad heir Archer Milton Huntington. However, Huntington was apparently untouched by the "Nobel effect" and refused to allow any of the Academy's prizes to bear his name. (The same cannot be said of Russell H. Loines, the attorney and philanthropist for whom the Academy's Loines Award in Poetry was named.) The Poetry Society of America offers a $6,000 prize based rather ambiguously on "genius and need," awarded continuously since 1929, and named not for a millionaire philanthropist but for Percy Bysshe Shelley. The Society's more generic lifetime achievement award, the $2,500 Frost Medal, dates from 1941 and is also named for a poet, the prize's first winner, Robert Frost. Other, more recent lifetime achievement awards administered by literary societies include the Academy of American Poets' Fellowship for Distinguished Achievement in Poetry, first presented in 1993, and the PEN/Voelcker award, a biennial award first presented by the PEN American Center in 1994. Finally, there is the National Laureateship, an honorary title and office rather than a prize as such but nonetheless an important feature of the poetry awards landscape. Owing to the fiasco of the Pound Bollingen, Congress long withheld its support from any high-profile government endorsement of a living poet. For almost 50 years, the closest thing to an American laureateship was the relatively neglected and lackluster position, created in 1937, of Consultant in Poetry at the Library of Congress. The first American actually to hold the title of "poet laureate" at the federal level was Robert Penn Warren in 1986–87. However, the position has rapidly become one of significant visibility, from which a poet may undertake rather ambitious public initiatives, such as Robert Pinsky's Favorite Poem Project in 1997–99.

Along with the major societies, academies, and government entities, some of the most important sponsors of poetry prizes are publishers. In fact, the Modern Poetry Society, which administers the Ruth Lilly Prize, is actually the nonprofit arm of *Poetry* magazine, founded in 1941 to draw philanthropic funds into the magazine, which was itself founded by Harriet Monroe in 1912. *Poetry* has been awarding the Salman O. Levinson Prize, an annual prize for the best poem published in the magazine the preceding year, since 1914. One-time or short-lived poetry prizes can be found in American literary magazines a good deal earlier than this (the influential *Century* magazine, to give just one example, sponsored from 1897 to 1900 a $250 annual prize for "the best metrical writing of not fewer than fifty lines"), and certain later prizes had far more impact (notably the *Dial* Award from 1921 to 1928, whose huge $2,000 cash value enabled that magazine to secure Eliot's *The Waste Land* for publication in 1922 and inspired William Carlos Williams to write a poem of thanks when he won it in 1927). However, the Levinson enjoys special prestige as the oldest such prize continuously awarded. In addition, the status of *Poetry* as the country's leading poetry magazine and a key venue for emerging talent gives this prize, along with seven others it awards, considerable symbolic importance despite its nominal monetary value ($500 in recent years). Many other literary magazines sponsor their own poetry awards not only for individual poems they have published but even for lifetime achievement. The *Sewanee Review,* for example, a magazine that dates to 1892 but became important to American poetry only under the editorship of Allen Tate and Andrew Lytle in the 1940s, established the Aiken Taylor Award for Modern American Poetry in 1995. Howard Nemerov, whose discovery by Tate had been one of the *Sewanee*'s signal achievements in the mid-1940s and who had been publishing steadily in the magazine ever since, was a most fitting first winner.

Justifiably or not, a modern poet's career depends on the publication not only of outstanding individual poems but of books, and the publishing of these books, most of which are far more valuable as credentials than as sources of income, is done mostly by university presses and other small, independent presses. To attract worthy manuscripts, to assist with promotion and publicity, and, it must be said, to bring in much-needed revenue in the form of artificially elevated entry fees, these presses have found manuscript-competition prizes to be a boon. There are at least 50 such competitions each year, attracting upward of 500 to 1,000 entrants, paying anywhere from $10 to $25 apiece in fees—and all these numbers appear to be growing. The "prize" in this case consists of publication of the winner's manuscript, usually with a guaranteed print run somewhat larger than a typical poetry book and, if the prize is a well-established one, a much better chance of being reviewed in the leading literary publications. The oldest and most prestigious of these is the Yale Series of Younger Poets competition, which dates to 1919 and, like many although not all of the contests, is closed to poets who have previously published a book. Apart from its longevity, the prestige of this competition rests largely on its record as a barometer of emerging talent. This record, in turn, rests largely on the 13-year period (1947–59) during which W.H. Auden served as the series editor, that is, the judge of the prize competition. Among the unpublished poets whose manuscripts Auden singled out for the Yale prize were Adrienne Rich, W.S. Merwin, John Ashbery, James Wright, and John Hollander, five of the most esteemed poets of the second half of the century.

The example of Auden is instructive in that his relationship with the press was strained and even acrimonious. He would routinely refuse the shortlist of candidates that Yale's editors and preliminary judges offered to him, either selecting his winner from among the stacks of manuscripts they had rejected (as he did with Ashbery), going outside the field of official submissions altogether to choose a poet of his personal acquaintance (as he did in 1947 and 1948), or declaring no manuscript worthy of the prize and forcing a break in the annual series (as he did in 1950 and again in 1955). No judge in the history of the prize was so resented by the administrators or pressed so hard for a resignation. Yet it is precisely because Auden single-mindedly dominated the selection process for so many years that the Yale prize now enjoys such preeminence. Unlike the various book-of-the-year and lifetime-achievement awards, with their juries and advisory boards and academic committees, these small-press book prizes are usually left in the hands of a single judge, generally a poet who already has some laurels of his or her own. In addition, this concentration of the power of judgment appears to have made them on the whole the boldest and least consensus-driven form of prize, the most likely to move the field of American poetry in new directions.

This is an important consideration since prizes have justifiably been accused of an inherent conservatism or backwardness of outlook. They have served for the most part as trailing rather than leading indicators, consecrating poets whose reputations were made at least a decade or two before, and often failing to appreciate the significance of new movements and voices as these have emerged into prominence. The American Academy of Arts and Letters held out firmly against Modernism all through the 1920s, resisting even the election of such poets as Robinson and Frost to its membership and preferring, when the Gold Medal revolved to literature at the midpoint of that decade, to express a general displeasure with the state of literary affairs by not making any award at all. Today, the Language poets, whose work has been one of the principal energizing forces in contemporary poetry for 25 years, are still positioned as too avant-garde or experimentalist to contend for the major poetry awards.

Perhaps nowhere is the conservatism of America's poetry prizes more apparent than in their neglect of women poets. The exceptions, once again, are the manuscript-competition prizes, especially those for unpublished authors such as the Yale prize, which have tended to be won by women as often as by men. However, if we survey the whole range of prizes, we find a staggering bias toward men. From its founding in 1914 until the turn of the century, the Levinson Prize has gone to men four times as often as to women, and, contrary to what we might expect, this ratio has not greatly narrowed in more recent times; of the last 20 winners, just five have been women. Moreover, the Ruth Lilly Prize, which in 1986 succeeded the Levinson as the most important award affiliated with *Poetry* magazine, has offset even this slight erosion of cultural patriarchy, being won by women just three times in the first 15 years of its existence. The Pulitzer's record is only marginally more balanced, with 18 women versus 60 men receiving the poetry prize between 1922 and 2000: a ratio of one in four, which has closed to about one in three since 1970. To take one more example, of the 40 poets who have held the post now known as Poet Laureate, only eight have been women, and only five have been women since 1950.

Although these sorts of evident biases might seem, by discrediting prizes as objective indicators of poetic value, to limit their symbolic efficacy and thereby to discourage their proliferation, they may well have the opposite effect. So far, America has not produced prizes specifically for women poets, judged by exclusively female juries, or administered by groups of women writers and readers. The rhetoric of universal values has dominated the scene of poetry awards to a greater extent than it has that of fiction awards. However, a trend toward more narrowly and counter-traditionally defined prizes is gradually becoming discernible, as, for example, in the rise of prizes for gay and lesbian poets (notably the Lambda Literary Awards, founded in 1989) and for poets of ethnic minorities (such as the Chicano/Latino Literary Contest, first held in 1977 and revolving to poetry every fourth year, and the First Book Poetry Award of the Native Writers Circle of the Americas, an annual prize founded in 1992). It appears likely that this trend will define the course of poetry prizes in the immediate future, sustaining the rapid proliferation that has characterized them in the 20th century at least into the early decades of the 21st.

JAMES F. ENGLISH

**Further Reading**

Bradley, George, "Introduction," in *The Yale Younger Poets Anthology*, edited by Bradley, New Haven, Connecticut: Yale University Press, 1998

Current, Richard Nelson, *Phi Beta Kappa in American Life: The First Two Hundred Years*, Oxford and New York: Oxford University Press, 1990

Hohenberg, John, *The Pulitzer Prizes: A History of the Awards in Books, Drama, Music, and Journalism, Based on the*

*Private Files over Six Decades,* New York: Columbia University Press, 1974
McGuire, William, "The Bollingen Foundation: Ezra Pound and the Prize in Poetry," *Quarterly Journal of the Library of Congress* 40, no. 3 (1983)
Morrone, John, editor, *Grants and Awards Available to American Writers, 2000–2001,* New York: PEN American Center, 2000
Thompson, Lawrence, "An Inquiry into the Importance of Boston Prize Poems," *The Colophon* (new series) 1, no. 4 (1940)
Updike, John, editor, *A Century of Arts and Letters,* New York: Columbia University Press, 1998
Waller, James, "The Culture of Competition: The Scoop on Poetry First-Book Awards," *Poets and Writers* 27, no. 4 (1999)

## Projective Verse. *See* Black Mountain School; Charles Olson

## Prosody and Versification

Originating in a Greek word meaning the song accompaniment to words and the accent marks used to indicate the tone, "prosody" has come to have various meanings. It refers to the theory and analysis of sound in language in general, to the theory and analysis of sound patterning in verse, and to actual patterns or systems of patterning in individual poems or writing styles. "Versification" simply means making verse, or making lines, as verse is language put into lines. The distinctions between prosody (the formal study of sound patterning) and versification (the making of sound patterns) have been blurred for some time because the rules for making and marking sound structure in verse have not been articulated distinctly, outside of some late-20th-century linguistic theory. With the growing emphasis in the Renaissance on developing and writing verse in meters that could be identified as English, "prosody" became almost synonymous with "versification," a more general term referring to the craft or act of composing poems.

The aim of prosodic study is to understand the principles upon which sound in verse is structured in order to create a theory of prosody and tools for critical judgment. Since the modern field of linguistics began more than a century ago, prosodists have been working toward a theory that joins literary and linguistic concepts and explanations, but no unified theory has been developed. Nevertheless, this work has produced a better understanding of the interaction of verse traditions and the possibilities for verse practice.

Descriptive understanding of language both expands and limits what can be written in verse. During the Renaissance, medieval grammar and rhetoric succumbed gradually to replacement by classical Greek and Roman systems. However inadequate these systems were when applied to English, they nevertheless shaped what poets wrote and became the predominant means by which poets, critics, and teachers understood accentual structures in poetry. What emerged was a lasting system of metrics used for description, analysis, and composition. Developed when classical Greek and Roman literary principles were being worked into English versecraft, classical versification centered on metricality; more often than not, metrical forms belonged to specific kinds of patterns and their distinctive verse and stanza types.

Poets writing in English in the 20th century could draw on more than a thousand years of verse tradition. Influence from other languages produced verse forms such as the ballad, sonnet, sestina, ode, and villanelle, as well as line forms such as iambic pentameter, to give a few examples. As abstractions, these forms continued to change and develop as poets wrote specific poems that accomplished something never before done with the form and as other poets picked up and modified those innovations. In stanza form, for example, the sonnet has a long history, beginning in the Renaissance with Italian models. The differences between the Italian and the English language sound structure necessitated a distinctly English verse in rhythm and line, however, and Shakespeare and Spenser developed alternative interlocking rhetorical and rhyme structures. Over the past 500 years poets turned the form to new organizations of rhyme, line, and rhythm. Despite the predominance of free verse in 20th-century American poetry, formal verse and the sonnet in particular remained very popular. Most free-verse poets composed striking free-form variations of sonnets, including Whitman, who composed one intended as the lead poem for the 1867 edition of *Leaves of Grass.*

For metrical choice, 20th-century poets writing in English could draw on three long traditions of prosody: an accentual alliterative strong stress line, the oldest, inherited from the Anglo-Saxon poets; a ballad rhythm, descended from the medieval period; and an accentual/syllabic line developed over several centuries from the time of Chaucer. Iambic pentameter reigned as the favorite of verse writers until the 20th century, undoubtedly because of its potential for achieving variations: the uneven number of metrical feet gives it a tendency to be divided off-center.

In accentual/syllabic verse the number of syllables together with the number and location of accents in a line must be organized on an underlying pattern of repetition over which the actual pattern of accents plays—a baseline going under a melody, so to speak. This play of the actual rhythm (the melody) over a basic regular pattern (such as weak strong weak strong) allows for a wide range of expressiveness. Once the rhythm is initiated the reader expects the repetition of syllable grouping, such as a succession of iambs. Variations are also part of a metrical tradition. To be recognized as metrical the kinds of divergences from the underlying pattern have been built up over centuries and are themselves part of the metrical code along with the underlying metrical regularity. Thus, permissible locations for substitutions—the line initial trochaic substitution, for instance—are as much a part of the tradition as is the underlying iambic pattern. Of course a poet deviating from the tradition may be attempting to change the possibilities for metricality and may not be recognized for some time as writing metrical poetry, as in the case of John Donne.

In addition to these three rich traditions, 20th-century poets inherited a fourth alternative: free verse, which by definition was freed from metrical convention for the poet to discover structural principles on some other basis. Without the poetic tradition, this other basis had to be the rhythmic resources available in the language itself. The most common American free verse by the beginning of the 20th century had a structural basis in rhythmic phrasing. It was initiated by Walt Whitman in 1855 and widely copied, albeit with less power and success than Whitman achieved.

Although analysts have seen a good deal of prosodic structure in Whitman's verse, to late-19th-century readers the verse was reminiscent of the Biblical psalms and recognizable in terms of English verse as little more than heightened prose. However, prosodic analysis reveals a richly structured verse organized on repetition and variation of a set of phrasal groupings accompanied by repetition of same words and same sounds and with the occasional occurrence of patterns familiar to readers of metrical verse. Whitman and the early Modernist free-verse poets were knowledgeable writers of traditional verse forms before they turned to free verse. An important dimension of meaning and of the actual prosody of their verse is that it was written *against* traditional formal verse; hence, it constituted a rejection of traditional metrical verse even as it depended on a "ghost" of meter below the surface: an invocation of the tradition necessary for its own recognition as poetry.

Both traditional and free-verse prosodies work by establishing patterns of expectation and surprise. Patterns of sound are of two types: quantitative and qualitative. The qualitative sound structure includes rhyme and all other sound repetition of vowels and consonants, and whole and partial words. The quantitative sound structure is established through repeated groupings of syllables that are in some way the same (type of metrical foot, number of syllables or accents per line, or number of accents per phrase). In metrical verse the syntactic organization works both with and against the underlying metrical pattern in various ways and at various places as the poem proceeds. The reader's sense of the metrical pattern derives from the repetition itself, from the reader's knowledge of the metrical code (the cultural tradition of literary sound structures), and from the poet's particular use of the code to coincide with and interrupt the rhythmic patterns governing some other pattern of the language, usually syntax. Because syntactic units are thought units (semantic units) as well as units of sound organization, and because emotion and drama can also be cued through a language's sound system, the poet can vary the metrical pattern for interesting effects in meaning and affect.

For example, the most complex and interesting line in English-language poetry is iambic pentameter. One way of describing the line is to say that it has a general underlying accentual pattern of five sequential iambs; that is, a metrical foot constituted by one weak syllable followed by one accented syllable (an iamb) is repeated in succession five times over the line for a total of ten syllables. A strict iambic pentameter will have, in most of the poem's lines, four or five of the potentially accentable syllabic positions filled with accents. Trochaic reversals will occur only where past use has made it acceptable: the fifth foot may not be reversed with a trochee; anapests and dactyls, which have three syllables to the foot, cannot replace iambs. Metrical verse assumes line integrity, a reason for being a line apart from metricality. The line must be an entity where sound and meaning work to advance additional meaning and effects beyond the meanings that would accrue if it were prose. In the formal tradition, lines are distinctively shaped rhythms, made strong by strong words (in accent force and meaning) at line end and often strategically at line onset. Line breaks and all other features of the entire sound system exploit the linguistic system and the poetic tradition so as to contribute to meaning and effect. A strong poet can expand the possibilities for variations on the tradition.

Robert Frost, for example, wrote almost entirely in traditional verse forms and expanded the iambic pentameter line tradition by loosening its regularity to accommodate a casual conversational tone. Asserting that there were only two kinds of meters, "strict iambic and loose iambic" ("The Figure a Poem Makes"), he added extra syllables to lines and placed accented syllables in new positions. He never interrupted the metrical pattern for long before returning to the familiar "strict" iambic readers recognized, however. Given such statements on his own verse practice, he clearly worked to shape a subject to aesthetic form. The majority of his poems are written in the strict iambic pentameter of traditional blank verse, as here, in "Birches":

> When I see birches bend from left and right
> Across the lines of straighter darker trees,
> I like to think some boy's been swinging them.
> But swinging doesn't bend them down to stay
> As ice-storms do. Often you must have seen them
> Loaded with ice a sunny winter morning
> After a rain. They click upon themselves. . . .

The opening of Frost's poem follows formal conventions for strict meter. The first four and a half lines are very regular, with most of the even-numbered syllabic positions strongly accented. In the middle of line five, "Often" disrupts this rhythm in the beat, and does so on the fifth syllable, uncharacteristic of the poetic tradition. Here the speaker turns to the reader to speak directly, as in a conversation; this is poetry heard, not overheard, another 19th-century convention disrupted (although first strongly disrupted by Walt Whitman and Robert Browning). The line has an extra syllable, which in itself would still fit the pentameter convention, except that here the syllable at line end comprises a separate word, not merely an unstressed final syllable of the last word in the line. The next line picks up with a strong beginning characteristic of the pentameter: "Loaded with ice." It mirrors line two in this onset and in the way the rhythm of the language cuts across the iambic pattern with the succession of trochaic stresses on "Straighter," "darker," "sunny," "winter," and "morning." The underlying iambic rhythm is set nearly into syncopation by the slight delay of downbeat created by the unstressed syllable's following immediately on end of the iambic foot. The unstressed syllables of the iambs arrive slightly earlier than if a separate word occupied that syllabic position.

Here lies the usefulness of prosody both for verse practice and for critical analysis, in determining whether the variation is effective in supporting or undercutting the meaning carried by the lines by way of drama or affect. In lines two and six the rhythm matches the sense—a cutting across the background, a contrast of ice with warmth. In line seven the final six syllables exactly match the iambic pattern, adding to the strong sound and sense of hard ice clicking.

"The Death of the Hired Man," by contrast, offers an unconventional beginning: the iambic pentameter is as uneasy and unsettled as Mary's state of mind:

Mary sat musing on the lamp-flame at the table
Waiting for Warren. When she heard his step,
She ran on tip-toe down the darkened passage. . . .

In fact, the first line cannot be considered iambic pentameter at all, unless one considers it both in the context of the rest of the poem *and* in the context of a developing tradition, as other poets come to accept Frost's variations and use them. What is unconventional about the first line? First, it is 13 syllables long, effectively imbuing the sound with the leisurely unfocused sense of musing, but it is not iambic pentameter unless the two unstressed syllables in a row in two places—"on the lamp-flame" and "at the table"—are considered "loose iambs" instead of anapests.

The qualitative aspect of the rhythm in "The Death of the Hired Man" is heavily textured, contributing to a tighter cohesion even as the iambic takes some time to begin: the four "m" sounds in line one, the two "s" sounds that occur closely together, and the echo in "table" of the "a" begun in "flame." In line two, "Wait" immediately echoes with the "a" again, and the occurrence of "w" three times in successive stressed words followed by another two occurrences of the "s" begun in line one, makes for a tight joining. The iambic regularity of line three and its repetition of initial "t" and "d" give a feeling of careful but definite and steady going, which underlines the progress of Mary's feet in the hallway.

The foregoing qualitative and quantitative sound analysis is based on classical metrics. It is suited to critical discussion of how poets think as they write and how readers who know classical metrics read. It is not, however, suited to an explanation of sound structure in terms of reader perception nor of the roles and interaction of the phonological, grammatical, and semantic systems. It cannot explain most types of free verse, nor the visual dimensions of modern poetry that impinge on sound structure. In fact no adequate theory of prosody has been developed that can satisfactorily explain poetry as rule-governed, and it may well be impossible to arrive at a unified theory. Nevertheless, the use of linguistic theory has made good progress toward understanding both metrical and nonmetrical systems in poetry. In free verse, classical literary prosody is wholly inadequate to describe anything more than fragments of the verse. In American poetry free verse is so prominent that to neglect study of its rhythmic structure would create a serious gap in understanding the nation's original contribution to 20th-century poetry around the world.

The type of free verse that quickly dominated American poetry was initiated by Whitman and based on the phonological phrase. The structure is made from repetition and variation of a few regularized unit types, each characterized by a pattern of prominence points. The phrasal unit is bounded by pauses; the shorter it is, the more syllables can rise into prominence, which signals the relative importance of each word with respect to the others. Here is an example from the opening of Whitman's "Song of Myself":

I celebrate myself,
And what I assume, you shall assume,
For every atom belonging to me as good belongs to you.

The first line is a single phrasal unit bearing two points of prominence; *cel-* and *-self* bear secondary and primary prominence, respectively. The first line could also be iambic in a context of iambic poetry, but only the last eight syllables of the last line are iambic pattern. The second line is made of two units, each with two points of prominence (*I* and *-sume, you* and *-sume*), in a falling pattern of primary to secondary prominence. The second line, as well as the third, could be scanned as a mix of iambics and anapests, but that will tell only why the lines sound familiar as poetry; it will not explain the prosody as a cohesive structure. In a long line like the following, many syllables fall into the nonprominent level, but the line has two phrases, a 3–2-1 contour and a 2–1 contour, Whitman's two most frequent unit types: "The distillation would intoxicate me also, but I shall not let it."

Much of 20th-century poetry is organized like Whitman's, by the poet's settling on a few rhythmic phrase patterns that are used over and over to create a fabric of expectation and variation. A few poets write long Whitman-like lines, with their own characteristic patterning. Others write shorter lines that could be described as a mix of metrical feet in which the characteristic binding structure needs phrasal explanation. Others rely on the visual aspect of the poem to indicate line boundaries, which are the markers of semantic boundaries as well. As Whitman's free-verse successors broke up his long oratorical line and eschewed rhyme and meter, they lost aural line boundaries and increasingly had to rely on this visual line.

ROSEMARY GATES WINSLOW

*See also* Free Verse

**Further Reading**

Attridge, Derek, *The Rhythms of English Poetry,* London and New York, Longman, 1982

Finch, Annie, *The Ghost of Meter: Culture and Prosody in American Free Verse,* Ann Arbor: University of Michigan Press, 1993

Fussell, Paul, *Poetic Meter and Poetic Form,* New York: Random House, 1965; revised edition, New York and London: McGraw-Hill, 1979

Gates, Rosemary L., "T.S. Eliot's Prosody and the Free Verse Tradition: Restricting Whitman's 'Free Growth of Metrical Laws,'" *Poetics Today* 11, no. 3 (1990)

Gross, Harvey, *Sound and Form in Modern Poetry,* Ann Arbor: University of Michigan Press, 1964; 2nd edition, 1996

Hartman, Charles O., *Free Verse: An Essay on Prosody,* Princeton, New Jersey: Princeton University Press, 1980

McCorkle, James, editor, *Conversant Essays: Contemporary Poets on Poetry,* Detroit, Michigan: Wayne State University Press, 1990

Steele, Timothy, *Missing Measures: Modern Poetry and the Revolt against Meter,* Fayetteville: University of Arkansas Press, 1990

Tarlinskaya, Marina, "Beyond 'Loose Iamb': The Form and Themes of the English 'Dolnik,'" *Poetics Today* 16, no. 3 (1995)

---

# R

## Carl Rakosi 1903–

Avowed enemy of generalization, Carl Rakosi has always been ambivalent about being categorized as an "Objectivist" poet, although his association with that grouping has assured him a place in the annals of American poetry, and his long tenure as the sole survivor of an illustrious list of avant-garde poets has made him a literary elder statesman.

The provenance of the "Objectivist" moniker bears out Rakosi's cautiousness, as it was adopted by Louis Zukofsky under pressure from editor Harriet Monroe, who wanted a catchy title for a special February 1931 issue on young avant-garde poets for her influential magazine *Poetry.* The term was to suggest a preference for clarity, precision, particularity, and scientific observation over what was felt to be the messiness of late Romantic or Victorian verse, with its ornate imagery, stilted diction, and privileging of the lyrical "I." Rakosi, who had been proposed for inclusion by Ezra Pound, agreed to the term, and four of his poems led off the Objectivist issue, and he also appeared in the 1932 *An "Objectivists" Anthology,* also edited by Zukofsky. Other notable writers included in these publications were William Carlos Williams, Basil Bunting, George Oppen, Charles Reznikoff, and Zukofsky. Although some of the poets had been or would become friends, the grouping never became an active movement; it can, however, be seen as one strand of the 1930s neorealist tradition in the arts, which included such disparate tendencies as social realism, precisionism, "Neue Sachlichkeit" (the New Objectivity), and so on. Zukofsky quickly distanced himself from the Objectivist designation, but Rakosi, paradoxically, warmed to it as a hedge "against psychological slush and sentimentality in any period" (*Man and Poet,* 1988 interview).

Rakosi has stated often that he seldom writes an "Objectivist" poem. The following poem is close to the original Objectivist goal of portraying nature in its dazzling specificity without letting the human ego intrude:

"ZZZZZ"

nasturtium petals alight:
                    20 watts of tangerine
shaded by green
                    leaf
meticulous parasol
                    by Hokusai
the orangey alpha
                    and the green omega
of the bee's world.

However, even here there is an aestheticizing that is more characteristic of the Japanese art allusions of Pound's Imagist period than of Objectivism proper. Rakosi does not, however, let us linger in one mode of perception. We move rapidly from the initial naturalist perspective to the electric conceit of "20 watts of tangerine" to the Hokusai analogy and end by looking at the nasturtium from the bee's perspective, in which the flower is indeed the "orangey alpha / and the green omega." Thus, the human gaze that one would expect to be privileged gives way to a shift to the animal realm—yet alternately, this can be considered a shift from the visual to the metaphysical (alpha/omega) and perhaps the comical. The strength of this poem's closing is consistent with a major feature of his work, closure, "which brings the poem full circle back to its title" (Pacernik, 1997).

Like the salamander to whom he says he will drink ("Nine Natures of Metaphor"), Rakosi is capable of a surprising array of tonal colors, often in the same poem; he is alternately an ironist, a meditative poet, a domestic lyricist, a social satirist, an erudite reveler in language's complexities, and a simple, compassionate voice. This eclecticism shows that he never completely abandoned the early formalism that he had learned from Yeats, Eliot, and especially Stevens, even as he moved to a more stripped-down approach.

He is best known for his short poems, whose tones range from light witticism to philosophical paradox and cosmic irony; he is a master of the epigrammatic mode, as in "Old Lovers":

Bubelah,
          if you will be
good-natured,
          I can be
wise.

Utilizing the staccato effect of his characteristic "line-weave" or cross-hatched lines, Rakosi often pokes gentle fun at the human condition, as in the following poem, where the lines of experience that divide young from old or even old from older can be seen at a glance:

"Walkers Passing Each Other in the Park"

Had I been eighty-five,
he would have stopped
to compare notes,
but what was there
to talk about
with a man of only sixty-five?

Rakosi's debt to the American vernacular tradition of Whitman, Sandburg, and Williams shows in poems written in colloquial diction, as in his "Americana" poems portraying both historical figures, such as Calvin Coolidge (whose "lips were sealed / tighter than an old man's / scrotum"), and ordinary people, such as "The American Girl," who complains, "These guys / are so fast / I don't know / what I'm doing / until I've / done it." Other poems possess a "found" quality, perhaps gleaned from his social work career in the way that Williams drew from his doctor's life; examples can be found in his "American Nymphs" series of letters to the Welfare Department:

"IV The Real Penelope"

'Madam,
I am glad
to report
that my husband
who is missing
is dead!'

A secular writer informed by Marxist sociology and Rankian psychology, Rakosi chose not to identify himself as a distinctly "Jewish" poet, although his heritage has come more to the fore in recent decades with translations of medieval Hebrew verse. There have always been echoes of Jewish life and heritage, however, as in quite moving poems to his father; wife, Leah; children; and grandchildren. A good illustration is the poem "L'Chayim," which combines a nod to tradition with familial emotions, humor, and Objectivist precision:

I felt
the foetus stir
a foot
below my wife's
breast

and woke
the neighbors
with my shouting
(a day
for silly asses)

and greeted
my first-born:
"Listen, I am
your provider,

Let us get to know
each other."

Rakosi's return to writing in 1965, after a quarter-century moratorium, cannot but recall the salamander's mythical rebirth. His creative fires having been rekindled by the letter of a young English poet, Andrew Crozier, then studying with Charles Olson at the University of Buffalo, Rakosi reentered the scene at a time of great ferment and was perfectly situated to be a link between the 1930s avant-garde and the new experimental tradition of Black Mountain, Beat, and New York School writers (and later the Language poets). There followed 35 years of productivity, with much-deserved awards, residencies, and senior editorship of the important poetry journal *Sagetrieb*. At age 97, Rakosi continues to be an inspiration to younger writers.

JOHN F. ROCHE, JR.

*See also* Objectivism

**Biography**
Born in Berlin, Germany, 6 November 1903; emigrated to the United States in 1910. Attended the University of Wisconsin, Madison, B.A. 1924, M.A. 1926; University of Pennsylvania, Philadelphia, M.S.W. 1940; attended law school briefly, University of Texas, Austin; Instructor, University of Texas, 1928–29; social worker, Cook County Bureau of Public Welfare, Chicago, 1932–33; supervisor, Federal Transient Bureau, New Orleans, 1933–34; field work supervisor, Graduate School of Social Work, Tulane University, New Orleans, 1934–35; caseworker, Jewish Family Welfare Society, Brooklyn, New York, 1935–40; case supervisor, Jewish Social Service Bureau, St. Louis, 1940–43; assistant director, Jewish Children's Bureau, and Bellefaire, both Cleveland, 1943–45; executive director, Jewish Family and Children's Service, Minneapolis, 1945–68; writer-in-residence, Yaddo Colony, 1968–75, University of Wisconsin, Madison, 1969–70, and Michigan State University, East Lansing, 1974; in private practice of psychotherapy, Minneapolis, 1958–68; since 1986 senior editor, *Sagetrieb*. Received National Endowment for the Arts Award, 1969, fellowship, 1972, 1979; Fund for Poetry Award, 1988; National Poetry Association Award, 1988; PEN Award, 1995. Living in San Francisco, California.

**Poetry**
*Two Poems*, 1933
*Selected Poems*, 1941
*Amulet*, 1967
*Ere-VOICE*, 1971
*Ex Cranium, Night*, 1975
*My Experiences in Parnassus*, 1977
*Droles de journal*, 1981
*History*, 1981
*Spiritus I*, 1983
*Meditation*, 1985
*The Collected Poems of Carl Rakosi*, 1986
*The Beasts* (with others), 1994
*Eight Songs and Meditations*, 1995
*Poems, 1923–1941*, 1995
*The Earth Suite*, 1997

**Other Writings:** essays (*The Collected Prose of Carl Rakosi*, 1984).

**Further Reading**

Hatlen, Burton, "Carl Rakosi and the Re-Invention of the Epigram," in *Collected Prose of Carl Rakosi,* by Carl Rakosi, Orono, Maine: National Poetry Foundation, 1983

Heller, Michael, *Conviction's Net of Branches: Essays on the Objectivist Poets and Poetry,* Carbondale: Southern Illinois University Press, 1985

Heller, Michael, editor, *Carl Rakosi: Man and Poet,* Orono, Maine: National Poetry Foundation, 1993

Ma, Ming-Qian, "Be Aware of 'The Medusa's Glance': The Objectivist Lens and Carl Rakosi's Poetics of Strabismal Seeing," in *The Objectivist Nexus: Essays in Cultural Poetics,* edited by Rachel Blau DuPlessis and Peter Quartermain, Tuscaloosa: University of Alabama Press, 1999

Pacernik, Gary, "Carl Rakosi: An Interview," *American Poetry Review* 26 (1997)

Perloff, Marjorie, "Looking for the Real Carl Rakosi: Collecteds and Selecteds," *Journal of American Studies* 30 (1996)

---

## John Crowe Ransom 1888–1974

John Crowe Ransom distinguished himself as poet, critic, essayist, and teacher, but his career as a poet was brief: his final volume, *Two Gentlemen in Bonds,* was published in 1927. After this publication his poetry appeared solely in selected editions of his verse: *Selected Poems* (1945) contains only five poems written after 1925 and omits entirely a sequence of 21 sonnets from *Chills and Fever* (1924) as well as the poems of *Two Gentlemen in Bonds. Selected Poems: Revised and Enlarged* (1969), in effect his offering to posterity, reprints only 80 of the 153 poems he had previously published. (His friend and "Fugitive" colleague, Allen Tate, was mercilessly critical of "the destructive revisions" that Ransom had made to some of his more important poems, and Tate recommended the text of the first editions.) His first volume, *Poems about God* (1919), was published, on Robert Frost's recommendation, while Ransom was coming to the end of his service as a first lieutenant in field artillery in France in World War I. The poems are immature and inconsequential efforts, but they do address many of Ransom's most basic themes and express the frequently contradictory and paradoxical nature of his religious belief (the title, however, suggesting as it does a volume of essentially spiritual lyrics, is misleading, for few of the poems are about God, although, as Ransom writes in his introduction, they make "considerable use of the term God"). None of the poems from this volume was included in the selected editions of his work, and he regarded *Chills and Fever* and *Two Gentlemen in Bonds* as his principal contributions to modern poetry; in effect, Ransom deemed his "Fugitive" period, roughly coextensive with the three years of the publication of *The Fugitive* magazine (1922–25), as coinciding with the years of his most significant writing (a selection of his verse for the English audience was published as *Grace after Meat* in 1924 and carried an introduction by Robert Graves).

Ransom's poetry was nurtured by the poetical movement that developed around *The Fugitive* magazine, edited and published at Vanderbilt University in Nashville, Tennessee, between 1922 and 1925. Following the demise of the magazine, much of the intellectual energy of the poets associated with it (Donald Davidson, Allen Tate, and Robert Penn Warren are the most considerable of them alongside Ransom) went into *I'll Take My Stand,* published in 1930, an influential collection of essays of what might be called "southern apologetics," although Ransom anticipated much of the mood of these essays in *God without Thunder: An Unorthodox Defense of Orthodoxy* (1930), written in the summer of 1929, a spirited if not entirely argumentatively coherent defense of southern fundamentalism prompted by the ridicule poured on the South by the northern press during the trial of John Scopes in 1925. Despite the tendency of Fugitive poets to be backward looking, conservative both in their politics and in their socioeconomic thought, Ransom, like his southern contemporaries, is very much the product of the Modernist sensibility; his poetry strains after the kind of anti-Romantic, anti-subjectivist register and studied impersonality found in T.S. Eliot's greatest poetry, but there is occasionally a lightness of touch (Randall Jarrell wrote of "the Mozartian" quality of some of his major poems) and a wry, ironical posturing in many of the conceits Ransom employs that betrays his sense of himself as an amateur poet. (Robert Penn Warren intelligently illustrated the "occasional" character of Ransom's verse by calling on Jarrell's remark that "being a poet is like standing out in the rain, waiting for lightning to hit you. If it hits you once—that is, if you write only one fine poem—you are good; if it hits you six times you're great.") This amateurishness, nevertheless, is another part of his posture, and it should not blind us to the fact that Ransom's small body of verse is of a very high order and takes its place among the most important contributions of modern southern culture to the literature of the United States.

Ransom's themes are those that we characteristically associate with the central traditions of lyric poetry in the English language, and his favored form is the quatrain. He writes much about mutability, death, the sorrows and paradoxes of love, and the frailty of the human condition. For someone so closely identified with Fugitive and Agrarian circles, there is surprisingly little verse that is unambiguously about the South (unlike that of fellow Fugitives such as Donald Davidson and Allen Tate) and little in the way of what we might deem overtly ideological or political rhetoric. An early poem such as "Necrological" may tempt us to think that its antiquarianism (the invocation of imagery and terminology from knighthood and heraldry) and its Latinate constructions are the residues of Ransom's "southernness" and are part of a studied revival of a more ornate way of writing in the face of the dissociations of the Modernist sensibility. However, the manner is both scholarly and ironic (Ransom was steeped in late medieval and early Renaissance English poetry), and there is little that is sentimentally nostalgic about either his material or his tone:

The friar had said his paternosters duly
And scourged his limbs, and afterwards would have slept;
But with much riddling his head became unruly,
He arose, from the quiet monastery he crept.

Dawn lightened the place where the battle had been won.
The people were dead—it is easy he thought to die—
These dead remained, but the living were all gone,
Gone with the wailing trumps of victory.

The friar introduced in the first line of the poem observes the bodies on a battlefield as "some gory and fabulous / Whom the sword had pierced and then the grey wolf eaten . . ." so that the "postured bones lie weather-beaten." The mannerism in "postured bones" is recognizably "Ransomian": violence is frequently deflated by the decorum and archaism of Ransom's language (although he criticized the archaism of some of Thomas Hardy's verse), so much so that what he calls the "texture" of the verse sometimes (and deliberately) works against the argument (what he calls the "structure"). In "Armageddon," a poem with obvious debts to Bunyan's *Pilgrim's Progress* and Milton's *Paradise Lost,* the ancient struggle between good and bad, Christ and Antichrist, although elemental in its ferocity and savagery, is rendered in a mock-heroic, almost farcical voice, as, for example, in the concluding stanzas:

Christ and his myrmidons, Christ at the head,
Chanted of death and glory and no complaisance;
Antichrist and the armies of malfeasance
Made songs of innocence and no bloodshed.

The immortal Adversary shook his head:
If now they fought too long, then he would famish;
And if much blood was shed, why, he was squeamish:
"These Armageddons weary me much," he said.

The ironic reversal—Christ as the violent, retributive wolf, Satan his lamblike adversary—inverts the reader's conventional expectations and gives the poem its quality of surprise and moral unpredictability. However, like many modern poets, Ransom seems unaware of the limitations of the ironic register, overworking it to the extent that the reader can become cynically insensitive to its cruelties. Terrible things happen in Ransom's poetry, notably the deaths of young children (his most well-known treatment of this is "Bells for John Whiteside's Daughter"), and even in such a carefully wrought and unsentimental poem as "Dead Boy," the opening stanza effects a rhyme that sits uneasily with the subject it enacts:

The little cousin is dead, by foul subtraction,
A green bough from Virginia's aged tree,
And none of the country kin like the transaction,
Nor some of the world of outer dark, like me.

In "Janet Waking," however, the ironic register is more appropriate to the droll comedy of the subject, the death of Janet's favorite "dainty-feathered hen" from the sting of a "transmogrifying bee":

So there was Janet
Kneeling on the wet grass, crying her brown hen
(Translated far beyond the daughters of men)
To rise and walk upon it.

And weeping fast as she had breath
Janet implored us, "Wake her from her sleep!"
And would not be instructed in how deep
Was the forgetful kingdom of death.

Ransom's love poems, many of which are numbered among his best, juxtapose the demands of honor and physical desire, irreconcilable demands that can only find "equilibrium" in art. The lovers of "The Equilibrists" find that the choice of one excludes the other:

In Heaven you have heard no marriage is,
No white flesh tinder to your lecheries,
Your male and female tissue sweetly shaped
Sublimed away, and furious blood escaped.

Great lovers lie in Hell, the stubborn ones
Infatuate of the flesh upon the bones;
Stuprate, they rend each other when they kiss,
The pieces kiss again, no end to this.

The speaker of the poem watches the lovers "spinning, orbited nice . . . ," letting them lie "perilous and beautiful" in his epitaph. Similarly, the lovers of "Spectral Lovers" move through an Eliotic landscape and seem more like strangers than intimates,

By night they haunted a thicket of April mist
Out of that black ground suddenly come to birth,
Else angels lost in each other and fallen on earth.
Lovers they knew they were, but why unclasped, unkissed?
Why should two lovers go frozen apart in fear?
And yet they were, they were.

while in "Winter Remembered" the speaker's memory of the loss of his beloved is described, in the concluding stanza, in one of Ransom's most extravagant images:

Dear love, these fingers that had known your touch,
And tied our separate forces first together,
Were ten poor idiot fingers not worth much,
Ten frozen parsnips hanging in the weather.

In a body of important and influential critical essays, Ransom drew a distinction between what he called the "texture" and the "structure" of a poem; the former is made up of its detail—the imagery, diction, values; the latter is the poem's argument, although to say that a poem is "argumentative" is not to say of it that its way of reasoning follows that of the sciences or other modes of logical discourse. Science, for Ransom, has no texture, no concrete particularity, and is, in effect, all structure; its argument is its very ontology. The structure of a poem, on the other hand, is inconceivable without its texture, although this is not to say that texture and structure are harmonious, and, indeed, Ransom is insistent on the degree to which the texture of a poem may *impede* its structure and thus create tension and paradox, irony, and ambiguity; the language of poetry has somehow a reality that other languages do not have, and it manifests itself as an affective aspect of (as Ransom puts it in the title of one of his critical books) "the world's body." There are, however, limitations to Ransom's theory of poetry, not least of which is that it is developed in essays that have the character of "occasional" pieces, and thus the theory as a whole is fragmentary, diffuse, and inchoate. The very notion of poetry's "ontology," a word by which Ransom's criticism is often identified (his rallying call to the New Criticism was of the need for "ontological critics"), is unsatisfactorily articulated, and when Ransom speaks of poetry's representation of the world (and he does not mean this in a mimetic sense), it is difficult to see precisely in what the representation consists. His notion of the "concrete universals" of poetry (in particular the essay "The Concrete Universal: Observations on the Understanding of Poetry") is Kantian in origin and nature, but Ransom gives us very little sense of the concreteness to which he adverts. We can read Ransom's poetry without familiarizing ourselves with his criticism, and it is likely that the poetry will survive in a way that even criticism of great importance will not. However, his criticism helps us understand the kind of scholarly intelligence that went into the poetry. For Ransom, as for so many of his contemporaries (Eliot most notably), writing poetry was a matter of reading other poets, and the "bookishness" of his verse (although he is rarely, if ever, pedantic) bespeaks his careful cultivation of the technical virtuosity and artifice that he saw as indispensable to serious literature.

Henry Claridge

*See also* Fugitives and Agrarians; New Criticism

**Biography**

Born in Pulaski, Tennessee, 30 April 1888. Attended Vanderbilt University, Nashville, Tennessee, 1903–04, 1907–09, A.B. 1909 (Phi Beta Kappa); Christ Church, Oxford (Rhodes Scholar), 1910–13, B.A. 1913; served in the United States Army, 1917–19; teacher in Mississippi, 1905, Tennessee, 1906, in private school, 1909–10, and at Hotchkiss School, Lakeville, Connecticut, 1913–14; Instructor, 1914–16, Assistant Professor, 1919–26, and Professor of English, 1927–37, Vanderbilt University; Carnegie Professor of Poetry, 1937–58, and Professor Emeritus, 1958–74, Kenyon College, Gambier, Ohio; Visiting Lecturer in English, Chattanooga University, Tennessee, 1938; Visiting Lecturer in language and criticism, University of Texas, Austin, 1956; member of the Fugitive group of poets; cofounder, *The Fugitive,* 1922–25; founding editor, *Kenyon Review,* 1937–59; honorary consultant in American letters, Library of Congress, Washington, D.C. Received Guggenheim fellowship, 1931; Bollingen Prize, 1951; Loines Award, 1951; Brandeis University Creative Arts Award, 1958; Academy of American Poets fellowship, 1962; National Book Award, 1964; National Endowment for the Arts Award, 1966; Emerson-Thoreau Medal, 1968; American Academy Gold Medal, 1973; member, American Academy, and American Academy of Arts and Sciences. Died in Gambier, Ohio, 3 July 1974.

**Poetry**

*Poems about God,* 1919
*Armageddon* (with *A Fragment,* by William Alexander Percy, and *Avalon,* by Donald Davidson), 1923
*Chills and Fever,* 1924
*Grace after Meat,* 1924
*Two Gentlemen in Bonds,* 1927
*Selected Poems,* 1945; revised editions, 1963, 1969
*Poems and Essays,* 1955

**Selected Criticism**

*American Poetry at Mid-Century* (with Delmore Schwartz and John Hall Wheelock), 1958

**Other Writings:** essays (*God without Thunder: An Unorthodox Defense of Orthodoxy,* 1930; *I'll Take My Stand: The South and the Agrarian Tradition* [with others], 1930; *Selected Essays of John Crowe Ransom,* edited by Thomas Daniel Young and John J. Hindle, 1984), correspondence (*Selected Letters of John Crowe Ransom,* edited by Thomas Daniel Young and George Core, 1985); edited collections of poetry (*Selected Poems,* by Thomas Hardy, 1961).

**Further Reading**

Buffington, Robert, *The Equilibrist: A Study of John Crowe Ransom's Poems, 1916–1963,* Nashville, Tennessee: Vanderbilt University Press, 1967
Quinlan, Kieran, *John Crowe Ransom's Secular Faith,* Baton Rouge: Louisiana State University Press, 1989
Schwartz, Delmore, "Instructed of Much Mortality," *Sewanee Review* 54 (Summer 1946)
Stewart, John L., *John Crowe Ransom,* Minneapolis: University of Minnesota Press, 1962
Warren, Robert Penn, "John Crowe Ransom: A Study in Irony," *Virginia Quarterly Review* 11 (January 1935)
Young, Thomas Daniel, *Gentleman in a Dustcoat: A Biography of John Crowe Ransom,* Baton Rouge: Louisiana State University Press, 1976

## Bells for John Whiteside's Daughter

"Bells for John Whiteside's Daughter" is easily John Crowe Ransom's most anthologized poem. First published in 1923, it is one of the many outstanding poems Ransom published that year. Other poems that appeared in 1923 include "Philomela," "Conrad at Twilight," "Here Lies a Lady," and "Vaunting Oak." Critics often point to this phase of Ransom's career as a prolific period in which his poetry noticeably matured. Although the voice of the poem is completely believable, "Bells for John Whiteside's Daughter" came entirely from the poet's imagination. The idea occurred to him as he watched a neighborhood girl playing in piled leaves, a sight that became the poem's image of the girl playing with the geese.

Although "Bells for John Whiteside's Daughter" may appear to be about the little girl who has died so young, it is actually about the speaker's reaction to this event. Told from the perspective of a neighbor, the poem centers on two images—the child in death and the child in life. The speaker, however, did not really know the girl when she was alive. In fact, his impression of her had been that she was a somewhat annoying child who chased her own shadow and disrupted geese in her noisy play. As he muses on the wastefulness of a child dying so young, his tone is detached and unemotional. To many readers, this distance seems inappropriate. Tragedy is generally accompanied by heightened emotion and deep despair, but here the speaker responds with a reflective, almost aloof tone. Because the speaker did not really know the child at all (her name is never mentioned, even in the title, suggesting that he did not know it), his reaction is understandably subdued in its sadness. The complexity of the poem, therefore, is in the emotional realism of the speaker's attitude. He is not deeply grieved at the child's loss but instead is bewildered, shocked, and disturbed.

Ransom utilizes contrast throughout the poem to emphasize the unnatural event of a child's death. Essentially, the contrast of the poem is between life and death, a theme frequently visited by poets and authors. Recalling the little girl's life, the speaker mentions the "lightness in her footfall" along with descriptions of her energetic play. In the first stanza, Ransom sets up the "astonishing" contrast between the "speed" and "lightness" of her play and the stillness of her "brown study." The next three stanzas describe the little girl playing outside, play-fighting with her own shadow, running into the pond, and chasing geese. The last stanza returns to the original image of the child, perfectly still in death, an image that vexes the speaker. To heighten the contrast, the last words of the poem are, "Lying so primly propped," calling to mind a lifeless but pretty doll. Despite the girl's boundless energy, she is as vulnerable to death as anyone else is. Thus, when the speaker sees her still body, he is astonished because what he sees before him is the exact opposite of what he is accustomed to seeing out his window. At the end of the poem, he is vexed. Although he had been annoyed by the child's boisterous playing, he sees her death as a senseless waste of youth and vitality. The juxtaposition of the two images of the little girl touches the very core of his view of the world. He is forced to consider the possibility that the world is unfair and unfeeling. The child's body comes to represent much more than the wastefulness of a single death; it represents the inherent injustice of life. Another, subtler example of contrast is how the speaker portrays the girl's play as a complete lack of self-consciousness, whereas Ransom portrays the speaker as completely self-conscious and introspective.

Various poetic devices are used in "Bells for John Whiteside's Daughter," most notably imagery. As previously discussed, the image of the "propped" child is gloomy, unnatural, and horrifying. The image of the girl taking "arms against her shadow" is both daunting and prophetic. The shadow is dark and one-dimensional, so that it resembles a person but has an unknowable and inescapable quality. It is an intangible that is tied to the girl by the laws of nature, much like her fate. That Ransom depicts the girl battling her shadow seems to foreshadow the upcoming struggle she will lose. In line 13, the speaker refers to the child's "tireless heart," which is an example of irony, considering that the occasion of the poem is her death. In the last stanza, Ransom introduces alliteration in the phrases "sternly stopped" and "primly propped." The effect is that the stanza reads a bit haltingly, which complements the moment of the last stanza. Just as the speaker and the others in the house are "ready" and "stopped" on hearing the bells, the reader feels the tempo of the poem become unstable.

"Bells for John Whiteside's Daughter" is a good exemplary poem for Ransom, which is why students so often analyze it. It contains many elements that are typical of Ransom's poetry, but it is also a strong enough poem to stand on its own without reference to the poet's entire canon. The remoteness of the speaker to the tragedy is typical of Ransom, whose poetry is not grounded in sprawling human emotion. In fact, some critics suggest that he intentionally chose to tell the story from the point of view of a detached neighbor in order to avoid a heavily sentimental and emotional composition. Ransom's poetry is characterized by its ability to depict a nuance of a feeling or experience rather than delving into the depths of human emotion. His poetry is poised and often a bit impersonal, yet readers almost always find honesty and sympathy in its lines. In all these ways, "Bells for John Whiteside's Daughter" represents the strengths of Ransom's poetry as a whole while offering the reader a unique opportunity to explore the complexities of human experience and the impulse to understand the workings of the world.

JENNIFER A. BUSSEY

**Further Reading**

Buffington, Robert, *The Equilibrist: A Study of John Crowe Ransom's Poems, 1916–1963,* Nashville, Tennessee: Vanderbilt University Press, 1967

Coulthard, A.R., "Ransom's 'Bells for John Whiteside's Daughter,'" *The Explicator* 54, no. 2 (1996)

Fowler, Douglas, "Ransom's 'Bells for John Whiteside's Daughter,'" *The Explicator* 52, no. 2 (1994)

Gray, Richard, *The Literature of Memory: Modern Writers of the American South,* Baltimore, Maryland: Johns Hopkins University Press, and London: Arnold, 1977

Rubin, Louis D., Jr., *The Wary Fugitives: Four Poets and the South,* Baton Rouge: Louisiana State University Press, 1978

Warren, Robert Penn, "John Crowe Ransom: A Study in Irony," *Virginia Quarterly Review* 11 (January 1935)

Williams, Miller, *The Poetry of John Crowe Ransom,* New Brunswick, New Jersey: Rutgers University Press, 1972

Young, Thomas Daniel, *Gentleman in a Dustcoat: A Biography of John Crowe Ransom,* Baton Rouge: Louisiana State University Press, 1976

Young, Thomas Daniel, editor, *John Crowe Ransom: Critical Essays and a Bibliography,* Baton Rouge: Louisiana State University Press, 1968

# Here Lies a Lady

The subject of death has been addressed, bemoaned, mocked, and personified in numerous ways by poets over the years. In "Here Lies a Lady," John Crowe Ransom creates a brief sketch of a young woman who died after a fitful illness. Ransom's poetry is characterized by poise and controlled emotion, and here the speaker reflects emotional detachment while simultaneously affording the reader a glimpse of the woman's experience. The poem was written in 1923, a year in which Ransom published 23 poems. Many of these are among his best-regarded work, including "Bells for John Whiteside's Daughter," "Philomela," and "Vaunting Oak." Without shirking his academic responsibilities, Ransom focused as much effort as possible on writing poetry during this time. He sought to write clearly about the uncertainties and ironies of the world without resorting to image-centered poetry. "Here Lies a Lady" attests to Ransom's success in creating richly textured and complex verse.

The issue of the narrator continues to engage critics in debate over whether the ambiguity of the speaker is a compositional strength or a weakness. Most scholars consider it a sticking point because the identity of the voice is difficult to ascertain on the basis of the text. The detached tone reads almost like reportage:

Here lies a lady of beauty and high degree.
Of chills and fever she died, of fever and chills,
The delight of her husband, her aunt, an infant of three,
And of medicos marveling sweetly on her ills.

In fact, this opening stanza strikes the reader as almost disrespectful when the second line reveals the pun ("high degree") in the first line. Further, the reference to carefree doctors in the last line contrasts with what should be a troubling scene of doctors striving to save this poor woman. Still, the tone never becomes altogether flippant or coarse.

The remaining stanzas focus on her sickness and not on the woman herself, making it unlikely that the speaker is a family member or a friend. The tone is not somber enough for a minister or other speaker at a funeral, yet the speaker is present and is privy to the details of her behavior during her spells. The speaker is involved, with limitations, and is also distant, but not completely. Some scholars find this an intriguing "hook" that compels the reader to delve deeply into the text. Others, however, find that it deprives the poem of grounding and authenticity, thus alienating the reader, whose natural tendency is to identify the speaker as a way to understand the poem. In the end, the reader is left unsure how to feel about the woman, and while there seems to be an attempt at a lesson learned (in the last stanza), the lesson lacks clarity. The images of the woman in the throes of her fits are woeful and frightening, but without the human connection to either the woman or the speaker, the reader is left solely responsible for his or her reaction. The poet does not guide the reader's emotion, which makes reading this poem an experience that is both challenging and personal.

The opening of "Here Lies a Lady" is reminiscent of a eulogy honoring a woman who suffered before she died. The middle of the poem, however, does not seem at all ceremonial, instead offering an account of the illness:

For either she burned, and her confident eyes would blaze,
And her fingers fly in a manner to puzzle their heads—
What was she making? Why, nothing; she sat in a maze
Of old scraps of laces, snipped into curious shreds—

Or this would pass, and the light of her fire decline
Till she lay discouraged and cold, like a stalk white and blown,
And would not open her eyes, to kisses, to wine;
The sixth of these states was her last; the cold settled down.

Her death came after her sixth fit, and as the speaker considers her mourners in the final stanza, the question is asked, "But was she not lucky?" This question is puzzling, as it is not at all clear what the speaker means:

Sweet ladies, long may ye bloom, and toughly I hope ye
  may thole,
But was she not lucky? In flowers and lace and mourning,
In love and great honor we bade God rest her soul
After six little spaces of chill, and six of burning.

Perhaps the idea behind the question is that she is lucky to be peaceful now that she is no longer subject to the extremes of her illness, or maybe the speaker wishes to call the reader's attention to the mourners who will miss her. It could be that she was lucky to have lived at all, which is why the speaker wishes the "sweet ladies" long lives.

The simple rhyme scheme of the poem offers no additional insights, yet it keeps the poem rhythmic and composed. There is no point at which the scheme is altered to alert the reader to a turn in the poem. Ransom is well known for his careful use of rhyme, and although many of America's most prominent poets relied on the conventions of rhyme, including T.S. Eliot, Robert Frost, and E.E. Cummings, Ransom has the distinction of never having written an outstanding unrhymed poem. In 1923, when this poem was written, Ransom grappled with finding just the right form for each poem. In "Here Lies a Lady," Ransom utilizes a series of four quatrains with the typical *abab* rhyme scheme.

"Here Lies a Lady" is not specific to a particular time or place, and this enhances the universal quality of the theme of death. Although Ransom was a southern poet, this poem speaks to an all-encompassing readership. The poem's many ambiguities allow the reader to engage the poem in his or her own way, and the complexities of the poem give the careful reader much to examine.

JENNIFER A. BUSSEY

**Further Reading**

Abbott, Craig S., *John Crowe Ransom: A Descriptive Bibliography,* Troy, New York: Whitson, 1999

Leithauser, Brad, "Selected Poems," *The New Republic* 36, no. 5 (5 August 1991)

Malvasi, Mark G., *The Unregenerate South: The Agrarian Thought of John Crowe Ransom, Allen Tate, and Donald Davidson,* Baton Rouge: Louisiana State University Press, 1997

Ransom, John Crowe, *Selected Essays of John Crowe Ransom,* edited by Thomas Daniel Young and John J. Hindle, Baton Rouge: Louisiana State University Press, 1984

Ransom, John Crowe, *Selected Letters of John Crowe Ransom,* edited by Thomas Daniel Young and George Core, Baton Rouge: Louisiana State University Press, 1985

Romine, Scott, "The Invisible I: John Crowe Ransom's Shadowy Speaker," *The Mississippi Quarterly* 46, no. 4 (Fall 1993)

# Ishmael Reed 1938–

Known primarily as an experimental novelist, Ishmael Reed is also a talented poet. Like his novels, many of Reed's poems are satirical. The New York art scene, the American academy, the East Coast literary establishment, critics, and even other poets are all fair game for Reed's acerbic wit. To his credit, Reed's poetry is not merely critical; it is affirmative. Reed's poems celebrate African-American folk culture (particularly hoodoo and the blues), histories of the American West (native, black, Hispanic, and Anglo), and more obscure facets of Americana. Through his work as a writer and editor, Reed was one of the earliest advocates of multiculturalism and canon revision in literary studies. Although much of Reed's poetry is sardonic and antagonistic, he has also written many imaginative and under-appreciated love poems.

Reed's first book of poetry, *Catechism of D Neoamerican Hoodoo Church* (1970), is in many ways a manifesto. Written to challenge the narrow perspectives of Eurocentric and black aesthetic critics and to introduce Reed's playful neo-hoodoo aesthetic, the book begins with a parody of Marx and Engels' *The Communist Manifesto.* Reed's claim that "A spectre is haunting America—the spectre of neo-hoodooism" prefigures the kind of mock seriousness that runs through many of the poems in this book. "I Am a Cowboy in the Boat of Ra" draws on Reed's interest in Egyptology and the American West to conjure the figure of an outlaw poet and aesthetician, a black badman preparing for a final showdown with Set, the embodiment of all that is staid, repressive, and monolithic in Western culture. "Badman of the Guest Professor" chides a Eurocentric English professor for his faithfulness to a dead culture: "listen man, i cant help it if / yr thing is over, kaput, / finis." "Dualism in Ralph Ellison's Invisible Man" parodies Ellison's depiction of the young zoot suit–wearing jitterbugs of the 1940s as "outside of history" by refiguring History as a hungry circus animal devouring all who claim to transcend it. "Catechism of D Neoamerican Hoodoo Church" is a skillful polemic against an academic who asks the speaker to "deform d works of ellison & wright . . . to accommodate a viewpoint [he] thought irresistible."

Reed's next book of poetry, *Conjure* (1972), picks up where *Catechism* left off. Only now, Reed has formulated a real "Neo-HooDoo Manifesto." In this extended prose poem, Reed offers the most detailed account to date of his neo-hoodoo philosophy. Referring to neo-hoodoo as a "Lost American Church," Reed suggests the myriad ways in which neo-hoodoo (i.e., black folk culture) has impacted American popular culture and posits a continuity between contemporary African-American cultural practices and those deriving from Africa (particularly Egypt) by way of New Orleans. "The Black Cock," dedicated to Jimi Hendrix, refers to an animal that is frequently used in voodoo ceremonies because of its ritual power and to the ludic sexuality that Hendrix displayed in his performances. "Betty's Ball Blues," a risqué blues lyric, is filled with double entendres. The poem rhapsodizes over the love relationship of fictional characters Betty and Dupree. Sentimental (in a good sense) and erotic, the poem scintillates with colorful lines, such as "China China China / Come blow my China horn / Telegraph my indigo skyship / and make its voyage long."

Reed's third book of poetry, *Chattanooga* (1973), is named after the town of his birth. The title poem, an ode to Chattanooga, speaks of the city's hybrid nature—its Native American name, its Civil War history, and its reputation as a center of industry in the South. "Railroad Bill, A Conjure Man" celebrates the life and exploits of the legendary badman, Railroad Bill. "Kali's Galaxy" uses astral metaphors to describe a love affair between a man and a woman that spans galaxies. Reed toasts poet Robert Hayden in "Swift, Tiny and Fine" by attributing various mythical feats to him. The poem ends with the couplet "A hummingbird standing still in mid air, / Robert Hayden is The Great Aware."

*A Secretary to the Spirits* (1978) is based on Reed's claim that he is "Mostly an errand boy for the spirits." "Pocadonia," written in AAB blues fashion, comically describes the anguish the speaker feels after being left by his love, Pocadonia. In "Sputin," the Russian mystic and courtier Rasputin serves as a trope for one of Reed's favorite themes, namely, that of the outsider who, against the predictions of naysayers, achieves unlikely success. "Soul Proprietorship," a tribute to jazz vocalist Billy Eckstine, is a celebration not only of his musicianship but of his courage, business acumen, and independence in starting a solo career late in life. The protagonist of "The Reactionary Poet" critiques Marxist aesthetics by enumerating all the things that he would recover from the past rather than inhabit a future peopled with pseudo-revolutionaries.

*New and Collected Poems* (1988) contains poems from all of Reed's previous books as well as a new section titled "Points of View." Most of the poems in "Points of View" are blues, ballads, or dramatic monologues. "Petite Kid Evrett" pokes fun at poet Amiri Baraka, whose birth name is Evrett Leroi Jones. In the poem, Kid Evrett is a punch-drunk boxer from Newark who lapses from professional boxing into street brawling. "Epistolary Monologue," written in the form of a letter from Queen Elizabeth to her working-class lover, lampoons England's royal family. The poem manages to take jabs at Prince Charles, Princess Anne, the late Princess Diana, and Ronald and Nancy Reagan. Continuing in this same vein, "The Pope Replies to the Ayatollah Khomeini" pretends to be a secret apology from the pope for sending an envoy to complain about conditions in Iran while remaining silent about the shah's earlier, more oppressive regime. In "Judas," Reed updates the story of Judas' betrayal of Jesus. The story gains much in the way of humor and immediacy from Reed's embellishments. Judas sports a corduroy suit made in Poland, Christ's passion involves electroshock therapy, Napa Valley champagne is served with every meal in heaven, and, in hell, the biscuits taste like baking soda.

More than any other American poet, Reed possesses the "built-in shit-detector" that Ernest Hemingway thought so crucial to the professional writer. While Reed's poetic persona suggests something of the showman, the ringmaster, or even the stage magician, his deep-seated democratic impulses display little tolerance for those who use the tricks of the trade for personal gain. Like a renegade magician pulling the rug out from under his fellow practitioners, Reed relentlessly satirizes poets, academics, religious leaders, politicians, and corporations. Reed's irreverence and idiosyncrasy, his humor and pragmatic common sense, his love for the best in American culture, as well as the hearty laughter that he inspires toward the worst make him one of the most essential voices in contemporary American poetry.

DOUGLAS TAYLOR

**Biography**
Born in Chattanooga, Tennessee, 22 February 1938. Attended the University of Buffalo, New York, 1956–60; staff writer, *Empire Star Weekly,* Buffalo, 1960–62; freelance writer, New York, 1962–67; co-founder, *East Village Other* and *Advance,* 1965; teacher, St. Mark's in the Bowery prose workshop, New York, 1966; since 1971 chair and president, Yardbird Publishing Company, Berkeley, California; editor, *Yardbird Reader,* 1972–76; since 1973 director, Reed Cannon and Johnson Communications, Berkeley; since 1981 founder and editor, with Al Young, *Quilt* magazine; since 1967 Lecturer, University of California, Berkeley; Lecturer, University of Washington, Seattle, 1969–70, State University of New York, Buffalo, 1975, 1979, Sitka Community Association, summer 1982, University of Arkansas, Fayetteville, 1982, Columbia University, New York, 1983, Harvard University, Cambridge, Massachusetts, 1987, and University of California, Santa Barbara, 1988; Visiting Professor, fall 1979, and since 1983 Associate Fellow of Calhoun House, Yale University, New Haven, Connecticut; Visiting Professor, Dartmouth College, Hanover, New Hampshire, 1980; since 1987 Associate Fellow, Harvard University Signet Society; since 1976 president, Before Columbus Foundation; chair, Berkeley Arts Commission, 1980, 1981; associate editor, *American Book Review.* Received National Endowment for the Arts grant, 1974; Rosenthal Foundation Award, 1975; Guggenheim fellowship, 1975; American Academy Award, 1975; Michaux Award, 1978. Living in Oakland, California.

**Poetry**
*Catechism of D Neoamerican Hoodoo Church,* 1970
*Conjure: Selected Poems, 1963–1970,* 1972
*Chattanooga,* 1973
*A Secretary to the Spirits,* 1978
*New and Collected Poems,* 1988
*The Reed Reader* (includes prose), 2000

**Other Writings:** novels (*The Terrible Twos,* 1982), essays (*Writin' Is Fightin': Thirty-Seven Years of Boxing on Paper: Essays,* 1988; *Airing Dirty Laundry,* 1993); edited collections of literature (*Calafia: The California Poetry,* 1979).

**Further Reading**
Boyer, Jay, *Ishmael Reed,* Boise, Idaho: Boise State University, 1993
Dick, Bruce Allen, and Pavel Zemliansky, *The Critical Response to Ishmael Reed,* Westport, Connecticut, and London: Greenwood Press, 1999
Fox, Elliot Robert, *Conscientious Sorcerers: The Black Postmodernist Fiction of LeRoi Jones/Amiri Baraka, Ishmael Reed, and Samuel R. Delany,* New York and London: Greenwood Press, 1987
Martin, Reginald, *Ishmael Reed and the New Black Aesthetic Critics,* London: Macmillan Press, and New York: St. Martin's Press, 1988
McGee, Patrick, *Ishmael Reed and the Ends of Race,* New York: St. Martin's Press, and London: Macmillan, 1997

---

# Lizette Woodworth Reese 1856–1935

Born outside Baltimore, Maryland, in Waverly, Lizette Woodworth Reese once described her childhood as "an unhurried and secure affair" (*A Victorian Village,* 1929). Later referred to as "Lady Baltimore" (Hahn, 1980), Reese taught for 48 years until her retirement in 1921. Her occupation had a definite impact on her writing style. In *A Victorian Village,* Reese notes how, as a student herself, writing in school was something she found difficult because she wrote slowly compared with her classmates. This anxiety is evident in her description of the composition of her first poem, "The Deserted House": "It took me weeks to write this poem, to select words or eliminate them, rubbing it up here, or letting it alone there, until in a sense it was something like what I wished it to be" (*A Victorian Village*). As she continued to balance writing and teaching, however, Reese found that time constraints prevented such lengthy written revision, so she devised a method of mental composition, eventually finding that "it grew into such a habit that even now when I have leisure, I must have the exact words which I wish to write all intact in my brain before I venture to trace them with pencil or pen" (*A Victorian Village*). This careful planning resulted in intensely rich poetry, most notable for its keen imagery.

Reese's first collection of poetry was her 1887 work *A Branch of May,* followed by *A Handful of Lavender* (1891) and *A Quiet Road* (1896). Reese did not publish again until her 1909 work *A Wayside Lute,* which contains her most famous work, "Tears." Reese shows how important it was to be deliberate in her writing when she explains the 13-year absence: "I had nothing to say, except at long intervals, and therefore did not try to say it" (*A Victorian Village*). She continued to write several more collections of poetry: *Spicewood* (1920), *Wild Cherry* (1923), *The Selected Poems* (1926), *Little Henrietta* (1927), *White April, and Other Poems* (1930), *Pastures, and Other Poems* (1933), and *The Old House in the Country* (1936). She also published a fictional piece, *Worleys* (1936), and two prose works: *A Victorian Village: Reminiscences of Other Days* (1929) and *The York Road* (1931), both of which contain poetry as well as sketches of her experience in her birthplace of Waverly.

Reese once wrote, "Art, like life, is hard. The poet, like any other individual, must work out his own redemption" (*A Victorian Village*). This statement provides a useful introduction to Reese's work not only because it illustrates her view that writing involves struggle but also because it suggests that the poet's search is often a solitary, personal one. Reese's writing often emphasizes individuality with the use of a single poetic speaker. Perhaps because of this interest in subjectivity, her writing does not reflect an overtly political purpose; instead, Reese explores traditional themes through regular poetic forms, such as sonnets and lyrics. Her focus on form and prosody have led critics such as H.L. Mencken to note the musical qualities of her work and Jessie Rittenhouse to label her as a "poet-*singer,*" an image echoed in one of her requested tombstone inscriptions based on Isaiah 42:10: "I will sing a new song unto the Lord."

"What go into the making of a song?" is one of the questions Reese asks in "Today" (1909). A review of her poems quickly reveals several answers. Explorations of nature appear frequently, and she illustrates both celebratory and stark representations. With its suggestions of rebirth and renewal, the month of April is a frequent image seen in such poems as "White April" (1930) and "The Thrush in the Orchard" (1896). For Reese, April is certainly not the cruelest month but a dramatic time of energetic renewal and reflection. Images of spring also often connect with spirituality. In "Trust" (1896), she equates herself with grass to represent her spiritual growth. Sometimes nature becomes threatening in its glory. In "Spring Ecstasy" (1923), the speaker wants to hide in God because "The weather has gone mad with white," and in "The White Fury of the Spring" (1930), she states that she knows that "certainly it will rush in at last, / And in my own house seize me at its will, / And drag me out to the white fury there." Occasionally, her writing focuses on more physical aspects, such as in her 1933 "After Spring": "Naked am I, stark naked of the spring, / Stripped to the very marrow of each bone" and that "To think of spring is of a dream that broke." Not all her nature poems, however, are so energetic; she frequently uses "dust" not only to point to humans' elemental state but also to capture a stagnant or arid atmosphere, as in her powerful "Drought" (1920). Bees, fog, and flowers are other frequent images.

Human relationships form another area of Reese's themes, and often issues of memory or time become involved. For example, ghosts appear frequently. Family dynamics are often treated by examining the grieving process of people who have lost children, as in *Little Henrietta* (1927). Women who have lost lovers or who feel rejected appear as well, as in "The Second Wife" (1930). Another interest is reflected in several poems that speak of relationships to God. In her 1909 poem "The Wayfarer," Reese writes, "Life is but a small rainy day / Betwixt two dusks; but in its gray / Enough of light for me, for you." Reflecting her optimistic spirit, this message encourages readers to focus on the possibilities that surround them.

Despite her accomplishments, Reese's work has been largely overlooked since her death in 1935, as clearly seen in the little critical work that has been done. As Carlin T. Kindilien (1957) argues, perhaps one reason for this exclusion is the difficulty of classifying Reese. Working in both the 19th and the 20th century, she employs a concise writing style and uses intense imagery—clear connections with Modernist concerns; however, her dislike of free verse illustrates her interest in continuing a poetic tradition. This traditional focus may have stemmed from her reading of other poets. She greatly admired Poe and was well versed in English literature. While she did state that many 20th-century poems show a great deal of quality, she notes "a disturbing ignorance of older poetic literature" and "a lack of feeling" (*A Victorian Village*). She also has been quoted as saying to Louis Untermeyer that she thought "Pound and Eliot were charlatans who had devised an elaborate hoax" (Jones, 1992). While most would probably argue with Reese about such a statement, it nevertheless shows her awareness of contemporary poetic issues. Much of her writing reflects her interest in other authors, and her work resonates with such diverse poets as Lydia Sigourney, Emily Dickinson, Walt Whitman, Edna St. Vincent Millay, Sara Teasdale, Louise Bogan, and Robert Frost. Overall, Reese's strong imagery, range of writing, and connections with other writers suggest that she should not be considered simply a writer of America's "twilight interval" but a powerful singer in the poetic landscape of the 20th century.

Kelly L. Richardson

**Biography**

Born in Huntingdon (now Waverly), Maryland, 9 January 1856. Teacher, St. John's Episcopal Parish School, Waverly, Maryland, 1873–76; Baltimore public schools, 1876–1901; Western High School, Baltimore, 1901–21. Received Mary L. Keats Memorial Prize, 1931; Poet Laureate of Maryland, 1931. Died in Waverly, Maryland, 17 December 1935.

**Poetry**

*A Branch of May,* 1887
*A Handful of Lavender,* 1891
*A Quiet Road,* 1896
*A Wayside Lute,* 1909
*Spicewood,* 1920
*Wild Cherry,* 1923
*The Selected Poems of Lizette Woodworth Reese,* 1926
*Little Henrietta,* 1927
*White April, and Other Poems,* 1930
*Pastures, and Other Poems,* 1933
*The Old House in the Country,* 1936

**Other Writings:** memoirs (*A Victorian Village: Reminiscences of Other Days,* 1929), novel (*Worleys,* 1936), short stories and sketches (*The York Road,* 1931).

**Further Reading**

Dietrich, Mae, "Lizette Woodworth Reese," *Emily Dickinson Bulletin* 15 (1970)
Giles, Ronald Kelley, "Lizette Woodworth Reese: The Quality and Influence of Her Poetic Voice," Ph.D. Diss., Auburn University, 1981
Gregory, Horace, and Marya Zaturenska, *A History of American Poetry, 1900–1940,* New York: Harcourt Brace, 1942
Hahn, H. George, "Twilight Reflections: The Hold of Victorian Baltimore on Lizette Woodworth Reese and H.L. Mencken," *Maryland Historian* 11 (1980)
Harris, R.P., "April Weather: The Poetry of Lizette Woodworth Reese," *South Atlantic Quarterly* 29 (1930)
Jones, Robert J., editor, *In Praise of Common Things: Lizette Woodworth Reese Revisited,* Westport, Connecticut: Greenwood Press, 1992
Kilcup, Karen L., *Robert Frost and Feminine Literary Tradition,* Ann Arbor: University of Michigan Press, 1998
Kindilien, Carlin T., "The Village World of Lizette Woodworth Reese," *South Atlantic Quarterly* 56 (1957)
Rittenhouse, Jessie B., *The Younger American Poets,* Boston: Little, Brown, 1904; reprint, Freeport, New York: Books for Libraries Press, 1968
Scholnick, Robert J., "Lizette Woodworth Reese," *Legacy* 15, no. 2 (1998)

Walker, Cheryl, *The Nightingale's Burden: Women Poets and American Culture before 1900,* Bloomington: Indiana University Press, 1982

Watts, Emily Stipes, *The Poetry of American Women from 1632 to 1945,* Austin: University of Texas Press, 1977

---

# Religion and Poetry

"Faith is *doubt,*" wrote Emily Dickinson to her sister-in-law in 1884, forecasting the temper of religious poetry in modern times (including her own). Faith was doubt also for the Psalmists and for Herbert and Donne, and a reader seeking unquestioned faith in 20th-century poetry would find little to delight her. Many academic critics, supposing that doubt is incompatible with faith, have missed the spiritual dimension in modern poetry. Nevertheless, religious poetries have persisted through the years of the modern, and "nevertheless" is their operative word.

The orthodox spiritual temperament of the century was a chastened Transcendentalism. To rebalance Carlyle's phrase, it was a naturalism with an irreducible element of supernaturalism. In spite of Darwin, in spite of the empiricism and even the principled uncertainty of modern science, a strain of American poets continued to look to "nature" with the same religious expectancy with which Thoreau had studied his beans at Walden. Every natural fact, Emerson had written in *Nature,* is a symbol of some spiritual fact; and although Emerson himself left open the question of whether the symbol's potency came from the divine powers of the human mind or from an Oversoul, the Transcendentalists put their faith in the doubleness of nature, physical and spiritual, to impart philosophical and ethical meaning to their experience—which is all they asked of religion.

Two early Modernists, Robert Frost and Wallace Stevens, had been evangelized by Emerson, and to his vision they maintained a skeptic fidelity. Is there a spiritual presence in nature? In "The Most of It," Frost articulated the hope behind *Nature:* what the lonely human spirit "wants / Is not its own love back in copy speech, / But counter-love, original response." However, "Nothing ever came of what he cried / Unless" (*Unless!*) the great buck that swims the lake and stalks away, ignoring him, is the incomprehensible "embodiment" of a response. This is quintessential Frost: is the gleam at the bottom of the well a pebble of quartz, or Truth? Or an answering "something"? Elsewhere, as in "Forgive, O Lord," Frost harangues a more personal "God," but his poems typically watch for a sign out of the depths of nature and occasionally, as in "Two Look at Two" and "Take Something Like a Star," get at least a hint of a corresponding Being.

Stevens' poetry often hovered over that rift between mind and matter that Emerson hoped he had "soldered" with Spirit in *Nature:* whatever correspondence we find in nature, he knew, arises wholly from our imagination. In "Nuances of a Theme by Williams," he invoked the impersonal, irresonant stars: "Shine like bronze, / that reflects neither my face nor any inner part / of my being." However, late in life he was still talking to them: "I am the archangel of evening and praise / This one star's blaze. / Suppose it was a drop of blood" ("One of the Inhabitants of the West"). Stevens was not Williams: the ghost in nature was one that he could never lay altogether.

The work of A.R. Ammons typified supernatural naturalism in the final third of the 20th century. Although he once said, "Overall is beyond me," his poems cannot desist from describing small arcs of the fleeting Oversoul. Emerson wrote in "Circles" that "every ultimate fact is only the first of a new series," and "Corson's Inlet" ends with a vow to "try / to fasten into order enlarging grasps of disorder" while accepting with Emersonian "serenity" the endlessness of this task. Like Frost and Stevens, Ammons sometimes feels the opacity of nature: "having been brought this far by nature I have been / brought out of nature / and nothing here shows me the image of myself" ("For Harold Bloom"). However, not finding the Self there, he may find something Other. On another walk, in another poem, nature—"snow or shale, squid or wolf, rose or lichen"—is suffused with "radiance," "and the dark / work of the deepest cells is of a tune with May bushes / and fear lit by the breadth of such calmly turns to praise" ("The City Limits"). In their attention to physical detail, his poems praise the Absolute under many names: "love" ("Prodigal"), "being" ("Still"), or, most characteristically, "*flowing*" ("Guide"). Bards in the wake of Romanticism—H.D., Robert Duncan, and Annie Dillard—still pursue the light that never was on land or sea, however protean or fleeting or problematic its gleam may be.

For poets such as Hart Crane and Theodore Roethke, this ambivalently supernatural naturalism was married to a Modernist preoccupation with myth. From the poetic practice of W.B. Yeats, T.S. Eliot, and David Jones and the criticism of conservatives such as Cleanth Brooks, mythic patterning was taken as a principle of "order"—in the chaos of the personal psyche, in the seemingly anarchic sphere of literature, and in the realm of public life. To some, religion provided an ordering myth, both social (invoking, often, a simplified Middle Ages) and literary (invoking, always, the *Divine Comedy*). Hart Crane, seeking in *The Bridge* (1930) a "myth" to unify both a disunited America and a recalcitrantly fragmentary poetic project, followed a technique of his master Walt Whitman, using liturgical forms such as prayer and invocation and imputing mythological significance to the physical landscape of America and to the creations of science and technology. Brooklyn Bridge, he prayed, would "lend a myth to God"—a spirit that was perhaps just the hypostasis of that cosmic consciousness attained by Whitman in "Passage to India" but whom Crane invoked, in the mouth of Columbus, as "Word," "Elohim," and finally as "Love." Crane acknowledged that although "I have never consciously approached any subject in a religious mood," in his poems there was nonetheless "a prevalent piety" (*The Letters of Hart Crane, 1916–1932,* edited by Brom Weber, 1965).

Roethke was seldom so programmatic about "myth," but Yeats and Eliot (and Jung) were his tutelaries, and his best-known poems retell the Night Journey, questing into the recesses of the unconscious, in search of the lost Father (or Mother), the master of death and life. This he sometimes found in the vegetal and neural beginnings of consciousness, often announcing his discovery in the language of religious mysticism: "The redeemer comes a dark way" ("The Shape of the Fire"). It is never clear whether this "redeemer" is anything more than a wished-for resolution to the poet's psychological distress. However, as his later poems moved out of the subconscious and the subjective and into a recognition of beings other than himself, they become more certainly religious. "North American Sequence" discovers, in the land's-end, sundown landscapes of the Northwest, glimpses of a spiritual presence other than his own—a presence that his final poems call by the name of God.

The romantic religious vision is always a private one and so nagged by introspective doubt. Is the vision genuine, or is it a self-induced illusion? "Do we move toward God, or merely another condition?" wondered Roethke ("The Abyss"). An alternative strand of modern American poetry sought to deliver itself from what Dickinson had called the "magic prison" of subjectivity, situating personal spiritual experience within the larger contexts provided by faith traditions and communities of belief and worship.

Those traditions were never absent from the early modern skeptics, Frost and Stevens. Frost kept on good terms with Scripture, using its images to phrase his own Job-like interrogation of God. Stevens, on the other hand, subjected Christian beliefs and figures to a relentless Emersonian critique, calling them "darkened ghosts of [an] old comedy" ("Of Heaven Considered as a Tomb") and insisting that "divinity must live with [ourselves]" ("Sunday Morning") as the creative, if fictive, power of imagination. The Christian mythos pervaded Stevens' poetry to the end as a challenge he could not dismiss: projecting his own spiritual state into Santayana's in "To an Old Philosopher in Rome," Stevens portrays him on the threshold between two worlds, "The extreme of the known in the presence of the extreme / Of the unknown." It is hard not to read Stevens' poetry as the embodiment of a negative theology, a lifelong process of casting off false images of God in pursuit of a divinity that lies always just beyond the final imagining.

T.S. Eliot also was an heir of supernatural naturalism. A constant throughout his poems is the Wordsworthian spot in time, a moment of vision unsummoned and irretrievable, often occurring in a garden. Garden, child, birdsong, flower: the nuclei of Eliot's interior life are unmistakably romantic; his struggles to contextualize those private experiences are not. His treatment of time and of language typify the ways poets throughout the 20th century kept in touch with religious traditions and communities.

All about the sacred moment in the garden stretches a waste of unintelligible profane time. In Eliot's early poetry, that moment is always in the irrecoverable past, both personal and cultural. To some companion of Jesus (Lazarus or John), to a painter of the Umbrian school, to Dante, the vision was near at hand, and assent in those days came readily. Eliot must have found this easy to believe; hence the reactionary posture of some of his prose. His poems present this attitude more critically. Paralyzed by their sense of living in the withered aftertime, his personae shrink from present summonses to step into time. "Hurry up please its time" is countered by "time . . . for a hundred indecisions." In the myth-world of "The Waste Land," the gods are forever reborn and so forever absent. How to "redeem / The time" from emptiness?—"Ash Wednesday" counsels a penitentiary but expectant quietude. The later poems embrace a Christian view of time, according to which God, through Christ, has entered time and made its every moment latently holy. Time is a dance, each end a new beginning, a new opening on the numinous: "the end of all our exploring / Will be to arrive where we started / And know the place for the first time" ("Little Gidding"). The *Quartets* look attentively to the future, saying with Krishna, "Fare forward, / O voyagers," and with Julian of Norwich, the 14th-century mystic, "All manner of thing shall be well."

Versions of this view of time are found in other poets in the Christian tradition, such as Countee Cullen, Allen Tate, Robert Lowell, and Richard Wilbur. In Cullen's "The Black Christ," Christ is re-figured in the lynching and the resurrection of a young black man—not by a figure of speech, as in many other African-American poems, but as an actual "miracle." The prevailing religious theme in Tate's poetry was the fall from innocence, a Calvinist conviction of the fallibility and depravity of humans that in its political form underlay the writings of T.E. Hulme, Eliot, and the Fugitives and as a literary donnée governed the New Critics and the writers they favored. Following patterns he had learned from Tate, Lowell in his early poems would first depict a corrupt and repulsive 20th-century scene and then invoke God, Christ, or the Virgin Mary, pleading for its redemption. In the best of them, "The Quaker Graveyard in Nantucket," surveying man's violence against man and nature, he prays, "Hide, / Our steel, Jonas Messias, in Thy side." Lowell's discomfort with the physical is the opposite of Wilbur's conviction that it is only in the "things of this world" that the sacred is to be found: his "Christmas Hymn" praises "the child / By whose descent among us / The worlds [of flesh and spirit] are reconciled." Robert Hayden, drawing on a different tradition of divine oversight in history, in "'From the Corpse Woodpiles, from the Ashes'" and "Words in the Mourning Time" looked beyond the racial violence, wars, and assassinations of his time to an era of reconciliation foreseen by the founder of Bahai, Bahá'u'lláh:

> I bear Him witness now:
> toward Him our history in its disastrous quest
> for meaning is impelled.

Poets in the tradition of Judaism build on a different sense of time, characterized by Jonathan Barron (2000) as "pre-messianic." Eschewing the immanentist religious vision of both the supernatural naturalists and the Christian poets, Jewish poets often have adopted the mode of remembrance. Delmore Schwartz, Marcia Falk, and Alicia Ostriker recast stories from the Torah. Among the myriad poems remembering the Holocaust, many (e.g., Robert Mezey's "The Wandering Jew") set it against the genocidal catastrophes suffered by ancient Israel, questioning the acquiescence—or the absence—of God in all this iniquity. The time measures of Judaism appear in poems about the Sabbath and the Holy Days, especially Yom Kippur, whether taken traditionally, as in Charles Reznikoff ("All wickedness shall go in smoke. / It must, it must!"), or rebelliously, as in Cynthia Ozick ("Let God renounce what's done / And for his absence and my doubt / Atone").

Prophetic anticipation has been a poetic mode used by many modern religious poets. In prophecy, the poet condemns his dissolute age, usually in a city, and foresees God's retribution. Eliot's unedited "The Waste Land" is a prophecy, as are Ginsberg's "Howl" (denouncing "Moloch") and "Wichita Vortex Sutra" (invoking God through avatars both Western and Eastern). Wendell Berry, Thomas Merton, Lucille Clifton, and Denise Levertov sustained the prophetic voice through the latter half of the century, condemning industrialism, racism, and militarism from explicitly religious points of view. Robert Hayden wrote several poems on spiritual visionaries associated with the African-American struggle: "The Ballad of Nat Turner," "Frederick Douglass," "John Brown," and "El-Hajj Malik El-Shabazz." The latter memorializes Malcolm X:

He fell upon his face before
Allah the raceless in whose blazing Oneness all
were one. He rose renewed renamed, became
much more than there was time for him to be.

Profane language is a correlative of profane time. In *Nature*, Emerson had created a theory of symbols, binding words with things and with meanings, and invoked the authorship of "God" to guarantee that nature spoke the same truths to everyone. Stevens relocated this power in the human imagination, conceding its provisionality: "Thou art not August unless I make thee so" ("Asides on the Oboe"). However, for the men and women of Eliot's Waste Land, the withdrawal of God had stripped words of their potency to represent and to elicit response. With the failure of language, objects lost their magic. The "splendour" of St. Magnus Martyr is "inexplicable," the city "Unreal," a babel of voices. "Ash Wednesday" invokes a vacant symbology of leopards, unicorns, and juniper trees. However, that poem contrives to name what is wrong, that the world has lost its Logocentricity—or at least lost touch with it. If words are empty, it is because "the Word [is] unheard." Yet the Word is still "within / The world and for the world," so the poem revisits the apparently exhausted words and cadences of prayer, beseeching a silent God to "speak the word." In the *Quartets*, fear of time and doubts about language are no less present, but they are counterpoised by a faith that there still are times and places "where prayer has been valid." These poems invoke religious traditions (mostly Christian, but with elements of Buddhism that always fascinated Eliot) as a way of maintaining continuity across time and escaping the solipsism of romantic spirituality. The prevailing mood of the *Quartets* is not affirmative but skeptical and expectant, finding that the modern way to God involves "no ecstasy," no certainty that one has found God. Nevertheless, these poems do resuscitate religious forms of discourse, such as the prayer and the meditation on place, and they reinvest commonplace things, such as water and fire, with sacramental power. Through the "Incarnation"—the coming of the Word into the world—"the impossible union / Of spheres of existence is actual" ("The Dry Salvages").

In the poetics of Judaism, only the words of the Torah—perhaps only the ineffable word of YHWH—enjoy such spiritual privilege. Harvey Shapiro depicts Moses the "aniconic Jew" confronted with the "pronominal" name of God and from it "spell[ing] mystery" ("Mountain, Fire, Thornbush"). Like Moses, poets work pronominally, sometimes eschewing re-presentation (Gertrude Stein and the Objectivists), sometimes writing in a spirit of commentary or translation (Jerome Rothenberg). In "The Alphabet," Karl Shapiro reflects on the otherness of Hebrew and its writing systems: "The letters of the Jews are black and clean / And lie in chain-line over Christian pages." The Jewish poet, writing in English, suspends his or her words over the abyss between Being and utterance.

Since midcentury, poets have revisited some traditional religious forms of speech, especially liturgical prayer. In "Horae Canonicae," W.H. Auden followed the daylong sequence of monastic prayer, specifically on Good Friday, meditating on the deadliness of the modern state, its persecution of the weak, and the need for arrogant "spirit" and pitiful "flesh" alike to be redeemed and reunified. "God bless this green world temporal," it ends. Jewish poets have turned to the Kaddish prayer, often as a remembrance of a dead loved one but sometimes with a more religious intent, as seen in Ginsberg's, Reznikoff's, and David Ignatow's memories of their mothers and Reznikoff's lament and prayer for the peace and safety of "Israel and . . . all who live / as the sparrows of the streets." In *God's Trombones* (1927), James Weldon Johnson caught some of the oral poetry of the African-American sermon:

In that great day,
People, in that great day,
God's a-going to rain down fire.
God's a-going to sit in the middle of the air
To judge the quick and the dead. ("The Judgment Day")

Later in the century, such evocations of sermon and hymn would usually be ironic dismissals of piety by secularized black poets. Lucille Clifton, however, often retrieves their original fervent spirit: in "atlantic is a sea of bones," she quotes from the spiritual "Dry Bones" before commemorating the deaths in the Middle Passage, and ends on a modern note: "i call my name into the roar of surf / and something awful answers." The poems John Coltrane wrote for *A Love Supreme* were formed from traditional prayer, and gospel music throughout the century was one of the most popular forms of religious poetry.

Denise Levertov is the poet who encompassed most fully the varieties of religious poetry in the 20th century. Her father a Hasidic Jew who had become an Anglican clergyman, her mother descended from Welsh mystics and bards, she pursued through the second half of the century a life that was at once a career in poetry and a spiritual pilgrimage. Hers was always a poetry of this world, reflecting her conviction that "the strawness of straw, the humanness of the human, is their divinity; in that intensity is the 'divine spark' Hasidic lore tells us dwells in all created things" ("Origins of a Poem"). "The Jacob's Ladder" represents the poem as a passage joining spirit with matter, not "a thing of gleaming strands" but solid rosy stone that "bring[s] the grip of . . . hands into play." Eros was the muse of many of her poems, rejoicing that the sexual is also the spiritual. Combining her memories of the Welsh countryside with her lifelong love of travel and with her readings in American romantics such as Emerson, Thoreau, Duncan, and H.D., she treated natural things as "holy" presences, all bound up in "the great / web of analogy" ("Conversation in Moscow"). To her, words were seeds of virtue, "sweet / to eat and sweet / to be given, to be eaten / in common" ("A Common Ground"). Out of her conviction of the holiness of life came a fierce prophetic stance, in deed as well as in word, condemning and resisting the American war in Vietnam and the development of nuclear weapons. In her middle life, hints of more formal religious belief began to appear in her work. A sequence in *Breathing the Water* (1987) meditates on religious works of art and addresses Julian of Norwich, whose visions never lost their grip on the homely stuff of life. Later she wrote a book of *Oblique Prayers* (1984) and a set of prayers for a mass—significantly, a mass for St. Thomas, the doubter. It confesses that "our hope lies / in the unknown, / in our unknowing." In modern times, faith incorporates doubt.

James Dougherty

**Further Reading**

Barron, Jonathan N., "Commentary in Contemporary Jewish American Poetry," in *Jewish American Poetry,* edited by Barron and Eric Murphy Selinger, Hanover, New Hampshire: University Press of New England, 2000

Blackmur, R.P., "Religious Poetry in the United States," in *Religious Perspectives in American Culture,* edited by James Ward Smith and A. Leland Jamison, Princeton, New Jersey: Princeton University Press, 1961

Buckley, Vincent, *Poetry and the Sacred,* New York: Barnes and Noble, and London: Chatto and Windus, 1968

Eliot, T.S., "Religion and Literature," in *Selected Prose of T.S. Eliot,* edited by Frank Kermode, New York: Harcourt Brace Jovanovich, and London: Faber, 1975

Gunn, Giles B., *The Interpretation of Otherness: Literature, Religion, and the American Imagination,* New York: Oxford University Press, 1979

Gunn, Giles B., editor, *Literature and Religion,* New York: Harper and Row, and London: SCM Press, 1971

Impastato, David, editor, *Upholding Mystery: An Anthology of Contemporary Christian Poetry,* Oxford and New York: Oxford University Press, 1995

Scott, Nathan A., Jr., *The Wild Prayer of Longing,* New Haven, Connecticut: Yale University Press, 1971

Scott, Nathan A., Jr., *Visions of Presence in Modern American Poetry,* Baltimore, Maryland: Johns Hopkins University Press, 1993

---

# Kenneth Rexroth 1905–82

For a poet deeply involved in many poetic movements and in contact with dozens of significant poets both as peer and mentor, Kenneth Rexroth remains somewhat invisible in American poetic history. Various factors account for his marginal status, spanning the geographic, political, personal, and aesthetic. He spent his career far from the established centers of literary culture on the East Coast (after leaving his native Midwest at age 21, he lived the rest of his life in California, mostly in San Francisco). On principle, Rexroth believed that poets were enemies of the state, and so he spent his life among the radical and disenfranchised rather than the powerful and connected. A fierce advocate of the work of friends and younger poets, his passionate support could just as easily focus on a petty personal conflict and sour into a long-held grudge. Associated with the Objectivists, the San Francisco Renaissance poets, and the Beats, he distanced himself from such groups as soon as they achieved notoriety or popularity. During the midcentury dominance of the New Criticism in academia, which transmitted the values of difficulty, irony, and impersonality to a generation of poets and readers, Rexroth wrote poetry distinctive for its accessibility, commitment, and personal voice. However, these liabilities will diminish as the history of American poetry in the 20th century consolidates, and the remarkable body of work that Rexroth produced, both original poetry and translations, as well as his literary essays and cultural criticism, will gain him a deserved visibility.

Rexroth was born in South Bend, Indiana. He was raised in an atmosphere of middle-class bohemianism and socialism, was educated largely by his independent and protofeminist mother, and was orphaned by his early teens. In Chicago, Rexroth married Andrée Schafer, a painter, and the couple hitchhiked to California in 1927. The next decade was spent exploring California's mountains and coastline, painting (both wife and husband painted in the same Cubist-derived style, often collaborating on the same canvas), writing experimental poetry, working for the Federal Writers' Project on the State Guide series, organizing workers, and carrying on extramarital affairs. Although he considered his poetics at the time Cubist, Rexroth's early experimental poetry was included in *An "Objectivists" Anthology* (1932) and the Objectivist issue of *Poetry* (February 1931), both edited by Louis Zukofsky. In the 1930s, his style shifted from the abstract and fragmented Cubism to a plain-style poetics that was discursive, descriptive, and immediate. His first book, *In What Hour* (1940), collected poems written in both modes and received a California Silver Medal Award. Robert Hass (1984) says that this book "seems . . . to have invented the culture of the West Coast."

Rexroth had been carrying on an affair and living with Marie Kass, a nurse, during a long separation from Andrée. Marie became his second wife, and many of the love poems and nature poems of his finest volumes of original poetry—*In What Hour, The Phoenix and the Tortoise* (1944), and *The Signature of All Things* (1950)—are dedicated to or feature her. Rexroth's erotic mysticism and ecological perspective are embodied in the lyrics of this period, written in his middle style that uses a syllabic line (usually seven to nine syllables), precise diction drawn from natural history, restrained figurative language, and conventional syntax and punctuation. The most enduring of these poems include "Toward an Organic Philosophy," "When We with Sappho," "Lyell's Hypothesis Again," and "The Signature of All Things." Additionally, Rexroth continued to write long, philosophical poems, a form he used as early as "The Homestead Called Damascus" (written in 1920–25). "The Phoenix and the Tortoise" presents a nightlong meditation on the themes of history and the individual, fact and value, the many and the one, set on the California coast during holy week in the midst of World War II. *The Dragon and the Unicorn* (1952) is a philosophical travel poem, taking the poet on a journey across the United States, through Europe, and back again to California. Fine set pieces were excerpted from this poem and individually titled for his *Collected Shorter Poems* (1966), including "Golden Section," "Time Spirals," and "Only Years."

Rexroth's companion for part of his stay in Europe in 1949 was Marthe Larsen, who would soon become his third wife. The couple had two daughters in the early 1950s, and their presence, combined with the tenor of the Cold War years and Eisenhower's America, shaped the style and content of *In Defense of the Earth* (1956). The volume contains more of Rexroth's fine love lyrics, a sequence of numbered poems called "Seven Poems for Marthe, My Wife," which were later given individual titles and stripped of their dedication after the marriage broke up. Also, the familiar nature poems continue, but now the beloved Other accompanying the speaker is a young daughter. The salient poem is the memorial for Dylan Thomas, "Thou Shalt Not Kill." Using Thomas' death as a reason to lament the ruinations of various artists and revolutionaries, the poem becomes a rant against the conformity and affluence of the 1950s, prefiguring the Beat ethos. However, Rexroth's lasting contribution to American poetry in the 1950s was not this book. In 1955, New Directions published *One Hundred Poems from the Japanese,* and *One Hundred Poems from the Chinese* followed a year later. These anthologies, edited and translated by Rexroth, went through multiple printings and introduced many young poets and general readers to the classical lyric traditions of Asia.

In 1968, Rexroth began teaching at the University of California, Santa Barbara; until then, he had supported himself through grants, book royalties, and literary journalism. For this reason, Rexroth's prose is eclectic, wide ranging, and written for a general audience. Topics include literature, music, art, politics, the counterculture, religion, anthropology, architecture, and communalism. Rexroth would write on almost any topic that paid. His prose style is offhand and colloquial, and he often dictated his thoughts on tape for transcription; his autobiography, *An Autobiographical Novel* (1966), was composed this way. Rexroth produced two major statements on the poetry of his time in these years. "Poetry in the Sixties" comments on the post-1945 poets. He dismisses the idea that the Beats were major contributors to the San Francisco Renaissance and proclaims Snyder, Levertov, and Creeley "our three leading post-war poets" (1970). *American Poetry in the Twentieth Century* (1971) ranges from the Modernists to the contemporary poets, offering Rexroth's commentary on everything from the small publications produced by the avant-garde to the "lost" poets of the "red" 1930s to African-American poets of the 1960s.

Rexroth took two extended trips to Japan in his later years, and from his experiences visiting monasteries and his deep involvement with Japanese traditions his most remarkable late work emerged. *The Morning Star* (1979) included new translations, a sequence called "On Flower Wreath Hill" (also published in a 1976 volume of the same title), and "The Love Poems of Marichiko." The Marichiko poems, a group of supposed translations, has become one of Rexroth's most widely known works. These explicitly erotic lyrics, which a note says are by "a contemporary young woman who lives near the temple of Marishi-ben in Kyoto," are actually Rexroth's own invention. An aging, Western, white male poet assumes the persona of a young, Asian, female poet and writes compelling and graceful poetry of physical and spiritual desire: there is nothing else like it in American poetry. In his final major poetic statement, Rexroth inscribed his own "invisibility" while he continued his lifelong exploration of the interdependence of love, nature, and lyric identity.

George Hart

*See also* San Francisco Renaissance

**Biography**

Born in South Bend, Indiana, 22 December 1905. Attended the Art Institute, Chicago; Art Students' League, New York; conscientious objector during World War II; Forest Service patrolman in Washington State, farm worker, factory hand, and seaman, 1920s; active in libertarian and anarchist movements, San Francisco, California, 1930s and 1940s; orderly, San Francisco County Hospital, 1939–45; painter, individual shows in Los Angeles, New York, Chicago, San Francisco, and Paris; San Francisco correspondent, *The Nation,* from 1953; columnist, San Francisco *Examiner,* 1958–68, *San Francisco Magazine,* and *San Francisco Bay Guardian,* from 1968; teacher, San Francisco State College, 1964, and University of Wisconsin, Madison; part-time Lecturer, University of California, Santa Barbara, from 1968. Received Guggenheim fellowship, 1948; Shelley Memorial Award, 1958; Amy Lowell fellowship, 1958; American Academy grant, 1964; Fulbright fellowship, 1974; National Endowment for the Arts grant, 1977; member, American Academy. Died in Montecito, California, 6 June 1982.

**Poetry**

*In What Hour,* 1940
*The Phoenix and the Tortoise,* 1944
*The Art of Worldly Wisdom,* 1949
*The Signature of All Things: Poems, Songs, Elegies, Translations, and Epigrams,* 1950
*The Dragon and the Unicorn,* 1952
*A Bestiary for My Daughters Mary and Katharine,* 1955
*Poems,* 1955
*In Defense of the Earth,* 1956
*The Homestead Called Damascus,* 1963
*Natural Numbers: New and Selected Poems,* 1963
*Collected Shorter Poems,* 1966
*Penguin Modern Poets 9* (poems by Rexroth, Denise Levertov, and William Carlos Williams), 1967
*The Heart's Garden, the Garden's Heart,* 1967
*Collected Longer Poems,* 1968
*The Spark in the Tinder of Knowing,* 1968
*Sky Sea Birds Trees Earth House Beasts Flowers,* 1970
*New Poems,* 1974
*On Flower Wreath Hill,* 1976
*The Silver Swan: Poems Written in Kyoto, 1974–75,* 1976
*The Morning Star: Poems and Translations,* 1979
*Between Two Wars: Selected Poems Written Prior to the Second World War,* 1982
*Selected Poems,* edited by Bradford Morrow, 1984
*Sacramental Acts: The Love Poems of Kenneth Rexroth,* edited by Sam Hamill and Elaine Laura Kleiner, 1997

*Swords that Shall Not Strike: Poems of Protest and Rebellion,* edited by Geoffrey Gardner, 1999

**Selected Criticism**
*With Eye and Ear,* 1970
*American Poetry in the Twentieth Century,* 1971
*The Elastic Retort: Essays in Literature and Ideas,* 1973

**Other Writings:** plays, essays (*World Outside the Window: The Selected Essays of Kenneth Rexroth,* edited by Bradford Morrow, 1987), autobiography (*An Autobiographical Novel,* 1966), translations of Japanese, Chinese, Greek, Spanish, and French literature (*One Hundred Poems from the Japanese,* 1955; *One Hundred Poems from the Chinese,* 1956; *Complete Poems,* by Li Ch'ing-chao, translator with Ling O. Chung, 1979); edited collections of literature (*Seasons of Sacred Lust,* by Kazuko Shiraishi, 1978).

**Further Reading**

Bartlett, Lee, *Kenneth Rexroth,* Boise, Idaho: Boise State University Press, 1988
Bartlett, Lee, *The Sun Is but a Morning Star: Studies in West Coast Poetry and Poetics,* Albuquerque: University of New Mexico Press, 1989
Davidson, Michael, *The San Francisco Renaissance: Poetics and Community at Mid-Century,* Cambridge and New York: Cambridge University Press, 1989
Gibson, Morgan, *Revolutionary Rexroth: Poet of East-West Wisdom,* Hamden, Connecticut: Archon Books, 1986
Gutierrez, Donald, *"The Holiness of the Real": The Short Verse of Kenneth Rexroth,* Madison, New Jersey: Fairleigh Dickinson University Press, and London: Associated University Presses, 1996
Hamalian, Linda, *A Life of Kenneth Rexroth,* New York: Norton, 1991; London: Norton, 1992
Hass, Robert, *Twentieth Century Pleasures: Prose on Poetry,* New York: Ecco Press, 1984; 3rd edition, 1997
Kodama, Sanahide, *American Poetry and Japanese Culture,* Hamden, Connecticut: Archon Books, 1984
O'Grady, John P., "Kenneth Rexroth," in *Updating the Literary West,* Fort Worth: Texas Christian University Press, 1997
Rexroth, Kenneth, *With Eye and Ear,* New York: Herder and Herder, 1970
Smith, Richard Càndida, *Utopia and Dissent: Art, Poetry, and Politics in California,* Berkeley: University of California Press, 1995

## On Flower Wreath Hill

Kenneth Rexroth began his career as a second-generation Modernist who wrote experimental verse, developed a middle-period style of direct statement poetics in which he wrote his most famous love and nature poetry, and became a purveyor of world poetry through his work translating and anthologizing French, Spanish, Greek, Chinese, and Japanese lyric poetry. Throughout his long career as a poet and literary journalist, religious and philosophical subjects were central to his writing. Although for most of his life he identified himself as an Anglo-Catholic, his religious vision drew from a wide and eclectic range of sources: Christian mysticism, Hinduism, and Chinese and Japanese Buddhism. Late in life, he more fully embraced Buddhism and its religious traditions, and he made four extended trips to Kyoto, Japan, staying in monasteries or a farmhouse near the mountains. The original poetry that he wrote during this period was greatly influenced by the Chinese and Japanese poetry that he translated while still bearing a similarity to Western contemplative-religious poetry, such as T.S. Eliot's *Four Quartets.* The first of these poems, "The Heart's Garden, the Garden's Heart" (1967), resembles the long philosophical poems he published throughout his career, such as "The Phoenix and the Tortoise" (1944) and "The Dragon and the Unicorn" (1952), written in his syllabic line and consisting of long verse paragraphs in numbered sections that discursively present his philosophical meditations. "On Flower Wreath Hill" (1976) reveals an even deeper response to the Asian lyric tradition in the brevity of its sections compared to the other long poems and its more elliptical and compressed narrative. In fact, as Rexroth points out in his notes to the sequence, some of the poems are actually translations he has made from the classical Japanese poets. So, in one of his last major poems, Rexroth the poet and Rexroth the translator merge in a contemplation of aging, death, and impermanence.

"On Flower Wreath Hill" consists of eight numbered sections, all of which, except the last, range in length from 10 to 20 lines; section eight is made up of six verse paragraphs, the longest of which contains over 30 lines. All the poems describe the speaker's evening walks along a leaf-strewn path up the hillside and through a graveyard. Section one reads,

> An aging pilgrim on a
> Darkening path walks through the
> Fallen and falling leaves, through
> A forest grown over the
> Hilltop tumulus of a
> Long dead princess, as the
> Moonlight grows and the daylight
> Fades and the Western Hills turn
> Dim in the distance and the
> Lights come on, pale green
> In the streets of the hazy city.

This poem sounds many of the keynotes of the whole sequence: the pilgrim-speaker's aging, the transience of human existence, and the seasonal and diurnal cycles. As Rexroth notes, "Flower Wreath Hill is also a Chinese and Japanese euphemism for a cemetery," and so the poem looks back to the tradition of graveyard ruminations, such as Gray's "Elegy in Country Churchyard." However, Rexroth also draws on a wide range of Eastern religious traditions and texts, most prominently the Kegon, or Flower Wreath, Sutra of Buddhism. This sutra, supposedly Buddha's first teaching after he had attained enlightenment, emphasizes the interpenetration of all beings. The image of the wreath of lotus blossoms symbolizes the multiplicity and mutability of life—each petal representing a universe with millions of worlds, all reflecting and changing into one another in an endless chain.

The "plot" of the poem reveals the speaker's interior journey from attachment to memory and the past, through the "Great Purification" of his 70th birthday, to enlightenment and acceptance of the mutability of personal identity. In the second section, the speaker wonders about the "dead princess" buried under the mound and dwells on his own past: "Until / Life goes out memory will / Not vanish, but grow stronger / Night by night." In this section, Rexroth interpolates lyrics from his Japanese translations, blending his own subjectivity with ancient and anonymous lyric emotion. The final lines of this section read,

Aching nostalgia—
In the darkness every moment
Grows longer and longer, and
I feel as timeless as the
Two thousand year old cypress.

In *One Hundred More Poems from the Japanese,* he included this anonymous lyric as number LXXX and translated it: "Aching nostalgia—/ As evening darkens / And every moment grows / Longer and longer, I feel / Ageless as the thousand year pine." Such "conflation," as Rexroth calls it in his notes, serves to express the speaker's feeling, simultaneously depersonalizing and connecting it to tradition. An act of appropriation, the Western poet borrowing from the Eastern canon, it grounds the poet in the culture and character of the country he is visiting.

The climax of section eight is the speaker's realization of the insight of the Flower Wreath Sutra, and it begins with one of Rexroth's signature images:

Oborozuki,
Drowned Moon,
The half moon is drowned in mist
Its hazy light gleams on leaves
Drenched with warm mist. The world
Is alive tonight. I am
Immersed in living protoplasm,
That stretches away over
Continents and seas.

Infusions of light signify mystical experience throughout Rexroth's poetry, and here the climatic conditions create an immersion in which the speaker's being expands in an "oceanic" moment. However, the poem does not conclude on this ephemeral and subjective experience, but the next four verse paragraphs recapitulate the themes of the whole sequence—the speaker sits on a tumbled grave marker, imagines the dead princess, and remembers his many walks on the hill; but, in the suffused light of the "Drowned Moon," "the / Hundreth night and the first night / Are the same night. The night / Known prior to consciousness, / Night of ecstasy, night of / Illumination so complete / It cannot be called perceptible."

In the last verse paragraph, the speaker encounters the web of an orb-weaver spider in his path, and the drops of mist condensed on the strands become a final image of the interpenetration that is the lesson of the Kegon Sutra. The web "Is itself the Net of Indra" and "The Flower Wreath," and the moonlight reflected in the droplets is "Each universe reflecting / Every other." As the Buddha himself did, the poet returns from his ineffable moment of enlightenment with an image meant to guide those who follow to the same realization.

GEORGE HART

**Further Reading**

Bartlett, Lee, *Kenneth Rexroth,* Boise, Idaho: Boise State University Press, 1988

Hamalian, Linda, *A Life of Kenneth Rexroth,* New York: Norton, 1991; London: Norton, 1992

Kern, Robert, *Orientalism, Modernism, and the American Poem,* Cambridge and New York: Cambridge University Press, 1996

Lockwood, William J., "Toward a Reappraisal of Kenneth Rexroth: The Poems of His Middle and Late Periods," *Sagetrieb* 2, no. 3 (1983)

Rexroth, Kenneth, compiler and translator, *One Hundred More Poems from the Japanese,* New York: New Directions, 1976

Robertson, David, "Kenneth Rexroth in Devil's Gulch," *American Poetry* 8 (1990)

# Charles Reznikoff 1894–1976

Charles Reznikoff's early-20th-century urban poetics has had a profound influence on the ethical as well as ethnic expansiveness of American poetry. A wide range of contemporary poets, including Charles Bernstein, Robert Duncan, Robert Creeley, Allen Ginsberg (who in late career sought to claim Reznikoff as a sort of poetic father), and Elaine Feinstein, were profoundly influenced by Reznikoff's compassionate voice, extraordinary understatement, and incisive arrangement of detail. At various times these poets have admired the anti-essentialist quality with which Reznikoff demonstrated the way a poet of "common experience" might challenge the Wordsworthian notion of "voice" as common language. He introduced a paradigm of the poet who is self-conscious of origins, ethnicity, and the particularity of inflection. A general indebtedness to Ezra Pound, as well as the unique, almost uninterrupted milieu of Reznikoff's urban environment, combined to shape what has become known as "urban Imagism."

In his formative years as an urban poet Reznikoff was a voracious reader of French, German, and Japanese poetry translations. In his 20s he began to study Hebrew and translate the Hebrew Bible. During the Depression Reznikoff worked briefly as editor for the *Corpus Juris* law encyclopedia but was fired for being too slow and meticulous. Reznikoff's study of the law nevertheless inspired him to explore the "plainspoken" possibilities of language, a paradigm that had increasing influence on his poetic mission to "redirect modernism's emphasis on the materiality of aesthetic language to the materiality of social speech" (Davidson,

1997). Moreover, this experience inspired his poetic disavowal of a monolithic national identity during the years of America's most xenophobic period. During the 1950s Reznikoff determined to write a projected four-volume poetic epic history of the nation between 1885–1915, the years he apparently considered the most representative of America's social and psychic fragmentation. The history was to be written in free verse and based entirely on the testimony that the poet encountered in law books as a young man. As he later recalled,

> Working for a publisher of law books, reading cases from every state and every year (since this country became a nation). Once in a while I could see in the facts of a case details of the time and place, and it seemed to me that out of such material the century and a half during which the U.S. has been a nation could be written up, not from the standpoint of an individual, as in diaries, nor merely from the angle of the unusual, as in newspapers, but from every standpoint—as many standpoints as were provided by the witnesses themselves. (*Testimony,* 1978–79)

As Michael Davidson (1997) cogently observes, in the poet's eagerness to write poetry from "as many standpoints as were provided by the witnesses themselves," Reznikoff must be appreciated as one of the age's most thoughtful innovators in "reading American history not as a narrative of Adamic discovery and perfectibility but as a material record of diverse constituencies."

In 1931 Reznikoff joined with Louis Zukofsky, George Oppen, and William Carlos Williams (the only non-Jewish member of the group), poets he had first met in the late 1920s, to form the short-lived "Objectivist" movement. Zukofsky drafted their manifesto, then Reznikoff's friend Oppen established a press. The Objectivist Press was based less on aesthetic coherence than on an opposition to the mainstream world of commercial publishing, as the editorial on the back of the dust wrapper of their inaugural venture suggests: "The Objectivist Press is an organization of writers who are publishing their own work and that of other writers whose work they think ought to be read." Surprisingly, this predominantly Jewish group included an Advisory Board headed by Ezra Pound and published T.S. Eliot's "Marina," apparently indifferent to the ostensible anti-Semitism of the High Modernists. In 1932 Oppen published *An "Objectivist" Anthology* in France, largely based on Zukofsky's editorial work on the "Objectivist" special issue of Harriet Monroe's *Poetry* (February 1931). Before going out of business the Objectivists' imprint, "TO, Publishers," produced work by Williams and Oppen as well as Reznikoff's own *Testimony* (with a preface by Kenneth Burke) and *Jerusalem the Golden* (both 1934). Zukofsky, who consistently praised the virtues of Reznikoff's work to Pound and others, pointed to Reznikoff as the exemplar of what he hoped would emerge as a new movement in American poetics in his lengthy essay "Sincerity and Objectification" (1931). As a movement, however, Objectivism remained an obvious offshoot of Pound's Imagism, conforming closely to such famous directives as "Go in fear of abstractions" and "The natural object is always the adequate symbol."

Alive to his family origins in the Russian-Jewish diaspora, Reznikoff's lyrics bear witness to the displacements, traumas, and cosmopolitan identities of other city dwellers. Dispersion, human vulnerability, and resilience are the chief tropes that drive his poetry. An attentive "walker in the city" years before Alfred Kazin popularized this paradigm, Reznikoff's intimate knowledge of, even affection for the urban environment is juxtaposed with an acute sense of never quite being at home. In Reznikoff's case this creates a poetics of witness, a respect for the reader's moral imagination, and an abiding interest in the decaying, lonely environment of the city and its resilient inhabitants:

> When I was four years old my mother led me to the park.
> The spring sunshine was not too warm. The street was
> almost empty.
> The witch in my fairy-book came walking along.
> She stooped to fish some mouldy grapes out of the gutter.
> ("Beggar Woman")

Reznikoff's childhood in the Brownsville ghetto of Brooklyn exposed him to the immigrant struggle of his parents, relatives, and numerous strangers who sought refuge from the czarist pogroms of the 1880s. Hence "Early History of a Writer" emphasizes the frequency of his family's moves around the city of New York, their economic struggles, and memorable accounts of their ugly, sometimes violent encounters with anti-Semitism in the New World. Reznikoff's compassionate interest in the fractured identities of urban Others and his sense of the past as weighing on the present derive from an acute awareness of his own history and identity: the paternalistic doctor who attended his birth named him "Charles" in place of the "Ezekial"—more befitting his Jewish surname—that his immigrant mother intended. In *Inscriptions* (1959) he comments on his early sense of dual-consciousness, which would grow to inflect much of his poetry:

> Because, the first born, I was not redeemed,
> I belong to my Lord, not to myself or you:
> by my name, in English, I am of His house,
> one of the carles—a Charles, a churl;
> and by my name in Hebrew which is Ezekial
> (whom God strengthened)
> my strength, such as it is, is His.

Reznikoff's poetry is haunted by the ghost of this grandfather, a poet whose entire body of work was burned by his illiterate widow, who feared that the writing might contain subversive elements that might prove dangerous to her family. This burnt manuscript, emblematic of greater catastrophes in Jewish history, lived with Reznikoff in the present moment, as a sign that he must take responsibility for printing his own work, even if there was no market for it. For years his poems appeared only in limited editions of hand-set type that Reznikoff privately printed and distributed from his parents' basement. As a poet fated to labor in obscurity almost until the end, Reznikoff worked for long stretches at various occupations including as a lawyer, millinary salesman, and freelance writer. For a brief time in the 1930s he worked at Paramount Pictures in Hollywood, one of his rare ventures outside New York City.

Although primarily a poet, Reznikoff wrote a surprising number of prose narratives over the years, ranging from historical sketches for the *Menorah Journal,* to his nine dramas modeled on German Expressionism (self-published, 1927), to his memoir of his parents' immigrant struggle in the millinery trade (*By the Waters of Manhattan,* 1930). *The Lionhearted: A Story about the Jews in Medieval England* (1944), a novel about the endurance of the Jews in spite of persecution, like the poet's "A Compassionate People," was explicitly composed as a response to the plight of the Jews of Europe during World War II. A later novel, *The Manner "Music"* (1977), an uncharacteristically bitter meditation on the plight of the alienated and neglected artist (reputedly written in response to William Carlos Williams' urging that he continue to write at any cost), was published posthumously by Black Sparrow Press.

Reznikoff's work failed to make the kind of commercial impact in his lifetime that other Modernist Jewish-American artists such as Mike Gold and Henry Roth enjoyed, but his early works were well reviewed by critics such as Leonard Ehrlich and Lionel Trilling. Moreover, in an important sense his poetry helped to create the very possibility of the Jewish-American poetic tradition that Karl Shapiro and Jerome Rothenberg later continued. His poetry is replete with the historical consciousness of the Jewish writer, and some of his best work includes dramatic monologues set in times of crisis: Samaria of 722 B.C.E., Spain of 1492, Russia of 1905. These works, composed in the 1930s, underscore the shadow of European genocide.

Later generations of non-Jewish poets, particularly the Black Mountain group, felt similarly indebted to Reznikoff's anti-essentialism as well as the lyrical tension between recapturing lost territory (whether linguistic or territorial) and the instability of habitation. The early enthusiasm of poets like William Carlos Williams and Ezra Pound led to the approval of critics such as Hugh Kenner. In his introduction to *The Manner "Music"* Robert Creeley called him a genius; in his review of Reznikoff's poetry Hayden Carruth gushed: "I was captivated, enthralled, swept away—what is the word? Delighted, awed, roused. . . . I cannot exaggerate the degree of my enthusiasm for this book" (see Carruth's article in Hindus, 1984). Allen Ginsberg, who often praised Reznikoff's neglected oeuvre to his own audiences, dedicated his *Plutonium Ode,* "After Whitman and Reznikoff."

During the last years of his life Reznikoff occupied himself with writing *Holocaust* (1975), a major work that employed the technique of the long sequential work *Testimony* and consisted of his "translation" of the transcripts of the Eichmann and Nuremberg trials into condensed, bare, appalling narratives. Although Reznikoff had always been something of a poet's poet, providing private pleasure to a small circle of writers and friends, public recognition did eventually come. At the age of 69 he received an award for his poetry from the National Institute of Arts and Letters that simply read:

> To Charles Reznikoff, born by the waters of Manhattan. Mr. Reznikoff was educated for the law but has instead dedicated his life to giving sworn testimony in the court of poetry against the swaggering injustices of our culture and on behalf of its meek wonders.

Thanks to Black Sparrow Press, a rush of publications followed and Reznikoff lived to see several volumes of his poetry published: *By the Well of Living and Seeing: New and Selected Poems, 1918–1973* (1974), *Holocaust,* and *The Complete Poems.* On the evening of 22 January 1976 Reznikoff remarked to Marie Syrkin—his wife, the daughter of Nachman Syrkin, an important theoretician and idealogue of Labor Zionism—"You know, I never made money but I have done everything that I most wanted to do" and died of a heart attack. Reznikoff was buried in the Old Mount Carmel Cemetery in Brooklyn, where his epitaph from *Separate Way* (1936) reads: "And the days brightness dwindles into stars."

RANEN OMER SHERMAN

*See also* Objectivism

**Biography**

Born in Brooklyn, New York, 31 August 1894. Attended University of Missouri, Columbia, 1910–11; New York University Law School, New York City, LL.B. 1915; Columbia University Law School, 1918; practiced law, 1916–18; hat salesman, family-owned business, 1918; editor, *Corpus Juris,* 1930–34; personal assistant to producer Albert Lewin, Paramount Studios, Hollywood, California, 1937–40; freelance writer, editor, and translator, New York City. Received Jewish Book Council of America Award, 1963; National Institute of Arts and Letters Award, 1971. Died in New York City, 22 January 1976.

**Poetry**

*Poems,* 1920
*By the Waters of Manhattan: An Annual,* 1927
*Five Groups of Verse,* 1927
*Testimony,* 1934
*In Memoriam: 1933,* 1934
*Jerusalem the Golden,* 1934
*Separate Way,* 1936
*Going To and Fro and Walking Up and Down,* 1941
*Inscriptions: 1944–1956,* 1959
*By the Waters of Manhattan: Selected Verse,* 1962
*Testimony: The United States, 1885–1890: Recitative,* 1965
*Testimony: The United States, 1891–1900: Recitative,* 1968
*By the Well of Living and Seeing, and the Fifth Book of the Maccabees,* 1969
*By the Well of Living and Seeing: New and Selected Poems, 1918–1973,* 1974
*Holocaust,* 1975
*Poems, 1918–1936,* 1976
*Poems, 1937–1975,* 1977
*Testimony: The United States, 1885–1915: Recitative* (2 vols.), 1978–79
*Poems, 1918–1975: The Complete Poems of Charles Reznikoff,* 1989

**Other Writings:** novels (*By the Waters of Manhattan,* 1930), plays (*Chatterton, The Black Death, and Meriwether Lewis: Three Plays,* 1922), correspondence (*Selected Letters of Charles Reznikoff, 1917–1976,* 1997), historiography (*The Jews of Charleston: A History of an American Jewish Community,* 1950), memoirs (*Early History of a Sewing-Machine Operator,* 1936), translations of German literature (*Stories and Fantasies from the Jewish Past,* by Emil Cohn, 1951).

**Further Reading**

Bernstein, Charles, "Reznikoff's Nearness," *Sulfur* 32 (Spring 1993)

Davidson, Michael, *Ghostlier Demarcations: Modern Poetry and the Material World,* Berkeley: University of California Press, 1997

Finkelstein, Norman, "Tradition and Modernity, Objectivism and Judaism: The Poetry of Charles Reznikoff," in *The Objectivist Nexus: Essays in Cultural Poetics,* edited by Rachel Blau DuPlessis and Peter Quartermain, Tuscaloosa: University of Alabama Press, 1999

Fredman, Stephen, *A Menorah for Athena: Charles Reznikoff and the Jewish Dilemmas of American Objectivist Poetry,* Chicago: University of Chicago Press, 2001

Hindus, Milton, "Charles Reznikoff," in *The "Other" New York Jewish Intellectuals,* edited by Carole S. Kessner, New York: New York University Press, 1994

Hindus, Milton, editor, *Charles Reznikoff: Man and Poet,* Orono, Maine: National Poetry Foundation, 1984

Omer, Ranen, "The Stranger and the Metropolis: Partial Visibilities and Manifold Possibilities of Identity in the Poetry of Charles Reznikoff," *Shofar* 16, no. 1 (Fall 1997)

Omer, Ranen, "'Palestine Was a Halting Place, One of Many': Transnationalism and the Poet," *MELUS* 25, no. 1 (Spring 2000)

*Sagetrieb* 13, nos. 1–2 (Spring/Fall 1994) (special issue on Reznikoff edited by Burton Hatlen)

## Autobiography: New York/ Autobiography: Hollywood

In Charles Reznikoff's New York City poetry, there is never any doubt that the city is properly the center of the human world. Modern sources, from Hegel to Jung to certain trends in contemporary environmental philosophy, erroneously contend that Judaism's story of the Garden in Genesis is responsible for our unhappy relationship with the natural world, but Reznikoff draws on the Hebrew Bible to imaginatively promote the attunement of the individual to his or her environment, suggesting that Paradise is wherever one lives fully in the present. As Robert Alter (1977) has said of the poet, "No one has gone further than he in the explicit effort to be a conscious Jewish writer and an emphatically American one." Throughout Reznikoff's struggle to set forth his relation to the urban environment in "Autobiography: New York" and "Autobiography: Hollywood" (two of the five lyrical sequences that compose *Going To and Fro and Walking Up and Down* [1941]), we experience the startlingly acerbic pleasures that follow when an ancient Hebraic and modern urban identity insistently brush up against each other:

This pavement barren
as the mountain
on which God spoke to Moses—
suddenly in the street
shining against my legs
the bumper of a motor car. (*CP* II.30)

Here, Reznikoff's great skill with the free-verse form is manifest (as is his ability to keep faith with both the Poundian idiom and the "Hebrew") as he moves from troubled enjambment to ironic completion. In a volume dedicated "to the memory of Sarah Yetta Reznikoff, my mother, who was born in the city of Elizavetgrad, Russia, the daughter of Ezekial and Hannah Wolvovsky, and who died in New York City, sixty-eight years of age, February 12, 1937," Reznikoff explores a variety of displacements and homelessness through the prism of Jewish immigration and loss. Yet the paradox at the heart of Reznikoff's artless and unassuming work is that the fragmentary and dangerous nature of modernity also opens up the gates of wholeness redemption, as they compel the poet and the reader's sympathy for and urgent witnessing of that environment and the vulnerable state of its inhabitants, as in this fragment of Reznikoff's poetry from the Great Depression of the 1930s, titled "Cooper Union Library":

Men and women with open books before them—
and never turn a page: come
merely for warmth
not light. (*CP* II.32)

Often strikingly congruent with Emanuel Levinas' ethics, Reznikoff's lyrics, revealing his true vocation as a walker in the city, never are acts of self-containment but instead reveal a modest "me" that is always subject to the disruption of and exposure to disturbances caused by other beings. The Other is always a disruptive presence that compels the most ethical attention, transforming the self-assurance and wholeness of the Self into a radical questioning. Such attention sometimes leads to small urban miracles of communion in which the poet's compassionate Jewishness fully merges with his New York milieu:

The young fellow walks about
with nothing to do: he has lost his job.
"If I ever get another, I'll be hard!
You've got to be hard
to get on. I'll be hard, all right,"
he says bitterly. Takes out his cigarettes.
Only four or five left.
Looks at me out of the corner of his eye—
a stranger he has just met; hesitates;
and offers me a cigarette. (*CP* II.33)

This is not to say that these straightforward poems are devoid of interiority. Indeed, many of the lyrics reveal poignant hints of the loneliness and obscurity that Reznikoff endured during his most creative years: "I like the sound of the street / but I, apart and alone / beside an open window / and behind a closed door" (*CP* II.27). This rueful validation of the isolated Jewish poet's fate in Christian society conjures up Kafka's similar judgment that "you have always relied only upon yourself and thus built up the strength to be alone." Occasionally, there is a movement away from the stoicism of Objectivist witnessing toward a warm Yiddish wit, as in his frequent midrashic takes on episodes from the Hebrew Bible, whose diction he sought to emulate in his sparse English lines:

I do not believe that David killed Goliath.
It must have been—
you will find the name in the list of David's captains.
But, whoever it was, he was no fool
when he took off the helmet
and put down the sword and the spear and the shield
and said, "these weapons you have given me are good.
but they are not mine."
I will fight in my own way
with a couple of pebbles and a sling. (*CP* II.29)

Reznikoff deflects our interest from the usual highlights conjured up by this scene—martial victory, the gore, a fallen giant, a jubilant mob, and the ascendancy to power—pointing instead to images of resiliency and adaptation, the peculiar triumphs of smallness. Of course, our reading might also lead us to think a little more about the identity of this profoundly humble poet—nearly unknown then as now but for the enduring affection of a small critical circle—who has done his best with a couple of pebbles and a sling. Besides providing a pleasurable moment of whimsy, this lyric is characteristic of Reznikoff's indifference to the mythic significance of messianic/nationalist narratives.

"Autobiography: Hollywood" contains some of the most luminous, if melancholy, poems in the poet's oeuvre. In 1938, an impoverished Reznikoff temporarily uprooted himself from his beloved New York City to join his lifelong friend Albert Lewin (1894–1968), who had joined MGM in 1924 as a personal assistant to Irving Thalberg, eventually overseeing the production of Academy Award–winning *The Good Earth* (1937) and several other well-received films for Paramount. Lewin brought Reznikoff to Hollywood to work as his personal researcher and reader. However, the poet's profound frustration, alienation, and growing contempt for his role as a "stooge" within the worldly prosperity of "Lotus Land" (his phrase) are readily apparent in his lyrics from this sequence:

> These gentlemen are great; they are paid
> a dollar a minute. They will not answer
> if you say, Good morning;
> will neither smile nor nod—
> if you are paid only a dollar or two
> an hour (Study
> when to be silent, when to smile.)
> The director who greets my employer loudly
> and smiles broadly, reaching for his hand and back,
> scowls and glares at my greeting. Now I understand
> why he managed to give me only his fingers
> when we were introduced. Why do you go to such trouble
> to teach me that you are great?
> I never doubted it until now. (*CP* II.43)

At the same time, Reznikoff finds comfort in juxtaposing his unease and uprootedness in his new surroundings (not to mention his absence from his wife, Marie Syrkin, whom he had just married) in relation to an entire genealogy of upheavals and dispersions:

> I like the streets of New York City, where I was born,
> better than these streets of palms.
> No doubt, my father liked his village in Ukrania
> better than the streets of New York City;
> and my grandfather the city and its synagogue,
> where he once read aloud the holy books,
> better than the village
> in which he dickered in the market place. (*CP* II.38)

Reconciled to the inevitability of change and the challenge to prove one's better enduring worth in spite of an indifferent world, Reznikoff offers a direct and unadorned poetry rooted in humility and concern for the disenfranchised. The cumulative effect of these lucid poems offers us a sense of a poet content to be himself, offering up existential, deeply felt truths about the human condition and, despite his reputation as a poet of the eye, a faith in the fundamentally spiritual nature of the world.

Ranen Omer Sherman

**Further Reading**


Alter, Robert, "Charles Reznikoff: Between Past and Present," in *Defenses of the Imagination,* Philadelphia, Pennsylvania: Jewish Publication Society, 1977

Franciosi, Robert, "A Story of Vocation: The Poetic Achievement of Charles Reznikoff," Ph.D. Diss., University of Iowa, 1985

Fredman, Stephen, *A Menorah for Athena: Charles Reznikoff and the Jewish Dilemmas of American Objectivist Poetry,* Chicago: University of Chicago Press, 2001

Heller, Michael, *Conviction's Net of Branches: Essays on the Objectivist Poets and Poetry,* Carbondale: Southern Illinois University Press, 1985

Hindus, Milton, editor, *Charles Reznikoff: Man and Poet,* Orono, Maine: National Poetry Foundation, 1984

Omer, Ranen, "'Palestine Was a Halting Place, One of Many': Transnationalism and the Poet," *MELUS* 25, no. 1 (Spring 2000)

*Sagetrieb* 13, nos. 1–2 (Spring/Fall 1994) (special issue on Reznikoff edited by Burton Hatlen)


---

# Adrienne Rich 1929–

To a significant extent, all poets are concerned with transformation. The very making of a poem involves a transformation from perceived reality or experience into a verbal utterance shaped by the poet's imagination and craft. For Adrienne Rich, however, transformation goes beyond the act of writing; it extends to the culture at large through the poem's ability to challenge given assumptions and offer new visions.

Rich delineated her poetics relatively early in her career in a 1971 essay, "When We Dead Awaken: Writing as Re-Vision":

> For a poem to coalesce, for a character or an action to take shape, there has to be an imaginative transformation of reality which is in no way passive. . . . Moreover, if the imagination is to transcend and transform experience, it has to

> question, to challenge, to conceive of alternatives, perhaps to the very life you are living at that moment.

Transformation is thus private as well as public, and Rich's poetry and essays have explored the space where these realms intersect, incorporating feminist, lesbian, historical, non-capitalist, humanitarian, multi-racial, and multi-cultural points of view. The form of her poems has evolved with her content, moving from tight formalist lyrics to more experimental poems using a combination of techniques: long lines, gaps in the line, interjections of prose, juxtaposition of voices and motifs, didacticism, and informal expression. Indeed, no poet's career reflects the cultural and poetic transformations undergone in the United States during the 20th century better than that of Adrienne Rich.

Rich demonstrated talent early in life, writing poems under her father's tutelage as a child. By the time she graduated from Radcliffe College her first book, *A Change of World* (1951), had been selected by W.H. Auden for the Yale Younger Poets Prize. This and her second book, *The Diamond Cutters* (1955), capture alienation and loss through the distancing devices of Modernist formalism, but both books contain poems that hint at her future thematic concerns. "Storm Warnings," from *A Change of World*, speaks of people "Who live in troubled regions" and foreshadows unspecified but disturbing change:

> Weather abroad
> And weather in the heart alike come on
> Regardless of prediction.

"Aunt Jennifer's Tigers" offers an image of power revealed and restrained by domestic arts. Three poems in *The Diamond Cutters*—"Picture by Vuillard," "Love in the Museum," and "Ideal Landscape"—question the version of reality offered by art, while "Living in Sin" depicts a woman's growing dissatisfaction with her lover and living situation.

*Snapshots of a Daughter-in-Law* (1963), which reflects the tensions she experienced as a wife and mother in the 1950s, marks a substantial change in Rich's style and subject matter. "The experience of motherhood," Rich wrote in "Split at the Root: An Essay on Jewish Identity" (1982), "was eventually to radicalize me." Part of that radicalizing process involved Rich's relationship to both poetry and history. In 1956 she began dating her poems by year:

> I did this because I was finished with the idea of a poem as a single, encapsulated event, a work of art complete in itself; I knew my life was changing, my work was changing, and I needed to indicate to readers my sense of being engaged in a long, continuous process.

The act of dating her poems amounted to a rejection of New Critical values that placed the poem outside of its cultural and historical contexts. Informed by a feminist sensibility, many of the poems in *Snapshots* use free verse and a more personal voice to express anger, to acknowledge a need for change, and to address or recover other women writers. The book's title piece, a ten-poem sequence written in free verse, creates an album of women's lives under male domination. The sequence moves back and forth in time and content, generalizing about the domestic repression of contemporary women and referring to female historical figures. To many critics "Snapshots of a Daughter-in-Law" presented a radical and problematic departure from Rich's earlier formalism, but in "When We Dead Awaken" Rich rejected the poem as "too literary, too dependent on allusion" and male literary authorities. Nevertheless, Rich's later poetry would rely heavily on allusions to literary, historical, and contemporary events and persons.

Rich's next three books—*Necessities of Life* (1966), *Leaflets* (1969), and *The Will to Change* (1971)—reflect the social upheaval of the late 1960s and early 1970s. Like other poets of her generation, such as Denise Levertov, Robert Bly, and W.S. Merwin, she wrote poems protesting the Vietnam War, particularly in *Leaflets*. Images of death pervade *Necessities of Life* as the poet struggled to create a life no longer shaped by predetermined rituals and social roles. Emily Dickinson became a recurring figure in her poems, foreshadowing her influential essay, "Vesuvius at Home: The Power of Emily Dickinson" (1975). Rich's poems also became increasingly experimental, employing longer, contrapuntal lines. She adapted the ghazal, a Persian form traditionally used for expressions of love, to convey social and political comment. At the same time, Rich began to distrust her medium because of its close ties to patriarchal culture. "This is the oppressor's language // yet I need it to talk to you," she writes in "The Burning of Paper Instead of Children," a five-poem sequence with prose segments in *The Will to Change*.

Informed more distinctly by a feminist analysis of history and culture, *Diving into the Wreck* (1973) marks another turning point in Rich's career. In it she expresses her anger regarding women's position in Western culture more directly and alludes to problematic dualities or images of Otherness. Language, too, remains on trial for its duplicitous nature. The book's title poem, one of the 20th century's most significant poems, uses an androgynous diver to examine a culture wrecked by its limited view of history and myth. As with *Leaflets* and *The Will to Change*, this book's tone ranges from critical to accusatory. When *Diving into the Wreck* was awarded the National Book Award in 1974, Rich rejected the prize as an individual but accepted it, with a statement coauthored by Audre Lorde and Alice Walker, on behalf of all unknown women writers.

Rich's essays and poetry from the mid-1970s to the early 1980s have been considered her most radical, in part because in them she rejects her earlier use of androgyny and seems to make a case for feminist separatism. "There are words I cannot choose again: / *humanism androgyny*," she writes in "Natural Resources," in which a female miner replaces the androgynous diver of "Diving into the Wreck." Rich defines and addresses her villain more clearly: a patriarchal culture that inherently devalues anything female or feminine. The impulse behind the search, however, remains the same: finding a way to "reconstitute the world" (*The Dream of a Common Language*, 1978). Rich advocates a woman-centered vision of creative energies that she aligns with lesbianism in her essays "'It Is the Lesbian in Us'" (*On Lies, Secrets, and Silence*, 1979) and "Compulsory Heterosexuality and Lesbian Experience" (*Blood, Bread, and Poetry*, 1986). She also criticizes the impact of patriarchal culture on motherhood in *Of Woman Born: Motherhood as Experience and Institution* (1976). Other essays as well as poems in *The Dream of a Common Language* and *A Wild Patience Has Taken Me This Far* (1981) offer important new readings of female literary and historical figures. Rich's lesbian love sequence, "Twenty-One Love Poems," also dates from this time and is as striking for its sensuousness as it is for its philosophical probing.

The poems and essays from this period contributed greatly to contemporary understanding of the social construction of gender; they also generated controversy. Critics objected to the didacticism in her poetry and considered her feminist/lesbian vision too narrow. Rich's strategies are more usefully seen as a counterpoint to the pervasiveness of patriarchal culture, which harms men as well as women. While Rich may claim, for example, that women together create "a whole new poetry" in poems such as "Transcendental Etude," her ultimate vision is broader. The "lost brother" Rich describes in "Natural Resources" "was never the rapist," but rather "a fellow creature / with natural resources equal to our own" (*The Dream of a Common Language*).

Rich's books published in the mid- to late 1980s, *Your Native Land, Your Life* (1986) and *Time's Power* (1989), examine her relationship to her Jewish origins and to the men in her life, as well as what it means to be a feminist in the Reagan era. Her landscapes include not only Southern California, to which she moved in 1984, but also South Africa, Lebanon, Poland, and Nicaragua. She addresses a public "you" held accountable for her quality of life: her parents, her former husband, her current lover, and a self wracked with arthritic and psychic pain. What remains consistent is Rich's insistence that poetry remain linked to a political and social context. "Poetry never stood a chance / of standing outside history," she writes in the second poem of her sequence "North American Time" (1986). "Living Memory" in *Time's Power* is a transitional piece, recalling the poet's past explorations in "Diving into the Wreck" and looking ahead to her future work. The poem instructs:

> Open the book of tales you knew by heart,
> begin driving the old roads again,
> repeating the old sentences, which have changed
> minutely from the wordings you remembered.

Rich follows her instructions in *An Atlas of the Difficult World* (1991), one of her most accomplished books of poetry. The title piece, a 13-poem sequence, invites comparison with other long poems of the American experience by Walt Whitman, Muriel Rukeyser, Allen Ginsberg, and Robert Pinsky. Its general theme of knowing one's country, however painful and disappointing, continues in *Dark Fields of the Republic* (1995), in which the poet's examination of America's problems uses the phrase "not somewhere else, but here" from *The Dream of a Common Language*. In 1995 she increases the load this phrase must bear, claiming in "What Kind of Times Are These" that "the edge of dread" along which she walks is

> not somewhere else, but here,
> our country moving closer to its own truth and dread,
> its own ways of making people disappear.

Rich sees undercurrents of violence in the materialism of the 1980s and 1990s that neither poets nor individuals can afford to ignore. These themes, as well as the role of poetry in political and social life, are also explored in her book of essays *What Is Found There: Notebooks on Poetry and Politics* (1993).

In her latest book of poems, *Midnight Salvage* (1999), Rich continues this discussion from the perspective of an aging activist poet looking back on her life. She alludes to several of her previous poems and books, and poses several questions: Has anything useful been salvaged from the wreck of culture Rich has been exploring for more than 30 years? Have art and language served society and the poet well? Do material comforts blind Americans to the lessons of the past? Her questions are not easily answered, and the book's tone borders on despair. "I wanted to go somewhere / the brain had not yet gone," she writes in "Letters to a Young Poet," "I wanted not to be / there so alone." The "wild patience" that helped Rich to survive into the late 1970s and early 1980s has become the "horrible patience" the poet needs to find language she can use effectively. Images of windows appear throughout the book as if the poet, enclosed and cut off from the world, were struggling to see it clearly. In the book's closing sequence, "A Long Conversation," Rich wonders if it is the "charred, crumpled, ever-changing human language" that "sways and presses against the pane," blocking her view.

Rich is best known as a key figure in feminist poetry. Her dream of a better language and a better world, however, aligns her with the visionary poetics of Shelley and Whitman, and with American transcendentalists such as Emerson. The documentary nature of her work—her poetry of witness and protest—is in keeping with the work of poets such as Carl Sandburg, Robert Hayden, Muriel Rukeyser, Gwendolyn Brooks, Carolyn Forché, and the lesser-known 19th-century women poets in England and the United States who wrote about social and domestic injustice. Rich's exploration of the points where private lives and public acts intersect, as well as the confessional mode her poems sometimes employ suggests the work of Robert Lowell, Sylvia Plath, and Anne Sexton. Her frank discussion and celebration of lesbian sexuality have contributed to a more open discussion of homosexuality today, not only within the walls of the academy but in the culture at large: it is difficult to imagine the work of Marilyn Hacker or Minnie Bruce Pratt without Rich as a precursor. Finally, her insistence in the 1980s that feminism move beyond the white middle class and be more sensitive to the needs of women of color and of varying economic classes aligns her with a number of poets: Audre Lorde, June Jordan, Joy Harjo, Judy Grahn, and Irish poet Evan Boland. This is a *short* list of links and influences, suggesting the complex and generative quality a poetics of transformation can possess. Her uses of anger, domestic imagery, and the poetic sequence or long poem suggest other possibilities.

RHONDA PETTIT

**Biography**

Born in Baltimore, Maryland, 16 May 1929. Attended Radcliffe College, Cambridge, Massachusetts, A.B. (cum laude) 1951 (Phi Beta Kappa); taught at the YM-YWHA Poetry Center Workshop, New York, 1966–67; visiting poet, Swarthmore College, Pennsylvania, 1966–68; Adjunct Professor, Graduate Writing Division, Columbia University, New York, 1967–69; Lecturer, 1968–70, Instructor, 1970–71, Assistant Professor, 1971–72, and Professor, 1974–75, City College of New York; Fannie Hurst Visiting Professor, Brandeis University, Waltham, Massachusetts, 1972–73; Professor of English, Douglass College, New Brunswick, New Jersey, 1976–78; A.D. White Professor-at-Large, Cornell University, Ithaca, New York, 1981–85; Visiting Professor, San Jose State University, California, 1985–86; since 1986 Professor of English and feminist studies,

Stanford University, California; Clark Lecturer and Distinguished Visiting Professor, Scripps College, Claremont, California, 1983; Burgess Lecturer, Pacific Oaks College, Pasadena, California, 1986; columnist, *American Poetry Review,* 1972–73; coeditor, *Sinister Wisdom,* 1980–84; since 1989 member of editorial collective, *Bridges: A Journal for Jewish Feminists and Our Friends.* Received Yale Series of Younger Poets Prize, 1951; Guggenheim fellowship, 1952, 1961; Ridgely Torrence Memorial Award, 1955; American Academy Award, 1961; Amy Lowell traveling scholarship, 1962; Bollingen Foundation grant, for translation, 1962; Bess Hokin Prize, 1963, and Eunice Tietjens Memorial Prize, 1968 (*Poetry,* Chicago); National Translation Center grant, 1968; National Endowment for the Arts grant, 1970; Shelley Memorial Award, 1971; Ingram Merrill Foundation grant, 1973; National Book Award, 1974; Donnelly fellowship, Bryn Mawr College, Pennsylvania, 1975; Fund for Human Dignity Award, 1981; Ruth Lilly Prize, 1986; Brandeis University Creative Arts Medal, 1987; Elmer Holmes Bobst Award, 1989; Academy of American Poets fellowship, 1992; Lenore Marshall Prize, 1992; MacArthur fellowship, 1994; Tanning Prize, 1996; Lifetime Achievement Award, Lannen Foundation, 1999; Chancellor, Academy of American Poets, 1999; honorary Litt.D., Wheaton College, Norton, Massachusetts, 1967; Smith College, Northampton, Massachusetts, 1979; Brandeis University, 1987; City College of New York, 1990; and Howard University, Washington, D.C., 1990. Living in northern California.

**Poetry**

*A Change of World,* 1951
*The Diamond Cutters, and Other Poems,* 1955
*Snapshots of a Daughter-in-Law: Poems, 1954–1962,* 1963
*Necessities of Life: Poems, 1962–1965,* 1966
*Selected Poems,* 1967
*Leaflets: Poems, 1965–1968,* 1969
*The Will to Change: Poems, 1968–1970,* 1971
*Diving into the Wreck: Poems, 1971–1972,* 1973
*Poems Selected and New, 1950–1974,* 1975
*Adrienne Rich's Poetry,* edited by Barbara Charlesworth Gelpi and Albert Gelpi, 1975; revised edition, as *Adrienne Rich's Poetry and Prose* (includes prose), 1993
*Twenty-One Love Poems,* 1976
*The Dream of a Common Language: Poems, 1974–1977,* 1978
*A Wild Patience Has Taken Me This Far: Poems, 1978–1981,* 1981
*Sources,* 1983
*The Fact of a Doorframe: Poems Selected and New, 1950–1984,* 1984
*Your Native Land, Your Life,* 1986
*Time's Power: Poems, 1985–1988,* 1989
*An Atlas of the Difficult World: Poems, 1988–1991,* 1991
*Collected Early Poems: 1950–1970,* 1993
*Dark Fields of the Republic: Poems, 1991–1995,* 1995
*Midnight Salvage: Poems, 1995–1998,* 1999

**Other Writings:** essays (*Of Woman Born: Motherhood as Experience and Institution,* 1976; *On Lies, Secrets, and Silence: Selected Prose, 1966–1978,* 1979; *Blood, Bread, and Poetry: Selected Prose, 1979–1985,* 1986; *What Is Found There: Notebooks on Poetry and Politics,* 1993), translations of Urdu and Flemish literature.

**Further Reading**

DuPlessis, Rachel Blau, "The Critique of Consciousness and Myth in Levertov, Rich, and Rukeyser," in *Shakespeare's Sisters: Feminist Essays on Women Poets,* edited by Sandra M. Gilbert and Susan Gubar, Bloomington: Indiana University Press, 1979
Friedman, Susan Stanford, "'I Go Where I Love': An Intertextual Study of H.D. and Adrienne Rich," in *Coming to Light: American Women Poets in the Twentieth Century,* edited by Diane Wood Middlebrook and Marilyn Yalom, Ann Arbor: University of Michigan Press, 1985
Martin, Wendy, *An American Triptych: Anne Bradstreet, Emily Dickinson, Adrienne Rich,* Chapel Hill: University of North Carolina Press, 1984
Ostriker, Alicia, "Her Cargo: Adrienne Rich and the Common Language," in *Writing Like a Woman,* by Ostriker, Ann Arbor: University of Michigan Press, 1983
Rich, Adrienne, *Adrienne Rich's Poetry,* edited by Barbara Charlesworth Gelpi and Albert Gelpi, New York and London: Norton, 1975; revised edition, as *Adrienne Rich's Poetry and Prose,* 1993
Rich, Adrienne, "Introduction," in *The Best American Poetry, 1996,* edited by Rich, New York: Scribner Paperback Poetry, 1996
Werner, Craig, *Adrienne Rich: The Poet and Her Critics,* Chicago and London: American Library Association, 1988
Whitehead, Kim, *The Feminist Poetry Movement,* Jackson: University Press of Mississippi, 1996

## An Atlas of the Difficult World

In *What Is Found There: Notebooks on Poetry and Politics* (1993), Adrienne Rich discusses seeing a great blue heron, then entering her house to look up its picture in a book. This desire to name what she sees surfaces in much of her work. Rich believes that language names and "fixes" people, turning them into symbols rather than independent beings—a false and disempowering transformation. For Rich, "Neither of us—woman or bird—is a symbol, despite efforts to make us that." In *An Atlas of the Difficult World* (1991), her 13th collection, Rich upends symbols to show how poetry fosters

> the crossing of trajectories of two (or more) elements that might not otherwise have known simultaneity. When this happens, a piece of the universe is revealed as if for the first time.

The desire to reveal the universe is not new to Rich. In *Snapshots of a Daughter-in-Law* (1963) she presented chilling images of enclosure created by her responsibilities as a wife, mother, and daughter-in-law. She addressed women's identities and the need for community in *The Dream of a Common Language* (1978). From there, she explored the effects of race, class, and gender in *A Wild Patience Has Taken Me This Far* (1981). In *Atlas* Rich moves from personal to public concerns, urging readers to accept shared responsibility for their country. As Mary Hussman's 1992 review of *Atlas* suggests,

> with *An Atlas of the Difficult World* [Rich] steps fully back into contemporary society bent on fathoming what it means to love [her] country. . . . Rich has discovered who she is; now she tries to show us where we are.

The first poem in *Atlas,* "a road poem bearing witness" (Hussman, 1992), alerts the reader to a speaker who has changed since Rich's earlier works:

> this is where I live now. If you had known me
> once, you'd still know me now though in a different
> light and life. This is no place you ever knew me.

Rich occupies new land in this collection and moves to explore unfamiliar areas. While she has no desire to sift through the decay she encounters, she realizes that poetry provides a way to reimagine the constructs of society.

Rich believes "poetry can break open locked chambers of possibility, restore numbed zones to feeling, recharge desire" (Rich, 1993). This belief in possibility sparks her desire to remap the world in the first poem. Accordingly, while she does not want to know "wreckage, dreck and waste," she knows that "these are the materials: with which we must work." In delving through that material Rich uncovers images of despair. In its panoramic sweep of the United States, the second poem highlights poverty, uneducated citizens and children, and a loss of well-paying jobs. Images of foreclosed farms, bankrupt fisheries, and unemployed auto workers indicate a land where financial stability and the American dream have been lost. Children are homeless, women and men out of work, forests clearcut. Rich holds out hope, however; she ends the poem dismissing small distinctions, calling upon people to recognize North America as more than a map of failures:

> I promised to show you a map you say but this is a mural
> then yes let it be these are small distinctions
> where do we see it from is the question[.]

As a mural, the map of America includes all people. For Rich, one must understand one's own position and perspective upon and within that mural before change can take place.

*Atlas* suggests that lack of attachment to land and lack of self-understanding affect cultural stability, and poems V and XI ask questions that echo throughout the collection:

> Where are we moored?
> What are the bindings?
> What behooves us?

Rich asserts her authority to ask such questions in terms of the reader's own search for answers within Rich's poetry:

> there is nothing else
> left to read
> there where you have landed, stripped as you are.

Rich insists that poetry can reimagine the world, and she pushes readers to see the world afresh. Such experience makes a difference, she explains in *What Is Found There:* "an 'I' can become a 'we' without extinguishing others . . . a partly common language exists to which strangers can bring their own heartbeat, memories, images." This language—Rich's poetry—calls upon readers to look into memories and images to understand a shared need for communal responsibility and inclusion.

For Rich, viewing a country's people as a mural provides the chance to discover new roads. In poem V, Rich calls upon Muriel Rukeyser's belief that "*There are roads to take . . . When you think of your country.*" Americans, she suggests, must find the best route amid the foreclosed farms and closed auto factories so as to co-exist in one country. Words and images can bring change when individuals understand what moors, binds, and behooves their culture. As Rich concludes *Atlas,* she talks about how "you," her reader, are coming into "places never planned." This journey will not "be short," "will not be simple," yet "it will become your will." She celebrates poetry's power to effect change on a national level. *An Atlas of the Difficult World* asserts that those who learn to understand their own politics of location will be able to change not just their lives, but the world.

Jeannette E. Riley

**Further Reading**


Dickie, Margaret, *Stein, Bishop, and Rich: Lyrics of Love, War, and Place,* Chapel Hill: University of North Carolina Press, 1997

Estrin, Barbara L., "Re-Versing the Past: Adrienne Rich's Postmodern Inquietude," *Tulsa Studies in Women's Literature* 16, no. 2 (1997)

Hussmann, Mary, "On Adrienne Rich," *The Iowa Review* 22, no. 1 (1992)

Rich, Adrienne, *What Is Found There: Notebooks on Poetry and Politics,* New York and London: Norton, 1993; new edition, London: Virago, 1995

Shreiber, Maeera, "'Where Are We Moored?' Adrienne Rich, Women's Mourning, and the Limits of Lament," in *Dwelling in Possibility: Women Poets and Critics on Poetry,* edited by Shreiber and Yopie Prins, Ithaca, New York: Cornell University Press, 1997

Templeton, Alice, "Contradictions: Tracking Adrienne Rich's Poetry," *Tulsa Studies in Women's Literature* 12, no. 2 (1993)

Templeton, Alice, *The Dream and the Dialogue: Adrienne Rich's Feminist Poetics,* Knoxville: University of Tennessee Press, 1994

Vandersee, Charles, "Rich's *An Atlas of the Difficult World,* 2 and 7," *Explicator* 57, no. 2 (1999)

Van Duyn, Mona, "The Lenore Marshall/*Nation* Poetry Prize–1992," *Nation* 255, no. 18 (1992)


## Diving into the Wreck

*Diving into the Wreck* (1973), Adrienne Rich's seventh collection, explores her growing opposition to the patriarchal order influencing her identity as a woman and a poet. In *The Dream and the Dialogue* (1994), Alice Templeton points out that even though many of Rich's early works handle themes about women's lives, those works cannot accurately be termed "feminist." Although earlier poems "individually experiment with fragmented forms and challenge the confines of interior lyric consciousness and traditional lyric form," they are not "consistently directed by a feminist vision." Templeton's observation rings true since much of Rich's early work accepts the expectations of literary tradition or at most expresses ambivalence. Furthermore, her attempt to adhere to neutrality and objectivity in her poetry prevented her from challenging the patriarchal values that structured her life. With *Diving into the Wreck,* however, Rich finally allowed her anger to shape her poetry, in effect joining the growing women's movement of the day and confronting what "Waking in the Dark" describes as "a man's world. But finished." Many critics view *Diving into the Wreck,* along with *Snapshots of a Daughter-in-Law* (1963), as the pivotal work that grounds much of Rich's later subject matter.

The poem "Incipience" provides a fruitful entry into the collection. It begins with a description of a woman trapped under plaster, a visceral metaphor for oppression under a patriarchal system. Aware of her paralyzed, dependent state, the woman describes her desire to "feel the fiery future / of every matchstick in the kitchen." Breaking out of the plaster will not be easy, however, for "Nothing can be done / but by inches." As the woman writes out her life "hour by hour, word by word," she struggles to imagine the

> existence
> of something uncreated
> this poem
> our lives[.]

If re-creation is to take place, "Incipience" argues, women must break loose from traditional images and roles perpetuated by patriarchal culture, struggling against a social order that is described in "Merced" as

> too numb to get the message
> in a world masculinity made
> unfit for women or men[.]

To deal with this numbed world, Rich turns to androgyny. On the cover from the first printing of *Diving into the Wreck,* Rich wrote that the collection

> continues the work I've been trying to do—breaking down the artificial barriers between private and public, between Vietnam and the lovers' bed, between the deepest images we carry out of our dreams and the most daylight events "out in the world." This is the intention and longing behind everything I write. (Keyes, 1986)

This longing for a breaking down of barriers comes in the shape of the androgyne, the ultimate dissolution of conflict between the sexes: the being that could encompass both poet and wife, poet and mother, poet and the son her father wished he had. This androgynous voice surfaces most vividly in the title poem, in which, as Betty Flowers argues in "The 'I' in Adrienne Rich: Individuation and the Androgyne Archetype" (1982), Rich tries to fuse masculine and feminine into one voice to circumvent the inevitable power struggle in any either/or structure. As the title poem draws to a close, she asserts "I am she: I am he"—she becomes "the androgyne—a man-woman, woman-man" (Keyes, 1986).

In search of wholeness Rich's androgynous being dives deep into the sea, hoping to see "the wreck and not the story of the wreck / the thing itself and not the myth," only to discover that ongoing social conflict has left him/her "half-destroyed." Ultimately Rich's hope to achieve unity through androgyny fails. The problem lies not in the speaker or in the subject of the poem but more insidiously in language itself and the power that language holds, for "words are purposes" and "words are maps." The damage done to both men and women cannot be fixed simply by merging the two together. The final lines of the poem indicate that Rich sees danger for women in such a merger, since women's stories are not written down and women's names "do not appear" in books or images created by patriarchal society.

In 1973 the androgyne offered only a temporary solution. In a later poem Rich herself said, "There are words I cannot choose again: / *humanism androgyny*" ("Natural Resources"). The oppositions created by language, and the hierarchies created in and through language, kept Rich from achieving the fulfillment and wholeness she desired. This discovery of language as the fundamental barrier, however, led to the transformational and powerful poetry in her 1978 volume *The Dream of a Common Language.*

JEANNETTE E. RILEY

**Further Reading**

Atwood, Margaret, "Review of *Diving into the Wreck,*" in *Adrienne Rich's Poetry and Prose,* by Adrienne Rich, edited by Barbara Charlesworth Gelpi and Albert Gelpi, revised edition, New York and London: Norton, 1993

Cooper, Jane Roberta, editor, *Reading Adrienne Rich: Reviews and Re-Visions, 1951–81,* Ann Arbor: University of Michigan Press, 1984

Díaz-Diocaretz, Myriam, *The Transforming Power of Language: The Poetry of Adrienne Rich,* Utrecht: HES, 1984

Flowers, Betty S., "The 'I' in Adrienne Rich: Individuation and the Androgyne Archetype, " in *The Theory and Practice of Feminist Literary Criticism,* edited by Gabriela Mora and Karen S. Van Hooft, Ypsilanti, Michigan: Bilingual Press, 1982

Keyes, Clare, *The Aesthetics of Power: The Poetry of Adrienne Rich,* Athens: University of Georgia Press, 1986

Slowik, Mary, "The Friction of the Mind: The Early Poetry of Adrienne Rich," *Massachusetts Review* 25, no. 1 (1984)

Templeton, Alice, "The Dream and the Dialogue: Rich's Feminist Poetics and Gadamer's Hermeneutics," *Tulsa Studies in Women's Literature* 7, no. 2 (1988)

Werner, Craig, *Adrienne Rich: The Poet and Her Critics,* Chicago and London: American Library Association, 1988

## Snapshots of a Daughter-in-Law

Looking back at "Snapshots of a Daughter-in-Law" in her 1971 essay "When We Dead Awaken," Adrienne Rich characterized the poem as marking a crucial shift away from the comparative impersonality of her earlier works and toward a poetry of personal experience—of herself "as a woman" (Rich, 1975).

The ten sections of "Snapshots" offer keen insights into the kinds of cultural baggage burdening women writing, as Rich had been, within the traditions of Western culture before feminism. The poem transforms this baggage, literalized in section three as the "commodious / steamer-trunk" of nature, into the far more positive "cargo" that is "delivered"—a word evoking pregnancy and birth—at the end of the poem.

The poem opens with a painful portrait of the emotional effects of aging on women, contrasting the remembered beauty of a Southern belle "with henna-colored hair, skin like a peachbud" with her present reality at middle age, "moldering like wedding-cake." Her efforts to live in the past seem pathetic. The "Nervy, glowering" daughter who closes this first section "grows another way," but her anger offers little hope of constructive change for either woman.

Although she has not yet suffered the loss of her beauty and youth, the woman in the second section (most likely the daughter who "wipe[d] the teaspoons" in the first section, now "Banging the coffee-pot into the sink") is still burdened by anger. Her only dragons are domestic, but they threaten her with the destruction of fiery self-mutilation (aimed tellingly at arm, thumb, and hand—the writer's body) even as she pursues her chores:

> she's let the tapstream scald her arm,
> a match burn to her thumbnail,
>
> or held her hand above the kettle's snout
> right in the woolly steam.

No knight comes to save her, although she does hear voices that "are probably angels." "[N]othing hurts her anymore," but she is not miraculously freed from pain; rather, she has grown increasingly numb to her own suffering. The angels advise her to break out of her angry prison, but like her mother she is unable to move.

All self-aware women, in the speaker's astute analysis, are subject to self-entrapment: "A thinking woman sleeps with monsters. / The beak that grips her, she becomes." Pursued by monsters, such a woman resists by becoming monstrous herself. As Craig Werner (1988) suggests, this passage bears reading against an important precursor text for Rich, Yeats' "Leda and the Swan." Yeats portrays Leda as "helpless," "terrified," and finally caught up by the "beak" and "mastered by" the power of the overwhelming vision and violence of the god who rapes her. In an earlier poem, "Aunt Jennifer's Tigers," Rich used Yeats' own language to offer an alternative to the absolute subjugation of the female: the triumph of women's art. In "Snapshots" Rich continues to loosen the grip of patriarchy and refines her alternative, suggesting counter-metamorphosis (rather than death, as in "Aunt Jennifer's Tigers") as a better response to the unbearable force of patriarchy's oppression.

The second stanza of this section laments another "grip" that traps women: each other. Instead of turning against the monstrous, instead of offering one another support or sisterhood, they project their anger onto one another. Monstrously, women knife one another in the back. Part of their anger, Rich suggests, comes from their frustrated creativity. The "Two handsome women" who were "gripped in argument" with one another "like Furies" earlier in the poem form a composite portrait of several women artists by the fourth section, "their gifts no pure fruition, but a thorn, / the prick filed sharp against a hint of scorn[.]" Rich evokes Emily Dickinson explicitly by quoting "*My Life had stood—a Loaded Gun—*." Possible implicit references include Tillie Olsen's "I Stand Here Ironing" and Mary Austin's *Earth Horizon,* with its uncontrolled anger against art reduced to a mere whatnot, a piece of decorous furniture in the parlor. For the women in Rich's poem, the significant activities of "Knowing," "Reading," and "writing" take place in fragmented moments "while waiting / for the iron to heat," "while the jellies boil and scum," or while "dusting everything on the whatnot every day of life." Repetition and confinement threaten to reduce their creative energies to little more than the "prick" of a "beaked . . . bird."

Even seemingly pleasant private moments have a subtext that women may or may not be aware of, as in the short but telling close-up of an unnamed woman shaving her legs "until they gleam / like petrified mammoth-tusk." At this point in the poem the familiar ritual takes on the unmistakable aura of ritual sacrifice. The sacrificial maiden prepares herself for the dragon, laughing sweetly (in the Latin of a Horatian ode) as she beautifies herself for death.

Rich rejects the normalcy of such scenes of self-destruction, at least for the woman artist. The sixth section notes that "When to her lute Corinna sings / neither words nor music are her own." She sings, that is, as a caged bird, a prisoner in the silken bonds of love, perhaps, but a prisoner nonetheless. The daughter-in-law is identified here as the caged bird; the mother-in-law is Mother Nature, who *may* offer her daughter-in-law privileged glimpses into "her household books . . . that her sons never saw." But the possibility is offered as a question, and no answer is given. Love is a trap, at least when Corinna sings songs not her own.

Women who dare to sing their own songs, however, meet with derision. The very different figure of Mary Wollstonecraft replaces Corinna in section seven. In the poem Wollstonecraft is both success and failure; she protests against the wrongs of women but as a result is "labeled harpy, shrew and whore," words charged with sexist oppression. Against this "scorn" Rich pits Wollstonecraft's call for "*some stay / which cannot be undermined.*" Printed in italics, enclosed in quotation marks, and documented by Rich's own note identifying their source (*Thoughts on the Education of Daughters*), these words are undeniably Wollstonecraft's "own," unlike Corinna's.

The scorn may take various forms in its attempts to undermine women. In section eight the middle-aged woman who opened the poem is now framed by a disparaging remark about women's physical beauty: "'You all die at fifteen,' said Diderot." Rich's speaker takes this threat seriously, as she knows that the aging belle dreams "inaccurately" of a romanticized past, and that her dream therefore imprisons her in the past.

Rich grapples with more aggressive attacks on women by responding to Samuel Johnson's famously contemptuous dismissal of women who preach. Rich transforms the apparent closure of Johnson's *bon mot* by punctuating it with a question mark: "Not that it is done well, but / that it is done at all?" The poem calls the "ladies" to a stricter accounting:

> Our blight has been our sinecure:
> mere talent was enough for us—
> glitter in fragments and rough drafts.

Johnson's remark describes the patriarchal world's condescending "gallantry" toward women's utterances. Rich envisions something different, something better; an "honor" for women willing to commit the "crime" of rising above patriarchy's low expectations.

The final section of the poem opens with an unexpectedly calm tone, an almost offhand sigh: "Well, / she's long about her coming." But the lines move swiftly to an astonishing vision of the "coming" woman artist who will at last be brave and strong enough to "smash the mold straight off":

> Her mind full to the wind, I see her plunge
> breasted and glancing through the currents,
> taking the light upon her
> at least as beautiful as any boy
> or helicopter

Rich's note identifies Simone de Beauvoir as her source for the strange simile of the helicopter. Some readers have remarked with dissatisfaction that the "boy" here replaces de Beauvoir's original "bird." These readers see Rich's substitution as a defeat; she seems unable to find the "powerful" "womanly" language appropriate to her prophetic vision (Rich, "Sources," 1986) and falls back upon patriarchal standards of perfection: "any boy." Still, the visionary woman is emphatically female, "breasted," associated with water: not Aphrodite, but someone vitally different, someone with a "mind full" of precious "cargo."

What this wonderful vision brings with her, the poem does not say. Her arrival is foretold, and her success guaranteed. That is all. The triumph of the poem—as Rich herself observed—is its sustained assumption of a female voice. Men speak in this poem only as the voice of the Other. The self is female, like the speaker and the figures in the poem's snapshots. Rich's readers have been almost unanimous in repeating her estimate of the poem's importance. It marks Rich's turn from Modernist formalism toward a poetry in which the personal is political, and both are important.

The discontinuity of the series of portraits offered in "Snapshots"—evocative of Pound's *Hugh Selwyn Mauberley* (1920)—may suggest the poem's limitation or even failure. But this discontinuity also illustrates a necessary stage in Rich's development as a poet, for the portraits bring Rich significantly closer to finding the powerful womanly language of her later work. Finally, it is perhaps more important to note the poem's steady movement from the bickering, repression, and failures of sections one through nine to the perfect vision of its final lines. "Snapshots" takes the reader from the alienation of the speaker, who opens section one with her oppositional and accusatory "You," to the triumphantly inclusive certainty of its last line: "ours."

CHERYL SPECTOR

**Further Reading**


Keyes, Clare, "'The Angels Chiding': Snapshots of a Daughter-in-Law," in *Reading Adrienne Rich: Reviews and Re-Visions, 1951–81,* edited by Jane Roberta Cooper, Ann Arbor: University of Michigan Press, 1984

Keyes, Clare, *The Aesthetics of Power: The Poetry of Adrienne Rich,* Athens: University of Georgia Press, 1986

Martin, Wendy, *An American Triptych: Anne Bradstreet, Emily Dickinson, Adrienne Rich,* Chapel Hill: University of North Carolina Press, 1984

Ostriker, Alicia, *Writing Like a Woman,* Ann Arbor: University of Michigan Press, 1983

Rich, Adrienne, *Adrienne Rich's Poetry,* edited by Barbara Charlesworth Gelpi and Albert Gelpi, New York and London: Norton, 1975; revised edition, as *Adrienne Rich's Poetry and Prose,* 1993

Rich, Adrienne, "Blood, Bread, and Poetry: The Location of the Poet," in *Blood, Bread, and Poetry: Selected Prose, 1979–1985,* New York and London: Norton, 1986

Rich, Adrienne, "Sources," in *Your Native Land, Your Life,* by Rich, New York and London: Norton, 1986

Werner, Craig, *Adrienne Rich: The Poet and Her Critics,* Chicago and London: American Library Association, 1988


## A Valediction Forbidding Mourning

In "A Valediction Forbidding Mourning," Adrienne Rich announces the irrevocability of her journeying away from both traditional language and heterosexual love. Published in 1971 as the concluding poem in the first section of *The Will to Change*—a title naming the process of conscious transformation that is also this poem's theme—"Valediction" measures Rich's distance from her esteemed precursor John Donne and his poem "A Valediction Forbidding Mourning." Departing from metaphysical poetry's demonstrations of the power of bravura language and artistic control, Rich questions assumptions about the certainties of language, of love, and even of her own poetic powers. This is a poem of exploration, not discovery—a voyage out, not a promise to return.

As described in Rich's poem, the speaker's departure from familiar patterns of desire, language, and poetry is apparently imminent. Yet, she says, there is enough time "before I leave" to make "A last attempt" to communicate with her lover, to explain why this "trip" will be "forever." The poem's first line establishes its themes of dissonance and failure, for it divides the lovers definitively with a midline caesura marked by a period: "My swirling wants. Your frozen lips." Donne's "stiffe twin compasses" are not here; there is no promise of a joyous homecoming. Instead, the speaker represents herself metonymically by her "swirling wants"; her emphasis is on process and unfulfilled desire, not on return and repetition (which the poem explicitly defines as "death"). On the other side of the caesura and the full stop is her lover—not named but surely representative of Rich's husband, Alfred Conrad, who committed suicide sometime after Rich left their troubled marriage in 1970, the year of composition that Rich assigns to this poem. Reduced metonymically like the speaker, he is present only as "frozen lips," a phrase suggesting not only the absence of desire and of speech but also the presence of a corpse, of death.

Stanza 1 offers further figurative versions of the death of speech and poetry, notably in the difficult second line—"The grammar turned and attacked me"—and in the fourth line's fragmentary lament, "Emptiness of the notations." The traditional rules of "grammar" no longer serve the poet; what she writes is meaningless. The theme of loss is echoed by a pattern of additional references: "wounds," "death," "failure," "pain," "*bleeding,*" "cemetery," "glacier," and "forever."

Syntactic fragments flout conventional grammar throughout this poem. The daunting effort to explain and compose is reflected in the speaker's style, which alternates between grammatically complete statements and incomplete noun phrases. Again, Rich turns sharply away from Donne's persuasive language of logical certainty and coherence, marked for us in the well-known rhetorical gestures of "therefore" and "though" that he uses to structure his own "Valediction." In place of Donne's beautiful gold circles,

Rich's poem offers the disturbingly empty perfection of "plastic wreaths," artificial tributes to the dead. The lovers' failed relationship here is accompanied by the failure of composition: "Themes, written under duress. / Emptiness of the notations." Nor does the more public world beyond the lovers' private one offer a refuge from personal disaster: it is represented by the nameless and therefore powerful "They" in line five who "gave me a drug that slowed the healing of wounds," surely a hostile prescription, and again by "the poster in the bus that said: / *my bleeding is under control*," presumably an advertisement for the kind of controlling pills that "They" likewise offered in Rich's "5:30 A.M." (*Leaflets*, 1969). In both cases, the speaker rejects a treatment that she regards as false and destructive of authenticity. Liberated from "the oppressor's language" ("The Burning of Paper Instead of Children," also in *The Will to Change*), menstrual bleeding becomes "A red plant in a cemetery of plastic wreaths"—a positive sign of life in an otherwise artificial world of death.

The irregular meter and form of this poem obscure the remarkable fact that it concludes with a rhymed couplet:

I could say: those mountains have a meaning
but further than that I could not say.

To do something very common in my own way.

Although the break between stanzas threatens to undo the couplet (in the same way that the human couple are undone), the rhyming of "say" and "way" surprisingly signals the familiar elegiac trope of the orderly turning from death to a new beginning: the speaker holds before us her determination to move beyond "those mountains" and "To do"—to make—"something," presumably poems. (Rich's 1978 volume *The Dream of a Common Language* is our proof that she succeeds in this effort.) The poem's structure, irregular though it is, offers additional and more immediate support for the turn away from failure. The odd-numbered stanzas of the poem (1, 3, and 5) alternate with its three single-line stanzas (2, 4, and 6) in a progression that shows us that "the will to change" is already at work here. Each even-numbered stanza is one line longer than its predecessor, suggesting in a small way a pattern of persistence and growth. The three single-line stanzas close with nouns connected by visual alliteration—"wounds," "wreaths," and "way"—and are connected also as a series of progressively more hopeful possibilities. Then, too, the presence of the "flashlight" in the trio of "images" that "go unglossed" (line 13) inevitably invites glossing: in Rich's next volume, *Diving into the Wreck* (1973), the poet's journey in the title poem succeeds spectacularly as she finds that "the beam of my lamp" reveals "the thing I came for: / the wreck and not the story of the wreck." Thus, "Valediction" gives us, finally, ample reason not to mourn Rich's farewell to the past as she turns, in her "own way," to the next stage in her changeful poetic and personal career.

Cheryl Spector

**Further Reading**


Donne, John, "A Valediction Forbidding Mourning," in *The Complete Poetry of John Donne,* edited by John T. Shawcross, Garden City, New York: Anchor Doubleday, 1967

Gould, Jean, "Adrienne Rich," in *Modern American Women Poets,* by Gould, New York: Dodd Mead, 1984

Kalstone, David, *Five Temperaments: Elizabeth Bishop, Robert Lowell, James Merrill, Adrienne Rich, John Ashbery,* New York: Oxford University Press, 1977

Kalstone, David, "Review of *The Will to Change: Poems, 1968–1970,*" in *Reading Adrienne Rich: Reviews and Re-Visions, 1951–1981,* edited by Jane Roberta Cooper, Ann Arbor: University of Michigan Press, 1984

Martin, Wendy, *An American Triptych: Anne Bradstreet, Emily Dickinson, Adrienne Rich,* Chapel Hill: University of North Carolina Press, 1984

Proffitt, Edward, "Allusion in Adrienne Rich's 'A Valediction Forbidding Mourning,'" *Concerning Poetry* 15, no. 1 (1982)

Rich Adrienne, *Adrienne Rich's Poetry,* edited by Barbara Charlesworth Gelpi and Albert Gelpi, New York and London: Norton, 1975; revised edition, as *Adrienne Rich's Poetry and Prose,* 1993

Rothschild, Matthew, "Interview with Adrienne Rich," *The Progressive* 58, no. 1 (1994)

Zivley, Sherry Lutz, "Adrienne Rich's Contemporary Metaphysical Conceit," *Notes on Contemporary Literature* 12, no. 3 (1982)


---

## Laura Riding 1901–91

In the preface to the 1938 edition of her *Collected Poems,* Laura Riding admonishes her readers that her work will be indecipherable to those who approach her poems for the wrong reasons. So bold a poet as to instruct readers not only on fine points of apprehension but also on their very moral states, Riding stood secure in her own reasons for producing poetry. She demands to be understood in her entirety: her poetry, fiction, and criticism as well as her eventual quest for a spiritually exact language. Riding wanted to renew the word itself, making our language sound enough to render with accuracy the most important of human concerns, to create a truth not possible through current means of discourse. She believed with a religious zeal that such a transformation of language was possible and necessary, and at first she thought the way was through poetry. Setting out to create for poetry a basis in solid truth, just as the visual arts have in the color spectrum or geometry, she suddenly turned away from her chosen realm at the height of her career. She spent the rest of her life developing a new lexicography aimed at elevating human communication to a higher spiritual level.

Riding's public career was set in motion by a newspaper advertisement. In 1923, while living in Louisville, Kentucky, she answered a notice for submissions to a poetry contest sponsored by the Fugitives, a literary movement out of Vanderbilt University headed by poet John Crowe Ransom. Winning the contest put her in print for the first time, but more important it brought her to Vanderbilt and into contact with a coterie of like-minded artists. Her burgeoning confidence caused her to leave behind an early marriage and move to New York, into the fertile literary territory of Greenwich Village in the 1920s. Her first book, *The Close Chaplet,* appeared under her married name, Laura Riding Gottschalk, and was not widely reviewed, although it did receive the support of influential friends such as Allen Tate. By the time the book appeared in 1926, the poet had already departed for England and a new phase of development. Riding's friendship with English poet Robert Graves resulted in a collaborative period that would be mutually beneficial, at least professionally, for some of the most important work of both their careers. This period included, among other works, most of Riding's major poetry, Graves' *The White Goddess,* and their influential *A Survey of Modernist Poetry* (1927), the precursor to William Empson's *The Seven Types of Ambiguity* and thus a founding element of the New Criticism. In addition to poetry and criticism, Riding produced novels and short stories, often through Seizin Press, the company founded by Graves and Riding to publish the new style of literature they were developing.

Upon the publication of her *Collected Poems* (1938), Riding appeared to be at midcareer as a poet; although she expressed frustration in her preface at the inexact literary education and improper motivations of poets and readers of poetry, she gives no notice of abandoning the art. The book is divided into sections: "Poems of Mythic Occasion," mostly written in the United States; "Poems of Immediate Occasion," from her time in England; and "Poems of Final Occasion," written primarily in Spain—that section's title being the only hard clue to her future plans. Although there is little in Riding's work to place her within any movements of her day, she was a modernist in her rejection of the past in form and subject matter. Her association with the Fugitives was brief, and she lacked their regional concerns. She was not an Imagist, ignoring Ezra Pound's famous advice to poets to "go in fear of abstractions." In fact, she could focus as acutely and vividly on an abstraction as the Imagists would focus on a physical object. For example, even in a poem such as "Prisms," Riding chooses a transparent image: "What is beheld through glass seems glass." This poem appears in the section "Poems of Mythic Occasion," which also contains what may be one of the only abstract narrative poems ever constructed, "The Quids."

In "Poems of Immediate Occasion," Riding's verse becomes even more spare and exact, often displaying, as in the poem "Beyond," the influence of Gertrude Stein, whose work Riding reviewed when most critics were still interpreting Stein's public persona. In "Poem Only," we again see Riding's acute interest in word sound and rhythm, too serious to be called wordplay, as it might be in other verse. In this manner, she differs from Stein—her repetitions and echoes evoke a quest rather than an experiment, a sense of fervent desire for accuracy of meaning. "Poem talking silence not dead death"—for Riding, "death" often meant a kind of stillness outside of time rather than mortality—and the final lines, "Cruel if kind and kind if cruel / And all if nothing," reveal much of Riding's theoretical bent. Through the strict truth of poetry, Riding sought to make the language pure enough to encompass ourselves, our stories as individuals, and the universe as well, reflecting all with a clarity never before produced in the written arts. The obstacles were readers who looked to poetry for incorrect reasons, those who believed that poetry was merely "fancy," an escape. Her ambition would take her to the ends of poetry, all the way to the other side of it.

Although their abstract quality prevents them from being overtly didactic, Riding's poems are imbued with a stillness; she weights the words with a kind of linguistic morality derived from her own belief in each word's sacred power. She holds out a friendly but stern hand to the reader by the end of the preface to the 1938 *Collected Poems,* saying, "I have learned from my poems what, completely and precisely, the scope of poetry is; and any reader may learn the same." As if realizing her own lack of humility, she asks immediately whether this claim is "too much," although Riding was often up to the task of absolving herself of excesses on the road to her higher goal.

After the 1930s, that goal was to be sought through prose and through collaboration with a sympathetic reviewer whom Riding would later meet and marry, Schuyler Jackson. She published little but corresponded widely, particularly after her husband's death in 1968. *The Telling* appeared in 1972, a prose work incorporating excerpts from these letters. In explanatory prefaces to reprints of her poems and in works-in-progress published in journals, she discussed her abandonment of poetry and her developing linguistic theories, particularly her work in renewing the meaning of vocabulary. All the new work came with a new authorial signature, Laura (Riding) Jackson, one that embraced her past as a poet yet separated that persona from her newer, more theoretical one.

Riding has suffered the same fate as her friend Gertrude Stein, being reviewed and discussed primarily for a lifestyle rather than a life's work—the extent of her influence on Graves' work, for example, has been debated widely. Her austere, compressed verse has been called sterile and unfeeling, and her poetic reputation wavered toward obscurity. Then, in the 1990s, new interest in her work was stirred by the republication of her *Collected Poems* as *The Poems of Laura Riding,* which won the Bollingen Prize in 1991. Her manuscript detailing her years of work on lexicography, *Rational Meaning: A New Foundation for the Definition of Words,* appeared for the first time in 1997, edited by friend and fellow poet William Harmon. Her letters are currently being edited for publication. Riding aspired to a role beyond her literary one, longing to speak not only to matters of art but also to matters of being human. Her legacy continues to evolve.

NICOLE SARROCCO

**Biography**

Born Laura Reichenthal in New York City, 16 January 1901; adopted the surname Riding in 1926. Attended Cornell University, Ithaca, New York; associated with the Fugitive group of poets; with Robert Graves established the Seizin Press, 1928, and *Epilogue* magazine, 1935. Received Fugitive Prize, 1925; Mark Rothko Appreciation Award, 1971; Guggenheim fellowship, 1973; National Endowment for the Arts fellowship, 1979; Bollingen Prize, 1991. Died 2 September 1991.

**Poetry**

*The Close Chaplet* (as Laura Riding Gottschalk), 1926
*Voltaire: A Biographical Fantasy* (as Laura Riding Gottschalk), 1927

*Love as Love, Death as Death,* 1928
*Poems: A Joking Word,* 1930
*Twenty Poems Less,* 1930
*Though Gently,* 1930
*Laura and Francisca,* 1931
*The Life of the Dead* (in French and English), 1933
*The First Leaf,* 1933
*Poet: A Lying Word,* 1933
*Americans,* 1934
*The Second Leaf,* 1935
*Collected Poems,* 1938; revised edition, as *The Poems of Laura Riding,* 1980
*Selected Poems: In Five Sets,* 1970
*A Poem,* 1980
*Laura (Riding) Jackson, 1901–1991: A Portfolio,* with others (includes prose), 1991
*First Awakenings: The Early Poems,* 1992
*A Selection of the Poems of Laura Riding,* edited by Robert Nye, 1994

**Selected Criticism**
*A Survey of Modernist Poetry* with Robert Graves, 1927

**Other Writings:** novels (*A Trojan Ending,* 1937), short stories (*Lives of Wives,* 1939), essays, translations of French literature; edited collections of letters (*The World and Ourselves: Letters about the World Situation from 65 People of Different Professions and Pursuits,* 1938).

**Further Reading**
Adams, Barbara Block, *The Enemy Self: Poetry and Criticism of Laura Riding,* Ann Arbor, Michigan: UMI Research Press, 1990
Baker, Deborah, *In Extremis: The Life of Laura Riding,* New York: Grove Press, and London: Harnish Hamilton, 1993
*Chelsea* 35 (1977) (special issue on Riding)
Wexler, Joyce Piell, *Laura Riding's Pursuit of Truth,* Athens: Ohio University Press, 1973

---

# Alberto Ríos 1952–

In an interview titled "Discovering the Alphabet of Life" (1997) with Sheilah Britton, Alberto Ríos explains that, in the interviewer's words, "his alphabet is made up not only of letters, which in and of themselves have meaning, but also of words and images. His realm as a writer is not only the alphabet he has used, but also the alphabet he has lived." Ríos' relationship with language, a product of growing up in the borderlands/la frontera between Mexico and Arizona, is a central theme in his seven books of poetry. Writing as part of a new generation of Latino voices, Ríos, known for his beautiful images and narrative poems, writes using the very best tradition of magical realism and storytelling.

Born on 18 September 1952 to a Mexican father, Alberto Alvaro, from Tapachula, Chiapas, Mexico, and Agnes (née Fogg), a British mother from Warrington, Lancashire, England, Ríos was influenced by the stories and languages of Mexico and England while also living in the United States. William Barillas (1996) notes that Ríos' connection to Mexico is particularly strong through the history of his paternal grandfather, Margarito Calderón Ríos, "a prominent figure in the Mexican Revolution and advisor to Mexican president Alvaro Obregón." Barillas explains that much of Ríos' work centers on his heritage and the rich cultural complexities of belonging to more than one place. He was "'born of people who were outside of time and place, people who were displaced and unsure' for whom borders were less external geographical realities than dimensions of their emotional lives." Like other prominent Chicano/Chicana poets, such as Gloria Anzaldúa, Martín Espada, Sandra Cisneros, and Lorna Dee Cervantes, Ríos uses his narrative, lyric poems to tell the stories of those caught between two conflicting worlds with sometimes violently opposed cultural traditions. Ríos has always worked to understand his world through words and language. He began to write early, exploring the liminal space between Spanish and English in his first poems in the second grade. While Ríos enjoyed school, he has noted in many interviews that his American schooling forced him to forget and then relearn Spanish as a condition of cultural assimilation.

Ríos' professional writing career began after his formal schooling. He earned a bachelor of arts in literature and creative writing (1974), a bachelor of arts in psychology (1975), and a master of fine arts (1979), all from the University of Arizona. He attended law school briefly in 1975–76. He won first place in the Academy of American Arts poetry contest for "A Man Then Suddenly Stops Moving" (1977), a writer's fellowship in poetry from the Arizona Commission on the Arts (1979), and a fellowship grant in creative writing from the National Endowment for the Arts (1980). His first significant national recognition came after he published two chapbooks: *Elk Heads on the Wall* (1979) and *Sleeping on Fists* (1981).

Ríos was honored with the Walt Whitman Award from the National Academy of American Poets (1981) for his first book-length collection, *Whispering to Fool the Wind* (1982). In this collection, as in subsequent work, Ríos presented a clear vision of living between two cultures through his people-centered poems, telling the lives of himself and those he knew and observed in his community. He explained to interviewer Susan McInnis (1998),

> For me, it's more than straddling two cultures. It's really three. There is an in-between state, a very messy, wonderful middleness to the culture I come from. It is a culture of capillaries, a culture of exchange, of the small detail that is absorbed the way oxygen enters blood. On the border we're dealing with several languages, several cultures, different sets

of laws, and everything else you can imagine. Nevertheless, you've got to live side-by-side. What results isn't neatly anybody's law, anybody's language. It's more a third way of living, and that time, or place of exchange, reckons with the world a little differently.

No poem more poignantly and fiercely demonstrates this than the now widely anthologized "Nani." Indicative of the language style and theme in Ríos' future poems, "Nani" represents Ríos' experimentation with oral culture and the language and stories he learned from his grandmother:

Sitting at her table, she serves
the sopa de arroz to me
instinctively, and I watch her,
the absolute mamá, and eat words
I might have had to say more
out of embarrassment. To speak,
now-foreign words I used to speak,
too, dribble down her mouth as she serves
me albóndigas. No more
than a third are easy to me.

He explores here the pain of forgetting Spanish, a facet of his American education, and the way in which this represented a cultural and emotional schism between him and his grandmother. Inherent in this poem is Ríos' adult dedication to recapturing his cultural identity through his writing.

Since 1982 and the wide success of *Whispering to Fool the Wind,* Ríos has taught creative writing at Arizona State University. He published four subsequent volumes of poetry, each drawing on the strengths represented in "Nani": *Five Indiscretions* (1985), *The Lime Orchard Woman* (1988), *The Warrington Poems* (1989), and *Teodoro Luna's Two Kisses* (1990). He was honored with a Pushcart Prize for fiction (1986) and poetry (1988, 1989) and received the Chicanos Por La Causa Community Appreciation Award (1988).

The title poem of Ríos' most recent collection, "Teodoro Luna's Two Kisses," again demonstrates his captivation with language and the way people express themselves: "Mr. Teodoro Luna in his later years had taken to kissing / His wife / Not so much with his lips as with his brows." Ríos reveals himself as observer-poet, drinking in the stories of those around him.

As Ríos has gained popularity, his work has been translated into many venues beyond individual poem and book-length collections. He was featured in the documentary *Birthwrite: Growing Up Hispanic.* His poetry has been set to music in a cantata by James DeMars called "Toto's Say" and on an EMI release, *Away from Home.* His work has been included in more than 90 major national and international literary anthologies, including the *Norton Anthology of Modern Poetry.* Ríos has expanded his genre focus with four recent publications: a memoir, *Capirotada: A Nogales Memoir* (1999), and three short-story collections, *The Iguana Killer* (1984), *Pig Cookies* (1995), and *The Curtain of Trees* (1999). His prose work has been equally well received with a second place award in the *New York Times* annual fiction competition for "The Way Spaghetti Feels" (1983), a New Times Fiction Award (1983), and a Western States Book Award for *The Iguana Killer* (1984).

J. Elizabeth Clark

**Biography**

Born in Nogales, Arizona, 18 September 1952. Attended University of Arizona, Tucson, B.A. in literature and creative writing 1974, B.A. in psychology 1975, law school 1975–76, M.F.A. in creative writing 1979; artist-in-the-schools, Phoenix, Arizona, 1978–83, consultant, 1983–; writer-in-residence, Central Arizona College, Coolidge, 1980–82; Assistant Professor, 1982–85, Associate Professor, 1985–89, and since 1989 Professor, Arizona State University, Tempe; Director, Creative Writing Program, Arizona State University, Tempe, 1986–89; board of directors, 1988–92, secretary, 1989, Associated Writing Programs. Received Arizona Commission on the Arts fellowship, 1979; National Endowment for the Arts fellowship, 1980; Academy of American Poets Walt Whitman Award, 1981; New Times Fiction Award, 1983; Western States Book Award (fiction), 1984; Chicanos Por La Causa Community Appreciation Award, 1988; Guggenheim fellowship, 1988; Arizona Governor's Arts Award, 1991. Living in Chandler, Arizona.

**Poetry**

*Elk Heads on the Wall,* 1979
*Sleeping on Fists,* 1981
*Whispering to Fool the Wind,* 1982
*Five Indiscretions,* 1985
*The Lime Orchard Woman: Poems,* 1988
*The Warrington Poems,* 1989
*Teodoro Luna's Two Kisses,* 1990

**Other Writings:** short stories (*The Iguana Killer: Twelve Stories of the Heart,* 1984), memoir (*Capirotada: A Nogales Memoir,* 1999).

**Further Reading**

Barillas, William, "'Words Like the Wind': An Interview with Alberto Ríos," *Americas Review* 24, no. 3 (1996)
Britton, Sheilah, "Discovering the Alphabet of Life," *Research* 11, no. 2 (1997)
Cárdenas, Lupe, and Justo Alarcón, "Entrevista: An Interview with Alberto Ríos," *Confluencia* 6, no. 1 (1990)
McDowell, Robert, "Alberto Ríos," in *Contemporary Poets,* 6th edition, edited by Thomas Riggs, New York and London: St. James Press, 1996
McInnis, Susan, "Interview with Alberto Ríos," *Glimmer Train* 26 (1998)
Saldívar, José David, "The Real and the Marvelous in Nogales, Arizona," *Denver Quarterly* 17, no. 2 (1982)
Saldívar, José David, "Towards a Chicano Poetics: The Making of the Chicano-Chicana Subject, 1969–1982," *Confluencia* 1 (1985)
Wild, Peter, *Alberto Ríos,* Boise, Idaho: Boise State University, 1998

# Edwin Arlington Robinson 1869–1935

Living half of his life in the 19th century and half in the 20th, Edwin Arlington Robinson is best understood as a transitional poet. In his verse he reflects the 19th-century interest in traditional poetic forms, meters, and rhymes; his poetry abounds in sonnets, iambic tetrameter, fixed rhyme schemes, rhyming couplets, and (in his longer work) blank verse. His voice is not passionless, but it is controlled, even, and moderate. His poems are easily read and generally accessible. In his vision of the world and the lives of men and women, however, Robinson is a poet of the 20th century. He shares the Modernist view that the world is a dark and confusing place in which all men and women struggle for individuality and identity, cut off from the traditional values that sustained earlier generations. For Robinson the idea of community is frequently stifling. If God exists his will is not knowable, and suffering, weakness, and isolation are the common elements of life. In his own life Robinson strove for understanding and peace, largely through Emersonian transcendentalism. Although he lived his life without the comforts or support of church, close family ties, or marital love, he valued his friendships and the kindness of many individuals who took benefit in knowing him and supporting his life and work.

Robinson was raised in Gardiner, Maine, a small river community. Although opportunities for culture and beauty were few there, he benefited from friendships with Alanson T. Schumann, a homeopathic physician and poet, and Harry de Forest Smith, a boyhood friend who became Professor of Greek at Amherst College. These men instilled a love of poetry and classical literature in Robinson through conversation and mutual studies. From Schumann he learned the craft of older forms of poetry: the rondeau, sestina, sonnet, and villanelle. With Smith he read the classics and translated Sophocles, developing an appreciation for classical moderation and restraint as well as a commitment to precision and order in writing. Two years at Harvard broadened his intellectual horizons with study of Wordsworth's meditative poetry, George Crabbe's realistic verse, the poetry of Whitman, Rudyard Kipling, and Thomas Hardy, the fiction of Hawthorne and Henry James, and the essays of Emerson.

Gardiner, Maine, eventually became the model for Tilbury Town, Robinson's poetic world populated with sad, broken people and confused, lonely romantics who succumb to alcohol or suicide. The townspeople he knew in Gardiner, as well as members of his own dysfunctional family—a bankrupt father, an alcoholic brother, another brother addicted to morphine—became models for the numerous piercing character studies in his poems. Introspective and morose by nature, acutely sensitive to the materialism, greed, and instability of his times, Robinson combined the sweet forms of a long-gone romantic age with the painful truths of a modern, industrialized, Darwinian world.

In 40 years of serious writing Robinson published 20 books. Although he was awarded three Pulitzer Prizes, two for later works, it is mostly for his early collections that he is best remembered. His earliest volumes—*The Torrent and the Night Before* (1896), *The Children of the Night* (1897), *The Town Down the River* (1910), and *The Man against the Sky* (1916)—contain some of his most memorable portraits. Robinson's second volume holds the distinction of being the only book of poetry ever to have received a published review by an American president. A friend of Robinson's, a teacher at the Groton School, introduced Kermit Roosevelt to *The Children of the Night*. The young man shared his interest in the book with his father, President Theodore Roosevelt, who admired it so much that he reviewed it in *The Outlook* (1905), referring to it as a work of genius. President Roosevelt's favorable attention was the start of the upward curve in Robinson's life and career. Scribner's decided to issue an edition of *The Children of the Night* in October 1905, bringing Robinson a surge of national attention, and the President offered Robinson a sinecure in the United States Customs Service in New York, giving him a secure income with plenty of time to write. He held the position for four years, enough time for him to gain the confidence of a working writer. Many years later Robinson confided in Kermit Roosevelt that his father's attention had rescued him from his habit of excessive drinking and a feeling of despair about his future.

These early volumes of shorter lyrics contain such memorable character studies as "Aaron Stark," "Cliff Klingenhagen," "Fleming Helpenstine," "Reuben Bright," "Luke Havergal," "Bewick Finzer," "Miniver Cheevy," and the most famous of all, "Richard Cory." Each poem presents a sharp, insightful portrait of a man whose life is circumscribed by pain or loss. The poem may attribute his strange or self-destructive behavior to deep-seated, twisted motivations or simply depict it without explanation. Robinson's voice in these poems is often a mixture of sympathy and irony, offering at once a poet's understanding of the character's human frailty with a moralist's detached evaluation of human failure.

Aaron Stark, for example, is "cursed and unkempt, shrewd, shrivelled, and morose," a miser who speaks only "through scattered fangs a few snarled words" and lives, therefore, "a loveless exile." Lacking human warmth and sympathy, he laughs at those who offer him words of pity "touched with tears." Cliff Klingenhagen and Fleming Helpenstine demonstrate behavior that is harmless but strange enough to leave the poem's speaker baffled with misunderstanding. Cliff Klingenhagen offers wine to his dinner guest but drinks a glass of bitter wormwood himself. Fleming Helpenstine at first enjoys laughter and conversation with the poem's speaker, but then "with a queer, quick frown" begins to stare "In a strained way that made us cringe and wince." Suddenly he withdraws, offering only "a wordless clogged apology," and disappears, never to be seen again. Reuben Bright, the butcher, cries "like a great baby" upon hearing of his wife's impending death. After her death, in sorrow and rage, he tears down his slaughterhouse. Each of these four portraits is written in the form of a Petrarchan sonnet with a traditional rhyme scheme and a clear division between the octave and the sestet. Robinson uses the two-part form of the sonnet to great advantage: in the octave he gives a generalized description of the character, then in the sestet he shows a specific action or situation that details each one's unique oddity or suffering. Robinson may have intended to moderate these critiques of character somewhat by using the Petrarchan sonnet, as the sonnet's traditional association with love and friendship suggests the reader should view these characters with sympathy rather than disgust.

Other portraits include Luke Havergal, who appears to be haunted by thoughts of suicide because of a long-lost love. A ghost, perhaps the spirit of a deceased lover, tells him, "Go to the western gate . . . and if you listen she will call." Bewick Finzer had been rich, but "something crumbled in his brain / When his half million went." Now indigent, he has only "The broken voice, the withered neck, / The coat worn out with care." All his "dreams and schemes" amounted to nothing, and he now depends upon handouts and loans that he can never repay. The poem's speaker warns that Finzer will be there for many years to come, "Familiar as an old mistake, / And futile as regret." Miniver Cheevy, a man out of tune with the times, longs for an ideal past that he is capable of understanding in only an unschooled, fragmented way and drowns his sorrow over his present condition in alcohol. The poem's speaker highlights Miniver Cheevy's befuddled condition by describing how he "Scratched his head and kept on thinking; . . . And kept on drinking."

"Richard Cory," perhaps the best known of Robinson's portraits, is a subtle masterpiece of image and word choice. Wealthy and admired by the common townspeople, the title character is associated with royalty in such phrases as "a gentleman from sole to crown," "imperially slim," and "richer than a king." The common folk, on the other hand, humbly "worked, and waited for the light, / And went without the meat, and cursed the bread." In contrast to Richard Cory, they have little in the way of material benefits, but they have two very important things that sustain them: "work" and belief in "the light." Lacking both of these, Richard Cory "Went home and put a bullet through his head." The surprise ending reminds the reader that belief in spiritual values, represented by "the light," and a daily commitment to positive action, represented by "work," are necessary to sustain life. The leisured wealthy classes may appear happy and self-contained on the outside, Robinson implies, but their emptiness within is the cause of irretrievable despair.

Every summer from 1911 until his death in 1935, Robinson was a guest at the MacDowell Colony in Peterborough, New Hampshire, a private institution devoted to subsidizing creative artists to work in a rural environment uninterrupted by outside distractions. Robinson became its most celebrated resident and benefited from the cyclical regularity of creative writing during the summers in Peterborough, and revising, editing, and proofreading in New York during the winters. During these years, with the help of friends and the income from his writings and awards, his financial worries vanished. His reputation as one of America's important literary figures gradually developed over two decades and found endorsement with awards, prizes, and honorary degrees from such prestigious institutions as Yale and Bowdoin.

Although Robinson continued to write important shorter poems, such as "Eros Turannos," "The Mill," and "Mr. Flood's Party," all of which emphasize character and the painful relations between modern life's broken people, more and more he turned toward the long narrative poem written in blank verse. In a trilogy of book-length poems Robinson used Arthurian legend as a source of imagery and value to explore the times in which he lived. In *Merlin: A Poem* (1917), *Lancelot: A Poem* (1920), and *Tristram* (1927), sweeping narratives emphasize broad social issues; the individual's actions are depicted not as unique personal phenomena but as events with wide public consequences. Robinson implies parallels between the world after World War I, with its rising imperialism, capitalistic materialism, and spiritual emptiness, and the world of King Arthur's faded Camelot. In these poems failure and emptiness prevail, and Robinson's modest efforts at offering signs of hope or optimism appear contrived.

Of his contemporaries, the most useful comparisons can be made with Robert Frost. Like Robinson, Frost saw himself as part of the tradition of English poetry and adapted older poetic forms and traditional metrics to write about the modern temperament. Both poets capitalized upon the New England region they occupied and used its Yankee language and rural setting to probe the troubled human mind and heart. Both excelled in wit and irony and shared what appeared to be an objective detachment from their subjects. The differences between the two, however, may help explain Frost's greater appeal. Unlike Robinson, who wrote 13 long narrative poems that were criticized for their wordiness and lack of action, Frost did not stray far from what he did best: the shorter lyric. He worked on it throughout his career, refining and developing his skill, making very successful use of nature as a source of inspiration and imagery, until he mastered the lyric's demand for condensation and intensity. In addition, while both wrote frequently about loss, loneliness, and human torment, Robinson's voice is more pessimistic and despairing than Frost's. In Frost's poetry there is an energetic self-confidence and will to endure despite life's pain and absurdity. Finally, although Frost was only five years younger than Robinson, he lived 28 years longer into the age of mass media. Films and recordings of the old, noble, white-haired poet speaking about literature, politics, and people during personal interviews and reciting poetry before large college audiences and on the inauguration platform of President John F. Kennedy provided Frost with a longevity and accessibility not available to Robinson.

Edwin Arlington Robinson's position in American literature is nonetheless assured, because he probed the hearts and minds of men and women with sincerity and sensitivity, using expert metrical language and forms to penetrate ideas and feelings universal to the human condition. While he may lack followers or imitators among poets, or champions among literary critics, he has never lacked readers.

Paul J. Ferlazzo

**Biography**

Born in Head Tide, Maine, 22 December 1869. Attended Harvard University, Cambridge, Massachusetts, 1891–93; freelance writer in Gardiner, Maine, 1893–96; secretary to the President of Harvard University, 1899; held various jobs including subway-construction inspector, New York, 1903–04; through patronage of Theodore Roosevelt, admirer of his poetry, clerk in United States Customs House, New York, 1905–09. Received Pulitzer Prize, 1922, 1925, 1928; Levinson Prize (*Poetry*, Chicago), 1923; American Academy Gold Medal, 1929; honorary Litt.D., Yale University, New Haven, Connecticut, 1922, Bowdoin College, Brunswick, Maine, 1925; member, American Academy. Died in New York City, 6 April 1935.

**Poetry**

*The Torrent and the Night before*, 1896; revised edition as *The Children of the Night*, 1897
*Captain Craig*, 1902; revised edition, 1915
*The Town Down the River*, 1910
*The Man against the Sky*, 1916
*Merlin: A Poem*, 1917
*Lancelot: A Poem*, 1920

*The Three Taverns,* 1920
*Avon's Harvest,* 1921
*Collected Poems,* 1921
*Roman Bartholow,* 1923
*The Man Who Died Twice,* 1924
*Dionysus in Doubt,* 1925
*Tristram,* 1927
*Collected Poems,* 5 vols., 1927
*Sonnets, 1889–1927,* 1928
*The Prodigal Son,* 1929
*Cavender's House,* 1929
*The Glory of the Nightingales,* 1930
*Matthias at the Door,* 1931
*Poems,* edited by Bliss Perry, 1931
*Nicodemus,* 1932
*Talifer,* 1933
*Amaranth,* 1934
*King Jasper,* 1935
*Collected Poems,* 1937
*Tilbury Town: Selected Poems,* edited by Lawrance Thompson, 1953
*Selected Early Poems and Letters,* edited by Charles T. Davis, 1960
*Selected Poems of Edwin Arlington Robinson,* edited by Morton Dauwen Zabel, 1965
*Uncollected Poems and Prose,* edited by Richard Cary, 1975
*Collected Poems of Edwin Arlington Robinson,* 1977
*Edwin Arlington Robinson,* 1990
*The Essential Robinson,* edited by Donald Hall, 1994
*Miniver Cheevy, and Other Poems,* 1995
*Selected Poems,* 1997
*The Poetry of E.A. Robinson,* 1999

**Other Writings:** plays (*The Porcupine,* 1915), correspondence (*Letters to Edith Brower,* edited by Richard Cary, 1968); edited collections of letters (*Selections from the Letters of Thomas Sergeant Perry,* 1929).

**Further Reading**

Anderson, Wallace L., *Edwin Arlington Robinson: A Critical Introduction,* Boston: Houghton Mifflin, 1967
Barnard, Ellsworth, *Edwin Arlington Robinson: A Critical Study,* New York: Macmillan, 1952
Bloom, Harold, editor, *Edwin Arlington Robinson,* New York: Chelsea House, 1988
Coxe, Louis, *Edwin Arlington Robinson: The Life of Poetry,* New York: Pegasus, 1969
Fussell, Edwin S., *Edwin Arlington Robinson: The Literary Background of a Traditional Poet,* Berkeley: University of California Press, 1954
Kaplan, Estelle, *Philosophy in the Poetry of Edwin Arlington Robinson,* New York: Columbia University Press, 1940
Murphy, Francis, editor, *Edwin Arlington Robinson: A Collection of Critical Essays,* Englewood Cliffs, New Jersey, and Hemel Hempstead, Hertfordshire: Prentice Hall, 1970
Neff, Emery, *Edwin Arlington Robinson,* New York: Sloane, and London: Methuen, 1948
Smith, Chard Powers, *Where the Light Falls: A Portrait of Edwin Arlington Robinson,* New York: Macmillan, 1965
Winters, Yvor, *Edwin Arlington Robinson,* Norfolk, Connecticut: New Directions, 1946; revised edition, 1971

## Eros Turannos

In his introduction to *Selected Poems of Edwin Arlington Robinson* (1965), the poet James Dickey proposes that Robinson "has been perhaps the only American poet—certainly the only one of major status—interested *exclusively* in human beings as subject matter for poetry—in the psychological, motivational aspects of living, in the inner life as it is projected upon the outer." In such lyrics as "Richard Cory" and "Reuben Bright," the speakers of Robinson's poems confront characters whose actions seem to contradict the outer image they have projected (or have had imposed on them by the community). In these poems, the speakers encounter the possibility that the inner lives of others may be not only complex and dissonant but also only partly knowable. The inner life projected on the outer is less a revelation of the inner life itself than its distorted or partial image. The action of the character that compels the speaker's attention testifies to the existence of this inner life, but as a cipher to be contemplated rather than a revelation. As such, these poems are not just descriptions of the various characters, of Cory, of Bright, whose actions startle the speakers and at first seem out of character; they are also implicitly representations of the speakers' sense of what they cannot know about the characters they describe, and they suggest—to us as readers and perhaps to the speakers as well—that the inner lives of their speakers may also be complex, unknown, and perhaps unknowable, both to others and to themselves.

"Eros Turannos," a poem from the middle of Robinson's career collected in *The Man against the Sky* (1916), both extends and modifies this pattern. It describes a marriage where the husband and wife seem inextricably bound together yet are deeply isolated from each other. The speaker of this poem is not the puzzled individual mulling the unexpected actions of another; rather, it is a kind of collective awareness of the town reflecting on the slow, seemingly inevitable process by which the couple has reached a state where they are suspended between almost recognizing the loss and emptiness they have made from their fear of each other and almost recognizing that this isolation within the relationship is finally less terrifying than what they would each face separately if they consciously acknowledged the emptiness of their relationship to themselves and each other. The first stanza outlines the situation:

> She fears him, and will always ask
> What fated her to choose him . . .
> But what she meets and what she fears
> Are less than the downward years . . .
> Of age, were she to lose him.

The next three stanzas elaborate the portrait. We discover that the husband is a "Judas" yet that "Love" has kept the wife from quite acknowledging this; and, although Robinson focuses mostly on the wife, we learn that the husband has also been "secure[d]" and is similarly trapped, passive, and suspended. Neither character understands the inner life of the other or how they have shaped each other's inner life, nor are they able to find a vantage point to see either themselves or their relationship—a situation Robinson deftly underscores with the rhymes of the fourth stanza ("confusion," "illusion," and "seclusion" and "died and "hide").

If "Richard Cory" and "Reuben Bright" are short stories in verse, a moment of action and response, the first four stanzas of "Eros Turannos" are like a novel in their attention to the history, context, and process of the relationship. Had Robinson ended with the fourth stanza, the poem would still be a compelling psychological portrait of emotional isolation, but "Eros Turannos" continues for two more stanzas beyond the four that present the story. Here, too, it alters the pattern of Robinson's earliest great poems. In this case, the speaker is not another character in the poem (as in "Richard Cory"), nor does it seem to be quite the poet. Rather, the narrator is a kind of collective voice that seems to synthesize the community's guesses about the couple. This "we" "tells" the story "as it should be. . . . As if we guessed what hers [her visions] have been / Or what they are or would be." The inner life that the "we" imagines from the outer life it observes ("all the town and harbor side / Vibrate with her [the wife's] seclusion") is largely hypothetical, and it stands in the poem not only as an interpretation of the marriage but also as a reflection of the need of those around the couple to imagine a way behind "the kindly veil between / Her visions and those we have seen."

In "Eros Turannos," that is, Robinson brings the problem of knowing the "inner life" more to the fore than in poems such as "Richard Cory." The inner life is envisioned, not perceived. The story is based as much on imagination as on perception, and the story that is constructed is as much a revelation of, a witness to, the inner life of the "we" as the inner lives of the couple. The poem asserts the reality of psychological depth but also implies its impenetrability. The richness, then, of "Eros Turannos" is to be found not only in the evocation and analysis of the couple but also in the way this complex portrait reflects on and partially reveals the "we" that has painted it. This chorus-like voice, it seems, sees the cost of the couple's imaginative and emotional compromises and the couple's dialectic of blindness and insight, yet it fails to see its own stake in what it portrays. Perhaps this is why the syntax of the final line allows "the blind" to refer to more than just the husband and wife of the first four stanzas and hints that this condition is broad and even universal.

TIM HUNT

**Further Reading**


Anderson, Wallace L., *Edwin Arlington Robinson: A Critical Introduction,* Boston: Houghton Mifflin, 1967

Bernard, Ellsworth, *Edwin Arlington Robinson: Centenary Essays,* Athens: University of Georgia Press, 1969

Dickey, James, "Introduction: Edwin Arlington Robinson: The Many Truths," in *Selected Poems of Edwin Arlington Robinson,* by Robinson, edited by Morton Dauwen Zabel, New York and London: Collier Books, 1965

Faggen, Robert, "Introduction," in *Selected Poems: Edwin Arlington Robinson,* by Robinson, edited by Faggen, London and New York: Penguin, 1997

Joyner, Nancy Carol, *Edwin Arlington Robinson: A Reference Guide,* Boston: G.K. Hall, 1978

Murphy, Francis, editor, *Edwin Arlington Robinson: A Collection of Critical Essays,* Englewood Cliffs, New Jersey, and Hemel Hempstead, Hertfordshire: Prentice Hall, 1970


# Miniver Cheevy

From its first appearance in the March issue of *Scribner's Magazine* in 1907 but especially after its inclusion in the financially successful *The Town Down the River* (1910), "Miniver Cheevy" proved so popular that it became Robinson's most anthologized work. Several of his contemporaries and later critics detected autobiographical implications in the poem that possibly spoofed the poet's proneness to depression, drink, and outmoded romantic inclinations. However, the more lasting appeal of the poem, which may have been influenced by Robert Browning's "Pictor Ignotus" (1845), derived from its humorous portrait presented in nearly singable stanzas that slightly revise the folk ballad form. So deft are Robinson's strokes of poetic nuance in this work that the reader's judgment of Miniver Cheevy is left suspended, uncertain whether this denizen of Tilbury Town is merely a dreamer whose disappointments in life have led him to drink or whether he is just a drunk whose talk of disappointments is a sorry excuse for his preferred behavior.

As the medieval-sounding title playfully suggests, Miniver Cheevy is a person of minimal achievement. Instead of engaging life, he withdraws from it because (he claims) opportunities for a person like him no longer exist. He believes that he was "born too late," that in an earlier, more romantic time he would have excelled. The past he dreams about ranges from the Greeks' assault on Troy, to Alexander the Great's siege of Thebes, to King Arthur's exploits in Camelot. His mind is full of unrealistic images of war, and so he "eye[s] a khaki suit with loathing" because military service in his own time does not suit his fantasy of grand human action. With tongue in cheek, the narrator further observes that Miniver "missed the mediaeval grace / Of iron clothing," which implies not only that Miniver is outlandish in thinking that war was ever a beautiful affair (iron clothing is hardly graceful) but also that he may have another, undeclared reason to eschew military service in his own time (a khaki uniform is not as protective as armor).

Warfare is hardly the only feature of contemporary human endeavor that Miniver debunks. Contemporary politics also strikes him as a mere shadow of the potency of the Medici family's rule in Florence from the 15th to the 18th century. Miniver, we are told, "would have sinned incessantly / Could he have been" a Medici. Not only the opportunity to engage life through passion but also the storybook inheritance of wealth appeals to him more than working for wages, and so he "scorned the gold he sought, / But sore annoyed was he without it."

Large-scale warfare, intrigue-ridden political power, socially transgressive sin, and hostility toward the wealthy—all these particular features of Miniver's plaint suggest deep-seated aggression. Ironically, this aggression fails to hit its mark; instead, it undercuts Miniver, whose life is futile in comparison to the high-flown or mythic behavior typical of the figments of his romantic imagination. Miniver "assailed the seasons," and what could be more futile than railing against something as natural and inevitable as the four seasons or, by metaphoric extension, against the passing of one age to another? Futility is evident, too, in the fact that sometimes Miniver's rage collapses into grief: "He wept that he was ever born, / And he had reasons." The narrator intimates here that the real doubt about Miniver's ever being born may have less to do with his living in the wrong era than with his being a person who would have amounted to nothing during any historical period.

The minimalness of Miniver's life is emphasized in the closing stanza, where "Miniver cough[s], and call[s] it fate." To what does *it* refer? Miniver points to his life, but the syntax of the narrator's line makes *it* refer to *cough*. A cough is such a slight, transient event that to associate it with the outcome of fate is laughable. Equally risible is Miniver's life, which is equated to an insignificant cough by the ambiguity of the referent of *it*.

In the last stanza, as throughout the poem, lines ending with rhyming words of two syllables, with the "weak" second syllable unstressed, reinforce this impression of Miniver's impotence. There is also a related suggestion of unproductive circularity implied in the last stanza, where we are told that Miniver "Scratched his head and kept on thinking" and "kept on drinking." His ridiculous thoughts drive him to drink, which in turn fuels his useless fantasy-imbued thoughts. Going nowhere, in his head or in his arrested life, "Miniver thought, and thought, and thought, / And thought about it."

As such details suggest, the poem criticizes Miniver, but it also hints that Miniver's dreams in some sense recall youth's general attraction to myth and romance. If the poem lampoons Miniver's response to an adult reality that does not conform to childhood fantasy, it does not repudiate myth or romance. The fact that such dream-like tales, with their vision of transcendent human possibilities, appear to be "on the town" (in disrepute) in the early 20th century may indeed be a loss. So, finally, whereas "Miniver Cheevy" is not sympathetic with its protagonist's behavior, it does not make clear whether he has experienced actual setbacks in his life or merely alleges disappointments to justify his personal malaise and dereliction.

WILLIAM J. SCHEICK

**Further Reading**

Anderson, Wallace L., *Edwin Arlington Robinson: A Critical Introduction*, Boston: Houghton Mifflin, 1967 (see pages 107–08)

Boswell, Jeanetta, *Edwin Arlington Robinson and the Critics: A Bibliography of Secondary Sources with Selective Annotations,* Metuchen, New Jersey, and London: Scarecrow Press, 1987

Joyner, Nancy Carol, *Edwin Arlington Robinson: A Reference Guide,* Boston: G.K. Hall, 1978

Miller, Michael G., "Miniver Grows Lean," *Colby Quarterly* 12 (1976)

Perrine, Laurence, *The Art of Total Relevance,* Rowley, Massachusetts: Newbury House, 1976 (see pages 89–96)

## Mr. Flood's Party

Edwin Arlington Robinson's poem "Mr. Flood's Party" was first published in 1920 and later appeared in *Avon's Harvest* (1921). The title's Eben Flood is a late-arriving denizen of that eccentric, picturesque yet representative and modern New England Tilbury Town that Edwin Arlington Robinson had peopled with poetic characterizations like Miniver Cheevy, Bewick Finzer, Richard Cory, Pamela, and Luke Havergal since the 1890s. Even in the 19th century Robinson's portrayals were notable for their intriguing mix of the traditional and the new, but his regional realism was eventually affected by an international Modernism. His time-tested poetic forms often expressed contemporary uncertainty and angst. Robinson's literary ties to the past and Eastern tradition seem even more pointed in a poem published after experiments in Modern verse appeared in arty American periodicals like Harriet Monroe's *Poetry: A Magazine of Verse*. Monroe's avant-garde magazine notwithstanding, "Mr. Flood's Party" does parallel the portraits of Midwesterners in Edgar Lee Masters' *Spoon River Anthology* (1915). The poem is also timely in its post–World War I depiction of malaise and loss.

The pathos of Eben Flood's life and circumstances is introduced by an opening line in which key mood-setting words include "old," "alone," and "night." (Robinson's 1897 volume was called *The Children of the Night.*) This is to be a small party, indeed. His home a "forsaken upland hermitage," Flood nonetheless climbs and manages conversation, albeit with himself. Seasonal images of autumn and harvest time reinforce the dark tone. As Flood talks aloud, asking and answering his own questions, he—and Robinson in his own "voice"—alludes to poets like Edward Fitzgerald and Robert Burns, writers whom the reader might consider outdated like Flood himself or stylistically old-fashioned like Robinson, who wrote the poem in seven metrical, rhyming octaves. Fitzgerald's "Rubaiyat of Omar Khayyam" and Burns' "Auld Lang Syne" furnish nostalgic references to time passing and give Flood more than ample excuse for yet another toast and deep swig from his jug. Robinson contrasts this mock-epic image of the lifted jug with the heroic scene in the medieval *Song of Roland,* in which Roland dies shortly after blowing his horn to warn Charlemagne of impending threat. Mr. Flood ("Roland's ghost") will also die soon, his own "scarred hopes outworn," but his ineffectual "silent horn" can warn or summon no one, for those who "had honored him" are "friends of other days."

The detail of the jug and its effects is germane to the plight of Flood as well as Robinson and his times. The beginning of Prohibition in the very year of the poem reminds the reader that this particular escape from woes had become illegal. Robinson had complained about the Volstead Act and proposed a home recipe for hard cider that possessed "a regular reservoir of possibilities" (Baker, 1974). In his very private party, Flood treasures his companion, handling it "tenderly," "knowing that most things break." Indeed, in an existentially troubling world he conducts himself with the sort of dignity exhibited by older men in Hemingway fiction like "A Clean Well-Lighted Place" and *The Old Man and the Sea.* Alone, Flood drinks to the past, but does so almost ritualistically, "enduring to the end." The jug and the past are realities, dependable and tangible.

The often discussed line 47 seems at first an oxymoron: as Flood takes another drink, he sings, "Secure, with only two moons listening." Can one be stable and inebriated simultaneously? Instead of considering the image a sign of drunkenness, however, Harkey (1971) cites the earlier clause "we have the harvest moon / again" and argues that the moons represent a composite and "secure" image of the present alongside a past harvest moon. Certainly the entire poem is replete with doubles: Flood's jug and the "jug of wine" of the "Rubaiyat"; the jug and Burns' "cup o' kindness"; the jug and Roland's medieval horn. The dead and the living, friends and strangers, and, always, the past and the present act as foils to each other. Identity itself suggests this duality: Roland may also refer to Browning's Victorian Childe Roland, and Flood serves as both commentator and as respondent ("many a change has come / to both of us," he says). The protagonist's very name communicates his fate: Eben Flood also reads as "ebb and flood," designations for outgoing and incoming tides. His life seems on the wane:

> There was not much that was ahead of him,
> And there was nothing in the town below—
> Where strangers would have shut the many doors
> That many friends had opened long ago.

Benjamin S. Lawson

**Further Reading**

Baker, Carlos, "'The Jug Makes the Paradise': New Light on Eben Flood," *Colby Library Quarterly* 10, no. 6 (1974)

Bloom, Harold, editor, *Edwin Arlington Robinson*, New York: Chelsea House, 1988

Brasher, Thomas L., "Robinson's 'Mr. Flood's Party,'" *The Explicator* 29 (1971)

Davis, William V. "'Enduring to the End': Edwin Arlington Robinson's 'Mr. Flood's Party,'" *Colby Quarterly* 12 (1976)

Harkey, Joseph H., "Mr. Flood's Two Moons," *Mark Twain Journal* 15, no. 4 (1971)

Joyner, Nancy Carol, *Edwin Arlington Robinson: A Reference Guide*, Boston: G.K. Hall, 1978

Murphy, Francis, editor, *Edwin Arlington Robinson: A Collection of Critical Essays*, Englewood Cliffs, New Jersey, and Hemel Hempstead, Hertfordshire: Prentice Hall, 1970

Stanford, Donald E., *Revolution and Convention in Modern Poetry: Studies in Ezra Pound, T.S. Eliot, Wallace Stevens, Edwin Arlington Robinson, and Yvor Winters*, Newark: University of Delaware Press, 1983

---

# Theodore Roethke 1908–63

Theodore Roethke stands alone in American poetry as a true original; his work does not bear much comparison to his contemporaries, although like many other postwar, post-Freudian poets, Roethke suffered throughout his adult life from varieties of psychological injury and trauma, including manic depression, paranoid schizophrenia, and alcoholism. Poetically, however, he is in many ways a maverick figure who resisted assimilation into any school or movement and who developed according to his own instincts and desires rather than the dictates of any particular mentor; influences would come and go, but the voice persisting throughout his work is determinedly his own.

In his family life and early education, Roethke never received any specific encouragement toward literature, nor did he appear to be particularly interested in it; however, by the time he was attending the University of Michigan, he had become increasingly intrigued with writing as an alternative to a conventional career. Once convinced of his vocation, Roethke found his poetic subject early and persevered with it. Technically, he experimented with form, idiom, and rhythm continually, often producing poems in the same volume that could manifest Roethke as either elegist or bardic visionary or folk balladeer or comic rhymester. He could write extraordinary free verse and brutally condensed songs, his rhetoric could be erudite, and he could write in baby talk.

The psychological and environmental circumstances of Roethke's pre-adolescence were to be the profoundest resource for his writing. He was born in Saginaw, Michigan, a town that had prospered during the lumber boom of the 19th century and had then converted to an agricultural economy out of necessity when deforestation was complete. Theodore's grandfather, Wilhelm Roethke, had emigrated from Germany in 1872. Wilhelm was an accomplished horticulturist, and he established a prosperous market garden; he used the considerable profits from this venture to fulfill his ambition of building a massive greenhouse for flower cultivation. Wilhelm had three sons, the youngest of whom was Theodore's father, Otto. When Wilhelm died, Otto took over the horticultural aspect of the business and his brother Charles the financial side. The Roethke house was dwarfed by the greenhouse complex, and it was in this unique environment that Theodore grew up. The world of botany was to be the most vital context for his writing, the greenhouse his most privileged imaginative site. The greenhouse was also a site of conflict, however, where Roethke had to contend with the authoritative presence of his father: "I was born under a glass heel and have always lived there."

Otto the master gardener would die in tragic circumstances when his son was 14, and the greenhouse was inevitably involved; Otto and Charles had quarreled over the running of the business, which led to Otto signing over his shares to his brother. It transpired that Charles was both an embezzler and a bankrupt. The greenhouse had to be taken down and sold, then Otto Roethke fell ill. Charles shot himself, and three months afterward Otto was dead from bowel cancer.

Roethke began publishing poetry in 1930, just as he was beginning his postgraduate work. By the end of 1934, he had published 23 poems and had studied briefly under I.A. Richards; he also had to find a teaching job to support himself as a writer. At Michigan State University in 1935 he began creating a reputation for himself as a charismatic teacher that would equal his poetic standing, yet his time there was curtailed by the first of what were to be many breakdowns, having had a "mystical experience" with a tree.

Having to leave after one academic year at Michigan State, Roethke found work at Pennsylvania State University, where he would compile the poems for his first book, *Open House* (1941). It is the beginning of his poetic growth, which he memorably conceptualized as an evolutionary struggle: "a struggle out of the slime." *Open House* is formally conservative and tersely lyrical, but the vocabulary and themes discovered in the book were the substance of his originality. As the opening stanza of "Open House" declares, no form or language is adequate to contain the urges of his imagination:

My secrets cry aloud.
I have no need for tongue.
My heart keeps open house,
My doors are widely swung.
An epic of the eyes
My love, with no disguise.

This openness also entailed vulnerability, and in poems such as "Feud" and "Premonition," Roethke began what would be a career-long attempt to comprehend what had happened to his family: "Darling of an infected brood, / You feel disaster climb the vein." In "Sale" and "The Auction," Roethke writes of dispossession and disinheritance; in "Long Live the Weeds," he demarcates what was to be the geography of his verse, his "narrow vegetable realm" afflicted by "The ugly of the universe." Elsewhere in the volume, Roethke had begun exhibiting a tendency toward the jocosely macabre balladry that would persist throughout his work.

*Open House* had suggested that Roethke was on the verge of writing something extraordinary; *The Lost Son* (published seven years later in 1948) was extraordinary, an awesomely concentrated and original book of 25 short and three long poems. The majority of the book was taken up with "greenhouse poems," which Roethke had been writing while teaching at Bennington College, Vermont, in 1943; with Kenneth Burke's encouragement, the poems came thick and fast. Although lyric in form, Roethke conceived of the "greenhouse" poems as a long poem-in-progress, describing the continuing struggle of a psychologically responsive imagination to find selfhood within the simulated paradise of the paternal greenhouse. This is the beginning of Roethke's "spiritual biography," a visionary quest that was nevertheless contained within an environment that the poet had inherited rather than discovered; Roethke's nomadic impulse leads him downward rather than outward, into a microscopic intimacy with the subterranean that nevertheless fails to comprehend the secrecy and mysterious animation of the plants. As the ingenuity and tenacity of plant life were fascinating for Roethke, they were also a challenge to him to comprehend the secrets of his own psyche. He draws heavily on Freud and Jung to do so; the book's opening pair of poems, "Cuttings" and "Cuttings *(later)*," demonstrate, respectively, the agencies of id and ego. "Cuttings" is full of limpid, fragile violence:

One nub of growth
Nudges a sand-crumb loose,
Pokes through a musty sheath
Its pale tendrilous horn.

"Cuttings *(later)*" shows the ego questioning and exerting itself to counter the first poem, terminating in a knowledge that it might have been better to do without:

I can hear, underground, that sucking and sobbing,
In my veins, in my bones I feel it,—
The small waters seeping upward,
The tight grains parting at last.
When sprouts break out,
Slippery as fish,
I quail, lean to beginnings, sheath-wet.

Formally, the controls of *Open House* had been relaxed, and Roethke's irregular lines and rhythms in *The Lost Son* appear to be emulating the protean unpredictability of the minute world he describes. The book is also remarkable for its environmental awareness, as in "Moss-Gathering," where the speaker realizes that he does not live in a human-centered universe:

And afterwards I always felt mean, jogging back over the logging road,
As if I had broken the natural order of things in that swampland,
Disturbed some rhythm, old and of vast importance,
By pulling off flesh from the living planet;
As if I had committed, against the whole scheme of life, a desecration.

By intervening in the world of nature outside the greenhouse, Roethke doubly transgresses, first in abandoning his man-made paradise and second by violating the natural world as if it were his own. Throughout the volume, there is a profound sense that the greenhouse is a wonderful but profligate and unnatural space that pervades the excremental detail of "Flower Dump" in particular.

In 1947, Roethke went to Seattle to begin teaching at the University of Washington; apart from intervening institutionalizations or trips abroad, he would stay there for the rest of his life. In 1951, he published *Praise to the End!*, which renewed his quest for identity (the title was taken from *The Prelude*); in these poems, however, Roethke attempted to "face up to genuine mystery" and "speak in a kind of psychic shorthand" by addressing the self directly and less through the medium of nature. The result was a thorough engagement with the infantile self, using nursery rhyme and child fantasy to explore derangement:

A deep dish. Lumps in it.
I can't taste my mother.
Hoo. I know the spoon.
Sit in my mouth.

Baby talk combines with visionary writing in an attempt to produce a compulsive awareness of self; in this sense, the poems of this volume are ritualistic, attempting to evoke euphoric epiphanies at their close:

I'm an otter with only one nose:
I'm all ready to whistle;
I'm more than when I was born;
I could say hello to things;
I could talk to a snail;
I see what sings!
What sings!

Roethke married Beatrice O'Connell, a former student, in January 1953. They honeymooned in Italy, and Roethke began writing the title poem for his 1957 collection *Words for the Wind* (published in the United States in 1958). Meanwhile, he published a volume of selected poems, *The Waking* (1953), which also featured eight new poems, including a new departure for Roethke in the erotic dream narrative of "The Visitant" and an important return to the mode of his earlier work in "Four for Sir John Davies." In early 1954, Roethke's mother, Helen, died; a few weeks later, he heard that he had won the Pulitzer Prize.

In 1956, the Roethkes returned to Europe, and the design of *Words for the Wind* was finalized; the volume read like a compendium of Roethke's multivalent voices and abilities; the first section showed his capacity for fantasy and ludic narrative as well as a revealing debt to D.H. Lawrence in the poems about animals ("The Serpent" and "The Sloth"), and the second section's love poems are full of mysticism, eroticism, communion, and indolence, a contemporary *Song of Solomon:*

> A lazy natural man,
> I loll, I loll, all Tongue.
> She moves, and I adore:
> Motion can do no more.

In section 3, "Voices and Creatures," Roethke countenances the schizoid projections of his writing—"I see my several selves / Come running from the leaves"—while sections 4 and 5 are extended elegiac sequences, one for W.B. Yeats and another for his mother.

In 1960, Roethke visited Europe for the last time; he made a prolonged visit to Ireland and worked on the poems that would go into his next book. The ranging confidence of *Words for the Wind* was confirmed with the posthumous publication of *The Far Field* (1964), a year after Roethke's death from a heart attack in Seattle. The sequences of his last volume—"The North American Sequence," "Love Poems," "Mixed Sequence," and "Sequence, Sometimes Metaphysical"—are without precedent in American poetry; in the drive toward maturation and realization, in the epic projection of his self onto the landscape from Michigan to the Northwest, Roethke transcends the Freudian determinisms of gardens and greenhouses and achieves both a spiritual and a geopolitical vision, finally replacing his father with a pantheistic God as his adversary and guide.

Roethke's appreciation of seriality further emphasizes the epic strategy of his poetic career and marks him out as a great late Romantic poet; Roethke is vital because of his vision, his detail and range, and the thorough integrity of his individuality: "I learned not to fear infinity."

MICHAEL HINDS

**Biography**

Born in Saginaw, Michigan, 25 May 1908. Attended the University of Michigan, Ann Arbor, 1925–29, B.A. 1929 (Phi Beta Kappa), M.A. 1936; Harvard University, Cambridge, Massachusetts, 1930–31; Instructor in English, 1931–35, director of public relations, 1934, and varsity tennis coach, 1934–35, Lafayette College, Easton, Pennsylvania; Instructor in English, Michigan State University, East Lansing, 1935; Instructor, 1936–40, Assistant Professor, 1940–43, and Associate Professor of English Composition, 1947, Pennsylvania State University, University Park; Instructor, Bennington College, Vermont, 1943–46; Associate Professor, 1947–48, Professor of English, 1948–62, and honorary poet-in-residence, 1962–63, University of Washington, Seattle. Received Yaddo fellowship, 1945; Guggenheim fellowship, 1945, 1950; American Academy grant, 1952; Fund for the Advancement of Education fellowship, 1952; Ford grant, 1952, 1959; Pulitzer Prize, 1954; Fulbright fellowship, 1955; Borestone Mountain Award, 1958; National Book Award, 1959, 1965; Bollingen Prize, 1959; Poetry Society of America Prize, 1962; Shelley Memorial Award, 1962; honorary L.H.D., University of Michigan, 1962. Died in Seattle, Washington, 1 August 1963.

**Poetry**

*Open House,* 1941
*The Lost Son, and Other Poems,* 1948
*Praise to the End!* 1951
*The Waking: Poems, 1933–1953,* 1953
*The Exorcism,* 1957
*Words for the Wind: The Collected Verse,* 1957
*Sequence, Sometimes Metaphysical,* 1963
*The Far Field,* 1964; selections republished as *The Rose,* 1975
*Two Poems,* 1965
*The Achievement of Roethke: A Comprehensive Selection of His Poems,* edited by William J. Mortz, 1966
*Collected Poems,* 1966
*Selected Poems,* edited by Beatrice Roethke, 1969
*Dirty Dinky and Other Creatures: Poems for Children,* edited by Beatrice Roethke and Stephen Lushington, 1973

**Other Writings:** children's literature, journals, letters (*Selected Letters,* edited by Ralph J. Mills, Jr., 1968), essays (*On the Poet and His Craft: Selected Prose,* edited by Ralph J. Mills, Jr., 1965).

**Further Reading**

Balakian, Peter, *Theodore Roethke's Far Fields: The Evolution of His Poetry,* Baton Rouge: Louisiana State University Press, 1989
Bowers, Neal, *Theodore Roethke: The Journey from I to Otherwise,* Columbia: University of Missouri Press, 1982
Heaney, Seamus, *Preoccupations: Selected Prose,* London and Boston: Faber and Faber, 1980
Kusch, Robert, *My Toughest Mentor: Theodore Roethke and William Carlos Williams (1940–48),* Lewisburg, Pennsylvania: Bucknell University Press, and London: Associated University Presses, 1999
Scott, Nathan A., Jr., *Visions of Presence in Modern American Poetry,* Baltimore, Maryland: Johns Hopkins University Press, 1993
Seager, Allan, *The Glass House: The Life of Theodore Roethke,* New York: McGraw-Hill, 1968

## Greenhouse Poems

The first section of Theodore Roethke's *The Lost Son, and Other Poems* (1948), commonly known as the "Greenhouse Poems," is a 14-poem sequence in which the poet, remembering various aspects of the world within the Michigan greenhouses kept by his father, re-creates his own coming to life as a child. Composed mainly of short, descriptive poems, the sequence explores what sort of information can be discovered and what sort of speculative freedom can be generated through intense, empathic looking. The final poem of the sequence, "Frau Bauman, Frau Schmidt, and Frau Schwartze," added in 1952, makes explicit the central role of memory in this sequence. Writing as an adult, "alone and cold in my bed," the poet remembers three greenhouse workers, the "three ancient ladies" who "teased out the seed [of his life] that the cold kept asleep." As he remembers, those three fates seem to hover over him once again, returning him to the smells and sounds and intuitions of his formative years—what the poem calls his "first sleep." What marks this as a breakthrough poem is Roethke's verbal re-creation of the sights and feelings associated with the different "stations" of that returned-to greenhouse world—his charting of the way one thinks with the eye and the body. The verbal patterns developed in this sequence were expanded on by the poet throughout his career and taken in new directions by writers such as Sylvia Plath, Seamus Heaney, and Robert Hass in recent years.

The first two poems in the sequence, "Cuttings" and "Cuttings (*later*)," sketch the discovery of this new use of language. "Cuttings" is composed of a series of descriptions of plant cuttings coming back to life, with the poet, in memory, examining the process as if it is taking place before his eyes. Starting from a disengaged distance—"Sticks-in-a-drowse droop over sugary loam"—Roethke's eye moves gradually closer so that it finally sees the cuttings' "small cells bulge" and, underground, one "pale tendrilous horn" poking "through a musty sheath." What is implied, although never stated directly, is that as the poet engages with the cuttings, himself coming imaginatively awake as the "dry sticks" come back to life, he is reexperiencing an earlier awakening when he first was teased into awareness. "Cuttings (*later*)" asks what can be made verbally out of that act of identification. Its first stanza proposes creating a metaphor to memorialize the cuttings' resurrection: they are like straining saints, rising on "lopped limbs to a new life." However, the poem's second stanza turns away from that appreciative assessment and bursts out with a new sort of language—one that merges poet and cuttings and relives the feelings generated by the movement of his eye:

I can hear, underground, that sucking and sobbing,
In my veins, in my bones I feel it,—
The small waters seeping upward,
The tight grains parting at last.
When sprouts break out,
Slippery as fish,
I quail, lean to beginnings, sheath-wet.

The poems that follow all begin from this point. Remembering back, gazing intently at some aspect of the greenhouse that lifts to visibility the poet's early life, they are written in the immediate, empathic language of "In my veins, in my bones I feel it."

While related, the poems are also independent of each other and can be grouped in a variety of ways. For example, one set of poems focuses on different parts of the greenhouse and invites the reader to read the poems against each other in a sort of back-and-forth conversation. "Root Cellar" captures a powerful, contradictory mixture of responses to the greenhouse's lower area. In his mind, the poet opens a door and encounters something "dank as a ditch," "ripe as old bait"—a world of obscenely lolling and dangling roots and shoots. At the same time, the darkness is stubbornly alive: "Nothing would sleep," "Nothing would give up life: / Even the dirt kept breathing a small breath." Looking back, one might say, the poet feels again, in his veins and bones, that peculiar mixture of energy and rankness shared by both the cellar and the adolescent body. "Weed Puller" separates into two planes the mixed feelings it brings into focus. The poet remembers both "The indignity" of "Crawling on all fours" like an infant under the benches, "Hacking at black hairy roots" with his world reduced to the barest of unformed webs and weeds and shapes, and his desperate sense of a fully developed, inaccessible world above him: "everything blooming above me, / Lilies, pale-pink cyclamen, roses / Whole fields lovely and inviolate—." In this poem, to be alive is to be torn, reduced, ashamed, and sick with yearning. At the same time, "Child on Top of a Greenhouse" suggests, in a dizzying rush of participles, that being alive was also the opposing (and equally disturbing) feeling of release and loss of control brought about by the virtual erasure of self in a whirl of expanding overbright sensations: "The wind billowing out the seat of my britches, / . . . The half-grown chrysanthemums staring up like accusers, / . . . A line of elms plunging and tossing like horses, / And everyone, everyone pointing up and shouting!" As the poet works his way through such encounters, the self that he re-creates is strikingly multiple and various.

Another set of poems can be thought about in terms of energies brought into play. "Forcing House" remembers a scene of pulsing and knocking pipes, heat and water and fertilizer being forced through the young plants—"Swelling the roots with steam and stench"—to stimulate growth. "Orchids," in a peculiar mixture of childlike and fearful images, remembers its way back to one aspect of that pulsing world that the poet was brought into—the "musky smell" of sexuality "Drifting down from their mossy cradles":

So many devouring infants!
Soft luminescent fingers,
Lips neither dead nor alive,
Loose ghostly mouths
Breathing.

"Moss-Gathering" describes a journey outside the greenhouse to pull up from swamps and green carpets patches of moss "for lining cemetery baskets." Its terms are reminiscent of Shakespeare's "expense of spirit in a waste of shame": "As if I had broken the natural order of things in that swampland; / Disturbed some rhythm, old and of vast importance, / By pulling off flesh from the living planet." "Carnations" imagines a brief transcendence of that sexual confusion in the cool air, seemingly "drifting down from wet hemlocks, / Or rising out of ferns not far from water," that moved about the pale blossoms and Corinthian-scrolled leaves of those flowers. One thinks of the spirit moving in the gospels—the flowers seemingly poised in the "clear autumnal weather of eternity." What these poems suggest, then, is that the self is composed of intertwining flows of energy—cool, charged, balked, and frightening.

A final set of poems touches on the presence, in the greenhouse, of an older guiding spirit, a presence whose loss Roethke's later "Lost Son" poems richly explore. In these poems, the father sails the greenhouse all night through "The core and pith of [an] ugly storm" ("Big Wind"). He "fan[s] life into wilted sweet-peas with his hat" and "stand[s] all night watering roses, his feet blue in rubber boots" ("Old Florist"); and, most powerfully, as if the poet is watching himself across the gap of time, the father's hands stroke and nurture:

Turning and tamping,
Lifting the young plants with two fingers,
Sifting in a palm-full of fresh loam,—
. . . .
The underleaves, the smallest buds
Breaking into nakedness,
The blossoms extending
Out into the sweet air. ("Transplanting")

The sequence's conflicting energies and differing accounts of what it is to be alive suggest that such delicate moments are both fragile and easily erased yet also continually available to the eye that has learned to look and remember and feel again.

THOMAS GARDNER

**Further Reading**


Balakian, Peter, *Theodore Roethke's Far Fields: The Evolution of His Poetry,* Baton Rouge: Louisiana State University Press, 1989

Blessing, Richard Alan, "The *Greenhouse Sequence,*" in *Theodore Roethke's Dynamic Vision,* by Blessing, Bloomington: Indiana University Press, 1974

Burke, Kenneth, "The Vegetal Radicalism of Theodore Roethke," *Sewanee Review* 58 (Winter 1950)

Heyen, William, editor, *Profile of Theodore Roethke,* Columbus, Ohio: Merrill, 1971

Martz, Louis, "A Greenhouse Eden," in *Theodore Roethke: Essays on the Poetry,* Arnold Stein, editor, Seattle: University of Washington Press, 1965

Seager, Allan, *The Glass House: The Life of Theodore Roethke,* New York: McGraw-Hill, 1968


## My Papa's Waltz

Composed in 1941 and first published in the author's second collection of poetry, *The Lost Son, and Other Poems* (1948; England 1949), "My Papa's Waltz" has not fared well with Theodore Roethke's critics, who do not find it representative of his particular stylistic or thematic achievements and consequently give it, at best, passing comment in most major studies of the poet. Roethke himself, however, when asked to contribute poems to the anthology *Mid-Century American Poets* (1950), told editor John Ciardi that he thought "a smart move would be to bear down on those with the widest appeal," mentioning "My Papa's Waltz" as his finest dramatic piece (Roethke, 1968). Despite the opinion of Roethke scholars, the poem continues to be widely anthologized and to appeal to readers because of its accessibility, the inherent interest of its subject matter, and the way the poem rewards close analysis.

"My Papa's Waltz" concerns a time when Roethke's father, Otto, came home drunk, "romped" with his son in a clumsy dance, and eventually "waltzed" the boy off to bed. In the details comprising this 16-line vignette, readers are often tempted to find either a fond recollection of filial love or a bitter denunciation of an abusive, terror-inspiring father. The poem, however, is more complex than either of these interpretations. In fact, as John J. McKenna's (1998) examination of the manuscript drafts reveals, Roethke worked hard to create a poem that held these very different attitudes in a complex tension.

Those who believe that the poem dramatizes a painful memory note that the poet's father was a heavy and habitual drinker who may have abused his son psychologically. In later life, Roethke remembered Otto "as a stern, short-tempered man whose love [I] doubted" (Seager, 1968), and "My Papa's Waltz" in fact pictures a father who has been drinking heavily and whose rowdy behavior is sufficient to knock pans "from the kitchen shelf." The poet's mother, although disturbed, can only frown at this inebriated spectacle, too cowed, perhaps, to intervene. The boy, meanwhile, has his ear scraped by an oblivious or indifferent father preoccupied with beating time on his small son's head as though it were a drum.

From such details emerges, in John Ciardi's phrase, a "poem of terror" (quoted in Fong, 1990): father drunk and reckless, unconcerned about the effects, both physical and psychological, he is having on those around him; mother angry, possibly frightened, and silently fuming; the boy desperate in the midst of his dysfunctional family, playing along with father rather than risking the consequences of resistance. In terms of this reading, when Roethke writes that he "hung on like death," he is offering not a comically hyperbolic cliché but a confession of real fear regarding what might have happened had he let go—giving father more room to swing or a reason to turn on mother?—and his observation that "such waltzing was not easy" must be read as a painfully understated reflection on life with father.

Yet to remain satisfied with this negative reading is perhaps to overestimate certain biographical facts and unfairly to apply current cultural assumptions to a work written when other attitudes prevailed. For example, papa's battered, dirt-caked hands may signify for the poet his father's life of manual labor as a florist and greenhouse gardener (not emotional coarseness or a penchant for violence), and alcohol may not symbolize destructive addiction but, rather, an indulgence common to working men at the end of a long day. Although the poem is in crucial respects autobiographical, it may give one pause to learn that in the earliest handwritten drafts of this poem the gender of the child was female, "boy" replacing "girl" only in penciled changes to the second draft (McKenna, 1998).

Moreover, support for those who find the poem a playful, gentle recollection can be found in textual details the negative reading must slight. First, rather than "father," the poet has chosen the more affectionate "papa," just as his choice of "waltz" to characterize the father's roughhousing adds a comic dimension as one imagines this squiffed workman in his dirty clothes attempting the moves of this elegant, formal dance. Adding to a tone of amused fondness is the hyperbole of asserting that the father's breath alone could inebriate the boy, the image of mother's face unable to "unfrown itself" (certainly an unserious way of describing genuine anger or upset), the use of "romped," and the final image of a child so enjoying this horseplay that he clings to papa's shirt while being "waltzed . . . off to bed" (waltzing here carrying the sense of something done effortlessly).

The scraped ear now reads as a harmless accident resulting from the boy's size and happy closeness to his dancing partner and his beaten head as a comic touch. Further, lightheartedness resides in

Roethke's occasional use of feminine rhymes (dizzy/easy, knuckle/buckle) that are conventionally thought to provide a comic effect. Finally, the poem's three-beat line mimics the waltz's 3/4-time gaiety, while the frequent irregularities of the iambic trimeter humorously evoke papa's unsteadiness while creating a cozy informality.

Even a reader ignorant of pertinent biographical details can understand how a parent loudly happy but out of control might prove both distressful and memorably delightful to a young child. Otto died shortly before his son's 15th birthday, and when the poet looked back on this childhood moment with a father whom he had never ceased to admire despite their often troubled relationship (see Malkoff, 1966), it is no surprise the poem commemorating his papa's waltz should embody conflicted feelings. The poetic result is an interlacing of fondly comic reminiscence with a snapshot of "childhood trauma" of a sort, according to Timothy Rivinus (1993), typically experienced by children of alcoholics. Ultimately, what "My Papa's Waltz" achieves is poetry that refuses to simplify the complexity of any close relationship, especially a troubled one.

BROOKE HORVATH

**Further Reading**

Fong, Bobby, "Roethke's 'My Papa's Waltz,'" *College Literature* 17, no. 1 (1990)

Janssen, Ronald R., "Roethke's 'My Papa's Waltz,'" *Explicator* 44, no. 2 (1986)

Malkoff, Karl, *Theodore Roethke: An Introduction to the Poetry,* New York: Columbia University Press, 1966

McKenna, John J., "Roethke's Revisions and the Tone of 'My Papa's Waltz,'" *ANQ* 11, no. 2 (1998)

"My Papa's Waltz," in *Poetry for Students,* volume 3, edited by Marie Rose Napierkowski and Mary K. Ruby, Detroit, Michigan: Gale Research, 1998

Rivinus, Timothy, "Waltzing with Papa, Dancing with the Bears: Illness, Alcoholism, and Creative Rebirth in Theodore Roethke's Poetry," in *Beyond the Pleasure Dome: Writing and Addiction from the Romantics,* edited by Sue Vice, Matthew Campbell, and Tim Armstrong, Sheffield, South Yorkshire: Sheffield Academic Press, 1993

Roethke, Theodore, *Selected Letters of Theodore Roethke,* edited by Ralph J. Mills, Jr., Seattle: University of Washington Press, 1968; London: Faber, 1970

Seager, Allan, *The Glass House: The Life of Theodore Roethke,* New York: McGraw-Hill, 1968

Stein, Arnold, editor, *Theodore Roethke: Essays on the Poetry,* Seattle: University of Washington Press, 1965

Wolff, George, *Theodore Roethke,* Boston: Twayne, 1981

## North American Sequence

"North American Sequence" opens Theodore Roethke's posthumous book *The Far Field* (1964). Its six poems, which appeared separately in magazines between 1959 and 1963, were arranged as a sequence by Roethke before his death. It culminates his later career and makes a counter-statement to the monologues of *The Lost Son* (1948) and *Praise to the End!* (1951). Those monologues were journeys to the interior, reiterated descents into the subconscious in search of some vanished person or event, often the dead father, whose loss had crippled the speaker's conscious life. Their imagery can fairly be called archetypal, translating the particulars of Roethke's greenhouse childhood into more universal symbols of fear, disintegration, and psychic recovery.

"North American Sequence" poses a different relationship between consciousness and imagery, exploring not the psychic interior but rather the outward circumstances of Roethke's life, specifically his dwelling in Seattle and his intuition of oncoming death. This exploration had begun earlier in the love poems of *The Waking* (1953) and *Words for the Wind* (1957), in which a beloved woman emerged at times as a distinct, autonomous person rather than as an archetype of forces within the poet's mind. In the "Sequence" Roethke recognizes the presence of beings distinct from himself: the landscapes of the Pacific Northwest, the Great Plains, and the Midwest; competitor poets like Whitman and Eliot; and a dimly sensed spiritual reality beyond death.

Negotiating constantly between the otherness of these forces and Roethke's own spiritual quest, "North American Sequence" can be described as a modern instance of the genre that Meyer Abrams named the Greater Romantic Lyric: a meditation based on an encounter with a landscape, like "Tintern Abbey." Through seeming digressions and regressions, disquiet and alienation develop into a sense of harmony. Although the "Sequence" invites comparison with Whitman's two great shoreside meditations, "As I Ebb'd with the Ocean of Life" and "Out of the Cradle, Endlessly Rocking," T.S. Eliot is the more audible predecessor, as Roethke occasionally quotes from, and sometimes ventriloquizes, *Four Quartets.* Like *Four Quartets,* "North American Sequence" reflects upon specific landscapes with a mind trammeled in memories but in quest of the eternal, arriving at a resolution figured by a rose. Roethke emphasized his link with Whitman; Eliot's presence as adversary is typical of the spirit of the "Sequence," however, confronting forces that cannot be dissolved into projections of the poet's psychic struggle.

The "Sequence" begins in spiritual despondency, "a bleak time, when a week of rain is a year." Rallying himself to seek a new life, the poet paraphrases Eliot—"Old men should be explorers"—but counters "I'll be an Indian," that is, someone who renews his current world rather than seeking novelty beyond it. In "Meditation at Oyster River" Roethke looks attentively at that world, describing a river's mouth on the east coast of Vancouver Island just before sunset, as the tide begins to come in. His language seeks the particular, not the archetype, naming the "elephant-colored" rocks and a "fish raven" in a dead tree, recreating the stillness of sea and land. The quieted eye, of course, sees into the heart of things: out of the scene "Death's face rises afresh," and the meditation shifts into memory, taking the poet back across the continent to his Michigan childhood. He returns not to his father's greenhouse, however, but to Saginaw's Tittebawasee River, as its winter ice-jam breaks up and "the spirit" begins to "run . . . / In and out of the small waves." The next three poems journey deeper into the American interior and into personal and national memory, describing automobile travels around Saginaw and across the Great Plains and the Rockies before returning to the "long waters" of the Northwest.

Although Roethke read extensively in the mystics, and critics trace the stages of mystical enlightenment in the "Sequence," spiritual insight and deliverance from the egoistic self seem to come not from ascetic detachment but from the plenitude of his experience of nature. At this point the poem often sounds like the Eliot of the *Quartets,* but its eye is on the details of "a country of bays and inlets," apprehended not as phenomena of memory or sensation but as selved entities. The tide resists the river's flow: consciousness acknowledges how reality limits it. "All finite things," Roethke sees, "reveal infinitude," and he finds himself "renewed by death, thought of my death" because "What I love is near at hand, / Always, in earth and air." The "Sequence" culminates in "The Rose," which opens with another challenge to *East Coker:*

> There are those to whom place is unimportant,
> But this place, where sea and fresh water meet,
> Is important.

Watching the tide and a sun sinking into the sea, he sways "outside [him]self" into the processes of nature, and encounters a visionary rose. The traditional figure of spiritual fulfillment, the rose is also an emblem of his florist father (seen, for perhaps the first time, as a person rather than as a psychological symbol) as well as an actual flower, blooming "out of the briary hedge . . . / Beyond . . . the wind-tipped madrona [trees]," swaying in the sea wind. Approaching the rose, he says,

> I came upon the true ease of myself,
> As if another man appeared out of the depths of my being,
> And I stood outside myself,
> Beyond becoming and perishing,
> A something wholly other.

The presence that has summoned him out of his self goes unnamed in the "Sequence," although later in *The Far Field* Roethke called it God or (echoing Tillich) "Godhead above my God."

Praise for the "Sequence" usually emphasizes its position near the end of Roethke's career. Readers troubled by the near solipsism of his earlier work—its scarcity of other human figures and seeming indifference to social and historical situation—have often been moved by the sensory richness of the "Sequence" and by its journey, literal and spiritual. "North American Sequence" speaks for a poet who, if he had lived, would surely have opened a newly expansive chapter in his work. Dying, Roethke left the "Sequence" as his spiritual testament, intimations of immortality within an American landscape.

James Dougherty

**Further Reading**

Abrams, Meyer, "Structure and Style in the Greater Romantic Lyric," in *From Sensibility to Romanticism: Essays Presented to Frederick R. Pottle,* edited by Frederick W. Hilles and Harold Bloom, New York: Oxford University Press, 1965; London: Oxford University Press, 1970

Balakian, Peter, *Theodore Roethke's Far Fields: The Evolution of His Poetry,* Baton Rouge: Louisiana State University Press, 1989

Bowers, Neal, *Theodore Roethke: The Journey from I to Otherwise,* Columbia: University of Missouri Press, 1982

La Belle, Jenijoy, *The Echoing Wood of Theodore Roethke,* Princeton, New Jersey: Princeton University Press, 1976

Nelson, Cary, "Theodore Roethke's 'North American Sequence,'" in *Our Last First Poets: Vision and History in Contemporary American Poetry,* Urbana: University of Illinois Press, 1981

Parini, Jay, *Theodore Roethke: An American Romantic,* Amherst: University of Massachusetts Press, 1979

Ross-Bryant, Lynn, *Theodore Roethke: Poetry of the Earth, Poet of the Spirit,* Port Washington, New York, and London: Kennikat Press, 1981

Scott, Nathan, "The Example of Roethke," in *The Wild Prayer of Longing: Poetry and the Sacred,* by Scott, New Haven, Connecticut: Yale University Press, 1971

Sullivan, Rosemary, *Theodore Roethke: The Garden Master,* Seattle: University of Washington Press, 1975

---

# Jerome Rothenberg 1931–

Multifarious, this Rothenberg: editor of *Technicians of the Sacred* (1968), the first publication to present "primitive" poetry on anything like its own terms, groundbreaking for its commentaries by Rothenberg that linked the archaic to contemporary experimental, avant-garde, radical poetry; author of *Poland/1931* (1969, 1974) and *Khurbn, and Other Poems* (1989), remarkable, unsentimental sequences of Jewish poetry to be read both for their irreverence and for their sense of the sacred; lower-east-side small-press pioneer of the late 1950s to early 1960s, when, as publisher of Hawk's Well Press books, including his first book, *White Sun, Black Sun* (1960), and the first books of Diane Wakoski and Robert Kelly, he edited *Poems from the Floating World* magazine, a venue for his ideas on "deep image" and "ethnopoetics," two terms that are of his coinage; inventor of "total translation," a technique that reevaluates so-called ambient sounds, not dismissing them as meaningless noise, locating them at the epicenter of the translation, an act of attempting "to restore what has been torn apart," as in the exemplary *Horse Songs* (1977); performance poet conversant in intermedia, multimedia mix, and creation of event/ritual/process-oriented poetry; anthologist supreme (e.g., *Shaking the Pumpkin* [1972; revised 1986, 1991], *A Big Jewish Book* [1978], and *Poems for the Millennium* [2 vols., 1995, 1998]), for no other poet in the 20th century used the anthology so effectively to promote his poetics; practitioner of aleatory verse, like colleagues John Cage and Jackson Mac Low, his *Gematria* (1994) constituting one of the finest examples of this form, hearkening back to ancient Jewish composition practices and those of the Dadaists, whom he has acknowledged for their "'discovery' that chance & accident could themselves create poems & structures" (Rothenberg, 1981).

To paraphrase Yeats—how to separate poet from anthologist, anthologies from their procedures of assembly, poetics of body from that of mind, measure from open field, meaning from chance, book from hands in which it lay open, concrete vision from abstract sublime, eschatology from everyday meaning, flux from repose, maverick from professor, lineages—what he calls "strain" (Mallarmé, Stein, Lorca, Seneca, Navajo, Jewish, Dada)—from himself?

Rothenberg has written,

> Everything & everyone around here are welcome to come into the poem—in particular what has been hidden for so long that the poem has almost to create it (or to seem to do so) to make it visible again. This is the open invitation of our poetry since Whitman. (Rothenberg, 1986)

Rothenberg's poetry is marked by an eschewal of the "lyrical I," a fearless use of repetition and nonsense, promulgation of multiple narratives, an incurable surrealistic bent, and lowercase informality and idiosyncratic punctuation, including his signature use of the ampersand. He is a poet "mad for content," for whom the experience of the poem is both on and off the page. He has reinvigorated the oral tradition:

> My experience is the experience of everything that happens to me in that act [performing a poem]: the movement of my arm, the sound (& feel) of pebbles against horn, the way that breaks across my voice, the tension in my throat, the full release of breath, the emptying that leaves me weak & ready to receive the next song, the song occurring, rising out of memory, becoming voice, becoming sound, becoming physical again, & then returning into silence. And it is also this room, this time & place, these others here with me. . . . The poem is everything-that-happens . . . : to insist that it is only part of it (the words), is to mistake the event, to miss that total presence. (Rothenberg, 1981)

Consistently and directly stated, Rothenberg's poetics appears as "pre-faces," "post-faces," or "commentaries" in his collections. This is contrary to the view that poems are superior to poetics, that nothing can explain the poem but the poem itself.

Rothenberg has positioned himself in the center of the rebellion against "familiar Anglo-Saxon & class-oriented view of language & high culture" (Rothenberg, 1981):

> Ethnopoetics . . . investigate[s] on a transcultural scale the range of possible poetries that have not only been imagined but put into practice by other human beings. It was premised on the perception that western definitions of poetry & art were no longer, indeed, had never been, sufficient. . . . The focus was . . . on those stateless & classless societies that an earlier ethnology had classified as "primitive." That the poetry & art of those cultures were complex in themselves & in their interconnections with each other was a first point that I found it necessary to assert. . . . *There are no primitive languages.* (Clay and Phillips, 1998)

Translation (in all of its meanings) is key:

> By its very nature, translation asserts or at least implies a concept of psychic & biological unity, weird as such assertion may seem in a time of growing dis-integration. Each poem, being made present & translated, flies in the face of divisive ideology. (Rothenberg, 1981)

If we are to be saved, it is through poetry. This has led to a notion of "a paradise of poets,"

> like that which Dante found outside of hell & heaven, in the position in mind's space that he called Limbo. I do not of course believe that such a paradise exists in any supernatural or mystical sense, but I have sometimes felt it come to life among my fellow poets and, even more, in writing—in the body of the poem. (Rothenberg, 1999)

For Rothenberg, there is a vital link between the literary avant-garde and a poetics of nonclosure, as alternative to expressions of a closed mind:

> If there's still any sense in talking of an avant-garde, then that must be it for me: an insistence that the work deny itself the last word, because the consequences of closure & closed mind have been & continue to be horrendous in the world we know. (Rothenberg, 1981)

Reading Rothenberg on his terms is to believe that humanity is on the upswing, even though we live in such a dark time of hyperfamiliarization with peril and terror. His idealism takes its cues from a number of sources, not the least of which is Mallarmé's notion of the book as "spiritual instrument . . . the [single] Book that every writer worked at even without knowing . . . the Orphic explanation of the Earth, which is the poet's only duty" (quoted by Rothenberg, 1996).

MARK MELNICOVE

*See also* Deep Image Poetry

**Biography**

Born in New York City, 11 December 1931. Attended City College of New York, B.A. 1952; University of Michigan, Ann Arbor, M.A. 1953; served in the United States Army, 1954–55; Instructor, City College of New York, 1959–60; Lecturer in English, Mannes College of Music, New York, 1961–70; Regents Professor, University of California, San Diego, 1971; Visiting Lecturer in anthropology, New School for Social Research, New York, 1971–72; Visiting Professor, University of Wisconsin, Milwaukee, 1974–75, San Diego State University, 1976–77, University of California, San Diego, 1977–79, 1980–84, University of California, Riverside, 1980, University of Oklahoma, Norman, 1985, State University of New York, Albany, 1986, and Binghamton, 1986–88; since 1988 Professor of visual arts and literature, University of California, San Diego; Distinguished Aerol Arnold Chair in English, University of Southern California, Los Angeles, 1983; distinguished writer-in-residence, New York State Writers Institute, Albany, 1986; founding publisher, Hawk's Well Press, New York, 1958–65; editor or co-editor, *Poems from the Floating World,* 1960–64, *Some/Thing,* 1965–68, *Alcheringa,* 1970–76, and *New Wilderness Letter,* 1976–85; contributing editor, *Stony Brook, Change International, Dialectical Anthropology,* and *Sulfur.*

Received Longview Foundation Award, 1960; Wenner-Gren Foundation grant, 1968; Guggenheim grant, 1974; National Endowment for the Arts grant, 1976; American Book Award, 1982; PEN Center USA West Translation Award, 1994; PEN Oakland Josephine Miles Literary Award, 1994, 1996. Living in San Diego, California.

**Poetry**

*White Sun, Black Sun,* 1960
*The Seven Hells of the Jigoku Zoshi,* 1962
*Sightings I–IX* (with *Lunes* by Robert Kelly), 1964
*The Gorky Poems* (bilingual edition), 1966
*Between: Poems, 1960–1963,* 1967
*Conversations,* 1968
*Poems, 1964–1967,* 1968
*Sightings I–IX and Red Easy a Color* (with Ian Tyson), 1968
*Poland/1931,* 1969
*Poems for the Game of Silence, 1960–1970,* 1971
*A Book of Testimony,* 1971
*Poems for the Society of the Mystic Animals* (with Ian Tyson and Richard Johnny John), 1972
*Seneca Journal I: A Poem of Beavers,* 1973
*Esther K. Comes to America, 1931,* 1974
*The Cards,* 1974
*Poland/1931* (complete edition), 1974
*The Pirke and the Pearl,* 1975
*Seneca Journal: Midwinter* (with Philip Sultz), 1975
*The Notebooks,* 1976
*Narratives and Realtheater Pieces* (with Ian Tyson), 1977
*Seneca Journal: The Serpent* (with Philip Sultz), 1978
*A Seneca Journal* (complete edition), 1978
*B*R*M*Tz*V*H,* 1979
*Abulafia's Circles,* 1979
*Letters and Numbers,* 1979
*Vienna Blood, and Other Poems,* 1980
*Altar Pieces,* 1982
*That Dada Strain,* 1983
*15 Flower World Variations* (with Harold Cohen), 1984
*A Merz Sonata,* 1985
*New Selected Poems, 1970–1985,* 1986
*Khurbn, and Other Poems,* 1989
*Further Sightings and Conversations,* 1989
*The Lorca Variations (1–8),* 1990
*Improvisations,* 1991
*Six Gematria,* 1992
*The Lorca Variations: I–XXXIII,* 1993
*In a Time of War: The Lorca Variations,* 1993
*Poems, Performance Pieces, Proses, Plays, Poetics,* 1993
*Gematria,* 1994
*An Oracle for Delphi,* 1995
*Pictures of the Crucifixion: Poems,* 1995
*Seedings, and Other Poems,* 1996
*Delight/Délices, and Other Gematria* (bilingual edition, French translations by Nicole Peyrafitte), 1998
*A Paradise of Poets: New Poems and Translations,* 1999

**Other Writings:** plays (*Poland/1931,* 1988), radio plays, translations of Spanish, Czechoslovakian, and German literature (*The 17 Horse Songs of Frank Mitchell, Nos. X–XIII,* 1969); edited collections of literature (*Symposium of the Whole: A Range of Discourse Toward an Ethnopoetics* [with Diane Rothenberg], 1983).

**Further Reading**

Clay, Steven, and Rodney Phillips, editors, *A Secret Location on the Lower East Side: Adventures in Writing, 1960–1980,* New York: New York Public Library, 1998
Paul, Sherman, *In Search of the Primitive: Rereading David Antin, Jerome Rothenberg, and Gary Snyder,* Baton Rouge: Louisiana State University Press, 1986
Polkinhorn, Harry, *Jerome Rothenberg: A Descriptive Bibliography,* Jefferson, North Carolina, and London: McFarland, 1988
Rothenberg, Jerome, *Pre-Faces and Other Writings,* New York: New Directions, 1981
Rothenberg, Jerome, "Poetry in the 1950s as a Global Awakening: A Recollection & Reconstruction," paper delivered at "American Poetry in the 1950s," University of Maine, Orono, 1996 (*http://wings.buffalo.edu/epc/authors/rothenberg/50s.html*)
Rothenberg, Jerome, and David Guss, editors, *The Book, Spiritual Instrument,* revised edition, New York: Granary Books, 1996
Rothenberg, Jerome, and Steven Clay, editors, *A Book of the Book,* New York: Granary Books, 2000
Selerie, Gavin, and Eric Mottram, editors, *Jerome Rothenberg,* London: Binnacle Press, 1984

---

## Muriel Rukeyser 1913–80

Muriel Rukeyser was a prolific poet whose works astonish by their variety of form, theme, tone, and subject. She also flourished as a journalist, a single mother, a biographer, a translator, a playwright, a university professor, and a lover whose eroticism was "democratic" in its inclusiveness (Kaufman, 1994). The distinguishing feature of her poems, in fact, is their insistent celebration of eroticism, passion, poetry, and love as necessary human responses to war, oppression, hatred, and death. Through poetry, she suggests, we are transformed, transfigured—and rescued.

Rukeyser proclaims her faith in the power of poetry to shape history and save lives in her visionary prose work *The Life of Poetry* (1949). For her, poetry is above all a form of protest and resistance against death, injustice, and oppression; it offers the possibility of transformation and connection. Poetry, she contends, is what Americans most fear and what they most need. It has the potential to save us from death, silence, and forgetting, which in Rukeyser's poetic world signify a kind of secular hell, an inner world without the full responsiveness that she believes should characterize human life.

The religious fervor of Rukeyser's beliefs is characteristic of her strong views. The courage of her convictions is evident in the often-anthologized poem "To be a Jew in the twentieth century," a sonnet in which she proclaims publicly, in print, her personal identity as Jew at the height of Hitler's Holocaust ("Letter to the Front," VII, *Beast in View,* 1944). The poem celebrates Jewish identity as "a gift" that enables those who accept the gift to "resist" death and oppression and to transform "suffering" into "human freedom" by "Daring to live for the impossible."

Rukeyser was a fearless poet from the beginning of her long career, as is evident in "The Book of the Dead" (*U.S. 1,* 1938). This long, complex poem commemorates and protests the deaths of West Virginia miners from silicosis in the mid-1930s. These victims of corporate greed become tragic figures who nonetheless are heroic in their embodiment of their gift to the rest of us: the chance to resist death and greed and oppression in the future, to learn and live by the poet's catechism:

> What three things can never be done?
> Forget.   Keep silent.   Stand alone.

We do not forget because the poem ensures that we will remember. It breaks the silence of the dead miners and offers us the chance to stand with them in solidarity against suffering and injustice—against "A corporation," which the poem defines punningly as "a body without a soul" ("The Dam").

Throughout her career, Rukeyser repeats this three-part response of remembering, speaking, and standing together in protest. Her poems memorialize the oppressed who have been prisoners of conscience, political prisoners, and victims of wars (from the Spanish resistance against Fascism in 1936 through World War II and Korea to the Vietnam War) and include those figuratively imprisoned because of their gender, color, religion, ethnicity, age, or sexual preference, as in "What Do We See?" This poem repeatedly challenges the reader and ends with a pair of widely spaced questions:

> Will we never see?      Will we never know?

Clearly, Rukeyser means to engage her readers on the side of justice.

The range of Rukeyser's subjects and forms reflects the breadth of her intellectual and emotional interests as well as her thematic and personal goal of joining separate selves through the process of poetic creation. The titles of her collections offer evidence of this goal with their references to "waking," "breaking," "turning," "speed," "motion," "movement," "colors," and "fire." The pattern coruscates, but the route, indicated literally in her title *U.S. 1,* is anything but evanescent. Her insistence on the possibility of forming unity from multiplicity and difference has invited comparison with Whitman. Like her, he is a poet of inclusiveness, democracy, movement, radical innovation, and grand scope. However, Rukeyser's remarkable stylistic range sets her apart from him. She moves so effortlessly between traditional received forms and highly experimental verse that she used a custom-made rubber stamp to implore editors and publishers, "PLEASE BELIEVE THE PUNCTUATION" (quoted in Daniels, 1992, and elsewhere). The anecdote is both characteristic and unforgettable.

Rukeyser's work in traditional forms is epitomized by the sonnet sequence "Nine Poems: For the Unborn Child" (*The Green Wave,* 1948) and by "Sestina," section 4 of "Letter to the Front." Both works, however, are equally notable for their nontraditional content: the poetry of pregnancy (her subject in "Nine Poems") was not even in its infancy in 1948, and her "Sestina" centers on "Free Catalonia" and its resistance to Fascist oppression.

Rukeyser's formal and stylistic innovations are visually obvious even to a casual reader. Colons appear disconcertingly at the start of lines; large spaces loom like visible caesuras; without warning, we must perform a "Cadenza for the reader" in "What Do We See?" (as Kaufman [1994] observes). Rukeyser discusses punctuation in this often-quoted passage from *The Life of Poetry:*

> Punctuation is biological. It is the physical indication of the body-rhythms which the reader is to acknowledge; and, as we know it, punctuation in poetry needs several inventions. Not least of all, we need a measured rest.

Clearly, Rukeyser's poetry offers many examples of her own effort to supply some of these "inventions." However, it is not her punctuation alone that is unconventional. Consider "St. Roach" (*The Gates,* 1976), a comic celebration of the serious possibilities of communion with the lowly roach, glorified in the poem as "lovely," "Fast as a dancer," and (most improbably) "witty." Yet even this poem is firmly linked to the history of poetry in English in its self-conscious echoing of Christopher Smart's memorable paean to "my cat Jeoffry" in *Jubilate Agno.* The structural movement of Rukeyser's poem from "I never knew you" to "Yesterday I looked at one of you" to "Today I touched one of you for the first time" represents comically the very serious enterprise at the heart of her poetry: to enable sympathetic communication between herself and her readers and all those others imaged as Other.

Another well-known poem, "Then" (also from *The Gates*), exemplifies Rukeyser as both a poetic descendant of Whitman and a believer in the power of poetry.

> When I am dead, even then,
> I will still love you, I will wait in these poems,
> When I am dead, even then
> I am still listening to you.

The echoes of Whitman's conclusion to "Song of Myself"—"I stop some where waiting for you"–are indisputable. In both cases, poetry offers a transcendent possibility of communication.

Rukeyser's work has been especially important to feminist poets and readers. Two poetry anthologies published in the 1970s took their titles from her lines: "No more masks!" from "The Poem as Mask" and "The world split open," a phrase adapted from the poem "Käthe Kollwitz" (both in *The Speed of Darkness,* 1968). Both poems explore the neglected, obscured power of the woman artist—something that Rukeyser knew well from personal experience. Anne Sexton's famous tribute to Rukeyser as "Muriel, mother of everyone" (quoted in Kertesz, 1980) perhaps sums up her importance to later women writers as a poetic foremother who made artistic life possible for Sexton as well as for Adrienne Rich and Alice Walker, among others.

A last feature central to Rukeyser's work is its startling transformation of two realms ordinarily far removed from poetry into metaphors of great power and beauty: her father's concrete-mixing business and the work of the scientist Willard Gibbs, who discovered the phase rule. The phase rule is beyond the scope of this discussion; suffice it to say that it appealed to Rukeyser as a mathematical description of the stunning metamorphosis from pourable liquid to enduring solid represented by concrete—and the equally stunning metamorphosis from breathable air to enduring verse form represented by poetry. Rukeyser celebrated these figurative parallels—between science and poetry and between city building and poetry—throughout her career, describing not only Käthe Kollwitz but also herself as "A woman pouring her opposites." The implicit comparison returns in the first and final lines of "Concrete" (section 4 of "Searching/Not Searching," *Breaking Open*, 1973): "They are pouring the city," and "I am pouring my poems." The appeal of the parallels is their emphasis on the art and science of metamorphosis—a topic that Rukeyser treats as central to the life of her poetry.

CHERYL SPECTOR

*See also* San Francisco Renaissance

**Biography**
Born in New York City, 15 December 1913. Attended Vassar College, Poughkeepsie, New York; Columbia University, New York, 1930–32; vice president, House of Photography, New York, 1946–60; teacher, Sarah Lawrence College, Bronxville, New York, 1946, 1956–57; member of board of directors, Teachers-Writers Collaborative, New York, from 1967; President, PEN American Center, 1975–76. Received Yale Series of Younger Poets Award, 1935; Harriet Monroe Award, 1941; American Academy Award, 1942; Guggenheim fellowship, 1943; American Council of Learned Societies fellowship, 1963; Swedish Academy Translation Award, 1967; Copernicus Award, 1977; Shelley Memorial Award, 1977; honorary Litt.D., Rutgers University, New Brunswick, New Jersey, 1961; member, American Academy. Died in New York City, 12 February 1980.

**Poetry**
*Theory of Flight*, 1935
*U.S. 1*, 1938
*Mediterranean*, 1938
*A Turning Wind*, 1939
*The Soul and Body of John Brown*, 1940
*Wake Island*, 1942
*Beast in View*, 1944
*The Children's Orchard*, 1947
*The Green Wave*, 1948
*Orpheus*, 1949
*Elegies*, 1949
*Selected Poems*, 1951
*Body of Waking*, 1958
*Waterlily Fire: Poems, 1935–62*, 1962
*The Outer Banks*, 1967
*The Speed of Darkness*, 1968
*29 Poems*, 1972
*Breaking Open*, 1973
*The Gates*, 1976
*The Collected Poems of Muriel Rukeyser*, 1978
*Out of Silence: Selected Poems*, edited by Kate Daniels, 1992

**Other Writings:** plays (*Houdini*, produced 1973), fiction (*More Night*, 1981), nonfiction (*The Life of Poetry*, 1949), children's literature, biography (*Willard Gibbs*, 1942), translations of French, German, Italian, Spanish, and Swedish literature (*Three Poems by Gunnar Ekelöf*, 1967; *Early Poems, 1935–1955*, by Octavio Paz, 1973).

**Further Reading**

Daniels, Kate, "In Order to Feel" (preface), *Out of Silence: Selected Poems*, edited by Daniels, Evanston, Illinois: Northwestern University Press, 1992

Herzog, Anne F., and Janet E. Kaufman, editors, *"How Shall We Tell Each Other of the Poet?": The Life and Writing of Muriel Rukeyser*, New York: St. Martin's Press, 1999

Kaufman, Janet E., "Muriel Rukeyser," in *Jewish American Women Writers: A Bio-bibliographical and Critical Sourcebook*, edited by Ann R. Shapiro, et. al., Westport, Connecticut, and London: Greenwood Press, 1994

Kertesz, Louise, *The Poetic Vision of Muriel Rukeyser*, Baton Rouge: Louisiana State University Press, 1980

Rukeyser, Muriel, "The Education of a Poet," in *The Writer on Her Work*, 2 vols., edited by Janet Sternburg, New York and London: Norton, 1980–91

Rukeyser, Muriel, *A Muriel Rukeyser Reader*, edited by Jan Heller Levi, New York and London: Norton, 1994

Rukeyser, Muriel, *The Life of Poetry*, New York: Current Books, 1949

Whitehead, Kim, *The Feminist Poetry Movement*, Jackson: University Press of Mississippi, 1996


## The Book of the Dead

Muriel Rukeyser's early long poem "The Book of the Dead" is a work of documentary witness. It was first published as the opening 63-page sequence of 20 lyrics from Rukeyser's second volume of poetry, *U.S. 1* (1938). In it Rukeyser adopts and adapts the documentary techniques and reform-minded politics that are central to the projects of other experimental documentary works of the 1930s, including the WPA photographs of Walker Evans and Margaret Bourke-White, Charles Reznikoff's testimonial poems, and John Dos Passos' experiments with newsreel-style writing. But more than a documentary representation of what is or was, "The Book of the Dead" is also an epic work that aspires to voice its audience's shared heritage, identity, and sensibility. From its opening lines, in which the poet intones, "These are the roads to take when you think of your country," it is a forward-looking attempt to reclaim for poetry the prerogative of fashioning what Pound called "the tale of the tribe." "The Book of the Dead" is Rukeyser's refashioning of the epic for modern times: she gives new life to a seemingly archaic form by fusing it with the transformative possibilities of new documentary technologies.

"The Book of the Dead" focuses attention on a mining disaster that took place in West Virginia in the 1930s. While drilling a tunnel for a hydro-electric project, miners discovered silica, a valuable but dangerous mineral. The directors of the project increased the size of the excavation to maximize the amount of silica removed, but they neglected the safety of the workers, many of whom consequently died of silicosis. The glass-like dust of the silica invaded workers' lungs, and, as the dust caused scars to form, the affected workers slowly suffocated. At least several hundred and perhaps as many as several thousand workers died. Company doctors diagnosed many of the affected as suffering from pneumonia so that the company would not appear responsible, and some were buried in mass graves to hide the extent of the disaster. Several lawsuits were filed and a Congressional investigation took place, but few reparations ended up in the hands of the survivors, and Congress did not pass any laws to reform mining practices or change disability compensation laws. Rukeyser's documentary poem reveals and challenges this institutional failure to protect human life.

The language and sensibility of the camera frames many sections of the poem. The poem "Gauley Bridge," for instance, opens with a "Camera at the crossing" that "sees the city," and the remainder of the poem chronicles what is seen by this "camera eye." When, at the end of this poem, Rukeyser asks, "What do you want—a cliff over a city? / . . . These people live here," her poetic lens sees through Romantic expectations to the hard reality. To further ground her poem in the reality of things, Rukeyser also includes snippets of Congressional testimony, stock quotes, and even scientific formulas. Perhaps the most moving of her documentary techniques is her use of testimonials to convey the suffering of the victims. The poem "Absalom," for instance, is in the voice of a woman who lost her husband and three sons. At one point the mother recalls the words of her youngest son:

> "Mother, when I die,
> I want you to have them open me up and
> see if that dust killed me.
> Try and get compensation,
> you will not have any way of making your living
> when we are gone,
> and the rest are going too."

With these techniques Rukeyser crafts a reality-making poem that pierces the complacencies of the official histories of the disaster. She creates a more convincing story than those told by the doctors, stockholders, and Congressmen whose authority to initially determine the meaning and consequences of the disaster depended on their institutional location. Rukeyser's poem attempts to formulate a more democratic access to power in which a collective participation in the discovery of the real takes precedence over any individual authority.

The language of witness so central to the documentary aspects of the poem also impacts the significance and function of its more traditional epic machinery. Rukeyser's facts, figures, and voices are entwined within a mythic structure that invests this single disaster with more than a local, temporary importance. In "Power," for instance, Rukeyser revisits the epic descent into the underworld. She meditates on the power of man and the power of the natural world as she leads the reader on a tour into the nearly finished tunnels beneath the dam. When the poet and her Milton-quoting guide of an engineer pause in a subterranean tunnel, the poet writes:

> This is the midway between water and flame,
> this is the road to take when you think of your country,
> between the dam and the furnace, terminal.

Here she not only describes the power of the engineering feat realized in the dam but also invokes her own poetic method: the structure of conservation is tied to that of transformation. The poem builds authority through the accumulation of dissenting voices, an epic that accesses not just traditional languages of power but also new possibilities that lie at the intersection of these multiple voices. As she writes in the final poem of the sequence:

> Defense is sight; widen the lens and see
> standing over the land myths of identity,
> new signals, processes:
>
> Alloys begin: certain dominant metals.
> Deliberate combines add new qualities,
> sums of new uses.

Whereas Pound, Eliot, and Williams turned to the epic to freeze a tradition into place, for Rukeyser it served as the best resource to use against stasis and exclusion because of its capacity to effect new alloys of dominant traditions. Rukeyser's "The Book of the Dead," when read against the dominant tradition of the Modernist epic, debunks the limited masculine uses of epic as only one of many possible poetic articulations of the social. This transformative engagement with a purportedly dead form is the lesson of Rukeyser's work for contemporary attempts at reconstructing the epic.

SCOTT MACPHAIL

**Further Reading**


Davidson, Michael, *Ghostlier Demarcations: Modern Poetry and the Material World,* Berkeley: University of California Press, 1997

Herzog, Anne F., and Janet E. Kaufman, editors, *"How Shall We Tell Each Other of the Poet?" The Life and Writing of Muriel Rukeyser,* New York: St. Martin's Press, 1999

Kadlec, David, "X-Ray Testimonials in Muriel Rukeyser," *Modernism/Modernity* 5 (1998)

Kalaidjian, Walter, *American Culture between the Wars: Revisionary Modernism and Postmodern Critique,* New York: Columbia University Press, 1993

Kertesz, Louise, *The Poetic Vision of Muriel Rukeyser,* Baton Rouge: Louisiana State University Press, 1980

Thurston, Michael, "Documentary Modernism as Popular Front Poetics: Muriel Rukeyser's 'Book of the Dead,'" *Modern Language Quarterly* 60, no. 1 (1999)

# S

## Mary Jo Salter 1954–

In her epigraph to *Sunday Skaters* (1994), her third collection of poems, Mary Jo Salter quotes from W.H. Auden's "New Year Letter":

> . . . each for better or for worse
> Must carry round with him through life,
> A judge, a landscape, and a wife.

These lines provide a synopsis of Salter's predominant subjects. She frequently references artists (Purcell to Lennon, Dickinson to Frost) she "judges" to be of merit; she describes the various landscapes she has inhabited; she writes stirringly about being a wife and a mother; and, increasingly, she documents moving "through life," discovering its glorious, grave, and transient nature.

Although Salter has never painted a wholly sanguine picture of domestic life, in her earlier poems about courtship, the early years of marriage, and pregnancy her tone is predominantly celebratory, although at times arch. In "Aubade for Brad," from *Henry Purcell in Japan* (1985), she lovingly chides her diligent husband who has risen early to write:

> . . . I'd joyfully disprove
> that formula by which all Energy
> converts to (printed) Matter
> and devote, this morning, some of it to Love.
> Darling, if you'll untie
> your shoes again and lie
> for a moment here, while the sun turns all to gold,
> I may grow very bold.

In later poems, such as "What Do Women Want?," the opening poem of *Sunday Skaters,* Salter continues to celebrate the comforts of domesticity but begins to admit its inadequacies. In "A Leak Somewhere," from *A Kiss in Space* (1999), her tone takes on a plangent, even poignant, quality. After watching a poorly made film on the Titanic disaster, Salter writes:

> Oh, you and I can laugh. But having
> turned off the set, and led the kids
> upstairs into dry beds, we sense
>
> that hidden in the house a fine
> crack—nothing spectacular,
> only a leak somewhere—is slowly
> widening to claim each of us
> in random order, and we start to rock
> in one another's arms.

Salter recognizes the cyclical nature of life: relationships, families, and even civilizations continually form, fall, and reconfigure. The fact that life is transient does not necessitate that it be trivial, however. In *Sunday Skaters* Salter quotes Thomas Jefferson: "Young poets complain often that life is fleeting and transient. We find in it seasons and situations however which move heavily enough." The "fleeting and transient" yet "heavy" seasons of life are manifest in "The Twelfth Year":

> Now, as we talked in circles, grim, accusing,
> we watched the green trees turning too and losing
> one by one every leaf, those bleeding hearts.
> . . . .
> When the circle broke at last it wasn't silence
> or speech that helped us, neither faith not will
> nor anything that people do at all;
> love made us green for no sure cause on earth
> and grew, like our children, from miracle.

She attests elsewhere in the same volume: "Love is reborn by surprise, / and increasingly as we get older."

In "Fire-Breathing Dragon," the opening poem of *A Kiss in Space,* Salter describes a hot-air balloon ride over Chartres. The ride proves a microcosm of the life cycle, as Salter views it. During the balloon's ascent, well-wishers on the ground shout greetings and send "a wave of blessing," and the riders feel

> already it's impossible
>
> we'd ever assent to landing, or
> follow any command but those
> of the puffed-up, roaring heart.

During the descent, Salter feels "deflated," but "who wouldn't?" Nonetheless, this phase of the ride also brings unexpected joys:

> Now,
> as if cabled to the sun that drops

off the rim of the world, we start
to descend; the snap of treetops

snagging under our basket turns
the stomach a little; the pilot turns
to me gallantly with a leaf bouquet
snatched in midair and suddenly
we're kissing (as he says) the tall
grasses hissing under us,
before we buck like a bronco to
a halt that is not a fall.

The poem concludes on a note of unequivocal celebration: "we fill our glasses with champagne / whose balloons by the hundreds rise."

Naturally, many of Salter's endings prove less sanguine. As she grows older, death becomes a more prominent subject in her work. In *Unfinished Painting* (1989) Salter tenderly records the deaths of her mother, father-in-law, and 28-year-old friend Etsuko, a suicide. Although Salter acknowledges that life will continue—her own children and Etsuko's have already been born—death nonetheless proves inexorable and irrevocable. Even the "monumental" rainbow shining over Paris in "A Rainbow over the Seine" (*A Kiss in Space*) seems ironic in that it promises nothing but its own demise:

the triumph of this *arc-
en-ciel,* the dazzle
of this monumental
prism cut by drizzle, is
that it vanishes.

Salter's emotional range has sometimes been criticized as narrow, perhaps because many contemporary readers have grown accustomed to stridency. Her tone is complex; its celebratory and witty qualities bear similarity to Emily Dickinson's and Elizabeth Bishop's. Salter rejoices in the moments in which the quotidian is transformed into the wondrous. Nor should one overlook her ironic, Elizabethan-style wit; she manages to smirk at painful truths. In "Brownie Troop *722 Visits the Nursing Home" (*Sunday Skaters*), for instance, she begins humorously—

As if being eight-five or ninety
and terrified and talked down to loudly
and pushed around in wheelchairs by the staff
all day weren't bad enough,

for tonight's entertainment the local Brownies
have come to sing Christmas carols. Nice
youngsters, all of them, but so off-
key that it could kill you off

just listening. Didn't they ever practice?

—only to conclude on a serious note: the only gift the seniors desire is "another spring . . . only to see the spring."

Similarly, Salter uses wit to grapple with the horrific, to disarm readers, thus startling them into recognizing the ways they overlook horror and forcing them to contemplate its full import. In "Welcome to Hiroshima" the poet describes the city as she finds it in the 1980s when she comes to see the memorial museum:

. . . a channel
silent in the TV of the brain

projects those flickering re-runs of a cloud
that brims its risen columnful like beer
and, spilling over, hangs its foamy head,
you feel a thirst for history: what year

it started to be safe to breathe the air,
and when to drink the blood and scum afloat
on the Ohta River. But no, the water's clear,
they pour it for your morning cup of tea

in one of the countless sunny coffee shops
whose plastic dioramas advertise
mutations of cuisine behind the glass:
a pancake sandwich; a pizza someone tops

with a maraschino cherry.

Salter considers writing a sacred act. In "The Rebirth of Venus," a poem about a sidewalk artist rendering Botticelli's masterpiece in chalk, Salter implores the Muses: "Slow gods of Art, late into afternoon // let there be light." She asserts that one of the primary functions of art is to document all that is meaningful and notable in life:

Let's face it: life means precious little.
Which is why we keep staring at it, and the beautiful
is the ideal, why pictures have to be painted.

As her poems attest, she finds pain as meaningful as beauty; in Frost's phrase, her poems provide only a "momentary stay against confusion." Defeat, tragedy, and loss always linger and sometimes prevail. Although her tone has grown darker, Salter continues to shun nihilism and to depict instead "a world I've pieced / together with a kind of faith."

SHERRI LYNN VANDENAKKER

**Biography**

Born in Grand Rapids, Michigan, 15 August 1954. Attended Harvard University, Cambridge, Massachusetts, B.A. 1976; New Hall, University of Cambridge, England, M.A. 1978; Instructor, Harvard University, 1978–79; staff editor, *Atlantic Monthly,* 1978–80; Instructor in English at various institutions in Japan, 1980–83; Lecturer, Mount Holyoke College, South Hadley, Massachusetts, 1984–85, 1987–88, and since 1990; poet-in-residence, Robert Frost Place, Franconia, New Hampshire, 1981; visiting artist, American Academy in Rome, 1985; Instructor, University of Iceland, Reykjavík, 1989–90; poetry editor, *New Republic,* from 1992; monthly columnist, *The Read* (online magazine). Received Discovery Prize from *The Nation,* 1983; National Endowment of the Arts fellowship, 1983–84; Lamont Poetry Prize, Academy of American Poets, 1988; Ingram Merrill Foundation fellowship, 1989; Witter Bynner Foundation Poetry Prize, from American Academy of Arts and Letters, 1989; Peter I.B. Lavan Award, from Academy of American Poets, 1990; Guggenheim fellowship, 1993; Amy Lowell Poetry traveling scholarship; Bogliasco fellowship, the Liguria Study Center for the Arts and Humanities, Bogliasco, Italy, 1998. Living in Amherst, Massachusetts.

**Poetry**
*Henry Purcell in Japan,* 1985
*Unfinished Painting,* 1989
*Sunday Skaters,* 1994
*A Kiss in Space,* 1999

**Other Writings:** children's literature (*The Moon Comes Home,* 1989); edited anthology of poetry (*The Norton Anthology of Poetry,* 4th edition [with Margaret Ferguson and Jon Stallworthy], 1996).

**Further Reading**

Benfey, Christopher, "Dickinson's Children," *New Republic* (17 and 24 July 1989)
Cole, Henri, "Short Reviews," *Poetry* 156 (April 1990)
Logan, William, "*Henry Purcell in Japan,*" *Parnassus* 12, no. 2 (1985)
Phillips, Robert, "Utterly Unlike," *Hudson Review* 52, no. 4 (Winter 2000)
Shaw, Robert B., "*Sunday Skaters,*" *Poetry* 166, no. 2 (May 1995)

---

## Sonia Sanchez 1934–

For Sonia Sanchez, art and politics are inseparable. As a result, she writes poetry that is both politically and linguistically revolutionary. Sanchez is a poet, activist, teacher, and scholar who has worked in every aspect of her life to liberate African-Americans from oppression. Her poetry reflects this struggle, demanding accountability for the past and producing hope for the future.

Born Wilsonia Driver in Birmingham, Alabama, Sanchez stuttered as a child, making her shy but at the same time giving her an increased appreciation for language and communication. She overcame this difficulty to earn a B.A. degree in political science from Hunter College in 1955. She then attended New York University for one year, doing graduate work in poetry under the mentorship of Louise Bogan.

Sanchez's career as a writer blossomed in the 1960s when she joined the Black Arts movement with Amiri Baraka (then LeRoi Jones), Don L. Lee (later Haki Madhubuti), Nikki Giovanni, and Dudley Randall, among others. Her work reflects her belief that poets have "got to make statements about what is happening in the world." Her first volume of poetry, *Homecoming* (1969), features a militant black voice and an unflinching gaze at racial prejudice in America. Overtly political, *Homecoming* seeks to awaken black culture to its oppression by white America. The title poem "homecoming," one of her most famous works, contains the major themes that mark her career: the return to black culture, the need for political action and spirituality in American life, and the question of black identity. In this volume Sanchez experiments with words, space, and typography, liberating poetry from white rationality while providing textual clues for performance. For instance, "to Chuck" offers a humorous yet scathing parody of an E.E. Cummings poem, pushing the limits of language through word division and line breaks while also playing with female sexual desire. Sanchez is concerned with female identity, including being able to express sexuality in its diverse forms. Her poems always reflect her personal journey as a black woman in America, and she is critical of men, black or white, who seek to reinstall patriarchal norms in the black community.

*We a BaddDDD People* (1970), Sanchez's next volume, also labels the enemies and celebrates the heroes of black culture. She celebrates Malcolm X, John Coltrane, and Billie Holiday, fellow African-Americans who sought to communicate the black experience through their words and their music. In this insurgent volume, she again mixes the political and the personal to great effect. *Love Poems* (1973), a volume of less strident lyrics, signals her maturation in content and technique as she distills the emotion of her earlier work into strict form poems, including sonnets and haikus. *A Blues Book for Blue Black Magical Women* (1974) asks the "Queens of the Universe" to resist racist Western life and to follow her in a spiritual journey into the past, enacting the symbolic rebirth of all African-American women. This volume in particular reflects her conversion to Islam, which coincided with her marriage to Etheridge Knight.

Sanchez's most recognized work is *Homegirls and Handgrenades* (1984), a collection that won the American Book Award in 1985. A combination of free verse, prose poems, haikus, and tankas, the collection applies the emotional force of the earlier books to social action. These poems are public utterances that evoke the struggle of the past and exhort readers to fight for the future. Sanchez wants to explode the traditional myths that people hold about themselves and the world. She travels through the anger and pain of oppression to find a productive space from which to change the present. In "Bluebirdbluebirdthrumywindow," she details an encounter with a homeless woman, asking readers to see the poor woman's humanity. "MIAs" depicts the murders of blacks in Atlanta, Johannesburg, and El Salvador, ending with an exhortation for freedom, the goal of all Sanchez's work. *Under a Soprano Sky* (1987) also reflects her spiritual and artistic growth. The title poem is both an elegy for her brother and slaughtered black men in Philadelphia and a lyric poem of her body and the natural world. Accounts of racial oppression mingle with heroic tributes. A diverse group of voices is used to represent the past, reflecting the oral traditions of black culture and of her poetry. The final section, "Endings," provides a promising vision of the future through new poets' work and her sons' high school graduations. Her later poetry heralds a combination of love and justice that will energize America's future.

Sanchez's poetry is oral by nature. To fully appreciate her poems requires hearing them read aloud. She has developed a unique reading style for her performances, a style based on the tradition of call and response in African-American culture. She uses traditional chants, screams, songs, and other sound elements to add a musical quality to her lyrical poems. The blues and jazz are also natural influences for Sanchez; she mimics their structures and their improvisational style in her work.

Sanchez is also a teacher. She began her teaching career in San Francisco at the Downtown Community School and then at San Francisco State College, where she helped create the first Black Studies program. She has taught at many schools, including Temple University, where she teaches today. She continues to write and to perform, having published recent three volumes of poetry: *Does Your House Have Lions?* (1997), *Like the Singing Coming Off the Drums: Love Poems* (1998), and *Shake Loose My Skin: New and Selected Poems* (1999). These volumes combine the political activism and fluid lyricism of her earlier work with a tempered quality of experience and wisdom. The political advocacy contained in her poetry, her pedagogy, and her philosophy seeks to eradicate black oppression and to spread love and inspiration in America.

DAVID E. MAGILL

*See also* Black Arts Movement

**Biography**

Born Wilsonia Benita Driver in Birmingham, Alabama, 9 September 1934. Attended Hunter College, New York, B.A. in political science 1955; New York University, 1959–60; on staff, Downtown Community School, 1965–67, and Mission Rebels in Action, 1968–69, San Francisco; Instructor, San Francisco State College, 1967–69; Lecturer in black literature, University of Pittsburgh, 1969–70, Rutgers University, New Brunswick, New Jersey, 1970–71, Manhattan Community College, New York, 1971–73, and City University of New York, 1972; Assistant Professor, Amherst College, Massachusetts, 1972–73, and University of Pennsylvania, Philadelphia, 1976–77; Associate Professor of English, 1977–79, since 1979 Professor of English, Provost's Office Faculty Fellow, 1986–87, Presidential Fellow, 1987–88, and Laura Carnell Chair in English, 1988–99, Temple University, Philadelphia; columnist, *American Poetry Review,* 1977–78, and Philadelphia *Daily News,* 1982–83. Received PEN Award, 1969; American Academy grant, 1970; National Endowment for the Arts Award, 1978; Smith College Tribute to Black Women Award, 1982; Lucretia Mott Award, 1984; American Book Award, 1985; Before Columbus Foundation Award, 1985; Pew fellowship in the arts, 1993; honorary Ph.D. in fine arts, Wilberforce University, Ohio, 1972. Living in Philadelphia, Pennsylvania.

**Poetry**

*Homecoming,* 1969
*We a BaddDDD People,* 1970
*It's a New Day: Poems for Young Brothas and Sistuhs,* 1971
*Love Poems,* 1973
*A Blues Book for Blue Black Magical Women,* 1974
*I've Been a Woman: New and Selected Poems,* 1978; revised edition, 1985
*Homegirls and Handgrenades,* 1984
*Generations: Selected Poetry, 1969–1985,* 1986
*Under a Soprano Sky,* 1987
*Wounded in the House of a Friend,* 1995
*Does Your House Have Lions?* 1997
*Like the Singing Coming Off the Drums: Love Poems,* 1998
*Shake Loose My Skin: New and Selected Poems,* 1999

**Other Writings:** plays (*I'm Black When I'm Singing, I'm Blue When I Ain't,* 1982), short stories (*A Sound Investment,* 1980), children's literature, speeches (*Crisis in Culture,* 1983); edited collections of literature (*We Be Word Sorcerers: 25 Stories by Black Americans,* 1973).

**Further Reading**

Baker, Houston A., Jr., "Our Lady: Sonia Sanchez and the Writing of a Black Renaissance," in *Black Feminist Criticism and Critical Theory,* edited by Baker and Joe Weixlmann, Greenwood, Florida: Penkevill, 1988

Cook, William, "The Black Arts Poets," in *The Columbia History of American Poetry,* edited by Jay Parini and Brett C. Millier, New York: Columbia University Press, 1993

Evans, Mari, editor, *Black Women Writers (1950–1980): A Critical Evaluation,* Garden City, New York: Anchor Press/ Doubleday, 1983

Gabbin, Joanne, "The Southern Imagination of Sonia Sanchez," in *Southern Women Writers: The New Generation,* edited by Tonette Bond Inge, Tuscaloosa: University of Alabama Press, 1990

Melhem, D.L., *Heroism in the New Black Poetry: Introductions and Interviews,* Lexington: University Press of Kentucky, 1990

Palmer, R. Roderick, "The Poetry of Three Revolutionists: Don L. Lee, Sonia Sanchez, and Nikki Giovanni," *CLA Journal* 15, no. 1 (September 1971)

Sitter, Deborah Ayer, "Sonia Sanchez," in *The Oxford Companion to African American Literature,* edited by William L. Andrews, Frances Smith Foster, and Trudier Harris, Oxford and New York: Oxford University Press, 1997

Tate, Claudia, editor, *Black Women Writers at Work,* New York: Continuum, and Harpenden, Hertfordshire: Oldcastle, 1983

---

# Carl Sandburg 1878–1967

With his *Chicago Poems* (1916), Carl Sandburg initiated the free-verse trend of 20th-century American poetry. He exemplified what Yeats considered the role of the poet, conveying the thoughts of the wise man in the speech of the common people. For the first time verse was truly "plain speech," describing the modern world in a savvy vernacular that was not intellectual imitation of colloquial talk, but the talk of a man who knew the rough and reckless streets, railroads, factories, and farms of American life. Laboring beside the working poor, sharing their sweat and strain, became Sandburg's life's mission and the subject matter of his poetry and prose. His plain technique and plain talk started a poetic revolution.

Born in Galesburg, Illinois, to recent Swedish immigrants, Sandburg was raised to be a worker by necessity, following the example of his father, a machinist's blacksmith. Sandburg was filled with a sense of adventure, however; he volunteered for the Spanish-American War in 1898, and his "letters" home became news for the Galesburg newspaper. On his return to the United States he pursued opportunities to write while mostly doing odd jobs and wandering about. The common men and women, always underdogs in Sandburg's view, became the heroes of his America. An active socialist, for many years Sandburg worked alongside his heroes doing whatever he could to make ends meet.

In 1912 Harriet Monroe founded *Poetry* magazine in Chicago, and it became the preeminent influence on American verse as Monroe herself became the patroness of modern poetry, introducing many of the poets who would dominate the century, including Sandburg. In a 1914 issue Monroe published a sequence of Sandburg's poems about Chicago's diverse urban-industrial landscape. Sandburg's poems used prose sensitized by the convention of "poetic" line breaks to enhance the natural colloquial rhythms of someone simply talking. Whitman was Sandburg's model and inspiration, but by 1914 Whitman had faded into the background of American poetry, obscured by the excessively genteel verbiage of *fin-de-siècle* floridity that emphasized artifice over reality.

Sandburg's style could not have been more different. Words such as "Hog Butcher," "railroads," "painted women," "gunman," "tool maker," "sweating," "building," "breaking," and "rebuilding" were not unique as single entities, but their use in the staccato cadences of pub talk, stacked together in a rush of stark and dusty "citified" images rather than green "countrified" images, became a sensation. Some readers were shocked at many of the brutal images and protested; more were moved by the contrasting underlying respect and tenderness. One of the poems published in *Poetry,* "Chicago," earned the Levinson Prize as the best single poem published in the magazine for that year.

World War I was in progress when the October 1915 edition of *Poetry* included 17 poems by Sandburg, unprecedented for a single poet. This success led to Sandburg's first volume of verse, *Chicago Poems,* the following year. Here was poetry that did not require an audience of intellectuals and academics; it was poetry that had come down from the ivory tower and found a place next to the daily news of the working-class American. Nonetheless, the majority of literary critics praised the groundbreaking book. The Sandburg era in American (and British) poetry had begun. He became a celebrity, befriending other important writers of the era and traveling around the country with the same wanderlust of his younger days.

*Cornhuskers* (1918), Sandburg's next volume, employed the same style, vocabulary, and subject matter as its predecessor. From 1915 to 1918 Sandburg also published poems in leftist periodicals such as the *International Socialist Review;* many of these poems dealt with the tumult and tragedy of World War I, particularly after America's entry in 1917. Titles included "Killers," "Statistics," and "Ashes and Dreams," a lament for the mothers of the world who had lost their sons in war.

Sandburg became increasingly popular with his pungent and direct evocations of "real life." He was also a savvy self-promoter who used his popularity to solidify both his reputation and his audience. In 1920 Sandburg teamed with friend and fellow poet Lew Sarett for a reading tour modeled after that of poet Vachel Lindsay, who was renowned for reciting his poetry with the flair of a very capable thespian. Sarett wrote of the wilds and the plight of Native Americans while Sandburg was known for his Chicago poems; consequently, they were billed as the "city" poet and the "wilderness" poet. Sandburg read his poems and also played guitar and sang folk songs. He would become a champion of preserving America's folk heritage. Sandburg and Sarett's tour was well reviewed and highly successful, but thereafter Sandburg toured alone, guitar in hand.

In the 1920s more traditional critics posited that Sandburg's poems were actually prose and that his rough subjects were antithetical to the esoteric sublimity of true verse. Aldous Huxley, at this time still a cult figure among the intellectual *cognoscenti,* defended Sandburg and the "new" poetry in a 1923 essay called "The Subject Matter of Poetry." Huxley asserted that urban and industrial subjects were merely an extension of a reporting on reality as old as Homer and, therefore, not so new after all:

> Translated into practice this means that contemporary poets can now write, in the words of Mr. Sandburg, of the "harr and boom of the blast fires," of "wops and bohunks. . . ." Where Homer wrote of horses and tamers of horses, our contemporaries write of trains, automobiles, and the various species of wops and bohunks who control the horsepower. . . . The critics who would have us believe that there is something essentially unpoetical about a bohunk (whatever a bohunk may be) and something essentially poetical about Sir Lancelot of the Lake are, of course, simply negligible.

Huxley and the more progressive critics won out.

Even among his supporters, however, Sandburg's efforts through the 1920s and 1930s were considered to be static renditions of his early verse—poetry that still pleased but did not develop his talent further. By the 1930s, Sandburg had become devoted to writing his voluminous biography of Abraham Lincoln; this effort did not replace poetry but left no time for trying new approaches or techniques. Indeed, except for one notable volume in 1937, Sandburg's poetry remained the same for the rest of his career. Moreover, the fact that many poets were now writing like Sandburg also diminished his uniqueness.

Sandburg's last great poetic work, *The People, Yes* (1937), may have been inspired by the poet Haniel Long's *Pittsburgh Memoranda* (1935), which featured mystical homilies on Americana and for which Sandburg contributed to the book's jacket copy: "Black soot smudged some pages and blue mists float idly on others." Whether Long's book inspired Sandburg's next work or solidified his ideas for a work in progress, one thing is certain: both books contain a profoundly monumental exposition of the American Everyman.

In 1937 the United States was emerging from the Great Depression and also starting to take notice of the rise of fascism in Europe and Asia. The former was cause for celebration, for America had persevered to overcome a grave economic crisis; the latter prompted Sandburg to remind his fellow citizens that

American democracy should not be taken for granted. Sandburg's voluminous collection of folk wit and wisdom saved through the years (he had made a practice of writing down every generic saying, anecdote, or story that struck his fancy) became the core of *The People, Yes,* which is dedicated to "contributors dead and living." In a prologue Sandburg describes *The People, Yes* as "being several stories and psalms nobody would want to laugh at / interspersed with memoranda variations worth a second look."

While the folk material serves as the core of the volume, Sandburg's own words comprise the majority of verse so that the core radiates with a sense of drama underscored with a philosophy about the "family of man." Sandburg's family is American by description, universal by implication. Sandburg's "variations"—reiterations rather than repetitions—add layer upon layer, building to a powerful paean to the "common man." *The People, Yes* is Sandburg's greatest achievement and stands as perhaps the single most definitive verse epic about an idealized American way of life. This is not to say that Sandburg's epic does not recognize faults in this way of life or chastise the "robber barons" who live well from the labor of others, but Sandburg's overall message is that America's great experiment in democracy will prevail. He ends his epic as he begins it: "Where to . . . ? What next?"

After 1937 Sandburg's output declined and he began to write poems about children and nature rather than social issues. He dabbled in music, autobiography, and fiction to much less effect. A public figure, he enjoyed his many public appearances and recitals, eventually becoming, along with Frost, a grand old man of American poetry. He is one of the major figures in 20th-century American poetry.

DAVID GARRETT IZZO

*See also* Midwestern Poetry Renaissance

**Biography**

Born in Galesburg, Illinois, 6 January 1878. Attended Lombard College, Galesburg (editor, *Lombard Review*), 1899–1902; served in the Sixth Illinois Volunteers during the Spanish-American War, 1899, Private; on staff of *Tomorrow* magazine, 1906; associate editor, *Lyceumite,* 1907–08; district organizer, Social-Democratic Party, Appleton, Wisconsin, 1908; city hall reporter, Milwaukee *Journal,* 1909–10; secretary to Mayor of Milwaukee, 1910–12; city editor, Milwaukee *Social Democratic Herald,* 1911; on staff of Milwaukee *Leader* and Chicago *World,* 1912, and *Day Book,* 1912–17; associate editor, *System: The Magazine of Business,* 1913; Stockholm correspondent, 1918, and manager of the Chicago office, 1919, Newspaper Enterprise Association; reporter, editorial writer, and motion picture editor, 1917–30, and syndicated columnist, 1930–32, Chicago *Daily News;* Lecturer, University of Hawaii, Honolulu, 1934; Walgreen Foundation Lecturer, University of Chicago, 1940; weekly columnist, syndicated by the Chicago *Daily Times,* from 1941. Received Poetry Society of America Award, 1919, 1921; Friends of Literature Award, 1934; Roosevelt Memorial Association Prize, for biography, 1939; Pulitzer Prize, for history, 1940, for poetry, 1951; American Academy Gold Medal, 1952; National Association for the Advancement of Colored People Award, 1965; honorary degrees from 15 colleges and universities; member, American Academy, 1940; Commander, Order of the North Star (Sweden), 1953. Died in Flat Rock, North Carolina, 22 July 1967.

**Poetry**

*Chicago Poems,* 1916
*Cornhuskers,* 1918
*Smoke and Steel,* 1920
*Slabs of the Sunburnt West,* 1922
*(Poems),* edited by Hughes Mearns, 1926
*Selected Poems,* edited by Rebecca West, 1926
*Good Morning, America,* 1928
*Early Moon* (for children), 1930
*The People, Yes,* 1937
*Bronze Wood,* 1941
*Harvest Poems, 1910–1960,* 1960
*Six New Poems and a Parable,* 1961
*Honey and Salt,* 1963
*The Complete Poems of Carl Sandburg,* 1969; revised and expanded edition, 1970
*Breathing Tokens,* edited by Margaret Sandburg, 1978
*Rainbows Are Made* (for children), 1982
*Arithmetic* (for children), 1993
*Billy Sunday, and Other Poems,* 1993
*Grassroots: Poems* (for children), 1998
*Not Everyday an Aurora Borealis for Your Birthday: A Love Poem* (for children), 1998
*Poems for Children: Nowhere Near Old Enough to Vote,* 1999
*Poems for the People,* 1999

**Other Writings:** novel (*Remembrance Rock,* 1948), biography (*Abraham Lincoln: The War Years,* 4 vols., 1939; revised edition as *Storm over the Land,* 1942), autobiography (*Always the Young Strangers,* 1953), correspondence (*The Letters of Carl Sandburg,* edited by Herbert Mitgang, 1968), screenplay, film reviews (*Sandburg at the Movies: A Poet in the Silent Era, 1920–1927,* edited by Dale Fetherling and Doug Fetherling, 1985); edited collections of papers (*A Lincoln and Whitman Miscellany,* 1938).

**Further Reading**

Huxley, Aldous, "The Subject Matter of Poetry," in *Collected Essays,* by Huxley, New York: Harper, 1958; London: Chatto and Windus, 1959
Long, Haniel, *Pittsburgh Memoranda,* Santa Fe, New Mexico: Writers' Editions, 1935
MacLeish, Archibald, "Introduction," in *The Complete Poems of Carl Sandburg,* by Sandburg, New York: Harcourt Brace Jovanovich, 1969; revised and expanded edition, 1970
Niven, Penelope, *Carl Sandburg: A Biography,* New York: Scribners, 1991
Sandburg, Carl, *The Letters of Carl Sandburg,* edited by Herbert Mitgang, New York: Harcourt Brace and World, 1968
Untermeyer, Louis, *From Another World: The Autobiography of Louis Untermeyer,* New York: Harcourt Brace, 1939 (contains an extended profile on Sandburg)
Van Doren, Carl, "Carl Sandburg: Flame and Slag," in *Many Minds,* by Van Doren, New York: Knopf, 1924; reprint, Port Washington, New York: Kennikat Press, 1966

## Chicago Poems

The last of his books to be published while Carl Sandburg was a member of the Socialist Party, *Chicago Poems* (1916) assured the poet of a wide national audience as well as critical attention for the first time, thanks to the important publisher Henry Holt and Company (Sandburg's other volumes had, so far, been published by small presses). Critic Mark Van Wienen (1991) has defined the poems in the collection as "protests both against much of conventional American political life and against established literary practice," revealing that "Sandburg was busy propagating American socialism not only in his work as an organizer and a newspaperman, but also in the supposedly apolitical realm of literature."

*Chicago Poems* exposes the plight of the working classes in the growing metropolis and their exploitation at the hands of capitalists driven only by profit. Sandburg's effort to capture the lives of the urban workers is apparent in poems such as "Halsted Street Car," where the poet asks the cartoonists to follow him in his morning observations of people going to work:

> Try with your pencils for these crooked faces,
> That pig-sticker in one corner—his mouth—
> That overall factory girl—her loose cheeks.

The promise of opportunity and social mobility within the urban context has revealed itself to be a falsehood, and Sandburg paints the faces of the workers as "Tired of wishes / Empty of dreams." The typical Modernist pose of the poet as observer of the masses is coupled in Sandburg with progressive political commitment. Sandburg meditates on the contrast between the apparent promise of limitless possibility for all in the city and the boundaries and constriction forced by the upper classes on the lower ones. For example, take these lines from "A Fence":

> As a fence, it is a masterpiece, and will shut off the rabble and all vagabonds and hungry men and all wandering children looking for a place to play

Within this sympathetic portrayal of the working classes, *Chicago Poems* also displays awareness of the ethnic fragmentation of Chicago. "Onion Days" follows Mrs. Gabrielle Giovannitti while she goes to her work as onion picker for Jasper, a member of the Episcopalian church in Ravenswood, whose mind during sermons "wanders to his 700-acre farm and how he can make it produce more efficiently." Immigrant groups are also pointed out as having spiritual qualities that can regenerate urban life. For example, in "Happiness," the poet claims that while he asked professors and famous executives what happiness was, it was only when he saw a "crowd of Hungarians under the trees with their women and children and a keg of beer and an accordion" that he understood the meaning of happiness.

This negative view of urban space is balanced by Sandburg's faith in the growth of Chicago and its leading role for the nation. "Chicago," a dialogue between the poet and the city, expresses this tension from the very beginning of the collection. On the one hand, the poet claims to have seen "the gunman kill and go free to kill again" or "the marks of wanton hunger" on the faces of women and children. Yet it is clear that the poet is an apologist of the city who "turn[s] once more to those who sneer at this my city, and I give them back the sneer." Tellingly, Chicago is compared to an adolescent, implying that there is still scope for development, although the city has already reached its role as leader of America:

> Laughing the stormy, husky, brawling laughter of Youth, half-naked, sweating, proud to be Hog Butcher, Tool Maker, Stacker of Wheat, Player with Railroads and Freight Handler to the Nation.

Sandburg's vision of the city can be compared to that of naturalist novelists, such as Dreiser, who condemned the decay of urban life but were fascinated by its complexity, its tempo and liveliness. This fascination with city life is embodied by Sandburg's positive depiction of the symbol of urban space: the skyscraper. In "Skyscraper," Sandburg claims that the building "has a soul" that is given to it by the people who work in it and by those who built it. As Carl Smith (1984) has argued, Sandburg "saw the skyscraper as the urban community in microcosm and pointed out that its highest purpose was to serve and express the spirit of the people who inhabited it." Yet another interpretation is also possible. It is the people who serve the skyscraper and at times sacrifice themselves for it:

> (One man fell from a girder and broke his neck at the end of a straight plunge—he is here—his soul has gone into the stones of the building)

Sandburg's sympathetic and almost celebratory attitude toward the common people inhabiting the city finds a clear equivalent in his style, which, as Richard Gray (1990) has noticed, tends to devise "a poetic equivalent of folk speech." Sandburg's syntax is mainly paratactical (notice, in the examples given here, the recurrence of the conjunction "and"), and his different sentences are therefore not organized according to a hierarchy of main and subordinate clauses. Gray also observes Sandburg's distinctively insistent use of participles, "so as to dramatise the idea of life as a process." Tellingly, Sandburg's style becomes itself a popular hero as the poet claims, "Kill my style / and you break Pavlowa's legs / and you blind Ty Cobb's batting eye."

As Van Wienen (1991) has concluded, Sandburg brings together in *Chicago Poems* both the "language of poetic art removed from praxis and the diction of a politically committed poetry," thus bridging the gap between the two.

LUCA PRONO

**Further Reading**

Duffey, Bernard, *The Chicago Renaissance in American Letters: A Critical History,* East Lansing: Michigan State University Press, 1954

Gray, Richard, *American Poetry of the Twentieth Century,* London and New York: Longman, 1990

Smith, Carl S., *Chicago and the American Literary Imagination, 1880–1920,* Chicago: University of Chicago Press, 1984

Van Wienen, Mark, "Taming the Socialist: Carl Sandburg's *Chicago Poems* and Its Critics," *American Literature* 63, no. 1 (March 1991)

# San Francisco Renaissance

The San Francisco Renaissance seemed to burst upon the American scene in the 1950s like a tempest. Its defining characteristics—an intentional "provincialism," political and ecological awareness, a desire to broaden and democratize poetry's readership, and commitment to the performance or spoken aspect of poetry—had been developing over many years, however. It could be argued that "The Berkeley Renaissance" is a more appropriate designation since much of the activity revolved around poets associated with the University of California at Berkeley. As Edward Halsey Foster observes in *Jack Spicer* (1991), the movement was not really a renaissance: nothing was reborn, yet "the name seemed to call for manifestos and revolution, and indeed the poems and theories changed the direction of American poetry dramatically."

An early omen of the San Francisco Renaissance was a new collection of essays and poems sponsored by the northern California branch of the Federal Writers Project (*Material Gathered on the Federal Writers Project, San Francisco,* 1936). Kenneth Rexroth, who had moved to San Francisco in 1927, declared that such creative writing magazines of a regional nature would tap a large source of potential readers who were "too poor or too illiterate" to buy glossy national publications filled with stories and poems unrelated to their lives. In 1936 several writers' conferences encouraged writers to identify with their native region and to develop a strong sense of place. In Chicago Meridel LeSueur argued that rooting oneself in a particular region led to confident writers and receptive audiences (Aaron, 1961). Rexroth supported her views in a paper ("The Function of the Poet in Society"), contending that artists and writers should not only be supported with money but should also be provided with local outlets for distributing their work. Rexroth and others argued for a more democratic approach to the writing and reading of poetry, one that would nurture an artistic sensibility in all people, irrespective of race, region, or class (a position Walt Whitman had articulated in "Democratic Vistas" that had not been taken up by his contemporaries). All of this went against the grain of Modernism and New Criticism, which held that poetry should be written in an impersonal voice, in language of preconceived and historical order, in order to rise above ingenuous provincialism.

Signs of the new movement surfaced in California's Bay Area as poetry workshops and readings enlivened its cultural life. As early as 1919, Witter Bynner, poet and translator of Chinese poetry, conducted classes in the Extension Division of the University of California, Berkeley. James Hart, who would become director of the Bancroft Library, also led workshops in 1936. As many as 100 students attended James Caldwell's weekly poetry readings, which began in 1936 on the Berkeley campus. There were no major bookstores in San Francisco that could serve as meeting grounds for writers and their readers, however, and the few local publishers had little interest in poetry. No local literary magazines existed. Whatever momentum had developed was dissipated temporarily with the onset of World War II.

Ironically, the war played a substantial role in making the Bay Area an important literary region. Many conscientious objectors (COs) were living at the Civilian Public Service Camp at Waldport, Oregon, one of several camps established through the efforts of various churches to ensure humane treatment for COs. At special schools in these camps COs could request assignment according to their particular interests. Waldport became a fine arts center, with workshops for printers, writers, painters, musicians, and actors. Several artists from other camps transferred to Waldport, including Martin Ponch, who brought *The Compass* with him from the East Coast. Fresno-born poet William Everson was there, printing *Untide,* an arts and pacifist-anarchist newsletter that served as an alternative to the official newsletter of the camp, *The Tide.* On furloughs the men caught the bus to San Francisco, where many of them would call on Rexroth, who by the mid-1940s had become a man of letters with a volume of lyrical and political poems (*In What Hour,* 1940) to his credit. When the war ended many of the COs settled in San Francisco and Berkeley, bringing with them the little magazines and printing presses that would help create new outlets for linking the life of the imagination to a pacifist-anarchist consciousness.

Rexroth was "at home" on Potrero Hill Friday evenings. Started as a literary soiree of sorts, this occasion grew into regular gatherings for poetry readings, philosophical debate, storytelling, and social banter. These sessions provided what Tom Parkinson described as "genuinely intellectual discussions" and a sense of community for Bay Area poets and philosophical anarchists (see *The Literary Review* [Fall 1988]). Several of the poets who attended these gatherings, among them Muriel Rukeyser, William Everson, Jack Spicer, Tom Parkinson, and Robert Duncan, also attended meetings of the Libertarian Circle, a group of philosophical anarchists. Duncan organized additional programs at a rundown rooming house on Telegraph Avenue called Throckmorton Manor. On the Berkeley campus Josephine Miles coordinated poetry readings and classes, some of them conducted by her own graduate students, including Spicer, Duncan, and Robin Blaser. In San Francisco Madeline Gleason arranged a series of readings that many Berkeley poets attended.

By 1954 Ruth Witt-Diamant had founded the Poetry Center at San Francisco State College; she made sure that it was funded in part with private money so that she could schedule readings off campus for audiences disinclined to hear poetry in an academic setting. Yvor Winters attracted high-powered graduate students to his Stanford classroom, among them Thom Gunn, J.V. Cunningham, and Herbert Blau, who would become the co-director of the Actors Workshop. More informally, the literary scene could be observed in coffeehouses and clubs like the Black Cat, The Cellar, Cafe Trieste, The Place, Gino & Carlo's, and Vesuvio's.

Among the new magazines that offered a forum for postwar West Coast literary energy, *Circle* was the earliest and perhaps the best known. It was anti-war, anti-authoritarian, and committed to new art forms. Its editor, George Leite, owned a bookstore called Daliel's, which acted like a literary center, celebrating with parties and readings the books sold there by Bay Area poets. In the first issue Leite declared that the journal would look to Europe and the Surrealists for inspiration but would welcome native writers. West Coast poets in the ten published issues of the magazine included Rexroth, Philip Lamantia, Everson, Duncan, Miles, and Kenneth Patchen. Other magazines that would contribute to the Bay Area's growing avant-garde, politically hip reputation were *Ark, City Lights, Goad, Inferno, Golden Goose,* and *Beatitude.*

Adding to the furor created by the new movement was an article published in *Harper's* of April 1947, "The New Cult of Sex and Anarchy," by Mildred Edie Brady, a freelancer living in Berkeley.

Denigrating both the art and intellectual activity that had emerged in the Bay Area, she divided these new bohemians into two camps: the Henry Millers and the Kenneth Rexroths. Those who gravitated toward Miller did so because of his pacifist booklet *Murder the Murderers,* and because they admired his uncensored books such as *The Colossus of Maroussi* and *The Air Conditioned Nightmare,* from which they "imbibed an engaging potpourri of mysticism, egoism, sexualism, surrealism and anarchism." This group emulated Miller's lifestyle, living in ramshackle cabins along the coast near Monterey.

Rexroth's group was more bookish: they discussed English anarchists and Kropotkin, "leavening the politics liberally with psychoanalytic interpretations from [Wilhelm] Reich," the inventor of orgone therapy. Brady insisted that their poetry was incomprehensible and was convinced that both groups placed their faith in the irrational and measured their spiritual and psychological health by the number of orgasms they could achieve. Her remarks stirred up things in the Bay Area, although not everyone took her seriously.

For many Bay Area poets the life of the imagination became intertwined with political consciousness, defining what William Everson described as a "distinct West Coast literary situation" in which the "poet's role as *vates* was affirmed, [and] his prophetic stance as refresher and invigorator of stultified literary social forms was asserted" (Everson, 1976). These poets made no attempt to separate poetry and politics, nor did they use the front of masques or personae in their poems. Many of them wanted ecological awareness and the West Coast landscape—the Pacific Ocean and California's mountains and forests—to assume an increasingly vital role in their work, as indeed it did in the case of Rexroth, Everson, and later Gary Snyder. The sense of sacramental presence in all things, reminiscent of Walt Whitman's discovery that each particle of matter contains an immensity, is evident in Rexroth's "Spring, Coast Range" from *In What Hour* (1940).

The writers of this period really thought that their poetry would make the world a better place. Although these poets risked sounding polemical, they often succeeded in articulating their pacifist, anti-imperialist politics because they approached their writing organically, as part of a larger creative act inspired by the rhythms of the natural world and their particular region. For all their confidence in their own political positions and their determination to be poets, they were humble about language and vision, aware that words and the world around them were not commodities. Moreover, their willingness to experiment with ways of perception and coherence itself encouraged younger generations of writers to trust their fresh visions of the world.

In this atmosphere of public concern, the concept of poetry as performance was revived and poetry/jazz became popular. Soon a radio station, KPFA, the first listener-sponsored station in the country, was founded. It created yet another outlet for poetry readings and book reviews, and also enabled poets to protest against the Korean War and rampant McCarthyism. Those associated with this revolution sought to mesh their art with their lifestyle, working to build a community that nurtured and supported all its inhabitants, whatever their vocation. Since they were not a homogenous group, tensions and ideological differences often surfaced. Nonetheless, these poets who made the Renaissance happen embodied the romantic spirit in their desire and determination to shape a new sense of community and a pluralistic social order.

Robert Duncan, one of the true stars of this group, opposed the implication that regionalism bound him to the other poets who happened to be writing in the Bay Area. It was coincidental, he thought, that he was grouped with the San Francisco poets. For Duncan "place" was "an imaginative construct, the boundaries of which are constantly under revision" (Davidson, 1989). He felt bound less by region and more by "coterie," the particular group of poets with whom he associated, many of them homosexual (Faas, 1978). His disclaimed ties to Modernism, however, put him at home with his San Francisco colleagues, as did his interest in non-Western cultures. Moreover, Duncan assumed a similar nonhierarchical stance toward his environment as a source of inspiration. In "Towards an Open Universe" Duncan states:

> [T]he imagination of this cosmos is as immediate to me as the imagination of my household or my self, for I have taken my being in what I know of the sun and of the magnitude of the cosmos, as I have taken my being in what I know of domestic things. (Nemerov, 1966)

A general air of optimism prevailed through the mid-1960s as the city received a whole new generation of writers who wanted to write poetry of hope and responsibility that articulated the human experience in fresh terms. Their strong sense of place became "the ground of numinous presence . . . a vehicle for participating directly in ecological orders" (Davidson, 1989). Their intentions were distorted and initially misunderstood by the inordinate attention East Coast media gave the Renaissance, however, largely in the form of sensational accounts of their frequent public readings in smoke-filled jazz clubs. The most memorable of these readings occurred on 13 October 1955 when Allen Ginsberg, Michael McClure, Philip Whalen, Philip Lamantia, and Gary Snyder read their poetry at the Six Gallery, an auto-repair garage converted into a space for young Bay Area artists. The Six Gallery Reading became one of the most celebrated events in San Francisco literary history, and with it the media announced that the Beat Generation had arrived. Ginsberg's "Howl" got the greatest attention at the reading. While San Francisco is only part of its locale, its evocative, incantatory qualities, its politics, its blatantly personal style, its very openness put it at home in the Bay Area.

Rexroth's early defense of the Beats ("Disengagement and the Art of the Beat Generation") helped define their niche in literary history and reiterated the mission of Bay Area poets, for whom the act of creation was an effective defense against despair and hopelessness. Their heroes, most notably Blake, Lawrence, and Whitman, were not sanctioned by the East Coast culture. Like their mentors', their poetry grew out of personal vision combined with everyday experience. The Beats were part of the San Francisco Renaissance, nurtured by it, in praise of it—see Kerouac's fictional account of the period, *Dharma Bums* (1958)—but they were not all of it.

The first publisher of *Howl* was Lawrence Ferlinghetti's City Lights Books. With Peter Martin, Ferlinghetti had opened the City Lights Pocket Book Shop, and it soon became a gathering place for local writers. After Martin returned to New York, Ferlinghetti pushed his project to print small, inexpensive editions of avant-garde poetry with the bookstore as a major outlet for publicity and distribution. The United States had no agency ready to serve people interested in serious reading who could afford only inexpensive editions. Ferlinghetti met this need: City Lights Books began publishing its Pocket Poets series in 1955, the idea behind the name being that people could conveniently carry these small volumes in their handbags or back pockets. This egalitarian perspective toward literature, this belief that appreciative audiences for poetry existed locally was squarely in the spirit of the Renaissance.

The first volume in the series was Ferlinghetti's *Pictures of the Gone World* (1955). In this volume and the others that would follow, Ferlinghetti demonstrated his interest in and talent for writing populist or street poetry that was political, dramatic, idiomatic, and meant to be read aloud to jazz accompaniment. "One Thousand Fearful Words for Fidel Castro," performed effectively at The Cellar, shows that all San Francisco poets did not feel compelled to write about nature. Living in western spaces where there was a recognizable audience for new kinds of poetry stimulated some to explore new boundaries of composition, whether in form or content.

The second volume in the Pocket Poets series was Rexroth's *Thirty Spanish Poems of Love and Exile* (1956), the third Patchen's *Poems of Humor and Protest* (1956). After the Six Gallery reading Ferlinghetti got permission to publish Ginsberg, and *Howl, and Other Poems* (1956) became the fourth in the series. It did well until the second printing was seized by U.S. customs officials in March 1957 on charges of obscenity. City Lights printed a new edition, removing it from their jurisdiction. In retaliation the police arrested Ferlinghetti and Shig Murao, the bookstore's manager, for selling obscene literature. After a protracted trial Judge Clayton Horn ruled that the book had redeeming social value and was not obscene. Many San Francisco professors and poets had testified on behalf of the defense, including Patchen, Duncan, Rexroth, Mark Shorer, and Herbert Blau. Its success was evidence that the Bay Area had developed a strong sense of community and allegiance to its writers.

City Lights also published four volumes of work by the now legendary Bob Kaufman, one of the original Beat poets who sometimes hung out at the Co-Existence Bagel Shop. Essentially improvisational, his style owes something to the Surrealist automatic writing. His visionary lyrics were satirical and full of social protest. Both Amiri Baraka and Ed Bullins, who spent time in the Bay Area, were influenced by Kaufman's extemporaneous technique, best seen in *Golden Sardine* (1967).

With the exception of Lenore Kandel, whose "First They Slaughtered the Angels" made her briefly a cult figure on North Beach, women poets such as Mary Fabilli and Eve Triem did not draw the same kinds of audiences as the men. Helen Adam, who studied with Duncan in the early 1950s, revived the ballad tradition and redefined classic images of witches and shining knights in armor from a woman's perspective. She contributed to the growing interest in poetry as performance by singing her poems, which often had a political edge to them. Joanne Kyger, closely linked with the Renaissance in the late 1950s, was apparently as comfortable with Duncan's circle as with Beat writers. Her poetry is conversational and personal, grounded in her everyday experiences: she did not hesitate to transform the domestic scenes of her life into poetry.

Muriel Rukeyser's experience had been somewhat different. She had first come to San Francisco in 1937 to celebrate the opening of the Golden Gate Bridge and returned in the mid-1940s to teach poetry at the California Labor School, where she could escape what she called the "wit writing" that was being promoted on East Coast campuses. She participated in Rexroth's literary evenings and became friends with Duncan. Although she would return to New York in 1954, her decade in California gave birth to *The Green Wave* (1948), *Orpheus* (1949), and sections of *Body of Waking* (1958). In San Francisco she felt encouraged to write poetry that Louise Kertesz (1980) describes as "open and direct." Although she was very much on the San Francisco scene and in tune with left-wing politics and the anti-Modernist ethos, she believed that her identification with the Renaissance went unrecognized because she was not a "group person" and because, as a single parent at the time, she was always "pushing a baby carriage" (Kertesz, 1980).

The San Francisco Renaissance suspended the looming homogenization of the United States, and a kind of multi-regionalism took over. The flowering of countless poetry journals and quality private presses on the West Coast (and throughout the country) was one impressive result. Many of the writers whom these journals and presses published anchored their work in political conscience, personal vision, and experience lived at home. They wanted to move into interpersonal communication, to create acts of imaginative identification between themselves and the men and women who live nearby and afar. They believed that poets are indispensable to the rediscovery of a world community and a common literary sensibility.

Linda Hamalian

*See also* Beat Poetry

**Further Reading**

Aaron, Daniel, *Writers on the Left: Episodes in American Literary Communism,* New York: Harcourt Brace and World, 1961

Allen, Donald, and Warren Tallman, editors, *The Poetics of the New American Poetry,* New York: Grove Press, 1973

Bartlett, Lee, *The Sun Is but a Morning Star: Studies in West Coast Poetry and Poetics,* Albuquerque: University of New Mexico Press, 1989

Davidson, Michael, *The San Francisco Renaissance: Poetics and Community at Mid-Century,* Cambridge and New York: Cambridge University Press, 1989

Everson, William, *Archetype West: The Pacific Coast as a Literary Region,* Berkeley, California: Oyez, 1976

Faas, Ekbert, editor, *Towards a New American Poetics,* Santa Barbara, California: Black Sparrow Press, 1978

Ferlinghetti, Lawrence, and Nancy J. Peters, *Literary San Francisco,* San Francisco: City Lights Books, 1980

Foster, Edward Halsey, *Jack Spicer,* Boise State University Press, 1991

Gelpi, Albert, *A Coherent Splendor: The American Poetic Renaissance, 1910–1950,* Cambridge and New York: Cambridge University Press, 1987

Hamalian, Linda, "Regionalism Makes Good: The San Francisco Renaissance," in *Reading the West: New Essays on the Literature of the American West,* edited by Michael Kowalewski, New York: Cambridge University Press, 1996

Kertesz, Louise, *The Poetic Vision of Muriel Rukeyser,* Baton Rouge: Louisiana State University Press, 1980

*The Literary Review* (Fall 1988) (collection of essays on the San Francisco Renaissance)

McClure, Michael, *Scratching the Beat Surface,* San Francisco: North Point Press, 1982

Meltzer, David, *The San Francisco Poets,* New York: Ballantine, 1971; revised edition, as *Golden Gate: Interviews with Five San Francisco Poets,* Berkeley, California: Wingbow Press, 1976

Nemerov, Howard, editor, *Poets on Poetry,* New York: Basic Books, 1966

Parkinson, Thomas, *Poets, Poems, Movements,* Ann Arbor, Michigan: UMI Research Press, 1987

Rexroth, Kenneth, *American Poetry in the Twentieth Century,* New York: Herder, 1971

Rexroth, Kenneth, "The Function of the Poet in Society," in *World Outside the Window: The Selected Essays of Kenneth Rexroth,* edited by Bradford Morrow, New York: New Directions, 1987

---

# Leslie Scalapino 1947–

Leslie Scalapino was born in Santa Barbara, California, to Dee Jessen, a singer, and Robert Scalapino, a professor of political science (politics of Asia). As a youth, Scalapino traveled extensively with her family throughout Asia, Africa, and Europe. She was deeply impressed at a young age by Asian thought, which is as great an influence on her work as are modern and postmodern European writers. She stated in an interview,

> Phenomenology and Stein's view of the continuous present and her view of perception have some similarity to views of perception and phenomena in Tibetan and Zen Buddhist philosophy (such as that of the early Indian philosopher Nagarjuna), which writings seem to me far more radical than Stein's, and which had already influenced me before I came to read her. (Frost, 1996)

Scalapino attended Reed College with poets Mei Mei Berssenbrugge and James Sherry, more than a decade and a half after the 1950–51 graduation of Gary Snyder, Philip Whalen, and Lew Welch. Although she shares deep commonalities with all her fellow alumni, Whalen's work has been of central interest to Scalapino, who has written a number of essays on his poetry. Scalapino continued her literature studies at the University of California, Berkeley, where she received an M.A. The political activism in Berkeley stood in stark contrast to the academic conservatism of the English Department. Her graduate school experience was deeply troubling and perhaps radicalized Scalapino's relationship to academic and literary conventions. It was after graduation that she began writing poetry.

Scalapino's oeuvre is a radical examination of reality by way of writing and a struggle to be fully present in the world. The term "radical" here serves an appropriate double purpose, as it connotes both an unconventional practice as well as the sense of primality, roots, or origins. Her work is both contemporary cutting edge and concerned with aboriginal human experience. There is a duality at the heart of her project, although not in the dualistic philosophical sense as most influentially articulated in Western thought by Descartes. In fact, Scalapino's work reevaluates traditional conceptions of dualistic opposition as it takes as central themes the relations of inside and outside, dream and waking, human and animal, singularity and sociality, reader and writer, as well as history and the present.

While Scalapino's work reveals a wide range of influences, from ancient Zen writing to contemporary post-Einsteinian physics, in her own critical writing she examines and rejects the idea of lineage altogether. "There shouldn't be lineage at all" because lineage makes it seem "as if history or thought is hierarchical and a poet's body of work is only seen *in* that hierarchy" (Scalapino, 1999). Thus, we might say that her work shares an affinity with that of Gertrude Stein, the Objectivists, and contemporary poets associated with Language writing.

While her work can be seen within the context of a human condition beyond the bounds of society, nation, and historical period, she is particularly an American writer writing in response to American culture. For Scalapino, the United States is an imperialist nation, from its inception up to the present (as opposed to, e.g., a Native American or other non-imperialist culture). Because domination and oppression on a mass scale are so central to the existence of the United States as we know it, what takes precedence in Scalapino's epistemological inquiry is the relation of knowledge to systems of power, authority, and convention. Her work studies the linguistic and imagistic mechanisms by which authority and convention subtly create a version of reality within each individual. Reading her work, we must ask ourselves, Is the world that appears to us as self-evident in fact a projection of an imposed order that has been internalized? As she writes in her novel *Defoe,* "I'm seeing what we call normal life as *being* a vision. So this is making another vision of their vision."

In order to scrutinize the difference between reality and imposed "visions," Scalapino's work meditates continually on the nature of perception. From her first major publication, *Considering How Exaggerated Music Is* (1982), Scalapino writes herself and her reader into an impossibility of reducing the experience of reading. Always a challenging and difficult project (and often joyful and liberatory), reading her work constantly makes us aware that we are reading a text in the moment; we do not get lost in a virtual world of narrative vistas or authorial projections. Although her work, in some important sense, is involved in the telling of stories and is based on her own experience, we as readers are, at every turn, made aware of our presence in meaning-making on every level.

Reality in Scalapino's work is in the ever ambiguous present, which creates the past (as much as it is created by the past) as well as the future. Reality is beyond reduction and is constantly changing and unstable. This is not to say the world and our experience of it are fantastical; rather, the fantasy of a stable and constant reality that can be reproduced in a regular fashion is. How do we interpret "on the rear her lacquer has a rose cloud / green fluid emerging is from the outside" from *The Line* (1994), an essay that is also a poem? *The Line* is a study of Aaron Shurin's *Into Distances* (1993) as well as a study of a number of other writers' work, including Robert Creeley, Herbert Spencer, H.D., and Jena Osman. It includes meditations on phenomenology and its relation to writing ("Narrative 'solely' is the same as hanging within the 'visible' horizon *as being* its existence") as well as political reportage ("A Moslem man in mid-age in Bosnia incarcerated in a camp where they're tortured later said the daughter of a town prostitute would gouge the men's intestines"). While her work is considered poetry first and foremost, it ranges in and out of all written genres, including the novel, essay, philosophical tract, literary criticism, reportage, and interviews, as well as performance and art genres, such as the play, calligraphy, and photography.

Regardless of the mode of Scalapino's work in specific instances, all her work defies generic categorization. Her focus on the experience of being present in the moment of writing—writing ahead of an ordering of genre or experience—is unrelenting. Scalapino's refusal to work in a preordained or conventional mode compares to the practice of American authors such as Emily Dickinson, Henry Thoreau, and William James. By crossing generic boundaries and breaking genre rules, these authors subvert a dominant paradigm that enforces hard-and-fast distinctions between fact and fiction, art and science: distinctions that serve to disempower artists' and other nonscientists' claims to knowledge and to overvalue scientific or "factual" claims to understanding the objective world. Scalapino's writing works to reveal the extent to which both fact and fiction are fantastical yet simultaneously real. While her work dismantles conventional binaries by exploding the distinction between fact and fiction, she does not "argue" for this state of affairs. If that were all she did, her work would not be of serious interest and would not be distinct from many 20th-century attempts to clarify this epistemological condition; rather, she writes the reader into an experience of the nakedness of perception and knowing. Reading her, we find ourselves as we create meaning and see the lucid illustration of the world as a visionary practice.

Alicia Cohen

**Biography**

Born in Santa Barbara, California, 25 July 1944. Attended Reed College, Portland, Oregon, B.A. 1966; University of California, Berkeley, M.A. 1969; English faculty member, College of Marin, Kentfield, California, fall 1973, New College of California, San Francisco, 1982, 1983–84, San Francisco State University, 1984, Bard College, Annandale-on-Hudson, New York, summers 1991–, San Francisco Art Institute, 1995–99, and the Naropa Institute, Boulder, Colorado, summers 1985, 1991, 1996, 1999; co-editor, *Foot,* 1979; since 1986 co-publisher, 0 Books. Received National Endowment for the Arts fellowship, 1976, 1986; Before Columbus Foundation Award, 1988; Lawrence Lipton Prize, 1988; San Francisco State University Poetry Center Award, 1988; Woodrow Wilson fellowship, 1996. Living in Oakland, California.

**Poetry**

*0, and Other Poems,* 1976
*The Woman Who Could Read the Minds of Dogs,* 1976
*Instead of an Animal,* 1977
*This Eating and Walking at the Same Time Is Associated Alright,* 1979
*Considering How Exaggerated Music Is,* 1982
*That They Were at the Beach,* 1985
*Way,* 1988
*Clarinet Part I Heard: For Tom White,* 1988
*War,* 1991
*Crowd and Not Evening or Light,* 1992
*The Line,* 1994
*The Front Matter, Dead Souls,* 1996
*Green and Black: Selected Writings* (includes prose), 1996
*Hearing* (with Lyn Hejinian), 1998
*Sight* (with Lyn Hejinian), 1999
*New Time,* 1999
*Seamless Antilandscape* (includes prose), 1999

**Other Writings:** novels (*The Return of Painting, The Pearl, and Onion/3 Novels,* 1991; *Defoe,* 1994), nonfiction (*How Phenomena Appear to Unfold,* 1990).

**Further Reading**

Frost, Elizabeth A., "An Interview with Leslie Scalapino," *Contemporary Literature* 37, no. 1 (1996)
Jarolim, Edith, "No Satisfaction: The Poetry of Leslie Scalapino," *North Dakota Quarterly* 55 (1987)
Murphy, Rosalie, editor, *Contemporary Poets of the English Language,* Chicago: St. James Press, 1970; 7th edition, as *Contemporary Poets,* edited by Thomas Riggs, Detroit, Michigan, and London: St. James Press, 2000
Scalapino, Leslie, "Secret Occurrence," *Jacket* 7 (April 1999) (*www.jacket.zip.com.au/jacket07/index.html*)
Smith Nash, Susan, "Magic and Mystery in Poetic Language: A Response to the Writings of Leslie Scalapino," *Talisman* 14 (1995)
Watten, Barrett, "Political Economy and the Avant-Garde: A Note on Haim Steinbach and Leslie Scalapino," *Talisman* 8 (1992) (special issue on Scalapino)

# Gjertrud Schnackenberg 1953–

The poetry of Gjertrud Schnackenberg elicits great admiration for its technical accomplishment and its scope of historical and cultural knowledge. Since her debut chapbook, *Portraits and Elegies,* appeared in 1982, Schnackenberg has been regarded by many as the future of formal verse. The long spaces between subsequent volumes add to the eager anticipation felt by Schnackenberg's admirers, who cherish her mastery of intricate metrical combinations and her unabashed use of rhyme. Equally eager are her detractors, who view her as a throwback to a mannered, superficial kind of poetry long made obsolete by the late-20th-century poets.

Schnackenberg's poems weave details from history, religion, biography, and the arts and have much in common with the work of American poets such as Richard Howard and W.S. Merwin in their historical narratives or British poet Geoffrey Hill in his *Mercian Hymns* sequence. Beginning in *Portraits and Elegies* and continuing through *The Lamplit Answer* (1985), she employs the post-Einsteinian view of time seen in Modernist poets such as Eliot and Pound as well as novelists such as Proust and Faulkner: the notion that the past, present, and future are knit together in a simultaneous reality. Her technique of placing great figures of the past in intimate, domestic contexts makes this abstract idea tangible in tactile and visual imagery. *Portraits and Elegies* consists of three sequences, beginning with "Laughing with One Eye," a series of poems in memory of her late father, a professor of history, and ending with "19 Hadley Street," a sequence reaching back through time by recounting the various inhabitants of a house over many years. The middle piece, "Darwin in 1881," is a meditative, narrative poem based on the last days of Charles Darwin and was reprinted in her first full volume, *The Lamplit Answer.* Although it begins with a formal, dramatic flourish, comparing the subject to Shakespeare's Prospero, the poet guides us closer and closer to the great man's most human and modest thoughts and actions. He stays away from an award presentation to play backgammon at home; he ponders for his memoirs his own identity as a boy, "a lazy, strutting liar" with a "bossy sister, twitching with desire / To tattletale—yes, that was good," his own judgment interrupting our secondary view of his personal past, reminding us of the layers of time and history present in the poem.

Although *The Lamplit Answer* was Schnackenberg's first full-length book, her name was already known to the poetry world as the newest New Formalist, and expectations ran accordingly. She had won a fellowship from the American Academy of Arts and Letters and the Lavan Younger Poets Award from the American Academy of Poets. Reviewers of the volume discussed her use of a wide range of forms, occasionally even misidentifying them. Much argument was made over the relevance of form, of rhyme and metrical soundness. Some critics argued that Schnackenberg's verses lacked a sense of urgency, never fully convincing readers of their necessity. Others called not only for praise of her works but for imitation as well, hailing her as the beginning of a new age of well-crafted, thoughtful poetry recognizing the specificity of fact and order over the vagueness of feeling and free verse. A series of painfully open love poems, called "light verse" by the publishers in a gambit perhaps to deflect the oncoming criticism, were singled out as indulgent and unsuitable for print by the anti-formalists, while others characterized the works as brave and brilliant. The rhyme and meter raised more controversy in poems of sentiment than in the poems on more academic subjects; her choice of form risked criticism in the context of a post-confessional poetry world more comfortable with expression of extreme emotions than with those of a more predictable variety.

Even as charges of sentimentality came up on occasion, Schnackenberg's dazzling technical ability confirmed her status as one of the most important contemporary poets. Her next book, *A Gilded Lapse of Time,* came seven years after *The Lamplit Answer,* in 1992. Its very structure seemed to be an answer to critical attacks of her overly academic subject matter—three sections, "A Gilded Lapse of Time," "Crux of Radiance," and "A Moment in Utopia," addressing the life of Dante, Christ's passion as represented in works of art, and the life of Russian poet Osip Mandelstam. Demonstrating further independence from any particular movement, Schnackenberg pared down her style to a modified free-verse form in some passages, prompting cries of desertion from some formalists.

In the seven years between *The Lamplit Answer* and *A Gilded Lapse of Time,* her readers were given only two opportunities to gain insight into her aesthetic principles. In 1989, her article on T.S. Eliot's "Marina" appeared in the *Yale Review.* In it, Schnackenberg sympathizes with Eliot, seeing how at that point in his life he might find emotional resonance not only in Shakespeare's *Pericles* but also in contemporary G. Wilson Knight's criticism of the play. Schnackenberg speaks with authority as a poet who culls from literature and history the metaphors for her own inner life, noting the aptness of the bewildered Pericles, unable to identify and name the world to which he is resurrected, as a sympathetic persona for the Modernist suffering his own feelings of bewilderment and alienation.

Another article was published in 1990 in Alfred Corn's *Incarnation: Contemporary Writers on the New Testament.* As Schnackenberg discusses Paul's letter to the Colossians, she talks of perspective, looking down into the ruins of Rome, where it can seem "that it is the dead who have been made real by death, whereas, before the massive, impenetrable finality, that monumental consequence, the living are changed into transitory ghosts." Seeing the living world as transitory and ghost-like has been a major part of 20th-century poetry; here, Schnackenberg hints at the source of her own ability to create "monumental consequence" out of the fixed past. By bringing that fixedness to the present, a sense of the continual emerges. The same is true for her use of form as a means to echo the past, to create in the present, and to resonate in the future.

Schnackenberg's *The Throne of Labdacus,* a retelling of the Oedipus myth, was released in 2000, along with *Supernatural Love: Poems, 1976–1992,* a reprinting of her first three books in one volume. Again Schnackenberg employs a tale from the past to explore contemporary concerns. In the long poem that makes up the volume, the god Apollo works at his own telling of Oedipus' story. In a key scene, the Greek alphabet is created in order to relate the myth. By focusing on this process of telling, Schnackenberg suggests that language itself is the greatness of literary art and our closest connection to the divine, while the stories themselves are at best secondary, always questionable in their worthiness. Her inspiration may have come from enduring the questions raised with regard to her own worthiness, the questions addressed to all poets who carve their own path against conventional expectation.

NICOLE SARROCCO

**Biography**

Born in Tacoma, Washington, 27 August 1953. Attended Mount Holyoke College, South Hadley, Massachusetts, B.A. (summa cum laude) 1975. Received Glascock Award for Poetry, 1973, 1974; Radcliffe College Bunting Institute fellowship, 1979–80; Lavan Award, 1983; American Academy of Arts and Letters Rome fellowship, 1983; Amy Lowell traveling fellowship, 1984–1985; National Endowment for the Arts fellowship, 1986; Guggenheim fellowship, 1987; American Academy of Arts and Letters Award in Literature, 1998; Ingram Merrill Foundation fellowship; Brandeis University Creative Arts Citation in Poetry; H.D.L., Mount Holyoke College, 1985. Living in Boston, Massachusetts.

**Poetry**

*Portraits and Elegies,* 1982; revised edition, 1986
*The Lamplit Answer,* 1985
*A Gilded Lapse of Time,* 1992
*The Throne of Labdacus,* 2000
*Supernatural Love: Poems, 1976–1992,* 2000

**Further Reading**

Harmon, William, "A Poetry Odyssey," *Sewanee Review* 41, no. 3 (1983)
McPhillips, Robert, "Gjertrud Schnackenberg," in *The Dictionary of Literary Biography,* volume 120: *American Poets Since World War II,* Detroit, Michigan: Gale Research, 1992
Schnackenberg, Gjertrud, "Marina," *Yale Review* 78, no. 2 (1989)
Schnackenberg, Gjertrud, "The Letter of Paul to the Colossians," in *Incarnation: Contemporary Writers on the New Testament,* edited by Alfred Corn, New York: Viking, 1990
Stitt, Peter, "Contemporary American Poetry: Does the Material World Exist?" *Georgia Review* 39, no. 2 (1985)

---

# James Schuyler 1923–91

At one point in James Schuyler's long poem "A Few Days," the narrator, Schuyler himself, remembers a sexual escapade from his youth, a lustily related incident that took place in the shower room at New York's Twenty-Third Street YMCA. The recollection continues:

> Sure was
> a change from West Virginia. When I told Alex Katz I
> went to college in West
> Virginia, he said in that way of his, "Nah,
> you're Harvard." Wish I
> were, but I'm a lot more panhandle than I am Cambridge,
> Mass.

This reminiscence may not, from one perspective, seem particularly remarkable. Indeed, little in Schuyler—who is more likely to find poetry in the ordinary, even slightly dull, quotidian events than in weighty abstractions or highly significant moments of great intensity—ever seems "remarkable," in the usual sense of that word. As he rather flatly puts it in "Dreams," "The said to be boring things / dreams, weather, a bus trip / are so fascinating." He expresses the same idea with his characteristic wry humor in "December": "A smile on the street may be loads! you don't have to undress everybody."

Nevertheless, the lines from "A Few Days" are worthy of comment and point toward aspects of the poetry that make Schuyler's one of the most interesting and genuinely human, if not most famous, voices in 20th-century American poetry. The fact that Schuyler is recounting the story to Alex Katz is telling. Katz is a New York painter who strongly influenced the work of Fairfield Porter, another painter and Schuyler's closest friend and, at one point, lover. (Off and on, Schuyler lived in Maine and Southampton with Porter and his wife, Anne. Anne remarked that Schuyler came for lunch one day and stayed for 11 years.) Schuyler's close associations with painters and his deep interest in painting often surface in the poetry, and Schuyler's eye for color and texture is remarkable:

> After two rainy days, a sunny one
> of cloud curds breaking up in blue.
> Now the sky is peach ice cream. ("Evenings in Vermont")

Furthermore, the "panhandle"/"Cambridge, Mass." distinction from "A Few Days" is of special importance. It points to a tension between the rural and the urban, between the wild and the civilized, or, to use the critic Philip Rahv's terms, between the literary "paleface" and "redskin"—the very tension that has characterized American literature from its beginnings. Schuyler is associated with the New York School poets, a group including John Ashbery, Frank O'Hara, and Kenneth Koch. These poets, who never constituted a formal school, were rather a group of friends closely connected with the New York art world of the middle and later decades of the 20th century. The poets often worked in collaboration (e.g., Schuyler and Ashbery co-wrote *A Nest of Ninnies* [1969], a hilarious novel of manners in which almost nothing happens) and looked toward one another for inspiration. However, as David Lehman (1998) notes, Schuyler has often remained "the odd man out" in critical evaluations of the New York School. The reasons are varied: Schuyler was the least prolific of the group; he was a late bloomer, his first commercially published collection, *Freely Espousing,* not appearing until 1969, three years after Frank O'Hara's death and a decline in the group's cohesiveness; he was often painfully shy and reclusive, not nearly as adept at promoting himself as the others; and, tellingly, Ashbery, Koch, and O'Hara were Harvard men, and Schuyler was not. It is not that Schuyler was ostracized on that basis, but his sensibilities were, indeed, "a lot more panhandle" than those of the more self-consciously urban (and urbane) New York School poets. As Helen Vendler (1995) writes, "James Schuyler is that unlikely writer in contemporary New York, a pastoral poet."

Pastoral poetry is, by its nature, contemplative, quiet, and reclusive. The poet's voice is characteristically lonely, that of a person who recognizes the essential isolation of the individual. If the voice is not dark, exactly, the overtones are melancholy:

> I have reached, alas, the long shadow
> and short day of whitening hills
> when color is lost in the grass. ("Sestina")

> I am as shy as you. Try as we may,
> only by practice will our talks prolong.
> What is, is by its nature, on display. ("Poem")

And this, from "The Payne Whitney Poems," written during one of Schuyler's many stays at a psychiatric hospital:

> The friends who come to see you and
> and the friends who don't.
> The weather in the window.
> A pierced ear.
> The mounting tension and the spasm.
> . . . .
> Give my love to, oh, anybody. ("Sleep")

Schuyler's work merits special interest, especially in the context of his association with the New York School poets, because of his intense interest in nature. Although he lived much of his adult life in Manhattan in association with a sophisticated, cutting-edge circle of peers and friends, much of his poetry, oddly and delightfully, focuses on changes of weather and the color of the sky, aspects of the natural world that seem out of place in an urban milieu. That is not to say that the city never surfaces in his poems. New York landmarks and aspects of urban life are, indeed, recounted frequently, but even Schuyler's most urban images are usually transformed by the "panhandle" lens through which he views the world:

> One green wave moved in the violet sea
> like the UN building on big evenings
> green and wet
> while the sky turns violet.
> A few almond trees
> had a few flowers, like a few snowflakes
> out of the blue looking pink in the light. ("February")

In an influential piece in the *American Poetry Review,* Howard Moss (1981) wrote, "How Schuyler manages to be absolutely truthful and an obsessed romantic at the same time is his secret." Moss' comment points toward the central paradox in Schuyler's work, the paradox that renders the poetry elusive but that also accounts for its capacity to inhabit, simultaneously, two realms: that of the earth, grounded and often gritty, and that of the imagination, soaring and free.

DOUGLAS BRANCH

*See also* New York School

**Biography**

Born in Chicago, Illinois, 9 November 1923. Attended Bethany College, West Virginia, 1941–43; University of Florence, 1947–48; staff member, Museum of Modern Art, New York, 1955–61; critic, *Art News,* New York, 1955–78. Received Longview Foundation Award, 1961; Frank O'Hara Prize (*Poetry,* Chicago), 1969; National Endowment for the Arts grant, 1969, 1972; American Academy Award, 1977; Pulitzer Prize, 1981; Guggenheim fellowship, 1981; Academy of American Poets fellowship, 1983; Whiting Award, 1985. Died 12 April 1991 in New York City.

**Poetry**

*Salute,* 1960
*May 24th or So,* 1966
*Freely Espousing,* 1969
*The Crystal Lithium,* 1972
*A Sun Cab,* 1972
*Penguin Modern Poets 24* (poems by Schuyler, Kenward Elmslie, and Kenneth Koch), 1973
*Hymn to Life,* 1974
*Song,* 1976
*Fireproof Floors of Witley Court: English Songs and Dances,* 1976
*The Home Book: Prose and Poems, 1951–1970,* edited by Trevor Winkfield, 1977
*The Morning of the Poem,* 1980
*A Few Days,* 1985
*Selected Poems,* 1988
*Poems and Diaries* (includes prose), 1991
*James Schuyler, Poems: Andrew Lord, Sculptures* (with others), 1992
*Collected Poems,* 1993
*Last Poems,* afterword by Lee Harwood, 1999

**Other Writings:** plays, novels (*A Nest of Ninnies* [with John Ashbery], 1969; *What's for Dinner?* 1978), journals (*Early in '71,* 1982; *The Diary of James Schuyler,* edited by Nathan Kernan, 1997), essays (*Selected Art Writings,* edited by Simon Petit, 1998); edited collections of literature (*Broadway: A Poets and Painters Anthology* [with Charles North], 1979).

**Further Reading**

Crase, Douglas, "A Voice Like the Day," *Poetry* 136, no. 4 (1994)
Lehman, David, *The Last Avant-Garde: The Making of the New York School of Poets,* New York and London: Doubleday, 1998
Moss, Howard, "James Schuyler: Whatever Is Moving," *American Poetry Review* 10, no. 3 (1981)

Rudman, Mark, "James Schuyler's Changing Skies," *Denver Quarterly* 24, no. 4 (1990)

Vendler, Helen, *Soul Says: On Recent Poetry,* Cambridge, Massachusetts: Harvard University Press, 1995

Ward, Geoff, *Statutes of Liberty: The New York School of Poets,* New York: St. Martin's Press, and London: Macmillan, 1993

---

# Delmore Schwartz 1913–66

Smiling confidently in the foreground of the famous photograph taken at a gathering to honor Sir Osbert and Dame Edith Sitwell at the Gotham Book Mart in 1948, Delmore Schwartz gave the impression that he still had every reason to believe that he was the foremost poet of his generation. His first book, a collection of poems and short stories titled *In Dreams Begin Responsibilities* (1938), had been universally well received, with Allen Tate remarking that it was "beyond doubt the first real innovation that we've had since Eliot and Pound," while Mark Van Doren described it as "one of the most valuable and enjoyable books published in its generation" (Atlas, 1977). In the three decades that followed his brilliant debut, however, the course of Schwartz's career was one of astonishing decline. Writing on his second book, a translation of Rimbaud's *Un saison en enfer* (*A Season in Hell*) first published in 1939, the critic Mary Colum suggested that Schwartz presented Rimbaud "in the English of a schoolboy tackling a 'sight' translation" (Atlas, 1977); his second book of poetry, *Genesis* (published in 1943 as the first part of a long autobiographical poem that Schwartz was working on until the last decade of his life), was also poorly received, described by one critic as "a dour chronicle" and as "a combination of ineptitude and earnestness" by another (Atlas, 1977). Schwartz's later books of poetry (he also wrote two full-length collections of stories, *The World Is a Wedding* and *Successful Love,* published in 1948 and 1961, respectively) never received anything approaching the level of praise that had greeted his remarkable debut. To put it simply and to paraphrase John Berryman's words in Dream Song 150 (one of a ten-song elegiac "block of agony" he wrote for Schwartz), Schwartz did not build on his early promise, and his work did not improve. Although he is still read, especially those early poems of *In Dreams Begin Responsibilities,* there is a strong sense that Schwartz's place in the history of American literature has more to do with his personal and professional involvement with other figures (such as Berryman, Robert Lowell, and the novelist Saul Bellow) than with the quality of his work. Although it is frequently placed alongside the work of other middle-generation poets, Schwartz's poetry has certainly been the focus of less critical attention than that of other members of that group, a point attested to by Thomas Travisano's exclusion of Schwartz from his recent study *Midcentury Quartet* (1999).

In a sense, Schwartz's problem from the start concerned his indulgence in too many forms and genres: he wrote poems (lyric, narrative, and dramatic), short stories, novels, plays, translations, and essays. A serious student of philosophy—in which he pursued a graduate program at Harvard University from 1935 until 1937, where he was taught by the influential philosopher Alfred North Whitehead—Schwartz was also a dedicated disciple of Marxism and, later, psychoanalysis as well as an incisive film critic and, like Marianne Moore, a baseball fanatic (his team was the New York Giants). As poetry editor at *The Partisan Review* during the 1940s and into the 1950s, Schwartz was responsible for encouraging many younger poets to develop their craft (while, one must add, his own floundered). With figures such as Philip Rahv and Mary McCarthy, Schwartz instigated many important intellectual discussions in *The Partisan Review* while simultaneously using those occasions to elaborate his own frequently contrary positions. A survey of Schwartz's contributions to *The Partisan Review* (and other journals) during this period reveals an intelligent, often formidable literary and cultural critic, coming closer than any other American poet in the post–World War II generation to the role of the poet as social commentator as described and defined by Ezra Pound 20 years before. Schwartz, however, never fully obtained the degree of fluency and control that marked his precursor's efforts. The reasons for his failure had less to do with a lack of talent or ability than with the mental and emotional instability that caused his eventual alienation not only from those people who once made up the intellectual milieu of which he had been a central player but also from himself. When Schwartz died in July 1966, his body lay for three days in a morgue in New York City before anyone came to claim it.

To describe Schwartz's career, then, is to come very close to describing the onset and development of mental illness (in his case schizophrenia) and the destructive effects that it can have on a highly talented and intelligent individual and those who surround him. However, to concentrate on this aspect of Schwartz's life alone is to do an injustice to the highlights of his career: in particular, the high praise that welcomed *In Dreams Begin Responsibilities* in 1938 needs to be taken seriously. In that book, Schwartz indicated something of the enormity of the project that he had set for himself from adolescence—he sent his first poems to *The Nation* and *The American Mercury* when he was 12 years old. It was a project that he might well have lacked the resources to complete in any case, even if he had not succumbed to schizophrenia in the last decade of his life. In short, Schwartz set out to describe and define what it means to be American, with particular emphasis on Jewish immigrant experience. Of recent Romanian ancestry himself, Schwartz boldly declared at a very early stage in his career that he was "the poet of the Atlantic migration"—the poet, in other words, for whom the question of identity was necessarily fractured, bifurcated, and heterogeneous (Atlas, 1977). It was, perhaps, Schwartz's attempt to mold this sense of cultural heterogeneity into a single and unified poetic theme that drove him forward on many failed quests for an adequate form of expression through various modes of poetry, drama, and prose. In doing this, Schwartz set for himself the task that many admittedly better writers have been content to examine only a small portion of: there is a sense in which Schwartz bit off a little more than he could chew. A lifelong reader and admirer of James Joyce's *Finnegans Wake,* Schwartz lacked the necessary focus to produce a literary work so engagingly and extravagantly encyclopedic.

If Schwartz failed in his lifelong attempt to produce a work of such enormous cultural significance as *Finnegans Wake,* one must admit that some of his work does present very important questions and issues that, although they never found satisfactory resolution in his later writing, are worth remembering and reading today. "The Ballad of the Children of the Czar," for example, explores the relationship between history and memory and suggests connections between the individual's sense of self and what might be called the larger social psyche:

While I ate a baked potato
Six thousand miles apart,

In Brooklyn, in 1916,
Aged two, irrational,

When Franklin D. Roosevelt
Was an Arrow Collar ad.

O Nicholas! Alas! Alas!
My grandfather coughed in your army,

Hid in a wine-stinking barrel,
For three days in Bucharest

Then left for America
To become a king himself.

Moreover, Schwartz's probing of the dilemma of immigrant (i.e., American) selfhood is bound up with his critique of modernity and his writing of the city.

In "In the Naked Bed, in Plato's Cave" Schwartz (an insomniac) rewrote Plato's parable of the figures who are chained inside a cave so that they can perceive life outside only as a series of shadows projected onto the walls of their prison (Plato, *The Republic,* Book VII). In his version of the parable, Schwartz compares the life of an urban dweller to that of the Platonic prisoner, *forced* to partake in the ceaseless life of the city while remaining alienated from it. In fact, this poem offers a subtle critique of the pervasiveness of modernity, with the speaker expressing an unforgettable sense of exhaustion and estrangement:

In the naked bed, in Plato's cave,
Reflected headlights slowly hid the wall,
Carpenters hammered under the shaded window,
Wind troubled the window curtains all night long,
A fleet of trucks strained uphill, grinding,
Their freights covered, as usual.
The ceiling lightened again, the slanting diagram
Slid slowly forth.
Hearing the milkman's chop,
His striving up the stair, the bottle's chink,
I rose from bed, lit a cigarette,
And walked to the window. The stony street
Displayed the stillness in which buildings stand,
The street-lamps vigil and the horse's patience.
The winter sky's pure capital
Turned me back to bed with exhausted eyes.

Poems such as "In the Naked Bed, in Plato's Cave" and "The Ballad of the Children of the Czar" seem to exemplify Hannah Arendt's claim that homelessness is the fundamental condition of modernity. For Schwartz, that concept also embodies an important sense of unease with and distance from the self, both physically and psychologically. The body, in a poem such as "The Heavy Bear Who Goes with Me," becomes a site of conflict where the thinking subject finds that he cannot escape the "hungry beating brutish one / In love with candy, anger, and sleep" and must always "stumble, flounder and strive to be fed" in "the hate-ridden city." In many of Schwartz's best early poems, such expansive use of imagery enables an enlargement of his thematic concerns, from melancholic self-examination to pertinent social critique. Of course, this process is also the result of a learned and scholarly imagination, which accounts for the frequent allusions in Schwartz's poetry not only to the greater literary tradition in English and other languages but also to the history of philosophy ranging from Plato to Heidegger and Sartre.

Schwartz does not always wear his learning lightly, however. Such heavy-handed titles as "Philology Recapitulates Ontology, Poetry Is Ontology," collected in *Last and Lost Poems* (1979), have surely put some readers off. More important, however, is the fact that many of Schwartz's earlier poems suffered from what might be described as a surfeit of style. In a critical climate where "rhapsody is no longer recognised as a form," as Douglas Dunn has written of Schwartz's long poem "Seurat's Sunday Afternoon along the Seine" in his introduction to the Carcanet *Selected Poems* (1976), a good number of Schwartz's poems seem too ecstatic and spontaneous, and they frequently tend toward verbosity and self-indulgence. This is evident in poems such as "All Clowns Are Masked and All Personae" and "Calmly We Walk through This April's Day," poems that seem to delight in the very occasion of their saying, but it may also account for the lack of power in some of Schwartz's longer works, "Coriolanus and His Mother" and "Narcissus" in particular, both collected in *Summer Knowledge: New and Selected Poems* (1959). At their best, however, when they do have something important to say, Schwartz's poems certainly repay attention. In poems such as those quoted earlier and others, including the posthumously published "The Greatest Thing in North America," "Overture," "America! America!" (not to be confused with the story of the same title), and "Love and Marilyn Monroe," Schwartz not only raises issues concerning his sense of disaffection from American culture but also offers an engaging critique of postmodern American society. In his best poems (early or late), Schwartz emerges as an important promoter of what Karl Shapiro in a foreword to a collection of Schwartz's letters (edited by Robert Phillips) called the "Euro-cultural dispensation" in the history of American literature in the 20th century, that group of American poets who strenuously opposed the "Whitman-Williams isolationist" line and in doing so reacted against the dominant (exceptionalist) cultural hegemony (Phillips, 1993).

If Schwartz's work is to be read and written about in the future, one suspects that this last point might provide a useful introduction.

Taking into account Schwartz's treatment of the themes of isolation and alienation, disaffection and dispossession, it would be interesting to examine how his work embodies and enforces various political strategies. The failure of Schwartz's career, however, might be read symbolically as the failure of the American dream. Moreover, Schwartz's failure may be read in those terms suggested by Denis Donoghue, who, writing on American literature ten years after Schwartz's death, asked, "Do we not feel that American literature thrives upon the conditions of failure and that it would lose its character, if not its soul, were it given the conditions of success?" (Donoghue, *The Sovereign Ghost,* 1976). Despite the contentiousness of this claim in itself, anyone who reads Schwartz's poetry seriously must ask this fundamental question: would we be reading Schwartz today at all if he had not—so enigmatically—failed?

Philip Coleman

**Biography**

Born in Brooklyn, New York, 8 December 1913. Attended University of Wisconsin, Madison, 1931; New York University, New York City, B.A. 1935; Harvard University, Cambridge, Massachusetts, 1935–37; Briggs-Copeland Instructor, 1940, and Assistant Professor, 1946–47, Harvard University; Visiting Professor, Syracuse University, New York, 1962–65; editor, 1943–47, and associate editor, 1947–55, *Partisan Review;* poetry editor, *New Republic,* 1955–57; Visiting Lecturer, Kenyon School of English, Kenyon College, 1950, Indiana School of Letters, summer 1951, Princeton University, New Jersey, 1952–53, University of Chicago, Illinois, spring 1954, New York University, 1966. Received Guggenheim fellowship, 1940, 1941; National Institute of Arts and Letters grant, 1953; *Kenyon Review* fellow, 1957; Levinson Prize, 1959; Bollingen Prize, 1960; Shelley Memorial Award, 1960. Died in New York City, 11 July 1966.

**Poetry**

*In Dreams Begin Responsibilities* (includes short stories), 1938
*Genesis: Book One,* 1943
*Vaudeville for a Princess, and Other Poems,* 1950
*Summer Knowledge: New and Selected Poems, 1938–1958,* 1959; revised edition, as *Selected Poems: Summer Knowledge, 1938–1958,* 1967
*What Is to Be Given: Selected Poems,* 1976
*I Am Cherry Alive, the Little Girl Sang,* 1979
*The Ego Is Always at the Wheel: Bagatelles,* 1986
*Last and Lost Poems of Delmore Schwartz,* 1979; revised edition, as *Last and Lost Poems,* 1989

**Selected Criticism**

*American Poetry at Mid-Century* (with John Crowe Ransom and John Hall Wheelock), 1958

**Other Writings:** plays (*Shenandoah,* 1940), short stories (*The World Is a Wedding,* 1948), essays (*Selected Essays of Delmore Schwartz,* 1970), memoirs (*Portrait of Delmore: Journals and Notes of Delmore Schwartz, 1939–1959,* 1986), correspondence (*Letters of Delmore Schwartz,* 1984), translation of French literature (*A Season in Hell,* by Arthur Rimbaud, 1939; revised edition, 1940).

**Further Reading**

Atlas, James, *Delmore Schwartz: The Life of an American Poet,* New York: Farrar, Straus and Giroux, 1977
Barrett, William, "The Truants: *Partisan Review* in the Forties," *Commentary* 49 (June 1974)
Bawer, Bruce, *The Middle Generation: The Lives and Poetry of Delmore Schwartz, Randall Jarrell, John Berryman, and Robert Lowell,* Hamden, Connecticut: Archon, 1986
Dunn, Douglas, "Introduction," in *What Is to Be Given: Selected Poems,* by Schwartz, Manchester: Carcanet New Press, 1976
Phillips, Robert, "Introduction," in *Last and Lost Poems of Delmore Schwartz,* by Schwartz, edited by Phillips, New York: Vanguard Press, 1979; revised edition, as *Last and Lost Poems,* New York: New Directions, 1989
Phillips, Robert, editor, *Letters of Delmore Schwartz,* Princeton, New Jersey: Ontario Review Press, 1984
Phillips, Robert, editor, *Delmore Schwartz and James Laughlin: Selected Letters,* New York and London: Norton, 1993
Rahv, Philip, "Delmore Schwartz: The Paradox of Precocity," *New York Review of Books* (20 May 1971)
Schwartz, Delmore, *Portrait of Delmore: Journals and Notes of Delmore Schwartz, 1939–1959,* edited by Elizabeth Pollett, New York: Farrar, Straus and Giroux, 1986
Simpson, Eileen, *Poets in Their Youth: A Memoir,* New York: Random House, and London: Faber, 1982

---

# Armand Schwerner 1927–99

Starting out in the late 1950s as a member of the original New York group of "deep image" poets, Armand Schwerner proved himself a savvy, sophisticated poet of the short forms. Over the next several decades, his work in open, experimental lyric brought to poetry a rich new lode of psychological matter based on Jung's theories of the mythic imagination and Western Buddhism's notion of the open self.

By the mid-1960s, Schwerner was at work on *The Tablets,* which he began publishing in installments in 1968. The title refers to actual Sumero-Akkadian cuneiform tablets representing some of the earliest writing in human history and now preserved in various museums. Many of these tablets are fragmented or indecipherable, and only parts of each "text" have been translated, with many gaps filled cautiously with speculative reconstructions by paleolinguists.

All this is the setting for a long, ironic poem that presumes to offer a scholarly new translation, but the "tablets" are entirely made up, even though the ruse set for the reader is obvious after the first few lines of Schwerner's opening tablet. *The Tablets* is in accord with other 20th-century long poems in attempting to construct a synchronic text dwelling on an earlier culture as the template against which the modern era can be measured and compared. In this case, Sumerian culture offers Schwerner a putative glimpse into the undifferentiated pre-individual intellect at the dawn of Western civilization, viewed from our own era of overweening egoism and self-indulgence.

The result is the collision of opposing cultures, the before and after of a history of the self, with hilarious consequences that are lost on the "scholar-translator," Schwerner's bumbling, academically myopic, overintellectualizing interpreter, who lavishes his textual reconstructions with elaborate footnote commentaries and bracketed interruptions—all of it a rich parody of the excesses of contemporary scholarship and cultural misreadings of otherness, including the Jew. Tablet XXVI quotes Dachau's motto, "Work makes freedom."

As the poem progresses, the textual content becomes more various and difficult, reminiscent of a Pynchon novel's codes and plot mazes, offering not only lacunae and missing parts but also reversed messages and increasingly arcane ideographs resembling Mayan hieroglyphs. Tablet XXVI introduces what are obviously computer-generated icons from a standard Macintosh word-processing program that begin to form a second textual layer of the poem, growing ever more intricate and complex in the closing tablets of the work. Sometimes whole poems are made of editorial devices (ellipses and plus signs) or iconic paragraphs. The symbols—bugle-like figures, circles, snake figures, and the like—are gathered into text boxes and floated among the "written" strophes. These iconic passages provoke wild ruminations from the scholar-translator and are meant to distance us from the "originals" while connecting them to the emerging language(s) of the computer age.

*The Tablets* opens with the fragments of a creation myth narrating the origins of a people through images of water, death, and regeneration. The first tablet introduces the principle of the *pluriloge*, Schwerner's invented term for the poetry of multiple voices and languages. Made-up words are sifted into the text little by little, building up a mythology of guardian and menacing spirits ruling over mortal life: the *pintprit* (a priapic god), the *knom* (or "Spirit which denies"), and so on. The poem moves on to the agonizingly slow but inexorable birth of individualized consciousness, a menacing figure who nonetheless fascinates the poem's narrator as the world shrinks behind him. A key line near the close of the poem has this figure announce, "In my ending, prone, I inhabit the great silence // harvest of the mouth" (Tablet XXVII).

If the poem were only a parody, a satiric look at the current veneration of early native cultures and their epics, *The Tablets* might have been dismissed long ago as a clever knockoff of post-modern epics. However, *The Tablets,* like Edward Dorn's satiric long poem *Slinger,* transcends its immediate satiric purpose by pursuing hilarious exaggeration while beguiling us with an intriguing look at the virtues of tribal identity and collective living. We are given glimpses into a primordial consciousness that cannot separate itself from nature or society and that lives in a larger, some might say richer, dynamic of life than does the modern individual.

Schwerner is keenly aware of his double purpose as satirist and idealist, and he manages to sustain the delicate balance of his text by never relaxing his deadpan delivery or the dogged labors of his scholar-translator, who increasingly reminds us of ourselves as he attempts to translate one age to another. The poem reveals how much we have lost in the process of evolving into a "higher" culture. The poem's most rueful point is to debunk the notion of "progress," or the illusion that human civilization grows as it moves through time. In *The Tablets,* the modern age is viewed as a decline into chaos and anarchy, holocaust, and world wars from a time that cherished community and the sacred world.

From that perspective, *The Tablets* points toward an Old Testament world of small, intimate village cohesion governed by the laws of Moses or their antecedents. Even if the poem has made up its history, the parallels between what may have been and what the poem invents are close enough to persuade the attentive reader that *The Tablets* is a thoughtful and deliberate meditation on squandered social ideals. Like other long poems of the century, it too is concerned mainly with ethics and metaphysics and the dilemma of being cut off from the religious past. *The Tablets* is ultimately a dissertation on religious ideas that once bound society into a coherent whole and elevated the realm of nature to the sacred—principles, the poem seems to argue, that have been abandoned in order to evolve into the post-industrial order of the present.

PAUL CHRISTENSEN

*See also* Deep Image Poetry

**Biography**

Born in Antwerp, Belgium, 11 May 1927. Attended Cornell University, Ithaca, New York, 1945–47; Université de Genève, Switzerland, 1947–48; Columbia University, New York City, B.S. 1950, M.A. 1964; teacher, Eron Preparatory School, New York City, 1955–59; instructor, Barnard School for Boys, Riverdale, New York, 1959–64; Instructor, Long Island University, New York City, 1963–64; Instructor, 1964–66, Assistant Professor, 1966–69, Associate Professor, 1969–73, and since 1973 Professor, Staten Island Community College. Received National Endowment for the Arts grant, 1973; New York State Council on the Arts fellowship, 1973, 1975; National Education Association fellowship, 1973, 1979; National Endowment for the Arts fellowship, 1987. Died 4 February 1999 in Staten Island, New York.

**Poetry**

*The Lightfall,* 1963
*The Tablets I–VIII,* 1968
*Seaweed,* 1968
*The Tablets I–XV,* 1971
*The Tablets XVI, XVII, XVIII,* 1975
*The Work, the Joy, and the Triumph of the Will,* 1977

*Sounds of the River Naranjana [and] The Tablets I–XXIV,* 1983
*The Tablets I–XXVI,* 1989
*Selections: 1999 (Selected Shorter Poems),* 1999

**Other Writings:** study guides (*John Steinbeck's "Of Mice and Men,"* 1965), translation of Native American poetry (*Redspel: Eleven American Indian Adaptations,* 1974).

**Further Reading**

Alpert, Barry, editor, *Jackson Mac Low, Armand Schwerner,* Silver Spring, Maryland: Alpert, 1975
Christensen, Paul, "Some Bearings on Ethnopoetics: Rothenberg, Schwerner, and Others," *Parnassus* 15 (1989)
Doria, Charles, "The Poetry of Memory," *Parnassus* 7 (1979)
Paul, Sherman, *In Love with the Gratuitous: Rereading Armand Schwerner,* Grand Forks: North Dakota Quarterly, 1986

---

## Anne Sexton 1928–74

During her life Anne Sexton produced seven volumes of poetry, beginning with *To Bedlam and Part Way Back* (1960), winning the Pulitzer Prize for *Live or Die* (1966), and concluding in *The Death Notebooks* (1974). Further collections appeared posthumously, most notably *The Awful Rowing toward God* (1975) and *Words for Dr. Y.* (1978). A contemporary of Plath's—both attended poetry workshops directed by Robert Lowell—Sexton's connection to the Middle Generation poets of the United States is as vexed as that of this grouping's other "members." As with Lowell and Berryman, for instance, she rejected the "Confessional" tag that was applied to their work, even though she shared some biographical details with these writers (depression, alcohol dependency).

Sexton is primarily a poet of the family and of family relations, although not necessarily of either her own family or of her own experiences. She conceived of herself as a storyteller, and her public readings were as much performances of her constructed personae as they were introductions to her writing. The register of female subjectivities, placed in both mundane and extreme situations, that runs through her work is central to any understanding of her poetry: the "I" is neither stable nor equivalent to Sexton herself. She remarked to one interviewer, "I tend to lie a lot," and this is evident in her poetic constructions. Her narrators are not reliable, the "I" shifts position and its versions of the world. Sexton continues exploring the crisis of the individual and the collapse of the psyche mapped by the Middle Generation writers, particularly in her later collections in which the shadow and dominance of Plath is notable. Her earlier work is arguably more formal and structured. One collection deserving of renewed attention is *Transformations* (1971), a volume dedicated to reworkings and adaptations of traditional fairy tales in which the poetic imagery Sexton developed in the earlier collections, particularly its application and appropriateness during times of mental disorder and breakdown, rewards continued reading.

Although certain aspects of the Sexton poetic are akin to those of her contemporary Sylvia Plath, she stands alone for her command of rhythm, rhyme, and imagery. Her first volumes contain a series of poetic narratives concerning the position and role of women within American society. An early, uncollected poem entitled "An Obsessive Combination of Ontological Inscape, Trickery and Love" maps out the territory her later work would investigate. In the opening lines

> Busy, with an idea for a code, I write
> signals hurrying from left to right,
> or right to left, by obscure routes,
> for my own reasons

Sexton suggests her particular methods of inquiry and her modes of poetic construction; her poems function as codes that the reader must decipher in order to uncover the personal, individual voices. Sexton's work is fertile territory for the application of feminist readings and theoretical positions. The surface text presented to the reader is, as Sexton wrote in a fragment entitled "June 6 1960" (published after her death), "Words waiting, angry, masculine, / with their fists in a knot." Sexton encodes this language of patriarchy with female significations that require deciphering by the sensitive and alert reader; then the subsumed subjectivities of her female speakers may be unraveled and the male constructs of language and meaning interrogated. The internalized female voice is an uncharted phenomenon for Sexton because it belies the factuality of male systems of language and categorization, which cannot map the geography of the concealed female self. In "January 24th" from *Words for Dr. Y.* she writes,

> I am alone here in my own mind.
> There is no map
> and there is no road.

This speaker experiences isolation because of the absence of known routes of access or indicators of direction, the lack of adequate examples of textual mappings of this internal female region.

The impulse to construct autobiographical readings of the work of the Middle Generation poets is tempting, particularly so with Sexton, as writing poetry was suggested as a method of therapy following her suicidal breakdown in 1956. Moreover, much of her work deals with intensely personal subjects (relationships, love, children, parents, death) and can be interpreted as an ordered approach to the reconstruction of her disintegrating life. Such purely biographical readings are reductionist in scope, however, and negate a large and unexplored field of inquiry into the Sexton canon. Biographical readings analyze the surface text and relate the "personal" signals of the poetic narratives without attempting to decipher the codes Sexton explicitly tells us that she has employed in her writing. These codes, once understood, allow the reader access to the multiplicity of (female) narratives and voices suppressed by the linear and monologic (male) surface text. Sexton's poetry operates to deconstruct (male) language from within; the empowered positions within her writing are ultimately those of the female voices realized through the codes and strategies of her concentrated poetic style.

In a broader view the Sexton corpus is bracketed by poetry written to, or in relation with, doctors and analysts. *To Bedlam and Part Way Back* opens with "You, Doctor Martin" and also includes such poems as "Said the Poet to the Analyst." The first section of *Words for Dr. Y.,* "Letters for Dr. Y.," contains a series of pieces written between 1960 and 1970 that Sexton insisted should not be published until after her death. Comparisons between her published work and these posthumous collections are not only inevitable but also highly rewarding. "Letters for Dr. Y." operates as a sublimated text within Sexton's poetic career, its short pieces paralleling the publicly released narratives in the collections of the period. Reading them in correlation with the earlier published work establishes a useful dynamic between Sexton's private and public voices. The individual, untitled segments of "Letters for Dr. Y." are differentiated only by Sexton's exact dating of each piece and read, therefore, as historically situated subtexts within the Sexton canon, similar to entries in a journal.

Possibly the most recurring strategy within Sexton's poetry is that of the lone or isolated female speaker; important examples of this are "Unknown Girl in the Maternity Ward" from her first collection and "The Abortion" from *All My Pretty Ones* (1962). Many of the characters inhabiting the Sexton poetic world are precisely just that, characters, constructed personae, fictitious selves. In an interview with Patricia Marx, Sexton made this point with particular reference to "Unknown Girl in the Maternity Ward":

> You can even lie (one can confess and lie forever) as I did in the poem of the illegitimate child that the girl had to give up. It hadn't happened to me. It wasn't true, yet it was indeed the truth. (Sexton, 1985)

As with many of Sexton's poems, at the textual center of this poem there is an opposition, a tension, between female and male texts, between competing versions of history, different and gendered interpretations of reality. In the poem the girl's "case history / stays blank" when she does not answer the doctors, who are presumably male, given their interest in factual rather than emotional detail. Sexton dislocates this particular female voice from male textualizations of it; although the girl is institutionalized, her history is not. Instead it functions as a silent narrative withheld from the official (male) record and social systems of recording, for although the girl says nothing, a male version of her history attempting to chart the riddle of her life will appear in the official text anyway. The poem provides a textual space to counter the institutional text of patriarchal America.

This legitimizing of female identity, intertwined as it is in Sexton with the sublimation of an accurate account of female experience, lies at the core of "The Abortion." This poem traces her internal conflict by contrasting poetic renditions of a traumatic experience and a stark realism concerning the event. Sexton juxtaposes a rhythmic writing of an intensely female experience, established throughout the poem, with the deliberately open-ended last line ("this baby that I bleed . . ."), which reveals the actual horror that the poetic conventions of meter and rhyme had been seeking to conceal. Further, the surface text, with its poetic devices and euphemisms that overwrite what the speaker actually meant to say, is physically constructed to figure a descent down the female form. Absent from it, however, are emotional considerations and responses to the abortion itself; these are concealed, within the speaker as well as within poetic conventions.

Sexton's collections and the writings of other Middle Generation writers map what Berryman termed "the geography of grief": the internal spaces of fragmenting subjectivities, the patterns of an individual's psyche in the America of the middle decades of the 20th century. In these inscapes fuller narratives of despair, loss, depression, and dependency are hidden for the reader prepared to work at decoding the surface text. The bleeding female form from "The Abortion" is one obvious example of such geographies of grief: the conjunction of the speaker's journey and body with the landscape of the country configures the words on the page. To gain access to the register of grief the reader must break through the individual details of the lines to decipher Sexton's coded use of patriarchal language. By reappropriating language for her own needs, Sexton reveals the intimate, interdependent connection in her poetry between the writing of texts and the discourses of love, a concept that Julia Kristeva postulates in "Stabat Mater" (1977) is "for a woman, the same thing as writing."

PHILIP MCGOWAN

*See also* Confessional Poetry

**Biography**

Born in Newton, Massachusetts, 9 November 1928. Attended Garland Junior College, Boston, Massachusetts, 1947–48; Radcliffe Institute, Cambridge, Massachusetts (Scholar), 1961–63; worked as a fashion model, Boston, 1950–51; teacher, Wayland High School, Massachusetts, 1967–68; Lecturer, 1970–71, and Professor of Creative Writing, 1972–74, Boston University; Crawshaw Professor of Literature, Colgate University, Hamilton, New York, 1972. Received Bread Loaf Writers Conference Robert Frost fellowship, 1959; American Academy traveling fellowship, 1963; Ford grant, 1964; Shelley Memorial Award, 1967; Pulitzer Prize, 1967; Guggenheim fellowship, 1969; honorary Litt.D., Tufts University, Medford, Massachusetts, 1970, Regis College, Weston, Massachusetts, 1971, and Fairfield University, Connecticut, 1971; Fellow, Royal Society of Literature (London). Died in Weston, Massachusetts, 4 October 1974.

**Poetry**

*To Bedlam and Part Way Back,* 1960
*All My Pretty Ones,* 1962
*Selected Poems,* 1964
*Live or Die,* 1966
*Love Poems,* 1969
*Transformations,* 1971
*The Book of Folly,* 1972
*The Death Notebooks,* 1974
*The Awful Rowing toward God,* 1975
*Words for Dr. Y.: Uncollected Poems with Three Stories,* edited by Linda Gray Sexton, 1978
*The Complete Poems,* 1981

*Selected Poems of Anne Sexton,* edited by Diane Wood Middlebrook and Diana Hume George, 1988

**Other Writings:** play (*Mercy Street,* 1969), children's literature, nonfiction (*No Evil Star: Selected Essays, Interviews, and Prose,* edited by Steven E. Colburn, 1985), correspondence (*Anne Sexton: A Self-Portrait in Letters,* edited by Linda Gray Sexton and Lois Ames, 1977).

**Further Reading**


Bixler, Frances, editor, *Original Essays on the Poetry of Anne Sexton,* Conway: University of Central Arkansas Press, 1988

George, Diana Hume, *Oedipus Anne: The Poetry of Anne Sexton,* Urbana: University of Illinois Press, 1987

George, Diana Hume, editor, *Sexton: Selected Criticism,* Urbana: University of Illinois Press, 1988

Hall, Caroline King Barnard, *Anne Sexton,* Boston: Twayne, 1989

McGowan, Philip, "Uncovering the Female Voice in Anne Sexton," *Revista canaria de estudios ingleses* 37 (1998)

Middlebrook, Diane Wood, *Anne Sexton: A Biography,* Boston: Houghton Mifflin, and London: Virago, 1991

Morris, Pam, *Literature and Feminism: An Introduction,* Oxford and Cambridge, Massachusetts: Blackwell, 1993

Morton, Richard Everett, *Anne Sexton's Poetry of Redemption: The Chronology of a Pilgrimage,* Lewiston, New York, and Lampeter, Wales: Mellen Press, 1989

Sexton, Anne, *No Evil Star: Selected Essays, Interviews, and Prose,* edited by Steven E. Colburn, Ann Arbor: University of Michigan Press, 1985

Wagner-Martin, Linda, editor, *Critical Essays on Anne Sexton,* Boston: G.K. Hall, 1989


## All My Pretty Ones

The title poem of Anne Sexton's second collection (published 1962), "All My Pretty Ones" is a pivotal work in Sexton's career as it explores opposed versions of male and female writing and textuality, a recurrent theme in her writing. The five ten-line stanzas figure Sexton sifting through the photographs and mementos of her recently dead parents' lives, deciding whether or not she should discard these incidents and texts from the past. Although momentarily intrigued by the "boxes of pictures of people I do not know," she resolves that it is not her task either to reconnect the histories of these people and to know their identities, or to use her poetry to write purely (auto)biographic accounts: "I'll never know what these faces are all about. / I lock them into their book and throw them out."

The impulse to read Sexton and her contemporaries as "Confessional" poets overlooks the important socially based and historically situated nature of their writing. Sexton here connects her life with the historical narratives of the United States. She discards the family photographs because she is writing her own version of her history, intertwining the first recorded moments of her life with the social and political events of the United States at that time. The text examines a literal scrapbook assembled by her father, juxtaposing images of her life with clippings from newspapers; personal and political history are equated in this textual space. Sexton provides specifics of American history in 1928, the year of her birth: Hoover's election victory for the Republicans, the continuation of Prohibition legislation that his "dry" victory ensured, and the later movements toward World War II. The fragments of her life that have been shored up are intricately interwoven with the cultural and political life of America.

In contrast to her mother's diary, discovered later in the poem, the scrapbook contains unnarrated images. It does not detail a purely personal life or relate an autobiographic point of view but rather presents a collection of unexplained photographs of life and "snapshots of marriage, stopped in places"; the daughter must question the identities contained therein as she has no frame of reference. The stasis and inertia of the stored images speak simultaneously of the married life of her parents and the between-wars history of America. Autobiographic commentaries are wholly absent; indeed, in this text of Sexton's early life her own identity is specifically implicated in the shifts and developments of the outside world. Although in later volumes this perception of an intimate connection with external political events would change for Sexton, her impulse to withhold her own self's most personal narratives from her texts remained central to her poetic narratives.

Sexton's linking of her birth with Hoover's victory and Prohibition is important in understanding this poem and in decoding large sections of her work. Concealed narratives of alcohol dependence recur throughout the texts of a range of American writers at this time; in this regard Sexton was no different. Her father, a recurring figure throughout her work, was an alcoholic, and she herself used alcohol heavily, yet her writings in relation to herself and her father conceal explicit references to continued or even problem alcohol use. This is a learned behavior for Sexton within the context of America's relation to such drinking; in "All My Pretty Ones," however, it functions as an inherited trait from her mother:

> I hold a five-year diary that my mother kept
> for three years, telling all she does not say
> of your alcoholic tendency. You overslept,
> she writes.

The mother's text is centered in euphemism and structured by the necessity of concealment. Sexton is clearly aware of the textual conflicts and, in producing her version of that history, writes against such inherited female traits. She opposes one female text (the mother's diary) with her own, providing for a contended textual space that the reader is asked to decipher and decode. Sexton reveals the instability and duplicity of the written word: the diary is not to be trusted; its writings are those that seek occlusion. The written (female) word and the messages that it transmits are open to manipulation and falsification. The daughter's confrontation with her mother's wrong versions of the past is set against her own remembered knowledge of her father. Sexton's pinpointing of the truth about his "alcoholic tendency" is the telling of what the mother's text refuses to say. The roles of storytelling and truth telling are juxtaposed in this moment as the two female texts intersect to reveal a fuller version of the past.

Sexton's narrators are women encountering a variety of interpretations of the world, a range of versions of history; they function to reveal the duplicitous nature of the written word, of the surface text on the page. In "All My Pretty Ones" the mother's diary "goes to my shelf" and is retained; this female text, wrong, euphemistic, economic with the truth as it may be, is about the father ("The diary of your hurly-burly years"). Female writing, certainly in terms of the mother in this poem and arguably throughout Sexton's collections, is not the site for autobiographic renditions of the self: her mother absents herself from her own diary. What such writing does accomplish is the encoding of a surface text, a surface text that is wrong, is not telling the truth, is subsuming all of the information. The mother's importance in this poem is solely as the writer of the diary, the encoder of a wrong, manipulated version of the past. Sexton preserves this account because here is the only space where love can be found, although it must be uncovered and decoded first: "Only in this hoarded span will love persevere."

PHILIP MCGOWAN

**Further Reading**


Bixler, Frances, editor, *Original Essays on the Poetry of Anne Sexton,* Conway: University of Central Arkansas Press, 1988

George, Diana Hume, *Oedipus Anne: The Poetry of Anne Sexton,* Urbana: University of Illinois Press, 1987

George, Diana Hume, editor, *Sexton: Selected Criticism,* Urbana: University of Illinois Press, 1988

Hall, Caroline King Barnard, *Anne Sexton,* Boston: Twayne, 1989

McGowan, Philip, "Uncovering the Female Voice in Anne Sexton," *Revista canaria de estudios ingleses* 37 (1998)

Middlebrook, Diane Wood, *Anne Sexton: A Biography,* Boston: Houghton Mifflin, and London: Virago, 1991

Morris, Pam, *Literature and Feminism: An Introduction,* Oxford and Cambridge, Massachusetts: Blackwell, 1993

Morton, Richard Everett, *Anne Sexton's Poetry of Redemption: The Chronology of a Pilgrimage,* Lewiston, New York, and Lampeter, Wales: Mellen Press, 1989

Sexton, Anne, *No Evil Star: Selected Essays, Interviews, and Prose,* edited by Steven E. Colburn, Ann Arbor: University of Michigan Press, 1985

Wagner-Martin, Linda, editor, *Critical Essays on Anne Sexton,* Boston: G.K. Hall, 1989


# The Double Image

In the early months of 1958, Anne Sexton drafted "The Double Image," one of several early poems composed for John Holmes' workshop. Sexton revised "The Double Image" from September through Thanksgiving of that year, based in part on the correspondence she had with W.D. Snodgrass, her workshop leader during the 1958 summer Writers' Conference at Antioch College. Sexton was deeply gratified by her poem's acceptance for publication in December 1958 in *The Hudson Review,* an unusual occurrence given the length of the poem and Sexton's status as a virtual unknown in literary circles.

"The Double Image" forms a critical nexus for Sexton's first book, *To Bedlam and Part Way Back* (1960), which borrows its title from a line in section two of "The Double Image." The book, like the poem, chronicles Sexton's bouts of depression and suicide attempts. In "The Double Image," as in future poems, Sexton explores the effects that these incidents had on her family, particularly on her two young daughters. "The Double Image" is an important poem both in Sexton's body of work and in an understanding of American Confessionalism.

Critical reaction to Sexton's poetry was typified by the response to "The Double Image": some critics dismissed it as too biographical, others embraced it for its honesty and the new direction it suggested for American poetry. Poet Maxine Kumin (1981) quotes Hayden Carruth's kind summary of Sexton's work, that her poems "raise the never-solved problem of what literature really is, where you draw the line between art and documentary." The poem incorporates many factual details from Sexton's life between 1956 and 1958, including her separation from her younger child, Joyce, who lived with George and Billie Sexton, her paternal grandparents; her two suicide attempts; her mother's cancer; her institutionalization; her brief stay at her mother's house; her return to her husband's home; and Joyce's return home. Sexton's real-life struggles, as they came to be poetically rendered in *To Bedlam and Part Way Back,* challenged the content of American poetry in much the same way as did other members of the new Confessional movement.

At 211 lines, "The Double Image" is an impressive poetic venture. As with many of her early poems, Sexton imposed a rigid formality on the poem, creating for it an elaborate rhyme scheme and system of repetitive lines. The poem is an explanation of Sexton's life in these years, telling Joyce why she was separated from her mother during her early life and why Sexton's suicide attempts made it impossible for her to offer a stable, loving home for Joyce. The poem is written after Sexton and Joyce are reunited; Sexton believes that she has conquered depression, as she states, "I checked out for the last time / on the first of May; / graduate of the mental cases, / with my analyst's okay." Through her chronicle of the time spent apart, Sexton seeks to communicate to Joyce and to the reader a larger explanation for what she perceives as her failings as a mother and the renewed possibilities for becoming a good mother.

Section one begins in the present, with Sexton watching the now four-year-old Joyce in the house. Presumably, they are together permanently, as the poet uses the past tense as the voice of madness. As Sexton looks at Joyce, she writes, "And I remember / mostly the three autumns you did not live here. / They said I'd never get you back again." Sexton expresses regret for the separation but moves on to link the separation not only to her madness and depression but also to Joyce herself. She explains suicide as the cause for separation, "letting doom / leak like a broken faucet; / as if doom had flooded my belly and filled your bassinet, / an old debt I must assume." Sexton intimates here that Joyce's presence is not enough to stop her from killing herself. Neither the child nor what her nickname represents, "Joy," has been enough to stay Sexton from her course of suicide. Instead, the doom prevails and calls to Sexton.

Sexton attempts to explain her madness to the child, writing, "I pretended I was dead / until the white men pumped the poison out." In a move that prefigured Sexton's award-winning poeticization of traditional fairy tales in *Transformations* (1971), Sexton blames her madness on "ugly angels" and "witches in my head." Through these voices, Sexton finds release. Joyce, through the poem, is to understand that the witches represent madness as well as compassion and love. Sexton tries to use her institutionalization and separation from Joyce as a moment of instruction for the child, explaining, "love your self's self where it lives."

In sections two to four, Sexton explains her move from the institution to her mother and father's home and back to the institution. As Sexton searches for health, she also searches for home. In her parents' home, "I lived like an angry guest / like a partly mended thing, an outgrown child." This is not a home, anymore than the institution is a home. Yet Sexton seems to be seeking her place and role and, by extension, a place for her child. In section five, she returns to her husband's home and to her role as a wife where she "served cocktails as a wife / should, made love among my petticoats." Into this domestic tranquility, the young Joyce enters as a "butterfly / girl with jelly bean cheeks, / disobedient three, my splendid / stranger." Mother and child are separated by time and emotional distance.

"You seldom came," Sexton tells Joyce. "I could not get you back / except for weekends." Sexton can understand her own child only as a stranger in her life. In the final stanza, Sexton reminds Joyce, "The first visit you asked my name" and "how we bumped away from each other like marionettes / on strings. It wasn't the same / as love." This distance is echoed in Sexton's relationship with her mother, who believes that her child, the adult Sexton, has given her cancer. The poem probes the meaning and form of mother/daughter relationships. Physically, "The Double Image" is a pair of portraits taken in the poem of Sexton and her mother, hung across from each other. Metaphorically, "The Double Image" represents Mary Gray's ability to be a mother to Sexton, even when battling cancer, while Sexton herself cannot be a good mother to Joyce. Sexton recalls literary madness as she says of her own portrait, "I rot on the wall, my own / Dorian Gray." Inherent in her own image, however, is Joyce's image. As Sexton reveals her guilt in abandoning her mother and her child, the poem ironically reveals that there are three images: Sexton's, Joyce's, and Mary Gray's. In the triplicate image, Sexton's guilt multiplies. The small Joyce, the daughter, represents Sexton's inability to choose to remain a daughter. Sexton realizes that she must choose a role—mother or daughter—thus pitting Joyce against her own grandmother, Mary Gray. Sexton realizes that she has abandoned her daughter in her infancy and her mother in her illness, and her suicide attempts serve as the primary loci of her guilt. Sexton ends the poem addressing Joyce: "And this was my worst guilt; you could not cure / nor soothe it. I made you to find me." This sad echo of section one leaves the reader to wonder whether the suicide that Sexton maintains so vigorously is behind her in "The Double Image" still lingers even in her own words of recovery—especially given the benefit of hindsight, through which we know of her eventual suicide.

J. ELIZABETH CLARK

**Further Reading**

Clark, Hilary, "Depression, Shame, and Reparation: The Case of Anne Sexton," in *Scenes of Shame: Psychoanalysis, Shame, and Writing,* edited by Joseph Adamson and Hilary Clark, Albany: State University of New York Press, 1999

Colburn, Steven E., "Anne Sexton: A Supplemental Bibliography, 1945–1990," *Bulletin of Bibliography* 48, no. 2 (1991)

Honton, Margaret, "The Double Image and the Division of Parts: A Study of Mother/Daughter Relationships in the Poetry of Anne Sexton," *Journal of Women's Studies in Literature* 1 (1979)

Johnson, Greg, "The Achievement of Anne Sexton," *Hollins Critic* 21, no. 3 (1984)

Kumin, Maxine, "How It Was: Maxine Kumin on Anne Sexton," in *The Complete Poems,* by Sexton, Boston: Houghton Mifflin, 1981

Long, Mikhail Ann, "As If Day Had Rearranged into Night: Suicidal Tendencies in the Poetry of Anne Sexton," *Literature and Psychology* 39, nos. 1–2 (1993)

Middlebrook, Diane Wood, "1957: Anne Sexton's Bedlam," *Pequod: A Journal of Contemporary Literature and Literary Criticism* 23–24 (1987)

Middlebrook, Diane Wood, *Anne Sexton: A Biography,* Boston: Houghton Mifflin, and London: Virago, 1991

Phillips, Robert, "Anne Sexton: The Blooming Mouth and the Bleeding Rose," in *The Confessional Poets,* by Phillips, Carbondale: Southern Illinois University Press, and London: Feffer and Simons, 1973

Wagner-Martin, Linda, editor, *Critical Essays on Anne Sexton,* Boston: G.K. Hall, 1989

# Housewife

Anne Sexton's ten-line poem "Housewife" first appeared in her collection *All My Pretty Ones* (1962), which includes an epigram from a letter by Kafka asserting that "a book should serve as the ax for the frozen sea within us." Sexton's poem, the shortest one in her second book, functions as a verbal ax, cutting through and deconstructing the frozen compound of the poem's title to reveal a biting psychological insight.

The first statement the poem makes ("Some women marry houses.") seems a humorous extension of the literal meaning of "housewife," the joke flashing from the unexpected object of "marry," but the next four statements move into the territory limned by the famous James Thurber cartoon in which the bodies of a woman and a house conflate as an ominous threat to the tiny man standing on the outside. Thurber connected the origin of his image with the "Subconscious of Man" (Thurber, 1948); Sexton's poem shows that the "house-woman," as Thurber called it, haunts women as well. The poem's second statement shifts the subject from "women" to a singular house, referred to as an "it" with a skin, internal organs, and "bowel movements." By means of metonymy, the transformation from womanhood to houseness seems inevitable. The disconcerting play between the funny and the frightening continues in the fourth statement, where the walls of the house are "permanent" (suggesting a rigid prison) and "pink" (obviously feminine, perhaps even cute). The fifth statement, a complex command to the reader to "see," verbalizes the total conflation of house and woman, as the "it" morphs into a "she" who "sits on her knees all day, / faithfully washing herself down." The reference to men who "enter by force, drawn back like Jonah / into their fleshy mothers" alludes to the biblical story of the unwilling prophet who was swallowed by a divinely sent whale as he tried to avoid his missionary call. The inevitable works on men as well as on women, but the distance between men and their "mothers" sharply contrasts with the union of a woman and her mother, a claim argued by contemporary psychoanalysts such as Nancy Chodorow (1978). Chodorow cites Sexton's poem as she claims that "a girl retains her pre-oedipal tie to her mother" and "she becomes the mother (phylogenetically the all-embracing sea, ontogenetically the womb)." Sexton's statement is more ambiguous than it appears, for "A woman is her mother" may also mean that a woman must mother herself because there will be no one else to fill that role. Sexton expressed this view in prose in her journal on New Year's Day 1972: "Now I am the wife. I am the mother" (Sexton, 1985). The last statement of the poem, "That's the main thing," abandons the audience to the discomforting realm of vague uncertainty, and ends with a noun more abstract than "truth" and more chilling for its inchoateness. The concluding "thing," nevertheless, names the dehumanization that happens to the "some women" with which the poem began.

Elizabeth Mills

**Further Reading**

Alkalay-Gut, Karen, "Sexton's 'Housewife,'" *The Explicator* 47, no. 2 (1989)

Chodorow, Nancy, *The Reproduction of Mothering: Psychoanalysis and the Sociology of Gender,* 2nd edition, Berkeley: University of California Press, 1978

George, Diana Hume, *Oedipus Anne: The Poetry of Anne Sexton,* Urbana: University of Illinois Press, 1987

Ostriker, Alicia, *Stealing the Language: The Emergence of Women's Poetry in America,* Boston: Beacon, 1986

Sexton, Anne, *No Evil Star: Selected Essays, Interviews, and Prose,* edited by Steven E. Colburn, Ann Arbor: University of Michigan Press, 1985

Thurber, James, *The Beast in Me and Other Animals,* New York: Harcourt Brace, 1948

---

# Karl Shapiro 1913–2000

Karl Shapiro, American poet, critic, and editor, received national attention after the publication of his second book of poetry, *V-Letter, and Other Poems*. Published in 1944 while he was stationed in the South Pacific during World War II, this slim volume of poetry received critical acclaim for his treatment of war themes. Evalyn Katz, his fiancee and literary agent at the time, received his poetry through V-Mail, the system used by the United States Armed Forces, and coordinated the publication of *V-Letter*. "Elegy for a Dead Soldier" is one of the most well-known poems from this book. Joseph Reino (1981) described *V-Letter* as having "just the appropriate touches of ethnic anguish, sentimental Christianity and wartime self-questioning" for it to be awarded the Pulitzer Prize in 1945. Shapiro was also offered the position of Consultant in Poetry to the Library of Congress and a tenured associated professorship in creative writing at Johns Hopkins University after its publication.

Shapiro's success as a poet had actually started years earlier, before he was sent overseas. His poem "Self History" was republished in five different newspapers on the East Coast, and by November 1941 *Poetry* magazine had accepted more than a dozen of his poems. Similarly, when he published *Person, Place, and Thing* (1942), Louise Bogan, the *New York Times* poetry editor, praised his work and called him "the finest young American talent to appear in many seasons" (*New Yorker* [9 January 1943]). She extolled the emotional depth of his poetry, which set him apart from those who wrote poetry of the mind alone.

Critics describe Shapiro's work as honest and meticulous in style, using middle-class themes with an undercurrent of the anguish felt by a Jewish man living in a conservative southern environment. He was characterized as a post-Fugitive poet with Romantic influences. Allen Tate, a leader of the Fugitive movement (1922–25) wrote in "Letter to a Poet" (*Common Sense* [February 1943]) that "common humanity of poets is not found in sympathy of views or politics, but in that special savagery of attack...." In particular Tate praised Shapiro's "Dome of Sunday" and "Love Poem" as having those unique qualities.

Although Shapiro's poetry had some of the characteristics of Fugitive poetry, he did not consider himself an intellectual. He often criticized highly cerebral poets and critics whom he believed did not understand the true nature of poetry. *In Defense of Ignorance* (1952) explains Shapiro's position on intellectuals:

> The position I take is anti-intellectual.... What is anti-intellectual? The best way to define it is through its opposite. An intellectual is a person who reduces all experience to abstract ideas.

He berated T.S. Eliot and Ezra Pound, describing them as "weak poets" despite the influence they had on American poetry, explaining that every poet of his generation "grew up in the shadow of the criticism of T.S. Eliot." According to Shapiro, criticism was detrimental to good poetry because critics did not comprehend the sensual nature of poetry. He believed that poetry was best expressed in the language of the common man, which was more precise and true, and preferred William Carlos Williams and Hart Crane, who were then considered rustics. Not until he started teaching and editing himself was he able to break from the influences of Eliot and Pound.

Shapiro's disdain for intellectuals may have stemmed from his background. He was not nearly as successful in school as his older brother. Shapiro's troublesome history in public schools and at the University of Virginia inspired him to write "University," which verbally flays the stuffiness of his professors and even the Jewish community he encountered at the school. Jews of Russian descent were considered inferior to German Jews, a fact that led him in earlier years to change the spelling of his name from Carl to Karl. The ethnic anguish and muted rage in his poetry made it seem similar to Fugitive poetry, but Shapiro heartily embraced the anti-intellectual poetry of William Carlos Williams and Beat poets—until he grew tired of their particular styles. Examples of his own poetry written in Beat style in addition to "University" include "Southerner," "Reading Keats in Wartime," and "Death of Emma Goldman." The Beat influence, which Shapiro adopted and then condemned, allowed him to criticize academic and mainstream poetry. In his essay *To Abolish Children* (1968), however, Shapiro described Beat poets as dissidents who "simply supply additional dry rot to the cultural fabric."

Like Shapiro, the Confessional poets—Sylvia Plath and Robert Lowell, among others—were never self-pitying and revealed almost too much about themselves in their poetry, leaving only a hint of mystery, as in Shapiro's own *The Bourgeois Poet* (1964). The Romantic influences, which seem contrary to the rage exhibited in much of Shapiro's poetry, are evident in "Olive Tree," "Cut Flower," and "Jew at Christmas Eve."

Shapiro's works of criticism, although they were not popular, were consistent with his style: to express himself with brutal honesty. His critical works include: *Beyond Criticism* (1953), *English Prosody and Modern Poetry* (1947), *Bibliography of Modern Prosody* (1948), and *Essay on Rime* (1945), which was written in verse. After publishing *Essay on Rime,* he lost favor with many of the same critics who had earlier praised *V-Letter*. He further lambasted intellectuals in *Beyond Criticism* and espoused his controversial views in a front-page article of the *New York Times Book Review* in 1959. He voiced his opinion about modern poetry and even cited names of particular poets.

Shapiro edited *Poetry* magazine from 1950 to 1956, but he described the experience as not really editing at all, but rather carrying on a long-held tradition:

> For five years I edited *Poetry* magazine and was forced to read a great deal of book-review criticism for publication. My only aim as editor of this famous magazine was to keep its reputation and what it was reputed to be. Editing poetry was a job for me, not a vocation. I let the magazine coast as it had for forty years. I was afraid to tamper with its respectability. (*In Defense of Ignorance*)

Shapiro also edited *Prairie Schooner* from 1956 to 1966.

Despite his lack of a formal college education, Shapiro taught at several universities. He published ten books of poetry, three collected works, one book of fiction, *Edsel* (1971), and six scholarly works. In particular, *Trial of a Poet* (1947), *Poems, 1940–1953* (1953), and *Poems of a Jew* (1958) focus on his ethnic heritage. He was the recipient in April 1944 of a Guggenheim post-service fellowship, one of the first grants given by the foundation for men and women in the armed services. He also received a special award in 1944 from the American Academy of Arts and Letters.

SARAH SCHOON

**Biography**

Born in Baltimore, Maryland, 10 November 1913. Attended the University of Virginia, Charlottesville, 1932–33; Johns Hopkins University, Baltimore, 1937–39; Pratt Library School, Baltimore, 1940; served in the United States Army, 1941–45; clerk in family business, mid-1930s; Associate Professor, Johns Hopkins University, 1948–50; Visiting Professor, University of Wisconsin, Madison, 1948, Loyola University, Chicago, 1951–52, University of California, Berkeley and Davis, 1955–56, and Indiana University, Bloomington, 1956–57; Professor of English, University of Nebraska, Lincoln, 1956–66, University of Illinois, Chicago Circle, 1966–68, and University of California, Davis, 1968–84; editor, *Poetry,* Chicago, 1950–56, *Newberry Library Bulletin,* 1953–55, and *Prairie Schooner,* 1956–66; Consultant in Poetry, 1946–47, and Whittall Lecturer, 1964, 1967, Library of Congress, Washington, D.C.; Lecturer, Salzburg Seminar in American Studies, 1952; State Department Lecturer, India, 1955; Elliston Lecturer, University of Cincinnati, 1959. Received American Academy grant, 1944; Guggenheim fellowship, 1944, 1953; Pulitzer Prize, 1945; Shelley Memorial Award, 1946; Kenyon School of Letters fellowship, 1956, 1957; Bollingen Prize, 1969; *Los Angeles Times* Kirsch Award, 1989; Charity Randall citation, 1990; honorary D.H.L., Wayne State University, Detroit, 1960; honorary Litt.D., Bucknell University, Lewisburg, Pennsylvania, 1972; fellow in American Letters, Library of Congress; member, American Academy of Arts and Sciences, and American Academy, 1959. Died in New York City, 14 May 2000.

**Poetry**

*Poems,* 1935
*Five Young American Poets* (with others), 1941
*The Place of Love,* 1942
*Person, Place, and Thing,* 1942
*V-Letter, and Other Poems,* 1944
*Essay on Rime,* 1945
*Trial of a Poet, and Other Poems,* 1947
*Poems, 1940–1953,* 1953
*Poems of a Jew,* 1958
*The Bourgeois Poet,* 1964
*Selected Poems,* 1968
*White-Haired Lover,* 1968
*Adult Bookstore,* 1976
*Collected Poems, 1940–1978,* 1978
*Love and War, Art and God,* 1984
*Adam and Eve,* 1986
*New and Selected Poems, 1940–1986,* 1987
*The Old Horsefly,* 1992
*The Wild Card: Selected Poems, Early and Late,* edited by Stanley Kunitz and David Ignatow, 1998

**Selected Criticism**

*Essay on Rime,* 1945
*English Prosody and Modern Poetry,* 1947
*Poets at Work* (with others), edited by Charles D. Abbott, 1948
*Beyond Criticism,* 1953

**Other Writings:** plays, novel (*Edsel,* 1971), essays (*In Defense of Ignorance,* 1952; *To Abolish Children,* 1968; *The Poetry Wreck: Selected Essays, 1950–1970,* 1975), writing handbooks, autobiography (*An Autobiography in Three Parts,* 1988); edited collections of poetry (*American Poetry,* 1960).

**Further Reading**

Bartlett, Lee, *Karl Shapiro: A Descriptive Bibliography, 1933–1977,* New York and London: Garland, 1979
Malkoff, Karl, "The Self in the Modern World: Karl Shapiro's

Jewish Poems," in *Contemporary American-Jewish Literature,* edited by Irving Malin, Bloomington: Indiana University Press, 1973
Reino, Joseph, *Karl Shapiro,* Boston: Twayne, 1981
Richman, Robert, "The Trials of a Poet," *New Centurion* 6, nos. 74–81 (1988)
Shapiro, Karl, *Poet: An Autobiography in Three Parts,* Chapel Hill, North Carolina: Algonquin, 1988

---

# Ron Silliman 1946–

One of the major theorists and practitioners of Language poetry, Ron Silliman studied at Berkeley and San Francisco State between 1966 and 1971 during the inception of the Language poetry movement, which seeks political and social change through its rejection of stock lyricism, its questioning of referentiality, and its readers' participation in making meaning. A prolific writer, Silliman has published over 20 books of poetry, a book of criticism called *The New Sentence* (1987), and the anthology *In the American Tree* (1986). His awards include a National Endowment for the Arts and a Pew fellowship.

Silliman is noted for his use of prose sentences and "random" collages of phrases and descriptions, as well as his lack of linear plot or characterization associated with traditional narrative; his narratives are about the creation of narrative itself. Silliman employs a wide variety of forms. "The Chinese Notebook" and "Sunset Debris" (*The Age of Huts,* 1986) are structured around an extended number of unanswered questions, an interrogative form that Charles Bernstein sees as derived from Wittgenstein's *Philosophical Investigations.* The cumulative form of *Paradise* (1985) is based on adding elements to the work in equal installments, such as writing one sentence per day; mathematically generated forms, as in *Ketjak* (1978) and *Tjanting* (1981), utilize the Fibonacci numbering series. A kind of wild or impure mixture of forms dominates books such as *Lit* (1987) and *Jones* (1993). "Jones," for example, contains seven prose sections (one prose section lined up margin right), one section in quatrains, one section in three-line stanzas, and one section of "sentence" in which Silliman collages the language of writing with objects from the natural world:

> An idea that a walk is raised makes curbs.
> Bridge gone in the dawn haze.
> Grease stains in the gutter shimmer with the morning sun.
> What's in that sack, sticking out beneath the bush?
> Ink runs in the gutter, downhill to the margin.

Most of Ron Silliman's books of poems are part of a larger work, the Alphabet, a unifying system that makes a whole out of the parts into an alphabetical epic. The influence of High Modernist Pound's *Cantos,* of Objectivist poet Louis Zukofsky's *"A,"* and of Projectivist poet Charles Olson's *Maximus Poems* is evident. This large work—a proposed 1,200 pages—suggests a systematic approach: reduce writing to the level of the paragraph, the new sentence, in order to focus on the essence of language; reduce further to words, which are in turn reducible to individual letters. Paradoxically, the letters make up the alphabet as a larger work.

Silliman's anthology of Language poetry *In the American Tree* offers a brief history of Language poetry. The book is arranged, according to Silliman in his introduction, as

> three sections and a coda. The first sequence addresses the poem's relation to society, the second the terrain of the poem itself, and the third the "mapping" which has been the site for my own practice as a poet.

The result is a landmark anthology, edited by an important theorist and practitioner working from the inside of the Language movement.

Since poetry and theory are joined in a symbiotic relationship, Silliman, working as a poetic theorist, believes that "The goal of poetry can never be the proof of theory, although it is inevitably a test of the poet's belief" (*The New Sentence*). As a Language writer Silliman sought both to reconsider long-standing literary terminology and dichotomies and to move literary theory forward with technological advances, arguing that historically

> the sentence, as distinct from the utterance of speech, is a unit of prose, and if prose as literature and the rise of the printing press are inextricably interwoven, then the impact of printing on literature, not just the presentation of literature, but on how writing itself is written, needs to be addressed.

Drawing from Modernist Gertrude Stein's books and lectures from the early 1930s, Silliman merges the compartmentalized limitations of poetry and prose into a general concept of writing. Because "the paragraph organizes the sentences fundamentally the same way a stanza does lines of verse," and since "at one level, the completed sentence . . . has become equivalent to a line, a condition not previously imposed on sentences," Silliman identifies the qualities of the new sentence:

1) The paragraph organizes the sentences;
2) The paragraph is a unity of quantity, not logic or argument;
3) Sentence length is a unit of measure;
4) Sentence structure is altered for torque, or increase polysemy/ambiguity;
5) Syllogistic movement is: (a) limited; (b) controlled;
6) Primary syllogistic movement is between the preceding and following sentences;
7) Secondary syllogistic movement is toward the paragraph as a whole, or the total work;

8) The limiting of syllogistic movement keeps the reader's attention at or very close to the level of language, that is, most often at the sentence level or below.

In articulating this new sentence Silliman both offers a rubric for readers new to Language poetry and creates a framework in which the poem—and its writing—becomes the narrative of the poem, centering the language rather than the writer's "voice." Additionally he creates a tool for writers that allows them to craft language-centered poems that ask the reader to interact with the text, creating an aesthetic in which readers and writers share equally in the production of literature rather than accept the social hierarchies commodified by commercial and academic concerns.

Determined to make such incursions across the borders between poetry and prose, and able to articulate the theoretical basis not only for what he has already written, but also for what he expects to try next, Silliman has emerged from the generation of Language poets as one of its foremost theorists and spokespersons, one whose impact is spreading throughout the world of poetry. As critic Hank Lazar (1988) reminds readers, however,

> Silliman's writing is fun to read: Its pleasure lies in the gradual unfolding of intricate forms and in the mix of puns, declarations, sounds and sights from our daily environment, the range of references from philosophy to baseball.

In the tradition of American writers who create a unified large work, Silliman, having worked to develop and define the new sentence, lets his work move simultaneously in what appear to be opposing directions: to the minute and specific—reducing language to words to the letters—and to the general and "epic," building toward his own Alphabet.

ROBERT MILTNER

*See also* Language Poetry

**Biography**

Born in Pasco, Washington, 8 May 1946. Attended Merritt College, 1965, 1969–72; San Francisco State College (now University), 1966–69; University of California, Berkeley, 1969–71; editorial assistant, Mecca Publications, San Francisco, 1972; director of research and education, Committee for Prisoner Humanity and Justice, San Rafael, California, 1972–76; project manager, Tenderloin Ethnographic Research Project, San Francisco, 1977–78; director of outreach, Central City Hospitality House, San Francisco, 1979–81; Lecturer, San Francisco State University, 1981; Visiting Lecturer, University of California, San Diego, 1982; writer-in-residence, New College of California, San Francisco, 1982; director of public relations and development, 1982–86, and poet-in-residence, 1983–90, California Institute of Integral Studies, San Francisco; currently marketing communications specialist for computer firm; editor, *Tottel's*, 1970–81; executive editor, 1986–89, and currently member of the editorial collective, *Socialist Review;* from 1989 managing editor, *Computer Land*. Received Hart Crane and Alice Crane Williams Award, 1968; Joan Lee Yang Award, 1970, 1971; National Endowment for the Arts fellowship, 1979; California Arts Council grant, 1979, 1980; Poetry Center Book Award, 1985. Living in Valley Forge, Pennsylvania.

**Poetry**

*Moon in the Seventh House,* 1968
*Three Syntactic Fictions for Dennis Schmitz,* 1969
*Crow,* 1971
*Mohawk,* 1973
*Nox,* 1974
*Sitting Up, Standing Up, Taking Steps,* 1978
*Ketjak,* 1978
*Tjanting,* 1981
*Bart,* 1982
*ABC,* 1983
*Paradise,* 1985
*The Age of Huts,* 1986
*Lit,* 1987
*What,* 1988
*Manifest,* 1990
*Leningrad* (with Michael Davidson, Lyn Hejinian, and Barrett Watten), 1991
*Demo to Ink,* 1992
*Toner,* 1992
*Jones,* 1993
*N/O,* 1994
*R,* 1995
*Xing,* 1996
*Quindecagon,* 1998

**Selected Criticism**

*The New Sentence,* 1987

**Other Writings:** screen play; edited poetry anthology (*In the American Tree,* 1986).

**Further Reading**

Amnasan, Michael, "Ron Silliman Interviewed," *Ottotole* 3 (Spring 1989)
Delville, Michel, *The American Prose Poem: Poetic Form and the Boundaries of Genre,* Gainesville: University Press of Florida, 1998
*The Difficulties* 2, no. 2 (1985) (special issue on Silliman)
Fredman, Stephen, *Poet's Prose: The Crisis in American Verse,* Cambridge and New York: Cambridge University Press, 1983; 2nd edition, 1990
Lazar, Hank, "Radical Collages," *Nation* (2–9 July 1988)
McCaffery, Larry, and Sinda Gregory, "An Interview with Ron Silliman," in *Alive and Writing: Interviews with American Authors of the 1980s,* Urbana: University of Illinois Press, 1987
Silliman, Ron, "Ron Silliman on the Alphabet," *Quarry West* 34 (1998)
Tanner, Ron, and Valerie Ross, "The Politics of Poetry: An Interview with Ron Silliman," *Cream City Review* 13, no. 2 (Fall 1989)

# Charles Simic 1938–

"Little said, much meant, is what poetry is all about," Charles Simic observes in the introduction to his anthology of Serbian poetry (*The Horse Has Six Legs,* 1992). As easily as one could apply this dictum to any number of contemporary American poets, it seems an especially apt description of Simic's own work, which combines haunting, suggestive images with an often surprising economy of language. His work bears the ready mark of French Surrealism as well as Yugoslav folklore and poetry, of which he is an avid and prolific translator. Cunning in their execution and unapologetic for their faith in conceit, Simic's poems trace the delicate boundary between experience and fancy, which Simic treats as equally tenuous mediations between the world and consciousness. Accordingly, his work is often characterized as dark, dream-like, or macabre, although such formulations fail to convey the humor and sophistication with which he addresses topics of universal significance, from the perception of objects (in poems like "Knife" and "Bestiary for the Fingers of My Right Hand") and the failure of utterance ("*errata*") in his early work to the prose meditations on personal and national histories in *The World Doesn't End,* which received the Pulitzer Prize in 1990.

Simic was born in Belgrade, Yugoslavia in 1938 and survived the Allied bombing of his native city. (The poet Richard Hugo, one of the bombardiers in that campaign, addresses this peculiar circumstance in his poem "Letter to Simic from Boulder.") The war left him a refugee, and he wandered through Western Europe with his family before arriving in the United States in the early 1950s. These peregrinations have had an almost palpable influence on Simic's poems and worldview: a creature of the city, raised in such cultural capitals as Paris, New York, and Chicago, Simic nevertheless imagines such oddities as a child whose head is made out of leftover black bread ("Austerities"), Death fumbling through bad weather to perform his thankless tasks ("Eyes Fastened with Pins"), and a displaced boy who learns early that war and chess are best played blindfolded ("Prodigy"). Many of Simic's poems take a provincial, superstitious sensibility that lends itself to the bizarre tricks of mind and dislocation of Old World belief and relocates it in the knowable, post-industrial, postmodern metropolis. In more recent poems like "Shadow Publishing Company" (*Walking the Black Cat,* 1996) and "Childhood at the Movies" (*A Wedding in Hell,* 1994) the details drawn from fantasy and reality create a remarkable balance: the odd or unsettling conceit (for example, an old widow inviting a strange couple to lie down on her marriage bed) displaces what is otherwise a plausible, quotidian narrative plane, but the potentially realistic, less fantastic details ("the street of overgrown lilacs"; "Her late husband was an eye doctor") also anchor the scene in the world of everyday experience. At the same time that the poems displace the reader from accepted reality, they make it impossible for the reader to surrender entirely to the dreamscape that exists within—not against—its recognizable details.

Simic's work has, with necessary exceptions, followed a trajectory toward this dual perspective. Those earlier poems that have been widely anthologized, including many of the poems in *Dismantling the Silence* (1971), his first full-length collection, and such famous pieces as "Watermelon" and "Breasts" (*Return to a Place Lit by a Glass of Milk,* 1974), are marked by the direct statement of metaphor. "Watermelons" are, quite simply, "Green Buddhas / On the fruit stand." The image is surprising and carefully executed but does not subject itself to much wider complication. The speaker is clearly engaging in an act of metaphor-making, establishing an artifice against which the reader must reconsider the object without the risk of becoming entangled in the conceit: the reader enjoys the puppet show but also sees the strings.

With *Charon's Cosmology* (1977) and *Classic Ballroom Dances* (1980), however, Simic began to animate his images, furnishing them with idiosyncratic behavior that often relegates the narrative voice to the position of commentator rather than magician. No longer asking the reader to accept a temporarily skewed perception, the poems from this period enact their metaphors without stating them, and the resulting narrative plane seems to follow its own peculiar rules. Subsequent collections, including among others *Unending Blues* (1986) and *The Book of Gods and Devils* (1990), develop this technique and place it in a contemporary cosmopolitan context with increasing frequency (see, for example, "Against Whatever It Is That's Encroaching" and "Le Beau Monde"). Like his later work, these poems deliver the sense of a partially rendered translation, one that allows only sporadic and often puzzling glimpses of the unseen original at the same time that it affords great pleasure in its half-revealed truths.

It is not difficult to trace Charles Simic's influences. He has published many essays, memoirs, and interviews, and he bears a close affinity to the several 20th-century Serbian and Slovene poets he has translated into English, among them Vasko Popa, Ivan V. Lalić, Novica Tadić, and Tomaž Šalamun. Like Simic, these poets combine post-Surrealist interests with stripped-down language and an often latent, occasionally overt preoccupation with the eerie mythologies and troubled history of the Balkans. The translations themselves, which earned Simic PEN translation awards in 1970 and 1980, convey both his admiration for the rhetoric of the originals as well as his precision and care in selecting faithful, natural English equivalents. But as much as poems in Simic's translation sound like Simic—an almost deliberate consequence of his approach to translation—they nevertheless remain exotic and imported in a way that Simic's own work never is.

This difference highlights just how American Simic is, regardless of where his worldview originates. His poems present glimpses of a Southern European tradition wholly imported into American language and culture, then tinged with Simic's unique touch; the end product is a complex set of implications within an aural simplicity and straightforwardness. This not only lends itself to his inimitability, as many critics have remarked, but also places him squarely within a contemporary poetic tradition alongside such distinctly American poets as Mark Strand, James Tate, and Bill Knott.

Benjamin Paloff

*See also* Surrealism

**Biography**

Born in Belgrade, Yugoslavia, 9 May 1938; emigrated to the United States in 1954; naturalized, 1971. Attended the University of Chicago, 1956–59; New York University, 1959–61, 1963–65, B.A. 1967; served in the United States Army, 1961–63; proofreader, Chicago *Sun-Times;* member of the Department of English, California State College, Hayward,

1970–73; since 1973 Professor of English, University of New Hampshire, Durham; editorial assistant, *Aperture* magazine, 1966–69. Received PEN Award for translation, 1970, 1980; Guggenheim fellowship, 1972; National Endowment for the Arts fellowship, 1974, 1979; Edgar Allan Poe Award, 1975; American Academy Award, 1976; Harriet Monroe Poetry Award, 1980; Poetry Society of America di Castignola Award, 1980; Fulbright fellowship, 1982; Ingram Merrill fellowship, 1983; MacArthur fellowship, 1984; Pulitzer Prize, 1990; Academy of American Poets fellowship, 1998; Chancellor, Academy of American Poets, 2000. Living in Durham, New Hampshire.

**Poetry**

*What the Grass Says*, 1967
*Somewhere Among Us a Stone Is Taking Notes*, 1969
*Dismantling the Silence*, 1971
*White*, 1972; revised edition, 1980
*Return to a Place Lit by a Glass of Milk*, 1974
*Charon's Cosmology*, 1977
*Classic Ballroom Dances*, 1980
*Austerities*, 1982
*Weather Forecast for Utopia and Vicinity: Poems, 1967–1982*, 1983
*Selected Poems, 1963–1983*, 1985; revised edition, 1990
*Unending Blues*, 1986
*The World Doesn't End: Prose Poems*, 1989
*The Book of Gods and Devils*, 1990
*Hotel Insomnia*, 1992
*A Wedding in Hell*, 1994
*Walking the Black Cat*, 1996
*On the Music of the Spheres* (with photographs by Linda Connor), 1996
*Looking for Trouble*, 1997
*Jackstraws*, 1999
*Charles Simic: Selected Early Poems*, 1999

**Selected Criticism**

*The Uncertain Certainty: Interviews, Essays, and Notes on Poetry*, 1985
*Wonderful Words, Silent Truth: Essays on Poetry, and a Memoir*, 1990
*Orphan Factory: Essays and Memoirs*, 1997

**Other Writings:** translations of French, Serbian (*The Horse Has Six Legs: An Anthology of Serbian Poetry*, 1992), Croatian, Macedonian, and Slovenian poetry (*Some Other Wine and Light*, by Aleksandar Ristović, 1989); edited collections of poetry (*Another Republic: 17 European and South American Writers* [with Mark Strand], 1976; *The Best American Poetry 1992*, 1992).

**Further Reading**

Corbett, William, "Charles Simic" (interview), *Poets and Writers* 24 (May/June 1996)
Jackson, Richard, *The Dismantling of Time in Contemporary American Poetry*, Tuscaloosa: University of Alabama Press, 1988
McQuade, Molly, *Stealing Glimpses: Of Poetry, Poets, and Things in Between*, Louisville, Kentucky: Sarabande, 1999
Stitt, Peter, *Uncertainty and Plenitude: Five Contemporary Poets*, Iowa City: University of Iowa Press, 1997
Vendler, Helen, *Soul Says: On Recent Poetry*, Cambridge, Massachusetts: Harvard University Press, 1995
Weigl, Bruce, editor, *Charles Simic: Essays on the Poetry*, Ann Arbor: University of Michigan Press, 1996

## Bestiary for the Fingers of My Right Hand

In his early five-part poem "Bestiary for the Fingers of My Right Hand," Charles Simic carefully destabilizes the reader's assumptions about the objects of mundane reality. This is not to say that the eponymous digits misbehave in a dark and radical manner, a signature of Simic's later work. In "Bestiary" Simic strikes a compromise between the vision he is soon to develop, one in which objects seem to take on a mischievous, self-determined life, and the manipulation of common articles as received, perhaps, from the American Modernist tradition. Simic's approach recalls such noteworthy models as William Carlos Williams' "The Red Wheelbarrow" and Wallace Stevens' "Study of Two Pears."

Besides Simic's radical recasting of each finger's role, however, "Bestiary" presents a subtler, more significant departure from the Modernist approach: in the Williams and Stevens examples, even in the absence of a first-person utterance, the speaker stands in relation to the object and inscribes himself within the description. He speaks with certainty and authority and thus remains at least as central a feature of the poem as the object itself. But Simic's poem suggests a degree of slippage, for while the reader understands the bizarre portrait as the mutterings of an idiosyncratic voice, that voice minimizes itself, showcasing the fantastic reality it has offered. There is a sense of this even in the first stanza of part one:

> Thumb, loose tooth of a horse.
> Rooster to his hens.
> Horn of a devil. Fat worm
> They have attached to my flesh
> At the time of my birth.
> It takes four to hold him down,
> Bend him in half, until the bone
> Begins to whimper.

The speaker intrudes in this portrait only insofar as it is his "flesh" and "birth" that bring the thumb. Otherwise, each version of the image is an even-toned statement of fact. Simic's characteristic gestures toward concision, in this case by eliminating the linking verb, enhance this metaphor-making. Instead of saying *A* is equal to *B*, Simic eliminates the first half of the comparison altogether: "Rooster to his hens. / Horn of a devil." He repeats the effect later while depicting the middle finger: "Stiff, still unaccustomed to this life; / An old man at birth."

The speaker's effort to imbue each finger with unique fanciful features is, in some measure, an act of self-abnegation. Because the narrative voice and poem's subject exist here in a balance made delicate by Simic's spare language, lines devoted to rounding out a finger's details are lines in which the speaker is not talking about himself. This would not be a productive feature of the poem's strategy—the reader would be perfectly content to omit the question of the "I" altogether, as many of Simic's later poems do—but for the puzzling intrusion of the first-person voice in part four: "After each bone, finger, / I come to him, troubled." The "him," of course, is the fourth finger, whom the speaker describes as "mystery." It is to this "mystery" that the speaker returns after considering what a finger is, presumably to find some solace for his "troubled" soul. While the relationship between the speaker and the imagined reader is didactic, with two imperatives (in part one, "Cut him off"; in part two, "Watch, he points further"), there is also a self-instructive element in these lines. The imagined animals of the "bestiary" are as difficult to interpret for the reader as for the speaker who, by offering these details, might arrive at his own understanding.

In this way "Bestiary" typifies Simic's early work. It appeared in his first full-length collection, *Dismantling the Silence* (1971), which Peter Stitt (1997) has justly described as thematic in its attempt to pare description down to almost pure silence. For the reader such a project means that the book's cryptic pockets of language appear as a symbolic network wherein many pathways have been severed or lost. These poems resemble religious icons with so much missing as to frustrate direct parallels with the experienced world. This points to the significance of the elusive "I," who cannot clarify meaning but instead grasps at evidence, as in the closing stanza:

> Something stirs in the fifth
> Something perpetually at the point
> Of birth. Weak and submissive,
> His touch is gentle.
> It weighs a tear.
> It takes the mote out of the eye.

The speaker cannot pinpoint what is special about the smallest finger, identifying it only as "Something perpetually at the point / Of birth." The rest is easily recognizable: the finger is "weak" and used to brush obstructions from the eyes. There is, however, a pleasing double entendre in the way the finger "weighs a tear," perhaps evaluating the sadness inherent in the moment, or in how it clears the eye to improve vision, both physical and spiritual. In these last lines Simic tempers a hope for understanding, the last finger offering clarity and rebirth, with the anxiety (of being feeble, small, or uncertain) that runs throughout the poem. The word "mote" stands out, denoting minuteness or insignificance even as the monosyllable evokes the murkiness of its medieval Saxon origins. The echoes of preceding material are essential here, especially given the poem's overall compactness. The difficulty determining what "stirs in the fifth" finger recalls the "mystery" of the fourth, while its weakness mirrors the "backache" of the middle finger and contrasts the strength of the thumb ("It takes four to hold him down"). "Birth" has already appeared (the middle finger is "An old man at birth"; the thumb was "attached to my flesh / At the time of my birth"), but it is uncertain what will be born. The homonymic cousin of "point" first appeared in part two, in which the index finger "points the way" and "points to himself." Ultimately a whole emerges, a hand whose constituent parts remain distinct in their temperament and agency, but who must work together in spite of themselves. This is as apt a description of the physical act of writing as it is of a soul in conflict.

Compared to other object-oriented poems from the same period of his career, "Bestiary for the Fingers of My Right Hand" has been more an anthology piece than the subject of critical attention. It is, however, representative of both Simic's early poems and the direction his work took in later collections. Simic's early poems tentatively mediate the separation between the world of mundane experience and that of imagination, metaphysics, and nightmare. The images are fantastic and to an extent surreal, but the speaker holds back enough to keep from offering this inverse reality as literal fact, a restraint Simic eventually abandons in favor of finding new meanings in his own peculiar world.

Benjamin Paloff

**Further Reading**

Corbett, William, "Charles Simic" (interview), *Poets and Writers* 24 (May/June 1996)

Simic, Charles, *The Uncertain Certainty: Interviews, Essays, and Notes on Poetry,* Ann Arbor: University of Michigan Press, 1985

Stitt, Peter, *Uncertainty and Plenitude: Five Contemporary Poets,* Iowa City: University of Iowa Press, 1997

Vendler, Helen, *Soul Says: On Recent Poetry,* Cambridge, Massachusetts: Harvard University Press, 1995

Weigl, Bruce, editor, *Charles Simic: Essays on the Poetry,* Ann Arbor: University of Michigan Press, 1996

---

# Louis Simpson 1923–

In his 1972 autobiography *North of Jamaica,* Louis Simpson admonishes readers that "every true poet is essentially different" and should take pains to avoid "artistic circles," but he makes the qualification that each poet also needs "companions" that form provisional groups. Simpson notes that both his disposition and his World War II experiences led him to write as a thoroughgoing realist, although he also situates himself squarely within a literary tradition that explores surreal scenes, dream narratives, and the efficacy of unconscious, archetypal images. He traces this literary lineage from Symbolism to Imagism to Surrealism to American "deep image" poetry, as it emerged in Robert Bly's literary journal *The Fifties,* to which Simpson and his contemporaries James Wright and Donald Hall contributed.

Although less socially and intellectually affiliated than other schools of poets, Simpson and his colleagues together employed Surrealist techniques and shared their generation's alienation from the conventionality of 1950s Modernism as well as from the impersonality of Objectivist poetics, one branch of William Carlos Williams' legacy. Simpson's posture toward the New Criticism becomes clear when he notes that he wanted to write "bad poems," or "extraordinary poems about being ordinary," largely in response to Eliot's followers as well as to the "Oxford Poets" who influenced his early development. In his poetry and criticism, he recoiled from the sense of exhaustion, imitation, loss of touch with humanity, abstract reference, and literary diction that he found in these schools.

Although colloquial, Simpson indulges neither "just personal" nor visionary urges. His insights remain more tightly controlled than Beat, apocalyptic expression, and although he addresses societal ills through inwardness, he is not a "confessional poet." Rather, he finds the character of the poet to consist in the exploration of personality, insofar as this process gives access to images that open readers' shared, emotive imagination. Like his friend Wright, Simpson begins with a fastidious scrutiny of mundane objects or scenes and makes an imaginative leap from the object or image to an interior world in order to retrieve mysterious, disturbing, or healing images. For Simpson, poetry intensifies as it approaches and expresses the deep regions of the collective psyche. Although the poem marks a movement from the outward, objective world toward the inner world, this interior consciousness is collective rather than egoistic or isolated.

For Simpson, Surrealism "created images and therefore realities," but Surrealist poets themselves still offered only a heap of broken, often remotely exotic images. He is suspicious of Surrealist poetry as it threatened to become "just a series of ecstatic exclamations," and his response involves giving the deep image a narrative direction that still follows the logic of dreams. Simpson's ideal poet could reject, on the one hand, unimaginative ratiocination, and on the other, gratuitous irrational images, in order to reveal the drama, rhythm, and narrative motion of the unconscious.

In his memoirs, Simpson recounts how in his youth he wanted "to tell stories and to write poems." Fittingly, his poetry is lyric in manner and intensity of focus but dramatic in human situation, using narrative to organize incidents and to present character. Simpson credits Chekhov with having helped him to the narrative conception of his poems. Narrative itself, especially Simpson's lyric-memoir form of autobiography, seems to provide the space for "the movement of the imagination," a movement of empathy that he praises in Sonnevi, among others, and that allows for deeper, shared experiences among his audiences.

Although Simpson's hard-realist and surreal worlds seem incommensurate, throughout his career he urges that imaginative evocation and close attention to mundane details remain interdependent; thus one encounters, for instance, a poem called "The Psyche of Riverside Drive." The logic of dreams facilitates both modes of reckoning reality, and imaginative narrative opens the space in which law-like reality and the dream-like images of the unconscious meet. For example, in "My Father in the Night Commanding No," the speaker recalls an everyday experience in detail, drawing a sharp contrast between his own parents, but through a dream narrative he can abstract this experience to a level of familiarity that tends toward the universal.

Although his characters have limitations, most often an uncritical acceptance of tradition and a lack of imagination, he treats them sympathetically. From his earliest work on, his compositional posture remains personally invested and his approach is meticulously straightforward. He says, "in poems I try to generate mystery and excitement; I have even dealt in general ideas. But I retain the dog-face's suspicion of the officer class, with their abstract language and indifference to individual human suffering." His treatment of everyday situations allows the contemporary ironies of American life their full scope while seeking renewed sources of empathy. Simpson contrasts the materialistic civilization of the United States with the ideal nation that Walt Whitman had prophesied, especially in a poem like "Walt Whitman at Bear Mountain." And with the American involvement in Vietnam, his protests and critique became more pronounced.

Over the course of his career, Simpson's verse technique remains conspicuously formed, and he produces finely crafted, humanely ironic, and witty poems, composed in understated language. Through the 1950s, Simpson composed detached poems in regular meters, rhyme schemes, and stanza form, usually treating war, love, and America as his subjects. Among the many poems relating his war experiences, "Carentan O Carentan" remains especially memorable. But with the publication of *At the End of the Open Road* (1963; 1964 Pulitzer Prize), Simpson began to sharpen the link between imagery and shared sensibility by using free form, colloquial language, and conversational rhythms. He found this style suited to his desire to reject America's sterile public façade, and it furthered his turn to a "deep inwardness." Through this approach, he could temper the idealization of the primitive that was becoming common in American poetry with alert images and striking juxtapositions. As he became less formal, he continued to take his material from "images that correspond to the lives we really have." This turn, helped along by Bly, made Simpson's form as fresh as his content had been.

As his poetry enjoys increasing critical esteem, Simpson continues to translate poetic works, especially the writings of French Symbolists, and his roles as astute critic of American life and literary historian complement his many other roles—editor, teacher, scholar, novelist, and literary critic. Currently he teaches at the Stony Brook School, a college preparatory near his home in Setauket, Long Island.

JIM KELLER

*See also* War and Anti-War Poetry

**Biography**

Born in Kingston, Jamaica, British West Indies, 27 March 1923. Attended Columbia University, New York, B.S. 1948, A.M. 1950, Ph.D. 1959; served in the United States Army, 1943–45, received Purple Heart twice and Bronze Star with oak leaf cluster; editor, Bobbs-Merrill Publishing Company, New York, 1950–55; Instructor, Columbia University, 1953–59; Instructor in English, New School for Social Research, 1955–59; Professor of English, University of California, Berkeley, 1959–67; Professor of English and Comparative Literature, State University of New York, Stony Brook, 1967–91, Distinguished Professor, 1991–93, and Professor Emeritus, 1993–. Received American Academy in Rome Prix de Rome fellowship in literature, 1957; *Hudson Review* fellowship, 1957; Edna St. Vincent Millay Award, 1960; Guggenheim fellowship, 1962, 1970; American Council of Learned Societies grant, 1963; Pulitzer Prize, 1964; Columbia University Medal for Excellence,

1965; American Academy Award, 1976; Institute of Jamaica Centenary Award, 1980; National Jewish Book Award, 1981; Elmer Holmes Bobst Award, 1987; Harold Morton Landon Award, for translation, 1998; honorary L.H.D., Eastern Michigan University, Ypsilanti, 1977; D.Litt., Hampden Sydney College, 1990. Living in Setauket, New York.

**Poetry**
*The Arrivistes: Poems, 1940–1949,* 1949
*Good News of Death, and Other Poems,* 1955
*A Dream of Governors,* 1959
*At the End of the Open Road,* 1963
*Five American Poets* (with others), edited by Thom Gunn and Ted Hughes, 1963
*Selected Poems,* 1965
*Adventures of the Letter I,* 1971
*Searching for the Ox,* 1976
*Armidale,* 1979
*Caviare at the Funeral,* 1980
*The Best Hour of the Night,* 1983
*People Live Here: Selected Poems, 1949–1983,* 1983
*Collected Poems,* 1988
*In the Room We Share,* 1990
*There You Are,* 1995

**Selected Criticism**
*James Hogg: A Critical Study,* 1962
*Three on the Tower: The Lives and Works of Ezra Pound, T.S. Eliot, and William Carlos Williams,* 1975
*A Revolution in Taste: Studies of Dylan Thomas, Allen Ginsberg, Sylvia Plath, and Robert Lowell,* 1978
*A Company of Poets,* 1981
*The Character of the Poet,* 1986
*Ships Going into the Blue: Essays and Notes on Poetry,* 1994

**Other Writings:** novel (*Riverside Drive,* 1962), plays, essays (*Selected Prose,* 1989), autobiography (*North of Jamaica,* 1972), poetry textbook (*An Introduction to Poetry,* 1967), translations of French poetry (*Modern Poets of France: A Bilingual Anthology,* 1998); edited poetry anthology (*New Poets of England and America* [with Donald Hall and Robert Pack], 1957).

**Further Reading**

Bawer, Bruce, "Louis Simpson and American Dreams," *Arizona Quarterly* 40, no. 2 (Summer 1984)
Cox, James M., "Re-Viewing Louis Simpson," *Southern Review* 31, no. 1 (Winter 1995)
Drury, John, and Mark Irwin, "An Interview with Louis Simpson," *Iowa Journal of Literary Studies* 3, no. 1–2 (1981)
Ginsberg, Allen, *Howl: Original Draft Facsimile, Transcript, and Variant Versions, with Correspondence,* New York: HarperPerennial, 1995
Lazer, Hank, "Louis Simpson and Walt Whitman: Destroying the Teacher," *Walt Whitman Review* 1, no. 3 (December 1983)
Lazer, Hank, editor, *On Louis Simpson: Depths beyond Happiness,* Ann Arbor: University of Michigan Press, 1988
Lensing, George S., and Ronald Moran, *Four Poets and the Emotive Imagination: Robert Bly, James Wright, Louis Simpson, and William Stafford,* Baton Rouge: Louisiana State University Press, 1976
Moran, Ronald, *Louis Simpson,* New York: Twayne, 1972
Moran, Ronald, "Louis Simpson: An Interview," *Five Points* 1, no. 1 (Fall 1996)
Schneider, Steven, "An Interview with Louis Simpson," *Wordsworth Circle* 13, no. 2 (Spring 1982)
Taylor, Henry, "Great Experiments: The Poetry of Louis Simpson," *Hollins Critic* 27, no. 3 (June 1990)


---

# Slams. *See* Performance Poetry

---

# Small Presses. *See* Little Magazines and Small Presses

---

# W.D. Snodgrass 1926–

W.D. Snodgrass was among the first Americans to write "Confessional" poetry and one of the first to move beyond it. Other poets with whom Snodgrass associated during graduate school were inventing the poetry that evolved in the 1960s as "Confessional" (M.L. Rosenthal, *The Modern Poets,* 1960) or "introspective" (Williamson, 1984). Innovators such as Sylvia Plath and Robert Lowell brought patrician sensibilities to this new poetry. By contrast, aspiring writers such as James Wright, James Dickey, and Snodgrass, who went to college on the G.I. Bill, brought the perspective of working-class families and military service, sometimes including combat. After completing their undergraduate educations (Snodgrass at Geneva College), these poets looked to mentors in graduate school who sought to escape the legacy of T.S. Eliot, Ezra Pound, William Carlos Williams, and Robert Frost. Eschewing the obscurity and "impersonality" that Pound and Eliot had elevated to poetic orthodoxy, these writers set directness and sincerity as their goal. At the University of Iowa, Snodgrass studied under Lowell, who credits his pupil with liberating Lowell's poetics.

Snodgrass' first collection, *Heart's Needle, and Other Poems* (1959), earned a Pulitzer Prize. Although personal, the poems in this volume feature a different kind of directness from that of other Confessional writers. Lowell confesses his patrician angst, wryly admitting, "My mind's not right"; Ginsberg challenges readers by flaunting his eschewal of mainstream American values; and Plath and Sexton create impassioned lyrics from their suppression in patriarchal culture. By contrast, Snodgrass practices a bittersweet lyricism that confesses personal weakness and idiosyncrasy while simultaneously projecting those oddities as therapeutic in a complacent, conformist society. "April Inventory" is organized around a list of the poet-speaker's liabilities: he needs psychoanalysis, he has failed to advance toward tenure, his hair is thinning and his teeth are decaying, and even his libido is diminished. By the standard of "solid scholars" building their careers, these liabilities are substantial. With a twist of phrase, however, he announces that he has not "read one book about / A book or memorized one plot," challenging the rote actions and secondhand knowledge that American education rewards. The poet challenges the tendencies toward selfishness and mediocrity in American education by confessing how short he falls when measured against these expectations. Similarly, "The Campus on the Hill" laments the university's serving status quo sociopolitical interests rather than encouraging social or ethical commitment. Snodgrass' assets in "April Inventory" are independence of mind, creativity, and other-directedness. Throughout *Heart's Needle,* this tension between mendacity in American public life and the inadequacy of any individual's private response to the wastelands of modern suburbia, academia, and America in general constitutes a central theme. Several poems deal with soldiers coming home from World War II to find America unchanged, still trapped in routines of getting and spending. Others treat failed love relationships.

In the essay "Finding a Poem," Snodgrass identifies directness and authenticity as measures of poetic excellence, seeking a "depth of sincerity" that rescues poems from the intellection that followed on emulating Eliot's poetics. His double insistence, on formal precision resembling W.H. Auden and Marianne Moore and on directness of subject matter, contains the paradox that organizes his greatest achievement in the Confessional mode, "Heart's Needle." Like Ginsberg's "Howl," the sequence is among the authentically original American poems of the 1950s. Unlike "Howl," Snodgrass restrains powerful emotions through the complex forms he chooses for each section. Each has a different, usually original meter and rhyme pattern. The poems explore a divorce in 1953, but they emphasize the poet's guilt over inflicting his need for freedom on his daughter, a dilemma articulated in poem six: "Child, I have another child, another wife. / We try to choose our life." His theme is that one must endure the life one has created. In addition, parents create their children's lives by the choices they make and must accept responsibility for the consequences of those choices. The "depth of sincerity" is accepting one's responsibility for imposing his personal happiness on others. Throughout the cycle, animal and nature images become correlatives for the characters' emotional states. A fox chews off a paw to escape a trap, suggesting an analogy for the poet's anguish over leaving his daughter to secure his freedom, in poem five. This sequence, within a masterful first volume, established Snodgrass among the enduring artists in Confessional poetry.

After completing *Heart's Needle,* Snodgrass played a joke on his readers that in fact initiated his creation of a poetic alter ego. His biographical note in the anthology *A Century of American Poetry* states that Snodgrass taught English at Wayne State University, and that the poet who influenced him the most was S.S. Gardons, who was also a Texas rock musician (Howard, 1969). "S.S. Gardons," the author of *Remains* (1970), is an anagram for "Snodgrass," who accepted authorship with his 1987 *Selected Poems.* Like *Heart's Needle, Remains* is a cycle about loss, the death of a young woman whose circumstances resemble those of the poet's sister; Snodgrass insists that the woman's asthma was insufficient to cause death "if she had really wanted to go on." From portraits such as "The Mother" and "Diplomacy: The Father" to anguished personal reflections such as "The Mouse," "Fourth of July," and "The Survivors," *Remains* indicts a dysfunctional family that inadvertently victimized the daughter. As a poet, "Gardons" paints a grim picture of his family's role in his sister's despair; as a son, Snodgrass kept the volume relatively secret by publishing an expensive limited edition under an anti-name.

The second volume by "Snodgrass" is less directly personal, suggesting Snodgrass' repudiation of Confessional techniques. As Richard Howard (1969) noted, *After Experience* (1968) resonates with "dialectical energy"; Paul Gaston (1978) argued that the poems are more directly concerned with exterior reality than with subjectivity. Several of the poems continue themes from *Heart's Needle* but from a more detached perspective. "Leaving the Motel" dramatizes the moment during which lovers complete their adulterous tryst. Mundane precautions, such as disposing of objects that might arouse suspicion, imply a meditation on the transience of adulterous love. After a series of poems about furtive, failed love relationships, *After Experience* contains portraits that are among Snodgrass' finest work. "Old Fritz" describes a veteran's agonizing death, over seven months, in a V.A. hospital. The observer is torn between admiration for the old man's tenacity and trying to figure out why Fritz refuses to give up his wretched life. A companion poem, "The Examination," which describes a scene in a hospital operating room, comments on the power of science to save lives but also to alter our perceptions of reality.

*After Experience* concludes with five poems based on paintings, by Matisse, Vuillard, Monet, Manet, and Van Gogh. Like Williams' *Pictures from Brueghel* (1962), these poems interpret the paintings' themes and contexts. For "Manet: The Execution of Emperor Maximilian," Snodgrass creates two voices, one that prosaically summarizes the execution and its consequences, and another that shifts between amusement, sober reflection, and a searching investigation of Manet's treatment of this execution as another European effort to impose its power on the New World.

The most striking poems in *After Experience,* the title poem and "A Visitation," are dialogues about violence, self-preservation, and collective as well as individual responsibility. "A Visitation" is a dialogue between the poet-speaker and Nazi war criminal Adolf Eichmann. Similarly, the title poem juxtaposes three voices, unpunctuated except for distinctive margins identifying each. The first voice, that of a philosopher, makes an argument, based on a Spinoza meditation, for the necessity of self-preservation. The sections spoken by the philosopher argue that preserving one's existence is the essential condition of any action. Interspersed between these stanzas are a soldier's instructions on how to engage in hand-to-hand combat. The dialogue that develops reveals common ground between the warrior's graphic instructions for ripping off an enemy's face and the philosopher's abstract argument for self-defense, which avoids gruesome applications. The final stanza, spatially distinct from the voices of the philosopher and soldier, challenges readers to reflect on what "unspeakable crime" we might condone to save ourselves.

Snodgrass' most controversial collection is *The Führer Bunker* (1977). In *Selected Poems* (1987), he claims that he has written 70 dramatic monologues that capture the final moments of Hitler's inner circle as they watch the Third Reich collapse around them. The 15 included in *Selected Poems* feature voices that range widely. Snodgrass employs the rigid, ordered sestina form and echoes the repetitions and diction of nursery rhymes to provide sharp contrast for the content of Magda Goebbels' lullaby to her children, as she prepares them to receive an injection of potassium cyanide. By contrast, Hitler's mistress joyfully accepts her suicide as his "chosen," taking pride in vanquishing other mistresses and defying her conventional family. Snodgrass punctuates her monologue with couplets from "Tea for Two," each linked thematically with the content of the subsequent stanza. At another extreme, Heinrich Himmler's monologues are printed on graph paper, with no punctuation, visually symbolizing the simultaneous order and chaos of the SS leader's mind.

At the cycle's core are Hitler's monologues; it is tempting to say that Snodgrass loans the devil his voice. Hitler remains a moral monster, confessing to sexual degeneracy and cruelty to his family as well as paranoid disgust for his generals, his inner circle, and even his bride. In his final monologue, Hitler's dementia intensifies as he approaches suicide. Ranting about enemies, facing eternity, Hitler boasts of the millions of Jews, Poles, gypsies, French, and Yugoslavians whom his death camps have destroyed, insanely equating himself with the big bad wolf, the little tailor of folklore, and the Grail Knight of myth. As Hitler's dementia intensifies, Snodgrass dissolves any semblance of ordered form into a relative visual and auditory chaos, a chaos resembling the horrors of the leader's mind. As with villains in Shakespearean tragedy, we begin to understand Hitler's madness and evil; and if we can understand him, we must acknowledge our shared humanity without condoning his malice.

In general, Snodgrass uses the dramatic monologue in a much different way than did Robert Browning or T.S. Eliot, who used the genre to offer ironic, judgmental perspectives on their speakers. Because the Nazis stand universally condemned, Snodgrass employs the soliloquy to illuminate the ways in which their various self-deceptions, vanities, and pettinesses resemble our own. His epigraph to *The Führer Bunker* quotes Mother Teresa of Calcutta, who traced the inspiration behind her life's mission to her discovery that "I had a Hitler inside me." Snodgrass' monologues are reminders to a world in need of reminding: it can happen again. We cannot be "good" unless we have a specific understanding of evil, and to dismiss the Nazi atrocities as "other" or "inhuman" ignores our connection with the worst in our species. Like Mother Teresa, we must recognize humanity's capacity for evil and train ourselves to do good in spite of it.

After *The Führer Bunker,* Snodgrass resumed the controlled, generally detached lyricism of *After Experience* in *Each in His Season* (1993). In addition to lyrics such as "Birds Caught, Birds Flying" and the sequence "In Flower," the book features direct, satiric pieces such as "The Ballad of Jesse Helms," an indictment of the New Right, and "In Memory of Lost Brain Cells." Snodgrass has also begun to produce light verse and children's verse. *W.D.'s Midnight Carnival* (1988) collects poems about oddities one might encounter in the sideshow that is America. Among the most charming of his recent works is a book for children, *The Death of Cock Robin* (1989), in which several titles include comic variations on the poet's identity, such as "W.D. Sits in Kafka's Chair and Is Interrogated Concerning the Assumed Death of Cock Robin."

Snodgrass' legacy is varied; although he has published comparatively few volumes, his achievements in the Confessional mode remain among the best manifestations of that genre, whereas his movement beyond Confessionalism into dramatic poems challenges our complacency about who we are. We can ask no more of a poet.

DAVID C. DOUGHERTY

*See also* Confessional Poetry

**Biography**

Born William Dewitt Snodgrass in Wilkinsburg, Pennsylvania, 5 January 1926. Attended Geneva College, Beaver Falls, Pennsylvania, 1943–44, 1946; University of Iowa, Iowa City, 1946–55, B.A. 1949, M.A. 1951, M.F.A. 1953; served in the United States Navy, 1944–46; Instructor in English, Cornell University, Ithaca, New York, 1955–57, University of Rochester, New York, 1957–58, and Wayne State University, Detroit, Michigan, 1959–67; Professor of English and speech, Syracuse University, New York, 1968–77; Visiting Professor, 1979, Distinguished Professor of creative writing and contemporary literature, 1980–94, and Distinguished Professor Emeritus, 1994–, University of Delaware, Newark; visiting teacher, Morehead Writers Conference, Kentucky, summer 1955, Antioch Writers Conference, Yellow Springs, Ohio, summers 1958–59, Narrative Poetry Workshop, State University of New York, Binghamton, 1977, Old Dominion University, Norfolk, Virginia, 1978–79, and Cranbrook Writers' Conference, Birmingham, Michigan, 1981. Received Ingram Merrill Foundation Award, 1958; *Hudson Review* fellowship, 1958; Longview Award, 1959; Poetry Society of America special citation, 1960; Yaddo Resident Award, 1960, 1961, 1965, 1976, 1977; American Academy grant, 1960; Pulitzer Prize, 1960; Guinness Award (U.K.), 1961; Ford fellowship, for drama, 1963; Miles Award, 1966; National Endowment for the Arts grant, 1966; Guggenheim fellowship, 1972; Academy of American Poets fellowship, 1972; Centennial Medal (Romania), 1977; Harold Morton Landon Award, for translation, 1998; member, American Academy, 1972. Living in Erieville, New York, and San Miguel de Allende, Mexico.

**Poetry**

*Heart's Needle, and Other Poems,* 1959
*After Experience: Poems and Translations,* 1968
*Remains* (as S.S. Gardons), 1970; revised edition (as W.D. Snodgrass), 1985
*The Führer Bunker: A Cycle of Poems in Progress,* 1977
*W.D. Meets Mr. Evil . . . ,* 1985
*The House the Poet Built,* 1986
*Selected Poems, 1957–1987,* 1987
*W.D.'s Midnight Carnival,* 1988
*The Death of Cock Robin,* 1989
*Each in His Season,* 1993
*Spring Suite,* 1994
*The Führer Bunker: The Complete Cycle,* 1995

**Selected Criticism**

*In Radical Pursuit: Critical Essays and Lectures,* 1975

**Other Writings:** play, translations of Italian, Hungarian, and other literature (*The Four Seasons,* 1984); edited collections of poetry (*Syracuse Poems 1969,* 1969).

**Further Reading**

Gaston, Paul L., *W.D. Snodgrass,* Boston: Twayne, 1978
Goldstein, Laurence, "*The Führer Bunker* and the New Discourse about Nazism," *Southern Review* 24 (Winter 1988)
Haven, Stephen, editor, *The Poetry of W.D. Snodgrass: Everything Human,* Ann Arbor: University of Michigan Press, 1993
Heyen, William, "Fishing the Swamp: The Poetry of W.D. Snodgrass," in *Modern American Poetry: Essays in Criticism,* compiled by Jerome Mazzaro, New York: McKay, 1970
Howard, Richard, "W.D. Snodgrass," in *Alone with America: Essays on the Art of Poetry in the United States since 1950,* by Howard, New York: Atheneum, 1969; London: Thames and Hudson, 1970; enlarged edition, New York: Atheneum, 1980
Phillips, Robert S., *The Confessional Poets,* Carbondale: Southern Illinois University Press, and London: Feffer and Simons, 1973
Williamson, Alan, *Introspection and Contemporary Poetry,* Cambridge, Massachusetts: Harvard University Press, 1984

---

# Gary Snyder 1930–

The appearance of Gary Snyder's *Mountains and Rivers without End* (*MRWE*) in 1996 marks an important point in contemporary American poetry. Begun in Berkeley in 1956, *MRWE* is a collection of poems Snyder produced during those 40 years. If *Myths and Texts* (1960), a collection it resembles, confirmed Snyder's significance as a contemporary poet, a reputation that had begun with *Riprap* (1959), *MRWE* represents the culmination of a long career.

According to Snyder, *Myths and Texts* was his "first venture into the long poem and the challenge of interweaving physical life and inward realms" (*MRWE*), something of a preoccupation in his work. Raised in the Pacific Northwest, Snyder claimed that he was "forever changed by that place of rock and sky" (*MRWE*), so much so that a shock of recognition occurred when he discovered in Asian landscape painting the space of Western vistas. Having worked as a fire lookout on Crater and Sourdough Mountains and having experienced the alpine's ceaseless change in sunlight and shadow, wind, and cloudscape, Snyder's contact with *shou-chan,* or hand scrolls, particularly one titled "Mountains and Rivers without End," profoundly inspired him, and in 1956 he began the "long poem" that eventuated 40 years later in the text of the same name. As a student at Reed College and later at the University of California, Snyder had studied Native American and Asian cultures, deepening his regard for Amerindian lore and especially Buddhism to the point where he studied Zen in Japan. There he attended Nō drama and began to further envision his long poem in terms of Nō, but without relinquishing his sense of connection with the ancient landscapes of his homeland, Turtle Island.

In the 1960s, Snyder worked as a seaman, alternating between California, where he visited the high Sierra Nevada wilderness, and Japan, where he met Yamabushi, or Mountain Buddhists, for whom, as he remarked, "walking the landscape can become both ritual and meditation" (*MRWE*). Throughout the 1960s, according to Snyder, poems for the collection continued to appear at a rate of about one per year, while on poetry reading tours he visited museums and collections, viewing Asian landscape scrolls, such as the one in Cleveland: Lu Yüan Ch'ing's "Mountains and Rivers without End." By the 1970s, texts by Dōgen, sometimes considered the Zen father of Japanese literature, began to be translated and published. Snyder cites "The Waters and Mountain Sutra" as of particular importance to him and in fact has considered his *MRWE* itself as "a sort of sutra," that is, "an extended poetic, philosophic, and mythic narrative of the female Buddha Tārā" (*MRWE*). Dōgen's influence on him is considerable. Snyder has said, "I predict that the discovery of Dōgen's work will have a profound intellectual effect. It's . . . coming into the postmodernist deconstructive European line of thinking. They're going to discover what deconstruction could *really* mean and what happens when you deconstruct not only the object but the subject, namely your own thinking" (Rossiter and Evans, in Murphy, 1999).

In *MRWE,* one finds Snyder's usual syncretism of Amerindian mythology (the trickster coyote, Wovoka and Ghost Dance, and the Hopi kokopele) and Asian traditions, especially Mayahana Buddhism, as well as Chinese poetics derived from Han Shan or Cold Mountain, among other Chinese poets, and late Modernist poetics from poets as diverse as Pound, Olson, Williams, Rexroth, and Jeffers. Like Eliot's *The Waste Land,* Snyder's *MRWE* is syncretic in its synthesis of diverse traditions into a whole, but while *The Waste Land* presented an urban, 20th-century wasteland, Snyder's *MRWE* taps into the dominant wilderness of a "globalized Turtle Island." Snyder's concern is to "translate space from its physical sense to the spiritual sense of space as emptiness—spiritual transparency—in Mayahana Buddhist philosophy" (O'Grady, 1998). In important ways, *MRWE* revises western frontier traditions of domination, conquest, and resource extraction by rendering the landscape's spiritual richness instead of its wealth of materials. The West of the argonauts of 1849, the gold rushes of Colorado and California, and the silver rushes of Arizona, Nevada, and South Dakota give way to a sacralized landscape—Turtle Island as spiritual ground—more in keeping with Native Americans than with the forty-niners.

In this sense, *MRWE* is a monumental poem in its rendering of the Great Basin and mountain ranges, especially the Sierra Nevadas, as well as the animals and humans inhabiting them. Each of the poem's four sections contains some of Snyder's best and most representative poetry. For example, in Part I, "Endless Streams and Mountains," "Bubbs Creek Haircut," "Night Highway 99," and "The Blue Sky" stand out, and in Part II, the celebrated poems with historic value, such as "The Circumambulation of Mt. Tamalpais," recount Snyder's walking meditation (*pradakshina*) and hike around the famous Bay Area landmark together with Philip Whalen, Allen Ginsberg, and Jack Kerouac. If walking meditation, or *pradakshina,* is present in "Circumambulation," movement and evident motion—perhaps metonymy for change, as in Dōgen's walking mountains—is present in "Endless Streams and Mountains," where the unfurling of the scroll with its colophons, seals, and annotations, accumulated over time by its owners and onlookers, is in a different way replicated in "Night Highway 99" with the fragmented commentary on hitchhikers and residents and the staccato of place names and locales. Snyder's poems often unfold landscape and voice in paratextual maneuvers that conflate the reader's passage through space with his or her movement through the poetic text. In "Night Highway 99," for example, as one travels south from the Pacific Northwest to San Francisco, encapsulated, elliptical "events" and "epiphanies" erupt in the anecdotal presence of voices of riders, residents, and travelers en route. This is the experience of motion through landscape as being. "Three Worlds, Three Realms, Six Roads" continues such movement, as do the lists in "Things to Do"—around Seattle, a fire lookout; around San Francisco, a "ship at sea"; and so on. Here compression, ellipsis, and concrete diction (in part derived from the rendering of the Chinese calligraphic poetry of Han Shan and others into English syntax) work to direct the reader toward Buddhist mindfulness, playfulness, and suchness, where the apprehension of the thing is nothing more than itself.

As Snyder himself put it, *MRWE* "had a very strong, self defining energy of its own from the time I first started it when I was about twenty-seven" (Rossiter and Evans, in Murphy, 1999). In this as in his other poetry, Snyder's is a particular "double vision of the West, seeing it simultaneously from the Native American angle and from the white settler angle, which I think is typical of many imaginative people of the West—they see both sides of the picture in their mind's eye," as he put it in an interview (O'Grady, 1998). However, if Buddhism and Native American lore permeate the landscape of his poetry with spirituality and a particularly animistic sense of the natural world, Snyder's political affiliations color how this landscape is inhabited by humans. "I am deeply imbued with a lot of western American political and literary lore . . . I grew up in the left-wing branch of the western culture. So labor history, strikes, IWW, early socialism, people [like] Charles Erskine Scott Wood and Joe Hill were part of . . . our [family's] thoughts" (O'Grady, 1998). Throughout Snyder's poetry, one hears the vernacular in diction, syntax, and tone—the intonations, figurations, and slang of ordinary working men and women.

In effect, then, Snyder's project has been to rewrite the western American landscape. Place becomes a source of loyalty that precedes political commitment. This sense of place is part of what Snyder calls "the old ways" (O'Grady, 1998). As he put it in an interview, "There [is] a distinction between finding your membership in a natural place, and locating your identity in terms of a social or political group. The landscape was my natural nation, and I could see that as having a validity and permanence that would outlast the changing political structures. It enabled me to be critical of the United States without feeling that I wasn't at home in North America" (O'Grady, 1998). Snyder says, finally, that *MRWE* "starts and ends in the West, and is never far from it but uses the western landscape as a metaphor for the whole planet." In sum, Snyder's comment about *MRWE* may be just as appropriate to his entire output as his stature as a poet continues to gain worldwide attention: "In a sense what I have done is globalize the West" (O'Grady, 1998).

MICHAEL W. VELLA

**Biography**

Born in San Francisco, California, 8 May 1930. Attended Reed College, Portland, B.A. in anthropology 1951; Indiana University, Bloomington, 1951–52; University of California, Berkeley, 1953–56; studied Buddhism in Japan, 1956, 1959–64, 1965–68; general lookout, Mt. Baker Forest, 1952–53; seaman, 1957–58; Lecturer in English, University of California, Berkeley, 1964–65; since 1985 Professor of English, University of California, Davis. Received Bess Hokin Prize, 1964, and Levinson Prize, 1968 (*Poetry,* Chicago); Bollingen grant, for Buddhist Studies, 1965; American Academy Prize, 1966; Guggenheim fellowship, 1968; Pulitzer Prize, 1975; Before Columbus Foundation Award, 1984; Bollingen Prize, 1997. Living in San Francisco, California.

**Poetry**
*Riprap*, 1959
*Myths and Texts*, 1960
*Riprap, and Cold Mountain Poems*, 1965
*Six Sections from Mountains and Rivers without End*, 1965
*A Range of Poems*, 1966
*Three Worlds, Three Realms, Six Roads*, 1966
*The Back Country*, 1967
*Regarding Wave*, 1969; enlarged edition, 1970
*Anasazi*, 1971
*Manzanita*, 1972
*Turtle Island*, 1974
*Axe Handles*, 1983
*Left Out in the Rain: New Poems, 1947–1985*, 1986
*No Nature: New and Selected Poems*, 1992
*North Pacific Lands and Waters: A Further Six Sections*, 1993
*Mountains and Rivers without End*, 1996
*The Gary Snyder Reader: Prose, Poetry, and Translations*, 1999

**Other Writings:** essays (*The Practice of the Wild*, 1990; *A Place in Space: Ethics, Aesthetics, and Watersheds: New and Selected Prose*, 1995), interviews (*The Real Work: Interviews and Talks, 1964–1979*, edited by William Scott McClean, 1980); edited collections of Buddhist writings (*The Wooden Fish: Basic Sutras and Gathas of Rinzai Zen* [with Gutetsu Kanetsuki], 1961).

**Further Reading**
Davidson, Michael, *The San Francisco Renaissance: Poetics and Community at Mid-Century*, Cambridge and New York: Cambridge University Press, 1989
Hunt, Anthony, "'The Hump-Backed Flute Player': The Structure of Emptiness in Gary Snyder's *Rivers and Mountains without End*," *Isle: Interdisciplinary Studies in Literature and Environment* 1, no. 2 (Fall 1993)
Hunt, Anthony, "Singing the Dyads: The Chinese Landscape Scroll and Gary Snyder's *Mountains and Rivers without End*," *Journal of Modern Literature* 23, no. 1 (Summer 1999)
Johnson, Kent, and Craig Paulenich, editors, *Beneath a Single Moon: Buddhism in Contemporary American Poetry*, Boston: Shambala, 1991 (contains an introduction by Snyder)
Murphy, Patrick D., *A Place for Wayfaring: The Poetry and Prose of Gary Snyder*, Corvallis: Oregon State University Press, 2000
Murphy, Patrick D., editor, *Critical Essays on Gary Snyder*, Boston: G.K. Hall, 1990
Murphy, Patrick D., editor, "Gary Snyder: An International Perspective," special issue of *Studies in the Humanities* 26, no. 1–2 (June–December 1999)
O'Grady, John P., "Living Landscape: An Interview with Gary Snyder," *Western American Literature* 33, no. 3 (Fall 1998)
Robertson, David, "Real Matter, Spiritual Mountain: Gary Snyder and Jack Kerouac on Mt. Tamalpais," *Western American Literature* 27, no. 3 (Fall 1992)
Robertson, David, "The Circumambulation of Mt. Tamalpais," *Western American Literature* 30, no. 1 (Spring 1995)

## Myths and Texts

Gary Snyder's best poetry exhibits two important thematic interests: an engagement with the natural world and its indigenous peoples, whether as observer, laborer, or storyteller, and an articulation of a mythical, numinous, and usually Buddhist perspective on reality. *Myths and Texts* (1960) is rife with both of these themes, which generate the myths and texts that make up the poem. Nothing illustrates this better than the opening section:

> The morning star is not a star
> Two seedling fir, one died
>                         Io, Io,
> Girdled in wistaria
> Wound with ivy
>                 "The May Queen
> Is the survival of
> A pre-human
> Rutting season"

The first line is a paraphrase from Thoreau's *Walden*, thus a text. However, as a text, it alludes to Venus—who is both Hesperus and Lucifer—as mythical avatar of morning. The second line speaks directly to the life cycle of birth and death, a text that constitutes a myth by way of the metaphor of the seed. The myth is confirmed in the choral invocation of the goddess Io in line three (Io is the daughter of Inachus, loved by Zeus and transformed into a cow by Hera, who tormented her with a gadfly; here she represents a version of a telluric deity). Lines four and five are descriptive texts; the quotation that concludes this selection appears to be a further text. On inspection, however, it is a text that comments on a myth, namely, that of the May Queen. Io, who was worshiped as a kind of earth goddess, is a stand-in for the May Queen; so is Venus, goddess of human and animal rutting seasons. The last quotation posits a spiritual, biological reality that is continuous with human evolution from earlier species. In this sense, it intertwines both of Snyder's thematic interests described previously: a reverence toward the natural world, which is best understood in terms of a mythical reality. Snyder's typically and deceptively plain style, it can be seen, is rich with cultural detail, a facet of his poetry that should be regarded as one of its chief strengths.

This book-length poem was written between 1952 and 1956, when Snyder was between 22 and 26 years old, and was first published as a stapled pamphlet by Totem Press in association with Corinth Press in 1960, when he was 30. In the same year, the final section of the poem was printed, along with a statement of poetics, dated 1959, in Donald Allen's seminal anthology for Grove Press, *The New American Poetry*. At the time he began writing the poem, nearly eight years earlier, Snyder had recently graduated from Reed College with a bachelors degree in anthropology, having written a thesis on Kwakiutl myths, later itself published as a book, *He Who Hunted Birds in His Father's Village* (1979).

*Myths and Texts* begins with a section titled "Logging," which is a series of poems concerning Snyder's experiences cutting timber in the Pacific Northwest; these poems express Snyder's sympathy for those men who made their living outdoors sawing down trees. It continues with "Hunting," which serializes a kind of shamanism expressed through connection with the natural and animal world, in which stories of the Native American coyote trickster run rampant. It concludes with "Burning," a series of Buddhist exercises and meditations that unite all three sections. Prosodically, the poem owes something to the influence of Ezra Pound, especially in the clipped rhythms of the poetry, and even more to the influence of Kenneth Rexroth, whose reflective meditations on the natural world of the Pacific Rim were clearly a model for the young Snyder. However indebted he might be to these influences, Snyder establishes what can be regarded irrefutably as the Snyder voice in *Myths and Texts,* and this voice, in turn, should be regarded as one of the most influential voices on American poetry written since its publication, both mainstream and experimental. *Myths and Texts* is impressive for the subtlety and confidence with which Snyder writes, matched only by the clarity of the verse itself.

Perhaps the most striking section of *Myths and Texts* is "Burning," a series of poems enhanced by a Buddhist, apocalyptic sense of things that is reminiscent of T.S. Eliot in "The Waste Land" but ultimately evocative of the figure of Thoreau, whose Asian-inflected thoughts on the natural world and virtuous living are a credo for Snyder's own life and writing. Indeed, the last line of *Myths and Texts* (prior to the place name and the date, marking and closing its composition), which is a variation on the first line, is a quotation of the last line of Thoreau's *Walden:* "The sun is but a morning star." Where Thoreau stands for an identification of the writer with the natural world—as in "Fire up Thunder Creek and the mountain— / troy's burning! / The cloud mutters / The mountains are your mind"—Eliot stands for a conflagrational desire to burn the world to purity, through an explicitly spiritual position, as in the "Fire Sermon" and "What the Thunder Said" in "The Waste Land." Snyder himself envisions the burning up of the city of the gandharvas, "not a real city." In Buddhist representations, the gandharvas are demigods, usually poets and musicians who herald the banquet of the gods and the preparation of soma, the heavenly drink. Snyder sees their city reflected in the burning of this world:

Smoke
From Tillamook a thousand miles
Soot and hot ashes. Forest fires.
Upper Skagit burned I think 1919
Smoke covered all northern Washington.
        lightning strikes, flares,
Blossoms a fire on the hill.
Smoke like clouds. Blotting the sun
Stinging the eyes.
The hot seeds steam underground
        still alive.

Here life is in cycle, seen in Pacific Oregon and Washington, west of the Cascades. Snyder as a kind of shaman is its observer: impartially, placidly Buddhist in his perception of the cycle of destruction and creation revealed in a huge forest fire. Like "The Waste Land," *Myths and Texts* can be regarded as a response to the poet's sense of civilization in crisis, which in Snyder's case is not war but the desolation of the natural world and people's increasing distance from that world. What is curious about Snyder's position in regard to this perception is that he is never judgmental about it. Rather, he uses this perception to fuel the burning of perception itself, a very Buddhist move on his part. In this sense, the myth of the destruction of the natural world is demonstrated in a polysemic text, whose signs are as much witnessed in the trees, mountains, and laborers as in the records of human learning and wisdom drawn on for inspiration and clarity. Steadfastly spiritual in its aspirations, *Myths and Texts* is thus both of these, a myth and a text of that myth, and one of the great religious poems of the 20th century.

PETER O'LEARY

**Further Reading**

Bartlett, Lee, "Gary Snyder's *Myths and Texts* and the Monomyth," *Western American Literature* 17, no. 2 (August 1982)

Bedrosian, Margaret, "Grounding the Self: The Image of the Buddha in Gary Snyder's *Myths and Texts,*" *South Asian Review* 17, no. 14 (December 1993)

Davidson, Michael, *The San Francisco Renaissance: Poetics and Community at Mid-Century,* Cambridge and New York: Cambridge University Press, 1989

Halper, Jon, editor, *Gary Snyder: Dimensions of a Life,* San Francisco: Sierra Club, 1991

Murphy, Patrick D., "Mythic Fantasy and Inhumanist Philosophy in the Long Poems of Robinson Jeffers and Gary Snyder," *American Studies* 30, no. 1 (Spring 1989)

Murphy, Patrick D., "Alternation and Interpretation: Gary Snyder's *Myths and Texts,*" in *Critical Essays on Gary Snyder,* edited by Murphy, Boston: G.K. Hall, 1990

# Riprap

*Riprap* (1959), Gary Snyder's first published book of poetry, is a striking combination of practical and metaphysical concerns. He condenses these concerns in the epigraph/definition that begins the book, describing "riprap" as "a cobble of stone laid on steep slick rock / to make a trail for horses in the mountains." The practicalities of making pathways through mountains and wilderness occupied Snyder during his frequent employment as a forester in the Pacific Northwest when the poet was in his 20s, at which time these poems were written. The idea of riprap becomes then a poetic construct; or, more precisely, it becomes a practical, poetic process for cobbling ideas up the steep slope of sometimes abstract, philosophical, or emotional concerns. This is most clearly demonstrated in the poem that opens the collection, "Mid-August at Sourdough Mountain Lookout," perhaps Snyder's best single lyric:

Down valley a smoke haze
Three days heat, after five days rain
Pitch glows on the fir-cones
Across rocks and meadows
Swarms of new flies.

I cannot remember things I once read
A few friends, but they are in cities.
Drinking cold snow-water from a tin cup
Looking down for miles
Through high still air.

The clear statement and unmeasured free verse mask the formalism of the poem, which is a nature meditation in the mode of

Wordsworth's "Tintern Abbey" or a compressed travelogue in the mode of Yeats' "Sailing to Byzantium." Like these forebears, Snyder deftly evokes a scene that feels familiar and exotic at the same time. The reader also gains a sense of time passing in solitude, especially when looking down from the last, lonely vista of the poem. However, the reflectiveness of the poem is carefully matched with precise detail: the smoke haze, the black on the pinecones, and the humidity coming up from the valley. The poet, who is looking for forest fires, is as watchful as he is reminiscent. The details come into precise focus with the swarming flies. The reader sees the valley laid out below the poet. The poem, however, shifts focus dramatically with the poet's apostrophe at the beginning of the second stanza. Whom is he addressing? Why is this thought included in this verbal landscape painting? The nostalgia of these two lines is matched with a sense of transience—friends in cities (where the poet conspicuously is not) and forgotten books. Snyder concludes the poem by introducing two new features: a sensation, in the form of the ice-cold water he is swallowing, and a vision, which telescopes downward from his vantage, taking in a momentarily harmonious world. The entire effect is that of a Chinese landscape painting in which the poet becomes but one element among many interacting, interdependent elements, so that even the cities beyond the vision of the poem must be included to best contemplate this scene. Snyder's practical concerns as a forest lookout are thus represented in metaphysical, even cosmological, terms.

*Riprap* was first published in Kyoto in a 30-page edition by Cid Corman's Origin Press in 1959 (at which time the poet was living in Japan and studying Zen Buddhism) and was later republished with *Cold Mountain Poems* (1965), Snyder's translations of the Chinese Chan (Zen) recluse Han Shan, by Grey Fox Press, and later North Point Press. The book could very easily be seen as a record of Snyder's jobs during the 1950s and the concerns that these jobs raised for him. In fact, *Riprap* is dedicated to a long list of co-workers who were foresters, lookouts, and tankermen. Titles such as "The Late Snow & Lumber Strike of the Summer of Fifty-Four" and "T-2 Tanker Blues" describe locations such as Mount Baker and the Midway Islands. Other poems are dated and given locations, such as "Red Sea" and "Columbia 1948–Arabia 1958." *Riprap* shows the poet belonging in the company of other adventure poets, whether Basho, Camões, or Sir Richard Burton. In this respect, the exigencies of difficult labor are constantly interfered with by the concerns of poetry, at least in the mind of this poet. Snyder demonstrates this problem succinctly in "Milton by Firelight," which begins with a quotation from *Paradise Lost*—"O hell, what do mine eyes / with grief behold"—in which Snyder drives a wedge into Milton's pentameter to make an enjambment. This he follows with a description of "an old / Singlejack miner" who has been blasting granite and making switchbacks up the sides of mountains "that last for years." The poet, elliptically, asks, "What use, Milton, a silly story / Of our lost general parents, / eaters of fruit?" His question leads him to reflect,

> In ten thousand years the Sierras
> Will be dry and dead, home of the scorpion.
> Ice-scratched slabs and bent trees.

The slabs and trees, without verbs, are viewed as permanent facts, outlasting Milton by millennia. Yet the poet cannot shake Milton, cannot shake the thought of Satan. At the end of the day, there is a bittersweet lament, when the fire dies down, that it is "Too dark to read." Milton's uselessness in this wilderness tugs on the poet as compellingly as the work he is doing there. How to bring these two facts of life into harmony?

Snyder builds his poems on the tensions between the need to work and the need to write, challenging the reader to turn poetry into work just as the poet himself has done. "Riprap," the poem that concludes this volume, is, like Snyder's much later poem "Axe Handles," an exemplary *ars poetica,* a poem that demonstrates its position as much as it explains it. Where the poet has been earning his living laying down riprap trails in the mountains, now he builds poems in the hills of language and speech:

> Lay down these words
> Before your mind like rocks.
>             placed solid, by hands
> In choice of place, set
> Before the body of the mind
>             in space and time:

The Buddhist principle of the mind as the sixth sense is evoked in this opening: Snyder's poems, like trails, are before the mind—not only in front of the mind but prior to the mind—the solid work of hands. The internal rhymes of "placed," "place," and "space," echoing "choice," set off the conspicuous but off-rhymed "mind" and "time." These abstractions form into a vision of the poem or, more properly, the work at hand. There is the "Cobble of milky way, / straying planets, / These poems, people . . ." There are "The worlds like an endless / four-dimensional / Game of *Go*." There are minute "ants and pebbles," and there is "Granite: ingrained / with torment of fire and weight . . ." It is this image of the compression of stone, of solid matter—the material that makes the trails of riprap—that concludes the poem, inhering solidity with poetic craft. Snyder envisions,

> Crystal and sediment linked hot
>             all change, in thoughts,
> As well as things.

These linkages, despite their changeability and despite the capriciousness of thought, when carefully composed, make for something solid and, if not as lasting as stone itself, perhaps are as useful in the long run as the "rocky sure-foot trails" we make to cross the wilderness we live in.

Peter O'Leary

**Further Reading**

Carpenter, David A., "Gary Snyder's Inhumanism, from Riprap to Axe Handles," *South Dakota Review* 26, no. 1 (Spring 1988)

Géfin, Laszlo, "Ellipsis and Riprap: Gary Snyder," in *Critical Essays on Gary Snyder,* edited by Patrick D. Murphy, Boston: G.K. Hall, 1990

Halper, Jon, editor, *Gary Snyder: Dimensions of a Life,* San Francisco: Sierra Club, 1991

Parkinson, Thomas, "The Poetry of Gary Snyder," in *Critical*

*Essays on Gary Snyder,* edited by Patrick D. Murphy, Boston: G.K. Hall, 1990

Paul, Sherman, "Arbeiten und Lieben: Gary Snyder," in *In Search of the Primitive: Rereading David Antin, Jerome Rothenberg, and Gary Snyder,* by Paul, Baton Rouge: Louisiana State University Press, 1986

Robertson, David, "Gary Snyder Riprapping in Yosemite, 1955," *American Poetry* 2, no. 1 (Fall 1984)

---

# Gustaf Sobin 1935–

The poetry of Gustaf Sobin is nothing less than the attempt to trace the movement of the unutterable silence at the heart of Being as it enters into language. For Sobin, language creates the possibilities and postulates of human experience, and the poet is a conduit through whom the creative forces of the universe flow. The poem embodies the motion of these forces as it emerges through the breath as a living organism born of a single germinal image. In Sobin's poetics, the poet strives to eliminate all traces of the personality in order that the poem move from the realm of the experiential toward its origin in the realm of the potential.

Gustaf Sobin was born in Boston in 1935, but after traveling to Provence and meeting the French poet René Char in 1962, he moved there permanently the following year. Sobin met the German philosopher Martin Heidegger when Heidegger came to visit Char in 1965 or 1966. For Heidegger, the idea of a nothingness at the source of all that exists is of central importance, and this generative nothingness is also fundamental to Sobin's poetry and poetics. Among Sobin's poetic influences are Blake, Duncan, McClure, Creeley, Oppen, Mallarmé, and of course Char.

Sobin describes his poems as including a "term of omission," a "crystal" that both is and is not. In *Wind Chrysalid's Rattle* (1980), this silence within speech is envisioned as a cosmic force. In "Isn't That's Almost," a "glint in the voice's wondrous shadows" conjures forth both word and world, and in "Notes on Sound, Speech, Speech-Crystals and the Celestial Echo," the entire universe is "spoken" into existence by a "Speech, that's never pronounced, but cast, diffused, exuded." In "That the Universe Is Chrysalid," creation is envisioned as a process of continuing emanation within which our very dwelling space is made of the "infinitesimal crystals we murmur." In "Making the Mirror," "breath crystals alighting . . . constitute the mirror," which in Sobin's somewhat idiosyncratic usage is the image that depicts a nexus within which self and other come into relation.

The poetry in Sobin's second book of poems, *Celebration of the Sound Through* (1982), is a movement of language in the direction of its origin. In "Way," the voice reflects on "letting the words take you towards wherever they'd come from." In "Draft: For Santa Cruz," this journey leads "past / myself, and into the / null's / suspended accelerant." "Ode," the collection's most ambitious poem, describes a fallen language, "darkened" and "circumscribed," yet the undiminished source of language, the null, "draws at the divided voice" so that words may still "spread radiant." The collection also contains some of Sobin's most beautiful flower poetry, in which flowers become a kind of poetic language. "Flowering Cherries" become "earth-the-word," "releasing" the earth itself as poetry growing in the direction of its own ongoing origin in what is about to be.

The poetic landscape of *The Earth as Air* (1984) is dominated by Sobin's metapoetic masterpiece "The Earth as Air: An Ars Poetica." In this poem, poetry is envisioned as a "passage" of "substance" into "sound," earth into breath and air. The poem is a "conveyed omission" channeling pure generative nothingness to create a "space" of absolute potential, "a dimension that we've metrically fashioned, projected past us, and assembled forever to our own exclusion." This dimension, forever just beyond us and "addressed away," is our eternal mirror within which language, our most "perilous" and "god-like" possession, is regenerated, as the "word-errant . . . touches upon the silence of the word-inceptive." We see this process at work in "Irises" when flowers are teased into "mass gutted for the sake of an inference."

The poems in *Voyaging Portraits* (1988) often move through space and time as they transform place into poetry and poetry into place. In "Road, Roadsides, and the Disparate Frames of Sequence," a drive through the desert of the western United States reveals that roads begin wherever words first rush "irrepressible" out of the "broken word." "Lineage," dedicated to Sobin's children, moves through time to "trace forwards" in order that the "still- / moving rumors of the otherwise / ob- / literated" might "emerge." "What the Music Wants" explores poetry's fashioning of "somewhere to stand," place itself created by the music of language, that "miracle" in the "bulb of its voices." "A Portrait of the Self as Instrument of Its Syllables" is one of Sobin's most important works. It is the "portrait" of the disappearance of self as the emergence of poetry. The culminating section of this work depicts a morning's journey into a cave in which Heidegger labors over a "translation of the waves" in a Hölderlin poem. It is in this context that the poet realizes his vocation: "impelled that I urge, herd, drive the / words into / that // luminous salvage."

*Breaths' Burials* (1995) contains some of Sobin's most powerful meditations on the nature of poetry. In "Tracing a Thirst," a poem "sluices a passage" even as it moves toward a "source" that is both its own and the world's. "Transparent Itineraries: 1992" speaks of the divine as "the nominal substitute for those wordless expanses," and it is this wordless "nihil," or nothingness, that provides the "nudge syllable" for the poem in "Domino." In "Fifth Ode: Potentia," the voice of the poem awaits "conveyance" through poetry into "the ever- / narrowing / coils // of some tenuous 'could.'"

In *Towards the Blanched Alphabets* (1998), the poems often move toward a past that might still possess the power for new possibilities. In "The Archeologist," the speaker scatters his own words in the "very updrafts" from which words had first "arisen." In a major poem, "Late Bronze, Early Iron," the archeologist speaker envisions an age before language became "circumscribed" like a commodity, an "âge d'or" when people lived in the "glow of their own voices." For Sobin, to "reach back" is a way of "projecting forwards" into the future. The poetry of Sobin bears the "open vocable" of origin into our increasingly constrained world and with it the possibility of the word regenerated and regenerating.

ROBERT BAKER

**Biography**

Born in Boston, Massachusetts, 15 November 1935. Attended Brown University, Providence, Rhode Island, 1954–58, B.A. 1958. Living in Provence and Languedoc, France.

**Poetry**

*Wind Chrysalid's Rattle,* 1980
*Celebration of the Sound Through,* 1982
*The Earth as Air,* 1984
*Voyaging Portraits,* 1988
*By the Bias of Sound: Selected Poems, 1974–1994,* 1995
*Breaths' Burials: Poems,* 1995
*Towards the Blanched Alphabets,* 1998

**Other Writings:** novels (*Venus Blue,* 1991; *Dark Mirrors: A Novel of Provence,* 1992; *The Fly-Truffler,* 1999), children's literature, translations of Chinese literature, essays (*Luminous Debris: Reflecting on Vestige in Provence and Languedoc,* 2000).

**Further Reading**

Baker, Robert, "The Manifestation of the Particular: The Thing in Sobin and Heidegger," *Talisman* 18 (1998)
Baker, Robert, "The Open Vocable," *American Book Review* 20, no. 2 (1999)
Foster, Edward Halsey, "Gustaf Sobin Interview," in *Postmodern Poetry: The Talisman Interviews,* by Foster, Hoboken, New Jersey: Talisman House, 1994
Foster, Edward Halsey, "Review of *Voyaging Portraits,*" in *Answerable to None,* by Foster, New York: Spuyten Duyvil, 1999
Zawacki, Andrew, "Review of *Towards the Blanched Alphabets,*" *Boston Review* 24, no. 5 (1999)

---

# Cathy Song 1955–

True to the title of her first major accolade as a writer, Cathy Song was just 27 years old when her first collection of poetry, *Picture Bride* (1983), was selected for recognition through the prestigious Yale Younger Poets series. This award introduced Song to the literary limelight, where she remains to this day. Such early acclaim can daunt as easily as stimulate a newcomer, but for Song it marked the beginning of a distinguished writing career.

As the product of study at the University of Hawaii, an undergraduate literary degree from Wellesley College, and an M.F.A. in creative writing from Boston University, Song asserts the primacy of her craft over the circumstances of her culture. Therefore, while she deals in subject matter that recalls the Chinese and Korean legacies of her biracial origin, recounts familial history, and situates herself as a woman of color in the United States, it is for her identity and practices as a poet that Song seeks attention. Resolute that she be thought of as a poet rather than as an Asian-American poet, Song claims a writing life that resists category. She wishes her work to be received on its own terms rather than read first or exclusively through the interpretive lens of ethnicity.

In so doing, Song has been successful in reaching a broad audience of readers and critics. She has published three collections: *Picture Bride* (1983), *Frameless Windows, Squares of Light* (1988), and *School Figures* (1994). Recurrent themes in her poetry include interpersonal relationships, particularly within a family; the immigration experience and attendant pressures for cultural assimilation; the sense of place as it grounds human action and affiliation; and the efforts to both recall and recast the cultural past.

Most likely as a result of these themes, Song's work is often compared to that of Maxine Hong Kingston. Song's "Picture Bride," for example, has been likened to Kingston's short story "No Name Woman" as a tale of a woman whose name has fallen away from the teller's tongue but whose fate must not. Both writers are capable of compellingly intimate testimony about women's lives. Overall, critics have found Song's work to be most powerful when it transcends circumstance—striking at recognizable feelings without sentimentality, establishing a context uncluttered by cliché.

Song's poetic style is, for the most part, spare and understated. Critics note the economy of language, quietness of tone, and stillness of mood in Song's poems. These qualities correspond to the reflective, even contemplative, work the poetry conducts and invites from readers. This pensiveness, along with the precision of images and their arrangement, helps define Song's technique as a poet. It is no surprise, then, that while critics seek to compare her to Rita Dove, Lorna Dee Cervantes, and Yoshiko Uchida, Song's influences come from visual art as much as, if not more than, from other writers of poetry. The two most prominent among these artistic figures are the Japanese printmaker Kitagawa Utamaro and the modern American painter Georgia O'Keeffe. Both poets and painters, after all, excel at composition.

Indeed, each of the five sections in Song's debut, *Picture Bride,* bears the title of one of O'Keeffe's painted studies of flowers, such as "Red Poppy" and "Black Iris." The homage does not stop there. Song even adopts the painter's speaking voice in "Blue and

White Lines after O'Keeffe" as she portrays the familiar tension of a daughter's struggle to live differently than her mother.

The visual medium as well as a preoccupation with the implications of color reappears in Song's second collection of poems, *Frameless Windows, Squares of Light.* In "A Child's Painting," for example, the speaker lingers over the intentions behind a youngster's picture and the message his image conveys. Once more securing the analogy between verbal and visual modes, Song ends the poem with a reference to "the colors of a private alphabet." In this phrase, Song could as easily be referring to her own images, sketched with visual acuity and rich hue.

In fact, in another piece from Song's second book, "Humble Jar," a poem generally understood as a tribute to the mother who keeps at the ready items ranging from sewing kits to chewing gum, Song simultaneously conjures a vision of the poet. Such a writer, like the mother with her collection of buttons, marshals this vocabulary of plainspoken objects, or words, to minister to the dilemmas of the present by calling on useful vestiges of the past.

Song's third collection, *School Figures,* finds the poet extending her meditations on kinship. In this volume, Song, now writing from the vantage point of a parent, seeks to reach terms with both the generations that preceded her and the one that follows, her children. This volume carries markers of both the contemporary moment (such as karaoke) and the historical past (such as bits of pidgin, a language surviving Hawaii's plantation era), as Song depicts the challenges of life among Hawaii's middle class. While some reviewers regard Song's poetry as insufficiently confrontational, even accommodationist in terms of its cultural politics, others sense the passion and anger underlying her poetic restraint.

In addition to receiving the Yale Younger Poets Award, Song has been honored with the Poetry Society of America's Shelley Memorial Award, the Hawaii Award for Literature, and a fellowship from the National Endowment for the Arts. Her works are frequently anthologized in surveys of American literature as well as multicultural and women's writing. Song maintains residence in her native Hawaii, where she continues her writing. She conducts college-level instruction in creative writing, sometimes at the same institution where her higher education began. In her efforts as an educator, she reaches emerging poets, both through the university classroom and the Poets in the Schools program, to which she remains devoted. "We desperately need our imagination," explains Song, and with her guidance, fledgling writers will continue to explore, as Song herself discovered before them, the depth of that need and its expression.

LINDA S. WATTS

*See also* Asian American Poetry

**Biography**

Born in Honolulu, Hawaii, 20 August 1955. Attended the University of Hawaii, Manoa, 1973–75; Wellesley College, B.A. 1977; Boston University, M.F.A., 1981; since 1987 teacher, Poet in the Schools program, Hawaii; visiting writer, University of Hawaii; editor, Bamboo Ridge Press, Honolulu, Hawaii. Received Yale Younger Poets Award, 1982; Hawaii Award for Literature, 1994; Shelley Memorial Award, 1994; National Endowment for the Arts fellowship. Living in Honolulu, Hawaii.

**Poetry**

*Picture Bride,* 1983
*Frameless Windows, Squares of Light,* 1988
*School Figures,* 1994

**Other Writings:** co-edited anthology of women's fiction and poetry (*Sister Stew,* 1991).

**Further Reading**

Chock, Eric, et al., editors, *Talk Story: An Anthology of Hawaii's Local Writers,* Honolulu, Hawaii: Petronium Press/ Talk Story, 1978

Fujita-Sato, Gayle K., "'Third World' as Place and Paradigm in Cathy Song's 'Picture Bride,'" *MELUS* 15, no. 1 (Spring 1988)

Greenbaum, Jessica, "Cathy Song," in *Asian American Literature: Reviews and Criticism of Works by American Writers of Asian Descent,* edited by Lawrence J. Trudeau, Detroit, Michigan, and London: Gale Research, 1995

Kyhan, Lee, "Korean American Literature: The Next Generation," *Korea Journal* 34, no. 1 (Spring 1994)

Nomaguchi, Debbie Murakami, "Cathy Song: 'I'm a Poet Who Happens to Be Asian American,'" *International Examiner* 2, no. 11 (2 May 1984)

Schultz, Susan M., "Cathy Song," in *American Poets since World War II,* fifth series, edited by Joseph Conte, Detroit, Michigan, and London: Gale Research, 1996

Shelton, Pamela L., editor, *Contemporary Women Poets,* Detroit, Michigan, and London: St. James Press, 1998

Sumida, Stephen H., *And the View from the Shore: Literary Traditions of Hawai'i,* Seattle: University of Washington Press, 1991

Wallace, Patricia, "Divided Loyalties: Literal and Literacy in the Poetry of Lorna Dee Cervantes, Cathy Song, and Rita Dove," *MELUS* 18, no. 3 (Fall 1993)

## Heaven

"Heaven" first appeared in Cathy Song's second book of poetry, *Frameless Windows, Squares of Light* (1988), and is one of five poems to represent Song in the influential *Norton Anthology of American Literature.* The poem's lucid and straightforward style, in which sentimentalism and rhetorical flourish play no part, reflects Song's celebration of the rhythms of ordinary speech. The poem's presentation of simple yet memorable images, indicative of the influence of William Carlos Williams and of the visual arts on Song's work, is in keeping with Song's commitment to exploring the mundane world in order to promote speculation and to spur the workings of memory. Thematically, "Heaven" typifies Song's concerns with the disruptions of immigrant experience, with humans' yearnings for escape, with cultural and historical gaps, and with the intricate, seemingly mystical ties that bind family members together across generations. A meditation on cultural difference and on the sense of one's place in a changing world, "Heaven" is more overtly political than much of Song's work. Appearing at a crucial moment in the history of Asian-American literature, the poem serves as a sounding board for theoretical debates revolving around issues of multiculturalism, nationality, and self-identity.

"Heaven" records a mother's reflections on the connection between her Asian-American son and his Chinese forefather. The young boy's physical appearance—Chinese features mixed with blond hair—renders him a sign of dichotomous origins and a symbol of cultural and racial hybridity. The boy is a reminder, both to the poem's speaker and to Song's readers, of the actual or potential conflicts of identity that underlie conceptions of the self, particularly for immigrants. The boy's hybrid character, along with his idealistic view of a supranational "Chinese heaven," destabilizes common notions of race, culture, and nation. It is with such instabilities that the mother/poet figure seeks to come to terms; like the alpine aspens that serve as "equivalents" for Chinese bamboo trees, the boy can be considered the equivalent of his forefather only by an act of the poetic imagination.

The imagination, however, may be liberating or disillusioning, and it becomes clear that the poem's speaker is disappointed with American life. In contrast to the "blue flower" of China, her town in the American West is a "black dot," like the period at the end of a sentence, where "the air is so thin, you can starve on it." One of those "landlocked, makeshift ghost towns" characterized by "broken fences, the whiny dogs, the rattletrap cars," her town is "mean and grubby," "still the wild west" portrayed in popular representations of the American frontier. Song's negative portrayal of this unnamed American town, as well the implication that minorities are relegated to such environments, disputes the widespread notion that most Asian-Americans have successfully integrated into the mainstream of American life and prosperity.

While deflating any idealization of the American present, "Heaven" also delves into the past, reminding the reader of the deprivations suffered by anonymous immigrants, such as the Chinese forefather, who were exploited in order to build the railroads so important to the nation's infrastructure. Song has often been praised for her superb handling of such confrontational material; avoiding both the maudlin and the preachy, she establishes a complex identification of the mother/speaker with the forefather and of the forefather with the speaker's own young son. Such cross-generational affiliations are accomplished by a pensive act of empathy on the part of the mother/speaker; she attempts to re-create or reimagine the mind-set of her forefather, a youth emigrating from a seaport city in southeastern China:

> Did a boy in Guangzhou dream of this
> as his last stop?
> . . . .
> He had always meant to go back.
> When did he finally know
> that each mile of track led him further away,
> that he would die in his sleep,
> dispossessed . . . ?

It is her evocative poetic vision that allows the speaker to re-experience and to empathize with the longings and disappointments of an ancestor whose life remains remote from her own. Yet the cyclical nature of such yearnings and disillusionments is unmistakable, and here the poem reaches a thematic climax. In understanding the experiences of her ancestors, the speaker of the poem arrives at a new knowledge of herself. On the one hand, she is already aware that her only access to China has been in her imagination—"I've never seen it. / It's as if I can't sing that far"—and she now recognizes parallels among her and her son's idealization of China and her forefather's dreams of the "Gold Mountain" of America. The realization that she is now living out her grandfather's dream leads to a central irony of the poem. For first-generation immigrants, the hope was that their offspring would serve to tie them to their new land, to America; in stark contrast, the speaker of "Heaven" is alienated from American life and feels, like her son, an inexplicable affinity with China. The celebration of such an affinity with one's cultural roots, however, is tempered by the sobering realization that any decision to return to one's ancestral origins might be as disenchanting as her forefather's original decision to emigrate two generations earlier.

The poem's final images, which figure the speaker and her son as sailing past "mountains / shimmering blue above the air," suggest that poetry serves as a vehicle for contemplative voyages that are emotionally valuable and spiritually uplifting. At the very least, straddling the divide between poetry as imagination and poetry as ideology, Song's "Heaven" underscores two dominant critical attitudes toward representation of the Far East: one that sees it as an ideal or Orientalist space of the imagination and one that views it as a thoroughly historicized and culturally relative reality. While, like much of Song's work, the poem devotes itself to unearthing a questionable past and present, "Heaven" is also aware of the complexity of learning from others' life stories and of the necessity for reimagining families, cultures, and histories. In seeking values that transcend generations, nations, and cultures, "Heaven" reinforces the Asian-American writing community's commitment to representing immigrant history, coming to terms with a multicultural present, and tentatively applying conclusions in order to better the future.

JOHN PARRAS

**Further Reading**

Chang, Juliana, "Reading Asian American Poetry," *MELUS* 21, no. 2 (Spring 1996)

Fujita-Sato, Gayle K., "'Third World' as Place and Paradigm in Cathy Song's 'Picture Bride,'" *MELUS* 15, no. 1 (Spring 1988)

Gottesman, Ronald, et al., editors, "Cathy Song," in *The Norton Anthology of American Literature,* 2 vols., New York and London: Norton, 1979

Hugo, Richard, "Foreword," in *Picture Bride,* by Cathy Song, New Haven, Connecticut: Yale University Press, 1983

Kyhan, Lee, "Korean American Literature: The Next Generation," *Korea Journal* 34, no. 1 (Spring 1994)

Lim, Shirley Geok-lin, "Review of 'Picture Bride' by Cathy Song," in *The Forbidden Stitch: An Asian-American Women's Anthology,* edited by Lim, Mayumi Tsutakawa, and Margarita Donnelly, Corvallis, Oregon: Calyx Books, 1989

Usui, Masami, "Women Disclosed: Cathy Song's Poetry and Kitagawa Utamaro's 'Ukiyoe,'" *Studies in Culture and the Humanities* (1995)

Wallace, Patricia, "Divided Loyalties: Literal and Literacy in the Poetry of Lorna Dee Cervantes, Cathy Song, and Rita Dove," *MELUS* 18, no. 3 (Fall 1993)

## Gary Soto 1952–

Like the 19th-century American transcendentalists, Gary Soto writes with vivid details about both nature and human conditions, employing concrete natural imagery to sketch lively pictures of the outdoors and the human presence in nature. Born and raised in Fresno, California, Soto is one of the youngest poets to appear in *The Norton Anthology of Modern Poetry.* Recipient of the 1976 United States Award of the International Poetry Forum, *The Elements of San Joaquin* (1977) elevated Soto from an obscure poet to a place among the most notable in contemporary American poetry. In an interview, Soto remarked, "What I felt was that I knew something about life that other people didn't realize. I thought I had a mystical sight" (Binder, 1985). This "mystical sight" and a sustained interest in not only the Chicano condition but also the human condition have defined his career. Soto is the author of ten poetry collections for adults, most significant among them *New and Selected Poems,* a 1995 finalist for both the *Los Angeles Times* Book Award and the National Book Award.

As a young poet, Soto was influenced by the poems of Allen Ginsberg and Edward Field. However, it was not until the fall of 1972, when he enrolled in Philip Levine's creative writing class at Fresno State University, that Soto began to recognize his passion and potential for writing poetry. By the summer of 1973, Soto had already written about two-thirds of *The Elements of San Joaquin,* inspired by an ethnic writers workshop in Wisconsin. Soto's use of language, primarily English, is direct, with concrete images and a flare for succinctness; it produces a style that is impeccable, down to earth, yet emotionally penetrating and provocative at the same time. However, the suppleness and simplicity of his diction and syntax often camouflages a profundity of ideas and emotions lurking beneath the surface of the poems. For instance, in one of his most anthologized poems, "Oranges," originally published in *Black Hair* (1985), Soto uses his unique narrative style to capture the tender memory of a first crush: a porch light that burned yellow, a barking dog, and bringing the 12-year-old girl a chocolate that he paid for with a nickel and an orange. The poem ends with a striking last line as Soto describes the act of peeling the bright orange: "Someone might have thought / I was making a fire in my hands."

Soto deals with a plethora of conditions in his poems, and his subjects include industrial and urban sprawl and the bleak predicament of urban violence. Noting the irony, he compares such postmodern industrial realities with the beauty of the agricultural fields that have extracted the sweat and humanity of young migrant farm workers (a dominant theme in *San Joaquin*). Soto's imagistic approach to characterization is a technique he first developed in *San Joaquin* and later refined in *The Tale of Sunlight* (1978). Soto manages to create vivid characters by stringing together seemingly random images and bits of information.

The poems in *San Joaquin* that are set in farm labor fields mesh the raw physicality of the fields with the mood of the workers who work the land. The speaker of "Hoeing" is a worker for whom the land is a pervasive part of his being: "Dirt . . . entering my nostrils / and eyes / The yellow under my fingernails." We see what the speaker sees as he works the hoe across his "shadow" to chops weeds. The wind blows the "thick caterpillars" into "shriveled rings" and the sun warms the left side of the worker's face.

*San Joaquin* resembles T.S. Eliot's *The Waste Land:* winds erode everything to dust, which in turn permeates all that survives. Clouds cover the sky and violence looms. Soto describes the gruesome details of several rapes and at least one murder in the first section of the book and a baby drowns in the third section. Soto treats violence and the threat of violence as a widespread phenomenon in modern urban society. He is not concerned with punishment for violent crime, which he suggests only aggravates the assaulter's pathology. He is only interested in transformation through kindness.

In an interview, Soto remarked, "Literature doesn't get better. What it does is, it changes its philosophy and it changes style. Chicano literature is one of the rare exceptions, because we began with people with heart and emotion, but sadly without any style, any craft" (Binder, 1985). Soto's credibility in both American and Chicano literary circles stems from his exploration of self-identity, human experience, and the craft of making poetry. His artistic control over language and imagination is indeed rare.

Reshmi Dutt

*See also* Hispanic American Poetry

**Biography**

Born in Fresno, California, 12 April 1952. Attended California State University, Fresno, B.A. 1974; University of California, Irvine, M.F.A. 1976; member of the Department of English, San Diego State University, California; since 1985 Associate Professor of English and ethnic studies, University of California, Berkeley; Elliston Poet, University of Cincinnati, Ohio, spring 1988. Received Academy of American Poets Prize, 1975; *The Nation* Award, 1975; International Poetry Forum Award, 1976; Bess Hokin Prize, 1977, and Levinson Award, 1984 (*Poetry,* Chicago); Guggenheim fellowship, 1979; National Education Association fellowship, 1982; Before Columbus Foundation Award, for prose, 1985; American Academy Award, 1985; California Arts Council fellowship, 1989; Andrew Carnegie Medal, 1993. Living in northern California.

**Poetry**

*Entrance: Four Chicano Poets* (with others), edited by Soto, 1976
*The Elements of San Joaquin,* 1977
*The Tale of Sunlight,* 1978
*Where Sparrows Work Hard,* 1981
*Black Hair,* 1985
*Who Will Know Us?* 1990
*A Fire in My Hands,* 1990
*Home Course in Religion,* 1991
*Neighborhood Odes,* 1992
*Canto Familiar/Familiar Song,* 1994
*New and Selected Poems,* 1995
*The Sparrows Move South: Early Poems,* 1995
*Super-Eight Movies: Poems* (illustrated by John Digby), 1996
*Junior College,* 1997
*A Natural Man,* 1999

**Other Writings:** prose (*Living Up the Street: Narrative Recollections,* 1985), essays (*A Summer Life,* 1990), children's literature (*Baseball in April, and Other Stories,* 1990); edited collections of literature (*California Childhood: Recollections and Stories of the Golden State,* 1988).

**Further Reading**

Binder, Wolfgang, *Partial Autobiographies: Interviews with Twenty Chicano Poets,* Erlangen, Germany: Palm and Enke, 1985

De La Fuente, Patricia, "Entropy in the Poetry of Gary Soto: The Dialectics of Violence," *Discurso literario: Revista de temas hispanicos* 5, no. 1 (Autumn 1987)

De La Fuente, Patricia, "Mutability and Stasis: Images of Time in Gary Soto's *Black Hair,*" *Americas Review: A Review of Hispanic Literature and Art of the USA* 17, no. 1 (Spring 1989)

Erben, Rudolf, "Popular Culture, Mass Media, and Chicano Identity in Gary Soto's *Living Up the Street* and *Small Faces,*" *MELUS* 17, no. 3 (Fall 1991–92)

Lee, Don, "About Gary Soto," *Ploughshares* 21, no. 1 (Spring 1995)

Soto, Gary, "The Childhood Worries; or, Why I Became a Writer," *Iowa Review* 25, no. 2 (Spring–Summer 1995)

---

# Jack Spicer 1925–65

Jack Spicer's poetry and poetics are among the most radical in the 20th century. Spicer claimed that his poetry originated through an encounter with an otherness, an outside of himself, that "dictated" his poems to him. For Spicer, the writing of poetry was a form of spiritual exercise in which the poet emptied himself of personal volition in order that he might become a conveyor of messages, a radio receiver of broadcasts from beyond. Spicer's poetry of dictation envisions poems existing before their emergence into a language that inevitably fails to bring their full presence through from the outside.

Jack Spicer was born in Los Angeles in 1925 but often claimed that his true birth was the period of time in 1945–46 when he met the poets Robert Duncan and Robin Blaser. Together with these poets, Spicer sought to form a *kreis,* a circle, based on the principle of *agape,* or communal love. Spicer, a linguist by training and profession, lived most of his life in the communities in and around San Francisco, and his poetry is filled with images of seagulls, oceans, waves, and fish as well as images from games such as chess and his beloved baseball. Among Spicer's influences are Yeats, Blake, Lorca, Rilke, Rimbaud, Poe, and of course Duncan.

Spicer's early poetry, written between 1945 and 1956, is collected in *One Night Stand, and Other Poems* (1980). The early poetry is more rooted in personal emotion and sexuality than the later work. Poems such as "The Dancing Ape" and "When Your Body Brushed Against Me" begin in erotic longings and isolation. Spicer's "Imaginary Elegies," written between 1950 and 1959, is his first major work and his first serial poem, a community of individual poems created through dictation to form an organic whole, or book. Spicer came to believe that great poetry could not be achieved within the boundaries of a single poem. With his "Imaginary Elegies," Spicer incorporates dictation and seriality. The resulting elegies exhort the poet to "be like god" and compare poetry to a speeding train with "alien cargo."

Spicer began his "Poetry as Magic Workshop" in 1957, and the community and energy created by this venture propelled Spicer into the major phase of his poetry. *After Lorca* (1957) is a collection of "translations" and letters from Spicer to the dead poet. In this book, Spicer plays a "game" with the "ghost" of Lorca and past poetic tradition, a game made out of a "need for a poetry that is more than the expression of my hatreds and desires." If *After Lorca* draws past tradition into Spicer's community of poetry, *Admonitions* (1958, published 1974) draws in his contemporaries. The book is a "hall of mirrors" in which poems reflect specific individuals and each other, creating a decentered "fun house" designed to lure the reader to the looking glass. *A Book of Music* (1958, published 1979) explores language's possibilities and limitations. "Duet for a Chair and a Table" explains how things named "assume identities," yet in "Improvisations on a Sentence by Poe," Spicer evokes "The grand concord of what / Does not stoop to definition." Poetry may approach the "indefiniteness" of "the true music," but, as "A Book of Music" states, it ultimately "ends like a rope," with its "twists" and "endings" exposed, and its connection to the "grand concord" is severed, leaving the poem as testimony to an incomplete union with the inexpressible.

*The Heads of the Town Up to the Aether* (1962) is Spicer's attempt to render *logos,* Apollonian truth, into language. According to Spicer, the book's three-part structure corresponds to the three parts of Dante's *Divine Comedy.* The first section of the book, "Homage to Creeley," is also divided into three parts, each named for a character from Cocteau's movie *Orpheus* (1949). In *Orpheus,* poetry is used to deceive and seduce the poet Orpheus into the realm of death. In Spicer's Inferno, the poet is similarly betrayed by poetry and language. The "ghosts" that dictate poetry go "All the way to the heart" in the "explanatory notes" to "Partington Ridge." However, as we hear in "Sheep Trails Are Fateful to Strangers," "words / turn mysteriously against those who use them," leaving the poet unsatisfied and apart. Spicer's Purgatorio is "A Fake Novel about the Life of Arthur Rimbaud." Rimbaud sought to re-create the world through poetry. However, in "Where and When," Rimbaud is edged away by a ghost who says, "I is the river." For Spicer, the "river" and "ghosts" of history and tradition are more significant than any re-creation of the world through poetry. Spicer claimed that his Paradiso, "A Textbook of Poetry," was his most completely dictated book. Here a word is "A vessel, a vesicle of truth," and yet "Nothing comes through." With sorrow, Spicer proclaims the death "Of every poem in every line." *Logos,* it seems, cannot be incarnated without becoming "Lowghost when He is pinned down to words."

Spicer's *The Holy Grail* (1964) combines grail myth with comic voices to create what Arthur calls "this uncomfortable music." Spicer even uses Galahad to mock the optimism of poetry in the Whitman/Ginsberg tradition as "fool-ish as if / words or poetry could save you." *Language* (1965) contains many of Spicer's bleakest pronouncements on language and the possibility of poetry. The book's first poem bluntly states, "No one listens to poetry." The poet's lips cannot even speak truly of love because "language / Has so misshaped them." Yet the book ends on a strangely positive note: "The dark / forest of words lets in some light from its branches." However, in "Ten Poems for Downbeat" from *Book of Magazine Verse* (1966), Spicer seems finally to realize the limits of dictated poetry; "identity" cannot be completely eliminated, and poets cannot "sing songs like nightingales."

In 1965, Spicer gave his famous Vancouver and Berkeley lectures, later published in *The House That Jack Built* (1998). These lectures describe the essential premises of Spicer's poetry. Spicer died of alcoholism that same year; his last words were, "My vocabulary did this to me." He remains a powerful influence on poets who strive to move beyond the personal voice in their work.

ROBERT BAKER

*See also* Symbolism

**Biography**

Born in Los Angeles, California, 30 January 1925. Attended the University of the Redlands, California; University of California, Berkeley, M.A. 1950; worked as a linguist. Died in San Francisco, California, 17 August 1965.

**Poetry**

*After Lorca,* 1957; revised edition, 1974
*The Heads of the Town Up to the Aether,* 1962
*The Holy Grail,* 1964; revised edition, 1970
*Language,* 1965
*Book of Magazine Verse,* 1966; revised edition, 1970
*Admonitions,* 1974
*The Collected Books of Jack Spicer,* 1975
*A Book of Music,* 1979
*One Night Stand, and Other Poems,* 1980
*Collected Poems, 1945–1946,* 1981

**Other Writings:** novels (*Tower of Babel,* 1994), correspondence (*Dear Ferlinghetti/Dear Jack: The Spicer-Ferlinghetti Correspondence,* 1962), lectures (*The House That Jack Built: The Collected Lectures of Jack Spicer,* 1998).

**Further Reading**


Blaser, Robin, "The Practice of Outside," in *The Collected Books of Jack Spicer,* by Spicer, edited by Blaser, Santa Rosa, California: Black Sparrow Press, 1975

Duncan, Robert, "Preface," in *One Night Stand, and Other Poems,* by Spicer, edited by Donald Allen, San Francisco: Grey Fox Press, 1980

Ellingham, Lewis, and Kevin Killian, *Poet Be Like God,* Hanover, New Hampshire: University Press of New England, 1998

Foster, Edward Halsey, *Jack Spicer,* Boise, Idaho: Boise State University Press, 1991

Foster, Edward Halsey, "Erosion in Paradise," in *Answerable to None,* by Foster, New York: Spuyten Duyvil, 1999

Gizzi, Peter, "Jack Spicer and the Practice of Reading," in *The House That Jack Built: The Collected Lectures of Jack Spicer,* by Spicer, edited by Gizzi, Hanover, New Hampshire: University Press of New England, 1998


## After Lorca

Jack Spicer regarded *After Lorca* (1957) as the true beginning of his career, although he had been writing poetry seriously for at least ten years before. Originally published in a small edition by Spicer's White Rabbit Press, it opens his *Collected Books* (1975), the standard edition of his works. On one level, the book can be read as a hoax: it consists of a set of poems, some of which are Spicer's, some of which are his translations of poems by the Spanish poet Federico García Lorca (1898–1936), and some of which are combinations of the two. Interspersed with the poems are crucial "programmatic letters" addressed to Lorca, in which Spicer presents, in his typically witty, conversational style, the ideas by which he will refashion his poetry. The entire production is rather resentfully introduced by the ghost of Lorca himself, speaking from "Outside Granada," that is, from his grave.

After composing *After Lorca,* Spicer thought of nearly all his earlier poetry as "foul" since "the poems belong nowhere." This harsh judgment, expressed in a letter to his fellow poet Robin Blaser included in Spicer's book *Admonitions* (1958, published 1974), is understandable given the severe principles of composition developed in *After Lorca,* which would determine the shape of Spicer's subsequent poetry. Chief among these, as he explains in the letter to Blaser, is the notion that "poems should echo and reecho against each other. They should create resonances." These resonances can be achieved only through serial composition and the organization of the writing into books rather than discrete lyrics, with their momentary, ephemeral expressions of emotion. *After Lorca* is just such a book, and the poems in the volume resonate powerfully against each other to produce a total aesthetic effect beyond that of any single poem.

It is also the first of Spicer's works composed through a process that later, in his Vancouver lectures, he will call "dictation." For Spicer, the poem must come from "outside," presenting itself as a radically other linguistic entity apart from the poet's personal concerns. Communing (or perhaps wrestling) with the spirit of Lorca enables Spicer to overcome this "big lie of the personal" and to align his poetry with "tradition," which he defines as "generations of different poets in different countries patiently telling the same story, writing the same poem, gaining and losing something with each transformation—but, of course, never really losing anything." Spicer's (mis)treatment of Lorca's poetry perfectly represents this notion of tradition: although he often distorts the original words or conflates them with his own, he also demonstrates their lasting importance to his midcentury San Francisco literary culture, possessed of a very different sensibility from that of Lorca's Andalusia.

Just as important, beginning with the Lorca project, the original poetry that Spicer writes becomes more direct and confident, what Clayton Eshleman (1977) describes as "a sharper, more forceful version of itself." A good example is "Ballad of Sleeping Somewhere Else," which for Eshleman "seems to be written by one poet called Garcia Spicer":

> The pine needles fall
> Like an ax in the forest.
>
> Can you hear them crumble
> There where we are sleeping?

The windows are close to the wall
Here in the darkness they remain open

(When I saw you in the morning
My arms were full of paper.)

Five hundred miles away
The moon is a hatchet of silver.

(When I saw you in the morning
My eyes were full of paper).

Five hundred miles away
The stars are glass that is breaking.

The windows sag on the wall
I feel cold glass in the blankets.

Child, you are too tall for this bed.

The pine needles fall
Like an ax in the forest.

Can you hear them crumble
There where we are sleeping?

Although this poem could be regarded simply as an imitation of the earlier poet's style, like much of *After Lorca* it exemplifies the notion of correspondence so important to Spicer's developing poetics. As he explains in one of the letters (and the pun on "correspondence" is quite intentional),

> Things do not connect; they correspond. That is what makes it possible for a poet to translate real objects, to bring them across language as easily as he can bring them across time. That tree you saw in Spain is a tree I could never have seen in California, that lemon has a different smell and a different taste, BUT the answer is this—every place and every time has a real object to *correspond* with your real object—that lemon may become this lemon, or it may even become this piece of seaweed, or this particular color of gray in this ocean. One does not need to imagine that lemon; one needs to discover it.

This passage is close to the heart of Spicer's project. Deeply distrustful of the Modernist emphasis on the image ("We have both tried to be independent of images," he writes to Lorca), Spicer tries instead to achieve a poetry "utterly independent of images," a poetry that would enable him "to point to the real." His notion that objects in a poem correspond to objects in the real world is premised on the belief, as Gilbert Sorrentino (1984) puts it, "that the world is there, regardless of what we think it is; it is the poet's task to reveal it." In *After Lorca,* Spicer takes his place in an Objectivist tradition that includes William Carlos Williams, Charles Olson, and Robert Duncan, a tradition of poets who understood that Imagism, which merely pictures the real, was an important but insufficient beginning for a new kind of poetry. This poetry, in Spicer's words, would be written in the belief that "objects, words, must be led across time not preserved against it." This insight, along with many of the others articulated in *After Lorca,* are fundamental to the generation of poets who follow Spicer, many of whom are active today.

Norman Finkelstein

**Further Reading**

Chamberlain, Lori, "Ghostwriting the Text: Translation and the Poetics of Jack Spicer," *Contemporary Literature* 26, no. 4 (1985)

Eshleman, Clayton, "The Lorca Working," *Boundary 2* 6, no. 1 (1977)

Finkelstein, Norman, "Jack Spicer's Ghosts and the Gnosis of History," *Boundary 2* 9, no. 2 (1981)

Finkelstein, Norman, *The Utopian Moment in Contemporary American Poetry,* Lewisburg, Pennsylvania: Bucknell University Press, and London: Associated University Presses, 1988; revised edition, 1993

Foster, Edward Halsey, *Jack Spicer,* Boise, Idaho: Boise State University Press, 1991

Hatlen, Burton, "Crawling into Bed with Sorrow: Jack Spicer's *After Lorca,*" *Ironwood* 14, no. 2 (1986)

Sorrentino, Gilbert, *Something Said,* San Francisco: North Point Press, 1984

Spicer, Jack, *The Collected Books of Jack Spicer,* edited by Robin Blaser, Santa Rosa, California: Black Sparrow Press, 1975

Spicer, Jack, *The House That Jack Built: The Collected Lectures of Jack Spicer,* edited by Peter Gizzi, Hanover, New Hampshire: University Press of New England, 1998

---

## Spoken Word. *See* Performance Poetry

---

# William Stafford 1914–93

Born in Hutchinson, Kansas, in 1914, William Edgar Stafford was a contemporary of Robert Lowell, John Berryman, and Elizabeth Bishop, but he did not publish his first book of poetry, *West of Your City,* until 1960. Consequently, his work was also contemporary with the work of poets such as Sylvia Plath, Robert Duncan, and Frank O'Hara. Although *West of Your City* received encouraging reviews and his second book *Traveling through the Dark* (1962) won a National Book Award, Stafford did not receive the same critical attention as other major poets. In part, this was due to his individual themes and style; he did not easily fit among the Confessional poets, the Black Mountain poets, the Beats, or other prevalent groups. Nonetheless, Stafford has usually been associated with poets such as Richard Hugo, Donald Hall, and James Wright, especially in his attachment to local, ordinary subjects; to the potency of imagination and memory; and to a conversational poetic style that privileges exploration and process.

Critics such as Judith Kitchen attribute much of Stafford's unique poetic vision to his experiences growing up. During the 1930s, his family moved from one small Kansas town to another in search of work. Stafford helped his parents by taking a number of different jobs, from field work to construction; he waited tables while earning his B.A. from the University of Kansas. These experiences introduced him to the people and places of the West, frequent subjects in his poetry. When the United States joined World War II, Stafford, a pacifist, filed as a conscientious objector and spent the years 1942–46 in the Civilian Public Service. In *You Must Revise Your Life* (1986), he recalled this period of alienation from the rest of the country as formative in his life: "My four years of 'alternative service under civilian direction' turned my life sharply into that independent channel of the second river—a course hereafter distinguished from any unexamined life, from the way it might have been in any of my hometowns."

If Stafford wanted a more circumspect life, he did not want the literary life of the writers whom he had met while getting his Ph.D. at the University of Iowa. Stafford recalled his years at Iowa as the "principal reference point I have for the literary life as lived by others." Following his own channel, he returned to the West and accepted a position in English at Lewis and Clark College in Portland, Oregon, where he remained until he retired in 1980. During his career, he authored 67 volumes, including *Allegiances* (1970), which helped solidify his reputation as a significant poet; *Stories That Could Be True* (1977); and *Writing the Australian Crawl* (1978), a mixture of poetry and advice about writing. Stafford's poetic vision remained consistent throughout his career, in large part because his vision privileges flexibility and change. Beginning in observation, his poems move tentatively; they probe outward and inward, offering impressions about the subject that refuse ultimately to harden into definitive explanations.

In a 1991 interview with Steven Ratiner, Stafford described his writing time as primarily exploratory: "I'm lying there relaxed. I have a blank sheet in front of me. I put the date on top, and I start letting whatever swims into my attention get written down on the page. . . . I welcome anything that comes along" (Stafford, *Crossing Unmarked Snow,* 1998). These initial observations are often grounded in what Stafford calls in "Allegiances" "the real things we live by." In "Traveling through the Dark," he begins with an event: "Traveling through the dark I found a deer dead on the edge of the Wilson River road." In "Is This Feeling about the West Real?," he begins with an observation: "All their lives out here some people know they live in a hemisphere beyond what Columbus discovered."

In both poems, the poet moves quickly outward, however, using imagination to expand the scope of his vision. As he touches the deer, he hesitates, seeing in the place and moment signs of a deeper mystery: "around our group I could hear the wilderness listen." This mystery is frequently embodied in Stafford's poems as wilderness, legend, or ocean, just as the poet's relation to that mystery is one of wandering or listening. "Is This Feeling about the West Real?" ends with just such a characteristic moment: "Listen—something else hovers out here, not color, not outlines or depth when air relieves distance by hazing far mountains, but some total feeling or other world almost coming forward, like when a bell sounds and then leaves a whole countryside waiting." Although the poet's efforts to see ordinary things in all their strangeness can be disquieting—which is why we follow daily routines and accepted ways of relating to experience—it can also be liberating. In "The Day Millicent Found the World," a young girl wanders into a forest until she is lost. Only when she must make her way moment by moment does she make the happy discovery of "a mysterious world where any direction would yield only surprise."

The idea that writing, like life, proceeds moment by moment without foreknowledge also underlies Stafford's poetic style. Using plain language, flat diction, and normal speech rhythms, his poetry often approximates prose. In poems such as "Ceremony," in which "a muskrat whirled and bit to the bone," this style is joined with clichés to suggest that poetry comes out of our daily experiences; the language is that of everyday usage. However, just as his vision becomes more associative, so his language begins to push against the patterns of everyday usage. Personification, shifting verb tenses, and fused sentences are characteristic of his poetry. The muskrat in "Ceremony," for example, trembles "with meaning my hand would wear forever." Syntactically joining the animal's purposeful trembling with the symbolic bite on the poet's hand illustrates the "kind of marriage" between him and nature suggested by the incident. Vague words such as "meaning," also common in Stafford's poetry, only emphasize the difficulty of understanding the deeper mysteries behind such incidents.

Poetry for Stafford is more than a record of lived experience. Language can re-create the experiences, calling attention to their inherent strangeness, even though the limitations of language's vocabulary and structure make it a crude tool. As he writes in "With My Crowbar Key," "I do tricks in order to know: careless I dance, then turn to see the mark to turn God left for me." As the lines of Stafford's poems wander, tricking perception into new channels, the poem itself becomes the trail, the mark to which the poet can return to see what has been left of the mystery he tried to approximate.

MICHAEL D. BERNDT

**Biography**

Born in Hutchinson, Kansas, 17 January 1914. Attended the University of Kansas, Lawrence, B.A. 1937, M.A. 1946;

University of Iowa, Iowa City, Ph.D. 1955; worked in civilian public service camps as conscientious objector, 1942–46; active in pacifist organizations, and from 1959 member, Oregon Board, Fellowship of Reconciliation; member of the English Department, 1948–54, 1957–60, Professor of English, 1960–80, and Emeritus Professor, 1980–1993, Lewis and Clark College, Portland, Oregon; Assistant Professor of English, Manchester College, Indiana, 1955–56; Professor of English, San Jose State College, California, 1956–57; consultant in poetry, Library of Congress, Washington, D.C., 1970–71; United States Information Agency Lecturer in Egypt, Iran, Pakistan, India, Nepal, and Bangladesh, 1972. Received Yaddo Foundation fellowship, 1955; Oregon Centennial Prize, for poetry and for short story, 1959; Union League Civic and Arts Foundation Prize (*Poetry,* Chicago), 1959; National Book Award, 1963; Shelley Memorial Award, 1964; American Academy Award, 1966, 1981; National Endowment for the Arts grant, 1966; Guggenheim fellowship, 1966; Melville Cane Award, 1974; Western States Book Award, 1992; Frost Medal, 1993; honorary Litt.D., Ripon College, Wisconsin, 1965, and Washington College, Chesterton, Maryland, 1981; honorary L.H.D., Linfield College, McMinnville, Oregon, 1970; Poet Laureate for Oregon, 1975–93. Died 28 August 1993 in Lake Oswego, Oregon.

**Poetry**

*West of Your City,* 1960
*Traveling through the Dark,* 1962
*Five American Poets* (with others), edited by Thom Gunn and Ted Hughes, 1963
*Five Poets of the Pacific Northwest* (with others), edited by Robin Skelton, 1964
*The Rescued Year,* 1966
*Eleven Untitled Poems,* 1968
*Weather,* 1969
*Allegiances,* 1970
*Temporary Facts,* 1970
*Poems for Tennessee* (with Robert Bly and William Matthews), 1971
*In the Clock of Reason,* 1973
*Someday, Maybe,* 1973
*That Other Alone,* 1973
*Going Places,* 1974
*North by West* (with John Haines), edited by Karen and John Sollid, 1975
*Late, Passing Prairie Farm,* 1976
*Braided Apart* (with Kim Robert Stafford), 1976
*Stories That Could Be True: New and Collected Poems,* 1977
*The Design on the Oriole,* 1977
*Writing the Australian Crawl* (poetry and advice on writing), 1978
*Two about Music,* 1978
*All about Light,* 1978
*Tuft by Puff,* 1978
*A Meeting with Disma Tumminello and William Stafford,* 1978
*Tuned in Late One Night,* 1978
*Around You, Your House, and A Catechism,* 1979
*The Quiet of the Land,* 1979
*Things That Happen Where There Aren't Any People,* 1980
*Wyoming Circuit,* 1980
*Sometimes Like a Legend: Puget Sound Country,* 1981
*A Glass Face in the Rain: New Poems,* 1982
*Roving across Fields: A Conversation, and Uncollected Poems, 1942–1982,* edited by Thom Tammaro, 1983
*Segues: A Correspondence in Poetry* (with Marvin Bell), 1983
*Smoke's Way: Poems from Limited Editions (1968–1981),* 1983
*Listening Deep,* 1984
*Stories, Storms, and Strangers,* 1984
*Wyoming,* 1985
*Brother Wind,* 1986
*You and Some Other Characters,* 1987
*An Oregon Message,* 1987
*Annie-Over* (with Marvin Bell), 1988
*Fin, Feather, Fur,* 1989
*A Scripture of Leaves,* 1989
*How to Hold Your Arms When It Rains: Poems,* 1990
*Kansas Poems of William Stafford,* edited by Denise Low, 1990
*Passwords,* 1991
*Seeking the Way: Poems,* 1991
*History Is Loose Again: Poems,* 1991
*The Long Sigh the Wind Makes: Poems,* 1991
*My Name Is William Tell: Poems,* 1992
*Holding onto the Grass: Poems,* 1992
*The Animal That Drank Up Sound* (for children), 1992
*Words in the Cold Air,* 1993
*Who Are You Really, Wanderer? Pages in the Language of Respect and Conciliation,* 1993
*The Darkness around Us Is Deep: Selected Poems,* edited by Robert Bly, 1993
*Learning to Live in the World: Earth Poems,* edited by Jerry Watson and Linda Obbink, 1994
*Wildfire,* edited by Peter Whalen, 1994
*The Methow River Poems,* 1995
*Even in Quiet Places: Poems,* 1996
*The Way It Is: New and Selected Poems,* 1998

**Selected Criticism**

*Friends to This Ground: A Statement for Readers, Teachers, and Writers of Literature,* 1967

**Other Writings:** essays (*You Must Revise Your Life,* 1986), translation of Urdu poetry (*Poems by Ghalib* [with Aijaz Ahmad and Adrienne Rich], 1969); edited collections of poetry (*Modern Poetry of Western America* [with Clinton F. Larson], 1975).

**Further Reading**

Andrews, Tom, editor, *On William Stafford: The Worth of Local Things,* Ann Arbor: University of Michigan Press, 1993
Carpenter, David A., *William Stafford,* Boise, Idaho: Boise State University Press, 1986
Holden, Jonathan, *The Mark of Turn: A Reading of William Stafford's Poetry,* Lawrence: University Press of Kansas, 1976

Kitchen, Judith, *Understanding William Stafford*, Columbia: University of South Carolina Press, 1989
Lauber, John, "The World's Guest—William Stafford," *Iowa Review* 5 (1974)
Pinsker, Sanford, *Three Pacific Northwest Poets: William Stafford, Richard Hugo, and David Wagoner*, Boston: Twayne, 1987
Stitt, Peter, *The World's Hieroglyphic Beauty: Five American Poets*, Athens: University of Georgia Press, 1985

---

# Timothy Steele 1948–

Timothy Steele is as well known for his critical stance toward poetry as for his poetry itself. Often designated as a member of "New Formalism," Steele is one of the few poets today to operate primarily within traditional forms and meters. His questioning, some would say criticizing, of free verse has led to a controversial career. As a professor at several universities in California over the past 20 years (including Stanford and UCLA), Steele has had the opportunity to pass on his "unconventional" views. Steele claims that meter is part of the "feel" of poetry and cannot be separated from the passion of the experience: "My keenest pleasure in reading poetry has from the beginning been bound up with the metrical experience; and I write in meter because only by doing so can I hope to give someone else the same degree of pleasure that the poetry I most love has given me." Those who read Steele's poetry as manifesto instead of what it is—enjoyable verse—miss the power of the experience.

Steele's first collection of verse, *Uncertainties and Rest* (1979), is ambitious for a first effort. Containing sonnets, quatrains, and many other kinds of verse-stanza forms, *Uncertainties and Rest* presented a young poet with a burgeoning interest in mastering a craft no longer widely practiced. In "Jogging in the Presidio," the rhythm and meter of the poem seem to suggest the thump of the jogger's feet:

> Though wayside skeptics eye me, I pursue
> Nothing particular, nothing that's mine,
> But merely leaves brought down by a hard rain
> Last evening, the clear wind the swallows ride,
> And the grass over which my shadow bends
> Evenly uphill as I hit my stride

*Uncertainties and Rest* was praised by several critics but did not attract the attention it deserved. Those who reviewed it noted its passion and clarity, especially for an initial effort. Besides the limitation of using only traditional verse, it was criticized for its occasional conversational tone and, as critic John Miller (1980) suggests, its "unrelieved privatism." It is important to note that when critics refer to Steele's "classical" or "traditional" approach, this references form only. The content of his work has always included everyday experience, a more personal poetry than most "traditional" poets utilize.

Over the next seven years, Steele continued to develop his formal technique. His next large collection of verse, *Sapphics Against Anger, and Other Poems* (1986), exhibited a tighter grasp of form. Many of these poems continue in the personal vein of Steele's first collection, examining everyday sensory experience of a highly personal nature. The fact that such writing is set to highly structured meter is unusual, but it can be just as moving as free verse, the more typical form for contemporary personal writing. Although many of the poems seem to involve Steele's adult life in California, there are nostalgic glances back to the poet's youth in New England. In "Timothy," a poem about the harvesting of autumn hay, Steele remembers with fondness working in the fields:

> Although the field lay cut in swaths,
> Grass at the edge survived the crop:
> Stiff stems, with lateral blades of leaf,
> Dense cattail flower-spikes at the top.
>
> If there was breeze and open sky,
> We raked each swath into a row;
> If not, we took the hay to dry
> To the barn's golden-showering mow.
>
> The hay we forked there from the truck
> Was thatched resilience where it fell,
> And I took pleasure in the thought
> The fresh hay's name was mine as well.

"Timothy" and many other poems in *Sapphics Against Anger, and Other Poems* crystallize Steele's progression as a poet, with increasingly personal sensory images housed within more firmly controlled formal verse. This cohesion of flawless form and content, which Steele feels negates the tag of "formalist," is wholly evident in the poem "Waiting for the Storm," quoted in its entirety here:

> Breeze sent a wrinkling darkness
> Across the bay. I knelt
> Beneath an upturned boat,
> And, moment by moment, felt
>
> The sand at my feet grow colder,
> The damp air chill and spread.
> Then the first raindrops sounded
> On the hull above my head.

In poems such as "Waiting for the Storm," Steele shows how brilliant, simple, and unpretentious "traditional" poetry can be and how it can be just as powerful as free verse, a form that revolted against the supposed stagnancy and rigidity of the traditional. Steele's mastery of personal content within traditional form continued in his third full collection of poetry, *The Color Wheel* (1994).

Steele is perhaps most noted for his critical views. In *Missing Measures: Modern Poetry and the Revolt Against Meter* (1990), he examines the history of poetry from the Greeks to the present, including discussion of the various avenues taken by poetry and prose and by traditional and free verse. In the book's most interesting section, Steele indicts the Modernist poets not so much for breaking away from traditional verse but rather for breaking away without setting up a new paradigm as a substitute (his reasoning here is that the lack of a pattern does not constitute a pattern itself). Steele argues that the project of Pound, Eliot, and Williams, perhaps rooted in a genuine effort to expand the boundaries of poetry and create new alternatives, was ultimately destructive, tearing down conventions without setting up any new ones in place, especially since those who have followed these pioneers have done little if nothing to advance their initial project. Steele continues by arguing that free verse is too subjective and often lacks the reality of human existence. *Missing Measures* advances a line of argument quite unpopular within academia, and the critical work has been as much pilloried as praised. Critic Stephen Matterson sees *Missing Measures* as a "polemical essay," questioning the quality of the scholarship. Steele's other critical work, *All the Fun's in How You Say a Thing* (1999), represents a study of literature through verse, also advancing Steele's controversial claims.

ANDREW HOWE

**Biography**
Born in Burlington, Vermont, 22 January 1948. Attended Stanford University, California, B.A. 1970; Brandeis University, Waltham, Massachusetts, Ph.D. 1977; Lecturer, California State University, Hayward, 1973–74, Stanford University, 1975–77, University of California, Los Angeles, 1977–83, and University of California, Santa Barbara, 1986; since 1987 Associate Professor, California State University, Los Angeles. Received Wallace Stegner fellowship (Stanford University), 1972–73; Guggenheim fellowship, 1984–85; Lavan Award, 1986; Commonwealth Club of California Medal, 1986; Los Angeles PEN Center Literacy Award, 1987. Living in Los Angeles, California.

**Poetry**
*Uncertainties and Rest,* 1979
*The Prudent Heart,* 1983
*On Harmony,* 1984
*Sapphics Against Anger, and Other Poems,* 1986
*The Color Wheel,* 1994
*Sapphics and Uncertainties: Poems, 1970–1986,* 1995

**Selected Criticism**
*Missing Measures: Modern Poetry and the Revolt Against Meter,* 1990
*All the Fun's in How You Say a Thing,* 1999

**Other Writings:** edited selections of poetry (*The Poems of J.V. Cunningham,* 1997).

**Further Reading**
Gwynn, R.S., "Second Gear," *New England Review and Bread Loaf Quarterly* 9 (Fall 1986)
Harvey, Gordon, "Illusions Not Illusions Any Longer," *Sequoia* 28 (Spring 1984)
Kinzie, Mary, "The Overdefinition of the Now," *American Poetry Review* 11 (March–April 1982)
Lake, Paul, "Toward a Liberal Poetics," *Threepenny Review* 8 (Winter 1988)
McPhillips, Robert, "What's New about the New Formalism," *Crosscurrents* 8 (1989)
Miller, John N., "A Renewable Disguise," *Chowder Review* 14 (Spring–Summer 1980)
Prunty, Wyatt, "Reciprocals," *Southern Review* 17 (Summer 1981)

---

## Gertrude Stein 1874–1946

Although Gertrude Stein remains a somewhat mysterious figure in the history of American poetry, her name nonetheless carries the recognition accorded a literary icon. It was always Stein's contention that her writing would find real acceptance only with the passing decades. She insisted that once society caught up with what she was doing in her work, she would be recognized and glorified as a literary lion. While for reasons both biographical and bibliographical Stein still does not stand in the High-Modernist canon, her place in literary and women's history, particularly as a poet, nonetheless now seems assured. Still more often quoted than read, her works represent a substantial investigation into the thematic, linguistic, poetic, and subtextual work performed and promoted by traditional literary writing.

Stein is best known as an expatriate writer. Her life began in Allegheny, Pennsylvania, although much of her childhood would be spent in Austria, France, and the western United States. Having lost both parents during her youth, Gertrude became especially close to older brother and fellow intellectual Leo Stein. After an uneven primary and secondary education, in 1893 Stein followed Leo to Harvard University. There, as a special student without a high school diploma, she entered Harvard Annex (later renamed Radcliffe), studying with such luminaries as William James. Despite pursuing a fascination with laboratory psychology as a student of Hugo Münsterberg, Stein left Cambridge, refusing her degree after failing a Latin examination. She spent the following four years studying medicine at Johns Hopkins Medical School, where Leo was conducting studies in biology. By 1898 Stein had received her undergraduate degree, but she would never conclude her medical studies. Her university studies in composition, philosophy, psychology, and medicine would later inform the way much of her writing, especially the early pieces, explores human impulse and represents human character.

In 1902 Stein moved to London with Leo and then followed him to Paris, where she met Alice B. Toklas, the partner with whom she would share her life and work. By 1908 Toklas began her involvement in Stein's writing career, moving in with Gertrude and Leo Stein in 1909. For a time, the three presided over a literary and artistic salon and started a collection of contemporary art, including works by Picasso and Matisse. In 1913, however, Leo moved out of the residence, decisively marking a break in his previous relationship with his sister. Paris would remain the primary home to Stein and Toklas, a place where they sustained a domestic life and held sway among artists, writers, and bohemians, anchoring Stein's career as a woman of letters. Toklas learned to type and, in close collaboration with Stein, helped in readying texts—poems, plays, stories, essays, and more—for a reading audience.

As something of a writer's writer, Stein has influenced a wide range of experimental authors. There can be little question that Stein's writing shapes the work of her contemporaries and later figures as well, including Kathy Acker, Sherwood Anderson, Djuna Barnes, Jean Rhys, Christine Brooke-Rose, Louis Zukofsky, Robert Duncan, Steve McCaffery, George Bowering, bpNichol, and Diane Ward. She also could be said to guide the hands of "Language" poets of the 1970s and 1980s. With their premise that reading and writing together constitute a single practice, the Language poets found in Stein a prophet and a precedent. Like the Language poets, Stein continuously reminded her readers how many rules have come to delimit and police the contact possible between writer and reader: one is never so aware of the stipulations of that tacit writer-reader contract as when one senses its violation or rupture. Under such transgressive circumstances, one is tempted to extract (even invent) a new set of laws from Stein's texts, to make a code of them. Such an interpretive strategy raises questions not of accuracy so much as of implication. What is at stake in making a Stein text regular? Is it a form of regulation imposed on the text by the reader?

Operating at the 'meta'-level, chiefly by looking at how the act of reading happens, the trend in Stein scholarship toward discussions of reading practices also acknowledges that the experience of reading Stein may represent a situationally bounded process, and so one best conducted self-consciously. Whether or not critics choose to recognize or identify the awareness contexts in which they act, these contexts shape critical outcomes, both in terms of vision and oversight. That is to say, during Stein's lifetime, readings of Stein seemed to remain squarely within the boundaries of a single dynamic: its hidden meaning versus its hidden meaninglessness. This construction of Stein's work reduced it to either a riddle or a hoax. Later inquiries into Stein's work refined the dynamic of referential versus reflexive writing to allow for more (and more subtle) interpretations. While there is no consensus among writers and critics on how exactly to move beyond simple dualities, few are satisfied today merely to render a verdict on the legitimacy of Stein's project. Such pronouncements, like assessments of greatness, are transitory at best.

For this and other reasons, with Stein one has the sensation of reading a solitary writer on her own terms, a writer who has managed to disrupt literary formulas of creation and reception. For the most part Stein declined association with literary schools and movements. She took greatest exception to the notion that her compositions were experimental, for she insisted there was nothing speculative about it. She maintained that she knew precisely what she was doing and why. Indeed, she claimed that she was creating a movement rather than taking part in one. If she mentioned the writers of her day, her comments were generally comparative or disparaging. Living writers were potential scavengers or competitors. Dead ones only overshadowed her creative force; theirs was not a legacy she prized, so when Stein took up Ezra Pound's Modernist call to "make it new," she sought to assure that her work would be read through new eyes, as well. She did not wish readers to receive her work only on the terms of literary precedent and artistic protocol. In order for her words to carry more than the usual associations of a "worn-out, literary" language, and in order for her work to be seen as anything but derivative, they (and she) must be taken in a new context of reading, one cleansed of convention and formula.

By insisting on having her language read on its own terms or not at all, Stein removed her readers' expectations for the ways in which "good" literature performs. This suspension of reader rules of textual conduct (however fleeting) allows Stein's work to traverse literary and social boundaries into a literary out-land. She preempts the usual forms of judgment that would be the grounds for dismissing both the writer and her texts. Without expectations, the reader must become a participant in the reading-writing process. Roles are not rigid, and so the contract may have new terms. Each text calls upon the reader to perform the labor of reflection in a distinctive manner deserving of closer attention.

Three works of poetry help dramatize the power and implication of Stein's enterprise: *Tender Buttons,* "Lifting Belly," and "Patriarchal Poetry." All three employ the signature uses of language for which Stein became notorious and for which the critics often mocked her. Each of the three compositions shows a writer hard at the work of contesting convention and jostling readers from their complacency.

*Tender Buttons,* a book-length poem for which she would later become better known, appeared in print in 1914. The volume was divided into three sections of poems: "Objects," "Food," and "Rooms." Through this startling assembly of poems, a kind of early word collage, Stein frees herself from the conventions of narrative prose or expressive verse. These verbal portraits of ordinary things and their interrelationships provide the reader with an abstract, associative, and sensory-charged set of objects to contemplate. In something like the language equivalent of the painter's still life, Stein casts the portraits of household items, fusing them into an intimate domestic space. Many critics have construed it as a celebration of the Stein-Toklas alliance and all its features of literal and symbolic homecoming.

It would fall to other texts, notably her erotic poems, to populate the distinctive domestic space Stein constructed with *Tender Buttons.* In 1917 Stein wrote "Lifting Belly," an extended erotic poem to which critics have directed considerable attention. "Lifting Belly," while frequently noted as exemplary of Stein's erotic writings, is but one of a number of such compositions from 1913 to 1919, including "Pink Melon Joy" and "If You Had Three Husbands." Furthermore, although the period from 1913 to 1919 proved most prolific, she continued to write in this intimate mode throughout her literary career. During the 1920s she wrote such noteworthy and related compositions as "As a Wife Has a Cow a Love Story" and "A Lyrical Opera Made by Two to Be Sung."

In these works Stein presents an affirmative view of women's sexuality, particularly as expressed between women.

Having fashioned a creative home and forged an intimate partnership with *Tender Buttons* and poems such as "Lifting Belly," it remained for Stein to position herself in the context of American letters, largely as a source of literary counter-statement. Stein lamented the way "Patriarchal poetry makes it as usual," suggesting the depth of its conventionality with such lines as "Patriarchal poetry one two three." "Patriarchal Poetry" (1927) outlined a treatise on the androcentric poetic tradition. Stein's objection to literary inheritance is not simply an objection to poetic clichés, but rather an objection to the conservative function a literary canon serves: to reflect the class and gender hierarchies of society. When honoring that canon, writers defer to and perpetuate not only literary styles, but also the social and political ideologies those styles encode. In this respect Stein's indictment of patriarchal poetry anticipates feminist challenges to the literary canon by both Anglo and French writers and critics.

Stein identifies this literary inheritance as masculinist and is quick to note that her own language, literary standards, and literary influences are largely if not exclusively male in origin. While such women as George Eliot, Charlotte Perkins Gilman, and Louisa May Alcott impress Stein, the bulk of her references are to men: Carlyle, Dante, Defoe, Fielding, Flaubert, Scott, Smollett, Shakespeare, Sterne, Swift, Wordsworth, Meredith, Hardy, and Trollope. While Gertrude Stein's immersion in male writing is indisputable, some would say inescapable, she does not accept blindly their techniques, perceptions, models, or hierarchies. Stein writes as one keenly aware not only of the possibilities opened by past writers, but also of the options their language and actions deny to her. "Patriarchal Poetry" stands as her manifesto to these limitations and her blueprint to alternative possibilities.

Stein functions as both a literary and a cultural legend. Although her work is still under-read, its implications are etched across literature, culture, and art well beyond her own time. Her writing crosses cultural boundaries and literary genres—from poetry, drama, autobiography, fiction, philosophical treatise, and art manifesto to fairy tale, love story, memoir, essay, lecture, and opera—and challenges readers to reinvent literary study.

LINDA S. WATTS

**Biography**

Born in Allegheny, Pennsylvania, 3 February 1874. Attended Radcliffe College, Cambridge, Massachusetts, 1893–97; Harvard University, Cambridge, 1897; Johns Hopkins Medical School, Baltimore, Maryland, 1897–1901; center of circle of artists, including Picasso, Matisse, and Braque, and of writers, including Hemingway and Fitzgerald; worked with American Fund for French Wounded, 1917–18; founder, Plain Edition, Paris, 1930–33; lectured in the United States, 1934–35. Died in Neuilly-sur-Seine, France, 27 July 1946.

**Poetry**

*Tender Buttons: Objects, Food, Rooms,* 1914
*Two (Hitherto Unpublished) Poems,* 1948
*Stanzas in Meditation, and Other Poems (1929–1933),* edited by Carl Van Vechten, 1956
*Gertrude Stein's America* (includes prose), 1965
*A Stein Reader* (includes prose), edited by Ulla E. Dydo, 1993
*Writings, 1903–1932* (includes prose), 1998

**Selected Criticism**

*Descriptions of Literature,* 1926

**Other Writings:** novels (*Things as They Are: A Novel in Three Parts,* 1950), short stories (*Three Lives: Stories of the Good Anna, Melanctha, and the Gentle Lena,* 1909), plays (*Lucretia Borgia,* 1968), operas, correspondence (*On Our Way,* 1959), nonfiction, biography (*The Autobiography of Alice B. Toklas,* 1933), children's literature, lectures.

**Further Reading**

Chessman, Harriet Scott, *The Public Is Invited to Dance: Representation, the Body, and Dialogue in Gertrude Stein,* Stanford, California: Stanford University Press, 1989
DeKoven, Marianne, *A Different Language: Gertrude Stein's Experimental Writings,* Madison: University of Wisconsin Press, 1983
Dickie, Margaret, *Stein, Bishop, and Rich: Lyrics of Love, War, and Place,* Chapel Hill: University of North Carolina Press, 1997
Grahn, Judy, *Really Reading Gertrude Stein: A Selected Anthology with Essays by Judy Grahn,* Freedom, California: Crossing Press, 1989
Gray, Nancy, *Language Unbound: On Experimental Writings by Women,* Urbana: University of Illinois Press, 1992
Kellner, Bruce, editor, *A Gertrude Stein Companion,* New York and London: Greenwood Press, 1988
Levin, Jonathan, *The Poetics of Transition: Emerson, Pragmatism, and American Literary Modernism,* Durham, North Carolina: Duke University Press, 1999
Quartermain, Peter, *Disjunctive Poetics: From Gertrude Stein and Louis Zukofsky to Susan Howe,* Cambridge: Cambridge University Press, 1992
Weiss, M. Lynn, *Gertrude Stein and Richard Wright: The Poetics and Politics of Modernism,* Jackson: University Press of Mississippi, 1998

# Tender Buttons

*Tender Buttons* (1914) is perhaps Gertrude Stein's most notorious and challenging work. A collection of wildly disjunctive prose poems arranged into three sections entitled "Objects," "Food," and "Rooms," it continues to be widely celebrated and attacked. Contemporary poets and writers associated with the avant-garde mark *Tender Buttons* as a highly significant and original turning point in American poetry against consistently offhand dismissals by more conservative critics. Indeed, a three-sentence review of *Tender Buttons* in *Library Journal* quickly buried the text by stating blandly that the "average person" would find *Tender Buttons* "makes no sense at all" (Rogers, 1999).

However, if seduced by the charming and sensual word-arrangements in the series, the reader can produce a variety of narratives for the text. *Tender Buttons* refers consistently to household objects and domestic practices. Various critics have focused on these references to suggest that domesticity itself is a kind of consistently interrogated theme in the work. Rachel Hadas (1978) has pointed out that *Tender Buttons* was written during a time that found Stein going through major personal changes; her lover Alice B. Toklas moved into her Paris apartment in 1909, and her brother Leo would leave the apartment in 1913 due to increasing animosity with his sister. Considering Stein's actual domestic situation while writing *Tender Buttons,* one can read the fractured nature of the text as a reflection of a household undergoing disruptive, if at times stimulating and welcome, change.

Outside of relating *Tender Buttons* to Stein's own biography, the reader can also see the work's correlation to other experimental art occurring around the same time. *Tender Buttons* was published in the same year as the legendary Armory Show, at which American audiences for the first time were introduced to Cubism and Dada via the work of Picasso, Marcel Duchamp, Cézanne, and others. An article on Stein's work written by Stein's friend Mabel Dodge was published in the March 1913 *Arts and Decoration,* an issue devoted entirely to the Armory exhibition. Dodge linked Gertrude Stein's aesthetic as a writer with that of Picasso as a painter, suggesting that Stein's language could be understood as a series of rhythmical and cadenced sounds existing outside the realm of linguistic reference. With artists like Picasso (a close friend of Stein's) creating work that had an intentionally disorienting effect on its audience, Stein's linguistic experimentation has a clear historical basis as a kind of partner to the visual disjunction of Cubism.

Readings of *Tender Buttons* include interpreting the book as lesbian love poem (the phrase "tender buttons" suggests a French slang term for nipples), as a revision of syntax, as celebration of domesticity, or as ritualistic display of alienation. The first section, "Objects," introduces Stein's concerns with diminished referentiality. In the final line of "A carafe, that is a blind glass" (the first prose poem in the book), Stein provides the reader with the overall poetic slogan for the book: "The difference is spreading." "Difference" in this sense is perspective, and the fact that difference is "spreading" indicates the conception of perspective as multivalent and arbitrary. "A carafe, that is a blind glass" can be read as the first among many Cubist-style still-lifes in the book; the first line reads in part "a spectacle and nothing strange . . . an arrangement in a system to pointing." The prose poem is not "strange" because, congruent with the Cubist painterly aesthetic, there is no primary underlying meaning or symbolism beyond the surface arrangement of things that make up the "spectacle."

At the same time as Stein transgresses meaning, she commits a cultural transgression: lesbianism. This theme runs in conjunction with the linguistic concerns of the book and thus invites a reading of lesbian sexuality and linguistic innovation working together to forcefully threaten or even implode stable notions of gender. The poem in "Objects" entitled "Peeled pencil, choke" reads, in its entirety, "Rub her coke." Here Stein uses loose homophones to cut up and graft male and female body parts. Perhaps "Peeled pencil" is intended to suggest the naked ("Peeled") and laughably small ("pencil"-dick) penis. In Stein's shifting sexual panorama, one might laugh at the pencil-dick as a "joke" ("joke" sounds somewhat like "choke"). Once invited to imagine the penis as a joke, the reader is encouraged to "Rub *her* coke"—that is, to rub and enjoy the female penis (cock/coke). Then again, this kind of imposition of absolutist interpretation related to *Tender Buttons* should be held under suspicion, as part of the joy of reading a Stein text arises from the shifting play of meaning.

Prose poems in "Food," the second section of *Tender Buttons,* are even more sensual and linguistically disruptive. Two poems in the series, both entitled "Milk," at once undermine the reader's expectations for poems "about" milk as they associate milk with motherhood and sexuality. In the second "Milk" the word "needles" may approximate the word "nipples," for example; this is suggested particularly since the word "utter" (homophone of "udder") precedes "needles." However, "needles" also have a phallic aspect in that they are designed to pierce. Despite the suggestions of lesbianism throughout the book, the agents in this poem are not categorically male or female, and thus lesbianism itself is destabilized as a referent.

"Rooms," the conclusive text in the *Tender Buttons* series, is a long, uninterrupted prose poem beginning with the phrase, "Act so that there is no use in a centre." The reader is now afforded the opportunity to see *Tender Buttons* as a musical form containing theme and variations, the theme being the continuous challenge to and rejuvenation of meaning-in-language. "Rooms" recalls the earlier slogan "The difference is spreading," both by the conceptual similarity of "Act so that there is no use in a centre" and phrases suggesting or repeating the word "spreading": "And then the spreading"; "If the center has the place then there is distribution"; and "Now when there is separation there is the division." Stein's advice to "Act so that there is no use in a centre" invites the reader to collaborate in a subversive and anarchistic discourse that re-imagines words as material which can at once fracture and revitalize an enervated language.

DANIEL KANE

**Further Reading**

DeKoven, Marianne, "Transformations of Gertrude Stein," *Modern Fiction Studies* 42, no. 3 (1996)

Hadas, Rachel, "Spreading the Difference: One Way to Read Gertrude Stein's *Tender Buttons,*" *Twentieth Century Literature* 24 (1978)

Hawkins, Susan E., "Sneak Previews: Gertrude Stein's Syntax in *Tender Buttons,*" in *Gertrude Stein and the Making of Literature,* edited by Shirley Neuman and Ira B. Nadel, Boston: Northeastern University Press, and Basingstoke, Hampshire: Macmillan, 1988

Knapp, Bettina L., *Gertrude Stein,* New York: Continuum, 1990

Knight, Christopher J., "Gertrude Stein, *Tender Buttons,* and the Premises of Classicalism," *Modern Language Studies* 21, no. 3 (Summer 1991)

Mellow, James R., *Charmed Circle: Gertrude Stein and Company,* New York: Praeger, and London: Phaidon Press, 1974

Mitrano, Mena, "Linguistic Exoticism and Literary Alienation: Gertrude Stein's *Tender Buttons,*" *Modern Language Studies* 28, no. 2 (1998)

Murphy, Margueritte S., "'Familiar Strangers': The Household Words of Gertrude Stein's *Tender Buttons,*" *Contemporary Literature* 32, no. 3 (1991)

Perloff, Marjorie, *The Poetics of Indeterminacy: Rimbaud to Cage,* Princeton, New Jersey: Princeton University Press, 1981

Rogers, Michael, "Rogers Reviews *Tender Buttons* by Gertrude Stein," *Library Journal* 124, no. 6 (1999)

Walker, Jayne L., *The Making of a Modernist: Gertrude Stein from "Three Lives" to "Tender Buttons,"* Amherst: University of Massachusetts Press, 1984

# Gerald Stern 1925–

A winner of major awards, including the National Book Award for Poetry for *This Time: New and Selected Poems* (1998), Gerald Stern has been a strong and independent voice in later 20th-century American poetry. Not associated with any one school or group of poets, his work is both ecstatic and sorrowful as it celebrates the mystery of life and experience and mourns the death and suffering of people and other living things. His is a poetry of compassion, emotionally evocative and serious, but also laced with humor. While the first-person pronoun is predominant, his poetry treats the poet's observations of both the world and himself in such a way that his persona is not limited to strictly personal revelation. Jane Somerville (1990) maintains that Stern "creates the effect of dramatic presence" and that his "speaker-hero is a tragi-comic character."

Many of his poems are in free verse, strung with iambs. Some incorporate a good deal of repetition and parallelism. Stern's poetry celebrates the physical world and emphasizes the poet's emotional response, moving many critics, including Peter Stitt (1997), to align him with Whitman. However, there are important differences, including Stern's Eastern European Jewish background. Born into an immigrant family, Stern was raised in a strong Jewish cultural and religious environment. He also observed that anti-Semitism existed locally in Pittsburgh in the 1920s and 1930s with street gangs, nationally with job discrimination in academia and elsewhere, and internationally with pogroms and later the Holocaust.

Stern was drawn to American and British poetry, receiving a B.A. from the University of Pittsburgh and an M.A. from Columbia University. He also spent about a year in the U.S. Army in counterintelligence and several years afterward in Europe before he took the first of a series of college teaching jobs at Temple University in 1956; his teaching career culminated 40 years later at the University of Iowa's Writers' Workshop.

Stern's second book, *Rejoicings* (1973), features some of his enduring themes and structural preferences, including his focus on nature and use of parallelism. His next publication, *Lucky Life* (1977), which includes the widely discussed poems "Behaving Like a Jew," "Burying an Animal on the Way to New York," and "Lucky Life," attracted major attention and received the Lamont Poetry Prize. Critics noted that both "Behaving Like a Jew" and "Burying an Animal on the Way to New York" convey, first, the poet's empathy with the injured and suffering and, second, his drive to confront the pain of death and his refusal to embrace the consolation of such concepts as eternal life.

The Holocaust is treated in several poems in *Paradise Poems* (1984). "The Dancing," in a painful, half-joking way, describes his father in Pittsburgh in 1945 mimicking a Ukrainian song, but it ends with the profoundly serious observation that his father's dance is

> . . . 5,000 miles away
> from the other dancing—in Poland and Germany—
> oh God of mercy, oh wild God.

"Soap," in the same collection, has received both praise and criticism. Using surreal imagery, the poet mourns the Jews lost in Europe by focusing on one man, his counterpart in Poland. Stern discusses this poem and many others in an interview with Gary Pacernick (1998) that treats his thoughts on various definitions of Jewish-American poetry and his relationship to literary tradition.

In addition to history, Stern's sensibility is informed by the world of literature, music, and the visual arts. He alludes to writers, composers, and artists in poems including "Thinking About Shelley," "The Red Coal," and "Magritte Dancing" in *The Red Coal* (1981) and "Stopping Schubert," "Béla," "Vivaldi Years," and "Kissing Stieglitz Goodbye" in other books. In "Hot Dog," a 55-page poem in *Odd Mercy* (1995), Stern portrays an encounter with Whitman and advocates a sociopolitical message akin to Whitman's. Expressing deep empathy for a homeless African-American woman, "Hot Dog" indicts Reagan's America and its harm to the underclass.

Stern also has affinities with Whitman and other Romantic poets in his celebration of and identification with nature. Nature imagery and meditations on nature appear in all the volumes noted previously and in others: *Lovesick* (1987), *Leaving Another Kingdom: Selected Poems* (1990), *Bread without Sugar* (1992), *This Time: New and Selected Poems* (1998), and *Last Blue* (2000). He praises birds and plants in such poems as "Small Sunflowers," "Sycamore," and "My First Kinglet." In incantatory phrases, he often celebrates their vitality and beauty and mourns their failure or destruction. As in the paintings of Marc Chagall, the natural world has a central place in Stern's psychological and mythic framework. However, urban landscapes also emerge in such poems as "The Rose Warehouse," "The Same Moon above Us," and "The Music."

Stern is preoccupied both with loss—the death of loved ones and the death of peoples—and with memory—the recollection, the record. This is partly the result of the psychological trauma caused by the childhood death of his sister. He has written a number of poems mourning the loss or the painful lives of various friends and family members, including Larry Levis, Bob Summers, Allen Ginsberg, his sister, and his parents. In "Joseph's Pockets," Stern as a middle-aged man stands in front of his sister's grave and recalls her death 40 years earlier. He writes, "I ask her to think again about the two peach trees, / how close together they were, how tiny their fruit was." Every glimmer of memory is significant for Stern. "Bread without Sugar," an elegy for his father, also treats cultural memory. It is a meditative poem considering, in retrospect, the burial of his father and the circumstance of the Jewish people. It ends with a prayer-like invocation:

> . . . May the turtles escape
> the nets! May I find my ocean! May
> the salt preserve me! May the black clouds instruct me!

For Stern, redemption lies in an all-encompassing engagement with people and with the world.

Memory, history, and community are values emphasized in Judaism. Somerville (1990) argues that "the Stern poem is a quest and lesson rooted steadfastly in the Bible." She discusses biblical allusions and imagery related to Jewish history and tradition found in his poetry. Stern's inheritance from American literary Romanticism and from Jewish cultural tradition provides the background for his vision and the underpinning for his important place in American poetry published since World War II.

KATHY RUGOFF

**Biography**

Born in Pittsburgh, Pennsylvania, 22 February 1925. Attended the University of Pittsburgh, B.A. 1947; Columbia University, New York, M.A. 1949; served in the United States Army Air Corps; Instructor, Temple University, Philadelphia, 1957–63; Professor, Indiana University of Pennsylvania, Indiana, 1963–67, and Somerset County College, Somerville, New Jersey, 1968–82; from 1982 faculty member, Writers' Workshop, University of Iowa, Iowa City; visiting poet, Sarah Lawrence College, Bronxville, New York, 1977; Visiting Professor, University of Pittsburgh, 1978, Columbia University, 1980, Bucknell University, Lewisburg, Pennsylvania, spring 1988, and New York University, fall 1989; Distinguished Chair in Creative Writing, University of Alabama, Montgomery, 1984; Fanny Hurst Professor, Washington University, St. Louis, Missouri, fall 1985; Bain Swiggert Chair, English Department, Princeton University, New Jersey, fall 1989; from 1973 consultant in literature, Pennsylvania Arts Council, Harrisburg. Received National Endowment for the Arts grant, 1976, 1981, 1987; Lamont Poetry Selection Award, 1977; State of Pennsylvania creative writing grant, 1979; Pennsylvania Governor's Award, 1980; Guggenheim fellowship, 1980; Bess Hokin Award (*Poetry*, Chicago), 1980; Bernard F. Connor Award, 1981; Melville Cane Award, 1982; Jerome J. Shestack Prize, 1984; Paterson Poetry Prize, 1992; Academy of American Poets fellowship, 1993; Ruth Lilly Poetry Prize, 1996; National Book Award, 1998. Living in Easton, Pennsylvania, and New York City.

**Poetry**

*The Naming of Beasts, and Other Poems,* 1973
*Rejoicings,* 1973; republished as *Rejoicings: Poems, 1966–1972,* 1984
*Lucky Life,* 1977
*The Red Coal,* 1981
*Paradise Poems,* 1984
*Lovesick,* 1987
*Leaving Another Kingdom: Selected Poems,* 1990
*Bread without Sugar,* 1992
*Odd Mercy,* 1995
*This Time: New and Selected Poems,* 1998
*Last Blue: Poems,* 2000

**Other Writings:** essays.

**Further Reading**

Garber, Frederick, "Pockets of Secrecy, Places of Occasion: On Gerald Stern," *American Poetry Review* 15, no. 4 (1986)
Hillringhouse, Mark, "The Poetry of Gerald Stern," *Literary Review: An International Journal of Contemporary Writing* 40, no. 2 (1997)
Pacernick, Gary, "Gerald Stern: An Interview," *American Poetry Review* 27, no. 4 (July/August 1998)
Pinsker, Sandford, "Weeping and Wailing: The Jewish Songs of Gerald Stern," *Studies in American Jewish Literature* 9, no. 2 (1990)
Somerville, Jane, "Gerald Stern among the Poets: The Speaker as Meaning," *American Poetry Review* 17, no. 6 (November/December 1988)
Somerville, Jane, *Making the Light Come: The Poetry of Gerald Stern,* Detroit, Michigan: Wayne State University Press, 1990
Stitt, Peter, *Uncertainty and Plentitude: Five Contemporary Poets,* Iowa City: University of Iowa Press, 1997

---

## Wallace Stevens 1879–1955

Not until he was nearly 44 years old did Wallace Stevens publish his first volume of poetry, *Harmonium* (1923), containing poems written in his 30s and early 40s. It was another 12 years before his second volume, *Ideas of Order* (1935), appeared. Before his death in 1955 Stevens published (in addition to several small-press editions of long, multi-poem sequences) *Owl's Clover* (1936), *The Man with the Blue Guitar, and Other Poems* (1937), *Parts of a World* (1942), *Transport to Summer* (1947), *The Auroras of Autumn* (1950), and *The Collected Poems of Wallace Stevens* (1954), which included a section of new poems entitled "The Rock." A collection of essays, *The Necessary Angel: Essays on Reality and the Imagination,* appeared in 1951. *Opus Posthumous* (1957) published his uncollected poetry and prose.

Stevens' late start can be attributed at least in part to his other career, first as a lawyer and then as an executive with the Hartford Accident and Indemnity Company, in Hartford, Connecticut (where he moved in 1916). Although he participated in the bohemian literary and art scene that thrived in New York City in the 1910s, he was somewhat marginal to it. Critics have long been intrigued by Stevens' double life as businessman-poet, often linking him with his contemporary William Carlos Williams, the physician-poet. Both Stevens and Williams advocated a poetics of the actual, grounded in the concrete particulars of the local environment and voiced in a distinctively American idiom. Where Williams looked to pare away the sentimental and even ideational resonances of his poetic language, Stevens developed a meditative poetry that sought to understand the interconnections between ideas and things. Often difficult and elusive, Stevens' poetry elucidates the dynamics of the human imagination's constantly changing relationship to the actual world.

Stevens' place among the Modernists has been the topic of some dispute. While his earliest published poems, which began appearing in small literary magazines in 1914, generally read like other Modernist poems of the era, especially in their highly developed irony, his poems reveal a strong affinity with Romantic traditions, both British and American. Where Pound and Eliot forcefully (and somewhat misleadingly) declared their break with their Romantic precursors, Stevens pursued what he once described to a correspondent as an "updated Romanticism." In part this reflects his continuing preoccupation with the visionary imperative of the poet. Stevens' habitual themes characterize him as a late Romantic: poems written to or about his muse, poems about mountains, rivers, flowers, the aurora borealis, and other inspirational topos, poems describing paintings and deliberating the value and role of art, poems examining the figure of the hero in the modern age. Even his characteristic line and stanza have more in common with Keats and Shelley than with his more formally experimental contemporaries: especially after *Harmonium,* Stevens favored an unrhymed iambic pentameter line, often set in regular two-, three-, or four-line stanzas. Above all, his lifelong preoccupation with the poetic imagination allies him with the Romantic tradition. Nevertheless, Stevens often sought to distinguish his poetics from what he regarded as the failed project of the Romantics. In his essay "Imagination as Value" he comments that "[W]e must somehow cleanse the imagination of the romantic," further clarifying,

> The imagination is one of the great human powers. The romantic belittles it. The imagination is the liberty of the mind. The romantic is a failure to make use of that liberty. It is to the imagination what sentimentality is to feeling.

As he comments elsewhere, imagination "has the strength of reality or none at all." This sense of the finely calibrated interdependence of reality and imagination led Stevens to develop a unique voice in modern poetry. Just as his poems seek the elusive point at which imagination and reality converge, so his poetic style shuttles between an expansive eloquence appropriate to a Romantic, visionary poetics and a reductive minimalism more characteristic of the disillusioned, skeptical temper of the Modernists. Given these somewhat different poetic imperatives, it is not surprising that critics have disagreed about how to label Stevens' poetry or measure his influence.

Stevens' earliest poetic innovations are primarily a matter of sound and irony, as in "The Emperor of Ice-Cream":

> Call the roller of big cigars,
> The muscular one, and bid him whip
> In kitchen cups concupiscent curds.

"The Emperor of Ice-Cream" is a characteristic early Stevens production in many respects: its juxtaposition of antithetical elements, unexpected thematic and imagistic turns, vaguely philosophical vocabulary, skillful play of sounds, and, above all, its abiding elusiveness. The juxtaposition of antithetical elements is evident in the poem's title: ice-cream does not suggest much of an empire, especially if one considers its propensity to melt. So too the muscular cigar roller seems out of place whipping curds in kitchen cups. The philosophical vocabulary of the poem emerges near the end of the first stanza: "Let be be finale of seem. / The only emperor is the emperor of ice-cream." One senses in the background a philosophical reflection on appearance and reality: the speaker suggests that this world's physical being is its final reality, that no more permanent or eternal being is likely to emerge. In this sense, the only emperor—the only permanent authority—is one that is itself subject to an all-too-human finitude.

Having stated this theme, it must be admitted that much if not even most of the language and imagery of this poem remains indistinct or indeterminate. As Stevens comments in "Man Carrying Thing," "The poem must resist the intelligence / Almost successfully." "The Emperor of Ice-Cream" would seem to be about the preparation of a corpse for burial. While almost nothing in the first stanza suggests this, the cigars, curds, flowers, newspapers, and ice cream do variously suggest the theme of perishables. The second stanza seems to describe a corpse and the room in which it is laid out: "If her horny feet protrude, they come / To show how cold she is, and dumb." The poem then concludes: "Let the lamp affix its beam. / The only emperor is the emperor of ice-cream." The details, and the stop brought on by the caesura before "and dumb," suggest that death is final; there is no expectation here of an afterlife, only an end of life. The poem is never sad or disappointed in such finality, however, but is full of life, reflected both in the activity going on in the house and in Stevens' characteristically vivid rhythm and diction. The lamp suggests the expressive Romantic tradition, but here it is invited to affix its beam on a corpse. The repetition, three times including the poem's title, of "the emperor of ice-cream" suggests something more than chaos and dark night: despite the finality of mortality, earthly experience remains the source of considerable delight.

Stevens' poems, especially in his first volume, are often obliquely evocative in this way. He opens "Anecdote of the Jar" with the odd assertion, "I placed a jar in Tennessee." Here Stevens takes a perfectly mundane topic and uses it to speculate about the nature of art and poetry. The round jar, placed on a hill, "made the slovenly wilderness / Surround that hill." Art, in other words, brings order to the random, chaotic nature that is the Tennessee wilderness: "The wilderness rose up to it, / And sprawled around, no longer wild." Most strikingly, Stevens' playful meditation on art and nature underscores the unresolvable nature of their relationship. The poem concludes:

> It took dominion everywhere.
> The jar was gray and bare.
> It did not give of bird or bush,
> Like nothing else in Tennessee.

Unlike the previous two stanzas, the concluding stanza emphasizes the abiding difference between jar and wilderness, especially in the declaration that the jar "did not give of bird or bush." There is something decidedly unnatural about the jar, something vaguely "jarring" about its "dominion." The tension between jar and wilderness exemplifies the balance Stevens constantly sought between imagination and reality. Stevens would return to the themes of order and chaos, and the mediating role of art and imagination in relation to them, in such later poems as "The Idea of Order at Key West," "Connoisseur of Chaos," "The Poems of Our Climate," and "Notes Toward a Supreme Fiction," all of which attempt to locate order emerging on the edge of chaos.

For all his emphasis on the poetic imagination, Stevens always underscores the value of sensuous responsiveness to the physical world. As he put it in "Esthétique du Mal,"

> The greatest poverty is not to live
> In a physical world, to feel that one's desire
> Is too difficult to tell from despair.

"Sunday Morning," with its sustained criticism of spiritualizing religious traditions, is among Stevens' best-known celebrations of the natural world. In it, he takes up traditional religious themes, especially the desire to transcend mortality, only to displace such other-worldly yearnings back onto this imperfect, fleeting, but sensuously compelling world. His aim here as elsewhere is to heighten the reader's appreciation of this world, in part because there is no other, more eternal or spiritual world beyond it. "The imperfect is our paradise," as he comments in "The Poems of Our Climate."

"Peter Quince at the Clavier" similarly demonstrates Stevens' feeling for physical detail, emphasizing the human body as well as the concrete sound effects that complement the events described in the poem. In "Evening without Angels" Stevens attempts to forge a language that can describe qualities of air and sky devoid of any of the supernatural beings with which artists and others have traditionally filled them:

> Air is air,
> Its vacancy glitters round us everywhere.
> Its sounds are not angelic syllables
> But our unfashioned spirits realized
> More sharply in more furious selves.

The poem eventually becomes a celebration of bareness, not as a negative or destructively chaotic principle, but rather as a space in which posited values might emerge:

> Bare night is best. Bare earth is best. Bare, bare,
> Except for our own houses, huddled low
> Beneath the arches and their spangled air,
> Beneath the rhapsodies of fire and fire,
> Where the voice that is in us makes a true response,
> Where the voice that is great within us rises up
> As we stand gazing at the rounded moon.

Such "true response" for Stevens does not evoke supernatural beings or metaphysical abstractions but rather emerges from the passionate responsiveness of the human encounter with the perishable, imperfect things of this earth.

Stevens offers a formula for this true response in "Chocorua to Its Neighbor":

> To say more than human things with human voice,
> That cannot be; to say human things with more
> Than human voice, that, also, cannot be;
> To speak humanly from the height or from the depth
> Of human things, that is acutest speech.

No "more-than-human" speech, poetry is pitched to the actual range of human experience, from the full height or depth of passionately engaged interest. In "Esthétique du Mal" Stevens rejects "the inventions of sorrow or the sob / Beyond invention" in favor of a language binding him to this world and others in it:

> Within what we permit,
> Within the actual, the warm, the near,
> So great a unity, that it is bliss,
> Ties us to those we love.

The human language of this actual world is a language at once intimate and abstract:

> Be near me, come closer, touch my hand, phrases
> Compounded of dear relation, spoken twice,
> Once by the lips, once by the services
> Of central sense, these minutiae mean more
> Than clouds, benevolences, distant heads.

Here Stevens rejects language that spiritualizes or otherwise detaches him from the world and cultivates instead a language that allows him passionately to engage the concrete particulars of this world.

As the decidedly obscure language of these last lines suggests, Stevens' way of celebrating the natural is altogether singular. Stevens writes as a realist, but as a special kind of realist, one preoccupied with the mental and aesthetic processes that accompany human perception of and response to the world of things. This phenomenological disposition accounts for his occasional characterization by critics as an idealist poet, one who ultimately shows more faith in powers of mind than in things of the world. In fact, Stevens' emphasis is on the always dialectical relationship between the concrete particulars of the world and the perceptual and aesthetic processes that those particulars stimulate. This, again, is what makes his poetry so hard to characterize: it is seemingly drawn in quite antithetical directions, to the real that is the base of things and the unreal that invariably emerges in any response to the real. As he put it in the late poem "An Ordinary Evening in New Haven,"

> We seek
> Nothing beyond reality. Within it,
>
> Everything, the spirits's alchemicana
> Included. . . .

In these lines, Stevens' language loosely invokes the religious traditions that his characteristic naturalism aims to displace.

By the mid-1920s Stevens stopped publishing, most likely in order to focus on family and career. When he began writing again in the early 1930s, he attempted to respond to the social conditions of his time, the Great Depression (from which he was effectively protected by his employment in the relatively prosperous insurance industry). Stevens often insisted that poetry must respond to the world from which it emerges. As he put it a little later in "Of Modern Poetry," poetry

> . . . has to be living, to learn the speech of the place.
> It has to face the men of the time and to meet
> The women of the time.

The two major sequences Stevens wrote in the 1930s, "Owl's Clover" (1936) and "The Man with the Blue Guitar" (1937), offer very different approaches to this poetics of the actual. "Owl's Clover," which Stevens later chose not to reprint in the *Collected Poems,* directly and somewhat discursively addresses the social issues of the day. "The Man with the Blue Guitar," on the other hand, attempts to forge a poetics responsive to the demands of the actual and to the imperative of imagination. Following the lead of the later sequence, Stevens' poetry in the 1940s and 1950s increasingly explores the function of poetic imagination in a disenchanted, dispirited modern world. For the later Stevens, poetry is the space in which imagination survives in this world, but it would be inadequate if it merely sought to temper or otherwise evade the often terrible social and historical conditions from which it emerges. Hence Stevens' recourse to a dialectical vocabulary, as in the constant shuffling in "Blue Guitar" between "things as they are" and things as they are "changed upon the blue guitar."

The "supreme fiction" emerges as one of the central themes of Stevens' late visionary realism. The "supreme fiction," which critics have sometimes linked to William James' "will to believe," is a belief adopted in full awareness of its status as fictional or metaphorical. The supreme fiction is a kind of god-substitute for a world without gods, emerging only after all other received, discredited fictions about the world have been suspended. He describes the belief in a supreme fiction in a notebook of aphorisms titled "Adagia":

> The final belief is to believe in a fiction, which you know to be a fiction, there being nothing else. The exquisite truth is to know that it is a fiction and that you believe in it willingly.

In fact, however, Stevens only composes *notes toward* his supreme fiction, a distinction underscored when he comments in "Notes" that the "first idea," as he somewhat obscurely calls it,

> . . . knows that what it has is what is not
> And throws it away like a thing of another time,
> As morning throws off stale moonlight and shabby sleep.

Stevens' open embrace of fiction is tempered, paradoxically enough, by a skepticism of all fictions, his own imagination's included. As he puts it in "Imagination as Value," the imagination cannot remain content with "any image of the world, even though it was an image with which a vast accumulation of imaginations had been content." The imagination is, he adds, "the irrepressible revolutionist."

As indicated earlier, Stevens' emphasis on imagination has led some critics to dismiss him as insufficiently Modernist or avant-garde. Others, influenced by new critical and theoretical approaches to the rhetoric of Romanticism that emerged in the 1960s and 1970s, have looked to Stevens' own discussion of the "effects of analogy," as well as to his distinctive poetic style, for their radical linguistic implications. Anticipating later poststructuralist theories of language in "Effects of Analogy," the prose section of "Three Academic Pieces," and other essays, Stevens suggests that meanings are produced by the relational or differential play among words and ideas. Stevens thus rejects a "correspondence theory" of language—one in which meaning derives from the correspondence between words and things in the external world—in favor of one modeled on the unbounded relational play among words, thus making reference a function of internal reference within a system of words, sounds, and marks. If one understands the world primarily by means of analogies, poems are not exaggerated or distorted forms of some ideal of rational understanding, but rather the normative model by which meanings are generated. Stevens further suggests that all "normal" understanding is constituted by the force of analogy: the world, he suggests, is constituted by analogy, and one's priorities and dispositions within the world are themselves a function of those analogies. While Stevens has sometimes been criticized for his relative disengagement from social and historical contexts, his reflection on poetic language is itself a product of his intense engagement with one material out of which social and historical participation is necessarily forged: language.

Stevens' last poems, collected in *The Auroras of Autumn* and "The Rock" section of the *Collected Poems,* offer a sustained reflection on the approach of death by one who remains skeptical of the conventional solaces the Western imagination has used to habituate itself to it. In other words, Stevens' late poems embrace the particularities of this world knowing that they do not point beyond themselves, that like the self perceiving them, they too are destined to recede into nothingness. Stevens had been fascinated by the reductive seductions of this nothingness from the very beginning of his public career as poet, most notably in the remarkable condensed lyric "The Snow Man," with its concluding vision of "Nothing that is not there and the nothing that is." In the late poem "The Plain Sense of Things" Stevens squarely faces a diminished world:

> The greenhouse never so badly needed paint.
> The chimney is fifty years old and slants to one side.
> A fantastic effort has failed, a repetition
> In a repetitiousness of men and flies.

The vision is wistful, bordering, in its reference to men and flies, on horrific. As is so often the case in Stevens' poetry, however, this vision is merely a prelude to an all-important qualifying "yet": "Yet the absence of the imagination had / Itself to be imagined." The plain sense of things is itself an imagined state, and so instead of an imaginative collapse, Stevens offers the sense of an always sustaining imagination.

The Reverend Arthur Hanley, Chaplain at the hospital in which Stevens died, claimed (some time after the fact) that Stevens elected to convert to Catholicism before dying. Stevens' daughter Holly reports that Stevens actually complained to her about being bothered by clergy in the hospital. The facts will probably never be known for sure. Still, the evidence of the poetry suggests that, while conversion seems unlikely, Stevens nevertheless valued the "supreme fiction" of ritual, embraced for what limited human satisfaction it would allow. Stevens' late attitudes toward the actual world and prospects for belief within that world emerge most compellingly in "To an Old Philosopher in Rome," the elegy Stevens composed to the recently deceased philosopher George Santayana (his friend at Harvard some 50 years earlier). The poem describes Santayana's own efforts to devise a human philosophy that would remain responsive to the actual conditions of his world. The poem alludes to Santayana's death as

> . . . a kind of total grandeur at the end,
> With every visible thing enlarged and yet
> No more than a bed, a chair and moving nuns.

As he dies, crossing the threshold from life to death, Santayana

> stops upon this threshold,
> As if the design of all his words takes form
> And frame from thinking and is realized.

This imagined world is Santayana's heaven, real by virtue not of any physical or metaphysical actuality but rather by virtue of its wholly human imaginative projection.

By the time of his death in 1955, Stevens had achieved a new level of influence among critics, scholars, and younger poets. He was awarded the Bollingen Prize in Poetry for 1950. He twice received the National Book Award in Poetry, for *The Auroras of Autumn* in 1951 and again for *The Collected Poems of Wallace Stevens,* which was also awarded a Pulitzer Prize in 1955. By the late 1950s critical studies of Stevens' poetry began to appear, highlighting his leading role as a Modernist writing outside the influence of Pound and Eliot. To some extent this mounting critical interest complemented a renewal of interest in Romanticism, which had for some time suffered neglect among scholars and critics. As critics studying the rhetoric of Romanticism began to incorporate new theoretical models in the 1960s and 1970s, Stevens' poetry was reinterpreted in light of the new theoretical paradigms, especially structuralist and poststructuralist theories of language. By the 1980s and 1990s, with the return of historical criticism, critics shifted their emphasis to the historical and cultural contexts of Stevens' poetry. While evaluations and interpretations of Stevens' work have fluctuated somewhat with changing critical fashions, he continues to be regarded as one of the leading poets of his age.

JONATHAN LEVIN

*See also* Long Poem; Religion and Poetry; Symbolism

**Biography**

Born in Reading, Pennsylvania, 2 October 1879. Attended Harvard University, Cambridge, Massachusetts, 1897–1900; New York University Law School, 1901–03; admitted to New York bar, 1904; reporter, New York *Herald Tribune,* 1900–01; lawyer in New York, 1904–16; worked for Hartford Accident and Indemnity Company, Connecticut, 1916, Vice President, 1934–55. Received Levinson Prize (*Poetry,* Chicago), 1920; *Nation* Poetry Prize, 1936; Harriet Monroe Poetry Award, 1946; Bollingen Prize, 1950; Poetry Society of America Gold Medal, 1951; National Book Award, 1951, 1955; Pulitzer Prize, 1955; received honorary degrees from seven colleges and universities; member, American Academy, 1946; member, National Institute of Arts and Letters, 1946. Died in Hartford, Connecticut, 2 August 1955.

**Poetry**

*Harmonium,* 1923; revised edition, 1931
*Ideas of Order,* 1935
*Owl's Clover,* 1936
*The Man with the Blue Guitar, and Other Poems,* 1937
*Parts of a World,* 1942
*Transport to Summer,* 1947
*The Auroras of Autumn,* 1950
*Selected Poems,* 1953
*The Collected Poems of Wallace Stevens,* 1954
*Opus Posthumous* (includes prose and plays), edited by Samuel French Morse, 1957; revised edition, edited by Milton J. Bates, 1989
*Poems by Wallace Stevens,* edited by Samuel French Morse, 1959
*The Palm at the End of the Mind: Selected Poems and a Play,* edited by Holly Stevens, 1971
*Collected Poetry and Prose,* 1997

**Other Writings:** plays, essays (*The Necessary Angel: Essays on Reality and the Imagination,* 1951), correspondence (*Letters of Wallace Stevens,* edited by Holly Stevens, 1966).

**Further Reading**

Bates, Milton J., *Wallace Stevens: A Mythology of Self,* Berkeley: University of California Press, 1985
Berger, Charles, *Forms of Farewell: The Late Poetry of Wallace Stevens,* Madison: University of Wisconsin Press, 1985
Bloom, Harold, *Wallace Stevens: The Poems of Our Climate,* Ithaca, New York: Cornell University Press, 1977
Filreis, Alan, *Wallace Stevens and the Actual World,* Princeton, New Jersey: Princeton University Press, 1991
Gelpi, Albert, editor, *Wallace Stevens: The Poetics of Modernism,* Cambridge and New York: Cambridge University Press, 1985
Longenbach, James, *Wallace Stevens: The Plain Sense of Things,* New York: Oxford University Press, 1991
Richardson, Joan, *Wallace Stevens,* 2 vols., New York: Beech Tree, 1986–88
Riddel, Joseph N., *The Clairvoyant Eye: The Poetry and Poetics of Wallace Stevens,* Baton Rouge: Louisiana State University Press, 1965
Vendler, Helen, *On Extended Wings: Wallace Stevens' Longer Poems,* Cambridge, Massachusetts: Harvard University Press, 1969

# The Idea of Order at Key West

Wallace Stevens' "The Idea of Order at Key West" is one of the most accomplished poems of the 20th century. The poem was first published in the 1935 volume *Ideas of Order,* which earned Stevens a place in the pantheon of major American poets. Frequently anthologized, "The Idea of Order at Key West" captures the Modernist sense of the poem as a self-reflexive investigation of poetry and life; more important, however, it is one of the most succinct and compelling statements about the act and the place of poetry—an achievement of poetry and philosophy at once.

Like many of his poems, "The Idea of Order at Key West" is set in Florida, where Stevens made frequent business and pleasure trips. At the time of composition—1935, according to one of Stevens' letters—Florida was not yet an overdeveloped tourist haven; rather, it embodied a wildness that provoked the desire to impose human order on a seemingly "unordered" natural world. The poem examines the issue of human and natural order as well as the vitality of the creative process and artistic representation, all of which are implicit in the famous opening line: "She sang beyond the genius of the sea." Moreover, the sea's depiction in the first stanza as being "like a body" and its "mimic motion" emphasize matters of representation and foreground the question of whether poetry, as in Plato's derogatory remarks in *The Republic,* is mere imitation and artifice or serves a greater purpose.

The poem pursues the question of representation and the relationship between art and the world through the central female singer, who is frequently interpreted as a figure of poetry: "It may be that in all her phrases stirred / The grinding water and the gasping wind; / But it was she and not the sea we heard." The stress falls on the singer as "the maker of the song she sang" and on her rendering of the sea and not the sea itself, which bolsters the identification of the singer with poetry since the word "maker," in its Greek equivalent, refers to the poet. The first four stanzas of the poem establish the vital relationship between the singer and the world rendered by the song.

The second half of the poem offers Stevens' most passionate and resounding articulation of the role of poetry, beginning with the observation that

> It was her voice that made
> The sky acutest at its vanishing.
> She measured to the hour the solitude.
> She was the single artificer of the world
> In which she sang. And when she sang, the sea,
> Whatever self it had, became the self
> That was her song, for she was the maker.

The emphasis is on the creative act—the "making" of the song and the role of the maker—which transforms the world into poetic vision. Subsequently, the song heightens perception, making aspects of the world more vibrant and acute: for it is "her voice that made / The sky acutest."

The creative power of the poem is accentuated further in the penultimate stanza, which is couched as a rhetorical question:

> Ramon Fernandez, tell me, if you know,
> Why, when the singing ended and we turned
> Toward the town, tell why the glassy lights,
> The lights in the fishing boats at anchor there,
> As the night descended, tilting in the air,
> Mastered the night and portioned out the sea,
> Fixing emblazoned zones and fiery poles,
> Arranging, deepening, enchanting night.

The song not only arranges, deepens, and makes night more enchanting but also transforms the listeners, who remain under the sway of the song and its "idea" of order. In this regard, the poem testifies to the power of the song to alter the listeners' perception of the world.

Although Stevens insisted that the name Ramon Fernandez "was not intended to be anyone" and that the name is "arbitrary . . . two everyday names" (*Letters of Wallace Stevens,* 1966), it is difficult to overlook the fact that Ramon Fernandez was a literary critic and philosopher of some renown with whom Stevens was familiar. More, both Fernandez and Stevens were published in the October 1924 issue of *The Criterion.* Therefore, the reference to Fernandez might be read as part of the poem's argument that poetic representation is more than mere imitation, speaking to the inherent value in poetry as well as to the subservient role of criticism in the face of poetry. In the final stanza, Fernandez is reduced to merely "pale Ramon" in the face of the fullness of the "maker's rage to order words of the sea":

> Words of the fragrant portals, dimly-starred,
> And of ourselves and of our origins,
> In ghostlier demarcations, keener sounds.

The "maker" creates the "order" of life through language and "keener sounds"—the tools of poetry. As Stevens remarked about this poem,

> It may be that every man introduces his own order into the life about him and that the idea of order in general is simply what Bishop Berkeley might have called a fortuitous concourse of personal orders. But there is still order . . . it is a fixed philosophical proposition that every man introduces into his own order as part of a general order. These are tentative ideas for the purposes of poetry. (*Letters of Wallace Stevens*)

In this light, any creative act is an idea of order, but Stevens' great poem articulates how art and poetry are "supreme" forms of ordering one's world and life. "The Idea of Order at Key West" is a compelling demonstration of the vitality of poetry and the sheer force of poetic imagination.

DAVID CLIPPINGER

**Further Reading**

Bloom, Harold, *Wallace Stevens: The Poems of Our Climate,* Ithaca, New York: Cornell University Press, 1977

Cleghorn, Angus, "Questioning the Composition of Romance in 'The Idea of Order at Key West,'" *Wallace Stevens Journal* 22, no. 1 (Spring 1998)

Miller, J. Hillis, "Reading and Periodization: Wallace Stevens' 'The Idea of Order at Key West,'" in *The Challenge of Periodization: Old Paradigms and New Perspectives,* edited by Lawrence Besserman, New York: Garland, 1996

Pearce, Roy Harvey, and J. Hillis Miller, editors, *The Act of the Mind: Essays on the Poetry of Wallace Stevens,* Baltimore, Maryland: Johns Hopkins University Press, 1965

Ryan, Michael, "Disclosures of Poetry: On Wallace Stevens and 'The Idea of Order at Key West,'" *American Poetry Review* 11, no. 5 (September–October 1982)

Vendler, Helen, *On Extended Wings: Wallace Stevens' Longer Poems,* Cambridge, Massachusetts: Harvard University Press, 1969

## Notes Toward a Supreme Fiction

Wallace Stevens' long poem "Notes Toward a Supreme Fiction" concentrates and extends his lifelong concern with the imagination's vigorous and necessary role in our earthly, human world. "Notes" contains some of Stevens' most emotional and memorable lyrics; the final cantos are a rare example of Stevens using a voice overtly his own. However, perhaps what most distinguishes "Notes" are the fables it contains—the 15 or so figures who color, sometimes playfully, the poem's otherwise meditative tenor: the Ephebe, the Arabian, MacCullough, the Man in the Old Coat, the President, General du Puy, the Planter, Nanzio Nunzio, the Blue Woman, the Lasting Visage, the Captain and Bawda, Canon Aspirin and his Sister, the Angel, and the Fat Girl. Stevens chooses ordinary figures and makes them fantastic; they serve as allegories, illustrating or challenging or complicating the more doctrinal language of the poem.

Stevens organizes his discursive poem in stanzaic triads, the first major example of a form on which he would later depend. The poem is divided into three parts of ten cantos each, titled "It Must

Be Abstract," "It Must Change," and "It Must Give Pleasure." The "It" here refers to the "Supreme Fiction" of the poem's title—the consummate poem, the imagined idea come to fruition, the Platonic form made tangible. However, the "Toward" of the poem's title emphasizes that what is purely imagined can never be reached. "Toward" signifies both *in the direction of* and *as a means of achieving;* that is, the poem itself serves as a way to reach the supreme fiction. However, as the "red robin" near the end of the poem suggests, movement is circulatory, "One of the vast repetitions final in / Themselves and, therefore, good, the going round." "Notes" celebrates human experience rooted in the colors, seasons, and weather of this world—experience that circles and returns to the earth.

Stevens explained, "The poem is a struggle with the inaccessibility of the abstract" (*Letters of Wallace Stevens,* 1966). Canto VI of the first part of the poem addresses the question, Can what is abstract be seen? Weather illustrates how the abstract exists in our earthly world yet exists out of our reach. Although "brushy clouds" denote "brushy winds," the winds themselves are invisible. Furthermore, while we can see how the sun alters appearance and we can detect the "fragrance of magnolias," light and scent are not completely tangible: "Invisible or visible or both: / A seeing and unseeing in the eye." Weather epitomizes the "supreme fiction": the abstract infused with the earthly. Stevens' poetic credo, conceived in *Harmonium* (1923), takes full form in "Notes": we need not believe in the spiritual or the sublime but should take pleasure in how we imaginatively transform the things of this world.

The poem is dedicated to Henry Church, a wealthy American expatriate who co-edited the Paris review *Mesures,* but Stevens claimed that the first eight lines of the poem are not addressed specifically to Church (*Letters of Wallace Stevens*). Rather, the "you" for which the speaker "feel[s] love" is the "Notes" that follow—the poetry that brings, just for a moment, "rest" and "peace." In the first ten cantos of "Notes," Stevens affirms a return to the "first idea"—a washing away of all that one has been taught in order to imagine the world as seen for the first time. The "ephebe," or young poet, must continually reimagine: "The poem refreshes life so that we share, / For a moment, the first idea." In the second part of the poem, "It Must Change," variation is set up against the ideals of Platonism; inconstancy is a positive force in our world. Repetition and stasis are sources of boredom and death. For instance, the monotony of the sound made by all birds ("ké-ké") is broken by the sound the sparrow sings ("bethou me"). However, the sparrow's sound, if it never changes, also can become monotonous: "It is / A sound like any other. It will end." The sparrow must reinvent his sound as the "ephebe" must imaginatively transform what he sees.

The third part of "Notes," "It Must Give Pleasure," emphasizes what Stevens wrote in his "Adagia": "The purpose of poetry is to contribute to man's happiness" (*Opus Posthumous,* 1957). Many critics have argued that this section of the poem contains the finest lyrics Stevens ever wrote. In Canto I, the "difficultest rigor" of playing music "in more than sensual mode" contrasts with the "facile exercise" of singing the same hymns as the "multitude." The figure of Canon Aspirin represents someone who zealously searches for a satisfying fiction but has not found one. The Canon "impose[s]" his fictions; he does not "discover" them. The emphatic and excited tone of Canto VII, where the poet himself wants to discover a fiction of his own, leads into the glorious Canto VIII ("What am I to believe?"), where the poet questions whether his joy is not equal to the angel's joy since he himself has created the angel through an act of his imagination:

> . . . Am I that imagine this angel less satisfied?
> Are the wings his, the lapis-haunted air?
>
> Is it he or is it I that experience this?
> Is it I then that keep saying there is an hour
> Filled with inexpressible bliss, in which I have
>
> No need, am happy, forget need's golden hand,
> Am satisfied without solacing majesty . . .

Stevens thought of adding a fourth section to "Notes" called "It Must Be Human" (*Letters of Wallace Stevens*). His coda to the poem, addressed to the "Soldier," perhaps fulfills his desire for a more humanist ending. "Notes" was first published in 1942, and the coda openly explains poetry's necessity in a time of war. However, after the stunning image of the last canto—a green "fluent mundo . . . revolving except in crystal"—the coda is arguably anticlimactic, an elegiac turn away from the forceful first person of the last stanzas. The poet, most human, is satisfied with what he is capable of imagining. "Flicked by feeling," he celebrates "twilight" understandings, not academic abstractions.

Liesl Marie Olson

**Further Reading**


Bloom, Harold, "'Notes Toward a Supreme Fiction': A Commentary," in *Wallace Stevens: A Collection of Critical Essays,* edited by Marie Borroff, Englewood Cliffs, New Jersey: Prentice Hall, 1963

Doggett, Frank, "This Invented World: Stevens' 'Notes Toward a Supreme Fiction,'" in *The Act of the Mind: Essays on the Poetry of Wallace Stevens,* edited by Roy Harvey Pearce and J. Hillis Miller, Baltimore, Maryland: Johns Hopkins University Press, 1965

Kermode, Frank, *Wallace Stevens,* Edinburgh: Oliver and Boyd, and New York: Grove Press, 1960

Perloff, Marjorie, "Revolving in Crystal: The Supreme Fiction and the Impasse of Modernist Lyric," in *Wallace Stevens: The Poetics of Modernism,* edited by Albert Gelpi, Cambridge and New York: Cambridge University Press, 1985

Stevens, Wallace, "The Noble Rider and the Sound of Words," in *The Necessary Angel: Essays on Reality and the Imagination,* New York: Knopf, 1951; London: Faber and Faber, 1960

Stevens, Wallace, *Opus Posthumous,* edited by Samuel French Morse, New York: Knopf, 1957; London: Faber and Faber, 1959; revised, enlarged, and corrected edition, edited by Milton J. Bates, New York: Knopf, 1989; London: Faber, 1990

Stevens, Wallace, *Letters of Wallace Stevens,* edited by Holly Stevens, Berkeley: University of California Press, and London: Faber, 1966

Vendler, Helen, *On Extended Wings: Wallace Stevens' Longer Poems,* Cambridge, Massachusetts: Harvard University Press, 1969

## Peter Quince at the Clavier

During a series of job changes in 1914–15, Wallace Stevens wrote two of his most famous poems, "Peter Quince at the Clavier" (published in the magazine *Others* in 1915) and "Sunday Morning" (published in *Poetry* in 1915). These two poems, the earliest of his mature work, were later collected in *Harmonium* (1923).

Peter Quince is the foppish director of "The Most Lamentable Comedy and Most Cruel Death of Pyramus and Thisbe" in Shakespeare's *A Midsummer Night's Dream*. In Shakespeare, Quince is a complete buffoon. Dull-witted players mutilate their lines and add an insipid explanatory prologue to the play; Nick Bottom makes an ass of himself, and the aristocratic audience heckles the players. Ultimately, Quince is not even allowed to demonstrate his talent in his role as Thisbe's father because Theseus, the Duke of Athens, a passionate man in his own right, is eager to bed his new Amazon wife and thus forbids the play's completion.

In Stevens' poem, however, Quince assumes the much more serious role of the lusty musician and narrator, who is attempting to woo a beautiful woman in blue. In so doing he recounts another—failed—seduction, the apocryphal story of Susanna and the Elders. In the story, two lusting elders spy on Susanna while she bathes and then insist that she have sexual relations with them; her refusal angers them, and they spread the rumor that she had committed adultery. Just before her execution Daniel proves the elders' perjury, however, and they are executed instead.

In this poem Stevens creates a kind of symphony in words, adapting the poem to the sonata form: exposition, development of the theme, recapitulation, and coda. In the poem's first section Peter Quince, the maestro of the imagination, establishes the theme: "Music is feeling, then, not sound." Art is not a physical thing, but feeling; what is important is its effect on the audience. The artist's imagination becomes that of the audience: as Quince's fingers produce music, so he, reciprocally, becomes the instrument when his emotions are played on by the music. In suggesting a complex relationship between sexual and aesthetic experience, Quince insists that if music is feeling, then feeling is music, feelings including his desire for the woman dressed in blue-shadowed silk. This relationship or reciprocity between art and feeling, music and sexual desire, becomes a component of the poem's major theme.

Susanna serves as the idealized prototype of the woman in blue, the object of Quince's desire, archetypal beauty that inspires feeling and leads to the creation of art. For their part, the elders are vicariously associated with Quince himself because they desire Susanna, and, hence, become participants in the music/desire symbiosis. The elders' lust is a "strain," music awakened in them by the bathing girl, the sight of whom makes the "basses of their beings throb."

The music Susanna evokes takes the form of religious praise, "[pulsing] pizzicati of Hosanna," in keeping with the elders' historical role. Their desires recapitulate the theme of the opening lines and are proleptic of the symphony's final coda: that a response to beauty constitutes a religious experience, a "sacrament of praise." The ominous yet "witching" bass chords, the heartbeats of the elders, suggest transcendence as Peter Quince applies the language of religion to aesthetics.

In the second section of the poem, Stevens switches to short lines with a livelier tempo. In a sort of cadenza (which re-states the theme with variations), Peter Quince muses upon the music of Susanna's feelings, suggesting that her own languorous imaginings are a brighter, sweeter, more melodic mode, in contrast to the throbbing music of the elders. In her bath, in "the green water, clear and warm," Susanna achieves a perfect oneness and harmony with the external world. Her reverie produces highly erotic "Concealed imaginings." Melody and the imagination again become one, and the power of that union enables her to achieve perfect equanimity in a world in which even the winds are "like her maids." Susanna is the world in which she moves, the eternal feminine, a personification of the beauty and pleasure, music and feeling that Peter Quince as artist seeks to synthesize but can only approximate. As she walks "upon the grass, / Still quavering," her melody is interrupted by cacophony—"A cymbal crashed, / And roaring horns"—as the elders intrude upon the melody of her reverie.

In the third section's macabre and cacophonous 3/4 time waltz tempo, Quince provides what may be a choral statement of the elders' accusation that Susanna is an adulteress: "a noise like tambourines" mocks her outraged modesty. In regular couplets, Quince details the desertion of their mistress by her previously faithful servants, the Byzantines. Their whispers produce a refrain "like a willow swept by rain," only to be once again overcome by the confusion of "a noise like tambourines"; harmony is destroyed as Susanna stands naked and ashamed, her servants believing the elders' accusation. The elders' experience is analogous to the artist's, whose attempt to capture beauty can result only in a momentary glimpse of the perfection of his subject. Once again, Peter Quince leaves his story unfinished, however; he does not mention the dénouement to the traditional story.

A tribute to physical beauty, the fourth movement opens with a surprising refutation of the Platonic notion that earthly beauty is simply an evanescent reflection of the "ideal form" originating in the mind:

> Beauty is momentary in the mind—
> The fitful tracing of a portal;
> But in the flesh it is immortal.

The mind plays a role in the appreciation of beauty, the poem argues, but only momentarily. Beauty most efficiently reveals itself in the flesh; art, which bases its aesthetic on the real world, becomes, then, the religion of beauty. As such art provides an immortality more satisfying than any spiritual immortality: "The body dies; the body's beauty lives."

The final stanza recapitulates the main theme, referring back to the "bawdy strings" and "ironic scraping" of the elders' lust and demise before the crystalline coda of the "clear viol of her memory." Quince's (and Stevens') answer to Plato's dualism is neither to deny the flesh nor to endow the mind with godlike qualities. He sees the eternality of the physical world as a fitting substitute for the immortality of the soul. It is in the ongoing regeneration of human beauty, as in the dawn of a new day after the darkness of night, the renewed fertility of a garden in spring, the neverending "auroral / Celebration" of marriage—in short, the recapitulation of all things—that true immortality exists. Beauty, an abstraction, finds its true source in human experience—in the human form, gardens, evenings, the change of seasons. The totality of that experience becomes a "wave, interminably flowing." It is the "maiden's choral," not the maiden, that is immortal. Death is indeed, then, the "mother of beauty," and Susanna's beauty is reborn in memory and in contemporary Susannas, of whom the woman in the blue-shadowed silk is one. Susanna's beauty, like poetry, is a "constant sacrament," a religious outpouring of praise celebrating the immutable verities of a world in flux.

RICHARD BUCKSTEAD

**Further Reading**


Carroll, Joseph, *Wallace Stevens' Supreme Fiction: A New Romanticism,* Baton Rouge: Louisiana State University Press, 1987

Longenbach, James, *Wallace Stevens: The Plain Sense of Things,* New York: Oxford University Press, 1991

MacLeod, Glen, *Wallace Stevens and Modern Art,* New Haven, Connecticut: Yale University Press, 1993

Rehder, Robert, *The Poetry of Wallace Stevens,* New York: St. Martin's Press, and Basingstoke, Hampshire: Macmillan, 1988

Richardson, Joan, *Wallace Stevens: The Early Years, 1879–1923,* New York: Beech Tree, 1986

Schwarz, Daniel R., *Narrative and Representation in the Poetry of Wallace Stevens,* New York: St. Martin's Press, and London: Macmillan, 1993

Weston, Susan, *Wallace Stevens: An Introduction to the Poetry,* New York: Columbia University Press, 1977

Whiting, Anthony, *The Never-Resting Mind: Wallace Stevens' Romantic Irony,* Ann Arbor: University of Michigan Press, 1996


## The Snow Man

"I shall explain 'The Snow Man,'" Wallace Stevens wrote in 1944, "as an example of the necessity of identifying oneself with reality in order to understand it and enjoy it" (*Letters of Wallace Stevens,* 1966). With this simple, almost offhand remark, Stevens belies the remarkable richness and paradoxical nature of this early lyric poem, first published in 1921 and later collected in his first book of poetry, *Harmonium* (1923).

What makes the poem unique, both in itself and as part of *Harmonium,* is its spare language and apparent simplicity, traits that would come to distinguish Stevens' poems of "winter" from his poems of "summer." This distinction is not merely one of style; it stems from his longstanding examination of the conflicting, dynamic relationship between "essential realities" and the "lush figurations" of the imagination, themes that engaged Stevens from the early lyrics of *Harmonium* to his late poems.

"The Snow Man" offers one of the most concise and penetrating introductions to that theme of reality and the imagination. In five short tercets that form one long, ruminative sentence, the poem posits a listener in winter who attempts to see and hear only what is there in the world around him, without adding to or imposing anything onto what he perceives. "One must have a mind of winter," the narrator suggests, to achieve this vantage of pure objectivity and perceive reality without the filter of human emotion or interpretation: to "behold" this wintry world of frost and snow and ice-laden trees and not hear "any misery in the sound of the wind."

Reality, the world of the poem, is a "bare place" and no less austere for the subtraction of human emotion from its landscape. The speaker desires to know it truly, however, to perceive only its essence and discard his own emotional projections. The imaginary listener's attempts to strip away the interventions of the imagination seem to be rewarded in the final stanza's epiphany, where, having become "nothing himself," he beholds "Nothing that is not there and the nothing that is."

Is this really a moment of union with nature? Has the mind succeeded in erasing itself and its own impositions of language, invention, feeling, in order to attain objective purity, or is Stevens, even as he articulates this apparent ideal, complicating its very possibility?

The more the reader examines this simple poem, the more intricate and ambiguous its language becomes. Indeed, in many ways it is a poem *about* language—its centrality to human thought and understanding, the inescapable linguistic impetus of the human mind. In this regard "The Snow Man" mirrors so many of Stevens' poems of process in which he attempts both to reflect and reflect upon the activity of thought, "the poem of the act of the mind."

In "The Snow Man," despite the poem's apparent resolution, the mind may be caught in the act of attempting the impossible. Although one may attempt to become "nothing" through an act of will, the very gesture of imagining oneself to be nothing (and stating so in language) is already a return to the creating mind, the poem suggests. Language itself holds the reader in thrall; Stevens' words "*not* to think / Of any misery" themselves evoke thoughts of misery. Language seems to have its own life in the poem, breeding meaning, evoking reference, multiplying interpretation.

The paradoxes of this endeavor accrue toward the enigmatic final stanza. Even if the listener *has* become "nothing himself," by subsequently beholding "nothing" in the world around him, he might again be reflecting himself onto the landscape, a "nothing" imagining a "nothing" as its counterpoint. The "mind of winter," too, projects its own inventions.

That this poem of negation ends, paradoxically, on the word "is"—an assertion of sheer existence—might seem to suggest that the listener has finally achieved oneness with an unembellished reality. But the existence is paradoxical, since it is that of *nothingness,* an "is" that is at once endlessly empty and endlessly full of meaning. In this reading nature is not the only thing that abhors a vacuum; the human mind simply cannot figure nothingness without inevitably turning it back into something.

The delight of "The Snow Man" lies in its ability to challenge ideas about language, reality, perception, and invention. Stevens' own position on these issues was anything but fixed. The publication history of "The Snow Man" reveals Stevens' interesting penchant for "pairing" poems, often representing two sides of an issue. In its 1921 printing "The Snow Man" had a companion piece, another short lyric, "Tea at the Palace of Hoon." Although the pairing was lost in subsequent publications—the two poems were separated in *Harmonium* and *The Collected Poems of Wallace Stevens* (1954)—they were brought together again in *The Palm at the End of the Mind* (1971). If "The Snow Man" is a poem of winter, "Tea at the Palace of Hoon" is a poem of summer. In this poem the chilly "January sun" has given way to the "golden ointment" of a summer sunset, and the speaker not only concedes but rather celebrates that he himself is the source of all he perceives and understands. Together the two poems create a unified picture of Stevens' early ideas about language, landscape, and the self.

Themes of imagination and reality, inner and outer, subjective and objective perception, "making" versus "finding" resonated throughout Stevens' career, often as irreconcilable dualities or, at the very least, as ideas to be taken up again and again. In the end the imagination and reality exist in Stevens' work not so much in opposition as in correlation: just as the seasons change from winter to summer and back again, each "no" in Stevens seems to spawn a "yes." So too the cycle of stripping away the mind's projections to achieve a nearer sense of reality inevitably precedes a return to the necessary delights of human language and invention.

Melita C. Schaum

**Further Reading**

Bevis, William W., *Mind of Winter: Wallace Stevens, Meditation, and Literature,* Pittsburgh, Pennsylvania: University of Pittsburgh Press, 1988

Bloom, Harold, *Wallace Stevens: The Poems of Our Climate,* Ithaca, New York: Cornell University Press, 1977

Burr, Robert Bell, "Wallace Stevens: Gaining the Light," *Wallace Stevens Journal* 23, no. 1 (Spring 1999)

Hesla, David, "Singing in Chaos: Wallace Stevens and Three or Four Ideas," *American Literature* 57, no. 2 (1985)

Kermode, Frank, "The Plain Sense of Things," in *Midrash and Literature,* edited by Geoffrey Hartman and Sanford Budick, New Haven, Connecticut: Yale University Press, 1986

Leckie, Ross, "Reading 'The Snow Man': Stevens' Structures of Undecidability," *Weber Studies* 13, no. 2 (Spring/Summer 1996)

Leonard, J.S., and C.E. Wharton, *The Fluent Mundo: Wallace Stevens and the Structure of Reality,* Athens: University of Georgia Press, 1988

Litz, A. Walton, *Wallace Stevens: The Poetry of Earth,* Washington, D.C.: Library of Congress, 1981

Schaum, Melita, *Wallace Stevens and the Critical Schools,* Tuscaloosa: University of Alabama Press, 1988

Schwarz, Daniel R., "'Spiritually Inquisitive Images': Wallace Stevens' Lyric Sequence about the Poetic Process," *Soundings* 74, no. 1 (Spring/Summer 1991)

## Sunday Morning

When "Sunday Morning" first appeared in 1915 in *Poetry,* the editor, Harriet Monroe, had cut three of the poem's original eight 15-line stanza sections and reordered them so that the last stanza had become the second one (I, VIII, IV, VI, and VII). Stevens restored the poem to its original form in his first volume, *Harmonium,* in 1923. "Sunday Morning" is Stevens' most famous poem, his first major poem, and ranks among the greatest poems of the 20th century. Often anthologized, the poem is a watershed both in modern poetry and in Stevens' opus. By turns perceived as "epicurean" or "spiritual," the poem resounds with Nietzsche's fervored cry that "God is dead." Neither experimental nor truly original, the poem is written in dignified blank verse; yet, despite its use of a traditional English poetic mode, the poem rejects the old pieties.

"Sunday Morning" is an early move toward satisfying Stevens' ambition to write a great poem of the earth rather than of the heavens. With the exception of Eliot, the poets of Stevens' generation were not writing poems that overtly grappled with the larger philosophical predicaments of the modern age. Written during World War I, the poem is highly cognizant of the "men who perish"; at the same time, the poem's stately composition and universalizing tone belie the violence of the contemporary world.

For all its exuberance, "Sunday Morning" does not possess the irony or flamboyant playfulness that characterizes many poems in *Harmonium.* Nevertheless, it reverberates with the volume's obsessive questioning of ontological sureties. The meditational quality of "Sunday Morning," its focus on a mind "in the act of finding what will suffice," as another poem puts it, becomes an important mode for Stevens. As his first longish articulation of a "philosophy," "Sunday Morning" launches the poet's restlessness with final formulations and his pleasure in continual metamorphosis. Like many of Stevens' long poems, its sections, linked through repetition, present variations on a theme. The poem rejects faith in permanence and forthrightly embraces transience and flux.

"Sunday Morning" opens with a female figure enjoying her "Complacencies of the peignoir, and late / Coffee and oranges in a sunny chair / And the green freedom of a cockatoo" instead of keeping the Sabbath at church. Stevens unsettles the "complacencies" of this painterly scene as her meditation leads seamlessly from "the green freedom of a cockatoo" to "the dark / Encroachment of that old catastrophe." As she "dreams" of the Crucifixion, her earthly pleasures "dissipate." The poem becomes an exercise in dialectical counterpoint: the desire to escape the "Dominion of the blood and sepulchre" with the woman's "need for some imperishable bliss."

The first stanza presents the eclipsing of the sensory as a muting of sound; at risk, then, is not only the woman's slippage into a disembodied stasis but also the poet's music. As an early muse for Stevens, the woman suffers an artistic crisis; in casting off a religious ethos, she embodies what Walter Pater had earlier dubbed the "aesthetic life." However, this is by no means the poem's entire scope. Building on the initial contest between the sensual and the dogmatic, it searches for a means to bestow significance on the ephemeral.

Stevens forges his female alter ego in the American tradition of self-reliance: "Divinity must live within herself" (II). Rather than adhering to an institutional order, the woman's emotions correspond to changes in weather and season: "Passions of rain, or moods in falling snow; / Grievings in loneliness, or unsubdued / Elations when the forest blooms" (II). In the center of the poem, Stevens negates all unearthly paradises (and the woman's craving for one) in this rhapsodically enjambed passage:

> There is not any haunt of prophecy,
> Nor any old chimera of the grave,
> Neither the golden underground, nor isle
> Melodious, where spirits gat them home,
> Nor visionary south, nor cloudy palm
> Remote on heaven's hill, that has endured
> As April's green endures; or will endure
> Like her remembrance of awakened birds,
> Or her desire for June and evening, tipped
> By the consummation of the swallow's wings. (IV)

This is as much an elegy for a literary tradition as it is for the death of the gods. Between memory and desire, we have "April's green," enduring in its very expiring, a vision that Eliot will completely reverse in *The Waste Land.*

Stevens amply alludes to his Romantic predecessors. "Death is the mother of beauty," the poem's pivotal declaration, echoes both Whitman and Keats. However, neither poet is as stark as Stevens in his acceptance of timeliness, exemplified by stanza VI, which deliberately revises "Ode on a Grecian Urn." Stevens jeeringly dismantles perfection and stasis:

> Is there no change of death in paradise?
> Does ripe fruit never fall? Or do the boughs
> Hang always heavy in that perfect sky,
> Unchanging, yet so like our perishing earth

Stanza VII in Monroe's rearrangement of the poem became the concluding one. It makes a radical (especially if made the last stanza) turn from the woman's "comforts of the sun" to a communal solar ritual: "Supple and turbulent, a ring of men / Shall chant in orgy on a summer morn / Their boisterous devotion to the sun." The appeal of stanza VII has been its affirmation of masculine fellowship and might account for Monroe's placement of it as the poem's finale. However, such placement undermines Stevens' more subdued ending.

The final stanza returns to the woman's crisis of belief, and its repeated images from the first stanza elegantly frame the poem. Counterpoised to section VII, it poses a more sober appraisal of mortality that also tempers the first stanza's epicurean strains. Instead of the "green freedom of a cockatoo," we have "casual flocks of pigeons." The buoyancy of stanzas IV through VII pivots on this indeterminate estimate of the human condition: "We live in an old chaos of the sun, / Or old dependency of day and night, / Or island solitude, unsponsored, free." The natural world no longer even presides as emotional concordance:

> Deer walk upon our mountains, and the quail
> Whistle about us their spontaneous cries;
> Sweet berries ripen in the wilderness;
> And, in the isolation of the sky,
> At evening, casual flocks of pigeons make
> Ambiguous undulations as they sink,
> Downward to darkness, on extended wings.

In its stark melancholy, this ending is purposefully anticlimactic, distinctively modern. "Sunday Morning" ushers in a world without hieroglyphic immanence.

Susan McCabe

**Further Reading**

Bates, Milton J., *Wallace Stevens: A Mythology of Self,* Berkeley: University of California Press, 1985

Bloom, Harold, *Wallace Stevens: The Poems of Our Climate,* Ithaca, New York: Cornell University Press, 1977

Buttel, Robert, *Wallace Stevens: The Making of Harmonium,* Princeton, New Jersey: Princeton University Press, 1967

Gelpi, Albert, editor, *Wallace Stevens: The Poetics of Modernism,* Cambridge and New York: Cambridge University Press, 1985

Lensing, George S., *Wallace Stevens: A Poet's Growth,* Baton Rouge: Louisiana State University Press, 1986

Longenbach, James, *Wallace Stevens: The Plain Sense of Things,* New York: Oxford University Press, 1991

Richardson, Joan, *Wallace Stevens: The Early Years, 1879–1923,* New York: Beech Tree, 1986

Riddel, Joseph N., *The Clairvoyant Eye: The Poetry and Poetics of Wallace Stevens,* Baton Rouge: Louisiana State University Press, 1965

Vendler, Helen, *On Extended Wings: Wallace Stevens' Longer Poems,* Cambridge, Massachusetts: Harvard University Press, 1969

---

## Mark Strand 1934–

Perhaps the most salient contribution that Mark Strand has made to contemporary American poetry can be found in the unique lucidity of his style. Since the mid-1960s, a Strand poem has been immediately identifiable by its simple, starkly elegant diction; its relaxed free verse, often shaped into tercets and quatrains; its melange of surprising concrete and abstract apothegms about the self (and its contexts); natural imagery full of chiaroscuro; and flares of surrealistic vision. Consummately lyrical, Strand's poetry frequently offers compact narratives with psychological intensity and self-reflexive irony. Although Strand typically writes one- or two-page poems, such poems as the eight-page "Elegy for My Father" (1973) and the book-length *Dark Harbor* (1993) provide the considerable rewards of stylistic and thematic repetition with intriguing variations.

Born of American parents in Summerside, Prince Edward Island, Canada, Strand spent his childhood in a variety of places in Canada, the United States, and South and Central America. He was educated at Antioch College, briefly studied painting at Yale University, and studied at the Iowa Writers' Workshop. Early in his career, he absorbed the influence of Wallace Stevens and Elizabeth Bishop as well as Carlos Drummond de Andrade, whose book he was to translate (1986), and other South American poets. The fiction of Kafka and Borges has had a strong impact on Strand's explorations of the dilemmas of the self.

In his highly influential reading of Strand's work of the 1960s, Harold Bloom (1976) perceives the poet as a major carrier of the torch of late Romanticism, a descendent of Stevens. Calling him "a quester engulfed by phantasmagoria" with an "overtly

Freudian" vision, Bloom asserts that "Strand's affliction is the family romance, and his main resource the transformations of the self as it dodges" a foreshadowing "of its own death in an outward world that seems not to exist." Robert von Hallberg (1977), speaking in an interview with Strand, notes the "dialectic" operations of "this divided or double self that everyone recognizes in [his] poems." Strand's first book, *Sleeping with One Eye Open* (1964), which was privately printed, introduces this dialectic. In "Keeping Things Whole," which was reprinted in Strand's second volume, *Reasons for Moving* (1968), the self paradoxically presents itself as an absence: "In a field / I am the absence of field. . . . / Wherever I am / I am what is missing." The triple assertion "I am" suggests that this insistent self is an intruder on the "presence" of the field; the speaker "parts the air" and thus finds an ethical reason for his inevitable movement: "I move / to keep things whole." "The Accident," "The Man in the Tree," and "The Dirty Hand" are other significant poems in *Reasons for Moving* that probe concepts of self-division.

Various poems in *Darker* (1970), including "The Remains," "Letter," and "Giving Myself Up," present a speaker who seeks to empty himself of the otherness that fills his "life." In "The Remains," the persona tries to divest himself of items such as "the names of others," "pockets," "shoes," and his "wife" so that he can return to the seemingly protected atmosphere of an early state: "I open the family album and look at myself as a boy. // What good does it do? The hours have done their job. . . . // My parents rise out of their thrones / into the milky rooms of clouds. How can I sing? / Time tells me what I am. / I change and I am the same. / I empty myself of my life and my life remains." The image of the speaker's "rising" parents exemplifies Strand's mastery of a wistful surrealism. If, in Strand's first three books, the remainder of self is frequently a "remains," a corpse embodying the withering consciousness of the movement toward death, gloom is substantially offset by the sublimity of the music.

The most remarkable poetic performance in Strand's fourth book, *The Story of Our Lives* (1973), is not a self-elegy but "Elegy for My Father (Robert Strand 1908–68)." Spare, emotionally restrained description, insistent patterns of repetition, and end-stopped lines of varying lengths poignantly convey the tension between the father's sudden absence and the environment, which includes every part of the body he has left behind. Part I begins,

> The hands were yours, the arms were yours,
> But you were not there.
> The eyes were yours, but they were closed and would not open.
> The distant sun was there.
> The moon poised on the hill's white shoulder was there.
> The wind on Bedford Basin was there.
> The pale green light of winter was there.
> Your mouth was there,
> But you were not there.
> When someone spoke, there was no answer.

Strand's presentation of "obvious" information has a potent impact not only because of his stylistic acuity but also because such fundamental details are so often overlooked or repressed. In part III, haunting repetition of the sentence "You went on with your dying" underscores the inevitability of the father's process of departure: "Nothing could stop [him]," including "the best day," "the ocean rocking," "the white-haired young doctor who saved [him] once," the "daughter / Who fed [him]," and the son "who thought [he] would live forever." Another central poem in *The Story of Our Lives,* "In Celebration," searches for a way to overcome the despair implied in the reiterated naming of absence in "Elegy for My Father" and to reach acceptance of mortality. Realizing that "desire leads only to sorrow, that sorrow / leads to achievement which leads to emptiness," the speaker enjoins his audience and himself to focus on "the only celebration," to believe "that by giving yourself over to nothing, you shall be healed."

Comparing and contrasting Strand's poetic "mode" in *The Late Hour* (1978) and in the prose text *The Monument* (1978), Richard Jackson (1980) suggests that the poet expands "with [the] region" of absence or emptiness and then attempts "a reconstruction of presence." The resultant "transcendental vision," transcending "Nothing as well as everything," may "grasp the problem of the absent Other." "White," one instance of such "vision" in *The Late Hour,* assembles a lyric catalog of experiential correspondences associated with the all-embracing color and concludes with an Emersonian widening of "the circle of light": "All things are one. / All things are joined / even beyond the edge of sight." In "For Jessica, My Daughter," Strand speaks of the difficulty of thinking "of how it is / such small beings as we / travel in the dark / with no visible way / or end in sight," but he closes the poem with an imaginative prayer for some lucid, secure source of continuity between the generations:

> I imagine a light
> that would not let us stray too far apart,
> a secret moon or mirror,
> a sheet of paper,
> something you could carry
> in the dark
> when I am away.

Between the publication of his *Selected Poems* (1980) and 1985, Strand wrote no poetry. However, during that time, he wrote art criticism, children's stories, and *Mr. and Mrs. Baby* (1985), a book of short stories. In the poetry collected after his break from verse in *The Continuous Life* (1990), Harold Bloom (1991) perceives a new development. Praising the "capacity" of "Strand's poetry . . . first to empty out, and then to renew or even reinvent the self," Bloom finds, in "Orpheus Alone," "Luminism," and *The Continuous Life*'s title poem, uncanny affirmation, "a Sublime apotheosis" of a noble voice. This development was already occurring in such poems as "In Celebration," "For Jessica, My Daughter," and "White," but it is more consistently evident in *The Continuous Life.* The title poem imagines its audience

> . . . learning to lean down close and hear
> The careless breathing of earth and feel its available
> Languor come over you, wave after wave, sending
> Small tremors of love through your brief,
> Undeniable selves, into your days, and beyond.

Another feature of Strand's poetry of the 1980s, exemplified by the prose poem "Translation," is the humor and play of writing that reflects on its own precarious status as representation. In "Translation," various likely and unlikely "translators," including Jorge Luis Borges, stumble into each other and offer pet theories about the vexations and pleasures of translating.

*Dark Harbor* (1993), a poem of 45 sections, each comprising six to eight tercets, is a contemporary rewriting of the Romantic quest poem. The speaker wishes to leave his town's "Main Street" to others in order to explore the sublime, to probe grand meanings of love, happiness, despair, and mortality. However, especially in the poem's early sections, he often returns, fascinated, to observe images of domesticity, such as "the rows of houses / Aglow with an icy green from TVs, spreading // A sheen of familiarity, of deliverance," as well as the fashion world's strange pseudo-sublime vicissitudes.

One aspect of the poet's quest is posited as the development of aesthetic compensation for suffering, "urging the harsh syllables of disaster into music." Thus, "pain" is turned "into its own memorial" and "into itself as witnessed / Through pleasure, so it can be known, even loved." Also, Strand notes enigmatic moments in which "a prodigal overflowing of mildness," figured as uncanny natural events, relieves intense pain and dread of immanent mortality:

> And later when the rain fell and flooded the streets
> And we heard the dripping on the porch and the wind
> Rustling the leaves like paper, how to explain
> Our happiness then, the particular way our voices
> Erased all signs of the sorrow that had been,
> Its violence, its terrible omens of the end?

In the song of Orpheus, Strand imagines a poetic vision capable of ennobling the imperfect world "as trees, / Rivers, mountains, animals, all find their true place," yet "when the song is over, / The world resumes its old flaws." Orpheus' "despair," the idea that "he cannot save" the world that he has temporarily changed, "is a brilliant limitation" that causes his song—and those of later poets—to be fundamentally "mournful." He imagines the self-disciplined cultivation of "a growing appetite // For littleness, a piece of ourselves, a bit of the world, / An understanding that remains unfinished, unentire, / Largely imperfect so long as it lasts," as an antidote to the frustration of harboring grand Orphic ambitions. In *Dark Harbor,* however, sublime longings cannot be erased; the poem ends with a Dantesque fantasy of a gathering of "many poets / . . . who wished to be alive again," since now "they were ready to say . . . / Words whose absence had been the silence of love, / Of pain, and even of pleasure." "Above the river, where the golden lights of sunset // And sunrise are one and the same," the speaker sees "an angel" stopping "in mid-air, / . . . one of the good ones, about to sing."

The short poems and midsize sequences of *Blizzard of One* (1998) effectively pursue the themes and stylistic mode of Strand's earlier work of the 1980s and 1990s. Poems such as "Precious Little," "The Great Poet Returns," and "A Piece of the Storm" deftly and concisely revisit some of the themes and imagery of *Dark Harbor.* In "The Night, the Porch," the speaker ponders the best way to "learn" the "lesson" of his mortality: "To stare at nothing is to learn by heart / What all of us will be swept into, and baring oneself / To the wind is feeling the ungraspable somewhere close by." Revising the sense in his early work of the anxieties of self-division, he perceives "our" greatest "desire" as "the comfort / Of being strangers, at least to ourselves"; nothingness, written in "the book out there," which "was never written with us in mind," is faced and, to some degree, embraced as inevitability.

Strand has gained many honors, including a MacArthur fellowship, the position of poet laureate of the United States, and the Bollingen Prize in Poetry (for *Dark Harbor*). These awards testify to Strand's accomplishments as a consummate stylist who, along with A.R. Ammons and a handful of others, has revitalized the enduring concerns of Romantic poetry inherited from Emerson, Whitman, Dickinson, and Stevens.

THOMAS FINK

**Biography**

Born in Summerside, Prince Edward Island, Canada, 11 April 1934; came to the United States in 1938. Attended Antioch College, Yellow Springs, Ohio, B.A. 1957; Yale University, New Haven, Connecticut (Cook Prize and Bergin Prize, 1959), B.F.A. 1959; University of Florence (Fulbright fellow), 1960–61; University of Iowa, Iowa City, M.A. 1962; Instructor, University of Iowa, 1962–65; Fulbright Lecturer, University of Brazil, Rio de Janeiro, 1965–66; Assistant Professor, Mount Holyoke College, South Hadley, Massachusetts, 1967; Visiting Professor, University of Washington, Seattle, 1968, 1970; Adjunct Associate Professor, Columbia University, New York, 1969–72; Visiting Professor, Yale University, 1969; Associate Professor, Brooklyn College, New York, 1970–72; Bain Swiggert Lecturer, Princeton University, New Jersey, 1973; Hurst Professor, Brandeis University, Waltham, Massachusetts, 1974–75; Visiting Professor, University of Virginia, Charlottesville, 1976, 1978, California State University, Fresno, 1977, University of California, Irvine, 1978, Wesleyan University, Middletown, Connecticut, 1979, and Harvard University, Cambridge, Massachusetts, 1980; Visiting Professor, University of Utah, Salt Lake City, 1981–1993; Elliott Coleman Professor of Poetry, Johns Hopkins University, Baltimore, Maryland, 1993–98; since 1998 Professor in the Committee on Social Thought at the University of Chicago. Received Ingram Merrill Foundation fellowship, 1966; National Endowment for the Arts grant, 1967, 1977, 1986; Rockefeller Award, 1968; Guggenheim fellowship, 1974; Edgar Allan Poe Award, 1974; American Academy Award, 1975; Academy of American Poets fellowship, 1979; MacArthur Foundation fellowship, 1987; United States Poet Laureate, 1990–91; Rebekah Johnson Bobbitt Prize for Poetry, 1992; Bollingen Prize, 1993; Pulitzer Prize, 1999; member, American Academy; Chancellor, Academy of American Poets, 1995. Living in Chicago, Illinois.

**Poetry**

*Sleeping with One Eye Open,* 1964
*Reasons for Moving,* 1968
*Darker,* 1970
*The Story of Our Lives,* 1973
*The Sargentville Notebook,* 1973
*Elegy for My Father,* 1973
*The Late Hour,* 1978
*Selected Poems,* 1980
*The Continuous Life,* 1990
*Explain That You Live* (with Karl Elder), 1992
*Dark Harbor,* 1993
*A Poet's Alphabet of Influences,* 1993
*A Suite of Appearances,* 1993

*Blizzard of One,* 1998
*Chicken, Shadow, Moon, and More,* 2000

**Selected Criticism**
*Hopper,* 1994

**Other Writings:** short stories (*Mr. and Mrs. Baby, and Other Stories,* 1985), essays (*The Weather of Words: Poetic Invention,* 2000), children's literature, translations of Spanish and Quecha literature (*Texas,* by Jorge Luis Borges, 1975); edited and translated collections of poetry (*Travelling in the Family: Selected Poems of Carlos Drummond de Andrade* [with Thomas Colchie], 1986).

**Further Reading**

Berger, Charles, "Poetry Chronicle," *Raritan* 10, no. 3 (Winter 1991)

Bloom, Harold, "Dark and Radiant Peripheries: Mark Strand and A.R. Ammons," in *Figures of Capable Imagination,* by Bloom, New York: Seabury, 1976

Bloom, Harold, "Mark Strand," *Gettysburg Review* 4, no. 2 (1991)

Donaldson, Jeffrey, "The Still Life of Mark Strand's Darkening Harbor," *Dalhousie Review* 74 (1994)

Gregerson, Linda, "Negative Capability," *Parnassus* 9 (1981)

Howard, Richard, "Mark Strand," in *Alone with America: Essays on the Art of Poetry since 1950,* by Howard, New York: Atheneum, 1969; enlarged edition, 1980

Jackson, Richard, "Charles Simic and Mark Strand: The Presence of Absence," *Contemporary Literature* 21, no. 1 (1980)

Kirby, David, *Mark Strand and the Poet's Place in Contemporary Culture,* Columbia: University of Missouri Press, 1990

Stitt, Peter, "Stages of Reality: The Mind/Body Problem in Contemporary Poetry," *Georgia Review* 37, no. 1 (1983)

Vine, Richard, and Robert von Hallberg, "A Conversation with Mark Strand," *Chicago Review* 28, no. 4 (1977)


---

# Surrealism

"For America *is* Dada," wrote Waldo Frank in the early decades of the 20th century. That there is much in American culture that is surreal and Dadaist is no less true today than it was then. The affinities of American culture with the surreal may in part explain why European Surrealist and Dadaist aesthetic strategies and the artists propounding them were generally received with open arms. Much of contemporary expression in American popular culture, film, poetry, painting, and fiction is best appreciated only with foundational knowledge of Dada and Surrealism, especially the emigration of major European Surrealists and Dadaists and the creative strategies they brought with them to New York City during and after World War II. The poet John Ashbery has said, "Surrealism has become a part of our daily lives: its effects can be seen everywhere, in the work of writers and artists who have no connection with the movement." These widespread effects originated when European artists and writers were exiled during the Nazi occupation of Paris.

In fact, Dadaism and Surrealism arose out of a militant resistance to warfare. Repulsed by the 20th century's mass industrialized violence—first World War I and then World War II with its holocausts and atomic bombs—artists and intellectuals revolted against Europe's inability to restrain war and Fascism. Dadaism began in Switzerland in 1916 among artists and writers, such as Tristan Tzara and Jean Arp, who frequented the legendary Cabaret Voltaire, run by the exiled German pacifist Hugo Ball. Although the early Dadaists claimed to be anti-political, their revolt against the economic and political conditions leading to war was itself a "politics" that was passed down to their followers, the Surrealists. Like the Dadaists, the Surrealists were anti-militarist, anti-nationalist, anti-capitalist, and anti-imperialist. From the start, both Dadaists and Surrealists emphasized anti-art and internationalism. Their anti-art consisted of collectively devised and collaboratively executed expression. Such an emphasis on collective expression gave coherence to their movement and, paradoxically, helps explain later factionalism and schisms among them.

Collage, assemblage, sound poems, and ready-mades all involved a rejection of the artist as individual creator and craftsman, replacing individual artistic volition with notions of group production and promoting the unstable and spontaneously generated art piece over the crafted art object. Spontaneity and chance were operative principles. If the Dadaists downplayed being a "movement" with a "politics" in favor of anarchy and anti-politics, their successors, the Surrealists, tipped the scales in the other direction, making their avant-garde a politically engaged movement, particularly under the aegis of André Breton.

After the armistice that ended World War I, European and New York Dadaists moved to Paris, which became the capital of Surrealism. Marcel Duchamp, Francis Picabia, and Man Ray all migrated from New York to Paris. From Zurich came Tristan Tzara. From Germany came Max Ernst. By 1920, Paris was the center of the avant-garde, and artists clustered around *Littérature,* a review put out by Paul Eluard, Benjamin Peret, Jacques Rigaut, and Philippe Soupault. "Lost Generation" American writers then living in Paris included Henry Miller, Matthew Josephson, Djuna Barnes, Nathanael West, Malcolm Cowley, Ernest Hemingway, William Faulkner, F. Scott Fitzgerald, Anaïs Nin, and Gertrude Stein, whose works are touched by Surrealism to widely varying degrees, although in general the American writers were attentive observers rather than participants in the movement.

In 1924, the *First Manifesto of Surrealism* appeared, a landmark in the movement's history. In it, Breton defined "Surrealism" as follows: "SURREALISM: n. Pure psychic automatism by whose means it is intended to express verbally, or in writing, or in any other manner, the actual functioning of thought. Dictation of thought, in the absence of all control by reason and outside of all aesthetic or moral preoccupations." As early as 1919, *Littérature* had published *Les Champs magnétiques,* a piece collaboratively produced by Breton and Soupault, an early experiment with "automatic writing" derived from Freud's theories of the unconscious. Adapting such theories, the Surrealists opted for a "psychic automatism" as a liberatory strategy for art, music, and literature. Automatism enabled artists to exploit dreams, the fantastic, the marvelous—in short, the *surreal.* Salon and café literary games such as *le cadavre exquis* (exquisite corpse) were based on automatism, chance, and the spontaneous. The production of poetry via group production and "poetic anonymity" became the Surrealist activity par excellence.

Growing political turmoil in France between the wars provoked the Surrealists to align with the Left, and the Surrealists' critique of Western bourgeois culture became more explicitly aligned with communist and Marxist movements, especially the coalition of pacifist, internationalist, socialist, and humanitarian writers and intellectuals contributing to *Clarté.* Such leftist proclivities among the Surrealists did not escape the attention of fascists, whose numbers also were increasing between the wars.

Events moved fast toward World War II. As the German Blitzkrieg approached Paris on 10 June 1940, the French government abandoned the capital. Four days later, the city was under Nazi occupation, and those Parisians who could flee did so. Among them were the avowed enemies of Fascism, revolutionary Surrealist artists, intellectuals, and writers, most of whom fled to Provence and Marseilles. The American government reacted. In August 1940, the U.S. government and the Emergency Rescue Committee sent Varian Fry (a foreign correspondent for *The New Republic*) to establish the Centre Americain de Secours and help anti-Nazi artists, intellectuals, and writers escape. President Roosevelt pushed through the visas that Fry granted to many Surrealist artists and writers, enabling their exile in New York City during the occupation. The face of American cultural expression was forever changed as a result.

In Marseilles, Fry had successfully solicited the help of wealthy American expatriates, especially Peggy Guggenheim and Mary Jane Gold, and arranged for the departure of more than 1,000 exiles—including intellectuals Claude Lévi-Strauss, André Breton, and Max Ernst. Fry's ability to elicit the support of Guggenheim and Gold modeled the patronage that would burgeon later in New York City, networking these artists into New York museum, gallery, and art circles. Although the Surrealists, like the Dadaists, hoped to dismantle Western civilization, especially its bourgeoisie and war machinery, they were complicit with the government agencies and cultural elites in New York City that were busy saving and appropriating them.

This was not the only ambiguity in their movement. Despite their overt commitment to eroticism, unshackled sexuality, and the redefinition of the "feminine," their connections with Guggenheim and Gold and other female patrons were imbued with patriarchy and sexism. Throughout their history, the Surrealists had ambiguous relations with the female artists, writers, and patrons who were their wives, mistresses, and benefactors. More important, these women were often their unacknowledged artistic collaborators. During the 1920s, a large number of American women fled oppressive American Puritanism and Victorianism for the liberated, heady atmosphere of Paris, many of them becoming wives and lovers of Surrealists: Kay Sage married Yves Tanguy, Ann Albert married Matta, Lee Miller married Man Ray, and Peggy Guggenheim and Dorothy Tanning had relationships with Max Ernst. Although women of other nationalities were part of the movement, it was the American female cohorts who helped the Surrealists and Dadaists influence the New York cultural scene once they were in exile there.

The literary reception of Surrealism and Dada in New York City had been long in the making, however. New York had hosted the Armory Show in 1913 and the First Annual Exhibition of the Society of Independent Artists in 1917 (the show to which Marcel Duchamp submitted his ready-made urinal entitled "Fountain" and signed "R. Mutt"). Alfred H. Barr, director of the Museum of Modern Art, and James Thrall Sobey had been interested in and, more important, had been collecting Dada and Surrealist art well before the exiles arrived in New York City. In 1935, Sobey had published *After Picasso,* the first American book primarily about Surrealism, and in 1936 Barr and Sobey worked together on an exhibition at the Museum of Modern Art entitled "Fantastic Art, Dada, and Surrealism." Barr and Sobey, the presence of Picabia and Duchamp among New York artists and intellectuals, the patronage of Walter Arensberg and the stimulation of his salon, and the Société Anonyme founded by Man Ray and Katerine Dreier (the first museum of modern art in New York City) made up a long New York prehistory of Dada and Surrealism that prepared the reception of the exiles. Their presence during the 1940s became a watershed for American cultural transformation.

As events spiraled into World War II, certain American editors and writers had been attentive to the movement. In *Poetry,* H.R. Hays argued in favor of Surrealism: "The revolutionaries of the word have gained us a freedom from orthodox technique. . . . The real revolution is still in progress." *Poetry* also editorialized, "Surrealism . . . widened the boundaries of association and made all types of materials available, restricting the poet to no one type of reality." Writing in 1940, Eugene Jolas, founding editor of *transition,* which published Surrealists in the 1920s and 1930s, remarked on the "militancy of the American Surrealist movement." In the writing of Parker Tyler, Charles Henri Ford, and Harold Rosenberg, he saw the promise that "the American poets may build on [Surrealism's] general libertarian foundation, but they will have to go beyond it. They will have to become *verticalist,* seek the cosmic consciousness in sidereal fantasies, reconstruct the myth of flying."

The literary reception of Surrealism and Dada in America during and after World War II is evident in two literary magazines published in New York City during the 1940s: *V.V.V.* and *View.* These avant-garde magazines became important vehicles for spreading the Surrealist message as well as venues where young American artists and writers could publish literary experiments.

*V.V.V.,* edited by David Hare, André Breton, and Max Ernst, proved fertile ground for American writers and artists. William Carlos Williams' "Catastrophic Birth" appeared in the first number in June 1942, just as Lionel Abel wrote that *V.V.V.* needed the skills of a "coroner and midwife" because impoverished traditions were dying on the one hand and an avant-garde was being born on the other. Williams' poem reads,

> Each age brings new calls upon violence
> for new rewards, variants of the old.
> Unless each hold firm
> Unless each remain inflexible
> there can be no new. The new opens
> new ways beyond all known ways.

*V.V.V.* put American writers such as Williams in the company of Claude Lévi-Strauss, Robert Motherwell, and Leonora Carrington. Later issues offered literary culture the same enrichment—a story, "Blind Date," by Dorothy Tanning; poems by a very young Philip Lamantia; essays by Patrick Waldenberg and Harold Rosenberg; poetry by Charles Henri Ford; and essays by Parker Tyler.

*View* numbers ran through the 1940s and published many American writers as well. Paul Bowles' translation of de Chirico's Surrealist novel *Hebdomeros* appeared in 1944 along with an article by Robert Melville analyzing a de Chirico painting and an essay by Parker Tyler analyzing the eroticism in a painting by Audrey Butler (appearing in an issue with a cover by Georgia O'Keeffe). Wallace Stevens contributed to *View,* as did Wallace Fowlie, commenting on Max Jacob; Henry Miller wrote book reviews for the magazine, and Charles Henri Ford published a Surrealistic poem for Billie Holiday in it:

> Like a baptized woman in a moment of depravity
> Your voice rings out, headstrong and dreamy
>
> On a night of desperadoes
> You deliver the clear cut message
> From the anti-suicides. . . .

In the fall of 1942, Peggy Guggenheim opened "Art of This Century," a permanent show and gallery on 57th Street in New York City dedicated to Surrealism. In October 1944, Duchamp designed the catalog for the only group exhibit during this period, titling it *First Papers of Surrealism,* named after the "first papers" that Surrealists acquired as immigrants to the United States. A famous 1945 group portrait of exiles taken in Matisse's New York apartment shows André and Elisa Breton, Marcel and Teeny Duchamp, Aimé Césaire, Matta and his wife, and Yves Tanguy.

If Surrealism affected American painting, chiefly Abstract Expressionism, it also affected American literary history, and if Surrealist automatism yielded gestural painting, it also yielded formal literary innovations among many poets. The relationship between the Dadaist "the gratuitous act" and the spontaneity of action painting or that between the Surrealist "event" and the vogue of "Happenings" in New York City in the 1950s and 1960s emerges directly out of the Surrealists' presence. The emphasis on both automatism and *hasard* (chance, accident) as artistic strategies challenged formalist assumptions by emphasizing the unconscious as a wellspring of creativity and energized the generations of American writers, artists, and poets coming of age in the 1940s and early 1950s, as well as thereafter.

The American literary use of Surrealism has varied. Charles Simic has argued that there are two major lines of influence—poets such as Jackson Mac Low and composers such as John Cage, more radical in their acceptance of chance in composition and creativity, and then those like Simic himself and others who "cheat on chance." Simic elaborates, "The reputation of the unconscious as the endless source of poetry is overrated. The first rule for the poet must be: cheat on your unconscious and your dreams." Simic's point is that, while the use of chance, spontaneity, and automatism is indeed liberatory, it must be tempered with craft and workmanship. John Ashbery makes a similar point about automatism: "In literature," Surrealist freedom "means automatic writing, but what is so free about that? Real freedom would be to use this method where it could be of service and to correct it with the conscious mind where indicated." Writers as diverse as Gertrude Stein, William Carlos Williams, Elizabeth Bishop, John Ashbery, Frank O'Hara, Robert Bly, Allen Ginsberg, Lawrence Ferlinghetti, Philip Lamantia, Bob Kaufman, Ann Waldman, Bob Dylan, Charles Simic, James Tate, and Jackson Mac Low have all used Surrealist techniques in their work. Ashbery's attitude that these techniques are often "unsatisfactory" is widespread among American poets, but so too is his idea that "we are all indebted to Surrealism; the significant art of our time could not have been produced without it."

If, as some have argued, the 1947 International Surrealist Exhibit in Paris marked the end of the movement in a French cultural scene that was turning increasingly to Camus, Sartre, existentialism, and those literary figures who were part of the Resistance movement rather than those writers who fled France in exile, and if future Parisian exhibits of the Surrealists and Dadaists seemed retrospective and nostalgic rather than avant-garde, the same was not true in New York City in the late 1940s and early 1950s, when young American artists and writers found in Surrealist strategies opportunities for liberation, resistance, and expression that enabled their creativity. Gallery and museum exhibitions of Surrealism generated excitement and enthusiasm among Americans for what to them still seemed new and pertinent to social reality. In the 1950s, Abstract Expressionists and the Beats and writers of the San Francisco Renaissance were often inspired by the Surrealists' radical suspicions of bourgeois culture, their resistance to militarism, and their revulsion at destructive technologies. The Korean War, the Cold War, and the rise of nuclear weaponry made the Surrealist critique of culture viable throughout the 1950s. For some, Jackson Pollock's action painting and Jack Kerouac's spontaneous prose became American apotheoses of Surrealism. The Vietnam War and the Civil Rights movement, in a similar vein, gave Surrealist strategies and resistance to militarism a continued pertinence in the 1960s. In 1968 John Ashbery could claim that Surrealism still was "what's happening."

Charles Simic has conducted collaborative, free-association experiments with James Tate; a young Allen Ginsberg was quoted expressing enthusiasm for *V.V.V.;* Gerald Nicosia has remarked on Bob Kaufman's use of Surrealist chance in his poetry; and John Ashbery has written extensively on Surrealism and the avant-garde, teasing out implications for his and others' poetry. Robert Bly has studied and written about the "leaping associations" of Spanish and French Surrealist poets. The list of American poets responsive to Surrealism is lengthy. Much like their counterpart artists—the painters in the New York scene—many writers, youthful in the 1940s and 1950s, were released from formalist shackles and academicism by automatism and the avant-garde. From the example of the Surrealists, they learned linguistic experimentation of the most revolutionary sort.

That avant-garde is not dead. Between 1993 and 1995 an exhibition entitled "The Return of the Cadavre Exquis" toured in New York; Washington, D.C.; Santa Monica, California; St. Louis; and Paris. "The Return of the Cadavre Exquis" first opened at the Drawing Center in New York City, involving more than 1,000 artists from cities worldwide in collaborative drawing games. As that international *cadavre exquis* unfolded, exile-poet Ted Joans was still working on "the world's longest cadavre exquis," entitled "Long Distance." Joans began it when he found computer paper in London in 1975 and continued the Surrealist experiment through 1993. Among its contributors are Paul Bowles and Allen Ginsberg.

Surrealism is now woven into the very warp and woof of American literary history, adapted as much by advertisers and pop culturalists as by poets and merging with the complexities of postmodern culture.

MICHAEL W. VELLA

*See also* Dada

**Further Reading**


Ades, Dawn, *Dada and Surrealism Reviewed,* London: Arts Council of Great Britain, 1978

Ashbery, John, *Reported Sightings: Art Chronicles, 1957–1987,* edited by David Bergman, New York: Knopf, and Manchester: Carcanet, 1989

Balakian, Anna, *Literary Origins of Surrealism: A New Mysticism in French Poetry,* New York: King's Crown Press, and London: University Press, 1947; new edition, London: University of London Press, and New York: New York University Press, 1967

Barr, Alfred H., Jr., editor, *Fantastic Art, Dada, Surrealism,* New York: Museum of Modern Art, 1936; 3rd edition, 1947

Chadwick, Whitney, *Women Artists and the Surrealist Movement,* London: Thames and Hudson, and Boston: Little Brown, 1985

Chénieux-Gendron, Jacqueline, *Le surréalisme,* Paris: Presses Universitaires de France, 1984; as *Surrealism,* translated by Vivian Folkenflik, New York: Columbia University Press, 1990

Freeman, Judi, *The Dada and Surrealist Word-Image,* Cambridge, Massachusetts: MIT Press, 1989

Gershman, Herbert S., *The Surrealist Revolution in France,* Ann Arbor: University of Michigan Press, 1969

Krauss, Rosalind E., *The Originality of the Avant-Garde and Other Modernist Myths,* Cambridge, Massachusetts: MIT Press, 1985

Lewis, Helena, *The Politics of Surrealism,* New York: Paragon House, 1988

Nadeau, Maurice, *Histoire du surréalisme,* 3 vols., Paris: Seuil, 1945–59; as *The History of Surrealism,* translated by Richard Howard, London: Cape, 1964; New York: Macmillan, 1965

Philbrick, Jane, editor, *The Return of the Cadavre Exquis* (exhib. cat.), New York: Drawing Center, 1993

Rubin, William S., *Dada, Surrealism, and Their Heritage* (exhib. cat.), New York: Museum of Modern Art, 1968

Tashjian, Dickran, *Skyscraper Primitives: Dada and the American Avant-Garde, 1910–1925,* Middleton, Connecticut: Wesleyan University Press, 1975

Waldberg, Patrick, *Le surréalisme,* Geneva: Skira, 1962; as *Surrealism,* translated by Stuart Gilbert, London: Thames and Hudson, 1965; New York: McGraw Hill, 1966


---

# May Swenson 1919–89

In a 1983 interview with Lee Hudson, May Swenson stated that she thought of her poems as "things" and that when she talked about her work she said she "made poems" or that "I am making poems." Her poems, she suggested, were like "three dimensional objects instead of just words on a page"; indeed, some of her poems were printed in shapes on the page. Throughout her career Swenson "made" both traditional and experimental verse, publishing ten volumes of poetry as well as works for young people, plays, and translations. Her many awards include a Rockefeller fellowship (1955), a Ford Foundation grant (1964), the Bollingen Prize (1981), and a MacArthur Foundation fellowship (1987).

Critics have noted Swenson's use of sound in her early volumes, *Another Animal* (1954), *A Cage of Spines* (1958), and *To Mix with Time: New and Selected Poems* (1963). In these early works she gained praise for her use of conventional poetic techniques as well as playful language. One of Swenson's best-known poems, "The Centaur," combines fantasy and reality when a child and willow branch horse meld together:

My head and my neck were mine
yet they were shaped like a horse
My hair flopped to the side
like the mane of a horse in the wind.

The child returns to reality when she enters the house, where her interactions with her mother reveal their relationship. The child is allowed a last bit of fantasy with her description of Rob Roy pulling clover in the field.

Swenson's inventiveness with language often turned her poems into riddles. Describing an object without naming it is in fact one of her recurring strategies. In "At Breakfast" (from *To Mix with Time*), for example, the first stanza reads:

Not quite
spherical
White
Oddly closed
and without a lid.

The poem continues its detailed description of an egg but never names it.

May Swenson's friendship with Elizabeth Bishop is documented in correspondence and through the poems that Swenson wrote for Bishop. Critics claim that Bishop was one of the influential poets in Swenson's career, but in a 1978 interview with Karla Hammond, Swenson denied the influence. Rather, Swenson said that she "shared the same basic perceptive equipment" with Bishop. "Dear Elizabeth," which first appeared in *The New Yorker,* was written in reply to a letter from Bishop who was then living in Brazil. The poem is notable for its treatment of sexuality and the exotic, using Bishop's words from letters to build a dialogue on lesbianism without ever naming it directly.

The poems in *Iconographs* (1970), Swenson's fifth collection, appear in shapes on the page. Treating poems as objects was not a new concept, but Swenson gave it a freshness, explaining in a note to the volume that she wanted to "give for each an individual arrangement in the space of the page." The shapes cause the reader to experience the poem visually, an effect that most traditional verse forms do not achieve. When many of the poems were reprinted in *New and Selected Things Taking Place* (1978), the format did not allow for all the shapes to be retained, thus altering the ways in which the poems could be interpreted. For example, "Feel Me" relates a father's dying words to his children. In the original, a diagonal slash through the poem, made by extra spaces between certain words, makes for a powerful visual representation of the chasm between life and death. The rhyme throughout the poem keeps its construction tightly knit.

*Nature,* published posthumously in 1994, draws together old and new poems. In the foreword poet Susan Mitchell compares Swenson to Gerard Manley Hopkins, who was as immersed in the world and in nature as she.

No definitive biography has been written about May Swenson, although a handful of critical pieces and dissertations exist. Roxana Knudson, her longtime companion, wrote a biography for young adults, *The Wonderful Pen of May Swenson* (1993). Although Swenson was a gifted poet, she does not enjoy the recognition that contemporaries such as Elizabeth Bishop, E.E. Cummings, and Marianne Moore do. She is nonetheless worth rediscovering for her use of language and her adventurous spirit.

MILLIE JACKSON

**Biography**

Born in Logan, Utah, 28 May 1919. Attended Utah State University, Logan, B.A. 1939; editor, New Directions Press, New York City, 1959–66; poet-in-residence, Purdue University, West Lafayette, Indiana, 1966–67; Instructor, University of North Carolina, Greensboro, 1968–69, 1974, Lethbridge University, Alberta, Canada, 1970, and University of California, Riverside, 1976; Chancellor, Academy of American Poets, 1980–89; staff, Bread Loaf Writers' Conference, Middlebury, Vermont, 1976. Received Rockefeller fellowship, 1955; Bread Loaf Writers' Conference fellowship, 1957; Poetry Society of America Award, 1957; Guggenheim fellowship, 1959; Amy Lowell traveling scholarship, 1960; National Institute of Arts and Letters Award, 1960; Ford Foundation grant, 1964; Rockefeller Foundation grant, 1967; Brandeis University Creative Arts Award, 1967; Shelley Memorial Award, 1968; National Endowment for the Arts grant, 1974, 1976; Academy of American Poets fellowship, 1979; Bollingen Prize, 1981; MacArthur Foundation fellowship, 1987. Died in Oceanview, Delaware, 4 December 1989.

**Poetry**

*Another Animal,* 1954
*A Cage of Spines,* 1958
*To Mix with Time: New and Selected Poems,* 1963
*Half Sun Half Sleep: New Poems,* 1967
*Iconographs,* 1970
*New and Selected Things Taking Place,* 1978
*In Other Words,* 1987
*The Love Poems of May Swenson,* 1991
*Nature: Poems Old and New,* 1994
*May Out West,* 1996

**Selected Criticism**

*The Contemporary Poet as Artist and Critic,* 1964
*Made with Words,* 1998

**Other Writings:** plays (*The Floor,* 1967), children's poetry (*Poems to Solve,* 1966), translations of Swedish poetry (*Windows and Stones: Selected Poems of Tomas Tranströmer,* 1972), correspondence (*Dear Elizabeth: Five Poems and Three Letters to Elizabeth Bishop,* 2000); edited collections of poetry (*New Voices: Selected University and College Prize-Winning Poems, 1979–83,* 1984).

**Further Reading**

"Craft Interview with May Swenson," *New York Quarterly* 19 (1977)
Gadomski, Kenneth E., "May Swenson: A Bibliography of Primary and Secondary Sources," *Bulletin of Bibliography* 44, no. 4 (1987)
Hammond, Karla, "An Interview with May Swenson, July 14, 1978," *Parnassus* 7 (1978) Hudson, Lee, "Interview: A Conversation with May Swenson," *Literature in Performance* 3, no. 2 (1983)
Ostriker, Alicia, "May Swenson and the Shape of Speculation," in *Writing Like a Woman,* by Ostriker, Ann Arbor: University of Michigan Press, 1983
Russell, Sue, "A Mysterious and Lavish Power: How Things Continue to Take Place in the Work of May Swenson," *Kenyon Review* 16, no. 3 (1994)
Zona, Kirstin Hotelling, "A 'Dangerous Game of Change': Images of Desire in the Love Poems of May Swenson," *Twentieth Century Literature* 44, no. 2 (1998)

# Symbolism

Symbolism, although traceable in part to Edgar Allan Poe (1809–49) by way of Charles Baudelaire (1821–67), was by origin a French movement, but its influence on other literatures was early and profound. The movement had been named by Jean Moreas (1856–1910) in "Symbolism—a Manifesto" (1886), which argued that the new poetry was neither didactic nor descriptive. Suggestive rather than explicit, Symbolist poetry evoked what were understood to be primal ideas or truths through the subtle manipulation of cadence, music, and imagery. The effect was to suggest rather than to state.

The term "Symbolism," as employed by French critics and poets in the late 19th century, did not mean what it did when applied, for example, to the literature of the Middle Ages. In that case, a symbol was understood to be an equivalent to another reality or thing. In the fully realized Symbolist work, however, the poem embodied or was exactly that which it named.

Romantic symbolism had been central to the poetry and fiction of the American Renaissance, where a symbol was seen as expressive of a primarily personal or subjective awareness. Stéphane Mallarmé (1842–98), however, argued in "Crisis in Poetry" (1886) that "[t]he pure work implies the disappearance of the poet as speaker, yielding his initiative to words" (translated by Mary Ann Caws, from Stéphane Mallarmé, *Selected Prose and Poetry,* 1982). In this, he reflected the belief advanced by Poe that a poem should not be the personal expression of the artist but an essentially impersonal linguistic structure. "Poésie pure" in the Symbolist aesthetic replaced the egocentric symbolic poem of the Romantics with what Mallarmé called an "Orphic explication of the earth."

Behind Mallarmé and other Symbolists, such as Arthur Rimbaud (1854–91) and Paul Verlaine (1844–96), is the "doctrine of correspondence" of Emanuel Swedenborg (1688–1772), which asserts that all spiritual realities correspond to material realities and that spirit, therefore, can be stated as matter, transcendent truth as art. In Symbolist aesthetics, this means that the poem can function much like the Eucharist, through which matter becomes spirit. In the increasingly agnostic culture of *fin de siècle,* this suggested that art could assume the role of religion, and the poet performed the function of the priest.

Stuart Merrill (1863–1915) is among the earliest American poets who grounded their work in Symbolist aesthetics. Born on Long Island, he spent most of his childhood in Paris, where his father was a counselor to the American legation. Merrill attended French schools, including the Lycée Fontaines, where his teachers included Mallarmé. Among the second generation of French Symbolists were several of Mallarmé's students—René Ghil (1862–1925) and Ephraïm Mikhaël (1866–90), among others—of whom Merrill was the most celebrated. Merrill was also an important translator of French Symbolist poetry into English, and his collection of French prose poetry, *Pastels in Prose* (1890), provided many Americans, including T.S. Eliot (1888–1965), with one of their first encounters with the new poetry.

In his "Credo" (1906), Merrill reveals himself as a classic French Symbolist, seeing poetry as "simultaneously Word and Music, . . . miraculously able to suggest the infinite in what is often only the indefinite" (translated by Elaine F. Corts, from Stuart Merrill, *The White Tomb: Selected Writings,* 1999). In a letter to his fellow American poet Francis Vielé-Griffin (1864–1937), who also played a significant role among the French Symbolists, although he was much less known in the United States, Merrill noted that "to express the idea by words, to suggest emotion by the music of these words,—such are, I think, the alpha and the omega of our doctrine" (Theodore Stanton, "A French-American Poet," *The Dial* [20 January 1916]).

Merrill was the most accomplished American poet of the late 19th and early 20th centuries and the most acclaimed of American Symbolists. Kenneth Rexroth argued that "in the whole period, from Walt Whitman and Emily Dickinson to Edwin Arlington Robinson and Robert Frost, the greatest American poet is Stuart Merrill" (*American Poetry in the Twentieth Century,* 1971). Aside from *Pastels in Prose* and two early poems, however, all Merrill's work is in French, making it unavailable, except in translation, to most American readers. William Dean Howells, who wrote the preface to *Pastels in Prose,* told him, "I want you to be an American poet, and to write in English, or, if you must write first in French, to reinstate yourself afterwards. A man is not born in his native place for nothing" (Marjorie Louise Henry, *Stuart Merrill: la contribution d'un américain au symbolisme français,* 1927).

Merrill not only rejected Howells' counsel and wrote all his important poems in French but also lived most of his life in and around Paris. The implication was clear: to succeed as a poet, at least within the Symbolist milieu as Merrill understood it, one worked in French and in France no matter what one's nationality. Nonetheless, Merrill's later poetry is modeled on Walt Whitman's long cadenced lines, and his work is far more political than that of any French Symbolist. Mallarmé's work is essentially apolitical, but Merrill's is deeply cognizant of social injustice, notably in his last major work, an anti-war poem, "A Tommy Atkins" (1915).

Merrill's writings were well known to the next generation of American poets, including High Modernists such as Eliot and Ezra Pound (1885–1972), who quotes him in *The Pisan Cantos.* The difference between them and Merrill has less to do with ability—for he was after all an exceptionally fine poet, if not their equal—than with ways in which an initially foreign aesthetic could be assimilated by an American poet. Merrill wished his work to find a place within the French poetical tradition, whereas American High Modernists such as Eliot wished to borrow from Symbolism only what was useful for their own ends.

Although there have been writers such as Merrill bred in one language who have become masters of another, they are exceptions. Eliot, who himself wrote some of his early poems in French, knew this, saying in an interview for *The Paris Review* (1959) that he had once, when he was a young man living in Paris, considered following Merrill's example and becoming a Symbolist poet working in French but believed that English offered "more resources." Further, it was not possible to be a poet in two languages: "I don't think that one can be a bilingual poet," he said.

When poets such as Eliot and Pound, who would dominate American Modernism, were still students, avant-garde American periodicals were publishing work by poets who had begun the assimilation of Symbolist poetics into American poetry. The conventional picture of American poets as working in isolation, innocent of developments in British and French literature, is not accurate. A great many American writers in addition to Merrill and Vielé-Griffin—Trumbull Stickney (1874–1904), Francis S. Saltus (1849–89), his half-brother Edgar Saltus (1855–1921),

James Huneker (1860–1921), Vance Thompson (1863–1925), and Vincent O'Sullivan (1868?–1940), among many others well known in their own day—lived in Paris, at least briefly, and were friendly with poets in the Symbolist community. These Americans brought Symbolist aesthetics back home and joined popular American poets such as Richard Hovey (1864–1900), Madison Cawein (1865–1914), and George Sylvester Viereck (1884–1962) in establishing an American audience for Symbolist poetry at a time when conservative American critics and readers still saw realism and naturalism as the defining tendencies in American writing. In fact, by 1895 Richard Hovey was able to argue in "Modern Symbolism and Maurice Maeterlinck" that Symbolism had already become an international movement, a general shift in the *Weltanschauung* that involved the British as much as the Belgians, the Americans as much as the French.

Much early American Symbolist poetry is weak (Hovey, for one, was a good translator of Mallarmé, but his own poems are routine), yet there are fine moments, as in Stickney's "The Melancholy Year Is Dead with Rain" (1902):

So in a mountain desolation burns
Some rich belated flower, and with the gray
Sick weather, in the world of rotting ferns
From out the dreadful stones it dies away.

Symbolist aesthetics were promoted in *fin-de-siècle* American journals such as *The Chap-Book, The Lark,* and *M'lle New York.* Also important was Arthur Symons' *The Symbolist Movement in Literature* (1899), which Eliot read in 1908, noting that it had led him to Rimbaud, Jules Laforgue (1860–87), and Verlaine, whose work in turn led him to Tristan Corbière (1845–75). Laforgue's polished irony would be especially important to Eliot, as such Symbolist-inflected lines from his "Preludes" (1915) as these indicate:

His soul stretched tight across the skies
That fade behind a city block,
Or trampled by insistent feet
At four and five and six o'clock;
And short square fingers stuffing pipes,
And evening newspapers, and eyes
Assured of certain certainties,
The conscience of a blackened street
Impatient to assume the world.

René Taupin's *L'influence du symbolisme français sur la poésie américaine* (1929) traces the early development of American Symbolism before Eliot without finding much to recommend but then argues that Imagism, as formulated by Ezra Pound, was an outgrowth of Symbolist poetics. Pound vehemently denied this, and indeed the clarity and directness sought by the Imagists is contrary to the Symbolist practice of poetry as suggestion. Pound defined an image, however, not merely as the depiction or representation of an object but as "that which presents an intellectual and emotional complex in an instant of time," a definition that could as well apply to the symbol within Mallarmé's poetics.

Emotion, Pound asserted in "As for Imagisme," creates "the Image," which is "more than an idea. It is a vortex or cluster of fused ideas and is endowed with energy." This was accomplished through various expressive or suggestive means, prominently including—as in Symbolist aesthetics—"melopoeia," or the music of language.

Imagism is not Symbolism, but the debt to Symbolism is clear. Desiring a more hard-edged, sculptural poetry than Mallarmé and his acolytes practiced, Pound worked within the poetic possibilities they had cultivated. "Melopoeia" is also central to the work of several of Pound's contemporaries, such as Amy Lowell (1874–1925), John Gould Fletcher (1886–1950), and Conrad Aiken (1889–1973). Aiken, for example, wrote in "The House of Dust" (1920),

We hear him and take him among us, like a wind of music,
Like a ghost of music we have somewhere heard.

In contrast, Pound wrote in the best known of his Imagist poems, "In a Station of the Metro" (1913),

The apparition of these faces in the crowd;
Petals on a wet, black bough.

The differences between Pound's primarily sculptural, visual poem and the more self-evidently musical lines from Aiken indicate two related but distinct traditions in American Modernism, both indebted to Symbolism.

Disentangling lines of influence between Symbolism and High Modernism can be daunting. Poets such as Eliot acquired the Symbolist aesthetic directly from its source, but younger poets absorbed it from various directions. Echoes of Verlaine can be found, for example, in poems by Samuel Greenberg (1893–1917) (e.g., "the street one color set, / Like a huge grey cat" from "Serenade in Grey," first published in 1920). His poetry was in turn read in manuscript by Hart Crane (1899–1932) and helped draw Crane's work into the Symbolist tradition.

Wallace Stevens (1879–1955) remarked that the French Symbolists were simply what people were reading when he was learning to write. He began working, that is, in a poetic milieu in which European rather than American literature provided the principal impetus, but by the second decade of the century, American poets were as often responding to each other as to European models. In 1916, for example, "Voyage à l'Infini," by Walter Conrad Arensberg, one of Stevens' close friends, included such Symbolist images as

At night
The lake is a wide silence
Without imagination.

A year earlier, Stevens had published "Sunday Morning" (1915), which contains the line "The day is like wide water, without sound." Arensberg's image may be a variant of Stevens', or, given the fact that "Voyage à l'Infini" may have circulated in manuscript while "Sunday Morning" was being written, Stevens' conceivably was "improving" Arensberg's. Symbolist aesthetics, textures, and images spread so freely in High-Modernist poetry that it is no longer meaningful to talk about "influence," as it is when discussing Merrill. By the time Stevens began writing major works such as "Sunday Morning" (published the same year that Merrill died), Symbolism had been fully naturalized.

In 1931, Edmund Wilson's *Axel's Castle* gave Americans a historical and theoretical framework in which to understand Symbolism, but Wilson was critical of the movement, which had by that time deeply penetrated American poetry. The result, it seemed, was an elitist poetry that seemingly held itself above political regard. The 1930s saw the rise of politically aligned poetry, and poets and critics attacked Stevens, among others, for alleged failure to confront social issues. William Carlos Williams (1883–1963), for example, declared in "Against the Weather: A Study of the Artist" (1939), "No symbolism can be permitted to obscure the real purpose, to lift the world of the senses to the level of the imagination and so give it new currency."

One direction American Symbolism followed at this time has come to be known as the academic tradition, rooted in part in the work of Allen Tate (1899–1979). Tate translated Mallarmé and other Symbolists in the 1920s but was drawn to Symbolism as much by reading Crane and Eliot. Tate's "Ode to the Confederate Dead" (1928) is self-consciously a Symbolist poem, and the poem, together with the essay Tate wrote about it, "Narcissus as Narcissus" (1938), became a textbook guide to Symbolist poetics for a younger generation that included Robert Lowell. In turn, Lowell's early work, such as "The Quaker Graveyard in Nantucket" (1945), helped inspire a tradition of complexly modulated Symbolist poetry that dominated anthologies and literature classrooms in the 1950s.

The academic tradition in which Tate and Lowell were central figures is sometimes seen as challenged and ultimately deposed by the innovative work collected in Donald Allen's *The New American Poetry: 1945–1960* (1960). As different as this poetry was from the prevailing academic taste, much of it depended on further permutations in the Symbolist tradition and provided new poetic grounds that have yet to run their course.

Several of the poets anthologized by Allen had roots in the San Francisco Renaissance, the poetic movement that arose in the Bay Area in the 1940s. Symbolist poetry, both as originally conceived and in the work of William Butler Yeats (1865–1939), Federico García Lorca (1898–1936), Rainer Maria Rilke (1898–1936), H.D. (1886–1961), Crane, Pound, Stevens, and Eliot, was mined by younger poets living in the area. Little magazines such as *Circle* carried essays on Rilke and other Symbolists and post-Symbolists, and C.F. MacIntyre worked on translations that would culminate in his anthology *French Symbolist Poetry* (1958). Lawrence Hart (1901–96) promulgated an aesthetic heavily indebted to Crane, Eliot, and other Symbolists. He and his followers, named the "Activists" by W.H. Auden, enjoyed much prestige at midcentury.

At the center of the San Francisco Renaissance were Robert Duncan (1919–88) and Jack Spicer (1925–65), who were drawn to Orphic traditions in poetry. Spicer was especially interested in Yeats, a dominant presence in his early poems. He also translated Rilke, and in his later work, beginning with "The Imaginary Elegies," modeled on Rilke's "Duino Elegies," he developed a poetics of dictation that would make possible "the disappearance of the poet as speaker," as Mallarmé had wished. Spicer saw the poet as a kind of "radio," a mere transmitter rather than creator of poems.

A linguist by training, Spicer, as much as Mallarmé, wished to yield the "initiative to words," and in *After Lorca* (1957), his first major book, he argued for a "pure poetry" in which things would be "caught forever in the structure of words." Pursuing similar notions, Duncan argued that the poet was a priest—not a creator but the means through whom the poem could enact itself.

Spicer's importance to later generations of American poets, including "Language writers" and those working in gnostic and hermetic traditions, is considerable, but whatever his work owes to the Symbolists, it is radically different from theirs. Spicer's poetry investigates inadequacies of language in ways that depend on 20th-century linguistics. Mallarmé saw all experience eventually contained in a book; for Spicer, language is so fraught with deficiencies that an ideal poem should have no words at all. "A really perfect poem," he wrote in *After Lorca,* would have "an infinitely small vocabulary."

The deltas of Symbolist influence in postmodern American poetry are considerable. Poets such as Johanna Drucker (1952–) and Susan Howe (1937–), for example, have explored the effect of typefaces and the arrangement of letters on the page, much as Mallarmé did in *A Coup de dés.* Gustaf Sobin (1935–), in "A Portrait of the Self as Instrument of Its Syllables" (1988), cites Mallarmé's "rush // of crushed / shadow" as fundamental to his poetic training. Among Sobin's formative teachers was René Char, who in turn was much indebted to Symbolism.

It would be incorrect, however, to consider these poets Symbolists. Sobin, like Merrill, has chosen to spend most of his life as a poet living in France, but Symbolism reached him through the long complexities of the 20th century, and if Mallarmé is important to his work, so are Robert Creeley, William Bronk, and others far removed from Symbolist aesthetics. Symbolism remains inextricably woven into American poetry, but it has merged with, and been transformed by, so many other strains and concerns that it rarely operates in ways that its original practitioners would endorse.

EDWARD HALSEY FOSTER

**Further Reading**

Benamou, Michel, *Wallace Stevens and the Symbolist Imagination,* Princeton, New Jersey: Princeton University Press, 1972

Foster, Edward, *Decadents, Symbolists, and Aesthetes in America: Fin-de-siécle American Poetry: An Anthology,* Jersey City, New Jersey: Talisman House, 2000

Smith, Richard Cándida, *Mallarmé's Children: Symbolism and the Renewal of Experience,* Berkeley: University of California Press, 1999

Taupin, René, *L'influence du symbolisme français sur la poésie américaine (de 1910 a 1920),* Paris: Champion, 1929; as *The Influence of French Symbolism on Modern American Poetry,* revised and edited by William Pratt, translated by William Pratt and Anne Rich Pratt, New York: AMS Press, 1985

Wilson, Edmund, *Axel's Castle: A Study in the Imaginative Literature of 1870–1930,* New York and London: Scribner, 1931; new edition, New York: Scribner, 1942

# T

## Genevieve Taggard 1894–1948

"It takes very few individuals to make a new age or explode an old one. That is, if the individuals themselves have hold on a vital substance," Genevieve Taggard wrote in her introduction to *May Days: An Anthology of Verse* (1925), dramatizing her belief in the capacity of individual acts of conscience to transform a nation. In works chiefly characterized by her conviction that writing itself might function as an agent of social and political change, Genevieve Taggard turned her poetry to the tasks that guided her life: socialism, labor, suffrage, equality, and, more generally, radical movements for social change. In a writing career that spanned some 29 years Taggard never retreated from her statements of principled dissent.

Genevieve Taggard's poetry has been largely overlooked in literary histories and anthologies, however. She is better known for her risk-taking biography of another woman poet, *The Life and Mind of Emily Dickinson* (1930). In this work of bio-criticism, Taggard explored the psychological context of Dickinson's verse, looking with particular care at the father-daughter relationship and its implications for the poet. Although Dickinson criticism has advanced considerably in the decades since this volume appeared, it still bears reading for those who are fascinated by the writer's mind and seek out the psychology behind the poetry. In addition to her critical writing Taggard generated an impressive body of poetic work. Like many writers of her era she was rescued from literary obscurity by the women's movement and its search for feminist precursors. In Taggard the women's movement found not merely evidence of a female voice, but also a champion of feminist causes during the first half of the 20th century. In this sense Taggard takes her place alongside rediscovered, politically aware, and activist women writers such as Muriel Rukeyser, Tess Slesinger, Josephine Herbst, and Meridel LeSueur.

Although many of her counterparts in leftist and literary circles emerged from the upper middle class, Taggard's radicalism was forged through experience. Her family's limited means were inspiration enough to convince her of the divide between "haves" and "have-nots." Although she was raised in a family of Christian missionaries, her emerging consciousness of class and privilege caused her to leave behind such progressive reforms for the prospect of revolution. Taggard preferred to become a socialist agitator rather than a Christian gentlewoman. Her poem "The Little Girl with Bands on Her Teeth" addresses this choice obliquely. It opens:

> I was far forward on the plain, the burning swamp,
> When the child called. And she was far behind.
> She was not my child, my charge. By chance I heard.

Eventually the speaker comes to the conclusion that "Any cry is the concern of all; we are all in a swamp. . . ." Of saintly pity, she notes, "The windows of pity shine, holy and vapid. / We need an essential plinth in the gap of that pity," suggesting that pity alone is an inadequate response to the call of those in need.

Escaping from the expectations of family and convention, in 1914 Taggard began study at the University of California at Berkeley. There she became involved with writing and, as a senior, assumed the role of editor of the campus literary magazine, *The Occident*. This work would launch her long association with literary and political magazines, as well as her career as a writer and poet. Shortly before graduating from Berkeley, Taggard published her first poem in a nationally distributed magazine: "An Hour on the Hill" appeared in *Harper's* in 1920.

After graduation Taggard's ambition as a writer and critic carried her to New York City, where she became involved in radical periodicals of the day, such as *The Masses*, *The Freeman*, and *The Liberator*. She soon joined forces with Maxwell Anderson to found *The Measure: A Journal of Poetry*, a "little magazine" that would publish monthly until 1926.

This hardly marked the end of Taggard's productivity as a poet. Following the release of *For Eager Lovers* in 1922, she published a series of collections of poetry, including the strident *Calling Western Union* (1936) and *Collected Poems, 1918–1938* (1938). The most praised volumes in this body of work are perhaps *Words for the Chisel* (1926), *Traveling Standing Still* (1928), and the poet's own professed favorite, *Slow Music* (1946). Reviewers such as Edmund Wilson, Allen Tate, and Katherine Anne Porter noted in particular the acuity of Taggard's visual images. Taggard herself admired a wide range of writers, from the contributors to a radically engaged press (Max Eastman, John Reed, Floyd Dell) to the socially minded writings of Upton Sinclair and John Dos Passos. As a poet, however, she perhaps owed most to the language of her friend and colleague Wallace Stevens.

Not content just to continue the work of her antecedents and contemporaries, however, Taggard set about extending the line of poetic influence. By the second decade of her career as a published poet, she began teaching in some of the most prestigious women's institutions in the East: Mount Holyoke College (1929–31), Bennington College (1932–35), and Sarah Lawrence College (1935–46). Through her efforts in and beyond the classroom Taggard reached out to the next generation of women's voices for social change. Much of her work remains out of print, but her complete writings are available in microform for those who wish a comprehensive look at her literary career. Her words also survive as lyrics set to music by such composers as William Schuman and Aaron Copland.

While not all of Taggard's verse addresses itself to politics, her bold advocacy of change serves as the signature of her poetry. She tackled the full range of her personal experience and dedicated her life and profession to battling social injustice. As a poet, critic, editor, biographer, and teacher, she did indeed "take hold on a vital substance," in terms of articulating the human cost of complacency, raising awareness of political issues, and calling for the eradication of social problems such as hunger, inequality, and exploitation.

LINDA S. WATTS

**Biography**

Born in Waitsburg, Washington, 28 November 1894. Attended Oahu College, Honolulu, Hawaii; University of California, Berkeley, A.B. 1920; co-founder and editor of *The Measure,* 1920–26; Instructor, Mount Holyoke College, South Hadley, Massachusetts, 1929–31; Professor, Bennington College, Bennington, Vermont, 1932–35; Professor, Sarah Lawrence College, Bronxville, New York, 1935–46. Received Guggenheim Memorial Foundation fellowship, 1931–32. Died in New York City, 8 November 1948.

**Poetry**

*For Eager Lovers,* 1922
*Words for the Chisel,* 1926
*Traveling Standing Still: Poems, 1918–1928,* 1928
*Not Mine to Finish: Poems, 1928–1934,* 1934
*Calling Western Union,* 1936
*Collected Poems, 1918–1938,* 1938
*Slow Music,* 1946
*Origin: Hawaii,* 1947

**Other Writings:** biography (*The Life and Mind of Emily Dickinson,* 1930), lyrics (*Prologue,* by William Schuman); edited anthology of poetry (*Continent's End* [co-editor with George Sterling and James Rorty], 1925).

**Further Reading**


Aaron, Daniel, *Writers on the Left: Episodes in Literary Communism,* New York: Harcourt Brace and World, 1961; Oxford: Oxford University Press, 1977

Blain, Virginia, Patricia Clements, and Isobel Grundy, *The Feminist Companion to Literature in English: Women Writers from the Middle Ages to the Present,* New Haven, Connecticut: Yale University Press, and London: Batsford, 1990

McCann Janet, "Genevieve Taggard," in *Dictionary of Literary Biography,* volume 45: *American Poets, 1880–1945, First Series,* edited by Peter Quartermain, Detroit, Michigan: Gale Research, 1986

Mille, Nina, "The Bonds of Free Love: Constructing the Female Bohemian Self," *Genders* 11 (Fall 1991)

Showalter, Elaine, "Women Writers Between the Wars," in *Columbia Literary History of the United States,* edited by Emory Elliott, New York: Columbia University Press, 1988

Wilson, Edmund, "A Poet of the Pacific," in *The Shores of Light: A Literary Chronicle of the Twenties and Thirties,* by Wilson, New York: Farrar Straus and Young, and London: Allen, 1952

Wilson, Martha A., and Gwendolyn Sell, "Lola Ridge and Genevieve Taggard: Voices of Resistance," *The Arkansas Quarterly: A Journal of Criticism* 2, no. 2 (Spring 1993)


---

# John Taggart 1942–

John Taggart is one of the most important figures of the third generation of 20th-century American experimental poets. His work, which builds on the achievements of the High Modernists (Pound, Eliot, and Stevens) but is more directly influenced by poets born in the first decade of the century (Louis Zukofsky and Charles Olson), has avoided both the chattiness of the poetry workshop and the hypertheoretical technicalization of the art advocated by the Language poets. Instead, Taggart has single-mindedly pursued a poetics of both musicality and vision, exploring aspects of the spiritual that have almost disappeared from contemporary experimental verse.

The poems in Taggart's earliest collection, *To Construct a Clock* (1971), are terse, specific, and taut, clearly indebted to Zukofsky's shorter poems and statements of poetics. Zukofsky's influence is most apparent in the poem "Liveforever: Of Actual Things in Expansion," which draws on Zukofsky's repeated image of "liveforever," a plant of the *Sedum* genus, and is preceded by a lengthy Zukofsky epigraph. Taggart's interest in the visual arts is also evident in poems based on works by Miro, Corot, and Edward Weston, and Taggart's long-standing investment in jazz results in "The Drum Thing," a poem inspired by a performance on John Coltrane's *Crescent* album.

*The Pyramid Is a Pure Crystal* (1974) and *Dodeka* (1979) were each produced by complex procedural compositional methods. (Taggart's volume *Prism and the Pine Twig* [1977] is subtitled "An Interlude" and indeed seems a return to the relatively straightforward presentational style of *To Construct a Clock.*) *The Pyramid Is a Pure Crystal,* which is dedicated to Zukofsky, is a large-scale canon (in the musical sense), taking as its foundation, or "cantus firmus," the single sentence "the pyramid is a pure crystal." The long poem *Dodeka* is based on an array of Pythagorean lore, central among it the geometric figure of the dodecahedron, held by the early Greeks to represent the earth. Although Taggart's compositional devices resemble those of such procedural poets as John Cage or Jackson Mac Low, he is invested more in the poem than in the procedure: while his generative scheme is important to him, he does not hesitate to alter the resulting poems if he is not pleased with them. *Dodeka* can be seen as marking the end of Taggart's midperiod poetics, but the poem's concern with music, color, and in particular the image of the laceration of the face followed by the *sparagmos*—the ritual spilling of seed ("Face cut: seeds spill")—reappears throughout his later work. In a retrospective introduction to *Prompted* (1991), a collection of his "jazz" poems, Taggart writes of the "voice"—in particular the voice of the jazz saxophone—that "eats the face away," and this terrifying image recurs again and again in his writings as a figure for the rapt attention of the listener (or viewer) who finds his own identity being eroded in the presence of the numinous.

*Peace on Earth* (1981) marks Taggart's emergence into his fully developed mature style, a mode that openly acknowledges its reliance on the models of jazz. Taggart telegraphs this connection in such titles as "Giant Steps," which is taken directly from a Coltrane tune. This is a poetry that relies overwhelmingly on repetition. Each of the four poems of *Peace on Earth* is composed not in the unit of the stanza but in the unit of the page. There is considerable repetition from line to line, and each succeeding page is nearly identical to the one before it; changes are incremental, but by the end of, say, "Peace on Earth," the final page is considerably altered from the first. The poetics of *Peace on Earth* and Taggart's succeeding works—*Dehiscence* (1983), *Loop* (1991), *Standing Wave* (1993), and *When the Saints* (1999)—are founded on both the Zukofskyan notion of the poem as melody, as musical composition, and Olson's Projectivist emphasis on the poet's voice as active performer of the poem. These are poems explicitly designed for reading aloud, poems in which "if not enacted by the voice, the cadence makes no sense; its shifting motion only confuses and irritates the eye." Such a shifting, incremental cadence owes much to the models not only of jazz and rhythm and blues but of the "minimalist" music of Terry Riley, Steve Reich, and Philip Glass.

The poems of *Peace on Earth* work on a principle of repetition from page to page. In more recent poems, Taggart has developed his poetic so that it works on a remarkably subtle and compelling compositional principle, generating poems as brief as eight lines or as long as dozen of pages and holding even the silent reader's attention. Each of his successive collections—*Loop* perhaps most impressive of them, if only because it is the longest—has shown Taggart more and more comfortable with his style, able to adapt it to a wider range of subjects and emotions: the musics of Coltrane, Thelonious Monk, Jerry Lee Lewis, Olivier Messiaen; the painting of Mark Rothko and Francis Bacon; the writings of Melville, Traherne, and Thomas Bernhard; and much else. His most recent volume, *When the Saints,* is a moving tribute to his late friend and collaborator, the sculptor Bradford Graves.

Taggart is also a fine and original critic. His *Remaining in Light: Ant Meditations on a Painting by Edward Hopper* (1993) begins as an examination of a single Hopper canvas and expands into a meditation on the nature of reading or writing itself, of opening oneself to an outside that includes both "spirit" and the other. In 1994, the University of Alabama Press published *Songs of Degrees,* Taggart's collected essays and reviews, making available most of his critical writings and bestowing on them an academic imprimatur. Taggart's poetry is widely respected among poets and critics, and while that work has yet to prove itself a central influence on younger writers, it has solidly established itself as a body of achievement utterly unlike any of its contemporaries. Taggart has pursued a rigorously individual path in developing his poetics, and in consequence he has received little recognition from either the mainstream establishment of American poetry or the establishment of the avant-garde. However, through that individual vision, he has achieved a poetry of remarkable presence and power, a poetry that gives the lie to any conception of the experimental as arid, vapid, or ultimately without spirit.

MARK SCROGGINS

**Biography**

Born in Perry, Iowa, 5 October 1942. Attended Earlham College, Richmond, Indiana, B.A. 1965; University of Chicago, Illinois, M.A. 1966; Syracuse University, Syracuse, New York, Ph.D. 1974; founder and editor, *MAPS* (literary magazine), 1966–74; since 1969 Assistant Professor, Shippensburg State College. Received Ford Foundation fellowship, 1965; National Endowment for the Arts grant, 1976. Living in Shippensburg, Pennsylvania.

**Poetry**

*To Construct a Clock,* 1971
*The Pyramid Is a Pure Crystal,* 1974
*Prism and the Pine Twig: An Interlude,* 1977
*Dodeka,* 1979
*Peace on Earth,* 1981
*Dehiscence,* 1983
*Loop,* 1991
*Prompted,* 1991
*Standing Wave,* 1993
*When the Saints,* 1999
*Crosses,* 2001

**Selected Criticism**

*Remaining in Light: Ant Meditations on a Painting by Edward Hopper,* 1993
*Songs of Degrees: Essays on Contemporary Poetry and Poetics,* 1994

**Further Reading**


Daly, Lew, *Swallowing the Scroll: Late in a Prophetic Tradition with the Poetry of Susan Howe and John Taggart,* Buffalo, New York: M Press, 1994

Howe, Susan, "Light in Darkness: John Taggart's Poetry," *Hambone* 2 (Spring 1982) Metcalf, Paul, Craig Watson, and Bruce Andrews, "Dodeka: 3 Views," *Paper Air* 4 (Spring 1978)

Miller, David, "The Poetry of John Taggart," *Paper Air* 4 (Spring 1978)

Olson, Toby, "Spirit Image, Kerry Clouds, Peace on Earth: A Few Old Memories and New Thoughts about John Taggart," *Paper Air* 4 (Spring 1978)

Ratner, Rochelle, "The Poet as Composer: An Inquiry into the Work of John Taggart," *Paper Air* 4 (Spring 1978)
Watson, Craig, "The Poetics of Community," *Northwest Review* 29 (1981)
Weinberger, Eliot, "Peace on Earth," in *Works on Paper, 1980–1986,* by Weinberger, New York: New Directions, 1986
Young, Karl, "Towards 'Peace on Earth,'" *Paper Air* 4 (Spring 1978)

---

# Allen Tate 1899–1979

In 1950, Allen Tate wrote of his poetry that "its main theme is man suffering from unbelief." His abiding concerns were the search for religious faith and the defense of a high culture that he associated with the agricultural South. His first collection, *Mr. Pope, and Other Poems* (1928), dealt with these themes (particularly in his best-known poem, "Ode to the Confederate Dead") and established the style that he would keep with minor variations throughout his career. His *Selected Poems* (1937) included the poems that he wished to preserve up to that date. The religious imagery (derived chiefly from Dante) that dominates *The Winter Sea* (1944) anticipates his conversion to Catholicism in 1950. He subsequently wrote little poetry. His *Poems* (1960) includes two of the three terza rima poems, written in 1952–53, that form his last considerable poetic achievement. *The Swimmers* (1971) and *Collected Poems* (1977) added the third terza rima poem and some poems from the early 1920s.

Tate's dense and allusive poetic style was derived from French Symbolist poetry. John Crowe Ransom recalled that Tate as an undergraduate at Vanderbilt College knew more about Charles Baudelaire and Stéphane Mallarmé than did his instructors. His two translations from Baudelaire suggest what he took from the Symbolists for his own poetry and also what he brought to his reading of their works. The sonnet "Correspondences" is a key early Symbolist text in which Baudelaire sees Man forever wandering through "des forets de symboles." This journey is intoxicating and frightening. Tate's poems occupy a similar symbolic landscape, but his narrators feel fear rather than intoxication. In "The Cross," the protagonist's inability to see the whole of his surroundings, revealed in the first lines, is directly related to his inability to understand the Christian symbols (a "blinding rood" and "world-destroying pit") that confront him:

> There is a place that some men know,
> I cannot see the whole of it
> Nor how I came there.

The speaker's horror intensifies as he realizes that modern life excludes any hope of salvation; it is merely a preparation for Hell during which man gradually becomes "a fiend" under the tutelage of "the fiery dead."

The same concern with mortality and horror dominates Tate's translation of Baudelaire's "Une Charogne" (A Carrion). The narrator and his mistress encounter an animal's carcass. He compares the splayed-out body to a beautiful woman seductively reclining and declares, "The flies swarmed on the putrid vulva." With its suggested revulsion toward female sexuality, this is the poem's most disturbing image, but it is not in Baudelaire. The original has flies on "ce ventre putride" (literally, "that putrid stomach"); the explicit sexual content is Tate's own. This quality of horror permeates Tate's poetry and is associated with a feeling of spiritual abandonment. In "Last Days of Alice," Lewis Carroll's Alice has lost touch with tangible reality; she has been "Turned absent-minded by infinity" and now exists in a universe of abstractions. She symbolizes the loss of religious faith in an age of excessive rationality. Modern man has fallen away from God; this is worse than damnation because it excludes him from the Christian universe. The last stanza is a prayer to God to damn us if He must rather than abandon us to a purposeless existence:

> O God of our flesh, return us to Your wrath,
> Let us be evil could we enter in
> Your grace, and falter on the stony path!

Tate's spiritual landscape is populated with sinister creatures that give his work a Gothic quality. Wolves, spiders, and predatory birds are plentiful, but the snake with its rich symbolism dominates his poetry. "Ode to the Confederate Dead" ends with a serpent symbolizing time. In "Mr. Pope," Alexander Pope "dribbles couplets like a snake / Coiled to a lithe precision"; his satires are as unerring in their technique and as deadly in their effect as a striking snake. In a letter to Donald Davidson (25 July 1925), Tate describes his poetic method as the attempt to "articulate the movement of thought, as if it were some vast snake which we must put together synthetically before we can look at the marvellous beauty and rhythm of the whole." Whenever this snake is particularized, it is as a lethal copperhead, a species that has strong associations with the South.

The South was essential to Tate's identity as a poet and a critic. In "Emblems," he describes it as his inheritance (his maternal ancestors had been plantation owners and slaveholders until the Civil War); it almost literally runs in his blood:

> Maryland, Virginia, Caroline
> Pent images in sleep
> Clay valleys rocky hills old fields of pine
> Unspeakable and deep
>
> Out of that source of time my farthest blood
> Runs strangely to this day

However, the South stood for a complex set of values that Tate both fiercely upheld and sometimes condemned. In the 1920s, the

Civil War and the period of Reconstruction were still in living memory and the source of much bitterness. It was an impoverished land in comparison to the North; in an essay on William Faulkner, Tate called it "Uncle Sam's Other Province." For many politicians, salvation lay in industrialization, which would create a prosperous New South. Tate, with his colleagues in the Fugitive and Agrarian movements, abhorred this idea. He argued in essays such as "The Man of Letters in the Modern World" that industrialization severed people from their regional identities and their traditional beliefs; it had a brutalizing effect:

> It is a tragedy of contemporary society that so much of democratic social theory reaches us in the language of "drive," "stimulus," and "response." This is not the language of freemen, it is the language of slaves.

His reference to slaves is provocative: the southern states were notorious for racism, and Tate's advocacy of an agrarian South could carry him too far. In his first book, *Stonewall Jackson* (1928), he argued that slavery had been partially defensible as a "form of benevolent protection": "The Black man, 'free,' would have been exploited." However, his subsequent work includes several condemnations of slavery and racial bigotry. In his novel *The Fathers* (1938), a knightly tournament, representing the antebellum South's flattering vision of itself as a chivalrous society, takes place simultaneously with the sexual exploitation of a mulatto girl by a white youth. Tate's late poem "The Swimmers" evokes his childhood memory of a lynching. The poem begins with an evocation of the innocence of a child's sight, but his boyhood self immediately sees an act of predatory evil:

> And give me back the eye that looked and fled
> When a thrush idling in the tulip tree
> Unwound the cold dream of the copperhead.

The snake's pursuit of the thrush anticipates the lynching party's pursuit of their victim. At the poem's conclusion, the black man's corpse is dragged back to town, where it becomes the embodiment of an unconfessed collective guilt:

> My breath crackled the dead air like a shotgun
> As, sheriff and the stranger disappearing,
> The faceless head lay still. I could not run
>
> Or walk, but stood. Alone in the public clearing
> This private thing was owned by all the town,
> Though never claimed by us within my hearing.

Despite this legacy of racial prejudice, the South gave Tate a code of conduct that informs his poetry. This code emphasized restraint and dignity as a way of holding the existential horrors of modern civilization at bay. He states in *The Fathers,* "You came to believe in honor and dignity for their own sake since all proper men knew what honor was and could recognize dignity; but nobody knew what human nature was or could presume to mete out justice to others." This concern with "honor and dignity" characterizes Tate's heroes, such as Aeneas in "Aeneas at Washington":

> In that extremity I bore me well,
> A true gentleman, valorous in arms,
> Disinterested and honourable. Then fled:
> That was a time when civilization
> Run by the few fell to the many, and
> Crashed to the shout of men, the clang of arms:

Aeneas is simultaneously a survivor of the fall of Troy and a southern veteran of the Civil War. He is an example of how Tate repeatedly fuses regional themes with international cultural concerns.

Tate's flaws as a poet reflect his virtues. His obsession with difficult metrical forms led to the achievement of "The Swimmers" written in terza rima, but it also results in the failure of "The Seasons of the Soul" and its companion piece "Winter Mask to the Memory of W.B. Yeats." Despite some fine passages, these works are sabotaged by Tate's employment of iambic trimeters arranged in ten-line stanzas with a fixed rhyme scheme and a refrain. The poet is not equal to these formal demands: some stanzas are padded with superfluous details, whereas others are overly terse. His use of rhyme is occasionally forced. "Winter Mask," for instance, includes the trite remark that cannibalism is "not nice" because Tate needs a rhyme for "ice."

Tate's role as a regional traditionalist sometimes degenerates into reactionary provincial grumbling. "Causerie" is one of his less successful meditations on an era that regards sex as a substitute for religion:

> In an age of abstract experience, fornication
> Is self-expression, adjunct to Christian euphoria,
> And whores become delinquents; delinquents, patients;
> Patients, wards of society. Whores, by that rule,
> Are precious.

Tate's "whores" have no existence except as a reference to Elizabethan and Jacobean tragedy (the dramatist Thomas Kyd is mentioned immediately after this extract). He cannot "see" them (how old are they? how do they dress? how much do they earn?); they are a literary convention. He can claim that prostitutes should be denounced rather than helped to leave their profession because he is so concerned with the Jacobean texture of his language that he neglects what he is saying. At his worst, Tate does not assimilate his literary influences; he is controlled by them.

Tate's reputation has declined since his death. Memoirs and academic studies occasionally appear, but his work has not spawned an academic industry comparable to that surrounding T.S. Eliot, the poet who had the greatest contemporary influence on his work. Although poetry anthologies provide only an impressionistic idea of a poet's standing, it is noteworthy that F.O. Mathiessen included nine of Tate's poems (21 pages) in his *Oxford Book of American Verse* (1950), whereas the *Penguin Book of American Poetry* (1977) includes only "Ode to the Confederate Dead" and the fifth edition of the *Norton Anthology of American Literature: Volume 2* (1998) excludes his work. He is better known because of his substantial influence on Robert Lowell and (as a critic) on Randall Jarrell than through his own writings.

In *Lives of the Poets* (1998), Michael Schmidt argues that Tate is a "poet's poet" and will never be widely appreciated. This is unfortunate. Tate's finest work resembles that of Matthew Arnold. As essayists, both writers attacked contemporary materialism with audacity and elegance. If Arnold brought the discussion of the Romantic poets to a new level of critical intelligence, Tate did the same as a prominent New Critic for Edgar Allan Poe, Emily Dickinson, and Hart Crane. As poets, Arnold and Tate longed to believe in Christianity but wrote their best poems from a standpoint of religious doubt. Tate's "Shadow and Shade" poignantly shares Arnold's recognition that even the most passionate sexual relationship cannot compensate for the absence of God:

> We lay long in the immense tide
> Of shade and shadowy desire
>
> And saw the dusk assail the wall,
> The black surge, mounting crush the stone!
> Companion of this lust, we fall,
> I said, lest we should die alone.

Although Tate is not a major poet, he wrote two or three poems that stand with the best of 20th-century American poetry as well as several perfectly realized minor works. He may be remembered as a "poet's poet," but his work is distinguished by a passionate concern with craftsmanship united with a deeply personal religious vision.

SEAN ELLIOTT

*See also* Fugitives and Agrarians; New Criticism; Symbolism

**Biography**

Born in Winchester, Kentucky, 19 November 1899. Attended Vanderbilt University, Nashville, Tennessee, 1918–22, B.A. 1923; member of the Fugitive group of poets; co-founder, *The Fugitive,* Nashville, 1922–25; high school teacher, Lumberport, West Virginia, 1924; assistant to the editor, *Telling Tales* magazine, 1925; Lecturer in English, Southwestern College, Memphis, Tennessee, 1934–36; Professor of English, The Woman's College, Greensboro, North Carolina, 1938–39; poet-in-residence, Princeton University, New Jersey, 1939–42; consultant in poetry, Library of Congress, Washington, D.C., 1943–44; editor, *Sewanee Review,* 1944–46; editor, Belles Lettres series, Henry Holt, publishers, 1946–48; Lecturer in humanities, New York University, 1948–51; Professor of English, from 1951, Regents' Professor, 1966, Professor Emeritus, 1968, University of Minnesota, Minneapolis; Visiting Professor in the Humanities, University of Chicago, 1949; Fulbright Lecturer, Oxford University, 1953, University of Rome, 1953–54, and Oxford and Leeds universities, 1958–59; Department of State Lecturer at universities of Liège and Louvain, 1954, Delhi and Bombay, 1956, the Sorbonne, Paris, 1956, Nottingham, 1956, and Urbino and Florence, 1961; Visiting Professor of English, University of North Carolina, Greensboro, 1966, and Vanderbilt University, 1967; Fellow, 1948, and Senior Fellow, 1956, Kenyon School of English, Kenyon College, Gambier, Ohio (now Indiana University School of Letters, Bloomington); member, Phi Beta Kappa Senate, 1951–53. Received Guggenheim fellowship, 1928, 1929; American Academy grant, 1948; Bollingen Prize, 1957; Brandeis University Creative Arts Award, 1960; Dante Society Gold Medal (Florence), 1962; Academy of American Poets fellowship, 1963; National Medal for Literature, 1976; received honorary degrees from six colleges and universities; member, American Academy, 1964; Chancellor, Academy of American Poets, 1964; member, American Academy of Arts and Sciences, 1965; President, National Institute of Arts and Letters, 1968. Died in Nashville, Tennessee, 9 February 1979.

**Poetry**

*Mr. Pope, and Other Poems,* 1928
*Three Poems,* 1930
*Poems, 1928–1931,* 1932
*The Mediterranean, and Other Poems,* 1936
*Selected Poems,* 1937
*The Winter Sea: A Book of Poems,* 1944
*Poems, 1920–1945: A Selection,* 1947
*Poems, 1922–1947,* 1948
*Two Conceits for the Eye to Sing, If Possible,* 1950
*Poems,* 1960
*The Swimmers, and Other Selected Poems,* 1971
*Collected Poems, 1919–1976,* 1977

**Selected Criticism**

*On the Limits of Poetry: Selected Essays, 1928–1948,* 1948
*The Poetry Reviews of Tate, 1924–1944,* edited by Ashley Brown and Frances Neel Cheney, 1983

**Other Writings:** play, novel (*The Fathers,* 1938), short stories, biography (*Jefferson Davis: His Rise and Fall: A Biographical Narrative,* 1929), nonfiction (*I'll Take My Stand: The South and the Agrarian Tradition* [with others], 1930), essays (*Essays of Four Decades,* 1969), translation of Latin literature (*The Vigil of Venus/Pervigilium Veneris,* 1943); edited collections of literature (*The Complete Poems and Selected Criticism of Edgar Allan Poe,* 1968).

**Further Reading**

Davidson, Donald, *The Literary Correspondence of Donald Davidson and Allen Tate,* edited by John Tyree Fain and Thomas Daniel Young, Athens: University of Georgia Press, 1974
Doreski, William, *The Years of Our Friendship: Robert Lowell and Allen Tate,* Jackson: University Press of Mississippi, 1990
Dupree, Robert S., *Allen Tate and the Augustinian Imagination,* Baton Rouge: Louisiana State University Press, 1983
Hammer, Langdon, *Hart Crane and Allen Tate: Janus-Faced Modernism,* Princeton, New Jersey: Princeton University Press, 1993
Meiners, Roger K., *The Last Alternatives: A Study of the Works of Allen Tate,* Denver, Colorado: Swallow, 1963
Rubin, Louis D., Jr., *The Wary Fugitives: Four Poets and the South,* Baton Rouge: Louisiana State University Press, 1978
Schmidt, Michael, "The Troubles of a Book," in *Lives of the Poets,* by Schmidt, London: Weidenfeld and Nicolson, 1998; New York: Knopf, 1999
Squires, Radcliffe, *Allen Tate: A Literary Biography,* New York: Pegasus, 1971
Squires, Radcliffe, editor, *Allen Tate and His Work: Critical Evaluations,* Minneapolis: University of Minnesota Press, and London: Oxford University Press, 1972

## Ode to the Confederate Dead

Allen Tate's "Ode to the Confederate Dead" was first published in *Fugitives: An Anthology of Verse* (January 1928) and later that year in Tate's first collection, *Mr. Pope, and Other Poems*. Its appearance with the work of Tate's fellow Tennessee-based poets emphasizes its position as a key text of the Southern Renaissance. Inspired by T.S. Eliot's "The Waste Land" (1922), it is a High Modernist treatment of man's deteriorating relationship with his own history and culture and rapidly became Tate's most influential poem. It has strong thematic affinities with Paul Valéry's *Le Cimetière marin* (1920; *The Graveyard by the Sea*) and influenced Robert Lowell's "For the Union Dead." After extensive revision (including the addition of the refrain about falling leaves that acts as a continuing reminder of human mortality) its final version appeared in Tate's *Selected Poems* (1937). In 1938 Tate wrote "Narcissus as Narcissus," an essay that defines in detail the predicament of the poem's narrator:

> That poem is "about" solipsism, a philosophical doctrine which says that we create the world in the act of perceiving it; or about Narcissism, or any other *ism* that denotes the failure of the human personality to function objectively in nature and society.

"Ode to the Confederate Dead" is about failure. Its speaker fails to understand the ideals of the Confederates and fails to create an authentic ode (a poem with a public theme). Even his vocabulary fails him; the adjectives in such phrases as "immitigable pines," "inscrutable infantry," and "improbable mist" obscure the meanings of his nouns. Tate himself called the "Ode" a "baroque poem." Its deliberate stylistic artificiality is embodied in the narrator's histrionic use of imperatives:

> Turn your eyes to the immoderate past,
> Turn to the inscrutable infantry rising
> Demons out of the earth—

Trapped in a world of decay, between the eroding tombstones at the poem's beginning and the "decomposing wall" at its end, the speaker (rather than the "past") becomes "immoderate" in despair. His lament is not for the dead Confederates but rather for his own spiritual bankruptcy. As the Fugitive poet Donald Davidson wrote in a letter to Tate (15 February 1927) about an early draft of the poem, "Your *elegy* is not for the Confederate Dead, but for your own dead emotion, or mine" (Davidson, 1974).

The opening passage employs a series of words with religious connotations ("sacrament," "eternity," "heaven," "election," "mortality") that are intentionally trivialized: "heaven," for instance, is only a stormy sky. These suppressed spiritual interpretations suggest the idealism that inspired the Confederates, but the speaker cannot recognize these ideals, relying instead on his memory. Although memory distinguishes him as human—the wind is "without recollection" and the numerous carnivorous animals in the "Ode" live by instinct—the speaker finds "the twilight certainty of an animal" tempting. He evasively uses the second person to compare himself to a "blind crab," recalling T.S. Eliot's "The Love Song of J. Alfred Prufrock" in which Prufrock wishes to become "a pair of ragged claws / Scuttling across the floors of silent seas." Tate's speaker is transfixed by "The brute curiosity of an angel's stare." The substitution of "brute" for the conventional "brutal" suggests his position: he is neither animal nor angel.

The speaker repeatedly tries to understand the dead Confederates. He attempts a formal elegy—

> these memories grow
> From the inexhaustible bodies that are not
> Dead, but feed the grass row after rich row

—but these lines parody the conventional heroic ode. Wishing to claim that the Confederates survive as an inspiration to future deeds of heroism, he merely suggests their biological continuance as fertilizer for grass. The awkward enjambment, spilling "Dead" into the next line, conveys his disillusionment with this approach even as he uses it. He remembers Parmenides and Zeno, pre-Socratic philosophers who explored the gap between absolute truth (arrived at through logic) and the plausible illusions provided by the senses. By their standards he lacks a logical structure for his meditation and is condemned to a world of subjective illusion. He makes a final effort, evoking the soldiers' contempt, sustained by their ethical "vision," for "the unimportant shrift of death." He cannot share this vision, however; as the cemetery is bounded by a literal wall, so is the speaker metaphorically walled in by his "modern" temperament. He is reduced to mechanically listing Civil War battles without understanding their historical or cultural meaning.

The final part of the poem is concerned with the nature of knowledge. The juxtaposition of the "serpent" and "knowledge" suggests that the falling leaves of the refrain are more than symbols of mortality. As the leaves of the tree of knowledge they are a reminder of the original sin which ensures that humankind remains more than brutes but less than angels. In the modern industrial era, the poem suggests, humanity possesses more information than ever before but less knowledge, having lost the "knowledge / Carried to the heart" implicit in the Christian ideal of self-sacrifice that inspired the dead Confederates.

Ultimately the protagonist's only knowledge is of his own mortality. He foresees no afterlife except the biological return of "the salt" in his blood to "the saltier oblivion of the sea." In "Narcissus" Tate claims that the Confederates represent "not merely moral heroism but heroism in the grand style, elevating even death from mere physical dissolution into a formal ritual." But, like George Posey in Tate's novel *The Fathers* (1938), who becomes hysterical at a funeral, the man at the cemetery cannot regard death as part of a traditional and ritualistic pattern of life. Instead the "ravenous grave" threatens to devour his sanity (the cemetery is "the insane green"). The "Ode," like John Milton's "Lycidas," concludes with the anticipated departure of the speaker. While Milton's swain leaves with a renewed sense of poetic and political purpose, however, Tate's hero flees from insanity and his "inscrutable" ancestors.

SEAN ELLIOTT

**Further Reading**

Davidson, Donald, *The Literary Correspondence of Donald Davidson and Allen Tate*, edited by John Tyree Fain and Thomas Daniel Young, Athens: University of Georgia Press, 1974

Dupree, Robert S., *Allen Tate and the Augustinian Imagination,* Baton Rouge: Louisiana State University Press, 1983

Fry, Paul H., "Introduction: The Man at the Gate," in *The Poet's Calling in the English Ode,* by Fry, New Haven, Connecticut: Yale University Press, 1980

Hammer, Langdon, *Hart Crane and Allen Tate: Janus-Faced Modernism,* Princeton, New Jersey: Princeton University Press, 1993

Helmick, E.T., "The Civil War Odes of Lowell and Tate," *Georgia Review* 25 (1971)

Humphries, Jefferson, "The Cemeteries of Allen Tate and Paul Valéry: The Ghosts of Aeneas and Narcissus," *The Southern Review* 20, no. 1 (1984)

Rubin, Louis D., Jr., *The Wary Fugitives: Four Poets and the South,* Baton Rouge: Louisiana State University Press, 1978

Squires, Radcliffe, *Allen Tate: A Literary Biography,* New York: Pegasus, 1971

---

# James Tate 1943–

James Tate first received critical attention when at 23 he became the youngest recipient of the Yale Younger Poets Prize. The winning collection of verse, *The Lost Pilot* (1967), was highly acclaimed and has remained one of Tate's most noted works. Tate's early style showed much promise, employing powerful surreal imagery tempered with a restraint usually exhibited by more mature writers. The title poem is perhaps the collection's best; "The Lost Pilot" refers to Tate's father, who was missing in action and presumed shot down while flying a bomber mission over Germany in 1943. The poem laments the disconnection between the two, as the father orbits the earth in his craft, cut off from the son he will never know. Through the son's desire for history, however, a connection with the father is established, one that allows for the void in between them:

My head cocked toward the sky,
I cannot get off the ground,
and, you, passing over again,

fast, perfect, and unwilling
to tell me that you are doing
well, or that it was mistake

that placed you in that world,
and me in this; or that misfortune
placed these worlds in us.

Tate returned to the theme of the absent father on several other occasions, in more sophisticated poems. Perhaps because of its biographical relevancy and the fact that it was written at such a young age, however, "The Lost Pilot" has remained one of Tate's most noted poems.

After *The Lost Pilot* Tate published several chapbooks. Many of these poems were then published in *The Oblivion Ha-Ha* (1970), Tate's second full-length collection. Critics largely panned this volume, finding Tate's surreal imagery a little too bizarre. Unlike *The Lost Pilot,* in which Tate had worked to control his metaphors, *The Oblivion Ha-Ha* represented an attempt to break free from easily identifiable associations. Although Tate was beginning to develop a new style and voice, employing increasingly complicated forms of language, he was slipping into sillier strains of Surrealism that most critics considered esoteric. These critics overlooked, however, that Tate's wild experimentation did not extend to all of his poetry; many of his poems still exhibited the restraint for which he had previously been praised. Poems such as "The Blue Booby," "Prose Poem," and "The Wheelchair Butterfly" spring from a vein similar to those found in *The Lost Pilot.*

In his next two collections—*Hints to Pilgrims* (1971) and *Absences* (1972)—Tate continued to experiment with form and content, although he was increasingly able to control his often bizarre imagery. His metaphors were no longer quite so convoluted, establishing a simplicity and clarity similar to that displayed in *The Lost Pilot,* although some still found his occasional use of free association to be "inscrutable." *Absences* in particular represented a new direction for Tate, a cultivation of cynicism rooted in the identification of the individual's isolation. Tate partially undermines this pessimism, however, through his widespread use of humor, such as in the poem "Teaching the Ape to Write Poems":

They didn't have much trouble
teaching the ape to write poems:
first they strapped him into the chair,
then tied the pencil around his hand
(the paper had already been nailed down).
Then Dr. Bluespire leaned over his shoulder
and whispered into his ear:
"You look like a god sitting there.
Why don't you try writing something?"

Tate's next two collections of verse—*Viper Jazz* (1976) and *Riven Doggeries* (1979)—continued to explore the isolation of the individual. Panning these works as "dispassionate" and "unattractively negative" despite their humor, most critics pronounced Tate's new style overbearing.

During the 1980s and 1990s, however, Tate slowly but surely won over many of his detractors, with poems once again exhibiting the intense passion of his earlier work. *Constant Defender* (1983) turns the critical eye on poetry, focusing on the individual's power to operate within the medium. *Reckoner* (1986) represented a turn away from just the individual, focusing more on societal problems, while *Distance from Loved Ones* (1990) focuses primarily on relationships. In 1992 Tate was awarded the Pulitzer Prize for *Selected Poems,* a compilation of previously published poetry. In two later collections Tate reached the zenith of his ability as a poet. *The Worshipful Company of Fletchers* (1994), perhaps Tate's most critically acclaimed work, represents the culmination of his ability to construct a verse built on power and clarity. In "Never Again the Same" Tate enjoys the terrible beauty of a sunset:

> peaches dripping opium,
> pandemonium of tangerines,
> inferno of irises,
> plutonian emeralds,
> and the wonder of discovery:
> And then the streetlights come on as always
> and we looked into one another's eyes—
> ancient caves with still pools
> and those little transparent fish
> who have never seen even one ray of light.
> And the calm that returned to us
> was not even our own.

Tate's 1997 collection, *Shroud of the Gnome*, weaves together the serious and the humorous, effortlessly examining complicated themes in simple ways. The surreal imagery in *Shroud of the Gnome*—on occasion reminiscent of Lewis Carroll—does not harm the clarity of Tate's verse.

Andrew Howe

**Biography**
Born in Kansas City, Missouri, 8 December 1943. Attended the University of Missouri, Kansas City, 1963–64; Kansas State College, Pittsburg, B.A. 1965; University of Iowa, Iowa City, M.F.A. 1967; Visiting Lecturer, University of Iowa, 1965–67, and University of California, Berkeley, 1967–68; Assistant Professor, Columbia University, New York, 1969–71, and Emerson College, Boston, 1970–71; since 1971 member of the English Department, University of Massachusetts, Amherst; since 1967 poetry editor, *Dickinson Review*, North Dakota; currently associate editor, Pym Randall Press, Cambridge, Massachusetts, and Barn Dream Press; consultant, Coordinating Council of Literary Magazines. Received Yale Series of Younger Poets Prize, 1966; National Endowment for the Arts grant, 1968, 1969; American Academy Award, 1974; Guggenheim fellowship, 1976; Pulitzer Prize, 1992; National Book Award, 1994; Tanning Prize, 1995; National Institute for Arts and Letters Award for Poetry. Living in Amherst, Massachusetts.

**Poetry**
*Cages*, 1966
*The Destination*, 1967
*The Lost Pilot*, 1967
*The Torches*, 1968; revised edition, 1971
*Notes of Woe*, 1968
*Mystics in Chicago*, 1968
*Camping in the Valley*, 1968
*Row with Your Hair*, 1969
*Is There Anything*, 1969
*Shepherds of the Mist*, 1969
*The Oblivion Ha-Ha*, 1970
*Amnesia People*, 1970
*Deaf Girl Playing*, 1970
*Are You Ready Mary Baker Eddy?* with Bill Knott, 1970
*The Immortals*, 1970
*Wrong Songs*, 1970
*Hints to Pilgrims*, 1971; revised edition, 1982
*Nobody Goes to Visit the Insane Anymore*, 1971
*Absences: New Poems*, 1972
*Apology for Eating Geoffrey Movius' Hyacinth*, 1972
*Viper Jazz*, 1976
*Riven Doggeries*, 1979
*The Land of Little Sticks*, 1981
*Constant Defender*, 1983
*Just Shades*, 1985
*Reckoner*, 1986
*Bewitched*, 1989
*Distance from Loved Ones*, 1990
*Selected Poems*, 1992
*The Worshipful Company of Fletchers*, 1994
*Shroud of the Gnome*, 1997

**Other Writings:** novel (*Lucky Darryl*, with Bill Knott, 1977), short stories (*Hottentot Ossuary*, 1974); edited collection of poetry (*The Best American Poetry 1997*, 1997).

**Further Reading**
Bellamy, Joe David, editor, *American Poetry Observed*, Chicago: Illinois University Press, 1984
Logan, William, "Language Against Fear," *Poetry* 80, no. 4 (July 1977)
Revell, Donald, "The Desperate Buck and Wing: James Tate and the Failure of Ritual," *Western Humanities Review* 38 (Winter 1984)
Rosen, R.D., "James Tate and Sidney Goldfarb and the Inexhaustible Nature of the Murmur," in *American Poetry since 1960: Some Critical Perspectives*, edited by Robert B. Shaw, Cheadle, Manchester: Carcanet Press, 1973; Chester Springs, Pennsylvania: Dufour, 1974
Rudman, Mark, "Private but No Less Ghostly Worlds," *The American Poetry Review* 10, no. 4 (July–August 1981)
Stryk, Lucien, editor, *Heartland: Poets of the Midwest*, Dekalb: Northern Illinois University Press, 1967
Tate, James, and Alberta Turner, "A Box for Tom," in *Fifty Contemporary Poets: The Creative Process*, edited by Alberta Turner, New York: McKay, and London: Longman, 1977
Upton, Lee, "The Masters Can Only Make Us Laugh," *South Atlantic Review* 55 (November 1990)
Upton, Lee, *The Muse of Abandonment: Origin, Identity, Mastery, in Five American Poets*, Lewisburg, Pennsylvania: Bucknell University Press, and London: Associated University Presses, 1998

# Sara Teasdale 1884–1933

An extremely popular poet during her lifetime, Sara Teasdale is noted for her fidelity to traditional poetics and her mastery of the short lyric. She embraced neither the Modernist movement of her generation nor the strict tenets of her Baptist roots. Teasdale's lyrics, infused by her own romantic inclinations and influenced initially by her admiration of Sir Walter Scott, Christina Rossetti, Swinburne, Keats, and later Yeats, strive for the "music of stillness holy and low" ("There Will Be Rest").

Music came early to Teasdale. Born in St. Louis on 8 August 1884 to John and Mary Teasdale, she was the fourth child in the family and much younger than her siblings. At the time of her birth, her brothers were 19 and 14, and her sister was 17. A frail and coddled child, Teasdale immersed herself in Victorian poetry, recognizing even then the healing virtues of reading and writing poetry. Years later, she would write to a friend, "As soon as a thing is nicely arranged in meter, it ceases to bother one" (Drake, 1984).

After graduating from Hosmer Hall School in 1903, Teasdale joined a group of artistic women who produced *Potter's Wheel* magazine, a monthly venture that focused primarily on medieval arts. Teasdale combined her fascination with the medieval and her interest in women artists in her first collection of poems, *Sonnets to Duse, and Other Poems,* published in 1907. In Petrarchan sonnets, she pays tribute to the actress Eleanor Duse, who gave life on the stage to many ancient and medieval figures.

One of the sonnets in this collection, "To Joy," is intriguing for its use of religious and biblical language to describe physical pleasure in an almost metaphysical way. Although Marya Zaturenska, in her introduction to *The Collected Poems of Sara Teasdale* (1937), sees "no trace" of the metaphysical poets in Teasdale's work, the fusion of the religious and the sensual, the personification of Joy (possibly as Cupid), and the line "And by my glimpse of joy my soul shall live" suggest that the young poet was willing to experiment with the metaphysical practices of the 17th century. George Herbert's poem "The Glimpse," for example, presents a speaker who regrets that he cannot recall the delightful, heaven-sent glimpse that once awakened his soul.

In "The Gift," the speaker who wishes to respond appropriately to her lover, "You who have given the world to me," protests that she has no gifts that are not "gifts of your giving." This exchange was a frequent dilemma for Herbert's speaker(s) who, addressing the deity, hoped to match his gifts before confessing that the quest was impossible. The only solution was to submit. Here, however, in a witty turn, Teasdale's speaker does not surrender but says, "I bid you awake at dawn and discover / I have gone my way and left you free." The speaker claims that this gift breaks her heart, but it also guarantees her the freedom to pursue the laurel and not the rose, whatever regrets follow in "Roses and Rue." The poems in this slim volume reveal a poet who is learning her craft.

Four years later, Teasdale published *Helen of Troy, and Other Poems.* The monologues that open this set in the *Collected Poems* present five "historical" women who address their situations from their own perspectives. Their versions are telling. Helen, who begins by asking the gods to let her die, recants and vows that she will no longer cry in anguish or in anger because her beauty is a gift and a curse. Accepting her present self, she declares, "I shall live on to conquer Greece again." The dying Beatrice whispers her regret for not loving the boy who "sang so many songs for love of me," yet still she reaches out to heaven to claim her reward. Marianna Alcoforano (a fictional nun who broke her vow of chastity), proclaiming that her life was enriched by her love affair, believes that both God and his Virgin Mother accept her as she is. In her monologue, she explains that the Virgin, for all her sorrows, knew a joy that no nun has experienced: the love of her own child. Guenevere, although married to Arthur, admits that she was surprised by the intensity of her feeling for Launcelot. She is disturbed because no one in Camelot can forgive her transgression. Through these personae, the fledgling poet articulates a woman's need to speak for herself even as Teasdale tests her own voice and tries on poetic forms.

In the "Love Songs" that follow the monologues, Teasdale's singers reveal an almost adolescent approach to love, along with their infatuation for New York City. The speaker of the memorable "I Would Live in Your Love" promises to lose herself in her lover. This concept accords with Teasdale's view at the time; she "began by accepting the 'truth' that a woman's life was created chiefly to love a man" (Drake, 1984). A few poems later, in "Union Square," a wiser but still inarticulate speaker regrets her inability to tell her lover of her needs, comparing herself unfavorably to the prostitutes "who ask for love / In the lights of Union Square." This "explicit" poem, which was reviewed in the *New York Times,* brought her some notoriety but also increased her determination to find a genuine poetic voice.

By this time, Teasdale was engaged with the literary world. She had joined the Poetry Society of America, located in New York City, where she met frequently with Jessie Rittenhouse, Edna St. Vincent Millay, Jean Untermeyer, Elinor Wylie, and John Hall Wheelock, whom she believed she loved. By 1913, she had established herself with the Chicago literati, among them Harriet Monroe, eventual editor of *Poetry: A Magazine of Verse;* Vachel Lindsay; Carl Sandburg; and Eunice Tietjens. Although still in love with Wheelock, she spent time with two suitors, Vachel Lindsay and Ernst Filsinger, the latter a businessman from St. Louis, whom she married in December 1914.

The volume *Rivers to the Sea* (1915) brought Teasdale more fame, completely selling out within three months. "I Shall Not Care," one of several poems with April in mind, earned critical as well as popular acclaim. This collection, which she revised several times before its publication, shows her development as an artist who has found her voice and form: her arrangement of the poems is deliberate, and her treatment of subject matter and meter is more sophisticated and less predictable than in her earlier work. She enjoys the facets of her imagery and plays with the measures of her lines.

In 1917, Teasdale edited *The Answering Voice: One Hundred Love Lyrics by Women,* a volume she revised and expanded in 1928. She also published *Love Songs,* which was awarded the Columbia Poetry Prize (later the Pulitzer Prize for Poetry) for 1918. "Barter," the poem that opens *Love Songs,* is one of her most familiar works. It tells of the beautiful and sensuous items that life offers but does not give away. One must barter with life to attain these treasures, and the cost, although dear, cannot be recalled. To purchase loveliness, one must surrender everything else; the poet who wishes to create this loveliness must surrender his or her life. As Yeats, the living poet she admired most, would have it, "we must labour to be beautiful" ("Adam's Curse").

Most readers see Teasdale's next volume, *Flame and Shadow* (1920), as the fruition of her labors. Her regard for Emily Dickinson is apparent in "The Unseen," "A Little While," and "The Long Hill," among other poems. These pieces are not imitations of Dickinson's poems, but they shine with the self-knowledge and self-possession that distinguish Dickinson's poetry. Unable to find the joy she longed for in love and marriage and not anticipating any compensation in religion, Teasdale turns again to Beauty. In "The Wind in the Hemlock," the poem that concludes the volume, the speaker recalls the advice of the tree:

If I am peaceful, I shall see
Beauty's face continually
Feeding on her wine and bread
I shall be wholly comforted,
For she can make one day for me
Rich as my lost eternity.

During the 1920s, Teasdale issued *Rainbow Gold* (1922), an anthology of poems for children; published *Dark of the Moon* (1926); and revised *The Answering Voice* (1928). She traveled to England (twice) and France and established a close friendship with Margaret Conklin, the young woman who would become the literary executor of her estate. Despite this appearance of activity, she coped with her continued ill health, the long absences of her husband, and the loss of dear friends. Growing more and more withdrawn, she filed for divorce in 1929. In 1930, she published *Star To-night,* a book of poems for children, and began a biography of Christina Rossetti while working on some new poems.

The suicide of Vachel Lindsay in December 1931, just a few weeks after he had visited her, took a terrible toll on Teasdale's emotional health. Weak and distraught after recovering from pneumonia, she used an overdose of pills to end her own life in January 1933. *Strange Victory,* her final volume, was published posthumously that same year. While it records her preoccupation with farewells and death, it also reaches a sense of closure, especially in the touching "All That Was Mortal." In *Strange Victory,* "she detailed with rare honesty the varied emotional responses that spring from the acceptance of the human condition and its inevitable ending in death" (Schoen, 1986). The "shadow side" of Teasdale is featured in *Mirror of the Heart* (1984), edited by William Drake: it includes 51 previously unpublished poems along with 15 uncollected poems from magazines and five poems not included in *The Collected Poems of Sara Teasdale.*

Teasdale has a place in 20th-century American poetry. Many of her models were British poets dedicated to the centuries-old tradition of rhyme, meter, and form, but her associates, those artists with whom she lived and breathed the literary spirit and from whom she learned precision and austerity, were American poets whose work she studied and admired.

Jeannie Sargent Judge

*See also* Midwestern Poetry Renaissance

**Biography**
Born in St. Louis, Missouri, 8 August 1884. Graduated from Hosmer Hall School, 1903. Received Columbia Poetry Prize (later Pulitzer Prize), 1918; Poetry Society of America Prize, 1918. Died in New York City, 29 January 1933.

**Poetry**
*Sonnets to Duse, and Other Poems,* 1907
*Helen of Troy, and Other Poems,* 1911; revised edition, 1922
*Rivers to the Sea,* 1915
*Love Songs,* 1917
*Vignettes of Italy: A Cycle of Nine Songs for High Voice,* 1919
*Flame and Shadow,* 1920; revised edition, 1924
*Dark of the Moon,* 1926
*Stars To-night: Verses New and Old for Boys and Girls,* 1930
*A Country House,* 1932
*Strange Victory,* 1933
*The Collected Poems of Sara Teasdale,* 1937
*Mirror of the Heart: Poems of Sara Teasdale,* edited by William Drake, 1984
*Christmas Carol* (for children), illustrated by Dale Gottlieb, 1993

**Other Writings:** edited collections of literature (*The Answering Voice: One Hundred Love Lyrics by Women,* 1917, revised 1928; *Rainbow Gold: Poems Old and New for Boys and Girls,* 1922).

**Further Reading**
Bogan, Louise, *Achievement in American Poetry, 1900–1950,* Chicago: Regnery, 1951
Drake, William, editor, *Mirror of the Heart: Poems of Sara Teasdale,* New York: Macmillan, and London: Collier Macmillan, 1984
Schoen, Carol B., *Sara Teasdale,* Boston: Twayne, 1986
Waggoner, Hyatt H., *American Poets, from the Puritans to the Present,* Boston: Houghton Mifflin, 1968; revised edition, Baton Rouge: Louisiana State University Press, 1984
Watts, Emily Stipes, *Poetry of American Women from 1632 to 1945,* Austin: University of Texas Press, 1977

---

# Melvin B. Tolson 1898–1966

There is no clear consensus on how to evaluate Melvin Tolson's "bifacial" poetry, to use his characterization of Hideho Heights, a poet of "split identity," in *Harlem Gallery: Book I, The Curator* (1965). Tolson's poems from the 1930s—many posthumously published as *A Gallery of Harlem Portraits* (1979)—were influenced by Edgar Lee Masters, although the more difficult work he wrote after 1944 links him with High Modernism. Before he died in 1966, Tolson had been recognized by a reading at the Library of Congress (1965), by the Avalon Chair in Humanities at the Tuskegee Institute (1965), and by an award from the

American Academy of Arts and Letters (1966), among other honors. However, he found it difficult to publish his first book, *Rendezvous with America* (1944); by 1987—despite two major book-length poems, *Libretto for the Republic of Liberia* (1953) and *Harlem Gallery*—his books were out of print and remained so until 1999.

Born on 6 February 1898 in Moberly, Missouri, Tolson published his first poem in 1912; he claimed that he originally wanted to be a visual artist, and his poems—from "Dark Symphony," which won a prize from the American Negro Exposition in Chicago in 1940, through *Harlem Gallery*—synchronize the visual, oral, and literary, or "sight, sound and sense" (King, 1966). Attending Fisk University for one year (1918–19) before transferring to Lincoln University, from which he graduated with honors in 1923, Tolson taught from 1924 to 1947 at Wiley College in Marshall, Texas, after which he became a professor at Langston University in Oklahoma. Except for two years (1930–31) in which the Rockefeller Foundation funded his work on a masters degree at Columbia University (where his thesis was on figures of the Harlem Renaissance), Tolson's life in education took place within black institutions. He was also committed to the public sphere. From 1937 to 1944, he wrote a newspaper column—"Caviar and Cabbage"—addressing topics concerning black life for the *Washington Tribune;* he served four terms as mayor of Langston, Oklahoma, and, in the 1930s, helped organize sharecroppers.

As an undergraduate, Tolson won prizes in oratory and debate, interests that, like his social activism and ties to the black community, inform the work that followed, from his successes as a debate coach at Wiley and a theater director at Langston to his poetry, which is often staged as dialogue and has designs on its readers (as a form of persuasion and education), even as it draws on—or reenacts—various classical traditions. The 24 sections of *Harlem Gallery* take their titles from the Greek alphabet; the notes that accompany *Libretto* and "E. & O. E." ("Errors and Omissions Excepted"), which won the 1952 Bess Hokim Award from *Poetry* magazine, like the references in *Harlem Gallery,* send readers to sources ranging from African proverbs to French Renaissance history, from Goya to Archimedes to E. Franklin Frazier's *Black Bourgeoisie.*

By 1947, Tolson became poet laureate of Liberia and wrote *Libretto*—a poem on black history in eight sections titled with the notes of the musical scale—which appeared in 1953 with an introduction by Allen Tate. Tolson's connection with Liberia is not surprising, given his association with Lincoln University, which was founded as the Ashmun Institute for the purpose of training future leaders of Liberia. It is more surprising to find Tate championing *Libretto* as "an English Pindaric ode" in the style of Hart Crane, separating Tolson's work from the "'folk' idiom" of others, such as Langston Hughes and Gwendolyn Brooks, and concluding that Tolson properly subordinated race to poetry, a form of praise that did not recommend Tolson to readers and writers increasingly committed to a Black Aesthetic by the 1960s.

*Harlem Gallery* appeared in 1965, the first of five proposed parts of an epic tracing the odyssey of the black man in America that Tolson did not live to complete. The poem is narrated by "the Curator," a man of "Afroirishjewish origins," and (among other things) delineates the biographies of three black artists (John Laugart, Hideho Heights, and Mister Starks) in ways that suggest the poem's self-consciousness about the dilemma of the black artist in American culture. *Harlem Gallery* was introduced by Karl Shapiro, who argued (against Tate) that Tolson was "a great poet" in part because he wrote and thought "in Negro" even while "outpounding Pound." Tate and Shapiro shaped responses to Tolson's work thereafter; an article by the poet Sarah Webster Fabio (1966) complained that Tolson's language was "not 'Negro'" and that no one could read his "bizarre, pseudo-literary diction," while Langston Hughes was quoted on the back cover of *Harlem Gallery:* "Tolson is no highbrow. . . . Kids from the cotton fields like him. Cowpunchers understand him."

The reception of Tolson's work mirrors larger arguments over African-American literature. In part, the question is whether Tolson is "the enemy of the dominant culture" (*Harlem Gallery: Book I, The Curator*) or a literary sharecropper (Nielsen, 1992). Despite obvious affiliations and arguments with both black and white cultural heritages, his major poetry appeared too late for both the Harlem Renaissance and the Black Arts movement and raised problems with its (equally belated) uses of Modernist techniques. As Fabio (1966) understood it, Tolson was "victimized by the cultural lag" between black and white culture. More recently, critics have proposed that Tolson did not mimic white culture but changed the face of High Modernism (Bérubé, 1992; Nielsen, 1992; Dove's introduction to *"Harlem Gallery," and Other Poems of Melvin B. Tolson,* 1999). Certainly *Harlem Gallery* focuses on black culture from the Harlem Renaissance forward and features standard African-American rhetorical forms, from blues to toasts, testifying, and riffs, even as its condensed language and wide-ranging references pose difficulties more typical of Modernists such as Pound or Crane. Critics are still coming to terms with just how Tolson's final poem signifies thematically and stylistically on African, African-American, and white Anglo-American culture.

LISA M. STEINMAN

**Biography**

Born in Moberly, Missouri, 6 February 1898. Attended Fisk University, Nashville, Tennessee, 1918–19; Lincoln University, Oxford, Pennsylvania, 1919–23, B.A. 1923; Columbia University, New York, 1930–31, M.A. 1940; Instructor, Wiley College, Marshall, Texas, 1924–47; Professor of English and drama, Langston University, Oklahoma, 1947–66; Avalon Professor of Humanities, Tuskegee Institute, Alabama, 1965; columnist ("Caviar and Cabbage"), *Washington Tribune,* 1937–44; Mayor, Langston, 1954, re-elected 1956, 1958, 1960. Received Bess Hokin Award, 1952; American Academy of Arts and Letters Award, 1966; Order of the Star of Africa (Liberia), 1954; honorary Doctor of Letters, 1954, and honorary Doctor of Humane Letters, 1965, Lincoln University. Died in Dallas, Texas, 29 August 1966.

**Poetry**

*Rendezvous with America,* 1944
*Libretto for the Republic of Liberia,* 1953
*Harlem Gallery: Book I, The Curator,* 1965
*A Gallery of Harlem Portraits,* edited by Robert M. Farnsworth, 1979
*"Harlem Gallery," and Other Poems of Melvin B. Tolson,* edited by Raymond Nelson, 1999

**Other Writings:** play (*Fire in the Flint,* from the novel by Walter F. White, produced 1952), essays (*Caviar and Cabbage:*

*Selected Columns from the Washington Tribune, 1937–1944,* edited by Robert M. Farnsworth, 1982).

**Further Reading**


Bérubé, Michael, *Marginal Forces/Cultural Centers: Tolson, Pynchon, and the Politics of the Canon,* Ithaca, New York: Cornell University Press, 1992

Dove, Rita, "Telling It Like It I-S IS: Narrative Techniques in Melvin Tolson's *Harlem Gallery,*" *New England Review and Bread Loaf Quarterly* 8, no. 1 (Autumn 1985)

Fabio, Sarah Webster, "Who Speaks Negro?" *Negro Digest* 16, no. 2 (December 1966)

Farnsworth, Robert M., *Melvin B. Tolson, 1898–1966: Plain Talk and Poetic Prophecy,* Columbia: University of Missouri Press, 1984

Flasch, Joy, *Melvin B. Tolson,* New York: Twayne, 1972

King, M.W., interviewer, "A Poet's Odyssey" (1965 interview with Tolson), in *Anger, and Beyond,* edited by Herbert Hill, New York: Harper and Row, 1966

Nielsen, Aldon L., "Melvin B. Tolson and the Deterritorialization of Modernism," *African American Review* 26, no. 2 (Summer 1992)

Russell, Mariann, *Melvin B. Tolson's "Harlem Gallery": A Literary Analysis,* Columbia: University of Missouri Press, 1980

Thompson, Gorden E., "Ambiguity in Tolson's *Harlem Gallery,*" *Callaloo* 9, no. 1 (Winter 1986)


## Harlem Gallery

Melvin B. Tolson's *Harlem Gallery: Book I, The Curator* (1965) is one of the more ambitious poems in American literature. Conceived by Tolson as "an attempt to picture the Negro in America before he becomes the great auk of the melting-pot in the dawn of the twenty-second century," it presents the furthest evolution of the oblique, allusive style of Tolson's late poetry, which incorporates the innovations of Modernism into an African-American aesthetic rooted in the blues and in folk traditions such as the toast and the trickster story. It is also the culmination of Tolson's lifelong engagement with Harlem. Tolson lived in Harlem while a graduate student at Columbia University and was a frequent visitor throughout his life. His master's thesis evaluated the writers of the Harlem Renaissance, and his first important poetic work, *A Gallery of Harlem Portraits* (a distant ancestor of *Harlem Gallery*), uses Harlem as its setting. In his thesis, Tolson wrote that "alien ideas and native ideas, alien customs and native customs, sometimes remaining unchanged, but often coalescing and producing startling hybrids—these have colored the literature dealing with Harlem." Three decades later, the vital cultural syncretism of Harlem would be foregrounded in *Harlem Gallery.*

Unfortunately, Tolson's achievement has too frequently been overlooked. Until it was reprinted in 1999, *Harlem Gallery* had long been unavailable. This is not to say that Tolson's work was not recognized during his lifetime. He was named poet laureate of Liberia in 1947, won a *Poetry* magazine prize in 1952 for his poem "E. & O.E.," and was praised by poets such as Karl Shapiro, whose introduction to *Harlem Gallery* declared that "a great poet has been living in our midst for decades." Shapiro's introduction, however, was problematic. Addressed in part to Allen Tate, who had claimed that Tolson was the first African-American poet to assimilate "the language of the Anglo-American tradition," Shapiro countered that "Tolson writes and thinks in Negro." Whatever Shapiro's intentions, his debate with Tate has proved distracting. Critics such as Sarah Webster Fabio (1966) have taken exception to the description of Tolson's language as "Negro," although this claim was Shapiro's, not Tolson's.

Tolson conceived *Harlem Gallery* as a five-book epic but was only able to complete *Book I, The Curator* because of failing health. He died before he could shed much light on the poem through essays and interviews. This has affected the poem's long-term reception. It is a difficult poem with a wide range of allusion, but unlike the similarly demanding *Libretto for the Republic of Liberia* (1953), it was not accompanied by notes. Raymond Nelson's *"Harlem Gallery," and Other Poems of Melvin B. Tolson* (1999) is the first annotated edition of the poem to be widely available.

The poem is divided into 24 sections, each named for a letter of the Greek alphabet. The first five sections introduce the Curator, the restless, probing speaker of the poem. Awakened at "a people's dusk of dawn" as "alarm bells bedevil the Great White World," he nonetheless laments:

> but often I hear a dry husk-of-locust blues
> descend the tone ladder of a laughing goose,
> syncopating between
> the faggot and the noose:
> "Black Boy, O Black Boy,
> is the port worth the cruise?"

Here, as throughout the poem, the Curator is alternately hopeful and despairing about the future of racial conflict in America. *Harlem Gallery*'s final lines celebrate "a people's New World odyssey / from chattel to Esquire!" but only after invoking the history of enslavement, rape, and violence that has accompanied that odyssey.

The Curator focuses on two broad themes: the nature of art and the complexities of identity. The Curator reflects on art's revolutionary potential, its unique mode of insight into human nature, and its irreducible mysteriousness. He quarrels with critics for their arrogance. He bitterly acknowledges the artist's quixotic struggle against the demands of the powerful, the "Bulls of Bashan," whose hierarchical categories and equivocal definitions fortify (borrowing Bacon's phrase) "the idols of the tribe." Here the Curator's concerns about art and identity merge: art should obliterate rather than reinforce false categories. Whites have suppressed the history of rape and miscegenation in America to indulge in fantasies of racial purity; the "afroirishjewish" Curator, in contrast, recognizes and celebrates his own variousness, part and parcel of the synthesizing energy of Harlem.

In addition to the Curator's monologues, the poem contains narrative episodes involving a few central characters. The impoverished painter John Laugart is an exemplary figure of artistic integrity and defiance. Dr. Obi Nkomo, the cosmopolitan African and "alter ego / of the Harlem Gallery," provides wise (if often cryptic) counterpoint to the Curator's reflections. Mister Starks is a Modernist composer and poet whose manuscript, *Harlem*

*Vignettes,* is given to the Curator after Starks' death (whether a result of suicide or murder is unclear). Starks' poems, portraits of *Harlem Gallery*'s most significant figures, provide an alternative view of the action and characters of *Harlem Gallery.*

Then there is Hideho Heights, the "vagabond bard of Lenox Avenue." Heights makes his grand, funny, and scornful entrance after an opening at the Harlem Gallery; later he holds court at the Zulu Club to the jazz accompaniment of the Indigo Combo. Reciting his version of the John Henry ballad, Heights' call is interspersed with the spirited response of the Club's audience, who "whoop and stomp, / clamp thighs and back and knees: / the poet and the audience one, / each gears itself to please." He delights the Club with his fable of a sea turtle that eats his way out of a shark's belly, an allegory of African-American resistance to assimilation. Heights' career, however, is complicated by a Modernist phase in Paris during the 1920s. The Curator, finding a manuscript of "E. & O.E." in Heights' apartment, discovers the secret "split identity / of the People's Poet—/ the bifacial nature of his poetry: / the racial ballad in the public domain / and the private poem in the modern vein."

Heights' "bifacial" poetry allows Tolson to explore the tensions between Modernism and populist writing—of crucial importance to Tolson, given his own aim of writing "difficult" works that would, he hoped, eventually gain a popular audience. Heights' response to the dilemma is simply to fashion two distinct personae. Tolson himself was more ambitious. Recently, there has been a surge of interest in *Harlem Gallery.* We may be catching up with Tolson at last.

James Gibbons

**Further Reading**

Bérubé, Michael, *Marginal Forces/Cultural Centers: Tolson, Pynchon, and the Politics of the Canon,* Ithaca, New York: Cornell University Press, 1992

Dove, Rita, "Telling It Like It I-S IS: Narrative Techniques in Melvin Tolson's *Harlem Gallery,*" *New England Review and Bread Loaf Quarterly* 8, no. 1 (Autumn 1985)

Fabio, Sarah Webster, "Who Speaks Negro?" *Negro Digest* 16, no. 2 (December 1966)

Farnsworth, Robert M., *Melvin B. Tolson, 1898–1966: Plain Talk and Poetic Prophecy,* Columbia: University of Missouri Press, 1984

Hansell, William H., "Three Artists in Melvin B. Tolson's *Harlem Gallery,*" *Black American Literature Forum* 18, no. 3 (Fall 1984)

Nielsen, Aldon L., "Melvin B. Tolson and the Deterritorialization of Modernism," *African American Review* 26, no. 2 (Summer 1992)

Russell, Mariann, *Melvin B. Tolson's "Harlem Gallery": A Literary Analysis,* Columbia: University of Missouri Press, 1980

Russell, Mariann, "Langston Hughes and Melvin Tolson: Blues People," in *The Furious Flowering of African American Poetry,* edited by Joanne V. Gabbin, Charlottesville: University of Virginia Press, 1999

Thompson, Gordon E., "Ambiguity in Tolson's *Harlem Gallery,*" *Callaloo* 9, no. 1 (Winter 1986)

Werner, Craig, "Blues for T.S. Eliot and Langston Hughes: The Afro-Modernist Aesthetic of *Harlem Gallery,*" *Black American Literature Forum* 24 (1990)

---

# Jean Toomer 1894–1967

Jean Toomer gained high visibility and popularity during the "Jazz Age." His best-known work, *Cane* (1923), interlaced poetry and prose in a brilliant representation of African-American life in the South. Although Toomer worked longest on issues of personal growth and spirituality for Americans of any heritage, he is remembered as a spokesman for the Harlem Renaissance or New Negro movement of the 1920s.

Toomer was the grandson of Pinckney B.S. Pinchback, a Reconstruction-era politician who rose to power in Louisiana and Washington, D.C. Pinchback, who claimed to be of mixed African- and Euro-American blood, was rumored to have falsely identified himself as "colored" in order to further his political career. In any case, Pinchback officially claimed Negro as his race, even though he instilled in his family an awareness of the range of nationalities contributing to their makeup. Toomer himself always referred to his own combination of "seven blood mixtures: French, Dutch, Welsh, Negro, German, Jewish, and Indian." He regularly noted that he lived without difficulty in both white and black worlds throughout his childhood and adolescence because the family was so light-skinned (*The Wayward and the Seeking,* 1980).

Writing was not foremost in Toomer's mind as he knocked about for a career as a youth. He initially sought training in a variety of fields, including agriculture, physical fitness, and music before settling on a future as a writer in his late 20s and developing associations with leading writers of the time, particularly Waldo Frank and Sherwood Anderson. Influenced by both the emerging Modernist literature and the popular Imagist poetry of the day, Toomer began to hone his skill as a poet and an essayist. His most important inspiration came in 1921 when he accepted a post as the head of an all-black agricultural college in Georgia. Experiencing life himself for the first time as categorically black (despite his appearance), Toomer found himself especially drawn to the lives of Georgia's rural black folk. In a 1922 letter to *The Liberator,* Toomer explained: "A deep part of my nature, a part that I had repressed, sprang suddenly to life and responded to them" (Toomer, 1988). This complex response energized *Cane.*

Published by New York's Boni and Liveright, *Cane* is an eclectic blend of verse, short stories, and dramatic hybrids. True to the Modernist literary tradition of fragmentary style, *Cane* is very much a collage or montage of African-American life in the early 20th century. Divided into three sections, each headed by the visual image of an arc, it deals with a culture in transition, covering the individual psychological developments occurring in African-American folk communities. Through sensitive poetry that incorporates slave spirituals, surviving Africanisms, and bittersweet descriptions of African-American life, *Cane* highlights the complicated and ultimately inspiring way that rural blacks negotiated their space in a larger American culture. The poem "Georgia Dusk" tells how Toomer's black community made "folk-songs from soul sounds," most notably in the fifth, sixth, and seventh stanzas:

Meanwhile, the men, with vestiges of pomp,
Race memories of king and caravan,
High-priests, an ostrich, and a juju-man,
Go singing through the footpaths of the swamp.

Their voices rise . . the pine trees are guitars,
Strumming, the pine-needles fall like sheets of rain . .
Their voices rise . . the chorus of the cane
Is caroling a vesper to the stars . .

O singers, resinous and soft your songs
Above the sacred whisper of the pines,
Give virgin lips to cornfield concubines,
Bring dreams of Christ to dusky cane-lipped throngs.

These "folk songs" and "soul sounds" would not remain in the South, however, and in *Cane*'s second section Toomer focused on the great migration of blacks to Northern cities, highlighting their difficulty in navigating a new urban landscape. *Cane* ends with "Kabnis," a prose-play hybrid that tells the story of a fair-skinned black man from the North who seeks his sanity and his salvation among the rural black folks who befriend him. This section is as much a general allegory as it is a thinly veiled summary of Toomer's own experiences while living in the deep South.

*Cane* was a critical success at its initial publication despite somewhat modest sales and distribution. Literary scholars hail it as one of the earliest publications to have effectively ushered in the New Negro movement. It is commonly associated with the Harlem Renaissance, even though Toomer initially submitted it while living in Washington, D.C. and actually had very little interaction with the Harlem intelligentsia. The gap between Toomer and black literary circles is important: Toomer admitted to creating *Cane* while the Negro part of him had been spiritually motivated, but he never described himself as exclusively Negro. Toomer insistently referred to himself as "American," although he would occasionally neglect to correct others when they emphasized a single part of his complex heritage (according to his biographer, Darwin T. Turner, he was particularly silent when, at the height of *Cane*'s popularity, critics and celebrants called him Negro). Although he never chose to align himself with a "movement," the most important literary influences on Toomer were popular white Modernists like Frank, Anderson, Van Wyck Brooks, Kenneth Burke, Alfred Stieglitz, and Hart Crane. One could also place him with such "Lost Generation" greats as Stein, Fitzgerald, and Hemingway. Wanting to represent the full complexity of all American life, Toomer found guidance and inspiration through his interactions with these and other early 20th-century writers.

*Cane*'s success aside, Toomer continued to author scores of poems, essays, short stories, and plays; he even wrote seven autobiographies. Relatively few of these were published, and none in book form. His only other book-length publication was the privately issued *Essentials: Definitions and Aphorisms* (1931). There are many theories on why Toomer's literary prominence waned in his lifetime, the most interesting being because of his own shift in purpose. With a long-standing interest in Western spirituality and phenomenology, Eastern religion and philosophy, and a measure of general social reform, in 1924 Toomer devoted himself to the teachings of noted mystic Georges Gurdjieff, becoming a disciple and eventual teacher of Gurdjieff's philosophy of altered consciousness. From then on Toomer's creative work took on an almost instructional quality, encouraging readers to heighten their self-awareness and spirituality through a deliberate engagement with individual consciousness and artistic expression. The short poem "White Arrow" (published in *The Dial* in 1929) poignantly makes this point:

Your force is greater than your use of it.
Existing, yet you dream that breath depends
On bonds I once contracted for. It is
A false belief induced by sleep and fear.
In faith and reason you were swift and free,
White arrow, as you were, awake and be!

Eventually Toomer moved away from Gurdjieff's teachings, finding a more religious than philosophical inspiration in Quakerism. A synthesis of his Quaker beliefs can be seen in the undated "Desire":

Through this suffering and the opened heart
I seek the universal love of beings;
May I be made one with that love
And extend to everything;
I turn towards that love,
In this new season of a forgotten life
I move towards the heart of love
Of all that breathes;
I would enter that radiant center
and from that center live.

He continued to write largely unpublished poetry and essays until his death in 1967.

Brilliant and enigmatic—such was the literary genius of Jean Toomer. His work *Cane* provides one of the most poignant representations of the strength, spirituality, and integrity of African-American folk communities. Toomer himself remains an example of one writer's quest for an American blend of ethnic and spiritual wholeness, pursued ironically through the fragmentary nature of Modernist literary style.

ROXANE V. PICKENS

*See also* Harlem Renaissance

**Biography**

Born in Washington, D.C., 26 December 1894. Attended the University of Wisconsin, Madison, 1914; Massachusetts College of Agriculture; American College of Physical Training, Chicago, 1916; New York University, summer 1917; City College, New York, 1917; physical education teacher in a school near

Milwaukee, 1918; clerk, Acker Merrall and Conduit grocery company, New York, 1918; shipyard worker, New York; worked at Howard Theatre, Washington, D.C., 1920; substitute principal, Sparta Agricultural and Industrial Institute, Sparta, Georgia, 1921; studied at Gurdjieff's Institute in Fontainebleau, France, 1924, 1926; led Gurdjieff groups in Harlem, 1925, and Chicago, 1926–33. Died in Doylestown, Pennsylvania, 30 March 1967.

**Poetry**

*Cane* (includes prose), 1923

*The Collected Poems of Jean Toomer,* edited by Robert B. Jones and Margery Toomer Latimer, 1980

*The Wayward and the Seeking: A Collection of Writings by Toomer,* edited by Darwin T. Turner, 1980

**Selected Criticism**

*Jean Toomer: Selected Essays and Literary Criticism,* edited by Robert B. Jones, 1996

**Other Writings:** play (*Balo,* in *Plays of Negro Life,* edited by Alain Locke and Montgomery Gregory, 1927), aphorisms (*Essentials,* 1931).

**Further Reading**

Byrd, Rudolph P., *Jean Toomer's Years with Gurdjieff: Portrait of an Artist, 1923–1936,* Athens: University of Georgia Press, 1990

Hutchinson, George, "Jean Toomer and American Racial Discourse," *Texas Studies in Literature and Language* 35, no. 2 (1993)

Jones, Robert B., *Jean Toomer and the Prison-House of Thought: A Phenomenology of the Spirit,* Amherst: University of Massachusetts Press, 1993

Kerman, Cynthia Earl, and Richard Eldridge, *The Lives of Jean Toomer: A Hunger for Wholeness,* Baton Rouge: Louisiana State University Press, 1997

Toomer, Jean, *Cane: An Authoritative Text, Backgrounds, and Criticism,* edited by Darwin T. Turner, New York and London: Norton, 1988

# U

## John Updike 1932–

There are two views of John Updike's poetry: either it has been critically ignored because of the author's towering international reputation as a novelist and short-story writer, or it has received any attention at all, maybe even its very publication, because of his reputation as a prose writer. Indeed, his most anthologized poem, "Ex-Basketball Player," is often collected not for its own merits as a poem but for its inclusion of an early version of the character Harry Angstrom, the focus of *Rabbit Angstrom: A Tetralogy,* his most famous and accomplished work of fiction. Lack of critical attention has not dissuaded Updike from writing poetry, however. His first book of poems, *The Carpentered Hen and Other Tame Creatures,* appeared in 1958, and until the end of the 20th century he produced a new collection every decade, culminating in his *Collected Poems, 1953–1993* (1993).

Hamilton Hammish (1994), while granting that Updike's poems ought to be read for their own sake, admits they hold equal value as "commentary upon his life and his work as a prose-writer." *The Library Journal* finds that "Many of the poems read like limbering-up exercises for the intricately wrought prose of his novels." According to X.J. Kennedy (1963) in a review of *Telephone Poles* (1963), Updike is "like some designer of Explorer rockets who hasn't enough to do, in his spare time touching off displays of Roman candles."

Even when noting that "Updike's ear tends to falter, his judgment often errs and the poetry wanders into dangerously trivial territory," critics address these weaknesses only in terms of how puzzling they are since "Updike's sense of rhythm in prose is exceptional, and his perceptions are bound so intimately with those rhythms" (*Publisher's Weekly*). Updike himself in the preface to his *Collected Poems* (1993)—employing exactly the kind of startlingly precise and original imagery that marks his best writing—remarks that his poetry forms "the thready backside of my life's fading tapestry" and describes his poems as "my oeuvre's beloved waifs."

In a review of *Facing Nature* (1985), Gavin Ewart (1985) places Updike not among the novelists who also write good poetry, such as Vladimir Nabokov and Kingsley Amis, but among Victorians such as Bronte, Thackeray, and Meredith: those who have "a tendency toward parody and light verse." Updike himself applies this designation to more than half of his poetry in *Collected Poems;* since light verse as a subgenera is generally immune from serious literary consideration in post–World War II America, this bent has not helped his reputation.

When critics do confront the poems directly, they rightly, if offhandedly, praise what Kennedy calls their "pyrotechnics": an acrobatic fondness for the language and an edgy, nearly metaphysical wit. It is almost as if by granting Updike a certain level of technical proficiency as a "comic," "light," or "humorous" poet, critics and reviewers are excused from addressing his poetry with any seriousness at all. Such a stance ignores the obvious fact that the best of light or comic verse is no less important than any other kind of poetry. Kronenberger (1935) puts it best:

> The best light verse must have human qualities, however madly they may have been reshuffled. Something beyond a corner of our minds must be affected—whether by sheer nonsense, which gets its effect beyond the mind, or by wit which floods the mind with an enlarging light, or by warmth or spontaneity of the laughter of the body or a pleasantly sensuous appeal.

Readers who are prepared to go beyond the artificial distinction between light verse and other kinds of verse will find more to praise in Updike's poetry than mere technique.

Updike does have his admirers among critics, who describe him as an "Urbane, controlled, contemplative and original" poet who writes about "dying and madness and loss of love with coolness and great technical aplomb" (Ewart, 1985). *Publisher's Weekly* notes how Updike "polishes and polishes a passing subject with a certain modesty, until it shimmers," while Hammish (1994) sees the poems capturing "those fleeting moments of intense feeling about some of life's great generalities." This passage from "Sea Gulls" confirms Hammish's observation:

> It is also this hour when plump young couples
> walk down to the water, bumping together,
> and stand thigh-deep in the rhythmic glass.
> Then they walk back towards the car,
> tugging as if at a secret between them,
> but which neither quite knows—
> walk capricious paths through the scattering gulls,
> as in some mythologies

beautiful gods stroll unconcerned
among mortal apprehensions.

Of the critics willing to address Updike's poetry, Donald Greiner (1981) has made the most sustained examination, albeit of only his first four collections: *The Carpenter Hen, Telephone Poles, Midpoint* (1969), and *Tossing and Turning* (1977). Although Greiner also praises Updike's "uncommon pleasure in common objects," he advises that the "comic surfaces mask serious intent." According to Greiner,

> Even the lightest verse takes on with reflection the weight of religious query when Updike rejoices in the imperfect quality which all things share and which thus links all things.

Greiner finds the poems gathering thematically around a "distrust of the assault of the rational upon the imagination" and "a confrontation with the immensity of non-human otherness."

Ultimately, if a poet should not be critically ignored for not ever appearing on a bestsellers list, then it seems to follow that one should not be dismissed so quickly simply because he has.

BRUCE TAYLOR

**Biography**

Born in Shillington, Pennsylvania, 18 March 1932. Attended Harvard University, Cambridge, Massachusetts, A.B. (summa cum laude) 1954; Ruskin School of Drawing and Fine Arts, Oxford (Knox Fellow), 1954–55; staff reporter, *New Yorker*, 1955–57. Received Guggenheim fellowship, 1959; Rosenthal Award, 1960; National Book Award, 1964; O. Henry Award, 1966; Foreign Book Prize (France), 1966; New England Poetry Club Golden Rose, 1979; MacDowell Medal, 1981; Pulitzer Prize, 1982, 1990; American Book Award, 1982; National Book Critics Circle Award, for fiction, 1982, for criticism, 1984; Union League Club Abraham Lincoln Award, 1982; National Arts Club Medal of Honor, 1984; National Medal of the Arts, 1989; National Book Foundation Medal, 1998; member, American Academy, 1976. Living in Beverly Farms, Massachusetts.

**Poetry**

*The Carpentered Hen and Other Tame Creatures*, 1958; as *Hoping for a Hoopee*, 1959
*Telephone Poles, and Other Poems*, 1963
*Midpoint, and Other Poems*, 1969
*Tossing and Turning*, 1977
*Facing Nature*, 1985
*Collected Poems, 1953–1993*, 1993

**Selected Criticism**

*Ego and Art in Walt Whitman*, 1978
*Hugging the Shore: Essays and Criticism*, 1983
*More Matter: Essays and Criticism*, 1999

**Other Writings:** plays, short stories, essays, novels (*Rabbit, Run*, 1960; *The Witches of Eastwick*, 1984), children's literature; edited collections of literature (*The Best American Short Stories 1984* [with Shannon Ravenel], 1984).

**Further Reading**

Burchard, Rachael C., *John Updike: Yea Sayings*, Carbondale: Southern Illinois University Press, and London: Feffer and Simons, 1971
Ewart, Gavin, "Making It Strange," *New York Times* (28 April 1985)
Greiner, Donald J., *The Other John Updike: Poems, Short Stories, Prose, Play*, Athens: Ohio University Press, 1981
Hammish, Hamilton, "His Other Hand: Complete Poems by John Updike," *The Economist* 330, no. 7848 (1994)
Kennedy, X.J., "A Light Look at Today," *New York Times* (22 September 1963)
Kronenberger, Louis, editor, *An Anthology of Light Verse*, New York: Modern Library, 1935
Matson, Elizabeth, "A Chinese Paradox, But Not Much of One: John Updike in His Poetry," *Minnesota Review* 7 (1967)
Updike, John, "On One's Own Oeuvre," in *Hugging the Shore: Essays and Criticism*, by Updike, New York: Vintage Books, and London: Deutsch, 1983

# V

## Mona Van Duyn 1921–

Even as early as the first poem, "Three Valentines to the Wide World," in her first volume of poetry, Mona Van Duyn had determined the direction her poetry would take:

I have never enjoyed those roadside overlooks from which
you can see the mountains of two states. The view keeps
  generating
a kind of pure, meaningless exaltation
that I can't find a use for. It drifts away from things.
(*Valentines to the Wide World,* 1959)

In addition to demonstrating her preference for the concrete rather than the abstract, Van Duyn's first book introduces many themes that would remain central to her poetry: the romantic concept of the child as "father to the man," the child's inevitable loss of innocence, the possibility of restoring innocence through art, the intimate relation between nature and human nature, and the stages of love.

"Three Valentines to the Wide World" concerns a little girl who, unlike the adults around her, is able to conceive of a loving God despite several pieces of evidence to the contrary—the cold snow "that tricked the earth to death," her friend's abusive father, a milkman who always kicks the dog. She asks her mother if love is "God's hobby," leaving Van Duyn to marvel at her childlike assumption that "Loving is easy, and hatred, hard work." Recalling the etymology of "amateur"—someone who engages in a pursuit as a hobby rather than as a profession but also a lover, someone who does something for the sheer pleasure of it—Van Duyn arrives at a fresh conception of God as a mild-mannered elderly gardener who is genuinely devoted to his creation, compelled to nurture and tend to it continually and unassumingly not because he has to but because he wants to: "In the freeness of time He gardens, and to His leisure old stems entrust new leaves all winter long." By presenting the world through a child's eyes, Van Duyn invites readers to reenvision their own world.

In *Merciful Disguises* (1973), Van Duyn aptly captures the interplay between nature and human nature, mind and body, in a single line: "Out of a dream I fished / the ache that feeds in my stomach's weedy slough." Studying nature is for Van Duyn, as it was for Emerson, a way of knowing oneself, while failure to examine it closely is tantamount to contempt for a realm of feeling. Van Duyn shares with her Modernist predecessors a distrust of the abstract that leads her to render particulars exactly and to concentrate on compressed images rather than on nebulous symbols. She consistently strives to depict what Seamus Heaney has described as "the god within the tree"—the universal within the particular, the essence within the form. In his book *"Fallen from the Symboled World": Precedents for the New Formalism* (1990), Wyatt Prunty observes that Van Duyn's figures of speech allow her "at once to examine the world around her and to avoid becoming one of the 'self-examined / Who've killed the self.'" By confining her attention to specific details in the landscape, Van Duyn avoids abstractions and also draws attention to the formal elements of her poems.

*Letters from a Father, and Other Poems* (1982) is written in the form of six letters from the poet's aging parents, whose physical ailments have led them to be resigned to death. The poet's gift of a bird feeder, however, gives them renewed interest in nature and hence in life.

In her Pulitzer Prize–winning book *Near Changes* (1990), Van Duyn relies on the same themes as in her earlier work, although her tone is lighter. In "A Bouquet of Zinnias," she pays homage to a common flower that is invariably excluded from floral arrangements. Zinnias remind her of her grandmother, whose love for her was strong albeit unrefined; the details that she provides about the often-overlooked zinnias lead the reader to contemplate a kind of love that is similarly overlooked, the love of women kin for each other. Van Duyn's subject is simply the love that exists between family members, a love that, although commonly regarded as secondary to selfless connubial love, romantic love, or maternal love, proves much more powerful and lasting. As she describes the zinnias, she simultaneously describes the few who are capable of this kind of love. While poems about nature furnish Van Duyn with a degree of objectivity and specificity, they are also ironically the means by which she chronicles women's inner lives—her own, those around her, and the poet's—with great control and eloquence. Her fidelity to the details of the landscape enables her to render pure emotion as opposed to "pure, meaningless exaltation." Instead of presenting the broad view, Van Duyn concentrates on particular aspects of the landscape; as she explains in one poem, the bird's-eye view invariably is preferable to the truck driver's.

In "Falls," a longer poem from which Van Duyn's title for *Firefall* (1992) is taken, the choice that she makes as a teenager during her family's visit to Niagara Falls is emblematic of the choices she later makes as a poet:

> We drove to see
> the American lip from Canada's side, but the whole
> was beyond the grasp of my lens and I snapped instead
> a family of swans, a simpler sight,
> father, mother, puffball babies, strolling.

"Falls" renders nature as the force that frees her from various societal pressures—parental pressure, the pressure of adolescence, and the pressure to marry. She recounts visits to the Fire Falls in California and later to Niagara Falls as a teenager on a family vacation. Although she recalls wanting to be a writer at the time, her Iowa relatives consider her ambitions foolish and expect her to marry and raise a family. The falls come to represent her own untapped creative potential but also the falls that we take as human beings. Van Duyn renders emotions by translating them into the concrete terms of landscape poetry; physical space suggests emotional distance.

*Firefall* represents a culmination of Van Duyn's long effort to present things as they are, stripped of easy abstraction and glib moralizing. In each carefully crafted poem, she presents a "simpler sight" that rewards the reader's close attention. "Double Sonnet for Minimalists" (*Near Changes*) uses a form called the minimalist sonnet, first used in *Near Changes* and explored more extensively in *Firefall*. "Double Sonnet" is a type of curtal sonnet—iambic dimeter instead of iambic pentameter—that demands precise diction and total attention to an essential image. In this poem about a shell, a small object that nonetheless seems to contain the sounds of a vast ocean, the form is especially appropriate. While the shell's color and shape summon memories that engage the senses, the multiplicity of images is carefully confined within the shell's "single-mindedness." Van Duyn's depiction of nature is reminiscent of Dickinson's: when the "certain slant of light" comes, "the landscape listens"; that is, it responds in a characteristically human way. Both Dickinson and Van Duyn employ synesthesia to suggest the kind of comprehensive experience of which an attentive observer is capable. *Firefall* is described by William Logan as "very much a book of elegy and farewell, a catalogue of the ills and complaints of age, the losses to be endured and the losses still to be faced." Its inclusion of responses to well-known poems by W.B. Yeats, T.S. Eliot, W.H. Auden, and Robert Frost suggests some of the major influences on Van Duyn's poetry.

*If It Be Not I: Collected Poems, 1959–1982* (1993) includes all of Van Duyn's previously published works prior to *Near Changes*. Critical response to the collection emphasized Van Duyn's reaction against confessionalism, Beat poetry, and antiwar poetry as well as her sustained commitment over three decades to the themes introduced in her first volume of poetry. While early critics such as James Dickey and David Kalstone had overemphasized the domestic images in her poems, later critics have valued her tough-minded rendering of experience and her affirmations of the power of love and art.

DONNA POTTS

**Biography**

Born in Waterloo, Iowa, 9 May 1921. Attended the University of Northern Iowa, Cedar Falls, B.A. 1942; University of Iowa, Iowa City, M.A. 1943; Instructor in English, University of Iowa, 1944–46, and University of Louisville, Kentucky, 1946–50; Lecturer in English, 1950–67, Adjunct Professor of poetry workshops, 1983, and Visiting Hurst Professor, 1987, Washington University, St. Louis, Missouri; Lecturer, Salzburg Seminar in American Studies, 1973; poetry consultant, Olin Library Modern Literature Collection, Washington University; editor, with Jarvis Thurston, *Perspective: A Quarterly of Literature,* 1947–70. Received Eunice Tietjens Memorial Prize, 1956, and Harriet Monroe Memorial Prize, 1968 (*Poetry,* Chicago); Helen Bullis Prize (*Poetry Northwest*), 1964; National Endowment for the Arts grant, 1966, 1985; National Council for the Arts grant, 1967; Borestone Mountain Poetry Prize, 1968; Hart Crane Memorial Award, 1968; Bollingen Prize, 1971; National Book Award, 1971; Guggenheim fellowship, 1972; Loines Award, 1976; Academy of American Poets fellowship, 1981; Cornell College Sandburg Prize, 1982; Shelley Memorial Award, 1987; Ruth Lilly Poetry Prize, 1989; Pulitzer Prize, 1991; United States Poet Laureate, 1992; honorary Litt.D., Washington University, 1971; Cornell College, Mt. Vernon, Iowa, 1972; member, American Academy, 1983; chancellor, Academy of American Poets, 1985. Living in St. Louis, Missouri.

**Poetry**

*Valentines to the Wide World,* 1959
*A Time of Bees,* 1964
*To See, to Take,* 1970
*Bedtime Stories,* 1972
*Merciful Disguises: Poems Published and Unpublished,* 1973
*Letters from a Father, and Other Poems,* 1982
*Near Changes,* 1990
*Lives and Deaths of the Poets and Non-Poets,* 1991
*Firefall,* 1992
*If It Be Not I: Collected Poems, 1959–1982,* 1993

**Further Reading**

Burns, Michael, editor, *Discovery and Reminiscence: Essays on the Poetry of Mona Van Duyn,* Fayetteville: University of Arkansas Press, 1998

Corn, Alfred, "A Review of *Near Changes,*" *Poetry* 157, no. 1 (October 1990)

Goldensohn, Lorrie, "Mona Van Duyn and the Politics of Love," *Ploughshares* 4, no. 3 (March 1978)

Hall, Judith, "Strangers May Run: The Nation's First Woman Poet Laureate," *The Antioch Review* 52, no. 1 (Winter 1994)

Hunting, Constance, "Methods of Transport," *Parnassus* 16, no. 2 (1991)

Oberg, Arthur, "Deer, Doors, Dark," *Southern Review* 9, no. 1 (Winter 1973)

Prunty, Wyatt, *"Fallen from the Symboled World": Precedents for the New Formalism,* New York and Oxford: Oxford University Press, 1990

Shaw, Robert B., "Life Work," *Shenandoah* 44 (Spring 1994)

# W

## Diane Wakoski 1937–

Diane Wakoski rejects the idea of herself as a confessional or feminist poet, although many of her readers might be surprised by this self-assessment. Wakoski, who has written over three score volumes of verse, beginning with *Coins and Coffins* in 1962, sees her craft as distinct from the scorched-earth intimacy of the poetry of Anne Sexton and Robert Lowell, and as outside of any feminist ideological penumbra. While her poems are personal and lyrical, their narrative thread is based on an idiosyncratic—at times even surreal—personal mythology. In this mythology George Washington represents an archetypal absent father romanticized by the daughter, and figures such as the King of Spain, the Motorcycle Man, and the Mechanic represent men as sexual objects and betrayers. Even the landscape of her poems takes on mythic tones, with Wakoski using such exotic locales as the Rings of Saturn to suggest the terrain of internal isolation.

In her 1974 essay "Creating a Personal Mythology," Wakoski states, "The poem is as interesting as the person who writes it," implying that all poetry is in one way or another autobiographical and thus to some degree confessional. She goes on to say:

> Of course I meant that the poet either invents his autobiography by selecting what is most important or interesting about his life to write about, or he in fact is smart enough to know that his life is dull but his mind isn't and he then gives his reader a fantasy self which is interesting. At any rate, you will never read a good poem that doesn't also make you think the poet was a fascinating person.

To this end Wakoski creates verbal projections of self that indeed become the objective correlatives of the existential self. She describes this process in her essay "Color Is a Poet's Tool":

> What I needed, then, was some system for presenting this material [personal emotion and abstract ideas] in poems. And it was a combination of poets and poetry which assaulted me during my first two years of college, teaching me about images, surrealism, big metaphors, incantation. And it was reading poems and imitating them which finally led to my own prosody and craft.

She credits Lorca's poem "Somnambule Ballad" with teaching her "simplification of images and symbolic speech" as well as the use of color as an organizing device. In the poem "The Pink Dress," for example, Wakoski repeats "I could not wear that pink dress tonight" to express the deep emotional pain of being betrayed and rejected. The color pink suggests a tinge of blood, or diluted anger, or even the speaker's diluted sense of self. In Wakoski's interpretation,

> The whole poem works with symbol. The dress itself is a symbol for woman as she is seen by most men, a decorative object, and as she chooses to present herself through her clothes.

While "The Pink Dress" arguably falls into the category of a typical feminist critique of male-female relations, many of Wakoski's other poems are not so easily categorized. The much-anthologized "Uneasy Rider" from *The Motorcycle Betrayal Poems* (1971) is a good example. In this poem the speaker admits to the ironic paradox of human (and especially female) sexuality:

> Falling in love with a mustache
> is like saying
> you can fall in love with
> the way a man polishes his shoes
> which,
> of course,
> is one of the things that turns on
> my tuned-up engine.

There is something fundamental about this kind of sexuality that is beyond politics and ideology. Wakoski's Motorcycle Man is an archetypal male representing both physical need and ultimate betrayal:

> wanting to touch your arms and feel the muscles
> that make a man's body have so much substance,
> that makes a woman
> lean and yearn in that direction
> that makes her melt.

This speaker has become subsumed in her desire, finding herself "a bad moralist" and "a sad poet" being brutalized, "blood spotting her legs / from the long ride." This stark admission of lust is an ironic counterpoint to the dedication of *The Motorcycle Betrayal Poems:* "This book is dedicated to all those men who betrayed me at one time or another, in hopes that they will fall off their motorcycles and break their necks."

In 1984 Wakoski published *The Collected Greed: Parts 1–13,* which documents her struggles with self-definition and ambivalent desires (themes that had always been a part of her poetry, as in "I Have Had to Learn to Live with My Face" from *The Motorcycle Betrayal Poems*). By the 1990s Wakoski's poetry had matured to include not only long narratives (which some critics consider her best work), but also poems featuring letters and prose fragments with topics ranging from popular films and literature to quantum physics. These later volumes include *Medea the Sorceress* (1990), *Jason the Sailor* (1993), *The Emerald City of Las Vegas* (1995), and *Argonaut Rose* (1998).

GARY P. WALTON

**Biography**

Born in Whittier, California, 3 August 1937. Attended the University of California, Berkeley, B.A. in English 1960; clerk, British Book Centre, New York, 1960–63; English teacher, Junior High School 22, New York, 1963–66; Lecturer, New School for Social Research, New York, 1969; poet-in-residence, California Institute of Technology, Pasadena, spring 1972, University of Virginia, Charlottesville, fall 1972, 1973, Willamette University, Salem, Oregon, spring 1974, University of California, Irvine, fall 1974, Hollins College, Virginia, 1974, Lake Forest College, Illinois, 1974, Colorado College, Colorado Springs, 1974, Macalester College, St. Paul, Minnesota, 1975, Michigan State University, East Lansing, spring 1975, University of Wisconsin, Madison, fall 1975, Whitman College, Walla Walla, Washington, fall 1976, University of Washington, Seattle, spring and summer 1977, University of Hawaii, Honolulu, fall 1978, and Emory University, Atlanta, Georgia, 1980–81; since 1976 writer-in-residence, Michigan State University; United States Information Agency lecturer, Romania, Hungary, and Yugoslavia, 1976. Received Bread Loaf Writers Conference Robert Frost fellowship, 1966; Cassandra Foundation Award, 1970; New York State Council on the Arts grant, 1971; Guggenheim grant, 1972; National Endowment for the Arts grant, 1973; Fulbright fellowship, 1984; Michigan Arts Council grant, 1988; Michigan Arts Foundation Award, 1989; William Carlos Williams Prize, 1989. Living in East Lansing, Michigan.

**Poetry**

*Coins and Coffins,* 1962
*Four Young Lady Poets* (with others), edited by LeRoi Jones, 1962
*Dream Sheet,* 1965
*Discrepancies and Apparitions,* 1966
*The George Washington Poems,* 1967
*Greed Parts One and Two,* 1968
*The Diamond Merchant,* 1968
*Inside the Blood Factory,* 1968
*A Play and Two Poems* (with Robert Kelly and Ron Loewinsohn), 1968
*Thanking My Mother for Piano Lessons,* 1969
*Greed Parts 3 and 4,* 1969
*The Moon Has a Complicated Geography,* 1969
*The Magellanic Clouds,* 1970
*Greed Parts 5–7,* 1970
*The Lament of the Lady Bank Dick,* 1970
*Love, You Big Fat Snail,* 1970
*Black Dream Ditty for Billy "The Kid" Seen in Dr. Generosity's Bar Recruiting for Hell's Angels and Black Mafia,* 1970
*The Wise Men Drawn to Kneel in Wonder at the Fact So of Itself,* 1970
*Exorcism,* 1971
*This Water Baby: For Tony,* 1971
*On Barbara's Shore,* 1971
*The Motorcycle Betrayal Poems,* 1971
*The Pumpkin Pie; or, Reassurances Are Always False, Tho We Love Them, Only Physics Counts,* 1972
*The Purple Finch Song,* 1972
*Sometimes a Poet Will Hijack the Moon,* 1972
*Smudging,* 1972
*The Owl and the Snake: A Fable,* 1973
*Greed Parts 8, 9, 11,* 1973
*Dancing on the Grave of a Son of a Bitch,* 1973
*Stillife: Michael, Silver, Flute, and Violets,* 1973
*Winter Sequences,* 1973
*Trilogy: Coins and Coffins, Discrepancies and Apparitions, The George Washington Poems,* 1974
*Looking for the King of Spain,* 1974
*The Wandering Tattler,* 1974
*Abalone,* 1974
*Virtuoso Literature for Two and Four Hands,* 1975
*The Fable of the Lion and the Scorpion,* 1975
*Waiting for the King of Spain,* 1976
*The Laguna Contract of Diane Wakoski,* 1976
*George Washington's Camp Cups,* 1976
*The Last Poem* (with *Tough Company,* by Charles Bukowski), 1976
*The Ring,* 1977
*Overnight Projects with Wood,* 1977
*Spending Christmas with the Man from Receiving at Sears,* 1977
*The Man Who Shook Hands,* 1978
*Pachelbel's Canon,* 1978
*Trophies,* 1979
*Cap of Darkness, Including "Looking for the King of Spain" and "Pachelbel's Canon,"* 1980
*Making a Sacher Torte: Nine Poems, Twelve Illustrations* (with Ellen Lanyon), 1981
*Saturn's Rings,* 1982
*The Lady Who Drove Me to the Airport,* 1982
*Divers,* 1982
*The Magician's Feastletters,* 1982
*Looking for Beethoven in Las Vegas,* 1983
*The Collected Greed: Parts 1–13,* 1984
*The Managed World,* 1985
*Why My Mother Likes Liberace,* 1985
*The Rings of Saturn,* 1986
*Emerald Ice: Selected Poems, 1962–1987,* 1988
*Medea the Sorceress,* 1990
*Jason the Sailor,* 1993
*The Ice Queen,* 1994

*The Emerald City of Las Vegas,* 1995
*Argonaut Rose,* 1998
*The Butcher's Apron: New and Selected Poems, Including "Greed Part 14,"* 2000

**Other Writings:** essays (*Toward a New Poetry,* 1980).

**Further Reading**


Allred, Joanne, "Diane Wakoski," in *Updating the Literary West,* edited by Thomas J. Lyon, Fort Worth: Texas Christian University Press, 1997

Bartlett, Lee, "Diane Wakoski," in *Talking Poetry: Conversations in the Workshop with Contemporary Poets,* compiled by Lee Bartlett, Albuquerque: University of New Mexico Press, 1987

Jacobsen, Sally A., Gary P. Walton, and Paul Goodin, "Diane Wakoski on the Whitman Tradition in Beat and Later Poetry: An Interview," *Journal of Kentucky Studies* 17 (2000)

Wagner, Linda W., "Wakoski's Early Poems: Moving Past Confession," in *Still the Frame Holds: Essays on Women Poets and Writers,* edited by Sheila Roberts, San Bernadino, California: Borgo Press, 1993

Wakoski, Diane, "Color Is a Poet's Tool," in *Poets' Perspectives: Reading, Writing, and Teaching Poetry,* edited by Charles R. Duke and Sally A. Jacobsen, Portsmouth, New Hampshire: Boyton/Cook, 1992

Wakoski, Diane, "How My Green Silk Dreams Led to the Concept of Personal Mythology," in *Night Errands: How Poets Use Dreams,* edited by Roderick Townley, Pittsburgh, Pennsylvania: University of Pittsburgh Press, 1998


---

# Derek Walcott 1930–

One of the most visible representatives of Caribbean and post-colonial literature, Derek Walcott has always been aware of his place in the tradition of British, world, and American literature. He has never tried to hide his influences, which range from the Greek and Roman classics to such modern authors as Hardy, Yeats, Joyce, Dylan Thomas, and Robert Lowell; indeed, they often form one layer of his subject matter. As Rei Terada (1992) has argued, the self-conscious intertextuality of Walcott's poetry enacts a specifically "American mimicry" that "tips the hand of its non-originality *and* implies the non-originality of that which it mimics." Thus, while ever at the margins of poetic fashions, Walcott is also a postmodernist who deconstructs the literary tradition with and in his own work. A virtuoso of prosodic resourcefulness, he has mastered many forms, from erotic and political lyrics to the long narrative poem in *Another Life* (1973) and *Omeros* (1990). While a good overview of his poetry can be gleaned from his *Collected Poems, 1948–1984* (1986), the selection tends toward poems with universal themes, which may obscure the local and personal flavors of much of his poetry. Readers would thus do well to explore his works wherever possible in their entirety, especially the sequences *Midsummer* (1984) and *The Bounty* (1997).

Born in 1930 on the island of St. Lucia in the British West Indies, Walcott was a twin, and both his grandfathers were white. His identity was thus "divided to the vein" in more ways than one. Receiving a "sound colonial education" in school and at the University of the West Indies in Jamaica, Walcott intended to become a painter but soon found himself drawn to literary work as a book reviewer, art critic, playwright, artistic director of a theatre workshop, and later professor of literature at Boston University. He has written numerous plays, and his prose has been collected in *What the Twilight Says* (1998). Elected to the American Academy and Institute of Arts in 1979, he has received numerous awards, including the Welsh Arts Council's International Writers Prize (1980), the MacArthur fellowship (1981), and the Nobel Prize for literature (1992).

From the beginning Walcott's poetry has been rich in diction, literary allusion, and natural metaphor, drawing upon the landscape and language of his traditional education and his tropical experience. The volumes *In a Green Night* (1962) and *The Castaway* (1965) often reveal an almost drunken immersion in the life of the senses, as though the poet is leaving his own body to inhabit the material world around him. In such poems as "Tarpon" and "Nights in the Gardens of Port of Spain," his view is not simply objective or descriptive, but a full body empathy with the natural, tactile, odorous world. In "Coral" this becomes the impossible attempt "To claim what lovers' hands have never known: // The nature of the body of another."

Widely traveled, Walcott first visited America in the 1950s, and his poetry immediately reflected the geographical and psychic closeness of the West Indies with the American mainland, especially the South and those urban areas with large West Indian populations. In "The Glory Trumpeter," for example, the young narrator remembers island men who had traveled like epic heroes to the American South to work as waiters or musicians, men who "sighed as if they spoke into their graves / About the Negro in America." In "Blues" the narrator takes a walk in New York, where he is beaten up by a gang of youths, even though "we were all / one, wop, nigger, jew." His reaction is an almost lighthearted conclusion:

> You know they wouldn't kill
> you. Just playing rough,
> like young America will.
> Still, it taught me something
> about love. If it's so tough,
> forget it.

*Another Life* (1973), Walcott's autobiographical novel in verse, consists of 23 "chapters" divided into four chronological parts: "The Divided Child" (chapters 1–7; childhood), "Homage to Gregorias" (8–12; teenage years), "A Simple Flame" (13–17;

young manhood), and "The Estranging Sea" (18–23; adulthood). While its structure has been seen as dramatic, this narrative exploration of his childhood, like George Seferis' *Mythistorema,* borrows even more significantly from novel and epic, grand forms that Walcott self-consciously admits his poem falls short of, just as his poem's 23 chapters fall short of the epic's customary 24. As though anticipating the critical reviews of Helen Vendler and Calvin Bedient, Walcott is conscious of painting a limited personal subject on a vast canvas, a grandeur of vision that may not fit the homely subject:

> Provincialism loves the pseudo-epic,
> so if these heroes have been given a stature
> disproportionate to their cramped lives,
> remember that I beheld them at knee-height,
> and that their thunderous exchanges
> rumbled like gods about another life.

Like Dylan Thomas' *Under Milkwood,* Walcott's group portrait of the community in which he grew up comes off as bigger than life, mimicking the epic because the child's perspective turns humans into heroes and examples into exemplars: "then pardon, life, / if he saw autumn in a rusted leaf."

In his next three volumes, *Sea Grapes* (1976), *The Star-Apple Kingdom* (1979), and *The Fortunate Traveller* (1981), Walcott seems fluently at play in the currents of traditional and experimental discourses, mixing the various voices and tonalities of British literature, Caribbean orality, and American informality. With a new emphasis on the value of life lived in the present, Walcott concludes the title poem of *Sea Grapes* with a partial rejection of the tradition: "The classics can console. But not enough." Providing a counterbalance to the European tradition, he includes in "Ste. Lucie" a "St. Lucian *conte,* or narrative Creole song" in the original Creole French, along with a translation into St. Lucian English, as though he, "like a relative who is tired of America," has come back home, able to see in the island's chapel not the imported angels of Giotto but "the real faces of angels."

*The Star-Apple Kingdom* continues this return to West Indian roots and its transformation and appropriation of the European literary tradition. In "The Schooner *Flight,*" Walcott writes his version of a Joseph Conrad sea story, from the point of view of a deck hand

> that they nickname Shabine, the patois for
> any red nigger, and I, Shabine, saw
> when these slums of empire was paradise.
> I'm just a red nigger who love the sea,
> I had a sound colonial education,
> I have Dutch, nigger, and English in me,
> and either I'm nobody, or I'm a nation.

The echo of Whitman's "Song of Myself" is deliberate, an American attitude of democratic all-inclusiveness that Walcott strikes to counterbalance the worth of the indigenous individual against the ideological elitism without which empire would be impossible. The volume's title poem begins as a lyrical meditation on childhood in the manner of Dylan Thomas' "Fern Hill" and ends with a political vision of a black woman, an allegorical figure of the Caribbean, "the darker, older America" who whispers in the keyhole of a dream: "Let me in, I'm finished praying, I'm the Revolution." But the dreamer rejects this alternative to action, preferring "a revolution without any bloodshed,"

> a history without any memory,
> streets without statues,
> and a geography without myth.

He wants instead to create his own persona outside history. Like the character in "Koenig of the River," Walcott seems to be playing upon the postmodern idea of constructed identity: "If I'm a character called Koenig, then I / shall dominate my future like a fiction."

The fictionalized self is reflected in the theme of exile that dominates *The Fortunate Traveller* and indeed all of Walcott's subsequent work. Exile is geographical, but it is also the internal fate of all writers who cannot dedicate themselves to a political agenda. Ironically echoing Thomas Nashe's picaresque romance *The Unfortunate Traveller* (1594) in the volume's title, Walcott examines both the psychic gains of being widely traveled and the accompanying psychic losses. As Ned Thomas (1980) comments on Shabine's "I had no country now but the imagination," Walcott's identity as an "international poet" may have lost him his "natural audience" and limited him to an audience of those "whose contrastive sense is honed by international travel." This limitation, however, seems less constrictive in a world increasingly internationalized through the media, multicultural awareness, and the democratization of tourism. Indeed, tourism becomes a major thematic chord in Walcott's subsequent work, not only as a cultural extension of imperialism but also as a facet of his own exile, so that when he returns as a tourist to an island, it can seem, as in *Omeros,* "a souvenir / of itself."

The 54 poems of *Midsummer* mark a departure from Walcott's earlier work and a new focus on his work in midlife. Written during the summer of 1983 while on holiday with his daughters in Trinidad, the meditative, even metapoetic poems in this volume reflect on where he has come from and, having passed the age of 50, where he is going. While he is able to cherish his face's wrinkles "as much as those on blue water," he feels the wear of having worked at "the craft I have pulled at for more than forty years." Likewise, he finds changes in the islands, where "Certain things" have become "quietly American"; cultural imperialism has replaced the old British colonialism, and he seems to hear the word "umpire instead of empire."

*The Arkansas Testament* (1987) contains his most accessible poems, perhaps because, after many years dividing his time between Boston and the West Indies, Walcott seems to have mastered the North American poetic idiom. The volume is again structured in such a way—Here/Elsewhere—as to emphasize his divided nature, "Here" containing poems that focus on his island "home," and "Elsewhere" focusing on his sojourns abroad. Echoing François Villon in the title poem, Walcott confronts his fear of the South and its racial tensions, Villon's hanged men like the shadows of modern lynchings:

> Villon and his brothers cower
> at the shadow of the still knot.
> There are things that my craft cannot
> wield, and one is power.

Having said that, however, Walcott powerfully analyzes the racial tension he feels as a black man in America, where "the bars of a flag whose cloth— / over motel, steeple, and precinct—must heal the stripes and the scars."

After the monumental *Omeros,* considered his masterpiece, Walcott returned in *The Bounty* to the sequence form so successfully employed in *Midsummer*. Part one consists of the title poem in the variably rhymed tercets of *Omeros,* while part two's untitled sequence of 37 poems uses the flexible *Midsummer* stanza. "The Bounty" acts as a musical prelude introducing the motifs and themes of the volume: coming to terms with nature's bounty in the face of old age and death. The title plays upon several meanings of the leitmotif "bounty," as nature's richness, the word's wealth, and life's reward. The colonialist theme is invoked in terms of tourism's exploitation of the islands' natural bounty: "Between the vision of the Tourist Board and the true / Paradise lies the desert" of the poet's exile from the islands, "where Isaiah's elations / force a rose from the sand." The poet comes to a religious appreciation of nature's bounty, "and the heart kneels to the sea-light. Its task? To adore." These fugues of figurative language seem designed "to exhaust the metaphor in the way that too much prayer / exhausts us," sensitizing the reader for the kind of spiritual appreciation that the mad rustic poet John Clare experienced as nature's wealth. Thus one prepares to return to nature in death:

> I see myself as blessedly invisible,
> anonymous and transparent as the wind, a leaf-light
> traveller
> between branches and stones, the clear, the unsayable
> voice.

In "Six Fictions" Walcott imagines returning to his island home and longs for "a day without narrative" because he is still dealing with "the pain of exile" and "mutters to himself in the old colonial diction." Eventually, however, he comes to realize: "I myself am a fiction, / remembering the hills of the island as it gets dark."

An extraordinary continuity informs Walcott's poetry, causing Peter Balakian to place Walcott "among the greatest poets of our century—Yeats, Neruda, Rilke, Williams, Elytis, for example—poets who write out of their obsessions without repeating themselves" (Hamner, 1993b). Thus, although the long narrative poems and poetic sequences are appreciable for their unity and individual design, the reader can profitably consider Walcott's complete works as an ongoing epic in which a voice from the marginal outpost of the Caribbean has managed to appropriate the poetic discourse of the tradition, to decenter it in a way that speaks both locally and universally. While placing the center back in the liberal humanist tradition of representative personal experience, Walcott continues to question the center uncompromisingly.

RICHARD COLLINS

*See also* Caribbean Poetry

**Biography**

Born in Castries, St. Lucia, West Indies, 23 January 1930. Attended St. Mary's College, Castries, 1941–47; University College of the West Indies, Mona, Jamaica, 1950–54, B.A. 1953; teacher, St. Mary's College, Castries, 1947–50 and 1954, Grenada Boy's Secondary School, St. George's, Grenada, 1953–54, and Jamaica College, Kingston, 1955; feature writer, *Public Opinion,* Kingston, 1956–57; feature writer, 1960–62, and drama critic, 1963–68, *Trinidad Guardian,* Port-of-Spain; co-founder, St. Lucia Arts Guild, 1950, and Basement Theatre, Port-of-Spain; founding director, Little Carib Theatre Workshop (later Trinidad Theatre Workshop), 1959–76; Assistant Professor of creative writing, 1981, and since 1985 Visiting Professor, Boston University; Visiting Professor, Columbia University, New York, 1981, and Harvard University, Cambridge, Massachusetts, 1982, 1987. Received Rockefeller grant, 1957, 1966, and fellowship, 1958; Arts Advisory Council of Jamaica Prize, 1960; Guinness Award, 1961; Ingram Merrill Foundation grant, 1962; Borestone Mountain Award, 1964, 1977; Royal Society of Literature Heinemann Award, 1966, 1983; Cholmondeley Award, 1969; Audrey Wood fellowship, 1969; Eugene O'Neill Foundation fellowship, 1969; Gold Hummingbird Medal (Trinidad), 1969; Obie Award, for drama, 1971; Jock Campbell Award (*New Statesman*), 1974; Guggenheim grant, 1977; *American Poetry Review* Award, 1979; Welsh Arts Council International Writers Prize, 1980; MacArthur fellowship, 1981; *Los Angeles Times* Prize, 1986; Queen's Gold Medal for Poetry, 1988; Nobel Prize for literature, 1992; Litt.D., University of the West Indies, Mona, 1973; fellow, Royal Society of Literature, 1966; O.B.E. (Officer, Order of the British Empire), 1972; honorary member, American Academy, 1979. Living in Diego Martin, Trinidad, and Boston, Massachusetts.

**Poetry**

*25 Poems,* 1948
*Epitaph for the Young: XII Cantos,* 1949
*Poems,* 1951
*In a Green Night: Poems, 1948–1960,* 1962
*Selected Poems,* 1964
*The Castaway, and Other Poems,* 1965
*The Gulf, and Other Poems,* 1969; as *The Gulf,* 1970
*Another Life,* 1973
*Sea Grapes,* 1976
*The Star-Apple Kingdom,* 1979
*Selected Poetry,* edited by Wayne Brown, 1981
*The Fortunate Traveller,* 1981
*The Caribbean Poetry of Derek Walcott and the Art of Romare Bearden,* 1983
*Midsummer,* 1984
*Collected Poems, 1948–1984,* 1986
*The Arkansas Testament,* 1987
*Omeros,* 1990
*Collected Poems,* 1990
*The Poet in the Theatre,* 1990
*Poems, 1965–1980,* 1992
*Black in America* (with others), 1996
*The Bounty,* 1997
*Tiepolo's Hound,* 2000

**Other Writings:** plays (*Dream on Monkey Mountain,* produced 1967; *The Snow Queen,* excerpt published in *People* [April 1977]), essays (*What the Twilight Says: Essays,* 1998).

**Further Reading**

Baugh, Edward, *Derek Walcott: Memory as Vision: Another Life,* London: Longman, 1978

Brown, Lloyd W., editor, *West Indian Poetry*, Boston: Twayne, 1978; 2nd edition, London: Heinemann, and Exeter, New Hampshire: Heinemann Educational, 1984
Brown, Stewart, editor, *The Art of Derek Walcott*, Chester Springs, Pennsylvania: Dufour, and Bridgend, Mid Glamorgan, Wales: Seren, 1991
Hamner, Robert D., *Derek Walcott*, Boston: Twayne, 1981; updated edition, New York: Twayne, and Toronto: Macmillan Canada, 1993
Hamner, Robert D., editor, *Critical Perspectives on Derek Walcott*, Washington, D.C.: Three Continents Press, 1993
Parker, Michael, and Roger Starkey, editors, *Postcolonial Literatures: Achebe, Ngugi, Desai, Walcott*, New York: St. Martin's Press, and London: Macmillan, 1995
Terada, Rei, *Derek Walcott's Poetry: American Mimicry*, Boston: Northeastern University Press, 1992
Thieme, John, *Derek Walcott*, Manchester and New York: Manchester University Press, 1999
Thomas, Ned, *Derek Walcott: Poet of the Islands*, Cardiff, Wales: Welsh Arts Council, 1980
Walcott, Derek, *Conversations with Derek Walcott*, edited by William Baer, Jackson: University Press of Mississippi, 1996

## Another Life

Derek Walcott's long autobiographical poem *Another Life* is a testament to his maturity as an artist. Published in 1973, it is a personal account of his life in the West Indies, specifically the island of his birth, St. Lucia. Thematically, the poem is a bildungsroman—a story about a poet's growth from boyhood into reflective adulthood—as well as a portrait of the artist as a young man. Although the poem ostensibly is an autobiography, Walcott suggests in an interview that it is actually the biography of a West Indian "intelligence," which he defines in terms of the Latin sense of "spirit." The autobiographical elements reflect the poem's public themes of the clash of cultures between England and its backwater colony, the role of history and memory, and the plight of the artist in West Indian society. As many friends have noted, Walcott's references to his life are not always accurate, but his purpose is not accuracy as memory and the exigencies of the narrative transform the quotidian into a personal and cultural odyssey.

The poem may have had its impetus in a magazine article that Walcott wrote in 1965, reminiscing about his life in St. Lucia. Manuscript evidence suggests that it began as a prose memoir and did not take poetic form until 1966 and that it went through many revisions before achieving its final form. An early long poem, "Epitaph for the Young" (1949), considered by Walcott to be a prototype or earlier version of *Another Life*, is obviously the apprentice work of a talented young artist attempting to negotiate his major European literary influences from Homer to T.S. Eliot. As such, it is a pastiche of different styles, direct allusions, and obvious puns. In *Another Life*, Walcott is in command of the form, as the allusions and images are organic to its overall theme.

*Another Life* is divided into four parts. Book One, titled "The Divided Child," opens at twilight and introduces one of the major themes of the poem: memory and history. The odyssey of the past is personal and public, as Walcott's life reflects the divided history and culture of the West Indies. The poem begins with Walcott as a young boy, showing his finished painting to his teacher, mentor, and substitute father, Harry Simmons, since his father died when he was one year old. Book Two, "Homage to Gregorias," focusing on Walcott's teenage years, emphasizes his friendship with a young painter, his contemporary Dunstan St. Omer (Gregorias in the poem), who provides him with a model for all struggling young artists. At the same time, the two books encompass his family life: the house he grew up in, the memory of his father, and his mother, who embodies a sense of order and a capacity to endure through her strength of character and fidelity to her dead husband. Although the poem contains a sense of the present and of immediacy, memory dominates these sections as Walcott develops domestic motifs such as sewing, washing, and ironing. However, the domestic world also parallels the public sphere as the young boy confronts English imperialism and culture, especially in relation to his art. Steeped in the European tradition, Walcott and Gregorias are without the means to express their native art, that of the Arawak and Carib Indians and the former slaves of Africa.

In Book Three, "A Simple Flame," the conflagration that burned away most of Castries, the capital of St. Lucia and Walcott's boyhood city, becomes the dominant symbol. The past is literally burned ruins. Having reached adulthood, the poet is ready to leave the "cement phoenix" of Castries as it begins to rise from its destruction. His infatuation with Anna, a nurse with whom he eventually falls in love, comes to the fore in this book as she also becomes his muse and embodiment of the island, "all Annas, enduring all goodbyes." Having outgrown his childhood home, he must take formal leave of her, Gregorias, and Harry Simmons to further his education in Trinidad. Unlike the first three books, in the last book, "The Estranging Sea," Walcott incorporates direct social criticism. This section is less autobiographical and more lyrical. At the same time, it includes two major events in Walcott's life: Dunstan's failed attempt to commit suicide and Simmons' successful attempt, both of which led to Walcott's increased disillusionment with the world. This book critiques the problems caused by slavery, the continued practice of colonial servitude, and the current bureaucrats and radicals who stand in the way of authentic change ("of toms, of traitors, of traditionalists and AfroSaxons / . . . they measure and divide"). The poem ends as an elegy to Gregorias and celebrates their mission as artists, which is having "Adam's task of giving things their names."

In *Another Life*, Walcott affirms the authenticity of Caribbean literary culture even as he melds it with the European tradition. The poet is the possessor and transmitter of knowledge about his culture. The Confessional genre in poetry made famous by Robert Lowell and Sylvia Plath becomes in Walcott's hands a unique amalgam of different styles as he makes it his own to incorporate Third World issues and values. His work as a whole includes a strong sense of the emerging Caribbean nationalism as it also legitimizes the multiplicity of African-Caribbean art and culture.

YMITRI JAYASUNDERA

**Further Reading**

Baugh, Edward, *Derek Walcott: Memory as Vision: Another Life*, London: Longman, 1978
Casteel, Sarah Phillips, "Autobiography as Rewriting: Derek Walcott's *Another Life* and *Omeros*," *Journal of Commonwealth Literature* 34 (1999)

Hamner, Robert D., *Derek Walcott,* Boston: Twayne, 1981; updated edition, New York: Twayne, and Toronto: Macmillan Canada, 1993

Pouchet Paquet, Sandra, "The Poetics of Memory and Authenticity in Derek Walcott's *Another Life,*" in *Memory and Cultural Politics: New Approaches to American Ethnic Literatures,* edited by Amritjit Singh, Joseph T. Skerrett, Jr., and Robert E. Hogan, Boston: Northeastern University Press, 1996

Wilson-Tagoe, Nana, "History and Style in *Another Life,*" in *The Art of Derek Walcott,* edited by Stewart Brown, Chester Springs, Pennsylvania: Dufour, and Bridgend, Mid Glamorgan, Wales: Seren, 1991

## A Far Cry from Africa

"A Far Cry from Africa" was first published in *Public Opinion* in Jamaica (15 December 1956) and later revised for the collections *In a Green Night: Poems, 1948–1960* (1962) and *Selected Poems* (1964). In this, his best-known early poem, Derek Walcott sets out his essential conflict between two cultures: the lived Caribbean heritage with its roots in faraway Africa and the English linguistic and literary inheritance that provides him the medium to express himself forcefully about the injustices of British rule. Walcott's distinctive combination of literary English and West Indian dialect has led J.D. McClatchy to suggest that Walcott "thinks in one language and moves in another" and Walcott to characterize himself as "the mulatto of style."

Walcott's verbal resourcefulness and lyrical complexity reflect his cultural conflict. Deft in his use of the armory of literary techniques available in English, he is particularly fond of puns. The pun in the "far cry" of the title, for example, embodies his felt dichotomy in a colloquial expression that harkens back to an oral culture (distance being measured by how far a voice can carry), while also suggesting the pain, both historical and personal, of the black man's removal from his cultural identity in Africa (with many tears shed along the way). Echoing "brutish necessity" with "British rule," or "colonel of carrion" with "colonial policy," Walcott evokes not only the double meanings in his own identity but also the hegemony of ideas hidden in language, just as the politics of colonialism has been justified by supposedly innocent natural metaphors. He also incorporates the Afrikaans word "veldt" and references to the Kikuyu, an East African tribe who fought as Mau Maus in the eight-year terrorist campaign against British settlers in Kenya, thus embodying the lexical and the historical in a rich verbal texture.

The first stanza begins with an image of a natural scene, the wind "ruffling the tawny pelt / Of Africa," but the reader quickly realizes that this superficially idyllic metaphor equates Africa with the corpse of a dead animal. In fact, the reader has happened upon a scene of slaughter, *in medias res:* "Corpses are scattered through a paradise." Both the Kikuyu and the colonists engage in the slaughter, fighting over the "carrion" corpse of Africa. The black flies of the Kikuyu and the white worms of colonialists are not fighting each other but exist symbiotically, one breeding the other. Both factions put aside "compassion" for the "separate dead" of individuals, whether these are "the white child hacked in bed" or the "savages, expendable as Jews," in favor of political goals. The factions differ only in the justifications for their violence. The Kikuyu "*batten* upon the bloodstreams of the veldt" to show that they are not *beaten* and that they do not act as the subaltern "beaters" for the white hunters. The colonialist worm, "colonel of carrion," is particularly articulate about the need to put the cause above the individual, just as others justify the slaughter with the scientific data of "statistics" and the supposedly objective arguments of "scholars." Similar justifications, after all, were offered by the Nazis for the European holocaust that Walcott alludes to by comparing the natives to Jews.

The second stanza explores the justifications offered by the colonialism of the Victorian period. Alluding to Tennyson's view that nature is "red in tooth and claw," Walcott suggests that this metaphor is an ideological construction that has been used to justify colonialism as survival of the fittest. Walcott thus deconstructs the hidden Tennysonian ideology in the "red/read" echo: "The violence of beast on beast is read / As natural law." Unlike the beasts, however, only "upright man" presumes to justify his violence by attributing to his goals a divine purpose, seeking "his divinity by inflicting pain." To play God by killing those individuals who get in the way of the divine plan is the hubris of colonialism, the poem suggests. The hypocrisy of this view is illustrated by the image of the colonialists who undertake their wars by dancing, like savages, "to the tightened carcass of a drum." Any resistance to the "white peace" that is offered—or actually paid for ("contracted") with the lives of the indigenous people—is not considered courage but simply the "native dread" of a backward and superstitious race.

If the poem ended here it would be a powerful indictment of colonialist intervention in Africa, but in the final stanza Walcott brings his theme back to the Caribbean and to his own identity, "divided to the vein." Because "brutish necessity" will always try to wipe its bloody hands on the justifications provided by "the napkin of a dirty cause," he suggests, indigenous peoples will always be at war with an articulate if violent oppressor, "as with Spain." Whether Walcott's allusion to Spain refers to the violent Spanish colonization of the New World or to the Spanish Civil War against Fascism, "the gorilla wrestles with the superman": the indigenous "gorilla" becomes a "guerilla" fighting the upright colonialist as "superman," the *Ubermensch* of European Fascism. Here again Walcott evokes a double meaning, an echo that transcends the historical and geographical to become personal and psychological, because Walcott recognizes that he is "poisoned with the blood of both" and is thus "divided to the vein."

Walcott does not settle the last stanza's concluding series of questions about his deeply conflicted loyalties between "this Africa and the British tongue I love" because the issue is too complex to be settled by a simple either/or choice. Given the complexity of politics and ethics, he cannot justify "the white child hacked in bed" through the abstractions of a resistance to colonial policy, but neither can he simply identify with the oppressor. To choose one culture over another is to betray both, yet not to choose is equally a double betrayal. The way Walcott frames his questions suggests a third way that navigates between denouncing and embracing the effects of cultural imperialism: to embrace the best of both cultures while denouncing the slaughter. "A Far Cry from Africa" questions the very nature of Walcott's art early in its development, examining its motives and purpose, and suspends the conflict only to suggest that the issues raised here must be undertaken in his future work. His later poetry takes the third path, negotiating the extremes of his divided cultural heritage so that he might "give back what they give."

RICHARD COLLINS

**Further Reading**

Baugh, Edward, *Derek Walcott: Memory as Vision: Another Life,* London: Longman, 1978

Brown, Lloyd W., editor, *West Indian Poetry,* Boston: Twayne, 1978; 2nd edition, London: Heinemann, and Exeter, New Hampshire: Heinemann Educational, 1984

Brown, Stewart, editor, *The Art of Derek Walcott,* Chester Springs, Pennsylvania: Dufour, and Bridgend, Mid Glamorgan, Wales: Seren, 1991

Hamner, Robert D., *Derek Walcott,* Boston: Twayne, 1981; updated edition, New York: Twayne, and Toronto: Macmillan Canada, 1993

Hamner, Robert D., editor, *Critical Perspectives on Derek Walcott,* Washington, D.C.: Three Continents Press, 1993 (see especially essay entitled "Divided Child" by J.D. McClatchy)

Parker, Michael, and Roger Starkey, editors, *Postcolonial Literatures: Achebe, Ngugi, Desai, Walcott,* New York: St. Martin's Press, and London: Macmillan, 1995

Terada, Rei, *Derek Walcott's Poetry: American Mimicry,* Boston: Northeastern University Press, 1992

Thieme, John, *Derek Walcott,* Manchester and New York: Manchester University Press, 1999

Thomas, Ned, *Derek Walcott: Poet of the Islands,* Cardiff, Wales: Welsh Arts Council, 1980

## Omeros

Derek Walcott's long narrative poem *Omeros,* published in 1990, clearly resembles his earlier poetry in its lyrical yet playful language, its rich allusiveness, and its engagement with problems of identity and history in the Caribbean. It is markedly different from his earlier work, however, in its ambitious scope. In *Omeros,* Walcott attempts nothing less than a New World epic. Adapting elements from various foundational texts of the Western literary tradition, including Homer's *Iliad* and *Odyssey,* Virgil's *Aeneid,* and Dante's *Inferno,* Walcott seeks to establish his own subject matter—the often marginalized Caribbean and its people—as equally worthy of epic representation.

Like the very name *Omeros,* Greek for "Homer," the poem's meter and stanzaic structure reinforce Walcott's epic intentions. Although the rhythm is variable enough to resemble free verse, Walcott himself claims that the lines of *Omeros* are "roughly hexametrical," thus positioning the poem in the Homeric tradition. The poem's three-line stanzas also pay homage to the *terza rima* stanzas of Dante's *Inferno.* As in the case of *Omeros*' "roughly hexametrical" lines, however, Walcott often deviates from the strictly interlocking rhyme scheme of *terza rima* (aba, bcb, and so on), switching frequently to unrhymed and sometimes rhymed triplets. At one point in chapter 33, he even inserts 17 rhymed couplets in iambic quatrimeter in order to emphasize, in semicomical fashion, the sterility of the poet-narrator's life in Boston.

Walcott's poem differs most significantly from its epic predecessors in that it does not focus on the adventures of a single "epic hero," such as Homer's Achilles or Virgil's Aeneas. Instead, the poem consists of narratives about various interrelated characters, all residents of Walcott's native St. Lucia, whose stories overlap to create a multi-layered sense of place.

The character Philoctete, encountered in the poem's first lines posing for tourists' cameras, is modeled on Philoctetes, a character from Greek mythology who is abandoned by his shipmates on an island because of a festering leg wound. Walcott's Philoctete, too, suffers from a leg wound that refuses to heal, but Walcott transforms the wound into "the cross . . . of his race," a visible symbol of the painful legacy of slavery. Philoctete's wound is eventually healed by Ma Kilman, proprietress of the No Pain Café: while returning from Mass one day, she experiences a kind of ancestral memory that enables her to discover a curative vine whose seed had been carried across the Atlantic from Africa in the belly of a bird (a swift), a recurring symbol in the poem.

The discovery of the vine links Catholicism, imported from Europe, and the island's African heritage, just as Ma Kilman is compared to both the Greek *sybil* at Cumae and an African obeah woman. By mingling European and African cultural references in this way, Walcott emphasizes (as he does throughout the poem) the hybridity of the Caribbean and presents the aftereffects of colonialism and slavery as a source of the region's distinctive cultural identity. Like the "self-healing coral" in chapter 59, the "patient, hybrid organism" that is Caribbean culture is self-renewing: "where coral died / it feeds on its death, the bones branch into more coral."

Like Philoctete, various other central characters in the poem experience epiphanies or rites of passage that enable them to come to terms with the past or with the Caribbean and their place in it. The fisherman Achille, for example, who is engaged in a struggle with Hector over Helen, experiences a dream vision in which he crosses the Atlantic to Africa. While there, he witnesses a village decimated by slave traders, meets his father, and learns his African name. Later in the poem, disgusted by tourism on the island, Achille flees south in his boat with Philoctete until an encounter with a whale, symbolizing the forces of raw nature, brings about his acceptance of the island as it actually is and an end to his resentment of what he sees as its degradation.

Major Plunkett, a British expatriate whose hobby is history, looks to the past for a sense of truly belonging to his adopted island home. He finds it in the discovery of a young midshipman Plunkett, who died in the Battle of the Saints, fought in 1782 by the English and the French, who were vying for supremacy in the region. While the discovery of this long-desired "son" in the historical archives of the local museum provides him with an imaginative personal link to the island's past, Plunkett comes to question his larger historical project. His obsession with writing the island's "History," he comes to realize, has quasi-imperialistic tendencies, seen most readily in his desire to make Helen, his former maid, the embodiment of the island rather than allowing her to exist simply as a beautiful, flesh and blood inhabitant of it: in the end, "when he thought of Helen / she was not a cause or a cloud, only a name / for a local wonder."

In much the same way, the poet figure, whose childhood and family as recalled in the poem bear a striking resemblance to Walcott's, questions his own allegiance to Western literary classics:

> All that Greek manure under the green bananas,
> under the indigo hills, the rain-rutted road,
> the galvanized village, the myth of rustic manners,

glazed by the transparent page of what I had read.
What I had read and rewritten till literature
was guilty as History. When would the sails drop

from my eyes, when would I not hear the Trojan War
in two fishermen cursing in Ma Kilman's shop?

By the end of the poem, however, the poet has come to terms with his relationship to literary history, and the poem ends with the hopeful image of Helen pregnant and with Achille, just in from the sea, peacefully ending his workday.

Walcott had struggled with issues of literary influence and Caribbean history throughout his career, most overtly in two essays written in 1974: "The Caribbean: Culture or Mimicry?" and "The Muse of History." In *Omeros,* he returns to these questions as a mature poet, finding in the epic a form capacious and flexible enough to accommodate ideas developed over decades.

ANNE BAKER

**Further Reading**


Farrell, Joseph, "Walcott's *Omeros:* The Classical Epic in a Postmodern World," in *Epic Traditions in the Contemporary World: The Poetics of Community,* edited by Margaret Beissinger, Jane Tylus, and Susanne Wofford, Berkeley: University of California Press, 1999

Hamner, Robert D., *Epic of the Dispossessed: Derek Walcott's "Omeros,"* Columbia: University of Missouri Press, 1997

Ramazani, Jahan, "The Wound of History: Walcott's *Omeros* and the Postcolonial Poetics of Affliction," *PMLA* 112 (1997)

Terada, Rei, *Derek Walcott's Poetry: American Mimicry,* Boston: Northeastern University Press, 1992

Thieme, John, *Derek Walcott,* Manchester and New York: Manchester University Press, 1999

Walcott, Derek, *What the Twilight Says: Essays,* New York: Farrar Straus and Giroux, and London: Faber, 1998


## Anne Waldman 1945–

Writer, performer, teacher, and administrator of poetic projects, Anne Waldman is one of the most prolific activists in the American poetry scene. Born in 1945 to an English professor and a translator of poetry, Waldman was raised in Greenwich Village, where she was exposed to poetry through her acquaintances with writers such as Allen Ginsberg, Robert Duncan, Gary Snyder, and William Burroughs. It is in part through these influences that Waldman eventually became what *Newsweek* described as "the reigning queen of the downtown New York poetry scene." Although she was a latecomer to the Beat scene, she was instrumental in creating a renewed interest in poetry. Waldman's poetry, Allen Ginsberg noted, "vocalizes, rhapsodizes, and defines metaphysics of a whole spectrum of modern consciousness." Her involvement in the poetic community extends from directing the St. Mark's Church-in-the-Bowery Project (1968–78) and founding *Angel Hair* literary magazine to more recently becoming the cofounder and director of the Jack Kerouac School of Disembodied Poetics at the Naropa Institute in Boulder, Colorado (1974–). She is a prolific writer with over 30 volumes of poetry as well as seven anthologies to her credit, most notably *The Beat Book: Poems and Fiction from the Beat Generation* (1996). Recently recognized in Brenda Knight's *Women of the Beat Generation* (1996), Waldman is a major writer within that literary movement, best known for dynamic performances of her work, often in conjunction with music.

Much of Waldman's work, like that of other Beat writers, especially Jack Kerouac, finds its origin in the intellectually challenging tenets of Buddhism. After embarking on several Buddhist pilgrimages to Asia, Waldman began writing in what she describes as "expansive chant-like structures." In one of her essays, she explains that her work is propelled by the Buddhist religious experience of *satori,* the "realization of impermanence, of the terrible beauty and fragility of existence" ("Poetry as Siddhi"). While her narrative style ranges from the classical epic (in *Iovis*) to Native American chants (in "skin Meat BONES"), Buddhism remains the ethical and philosophical foundation of Waldman's poetry—a poetry that not only serves as a form of entertainment but also politically engages issues such as feminism, pacifism, and environmentalism.

Waldman's best-known work is *Fast Speaking Woman, and Other Chants* (1975), a volume that was republished in an expanded edition in 1996. In the title poem, she fills 31 pages chanting with her "woman's tongue split in ten directions" as she encyclopedically catalogs the multiple roles of women. Declaring "my mouth breathes holy fire," Waldman writes a performative, feminist manifesto in order to demonstrate the power of women to change and control their own identities. "I'm the woman who scribes this text," Waldman declares. "I write down my messages to the world / The wind carries them away invisibly, / staccato impulses to the world." According to Waldman, a poem that invokes and employs female energy is capable of changing the world because the energies that go into writing are "sending out impulses" that purposefully lead women to a sense of personal empowerment. In her expansive chant-like lines that capture the urgency of the visionary state, Waldman seeks to speak to larger issues, promoting feminist politics and championing the strength and diversity of female existence.

Described by Waldman as a "printed text for an oral performance" after "Native American pieces which have instruction for an event or performance or ritual enactment," "skin Meat BONES" (1985) was published to be read aloud. The word "skin" is to be sung in a high soprano register, "Meat" in tenor, and "BONES" basso profundo. While effective as an emotionally captivating performance, this poem also articulates Waldman's raw political passions. Her final lines implore the reader "in the name of all female deities wrathful & compassionate" to make musical instruments out of her bones after death and to "PROTECT ENDANGERED SPECIES ALSO!"

Considered to be part of the recent tradition of Language poetry, Waldman's *Iovis* (Book I, 1993; Book II, 1997) consciously and actively critiques the genre of the male-dominated epic. The *Iovis* epic, according to Waldman, functions as an "all-encompassing exploratory collage argument with male energy" in both its harmful and its harmless forms. The poem may be considered personal and confessional, but, as Heather Thomas (2001) has argued at length, Waldman broadens these concerns by juxtaposing the mythic and ordinary to produce a feminist poem in the masculine tradition. Waldman "grabs the power of male deities" and then "transmutes their form . . . to her own." Later she claims that her femininity is "the window of her world," applying the energy previously concentrated on the mythical male gods to the feminine power of creation. Waldman thus affirms the natural right and power of femaleness that has for so long been left out of Western mythic consciousness. At the same time as she calls forth a mythic re-vision, Waldman contemplates the everyday modern world: "Check this out: A long way back, & now in Saudi women can't drive cars. They can, of course, but may they? May they? Does anyone, (they), care?" Through such insistent questions, she draws the reader into a context in which energy and commitment for political action are sorely needed, and while Waldman lays the responsibility for the mistreatment of women at our feet, she also acknowledges the complicity of those oppressed women, even if they do not have the same freedom as Western women to rebel against their oppressors.

The *Iovis* epic is not organized into a traditional plot but is written in a postmodern style, weaving fragments of the commonplace together with the mythic. Both *Iovis* books end on notes of misfortune—Book I with a divorce and Book II with aging and illness—but the poems' fragmentation and dismal closures do not lead to despair. Wholeness is found in the underlying Buddhist ethics, exemplified in this conjecture from Book II: "all experience & phenomena have the same inherent quality of energy, whether it be negative or positive, painful or pleasurable." Despite the painful events of Waldman's own life or of women's lives as they struggle for equality and peace, *Iovis* concludes with a sense of completeness and even with a utopian vision. Alice Notley (1998) praises the redemptive effect of *Iovis;* for Waldman, she claims, "myth is used in the search for harmless and healing ways to be grand, and in the search for ways to free one from the quotidian, as we are expected to live in a society grown away from myth and religion." This may be the reason for Waldman's prolificacy as a poet and for her authority as a teacher and leader in the poetic community as a whole. Waldman has enormous faith in the redemptive and revolutionary powers of poetry on both the personal and the societal level.

KATEY KUHNS CASTELLANO

*See also* New York School

**Biography**

Born in Millville, New Jersey, 2 April 1945. Attended Bennington College, Vermont, B.A. 1966; assistant director, 1966–68, and director, 1968–78, St. Mark's Church-in-the-Bowery Poetry Project, New York; since 1974, founding co-director, with Allen Ginsberg, Jack Kerouac School of Disembodied Poetics, Naropa Institute, Boulder, Colorado; associated with Stevens Institute of Technology, Hoboken, New Jersey, 1981–82, New College of California, San Francisco, 1982, York University, Toronto, 1984, Institute of American Indian Arts, Santa Fe, New Mexico, 1985, University of Maine, Portland, summer 1986, and Naropa Institute of Halifax, Nova Scotia, summers 1986, 1987; member of the board of directors, Giorno Poetry Systems Institute, and Eye and Ear Theatre, both New York. Received Dylan Thomas Award, 1967; Cultural Artists grant, 1976; National Endowment for the Arts grant, 1980; Shelley Memorial Award, 1996. Living in Boulder, Colorado.

**Poetry**

*On the Wing,* 1967
*Giant Night,* 1968
*O My Life!* 1969
*Baby Breakdown,* 1970
*Up through the Years,* 1970
*Giant Night: Selected Poems,* 1970
*Icy Rose,* 1971
*No Hassles,* 1971
*Memorial Day* (with Ted Berrigan), 1971
*Spin Off,* 1972
*Life Notes: Selected Poems,* 1973
*Fast Speaking Woman, and Other Chants,* 1975; expanded edition, 1996
*Journals and Dreams,* 1976
*Shaman,* 1977
*Cabin,* 1982
*First Baby Poems,* 1982; augmented edition, 1983
*Make-Up on Empty Space,* 1984
*Skin Meat Bones,* 1985
*Helping the Dreamer: Selected Poems, 1966–1988,* 1989
*Not a Male Pseudonym,* 1990
*Lokapala,* 1991
*Fait Accompli,* 1992
*Iovis: All Is Full of Jove,* 1993–97
*Kill or Cure,* 1994
*Kin,* 1997
*Polemics* (with Anselm Hollo and Jack Collom), 1998
*Marriage: A Sentence,* 2000

**Other Writings:** edited collections of poetry (*The Beat Book: Poems and Fiction from the Beat Generation,* 1996).

**Further Reading**

Foster, Edward, "An Interview with Anne Waldman," *Talisman* 13 (Winter 1995)
Knight, Brenda, *Women of the Beat Generation: The Writers, Artists, and Muses at the Heart of the Revolution,* Berkeley, California: Conari Press, 1996
Notley, Alice, "Iovis Omnia Plena: A Review of Anne Waldman's *Iovis,* Books I and II," *Chicago Review* 44, no. 1 (1998)
Rasula, Jed, "Ten Different Fruits on One Different Tree: Experiment as the Claim of the Book," *Chicago Review* 43, no. 4 (1997)

Ritkes, Dan, "Interview with Anne Waldman," *Onthebus* 3, no. 2 (1991)
Thomas, Heather H., "'Eyes in All Heads': Anne Waldman's Performance of Bigendered Imagination in *Iovis,*" in *"We Who Love to Be Astonished": Experimental Feminist Poetics and Performance Art,* edited by Laura Hinton and Cynthia Hogue, Tuscaloosa: University of Alabama Press, 2001
Tonkinson, Carole, editor, *Big Sky Mind: Buddhism and the Beat Generation,* New York: Riverhead, 1995; London: Thorsons, 1996

---

# Rosmarie Waldrop 1935–

Perhaps it is an irony that Rosmarie Waldrop's career as a major American poet has been built on her contributions to international literature. Born on 24 August 1935 in Kitzingen-am-Main, Germany, Waldrop was the youngest daughter of Josef Sebald and Friederike Wuhlgemuth. During her early childhood, Waldrop suffered several traumatic experiences pertaining to World War II. In addition to encountering the restrictions of German Nationalism and the Nazi regime, her family endured the ongoing threat of Allied bombings. Although the war ended when Waldrop was ten years old, throughout her adolescence she witnessed the aftermath of the devastating conflict in the form of the occupation and rebuilding of Germany. During these years, she began to formulate questions about her country's role in the atrocities of World War II and the Holocaust. By high school, she had begun to spend a good deal of time reading.

Through her father's interest in literature and her mother's interest in music, Waldrop found herself in an atmosphere conducive to intellectual activity. In the fall of 1954, she began college, briefly attending the University of Würzburg. That winter she met the poet Bernard Keith Waldrop, who was then an American soldier stationed near Kitzingen. Between 1956 and 1957, the two lived together in France, where they studied at the University of Aix-Marseille. In December 1958, she moved to the United States, where she married Keith Waldrop and later began graduate studies at the University of Michigan in Ann Arbor. There she completed a doctorate in comparative literature and met many poets and composers who would later influence her work. It was around this time that Waldrop began to compose poetry in English. In 1961, she and her husband established Burning Deck Press and began publishing poetry first through *Burning Deck* magazine and later in the form of complete volumes of writing by a number of young writers whose work Waldrop has described as "eclectic." Burning Deck Press is now recognized as one of the most longstanding and influential publishers of experimental poetry in the United States. In 1964, Waldrop was appointed to a teaching position at Wesleyan University in Connecticut, and until 1970 she was a professor in the school's Departments of German and Comparative Literature. Waldrop then joined her husband in Providence, Rhode Island, beginning her career as a writer in earnest and continuing to expand the parameters of Burning Deck Press. Through two editorial projects, Série d'Écriture and Dichten, she has been responsible for making a number of contemporary French and German poetry texts available to an English-speaking audience for the first time.

The early part of Waldrop's writing career was in fact marked by her crucial work as a translator of French and German poetry. During the 1970s, her major focus was on the work of Edmond Jabès, whose four-volume collection *Book of Questions* she translated into English over the course of a number of years. Jabès, an Egyptian-born Jew, was a key figure in French literature during the postwar era. In addition to translating his work, Waldrop also has translated books by major European writers, such as Paul Celan, Friederike Mayröcker, Jacques Roubaud, Emmanuel Hocquard, and Anne-Marie Albiach. At the same time, she has been associated with an American poetry movement known as the Language School, whose members take up theoretical and political concerns regarding language in their work. While it would be inaccurate to confine Waldrop to any particular movement of American poetry, her work has formed an ample contribution to Language poetry, as reflected in her critical book *Against Language?,* which was published in 1971. A year later, her first major collection of poems, *The Aggressive Ways of the Casual Stranger,* was published. During the late 1970s and early 1980s, Waldrop continued her work as a translator and also continued to expand her own methods as a writer. In 1986, she published *The Hanky of Pippin's Daughter,* a novel in which she made use of autobiographical information related to her childhood and the effects that World War II had on her family. In 1987, with the publication of *The Reproduction of Profiles,* Waldrop began a project that has been crucial to her career. In it, she explored the use of collage techniques, drawing from the ideas of German philosopher Ludwig Wittgenstein. Two subsequent books, *Lawn of Excluded Middle* (1993) and *Reluctant Gravities* (1999), continued this project. By using direct quotations and paraphrases from Wittgenstein's *Philosophical Investigations,* she created a dialogue between texts of philosophy and poetry. Metaphors for the body are a common theme in her work, as are commentaries on the role of women in society. Science, philosophy, and literature all intersect with fragments of a more autobiographical narrative.

In these books, as in much of her work of the last 20 years, Waldrop focused primarily on the form known as prose poetry, and she is now recognized as one of the major innovators in that field. Waldrop blurred the distinctions between poetry and prose even further in her second novel, *A Form / of Taking / It All* (1990). In this novel, she again employed collage techniques and repetitions to build an experimental narrative, incorporating an exploration of history and the ways in which history is recorded. Like that of Modernist writers Gertrude Stein and James Joyce, her writing style makes the reader more conscious of the nature of narrative structures, language, and communication. In *A Form / of Taking / It All,* she also examined the perspective from which narratives of history are written and how history might be viewed from the perspective of peoples whose voices are absent from the official historical record. In this way her work brings forward questions about the nature of power relations and conquest in world history, the very same issues that puzzled her as a child in Nazi Germany. She continued this work in *A Key into the Language of America* (1994), a book of poetry that focuses on the relationship between the Narragansett Indians of Rhode Island and the English inhabitants who attempted to interpret their culture.

LISA JARNOT

**Biography**
Born in Kitzingen-am-Main, Germany, 24 August 1935. Attended University of Würzberg 1954–56; University of Aix-Marseille, 1956–57, University of Freiburg, B.A. 1958; University of Michigan, Ann Arbor, M.A. 1960, Ph.D. 1966; Assistant Professor, Wesleyan University, Middletown, Connecticut, 1964–70; freelance translator, 1971–77; Visiting Poet, Southeastern Massachusetts University, North Dartmouth, 1977; Visiting Lecturer, Brown University, Providence, Rhode Island, 1977–78, and Tufts University, Medford, Massachusetts, 1979–81; Visiting Associate Professor, Brown University, 1983, 1990–91; since 1983 freelance translator; since 1968 editor, Burning Deck Press; co-founder, Wastepaper Theater, Providence, Rhode Island, 1973–83. Received Major Hopwood Award, 1963; Humboldt fellowship, 1970–71; Howard Foundation fellowship, 1974–75; Columbia Translation Center Award, 1978; National Endowment for the Arts grant, 1980, 1994; Rhode Island Governor's Arts Award, 1988; Fund for Poetry Award, 1990; PEN Book of the Month Club citation, 1991; DAAD Berlin Artists Program Award, 1993; Harold Morton Landon Translation Award, 1994; Chevalier of Arts and Letters, 2000. Living in Providence, Rhode Island.

**Poetry**
*The Aggressive Ways of the Casual Stranger,* 1972
*The Road Is Everywhere or Stop This Body,* 1978
*When They Have Senses,* 1980
*Nothing Has Changed,* 1981
*Differences for Four Hands,* 1984
*Streets Enough to Welcome Snow,* 1986
*The Reproduction of Profiles,* 1987
*Shorter American Memory,* 1988
*Peculiar Motions,* 1990
*Lawn of Excluded Middle,* 1993
*A Key into the Language of America,* 1994
*Another Language: Selected Poems,* 1997
*Split Infinities,* 1998
*Well Well Reality* (with Keith Waldrop), 1998
*Reluctant Gravities,* 1999

**Selected Criticism**
*Against Language?: Dissatisfaction with Language as Theme and as Impulse towards Experiments in Twentieth Century Poetry,* 1971

**Other Writings:** chapbooks (*A Dark Octave,* 1967), novels (*The Hanky of Pippin's Daughter,* 1986; *A Form / of Taking / It All,* 1990), translations from German (*Mountains in Berlin,* by Elke Erb, 1995) and French (*The Death of God,* by Edmond Jabès, 1979); edited anthologies of poetry (*A Century in Two Decades: A Burning Deck Anthology, 1961–1981* [with Keith Waldrop], 1982).

**Further Reading**
Foster, Edward, "An Interview with Rosmarie Waldrop," *Talisman* 6 (Spring 1991)
Perloff, Marjorie, *Wittgenstein's Ladder: Poetic Language and the Strangeness of the Ordinary,* Chicago: University of Chicago Press, 1996
Retallack, Joan, "Non-Euclidean Narrative Combustion (or, What the Subtitles Can't Say)," in *Conversant Essays: Contemporary Poets on Poetry,* edited by James McCorkle, Detroit, Michigan: Wayne State University Press, 1990
Retallack, Joan, "A Conversation with Rosmarie Waldrop," *Contemporary Literature* 40, no. 3 (Fall 1999)

---

# Margaret Walker 1915–98

Margaret Walker was one of the most formidable voices to emerge in the 20th century. Her landmark volume *For My People* celebrated ordinary life and poignantly described the joys, heartaches, and triumphs of African-Americans in the United States, using distinctive sounds and rhythms to capture a wide range of emotion. Walker's call for spiritual, emotional, and political transformation in her poetry made her a historian for her race.

The daughter of a college professor, Walker was raised in the Jim Crow South; a drunken white policeman who resented a fountain pen in a black man's pocket once chased her father home. She attended New Orleans University (now Dillard University) for two years before transferring to Northwestern University on the advice of acclaimed poet Langston Hughes, who recognized her talents and encouraged her to seek training in the North. In 1936 she began full-time work with the Federal Writer's Project in Chicago under Franklin D. Roosevelt's Works Project Administration (WPA). During this time she befriended such noted artists as Richard Wright, Gwendolyn Brooks, and Katherine Dunham. Walker's involvement with the WPA gave her an inside glimpse of the struggles of her fellow African-Americans who were involved in the Great Migration from the rural South to the industrialized North.

In 1942 Walker published *For My People,* her first volume of poems. Published in *Poetry* magazine in 1937 and anthologized in *The Negro Caravan* in 1941, the title poem quickly became her signature piece, moving her toward literary success. In 1942 Walker became the first African-American to win the coveted Yale Younger Poets Prize. Walker also established one of the first Black Studies centers in the nation while teaching at Mississippi's Jackson State College. She returned to school to earn a master of arts in 1949 and a doctorate in 1965.

Walker's greatest literary task was to "write the songs of my people—to frame their dreams into words, their souls into notes." The opening stanzas of "For My People" ring with Walker's distinctive lyrical tone. The poem chronicles the day-to-day life of a dispirited people, the mundane rewards for hard labor. "For My People" also makes blacks complicit in their own misery, however, and calls for a new day for the masses. Walker's lack of punctuation establishes a rhythmic sense of a ceaseless and tiring existence that has come to wear down even the most resilient of black people, "who are praying their prayers nightly to an unknown god / bending their knees humbly to an unseen power." Their lives are filled with uncertainty and mixed feelings, evident in their songs, their "dirges and their ditties and their blues / and jubilees." "For My People" employs a cadence and rhythm that evoke the experience of the "plowing digging planting pruning patching / of a people in distress."

"We Have Been Believers," another poem from Walker's first collection, is also written in free verse. In this piece she writes about sustaining the power of African-American belief, whether it be in "the black gods of an old land," "the white gods of a new land," or the "conjure of the humble / and the faithful and the pure." Believing that faith fosters the survival of African-Americans, she wrote: "Neither the slavers' whip nor the lynchers' rope nor the / bayonet could kill our black belief."

"Sorrow Home" establishes the southern United States as the native residence of African-Americans. Walker boasts that her "roots are deep" in Southern culture, "deeper than John Brown / or Nat Turner or Robert Lee." She further proclaims that "Warm skies and gulf blue streams are in my blood." She denounces the "steam-heated flats and the music of El and subway" of the North and refuses to be "walled in / by steel and wood and brick far from the sky." Despite her Southern heritage, Walker mourns the South as her beloved "sorrow home" and the "Klan of hate, the hounds and / the chain gang [that] keep [her] from [her] own."

Walker's poetry helped fuel the Civil Rights movement. During the 1960s she was an outspoken political activist and a role model for a new generation of writers in the Black Arts movement, including poets Sonia Sanchez and Nikki Giovanni. Following retirement Walker remained active. Sanchez, who visited the writer a week before her death, described her as "a woman of ideas, a first-rate philosopher and thinker." During Walker's final appearance at the Gwendolyn Brooks Writers' Conference at Chicago State University, she was inducted into the African-American Literary Hall of Fame. On 30 November 1998, after suffering for some time from breast cancer, Walker died at the age of 83, leaving several projects incomplete. She will be remembered as one of the greatest contributors to African-American heritage.

CANDICE MAUREEN MOTON

**Biography**

Born in Birmingham, Alabama, 7 July 1915. Attended Northwestern University, Evanston, Illinois, B.A. 1935; University of Iowa, Iowa City, M.A. 1949, Ph.D. 1965; Yale University, New Haven, Connecticut (Ford fellow), 1954; worked as a social worker, reporter, and magazine editor; teacher at Livingstone College, Salisbury, North Carolina, 1941–42, 1945–46, and West Virginia State College, Institute, 1942–43; from 1949 Professor of English and Emeritus Professor, and from 1968 director of the Institute for the Study of the History, Life, and Culture of Black Peoples, Jackson State College, Mississippi; Lecturer, National Concert and Artists Corporation Lecture Bureau, 1943–48; Visiting Professor, Northwestern University, 1969. Received Yale Series of Younger Poets Prize, 1942; Rosenwald fellowship, 1944; Houghton Mifflin fellowship, 1966; Fulbright fellowship, 1971; National Endowment for the Arts grant, 1972; honorary Litt.D., Northwestern University, 1974; Rust College, Holly Springs, Mississippi, 1974; Morgan State University, Baltimore, 1976; D.F.A., Denison University, Granville, Ohio, 1974. Died in Chicago, Illinois, 30 November 1998.

**Poetry**

*For My People,* 1942
*Ballad of the Free,* 1966
*Prophets for a New Day,* 1970
*October Journey,* 1973
*This Is My Century: New and Collected Poems,* 1989

**Other Writings:** novels (*Jubilee,* 1966), essays (*How I Wrote Jubilee, and Other Essays on Life and Literature,* 1989).

**Further Reading**

Baker, Houston, Elizabeth Alexander, and Patricia Redmond, editors, *Workings of the Spirit: The Poetics of Afro-American Women's Writings,* Chicago: University of Chicago Press, 1990
Christian, Barbara, *Black Feminist Criticism: Perspectives on Black Women Writers,* New York: Pergamon Press, 1985; 2nd edition, New York: Teacher's College Press, 1997
Freeman, Roland, *Margaret Walker's "For My People": A Tribute,* Jackson: University of Mississippi Press, 1992
Henry, Aaron, and Constance Curry, *Aaron Henry: The Fire Ever Burning,* Jackson: University of Mississippi Press, 2000

# War and Anti-War Poetry

At the birth of the English language, the Beowulf poet made an epic war poem in Anglo-Saxon, and in the Renaissance, Shakespeare thrust war into plays. Through the Enlightenment and on into the Romantic revolution, Dryden, Byron, and others waxed at ceremonial length about the glories of war. Even so late as 1937, David Jones shaped a long, albeit prickly, narrative poem on World War I, *In Parenthesis*. However, for 20th-century American war poets, novels and films have thoroughly preempted the imaginative energy that might have gone into epic or drama. In its briefer national trajectory, American war poetry truly began with Walt Whitman's lyric and elegiac pieces in *Drum Taps* (1865), and settling for immediacy, compression, and intensity, 20th-century war poets continue to favor the shorter lyric poem.

This choice is visible from Alan Seeger's "Rendezvous" (1916) all the way to Doug Anderson's "Ambush" (1991). Typically, Louis Simpson, after a grueling campaign, distills an instant of his stunned survival at Bastogne in World War II for a poem called simply "The Battle":

Most clearly of that battle I remember
The tiredness in eyes, how hands looked thin
Around a cigarette, and the bright ember
Would pulse with all the life there was within.

As industrial warfare intensified throughout the 19th and 20th centuries, mass conscription, mass death, and the arrival of mass communications have redefined the experience of war for both battlefield and home front. The 20th-century war poem shifts even the elegiac mode toward a greater skepticism about the utility of the ultimate sacrifice and toward a content that is dominantly anti-war: the poems argue more, console less, and celebrate heroic action with a distinctly heavier heart.

While American war poetry makes its first major statement in the mourning and reconciliatory Civil War poems of Walt Whitman, the subsequent poems of World War II and of Korea and Vietnam begin to bristle with the energy of anti-elegy and with moods of defiance, helpless anger, accusation, and provocative shame. However, in Whitman's "Ashes of Soldiers," a confident assumption of the justice of his war allows Whitman to say, "What love, O comrades! / Perfume from the battle-fields rising, up from the foetor rising." The fellowship of comrades on the field—a bond transcending death—perfumes, or sanitizes, the distresses of battle—their "foetor," or literal stink—into something sublime. Throughout the 19th and 20th centuries, war elegies will veer back and forth between seeing the tragedy of war death as part of nature, human and otherwise, or seeing it as aberrant. In 1899, Stephen Crane set the tone of anti-elegy, providing the basis for modern responses such as Allen Tate's "Ode to the Confederate Dead" (1928) and Robert Lowell's "For the Union Dead" (1961), poems that rewrote the Civil War for modern ears, removing the sublime. In Crane's "War Is Kind," regimental glory is bitterly "unexplained" to babe, maiden, and mother. As Crane juxtaposes rationalization and result, a crushing irony alone is clear:

These men were born to drill and die.
Point for them the virtue of slaughter,
Make plain to them the excellence of killing
And a field where a thousand corpses lie.

The traditional response, which alleges the restorative continuity of nature or comfortably explains battlefield death as a stoical shouldering of duty, mutates here into 20th-century mistrust and disbelief.

Yet the survivor's need to fit war's human destruction into a hopeful pattern of event reparable by the organic world and subordinate to it persists. In 1918, Carl Sandburg's "Grass" says, half soothing and half sardonic, to the piled bodies at Austerlitz, Waterloo, Gettysburg, Ypres, and Verdun, "I am the grass; I cover all." In the same year, Wallace Stevens' "The Death of a Soldier" declares,

Life contracts and death is expected,
As in a season of autumn,
The soldier falls.

However, even after granting nature its repeating season, Stevens concludes, "Death is absolute and without memorial." For Sandburg, nature blankets; for Stevens, it obliterates.

The sense of the bad fit between mourning war death and commemorating its ritual proprieties only intensifies. When Robert Lowell writes "For the Union Dead" in 1961, nearly a century after the Boston monument for "Colonel Shaw / and his bell-cheeked Negro infantry" was erected, he asserts, "Their monument sticks like a fishbone / in the city's throat." While Colonel Shaw, or Robert Lowell, may rejoice "in man's lovely, / peculiar power to choose life and die—" this style of heroism remains a choice of the past. The ignominious present is faced with total war and nuclear extinction:

The ditch is nearer.
There are no statues for the last war here;
on Boylston Street, a commercial photograph
shows Hiroshima boiling

over a Mosler Safe, the "Rock of Ages"
that survived the blast.

In a society that cares more for the preservation of its material assets than for its living flesh, a brutal and mechanized nature prevails:

Everywhere,
giant finned cars nose forward like fish;
a savage servility
slides by on grease.

As the killing power of modern weapons accelerates and technology takes over, the part played by the machine amplifies and the part played by the soldier declines, radically redefining the terms of the heroic. Generally literate, a soldier of the modern industrial state has some sense of his rights and duties. However, for the mass recruit on the field, as his initiative within a complex technological enterprise shrinks while his education and knowledge swell beyond that of earlier generations of soldiers, so does his frustration grow at his inability to direct the wars that so powerfully and pitilessly immerse him. Increasingly, war death is seen as passive sacrifice lacking in dignity: the corpse of Randall Jarrell's ball turret gunner is "washed . . . out of the turret with a hose." In "The Heroes" (1955), Louis Simpson dreams of dead war heroes as "scrap metal" and of disposable men "packaged and sent home in parts." In "The Fury of Aerial Bombardment" (1944), Richard Eberhart closes a poem for his replaceable gunnery students with these lines:

> Names on a list, whose faces I do not recall
> But they are gone to early death, who late in school
> Distinguished the belt feed lever from the belt-holding
> pawl.

Irony becomes the chosen defense against grief and horror—although by 1977, in Gerald McCarthy's "War Story," irony gives way to something less easily mastered by attitude:

> They . . . tried to piece the bodies back together,
> shoved them in plastic bags
> to be sent home.
> Sometimes there was an arm or leg
> leftover,
> it lay around until the next shipment;
> they made it fit in somewhere.

While resistance to war has been consistently expressed by civilian American poets, a growing number of war poems bring in anger or pain from the experience of poets in uniform. In the 20th century, more sizable armies with more literate recruits have increasing access to print. Because of the huge number of people mobilized and their lengthy deployment, the first surge of American poets in uniform begins in World War II with Randall Jarrell, Karl Shapiro, Louis Simpson, Howard Nemerov, and Richard Eberhart. A second wave of soldier poets flows from the Vietnam War, while anthologies such as *Visions of War, Dreams of Peace: Writings of Women in the Vietnam War* (Van Devanter and Furey, 1991) further widen the literary witness.

Modern war poets, in uniform or out of it, struggle with the practices of total war that involve whole populations. When bombing campaigns flatten cities and military strategists treat the munitions worker as a threat equal to an infantryman, the line separating home front and battlefield or determining who wages war or who suffers its consequences begins to blur. In Randall Jarrell's "Losses" (1944), the dead civilians query the dead pilots, "but why did I die?" Global war spills over space and time. The periods building up to war, and then the unfolding of the aftermath of occupation, with its displaced persons and destroyed facilities, make it more difficult to sustain the traditional binaries—war zone/home front, combatant/noncombatant, wartime/peacetime—that delineate war narrative.

A consequence of women entering the labor force in World War I was women's suffrage. As women, too, become munitions and medical workers and journalists and refugees who publish memoirs, they alter the balance of gender in wartime activity and begin to actively redesign their political and social roles in remembering war. When a poet such as Gertrude Stein publishes *Wars I Have Seen* (1945) about life in occupied France and H.D. (Hilda Doolittle) writes about surviving the Blitz in *Trilogy* (1973), their knowledge achieves parity with that of poets such as Wallace Stevens and Randall Jarrell, who remained in the United States, or T.S. Eliot, who served as a fire warden in England.

Yet the appalling volume of soldier death in action from the Ardennes to Normandy and on through the Tet offensive has led Americans to find direct battlefield witness the most compelling. The preference for this perspective may stem from historical positioning: during the wars of the 20th century, most Americans were out of harm's way. Their Civil War was the last to strike Americans on home soil; if 20th-century war meant bombed cities as well as decimated armies, thrilled and terrified Americans heard of these conditions secondhand. In "Smoke," Carl Sandburg observed,

> Millions of men go to war, acres of them are buried, guns
> and ships broken, cities burned, villages sent up in
> smoke,
> and children where cows are killed off amid hoarse
> barbecues
> vanish like finger-rings of smoke in a north wind.
>
> I sit in a chair and read the newspapers.

Writing in the years of the Vietnam War, Margaret Atwood blazed less passively in "It Is Dangerous to Read Newspapers":

> Each time I hit a key
> on my electric typewriter,
> speaking of peaceful trees
>
> another village explodes.

In poems such as "The Teeth Mother Naked at Last," Robert Bly and others began to write disturbing and unflattering civic portraits of the connections between American profits in armaments and its worldwide pursuit of war.

A remote American involvement may explain the growing self-consciousness about describing war, a trait that begins in World War II poetry and strengthens during the Vietnam War. Howard Nemerov uneasily dismissed the "high heroic" ("Who Did Not Die in Vain," 1947), with its soldier's "death the death of movies." In "Norman Morrison" (1967), David Ferguson remarks, "Other people's pain / can turn so easily / into a kind of play." Later poets pick up on the soldier's sense of being imprisoned within someone else's movie shoot, of vulnerably inhabiting a familiar unreality, as if after millennia, all war stories, even your own, evoke a spasm of mythic déjà vu. However, for the World War II generation, whatever the political stance, global conflict was contained within precise poems of great formal elegance and a usually severe ironic detachment.

Both English and American poets of World War II were also oppressed by the idea that the previous generation of poets—Wilfred Owen, Siegfried Sassoon, and Isaac Rosenberg—had said and done it all. Yet a large difference between the English poetry of World War I and American poetry of World War II lies in the attribution of guilt for war's victimizations. Owen and Sassoon gave poignant images of the trench soldier seen as victim: he rarely shoots but is always shot at. Randall Jarrell changed the angle of perception. Poems such as "Eighth Air Force," "Losses," and "Siegfried" meticulously preserve the moral ambiguities and tensions of saving one's country through the taking of human life. Jarrell's boyish pilots, who burn the cities they learned about in school, troop into their quarters as "murderers." In murderous irony, "Eighth Air Force" concludes, "Men wash their hands, in blood, as best they can: / I find no fault in this just man." When the legless pilot of "Siegfried" returns home to take up his civilian life, he says climactically, "you have understood / Your world at last: you have tasted your own blood." As Thomas Travisano (*Midcentury Quartet,* 1999) points out, in the Wagnerian legend to which Jarrell refers, when the warrior Siegfried kills the monster Fafnir, he tastes the dragon's blood and comes to know its evil; Jarrell's Siegfried, slayer and slain, tastes his own blood and understands himself as both victim and source of the malevolence of war.

Randall Jarrell's poems of World War II cover the widest territory. Although no one wrote as well of the strange terrors and beauties of the air war, evoking its epic and elemental scope, Jarrell also put on his canvas the people who died under the bombers and the children who went up in smoke through the chimneys of the death camps. For Birkenau and Odessa, Jarrell wrote "Protocols"; for bombed children wounded in mind and body, he wrote "The Truth" and "Come to the Stone . . . ," in which the dead child asks,

> In the sky the planes are angry like the wind.
> The people are punishing the people—why?
>
> He answers easily, his foolish eyes
> Brightening at that long simile, the world.
> The angels sway above his story like balloons.
> A child makes everything—except his death—a child's.
> *Come to the stone and tell me why I died.*

When others praised Marianne Moore's poem "In Distrust of Merits" for its self-effacing tribute to heroism, Jarrell chided her for "blindingly moral terms" (*Kipling, Auden and Co,* 1980), in which humility retreats before the effort to understand, an effort that Jarrell sees all, combatant and noncombatant alike, needing to make. Moore is

> afraid to question [the merits] of the heroic soldiers of her poem. She does not understand that they are heroes in the sense that the chimney sweeps, the factory children in the blue books, were heroes: routine loss in the routine business of the world. [. . .] she does not remember that most of the people in a war never fight for even a minute—though they bear for years and die forever. They do not fight, but only starve, only suffer, only die: the sum of all this passive misery is that great activity, War.

Unlike the English poetry of World War I, the American poetry of World War II did not initiate or define a genre; yet poems by Randall Jarrell, Louis Simpson, Richard Eberhart, and Gwendolyn Brooks enlarged the subject area of war literature. Each of them made way for what was yet more powerfully developed in the multiple textures of Vietnam War poetry.

The tough, astringent originality of Gwendolyn Brooks' poems from the 1940s, including "Gay Chaps at the Bar," "Memorial to Ed Bland," and "Negro Hero," registers the cracks and dents of race in the facade of wartime unity. "Negro Hero" opens bluntly: "I had to kick their law into their teeth in order to save them." And yet

> I loved. And a man will guard when he loves.
> Their white-gowned democracy was my fair lady.
> With her knife lying cold, straight, in the softness of her
> sweet-flowing sleeve.
> But for the sake of the dear smiling mouth and the stuttered
> promise I toyed with my life.

Like Robert Lowell's Colonel Shaw, this later soldier, toying with his life, "rejoices in man's lovely, / peculiar power to choose life and die." Knowing how little value the gift of his life holds for some, Gwendolyn Brooks' anonymous hero still clings fiercely to belief in the value of his gift for all. While Lowell's "For the Union Dead" keeps his black soldiers mute, Gwendolyn Brooks gives her "Negro Hero" both active voice and integrity. However, it is not until black soldier poets from the Vietnam War start to speak for themselves that the black voice acquires its full range and dimension in print.

In Yusef Komunyakaa's *Dien Cai Dau* (1988), black soldiers on long nights listen wryly to the seductive broadcasts of Hanoi Hannah, addressing her "soul brothers" and calling on them to desert the army of the country that has denied them equality. "You know you're dead men / don't you? You're dead / as King today in Memphis." "Tu Do Street," describing the segregated brothels in Saigon, notes that "only machine gun fire" brings American soldiers together, yet their ties to the Vietnamese prostitutes are equally illogical and deadly in their racial inflection:

> Back in the bush at Dak To
> & Khe Sanh, we fought
> the brothers of these women
> we now run to hold in our arms.

Exquisitely probing the balance of his tense and layered allegiances, Komunyakaa's soldier accepts the grip by which language and nationhood trump the loyalties of skin color. Other poems by Komunyakaa and Horace Coleman reflect on the children of soldiers whose mixed parentage will leave them unwelcome orphans in either Vietnam or America.

The biggest contrast between Vietnam War poets and the poets of other wars is the large show of cruelly direct interaction between soldiers and civilians. Bryan Alec Floyd's "Sergeant Brandon Just. U.S.M.C." records horrific damage to a child because of Just's "slightest mistake of degrees." The conscience-stricken artillery sergeant visits her regularly in the hospital; when he starts to leave, she tries to speak to him:

> Her tongue, bitten in two while she had burned,
> strafing his ears
> saying, without mercy,
> I love you.

Without comment, Doug Anderson's "Two Boys" describes an American Marine sighting in a machine gun by training it on a group of children. The first rounds hit high, and all but two boys get away. As the gunner sights in on a remaining boy,

> this eight year old, with wisdom perhaps
> from the dead, yanks off his red shirt, becomes
> the same color as the fields, the gunner lowering
> the muzzle now, whispering a wistful, *damn.*

The war being told here leaves indelible marks on all its survivors. W.D. Ehrhart remarks, "Ethics and war are mutually exclusive. You can have one or you can have the other, but you can't have both. . . . And my poetry is an ongoing attempt to atone for the unethical, for my loss of a moral compass when I was a young man" (see "War, Poetry, and Ethics: A Symposium," *War, Literature, and the Arts* 10, no. 2 [Fall/Winter 1998]). Early in the 20th century, Wallace Stevens and Carl Sandburg, bystanders of war, saw public memory of the burial mounds of World War I yield to the grass of nature's forgetfulness. For later veteran poets haunted by the apocalyptic burn of the Vietnam War, grief and guilt-ridden personal memory will not heal over. In "The Dead at Quang Tri," Yusef Komunyakaa says of a Buddhist monk, "He won't stay dead, dammit! / . . . the grass we walk on / won't stay down."

Relations with women are an integral part of these memories. Soldiers, powerless in the disposition of their lives and watching their friends picked off by an invisible guerilla enemy, attempt to regain or test manhood on women who, often enough, were involved in their own antagonistic wars for survival. For a younger army of adolescents far from home, women become the source of painfully labile emotions. All the many poems remembering laundresses, bar girls, mama-sans, nuns, and peasants, as well as the poems written by American women serving in Vietnam, uniquely cluster the problems of war and violence within the flammable arenas of sex, power, desire, and fear.

In sharp contrast to the formal rhyme and meter of earlier war poetry, this work is enormously heterogeneous in style and literary orientation. The first soldier poems of the Vietnam War, published in *Winning Hearts and Minds* (Barry, Rottman, and Paquet, 1972), locate the range, with their flat, colloquial diction, their forms close to joke, savage anecdote, and prose collage. However, the poems by veterans such as Bruce Weigl, Yusef Komunyakaa, and Doug Anderson, who published in the 1980s and 1990s, uncoil a whiplash lyric intensity. Their poetry, honed in the writing workshops that have flourished since the 1950s, draws energy from the post-Beat loosening of forms, the cultural increase in sexual and personal candor, and a subtler language more deftly nuanced and musical.

Since the war's end in 1975, poetry published in English has opened to include Vietnamese refugees in America, children of soldiers, ex-nurses, and medical workers. The story keeps unfolding and expanding: its style always more richly and riskily various. Today, many veteran poets, home again, begin to reclaim their ties with communities of poetic tradition. Poets such as Bruce Weigl salt their poems with reference to earlier war poets. After publishing *Song of Napalm* (1988), Weigl also collaborated with Thanh T. Nguyen to produce *Poems from Captured Documents* (1994). R.L. Barth draws on parallels with Greek myth in *Forced Marching to The Styx* (1983), and Doug Anderson, in his 1994 sequence *Raids on Homer*, brilliantly interpolates archaic Greek and contemporary American war experience.

As decades pass and the meanings of the conflict in Vietnam are absorbed, other poets begin to reinterpret their own wars in its light. Keith Wilson's *Graves Registry, and Other Poems* (1969), based on his Korean War experience, and Rolando Hinojosa's *Korean Love Songs* (1978), for instance, make points about racism, imperial politics, and war guilt that only demonstrate how the wisdom gained in literature about the Vietnam War has come to shape our evolving understanding of other wars, past or future.

LORRIE GOLDENSOHN

**Further Reading**


Anderson, Doug, *The Moon Reflected Fire: Poems*, Florence, Maryland: Anderson, 1994

Ehrhart, W.D., "Soldier Poets of the Korean War," *War, Literature, and the Arts* 9, no. 2 (Fall/Winter 1997)

Ehrhart, W.D., editor, *Carrying the Darkness: The Poetry of the Vietnam War*, Lubbock: Texas Tech University Press, 1985

Forché, Carolyn, editor, *Against Forgetting: Twentieth Century Poetry of Witness*, New York: Norton, 1993

Goldensohn, Lorrie, "Randall Jarrell's War," *War, Literature, and the Arts* 11, no. 1 (Spring/Summer 1999)

Jarrell, Randall, *The Complete Poems*, New York: Farrar, Straus and Giroux, 1969; London: Faber and Faber, 1971

Komunyakaa, Yusef, *Dien Cai Dau*, Middleton, Connecticut: Wesleyan University Press, 1988

Mahony, Phillip, editor, *From Both Sides Now: The Poetry of the Vietnam War and Its Aftermath*, New York: Scribner, 1998

Nemerov, Howard, *War Stories*, Chicago: University of Chicago Press, 1987

Van Devanter, Lynda, and Joan A. Furey, editors, *Visions of War, Dreams of Peace: Writings of Women in the Vietnam War*, New York: Warner, 1991

"War, Poetry, and Ethics: A Symposium," *War, Literature, and the Arts* 10, no. 2 (Fall/Winter 1998)

Weigl, Bruce, *Song of Napalm*, New York: Atlantic Monthly Press, 1988


---

## Robert Penn Warren 1905–89

One of the most prolific and versatile American writers of the 20th century, Robert Penn Warren published 17 volumes of poetry and 10 novels, along with numerous books of literary, historical, and social criticism. He is the only American writer to date to have won Pulitzer Prizes in two genres—one for fiction (in 1947 for *All the King's Men*) and two for poetry (in 1958 for *Promises* and in 1979 for *Now and Then*). Despite the fact that most Americans know him as the author of *All the King's Men*, Warren came to consider himself a poet first and foremost, and literary critics today generally agree that his lasting reputation will rest on his extensive canon of poetry. *The Collected Poems of Robert Penn Warren*, published in 1998, attests to the breadth, scope, and diversity of that canon. Even though it does not contain the two versions of Warren's long narrative poem *Brother to Dragons* (1953 and 1979), this posthumous edition contains over 600 pages of verse spanning more than six decades. Reflecting upon the publication of this impressive volume, Harold Bloom asserted that Warren is surely among "the modern American poets who will be permanent in our literature" (foreword to *The Collected Poems of Robert Penn Warren,* edited by John Burt, 1998).

In contrast to the work of poets like Eliot, Pound, Williams, and Lowell, Warren's poetry mirrored trends in Modern and contemporary American poetry more than it created them; however, this is not to say that Warren did not influence the course of American poetry. Indeed, the textbook and anthology *Understanding Poetry* (1938), which Warren co-authored with Cleanth Brooks, taught an entire generation of college students to read and analyze poetry according to the formalist standards of the New Criticism. For his association with the New Criticism, as well as for his early alliance with the conservative Agrarian writers of the South, some might dismiss Warren as a right-wing defender of the old guard of American poetry, but his career and his canon of poetry are much more complex than such a view allows. Over the course of his career Warren continually re-shaped himself as a poet, moving from the High Modernist principles of Eliot and Pound toward a more open, subjective, and Romantic aesthetic, and finally toward Postmodernism.

As a 16-year-old freshman at Vanderbilt University, Warren originally hoped to pursue a degree in chemical engineering but soon became more interested in his English classes. Over the next few years he became closely associated with the Fugitives, a group of Nashville-based poets who in 1922 launched a literary magazine titled *The Fugitive: A Journal of Poetry*. Warren formed close friendships with Allen Tate, John Crowe Ransom, and Donald Davidson, and through them later became involved with a group of conservative Southern intellectuals known as the Agrarians, who in 1930 published a controversial collection of essays titled *I'll Take My Stand: The South and the Agrarian Tradition*. The youngest member of the group, Warren nonetheless had the most difficult task: to write a defense of racial segregation in the South. Warren's pro-segregation essay, "The Briar Patch," has provoked sharply conflicting critical response, and as biographer Joseph Blotner (1997) succinctly puts it, the young Warren "could not know how 'The Briar Patch' would haunt him, or how he would be judged a racist by people ignorant of his later repudiation of the 'separate but equal' doctrine." Warren's public repudiation of segregation and his adoption of a more liberal, integrationist position came in two later books published against the backdrop of the Civil Rights movement: *Segregation: The Inner Conflict of the South* (1955) and *Who Speaks for the Negro?* (1965). Significantly, Warren's political evolution from conservative segregationist to liberal integrationist coincides with his poetic evolution from Modernism to a chastened form of Romanticism.

Warren's first three volumes of poetry—*Thirty-Six Poems* (1936), *Eleven Poems on the Same Theme* (1942), and *Selected Poems, 1923–1943* (1944)—generally adhere to the High Modernist principles established by Eliot and Pound, displaying a detached, impersonal formalism and portraying the modern individual as cut off from the sustaining beliefs and traditions of the past, living a spiritually dead, naturalistic existence. That his early themes echo the pre-conversion Eliot should come as no surprise: while a student at Vanderbilt the young Warren was simply overwhelmed by *The Waste Land*. He covered his dormitory room walls with murals depicting scenes from the poem, and he was also capable of reciting it in its entirety. In "Tradition and the Individual Talent" (1920), Eliot had demanded that in order to be original a young poet must first establish his or her own unique relationship with the tradition. Not surprisingly then, many of Warren's early poems clearly seem derivative, echoing on the one hand Eliot—as in "The Return: An Elegy" and "Kentucky Mountain Farm"—and on the other hand the Metaphysical poets: "Bearded Oaks," "Love's Parable," and "Picnic Remembered." In either vein Warren proved himself an astute technician. Perhaps the most original of Warren's early poems is "The Ballad of Billie Potts," a long narrative poem that oscillates between violent folk ballad and interpolated commentary from a modern perspective. At the time of its publication in 1944, the poem provoked both high praise and condemnation, and since then many critics have come to view it as an important step in Warren's overall development due to its original formal qualities and its potentially redemptive conclusion.

Following the publication of *Selected Poems, 1923–1943,* Warren entered into a period of nearly ten years during which he published no new poetry. Some critics have suggested that Warren was simply more focused on his fiction at this point in his career, producing his two best novels during these years: *All the King's Men* (1946) and *World Enough and Time* (1949). Warren's own comments, however, suggest that he was experiencing a deeper aesthetic crisis or conflict regarding his poetry; he explained that he was still trying to write poetry during this period, but that he simply "lost the capacity for finishing the short poem" (Watkins, et al., 1990). Significantly, Warren explained that it was during this same period that Agrarianism began to seem "irrelevant" to him (Watkins, et al., 1990). As he lost faith in the conservative values of Agrarianism, he seems to have similarly lost faith in the tradition-oriented Modernist aesthetic to which he had earlier aligned himself. The aesthetic principles of Romanticism would eventually provide a way out of this drought, and as Lesa Carnes Corrigan (1999) has argued, Warren's 1946 essay on Coleridge's *Rime of the Ancient Mariner,* "A Poem of Pure Imagination: An Experiment in Reading," provided a "catalyst" for this "conversion" to Romanticism.

Warren returned to poetry in dramatic fashion with the publication of *Brother to Dragons* (1953) and the Pulitzer Prize–winning volume *Promises: Poems, 1954–1956* (1957). In contrast to the impersonal formalism of his earlier poetry, Warren now presents a more subjective and seemingly Romantic concept of poetry, the poet, and the social function of art. Despite its occasional rhetorical excesses and feverish pitch, *Brother to Dragons* is a disturbing tour de force that exposes the heart of darkness that lies at the center of American experience. The poem focuses on the brutal axe murder of a slave by Lilburn and Isham Lewis, nephews of Thomas Jefferson, and unfolds as a dialogue between R.P.W.—the poet himself—and the disembodied voices from the historical past. Warren's decision to include himself in the poem raises a complex knot of issues, for R.P.W.'s often heated exchanges with Jefferson form an interrogation of Warren's own Agrarian past, since Jefferson is the quintessential Agrarian icon. Despite its dark subject and often brooding tone, Warren emerges from the poem a chastened Romantic with a redemptive vision of experience:

Fulfillment is only in the degree of recognition
Of the common lot of our kind. And that is the death of
vanity,
And that is the beginning of virtue.

The recognition of complicity is the beginning of innocence.
The recognition of necessity is the beginning of freedom.
The recognition of the direction of fulfillment is the death
of the self.
And the death of the self is the beginning of selfhood.
All else is surrogate of hope and destitution of spirit.

Warren solidified his new allegiance to Romanticism with his 1955 essay "Knowledge and the Image of Man," in which he transforms Coleridge's concept of "One Life" into his own theory of an "osmosis of being" that unites all human experience. The influence of the Romantics is also evident in the poems of *Promises,* which are more autobiographical than anything he had written to this date. Warren increasingly wrote of personal memories and the effort to connect his past with his present, and some of the best poems in the volume—such as the sequence "To a Little Girl, One Year Old, in a Ruined Fortress"—focus on his two young children, the result of his second, happier marriage.

While his poetry of the 1950s and early 1960s still betrays some signs of his early Modernist influences, by the time he published his 1966 essay *A Plea in Mitigation: Modern Poetry and the End of an Era,* Warren could proclaim that Modernism was definitely dead. Accordingly, the poems published in the last two decades of his career are more in line with the poetics of the "New American Poetry": more personal expression in looser, more open forms, which results in greater accessibility. In *Audubon: A Vision* (1969), *Or Else: Poem/Poems, 1968–1974* (1974), and *Now and Then: Poems, 1976–1978* (1978), Warren is at his best: technically challenging but personal and approachable, sublime yet earthy, and more often than not, affirmative and redemptive. In the post-*Audubon* poetry Warren also settles more certainly upon a thematic center involving a matrix of issues related to identity, particularly time, memory, and language. In contrast to the autobiographical poems of *Promises,* the issue of identity becomes more unsettled and problematic in Warren's later verse. As he writes in "Interjection #1: The Need for Re-Evaluation" in *Or Else,*

*Is this really me?* Of course not, for Time
Is only a mirror in the fun-house.

You must re-evaluate the whole question.

The negotiation between memory, language, and identity produces some of Warren's finest individual poems: "The True Nature of Time," "I Am Dreaming of a White Christmas: The Natural History of a Vision," "Sunset Walk in Thaw-Time in Vermont," "Rattlesnake Country," "Reading Late at Night, Thermometer Falling," "Red-Tail Hawk and Pyre of Youth," and "Old Nigger on One-Mule Cart Encountered When Driving Home From Party in the Back Country."

As Warren's poetry increasingly focused on the nuances of memory and the autobiographical act, he moved inevitably closer to the conclusion he draws in his 1975 poem "Brotherhood in Pain": "You exist only in the delirious illusion of language." Similarly, in the "Afterthought" of *Being Here: Poetry, 1977–1980* (1980), Warren describes his poems as a "shadowy autobiography . . . a fusion of fiction and fact." He goes on to explain, however, that "fiction may often be more deeply significant than fact. Indeed, it may be said that our lives are our own supreme fiction." While this statement echoes and extends Wallace Stevens' definition of poetry as the supreme fiction, it also places Warren at the threshold of Postmodernism. Warren's poetry does not engage in the radical, often remote forms sometimes associated with Postmodernism. In Postmodern fashion, however, his late views regarding the self, language, and time are marked by uncertainty and instability, and he continually undermines the notion of some absolutely verifiable, objective, and universal truth. This is readily seen in such fine poems as "Language Barrier," "Mountain Plateau," "The Whole Question," "Inevitable Frontier," and "Fear and Trembling." Warren's career successfully bridges the Modern and the Postmodern, and even though his career reflects the changing trends in American poetry more than it created them, his best poems are uniquely his own. Fittingly, Warren's highest honor came when he was named the nation's first Poet Laureate in 1986. He died three years later.

ANTHONY SZCZESIUL

*See also* Fugitives and Agrarians; New Criticism

**Biography**

Born in Guthrie, Kentucky, 24 April 1905. Attended Vanderbilt University, Nashville, Tennessee, 1921–25, B.A. (summa cum laude) 1925; University of California, Berkeley, M.A. 1927; Yale University, New Haven, Connecticut, 1927–28; Oxford University (Rhodes scholar), B.Litt. 1930; Assistant Professor, Southwestern College, Memphis, Tennessee, 1930–31, and Vanderbilt University, 1931–34; Assistant Professor, then Associate Professor, Louisiana State University, Baton Rouge, 1934–42; Professor of English, University of Minnesota, Minneapolis, 1942–50; Professor of Playwriting, 1950–56, Professor of English, 1962–73, and from 1973 Professor Emeritus, Yale University; member of the Fugitive group of poets; co-founder, *The Fugitive,* 1922–25; founding editor, *Southern Review,* Louisiana, 1935–42; advisory editor, *Kenyon Review,* 1942–63; consultant in poetry, Library of Congress, Washington, D.C., 1944–45; Jefferson Lecturer, National Endowment for the Humanities, 1974. Received Caroline Sinkler Award, 1936, 1937, 1938; Houghton Mifflin fellowship, 1939; Guggenheim fellowship, 1939, 1947; Shelley Memorial Award, 1943; Pulitzer Prize, for fiction, 1947, for poetry, 1958, 1979; Screenwriters Guild Meltzer Award, 1949; Foreign Book Prize (France), 1950; Sidney Hillman Prize, 1957; Edna St. Vincent Millay Memorial Prize, 1958; National Book Award, for poetry, 1958; Bollingen Prize, for poetry, 1967; National Endowment for the Arts grant, 1968, and lectureship, 1974; Bellamann Award, 1970; Van Wyck Brooks Award, for poetry, 1970; National Medal for Literature, 1970; Emerson-Thoreau Medal, 1975; Copernicus Award, 1976; Presidential Medal of Freedom, 1980; Common Wealth Award, 1981; MacArthur fellowship, 1981; Brandeis University Creative Arts Award, 1983; received honorary degrees from 17 colleges and universities; member, American Academy, and American Academy of Arts and Sciences; Chancellor, Academy of

American Poets, 1972; United States Poet Laureate, 1986. Died 15 September 1989.

**Poetry**
*Thirty-Six Poems,* 1936
*Eleven Poems on the Same Theme,* 1942
*Selected Poems, 1923–1943,* 1944
*Brother to Dragons: A Tale in Verse and Voices,* 1953; revised edition, 1979
*Promises: Poems, 1954–1956,* 1957
*You, Emperors, and Others: Poems, 1957–1960,* 1960
*Selected Poems: New and Old, 1923–1966,* 1966
*Incarnations: Poems, 1966–1968,* 1968
*Audubon: A Vision,* 1969
*Or Else: Poem/Poems, 1968–1974,* 1974
*Selected Poems, 1923–1975,* 1977
*Now and Then: Poems, 1976–1978,* 1978
*Being Here: Poetry, 1977–1980,* 1980
*Rumor Verified: Poems, 1979–1980,* 1981
*Chief Joseph of the Nez Perce,* 1983
*New and Selected Poems, 1923–1985,* 1985
*A Robert Penn Warren Reader* (includes prose), 1987
*The Collected Poems of Robert Penn Warren,* edited by John Burt, 1998

**Selected Criticism**
*Understanding Poetry: An Anthology for College Students* (with Cleanth Brooks), 1938; revised editions, 1950, 1960, 1976
*John Greenleaf Whittier's Poetry: An Appraisal and a Selection,* 1971

**Other Writings:** novels (*All the King's Men,* 1946; *World Enough and Time,* 1949), plays (*Proud Flesh,* 1947), nonfiction (*Segregation: The Inner Conflict of the South,* 1955; *Selected Essays,* 1958; *Who Speaks for the Negro?* 1965), screenplays (*Bonnie and Clyde,* 1972), children's literature, writing handbooks; edited collections of literature and essays (*Selected Poems of Herman Melville,* 1970; *The Essential Melville,* 1987).

**Further Reading**
Bedient, Calvin, *In the Heart's Last Kingdom: Robert Penn Warren's Major Poetry,* Cambridge, Massachusetts: Harvard University Press, 1984
Blotner, Joseph, *Robert Penn Warren: A Biography,* New York: Random House, 1997
Burt, John, *Robert Penn Warren and American Idealism,* New Haven, Connecticut: Yale University Press, 1988
Clark, William Bedford, *The American Vision of Robert Penn Warren,* Lexington: University Press of Kentucky, 1991
Corrigan, Lesa Carnes, *Poems of Pure Imagination: Robert Penn Warren and the Romantic Tradition,* Baton Rouge: Louisiana State University Press, 1999
Justus, James, *The Achievement of Robert Penn Warren,* Baton Rouge: Louisiana State University Press, 1981
Koppelman, Robert S., *Robert Penn Warren's Modernist Spirituality,* Columbia: University of Missouri Press, 1995
Runyon, Randolph Paul, *The Braided Dream: Robert Penn Warren's Late Poetry,* Lexington: University Press of Kentucky, 1990
Strandberg, Victor, *The Poetic Vision of Robert Penn Warren,* Lexington: University Press of Kentucky, 1977
Watkins, Floyd, John T. Hiers, and Mary Louise Weaks, editors, *Talking with Robert Penn Warren,* Athens: University of Georgia Press, 1990

# Audubon: A Vision

Robert Penn Warren's long poem *Audubon: A Vision* (1969) has been designated as a watershed moment in his career, his greatest poetic achievement, and one of the finest poetic sequences published in the second half of the 20th century. Both a summary statement of Warren's late themes and one of his most affirmative poems, *Audubon: A Vision* presents a high-Romantic vision of art and poetry while at the same time underscoring the ironic limitations inherent in artistic and linguistic representation.

Warren first became interested in the naturalist and painter John James Audubon in the 1940s while researching for his novel *World Enough and Time* (1949), but early attempts at the poem failed because he could not see his way out of what he described as a "narrative trap." It was not until 1968, after reimmersing himself in Audubon during work on an American literature anthology, that he solved his problem. Warren explained that one morning as he was making his bed, a fragment of the earlier failed poem came to mind, and he suddenly conceived of portraying Audubon in a sequence of "snapshots." That remembered fragment, "Was not the lost dauphin," became the opening line of his remarkable sequence. Warren's 1944 essay "Love and Separateness in Eudora Welty" provides evidence of his early interest in Audubon, particularly his discussion of her short story "A Still Moment," in which Audubon is a character. The essay reveals the poem's themes in nascent form and also foreshadows the eventual solution to the question of form: to portray Audubon through a series of snapshots, or still moments.

*Audubon: A Vision* is a poem about identity and the transformative powers of the creative imagination, which, according to Warren, is essential not only to the creation of a painting or a poem but also to the construction of the self. Although the poem pays homage to the historical Audubon's achievements, Warren's hero is actually more fiction than fact, as seen in the sequence's long second section, "The Dream He Never Knew the End of." This section, the only extended narrative in the sequence, is based on an incident described in Audubon's *Ornithological Biography,* but Warren transforms the real-life Audubon's straightforward account of a near-death experience into a dark fairy tale of archetypal significance. The result is that Warren's fictional Audubon, both here and throughout the sequence, is more psychologically complex than the naturalist ever let on.

The opening lines of the poem's first section strip away the legends that surrounded Audubon—most notably, that he was the lost dauphin of France. As a Romantic hero, Warren's Audubon instead achieves identity by giving himself over to his passion, his love for birds:

Was not the lost dauphin, though handsome was only
Base-born, and not even able
To make a decent living, was only

Himself, Jean Jacques, and his passion—What
Is man but his passion?

The first snapshot image that follows places Audubon in a southern cypress swamp at dawn, watching a white heron glide across the sky, a scene reminiscent of Welty's "A Still Moment":

Saw
It proceed across the inflamed distance.

Moccasins set in hoar frost, eyes fixed on the bird,
Thought: "On that sky it is black."
Thought: "In my mind it is white."
Thinking: "*Ardea occidentalis,* heron, the great one."
Dawn: his heart shook in the tension of the world.

Audubon seems like a new Adam, naming his world and the object of his passion; however, Warren's hero cannot achieve identity simply through immersing himself in nature. Audubon's naming of the bird, rather than uniting him with it, makes him more acutely aware of his inevitable separateness from it. As he continues to reflect on his natural surroundings, he senses the "thin . . . membrane between himself and the world." Moreover, although Audubon here can name the heron with some degree of confidence, later in the sequence he is unable to name himself: "he stood / At dusk, in the street of the raw settlement, . . . and did not know / What he was. Thought: I do not know my own name." Warren shows that we must rely on language to create order and understanding of both the world around us and ourselves, yet he also acknowledges that language is an imperfect filter for experience, separating us from the world and even from ourselves.

Similarly, while Warren celebrates Audubon's willingness to pursue his love for birds, he also emphasizes the ironic limitations of his art. In order to act out his fate—to create his magnificent *Birds of North America*—Audubon destroyed the objects of his passion: he was an excellent marksman who slaughtered thousands of birds for specimens. Warren underscores this irony in the poem's penultimate section, titled "Love and Knowledge." The section opens with a beautiful linguistic portrait of the birds but then shifts abruptly to the destruction necessary for their representation:

He slew them, at surprising distances, with his gun.
Over a body held in his hand, his head was bowed low,
But not in grief.

He put them where they are, and there we see them:
In our imagination.

What is love?

One name for it is knowledge.

Warren reminds the reader that the creative act always carries with it a sense of estrangement and separateness. Audubon's timeless paintings are not the birds themselves but mere shadows, and in the end they are mute. Similarly, the poem's second epigraph suggests that Warren's own poetic vision of Audubon is similarly silent: "I caught at his strict shadow and the shadow released itself with neither haste nor anger. But he remained silent." Despite these limitations, however, *Audubon: A Vision* still celebrates the human capacity to create, and in the poem's final section the poet enters into the sequence and affirms the human need for myth, for stories that remind us of our creative possibilities:

Tell me a story.

In this century, and moment, of mania,
Tell me a story.

Make it a story of great distances, and starlight.

The name of the story will be Time.
But you must not pronounce its name.

Tell me a story of deep delight.

ANTHONY SZCZESIUL

**Further Reading**


Bedient, Calvin, *In the Heart's Last Kingdom: Robert Penn Warren's Major Poetry,* Cambridge, Massachusetts: Harvard University Press, 1984

Burt, John, *Robert Penn Warren and American Idealism,* New Haven, Connecticut: Yale University Press, 1988

Cluck, Nancy, "'Audubon': Images of the Artist in Eudora Welty and Robert Penn Warren," *Southern Literary Journal* 17, no. 2 (Spring 1985)

Corrigan, Lesa Carnes, *Poems of Pure Imagination: Robert Penn Warren and the Romantic Tradition,* Baton Rouge: Louisiana State University Press, 1999

Hummer, T.R., "Robert Penn Warren: 'Audubon' and the Moral Center," *Southern Review* 16, no. 4 (Autumn 1980)

Ruppersburg, Hugh, *Robert Penn Warren and the American Imagination,* Athens: University of Georgia Press, 1990

Strandberg, Victor, *The Poetic Vision of Robert Penn Warren,* Lexington: University Press of Kentucky, 1977

Szczesiul, Anthony, "Robert Penn Warren's 'Audubon': Vision and Revision," *Mississippi Quarterly* 47, no. 1 (Winter 1993–94)

Walker, Marshall, *Robert Penn Warren: A Vision Earned,* Edinburgh: Harris, and New York: Barnes and Noble, 1979

Webb, Max, "'Audubon: A Vision': Robert Penn Warren's Response to Eudora Welty's 'A Still Moment,'" *Mississippi Quarterly* 34, no. 4 (Fall 1981)

# Philip Whalen 1923–

Ezra Pound's Imagism has come a long way from its debut early in the 20th century as a poetry of small, tersely worded perceptions of form in nature to the sprawling, colloquial humor of Philip Whalen's "manufactured" poems. One thing remains constant across the century of avant-garde poetry, however: the use of imagination as a faculty for tuning into nature's own creativity. Whalen's breezier versions of this kind of lyric testimony to the unity of the natural world do not depart from early Imagism so much as festoon the process with more atmosphere and chitchat, much of it funny, outrageous, or merely witty.

For Whalen, poetry is the language of intelligence, and a poem is, by his coinage, "brain candy." After years of writing fairly disciplined short lyrics, he began experimenting with a more open method in which the poem's basis was no longer the perception of a formal event in isolation, but also included seemingly irrelevant details that nonetheless constitute the reality in which ideas occur. Whalen's poems are like Persian carpets compared to Pound's Japanese scroll-like lyrics. Once liberated from the haiku model of poetry, Whalen could incorporate the colloquial speech of his time and much of the cluttered but exciting atmosphere of the San Francisco Renaissance, the movement that swept him up and associated him with Beat poetry.

Getting to the open poem required diligent practice until he stumbled upon his method of cut-and-paste in "If You're So Smart Why Ain't You Rich?," composed in 1955. If the language of verse is necessarily the climax of perceptive attention, then Whalen would cull such moments from his voluminous notebooks, in which he hastily threw down perceptions in verse form. Cutting out the best phrases meant finding a fit for them with other phrases in a mosaic method of "manufacture," as he once called it. The result is a high-powered flow of chatter in which ideas and relations among things pop off the surface of the page.

Asked once why he dated all of his poems, both in manuscript and in published form, Whalen answered that he wanted to demonstrate his right to speak on issues that would later become common property; the date would show his prescience. The more likely, less witty explanation is that all writers absorbed with "organic" poetry wish to track the flow and formation of ideas by means of the calendar.

Whalen has been in love with cities throughout his career, discovering the joys of Berkeley first, during the 1950s, when the University of California seemed like the center of an important intellectual revolution calling visionaries and scholars from all parts of the globe. His poetry may be said to be a celebration of the talk he first heard there among the literary stars of his social circle, the Beat poets. A Whalen lyric typically features fast, high-octane talk from a powerful speaker, his imitation of the Gatling-gun volubility of Neal Cassady, Jack Kerouac, and Allen Ginsberg. It was Ginsberg, Whalen recalled recently, whose mind went "5,000 miles an hour." Kerouac, another of Whalen's close friends and an influence on his two novels, also had the gift of driving speech, and a similar breakneck tempo in his prose. All this pours over the surface of Whalen's best poetry as a tribute to the open mind that flourished briefly on the West Coast during the early days of the Vietnam War and into the so-called hippie era.

To parse a typical short poem by Whalen is to discover a kind of latticework of brilliant observations carefully edited to flow in a melodious unity of rhythm and sound. These poems are best enjoyed read aloud. Whalen was self-schooled in music and read widely in the subject, and some of his learning about composition theory comes into his poetry by reference, if not outright by modes of composition. The alert reader will detect a certain amount of "orchestration" in the lines, as if the model might be the scherzo for short lyrics and the fugue for longer pieces.

Since 1972, when he became a Buddhist monk, Whalen has diverted his energies almost entirely to his religious life. Meditation has taken the place of writing lyrics, but he remains attentive to publishing editions of his work and to readings around the United States. Failing eyesight may also have contributed to his early retirement from writing. His contributions to poetry were modest but resilient and have contributed to an ongoing openness in lyric forms, particularly in West Coast writing. If his poetry has a unique edge, that edge may lie in his celebration of an often-overlooked subject, the love of intelligence itself. Whalen has overtly relished ideas and the fertile minds that throw them off like sparks from a grinding wheel. The implicit ideal underlying the mosaic method of his poems may be the desire to reenact the joys of hearing a fully alert mind discourse on the world around it with flawless attention and unguarded, brilliant speech.

In that regard, all Beat writing is a celebration of the unrestrained intellect in a state of elated response to the world. Much of what Whalen wrote follows closely the textures and formal fluidity of Ginsberg and Kerouac at their best, and all three writers may be said to translate into poetry the pyrotechnic genius of bebop and the electrifying riffs of Charlie "Bird" Parker. Although still considered a difficult poetry for younger readers, Whalen's best poems are lucid and compelling demonstrations of living joyfully.

PAUL CHRISTENSEN

*See also* Beat Poetry

**Biography**

Born in Portland, Oregon, 20 October 1923. Attended Reed College, Portland, B.A. in literature and languages 1951; served in the United States Army Air Corps, 1943–46; worked as lecturer and teacher; ordained as Zen Buddhist priest, 1973; Shuso (Acting Head Monk), Zen Mountain Center, 1975; Lecturer, San Francisco Zen Center and Zen Mountain Center, Tassajara Springs, California; Head Monk, Dharma Sangha, Santa Fe, New Mexico, 1984; since 1989 head of practice, One Mountain Temple, San Francisco. Received Poets Foundation Award, 1962; Ratcliff Award, 1964; American Academy grant, 1965; Commission on Poetry grant, 1968, 1970, 1971; Morton Dauwen Zabel Award, 1986; Fund for Poetry Award, 1987. Living in San Francisco.

**Poetry**

*Three Satires,* 1951
*Self-Portrait, from Another Direction,* 1959
*Like I Say,* 1960
*Memoirs of an Interglacial Age,* 1960
*Hymnus ad Patrem Sinensis,* 1963
*Monday in the Evening: 21 VIII 61,* 1963

*Three Mornings,* 1964
*Goddess,* 1964
*Every Day,* 1965
*Dear Mr. President* (with Gary Snyder), 1965
*Highgrade: Doodles, Poems,* 1966
*The Education Continues Along,* 1967
*T/O,* 1967
*On Bear's Head: Selected Poems,* 1969
*Severance Pay: Poems, 1967–1969,* 1970
*Scenes of Life at the Capital,* 1971
*The Kindness of Strangers: Poems, 1969–1974,* 1975
*Decompressions: Selected Poems,* 1977
*Enough Said: Fluctuat nec Mergitur: Poems, 1974–1979,* 1980
*Heavy Breathing,* 1983
*Canoeing up Cabarga Creek: Buddhist Poems, 1955–1986,* 1996
*Some of these Days: Poems,* 1999
*Overtime: Selected Poems,* 1999

**Selected Criticism**
*On Bread and Poetry: A Panel Discussion with Gary Snyder, Lew Welch, and Philip Whalen,* edited by Donald Allen, 1977

**Other Writings:** novels (*The Diamond Noodle,* 1980; *Two Novels,* 1985), children's literature.

**Further Reading**
Smith, Dale, editor, "The Whalen Issue," *Jacket 11* website, (*www.jacket.zip.com.au/jacket11*)
Snyder, Gary, *On Bread and Poetry: A Panel Discussion with Gary Snyder, Lew Welch, and Philip Whalen,* edited by Donald Allen, Bolinas, California: Grey Fox Press, 1977
Thomas, Bill, editor, *Intransit* (1967) (special issue on Philip Whalen)
Whalen, Philip, *Off the Wall: Interviews with Philip Whalen,* edited by Donald Allen, Bolinas, California: Four Seasons Foundation, 1978

---

# John Wieners 1934–

Neither John Wieners' poetry nor his life admit to easy outline. His life and verse are of one piece, a corpus of words and of spirit Charles Olson called "poetry of affect," a description refined by Robert Creeley (1988) as poem-making "in the process of a life being lived, literally, as Keats' was, or Hart Crane's, or Olson's own." The legend and rumor that surround Wieners distort his troubled, mostly solitary life and a body of work that is intensely focused on poetic tradition, work that in turn attempts to redeem both the tradition and the life it projects.

One point is not in doubt. Wieners' person and work are conjoint to his peers, earning highest praise. To Allen Ginsberg (1986), Wieners is "pure poet . . . a man become one with his poetry." In "To John Wieners," Frank O'Hara asks, "Whose heart is beating in this shell? the pulse of poetry[.]" Fanny Howe (1996) hears Wieners' voice as "a new form of speech, one that narrows the gap between longing and calling."

John Wieners grew up in a working-class family south of Boston. The "legend" begins in September 1954 when he attended his first public poetry event, Olson's marathon reading at Charles Street Meeting House during Hurricane Hazel. This was a life-defining moment for Wieners: "Charles put his hand on me and ordained me a priest." Olson assumed the role of stimulus and, in Tom Clark's (1991) description, Wieners, "a twenty-year-old waif of the night," responded, following Olson to Black Mountain, becoming "Olson's acknowledged favorite." At Black Mountain Wieners was befriended by Creeley and Robert Duncan among others. By 1956 Wieners moved to San Francisco, meeting Jack Kerouac, Allen Ginsberg, Joanne Kyger, Jack Spicer, Michael McClure, and many more writers and artists.

In 1958 Wieners solidified his reputation with his very first book, *The Hotel Wentley Poems,* a slim volume of eight poems composed in less than a week and occasioned by the end of a six-year affair. While holed up in a rundown boarding house Wieners sounds an enduring theme:

> One needs no defense.
>
> Only the score of a man's
> struggle to stay with
> what is his own, what
> lies within him to do.

Ginsberg (1986) sees "commitment" in *The Hotel Wentley Poems* "to the moment of Love, of Street, of Drug, glamors of the Underworld," pronouncing this "the work of a naked flower, a tragic *maudit.*" More than tragic, Wieners is defiant ("I . . . hang on the Demon") and foreboding ("a bed . . . it looks like a / casket"). He prophesies lifelong chaos and struggle. "A poem for record players" wrestles a deity that would purloin love: "I am engaged in taking away / from God his sound," the speaker asserts, taunting

> . . . oh clack your
> metal wings, god, you are
> mine now[.]

"A poem for vipers" concerns drug habits, and in "A poem for the old man" Wieners says good-bye to his companion:

> God love you
> Dana my lover
> lost in the horde
> on this Friday night[.]

The poem concludes,

Let blond hair burn
on the back of his
neck, let no ache
screw his face
up in pain, his soul
  is so hooked.
Not heroin.
Rather fix these
hundred men as his
lovers & lift him
with the enormous bale
of their desire.

The poems complain and call out to God, any god, audacious even decades after their composition. Wieners transmutes pain into incantation, his hallmark. This pain-to-prayer alchemy stays with Wieners as his poetry traces periods of severe depression and hospitalization for mental illness as well as relatively placid phases in his life. He moved back to the East Coast in 1959, resettling in his native Boston by the late 1960s, maintaining long stretches of silence but refusing self-pity; he declared in one interview that he was merely "living out the logical conclusion of my books" (Foye, 1988).

Although Wieners is associated with the Beats and Black Mountain, his achievements are beyond those categories. Restrained ire and his interest in revision set him apart from many Beats, as Wieners' editor Raymond Foye (1988) notes. Critic Jeremy Reed (1994) argues that "personalized lyric" distinguishes Wieners from Black Mountain writers' "transpersonal ethos." Some commentators dwell on campy fantasy as a unique feature, citing his personae of glamorous aggrieved women ("The Imperatrice," "The Garbos and Dietrichs") and Odyssean travelogues ("Playboy," "Hotels").

Wieners is most revelatory confronting homosexual desire and vulnerability, and documenting "staying with what is his own" through experiment. Risk-taking with form in *Ace of Pentacles* (1964) engenders sonnets, pristine homoerotic ballads like "Act #2"—

I blew him like a symphony,
it floated and
    he took me
down the street and
    left me here

—as well as "The Acts of Youth," another incantation of agonized enjambment set mostly in quatrains:

Pain and suffering. Give me the strength
to bear it, to enter those places where the
great animals are caged. And we can live
at peace by their side. A bride to the burden[.]

Elaborate collage sets *Behind the State Capitol* (1975) apart. Judged by some as psychotically incoherent, others see its upended syntax as implicit social critique, extolling political poems like "Children of the Working Class." In *Cultural Affairs in Boston* (1988) Wieners raises questions of birth and birthrights, conflicts of personal and poetical inheritance. In "W O W" Wieners remembers

I wanted to write a Thanksgiving poem about
  my mother how did
  she get in here and
  drunk too always on
  holidays how will I
  go about getting her
out.

"Waste" opens:

*Poetry* a noble art, it
comes from well born sons.
Futile for me[.]

At bottom, however, Wieners apprehends quite the opposite. In "The Lanterns Along the Wall," Wieners writes that "poets are under magical orders" and describes his poetry as "form wherein or by I may attain some soft definition of myself." He continues: "There are words and they govern. I wrote go on."

Jack Kimball

*See also* Black Mountain School

**Biography**

Born in Boston, Massachusetts, 6 January 1934. Attended Boston College, A.B. in English 1954; Black Mountain College, North Carolina, 1955–56; State University of New York, Buffalo (Teaching fellow), 1965–67; library clerk, Lamont Library, Harvard University, Cambridge, Massachusetts, 1955–57; actor and stage manager, Poets Theatre, Cambridge, 1956; assistant bookkeeper, 8th Street Bookshop, New York, 1962–63; subscriptions editor, Jordan Marsh Company, Boston, 1963–65; class leader, Beacon Hill Free School, Boston, 1973; co-founding editor, *Measure,* 1957–63. Received Poets Foundation grant, 1961; New Hope Foundation Award, 1963; National Endowment for the Arts grant, 1966, 1968, fellowship, 1986; American Academy Award, 1968; Committee on Poetry grant, 1970, 1971, 1972; Guggenheim fellowship, 1986. Living in Boston, Massachusetts.

**Poetry**

*The Hotel Wentley Poems,* 1958; revised edition, 1965
*Ace of Pentacles,* 1964
*Pressed Wafer,* 1967
*Selected Poems,* 1968
*Unhired,* 1968
*Asylum Poems,* 1969
*Invitation,* 1970
*Youth,* 1970
*Nerves,* 1970
*Selected Poems,* 1972
*Behind the State Capitol; or, Cincinnati Pike,* 1975
*Selected Poems, 1958–1984,* 1986
*Cultural Affairs in Boston: Poetry and Prose, 1956–1985,* 1988

**Other Writings:** plays, television documentary (*The Spirit of Romance* [with Robert Duncan], 1965), journals (*The Journal of John Wieners Is to Be Called 707 Scott Street for Billie Holiday, 1959,* 1996).

**Further Reading**

Clark, Tom, *Charles Olson: The Allegory of a Poet's Life,* New York and London: Norton, 1991

Creeley, Robert, "Preface," in *Cultural Affairs in Boston,* by John Wieners, edited by Raymond Foye, Santa Rosa, California: Black Sparrow Press, 1988

Foye, Raymond, "Introduction," in *Cultural Affairs in Boston,* by John Wieners, edited by Foye, Santa Rosa, California: Black Sparrow Press, 1988

Ginsberg, Allen, "Foreword," in *Selected Poems, 1958–1984,* by John Wieners, edited by Raymond Foye, Santa Barbara, California: Black Sparrow Press, 1986

Kimball, Jack, "On the Rugged Path with John Wieners," *Readme* 1 (1999) (*http://www.jps.net/nada/wieners.htm*)

Reed, Jeremy, "Splashed in Cinematic Jewels: Jeremy Reed on John Wieners," *Angel Exhaust* 11 (1994)

Shively, Charley, "Charley Shively Interviews John Wieners," in *Selected Poems, 1958–1984,* by John Wieners, edited by Raymond Foye, Santa Barbara, California: Black Sparrow Press, 1986

Von Hallberg, Robert, "A Talk with John Wieners," in *Selected Poems, 1958–1984,* by John Wieners, edited by Raymond Foye, Santa Barbara, California: Black Sparrow Press, 1986

Warsh, Lewis, and Fanny Howe, "How This Book Came to Be: Two Short Histories," in *The Journal of John Wieners Is to Be Called 707 Scott Street for Billie Holiday, 1959,* by John Wieners, Los Angeles: Sun and Moon Press, 1996

---

# Richard Wilbur 1921–

Richard Wilbur has been one of the most consistently impressive voices in American poetry since the late 1940s, when he began publishing his verse, but he has received little of the critical fame or celebrity enjoyed by contemporaries such as Allen Ginsberg, Robert Lowell, or Sylvia Plath. This can be explained by the "directions" that American poetry (and the criticism of it) has taken over the past 50 years, directions that Wilbur's verse, in large part, has eschewed. The experimental Modernism of Ezra Pound and T.S. Eliot was recast in the United States by poets such as Charles Olson, William Carlos Williams, Louis Zukofsky, and, in more recent years, Ed Dorn and John Wieners; the model offered by Williams, in particular, offered an alternative to the Modernism of Eliot and Pound, whose recondite and allusive "learnedness" seemed to lock modern poetry into an essentially European cultural tradition (continuing, especially, its subservience to English models) far removed from the demotic and democratic possibilities of verse built from the idioms and cadences of American speech. Another tradition of postwar verse takes a "confessional" mode, exemplified above all in the writings of Robert Lowell and Sylvia Plath but found also in poets such as John Berryman and Theodore Roethke. In the "confessional poets," there is little or no ironic distance between the personae of the poems and the poet him- or herself; the verse is frequently transparently psychological or historical (retailing the "inner" as well as the outer history of the writer) and just as frequently combative or rebellious. The limitations of autobiographical intensity, however, are all too apparent, even to the most sympathetic readers, and at its worst the "confessional" mode can seem to make a poetic virtue out of the hysterical or pathological. Wilbur has resisted the inducements of both traditions while simultaneously absorbing their lessons.

"Most American poets of my generation were taught to admire the English metaphysical poets of the seventeenth century and such contemporary masters of irony as John Crowe Ransom. We were led by our teachers and by the critics whom we read to feel that the most adequate and convincing poetry is that which accommodates mixed feelings, clashing ideas, and incongruous images" (*Responses: Prose Pieces, 1953–1976,* 1976); thus, Wilbur acknowledged his indebtedness to English metaphysical verse and to the invariably ironic registers of modern American poets, such as Ransom and Allen Tate. Wilbur's admiration of the metaphysical poets was shaped by Eliot's reassessment of them and those influential critical writings in which Eliot articulated his belief that when the poet's mind "is perfectly equipped for its work, it is constantly amalgamating disparate experience." Wilbur's remarks on his indebtedness to Ransom remind us, moreover, of the degree to which he belongs to a generation of poets whose work was shaped by its teachers: Eliot, Wallace Stevens, and William Carlos Williams had all followed careers that had no direct relationship to their writing, but poets such as Wilbur were taught by distinguished poets (who were often also distinguished critics; Wilbur was a student at Amherst College, where Robert Frost gave frequent readings and periodically taught) and promoted their verse through public readings and the teaching posts (often in English and creative writing) that gave them both employment and direct access to future generations of readers. This public "posture" was evidenced again in Wilbur's acceptance of the position of United States poet laureate for 1987–88.

Wilbur's early poems were written in response to what he called "the inner and outer disorders of the Second World War and they helped me . . . to take hold of raw events and convert them, provisionally, into experience" (*Responses*). His first volume, *The Beautiful Changes, and Other Poems* (1947), draws on his wartime experience, but the experiences themselves are rarely recorded in any direct sense; instead, they are shaped by an imaginative vision that looks for metaphorical and philosophical meaning at the expense of systematic order and coherence. "On the Eyes of an SS Officer," for example, presents its controlling idea through comparisons that articulate the poet's discoveries in metaphors rather than in paraphraseable statement:

> I think of Amundsen, enormously bit
> By arch-dark flurries on the ice plateaus,

An amorist of violent virgin snows
At the cold end of the world's spit.

Or a Bombay saint asquat in the market place,
Eyes gone from staring the sun over the sky,
Who still dead-reckons that acetylene eye,
An eclipsed mind in a blind face.

But this one's iced or ashen eyes devise,
Foul purities, in flesh their wilderness,
Their fire; I ask my makeshift God of this,
My opulent bric-a-brac earth to damn his eyes.

Poems such as this lend support to Wilbur's statement that "the relation between the artist and reality is an oblique one, and indeed there is no good art which is not consciously oblique. If you respect the reality of the world, you know that you can approach that reality only by indirect means" (*Responses*). Wilbur's two subsequent volumes, *Ceremony, and Other Poems* (1950) and *Things of This World* (1956), for which he won the Pulitzer Prize for Poetry in 1957, confirmed his presence for the ironic, reflective lyric poem cast in stanzas of strict metrical regularity. The title poem of the earlier volume exploits the oblique approach admirably:

A striped blouse in a clearing by Bazille
Is, you may say, a patroness of boughs
Too queenly kind toward nature to be kin.
But ceremony never did conceal,
Save to the silly eye, which all allows,
How much we are the woods we wander in.

The regular sestets of "Ceremony" lend formality to Wilbur's witty, mock-pastoral treatment of Jean Frederic Bazille's impressionist paintings of figures in forest settings. The second stanza rises to Miltonic (with its echoes of *Comus*) and metaphysical effects as the poet's "reading" of the painting translates it into something more than a mere "picture":

Let her be some Sabrina fresh from stream,
Lucent as shallows slowed by wading sun,
Bedded on fern, the flowers' cynosure:
Then nymph and wood must nod and strive to dream
That she is airy earth, the trees, undone,
Must ape her languor natural and pure.

Ho-hum. I am for wit and wakefulness,
And love this feigning lady by Bazille.
What's lightly hid is deeply understood,
And when with social smile and formal dress
She teaches leaves to curtsey and quadrille,
I think there are most tigers in the wood.

Being "for wit and wakefulness" entails both an eye for the comic and a celebratory vision of the "things of this world." The comic is never very far from the surface of many of Wilbur's poems, although the comedy sometimes partakes of absurdist and surrealist qualities, as, for example, in "A Hole in the Floor" from *Advice to a Prophet* (1961), with its dedication to the Belgian painter René Magritte:

The carpenter's made a hole
In the parlor floor, and I'm standing
Staring down into it now
At four o'clock in the evening,
As Schliemann stood when his shovel
Knocked on the crowns of Troy.

The extravagance of the comparison between the poet's peering into the hole in his "parlor floor" and the great German archaeologist's excavations in Asia Minor for the site of Troy adverts to the absurdity of scale with which we contemplate some of life's quotidian trivialities, but the poem still persuades us to translate everyday objects into figures of the unconscious (as, indeed, Magritte sought to enact in his paintings):

The radiator-pipe
Rises in middle distance
Like a shuttered kiosk, standing
Where the only news is night.
Here it's not painted green,
As it is in the visible world.

For God's sake, what am I after?
Some treasure, or tiny garden?
Or that untrodden place,
The house's very soul,
Where time has stored our footbeats
And the long skein of our voices?

The title poem of this 1961 collection, "Advice to a Prophet" is often considered one of Wilbur's finest. The poet's address to the prophet concerns itself with man's folly; he advises the prophet to find some appropriate form of admonition or punishment by which man might understand the consequence of his ways. Characteristically, for Wilbur, even threats of man's total demise in some universal cataclysm or conflagration do little to upset his misplaced confidence in his centrality to some metaphysical scheme of things:

Nor shall you scare us with talk of the death of the race.
How should we dream of this place without us?—
The sun mere fire, the leaves untroubled about us,
A stone look on the stone's face?

Speak of the world's own change. Though we cannot
conceive
Of an undreamt thing, we know to our cost
How the dreamt cloud crumbles, the vines are blackened by
frost,
How the view alters. We could believe,

If you told us so, that the white-tailed deer will slip
Into perfect shade, grown perfectly shy,
The lark avoid the reaches of eye
The jack-pine lose its knuckled grip

These reflections have something of the quality of Robert Frost's meditations on the universe revealed by modern physics and astronomy (one thinks, particularly, of his "Desert Places") refracted through the aestheticism of Wallace Stevens but without, finally, Stevens' confidence in the transcendent power of art to shield us against the world's terrors, especially those of mutability and decay.

Wilbur's great gifts in comic and satiric verse equipped him admirably for his translations of Molière into English couplets (notably *Tartuffe*) and his lyrics for Leonard Bernstein's and Lillian Hellman's adaptation of Voltaire's *Candide* for the Broadway stage in 1956 (although the show was not a commercial or critical success, it ran for 73 performances in New York). Wilbur blamed himself for being "too literary and stubborn" in his approach to *Candide,* but his lyrics remain a poetical "high point" of the musical, as exemplified by "Pangloss's Song: A Comic-Opera Lyric," chosen for inclusion in *Advice to a Prophet.* Dr. Pangloss' boundless optimism overwhelms the realization that he is disfigured by syphilis:

Dear boy, you will not hear me speak
With sorrow or with rancor
Of what has shrivelled up my cheek
And blasted it with canker;
'Twas Love, great Love, that did the deed.
Through Nature's gentle laws,
And how should ill effects proceed
From so divine a cause?

Sweet honey comes from bees that sting
As you are well aware:
To one adept in reasoning,
Whatever pains disease may bring
Are but the tangy seasoning
To Love's delicious fare.

The words here (effortlessly shaped as they are to their musical setting) provide some of those pleasures we associate with American popular song in lyricists such as Cole Porter and Lorenz Hart (e.g., the insistent rhyme of the third, fourth, and fifth lines of the second stanza), and they reveal, again, the confidence with which Wilbur can work, with admirable regularity and metrical strictness, in the various registers of sound and diction that lyric poetry calls on. Despite his dissatisfaction with *Candide,* Wilbur returned to the composition of words for music in the 1980s, just prior to his assumption of the poet laureateship, with the text of a cantata, "On Freedom's Ground," written in collaboration with the American composer William Schuman and performed at Lincoln Center in October 1986 as part of the celebrations for the centennial of the Statue of Liberty—an "effort," as he puts it in his "Introduction" to *New and Collected Poems* (1988), "to say something clear and acceptable, yet not wholly predictable, on a national occasion." *Advice to a Prophet* offered translations from Jorge Guillen, Salvatore Quasimodo, Gerard de Nerval, as well as Molière, but the place of translation in Wilbur's poetic output assumed even greater proportions in the poetry published between 1969 and 1976. *Walking to Sleep: New Poems and Translations* (1969) includes a section of translations from Jorge Luis Borges, Anna Akhmatova, Andrei Voznesensky, Charles D'Orleans, and François Villon, and *The Mind-Reader: New Poems* (1976) added translations from Jean de la Fontaine, Voltaire, Joseph Brodsky, and Nikolai Morshen to what was already a considerable body of the re-creation of others' work. As Ralph J. Mills (1983) has remarked of Wilbur's translations, "Each of them seems chosen because of a certain kinship of spirit between the foreign poem and the artistic personality of the translator. In other words, they are poems of a kind Wilbur himself might conceivably have written; in the act of translating he has apparently entered so intimately into an experience of the original that a new poem has been born of it in another language."

It is possible to say of Wilbur that his poetry shows little development, but to say this is to point to a strength and not a weakness. He himself has argued that in his later writing he discovered a "plainer and more straightforward way of writing" and that he moved, sometime in the late 1950s, from the use of a "single meditative voice balancing argument and counter-argument" to the more dramatic registers of a poem such as "Two Voices in a Meadow." However, like Frost, who also "discovered" the poetical and philosophical possibilities of the dramatic form, Wilbur has never been a formulaic poet, and he has, above all, resisted the instincts of many of his generation to use poetry for oppositional or polemical purposes. In many ways, for all the Romantic seriousness of his writing, his affinities are with the 18th century and its belief that poetry is a rational activity that, through wit and the play of sound and delight in the "things of this world," reminds us of both the pleasures of life and the folly of our ambitions. In his characteristically pointed way, Wilbur articulates this better than any of his critics in a recent poem, "On Having Mis-Identified a Wild Flower":

A thrush, because I'd been wrong,
Burst rightly into song
In a world not vague, not lonely,
Not governed by me only.

Henry Claridge

**Biography**

Born in New York City, 1 March 1921. Attended Amherst College, Massachusetts, B.A. 1942, A.M. 1952; Harvard University, Cambridge, Massachusetts, A.M. 1947; served in the United States Army, 1943–45; member of the Society of Fellows, 1947–50, and Assistant Professor of English, 1950–54, Harvard University; Associate Professor of English, Wellesley College, Massachusetts, 1955–57; Professor of English, Wesleyan University, Middletown, Connecticut, 1957–77; writer-in-residence, Smith College, Northampton, Massachusetts, 1977–86; general editor, Laurel Poets series, Dell Publishing Company, New York; State Department cultural exchange representative to the U.S.S.R., 1961. Received Guggenheim fellowship, 1952, 1963; American Academy in Rome fellowship, 1954; Pulitzer Prize, 1957, 1989; National Book Award, 1957; Edna St. Vincent Millay Memorial Award, 1957; Ford fellowship, for drama, 1960; Melville Cane Award, 1962; Bollingen Prize, for translation, 1963, for poetry, 1971; Sarah Josepha Hale Award, 1968; Brandeis University Creative Arts Award, 1970; Henri Desfeuilles Prize, 1971; Shelley Memorial Award, 1973; Harriet Monroe Award, 1978; PEN Translation Award, 1983; Drama Desk Award, for translation, 1983; St. Botolph's Club Foundation Award, 1983; Camargo Foundation fellowship, 1985; *Los Angeles Times* Prize, 1988; Birmingham-Southern University Grand Master Award, 1989; Frost Medal, 1996; member, American Academy of Arts and Sciences; President, 1974–76, and Chancellor, 1976–78, 1980–81, American Academy; Chancellor, Academy of American

Poets, 1961–95; Chevalier, Ordre National des Palmes Académiques, 1983; United States Poet Laureate, 1987–88; has received honorary degrees from 13 colleges and universities. Living in Cummington, Massachusetts.

**Poetry**

*The Beautiful Changes, and Other Poems,* 1947
*Ceremony, and Other Poems,* 1950
*Things of This World,* 1956; one section reprinted as *Digging to China,* 1970
*Poems, 1943–1956,* 1957
*Advice to a Prophet, and Other Poems,* 1961
*The Poems of Richard Wilbur,* 1963
*Walking to Sleep: New Poems and Translations,* 1969
*The Mind-Reader: New Poems,* 1976
*New and Collected Poems,* 1988
*About Sylvia: Poems* (with others), 1996
*Mayflies: New Poems and Translations,* 2000

**Selected Criticism**

*Emily Dickinson: Three Views* (with Louise Bogan and Archibald MacLeish), 1960
*Responses: Prose Pieces, 1953–1976,* 1976

**Other Writings:** plays (*On Freedom's Ground* [with William Schuman], produced 1986), children's literature (*Loudmouse, Opposites,* 1973), translation of French (*The Misanthrope: Comedy in Five Acts,* by Molière, 1955) and Russian literature (*The Funeral of Bobo,* by Joseph Brodsky, 1974); edited collections of poetry (*Poe: Complete Poems,* 1959).

**Further Reading**

Cummins, Paul F., *Richard Wilbur: A Critical Essay,* Grand Rapids, Michigan: Eerdmans, 1971
Hougen, John B., *Ecstasy within Discipline: The Poetry of Richard Wilbur,* Atlanta, Georgia: Scholars Press, 1995
Jarrell, Randall, *Poetry and the Age,* New York: Knopf, and London: Faber and Faber, 1953
Jarrell, Randall, *The Third Book of Criticism,* New York: Farrar, Straus and Giroux, 1965; London: Faber, 1975
Michelson, Bruce, *Wilbur's Poetry: Music in a Scattering Time,* Amherst: University of Massachusetts Press, 1991
Mills, Ralph J., Jr., *Contemporary American Poetry,* New York: Random House, 1965
Salinger, Wendy, editor, *Richard Wilbur's Creation,* Ann Arbor: University of Michigan Press, 1983

## Love Calls Us to the Things of This World

Richard Wilbur's great praise of domestic sublimity originally appeared in the Pulitzer Prize–winning 1956 collection to which it gives a title: *Things of This World.* "Love Calls Us to the Things of This World" is among Wilbur's best-known works, one of only a handful of poems by living writers in Columbia University's 1992 *Top 500 Poems* anthology (a ranking based solely on the number of times a poem has been anthologized). The poem puts forward, simply and in a startlingly common image, one of Wilbur's major themes: the capacity of metaphor to wed the spiritual and material worlds. In this poem, a man's soul, preceding the wakening body in awareness, sees a clothesline populated not by laundry but by bodiless angels; then, as if caught by the dawn's light, the soul returns to the human body, wishing that the laundry, too, will come down to its wearers, to clothe the material with what has been clean and impersonal.

Like Wilbur's early "Praise in Summer," his very recent "A Digression" and "Mayflies," or his "Digging for China" (also in *Things of This World*), this poem relies on the metaphor-making capacities of a mind (or "soul") taken by surprise: the poem opens bleary-eyed, startled awake by "the cry of pulleys," with the soul abruptly "spirited from sleep." The brilliant and apt descriptions of the clothes' angelic laundry-line dance—sometimes "calm swells / of halycon feeling," sometimes a "terrible speed . . . moving and staying like white water," varying with the wind—seem to depend on the "bodiless" soul's unconditioned, almost childlike sight. As if to preserve this literally ecstatic (i.e., out-of-place) vision, the soul cries,

> Oh, let there be nothing on earth but laundry,
> Nothing but rosy hands in the rising steam
> And clear dances done in sight of heaven.

Those rosy hands, one suspects, echo Homer's "rosy-fingered dawn." Yet, as the sun brings color to the dawning world, the soul "descends once more in bitter love / to accept the waking body" and, from the body, speaks a different injunction, "in a changed voice." Instead of wishing solely for the cleanliness and clarity of dawn, the embodied soul asks that the bedsheets, blouses, and smocks be brought down "from their ruddy gallows," an image suffused at once with the blood of life and the shadow of its loss. "Let there be," he calls out,

> . . . clean linen for the backs of thieves;
> Let lovers go fresh and sweet to be undone,
> And the heaviest nuns walk in a pure floating
> Of dark habits,
> keeping their difficult balance.

This "difficult balance," between the material and the spiritual, is one of Wilbur's central tropes, as Peter Harris has pointed out in his essay "Forty Years of Richard Wilbur: The Loving Work of an Equilibrist" (1990). May Swenson identifies the poem as "an epitome of relative weight and equipoise," formally and thematically (in Ostroff, 1964). Wilbur himself explains the final image of the nuns in two ways: first, the city of the poem is Rome, where he lived in the mid-1950s under the auspices of the Prix de Roma fellowship, "and, of course, the streets of Rome are full of monks and sisters." Wilbur's less occasional reason, however, is that "it's always seemed to me that nuns have a particularly difficult job of balancing the claims of this world against the next" (Madden, 1968). The three groups that Wilbur counterpoises—thieves, lovers, and nuns—seem to possess their own balance, as a catalog: of virtue against vice, greed against love, and lightness (the "clean linen" and the sweetness of the lovers) against doom (the nuns' "dark habits" and the suggestion that the clothes' "ruddy gallows" might also serve for the thieves that wear them). Equally, of course, all three groups must balance the concerns of the spirit against "the things of this world," as the poem's title reminds us.

(The title comes from St. Augustine, who takes issue with the Book of John's proscription, "Love not the world, neither the things that are in the world.") This is perhaps clearest for the briefly described lovers, who by their very occupation recall the title and the bedsheets of the second stanza and who (on their way to being "undone") seem to relish each other not only as souls but also as beings of this world. Wilbur reminds us here that love demands a bridge between the soul and the world around it, that it is perhaps "bitter love," but love nonetheless, that brings the soul back into the body to witness the shocking "punctual rape of every blessèd day."

The soul's transit, in this poem, from sleep through poetic metaphor to full awakening seems familiar from such well-known poems as Keats' "Ode to a Nightingale" or (perhaps) Frost's "Birches"—the difference here being that where Keats' is a midnight drowsiness, Wilbur's is one of praise at dawn; where Keats travels imaginatively into the realm of pure poetry (even to the magical casements of a fairy tale), Wilbur remains happily in the urban world around him. The connection to Frost—the poems' similarity of trajectory—is less clear, perhaps, but is suggested by Wilbur's essay "Poetry and Happiness" (1966), in which he praises Frost for recommending "limited aspiration, or high-minded earthliness," an equipoise not unlike the one Wilbur himself achieves. Like Wilbur, the narrator of "Birches" travels briefly up away from the world, fashioning a metaphor as means for this transit; like Wilbur, too, he returns, acknowledging that "Earth's the right place for love." Thus, Wilbur contends in his essay, Frost's poem "is happy in all the ways in which a poem can be happy": doing justice to the poet's personal "temper" (for Wilbur, one most often of praise), to the "practical idealism of the New England spirit," and to the poetic tradition that he subtly engages. Much the same credit could be granted to Wilbur, who here strikes the "difficult balance" to which he continually aspires.

Isaac Cates

**Further Reading**


Edgecombe, Rodney Stenning, *A Reader's Guide to the Poetry of Richard Wilbur,* Tuscaloosa: University of Alabama Press, 1995

Harris, Peter, "Forty Years of Richard Wilbur: The Loving Work of an Equilibrist," *Virginia Quarterly Review* 66 (1990)

Littler, Frank, "Wilbur's 'Love Calls Us to the Things of This World,'" *Explicator* 40, no. 3 (1982)

Madden, Charles F., editor, *Talks with Authors,* Carbondale: Southern Illinois University Press, 1968

Ostroff, Anthony, editor, *The Contemporary Poet as Artist and Critic,* Boston: Little Brown, 1964

Wilbur, Richard, "My Own Work" and "Poetry and Happiness," in *Responses: Prose Pieces, 1953–1976,* New York and London: Harcourt Brace Jovanovich, 1976; expanded edition, Ashland, Oregon: Storyline Press, 2000


## The Writer

"The Writer," one of the gems in Richard Wilbur's *The Mind-Reader: New Poems* (1976), is noteworthy among 20th-century poems for its uncommon subject: a father's meditation on his daughter and her future. It is also significant for being both unusual and canonical: it is unusual in that, like two other poems in this grouping, it is unrhymed; it is canonical in that it meets, in its dramatic change of heart and metaphor, Wilbur's passionate request in "The Eye," that his poetic vision will always be a "giver of due regard" to the object of contemplation. Adhering to this principle, Wilbur divides "The Writer" into three sections, creating a "reinvented poem," to use the term that Helen Vendler applies to many lyrics by George Herbert, a metaphysical poet to whom Wilbur is sometimes compared.

"The Writer" consists of 11 prow-shaped tercets and three thematic sections: the first five stanzas establish the metaphor of a ship; the second five focus on the endangered starling; and the last transforms the narrative poem *about* his daughter into an address *to* his daughter and a heartfelt prayer for her success.

The poem begins straightforwardly as the speaker-father directs us to a room "at the prow of the house" where his "daughter is writing a story." She is not writing in silence; in fact, at that moment she is the center and source of a "commotion of type-writer keys," which the speaker likens to the sound of a "chain hauled over a gunwale." As he stands outside her "shut door," very much aware of the noise, the scene that he imagines does not romanticize the artist or the process of creation. In his next observation, he assumes a mock serious tone as he describes her material and her efforts: "the stuff / Of her life is a great cargo, and some of it heavy." Fondly then, but cavalierly still, he wishes her "a lucky passage."

His amusement falters, however, when the jarring sound stops; he recognizes the moment, the troubling silence in which the trapped writer struggles for the word, the precise word, the only word that matters. Her silence brings him to a discovery about himself and her plight. Despite his commitment, he has not prepared himself to become for his writer-daughter a "giver of due regard." Although she is young and inexperienced, he suspects that she, on her side of the "shut door," would reject the conventional metaphor, the "easy figure" of the ship with a place to go and a message (cargo) to carry. The trite metaphor violates his aesthetic. In a letter that became part of a book, Wilbur claims that a poem cannot be "a message"; a poem should "'bring the whole soul . . . into activity'" (Ostroff, 1964). Yet the ship figure that he chooses for her is facile and inappropriate: it not only trivializes the "whole soul" that she as an artist, however fledgling, yearns to express but also denies the beating spirit of the writer in the room.

The pause sets him straight and redirects the emotional curve of the poem. Perhaps his first response incorporates the attitude of a poet whose "important" work was interrupted by the "commotion" made by the other writer in the house. Perhaps his arch tone is merely a cover for his true feelings and fears; it reflects his desire to protect his daughter from a future with which he is too familiar. While he respects the ambition and courage of his daughter, whose soul longs to clear "the sill of the world," he realizes that for the true artist this venture is a "life or death" struggle. Chastened, he reconsiders her situation. His second apprehension admits that the challenge is painful and passionate, not a matter of noise but spirit, not a measured distance to be traveled but a flight, not a matter of choice but survival.

In the second section of the poem, the speaker turns to a fitting metaphor, seeing his daughter as the trapped starling whose heroic struggle for freedom impressed both father and daughter (and he establishes the only end rhyme in the poem with "starling" and "darling"):

I remember the dazed starling
Which was trapped in that very room, two years ago;
How we stole in, lifted a sash

And retreated, not to affright it;
And how for a helpless hour, through the crack of the door,
We watched the sleek, wild, dark

And iridescent creature
Batter against the brilliance, drop like a glove
To the hard floor, or the desk-top

And wait then, humped and bloody,
For the wits to try it again; and how our spirits
Rose when, suddenly sure,

It lifted off from a chair-back,
Beating a smooth course for the right window
And clearing the sill of the world.

The memory draws him closer to her, as he knows that his daughter will attempt to launch herself through many brilliant but deceptively closed windows before she sees with certainty the window "open" for her; moreover, she will encounter this challenge with each work.

In his three-line benediction that concludes the poem, the speaker appears to anoint his daughter as a prophet in her own right:

It is always a matter, my darling,
Of life or death, as I had forgotten. I wish
What I wished before, but harder.

Wilbur's use of the word "harder" is telling and personal. It is "harder," he says, in poetry to "assess the signs of the soul" because "poetic technique translates all signs into a new and condensed language"; here he embodies his passionate blessing in this precise word (Ostroff, 1964).

Although Wilbur breaks his poem into divisions based on inappropriate and appropriate metaphor (and he uses the past tense in the second section), the turn from the ship to the starling does not alter the poetic elements dramatically (except that the sprightly, anapestic rhythm of the opening line disappears quickly). The meticulous craftsmanship for which he is noted is as evident in the first five stanzas as in the remainder of the poem. Assonance and alliteration in prominent words (prow, house; chain, gunwale; reject, easy; whole, house; how, helpless; what, wished) contribute the sound effects of the poem, emphasizing first the place and time of the daughter's decision and then the father's acceptance of her choice. The beauty of the poem lies in the power of the subject with the father embracing the spirit and profession of his daughter. As Eavan Boland points out, "[T]he intimacy and grace of Richard Wilbur's beautiful poem for his writer-daughter shows how skillfully he blends those inward and indoor elements: the trapped starling and the old authorities of father versus daughter shimmering and dissolving as one writer listens for the emergence of another" (*http://www.poets.org/exh/Exhibit.cfm?prmID=9*).

Jeannie Sargent Judge

**Further Reading**

Hill, Donald Louis, *Richard Wilbur,* New York: Twayne, 1967
Nemerov, Howard, editor, *Poets on Poetry,* New York: Basic Books, 1966
Ostroff, Anthony, editor, *The Contemporary Poet as Artist and Critic,* Boston: Little Brown, 1964
Salinger, Wendy, editor, *Richard Wilbur's Creation,* Ann Arbor: University of Michigan Press, 1983
Waggoner, Hyatt H., editor, *American Poets, from the Puritans to the Present,* Boston: Houghton Mifflin, 1968; revised edition, Baton Rouge: Louisiana State University Press, 1984
Wilbur, Richard, *The Catbird's Song: Prose Pieces, 1963–1995,* New York: Harcourt Brace, 1997

---

## William Carlos Williams 1883–1963

Within the past 40 years William Carlos Williams has emerged as arguably the single most influential of 20th-century American poets. The publication of Donald Allen's landmark anthology *The New American Poetry* in 1960 confirmed Williams' impact. The work of poets such as Charles Olson, Robert Creeley, Denise Levertov, and Allen Ginsberg, all included in the anthology, demonstrated the influence Williams had exercised on content—the idea of what sort of material or subject might make up a poem—and on form, particularly the more open, "organic" notion of language, the poetic line, and the overall appearance of a poem on the page. Robert Lowell, John Ashbery, and diverse contemporary postmodernists have professed a debt to Williams, a prolific writer who in over 40 books in a variety of genres never lost the motivation to experiment with pushing generic boundaries and the notion of what constituted an "American" poetry. Although he published short stories, plays, essays, reviews, experimental novels, and other types of prose, Williams is best remembered for his large body of poetry, which began inauspiciously with the publication of *Poems* (1909), a highly derivative volume written in romantic Keatsian language. Williams sought to suppress this apprentice work by refusing to reprint any of the poems during his lifetime. *The Tempers* (1913), while rhythmically less contrived than the earlier poems, remained imitative in many ways, particularly in diction and phrasing. Williams had at this point, however, begun what was to be a lifelong correspondence with his former classmate at the University of Pennsylvania, the poet Ezra Pound. Now living in England, in addition to publishing Williams in London literary magazines, Pound sent regular missives on the state of the art in Europe. Williams had already visited Pound and met Yeats through him, and by the time of the publication of *The Tempers,* Pound was formulating his aesthetic of Imagism, a pared-down form of poetry stressing "direct treatment of the thing," which so influenced Williams' work for decades to come. In addition, Pound's interest in the poetries of Europe may have influenced Williams' decision to include some of his own translations of Spanish ballads in *The Tempers*.

Many scholars consider *Al Que Quiere!* (1917) Williams' breakthrough volume, the first to contain several poems distinct in style and voice. Williams had considered the alternative title "The Pleasures of Democracy," but opted for the Spanish title, which translates as "to him who wants it," alluding to what would become a major theme for Williams, the relationship between artist and audience. This theme is certainly evident in the often-anthologized "Tract," which presents a speaker instructing "my townspeople" in how to perform a less ostentatious funeral, one more honest and authentic, with the "ground sense necessary" to openly express grief and honor the deceased. Another poem, "Apology," written in the short lines that characterize most of *Al Que Quiere!,* begins with the question "Why do I write today?" The poem goes on to contrast the "beauty" of the "nonentities" of society—people of color, laborers, the elderly—with the less inspiring faces of the "leading citizens." In one of several early poems titled "Pastoral" ("When I was younger"), the poet walks the "back streets" and admires the houses of the poor; their "weathered" colors and "out of line" dilapidation please the speaker and strike him as being "of vast import to the nation." This illustrates another of Williams' central themes, the idea that it is up to the artist to take the commonplace, the everyday, and make it the material of art. Many commentators have seen this theme as one of Williams' vital links to Whitman.

Williams' next volume, *Sour Grapes* (1921), experimented with slightly longer lines and more poems on images of and responses to nature, as well as poems of sensuality such as "Queen-Anne's-Lace," which compares the flower to a woman's body. One poem of particular note is "The Great Figure," evoking the sight and sound of a fire truck roaring down a city block in New York City. The poem inspired the famous painting by Williams' friend Charles Demuth, "I Saw the Figure Five in Gold," which visually pays homage to the poem and its author. Williams had for several years been going to New York from his home in Rutherford, New Jersey, to visit galleries and museums, and to spend time in studios and restaurants with artists such as Alfred Stieglitz, Demuth, Man Ray, Charles Sheeler, and others. Later, in 1939, he would write the catalogue copy for an exhibition of Sheeler's work, but in his autobiography Williams highlighted as crucial to his development as a writer the famous Armory Show of 1913, the first American exhibition of post-Impressionist European painting. (His wife contended that he did not actually attend.) He claimed that the famous sculpture by Marcel Duchamp titled "Fountain," an upside-down men's urinal signed "R. Mutt," made him laugh with relief. If this could make its way into a serious exhibition of art, then surely an American poet could experiment by dispensing with regular meter and rhyme. In his "Prologue to *Kora in Hell*" (1918) and in the prose sections of *Spring and All* (1923), Williams devoted several passages to discussing the importance of innovations made by European artists such as Duchamp, Wassily Kandinsky, Juan Gris, and Paul Cézanne.

*Kora in Hell: Improvisations* (1920) is Williams' first experimental text using prose to lend insight as to how the poet's mind works. In Kora, the Greek goddess of spring who was captured and transported to hell, Williams saw an analogue for the contemporary American artist, eager to create something new, but disregarded and cast aside by his fellow citizens. This is a recurring theme among the short aphoristic passages that comprise the text. Many of the short passages could be described as prose poems, with other passages speculating on the role of the poet or the poem. The "Prologue," first published in 1918 but not in conjunction with the complete text of *Kora* until 1957, discusses the methods of an avant-garde artist such as Duchamp in ways that lend useful insight into the Williams aesthetic. *Spring and All* is perhaps the most vital of any Williams text in this regard. Initially published in France in a limited edition of just 300 copies, the full text became available to American readers only in 1970, although in the interval several of its poems became among Williams' best known due to their inclusion in anthologies and the various editions of *Selected Poems* published by Williams during his lifetime. One of the essential texts of American Modernism, *Spring and All* blends passages of prose with untitled poems, offering some of Williams' most complete statements on his philosophy of poetry. On the first page of the book Williams states the central aim of his art, to break down the "constant barrier between the reader and his consciousness of immediate contact with the world." Professing himself a writer addressed "to the imagination," Williams stresses an art of immediacy and vitality, a distinctly "NEW" sort of American poetry, one not concerned with "crude symbolism" and "strained associations." (Clearly, Williams had in mind the work of T.S. Eliot, which he elsewhere railed against as antithetical to his own aims.)

Among the major poems included in *Spring and All* are those that later came to bear the titles "Spring and All," "The Red Wheelbarrow," and "To Elsie." One of Williams' major themes in the poems is the emergence of the new in art, as reflected by nature: "One by one objects are defined— / It quickens: clarity, outline of leaf[.]" In addition, several poems continue his attempt to capture the significance of the everyday, including what may be his most famous poem: "so much depends / upon // a red wheel / barrow // glazed with rain / water // beside the white / chickens[.]"

Another text first published in a limited edition in France in 1923 was *The Great American Novel,* which Williams later termed "a satire on the novel form." In this book as well as in his other major prose work of the period, an examination of American history and folklore titled *In the American Grain* (1925), Williams reveals his ongoing fascination with American culture and the American character.

"The Descent of Winter" (1928), which appeared in *The Exile,* the little magazine edited by Pound, is a journal-like collage of short passages of poetry and prose, again including many statements concerning the function of poetry. While much shorter than *Spring and All,* some critics see the sequence as crucial to an understanding of Williams' evolving aesthetic. The two volumes of the 1930s, *An Early Martyr, and Other Poems* (1935) and *Adam and Eve and the City* (1936), have not received extensive critical attention. The first volume contains the well-known "The Yachts," sometimes read as a symbolic commentary on the proletarian cause, and "Young Love," a collage poem of anguished physical desire set in the midst of the modern city. "Perpetuum Mobile: The City," from the latter volume, is one of several Williams poems of the 1930s reflecting his attempt to work toward a theory of the individual in relation to the city, a dynamic more fully explored in *Paterson*. Another poem of note from *Adam and Eve* is "The Crimson Cyclamen," dedicated to the memory of Demuth, which continues Williams' theme of the organic emergence of form in a work of art through the function of the imagination. Williams also began his long association with James Laughlin and his New Directions publishing house during this period.

In the 1930s Williams also wrote several passages of poetry that would make their way into *Paterson,* the long poem that would appear in separate volumes in 1946, 1948, 1949, and 1951. A fifth volume would appear in 1958, but many Williams scholars consider it less integral to the poem as a whole than the first four books, all of which were published before the series of strokes that began debilitating Williams in the early 1950s. One of the most significant long poems in American literature, *Paterson* takes as its central metaphor the city of Paterson, New Jersey, and in particular the Passaic Falls. The falls seems to serve as an analogue for native but unrecognized imaginative power, perhaps poetic power, and the city is increasingly conflated with a doctor-poet figure named Paterson, a figure resembling Williams in his imaginative quest for form and vision for his poem. The collage structure of the poem finds room for not just varied stanzas of verse, but also documentary histories of the region, newspaper accounts of local events, and letters Williams received from various figures, including a young woman named Marcia Nardi, identified in the poem as Cress, who solicited Williams' support for her work. Many Williams scholars regard *Paterson* as his major achievement. Among the poem's many themes are the significance of the local as native material for the imagination, the connection between history and the writing process, the quest for an adequate language, the role of the individual within the city, violence as part of the national character, and the channeling of sexual energy. The five books of *Paterson,* with fragments of a sixth, were first published as a whole in 1963. Poems written during the 1940s that did not make their way into *Paterson* were published by Williams in individual volumes titled *The Wedge* (1944), *The Clouds* (1948), and *The Pink Church* (1949), the latter a chapbook of 11 poems.

The poetry of the 1950s, particularly in *The Desert Music* (1954) and *Journey to Love* (1955), is more reflective in tone than the work of Williams' early and mid-career. Gone is the sense of urgency and the search for a fresh poetic language, due in part to the strokes and an ensuing depression. Williams continued as an innovator during this period, however, in large part because of his extensive use of what he called the "variable foot," a new sort of measure aimed at capturing the rhythms of everyday American speech. The form is essentially a tercet with a "stepped" left margin, each line being brought further to the right of the page, with extensive enjambment, and capitalization used only at the beginning of a new sentence. Williams had introduced the form in *Paterson,* Book II, but it came to dominate both his late poetry and his theoretical statements on poetry from this period. Many readers and scholars have commented upon the increased accessibility of these late poems, with "Asphodel, That Greeny Flower," the final poem from *Journey to Love,* receiving special attention. The long poem is both a love poem and apology to Williams' wife, and, in the wake of World War II and the potential of "the bomb" to end human life, a reflection on human mortality. Williams' final volume of poems, *Pictures from Brueghel* (1962), returns to the form of the short lyric, with many poems employing the triadic, stepped-line form. This volume was awarded the Pulitzer Prize in 1963, shortly after the poet's death.

Although most noted for his poetry, Williams' experimental work in prose and drama should not be overlooked. In addition, his essays, letters, and autobiography offer fascinating insights into both his life and poetic practice. His reputation among the major American Modernists is secure, as evidenced by the publication of scholarly editions of his *Collected Poems* (2 vols., 1986, 1988) and of *Paterson* (1992).

ERNEST J. SMITH

**Biography**

Born in Rutherford, New Jersey, 17 September 1883. Attended the University of Pennsylvania, Philadelphia, 1902–06, M.D. 1906; intern at hospitals in New York City, 1906–08; post-graduate work in pediatrics, University of Leipzig, 1908–09; practiced medicine in Rutherford, 1910 through mid-1950s; editor, *Others,* 1919; editor, with Robert McAlmon, *Contact,* 1920–23; editor, *Contact: An American Quarterly,* 1931–33; appointed consultant in poetry, Library of Congress, Washington, D.C., 1952 (not accepted). Received Loines Award, 1948; National Book Award, 1950; Bollingen Prize, 1952; Academy of American Poets fellowship, 1956; Brandeis University Creative Arts Award, 1958; American Academy Gold Medal, 1963; Pulitzer Prize, 1963; honorary L.L.D., State University of New York, Buffalo, 1956, and Fairleigh Dickinson University, Teaneck, New Jersey, 1959; honorary Litt.D., Rutgers University, New Brunswick, New Jersey, 1948, Bard College, Annandale-on-Hudson, New York, 1948, and University of Pennsylvania, 1952; member, American Academy. Died in New Jersey, 4 March 1963.

**Poetry**

*Poems,* 1909
*The Tempers,* 1913
*Al Que Quiere!* 1917
*Sour Grapes,* 1921
*Spring and All,* 1923
*Collected Poems, 1921–1931,* 1934
*An Early Martyr, and Other Poems,* 1935
*Adam and Eve and the City,* 1936
*The Complete Collected Poems, 1906–1938,* 1938
*The Wedge,* 1944
*Paterson, Book I,* 1946
*Paterson, Book II,* 1948
*The Clouds,* 1948
*Paterson, Book III,* 1949
*Selected Poems,* 1949
*The Collected Later Poems,* 1950; revised edition, 1963
*Paterson, Book IV,* 1951
*The Collected Earlier Poems,* 1951
*The Desert Music, and Other Poems,* 1954
*Journey to Love,* 1955
*Paterson, Book V,* 1958
*Pictures from Brueghel, and Other Poems,* 1962
*Paterson, Books I–V,* 1963; as *Paterson,* 1992

*The Williams Reader* (includes prose), edited by M.L. Rosenthal, 1966
*Penguin Modern Poets 9* (poems by Williams, Denise Levertov, and Kenneth Rexroth), 1967
*Imaginations,* 1970; as *Imaginations: Five Experimental Prose Pieces,* 1970
*Selected Poems,* edited by Charles Tomlinson, 1976
*Collected Poems, Volume I: 1909–1939,* edited by A. Walton Litz and Christopher MacGowan, 1986
*Collected Poems, Volume II: 1939–1962,* 1988
*Asphodel, That Greeny Flower, and Other Love Poems,* 1994
*Early Poems,* 1997
*Autumn: A Poem,* 1998

**Selected Criticism**
*Something to Say: Williams on Younger Poets,* edited by James E.B. Breslin, 1985

**Other Writings:** plays, novels (*The Great American Novel,* 1923), short stories (*The Farmers' Daughters: The Collected Stories,* 1961), improvisational prose (*Kora in Hell: Improvisations,* 1920), essays, autobiography (*The Autobiography of William Carlos Williams,* 1951), correspondence (*Pound/Williams: Selected Letters of Ezra Pound and William Carlos Williams,* edited by Hugh Witemeyer, 1996), translations of French literature (*Last Nights of Paris,* by Philippe Soupault, 1929).

**Further Reading**
Ahearn, Barry, *William Carlos Williams and Alterity: The Early Poetry,* Cambridge and New York: Cambridge University Press, 1994
Axelrod, Steven Gould, and Helen Deese, *Critical Essays on William Carlos Williams,* New York: G.K. Hall, and Oxford: Macmillan, 1995
Crawford, Hugh T., *Modernism, Medicine, and William Carlos Williams,* Norman: University of Oklahoma Press, 1993
Halter, Peter, *The Revolution in the Visual Arts and the Poetry of William Carlos Williams,* Cambridge and New York: Cambridge University Press, 1994
Lowney, John, *The American Avant-Garde Tradition: William Carlos Williams, Postmodern Poetry, and the Politics of Cultural Memory,* Lewisburg, Pennsylvania: Bucknell University Press, and London: Associated University Presses, 1997
MacGowan, Christopher, editor, *The Letters of Denise Levertov and William Carlos Williams,* New York: New Directions, 1998
Mariani, Paul, *William Carlos Williams: A New World Naked,* New York: McGraw Hill, 1981
Pound, Ezra, *Pound/Williams: Selected Letters of Ezra Pound and William Carlos Williams,* edited by Hugh Witemeyer, New York: New Directions, 1996
Schmidt, Peter, *William Carlos Williams, the Arts, and Literary Tradition,* Baton Rouge: Louisiana State University Press, 1988
Witemeyer, Hugh, *William Carlos Williams and James Laughlin: Selected Letters,* New York and London: Norton, 1989

## Al Que Quiere!

*Al Que Quiere!,* William Carlos Williams' second major book of verse, appeared in November 1917 after some delay. He had submitted the manuscript in February 1917, and in a late April letter to Harriet Monroe said he had been told the book would be out in a few weeks. In another letter to Monroe dated 15 May, he complained that the book had been announced twice by the publisher and that he did not know when it would finally appear (Monroe Papers). In the end he did not receive his first copy until November, and review copies were not distributed until January 1918. After all that, *Al Que Quiere!* received little critical attention (Mariani, 1981).

Williams' first book after *The Tempers* (1913) and *Poems* (1909, privately printed), *Al Que Quiere!* was a much larger and more substantial collection than either of its predecessors, in which the distinctive spare verse of short lines and plain words of *Sour Grapes* (1921) and *Spring and All* (1923) emerges clearly. At the same time the collection marks an important phase in Williams' career during which he was redefining his role as a poet: a poet of the local, a member of a democracy, but one increasingly solitary and alienated from his townspeople, his readers. Williams ends the collection with a new version of "The Wanderer," his early Whitmanesque vision of the poet in a modern industrialized landscape. More explicitly retrospective than the 1914 *Egoist* piece, this version still concludes with "the filthy Passaic" entering the poet's "heart" until, he writes,

> I felt the utter depth of its rottenness
> The vile breadth of its degradation
> And dropped down knowing this was me now.

In context, his immersion in this polluted landscape resonates with

> the old man who goes about
> gathering dog-lime
> . . . in the gutter

in "Pastoral" and "the young doctor" in "January Morning" who

> notices
> the curdy barnacles and broken ice crusts
> left at the [ferry] slip's base by the low tide.

In fact, as far as Williams had come from his early anachronistic style, he does not so much reinvent the role of poet in *Al Que Quiere!* as recast familiar roles in a new poetic idiom. The solitary visionary of "The Wanderer" now takes "strange courage" from the morning star, which he commands, "Shine alone in the sunrise / To which you lend no part" ("El Hombre"). He dances alone, "naked, grotesquely," before his mirror to see himself as "the happy genius of [his] household" ("Danse Russe"), or compares himself to

> young girls [who] run giggling
> on Park Avenue after dark
> when they ought to be home in bed. ("January Morning")

The poet who described "toilers after peace and after pleasure" now directly addresses his "townspeople," calling their attention to "the strange birds . . . that sometimes / rest upon our river in winter" ("Gulls"), exhorting them to build "[a] rough plain hearse . . . / with gilt wheels and no top at all." On it, a coffin will lie "by its own weight" ("Tract"). The townspeople themselves he represents directly in their specific conditions: an impoverished prostitute living unapologetically as a squatter in an abandoned house ("Portrait of a Woman in Bed"), old men

who have studied
every leg show
in the city ("The Old Men")

and

dirt-colored men
about a fire bursting from an old
ash can. ("January Morning")

Of those with middle-class pretensions (especially church-goers), Williams is consistently critical ("Tract," "History"). About those too poor or uneducated to pretend to anything, he is unsentimental and indiscriminate but always interested (as in "Virtue" or "K. McB.," whose subject later provides the model for "To Elsie" in *Spring and All*).

In fact, Williams reconfigured the role of the poet and the function of poetry around a kind of purposeful indiscrimination in *Al Que Quiere!*—nothing is off limits, all senses operate all the time to produce subject matter. In "Smell!" he and his nose are "tactless asses . . . / always indiscriminate, always unashamed." In "Sub Terra," the first poem in the collection, which should be read against "The Wanderer," Williams invokes as his muse "grotesque fellows," "seven year locusts / with cased wings," who will accompany him "in among children / leaping around a dead dog."

Often, though, Williams' imagery is more pointed. In some poems nature is explicitly sexual: "the fences watch where the ground / has humped an aching shoulder for the ecstasy" ("Winter Quiet"), or, in "Love Song,"

a honey-thick stain
. . . drips from leaf to leaf
and limb to limb.

In other poems his urban imagery can be sight-centered and painterly. He commands his "solitary disciple" to look at the church and

See how the converging lines
of the hexagonal spire
escape upward

and to

Observe
how motionless
the eaten moon
lies in the protecting lines.

In "Pastoral," the second poem of the collection, he admires "the houses / of the very poor," especially when "smeared a bluish green / . . . properly weathered." He appreciates their disorder:

roof out of line with sides
the yards cluttered
with old chicken wire, ashes,
furniture gone wrong.

This sense of disorder, irregularity, and destabilization is one of the identifying marks for both style and subject matter in *Al Que Quiere!* In letters to Harriet Monroe around this time, Williams repeatedly chafes against her attempts to regularize or sanitize his verse in any way. (She insists, for example, on capitalizing the initial letter of each line of poetry.) By this point in his career the jagged, rough edges of the present's break from the past have become central qualities of Williams' "mirror to modernity" ("The Wanderer").

Williams further differentiated his style here through the use of foreign words and phrases, particularly Spanish ones, which provide an important frame for his "local" poetry. He understood and resisted the pull of European culture to legitimize life in the New World (see "Gulls" and 1925's *In the American Grain*). His use of Spanish in "Mujer" (which concerns his cat) and "El Hombre" redefines the Spanish as much as it elevates the commonplace. In "Dedication for a Plot of Ground" he invokes his grandmother's "living presence" on the "grass plot" that she "grubbed . . . with her own hands," tracing her migration from England to the Azores to Brooklyn to the Caribbean and back to New York to live out her life on the small plot "facing the waters of this inlet." Williams roots her through her labor in the New World, albeit at its edge. As a first-generation American himself, he was on the margins of the dominant culture as well as within it.

Williams wrote Marianne Moore in February 1917 that he had decided to title his collection *A Book of Poems: Al Que Quiere! or The Pleasures of Democracy*. He liked the Spanish, he said, "just as I like a Chinese image cut of stone: it is decorative and has a certain integral charm." By itself, however, the Spanish phrase was "not democratic"; Williams liked the "conglomerate title" because it was "nearly a perfect image of my own grinning mug (seen from the inside)" (*Selected Letters*, 1957). His poetry, too, is a conglomeration, a *bricolage,* especially in the central sequence "January Morning" (subtitled "A Suite"). He ends by addressing his mother:

All this—
        was for you, old woman.
I wanted to write a poem
that you would understand.
For what good is it to me
if you can't understand it?
                But you got to try hard—

He knows that the language he must find to mediate the world can be neither entirely hers nor his, but hybrid, irregular, tenuous. In the end Williams shortened the title to *Al Que Quiere!,* but he continued for at least another ten years to search for an audience that would want to read what he had written there.

RANDOLPH CHILTON

**Further Reading**

Breslin, James E.B., *William Carlos Williams, an American Artist,* New York: Oxford University Press, 1970; with a new preface, Chicago: University of Chicago Press, 1985

MacGowan, Christopher, *William Carlos Williams' Early Poetry: The Visual Arts Background,* Ann Arbor, Michigan: UMI Research Press, and Epping, Essex: Bowker, 1984
Mariani, Paul, *William Carlos Williams: A New World Naked,* New York: McGraw Hill, 1981
Perloff, Marjorie, *The Poetics of Indeterminacy: Rimbaud to Cage,* Princeton, New Jersey: Princeton University Press, 1981
Rapp, Carl, *William Carlos Williams and Romantic Idealism,* Hanover, New Hampshire: University Press of New England, 1984

## Asphodel, That Greeny Flower

William Carlos Williams' long, late poem "Asphodel, That Greeny Flower" is remarkable in several regards. It is the fullest example of his work in the variable foot and in the triadic (or three-foot, stepped-down) line, a breakthrough form he discovered in *Paterson, II* ("The descent beckons . . .") and utilized for many of his poems from the 1950s. It is also one of the most beautiful affirmations of the power of love in—and against—the nuclear age, and one of the few memorable love poems in English written not for a mistress but for a wife: his spouse of 40 years, Florence Herman Williams, or Flossie.

First published in *Journey to Love* (1955), "Asphodel, That Greeny Flower" came into existence during a time of nearly overwhelming crisis in Williams' life. Originally he thought of it as the fifth book of *Paterson,* gave it the working title "The River of Heaven," and planned for it to include "Everything left over that wasn't done or said—*at ease.*" He began the poem in March 1952, on a hotel menu in New York City, and worked on it for nearly two years. During those years his health, which had begun to break with his heart attack in 1948 and strokes in 1949 and 1951, continued to deteriorate. He suffered another major stroke in August 1952, and knew that he could expect further strokes—any one of them possibly fatal—at any time from then on. His mental condition was likewise precarious. A bout with depression was exacerbated both by the recent stroke and by the injustices surrounding Williams' appointment as Poetry Consultant to the Library of Congress. The position was first offered, then withdrawn owing to allegations of Communist sympathizing, then offered again contingent upon further loyalty investigations, which were conducted but never evaluated, so that the year's term was up before Williams was able to serve. The situation tormented him with feelings of rage, powerlessness, and humiliation. On 21 February 1953, he was admitted to a private mental hospital in Queens, where he underwent psychiatric treatment until his release on 18 April.

Most painful of all, the old uneasy balance between confession and deceit in Williams' marriage to Flossie finally gave way. During his stay in the mental hospital, threatened by death and ready at last to let Flossie truly know him, he worked on poems, including "Asphodel," and wrote letters confessing past adulteries that finally compelled Flossie's full belief. The process must have been immeasurably painful for them both. Needing his wife to hold firm now more than ever, the poet must test her by buffeting and shaking her. "Having your love / I was rich," he tells her in "Asphodel." "Thinking to have lost it / I am tortured / and cannot rest." And so, in three "Books" and a "Coda," he writes to Flossie about the flower of the Elysian fields, the flower that grows also "in hell." The flower has a central meaning: "Of love, abiding love / it will be telling." In the first two Books he speaks of their marriage, their past, shared projects, triumphs, and griefs; in Book III he begs for forgiveness, but also writes movingly of desire, giving "the steps / if it may be / by which you shall mount, / again to think well / of me." The "Coda," then, is his gift to Flossie, made possible by her forgiveness of him. They approach the end, the "thunderstroke," together, and tenderly he seeks to reassure her:

Inseparable from the fire
        its light
                takes precedence over it.
Then follows
        what we have dreaded—
                but it can never
overcome what has gone before.

Reassuring her, he also reassures himself. Without Flossie's love, any attempt at final affirmation would be whistling in the dark; with it, although the dark remains real, the poet's voice rings with authority, soars in celebration, and nearly breaks in a quiet hymn of praise.

The threats of both physical death and the death of love are right at the center of "Asphodel"—and not just at the personal level, but also at the level of global destruction. The poem has a strong dimension of public, as well as private, utterance. Throughout, it confronts what Williams calls "the bomb," both the nuclear threat itself and all forms of "avarice / breeding hatred / through fear," all forms of cruelty, oppression, and repression. But against *thanatos,* the death instinct, again and again the poet sets *eros;* whether it take the form of art, medicine, discovery, or desire, *eros* is the force that drives the imagination, the force that counters death:

If a man die
        it is because death
                has first
possessed his imagination.
        But if he refuse death—
                no greater evil
can befall him
        unless it be the death of love
                meet him
in full career.
        Then indeed
                for him
the light has gone out.
But love and the imagination
        are of a piece,
                swift as the light
to avoid destruction.
        So we come to watch time's flight
                as we might watch
summer lightning
        or fireflies, secure,
                by grace of the imagination,
safe in its care.

"Asphodel, That Greeny Flower" is not, perhaps, a perfect poem. Some have felt its final vision of Flossie as bride, "a girl so pale / and ready to faint / that I pitied / and wanted to protect you," to be condescending. Furthermore, as a philosophy of life the "Coda" is problematic, for Williams cannot quite articulate what he means by "the light." But "Asphodel" is a great poem. It was written by a man in his 70s who had to type it with the fingers of one hand, who could sometimes barely see. Yet it is one of those extraordinary utterances that proves the truth of Keats' contention that the world is a "vale of Soul-making." As a young man, in *Spring and All,* Williams wrote, "Life is valuable—when completed by the imagination. And then only." Thirty years later, "Asphodel, That Greeny Flower" reveals a life completed by the imagination. Despite the ruin of the body, the made soul shines out indestructibly.

Ann Fisher-Wirth

**Further Reading**

Breslin, James E.B., *William Carlos Williams, an American Artist,* New York: Oxford University Press, 1970; with a new preface, Chicago: University of Chicago Press, 1985

Cushman, Stephen, *William Carlos Williams and the Meanings of Measure,* New Haven, Connecticut: Yale University Press, 1985

Fisher-Wirth, Ann, *William Carlos Williams and Autobiography: The Woods of His Own Nature,* University Park: Pennsylvania State University Press, 1989

Giorcelli, Cristina, and Maria Anita Stefanelli, editors, *The Rhetoric of Love in the Collected Poems of William Carlos Williams,* Rome: Edizioni Associate, 1993

Graham, Theodora Rapp, "Review of *The Rhetoric of Love,*" *William Carlos Williams Review* 21, no. 2 (Fall 1995)

Kallet, Marilyn, *Honest Simplicity in William Carlos Williams's "Asphodel, That Greeny Flower,"* Baton Rouge: Louisiana State University Press, 1985

Koehler, G. Stanley, *Countries of the Mind: The Poetry of William Carlos Williams,* Lewisburg, Pennsylvania: Bucknell University Press, and London: Associated University Presses, 1998

Mariani, Paul, *William Carlos Williams: A New World Naked,* New York: McGraw Hill, 1981

Mazzaro, Jerome, *William Carlos Williams: The Later Poems,* Ithaca, New York: Cornell University Press, 1973

Schmidt, Peter, *William Carlos Williams, the Arts, and Literary Tradition,* Baton Rouge: Louisiana State University Press, 1988

# The Desert Music

"The Desert Music" (1954) is a culminating point in William Carlos Williams' career and a crucial work for understanding the status of poetry under the conditions of modernity. The poem was written in May 1951, based on a visit that Williams and his wife had made to El Paso and Juarez the previous November, at the end of a successful reading tour in the West. They had stopped in El Paso to visit Williams' compatriot, Robert McAlmon, and crossed the bridge with him, his brothers, and their wives to spend an evening in Juarez. It was the last time Williams was to see McAlmon, who was alcoholic, tubercular, and worn out. Williams, by contrast, was finally achieving some official recognition. Unfortunately, he suffered a stroke on 28 March and was still recovering when he composed "The Desert Music" in response to an invitation from Harvard's Alpha Chapter of Phi Beta Kappa to read a "fifteen minute poem" at the group's commencement exercises. The enthusiastic reception Williams received in the West was counterbalanced by his anxiety over the upcoming performance at the center of the Eastern academic establishment, which he regarded as repressed and moribund. The reading produced both anxiety and revolutionary fervor: anxiety at "facing those who were synonymous for him with the academy," and fervor from "performing his own rebellious strip in church, singing about—of all things—a whore in a cheap Mexican joint in his own rendition of the American West" (Mariani, 1981).

Written under the sign of mortality, "The Desert Music" raises the issue of artistic success and fame. Its motifs, held in a masterful fugal structure, continually point out both the inadequacy and the inescapability of the poetic vocation. The strange figure on the bridge, the beggar children, the stripper, the conversation at dinner, and, above all, the references to music and dance become the matter of a desperate dialogue that the poet conducts with himself and his audience. Does the poet even have an audience apart from himself? As his dinner companions imply, wanting to write a poem (Williams names this urge "necessity"), much less poetry itself, is incomprehensible to average people. Although Williams seems "quite normal" to his fellow diners, he cannot avoid the *abnormality* of writing poetry.

This episode adumbrates the modern problem of poetic identity. Williams' ambivalent declarations come from his awareness that the poetry necessary to him is often remote from those common readers he hopes to reach. The music that Williams cannot escape while visiting Juarez seems to come from beyond him and to demand "the made poem," yet its power still raises doubts. Even before dinner, after watching the striptease, he asks

> [A]m I merely playing the poet? Do I merely invent
> it out of whole cloth? I thought
>
> > What in the form of an old whore in
> > a cheap Mexican joint in Juarez, her bare
> > can waggling crazily can be
> > so refreshing to me, raise to my ear
> > so sweet a tune, built of such slime?

Williams identifies with this "old whore," for, like her, he cannot relinquish his art. In her presence he feels the pulse of his own rhythms, and the section of the poem in which he describes her performance is a perfect example of the enjambed, syncopated measure he had developed over his long career. Yet like his other fallen muse figures, she leads him to question whether his vocation is a delusion, a cheap performance providing nothing more than a momentary thrill. How can there be "so sweet a tune, built of such slime?" One thinks of all the other common subjects of Williams' verse, for his entire project was based on a reversal of traditional aesthetic values. Nevertheless, he still holds to the old notion of the poet who heeds a music beyond him.

"The Desert Music," then, is a crisis-poem: Williams' anxiety has to do both with his belief in himself as a poet and with his understanding of poetic language. For Williams, poetic language is born out of slime, which he associates with feminine sexuality. The poem continually returns to the egg-shaped figure on the bridge, "an inhuman shapelessness" that seems at first to defy description. By the end of the poem, Williams is able to speak of it as

a child in the womb prepared to imitate life,
warding its life against
a birth of awful promise. The music
guards it, a mucus, a film that surrounds it[.]

What the mucus or amniotic fluid is to the child about to be born, the music is to the poet: the child emerges from the womb into the world; the poet emerges from "insensate" sound into language. In each case the stuff from which form emerges has a primal materiality.

This accounts for Williams' concern for linguistic form, which maintains the link to material reality while simultaneously asserting its imaginative autonomy. Williams insists on the materiality of language, always seeking to produce a greater sense of immediacy. He argues that poetry, despite its intimate relation to the material world, should in no way conform to any simple notion of realism. Thus in "The Desert Music" word and thing must be united through the verbal act of "imitation," producing "the made poem," called into being by the verb in its response to the music of reality.

But if writing poetry truly produces such transformations, resulting in the enlarged and dignified status of the artist and the work, why then does Williams remain in doubt throughout "The Desert Music," "ashamed" in his self-affirmation even as he stands in awe of

the brain that
hears that music and of our
skill sometimes to record it[?]

Like "those insistent fingers" of the Mexican children, which tap on the poet's "naked wrist," this question will not go away. Like those children, poetry itself is impoverished, subsisting on handouts, the scraps of language drawn from the tawdry materials of the world. Ironically, out of such reduced circumstances, language is able to assume a dignity and beauty hitherto unknown, a state in which reality is as crude as a stripper with "her bare / can waggling crazily."

Yet however compelling this modern aesthetic may be, Williams never accepts it fully. Regret over the loss of the transcendental sublime remains with him, although the "changeless, endless / inescapable and insistent music" of sensual life brings the poem into being. The inspiring experience of such spiritualized sensuality redeems the gross condition in which the poet too often finds himself and his language. Although there are times when, like the "Latins" of Juarez, Williams seeks "relief" from the music that he hears, ultimately he cannot do without it. In its presence, language is wholly inadequate,

as when Casals struck
and held a deep cello tone
and I am speechless

But when "The verb detaches itself / seeking to become articulate," out of that speechlessness poetry is reborn.

"The Desert Music," then, is composed in a state of profound attentiveness, which is simultaneously a condition of great risk. Attempting to hear the music of reality, the poet may be engulfed by the unvoiced sound and struck dumb; or, following the impetus to act, he may bring that music into utterance. The word "sometimes" in the last line takes on great weight: *sometimes* he has the skill to record the music, but sometimes he does not. Then the poem fails to achieve form, and the poet, whose identity is at risk each time he tries to listen to the music, ceases, in effect, to be a poet. Thus at its deepest level, "The Desert Music" is not about Williams, man or poet: it is about the music.

NORMAN FINKELSTEIN

**Further Reading**

Creeley, Robert, "A Character for Love," in *The Collected Essays of Robert Creeley,* Berkeley: University of California Press, 1989

Duffey, Bernard, *A Poetry of Presence: The Writing of William Carlos Williams,* Madison: University of Wisconsin Press, 1986

Mariani, Paul, *William Carlos Williams: A New World Naked,* New York: McGraw Hill, 1981

Paul, Sherman, *The Music of Survival: A Biography of a Poem by William Carlos Williams,* Urbana: University of Illinois Press, 1968

## Paterson

William Carlos Williams' *Paterson* is a long poem in five books published between 1946 and 1958; fragments of a sixth book were found among the poet's papers at his death, and these were added as an appendix to the work when it was published in its entirety by New Directions in 1963. The project was conceived sometime in 1942 (although as early as 1927 Williams had published a short poem titled "Paterson" in *The Dial*), and in *The Autobiography of William Carlos Williams* (1951) the author writes, "The first idea centering on the poem, Paterson, came alive very early: to find an image large enough to embody the whole knowable world about me. The longer I lived in my place, among the details of my life, I realized that these isolated observations and experiences needed pulling together to gain 'profundity.'" Williams had attempted a poem in an extended form as early as 1920 in *Kora in Hell: Improvisations,* but this work of "prose poetry," for all Williams' concerted efforts to make poetry amenable to the "antipoetical" truths of quotidian reality, suffers, argumentatively, from the very spontaneity it seeks to enact. With *Paterson,* however, Williams found an organizing principle: the industrial New Jersey town with its landmark of the Passaic Great Falls (the second-largest waterfall by volume east of the Mississippi River). The city in Williams' imagination becomes coextensive with the man, and, as he explains in his "Author's Note," the structure of the poem, its argument, seeks to show

> that a man in himself is a city, beginning, seeking, achieving and concluding his life in ways which the various aspects of a city may embody—if imaginatively conceived—any city, all the details of which may be made to voice his most intimate convictions. Part One introduces the elemental character of

> the place. The Second Part comprises the modern replicas. Three will seek a language to make them vocal, and Four, the river below the Falls, will be reminiscent of episodes—all that any one may achieve in a lifetime.

(At this point, Williams had conceived of a long poem in four books only.)

The Passaic Falls provide both the physical energy (harnessed as hydroelectric power) on which the city of Paterson built its industrial economy and the metaphoric energy of a language that originates in the falls and the landscape around them:

> (What common language to unravel?
> combed into straight lines
> from that rafter of a rock's
> lip.)
> (*Paterson,* Book I)

The figure of Paterson himself assumes many forms: he is at once a kind of mythical giant, lying "in the valley of the Passaic Falls / its spent waters forming the outline of his back," but he is also the city itself and its history, as well as an extension of the poet, a doctor (as Williams was) whose poem records his attempt to dismantle the barriers that separate the self from the city. Williams' development of the various "energies" of his poem frequently assumes a gendered form: Paterson, both man and city, is masculine, while the landscape surrounding the falls is feminine, and in Book IV masculine and feminine meet (and separate) in a series of sexual failures (foreshadowed in the poet's walk through the park in Book II, subtitled "Sunday in the Park"). The very idea of separation—the word "Passaic" derives from an Indian verb meaning "to split" or "to divide"—and of the failure to integrate or harmonize bespeak something of Williams' moral purpose in *Paterson* and are articulated repeatedly in the early stages of the poem:

> They turn their backs
> and grow faint—but recover!
> Life is sweet
> they say: the language
> is divorced from their minds
> the language . . the language!
> (Book I)

and

> a bud forever green
> tight-curled, upon the pavement, perfect
> in juice and substance but divorced, divorced
> from its fellows, fallen low—
>
> Divorce is
> the sign of knowledge in our time,
> divorce! divorce!
> (Book I)

Redemption, in the forms of harmony and renewal, comes through art and through the role of the poetic imagination in shaping historical memory to the "particulars" of contemporary reality. In Williams' poetics, the particulars always have a special place, for they are what the writer most intimately knows, and yet, if he or she is up to the job, they become universals, as he announces in the "Preface" to the poem:

> To make a start,
> out of particulars
> and make them general, rolling
> up the sum, by defective means—
> (Book I)

Williams remained surprisingly faithful to this dictum throughout his poetic career.

The form of *Paterson* has elicited a good deal of commentary. Many critics have seen it as an approximation to an American epic, although one whose materials are democratic and familiar rather than heroic, martial, or aristocratic. Of central importance, of course, is Williams' affinity with Whitman, and the degree to which "Song of Myself" acts as a precursor to *Paterson* in its insistence on both the validity of the poetic voice as an epic subject and the belief that American speech, especially its demotic forms, constitutes a new language. Other commentators have suggested a Joycean model in which Paterson assumes the role that Dublin had for Joyce in *Ulysses,* another city by a river where characters, incidents, scenes, and historical events are interwoven in the consciousness of a reflective intelligence. It is ultimately futile, however, to look too closely for a governing structure or the evidence of "through composition" (as in the case of Ezra Pound's *Cantos*); like *Kora in Hell, Paterson* is an improvisation, a collage of anecdotes, letters, fragments of news, historical records, and other nonliterary documents held together by a poetic sensibility that is registered in symbolic tropes rather than narrative coherence, so much so that the looseness of the accomplished work, its essential "unfinishedness," is the very condition of its being.

HENRY CLARIDGE

**Further Reading**

Lloyd, Margaret Glynne, *William Carlos Williams's "Paterson": A Critical Reappraisal,* Rutherford, New Jersey: Fairleigh Dickinson University Press, and London: Associated University Presses, 1980

Mariani, Paul, *William Carlos Williams: A New World Naked,* New York: McGraw Hill, 1981

Martz, Louis L., "The Unicorn in *Paterson:* William Carlos Williams," in *Modern Poetry: Essays in Criticism,* edited by John Hollander, London and New York: Oxford University Press, 1968

Mazzaro, Jerome, *William Carlos Williams: The Later Poems,* Ithaca, New York: Cornell University Press, 1973

Pearce, Roy Harvey, *The Continuity of American Poetry,* Princeton, New Jersey: Princeton University Press, 1961

Quinn, Sister Bernetta, "*Paterson:* Listening to Landscape," in *Modern American Poetry: Essays in Criticism,* edited by Jerome Mazzaro, New York: McKay, 1970

Sankey, Benjamin, *A Companion to William Carlos Williams's "Paterson,"* Berkeley: University of California Press, 1971

Weaver, Mike, *William Carlos Williams: The American Background,* London: Cambridge University Press, 1971

## Spring and All

As Webster Schott points out, William Carlos Williams' *Spring and All* "was printed in Dijon and first published in Paris in 1923 (around 300 copies) by Robert McAlmon's Contact Publishing Co." (see Williams, 1970). Unfortunately, however, *Spring and All* remained unavailable as a complete book for many years. Because it was published as a limited edition and because, as Paul Mariani (1981) points out, "most of the copies that were sent to America were simply confiscated by American customs officials[,] . . . *Spring and All* all but disappeared as a cohesive text until its republication nearly ten years after Williams' death." Despite this fact, the appearance of the book represented an important personal success for Williams, for until McAlmon generously published *Spring and All* at his own expense, Williams had only been able to publish the poems from the book, without the prose. The publication of *Spring and All* marked a new stage in the development of his style, but the work also continued the improvisatory method of *Kora in Hell* (1920). Prose passages alternate with poetry throughout *Spring and All,* and the entire book reflects Williams' experimentation in both forms as well as his passionate questioning of the division between them. *Spring and All* is not only a collection of important lyrics but also Williams' personal manifesto of the Modernist imagination. The prose sections of the book, which sometimes break off in the middle of a sentence, represent the poet's ruminations on imagination, reality, and the role of art, and the poems often serve as examples of his unfolding "argument." In the course of the book, Williams works out his view that the imagination remakes rather than reflects reality.

Williams opens his book with a prose passage that identifies the imagination as both his subject and his muse and that addresses the reader in intimate terms reminiscent of Whitman: "I myself," writes Williams, "invite you to read and to see." "In the imagination," he continues, "we are from henceforth (so long as you read) locked in a fraternal embrace, the classic caress of author and reader. We are one" (Williams, 1970). Williams' bold invitation sets the tone for the playful and often funny extravagances that follow, but it also expresses his sense of the importance of contact and communion in the creation of poetry. For Williams, vital art must clutch the world as well as convey it.

As Williams repeatedly insists throughout *Spring and All,* imagination is a reconstitution of reality, the force through which the artist conceives and creates his work. "It is not a matter of 'representation,'" Williams writes, "but of separate existence." Like the Cubist painters, Williams sought an art that created its own vivid world rather than one that merely imitated reality. What Williams wanted to convey in his poetry was "not 'realism,' but reality itself" (1970). By conceiving the imagination as a mediating force between human beings and the world, Williams figures the art object as an imaginative response to reality rather than a mimetic adjunct to it. "Poetry," he insists, "does not tamper with the world but moves it—It affirms reality most powerfully" (1970). The material existence of the poem gives it an independence from the chaos of reality, an integrity that Williams deeply values. For him, the artist, like the farmer in the third poem of *Spring and All* ("The farmer in deep thought / is pacing through the rain"), is an "antagonist" who wrestles with the world in order to wrest meaning from it (1970). The artist struggles to register his experience in the shape and substance of his art, to make something that embodies his response to reality. In the successful poem, the poet presents an imagined world that conveys a clear sense of himself in relation to everything else. Through the power of the imagination, the poet infuses the world with his personality in the material form of his poems.

Williams insists that imagination reorders experience; his theory of imagination authorizes his work as a poet by supporting his claim that the art work is a new object added to the world rather than a mirror that represents it: "The value of the imagination to the writer consists in its ability to make words. Its unique power is to give created forms reality, actual existence" (1970). In "great works of the imagination," he writes,

> A CREATIVE FORCE IS SHOWN AT WORK MAKING OBJECTS WHICH ALONE COMPLETE SCIENCE AND ALLOW THE INTELLIGENCE TO SURVIVE—his picture lives anew. It lives as pictures only can: by their power to ESCAPE ILLUSION and stand between man and nature as saints once stood between man and the sky—their reality in such work, say, as that of Juan Gris. (1970)

His description of the imagination in this passage echoes his characterization of the farmer as an "artist figure" whose work involves a "composing" of himself as well as his poetry. Williams defines the work of the imagination as a direct elemental struggle with reality: "Bare handed the man contends with the sky without experience of existence seeking to invent and design" (1970).

In a poem that, like the prose passages quoted previously, turns on the opposition between earth and sky, Williams dramatizes the mediating work of the imagination by showing its ability to soar from earth into space and to connect the two elements through its tensile force. In "The Rose Is Obsolete," Williams displaces the rose of traditional English poetry with a Cubist portrait of a strange new flower. "From the petal's edge" of this flower,

> a line starts  
> that being of steel  
> infinitely fine, infinitely  
> rigid penetrates  
> the Milky Way  
> without contact—lifting  
> from it—neither hanging  
> nor pushing—
>
> The fragility of the flower  
> unbruised  
> penetrates space

The poet reconceives the roses of reality and poetic tradition in the new form of his "infinitely fine" yet durable line that rises through the roof of the world. In the soaring paradox of a "fragility" that "penetrates space," Williams dramatizes the transfiguring power of the imagination.

JEFF WESTOVER

**Further Reading**

Brogger, Fredrik, "Design and Disconnection in W.C. Williams' 'Spring and All,'" in *Excursions in Fiction,* edited by Andrew Kennedy and Orm Øverland, Oslo: Novus, 1994

Bufithis, Philip, "William Carlos Williams Writing against *The Waste Land,*" *Sagetrieb* 8, nos. 1/2 (1989)
Dolin, Sharon, "Enjambment as Modernist Metaphor in Williams' Poetry," *Sagetrieb* 9, no. 3 (1990)
Dolin, Sharon, "Enjambment and the Erotics of the Gaze in Williams' Poetry," *American Imago* 50 (1993)
Dunn, Allen, "Williams's Liberating Need," *Journal of Modern Literature* 16 (1989)
Frye, Richard, "'Ascent to a Higher Plane': The Fourth Dimension and the Imagination in Williams' 'Kora in Hell' and 'Spring and All,'" *Sagetrieb* 12, no. 2 (1993)
Hatlen, Burton, "Openess and Closure in Williams' 'Spring and All,'" *William Carlos Williams Review* 20, no. 2 (1994)
Mariani, Paul, *William Carlos Williams: A New World Naked,* New York: McGraw Hill, 1981
Palatella, John, "But If It Ends the Start Is Begun: 'Spring and All,' Americanism, and Postwar Apocalypse," *William Carlos Williams Review* 21, no. 1 (1995)
Williams, William Carlos, *Imaginations,* edited by Webster Schott, New York: New Directions, 1970; as *Imaginations: Five Experimental Prose Pieces,* London: MacGibbon and Kee, 1970

---

# Yvor Winters 1900–68

While earning a good living as an English professor at Stanford University for almost 40 years, Yvor Winters earned little admiration in his dual roles as poet and literary critic. As a critic, Winters enraged many of his peers at Stanford with his attacks on the works of some of the most revered names in the literary canon, among them Shakespeare, William Wordsworth, and Samuel Taylor Coleridge. Winters' primary complaint was that these and other writers allowed emotion to reign superior over logic and reason in their works. As a poet, Winters is hardly remembered and rarely praised.

Born on 17 October 1900 in Chicago, Arthur Yvor Winters grew up in Eagle Rock, California. A prodigious child, he was delving into Macaulay at the age of four. It should come as no surprise, then, that Winters excelled academically, receiving his B.A. and M.A. in Romance languages and Latin from the University of Colorado, Boulder, in 1925. In the fall of 1918, however, his studies were interrupted when he contracted tuberculosis. He convalesced at sanatoriums in New Mexico, spending his time writing poetry. After recovering, he married poet and novelist Janet Lewis in 1926, taught at the University of Idaho in Pocatello for two years, and then entered Stanford University as a graduate student in 1927. He earned his Ph.D. at Stanford in 1934, continuing to teach there in the English Department from 1928 until his retirement in 1966.

At Stanford, Winters raised many eyebrows among his colleagues and contemporaries, mostly for what Kenneth Fields calls his "critical iconoclasm." For example, Winters declared the obscure Charles Churchill "the greatest poetic talent" of the mid-18th century; named Frederick G. Tuckerman, Jones Very, and Emily Dickinson the three best poets of the 19th century; called Edith Wharton's *The Age of Innocence* better than any novel by Herman Melville or Henry James; and identified Robert Bridges as a far better poet than T.S. Eliot. Winters also wrote that Tennyson "has nothing to say, and his style is insipid."

For Winters, poets and novelists who demonstrated unchecked emotion in their works were guilty of bad poetry and moral irresponsibility. In *Notes on Contemporary Criticism* (1929), Winters writes, "The basis of evil is in emotion; Good rests in the power of rational selection in action." For this reason, he was obviously not a big fan of the likes of Wordsworth and Keats (among other Romantics). Winters sought in poetry a classical sense of order, reason, and balance; poetry had to be linguistically, formally, and structurally restrained. In *Primitivism and Decadence* (1937), he states, "The theory of literature I defend . . . is absolutist. I believe that the work of literature, in so far as it is valuable, approximates a real apprehension and communication of a particular kind of objective truth."

Although best known for his wildly iconoclastic critical explorations, Winters also gained some degree of fame with his poetry. While his early poems were experimental and ranged beyond the pale of poetic restraint, Winters soon began writing poetry in the formalist mold, which held reason and logic to be supreme over emotion. In "To a Young Writer—Achilles Holt, Stanford, 1930," Winters clearly expresses this formalist philosophy of poetry:

Here for a few short years
Strengthen affections; meet,
Later, the dull arrears
Of age, and be discreet.

The angry blood burns low.
Some friend of lesser mind
Discerns you not; but so
Your solitude's defined.

Write little; do it well.
Your knowledge will be such,
At last, as to dispel
What moves you overmuch.

Knowledge—or reason and faith—will temper that which "moves you overmuch" or causes excessive emotion, which can overshadow the true intent of a poem, namely, according to Winters, to advocate morality. We see this theme again in "For the Opening of the William Dinsmore Briggs Room Stanford University, May 7, 1942":

Because our Being grows in mind,
And evil in imperfect thought,
And passion running undefined
May ruin what the masters taught;

Within the edge of war we meet
To dedicate this room to one
Who made his wisdom more complete
Than any save the great have done.

That in this room, men yet may reach,
By labor and wit's sullen shock,
The final certitude of speech,
Which Hell itself cannot unlock.

Winters values certitude above the wandering uncertainty of imagination and emotion. As he writes in "On Teaching the Young," "The poet's only bliss / Is in cold certitude— / Laurel, archaic, rude."

As Elizabeth Isaacs notes in *An Introduction to the Poetry of Yvor Winters* (1981), his "favorite theme for his life and his poetry" was "the search for self-identity in the battle between reason and sensation":

> This theme, recurrent throughout the entire body of his poetry, involves the sensitive human being's temptation to immersion in sensation; a detailed description of particulars to the point of near disintegration; and finally the successful recovery to a life of rational order.

However, in the end it is not his poetry that had people talking. Instead, Winters' legacy is his unabashed criticism of some of literature's greatest names. In his playful "Essay on Psychiatrists," poet Robert Pinsky, a student of Winters, portrays his former teacher in an honest yet lighthearted manner. Here, the narrator is a not-so-veiled representation of Winters:

. . . I know why you are here.
You are here to laugh. You have heard of a crazy
Old man who believes that Robert Bridges
Was a great poet; who believes that Fulke

Greville was a great poet, greater than Philip
Sidney; who believes that Shakespeare's Sonnets
Are not all that they are cracked up to be. . . .

When Winters died on 25 January 1968 in Palo Alto, California, he would be remembered primarily as just that: a "crazy / Old man." He was notorious for and arguably random in his criticism of poets and novelists, and he was something of a Johnny-one-note in his poetry, advocating expressions of morality over those of imagination and emotion.

JEFF FOSTER

**Biography**
Born in Chicago, Illinois, 17 October 1900. Attended the University of Chicago, 1917–18; University of Colorado, Boulder, 1923–25, B.A. and M.A. in Romance languages, 1925; Stanford University, California, Ph.D. 1934; tuberculosis patient in sanatorium, Santa Fe, New Mexico, 1919–21; teacher, Madrid and Los Cerillos, New Mexico, 1921–22; Instructor in French and Spanish, University of Idaho, Pocatello, 1925–27; Instructor, 1928–37, Assistant Professor, 1937–40, Associate Professor, 1941–48, Professor, 1948–61, and Albert Guerard Professor, 1961–66, Stanford University; founding editor, with Howard Baker and Janet Lewis, *Gyroscope*, 1929–30; regional editor, *Hound and Horn*, 1932–34; fellow, Kenyon School of English, Gambier, Ohio, 1948–50. Received American Academy grant, 1952; Brandeis University Creative Arts Award, 1959; Harriet Monroe Poetry Award, 1960; Bollingen Prize, 1961; National Endowment for the Arts grant, 1967; member, American Academy of Arts and Sciences. Died in Palo Alto, California, 25 January 1968.

**Poetry**
*The Immobile Wind*, 1921
*The Magpie's Shadow*, 1922
*The Bare Hills: A Book of Poems*, 1927
*The Proof*, 1930
*The Journey, and Other Poems*, 1931
*Before Disaster*, 1934
*Poems*, 1940
*The Giant Weapon*, 1943
*To the Holy Spirit: A Poem*, 1947
*Three Poems*, 1950
*Collected Poems*, 1952; revised edition, 1960
*The Early Poems of Yvor Winters, 1920–28*, 1966
*The Collected Poems of Yvor Winters*, edited by Donald Davie, 1978; republished as *The Poetry of Yvor Winters*, 1980
*The Uncollected Poems of Yvor Winters, 1929–1957*, edited by R.L. Barth, 1997
*The Selected Poems of Yvor Winters*, edited by R.L. Barth, 1999

**Selected Criticism**
*Primitivism and Decadence: A Study of American Experimental Poetry*, 1937
*Edwin Arlington Robinson*, 1946
*On Modern Poets: Stevens, Eliot, Ransom, Crane, Hopkins, Frost*, 1959
*Forms of Discovery: Critical and Historical Essays on the Forms of the Short Poem in English*, 1967

**Other Writings:** fiction (*The Book of Darkness*, 1947), essays, correspondence (*The Selected Letters of Yvor Winters*, edited by R.L. Barth, 2000), translation of Portuguese poetry (*The Last Sonnets of Pierre de Ronsard* [with *Diadems and Fagots*, by Olavo Bilac, translated by John Meem], 1921); edited collections of literature (*Twelve Poets of the Pacific*, 1937).

**Further Reading**
Carnochan, Brigitte Hoy, *The Strength of Art: Poets and Poetry in the Lives of Yvor Winters and Janet Lewis*, Stanford, California: Stanford University Press, 1984
Comito, Terry, *In Defense of Winters: The Poetry and Prose of Yvor Winters*, Madison: University of Wisconsin Press, 1986

Isaacs, Elizabeth, *An Introduction to the Poetry of Yvor Winters,* Athens: Ohio University Press, 1981
Powell, Grosvenor, *Language as Being in the Poetry of Yvor Winters,* Baton Rouge: Louisiana State University Press, 1980
Trimpi, Helen Pinkerton, "Introduction," in *The Selected Poems of Yvor Winters*, edited by R.L. Barth, Athens: Ohio University Press, 1999
Winters, Yvor, *The Selected Letters of Yvor Winters,* edited by R.L. Barth, Athens: Ohio University Press, 2000

---

# Charles Wright 1935–

Throughout much of his poetry, Charles Wright focuses on the relationship between what he calls "landscape," or images, and language. In "Silent Journal" (*Zone Journals,* 1988), we see the two intertwine:

Inaudible consonant inaudible vowel
The word continues to fall
                              in splendor around us
Window half shadow window half moon
                                    back yard like a book of snow
That holds nothing and that nothing holds
Immaculate text
                    not too prescient not too true

The snow, a metaphor for words, blankets the world allowing us to see nature as a text itself. We see the image of snow, and we see the words on the page. Both images are "inaudible," yet they can and do speak volumes. Working together and working off one another, landscape and language help to explain life's mysteries. Language serves to bridge the gap between a visible, tangible world and an abstract, unseen mystery.

Widely regarded as one of the most important and innovative American poets, Wright eloquently and evocatively renders the invisible feelings of the human condition into concrete, precise images. From his first of 13 collections, *The Grave of the Right Hand* (1970), to later books such as *The World of the Ten Thousand Things* (1990) and his trilogy, *Chickamauga* (1995), *Black Zodiac* (1997), and *Appalachia* (1998), Wright's Imagist narratives continue to articulate questions on the state of being, personal salvation, the sublime, and the uses of memory and the past. Wright's visionary lyricism uses the particularity of ordinary individual existence to evoke a universal experience and spiritual transcendence, translating emotion into form. For Wright, poetry uses the structure of the image and the musicality of sounds and rhythms from the familiar world to explore the metaphysical. Through his meditative engagement with logic and reasoning, religion, memory, and mortality, Wright—and his reader—may contemplate transcendence and the possibility of universal truths.

Wright spent his childhood moving around the rural South. Out of the landscape of Tennessee, and later North Carolina, Wright developed a deep concern for history and a correspondence with nature and spirituality. After graduating from Davidson College with a B.A. in history, Wright served in the Army Intelligence Corps stationed in Italy, where he read Ezra Pound's *Cantos* in Sirmione, a town on Lake Garda, the exact spot where Pound wrote about looking at the Alps. Wright credits Pound's image of the beauty of the place as an epiphany. In the course of his professional career he has received a Guggenheim fellowship, an Edgar Allan Poe Award, a PEN Translation Award, a National Book Award in poetry, a Lenore Marshall Poetry Prize, and a Pulitzer Prize in poetry.

Wright's first collection of poems, *The Grave of the Right Hand* (1970), highlights much of Pound's initial influence. Wright impresses the symbolic upon his readers through plain style speech and precise images, in which he notes that lucidity, attention to detail, and vision are virtues of any art. This collection introduces Wright's themes of mortality, painful memory, and personal salvation, constructing verbal meanings out of inarticulate feelings. His next collections, *Hard Freight* (1973), *Bloodlines* (1975), and *China Trace* (1977), comprise his first of three trilogies in which individual poems serve as parts of a whole, each commenting and building on another's images and metaphors. These works demonstrate Wright's developing technique of accumulating fragmented images, details, and metaphors.

A collection of four volumes of previous work, *The World of the Ten Thousand Things* departs from Wright's earlier short lyrics and moves into journal-type poems that extend the line, play with stanza arrangement and syntactic patterns, and evoke descriptions from landscape. Each poem charts Wright's thoughts on language, landscape, and questions of the self; at the same time it constructs intense verbal discourse with variations in internal rhyme, building successions of stanzas, and looser and more open structures. *The Southern Cross* (1981) focuses on images of the past in which the poet relies heavily on memory as a way of conjuring particular images in poems such as "Spring Abstract" and "Childhood's Body." "The notes I fall for fall from the lip of the sky, / A thousand years of music unstrung by the wind. / What do I care for the noun and its adjective?" he writes in "Spring Abstract." In this long span of time, Wright questions the relevance of the smallness of language to the hugeness of a thousand years. As in "Spring Abstract," "Childhood's Body" also touches on language's dependence upon the image: "Keeping the world alive, / My poems in a language now / I finally understand, / Little tablets of salt rubbed smooth by the wind." *The Other Side of the River* (1984) meditates on experience and how language enables perception. Both of these volumes emphasize the exterior aspect of experience over inner thoughts, words "looming phosphorescent against the dark," he notes in "Cryopexy." The second half of the collection moves into a deeper, more insightful and personal exploration of language over images. In *Zone Journals* (1988) Wright observes ordinary events or what he calls the "quotidian." Diary-like, each poem records Wright's isolated thoughts on language and events organized into areas or zones while still relating to the larger thematic concerns of the whole work. The written word, "an architecture of absence," he writes in "Yard Journal," traces the dissolved moment in time in order to help the reader return to a point of origin. By the last volume, *Xionia* (1990), Wright accepts the arbitrariness of language as a link to the invisible, despite his perpetual hunger to answer larger philosophical questions.

A later trilogy, *Chickamauga, Black Zodiac,* and *Appalachia,* continues to meditate upon language's contingent link to the unseen. In these volumes, however, Wright begins to push abstraction into more oblique associations. Rather than focus on the particulars of a specific and mundane image as he had practiced in earlier collections, Wright refrains from direct figurative relationships, opting for less detail. Most of the poems hover near the sublime and avoid explicit history, memory, or past experience. He uses what amount to small epiphanies in the landscape to sketch personal impressions addressing philosophical questions, religious doubts, and a vision of unity. Wright creates new variations and structures on a limited number of subjects. Poems, as he puts it, are translations that basically revolve around the same things: life, death, love, the divine. Hence, he augments the form of the poem rather than the content: he breaks syntax, varies line lengths and breaks, and shifts the tempo of his poems. These techniques become tools for innovative presentations of the invisible world. "Disjecta Membra" from *Black Zodiac* relates Wright's urgency to translate the world:

> Backyard, dry flower half-border, unpeopled landscape
> Stripped of embellishment and anecdotal concern:
> A mirror of personality,
> unworldly and self-effacing,
> The onlooker sees himself in,
> a monk among the oak trees . . .

Wright's best technique is his creation of images to translate the spiritual into words. He attributes his musicality to the works of Dante and of Eugenio Montale, the Italian poet whom Wright translates in two collections, *The Storm* (1978) and *Motets* (1981). Both poets compose lush, sonata-like works evoking the landscape of Italy; their images lend the context of place, in Wright's case California, the South, and the Italian peninsula, to Wright's lyric desire and memory. The Imagist movement exemplified by Ezra Pound and William Carlos Williams also influences Wright's poetry. Imagism stresses the objective, the particular, and the visual. The poets who practice in this vein employ precise language to close the gap between language and the object they intend to represent. Wright explores this breach between the word and the object in many of his later poems, attempting to connect the underlying and invisible human condition with the external world of nature and the quotidian life as a way of transcendence into a divine, sublime realm.

Wright's influence on American life and letters continues to generate fresh and innovative contexts and forms for examining daily life. His technical and stylistic originality, his search for the absolute, his poignant lyricism, and his lucid imagery push his readers to contemplate how they may articulate and transcend the lived world by engaging with memory, imagination, and spirituality. He leaves open the possibility for universal truth while celebrating the particularity of experience.

NICOLE E. CORTZ

**Biography**

Born in Pickwick Dam, Tennessee, 25 August 1935. Attended Davidson College, North Carolina, 1953–57, B.A. 1957; University of Iowa, Iowa City, 1961–63, M.F.A. 1963; University of Rome (Fulbright fellow), 1963–64; served in the United States Army Intelligence Corps, 1957–61; Professor of English, University of California, Irvine, 1966–83; since 1983 Professor, currently Souder Family Professor of English, University of Virginia, Charlottesville; Fulbright Lecturer, University of Padua, 1968–69; Visiting Lecturer, University of Iowa, 1974–75, Princeton University, New Jersey, 1978, and Columbia University, New York, 1978. Received Eunice Tietjens Award (*Poetry,* Chicago), 1969; National Endowment for the Arts grant, 1974; Guggenheim fellowship, 1975; Melville Cane Award, 1976; Edgar Allan Poe Award, 1976; American Academy grant, 1977; PEN Translation Award, 1979; Ingram Merrill fellowship, 1980; American Book Award, 1983; Brandeis University Creative Arts Award, 1987; Ruth Lilly Poetry Prize, 1993; Lenore Marshall Poetry Prize, 1996; Pulitzer Prize, 1997; *Los Angeles Times* Book Prize, 1998; National Book Critics Circle Award, 1998; Chancellor, Academy of American Poets, 1999. Living in Charlottesville, Virginia.

**Poetry**

*The Grave of the Right Hand,* 1970
*Hard Freight,* 1973
*Bloodlines,* 1975
*China Trace,* 1977
*The Southern Cross,* 1981
*Country Music: Selected Early Poems,* 1982
*The Other Side of the River,* 1984
*Five Journals,* 1986
*Zone Journals,* 1988
*The World of the Ten Thousand Things,* 1990
*Xionia,* 1990
*Chickamauga,* 1995
*Black Zodiac,* 1997
*Appalachia,* 1998
*Negative Blues: Selected Later Poems,* 2000

**Selected Criticism**

*Quarter Notes: Improvisations and Interviews,* 1995
*Halflife,* 1998

**Other Writings:** essays, translations of Italian literature (*The Storm* [1978] and *Motets* [1981], both by Eugenio Montale).

**Further Reading**

Andrews, Tom, editor, *The Point Where All Things Meet: Essays on Charles Wright,* Oberlin, Ohio: Oberlin College Press, 1995
Collins, Floyd, "Metamorphosis within the Poetry of Charles Wright," *Gettysburg Review* 4, no. 3 (1991)
Collins, Floyd, "A Poetry of Transcendence," *Gettysburg Review* 10, no. 4 (1997)

Garrison, David, "From Feeling to Form: Image as Translation in the Poetry of Charles Wright," *Midwest Quarterly* 4, no. 1 (1999)
Gitzen, Julian, "Charles Wright and Presences in Absence," *Mid-American Review* 14, no. 2 (1994)
Suarez, Ernest, "Charles Wright," *Five Points* 2, no. 3 (1998)
Van Winckel, Nance, "Charles Wright and the Landscape of the Lyric," *New England Review* 12, no. 3 (1988)
Vendler, Helen, *The Music of What Happens,* Cambridge, Massachusetts: Harvard University Press, 1988
Young, David, "The Blood Bees of Paradise," *Field* 44 (1991)

---

## James Wright 1927–80

Possessed of one of the most distinctive and clearest voices of his generation of poets, James Wright embodied a series of interesting tensions. Born and raised in the rugged, working-class town of Martins Ferry, Ohio, Wright was a physically imposing, hard-drinking man who wrote some of the most tender, beautiful lyrics of midcentury American poetry. Acclaimed by critics for the formal skill of his first two books—tight iambs, rhyme, sonority—Wright abruptly labeled such work "the poetry of calcium" and turned to experiments in free verse, Robert Bly's "deep image" surrealism, and prose poems. As a reader Wright's preferences embraced both traditional writers and those contemporary poets who most directly challenged the traditional. Although he is best known as a poet, Wright thought of himself primarily as a teacher whose specialty was the 19th-century English novel.

Wright grew up amid the Great Depression in the Ohio River Valley. Neither of his parents graduated from high school, and his father endured repeated lay-offs at the Hazel-Atlas glass factory in Wheeling, West Virginia. Wright suffered his first nervous breakdown at age 16 and missed an entire year of high school. Depression, or perhaps what doctors today call bipolar mood disorder, would remain with him for much of the rest of his life. This condition was compounded by a serious alcohol problem. Given this background, it is not surprising that in so many of his poems Wright's subjects are the dispossessed, the downtrodden, the reviled: violent criminals ("A Poem about George Doty in the Death House"), prostitutes ("In Response to a Rumor That the Oldest Whorehouse in Wheeling, West Virginia, Has Been Condemned"), broken men ("Old Man Drunk"), the poor ("In Terror of Hospital Bills"), the victimized ("Split-lipped homosexuals limp in terror of assault"). These recurrent themes of human suffering, loneliness, and alienation are balanced by a delight in the natural world, in certain landscapes, in particular people, and finally in the redemptive power of love.

After serving with the U.S. Army's occupation force in Japan in 1946–47, Wright entered Kenyon College on the G.I. bill, where he studied with John Crowe Ransom. Ransom's New Critical emphasis on structural complexity and questions of form taught Wright to value such traditional poets as Edwin Arlington Robinson, Thomas Hardy, and Robert Frost. In his senior year Wright published two poems in the *Kenyon Review,* a rare achievement for an undergraduate. Wright spent 1952–53 as a Fulbright scholar at the University of Vienna, where he studied Theodor Storm's fiction and Georg Trakl's poetry. Trakl's surreal imagery did not have an immediate influence, but it would resurface when Wright began his collaboration with Robert Bly. From Vienna Wright went to the University of Washington, where he studied creative writing with Theodore Roethke and Stanley Kunitz, and also pursued a Ph.D. in literature. Like Ransom, Roethke valued traditional poetic forms, but Roethke's poems were far more intensely personal than Ransom's, and Wright absorbed the examples of both. He defended his Ph.D. dissertation, "The Comic Imagination of the Young Dickens," in 1959, and one senses that prose rhythms were important for Wright well before his prose poems of the 1970s.

Wright's first book, *The Green Wall* (1957), was selected by W.H. Auden for publication in the Yale Series of Younger Poets. Heavily influenced by Robinson and Frost, these are elegant, carefully made poems, similar in their formalism to the poems of Wilbur, Lowell, and Nemerov, and remarkable for their subtle, supple iambic rhythms; Wright's ear was his greatest strength at this point in his career. The poems of *Saint Judas* (1959) are also polished and intricate, although Wright was beginning to work with a more colloquial diction and looser forms, as in "At the Executed Murderer's Grave." The title poem is perhaps the best known, a first-person sonnet in which Judas, on his way to hang himself, stops to aid a beaten man and thereby attains a stunned awareness of his (and perhaps also the human) condition: ". . . Flayed without hope, / I held the man for nothing in my arms."

Despite the success of his first two books, the completion of his dissertation, and his tenure-track position at the University of Minnesota, however, Wright felt that he had reached a crisis, both personally and creatively. He and his wife separated in 1959 and divorced in 1962, and Wright's struggles with depression led to electroshock and psychotherapy. His poem "Having Lost My Sons, I Confront the Wreckage of the Moon: Christmas, 1960" suggests the loneliness and desolation of this point in his life. Moreover, he felt he had reached an aesthetic dead end; he could no longer write in the formalist mode of his first two books. But amid the failing marriage, the depression, and the alcoholism (a major factor in his being denied tenure at Minnesota), Wright discovered Robert Bly's journal *The Fifties,* wrote Bly a 16-page letter, and was invited to Bly's farm in western Minnesota. Bly was exactly what Wright needed, for their conversations on poetry led to collaborative translations of such poets as Pablo Neruda, Cesar Vallejo, and Jorge Guillen, and rekindled Wright's interest in Trakl, from whom Wright said he learned to look, listen, and wait. These translations helped Wright to extend his understanding of the poetic resources of his own language and showed him that patterns of juxtaposed images can carry the burden of poetic form in powerful and liberating ways. Although Wright is often grouped with Bly, Louis Simpson, and William Stafford as a Deep Image poet, and his affiliation with Bly is often taken as signaling a repudiation of his earlier formalism, this oversimplifies the truth. Wright never fully repudiated his formalist concerns, and, unlike Bly, he evinced no real interest in the deep images of the Jungian unconscious. It is clear, however, that his contact with Bly, their translations, and the time Wright spent simply living on Bly's farm instead of in Minneapolis were seminal elements in the creation of his next, and perhaps his very best, book of poems, *The Branch Will Not Break* (1963).

*The Branch Will Not Break* is probably Wright's most critically admired book; it certainly contains his most widely anthologized and best-known poems, including "Autumn Begins in Martins Ferry, Ohio," "Lying in a Hammock at William Duffy's Farm in Pine Island, Minnesota," "The Jewel," "Eisenhower's Visit to Franco, 1959," and "A Blessing."

Although Wright regularly described himself as a "conservative" and a "Horatian" in his prosodic principles, the strongest poems in this book are in free verse structured in parallel or juxtaposed images: for example, in "Lying in a Hammock at William Duffy's Farm in Pine Island, Minnesota," the image of an empty house is set against images of domestic and wild animals, each of which is at home in the world, and against the image of the alienated speaker. The speaker simply describes the various things he sees and hears from his hammock, and then culminates his observations with a surprising, enigmatic assertion—"I have wasted my life"—a line that has occasioned considerable disagreement among its readers. Similarly, "A Blessing" describes the speaker and a friend watching two ponies in a Minnesota pasture, and concludes,

> Suddenly I realize
> That if I stepped out of my body I would break
> Into blossom.

That kind of ecstatic, visionary consciousness strikes some readers as unearned, sentimental, or self-indulgent, and Wright risks such responses because of the non sequitur progression of his images and statements. Other readers, however, find these poems enacting a kind of self-transcendence, a rendering of lived experience so vividly intense as to be genuinely revelatory. The poems of *Shall We Gather at the River* (1968) are also in free verse, but they tend to be set in Minneapolis or Ohio rather than rural, western Minnesota, and their emotional color is darker, closer in some ways to Wright's first two books than to the life-affirming poems of *The Branch Will Not Break*.

Although Wright's *Collected Poems* (1971) was awarded the 1972 Pulitzer Prize, none of its 33 new poems stands out as a significant advance on his earlier work. In fact, Wright sounds somewhat dissatisfied with himself and his work:

> The kind of poetry I want to write is
> The poetry of a grown man.
> The young poets of New York come to me with
> Their mangled figures of speech,
> But they have little pity
> For the pure clear word.
> I know something about the pure clear word,
> Though I am not yet a grown man.

The new poems of *Collected Poems* and Wright's next book, *Two Citizens* (1973), are perhaps his weakest, for they lack the formal virtuosity of his poems of the 1950s as well as the emotional intensity and arresting imagery of his poems of the 1960s. Here Wright comes close to being merely colloquial in his diction, merely quotidian in his concerns, and the accusation of sentimentality is, sometimes, valid.

In 1967 Wright remarried and began spending considerable time in Europe, especially France and Italy. If Robert Bly helped to save Wright, as a poet, in the late 1950s and early 1960s, then Annie, his second wife, did the same in the mid-1970s. Annie and Europe were major subjects of *Two Citizens*, but in that book Wright had not learned how to use his new material, nor had he found his voice. In 1974, shortly after the deaths of both his parents, Wright suffered another nervous breakdown, and in 1975 his drinking finally led him to Alcoholics Anonymous. Cancer of the tongue would kill him in 1980, but in the last five years of his life he entered the third major phase of his work and produced two excellent books, *To a Blossoming Pear Tree* (1977) and the posthumous *This Journey* (1982). These poems reflect a profound re-engagement with the world, or what Nathan Scott (1993) has called a posture of *pietas* toward the world. Wright continues to employ colloquial diction and direct address, but here his remarkable ear for rhythm is again evident as it had not been since his first two books: his prose poems are among the finest in American literature. Wright's attentiveness and receptiveness to the sensuous beauty of the natural world—certain Italian landscapes, certain qualities of light, flowers, insects, human faces—are as full and rich as they were in *The Branch Will Not Break*. His wife Annie and Italy, the two great loves of the final decade of his life, were the kind of creative catalyst that Robert Bly and rural Minnesota had been earlier, and before he died, James Wright produced the poetry of a grown man:

> Many men
> Have searched all over Tuscany and never found
> What I found there, the heart of the light

There is no critical consensus on Wright. For every Calvin Bedient, who finds an overly mannered, tough-guy sentimentalism in his poems, there is a Marjorie Perloff, who places him among American literature's finest visionary poets. James E.B. Breslin situates Wright firmly in the Deep Image school of poetry, while *The Columbia History of American Poetry* labels him—along with Philip Levine and Adrienne Rich—a post-Confessional poet. Wright was a gifted reader of other poets, as the essays in his *Collected Prose* (1983) make clear, but he wrote no manifestos on poetics. He was neither a theoretician, nor the founder of a school of poetry, nor a follower. Although his teachers Ransom and Roethke are important influences, no one has seriously accused Wright of being merely derivative, and although his friend Robert Bly was another major influence, Wright was careful to hide from Bly the sonnets and other formalist poems he sometimes wrote while staying at Bly's farm. Like Robert Lowell and Adrienne Rich, James Wright stands as an important example of how a strong poet can re-invent an aesthetic. Like theirs, Wright's clear, distinctive voice is central to the canon of mid-20th-century American poetry.

GARY GRIEVE CARLSON

**Biography**

Born in Martins Ferry, Ohio, 13 December 1927. Attended Kenyon College, Gambier, Ohio, B.A. (cum laude, Phi Beta Kappa) 1952; University of Vienna (Fulbright fellow), 1952–53; University of Washington, Seattle, M.A. 1954, Ph.D. 1959; served in the United States Occupation Forces, Japan, 1946–47; teacher, University of Minnesota, Minneapolis, 1957–64, Macalester College, St. Paul, Minnesota, 1963–65, and Hunter College, New York City, 1966–80. Received Robert Frost Poetry Prize, 1952; Borestone Mountain Poetry Award, 1954, 1955; Eunice Tietjens Memorial Award (*Poetry,* Chicago), 1955; American Academy grant, 1959; Guggenheim fellowship, 1964, 1978; Brandeis University Creative Arts Award, 1970; Academy of American Poets fellowship, 1971; Melville Cane Award, 1972; Pulitzer Prize, 1972; member, American Academy, 1974. Died in New York City, 25 March 1980.

**Poetry**

*The Green Wall,* 1957
*Saint Judas,* 1959
*The Branch Will Not Break,* 1963
*Shall We Gather at the River,* 1968
*Collected Poems,* 1971
*Two Citizens,* 1973
*Moments of the Italian Summer,* 1976
*To a Blossoming Pear Tree,* 1977
*This Journey,* 1982
*The Shape of Light,* 1986
*Above the River: The Complete Poems,* 1990

**Other Writings:** essays (*Collected Prose,* 1983), selected correspondence (*With the Delicacy and Strength of Lace: Letters Between Leslie Marmon Silko and James Wright,* edited by Annie Wright, 1986), translations of German and Spanish poetry (*The Rider on the White Horse,* by Theodor Storm, 1964); edited collections of poetry (*Poems,* by Hermann Hesse [Wright also translated], 1970).

**Further Reading**

Breslin, James E.B., *From Modern to Contemporary: American Poetry, 1945–1965,* Chicago: University of Chicago Press, 1984
Dougherty, David, *James Wright,* Boston: Twayne, 1987
Hass, Robert, "James Wright," *Ironwood* 10 (1977)
Scott, Nathan A., Jr., *Visions of Presence in Modern American Poetry,* Baltimore, Maryland: Johns Hopkins University Press, 1993
Smith, Dave, editor, *The Pure Clear Word: Essays on the Poetry of James Wright,* Urbana: University of Illinois Press, 1982
Stein, Kevin, *James Wright: The Poetry of a Grown Man,* Athens: Ohio University Press, 1989
Stitt, Peter, and Frank Graziano, editors, *James Wright: The Heart of the Light,* Ann Arbor: University of Michigan Press, 1990
Taylor, Henry, *Compulsory Figures: Essays on Recent American Poets,* Baton Rouge: Louisiana State University Press, 1992

---

# Elinor Wylie 1885–1928

Elinor Wylie's poetic style evolved from a finely chiseled *fin-de-siècle* aesthetic elegance and presented its content—declarations of feminist independence—subtly, in gilded frames. Wylie was considered a beautiful *femme fatale* and a "notorious" woman because she was married three times, initiated divorce twice, and twice married to further her artistic career rather than for love. She was an Edith Wharton (to whom Edmund Wilson compared her) or Henry James heroine, born into a blue-blood world of hypocritical strictness and inevitable tragedies, including several suicides. In the seven years before her early death, she published four volumes of verse and four novels. Shelley was her hero, and she emulated him in technique, free spiritedness, and short life. Her female peers included Sara Teasdale, Edna St. Vincent Millay, and Dorothy Parker. While all three are better remembered, Wylie is the better poet.

Her first volume of poems, *Incidental Numbers* (1912), was a private printing (60 copies) that merely hinted at her future skill. The poem "From Whom No Secrets Are Hid" concerns her guilt over leaving her first husband and infant son for Horace Wylie, who represented the intellectual life to which she aspired. *Nets to Catch the Wind* (1921), her first commercial volume, generated high praise from critics for its technical virtuosity (critics began to compare Wylie to Blake and Wordsworth) and from poets such as Yeats, a Wylie favorite, who admired "The Eagle and the Mole" for its Romantic images and yearnings. Themes enunciated in this volume became mainstays in her work: the rebukes suffered by the sensitive artist from an insensitive society; the wish to withdraw from this pain through beautiful nature, sleep, or death; and the spiritual regeneration to be gained from loving art and creating it.

In 1923 Wylie divorced Horace Wylie to marry William Rose Benét, editor of *The Literary Review* and a poet with numerous connections in New York's literary circle. Wylie herself became literary editor of *Vanity Fair,* published her first novel (*Jennifer Lorn,* a play on "Jennie forlorn") to great acclaim as a clever satire of vapid aestheticism, and also published a book of poetry, *Black Armour.* In *Black Armour* Wylie achieved a technical brilliance, particularly in her sonnets, that surpassed even the precision of *Nets to Catch the Wind.* Critics considered the crystalline sheen a formidable contrast to the understated emotional conflicts, guilt, fear of failure, and fear of death. After Wylie's death her admirer and friend Millay would imitate the sonnets in *Fatal Interview* (1931), which is dedicated to Wylie.

Wylie had now achieved fame for herself as an artist and not merely as a man's adornment (a theme of *Jennifer Lorn*). She was erratic, eccentric, and vain, with devoted admirers and as many detractors. Her public life matched her poetry: she wished to appear as the height of stylish fashion and as a leading intellectual in New York's Greenwich Village, but at the same time she hardly disguised her insecurity and anxiety. Much of her anxiety, in addition to psychological causes, resulted from severe hypertension, an illness that was barely treatable in her era. Moreover, her compulsion to prove herself as an artist pushed her to an unrelenting work schedule that seemed to be motivated by a prescient fear of early death.

Wylie's next novel, *The Venetian Glass Nephew* (1924), which she called a "kind of moral fairy tale" in the preface, focused on themes developed in her poetry. In the novel a lovely and ebullient girl agrees to become a porcelain *objet d'art* in order to satisfy a husband made of glass. This theme echoes those in *Jennifer Lorn* as well as those in Pound's *Hugh Selwyn Mauberley* (1920), in which "the glow of porcelain" is presented as all show with no substance.

Wylie's obsession with Shelley—she befriended Aldous Huxley because she thought him the *new* Shelley—became the subject of her next two novels, *The Orphan Angel* (1926) and *Mr. Hodge and Mr. Hazard* (1928). These are fantasies in which Wylie wishes she were Shelley himself, the protagonist in both stories. These novels were important preludes to her 1928 volume of poetry *Trivial Breath*.

A heart attack had left Wylie frail yet determined to honor her hero in verse. The poems in *Trivial Breath* are not about Shelley per se, but rather about what Wylie perceived to be the themes he might have chosen had he been disillusioned, as she was. She believed Shelley had the attributes she lacked for fulfillment. "Dedication" has more meaning when the reader understands that Shelley is the poem's object, while the four sonnets of "A Red Carpet to Shelley" are direct rather than allusive. A cynicism within the typically delicate technique matches the sarcasm of her friend Dorothy Parker, while a coldness suggests disappointment in her failure to achieve a truly mystical love that could fuse affection and desire. The often-anthologized "Puritan's Ballad" revels in opposites and humorously satiric rhymes to hide her pain.

While writing *Trivial Breath* Wylie met a man whom she believed was the one person who could give her spiritual love: Clifford Woodhouse, who was happily married. Her affection went unrequited and Wylie, after repeated heart attacks, began to consider death her only hope for peaceful respite. She addresses Woodhouse, rejection, and death in her greatest poetic achievement, the posthumous *Angels and Earthly Creatures* (1929). The title from Donne signifies her metaphysical intent. The centerpiece is the 19-sonnet sequence "One Person," which details Wylie's friendship with Woodhouse, a sympathetic listener who seemed to Wylie to provide the spiritual solace that others—Shelley notwithstanding—could not. He also made it clear that their friendship could be no more than that. Bereft, Wylie died of a stroke in 1928. Her gravestone quotes Shelley: "Well done thou good and faithful servant / An image of some bright eternity."

DAVID GARRETT IZZO

**Biography**

Born in Somerville, New Jersey, 7 September 1885. Poetry editor, *Vanity Fair,* 1923–25; editor, Literary Guild, New York, 1926–28; contributing editor, *New Republic,* 1926–28. Received Julia Ellsworth Ford Prize, 1921. Died in New York City, 16 December 1928.

**Poetry**

*Incidental Numbers,* 1912
*Nets to Catch the Wind,* 1921
*Black Armour,* 1923
*(Poems),* edited by Laurence Jordan, 1926
*Trivial Breath,* 1928
*Angels and Earthly Creatures: A Sequence of Sonnets,* 1928
*Angels and Earthly Creatures* (collection), 1929
*Collected Poems,* edited by William Rose Benét, 1932
*Nadir,* 1937
*Last Poems,* edited by Jane D. Wise, 1943
*Collected Poems of Elinor Wylie,* 1947

**Other Writings:** novels (*Jennifer Lorn,* 1923; *The Venetian Glass Nephew,* 1924; *The Orphan Angel,* 1926; *Mr. Hodge and Mr. Hazard,* 1928), essays (*Collected Prose,* 1933).

**Further Reading**

Benét, William Rose, *The Dust Which Is God,* New York: Dodd Mead, 1941
Farr, Judith, *The Life and Art of Elinor Wylie,* Baton Rouge: Louisiana State University Press, 1983
Gray, Thomas, *Elinor Wylie,* New York: Twayne, 1969
Jones, Phyllis M., "Amatory Sonnet Sequences and the Female Perspective of Elinor Wylie and Edna St. Vincent Millay," *Women's Studies* 10, no. 1 (1983)
Olson, Stanley, *Elinor Wylie: A Life Apart: A Biography,* New York: Dial Press, 1979

# Z

## Louis Zukofsky 1904–78

Born in New York City, Louis Zukofsky grew up in a Yiddish-speaking family environment that figured significantly in his later writing, often as a source for an agonized relationship with Judaism. An accomplished poet and writer by his early 20s, he had gained the admiration and support of Ezra Pound, William Carlos Williams, and T.S. Eliot. Williams in particular gradually came to rely on Zukofsky as a reader and editor of his own poetry and to help him through the tricky political waters of literary Modernism in New York in the 1930s and 1940s. However, it was at the instigation of Ezra Pound that Harriet Monroe asked Zukofsky to accept editorial responsibility for an issue of *Poetry,* focusing on contemporary developments in modern poetry. Despite Zukofsky's protestations to the contrary, this volume effectively created the Objectivist movement, which centered mainly on the work of George Oppen, Charles Reznikoff, and Carl Rakosi and, to a lesser extent, poets such as Lorine Niedecker and William Carlos Williams. In the now famous February 1931 "Objectivist" volume of *Poetry,* Zukofsky reluctantly offered the label "Objectivist" to describe the poetic tendencies that he outlined in his significant prefatory essay "Sincerity and Objectification." The principal characteristic of Objectivist poetry was an attempt to find a non-predatory mode of representing objects that resisted the intrusion of a controlling, dominating ego that enforced its own perception on objects. In the famous prefatory statement, Zukofsky maintained, "In sincerity shapes appear concomitants of word combinations, precursors of . . . completed sound structure, melody or form. Writing occurs which is the detail, not mirage, of seeing, of thinking with things as they exist, and of directing them along a line of melody. Shapes suggest themselves and the mind senses and receives awareness" ("An Objective," in *Prepositions: The Collected Critical Essays,* 1967, 1981). "Sincerity" then leads to "objectification," the structure or "rested totality" of the poem: "objectification—the apprehension satisfied completely as to the appearance of the art form as an object . . . its character may be simply described as the arrangement, into one apprehended unit, the resolving of words and their ideation into structure" ("An Objective," in *Prepositions*). Objectification is making the poem into a thing, an object in the world, which, although rare in poetry, is nevertheless the goal of an ethical vision and composition.

Developing a reputation as one of the most musical poets of the Modernist era, Zukofsky was also one of the more intellectually difficult writers. Yet he was an extremely versatile and metrically proficient poet, as testified by the variety of his work, which includes short lyrics, sonnet sequences, and longer epic sequences. Most of his shorter poems have been collected in *All: The Collected Short Poems* (1965–66), which includes such witty lyrics as his Valentine poems to his wife, Celia, as well as his more politicized poems, such as "Song—3/4 time," "Memory of V.I. Ulianov," and "The Immediate Aim." Many of the preoccupations of his later work are evident in two significant early poems, "Poem Beginning 'The'" and "'Mantis': An Interpretation." These poems demonstrate his adept interweaving of social commentary and the philosophy of his developing poetics. "Poem Beginning 'The'" concerns cultural assimilation, ethnic identity, and the subject's ease with the values of a different literary tradition and culture. It is written in a fragmented style, the numeration of each line parodying the fragmented texts of European Modernism. It incorporates extracts from the emerging important "Modernist" texts (Woolf's *Mrs. Dalloway,* Joyce's *Ulysses,* Lawrence's *Kangaroo,* and Pound's *Hugh Selwyn Mauberley*) as well as important American Modernist writing (E.E. Cummings' *Is Five* and Marianne Moore's poetry). All these works are enmeshed with quotations from other eras and from other cultures and languages in a typically Eliotic manner. One of the principal differences, however, is that Zukofsky's quotations are much more heterogeneous than Eliot's selective tradition that appears in *The Waste Land.* Zukofsky's quotations read like an attempt to challenge the prevailing selectivism of Eliot and to reveal alternative popular currents and ethnic traditions.

"Poem Beginning 'The'" also firmly locates Zukofsky's early poetics within the matrix of the major debate concerning the relationship between aesthetics and politics that was occurring in the 1930s and 1940s. Clearly preoccupied with developing and exploring techniques of literary experimentalism and aesthetic formalism, the poem nevertheless also shows an engagement in a political and sociocultural critique of traditional and reactionary cultures. In "'Mantis': An Interpretation," Zukofsky's observation of a praying mantis in a New York subway becomes the occasion for an extended exploration of the acts of cognition and perception and the transformative mechanics of interpretation and representation. The two poems—a sestina and an interpretation—focus on the way something can accrue various mythical, symbolic, literal, and metaphoric significances. Zukofsky's dilemma was whether his symbolic association of the mantis with "the growing oppression of the poor" removed the latter from its social and historical particulars: in other words, whether representation aestheticizes politics. Zukofsky wrestles with the same problem he confronted in "Poem Beginning 'The'": how to construct a form that keeps history vibrant and current rather than as some ossified, monumental structure.

Zukofsky's principal work was his long poem *"A,"* which is structured as 24 movements composed throughout his life. An epic collage of autobiography, history, popular culture, reflections on daily and family life, theater pieces, music, wordplay, and puns, like Pound's *Cantos,* the poem resists easy exegesis. Nevertheless, it develops many of the issues raised in his early work, and it has emerged as a significant and defining poem of American Modernism. Published in a series of stages over the decades, the entire poem amounts to a sustained 50-year investigation of the political, ethical, social, poetic, philosophical, musical, and literary issues that preoccupied 20th-century America. Written in an "open form" similar to that of the Imagistic *Cantos* and the experiments with the "open field" poetics by the poets allied to the Black Mountain School, *"A"* becomes increasingly concerned with form and its ideological implications. The poem begins as a particularly careful examination of the phenomenological relationship of words to things and gradually develops into a more emphatic investigation into the relationship of words to other words and of English to other languages. This trajectory of the poem has meant that it has appealed to a variety of radical critical positions, both Marxist and poststructuralist critics finding the poem amenable to their critical perspectives.

*"A"*'s vigorous development of a new structure of poetic expression that attends to the *aural* dimensions of words, while not forgetting the Objectivist eye on the detail of things represented in language, demonstrated Zukofsky's perennial interest in translation. Evident in many of his shorter poems and sections of *"A,"* such as movement 21, his main work of translation, *Catullus* (1969), was completed with Celia. This work manifests Zukofsky's attention to the musical properties of language, maintaining a delicate balance in the poetry between an emphasis on the eye and the ear. Often criticized for its idiosyncratic approach, it is actually a transliteration, the sound of the original Latin being echoed in the English translation. For example, "Vivamus, mea Lesbia, atque amemus" (Catullus, *Odes,* V) becomes "We warm us may ah Lesbia what cue / may maim us" in *"A"*-18 and "May we live, my Lesbia, love while we may" in *Catullus.* Such ornamentation, embellishment, and adornment are related to improvisation, as an art of performing on something that has been previously accomplished. Yet improvisation in this case is not an art of free origination: instead, it commences with the given, which it then proceeds to amplify, alter, or embellish.

The attention to the sounding of words, or the breath of the "literal meaning" (Zukofsky in *Catullus*), is a central facet of the adjustment of the eye as the main structural and epistemological metaphor. The text suggests a new interrelationship where the visual and the aural are complementary rather than exclusive: "one to one, ear to / eye loving song greater than / anything—" (*"A"*-23). The interconnection of the ear and eye opens an exploration of syntax, typography, and sentences and their relation to space. Zukofsky's poetry investigates a variety of syntactic constructions, always considering how different syntactic forms alter or disrupt the constitution of meaning. For example, experiments with lineation occur in the syllabic count of section IV in *"A"*-13, in the two-word lines of *"A"*-19, in the five-word lines of *"A"*-22 and *"A"*-23, and in many of his shorter poems. Zukofsky produces a poetics in which "each sound of a word is weighed" (*Prepositions*) to foreground how certain patterns or arrangements of words can prescribe meaning. By not conforming to the conventional typography of the printed page with its close print, quickly organized as compact units of exchangeable meaning, Zukofsky highlights how meaning arrives after a process of *material* engagement with a text (on the barest level, one is forced to turn four or more pages for what amounts to two or three sentences). "One is brought back to the entirety of the *single* word which is in itself a relation, an implied metaphor, an arrangement, harmony or dissonance" (*Prepositions*). Meaning is literally—or *letterally*—drawn out, extended beyond the boundaries of the conventional page and typographical framework.

Zukofsky's other major poetic work is *80 Flowers* (1978), a sequence of 80 sonnets, each centered on a different flower, written in anticipation of his 80th birthday and to celebrate his interest in botany. The sonnets are highly wrought and densely woven pieces: they frequently contain puns and wordplay based on allusions to the mythical connotations of the flower, transliterations of the Latin species name, and other sources of often obscure and eclectic botanical knowledge. Toward the end of his life, he began *Gamut: 90 Trees,* a similar sonnet sequence for his 90th birthday, this time based on trees, although it was never finished, and only a few sonnets survive in draft form. In addition, Zukofsky wrote the massive critical study *Bottom: On Shakespeare* (1963), which brings together Wittgenstein, Spinoza, Aristotle, and a host of other literary, philosophical, and cultural texts in a highly original (some say eccentric) reading of the key tropes of the Shakespearean canon. Conceived of as a study of the relationships between love, sight, and language in the plays of Shakespeare, *Bottom* is really a major articulation of the principles informing Zukofsky's own poetics:

> The love of sound becomes excessively involved in an interplay of conceptual words. The tendency then is for the sound to persist as poem or tenuous intellectual echo, unless these words are spoken over and over again or, what amounts to the same process, unless the actual print preserves them for the eye to fathom but not to see. A good deal of the sound of this writing is thus gone as quickly as the processes of an imagination difficult to sound or to hear. The apprehensions of the eyes render the "simpler" words "concrete" and their sound less "interesting," that is, verbally less complicated.

Other prose works include essays on Henry Adams, Ezra Pound, William Carlos Williams, and Wallace Stevens, all of which are collected in *Prepositions,* as well as a series of minor prose works collected in *Collected Fiction* (1990). These prose works attest to the wryness and humor in Zukofsky's vision as well as his continuing interest in linguistic play and verbal relationships.

Despite a period of languishing in a certain amount of obscurity in the 1930s and 1940s, Zukofsky's poetry was "rediscovered" and championed in the 1950s by poets such as Robert Creeley, Robert Duncan, Cid Corman, and Allen Ginsberg. Today, his reputation is especially high among the Language poets, who regard him as one of the founding figures of Modernist poetry and an important precursor to their own poetic practices. Objectivist poetics, and its influence on Language poetry, was first and foremost an indigenous redefinition and rerouting of American poetic Modernism. As David Antin has suggested, this significant poetic lineage has shifted poetics from questions of personal expression to matters of construction and composition; it has reinvented the techniques of collage central to European Modernism while, at the same time, incorporating, as Olson says, the example of Williams' and Pound's use of "nonpoetic" narrative materials in the making of poetry. Always self-reflexively engaged in writing the self (or selves), constructing a process of confronting, negotiating, and engaging the limits of the self and other, music has been the dominant potential paradigm for Zukofsky's poetry since "music does not depend mainly on the human voice, as poetry does, for rendition" (*Prepositions*). As Zukofsky speculates in "A Statement for Poetry," the possibility of allowing speech to "become a movement of sounds" is only a "musical horizon of poetry (which incidentally poems perhaps never reach)" (*Prepositions*).

TIM WOODS

*See also* Objectivism

**Biography**

Born in New York City, 23 January 1904. Attended Columbia University, New York, M.A. 1924; teacher, University of Wisconsin, Madison, 1930–31, Colgate University, Hamilton, New York, 1947, and Polytechnic Institute of Brooklyn, New York, 1947–66; worked for Federal Writers' Project, Works Progress Administration, 1935–42; poet-in-residence, San Francisco State College (now California State University), 1958. Received Longview Foundation Award, 1961; Oscar Blumenthal/Charles Leviton Prize (*Poetry*, Chicago), 1966; National Endowment for the Arts grant, 1966, 1968; American Academy Award, 1976; honorary degree, Bard College, Annandale-on-Hudson, New York, 1977. Died in Port Jefferson, New York, 12 May 1978.

**Poetry**

*55 Poems*, 1941
*Anew*, 1946
*Some Time: Short Poems*, 1956
*Barely and Widely*, 1958
*"A" 1–12*, 1959; corrected edition, 1966
*16 Once Published*, 1962
*I's Pronounced Eyes*, 1963
*Found Objects, 1962–1926*, 1964
*Iyyob*, 1965
*All: The Collected Short Poems, 1923–1958 and 1956–1964*, 2 vols., 1965–66
*"A"-14*, 1967
*"A" 13–21*, 1968
*The Gas Age: A Poem*, 1969
*"A"-24*, 1972
*"A"-22 and 23*, 1975
*"A"* (complete version), 1978
*80 Flowers*, 1978
*Complete Short Poetry*, 1991

**Selected Criticism**

*Bottom: On Shakespeare*, 1963
*Prepositions: The Collected Critical Essays*, 1967; revised edition, 1981

**Other Writings:** play (*Arise, Arise*, 1973), short stories (*Ferdinand, Including It Was*, 1968), memoirs, translations of Latin literature (*Catullus* [with Celia Zukofsky], 1969); edited collections of literature (*A Test of Poetry*, 1948).

**Further Reading**

Ahearn, Barry, *Zukofsky's "A": An Introduction*, Berkeley: University of California Press, 1983
Leggott, Michele J., *Reading Zukofsky's "80 Flowers,"* Baltimore, Maryland: Johns Hopkins University Press, 1989
Scroggins, Mark, editor, *Upper Limit Music: The Writing of Louis Zukofsky*, Tuscaloosa: University of Alabama Press, 1997
Scroggins, Mark, *Louis Zukofsky and the Poetry of Knowledge*, Tuscaloosa: University of Alabama Press, 1998
Stanley, Sandra Kumamoto, *Louis Zukofsky and the Transformation of a Modern American Poetics*, Berkeley: University of California Press, 1994
Terrell, Carroll F., editor, *Louis Zukofsky: Man and Poet*, Orono, Maine: National Poetry Foundation, 1979

## "A"

Louis Zukofsky called his 24-section poem *"A"* (1978), begun in 1928 and completed in 1974, "the poem of a life." While the most obvious thread running through this 800-page work is the life of its author, the poem is not a simple autobiography; *"A"* presents its reader with a rich variety of forms and subject matters and at the same time offers a wide range of lasting pleasures. *"A"* has too often been dismissed as derivative of Ezra Pound's *Cantos*, another Modernist poem of similar length. While *"A"* certainly begins under the influence of the *Cantos*, it opens itself up to a far wider range of forms and methods and ultimately exhibits an overall coherence that surpasses that of Pound's unfinished poem. Of the long poems produced by the American Modernists, *"A"* is unique in the firmness of its conceptual architecture, the range of its personal and social vision, and the variety of its formal invention.

*"A"*-1 through *"A"*-7, which Zukofsky wrote between 1928 and 1930, were first published as a unit in his *An "Objectivists" Anthology* (1932). The poem's initiatory moment is a 1928 performance of Bach's *St. Matthew Passion* at Carnegie Hall. In *"A"*-1 (1928) Zukofsky compares this performance of the *Passion* to its 1729 premiere, then counterpoints passages from the work's libretto with various manifestations of social unrest and economic distress in contemporary America. For the poet the transcendent beauty of the music represents an artistic ideal continually stymied by the brutal conditions of everyday existence. The *Passion*'s themes of death and expected resurrection continue through *"A"*'s first seven movements. *"A"*-3 (1928) is an elegy to Zukofsky's friend Richard Chambers, who had committed suicide in 1926. *"A"*-4 (1928) explores Zukofsky's own immigrant Jewish roots

and contrasts the cultural backwardness of New York's Orthodox community to the vital Yiddish poetry recently written by Yehoash (pen name of Solomon Bloomgarden).

The first five movements of *"A"* are highly compressed, shifting subjects rapidly in a collage. *"A"*-6 (1930) is somewhat more relaxed, and among much else chronicles a cross-country trip by Zukofsky. At the very end, however, this movement gives an important signal as to Zukofsky's formal intentions:

*Can*
The design
Of the fugue
Be transferred
To poetry?

Zukofsky's formal model for *"A,"* and especially for its earlier movements, is the baroque fugue, in which melodic "subjects" and "countersubjects" are counterpointed against one another. It is an imprecise model—really only an allegory, for a poem cannot reproduce the simultaneous voices of a musical fugue—but the fugue gives Zukofsky a powerful analogy for the sort of weaving of images, sounds, and ideas that he wants to accomplish in his work.

*"A"*-7 (1928–30) is the culmination of the poem thus far, a series of seven Shakespearean sonnets that recapitulate almost all of the themes that have previously appeared in the poem. *"A"*-8 (1935–37), longer than all seven preceding movements, is a dauntingly complex attempt to write a "mirror" fugue, deploying no fewer than eight primary themes, including Bach's *St. Matthew Passion,* Bach's own biography, economic and historical theories of Marx and Henry Adams, Spinoza's philosophy, and contemporary science. The first third of *"A"* is heavily influenced by leftist political theory, but after the first half of *"A"*-9 (1938–40), politics largely disappear from the poem. *"A"*-9 is Zukofsky's translation of Guido Cavalcanti's canzone "Donna mi priegha," a formally complex work that Pound had repeatedly struggled to render into English. The first half of *"A"*-9 translates the canzone using phrases from Marx's *Das Kapital,* advancing an interpretation of the relationship of use-value and exchange-value. The second half (1948–50) retains the same rhyme sounds (and many of the same rhyme words), but uses phrases from Spinoza's *Ethics* instead of Marx, delineating a theory of love.

After Zukofsky's marriage in 1939 and the birth of his son in 1943, *"A"* turns increasingly toward the familial rather than the social sphere. *"A"*-11 (1950) is an adaptation of another Cavalcanti poem, "Perch'io non spero," addressed to his wife and son. *"A"*-12 (1950–51) is an enormous, loosely fugally-structured grab-bag of materials reflecting Zukofsky's reading and the day-to-day interactions of his family. His method in the second half of *"A"* is to weave together materials from his daily life and from the entire storehouse of Western culture; it is a poetics of quotation, translation, and paraphrase. The latter movements of the poem, like the earlier "fugal" passages, often take musical forms for their formal inspiration. *"A"*-10 (1940) is an inverted mass lamenting the fall of Paris to the Germans. *"A"*-13 (1960), subtitled "partita," is comprised of five parts, each written in a different stanzaic form; these shifts in stanza and meter are meant to parallel the shifts in rhythm and tempo of Bach's Violin Partita in D Minor.

Near the beginning of *"A"*-14 (1964) Zukofsky announces that this is the

*First of*
*eleven songs*
*beginning An.*

Each of these 11 movements does indeed begin with the syllable "an," but the individual forms of each movement are very diverse indeed. Most of *"A"*-14 consists of three-line stanzas with three words in each line. *"A"*-15 (1964) begins with a translation of a passage from Job in which Zukofsky reproduces as closely as possible the sounds of the Hebrew, then proceeds to mourn the death of John F. Kennedy, which is counterpointed with passages from Gibbon's *Decline and Fall of the Roman Empire. "A"*-16 (1963) is a four-word elegy to Robert Frost:

An
inequality

wind flower.

*"A"*-17 is also an elegy, "A CORONAL for Floss" that collages passages from Zukofsky's writings that deal with his recently dead friend William Carlos Williams.

The remaining movements of *"A"* are equally formally diverse—*"A"*-21 (1967), for instance, is a translation of Plautus' *Rudens*—but the poem culminates in two matched movements, *"A"*-22 and 23 (1970–74). (Zukofsky's wife Celia had given him *"A"*-24 as a present in 1968; her arrangement of passages from the whole range of his writings in five-voiced counterpoint to Handel's harpsichord music is published in *"A"* as a musical score.) *"A"*-22 and 23 each consist of 1,000 five-word lines and chart 6,000 years of history by means of quotation, paraphrase, and translation.

Most of the movements of *"A"* were published in periodicals, especially *Poetry* magazine. Its first single volume collection was *"A" 1–12* (1959; corrected edition, 1966), followed by *"A" 13–21* in 1968. *"A"* was published as a single volume in 1978, the year of Zukofsky's death. Zukofsky's poetry is difficult; he himself was fond of referring to his work as "crabbed." Nonetheless, *"A"* is a towering achievement in 20th-century American poetry, not merely for its musical and intellectual pleasures and the variety of its formal invention, but for the breadth of its learning and the depth of its humane vision.

MARK SCROGGINS

**Further Reading**

Ahearn, Barry, *Zukofsky's "A": An Introduction,* Berkeley: University of California Press, 1983

Comens, Bruce, *Apocalypse and After: Modern Strategy and Postmodern Tactics in Pound, Williams, and Zukofsky,* Tuscaloosa: University of Alabama Press, 1995

Perelman, Bob, *The Trouble with Genius: Reading Pound, Joyce, Stein, and Zukofsky,* Berkeley: University of California Press, 1994

Quartermain, Peter, *Disjunctive Poetics: From Gertrude Stein and Louis Zukofsky to Susan Howe,* Cambridge and New York: Cambridge University Press, 1992

Rieke, Alison, *The Senses of Nonsense,* Iowa City: University of Iowa Press, 1992

Scroggins, Mark, *Louis Zukofsky and the Poetry of Knowledge,* Tuscaloosa: University of Alabama Press, 1998

Scroggins, Mark, editor, *Upper Limit Music: The Writing of Louis Zukofsky,* Tuscaloosa: University of Alabama Press, 1997

Stanley, Sandra Kumamoto, *Louis Zukofsky and the Transformation of a Modern American Poetics,* Berkeley: University of California Press, 1994

Taggart, John, *Songs of Degrees: Essays on Contemporary Poetry and Poetics,* Tuscaloosa: University of Alabama Press, 1994

Terrell, Carroll F., editor, *Louis Zukofsky: Man and Poet,* Orono, Maine: National Poetry Foundation, 1979

---

# INDEXES

# TITLE INDEX

This index lists all the titles in the Poetry section of the entries on individual writers. The name in parentheses directs the reader to the appropriate entry, where more complete information is available.

# GENERAL INDEX

Page numbers in **boldface** indicate subjects with their own entries.

# NOTES ON ADVISERS AND CONTRIBUTORS

**Abramson, Edward A.** Senior Lecturer, American Studies, University of Hull, Kingston upon Hull, UK. Author of *The Immigrant Experience in American Literature* (1982), *Chaim Potok* (1986), and *Bernard Malamud Revisited* (1993). Contributor to *Studies in American Jewish Literature* (1975, 1996), *Yearbook of English Studies* (1994), edited by Andrew Gurr, and *Reader's Guide to Literature in English* (1996), edited by Mark Hawkins-Dady. **Essay:** Frost: The Road Not Taken.

**Abravanel, Genevieve.** Ph.D. candidate, Department of English, Duke University, Durham, NC. Contributor to *Wilson Quarterly* (Fall 1995; Fall 1996), *Harvard Review* (1995– ), *Postmodern Culture* (Spring 2000), *Virginia Woolf Out of Bounds* (2001), edited by Jessica Berman and Jane Goldman, and *Journal of Caribbean Literatures* (forthcoming). **Essay:** Hacker, Marilyn.

**Albright, Alex.** Professor, Department of English, East Carolina University, Greenville, SC. Contributor to *Southern Quarterly* (1986), *Raleigh News and Observer* (1986), *North Carolina Literary Review* (1992), *North Carolina Humanities* (1993), and *Encyclopedia of Urban America: The Cities and Suburbs* (1998), edited by Neil Larry Shumsky. **Essay:** Ammons, A.R.

**Alkalay-Gut, Karen.** Ph.D., Department of English, Tel Aviv University, Ramat Aviv, Israel. Author of *Alone in the Dawn: The Life of Adelaide Crapsey* (1988). Editor of *English Poetry in Israel* (1996) and *PEN Israel Anthology* (1997). Contributor to *Journal of Modern Literature* (1996), *Journal of Pre-Raphaelite Studies* (1997), *Victorian Poetry* (1997), and *Poetics Today* (2000). **Essay:** Crapsey, Adelaide.

**Arnold, Elizabeth.** Poet and Visiting Assistant Professor, Department of English, University of Maryland, College Park. Author of *The Reef* (1999), edited by Alan Shapiro. Editor of *Mina Loy's Insel* (1991). Contributor to *TriQuarterly* (1996), *Kalliope* (1999), *Poetry Daily* (1999), *Chicago Review* (2001), and *Slate.com* (2001). **Essay:** Niedecker, Lorine.

**Atkins, G. Douglas.** Professor, Department of English, University of Kansas, Lawrence. Author of *The Faith of John Dryden* (1980), *Reading Deconstruction/Deconstructive Reading* (1986), *Quests of Difference: Reading Pope's Poems* (1986), *Geoffrey Hartman: Criticism as Answerable Style* (1990), and *Estranging the Familiar: Toward a Revitalized Critical Writing* (1992). Coeditor of *Writing and Reading Differently* (1985), *Contemporary Literary Theory* (1988), and *Shakespeare and Deconstruction* (1988). **Essay:** Eliot: The Waste Land.

**Axelrod, Steven Gould.** Full Professor, Department of English, University of California, Riverside. Author of *Robert Lowell: Life and Art* (1978) and *Sylvia Plath: The Wound and the Cure of Words* (1990). Coauthor with Helen Deese of *Robert Lowell: A Reference Guide* (1982). Editor of *The Critical Response to Robert Lowell* (1999). Coeditor with Helen Deese of *Robert Lowell: Essays on the Poetry* (1986). Contributor to *Twentieth Century Literature* (1972, 1985), *Contemporary Literature* (1977, 1985), *Modern Philology* (1984, 2000), *New England Quarterly* (1999), and *War, Literature and the Arts* (1999). **Essays:** Bidart, Frank; Lowell, Robert.

**Baker, Anne.** Visiting Assistant Professor, Department of English, Reed College, Portland, OR. Contributor to *ESQ: A Journal of the American Renaissance* (1998) and *Fear Itself: Enemies Real and Imagined in American Culture* (1999). **Essay:** Walcott: Omeros.

**Baker, Robert.** Ph.D. Contributor to *Talisman* (Fall 1998), *American Book Review,* and *Rain Taxi.* **Essays:** Lansing, Gerrit; Sobin, Gustaf; Spicer, Jack.

**Barbera, Jack.** Professor, Department of English, University of Mississippi. Coauthor with William McBrien of *Stevie: A Biography of Stevie Smith* (1985). Coeditor with William McBrien of *Me Again: Uncollected Writings of Stevie Smith* (1981) and *Stevie Smith: A Bibliography* (1987). Guest editor of special Athol Fugard issue of *Twentieth Century Literature* (Winter 1993). Contributor to *Modern Drama* (September 1981), *The South and Film* (1981), edited by Warren French, *Modern Language Studies* (Fall 1984), *Journal of Modern Literature* (July 1985), *College English* (September 1991), *The Nation* (January 1996), *American Drama* (Fall 1997), and *Southern Quarterly* (Fall 1999). **Essay:** Frost: Design.

**Basinski, Michael.** Associate Curator, the Poetry/Rare Books Collection, State University of New York, Buffalo. **Essay:** Bukowski, Charles.

**Beach, Christopher (Adviser).** Author of *ABC of Influence* (1992), *The Politics of Distinction* (1996), and *Poetic Culture* (1999). Editor of *Artifice and Indeterminacy* (1998). Editorial board member of *Journal X.* Contributor to *English Literary History* (1989), *Contemporary Literature* (1991), *Western Humanities Review* (1997), and *Beauty and the Critic* (1998), edited by Eric L. Haralson. **Essay:** Pound, Ezra.

**Berger, Charles (Adviser).** Chair, Department of English, University of Utah, Salt Lake City. Author of *Forms of Farewell: The Late Poetry of Wallace Stevens* (1985). Coeditor of *James Merrill: Essays in Criticism* (1983). Contributor to *Raritan.*

**Berndt, Michael D.** Teaching Specialist, Department of English, University of Minnesota, MN. Contributor to *Proceedings from Sixth National Conference on Undergraduate Research* (1992), edited by Robert Yearout, *Western American Literature* (1996, 1998), *Interdisciplinary Studies in Literature and the Environment* (1998), *Kairos: A Journal for Teachers of Writing in a Webbed Environment* (1998), and *The Robert Frost Encyclopedia* (2000), edited by Nancy Tuten and John Zubizaretta. **Essay:** Stafford, William.

**Bertholf, Robert.** Curator, the Poetry/Rare Books Collection, State University of New York, Buffalo. Author of *A Descriptive Catalog of the Private Library of Thomas B. Lockwood* (1983) and *Robert Duncan: A Descriptive Bibliography* (1986). Editor of *Credences* (1974–83), *Robert Duncan: Selected Poems* (1993), *Robert Duncan: A Selected Prose* (1995), and *Joel Oppenheimer: Collected Later Poems* (1997). Editorial board member of *Journal of American Studies in Turkey* (2001), *Gravesiana* (2001), *William Carlos Williams Review* (2001), and *Journal of Modern Literature* (2001). **Essay:** Duncan, Robert.

**Bettridge, Joel.** Ph.D. candidate, Department of English, State University of New York, Buffalo. **Essay:** Creeley: The Door.

**Boughn, Michael.** Writer, Toronto, Canada. Author of *H.D.: A Bibliography, 1905–1990* (1993), *Iterations of the Diagonal* (1995), and *one's own MIND* (1999). Coeditor of *Intent: Newsletter of Talk, Thinking, and Document* (1989–91). Editorial board member of *First Intensity* (1993–2001). Contributor to *Talisman, Arizona Quarterly,* and *Sagetrieb.* **Essays:** Blaser, Robin; Canadian Poetry (Anglophone); Dorn, Edward; Dorn: Gunslinger.

**Bradshaw, Melissa.** Department of English, State University of New York, Stony Brook. **Essay:** Lowell, Amy.

**Branch, Douglas.** Instructor, Department of English, Southwest Tennessee Community College, Memphis. **Essays:** Koch, Kenneth; Schuyler, James.

**Brooker, Jewel Spears.** Full Professor, Collegium of Letters, Eckerd College, St. Petersburg, FL. Author of *Mastery and Escape: T.S. Eliot and the Dialectic of Modernism* (1994). Coauthor with Joseph Bentley of *Reading "The Waste Land": Modernism and the Limits of Interpretation* (1990). Editor of *Approaches to Teaching Eliot's Poetry and Plays* (1988), *The Placing of T.S. Eliot* (1991), and *T.S. Eliot and Our Turning World* (2001). Contributor to *English Literary History* (1979), *Modern Philology* (1980), *Massachusetts Review* (1984), *Southern Review* (1985), and *South Atlantic Review* (1996). **Essay:** Eliot, T.S.

**Buckstead, Richard.** Ph.D., Department of English, St. Olaf College, Northfield, MN. **Essay:** Stevens: Peter Quince at the Clavier.

**Burris, Sidney J.** Associate Professor, Department of English, University of Arkansas, Fayetteville. Author of *The Poetry of Resistance: Seamus Heaney and the Pastoral Tradition* (1990). Contributor to *Atlantic Monthly, Poetry, Virginia Quarterly Review, Southern Review,* and *Kenyon Review.* **Essay:** Auden: September 1, 1939.

**Bushyeager, Peter J.** Poet, New York. Author of *Vital Wires* (1986), *Mute Dog* (1998), and *Single Gun* (2001). Editor of *Hot Water Review* (1976–86). Contributor to *Painted Bride Quarterly* (1993), *The World* (1993, 1995), *Synergism: An Anthology of Collaborative Writing* (1995), and *Talisman* (1998). **Essays:** Blackburn, Paul; New York School.

**Bussey, Jennifer A.** M.A. Independent writer specializing in literature. Sole proprietor, Dog Star Writing Services. Contributor to *Black and Hispanic Writers* (1999) and *Contemporary Authors* (1999, 2000). **Essays:** Parker, Dorothy; Ransom: Bells for John Whiteside's Daughter; Ransom: Here Lies a Lady.

**Cameros, Cynthia.** Instructor, Department of Communication Arts, Fairleigh Dickinson University, Teaneck, NJ. Contributor to *Village Voice* (1989), *Kirkus Reviews* (1994), *Contemporary Novelists* (2000), and *Dictionary of Literary Biography* (2001). **Essays:** Bishop: The Armadillo; Bishop: Crusoe in England.

**Castellano, Katey Kuhns.** M.A. candidate, Department of English, Bucknell University, Lewisburg, PA. **Essays:** Eliot: Ash-Wednesday; Hecht, Anthony; Waldman, Anne.

**Cates, Isaac.** Ph.D. candidate and chief organizer of the Contemporary Poetry Discussion Group, Department of English, Yale University, New Haven, CT. Contributor to *Analecta, Zirkus, Yale Literary Magazine, Cumberland Poetry Review* (Fall 1998), and *The Robert Frost Encyclopedia* (2000), edited by Nancy Tuten and John Zubizaretta. **Essays:** Belitt, Ben; Pinsky: The Figured Wheel; Wilbur: Love Calls Us to the Things of This World.

**Caws, Mary Ann.** Distinguished Professor, Department of English, French, and Comparative Literature, Graduate School, City University of New York. Author of *The Poetry of Dada and Surrealism* (1973), *Reading Frames in Modern Fiction* (1986), *The Surrealist Book* (1997), and *The Art of Interference* (1998). Coauthor with Sarah Wright of *Bloomsbury and France* (1999). Editor of *City Images* (1991), *Joseph Cornell's Theatre of the Mind* (1994), and *The Surrealist Painters and Poets* (2000). Contributor to *PMLA, Denver Quarterly, Nineteenth-Century French Poetry, Princeton Encyclopedia of Poetics,* and *Dictionary of Women Artists.* **Essays:** Dada; H.D. (Hilda Doolittle).

**Chilton, Randolph.** Professor, Department of English, University of St. Francis, Joliet, IL. Contributor to *George Oppen: Man and Poet* (1981), edited by Burton Hatlen, *Charles Reznikoff: Man* *and Poet* (1984), edited by Milton Hindus, *Twentieth Century Literature* (1990), and *The Heath Anthology of American Literature* (3rd edition, 1998), edited by Paul Lauter. **Essay:** Williams: Al Que Quiere!

**Christensen, Paul.** Professor, Department of English, Texas A&M University, College Station. Author of *In Love, In Sorrow: The Complete Correspondence of Charles Olson and Edward Dahlberg* (1990), *Minding the Underworld: Clayton Eshleman and Late Postmodernism* (1991), and *West of the American Dream: An Encounter with Texas* (2000). Editor of *Quartet Magazine, Affinities, Vortex, N.A.T.O.N. Review,* and *France Today.* Contributor to *Conversant Essays: Poets on Poetry* (1990), edited by James McCorkle, *Texas Women Writers* (1997), edited by Sylvia Grider and Lou Rodenberg, *Writing Work: Writers on Working Class Writing* (1999), edited by Larry Smith, and *Ethnic Eating* (2000), edited by Sherrie Inness. **Essays:** Cummings, E.E.; Deep Image Poetry; Dickey, James; Dickey: Drowning with Others; Eshleman, Clayton; Experimental Poetry/The Avant-Garde; Hoffman, Daniel; New Criticism; Olson, Charles; Oppen, George; Schwerner, Armand; Whalen, Philip.

**Claridge, Henry.** Senior Lecturer in English, University of Kent, Canterbury. Contributor to *Journal of American Studies* (1986), *Post-War American Studies* (1992), *English Review* (1993), *William Faulkner: Critical Assessments* (1999), and *Year's Work on English Studies* (2000). Editor of *F. Scott Fitzgerald: Critical Assessments* (1993). **Essays:** Fugitives and Agrarians; Ransom, John Crowe; Wilbur, Richard; Williams: Paterson.

**Clark, J. Elizabeth.** Assistant Professor, Department of English, Fiorello H. LaGuardia Community College, Long Island City, NY. Coauthor of *Instructor's Guide for Against the Current* (1998). Contributor to *A and U: America's AIDS Magazine* (August 1997), *Comstock Review* (Spring 1998), *Riversedge* (Spring 1999), and *New Writer* (October 2000). Member of editorial board for *Radical Teacher* (1998– ). **Essays:** Bogan: Medusa; Forché, Carolyn; Hadas, Rachel; Harper: Dear John, Dear Coltrane; Harper: Nightmare Begins Responsibility; Kennedy, X.J.; Ríos, Alberto; Sexton: The Double Image.

**Clarkson, William.** Professor, Department of English, University of the South, Sewanee, Tennessee. Contributor to *Contemporary Southern Writers* (1999), edited by Roger Matuz. **Essays:** Nemerov, Howard; Pound: Hugh Selwyn Mauberley.

**Clippinger, David.** Assistant Professor, Department of English, Penn State University, Monaca, PA. Author of *The Mind's Landscape: William Bronk and American Poetry* (forthcoming) and *Accumulating Position: Selected Letters of William Bronk* (forthcoming). Editor of *The Body of This Life: Reading William Bronk* (2000). Contributor to *International Review of Modernism* (1994, 1996, 1999), *Harvard Review* (1994), *Talisman* (1995), *Sagetrieb* (1996), and *Chicago Review* (1996, 1997). **Essays:** Antin, David; Bronk: The Force of Desire; H.D.: Helen in Egypt; Howe (Susan): Pythagorean Silence; Palmer, Michael; Stevens: The Idea of Order at Key West.

**Cohen, Alicia.** Doctoral candidate, Department of English, State University of New York, Buffalo. Author of *Bear* (2000). Editor of *Small Press Collective* (1990–92), *Kiosk* (1995), and *Curricle Patterns* (1999–2000). Contributor to *Lagniappe* (1999). **Essay:** Scalapino, Leslie.

**Colburn, Nadia Herman.** Graduate student, Department of English and Comparative Literature, Columbia University, New York, NY. Editor of *W.H. Auden Society Newsletter* (1999– ). Contributor to *W.H. Auden Society Newsletter* (1999, 2000). **Essay:** Eliot: Gerontion.

**Coleman, Philip.** Ph.D. candidate, School of English, University of Dublin, Trinity College, Ireland. Contributor to *Metre* (June 1999), *Thumbscrew* (January 2000), *Irish Association for American Studies Journal* (May 2000), and *Swansea Review* (September 2000). **Essays:** Berryman, John; Berryman: Homage to Mistress Bradstreet; Milosz: Ars Poetica?; Schwartz, Delmore.

**Collins, Richard.** Associate Professor, Department of English, Xavier University of Louisiana, New Orleans. Author of *John Fante: A Literary Portrait* (2000). Editor of *New Delta Review* (1986–92). Coeditor of *Xavier Review* (1999– ). Contributor to *John Fante: A Critical Gathering* (1999), *Studies in the Humanities* (2000), *Studies in Browning and His Circle* (2000), *Thus Spake the Corpse: An Exquisite Corpse Reader 1988–98* (2000, 2001), *Transgressive Wilkie Collins* (2001), *Rebuilding the Bayou: Post-Bellum Louisiana Authors* (2001), *Wilkie Collins Society Journal, George Gissing Journal, MELUS, Spillway, Yellow Silk, Negative Capability, Literary Review, Rosebud,* and *Asylum.* Translator for *Fifty Novels and Other Utopias by Ioan Flora* (1996). **Essays:** Auden: In Memory of W.B. Yeats; Merrill, James; Walcott, Derek; Walcott: A Far Cry from Africa.

**Cortz, Nicole E.** Ph.D. candidate, Department of English, University of California, Riverside. Instructor of English at Long Beach City College, CA. **Essays:** Armantrout, Rae; Hak Kyung Cha, Theresa; Wright, Charles.

**Crown, Kathleen.** Assistant Professor, Department of English, Kalamazoo College, MI. Contributor to *Sagetrieb* (1995, 1996), *Virginia Woolf: Texts and Contexts* (1996), edited by Beth Rigel Daugherty and Eileen Barrett, *Contemporary Literature* (1998), *Women's Studies: An Interdisciplinary Journal* (1998), *H.D. and Poets After* (2000), edited by Donna Hollenberg, *Poetics Today* (2000), *We Who "Love to Be Astonished": Feminist Experimental Fiction, Poetry, and Performance* (2001), edited by Cynthia Hogue and Laura Hinton, and *Assembling Alternatives: Essays on the Problems of Reading Postmodern Poetries* (2001), edited by Romana Huk. **Essay:** Performance Poetry.

**Cucinella, Catherine.** Editor of *Contemporary American Women Poets: A Bio-Bibliographical Critical Sourcebook* (2002). Contributor to *American Women Writers, 1900–1945: A Bio-Bibliographical Critical Sourcebook* (2000), *MELUS* (2001), and *Contemporary American Fiction Writers: A Bio-Bibliographical Critical Sourcebook* (2001). **Essay:** Millay, Edna St. Vincent.

**Cushman, Stephen.** Full Professor, Department of English, University of Virginia, Charlottesville. Contributor to *Poetry, American Literary History, American Literature,* and *New Literary History.* Editorial board member of *Virginia Quarterly Review.* **Essay:** Frost: Home Burial.

**Davidson, Adenike Marie.** Assistant Professor, Department of English, University of Central Florida, Orlando. **Essays:** Brown, Sterling A.; Johnson, Georgia Douglas; McKay: The Lynching.

**Davis, William V.** Full Professor, Writer-in-Residence, Department of English, Baylor University, Waco, TX. Author of *One Way to Reconstruct the Scene* (1980), *Understanding Robert Bly* (1988), and *Robert Bly: The Poet and His Critics* (1994). Editor of *Critical Essays on Robert Bly* (1992) and *Miraculous Simplicity: Essays on R.S. Thomas* (1993). Contributor to *New Criterion, Atlantic Monthly, Hudson Review, Poetry* (Chicago), and *Sewanee Review*. **Essays:** Bly, Robert; Bly: Counting Small-Boned Bodies; Bly: Driving Toward the Lac Qui Parle River; Bly: The Teeth Mother Naked at Last.

**Dawahare, Anthony.** Associate Professor, Department of English, California State University, Northridge. Contributor to *Criticism: A Quarterly for Criticism and the Arts* (Summer 1997), *College Literature* (Fall 1997), *Twentieth Century Literature* (Fall 1998), *MELUS* (Fall 1998), and *African American Review* (Fall 1999). **Essays:** Brown: Southern Road; Cullen, Countee; Hughes, Langston.

**Doerr, Joe Francis.** Ph.D. candidate, poet, Department of English, University of Notre Dame, South Bend, IN. Contributor to *PN Review* (July/August 1997), *Old English Newsletter* (Fall 1998), *Samizdat* (1999), *The Possibility of Language: Seven Younger Poets* (2001), edited by Jeff Roessner, and *Notre Dame Review* (Summer 2001). **Essays:** Ashbery: The Tennis Court Oath; Creeley, Robert; New Formalism.

**Dougherty, David C.** Professor, English Department, and Director, Graduate Program, Loyola College, Baltimore, MD. Author of *James Wright* (1987) and *Stanley Elkin* (1991). Contributor to *Old Northwest* (1975, 1985, 1987), *Contemporary Poetry* (1977), *Modern Fiction Studies* (1979), *Literary Review* (1991), *Teaching Wallace Stevens: Practical Essays* (1994), edited by John Serio and B.J. Leggett, and *South Carolina Review* (1996, 1997). **Essay:** Snodgrass, W.D.

**Dougherty, James.** Professor, Department of English, The University of Notre Dame, IN. Author of *The Fivesquare City: The City in the Religious Imagination* (1980) and *Walt Whitman and the Citizen's Eye* (1993). Editor of *Religion and Literature* (1984– ). Contributor to *Yale Review* (1982) and *Soundings* (1986). Editorial board member of *Literature and Belief* (1990– ). **Essays:** Religion and Poetry; Roethke: North American Sequence.

**Dungy, Camille.** Assistant Professor, Department of English, Randolph-Macon Woman's College, Lynchburg, VA. Contributor to *Louisville Review* (Spring 1997), *Obsidian III* (Spring/Summer 2000), *African Voices* (Spring 2000), *Cider Press Review* (Spring 2000), and *Rattle* (Spring 2001). **Essays:** Brooks: A Street in Bronzeville; Cullen: Heritage; Giovanni, Nikki; O'Hara: The Day Lady Died.

**Dutt, Reshmi.** Ph.D. candidate, Department of English, University of Minnesota, Minneapolis. Editor of *Research in the Teaching of Writing* (1997–98). Contributor to *Journal of the Asian American Renaissance* (1995) and *Nature and the Self* (2000), edited by Michael Aleksnik. **Essay:** Soto, Gary.

**Dworkin, Craig.** Assistant Professor, Department of English, Princeton University, Princeton, NJ. Author of *Signature-Effects* (1997). Contributor to *Contemporary Literature* (1995) and *Word and Image* (1996). **Essay:** Andrews, Bruce.

**Elliott, Sean.** Visiting Tutor, English Department, Goldsmiths College, London University, UK. Contributor to *Seam* (1998), *London Magazine* (1998), *Agenda* (1999), and *PN Review* (2000). **Essays:** Crane: Voyages; Tate, Allen; Tate, Allen: Ode to the Confederate Dead.

**English, James F.** Associate Professor, Department of English, University of Pennsylvania, Philadelphia. Author of *Comic Transactions: Literature, Humor, and the Politics of Community in 20th-Century Britain* (1994). Editor of *Postmodern Culture* (1999). Contributor to *Modern Fiction Studies* (1992, 1999), *Modernism/Modernity* (1999), *Textual Practice* (2000), *Directed by Allen Smithee* (2001), edited by Jeremy Braddock and Stephen Hock, and *New Literary History* (2001). **Essay:** Prizes.

**Epstein, Andrew.** Lecturer, Department of English, Barnard College, NY. Contributor to *Keats-Shelley Journal* (1999), *American Book Review* (2000), *World Poets* (2000), edited by Ron Padgett, *Lingua Franca* (2000), *Raritan* (2000), *Who's Who in Twentieth-Century World Poetry* (2001), edited by Mark Willhardt and Alan Michael Parker, *The Scene of My Selves: New Work on New York School Poets* (2001), edited by Terence Diggory and Stephen Paul Miller, and *W.H. Auden Society Newsletter* (2001). **Essays:** Ashbery, John; Moore: Marriage.

**Featherston, Dan.** Poet. Author of *Anatomies* (1998), *Rooms* (1998), and *26 Islands* (1999). Editor of *A.BACUS* (2001– ). Contributor to *Sulfur, New American Writing, First Intensity, The World in Time and Space: Toward a History of Innovative American Poetry: 1970–2000,* edited by Edward Foster and Joe Donahue, and *Talisman*. **Essays:** Olson: As the Dead Prey Upon Us; Olson: The Kingfishers.

**Ferlazzo, Paul J.** Full Professor, Department of English, Northern Arizona University, Flagstaff. Author of *Emily Dickinson* (1976). Editor of *Critical Essays on Emily Dickinson* (1984). Contributor to *American Quarterly* (1973), *Walt Whitman Review* (1977), *The Transcendentalists* (1984), edited by Joel Myerson, *Association of Departments of English Bulletin* (1986), *Dictionary of Literary Biography* (1988), edited by Bobby Ellen Kimbel, *Western American Literature* (1994), and *Encyclopedia of American Poetry: The Nineteenth Century* (1998), edited by Eric L. Haralson. **Essays:** Frost, Robert; Robinson, Edwin Arlington.

**Fink, Thomas.** Full Professor, Department of English, City University of New York, Long Island City. Author of *The Poetry of David Shapiro* (1993), *Surprise Visit* (1993), and *"A Different Sense of Power": Problems of Community in Late Twentieth Century U.S. Poetry* (2001). Coeditor of *Literature around the Globe* (1994). Contributor to *American Poetry Review* (1988), *Contemporary Literature* (1996), *Confrontation* (1998, 1999, 2000), *Americas Review* (1999), and *Rain Taxi* (2000). **Essays:** Ammons: Garbage; Strand, Mark.

**Finkelstein, Norman.** Professor, Department of English, Xavier University, Cincinnati, OH. Author of *The Utopian Moment in*

*Contemporary American Poetry* (1988, 1993), *The Ritual of New Creation: Jewish Tradition and Contemporary Literature* (1992), *Restless Messengers* (1992), *Track* (1999), and *Not One of Them in Place: Modern Poetry and Jewish American Identity* (2001). Contributor to *Contemporary Literature* (1998), *Religion and Literature* (1998), *Denver Quarterly* (2000), and *Colorado Review* (2001). Editorial board member of *Sagetrieb*. **Essays:** Oppen: Of Being Numerous; Palmer: Sun; Spicer: After Lorca; Williams: The Desert Music.

**Fisher-Wirth, Ann.** Professor, Department of English, University of Mississippi, University. Author of *William Carlos Williams and Autobiography: The Woods of His Own Nature* (1989). Contributor to *Cather Studies I, Cather Studies II* (1990, 1993), edited by Susan J. Rosowski, *Twentieth Century Literature* (1990, 1995), *Georgia Review* (1996), *ISLE (Interdisciplinary Studies in Literature and Environment)* (1997, 1998, 1999), *Kenyon Review* (2000), *Value and Vision: Literary Essays in Honor of Ray Lewis White* (2000), edited by Joseph Candido, *Journal X* (2000), and *Willa Cather and the Southwest* (2001), edited by John Swift and Joseph Urgo. **Essays:** Kinnell, Galway; Kinnell: Little Sleep's-Head Sprouting Hair in the Moonlight; Olds, Sharon; Williams: Asphodel, That Greeny Flower.

**Flanzbaum, Hilene.** Associate Professor, Department of English, Butler University, Indianapolis. Editor of *The Americanization of the Holocaust* (1999) and *Jewish American Literature: A Norton Anthology* (2001). Contributor to *New England Quarterly* (1996), *English Literary History* (1999), *Robert Lowell: A Critical History* (2000), edited by Steven Gould Axelrod, *Genocide Studies* (2000), and *Yale Journal of Criticism* (2001). **Essays:** Anthologies, Textbooks, and Canon Formation; Lowell, Robert: Life Studies.

**Foster, Edward Halsey (Adviser).** Professor and poet, Department of Humanities, Stevens Institute of Technology, Hoboken, NJ. Author of *Jack Spicer* (1991), *Understanding the Black Mountain Poets* (1995), *Boy in the Key of E* (1998), and *Answerable to None: Berrigan, Bronk, and the American Real* (1999). Editor of *Talisman* (1988– ) and *Decadents, Symbolists, and Aesthetes in America* (2000). Contributor to *American Book Review, Sagetrieb,* and *Boston Review of Books*. Editorial board member of *MultiCultural Review* (1991–95). **Essays:** Bronk, William; Little Magazines and Small Presses; Symbolism.

**Foster, Jeff.** Ph.D., The University of Rhode Island. Contributor to *Connecticut Review* and *Puck*. Short stories have appeared in such journals as *Confluence, Kimera,* and *Mind in Motion*. **Essay:** Winters, Yvor.

**Gardner, Thomas.** Professor, Department of English, Virginia Tech, Blacksburg. Author of *Discovering Ourselves in Whitman: The Contemporary American Long Poem* (1989), *The Mime Speaking* (1992), and *Regions of Unlikeness: Explaining Contemporary Poetry* (1999). Editorial board member of *Contemporary Literature* (1985– ). Contributor to *Sagetrieb* (1985), *Hollins Critic* (1987), *Denver Quarterly* (1992), *Talisman* (1993), and *Wallace Stevens Journal* (1995). **Essays:** Graham, Jorie; Hass, Robert; Long Poem; Roethke: Greenhouse Poems.

**Gibbons, James.** Assistant Editor, The Library of America. Contributor to *Aethlon* (1997), *Raritan* (2000), and *Poets: A Student Encyclopedia* (forthcoming). **Essays:** Milosz, Czeslaw; Kees: Robinson Poems; Tolson: Harlem Gallery.

**Gibson, Dobby.** M.F.A., poet, St. Paul, MN. Contributor to *New England Review* (1997), *Crazyhorse* (1998), *Third Coast* (1999, 2000), *Another Chicago Magazine* (2000), *Crazy People without Insurance* (2001), edited by John Colburn, and *Conduit* (2001). **Essays:** Ashbery: Flow Chart; Merwin: The Chinese Mountain Fox.

**Gill, Jonathan.** Associate Professor, Department of English, Columbia University, New York, NY. Contributor to *Boston Review* (1999), *T.S. Eliot's Orchestra* (2000), edited by John Xiros Cooper, *Naming the Father* (2000), edited by Eva Paulino Bueno, *American Modernism across the Arts* (2000), edited by Justin Kaplan, and *American Book Review* (2000). **Essay:** Pound: The Pisan Cantos.

**Gioia, Dana (Adviser).** Writer, poet, critic, and translator, Sonoma County, CA. Author of *Two Poems* (1982), *Letter to the Bahamas* (1983), *Summer* (1983), *Journeys in Sunlight* (1986), *Daily Horoscope* (1986), *Words for Music* (1987), *Two Poems/Due Poesie* (1987), *Planting a Sequoia* (1991), *The Gods of Winter* (1991), *Can Poetry Matter?: Essays on Poetry and American Culture* (1992), *Juno Plots Her Revenge* (1993), *The Litany* (1999), *The Barrier of a Common Language: Essays on Contemporary British Poetry* (2001), *Interrogations at Noon* (2001), and *Nosferatu* (2001). Coeditor with William Jay Smith of *Poems from Italy* (1985); with Michael Palma of *New Italian Poets* (1991); with William Logan of *Certain Solitudes: Essays on the Poetry of Donald Justice* (1997); with X.J. Kennedy of *An Introduction to Poetry* (1998), *Literature: An Introduction to Fiction, Poetry and Drama* (1999), and *An Introduction to Fiction* (1999); and with R.S. Gwynn of *The Longman Anthology of Short Fiction: Stories and Authors in Context* (2001). Contributed an introduction to *The Ceremony and Other Stories* (1983–84). Translator of *Mottetti: Poems of Love* (1990), written by Eugenio Montale, and *The Madness of Hercules* (1995), written by Seneca.

**Goldensohn, Lorrie.** Associate Professor, Department of English, Vassar College, Poughkeepsie, NY. Author of *The Tether* (1983) and *Elizabeth Bishop: The Biography of Poetry* (1991). Coauthor with Barry Goldensohn of *East Long Pond* (1997). Coordinating editor (1981) and editorial board member (1981– ) of *Ploughshares*. Contributor to *Elizabeth Bishop: Geography of Gender* (1993), edited by Marilyn Oray Lombardi, *Contemporary Poets* (1995), edited by Tracy Chevalier, *Critical Essays on Galway Kinnell* (1996), edited by Nancy Tuten, *In Worcester, Massachusetts/ Essays on Elizabeth Bishop* (1999), edited by Laura Menides, and *Essays on Muriel Rukeyser* (1999), edited by Anne Herzog and Janet Kaufman. **Essays:** Bishop, Elizabeth; Jarrell, Randall; War and Anti-War Poetry.

**Gordon, Maggie.** Postdoctoral Fellow, Department of English, University of Mississippi, Oxford. Contributor to *ISLE (Interdisciplinary Studies of Literature and the Environment)* (Winter 1999), *Literature/Film Quarterly* (2000), *Clues: A Journal of Detection* (Spring/Summer 2001), and *Ecological Poetry: A Critical*

*Introduction* (forthcoming), edited by Scott Bryson. **Essays:** di Prima, Diane; Glück, Louise.

**Grainger, Elizabeth.** Graduate student, School of the Arts, Columbia University, New York, NY. **Essay:** Millay: Renascence.

**Gregory, Elizabeth L. (Adviser).** Associate Professor, Department of English, University of Houston, TX. Author of *Quotation and Modern American Poetry: "'Imaginary Gardens with Real Toads'"* (1996). Editor of *The Critical Response to Marianne Moore* (2002). Contributor to *Discourse* (1994), *William Carlos Williams Review* (1995), and *Women Writers of the First World War* (1997), edited by Suzanne Raitt and Trudi Tate.

**Grieve Carlson, Gary.** Professor, Department of English, Lebanon Valley College, Annville, PA. Contributor to *William Carlos Williams Review* (1986), *Classics in Cultural Criticism* (1990), edited by H. Heuermann, *Kindlers Neues Literatur Lexikon* (1990, 1991, 1992), edited by Rudolf Radler, *Contemporaries in Cultural Criticism* (1991), edited by H. Heuermann and B. Lange, and *Nobodaddies* (1994, 1995). **Essay:** Wright, James.

**Gwiazda, Piotr.** Adjunct Professor, Department of English and Speech, Fashion Institute of Technology, State University of New York. Editor of *Elm* (1995–97). Contributor to *Anticipating the End: The Experience of the Nineties* (1999), edited by Susan Blair Green, *XCP: Cross Cultural Poetics* (1999), and *W.H. Auden: A Legacy* (2000), edited by David Garrett Izzo. **Essays:** Auden: In Praise of Limestone; Merrill: The Changing Light at Sandover.

**Hall, James C.** Assistant Professor of African American Studies and English, University of Illinois at Chicago. Author of *Mercy, Mercy Me: African American Culture and the American Sixties* (forthcoming). Editor of *Teaching a New Canon? Students, Teachers, and Texts in TAE College Literature Classroom* (1995), *Approaches to Teaching Narrative of the Life of Frederick Douglass* (1998), and *Langston Hughes: A Collection of Poems* (1998). Editorial board member of *Journal X*. Contributor to *Approaches to Teaching Wright's "Native Son"* (1997), edited by James Miller, *Approaches to Teaching the Novels of Toni Morrison* (1997), edited by Nellie McKay and Kathryn Earle, *African American Review,* and *Langston Hughes Review.* **Essays:** Alexander, Will; Mackey, Nathaniel; Mullen, Harryette.

**Halpern, Nick.** Assistant Professor, Department of English, North Carolina State University, Raleigh. Author of *Everyday and Prophetic: Strategies of Power in Postwar and Contemporary American Poetry* (forthcoming). Contributor to *Centennial Review* (1999). **Essays:** Ammons: Sphere: The Form of a Motion; Kleinzahler, August.

**Hamalian, Linda.** Full Professor, Department of English, William Paterson University, Wayne, NJ. Author of *A Life of Kenneth Rexroth* (1991). Editor of *An Autobiographical Novel by Kenneth Rexroth* (1991). Coeditor with Leo Hamalian of *Solo: Women on Woman Alone* (1977). Contributor to *North Dakota Quarterly* (1988), *Obsidian II* (1988), *Literary Review* (1988), *African American Review* (1992), and *American Literature* (1997, 2000). **Essay:** San Francisco Renaissance.

**Haralson, Eric L. (Editor).** Assistant Professor, State University of New York at Stony Brook. Editor of *Encyclopedia of American Poetry: The Nineteenth Century* (1998).

**Hart, George.** Postdoctoral Fellow in Literature and Environment, University of Nevada, Reno. Contributor to *Sagetrieb* (1995), *ISLE (Interdisciplinary Studies in Literature and Environment)* (1998), *Women's Studies* (1998), and *Reading under the Sign of Nature* (2000), edited by John Tallmadge and Henry Harrington. **Essays:** Jeffers: Shine, Perishing Republic; Niedecker: Lake Superior; Niedecker: My Life by Water; Rexroth, Kenneth; Rexroth: On Flower Wreath Hill.

**Hatlen, Burton.** Professor, Department of English, University of Maine, Orono. Author of *I Wanted to Tell You* (1988). Editor of *George Oppen: Man and Poet* (1981) and *Sagetrieb* (1982–99). Contributor to *American Poetry Review* (1993), *William Carlos Williams Review* (1994), *Paideuma: A Journal of Pound Scholarship* (1996), *English Literary Renaissance* (1997), and *The Objectivist Nexus* (1999), edited by DuPlessis and Quartermain. **Essays:** Modernism; Objectivism.

**Haworth Hoeppner, Edward.** Full Professor, Department of English, Oakland University, Rochester, MI. Author of *Echoes and Moving Fields: Structure and Subjectivity in the Poetry of W.S. Merwin and John Ashbery* (1994) and *Rain through High Windows* (2000). Contributor to *Philological Quarterly* (1987), *Concerning Poetry* (1987), *Modern Language Quarterly* (1988), *Latin American Literary Review* (1992), and *Southern Humanities Review* (1997). **Essay:** Ashbery: Self-Portrait in a Convex Mirror.

**Hayot, Eric.** Assistant Professor, Department of English, University of Arizona, Tucson. Contributor to *Mediations* (1995), *Discourse* (1997), *Modern Chinese Literature* (1999), and *Twentieth Century Literature* (1999). **Essays:** Imagism; Pound: Cathay.

**Henson, Kristin K.** Ph.D., Birmingham, AL. **Essay:** Johnson, James Weldon: God's Trombones.

**Hickman, Trenton.** Assistant Professor of English, Brigham Young University, Provo, UT. Contributor to *La Marca Hispanica* (1996) and *Journal of Caribbean Studies* (2000). Translator for *The Space of Silence: Selected Poems by Rafael Cadenas* (1992). **Essays:** Algarín, Miguel; Alvarez, Julia; Bishop: In the Waiting Room; Hernández Cruz, Victor.

**Hillringhouse, Mark.** Writing Specialist, Academic Skills Center, Passaic County Community College, Paterson, NJ. Editor of *American Book Review* (1982–85). Coeditor of *Joe Soap's Canoe* (1989–94). Contributor to *New York Arts Journal* (1981–82). Poems, interviews, articles, essays, book reviews, and translations have appeared in: *American Poetry Review, American Poetry, Columbia, Hanging Loose, Literary Review, Little Magazine, New American Writing, New Jersey Monthly, New York Times Book Review,* and many other publications. **Essay:** Matthews, William.

**Hinds, Michael.** University of Dublin, Ireland. Contributor to *Element* (1991–92), *The Harp* (1997–99), and *American Studies* (1999). **Essays:** Dickey: Falling; Roethke, Theodore.

**Hoffman, Tyler.** Assistant Professor, Department of English, and Codirector of the American Studies Program, Rutgers University, Camden, NJ. Author of *Robert Frost and the Politics of Poetry* (2001). Coeditor of *Walt Whitman Quarterly Review* (1999) and *Robert Frost Review* (2001– ). Contributor to *Emily Dickinson Journal* (1994), *Journal of Imagism* (1998), *Robert Frost Review* (2000), *South Atlantic Review* (2000), *American Writers (Scribner's)* (2001), and *Modern Language Studies* (forthcoming). **Essays:** Gunn, Thom; Lindsay, Vachel; Lindsay: The Congo.

**Hollander, John, Jr. (Adviser).** Sterling Professor, Department of English, Yale University, New Haven, CT. Author of *Tesserae and Other Poems* (1993), *Selected Poetry* (1993), *The Gazer's Spirit* (1995), *The Work of Poetry* (1997), and *Figurehead and Other Poems* (1999). Contributor to *The New Yorker* (1956– ). Editorial board member of *Southwest Review* (1990– ), *Yale Review, Raritan* (1981– ), and *Harper's*.

**Horvath, Brooke.** Full Professor, Department of English, Kent State University, Canton, OH. Author of *Consolation at Ground Zero* (1996). Coeditor with Irving Malin and Paul Ruffin of *A Goyen Companion* (1997); with Irving Malin of *George Garrett: The Elizabethan Trilogy* (1998) and *Pynchon and "Mason and Dixon"* (2000); and with Joseph Dewey of *"The Finer Thread, the Tighter Weave": Essays on the Short Fiction of Henry James* (2001). Managing editor of *Modern Fiction Studies* (1984–87), associate editor of *Review of Contemporary Fiction* (1988–2001), and book-review editor of *Aethlon: The Journal of Sport Literature* (1991–95). Contributor to *American Literature* and *Denver Quarterly*. **Essays:** Frost: Desert Places; Ginsberg: Howl; Roethke: My Papa's Waltz.

**Howard, W. Scott.** Assistant Professor, Department of English, University of Denver, CO. Contributor to *Talisman* (1995), *Imprimatur* (1996), *Denver Quarterly* (2000), *Many Mountains Moving* (2001), and *Studying Cultural Landscapes* (2002), edited by Iain Robertson and Penny Richards. Member of editorial board for *English Language Notes* (2001). **Essays:** Hall, Donald; Hayden: Elegies for Paradise Valley; Howe, Susan; Levine: On the Murder of Lieutenant José Del Castillo by the Falangist Bravo Martinez, July 12th, 1936; Merwin, W.S.

**Howe, Andrew.** Graduate student, University of California, Riverside. **Essays:** Corso, Gregory; Mezey, Robert; Moss, Howard; Perelman, Bob; Steele, Timothy; Tate, James.

**Hunt, Tim.** Professor of English, Washington State University, Vancouver, WA. Author of *Kerouac's Crooked Road: Development of a Fiction* (1996). Editor of *The Collected Poetry of Robinson Jeffers: Volumes I–III* (1988, 1989, 1991). Contributor to *Review of Contemporary Fiction* (1982, 1983), *American Literary Scholarship: 1985* (1987), edited by J. Albert Robbins, *Critical Essays on Robinson Jeffers* (1990), edited by James Karman, *Robinson Jeffers: Centennial Essays* (1991), edited by Robert Zaller, *Robinson Jeffers: Dimensions of a Poet* (1995), edited by Robert Brophy, and *Text* (1995). **Essays:** Jeffers: Hurt Hawks; Masters, Edgar Lee; Robinson: Eros Turannos.

**Iadonisi, Richard A.** Visiting Assistant Professor, Department of English, Grand Valley State University, Allendale, MI. Contributor to *CEA Critic* (1995), *Robert Frost Review* (1996), and *American National Biography* (1999). **Essay:** Ginsberg, Allen.

**Izzo, David Garrett.** Independent scholar. Author of *Aldous Huxley and W.H. Auden on Language* (1998), *Christopher Isherwood: His Era, His Gang, and the Legacy of the Truly Strong Man* (2001), *Richard Stern: An Analysis of His Writings* (2001), and the play *The American World of Stephen Vincent Benét*. Editor of *W.H. Auden: A Legacy* (2001). Coeditor of *Thornton Wilder: New Essays* (1999). **Essays:** Aiken, Conrad; Benét, Stephen Vincent; MacLeish, Archibald; Sandburg, Carl; Wylie, Elinor.

**Jackson, Millie.** Associate Librarian, Zumberge Library, Grand Valley State University, Allendale, MI. Contributor to *Virginia English Bulletin* (1998), *Language Arts Journal of Michigan* (2000), and *The Louisa May Alcott Encyclopedia* (2001), edited by Gregory Eiselein and Anne K. Phillips. **Essays:** Expatriate Poetry; Kizer, Carolyn; Swenson, May.

**Jarnot, Lisa.** Poet, Brooklyn, NY. Author of *Some Other Kind of Mission* (1996) and *Ring of Fire* (2000). Editor of *Poetry Project Newsletter* (1996–98). Coeditor of *An Anthology of New American Poetry* (1998). Contributor to *Grand Street* (1996), *Colorado Review* (1998), *Shiny* (2000), and *The World* (2000). **Essays:** Creeley: Anger; Duncan: Doves; Duncan: A Poem Beginning with a Line by Pindar; Ginsberg: America; Mayer, Bernadette; Waldrop, Rosmarie.

**Jayasundera, Ymitri.** Visiting Assistant Professor, Department of English, Bridgewater State College, MA. Contributor to *Contemporary African American Novelists* (1999), edited by Emmanuel S. Nelson, *Asian American Novelists* (2000), edited by Emmanuel S. Nelson, *African American Authors, 1745–1945* (2000), edited by Emmanuel S. Nelson, and *An Encyclopedia of American War Literature* (forthcoming), edited by Mark A. Graves and Philip K. Jason. **Essay:** Walcott: Another Life.

**Jenkins, Lee M.** Ph.D., Department of English, University College of Cork, Ireland. Author of *Wallace Stevens: Rage for Order* (1999). Coeditor of *Locations of Literary Modernism* (2000). Contributor to *Wallace Stevens Journal* (1994), *Angel Exhaust* (1999), *Irish Review* (1999), *Nineteenth Century Studies* (1999), and *Ariel* (2000). **Essay:** McKay: America.

**Judge, Jeannie Sargent.** Assistant Professor, Department of English, University of Massachusetts, Lowell. Editor of *Vyü Magazine* (1999–2000). Contributor to *Mid-Hudson Language Studies: Journal of the Mid-Hudson MLA* (1988), *Cithara: Essays in the Judaeo-Christian Tradition* (1990), and *Literature and Belief* (1998). **Essays:** Millay: Justice Denied in Massachusetts; Teasdale, Sara; Wilbur: The Writer.

**Kane, Daniel.** Assistant Professor, Department of English, Kingsborough Community College, Brooklyn, NY. Author of *Improvising Community: The Lower East Side Poetry Scene in the 1960's* (2002). Contributor to *Contemporary Jewish-American Dramatists and Poets* (1999), edited by Michael Taub and Joel Shatzky, *Arshile Magazine* (1999), *New York Post* (December 2000), *Using American Literature to Teach Writing* (2001), edited by Chris Edgar, *Poetry Project Newsletter* (2001), and *MS Magazine* (2001). **Essays:** Ashbery: Clepsydra; Stein: Tender Buttons.

**Keller, Jim.** Ph.D. candidate, State University of New York, Stony Brook. **Essay:** Simpson, Louis.

**Kimball, Jack.** Poet, Program in Writing and Humanistic Studies, Massachusetts Institute of Technology, Cambridge. Author of *Quite Vacation* (1998) and *Nitric Oxide* (2000). Coauthor with Peter Ganick of *Witness Protection* (1997). Editor of *The East Village* (1998–2001). Contributor to *Jacket* (1999, 2000), *Readme* (1999, 2000), *Defib* (2000), and *Milk* (2000). **Essays:** Bronk: The World, the Worldless; Creeley: For Love: Poems, 1950–1960; Padgett, Ron; Wieners, John.

**Komunyakaa, Yusef (Adviser).** Professor, Council of Humanities and Creative Writing, Princeton University, Princeton, NJ. Author of *Copacetic* (1984), *I Apologize for the Eyes in My Head* (1986; winner of the San Francisco Poetry Center Award), *Dien Cai Dau* (1988; winner of the Dark Room Poetry Prize), *Magic City* (1992), *Neon Vernacular: New and Selected Poems* (1993; winner of the Pulitzer Prize and the Kingsley Tufts Poetry Award), *Thieves of Paradise* (1998; finalist for the National Book Critics Circle Award), *Talking Dirty to the Gods* (2000), and *Pleasure Dome: New and Collected Poems* (2001). Coeditor with Sascha Feinstein of *The Jazz Poetry Anthology* (2 vols., 1991, 1996). Cotranslator with Martha Collins of *The Insomnia of Fire* (1995). Honors include the William Faulkner Prize from the Université de Rennes, the Thomas Forcade Award, the Hanes Poetry Prize, and fellowships from the Fine Arts Work Center in Provincetown, the Louisiana Arts Council, and the National Endowment for the Arts. Elected a Chancellor of the Academy of American Poets (1999).

**Kuhl, Nancy.** Reference/Instruction Librarian, Robert Frost Library, Amherst College, MA. Author of *In the Arbor* (1997). Contributor to *American Studies International* (1998) and *The Journal, Ohio State University* (2001). **Essay:** Lee, Li-Young.

**Lamm, Kimberly.** Ph.D. candidate, Department of English, University of Washington, Seattle. Contributor to *How2*. **Essays:** Howe, Fanny; Lauterbach, Ann; Notley, Alice.

**Lawson, Benjamin S.** Full Professor, Department of English and Modern Languages, Albany State University, GA. Author of *Joaquin Miller* (1980) and *Rereading the Revolution: The Turn-of-the-Century American Revolutionary War Novel* (2000). Contributor to *South Dakota Review* (1974), *Extrapolation* (1984), *Southern Literary Journal* (1989), and *South Atlantic Review* (1999). **Essay:** Robinson: Mr. Flood's Party.

**Leahy, Anna.** Assistant Professor, Department of English, Missouri Western State College, Saint Joseph. Author of *The Insect Workbook* (1994) and *Hagioscope* (2000). Editor of *Quarter after Eight* (1996–97) and *Mochila Review* (2000– ). Contributor to *Facts on File: The American Short Story* and *American Studies International*. **Essays:** Lorde: Coal; Pinsky, Robert.

**Leddy, Michael.** Professor, Department of English, Eastern Illinois University, Charleston. Author of *Inventories* (1997). Contributor to *World Literature Today* (1991– ), *Modern Fiction Studies* (1992), *British Journal of Aesthetics* (1992), *Contemporary Literature* (1994), *The Gertrude Stein Awards in Innovative American Poetry, 1993–1994* (1995), edited by Douglas Messerli, *Cather Studies* (1996), edited by Susan J. Rosowski, and *World Poets* (2000), edited by Ron Padgett. Editorial board member of *Studies in the Novel* (1992– ). **Essays:** Berrigan, Ted; Coolidge, Clark; O'Hara, Frank.

**Lee, Cecilia Hae-Jin.** Writer, artist, and poet. **Essay:** Nash, Ogden.

**Levin, Jonathan.** Associate Professor, Department of English, Fordham University, New York, NY. Associate editor of *Raritan* (1991– ). Author of *The Poetics of Transition: Emerson, Pragmatism, and American Literary Modernism* (1999). Editor of *Walt Whitman* (1997). Contributor to *Arizona Quarterly* (1992), *American Literary History* (1994), *Henry James Review* (1997), Yearbook of Comparative and General Literature (1999), *ISLE (Interdisciplinary Studies in Literature and Environment)* (2000), and *Contemporary Literature* (2000). **Essay:** Stevens, Wallace.

**Lott, Deshae E.** Assistant Professor, Department of English, University of Illinois, Springfield. Contributor to *Encyclopedia of American Poetry: The Nineteenth Century* (1998), edited by Eric L. Haralson, *Walt Whitman: An Encyclopedia* (1998), edited by J.R. LeMaster and Donald D. Kummings, *Studia Mystica* (1999), *South Central Review* (2000), *American Women Prose Writers, 1820–1870: Dictionary of Literary Biography 239* (2001), edited by Amy Hudock and Katharine Rodier, *The American Renaissance in New England* (2001), edited by Wesley Mott, and *Embodied Rhetorics: Disability in Language and Culture* (2001), edited by James C. Wilson and Cynthia Lewiecki-Wilson. **Essays:** Angelou, Maya; Oppen: Discrete Series.

**MacPhail, Scott.** Visiting Assistant Professor, Department of English, Marquette University, Milwaukee, WI. Contributor to *Chicago Review* (1998), *African American Review* (1999), and *Texas Studies in Literature and Language* (2001). **Essays:** Hayden, Robert; Jordan, June; Rukeyser: The Book of the Dead.

**Magill, David E.** Ph.D. candidate, Department of English, University of Kentucky, Lexington. **Essays:** Bontemps, Arna; Sanchez, Sonia.

**Mao, Douglas.** Assistant Professor, Department of English and American Literature and Language, Harvard University, Cambridge, MA. Member of the Board of Directors, Center for Lesbian and Gay Studies at the City University of New York. Author of *Solid Objects: Modernism and the Test of Production* (1998). Contributor to *English Literary History* (1996) and *Modernism/Modernity* (2001). Member of the Executive Committee of the Division on Late Nineteenth- and Early Twentieth-Century English Literature, Modern Language Association. **Essays:** Auden, W.H; Auden: Musée des Beaux Arts.

**Mariani, Paul L. (Adviser).** Full Professor, Department of English, Boston College, Newton, MA. Author of *William Carlos Williams: A New World Naked* (1981), *Dream Song: The Life of John Berryman* (1990), and *Lost Puritan: A Life of Robert Lowell* (1994).

**Marriott, David.** Poet and Doctorate, School of English and Drama, University of London, Queen Mary College, London. Author of *Lative* (1992) and *On Black Men* (2000). Contributor to

*Textual Practice* (1994), *Psycho-Politics and Cultural Desires* (1998), *The Psychoanalysis of Race* (1999), and *New Formations* (2001). **Essay:** Baraka, Imamu Amiri (LeRoi Jones).

**Martin, Dawn Lundy.** Ph.D. candidate, Department of English, University of Massachusetts, Amherst. Contributor to *Callaloo* (1999, 2000) and *Fence* (Spring 2001). **Essay:** Fraser, Kathleen.

**Martin, Robert K.** Professor, Département d'études anglaises, Université de Montréal. Author of *Hero, Captain, and Stranger: Male Friendship, Social Critique, and Literary Form in the Sea Novels of Herman Melville* (1986) and *The Homosexual Tradition in American Poetry* (1979, 1998). Editor of *E.M. Forster: Centenary Revaluations* (1982, 1994), *The Continuing Presence of Walt Whitman* (1991), *Textual Studies in Canada* (1994), *Canadian Review of American Studies* (1994), *English Studies in Canada, ACUTE* (1994, 1995), *Queer Forster* (1997), and *American Gothic: New Interventions in a National Narrative* (1998). Contributor to *The Cambridge Companion to Herman Melville* (1998), edited by Robert Levine, and *The Portrait of a Lady* (1999), edited by John R. Bradley. **Essays:** Crane, Hart; Gay and Lesbian Poetry.

**Mason, David.** Poet, Department of English, The Colorado College, Colorado Springs. Author of *The Buried Houses* (1991), *The Country I Remember* (1996), and *The Poetry of Life and the Life of Poetry* (2000). Coeditor with Mark Jarman of *Rebel Angels: 25 Poets of the New Formalism* (1996).Contributor to *Shenandoah, Grand Street, Poetry,* and *Georgia Review*. Editorial board member of *Hudson Review* (1997– ). **Essay:** Gioia, Dana.

**McCabe, Susan.** Associate Professor, Department of English, University of Southern California, Los Angeles. Author of *Elizabeth Bishop: Her Poetics of Loss* (1994). Contributor to *Antioch Review* (1997), *Wallace Stevens Journal* (1998), *Women Poets of the Americas* (1999), edited by Jacqueline Vaught Brogan and Cordelia Chávez Candelaria, *Challenging Boundaries: Gender and Periodization* (2000), edited by Margaret Dickie and Joyce W. Warren, and *Mosaic* (2000). **Essays:** Moore, Marianne; Stevens: Sunday Morning.

**McCann, Janet.** Professor of English and Coordinator of Creative Writing, Texas A&M University, College Station. Author of *Wallace Stevens Revisited: The Celestial Possible* (1996). Coauthor with Hugh McCann and Edgar Moore of *Creative and Critical Thinking* (1985). Coeditor with David Craig of *Place of Passage: Contemporary Catholic Poetry* (2000). Contributor to *Southwest Review, Wallace Stevens Journal,* and *Dickinson Studies*. **Essays:** Merwin: The Drunk in the Furnace; Plath, Sylvia; Plath: Ariel; Plath: Daddy.

**McCay, Mary A.** Professor, Department of English, Loyola University, New Orleans, LA. Author of *Rachel Carson* (1993) and *Ellen Gilchurt* (1997). Book-review editor of *New Orleans Review* (1992–2000) and coeditor with B. Ewell of *Performance for a Lifetime* (1997). Contributor to *Global Perspectives in Teaching Literature* (1993), edited by S. Lott, et al., *Mississippi Quarterly* (1996), and *Writing Truths* (1998), edited by Hans Boh. **Essay:** Bogan, Louise.

**McGowan, Philip.** Doctorate, Department of English, Goldsmiths College, University of London. Author of *American Carnival: Seeing and Reading American Culture* (2001). Contributor to *Revista canaria de istudios ingleses* (1998), *A Babel of Bottles: Drink, Drinkers and Drinking Places in Literature* (January 2000), and *Saul Bellow Journal* (2000–01). **Essays:** Berryman: The Dream Songs; Sexton, Anne; Sexton: All My Pretty Ones.

**Melnicove, Mark.** Teacher, Department of English, Gardiner Area High School, ME. Author of *Advanced Memories* (1981, 1983). Coauthor with Kendall Merriam of *The Uncensored Guide to Maine* (1984) and with Margy Burns Knight of *Africa Is Not a Country* (2000). Editor of *Inside Vacationland: New Fiction from the Real Maine* (1985) and *Sounds That Arouse Me* (1992). Contributor to *Stony Hills* (1981), *Underground Forest* (1991), *Exquisite Corpse* (1995), and *Ruminator Review* (2001). Editorial board member of *Maine in Print* (1980–88). **Essays:** Ginsberg: Kaddish; Patchen, Kenneth; Rothenberg, Jerome.

**Merriweather, Sandra.** Graduate student, Department of English, Oakland University, Rochester, MI. **Essay:** Hughes: The Negro Speaks of Rivers.

**Mikkelsen, Ann-Marie.** Graduate student, University of California, Irvine. **Essays:** Guest, Barbara; Hejinian, Lyn.

**Mills, Bronwyn.** M.F.A., doctoral candidate, Department of Comparative Literature, and Caribbean and African Diasporic Literature, New York University. Contributor to *Atlantica internacional: revista de las artes* (1991), *Contemporary Literary Criticism* (1992), edited by Thomas Votteler, *Bloomsbury Review* (December 1995), and *Hispanic Literary Criticism* (1999), edited by Thomas Votteler. **Essay:** Caribbean Poetry.

**Mills, Elizabeth.** Professor, Department of English, Davidson College, Davidson, NC. Contributor to *Contemporary Women Poets*. **Essays:** Ammons: Easter Morning; Sexton: Housewife.

**Mills, Fiona.** Ph.D. candidate, Department of English, University of North Carolina, Chapel Hill. **Essays:** Brooks, Gwendolyn; Lorde, Audre.

**Miltner, Robert.** Assistant Professor, Department of English, Kent State University, Canton, OH. Author of *The Seamless Serial Hour* (1993), *Against the Simple* (1995), and *On the Off-Ramp* (1996). Contributor to *Journal of the Fantastic in the Arts* (1994), *Chiron Review* (1994), *No Exit* (1995), *Plerades* (1995), and *Associated Writing Programs Chronicle* (1998). **Essays:** Ignatow, David; Kunitz, Stanley; Silliman, Ron.

**Montgomery, Will.** Ph.D. candidate, Department of English and Drama, Queen Mary College, University of London. **Essay:** Olson: The Maximus Poems.

**Moore, Sharon L.** Assistant Professor, Department of English, University of Nevada, Las Vegas. **Essays:** Brooks: A Bronzeville Mother Loiters in Mississippi. Meanwhile, a Mississippi Mother Burns Bacon; Harlem Renaissance; Lorde: Walking Our Boundaries.

**Moton, Candice Maureen.** Teacher, K–12 Special Education, Spotsylvania County Public Schools, Fredericksburg, VA. Editor of a montly newsletter for youth. **Essay:** Walker, Margaret.

**Munich, Adrienne.** Full Professor, English and Women's Studies, State University of New York, Stony Brook. Author of *Andromeda's Chains* (1989) and *Queen Victoria's Secrets* (1996). Coauthor with Harold Bloom of *Robert Browning: A Collection of Critical Essays* (1979). Coeditor with Margaret Homans of *Victorian Literature and Culture* (1984– ), *Arms and the Woman* (1989), and *Remaking Queen Victoria* (1997). Editorial board member of *PMLA* (1993–96). **Essay:** Lowell, Amy: The Sisters.

**Nanes, Erika.** Ph.D. candidate, Department of English and Comparative Literature, University of California, Irvine. Contributor to *Journal X* (1997) and *ADE Bulletin* (2000). **Essay:** Pound: Homage to Sextus Propertius.

**New, Elisa (Adviser).** Professor, Department of English, Harvard University, Cambridge, MA. Author of *The Regenerate Lyric: Theology and Innovation in American Poetry* (1993) and *The Line's Eye: Poetic Experience, American Sight* (1998). Contributor to *Contemporary Literature* (1993), *Common Knowledge* (1993), *Early American Literature* (1995), and *Poetics Today* (Summer 1998). **Essay:** Grossman, Allen.

**Nickowitz, Peter.** Adjunct Assistant Professor, General Studies Program, New York University. Contributor to *Response: A Contemporary Jewish Review* (Spring 1997), *Out Magazine* (September 1998), and *Poets and Writers* (Summer 1999). **Essay:** Crane: At Melville's Tomb.

**O'Brien, Geoffrey (Adviser).** Writer; Editor-in-Chief, The Library of America, New York, NY. Author of *Dream Time: Chapters from the Sixties* (1988), *The Phantom Empire* (1993), *Floating City: Selected Poems, 1978–1995* (1996), *Bardic Deadlines: Reviewing Poetry, 1984–95* (1998), and *The Browser's Ecstasy: A Meditation on Reading* (2000). Contributor to *Film Comment, American Letters and Commentary, New Republic, New York Review of Books,* and *Michigan Quarterly Review.*

**O'Leary, Peter.** Poet, St. Louis, MO. Author of *Watchfulness* (2001) and *Gnostic Contagion: Robert Duncan and the Poetry of Illness* (forthcoming). Editor of *LVNG* (1990– ), *To Do as Adam Did: Selected Poems,* by Ronald Johnson (2000), and *The Shrubberies,* by Ronald Johnson (2001). **Essays:** Everson, William; Johnson, Ronald; Snyder: Myths and Texts; Snyder: Riprap.

**Olson, John.** Poet, Seattle, WA. Author of *Swarm of Edges* (1996), *Eggs and Mirrors* (1999), *Logo Lagoon* (1999), and *Echo Regime* (2000). Poetry editor of *Raven Chronicles* (1996). Contributor to *Talisman, Sulfur, New American Writing,* and *First Intensity.* **Essay:** Mac Low, Jackson.

**Olson, Liesl Marie.** Ph.D. candidate, Department of English and Comparative Literature, Columbia University, New York, NY. Contributor to *James Joyce Quarterly* (Spring 2000). **Essay:** Stevens: Notes Toward a Supreme Fiction.

**Olson, Ted.** Assistant Professor, Department of English, East Tennessee State University, Johnson City. Author of *So Far: Poems* (1994) and *Blue Ridge Folklife* (1998). Editor of *Cross Roads: A Journal of Southern Culture* (1992–96), *Writing about Identity in the South* (1993), *Mississippi Folklore Register* (1993), *Yalobusha Review* (1995), and *Encyclopedia of Appalachia* (1998–2000). Contributor to *Oxford Companion to African American Literature* (1997), edited by Andrews, Foster, and Harris, *Prospects: An Annual of American Cultural Studies* (1999), *Thoreau's Sense of Place: Essays in American Environmental Writing* (2000), edited by Richard Schneider, and *An Encyclopedia of American War Literature* (forthcoming), edited by Mark A. Graves and Philip K. Jason. **Essay:** Berry, Wendell.

**Omer Sherman, Ranen.** Assistant Professor, Department of English, University of St. Louis, Madrid Campus, Spain. Author of *Finding One's Own Jerusalem: The Diaspora Subject in Jewish American Literature* (2002). Coeditor of *Religion and Literature* (1997–98). Contributor to *Modern Jewish Studies* (Fall 1997), *Shofar* (1997), *Texas Studies in Literature and Language* (1997), and *MELUS* (1999). **Essays:** Reznikoff, Charles; Reznikoff: Autobiography: New York/Autobiography: Hollywood.

**Orem, William.** Ph.D. Author of *Zombi, You My Love* (1999). **Essay:** Cage, John.

**Oventile, Robert S.** Assistant Professor, English and Foreign Languages Division, Pasadena City College, CA. Contributor to *inside english: Journal of the English Council of California Two-Year Colleges* (2000) and *Comitatus: A Journal of Medieval and Renaissance Studies* (2000). **Essays:** Hollander: Kinneret; Kinnell: The Fundamental Project of Technology.

**Paloff, Benjamin.** Freelance writer. Editor of *2B: A Journal of Ideas* (1997– ). Contributor to *Encyclopedia of Life Writing* (2000), edited by Margaretta Jolly, *Harvard Review, Poet Lore,* and *2B.* **Essays:** Brodsky, Joseph; Hugo, Richard; Simic, Charles; Simic: Bestiary for the Fingers of My Right Hand.

**Parke, Catherine N.** Full Professor, Department of English, University of Missouri, Columbia. Author of *Samuel Johnson and Biographical Thinking* (1991), *Other People's Lives: Poems* (1994), and *Biography: Writing Lives* (1996). Editor of *In the Shadow of Parnassus: Zoe Akins's Essays on American Poetry* (1994). Coeditor of *Missouri Review* (1982–87). Contributor to *Modern Language Quarterly* (1989), *Philological Quarterly* (1989), and *Eighteenth-Century Life* (1992). Editorial board member of *The Age of Johnson: A Scholarly Annual* (2001– ). **Essays:** Guiney, Louise Imogen; Midwestern Poetry Renaissance.

**Parras, John.** Assistant Professor of Critical and Creative Writing, English Department, William Paterson University, Wayne, NJ. Contributor to *Virginia Woolf Miscellany* (Spring 1998), *Filipino Reporter* (December 1999), *CrossConnect: Writers of the Information Age* (1999), and *Eureka Literary Magazine* (Spring 2000). **Essays:** Milosz: Campo dei Fiori; Song: Heaven.

**Patell, Cyrus R.K.** Associate Professor, Department of English, New York University. Author of *Joyce's Use of History in "Finnegans Wake"* (1984) and *Negative Liberties: Morrison, Pynchon, and the Problem of Liberal Ideology* (2001). Coeditor with Sacvan Bercovitch of *The Cambridge History of American Liter-*

*ature, Volume 1: 1590–1820* (1994) and *Volume 2: Prose Writing, 1820–1865* (1994). Contributor to *Prospects* (1993), *Nineteenth Century Literature* (1994), *Journal of American Studies of Turkey* (1997), *The Cambridge History of American Literature, Volume 7: Prose Writing, 1940–1990* (1999), edited by Sacvan Bercovitch, and *American Literary History* (1999). **Essays:** Asian American Poetry; Brathwaite, Kamau; Hispanic American Poetry; Komunyakaa, Yusef.

**Paul, Catherine.** Assistant Professor, Department of English, Clemson University, SC. Author of *Poetry in the Museums of Modernism: Yeats, Pound, Moore, Stein* (2001). Contributor to *South Carolina Review* (1998, 1999, 2000), *Studies in the Literary Imagination* (1999), and *Yeats: An Annual* (2000). **Essay:** Moore: The Pangolin.

**Peddie, Ian.** Graduate student, University of Rochester, New York. **Essays:** Clampitt, Amy; McGrath, Thomas.

**Perloff, Marjorie G. (Adviser).** Sadie D. Patek Professor Emerita, Department of English, Stanford University, Stanford, CA. Author of *Frank O'Hara: Poet among Painters* (1977, 1987), *The Poetics of Indeterminacy: Rimbaud to Cage* (1981), *The Futurist Moment* (1986), *Wittgenstein's Ladder* (1996), and *Poetry On and Off the Page* (1998). Contributor to *New Literary History, Contemporary Literature, Modernism/Modernity, Critical Inquiry,* and *American Literature.*

**Peterson, Nancy J.** Associate Professor, English and American Studies, Purdue University, West Lafayette, IN. Author of *Against Amnesia: Contemporary Women Writers and the Crises of Historical Memory* (2001). Editor of *Toni Morrison: Critical and Theoretical Approaches* (1997). Coeditor of *Modern Fiction Studies* (1993–98). Contributor to *PMLA* (1994), *The Chippewa Landscape of Louise Erdrich* (1999), edited by Allan Chavkin, and *Contemporary Literature* (1999). Guest editor for the special issue "Native American Literature" of *Modern Fiction Studies* (Spring 1999). **Essay:** Harjo, Joy.

**Pettit, Rhonda.** Assistant Professor, Department of English, University of Cincinnati Raymond Walters College, OH. Author of *Joy Harjo* (1998) and *A Gendered Collision: Sentimentalism and Modernism in Dorothy Parker's Poetry and Fiction* (2000). Contributor to *Through the Gap: An Anthology of Contemporary Kentucky Poetry* (1990), *Working Papers in Irish Studies* (1998), and *American Women Writers, 1900–1945: A Bio-Bibliographical Critical Sourcebook* (2000). Editorial board member of *Kentucky Philological Review* (1998). **Essays:** Hayden: Middle Passage; Rich, Adrienne.

**Pickens, Roxane V.** Ph.D. candidate, American Studies Program, College of William and Mary, Williamsburg, VA. Doctoral scholar, Southern Regional Board of Education, part of the Compact for Faculty Diversity. **Essays:** Brown: Ma Rainey; Toomer, Jean.

**Potts, Donna.** Associate Professor, English, Kansas State University, Manhattan. Author of *Howard Nemerov and Objective Idealism* (1994). Contributor to *Studies: An Irish Quarterly Review* (1999), *Tulsa Studies in Women's Literature* (1999), *New Hibernia Review* (1999), *Border Crossings: Irish Women Writers and National Identities* (2000), edited by Kathryn Kirkpatrick, and *Terranglian Territories* (2000), edited by Susanne Hagemann. **Essays:** Hollander, John; Native American Poetry; Ortiz, Simon; Van Duyn, Mona.

**Prono, Luca.** Ph.D. candidate, School of American and Canadian Studies, University of Nottingham, UK. Deputy film review editor of *Scope: An Online Journal of Film Studies* (2000– ). Contributor to *Links and Letters* (1999), *Encyclopedia of Popular Culture* (1999), edited by Tom and Sara Pendergast, and *Encyclopedia of Life Writing* (2000), edited by Margaretta Jolly. **Essays:** Baraka: Black People: This Is Our Destiny; McKay: The White City; Sandburg: Chicago Poems.

**Rachman, Stephen.** Associate Professor, Department of English, Michigan State University, East Lansing. Coeditor of *The American Face of Edgar Allan Poe* (1995). Contributor to *Literature and Medicine* (Fall 1997), *American Literary History* (1997), *Walt Whitman: An Encyclopedia* (1998), edited by J.R. LeMaster and Donald D. Kummings, *Narrative Based Medicine* (1998), and *The Seventies: Age of Glitter* (1999), edited by Shelton Waldrep. **Essays:** Blackmur, R.P.; Justice, Donald.

**Raynor, Sharon.** Lecturer, Department of English, East Carolina University, Greenville, SC. Contributor to *Who's Who in Contemporary Women's Writing* (1999), edited by Marie Umeh. **Essays:** Baraka: A Poem Some People Will Have to Understand; Black Arts Movement; Komunyakaa: Facing It.

**Rhyne, Jeffrey.** Ph.D. candidate, Department of English, University of California, Riverside. Coeditor with Emory Elliott and Lou Caton of *Aesthetics in a Multicultural Age* (December 2001). **Essay:** Grimké, Angelina Weld.

**Richardson, Kelly L.** Doctoral candidate, Department of English, University of North Carolina, Greensboro. Contributor to *Such News of the Land: American Women Nature Writers* (2001), edited by Thomas S. Edwards and Elizabeth De Wolfe. **Essays:** Piercy, Marge; Reese, Lizette Woodworth.

**Righelato, Pat.** Doctorate, Department of English, University of Reading, UK. Contributor to *American Poetry: The Modernist Ideal* (1995), *Reader's Guide to Literature in English* (1996), edited by Mark Hawkins-Dady, *Year's Work in English Studies* (1997, 1998, 1999, 2000), and *Yearbook of English Studies* (2001). **Essays:** Dove, Rita; Dove: Ö.

**Riley, Jeannette E.** Assistant Professor, Department of English, Kent State University, Canton, OH. Contributor to *Encyclopedia of British Women Writers* (1997), *Irish University Review* (1998), *Blue Mesa Review* (1998), *Rocky Mountain MLA Review* (1999), *Nua: Studies in Contemporary Irish Literature* (1999), and *The Robert Frost Encyclopedia* (2000), edited by Nancy Tuten and John Zubizaretta. **Essays:** Rich: An Atlas of the Difficult World; Rich: Diving into the Wreck.

**Roberts, Gary.** Ph.D. candidate, Department of English and American Literature, Brandeis University, Waltham, MA. Editor-in-Chief of *Chicago Literary Review* (1989–90). Contributor to

*Contemporary Women Poets* (1998), edited by Pamela Shelton, *Essays in Criticism* (1997), *Dictionary of Literary Biography* (1998), edited by Joseph Conte, *The Nature of Cities* (1999), edited by Michael Bennet and David Teague, and *The Robert Frost Encyclopedia* (2000), edited by Nancy Tuten and John Zubizaretta. **Essay:** Cunningham, J.V.

**Robins, Corinne.** Visiting Associate Professor, Department of Painting and Drawing, Pratt Institute, Brooklyn, NY. Author of *The Pluralist Era: American Art 1968–81* (1984), *Art in the 7th Power* (1984), *Facing It* (1996), and *Marble Goddesses with Technicolor Skins* (2000). Editor of *American Book Review* (1988–2000). Contributor to *Arts Magazine* (1988), *Art Journal* (1996), *American Book Review* (1999, 2000), and *M/E/A/N/I/N/G: An Anthology of Artists' Writings, Theory, and Criticism* (2000), edited by Mira Schor and Susan Boo. **Essay:** Moore: The Steeple-Jack.

**Roche, John F., Jr.** Assistant Professor, Language and Literature, Rochester Institute of Technology, NY. Contributor to *Feminist Writers* (1996), edited by Pamela Shelton, *Contemporary Women Poets* (1998), edited by Pamela Shelton, *Walt Whitman: An Encyclopedia* (1998), edited by J.R. LeMaster and Donald D. Kummings, *Journal of Pre-Raphaelite Studies, Twentieth-Century Literary Criticism, Educational Theory, Walt Whitman Quarterly Review, American Transcendental Quarterly,* and *Choice: Current Reviews for College Libraries.* **Essay:** Rakosi, Carl.

**Rohrbach, Augusta.** Bunting Fellow, Radcliffe Institute for Advanced Study, Harvard University, Cambridge, MA. Author of *Keeping It Real: Material Contexts for Literary Realism from Abolition to the Harlem Renaissance* (forthcoming). Editorial board member of *Edith Wharton Review.* Contributor to *International Journey of Philosophy, Callaloo, Print Magazine, New England Quarterly,* and *American Literature.* **Essays:** Johnson, James Weldon; McKay, Claude.

**Rubinstein, Rachel.** Contributor to *Jewish Writers of the Twentieth Century* (2001), edited by Sorrel Kerbel. **Essay:** Levertov: A Woman Alone.

**Rugoff, Kathy.** Associate Professor, Department of English, University of North Carolina, Wilmington. Contributor to *Journal of American Humor* (new series, 1986), *Perspectives on Contemporary Literature* (1988), *Connecticut Review* (1991, 1992), *Ars Lyrica* (1993), *Multicultural Literatures through Feminist/Poststructuralist Lenses* (1993), edited by Barbara Frey Waxman, *Women on the Edge: Ethnicity and Gender in Short Stories by American Women* (1999), edited by Corinne H. Dale and J.H.E. Paine, and *Walt Whitman and Modern Music: War, Desire, and the Trials of a Nationhood* (2000), edited by Lawence Kramer. **Essays:** Black Mountain School; Stern, Gerald.

**Sarrocco, Nicole.** Editorial board member of *Carolina Quarterly* (1994–95). Contributor to *Encyclopedia of American Literature* (1999), edited by Steven Serafin, and *The Columbia Granger World of Poetry CD ROM* (1999), edited by William Harmon. **Essays:** Frost: Mending Wall; Hirsch, Edward; Light Verse; Riding, Laura; Schnackenberg, Gjertrud.

**Schaum, Melita C.** Professor of English, Department of Humanities, University of Michigan, Dearborn. Author of *Wallace Stevens and the Critical Schools* (1998). Editorial board member of *Wallace Stevens Journal* (1987– ). Editor of *Gender Images* (1992) and *Wallace Stevens and the Feminine* (1993). Contributor to *Genders* (1989), *Paideuma* (1995), *Journal of American Studies* (1995), and *Journal of Modern Literature* (2000). **Essay:** Stevens: The Snow Man.

**Scheick, William J.** Millikan Centennial Professor of American Literature, Department of English, University of Texas, Austin. Author of *The Half-Blood: A Cultural Symbol in Nineteenth-Century American Fiction* (1979), *Fictional Structure and Ethics: The Turn-of-the-Century English Novel* (1990), *Design in Puritan American Literature* (1992), *The Ethos of Romance at the Turn of the Century* (1994), and *Authority and Female Authorship in Colonial America* (1998). **Essays:** Lowell, Amy: Patterns; Robinson: Miniver Cheevy

**Schmid, Julie M.** Graduate student, University of Iowa, Iowa City. Contributor to *Performing Arts Journal* (1996), *Talisman* (Winter 1999), and *MELUS* (Summer 2000). **Essays:** Holman, Bob; Loy, Mina; Loy: Love Songs to Joannes.

**Schoon, Sarah. Essay:** Shapiro, Karl.

**Schwartz, Leonard.** Poet-in-Residence, Lacoste School of the Arts, France. Author of *Objects of Thought, Attempts at Speech* (1990), *Gnostic Blessing* (1992), *Words Before the Articulate: New and Selected Poems* (1997), and *A Flicker at the Edge of Things: Essays on Poetics, 1987–1997* (1998). Editor of *Literary Review* (Summer 1990). Coeditor with Lisa Jarnot and Chris Stroffolino of *An Anthology of New (American) Poets* (1998). Contributor to *Talisman* (1992–2000), *The World* (1995), *Cross Cultural Poetics* (1999), and *Conjunctions* (2000). **Essays:** H.D.: Trilogy; Kelly, Robert.

**Schweizer, Harold.** Full Professor, Department of English, Bucknell University, Lewisburg, PA. Author of *Suffering and the Remedy of Art* (1997). Editor of *The Poetry of Irving Feldman* (1992) and *History and Memory: Suffering and Art* (1998). Coeditor of *The Bucknell Lectures in Literary Theory* (1988–94). Contributor to *Literature and Psychology* (1991), *Profils Americains* (1993), *Literature and Medicine* (1995, 1997, 2000), *Blackwell Dictionary of Cultural and Critical Theory* (1996), and *Q/W/E/R/T/Y* (1999). **Essays:** Eliot: The Love Song of J. Alfred Prufrock; Literary Theory and Poetry.

**Scroggins, Mark.** Associate Professor, Department of English, Florida Atlantic University, Boca Raton. Author of *Louis Zukofsky and the Poetry of Knowledge* (1998). Editor of *Upper Limit Music: The Writing of Louis Zukofsky* (1997). Coeditor of *Diaeresis Chapbook Series in Poetry and Poetics.* **Essays:** Taggart, John; Zukofsky: "A."

**Shilts, Katrina.** Ph.D. candidate and Instructor, Department of English, Binghamton University, NY. **Essay:** Jarrell: Thinking of the Lost World.

**Smith, Ernest J.** Associate Professor, Department of English, University of Central Florida, Orlando. Author of *The Imaged Word:*

*The Infrastructure of Hart Crane's "White Buildings"* (1990). Contributor to *Studies in Short Fiction* (1993), *Millay at 100: A Critical Reappraisal* (1995), edited by Diane P. Freedman, *American Women Writers: 1900–1945* (2000), edited by Laurie Champion, *Literature and Homosexuality* (2000), edited by Michael J. Meyer, *Journal of Modern Literature* (2001), and *Lowell, Bishop, Jarrell, and Co.* (2002), edited by Suzanne Ferguson. **Essays:** Harper, Michael S.; Justice: Men at Forty; Williams, William Carlos.

**Spector, Cheryl.** Associate Professor, Department of English, California State University, Northridge. **Essays:** Kumin, Maxine; Rich: Snapshots of a Daughter-in-Law; Rich: A Valediction Forbidding Mourning; Rukeyser, Muriel.

**Spencer, Nicholas.** Assistant Professor, Department of English, University of Nebraska, Lincoln. Contributor to *Contemporary Literature* (1999) and *Angelaki* (2000). **Essay:** Kees, Weldon.

**Stearns, Thaine.** Ph.D., Department of English, Pacific Northwest College of Art, Portland, OR. Contributor to *William Carlos Williams Encyclopedia* (2001) and *Modernism/Modernity* (April 2001). **Essay:** Nabokov, Vladimir.

**Stein, Karen F.** Professor of English and Women's Studies, University of Rhode Island, Kingston. Author of *Margaret Atwood Revisited* (1999). Contributor to *University of Toronto Quarterly* (1992, 2001), *Studies in Canadian Literature* (1995), *Canadian Literature* (1996), *Understanding Toni Morrison's "Beloved" and "Sula"* (2000), edited by Solomon Iyasere and Marla Iyasere, *Margaret Atwood: Modern Critical Views* (2000), edited by Harold Bloom, and *Crone's Nest: Wisdom of the Elderwoman* (2000). **Essays:** Clifton, Lucille; Dove: Thomas and Beulah; Francis, Robert; Plath: Lady Lazarus.

**Steinman, Lisa M.** Kenan Professor of English and Humanities, Department of English, Reed College, Portland, OR. Author of *Lost Poems* (1976), *Made in America: Science, Technology, and American Modernist Poets* (1987), *All That Comes to Light* (1989), *A Book of Other Days* (1994), and *Masters of Repetition: Poetry, Culture, and Work* (1998). Coeditor of *Hubbub* (1983– ). Contributor to *American Literature* (1990, 1994, 2000) and *Modernism/Modernity* (1997, 2002). Editorial board member of *Wallace Stevens Journal* (1994– ) and *William Carlos Williams Review* (1991– ). **Essay:** Tolson, Melvin B.

**Stone, Derrick.** Instructor, Language Centre, Hong Kong Baptist University. **Essay:** Ferlinghetti, Lawrence.

**Szczesiul, Anthony.** Assistant Professor, Department of English, University of Massachusetts, Lowell. Contributor to *Walt Whitman Quarterly Review* (1993), *Mississippi Quarterly* (1994, 1999), and *ATQ: American Transcendental Quarterly* (1996). **Essays:** Warren, Robert Penn; Warren: Audubon: A Vision.

**Taylor, Bruce.** Full Professor, Department of English, University of Wisconsin-Eau Claire. Author of *This Day* (1993) and *Why That Man Talks That Way* (1994). Editor of *Wisconsin Poetry* (1993). Coeditor with Patti See of *Higher Learning: Reading and Writing about College* (2001). Contributor to *Poetry* (1994), *Northwest Review* (1996), *The Formalist* (1998), *Nerve* (2000), and *Exquisite Corpse* (2000). **Essays:** Confessional Poetry; Updike, John.

**Taylor, Douglas.** Ph.D. candidate, Department of English, University of North Carolina, Chapel Hill. **Essays:** Cortez, Jayne; Reed, Ishmael.

**Taylor, Michelle L.** Ph.D. candidate, Department of English, Rice University, Houston, TX. Contributor to *Dictionary of Literary Biography* (forthcoming), edited by David Zizzo. **Essays:** Hughes: Montage of a Dream Deferred; Hughes: The Weary Blues.

**Thibodeaux, Troy.** Graduate student, Department of English, New York University. Contributor to *Yeats-Eliot Review* (1996), *Hopkins Quarterly* (1996), *Dictionary of Literary Biography: American Short Story Writers since World War II* (2000), edited by Patrick Meanor and Richard Lee, and *Reader's Companion to Short Fiction* (2001). **Essay:** Lowell, Robert: After the Surprising Conversions.

**Tramontana, Catherine.** Ph.D., Department of Literatures in English, Rutgers University, New Brunswick, NJ. Contributor to *An Encyclopedia of American War Literature* (forthcoming), edited by Mark A. Graves and Philip K. Jason. **Essays:** Cummings: i sing of Olaf glad and big; Cummings: my father moved through dooms of love; Kilmer, Joyce; Moore: The Fish; Moore: Poetry.

**Vance, Jane Gentry.** Professor, Department of English and in the Honor's Program, University of Kentucky, Lexington. Author of *A Garden in Kentucky* (1995). Contributor to *American Women Writing Fiction: Memory, Identity, Family, Space* (1989), edited by Mickey Pearlman, *Savory Memories* (1998), edited by L. Elisabeth Beattie, *Encyclopedia of American Poetry: The Nineteenth Century* (1998), edited by Eric L. Haralson, *The Companion to Southern Culture* (2000), edited by Lucindo McKethan and Joseph Flora, *Southern Literary Journal, Iron Mountain Review, Mississippi Quarterly,* and *Kentucky Review.* **Essay:** Oliver, Mary.

**VandenAkker, Sherri Lynn.** Assistant Professor, Springfield College School of Human Services, MA. Coeditor with Bo Wiman and Angela Wiman of *The Art of Natural Resource Management: Poetics, Policy, and Practice* (1998). Contributor to *Computers and Composition* (1993), *The Norton Anthology of Poetry* (1996), *The Art of Natural Resource Management* (1998), and *Connecticut Poetry Review.* **Essays:** Bishop: One Art; Salter, Mary Jo.

**Van Egmond, Peter.** Associate Professor, Department of English, University of Maryland, College Park. Author of *The Critical Reception of Robert Frost* (1974) and *Robert Frost: A Reference Guide, 1974–1990* (1991). Coeditor of *The Major American Poets: An Introduction* (1989). Has published poems in such journals as *Calvert Review, Cumberland Poetry Review, Shenandoah, Laurel Review, CEA Critic,* and *Sou'wester.* **Essays:** Ciardi, John; Kerouac, Jack.

**Veladota, Christina.** Ph.D. candidate, Creative Writing, Ohio University, Athens. Editor of *Quarter after Eight: A Journal of Prose and Commentary* (1999– ). Contributor to *Alaska Quarterly*

*Review, Greensboro Review, Ascent,* and *Poem.* **Essay:** Carruth, Hayden.

**Vella, Michael W.** Professor of American Literature and American Studies, Indiana University of Pennsylvania. Editor of *The Meritorious Price of Our Redemption,* by William Pynchon (1992). Special guest editor of *Film Quarterly* and *Studies in the Humanities.* Editorial board member of *Studies in the Humanities.* Contributor to *Oxford Companion to American Women Writers* (1997), *Dictionary of Literary Biography* (1999), *Emerson Society Quarterly, Lost Generation Journal, Twentieth Century Literature, DELTA, Early American Literature,* and *Studies in the Humanities.* **Essays:** Snyder, Gary; Surrealism.

**Wagner-Martin, Linda C. (Adviser).** Hanes Professor, Department of English, University of North Carolina, Chapel Hill. Author of *Favored Strangers: Gertrude Stein and Her Family* (1995), *Sylvia Plath: A Literary Life* (1999), and *The Poisonwood Bible: A Commentary* (2001). Coeditor of *The Oxford Companion to Women's Writing in the United States* (1995). Editor of *Centennial Review* (1983–88). Editorial board member for *Studies in American Fiction* (1980– ), *American Literature* (1980–83), *Hemingway Review* (1990– ), and *Narrative* (1991–94).

**Walpert, Bryan.** Ph.D. candidate and poet, Department of English, University of Denver, CO. Coeditor with Janet Black of *Breaking Ground: Guide to First-Year English* (August 2000). Contributor to *Poet Lore* (Fall 1997), *Maryland Poetry Review* (1998), *Metropolitan Review* (Fall/Winter 1998), *Ravishing DisUnities: Real Ghazals in English* (2000), edited by Agha Shahid Ali, *The Lyric* (Winter 2000), and *Crab Orchard Review* (Spring/Summer 2000). **Essay:** Narrative Poetry.

**Walter, Krista.** Professor, Department of English, Pasadena City College, CA. Contributor to *African American Review* (2000) and *Literature/Film Quarterly* (2001). **Essay:** Jeffers, Robinson.

**Walton, Gary P.** Full-time Lecturer, Department of Literature and Language, Northern Kentucky University, Highland Heights. Author of *The Sweetest Song* (1989), *Cobwebs and Chimeras* (1994), *The Newt Phillips Papers* (1996), and *Effervescent Softsell* (1997). Editor of *Vermillion Literary Project* (1981–82), *Clifton Magazine* (1987–88), *Journal of Kentucky Studies* (1997– ), and *Kentucky Philological Review* (1998–99). Contributor to *Arkansas Quarterly* (1992, 1993, 1995), *Issues and Identities in Literature* (1997), edited by David Peck, and *Critical Survey of Long Fiction* (2000), edited by Carl Rollyson. **Essays:** Cummings: anyone lived in a pretty how town; Wakoski, Diane.

**Watts, Linda S.** Professor of American Studies and Director of Interdisciplinary Arts and Sciences Program, University of Washington, Bothell. Author of *Rapture Untold: Gender, Mysticism, and "The Moment of Recognition" in the Writings of Gertrude Stein* (1996) and *Gertrude Stein: A Study of the Short Fiction* (1999). Contributor to *Transformations: A Resource for Transformation and Scholarship* (1992– ), *Women and Language* (1993), *Journal of Feminist Studies in Religion* (1994), *Radical History Review* (1994), and *Radical Teacher: A Socialist and Feminist Journal on the Theory and Practice of Teaching* (1995– ). **Essays:** Ortiz Cofer, Judith; Song, Cathy; Stein, Gertrude; Taggard, Genevieve.

**Wenthe, Michael.** Ph.D. candidate, Department of English, Yale University, New Haven, CT. **Essay:** Bynner, Witter.

**Westover, Jeff.** Doctoral student, Boston College, Chestnut Hill, MA. Contributor to *Style* (1994), *Critical Essays on James Merrill* (1996), *Chaucer Review* (1998), *Classical and Modern Literature* (1998), and *Massachusetts Review* (1998). **Essays:** Bogan: Women; Merrill: Lost in Translation; Williams: Spring and All.

**Winslow, Rosemary Gates.** Associate Professor, Department of English, The Catholic University of America, Washington, DC. Contributor to *Language and Style* (1983–85), *Walt Whitman Review* (1987), *Poetics Today* (1987–91), *Journal of Advanced Composition* (1988–89), and *Composition Studies/Freshman English News* (1988–95). **Essays:** Free Verse; Levertov, Denise; Levertov: Olga Poems; Prosody and Versification.

**Woods, Tim.** Senior Lecturer, Department of English and American Studies, University of Wales, Aberystwyth. Author of *Beginning Postmodernism* (1999). Coauthor with D. Rainsford of *Critical Ethics* (1998), with A. Hadfield and D. Rainsford of *The Ethics of Literature* (1998), and with Peter Middleton of *Literatures of Memory* (2000). Contributor to *Parataxis* (1996), *Rethinking History* (1998), *English* (1999), *Poetry Now* (1999), edited by H. Klein, S. Coelsch-Foisner, and W. Gortschacher, and *Textual Practice* (2000). **Essays:** Bernstein, Charles; Eliot: Four Quartets; Language Poetry; Zukofsky, Louis.

**York, Jake Adam.** Poet, Assistant Professor, Department of English, University of Colorado, Denver. Contributor to *Southern Poetry Review* (1999), *Shenandoah* (2000), *Poet Lore* (2001), and *Southern Humanities Review* (2001). Editorial board member of *Shenandoah* (2001). **Essays:** Crane: The Bridge; Levine, Philip; Lowell, Robert: For the Union Dead; Lowell, Robert: The Quaker Graveyard in Nantucket.

**Zauhar, David R.** Lecturer, University of Illinois at Chicago. Assistant editor of *Exquisite Corpse* (1985) and *Symplotie* (1998–99). Contributor to *Electronic Books Review* (1999) and *How* (1999). **Essays:** Beat Poetry; Eberhart, Richard; Kaufman, Bob; Kerouac: Mexico City Blues.